Presented

to

Roxanne

by

Mom

on

March 28, 2003

CATHOLIC, Women's DEVOTIONAL BIBLE

NEW REVISED STANDARD VERSION
CATHOLIC EDITION

ZondervanPublishingHouse
Grand Rapids, MI 49530 USA

Table of Contents

Old Testament

New Testament

Study Helps

How to Use This Bible

While many Catholics grew up hearing the Word of God read during daily and Sunday Masses, few of us are as intimately acquainted with it as we would like to be.

Some of us may even feel a little intimidated by such strange-sounding names as Leviticus, Chronicles, Habakkuk, and Numbers—how readable could a book called "Numbers" be anyway? We may have Protestant friends who've studied the Bible and can locate in the blink of an eye I Samuel 2.1–10 or Romans 8.1–4. They may even be able to pronounce Potiphar, Uzziah, and Rizpah as though these are people they've known all their lives. But such names merely confirm our hesitancy about this mysterious book.

If only we could do with the Bible what the Emperor Charlemagne supposedly did with Augustine's lengthy masterpiece, *The City of God*, tucking it under his pillow in hopes of absorbing its contents while he was asleep. Still, we know that a regular habit of Scripture reading can deepen our spiritual lives and provide answers to some of life's most vexing questions. But where do we start—at Genesis, reading straight through to Revelation? A few hardy souls may make that journey, but most of us will drop out midway through Leviticus, confused and discouraged by a worldview that is often so foreign to our own.

Whether you have done a little or a lot of Bible reading, or even if you are opening the Bible for the first time, the *Catholic Women's Devotional Bible* can offer you insight and practical help for reading the Scripture and applying it to your life. This Bible has been developed to ease the confusion that so often accompanies Bible reading, so that you can experience a greater confidence in understanding and praying the Scriptures.

Because the church established the canon of the Bible and has the responsibility for authoritatively interpreting the Scripture, it is also helpful to see how various traditions and teachings of the Catholic Church are linked directly to the Scriptures. The *Catholic Women's Devotional Bible* will help deepen your understanding of holy days, sacraments, liturgy, and spiritual direction, as well as a host of other topics that are part of Catholic life and practice. More specifically, the features of this Bible have been developed in response to both the bishops' call to lay Catholics to read and study the Bible and to the directive given in the *Dogmatic Constitution on Divine Revelation* (paragraphs 22 and 25) of the Second Vatican Council, which says:

> Easy access to Sacred Scripture should be provided for all the Christian faithful . . . This sacred Synod earnestly and specifically urges all the Christian faithful . . . to learn by frequent reading of the divine Scriptures of the "excelling knowledge of Jesus Christ" (Philippians 3.8). "For ignorance of the Scriptures is ignorance of Christ" [St. Jerome]. Therefore, they should gladly put themselves in touch with the sacred text itself, whether it be through the liturgy . . . Or through devotional reading, or through instructions suitable for the purpose and other aids . . .

In order to help you better understand and apply Scripture to your life, this Bible offers certain features that focus on themes and characters in the Bible that may be of special interest to women. Too often, the role that women play in the story of salvation has been overlooked or underemphasized. By lifting these women up, we hope to provide fresh insight into the various ways God works with his people.

It should be mentioned that the emphasis of the *Catholic Women's Devotional Bible* is on spirituality rather than study. Though modern scholars have debated important matters concerning the authorship and development of various books of the Bible, these issues are not the primary focus of this Bible. Rather the stress is on helping lay people read and pray the Bible on a daily basis.

Special Features

Devotional Readings

Devotional readings, compiled by Louise Perrotta, have been drawn from a rich variety of authors and placed near the Scripture passage to which the devotional messages are linked. You can begin

on any day of the week simply by turning to the reading for that day. To find out where the next day's reading is, simply look at the bottom of the devo-

tion to find the page number for the next reading. In the top right corner of the reading is a suggested passage of Scripture to be read that day, as well as a particular verse or verses on which to meditate. Most, but not all, of the daily meditations were written by Catholic authors.

Weekend Meditations—Women's Stories

Each weekend's devotional reading focuses on a different woman in Scripture, retelling her story and then leading you into a time of prayer as you read the Scripture passages pertaining to her life. The section titled "Lift Your Heart" is meant to offer creative ways of responding to her story to make it more meaningful in your own life. Ann Spangler has written the weekend meditations, longer versions of which can be found in her book, co-authored with Jean Syswerda, titled *Women of the Bible: A One-Year Devotional Study of Women in Scripture.*

Book Introductions

Brief introductions, written by Ann Spangler, are provided for each of the 73 books of the Bible in order to highlight main themes and provide useful background information.

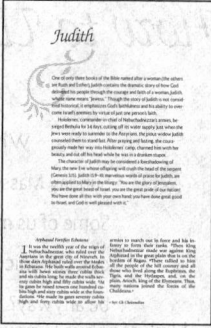

"The Tradition"

Louise Perrotta has written 50 articles that help show the connection between Scripture and Catholic life and teaching. These informative articles cover topics like purgatory, angels, sacra-

ments, the liturgy of the hours, the rosary, spiritual direction, and the saints. They are designed to deepen your understanding of your faith.

A Six-Year Reading Guide Keyed to the Catholic Lectionary

At the back of the Bible, starting on page 1713, is an easy-to-use six-year reading guide based on the lectionary of the Catholic Church. It allows you to quickly locate the Scripture readings on any given day for both the daily and Sunday Masses.

Topical Index

The topical index on page 1683 will help you locate devotions on topics of special interest to you.

Index of Women of the Bible

An index to the stories of 52 women of the Bible can be found on page vi. It will lead you to the weekend meditation that focuses on a particular woman, as well as to key Scripture passages pertaining to her.

Index of "The Tradition" Articles

A topical index to "The Tradition" articles can also be found on page vi.

Preface

This Catholic edition of the New Revised Standard Version of the Bible has been authorized by the National Conference of Catholic Bishops in the U.S.A. and by the National Council of the Churches of Christ in the U.S.A. It has received the ecclesiastical approval of the Catholic Bishops of both the United States and Canada. The undersigned, who prepared this edition, is a member of the Revised Standard Version Bible Translation Committee as well as an active member and past president of the Catholic Biblical Association of America.

Roman Catholics are already familiar with the accuracy and elegance of the New Revised Standard Version, first published in 1990. It has previously appeared in two major types of edition: an edition of the Old and New Testaments alone, the Bible of most Protestants; and an edition of the Old and New Testaments with the Apocryphal/Deuterocanonical Books placed between the two Testaments. The text of the latter edition received the Imprimatur (official approbation) of the United States and Canadian Catholic Bishops. The New Revised Standard Version is truly an ecumenical translation, for it was produced by Roman Catholic, Eastern Orthodox, Protestant, and Jewish scholars. Because of this Catholic presence no change in the translation was requested for this edition. The only exceptions are the Book of Esther, which exists in two different forms that are explained below, and the Book of Daniel, which includes the deuterocanonical portions that are listed below.

Regarding the number of the books of the Old Testament canon and their arrangement, however, Protestants and Jews on the one hand, and Roman Catholics and Orthodox Christians on the other, hold different beliefs. From the time of the Reformation in the sixteenth century, Protestants have adopted the Jewish canon of the Old Testament, which was established by the rabbis at the end of the first century of the Common Era. This canon includes only those books that were written in Hebrew and Aramaic. In addition to these books, however, Roman Catholics, following the ancient tradition of the Christian church, also hold the Deuterocanonical Books of the Old Testament to be sacred and inspired, and therefore canonical. Protestants and Jews call these books Apocrypha, a word that means "hidden or concealed," an inappropriate title for works that were part of the Greek Old Testament (the Septuagint) from pre-Christian times. The Roman Catholic canon, which was fixed by the time of the Council of Hippo in 393 and reaffirmed by the two Councils of Carthage in 397 and 419, was formally defined by the Council of Trent in 1546. This canon contains seven Deuterocanonical Books: Tobit, Judith, the Wisdom of Solomon, Sirach (the Wisdom of Ben Sira, also known as Ecclesiasticus), Baruch including the Letter of Jeremiah as chapter 6, and 1 and 2 Maccabees; and extra portions of two other books: the Additions to Esther; and the Prayer of Azariah and the Song of the Three Jews inserted between verses 23 and 24 of Daniel 3, Susanna as Daniel 13, and Bel and the Dragon as Daniel 14. Over and above these books and extra portions, the Bible of Greek and Slavonic Orthodox Christians includes 1 Esdras, the Prayer of Manasseh, Psalm 151, and 3 Maccabees. The Slavonic Bible also contains 2 Esdras, and an appendix to the Greek Bible includes 4 Maccabees.

Several of the Deuterocanonical Books were written originally in Hebrew or Aramaic, the rest in Greek. More than two-thirds of the Book of Sirach is now extant in Hebrew, and four fragments of the Book of Tobit in Hebrew and Aramaic were recovered from Qumran Cave IV. It seems certain that Judith and the additions to Daniel were also written originally in Hebrew. Hebrew is the original language of the prose parts of Baruch; the poetic parts were composed in Greek. The Wisdom of Solomon was written completely in Greek. The original language of 1 Maccabees was Hebrew while 2 Maccabees was composed in Greek.

The Book of Esther has two different forms: the short Hebrew original; and the longer Greek version that contains one hundred and seven additional verses comprising six distinct portions, A through F. It is the translation of the entire Greek version that appears in the Deuterocanonical section of the New Revised Standard Version. In this Catholic edition, however, the translation of the Greek portions has been inserted at the appropriate places of the translation of the Hebrew form of the book.

Some of the Greek portions apparently had a Hebrew origin; the others were written in Greek.

What is distinctive about this Catholic edition—as well as every other edition published by Roman Catholics—is that the Deuterocanonical Books and portions are placed in their proper order among the other books of the Old Testament. Thus, Tobit, Judith, the long form of Esther, and 1 and 2 Maccabees are found among the so-called historical books directly after Nehemiah. The Wisdom of Solomon and the Book of Sirach follow after the Song of Solomon among the wisdom books. Because Baruch, the well-known secretary of Jeremiah, is said to be the author of the work that bears his name, the book is placed after Jeremiah and Lamentations. This order of books comes from the Latin Vulgate translated by St. Jerome in the late fourth and early fifth centuries. It is essentially the same order as that found in the fourth-century Codex Vaticanus, one of the oldest extant manuscripts of the Septuagint.

Roman Catholics will welcome this edition of the New Revised Standard Version of the Bible for personal reading and study as well as liturgical usage. Based on the latest manuscript discoveries and critical editions, it offers the fruits of the best biblical scholarship in the idiom of today while being sensitive to the contemporary concern for inclusive language when referring to human beings.

ALEXANDER A. DI LELLA, O.F.M.
Andrews-Kelly-Ryan Distinguished Professor of Biblical Studies
The Catholic University of America

September 30, 1992
Feast of St. Jerome

To the Reader

This preface is addressed to you by the Committee of translators, who wish to explain, as briefly as possible, the origin and character of our work. The publication of our revision is yet another step in the long, continual process of making the Bible available in the form of the English language that is most widely current in our day. To summarize in a single sentence: the New Revised Standard Version of the Bible is an authorized revision of the Revised Standard Version, published in 1952, which was a revision of the American Standard Version, published in 1901, which, in turn, embodied earlier revisions of the King James Version, published in 1611.

In the course of time, the King James Version came to be regarded as "the Authorized Version." With good reason it has been termed "the noblest monument of English prose," and it has entered, as no other book has, into the making of the personal character and the public institutions of the English-speaking peoples. We owe to it an incalculable debt.

Yet the King James Version has serious defects. By the middle of the nineteenth century, the development of biblical studies and the discovery of many biblical manuscripts more ancient than those on which the King James Version was based made it apparent that these defects were so many as to call for revision. The task was begun, by authority of the Church of England, in 1870. The (British) Revised Version of the Bible was published in 1881–1885; and the American Standard Version, its variant embodying the preferences of the American scholars associated with the work, was published, as was mentioned above, in 1901. In 1928 the copyright of the latter was acquired by the International Council of Religious Education and thus passed into the ownership of the churches of the United States and Canada that were associated in this Council through their boards of education and publication.

The Council appointed a committee of scholars to have charge of the text of the American Standard Version and to undertake inquiry concerning the need for further revision. After studying the questions whether or not revision should be undertaken, and if so, what its nature and extent should be, in 1937 the Council authorized a revision. The scholars who served as members of the Committee worked in two sections, one dealing with the Old Testament and one with the New Testament. In 1946 the Revised Standard Version of the New Testament was published. The publication of the Revised Standard Version of the Bible, containing the Old and New Testaments, took place on September 30, 1952. A translation of the Apocryphal/Deuterocanonical Books of the Old Testament followed in 1957. In 1977 this collection was issued in an expanded edition, containing three additional texts received by Eastern Orthodox communions (3 and 4 Maccabees and Psalm 151). Thereafter the Revised Standard Version gained the distinction of being officially authorized for use by all major Christian churches: Protestant, Anglican, Roman Catholic, and Eastern Orthodox.

The Revised Standard Version Bible Committee is a continuing body, comprising about thirty members, both men and women. Ecumenical in representation, it includes scholars affiliated with various Protestant denominations, as well as several Roman Catholic members, an Eastern Orthodox member, and a Jewish member who serves in the Old Testament section. For a period of time the Committee included several members from Canada and from England.

Because no translation of the Bible is perfect or is acceptable to all groups of readers, and because discoveries of older manuscripts and further investigation of linguistic features of the text continue to become available, renderings of the Bible have proliferated. During the years following the publication of the Revised Standard Version, twenty-six other English translations and revisions of the Bible were produced by committees and by individual scholars—not to mention twenty-five other translations and revisions of the New Testament alone. One of the latter was the second edition of the RSV New Testament, issued in 1971, twenty-five years after its initial publication.

Following the publication of the RSV Old Testament in 1952, significant advances were made in the discovery and interpretation of documents in Semitic languages related to Hebrew. In addition to the information that had become available in the late 1940s from the Dead Sea texts of Isaiah and

Habakkuk, subsequent acquisitions from the same area brought to light many other early copies of all the books of the Hebrew Scriptures (except Esther), though most of these copies are fragmentary. During the same period early Greek manuscript copies of books of the New Testament also became available.

In order to take these discoveries into account, along with recent studies of documents in Semitic languages related to Hebrew, in 1974 the Policies Committee of the Revised Standard Version, which is a standing committee of the National Council of the Churches of Christ in the U.S.A., authorized the preparation of a revision of the entire RSV Bible.

For the Old Testament the Committee has made use of the *Biblia Hebraica Stuttgartensia* (1977; ed. sec. emendata, 1983). This is an edition of the Hebrew and Aramaic text as current early in the Christian era and fixed by Jewish scholars (the "Masoretes") of the sixth to the ninth centuries. The vowel signs, which were added by the Masoretes, are accepted in the main, but where a more probable and convincing reading can be obtained by assuming different vowels, this has been done. No notes are given in such cases, because the vowel points are less ancient and reliable than the consonants. When an alternative reading given by the Masoretes is translated in a footnote, this is identified by the words "Another reading is."

Departures from the consonantal text of the best manuscripts have been made only where it seems clear that errors in copying had been made before the text was standardized. Most of the corrections adopted are based on the ancient versions (translations into Greek, Aramaic, Syriac, and Latin), which were made prior to the time of the work of the Masoretes and which therefore may reflect earlier forms of the Hebrew text. In such instances a footnote specifies the version or versions from which the correction has been derived and also gives a translation of the Masoretic Text. Where it was deemed appropriate to do so, information is supplied in footnotes from subsidiary Jewish traditions concerning other textual readings (the *Tiqqune Sopherim*, "emendations of the scribes"). These are identified in the footnotes as "Ancient Heb tradition."

Occasionally it is evident that the text has suffered in transmission and that none of the versions provides a satisfactory restoration. Here we can only follow the best judgment of competent scholars as to the most probable reconstruction of the original text. Such reconstructions are indicated in footnotes by the abbreviation Cn ("Correction"), and a translation of the Masoretic Text is added.

For the Apocryphal/Deuterocanonical Books of the Old Testament the Committee has made use of a number of texts. For most of these books the basic Greek text from which the present translation was made is the edition of the Septuagint prepared by Alfred Rahlfs and published by the Württemberg Bible Society (Stuttgart, 1935). For several of the books the more recently published individual volumes of the Göttingen Septuagint project were utilized. For the book of Tobit it was decided to follow the form of the Greek text found in codex Sinaiticus (supported as it is by evidence from Qumran); where this text is defective, it was supplemented and corrected by other Greek manuscripts. For the three Additions to Daniel (namely, Susanna, the Prayer of Azariah and the Song of the Three Jews, and Bel and the Dragon) the Committee continued to use the Greek version attributed to Theodotion (the so-called "Theodotion-Daniel"). In translating Ecclesiasticus (Sirach), while constant reference was made to the Hebrew fragments of a large portion of this book (those discovered at Qumran and Masada as well as those recovered from the Cairo Geniza), the Committee generally followed the Greek text (including verse numbers) published by Joseph Ziegler in the Göttingen Septuagint (1965). But in many places the Committee has translated the Hebrew text when this provides a reading that is clearly superior to the Greek; the Syriac and Latin versions were also consulted throughout and occasionally adopted. The basic text adopted in rendering 2 Esdras is the Latin version given in *Biblia Sacra*, edited by Robert Weber (Stuttgart, 1971). This was supplemented by consulting the Latin text as edited by R. L. Bensly (1895) and by Bruno Violet (1910), as well as by taking into account the several Oriental versions of 2 Esdras, namely, the Syriac, Ethiopic, Arabic (two forms, referred to as Arabic I and Arabic 2), Armenian, and Georgian versions. Finally, since the Additions to the Book of Esther are disjointed and quite unintelligible as they stand in most editions of the Apocrypha, we have provided them with their original context by translating the whole of the Greek version of Esther from Robert Hanhart's Göttingen edition (1983).

For the New Testament the Committee has based its work on the most recent edition of *The Greek New Testament*, prepared by an interconfessional and international committee and published by the

United Bible Societies (1966; 3rd ed. corrected, 1983; information concerning changes to be introduced into the critical apparatus of the forthcoming 4th edition was available to the Committee). As in that edition, double brackets are used to enclose a few passages that are generally regarded to be later additions to the text, but which we have retained because of their evident antiquity and their importance in the textual tradition. Only in very rare instances have we replaced the text or the punctuation of the Bible Societies' edition by an alternative that seemed to us to be superior. Here and there in the footnotes the phrase, "Other ancient authorities read," identifies alternative readings preserved by Greek manuscripts and early versions. In both Testaments, alternative renderings of the text are indicated by the word "Or."

As for the style of English adopted for the present revision, among the mandates given to the Committee in 1980 by the Division of Education and Ministry of the National Council of Churches of Christ (which now holds the copyright of the RSV Bible) was the directive to continue in the tradition of the King James Bible, but to introduce such changes as are warranted on the basis of accuracy, clarity, euphony, and current English usage. Within the constraints set by the original texts and by the mandates of the Division, the Committee has followed the maxim, "As literal as possible, as free as necessary." As a consequence, the New Revised Standard Version (NRSV) remains essentially a literal translation. Paraphrastic renderings have been adopted only sparingly, and then chiefly to compensate for a deficiency in the English language—the lack of a common gender third person singular pronoun.

During the almost half a century since the publication of the RSV, many in the churches have become sensitive to the danger of linguistic sexism arising from the inherent bias of the English language towards the masculine gender, a bias that in the case of the Bible has often restricted or obscured the meaning of the original text. The mandates from the Division specified that, in references to men and women, masculine-oriented language should be eliminated as far as this can be done without altering passages that reflect the historical situation of ancient patriarchal culture. As can be appreciated, more than once the Committee found that the several mandates stood in tension and even in conflict. The various concerns had to be balanced case by case in order to provide a faithful and acceptable rendering without using contrived English. Only very occasionally has the pronoun "he" or "him" been retained in passages where the reference may have been to a woman as well as to a man; for example, in several legal texts in Leviticus and Deuteronomy. In such instances of formal, legal language, the options of either putting the passage in the plural or of introducing additional nouns to avoid masculine pronouns in English seemed to the Committee to obscure the historic structure and literary character of the original. In the vast majority of cases, however, inclusiveness has been attained by simple rephrasing or by introducing plural forms when this does not distort the meaning of the passage. Of course, in narrative and in parable no attempt was made to generalize the sex of individual persons.

Another aspect of style will be detected by readers who compare the more stately English rendering of the Old Testament with the less formal rendering adopted for the New Testament. For example, the traditional distinction between *shall* and *will* in English has been retained in the Old Testament as appropriate in rendering a document that embodies what may be termed the classic form of Hebrew, while in the New Testament the abandonment of such distinctions in the usage of the future tense in English reflects the more colloquial nature of the koine Greek used by most New Testament authors except when they are quoting the Old Testament.

Careful readers will notice that here and there in the Old Testament the word LORD (or in certain cases GOD) is printed in capital letters. This represents the traditional manner in English versions of rendering the Divine Name, the "Tetragrammaton" (see the notes on Exodus 3.14, 15), following the precedent of the ancient Greek and Latin translators and the long established practice in the reading of the Hebrew Scriptures in the synagogue. While it is almost if not quite certain that the Name was originally pronounced "Yahweh," this pronunciation was not indicated when the Masoretes added vowel sounds to the consonantal Hebrew text. To the four consonants YHWH of the Name, which had come to be regarded as too sacred to be pronounced, they attached vowel signs indicating that in its place should be read the Hebrew word *Adonai* meaning "Lord" (or *Elohim* meaning "God"). Ancient Greek translators employed the word *Kyrios* ("Lord") for the Name. The Vulgate likewise used the Latin word *Dominus* ("Lord"). The form "Jehovah" is of late medieval origin; it is a combination of the consonants of the Divine Name and the vowels attached to it by the Masoretes but belonging to an entirely different word. Although the American Standard Version (1901) had used "Jehovah" to render the Tetragrammaton (the sound of Y being represented by J and the sound of W by V, as in Latin), for two reasons the Committees that produced the RSV and the NRSV returned to the more familiar usage of the King James Version. (1) The word "Jehovah" does not accurately represent any form of the Name ever used in Hebrew. (2) The use of any proper name for the one and only God, as though there were other gods from whom the true God had to be distinguished, began to be discontinued in Judaism before the Christian era and is inappropriate for the universal faith of the Christian Church.

It will be seen that in the Psalms and in other prayers addressed to God the archaic second person singular pronouns (*thee, thou, thine*) and verb forms (*art, hast, hadst*) are no longer used. Although some readers may regret this change, it should be pointed out that in the original languages neither the Old Testament nor the New makes any linguistic distinction between addressing a human being and addressing the Deity. Furthermore, in the tradition of the King James Version one will not expect to find the use of capital letters for pronouns that refer to the Deity—such capitalization is an unnecessary innovation that has only recently been introduced into a few English translations of the Bible. Finally, we have left to the discretion of the licensed publishers such matters as section headings, cross-references, and clues to the pronunciation of proper names.

This new version seeks to preserve all that is best in the English Bible as it has been known and used through the years. It is intended for use in public reading and congregational worship, as well as in private study, instruction, and meditation. We have resisted the temptation to introduce terms and phrases that merely reflect current moods, and have tried to put the message of the Scriptures in simple, enduring words and expressions that are worthy to stand in the great tradition of the King James Bible and its predecessors.

In traditional Judaism and Christianity, the Bible has been more than a historical document to be preserved or a classic of literature to be cherished and admired; it is recognized as the unique record of God's dealings with people over the ages. The Old Testament sets forth the call of a special people to enter into covenant relation with the God of justice and steadfast love and to bring God's law to the nations. The New Testament records the life and work of Jesus Christ, the one in whom "the Word became flesh," as well as describes the rise and spread of the early Christian Church. The Bible carries its full message, not to those who regard it simply as a noble literary heritage of the past or who wish to use it to enhance political purposes and advance otherwise desirable goals, but to all persons and communities who read it so that they may discern and understand what God is saying to them. That message must not be disguised in phrases that are no longer clear, or hidden under words that have changed or lost their meaning; it must be presented in language that is direct and plain and meaningful to people today. It is the hope and prayer of the translators that this version of the Bible may continue to hold a large place in congregational life and to speak to all readers, young and old alike, helping them to understand and believe and respond to its message.

For the Committee,
BRUCE M. METZGER

The Old Testament

Genesis

The Jewish title for Genesis is *bereshith*, (the first word in Hebrew in the book of Genesis, which is translated "in the beginning"). Genesis tells the story of how everything began, how paradise was lost, and how God has promised to redeem the world. Through its stories it reveals patterns that have been repeated throughout history. Reading Genesis can help you understand God's original intention for human beings as well as the tragic consequences of sin—the condition that tears us away from God, separates us from each other, and divides our own souls.

Genesis contains many of the stories we have known and cherished since childhood: Adam and Eve; Cain and Abel; Noah's Ark; and Joseph, the dreamer who is sold into slavery by his jealous brothers. As we re-read the ancient stories, we may be surprised to discover how current they are, poignantly reflecting the condition of our hearts. Eve, Sarah, Hagar, Rebekah, Rachel, Leah—their unvarnished stories reveal much about the frailty of our faith and the depth of our need for God. Through their stories, we begin to see how God acts in our own lives.

Six Days of Creation and the Sabbath

1 In the beginning when God created[a] the heavens and the earth, [2] the earth was a formless void and darkness covered the face of the deep, while a wind from God[b] swept over the face of the waters. [3] Then God said, "Let there be light"; and there was light. [4] And God saw that the light was good; and God separated the light from the darkness. [5] God called the light Day, and the darkness he called Night. And there was evening and there was morning, the first day.

6 And God said, "Let there be a dome in the midst of the waters, and let it separate the waters from the waters." [7] So God made the dome and separated the waters that were under the dome from the waters that were above the dome. And it was so. [8] God called the dome Sky. And there was evening and there was morning, the second day.

9 And God said, "Let the waters under the sky be gathered together into one place, and let the dry land appear." And it was so. [10] God called the dry land Earth,

---

[a] Or *when God began to create* or *In the beginning God created* [b] Or *while the spirit of God* or *while a mighty wind*

and the waters that were gathered together he called Seas. And God saw that it was good. ¹¹Then God said, "Let the earth put forth vegetation: plants yielding seed, and fruit trees of every kind on earth that bear fruit with the seed in it." And it was so. ¹²The earth brought forth vegetation: plants yielding seed of every kind, and trees of every kind bearing fruit with the seed in it. And God saw that it was good. ¹³And there was evening and there was morning, the third day.

*B*reath of God

MONDAY

Scripture Reading
for Today:
Genesis 1.1–26

Verses for Today:
Genesis 1.1–2; 2.7

Emptiness. Darkness. Confusion. It was a world without a welcome, an earth that held no warmth.

The disarray waited for a breath that would waken it to life. To say that God created is to say that light flooded the darkness, that music and beauty broke into the emptiness, that energy swept through the confusion and gave it direction and meaning. The abyss, the symbol of complete desolation, was transformed into a home for all of God's best ideas.

All of these ideas shared something in common. All were connected at a most fundamental level by God's own breath. God the breath-sharer . . .

It is an image as intimate as it is mysterious. The God of the Israelites did not act from a distance, but rather, drew as close to the sleeping universe as possible, as close as breath. The Hebrew word for "breath" is *ruah*. It also means "wind" or "spirit." God's very breath reached and sustained all of creation. The breath of God became our breath.

God's very breath penetrated creatures! How do we understand a God who shares breath? How do we feel the awesome nearness of such a God?

Perhaps the type of breath-sharing that is closest to our own experiences is the act of mouth-to-mouth resuscitation. A few months ago, in a tragic accident in a nearby neighborhood, a 7-year-old boy was struck by a motorcycle. As he lay on the cement, bruised, bleeding, and without breath, his father ran out and instinctively pressed his mouth to his child's and began to breathe his own breath into his son's lungs. It was an effort to stir to life. It was saving action—the kind of saving action so characteristic of the parent God.

Sometimes at accident scenes and swimming pools one person literally puts his or her breath into another's lungs. At other times the breath that gives life is a word of encouragement, an hour of time, an expression of love. Whenever our words and actions energize one another, we are participating in the ongoing process of creation.

—FRAN FERDER

Go to page 5 for your next devotional reading.

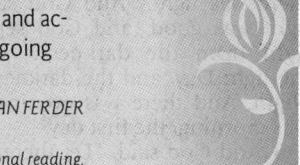

14 And God said, "Let there be lights in the dome of the sky to separate the day from the night; and let them be for signs and for seasons and for days and years, [15]and let them be lights in the dome of the sky to give light upon the earth." And it was so. [16]God made the two great lights— the greater light to rule the day and the lesser light to rule the night—and the stars. [17]God set them in the dome of the sky to give light upon the earth, [18]to rule over the day and over the night, and to separate the light from the darkness. And God saw that it was good. [19]And there was evening and there was morning, the fourth day.

20 And God said, "Let the waters bring forth swarms of living creatures, and let birds fly above the earth across the dome of the sky." [21]So God created the great sea monsters and every living creature that moves, of every kind, with which the waters swarm, and every winged bird of every kind. And God saw that it was good. [22]God blessed them, saying, "Be fruitful and multiply and fill the waters in the seas, and let birds multiply on the earth." [23]And there was evening and there was morning, the fifth day.

24 And God said, "Let the earth bring forth living creatures of every kind: cattle and creeping things and wild animals of the earth of every kind." And it was so. [25]God made the wild animals of the earth of every kind, and the cattle of every kind, and everything that creeps upon the ground of every kind. And God saw that it was good.

26 Then God said, "Let us make humankind[c] in our image, according to our likeness; and let them have dominion over the fish of the sea, and over the birds of the air, and over the cattle, and over all the wild animals of the earth,[d] and over every creeping thing that creeps upon the earth."

27 So God created humankind[c] in his image,
in the image of God he created them;[e]
male and female he created them.

[28]God blessed them, and God said to them, "Be fruitful and multiply, and fill the earth and subdue it; and have dominion over the fish of the sea and over the birds of the air and over every living thing that moves upon the earth." [29]God said, "See, I have given you every plant yielding seed that is upon the face of all the earth, and every tree with seed in its fruit; you shall have them for food. [30]And to every beast of the earth, and to every bird of the air, and to everything that creeps on the earth, everything that has the breath of life, I have given every green plant for food." And it was so. [31]God saw everything that he had made, and indeed, it was very good. And there was evening and there was morning, the sixth day.

2 Thus the heavens and the earth were finished, and all their multitude. [2]And on the seventh day God finished the work that he had done, and he rested on the seventh day from all the work that he had done. [3]So God blessed the seventh day and hallowed it, because on it God rested from all the work that he had done in creation.

4 These are the generations of the heavens and the earth when they were created.

Another Account of the Creation

In the day that the LORD[f] God made the earth and the heavens, [5]when no plant of the field was yet in the earth and no herb of the field had yet sprung up—for the LORD God had not caused it to rain upon the earth, and there was no one to till the ground; [6]but a stream would rise from the earth, and water the whole face of the ground— [7]then the LORD God formed man from the dust of the ground,[g] and breathed into his nostrils the breath of life; and the man became a living being. [8]And the LORD God planted a garden in Eden, in the east; and there he put the man whom he had formed. [9]Out of the ground the LORD God made to grow every tree that is pleasant to the sight and good for food, the tree of life also in the midst of the garden, and the tree of the knowledge of good and evil.

10 A river flows out of Eden to water the garden, and from there it divides and becomes four branches. [11]The name of the first is Pishon; it is the one that flows around the whole land of Havilah, where there is gold; [12]and the gold of that land is good; bdellium and onyx stone are there.

---

[c] Heb *adam*   [d] Syr: Heb *and over all the earth*
[e] Heb *him*   [f] Heb YHWH, as in other places where "LORD" is spelled with capital letters (see also Exod 3.14-15 with notes).   [g] Or *formed a man* (Heb *adam*) *of dust from the ground* (Heb *adamah*)

¹³The name of the second river is Gihon; it is the one that flows around the whole land of Cush. ¹⁴The name of the third river is Tigris, which flows east of Assyria. And the fourth river is the Euphrates.

15 The LORD God took the man and put him in the garden of Eden to till it and keep it. ¹⁶And the LORD God commanded the man, "You may freely eat of every tree of the garden; ¹⁷but of the tree of the knowledge of good and evil you shall not eat, for in the day that you eat of it you shall die."

18 Then the LORD God said, "It is not good that the man should be alone; I will make him a helper as his partner." ¹⁹So out of the ground the LORD God formed every animal of the field and every bird of the air, and brought them to the man to see what he would call them; and whatever the man called every living creature, that was its name. ²⁰The man gave names to all cattle, and to the birds of the air, and to every animal of the field; but for the man*ʰ* there was not found a helper as his partner. ²¹So the LORD God caused a deep sleep to fall upon the man, and he slept; then he took one of his ribs and closed up its place with flesh. ²²And the rib that the LORD God had taken from the man made into a woman and brought her to the man. ²³Then the man said,

"This at last is bone of my bones
    and flesh of my flesh;
this one shall be called Woman,*ⁱ*
    for out of Man *ʲ* this one was
        taken."

²⁴Therefore a man leaves his father and his mother and clings to his wife, and they become one flesh. ²⁵And the man and his wife were both naked, and were not ashamed.

The First Sin and Its Punishment

3 Now the serpent was more crafty than any other wild animal that the LORD God had made. He said to the woman, "Did God say, 'You shall not eat from any tree in the garden'?" ²The woman said to the serpent, "We may eat of the fruit of the trees in the garden; ³but God said, 'You shall not eat of the fruit of the tree that is in the middle of the garden, nor shall you touch it, or you shall die.' " ⁴But the serpent said to the woman, "You will not die; ⁵for God knows that when you eat of it your eyes will be opened, and you will be like God,*ᵏ* knowing good and

evil." ⁶So when the woman saw that the tree was good for food, and that it was a delight to the eyes, and that the tree was to be desired to make one wise, she took of its fruit and ate; and she also gave some to her husband, who was with her, and he ate. ⁷Then the eyes of both were opened, and they knew that they were naked; and they sewed fig leaves together and made loincloths for themselves.

8 They heard the sound of the LORD God walking in the garden at the time of the evening breeze, and the man and his wife hid themselves from the presence of the LORD God among the trees of the garden. ⁹But the LORD God called to the man, and said to him, "Where are you?" ¹⁰He said, "I heard the sound of you in the garden, and I was afraid, because I was naked; and I hid myself." ¹¹He said, "Who told you that you were naked? Have you eaten from the tree of which I commanded you not to eat?" ¹²The man said, "The woman whom you gave to be with me, she gave me fruit from the tree, and I ate." ¹³Then the LORD God said to the woman, "What is this that you have done?" The woman said, "The serpent tricked me, and I ate." ¹⁴The LORD God said to the serpent,

"Because you have done this,
    cursed are you among all animals
        and among all wild creatures;
upon your belly you shall go,
    and dust you shall eat
        all the days of your life.
15 I will put enmity between you and
        the woman,
    and between your offspring and
        hers;
he will strike your head,
    and you will strike his heel."

¹⁶To the woman he said,

"I will greatly increase your pangs in
        childbearing;
    in pain you shall bring forth
        children,
yet your desire shall be for your
        husband,
    and he shall rule over you."

¹⁷And to the man*ˡ* he said,

"Because you have listened to the
        voice of your wife,
    and have eaten of the tree
    about which I commanded you,

ʰ Or for Adam   *ⁱ Heb ishshah*   *ʲ Heb ish*
ᵏ Or gods   *ˡ Or to Adam*

A Psalm for Women

TUESDAY

Scripture Reading
for Today:
Genesis 2.18–25

Verse for Today:
Genesis 2.23

Divine Wisdom, out of love and compassion
You created me
   and called me "woman"
bone of bones and flesh of flesh
companion and partner with man.

You created me in your
own image to be fruitful
   and to fill the earth with life,
leading, ordering and empowering
   the created universe,
together with the holy women and men,
   created and infused with your spirit of love.

You have drawn me into a web
of woven threads with the ancient ones
Eve and Esther
   Ruth and Naomi
      Sarah and Rebecca.
You have drawn me into a sisterhood
of pieces and patterns
designed by holy women
Mary and Elizabeth
   Martha of Bethany and Mary of Magdala
      Priscilla and Lydia.
You have drawn me into a kinship
with the wild, daring, holy women
   whose lives flavor my own
Thérèse of Lisieux and Catherine of Siena
   Clare of Assisi and Teresa of Avila
      Margaret of Hungary and Briget of Kildare.
You have drawn me into a union
   with the wise women
      of my own time and culture
Dorothy Day and Thea Bowman
   Mother Teresa and Edith Stein
      Simone Weil and
      Catherine de Hueck Doherty.
In their company I will spring up, blossom and grow
into the woman of wisdom
   You have molded and formed
      from the beginning of time.

—*CAROL GURA*

Go to page 6 for your next devotional reading.

'You shall not eat of it,'
cursed is the ground because of
you;
in toil you shall eat of it all the
days of your life;
18 thorns and thistles it shall bring
forth for you;
and you shall eat the plants of the
field.
19 By the sweat of your face
you shall eat bread
until you return to the ground,
for out of it you were taken;
you are dust,
and to dust you shall return."

20 The man named his wife Eve,[m] because she was the mother of all living. [21]And the LORD God made garments of skins for the man[n] and for his wife, and clothed them.

22 Then the LORD God said, "See, the man has become like one of us, knowing good and evil; and now, he might reach out his hand and take also from the tree of life, and eat, and live forever"— [23]therefore the LORD God sent him forth from the garden of Eden, to till the ground from which he was taken. [24]He drove out the man; and at the east of the garden of Eden he placed the cherubim, and a sword flaming and turning to guard the way to the tree of life.

Cain Murders Abel

4 Now the man knew his wife Eve, and she conceived and bore Cain, saying, "I have produced[o] a man with the help of the LORD." [2]Next she bore his brother Abel. Now Abel was a keeper of sheep,

[m] In Heb *Eve* resembles the word for *living*
[n] Or *for Adam*　　[o] The verb in Heb resembles the word for *Cain*

---

*D*oubting

WEDNESDAY

Scripture Reading
for Today:
Genesis 3.1–7

Verse for Today:
Genesis 3.1

"Did God really say it?" "Are you sure?" "Surely he didn't." How often I am tempted to listen to those words—how often all of us are. God most definitely has spoken. His word, steadfast and unchanging, he means what he says. Does what he says. Never pulls a fast one. And still we question or disregard his heart. I, for one, have indulged in the rationalizing, the putting a stamp of okay on something that God has said is unholy. We need only look around today to see the effects of Satan's questions. Moral and spiritual decay. A rightness placed on what is so obviously wrong. A label of old-fashioned and barbaric attached to laws that are still the same in God's eyes and that he still cherishes. A bend toward our own philosophies. A turning from absolute truth to what our own truth happens to be.

So we are left believing the lies of the enemy and with the consequences of our choices. And it all takes place under the guise of love and honesty, goodness and fairness, open-mindedness and tolerance.

The serpent may come to you and say, "Did God really say that?" Your answer must be "yes." For no matter how many promises God has made, they are yes in Christ (see 2 Corinthians 1.20). "Yes!" to all he desires and "No!" to all he does not. Nothing is worth being out of the will of God. Take him at his word.

—*KATHY TROCCOLI*

Go to page 7 for your next devotional reading.
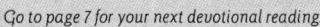

and Cain a tiller of the ground. ³In the course of time Cain brought to the LORD an offering of the fruit of the ground, ⁴and Abel for his part brought of the firstlings of his flock, their fat portions. And the LORD had regard for Abel and his offering, ⁵but for Cain and his offering he had no regard. So Cain was very angry, and his countenance fell. ⁶The LORD said to Cain, "Why are you angry, and why has your countenance fallen? ⁷If you do well, will you not be accepted? And if you do not do well, sin is lurking at the door; its desire is for you, but you must master it."

8 Cain said to his brother Abel, "Let us go out to the field." ᵖ And when they were in the field, Cain rose up against his brother Abel, and killed him. ⁹Then the

ᵖ Sam Gk Syr Compare Vg: MT lacks *Let us go out to the field*

THURSDAY

Scripture Reading
for Today:
Genesis 4.1–7

Verse for Today:
Genesis 4.6

What About Me?

Once I was standing with others at a quilt show. The piece before us was stunning. "Does that make you feel inferior or inspired?" someone asked. The question was more profound than she knew.

When we see that another person lives very close to God or has received particular gifts or seems to progress faster in spiritual life than we do, how do we respond? Do we feel small and ignored by the Spirit? Do we feel angry that God gives so much to that other one? Do we feel inferior? Do we wonder why that person was given so much and we were given so little? Or do we take inspiration from the beauty of another's life?

If we are able to rejoice in God's grace for all, without comparisons and without envy, we live in shared joy and tender appreciation for everyone. We then learn what it means to love both neighbor and enemy.

During Dante's vision of heaven in the *Paradiso*, he describes the universe-size rose of souls that surrounds the divine throne with utter beauty. He wonders aloud to a soul on the edge of this rose, farthest from the throne, whether he is content there. The soul replies that he so loves God he is thrilled to be in whatever place God has put him; he is filled with God's praise and God's love—how can he wish for more?

It is a rare person who loves enough to rejoice in *all* goodness, whether he or she benefits directly or not. Yet we can all practice this happy attitude. When we hear of something wonderful falling into another's life, we can set aside that nagging "But what about me?" and simply enjoy the beauty with that person. We may even celebrate it. It is recommended that we do this, even though in the beginning it may *feel* unreal, if we have habitually envied every good thing that happened to others. Our emotions carry on in their habits, but do our emotions tell us the truth? Rarely!

—MARILYN GUSTIN

Go to page 12 for your next devotional reading.

LORD said to Cain, "Where is your brother
Abel?" He said, "I do not know; am I my
brother's keeper?" 10And the LORD said,
"What have you done? Listen; your brother's blood is crying out to me from the
ground! 11And now you are cursed from
the ground, which has opened its mouth
to receive your brother's blood from your
hand. 12When you till the ground, it will
no longer yield to you its strength; you
will be a fugitive and a wanderer on the
earth." 13Cain said to the LORD, "My punishment is greater than I can bear! 14To-
day you have driven me away from the
soil, and I shall be hidden from your face;
I shall be a fugitive and a wanderer on the
earth, and anyone who meets me may kill
me." 15Then the LORD said to him, "Not
so![q] Whoever kills Cain will suffer a sevenfold vengeance." And the LORD put a
mark on Cain, so that no one who came
upon him would kill him. 16Then Cain
went away from the presence of the LORD,
and settled in the land of Nod,[r] east of
Eden.

Beginnings of Civilization

17 Cain knew his wife, and she conceived and bore Enoch; and he built a city,
and named it Enoch after his son Enoch.
18To Enoch was born Irad; and Irad was
the father of Mehujael, and Mehujael the
father of Methushael, and Methushael the
father of Lamech. 19Lamech took two
wives; the name of the one was Adah, and
the name of the other Zillah. 20Adah bore
Jabal; he was the ancestor of those who
live in tents and have livestock. 21His
brother's name was Jubal; he was the ancestor of all those who play the lyre and
pipe. 22Zillah bore Tubal-cain, who made
all kinds of bronze and iron tools. The
sister of Tubal-cain was Naamah.

23 Lamech said to his wives:
"Adah and Zillah, hear my voice;
you wives of Lamech, listen to
what I say:
I have killed a man for wounding
me,
a young man for striking me.
24 If Cain is avenged sevenfold,
truly Lamech seventy-sevenfold."

25 Adam knew his wife again, and she
bore a son and named him Seth, for she
said, "God has appointed[s] for me another child instead of Abel, because Cain
killed him." 26To Seth also a son was born,
and he named him Enosh. At that time
people began to invoke the name of the
LORD.

Adam's Descendants to Noah and His Sons

5 This is the list of the descendants of
Adam. When God created human-
kind,[t] he made them[u] in the likeness of
God. 2Male and female he created them,
and he blessed them and named them
"Humankind"[t] when they were created.

3 When Adam had lived one hundred
thirty years, he became the father of a son
in his likeness, according to his image,
and named him Seth. 4The days of Adam
after he became the father of Seth were
eight hundred years; and he had other
sons and daughters. 5Thus all the days
that Adam lived were nine hundred thirty
years; and he died.

6 When Seth had lived one hundred
five years, he became the father of Enosh.
7Seth lived after the birth of Enosh eight
hundred seven years, and had other sons
and daughters. 8Thus all the days of Seth
were nine hundred twelve years; and he
died.

9 When Enosh had lived ninety years,
he became the father of Kenan. 10Enosh
lived after the birth of Kenan eight hundred fifteen years, and had other sons and
daughters. 11Thus all the days of Enosh
were nine hundred five years; and he died.

12 When Kenan had lived seventy
years, he became the father of Mahalalel.
13Kenan lived after the birth of Mahalalel
eight hundred and forty years, and had
other sons and daughters. 14Thus all the
days of Kenan were nine hundred and ten
years; and he died.

15 When Mahalalel had lived sixty-five
years, he became the father of Jared. 16Ma-
halalel lived after the birth of Jared eight
hundred thirty years, and had other sons
and daughters. 17Thus all the days of Mahalalel were eight hundred ninety-five
years; and he died.

18 When Jared had lived one hundred
sixty-two years he became the father of
Enoch. 19Jared lived after the birth of
Enoch eight hundred years, and had other
sons and daughters. 20Thus all the days of
Jared were nine hundred sixty-two years;
and he died.

21 When Enoch had lived sixty-five

[q] Gk Syr Vg: Heb *Therefore* [r] That is *Wandering*
[s] The verb in Heb resembles the word for *Seth*
[t] Heb *adam* [u] Heb *him*

years, he became the father of Methuselah. 22Enoch walked with God after the birth of Methuselah three hundred years, and had other sons and daughters. 23Thus all the days of Enoch were three hundred sixty-five years. 24Enoch walked with God; then he was no more, because God took him.

25 When Methuselah had lived one hundred eighty-seven years, he became the father of Lamech. 26Methuselah lived after the birth of Lamech seven hundred eighty-two years, and had other sons and daughters. 27Thus all the days of Methuselah were nine hundred sixty-nine years; and he died.

28 When Lamech had lived one hundred eighty-two years, he became the father of a son; 29he named him Noah, saying, "Out of the ground that the LORD has cursed this one shall bring us relief from our work and from the toil of our hands." 30Lamech lived after the birth of Noah five hundred ninety-five years, and had other sons and daughters. 31Thus all the days of Lamech were seven hundred seventy-seven years; and he died.

32 After Noah was five hundred years old, Noah became the father of Shem, Ham, and Japheth.

The Wickedness of Humankind

6 When people began to multiply on the face of the ground, and daughters were born to them, 2the sons of God saw that they were fair; and they took wives for themselves of all that they chose. 3Then the LORD said, "My spirit shall not abide*v* in mortals forever, for they are flesh; their days shall be one hundred twenty years." 4The Nephilim were on the earth in those days—and also afterward—when the sons of God went in to the daughters of humans, who bore children to them. These were the heroes that were of old, warriors of renown.

5 The LORD saw that the wickedness of humankind was great in the earth, and that every inclination of the thoughts of their hearts was only evil continually. 6And the LORD was sorry that he had made humankind on the earth, and it grieved him to his heart. 7So the LORD said, "I will blot out from the earth the human beings I have created—people together with animals and creeping things and birds of the air, for I am sorry that I have made them."

8But Noah found favor in the sight of the LORD.

Noah Pleases God

9 These are the descendants of Noah. Noah was a righteous man, blameless in his generation; Noah walked with God. 10And Noah had three sons, Shem, Ham, and Japheth.

11 Now the earth was corrupt in God's sight, and the earth was filled with violence. 12And God saw that the earth was corrupt; for all flesh had corrupted its ways upon the earth. 13And God said to Noah, "I have determined to make an end of all flesh, for the earth is filled with violence because of them; now I am going to destroy them along with the earth. 14Make yourself an ark of cypress*v* wood; make rooms in the ark, and cover it inside and out with pitch. 15This is how you are to make it: the length of the ark three hundred cubits, its width fifty cubits, and its height thirty cubits. 16Make a roof*w* for the ark, and finish it to a cubit above; and put the door of the ark in its side; make it with lower, second, and third decks. 17For my part, I am going to bring a flood of waters on the earth, to destroy from under heaven all flesh in which is the breath of life; everything that is on the earth shall die. 18But I will establish my covenant with you; and you shall come into the ark, you, your sons, your wife, and your sons' wives with you. 19And of every living thing, of all flesh, you shall bring two of every kind into the ark, to keep them alive with you; they shall be male and female. 20Of the birds according to their kinds, and of the animals according to their kinds, of every creeping thing of the ground according to its kind, two of every kind shall come in to you, to keep them alive. 21Also take with you every kind of food that is eaten, and store it up; and it shall serve as food for you and for them." 22Noah did this; he did all that God commanded him.

The Great Flood

7 Then the LORD said to Noah, "Go into the ark, you and all your household, for I have seen that you alone are righteous before me in this generation. 2Take with you seven pairs of all clean animals, the male and its mate; and a pair

---

v Meaning of Heb uncertain   w Or window

of the animals that are not clean, the male and its mate; ³and seven pairs of the birds of the air also, male and female, to keep their kind alive on the face of all the earth. ⁴For in seven days I will send rain on the earth for forty days and forty nights; and every living thing that I have made I will blot out from the face of the ground." ⁵And Noah did all that the LORD had commanded him.

6 Noah was six hundred years old when the flood of waters came on the earth. ⁷And Noah with his sons and his wife and his sons' wives went into the ark to escape the waters of the flood. ⁸Of clean animals, and of animals that are not clean, and of birds, and of everything that creeps on the ground, ⁹two and two, male and female, went into the ark with Noah, as God had commanded Noah. ¹⁰And after seven days the waters of the flood came on the earth.

11 In the six hundredth year of Noah's life, in the second month, on the seventeenth day of the month, on that day all the fountains of the great deep burst forth, and the windows of the heavens were opened. ¹²The rain fell on the earth forty days and forty nights. ¹³On the very same day Noah with his sons, Shem and Ham and Japheth, and Noah's wife and the three wives of his sons entered the ark, ¹⁴they and every wild animal of every kind, and all domestic animals of every kind, and every creeping thing that creeps on the earth, and every bird of every kind—every bird, every winged creature. ¹⁵They went into the ark with Noah, two and two of all flesh in which there was the breath of life. ¹⁶And those that entered, male and female of all flesh, went in as God had commanded him; and the LORD shut him in.

17 The flood continued forty days on the earth; and the waters increased, and bore up the ark, and it rose high above the earth. ¹⁸The waters swelled and increased greatly on the earth; and the ark floated on the face of the waters. ¹⁹The waters swelled so mightily on the earth that all the high mountains under the whole heaven were covered; ²⁰the waters swelled above the mountains, covering them fifteen cubits deep. ²¹And all flesh died that moved on the earth, birds, domestic animals, wild animals, all swarming creatures that swarm on the earth, and all human beings; ²²everything on dry land in whose nostrils was the breath of life died. ²³He blotted out every living thing that was on the face of the ground, human beings and animals and creeping things and birds of the air; they were blotted out from the earth. Only Noah was left, and those that were with him in the ark. ²⁴And the waters swelled on the earth for one hundred fifty days.

The Flood Subsides

8 But God remembered Noah and all the wild animals and all the domestic animals that were with him in the ark. And God made a wind blow over the earth, and the waters subsided; ²the fountains of the deep and the windows of the heavens were closed, the rain from the heavens was restrained, ³and the waters gradually receded from the earth. At the end of one hundred fifty days the waters had abated; ⁴and in the seventh month, on the seventeenth day of the month, the ark came to rest on the mountains of Ararat. ⁵The waters continued to abate until the tenth month; in the tenth month, on the first day of the month, the tops of the mountains appeared.

6 At the end of forty days Noah opened the window of the ark that he had made ⁷and sent out the raven; and it went to and fro until the waters were dried up from the earth. ⁸Then he sent out the dove from him, to see if the waters had subsided from the face of the ground; ⁹but the dove found no place to set its foot, and it returned to him to the ark, for the waters were still on the face of the whole earth. So he put out his hand and took it and brought it into the ark with him. ¹⁰He waited another seven days, and again he sent out the dove from the ark; ¹¹and the dove came back to him in the evening, and there in its beak was a freshly plucked olive leaf; so Noah knew that the waters had subsided from the earth. ¹²Then he waited another seven days, and sent out the dove; and it did not return to him any more.

13 In the six hundred first year, in the first month, on the first day of the month, the waters were dried up from the earth; and Noah removed the covering of the ark, and looked, and saw that the face of the ground was drying. ¹⁴In the second month, on the twenty-seventh day of the month, the earth was dry. ¹⁵Then God said to Noah, ¹⁶"Go out of the ark, you

and your wife, and your sons and your sons' wives with you. ¹⁷Bring out with you every living thing that is with you of all flesh—birds and animals and every creeping thing that creeps on the earth—so that they may abound on the earth, and be fruitful and multiply on the earth." ¹⁸So Noah went out with his sons and his wife and his sons' wives. ¹⁹And every animal, every creeping thing, and every bird, everything that moves on the earth, went out of the ark by families.

God's Promise to Noah

20 Then Noah built an altar to the LORD, and took of every clean animal and of every clean bird, and offered burnt offerings on the altar. ²¹And when the LORD smelled the pleasing odor, the LORD said in his heart, "I will never again curse the ground because of humankind, for the inclination of the human heart is evil from youth; nor will I ever again destroy every living creature as I have done.
²² As long as the earth endures,
    seedtime and harvest, cold and
        heat,
    summer and winter, day and night,
        shall not cease."

The Covenant with Noah

9 God blessed Noah and his sons, and said to them, "Be fruitful and multiply, and fill the earth. ²The fear and dread of you shall rest on every animal of the earth, and on every bird of the air, on everything that creeps on the ground, and on all the fish of the sea; into your hand they are delivered. ³Every moving thing that lives shall be food for you; and just as I gave you the green plants, I give you everything. ⁴Only, you shall not eat flesh with its life, that is, its blood. ⁵For your own lifeblood I will surely require a reckoning: from every animal I will require it and from human beings, each one for the blood of another, I will require a reckoning for human life.
⁶ Whoever sheds the blood of a
        human,
    by a human shall that person's
        blood be shed;
    for in his own image
        God made humankind.
⁷And you, be fruitful and multiply, abound on the earth and multiply in it."
8 Then God said to Noah and to his sons with him, ⁹"As for me, I am estab-lishing my covenant with you and your descendants after you, ¹⁰and with every living creature that is with you, the birds, the domestic animals, and every animal of the earth with you, as many as came out of the ark.ˣ ¹¹I establish my covenant with you, that never again shall all flesh be cut off by the waters of a flood, and never again shall there be a flood to destroy the earth." ¹²God said, "This is the sign of the covenant that I make between me and you and every living creature that is with you, for all future generations: ¹³I have set my bow in the clouds, and it shall be a sign of the covenant between me and the earth. ¹⁴When I bring clouds over the earth and the bow is seen in the clouds, ¹⁵I will remember my covenant that is between me and you and every living creature of all flesh; and the waters shall never again become a flood to destroy all flesh. ¹⁶When the bow is in the clouds, I will see it and remember the everlasting covenant between God and every living creature of all flesh that is on the earth." ¹⁷God said to Noah, "This is the sign of the covenant that I have established between me and all flesh that is on the earth."

Noah and His Sons

18 The sons of Noah who went out of the ark were Shem, Ham, and Japheth. Ham was the father of Canaan. ¹⁹These three were the sons of Noah; and from these the whole earth was peopled.
20 Noah, a man of the soil, was the first to plant a vineyard. ²¹He drank some of the wine and became drunk, and he lay uncovered in his tent. ²²And Ham, the father of Canaan, saw the nakedness of his father, and told his two brothers outside. ²³Then Shem and Japheth took a garment, laid it on both their shoulders, and walked backward and covered the nakedness of their father; their faces were turned away, and they did not see their father's nakedness. ²⁴When Noah awoke from his wine and knew what his youngest son had done to him, ²⁵he said,
    "Cursed be Canaan;
        lowest of slaves shall he be to his
            brothers."
²⁶He also said,
    "Blessed by the LORD my God be
        Shem;
    and let Canaan be his slave.

ˣ Gk: Heb adds *every animal of the earth*

²⁷ May God make space for ʸ Japheth,
and let him live in the tents of
Shem;
and let Canaan be his slave."
28 After the flood Noah lived three
hundred fifty years. ²⁹All the days of Noah
were nine hundred fifty years; and he
died.

Nations Descended from Noah

10 These are the descendants of
Noah's sons, Shem, Ham, and Japheth; children were born to them after
the flood.

2 The descendants of Japheth: Gomer,
Magog, Madai, Javan, Tubal, Meshech,
and Tiras. ³The descendants of Gomer:
Ashkenaz, Riphath, and Togarmah. ⁴The
descendants of Javan: Elishah, Tarshish,
Kittim, and Rodanim.ᶻ ⁵From these the
coastland peoples spread. These are the
descendants of Japhethᵃ in their lands,

with their own language, by their families,
in their nations.
6 The descendants of Ham: Cush,
Egypt, Put, and Canaan. ⁷The descendants
of Cush: Seba, Havilah, Sabtah, Raamah,
and Sabteca. The descendants of Raamah:
Sheba and Dedan. ⁸Cush became the father of Nimrod; he was the first on earth
to become a mighty warrior. ⁹He was a
mighty hunter before the LORD; therefore it
is said, "Like Nimrod a mighty hunter before the LORD." ¹⁰The beginning of his kingdom was Babel, Erech, and Accad, all of
them in the land of Shinar. ¹¹From that
land he went into Assyria, and built Nineveh, Rehoboth-ir, Calah, and ¹²Resen between Nineveh and Calah; that is the great
city. ¹³Egypt became the father of Ludim,

ʸ Heb *yapht*, a play on *Japheth*   ᶻ Heb Mss Sam
Gk See 1 Chr 1.7: MT *Dodanim*   ᵃ Compare
verses 20, 31. Heb lacks *These are the descendants
of Japheth*

FRIDAY

Scripture Reading
for Today:
Genesis 9.8–17

Verse for Today:
Genesis 9.16

A Sign of Covenant

Nancy Trant, mourning the sudden death of her fiancé, traveled to
Colorado where they had planned to honeymoon. The trip was
picturesque but very lonely.

One day Nancy rented a car and drove to the top of Pikes Peak,
some fourteen thousand feet above sea level. At the summit, however, she began to feel dizzy. The entire peak was covered in a
dense cloud. "Since no one else was around and I couldn't see anything, I started back to my car," she says.

On the way, she heard an inner voice command: "Return to
where you were standing." Still light-headed, Nancy argued with
the voice, but it remained insistent within her spirit: "Go!"
Relenting, she hiked back to the guardrail.

Instantly, the clouds parted in front of her. "Before me stood a
rainbow three to four stories high, coming out of the mountain
and reaching into infinity," Nancy says. The air seemed tinged
with electricity, and she could see for miles. Nancy was trans-
fixed, filled with rapture. Wasn't the rainbow a sign of God's
covenant with his people, with her? The exquisite scene remained for several minutes, then clouds covered the summit again.
But Nancy has never forgotten the moment when God sent her
consolation in her grief and the promise of a happier tomorrow.

—JOAN WESTER ANDERSON

Go to page 14 for your next devotional reading.

Anamim, Lehabim, Naphtuhim, [14]Pathrusim, Casluhim, and Caphtorim, from which the Philistines come.[b]

15 Canaan became the father of Sidon his firstborn, and Heth, [16]and the Jebusites, the Amorites, the Girgashites, [17]the Hivites, the Arkites, the Sinites, [18]the Arvadites, the Zemarites, and the Hamathites. Afterward the families of the Canaanites spread abroad. [19]And the territory of the Canaanites extended from Sidon, in the direction of Gerar, as far as Gaza, and in the direction of Sodom, Gomorrah, Admah, and Zeboiim, as far as Lasha. [20]These are the descendants of Ham, by their families, their languages, their lands, and their nations.

21 To Shem also, the father of all the children of Eber, the elder brother of Japheth, children were born. [22]The descendants of Shem: Elam, Asshur, Arpachshad, Lud, and Aram. [23]The descendants of Aram: Uz, Hul, Gether, and Mash. [24]Arpachshad became the father of Shelah; and Shelah became the father of Eber. [25]To Eber were born two sons: the name of the one was Peleg,[c] for in his days the earth was divided, and his brother's name was Joktan. [26]Joktan became the father of Almodad, Sheleph, Hazarmaveth, Jerah, [27]Hadoram, Uzal, Diklah, [28]Obal, Abimael, Sheba, [29]Ophir, Havilah, and Jobab; all these were the descendants of Joktan. [30]The territory in which they lived extended from Mesha in the direction of Sephar, the hill country of the east. [31]These are the descendants of Shem, by their families, their languages, their lands, and their nations.

32 These are the families of Noah's sons, according to their genealogies, in their nations; and from these the nations spread abroad on the earth after the flood.

The Tower of Babel

11 Now the whole earth had one language and the same words. [2]And as they migrated from the east,[d] they came upon a plain in the land of Shinar and settled there. [3]And they said to one another, "Come, let us make bricks, and burn them thoroughly." And they had brick for stone, and bitumen for mortar. [4]Then they said, "Come, let us build ourselves a city, and a tower with its top in the heavens, and let us make a name for ourselves; otherwise we shall be scattered abroad upon the face of the whole earth."

[5]The LORD came down to see the city and the tower, which mortals had built. [6]And the LORD said, "Look, they are one people, and they have all one language; and this is only the beginning of what they will do; nothing that they propose to do will now be impossible for them. [7]Come, let us go down, and confuse their language there, so that they will not understand one another's speech." [8]So the LORD scattered them abroad from there over the face of all the earth, and they left off building the city. [9]Therefore it was called Babel, because there the LORD confused[e] the language of all the earth; and from there the LORD scattered them abroad over the face of all the earth.

Descendants of Shem

10 These are the descendants of Shem. When Shem was one hundred years old, he became the father of Arpachshad two years after the flood; [11]and Shem lived after the birth of Arpachshad five hundred years, and had other sons and daughters.

12 When Arpachshad had lived thirty-five years, he became the father of Shelah; [13]and Arpachshad lived after the birth of Shelah four hundred three years, and had other sons and daughters.

14 When Shelah had lived thirty years, he became the father of Eber; [15]and Shelah lived after the birth of Eber four hundred three years, and had other sons and daughters.

16 When Eber had lived thirty-four years, he became the father of Peleg; [17]and Eber lived after the birth of Peleg four hundred thirty years, and had other sons and daughters.

18 When Peleg had lived thirty years, he became the father of Reu; [19]and Peleg lived after the birth of Reu two hundred nine years, and had other sons and daughters.

20 When Reu had lived thirty-two years, he became the father of Serug; [21]and Reu lived after the birth of Serug two hundred seven years, and had other sons and daughters.

22 When Serug had lived thirty years, he became the father of Nahor; [23]and Serug lived after the birth of Nahor two hun-

b Cn: Heb *Casluhim, from which the Philistines come, and Caphtorim*   *c* That is *Division*   *d* Or *migrated eastward*   *e* Heb *balal,* meaning *to confuse*

Eve

Her Name Means *"Life-giving"* or
"Mother of All Who Have Life"

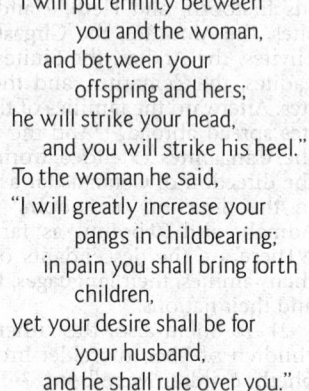

Her Character: *She came into the world at peace with God and with Adam, the only other person on the planet. She possessed every pleasure imaginable and never knew the meaning of embarrassment, misunderstanding, hurt, envy, bitterness, grief, or guilt—until she listened to her enemy Satan and began to doubt God.*

Her Sorrow: *That she and her husband were banished from Eden and that her first son was a murderer and her second son his victim.*

Her Joy: *That she had once tasted paradise and that God had promised her offspring would eventually destroy her enemy.*

Read Genesis 2—4

The woman stirred and stretched, her skin soft and supple as a newborn's. One finger then another moved in gentle exploration of the ground that cradled her. She felt warm and full inside, unable to contain the laughter that burst from her lips. Then a Touch quieted her.

Her eyes opened to a Brightness, her ears to a Voice. And then a smaller voice, echoing an elated response: "This at last is bone of my bones and flesh of my flesh; this one shall be called Woman, for out of Man this one was taken" (2.23). Adam took hold of her, and their laughter met like streams converging.

The man and the woman walked together naked and unashamed in their paradise, at ease with themselves and with God. Then one day a serpent spoke to the woman. "Did God say, 'You shall not eat from any tree in the garden'? ... You will not die; for God knows that when you eat of it your eyes will be opened, and you will be like God, knowing good and evil" (3.1, 4–5).

The woman listened. Doubt and desire pursued her until she ate the fruit and shared it with her husband. And darkness rushed into Eden.

God banished them from their garden paradise, pronouncing judgment on both Eve and her husband. Cursing the serpent, he added this promise:

"I will put enmity between
    you and the woman,
  and between your
    offspring and hers;
he will strike your head,
  and you will strike his heel."
To the woman he said,
"I will greatly increase your
    pangs in childbearing;
  in pain you shall bring forth
    children,
yet your desire shall be for
    your husband,
  and he shall rule over you."
                    (3.15–16)

Because of their sin, the curse of death fell suddenly upon the new world. So Adam and his wife fled paradise. And although Eve received her name because she was the mother of all living, her firstborn, Cain, became a murderer and her second son, Abel, his victim.

In our last glimpse of Eve, we imagine her, not as a creature springing fresh from God's hand, but as a woman in anguish. Her skin, damaged by sun and age, stretches like rough canvas across her limbs. Her hands are like restless spiders, clawing the stony ground beneath her, grasping for something to ease her pain. She can feel the child inside, filling her, his body pressing for a way of escape. The cries of mother and child meet like streams converging. And Seth is born.

With her child cradled against her breast, relief begins to spread across Eve's face. As she rests, a smile forms and then finally laughter rushes from her lips. For she remembers the Brightness and the Voice and the promise God gave: Sooner or later, despite many griefs, her offspring would crush the serpent. The woman would win.

Praying With Eve

So God created humankind in his image, in the image of God he created them; male and female he created them.—*Genesis 1.27*

Praise God: *Because he created you in his own image, making you a woman capable of reflecting his love, truth, strength, goodness, wisdom, and beauty.*

Offer Thanks: *That imbedded in God's judgment of Adam and Eve is the promise of a Redeemer who will crush the head of our enemy.*

Confess: *Your own tendency to mar God's image in you by preferring your will to his.*

Ask God: *To help you surrender your life to him so that he can fulfill his purpose for creating you.*

Lift Your Heart

Find a peaceful setting, surrounded by the beauty of creation, to meditate on what life must have been like in the Garden of Eden. Think about what your life would be like if you experienced peace in all your relationships, if you never suffered physical or emotional pain, if you were never confused or ashamed or guilty, if you always experienced God's love and friendship. Let your imagination run riot as it fills in the details of God's original intention for your life and for those you love. Then consider this: You were made for paradise. The joys you taste now are infinitesimal compared to those that await you in heaven.

Father, give me a greater understanding of your original plan for our world. Help me to envision its beauty so that I might live with a constant awareness that you intend to restore paradise to all who belong to you. May I surrender every sin and every sorrow to you, trusting that you will fulfill your purpose for my life.

Go to page 20 for your next devotional reading.

dred years, and had other sons and daughters.

24 When Nahor had lived twenty-nine years, he became the father of Terah; 25and Nahor lived after the birth of Terah one hundred nineteen years, and had other sons and daughters.

26 When Terah had lived seventy years, he became the father of Abram, Nahor, and Haran.

Descendants of Terah

27 Now these are the descendants of Terah. Terah was the father of Abram, Nahor, and Haran; and Haran was the father of Lot. 28Haran died before his father Terah in the land of his birth, in Ur of the Chaldeans. 29Abram and Nahor took wives; the name of Abram's wife was Sarai, and the name of Nahor's wife was Milcah. She was the daughter of Haran the father of Milcah and Iscah. 30Now Sarai was barren; she had no child.

31 Terah took his son Abram and his grandson Lot son of Haran, and his daughter-in-law Sarai, his son Abram's wife, and they went out together from Ur of the Chaldeans to go into the land of Canaan; but when they came to Haran, they settled there. 32The days of Terah were two hundred five years; and Terah died in Haran.

The Call of Abram

12 Now the LORD said to Abram, "Go from your country and your kindred and your father's house to the land that I will show you. 2I will make of you a great nation, and I will bless you, and make your name great, so that you will be a blessing. 3I will bless those who bless you, and the one who curses you I will curse; and in you all the families of the earth shall be blessed."*f*

4 So Abram went, as the LORD had told him; and Lot went with him. Abram was seventy-five years old when he departed from Haran. 5Abram took his wife Sarai and his brother's son Lot, and all the possessions that they had gathered, and the persons whom they had acquired in Haran; and they set forth to go to the land of Canaan. When they had come to the land of Canaan, 6Abram passed through the land to the place at Shechem, to the oak*g* of Moreh. At that time the Canaanites were in the land. 7Then the LORD appeared to Abram, and said, "To your offspring*h*

I will give this land." So he built there an altar to the LORD, who had appeared to him. 8From there he moved on to the hill country on the east of Bethel, and pitched his tent, with Bethel on the west and Ai on the east; and there he built an altar to the LORD and invoked the name of the LORD. 9And Abram journeyed on by stages toward the Negeb.

Abram and Sarai in Egypt

10 Now there was a famine in the land. So Abram went down to Egypt to reside there as an alien, for the famine was severe in the land. 11When he was about to enter Egypt, he said to his wife Sarai, "I know well that you are a woman beautiful in appearance; 12and when the Egyptians see you, they will say, 'This is his wife'; then they will kill me, but they will let you live. 13Say you are my sister, so that it may go well with me because of you, and that my life may be spared on your account." 14When Abram entered Egypt the Egyptians saw that the woman was very beautiful. 15When the officials of Pharaoh saw her, they praised her to Pharaoh. And the woman was taken into Pharaoh's house. 16And for her sake he dealt well with Abram; and he had sheep, oxen, male donkeys, male and female slaves, female donkeys, and camels.

17 But the LORD afflicted Pharaoh and his house with great plagues because of Sarai, Abram's wife. 18So Pharaoh called Abram, and said, "What is this you have done to me? Why did you not tell me that she was your wife? 19Why did you say, 'She is my sister,' so that I took her for my wife? Now then, here is your wife, take her, and be gone." 20And Pharaoh gave his men orders concerning him; and they set him on the way, with his wife and all that he had.

Abram and Lot Separate

13 So Abram went up from Egypt, he and his wife, and all that he had, and Lot with him, into the Negeb.

2 Now Abram was very rich in livestock, in silver, and in gold. 3He journeyed on by stages from the Negeb as far as Bethel, to the place where his tent had been at the beginning, between Bethel and Ai, 4to the place where he had made

---

f Or by you all the families of the earth shall bless themselves   g Or terebinth   h Heb seed

an altar at the first; and there Abram called on the name of the LORD. ⁵Now Lot, who went with Abram, also had flocks and herds and tents, ⁶so that the land could not support both of them living together; for their possessions were so great that they could not live together, ⁷and there was strife between the herders of Abram's livestock and the herders of Lot's livestock. At that time the Canaanites and the Perizzites lived in the land.

8 Then Abram said to Lot, "Let there be no strife between you and me, and between your herders and my herders; for we are kindred. ⁹Is not the whole land before you? Separate yourself from me. If you take the left hand, then I will go to the right; or if you take the right hand, then I will go to the left." ¹⁰Lot looked about him, and saw that the plain of the Jordan was well watered everywhere like the garden of the LORD, like the land of Egypt, in the direction of Zoar; this was before the LORD had destroyed Sodom and Gomorrah. ¹¹So Lot chose for himself all the plain of the Jordan, and Lot journeyed eastward; thus they separated from each other. ¹²Abram settled in the land of Canaan, while Lot settled among the cities of the Plain and moved his tent as far as Sodom. ¹³Now the people of Sodom were wicked, great sinners against the LORD.

14 The LORD said to Abram, after Lot had separated from him, "Raise your eyes now, and look from the place where you are, northward and southward and eastward and westward; ¹⁵for all the land that you see I will give to you and to your offspring^i forever. ¹⁶I will make your offspring like the dust of the earth; so that if one can count the dust of the earth, your offspring also can be counted. ¹⁷Rise up, walk through the length and the breadth of the land, for I will give it to you." ¹⁸So Abram moved his tent, and came and settled by the oaks^j of Mamre, which are at Hebron; and there he built an altar to the LORD.

Lot's Captivity and Rescue

14 In the days of King Amraphel of Shinar, King Arioch of Ellasar, King Chedorlaomer of Elam, and King Tidal of Goiim, ²these kings made war with King Bera of Sodom, King Birsha of Gomorrah, King Shinab of Admah, King Shemeber of Zeboiim, and the king of Bela (that is, Zoar). ³All these joined

forces in the Valley of Siddim (that is, the Dead Sea).^{k} ⁴Twelve years they had served Chedorlaomer, but in the thirteenth year they rebelled. ⁵In the fourteenth year Chedorlaomer and the kings who were with him came and subdued the Rephaim in Ashteroth-karnaim, the Zuzim in Ham, the Emim in Shaveh-kiriathaim, ⁶and the Horites in the hill country of Seir as far as El-paran on the edge of the wilderness; ⁷then they turned back and came to En-mishpat (that is, Kadesh), and subdued all the country of the Amalekites, and also the Amorites who lived in Hazazon-tamar. ⁸Then the king of Sodom, the king of Gomorrah, the king of Admah, the king of Zeboiim, and the king of Bela (that is, Zoar) went out, and they joined battle in the Valley of Siddim ⁹with King Chedorlaomer of Elam, King Tidal of Goiim, King Amraphel of Shinar, and King Arioch of Ellasar, four kings against five. ¹⁰Now the Valley of Siddim was full of bitumen pits; and as the kings of Sodom and Gomorrah fled, some fell into them, and the rest fled to the hill country. ¹¹So the enemy took all the goods of Sodom and Gomorrah, and all their provisions, and went their way; ¹²they also took Lot, the son of Abram's brother, who lived in Sodom, and his goods, and departed.

13 Then one who had escaped came and told Abram the Hebrew, who was living by the oaks^j of Mamre the Amorite, brother of Eshcol and of Aner; these were allies of Abram. ¹⁴When Abram heard that his nephew had been taken captive, he led forth his trained men, born in his house, three hundred eighteen of them, and went in pursuit as far as Dan. ¹⁵He divided his forces against them by night, he and his servants, and routed them and pursued them to Hobah, north of Damascus. ¹⁶Then he brought back all the goods, and also brought back his nephew Lot with his goods, and the women and the people.

Abram Blessed by Melchizedek

17 After his return from the defeat of Chedorlaomer and the kings who were with him, the king of Sodom went out to meet him at the Valley of Shaveh (that is, the King's Valley). ¹⁸And King Melchizedek of Salem brought out bread and wine;

i Heb *seed*   *j* Or *terebinths*   *k* Heb *Salt Sea*

he was priest of God Most High.[l] [19]He blessed him and said,

"Blessed be Abram by God Most High,[l]
    maker of heaven and earth;
[20] and blessed be God Most High,[l]
    who has delivered your enemies
        into your hand!"

And Abram gave him one-tenth of everything. [21]Then the king of Sodom said to Abram, "Give me the persons, but take the goods for yourself." [22]But Abram said to the king of Sodom, "I have sworn to the LORD, God Most High,[l] maker of heaven and earth, [23]that I would not take a thread or a sandal-thong or anything that is yours, so that you might not say, 'I have made Abram rich.' [24]I will take nothing but what the young men have eaten, and the share of the men who went with me—Aner, Eshcol, and Mamre. Let them take their share."

God's Covenant with Abram

15 After these things the word of the LORD came to Abram in a vision, "Do not be afraid, Abram, I am your shield; your reward shall be very great." [2]But Abram said, "O Lord GOD, what will you give me, for I continue childless, and the heir of my house is Eliezer of Damascus?"[m] [3]And Abram said, "You have given me no offspring, and so a slave born in my house is to be my heir." [4]But the word of the LORD came to him, "This man shall not be your heir; no one but your very own issue shall be your heir." [5]He brought him outside and said, "Look toward heaven and count the stars, if you are able to count them." Then he said to him, "So shall your descendants be." [6]And he believed the LORD; and the LORD[n] reckoned it to him as righteousness.

[7] Then he said to him, "I am the LORD who brought you from Ur of the Chaldeans, to give you this land to possess." [8]But he said, "O Lord GOD, how am I to know that I shall possess it?" [9]He said to him, "Bring me a heifer three years old, a female goat three years old, a ram three years old, a turtledove, and a young pigeon." [10]He brought him all these and cut them in two, laying each half over against the other; but he did not cut the birds in two. [11]And when birds of prey came down on the carcasses, Abram drove them away.

[12] As the sun was going down, a deep sleep fell upon Abram, and a deep and terrifying darkness descended upon him. [13]Then the LORD[n] said to Abram, "Know this for certain, that your offspring shall be aliens in a land that is not theirs, and shall be slaves there, and they shall be oppressed for four hundred years; [14]but I will bring judgment on the nation that they serve, and afterward they shall come out with great possessions. [15]As for yourself, you shall go to your ancestors in peace; you shall be buried in a good old age. [16]And they shall come back here in the fourth generation; for the iniquity of the Amorites is not yet complete."

[17] When the sun had gone down and it was dark, a smoking fire pot and a flaming torch passed between these pieces. [18]On that day the LORD made a covenant with Abram, saying, "To your descendants I give this land, from the river of Egypt to the great river, the river Euphrates, [19]the land of the Kenites, the Kenizzites, the Kadmonites, [20]the Hittites, the Perizzites, the Rephaim, [21]the Amorites, the Canaanites, the Girgashites, and the Jebusites."

The Birth of Ishmael

16 Now Sarai, Abram's wife, bore him no children. She had an Egyptian slave-girl whose name was Hagar, [2]and Sarai said to Abram, "You see that the LORD has prevented me from bearing children; go in to my slave-girl; it may be that I shall obtain children by her." And Abram listened to the voice of Sarai. [3]So, after Abram had lived ten years in the land of Canaan, Sarai, Abram's wife, took Hagar the Egyptian, her slave-girl, and gave her to her husband Abram as a wife. [4]He went in to Hagar, and she conceived; and when she saw that she had conceived, she looked with contempt on her mistress. [5]Then Sarai said to Abram, "May the wrong done to me be on you! I gave my slave-girl to your embrace, and when she saw that she had conceived, she looked on me with contempt. May the LORD judge between you and me!" [6]But Abram said to Sarai, "Your slave-girl is in your power; do to her as you please." Then Sarai dealt harshly with her, and she ran away from her.

[7] The angel of the LORD found her by a spring of water in the wilderness, the

---

[l] Heb El Elyon   [m] Meaning of Heb uncertain
[n] Heb he

spring on the way to Shur. [8]And he said, "Hagar, slave-girl of Sarai, where have you come from and where are you going?" She said, "I am running away from my mistress Sarai." [9]The angel of the LORD said to her, "Return to your mistress, and submit to her." [10]The angel of the LORD also said to her, "I will so greatly multiply your offspring that they cannot be counted for multitude." [11]And the angel of the LORD said to her,

> "Now you have conceived and shall
>   bear a son;
> you shall call him Ishmael,[o]
> for the LORD has given heed to
>   your affliction.
> [12] He shall be a wild ass of a man,
>   with his hand against everyone,
>   and everyone's hand against him;
> and he shall live at odds with all his
>   kin."

[13]So she named the LORD who spoke to her, "You are El-roi"; [p] for she said, "Have I really seen God and remained alive after seeing him?"[q] [14]Therefore the well was called Beer-lahai-roi;[r] it lies between Kadesh and Bered.

[15] Hagar bore Abram a son; and Abram named his son, whom Hagar bore, Ishmael. [16]Abram was eighty-six years old when Hagar bore him[s] Ishmael.

The Sign of the Covenant

17 When Abram was ninety-nine years old, the LORD appeared to Abram, and said to him, "I am God Almighty;[t] walk before me, and be blameless. [2]And I will make my covenant between me and you, and will make you exceedingly numerous." [3]Then Abram fell on his face; and God said to him, [4]"As for me, this is my covenant with you: You shall be the ancestor of a multitude of nations. [5]No longer shall your name be Abram,[u] but your name shall be Abraham;[v] for I have made you the ancestor of a multitude of nations. [6]I will make you exceedingly fruitful; and I will make nations of you, and kings shall come from you. [7]I will establish my covenant between me and you, and your offspring after you throughout their generations, for an everlasting covenant, to be God to you and to your offspring[w] after you. [8]And I will give to you, and to your offspring after you, the land where you are now an alien, all the land of Canaan, for a perpetual holding; and I will be their God."

[9] God said to Abraham, "As for you, you shall keep my covenant, you and your offspring after you throughout their generations. [10]This is my covenant, which you shall keep, between me and you and your offspring after you: Every male among you shall be circumcised. [11]You shall circumcise the flesh of your foreskins, and it shall be a sign of the covenant between me and you. [12]Throughout your generations every male among you shall be circumcised when he is eight days old, including the slave born in your house and the one bought with your money from any foreigner who is not of your offspring. [13]Both the slave born in your house and the one bought with your money must be circumcised. So shall my covenant be in your flesh an everlasting covenant. [14]Any uncircumcised male who is not circumcised in the flesh of his foreskin shall be cut off from his people; he has broken my covenant."

[15] God said to Abraham, "As for Sarai your wife, you shall not call her Sarai, but Sarah shall be her name. [16]I will bless her, and moreover I will give you a son by her. I will bless her, and she shall give rise to nations; kings of peoples shall come from her." [17]Then Abraham fell on his face and laughed, and said to himself, "Can a child be born to a man who is a hundred years old? Can Sarah, who is ninety years old, bear a child?" [18]And Abraham said to God, "O that Ishmael might live in your sight!" [19]God said, "No, but your wife Sarah shall bear you a son, and you shall name him Isaac.[x] I will establish my covenant with him as an everlasting covenant for his offspring after him. [20]As for Ishmael, I have heard you; I will bless him and make him fruitful and exceedingly numerous; he shall be the father of twelve princes, and I will make him a great nation. [21]But my covenant I will establish with Isaac, whom Sarah shall bear to you at this season next year." [22]And when he had finished talking with him, God went up from Abraham.

[23] Then Abraham took his son Ishmael and all the slaves born in his house

---

o That is *God hears*   *p* Perhaps *God of seeing* or *God who sees*   *q* Meaning of Heb uncertain   *r* That is *the Well of the Living One who sees me*   *s* Heb *Abram*   *t* Traditional rendering of Heb *El Shaddai*   *u* That is *exalted ancestor*   *v* Here taken to mean *ancestor of a multitude*   *w* Heb *seed*   *x* That is *he laughs*

or bought with his money, every male among the men of Abraham's house, and he circumcised the flesh of their foreskins that very day, as God had said to him. ²⁴Abraham was ninety-nine years old when he was circumcised in the flesh of his foreskin. ²⁵And his son Ishmael was thirteen years old when he was circumcised in the flesh of his foreskin. ²⁶That very day Abraham and his son Ishmael were circumcised; ²⁷and all the men of his house, slaves born in the house and those bought with money from a foreigner, were circumcised with him.

A Son Promised to Abraham and Sarah

18 The LORD appeared to Abraham *y* by the oaks*z* of Mamre, as he sat at the entrance of his tent in the heat of the day. ²He looked up and saw three men standing near him. When he saw them, he ran from the tent entrance to meet them, and bowed down to the ground. ³He said, "My lord, if I find favor with you, do not pass by your servant. ⁴Let a little water be brought, and wash your feet, and rest yourselves under the tree. ⁵Let me bring a little bread, that you may refresh yourselves, and after that you may pass on—since you have come to your servant." So they said, "Do as you have said." ⁶And Abraham hastened into the tent to Sarah, and said, "Make ready quickly three measures*a* of choice flour, knead it, and make cakes." ⁷Abraham ran to the herd, and took a calf, tender and good, and gave it to the servant, who hastened to prepare it. ⁸Then he took curds and milk and the calf that he had prepared, and set it before them; and he stood by them under the tree while they ate.

9 They said to him, "Where is your wife Sarah?" And he said, "There, in the tent." ¹⁰Then one said, "I will surely return to you in due season, and your wife Sarah shall have a son." And Sarah was listening at the tent entrance behind him. ¹¹Now Abraham and Sarah were old, advanced in age; it had ceased to be with Sarah after

y Heb *him*   *z* Or *terebinths*   *a* Heb *seahs*

For the Sake of a Promise

MONDAY

Scripture Reading for Today:
Genesis 17.15–22

Verse for Today:
Genesis 17.16

Letting go is no easy thing. I think of the story of Sarah in the book of Genesis. Sarah is a strong symbol of the part of us that has gotten secure and settled. Suddenly her life gets terribly messy—she hears an inner call to pack up and head into unknown territory. It is the call of skin-shedding. She hears that she has within her a source of new life. At first, all this seems so incredible that she simply laughs at the thought of it. Eventually, she does indeed set out and leaves her old life behind her.

Sarah's transition is often ignored alongside the call of Abraham's, but, in reality, I think hers was equally difficult. Sarah goes into dangerous, unmarked territory with the promise of a new generation in her womb. She risks the future because she believes in the call to uproot, to shed the skin, to leave behind the only life she has ever known.

In midlife, we also have the promise of new life within us if only we let go of some of the well-worn securities that bind us to the past. The midlife journey of transformation takes an enormous amount of trust in the Voice that urges us to shed the skin.

—*JOYCE RUPP*

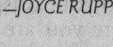

Go to page 21 for your next devotional reading.

the manner of women. ¹²So Sarah laughed to herself, saying, "After I have grown old, and my husband is old, shall I have pleasure?" ¹³The LORD said to Abraham, "Why did Sarah laugh, and say, 'Shall I indeed bear a child, now that I am old?' ¹⁴Is anything too wonderful for the LORD? At the set time I will return to you, in due season, and Sarah shall have a son." ¹⁵But Sarah denied, saying, "I did not laugh"; for she was afraid. He said, "Oh yes, you did laugh."

*S*mall *Gifts*

TUESDAY

Scripture Reading for Today:
Genesis 18.1–8

Verse for Today:
Genesis 18.5

My parents have always welcomed strays; people from their prayer group, many with serious problems, frequently crashed at our house until the crisis had passed. An elderly friend of Mom's came twice a year and stayed a week at a stretch, just because she was lonely. And Dad couldn't resist bringing home the parish priest on hot dog night, no matter how often Mom scolded him for not calling ahead.

The accommodations weren't first-rate in a house with two parents, one grandma, eight kids, and a dog. But the brave and the desperate soon learned that the discomforts took a back seat to the love they felt in my parents' willingness to listen, to pray and to counsel.

Scripture says much to recommend this virtue. In the Old Testament, we read of Abraham and Sarah showing hospitality to the Lord and his messengers, and the widow of Zarephath, giving her last bit of bread to Elijah (see 1 Kings 17). Whether we have an extra steer in the backyard, like Abraham, or are scraping together the family meal, like the widow of Zarephath, we can all practice hospitality.

I am also reminded of the scriptural admonition to "extend hospitality to strangers" (Romans 12.13). For me, this verse has nothing to do with financing hospitality, since I believe hot dogs served in love can be a feast. Rather, it means giving up some of my leisure time to welcome friends and strangers into my life, into my space, to minister God's mercy to them in the ways they most need it.

Small gifts, a special meal, a listening ear—these may seem a poor defense against the alienation and isolation of the modern world. But Scripture reveals their eternal magnitude. "I was hungry and you gave me food . . . a stranger and you welcomed me" (Matthew 25.35). Not only does hospitality minister to the needs of the human body and soul, it also prepares us for the day we will enjoy the hospitality of heaven: "Come, you that are blessed by my Father, inherit the kingdom prepared for you from the foundation of the world" (Matthew 25.34).

—LISA FERGUSON

Go to page 25 for your next devotional reading.

Judgment Pronounced on Sodom

16 Then the men set out from there, and they looked toward Sodom; and Abraham went with them to set them on their way. 17The Lord said, "Shall I hide from Abraham what I am about to do, 18seeing that Abraham shall become a great and mighty nation, and all the nations of the earth shall be blessed in him?*b* 19No, for I have chosen*c* him, that he may charge his children and his household after him to keep the way of the Lord by doing righteousness and justice; so that the Lord may bring about for Abraham what he has promised him." 20Then the Lord said, "How great is the outcry against Sodom and Gomorrah and how very grave their sin! 21I must go down and see whether they have done altogether according to the outcry that has come to me; and if not, I will know."

22 So the men turned from there, and went toward Sodom, while Abraham remained standing before the Lord.*d* 23Then Abraham came near and said, "Will you indeed sweep away the righteous with the wicked? 24Suppose there are fifty righteous within the city; will you then sweep away the place and not forgive it for the fifty righteous who are in it? 25Far be it from you to do such a thing, to slay the righteous with the wicked, so that the righteous fare as the wicked! Far be that from you! Shall not the Judge of all the earth do what is just?" 26And the Lord said, "If I find at Sodom fifty righteous in the city, I will forgive the whole place for their sake." 27Abraham answered, "Let me take it upon myself to speak to the Lord, I who am but dust and ashes. 28Suppose five of the fifty righteous are lacking? Will you destroy the whole city for lack of five?" And he said, "I will not destroy it if I find forty-five there." 29Again he spoke to him, "Suppose forty are found there." He answered, "For the sake of forty I will not do it." 30Then he said, "Oh do not let the Lord be angry if I speak. Suppose thirty are found there." He answered, "I will not do it, if I find thirty there." 31He said, "Let me take it upon myself to speak to the Lord. Suppose twenty are found there." He answered, "For the sake of twenty I will not destroy it." 32Then he said, "Oh do not let the Lord be angry if I speak just once more. Suppose ten are found there." He answered, "For the sake of ten I will not

destroy it." 33And the Lord went his way, when he had finished speaking to Abraham; and Abraham returned to his place.

The Depravity of Sodom

19 The two angels came to Sodom in the evening, and Lot was sitting in the gateway of Sodom. When Lot saw them, he rose to meet them, and bowed down with his face to the ground. 2He said, "Please, my lords, turn aside to your servant's house and spend the night, and wash your feet; then you can rise early and go on your way." They said, "No; we will spend the night in the square." 3But he urged them strongly; so they turned aside to him and entered his house; and he made them a feast, and baked unleavened bread, and they ate. 4But before they lay down, the men of the city, the men of Sodom, both young and old, all the people to the last man, surrounded the house; 5and they called to Lot, "Where are the men who came to you tonight? Bring them out to us, so that we may know them." 6Lot went out of the door to the men, shut the door after him, 7and said, "I beg you, my brothers, do not act so wickedly. 8Look, I have two daughters who have not known a man; let me bring them out to you, and do to them as you please; only do nothing to these men, for they have come under the shelter of my roof." 9But they replied, "Stand back!" And they said, "This fellow came here as an alien, and he would play the judge! Now we will deal worse with you than with them." Then they pressed hard against the man Lot, and came near the door to break it down. 10But the men inside reached out their hands and brought Lot into the house with them, and shut the door. 11And they struck with blindness the men who were at the door of the house, both small and great, so that they were unable to find the door.

Sodom and Gomorrah Destroyed

12 Then the men said to Lot, "Have you anyone else here? Sons-in-law, sons, daughters, or anyone you have in the city—bring them out of the place. 13For we are about to destroy this place, because

b Or *and all the nations of the earth shall bless themselves by him*　*c* Heb *known*　*d* Another ancient tradition reads *while the Lord remained standing before Abraham*

the outcry against its people has become great before the LORD, and the LORD has sent us to destroy it." ¹⁴So Lot went out and said to his sons-in-law, who were to marry his daughters, "Up, get out of this place; for the LORD is about to destroy the city." But he seemed to his sons-in-law to be jesting.

15 When morning dawned, the angels urged Lot, saying, "Get up, take your wife and your two daughters who are here, or else you will be consumed in the punishment of the city." ¹⁶But he lingered; so the men seized him and his wife and his two daughters by the hand, the LORD being merciful to him, and they brought him out and left him outside the city. ¹⁷When they had brought them outside, theyᵉ said, "Flee for your life; do not look back or stop anywhere in the Plain; flee to the hills, or else you will be consumed." ¹⁸And Lot said to them, "Oh, no, my lords; ¹⁹your servant has found favor with you, and you have shown me great kindness in saving my life; but I cannot flee to the hills, for fear the disaster will overtake me and I die. ²⁰Look, that city is near enough to flee to, and it is a little one. Let me escape there—is it not a little one?—and my life will be saved!" ²¹He said to him, "Very well, I grant you this favor too, and will not overthrow the city of which you have spoken. ²²Hurry, escape there, for I can do nothing until you arrive there." Therefore the city was called Zoar.ᶠ ²³The sun had risen on the earth when Lot came to Zoar.

24 Then the LORD rained on Sodom and Gomorrah sulfur and fire from the LORD out of heaven; ²⁵and he overthrew those cities, and all the Plain, and all the inhabitants of the cities, and what grew on the ground. ²⁶But Lot's wife, behind him, looked back, and she became a pillar of salt.

27 Abraham went early in the morning to the place where he had stood before the LORD; ²⁸and he looked down toward Sodom and Gomorrah and toward all the land of the Plain and saw the smoke of the land going up like the smoke of a furnace.

29 So it was that, when God destroyed the cities of the Plain, God remembered Abraham, and sent Lot out of the midst of the overthrow, when he overthrew the cities in which Lot had settled.

The Shameful Origin of Moab and Ammon

30 Now Lot went up out of Zoar and settled in the hills with his two daughters, for he was afraid to stay in Zoar; so he lived in a cave with his two daughters. ³¹And the firstborn said to the younger, "Our father is old, and there is not a man on earth to come in to us after the manner of all the world. ³²Come, let us make our father drink wine, and we will lie with him, so that we may preserve offspring through our father." ³³So they made their father drink wine that night; and the firstborn went in, and lay with her father; he did not know when she lay down or when she rose. ³⁴On the next day, the firstborn said to the younger, "Look, I lay last night with my father; let us make him drink wine tonight also; then you go in and lie with him, so that we may preserve offspring through our father." ³⁵So they made their father drink wine that night also; and the younger rose, and lay with him; and he did not know when she lay down or when she rose. ³⁶Thus both the daughters of Lot became pregnant by their father. ³⁷The firstborn bore a son, and named him Moab; he is the ancestor of the Moabites to this day. ³⁸The younger also bore a son and named him Ben-ammi; he is the ancestor of the Ammonites to this day.

Abraham and Sarah at Gerar

20 From there Abraham journeyed toward the region of the Negeb, and settled between Kadesh and Shur. While residing in Gerar as an alien, ²Abraham said of his wife Sarah, "She is my sister." And King Abimelech of Gerar sent and took Sarah. ³But God came to Abimelech in a dream by night, and said to him, "You are about to die because of the woman whom you have taken; for she is a married woman." ⁴Now Abimelech had not approached her; so he said, "Lord, will you destroy an innocent people? ⁵Did he not himself say to me, 'She is my sister'? And she herself said, 'He is my brother.' I did this in the integrity of my heart and the innocence of my hands." ⁶Then God said to him in the dream, "Yes, I know that you did this in the integrity of your heart; furthermore it was I who kept you from sinning against me. Therefore I

ᵉ Gk Syr Vg: Heb *he*   ᶠ That is *Little*

did not let you touch her. 7Now then, return the man's wife; for he is a prophet, and he will pray for you and you shall live. But if you do not restore her, know that you shall surely die, you and all that are yours."

8 So Abimelech rose early in the morning, and called all his servants and told them all these things; and the men were very much afraid. 9Then Abimelech called Abraham, and said to him, "What have you done to us? How have I sinned against you, that you have brought such great guilt on me and my kingdom? You have done things to me that ought not to be done." 10And Abimelech said to Abraham, "What were you thinking of, that you did this thing?" 11Abraham said, "I did it because I thought, There is no fear of God at all in this place, and they will kill me because of my wife. 12Besides, she is indeed my sister, the daughter of my father but not the daughter of my mother; and she became my wife. 13And when God caused me to wander from my father's house, I said to her, 'This is the kindness you must do me: at every place to which we come, say of me, He is my brother.' " 14Then Abimelech took sheep and oxen, and male and female slaves, and gave them to Abraham, and restored his wife Sarah to him. 15Abimelech said, "My land is before you; settle where it pleases you." 16To Sarah he said, "Look, I have given your brother a thousand pieces of silver; it is your exoneration before all who are with you; you are completely vindicated." 17Then Abraham prayed to God; and God healed Abimelech, and also healed his wife and female slaves so that they bore children. 18For the LORD had closed fast all the wombs of the house of Abimelech because of Sarah, Abraham's wife.

The Birth of Isaac

21 The LORD dealt with Sarah as he had said, and the LORD did for Sarah as he had promised. 2Sarah conceived and bore Abraham a son in his old age, at the time of which God had spoken to him. 3Abraham gave the name Isaac to his son whom Sarah bore him. 4And Abraham circumcised his son Isaac when he was eight days old, as God had commanded him. 5Abraham was a hundred years old when his son Isaac was born to him. 6Now Sarah said, "God has brought

laughter for me; everyone who hears will laugh with me." 7And she said, "Who would ever have said to Abraham that Sarah would nurse children? Yet I have borne him a son in his old age."

Hagar and Ishmael Sent Away

8 The child grew, and was weaned; and Abraham made a great feast on the day that Isaac was weaned. 9But Sarah saw the son of Hagar the Egyptian, whom she had borne to Abraham, playing with her son Isaac.8 10So she said to Abraham, "Cast out this slave woman with her son; for the son of this slave woman shall not inherit along with my son Isaac." 11The matter was very distressing to Abraham on account of his son. 12But God said to Abraham, "Do not be distressed because of the boy and because of your slave woman; whatever Sarah says to you, do as she tells you, for it is through Isaac that offspring shall be named for you. 13As for the son of the slave woman, I will make a nation of him also, because he is your offspring." 14So Abraham rose early in the morning, and took bread and a skin of water, and gave it to Hagar, putting it on her shoulder, along with the child, and sent her away. And she departed, and wandered about in the wilderness of Beer-sheba.

15 When the water in the skin was gone, she cast the child under one of the bushes. 16Then she went and sat down opposite him, a good way off, about the distance of a bowshot; for she said, "Do not let me look on the death of the child." And as she sat opposite him, she lifted up her voice and wept. 17And God heard the voice of the boy; and the angel of God called to Hagar from heaven, and said to her, "What troubles you, Hagar? Do not be afraid; for God has heard the voice of the boy where he is. 18Come, lift up the boy and hold him fast with your hand, for I will make a great nation of him." 19Then God opened her eyes and she saw a well of water. She went, and filled the skin with water, and gave the boy a drink.

20 God was with the boy, and he grew up; he lived in the wilderness, and became an expert with the bow. 21He lived in the wilderness of Paran; and his mother got a wife for him from the land of Egypt.

8 Gk Vg: Heb lacks *with her son Isaac*

Abraham and Abimelech Make a Covenant

22 At that time Abimelech, with Phicol the commander of his army, said to Abraham, "God is with you in all that you do; 23now therefore swear to me here by God that you will not deal falsely with me or with my offspring or with my posterity, but as I have dealt loyally with you, you will deal with me and with the land where you have resided as an alien." 24And Abraham said, "I swear it."

25 When Abraham complained to Abimelech about a well of water that Abimelech's servants had seized, 26Abimelech said, "I do not know who has done this; you did not tell me, and I have not heard of it until today." 27So Abraham took sheep and oxen and gave them to Abimelech, and the two men made a covenant. 28Abraham set apart seven ewe lambs of the flock. 29And Abimelech said to Abraham, "What is the meaning of these seven ewe lambs that you have set apart?" 30He said, "These seven ewe lambs you shall accept from my hand, in order that you may be a witness for me that I dug this well." 31Therefore that place was called Beer-sheba;*h* because there both of them swore an oath. 32When they had made a covenant at Beer-sheba, Abimelech, with Phicol the commander of his army, left and returned to the land of the Philistines. 33Abraham*i* planted a tamarisk tree in Beer-sheba, and called there on the name of the LORD, the Everlasting God.*j* 34And Abraham resided as an alien many days in the land of the Philistines.

The Command to Sacrifice Isaac

22 After these things God tested Abraham. He said to him, "Abraham!" And he said, "Here I am." 2He said, "Take your son, your only son Isaac, whom you love, and go to the land of Moriah, and offer him there as a burnt offering on one of the mountains that I

h That is *Well of seven* or *Well of the oath*   *i* Heb *He*   *j* Or *the* LORD, *El Olam*

Intelligent Trust

Love is not blind, despite the saying, and we cannot truly give our hearts to the unknown.

The story of Abraham and his only son Isaac has always been a daunting one. Abraham believed that God was calling him to sacrifice his son, and he was saved from this hideous action only at the last minute. I have a personal reading of this story: to me the only one that makes sense. It is that God would never ask us to do something that is evil, and Abraham must have known this. So what we have [are] two gigantic acts of trust, each based upon the knowledge of the other person, and of God. Abraham could only have gone ahead in the absolute belief that the horror would never happen. Isaac, for his part, submitted to being bound and laid on the altar, believing against all appearances that his father would not harm him.

If Abraham had not known God, if Isaac had not known his father, such trust would have been madness. Love insists that we make a true judgment and then cleave to it, whatever the appearances.

—*SISTER WENDY BECKETT*

WEDNESDAY

Scripture Reading for Today:
Genesis 22.1–14

Verse for Today:
Genesis 22.2

Go to page 39 for your next devotional reading.

shall show you." ³So Abraham rose early in the morning, saddled his donkey, and took two of his young men with him, and his son Isaac; he cut the wood for the burnt offering, and set out and went to the place in the distance that God had shown him. ⁴On the third day Abraham looked up and saw the place far away. ⁵Then Abraham said to his young men, "Stay here with the donkey; the boy and I will go over there; we will worship, and then we will come back to you." ⁶Abraham took the wood of the burnt offering and laid it on his son Isaac, and he himself carried the fire and the knife. So the two of them walked on together. ⁷Isaac said to his father Abraham, "Father!" And he said, "Here I am, my son." He said, "The fire and the wood are here, but where is the lamb for a burnt offering?" ⁸Abraham said, "God himself will provide the lamb for a burnt offering, my son." So the two of them walked on together.

9 When they came to the place that God had shown him, Abraham built an altar there and laid the wood in order. He bound his son Isaac, and laid him on the altar, on top of the wood. ¹⁰Then Abraham reached out his hand and took the knife to kill*ᵏ* his son. ¹¹But the angel of the Lord called to him from heaven, and said, "Abraham, Abraham!" And he said, "Here I am." ¹²He said, "Do not lay your hand on the boy or do anything to him; for now I know that you fear God, since you have not withheld your son, your only son, from me." ¹³And Abraham looked up and saw a ram, caught in a thicket by its horns. Abraham went and took the ram and offered it up as a burnt offering instead of his son. ¹⁴So Abraham called that place "The Lord will provide";*ˡ* as it is said to this day, "On the mount of the Lord it shall be provided."*ᵐ*

15 The angel of the Lord called to Abraham a second time from heaven, ¹⁶and said, "By myself I have sworn, says the Lord: Because you have done this, and have not withheld your son, your only son, ¹⁷I will indeed bless you, and I will make your offspring as numerous as the stars of heaven and as the sand that is on the seashore. And your offspring shall possess the gate of their enemies, ¹⁸and by your offspring shall all the nations of the earth gain blessing for themselves, because you have obeyed my voice." ¹⁹So Abraham returned to his young men, and

they arose and went together to Beersheba; and Abraham lived at Beer-sheba.

The Children of Nahor

20 Now after these things it was told Abraham, "Milcah also has borne children, to your brother Nahor: ²¹Uz the firstborn, Buz his brother, Kemuel the father of Aram, ²²Chesed, Hazo, Pildash, Jidlaph, and Bethuel." ²³Bethuel became the father of Rebekah. These eight Milcah bore to Nahor, Abraham's brother. ²⁴Moreover, his concubine, whose name was Reumah, bore Tebah, Gaham, Tahash, and Maacah.

Sarah's Death and Burial

23 Sarah lived one hundred twentyseven years; this was the length of Sarah's life. ²And Sarah died at Kiriatharba (that is, Hebron) in the land of Canaan; and Abraham went in to mourn for Sarah and to weep for her. ³Abraham rose up from beside his dead, and said to the Hittites, ⁴"I am a stranger and an alien residing among you; give me property among you for a burying place, so that I may bury my dead out of my sight." ⁵The Hittites answered Abraham, ⁶"Hear us, my lord; you are a mighty prince among us. Bury your dead in the choicest of our burial places; none of us will withhold from you any burial ground for burying your dead." ⁷Abraham rose and bowed to the Hittites, the people of the land. ⁸He said to them, "If you are willing that I should bury my dead out of my sight, hear me, and entreat for me Ephron son of Zohar, ⁹so that he may give me the cave of Machpelah, which he owns; it is at the end of his field. For the full price let him give it to me in your presence as a possession for a burying place." ¹⁰Now Ephron was sitting among the Hittites; and Ephron the Hittite answered Abraham in the hearing of the Hittites, of all who went in at the gate of his city, ¹¹"No, my lord, hear me; I give you the field, and I give you the cave that is in it; in the presence of my people I give it to you; bury your dead." ¹²Then Abraham bowed down before the people of the land. ¹³He said to Ephron in the hearing of the people of the land, "If you only will listen to me! I will give the price of the field; accept it from me, so

ᵏ Or to slaughter   ˡ Or will see; Heb traditionally transliterated Jehovah Jireh   ᵐ Or he shall be seen

that I may bury my dead there." 14Ephron answered Abraham, 15"My lord, listen to me; a piece of land worth four hundred shekels of silver—what is that between you and me? Bury your dead." 16Abraham agreed with Ephron; and Abraham weighed out for Ephron the silver that he had named in the hearing of the Hittites, four hundred shekels of silver, according to the weights current among the merchants.

17 So the field of Ephron in Machpelah, which was to the east of Mamre, the field with the cave that was in it and all the trees that were in the field, throughout its whole area, passed 18to Abraham as a possession in the presence of the Hittites, in the presence of all who went in at the gate of his city. 19After this, Abraham buried Sarah his wife in the cave of the field of Machpelah facing Mamre (that is, Hebron) in the land of Canaan. 20The field and the cave that is in it passed from the Hittites into Abraham's possession as a burying place.

The Marriage of Isaac and Rebekah

24 Now Abraham was old, well advanced in years; and the LORD had blessed Abraham in all things. 2Abraham said to his servant, the oldest of his house, who had charge of all that he had, "Put your hand under my thigh 3and I will make you swear by the LORD, the God of heaven and earth, that you will not get a wife for my son from the daughters of the Canaanites, among whom I live, 4but will go to my country and to my kindred and get a wife for my son Isaac." 5The servant said to him, "Perhaps the woman may not be willing to follow me to this land; must I then take your son back to the land from which you came?" 6Abraham said to him, "See to it that you do not take my son back there. 7The LORD, the God of heaven, who took me from my father's house and from the land of my birth, and who spoke to me and swore to me, 'To your offspring I will give this land,' he will send his angel before you, and you shall take a wife for my son from there. 8But if the woman is not willing to follow you, then you will be free from this oath of mine; only you must not take my son back there." 9So the servant put his hand under the thigh of Abraham his master and swore to him concerning this matter.

10 Then the servant took ten of his master's camels and departed, taking all kinds of choice gifts from his master; and he set out and went to Aram-naharaim, to the city of Nahor. 11He made the camels kneel down outside the city by the well of water; it was toward evening, the time when women go out to draw water. 12And he said, "O LORD, God of my master Abraham, please grant me success today and show steadfast love to my master Abraham. 13I am standing here by the spring of water, and the daughters of the townspeople are coming out to draw water. 14Let the girl to whom I shall say, 'Please offer your jar that I may drink,' and who shall say, 'Drink, and I will water your camels'—let her be the one whom you have appointed for your servant Isaac. By this I shall know that you have shown steadfast love to my master."

15 Before he had finished speaking, there was Rebekah, who was born to Bethuel son of Milcah, the wife of Nahor, Abraham's brother, coming out with her water jar on her shoulder. 16The girl was very fair to look upon, a virgin, whom no man had known. She went down to the spring, filled her jar, and came up. 17Then the servant ran to meet her and said, "Please let me sip a little water from your jar." 18"Drink, my lord," she said, and quickly lowered her jar upon her hand and gave him a drink. 19When she had finished giving him a drink, she said, "I will draw for your camels also, until they have finished drinking." 20So she quickly emptied her jar into the trough and ran again to the well to draw, and she drew for all his camels. 21The man gazed at her in silence to learn whether or not the LORD had made his journey successful.

22 When the camels had finished drinking, the man took a gold nose-ring weighing a half shekel, and two bracelets for her arms weighing ten gold shekels, 23and said, "Tell me whose daughter you are. Is there room in your father's house for us to spend the night?" 24She said to him, "I am the daughter of Bethuel son of Milcah, whom she bore to Nahor." 25She added, "We have plenty of straw and fodder and a place to spend the night." 26The man bowed his head and worshiped the LORD 27and said, "Blessed be the LORD, the God of my master Abraham, who has not forsaken his steadfast love and his faithfulness toward my master. As for me, the

LORD has led me on the way to the house of my master's kin."

28 Then the girl ran and told her mother's household about these things. 29 Rebekah had a brother whose name was Laban; and Laban ran out to the man, to the spring. 30 As soon as he had seen the nosering, and the bracelets on his sister's arms, and when he heard the words of his sister Rebekah, "Thus the man spoke to me," he went to the man; and there he was, standing by the camels at the spring. 31 He said, "Come in, O blessed of the LORD. Why do you stand outside when I have prepared the house and a place for the camels?" 32 So the man came into the house; and Laban unloaded the camels, and gave him straw and fodder for the camels, and water to wash his feet and the feet of the men who were with him. 33 Then food was set before him to eat; but he said, "I will not eat until I have told my errand." He said, "Speak on."

34 So he said, "I am Abraham's servant. 35 The LORD has greatly blessed my master, and he has become wealthy; he has given him flocks and herds, silver and gold, male and female slaves, camels and donkeys. 36 And Sarah my master's wife bore a son to my master when she was old; and he has given him all that he has. 37 My master made me swear, saying, 'You shall not take a wife for my son from the daughters of the Canaanites, in whose land I live; 38 but you shall go to my father's house, to my kindred, and get a wife for my son.' 39 I said to my master, 'Perhaps the woman will not follow me.' 40 But he said to me, 'The LORD, before whom I walk, will send his angel with you and make your way successful. You shall get a wife for my son from my kindred, from my father's house. 41 Then you will be free from my oath, when you come to my kindred; even if they will not give her to you, you will be free from my oath.'

42 "I came today to the spring, and said, 'O LORD, the God of my master Abraham, if now you will only make successful the way I am going! 43 I am standing here by the spring of water; let the young woman who comes out to draw, to whom I shall say, "Please give me a little water from your jar to drink," 44 and who will say to me, "Drink, and I will draw for your camels also"—let her be the woman whom the LORD has appointed for my master's son.'

45 "Before I had finished speaking in my heart, there was Rebekah coming out with her water jar on her shoulder; and she went down to the spring, and drew. I said to her, 'Please let me drink.' 46 She quickly let down her jar from her shoulder, and said, 'Drink, and I will also water your camels.' So I drank, and she also watered the camels. 47 Then I asked her, 'Whose daughter are you?' She said, 'The daughter of Bethuel, Nahor's son, whom Milcah bore to him.' So I put the ring on her nose, and the bracelets on her arms. 48 Then I bowed my head and worshiped the LORD, and blessed the LORD, the God of my master Abraham, who had led me by the right way to obtain the daughter of my master's kinsman for his son. 49 Now then, if you will deal loyally and truly with my master, tell me; and if not, tell me, so that I may turn either to the right hand or to the left."

50 Then Laban and Bethuel answered, "The thing comes from the LORD; we cannot speak to you anything bad or good. 51 Look, Rebekah is before you, take her and go, and let her be the wife of your master's son, as the LORD has spoken."

52 When Abraham's servant heard their words, he bowed himself to the ground before the LORD. 53 And the servant brought out jewelry of silver and of gold, and garments, and gave them to Rebekah; he also gave to her brother and to her mother costly ornaments. 54 Then he and the men who were with him ate and drank, and they spent the night there. When they rose in the morning, he said, "Send me back to my master." 55 Her brother and her mother said, "Let the girl remain with us a while, at least ten days; after that she may go." 56 But he said to them, "Do not delay me, since the LORD has made my journey successful; let me go that I may go to my master." 57 They said, "We will call the girl, and ask her." 58 And they called Rebekah, and said to her, "Will you go with this man?" She said, "I will." 59 So they sent away their sister Rebekah and her nurse along with Abraham's servant and his men. 60 And they blessed Rebekah and said to her,

"May you, our sister, become
    thousands of myriads;
may your offspring gain possession
    of the gates of their foes."

61 Then Rebekah and her maids rose up, mounted the camels, and followed the

man; thus the servant took Rebekah, and went his way.

62 Now Isaac had come from[n] Beer-lahai-roi, and was settled in the Negeb. [63]Isaac went out in the evening to walk[o] in the field; and looking up, he saw camels coming. [64]And Rebekah looked up, and when she saw Isaac, she slipped quickly from the camel, [65]and said to the servant, "Who is the man over there, walking in the field to meet us?" The servant said, "It is my master." So she took her veil and covered herself. [66]And the servant told Isaac all the things that he had done. [67]Then Isaac brought her into his mother Sarah's tent. He took Rebekah, and she became his wife; and he loved her. So Isaac was comforted after his mother's death.

Abraham Marries Keturah

25 Abraham took another wife, whose name was Keturah. [2]She bore him Zimran, Jokshan, Medan, Midian, Ishbak, and Shuah. [3]Jokshan was the father of Sheba and Dedan. The sons of Dedan were Asshurim, Letushim, and Leummim. [4]The sons of Midian were Ephah, Epher, Hanoch, Abida, and Eldaah. All these were the children of Keturah. [5]Abraham gave all he had to Isaac. [6]But to the sons of his concubines Abraham gave gifts, while he was still living, and he sent them away from his son Isaac, eastward to the east country.

The Death of Abraham

7 This is the length of Abraham's life, one hundred seventy-five years. [8]Abraham breathed his last and died in a good old age, an old man and full of years, and was gathered to his people. [9]His sons Isaac and Ishmael buried him in the cave of Machpelah, in the field of Ephron son of Zohar the Hittite, east of Mamre, [10]the field that Abraham purchased from the Hittites. There Abraham was buried, with his wife Sarah. [11]After the death of Abraham God blessed his son Isaac. And Isaac settled at Beer-lahai-roi.

Ishmael's Descendants

12 These are the descendants of Ishmael, Abraham's son, whom Hagar the Egyptian, Sarah's slave-girl, bore to Abraham. [13]These are the names of the sons of Ishmael, named in the order of their birth: Nebaioth, the firstborn of Ishmael; and Kedar, Adbeel, Mibsam, [14]Mishma, Dumah, Massa, [15]Hadad, Tema, Jetur, Naphish, and Kedemah. [16]These are the sons of Ishmael and these are their names, by their villages and by their encampments, twelve princes according to their tribes. [17](This is the length of the life of Ishmael, one hundred thirty-seven years; he breathed his last and died, and was gathered to his people.) [18]They settled from Havilah to Shur, which is opposite Egypt in the direction of Assyria; he settled down[p] alongside of[q] all his people.

The Birth and Youth of Esau and Jacob

19 These are the descendants of Isaac, Abraham's son: Abraham was the father of Isaac, [20]and Isaac was forty years old when he married Rebekah, daughter of Bethuel the Aramean of Paddan-aram, sister of Laban the Aramean. [21]Isaac prayed to the LORD for his wife, because she was barren; and the LORD granted his prayer, and his wife Rebekah conceived. [22]The children struggled together within her; and she said, "If it is to be this way, why do I live?"[r] So she went to inquire of the LORD. [23]And the LORD said to her,

> "Two nations are in your womb,
>   and two peoples born of you shall
>   be divided;
>   the one shall be stronger than the
>   other,
>   the elder shall serve the younger."

[24]When her time to give birth was at hand, there were twins in her womb. [25]The first came out red, all his body like a hairy mantle; so they named him Esau. [26]Afterward his brother came out, with his hand gripping Esau's heel; so he was named Jacob.[s] Isaac was sixty years old when she bore them.

27 When the boys grew up, Esau was a skillful hunter, a man of the field, while Jacob was a quiet man, living in tents. [28]Isaac loved Esau, because he was fond of game; but Rebekah loved Jacob.

Esau Sells His Birthright

29 Once when Jacob was cooking a stew, Esau came in from the field, and he was famished. [30]Esau said to Jacob, "Let me eat some of that red stuff, for I am

---

n Syr Tg: Heb *from coming to*   o Meaning of Heb word is uncertain   p Heb *he fell*   q Or *down in opposition to*   r Syr: Meaning of Heb uncertain   s That is *He takes by the heel* or *He supplants*

famished!" (Therefore he was called Edom.[t]) [31]Jacob said, "First sell me your birthright." [32]Esau said, "I am about to die; of what use is a birthright to me?" [33]Jacob said, "Swear to me first."[u] So he swore to him, and sold his birthright to Jacob. [34]Then Jacob gave Esau bread and lentil stew, and he ate and drank, and rose and went his way. Thus Esau despised his birthright.

Isaac and Abimelech

26 Now there was a famine in the land, besides the former famine that had occurred in the days of Abraham. And Isaac went to Gerar, to King Abimelech of the Philistines. [2]The LORD appeared to Isaac[v] and said, "Do not go down to Egypt; settle in the land that I shall show you. [3]Reside in this land as an alien, and I will be with you, and will bless you; for to you and to your descendants I will give all these lands, and I will fulfill the oath that I swore to your father Abraham. [4]I will make your offspring as numerous as the stars of heaven, and will give to your offspring all these lands; and all the nations of the earth shall gain blessing for themselves through your offspring, [5]because Abraham obeyed my voice and kept my charge, my commandments, my statutes, and my laws."

6 So Isaac settled in Gerar. [7]When the men of the place asked him about his wife, he said, "She is my sister"; for he was afraid to say, "My wife," thinking, "or else the men of the place might kill me for the sake of Rebekah, because she is attractive in appearance." [8]When Isaac had been there a long time, King Abimelech of the Philistines looked out of a window and saw him fondling his wife Rebekah. [9]So Abimelech called for Isaac, and said, "So she is your wife! Why then did you say, 'She is my sister'?" Isaac said to him, "Because I thought I might die because of her." [10]Abimelech said, "What is this you have done to us? One of the people might easily have lain with your wife, and you would have brought guilt upon us." [11]So Abimelech warned all the people, saying, "Whoever touches this man or his wife shall be put to death."

12 Isaac sowed seed in that land, and in the same year reaped a hundredfold. The LORD blessed him, [13]and the man became rich; he prospered more and more until he became very wealthy. [14]He had possessions of flocks and herds, and a great household, so that the Philistines envied him. [15](Now the Philistines had stopped up and filled with earth all the wells that his father's servants had dug in the days of his father Abraham.) [16]And Abimelech said to Isaac, "Go away from us; you have become too powerful for us."

17 So Isaac departed from there and camped in the valley of Gerar and settled there. [18]Isaac dug again the wells of water that had been dug in the days of his father Abraham; for the Philistines had stopped them up after the death of Abraham; and he gave them the names that his father had given them. [19]But when Isaac's servants dug in the valley and found there a well of spring water, [20]the herders of Gerar quarreled with Isaac's herders, saying, "The water is ours." So he called the well Esek,[w] because they contended with him. [21]Then they dug another well, and they quarreled over that one also; so he called it Sitnah.[x] [22]He moved from there and dug another well, and they did not quarrel over it; so he called it Rehoboth,[y] saying, "Now the LORD has made room for us, and we shall be fruitful in the land."

23 From there he went up to Beersheba. [24]And that very night the LORD appeared to him and said, "I am the God of your father Abraham; do not be afraid, for I am with you and will bless you and make your offspring numerous for my servant Abraham's sake." [25]So he built an altar there, called on the name of the LORD, and pitched his tent there. And there Isaac's servants dug a well.

26 Then Abimelech went to him from Gerar, with Ahuzzath his adviser and Phicol the commander of his army. [27]Isaac said to them, "Why have you come to me, seeing that you hate me and have sent me away from you?" [28]They said, "We see plainly that the LORD has been with you; so we say, let there be an oath between you and us, and let us make a covenant with you [29]so that you will do us no harm, just as we have not touched you and have done to you nothing but good and have sent you away in peace. You are now the blessed of the LORD." [30]So he made them a feast, and they ate and drank. [31]In the morning they rose early and exchanged

---

t That is *Red*   *u* Heb *today*   *v* Heb *him*
w That is *Contention*   *x* That is *Enmity*   *y* That is *Broad places* or *Room*

oaths; and Isaac set them on their way, and they departed from him in peace. ³²That same day Isaac's servants came and told him about the well that they had dug, and said to him, "We have found water!" ³³He called it Shibah;ᶻ therefore the name of the city is Beer-shebaᵃ to this day.

Esau's Hittite Wives

34 When Esau was forty years old, he married Judith daughter of Beeri the Hittite, and Basemath daughter of Elon the Hittite; ³⁵and they made life bitter for Isaac and Rebekah.

Isaac Blesses Jacob

27 When Isaac was old and his eyes were dim so that he could not see, he called his elder son Esau and said to him, "My son"; and he answered, "Here I am." ²He said, "See, I am old; I do not know the day of my death. ³Now then, take your weapons, your quiver and your bow, and go out to the field, and hunt game for me. ⁴Then prepare for me savory food, such as I like, and bring it to me to eat, so that I may bless you before I die."

5 Now Rebekah was listening when Isaac spoke to his son Esau. So when Esau went to the field to hunt for game and bring it, ⁶Rebekah said to her son Jacob, "I heard your father say to your brother Esau, ⁷'Bring me game, and prepare for me savory food to eat, that I may bless you before the LORD before I die.' ⁸Now therefore, my son, obey my word as I command you. ⁹Go to the flock, and get me two choice kids, so that I may prepare from them savory food for your father, such as he likes; ¹⁰and you shall take it to your father to eat, so that he may bless you before he dies." ¹¹But Jacob said to his mother Rebekah, "Look, my brother Esau is a hairy man, and I am a man of smooth skin. ¹²Perhaps my father will feel me, and I shall seem to be mocking him, and bring a curse on myself and not a blessing." ¹³His mother said to him, "Let your curse be on me, my son; only obey my word, and go, get them for me." ¹⁴So he went and got them and brought them to his mother; and his mother prepared savory food, such as his father loved. ¹⁵Then Rebekah took the best garments of her elder son Esau, which were with her in the house, and put them on her younger son Jacob; ¹⁶and she put the skins of the kids on his hands and on the smooth part of his neck. ¹⁷Then she handed the savory food, and the bread that she had prepared, to her son Jacob.

18 So he went in to his father, and said, "My father"; and he said, "Here I am; who are you, my son?" ¹⁹Jacob said to his father, "I am Esau your firstborn. I have done as you told me; now sit up and eat of my game, so that you may bless me." ²⁰But Isaac said to his son, "How is it that you have found it so quickly, my son?" He answered, "Because the LORD your God granted me success." ²¹Then Isaac said to Jacob, "Come near, that I may feel you, my son, to know whether you are really my son Esau or not." ²²So Jacob went up to his father Isaac, who felt him and said, "The voice is Jacob's voice, but the hands are the hands of Esau." ²³He did not recognize him, because his hands were hairy like his brother Esau's hands; so he blessed him. ²⁴He said, "Are you really my son Esau?" He answered, "I am." ²⁵Then he said, "Bring it to me, that I may eat of my son's game and bless you." So he brought it to him, and he ate; and he brought him wine, and he drank. ²⁶Then his father Isaac said to him, "Come near and kiss me, my son." ²⁷So he came near and kissed him; and he smelled the smell of his garments, and blessed him, and said,

> "Ah, the smell of my son
>   is like the smell of a field that the
>   LORD has blessed.
> 28 May God give you of the dew of
>   heaven,
>   and of the fatness of the earth,
>   and plenty of grain and wine.
> 29 Let peoples serve you,
>   and nations bow down to you.
> Be lord over your brothers,
>   and may your mother's sons bow
>   down to you.
> Cursed be everyone who curses you,
>   and blessed be everyone who
>   blesses you!"

Esau's Lost Blessing

30 As soon as Isaac had finished blessing Jacob, when Jacob had scarcely gone out from the presence of his father Isaac, his brother Esau came in from his hunting. ³¹He also prepared savory food, and

---

ᶻ A word resembling the word for *oath*   ᵃ That is *Well of the oath* or *Well of seven*

brought it to his father. And he said to his father, "Let my father sit up and eat of his son's game, so that you may bless me." [32]His father Isaac said to him, "Who are you?" He answered, "I am your firstborn son, Esau." [33]Then Isaac trembled violently, and said, "Who was it then that hunted game and brought it to me, and I ate it all[b] before you came, and I have blessed him?—yes, and blessed he shall be!" [34]When Esau heard his father's words, he cried out with an exceedingly great and bitter cry, and said to his father, "Bless me, me also, father!" [35]But he said, "Your brother came deceitfully, and he has taken away your blessing." [36]Esau said, "Is he not rightly named Jacob?[c] For he has supplanted me these two times. He took away my birthright; and look, now he has taken away my blessing." Then he said, "Have you not reserved a blessing for me?" [37]Isaac answered Esau, "I have already made him your lord, and I have given him all his brothers as servants, and with grain and wine I have sustained him. What then can I do for you, my son?" [38]Esau said to his father, "Have you only one blessing, father? Bless me, me also, father!" And Esau lifted up his voice and wept.

39 Then his father Isaac answered him:

"See, away from[d] the fatness of the
    earth shall your home be,
and away from[e] the dew of
    heaven on high.
40 By your sword you shall live,
    and you shall serve your brother;
but when you break loose,[f]
    you shall break his yoke from
        your neck."

Jacob Escapes Esau's Fury

41 Now Esau hated Jacob because of the blessing with which his father had blessed him, and Esau said to himself, "The days of mourning for my father are approaching; then I will kill my brother Jacob." [42]But the words of her elder son Esau were told to Rebekah; so she sent and called her younger son Jacob and said to him, "Your brother Esau is consoling himself by planning to kill you. [43]Now therefore, my son, obey my voice; flee at once to my brother Laban in Haran, [44]and stay with him a while, until your brother's fury turns away— [45]until your brother's anger against you turns away, and he forgets what you have done to him; then I will send, and bring you back from there. Why should I lose both of you in one day?"

46 Then Rebekah said to Isaac, "I am weary of my life because of the Hittite women. If Jacob marries one of the Hittite women such as these, one of the women of the land, what good will my life be to me?"

28 Then Isaac called Jacob and blessed him, and charged him, "You shall not marry one of the Canaanite women. [2]Go at once to Paddan-aram to the house of Bethuel, your mother's father; and take as wife from there one of the daughters of Laban, your mother's brother. [3]May God Almighty[g] bless you and make you fruitful and numerous, that you may become a company of peoples. [4]May he give to you the blessing of Abraham, to you and to your offspring with you, so that you may take possession of the land where you now live as an alien— land that God gave to Abraham." [5]Thus Isaac sent Jacob away; and he went to Paddan-aram, to Laban son of Bethuel the Aramean, the brother of Rebekah, Jacob's and Esau's mother.

Esau Marries Ishmael's Daughter

6 Now Esau saw that Isaac had blessed Jacob and sent him away to Paddan-aram to take a wife from there, and that as he blessed him he charged him, "You shall not marry one of the Canaanite women," [7]and that Jacob had obeyed his father and his mother and gone to Paddan-aram. [8]So when Esau saw that the Canaanite women did not please his father Isaac, [9]Esau went to Ishmael and took Mahalath daughter of Abraham's son Ishmael, and sister of Nebaioth, to be his wife in addition to the wives he had.

Jacob's Dream at Bethel

10 Jacob left Beer-sheba and went toward Haran. [11]He came to a certain place and stayed there for the night, because the sun had set. Taking one of the stones of the place, he put it under his head and lay down in that place. [12]And he dreamed that there was a ladder[h] set up on the earth, the top of it reaching to heaven; and the angels of God were ascending and de-

---

b Cn: Heb *of all*   *c* That is *He supplants* or *He takes by the heel*   *d* Or *See, of*   *e* Or *and of*   *f* Meaning of Heb uncertain   *g* Traditional rendering of Heb *El Shaddai*   *h* Or *stairway* or *ramp*

scending on it. [13]And the LORD stood beside him[i] and said, "I am the LORD, the God of Abraham your father and the God of Isaac; the land on which you lie I will give to you and to your offspring; [14]and your offspring shall be like the dust of the earth, and you shall spread abroad to the west and to the east and to the north and to the south; and all the families of the earth shall be blessed[j] in you and in your offspring. [15]Know that I am with you and will keep you wherever you go, and will bring you back to this land; for I will not leave you until I have done what I have promised you." [16]Then Jacob woke from

his sleep and said, "Surely the LORD is in this place—and I did not know it!" [17]And he was afraid, and said, "How awesome is this place! This is none other than the house of God, and this is the gate of heaven."

[18] So Jacob rose early in the morning, and he took the stone that he had put under his head and set it up for a pillar and poured oil on the top of it. [19]He called that place Bethel;[k] but the name of the city was Luz at the first. [20]Then Jacob made a vow, saying, "If God will be with

---

[i] Or *stood above it*   [j] Or *shall bless themselves*
[k] That is *House of God*

THE TRADITION

Sacramentals

So Jacob rose early in the morning, and he took the stone that he had put under his head and set it up for a pillar and poured oil on the top of it.

GENESIS 28.18

Jacob awoke from his dream in solemn wonder. Right here where he had slept, with a rock for a pillow, angels had moved up and down a stairway connecting heaven and earth. God had appeared and spoken. "Surely the LORD is in this place—and I did not know it!" Jacob exclaimed (28.16). Then he marked the spot by setting up his pillow-stone as a monument.

We can understand Jacob's desire to leave some visible sign of his meeting with God. If he had tried to carry off the stone, we could understand that too! We fill our homes with souvenirs, photos of people we love, food and music that evoke special memories. Things we can see, smell, hear, taste, and touch become reminders of what is past or far away. But we also seek everyday reminders—as physically real as Jacob's rock—of our relationship with God. We find them in the sacramentals.

Sacramentals are sacred signs—things, words, images, actions, and music—that direct us to God and through which God works. They do not have the same power and

importance as the seven sacraments. On the other hand, they are everywhere. Almost anything, if blessed and properly used, can become a sacramental.

Outward physical expressions of the life of grace, sacramentals are like a string around the finger—a reminder of unseen spiritual realities. Holy water recalls the waters of Baptism. Icons proclaim that God became man and that the Holy Spirit continues to live in human beings. Blessings verbalize God's desire for our welfare.

But, like the angels on Jacob's ladder, sacramentals move in two directions: They both point to God's presence and provide a means of response. The sign of the cross is both our remembrance of Christ's sacrifice and our declaration of intent to follow him. Medals mark us as disciples. A burning candle expresses our desire to pray always.

"Surely the LORD is in this place!"—that is, in the entire physical universe. Sacramentals open our eyes to the reality that, as Elizabeth Barrett Browning wrote, "earth's crammed with heaven."

me, and will keep me in this way that I go, and will give me bread to eat and clothing to wear, ²¹so that I come again to my father's house in peace, then the LORD shall be my God, ²²and this stone, which I have set up for a pillar, shall be God's house; and of all that you give me I will surely give one-tenth to you."

Jacob Meets Rachel

29 Then Jacob went on his journey, and came to the land of the people of the east. ²As he looked, he saw a well in the field and three flocks of sheep lying there beside it; for out of that well the flocks were watered. The stone on the well's mouth was large, ³and when all the flocks were gathered there, the shepherds would roll the stone from the mouth of the well, and water the sheep, and put the stone back in its place on the mouth of the well.

4 Jacob said to them, "My brothers, where do you come from?" They said, "We are from Haran." ⁵He said to them, "Do you know Laban son of Nahor?" They said, "We do." ⁶He said to them, "Is it well with him?" "Yes," they replied, "and here is his daughter Rachel, coming with the sheep." ⁷He said, "Look, it is still broad daylight; it is not time for the animals to be gathered together. Water the sheep, and go, pasture them." ⁸But they said, "We cannot until all the flocks are gathered together, and the stone is rolled from the mouth of the well; then we water the sheep."

9 While he was still speaking with them, Rachel came with her father's sheep; for she kept them. ¹⁰Now when Jacob saw Rachel, the daughter of his mother's brother Laban, and the sheep of his mother's brother Laban, Jacob went up and rolled the stone from the well's mouth, and watered the flock of his mother's brother Laban. ¹¹Then Jacob kissed Rachel, and wept aloud. ¹²And Jacob told Rachel that he was her father's kinsman, and that he was Rebekah's son; and she ran and told her father.

13 When Laban heard the news about his sister's son Jacob, he ran to meet him; he embraced him and kissed him, and brought him to his house. Jacob*l* told Laban all these things, ¹⁴and Laban said to him, "Surely you are my bone and my flesh!" And he stayed with him a month.

Jacob Marries Laban's Daughters

15 Then Laban said to Jacob, "Because you are my kinsman, should you therefore serve me for nothing? Tell me, what shall your wages be?" ¹⁶Now Laban had two daughters; the name of the elder was Leah, and the name of the younger was Rachel. ¹⁷Leah's eyes were lovely,*m* and Rachel was graceful and beautiful. ¹⁸Jacob loved Rachel; so he said, "I will serve you seven years for your younger daughter Rachel." ¹⁹Laban said, "It is better that I give her to you than that I should give her to any other man; stay with me." ²⁰So Jacob served seven years for Rachel, and they seemed to him but a few days because of the love he had for her.

21 Then Jacob said to Laban, "Give me my wife that I may go in to her, for my time is completed." ²²So Laban gathered together all the people of the place, and made a feast. ²³But in the evening he took his daughter Leah and brought her to Jacob; and he went in to her. ²⁴(Laban gave his maid Zilpah to his daughter Leah to be her maid.) ²⁵When morning came, it was Leah! And Jacob said to Laban, "What is this you have done to me? Did I not serve with you for Rachel? Why then have you deceived me?" ²⁶Laban said, "This is not done in our country—giving the younger before the firstborn. ²⁷Complete the week of this one, and we will give you the other also in return for serving me another seven years." ²⁸Jacob did so, and completed her week; then Laban gave him his daughter Rachel as a wife. ²⁹(Laban gave his maid Bilhah to his daughter Rachel to be her maid.) ³⁰So Jacob went in to Rachel also, and he loved Rachel more than Leah. He served Laban*n* for another seven years.

31 When the LORD saw that Leah was unloved, he opened her womb; but Rachel was barren. ³²Leah conceived and bore a son, and she named him Reuben;*o* for she said, "Because the LORD has looked on my affliction; surely now my husband will love me." ³³She conceived again and bore a son, and said, "Because the LORD has heard*p* that I am hated, he has given me this son also"; and she named him Simeon. ³⁴Again she conceived and bore a son, and said, "Now this time my hus-

---

l Heb *He*   *m* Meaning of Heb uncertain   *n* Heb
him   *o* That is *See, a son*   *p* Heb *shama*

band will be joined[q] to me, because I have borne him three sons"; therefore he was named Levi. [35]She conceived again and bore a son, and said, "This time I will praise[r] the LORD"; therefore she named him Judah; then she ceased bearing.

30 When Rachel saw that she bore Jacob no children, she envied her sister; and she said to Jacob, "Give me children, or I shall die!" [2]Jacob became very angry with Rachel and said, "Am I in the place of God, who has withheld from you the fruit of the womb?" [3]Then she said, "Here is my maid Bilhah; go in to her, that she may bear upon my knees and that I too may have children through her." [4]So she gave him her maid Bilhah as a wife; and Jacob went in to her. [5]And Bilhah conceived and bore Jacob a son. [6]Then Rachel said, "God has judged me, and has also heard my voice and given me a son"; therefore she named him Dan.[s] [7]Rachel's maid Bilhah conceived again and bore Jacob a second son. [8]Then Rachel said, "With mighty wrestlings I have wrestled[t] with my sister, and have prevailed"; so she named him Naphtali.

[9] When Leah saw that she had ceased bearing children, she took her maid Zilpah and gave her to Jacob as a wife. [10]Then Leah's maid Zilpah bore Jacob a son. [11]And Leah said, "Good fortune!" so she named him Gad.[u] [12]Leah's maid Zilpah bore Jacob a second son. [13]And Leah said, "Happy am I! For the women will call me happy"; so she named him Asher.[v]

[14] In the days of wheat harvest Reuben went and found mandrakes in the field, and brought them to his mother Leah. Then Rachel said to Leah, "Please give me some of your son's mandrakes." [15]But she said to her, "Is it a small matter that you have taken away my husband? Would you take away my son's mandrakes also?" Rachel said, "Then he may lie with you tonight for your son's mandrakes." [16]When Jacob came from the field in the evening, Leah went out to meet him, and said, "You must come in to me; for I have hired you with my son's mandrakes." So he lay with her that night. [17]And God heeded Leah, and she conceived and bore Jacob a fifth son. [18]Leah said, "God has given me my hire[w] because I gave my maid to my husband"; so she named him Issachar. [19]And Leah conceived again, and she bore Jacob a sixth son. [20]Then Leah said, "God has endowed me with a good dowry; now

my husband will honor[x] me, because I have borne him six sons"; so she named him Zebulun. [21]Afterwards she bore a daughter, and named her Dinah.

[22] Then God remembered Rachel, and God heeded her and opened her womb. [23]She conceived and bore a son, and said, "God has taken away my reproach"; [24]and she named him Joseph,[y] saying, "May the LORD add to me another son!"

Jacob Prospers at Laban's Expense

[25] When Rachel had borne Joseph, Jacob said to Laban, "Send me away, that I may go to my own home and country. [26]Give me my wives and my children for whom I have served you, and let me go; for you know very well the service I have given you." [27]But Laban said to him, "If you will allow me to say so, I have learned by divination that the LORD has blessed me because of you; [28]name your wages, and I will give it." [29]Jacob said to him, "You yourself know how I have served you, and how your cattle have fared with me. [30]For you had little before I came, and it has increased abundantly; and the LORD has blessed you wherever I turned. But now when shall I provide for my own household also?" [31]He said, "What shall I give you?" Jacob said, "You shall not give me anything; if you will do this for me, I will again feed your flock and keep it: [32]let me pass through all your flock today, removing from it every speckled and spotted sheep and every black lamb, and the spotted and speckled among the goats; and such shall be my wages. [33]So my honesty will answer for me later, when you come to look into my wages with you. Every one that is not speckled and spotted among the goats and black among the lambs, if found with me, shall be counted stolen." [34]Laban said, "Good! Let it be as you have said." [35]But that day Laban removed the male goats that were striped and spotted, and all the female goats that were speckled and spotted, every one that had white on it, and every lamb that was black, and put them in charge of his sons; [36]and he set a distance of three days' journey between himself and Jacob, while Jacob was pasturing the rest of Laban's flock.

---

[q] Heb *lawah*   [r] Heb *hodah*   [s] That is *He judged*
[t] Heb *niphtal*   [u] That is *Fortune*   [v] That is
Happy   [w] Heb *sakar*   [x] Heb *zabal*   [y] That is
He adds

37 Then Jacob took fresh rods of poplar and almond and plane, and peeled white streaks in them, exposing the white of the rods. 38He set the rods that he had peeled in front of the flocks in the troughs, that is, the watering places, where the flocks came to drink. And since they bred when they came to drink, 39the flocks bred in front of the rods, and so the flocks produced young that were striped, speckled, and spotted. 40Jacob separated the lambs, and set the faces of the flocks toward the striped and the completely black animals in the flock of Laban; and he put his own droves apart, and did not put them with Laban's flock. 41Whenever the stronger of the flock were breeding, Jacob laid the rods in the troughs before the eyes of the flock, that they might breed among the rods, 42but for the feebler of the flock he did not lay them there; so the feebler were Laban's, and the stronger Jacob's. 43Thus the man grew exceedingly rich, and had large flocks, and male and female slaves, and camels and donkeys.

Jacob Flees with Family and Flocks

31 Now Jacob heard that the sons of Laban were saying, "Jacob has taken all that was our father's; he has gained all this wealth from what belonged to our father." 2And Jacob saw that Laban did not regard him as favorably as he did before. 3Then the LORD said to Jacob, "Return to the land of your ancestors and to your kindred, and I will be with you." 4So Jacob sent and called Rachel and Leah into the field where his flock was, 5and said to them, "I see that your father does not regard me as favorably as he did before. But the God of my father has been with me. 6You know that I have served your father with all my strength; 7yet your father has cheated me and changed my wages ten times, but God did not permit him to harm me. 8If he said, 'The speckled shall be your wages,' then all the flock bore speckled; and if he said, 'The striped shall be your wages,' then all the flock bore striped. 9Thus God has taken away the livestock of your father, and given them to me.

10 "During the mating of the flock I once had a dream in which I looked up and saw that the male goats that leaped upon the flock were striped, speckled, and mottled. 11Then the angel of God said to me in the dream, 'Jacob,' and I said, 'Here I am!' 12And he said, 'Look up and see that all the goats that leap on the flock are striped, speckled, and mottled; for I have seen all that Laban is doing to you. 13I am the God of Bethel,z where you anointed a pillar and made a vow to me. Now leave this land at once and return to the land of your birth.' " 14Then Rachel and Leah answered him, "Is there any portion or inheritance left to us in our father's house? 15Are we not regarded by him as foreigners? For he has sold us, and he has been using up the money given for us. 16All the property that God has taken away from our father belongs to us and to our children; now then, do whatever God has said to you."

17 So Jacob arose, and set his children and his wives on camels; 18and he drove away all his livestock, all the property that he had gained, the livestock in his possession that he had acquired in Paddan-aram, to go to his father Isaac in the land of Canaan.

19 Now Laban had gone to shear his sheep, and Rachel stole her father's household gods. 20And Jacob deceived Laban the Aramean, in that he did not tell him that he intended to flee. 21So he fled with all that he had; starting out he crossed the Euphrates,a and set his face toward the hill country of Gilead.

Laban Overtakes Jacob

22 On the third day Laban was told that Jacob had fled. 23So he took his kinsfolk with him and pursued him for seven days until he caught up with him in the hill country of Gilead. 24But God came to Laban the Aramean in a dream by night, and said to him, "Take heed that you say not a word to Jacob, either good or bad." 25 Laban overtook Jacob. Now Jacob had pitched his tent in the hill country, and Laban with his kinsfolk camped in the hill country of Gilead. 26Laban said to Jacob, "What have you done? You have deceived me, and carried away my daughters like captives of the sword. 27Why did you flee secretly and deceive me and not tell me? I would have sent you away with mirth and songs, with tambourine and lyre. 28And why did you not permit me to kiss my sons and my daughters farewell?

z Cn: Meaning of Heb uncertain   a Heb *the river*

What you have done is foolish. ²⁹It is in my power to do you harm; but the God of your father spoke to me last night, saying, 'Take heed that you speak to Jacob neither good nor bad.' ³⁰Even though you had to go because you longed greatly for your father's house, why did you steal my gods?" ³¹Jacob answered Laban, "Because I was afraid, for I thought that you would take your daughters from me by force. ³²But anyone with whom you find your gods shall not live. In the presence of our kinsfolk, point out what I have that is yours, and take it." Now Jacob did not know that Rachel had stolen the gods.[b]

33 So Laban went into Jacob's tent, and into Leah's tent, and into the tent of the two maids, but he did not find them. And he went out of Leah's tent, and entered Rachel's. ³⁴Now Rachel had taken the household gods and put them in the camel's saddle, and sat on them. Laban felt all about in the tent, but did not find them. ³⁵And she said to her father, "Let not my lord be angry that I cannot rise before you, for the way of women is upon me." So he searched, but did not find the household gods.

36 Then Jacob became angry, and upbraided Laban. Jacob said to Laban, "What is my offense? What is my sin, that you have hotly pursued me? ³⁷Although you have felt about through all my goods, what have you found of all your household goods? Set it here before my kinsfolk and your kinsfolk, so that they may decide between us two. ³⁸These twenty years I have been with you; your ewes and your female goats have not miscarried, and I have not eaten the rams of your flocks. ³⁹That which was torn by wild beasts I did not bring to you; I bore the loss of it myself; of my hand you required it, whether stolen by day or stolen by night. ⁴⁰It was like this with me: by day the heat consumed me, and the cold by night, and my sleep fled from my eyes. ⁴¹These twenty years I have been in your house; I served you fourteen years for your two daughters, and six years for your flock, and you have changed my wages ten times. ⁴²If the God of my father, the God of Abraham and the Fear[c] of Isaac, had not been on my side, surely now you would have sent me away empty-handed. God saw my affliction and the labor of my hands, and rebuked you last night."

Laban and Jacob Make a Covenant

43 Then Laban answered and said to Jacob, "The daughters are my daughters, the children are my children, the flocks are my flocks, and all that you see is mine. But what can I do today about these daughters of mine, or about their children whom they have borne? ⁴⁴Come now, let us make a covenant, you and I; and let it be a witness between you and me." ⁴⁵So Jacob took a stone, and set it up as a pillar. ⁴⁶And Jacob said to his kinsfolk, "Gather stones," and they took stones, and made a heap; and they ate there by the heap. ⁴⁷Laban called it Jegar-sahadutha:[d] but Jacob called it Galeed.[e] ⁴⁸Laban said, "This heap is a witness between you and me today." Therefore he called it Galeed, ⁴⁹and the pillar[f] Mizpah,[g] for he said, "The LORD watch between you and me, when we are absent one from the other. ⁵⁰If you ill-treat my daughters, or if you take wives in addition to my daughters, though no one else is with us, remember that God is witness between you and me."

51 Then Laban said to Jacob, "See this heap and see the pillar, which I have set between you and me. ⁵²This heap is a witness, and the pillar is a witness, that I will not pass beyond this heap to you, and you will not pass beyond this heap and this pillar to me, for harm. ⁵³May the God of Abraham and the God of Nahor"—the God of their father—"judge between us." So Jacob swore by the Fear[c] of his father Isaac, ⁵⁴and Jacob offered a sacrifice on the height and called his kinsfolk to eat bread; and they ate bread and tarried all night in the hill country.

⁵⁵[h]Early in the morning Laban rose up, and kissed his grandchildren and his daughters and blessed them; then he departed and returned home.

32 Jacob went on his way and the angels of God met him; ²and when Jacob saw them he said, "This is God's camp!" So he called that place Mahanaim.[i]

Jacob Sends Presents to Appease Esau

3 Jacob sent messengers before him to his brother Esau in the land of Seir, the

---

[b] Heb *them*   [c] Meaning of Heb uncertain   [d] In Aramaic *The heap of witness*   [e] In Hebrew *The heap of witness*   [f] Compare Sam: MT lacks *the pillar*   [g] That is *Watchpost*   [h] Ch 32.1 in Heb   [i] Here taken to mean *Two camps*

country of Edom, [4]instructing them, "Thus you shall say to my lord Esau: Thus says your servant Jacob, 'I have lived with Laban as an alien, and stayed until now; [5]and I have oxen, donkeys, flocks, male and female slaves; and I have sent to tell my lord, in order that I may find favor in your sight.' "

6 The messengers returned to Jacob, saying, "We came to your brother Esau, and he is coming to meet you, and four hundred men are with him." [7]Then Jacob was greatly afraid and distressed; and he divided the people that were with him, and the flocks and herds and camels, into two companies, [8]thinking, "If Esau comes to the one company and destroys it, then the company that is left will escape."

9 And Jacob said, "O God of my father Abraham and God of my father Isaac, O LORD who said to me, 'Return to your country and to your kindred, and I will do you good,' [10]I am not worthy of the least of all the steadfast love and all the faithfulness that you have shown to your servant, for with only my staff I crossed this Jordan; and now I have become two companies. [11]Deliver me, please, from the hand of my brother, from the hand of Esau, for I am afraid of him; he may come and kill us all, the mothers with the children. [12]Yet you have said, 'I will surely do you good, and make your offspring as the sand of the sea, which cannot be counted because of their number.' "

13 So he spent that night there, and from what he had with him he took a present for his brother Esau, [14]two hundred female goats and twenty male goats, two hundred ewes and twenty rams, [15]thirty milch camels and their colts, forty cows and ten bulls, twenty female donkeys and ten male donkeys. [16]These he delivered into the hand of his servants, every drove by itself, and said to his servants, "Pass on ahead of me, and put a space between drove and drove." [17]He instructed the foremost, "When Esau my brother meets you, and asks you, 'To whom do you belong? Where are you going? And whose are these ahead of you?' [18]then you shall say, 'They belong to your servant Jacob; they are a present sent to my lord Esau; and moreover he is behind us.' " [19]He likewise instructed the second and the third and all who followed the droves, "You shall say the same thing to Esau when you meet him, [20]and you shall say,

'Moreover your servant Jacob is behind us.' " For he thought, "I may appease him with the present that goes ahead of me, and afterwards I shall see his face; perhaps he will accept me." [21]So the present passed on ahead of him; and he himself spent that night in the camp.

Jacob Wrestles at Peniel

22 The same night he got up and took his two wives, his two maids, and his eleven children, and crossed the ford of the Jabbok. [23]He took them and sent them across the stream, and likewise everything that he had. [24]Jacob was left alone; and a man wrestled with him until daybreak. [25]When the man saw that he did not prevail against Jacob, he struck him on the hip socket; and Jacob's hip was put out of joint as he wrestled with him. [26]Then he said, "Let me go, for the day is breaking." But Jacob said, "I will not let you go, unless you bless me." [27]So he said to him, "What is your name?" And he said, "Jacob." [28]Then the man [j] said, "You shall no longer be called Jacob, but Israel,[k] for you have striven with God and with humans,[l] and have prevailed." [29]Then Jacob asked him, "Please tell me your name." But he said, "Why is it that you ask my name?" And there he blessed him. [30]So Jacob called the place Peniel,[m] saying, "For I have seen God face to face, and yet my life is preserved." [31]The sun rose upon him as he passed Penuel, limping because of his hip. [32]Therefore to this day the Israelites do not eat the thigh muscle that is on the hip socket, because he struck Jacob on the hip socket at the thigh muscle.

Jacob and Esau Meet

33 Now Jacob looked up and saw Esau coming, and four hundred men with him. So he divided the children among Leah and Rachel and the two maids. [2]He put the maids with their children in front, then Leah with her children, and Rachel and Joseph last of all. [3]He himself went on ahead of them, bowing himself to the ground seven times, until he came near his brother.

4 But Esau ran to meet him, and embraced him, and fell on his neck and kissed him, and they wept. [5]When Esau

j Heb *he*   k That is *The one who strives with God or God strives*   l Or *with divine and human beings*   m That is *The face of God*

looked up and saw the women and children, he said, "Who are these with you?" Jacob said, "The children whom God has graciously given your servant." 6Then the maids drew near, they and their children, and bowed down; 7Leah likewise and her children drew near and bowed down; and finally Joseph and Rachel drew near, and they bowed down. 8Esau said, "What do you mean by all this company that I met?" Jacob answered, "To find favor with my lord." 9But Esau said, "I have enough, my brother; keep what you have for yourself." 10Jacob said, "No, please; if I find favor with you, then accept my present from my hand; for truly to see your face is like seeing the face of God—since you have received me with such favor. 11Please accept my gift that is brought to you, because God has dealt graciously with me, and because I have everything I want." So he urged him, and he took it.

12 Then Esau said, "Let us journey on our way, and I will go alongside you."

*C*ontending With God

THURSDAY

Scripture Reading
for Today:
Genesis 32.22–32

Verse for Today:
Genesis 32.30

My favorite Biblical example of conversion is the story of Jacob. Like his mother Rebekah, he is a master manipulator and controller, the kind of person who's good at looking out for Number One, which is what leads him to deceive his elderly father and cheat his brother out of an inheritance.

The thing Jacob had to learn is that reconciling with his brother means contending with God. And it also meant that he had to become a person who is willing to rely on God, and not just on himself. When Jacob awakens from his odd dream of wrestling with—a man, an angel, God himself, we are never told for sure—he is in awe once again. He says, "I have seen God face to face, and yet my life is preserved." Jacob names the place *Peniel*, which means "face of God." The next day, when he meets up with his brother Esau, the conversion of Jacob becomes complete. For instead of threatening him, his brother Esau runs to him and kisses him, and the two men weep. Jacob says to his brother, "for truly to see your face is like seeing the face of God" (Genesis 33.10). This story says to me that if we have ever truly been forgiven, we have seen the face of God. If we've ever been on the receiving end of an act of mercy that made a difference in our lives, we have seen the face of God.

Most of us have had family, mentors, friends, and even enemies who have wrestled with us through the important questions; who have helped us grow up, building something good out of the ruins we have made for ourselves. Like Jacob, maybe some of us have looked for a curse and received a blessing instead. Like Jacob, some of us have found the worst parts of ourselves converted into something better, our small expectations shattered in the presence of God's great abundance, or as the old hymn puts it, "the wideness of God's mercy."

—*KATHLEEN NORRIS*

Go to page 44 for your next devotional reading.

[13]But Jacob said to him, "My lord knows that the children are frail and that the flocks and herds, which are nursing, are a care to me; and if they are overdriven for one day, all the flocks will die. [14]Let my lord pass on ahead of his servant, and I will lead on slowly, according to the pace of the cattle that are before me and according to the pace of the children, until I come to my lord in Seir."

15 So Esau said, "Let me leave with you some of the people who are with me." But he said, "Why should my lord be so kind to me?" [16]So Esau returned that day on his way to Seir. [17]But Jacob journeyed to Succoth,[n] and built himself a house, and made booths for his cattle; therefore the place is called Succoth.

Jacob Reaches Shechem

18 Jacob came safely to the city of Shechem, which is in the land of Canaan, on his way from Paddan-aram; and he camped before the city. [19]And from the sons of Hamor, Shechem's father, he bought for one hundred pieces of money[o] the plot of land on which he had pitched his tent. [20]There he erected an altar and called it El-Elohe-Israel.[p]

The Rape of Dinah

34 Now Dinah the daughter of Leah, whom she had borne to Jacob, went out to visit the women of the region. [2]When Shechem son of Hamor the Hivite, prince of the region, saw her, he seized her and lay with her by force. [3]And his soul was drawn to Dinah daughter of Jacob; he loved the girl, and spoke tenderly to her. [4]So Shechem spoke to his father Hamor, saying, "Get me this girl to be my wife."

5 Now Jacob heard that Shechem[q] had defiled his daughter Dinah; but his sons were with his cattle in the field, so Jacob held his peace until they came. [6]And Hamor the father of Shechem went out to Jacob to speak with him, [7]just as the sons of Jacob came in from the field. When they heard of it, the men were indignant and very angry, because he had committed an outrage in Israel by lying with Jacob's daughter, for such a thing ought not to be done.

8 But Hamor spoke with them, saying, "The heart of my son Shechem longs for your daughter; please give her to him in marriage. [9]Make marriages with us; give your daughters to us, and take our daughters for yourselves. [10]You shall live with us; and the land shall be open to you; live and trade in it, and get property in it." [11]Shechem also said to her father and to her brothers, "Let me find favor with you, and whatever you say to me I will give. [12]Put the marriage present and gift as high as you like, and I will give whatever you ask me; only give me the girl to be my wife."

13 The sons of Jacob answered Shechem and his father Hamor deceitfully, because he had defiled their sister Dinah. [14]They said to them, "We cannot do this thing, to give our sister to one who is uncircumcised, for that would be a disgrace to us. [15]Only on this condition will we consent to you: that you will become as we are and every male among you be circumcised. [16]Then we will give our daughters to you, and we will take your daughters for ourselves, and we will live among you and become one people. [17]But if you will not listen to us and be circumcised, then we will take our daughter and be gone."

18 Their words pleased Hamor and Hamor's son Shechem. [19]And the young man did not delay to do the thing, because he was delighted with Jacob's daughter. Now he was the most honored of all his family. [20]So Hamor and his son Shechem came to the gate of their city and spoke to the men of their city, saying, [21]"These people are friendly with us; let them live in the land and trade in it, for the land is large enough for them; let us take their daughters in marriage, and let us give them our daughters. [22]Only on this condition will they agree to live among us, to become one people: that every male among us be circumcised as they are circumcised. [23]Will not their livestock, their property, and all their animals be ours? Only let us agree with them, and they will live among us." [24]And all who went out of the city gate heeded Hamor and his son Shechem; and every male was circumcised, all who went out of the gate of his city.

Dinah's Brothers Avenge Their Sister

25 On the third day, when they were still in pain, two of the sons of Jacob, Sim-

n That is Booths   o Heb one hundred qesitah
p That is God, the God of Israel   q Heb he

eon and Levi, Dinah's brothers, took their swords and came against the city unawares, and killed all the males. 26They killed Hamor and his son Shechem with the sword, and took Dinah out of Shechem's house, and went away. 27And the other sons of Jacob came upon the slain, and plundered the city, because their sister had been defiled. 28They took their flocks and their herds, their donkeys, and whatever was in the city and in the field. 29All their wealth, all their little ones and their wives, all that was in the houses, they captured and made their prey. 30Then Jacob said to Simeon and Levi, "You have brought trouble on me by making me odious to the inhabitants of the land, the Canaanites and the Perizzites; my numbers are few, and if they gather themselves against me and attack me, I shall be destroyed, both I and my household." 31But they said, "Should our sister be treated like a whore?"

Jacob Returns to Bethel

35 God said to Jacob, "Arise, go up to Bethel, and settle there. Make an altar there to the God who appeared to you when you fled from your brother Esau." 2So Jacob said to his household and to all who were with him, "Put away the foreign gods that are among you, and purify yourselves, and change your clothes; 3then come, let us go up to Bethel, that I may make an altar there to the God who answered me in the day of my distress and has been with me wherever I have gone." 4So they gave to Jacob all the foreign gods that they had, and the rings that were in their ears; and Jacob hid them under the oak that was near Shechem.

5 As they journeyed, a terror from God fell upon the cities all around them, so that no one pursued them. 6Jacob came to Luz (that is, Bethel), which is in the land of Canaan, he and all the people who were with him, 7and there he built an altar and called the place El-bethel,r because it was there that God had revealed himself to him when he fled from his brother. 8And Deborah, Rebekah's nurse, died, and she was buried under an oak below Bethel. So it was called Allon-bacuth.s

9 God appeared to Jacob again when he came from Paddan-aram, and he blessed him. 10God said to him, "Your name is Jacob; no longer shall you be called Jacob, but Israel shall be your

name." So he was called Israel. 11God said to him, "I am God Almighty:t be fruitful and multiply; a nation and a company of nations shall come from you, and kings shall spring from you. 12The land that I gave to Abraham and Isaac I will give to you, and I will give the land to your offspring after you." 13Then God went up from him at the place where he had spoken with him. 14Jacob set up a pillar in the place where he had spoken with him, a pillar of stone; and he poured out a drink offering on it, and poured oil on it. 15So Jacob called the place where God had spoken with him Bethel.

The Birth of Benjamin and the Death of Rachel

16 Then they journeyed from Bethel; and when they were still some distance from Ephrath, Rachel was in childbirth, and she had hard labor. 17When she was in her hard labor, the midwife said to her, "Do not be afraid; for now you will have another son." 18As her soul was departing (for she died), she named him Ben-oni;u but his father called him Benjamin.v 19So Rachel died, and she was buried on the way to Ephrath (that is, Bethlehem), 20and Jacob set up a pillar at her grave; it is the pillar of Rachel's tomb, which is there to this day. 21Israel journeyed on, and pitched his tent beyond the tower of Eder.

22 While Israel lived in that land, Reuben went and lay with Bilhah his father's concubine; and Israel heard of it.

Now the sons of Jacob were twelve. 23The sons of Leah: Reuben (Jacob's firstborn), Simeon, Levi, Judah, Issachar, and Zebulun. 24The sons of Rachel: Joseph and Benjamin. 25The sons of Bilhah, Rachel's maid: Dan and Naphtali. 26The sons of Zilpah, Leah's maid: Gad and Asher. These were the sons of Jacob who were born to him in Paddan-aram.

The Death of Isaac

27 Jacob came to his father Isaac at Mamre, or Kiriath-arba (that is, Hebron), where Abraham and Isaac had resided as aliens. 28Now the days of Isaac were one hundred eighty years. 29And Isaac

---

r That is God of Bethel　　s That is Oak of weeping
t Traditional rendering of Heb El Shaddai
u That is Son of my sorrow　　v That is Son of the right hand or Son of the South

breathed his last; he died and was gathered to his people, old and full of days; and his sons Esau and Jacob buried him.

Esau's Descendants

36 These are the descendants of Esau (that is, Edom). ²Esau took his wives from the Canaanites: Adah daughter of Elon the Hittite, Oholibamah daughter of Anah son*w* of Zibeon the Hivite, ³and Basemath, Ishmael's daughter, sister of Nebaioth. ⁴Adah bore Eliphaz to Esau; Basemath bore Reuel; ⁵and Oholibamah bore Jeush, Jalam, and Korah. These are the sons of Esau who were born to him in the land of Canaan.

6 Then Esau took his wives, his sons, his daughters, and all the members of his household, his cattle, all his livestock, and all the property he had acquired in the land of Canaan; and he moved to a land some distance from his brother Jacob. ⁷For their possessions were too great for them to live together; the land where they were staying could not support them because of their livestock. ⁸So Esau settled in the hill country of Seir; Esau is Edom.

9 These are the descendants of Esau, ancestor of the Edomites, in the hill country of Seir. ¹⁰These are the names of Esau's sons: Eliphaz son of Adah the wife of Esau; Reuel, the son of Esau's wife Basemath. ¹¹The sons of Eliphaz were Teman, Omar, Zepho, Gatam, and Kenaz. ¹²(Timna was a concubine of Eliphaz, Esau's son; she bore Amalek to Eliphaz.) These were the sons of Adah, Esau's wife. ¹³These were the sons of Reuel: Nahath, Zerah, Shammah, and Mizzah. These were the sons of Esau's wife, Basemath. ¹⁴These were the sons of Esau's wife Oholibamah, daughter of Anah son*x* of Zibeon: she bore to Esau Jeush, Jalam, and Korah.

Clans and Kings of Edom

15 These are the clans*y* of the sons of Esau. The sons of Eliphaz the firstborn of Esau: the clans*y* Teman, Omar, Zepho, Kenaz, ¹⁶Korah, Gatam, and Amalek; these are the clans*y* of Eliphaz in the land of Edom; they are the sons of Adah. ¹⁷These are the sons of Esau's son Reuel: the clans*y* Nahath, Zerah, Shammah, and Mizzah; these are the clans*y* of Reuel in the land of Edom; they are the sons of Esau's wife Basemath. ¹⁸These are the sons of Esau's wife Oholibamah: the clans*y* Jeush, Jalam, and Korah; these are the clans*y* born of Esau's wife Oholibamah, the daughter of Anah. ¹⁹These are the sons of Esau (that is, Edom), and these are their clans. *y*

20 These are the sons of Seir the Horite, the inhabitants of the land: Lotan, Shobal, Zibeon, Anah, ²¹Dishon, Ezer, and Dishan; these are the clans*y* of the Horites, the sons of Seir in the land of Edom. ²²The sons of Lotan were Hori and Heman; and Lotan's sister was Timna. ²³These are the sons of Shobal: Alvan, Manahath, Ebal, Shepho, and Onam. ²⁴These are the sons of Zibeon: Aiah and Anah; he is the Anah who found the springs*z* in the wilderness, as he pastured the donkeys of his father Zibeon. ²⁵These are the children of Anah: Dishon and Oholibamah daughter of Anah. ²⁶These are the sons of Dishon: Hemdan, Eshban, Ithran, and Cheran. ²⁷These are the sons of Ezer: Bilhan, Zaavan, and Akan. ²⁸These are the sons of Dishan: Uz and Aran. ²⁹These are the clans*y* of the Horites: the clans*y* Lotan, Shobal, Zibeon, Anah, ³⁰Dishon, Ezer, and Dishan; these are the clans*y* of the Horites, clan by clan*a* in the land of Seir.

31 These are the kings who reigned in the land of Edom, before any king reigned over the Israelites. ³²Bela son of Beor reigned in Edom, the name of his city being Dinhabah. ³³Bela died, and Jobab son of Zerah of Bozrah succeeded him as king. ³⁴Jobab died, and Husham of the land of the Temanites succeeded him as king. ³⁵Husham died, and Hadad son of Bedad, who defeated Midian in the country of Moab, succeeded him as king, the name of his city being Avith. ³⁶Hadad died, and Samlah of Masrekah succeeded him as king. ³⁷Samlah died, and Shaul of Rehoboth on the Euphrates succeeded him as king. ³⁸Shaul died, and Baal-hanan son of Achbor succeeded him as king. ³⁹Baal-hanan son of Achbor died, and Hadar succeeded him as king, the name of his city being Pau; his wife's name was Mehetabel, the daughter of Matred, daughter of Me-zahab.

40 These are the names of the clans*y* of Esau, according to their families and their localities by their names: the clans*y* Timna, Alvah, Jetheth, ⁴¹Oholibamah,

---

w Sam Gk Syr: Heb *daughter*   *x* Gk Syr: Heb *daughter*   *y* Or *chiefs*   *z* Meaning of Heb uncertain   *a* Or *chief by chief*

Elah, Pinon, ⁴²Kenaz, Teman, Mibzar, ⁴³Magdiel, and Iram; these are the clans*ᵇ* of Edom (that is, Esau, the father of Edom), according to their settlements in the land that they held.

Joseph Dreams of Greatness

3 7 Jacob settled in the land where his father had lived as an alien, the land of Canaan. ²This is the story of the family of Jacob.

Joseph, being seventeen years old, was shepherding the flock with his brothers; he was a helper to the sons of Bilhah and Zilpah, his father's wives; and Joseph brought a bad report of them to their father. ³Now Israel loved Joseph more than any other of his children, because he was the son of his old age; and he had made him a long robe with sleeves.*ᶜ* ⁴But when his brothers saw that their father loved him more than all his brothers, they hated him, and could not speak peaceably to him.

5 Once Joseph had a dream, and when he told it to his brothers, they hated him even more. ⁶He said to them, "Listen to this dream that I dreamed. ⁷There we were, binding sheaves in the field. Suddenly my sheaf rose and stood upright; then your sheaves gathered around it, and bowed down to my sheaf." ⁸His brothers said to him, "Are you indeed to reign over us? Are you indeed to have dominion over us?" So they hated him even more because of his dreams and his words.

9 He had another dream, and told it to his brothers, saying, "Look, I have had another dream: the sun, the moon, and eleven stars were bowing down to me." ¹⁰But when he told it to his father and to his brothers, his father rebuked him, and said to him, "What kind of dream is this that you have had? Shall we indeed come, I and your mother and your brothers, and bow to the ground before you?" ¹¹So his brothers were jealous of him, but his father kept the matter in mind.

Joseph Is Sold by His Brothers

12 Now his brothers went to pasture their father's flock near Shechem. ¹³And Israel said to Joseph, "Are not your brothers pasturing the flock at Shechem? Come, I will send you to them." He answered, "Here I am." ¹⁴So he said to him, "Go now, see if it is well with your brothers and with the flock; and bring word back

to me." So he sent him from the valley of Hebron.

He came to Shechem, ¹⁵and a man found him wandering in the fields; the man asked him, "What are you seeking?" ¹⁶"I am seeking my brothers," he said; "tell me, please, where they are pasturing the flock." ¹⁷The man said, "They have gone away, for I heard them say, 'Let us go to Dothan.' " So Joseph went after his brothers, and found them at Dothan. ¹⁸They saw him from a distance, and before he came near to them, they conspired to kill him. ¹⁹They said to one another, "Here comes this dreamer. ²⁰Come now, let us kill him and throw him into one of the pits; then we shall say that a wild animal has devoured him, and we shall see what will become of his dreams." ²¹But when Reuben heard it, he delivered him out of their hands, saying, "Let us not take his life." ²²Reuben said to them, "Shed no blood; throw him into this pit here in the wilderness, but lay no hand on him"—that he might rescue him out of their hand and restore him to his father. ²³So when Joseph came to his brothers, they stripped him of his robe, the long robe with sleeves*ᵈ* that he wore; ²⁴and they took him and threw him into a pit. The pit was empty; there was no water in it.

25 Then they sat down to eat; and looking up they saw a caravan of Ishmaelites coming from Gilead, with their camels carrying gum, balm, and resin, on their way to carry it down to Egypt. ²⁶Then Judah said to his brothers, "What profit is it if we kill our brother and conceal his blood? ²⁷Come, let us sell him to the Ishmaelites, and not lay our hands on him, for he is our brother, our own flesh." And his brothers agreed. ²⁸When some Midianite traders passed by, they drew Joseph up, lifting him out of the pit, and sold him to the Ishmaelites for twenty pieces of silver. And they took Joseph to Egypt.

29 When Reuben returned to the pit and saw that Joseph was not in the pit, he tore his clothes. ³⁰He returned to his brothers, and said, "The boy is gone; and I, where can I turn?" ³¹Then they took Joseph's robe, slaughtered a goat, and dipped the robe in the blood. ³²They had the long robe with sleeves*ᵈ* taken to their

---

b Or *chiefs*   *c* Traditional rendering (compare Gk): *a coat of many colors*; meaning of Heb uncertain   *d* See note on 37.3

father, and they said, "This we have found; see now whether it is your son's robe or not." 33He recognized it, and said, "It is my son's robe! A wild animal has devoured him; Joseph is without doubt torn to pieces." 34Then Jacob tore his garments, and put sackcloth on his loins, and mourned for his son many days. 35All his sons and all his daughters sought to comfort him; but he refused to be comforted, and said, "No, I shall go down to Sheol to my son, mourning." Thus his father bewailed him. 36Meanwhile the Midianites had sold him in Egypt to Potiphar, one of Pharaoh's officials, the captain of the guard.

Judah and Tamar

38 It happened at that time that Judah went down from his brothers and settled near a certain Adullamite

Broken Dreams

FRIDAY

Scripture Reading
for Today:
Genesis 37.5–11

Verse for Today:
Genesis 37.5

Joseph made the mistake of telling his brothers a dream he had, which seemed to imply that he would one day rule over them. In their envy, they plotted and schemed and eventually sold their younger brother as a slave to a caravan of merchants bound for Egypt.

Joseph had many years to wonder. Hadn't God promised he would one day be great? Then why was he a slave in Egypt? Had his magnificent dream turned into a nightmare?

Perhaps God has given you a dream or made a promise to you, which now seems impossible to fulfill. Like Joseph, you may have been sinned against by someone close to you: a family member who abused you, a husband who betrayed you, a person who spread lies about you. You may suffer emotional and physical scars from the sins of others. Perhaps the wounds are so deep that you feel as though you have been sold into a kind of emotional slavery, unable to break free from the hurts of the past. You may wonder why God allowed such evils to befall you.

If you feel this way, you may find comfort in Joseph's story. Through the long years of his bondage, Joseph did not lose faith in God. He must have suffered tremendous loneliness, rejection, depression, and confusion in the years before God fulfilled the dream. Still he clung to it. And his faithfulness was rewarded. The evil that Joseph suffered became the very thing God used to shape him into the kind of man capable of ruling. With infinite creativity, God once again transformed the malevolent intentions of others to fulfill his own plan.

If you have lived for any length of years, you will have suffered from the sins of someone close to you. Ask God for the grace to trust him even in the midst of your suffering. If you do, he will raise you up and use you for his purposes, making something beautiful out of every tear you shed.

—*ANN SPANGLER*

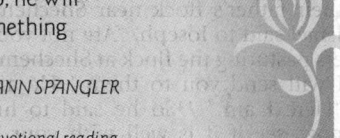

Go to page 46 for your next devotional reading.

whose name was Hirah. ²There Judah saw the daughter of a certain Canaanite whose name was Shua; he married her and went in to her. ³She conceived and bore a son; and he named him Er. ⁴Again she conceived and bore a son whom she named Onan. ⁵Yet again she bore a son, and she named him Shelah. She*ᵉ* was in Chezib when she bore him. ⁶Judah took a wife for Er his firstborn; her name was Tamar. ⁷But Er, Judah's firstborn, was wicked in the sight of the LORD, and the LORD put him to death. ⁸Then Judah said to Onan, "Go in to your brother's wife and perform the duty of a brother-in-law to her; raise up offspring for your brother." ⁹But since Onan knew that the offspring would not be his, he spilled his semen on the ground whenever he went in to his brother's wife, so that he would not give offspring to his brother. ¹⁰What he did was displeasing in the sight of the LORD, and he put him to death also. ¹¹Then Judah said to his daughter-in-law Tamar, "Remain a widow in your father's house until my son Shelah grows up"—for he feared that he too would die, like his brothers. So Tamar went to live in her father's house.

12 In course of time the wife of Judah, Shua's daughter, died; when Judah's time of mourning was over,*ᶠ* he went up to Timnah to his sheepshearers, he and his friend Hirah the Adullamite. ¹³When Tamar was told, "Your father-in-law is going up to Timnah to shear his sheep," ¹⁴she put off her widow's garments, put on a veil, wrapped herself up, and sat down at the entrance to Enaim, which is on the road to Timnah. She saw that Shelah was grown up, yet she had not been given to him in marriage. ¹⁵When Judah saw her, he thought her to be a prostitute, for she had covered her face. ¹⁶He went over to her at the roadside, and said, "Come, let me come in to you," for he did not know that she was his daughter-in-law. She said, "What will you give me, that you may come in to me?" ¹⁷He answered, "I will send you a kid from the flock." And she said, "Only if you give me a pledge, until you send it." ¹⁸He said, "What pledge shall I give you?" She replied, "Your signet and your cord, and the staff that is in your hand." So he gave them to her, and went in to her, and she conceived by him. ¹⁹Then she got up and went away, and taking off her veil she put on the garments of her widowhood.

20 When Judah sent the kid by his friend the Adullamite, to recover the pledge from the woman, he could not find her. ²¹He asked the townspeople, "Where is the temple prostitute who was at Enaim by the wayside?" But they said, "No prostitute has been here." ²²So he returned to Judah, and said, "I have not found her; moreover the townspeople said, 'No prostitute has been here.' " ²³Judah replied, "Let her keep the things as her own, otherwise we will be laughed at; you see, I sent this kid, and you could not find her."

24 About three months later Judah was told, "Your daughter-in-law Tamar has played the whore; moreover she is pregnant as a result of whoredom." And Judah said, "Bring her out, and let her be burned." ²⁵As she was being brought out, she sent word to her father-in-law, "It was the owner of these who made me pregnant." And she said, "Take note, please, whose these are, the signet and the cord and the staff." ²⁶Then Judah acknowledged them and said, "She is more in the right than I, since I did not give her to my son Shelah." And he did not lie with her again.

27 When the time of her delivery came, there were twins in her womb. ²⁸While she was in labor, one put out a hand; and the midwife took and bound on his hand a crimson thread, saying, "This one came out first." ²⁹But just then he drew back his hand, and out came his brother; and she said, "What a breach you have made for yourself!" Therefore he was named Perez.*ᵍ* ³⁰Afterward his brother came out with the crimson thread on his hand; and he was named Zerah.*ʰ*

Joseph and Potiphar's Wife

39 Now Joseph was taken down to Egypt, and Potiphar, an officer of Pharaoh, the captain of the guard, an Egyptian, bought him from the Ishmaelites who had brought him down there. ²The LORD was with Joseph, and he became a successful man; he was in the house of his Egyptian master. ³His master saw that the LORD was with him, and that the LORD caused all that he did to prosper

---

e Gk: Heb *He*   *f* Heb *when Judah was comforted*
g That is *A breach*   *h* That is *Brightness*; perhaps alluding to the crimson thread

Sarah

Her Name Means
"Princess"

Read Genesis 17.15–21; 18.1–15

Sarah was sixty-five, the age at which many of us retire, when she began a journey that would lead her into uncharted spiritual territory. She and her husband Abraham moved hundreds of miles south of her homeland to Canaan, a land fertile with the promises of God but barren of everything cherished and familiar. God had promised the land to Abraham and his offspring. From him would come an entire nation, a people who would belong to God as no other people had.

The promise spread like ripples from a stone pitched in water. If Abraham were to father a new nation, surely Sarah would be its mother. Yet she longed to give birth, not to a nation, but to one small child she could kiss and cradle.

But years passed and still there was no child. So Sarah took matters into her own hands, and following a practice common in the ancient world, asked Abraham to sleep with her Egyptian maid, Hagar. Sarah's slave would become a surrogate mother for the promised child. Before long Ishmael was born, and there was little peace between the two women.

One day the Lord appeared to Abraham while he was sitting at the entrance to his tent and told Abraham that Sarah would yet have a son.

Now Sarah, who had been eavesdropping from inside the tent, laughed and said, "After I have grown old, and my husband is old, shall I

Her Character: *Beautiful enough to attract rulers in the ancient world, she could be strong-willed and jealous. Yet Sarah was considered a loyal wife, who did what was right and didn't give in to fear.*
Her Sorrow: *That she remained childless for most of her life.*
Her Joy: *That at the age of ninety, she gave birth to Isaac, child of the promise.*

have pleasure?" But the Lord challenged Sarah through Abraham. "Why did Sarah laugh, and say, 'Shall I indeed bear a child, now that I am old?' Is anything too wonderful for the LORD? At the set time I will return to you, in due season, and Sarah shall have a son." Because Sarah was afraid, she lied and said, "I did not laugh." But God pressed her, saying, "Oh yes, you did laugh" (18.15).

A year later, Sarah gave birth to Isaac, whose name meant "laughter." Of course the joke was not lost on the ninety-year-old mother, who exclaimed: "God has brought laughter for me; everyone who hears will laugh with me" (21.6). God would keep his promise through Isaac, not Ishmael.

Did Sarah ever feel ashamed, perhaps years later, of her treatment of Hagar and Ishmael, whom she forced out of her household and into the harsh desert? Did she regret laughing when God told Abraham she would bear a child at the age of ninety? Did she appreciate the echoing irony in young Isaac's laughter? Did she have any idea she would one day be revered as the Mother of Israel, indeed, a symbol of the promise just as Hagar was to become a symbol of slavery under the law? Scripture does not say. But it is heartening to realize that God accomplishes his purposes despite our frailties, our weak faith, our entrenched self-reliance. Despite her jealousy, anxiety, and skepticism about God's ability to keep his promises, Sarah was a risk-taker of the first order, a woman who said goodbye to everything familiar in order to live an adventure that began with a promise and ended with laughter.

Praying With Sarah

God said to Abraham, "As for Sarai your wife, you shall not call her Sarai, but Sarah shall be her name. I will bless her, and moreover I will give you a son by her. I will bless her, and she shall give rise to nations; kings of peoples shall come from her."—*Genesis 17.15–16*

Praise God: Because he keeps his promises, come what may.
Offer Thanks: That God has a gracious plan for you that will unfold in his time, according to his way.
Confess: Your anxiety and self-reliance.
Ask God: To help you wait with a listening ear and a ready heart to do his will.

Lift Your Heart

God hints at his purpose for you by planting dreams within your heart. Sarah's dream was to give birth to a son. Find a quiet place and spend some time focusing on your dreams. Ask yourself what dreams you've been too busy, too afraid, or too disappointed to pursue. Write them down and pray about each one. Is God giving you the go-ahead to pursue one in particular? If you take the plunge, you might just find yourself joyfully echoing Sarah's words in Genesis 21.6: "God has brought laughter for me."

Father, thank you for loving me despite the fact that my soul still contains shadows that sometimes block the light of your Spirit. As I grow older, may I trust you more completely for the dreams you've implanted in my soul, the promises you've made to me. Like Sarah, may I be surrounded by laughter at the wonderful way you accomplish your purpose despite my weakness.

Go to page 52 for your next devotional reading.

in his hands. 4So Joseph found favor in his sight and attended him; he made him overseer of his house and put him in charge of all that he had. 5From the time that he made him overseer in his house and over all that he had, the LORD blessed the Egyptian's house for Joseph's sake; the blessing of the LORD was on all that he had, in house and field. 6So he left all that he had in Joseph's charge; and, with him there, he had no concern for anything but the food that he ate.

Now Joseph was handsome and good-looking. 7And after a time his master's wife cast her eyes on Joseph and said, "Lie with me." 8But he refused and said to his master's wife, "Look, with me here, my master has no concern about anything in the house, and he has put everything that he has in my hand. 9He is not greater in this house than I am, nor has he kept back anything from me except yourself, because you are his wife. How then could I do this great wickedness, and sin against God?" 10And although she spoke to Joseph day after day, he would not consent to lie beside her or to be with her. 11One day, however, when he went into the house to do his work, and while no one else was in the house, 12she caught hold of his garment, saying, "Lie with me!" But he left his garment in her hand, and fled and ran outside. 13When she saw that he had left his garment in her hand and had fled outside, 14she called out to the members of her household and said to them, "See, my husband[i] has brought among us a Hebrew to insult us! He came in to me to lie with me, and I cried out with a loud voice; 15and when he heard me raise my voice and cry out, he left his garment beside me, and fled outside." 16Then she kept his garment by her until his master came home, 17and she told him the same story, saying, "The Hebrew servant, whom you have brought among us, came in to me to insult me; 18but as soon as I raised my voice and cried out, he left his garment beside me, and fled outside."

19 When his master heard the words that his wife spoke to him, saying, "This is the way your servant treated me," he became enraged. 20And Joseph's master took him and put him into the prison, the place where the king's prisoners were confined; he remained there in prison. 21But the LORD was with Joseph and showed him steadfast love; he gave him favor in the sight of the chief jailer. 22The chief jailer committed to Joseph's care all the prisoners who were in the prison, and whatever was done there, he was the one who did it. 23The chief jailer paid no heed to anything that was in Joseph's care, because the LORD was with him; and whatever he did, the LORD made it prosper.

The Dreams of Two Prisoners

40 Some time after this, the cupbearer of the king of Egypt and his baker offended their lord the king of Egypt. 2Pharaoh was angry with his two officers, the chief cupbearer and the chief baker, 3and he put them in custody in the house of the captain of the guard, in the prison where Joseph was confined. 4The captain of the guard charged Joseph with them, and he waited on them; and they continued for some time in custody. 5One night they both dreamed—the cupbearer and the baker of the king of Egypt, who were confined in the prison—each his own dream, and each dream with its own meaning. 6When Joseph came to them in the morning, he saw that they were troubled. 7So he asked Pharaoh's officers, who were with him in custody in his master's house, "Why are your faces downcast today?" 8They said to him, "We have had dreams, and there is no one to interpret them." And Joseph said to them, "Do not interpretations belong to God? Please tell them to me."

9 So the chief cupbearer told his dream to Joseph, and said to him, "In my dream there was a vine before me, 10and on the vine there were three branches. As soon as it budded, its blossoms came out and the clusters ripened into grapes. 11Pharaoh's cup was in my hand; and I took the grapes and pressed them into Pharaoh's cup, and placed the cup in Pharaoh's hand." 12Then Joseph said to him, "This is its interpretation: the three branches are three days; 13within three days Pharaoh will lift up your head and restore you to your office; and you shall place Pharaoh's cup in his hand, just as you used to do when you were his cupbearer. 14But remember me when it is well with you; please do me the kindness to make mention of me to Pharaoh, and so get me out of this place. 15For in fact I was stolen out of the land of the Hebrews; and here also I have done noth-

i Heb *he*

ing that they should have put me into the dungeon."

16 When the chief baker saw that the interpretation was favorable, he said to Joseph, "I also had a dream: there were three cake baskets on my head, 17and in the uppermost basket there were all sorts of baked food for Pharaoh, but the birds were eating it out of the basket on my head." 18And Joseph answered, "This is its interpretation: the three baskets are three days; 19within three days Pharaoh will lift up your head—from you!—and hang you on a pole; and the birds will eat the flesh from you."

20 On the third day, which was Pharaoh's birthday, he made a feast for all his servants, and lifted up the head of the chief cupbearer and the head of the chief baker among his servants. 21He restored the chief cupbearer to his cupbearing, and he placed the cup in Pharaoh's hand; 22but the chief baker he hanged, just as Joseph had interpreted to them. 23Yet the chief cupbearer did not remember Joseph, but forgot him.

Joseph Interprets Pharaoh's Dream

41 After two whole years, Pharaoh dreamed that he was standing by the Nile, 2and there came up out of the Nile seven sleek and fat cows, and they grazed in the reed grass. 3Then seven other cows, ugly and thin, came up out of the Nile after them, and stood by the other cows on the bank of the Nile. 4The ugly and thin cows ate up the seven sleek and fat cows. And Pharaoh awoke. 5Then he fell asleep and dreamed a second time; seven ears of grain, plump and good, were growing on one stalk. 6Then seven ears, thin and blighted by the east wind, sprouted after them. 7The thin ears swallowed up the seven plump and full ears. Pharaoh awoke, and it was a dream. 8In the morning his spirit was troubled; so he sent and called for all the magicians of Egypt and all its wise men. Pharaoh told them his dreams, but there was no one who could interpret them to Pharaoh.

9 Then the chief cupbearer said to Pharaoh, "I remember my faults today. 10Once Pharaoh was angry with his servants, and put me and the chief baker in custody in the house of the captain of the guard. 11We dreamed on the same night, he and I, each having a dream with its own meaning. 12A young Hebrew was

there with us, a servant of the captain of the guard. When we told him, he interpreted our dreams to us, giving an interpretation to each according to his dream. 13As he interpreted to us, so it turned out; I was restored to my office, and the baker was hanged."

14 Then Pharaoh sent for Joseph, and he was hurriedly brought out of the dungeon. When he had shaved himself and changed his clothes, he came in before Pharaoh. 15And Pharaoh said to Joseph, "I have had a dream, and there is no one who can interpret it. I have heard it said of you that when you hear a dream you can interpret it." 16Joseph answered Pharaoh, "It is not I; God will give Pharaoh a favorable answer." 17Then Pharaoh said to Joseph, "In my dream I was standing on the banks of the Nile; 18and seven cows, fat and sleek, came up out of the Nile and fed in the reed grass. 19Then seven other cows came up after them, poor, very ugly, and thin. Never had I seen such ugly ones in all the land of Egypt. 20The thin and ugly cows ate up the first seven fat cows, 21but when they had eaten them no one would have known that they had done so, for they were still as ugly as before. Then I awoke. 22I fell asleep a second time*j* and I saw in my dream seven ears of grain, full and good, growing on one stalk, 23and seven ears, withered, thin, and blighted by the east wind, sprouting after them; 24and the thin ears swallowed up the seven good ears. But when I told it to the magicians, there was no one who could explain it to me."

25 Then Joseph said to Pharaoh, "Pharaoh's dreams are one and the same; God has revealed to Pharaoh what he is about to do. 26The seven good cows are seven years, and the seven good ears are seven years; the dreams are one. 27The seven lean and ugly cows that came up after them are seven years, as are the seven empty ears blighted by the east wind. They are seven years of famine. 28It is as I told Pharaoh; God has shown to Pharaoh what he is about to do. 29There will come seven years of great plenty throughout all the land of Egypt. 30After them there will arise seven years of famine, and all the plenty will be forgotten in the land of Egypt; the famine will consume the land. 31The plenty will no longer be known in

j Gk Syr Vg: Heb lacks I fell asleep a second time

the land because of the famine that will follow, for it will be very grievous. 32And the doubling of Pharaoh's dream means that the thing is fixed by God, and God will shortly bring it about. 33Now therefore let Pharaoh select a man who is discerning and wise, and set him over the land of Egypt. 34Let Pharaoh proceed to appoint overseers over the land, and take one-fifth of the produce of the land of Egypt during the seven plenteous years. 35Let them gather all the food of these good years that are coming, and lay up grain under the authority of Pharaoh for food in the cities, and let them keep it. 36That food shall be a reserve for the land against the seven years of famine that are to befall the land of Egypt, so that the land may not perish through the famine."

Joseph's Rise to Power

37 The proposal pleased Pharaoh and all his servants. 38Pharaoh said to his servants, "Can we find anyone else like this—one in whom is the spirit of God?" 39So Pharaoh said to Joseph, "Since God has shown you all this, there is no one so discerning and wise as you. 40You shall be over my house, and all my people shall order themselves as you command; only with regard to the throne will I be greater than you." 41And Pharaoh said to Joseph, "See, I have set you over all the land of Egypt." 42Removing his signet ring from his hand, Pharaoh put it on Joseph's hand; he arrayed him in garments of fine linen, and put a gold chain around his neck. 43He had him ride in the chariot of his second-in-command; and they cried out in front of him, "Bow the knee!"k Thus he set him over all the land of Egypt. 44Moreover Pharaoh said to Joseph, "I am Pharaoh, and without your consent no one shall lift up hand or foot in all the land of Egypt." 45Pharaoh gave Joseph the name Zaphenath-paneah; and he gave him Asenath daughter of Potiphera, priest of On, as his wife. Thus Joseph gained authority over the land of Egypt.

46 Joseph was thirty years old when he entered the service of Pharaoh king of Egypt. And Joseph went out from the presence of Pharaoh, and went through all the land of Egypt. 47During the seven plenteous years the earth produced abundantly. 48He gathered up all the food of the seven years when there was plentyl in the land of Egypt, and stored up food in the cities;

he stored up in every city the food from the fields around it. 49So Joseph stored up grain in such abundance—like the sand of the sea—that he stopped measuring it; it was beyond measure.

50 Before the years of famine came, Joseph had two sons, whom Asenath daughter of Potiphera, priest of On, bore to him. 51Joseph named the firstborn Manasseh,m "For," he said, "God has made me forget all my hardship and all my father's house." 52The second he named Ephraim,n "For God has made me fruitful in the land of my misfortunes."

53 The seven years of plenty that prevailed in the land of Egypt came to an end; 54and the seven years of famine began to come, just as Joseph had said. There was famine in every country, but throughout the land of Egypt there was bread. 55When all the land of Egypt was famished, the people cried to Pharaoh for bread. Pharaoh said to all the Egyptians, "Go to Joseph; what he says to you, do." 56And since the famine had spread over all the land, Joseph opened all the storehouses,o and sold to the Egyptians, for the famine was severe in the land of Egypt. 57Moreover, all the world came to Joseph in Egypt to buy grain, because the famine became severe throughout the world.

Joseph's Brothers Go to Egypt

42 When Jacob learned that there was grain in Egypt, he said to his sons, "Why do you keep looking at one another? 2I have heard," he said, "that there is grain in Egypt; go down and buy grain for us there, that we may live and not die." 3So ten of Joseph's brothers went down to buy grain in Egypt. 4But Jacob did not send Joseph's brother Benjamin with his brothers, for he feared that harm might come to him. 5Thus the sons of Israel were among the other people who came to buy grain, for the famine had reached the land of Canaan.

6 Now Joseph was governor over the land; it was he who sold to all the people of the land. And Joseph's brothers came

k Abrek, apparently an Egyptian word similar in sound to the Hebrew word meaning to kneel   l Sam Gk: MT the seven years that were   m That is Making to forget   n From a Hebrew word meaning to be fruitful   o Gk Vg Compare Syr: Heb opened all that was in (or, among) them

and bowed themselves before him with their faces to the ground. 7When Joseph saw his brothers, he recognized them, but he treated them like strangers and spoke harshly to them. "Where do you come from?" he said. They said, "From the land of Canaan, to buy food." 8Although Joseph had recognized his brothers, they did not recognize him. 9Joseph also remembered the dreams that he had dreamed about them. He said to them, "You are spies; you have come to see the nakedness of the land!" 10They said to him, "No, my lord; your servants have come to buy food. 11We are all sons of one man; we are honest men; your servants have never been spies." 12But he said to them, "No, you have come to see the nakedness of the land!" 13They said, "We, your servants, are twelve brothers, the sons of a certain man in the land of Canaan; the youngest, however, is now with our father, and one is no more." 14But Joseph said to them, "It is just as I have said to you; you are spies! 15Here is how you shall be tested: as Pharaoh lives, you shall not leave this place unless your youngest brother comes here! 16Let one of you go and bring your brother, while the rest of you remain in prison, in order that your words may be tested, whether there is truth in you; or else, as Pharaoh lives, surely you are spies." 17And he put them all together in prison for three days.

18 On the third day Joseph said to them, "Do this and you will live, for I fear God: 19if you are honest men, let one of your brothers stay here where you are imprisoned. The rest of you shall go and carry grain for the famine of your households, 20and bring your youngest brother to me. Thus your words will be verified, and you shall not die." And they agreed to do so. 21They said to one another, "Alas, we are paying the penalty for what we did to our brother; we saw his anguish when he pleaded with us, but we would not listen. That is why this anguish has come upon us." 22Then Reuben answered them, "Did I not tell you not to wrong the boy? But you would not listen. So now there comes a reckoning for his blood." 23They did not know that Joseph understood them, since he spoke with them through an interpreter. 24He turned away from them and wept; then he returned and spoke to them. And he picked out Simeon and had him bound before their eyes.

25Joseph then gave orders to fill their bags with grain, to return every man's money to his sack, and to give them provisions for their journey. This was done for them.

Joseph's Brothers Return to Canaan

26 They loaded their donkeys with their grain, and departed. 27When one of them opened his sack to give his donkey fodder at the lodging place, he saw his money at the top of the sack. 28He said to his brothers, "My money has been put back; here it is in my sack!" At this they lost heart and turned trembling to one another, saying, "What is this that God has done to us?"

29 When they came to their father Jacob in the land of Canaan, they told him all that had happened to them, saying, 30"The man, the lord of the land, spoke harshly to us, and charged us with spying on the land. 31But we said to him, 'We are honest men, we are not spies. 32We are twelve brothers, sons of our father; one is no more, and the youngest is now with our father in the land of Canaan.' 33Then the man, the lord of the land, said to us, 'By this I shall know that you are honest men: leave one of your brothers with me, take grain for the famine of your households, and go your way. 34Bring your youngest brother to me, and I shall know that you are not spies but honest men. Then I will release your brother to you, and you may trade in the land.' "

35 As they were emptying their sacks, there in each one's sack was his bag of money. When they and their father saw their bundles of money, they were dismayed. 36And their father Jacob said to them, "I am the one you have bereaved of children: Joseph is no more, and Simeon is no more, and now you would take Benjamin. All this has happened to me!" 37Then Reuben said to his father, "You may kill my two sons if I do not bring him back to you. Put him in my hands, and I will bring him back to you." 38But he said, "My son shall not go down with you, for his brother is dead, and he alone is left. If harm should come to him on the journey that you are to make, you would bring down my gray hairs with sorrow to Sheol."

The Brothers Come Again, Bringing Benjamin

43 Now the famine was severe in the land. 2And when they had eaten

up the grain that they had brought from Egypt, their father said to them, "Go again, buy us a little more food." ³But Judah said to him, "The man solemnly warned us, saying, 'You shall not see my face unless your brother is with you.' ⁴If you will send our brother with us, we will go down and buy you food; ⁵but if you will not send him, we will not go down, for the man said to us, 'You shall not see my face, unless your brother is with you.'" ⁶Israel said, "Why did you treat me so badly as to tell the man that you had another brother?" ⁷They replied, "The man questioned us carefully about ourselves and our kindred, saying, 'Is your father still alive? Have you another brother?' What we told him was in answer to these questions. Could we in any way know that he would say, 'Bring your brother down'?" ⁸Then Judah said to his father Is-

rael, "Send the boy with me, and let us be on our way, so that we may live and not die—you and we and also our little ones. ⁹I myself will be surety for him; you can hold me accountable for him. If I do not bring him back to you and set him before you, then let me bear the blame forever. ¹⁰If we had not delayed, we would now have returned twice."

11 Then their father Israel said to them, "If it must be so, then do this: take some of the choice fruits of the land in your bags, and carry them down as a present to the man—a little balm and a little honey, gum, resin, pistachio nuts, and almonds. ¹²Take double the money with you. Carry back with you the money that was returned in the top of your sacks; perhaps it was an oversight. ¹³Take your brother also, and be on your way again to the man; ¹⁴may God

$\mathcal{M}$ake Me Merciful, Lord!

MONDAY

Scripture Reading for Today:
Genesis 43.1–14

Verse for Today:
Genesis 43.14

Help me, O Lord, that my hands may be merciful and filled with good deeds, so that I may do only good to my neighbors and take upon myself the more difficult and toilsome tasks.

Help me, that my feet may be merciful, so that I may hurry to assist my neighbor, overcoming my own fatigue and weariness. My true rest is in the service of my neighbor.

Help me, O Lord, that my heart may be merciful so that I myself may feel all the sufferings of my neighbor. I will refuse my heart to no one. I will be sincere even with those who, I know, will abuse my kindness. And I will lock myself up in the most merciful heart of Jesus. I will bear my own suffering in silence. May your mercy, O Lord, rest upon me.

You yourself command me to exercise the three degrees of mercy. The first: the act of mercy, of whatever kind. The second: the word of mercy—if I cannot carry out a work of mercy, I will assist by my words. The third: prayer—if I cannot show mercy by deeds or words, I can always do so by prayer. My prayer reaches out even there where I cannot reach out physically. O my Jesus, transform me into yourself, for you can do all things.

—FAUSTINA KOWALSKA

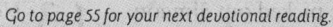

Go to page 55 for your next devotional reading.

Almighty*p* grant you mercy before the man, so that he may send back your other brother and Benjamin. As for me, if I am bereaved of my children, I am bereaved." 15So the men took the present, and they took double the money with them, as well as Benjamin. Then they went on their way down to Egypt, and stood before Joseph.

16 When Joseph saw Benjamin with them, he said to the steward of his house, "Bring the men into the house, and slaughter an animal and make ready, for the men are to dine with me at noon." 17The man did as Joseph said, and brought the men to Joseph's house. 18Now the men were afraid because they were brought to Joseph's house, and they said, "It is because of the money, replaced in our sacks the first time, that we have been brought in, so that he may have an opportunity to fall upon us, to make slaves of us and take our donkeys." 19So they went up to the steward of Joseph's house and spoke with him at the entrance to the house. 20They said, "Oh, my lord, we came down the first time to buy food; 21and when we came to the lodging place we opened our sacks, and there was each one's money in the top of his sack, our money in full weight. So we have brought it back with us. 22Moreover we have brought down with us additional money to buy food. We do not know who put our money in our sacks." 23He replied, "Rest assured, do not be afraid; your God and the God of your father must have put treasure in your sacks for you; I received your money." Then he brought Simeon out to them. 24When the steward*q* had brought the men into Joseph's house, and given them water, and they had washed their feet, and when he had given their donkeys fodder, 25they made the present ready for Joseph's coming at noon, for they had heard that they would dine there.

26 When Joseph came home, they brought him the present that they had carried into the house, and bowed to the ground before him. 27He inquired about their welfare, and said, "Is your father well, the old man of whom you spoke? Is he still alive?" 28They said, "Your servant our father is well; he is still alive." And they bowed their heads and did obeisance. 29Then he looked up and saw his brother Benjamin, his mother's son, and said, "Is this your youngest brother, of whom you

spoke to me? God be gracious to you, my son!" 30With that, Joseph hurried out, because he was overcome with affection for his brother, and he was about to weep. So he went into a private room and wept there. 31Then he washed his face and came out; and controlling himself he said, "Serve the meal." 32They served him by himself, and them by themselves, and the Egyptians who ate with him by themselves, because the Egyptians could not eat with the Hebrews, for that is an abomination to the Egyptians. 33When they were seated before him, the firstborn according to his birthright and the youngest according to his youth, the men looked at one another in amazement. 34Portions were taken to them from Joseph's table, but Benjamin's portion was five times as much as any of theirs. So they drank and were merry with him.

Joseph Detains Benjamin

44 Then he commanded the steward of his house, "Fill the men's sacks with food, as much as they can carry, and put each man's money in the top of his sack. 2Put my cup, the silver cup, in the top of the sack of the youngest, with his money for the grain." And he did as Joseph told him. 3As soon as the morning was light, the men were sent away with their donkeys. 4When they had gone only a short distance from the city, Joseph said to his steward, "Go, follow after the men; and when you overtake them, say to them, 'Why have you returned evil for good? Why have you stolen my silver cup?*r* 5Is it not from this that my lord drinks? Does he not indeed use it for divination? You have done wrong in doing this.' "

6 When he overtook them, he repeated these words to them. 7They said to him, "Why does my lord speak such words as these? Far be it from your servants that they should do such a thing! 8Look, the money that we found at the top of our sacks, we brought back to you from the land of Canaan; why then would we steal silver or gold from your lord's house? 9Should it be found with any one of your servants, let him die; moreover the rest of us will become my lord's slaves." 10He said,

---

p Traditional rendering of Heb *El Shaddai*
q Heb *the man*   *r* Gk Compare Vg: Heb lacks *Why have you stolen my silver cup?*

"Even so; in accordance with your words, let it be: he with whom it is found shall become my slave, but the rest of you shall go free." ¹¹Then each one quickly lowered his sack to the ground, and each opened his sack. ¹²He searched, beginning with the eldest and ending with the youngest; and the cup was found in Benjamin's sack. ¹³At this they tore their clothes. Then each one loaded his donkey, and they returned to the city.

14 Judah and his brothers came to Joseph's house while he was still there; and they fell to the ground before him. ¹⁵Joseph said to them, "What deed is this that you have done? Do you not know that one such as I can practice divination?" ¹⁶And Judah said, "What can we say to my lord? What can we speak? How can we clear ourselves? God has found out the guilt of your servants; here we are then, my lord's slaves, both we and also the one in whose possession the cup has been found." ¹⁷But he said, "Far be it from me that I should do so! Only the one in whose possession the cup was found shall be my slave; but as for you, go up in peace to your father."

Judah Pleads for Benjamin's Release

18 Then Judah stepped up to him and said, "O my lord, let your servant please speak a word in my lord's ears, and do not be angry with your servant; for you are like Pharaoh himself. ¹⁹My lord asked his servants, saying, 'Have you a father or a brother?' ²⁰And we said to my lord, 'We have a father, an old man, and a young brother, the child of his old age. His brother is dead; he alone is left of his mother's children, and his father loves him.' ²¹Then you said to your servants, 'Bring him down to me, so that I may set my eyes on him.' ²²We said to my lord, 'The boy cannot leave his father, for if he should leave his father, his father would die.' ²³Then you said to your servants, 'Unless your youngest brother comes down with you, you shall see my face no more.' ²⁴When we went back to your servant my father we told him the words of my lord. ²⁵And when our father said, 'Go again, buy us a little food,' ²⁶we said, 'We cannot go down. Only if our youngest brother goes with us, will we go down; for we cannot see the man's face unless our youngest brother is with us.' ²⁷Then your servant my father said to us, 'You know

that my wife bore me two sons; ²⁸one left me, and I said, Surely he has been torn to pieces; and I have never seen him since. ²⁹If you take this one also from me, and harm comes to him, you will bring down my gray hairs in sorrow to Sheol.' ³⁰Now therefore, when I come to your servant my father and the boy is not with us, then, as his life is bound up in the boy's life, ³¹when he sees that the boy is not with us, he will die; and your servants will bring down the gray hairs of your servant our father with sorrow to Sheol. ³²For your servant became surety for the boy to my father, saying, 'If I do not bring him back to you, then I will bear the blame in the sight of my father all my life.' ³³Now therefore, please let your servant remain as a slave to my lord in place of the boy; and let the boy go back with his brothers. ³⁴For how can I go back to my father if the boy is not with me? I fear to see the suffering that would come upon my father."

Joseph Reveals Himself to His Brothers

45 Then Joseph could no longer control himself before all those who stood by him, and he cried out, "Send everyone away from me." So no one stayed with him when Joseph made himself known to his brothers. ²And he wept so loudly that the Egyptians heard it, and the household of Pharaoh heard it. ³Joseph said to his brothers, "I am Joseph. Is my father still alive?" But his brothers could not answer him, so dismayed were they at his presence.

4 Then Joseph said to his brothers, "Come closer to me." And they came closer. He said, "I am your brother, Joseph, whom you sold into Egypt. ⁵And now do not be distressed, or angry with yourselves, because you sold me here; for God sent me before you to preserve life. ⁶For the famine has been in the land these two years; and there are five more years in which there will be neither plowing nor harvest. ⁷God sent me before you to preserve for you a remnant on earth, and to keep alive for you many survivors. ⁸So it was not you who sent me here, but God; he has made me a father to Pharaoh, and lord of all his house and ruler over all the land of Egypt. ⁹Hurry and go up to my father and say to him, 'Thus says your son Joseph, God has made me lord of all Egypt; come down to me, do not delay. ¹⁰You shall settle in the land of Goshen,

and you shall be near me, you and your children and your children's children, as well as your flocks, your herds, and all that you have. ¹¹I will provide for you there—since there are five more years of famine to come—so that you and your household, and all that you have, will not come to poverty.' ¹²And now your eyes and the eyes of my brother Benjamin see that it is my own mouth that speaks to you. ¹³You must tell my father how greatly I am honored in Egypt, and all that you have seen. Hurry and bring my father down here." ¹⁴Then he fell upon his brother Benjamin's neck and wept, while Benjamin wept upon his neck. ¹⁵And he kissed all his brothers and wept upon them; and after that his brothers talked with him.

*H*oly Reversals

TUESDAY

Scripture Reading for Today:
Genesis 45.1–15

Verse for Today:
Genesis 45.5

"Don't curse it, don't nurse it, don't rehearse it. Disperse it, and God will reverse it." This is more than a catchy jingle to Pastor Larry Lea. You see, this advice changed his life. [At an ecumenical conference I attended] Pastor Lea told of a crushing blow in his own life and ministry years ago. He explained how the Lord showed him that this very disappointment, difficulty and disillusionment with others could be a tombstone or a stepping stone for him, depending on his response to the offense.

And isn't that true for all of us who have been offended? If we take the offense and curse it, or curse God for it, then it becomes a tombstone. You know the scenario: "Why did this have to happen to me? I don't deserve this. I've tried so hard to be good. Poor me." We nurse our injuries. Throw a pity party. Brood. We wind up angry and bitter.

So if you're stuck in the "cursing it, nursing it, rehearsing it" stage, take heart! Cry out to the Lord in prayer. Disperse the offense to the Lord, and he *will* reverse it. That's an unfailing promise! Remember Romans 8.28? God makes "*all things* work together for good" for those who love him (italics added). Everything in your life, even the wrongs you have suffered, can have a redeeming value if you are surrendering to God and trying to grow in his love.

I once heard the story of a Christian woman who had been seriously wronged by someone. With God's grace she dispersed the offense to God in prayer, and he reversed it to her good. Many years later someone recalled to her the painful incident, but she acted as though she had no recollection of it. Her friend insisted, "But you must remember what he said. Don't you recall . . ." Before the details of the offense were rehearsed any further, the woman intervened, "No. I distinctly remember forgetting it." That Christian woman had a share of the wonderful forgetfulness God has toward our forgiven sins.

—PATTI GALLAGHER MANSFIELD

Go to page 65 for your next devotional reading.

16 When the report was heard in Pharaoh's house, "Joseph's brothers have come," Pharaoh and his servants were pleased. 17Pharaoh said to Joseph, "Say to your brothers, 'Do this: load your animals and go back to the land of Canaan. 18Take your father and your households and come to me, so that I may give you the best of the land of Egypt, and you may enjoy the fat of the land.' 19You are further charged to say, 'Do this: take wagons from the land of Egypt for your little ones and for your wives, and bring your father, and come. 20Give no thought to your possessions, for the best of all the land of Egypt is yours.' "

21 The sons of Israel did so. Joseph gave them wagons according to the instruction of Pharaoh, and he gave them provisions for the journey. 22To each one of them he gave a set of garments; but to Benjamin he gave three hundred pieces of silver and five sets of garments. 23To his father he sent the following: ten donkeys loaded with the good things of Egypt, and ten female donkeys loaded with grain, bread, and provision for his father on the journey. 24Then he sent his brothers on their way, and as they were leaving he said to them, "Do not quarrels along the way."

25 So they went up out of Egypt and came to their father Jacob in the land of Canaan. 26And they told him, "Joseph is still alive! He is even ruler over all the land of Egypt." He was stunned; he could not believe them. 27But when they told him all the words of Joseph that he had said to them, and when he saw the wagons that Joseph had sent to carry him, the spirit of their father Jacob revived. 28Israel said, "Enough! My son Joseph is still alive. I must go and see him before I die."

Jacob Brings His Whole Family to Egypt

46 When Israel set out on his journey with all that he had and came to Beer-sheba, he offered sacrifices to the God of his father Isaac. 2God spoke to Israel in visions of the night, and said, "Jacob, Jacob." And he said, "Here I am." 3Then he said, "I am God,t the God of your father; do not be afraid to go down to Egypt, for I will make of you a great nation there. 4I myself will go down with you to Egypt, and I will also bring you up again; and Joseph's own hand shall close your eyes."

5 Then Jacob set out from Beer-sheba; and the sons of Israel carried their father Jacob, their little ones, and their wives, in the wagons that Pharaoh had sent to carry him. 6They also took their livestock and the goods that they had acquired in the land of Canaan, and they came into Egypt, Jacob and all his offspring with him, 7his sons, and his sons' sons with him, his daughters, and his sons' daughters; all his offspring he brought with him into Egypt.

8 Now these are the names of the Israelites, Jacob and his offspring, who came to Egypt. Reuben, Jacob's firstborn, 9and the children of Reuben: Hanoch, Pallu, Hezron, and Carmi. 10The children of Simeon: Jemuel, Jamin, Ohad, Jachin, Zohar, and Shaul,u the son of a Canaanite woman. 11The children of Levi: Gershon, Kohath, and Merari. 12The children of Judah: Er, Onan, Shelah, Perez, and Zerah (but Er and Onan died in the land of Canaan); and the children of Perez were Hezron and Hamul. 13The children of Issachar: Tola, Puvah, Jashub,v and Shimron. 14The children of Zebulun: Sered, Elon, and Jahleel 15(these are the sons of Leah, whom she bore to Jacob in Paddan-aram, together with his daughter Dinah; in all his sons and his daughters numbered thirty-three). 16The children of Gad: Ziphion, Haggi, Shuni, Ezbon, Eri, Arodi, and Areli. 17The children of Asher: Imnah, Ishvah, Ishvi, Beriah, and their sister Serah. The children of Beriah: Heber and Malchiel 18(these are the children of Zilpah, whom Laban gave to his daughter Leah; and these she bore to Jacob—sixteen persons). 19The children of Jacob's wife Rachel: Joseph and Benjamin. 20To Joseph in the land of Egypt were born Manasseh and Ephraim, whom Asenath daughter of Potiphera, priest of On, bore to him. 21The children of Benjamin: Bela, Becher, Ashbel, Gera, Naaman, Ehi, Rosh, Muppim, Huppim, and Ard 22(these are the children of Rachel, who were born to Jacob—fourteen persons in all). 23The children of Dan: Hashum.w 24The children of Naphtali: Jahzeel, Guni, Jezer, and Shillem 25(these are the children of Bilhah, whom Laban gave to his daughter Rachel, and these she bore to Jacob—seven persons in all). 26All the persons belonging to

s Or be agitated   t Heb the God   u Or Saul
v Compare Sam Gk Num 26.24; 1 Chr 7.1: MT Iob
w Gk: Heb Hushim

Jacob who came into Egypt, who were his own offspring, not including the wives of his sons, were sixty-six persons in all. ²⁷The children of Joseph, who were born to him in Egypt, were two; all the persons of the house of Jacob who came into Egypt were seventy.

Jacob Settles in Goshen

28 Israel˟ sent Judah ahead to Joseph to lead the way before him into Goshen. When they came to the land of Goshen, ²⁹Joseph made ready his chariot and went up to meet his father Israel in Goshen. He presented himself to him, fell on his neck, and wept on his neck a good while. ³⁰Israel said to Joseph, "I can die now, having seen for myself that you are still alive." ³¹Joseph said to his brothers and to his father's household, "I will go up and tell Pharaoh, and will say to him, 'My brothers and my father's household, who were in the land of Canaan, have come to me. ³²The men are shepherds, for they have been keepers of livestock; and they have brought their flocks, and their herds, and all that they have.' ³³When Pharaoh calls you, and says, 'What is your occupation?' ³⁴you shall say, 'Your servants have been keepers of livestock from our youth even until now, both we and our ancestors'—in order that you may settle in the land of Goshen, because all shepherds are abhorrent to the Egyptians."

47 So Joseph went and told Pharaoh, "My father and my brothers, with their flocks and herds and all that they possess, have come from the land of Canaan; they are now in the land of Goshen." ²From among his brothers he took five men and presented them to Pharaoh. ³Pharaoh said to his brothers, "What is your occupation?" And they said to Pharaoh, "Your servants are shepherds, as our ancestors were." ⁴They said to Pharaoh, "We have come to reside as aliens in the land; for there is no pasture for your servants' flocks because the famine is severe in the land of Canaan. Now, we ask you, let your servants settle in the land of Goshen." ⁵Then Pharaoh said to Joseph, "Your father and your brothers have come to you. ⁶The land of Egypt is before you; settle your father and your brothers in the best part of the land; let them live in the land of Goshen; and if you know that there are capable men among them, put them in charge of my livestock."

7 Then Joseph brought in his father Jacob, and presented him before Pharaoh, and Jacob blessed Pharaoh. ⁸Pharaoh said to Jacob, "How many are the years of your life?" ⁹Jacob said to Pharaoh, "The years of my earthly sojourn are one hundred thirty; few and hard have been the years of my life. They do not compare with the years of the life of my ancestors during their long sojourn." ¹⁰Then Jacob blessed Pharaoh, and went out from the presence of Pharaoh. ¹¹Joseph settled his father and his brothers, and granted them a holding in the land of Egypt, in the best part of the land, in the land of Rameses, as Pharaoh had instructed. ¹²And Joseph provided his father, his brothers, and all his father's household with food, according to the number of their dependents.

The Famine in Egypt

13 Now there was no food in all the land, for the famine was very severe. The land of Egypt and the land of Canaan languished because of the famine. ¹⁴Joseph collected all the money to be found in the land of Egypt and in the land of Canaan, in exchange for the grain that they bought; and Joseph brought the money into Pharaoh's house. ¹⁵When the money from the land of Egypt and from the land of Canaan was spent, all the Egyptians came to Joseph, and said, "Give us food! Why should we die before your eyes? For our money is gone." ¹⁶And Joseph answered, "Give me your livestock, and I will give you food in exchange for your livestock, if your money is gone." ¹⁷So they brought their livestock to Joseph; and Joseph gave them food in exchange for the horses, the flocks, the herds, and the donkeys. That year he supplied them with food in exchange for all their livestock. ¹⁸When that year was ended, they came to him the following year, and said to him, "We can not hide from my lord that our money is all spent; and the herds of cattle are my lord's. There is nothing left in the sight of my lord but our bodies and our lands. ¹⁹Shall we die before your eyes, both we and our land? Buy us and our land in exchange for food. We with our land will become slaves to Pharaoh; just give us seed, so that we may live and not die, and that the land may not become desolate."

˟ Heb *He*

20 So Joseph bought all the land of Egypt for Pharaoh. All the Egyptians sold their fields, because the famine was severe upon them; and the land became Pharaoh's. ²¹As for the people, he made slaves of them[y] from one end of Egypt to the other. ²²Only the land of the priests he did not buy; for the priests had a fixed allowance from Pharaoh, and lived on the allowance that Pharaoh gave them; therefore they did not sell their land. ²³Then Joseph said to the people, "Now that I have this day bought you and your land for Pharaoh, here is seed for you; sow the land. ²⁴And at the harvests you shall give one-fifth to Pharaoh, and four-fifths shall be your own, as seed for the field and as food for yourselves and your households, and as food for your little ones." ²⁵They said, "You have saved our lives; may it please my lord, we will be slaves to Pharaoh." ²⁶So Joseph made it a statute concerning the land of Egypt, and it stands to this day, that Pharaoh should have the fifth. The land of the priests alone did not become Pharaoh's.

The Last Days of Jacob

27 Thus Israel settled in the land of Egypt, in the region of Goshen; and they gained possessions in it, and were fruitful and multiplied exceedingly. ²⁸Jacob lived in the land of Egypt seventeen years; so the days of Jacob, the years of his life, were one hundred forty-seven years. 29 When the time of Israel's death drew near, he called his son Joseph and said to him, "If I have found favor with you, put your hand under my thigh and promise to deal loyally and truly with me. Do not bury me in Egypt. ³⁰When I lie down with my ancestors, carry me out of Egypt and bury me in their burial place." He answered, "I will do as you have said." ³¹And he said, "Swear to me"; and he swore to him. Then Israel bowed himself on the head of his bed.

Jacob Blesses Joseph's Sons

48 After this Joseph was told, "Your father is ill." So he took with him his two sons, Manasseh and Ephraim. ²When Jacob was told, "Your son Joseph has come to you," he[z] summoned his strength and sat up in bed. ³And Jacob said to Joseph, "God Almighty[a] appeared to me at Luz in the land of Canaan, and he blessed me, ⁴and said to me,

'I am going to make you fruitful and increase your numbers; I will make of you a company of peoples, and will give this land to your offspring after you for a perpetual holding.' ⁵Therefore your two sons, who were born to you in the land of Egypt before I came to you in Egypt, are now mine; Ephraim and Manasseh shall be mine, just as Reuben and Simeon are. ⁶As for the offspring born to you after them, they shall be yours. They shall be recorded under the names of their brothers with regard to their inheritance. ⁷For when I came from Paddan, Rachel, alas, died in the land of Canaan on the way, while there was still some distance to go to Ephrath; and I buried her there on the way to Ephrath" (that is, Bethlehem).

8 When Israel saw Joseph's sons, he said, "Who are these?" ⁹Joseph said to his father, "They are my sons, whom God has given me here." And he said, "Bring them to me, please, that I may bless them." ¹⁰Now the eyes of Israel were dim with age, and he could not see well. So Joseph brought them near him; and he kissed them and embraced them. ¹¹Israel said to Joseph, "I did not expect to see your face; and here God has let me see your children also." ¹²Then Joseph removed them from his father's knees,[b] and he bowed himself with his face to the earth. ¹³Joseph took them both, Ephraim in his right hand toward Israel's left, and Manasseh in his left hand toward Israel's right, and brought them near him. ¹⁴But Israel stretched out his right hand and laid it on the head of Ephraim, who was the younger, and his left hand on the head of Manasseh, crossing his hands, for Manasseh was the firstborn. ¹⁵He blessed Joseph, and said,

"The God before whom my
     ancestors Abraham and Isaac
     walked,
the God who has been my shepherd
     all my life to this day,
¹⁶ the angel who has redeemed me
     from all harm, bless the boys;
and in them let my name be
     perpetuated, and the name of
     my ancestors Abraham and
     Isaac;

[y] Sam Gk Compare Vg: MT *He removed them to the cities*   [z] Heb *Israel*   [a] Traditional rendering of Heb *El Shaddai*   [b] Heb *from his knees*

and let them grow into a multitude
   on the earth."

17 When Joseph saw that his father
laid his right hand on the head of Ephraim, it displeased him; so he took his father's hand, to remove it from Ephraim's
head to Manasseh's head. 18Joseph said to
his father, "Not so, my father! Since this
one is the firstborn, put your right hand
on his head." 19But his father refused, and
said, "I know, my son, I know; he also
shall become a people, and he also shall
be great. Nevertheless his younger brother
shall be greater than he, and his offspring
shall become a multitude of nations." 20So
he blessed them that day, saying,
  "By you*c* Israel will invoke
    blessings, saying,
  'God make you*c* like Ephraim and
    like Manasseh.' "
So he put Ephraim ahead of Manasseh.
21Then Israel said to Joseph, "I am about
to die, but God will be with you and will
bring you again to the land of your ancestors. 22I now give to you one portion*d*
more than to your brothers, the portion*d*
that I took from the hand of the Amorites
with my sword and with my bow."

Jacob's Last Words to His Sons

49 Then Jacob called his sons, and
  said: "Gather around, that I may
tell you what will happen to you in days
to come.
  2 Assemble and hear, O sons of Jacob;
    listen to Israel your father.

  3 Reuben, you are my firstborn,
    my might and the first fruits of
      my vigor,
    excelling in rank and excelling in
      power.
  4 Unstable as water, you shall no
      longer excel
    because you went up onto your
      father's bed;
    then you defiled it—you*e* went
      up onto my couch!

  5 Simeon and Levi are brothers;
    weapons of violence are their
      swords.
  6 May I never come into their council;
    may I not be joined to their
      company—
    for in their anger they killed men,
    and at their whim they hamstrung
      oxen.

  7 Cursed be their anger, for it is fierce,
    and their wrath, for it is cruel!
  I will divide them in Jacob,
    and scatter them in Israel.

  8 Judah, your brothers shall praise
      you;
    your hand shall be on the neck of
      your enemies;
    your father's sons shall bow down
      before you.
  9 Judah is a lion's whelp;
    from the prey, my son, you have
      gone up.
  He crouches down, he stretches out
    like a lion,
    like a lioness—who dares rouse
      him up?
  10 The scepter shall not depart from
      Judah,
    nor the ruler's staff from between
      his feet,
  until tribute comes to him;*f*
    and the obedience of the peoples
      is his.
  11 Binding his foal to the vine
    and his donkey's colt to the
      choice vine,
  he washes his garments in wine
    and his robe in the blood of
      grapes;
  12 his eyes are darker than wine,
    and his teeth whiter than milk.

  13 Zebulun shall settle at the shore of
      the sea;
    he shall be a haven for ships,
    and his border shall be at Sidon.

  14 Issachar is a strong donkey,
    lying down between the
      sheepfolds;
  15 he saw that a resting place was
      good,
    and that the land was pleasant;
  so he bowed his shoulder to the
      burden,
    and became a slave at forced
      labor.

  16 Dan shall judge his people

---

c you here is singular in Heb   *d* Or *mountain
slope* (Heb *shekem,* a play on the name of the
town and district of Shechem)   *e* Gk Syr Tg:
Heb *he*   *f* Or *until Shiloh comes* or *until he comes
to Shiloh* or (with Syr) *until he comes to whom it
belongs*

as one of the tribes of Israel.

17 Dan shall be a snake by the
    roadside,
  a viper along the path,
that bites the horse's heels
  so that its rider falls backward.

18 I wait for your salvation, O LORD.

19 Gad shall be raided by raiders,
  but he shall raid at their heels.

20 Asher's*g* food shall be rich,
  and he shall provide royal
    delicacies.

21 Naphtali is a doe let loose
  that bears lovely fawns.*h*

22 Joseph is a fruitful bough,
  a fruitful bough by a spring;
  his branches run over the wall.*i*

23 The archers fiercely attacked him;
  they shot at him and pressed him
    hard.

24 Yet his bow remained taut,
  and his arms*j* were made agile
by the hands of the Mighty One of
    Jacob,
  by the name of the Shepherd, the
    Rock of Israel,

25 by the God of your father, who will
    help you,
  by the Almighty*k* who will bless
    you
with blessings of heaven above,
blessings of the deep that lies
    beneath,
blessings of the breasts and of the
    womb.

26 The blessings of your father
  are stronger than the blessings of
    the eternal mountains,
  the bounties*l* of the everlasting
    hills;
may they be on the head of Joseph,
  on the brow of him who was set
    apart from his brothers.

27 Benjamin is a ravenous wolf,
  in the morning devouring the
    prey,
  and at evening dividing the spoil."

28 All these are the twelve tribes of Israel, and this is what their father said to
them when he blessed them, blessing
each one of them with a suitable blessing.

Jacob's Death and Burial

29 Then he charged them, saying to
them, "I am about to be gathered to my
people. Bury me with my ancestors—in
the cave in the field of Ephron the Hittite,
30in the cave in the field at Machpelah,
near Mamre, in the land of Canaan, in the
field that Abraham bought from Ephron
the Hittite as a burial site. 31There Abraham and his wife Sarah were buried; there
Isaac and his wife Rebekah were buried;
and there I buried Leah— 32the field and
the cave that is in it were purchased from
the Hittites." 33When Jacob ended his
charge to his sons, he drew up his feet into
the bed, breathed his last, and was gathered to his people.

50 Then Joseph threw himself on his
father's face and wept over him
and kissed him. 2Joseph commanded the
physicians in his service to embalm his
father. So the physicians embalmed Israel;
3they spent forty days in doing this, for
that is the time required for embalming.
And the Egyptians wept for him seventy
days.

4 When the days of weeping for him
were past, Joseph addressed the household of Pharaoh, "If now I have found
favor with you, please speak to Pharaoh as
follows: 5My father made me swear an
oath; he said, 'I am about to die. In the
tomb that I hewed out for myself in the
land of Canaan, there you shall bury me.'
Now therefore let me go up, so that I may
bury my father; then I will return." 6Phar-
aoh answered, "Go up, and bury your father, as he made you swear to do."

7 So Joseph went up to bury his father.
With him went up all the servants of Pharaoh, the elders of his household, and all
the elders of the land of Egypt, 8as well as
all the household of Joseph, his brothers,
and his father's household. Only their
children, their flocks, and their herds were
left in the land of Goshen. 9Both chariots
and charioteers went up with him. It was
a very great company. 10When they came
to the threshing floor of Atad, which is
beyond the Jordan, they held there a very
great and sorrowful lamentation; and he
observed a time of mourning for his fa-

g Gk Vg Syr: Heb *From Asher*   *h* Or *that gives
beautiful words*   *i* Meaning of Heb uncertain
j Heb *the arms of his hands*   *k* Traditional
rendering of Heb *Shaddai*   *l* Cn Compare Gk:
Heb *of my progenitors to the boundaries*

ther seven days. ¹¹When the Canaanite inhabitants of the land saw the mourning on the threshing floor of Atad, they said, "This is a grievous mourning on the part of the Egyptians." Therefore the place was named Abel-mizraim;ᵐ it is beyond the Jordan. ¹²Thus his sons did for him as he had instructed them. ¹³They carried him to the land of Canaan and buried him in the cave of the field at Machpelah, the field near Mamre, which Abraham bought as a burial site from Ephron the Hittite. ¹⁴After he had buried his father, Joseph returned to Egypt with his brothers and all who had gone up with him to bury his father.

Joseph Forgives His Brothers

15 Realizing that their father was dead, Joseph's brothers said, "What if Joseph still bears a grudge against us and pays us back in full for all the wrong that we did to him?" ¹⁶So they approachedⁿ Joseph, saying, "Your father gave this instruction before he died, ¹⁷'Say to Joseph: I beg you, forgive the crime of your brothers and the wrong they did in harming you.' Now therefore please forgive the crime of the servants of the God of your father." Joseph wept when they spoke to him. ¹⁸Then his brothers also wept,ᵒ fell down before him, and said, "We are here as your slaves." ¹⁹But Joseph said to them, "Do not be afraid! Am I in the place of God? ²⁰Even though you intended to do harm to me, God intended it for good, in order to preserve a numerous people, as he is doing today. ²¹So have no fear; I myself will provide for you and your little ones." In this way he reassured them, speaking kindly to them.

Joseph's Last Days and Death

22 So Joseph remained in Egypt, he and his father's household; and Joseph lived one hundred ten years. ²³Joseph saw Ephraim's children of the third generation; the children of Machir son of Manasseh were also born on Joseph's knees. 24 Then Joseph said to his brothers, "I am about to die; but God will surely come to you, and bring you up out of this land to the land that he swore to Abraham, to Isaac, and to Jacob." ²⁵So Joseph made the Israelites swear, saying, "When God comes to you, you shall carry up my bones from here." ²⁶And Joseph died, being one hundred ten years old; he was embalmed and placed in a coffin in Egypt.

m That is *mourning* (or *meadow*) *of Egypt*   *n* Gk Syr: Heb *they commanded*   *o* Cn: Heb *also came*

Exodus

The second book of the Bible is called *Exodus*, which in Greek means "departure." It tells the dramatic story of the Israelites' escape from slavery in Egypt through a series of marvelous acts of one-upmanship that God performed through a man named Moses. As an infant, Moses had been delivered from death through the help of three women: his mother; his sister, Miriam; and the pharaoh's daughter.

We are familiar with the story of the plagues—the Nile River turning to blood, the devouring locusts, the sparing of the Israelite firstborn. We remember, too, the dramatic crossing of the sea, the giving of the commandments at Mount Sinai, the manna in the desert. But have we ever read the story in light of our own story of faith—realizing that Jesus is the one who frees us from bondage to sin, that the Eucharist helps sustain us in the wilderness of this life, and that Christ will fully and finally triumph over Satan, just as Moses triumphed over Pharaoh? As you read Exodus, try putting yourself into the story, realizing that the work of Moses foreshadows the saving work of Christ.

The book of Exodus is the story of how God shaped his people in the midst of great oppression, dealing with their own waywardness and leading them to freedom.

1 These are the names of the sons of Israel who came to Egypt with Jacob, each with his household: ²Reuben, Simeon, Levi, and Judah, ³Issachar, Zebulun, and Benjamin, ⁴Dan and Naphtali, Gad and Asher. ⁵The total number of people born to Jacob was seventy. Joseph was already in Egypt. ⁶Then Joseph died, and all his brothers, and that whole generation. ⁷But the Israelites were fruitful and prolific; they multiplied and grew exceedingly strong, so that the land was filled with them.

The Israelites Are Oppressed

8 Now a new king arose over Egypt, who did not know Joseph. ⁹He said to his people, "Look, the Israelite people are more numerous and more powerful than we. ¹⁰Come, let us deal shrewdly with them, or they will increase and, in the event of war, join our enemies and fight

against us and escape from the land." [11]Therefore they set taskmasters over them to oppress them with forced labor. They built supply cities, Pithom and Rameses, for Pharaoh. [12]But the more they were oppressed, the more they multiplied and spread, so that the Egyptians came to dread the Israelites. [13]The Egyptians became ruthless in imposing tasks on the Israelites, [14]and made their lives bitter with hard service in mortar and brick and in every kind of field labor. They were ruthless in all the tasks that they imposed on them.

15 The king of Egypt said to the Hebrew midwives, one of whom was named Shiphrah and the other Puah, [16]"When you act as midwives to the Hebrew women, and see them on the birthstool, if it is a boy, kill him; but if it is a girl, she shall live." [17]But the midwives feared God; they did not do as the king of Egypt commanded them, but they let the boys live. [18]So the king of Egypt summoned the midwives and said to them, "Why have you done this, and allowed the boys to live?" [19]The midwives said to Pharaoh, "Because the Hebrew women are not like the Egyptian women; for they are vigorous and give birth before the midwife comes to them." [20]So God dealt well with the midwives; and the people multiplied and became very strong. [21]And because the midwives feared God, he gave them families. [22]Then Pharaoh commanded all his people, "Every boy that is born to the Hebrews[a] you shall throw into the Nile, but you shall let every girl live."

Birth and Youth of Moses

2 Now a man from the house of Levi went and married a Levite woman. [2]The woman conceived and bore a son; and when she saw that he was a fine baby, she hid him three months. [3]When she could hide him no longer she got a papyrus basket for him, and plastered it with bitumen and pitch; she put the child in it and placed it among the reeds on the bank of the river. [4]His sister stood at a distance, to see what would happen to him.

5 The daughter of Pharaoh came down to bathe at the river, while her attendants walked beside the river. She saw the basket among the reeds and sent her maid to bring it. [6]When she opened it, she saw the child. He was crying, and she took pity on him. "This must be one of the Hebrews' children," she said. [7]Then his sister said to Pharaoh's daughter, "Shall I go and get you a nurse from the Hebrew women to nurse the child for you?" [8]Pharaoh's daughter said to her, "Yes." So the girl went and called the child's mother. [9]Pharaoh's daughter said to her, "Take this child and nurse it for me, and I will give you your wages." So the woman took the child and nursed it. [10]When the child grew up, she brought him to Pharaoh's daughter, and she took him as her son. She named him Moses,[b] "because," she said, "I drew him out[c] of the water."

Moses Flees to Midian

11 One day, after Moses had grown up, he went out to his people and saw their forced labor. He saw an Egyptian beating a Hebrew, one of his kinsfolk. [12]He looked this way and that, and seeing no one he killed the Egyptian and hid him in the sand. [13]When he went out the next day, he saw two Hebrews fighting; and he said to the one who was in the wrong, "Why do you strike your fellow Hebrew?" [14]He answered, "Who made you a ruler and judge over us? Do you mean to kill me as you killed the Egyptian?" Then Moses was afraid and thought, "Surely the thing is known." [15]When Pharaoh heard of it, he sought to kill Moses.

But Moses fled from Pharaoh. He settled in the land of Midian, and sat down by a well. [16]The priest of Midian had seven daughters. They came to draw water, and filled the troughs to water their father's flock. [17]But some shepherds came and drove them away. Moses got up and came to their defense and watered their flock. [18]When they returned to their father Reuel, he said, "How is it that you have come back so soon today?" [19]They said, "An Egyptian helped us against the shepherds; he even drew water for us and watered the flock." [20]He said to his daughters, "Where is he? Why did you leave the man? Invite him to break bread." [21]Moses agreed to stay with the man, and he gave Moses his daughter Zipporah in marriage. [22]She bore a son, and he named him Gershom; for he said, "I have been an alien[d] residing in a foreign land."

23 After a long time the king of Egypt

---

[a] Sam Gk Tg: Heb lacks *to the Hebrews*   [b] Heb *Mosheh*   [c] Heb *mashah*   [d] Heb *ger*

died. The Israelites groaned under their slavery, and cried out. Out of the slavery their cry for help rose up to God. ²⁴God heard their groaning, and God remembered his covenant with Abraham, Isaac, and Jacob. ²⁵God looked upon the Israelites, and God took notice of them.

Moses at the Burning Bush

3 Moses was keeping the flock of his father-in-law Jethro, the priest of Midian; he led his flock beyond the wilderness, and came to Horeb, the mountain of God. ²There the angel of the LORD appeared to him in a flame of fire out of a bush; he looked, and the bush was blazing, yet it was not consumed. ³Then Moses said, "I must turn aside and look at this great sight, and see why the bush is not burned up." ⁴When the LORD saw that he had turned aside to see, God called to him out of the bush, "Moses, Moses!" And he said, "Here I am." ⁵Then he said, "Come no closer! Remove the sandals from your feet, for the place on which you are standing is holy ground." ⁶He said further, "I am the God of your father, the God of Abraham, the God of Isaac, and the God of Jacob." And Moses hid his face, for he was afraid to look at God.

7 Then the LORD said, "I have observed the misery of my people who are in Egypt; I have heard their cry on account of their taskmasters. Indeed, I know their sufferings, ⁸and I have come down to deliver them from the Egyptians, and to bring them up out of that land to a good and broad land, a land flowing with milk and honey, to the country of the Canaanites, the Hittites, the Amorites, the Perizzites, the Hivites, and the Jebusites. ⁹The cry of the Israelites has now come to me; I have also seen how the Egyptians oppress them. ¹⁰So come, I will send you to Pharaoh to bring my people, the Israelites, out of Egypt." ¹¹But Moses said to God, "Who am I that I should go to Pharaoh, and bring the Israelites out of Egypt?" ¹²He said, "I will be with you; and this shall be the sign for you that it is I who sent you: when you have brought the people out of Egypt, you shall worship God on this mountain."

The Divine Name Revealed

13 But Moses said to God, "If I come to the Israelites and say to them, 'The God of your ancestors has sent me to you,' and they ask me, 'What is his name?' what shall I say to them?" ¹⁴God said to Moses, "I AM WHO I AM."ᵉ He said further, "Thus you shall say to the Israelites, 'I AM has sent me to you.' " ¹⁵God also said to Moses, "Thus you shall say to the Israelites, 'The LORD,ᶠ the God of your ancestors, the God of Abraham, the God of Isaac, and the God of Jacob, has sent me to you':

This is my name forever,

and this is my title for all generations.

¹⁶Go and assemble the elders of Israel, and say to them, 'The LORD, the God of your ancestors, the God of Abraham, of Isaac, and of Jacob, has appeared to me, saying: I have given heed to you and to what has been done to you in Egypt. ¹⁷I declare that I will bring you up out of the misery of Egypt, to the land of the Canaanites, the Hittites, the Amorites, the Perizzites, the Hivites, and the Jebusites, a land flowing with milk and honey.' ¹⁸They will listen to your voice; and you and the elders of Israel shall go to the king of Egypt and say to him, 'The LORD, the God of the Hebrews, has met with us; let us now go a three days' journey into the wilderness, so that we may sacrifice to the LORD our God.' ¹⁹I know, however, that the king of Egypt will not let you go unless compelled by a mighty hand.ᵍ ²⁰So I will stretch out my hand and strike Egypt with all my wonders that I will perform in it; after that he will let you go. ²¹I will bring this people into such favor with the Egyptians that, when you go, you will not go empty-handed; ²²each woman shall ask her neighbor and any woman living in the neighbor's house for jewelry of silver and of gold, and clothing, and you shall put them on your sons and on your daughters; and so you shall plunder the Egyptians."

Moses' Miraculous Power

4 Then Moses answered, "But suppose they do not believe me or listen to me, but say, 'The LORD did not appear to you.' " ²The LORD said to him, "What is that in your hand?" He said, "A staff." ³And he said, "Throw it on the ground." So he

ᵉ Or *I AM WHAT I AM* or *I WILL BE WHAT I WILL BE*
ᶠ The word "LORD" when spelled with capital letters stands for the divine name, YHWH, which is here connected with the verb *hayah*, "to be"
ᵍ Gk Vg: Heb *no, not by a mighty hand*

threw the staff on the ground, and it became a snake; and Moses drew back from it. [4]Then the LORD said to Moses, "Reach out your hand, and seize it by the tail"—so he reached out his hand and grasped it, and it became a staff in his hand— [5]"so that they may believe that the LORD, the God of their ancestors, the God of Abra-

God's Name

WEDNESDAY

Scripture Reading for Today:
Exodus 3.1–16

Verse for Today:
Exodus 3.14

"Hallowed be thy name . . ." We are asking that God's name be honored, that it be "set apart for special use." Evidently our prayers aren't being answered. We seldom hear God or Jesus mentioned, except as an expression of shock or disgust. "Oh, my God!" says Sue when it's drizzling, and she's left her umbrella in the car. "Oh, Jesus!" says Ron when he discovers that *Presumed Innocent* has moved to another theater. God's name punctuates the trivial.

Sometimes when I hear God's name misused, I fantasize [that] God may lose patience, and start appearing at the casual use of his name, producing the same result as the casual handling of the ark of the covenant (when bodies started dropping—see 2 Samuel 6.6–7). Or I picture a classroom: The student looks at the physics test and says, "Oh my God." The room is suddenly filled with angels: "You called?"

These are daydreams. God will use those who love his name to hallow it. How can we join in making God's name holy?

Several ways: Those of us who have experienced God's wholeness and forgiveness in our lives must use the name with great care, confessing God's presence in our lives with extreme sensitivity.

We can also pray for people who misuse God's name, that they may come to call him Lord.

Or this, though it takes nerve. The scene: I am having lunch with a colleague when she drops her fork and says, "Oh my God."

I wince or say, "Ouch."

"What's wrong?" she asks.

"Words are important to me, names are important to me, and God is important to me: It hurts to hear his name used like that."

"It does? I'm sorry, I didn't know you were religious."

Most important, we can hallow God's name by the holiness of our lives. Profanation of God's name in the Bible is linked not only to verbal abuse, but to a lack of obedience to God's commands (see Leviticus 22.31–32; Amos 2.7). Paul writes to the Romans that, "The name of God is blasphemed among the Gentiles because of you" (Romans 2.24). If our lives are hypocritical, unloving, or insensitive to the poor, then God's name is blasphemed.

—MARY ELLEN ASHCROFT

Go to page 70 for your next devotional reading.

ham, the God of Isaac, and the God of Jacob, has appeared to you."

6 Again, the LORD said to him, "Put your hand inside your cloak." He put his hand into his cloak; and when he took it out, his hand was leprous,[h] as white as snow. 7Then God said, "Put your hand back into your cloak"—so he put his hand back into his cloak, and when he took it out, it was restored like the rest of his body— 8"If they will not believe you or heed the first sign, they may believe the second sign. 9If they will not believe even these two signs or heed you, you shall take some water from the Nile and pour it on the dry ground; and the water that you shall take from the Nile will become blood on the dry ground."

10 But Moses said to the LORD, "O my Lord, I have never been eloquent, neither in the past nor even now that you have spoken to your servant; but I am slow of speech and slow of tongue." 11Then the LORD said to him, "Who gives speech to mortals? Who makes them mute or deaf, seeing or blind? Is it not I, the LORD? 12Now go, and I will be with your mouth and teach you what you are to speak." 13But he said, "O my Lord, please send someone else." 14Then the anger of the LORD was kindled against Moses and he said, "What of your brother Aaron the Levite? I know that he can speak fluently; even now he is coming out to meet you, and when he sees you his heart will be glad. 15You shall speak to him and put the words in his mouth; and I will be with your mouth and with his mouth, and will teach you what you shall do. 16He indeed shall speak for you to the people; he shall serve as a mouth for you, and you shall serve as God for him. 17Take in your hand this staff, with which you shall perform the signs."

Moses Returns to Egypt

18 Moses went back to his father-in-law Jethro and said to him, "Please let me go back to my kindred in Egypt and see whether they are still living." And Jethro said to Moses, "Go in peace." 19The LORD said to Moses in Midian, "Go back to Egypt; for all those who were seeking your life are dead." 20So Moses took his wife and his sons, put them on a donkey, and went back to the land of Egypt; and Moses carried the staff of God in his hand.

21 And the LORD said to Moses, "When you go back to Egypt, see that you perform before Pharaoh all the wonders that I have put in your power; but I will harden his heart, so that he will not let the people go. 22Then you shall say to Pharaoh, 'Thus says the LORD: Israel is my firstborn son. 23I said to you, "Let my son go that he may worship me." But you refused to let him go; now I will kill your firstborn son.' "

24 On the way, at a place where they spent the night, the LORD met him and tried to kill him. 25But Zipporah took a flint and cut off her son's foreskin, and touched Moses'[i] feet with it, and said, "Truly you are a bridegroom of blood to me!" 26So he let him alone. It was then she said, "A bridegroom of blood by circumcision."

27 The LORD said to Aaron, "Go into the wilderness to meet Moses." So he went; and he met him at the mountain of God and kissed him. 28Moses told Aaron all the words of the LORD with which he had sent him, and all the signs with which he had charged him. 29Then Moses and Aaron went and assembled all the elders of the Israelites. 30Aaron spoke all the words that the LORD had spoken to Moses, and performed the signs in the sight of the people. 31The people believed; and when they heard that the LORD had given heed to the Israelites and that he had seen their misery, they bowed down and worshiped.

Bricks without Straw

5 Afterward Moses and Aaron went to Pharaoh and said, "Thus says the LORD, the God of Israel, 'Let my people go, so that they may celebrate a festival to me in the wilderness.' " 2But Pharaoh said, "Who is the LORD, that I should heed him and let Israel go? I do not know the LORD, and I will not let Israel go." 3Then they said, "The God of the Hebrews has revealed himself to us; let us go a three days' journey into the wilderness to sacrifice to the LORD our God, or he will fall upon us with pestilence or sword." 4But the king of Egypt said to them, "Moses and Aaron, why are you taking the people away from their work? Get to your labors!" 5Pharaoh continued, "Now they are more numer-

---

h A term for several skin diseases; precise meaning uncertain   *i* Heb *his*

ous than the people of the land *j* and yet you want them to stop working!" ⁶That same day Pharaoh commanded the taskmasters of the people, as well as their supervisors, ⁷"You shall no longer give the people straw to make bricks, as before; let them go and gather straw for themselves. ⁸But you shall require of them the same quantity of bricks as they have made previously; do not diminish it, for they are lazy; that is why they cry, 'Let us go and offer sacrifice to our God.' ⁹Let heavier work be laid on them; then they will labor at it and pay no attention to deceptive words."

10 So the taskmasters and the supervisors of the people went out and said to the people, "Thus says Pharaoh, 'I will not give you straw. ¹¹Go and get straw yourselves, wherever you can find it; but your work will not be lessened in the least.' " ¹²So the people scattered throughout the land of Egypt, to gather stubble for straw. ¹³The taskmasters were urgent, saying, "Complete your work, the same daily assignment as when you were given straw." ¹⁴And the supervisors of the Israelites, whom Pharaoh's taskmasters had set over them, were beaten, and were asked, "Why did you not finish the required quantity of bricks yesterday and today, as you did before?"

15 Then the Israelite supervisors came to Pharaoh and cried, "Why do you treat your servants like this? ¹⁶No straw is given to your servants, yet they say to us, 'Make bricks!' Look how your servants are beaten! You are unjust to your own people."*k* ¹⁷He said, "You are lazy, lazy; that is why you say, 'Let us go and sacrifice to the LORD.' ¹⁸Go now, and work; for no straw shall be given you, but you shall still deliver the same number of bricks." ¹⁹The Israelite supervisors saw that they were in trouble when they were told, "You shall not lessen your daily number of bricks." ²⁰As they left Pharaoh, they came upon Moses and Aaron who were waiting to meet them. ²¹They said to them, "The LORD look upon you and judge! You have brought us into bad odor with Pharaoh and his officials, and have put a sword in their hand to kill us."

22 Then Moses turned again to the LORD and said, "O LORD, why have you mistreated this people? Why did you ever send me? ²³Since I first came to Pharaoh to speak in your name, he has mistreated this people, and you have done nothing at all to deliver your people."

Israel's Deliverance Assured

6 Then the LORD said to Moses, "Now you shall see what I will do to Pharaoh: Indeed, by a mighty hand he will let them go; by a mighty hand he will drive them out of his land."

2 God also spoke to Moses and said to him: "I am the LORD. ³I appeared to Abraham, Isaac, and Jacob as God Almighty,*l* but by my name 'The LORD'*m* I did not make myself known to them. ⁴I also established my covenant with them, to give them the land of Canaan, the land in which they resided as aliens. ⁵I have also heard the groaning of the Israelites whom the Egyptians are holding as slaves, and I have remembered my covenant. ⁶Say therefore to the Israelites, 'I am the LORD, and I will free you from the burdens of the Egyptians and deliver you from slavery to them. I will redeem you with an outstretched arm and with mighty acts of judgment. ⁷I will take you as my people, and I will be your God. You shall know that I am the LORD your God, who has freed you from the burdens of the Egyptians. ⁸I will bring you into the land that I swore to give to Abraham, Isaac, and Jacob; I will give it to you for a possession. I am the LORD.' " ⁹Moses told this to the Israelites; but they would not listen to Moses, because of their broken spirit and their cruel slavery.

10 Then the LORD spoke to Moses, ¹¹"Go and tell Pharaoh king of Egypt to let the Israelites go out of his land." ¹²But Moses spoke to the LORD, "The Israelites have not listened to me; how then shall Pharaoh listen to me, poor speaker that I am?"*n* ¹³Thus the LORD spoke to Moses and Aaron, and gave them orders regarding the Israelites and Pharaoh king of Egypt, charging them to free the Israelites from the land of Egypt.

The Genealogy of Moses and Aaron

14 The following are the heads of their ancestral houses: the sons of Reuben, the firstborn of Israel: Hanoch, Pallu, Hezron,

---

j Sam: Heb *The people of the land are now many*
k Gk Compare Syr Vg: Heb *beaten, and the sin of your people*   *l* Traditional rendering of Heb *El Shaddai*   *m* Heb *YHWH*; see note at 3.15
n Heb *me? I am uncircumcised of lips*

and Carmi; these are the families of Reuben. ¹⁵The sons of Simeon: Jemuel, Jamin, Ohad, Jachin, Zohar, and Shaul,^o the son of a Canaanite woman; these are the families of Simeon. ¹⁶The following are the names of the sons of Levi according to their genealogies: Gershon,^p Kohath, and Merari, and the length of Levi's life was one hundred thirty-seven years. ¹⁷The sons of Gershon:^p Libni and Shimei, by their families. ¹⁸The sons of Kohath: Amram, Izhar, Hebron, and Uzziel, and the length of Kohath's life was one hundred thirty-three years. ¹⁹The sons of Merari: Mahli and Mushi. These are the families of the Levites according to their genealogies. ²⁰Amram married Jochebed his fa-

ther's sister and she bore him Aaron and Moses, and the length of Amram's life was one hundred thirty-seven years. ²¹The sons of Izhar: Korah, Nepheg, and Zichri. ²²The sons of Uzziel: Mishael, Elzaphan, and Sithri. ²³Aaron married Elisheba, daughter of Amminadab and sister of Nahshon, and she bore him Nadab, Abihu, Eleazar, and Ithamar. ²⁴The sons of Korah: Assir, Elkanah, and Abiasaph; these are the families of the Korahites. ²⁵Aaron's son Eleazar married one of the daughters of Putiel, and she bore him Phinehas. These are the heads of the an-

o Or *Saul*   *p* Also spelled *Gershom;* see 2.22

THE TRADITION

God Loves the Poor

*"I have also heard the groaning of the Israelites
whom the Egyptians are holding as slaves."*

EXODUS 6.5

No doubt about it: God has a "weak" spot for the underdog.

Consider the exodus from Egypt. Moved by the groaning of the enslaved Israelites, God says, "I have given heed to you and ... I will free you" (Exodus 3.16; 6.6). And he follows up with a dazzling display of power. Later, when the Israelites settle in their own land, God outlines laws to protect the poor. He cautions the Israelites against exacting interest from poor people who borrow from them or treating the poor unfairly in lawsuits (22.25; 23.6). God asks that the Israelite farmers leave produce for the poor to glean (Leviticus 19.10). In such ways and by his command, God tells his people to open their hands to the poor (Deuteronomy 15.11). Later, God sends prophets to Israel and Judah to prophesy judgment on those who mistreat poor people (Amos 4.1–2; 5.11; Zechariah 7.10).

Most mind-boggling of all, though, is that God *identifies* with the poor. From manger to cross, Jesus, God's most perfect revelation

of himself, shared the life of the poor. In fact, Jesus identified so closely with the poor of every kind that he made actively loving them the way into his kingdom. "I was hungry and you gave me food ..." (see Matthew 25.31–46). This is why Dorothy Day, like other servants of the suffering, rightly insisted that the poor "are Jesus, and what you do for them you do for him."

God calls us through his Word to imitate him in his "weakness." The poor are "the object of a *preferential love* on the part of the Church," says the *Catechism of the Catholic Church* (2448). We all must find our own way of participating in the works of charity. And if ever we are tempted to begrudge our little services or think God's preferences unfair, we might ask: In God's eyes, who is *not* poor?

Shall I feel left out because Jesus came only for the sick, the lost, the sinner, the poor? Don't I fit those descriptions? Shouldn't I rather rejoice that God has a weak spot for me?

cestral houses of the Levites by their families. 26 It was this same Aaron and Moses to whom the LORD said, "Bring the Israelites out of the land of Egypt, company by company." 27It was they who spoke to Pharaoh king of Egypt to bring the Israelites out of Egypt, the same Moses and Aaron.

Moses and Aaron Obey God's Commands

28 On the day when the LORD spoke to Moses in the land of Egypt, 29he said to him, "I am the LORD; tell Pharaoh king of Egypt all that I am speaking to you." 30But Moses said in the LORD's presence, "Since I am a poor speaker,*q* why would Pharaoh listen to me?"

7 The LORD said to Moses, "See, I have made you like God to Pharaoh, and your brother Aaron shall be your prophet. 2You shall speak all that I command you, and your brother Aaron shall tell Pharaoh to let the Israelites go out of his land. 3But I will harden Pharaoh's heart, and I will multiply my signs and wonders in the land of Egypt. 4When Pharaoh does not listen to you, I will lay my hand upon Egypt and bring my people the Israelites, company by company, out of the land of Egypt by great acts of judgment. 5The Egyptians shall know that I am the LORD, when I stretch out my hand against Egypt and bring the Israelites out from among them." 6Moses and Aaron did so; they did just as the LORD commanded them. 7Moses was eighty years old and Aaron eighty-three when they spoke to Pharaoh.

Aaron's Miraculous Rod

8 The LORD said to Moses and Aaron, 9"When Pharaoh says to you, 'Perform a wonder,' then you shall say to Aaron, 'Take your staff and throw it down before Pharaoh, and it will become a snake.'" 10So Moses and Aaron went to Pharaoh and did as the LORD had commanded; Aaron threw down his staff before Pharaoh and his officials, and it became a snake. 11Then Pharaoh summoned the wise men and the sorcerers; and they also, the magicians of Egypt, did the same by their secret arts. 12Each one threw down his staff, and they became snakes; but Aaron's staff swallowed up theirs. 13Still Pharaoh's heart was hardened, and he would not listen to them, as the LORD had said.

The First Plague: Water Turned to Blood

14 Then the LORD said to Moses, "Pharaoh's heart is hardened; he refuses to let the people go. 15Go to Pharaoh in the morning, as he is going out to the water; stand by at the river bank to meet him, and take in your hand the staff that was turned into a snake. 16Say to him, 'The LORD, the God of the Hebrews, sent me to you to say, "Let my people go, so that they may worship me in the wilderness." But until now you have not listened. 17Thus says the LORD, "By this you shall know that I am the LORD." See, with the staff that is in my hand I will strike the water that is in the Nile, and it shall be turned to blood. 18The fish in the river shall die, the river itself shall stink, and the Egyptians shall be unable to drink water from the Nile.'" 19The LORD said to Moses, "Say to Aaron, 'Take your staff and stretch out your hand over the waters of Egypt—over its rivers, its canals, and its ponds, and all its pools of water—so that they may become blood; and there shall be blood throughout the whole land of Egypt, even in vessels of wood and in vessels of stone.'"

20 Moses and Aaron did just as the LORD commanded. In the sight of Pharaoh and of his officials he lifted up the staff and struck the water in the river, and all the water in the river was turned into blood, 21and the fish in the river died. The river stank so that the Egyptians could not drink its water, and there was blood throughout the whole land of Egypt. 22But the magicians of Egypt did the same by their secret arts; so Pharaoh's heart remained hardened, and he would not listen to them, as the LORD had said. 23Pharaoh turned and went into his house, and he did not take even this to heart. 24And all the Egyptians had to dig along the Nile for water to drink, for they could not drink the water of the river.

25 Seven days passed after the LORD had struck the Nile.

The Second Plague: Frogs

8*r* Then the LORD said to Moses, "Go to Pharaoh and say to him, 'Thus says the LORD: Let my people go, so that they may worship me. 2If you refuse to let

q Heb am uncircumcised of lips; see 6.12   *r Ch 7.26 in Heb* them go, I will plague your whole country with frogs. ³The river shall swarm with frogs; they shall come up into your palace, into your bedchamber and your bed, and into the houses of your officials and of your people,ˢ and into your ovens and your kneading bowls. ⁴The frogs shall come up on you and on your people and on all your officials.' " ⁵ᵗAnd the LORD said to Moses, "Say to Aaron, 'Stretch out your hand with your staff over the rivers, the canals, and the pools, and make frogs come up on the land of Egypt.' " ⁶So Aaron stretched out his hand over the waters of Egypt; and the frogs came up and covered the land of Egypt. ⁷But the magicians did the same by their secret arts, and brought frogs up on the land of Egypt.

8 Then Pharaoh called Moses and Aaron, and said, "Pray to the LORD to take

ˢ Gk: Heb *upon your people*   ᵗ Ch 8.1 in Heb

Stubborn Heart

THURSDAY

Scripture Reading for Today:
Exodus 8.1–15

Verse for Today:
Exodus 8.15

Pharaoh was stubborn. He refused to listen to Moses and Aaron when they promised a plague of frogs. So the frogs came in thousands. They were everywhere—in ovens, on beds, underfoot, and even in the bread and water. Then, just as suddenly as they had appeared, the frogs died. From one end of the nation to the other, Egypt reeked of them.

The Israelites must have enjoyed the irony of this plague. They knew that the Egyptians worshiped the frog as a sacred idol, the god of fecundity. Now the God of Israel was rubbing their noses in their idolatry. Where was this mighty god of Egypt when the true God displayed his power?

Scripture tells us that after the frogs died, Pharaoh hardened his heart. Throughout the Bible, "hardening the heart" involves rejecting God in favor of something else. While obedience softens the heart, sin hardens it. The more the heart disregards its Creator, the less susceptible it will be to grace. With each plague, Pharaoh's heart grew harder and more distant from God.

Clearly, Pharaoh was one of history's bad guys. If we identify with anyone in the story, it's likely to be Moses or the oppressed Israelites. Yet, in common with Pharaoh, we share a heart that is capable of either great good or enormous evil. And like him, we sometimes suffer judgment. We may not wake up with frogs on our pillow, but we will inevitably sample the consequences of our sin. If we drink too much, we will one day find that alcohol has robbed us of our family and our future. If we are disloyal, we may one day face betrayal. If we have judged harshly, we will search in vain for mercy when we need it most. True, we don't always get exactly what we deserve. But sooner or later we usually do get a taste of our own medicine. Bitter though it is, this is the medicine that has the power to deliver us from evil, to heal our hearts and keep them soft.

—ANN SPANGLER

Go to page 76 for your next devotional reading.

away the frogs from me and my people, and I will let the people go to sacrifice to the LORD." [9]Moses said to Pharaoh, "Kindly tell me when I am to pray for you and for your officials and for your people, that the frogs may be removed from you and your houses and be left only in the Nile." [10]And he said, "Tomorrow." Moses said, "As you say! So that you may know that there is no one like the LORD our God, [11]the frogs shall leave you and your houses and your officials and your people; they shall be left only in the Nile." [12]Then Moses and Aaron went out from Pharaoh; and Moses cried out to the LORD concerning the frogs that he had brought upon Pharaoh.[u] [13]And the LORD did as Moses requested: the frogs died in the houses, the courtyards, and the fields. [14]And they gathered them together in heaps, and the land stank. [15]But when Pharaoh saw that there was a respite, he hardened his heart, and would not listen to them, just as the LORD had said.

The Third Plague: Gnats

16 Then the LORD said to Moses, "Say to Aaron, 'Stretch out your staff and strike the dust of the earth, so that it may become gnats throughout the whole land of Egypt.'" [17]And they did so; Aaron stretched out his hand with his staff and struck the dust of the earth, and gnats came on humans and animals alike; all the dust of the earth turned into gnats throughout the whole land of Egypt. [18]The magicians tried to produce gnats by their secret arts, but they could not. There were gnats on both humans and animals. [19]And the magicians said to Pharaoh, "This is the finger of God!" But Pharaoh's heart was hardened, and he would not listen to them, just as the LORD had said.

The Fourth Plague: Flies

20 Then the LORD said to Moses, "Rise early in the morning and present yourself before Pharaoh, as he goes out to the water, and say to him, 'Thus says the LORD: Let my people go, so that they may worship me. [21]For if you will not let my people go, I will send swarms of flies on you, your officials, and your people, and into your houses; and the houses of the Egyptians shall be filled with swarms of flies; so also the land where they live. [22]But on that day I will set apart the land of Goshen, where my people live, so that no swarms of flies shall be there, that you

may know that I the LORD am in this land. [23]Thus I will make a distinction[v] between my people and your people. This sign shall appear tomorrow.'" [24]The LORD did so, and great swarms of flies came into the house of Pharaoh and into his officials' houses; in all of Egypt the land was ruined because of the flies.

25 Then Pharaoh summoned Moses and Aaron, and said, "Go, sacrifice to your God within the land." [26]But Moses said, "It would not be right to do so; for the sacrifices that we offer to the LORD our God are offensive to the Egyptians. If we offer in the sight of the Egyptians sacrifices that are offensive to them, will they not stone us? [27]We must go a three days' journey into the wilderness and sacrifice to the LORD our God as he commands us." [28]So Pharaoh said, "I will let you go to sacrifice to the LORD your God in the wilderness, provided you do not go very far away. Pray for me." [29]Then Moses said, "As soon as I leave you, I will pray to the LORD that the swarms of flies may depart tomorrow from Pharaoh, from his officials, and from his people; only do not let Pharaoh again deal falsely by not letting the people go to sacrifice to the LORD."

30 So Moses went out from Pharaoh and prayed to the LORD. [31]And the LORD did as Moses asked: he removed the swarms of flies from Pharaoh, from his officials, and from his people; not one remained. [32]But Pharaoh hardened his heart this time also, and would not let the people go.

The Fifth Plague: Livestock Diseased

9 Then the LORD said to Moses, "Go to Pharaoh, and say to him, 'Thus says the LORD, the God of the Hebrews: Let my people go, so that they may worship me. [2]For if you refuse to let them go and still hold them, [3]the hand of the LORD will strike with a deadly pestilence your livestock in the field: the horses, the donkeys, the camels, the herds, and the flocks. [4]But the LORD will make a distinction between the livestock of Israel and the livestock of Egypt, so that nothing shall die of all that belongs to the Israelites.'" [5]The LORD set a time, saying, "Tomorrow the LORD will do this thing in the land." [6]And on the next day the LORD did so; all the livestock of the

u Or frogs, as he had agreed with Pharaoh   v Gk Vg: Heb will set redemption

Egyptians died, but of the livestock of the Israelites not one died. 7Pharaoh inquired and found that not one of the livestock of the Israelites was dead. But the heart of Pharaoh was hardened, and he would not let the people go.

The Sixth Plague: Boils

8 Then the Lord said to Moses and Aaron, "Take handfuls of soot from the kiln, and let Moses throw it in the air in the sight of Pharaoh. 9It shall become fine dust all over the land of Egypt, and shall cause festering boils on humans and animals throughout the whole land of Egypt." 10So they took soot from the kiln, and stood before Pharaoh, and Moses threw it in the air, and it caused festering boils on humans and animals. 11The magicians could not stand before Moses because of the boils, for the boils afflicted the magicians as well as all the Egyptians. 12But the Lord hardened the heart of Pharaoh, and he would not listen to them, just as the Lord had spoken to Moses.

The Seventh Plague: Thunder and Hail

13 Then the Lord said to Moses, "Rise up early in the morning and present yourself before Pharaoh, and say to him, 'Thus says the Lord, the God of the Hebrews: Let my people go, so that they may worship me. 14For this time I will send all my plagues upon you yourself, and upon your officials, and upon your people, so that you may know that there is no one like me in all the earth. 15For by now I could have stretched out my hand and struck you and your people with pestilence, and you would have been cut off from the earth. 16But this is why I have let you live: to show you my power, and to make my name resound through all the earth. 17You are still exalting yourself against my people, and will not let them go. 18Tomorrow at this time I will cause the heaviest hail to fall that has ever fallen in Egypt from the day it was founded until now. 19Send, therefore, and have your livestock and everything that you have in the open field brought to a secure place; every human or animal that is in the open field and is not brought under shelter will die when the hail comes down upon them.'" 20Those officials of Pharaoh who feared the word of the Lord hurried their slaves and livestock off to a secure place. 21Those who did not regard the word of

the Lord left their slaves and livestock in the open field.

22 The Lord said to Moses, "Stretch out your hand toward heaven so that hail may fall on the whole land of Egypt, on humans and animals and all the plants of the field in the land of Egypt." 23Then Moses stretched out his staff toward heaven, and the Lord sent thunder and hail, and fire came down on the earth. And the Lord rained hail on the land of Egypt; 24there was hail with fire flashing continually in the midst of it, such heavy hail as had never fallen in all the land of Egypt since it became a nation. 25The hail struck down everything that was in the open field throughout all the land of Egypt, both human and animal; the hail also struck down all the plants of the field, and shattered every tree in the field. 26Only in the land of Goshen, where the Israelites were, there was no hail.

27 Then Pharaoh summoned Moses and Aaron, and said to them, "This time I have sinned; the Lord is in the right, and I and my people are in the wrong. 28Pray to the Lord! Enough of God's thunder and hail! I will let you go; you need stay no longer." 29Moses said to him, "As soon as I have gone out of the city, I will stretch out my hands to the Lord; the thunder will cease, and there will be no more hail, so that you may know that the earth is the Lord's. 30But as for you and your officials, I know that you do not yet fear the Lord God." 31(Now the flax and the barley were ruined, for the barley was in the ear and the flax was in bud. 32But the wheat and the spelt were not ruined, for they are late in coming up.) 33So Moses left Pharaoh, went out of the city, and stretched out his hands to the Lord; then the thunder and the hail ceased, and the rain no longer poured down on the earth. 34But when Pharaoh saw that the rain and the hail and the thunder had ceased, he sinned once more and hardened his heart, he and his officials. 35So the heart of Pharaoh was hardened, and he would not let the Israelites go, just as the Lord had spoken through Moses.

The Eighth Plague: Locusts

10 Then the Lord said to Moses, "Go to Pharaoh; for I have hardened his heart and the heart of his officials, in order that I may show these signs of mine among them, 2and that you may tell your

children and grandchildren how I have made fools of the Egyptians and what signs I have done among them—so that you may know that I am the LORD."

3 So Moses and Aaron went to Pharaoh, and said to him, "Thus says the LORD, the God of the Hebrews, 'How long will you refuse to humble yourself before me? Let my people go, so that they may worship me. ⁴For if you refuse to let my people go, tomorrow I will bring locusts into your country. ⁵They shall cover the surface of the land, so that no one will be able to see the land. They shall devour the last remnant left you after the hail, and they shall devour every tree of yours that grows in the field. ⁶They shall fill your houses, and the houses of all your officials and of all the Egyptians—something that neither your parents nor your grandparents have seen, from the day they came on earth to this day.' " Then he turned and went out from Pharaoh.

7 Pharaoh's officials said to him, "How long shall this fellow be a snare to us? Let the people go, so that they may worship the LORD their God; do you not yet understand that Egypt is ruined?" ⁸So Moses and Aaron were brought back to Pharaoh, and he said to them, "Go, worship the LORD your God! But which ones are to go?" ⁹Moses said, "We will go with our young and our old; we will go with our sons and daughters and with our flocks and herds, because we have the LORD's festival to celebrate." ¹⁰He said to them, "The LORD indeed will be with you, if ever I let your little ones go with you! Plainly, you have some evil purpose in mind. ¹¹No, never! Your men may go and worship the LORD, for that is what you are asking." And they were driven out from Pharaoh's presence.

12 Then the LORD said to Moses, "Stretch out your hand over the land of Egypt, so that the locusts may come upon it and eat every plant in the land, all that the hail has left." ¹³So Moses stretched out his staff over the land of Egypt, and the LORD brought an east wind upon the land all that day and all that night; when morning came, the east wind had brought the locusts. ¹⁴The locusts came upon all the land of Egypt and settled on the whole country of Egypt, such a dense swarm of locusts as had never been before, nor ever shall be again. ¹⁵They covered the surface of the whole land, so that the land was black; and they ate all the plants in the land and all the fruit of the trees that the hail had left; nothing green was left, no tree, no plant in the field, in all the land of Egypt. ¹⁶Pharaoh hurriedly summoned Moses and Aaron and said, "I have sinned against the LORD your God, and against you. ¹⁷Do forgive my sin just this once, and pray to the LORD your God that at the least he remove this deadly thing from me." ¹⁸So he went out from Pharaoh and prayed to the LORD. ¹⁹The LORD changed the wind into a very strong west wind, which lifted the locusts and drove them into the Red Sea;*ʷ* not a single locust was left in all the country of Egypt. ²⁰But the LORD hardened Pharaoh's heart, and he would not let the Israelites go.

The Ninth Plague: Darkness

21 Then the LORD said to Moses, "Stretch out your hand toward heaven so that there may be darkness over the land of Egypt, a darkness that can be felt." ²²So Moses stretched out his hand toward heaven, and there was dense darkness in all the land of Egypt for three days. ²³People could not see one another, and for three days they could not move from where they were; but all the Israelites had light where they lived. ²⁴Then Pharaoh summoned Moses, and said, "Go, worship the LORD. Only your flocks and your herds shall remain behind. Even your children may go with you." ²⁵But Moses said, "You must also let us have sacrifices and burnt offerings to sacrifice to the LORD our God. ²⁶Our livestock also must go with us; not a hoof shall be left behind, for we must choose some of them for the worship of the LORD our God, and we will not know what to use to worship the LORD until we arrive there." ²⁷But the LORD hardened Pharaoh's heart, and he was unwilling to let them go. ²⁸Then Pharaoh said to him, "Get away from me! Take care that you do not see my face again, for on the day you see my face you shall die." ²⁹Moses said, "Just as you say! I will never see your face again."

Warning of the Final Plague

11 The LORD said to Moses, "I will bring one more plague upon Pharaoh and upon Egypt; afterwards he will let you go from here; indeed, when he

ʷ Or Sea of Reeds

lets you go, he will drive you away. ²Tell the people that every man is to ask his neighbor and every woman is to ask her neighbor for objects of silver and gold." ³The LORD gave the people favor in the sight of the Egyptians. Moreover, Moses himself was a man of great importance in the land of Egypt, in the sight of Pharaoh's officials and in the sight of the people.

4 Moses said, "Thus says the LORD: About midnight I will go out through Egypt. ⁵Every firstborn in the land of Egypt shall die, from the firstborn of Pharaoh who sits on his throne to the firstborn of the female slave who is behind the handmill, and all the firstborn of the livestock. ⁶Then there will be a loud cry throughout the whole land of Egypt, such as has never been or will ever be again. ⁷But not a dog shall growl at any of the Israelites—not at people, not at animals—so that you may know that the LORD makes a distinction between Egypt and Israel. ⁸Then all these officials of yours shall come down to me, and bow low to me, saying, 'Leave us, you and all the people who follow you.' After that I will leave." And in hot anger he left Pharaoh.

9 The LORD said to Moses, "Pharaoh will not listen to you, in order that my wonders may be multiplied in the land of Egypt." ¹⁰Moses and Aaron performed all these wonders before Pharaoh; but the LORD hardened Pharaoh's heart, and he did not let the people of Israel go out of his land.

The First Passover Instituted

12 The LORD said to Moses and Aaron in the land of Egypt: ²This month shall mark for you the beginning of months; it shall be the first month of the year for you. ³Tell the whole congregation of Israel that on the tenth of this month they are to take a lamb for each family, a lamb for each household. ⁴If a household is too small for a whole lamb, it shall join its closest neighbor in obtaining one; the lamb shall be divided in proportion to the number of people who eat of it. ⁵Your lamb shall be without blemish, a year-old male; you may take it from the sheep or from the goats. ⁶You shall keep it until the fourteenth day of this month; then the whole assembled congregation of Israel shall slaughter it at twilight. ⁷They shall take some of the blood and put it on the two doorposts and the lintel of the houses in which they eat it. ⁸They shall eat the lamb that same night; they shall eat it roasted over the fire with unleavened bread and bitter herbs. ⁹Do not eat any of it raw or boiled in water, but roasted over the fire, with its head, legs, and inner organs. ¹⁰You shall let none of it remain until the morning; anything that remains until the morning you shall burn. ¹¹This is how you shall eat it: your loins girded, your sandals on your feet, and your staff in your hand; and you shall eat it hurriedly. It is the passover of the LORD. ¹²For I will pass through the land of Egypt that night, and I will strike down every firstborn in the land of Egypt, both human beings and animals; on all the gods of Egypt I will execute judgments: I am the LORD. ¹³The blood shall be a sign for you on the houses where you live: when I see the blood, I will pass over you, and no plague shall destroy you when I strike the land of Egypt.

14 This day shall be a day of remembrance for you. You shall celebrate it as a festival to the LORD; throughout your generations you shall observe it as a perpetual ordinance. ¹⁵Seven days you shall eat unleavened bread; on the first day you shall remove leaven from your houses, for whoever eats leavened bread from the first day until the seventh day shall be cut off from Israel. ¹⁶On the first day you shall hold a solemn assembly, and on the seventh day a solemn assembly; no work shall be done on those days; only what everyone must eat, that alone may be prepared by you. ¹⁷You shall observe the festival of unleavened bread, for on this very day I brought your companies out of the land of Egypt: you shall observe this day throughout your generations as a perpetual ordinance. ¹⁸In the first month, from the evening of the fourteenth day until the evening of the twenty-first day, you shall eat unleavened bread. ¹⁹For seven days no leaven shall be found in your houses; for whoever eats what is leavened shall be cut off from the congregation of Israel, whether an alien or a native of the land. ²⁰You shall eat nothing leavened; in all your settlements you shall eat unleavened bread.

21 Then Moses called all the elders of Israel and said to them, "Go, select lambs for your families, and slaughter the passover lamb. ²²Take a bunch of hyssop, dip it in the blood that is in the basin, and

touch the lintel and the two doorposts with the blood in the basin. None of you shall go outside the door of your house until morning. 23For the LORD will pass through to strike down the Egyptians; when he sees the blood on the lintel and on the two doorposts, the LORD will pass over that door and will not allow the destroyer to enter your houses to strike you down. 24You shall observe this rite as a perpetual ordinance for you and your children. 25When you come to the land that the LORD will give you, as he has promised, you shall keep this observance. 26And when your children ask you, 'What do you mean by this observance?' 27you shall say, 'It is the passover sacrifice to the LORD, for he passed over the houses of the Israelites in Egypt, when he struck down the Egyptians but spared our houses.' " And the people bowed down and worshiped.

28 The Israelites went and did just as the LORD had commanded Moses and Aaron.

The Tenth Plague: Death of the Firstborn

29 At midnight the LORD struck down all the firstborn in the land of Egypt, from the firstborn of Pharaoh who sat on his throne to the firstborn of the prisoner who was in the dungeon, and all the firstborn of the livestock. 30Pharaoh arose in the night, he and all his officials and all the Egyptians; and there was a loud cry in Egypt, for there was not a house without someone dead. 31Then he summoned Moses and Aaron in the night, and said, "Rise up, go away from my people, both you and the Israelites! Go, worship the LORD, as you said. 32Take your flocks and your herds, as you said, and be gone. And bring a blessing on me too!"

The Exodus: From Rameses to Succoth

33 The Egyptians urged the people to hasten their departure from the land, for they said, "We shall all be dead." 34So the people took their dough before it was leavened, with their kneading bowls wrapped up in their cloaks on their shoulders. 35The Israelites had done as Moses told them; they had asked the Egyptians for jewelry of silver and gold, and for clothing, 36and the LORD had given the people favor in the sight of the Egyptians, so that they let them have what they asked. And so they plundered the Egyptians.

37 The Israelites journeyed from Rameses to Succoth, about six hundred thousand men on foot, besides children. 38A mixed crowd also went up with them, and livestock in great numbers, both flocks and herds. 39They baked unleavened cakes of the dough that they had brought out of Egypt; it was not leavened, because they were driven out of Egypt and could not wait, nor had they prepared any provisions for themselves.

40 The time that the Israelites had lived in Egypt was four hundred thirty years. 41At the end of four hundred thirty years, on that very day, all the companies of the LORD went out from the land of Egypt. 42That was for the LORD a night of vigil, to bring them out of the land of Egypt. That same night is a vigil to be kept for the LORD by all the Israelites throughout their generations.

Directions for the Passover

43 The LORD said to Moses and Aaron: This is the ordinance for the passover: no foreigner shall eat of it, 44but any slave who has been purchased may eat of it after he has been circumcised; 45no bound or hired servant may eat of it. 46It shall be eaten in one house; you shall not take any of the animal outside the house, and you shall not break any of its bones. 47The whole congregation of Israel shall celebrate it. 48If an alien who resides with you wants to celebrate the passover to the LORD, all his males shall be circumcised; then he may draw near to celebrate it; he shall be regarded as a native of the land. But no uncircumcised person shall eat of it; 49there shall be one law for the native and for the alien who resides among you.

50 All the Israelites did just as the LORD had commanded Moses and Aaron. 51That very day the LORD brought the Israelites out of the land of Egypt, company by company.

13 The LORD said to Moses: 2Consecrate to me all the firstborn; whatever is the first to open the womb among the Israelites, of human beings and animals, is mine.

The Festival of Unleavened Bread

3 Moses said to the people, "Remember this day on which you came out of Egypt, out of the house of slavery, because

the LORD brought you out from there by strength of hand; no leavened bread shall be eaten. [4]Today, in the month of Abib, you are going out. [5]When the LORD brings you into the land of the Canaanites, the Hittites, the Amorites, the Hivites, and the Jebusites, which he swore to your ancestors to give you, a land flowing with milk and honey, you shall keep this observance in this month. [6]Seven days you shall eat unleavened bread, and on the seventh day there shall be a festival to the LORD. [7]Unleavened bread shall be eaten for seven days; no leavened bread shall be seen in your possession, and no leaven shall be seen among you in all your territory. [8]You shall tell your child on that day, 'It is because of what the LORD did for me when I came out of Egypt.' [9]It shall serve for you as a sign on your hand and as a reminder

Throw Off the Darkness

Scripture Reading
for Today:
Exodus 13.3–16

Verse for Today:
Exodus 13.3

"Remember this day on which you came out of Egypt, out of the house of slavery, because the LORD brought you out from there by strength of hand; no leavened bread shall be eaten" (Exodus 13.3). What does this mean?

You who wish to be imitators of my Son, turn your eyes from death to life and keep in mind the salvation of that Day which is my Son, who trampled death and gave life, so that you went forth from the wretched exile of perdition; you threw off the thick darkness of infidelity and tore yourselves away from the house of the Devil, to whom Adam's transgression had given you. Turn your eyes from earthly to heavenly actions, for by divine power I the Lord have led you out of evil; I who rule over all with such strength that no obstacle can stand against my might, but I sharply penetrate all things. So through my Son I have snatched you from the place where you shamefully lay in your wickedness, serving death by your infidelity instead of doing good works.

And now that you are freed in my Only-Begotten from that oppression, go from strength to strength. Do not follow the arts of the devil or the other fictions people devise for themselves, corrupted by philosophers, pagans and heretics; but imitate my Son as a mirror of faith, who delivered you from the prison of hell when he gave himself for you to the suffering of the cross. And, that you may more carefully follow in his steps, strengthen your hearts with the celestial bread, and so with faithful devotion receive his body. For he came from heaven and was born of the sweet and pure virgin, and, by suffering for you on the cross, gave you his very self; so that now you may receive the sweet and pure bread, which is his body, consecrated on the altar by divine invocation, without any bitterness but with sincere affection, and thus escape from humanity's inner hunger and attain to the banquet of eternal beatitude.

—*SAINT HILDEGARD OF BINGEN*

Go to page 80 for your next devotional reading.

on your forehead, so that the teaching of the LORD may be on your lips; for with a strong hand the LORD brought you out of Egypt. 10You shall keep this ordinance at its proper time from year to year.

The Consecration of the Firstborn

11 "When the LORD has brought you into the land of the Canaanites, as he swore to you and your ancestors, and has given it to you, 12you shall set apart to the LORD all that first opens the womb. All the firstborn of your livestock that are males shall be the LORD's. 13But every firstborn donkey you shall redeem with a sheep; if you do not redeem it, you must break its neck. Every firstborn male among your children you shall redeem. 14When in the future your child asks you, 'What does this mean?' you shall answer, 'By strength of hand the LORD brought us out of Egypt, from the house of slavery. 15When Pharaoh stubbornly refused to let us go, the LORD killed all the firstborn in the land of Egypt, from human firstborn to the first-born of animals. Therefore I sacrifice to the LORD every male that first opens the womb, but every firstborn of my sons I redeem.' 16It shall serve as a sign on your hand and as an emblem*x* on your forehead that by strength of hand the LORD brought us out of Egypt."

The Pillars of Cloud and Fire

17 When Pharaoh let the people go, God did not lead them by way of the land of the Philistines, although that was nearer; for God thought, "If the people face war, they may change their minds and return to Egypt." 18So God led the people by the roundabout way of the wilderness toward the Red Sea.*y* The Israelites went up out of the land of Egypt prepared for battle. 19And Moses took with him the bones of Joseph who had required a solemn oath of the Israelites, saying, "God will surely take notice of you, and then you must carry my bones with you from here." 20They set out from Succoth, and camped at Etham, on the edge of the wilderness. 21The LORD went in front of them in a pillar of cloud by day, to lead them along the way, and in a pillar of fire by night, to give them light, so that they might travel by day and by night. 22Neither the pillar of cloud by day nor the pillar of fire by night left its place in front of the people.

Crossing the Red Sea

14 Then the LORD said to Moses: 2Tell the Israelites to turn back and camp in front of Pi-hahiroth, between Migdol and the sea, in front of Baal-zephon; you shall camp opposite it, by the sea. 3Pharaoh will say of the Israelites, "They are wandering aimlessly in the land; the wilderness has closed in on them." 4I will harden Pharaoh's heart, and he will pursue them, so that I will gain glory for myself over Pharaoh and all his army; and the Egyptians shall know that I am the LORD. And they did so.

5 When the king of Egypt was told that the people had fled, the minds of Pharaoh and his officials were changed toward the people, and they said, "What have we done, letting Israel leave our service?" 6So he had his chariot made ready, and took his army with him; 7he took six hundred picked chariots and all the other chariots of Egypt with officers over all of them. 8The LORD hardened the heart of Pharaoh king of Egypt and he pursued the Israelites, who were going out boldly. 9The Egyptians pursued them, all Pharaoh's horses and chariots, his chariot drivers and his army; they overtook them camped by the sea, by Pi-hahiroth, in front of Baal-zephon.

10 As Pharaoh drew near, the Israelites looked back, and there were the Egyptians advancing on them. In great fear the Israelites cried out to the LORD. 11They said to Moses, "Was it because there were no graves in Egypt that you have taken us away to die in the wilderness? What have you done to us, bringing us out of Egypt? 12Is this not the very thing we told you in Egypt, 'Let us alone and let us serve the Egyptians'? For it would have been better for us to serve the Egyptians than to die in the wilderness." 13But Moses said to the people, "Do not be afraid, stand firm, and see the deliverance that the LORD will accomplish for you today; for the Egyptians whom you see today you shall never see again. 14The LORD will fight for you, and you have only to keep still."

15 Then the LORD said to Moses, "Why do you cry out to me? Tell the Israelites to go forward. 16But you lift up your staff, and stretch out your hand over the sea

---

x Or *as a frontlet*; meaning of Heb uncertain
y Or *Sea of Reeds*

and divide it, that the Israelites may go into the sea on dry ground. [17]Then I will harden the hearts of the Egyptians so that they will go in after them; and so I will gain glory for myself over Pharaoh and all his army, his chariots, and his chariot drivers. [18]And the Egyptians shall know that I am the Lord, when I have gained glory for myself over Pharaoh, his chariots, and his chariot drivers."

19 The angel of God who was going before the Israelite army moved and went behind them; and the pillar of cloud moved from in front of them and took its place behind them. [20]It came between the army of Egypt and the army of Israel. And so the cloud was there with the darkness, and it lit up the night; one did not come near the other all night.

21 Then Moses stretched out his hand over the sea. The Lord drove the sea back by a strong east wind all night, and turned the sea into dry land; and the waters were divided. [22]The Israelites went into the sea on dry ground, the waters forming a wall for them on their right and on their left. [23]The Egyptians pursued, and went into the sea after them, all of Pharaoh's horses, chariots, and chariot drivers. [24]At the morning watch the Lord in the pillar of fire and cloud looked down upon the Egyptian army, and threw the Egyptian army into panic. [25]He clogged[z] their chariot wheels so that they turned with difficulty. The Egyptians said, "Let us flee from the Israelites, for the Lord is fighting for them against Egypt."

The Pursuers Drowned

26 Then the Lord said to Moses, "Stretch out your hand over the sea, so that the water may come back upon the Egyptians, upon their chariots and chariot drivers." [27]So Moses stretched out his hand over the sea, and at dawn the sea returned to its normal depth. As the Egyptians fled before it, the Lord tossed the Egyptians into the sea. [28]The waters returned and covered the chariots and the chariot drivers, the entire army of Pharaoh that had followed them into the sea; not one of them remained. [29]But the Israelites walked on dry ground through the sea, the waters forming a wall for them on their right and on their left.

30 Thus the Lord saved Israel that day from the Egyptians; and Israel saw the Egyptians dead on the seashore. [31]Israel saw the great work that the Lord did against the Egyptians. So the people feared the Lord and believed in the Lord and in his servant Moses.

The Song of Moses

15 Then Moses and the Israelites sang this song to the Lord:

"I will sing to the Lord, for he has
    triumphed gloriously;
  horse and rider he has thrown
    into the sea.
[2] The Lord is my strength and my
    might,[a]
  and he has become my salvation;
this is my God, and I will praise
    him,
  my father's God, and I will exalt
    him.
[3] The Lord is a warrior;
  the Lord is his name.

[4] "Pharaoh's chariots and his army he
    cast into the sea;
  his picked officers were sunk in
    the Red Sea.[b]
[5] The floods covered them;
  they went down into the depths
    like a stone.
[6] Your right hand, O Lord, glorious in
    power—
  your right hand, O Lord, shattered
    the enemy.
[7] In the greatness of your majesty you
    overthrew your adversaries;
  you sent out your fury, it
    consumed them like stubble.
[8] At the blast of your nostrils the
    waters piled up,
  the floods stood up in a heap;
  the deeps congealed in the heart
    of the sea.
[9] The enemy said, 'I will pursue, I will
    overtake,
  I will divide the spoil, my desire
    shall have its fill of them.
  I will draw my sword, my hand
    shall destroy them.'
[10] You blew with your wind, the sea
    covered them;
  they sank like lead in the mighty
    waters.

[11] "Who is like you, O Lord, among
    the gods?

---

z Sam Gk Syr: MT *removed*   a Or *song*   b Or *Sea of Reeds*

Who is like you, majestic in
　　holiness,
　　awesome in splendor, doing
　　wonders?
12 You stretched out your right hand,
　　the earth swallowed them.

13 "In your steadfast love you led the
　　people whom you redeemed;
　　you guided them by your strength
　　　to your holy abode.
14 The peoples heard, they trembled;
　　pangs seized the inhabitants of
　　　Philistia.
15 Then the chiefs of Edom were
　　　dismayed;
　　trembling seized the leaders of
　　　Moab;
　　all the inhabitants of Canaan
　　　melted away.
16 Terror and dread fell upon them;
　　by the might of your arm, they
　　　became still as a stone
　　until your people, O LORD, passed
　　　by,
　　until the people whom you
　　　acquired passed by.
17 You brought them in and planted
　　them on the mountain of
　　　your own possession,
　　the place, O LORD, that you made
　　　your abode,
　　the sanctuary, O LORD, that your
　　　hands have established.
18 The LORD will reign forever and ever."

19 When the horses of Pharaoh with
his chariots and his chariot drivers went
into the sea, the LORD brought back the
waters of the sea upon them; but the Israelites walked through the sea on dry
ground.

The Song of Miriam

20 Then the prophet Miriam, Aaron's
sister, took a tambourine in her hand; and
all the women went out after her with
tambourines and with dancing. 21And
Miriam sang to them:
　　"Sing to the LORD, for he has
　　　triumphed gloriously;
　　horse and rider he has thrown into
　　　the sea."

Bitter Water Made Sweet

22 Then Moses ordered Israel to set out
from the Red Sea,*c* and they went into
the wilderness of Shur. They went three
days in the wilderness and found no wa-

ter. 23When they came to Marah, they
could not drink the water of Marah because it was bitter. That is why it was
called Marah.*d* 24And the people complained against Moses, saying, "What
shall we drink?" 25He cried out to the LORD;
and the LORD showed him a piece of
wood;*e* he threw it into the water, and
the water became sweet.

There the LORD *f* made for them a statute and an ordinance and there he put
them to the test. 26He said, "If you will
listen carefully to the voice of the LORD
your God, and do what is right in his
sight, and give heed to his commandments and keep all his statutes, I will not
bring upon you any of the diseases that I
brought upon the Egyptians; for I am the
LORD who heals you."

27 Then they came to Elim, where
there were twelve springs of water and seventy palm trees; and they camped there by
the water.

Bread from Heaven

16 The whole congregation of the Israelites set out from Elim; and Israel came to the wilderness of Sin, which
is between Elim and Sinai, on the fifteenth day of the second month after they
had departed from the land of Egypt. 2The
whole congregation of the Israelites complained against Moses and Aaron in the
wilderness. 3The Israelites said to them,
"If only we had died by the hand of the
LORD in the land of Egypt, when we sat by
the fleshpots and ate our fill of bread; for
you have brought us out into this wilderness to kill this whole assembly with hunger."

4 Then the LORD said to Moses, "I am
going to rain bread from heaven for you,
and each day the people shall go out and
gather enough for that day. In that way I
will test them, whether they will follow
my instruction or not. 5On the sixth day,
when they prepare what they bring in, it
will be twice as much as they gather on
other days." 6So Moses and Aaron said to
all the Israelites, "In the evening you shall
know that it was the LORD who brought
you out of the land of Egypt, 7and in the
morning you shall see the glory of the
LORD, because he has heard your complaining against the LORD. For what are we,

c Or *Sea of Reeds*　　*d* That is *Bitterness*　　*e* Or *a
tree*　　*f* Heb *he*

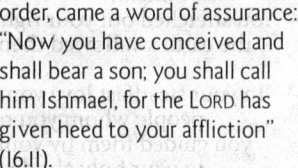

Hagar

*Her Name Is Egyptian and May
Mean "Fugitive" or "Immigrant".*

Her Character: *A foreigner and slave, she let
pride overtake her when
she became Abraham's
wife. A woman with few
resources, she suffered
harshly for her mistake.
She obeyed God's voice as
soon as she heard it and
was given a promise that
her son would father a
great nation.*

Her Sorrow: *That she
was taken from her
homeland to become a
slave in a foreign land.*

Her Joy: *To know that
God saw her suffering
and heard her cry and
that he helped her when
she needed him most.*

Read Genesis 21.8–21
An Egyptian slave and Sarah's bitter rival, Hagar still had one thing going for her that her mistress never enjoyed—a personal revelation of God, who lovingly intervened on her behalf, not once but twice. It happened when she was alone and afraid, without a shekel to her name—but that's getting ahead of the story.

You may remember that Abraham, whom we honor as the father of faith, showed little evidence of that faith when he and Sarah first entered Egypt to escape a famine in Canaan. Certain the Egyptians would kill him once they caught sight of his beautiful wife, he advised her to pose as his sister. (She actually was his half-sister.) Soon enough, Pharaoh added Sarah to his harem and rewarded Abraham with an abundance of livestock and servants. Possibly, Hagar was part of the booty Abraham and Sarah took with them when they left Egypt—a gift that later backfired.

Hagar was perhaps an innocent victim in this scheme, a slave with little power to resist. But as soon as she discovered her pregnancy, Hagar began lording it over her mistress.

Sarah retaliated by making life so difficult that Hagar fled into the desert—a desperate move for a young woman bearing a child so far from home. She hadn't gotten far before she heard a voice calling, "Hagar, slave-girl of Sarai . . . Return to your mistress, and submit to her" (16.8–9). But then, as if to sweeten the order, came a word of assurance: "Now you have conceived and shall bear a son; you shall call him Ishmael, for the LORD has given heed to your affliction" (16.11).

Remarkably, Hagar didn't argue but turned right around and retraced her steps. God's word penetrated the wilderness of her heart, like a spring nourishing a desert oasis. Her bondage, her bitterness, her anxiety—God had seen every bit of it. He knew about the child in her womb, naming him, *Ishmael*, meaning "God hears." In the future, every time Hagar would hold her son close, watch him play, or worry about his future, she would remember that God was near, listening for the child's cry.

Some 16 years later, Hagar found herself once again in the wilderness, this time by force not choice. In a crescendo of bitterness, Sarah had expelled Hagar and Ishmael from their home. Nearing death, Hagar placed her son under a bush and withdrew, unable to witness his agony.

Her weeping was soon broken by an angel's voice, "Do not be afraid; for God has heard the voice of the boy where he is" (21.17). With that, the angel of the Lord opened Hagar's eyes so that she discovered a well of water nearby that would save her son's life.

When we last read of Hagar, she is living in the desert in the Sinai Peninsula and is busy securing a wife, and therefore a future, for Ishmael. God had made a way in the wilderness for a single woman and her son, without friends, family, or resources to help her. God had seen; he had heard; he had indeed been faithful.

Praying With Hagar

"What troubles you, Hagar? Do not be afraid; for God has heard the voice of the boy where he is. Come, lift up the boy and hold him fast with your hand, for I will make a great nation of him." —Genesis 21:17–18

Praise God: Because he is a loving father who listens to the cries of his children. Nothing that happens to us can ever escape his notice.

Offer Thanks: That the Lord pursues the weak and the helpless, to show them his mercy and his plan of blessing for their lives.

Confess: Any pride, selfishness, or other sin that may have contributed to your present circumstances.

Ask God: To open your eyes to the way he is protecting and providing for you and your children. Ask him to help you live each day, not as a slave to the law but as a child of grace.

Lift Your Heart

Prepare a Middle Eastern feast with olives, figs, pita bread, nuts, *hummus, tabbouleh,* and your favorite drink. Invite a couple of close friends to share it with you and then pray a special grace, thanking God for providing so richly for you even when you felt you were living through a wilderness season in your life. Share stories with each other about how God has provided even when you weren't sure he was listening to your prayers.

Lord, sometimes I feel abandoned, as though no one understands or cares about me. Please show me that you really are near and that you see and hear everything that happens. Refresh me with your presence even when I am walking through a wilderness experience. And help me, in turn, to comfort others when they feel hopeless and alone.

Go to page 97 for your next devotional reading.

that you complain against us?" [8]And Moses said, "When the LORD gives you meat to eat in the evening and your fill of bread in the morning, because the LORD has heard the complaining that you utter against him—what are we? Your complaining is not against us but against the LORD."

9 Then Moses said to Aaron, "Say to the whole congregation of the Israelites, 'Draw near to the LORD, for he has heard your complaining.' " [10]And as Aaron spoke to the whole congregation of the Israelites, they looked toward the wilderness, and the glory of the LORD appeared in the cloud. [11]The LORD spoke to Moses and said, [12]"I have heard the complaining of the Israelites; say to them, 'At twilight you shall eat meat, and in the morning you shall have your fill of bread; then you shall know that I am the LORD your God.' "

13 In the evening quails came up and covered the camp; and in the morning there was a layer of dew around the camp. [14]When the layer of dew lifted, there on the surface of the wilderness was a fine flaky substance, as fine as frost on the ground. [15]When the Israelites saw it, they said to one another, "What is it?"[g] For they did not know what it was. Moses said to them, "It is the bread that the LORD has given you to eat. [16]This is what the LORD has commanded: 'Gather as much of it as each of you needs, an omer to a person according to the number of persons, all providing for those in their own tents.' " [17]The Israelites did so, some gathering more, some less. [18]But when they measured it with an omer, those who gathered much had nothing over, and those who gathered little had no shortage; they gathered as much as each of them needed. [19]And Moses said to them, "Let no one leave any of it over until morning." [20]But they did not listen to Moses; some left part of it until morning, and it bred worms and became foul. And Moses was angry with them. [21]Morning by morning they gathered it, as much as each needed; but when the sun grew hot, it melted.

22 On the sixth day they gathered twice as much food, two omers apiece. When all the leaders of the congregation came and told Moses, [23]he said to them, "This is what the LORD has commanded: 'Tomorrow is a day of solemn rest, a holy sabbath to the LORD; bake what you want to bake and boil what you want to boil,

and all that is left over put aside to be kept until morning.' " [24]So they put it aside until morning, as Moses commanded them; and it did not become foul, and there were no worms in it. [25]Moses said, "Eat it today, for today is a sabbath to the LORD; today you will not find it in the field. [26]Six days you shall gather it; but on the seventh day, which is a sabbath, there will be none."

27 On the seventh day some of the people went out to gather, and they found none. [28]The LORD said to Moses, "How long will you refuse to keep my commandments and instructions? [29]See! The LORD has given you the sabbath, therefore on the sixth day he gives you food for two days; each of you stay where you are; do not leave your place on the seventh day." [30]So the people rested on the seventh day.

31 The house of Israel called it manna; it was like coriander seed, white, and the taste of it was like wafers made with honey. [32]Moses said, "This is what the LORD has commanded: 'Let an omer of it be kept throughout your generations, in order that they may see the food with which I fed you in the wilderness, when I brought you out of the land of Egypt.' " [33]And Moses said to Aaron, "Take a jar, and put an omer of manna in it, and place it before the LORD, to be kept throughout your generations." [34]As the LORD commanded Moses, so Aaron placed it before the covenant,[h] for safekeeping. [35]The Israelites ate manna forty years, until they came to a habitable land; they ate manna, until they came to the border of the land of Canaan. [36]An omer is a tenth of an ephah.

Water from the Rock

17 From the wilderness of Sin the whole congregation of the Israelites journeyed by stages, as the LORD commanded. They camped at Rephidim, but there was no water for the people to drink. [2]The people quarreled with Moses, and said, "Give us water to drink." Moses said to them, "Why do you quarrel with me? Why do you test the LORD?" [3]But the people thirsted there for water; and the people complained against Moses and said, "Why did you bring us out of Egypt, to kill us and our children and livestock with

---

[g] Or *"It is manna"* (Heb *man hu*, see verse 31)
[h] Or *treaty* or *testimony*; Heb *eduth*

thirst?" ⁴So Moses cried out to the LORD, "What shall I do with this people? They are almost ready to stone me." ⁵The LORD said to Moses, "Go on ahead of the people, and take some of the elders of Israel with you; take in your hand the staff with which you struck the Nile, and go. ⁶I will be standing there in front of you on the rock at Horeb. Strike the rock, and water will come out of it, so that the people may drink." Moses did so, in the sight of the elders of Israel. ⁷He called the place Massah[i] and Meribah,[j] because the Israelites quarreled and tested the LORD, saying, "Is the LORD among us or not?"

Amalek Attacks Israel and Is Defeated

8 Then Amalek came and fought with Israel at Rephidim. ⁹Moses said to Joshua, "Choose some men for us and go out, fight with Amalek. Tomorrow I will stand on the top of the hill with the staff of God in my hand." ¹⁰So Joshua did as Moses told him, and fought with Amalek, while Moses, Aaron, and Hur went up to the top of the hill. ¹¹Whenever Moses held up his hand, Israel prevailed; and whenever he lowered his hand, Amalek prevailed. ¹²But Moses' hands grew weary; so they took a stone and put it under him, and he sat on it. Aaron and Hur held up his hands, one on one side, and the other on the other side; so his hands were steady until the sun set. ¹³And Joshua defeated Amalek and his people with the sword.

14 Then the LORD said to Moses, "Write this as a reminder in a book and recite it in the hearing of Joshua: I will utterly blot out the remembrance of Amalek from under heaven." ¹⁵And Moses built an altar and called it, The LORD is my banner. ¹⁶He said, "A hand upon the banner of the LORD![k] The LORD will have war with Amalek from generation to generation."

Jethro's Advice

18 Jethro, the priest of Midian, Moses' father-in-law, heard of all that God had done for Moses and for his people Israel, how the LORD had brought Israel out of Egypt. ²After Moses had sent away his wife Zipporah, his father-in-law Jethro took her back, ³along with her two sons. The name of the one was Gershom (for he said, "I have been an alien[l] in a foreign land"), ⁴and the name of the other, Eliezer[m] (for he said, "The God of my father was my help, and delivered me

from the sword of Pharaoh"). ⁵Jethro, Moses' father-in-law, came into the wilderness where Moses was encamped at the mountain of God, bringing Moses' sons and wife to him. ⁶He sent word to Moses, "I, your father-in-law Jethro, am coming to you, with your wife and her two sons." ⁷Moses went out to meet his father-in-law; he bowed down and kissed him; each asked after the other's welfare, and they went into the tent. ⁸Then Moses told his father-in-law all that the LORD had done to Pharaoh and to the Egyptians for Israel's sake, all the hardship that had beset them on the way, and how the LORD had delivered them. ⁹Jethro rejoiced for all the good that the LORD had done to Israel, in delivering them from the Egyptians.

10 Jethro said, "Blessed be the LORD, who has delivered you from the Egyptians and from Pharaoh. ¹¹Now I know that the LORD is greater than all gods, because he delivered the people from the Egyptians,[n] when they dealt arrogantly with them." ¹²And Jethro, Moses' father-in-law, brought a burnt offering and sacrifices to God; and Aaron came with all the elders of Israel to eat bread with Moses' father-in-law in the presence of God.

13 The next day Moses sat as judge for the people, while the people stood around him from morning until evening. ¹⁴When Moses' father-in-law saw all that he was doing for the people, he said, "What is this that you are doing for the people? Why do you sit alone, while all the people stand around you from morning until evening?" ¹⁵Moses said to his father-in-law, "Because the people come to me to inquire of God. ¹⁶When they have a dispute, they come to me and I decide between one person and another, and I make known to them the statutes and instructions of God." ¹⁷Moses' father-in-law said to him, "What you are doing is not good. ¹⁸You will surely wear yourself out, both you and these people with you. For the task is too heavy for you; you cannot do it alone. ¹⁹Now listen to me. I will give you counsel, and God be with you! You should represent the people before God, and you should bring their cases before God; ²⁰teach them the statutes and

i That is Test   j That is Quarrel   k Cn: Meaning of Heb uncertain   l Heb ger   m Heb Eli, my God; ezer, help   n The clause because . . . Egyptians has been transposed from verse 10

instructions and make known to them the way they are to go and the things they are to do. ²¹You should also look for able men among all the people, men who fear God, are trustworthy, and hate dishonest gain; set such men over them as officers over thousands, hundreds, fifties, and tens. ²²Let them sit as judges for the people at all times; let them bring every important case to you, but decide every minor case themselves. So it will be easier for you, and they will bear the burden with you. ²³If you do this, and God so commands you, then you will be able to endure, and all these people will go to their home in peace."

24 So Moses listened to his father-in-law and did all that he had said. ²⁵Moses chose able men from all Israel and appointed them as heads over the people, as officers over thousands, hundreds, fifties, and tens. ²⁶And they judged the people at all times; hard cases they brought to Moses, but any minor case they decided themselves. ²⁷Then Moses let his father-in-law depart, and he went off to his own country.

The Israelites Reach Mount Sinai

19 On the third new moon after the Israelites had gone out of the land of Egypt, on that very day, they came into the wilderness of Sinai. ²They had journeyed from Rephidim, entered the wilderness of Sinai, and camped in the wilderness; Israel camped there in front of the mountain. ³Then Moses went up to God; the LORD called to him from the mountain, saying, "Thus you shall say to the house of Jacob, and tell the Israelites: ⁴You have seen what I did to the Egyptians, and how I bore you on eagles' wings and brought you to myself. ⁵Now therefore, if you obey my voice and keep my covenant, you shall be my treasured possession out of all the peoples. Indeed, the whole earth is mine, ⁶but you shall be for me a priestly kingdom and a holy nation. These are the words that you shall speak to the Israelites."

7 So Moses came, summoned the elders of the people, and set before them all these words that the LORD had commanded him. ⁸The people all answered as one: "Everything that the LORD has spoken we will do." Moses reported the words of the people to the LORD. ⁹Then the LORD said to Moses, "I am going to come to you in a dense cloud, in order that the people may hear when I speak with you and so trust you ever after."

The People Consecrated

When Moses had told the words of the people to the LORD, ¹⁰the LORD said to Moses: "Go to the people and consecrate them today and tomorrow. Have them wash their clothes ¹¹and prepare for the third day, because on the third day the LORD will come down upon Mount Sinai in the sight of all the people. ¹²You shall set limits for the people all around, saying, 'Be careful not to go up the mountain or to touch the edge of it. Any who touch the mountain shall be put to death. ¹³No hand shall touch them, but they shall be stoned or shot with arrows;ᵒ whether animal or human being, they shall not live.' When the trumpet sounds a long blast, they may go up on the mountain." ¹⁴So Moses went down from the mountain to the people. He consecrated the people, and they washed their clothes. ¹⁵And he said to the people, "Prepare for the third day; do not go near a woman."

16 On the morning of the third day there was thunder and lightning, as well as a thick cloud on the mountain, and a blast of a trumpet so loud that all the people who were in the camp trembled. ¹⁷Moses brought the people out of the camp to meet God. They took their stand at the foot of the mountain. ¹⁸Now Mount Sinai was wrapped in smoke, because the LORD had descended upon it in fire; the smoke went up like the smoke of a kiln, while the whole mountain shook violently. ¹⁹As the blast of the trumpet grew louder and louder, Moses would speak and God would answer him in thunder. ²⁰When the LORD descended upon Mount Sinai, to the top of the mountain, the LORD summoned Moses to the top of the mountain, and Moses went up. ²¹Then the LORD said to Moses, "Go down and warn the people not to break through to the LORD to look; otherwise many of them will perish. ²²Even the priests who approach the LORD must consecrate themselves or the LORD will break out against them." ²³Moses said to the LORD, "The people are not permitted to come up to Mount Sinai; for you yourself warned us, saying, 'Set limits around the

---

ᵒ Heb lacks *with arrows*

mountain and keep it holy.' " 24The LORD
said to him, "Go down, and come up
bringing Aaron with you; but do not let
either the priests or the people break
through to come up to the LORD; otherwise
he will break out against them." 25So Moses went down to the people and told
them.

The Ten Commandments

20 Then God spoke all these words:
2 I am the LORD your God, who
brought you out of the land of Egypt, out
of the house of slavery; 3you shall have no
other gods before[p] me.
4 You shall not make for yourself an
idol, whether in the form of anything that
is in heaven above, or that is on the earth
beneath, or that is in the water under the
earth. 5You shall not bow down to them
or worship them; for I the LORD your God
am a jealous God, punishing children for
the iniquity of parents, to the third and
the fourth generation of those who reject
me, 6but showing steadfast love to the
thousandth generation[q] of those who
love me and keep my commandments.
7 You shall not make wrongful use of
the name of the LORD your God, for the
LORD will not acquit anyone who misuses
his name.
8 Remember the sabbath day, and keep
it holy. 9Six days you shall labor and do
all your work. 10But the seventh day is a
sabbath to the LORD your God; you shall
not do any work—you, your son or your
daughter, your male or female slave, your
livestock, or the alien resident in
your towns. 11For in six days the LORD
made heaven and earth, the sea, and all
that is in them, but rested the seventh day;
therefore the LORD blessed the sabbath day
and consecrated it.
12 Honor your father and your mother, so that your days may be long in the
land that the LORD your God is giving you.
13 You shall not murder.[r]
14 You shall not commit adultery.
15 You shall not steal.
16 You shall not bear false witness
against your neighbor.
17 You shall not covet your neighbor's
house; you shall not covet your neighbor's
wife, or male or female slave, or ox, or
donkey, or anything that belongs to your
neighbor.
18 When all the people witnessed the
thunder and lightning, the sound of the
trumpet, and the mountain smoking, they
were afraid[s] and trembled and stood at a
distance, 19and said to Moses, "You speak
to us, and we will listen; but do not let
God speak to us, or we will die." 20Moses
said to the people, "Do not be afraid; for
God has come only to test you and to put
the fear of him upon you so that you do
not sin." 21Then the people stood at a distance, while Moses drew near to the thick
darkness where God was.

The Law concerning the Altar

22 The LORD said to Moses: Thus you
shall say to the Israelites: "You have seen
for yourselves that I spoke with you from
heaven. 23You shall not make gods of silver alongside me, nor shall you make for
yourselves gods of gold. 24You need make
for me only an altar of earth and sacrifice
on it your burnt offerings and your offerings of well-being, your sheep and your
oxen; in every place where I cause my
name to be remembered I will come to
you and bless you. 25But if you make for
me an altar of stone, do not build it of
hewn stones; for if you use a chisel upon
it you profane it. 26You shall not go up by
steps to my altar, so that your nakedness
may not be exposed on it."

The Law concerning Slaves

21 These are the ordinances that you
shall set before them:
2 When you buy a male Hebrew slave,
he shall serve six years, but in the seventh
he shall go out a free person, without
debt. 3If he comes in single, he shall go
out single; if he comes in married, then
his wife shall go out with him. 4If his master gives him a wife and she bears him
sons or daughters, the wife and her children shall be her master's and he shall go
out alone. 5But if the slave declares, "I
love my master, my wife, and my children; I will not go out a free person," 6then
his master shall bring him before God.[t]
He shall be brought to the door or the
doorpost; and his master shall pierce his
ear with an awl; and he shall serve him for
life.
7 When a man sells his daughter as a
slave, she shall not go out as the male
slaves do. 8If she does not please her master, who designated her for himself, then

p Or *besides* q Or *to thousands* r Or *kill*
s Sam Gk Syr Vg: MT *they saw* t Or *to the judges*

he shall let her be redeemed; he shall have no right to sell her to a foreign people, since he has dealt unfairly with her. [9]If he designates her for his son, he shall deal with her as with a daughter. [10]If he takes another wife to himself, he shall not diminish the food, clothing, or marital rights of the first wife.[u] [11]And if he does not do these three things for her, she shall go out without debt, without payment of money.

The Law concerning Violence

12 Whoever strikes a person mortally shall be put to death. [13]If it was not premeditated, but came about by an act of God, then I will appoint for you a place to which the killer may flee. [14]But if someone willfully attacks and kills another by treachery, you shall take the killer from my altar for execution.

15 Whoever strikes father or mother shall be put to death.

16 Whoever kidnaps a person, whether that person has been sold or is still held in possession, shall be put to death.

17 Whoever curses father or mother shall be put to death.

18 When individuals quarrel and one strikes the other with a stone or fist so that the injured party, though not dead, is confined to bed, [19]but recovers and walks around outside with the help of a staff, then the assailant shall be free of liability, except to pay for the loss of time, and to arrange for full recovery.

20 When a slaveowner strikes a male or female slave with a rod and the slave dies immediately, the owner shall be punished. [21]But if the slave survives a day or two, there is no punishment; for the slave is the owner's property.

22 When people who are fighting injure a pregnant woman so that there is a miscarriage, and yet no further harm follows, the one responsible shall be fined what the woman's husband demands, paying as much as the judges determine. [23]If any harm follows, then you shall give life for life, [24]eye for eye, tooth for tooth, hand for hand, foot for foot, [25]burn for burn, wound for wound, stripe for stripe.

26 When a slaveowner strikes the eye of a male or female slave, destroying it, the owner shall let the slave go, a free person, to compensate for the eye. [27]If the owner knocks out a tooth of a male or female slave, the slave shall be let go, a free person, to compensate for the tooth.

Laws concerning Property

28 When an ox gores a man or a woman to death, the ox shall be stoned, and its flesh shall not be eaten; but the owner of the ox shall not be liable. [29]If the ox has been accustomed to gore in the past, and its owner has been warned but has not restrained it, and it kills a man or a woman, the ox shall be stoned, and its owner also shall be put to death. [30]If a ransom is imposed on the owner, then the owner shall pay whatever is imposed for the redemption of the victim's life. [31]If it gores a boy or a girl, the owner shall be dealt with according to this same rule. [32]If the ox gores a male or female slave, the owner shall pay to the slaveowner thirty shekels of silver, and the ox shall be stoned.

33 If someone leaves a pit open, or digs a pit and does not cover it, and an ox or a donkey falls into it, [34]the owner of the pit shall make restitution, giving money to its owner, but keeping the dead animal.

35 If someone's ox hurts the ox of another, so that it dies, then they shall sell the live ox and divide the price of it; and the dead animal they shall also divide. [36]But if it was known that the ox was accustomed to gore in the past, and its owner has not restrained it, the owner shall restore ox for ox, but keep the dead animal.

Laws of Restitution

22 [v]When someone steals an ox or a sheep, and slaughters it or sells it, the thief shall pay five oxen for an ox, and four sheep for a sheep.[w] The thief shall make restitution, but if unable to do so, shall be sold for the theft. [4]When the animal, whether ox or donkey or sheep, is found alive in the thief's possession, the thief shall pay double.

2[x]If a thief is found breaking in, and is beaten to death, no bloodguilt is incurred; [3]but if it happens after sunrise, bloodguilt is incurred.

5 When someone causes a field or vineyard to be grazed over, or lets livestock loose to graze in someone else's field, res-

---

u Heb of her   v Ch 21.37 in Heb   w Verses 2, 3, and 4 rearranged thus: 3b, 4, 2, 3a   x Ch 22.1 in Heb titution shall be made from the best in the owner's field or vineyard.

6 When fire breaks out and catches in thorns so that the stacked grain or the standing grain or the field is consumed, the one who started the fire shall make full restitution.

7 When someone delivers to a neighbor money or goods for safekeeping, and they are stolen from the neighbor's house, then the thief, if caught, shall pay double. [8]If the thief is not caught, the owner of the house shall be brought before God, [y] to determine whether or not the owner had laid hands on the neighbor's goods.

9 In any case of disputed ownership involving ox, donkey, sheep, clothing, or any other loss, of which one party says, "This is mine," the case of both parties shall come before God; [y] the one whom God condemns [z] shall pay double to the other.

10 When someone delivers to another a donkey, ox, sheep, or any other animal for safekeeping, and it dies or is injured or is carried off, without anyone seeing it, [11]an oath before the LORD shall decide between the two of them that the one has not laid hands on the property of the other; the owner shall accept the oath, and no restitution shall be made. [12]But if it was stolen, restitution shall be made to its owner. [13]If it was mangled by beasts, let it be brought as evidence; restitution shall not be made for the mangled remains.

14 When someone borrows an animal from another and it is injured or dies, the owner not being present, full restitution shall be made. [15]If the owner was present, there shall be no restitution; if it was hired, only the hiring fee is due.

Social and Religious Laws

16 When a man seduces a virgin who is not engaged to be married, and lies with her, he shall give the bride-price for her and make her his wife. [17]But if her father refuses to give her to him, he shall pay an amount equal to the bride-price for virgins.

18 You shall not permit a female sorcerer to live.

19 Whoever lies with an animal shall be put to death.

20 Whoever sacrifices to any god, other than the LORD alone, shall be devoted to destruction.

21 You shall not wrong or oppress a resident alien, for you were aliens in the land of Egypt. [22]You shall not abuse any widow or orphan. [23]If you do abuse them, when they cry out to me, I will surely heed their cry; [24]my wrath will burn, and I will kill you with the sword, and your wives shall become widows and your children orphans.

25 If you lend money to my people, to the poor among you, you shall not deal with them as a creditor; you shall not exact interest from them. [26]If you take your neighbor's cloak in pawn, you shall restore it before the sun goes down; [27]for it may be your neighbor's only clothing to use as cover; in what else shall that person sleep? And if your neighbor cries out to me, I will listen, for I am compassionate.

28 You shall not revile God, or curse a leader of your people.

29 You shall not delay to make offerings from the fullness of your harvest and from the outflow of your presses. [a]

The firstborn of your sons you shall give to me. [30]You shall do the same with your oxen and with your sheep: seven days it shall remain with its mother; on the eighth day you shall give it to me.

31 You shall be people consecrated to me; therefore you shall not eat any meat that is mangled by beasts in the field; you shall throw it to the dogs.

Justice for All

23 You shall not spread a false report. You shall not join hands with the wicked to act as a malicious witness. [2]You shall not follow a majority in wrongdoing; when you bear witness in a lawsuit, you shall not side with the majority so as to pervert justice; [3]nor shall you be partial to the poor in a lawsuit.

4 When you come upon your enemy's ox or donkey going astray, you shall bring it back.

5 When you see the donkey of one who hates you lying under its burden and you would hold back from setting it free, you must help to set it free. [a]

6 You shall not pervert the justice due to your poor in their lawsuits. [7]Keep far from a false charge, and do not kill the innocent and those in the right, for I will not acquit the guilty. [8]You shall take no bribe, for a bribe blinds the officials, and

---

[y] Or *before the judges*   [z] Or *the judges condemn*
[a] Meaning of Heb uncertain

subverts the cause of those who are in the right.

9 You shall not oppress a resident alien; you know the heart of an alien, for you were aliens in the land of Egypt.

Sabbatical Year and Sabbath

10 For six years you shall sow your land and gather in its yield; 11but the seventh year you shall let it rest and lie fallow, so that the poor of your people may eat; and what they leave the wild animals may eat. You shall do the same with your vineyard, and with your olive orchard.

12 Six days you shall do your work, but on the seventh day you shall rest, so that your ox and your donkey may have relief, and your homeborn slave and the resident alien may be refreshed. 13Be attentive to all that I have said to you. Do not invoke the names of other gods; do not let them be heard on your lips.

The Annual Festivals

14 Three times in the year you shall hold a festival for me. 15You shall observe the festival of unleavened bread; as I commanded you, you shall eat unleavened bread for seven days at the appointed time in the month of Abib, for in it you came out of Egypt.

No one shall appear before me empty-handed.

16 You shall observe the festival of harvest, of the first fruits of your labor, of what you sow in the field. You shall observe the festival of ingathering at the end of the year, when you gather in from the field the fruit of your labor. 17Three times in the year all your males shall appear before the Lord GOD.

18 You shall not offer the blood of my sacrifice with anything leavened, or let the fat of my festival remain until the morning.

19 The choicest of the first fruits of your ground you shall bring into the house of the LORD your God.

You shall not boil a kid in its mother's milk.

The Conquest of Canaan Promised

20 I am going to send an angel in front of you, to guard you on the way and to bring you to the place that I have prepared. 21Be attentive to him and listen to his voice; do not rebel against him, for he will not pardon your transgression; for my name is in him.

22 But if you listen attentively to his voice and do all that I say, then I will be an enemy to your enemies and a foe to your foes.

23 When my angel goes in front of you, and brings you to the Amorites, the Hittites, the Perizzites, the Canaanites, the Hivites, and the Jebusites, and I blot them out, 24you shall not bow down to their gods, or worship them, or follow their practices, but you shall utterly demolish them and break their pillars in pieces. 25You shall worship the LORD your God, and I[b] will bless your bread and your water; and I will take sickness away from among you. 26No one shall miscarry or be barren in your land; I will fulfill the number of your days. 27I will send my terror in front of you, and will throw into confusion all the people against whom you shall come, and I will make all your enemies turn their backs to you. 28And I will send the pestilence[c] in front of you, which shall drive out the Hivites, the Canaanites, and the Hittites from before you. 29I will not drive them out from before you in one year, or the land would become desolate and the wild animals would multiply against you. 30Little by little I will drive them out from before you, until you have increased and possess the land. 31I will set your borders from the Red Sea[d] to the sea of the Philistines, and from the wilderness to the Euphrates; for I will hand over to you the inhabitants of the land, and you shall drive them out before you. 32You shall make no covenant with them and their gods. 33They shall not live in your land, or they will make you sin against me; for if you worship their gods, it will surely be a snare to you.

The Blood of the Covenant

24 Then he said to Moses, "Come up to the LORD, you and Aaron, Nadab, and Abihu, and seventy of the elders of Israel, and worship at a distance. 2Moses alone shall come near the LORD; but the others shall not come near, and the people shall not come up with him."

3 Moses came and told the people all

b Gk Vg: Heb he   c Or hornets: Meaning of Heb uncertain   d Or Sea of Reeds the words of the Lord and all the ordinances; and all the people answered with one voice, and said, "All the words that the Lord has spoken we will do." 4And Moses wrote down all the words of the Lord. He rose early in the morning, and built an altar at the foot of the mountain, and set up twelve pillars, corresponding to the twelve tribes of Israel. 5He sent young men of the people of Israel, who offered burnt offerings and sacrificed oxen as offerings of well-being to the Lord. 6Moses took half of the blood and put it in basins, and half of the blood he dashed against the altar. 7Then he took the book of the covenant, and read it in the hearing of the people; and they said, "All that the Lord has spoken we will do, and we will be obedient." 8Moses took the blood and dashed it on the people, and said, "See the blood of the covenant that the Lord has made with you in accordance with all these words."

On the Mountain with God

9 Then Moses and Aaron, Nadab, and Abihu, and seventy of the elders of Israel went up, 10and they saw the God of Israel. Under his feet there was something like a pavement of sapphire stone, like the very heaven for clearness. 11God*e* did not lay his hand on the chief men of the people of Israel; also they beheld God, and they ate and drank.

12 The Lord said to Moses, "Come up to me on the mountain, and wait there; and I will give you the tablets of stone, with the law and the commandment, which I have written for their instruction." 13So Moses set out with his assistant Joshua, and Moses went up into the mountain of God. 14To the elders he had said, "Wait here for us, until we come to you again; for Aaron and Hur are with you; whoever has a dispute may go to them."

15 Then Moses went up on the mountain, and the cloud covered the mountain. 16The glory of the Lord settled on Mount Sinai, and the cloud covered it for six days; on the seventh day he called to Moses out of the cloud. 17Now the appearance of the glory of the Lord was like a devouring fire on the top of the mountain in the sight of the people of Israel. 18Moses entered the cloud, and went up on the mountain. Moses was on the mountain for forty days and forty nights.

Offerings for the Tabernacle

25 The Lord said to Moses: 2Tell the Israelites to take for me an offering; from all whose hearts prompt them to give you shall receive the offering for me. 3This is the offering that you shall receive from them: gold, silver, and bronze, 4blue, purple, and crimson yarns and fine linen, goats' hair, 5tanned rams' skins, fine leather,*f* acacia wood, 6oil for the lamps, spices for the anointing oil and for the fragrant incense, 7onyx stones and gems to be set in the ephod and for the breastpiece. 8And have them make me a sanctuary, so that I may dwell among them. 9In accordance with all that I show you concerning the pattern of the tabernacle and of all its furniture, so you shall make it.

The Ark of the Covenant

10 They shall make an ark of acacia wood; it shall be two and a half cubits long, a cubit and a half wide, and a cubit and a half high. 11You shall overlay it with pure gold, inside and outside you shall overlay it, and you shall make a molding of gold upon it all around. 12You shall cast four rings of gold for it and put them on its four feet, two rings on the one side of it, and two rings on the other side. 13You shall make poles of acacia wood, and overlay them with gold. 14And you shall put the poles into the rings on the sides of the ark, by which to carry the ark. 15The poles shall remain in the rings of the ark; they shall not be taken from it. 16You shall put into the ark the covenant*g* that I shall give you.

17 Then you shall make a mercy seat*h* of pure gold; two cubits and a half shall be its length, and a cubit and a half its width. 18You shall make two cherubim of gold; you shall make them of hammered work, at the two ends of the mercy seat.*i* 19Make one cherub at the one end, and one cherub at the other; of one piece with the mercy seat*i* you shall make the cherubim at its two ends. 20The cherubim shall spread out their wings above, overshadowing the mercy seat*i* with their wings. They shall face one to another; the faces of the cherubim shall be turned toward the mercy seat.*i* 21You shall put the

---

e Heb *He*   *f* Meaning of Heb uncertain   *g* Or *treaty,* or *testimony*; Heb *eduth*   *h* Or *a cover*   *i* Or *the cover*

mercy seat[j] on the top of the ark; and in the ark you shall put the covenant[k] that I shall give you. 22There I will meet with you, and from above the mercy seat,[j] from between the two cherubim that are on the ark of the covenant,[k] I will deliver to you all my commands for the Israelites.

The Table for the Bread of the Presence

23 You shall make a table of acacia wood, two cubits long, one cubit wide, and a cubit and a half high. 24You shall overlay it with pure gold, and make a molding of gold around it. 25You shall make around it a rim a handbreadth wide, and a molding of gold around the rim. 26You shall make for it four rings of gold, and fasten the rings to the four corners at its four legs. 27The rings that hold the poles used for carrying the table shall be close to the rim. 28You shall make the poles of acacia wood, and overlay them with gold, and the table shall be carried with these. 29You shall make its plates and dishes for incense, and its flagons and bowls with which to pour drink offerings; you shall make them of pure gold. 30And you shall set the bread of the Presence on the table before me always.

The Lampstand

31 You shall make a lampstand of pure gold. The base and the shaft of the lampstand shall be made of hammered work; its cups, its calyxes, and its petals shall be of one piece with it; 32and there shall be six branches going out of its sides, three branches of the lampstand out of one side of it and three branches of the lampstand out of the other side of it; 33three cups shaped like almond blossoms, each with calyx and petals, on one branch, and three cups shaped like almond blossoms, each with calyx and petals, on the other branch—so for the six branches going out of the lampstand. 34On the lampstand itself there shall be four cups shaped like almond blossoms, each with its calyxes and petals. 35There shall be a calyx of one piece with it under the first pair of branches, a calyx of one piece with it under the next pair of branches, and a calyx of one piece with it under the last pair of branches—so for the six branches that go out of the lampstand. 36Their calyxes and their branches shall be of one piece with it, the whole of it one hammered piece of pure gold. 37You shall make the seven lamps for it; and the lamps shall be set up so as to give light on the space in front of it. 38Its snuffers and trays shall be of pure gold. 39It, and all these utensils, shall be made from a talent of pure gold. 40And see that you make them according to the pattern for them, which is being shown you on the mountain.

The Tabernacle

26 Moreover you shall make the tabernacle with ten curtains of fine twisted linen, and blue, purple, and crimson yarns; you shall make them with cherubim skillfully worked into them. 2The length of each curtain shall be twenty-eight cubits, and the width of each curtain four cubits; all the curtains shall be of the same size. 3Five curtains shall be joined to one another; and the other five curtains shall be joined to one another. 4You shall make loops of blue on the edge of the outermost curtain in the first set; and likewise you shall make loops on the edge of the outermost curtain in the second set. 5You shall make fifty loops on the one curtain, and you shall make fifty loops on the edge of the curtain that is in the second set; the loops shall be opposite one another. 6You shall make fifty clasps of gold, and join the curtains to one another with the clasps, so that the tabernacle may be one whole.

7 You shall also make curtains of goats' hair for a tent over the tabernacle; you shall make eleven curtains. 8The length of each curtain shall be thirty cubits, and the width of each curtain four cubits; the eleven curtains shall be of the same size. 9You shall join five curtains by themselves, and six curtains by themselves, and the sixth curtain you shall double over at the front of the tent. 10You shall make fifty loops on the edge of the curtain that is outermost in one set, and fifty loops on the edge of the curtain that is outermost in the second set.

11 You shall make fifty clasps of bronze, and put the clasps into the loops, and join the tent together, so that it may be one whole. 12The part that remains of the curtains of the tent, the half curtain that remains, shall hang over the back of the tabernacle. 13The cubit on the one side, and the cubit on the other side, of

[j] Or *the cover* [k] Or *treaty*, or *testimony*; Heb *eduth*

what remains in the length of the curtains of the tent, shall hang over the sides of the tabernacle, on this side and that side, to cover it. ¹⁴You shall make for the tent a covering of tanned rams' skins and an outer covering of fine leather.*l*

The Framework

15 You shall make upright frames of acacia wood for the tabernacle. ¹⁶Ten cubits shall be the length of a frame, and a cubit and a half the width of each frame. ¹⁷There shall be two pegs in each frame to fit the frames together; you shall make these for all the frames of the tabernacle. ¹⁸You shall make the frames for the tabernacle: twenty frames for the south side; ¹⁹and you shall make forty bases of silver under the twenty frames, two bases under the first frame for its two pegs, and two bases under the next frame for its two pegs; ²⁰and for the second side of the tabernacle, on the north side twenty frames, ²¹and their forty bases of silver, two bases under the first frame, and two bases under the next frame; ²²and for the rear of the tabernacle westward you shall make six frames. ²³You shall make two frames for corners of the tabernacle in the rear; ²⁴they shall be separate beneath, but joined at the top, at the first ring; it shall be the same with both of them; they shall form the two corners. ²⁵And so there shall be eight frames, with their bases of silver, sixteen bases; two bases under the first frame, and two bases under the next frame.

26 You shall make bars of acacia wood, five for the frames of the one side of the tabernacle, ²⁷and five bars for the frames of the other side of the tabernacle, and five bars for the frames of the side of the tabernacle at the rear westward. ²⁸The middle bar, halfway up the frames, shall pass through from end to end. ²⁹You shall overlay the frames with gold, and shall make their rings of gold to hold the bars; and you shall overlay the bars with gold. ³⁰Then you shall erect the tabernacle according to the plan for it that you were shown on the mountain.

The Curtain

31 You shall make a curtain of blue, purple, and crimson yarns, and of fine twisted linen; it shall be made with cherubim skillfully worked into it. ³²You shall hang it on four pillars of acacia overlaid with gold, which have hooks of gold and rest on four bases of silver. ³³You shall hang the curtain under the clasps, and bring the ark of the covenant *m* in there, within the curtain; and the curtain shall separate for you the holy place from the most holy. ³⁴You shall put the mercy seat*n* on the ark of the covenant *m* in the most holy place. ³⁵You shall set the table outside the curtain, and the lampstand on the south side of the tabernacle opposite the table; and you shall put the table on the north side.

36 You shall make a screen for the entrance of the tent, of blue, purple, and crimson yarns, and of fine twisted linen, embroidered with needlework. ³⁷You shall make for the screen five pillars of acacia, and overlay them with gold; their hooks shall be of gold, and you shall cast five bases of bronze for them.

The Altar of Burnt Offering

27 You shall make the altar of acacia wood, five cubits long and five cubits wide; the altar shall be square, and it shall be three cubits high. ²You shall make horns for it on its four corners; its horns shall be of one piece with it, and you shall overlay it with bronze. ³You shall make pots for it to receive its ashes, and shovels and basins and forks and firepans; you shall make all its utensils of bronze. ⁴You shall also make for it a grating, a network of bronze; and on the net you shall make four bronze rings at its four corners. ⁵You shall set it under the ledge of the altar so that the net shall extend halfway down the altar. ⁶You shall make poles for the altar, poles of acacia wood, and overlay them with bronze; ⁷the poles shall be put through the rings, so that the poles shall be on the two sides of the altar when it is carried. ⁸You shall make it hollow, with boards. They shall be made just as you were shown on the mountain.

The Court and Its Hangings

9 You shall make the court of the tabernacle. On the south side the court shall have hangings of fine twisted linen one hundred cubits long for that side; ¹⁰its twenty pillars and their twenty bases shall be of bronze, but the hooks of the pillars

---

l Meaning of Heb uncertain　　*m* Or *treaty,* or *testimony;* Heb *eduth*　　*n* Or *the cover*

and their bands shall be of silver. ¹¹Likewise for its length on the north side there shall be hangings one hundred cubits long, their pillars twenty and their bases twenty, of bronze, but the hooks of the pillars and their bands shall be of silver. ¹²For the width of the court on the west side there shall be fifty cubits of hangings, with ten pillars and ten bases. ¹³The width of the court on the front to the east shall be fifty cubits. ¹⁴There shall be fifteen cubits of hangings on the one side, with three pillars and three bases. ¹⁵There shall be fifteen cubits of hangings on the other side, with three pillars and three bases. ¹⁶For the gate of the court there shall be a screen twenty cubits long, of blue, purple, and crimson yarns, and of fine twisted linen, embroidered with needlework; it shall have four pillars and with them four bases. ¹⁷All the pillars around the court shall be banded with silver; their hooks shall be of silver, and their bases of bronze. ¹⁸The length of the court shall be one hundred cubits, the width fifty, and the height five cubits, with hangings of fine twisted linen and bases of bronze. ¹⁹All the utensils of the tabernacle for every use, and all its pegs and all the pegs of the court, shall be of bronze.

The Oil for the Lamp

20 You shall further command the Israelites to bring you pure oil of beaten olives for the light, so that a lamp may be set up to burn regularly. ²¹In the tent of meeting, outside the curtain that is before the covenant,ᵒ Aaron and his sons shall tend it from evening to morning before the LORD. It shall be a perpetual ordinance to be observed throughout their generations by the Israelites.

Vestments for the Priesthood

28 Then bring near to you your brother Aaron, and his sons with him, from among the Israelites, to serve me as priests—Aaron and Aaron's sons, Nadab and Abihu, Eleazar and Ithamar. ²You shall make sacred vestments for the glorious adornment of your brother Aaron. ³And you shall speak to all who have ability, whom I have endowed with skill, that they make Aaron's vestments to consecrate him for my priesthood. ⁴These are the vestments that they shall make: a breastpiece, an ephod, a robe, a checkered tunic, a turban, and a sash. When they

make these sacred vestments for your brother Aaron and his sons to serve me as priests, ⁵they shall use gold, blue, purple, and crimson yarns, and fine linen.

The Ephod

6 They shall make the ephod of gold, of blue, purple, and crimson yarns, and of fine twisted linen, skillfully worked. ⁷It shall have two shoulder-pieces attached to its two edges, so that it may be joined together. ⁸The decorated band on it shall be of the same workmanship and materials, of gold, of blue, purple, and crimson yarns, and of fine twisted linen. ⁹You shall take two onyx stones, and engrave on them the names of the sons of Israel, ¹⁰six of their names on the one stone, and the names of the remaining six on the other stone, in the order of their birth. ¹¹As a gem-cutter engraves signets, so you shall engrave the two stones with the names of the sons of Israel; you shall mount them in settings of gold filigree. ¹²You shall set the two stones on the shoulder-pieces of the ephod, as stones of remembrance for the sons of Israel; and Aaron shall bear their names before the LORD on his two shoulders for remembrance. ¹³You shall make settings of gold filigree, ¹⁴and two chains of pure gold, twisted like cords; and you shall attach the corded chains to the settings.

The Breastplate

15 You shall make a breastpiece of judgment, in skilled work; you shall make it in the style of the ephod; of gold, of blue and purple and crimson yarns, and of fine twisted linen you shall make it. ¹⁶It shall be square and doubled, a span in length and a span in width. ¹⁷You shall set in it four rows of stones. A row of carnelian,ᵖ chrysolite, and emerald shall be the first row; ¹⁸and the second row a turquoise, a sapphire,�q and a moonstone; ¹⁹and the third row a jacinth, an agate, and an amethyst; ²⁰and the fourth row a beryl, an onyx, and a jasper; they shall be set in gold filigree. ²¹There shall be twelve stones with names corresponding to the names of the sons of Israel; they shall be like signets, each engraved with its name, for the twelve tribes. ²²You shall make for

---

ᵒ Or *treaty,* or *testimony;* Heb *eduth*   ᵖ The identity of several of these stones is uncertain   q Or *lapis lazuli*

the breastpiece chains of pure gold, twisted like cords; 23and you shall make for the breastpiece two rings of gold, and put the two rings on the two edges of the breastpiece. 24You shall put the two cords of gold in the two rings at the edges of the breastpiece; 25the two ends of the two cords you shall attach to the two settings, and so attach it in front to the shoulder-pieces of the ephod. 26You shall make two rings of gold, and put them at the two ends of the breastpiece, on its inside edge next to the ephod. 27You shall make two rings of gold, and attach them in front to the lower part of the two shoulder-pieces of the ephod, at its joining above the decorated band of the ephod. 28The breastpiece shall be bound by its rings to the rings of the ephod with a blue cord, so that it may lie on the decorated band of the ephod, and so that the breastpiece shall not come loose from the ephod. 29So Aaron shall bear the names of the sons of Israel in the breastpiece of judgment on his heart when he goes into the holy place, for a continual remembrance before the LORD. 30In the breastpiece of judgment you shall put the Urim and the Thummim, and they shall be on Aaron's heart when he goes in before the LORD; thus Aaron shall bear the judgment of the Israelites on his heart before the LORD continually.

Other Priestly Vestments

31 You shall make the robe of the ephod all of blue. 32It shall have an opening for the head in the middle of it, with a woven binding around the opening, like the opening in a coat of mail,r so that it may not be torn. 33On its lower hem you shall make pomegranates of blue, purple, and crimson yarns, all around the lower hem, with bells of gold between them all around—34a golden bell and a pomegranate alternating all around the lower hem of the robe. 35Aaron shall wear it when he ministers, and its sound shall be heard when he goes into the holy place before the LORD, and when he comes out, so that he may not die.

36 You shall make a rosette of pure gold, and engrave on it, like the engraving of a signet, "Holy to the LORD." 37You shall fasten it on the turban with a blue cord; it shall be on the front of the turban. 38It shall be on Aaron's forehead, and Aaron shall take on himself any guilt incurred in

the holy offering that the Israelites consecrate as their sacred donations; it shall always be on his forehead, in order that they may find favor before the LORD.

39 You shall make the checkered tunic of fine linen, and you shall make a turban of fine linen, and you shall make a sash embroidered with needlework.

40 For Aaron's sons you shall make tunics and sashes and headdresses; you shall make them for their glorious adornment. 41You shall put them on your brother Aaron, and on his sons with him, and shall anoint them and ordain them and consecrate them, so that they may serve me as priests. 42You shall make for them linen undergarments to cover their naked flesh; they shall reach from the hips to the thighs; 43Aaron and his sons shall wear them when they go into the tent of meeting, or when they come near the altar to minister in the holy place; or they will bring guilt on themselves and die. This shall be a perpetual ordinance for him and for his descendants after him.

The Ordination of the Priests

29 Now this is what you shall do to them to consecrate them, so that they may serve me as priests. Take one young bull and two rams without blemish, 2and unleavened bread, unleavened cakes mixed with oil, and unleavened wafers spread with oil. You shall make them of choice wheat flour. 3You shall put them in one basket and bring them in the basket, and bring the bull and the two rams. 4You shall bring Aaron and his sons to the entrance of the tent of meeting, and wash them with water. 5Then you shall take the vestments, and put on Aaron the tunic and the robe of the ephod, and the ephod, and the breastpiece, and gird him with the decorated band of the ephod; 6and you shall set the turban on his head, and put the holy diadem on the turban. 7You shall take the anointing oil, and pour it on his head and anoint him. 8Then you shall bring his sons, and put tunics on them, 9and you shall gird them with sashess and tie headdresses on them; and the priesthood shall be theirs by a perpetual ordinance. You shall then ordain Aaron and his sons.

10 You shall bring the bull in front of

r Meaning of Heb uncertain   s Gk: Heb sashes, Aaron and his sons

the tent of meeting. Aaron and his sons shall lay their hands on the head of the bull, [11]and you shall slaughter the bull before the LORD, at the entrance of the tent of meeting, [12]and shall take some of the blood of the bull and put it on the horns of the altar with your finger, and all the rest of the blood you shall pour out at the base of the altar. [13]You shall take all the fat that covers the entrails, and the appendage of the liver, and the two kidneys with the fat that is on them, and turn them into smoke on the altar. [14]But the flesh of the bull, and its skin, and its dung, you shall burn with fire outside the camp; it is a sin offering.

15 Then you shall take one of the rams, and Aaron and his sons shall lay their hands on the head of the ram, [16]and you shall slaughter the ram, and shall take its blood and dash it against all sides of the altar. [17]Then you shall cut the ram into its parts, and wash its entrails and its legs, and put them with its parts and its head, [18]and turn the whole ram into smoke on the altar; it is a burnt offering to the LORD; it is a pleasing odor, an offering by fire to the LORD.

19 You shall take the other ram; and Aaron and his sons shall lay their hands on the head of the ram, [20]and you shall slaughter the ram, and take some of its blood and put it on the lobe of Aaron's right ear and on the lobes of the right ears of his sons, and on the thumbs of their right hands, and on the big toes of their right feet, and dash the rest of the blood against all sides of the altar. [21]Then you shall take some of the blood that is on the altar, and some of the anointing oil, and sprinkle it on Aaron and his vestments and on his sons and his sons' vestments with him; then he and his vestments shall be holy, as well as his sons and his sons' vestments.

22 You shall also take the fat of the ram, the fat tail, the fat that covers the entrails, the appendage of the liver, the two kidneys with the fat that is on them, and the right thigh (for it is a ram of ordination), [23]and one loaf of bread, one cake of bread made with oil, and one wafer, out of the basket of unleavened bread that is before the LORD; [24]and you shall place all these on the palms of Aaron and on the palms of his sons, and raise them as an elevation offering before the LORD. [25]Then you shall take them from their hands, and turn them into smoke on the altar on top of the burnt offering of pleasing odor before the LORD; it is an offering by fire to the LORD.

26 You shall take the breast of the ram of Aaron's ordination and raise it as an elevation offering before the LORD; and it shall be your portion. [27]You shall consecrate the breast that was raised as an elevation offering and the thigh that was raised as an elevation offering from the ram of ordination, from that which belonged to Aaron and his sons. [28]These things shall be a perpetual ordinance for Aaron and his sons from the Israelites, for this is an offering; and it shall be an offering by the Israelites from their sacrifice of offerings of well-being, their offering to the LORD.

29 The sacred vestments of Aaron shall be passed on to his sons after him; they shall be anointed in them and ordained in them. [30]The son who is priest in his place shall wear them seven days, when he comes into the tent of meeting to minister in the holy place.

31 You shall take the ram of ordination, and boil its flesh in a holy place; [32]and Aaron and his sons shall eat the flesh of the ram and the bread that is in the basket, at the entrance of the tent of meeting. [33]They themselves shall eat the food by which atonement is made, to ordain and consecrate them, but no one else shall eat of them, because they are holy. [34]If any of the flesh for the ordination, or of the bread, remains until the morning, then you shall burn the remainder with fire; it shall not be eaten, because it is holy.

35 Thus you shall do to Aaron and to his sons, just as I have commanded you; through seven days you shall ordain them. [36]Also every day you shall offer a bull as a sin offering for atonement. Also you shall offer a sin offering for the altar, when you make atonement for it, and shall anoint it, to consecrate it. [37]Seven days you shall make atonement for the altar, and consecrate it, and the altar shall be most holy; whatever touches the altar shall become holy.

The Daily Offerings

38 Now this is what you shall offer on the altar: two lambs a year old regularly each day. [39]One lamb you shall offer in the morning, and the other lamb you shall offer in the evening; [40]and with the

first lamb one-tenth of a measure of choice flour mixed with one-fourth of a hin of beaten oil, and one-fourth of a hin of wine for a drink offering. 41And the other lamb you shall offer in the evening, and shall offer with it a grain offering and its drink offering, as in the morning, for a pleasing odor, an offering by fire to the LORD. 42It shall be a regular burnt offering throughout your generations at the entrance of the tent of meeting before the LORD, where I will meet with you, to speak to you there. 43I will meet with the Israelites there, and it shall be sanctified by my glory; 44I will consecrate the tent of meeting and the altar; Aaron also and his sons I will consecrate, to serve me as priests. 45I will dwell among the Israelites, and I will be their God. 46And they shall know that I am the LORD their God, who brought them out of the land of Egypt that I might dwell among them; I am the LORD their God.

The Altar of Incense

30 You shall make an altar on which to offer incense; you shall make it of acacia wood. 2It shall be one cubit long, and one cubit wide; it shall be square, and shall be two cubits high; its horns shall be of one piece with it. 3You shall overlay it with pure gold, its top, and its sides all around and its horns; and you shall make for it a molding of gold all around. 4And you shall make two golden rings for it; under its molding on two opposite sides of it you shall make them, and they shall hold the poles with which to carry it. 5You shall make the poles of acacia wood, and overlay them with gold. 6You shall place it in front of the curtain that is above the ark of the covenant,*t* in front of the mercy seat*u* that is over the covenant,*t* where I will meet with you. 7Aaron shall offer fragrant incense on it; every morning when he dresses the lamps he shall offer it, 8and when Aaron sets up the lamps in the evening, he shall offer it, a regular incense offering before the LORD throughout your generations. 9You shall not offer unholy incense on it, or a burnt offering, or a grain offering; and you shall not pour a drink offering on it. 10Once a year Aaron shall perform the rite of atonement on its horns. Throughout your generations he shall perform the atonement for it once a year with the blood of the atoning sin offering. It is most holy to the LORD.

The Half Shekel for the Sanctuary

11 The LORD spoke to Moses: 12When you take a census of the Israelites to register them, at registration all of them shall give a ransom for their lives to the LORD, so that no plague may come upon them for being registered. 13This is what each one who is registered shall give: half a shekel according to the shekel of the sanctuary (the shekel is twenty gerahs), half a shekel as an offering to the LORD. 14Each one who is registered, from twenty years old and upward, shall give the LORD's offering. 15The rich shall not give more, and the poor shall not give less, than the half shekel, when you bring this offering to the LORD to make atonement for your lives. 16You shall take the atonement money from the Israelites and shall designate it for the service of the tent of meeting; before the LORD it will be a reminder to the Israelites of the ransom given for your lives.

The Bronze Basin

17 The LORD spoke to Moses: 18You shall make a bronze basin with a bronze stand for washing. You shall put it between the tent of meeting and the altar, and you shall put water in it; 19with the water*v* Aaron and his sons shall wash their hands and their feet. 20When they go into the tent of meeting, or when they come near the altar to minister, to make an offering by fire to the LORD, they shall wash with water, so that they may not die. 21They shall wash their hands and their feet, so that they may not die: it shall be a perpetual ordinance for them, for him and for his descendants throughout their generations.

The Anointing Oil and Incense

22 The LORD spoke to Moses: 23Take the finest spices: of liquid myrrh five hundred shekels, and of sweet-smelling cinnamon half as much, that is, two hundred fifty, and two hundred fifty of aromatic cane, 24and five hundred of cassia—measured by the sanctuary shekel—and a hin of olive oil; 25and you shall make of these a sacred anointing oil blended as by the perfumer; it shall be a holy anointing oil. 26With it you shall anoint the tent of

---

t Or treaty, or *testimony;* Heb *eduth*   *u* Or *the cover*   *v* Heb *it*

meeting and the ark of the covenant,[w] [27]and the table and all its utensils, and the lampstand and its utensils, and the altar of incense, [28]and the altar of burnt offering with all its utensils, and the basin with its stand; [29]you shall consecrate them, so that they may be most holy; whatever touches them will become holy. [30]You shall anoint Aaron and his sons, and consecrate them, in order that they may serve me as priests. [31]You shall say to the Israelites, "This shall be my holy anointing oil throughout your generations. [32]It shall not be used in any ordinary anointing of the body, and you shall make no other like it in composition; it is holy, and it shall be holy to you. [33]Whoever compounds any like it or whoever puts any of it on an unqualified person shall be cut off from the people."

34 The LORD said to Moses: Take sweet spices, stacte, and onycha, and galbanum, sweet spices with pure frankincense (an equal part of each), [35]and make an incense blended as by the perfumer, seasoned with salt, pure and holy; [36]and you shall beat some of it into powder, and put part of it before the covenant[w] in the tent of meeting where I shall meet with you; it shall be for you most holy. [37]When you make incense according to this composition, you shall not make it for yourselves; it shall be regarded by you as holy to the LORD. [38]Whoever makes any like it to use as perfume shall be cut off from the people.

Bezalel and Oholiab

31 The LORD spoke to Moses: [2]See, I have called by name Bezalel son of Uri son of Hur, of the tribe of Judah: [3]and I have filled him with divine spirit,[x] with ability, intelligence, and knowledge in every kind of craft, [4]to devise artistic designs, to work in gold, silver, and bronze, [5]in cutting stones for setting, and in carving wood, in every kind of craft. [6]Moreover, I have appointed with him Oholiab son of Ahisamach, of the tribe of Dan; and I have given skill to all the skillful, so that they may make all that I have commanded you: [7]the tent of meeting, and the ark of the covenant,[w] and the mercy seat[y] that is on it, and all the furnishings of the tent, [8]the table and its utensils, and the pure lampstand with all its utensils, and the altar of incense, [9]and the altar of burnt offering with all its uten-

sils, and the basin with its stand, [10]and the finely worked vestments, the holy vestments for the priest Aaron and the vestments of his sons, for their service as priests, [11]and the anointing oil and the fragrant incense for the holy place. They shall do just as I have commanded you.

The Sabbath Law

12 The LORD said to Moses: [13]You yourself are to speak to the Israelites: "You shall keep my sabbaths, for this is a sign between me and you throughout your generations, given in order that you may know that I, the LORD, sanctify you. [14]You shall keep the sabbath, because it is holy for you; everyone who profanes it shall be put to death; whoever does any work on it shall be cut off from among the people. [15]Six days shall work be done, but the seventh day is a sabbath of solemn rest, holy to the LORD; whoever does any work on the sabbath day shall be put to death. [16]Therefore the Israelites shall keep the sabbath, observing the sabbath throughout their generations, as a perpetual covenant. [17]It is a sign forever between me and the people of Israel that in six days the LORD made heaven and earth, and on the seventh day he rested, and was refreshed."

The Two Tablets of the Covenant

18 When God[z] finished speaking with Moses on Mount Sinai, he gave him the two tablets of the covenant,[w] tablets of stone, written with the finger of God.

The Golden Calf

32 When the people saw that Moses delayed to come down from the mountain, the people gathered around Aaron, and said to him, "Come, make gods for us, who shall go before us; as for this Moses, the man who brought us up out of the land of Egypt, we do not know what has become of him." [2]Aaron said to them, "Take off the gold rings that are on the ears of your wives, your sons, and your daughters, and bring them to me." [3]So all the people took off the gold rings from their ears, and brought them to Aaron. [4]He took the gold from them, formed it in a mold,[a] and cast an image of a calf; and

---

[w] Or *treaty*, or *testimony*; Heb *eduth*   [x] Or *with the spirit of God*   [y] Or *the cover*   [z] Heb *he*   [a] Or *fashioned it with a graving tool*; Meaning of Heb uncertain

they said, "These are your gods, O Israel, who brought you up out of the land of Egypt!" 5When Aaron saw this, he built an altar before it; and Aaron made proclamation and said, "Tomorrow shall be a festival to the LORD." 6They rose early the next day, and offered burnt offerings and brought sacrifices of well-being; and the people sat down to eat and drink, and rose up to revel.

7 The LORD said to Moses, "Go down at once! Your people, whom you brought up

"What, Lord?"

MONDAY

Scripture Reading
for Today:
Exodus 32.1–8

Verse for Today:
Exodus 32.8

It was Ash Wednesday and a beautiful spring day in sunny Florida. I was on my lunch hour, driving up State Road 580 toward my favorite destination—the shopping mall. Shopping was my passion. In fact, I had to make at least one trip a day to the store and buy something—anything—it didn't matter.

I had turned on the radio to my favorite Christian station. My left arm was in the air praising the Lord, and I was singing at the top of my lungs. As the song came to an end, I began to tell the Lord how much I loved him. I told him I would do anything for him.

Quietly, deep within my spirit, I sensed a voice saying, "Johnette, do you really love me?"

"Yes, Lord. You know I love you. Haven't I been telling you this my whole way to the mall?"

"Johnette, if you love me," the voice said, "then don't go shopping today."

"Don't go shopping! It's Ash Wednesday, Lord, and I saw a dress yesterday that I'd like to have for Easter. I didn't know you'd ask me not to shop. I thought maybe you'd call me to the mission field or something. But, not shop—I don't know if I can do that!" I lamented.

"Johnette, I'd like you to give up shopping for Lent," he persisted.

"For Lent!" I cried. "Lent is forty days, Lord—and it's only Ash Wednesday! What about my Easter dress?"

"Johnette, you can't do this on your own, but through my grace all things are possible."

What could I say? Shopping had become an addiction for me, an attachment that came dangerously close to idolatry. I knew Jesus was offering me the grace in that moment to overcome this bondage in my life. And if I agreed, he would heal me of this lust for possessions and material goods. In that moment, I understood that my passion for shopping was a feeble attempt to fill up a hole in my heart that could only be filled with the presence of God.

—*JOHNETTE BENKOVIC*

Go to page 102 for your next devotional reading.

out of the land of Egypt, have acted perversely; [8]they have been quick to turn aside from the way that I commanded them; they have cast for themselves an image of a calf, and have worshiped it and sacrificed to it, and said, 'These are your gods, O Israel, who brought you up out of the land of Egypt!' " [9]The LORD said to Moses, "I have seen this people, how stiffnecked they are. [10]Now let me alone, so that my wrath may burn hot against them and I may consume them; and of you I will make a great nation."

11 But Moses implored the LORD his God, and said, "O LORD, why does your wrath burn hot against your people, whom you brought out of the land of Egypt with great power and with a mighty hand? [12]Why should the Egyptians say, 'It was with evil intent that he brought them out to kill them in the mountains, and to consume them from the face of the earth'? Turn from your fierce wrath; change your mind and do not bring disaster on your people. [13]Remember Abraham, Isaac, and Israel, your servants, how you swore to them by your own self, saying to them, 'I will multiply your descendants like the stars of heaven, and all this land that I have promised I will give to your descendants, and they shall inherit it forever.' " [14]And the LORD changed his mind about the disaster that he planned to bring on his people.

15 Then Moses turned and went down from the mountain, carrying the two tablets of the covenant[b] in his hands, tablets that were written on both sides, written on the front and on the back. [16]The tablets were the work of God, and the writing was the writing of God, engraved upon the tablets. [17]When Joshua heard the noise of the people as they shouted, he said to Moses, "There is a noise of war in the camp." [18]But he said,

"It is not the sound made by
     victors,
or the sound made by losers;
it is the sound of revelers that I
     hear."

[19]As soon as he came near the camp and saw the calf and the dancing, Moses' anger burned hot, and he threw the tablets from his hands and broke them at the foot of the mountain. [20]He took the calf that they had made, burned it with fire, ground it to powder, scattered it on the water, and made the Israelites drink it.

21 Moses said to Aaron, "What did this people do to you that you have brought so great a sin upon them?" [22]And Aaron said, "Do not let the anger of my lord burn hot; you know the people, that they are bent on evil. [23]They said to me, 'Make us gods, who shall go before us; as for this Moses, the man who brought us up out of the land of Egypt, we do not know what has become of him.' [24]So I said to them, 'Whoever has gold, take it off'; so they gave it to me, and I threw it into the fire, and out came this calf!"

25 When Moses saw that the people were running wild (for Aaron had let them run wild, to the derision of their enemies), [26]then Moses stood in the gate of the camp, and said, "Who is on the LORD's side? Come to me!" And all the sons of Levi gathered around him. [27]He said to them, "Thus says the LORD, the God of Israel, 'Put your sword on your side, each of you! Go back and forth from gate to gate throughout the camp, and each of you kill your brother, your friend, and your neighbor.' " [28]The sons of Levi did as Moses commanded, and about three thousand of the people fell on that day. [29]Moses said, "Today you have ordained yourselves[c] for the service of the LORD, each one at the cost of a son or a brother, and so have brought a blessing on yourselves this day."

30 On the next day Moses said to the people, "You have sinned a great sin. But now I will go up to the LORD; perhaps I can make atonement for your sin." [31]So Moses returned to the LORD and said, "Alas, this people has sinned a great sin; they have made for themselves gods of gold. [32]But now, if you will only forgive their sin— but if not, blot me out of the book that you have written." [33]But the LORD said to Moses, "Whoever has sinned against me I will blot out of my book. [34]But now go, lead the people to the place about which I have spoken to you; see, my angel shall go in front of you. Nevertheless, when the day comes for punishment, I will punish them for their sin."

35 Then the LORD sent a plague on the people, because they made the calf—the one that Aaron made.

---

[b] Or *treaty*, or *testimony*; Heb *eduth*   [c] Gk Vg
Compare Tg: Heb *Today ordain yourselves*

The Command to Leave Sinai

33 The LORD said to Moses, "Go, leave this place, you and the people whom you have brought up out of the land of Egypt, and go to the land of which I swore to Abraham, Isaac, and Jacob, saying, 'To your descendants I will give it.' 2I will send an angel before you, and I will drive out the Canaanites, the Amorites, the Hittites, the Perizzites, the Hivites, and the Jebusites. 3Go up to a land flowing with milk and honey; but I will not go up among you, or I would consume you on the way, for you are a stiff-necked people."

4 When the people heard these harsh words, they mourned, and no one put on ornaments. 5For the LORD had said to Moses, "Say to the Israelites, 'You are a stiff-necked people; if for a single moment I should go up among you, I would consume you. So now take off your ornaments, and I will decide what to do to you.' " 6Therefore the Israelites stripped themselves of their ornaments, from Mount Horeb onward.

The Tent outside the Camp

7 Now Moses used to take the tent and pitch it outside the camp, far off from the camp; he called it the tent of meeting. And everyone who sought the LORD would go out to the tent of meeting, which was outside the camp. 8Whenever Moses went out to the tent, all the people would rise and stand, each of them, at the entrance of their tents and watch Moses until he had gone into the tent. 9When Moses entered the tent, the pillar of cloud would descend and stand at the entrance of the tent, and the LORD would speak with Moses. 10When all the people saw the pillar of cloud standing at the entrance of the tent, all the people would rise and bow down, all of them, at the entrance of their tent. 11Thus the LORD used to speak to Moses face to face, as one speaks to a friend. Then he would return to the camp; but his young assistant, Joshua son of Nun, would not leave the tent.

Moses' Intercession

12 Moses said to the LORD, "See, you have said to me, 'Bring up this people'; but you have not let me know whom you will send with me. Yet you have said, 'I know you by name, and you have also found favor in my sight.' 13Now if I have found favor in your sight, show me your ways, so that I may know you and find favor in your sight. Consider too that this nation is your people." 14He said, "My presence will go with you, and I will give you rest." 15And he said to him, "If your presence will not go, do not carry us up from here. 16For how shall it be known that I have found favor in your sight, I and your people, unless you go with us? In this way, we shall be distinct, I and your people, from every people on the face of the earth."

17 The LORD said to Moses, "I will do the very thing that you have asked; for you have found favor in my sight, and I know you by name." 18Moses said, "Show me your glory, I pray." 19And he said, "I will make all my goodness pass before you, and will proclaim before you the name, 'The LORD';d and I will be gracious to whom I will be gracious, and will show mercy on whom I will show mercy. 20But," he said, "you cannot see my face; for no one shall see me and live." 21And the LORD continued, "See, there is a place by me where you shall stand on the rock; 22and while my glory passes by I will put you in a cleft of the rock, and I will cover you with my hand until I have passed by; 23then I will take away my hand, and you shall see my back; but my face shall not be seen."

Moses Makes New Tablets

34 The LORD said to Moses, "Cut two tablets of stone like the former ones, and I will write on the tablets the words that were on the former tablets, which you broke. 2Be ready in the morning, and come up in the morning to Mount Sinai and present yourself there to me, on the top of the mountain. 3No one shall come up with you, and do not let anyone be seen throughout all the mountain; and do not let flocks or herds graze in front of that mountain." 4So Moses cut two tablets of stone like the former ones; and he rose early in the morning and went up on Mount Sinai, as the LORD had commanded him, and took in his hand the two tablets of stone. 5The LORD descended in the cloud and stood with him there, and proclaimed the name, "The LORD."d

---

d Heb YHWH; see note at 3.15

⁶The LORD passed before him, and proclaimed,
"The LORD, the LORD,
a God merciful and gracious,
slow to anger,
and abounding in steadfast love and
    faithfulness,
⁷ keeping steadfast love for the
    thousandth generation,ᵉ
forgiving iniquity and transgression
    and sin,
yet by no means clearing the guilty,
but visiting the iniquity of the
    parents
upon the children
and the children's children,
to the third and the fourth
    generation."

⁸And Moses quickly bowed his head toward the earth, and worshiped. ⁹He said, "If now I have found favor in your sight, O Lord, I pray, let the Lord go with us. Although this is a stiff-necked people, pardon our iniquity and our sin, and take us for your inheritance."

The Covenant Renewed

10 He said: I hereby make a covenant. Before all your people I will perform marvels, such as have not been performed in all the earth or in any nation; and all the people among whom you live shall see the work of the LORD; for it is an awesome thing that I will do with you.

11 Observe what I command you today. See, I will drive out before you the Amorites, the Canaanites, the Hittites, the Perizzites, the Hivites, and the Jebusites. ¹²Take care not to make a covenant with the inhabitants of the land to which you are going, or it will become a snare among you. ¹³You shall tear down their altars, break their pillars, and cut down their sacred polesᶠ ¹⁴(for you shall worship no other god, because the LORD, whose name is Jealous, is a jealous God). ¹⁵You shall not make a covenant with the inhabitants of the land, for when they prostitute themselves to their gods and sacrifice to their gods, someone among them will invite you, and you will eat of the sacrifice. ¹⁶And you will take wives from among their daughters for your sons, and their daughters who prostitute themselves to their gods will make your sons also prostitute themselves to their gods.

17 You shall not make cast idols.

18 You shall keep the festival of unleavened bread. Seven days you shall eat unleavened bread, as I commanded you, at the time appointed in the month of Abib; for in the month of Abib you came out from Egypt.

19 All that first opens the womb is mine, all your maleᵍ livestock, the firstborn of cow and sheep. ²⁰The firstborn of a donkey you shall redeem with a lamb, or if you will not redeem it you shall break its neck. All the firstborn of your sons you shall redeem.

No one shall appear before me empty-handed.

21 Six days you shall work, but on the seventh day you shall rest; even in plowing time and in harvest time you shall rest. ²²You shall observe the festival of weeks, the first fruits of wheat harvest, and the festival of ingathering at the turn of the year. ²³Three times in the year all your males shall appear before the LORD God, the God of Israel. ²⁴For I will cast out nations before you, and enlarge your borders; no one shall covet your land when you go up to appear before the LORD your God three times in the year.

25 You shall not offer the blood of my sacrifice with leaven, and the sacrifice of the festival of the passover shall not be left until the morning.

26 The best of the first fruits of your ground you shall bring to the house of the LORD your God.

You shall not boil a kid in its mother's milk.

27 The LORD said to Moses: Write these words; in accordance with these words I have made a covenant with you and with Israel. ²⁸He was there with the LORD forty days and forty nights; he neither ate bread nor drank water. And he wrote on the tablets the words of the covenant, the ten commandments.ʰ

The Shining Face of Moses

29 Moses came down from Mount Sinai. As he came down from the mountain with the two tablets of the covenantⁱ in his hand, Moses did not know that the skin of his face shone because he had been talking with God. ³⁰When Aaron and all the Israelites saw Moses, the skin of his face was shining, and they were afraid

ᵉ Or for thousands   ᶠ Heb Asherim   ᵍ Gk
Theodotion Vg Tg: Meaning of Heb uncertain
ʰ Heb words   ⁱ Or treaty, or testimony; Heb eduth

to come near him. [31]But Moses called to them; and Aaron and all the leaders of the congregation returned to him, and Moses spoke with them. [32]Afterward all the Israelites came near, and he gave them in commandment all that the LORD had spoken with him on Mount Sinai. [33]When Moses had finished speaking with them, he put a veil on his face; [34]but whenever Moses went in before the LORD to speak with him, he would take the veil off, until he came out; and when he came out, and told the Israelites what he had been commanded, [35]the Israelites would see the face of Moses, that the skin of his face was shining; and Moses would put the veil on his face again, until he went in to speak with him.

Sabbath Regulations

35 Moses assembled all the congregation of the Israelites and said to them: These are the things that the LORD has commanded you to do:
[2] Six days shall work be done, but on the seventh day you shall have a holy sabbath of solemn rest to the LORD; whoever does any work on it shall be put to death. [3]You shall kindle no fire in all your dwellings on the sabbath day.

Preparations for Making the Tabernacle

[4] Moses said to all the congregation of the Israelites: This is the thing that the LORD has commanded: [5]Take from among you an offering to the LORD; let whoever is of a generous heart bring the LORD's offering: gold, silver, and bronze; [6]blue, purple, and crimson yarns, and fine linen; goats' hair, [7]tanned rams' skins, and fine leather;[j] acacia wood, [8]oil for the light, spices for the anointing oil and for the fragrant incense, [9]and onyx stones and gems to be set in the ephod and the breastpiece.
[10] All who are skillful among you shall come and make all that the LORD has commanded: the tabernacle, [11]its tent and its covering, its clasps and its frames, its bars, its pillars, and its bases; [12]the ark with its poles, the mercy seat,[k] and the curtain for the screen; [13]the table with its poles and all its utensils, and the bread of the Presence; [14]the lampstand also for the light, with its utensils and its lamps, and the oil for the light; [15]and the altar of incense, with its poles, and the anointing oil and the fragrant incense, and the screen

for the entrance, the entrance of the tabernacle; [16]the altar of burnt offering, with its grating of bronze, its poles, and all its utensils, the basin with its stand; [17]the hangings of the court, its pillars and its bases, and the screen for the gate of the court; [18]the pegs of the tabernacle and the pegs of the court, and their cords; [19]the finely worked vestments for ministering in the holy place, the holy vestments for the priest Aaron, and the vestments of his sons, for their service as priests.

Offerings for the Tabernacle

[20] Then all the congregation of the Israelites withdrew from the presence of Moses. [21]And they came, everyone whose heart was stirred, and everyone whose spirit was willing, and brought the LORD's offering to be used for the tent of meeting, and for all its service, and for the sacred vestments. [22]So they came, both men and women; all who were of a willing heart brought brooches and earrings and signet rings and pendants, all sorts of gold objects, everyone bringing an offering of gold to the LORD. [23]And everyone who possessed blue or purple or crimson yarn or fine linen or goats' hair or tanned rams' skins or fine leather,[j] brought them. [24]Everyone who could make an offering of silver or bronze brought it as the LORD's offering; and everyone who possessed acacia wood of any use in the work, brought it. [25]All the skillful women spun with their hands, and brought what they had spun in blue and purple and crimson yarns and fine linen; [26]all the women whose hearts moved them to use their skill spun the goats' hair. [27]And the leaders brought onyx stones and gems to be set in the ephod and the breastpiece, [28]and spices and oil for the light, and for the anointing oil, and for the fragrant incense. [29]All the Israelite men and women whose hearts made them willing to bring anything for the work that the LORD had commanded by Moses to be done, brought it as a freewill offering to the LORD.

Bezalel and Oholiab

[30] Then Moses said to the Israelites: See, the LORD has called by name Bezalel son of Uri son of Hur, of the tribe of Ju-

---

j Meaning of Heb uncertain   k Or the cover

dah; [31]he has filled him with divine spirit,[1] with skill, intelligence, and knowledge in every kind of craft, [32]to devise artistic designs, to work in gold, silver, and bronze, [33]in cutting stones for setting, and in carving wood, in every kind of craft. [34]And he has inspired him to teach, both him and Oholiab son of Ahisa-

[1] Or *the spirit of God*

*M*ake Something *Beautiful for God*

TUESDAY

Scripture Reading
for Today:
Exodus 35.30–35

Verse for Today:
Exodus 35.35

It was the most gorgeous fabric my 13-year-old eyes had ever seen—glossy, shimmering satin that fell in heavy folds of purest white. Dreamily, I stroked its baby-smooth surface as I watched my mother tackle her project.

First she built a cardboard frame. Then she snipped and stitched the satin into a padded, upholstered covering that fit it perfectly. Then the final elegant touches: lace edging and fine embroidery with silk thread and French knots. It took Mom days, but when it was over she had created a tabernacle interior that was a fitting dwelling for the King of kings, Jesus in the humble guise of consecrated hosts. Glimpsing it in church one day as the tabernacle door was opened, I caught my breath at its glowing beauty.

My mother, I think, had something in common with Bezalel and the other artisans who built the Israelites' worship tent. All had God-given skill in their crafts, as well as hearts that were "stirred to come to do the work" (Exodus 36.2). All gave generously of time and creative ability so that God's house could be beautiful.

Unlike my mother and Bezalel and company, I have never had the opportunity to use my creative gifts to adorn a place of worship. But I have learned that every skill offered with love builds something beautiful for God. Dresses for children and grandchildren, ornaments for the parish Christmas bazaar, quilts and hangings for friends and relatives—with love and prayer in every stitch, my handiwork, I like to think, also contributes to the beauty of God's house.

And isn't this what God asks of each of us? We may not hear a call (or be equipped) to build a worship tent or a tabernacle interior. But each of us can be like the Israelites whose hearts prompted them to contribute the raw materials for the artisans' use—gold and jewelry, spices, precious stones, yarn, thread (see Exodus 35.20–29).

Whatever our gifts, we too build and adorn God's house as we offer them in love.

—*ROMA BOURASSA*

Go to page 107 for your next devotional reading.

mach, of the tribe of Dan. ³⁵He has filled them with skill to do every kind of work done by an artisan or by a designer or by an embroiderer in blue, purple, and crimson yarns, and in fine linen, or by a weaver—by any sort of artisan or skilled designer.

36 Bezalel and Oholiab and every skillful one to whom the Lord has given skill and understanding to know how to do any work in the construction of the sanctuary shall work in accordance with all that the Lord has commanded.

2 Moses then called Bezalel and Oholiab and every skillful one to whom the Lord had given skill, everyone whose heart was stirred to come to do the work; ³and they received from Moses all the freewill offerings that the Israelites had brought for doing the work on the sanctuary. They still kept bringing him freewill offerings every morning, ⁴so that all the artisans who were doing every sort of task on the sanctuary came, each from the task being performed, ⁵and said to Moses, "The people are bringing much more than enough for doing the work that the Lord has commanded us to do." ⁶So Moses gave command, and word was proclaimed throughout the camp: "No man or woman is to make anything else as an offering for the sanctuary." So the people were restrained from bringing; ⁷for what they had already brought was more than enough to do all the work.

Construction of the Tabernacle

8 All those with skill among the workers made the tabernacle with ten curtains; they were made of fine twisted linen, and blue, purple, and crimson yarns, with cherubim skillfully worked into them. ⁹The length of each curtain was twenty-eight cubits, and the width of each curtain four cubits; all the curtains were of the same size.

10 He joined five curtains to one another, and the other five curtains he joined to one another. ¹¹He made loops of blue on the edge of the outermost curtain of the first set; likewise he made them on the edge of the outermost curtain of the second set; ¹²he made fifty loops on the one curtain, and he made fifty loops on the edge of the curtain that was in the second set; the loops were opposite one another. ¹³And he made fifty clasps of gold, and joined the curtains one to the other with clasps; so the tabernacle was one whole.

14 He also made curtains of goats' hair for a tent over the tabernacle; he made eleven curtains. ¹⁵The length of each curtain was thirty cubits, and the width of each curtain four cubits; the eleven curtains were of the same size. ¹⁶He joined five curtains by themselves, and six curtains by themselves. ¹⁷He made fifty loops on the edge of the outermost curtain of the one set, and fifty loops on the edge of the other connecting curtain. ¹⁸He made fifty clasps of bronze to join the tent together so that it might be one whole. ¹⁹And he made for the tent a covering of tanned rams' skins and an outer covering of fine leather.ᵐ

20 Then he made the upright frames for the tabernacle of acacia wood. ²¹Ten cubits was the length of a frame, and a cubit and a half the width of each frame. ²²Each frame had two pegs for fitting together; he did this for all the frames of the tabernacle. ²³The frames for the tabernacle he made in this way: twenty frames for the south side; ²⁴and he made forty bases of silver under the twenty frames, two bases under the first frame for its two pegs, and two bases under the next frame for its two pegs. ²⁵For the second side of the tabernacle, on the north side, he made twenty frames ²⁶and their forty bases of silver, two bases under the first frame and two bases under the next frame. ²⁷For the rear of the tabernacle westward he made six frames. ²⁸He made two frames for corners of the tabernacle in the rear. ²⁹They were separate beneath, but joined at the top, at the first ring; he made two of them in this way, for the two corners. ³⁰There were eight frames with their bases of silver: sixteen bases, under every frame two bases.

31 He made bars of acacia wood, five for the frames of the one side of the tabernacle, ³²and five bars for the frames of the other side of the tabernacle, and five bars for the frames of the tabernacle at the rear westward. ³³He made the middle bar to pass through from end to end halfway up the frames. ³⁴And he overlaid the frames with gold, and made rings of gold for them to hold the bars, and overlaid the bars with gold.

35 He made the curtain of blue, purple, and crimson yarns, and fine twisted

ᵐ Meaning of Heb uncertain

linen, with cherubim skillfully worked into it. [36]For it he made four pillars of acacia, and overlaid them with gold; their hooks were of gold, and he cast for them four bases of silver. [37]He also made a screen for the entrance to the tent, of blue, purple, and crimson yarns, and fine twisted linen, embroidered with needlework; [38]and its five pillars with their hooks. He overlaid their capitals and their bases with gold, but their five bases were of bronze.

Making the Ark of the Covenant

37 Bezalel made the ark of acacia wood; it was two and a half cubits long, a cubit and a half wide, and a cubit and a half high. [2]He overlaid it with pure gold inside and outside, and made a molding of gold around it. [3]He cast for it four rings of gold for its four feet, two rings on its one side and two rings on its other side. [4]He made poles of acacia wood, and overlaid them with gold, [5]and put the poles into the rings on the sides of the ark, to carry the ark. [6]He made a mercy seat[n] of pure gold; two cubits and a half was its length, and a cubit and a half its width. [7]He made two cherubim of hammered gold; at the two ends of the mercy seat[o] he made them, [8]one cherub at the one end, and one cherub at the other end; of one piece with the mercy seat[o] he made the cherubim at its two ends. [9]The cherubim spread out their wings above, overshadowing the mercy seat[o] with their wings. They faced one another; the faces of the cherubim were turned toward the mercy seat.[o]

Making the Table for the Bread of the Presence

10 He also made the table of acacia wood, two cubits long, one cubit wide, and a cubit and a half high. [11]He overlaid it with pure gold, and made a molding of gold around it. [12]He made around it a rim a handbreadth wide, and made a molding of gold around the rim. [13]He cast for it four rings of gold, and fastened the rings to the four corners at its four legs. [14]The rings that held the poles used for carrying the table were close to the rim. [15]He made the poles of acacia wood to carry the table, and overlaid them with gold. [16]And he made the vessels of pure gold that were to be on the table, its plates and dishes for incense, and its bowls and flagons with which to pour drink offerings.

Making the Lampstand

17 He also made the lampstand of pure gold. The base and the shaft of the lampstand were made of hammered work; its cups, its calyxes, and its petals were of one piece with it. [18]There were six branches going out of its sides, three branches of the lampstand out of one side of it and three branches of the lampstand out of the other side of it; [19]three cups shaped like almond blossoms, each with calyx and petals, on one branch, and three cups shaped like almond blossoms, each with calyx and petals, on the other branch—so for the six branches going out of the lampstand. [20]On the lampstand itself there were four cups shaped like almond blossoms, each with its calyxes and petals. [21]There was a calyx of one piece with it under the first pair of branches, a calyx of one piece with it under the next pair of branches, and a calyx of one piece with it under the last pair of branches. [22]Their calyxes and their branches were of one piece with it, the whole of it one hammered piece of pure gold. [23]He made its seven lamps and its snuffers and its trays of pure gold. [24]He made it and all its utensils of a talent of pure gold.

Making the Altar of Incense

25 He made the altar of incense of acacia wood, one cubit long, and one cubit wide; it was square, and was two cubits high; its horns were of one piece with it. [26]He overlaid it with pure gold, its top, and its sides all around, and its horns; and he made for it a molding of gold all around, [27]and made two golden rings for it under its molding, on two opposite sides of it, to hold the poles with which to carry it. [28]And he made the poles of acacia wood, and overlaid them with gold.

Making the Anointing Oil and the Incense

29 He made the holy anointing oil also, and the pure fragrant incense, blended as by the perfumer.

Making the Altar of Burnt Offering

38 He made the altar of burnt offering also of acacia wood; it was five cubits long, and five cubits wide; it was square, and three cubits high. [2]He made horns for it on its four corners; its

[n] Or a cover　　[o] Or the cover

horns were of one piece with it, and he overlaid it with bronze. ³He made all the utensils of the altar, the pots, the shovels, the basins, the forks, and the firepans: all its utensils he made of bronze. ⁴He made for the altar a grating, a network of bronze, under its ledge, extending halfway down. ⁵He cast four rings on the four corners of the bronze grating to hold the poles; ⁶he made the poles of acacia wood, and overlaid them with bronze. ⁷And he put the poles through the rings on the sides of the altar, to carry it with them; he made it hollow, with boards.

8 He made the basin of bronze with its stand of bronze, from the mirrors of the women who served at the entrance to the tent of meeting.

Making the Court of the Tabernacle

9 He made the court; for the south side the hangings of the court were of fine twisted linen, one hundred cubits long; ¹⁰its twenty pillars and their twenty bases were of bronze, but the hooks of the pillars and their bands were of silver. ¹¹For the north side there were hangings one hundred cubits long; its twenty pillars and their twenty bases were of bronze, but the hooks of the pillars and their bands were of silver. ¹²For the west side there were hangings fifty cubits long, with ten pillars and ten bases; the hooks of the pillars and their bands were of silver. ¹³And for the front to the east, fifty cubits. ¹⁴The hangings for one side of the gate were fifteen cubits, with three pillars and three bases. ¹⁵And so for the other side; on each side of the gate of the court were hangings of fifteen cubits, with three pillars and three bases. ¹⁶All the hangings around the court were of fine twisted linen. ¹⁷The bases for the pillars were of bronze, but the hooks of the pillars and their bands were of silver; the overlaying of their capitals was also of silver, and all the pillars of the court were banded with silver. ¹⁸The screen for the entrance to the court was embroidered with needlework in blue, purple, and crimson yarns and fine twisted linen. It was twenty cubits long and, along the width of it, five cubits high, corresponding to the hangings of the court. ¹⁹There were four pillars; their four bases were of bronze, their hooks of silver, and the overlaying of their capitals and their bands of silver. ²⁰All the pegs for the tab-

ernacle and for the court all around were of bronze.

Materials of the Tabernacle

21 These are the records of the tabernacle, the tabernacle of the covenant, ᴾ which were drawn up at the commandment of Moses, the work of the Levites being under the direction of Ithamar son of the priest Aaron. ²²Bezalel son of Uri son of Hur, of the tribe of Judah, made all that the LORD commanded Moses; ²³and with him was Oholiab son of Ahisamach, of the tribe of Dan, engraver, designer, and embroiderer in blue, purple, and crimson yarns, and in fine linen.

24 All the gold that was used for the work, in all the construction of the sanctuary, the gold from the offering, was twenty-nine talents and seven hundred thirty shekels, measured by the sanctuary shekel. ²⁵The silver from those of the congregation who were counted was one hundred talents and one thousand seven hundred seventy-five shekels, measured by the sanctuary shekel; ²⁶a beka a head (that is, half a shekel, measured by the sanctuary shekel), for everyone who was counted in the census, from twenty years old and upward, for six hundred three thousand, five hundred fifty men. ²⁷The hundred talents of silver were for casting the bases of the sanctuary, and the bases of the curtain; one hundred bases for the hundred talents, a talent for a base. ²⁸Of the thousand seven hundred seventy-five shekels he made hooks for the pillars, and overlaid their capitals and made bands for them. ²⁹The bronze that was contributed was seventy talents, and two thousand four hundred shekels; ³⁰with it he made the bases for the entrance of the tent of meeting, the bronze altar and the bronze grating for it and all the utensils of the altar, ³¹the bases all around the court, and the bases of the gate of the court, all the pegs of the tabernacle, and all the pegs around the court.

Making the Vestments for the Priesthood

39 Of the blue, purple, and crimson yarns they made finely worked vestments, for ministering in the holy place; they made the sacred vestments for Aaron; as the LORD had commanded Moses.

ᴾ Or *treaty,* or *testimony;* Heb *eduth*

2 He made the ephod of gold, of blue,
purple, and crimson yarns, and of fine
twisted linen. 3 Gold leaf was hammered
out and cut into threads to work into the
blue, purple, and crimson yarns and into
the fine twisted linen, in skilled design.
4 They made for the ephod shoulder-
pieces, joined to it at its two edges. 5 The
decorated band on it was of the same materials and workmanship, of gold, of blue,
purple, and crimson yarns, and of fine
twisted linen; as the LORD had commanded Moses.

6 The onyx stones were prepared, enclosed in settings of gold filigree and engraved like the engravings of a signet, according to the names of the sons of Israel.
7 He set them on the shoulder-pieces of
the ephod, to be stones of remembrance
for the sons of Israel; as the LORD had commanded Moses.

8 He made the breastpiece, in skilled
work, like the work of the ephod, of gold,
of blue, purple, and crimson yarns, and
of fine twisted linen. 9 It was square; the
breastpiece was made double, a span in
length and a span in width when doubled. 10 They set in it four rows of stones.
A row of carnelian,[q] chrysolite, and emerald was the first row; 11 and the second
row, a turquoise, a sapphire,[r] and a
moonstone; 12 and the third row, a jacinth,
an agate, and an amethyst; 13 and the
fourth row, a beryl, an onyx, and a jasper;
they were enclosed in settings of gold filigree. 14 There were twelve stones with
names corresponding to the names of the
sons of Israel; they were like signets, each
engraved with its name, for the twelve
tribes. 15 They made on the breastpiece
chains of pure gold, twisted like cords;
16 and they made two settings of gold filigree and two gold rings, and put the two
rings on the two edges of the breastpiece;
17 and they put the two cords of gold in the
two rings at the edges of the breastpiece.
18 Two ends of the two cords they had attached to the two settings of filigree; in
this way they attached it in front to the
shoulder-pieces of the ephod. 19 Then they
made two rings of gold, and put them at
the two ends of the breastpiece, on its inside edge next to the ephod. 20 They made
two rings of gold, and attached them in
front to the lower part of the two
shoulder-pieces of the ephod, at its joining above the decorated band of the
ephod. 21 They bound the breastpiece by
its rings to the rings of the ephod with a
blue cord, so that it should lie on the decorated band of the ephod, and that the
breastpiece should not come loose from
the ephod; as the LORD had commanded
Moses.

22 He also made the robe of the ephod
woven all of blue yarn; 23 and the opening
of the robe in the middle of it was like the
opening in a coat of mail,[s] with a binding around the opening, so that it might
not be torn. 24 On the lower hem of the
robe they made pomegranates of blue,
purple, and crimson yarns, and of fine
twisted linen. 25 They also made bells of
pure gold, and put the bells between the
pomegranates on the lower hem of the
robe all around, between the pomegranates; 26 a bell and a pomegranate, a bell
and a pomegranate all around on the lower hem of the robe for ministering; as the
LORD had commanded Moses.

27 They also made the tunics, woven of
fine linen, for Aaron and his sons, 28 and
the turban of fine linen, and the headdresses of fine linen, and the linen undergarments of fine twisted linen, 29 and the
sash of fine twisted linen, and of blue,
purple, and crimson yarns, embroidered
with needlework; as the LORD had commanded Moses.

30 They made the rosette of the holy
diadem of pure gold, and wrote on it an
inscription, like the engraving of a signet,
"Holy to the LORD." 31 They tied to it a blue
cord, to fasten it on the turban above; as
the LORD had commanded Moses.

The Work Completed

32 In this way all the work of the tabernacle of the tent of meeting was finished;
the Israelites had done everything just as
the LORD had commanded Moses. 33 Then
they brought the tabernacle to Moses, the
tent and all its utensils, its hooks, its
frames, its bars, its pillars, and its bases;
34 the covering of tanned rams' skins and
the covering of fine leather,[s] and the curtain for the screen; 35 the ark of the covenant[t] with its poles and the mercy seat;[u]
36 the table with all its utensils, and the
bread of the Presence; 37 the pure lamp-

[q] The identification of several of these stones is uncertain [r] Or *lapis lazuli* [s] Meaning of Heb uncertain [t] Or *treaty*, or *testimony*; Heb *eduth* [u] Or *the cover*

stand with its lamps set on it and all its utensils, and the oil for the light; ³⁸the golden altar, the anointing oil and the fragrant incense, and the screen for the entrance of the tent; ³⁹the bronze altar, and its grating of bronze, its poles, and all its utensils; the basin with its stand; ⁴⁰the hangings of the court, its pillars, and its bases, and the screen for the gate of the court, its cords, and its pegs; and all the utensils for the service of the tabernacle, for the tent of meeting; ⁴¹the finely worked vestments for ministering in the holy place, the sacred vestments for the priest Aaron, and the vestments of his sons to serve as priests. ⁴²The Israelites had done all of the work just as the LORD had commanded Moses. ⁴³When Moses saw that they had done all the work just as the LORD had commanded, he blessed them.

The Tabernacle Erected and Its Equipment Installed

40 The LORD spoke to Moses: ²On the first day of the first month you shall set up the tabernacle of the tent of meeting. ³You shall put in it the ark of the covenant,ᵛ and you shall screen the ark with the curtain. ⁴You shall bring in the table, and arrange its setting; and you shall bring in the lampstand, and set up its lamps. ⁵You shall put the golden altar for incense before the ark of the covenant,ᵛ and set up the screen for the entrance of the tabernacle. ⁶You shall set the altar of burnt offering before the entrance of the tabernacle of the tent of meeting, ⁷and place the basin between the tent of meeting and the altar, and put water in it.

ᵛ Or *treaty*, or *testimony*; Heb *eduth*

WEDNESDAY

Scripture Reading for Today:
Exodus 40.1–15

Verse for Today:
Exodus 40.3

Sanctuary

One of Mary's traditional titles is ark of the covenant. Since the ark of the covenant was the Hebrew container for the tablets of the Law that Moses brought down from Mount Sinai, calling Mary the ark of the covenant may strike us as being a little peculiar. The title seems to imply that she's like a gilded box with stone inside. Not a terribly appealing image until you understand what the title really indicates.

The ark of the covenant was the sanctuary for the material sign of God's contract with the Hebrews. Because of its close contact with the tablets of the Law, the ark itself was transformed into a holy object.

In traditional Christian belief, Mary's womb became the sanctuary for Jesus, who was the material sign of God's new contract with all people. Like the original ark, Mary was transformed through her contact with Jesus.

As Pope John Paul II said in an address on November 30, 1980, "Has man ever been able to attain to anything more exalted? Has he ever been able to experience about himself anything more profound? Has man been able through any achievement of his being man—through his intellect, the greatness of his mind, or through heroic deeds—to be lifted to a higher state than has been given him in this 'fruit of the womb' of Mary?"

—WOODENE KOENIG-BRICKER

Go to page 110 for your next devotional reading.

8You shall set up the court all around, and hang up the screen for the gate of the court. 9Then you shall take the anointing oil, and anoint the tabernacle and all that is in it, and consecrate it and all its furniture, so that it shall become holy. 10You shall also anoint the altar of burnt offering and all its utensils, and consecrate the altar, so that the altar shall be most holy. 11You shall also anoint the basin with its stand, and consecrate it. 12Then you shall bring Aaron and his sons to the entrance of the tent of meeting, and shall wash them with water, 13and put on Aaron the sacred vestments, and you shall anoint him and consecrate him, so that he may serve me as priest. 14You shall bring his sons also and put tunics on them, 15and anoint them, as you anointed their father, that they may serve me as priests: and their anointing shall admit them to a perpetual priesthood throughout all generations to come.

16 Moses did everything just as the LORD had commanded him. 17In the first month in the second year, on the first day of the month, the tabernacle was set up. 18Moses set up the tabernacle; he laid its bases, and set up its frames, and put in its poles, and raised up its pillars; 19and he spread the tent over the tabernacle, and put the covering of the tent over it; as the LORD had commanded Moses. 20He took the covenant*w* and put it into the ark, and put the poles on the ark, and set the mercy seat*x* above the ark; 21and he brought the ark into the tabernacle, and set up the curtain for screening, and screened the ark of the covenant;*w* as the LORD had commanded Moses. 22He put the table in the tent of meeting, on the north side of the tabernacle, outside the curtain, 23and set the bread in order on it before the LORD; as the LORD had commanded Moses. 24He put the lampstand in the tent of meeting,

opposite the table on the south side of the tabernacle, 25and set up the lamps before the LORD; as the LORD had commanded Moses. 26He put the golden altar in the tent of meeting before the curtain, 27and offered fragrant incense on it; as the LORD had commanded Moses. 28He also put in place the screen for the entrance of the tabernacle. 29He set the altar of burnt offering at the entrance of the tabernacle of the tent of meeting, and offered on it the burnt offering and the grain offering as the LORD had commanded Moses. 30He set the basin between the tent of meeting and the altar, and put water in it for washing, 31with which Moses and Aaron and his sons washed their hands and their feet. 32When they went into the tent of meeting, and when they approached the altar, they washed; as the LORD had commanded Moses. 33He set up the court around the tabernacle and the altar, and put up the screen at the gate of the court. So Moses finished the work.

The Cloud and the Glory

34 Then the cloud covered the tent of meeting, and the glory of the LORD filled the tabernacle. 35Moses was not able to enter the tent of meeting because the cloud settled upon it, and the glory of the LORD filled the tabernacle. 36Whenever the cloud was taken up from the tabernacle, the Israelites would set out on each stage of their journey; 37but if the cloud was not taken up, then they did not set out until the day that it was taken up. 38For the cloud of the LORD was on the tabernacle by day, and fire was in the cloud*y* by night, before the eyes of all the house of Israel at each stage of their journey.

w Or *treaty,* or *testimony;* Heb *eduth*   *x* Or *the cover*   *y* Heb *it*

Leviticus

Unlike Genesis and Exodus, the book of Leviticus has no strong story line to keep you reading. It consists primarily of the laws Moses received from God at Mount Sinai. It is entitled *Leviticus* because so much of it concerns the sacrificial and ritual laws prescribed for the priests, who came from the tribe of Levi. Though it contains hundreds of rules regulating the civil, social, and religious life of Israel, its main focus is on holiness. In fact, the word *holiness* occurs more than 80 times throughout the book.

To belong to God involves being holy as he is holy, being separated from everything that is foreign to his nature—anything impure, unloving, unrighteous. The laws of Leviticus were meant to set the Israelites apart from every other people on earth so that they could be in relationship with God.

The various kinds of sacrifices that comprise the temple liturgy foreshadow Christ's once-and-for-all sacrifice on the cross. Like the holocaust offering described in Leviticus, his life was entirely consumed. He became the peace offering that reconciles sinners to God, and he became the sin offering, bearing in his own body the punishment for our sins. In the Sacrifice of the Mass we are not only reminded of Christ's sacrificial role but also invited to share the benefits of his perfect sacrifice.

The Burnt Offering

1 The LORD summoned Moses and spoke to him from the tent of meeting, saying: 2Speak to the people of Israel and say to them: When any of you bring an offering of livestock to the LORD, you shall bring your offering from the herd or from the flock.

3 If the offering is a burnt offering from the herd, you shall offer a male without blemish; you shall bring it to the entrance of the tent of meeting, for acceptance in your behalf before the LORD. 4You shall lay your hand on the head of the burnt offering, and it shall be acceptable in your behalf as atonement for you. 5The bull shall be slaughtered before the LORD; and Aaron's sons the priests shall offer the blood, dashing the blood against all sides of the altar that is at the entrance of the tent

of meeting. ⁶The burnt offering shall be flayed and cut up into its parts. ⁷The sons of the priest Aaron shall put fire on the altar and arrange wood on the fire. ⁸Aaron's sons the priests shall arrange the parts, with the head and the suet, on the wood that is on the fire on the altar; ⁹but its entrails and its legs shall be washed with water. Then the priest shall turn the whole into smoke on the altar as a burnt offering, an offering by fire of pleasing odor to the LORD.

10 If your gift for a burnt offering is from the flock, from the sheep or goats, your offering shall be a male without blemish. ¹¹It shall be slaughtered on the north side of the altar before the LORD, and Aaron's sons the priests shall dash its blood against all sides of the altar. ¹²It shall be cut up into its parts, with its head and its suet, and the priest shall arrange them on the wood that is on the fire on the altar; ¹³but the entrails and the legs shall be washed with water. Then the priest shall offer the whole and turn it into smoke on the altar; it is a burnt offering, an offering by fire of pleasing odor to the LORD.

14 If your offering to the LORD is a burnt offering of birds, you shall choose your offering from turtledoves or pigeons. ¹⁵The priest shall bring it to the altar and wring off its head, and turn it into smoke on the altar; and its blood shall be drained out against the side of the altar. ¹⁶He shall remove its crop with its contents[a] and throw it at the east side of the altar, in the place for ashes. ¹⁷He shall tear it open by its wings without severing it. Then the priest shall turn it into smoke on the altar, on the wood that is on the fire; it is a burnt offering, an offering by fire of pleasing odor to the LORD.

---

a Meaning of Heb uncertain

Sacrifice

THURSDAY

Scripture Reading for Today:
Leviticus 1.1–9

Verse for Today:
Leviticus 1.9

In the time before Christ, the Jewish people offered blood sacrifices. An unblemished male animal was ceremonially killed and its blood sprinkled about the altar. The carcass was then placed on the altar and ignited, becoming consumed by the flames.

Since we no longer make blood sacrifices, what does God want from us?

A proper sacrifice to God is one that creates and restores, not one that tears down and destroys.

All too often, we think that God wants us to offer up our individuality, to become something other than who we are, but that's not what God desires at all. God wants the exact opposite: God wants us to sacrifice those things that keep us from becoming unique individuals.

God doesn't call us to sacrifice ourselves to an abusive relationship, for example. God doesn't ask us to sacrifice our talents or abilities in order to attempt to make someone else feel better. God *does* ask us to sacrifice our selfish desires and wishes in order to become more loving and giving. God does desire that we sacrifice our greedy natures so that we can share more freely.

God still wants sacrifices, but only those that change our hearts—not those that destroy our spirits.

—*WOODENE KOENIG-BRICKER*

Go to page 128 for your next devotional reading.

Grain Offerings

2 When anyone presents a grain offering to the Lord, the offering shall be of choice flour; the worshiper shall pour oil on it, and put frankincense on it, ²and bring it to Aaron's sons the priests. After taking from it a handful of the choice flour and oil, with all its frankincense, the priest shall turn this token portion into smoke on the altar, an offering by fire of pleasing odor to the Lord. ³And what is left of the grain offering shall be for Aaron and his sons, a most holy part of the offerings by fire to the Lord.

4 When you present a grain offering baked in the oven, it shall be of choice flour: unleavened cakes mixed with oil, or unleavened wafers spread with oil. ⁵If your offering is grain prepared on a griddle, it shall be of choice flour mixed with oil, unleavened; ⁶break it in pieces, and pour oil on it; it is a grain offering. ⁷If your offering is grain prepared in a pan, it shall be made of choice flour in oil. ⁸You shall bring to the Lord the grain offering that is prepared in any of these ways; and when it is presented to the priest, he shall take it to the altar. ⁹The priest shall remove from the grain offering its token portion and turn this into smoke on the altar, an offering by fire of pleasing odor to the Lord. ¹⁰And what is left of the grain offering shall be for Aaron and his sons; it is a most holy part of the offerings by fire to the Lord.

11 No grain offering that you bring to the Lord shall be made with leaven, for you must not turn any leaven or honey into smoke as an offering by fire to the Lord. ¹²You may bring them to the Lord as an offering of choice products, but they shall not be offered on the altar for a pleasing odor. ¹³You shall not omit from your grain offerings the salt of the covenant with your God; with all your offerings you shall offer salt.

14 If you bring a grain offering of first fruits to the Lord, you shall bring as the grain offering of your first fruits coarse new grain from fresh ears, parched with fire. ¹⁵You shall add oil to it and lay frankincense on it; it is a grain offering. ¹⁶And the priest shall turn a token portion of it into smoke—some of the coarse grain and oil with all its frankincense; it is an offering by fire to the Lord.

Offerings of Well-Being

3 If the offering is a sacrifice of well-being, if you offer an animal of the herd, whether male or female, you shall offer one without blemish before the Lord. ²You shall lay your hand on the head of the offering and slaughter it at the entrance of the tent of meeting; and Aaron's sons the priests shall dash the blood against all sides of the altar. ³You shall offer from the sacrifice of well-being, as an offering by fire to the Lord, the fat that covers the entrails and all the fat that is around the entrails; ⁴the two kidneys with the fat that is on them at the loins, and the appendage of the liver, which he shall remove with the kidneys. ⁵Then Aaron's sons shall turn these into smoke on the altar, with the burnt offering that is on the wood on the fire, as an offering by fire of pleasing odor to the Lord.

6 If your offering for a sacrifice of well-being to the Lord is from the flock, male or female, you shall offer one without blemish. ⁷If you present a sheep as your offering, you shall bring it before the Lord ⁸and lay your hand on the head of the offering. It shall be slaughtered before the tent of meeting, and Aaron's sons shall dash its blood against all sides of the altar. ⁹You shall present its fat from the sacrifice of well-being, as an offering by fire to the Lord: the whole broad tail, which shall be removed close to the backbone, the fat that covers the entrails, and all the fat that is around the entrails; ¹⁰the two kidneys with the fat that is on them at the loins, and the appendage of the liver, which you shall remove with the kidneys. ¹¹Then the priest shall turn these into smoke on the altar as a food offering by fire to the Lord.

12 If your offering is a goat, you shall bring it before the Lord ¹³and lay your hand on its head; it shall be slaughtered before the tent of meeting; and the sons of Aaron shall dash its blood against all sides of the altar. ¹⁴You shall present as your offering from it, as an offering by fire to the Lord, the fat that covers the entrails, and all the fat that is around the entrails; ¹⁵the two kidneys with the fat that is on them at the loins, and the appendage of the liver, which you shall remove with the kidneys. ¹⁶Then the priest shall turn these into smoke on the altar as a food offering by fire for a pleasing odor.

All fat is the Lord's. ¹⁷It shall be a perpetual statute throughout your generations, in all your settlements: you must not eat any fat or any blood.

Sin Offerings

4 The LORD spoke to Moses, saying, ²Speak to the people of Israel, saying: When anyone sins unintentionally in any of the LORD's commandments about things not to be done, and does any one of them:

3 If it is the anointed priest who sins, thus bringing guilt on the people, he shall offer for the sin that he has committed a bull of the herd without blemish as a sin offering to the LORD. ⁴He shall bring the bull to the entrance of the tent of meeting before the LORD and lay his hand on the head of the bull; the bull shall be slaughtered before the LORD. ⁵The anointed priest shall take some of the blood of the bull and bring it into the tent of meeting. ⁶The priest shall dip his finger in the blood and sprinkle some of the blood seven times before the LORD in front of the curtain of the sanctuary. ⁷The priest shall put some of the blood on the horns of the altar of fragrant incense that is in the tent of meeting before the LORD; and the rest of the blood of the bull he shall pour out at the base of the altar of burnt offering, which is at the entrance of the tent of meeting. ⁸He shall remove all the fat from the bull of sin offering: the fat that covers the entrails and all the fat that is around the entrails; ⁹the two kidneys with the fat that is on them at the loins; and the appendage of the liver, which he shall remove with the kidneys, ¹⁰just as these are removed from the ox of the sacrifice of well-being. The priest shall turn them into smoke upon the altar of burnt offering. ¹¹But the skin of the bull and all its flesh, as well as its head, its legs, its entrails, and its dung— ¹²all the rest of the bull—he shall carry out to a clean place outside the camp, to the ash heap, and shall burn it on a wood fire; at the ash heap it shall be burned.

13 If the whole congregation of Israel errs unintentionally and the matter escapes the notice of the assembly, and they do any one of the things that by the LORD's commandments ought not to be done and incur guilt; ¹⁴when the sin that they have committed becomes known, the assembly shall offer a bull of the herd for a sin offering and bring it before the tent of meeting. ¹⁵The elders of the congregation shall lay their hands on the head of the bull before the LORD, and the bull shall be slaughtered before the LORD. ¹⁶The anointed priest shall bring some of the blood of the bull into the tent of meeting, ¹⁷and the priest shall dip his finger in the blood and sprinkle it seven times before the LORD, in front of the curtain. ¹⁸He shall put some of the blood on the horns of the altar that is before the LORD in the tent of meeting; and the rest of the blood he shall pour out at the base of the altar of burnt offering that is at the entrance of the tent of meeting. ¹⁹He shall remove all its fat and turn it into smoke on the altar. ²⁰He shall do with the bull just as is done with the bull of sin offering; he shall do the same with this. The priest shall make atonement for them, and they shall be forgiven. ²¹He shall carry the bull outside the camp, and burn it as he burned the first bull; it is the sin offering for the assembly.

22 When a ruler sins, doing unintentionally any one of all the things that by commandments of the LORD his God ought not to be done and incurs guilt, ²³once the sin that he has committed is made known to him, he shall bring as his offering a male goat without blemish. ²⁴He shall lay his hand on the head of the goat; it shall be slaughtered at the spot where the burnt offering is slaughtered before the LORD; it is a sin offering. ²⁵The priest shall take some of the blood of the sin offering with his finger and put it on the horns of the altar of burnt offering, and pour out the rest of its blood at the base of the altar of burnt offering. ²⁶All its fat he shall turn into smoke on the altar, like the fat of the sacrifice of well-being. Thus the priest shall make atonement on his behalf for his sin, and he shall be forgiven.

27 If anyone of the ordinary people among you sins unintentionally in doing any one of the things that by the LORD's commandments ought not to be done and incurs guilt, ²⁸when the sin that you have committed is made known to you, you shall bring a female goat without blemish as your offering, for the sin that you have committed. ²⁹You shall lay your hand on the head of the sin offering; and the sin offering shall be slaughtered at the place of the burnt offering. ³⁰The priest shall take some of its blood with his finger

and put it on the horns of the altar of burnt offering, and he shall pour out the rest of its blood at the base of the altar. ³¹He shall remove all its fat, as the fat is removed from the offering of well-being, and the priest shall turn it into smoke on the altar for a pleasing odor to the LORD. Thus the priest shall make atonement on your behalf, and you shall be forgiven.

32 If the offering you bring as a sin offering is a sheep, you shall bring a female without blemish. ³³You shall lay your hand on the head of the sin offering; and it shall be slaughtered as a sin offering at the spot where the burnt offering is slaughtered. ³⁴The priest shall take some of the blood of the sin offering with his finger and put it on the horns of the altar of burnt offering, and pour out the rest of its blood at the base of the altar. ³⁵You shall remove all its fat, as the fat of the sheep is removed from the sacrifice of well-being, and the priest shall turn it into smoke on the altar, with the offerings by fire to the LORD. Thus the priest shall make atonement on your behalf for the sin that you have committed, and you shall be forgiven.

5 When any of you sin in that you have heard a public adjuration to testify and—though able to testify as one who has seen or learned of the matter—do not speak up, you are subject to punishment. ²Or when any of you touch any unclean thing—whether the carcass of an unclean beast or the carcass of unclean livestock or the carcass of an unclean swarming thing—and are unaware of it, you have become unclean, and are guilty. ³Or when you touch human uncleanness—any uncleanness by which one can become unclean—and are unaware of it, when you come to know it, you shall be guilty. ⁴Or when any of you utter aloud a rash oath for a bad or a good purpose, whatever people utter in an oath, and are unaware of it, when you come to know it, you shall in any of these be guilty. ⁵When you realize your guilt in any of these, you shall confess the sin that you have committed. ⁶And you shall bring to the LORD, as your penalty for the sin that you have committed, a female from the flock, a sheep or a goat, as a sin offering; and the priest shall make atonement on your behalf for your sin.

7 But if you cannot afford a sheep, you shall bring to the LORD, as your penalty for the sin that you have committed, two turtledoves or two pigeons, one for a sin offering and the other for a burnt offering. ⁸You shall bring them to the priest, who shall offer first the one for the sin offering, wringing its head at the nape without severing it. ⁹He shall sprinkle some of the blood of the sin offering on the side of the altar, while the rest of the blood shall be drained out at the base of the altar; it is a sin offering. ¹⁰And the second he shall offer for a burnt offering according to the regulation. Thus the priest shall make atonement on your behalf for the sin that you have committed, and you shall be forgiven.

11 But if you cannot afford two turtledoves or two pigeons, you shall bring as your offering for the sin that you have committed one-tenth of an ephah of choice flour for a sin offering; you shall not put oil on it or lay frankincense on it, for it is a sin offering. ¹²You shall bring it to the priest, and the priest shall scoop up a handful of it as its memorial portion, and turn this into smoke on the altar, with the offerings by fire to the LORD; it is a sin offering. ¹³Thus the priest shall make atonement on your behalf for whichever of these sins you have committed, and you shall be forgiven. Like the grain offering, the rest shall be for the priest.

Offerings with Restitution

14 The LORD spoke to Moses, saying: ¹⁵When any of you commit a trespass and sin unintentionally in any of the holy things of the LORD, you shall bring, as your guilt offering to the LORD, a ram without blemish from the flock, convertible into silver by the sanctuary shekel; it is a guilt offering. ¹⁶And you shall make restitution for the holy thing in which you were remiss, and shall add one-fifth to it and give it to the priest. The priest shall make atonement on your behalf with the ram of the guilt offering, and you shall be forgiven.

17 If any of you sin without knowing it, doing any of the things that by the LORD's commandments ought not to be done, you have incurred guilt, and are subject to punishment. ¹⁸You shall bring to the priest a ram without blemish from the flock, or the equivalent, as a guilt offering; and the priest shall make atonement on your behalf for the error that you committed unintentionally, and you shall

be forgiven. [19]It is a guilt offering; you have incurred guilt before the LORD.

6[b] The LORD spoke to Moses, saying: [2]When any of you sin and commit a trespass against the LORD by deceiving a neighbor in a matter of a deposit or a pledge, or by robbery, or if you have defrauded a neighbor, [3]or have found something lost and lied about it—if you swear falsely regarding any of the various things that one may do and sin thereby— [4]when you have sinned and realize your guilt, and would restore what you took by robbery or by fraud or the deposit that was committed to you, or the lost thing that you found, [5]or anything else about which you have sworn falsely, you shall repay the principal amount and shall add one-fifth to it. You shall pay it to its owner when you realize your guilt. [6]And you shall bring to the priest, as your guilt offering to the LORD, a ram without blemish from the flock, or its equivalent, for a guilt offering. [7]The priest shall make atonement on your behalf before the LORD, and you shall be forgiven for any of the things that one may do and incur guilt thereby.

Instructions concerning Sacrifices

[8][c]The LORD spoke to Moses, saying: [9]Command Aaron and his sons, saying: This is the ritual of the burnt offering. The burnt offering itself shall remain on the hearth upon the altar all night until the morning, while the fire on the altar shall be kept burning. [10]The priest shall put on his linen vestments after putting on his linen undergarments next to his body; and he shall take up the ashes to which the fire has reduced the burnt offering on the altar, and place them beside the altar. [11]Then he shall take off his vestments and put on other garments, and carry the ashes out to a clean place outside the camp. [12]The fire on the altar shall be kept burning; it shall not go out. Every morning the priest shall add wood to it, lay out the burnt offering on it, and turn into smoke the fat pieces of the offerings of well-being. [13]A perpetual fire shall be kept burning on the altar; it shall not go out.

[14] This is the ritual of the grain offering: The sons of Aaron shall offer it before the LORD, in front of the altar. [15]They shall take from it a handful of the choice flour and oil of the grain offering, with all the frankincense that is on the offering, and

they shall turn its memorial portion into smoke on the altar as a pleasing odor to the LORD. [16]Aaron and his sons shall eat what is left of it; it shall be eaten as unleavened cakes in a holy place; in the court of the tent of meeting they shall eat it. [17]It shall not be baked with leaven. I have given it as their portion of my offerings by fire; it is most holy, like the sin offering and the guilt offering. [18]Every male among the descendants of Aaron shall eat of it, as their perpetual due throughout your generations, from the LORD's offerings by fire; anything that touches them shall become holy.

19 The LORD spoke to Moses, saying: [20]This is the offering that Aaron and his sons shall offer to the LORD on the day when he is anointed: one-tenth of an ephah of choice flour as a regular offering, half of it in the morning and half in the evening. [21]It shall be made with oil on a griddle; you shall bring it well soaked, as a grain offering of baked[d] pieces, and you shall present it as a pleasing odor to the LORD. [22]And so the priest, anointed from among Aaron's descendants as a successor, shall prepare it; it is the LORD's—a perpetual due—to be turned entirely into smoke. [23]Every grain offering of a priest shall be wholly burned; it shall not be eaten.

24 The LORD spoke to Moses, saying: [25]Speak to Aaron and his sons, saying: This is the ritual of the sin offering. The sin offering shall be slaughtered before the LORD at the spot where the burnt offering is slaughtered; it is most holy. [26]The priest who offers it as a sin offering shall eat of it; it shall be eaten in a holy place, in the court of the tent of meeting. [27]Whatever touches its flesh shall become holy; and when any of its blood is spattered on a garment, you shall wash the bespattered part in a holy place. [28]An earthen vessel in which it was boiled shall be broken; but if it is boiled in a bronze vessel, that shall be scoured and rinsed in water. [29]Every male among the priests shall eat of it; it is most holy. [30]But no sin offering shall be eaten from which any blood is brought into the tent of meeting for atonement in the holy place; it shall be burned with fire.

b Ch 5.20 in Heb   *c* Ch 6.1 in Heb
d Meaning of Heb uncertain

7 This is the ritual of the guilt offering. It is most holy; ²at the spot where the burnt offering is slaughtered, they shall slaughter the guilt offering, and its blood shall be dashed against all sides of the altar. ³All its fat shall be offered: the broad tail, the fat that covers the entrails, ⁴the two kidneys with the fat that is on them at the loins, and the appendage of the liver, which shall be removed with the kidneys. ⁵The priest shall turn them into smoke on the altar as an offering by fire to the LORD; it is a guilt offering. ⁶Every male among the priests shall eat of it; it shall be eaten in a holy place; it is most holy.

7 The guilt offering is like the sin offering, there is the same ritual for them; the priest who makes atonement with it shall have it. ⁸So, too, the priest who offers anyone's burnt offering shall keep the skin of the burnt offering that he has offered. ⁹And every grain offering baked in the oven, and all that is prepared in a pan or on a griddle, shall belong to the priest who offers it. ¹⁰But every other grain offering, mixed with oil or dry, shall belong to all the sons of Aaron equally.

Further Instructions

11 This is the ritual of the sacrifice of the offering of well-being that one may offer to the LORD. ¹²If you offer it for thanksgiving, you shall offer with the thank offering unleavened cakes mixed with oil, unleavened wafers spread with oil, and cakes of choice flour well soaked in oil. ¹³With your thanksgiving sacrifice of well-being you shall bring your offering with cakes of leavened bread. ¹⁴From this you shall offer one cake from each offering, as a gift to the LORD; it shall belong to the priest who dashes the blood of the offering of well-being. ¹⁵And the flesh of your thanksgiving sacrifice of well-being shall be eaten on the day it is offered; you shall not leave any of it until morning. ¹⁶But if the sacrifice you offer is a votive offering or a freewill offering, it shall be eaten on the day that you offer your sacrifice, and what is left of it shall be eaten the next day; ¹⁷but what is left of the flesh of the sacrifice shall be burned up on the third day. ¹⁸If any of the flesh of your sacrifice of well-being is eaten on the third day, it shall not be acceptable, nor shall it be credited to the one who offers it; it shall be an abomination, and the one who eats of it shall incur guilt.

19 Flesh that touches any unclean thing shall not be eaten; it shall be burned up. As for other flesh, all who are clean may eat such flesh. ²⁰But those who eat flesh from the LORD's sacrifice of well-being while in a state of uncleanness shall be cut off from their kin. ²¹When any one of you touches any unclean thing—human uncleanness or an unclean animal or any unclean creature—and then eats flesh from the LORD's sacrifice of well-being, you shall be cut off from your kin.

22 The LORD spoke to Moses, saying: ²³Speak to the people of Israel, saying: You shall eat no fat of ox or sheep or goat. ²⁴The fat of an animal that died or was torn by wild animals may be put to any other use, but you must not eat it. ²⁵If any one of you eats the fat from an animal of which an offering by fire may be made to the LORD, you who eat it shall be cut off from your kin. ²⁶You must not eat any blood whatever, either of bird or of animal, in any of your settlements. ²⁷Any one of you who eats any blood shall be cut off from your kin.

28 The LORD spoke to Moses, saying: ²⁹Speak to the people of Israel, saying: Any one of you who would offer to the LORD your sacrifice of well-being must yourself bring to the LORD your offering from your sacrifice of well-being. ³⁰Your own hands shall bring the LORD's offering by fire; you shall bring the fat with the breast, so that the breast may be raised as an elevation offering before the LORD. ³¹The priest shall turn the fat into smoke on the altar, but the breast shall belong to Aaron and his sons. ³²And the right thigh from your sacrifices of well-being you shall give to the priest as an offering; ³³the one among the sons of Aaron who offers the blood and fat of the offering of well-being shall have the right thigh for a portion. ³⁴For I have taken the breast of the elevation offering, and the thigh that is offered, from the people of Israel, from their sacrifices of well-being, and have given them to Aaron the priest and to his sons, as a perpetual due from the people of Israel. ³⁵This is the portion allotted to Aaron and to his sons from the offerings made by fire to the LORD, once they have been brought forward to serve the LORD as priests; ³⁶these the LORD commanded to be given them, when he anointed them, as a perpetual due from the people of Israel throughout their generations.

37 This is the ritual of the burnt offering, the grain offering, the sin offering, the guilt offering, the offering of ordination, and the sacrifice of well-being, 38which the LORD commanded Moses on Mount Sinai, when he commanded the people of Israel to bring their offerings to the LORD, in the wilderness of Sinai.

The Rites of Ordination

8 The LORD spoke to Moses, saying: 2Take Aaron and his sons with him, the vestments, the anointing oil, the bull of sin offering, the two rams, and the basket of unleavened bread; 3and assemble the whole congregation at the entrance of the tent of meeting. 4And Moses did as the LORD commanded him. When the congregation was assembled at the entrance of the tent of meeting, 5Moses said to the congregation, "This is what the LORD has commanded to be done."

6 Then Moses brought Aaron and his sons forward, and washed them with water. 7He put the tunic on him, fastened the sash around him, clothed him with the robe, and put the ephod on him. He then put the decorated band of the ephod around him, tying the ephod to him with it. 8He placed the breastpiece on him, and in the breastpiece he put the Urim and the Thummim. 9And he set the turban on his head, and on the turban, in front, he set the golden ornament, the holy crown, as the LORD commanded Moses.

10 Then Moses took the anointing oil and anointed the tabernacle and all that was in it, and consecrated them. 11He sprinkled some of it on the altar seven times, and anointed the altar and all its utensils, and the basin and its base, to consecrate them. 12He poured some of the anointing oil on Aaron's head and anointed him, to consecrate him. 13And Moses brought forward Aaron's sons, and clothed them with tunics, and fastened sashes around them, and tied headdresses on them, as the LORD commanded Moses.

14 He led forward the bull of sin offering; and Aaron and his sons laid their hands upon the head of the bull of sin offering, 15and it was slaughtered. Moses took the blood and with his finger put some on each of the horns of the altar, purifying the altar; then he poured out the blood at the base of the altar. Thus he consecrated it, to make atonement for it. 16Moses took all the fat that was around

the entrails, and the appendage of the liver, and the two kidneys with their fat, and turned them into smoke on the altar. 17But the bull itself, its skin and flesh and its dung, he burned with fire outside the camp, as the LORD commanded Moses.

18 Then he brought forward the ram of burnt offering. Aaron and his sons laid their hands on the head of the ram, 19and it was slaughtered. Moses dashed the blood against all sides of the altar. 20The ram was cut into its parts, and Moses turned into smoke the head and the parts and the suet. 21And after the entrails and the legs were washed with water, Moses turned into smoke the whole ram on the altar; it was a burnt offering for a pleasing odor, an offering by fire to the LORD, as the LORD commanded Moses.

22 Then he brought forward the second ram, the ram of ordination. Aaron and his sons laid their hands on the head of the ram, 23and it was slaughtered. Moses took some of its blood and put it on the lobe of Aaron's right ear and on the thumb of his right hand and on the big toe of his right foot. 24After Aaron's sons were brought forward, Moses put some of the blood on the lobes of their right ears and on the thumbs of their right hands and on the big toes of their right feet; and Moses dashed the rest of the blood against all sides of the altar. 25He took the fat— the broad tail, all the fat that was around the entrails, the appendage of the liver, and the two kidneys with their fat—and the right thigh. 26From the basket of unleavened bread that was before the LORD, he took one cake of unleavened bread, one cake of bread with oil, and one wafer, and placed them on the fat and on the right thigh. 27He placed all these on the palms of Aaron and on the palms of his sons, and raised them as an elevation offering before the LORD. 28Then Moses took them from their hands and turned them into smoke on the altar with the burnt offering. This was an ordination offering for a pleasing odor, an offering by fire to the LORD. 29Moses took the breast and raised it as an elevation offering before the LORD; it was Moses' portion of the ram of ordination, as the LORD commanded Moses.

30 Then Moses took some of the anointing oil and some of the blood that was on the altar and sprinkled them on Aaron and his vestments, and also on his

sons and their vestments. Thus he consecrated Aaron and his vestments, and also his sons and their vestments.

31 And Moses said to Aaron and his sons, "Boil the flesh at the entrance of the tent of meeting, and eat it there with the bread that is in the basket of ordination offerings, as I was commanded, 'Aaron and his sons shall eat it'; 32and what remains of the flesh and the bread you shall burn with fire. 33You shall not go outside the entrance of the tent of meeting for seven days, until the day when your period of ordination is completed. For it will take seven days to ordain you; 34as has been done today, the LORD has commanded to be done to make atonement for you. 35You shall remain at the entrance of the tent of meeting day and night for seven days, keeping the LORD's charge so that you do not die; for so I am commanded." 36Aaron and his sons did all the things that the LORD commanded through Moses.

Aaron's Priesthood Inaugurated

9 On the eighth day Moses summoned Aaron and his sons and the elders of Israel. 2He said to Aaron, "Take a bull calf for a sin offering and a ram for a burnt offering, without blemish, and offer them before the LORD. 3And say to the people of Israel, 'Take a male goat for a sin offering; a calf and a lamb, yearlings without blemish, for a burnt offering; 4and an ox and a ram for an offering of well-being to sacrifice before the LORD; and a grain offering mixed with oil. For today the LORD will appear to you.' " 5They brought what Moses commanded to the front of the tent of meeting; and the whole congregation drew near and stood before the LORD. 6And Moses said, "This is the thing that the LORD commanded you to do, so that the glory of the LORD may appear to you." 7Then Moses said to Aaron, "Draw near to the altar and sacrifice your sin offering and your burnt offering, and make atonement for yourself and for the people; and sacrifice the offering of the people, and make atonement for them; as the LORD has commanded."

8 Aaron drew near to the altar, and slaughtered the calf of the sin offering, which was for himself. 9The sons of Aaron presented the blood to him, and he dipped his finger in the blood and put it on the horns of the altar; and the rest of the blood he poured out at the base of the altar. 10But the fat, the kidneys, and the appendage of the liver from the sin offering he turned into smoke on the altar, as the LORD commanded Moses; 11and the flesh and the skin he burned with fire outside the camp.

12 Then he slaughtered the burnt offering. Aaron's sons brought him the blood, and he dashed it against all sides of the altar. 13And they brought him the burnt offering piece by piece, and the head, which he turned into smoke on the altar. 14He washed the entrails and the legs and, with the burnt offering, turned them into smoke on the altar.

15 Next he presented the people's offering. He took the goat of the sin offering that was for the people, and slaughtered it, and presented it as a sin offering like the first one. 16He presented the burnt offering, and sacrificed it according to regulation. 17He presented the grain offering, and, taking a handful of it, he turned it into smoke on the altar, in addition to the burnt offering of the morning.

18 He slaughtered the ox and the ram as a sacrifice of well-being for the people. Aaron's sons brought him the blood, which he dashed against all sides of the altar, 19and the fat of the ox and of the ram—the broad tail, the fat that covers the entrails, the two kidneys and the fat on them,*e* and the appendage of the liver. 20They first laid the fat on the breasts, and the fat was turned into smoke on the altar; 21and the breasts and the right thigh Aaron raised as an elevation offering before the LORD, as Moses had commanded.

22 Aaron lifted his hands toward the people and blessed them; and he came down after sacrificing the sin offering, the burnt offering, and the offering of well-being. 23Moses and Aaron entered the tent of meeting, and then came out and blessed the people; and the glory of the LORD appeared to all the people. 24Fire came out from the LORD and consumed the burnt offering and the fat on the altar; and when all the people saw it, they shouted and fell on their faces.

Nadab and Abihu

10 Now Aaron's sons, Nadab and Abihu, each took his censer, put fire in it, and laid incense on it; and they

---

e Gk: Heb *the broad tail, and that which covers, and the kidneys*

offered unholy fire before the LORD, such as he had not commanded them. ²And fire came out from the presence of the LORD and consumed them, and they died before the LORD. ³Then Moses said to Aaron, "This is what the LORD meant when he said,

'Through those who are near me
  I will show myself holy,
and before all the people
  I will be glorified.' "
And Aaron was silent.

4 Moses summoned Mishael and Elzaphan, sons of Uzziel the uncle of Aaron, and said to them, "Come forward, and carry your kinsmen away from the front of the sanctuary to a place outside the camp." ⁵They came forward and carried them by their tunics out of the camp, as Moses had ordered. ⁶And Moses said to Aaron and to his sons Eleazar and Ithamar, "Do not dishevel your hair, and do not tear your vestments, or you will die and wrath will strike all the congregation; but your kindred, the whole house of Israel, may mourn the burning that the LORD has sent. ⁷You shall not go outside the entrance of the tent of meeting, or you will die; for the anointing oil of the LORD is on you." And they did as Moses had ordered.

8 And the LORD spoke to Aaron: ⁹Drink no wine or strong drink, neither you nor your sons, when you enter the tent of meeting, that you may not die; it is a statute forever throughout your generations. ¹⁰You are to distinguish between the holy and the common, and between the unclean and the clean; ¹¹and you are to teach the people of Israel all the statutes that the LORD has spoken to them through Moses.

12 Moses spoke to Aaron and to his remaining sons, Eleazar and Ithamar: Take the grain offering that is left from the LORD's offerings by fire, and eat it unleavened beside the altar, for it is most holy; ¹³you shall eat it in a holy place, because it is your due and your sons' due, from the offerings by fire to the LORD; for so I am commanded. ¹⁴But the breast that is elevated and the thigh that is raised, you and your sons and daughters as well may eat in any clean place; for they have been assigned to you and your children from the sacrifices of the offerings of well-being of the people of Israel. ¹⁵The thigh that is raised and the breast that is elevated they shall bring, together with the offerings by fire of the fat, to raise for an elevation

offering before the LORD; they are to be your due and that of your children forever, as the LORD has commanded.

16 Then Moses made inquiry about the goat of the sin offering, and—it had already been burned! He was angry with Eleazar and Ithamar, Aaron's remaining sons, and said, ¹⁷"Why did you not eat the sin offering in the sacred area? For it is most holy, and God*f* has given it to you that you may remove the guilt of the congregation, to make atonement on their behalf before the LORD. ¹⁸Its blood was not brought into the inner part of the sanctuary. You should certainly have eaten it in the sanctuary, as I commanded." ¹⁹And Aaron spoke to Moses, "See, today they offered their sin offering and their burnt offering before the LORD; and yet such things as these have befallen me! If I had eaten the sin offering today, would it have been agreeable to the LORD?" ²⁰And when Moses heard that, he agreed.

Clean and Unclean Foods

11 The LORD spoke to Moses and Aaron, saying to them: ²Speak to the people of Israel, saying:

From among all the land animals, these are the creatures that you may eat. ³Any animal that has divided hoofs and is cleft-footed and chews the cud—such you may eat. ⁴But among those that chew the cud or have divided hoofs, you shall not eat the following: the camel, for even though it chews the cud, it does not have divided hoofs; it is unclean for you. ⁵The rock badger, for even though it chews the cud, it does not have divided hoofs; it is unclean for you. ⁶The hare, for even though it chews the cud, it does not have divided hoofs; it is unclean for you. ⁷The pig, for even though it has divided hoofs and is cleft-footed, it does not chew the cud; it is unclean for you. ⁸Of their flesh you shall not eat, and their carcasses you shall not touch; they are unclean for you.

9 These you may eat, of all that are in the waters. Everything in the waters that has fins and scales, whether in the seas or in the streams—such you may eat. ¹⁰But anything in the seas or the streams that does not have fins and scales, of the swarming creatures in the waters and among all the other living creatures that are in the waters—they are detestable to

f Heb *he*

you ¹¹and detestable they shall remain. Of their flesh you shall not eat, and their carcasses you shall regard as detestable. ¹²Everything in the waters that does not have fins and scales is detestable to you.

13 These you shall regard as detestable among the birds. They shall not be eaten; they are an abomination: the eagle, the vulture, the osprey, ¹⁴the buzzard, the kite of any kind; ¹⁵every raven of any kind; ¹⁶the ostrich, the nighthawk, the sea gull, the hawk of any kind; ¹⁷the little owl, the cormorant, the great owl, ¹⁸the water hen, the desert owl, *ᵍ* the carrion vulture, ¹⁹the stork, the heron of any kind, the hoopoe, and the bat.*ʰ*

20 All winged insects that walk upon all fours are detestable to you. ²¹But among the winged insects that walk on all fours you may eat those that have jointed legs above their feet, with which to leap on the ground. ²²Of them you may eat: the locust according to its kind, the bald locust according to its kind, the cricket according to its kind, and the grasshopper according to its kind. ²³But all other winged insects that have four feet are detestable to you.

Unclean Animals

24 By these you shall become unclean; whoever touches the carcass of any of them shall be unclean until the evening, ²⁵and whoever carries any part of the carcass of any of them shall wash his clothes and be unclean until the evening. ²⁶Every animal that has divided hoofs but is not cleft-footed or does not chew the cud is unclean for you; everyone who touches one of them shall be unclean. ²⁷All that walk on their paws, among the animals that walk on all fours, are unclean for you; whoever touches the carcass of any of them shall be unclean until the evening, ²⁸and the one who carries the carcass shall wash his clothes and be unclean until the evening; they are unclean for you.

29 These are unclean for you among the creatures that swarm upon the earth: the weasel, the mouse, the great lizard according to its kind, ³⁰the gecko, the land crocodile, the lizard, the sand lizard, and the chameleon. ³¹These are unclean for you among all that swarm; whoever touches one of them when they are dead shall be unclean until the evening. ³²And anything upon which any of them falls when they are dead shall be unclean,

whether an article of wood or cloth or skin or sacking, any article that is used for any purpose; it shall be dipped into water, and it shall be unclean until the evening, and then it shall be clean. ³³And if any of them falls into any earthen vessel, all that is in it shall be unclean, and you shall break the vessel. ³⁴Any food that could be eaten shall be unclean if water from any such vessel comes upon it; and any liquid that could be drunk shall be unclean if it was in any such vessel. ³⁵Everything on which any part of the carcass falls shall be unclean; whether an oven or stove, it shall be broken in pieces; they are unclean, and shall remain unclean for you. ³⁶But a spring or a cistern holding water shall be clean, while whatever touches the carcass in it shall be unclean. ³⁷If any part of their carcass falls upon any seed set aside for sowing, it is clean; ³⁸but if water is put on the seed and any part of their carcass falls on it, it is unclean for you.

39 If an animal of which you may eat dies, anyone who touches its carcass shall be unclean until the evening. ⁴⁰Those who eat of its carcass shall wash their clothes and be unclean until the evening; and those who carry the carcass shall wash their clothes and be unclean until the evening.

41 All creatures that swarm upon the earth are detestable; they shall not be eaten. ⁴²Whatever moves on its belly, and whatever moves on all fours, or whatever has many feet, all the creatures that swarm upon the earth, you shall not eat; for they are detestable. ⁴³You shall not make yourselves detestable with any creature that swarms; you shall not defile yourselves with them, and so become unclean. ⁴⁴For I am the LORD your God; sanctify yourselves therefore, and be holy, for I am holy. You shall not defile yourselves with any swarming creature that moves on the earth. ⁴⁵For I am the LORD who brought you up from the land of Egypt, to be your God; you shall be holy, for I am holy.

46 This is the law pertaining to land animal and bird and every living creature that moves through the waters and every creature that swarms upon the earth, ⁴⁷to make a distinction between the unclean and the clean, and between the living

ᵍ Or *pelican*   *ʰ* Identification of several of the birds in verses 13-19 is uncertain

creature that may be eaten and the living creature that may not be eaten.

Purification of Women after Childbirth

12 The LORD spoke to Moses, saying: ²Speak to the people of Israel, saying:

If a woman conceives and bears a male child, she shall be ceremonially unclean seven days; as at the time of her menstruation, she shall be unclean. ³On the eighth day the flesh of his foreskin shall be circumcised. ⁴Her time of blood purification shall be thirty-three days; she shall not touch any holy thing, or come into the sanctuary, until the days of her purification are completed. ⁵If she bears a female child, she shall be unclean two weeks, as in her menstruation; her time of blood purification shall be sixty-six days.

6 When the days of her purification are completed, whether for a son or for a daughter, she shall bring to the priest at the entrance of the tent of meeting a lamb in its first year for a burnt offering, and a pigeon or a turtledove for a sin offering. ⁷He shall offer it before the LORD, and make atonement on her behalf; then she shall be clean from her flow of blood. This is the law for her who bears a child, male or female. ⁸If she cannot afford a sheep, she shall take two turtledoves or two pigeons, one for a burnt offering and the other for a sin offering; and the priest shall make atonement on her behalf, and she shall be clean.

Leprosy, Varieties and Symptoms

13 The LORD spoke to Moses and Aaron, saying:

2 When a person has on the skin of his body a swelling or an eruption or a spot, and it turns into a leprous*ⁱ* disease on the skin of his body, he shall be brought to Aaron the priest or to one of his sons the priests. ³The priest shall examine the disease on the skin of his body, and if the hair in the diseased area has turned white and the disease appears to be deeper than the skin of his body, it is a leprous*ⁱ* disease; after the priest has examined him he shall pronounce him ceremonially unclean. ⁴But if the spot is white in the skin of his body, and appears no deeper than the skin, and the hair in it has not turned white, the priest shall confine the diseased person for seven days. ⁵The priest shall examine him on the seventh day, and if

he sees that the disease is checked and the disease has not spread in the skin, then the priest shall confine him seven days more. ⁶The priest shall examine him again on the seventh day, and if the disease has abated and the disease has not spread in the skin, the priest shall pronounce him clean; it is only an eruption; and he shall wash his clothes, and be clean. ⁷But if the eruption spreads in the skin after he has shown himself to the priest for his cleansing, he shall appear again before the priest. ⁸The priest shall make an examination, and if the eruption has spread in the skin, the priest shall pronounce him unclean; it is a leprous*ⁱ* disease.

9 When a person contracts a leprous*ⁱ* disease, he shall be brought to the priest. ¹⁰The priest shall make an examination, and if there is a white swelling in the skin that has turned the hair white, and there is quick raw flesh in the swelling, ¹¹it is a chronic leprous*ⁱ* disease in the skin of his body. The priest shall pronounce him unclean; he shall not confine him, for he is unclean. ¹²But if the disease breaks out in the skin, so that it covers all the skin of the diseased person from head to foot, so far as the priest can see, ¹³then the priest shall make an examination, and if the disease has covered all his body, he shall pronounce him clean of the disease; since it has all turned white, he is clean. ¹⁴But if raw flesh ever appears on him, he shall be unclean; ¹⁵the priest shall examine the raw flesh and pronounce him unclean. Raw flesh is unclean, for it is a leprous*ⁱ* disease. ¹⁶But if the raw flesh again turns white, he shall come to the priest; ¹⁷the priest shall examine him, and if the disease has turned white, the priest shall pronounce the diseased person clean. He is clean.

18 When there is on the skin of one's body a boil that has healed, ¹⁹and in the place of the boil there appears a white swelling or a reddish-white spot, it shall be shown to the priest. ²⁰The priest shall make an examination, and if it appears deeper than the skin and its hair has turned white, the priest shall pronounce him unclean; this is a leprous*ⁱ* disease, broken out in the boil. ²¹But if the priest examines it and the hair on it is not white, nor is it deeper than the skin but has abat-

ⁱ A term for several skin diseases; precise meaning uncertain ed, the priest shall confine him seven days. 22If it spreads in the skin, the priest shall pronounce him unclean; it is diseased. 23But if the spot remains in one place and does not spread, it is the scar of the boil; the priest shall pronounce him clean.

24 Or, when the body has a burn on the skin and the raw flesh of the burn becomes a spot, reddish-white or white, 25the priest shall examine it. If the hair in the spot has turned white and it appears deeper than the skin, it is a leprous*j* disease; it has broken out in the burn, and the priest shall pronounce him unclean. This is a leprous*j* disease. 26But if the priest examines it and the hair in the spot is not white, and it is no deeper than the skin but has abated, the priest shall confine him seven days. 27The priest shall examine him the seventh day; if it is spreading in the skin, the priest shall pronounce him unclean. This is a leprous*j* disease. 28But if the spot remains in one place and does not spread in the skin but has abated, it is a swelling from the burn, and the priest shall pronounce him clean; for it is the scar of the burn.

29 When a man or woman has a disease on the head or in the beard, 30the priest shall examine the disease. If it appears deeper than the skin and the hair in it is yellow and thin, the priest shall pronounce him unclean; it is an itch, a leprous*j* disease of the head or the beard. 31If the priest examines the itching disease, and it appears no deeper than the skin and there is no black hair in it, the priest shall confine the person with the itching disease for seven days. 32On the seventh day the priest shall examine the itch; if the itch has not spread, and there is no yellow hair in it, and the itch appears to be no deeper than the skin, 33he shall shave, but the itch he shall not shave. The priest shall confine the person with the itch for seven days more. 34On the seventh day the priest shall examine the itch; if the itch has not spread in the skin and it appears to be no deeper than the skin, the priest shall pronounce him clean. He shall wash his clothes and be clean. 35But if the itch spreads in the skin after he was pronounced clean, 36the priest shall examine him. If the itch has spread in the skin, the priest need not seek for the yellow hair; he is unclean. 37But if in his eyes the itch is checked, and black hair has grown in it, the itch is healed, he is clean; and the priest shall pronounce him clean.

38 When a man or a woman has spots on the skin of the body, white spots, 39the priest shall make an examination, and if the spots on the skin of the body are of a dull white, it is a rash that has broken out on the skin; he is clean.

40 If anyone loses the hair from his head, he is bald but he is clean. 41If he loses the hair from his forehead and temples, he has baldness of the forehead but he is clean. 42But if there is on the bald head or the bald forehead a reddish-white diseased spot, it is a leprous*j* disease breaking out on his bald head or his bald forehead. 43The priest shall examine him; if the diseased swelling is reddish-white on his bald head or on his bald forehead, which resembles a leprous*j* disease in the skin of the body, 44he is leprous,*j* he is unclean. The priest shall pronounce him unclean; the disease is on his head.

45 The person who has the leprous*j* disease shall wear torn clothes and let the hair of his head be disheveled; and he shall cover his upper lip and cry out, "Unclean, unclean." 46He shall remain unclean as long as he has the disease; he is unclean. He shall live alone; his dwelling shall be outside the camp.

47 Concerning clothing: when a leprous*j* disease appears in it, in woolen or linen cloth, 48in warp or woof of linen or wool, or in a skin or in anything made of skin, 49if the disease shows greenish or reddish in the garment, whether in warp or woof or in skin or in anything made of skin, it is a leprous*j* disease and shall be shown to the priest. 50The priest shall examine the disease, and put the diseased article aside for seven days. 51He shall examine the disease on the seventh day. If the disease has spread in the cloth, in warp or woof, or in the skin, whatever be the use of the skin, this is a spreading leprous*j* disease; it is unclean. 52He shall burn the clothing, whether diseased in warp or woof, woolen or linen, or anything of skin, for it is a spreading leprous*j* disease; it shall be burned in fire.

53 If the priest makes an examination, and the disease has not spread in the clothing, in warp or woof or in anything

---

j A term for several skin diseases; precise meaning uncertain

of skin, ⁵⁴the priest shall command them to wash the article in which the disease appears, and he shall put it aside seven days more. ⁵⁵The priest shall examine the diseased article after it has been washed. If the diseased spot has not changed color, though the disease has not spread, it is unclean; you shall burn it in fire, whether the leprous^k spot is on the inside or on the outside.

56 If the priest makes an examination, and the disease has abated after it is washed, he shall tear the spot out of the cloth, in warp or woof, or out of skin. ⁵⁷If it appears again in the garment, in warp or woof, or in anything of skin, it is spreading; you shall burn with fire that in which the disease appears. ⁵⁸But the cloth, warp or woof, or anything of skin from which the disease disappears when you have washed it, shall then be washed a second time, and it shall be clean.

59 This is the ritual for a leprous^k disease in a cloth of wool or linen, either in warp or woof, or in anything of skin, to decide whether it is clean or unclean.

Purification of Lepers and Leprous Houses

14 The LORD spoke to Moses, saying: ²This shall be the ritual for the leprous^k person at the time of his cleansing:

He shall be brought to the priest; ³the priest shall go out of the camp, and the priest shall make an examination. If the disease is healed in the leprous^k person, ⁴the priest shall command that two living clean birds and cedarwood and crimson yarn and hyssop be brought for the one who is to be cleansed. ⁵The priest shall command that one of the birds be slaughtered over fresh water in an earthen vessel. ⁶He shall take the living bird with the cedarwood and the crimson yarn and the hyssop, and dip them and the living bird in the blood of the bird that was slaughtered over the fresh water. ⁷He shall sprinkle it seven times upon the one who is to be cleansed of the leprous^k disease; then he shall pronounce him clean, and he shall let the living bird go into the open field. ⁸The one who is to be cleansed shall wash his clothes, and shave off all his hair, and bathe himself in water, and he shall be clean. After that he shall come into the camp, but shall live outside his tent seven days. ⁹On the seventh day he shall shave all his hair: of head, beard,

eyebrows; he shall shave all his hair. Then he shall wash his clothes, and bathe his body in water, and he shall be clean.

10 On the eighth day he shall take two male lambs without blemish, and one ewe lamb in its first year without blemish, and a grain offering of three-tenths of an ephah of choice flour mixed with oil, and one log^l of oil. ¹¹The priest who cleanses shall set the person to be cleansed, along with these things, before the LORD, at the entrance of the tent of meeting. ¹²The priest shall take one of the lambs, and offer it as a guilt offering, along with the log^l of oil, and raise them as an elevation offering before the LORD. ¹³He shall slaughter the lamb in the place where the sin offering and the burnt offering are slaughtered in the holy place; for the guilt offering, like the sin offering, belongs to the priest: it is most holy. ¹⁴The priest shall take some of the blood of the guilt offering and put it on the lobe of the right ear of the one to be cleansed, and on the thumb of the right hand, and on the big toe of the right foot. ¹⁵The priest shall take some of the log^l of oil and pour it into the palm of his own left hand, ¹⁶and dip his right finger in the oil that is in his left hand and sprinkle some oil with his finger seven times before the LORD. ¹⁷Some of the oil that remains in his hand the priest shall put on the lobe of the right ear of the one to be cleansed, and on the thumb of the right hand, and on the big toe of the right foot, on top of the blood of the guilt offering. ¹⁸The rest of the oil that is in the priest's hand he shall put on the head of the one to be cleansed. Then the priest shall make atonement on his behalf before the LORD: ¹⁹the priest shall offer the sin offering, to make atonement for the one to be cleansed from his uncleanness. Afterward he shall slaughter the burnt offering; ²⁰and the priest shall offer the burnt offering and the grain offering on the altar. Thus the priest shall make atonement on his behalf and he shall be clean.

21 But if he is poor and cannot afford so much, he shall take one male lamb for a guilt offering to be elevated, to make atonement on his behalf, and one-tenth of an ephah of choice flour mixed with oil for a grain offering and a log^l of oil; ²²also two turtledoves or two pigeons,

---

^{k} A term for several skin diseases; precise meaning uncertain ^{l} A liquid measure

such as he can afford, one for a sin offering and the other for a burnt offering. [23]On the eighth day he shall bring them for his cleansing to the priest, to the entrance of the tent of meeting, before the LORD; [24]and the priest shall take the lamb of the guilt offering and the log[m] of oil, and the priest shall raise them as an elevation offering before the LORD. [25]The priest shall slaughter the lamb of the guilt offering and shall take some of the blood of the guilt offering, and put it on the lobe of the right ear of the one to be cleansed, and on the thumb of the right hand, and on the big toe of the right foot. [26]The priest shall pour some of the oil into the palm of his own left hand, [27]and shall sprinkle with his right finger some of the oil that is in his left hand seven times before the LORD. [28]The priest shall put some of the oil that is in his hand on the lobe of the right ear of the one to be cleansed, and on the thumb of the right hand, and the big toe of the right foot, where the blood of the guilt offering was placed. [29]The rest of the oil that is in the priest's hand he shall put on the head of the one to be cleansed, to make atonement on his behalf before the LORD. [30]And he shall offer, of the turtledoves or pigeons such as he can afford, [31]one[n] for a sin offering and the other for a burnt offering, along with a grain offering; and the priest shall make atonement before the LORD on behalf of the one being cleansed. [32]This is the ritual for the one who has a leprous[o] disease, who cannot afford the offerings for his cleansing.

[33] The LORD spoke to Moses and Aaron, saying:

[34] When you come into the land of Canaan, which I give you for a possession, and I put a leprous[o] disease in a house in the land of your possession, [35]the owner of the house shall come and tell the priest, saying, "There seems to me to be some sort of disease in my house." [36]The priest shall command that they empty the house before the priest goes to examine the disease, or all that is in the house will become unclean; and afterward the priest shall go in to inspect the house. [37]He shall examine the disease; if the disease is in the walls of the house with greenish or reddish spots, and if it appears to be deeper than the surface, [38]the priest shall go outside to the door of the house and shut up the house seven days. [39]The priest shall come again on the seventh day and make

an inspection; if the disease has spread in the walls of the house, [40]the priest shall command that the stones in which the disease appears be taken out and thrown into an unclean place outside the city. [41]He shall have the inside of the house scraped thoroughly, and the plaster that is scraped off shall be dumped in an unclean place outside the city. [42]They shall take other stones and put them in the place of those stones, and take other plaster and plaster the house.

[43] If the disease breaks out again in the house, after he has taken out the stones and scraped the house and plastered it, [44]the priest shall go and make inspection; if the disease has spread in the house, it is a spreading leprous[o] disease in the house; it is unclean. [45]He shall have the house torn down, its stones and timber and all the plaster of the house, and taken outside the city to an unclean place. [46]All who enter the house while it is shut up shall be unclean until the evening; [47]and all who sleep in the house shall wash their clothes; and all who eat in the house shall wash their clothes.

[48] If the priest comes and makes an inspection, and the disease has not spread in the house after the house was plastered, the priest shall pronounce the house clean; the disease is healed. [49]For the cleansing of the house he shall take two birds, with cedarwood and crimson yarn and hyssop, [50]and shall slaughter one of the birds over fresh water in an earthen vessel, [51]and shall take the cedarwood and the hyssop and the crimson yarn, along with the living bird, and dip them in the blood of the slaughtered bird and the fresh water, and sprinkle the house seven times. [52]Thus he shall cleanse the house with the blood of the bird, and with the fresh water, and with the living bird, and with the cedarwood and hyssop and crimson yarn; [53]and he shall let the living bird go out of the city into the open field; so he shall make atonement for the house, and it shall be clean.

[54] This is the ritual for any leprous[o] disease: for an itch, [55]for leprous[o] diseases in clothing and houses, [56]and for a swelling or an eruption or a spot, [57]to determine when it is unclean and when it is

---

[m] A liquid measure   [n] Gk Syr: Heb *afford*, [31]*such as he can afford, one*   [o] A term for several skin diseases; precise meaning uncertain

clean. This is the ritual for leprous *p* diseases.

Concerning Bodily Discharges

15 The LORD spoke to Moses and Aaron, saying: ²Speak to the people of Israel and say to them:

When any man has a discharge from his member, *q* his discharge makes him ceremonially unclean. ³The uncleanness of his discharge is this: whether his member *q* flows with his discharge, or his member *q* is stopped from discharging, it is uncleanness for him. ⁴Every bed on which the one with the discharge lies shall be unclean; and everything on which he sits shall be unclean. ⁵Anyone who touches his bed shall wash his clothes, and bathe in water, and be unclean until the evening. ⁶All who sit on anything on which the one with the discharge has sat shall wash their clothes, and bathe in water, and be unclean until the evening. ⁷All who touch the body of the one with the discharge shall wash their clothes, and bathe in water, and be unclean until the evening. ⁸If the one with the discharge spits on persons who are clean, then they shall wash their clothes, and bathe in water, and be unclean until the evening. ⁹Any saddle on which the one with the discharge rides shall be unclean. ¹⁰All who touch anything that was under him shall be unclean until the evening, and all who carry such a thing shall wash their clothes, and bathe in water, and be unclean until the evening. ¹¹All those whom the one with the discharge touches without his having rinsed his hands in water shall wash their clothes, and bathe in water, and be unclean until the evening. ¹²Any earthen vessel that the one with the discharge touches shall be broken; and every vessel of wood shall be rinsed in water.

13 When the one with a discharge is cleansed of his discharge, he shall count seven days for his cleansing; he shall wash his clothes and bathe his body in fresh water, and he shall be clean. ¹⁴On the eighth day he shall take two turtledoves or two pigeons and come before the LORD to the entrance of the tent of meeting and give them to the priest. ¹⁵The priest shall offer them, one for a sin offering and the other for a burnt offering; and the priest shall make atonement on his behalf before the LORD for his discharge.

16 If a man has an emission of semen, he shall bathe his whole body in water, and be unclean until the evening. ¹⁷Everything made of cloth or of skin on which the semen falls shall be washed with water, and be unclean until the evening. ¹⁸If a man lies with a woman and has an emission of semen, both of them shall bathe in water, and be unclean until the evening.

19 When a woman has a discharge of blood that is her regular discharge from her body, she shall be in her impurity for seven days, and whoever touches her shall be unclean until the evening. ²⁰Everything upon which she lies during her impurity shall be unclean; everything also upon which she sits shall be unclean. ²¹Whoever touches her bed shall wash his clothes, and bathe in water, and be unclean until the evening. ²²Whoever touches anything upon which she sits shall wash his clothes, and bathe in water, and be unclean until the evening; ²³whether it is the bed or anything upon which she sits, when he touches it he shall be unclean until the evening. ²⁴If any man lies with her, and her impurity falls on him, he shall be unclean seven days; and every bed on which he lies shall be unclean.

25 If a woman has a discharge of blood for many days, not at the time of her impurity, or if she has a discharge beyond the time of her impurity, all the days of the discharge she shall continue in uncleanness; as in the days of her impurity, she shall be unclean. ²⁶Every bed on which she lies during all the days of her discharge shall be treated as the bed of her impurity; and everything on which she sits shall be unclean, as in the uncleanness of her impurity. ²⁷Whoever touches these things shall be unclean, and shall wash his clothes, and bathe in water, and be unclean until the evening. ²⁸If she is cleansed of her discharge, she shall count seven days, and after that she shall be clean. ²⁹On the eighth day she shall take two turtledoves or two pigeons and bring them to the priest at the entrance of the tent of meeting. ³⁰The priest shall offer one for a sin offering and the other for a burnt offering; and the priest shall make atonement on her behalf before the LORD for her unclean discharge.

31 Thus you shall keep the people of

p A term for several skin diseases; precise meaning uncertain   *q* Heb *flesh*

Israel separate from their uncleanness, so that they do not die in their uncleanness by defiling my tabernacle that is in their midst.

32 This is the ritual for those who have a discharge: for him who has an emission of semen, becoming unclean thereby, 33for her who is in the infirmity of her period, for anyone, male or female, who has a discharge, and for the man who lies with a woman who is unclean.

The Day of Atonement

16 The LORD spoke to Moses after the death of the two sons of Aaron, when they drew near before the LORD and died. 2The LORD said to Moses:

Tell your brother Aaron not to come just at any time into the sanctuary inside the curtain before the mercy seat[r] that is upon the ark, or he will die; for I appear in the cloud upon the mercy seat.[r] 3Thus shall Aaron come into the holy place: with a young bull for a sin offering and a ram for a burnt offering. 4He shall put on the holy linen tunic, and shall have the linen undergarments next to his body, fasten the linen sash, and wear the linen turban; these are the holy vestments. He shall bathe his body in water, and then put them on. 5He shall take from the congregation of the people of Israel two male goats for a sin offering, and one ram for a burnt offering.

6 Aaron shall offer the bull as a sin offering for himself, and shall make atonement for himself and for his house. 7He shall take the two goats and set them before the LORD at the entrance of the tent of meeting; 8and Aaron shall cast lots on the two goats, one lot for the LORD and the other lot for Azazel.[s] 9Aaron shall present the goat on which the lot fell for the LORD, and offer it as a sin offering; 10but the goat on which the lot fell for Azazel[s] shall be presented alive before the LORD to make atonement over it, that it may be sent away into the wilderness to Azazel.[s]

11 Aaron shall present the bull as a sin offering for himself, and shall make atonement for himself and for his house; he shall slaughter the bull as a sin offering for himself. 12He shall take a censer full of coals of fire from the altar before the LORD, and two handfuls of crushed sweet incense, and he shall bring it inside the curtain 13and put the incense on the fire before the LORD, that the cloud of the incense may cover the mercy seat[r] that is upon the covenant,[t] or he will die. 14He shall take some of the blood of the bull, and sprinkle it with his finger on the front of the mercy seat,[r] and before the mercy seat[r] he shall sprinkle the blood with his finger seven times.

15 He shall slaughter the goat of the sin offering that is for the people and bring its blood inside the curtain, and do with its blood as he did with the blood of the bull, sprinkling it upon the mercy seat[r] and before the mercy seat.[r] 16Thus he shall make atonement for the sanctuary, because of the uncleannesses of the people of Israel, and because of their transgressions, all their sins; and so he shall do for the tent of meeting, which remains with them in the midst of their uncleannesses. 17No one shall be in the tent of meeting from the time he enters to make atonement in the sanctuary until he comes out and has made atonement for himself and for his house and for all the assembly of Israel. 18Then he shall go out to the altar that is before the LORD and make atonement on its behalf, and shall take some of the blood of the bull and of the blood of the goat, and put it on each of the horns of the altar. 19He shall sprinkle some of the blood on it with his finger seven times, and cleanse it and hallow it from the uncleannesses of the people of Israel.

20 When he has finished atoning for the holy place and the tent of meeting and the altar, he shall present the live goat. 21Then Aaron shall lay both his hands on the head of the live goat, and confess over it all the iniquities of the people of Israel, and all their transgressions, all their sins, putting them on the head of the goat, and sending it away into the wilderness by means of someone designated for the task.[u] 22The goat shall bear on itself all their iniquities to a barren region; and the goat shall be set free in the wilderness.

23 Then Aaron shall enter the tent of meeting, and shall take off the linen vestments that he put on when he went into the holy place, and shall leave them there. 24He shall bathe his body in water in a holy place, and put on his vestments; then

---

[r] Or *the cover*   [s] Traditionally rendered *a scapegoat*   [t] Or *treaty*, or *testament*; Heb *eduth*   [u] Meaning of Heb uncertain

he shall come out and offer his burnt offering and the burnt offering of the people, making atonement for himself and for the people. 25The fat of the sin offering he shall turn into smoke on the altar. 26The one who sets the goat free for Azazel*v* shall wash his clothes and bathe his body in water, and afterward may come into the camp. 27The bull of the sin offering and the goat of the sin offering, whose blood was brought in to make atonement in the holy place, shall be taken outside the camp; their skin and their flesh and their dung shall be consumed in fire. 28The one who burns them shall wash his clothes and bathe his body in water, and afterward may come into the camp.

29 This shall be a statute to you forever: In the seventh month, on the tenth day of the month, you shall deny yourselves,*w* and shall do no work, neither the citizen nor the alien who resides among you. 30For on this day atonement shall be made for you, to cleanse you; from all your sins you shall be clean before the LORD. 31It is a sabbath of complete rest to you, and you shall deny yourselves;*w* it is a statute forever. 32The priest who is anointed and consecrated as priest in his father's place shall make atonement, wearing the linen vestments, the holy vestments. 33He shall make atonement for the sanctuary, and he shall make atonement for the tent of meeting and for the altar, and he shall make atonement for the priests and for all the people of the assembly. 34This shall be an everlasting statute for you, to make atonement for the people of Israel once in the year for all their sins. And Moses did as the LORD had commanded him.

The Slaughtering of Animals

17 The LORD spoke to Moses: 2 Speak to Aaron and his sons and to all the people of Israel and say to them: This is what the LORD has commanded. 3If anyone of the house of Israel slaughters an ox or a lamb or a goat in the camp, or slaughters it outside the camp, 4and does not bring it to the entrance of the tent of meeting, to present it as an offering to the LORD before the tabernacle of the LORD, he shall be held guilty of bloodshed; he has shed blood, and he shall be cut off from the people. 5This is in order that the people of Israel may bring their sacrifices that they offer in the open field, that they may bring them to the LORD, to the priest at the entrance of the tent of meeting, and offer them as sacrifices of well-being to the LORD. 6The priest shall dash the blood against the altar of the LORD at the entrance of the tent of meeting, and turn the fat into smoke as a pleasing odor to the LORD, 7so that they may no longer offer their sacrifices for goat-demons, to whom they prostitute themselves. This shall be a statute forever to them throughout their generations.

8 And say to them further: Anyone of the house of Israel or of the aliens who reside among them who offers a burnt offering or sacrifice, 9and does not bring it to the entrance of the tent of meeting, to sacrifice it to the LORD, shall be cut off from the people.

Eating Blood Prohibited

10 If anyone of the house of Israel or of the aliens who reside among them eats any blood, I will set my face against that person who eats blood, and will cut that person off from the people. 11For the life of the flesh is in the blood; and I have given it to you for making atonement for your lives on the altar; for, as life, it is the blood that makes atonement. 12Therefore I have said to the people of Israel: No person among you shall eat blood, nor shall any alien who resides among you eat blood. 13And anyone of the people of Israel, or of the aliens who reside among them, who hunts down an animal or bird that may be eaten shall pour out its blood and cover it with earth.

14 For the life of every creature—its blood is its life; therefore I have said to the people of Israel: You shall not eat the blood of any creature, for the life of every creature is its blood; whoever eats it shall be cut off. 15All persons, citizens or aliens, who eat what dies of itself or what has been torn by wild animals, shall wash their clothes, and bathe themselves in water, and be unclean until the evening; then they shall be clean. 16But if they do not wash themselves or bathe their body, they shall bear their guilt.

Sexual Relations

18 The LORD spoke to Moses, saying: 2 Speak to the people of Israel

v Traditionally rendered *a scapegoat*   *w* Or *shall fast*

and say to them: I am the LORD your God.
³You shall not do as they do in the land of
Egypt, where you lived, and you shall not
do as they do in the land of Canaan, to
which I am bringing you. You shall not
follow their statutes. ⁴My ordinances you
shall observe and my statutes you shall
keep, following them: I am the LORD your
God. ⁵You shall keep my statutes and my
ordinances; by doing so one shall live: I
am the LORD.

6 None of you shall approach anyone
near of kin to uncover nakedness: I am the
LORD. ⁷You shall not uncover the nakedness of your father, which is the nakedness of your mother; she is your mother,
you shall not uncover her nakedness.
⁸You shall not uncover the nakedness of
your father's wife; it is the nakedness of
your father. ⁹You shall not uncover the
nakedness of your sister, your father's
daughter or your mother's daughter,
whether born at home or born abroad.
¹⁰You shall not uncover the nakedness of
your son's daughter or of your daughter's
daughter, for their nakedness is your own
nakedness. ¹¹You shall not uncover the
nakedness of your father's wife's daughter,
begotten by your father, since she is your
sister. ¹²You shall not uncover the nakedness of your father's sister; she is your father's flesh. ¹³You shall not uncover the
nakedness of your mother's sister, for she
is your mother's flesh. ¹⁴You shall not
uncover the nakedness of your father's
brother, that is, you shall not approach
his wife; she is your aunt. ¹⁵You shall not
uncover the nakedness of your daughter-
in-law: she is your son's wife; you shall
not uncover her nakedness. ¹⁶You shall
not uncover the nakedness of your brother's wife; it is your brother's nakedness.
¹⁷You shall not uncover the nakedness of
a woman and her daughter, and you shall
not take*ˣ* her son's daughter or her
daughter's daughter to uncover her nakedness; they are your*ʸ* flesh; it is depravity.
¹⁸And you shall not take*ˣ* a woman as a
rival to her sister, uncovering her nakedness while her sister is still alive.

19 You shall not approach a woman to
uncover her nakedness while she is in her
menstrual uncleanness. ²⁰You shall not
have sexual relations with your kinsman's
wife, and defile yourself with her. ²¹You
shall not give any of your offspring to sacrifice them*ᶻ* to Molech, and so profane
the name of your God: I am the LORD.

²²You shall not lie with a male as with a
woman; it is an abomination. ²³You shall
not have sexual relations with any animal
and defile yourself with it, nor shall any
woman give herself to an animal to have
sexual relations with it: it is perversion.

24 Do not defile yourselves in any of
these ways, for by all these practices the
nations I am casting out before you have
defiled themselves. ²⁵Thus the land became defiled; and I punished it for its iniquity, and the land vomited out its inhabitants. ²⁶But you shall keep my
statutes and my ordinances and commit
none of these abominations, either the
citizen or the alien who resides among
you ²⁷(for the inhabitants of the land,
who were before you, committed all of
these abominations, and the land became
defiled); ²⁸otherwise the land will vomit
you out for defiling it, as it vomited out
the nation that was before you. ²⁹For
whoever commits any of these abominations shall be cut off from their people.
³⁰So keep my charge not to commit any of
these abominations that were done before
you, and not to defile yourselves by them:
I am the LORD your God.

Ritual and Moral Holiness

19 The LORD spoke to Moses, saying:
2 Speak to all the congregation of
the people of Israel and say to them: You
shall be holy, for I the LORD your God am
holy. ³You shall each revere your mother
and father, and you shall keep my sabbaths: I am the LORD your God. ⁴Do not
turn to idols or make cast images for yourselves: I am the LORD your God.

5 When you offer a sacrifice of well-
being to the LORD, offer it in such a way
that it is acceptable in your behalf. ⁶It
shall be eaten on the same day you offer
it, or on the next day; and anything left
over until the third day shall be consumed
in fire. ⁷If it is eaten at all on the third day,
it is an abomination; it will not be acceptable. ⁸All who eat it shall be subject to
punishment, because they have profaned
what is holy to the LORD; and any such
person shall be cut off from the people.

9 When you reap the harvest of your
land, you shall not reap to the very edges
of your field, or gather the gleanings of
your harvest. ¹⁰You shall not strip your

x Or *marry*   *y* Gk: Heb lacks *your*   *z* Heb *to pass*
them over

vineyard bare, or gather the fallen grapes of your vineyard; you shall leave them for the poor and the alien: I am the LORD your God.

11 You shall not steal; you shall not deal falsely; and you shall not lie to one another. 12And you shall not swear falsely by my name, profaning the name of your God: I am the LORD.

13 You shall not defraud your neighbor; you shall not steal; and you shall not keep for yourself the wages of a laborer until morning. 14You shall not revile the deaf or put a stumbling block before the blind; you shall fear your God: I am the LORD.

15 You shall not render an unjust judgment; you shall not be partial to the poor or defer to the great: with justice you shall judge your neighbor. 16You shall not go around as a slanderer[a] among your people, and you shall not profit by the blood[b] of your neighbor: I am the LORD.

___

[a] Meaning of Heb uncertain   [b] Heb *stand against the blood*

Be Holy

FRIDAY

Scripture Reading for Today:
Leviticus 19.1–4

Verse for Today:
Leviticus 19.2

One night, I woke up with a start. I looked up at the ceiling and there, as though on a movie or television screen, was a picture of a beautiful garden. The garden had many flowers and among these flowers were little weeds.

The Lord said to me, "Briege, this is your soul." The flowers represented the virtues I was trying to cultivate in my efforts to become holy. But at the same time, as I walked around the garden admiring the flowers, I was looking at the weeds and saying, "Oh, they're just small and they won't do a bit of harm." I saw myself giving the weeds a little pat saying, "I'll not bother with you. You're just little weeds."

Then the Lord said to me, "Those weeds represent sin. You are comparing yourself with the world, with all the evil in the world."

You know how it is. We hear about all the terrible things that go on in the world and then we say, "Oh, but I don't kill or steal. I don't push drugs. I don't sell my body in prostitution," and so on.

The Lord said to me, "You are not called to compare yourself with the world. You are called to compare yourself with me. I am your model. Not the world. You must never accept sin."

As I continued to look at the image, I saw the gardener coming in. He looked at me and said, "If you let me, I'll eradicate those weeds for you. Then the flowers will have a brighter color and there will be greater growth in your garden."

The Lord showed me two things through this image. First, I cannot save myself. I cannot make my garden beautiful on my own; I cannot become holy on my own. I must acknowledge that I am a sinner. If I don't, I am self-righteous and proud. Second, I learned the value of repentance and the beauty of confession. Confession is coming to the Jesus who loves me.

—*BRIEGE MCKENNA, O.S.C.*

Go to page 146 for your next devotional reading.

17 You shall not hate in your heart anyone of your kin; you shall reprove your neighbor, or you will incur guilt yourself. ¹⁸You shall not take vengeance or bear a grudge against any of your people, but you shall love your neighbor as yourself: I am the LORD.

19 You shall keep my statutes. You shall not let your animals breed with a different kind; you shall not sow your field with two kinds of seed; nor shall you put on a garment made of two different materials.

20 If a man has sexual relations with a woman who is a slave, designated for another man but not ransomed or given her freedom, an inquiry shall be held. They shall not be put to death, since she has not been freed; ²¹but he shall bring a guilt offering for himself to the LORD, at the entrance of the tent of meeting, a ram as guilt offering. ²²And the priest shall make atonement for him with the ram of guilt offering before the LORD for his sin that he committed; and the sin he committed shall be forgiven him.

23 When you come into the land and plant all kinds of trees for food, then you shall regard their fruit as forbidden;ᶜ three years it shall be forbiddenᵈ to you, it must not be eaten. ²⁴In the fourth year all their fruit shall be set apart for rejoicing in the LORD. ²⁵But in the fifth year you may eat of their fruit, that their yield may be increased for you: I am the LORD your God.

26 You shall not eat anything with its blood. You shall not practice augury or witchcraft. ²⁷You shall not round off the hair on your temples or mar the edges of your beard. ²⁸You shall not make any gashes in your flesh for the dead or tattoo any marks upon you: I am the LORD.

29 Do not profane your daughter by making her a prostitute, that the land not become prostituted and full of depravity. ³⁰You shall keep my sabbaths and reverence my sanctuary: I am the LORD.

31 Do not turn to mediums or wizards; do not seek them out, to be defiled by them: I am the LORD your God.

32 You shall rise before the aged, and defer to the old; and you shall fear your God: I am the LORD.

33 When an alien resides with you in your land, you shall not oppress the alien. ³⁴The alien who resides with you shall be to you as the citizen among you; you shall

love the alien as yourself, for you were aliens in the land of Egypt: I am the LORD your God.

35 You shall not cheat in measuring length, weight, or quantity. ³⁶You shall have honest balances, honest weights, an honest ephah, and an honest hin: I am the LORD your God, who brought you out of the land of Egypt. ³⁷You shall keep all my statutes and all my ordinances, and observe them: I am the LORD.

Penalties for Violations of Holiness

20 The LORD spoke to Moses, saying: ²Say further to the people of Israel:

Any of the people of Israel, or of the aliens who reside in Israel, who give any of their offspring to Molech shall be put to death; the people of the land shall stone them to death. ³I myself will set my face against them, and will cut them off from the people, because they have given of their offspring to Molech, defiling my sanctuary and profaning my holy name. ⁴And if the people of the land should ever close their eyes to them, when they give of their offspring to Molech, and do not put them to death, ⁵I myself will set my face against them and against their family, and will cut them off from among their people, them and all who follow them in prostituting themselves to Molech.

6 If any turn to mediums and wizards, prostituting themselves to them, I will set my face against them, and will cut them off from the people. ⁷Consecrate yourselves therefore, and be holy; for I am the LORD your God. ⁸Keep my statutes, and observe them; I am the LORD; I sanctify you. ⁹All who curse father or mother shall be put to death; having cursed father or mother, their blood is upon them.

10 If a man commits adultery with the wife ofᵉ his neighbor, both the adulterer and the adulteress shall be put to death. ¹¹The man who lies with his father's wife has uncovered his father's nakedness; both of them shall be put to death; their blood is upon them. ¹²If a man lies with his daughter-in-law, both of them shall be put to death; they have committed perversion, their blood is upon them. ¹³If a man lies with a male as with a woman,

---

ᶜ Heb *as their uncircumcision*   ᵈ Heb
uncircumcision   ᵉ Heb repeats *if a man commits
adultery with the wife of*

both of them have committed an abomination; they shall be put to death; their blood is upon them. ¹⁴If a man takes a wife and her mother also, it is depravity; they shall be burned to death, both he and they, that there may be no depravity among you. ¹⁵If a man has sexual relations with an animal, he shall be put to death; and you shall kill the animal. ¹⁶If a woman approaches any animal and has sexual relations with it, you shall kill the woman and the animal; they shall be put to death, their blood is upon them.

17 If a man takes his sister, a daughter of his father or a daughter of his mother, and sees her nakedness, and she sees his nakedness, it is a disgrace, and they shall be cut off in the sight of their people; he has uncovered his sister's nakedness, he shall be subject to punishment. ¹⁸If a man lies with a woman having her sickness and uncovers her nakedness, he has laid bare her flow and she has laid bare her flow of blood; both of them shall be cut off from their people. ¹⁹You shall not uncover the nakedness of your mother's sister or of your father's sister, for that is to lay bare one's own flesh; they shall be subject to punishment. ²⁰If a man lies with his uncle's wife, he has uncovered his uncle's nakedness; they shall be subject to punishment; they shall die childless. ²¹If a man takes his brother's wife, it is impurity; he has uncovered his brother's nakedness; they shall be childless.

22 You shall keep all my statutes and all my ordinances, and observe them, so that the land to which I bring you to settle in may not vomit you out. ²³You shall not follow the practices of the nation that I am driving out before you. Because they did all these things, I abhorred them. ²⁴But I have said to you: You shall inherit their land, and I will give it to you to possess, a land flowing with milk and honey. I am the LORD your God; I have separated you from the peoples. ²⁵You shall therefore make a distinction between the clean animal and the unclean, and between the unclean bird and the clean; you shall not bring abomination on yourselves by animal or by bird or by anything with which the ground teems, which I have set apart for you to hold unclean. ²⁶You shall be holy to me; for I the LORD am holy, and I have separated you from the other peoples to be mine.

27 A man or a woman who is a medium or a wizard shall be put to death; they shall be stoned to death, their blood is upon them.

The Holiness of Priests

21 The LORD said to Moses: Speak to the priests, the sons of Aaron, and say to them:

No one shall defile himself for a dead person among his relatives, ²except for his nearest kin: his mother, his father, his son, his daughter, his brother; ³likewise, for a virgin sister, close to him because she has had no husband, he may defile himself for her. ⁴But he shall not defile himself as a husband among his people and so profane himself. ⁵They shall not make bald spots upon their heads, or shave off the edges of their beards, or make any gashes in their flesh. ⁶They shall be holy to their God, and not profane the name of their God; for they offer the LORD's offerings by fire, the food of their God; therefore they shall be holy. ⁷They shall not marry a prostitute or a woman who has been defiled; neither shall they marry a woman divorced from her husband. For they are holy to their God, ⁸and you shall treat them as holy, since they offer the food of your God; they shall be holy to you, for I the LORD, I who sanctify you, am holy. ⁹When the daughter of a priest profanes herself through prostitution, she profanes her father; she shall be burned to death.

10 The priest who is exalted above his fellows, on whose head the anointing oil has been poured and who has been consecrated to wear the vestments, shall not dishevel his hair, nor tear his vestments. ¹¹He shall not go where there is a dead body; he shall not defile himself even for his father or mother. ¹²He shall not go outside the sanctuary and thus profane the sanctuary of his God; for the consecration of the anointing oil of his God is upon him: I am the LORD. ¹³He shall marry only a woman who is a virgin. ¹⁴A widow, or a divorced woman, or a woman who has been defiled, a prostitute, these he shall not marry. He shall marry a virgin of his own kin, ¹⁵that he may not profane his offspring among his kin; for I am the LORD; I sanctify him.

16 The LORD spoke to Moses, saying: ¹⁷Speak to Aaron and say: No one of your offspring throughout their generations who has a blemish may approach to offer

the food of his God. [18]For no one who has a blemish shall draw near, one who is blind or lame, or one who has a mutilated face or a limb too long, [19]or one who has a broken foot or a broken hand, [20]or a hunchback, or a dwarf, or a man with a blemish in his eyes or an itching disease or scabs or crushed testicles. [21]No descendant of Aaron the priest who has a blemish shall come near to offer the LORD's offerings by fire; since he has a blemish, he shall not come near to offer the food of his God. [22]He may eat the food of his God, of the most holy as well as of the holy. [23]But he shall not come near the curtain or approach the altar, because he has a blemish, that he may not profane my sanctuaries; for I am the LORD; I sanctify them. [24]Thus Moses spoke to Aaron and to his sons and to all the people of Israel.

The Use of Holy Offerings

22 The LORD spoke to Moses, saying: [2]Direct Aaron and his sons to deal carefully with the sacred donations of the people of Israel, which they dedicate to me, so that they may not profane my holy name; I am the LORD. [3]Say to them: If anyone among all your offspring throughout your generations comes near the sacred donations, which the people of Israel dedicate to the LORD, while he is in a state of uncleanness, that person shall be cut off from my presence: I am the LORD. [4]No one of Aaron's offspring who has a leprous[f] disease or suffers a discharge may eat of the sacred donations until he is clean. Whoever touches anything made unclean by a corpse or a man who has had an emission of semen, [5]and whoever touches any swarming thing by which he may be made unclean or any human being by whom he may be made unclean— whatever his uncleanness may be— [6]the person who touches any such shall be unclean until evening and shall not eat of the sacred donations unless he has washed his body in water. [7]When the sun sets he shall be clean; and afterward he may eat of the sacred donations, for they are his food. [8]That which died or was torn by wild animals he shall not eat, becoming unclean by it: I am the LORD. [9]They shall keep my charge, so that they may not incur guilt and die in the sanctuary[g] for having profaned it: I am the LORD; I sanctify them.

[10] No lay person shall eat of the sacred donations. No bound or hired servant of the priest shall eat of the sacred donations; [11]but if a priest acquires anyone by purchase, the person may eat of them; and those that are born in his house may eat of his food. [12]If a priest's daughter marries a layman, she shall not eat of the offering of the sacred donations; [13]but if a priest's daughter is widowed or divorced, without offspring, and returns to her father's house, as in her youth, she may eat of her father's food. No lay person shall eat of it. [14]If a man eats of the sacred donation unintentionally, he shall add one-fifth of its value to it, and give the sacred donation to the priest. [15]No one shall profane the sacred donations of the people of Israel, which they offer to the LORD, [16]causing them to bear guilt requiring a guilt offering, by eating their sacred donations: for I am the LORD; I sanctify them.

Acceptable Offerings

17 The LORD spoke to Moses, saying: [18]Speak to Aaron and his sons and all the people of Israel and say to them: When anyone of the house of Israel or of the aliens residing in Israel presents an offering, whether in payment of a vow or as a freewill offering that is offered to the LORD as a burnt offering, [19]to be acceptable in your behalf it shall be a male without blemish, of the cattle or the sheep or the goats. [20]You shall not offer anything that has a blemish, for it will not be acceptable in your behalf.

21 When anyone offers a sacrifice of well-being to the LORD, in fulfillment of a vow or as a freewill offering, from the herd or from the flock, to be acceptable it must be perfect; there shall be no blemish in it. [22]Anything blind, or injured, or maimed, or having a discharge or an itch or scabs—these you shall not offer to the LORD or put any of them on the altar as offerings by fire to the LORD. [23]An ox or a lamb that has a limb too long or too short you may present for a freewill offering; but it will not be accepted for a vow. [24]Any animal that has its testicles bruised or crushed or torn or cut, you shall not offer to the LORD; such you shall not do within your land, [25]nor shall you accept any such animals from a foreigner to offer

---

f A term for several skin diseases; precise meaning uncertain   g Vg: Heb *incur guilt for it and die in it*

as food to your God; since they are mutilated, with a blemish in them, they shall not be accepted in your behalf.

26 The LORD spoke to Moses, saying: 27When an ox or a sheep or a goat is born, it shall remain seven days with its mother, and from the eighth day on it shall be acceptable as the LORD's offering by fire. 28But you shall not slaughter, from the herd or the flock, an animal with its young on the same day. 29When you sacrifice a thanksgiving offering to the LORD, you shall sacrifice it so that it may be acceptable in your behalf. 30It shall be eaten on the same day; you shall not leave any of it until morning: I am the LORD.

31 Thus you shall keep my commandments and observe them: I am the LORD. 32You shall not profane my holy name, that I may be sanctified among the people of Israel: I am the LORD; I sanctify you, 33I who brought you out of the land of Egypt to be your God: I am the LORD.

Appointed Festivals

23 The LORD spoke to Moses, saying: 2Speak to the people of Israel and say to them: These are the appointed festivals of the LORD that you shall proclaim as holy convocations, my appointed festivals.

THE TRADITION

The Church Year

These are the appointed festivals of the LORD that you shall proclaim as holy convocations, my appointed festivals.

LEVITICUS 23.2

Some things are too vast to take in all at once. Our eyes sweep over the Grand Canyon and the night sky, but our brains can process only so many impressions at a time. Our hearts enter into the miracles of human life and love, but not even in a lifetime will we penetrate their depths.

God's saving plan is like that. The eternal mysteries surrounding our redemption are unimaginably deep and dazzling. How can we—time-bound creatures of limited perceptions—ever approach them?

The Church's answer is the liturgical year. Like the Israelites who commemorated God's saving actions with fixed "festivals of the Lord," we consider the mysteries of our faith in stages, on a regular cycle. Week by week, the Church unfolds various aspects of the one Paschal mystery and invites us to view it from different angles.

We might compare this approach to visiting an enormous museum filled with paintings of the most exquisite appeal. Every year the Church travels through this collection together. We begin on a note of expectation for the Lord's return with Advent. We view the masterpiece of the incarnation at Christmas and Epiphany. Elsewhere in this interactive exhibit, we participate in Lent and Paschaltide. We are drawn into additional scenes from Jesus' life and teaching. We see portraits of his mother and his followers. But in the central hall is the masterpiece, a luminous work of art whose theme and radiance spill over into the entire collection. This is the sacred Triduum—the remembrance of Christ's death and resurrection, which fills and transfigures the whole year.

Interspersed among these feasts and seasons is "ordinary time" that glows with resurrection light. Each Sunday we return to that masterpiece in the main hall; we contemplate Christ's dying and rising; and we respond with praise and thanks.

The Church year guides us into inexhaustible mysteries. Eternal riches are opened up to us and "in some way made present for all time." We "lay hold of them and are filled with saving grace" (Vatican II, *Constitution on the Sacred Liturgy*, 102).

The Sabbath, Passover, and Unleavened Bread

3 Six days shall work be done; but the seventh day is a sabbath of complete rest, a holy convocation; you shall do no work: it is a sabbath to the LORD throughout your settlements.

4 These are the appointed festivals of the LORD, the holy convocations, which you shall celebrate at the time appointed for them. 5In the first month, on the fourteenth day of the month, at twilight,*h* there shall be a passover offering to the LORD, 6and on the fifteenth day of the same month is the festival of unleavened bread to the LORD; seven days you shall eat unleavened bread. 7On the first day you shall have a holy convocation; you shall not work at your occupations. 8For seven days you shall present the LORD's offerings by fire; on the seventh day there shall be a holy convocation: you shall not work at your occupations.

The Offering of First Fruits

9 The LORD spoke to Moses: 10Speak to the people of Israel and say to them: When you enter the land that I am giving you and you reap its harvest, you shall bring the sheaf of the first fruits of your harvest to the priest. 11He shall raise the sheaf before the LORD, that you may find acceptance; on the day after the sabbath the priest shall raise it. 12On the day when you raise the sheaf, you shall offer a lamb a year old, without blemish, as a burnt offering to the LORD. 13And the grain offering with it shall be two-tenths of an ephah of choice flour mixed with oil, an offering by fire of pleasing odor to the LORD; and the drink offering with it shall be of wine, one-fourth of a hin. 14You shall eat no bread or parched grain or fresh ears until that very day, until you have brought the offering of your God: it is a statute forever throughout your generations in all your settlements.

The Festival of Weeks

15 And from the day after the sabbath, from the day on which you bring the sheaf of the elevation offering, you shall count off seven weeks; they shall be complete. 16You shall count until the day after the seventh sabbath, fifty days; then you shall present an offering of new grain to the LORD. 17You shall bring from your set-

tlements two loaves of bread as an elevation offering, each made of two-tenths of an ephah; they shall be of choice flour, baked with leaven, as first fruits to the LORD. 18You shall present with the bread seven lambs a year old without blemish, one young bull, and two rams; they shall be a burnt offering to the LORD, along with their grain offering and their drink offerings, an offering by fire of pleasing odor to the LORD. 19You shall also offer one male goat for a sin offering, and two male lambs a year old as a sacrifice of well-being. 20The priest shall raise them with the bread of the first fruits as an elevation offering before the LORD, together with the two lambs; they shall be holy to the LORD for the priest. 21On that same day you shall make proclamation; you shall hold a holy convocation; you shall not work at your occupations. This is a statute forever in all your settlements throughout your generations.

22 When you reap the harvest of your land, you shall not reap to the very edges of your field, or gather the gleanings of your harvest; you shall leave them for the poor and for the alien: I am the LORD your God.

The Festival of Trumpets

23 The LORD spoke to Moses, saying: 24Speak to the people of Israel, saying: In the seventh month, on the first day of the month, you shall observe a day of complete rest, a holy convocation commemorated with trumpet blasts. 25You shall not work at your occupations; and you shall present the LORD's offering by fire.

The Day of Atonement

26 The LORD spoke to Moses, saying: 27Now, the tenth day of this seventh month is the day of atonement; it shall be a holy convocation for you: you shall deny yourselves*i* and present the LORD's offering by fire; 28and you shall do no work during that entire day; for it is a day of atonement, to make atonement on your behalf before the LORD your God. 29For anyone who does not practice self-denial*j* during that entire day shall be cut off from the people. 30And anyone who does any work during that entire day, such a one I will destroy from the midst of the

h Heb between the two evenings   i Or shall fast
j Or does not fast

people. [31]You shall do no work: it is a statute forever throughout your generations in all your settlements. [32]It shall be to you a sabbath of complete rest, and you shall deny yourselves;[k] on the ninth day of the month at evening, from evening to evening you shall keep your sabbath.

The Festival of Booths

33 The LORD spoke to Moses, saying: [34]Speak to the people of Israel, saying: On the fifteenth day of this seventh month, and lasting seven days, there shall be the festival of booths[l] to the LORD. [35]The first day shall be a holy convocation; you shall not work at your occupations. [36]Seven days you shall present the LORD's offerings by fire; on the eighth day you shall observe a holy convocation and present the LORD's offerings by fire; it is a solemn assembly; you shall not work at your occupations.

37 These are the appointed festivals of the LORD, which you shall celebrate as times of holy convocation, for presenting to the LORD offerings by fire—burnt offerings and grain offerings, sacrifices and drink offerings, each on its proper day— [38]apart from the sabbaths of the LORD, and apart from your gifts, and apart from all your votive offerings, and apart from all your freewill offerings, which you give to the LORD.

39 Now, the fifteenth day of the seventh month, when you have gathered in the produce of the land, you shall keep the festival of the LORD, lasting seven days; a complete rest on the first day, and a complete rest on the eighth day. [40]On the first day you shall take the fruit of majestic[m] trees, branches of palm trees, boughs of leafy trees, and willows of the brook; and you shall rejoice before the LORD your God for seven days. [41]You shall keep it as a festival to the LORD seven days in the year; you shall keep it in the seventh month as a statute forever throughout your generations. [42]You shall live in booths for seven days; all that are citizens in Israel shall live in booths, [43]so that your generations may know that I made the people of Israel live in booths when I brought them out of the land of Egypt: I am the LORD your God.

44 Thus Moses declared to the people of Israel the appointed festivals of the LORD.

The Lamp

24 The LORD spoke to Moses, saying: [2]Command the people of Israel to bring you pure oil of beaten olives for the lamp, that a light may be kept burning regularly. [3]Aaron shall set it up in the tent of meeting, outside the curtain of the covenant,[n] to burn from evening to morning before the LORD regularly; it shall be a statute forever throughout your generations. [4]He shall set up the lamps on the lampstand of pure gold[o] before the LORD regularly.

The Bread for the Tabernacle

5 You shall take choice flour, and bake twelve loaves of it; two-tenths of an ephah shall be in each loaf. [6]You shall place them in two rows, six in a row, on the table of pure gold.[p] [7]You shall put pure frankincense with each row, as a token offering for the bread, as an offering by fire to the LORD. [8]Every sabbath day Aaron shall set them in order before the LORD regularly as a commitment of the people of Israel, as a covenant forever. [9]They shall be for Aaron and his descendants, who shall eat them in a holy place, for they are most holy portions for him from the offerings by fire to the LORD, a perpetual due.

Blasphemy and Its Punishment

10 A man whose mother was an Israelite and whose father was an Egyptian came out among the people of Israel; and the Israelite woman's son and a certain Israelite began fighting in the camp. [11]The Israelite woman's son blasphemed the Name in a curse. And they brought him to Moses—now his mother's name was Shelomith, daughter of Dibri, of the tribe of Dan— [12]and they put him in custody, until the decision of the LORD should be made clear to them.

13 The LORD said to Moses, saying: [14]Take the blasphemer outside the camp; and let all who were within hearing lay their hands on his head, and let the whole congregation stone him. [15]And speak to the people of Israel, saying: Anyone who curses God shall bear the sin. [16]One who blasphemes the name of the LORD shall be

---

k Or *shall fast* l Or *tabernacles*: Heb *succoth*
m Meaning of Heb uncertain n Or *treaty*, or *testament*; Heb *eduth* o Heb *pure lampstand*
p Heb *pure table*

put to death; the whole congregation shall stone the blasphemer. Aliens as well as citizens, when they blaspheme the Name, shall be put to death. ¹⁷Anyone who kills a human being shall be put to death. ¹⁸Anyone who kills an animal shall make restitution for it, life for life. ¹⁹Anyone who maims another shall suffer the same injury in return: ²⁰fracture for fracture, eye for eye, tooth for tooth; the injury inflicted is the injury to be suffered. ²¹One who kills an animal shall make restitution for it; but one who kills a human being shall be put to death. ²²You shall have one law for the alien and for the citizen: for I am the Lord your God. ²³Moses spoke thus to the people of Israel; and they took the blasphemer outside the camp, and stoned him to death. The people of Israel did as the Lord had commanded Moses.

The Sabbatical Year

25 The Lord spoke to Moses on Mount Sinai, saying: ²Speak to the people of Israel and say to them: When you enter the land that I am giving you, the land shall observe a sabbath for the Lord. ³Six years you shall sow your field, and six years you shall prune your vineyard, and gather in their yield; ⁴but in the seventh year there shall be a sabbath of complete rest for the land, a sabbath for the Lord: you shall not sow your field or prune your vineyard. ⁵You shall not reap the aftergrowth of your harvest or gather the grapes of your unpruned vine: it shall be a year of complete rest for the land. ⁶You may eat what the land yields during its sabbath—you, your male and female slaves, your hired and your bound laborers who live with you; ⁷for your livestock also, and for the wild animals in your land all its yield shall be for food.

The Year of Jubilee

8 You shall count off seven weeks*q* of years, seven times seven years, so that the period of seven weeks of years gives forty-nine years. ⁹Then you shall have the trumpet sounded loud; on the tenth day of the seventh month—on the day of atonement—you shall have the trumpet sounded throughout all your land. ¹⁰And you shall hallow the fiftieth year and you shall proclaim liberty throughout the land to all its inhabitants. It shall be a jubilee for you: you shall return, every one of you, to your property and every one of you to

your family. ¹¹That fiftieth year shall be a jubilee for you: you shall not sow, or reap the aftergrowth, or harvest the unpruned vines. ¹²For it is a jubilee; it shall be holy to you: you shall eat only what the field itself produces.

13 In this year of jubilee you shall return, every one of you, to your property. ¹⁴When you make a sale to your neighbor or buy from your neighbor, you shall not cheat one another. ¹⁵When you buy from your neighbor, you shall pay only for the number of years since the jubilee; the seller shall charge you only for the remaining crop years. ¹⁶If the years are more, you shall increase the price, and if the years are fewer, you shall diminish the price; for it is a certain number of harvests that are being sold to you. ¹⁷You shall not cheat one another, but you shall fear your God; for I am the Lord your God.

18 You shall observe my statutes and faithfully keep my ordinances, so that you may live on the land securely. ¹⁹The land will yield its fruit, and you will eat your fill and live on it securely. ²⁰Should you ask, "What shall we eat in the seventh year, if we may not sow or gather in our crop?" ²¹I will order my blessing for you in the sixth year, so that it will yield a crop for three years. ²²When you sow in the eighth year, you will be eating from the old crop; until the ninth year, when its produce comes in, you shall eat the old. ²³The land shall not be sold in perpetuity, for the land is mine; with me you are but aliens and tenants. ²⁴Throughout the land that you hold, you shall provide for the redemption of the land.

25 If anyone of your kin falls into difficulty and sells a piece of property, then the next of kin shall come and redeem what the relative has sold. ²⁶If the person has no one to redeem it, but then prospers and finds sufficient means to do so, ²⁷the years since its sale shall be computed and the difference shall be refunded to the person to whom it was sold, and the property shall be returned. ²⁸But if there are not sufficient means to recover it, what was sold shall remain with the purchaser until the year of jubilee; in the jubilee it shall be released, and the property shall be returned.

29 If anyone sells a dwelling house in a walled city, it may be redeemed until a

q Or sabbaths

year has elapsed since its sale; the right of redemption shall be one year. [30]If it is not redeemed before a full year has elapsed, a house that is in a walled city shall pass in perpetuity to the purchaser, throughout the generations; it shall not be released in the jubilee. [31]But houses in villages that have no walls around them shall be classed as open country; they may be redeemed, and they shall be released in the jubilee. [32]As for the cities of the Levites, the Levites shall forever have the right of redemption of the houses in the cities belonging to them. [33]Such property as may be redeemed from the Levites—houses sold in a city belonging to them—shall be released in the jubilee; because the houses in the cities of the Levites are their possession among the people of Israel. [34]But the open land around their cities may not be sold; for that is their possession for all time.

35 If any of your kin fall into difficulty and become dependent on you,[r] you shall support them; they shall live with you as though resident aliens. [36]Do not take interest in advance or otherwise make a profit from them, but fear your God; let them live with you. [37]You shall not lend them your money at interest taken in advance, or provide them food at a profit. [38]I am the LORD your God, who brought you out of the land of Egypt, to give you the land of Canaan, to be your God.

39 If any who are dependent on you become so impoverished that they sell themselves to you, you shall not make them serve as slaves. [40]They shall remain with you as hired or bound laborers. They shall serve with you until the year of the jubilee. [41]Then they and their children with them shall be free from your authority; they shall go back to their own family and return to their ancestral property. [42]For they are my servants, whom I brought out of the land of Egypt; they shall not be sold as slaves are sold. [43]You shall not rule over them with harshness, but shall fear your God. [44]As for the male and female slaves whom you may have, it is from the nations around you that you may acquire male and female slaves. [45]You may also acquire them from among the aliens residing with you, and from their families that are with you, who have been born in your land; and they may be your property. [46]You may keep them as a

possession for your children after you, for them to inherit as property. These you may treat as slaves, but as for your fellow Israelites, no one shall rule over the other with harshness.

47 If resident aliens among you prosper, and if any of your kin fall into difficulty with one of them and sell themselves to an alien, or to a branch of the alien's family, [48]after they have sold themselves they shall have the right of redemption; one of their brothers may redeem them, [49]or their uncle or their uncle's son may redeem them, or anyone of their family who is of their own flesh may redeem them; or if they prosper they may redeem themselves. [50]They shall compute with the purchaser the total from the year when they sold themselves to the alien until the jubilee year; the price of the sale shall be applied to the number of years: the time they were with the owner shall be rated as the time of a hired laborer. [51]If many years remain, they shall pay for their redemption in proportion to the purchase price; [52]and if few years remain until the jubilee year, they shall compute thus: according to the years involved they shall make payment for their redemption. [53]As a laborer hired by the year they shall be under the alien's authority, who shall not, however, rule with harshness over them in your sight. [54]And if they have not been redeemed in any of these ways, they and their children with them shall go free in the jubilee year. [55]For to me the people of Israel are servants; they are my servants whom I brought out from the land of Egypt: I am the LORD your God.

Rewards for Obedience

26 You shall make for yourselves no idols and erect no carved images or pillars, and you shall not place figured stones in your land, to worship at them; for I am the LORD your God. [2]You shall keep my sabbaths and reverence my sanctuary: I am the LORD.

3 If you follow my statutes and keep my commandments and observe them faithfully, [4]I will give you your rains in their season, and the land shall yield its produce, and the trees of the field shall yield their fruit. [5]Your threshing shall overtake the vintage, and the vintage shall overtake the sowing; you shall eat

[r] Meaning of Heb uncertain

your bread to the full, and live securely in your land. 6And I will grant peace in the land, and you shall lie down, and no one shall make you afraid; I will remove dangerous animals from the land, and no sword shall go through your land. 7You shall give chase to your enemies, and they shall fall before you by the sword. 8Five of you shall give chase to a hundred, and a hundred of you shall give chase to ten thousand; your enemies shall fall before you by the sword. 9I will look with favor upon you and make you fruitful and multiply you; and I will maintain my covenant with you. 10You shall eat old grain long stored, and you shall have to clear out the old to make way for the new. 11I will place my dwelling in your midst, and I shall not abhor you. 12And I will walk among you, and will be your God, and you shall be my people. 13I am the LORD your God who brought you out of the land of Egypt, to be their slaves no more; I have broken the bars of your yoke and made you walk erect.

Penalties for Disobedience

14 But if you will not obey me, and do not observe all these commandments, 15if you spurn my statutes, and abhor my ordinances, so that you will not observe all my commandments, and you break my covenant, 16I in turn will do this to you: I will bring terror on you; consumption and fever that waste the eyes and cause life to pine away. You shall sow your seed in vain, for your enemies shall eat it. 17I will set my face against you, and you shall be struck down by your enemies; your foes shall rule over you, and you shall flee though no one pursues you. 18And if in spite of this you will not obey me, I will continue to punish you sevenfold for your sins. 19I will break your proud glory, and I will make your sky like iron and your earth like copper. 20Your strength shall be spent to no purpose: your land shall not yield its produce, and the trees of the land shall not yield their fruit.

21 If you continue hostile to me, and will not obey me, I will continue to plague you sevenfold for your sins. 22I will let loose wild animals against you, and they shall bereave you of your children and destroy your livestock; they shall make you few in number, and your roads shall be deserted.

23 If in spite of these punishments you

have not turned back to me, but continue hostile to me, 24then I too will continue hostile to you: I myself will strike you sevenfold for your sins. 25I will bring the sword against you, executing vengeance for the covenant; and if you withdraw within your cities, I will send pestilence among you, and you shall be delivered into enemy hands. 26When I break your staff of bread, ten women shall bake your bread in a single oven, and they shall dole out your bread by weight; and though you eat, you shall not be satisfied.

27 But if, despite this, you disobey me, and continue hostile to me, 28I will continue hostile to you in fury; I in turn will punish you myself sevenfold for your sins. 29You shall eat the flesh of your sons, and you shall eat the flesh of your daughters. 30I will destroy your high places and cut down your incense altars; I will heap your carcasses on the carcasses of your idols. I will abhor you. 31I will lay your cities waste, will make your sanctuaries desolate, and I will not smell your pleasing odors. 32I will devastate the land, so that your enemies who come to settle in it shall be appalled at it. 33And you I will scatter among the nations, and I will unsheathe the sword against you; your land shall be a desolation, and your cities a waste.

34 Then the land shall enjoys its sabbath years as long as it lies desolate, while you are in the land of your enemies; then the land shall rest, and enjoys its sabbath years. 35As long as it lies desolate, it shall have the rest it did not have on your sabbaths when you were living on it. 36And as for those of you who survive, I will send faintness into their hearts in the lands of their enemies; the sound of a driven leaf shall put them to flight, and they shall flee as one flees from the sword, and they shall fall though no one pursues. 37They shall stumble over one another, as if to escape a sword, though no one pursues; and you shall have no power to stand against your enemies. 38You shall perish among the nations, and the land of your enemies shall devour you. 39And those of you who survive shall languish in the land of your enemies because of their iniquities; also they shall languish because of the iniquities of their ancestors.

40 But if they confess their iniquity

s Or *make up for*

and the iniquity of their ancestors, in that they committed treachery against me and, moreover, that they continued hostile to me— ⁴¹so that I, in turn, continued hostile to them and brought them into the land of their enemies; if then their uncircumcised heart is humbled and they make amends for their iniquity, ⁴²then will I remember my covenant with Jacob; I will remember also my covenant with Isaac and also my covenant with Abraham, and I will remember the land. ⁴³For the land shall be deserted by them, and enjoyᵗ its sabbath years by lying desolate without them, while they shall make amends for their iniquity, because they dared to spurn my ordinances, and they abhorred my statutes. ⁴⁴Yet for all that, when they are in the land of their enemies, I will not spurn them, or abhor them so as to destroy them utterly and break my covenant with them; for I am the LORD their God; ⁴⁵but I will remember in their favor the covenant with their ancestors whom I brought out of the land of Egypt in the sight of the nations, to be their God: I am the LORD.

46 These are the statutes and ordinances and laws that the LORD established between himself and the people of Israel on Mount Sinai through Moses.

Votive Offerings

27 The LORD spoke to Moses, saying: ²Speak to the people of Israel and say to them: When a person makes an explicit vow to the LORD concerning the equivalent for a human being, ³the equivalent for a male shall be: from twenty to sixty years of age the equivalent shall be fifty shekels of silver by the sanctuary shekel. ⁴If the person is a female, the equivalent is thirty shekels. ⁵If the age is from five to twenty years of age, the equivalent is twenty shekels for a male and ten shekels for a female. ⁶If the age is from one month to five years, the equivalent for a male is five shekels of silver, and for a female the equivalent is three shekels of silver. ⁷And if the person is sixty years old or over, then the equivalent for a male is fifteen shekels, and for a female ten shekels. ⁸If any cannot afford the equivalent, they shall be brought before the priest and the priest shall assess them; the priest shall assess them according to what each one making a vow can afford.

9 If it concerns an animal that may be brought as an offering to the LORD, any such that may be given to the LORD shall be holy. ¹⁰Another shall not be exchanged or substituted for it, either good for bad or bad for good; and if one animal is substituted for another, both that one and its substitute shall be holy. ¹¹If it concerns any unclean animal that may not be brought as an offering to the LORD, the animal shall be presented before the priest. ¹²The priest shall assess it: whether good or bad, according to the assessment of the priest, so it shall be. ¹³But if it is to be redeemed, one-fifth must be added to the assessment.

14 If a person consecrates a house to the LORD, the priest shall assess it: whether good or bad, as the priest assesses it, so it shall stand. ¹⁵And if the one who consecrates the house wishes to redeem it, one-fifth shall be added to its assessed value, and it shall revert to the original owner.

16 If a person consecrates to the LORD any inherited landholding, its assessment shall be in accordance with its seed requirements: fifty shekels of silver to a homer of barley seed. ¹⁷If the person consecrates the field as of the year of jubilee, that assessment shall stand; ¹⁸but if the field is consecrated after the jubilee, the priest shall compute the price for it according to the years that remain until the year of jubilee, and the assessment shall be reduced. ¹⁹And if the one who consecrates the field wishes to redeem it, then one-fifth shall be added to its assessed value, and it shall revert to the original owner; ²⁰but if the field is not redeemed, or if it has been sold to someone else, it shall no longer be redeemable. ²¹But when the field is released in the jubilee, it shall be holy to the LORD as a devoted field; it becomes the priest's holding. ²²If someone consecrates to the LORD a field that has been purchased, which is not a part of the inherited landholding, ²³the priest shall compute for it the proportionate assessment up to the year of jubilee, and the assessment shall be paid as of that day, a sacred donation to the LORD. ²⁴In the year of jubilee the field shall return to the one from whom it was bought, whose holding the land is. ²⁵All assessments shall be by the sanctuary shekel: twenty gerahs shall make a shekel.

26 A firstling of animals, however, which as a firstling belongs to the LORD,

---

ᵗ Or *make up for*

cannot be consecrated by anyone; whether ox or sheep, it is the LORD's. [27]If it is an unclean animal, it shall be ransomed at its assessment, with one-fifth added; if it is not redeemed, it shall be sold at its assessment.

28 Nothing that a person owns that has been devoted to destruction for the LORD, be it human or animal, or inherited landholding, may be sold or redeemed; every devoted thing is most holy to the LORD. [29]No human beings who have been devoted to destruction can be ransomed; they shall be put to death.

30 All tithes from the land, whether the seed from the ground or the fruit from the tree, are the LORD's; they are holy to the LORD. [31]If persons wish to redeem any of their tithes, they must add one-fifth to them. [32]All tithes of herd and flock, every tenth one that passes under the shepherd's staff, shall be holy to the LORD. [33]Let no one inquire whether it is good or bad, or make substitution for it; if one makes substitution for it, then both it and the substitute shall be holy and cannot be redeemed.

34 These are the commandments that the LORD gave to Moses for the people of Israel on Mount Sinai.

Numbers

Author Evelyn Bence, a lover of words and not numbers, once said, "There is no grace in numbers." She meant of course that numbers are precise. Calculations are either right or wrong. An error of only one penny is still an error. But fortunately, there is grace in the book of Numbers, which is not primarily a list of numbers but the continuation of the story that began in Exodus. A combination of law and history, the book of Numbers covers a period of 38 years, during which time the Israelites were made to wander in the desert as punishment for the sin of unbelief. During this time, a new generation was born in the wilderness and was shaped into a people capable of taking hold of the promise God had made to lead them into a land of milk and honey.

The book of Numbers derives its title from the account of two different censuses that were taken. Chapter 1 describes a census taken of those who left Egypt. Chapter 26 describes a census of those who were born in the wilderness and who would enter the promised land. Only Joshua and Caleb were numbered in both, because they had confidence that God would do what he had promised.

The First Census of Israel

1 The LORD spoke to Moses in the wilderness of Sinai, in the tent of meeting, on the first day of the second month, in the second year after they had come out of the land of Egypt, saying: ²Take a census of the whole congregation of Israelites, in their clans, by ancestral houses, according to the number of names, every male individually; ³from twenty years old and upward, everyone in Israel able to go to war. You and Aaron shall enroll them, company by company. ⁴A man from each tribe shall be with you, each man the head of his ancestral house. ⁵These are the names of the men who shall assist you:

From Reuben, Elizur son of Shedeur.
⁶ From Simeon, Shelumiel son of Zurishaddai.
⁷ From Judah, Nahshon son of Amminadab.
⁸ From Issachar, Nethanel son of Zuar.
⁹ From Zebulun, Eliab son of Helon.
¹⁰ From the sons of Joseph:
from Ephraim, Elishama son of Ammihud;
from Manasseh, Gamaliel son of Pedahzur.
¹¹ From Benjamin, Abidan son of Gideoni.
¹² From Dan, Ahiezer son of Ammishaddai.

13 From Asher, Pagiel son of Ochran.

14 From Gad, Eliasaph son of Deuel.

15 From Naphtali, Ahira son of Enan.

16These were the ones chosen from the congregation, the leaders of their ancestral tribes, the heads of the divisions of Israel.

17 Moses and Aaron took these men who had been designated by name, 18and on the first day of the second month they assembled the whole congregation together. They registered themselves in their clans, by their ancestral houses, according to the number of names from twenty years old and upward, individually, 19as the LORD commanded Moses. So he enrolled them in the wilderness of Sinai.

20 The descendants of Reuben, Israel's firstborn, their lineage, in their clans, by their ancestral houses, according to the number of names, individually, every male from twenty years old and upward, everyone able to go to war: 21those enrolled of the tribe of Reuben were forty-six thousand five hundred.

22 The descendants of Simeon, their lineage, in their clans, by their ancestral houses, those of them that were numbered, according to the number of names, individually, every male from twenty years old and upward, everyone able to go to war: 23those enrolled of the tribe of Simeon were fifty-nine thousand three hundred.

24 The descendants of Gad, their lineage, in their clans, by their ancestral houses, according to the number of the names, from twenty years old and upward, everyone able to go to war: 25those enrolled of the tribe of Gad were forty-five thousand six hundred fifty.

26 The descendants of Judah, their lineage, in their clans, by their ancestral houses, according to the number of names, from twenty years old and upward, everyone able to go to war: 27those enrolled of the tribe of Judah were seventy-four thousand six hundred.

28 The descendants of Issachar, their lineage, in their clans, by their ancestral houses, according to the number of names, from twenty years old and upward, everyone able to go to war: 29those enrolled of the tribe of Issachar were fifty-four thousand four hundred.

30 The descendants of Zebulun, their lineage, in their clans, by their ancestral houses, according to the number of names, from twenty years old and up-

ward, everyone able to go to war: 31those enrolled of the tribe of Zebulun were fifty-seven thousand four hundred.

32 The descendants of Joseph, namely, the descendants of Ephraim, their lineage, in their clans, by their ancestral houses, according to the number of names, from twenty years old and upward, everyone able to go to war: 33those enrolled of the tribe of Ephraim were forty thousand five hundred.

34 The descendants of Manasseh, their lineage, in their clans, by their ancestral houses, according to the number of names, from twenty years old and upward, everyone able to go to war: 35those enrolled of the tribe of Manasseh were thirty-two thousand two hundred.

36 The descendants of Benjamin, their lineage, in their clans, by their ancestral houses, according to the number of names, from twenty years old and upward, everyone able to go to war: 37those enrolled of the tribe of Benjamin were thirty-five thousand four hundred.

38 The descendants of Dan, their lineage, in their clans, by their ancestral houses, according to the number of names, from twenty years old and upward, everyone able to go to war: 39those enrolled of the tribe of Dan were sixty-two thousand seven hundred.

40 The descendants of Asher, their lineage, in their clans, by their ancestral houses, according to the number of names, from twenty years old and upward, everyone able to go to war: 41those enrolled of the tribe of Asher were forty-one thousand five hundred.

42 The descendants of Naphtali, their lineage, in their clans, by their ancestral houses, according to the number of names, from twenty years old and upward, everyone able to go to war: 43those enrolled of the tribe of Naphtali were fifty-three thousand four hundred.

44 These are those who were enrolled, whom Moses and Aaron enrolled with the help of the leaders of Israel, twelve men, each representing his ancestral house. 45So the whole number of the Israelites, by their ancestral houses, from twenty years old and upward, everyone able to go to war in Israel— 46their whole number was six hundred three thousand five hundred fifty. 47The Levites, however, were not numbered by their ancestral tribe along with them.

48 The LORD had said to Moses: 49Only the tribe of Levi you shall not enroll, and you shall not take a census of them with the other Israelites. 50Rather you shall appoint the Levites over the tabernacle of the covenant,*a* and over all its equipment, and over all that belongs to it; they are to carry the tabernacle and all its equipment, and they shall tend it, and shall camp around the tabernacle. 51When the tabernacle is to be set out, the Levites shall take it down; and when the tabernacle is to be pitched, the Levites shall set it up. And any outsider who comes near shall be put to death. 52The other Israelites shall camp in their respective regimental camps, by companies; 53but the Levites shall camp around the tabernacle of the covenant,*a* that there may be no wrath on the congregation of the Israelites; and the Levites shall perform the guard duty of the tabernacle of the covenant.*a* 54The Israelites did so; they did just as the LORD commanded Moses.

The Order of Encampment and Marching

2 The LORD spoke to Moses and Aaron, saying: 2The Israelites shall camp each in their respective regiments, under ensigns by their ancestral houses; they shall camp facing the tent of meeting on every side. 3Those to camp on the east side toward the sunrise shall be of the regimental encampment of Judah by companies. The leader of the people of Judah shall be Nahshon son of Amminadab, 4with a company as enrolled of seventy-four thousand six hundred. 5Those to camp next to him shall be the tribe of Issachar. The leader of the Issacharites shall be Nethanel son of Zuar, 6with a company as enrolled of fifty-four thousand four hundred. 7Then the tribe of Zebulun: The leader of the Zebulunites shall be Eliab son of Helon, 8with a company as enrolled of fifty-seven thousand four hundred. 9The total enrollment of the camp of Judah, by companies, is one hundred eighty-six thousand four hundred. They shall set out first on the march.

10 On the south side shall be the regimental encampment of Reuben by companies. The leader of the Reubenites shall be Elizur son of Shedeur, 11with a company as enrolled of forty-six thousand five hundred. 12And those to camp next to him shall be the tribe of Simeon. The leader of the Simeonites shall be Shelumi-el son of Zurishaddai, 13with a company as enrolled of fifty-nine thousand three hundred. 14Then the tribe of Gad: The leader of the Gadites shall be Eliasaph son of Reuel, 15with a company as enrolled of forty-five thousand six hundred fifty. 16The total enrollment of the camp of Reuben, by companies, is one hundred fifty-one thousand four hundred fifty. They shall set out second.

17 The tent of meeting, with the camp of the Levites, shall set out in the center of the camps; they shall set out just as they camp, each in position, by their regiments.

18 On the west side shall be the regimental encampment of Ephraim by companies. The leader of the people of Ephraim shall be Elishama son of Ammihud, 19with a company as enrolled of forty thousand five hundred. 20Next to him shall be the tribe of Manasseh. The leader of the people of Manasseh shall be Gamaliel son of Pedahzur, 21with a company as enrolled of thirty-two thousand two hundred. 22Then the tribe of Benjamin: The leader of the Benjaminites shall be Abidan son of Gideoni, 23with a company as enrolled of thirty-five thousand four hundred. 24The total enrollment of the camp of Ephraim, by companies, is one hundred eight thousand one hundred. They shall set out third on the march.

25 On the north side shall be the regimental encampment of Dan by companies. The leader of the Danites shall be Ahiezer son of Ammishaddai, 26with a company as enrolled of sixty-two thousand seven hundred. 27Those to camp next to him shall be the tribe of Asher. The leader of the Asherites shall be Pagiel son of Ochran, 28with a company as enrolled of forty-one thousand five hundred. 29Then the tribe of Naphtali: The leader of the Naphtalites shall be Ahira son of Enan, 30with a company as enrolled of fifty-three thousand four hundred. 31The total enrollment of the camp of Dan is one hundred fifty-seven thousand six hundred. They shall set out last, by companies.*b*

32 This was the enrollment of the Israelites by their ancestral houses; the total enrollment in the camps by their companies was six hundred three thousand five

---

a Or *treaty*, or *testimony*; Heb *eduth*   *b* Compare verses 9, 16, 24: Heb *by their regiments*

hundred fifty. 33Just as the LORD had commanded Moses, the Levites were not enrolled among the other Israelites.

34 The Israelites did just as the LORD had commanded Moses: They camped by regiments, and they set out the same way, everyone by clans, according to ancestral houses.

The Sons of Aaron

3 This is the lineage of Aaron and Moses at the time when the LORD spoke with Moses on Mount Sinai. 2These are the names of the sons of Aaron: Nadab the firstborn, and Abihu, Eleazar, and Ithamar; 3these are the names of the sons of Aaron, the anointed priests, whom he ordained to minister as priests. 4Nadab and Abihu died before the LORD when they offered unholy fire before the LORD in the wilderness of Sinai, and they had no children. Eleazar and Ithamar served as priests in the lifetime of their father Aaron.

The Duties of the Levites

5 Then the LORD spoke to Moses, saying: 6Bring the tribe of Levi near, and set them before Aaron the priest, so that they may assist him. 7They shall perform duties for him and for the whole congregation in front of the tent of meeting, doing service at the tabernacle; 8they shall be in charge of all the furnishings of the tent of meeting, and attend to the duties for the Israelites as they do service at the tabernacle. 9You shall give the Levites to Aaron and his descendants; they are unreservedly given to him from among the Israelites. 10But you shall make a register of Aaron and his descendants; it is they who shall attend to the priesthood, and any outsider who comes near shall be put to death.

11 Then the LORD spoke to Moses, saying: 12I hereby accept the Levites from among the Israelites as substitutes for all the firstborn that open the womb among the Israelites. The Levites shall be mine, 13for all the firstborn are mine; when I killed all the firstborn in the land of Egypt, I consecrated for my own all the firstborn in Israel, both human and animal; they shall be mine. I am the LORD.

A Census of the Levites

14 Then the LORD spoke to Moses in the wilderness of Sinai, saying: 15Enroll the Levites by ancestral houses and by clans. You shall enroll every male from a month old and upward. 16So Moses enrolled them according to the word of the LORD, as he was commanded. 17The following were the sons of Levi, by their names: Gershon, Kohath, and Merari. 18These are the names of the sons of Gershon by their clans: Libni and Shimei. 19The sons of Kohath by their clans: Amram, Izhar, Hebron, and Uzziel. 20The sons of Merari by their clans: Mahli and Mushi. These are the clans of the Levites, by their ancestral houses.

21 To Gershon belonged the clan of the Libnites and the clan of the Shimeites; these were the clans of the Gershonites. 22Their enrollment, counting all the males from a month old and upward, was seven thousand five hundred. 23The clans of the Gershonites were to camp behind the tabernacle on the west, 24with Eliasaph son of Lael as head of the ancestral house of the Gershonites. 25The responsibility of the sons of Gershon in the tent of meeting was to be the tabernacle, the tent with its covering, the screen for the entrance of the tent of meeting, 26the hangings of the court, the screen for the entrance of the court that is around the tabernacle and the altar, and its cords—all the service pertaining to these.

27 To Kohath belonged the clan of the Amramites, the clan of the Izharites, the clan of the Hebronites, and the clan of the Uzzielites; these are the clans of the Kohathites. 28Counting all the males, from a month old and upward, there were eight thousand six hundred, attending to the duties of the sanctuary. 29The clans of the Kohathites were to camp on the south side of the tabernacle, 30with Elizaphan son of Uzziel as head of the ancestral house of the clans of the Kohathites. 31Their responsibility was to be the ark, the table, the lampstand, the altars, the vessels of the sanctuary with which the priests minister, and the screen—all the service pertaining to these. 32Eleazar son of Aaron the priest was to be chief over the leaders of the Levites, and to have oversight of those who had charge of the sanctuary.

33 To Merari belonged the clan of the Mahlites and the clan of the Mushites: these are the clans of Merari. 34Their enrollment, counting all the males from a month old and upward, was six thousand two hundred. 35The head of the ancestral house of the clans of Merari was Zuriel

son of Abihail; they were to camp on the north side of the tabernacle. ³⁶The responsibility assigned to the sons of Merari was to be the frames of the tabernacle, the bars, the pillars, the bases, and all their accessories—all the service pertaining to these; ³⁷also the pillars of the court all around, with their bases and pegs and cords.

38 Those who were to camp in front of the tabernacle on the east—in front of the tent of meeting toward the east—were Moses and Aaron and Aaron's sons, having charge of the rites within the sanctuary, whatever had to be done for the Israelites; and any outsider who came near was to be put to death. ³⁹The total enrollment of the Levites whom Moses and Aaron enrolled at the commandment of the LORD, by their clans, all the males from a month old and upward, was twenty-two thousand.

The Redemption of the Firstborn

40 Then the LORD said to Moses: Enroll all the firstborn males of the Israelites, from a month old and upward, and count their names. ⁴¹But you shall accept the Levites for me—I am the LORD—as substitutes for all the firstborn among the Israelites, and the livestock of the Levites as substitutes for all the firstborn among the livestock of the Israelites. ⁴²So Moses enrolled all the firstborn among the Israelites, as the LORD commanded him. ⁴³The total enrollment, all the firstborn males from a month old and upward, counting the number of names, was twenty-two thousand two hundred seventy-three.

44 Then the LORD spoke to Moses, saying: ⁴⁵Accept the Levites as substitutes for all the firstborn among the Israelites, and the livestock of the Levites as substitutes for their livestock; and the Levites shall be mine. I am the LORD. ⁴⁶As the price of redemption of the two hundred seventy-three of the firstborn of the Israelites, over and above the number of the Levites, ⁴⁷you shall accept five shekels apiece, reckoning by the shekel of the sanctuary, a shekel of twenty gerahs. ⁴⁸Give to Aaron and his sons the money by which the excess number of them is redeemed. ⁴⁹So Moses took the redemption money from those who were over and above those redeemed by the Levites; ⁵⁰from the firstborn of the Israelites he took the money, one thousand three hundred sixty-five

shekels, reckoned by the shekel of the sanctuary; ⁵¹and Moses gave the redemption money to Aaron and his sons, according to the word of the LORD, as the LORD had commanded Moses.

The Kohathites

4 The LORD spoke to Moses and Aaron, saying: ²Take a census of the Kohathites separate from the other Levites, by their clans and their ancestral houses, ³from thirty years old up to fifty years old, all who qualify to do work relating to the tent of meeting. ⁴The service of the Kohathites relating to the tent of meeting concerns the most holy things.

5 When the camp is to set out, Aaron and his sons shall go in and take down the screening curtain, and cover the ark of the covenant^c with it; ⁶then they shall put on it a covering of fine leather,^d and spread over that a cloth all of blue, and shall put its poles in place. ⁷Over the table of the bread of the Presence they shall spread a blue cloth, and put on it the plates, the dishes for incense, the bowls, and the flagons for the drink offering; the regular bread also shall be on it; ⁸then they shall spread over them a crimson cloth, and cover it with a covering of fine leather,^d and shall put its poles in place. ⁹They shall take a blue cloth, and cover the lampstand for the light, with its lamps, its snuffers, its trays, and all the vessels for oil with which it is supplied; ¹⁰and they shall put it with all its utensils in a covering of fine leather,^d and put it on the carrying frame. ¹¹Over the golden altar they shall spread a blue cloth, and cover it with a covering of fine leather,^d and shall put its poles in place; ¹²and they shall take all the utensils of the service that are used in the sanctuary, and put them in a blue cloth, and cover them with a covering of fine leather,^d and put them on the carrying frame. ¹³They shall take away the ashes from the altar, and spread a purple cloth over it; ¹⁴and they shall put on it all the utensils of the altar, which are used for the service there, the firepans, the forks, the shovels, and the basins, all the utensils of the altar; and they shall spread on it a covering of fine leather,^d and shall put its poles in place. ¹⁵When Aaron and his sons have finished covering the sanc-

---

^c Or *treaty*, or *testimony*; Heb *eduth* ^d Meaning of Heb uncertain

tuary and all the furnishings of the sanctuary, as the camp sets out, after that the Kohathites shall come to carry these, but they must not touch the holy things, or they will die. These are the things of the tent of meeting that the Kohathites are to carry.

16 Eleazar son of Aaron the priest shall have charge of the oil for the light, the fragrant incense, the regular grain offering, and the anointing oil, the oversight of all the tabernacle and all that is in it, in the sanctuary and in its utensils.

17 Then the LORD spoke to Moses and Aaron, saying: 18You must not let the tribe of the clans of the Kohathites be destroyed from among the Levites. 19This is how you must deal with them in order that they may live and not die when they come near to the most holy things: Aaron and his sons shall go in and assign each to a particular task or burden. 20But the Kohathites*e* must not go in to look on the holy things even for a moment; otherwise they will die.

The Gershonites and Merarites

21 Then the LORD spoke to Moses, saying: 22Take a census of the Gershonites also, by their ancestral houses and by their clans; 23from thirty years old up to fifty years old you shall enroll them, all who qualify to do work in the tent of meeting. 24This is the service of the clans of the Gershonites, in serving and bearing burdens: 25They shall carry the curtains of the tabernacle, and the tent of meeting with its covering, and the outer covering of fine leather*f* that is on top of it, and the screen for the entrance of the tent of meeting, 26and the hangings of the court, and the screen for the entrance of the gate of the court that is around the tabernacle and the altar, and their cords, and all the equipment for their service; and they shall do all that needs to be done with regard to them. 27All the service of the Gershonites shall be at the command of Aaron and his sons, in all that they are to carry, and in all that they have to do; and you shall assign to their charge all that they are to carry. 28This is the service of the clans of the Gershonites relating to the tent of meeting, and their responsibilities are to be under the oversight of Ithamar son of Aaron the priest.

29 As for the Merarites, you shall enroll them by their clans and their ancestral houses; 30from thirty years old up to fifty years old you shall enroll them, everyone who qualifies to do the work of the tent of meeting. 31This is what they are charged to carry, as the whole of their service in the tent of meeting: the frames of the tabernacle, with its bars, pillars, and bases, 32and the pillars of the court all around with their bases, pegs, and cords, with all their equipment and all their related service; and you shall assign by name the objects that they are required to carry. 33This is the service of the clans of the Merarites, the whole of their service relating to the tent of meeting, under the hand of Ithamar son of Aaron the priest.

Census of the Levites

34 So Moses and Aaron and the leaders of the congregation enrolled the Kohathites, by their clans and their ancestral houses, 35from thirty years old up to fifty years old, everyone who qualified for work relating to the tent of meeting; 36and their enrollment by clans was two thousand seven hundred fifty. 37This was the enrollment of the clans of the Kohathites, all who served at the tent of meeting, whom Moses and Aaron enrolled according to the commandment of the LORD by Moses.

38 The enrollment of the Gershonites, by their clans and their ancestral houses, 39from thirty years old up to fifty years old, everyone who qualified for work relating to the tent of meeting— 40their enrollment by their clans and their ancestral houses was two thousand six hundred thirty. 41This was the enrollment of the clans of the Gershonites, all who served at the tent of meeting, whom Moses and Aaron enrolled according to the commandment of the LORD.

42 The enrollment of the clans of the Merarites, by their clans and their ancestral houses, 43from thirty years old up to fifty years old, everyone who qualified for work relating to the tent of meeting— 44their enrollment by their clans was three thousand two hundred. 45This is the enrollment of the clans of the Merarites, whom Moses and Aaron enrolled according to the commandment of the LORD by Moses.

46 All those who were enrolled of the Levites, whom Moses and Aaron and the

e Heb *they*   *f* Meaning of Heb uncertain

Lot's Wife

Her Character: *She
was a prosperous
woman who may have
been more attached to
the good life than was
good for her. Though
there is no indication she
participated in the sin of
Sodom, her story implies
that she had learned to
tolerate it and that her
heart had become divid-
ed as a result.*

Her Tragedy: *That her
heart's choice led to judgment rather than mercy.
That she ultimately re-
fused God's attempts to
save her.*

Read Genesis 19

Lot's wife had only hours to live,
though she never suspected it.
She must have gone about her
business, heedless of the tragedy
about to unfold. Years earlier she
had married Abraham's nephew,
and the two had settled in Sodom—uncomfortably comfortable
in a city so wicked that heaven
had dispatched angels to investigate the allegations against it.

Lot happened to be at the city
gate just as the angels arrived.
Greeting the strangers, he begged
them to spend the night in his
home, anxious about what might
happen to them out in the open.

Just before bedtime, Lot's wife would have
heard the voices. At first a few muffled words
and then an ugly clamor as a noose of men
tightened around her house. Rough voices
shouted for Lot to open the door and surrender his guests to their pleasure.

Finally, the angels struck the men at the
door blind and urged Lot, "Have you anyone
else here? Sons-in-law, sons, daughters, or
anyone you have in the city—bring them out
of the place. For we are about to destroy this
place" (verses 12–13).

But Lot hesitated, until the angels grabbed
the family by their hands and dragged them
out, urging, "Flee for your life; do not look back
or stop anywhere in the Plain!" (verse 17).

By the time they reached safety, the sun
had risen over the land, and the city of
Sodom was in flames. Men, women, children,
and livestock—all were obliterated. Terrible
judgment for terrible sin.

But the judgment was even worse than

either Lot or his daughters first
realized. Safe at last, they must
have turned to each other in relief at their escape and then
turned again in shock, realizing
that one of their number was
missing. They would have
searched. They would have
hoped. They would have finally
caught sight of the white salt
pillar, silhouetted against the
sky, a lonely monument in the
shape of a woman turning round
toward Sodom.

If you have ever seen pictures of ancient Pompeii, destroyed by the eruption of
Mount Vesuvius in A.D. 79,
where human shapes are preserved to this day by the lava
that stopped them in their
tracks, you might imagine the
disaster that overtook Lot's wife.

Why did she turn, despite
the angels' clear warning? Was her heart still
attached to everything she left behind in the
city, a life of ease and pleasure? Was her love
of comfort and wealth a glue that caused her
feet to slow, her head to turn, and her body to
be overtaken by the punishment God had
meant to spare her? By her own choice, her
very last choice, she cast her lot with judgment rather than mercy.

Jesus urged his followers to remember
Lot's wife on the day of his second coming.
"On that day, anyone on the housetop who
has belongings in the house must not come
down to take them away; and likewise anyone in the field must not turn back. Remember Lot's wife. Those who try to make their
life secure will lose it, but those who lose
their life will keep it" (Luke 17:31–33). Sobering words recalling a sobering story, but
words meant to lead us away from the compelling illusions of wickedness and safe into
the arms of mercy.

Praying in Light of the Story of Lot's Wife

But [Lot] lingered; so the men seized him and his wife and his two daughters by the hand, the LORD being merciful to him, and they brought him out and left him outside the city. When they had brought them outside, they said, "Flee for your life; do not look back or stop anywhere in the Plain."—*Genesis 19.16–17*

Praise God: *That though he hates sin, he also loves mercy.*

Offer Thanks: *For ways that God has shown mercy to you and members of your family.*

Confess: *Any tendency to ignore God's voice because you prefer to go your own way.*

Ask God: *For the grace never to become rigid because of your attachments or your sin.*

Lift Your Heart

In a society like ours, it's rare to find someone who isn't attached to creature comforts. Test your own level of attachment by taking a weeklong retreat from television, newspapers, magazines, catalogs, and shopping malls. Instead, carve out a time and place in your home, even if it's only a few minutes in a small corner or a closet, for silent prayer and praise. Ask God to reveal any misplaced attachments or rigidity that may have developed in your spirit. Tell him you want to be a woman who is free and flexible enough to respond quickly to his direction.

Lord, you call me to live in the world without embracing the ways of the world. Help me to live in a way that preserves my freedom to follow you wherever and however you lead. If I should leave behind a monument, may it be a reminder to others of faith and not foolishness.

Go to page 158 for your next devotional reading.

leaders of Israel enrolled, by their clans and their ancestral houses, ⁴⁷from thirty years old up to fifty years old, everyone who qualified to do the work of service and the work of bearing burdens relating to the tent of meeting, ⁴⁸their enrollment was eight thousand five hundred eighty. ⁴⁹According to the commandment of the LORD through Moses they were appointed to their several tasks of serving or carrying; thus they were enrolled by him, as the LORD commanded Moses.

Unclean Persons

5 The LORD spoke to Moses, saying: ²Command the Israelites to put out of the camp everyone who is leprous,ᵍ or has a discharge, and everyone who is unclean through contact with a corpse; ³you shall put out both male and female, putting them outside the camp; they must not defile their camp, where I dwell among them. ⁴The Israelites did so, putting them outside the camp; as the LORD had spoken to Moses, so the Israelites did.

Confession and Restitution

5 The LORD spoke to Moses, saying: ⁶Speak to the Israelites: When a man or a woman wrongs another, breaking faith with the LORD, that person incurs guilt ⁷and shall confess the sin that has been committed. The person shall make full restitution for the wrong, adding one-fifth to it, and giving it to the one who was wronged. ⁸If the injured party has no next of kin to whom restitution may be made for the wrong, the restitution for wrong shall go to the LORD for the priest, in addition to the ram of atonement with which atonement is made for the guilty party. ⁹Among all the sacred donations of the Israelites, every gift that they bring to the priest shall be his. ¹⁰The sacred donations of all are their own; whatever anyone gives to the priest shall be his.

Concerning an Unfaithful Wife

11 The LORD spoke to Moses, saying: ¹²Speak to the Israelites and say to them: If any man's wife goes astray and is unfaithful to him, ¹³if a man has had intercourse with her but it is hidden from her husband, so that she is undetected though she has defiled herself, and there is no witness against her since she was not caught in the act; ¹⁴if a spirit of jealousy comes on him, and he is jealous of his wife who has defiled herself; or if a spirit of jealousy comes on him, and he is jealous of his wife, though she has not defiled herself; ¹⁵then the man shall bring his wife to the priest. And he shall bring the offering required for her, one-tenth of an ephah of barley flour. He shall pour no oil on it and put no frankincense on it, for it is a grain offering of jealousy, a grain offering of remembrance, bringing iniquity to remembrance.

16 Then the priest shall bring her near, and set her before the LORD; ¹⁷the priest shall take holy water in an earthen vessel, and take some of the dust that is on the floor of the tabernacle and put it into the water. ¹⁸The priest shall set the woman before the LORD, dishevel the woman's hair, and place in her hands the grain offering of remembrance, which is the grain offering of jealousy. In his own hand the priest shall have the water of bitterness that brings the curse. ¹⁹Then the priest shall make her take an oath, saying, "If no man has lain with you, if you have not turned aside to uncleanness while under your husband's authority, be immune to this water of bitterness that brings the curse. ²⁰But if you have gone astray while under your husband's authority, if you have defiled yourself and some man other than your husband has had intercourse with you," ²¹—let the priest make the woman take the oath of the curse and say to the woman—"the LORD make you an execration and an oath among your people, when the LORD makes your uterus drop, your womb discharge; ²²now may this water that brings the curse enter your bowels and make your womb discharge, your uterus drop!" And the woman shall say, "Amen. Amen."

23 Then the priest shall put these curses in writing, and wash them off into the water of bitterness. ²⁴He shall make the woman drink the water of bitterness that brings the curse, and the water that brings the curse shall enter her and cause bitter pain. ²⁵The priest shall take the grain offering of jealousy out of the woman's hand, and shall elevate the grain offering before the LORD and bring it to the altar; ²⁶and the priest shall take a handful of the grain offering, as its memorial portion, and turn it into smoke on the altar,

---

ᵍ A term for several skin diseases; precise meaning uncertain

and afterward shall make the woman drink the water. 27When he has made her drink the water, then, if she has defiled herself and has been unfaithful to her husband, the water that brings the curse shall enter into her and cause bitter pain, and her womb shall discharge, her uterus drop, and the woman shall become an execration among her people. 28But if the woman has not defiled herself and is clean, then she shall be immune and be able to conceive children.

29 This is the law in cases of jealousy, when a wife, while under her husband's authority, goes astray and defiles herself, 30or when a spirit of jealousy comes on a man and he is jealous of his wife; then he shall set the woman before the LORD, and the priest shall apply this entire law to her. 31The man shall be free from iniquity, but the woman shall bear her iniquity.

The Nazirites

6 The LORD spoke to Moses, saying: 2Speak to the Israelites and say to them: When either men or women make a special vow, the vow of a nazirite,*h* to separate themselves to the LORD, 3they shall separate themselves from wine and strong drink; they shall drink no wine vinegar or other vinegar, and shall not drink any grape juice or eat grapes, fresh or dried. 4All their days as nazirites*i* they shall eat nothing that is produced by the grapevine, not even the seeds or the skins.

5 All the days of their nazirite vow no razor shall come upon the head; until the time is completed for which they separate themselves to the LORD, they shall be holy; they shall let the locks of the head grow long.

6 All the days that they separate themselves to the LORD they shall not go near a corpse. 7Even if their father or mother, brother or sister, should die, they may not defile themselves; because their consecration to God is upon the head. 8All their days as nazirites*i* they are holy to the LORD.

9 If someone dies very suddenly nearby, defiling the consecrated head, then they shall shave the head on the day of their cleansing; on the seventh day they shall shave it. 10On the eighth day they shall bring two turtledoves or two young pigeons to the priest at the entrance of the tent of meeting, 11and the priest shall offer one as a sin offering and the other as a

burnt offering, and make atonement for them, because they incurred guilt by reason of the corpse. They shall sanctify the head that same day, 12and separate themselves to the LORD for their days as nazirites,*i* and bring a male lamb a year old as a guilt offering. The former time shall be void, because the consecrated head was defiled.

13 This is the law for the nazirites*i* when the time of their consecration has been completed: they shall be brought to the entrance of the tent of meeting, 14and they shall offer their gift to the LORD, one male lamb a year old without blemish as a burnt offering, one ewe lamb a year old without blemish as a sin offering, one ram without blemish as an offering of well-being, 15and a basket of unleavened bread, cakes of choice flour mixed with oil and unleavened wafers spread with oil, with their grain offering and their drink offerings. 16The priest shall present them before the LORD and offer their sin offering and burnt offering, 17and shall offer the ram as a sacrifice of well-being to the LORD, with the basket of unleavened bread; the priest also shall make the accompanying grain offering and drink offering. 18Then the nazirites*i* shall shave the consecrated head at the entrance of the tent of meeting, and shall take the hair from the consecrated head and put it on the fire under the sacrifice of well-being. 19The priest shall take the shoulder of the ram, when it is boiled, and one unleavened cake out of the basket, and one unleavened wafer, and shall put them in the palms of the nazirites,*i* after they have shaved the consecrated head. 20Then the priest shall elevate them as an elevation offering before the LORD; they are a holy portion for the priest, together with the breast that is elevated and the thigh that is offered. After that the nazirites*i* may drink wine.

21 This is the law for the nazirites*i* who take a vow. Their offering to the LORD must be in accordance with the nazirite*h* vow, apart from what else they can afford. In accordance with whatever vow they take, so they shall do, following the law for their consecration.

---

h That is *one separated* or *one consecrated*   *i* That is *those separated* or *those consecrated*

The Priestly Benediction

22 The LORD spoke to Moses, saying:
23Speak to Aaron and his sons, saying,
Thus you shall bless the Israelites: You
shall say to them,

24 The LORD bless you and keep you;
25 the LORD make his face to shine
         upon you, and be gracious to
         you;
26 the LORD lift up his countenance
         upon you, and give you
         peace.

27 So they shall put my name on the
Israelites, and I will bless them.

Offerings of the Leaders

7 On the day when Moses had finished
setting up the tabernacle, and had
anointed and consecrated it with all its
furnishings, and had anointed and consecrated the altar with all its utensils, 2the
leaders of Israel, heads of their ancestral
houses, the leaders of the tribes, who were
over those who were enrolled, made offerings. 3They brought their offerings before
the LORD, six covered wagons and twelve
oxen, a wagon for every two of the leaders,
and for each one an ox; they presented
them before the tabernacle. 4Then the
LORD said to Moses: 5Accept these from
them, that they may be used in doing the
service of the tent of meeting, and give
them to the Levites, to each according to
his service. 6So Moses took the wagons
and the oxen, and gave them to the Levites. 7Two wagons and four oxen he gave
to the Gershonites, according to their service; 8and four wagons and eight oxen he
gave to the Merarites, according to their
service, under the direction of Ithamar
son of Aaron the priest. 9But to the Kohathites he gave none, because they were
charged with the care of the holy things
that had to be carried on the shoulders.

10 The leaders also presented offerings
for the dedication of the altar at the time
when it was anointed; the leaders presented their offering before the altar. 11The
LORD said to Moses: They shall present
their offerings, one leader each day, for
the dedication of the altar.

12 The one who presented his offering
the first day was Nahshon son of Amminadab, of the tribe of Judah; 13his offering
was one silver plate weighing one hundred thirty shekels, one silver basin
weighing seventy shekels, according to the
shekel of the sanctuary, both of them full
of choice flour mixed with oil for a grain
offering; 14one golden dish weighing ten
shekels, full of incense; 15one young bull,
one ram, one male lamb a year old, for a
burnt offering; 16one male goat for a sin
offering; 17and for the sacrifice of well-
being, two oxen, five rams, five male
goats, and five male lambs a year old. This
was the offering of Nahshon son of Amminadab.

18 On the second day Nethanel son of
Zuar, the leader of Issachar, presented an
offering; 19he presented for his offering
one silver plate weighing one hundred
thirty shekels, one silver basin weighing
seventy shekels, according to the shekel of
the sanctuary, both of them full of choice
flour mixed with oil for a grain offering;
20one golden dish weighing ten shekels,
full of incense; 21one young bull, one ram,
one male lamb a year old, as a burnt offering; 22one male goat as a sin offering;
23and for the sacrifice of well-being, two
oxen, five rams, five male goats, and five
male lambs a year old. This was the offering of Nethanel son of Zuar.

24 On the third day Eliab son of Helon, the leader of the Zebulunites: 25his
offering was one silver plate weighing one
hundred thirty shekels, one silver basin
weighing seventy shekels, according to the
shekel of the sanctuary, both of them full
of choice flour mixed with oil for a grain
offering; 26one golden dish weighing ten
shekels, full of incense; 27one young bull,
one ram, one male lamb a year old, for a
burnt offering; 28one male goat for a sin
offering; 29and for the sacrifice of well-
being, two oxen, five rams, five male
goats, and five male lambs a year old. This
was the offering of Eliab son of Helon.

30 On the fourth day Elizur son of
Shedeur, the leader of the Reubenites:
31his offering was one silver plate weighing one hundred thirty shekels, one silver
basin weighing seventy shekels, according
to the shekel of the sanctuary, both of
them full of choice flour mixed with oil
for a grain offering; 32one golden dish
weighing ten shekels, full of incense;
33one young bull, one ram, one male
lamb a year old, for a burnt offering;
34one male goat for a sin offering; 35and
for the sacrifice of well-being, two oxen,
five rams, five male goats, and five male
lambs a year old. This was the offering of
Elizur son of Shedeur.

36 On the fifth day Shelumiel son of Zurishaddai, the leader of the Simeonites: [37]his offering was one silver plate weighing one hundred thirty shekels, one silver basin weighing seventy shekels, according to the shekel of the sanctuary, both of them full of choice flour mixed with oil for a grain offering; [38]one golden dish weighing ten shekels, full of incense; [39]one young bull, one ram, one male lamb a year old, for a burnt offering; [40]one male goat for a sin offering; [41]and for the sacrifice of well-being, two oxen, five rams, five male goats, and five male lambs a year old. This was the offering of Shelumiel son of Zurishaddai.

42 On the sixth day Eliasaph son of Deuel, the leader of the Gadites: [43]his offering was one silver plate weighing one hundred thirty shekels, one silver basin weighing seventy shekels, according to the shekel of the sanctuary, both of them full of choice flour mixed with oil for a grain offering; [44]one golden dish weighing ten shekels, full of incense; [45]one young bull, one ram, one male lamb a year old, for a burnt offering; [46]one male goat for a sin offering; [47]and for the sacrifice of well-being, two oxen, five rams, five male goats, and five male lambs a year old. This was the offering of Eliasaph son of Deuel.

48 On the seventh day Elishama son of Ammihud, the leader of the Ephraimites: [49]his offering was one silver plate weighing one hundred thirty shekels, one silver basin weighing seventy shekels, according to the shekel of the sanctuary, both of them full of choice flour mixed with oil for a grain offering; [50]one golden dish weighing ten shekels, full of incense; [51]one young bull, one ram, one male lamb a year old, for a burnt offering; [52]one male goat for a sin offering; [53]and for the sacrifice of well-being, two oxen, five rams, five male goats, and five male lambs a year old. This was the offering of Elishama son of Ammihud.

54 On the eighth day Gamaliel son of Pedahzur, the leader of the Manassites: [55]his offering was one silver plate weighing one hundred thirty shekels, one silver basin weighing seventy shekels, according to the shekel of the sanctuary, both of them full of choice flour mixed with oil for a grain offering; [56]one golden dish weighing ten shekels, full of incense; [57]one young bull, one ram, one male lamb a year old, for a burnt offering; [58]one male goat for a sin offering; [59]and for the sacrifice of well-being, two oxen, five rams, five male goats, and five male lambs a year old. This was the offering of Gamaliel son of Pedahzur.

60 On the ninth day Abidan son of Gideoni, the leader of the Benjaminites: [61]his offering was one silver plate weighing one hundred thirty shekels, one silver basin weighing seventy shekels, according to the shekel of the sanctuary, both of them full of choice flour mixed with oil for a grain offering; [62]one golden dish weighing ten shekels, full of incense; [63]one young bull, one ram, one male lamb a year old, for a burnt offering; [64]one male goat for a sin offering; [65]and for the sacrifice of well-being, two oxen, five rams, five male goats, and five male lambs a year old. This was the offering of Abidan son of Gideoni.

66 On the tenth day Ahiezer son of Ammishaddai, the leader of the Danites: [67]his offering was one silver plate weighing one hundred thirty shekels, one silver basin weighing seventy shekels, according to the shekel of the sanctuary, both of them full of choice flour mixed with oil for a grain offering; [68]one golden dish weighing ten shekels, full of incense; [69]one young bull, one ram, one male lamb a year old, for a burnt offering; [70]one male goat for a sin offering; [71]and for the sacrifice of well-being, two oxen, five rams, five male goats, and five male lambs a year old. This was the offering of Ahiezer son of Ammishaddai.

72 On the eleventh day Pagiel son of Ochran, the leader of the Asherites: [73]his offering was one silver plate weighing one hundred thirty shekels, one silver basin weighing seventy shekels, according to the shekel of the sanctuary, both of them full of choice flour mixed with oil for a grain offering; [74]one golden dish weighing ten shekels, full of incense; [75]one young bull, one ram, one male lamb a year old, for a burnt offering; [76]one male goat for a sin offering; [77]and for the sacrifice of well-being, two oxen, five rams, five male goats, and five male lambs a year old. This was the offering of Pagiel son of Ochran.

78 On the twelfth day Ahira son of Enan, the leader of the Naphtalites: [79]his offering was one silver plate weighing one hundred thirty shekels, one silver basin weighing seventy shekels, according to the shekel of the sanctuary, both of them full

of choice flour mixed with oil for a grain offering; 80one golden dish weighing ten shekels, full of incense; 81one young bull, one ram, one male lamb a year old, for a burnt offering; 82one male goat for a sin offering; 83and for the sacrifice of well-being, two oxen, five rams, five male goats, and five male lambs a year old. This was the offering of Ahira son of Enan.

84 This was the dedication offering for the altar, at the time when it was anointed, from the leaders of Israel: twelve silver plates, twelve silver basins, twelve golden dishes, 85each silver plate weighing one hundred thirty shekels and each basin seventy, all the silver of the vessels two thousand four hundred shekels according to the shekel of the sanctuary, 86the twelve golden dishes, full of incense, weighing ten shekels apiece according to the shekel of the sanctuary, all the gold of the dishes being one hundred twenty shekels; 87all the livestock for the burnt offering twelve bulls, twelve rams, twelve male lambs a year old, with their grain offering; 88and all the livestock for the sacrifice of well-being twenty-four bulls, the rams sixty, the male goats sixty, the male lambs a year old sixty. This was the dedication offering for the altar, after it was anointed.

89 When Moses went into the tent of meeting to speak with the LORD,j he would hear the voice speaking to him from above the mercy seatk that was on the ark of the covenantl from between the two cherubim; thus it spoke to him.

The Seven Lamps

8 The LORD spoke to Moses, saying: 2Speak to Aaron and say to him: When you set up the lamps, the seven lamps shall give light in front of the lampstand. 3Aaron did so; he set up its lamps to give light in front of the lampstand, as the LORD had commanded Moses. 4Now this was how the lampstand was made, out of hammered work of gold. From its base to its flowers, it was hammered work; according to the pattern that the LORD had shown Moses, so he made the lampstand.

Consecration and Service of the Levites

5 The LORD spoke to Moses, saying: 6Take the Levites from among the Israelites and cleanse them. 7Thus you shall do to them, to cleanse them: sprinkle the water of purification on them, have them shave their whole body with a razor and wash their clothes, and so cleanse themselves. 8Then let them take a young bull and its grain offering of choice flour mixed with oil, and you shall take another young bull for a sin offering. 9You shall bring the Levites before the tent of meeting, and assemble the whole congregation of the Israelites. 10When you bring the Levites before the LORD, the Israelites shall lay their hands on the Levites, 11and Aaron shall present the Levites before the LORD as an elevation offering from the Israelites, that they may do the service of the LORD. 12The Levites shall lay their hands on the heads of the bulls, and he shall offer the one for a sin offering and the other for a burnt offering to the LORD, to make atonement for the Levites. 13Then you shall have the Levites stand before Aaron and his sons, and you shall present them as an elevation offering to the LORD.

14 Thus you shall separate the Levites from among the other Israelites, and the Levites shall be mine. 15Thereafter the Levites may go in to do service at the tent of meeting, once you have cleansed them and presented them as an elevation offering. 16For they are unreservedly given to me from among the Israelites; I have taken them for myself, in place of all that open the womb, the firstborn of all the Israelites. 17For all the firstborn among the Israelites are mine, both human and animal. On the day that I struck down all the firstborn in the land of Egypt I consecrated them for myself, 18but I have taken the Levites in place of all the firstborn among the Israelites. 19Moreover, I have given the Levites as a gift to Aaron and his sons from among the Israelites, to do the service for the Israelites at the tent of meeting, and to make atonement for the Israelites, in order that there may be no plague among the Israelites for coming too close to the sanctuary.

20 Moses and Aaron and the whole congregation of the Israelites did with the Levites accordingly; the Israelites did with the Levites just as the LORD had commanded Moses concerning them. 21The Levites purified themselves from sin and washed their clothes; then Aaron presented them as an elevation offering before the LORD, and Aaron made atonement for them to

j Heb *him*   k Or *the cover*   l Or *treaty,* or *testimony;* Heb *eduth* cleanse them. 22Thereafter the Levites went in to do their service in the tent of meeting in attendance on Aaron and his sons. As the LORD had commanded Moses concerning the Levites, so they did with them.

23 The LORD spoke to Moses, saying: 24This applies to the Levites: from twenty-five years old and upward they shall begin to do duty in the service of the tent of meeting; 25and from the age of fifty years they shall retire from the duty of the service and serve no more. 26They may assist their brothers in the tent of meeting in carrying out their duties, but they shall perform no service. Thus you shall do with the Levites in assigning their duties.

The Passover at Sinai

9 The LORD spoke to Moses in the wilderness of Sinai, in the first month of the second year after they had come out of the land of Egypt, saying: 2Let the Israelites keep the passover at its appointed time. 3On the fourteenth day of this month, at twilight,m you shall keep it at its appointed time; according to all its statutes and all its regulations you shall keep it. 4So Moses told the Israelites that they should keep the passover. 5They kept the passover in the first month, on the fourteenth day of the month, at twilight,m in the wilderness of Sinai. Just as the LORD had commanded Moses, so the Israelites did. 6Now there were certain people who were unclean through touching a corpse, so that they could not keep the passover on that day. They came before Moses and Aaron on that day, 7and said to him, "Although we are unclean through touching a corpse, why must we be kept from presenting the LORD's offering at its appointed time among the Israelites?" 8Moses spoke to them, "Wait, so that I may hear what the LORD will command concerning you."

9 The LORD spoke to Moses, saying: 10Speak to the Israelites, saying: Anyone of you or your descendants who is unclean through touching a corpse, or is away on a journey, shall still keep the passover to the LORD. 11In the second month on the fourteenth day, at twilight,m they shall keep it; they shall eat it with unleavened bread and bitter herbs. 12They shall leave none of it until morning, nor break a bone of it; according to all the statute for the passover they shall keep

it. 13But anyone who is clean and is not on a journey, and yet refrains from keeping the passover, shall be cut off from the people for not presenting the LORD's offering at its appointed time; such a one shall bear the consequences for the sin. 14Any alien residing among you who wishes to keep the passover to the LORD shall do so according to the statute of the passover and according to its regulation; you shall have one statute for both the resident alien and the native.

The Cloud and the Fire

15 On the day the tabernacle was set up, the cloud covered the tabernacle, the tent of the covenant;n and from evening until morning it was over the tabernacle, having the appearance of fire. 16It was always so: the cloud covered it by dayo and the appearance of fire by night. 17Whenever the cloud lifted from over the tent, then the Israelites would set out; and in the place where the cloud settled down, there the Israelites would camp. 18At the command of the LORD the Israelites would set out, and at the command of the LORD they would camp. As long as the cloud rested over the tabernacle, they would remain in camp. 19Even when the cloud continued over the tabernacle many days, the Israelites would keep the charge of the LORD, and would not set out. 20Sometimes the cloud would remain a few days over the tabernacle, and according to the command of the LORD they would remain in camp; then according to the command of the LORD they would set out. 21Sometimes the cloud would remain from evening until morning; and when the cloud lifted in the morning, they would set out, or if it continued for a day and a night, when the cloud lifted they would set out. 22Whether it was two days, or a month, or a longer time, that the cloud continued over the tabernacle, resting upon it, the Israelites would remain in camp and would not set out; but when it lifted they would set out. 23At the command of the LORD they would camp, and at the command of the LORD they would set out. They kept the charge of the LORD, at the command of the LORD by Moses.

---

m Heb *between the two evenings*   n Or *treaty,* or *testimony;* Heb *eduth*   o Gk Syr Vg: Heb lacks *by day*

The Silver Trumpets

10 The LORD spoke to Moses, saying: ²Make two silver trumpets; you shall make them of hammered work; and you shall use them for summoning the congregation, and for breaking camp. ³When both are blown, the whole congregation shall assemble before you at the entrance of the tent of meeting. ⁴But if only one is blown, then the leaders, the heads of the tribes of Israel, shall assemble before you. ⁵When you blow an alarm, the camps on the east side shall set out; ⁶when you blow a second alarm, the camps on the south side shall set out. An alarm is to be blown whenever they are to set out. ⁷But when the assembly is to be gathered, you shall blow, but you shall not sound an alarm. ⁸The sons of Aaron, the priests, shall blow the trumpets; this shall be a perpetual institution for you throughout your generations. ⁹When you go to war in your land against the adversary who oppresses you, you shall sound an alarm with the trumpets, so that you may be remembered before the LORD your God and be saved from your enemies. ¹⁰Also on your days of rejoicing, at your appointed festivals, and at the beginnings of your months, you shall blow the trumpets over your burnt offerings and over your sacrifices of well-being; they shall serve as a reminder on your behalf before the LORD your God: I am the LORD your God.

Departure from Sinai

11 In the second year, in the second month, on the twentieth day of the month, the cloud lifted from over the tabernacle of the covenant.ᵖ ¹²Then the Israelites set out by stages from the wilderness of Sinai, and the cloud settled down in the wilderness of Paran. ¹³They set out for the first time at the command of the LORD by Moses. ¹⁴The standard of the camp of Judah set out first, company by company, and over the whole company was Nahshon son of Amminadab. ¹⁵Over the company of the tribe of Issachar was Nethanel son of Zuar; ¹⁶and over the company of the tribe of Zebulun was Eliab son of Helon. 17 Then the tabernacle was taken down, and the Gershonites and the Merarites, who carried the tabernacle, set out. ¹⁸Next the standard of the camp of Reuben set out, company by company; and over the whole company was Elizur son of Shedeur. ¹⁹Over the company of the tribe of Simeon was Shelumiel son of Zurishaddai, ²⁰and over the company of the tribe of Gad was Eliasaph son of Deuel.

21 Then the Kohathites, who carried the holy things, set out; and the tabernacle was set up before their arrival. ²²Next the standard of the Ephraimite camp set out, company by company, and over the whole company was Elishama son of Ammihud. ²³Over the company of the tribe of Manasseh was Gamaliel son of Pedahzur, ²⁴and over the company of the tribe of Benjamin was Abidan son of Gideoni.

25 Then the standard of the camp of Dan, acting as the rear guard of all the camps, set out, company by company, and over the whole company was Ahiezer son of Ammishaddai. ²⁶Over the company of the tribe of Asher was Pagiel son of Ochran, ²⁷and over the company of the tribe of Naphtali was Ahira son of Enan. ²⁸This was the order of march of the Israelites, company by company, when they set out.

29 Moses said to Hobab son of Reuel the Midianite, Moses' father-in-law, "We are setting out for the place of which the LORD said, 'I will give it to you'; come with us, and we will treat you well; for the LORD has promised good to Israel." ³⁰But he said to him, "I will not go, but I will go back to my own land and to my kindred." ³¹He said, "Do not leave us, for you know where we should camp in the wilderness, and you will serve as eyes for us. ³²Moreover, if you go with us, whatever good the LORD does for us, the same we will do for you."

33 So they set out from the mount of the LORD three days' journey with the ark of the covenant of the LORD going before them three days' journey, to seek out a resting place for them, ³⁴the cloud of the LORD being over them by day when they set out from the camp.

35 Whenever the ark set out, Moses would say,

"Arise, O LORD, let your enemies be
     scattered,
   and your foes flee before you."
³⁶And whenever it came to rest, he would say,

p Or *treaty*, or *testimony*; Heb *eduth*

"Return, O Lord of the ten thousand thousands of Israel."q

Complaining in the Desert

11 Now when the people complained in the hearing of the Lord about their misfortunes, the Lord heard it and his anger was kindled. Then the fire of the Lord burned against them, and consumed some outlying parts of the camp. 2But the people cried out to Moses; and Moses prayed to the Lord, and the fire abated. 3So that place was called Taberah,r because the fire of the Lord burned against them.

4 The rabble among them had a strong craving; and the Israelites also wept again, and said, "If only we had meat to eat! 5We remember the fish we used to eat in Egypt for nothing, the cucumbers, the melons, the leeks, the onions, and the garlic; 6but now our strength is dried up, and there is nothing at all but this manna to look at."

7 Now the manna was like coriander seed, and its color was like the color of gum resin. 8The people went around and gathered it, ground it in mills or beat it in mortars, then boiled it in pots and made cakes of it; and the taste of it was like the taste of cakes baked with oil. 9When the dew fell on the camp in the night, the manna would fall with it.

10 Moses heard the people weeping throughout their families, all at the entrances of their tents. Then the Lord became very angry, and Moses was displeased. 11So Moses said to the Lord, "Why have you treated your servant so badly? Why have I not found favor in your sight, that you lay the burden of all this people on me? 12Did I conceive all this people? Did I give birth to them, that you should say to me, 'Carry them in your bosom, as a nurse carries a sucking child,' to the land that you promised on oath to their ancestors? 13Where am I to get meat to give to all this people? For they come weeping to me and say, 'Give us meat to eat!' 14I am not able to carry all this people alone, for they are too heavy for me. 15If this is the way you are going to treat me, put me to death at once—if I have found favor in your sight—and do not let me see my misery."

The Seventy Elders

16 So the Lord said to Moses, "Gather for me seventy of the elders of Israel, whom you know to be the elders of the people and officers over them; bring them to the tent of meeting, and have them take their place there with you. 17I will come down and talk with you there; and I will take some of the spirit that is on you and put it on them; and they shall bear the burden of the people along with you so that you will not bear it all by yourself. 18And say to the people: Consecrate yourselves for tomorrow, and you shall eat meat; for you have wailed in the hearing of the Lord, saying, 'If only we had meat to eat! Surely it was better for us in Egypt.' Therefore the Lord will give you meat, and you shall eat. 19You shall eat not only one day, or two days, or five days, or ten days, or twenty days, 20but for a whole month— until it comes out of your nostrils and becomes loathsome to you—because you have rejected the Lord who is among you, and have wailed before him, saying, 'Why did we ever leave Egypt?'" 21But Moses said, "The people I am with number six hundred thousand on foot; and you say, 'I will give them meat, that they may eat for a whole month'! 22Are there enough flocks and herds to slaughter for them? Are there enough fish in the sea to catch for them?" 23The Lord said to Moses, "Is the Lord's power limited?s Now you shall see whether my word will come true for you or not."

24 So Moses went out and told the people the words of the Lord; and he gathered seventy elders of the people, and placed them all around the tent. 25Then the Lord came down in the cloud and spoke to him, and took some of the spirit that was on him and put it on the seventy elders; and when the spirit rested upon them, they prophesied. But they did not do so again.

26 Two men remained in the camp, one named Eldad, and the other named Medad, and the spirit rested on them; they were among those registered, but they had not gone out to the tent, and so they prophesied in the camp. 27And a young man ran and told Moses, "Eldad and Medad are prophesying in the camp." 28And Joshua son of Nun, the assistant of Moses, one of his chosen men,t said, "My lord

---

q Meaning of Heb uncertain   r That is Burning
s Heb Lord's hand too short?   t Or of Moses from his youth

Moses, stop them!" ²⁹But Moses said to him, "Are you jealous for my sake? Would that all the LORD's people were prophets, and that the LORD would put his spirit on them!" ³⁰And Moses and the elders of Israel returned to the camp.

The Quails

31 Then a wind went out from the LORD, and it brought quails from the sea and let them fall beside the camp, about a day's journey on this side and a day's journey on the other side, all around the camp, about two cubits deep on the ground. ³²So the people worked all that day and night and all the next day, gathering the quails; the least anyone gathered was ten homers; and they spread them out for themselves all around the camp. ³³But while the meat was still between their teeth, before it was consumed, the anger of the LORD was kindled against the people, and the LORD struck the people with a very great plague. ³⁴So that place was called Kibroth-hattaavah,ᵘ because there they buried the people who had the craving. ³⁵From Kibroth-hattaavah the people journeyed to Hazeroth.

Aaron and Miriam Jealous of Moses

12 While they were at Hazeroth, Miriam and Aaron spoke against Moses because of the Cushite woman whom he had married (for he had indeed married a Cushite woman); ²and they said, "Has the LORD spoken only through Moses? Has he not spoken through us also?" And the LORD heard it. ³Now the man Moses was very humble,ᵛ more so than anyone else on the face of the earth. ⁴Suddenly the LORD said to Moses, Aaron, and Miriam, "Come out, you three, to the tent of meeting." So the three of them came out. ⁵Then the LORD came down in a pillar of cloud, and stood at the entrance of the tent, and called Aaron and Miriam; and they both came forward. ⁶And he said,
"Hear my words:
When there are prophets among
    you,
I the LORD make myself known to
    them in visions;
I speak to them in dreams.
⁷ Not so with my servant Moses;
    he is entrusted with all my house.
⁸ With him I speak face to face—
    clearly, not in riddles;

and he beholds the form of the
    LORD.
Why then were you not afraid to speak against my servant Moses?" ⁹And the anger of the LORD was kindled against them, and he departed.

10 When the cloud went away from over the tent, Miriam had become leprous,ʷ as white as snow. And Aaron turned towards Miriam and saw that she was leprous. ¹¹Then Aaron said to Moses, "Oh, my lord, do not punish usˣ for a sin that we have so foolishly committed. ¹²Do not let her be like one stillborn, whose flesh is half consumed when it comes out of its mother's womb." ¹³And Moses cried to the LORD, "O God, please heal her." ¹⁴But the LORD said to Moses, "If her father had but spit in her face, would she not bear her shame for seven days? Let her be shut out of the camp for seven days, and after that she may be brought in again." ¹⁵So Miriam was shut out of the camp for seven days; and the people did not set out on the march until Miriam had been brought in again. ¹⁶After that the people set out from Hazeroth, and camped in the wilderness of Paran.

Spies Sent into Canaan

13 The LORD said to Moses, ²"Send men to spy out the land of Canaan, which I am giving to the Israelites; from each of their ancestral tribes you shall send a man, every one a leader among them." ³So Moses sent them from the wilderness of Paran, according to the command of the LORD, all of them leading men among the Israelites. ⁴These were their names: From the tribe of Reuben, Shammua son of Zaccur; ⁵from the tribe of Simeon, Shaphat son of Hori; ⁶from the tribe of Judah, Caleb son of Jephunneh; ⁷from the tribe of Issachar, Igal son of Joseph; ⁸from the tribe of Ephraim, Hoshea son of Nun; ⁹from the tribe of Benjamin, Palti son of Raphu; ¹⁰from the tribe of Zebulun, Gaddiel son of Sodi; ¹¹from the tribe of Joseph (that is, from the tribe of Manasseh), Gaddi son of Susi; ¹²from the tribe of Dan, Ammiel son of Gemalli; ¹³from the tribe of Asher, Sethur son of Michael; ¹⁴from the tribe of Naphtali, Nahbi son of Vophsi; ¹⁵from the tribe of

---

ᵘ That is *Graves of craving*   ᵛ Or *devout*   ʷ A term for several skin diseases; precise meaning uncertain   ˣ Heb *do not lay sin upon us*

Gad, Geuel son of Machi. [16]These were the names of the men whom Moses sent to spy out the land. And Moses changed the name of Hoshea son of Nun to Joshua.

17 Moses sent them to spy out the land of Canaan, and said to them, "Go up there into the Negeb, and go up into the hill country, [18]and see what the land is like, and whether the people who live in it are strong or weak, whether they are few or many, [19]and whether the land they live in is good or bad, and whether the towns that they live in are unwalled or fortified, [20]and whether the land is rich or poor, and whether there are trees in it or not. Be bold, and bring some of the fruit of the land." Now it was the season of the first ripe grapes.

21 So they went up and spied out the land from the wilderness of Zin to Rehob, near Lebo-hamath. [22]They went up into the Negeb, and came to Hebron; and Ahiman, Sheshai, and Talmai, the Anakites, were there. (Hebron was built seven years before Zoan in Egypt.) [23]And they came to the Wadi Eshcol, and cut down from there a branch with a single cluster of grapes, and they carried it on a pole between two of them. They also brought some pomegranates and figs. [24]That place was called the Wadi Eshcol,y because of the cluster that the Israelites cut down from there.

The Report of the Spies

25 At the end of forty days they returned from spying out the land. [26]And they came to Moses and Aaron and to all the congregation of the Israelites in the wilderness of Paran, at Kadesh; they brought back word to them and to all the congregation, and showed them the fruit of the land. [27]And they told him, "We came to the land to which you sent us; it flows with milk and honey, and this is its fruit. [28]Yet the people who live in the land are strong, and the towns are fortified and very large; and besides, we saw the descendants of Anak there. [29]The Amalekites live in the land of the Negeb; the Hittites, the Jebusites, and the Amorites live in the hill country; and the Canaanites live by the sea, and along the Jordan."

30 But Caleb quieted the people before Moses, and said, "Let us go up at once and occupy it, for we are well able to overcome it." [31]Then the men who had gone up with him said, "We are not able to go up against this people, for they are stronger than we." [32]So they brought to the Israelites an unfavorable report of the land that they had spied out, saying, "The land that we have gone through as spies is a land that devours its inhabitants; and all the people that we saw in it are of great size. [33]There we saw the Nephilim (the Anakites come from the Nephilim); and to ourselves we seemed like grasshoppers, and so we seemed to them."

The People Rebel

14 Then all the congregation raised a loud cry, and the people wept that night. [2]And all the Israelites complained against Moses and Aaron; the whole congregation said to them, "Would that we had died in the land of Egypt! Or would that we had died in this wilderness! [3]Why is the LORD bringing us into this land to fall by the sword? Our wives and our little ones will become booty; would it not be better for us to go back to Egypt?" [4]So they said to one another, "Let us choose a captain, and go back to Egypt."

5 Then Moses and Aaron fell on their faces before all the assembly of the congregation of the Israelites. [6]And Joshua son of Nun and Caleb son of Jephunneh, who were among those who had spied out the land, tore their clothes [7]and said to all the congregation of the Israelites, "The land that we went through as spies is an exceedingly good land. [8]If the LORD is pleased with us, he will bring us into this land and give it to us, a land that flows with milk and honey. [9]Only, do not rebel against the LORD; and do not fear the people of the land, for they are no more than bread for us; their protection is removed from them, and the LORD is with us; do not fear them." [10]But the whole congregation threatened to stone them.

Then the glory of the LORD appeared at the tent of meeting to all the Israelites. [11]And the LORD said to Moses, "How long will this people despise me? And how long will they refuse to believe in me, in spite of all the signs that I have done among them? [12]I will strike them with pestilence and disinherit them, and I will make of you a nation greater and mightier than they."

y That is Cluster

Moses Intercedes for the People

13 But Moses said to the LORD, "Then the Egyptians will hear of it, for in your might you brought up this people from among them, 14and they will tell the inhabitants of this land. They have heard that you, O LORD, are in the midst of this people; for you, O LORD, are seen face to face, and your cloud stands over them and you go in front of them, in a pillar of cloud by day and in a pillar of fire by night. 15Now if you kill this people all at one time, then the nations who have heard about you will say, 16'It is because the LORD was not able to bring this people into the land he swore to give them that he has slaughtered them in the wilderness.' 17And now, therefore, let the power of the LORD be great in the way that you promised when you spoke, saying,

18 'The LORD is slow to anger,
and abounding in steadfast love,
forgiving iniquity and transgression,
but by no means clearing the guilty,
visiting the iniquity of the parents
upon the children
to the third and the fourth
generation.'

19Forgive the iniquity of this people according to the greatness of your steadfast love, just as you have pardoned this people, from Egypt even until now."

20 Then the LORD said, "I do forgive, just as you have asked; 21nevertheless—as I live, and as all the earth shall be filled with the glory of the LORD— 22none of the

Gratitude

MONDAY

Scripture Reading
for Today:
Numbers 14.1–11

Verse for Today:
Numbers 14.2

The Israelites were slow to learn, short on patience, and quick to blame others for anything that did not immediately fall into place or make life easier for them. They were ungrateful, dismissing the gifts of God that sustained them, and they were bitter toward Moses and God. It is easy to see in retrospect how patient God was with them, and just as easy to see how stuck they were in their old ways of being slaves to their own immediate needs, even after seeing the power of God at work in their lives and history.

Do we at heart act like them? How mindful are we of God's actions in our lives and communities? Who defends God and stands up for God in our midst? We certainly complain a lot, as individuals, in parishes, religious communities, and churches. We moan and groan about finances, the pope, bishops, priests, deacons, leaders or the lack of them, corruption, lack of integrity, secrecy, mismanagement, and on and on. But as we point the finger at others, are we totally heedless of our own sin? Do we complain against God—who isn't to our liking, who doesn't fall into our categories? It has been said that all our spiritual problems stem from one reality: We are all bitterly angry that we are not God. Whom do we attack in the church and the world, because we can't get at God? Maybe we need to look at the consequences of our lack of gratitude and see what God does for us and who God really is, far beyond our narrow renderings of the Almighty.

—MEGAN MCKENNA

Go to page 174 for your next devotional reading.

people who have seen my glory and the signs that I did in Egypt and in the wilderness, and yet have tested me these ten times and have not obeyed my voice, 23shall see the land that I swore to give to their ancestors; none of those who despised me shall see it. 24But my servant Caleb, because he has a different spirit and has followed me wholeheartedly, I will bring into the land into which he went, and his descendants shall possess it. 25Now, since the Amalekites and the Canaanites live in the valleys, turn tomorrow and set out for the wilderness by the way to the Red Sea."z

An Attempted Invasion is Repulsed

26 And the LORD spoke to Moses and to Aaron, saying: 27How long shall this wicked congregation complain against me? I have heard the complaints of the Israelites, which they complain against me. 28Say to them, "As I live," says the LORD, "I will do to you the very things I heard you say: 29your dead bodies shall fall in this very wilderness; and of all your number, included in the census, from twenty years old and upward, who have complained against me, 30not one of you shall come into the land in which I swore to settle you, except Caleb son of Jephunneh and Joshua son of Nun. 31But your little ones, who you said would become booty, I will bring in, and they shall know the land that you have despised. 32But as for you, your dead bodies shall fall in this wilderness. 33And your children shall be shepherds in the wilderness for forty years, and shall suffer for your faithlessness, until the last of your dead bodies lies in the wilderness. 34According to the number of the days in which you spied out the land, forty days, for every day a year, you shall bear your iniquity, forty years, and you shall know my displeasure." 35I the LORD have spoken; surely I will do thus to all this wicked congregation gathered together against me: in this wilderness they shall come to a full end, and there they shall die.

36 And the men whom Moses sent to spy out the land, who returned and made all the congregation complain against him by bringing a bad report about the land— 37the men who brought an unfavorable report about the land died by a plague before the LORD. 38But Joshua son of Nun and Caleb son of Jephunneh alone remained alive, of those men who went to spy out the land.

39 When Moses told these words to all the Israelites, the people mourned greatly. 40They rose early in the morning and went up to the heights of the hill country, saying, "Here we are. We will go up to the place that the LORD has promised, for we have sinned." 41But Moses said, "Why do you continue to transgress the command of the LORD? That will not succeed. 42Do not go up, for the LORD is not with you; do not let yourselves be struck down before your enemies. 43For the Amalekites and the Canaanites will confront you there, and you shall fall by the sword; because you have turned back from following the LORD, the LORD will not be with you." 44But they presumed to go up to the heights of the hill country, even though the ark of the covenant of the LORD, and Moses, had not left the camp. 45Then the Amalekites and the Canaanites who lived in that hill country came down and defeated them, pursuing them as far as Hormah.

Various Offerings

15 The LORD spoke to Moses, saying: 2Speak to the Israelites and say to them: When you come into the land you are to inhabit, which I am giving you, 3and you make an offering by fire to the LORD from the herd or from the flock— whether a burnt offering or a sacrifice, to fulfill a vow or as a freewill offering or at your appointed festivals—to make a pleasing odor for the LORD, 4then whoever presents such an offering to the LORD shall present also a grain offering, one-tenth of an ephah of choice flour, mixed with one-fourth of a hin of oil. 5Moreover, you shall offer one-fourth of a hin of wine as a drink offering with the burnt offering or the sacrifice, for each lamb. 6For a ram, you shall offer a grain offering, two-tenths of an ephah of choice flour mixed with one-third of a hin of oil; 7and as a drink offering you shall offer one-third of a hin of wine, a pleasing odor to the LORD. 8When you offer a bull as a burnt offering or a sacrifice, to fulfill a vow or as an offering of well-being to the LORD, 9then you shall present with the bull a grain offering, three-tenths of an ephah of choice flour, mixed with half a hin of oil, 10and you shall present as a drink offering half a hin

z Or *Sea of Reeds*

of wine, as an offering by fire, a pleasing odor to the LORD.

11 Thus it shall be done for each ox or ram, or for each of the male lambs or the kids. 12According to the number that you offer, so you shall do with each and every one. 13Every native Israelite shall do these things in this way, in presenting an offering by fire, a pleasing odor to the LORD. 14An alien who lives with you, or who takes up permanent residence among you, and wishes to offer an offering by fire, a pleasing odor to the LORD, shall do as you do. 15As for the assembly, there shall be for both you and the resident alien a single statute, a perpetual statute throughout your generations; you and the alien shall be alike before the LORD. 16You and the alien who resides with you shall have the same law and the same ordinance.

17 The LORD spoke to Moses, saying: 18Speak to the Israelites and say to them: After you come into the land to which I am bringing you, 19whenever you eat of the bread of the land, you shall present a donation to the LORD. 20From your first batch of dough you shall present a loaf as a donation; you shall present it just as you present a donation from the threshing floor. 21Throughout your generations you shall give to the LORD a donation from the first of your batch of dough.

22 But if you unintentionally fail to observe all these commandments that the LORD has spoken to Moses— 23everything that the LORD has commanded you by Moses, from the day the LORD gave commandment and thereafter, throughout your generations— 24then if it was done unintentionally without the knowledge of the congregation, the whole congregation shall offer one young bull for a burnt offering, a pleasing odor to the LORD, together with its grain offering and its drink offering, according to the ordinance, and one male goat for a sin offering. 25The priest shall make atonement for all the congregation of the Israelites, and they shall be forgiven; it was unintentional, and they have brought their offering, an offering by fire to the LORD, and their sin offering before the LORD, for their error. 26All the congregation of the Israelites shall be forgiven, as well as the aliens residing among them, because the whole people was involved in the error.

27 An individual who sins unintentionally shall present a female goat a year old for a sin offering. 28And the priest shall make atonement before the LORD for the one who commits an error, when it is unintentional, to make atonement for the person, who then shall be forgiven. 29For both the native among the Israelites and the alien residing among them—you shall have the same law for anyone who acts in error. 30But whoever acts high-handedly, whether a native or an alien, affronts the LORD, and shall be cut off from among the people. 31Because of having despised the word of the LORD and broken his commandment, such a person shall be utterly cut off and bear the guilt.

Penalty for Violating the Sabbath

32 When the Israelites were in the wilderness, they found a man gathering sticks on the sabbath day. 33Those who found him gathering sticks brought him to Moses, Aaron, and to the whole congregation. 34They put him in custody, because it was not clear what should be done to him. 35Then the LORD said to Moses, "The man shall be put to death; all the congregation shall stone him outside the camp." 36The whole congregation brought him outside the camp and stoned him to death, just as the LORD had commanded Moses.

Fringes on Garments

37 The LORD said to Moses: 38Speak to the Israelites, and tell them to make fringes on the corners of their garments throughout their generations and to put a blue cord on the fringe at each corner. 39You have the fringe so that, when you see it, you will remember all the commandments of the LORD and do them, and not follow the lust of your own heart and your own eyes. 40So you shall remember and do all my commandments, and you shall be holy to your God. 41I am the LORD your God, who brought you out of the land of Egypt, to be your God: I am the LORD your God.

Revolt of Korah, Dathan, and Abiram

16 Now Korah son of Izhar son of Kohath son of Levi, along with Dathan and Abiram sons of Eliab, and On son of Peleth—descendants of Reuben—took 2two hundred fifty Israelite men, leaders of the congregation, chosen from

the assembly, well-known men,[a] and they confronted Moses. ³They assembled against Moses and against Aaron, and said to them, "You have gone too far! All the congregation are holy, every one of them, and the LORD is among them. So why then do you exalt yourselves above the assembly of the LORD?" ⁴When Moses heard it, he fell on his face. ⁵Then he said to Korah and all his company, "In the morning the LORD will make known who is his, and who is holy, and who will be allowed to approach him; the one whom he will choose he will allow to approach him. ⁶Do this: take censers, Korah and all your[b] company, ⁷and tomorrow put fire in them, and lay incense on them before the LORD; and the man whom the LORD chooses shall be the holy one. You Levites have gone too far!" ⁸Then Moses said to Korah, "Hear now, you Levites! ⁹Is it too little for you that the God of Israel has separated you from the congregation of Israel, to allow you to approach him in order to perform the duties of the LORD's tabernacle, and to stand before the congregation and serve them? ¹⁰He has allowed you to approach him, and all your brother Levites with you; yet you seek the priesthood as well! ¹¹Therefore you and all your company have gathered together against the LORD. What is Aaron that you rail against him?"

12 Moses sent for Dathan and Abiram sons of Eliab; but they said, "We will not come! ¹³Is it too little that you have brought us up out of a land flowing with milk and honey to kill us in the wilderness, that you must also lord it over us? ¹⁴It is clear you have not brought us into a land flowing with milk and honey, or given us an inheritance of fields and vineyards. Would you put out the eyes of these men? We will not come!"

15 Moses was very angry and said to the LORD, "Pay no attention to their offering. I have not taken one donkey from them, and I have not harmed any one of them." ¹⁶And Moses said to Korah, "As for you and all your company, be present tomorrow before the LORD, you and they and Aaron; ¹⁷and let each one of you take his censer, and put incense on it, and each one of you present his censer before the LORD, two hundred fifty censers; you also, and Aaron, each his censer." ¹⁸So each man took his censer, and they put fire in the censers and laid incense on them, and

they stood at the entrance of the tent of meeting with Moses and Aaron. ¹⁹Then Korah assembled the whole congregation against them at the entrance of the tent of meeting. And the glory of the LORD appeared to the whole congregation.

20 Then the LORD spoke to Moses and to Aaron, saying: ²¹Separate yourselves from this congregation, so that I may consume them in a moment. ²²They fell on their faces, and said, "O God, the God of the spirits of all flesh, shall one person sin and you become angry with the whole congregation?"

23 And the LORD spoke to Moses, saying: ²⁴Say to the congregation: Get away from the dwellings of Korah, Dathan, and Abiram. ²⁵So Moses got up and went to Dathan and Abiram; the elders of Israel followed him. ²⁶He said to the congregation, "Turn away from the tents of these wicked men, and touch nothing of theirs, or you will be swept away for all their sins." ²⁷So they got away from the dwellings of Korah, Dathan, and Abiram; and Dathan and Abiram came out and stood at the entrance of their tents, together with their wives, their children, and their little ones. ²⁸And Moses said, "This is how you shall know that the LORD has sent me to do all these works; it has not been of my own accord: ²⁹If these people die a natural death, or if a natural fate comes on them, then the LORD has not sent me. ³⁰But if the LORD creates something new, and the ground opens its mouth and swallows them up, with all that belongs to them, and they go down alive into Sheol, then you shall know that these men have despised the LORD."

31 As soon as he finished speaking all these words, the ground under them was split apart. ³²The earth opened its mouth and swallowed them up, along with their households—everyone who belonged to Korah and all their goods. ³³So they with all that belonged to them went down alive into Sheol; the earth closed over them, and they perished from the midst of the assembly. ³⁴All Israel around them fled at their outcry, for they said, "The earth will swallow us too!" ³⁵And fire came out from the LORD and consumed the two hundred fifty men offering the incense.

a Cn: Heb and they confronted Moses, and two hundred fifty men . . . well-known men   b Heb his

36cThen the LORD spoke to Moses, saying: 37Tell Eleazar son of Aaron the priest to take the censers out of the blaze; then scatter the fire far and wide. 38For the censers of these sinners have become holy at the cost of their lives. Make them into hammered plates as a covering for the altar, for they presented them before the LORD and they became holy. Thus they shall be a sign to the Israelites. 39So Eleazar the priest took the bronze censers that had been presented by those who were burned; and they were hammered out as a covering for the altar— 40a reminder to the Israelites that no outsider, who is not of the descendants of Aaron, shall approach to offer incense before the LORD, so as not to become like Korah and his company—just as the LORD had said to him through Moses.

41 On the next day, however, the whole congregation of the Israelites rebelled against Moses and against Aaron, saying, "You have killed the people of the LORD." 42And when the congregation had assembled against them, Moses and Aaron turned toward the tent of meeting; the cloud had covered it and the glory of the LORD appeared. 43Then Moses and Aaron came to the front of the tent of meeting, 44and the LORD spoke to Moses, saying, 45"Get away from this congregation, so that I may consume them in a moment." And they fell on their faces. 46Moses said to Aaron, "Take your censer, put fire on it from the altar and lay incense on it, and carry it quickly to the congregation and make atonement for them. For wrath has gone out from the LORD; the plague has begun." 47So Aaron took it as Moses had ordered, and ran into the middle of the assembly, where the plague had already begun among the people. He put on the incense, and made atonement for the people. 48He stood between the dead and the living; and the plague was stopped. 49Those who died by the plague were fourteen thousand seven hundred, besides those who died in the affair of Korah. 50When the plague was stopped, Aaron returned to Moses at the entrance of the tent of meeting.

The Budding of Aaron's Rod

17 dThe LORD spoke to Moses, saying: 2Speak to the Israelites, and get twelve staffs from them, one for each ancestral house, from all the leaders of their ancestral houses. Write each man's name on his staff, 3and write Aaron's name on the staff of Levi. For there shall be one staff for the head of each ancestral house. 4Place them in the tent of meeting before the covenant,e where I meet with you. 5And the staff of the man whom I choose shall sprout; thus I will put a stop to the complaints of the Israelites that they continually make against you. 6Moses spoke to the Israelites; and all their leaders gave him staffs, one for each leader, according to their ancestral houses, twelve staffs; and the staff of Aaron was among theirs. 7So Moses placed the staffs before the LORD in the tent of the covenant.e

8 When Moses went into the tent of the covenante on the next day, the staff of Aaron for the house of Levi had sprouted. It put forth buds, produced blossoms, and bore ripe almonds. 9Then Moses brought out all the staffs from before the LORD to all the Israelites; and they looked, and each man took his staff. 10And the LORD said to Moses, "Put back the staff of Aaron before the covenant,e to be kept as a warning to rebels, so that you may make an end of their complaints against me, or else they will die." 11Moses did so; just as the LORD commanded him, so he did.

12 The Israelites said to Moses, "We are perishing; we are lost, all of us are lost! 13Everyone who approaches the tabernacle of the LORD will die. Are we all to perish?"

Responsibility of Priests and Levites

18 The LORD said to Aaron: You and your sons and your ancestral house with you shall bear responsibility for offenses connected with the sanctuary, while you and your sons alone shall bear responsibility for offenses connected with the priesthood. 2So bring with you also your brothers of the tribe of Levi, your ancestral tribe, in order that they may be joined to you, and serve you while you and your sons with you are in front of the tent of the covenant.e 3They shall perform duties for you and for the whole tent. But they must not approach either the utensils of the sanctuary or the altar, otherwise both they and you will die. 4They are attached to you in order to perform the duties of the tent of meeting, for

c Ch 17.1 in Heb　　d Ch 17.16 in Heb　　e Or treaty, or testimony; Heb eduth all the service of the tent; no outsider shall approach you. ⁵You yourselves shall perform the duties of the sanctuary and the duties of the altar, so that wrath may never again come upon the Israelites. ⁶It is I who now take your brother Levites from among the Israelites; they are now yours as a gift, dedicated to the LORD, to perform the service of the tent of meeting. ⁷But you and your sons with you shall diligently perform your priestly duties in all that concerns the altar and the area behind the curtain. I give your priesthood as a gift; *f* any outsider who approaches shall be put to death.

The Priests' Portion

8 The LORD spoke to Aaron: I have given you charge of the offerings made to me, all the holy gifts of the Israelites; I have given them to you and your sons as a priestly portion due you in perpetuity. ⁹This shall be yours from the most holy things, reserved from the fire: every offering of theirs that they render to me as a most holy thing, whether grain offering, sin offering, or guilt offering, shall belong to you and your sons. ¹⁰As a most holy thing you shall eat it; every male may eat it; it shall be holy to you. ¹¹This also is yours: I have given to you, together with your sons and daughters, as a perpetual due, whatever is set aside from the gifts of all the elevation offerings of the Israelites; everyone who is clean in your house may eat them. ¹²All the best of the oil and all the best of the wine and of the grain, the choice produce that they give to the LORD, I have given to you. ¹³The first fruits of all that is in their land, which they bring to the LORD, shall be yours; everyone who is clean in your house may eat of it. ¹⁴Every devoted thing in Israel shall be yours. ¹⁵The first issue of the womb of all creatures, human and animal, which is offered to the LORD, shall be yours; but the firstborn of human beings you shall redeem, and the firstborn of unclean animals you shall redeem. ¹⁶Their redemption price, reckoned from one month of age, you shall fix at five shekels of silver, according to the shekel of the sanctuary (that is, twenty gerahs). ¹⁷But the firstborn of a cow, or the firstborn of a sheep, or the firstborn of a goat, you shall not redeem; they are holy. You shall dash their blood on the altar, and shall turn their fat into smoke as an offering by fire for a pleasing odor to the LORD; ¹⁸but their flesh shall be yours, just as the breast that is elevated and as the right thigh are yours. ¹⁹All the holy offerings that the Israelites present to the LORD I have given to you, together with your sons and daughters, as a perpetual due; it is a covenant of salt forever before the LORD for you and your descendants as well. ²⁰Then the LORD said to Aaron: You shall have no allotment in their land, nor shall you have any share among them; I am your share and your possession among the Israelites.

21 To the Levites I have given every tithe in Israel for a possession in return for the service that they perform, the service in the tent of meeting. ²²From now on the Israelites shall no longer approach the tent of meeting, or else they will incur guilt and die. ²³But the Levites shall perform the service of the tent of meeting, and they shall bear responsibility for their own offenses; it shall be a perpetual statute throughout your generations. But among the Israelites they shall have no allotment, ²⁴because I have given to the Levites as their portion the tithe of the Israelites, which they set apart as an offering to the LORD. Therefore I have said of them that they shall have no allotment among the Israelites.

25 Then the LORD spoke to Moses, saying: ²⁶You shall speak to the Levites, saying: When you receive from the Israelites the tithe that I have given you from them for your portion, you shall set apart an offering from it to the LORD, a tithe of the tithe. ²⁷It shall be reckoned to you as your gift, the same as the grain of the threshing floor and the fullness of the wine press. ²⁸Thus you also shall set apart an offering to the LORD from all the tithes that you receive from the Israelites; and from them you shall give the LORD's offering to the priest Aaron. ²⁹Out of all the gifts to you, you shall set apart every offering due to the LORD; the best of all of them is the part to be consecrated. ³⁰Say also to them: When you have set apart the best of it, then the rest shall be reckoned to the Levites as produce of the threshing floor, and as produce of the wine press. ³¹You may eat it in any place, you and your households; for it is your payment for your service in the tent of meeting. ³²You shall incur no guilt by reason of it, when

---

f Heb *as a service of gift*

you have offered the best of it. But you shall not profane the holy gifts of the Israelites, on pain of death.

Ceremony of the Red Heifer

19 The LORD spoke to Moses and Aaron, saying: 2This is a statute of the law that the LORD has commanded: Tell the Israelites to bring you a red heifer without defect, in which there is no blemish and on which no yoke has been laid. 3You shall give it to the priest Eleazar, and it shall be taken outside the camp and slaughtered in his presence. 4The priest Eleazar shall take some of its blood with his finger and sprinkle it seven times towards the front of the tent of meeting. 5Then the heifer shall be burned in his sight; its skin, its flesh, and its blood, with its dung, shall be burned. 6The priest shall take cedarwood, hyssop, and crimson material, and throw them into the fire in which the heifer is burning. 7Then the priest shall wash his clothes and bathe his body in water, and afterwards he may come into the camp; but the priest shall remain unclean until evening. 8The one who burns the heifer*g* shall wash his clothes in water and bathe his body in water; he shall remain unclean until evening. 9Then someone who is clean shall gather up the ashes of the heifer, and deposit them outside the camp in a clean place; and they shall be kept for the congregation of the Israelites for the water for cleansing. It is a purification offering. 10The one who gathers the ashes of the heifer shall wash his clothes and be unclean until evening.

This shall be a perpetual statute for the Israelites and for the alien residing among them. 11Those who touch the dead body of any human being shall be unclean seven days. 12They shall purify themselves with the water on the third day and on the seventh day, and so be clean; but if they do not purify themselves on the third day and on the seventh day, they will not become clean. 13All who touch a corpse, the body of a human being who has died, and do not purify themselves, defile the tabernacle of the LORD; such persons shall be cut off from Israel. Since water for cleansing was not dashed on them, they remain unclean; their uncleanness is still on them.

14 This is the law when someone dies in a tent: everyone who comes into the tent, and everyone who is in the tent, shall be unclean seven days. 15And every open vessel with no cover fastened on it is unclean. 16Whoever in the open field touches one who has been killed by a sword, or who has died naturally,*h* or a human bone, or a grave, shall be unclean seven days. 17For the unclean they shall take some ashes of the burnt purification offering, and running water shall be added in a vessel; 18then a clean person shall take hyssop, dip it in the water, and sprinkle it on the tent, on all the furnishings, on the persons who were there, and on whoever touched the bone, the slain, the corpse, or the grave. 19The clean person shall sprinkle the unclean ones on the third day and on the seventh day, thus purifying them on the seventh day. Then they shall wash their clothes and bathe themselves in water, and at evening they shall be clean. 20Any who are unclean but do not purify themselves, those persons shall be cut off from the assembly, for they have defiled the sanctuary of the LORD. Since the water for cleansing has not been dashed on them, they are unclean.

21 It shall be a perpetual statute for them. The one who sprinkles the water for cleansing shall wash his clothes, and whoever touches the water for cleansing shall be unclean until evening. 22Whatever the unclean person touches shall be unclean, and anyone who touches it shall be unclean until evening.

The Waters of Meribah

20 The Israelites, the whole congregation, came into the wilderness of Zin in the first month, and the people stayed in Kadesh. Miriam died there, and was buried there.

2 Now there was no water for the congregation; so they gathered together against Moses and against Aaron. 3The people quarreled with Moses and said, "Would that we had died when our kindred died before the LORD! 4Why have you brought the assembly of the LORD into this wilderness for us and our livestock to die here? 5Why have you brought us up out of Egypt, to bring us to this wretched place? It is no place for grain, or figs, or vines, or pomegranates; and there is no water to drink." 6Then Moses and Aaron went away from the assembly to the entrance of the tent of meeting; they fell on their faces,

g Heb *it*   *h* Heb lacks *naturally*

and the glory of the LORD appeared to them. 7The LORD spoke to Moses, saying: 8Take the staff, and assemble the congregation, you and your brother Aaron, and command the rock before their eyes to yield its water. Thus you shall bring water out of the rock for them; thus you shall provide drink for the congregation and their livestock.

9 So Moses took the staff from before the LORD, as he had commanded him. 10Moses and Aaron gathered the assembly together before the rock, and he said to them, "Listen, you rebels, shall we bring water for you out of this rock?" 11Then Moses lifted up his hand and struck the rock twice with his staff; water came out abundantly, and the congregation and their livestock drank. 12But the LORD said to Moses and Aaron, "Because you did not trust in me, to show my holiness before the eyes of the Israelites, therefore you shall not bring this assembly into the land that I have given them." 13These are the waters of Meribah,*i* where the people of Israel quarreled with the LORD, and by which he showed his holiness.

Passage through Edom Refused

14 Moses sent messengers from Kadesh to the king of Edom, "Thus says your brother Israel: You know all the adversity that has befallen us: 15how our ancestors went down to Egypt, and we lived in Egypt a long time; and the Egyptians oppressed us and our ancestors; 16and when we cried to the LORD, he heard our voice, and sent an angel and brought us out of Egypt; and here we are in Kadesh, a town on the edge of your territory. 17Now let us pass through your land. We will not pass through field or vineyard, or drink water from any well; we will go along the King's Highway, not turning aside to the right hand or to the left until we have passed through your territory."

18 But Edom said to him, "You shall not pass through, or we will come out with the sword against you." 19The Israelites said to him, "We will stay on the highway; and if we drink of your water, we and our livestock, then we will pay for it. It is only a small matter; just let us pass through on foot." 20But he said, "You shall not pass through." And Edom came out against them with a large force, heavily armed. 21Thus Edom refused to give Israel

passage through their territory; so Israel turned away from them.

The Death of Aaron

22 They set out from Kadesh, and the Israelites, the whole congregation, came to Mount Hor. 23Then the LORD said to Moses and Aaron at Mount Hor, on the border of the land of Edom, 24"Let Aaron be gathered to his people. For he shall not enter the land that I have given to the Israelites, because you rebelled against my command at the waters of Meribah. 25Take Aaron and his son Eleazar, and bring them up Mount Hor; 26strip Aaron of his vestments, and put them on his son Eleazar. But Aaron shall be gathered to his people,*j* and shall die there." 27Moses did as the LORD had commanded; they went up Mount Hor in the sight of the whole congregation. 28Moses stripped Aaron of his vestments, and put them on his son Eleazar; and Aaron died there on the top of the mountain. Moses and Eleazar came down from the mountain. 29When all the congregation saw that Aaron had died, all the house of Israel mourned for Aaron thirty days.

The Bronze Serpent

21 When the Canaanite, the king of Arad, who lived in the Negeb, heard that Israel was coming by the way of Atharim, he fought against Israel and took some of them captive. 2Then Israel made a vow to the LORD and said, "If you will indeed give this people into our hands, then we will utterly destroy their towns." 3The LORD listened to the voice of Israel, and handed over the Canaanites; and they utterly destroyed them and their towns; so the place was called Hormah.*k*

4 From Mount Hor they set out by the way to the Red Sea,*l* to go around the land of Edom; but the people became impatient on the way. 5The people spoke against God and against Moses, "Why have you brought us up out of Egypt to die in the wilderness? For there is no food and no water, and we detest this miserable food." 6Then the LORD sent poisonous*m* serpents among the people, and they bit the people, so that many Israelites died. 7The people came to Moses and said, "We

i That is *Quarrel*   *j* Heb lacks *to his people*
k Heb *Destruction*   *l* Or *Sea of Reeds*   *m* Or *fiery*; Heb *seraphim*

have sinned by speaking against the LORD and against you; pray to the LORD to take away the serpents from us." So Moses prayed for the people. 8And the LORD said to Moses, "Make a poisonous[n] serpent, and set it on a pole; and everyone who is bitten shall look at it and live." 9So Moses made a serpent of bronze, and put it upon a pole; and whenever a serpent bit someone, that person would look at the serpent of bronze and live.

The Journey to Moab

10 The Israelites set out, and camped in Oboth. 11They set out from Oboth, and camped at Iye-abarim, in the wilderness bordering Moab toward the sunrise. 12From there they set out, and camped in the Wadi Zered. 13From there they set out, and camped on the other side of the Arnon, in[o] the wilderness that extends from the boundary of the Amorites; for the Arnon is the boundary of Moab, between Moab and the Amorites. 14Wherefore it is said in the Book of the Wars of the LORD,

"Waheb in Suphah and the wadis.
The Arnon 15and the slopes of the
   wadis
that extend to the seat of Ar,
and lie along the border of Moab."[p]

16 From there they continued to Beer;[q] that is the well of which the LORD said to Moses, "Gather the people together, and I will give them water." 17Then Israel sang this song:

"Spring up, O well!—Sing to it!—
18 the well that the leaders sank,
that the nobles of the people dug,
   with the scepter, with the staff."

From the wilderness to Mattanah, 19from Mattanah to Nahaliel, from Nahaliel to Bamoth, 20and from Bamoth to the valley lying in the region of Moab by the top of Pisgah that overlooks the wasteland.[r]

King Sihon Defeated

21 Then Israel sent messengers to King Sihon of the Amorites, saying, 22"Let me pass through your land; we will not turn aside into field or vineyard; we will not drink the water of any well; we will go by the King's Highway until we have passed through your territory." 23But Sihon would not allow Israel to pass through his territory. Sihon gathered all his people together, and went out against Israel to the wilderness; he came to Jahaz, and fought

against Israel. 24Israel put him to the sword, and took possession of his land from the Arnon to the Jabbok, as far as to the Ammonites; for the boundary of the Ammonites was strong. 25Israel took all these towns, and Israel settled in all the towns of the Amorites, in Heshbon, and in all its villages. 26For Heshbon was the city of King Sihon of the Amorites, who had fought against the former king of Moab and captured all his land as far as the Arnon. 27Therefore the ballad singers say,

"Come to Heshbon, let it be built;
  let the city of Sihon be
    established.
28 For fire came out from Heshbon,
  flame from the city of Sihon.
It devoured Ar of Moab,
  and swallowed up[s] the heights of
    the Arnon.
29 Woe to you, O Moab!
  You are undone, O people of
    Chemosh!
He has made his sons fugitives,
  and his daughters captives,
    to an Amorite king, Sihon.
30 So their posterity perished
  from Heshbon[t] to Dibon,
and we laid waste until fire spread
    to Medeba."[u]

31 Thus Israel settled in the land of the Amorites. 32Moses sent to spy out Jazer; and they captured its villages, and dispossessed the Amorites who were there.

King Og Defeated

33 Then they turned and went up the road to Bashan; and King Og of Bashan came out against them, he and all his people, to battle at Edrei. 34But the LORD said to Moses, "Do not be afraid of him; for I have given him into your hand, with all his people, and all his land. You shall do to him as you did to King Sihon of the Amorites, who ruled in Heshbon." 35So they killed him, his sons, and all his people, until there was no survivor left; and they took possession of his land.

---

[n] Or *fiery;* Heb *seraph*   [o] Gk: Heb *which is in*
[p] Meaning of Heb uncertain   [q] That is *Well*
[r] Or *Jeshimon*   [s] Gk: Heb *and the lords of*
[t] Gk: Heb *we have shot at them; Heshbon has perished*   [u] Compare Sam Gk: Meaning of MT uncertain

Balak Summons Balaam to Curse Israel

22 The Israelites set out, and camped in the plains of Moab across the Jordan from Jericho. 2Now Balak son of Zippor saw all that Israel had done to the Amorites. 3Moab was in great dread of the people, because they were so numerous; Moab was overcome with fear of the people of Israel. 4And Moab said to the elders of Midian, "This horde will now lick up all that is around us, as an ox licks up the grass of the field." Now Balak son of Zippor was king of Moab at that time. 5He sent messengers to Balaam son of Beor at Pethor, which is on the Euphrates, in the land of Amaw,*v* to summon him, saying, "A people has come out of Egypt; they have spread over the face of the earth, and they have settled next to me. 6Come now, curse this people for me, since they are stronger than I; perhaps I shall be able to defeat them and drive them from the land; for I know that whomever you bless is blessed, and whomever you curse is cursed."

7 So the elders of Moab and the elders of Midian departed with the fees for divination in their hand; and they came to Balaam, and gave him Balak's message. 8He said to them, "Stay here tonight, and I will bring back word to you, just as the Lord speaks to me"; so the officials of Moab stayed with Balaam. 9God came to Balaam and said, "Who are these men with you?" 10Balaam said to God, "King Balak son of Zippor of Moab, has sent me this message: 11'A people has come out of Egypt and has spread over the face of the earth; now come, curse them for me; perhaps I shall be able to fight against them and drive them out.' " 12God said to Balaam, "You shall not go with them; you shall not curse the people, for they are blessed." 13So Balaam rose in the morning, and said to the officials of Balak, "Go to your own land, for the Lord has refused to let me go with you." 14So the officials of Moab rose and went to Balak, and said, "Balaam refuses to come with us."

15 Once again Balak sent officials, more numerous and more distinguished than these. 16They came to Balaam and said to him, "Thus says Balak son of Zippor: 'Do not let anything hinder you from coming to me; 17for I will surely do you great honor, and whatever you say to me I will do; come, curse this people for me.' "

18But Balaam replied to the servants of Balak, "Although Balak were to give me his house full of silver and gold, I could not go beyond the command of the Lord my God, to do less or more. 19You remain here, as the others did, so that I may learn what more the Lord may say to me." 20That night God came to Balaam and said to him, "If the men have come to summon you, get up and go with them; but do only what I tell you to do." 21So Balaam got up in the morning, saddled his donkey, and went with the officials of Moab.

Balaam, the Donkey, and the Angel

22 God's anger was kindled because he was going, and the angel of the Lord took his stand in the road as his adversary. Now he was riding on the donkey, and his two servants were with him. 23The donkey saw the angel of the Lord standing in the road, with a drawn sword in his hand; so the donkey turned off the road, and went into the field; and Balaam struck the donkey, to turn it back onto the road. 24Then the angel of the Lord stood in a narrow path between the vineyards, with a wall on either side. 25When the donkey saw the angel of the Lord, it scraped against the wall, and scraped Balaam's foot against the wall; so he struck it again. 26Then the angel of the Lord went ahead, and stood in a narrow place, where there was no way to turn either to the right or to the left. 27When the donkey saw the angel of the Lord, it lay down under Balaam; and Balaam's anger was kindled, and he struck the donkey with his staff. 28Then the Lord opened the mouth of the donkey, and it said to Balaam, "What have I done to you, that you have struck me these three times?" 29Balaam said to the donkey, "Because you have made a fool of me! I wish I had a sword in my hand! I would kill you right now!" 30But the donkey said to Balaam, "Am I not your donkey, which you have ridden all your life to this day? Have I been in the habit of treating you this way?" And he said, "No."

31 Then the Lord opened the eyes of Balaam, and he saw the angel of the Lord standing in the road, with his drawn sword in his hand; and he bowed down, falling on his face. 32The angel of the Lord said to him, "Why have you struck your donkey these three times? I have come out

---

v Or land of his kinsfolk

as an adversary, because your way is perverse[w] before me. 33The donkey saw me, and turned away from me these three times. If it had not turned away from me, surely just now I would have killed you and let it live." 34Then Balaam said to the angel of the LORD, "I have sinned, for I did not know that you were standing in the road to oppose me. Now therefore, if it is displeasing to you, I will return home." 35The angel of the LORD said to Balaam, "Go with the men; but speak only what I tell you to speak." So Balaam went on with the officials of Balak.

36 When Balak heard that Balaam had come, he went out to meet him at Ir-moab, on the boundary formed by the Arnon, at the farthest point of the boundary. 37Balak said to Balaam, "Did I not send to summon you? Why did you not come to me? Am I not able to honor you?" 38Balaam said to Balak, "I have come to you now, but do I have power to say just anything? The word God puts in my mouth, that is what I must say." 39Then Balaam went with Balak, and they came to Kiriath-huzoth. 40Balak sacrificed oxen and sheep, and sent them to Balaam and to the officials who were with him.

Balaam's First Oracle

41 On the next day Balak took Balaam and brought him up to Bamoth-baal; and from there he could see part of the people of Israel.[x] **23** 1Then Balaam said to Balak, "Build me seven altars here, and prepare seven bulls and seven rams for me." 2Balak did as Balaam had said; and Balak and Balaam offered a bull and a ram on each altar. 3Then Balaam said to Balak, "Stay here beside your burnt offerings while I go aside. Perhaps the LORD will come to meet me. Whatever he shows me I will tell you." And he went to a bare height.

4 Then God met Balaam; and Balaam said to him, "I have arranged the seven altars, and have offered a bull and a ram on each altar." 5The LORD put a word in Balaam's mouth, and said, "Return to Balak, and this is what you must say." 6So he returned to Balak,[y] who was standing beside his burnt offerings with all the officials of Moab. 7Then Balaam[z] uttered his oracle, saying:

"Balak has brought me from Aram,
　the king of Moab from the eastern
　　mountains:

'Come, curse Jacob for me;
　Come, denounce Israel!'
8 How can I curse whom God has not
　cursed?
　How can I denounce those whom
　　the LORD has not denounced?
9 For from the top of the crags I see
　him,
　from the hills I behold him.
Here is a people living alone,
　and not reckoning itself among
　　the nations!
10 Who can count the dust of Jacob,
　or number the dust-cloud[a] of
　　Israel?
Let me die the death of the upright,
　and let my end be like his!"

11 Then Balak said to Balaam, "What have you done to me? I brought you to curse my enemies, but now you have done nothing but bless them." 12He answered, "Must I not take care to say what the LORD puts into my mouth?"

Balaam's Second Oracle

13 So Balak said to him, "Come with me to another place from which you may see them; you shall see only part of them, and shall not see them all; then curse them for me from there." 14So he took him to the field of Zophim, to the top of Pisgah. He built seven altars, and offered a bull and a ram on each altar. 15Balaam said to Balak, "Stand here beside your burnt offerings, while I meet the LORD over there." 16The LORD met Balaam, put a word into his mouth, and said, "Return to Balak, and this is what you shall say." 17When he came to him, he was standing beside his burnt offerings with the officials of Moab. Balak said to him, "What has the LORD said?" 18Then Balaam uttered his oracle, saying:

"Rise, Balak, and hear;
　listen to me, O son of Zippor:
19 God is not a human being, that he
　should lie,
　or a mortal, that he should
　　change his mind.
Has he promised, and will he not
　do it?
Has he spoken, and will he not
　fulfill it?
20 See, I received a command to bless;

---

he has blessed, and I cannot
      revoke it.
21 He has not beheld misfortune in
      Jacob;
    nor has he seen trouble in Israel.
  The LORD their God is with them,
    acclaimed as a king among them.
22 God, who brings them out of Egypt,
    is like the horns of a wild ox for
      them.
23 Surely there is no enchantment
      against Jacob,
    no divination against Israel;
  now it shall be said of Jacob and
      Israel,
    'See what God has done!'
24 Look, a people rising up like a
      lioness,
    and rousing itself like a lion!
  It does not lie down until it has
      eaten the prey
    and drunk the blood of the slain."

25 Then Balak said to Balaam, "Do not
curse them at all, and do not bless them at
all." 26But Balaam answered Balak, "Did I
not tell you, 'Whatever the LORD says, that
is what I must do'?"

27 So Balak said to Balaam, "Come
now, I will take you to another place; perhaps it will please God that you may curse
them for me from there." 28So Balak took
Balaam to the top of Peor, which overlooks the wasteland.b 29Balaam said to
Balak, "Build me seven altars here, and
prepare seven bulls and seven rams for
me." 30So Balak did as Balaam had said,
and offered a bull and a ram on each altar.

Balaam's Third Oracle

24 Now Balaam saw that it pleased
the LORD to bless Israel, so he did
not go, as at other times, to look for
omens, but set his face toward the wilderness. 2Balaam looked up and saw Israel
camping tribe by tribe. Then the spirit of
God came upon him, 3and he uttered his
oracle, saying:

  "The oracle of Balaam son of Beor,
    the oracle of the man whose eye
      is clear,c
4 the oracle of one who hears the
      words of God,
    who sees the vision of the
      Almighty,d
    who falls down, but with eyes
      uncovered:
5 how fair are your tents, O Jacob,
    your encampments, O Israel!

6 Like palm groves that stretch far
      away,
    like gardens beside a river,
  like aloes that the LORD has planted,
    like cedar trees beside the waters.
7 Water shall flow from his buckets,
    and his seed shall have abundant
      water,
  his king shall be higher than Agag,
    and his kingdom shall be exalted.
8 God who brings him out of Egypt,
    is like the horns of a wild ox for
      him;
  he shall devour the nations that are
      his foes
    and break their bones.
  He shall strike with his arrows.e
9 He crouched, he lay down like a
      lion,
    and like a lioness; who will rouse
      him up?
  Blessed is everyone who blesses you,
    and cursed is everyone who curses
      you."

10 Then Balak's anger was kindled
against Balaam, and he struck his hands
together. Balak said to Balaam, "I summoned you to curse my enemies, but instead you have blessed them these three
times. 11Now be off with you! Go home!
I said, 'I will reward you richly,' but the
LORD has denied you any reward." 12And
Balaam said to Balak, "Did I not tell your
messengers whom you sent to me, 13'If
Balak should give me his house full of
silver and gold, I would not be able to go
beyond the word of the LORD, to do either
good or bad of my own will; what the
LORD says, that is what I will say'? 14So
now, I am going to my people; let me
advise you what this people will do to
your people in days to come."

Balaam's Fourth Oracle

15 So he uttered his oracle, saying:
  "The oracle of Balaam son of Beor,
    the oracle of the man whose eye
      is clear,c
16 the oracle of one who hears the
      words of God,
    and knows the knowledge of the
      Most High,f
  who sees the vision of the
      Almighty,d

b Or overlooks Jeshimon   c Or closed or open
d Traditional rendering of Heb Shaddai
e Meaning of Heb uncertain   f Or of Elyon

who falls down, but with his eyes
uncovered:

17 I see him, but not now;
   I behold him, but not near—
   a star shall come out of Jacob,
      and a scepter shall rise out of
         Israel;
   it shall crush the borderlands*g* of
         Moab,
      and the territory*h* of all the
         Shethites.
18 Edom will become a possession,
   Seir a possession of its enemies,*i*
      while Israel does valiantly.
19 One out of Jacob shall rule,
      and destroy the survivors of Ir."

20 Then he looked on Amalek, and uttered his oracle, saying:

"First among the nations was
   Amalek,
but its end is to perish forever."

21 Then he looked on the Kenite, and uttered his oracle, saying:

"Enduring is your dwelling place,
   and your nest is set in the rock;
22 yet Kain is destined for burning.
   How long shall Asshur take you
      away captive?"

23 Again he uttered his oracle, saying:
"Alas, who shall live when God
      does this?
24   But ships shall come from Kittim
   and shall afflict Asshur and Eber;
      and he also shall perish forever."

25 Then Balaam got up and went back to his place, and Balak also went his way.

Worship of Baal of Peor

25 While Israel was staying at Shittim, the people began to have sexual relations with the women of Moab. 2These invited the people to the sacrifices of their gods, and the people ate and bowed down to their gods. 3Thus Israel yoked itself to the Baal of Peor, and the LORD's anger was kindled against Israel. 4The LORD said to Moses, "Take all the chiefs of the people, and impale them in the sun before the LORD, in order that the fierce anger of the LORD may turn away from Israel." 5And Moses said to the judges of Israel, "Each of you shall kill any of your people who have yoked themselves to the Baal of Peor."

6 Just then one of the Israelites came and brought a Midianite woman into his family, in the sight of Moses and in the sight of the whole congregation of the Is-

raelites, while they were weeping at the entrance of the tent of meeting. 7When Phinehas son of Eleazar, son of Aaron the priest, saw it, he got up and left the congregation. Taking a spear in his hand, 8he went after the Israelite man into the tent, and pierced the two of them, the Israelite and the woman, through the belly. So the plague was stopped among the people of Israel. 9Nevertheless those that died by the plague were twenty-four thousand.

10 The LORD spoke to Moses, saying: 11"Phinehas son of Eleazar, son of Aaron the priest, has turned back my wrath from the Israelites by manifesting such zeal among them on my behalf that in my jealousy I did not consume the Israelites. 12Therefore say, 'I hereby grant him my covenant of peace. 13It shall be for him and for his descendants after him a covenant of perpetual priesthood, because he was zealous for his God, and made atonement for the Israelites.' "

14 The name of the slain Israelite man, who was killed with the Midianite woman, was Zimri son of Salu, head of an ancestral house belonging to the Simeonites. 15The name of the Midianite woman who was killed was Cozbi daughter of Zur, who was the head of a clan, an ancestral house in Midian.

16 The LORD said to Moses, 17"Harass the Midianites, and defeat them; 18for they have harassed you by the trickery with which they deceived you in the affair of Peor, and in the affair of Cozbi, the daughter of a leader of Midian, their sister; she was killed on the day of the plague that resulted from Peor."

A Census of the New Generation

26 After the plague the LORD said to Moses and to Eleazar son of Aaron the priest, 2"Take a census of the whole congregation of the Israelites, from twenty years old and upward, by their ancestral houses, everyone in Israel able to go to war." 3Moses and Eleazar the priest spoke with them in the plains of Moab by the Jordan opposite Jericho, saying, 4"Take a census of the people,*j* from twenty years old and upward," as the LORD commanded Moses.

---

g Or *forehead* *h* Some Mss read *skull* *i* Heb
Seir, its enemies, a possession *j* Heb lacks *take a
census of the people*: Compare verse 2

The Israelites, who came out of the land of Egypt, were:

5 Reuben, the firstborn of Israel. The descendants of Reuben: of Hanoch, the clan of the Hanochites; of Pallu, the clan of the Palluites; ⁶of Hezron, the clan of the Hezronites; of Carmi, the clan of the Carmites. ⁷These are the clans of the Reubenites; the number of those enrolled was forty-three thousand seven hundred thirty. ⁸And the descendants of Pallu: Eliab. ⁹The descendants of Eliab: Nemuel, Dathan, and Abiram. These are the same Dathan and Abiram, chosen from the congregation, who rebelled against Moses and Aaron in the company of Korah, when they rebelled against the Lord, ¹⁰and the earth opened its mouth and swallowed them up along with Korah, when that company died, when the fire devoured two hundred fifty men; and they became a warning. ¹¹Notwithstanding, the sons of Korah did not die.

12 The descendants of Simeon by their clans: of Nemuel, the clan of the Nemuelites; of Jamin, the clan of the Jaminites; of Jachin, the clan of the Jachinites; ¹³of Zerah, the clan of the Zerahites; of Shaul, the clan of the Shaulites.ᵏ ¹⁴These are the clans of the Simeonites, twenty-two thousand two hundred.

15 The children of Gad by their clans: of Zephon, the clan of the Zephonites; of Haggi, the clan of the Haggites; of Shuni, the clan of the Shunites; ¹⁶of Ozni, the clan of the Oznites; of Eri, the clan of the Erites; ¹⁷of Arod, the clan of the Arodites; of Areli, the clan of the Arelites. ¹⁸These are the clans of the Gadites: the number of those enrolled was forty thousand five hundred.

19 The sons of Judah: Er and Onan; Er and Onan died in the land of Canaan. ²⁰The descendants of Judah by their clans were: of Shelah, the clan of the Shelanites; of Perez, the clan of the Perezites; of Zerah, the clan of the Zerahites. ²¹The descendants of Perez were: of Hezron, the clan of the Hezronites; of Hamul, the clan of the Hamulites. ²²These are the clans of Judah: the number of those enrolled was seventy-six thousand five hundred.

23 The descendants of Issachar by their clans: of Tola, the clan of the Tolaites; of Puvah, the clan of the Punites; ²⁴of Jashub, the clan of the Jashubites; of Shimron, the clan of the Shimronites. ²⁵These are the clans of Issachar: sixty-four thousand three hundred enrolled.

26 The descendants of Zebulun by their clans: of Sered, the clan of the Seredites; of Elon, the clan of the Elonites; of Jahleel, the clan of the Jahleelites. ²⁷These are the clans of the Zebulunites; the number of those enrolled was sixty thousand five hundred.

28 The sons of Joseph by their clans: Manasseh and Ephraim. ²⁹The descendants of Manasseh: of Machir, the clan of the Machirites; and Machir was the father of Gilead; of Gilead, the clan of the Gileadites. ³⁰These are the descendants of Gilead: of Iezer, the clan of the Iezerites; of Helek, the clan of the Helekites; ³¹and of Asriel, the clan of the Asrielites; and of Shechem, the clan of the Shechemites; ³²and of Shemida, the clan of the Shemidaites; and of Hepher, the clan of the Hepherites. ³³Now Zelophehad son of Hepher had no sons, but daughters: and the names of the daughters of Zelophehad were Mahlah, Noah, Hoglah, Milcah, and Tirzah. ³⁴These are the clans of Manasseh; the number of those enrolled was fifty-two thousand seven hundred.

35 These are the descendants of Ephraim according to their clans: of Shuthelah, the clan of the Shuthelahites; of Becher, the clan of the Becherites; of Tahan, the clan of the Tahanites. ³⁶And these are the descendants of Shuthelah: of Eran, the clan of the Eranites. ³⁷These are the clans of the Ephraimites: the number of those enrolled was thirty-two thousand five hundred. These are the descendants of Joseph by their clans.

38 The descendants of Benjamin by their clans: of Bela, the clan of the Belaites; of Ashbel, the clan of the Ashbelites; of Ahiram, the clan of the Ahiramites; ³⁹of Shephupham, the clan of the Shuphamites; of Hupham, the clan of the Huphamites. ⁴⁰And the sons of Bela were Ard and Naaman: of Ard, the clan of the Ardites; of Naaman, the clan of the Naamites. ⁴¹These are the descendants of Benjamin by their clans; the number of those enrolled was forty-five thousand six hundred.

42 These are the descendants of Dan by their clans: of Shuham, the clan of the Shuhamites. These are the clans of Dan by their clans. ⁴³All the clans of the Shuham-

ᵏ *Or Saul . . . Saulites*

ites: sixty-four thousand four hundred enrolled.

44 The descendants of Asher by their families: of Imnah, the clan of the Imnites; of Ishvi, the clan of the Ishvites; of Beriah, the clan of the Beriites. 45Of the descendants of Beriah: of Heber, the clan of the Heberites; of Malchiel, the clan of the Malchielites. 46And the name of the daughter of Asher was Serah. 47These are the clans of the Asherites: the number of those enrolled was fifty-three thousand four hundred.

48 The descendants of Naphtali by their clans: of Jahzeel, the clan of the Jahzeelites; of Guni, the clan of the Gunites; 49of Jezer, the clan of the Jezerites; of Shillem, the clan of the Shillemites. 50These are the Naphtalites¹ by their clans: the number of those enrolled was forty-five thousand four hundred.

51 This was the number of the Israelites enrolled: six hundred and one thousand seven hundred thirty.

52 The LORD spoke to Moses, saying: 53To these the land shall be apportioned for inheritance according to the number of names. 54To a large tribe you shall give a large inheritance, and to a small tribe you shall give a small inheritance; every tribe shall be given its inheritance according to its enrollment. 55But the land shall be apportioned by lot; according to the names of their ancestral tribes they shall inherit. 56Their inheritance shall be apportioned according to lot between the larger and the smaller.

57 This is the enrollment of the Levites by their clans: of Gershon, the clan of the Gershonites; of Kohath, the clan of the Kohathites; of Merari, the clan of the Merarites. 58These are the clans of Levi: the clan of the Libnites, the clan of the Hebronites, the clan of the Mahlites, the clan of the Mushites, the clan of the Korahites. Now Kohath was the father of Amram. 59The name of Amram's wife was Jochebed daughter of Levi, who was born to Levi in Egypt; and she bore to Amram: Aaron, Moses, and their sister Miriam. 60To Aaron were born Nadab, Abihu, Eleazar, and Ithamar. 61But Nadab and Abihu died when they offered unholy fire before the LORD. 62The number of those enrolled was twenty-three thousand, every male one month old and upward; for they were not enrolled among the Israel-

ites because there was no allotment given to them among the Israelites.

63 These were those enrolled by Moses and Eleazar the priest, who enrolled the Israelites in the plains of Moab by the Jordan opposite Jericho. 64Among these there was not one of those enrolled by Moses and Aaron the priest, who had enrolled the Israelites in the wilderness of Sinai. 65For the LORD had said of them, "They shall die in the wilderness." Not one of them was left, except Caleb son of Jephunneh and Joshua son of Nun.

The Daughters of Zelophehad

27 Then the daughters of Zelophehad came forward. Zelophehad was son of Hepher son of Gilead son of Machir son of Manasseh son of Joseph, a member of the Manassite clans. The names of his daughters were: Mahlah, Noah, Hoglah, Milcah, and Tirzah. 2They stood before Moses, Eleazar the priest, the leaders, and all the congregation, at the entrance of the tent of meeting, and they said, 3"Our father died in the wilderness; he was not among the company of those who gathered themselves together against the LORD in the company of Korah, but died for his own sin; and he had no sons. 4Why should the name of our father be taken away from his clan because he had no son? Give to us a possession among our father's brothers."

5 Moses brought their case before the LORD. 6And the LORD spoke to Moses, saying: 7The daughters of Zelophehad are right in what they are saying; you shall indeed let them possess an inheritance among their father's brothers and pass the inheritance of their father on to them. 8You shall also say to the Israelites, "If a man dies, and has no son, then you shall pass his inheritance on to his daughter. 9If he has no daughter, then you shall give his inheritance to his brothers. 10If he has no brothers, then you shall give his inheritance to his father's brothers. 11And if his father has no brothers, then you shall give his inheritance to the nearest kinsman of his clan, and he shall possess it. It shall be for the Israelites a statute and ordinance, as the LORD commanded Moses."

Joshua Appointed Moses' Successor

12 The LORD said to Moses, "Go up this

¹ Heb *clans of Naphtali*

mountain of the Abarim range, and see the land that I have given to the Israelites. [13]When you have seen it, you also shall be gathered to your people, as your brother Aaron was, [14]because you rebelled against my word in the wilderness of Zin when the congregation quarreled with me.[m] You did not show my holiness before their eyes at the waters." (These are the waters of Meribath-kadesh in the wilderness of Zin.) [15]Moses spoke to the LORD, saying, [16]"Let the LORD, the God of the spirits of all flesh, appoint someone over the congregation [17]who shall go out before them and come in before them, who shall lead them out and bring them in, so that the congregation of the LORD may not be like sheep without a shepherd." [18]So the LORD said to Moses, "Take Joshua son of Nun, a man in whom is the spirit, and lay your hand upon him; [19]have him stand before Eleazar the priest and all the congregation, and commission him in their sight. [20]You shall give him some of your authority, so that all the congregation of the Israelites may obey. [21]But he shall stand before Eleazar the priest, who shall inquire for him by the decision of the Urim before the LORD; at his word they shall go out, and at his word they shall come in, both he and all the Israelites with him, the whole congregation." [22]So Moses did as the LORD commanded him. He took Joshua and had him stand before Eleazar the priest and the whole congregation; [23]he laid his hands on him and commissioned him—as the LORD had directed through Moses.

Daily Offerings

28 The LORD spoke to Moses, saying: [2]Command the Israelites, and say to them: My offering, the food for my offerings by fire, my pleasing odor, you shall take care to offer to me at its appointed time. [3]And you shall say to them, This is the offering by fire that you shall offer to the LORD: two male lambs a year old without blemish, daily, as a regular offering. [4]One lamb you shall offer in the morning, and the other lamb you shall offer at twilight;[n] [5]also one-tenth of an ephah of choice flour for a grain offering, mixed with one-fourth of a hin of beaten oil. [6]It is a regular burnt offering, ordained at Mount Sinai for a pleasing odor, an offering by fire to the LORD. [7]Its drink

offering shall be one-fourth of a hin for each lamb; in the sanctuary you shall pour out a drink offering of strong drink to the LORD. [8]The other lamb you shall offer at twilight[n] with a grain offering and a drink offering like the one in the morning; you shall offer it as an offering by fire, a pleasing odor to the LORD.

Sabbath Offerings

9 On the sabbath day: two male lambs a year old without blemish, and two-tenths of an ephah of choice flour for a grain offering, mixed with oil, and its drink offering— [10]this is the burnt offering for every sabbath, in addition to the regular burnt offering and its drink offering.

Monthly Offerings

11 At the beginnings of your months you shall offer a burnt offering to the LORD: two young bulls, one ram, seven male lambs a year old without blemish; [12]also three-tenths of an ephah of choice flour for a grain offering, mixed with oil, for each bull; and two-tenths of choice flour for a grain offering, mixed with oil, for the one ram; [13]and one-tenth of choice flour mixed with oil as a grain offering for every lamb—a burnt offering of pleasing odor, an offering by fire to the LORD. [14]Their drink offerings shall be half a hin of wine for a bull, one-third of a hin for a ram, and one-fourth of a hin for a lamb. This is the burnt offering of every month throughout the months of the year. [15]And there shall be one male goat for a sin offering to the LORD; it shall be offered in addition to the regular burnt offering and its drink offering.

Offerings at Passover

16 On the fourteenth day of the first month there shall be a passover offering to the LORD. [17]And on the fifteenth day of this month is a festival; seven days shall unleavened bread be eaten. [18]On the first day there shall be a holy convocation. You shall not work at your occupations. [19]You shall offer an offering by fire, a burnt offering to the LORD: two young bulls, one ram, and seven male lambs a year old; see

---

[m] Heb lacks *with me*   [n] Heb *between the two evenings*

that they are without blemish. [20]Their grain offering shall be of choice flour mixed with oil: three-tenths of an ephah shall you offer for a bull, and two-tenths for a ram; [21]one-tenth shall you offer for each of the seven lambs; [22]also one male goat for a sin offering, to make atonement for you. [23]You shall offer these in addition to the burnt offering of the morning, which belongs to the regular burnt offering. [24]In the same way you shall offer daily, for seven days, the food of an offering by fire, a pleasing odor to the LORD; it shall be offered in addition to the regular burnt offering and its drink offering. [25]And on the seventh day you shall have a holy convocation; you shall not work at your occupations.

Offerings at the Festival of Weeks

26 On the day of the first fruits, when you offer a grain offering of new grain to the LORD at your festival of weeks, you shall have a holy convocation; you shall not work at your occupations. [27]You shall offer a burnt offering, a pleasing odor to the LORD: two young bulls, one ram, seven male lambs a year old. [28]Their grain offering shall be of choice flour mixed with oil, three-tenths of an ephah for each bull, two-tenths for one ram, [29]one-tenth for each of the seven lambs; [30]with one male goat, to make atonement for you. [31]In addition to the regular burnt offering with its grain offering, you shall offer them and their drink offering. They shall be without blemish.

Family Traditions

The rituals and traditions of the Jewish holy days have their counterpart in the feasts of the Church. In the "domestic church" of the family, traditions likewise play a crucial role.

TUESDAY

Scripture Reading for Today:
Numbers 28.1–10

Verse for Today:
Numbers 28.2

Families who treasure their traditions and rituals seem automatically to have a sense of family. Traditions are the underpinning in such families, regarded as necessities, not frills. These are the families who explain that they can't come to a meeting because there's a family birthday, or they refuse an opportunity for overtime on the job because they always meet for a picnic and volleyball games with another family on the first weekend of August, or they allow their children to stay home from school because it's Saint Joseph's Day and the Italians like to celebrate on that day.

Families don't have to have a great backlog of traditions in order to pass them along. To children, once is a tradition, and many a parent after some simple family observance is dumbfounded to hear the children describe it by saying, "We always do it that way." This is a pretty good key to the depth and value placed on that experience by the children. It tells parents that the children want to repeat the experience as a family and indicates that they would welcome more such experiences, as original as those experiences might be. It's probably one of the best signals children send parents on the need for more traditions and rituals in the home.

—*DOLORES CURRAN*

Go to page 191 for your next devotional reading.

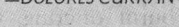

Offerings at the Festival of Trumpets

29 On the first day of the seventh month you shall have a holy convocation; you shall not work at your occupations. It is a day for you to blow the trumpets, ²and you shall offer a burnt offering, a pleasing odor to the LORD: one young bull, one ram, seven male lambs a year old without blemish. ³Their grain offering shall be of choice flour mixed with oil, three-tenths of one ephah for the bull, two-tenths for the ram, ⁴and one-tenth for each of the seven lambs; ⁵with one male goat for a sin offering, to make atonement for you. ⁶These are in addition to the burnt offering of the new moon and its grain offering, and the regular burnt offering and its grain offering, and their drink offerings, according to the ordinance for them, a pleasing odor, an offering by fire to the LORD.

Offerings on the Day of Atonement

7 On the tenth day of this seventh month you shall have a holy convocation, and deny yourselves;ᵒ you shall do no work. ⁸You shall offer a burnt offering to the LORD, a pleasing odor: one young bull, one ram, seven male lambs a year old. They shall be without blemish. ⁹Their grain offering shall be of choice flour mixed with oil, three-tenths of an ephah for the bull, two-tenths for the one ram, ¹⁰one-tenth for each of the seven lambs; ¹¹with one male goat for a sin offering, in addition to the sin offering of atonement, and the regular burnt offering and its grain offering, and their drink offerings.

Offerings at the Festival of Booths

12 On the fifteenth day of the seventh month you shall have a holy convocation; you shall not work at your occupations. You shall celebrate a festival to the LORD seven days. ¹³You shall offer a burnt offering, an offering by fire, a pleasing odor to the LORD: thirteen young bulls, two rams, fourteen male lambs a year old. They shall be without blemish. ¹⁴Their grain offering shall be of choice flour mixed with oil, three-tenths of an ephah for each of the thirteen bulls, two-tenths for each of the two rams, ¹⁵and one-tenth for each of the fourteen lambs; ¹⁶also one male goat for a sin offering, in addition to the regular burnt offering, its grain offering and its drink offering.

17 On the second day: twelve young bulls, two rams, fourteen male lambs a year old without blemish, ¹⁸with the grain offering and the drink offerings for the bulls, for the rams, and for the lambs, as prescribed in accordance with their number; ¹⁹also one male goat for a sin offering, in addition to the regular burnt offering and its grain offering, and their drink offerings.

20 On the third day: eleven bulls, two rams, fourteen male lambs a year old without blemish, ²¹with the grain offering and the drink offerings for the bulls, for the rams, and for the lambs, as prescribed in accordance with their number; ²²also one male goat for a sin offering, in addition to the regular burnt offering and its grain offering and its drink offering.

23 On the fourth day: ten bulls, two rams, fourteen male lambs a year old without blemish, ²⁴with the grain offering and the drink offerings for the bulls, for the rams, and for the lambs, as prescribed in accordance with their number; ²⁵also one male goat for a sin offering, in addition to the regular burnt offering, its grain offering and its drink offering.

26 On the fifth day: nine bulls, two rams, fourteen male lambs a year old without blemish, ²⁷with the grain offering and the drink offerings for the bulls, for the rams, and for the lambs, as prescribed in accordance with their number; ²⁸also one male goat for a sin offering, in addition to the regular burnt offering and its grain offering and its drink offering.

29 On the sixth day: eight bulls, two rams, fourteen male lambs a year old without blemish, ³⁰with the grain offering and the drink offerings for the bulls, for the rams, and for the lambs, as prescribed in accordance with their number; ³¹also one male goat for a sin offering, in addition to the regular burnt offering, its grain offering, and its drink offerings.

32 On the seventh day: seven bulls, two rams, fourteen male lambs a year old without blemish, ³³with the grain offering and the drink offerings for the bulls, for the rams, and for the lambs, as prescribed in accordance with their number; ³⁴also one male goat for a sin offering, besides the regular burnt offering, its grain offering, and its drink offering.

35 On the eighth day you shall have a

ᵒ Or *and fast*

solemn assembly; you shall not work at your occupations. 36You shall offer a burnt offering, an offering by fire, a pleasing odor to the LORD: one bull, one ram, seven male lambs a year old without blemish, 37and the grain offering and the drink offerings for the bull, for the ram, and for the lambs, as prescribed in accordance with their number; 38also one male goat for a sin offering, in addition to the regular burnt offering and its grain offering and its drink offering.

39 These you shall offer to the LORD at your appointed festivals, in addition to your votive offerings and your freewill offerings, as your burnt offerings, your grain offerings, your drink offerings, and your offerings of well-being.

40pSo Moses told the Israelites everything just as the LORD had commanded Moses.

Vows Made by Women

30 Then Moses said to the heads of the tribes of the Israelites: This is what the LORD has commanded. 2When a man makes a vow to the LORD, or swears an oath to bind himself by a pledge, he shall not break his word; he shall do according to all that proceeds out of his mouth.

3 When a woman makes a vow to the LORD, or binds herself by a pledge, while within her father's house, in her youth, 4and her father hears of her vow or her pledge by which she has bound herself, and says nothing to her; then all her vows shall stand, and any pledge by which she has bound herself shall stand. 5But if her father expresses disapproval to her at the time that he hears of it, no vow of hers, and no pledge by which she has bound herself, shall stand; and the LORD will forgive her, because her father had expressed to her his disapproval.

6 If she marries, while obligated by her vows or any thoughtless utterance of her lips by which she has bound herself, 7and her husband hears of it and says nothing to her at the time that he hears, then her vows shall stand, and her pledges by which she has bound herself shall stand. 8But if, at the time that her husband hears of it, he expresses disapproval to her, then he shall nullify the vow by which she was obligated, or the thoughtless utterance of her lips, by which she bound herself; and the LORD will forgive her. 9(But every vow

of a widow or of a divorced woman, by which she has bound herself, shall be binding upon her.) 10And if she made a vow in her husband's house, or bound herself by a pledge with an oath, 11and her husband heard it and said nothing to her, and did not express disapproval to her, then all her vows shall stand, and any pledge by which she bound herself shall stand. 12But if her husband nullifies them at the time that he hears them, then whatever proceeds out of her lips concerning her vows, or concerning her pledge of herself, shall not stand. Her husband has nullified them, and the LORD will forgive her. 13Any vow or any binding oath to deny herself,q her husband may allow to stand, or her husband may nullify. 14But if her husband says nothing to her from day to day,r then he validates all her vows, or all her pledges, by which she is obligated; he has validated them, because he said nothing to her at the time that he heard of them. 15But if he nullifies them some time after he has heard of them, then he shall bear her guilt.

16 These are the statutes that the LORD commanded Moses concerning a husband and his wife, and a father and his daughter while she is still young and in her father's house.

War against Midian

31 The LORD spoke to Moses, saying, 2"Avenge the Israelites on the Midianites; afterward you shall be gathered to your people." 3So Moses said to the people, "Arm some of your number for the war, so that they may go against Midian, to execute the LORD's vengeance on Midian. 4You shall send a thousand from each of the tribes of Israel to the war." 5So out of the thousands of Israel, a thousand from each tribe were conscripted, twelve thousand armed for battle. 6Moses sent them to the war, a thousand from each tribe, along with Phinehas son of Eleazar the priest,s with the vessels of the sanctuary and the trumpets for sounding the alarm in his hand. 7They did battle against Midian, as the LORD had commanded Moses, and killed every male. 8They killed the kings of Midian: Evi, Rekem, Zur, Hur, and Reba, the five kings of Midian, in addition to others who were slain by them;

p Ch 30.1 in Heb   q Or to fast   r Or from that day to the next   s Gk: Heb adds to the war and they also killed Balaam son of Beor with the sword. ⁹The Israelites took the women of Midian and their little ones captive; and they took all their cattle, their flocks, and all their goods as booty. ¹⁰All their towns where they had settled, and all their encampments, they burned, ¹¹but they took all the spoil and all the booty, both people and animals. ¹²Then they brought the captives and the booty and the spoil to Moses, to Eleazar the priest, and to the congregation of the Israelites, at the camp on the plains of Moab by the Jordan at Jericho.

Return from the War

13 Moses, Eleazar the priest, and all the leaders of the congregation went to meet them outside the camp. ¹⁴Moses became angry with the officers of the army, the commanders of thousands and the commanders of hundreds, who had come from service in the war. ¹⁵Moses said to them, "Have you allowed all the women to live? ¹⁶These women here, on Balaam's advice, made the Israelites act treacherously against the LORD in the affair of Peor, so that the plague came among the congregation of the LORD. ¹⁷Now therefore, kill every male among the little ones, and kill every woman who has known a man by sleeping with him. ¹⁸But all the young girls who have not known a man by sleeping with him, keep alive for yourselves. ¹⁹Camp outside the camp seven days; whoever of you has killed any person or touched a corpse, purify yourselves and your captives on the third and on the seventh day. ²⁰You shall purify every garment, every article of skin, everything made of goats' hair, and every article of wood."

21 Eleazar the priest said to the troops who had gone to battle: "This is the statute of the law that the LORD has commanded Moses: ²²gold, silver, bronze, iron, tin, and lead— ²³everything that can withstand fire, shall be passed through fire, and it shall be clean. Nevertheless it shall also be purified with the water for purification; and whatever cannot withstand fire, shall be passed through the water. ²⁴You must wash your clothes on the seventh day, and you shall be clean; afterward you may come into the camp."

Disposition of Captives and Booty

25 The LORD spoke to Moses, saying,

²⁶"You and Eleazar the priest and the heads of the ancestral houses of the congregation make an inventory of the booty captured, both human and animal. ²⁷Divide the booty into two parts, between the warriors who went out to battle and all the congregation. ²⁸From the share of the warriors who went out to battle, set aside as tribute for the LORD, one item out of every five hundred, whether persons, oxen, donkeys, sheep, or goats. ²⁹Take it from their half and give it to Eleazar the priest as an offering to the LORD. ³⁰But from the Israelites' half you shall take one out of every fifty, whether persons, oxen, donkeys, sheep, or goats—all the animals—and give them to the Levites who have charge of the tabernacle of the LORD."

31 Then Moses and Eleazar the priest did as the LORD had commanded Moses:

32 The booty remaining from the spoil that the troops had taken totaled six hundred seventy-five thousand sheep, ³³seventy-two thousand oxen, ³⁴sixty-one thousand donkeys, ³⁵and thirty-two thousand persons in all, women who had not known a man by sleeping with him.

36 The half-share, the portion of those who had gone out to war, was in number three hundred thirty-seven thousand five hundred sheep and goats, ³⁷and the LORD's tribute of sheep and goats was six hundred seventy-five. ³⁸The oxen were thirty-six thousand, of which the LORD's tribute was seventy-two. ³⁹The donkeys were thirty thousand five hundred, of which the LORD's tribute was sixty-one. ⁴⁰The persons were sixteen thousand, of which the LORD's tribute was thirty-two persons. ⁴¹Moses gave the tribute, the offering for the LORD, to Eleazar the priest, as the LORD had commanded Moses.

42 As for the Israelites' half, which Moses separated from that of the troops, ⁴³the congregation's half was three hundred thirty-seven thousand five hundred sheep and goats, ⁴⁴thirty-six thousand oxen, ⁴⁵thirty thousand five hundred donkeys, ⁴⁶and sixteen thousand persons. ⁴⁷From the Israelites' half Moses took one of every fifty, both of persons and of animals, and gave them to the Levites who had charge of the tabernacle of the LORD; as the LORD had commanded Moses.

48 Then the officers who were over the thousands of the army, the commanders of thousands and the commanders of hundreds, approached Moses, ⁴⁹and said

to Moses, "Your servants have counted the warriors who are under our command, and not one of us is missing. [50]And we have brought the LORD's offering, what each of us found, articles of gold, armlets and bracelets, signet rings, earrings, and pendants, to make atonement for ourselves before the LORD." [51]Moses and Eleazar the priest received the gold from them, all in the form of crafted articles. [52]And all the gold of the offering that they offered to the LORD, from the commanders of thousands and the commanders of hundreds, was sixteen thousand seven hundred fifty shekels. [53](The troops had all taken plunder for themselves.) [54]So Moses and Eleazar the priest received the gold from the commanders of thousands and of hundreds, and brought it into the tent of meeting as a memorial for the Israelites before the LORD.

Conquest and Division of Transjordan

32 Now the Reubenites and the Gadites owned a very great number of cattle. When they saw that the land of Jazer and the land of Gilead was a good place for cattle, [2]the Gadites and the Reubenites came and spoke to Moses, to Eleazar the priest, and to the leaders of the congregation, saying, [3]"Ataroth, Dibon, Jazer, Nimrah, Heshbon, Elealeh, Sebam, Nebo, and Beon— [4]the land that the LORD subdued before the congregation of Israel—is a land for cattle; and your servants have cattle." [5]They continued, "If we have found favor in your sight, let this land be given to your servants for a possession; do not make us cross the Jordan."

[6] But Moses said to the Gadites and to the Reubenites, "Shall your brothers go to war while you sit here? [7]Why will you discourage the hearts of the Israelites from going over into the land that the LORD has given them? [8]Your fathers did this, when I sent them from Kadesh-barnea to see the land. [9]When they went up to the Wadi Eshcol and saw the land, they discouraged the hearts of the Israelites from going into the land that the LORD had given them. [10]The LORD's anger was kindled on that day and he swore, saying, [11]'Surely none of the people who came up out of Egypt, from twenty years old and upward, shall see the land that I swore to give to Abraham, to Isaac, and to Jacob, because they have not unreservedly followed me— [12]none except Caleb son of Jephunneh the

Kenizzite and Joshua son of Nun, for they have unreservedly followed the LORD.' [13]And the LORD's anger was kindled against Israel, and he made them wander in the wilderness for forty years, until all the generation that had done evil in the sight of the LORD had disappeared. [14]And now you, a brood of sinners, have risen in place of your fathers, to increase the LORD's fierce anger against Israel! [15]If you turn away from following him, he will again abandon them in the wilderness; and you will destroy all this people."

[16] Then they came up to him and said, "We will build sheepfolds here for our flocks, and towns for our little ones, [17]but we will take up arms as a vanguard[t] before the Israelites, until we have brought them to their place. Meanwhile our little ones will stay in the fortified towns because of the inhabitants of the land. [18]We will not return to our homes until all the Israelites have obtained their inheritance. [19]We will not inherit with them on the other side of the Jordan and beyond, because our inheritance has come to us on this side of the Jordan to the east."

[20] So Moses said to them, "If you do this—if you take up arms to go before the LORD for the war, [21]and all those of you who bear arms cross the Jordan before the LORD, until he has driven out his enemies from before him [22]and the land is subdued before the LORD—then after that you may return and be free of obligation to the LORD and to Israel, and this land shall be your possession before the LORD. [23]But if you do not do this, you have sinned against the LORD; and be sure your sin will find you out. [24]Build towns for your little ones, and folds for your flocks; but do what you have promised."

[25] Then the Gadites and the Reubenites said to Moses, "Your servants will do as my lord commands. [26]Our little ones, our wives, our flocks, and all our livestock shall remain there in the towns of Gilead; [27]but your servants will cross over, everyone armed for war, to do battle for the LORD, just as my lord orders."

[28] So Moses gave command concerning them to Eleazar the priest, to Joshua son of Nun, and to the heads of the ancestral houses of the Israelite tribes. [29]And Moses said to them, "If the Gadites and the Reubenites, everyone armed for battle

t Cn: Heb *hurrying*

before the LORD, will cross over the Jordan with you and the land shall be subdued before you, then you shall give them the land of Gilead for a possession; ³⁰but if they will not cross over with you armed, they shall have possessions among you in the land of Canaan." ³¹The Gadites and the Reubenites answered, "As the LORD has spoken to your servants, so we will do. ³²We will cross over armed before the LORD into the land of Canaan, but the possession of our inheritance shall remain with us on this side of^u the Jordan."

33 Moses gave to them—to the Gadites and to the Reubenites and to the half-tribe of Manasseh son of Joseph—the kingdom of King Sihon of the Amorites and the kingdom of King Og of Bashan, the land and its towns, with the territories of the surrounding towns. ³⁴And the Gadites rebuilt Dibon, Ataroth, Aroer, ³⁵Atroth-shophan, Jazer, Jogbehah, ³⁶Beth-nimrah, and Beth-haran, fortified cities, and folds for sheep. ³⁷And the Reubenites rebuilt Heshbon, Elealeh, Kiriathaim, ³⁸Nebo, and Baal-meon (some names being changed), and Sibmah; and they gave names to the towns that they rebuilt. ³⁹The descendants of Machir son of Manasseh went to Gilead, captured it, and dispossessed the Amorites who were there; ⁴⁰so Moses gave Gilead to Machir son of Manasseh, and he settled there. ⁴¹Jair son of Manasseh went and captured their villages, and renamed them Havvoth-jair.^v ⁴²And Nobah went and captured Kenath and its villages, and renamed it Nobah after himself.

The Stages of Israel's Journey from Egypt

33 These are the stages by which the Israelites went out of the land of Egypt in military formation under the leadership of Moses and Aaron. ²Moses wrote down their starting points, stage by stage, by command of the LORD; and these are their stages according to their starting places. ³They set out from Rameses in the first month, on the fifteenth day of the first month; on the day after the passover the Israelites went out boldly in the sight of all the Egyptians, ⁴while the Egyptians were burying all their firstborn, whom the LORD had struck down among them. The LORD executed judgments even against their gods.

5 So the Israelites set out from Rameses, and camped at Succoth. ⁶They set out from Succoth, and camped at Etham, which is on the edge of the wilderness. ⁷They set out from Etham, and turned back to Pi-hahiroth, which faces Baal-zephon; and they camped before Migdol. ⁸They set out from Pi-hahiroth, passed through the sea into the wilderness, went a three days' journey in the wilderness of Etham, and camped at Marah. ⁹They set out from Marah and came to Elim; at Elim there were twelve springs of water and seventy palm trees, and they camped there. ¹⁰They set out from Elim and camped by the Red Sea.^w ¹¹They set out from the Red Sea^w and camped in the wilderness of Sin. ¹²They set out from the wilderness of Sin and camped at Dophkah. ¹³They set out from Dophkah and camped at Alush. ¹⁴They set out from Alush and camped at Rephidim, where there was no water for the people to drink. ¹⁵They set out from Rephidim and camped in the wilderness of Sinai. ¹⁶They set out from the wilderness of Sinai and camped at Kibroth-hattaavah. ¹⁷They set out from Kibroth-hattaavah and camped at Hazeroth. ¹⁸They set out from Hazeroth and camped at Rithmah. ¹⁹They set out from Rithmah and camped at Rimmon-perez. ²⁰They set out from Rimmon-perez and camped at Libnah. ²¹They set out from Libnah and camped at Rissah. ²²They set out from Rissah and camped at Kehelathah. ²³They set out from Kehelathah and camped at Mount Shepher. ²⁴They set out from Mount Shepher and camped at Haradah. ²⁵They set out from Haradah and camped at Makheloth. ²⁶They set out from Makheloth and camped at Tahath. ²⁷They set out from Tahath and camped at Terah. ²⁸They set out from Terah and camped at Mithkah. ²⁹They set out from Mithkah and camped at Hashmonah. ³⁰They set out from Hashmonah and camped at Moseroth. ³¹They set out from Moseroth and camped at Bene-jaakan. ³²They set out from Bene-jaakan and camped at Hor-haggidgad. ³³They set out from Hor-haggidgad and camped at Jotbathah. ³⁴They set out from Jotbathah and camped at Abronah. ³⁵They set out from Abronah and camped at Ezion-geber. ³⁶They set out from Ezion-geber and camped in the wilderness of Zin (that is, Kadesh). ³⁷They set out from Kadesh and

^u Heb *beyond*   ^v That is *the villages of Jair*   ^w Or *Sea of Reeds*

camped at Mount Hor, on the edge of the land of Edom.

38 Aaron the priest went up Mount Hor at the command of the LORD and died there in the fortieth year after the Israelites had come out of the land of Egypt, on the first day of the fifth month. ³⁹Aaron was one hundred twenty-three years old when he died on Mount Hor.

40 The Canaanite, the king of Arad, who lived in the Negeb in the land of Canaan, heard of the coming of the Israelites.

41 They set out from Mount Hor and camped at Zalmonah. ⁴²They set out from Zalmonah and camped at Punon. ⁴³They set out from Punon and camped at Oboth. ⁴⁴They set out from Oboth and camped at Iye-abarim, in the territory of Moab. ⁴⁵They set out from Iyim and camped at Dibon-gad. ⁴⁶They set out from Dibon-gad and camped at Almon-diblathaim. ⁴⁷They set out from Almon-diblathaim and camped in the mountains of Abarim, before Nebo. ⁴⁸They set out from the mountains of Abarim and camped in the plains of Moab by the Jordan at Jericho; ⁴⁹they camped by the Jordan from Beth-jeshimoth as far as Abel-shittim in the plains of Moab.

Directions for the Conquest of Canaan

50 In the plains of Moab by the Jordan at Jericho, the LORD spoke to Moses, saying: ⁵¹Speak to the Israelites, and say to them: When you cross over the Jordan into the land of Canaan, ⁵²you shall drive out all the inhabitants of the land from before you, destroy all their figured stones, destroy all their cast images, and demolish all their high places. ⁵³You shall take possession of the land and settle in it, for I have given you the land to possess. ⁵⁴You shall apportion the land by lot according to your clans; to a large one you shall give a large inheritance, and to a small one you shall give a small inheritance; the inheritance shall belong to the person on whom the lot falls; according to your ancestral tribes you shall inherit. ⁵⁵But if you do not drive out the inhabitants of the land from before you, then those whom you let remain shall be as barbs in your eyes and thorns in your sides; they shall trouble you in the land where you are settling. ⁵⁶And I will do to you as I thought to do to them.

The Boundaries of the Land

34 The LORD spoke to Moses, saying: ²Command the Israelites, and say to them: When you enter the land of Canaan (this is the land that shall fall to you for an inheritance, the land of Canaan, defined by its boundaries), ³your south sector shall extend from the wilderness of Zin along the side of Edom. Your southern boundary shall begin from the end of the Dead Sea*ˣ* on the east; ⁴your boundary shall turn south of the ascent of Akrabbim, and cross to Zin, and its outer limit shall be south of Kadesh-barnea; then it shall go on to Hazar-addar, and cross to Azmon; ⁵the boundary shall turn from Azmon to the Wadi of Egypt, and its termination shall be at the Sea.

6 For the western boundary, you shall have the Great Sea and its*ʸ* coast; this shall be your western boundary.

7 This shall be your northern boundary: from the Great Sea you shall mark out your line to Mount Hor; ⁸from Mount Hor you shall mark it out to Lebo-hamath, and the outer limit of the boundary shall be at Zedad; ⁹then the boundary shall extend to Ziphron, and its end shall be at Hazar-enan; this shall be your northern boundary.

10 You shall mark out your eastern boundary from Hazar-enan to Shepham; ¹¹and the boundary shall continue down from Shepham to Riblah on the east side of Ain; and the boundary shall go down, and reach the eastern slope of the sea of Chinnereth; ¹²and the boundary shall go down to the Jordan, and its end shall be at the Dead Sea.*ˣ* This shall be your land with its boundaries all around.

13 Moses commanded the Israelites, saying: This is the land that you shall inherit by lot, which the LORD has commanded to give to the nine tribes and to the half-tribe; ¹⁴for the tribe of the Reubenites by their ancestral houses and the tribe of the Gadites by their ancestral houses have taken their inheritance, and also the half-tribe of Manasseh; ¹⁵the two tribes and the half-tribe have taken their inheritance beyond the Jordan at Jericho eastward, toward the sunrise.

Tribal Leaders

16 The LORD spoke to Moses, saying:

---

x Heb *Salt Sea*   *y* Syr: Heb lacks *its*

17These are the names of the men who shall apportion the land to you for inheritance: the priest Eleazar and Joshua son of Nun. 18You shall take one leader of every tribe to apportion the land for inheritance. 19These are the names of the men: Of the tribe of Judah, Caleb son of Jephunneh. 20Of the tribe of the Simeonites, Shemuel son of Ammihud. 21Of the tribe of Benjamin, Elidad son of Chislon. 22Of the tribe of the Danites a leader, Bukki son of Jogli. 23Of the Josephites: of the tribe of the Manassites a leader, Hanniel son of Ephod, 24and of the tribe of the Ephraimites a leader, Kemuel son of Shiphtan. 25Of the tribe of the Zebulunites a leader, Eli-zaphan son of Parnach. 26Of the tribe of the Issacharites a leader, Paltiel son of Azzan. 27And of the tribe of the Asherites a leader, Ahihud son of Shelomi. 28Of the tribe of the Naphtalites a leader, Pedahel son of Ammihud. 29These were the ones whom the LORD commanded to apportion the inheritance for the Israelites in the land of Canaan.

Cities for the Levites

35 In the plains of Moab by the Jordan at Jericho, the LORD spoke to Moses, saying: 2Command the Israelites to give, from the inheritance that they possess, towns for the Levites to live in; you shall also give to the Levites pasture lands surrounding the towns. 3The towns shall be theirs to live in, and their pasture lands shall be for their cattle, for their livestock, and for all their animals. 4The pasture lands of the towns, which you shall give to the Levites, shall reach from the wall of the town outward a thousand cubits all around. 5You shall measure, outside the town, for the east side two thousand cubits, for the south side two thousand cubits, for the west side two thousand cubits, and for the north side two thousand cubits, with the town in the middle; this shall belong to them as pasture land for their towns.

6 The towns that you give to the Levites shall include the six cities of refuge, where you shall permit a slayer to flee, and in addition to them you shall give forty-two towns. 7The towns that you give to the Levites shall total forty-eight, with their pasture lands. 8And as for the towns that you shall give from the possession of the Israelites, from the larger tribes you shall take many, and from the smaller tribes

you shall take few; each, in proportion to the inheritance that it obtains, shall give of its towns to the Levites.

Cities of Refuge

9 The LORD spoke to Moses, saying: 10Speak to the Israelites, and say to them: When you cross the Jordan into the land of Canaan, 11then you shall select cities to be cities of refuge for you, so that a slayer who kills a person without intent may flee there. 12The cities shall be for you a refuge from the avenger, so that the slayer may not die until there is a trial before the congregation.

13 The cities that you designate shall be six cities of refuge for you: 14you shall designate three cities beyond the Jordan, and three cities in the land of Canaan, to be cities of refuge. 15These six cities shall serve as refuge for the Israelites, for the resident or transient alien among them, so that anyone who kills a person without intent may flee there.

Concerning Murder and Blood Revenge

16 But anyone who strikes another with an iron object, and death ensues, is a murderer; the murderer shall be put to death. 17Or anyone who strikes another with a stone in hand that could cause death, and death ensues, is a murderer; the murderer shall be put to death. 18Or anyone who strikes another with a weapon of wood in hand that could cause death, and death ensues, is a murderer; the murderer shall be put to death. 19The avenger of blood is the one who shall put the murderer to death; when they meet, the avenger of blood shall execute the sentence. 20Likewise, if someone pushes another from hatred, or hurls something at another, lying in wait, and death ensues, 21or in enmity strikes another with the hand, and death ensues, then the one who struck the blow shall be put to death; that person is a murderer; the avenger of blood shall put the murderer to death, when they meet.

22 But if someone pushes another suddenly without enmity, or hurls any object without lying in wait, 23or, while handling any stone that could cause death, unintentionallyz drops it on another and death ensues, though they were not enemies, and no harm was intended, 24then the

z Heb *without seeing*

congregation shall judge between the slayer and the avenger of blood, in accordance with these ordinances; 25and the congregation shall rescue the slayer from the avenger of blood. Then the congregation shall send the slayer back to the original city of refuge. The slayer shall live in it until the death of the high priest who was anointed with the holy oil. 26But if the slayer shall at any time go outside the bounds of the original city of refuge, 27and is found by the avenger of blood outside the bounds of the city of refuge, and is killed by the avenger, no bloodguilt shall be incurred. 28For the slayer must remain in the city of refuge until the death of the high priest; but after the death of the high priest the slayer may return home.

29 These things shall be a statute and ordinance for you throughout your generations wherever you live.

30 If anyone kills another, the murderer shall be put to death on the evidence of witnesses; but no one shall be put to death on the testimony of a single witness. 31Moreover you shall accept no ransom for the life of a murderer who is subject to the death penalty; a murderer must be put to death. 32Nor shall you accept ransom for one who has fled to a city of refuge, enabling the fugitive to return to live in the land before the death of the high priest. 33You shall not pollute the land in which you live; for blood pollutes the land, and no expiation can be made for the land, for the blood that is shed in it, except by the blood of the one who shed it. 34You shall not defile the land in which you live, in which I also dwell; for I the LORD dwell among the Israelites.

Marriage of Female Heirs

36 The heads of the ancestral houses of the clans of the descendants of Gilead son of Machir son of Manasseh, of the Josephite clans, came forward and spoke in the presence of Moses and the leaders, the heads of the ancestral houses of the Israelites; 2they said, "The LORD commanded my lord to give the land for inheritance by lot to the Israelites; and my lord was commanded by the LORD to give the inheritance of our brother Zelophehad to his daughters. 3But if they are married into another Israelite tribe, then their inheritance will be taken from the inheritance of our ancestors and added to the inheritance of the tribe into which they marry; so it will be taken away from the allotted portion of our inheritance. 4And when the jubilee of the Israelites comes, then their inheritance will be added to the inheritance of the tribe into which they have married; and their inheritance will be taken from the inheritance of our ancestral tribe."

5 Then Moses commanded the Israelites according to the word of the LORD, saying, "The descendants of the tribe of Joseph are right in what they are saying. 6This is what the LORD commands concerning the daughters of Zelophehad, 'Let them marry whom they think best; only it must be into a clan of their father's tribe that they are married, 7so that no inheritance of the Israelites shall be transferred from one tribe to another; for all Israelites shall retain the inheritance of their ancestral tribes. 8Every daughter who possesses an inheritance in any tribe of the Israelites shall marry one from the clan of her father's tribe, so that all Israelites may continue to possess their ancestral inheritance. 9No inheritance shall be transferred from one tribe to another; for each of the tribes of the Israelites shall retain its own inheritance.' "

10 The daughters of Zelophehad did as the LORD had commanded Moses. 11Mahlah, Tirzah, Hoglah, Milcah, and Noah, the daughters of Zelophehad, married sons of their father's brothers. 12They were married into the clans of the descendants of Manasseh son of Joseph, and their inheritance remained in the tribe of their father's clan.

13 These are the commandments and the ordinances that the LORD commanded through Moses to the Israelites in the plains of Moab by the Jordan at Jericho.

Deuteronomy

The title of this book comes from a Greek word that means "second law" because the law given to Moses on Mount Sinai is partially repeated here. Actually, the Hebrew title, *Debarim*, meaning "words" is more descriptive since this book is presented as the final words of Moses, spoken to the Israelites over a period of 40 days, just before they were to enter the promised land. The setting is the plains of Moab, the land where Moses was buried, just east of Canaan.

In the instruction known as the *shema* (6.4–5), Moses eloquently exhorted the people to be loyal to God: "Hear, O Israel: The LORD is our God, the LORD alone. You shall love the LORD your God with all your heart, and with all your soul, and with all your might." He also reminded them to make the most important choice any human being can ever make (30.19–20): "I call heaven and earth to witness against you today that I have set before you life and death, blessings and curses. Choose life so that you and your descendants may live, loving the LORD your God, obeying him, and holding fast to him."

As we reflect on our own history with God, we can see the parallels between our personal experience and the experience of the Israelites. Centuries later, we, too, are called to express our own passionate loyalty to God, understanding that obedience is an expression of love as well as a pathway for blessings.

Events at Horeb Recalled

1 These are the words that Moses spoke to all Israel beyond the Jordan—in the wilderness, on the plain opposite Suph, between Paran and Tophel, Laban, Hazeroth, and Di-zahab. ²(By the way of Mount Seir it takes eleven days to reach Kadesh-barnea from Horeb.) ³In the fortieth year, on the first day of the eleventh month, Moses spoke to the Israelites just as the LORD had commanded him to speak to them. ⁴This was after he had defeated King Sihon of the Amorites, who reigned in Heshbon, and King Og of Bashan, who reigned in Ashtaroth and*a* in Edrei. ⁵Beyond the Jordan in the land of Moab, Moses undertook to expound this law as follows:

a Gk Syr Vg Compare Josh 12.4: Heb lacks *and*

6 The LORD our God spoke to us at Horeb, saying, "You have stayed long enough at this mountain. 7Resume your journey, and go into the hill country of the Amorites as well as into the neighboring regions—the Arabah, the hill country, the Shephelah, the Negeb, and the seacoast—the land of the Canaanites and the Lebanon, as far as the great river, the river Euphrates. 8See, I have set the land before you; go in and take possession of the land that I[b] swore to your ancestors, to Abraham, to Isaac, and to Jacob, to give to them and to their descendants after them."

Appointment of Tribal Leaders

9 At that time I said to you, "I am unable by myself to bear you. 10The LORD your God has multiplied you, so that today you are as numerous as the stars of heaven. 11May the LORD, the God of your ancestors, increase you a thousand times more and bless you, as he has promised you! 12But how can I bear the heavy burden of your disputes all by myself? 13Choose for each of your tribes individuals who are wise, discerning, and reputable to be your leaders." 14You answered me, "The plan you have proposed is a good one." 15So I took the leaders of your tribes, wise and reputable individuals, and installed them as leaders over you, commanders of thousands, commanders of hundreds, commanders of fifties, commanders of tens, and officials, throughout your tribes. 16I charged your judges at that time: "Give the members of your community a fair hearing, and judge rightly between one person and another, whether citizen or resident alien. 17You must not be partial in judging: hear out the small and the great alike; you shall not be intimidated by anyone, for the judgment is God's. Any case that is too hard for you, bring to me, and I will hear it." 18So I charged you at that time with all the things that you should do.

Israel's Refusal to Enter the Land

19 Then, just as the LORD our God had ordered us, we set out from Horeb and went through all that great and terrible wilderness that you saw, on the way to the hill country of the Amorites, until we reached Kadesh-barnea. 20I said to you, "You have reached the hill country of the Amorites, which the LORD our God is giving us. 21See, the LORD your God has given

the land to you; go up, take possession, as the LORD, the God of your ancestors, has promised you; do not fear or be dismayed."

22 All of you came to me and said, "Let us send men ahead of us to explore the land for us and bring back a report to us regarding the route by which we should go up and the cities we will come to." 23The plan seemed good to me, and I selected twelve of you, one from each tribe. 24They set out and went up into the hill country, and when they reached the Valley of Eshcol they spied it out 25and gathered some of the land's produce, which they brought down to us. They brought back a report to us, and said, "It is a good land that the LORD our God is giving us."

26 But you were unwilling to go up. You rebelled against the command of the LORD your God; 27you grumbled in your tents and said, "It is because the LORD hates us that he has brought us out of the land of Egypt, to hand us over to the Amorites to destroy us. 28Where are we headed? Our kindred have made our hearts melt by reporting, 'The people are stronger and taller than we; the cities are large and fortified up to heaven! We actually saw there the offspring of the Anakim!' " 29I said to you, "Have no dread or fear of them. 30The LORD your God, who goes before you, is the one who will fight for you, just as he did for you in Egypt before your very eyes, 31and in the wilderness, where you saw how the LORD your God carried you, just as one carries a child, all the way that you traveled until you reached this place. 32But in spite of this, you have no trust in the LORD your God, 33who goes before you on the way to seek out a place for you to camp, in fire by night, and in the cloud by day, to show you the route you should take."

The Penalty for Israel's Rebellion

34 When the LORD heard your words, he was wrathful and swore: 35"Not one of these—not one of this evil generation—shall see the good land that I swore to give to your ancestors, 36except Caleb son of Jephunneh. He shall see it, and to him and to his descendants I will give the land on which he set foot, because of his complete fidelity to the LORD." 37Even with me

b Sam Gk: MT *the LORD*

the LORD was angry on your account, saying, "You also shall not enter there. [38]Joshua son of Nun, your assistant, shall enter there; encourage him, for he is the one who will secure Israel's possession of it. [39]And as for your little ones, who you thought would become booty, your children, who today do not yet know right from wrong, they shall enter there; to them I will give it, and they shall take possession of it. [40]But as for you, journey back into the wilderness, in the direction of the Red Sea."[c]

41 You answered me, "We have sinned against the LORD! We are ready to go up and fight, just as the LORD our God commanded us." So all of you strapped on your battle gear, and thought it easy to go up into the hill country. [42]The LORD said to me, "Say to them, 'Do not go up and do not fight, for I am not in the midst of you; otherwise you will be defeated by your enemies.' " [43]Although I told you, you would not listen. You rebelled against the command of the LORD and presumptuously went up into the hill country. [44]The Amorites who lived in that hill country then came out against you and chased you as bees do. They beat you down in Seir as far as Hormah. [45]When you returned and wept before the LORD, the LORD would neither heed your voice nor pay you any attention.

The Desert Years

46 After you had stayed at Kadesh as many days as you did, [1]we journeyed back into the wilderness, in the direction of the Red Sea,[c] as the LORD had told me and skirted Mount Seir for many days. [2]Then the LORD said to me: [3]"You have been skirting this hill country long enough. Head north, [4]and charge the people as follows: You are about to pass through the territory of your kindred, the descendants of Esau, who live in Seir. They will be afraid of you, so, be very careful [5]not to engage in battle with them, for I will not give you even so much as a foot's length of their land, since I have given Mount Seir to Esau as a possession. [6]You shall purchase food from them for money, so that you may eat; and you shall also buy water from them for money, so that you may drink. [7]Surely the LORD your God has blessed you in all your undertakings; he knows your going through this great wilderness. These forty years the

LORD your God has been with you; you have lacked nothing." [8]So we passed by our kin, the descendants of Esau who live in Seir, leaving behind the route of the Arabah, and leaving behind Elath and Ezion-geber.

When we had headed out along the route of the wilderness of Moab, [9]the LORD said to me: "Do not harass Moab or engage them in battle, for I will not give you any of its land as a possession, since I have given Ar as a possession to the descendants of Lot." [10](The Emim—a large and numerous people, as tall as the Anakim—had formerly inhabited it. [11]Like the Anakim, they are usually reckoned as Rephaim, though the Moabites call them Emim. [12]Moreover, the Horim had formerly inhabited Seir, but the descendants of Esau dispossessed them, destroying them and settling in their place, as Israel has done in the land that the LORD gave them as a possession.) [13]"Now then, proceed to cross over the Wadi Zered."

So we crossed over the Wadi Zered. [14]And the length of time we had traveled from Kadesh-barnea until we crossed the Wadi Zered was thirty-eight years, until the entire generation of warriors had perished from the camp, as the LORD had sworn concerning them. [15]Indeed, the LORD's own hand was against them, to root them out from the camp, until all had perished.

16 Just as soon as all the warriors had died off from among the people, [17]the LORD spoke to me, saying, [18]"Today you are going to cross the boundary of Moab at Ar. [19]When you approach the frontier of the Ammonites, do not harass them or engage them in battle, for I will not give the land of the Ammonites to you as a possession, because I have given it to the descendants of Lot." [20](It also is usually reckoned as a land of Rephaim. Rephaim formerly inhabited it, though the Ammonites call them Zamzummim, [21]a strong and numerous people, as tall as the Anakim. But the LORD destroyed them from before the Ammonites so that they could dispossess them and settle in their place. [22]He did the same for the descendants of Esau, who live in Seir, by destroying the Horim before them so that they could dispossess them and settle in their place even to this day. [23]As for the Avvim,

[c] Or *Sea of Reeds*

who had lived in settlements in the vicinity of Gaza, the Caphtorim, who came from Caphtor, destroyed them and settled in their place.) 24"Proceed on your journey and cross the Wadi Arnon. See, I have handed over to you King Sihon the Amorite of Heshbon, and his land. Begin to take possession by engaging him in battle. 25This day I will begin to put the dread and fear of you upon the peoples everywhere under heaven; when they hear report of you, they will tremble and be in anguish because of you."

Defeat of King Sihon

26 So I sent messengers from the wilderness of Kedemoth to King Sihon of Heshbon with the following terms of peace: 27"If you let me pass through your land, I will travel only along the road; I will turn aside neither to the right nor to the left. 28You shall sell me food for money, so that I may eat, and supply me water for money, so that I may drink. Only allow me to pass through on foot— 29just as the descendants of Esau who live in Seir have done for me and likewise the Moabites who live in Ar—until I cross the Jordan into the land that the LORD our God is giving us." 30But King Sihon of Heshbon was not willing to let us pass through, for the LORD your God had hardened his spirit and made his heart defiant in order to hand him over to you, as he has now done.

31 The LORD said to me, "See, I have begun to give Sihon and his land over to you. Begin now to take possession of his land." 32So when Sihon came out against us, he and all his people for battle at Jahaz, 33the LORD our God gave him over to us; and we struck him down, along with his offspring and all his people. 34At that time we captured all his towns, and in each town we utterly destroyed men, women, and children. We left not a single survivor. 35Only the livestock we kept as spoil for ourselves, as well as the plunder of the towns that we had captured. 36From Aroer on the edge of the Wadi Arnon (including the town that is in the wadi itself) as far as Gilead, there was no citadel too high for us. The LORD our God gave everything to us. 37You did not encroach, however, on the land of the Ammonites, avoiding the whole upper region of the Wadi Jabbok as well as the towns of the

hill country, just as^d the LORD our God had charged.

Defeat of King Og

3 When we headed up the road to Bashan, King Og of Bashan came out against us, he and all his people, for battle at Edrei. 2The LORD said to me, "Do not fear him, for I have handed him over to you, along with his people and his land. Do to him as you did to King Sihon of the Amorites, who reigned in Heshbon." 3So the LORD our God also handed over to us King Og of Bashan and all his people. We struck him down until not a single survivor was left. 4At that time we captured all his towns; there was no citadel that we did not take from them—sixty towns, the whole region of Argob, the kingdom of Og in Bashan. 5All these were fortress towns with high walls, double gates, and bars, besides a great many villages. 6And we utterly destroyed them, as we had done to King Sihon of Heshbon, in each city utterly destroying men, women, and children. 7But all the livestock and the plunder of the towns we kept as spoil for ourselves.

8 So at that time we took from the two kings of the Amorites the land beyond the Jordan, from the Wadi Arnon to Mount Hermon 9(the Sidonians call Hermon Sirion, while the Amorites call it Senir), 10all the towns of the tableland, the whole of Gilead, and all of Bashan, as far as Salecah and Edrei, towns of Og's kingdom in Bashan. 11(Now only King Og of Bashan was left of the remnant of the Rephaim. In fact his bed, an iron bed, can still be seen in Rabbah of the Ammonites. By the common cubit it is nine cubits long and four cubits wide.) 12As for the land that we took possession of at that time, I gave to the Reubenites and Gadites the territory north of Aroer,^{e} that is on the edge of the Wadi Arnon, as well as half the hill country of Gilead with its towns, 13and I gave to the half-tribe of Manasseh the rest of Gilead and all of Bashan, Og's kingdom. (The whole region of Argob: all that portion of Bashan used to be called a land of Rephaim; 14Jair the Manassite acquired the whole region of Argob as far as the border of the Geshurites and the Maacathites, and he named them—that is, Ba-

^{d} Gk Tg: Heb and all ^{e} Heb territory from Aroer

shan—after himself, Havvoth-jair,*f* as it is to this day.) ¹⁵To Machir I gave Gilead. ¹⁶And to the Reubenites and the Gadites I gave the territory from Gilead as far as the Wadi Arnon, with the middle of the wadi as a boundary, and up to the Jabbok, the wadi being boundary of the Ammonites; ¹⁷the Arabah also, with the Jordan and its banks, from Chinnereth down to the sea of the Arabah, the Dead Sea,*g* with the lower slopes of Pisgah on the east.

18 At that time, I charged you as follows: "Although the LORD your God has given you this land to occupy, all your troops shall cross over armed as the vanguard of your Israelite kin. ¹⁹Only your wives, your children, and your livestock— I know that you have much livestock— shall stay behind in the towns that I have given to you. ²⁰When the LORD gives rest to your kindred, as to you, and they too have occupied the land that the LORD your God is giving them beyond the Jordan, then each of you may return to the property that I have given to you." ²¹And I charged Joshua as well at that time, saying: "Your own eyes have seen everything that the LORD your God has done to these two kings; so the LORD will do to all the kingdoms into which you are about to cross. ²²Do not fear them, for it is the LORD your God who fights for you."

Moses Views Canaan from Pisgah

23 At that time, too, I entreated the LORD, saying: ²⁴"O Lord GOD, you have only begun to show your servant your greatness and your might; what god in heaven or on earth can perform deeds and mighty acts like yours! ²⁵Let me cross over to see the good land beyond the Jordan, that good hill country and the Lebanon." ²⁶But the LORD was angry with me on your account and would not heed me. The LORD said to me, "Enough from you! Never speak to me of this matter again! ²⁷Go up to the top of Pisgah and look around you to the west, to the north, to the south, and to the east. Look well, for you shall not cross over this Jordan. ²⁸But charge Joshua, and encourage and strengthen him, because it is he who shall cross over at the head of this people and who shall secure their possession of the land that you will see." ²⁹So we remained in the valley opposite Beth-peor.

Moses Commands Obedience

4 So now, Israel, give heed to the statutes and ordinances that I am teaching you to observe, so that you may live to enter and occupy the land that the LORD, the God of your ancestors, is giving you. ²You must neither add anything to what I command you nor take away anything from it, but keep the commandments of the LORD your God with which I am charging you. ³You have seen for yourselves what the LORD did with regard to the Baal of Peor—how the LORD your God destroyed from among you everyone who followed the Baal of Peor, ⁴while those of you who held fast to the LORD your God are all alive today.

5 See, just as the LORD my God has charged me, I now teach you statutes and ordinances for you to observe in the land that you are about to enter and occupy. ⁶You must observe them diligently, for this will show your wisdom and discernment to the peoples, who, when they hear all these statutes, will say, "Surely this great nation is a wise and discerning people!" ⁷For what other great nation has a god so near to it as the LORD our God is whenever we call to him? ⁸And what other great nation has statutes and ordinances as just as this entire law that I am setting before you today?

9 But take care and watch yourselves closely, so as neither to forget the things that your eyes have seen nor to let them slip from your mind all the days of your life; make them known to your children and your children's children— ¹⁰how you once stood before the LORD your God at Horeb, when the LORD said to me, "Assemble the people for me, and I will let them hear my words, so that they may learn to fear me as long as they live on the earth, and may teach their children so"; ¹¹you approached and stood at the foot of the mountain while the mountain was blazing up to the very heavens, shrouded in dark clouds. ¹²Then the LORD spoke to you out of the fire. You heard the sound of words but saw no form; there was only a voice. ¹³He declared to you his covenant, which he charged you to observe, that is, the ten commandments;*h* and he wrote them on two stone tablets. ¹⁴And

---

f That is *Settlement of Jair*   *g* Heb *Salt Sea*
h Heb *the ten words*

the LORD charged me at that time to teach you statutes and ordinances for you to observe in the land that you are about to cross into and occupy.

15 Since you saw no form when the LORD spoke to you at Horeb out of the fire, take care and watch yourselves closely, ¹⁶so that you do not act corruptly by making an idol for yourselves, in the form of any figure—the likeness of male or female, ¹⁷the likeness of any animal that is on the earth, the likeness of any winged bird that flies in the air, ¹⁸the likeness of anything that creeps on the ground, the likeness of any fish that is in the water under the earth. ¹⁹And when you look up to the heavens and see the sun, the moon, and the stars, all the host of heaven, do not be led astray and bow down to them and serve them, things that the LORD your God has allotted to all the peoples everywhere under heaven. ²⁰But the LORD has taken you and brought you out of the iron-smelter, out of Egypt, to become a people of his very own possession, as you are now.

21 The LORD was angry with me because of you, and he vowed that I should not cross the Jordan and that I should not enter the good land that the LORD your God is giving for your possession. ²²For I am going to die in this land without crossing over the Jordan, but you are going to cross over to take possession of that good land. ²³So be careful not to forget the covenant that the LORD your God made with you, and not to make for yourselves an idol in the form of anything that the LORD your God has forbidden you. ²⁴For the LORD your God is a devouring fire, a jealous God.

25 When you have had children and children's children, and become complacent in the land, if you act corruptly by making an idol in the form of anything, thus doing what is evil in the sight of the LORD your God, and provoking him to anger, ²⁶I call heaven and earth to witness against you today that you will soon utterly perish from the land that you are crossing the Jordan to occupy; you will not live long on it, but will be utterly destroyed. ²⁷The LORD will scatter you among the peoples; only a few of you will be left among the nations where the LORD will lead you. ²⁸There you will serve other gods made by human hands, objects of wood and stone that neither see, nor hear,

nor eat, nor smell. ²⁹From there you will seek the LORD your God, and you will find him if you search after him with all your heart and soul. ³⁰In your distress, when all these things have happened to you in time to come, you will return to the LORD your God and heed him. ³¹Because the LORD your God is a merciful God, he will neither abandon you nor destroy you; he will not forget the covenant with your ancestors that he swore to them.

32 For ask now about former ages, long before your own, ever since the day that God created human beings on the earth; ask from one end of heaven to the other: has anything so great as this ever happened or has its like ever been heard of? ³³Has any people ever heard the voice of a god speaking out of a fire, as you have heard, and lived? ³⁴Or has any god ever attempted to go and take a nation for himself from the midst of another nation, by trials, by signs and wonders, by war, by a mighty hand and an outstretched arm, and by terrifying displays of power, as the LORD your God did for you in Egypt before your very eyes? ³⁵To you it was shown so that you would acknowledge that the LORD is God; there is no other besides him. ³⁶From heaven he made you hear his voice to discipline you. On earth he showed you his great fire, while you heard his words coming out of the fire. ³⁷And because he loved your ancestors, he chose their descendants after them. He brought you out of Egypt with his own presence, by his great power, ³⁸driving out before you nations greater and mightier than yourselves, to bring you in, giving you their land for a possession, as it is still today. ³⁹So acknowledge today and take to heart that the LORD is God in heaven above and on the earth beneath; there is no other. ⁴⁰Keep his statutes and his commandments, which I am commanding you today for your own well-being and that of your descendants after you, so that you may long remain in the land that the LORD your God is giving you for all time.

Cities of Refuge East of the Jordan

41 Then Moses set apart on the east side of the Jordan three cities ⁴²to which a homicide could flee, someone who unintentionally kills another person, the two not having been at enmity before; the homicide could flee to one of these cities and live: ⁴³Bezer in the wilderness on the

tableland belonging to the Reubenites, Ramoth in Gilead belonging to the Gadites, and Golan in Bashan belonging to the Manassites.

Transition to the Second Address

44 This is the law that Moses set before the Israelites. 45These are the decrees and the statutes and ordinances that Moses spoke to the Israelites when they had come out of Egypt, 46beyond the Jordan in the valley opposite Beth-peor, in the land of King Sihon of the Amorites, who reigned at Heshbon, whom Moses and the Israelites defeated when they came out of Egypt. 47They occupied his land and the land of King Og of Bashan, the two kings of the Amorites on the eastern side of the Jordan: 48from Aroer, which is on the edge of the Wadi Arnon, as far as Mount Sirion[i] (that is, Hermon), 49together with all the Arabah on the east side of the Jordan as far as the Sea of the Arabah, under the slopes of Pisgah.

The Ten Commandments

5 Moses convened all Israel, and said to them:

Hear, O Israel, the statutes and ordinances that I am addressing to you today; you shall learn them and observe them diligently. 2The LORD our God made a covenant with us at Horeb. 3Not with our ancestors did the LORD make this covenant, but with us, who are all of us here alive today. 4The LORD spoke with you face to face at the mountain, out of the fire. 5(At that time I was standing between the LORD and you to declare to you the words[j] of the LORD; for you were afraid because of the fire and did not go up the mountain.) And he said:

6 I am the LORD your God, who brought you out of the land of Egypt, out of the house of slavery; 7you shall have no other gods before[k] me.

8 You shall not make for yourself an idol, whether in the form of anything that is in heaven above, or that is on the earth beneath, or that is in the water under the earth. 9You shall not bow down to them or worship them; for I the LORD your God am a jealous God, punishing children for the iniquity of parents, to the third and fourth generation of those who reject me, 10but showing steadfast love to the thousandth generation[l] of those who love me and keep my commandments.

11 You shall not make wrongful use of the name of the LORD your God, for the LORD will not acquit anyone who misuses his name.

12 Observe the sabbath day and keep it holy, as the LORD your God commanded you. 13Six days you shall labor and do all your work. 14But the seventh day is a sabbath to the LORD your God; you shall not do any work—you, or your son or your daughter, or your male or female slave, or your ox or your donkey, or any of your livestock, or the resident alien in your towns, so that your male and female slave may rest as well as you. 15Remember that you were a slave in the land of Egypt, and the LORD your God brought you out from there with a mighty hand and an outstretched arm; therefore the LORD your God commanded you to keep the sabbath day.

16 Honor your father and your mother, as the LORD your God commanded you, so that your days may be long and that it may go well with you in the land that the LORD your God is giving you.

17 You shall not murder.[m]

18 Neither shall you commit adultery.

19 Neither shall you steal.

20 Neither shall you bear false witness against your neighbor.

21 Neither shall you covet your neighbor's wife.

Neither shall you desire your neighbor's house, or field, or male or female slave, or ox, or donkey, or anything that belongs to your neighbor.

Moses the Mediator of God's Will

22 These words the LORD spoke with a loud voice to your whole assembly at the mountain, out of the fire, the cloud, and the thick darkness, and he added no more. He wrote them on two stone tablets, and gave them to me. 23When you heard the voice out of the darkness, while the mountain was burning with fire, you approached me, all the heads of your tribes and your elders; 24and you said, "Look, the LORD our God has shown us his glory and greatness, and we have heard his voice out of the fire. Today we have seen that God may speak to someone and the person may still live. 25So

i Syr: Heb *Sion*   *j* Q Mss Sam Gk Syr Vg Tg: MT *word*   *k* Or *besides*   *l* Or *to thousands*   *m* Or *kill*

now why should we die? For this great fire will consume us; if we hear the voice of the LORD our God any longer, we shall die. 26For who is there of all flesh that has heard the voice of the living God speaking out of fire, as we have, and remained alive? 27Go near, you yourself, and hear all that the LORD our God will say. Then tell us everything that the LORD our God tells you, and we will listen and do it."

28 The LORD heard your words when you spoke to me, and the LORD said to me: "I have heard the words of this people, which they have spoken to you; they are right in all that they have spoken. 29If only they had such a mind as this, to fear me and to keep all my commandments always, so that it might go well with them and with their children forever! 30Go say to them, 'Return to your tents.' 31But you, stand here by me, and I will tell you all the commandments, the statutes and the ordinances, that you shall teach them, so that they may do them in the land that I am giving them to possess." 32You must therefore be careful to do as the LORD your God has commanded you; you shall not turn to the right or to the left. 33You must follow exactly the path that the LORD your God has commanded you, so that you may live, and that it may go well with you, and that you may live long in the land that you are to possess.

The Great Commandment

6 Now this is the commandment—the statutes and the ordinances—that the LORD your God charged me to teach you to observe in the land that you are about to cross into and occupy, 2so that you and your children and your children's children may fear the LORD your God all the days of your life, and keep all his decrees and his commandments that I am commanding you, so that your days may be long. 3Hear therefore, O Israel, and observe them diligently, so that it may go well with you, and so that you may multiply greatly in a land flowing with milk and honey, as the LORD, the God of your ancestors, has promised you.

4 Hear, O Israel: The LORD is our God, the LORD alone.*n* 5You shall love the LORD your God with all your heart, and with all your soul, and with all your might. 6Keep these words that I am commanding you today in your heart. 7Recite them to your children and talk about them when you

are at home and when you are away, when you lie down and when you rise. 8Bind them as a sign on your hand, fix them as an emblem*o* on your forehead, 9and write them on the doorposts of your house and on your gates.

Caution against Disobedience

10 When the LORD your God has brought you into the land that he swore to your ancestors, to Abraham, to Isaac, and to Jacob, to give you—a land with fine, large cities that you did not build, 11houses filled with all sorts of goods that you did not fill, hewn cisterns that you did not hew, vineyards and olive groves that you did not plant—and when you have eaten your fill, 12take care that you do not forget the LORD, who brought you out of the land of Egypt, out of the house of slavery. 13The LORD your God you shall fear; him you shall serve, and by his name alone you shall swear. 14Do not follow other gods, any of the gods of the peoples who are all around you, 15because the LORD your God, who is present with you, is a jealous God. The anger of the LORD your God would be kindled against you and he would destroy you from the face of the earth.

16 Do not put the LORD your God to the test, as you tested him at Massah. 17You must diligently keep the commandments of the LORD your God, and his decrees, and his statutes that he has commanded you. 18Do what is right and good in the sight of the LORD, so that it may go well with you, and so that you may go in and occupy the good land that the LORD swore to your ancestors to give you, 19thrusting out all your enemies from before you, as the LORD has promised.

20 When your children ask you in time to come, "What is the meaning of the decrees and the statutes and the ordinances that the LORD our God has commanded you?" 21then you shall say to your children, "We were Pharaoh's slaves in Egypt, but the LORD brought us out of Egypt with a mighty hand. 22The LORD displayed before our eyes great and awesome signs and wonders against Egypt, against Pharaoh and all his household. 23He brought us out from there in order to bring us in, to

n Or *The LORD our God is one LORD,* or *The LORD our God, the LORD is one,* or *The LORD is our God, the LORD is one*   *o* Or *as a frontlet*

give us the land that he promised on oath to our ancestors. 24Then the LORD commanded us to observe all these statutes, to fear the LORD our God, for our lasting good, so as to keep us alive, as is now the case. 25If we diligently observe this entire commandment before the LORD our God, as he has commanded us, we will be in the right."

A Chosen People

7 When the LORD your God brings you into the land that you are about to enter and occupy, and he clears away many nations before you—the Hittites, the Girgashites, the Amorites, the Canaanites, the Perizzites, the Hivites, and the Jebusites, seven nations mightier and more numerous than you— 2and when the LORD your God gives them over to you and you defeat them, then you must utterly destroy them. Make no covenant with them and show them no mercy. 3Do not intermarry with them, giving your daughters to their sons or taking their daughters for your sons, 4for that would turn away your children from following me, to serve other gods. Then the anger of the LORD would be kindled against you, and he would destroy you quickly. 5But this is how you must deal with them: break down their altars, smash their pillars, hew down their sacred poles, *p* and burn their idols with fire. 6For you are a people holy

p Heb *Asherim*

A Prayer for Coming Home

WEDNESDAY

Scripture Reading
for Today:
Deuteronomy 6.4–15

Verses for Today:
Deuteronomy 6.4–5

O True and Ever-Living God
I repent of all my false and empty gods
I look again into the closets of my life
    my mind, my heart
        to see what rules me.
Whom do I serve?
What are the possessions
    the people, the opinions
    the events, that control my life?

O Welcoming One
I see you standing at the door
    of my heart
        waiting for me.
You gaze at my strange gods
    with an eye of compassion.
I am ashamed to invite you
    into my cluttered house
        yet my heart aches to be at home with you.

My hand is reaching for the door
I hear myself saying, Come on in
I have more room than I thought I had.
Come on in, and be the *only God* in my life.
May this moment of homecoming last forever.

—MACRINA WIEDERKEHR

Go to page 199 for your next devotional reading.

to the LORD your God; the LORD your God has chosen you out of all the peoples on earth to be his people, his treasured possession.

7 It was not because you were more numerous than any other people that the LORD set his heart on you and chose you— for you were the fewest of all peoples. 8It was because the LORD loved you and kept the oath that he swore to your ancestors, that the LORD has brought you out with a mighty hand, and redeemed you from the house of slavery, from the hand of Pharaoh king of Egypt. 9Know therefore that the LORD your God is God, the faithful God who maintains covenant loyalty with those who love him and keep his commandments, to a thousand generations, 10and who repays in their own person those who reject him. He does not delay but repays in their own person those who reject him. 11Therefore, observe diligently the commandment—the statutes and the ordinances—that I am commanding you today.

Blessings for Obedience

12 If you heed these ordinances, by diligently observing them, the LORD your God will maintain with you the covenant loyalty that he swore to your ancestors; 13he will love you, bless you, and multiply you; he will bless the fruit of your womb and the fruit of your ground, your grain and your wine and your oil, the increase of your cattle and the issue of your flock, in the land that he swore to your ancestors to give you. 14You shall be the most blessed of peoples, with neither sterility nor barrenness among you or your livestock. 15The LORD will turn away from you every illness; all the dread diseases of Egypt that you experienced, he will not inflict on you, but he will lay them on all who hate you. 16You shall devour all the peoples that the LORD your God is giving over to you, showing them no pity; you shall not serve their gods, for that would be a snare to you.

17 If you say to yourself, "These nations are more numerous than I; how can I dispossess them?" 18do not be afraid of them. Just remember what the LORD your God did to Pharaoh and to all Egypt, 19the great trials that your eyes saw, the signs and wonders, the mighty hand and the outstretched arm by which the LORD your God brought you out. The LORD your God

will do the same to all the peoples of whom you are afraid. 20Moreover, the LORD your God will send the pestilence*q* against them, until even the survivors and the fugitives are destroyed. 21Have no dread of them, for the LORD your God, who is present with you, is a great and awesome God. 22The LORD your God will clear away these nations before you little by little; you will not be able to make a quick end of them, otherwise the wild animals would become too numerous for you. 23But the LORD your God will give them over to you, and throw them into great panic, until they are destroyed. 24He will hand their kings over to you and you shall blot out their name from under heaven; no one will be able to stand against you, until you have destroyed them. 25The images of their gods you shall burn with fire. Do not covet the silver or the gold that is on them and take it for yourself, because you could be ensnared by it; for it is abhorrent to the LORD your God. 26Do not bring an abhorrent thing into your house, or you will be set apart for destruction like it. You must utterly detest and abhor it, for it is set apart for destruction.

A Warning Not to Forget God in Prosperity

8 This entire commandment that I command you today you must diligently observe, so that you may live and increase, and go in and occupy the land that the LORD promised on oath to your ancestors. 2Remember the long way that the LORD your God has led you these forty years in the wilderness, in order to humble you, testing you to know what was in your heart, whether or not you would keep his commandments. 3He humbled you by letting you hunger, then by feeding you with manna, with which neither you nor your ancestors were acquainted, in order to make you understand that one does not live by bread alone, but by every word that comes from the mouth of the LORD.*r* 4The clothes on your back did not wear out and your feet did not swell these forty years. 5Know then in your heart that as a parent disciplines a child so the LORD your God disciplines you. 6Therefore keep the commandments of the LORD your God, by walking in his ways and by fearing him.

q Or hornets: Meaning of Heb uncertain   r Or by anything that the LORD decrees

7For the LORD your God is bringing you into a good land, a land with flowing streams, with springs and underground waters welling up in valleys and hills, 8a land of wheat and barley, of vines and fig trees and pomegranates, a land of olive trees and honey, 9a land where you may eat bread without scarcity, where you will lack nothing, a land whose stones are iron and from whose hills you may mine copper. 10You shall eat your fill and bless the LORD your God for the good land that he has given you.

11 Take care that you do not forget the LORD your God, by failing to keep his commandments, his ordinances, and his statutes, which I am commanding you today. 12When you have eaten your fill and have built fine houses and live in them, 13and when your herds and flocks have multiplied, and your silver and gold is multiplied, and all that you have is multiplied, 14then do not exalt yourself, forgetting the LORD your God, who brought you out of the land of Egypt, out of the house of slavery, 15who led you through the great and terrible wilderness, an arid wasteland with poisonous[s] snakes and scorpions. He made water flow for you from flint rock, 16and fed you in the wilderness with manna that your ancestors did not know, to humble you and to test you, and in the end to do you good. 17Do not say to yourself, "My power and the might of my own hand have gotten me this wealth." 18But remember the LORD your God, for it is he who gives you power to get wealth, so that he may confirm his covenant that he swore to your ancestors, as he is doing today. 19If you do forget the LORD your God and follow other gods to serve and worship them, I solemnly warn you today that you shall surely perish. 20Like the nations that the LORD is destroying before you, so shall you perish, because you would not obey the voice of the LORD your God.

The Consequences of Rebelling against God

9 Hear, O Israel! You are about to cross the Jordan today, to go in and dispossess nations larger and mightier than you, great cities, fortified to the heavens, 2a strong and tall people, the offspring of the Anakim, whom you know. You have heard it said of them, "Who can stand up to the Anakim?" 3Know then today that the LORD your God is the one who crosses over

before you as a devouring fire; he will defeat them and subdue them before you, so that you may dispossess and destroy them quickly, as the LORD has promised you.

4 When the LORD your God thrusts them out before you, do not say to yourself, "It is because of my righteousness that the LORD has brought me in to occupy this land"; it is rather because of the wickedness of these nations that the LORD is dispossessing them before you. 5It is not because of your righteousness or the uprightness of your heart that you are going in to occupy their land; but because of the wickedness of these nations the LORD your God is dispossessing them before you, in order to fulfill the promise that the LORD made on oath to your ancestors, to Abraham, to Isaac, and to Jacob.

6 Know, then, that the LORD your God is not giving you this good land to occupy because of your righteousness; for you are a stubborn people. 7Remember and do not forget how you provoked the LORD your God to wrath in the wilderness; you have been rebellious against the LORD from the day you came out of the land of Egypt until you came to this place.

8 Even at Horeb you provoked the LORD to wrath, and the LORD was so angry with you that he was ready to destroy you. 9When I went up the mountain to receive the stone tablets, the tablets of the covenant that the LORD made with you, I remained on the mountain forty days and forty nights; I neither ate bread nor drank water. 10And the LORD gave me the two stone tablets written with the finger of God; on them were all the words that the LORD had spoken to you at the mountain out of the fire on the day of the assembly. 11At the end of forty days and forty nights the LORD gave me the two stone tablets, the tablets of the covenant. 12Then the LORD said to me, "Get up, go down quickly from here, for your people whom you have brought from Egypt have acted corruptly. They have been quick to turn from the way that I commanded them; they have cast an image for themselves." 13Furthermore the LORD said to me, "I have seen that this people is indeed a stubborn people. 14Let me alone that I may destroy them and blot out their name from under heaven; and I will make of you a nation mightier and more numerous than they."

s Or fiery; Heb seraph

15 So I turned and went down from the mountain, while the mountain was ablaze; the two tablets of the covenant were in my two hands. 16Then I saw that you had indeed sinned against the LORD your God, by casting for yourselves an image of a calf; you had been quick to turn from the way that the LORD had commanded you. 17So I took hold of the two tablets and flung them from my two hands, smashing them before your eyes. 18Then I lay prostrate before the LORD as before, forty days and forty nights; I neither ate bread nor drank water, because of all the sin you had committed, provoking the LORD by doing what was evil in his sight. 19For I was afraid that the anger that the LORD bore against you was so fierce that he would destroy you. But the LORD listened to me that time also. 20The LORD was so angry with Aaron that he was ready to destroy him, but I interceded also on behalf of Aaron at that same time. 21Then I took the sinful thing you had made, the calf, and burned it with fire and crushed it, grinding it thoroughly, until it was reduced to dust; and I threw the dust of it into the stream that runs down the mountain.

22 At Taberah also, and at Massah, and at Kibroth-hattaavah, you provoked the LORD to wrath. 23And when the LORD sent you from Kadesh-barnea, saying, "Go up and occupy the land that I have given you," you rebelled against the command of the LORD your God, neither trusting him nor obeying him. 24You have been rebellious against the LORD as long as he has*t* known you.

25 Throughout the forty days and forty nights that I lay prostrate before the LORD when the LORD intended to destroy you, 26I prayed to the LORD and said, "Lord GOD, do not destroy the people who are your very own possession, whom you redeemed in your greatness, whom you brought out of Egypt with a mighty hand. 27Remember your servants, Abraham, Isaac, and Jacob; pay no attention to the stubbornness of this people, their wickedness and their sin, 28otherwise the land from which you have brought us might say, 'Because the LORD was not able to bring them into the land that he promised them, and because he hated them, he has brought them out to let them die in the wilderness.' 29For they are the people of your very own possession, whom you brought out by your great power and by your outstretched arm."

The Second Pair of Tablets

10 At that time the LORD said to me, "Carve out two tablets of stone like the former ones, and come up to me on the mountain, and make an ark of wood. 2I will write on the tablets the words that were on the former tablets, which you smashed, and you shall put them in the ark." 3So I made an ark of acacia wood, cut two tablets of stone like the former ones, and went up the mountain with the two tablets in my hand. 4Then he wrote on the tablets the same words as before, the ten commandments*u* that the LORD had spoken to you on the mountain out of the fire on the day of the assembly; and the LORD gave them to me. 5So I turned and came down from the mountain, and put the tablets in the ark that I had made; and there they are, as the LORD commanded me.

6 (The Israelites journeyed from Beeroth-bene-jaakan*v* to Moserah. There Aaron died, and there he was buried; his son Eleazar succeeded him as priest. 7From there they journeyed to Gudgodah, and from Gudgodah to Jotbathah, a land with flowing streams. 8At that time the LORD set apart the tribe of Levi to carry the ark of the covenant of the LORD, to stand before the LORD to minister to him, and to bless in his name, to this day. 9Therefore Levi has no allotment or inheritance with his kindred; the LORD is his inheritance, as the LORD your God promised him.)

10 I stayed on the mountain forty days and forty nights, as I had done the first time. And once again the LORD listened to me. The LORD was unwilling to destroy you. 11The LORD said to me, "Get up, go on your journey at the head of the people, that they may go in and occupy the land that I swore to their ancestors to give them."

The Essence of the Law

12 So now, O Israel, what does the LORD your God require of you? Only to fear the LORD your God, to walk in all his ways, to love him, to serve the LORD your God with all your heart and with all your soul, 13and to keep the commandments of

t Sam Gk: MT *I have*   *u* Heb *the ten words*
v Or *the wells of the Bene-jaakan*

the LORD your God[w] and his decrees that I am commanding you today, for your own well-being. [14]Although heaven and the heaven of heavens belong to the LORD your God, the earth with all that is in it, [15]yet the LORD set his heart in love on your ancestors alone and chose you, their descendants after them, out of all the peoples, as it is today. [16]Circumcise, then, the foreskin of your heart, and do not be stubborn any longer. [17]For the LORD your God is God of gods and Lord of lords, the great God, mighty and awesome, who is not partial and takes no bribe, [18]who executes justice for the orphan and the widow, and who loves the strangers, providing them food and clothing. [19]You shall also love the stranger, for you were strangers in the land of Egypt. [20]You shall fear the LORD your God; him alone you shall worship; to him you shall hold fast, and by his name you shall swear. [21]He is your praise; he is your God, who has done for you these great and awesome things that your own eyes have seen. [22]Your ancestors went down to Egypt seventy persons; and now the LORD your God has made you as numerous as the stars in heaven.

Rewards for Obedience

11 You shall love the LORD your God, therefore, and keep his charge, his decrees, his ordinances, and his commandments always. [2]Remember today that it was not your children (who have not known or seen the discipline of the LORD your God), but it is you who must acknowledge his greatness, his mighty hand and his outstretched arm, [3]his signs and his deeds that he did in Egypt to Pharaoh, the king of Egypt, and to all his land; [4]what he did to the Egyptian army, to their horses and chariots, how he made the water of the Red Sea[x] flow over them as they pursued you, so that the LORD has destroyed them to this day; [5]what he did to you in the wilderness, until you came to this place; [6]and what he did to Dathan and Abiram, sons of Eliab son of Reuben, how in the midst of all Israel the earth opened its mouth and swallowed them up, along with their households, their tents, and every living being in their company; [7]for it is your own eyes that have seen every great deed that the LORD did.

8 Keep, then, this entire commandment that I am commanding you today,

so that you may have strength to go in and occupy the land that you are crossing over to occupy, [9]and so that you may live long in the land that the LORD swore to your ancestors to give them and to their descendants, a land flowing with milk and honey. [10]For the land that you are about to enter to occupy is not like the land of Egypt, from which you have come, where you sow your seed and irrigate by foot like a vegetable garden. [11]But the land that you are crossing over to occupy is a land of hills and valleys, watered by rain from the sky, [12]a land that the LORD your God looks after. The eyes of the LORD your God are always on it, from the beginning of the year to the end of the year.

13 If you will only heed his every commandment[y] that I am commanding you today—loving the LORD your God, and serving him with all your heart and with all your soul— [14]then he[z] will give the rain for your land in its season, the early rain and the later rain, and you will gather in your grain, your wine, and your oil; [15]and he[z] will give grass in your fields for your livestock, and you will eat your fill. [16]Take care, or you will be seduced into turning away, serving other gods and worshiping them, [17]for then the anger of the LORD will be kindled against you and he will shut up the heavens, so that there will be no rain and the land will yield no fruit; then you will perish quickly off the good land that the LORD is giving you.

18 You shall put these words of mine in your heart and soul, and you shall bind them as a sign on your hand, and fix them as an emblem[a] on your forehead. [19]Teach them to your children, talking about them when you are at home and when you are away, when you lie down and when you rise. [20]Write them on the doorposts of your house and on your gates, [21]so that your days and the days of your children may be multiplied in the land that the LORD swore to your ancestors to give them, as long as the heavens are above the earth.

22 If you will diligently observe this entire commandment that I am commanding you, loving the LORD your God, walking in all his ways, and holding fast

---

w Q Ms Gk Syr: MT lacks *your God*   x Or *Sea of Reeds*   y Compare Gk: Heb *my commandments*   z Sam Gk Vg: MT *I*   a Or *as a frontlet*

to him, 23then the LORD will drive out all these nations before you, and you will dispossess nations larger and mightier than yourselves. 24Every place on which you set foot shall be yours; your territory shall extend from the wilderness to the Lebanon and from the River, the river Euphrates, to the Western Sea. 25No one will be able to stand against you; the LORD your God will put the fear and dread of you on all the land on which you set foot, as he promised you.

26 See, I am setting before you today a blessing and a curse: 27the blessing, if you obey the commandments of the LORD your God that I am commanding you today; 28and the curse, if you do not obey the commandments of the LORD your God, but turn from the way that I am commanding you today, to follow other gods that you have not known.

29 When the LORD your God has brought you into the land that you are entering to occupy, you shall set the blessing on Mount Gerizim and the curse on Mount Ebal. 30As you know, they are beyond the Jordan, some distance to the west, in the land of the Canaanites who

THE TRADITION

Handing on the Faith

You shall put these words of mine in your heart and soul . . .
Teach them to your children.

DEUTERONOMY 11.18–19

Faith is a gift from God, but the content of that faith is passed on from one believer to another.

The content Moses imparts to us in the book of Deuteronomy differs in many respects from the New Testament Good News that fulfills it. But Deuteronomy's emphasis on why and how to hand on the faith challenges us to get serious about our call to *evangelization*. How? For starters:

Be a lifelong learner. We can't teach what we don't know. And learning God's law—taking it into "your heart and soul" (11.18)—sets a life agenda for each of us. For Catholics, one of the most important items on that agenda is frequent reading of the divine Scriptures—a goal to which Vatican II urged us.

Teach your children (verse 19). One of Moses' main themes, he expands on it by instructing parents to explain not just the laws but the "why" behind them (see also Deuteronomy 6.20–25). As their children's first teachers, Catholic mothers and fathers have the primary responsibility for explaining the faith, modeling prayer, and encouraging growth in the virtues. We are to be on the

lookout for teachable moments and creative ways to approach those moments. Godparents too can provide loving guidance as well as providing examples of faith.

Use special helps. Moses recommends string-around-the-finger-type memory aids: capsules holding Biblical verses and bound to the wrist, forehead, and doorpost (11.18, 20). Special feasts and public readings of God's Word supplement ordinary teaching times (see Deuteronomy 16; 31.9–13). Special helps for Catholics include sacramentals like the crucifix, which invite us to meditation and action. The Church year reviews key aspects of the Paschal mystery, one by one.

This means you! Moses addresses "all Israel" (5.1), not just an elite group. Each person is responsible to know, observe, and teach God's law. More than in-family evangelism is intended (the law is posted on the city gates [see 11.20]).

Out of love for Christ, each of us must take responsibility to proclaim the Good News everywhere in the world, handing it on from generation to generation.

live in the Arabah, opposite Gilgal, beside the oak[b] of Moreh.

31 When you cross the Jordan to go in to occupy the land that the LORD your God is giving you, and when you occupy it and live in it, 32you must diligently observe all the statutes and ordinances that I am setting before you today.

Pagan Shrines to Be Destroyed

12 These are the statutes and ordinances that you must diligently observe in the land that the LORD, the God of your ancestors, has given you to occupy all the days that you live on the earth. 2 You must demolish completely all the places where the nations whom you are about to dispossess served their gods, on the mountain heights, on the hills, and under every leafy tree. 3Break down their altars, smash their pillars, burn their sacred poles[c] with fire, and hew down the idols of their gods, and thus blot out their name from their places. 4You shall not worship the LORD your God in such ways. 5But you shall seek the place that the LORD your God will choose out of all your tribes as his habitation to put his name there. You shall go there, 6bringing there your burnt offerings and your sacrifices, your tithes and your donations, your votive gifts, your freewill offerings, and the firstlings of your herds and flocks. 7And you shall eat there in the presence of the LORD your God, you and your households together, rejoicing in all the undertakings in which the LORD your God has blessed you. 8 You shall not act as we are acting here today, all of us according to our own desires, 9for you have not yet come into the rest and the possession that the LORD your God is giving you. 10When you cross over the Jordan and live in the land that the LORD your God is allotting to you, and when he gives you rest from your enemies all around so that you live in safety, 11then you shall bring everything that I command you to the place that the LORD your God will choose as a dwelling for his name: your burnt offerings and your sacrifices, your tithes and your donations, and all your choice votive gifts that you vow to the LORD. 12And you shall rejoice before the LORD your God, you together with your sons and your daughters, your male and female slaves, and the Levites who reside in your towns (since they have no allotment or inheritance with you).

A Prescribed Place of Worship

13 Take care that you do not offer your burnt offerings at any place you happen to see. 14But only at the place that the LORD will choose in one of your tribes—there you shall offer your burnt offerings and there you shall do everything I command you.

15 Yet whenever you desire you may slaughter and eat meat within any of your towns, according to the blessing that the LORD your God has given you; the unclean and the clean may eat of it, as they would of gazelle or deer. 16The blood, however, you must not eat; you shall pour it out on the ground like water. 17Nor may you eat within your towns the tithe of your grain, your wine, and your oil, the firstlings of your herds and your flocks, any of your votive gifts that you vow, your freewill offerings, or your donations; 18these you shall eat in the presence of the LORD your God at the place that the LORD your God will choose, you together with your son and your daughter, your male and female slaves, and the Levites resident in your towns, rejoicing in the presence of the LORD your God in all your undertakings. 19Take care that you do not neglect the Levite as long as you live in your land.

20 When the LORD your God enlarges your territory, as he has promised you, and you say, "I am going to eat some meat," because you wish to eat meat, you may eat meat whenever you have the desire. 21If the place where the LORD your God will choose to put his name is too far from you, and you slaughter as I have commanded you any of your herd or flock that the LORD has given you, then you may eat within your towns whenever you desire. 22Indeed, just as gazelle or deer is eaten, so you may eat it; the unclean and the clean alike may eat it. 23Only be sure that you do not eat the blood; for the blood is the life, and you shall not eat the life with the meat. 24Do not eat it; you shall pour it out on the ground like water. 25Do not eat it, so that all may go well with you and your children after you, because you do what is right in the sight of the LORD. 26But the sacred donations that are due from you, and your votive gifts, you shall bring to the place that the LORD will choose.

---

b Gk Syr: Compare Gen 12.6; Heb *oaks* or *terebinths*   *c* Heb *Asherim*

27You shall present your burnt offerings, both the meat and the blood, on the altar of the LORD your God; the blood of your other sacrifices shall be poured out beside[d] the altar of the LORD your God, but the meat you may eat.

28 Be careful to obey all these words that I command you today,[e] so that it may go well with you and with your children after you forever, because you will be doing what is good and right in the sight of the LORD your God.

Warning against Idolatry

29 When the LORD your God has cut off before you the nations whom you are about to enter to dispossess them, when you have dispossessed them and live in their land, 30take care that you are not snared into imitating them, after they have been destroyed before you: do not inquire concerning their gods, saying, "How did these nations worship their gods? I also want to do the same." 31You must not do the same for the LORD your God, because every abhorrent thing that the LORD hates they have done for their gods. They would even burn their sons and their daughters in the fire to their gods. 32[f] You must diligently observe everything that I command you; do not add to it or take anything from it.

13 [g] If prophets or those who divine by dreams appear among you and promise you omens or portents, 2and the omens or the portents declared by them take place, and they say, "Let us follow other gods" (whom you have not known) "and let us serve them," 3you must not heed the words of those prophets or those who divine by dreams; for the LORD your God is testing you, to know whether you indeed love the LORD your God with all your heart and soul. 4The LORD your God you shall follow, him alone you shall fear, his commandments you shall keep, his voice you shall obey, him you shall serve, and to him you shall hold fast. 5But those prophets or those who divine by dreams shall be put to death for having spoken treason against the LORD your God—who brought you out of the land of Egypt and redeemed you from the house of slavery—to turn you from the way in which the LORD your God commanded you to walk. So you shall purge the evil from your midst.

6 If anyone secretly entices you—even

if it is your brother, your father's son or[h] your mother's son, or your own son or daughter, or the wife you embrace, or your most intimate friend—saying, "Let us go worship other gods," whom neither you nor your ancestors have known, 7any of the gods of the peoples that are around you, whether near you or far away from you, from one end of the earth to the other, 8you must not yield to or heed any such persons. Show them no pity or compassion and do not shield them. 9But you shall surely kill them; your own hand shall be first against them to execute them, and afterwards the hand of all the people. 10Stone them to death for trying to turn you away from the LORD your God, who brought you out of the land of Egypt, out of the house of slavery. 11Then all Israel shall hear and be afraid, and never again do any such wickedness.

12 If you hear it said about one of the towns that the LORD your God is giving you to live in, 13that scoundrels from among you have gone out and led the inhabitants of the town astray, saying, "Let us go and worship other gods," whom you have not known, 14then you shall inquire and make a thorough investigation. If the charge is established that such an abhorrent thing has been done among you, 15you shall put the inhabitants of that town to the sword, utterly destroying it and everything in it—even putting its livestock to the sword. 16All of its spoil you shall gather into its public square; then burn the town and all its spoil with fire, as a whole burnt offering to the LORD your God. It shall remain a perpetual ruin, never to be rebuilt. 17Do not let anything devoted to destruction stick to your hand, so that the LORD may turn from his fierce anger and show you compassion, and in his compassion multiply you, as he swore to your ancestors, 18if you obey the voice of the LORD your God by keeping all his commandments that I am commanding you today, doing what is right in the sight of the LORD your God.

Pagan Practices Forbidden

14 You are children of the LORD your God. You must not lacerate yourselves or shave your forelocks for the

---

[d] Or on   [e] Gk Sam Syr: MT lacks today   [f] Ch 13.1 in Heb   [g] Ch 13.2 in Heb   [h] Sam Gk Compare Tg: MT lacks your father's son or

dead. ²For you are a people holy to the LORD your God; it is you the LORD has chosen out of all the peoples on earth to be his people, his treasured possession.

Clean and Unclean Foods

3 You shall not eat any abhorrent thing. ⁴These are the animals you may eat: the ox, the sheep, the goat, ⁵the deer, the gazelle, the roebuck, the wild goat, the ibex, the antelope, and the mountain-sheep. ⁶Any animal that divides the hoof and has the hoof cleft in two, and chews the cud, among the animals, you may eat. ⁷Yet of those that chew the cud or have the hoof cleft you shall not eat these: the camel, the hare, and the rock badger, because they chew the cud but do not divide the hoof; they are unclean for you. ⁸And the pig, because it divides the hoof but does not chew the cud, is unclean for you. You shall not eat their meat, and you shall not touch their carcasses.

9 Of all that live in water you may eat these: whatever has fins and scales you may eat. ¹⁰And whatever does not have

Communion of Saints

THURSDAY

Scripture Reading for Today:
Deuteronomy 14.1–2

Verse for Today:
Deuteronomy 14.1

As Americans we are protected from contact with death. Most people die in hospitals. Funeral homes tend to dull our senses to the realities of death. As Catholics we believe that death is our birth into eternal life. When our children were growing up, I made a point of taking them to visit the sick and dying and to funerals and to houses of the bereaved. At an early age they became comfortable dealing with sad situations. I encouraged them to talk about death with their friends, especially with those who had lost a loved one. They tell me that they are very grateful for this. It never posed a problem and helped relieve anxiety all around.

For a family, death of a loved one will bring too much sorrow to think of celebration. But when that sorrow is abated, why not plant a rosebush in the garden in that person's memory? I started to do this several years ago and now have a magnificent rose garden. When I water the roses on summer mornings, I say a prayer for the person for whom it was planted. On the thirtieth anniversary of my own first holy communion, I planted a rose for all of those concerned with that day—the teacher who prepared me, the priest who administered the sacrament, the woman who made my dress, as well as my parents. Every summer morning brings me an opportunity to rejoice in the communion of saints, knowing that these people are not gone. They are merely in a different state—and I am spiritually connected to them forever.

Memorial Day provides an excellent opportunity to remember our dead loved ones. Tell the children about a grandmother, uncle or sibling who has died. Children love to hear these stories. Keep our communion of saints alive in their minds. Read the "for everything there is a season" poem in Ecclesiastes 3.1–8, and perhaps have the children learn it by heart.

—ELIZABETH MCNAMER

Go to page 201 for your next devotional reading.

fins and scales you shall not eat; it is unclean for you.

11 You may eat any clean birds. 12But these are the ones that you shall not eat: the eagle, the vulture, the osprey, 13the buzzard, the kite of any kind; 14every raven of any kind; 15the ostrich, the nighthawk, the sea gull, the hawk of any kind; 16the little owl and the great owl, the water hen 17and the desert owl,*i* the carrion vulture and the cormorant, 18the stork, the heron of any kind; the hoopoe and the bat.*j* 19And all winged insects are unclean for you; they shall not be eaten. 20You may eat any clean winged creature.

21 You shall not eat anything that dies of itself; you may give it to aliens residing in your towns for them to eat, or you may sell it to a foreigner. For you are a people holy to the LORD your God.

You shall not boil a kid in its mother's milk.

Regulations concerning Tithes

22 Set apart a tithe of all the yield of your seed that is brought in yearly from the field. 23In the presence of the LORD your God, in the place that he will choose as a dwelling for his name, you shall eat the tithe of your grain, your wine, and your oil, as well as the firstlings of your herd and flock, so that you may learn to fear the LORD your God always. 24But if, when the LORD your God has blessed you, the distance is so great that you are unable to transport it, because the place where the LORD your God will choose to set his name is too far away from you, 25then you may turn it into money. With the money secure in hand, go to the place that the LORD your God will choose; 26spend the money for whatever you wish—oxen, sheep, wine, strong drink, or whatever you desire. And you shall eat there in the presence of the LORD your God, you and your household rejoicing together. 27As for the Levites resident in your towns, do not neglect them, because they have no allotment or inheritance with you.

28 Every third year you shall bring out the full tithe of your produce for that year, and store it within your towns; 29the Levites, because they have no allotment or inheritance with you, as well as the resident aliens, the orphans, and the widows in your towns, may come and eat their fill so that the LORD your God may bless you in all the work that you undertake.

Laws concerning the Sabbatical Year

15 Every seventh year you shall grant a remission of debts. 2And this is the manner of the remission: every creditor shall remit the claim that is held against a neighbor, not exacting it of a neighbor who is a member of the community, because the LORD's remission has been proclaimed. 3Of a foreigner you may exact it, but you must remit your claim on whatever any member of your community owes you. 4There will, however, be no one in need among you, because the LORD is sure to bless you in the land that the LORD your God is giving you as a possession to occupy, 5if only you will obey the LORD your God by diligently observing this entire commandment that I command you today. 6When the LORD your God has blessed you, as he promised you, you will lend to many nations, but you will not borrow; you will rule over many nations, but they will not rule over you.

7 If there is among you anyone in need, a member of your community in any of your towns within the land that the LORD your God is giving you, do not be hard-hearted or tight-fisted toward your needy neighbor. 8You should rather open your hand, willingly lending enough to meet the need, whatever it may be. 9Be careful that you do not entertain a mean thought, thinking, "The seventh year, the year of remission, is near," and therefore view your needy neighbor with hostility and give nothing; your neighbor might cry to the LORD against you, and you would incur guilt. 10Give liberally and be ungrudging when you do so, for on this account the LORD your God will bless you in all your work and in all that you undertake. 11Since there will never cease to be some in need on the earth, I therefore command you, "Open your hand to the poor and needy neighbor in your land."

12 If a member of your community, whether a Hebrew man or a Hebrew woman, is sold*k* to you and works for you six years, in the seventh year you shall set that person free. 13And when you send a male slave*l* out from you a free person, you shall not send him out emptyhanded. 14Provide liberally out of your flock, your threshing floor, and your wine

---

i Or *pelican*   *j* Identification of several of the birds in verses 12-18 is uncertain   *k* Or *sells himself or herself*   *l* Heb *him*

press, thus giving to him some of the bounty with which the LORD your God has blessed you. [15]Remember that you were a slave in the land of Egypt, and the LORD your God redeemed you; for this reason I lay this command upon you today. [16]But if he says to you, "I will not go out from you," because he loves you and your household, since he is well off with you, [17]then you shall take an awl and thrust it through his earlobe into the door, and he shall be your slave[m] forever.

You shall do the same with regard to your female slave.[n]

18 Do not consider it a hardship when you send them out from you free persons, because for six years they have given you services worth the wages of hired laborers; and the LORD your God will bless you in all that you do.

The Firstborn of Livestock

19 Every firstling male born of your herd and flock you shall consecrate to the LORD your God; you shall not do work with your firstling ox nor shear the firstling of your flock. [20]You shall eat it, you together with your household, in the presence of the LORD your God year by year at the place that the LORD will choose. [21]But if it has any defect—any serious defect, such as lameness or blindness—you shall not sacrifice it to the LORD your God; [22]within your towns you may eat it, the unclean and the clean alike, as you would a gazelle or deer. [23]Its blood, however, you must not eat; you shall pour it out on the ground like water.

The Passover Reviewed

16 Observe the month[o] of Abib by keeping the passover to the LORD your God, for in the month of Abib the LORD your God brought you out of Egypt by night. [2]You shall offer the passover sacrifice to the LORD your God, from the flock and the herd, at the place that the LORD

m Or bondman   n Or bondwoman   o Or new moon

---

*G*iving

Jesus never instructed us to check into the background of the poor before we feed them. Indeed, Luke tells us Jesus said, "Do not judge, and you will not be judged; do not condemn, and you will not be condemned. Forgive, and you will be forgiven; give, and it will be given to you. A good measure, pressed down, shaken together, running over, will be put into your lap; for the measure you give will be the measure you get back" (Luke 6.37–38).

The last line is a bit scary, especially when we find ourselves judging the worthiness of others to be recipients of our time, energy and money. Grace comes when we give of ourselves unconditionally, just as God gives. Christian idealists don't ask for a background check on an idle worker before giving a bowl of soup or a bed.

When someone, reacting to such idealism, charges that helping the poor just keeps them poor, we can respond firmly that we would rather take the attitude that "There but for the grace of God go I." If a response like that doesn't change their perceptions a little, at least it tells them that we aren't ashamed of our own caring attitude.

—*DOLORES CURRAN*

Scripture Reading for Today:
Deuteronomy 15.1–11

Verse for Today:
Deuteronomy 15.10

Go to page 204 for your next devotional reading.

will choose as a dwelling for his name. ³You must not eat with it anything leavened. For seven days you shall eat unleavened bread with it—the bread of affliction—because you came out of the land of Egypt in great haste, so that all the days of your life you may remember the day of your departure from the land of Egypt. ⁴No leaven shall be seen with you in all your territory for seven days; and none of the meat of what you slaughter on the evening of the first day shall remain until morning. ⁵You are not permitted to offer the passover sacrifice within any of your towns that the LORD your God is giving you. ⁶But at the place that the LORD your God will choose as a dwelling for his name, only there shall you offer the passover sacrifice, in the evening at sunset, the time of day when you departed from Egypt. ⁷You shall cook it and eat it at the place that the LORD your God will choose; the next morning you may go back to your tents. ⁸For six days you shall continue to eat unleavened bread, and on the seventh day there shall be a solemn assembly for the LORD your God, when you shall do no work.

The Festival of Weeks Reviewed

9 You shall count seven weeks; begin to count the seven weeks from the time the sickle is first put to the standing grain. ¹⁰Then you shall keep the festival of weeks to the LORD your God, contributing a freewill offering in proportion to the blessing that you have received from the LORD your God. ¹¹Rejoice before the LORD your God—you and your sons and your daughters, your male and female slaves, the Levites resident in your towns, as well as the strangers, the orphans, and the widows who are among you—at the place that the LORD your God will choose as a dwelling for his name. ¹²Remember that you were a slave in Egypt, and diligently observe these statutes.

The Festival of Booths Reviewed

13 You shall keep the festival of booths *p* for seven days, when you have gathered in the produce from your threshing floor and your wine press. ¹⁴Rejoice during your festival, you and your sons and your daughters, your male and female slaves, as well as the Levites, the strangers, the orphans, and the widows resident in your towns. ¹⁵Seven days you shall keep the festival to the LORD your God at the place that the LORD will choose; for the LORD your God will bless you in all your produce and in all your undertakings, and you shall surely celebrate.

16 Three times a year all your males shall appear before the LORD your God at the place that he will choose: at the festival of unleavened bread, at the festival of weeks, and at the festival of booths. *p* They shall not appear before the LORD empty-handed; ¹⁷all shall give as they are able, according to the blessing of the LORD your God that he has given you.

Municipal Judges and Officers

18 You shall appoint judges and officials throughout your tribes, in all your towns that the LORD your God is giving you, and they shall render just decisions for the people. ¹⁹You must not distort justice; you must not show partiality; and you must not accept bribes, for a bribe blinds the eyes of the wise and subverts the cause of those who are in the right. ²⁰Justice, and only justice, you shall pursue, so that you may live and occupy the land that the LORD your God is giving you.

Forbidden Forms of Worship

21 You shall not plant any tree as a sacred pole*q* beside the altar that you make for the LORD your God; ²²nor shall you set up a stone pillar—things that the LORD your God hates.

17 You must not sacrifice to the LORD your God an ox or a sheep that has a defect, anything seriously wrong; for that is abhorrent to the LORD your God.

2 If there is found among you, in one of your towns that the LORD your God is giving you, a man or woman who does what is evil in the sight of the LORD your God, and transgresses his covenant ³by going to serve other gods and worshiping them—whether the sun or the moon or any of the host of heaven, which I have forbidden— ⁴and if it is reported to you or you hear of it, and you make a thorough inquiry, and the charge is proved true that such an abhorrent thing has occurred in Israel, ⁵then you shall bring out to your gates that man or that woman who has committed this crime and you shall stone the man or woman to death. ⁶On the evidence of two or three witnesses the death

p Or *tabernacles*; Heb *succoth*   *q* Heb *Asherah*

sentence shall be executed; a person must not be put to death on the evidence of only one witness. 7The hands of the witnesses shall be the first raised against the person to execute the death penalty, and afterward the hands of all the people. So you shall purge the evil from your midst.

Legal Decisions by Priests and Judges

8 If a judicial decision is too difficult for you to make between one kind of bloodshed and another, one kind of legal right and another, or one kind of assault and another—any such matters of dispute in your towns—then you shall immediately go up to the place that the LORD your God will choose, 9where you shall consult with the levitical priests and the judge who is in office in those days; they shall announce to you the decision in the case. 10Carry out exactly the decision that they announce to you from the place that the LORD will choose, diligently observing everything they instruct you. 11You must carry out fully the law that they interpret for you or the ruling that they announce to you; do not turn aside from the decision that they announce to you, either to the right or to the left. 12As for anyone who presumes to disobey the priest appointed to minister there to the LORD your God, or the judge, that person shall die. So you shall purge the evil from Israel. 13All the people will hear and be afraid, and will not act presumptuously again.

Limitations of Royal Authority

14 When you have come into the land that the LORD your God is giving you, and have taken possession of it and settled in it, and you say, "I will set a king over me, like all the nations that are around me," 15you may indeed set over you a king whom the LORD your God will choose. One of your own community you may set as king over you; you are not permitted to put a foreigner over you, who is not of your own community. 16Even so, he must not acquire many horses for himself, or return the people to Egypt in order to acquire more horses, since the LORD has said to you, "You must never return that way again." 17And he must not acquire many wives for himself, or else his heart will turn away; also silver and gold he must not acquire in great quantity for himself. 18When he has taken the throne of his kingdom, he shall have a copy of this law

written for him in the presence of the levitical priests. 19It shall remain with him and he shall read in it all the days of his life, so that he may learn to fear the LORD his God, diligently observing all the words of this law and these statutes, 20neither exalting himself above other members of the community nor turning aside from the commandment, either to the right or to the left, so that he and his descendants may reign long over his kingdom in Israel.

Privileges of Priests and Levites

18 The levitical priests, the whole tribe of Levi, shall have no allotment or inheritance within Israel. They may eat the sacrifices that are the LORD's portion[r] 2but they shall have no inheritance among the other members of the community; the LORD is their inheritance, as he promised them.

3 This shall be the priests' due from the people, from those offering a sacrifice, whether an ox or a sheep: they shall give to the priest the shoulder, the two jowls, and the stomach. 4The first fruits of your grain, your wine, and your oil, as well as the first of the fleece of your sheep, you shall give him. 5For the LORD your God has chosen Levi[s] out of all your tribes, to stand and minister in the name of the LORD, him and his sons for all time.

6 If a Levite leaves any of your towns, from wherever he has been residing in Israel, and comes to the place that the LORD will choose (and he may come whenever he wishes), 7then he may minister in the name of the LORD his God, like all his fellow-Levites who stand to minister there before the LORD. 8They shall have equal portions to eat, even though they have income from the sale of family possessions.[r]

Child-Sacrifice, Divination, and Magic Prohibited

9 When you come into the land that the LORD your God is giving you, you must not learn to imitate the abhorrent practices of those nations. 10No one shall be found among you who makes a son or daughter pass through fire, or who practices divination, or is a soothsayer, or an augur, or a sorcerer, 11or one who casts spells, or who consults ghosts or spirits, or who seeks oracles from the dead. 12For

---

r Meaning of Heb uncertain   s Heb *him*

Rebekah

*Her Name Probably Means
"Loop" or "Tie"*

Read Genesis 24; 27

The sun was dipping beyond the rim of the sky as the young woman approached the well outside a small town, five hundred miles northeast of Canaan. Rebekah hoisted the brimming jug to her shoulder, welcoming its cooling touch against her skin.

As she turned to go, a stranger approached, asking for a drink. Obligingly she offered to draw water for his camels as well. She noticed the look of surprised pleasure that flashed across his face. Had she overheard his whispered prayer moments earlier, her astonishment would have exceeded his: "Let the girl to whom I shall say, 'Please offer your jar that I may drink,' and who shall say, 'Drink, and I will water your camels'—let her be the one whom you have appointed for your servant Isaac" (24.14).

A simple gesture. A generous response. A woman's future altered in a moment. The man Rebekah encountered at the well, Abraham's servant, had embarked on a sacred quest—to find Isaac a wife from among Abraham's own people.

Like her great-aunt Sarah before her, Rebekah would make the journey south, embracing a future she could hardly glimpse. Betrothed to a man twice her age, whose name meant "laughter," she felt a sudden giddiness

Her Character: *Hardworking and generous, her faith was so great that she left home forever to marry a man she had never met. Yet she played favorites with her sons, failing to trust God fully for his promises.*
Her Sorrow: *That she was unable to have children for the first 20 years of her married life and that she never again set eyes on her favorite son, Jacob, after he fled from Esau.*
Her Joy: *That God had gone to extraordinary lengths to pursue her, inviting her to become part of his people and his promises.*

rise inside her. The God of Abraham and Sarah was calling her.

So Isaac and Rebekah were married, and Isaac loved his wife. But it was 20 years before she gave birth—to twins. During the delivery, the youngest grasped the heel of his brother, as though striving for first position even then. Though second by birth, Jacob was first in Rebekah's affections. But her husband, Isaac, loved Esau best.

Years later, when Isaac was old and blind, he summoned his firstborn, Esau, to receive his blessings. But the clever Rebekah devised a scheme to trick old Isaac in favor of Jacob. Disguised as Esau, Jacob presented himself to his father for the much-coveted blessing.

Afraid of Esau's wrath, Rebekah persuaded Isaac to send Jacob in search of a wife from among her brother Laban's daughters. She would send for him as soon as his brother's fury abated. But more than 20 years would pass before Jacob returned. And though Isaac would live to welcome his son, Rebekah would not.

As a young girl, Rebekah heard God's call to play a vital role in the story of his people. Like Sarah, she would become a matriarch of God's people. And like Sarah, her heart often would be divided between faith and doubt, often acting as though God's promise required her intervention. Finding it difficult to rest in the promise, she fostered a rivalry between her sons that separated them for most of their lives.

Praying With Rebekah

"May you, our sister, become thousands of myriads; may your offspring gain possession of the gates of their foes."—*Genesis 24.60*

Praise God: *Because unlike Isaac, who had only one blessing to give his children, God has blessings designed for each of us.*

Offer Thanks: *That God doesn't wait until we're perfect to involve us in his plans.*

Confess: *Your tendency to try to control the future, rather than trusting God to shape it according to his timetable.*

Ask God: *To help you avoid playing favorites with your own children and to trust that he has a generous plan for each one.*

Lift Your Heart

Take a few minutes to make a blessing card for each of your children. You can use a simple index card. You may want to dress it up with stickers, stencils, or line drawings. (If you don't have children of your own, you can do this for a niece or nephew or another special child in your life.) Start by praying for each child, asking God's blessing. Then write out the blessings you sense God wants for them. Tuck the blessing cards under their pillows or place them next to their dinner plates. Tell them these are some of the ways you are asking God to bless them. Be sure to keep a copy of each card for yourself so that you can make those blessings a subject of frequent prayer.

Lord, you give us the power to bless our children through our example, our teaching, our love, and our prayers. May our children surpass us in faith. In all their struggles may they sense your nearness and may their joy be renewed each morning. May each of them become the kind of person that attracts others to you.

Go to page 214 for your next devotional reading.

whoever does these things is abhorrent to the LORD; it is because of such abhorrent practices that the LORD your God is driving them out before you. ¹³You must remain completely loyal to the LORD your God. ¹⁴Although these nations that you are about to dispossess do give heed to soothsayers and diviners, as for you, the LORD your God does not permit you to do so.

A New Prophet Like Moses

15 The LORD your God will raise up for you a prophet^t like me from among your own people; you shall heed such a prophet.^u ¹⁶This is what you requested of the LORD your God at Horeb on the day of the assembly when you said: "If I hear the voice of the LORD my God any more, or ever again see this great fire, I will die." ¹⁷Then the LORD replied to me: "They are right in what they have said. ¹⁸I will raise up for them a prophet^t like you from among their own people; I will put my words in the mouth of the prophet,^v who shall speak to them everything that I command. ¹⁹Anyone who does not heed the words that the prophet^w shall speak in my name, I myself will hold accountable. ²⁰But any prophet who speaks in the name of other gods, or who presumes to speak in my name a word that I have not commanded the prophet to speak—that prophet shall die." ²¹You may say to yourself, "How can we recognize a word that the LORD has not spoken?" ²²If a prophet speaks in the name of the LORD but the thing does not take place or prove true, it is a word that the LORD has not spoken. The prophet has spoken it presumptuously; do not be frightened by it.

Laws concerning the Cities of Refuge

19 When the LORD your God has cut off the nations whose land the LORD your God is giving you, and you have dispossessed them and settled in their towns and in their houses, ²you shall set apart three cities in the land that the LORD your God is giving you to possess. ³You shall calculate the distances^x and divide into three regions the land that the LORD your God gives you as a possession, so that any homicide can flee to one of them.

4 Now this is the case of a homicide who might flee there and live, that is, someone who has killed another person unintentionally when the two had not been at enmity before: ⁵Suppose someone goes into the forest with another to cut wood, and when one of them swings the ax to cut down a tree, the head slips from the handle and strikes the other person who then dies; the killer may flee to one of these cities and live. ⁶But if the distance is too great, the avenger of blood in hot anger might pursue and overtake and put the killer to death, although a death sentence was not deserved, since the two had not been at enmity before. ⁷Therefore I command you: You shall set apart three cities.

8 If the LORD your God enlarges your territory, as he swore to your ancestors—and he will give you all the land that he promised your ancestors to give you, ⁹provided you diligently observe this entire commandment that I command you today, by loving the LORD your God and walking always in his ways—then you shall add three more cities to these three, ¹⁰so that the blood of an innocent person may not be shed in the land that the LORD your God is giving you as an inheritance, thereby bringing bloodguilt upon you.

11 But if someone at enmity with another lies in wait and attacks and takes the life of that person, and flees into one of these cities, ¹²then the elders of the killer's city shall send to have the culprit taken from there and handed over to the avenger of blood to be put to death. ¹³Show no pity; you shall purge the guilt of innocent blood from Israel, so that it may go well with you.

Property Boundaries

14 You must not move your neighbor's boundary marker, set up by former generations, on the property that will be allotted to you in the land that the LORD your God is giving you to possess.

Law concerning Witnesses

15 A single witness shall not suffice to convict a person of any crime or wrongdoing in connection with any offense that may be committed. Only on the evidence of two or three witnesses shall a charge be sustained. ¹⁶If a malicious witness comes forward to accuse someone of wrongdoing, ¹⁷then both parties to the dispute shall appear before the LORD, before the

---

^t Or prophets   ^u Or such prophets   ^v Or mouths of the prophets   ^w Heb he   ^x Or prepare roads to them

priests and the judges who are in office in those days, ¹⁸and the judges shall make a thorough inquiry. If the witness is a false witness, having testified falsely against another, ¹⁹then you shall do to the false witness just as the false witness had meant to do to the other. So you shall purge the evil from your midst. ²⁰The rest shall hear and be afraid, and a crime such as this shall never again be committed among you. ²¹Show no pity: life for life, eye for eye, tooth for tooth, hand for hand, foot for foot.

Rules of Warfare

20 When you go out to war against your enemies, and see horses and chariots, an army larger than your own, you shall not be afraid of them; for the LORD your God is with you, who brought you up from the land of Egypt. ²Before you engage in battle, the priest shall come forward and speak to the troops, ³and shall say to them: "Hear, O Israel! Today you are drawing near to do battle against your enemies. Do not lose heart, or be afraid, or panic, or be in dread of them; ⁴for it is the LORD your God who goes with you, to fight for you against your enemies, to give you victory." ⁵Then the officials shall address the troops, saying, "Has anyone built a new house but not dedicated it? He should go back to his house, or he might die in the battle and another dedicate it. ⁶Has anyone planted a vineyard but not yet enjoyed its fruit? He should go back to his house, or he might die in the battle and another be first to enjoy its fruit. ⁷Has anyone become engaged to a woman but not yet married her? He should go back to his house, or he might die in the battle and another marry her." ⁸The officials shall continue to address the troops, saying, "Is anyone afraid or disheartened? He should go back to his house, or he might cause the heart of his comrades to melt like his own." ⁹When the officials have finished addressing the troops, then the commanders shall take charge of them.

10 When you draw near to a town to fight against it, offer it terms of peace. ¹¹If it accepts your terms of peace and surrenders to you, then all the people in it shall serve you at forced labor. ¹²If it does not submit to you peacefully, but makes war against you, then you shall besiege it; ¹³and when the LORD your God gives it

into your hand, you shall put all its males to the sword. ¹⁴You may, however, take as your booty the women, the children, livestock, and everything else in the town, all its spoil. You may enjoy the spoil of your enemies, which the LORD your God has given you. ¹⁵Thus you shall treat all the towns that are very far from you, which are not towns of the nations here. ¹⁶But as for the towns of these peoples that the LORD your God is giving you as an inheritance, you must not let anything that breathes remain alive. ¹⁷You shall annihilate them—the Hittites and the Amorites, the Canaanites and the Perizzites, the Hivites and the Jebusites—just as the LORD your God has commanded, ¹⁸so that they may not teach you to do all the abhorrent things that they do for their gods, and you thus sin against the LORD your God.

19 If you besiege a town for a long time, making war against it in order to take it, you must not destroy its trees by wielding an ax against them. Although you may take food from them, you must not cut them down. Are trees in the field human beings that they should come under siege from you? ²⁰You may destroy only the trees that you know do not produce food; you may cut them down for use in building siegeworks against the town that makes war with you, until it falls.

Law concerning Murder by Persons Unknown

21 If, in the land that the LORD your God is giving you to possess, a body is found lying in open country, and it is not known who struck the person down, ²then your elders and your judges shall come out to measure the distances to the towns that are near the body. ³The elders of the town nearest the body shall take a heifer that has never been worked, one that has not pulled in the yoke; ⁴the elders of that town shall bring the heifer down to a wadi with running water, which is neither plowed nor sown, and shall break the heifer's neck there in the wadi. ⁵Then the priests, the sons of Levi, shall come forward, for the LORD your God has chosen them to minister to him and to pronounce blessings in the name of the LORD, and by their decision all cases of dispute and assault shall be settled. ⁶All the elders of that town nearest the body shall wash their hands over the heifer

whose neck was broken in the wadi, [7]and they shall declare: "Our hands did not shed this blood, nor were we witnesses to it. [8]Absolve, O LORD, your people Israel, whom you redeemed; do not let the guilt of innocent blood remain in the midst of your people Israel." Then they will be absolved of bloodguilt. [9]So you shall purge the guilt of innocent blood from your midst, because you must do what is right in the sight of the LORD.

Female Captives

[10] When you go out to war against your enemies, and the LORD your God hands them over to you and you take them captive, [11]suppose you see among the captives a beautiful woman whom you desire and want to marry, [12]and so you bring her home to your house: she shall shave her head, pare her nails, [13]discard her captive's garb, and shall remain in your house a full month, mourning for her father and mother; after that you may go in to her and be her husband, and she shall be your wife. [14]But if you are not satisfied with her, you shall let her go free and not sell her for money. You must not treat her as a slave, since you have dishonored her.

The Right of the Firstborn

[15] If a man has two wives, one of them loved and the other disliked, and if both the loved and the disliked have borne him sons, the firstborn being the son of the one who is disliked, [16]then on the day when he wills his possessions to his sons, he is not permitted to treat the son of the loved as the firstborn in preference to the son of the disliked, who is the firstborn. [17]He must acknowledge as firstborn the son of the one who is disliked, giving him a double portion[y] of all that he has; since he is the first issue of his virility, the right of the firstborn is his.

Rebellious Children

[18] If someone has a stubborn and rebellious son who will not obey his father and mother, who does not heed them when they discipline him, [19]then his father and his mother shall take hold of him and bring him out to the elders of his town at the gate of that place. [20]They shall say to the elders of his town, "This son of ours is stubborn and rebellious. He will not obey us. He is a glutton and a drunk-

ard." [21]Then all the men of the town shall stone him to death. So you shall purge the evil from your midst; and all Israel will hear, and be afraid.

Miscellaneous Laws

[22] When someone is convicted of a crime punishable by death and is executed, and you hang him on a tree, [23]his corpse must not remain all night upon the tree; you shall bury him that same day, for anyone hung on a tree is under God's curse. You must not defile the land that the LORD your God is giving you for possession.

22 You shall not watch your neighbor's ox or sheep straying away and ignore them; you shall take them back to their owner. [2]If the owner does not reside near you or you do not know who the owner is, you shall bring it to your own house, and it shall remain with you until the owner claims it; then you shall return it. [3]You shall do the same with a neighbor's donkey; you shall do the same with a neighbor's garment; and you shall do the same with anything else that your neighbor loses and you find. You may not withhold your help.

[4] You shall not see your neighbor's donkey or ox fallen on the road and ignore it; you shall help to lift it up.

[5] A woman shall not wear a man's apparel, nor shall a man put on a woman's garment; for whoever does such things is abhorrent to the LORD your God.

[6] If you come on a bird's nest, in any tree or on the ground, with fledglings or eggs, with the mother sitting on the fledglings or on the eggs, you shall not take the mother with the young. [7]Let the mother go, taking only the young for yourself, in order that it may go well with you and you may live long.

[8] When you build a new house, you shall make a parapet for your roof; otherwise you might have bloodguilt on your house, if anyone should fall from it.

[9] You shall not sow your vineyard with a second kind of seed, or the whole yield will have to be forfeited, both the crop that you have sown and the yield of the vineyard itself.

[10] You shall not plow with an ox and a donkey yoked together.

[y] Heb two-thirds

11 You shall not wear clothes made of wool and linen woven together.

12 You shall make tassels on the four corners of the cloak with which you cover yourself.

Laws concerning Sexual Relations

13 Suppose a man marries a woman, but after going in to her, he dislikes her [14]and makes up charges against her, slandering her by saying, "I married this woman; but when I lay with her, I did not find evidence of her virginity." [15]The father of the young woman and her mother shall then submit the evidence of the young woman's virginity to the elders of the city at the gate. [16]The father of the young woman shall say to the elders: "I gave my daughter in marriage to this man but he dislikes her; [17]now he has made up charges against her, saying, 'I did not find evidence of your daughter's virginity.' But here is the evidence of my daughter's virginity." Then they shall spread out the cloth before the elders of the town. [18]The elders of that town shall take the man and punish him; [19]they shall fine him one hundred shekels of silver (which they shall give to the young woman's father) because he has slandered a virgin of Israel. She shall remain his wife; he shall not be permitted to divorce her as long as he lives.

20 If, however, this charge is true, that evidence of the young woman's virginity was not found, [21]then they shall bring the young woman out to the entrance of her father's house and the men of her town shall stone her to death, because she committed a disgraceful act in Israel by prostituting herself in her father's house. So you shall purge the evil from your midst.

22 If a man is caught lying with the wife of another man, both of them shall die, the man who lay with the woman as well as the woman. So you shall purge the evil from Israel.

23 If there is a young woman, a virgin already engaged to be married, and a man meets her in the town and lies with her, [24]you shall bring both of them to the gate of that town and stone them to death, the young woman because she did not cry for help in the town and the man because he violated his neighbor's wife. So you shall purge the evil from your midst.

25 But if the man meets the engaged woman in the open country, and the man seizes her and lies with her, then only the man who lay with her shall die. [26]You shall do nothing to the young woman; the young woman has not committed an offense punishable by death, because this case is like that of someone who attacks and murders a neighbor. [27]Since he found her in the open country, the engaged woman may have cried for help, but there was no one to rescue her.

28 If a man meets a virgin who is not engaged, and seizes her and lies with her, and they are caught in the act, [29]the man who lay with her shall give fifty shekels of silver to the young woman's father, and she shall become his wife. Because he violated her he shall not be permitted to divorce her as long as he lives.

30[z]A man shall not marry his father's wife, thereby violating his father's rights.[a]

Those Excluded from the Assembly

23 No one whose testicles are crushed or whose penis is cut off shall be admitted to the assembly of the LORD.

2 Those born of an illicit union shall not be admitted to the assembly of the LORD. Even to the tenth generation, none of their descendants shall be admitted to the assembly of the LORD.

3 No Ammonite or Moabite shall be admitted to the assembly of the LORD. Even to the tenth generation, none of their descendants shall be admitted to the assembly of the LORD, [4]because they did not meet you with food and water on your journey out of Egypt, and because they hired against you Balaam son of Beor, from Pethor of Mesopotamia, to curse you. [5](Yet the LORD your God refused to heed Balaam; the LORD your God turned the curse into a blessing for you, because the LORD your God loved you.) [6]You shall never promote their welfare or their prosperity as long as you live.

7 You shall not abhor any of the Edomites, for they are your kin. You shall not abhor any of the Egyptians, because you were an alien residing in their land. [8]The children of the third generation that are born to them may be admitted to the assembly of the LORD.

z Ch 23.1 in Heb   a Heb *uncovering his father's skirt*

Sanitary, Ritual, and Humanitarian Precepts

9 When you are encamped against your enemies you shall guard against any impropriety.

10 If one of you becomes unclean because of a nocturnal emission, then he shall go outside the camp; he must not come within the camp. [11]When evening comes, he shall wash himself with water, and when the sun has set, he may come back into the camp.

12 You shall have a designated area outside the camp to which you shall go. [13]With your utensils you shall have a trowel; when you relieve yourself outside, you shall dig a hole with it and then cover up your excrement. [14]Because the Lord your God travels along with your camp, to save you and to hand over your enemies to you, therefore your camp must be holy, so that he may not see anything indecent among you and turn away from you.

15 Slaves who have escaped to you from their owners shall not be given back to them. [16]They shall reside with you, in your midst, in any place they choose in any one of your towns, wherever they please; you shall not oppress them.

17 None of the daughters of Israel shall be a temple prostitute; none of the sons of Israel shall be a temple prostitute. [18]You shall not bring the fee of a prostitute or the wages of a male prostitute[b] into the house of the Lord your God in payment for any vow, for both of these are abhorrent to the Lord your God.

19 You shall not charge interest on loans to another Israelite, interest on money, interest on provisions, interest on anything that is lent. [20]On loans to a foreigner you may charge interest, but on loans to another Israelite you may not charge interest, so that the Lord your God may bless you in all your undertakings in the land that you are about to enter and possess.

21 If you make a vow to the Lord your God, do not postpone fulfilling it; for the Lord your God will surely require it of you, and you would incur guilt. [22]But if you refrain from vowing, you will not incur guilt. [23]Whatever your lips utter you must diligently perform, just as you have freely vowed to the Lord your God with your own mouth.

24 If you go into your neighbor's vineyard, you may eat your fill of grapes, as many as you wish, but you shall not put any in a container.

25 If you go into your neighbor's standing grain, you may pluck the ears with your hand, but you shall not put a sickle to your neighbor's standing grain.

Laws concerning Marriage and Divorce

24 Suppose a man enters into marriage with a woman, but she does not please him because he finds something objectionable about her, and so he writes her a certificate of divorce, puts it in her hand, and sends her out of his house; she then leaves his house [2]and goes off to become another man's wife. [3]Then suppose the second man dislikes her, writes her a bill of divorce, puts it in her hand, and sends her out of his house (or the second man who married her dies); [4]her first husband, who sent her away, is not permitted to take her again to be his wife after she has been defiled; for that would be abhorrent to the Lord, and you shall not bring guilt on the land that the Lord your God is giving you as a possession.

Miscellaneous Laws

5 When a man is newly married, he shall not go out with the army or be charged with any related duty. He shall be free at home one year, to be happy with the wife whom he has married.

6 No one shall take a mill or an upper millstone in pledge, for that would be taking a life in pledge.

7 If someone is caught kidnaping another Israelite, enslaving or selling the Israelite, then that kidnaper shall die. So you shall purge the evil from your midst.

8 Guard against an outbreak of a leprous[c] skin disease by being very careful; you shall carefully observe whatever the levitical priests instruct you, just as I have commanded them. [9]Remember what the Lord your God did to Miriam on your journey out of Egypt.

10 When you make your neighbor a loan of any kind, you shall not go into the house to take the pledge. [11]You shall wait outside, while the person to whom you are making the loan brings the pledge out to you. [12]If the person is poor, you shall

---

b Heb *a dog*　　*c* A term for several skin diseases; precise meaning uncertain not sleep in the garment given you as[d] the pledge. 13You shall give the pledge back by sunset, so that your neighbor may sleep in the cloak and bless you; and it will be to your credit before the LORD your God.

14 You shall not withhold the wages of poor and needy laborers, whether other Israelites or aliens who reside in your land in one of your towns. 15You shall pay them their wages daily before sunset, because they are poor and their livelihood depends on them; otherwise they might cry to the LORD against you, and you would incur guilt.

16 Parents shall not be put to death for their children, nor shall children be put to death for their parents; only for their own crimes may persons be put to death.

17 You shall not deprive a resident alien or an orphan of justice; you shall not take a widow's garment in pledge. 18Remember that you were a slave in Egypt and the LORD your God redeemed you from there; therefore I command you to do this.

19 When you reap your harvest in your field and forget a sheaf in the field, you shall not go back to get it; it shall be left for the alien, the orphan, and the widow, so that the LORD your God may bless you in all your undertakings. 20When you beat your olive trees, do not strip what is left; it shall be for the alien, the orphan, and the widow.

21 When you gather the grapes of your vineyard, do not glean what is left; it shall be for the alien, the orphan, and the widow. 22Remember that you were a slave in the land of Egypt; therefore I am commanding you to do this.

25 Suppose two persons have a dispute and enter into litigation, and the judges decide between them, declaring one to be in the right and the other to be in the wrong. 2If the one in the wrong deserves to be flogged, the judge shall make that person lie down and be beaten in his presence with the number of lashes proportionate to the offense. 3Forty lashes may be given but not more; if more lashes than these are given, your neighbor will be degraded in your sight.

4 You shall not muzzle an ox while it is treading out the grain.

Levirate Marriage

5 When brothers reside together, and one of them dies and has no son, the wife of the deceased shall not be married outside the family to a stranger. Her husband's brother shall go in to her, taking her in marriage, and performing the duty of a husband's brother to her, 6and the firstborn whom she bears shall succeed to the name of the deceased brother, so that his name may not be blotted out of Israel. 7But if the man has no desire to marry his brother's widow, then his brother's widow shall go up to the elders at the gate and say, "My husband's brother refuses to perpetuate his brother's name in Israel; he will not perform the duty of a husband's brother to me." 8Then the elders of his town shall summon him and speak to him. If he persists, saying, "I have no desire to marry her," 9then his brother's wife shall go up to him in the presence of the elders, pull his sandal off his foot, spit in his face, and declare, "This is what is done to the man who does not build up his brother's house." 10Throughout Israel his family shall be known as "the house of him whose sandal was pulled off."

Various Commands

11 If men get into a fight with one another, and the wife of one intervenes to rescue her husband from the grip of his opponent by reaching out and seizing his genitals, 12you shall cut off her hand; show no pity.

13 You shall not have in your bag two kinds of weights, large and small. 14You shall not have in your house two kinds of measures, large and small. 15You shall have only a full and honest weight; you shall have only a full and honest measure, so that your days may be long in the land that the LORD your God is giving you. 16For all who do such things, all who act dishonestly, are abhorrent to the LORD your God.

17 Remember what Amalek did to you on your journey out of Egypt, 18how he attacked you on the way, when you were faint and weary, and struck down all who lagged behind you; he did not fear God. 19Therefore when the LORD your God has given you rest from all your enemies on every hand, in the land that the LORD your God is giving you as an inheritance to possess, you shall blot out the remem-

d Heb lacks *the garment given you as*

brance of Amalek from under heaven; do not forget.

First Fruits and Tithes

26 When you have come into the land that the LORD your God is giving you as an inheritance to possess, and you possess it, and settle in it, ²you shall take some of the first of all the fruit of the ground, which you harvest from the land that the LORD your God is giving you, and you shall put it in a basket and go to the place that the LORD your God will choose as a dwelling for his name. ³You shall go to the priest who is in office at that time, and say to him, "Today I declare to the LORD your God that I have come into the land that the LORD swore to our ancestors to give us." ⁴When the priest takes the basket from your hand and sets it down before the altar of the LORD your God, ⁵you shall make this response before the LORD your God: "A wandering Aramean was my ancestor; he went down into Egypt and lived there as an alien, few in number, and there he became a great nation, mighty and populous. ⁶When the Egyptians treated us harshly and afflicted us, by imposing hard labor on us, ⁷we cried to the LORD, the God of our ancestors; the LORD heard our voice and saw our affliction, our toil, and our oppression. ⁸The LORD brought us out of Egypt with a mighty hand and an outstretched arm, with a terrifying display of power, and with signs and wonders; ⁹and he brought us into this place and gave us this land, a land flowing with milk and honey. ¹⁰So now I bring the first of the fruit of the ground that you, O LORD, have given me." You shall set it down before the LORD your God and bow down before the LORD your God. ¹¹Then you, together with the Levites and the aliens who reside among you, shall celebrate with all the bounty that the LORD your God has given to you and to your house.

12 When you have finished paying all the tithe of your produce in the third year (which is the year of the tithe), giving it to the Levites, the aliens, the orphans, and the widows, so that they may eat their fill within your towns, ¹³then you shall say before the LORD your God: "I have removed the sacred portion from the house, and I have given it to the Levites, the resident aliens, the orphans, and the widows, in accordance with your entire command-

ment that you commanded me; I have neither transgressed nor forgotten any of your commandments: ¹⁴I have not eaten of it while in mourning; I have not removed any of it while I was unclean; and I have not offered any of it to the dead. I have obeyed the LORD my God, doing just as you commanded me. ¹⁵Look down from your holy habitation, from heaven, and bless your people Israel and the ground that you have given us, as you swore to our ancestors—a land flowing with milk and honey."

Concluding Exhortation

16 This very day the LORD your God is commanding you to observe these statutes and ordinances; so observe them diligently with all your heart and with all your soul. ¹⁷Today you have obtained the LORD's agreement: to be your God; and for you to walk in his ways, to keep his statutes, his commandments, and his ordinances, and to obey him. ¹⁸Today the LORD has obtained your agreement: to be his treasured people, as he promised you, and to keep his commandments; ¹⁹for him to set you high above all nations that he has made, in praise and in fame and in honor; and for you to be a people holy to the LORD your God, as he promised.

The Inscribed Stones and Altar on Mount Ebal

27 Then Moses and the elders of Israel charged all the people as follows: Keep the entire commandment that I am commanding you today. ²On the day that you cross over the Jordan into the land that the LORD your God is giving you, you shall set up large stones and cover them with plaster. ³You shall write on them all the words of this law when you have crossed over, to enter the land that the LORD your God is giving you, a land flowing with milk and honey, as the LORD, the God of your ancestors, promised you. ⁴So when you have crossed over the Jordan, you shall set up these stones, about which I am commanding you today, on Mount Ebal, and you shall cover them with plaster. ⁵And you shall build an altar there to the LORD your God, an altar of stones on which you have not used an iron tool. ⁶You must build the altar of the LORD your God of unhewn*ᵉ* stones. Then

---

ᵉ Heb whole

offer up burnt offerings on it to the LORD your God, 7make sacrifices of well-being, and eat them there, rejoicing before the LORD your God. 8You shall write on the stones all the words of this law very clearly.

9 Then Moses and the levitical priests spoke to all Israel, saying: Keep silence and hear, O Israel! This very day you have become the people of the LORD your God. 10Therefore obey the LORD your God, observing his commandments and his statutes that I am commanding you today.

Twelve Curses

11 The same day Moses charged the people as follows: 12When you have crossed over the Jordan, these shall stand on Mount Gerizim for the blessing of the people: Simeon, Levi, Judah, Issachar, Joseph, and Benjamin. 13And these shall stand on Mount Ebal for the curse: Reuben, Gad, Asher, Zebulun, Dan, and Naphtali. 14Then the Levites shall declare in a loud voice to all the Israelites:

15 "Cursed be anyone who makes an idol or casts an image, anything abhorrent to the LORD, the work of an artisan, and sets it up in secret." All the people shall respond, saying, "Amen!"

16 "Cursed be anyone who dishonors father or mother." All the people shall say, "Amen!"

17 "Cursed be anyone who moves a neighbor's boundary marker." All the people shall say, "Amen!"

18 "Cursed be anyone who misleads a blind person on the road." All the people shall say, "Amen!"

19 "Cursed be anyone who deprives the alien, the orphan, and the widow of justice." All the people shall say, "Amen!"

20 "Cursed be anyone who lies with his father's wife, because he has violated his father's rights."f All the people shall say, "Amen!"

21 "Cursed be anyone who lies with any animal." All the people shall say, "Amen!"

22 "Cursed be anyone who lies with his sister, whether the daughter of his father or the daughter of his mother." All the people shall say, "Amen!"

23 "Cursed be anyone who lies with his mother-in-law." All the people shall say, "Amen!"

24 "Cursed be anyone who strikes

down a neighbor in secret." All the people shall say, "Amen!"

25 "Cursed be anyone who takes a bribe to shed innocent blood." All the people shall say, "Amen!"

26 "Cursed be anyone who does not uphold the words of this law by observing them." All the people shall say, "Amen!"

Blessings for Obedience

28 If you will only obey the LORD your God, by diligently observing all his commandments that I am commanding you today, the LORD your God will set you high above all the nations of the earth; 2all these blessings shall come upon you and overtake you, if you obey the LORD your God:

3 Blessed shall you be in the city, and blessed shall you be in the field.

4 Blessed shall be the fruit of your womb, the fruit of your ground, and the fruit of your livestock, both the increase of your cattle and the issue of your flock.

5 Blessed shall be your basket and your kneading bowl.

6 Blessed shall you be when you come in, and blessed shall you be when you go out.

7 The LORD will cause your enemies who rise against you to be defeated before you; they shall come out against you one way, and flee before you seven ways. 8The LORD will command the blessing upon you in your barns, and in all that you undertake; he will bless you in the land that the LORD your God is giving you. 9The LORD will establish you as his holy people, as he has sworn to you, if you keep the commandments of the LORD your God and walk in his ways. 10All the peoples of the earth shall see that you are called by the name of the LORD, and they shall be afraid of you. 11The LORD will make you abound in prosperity, in the fruit of your womb, in the fruit of your livestock, and in the fruit of your ground in the land that the LORD swore to your ancestors to give you. 12The LORD will open for you his rich storehouse, the heavens, to give the rain of your land in its season and to bless all your undertakings. You will lend to many nations, but you will not borrow. 13The LORD will make you the head, and not the tail; you shall be only at the top, and not at the bottom—if you obey the command-

f Heb *uncovered his father's skirt*

ments of the LORD your God, which I am commanding you today, by diligently observing them, [14]and if you do not turn aside from any of the words that I am commanding you today, either to the right or to the left, following other gods to serve them.

Warnings against Disobedience

15 But if you will not obey the LORD your God by diligently observing all his commandments and decrees, which I am commanding you today, then all these curses shall come upon you and overtake you:

16 Cursed shall you be in the city, and cursed shall you be in the field.

17 Cursed shall be your basket and your kneading bowl.

18 Cursed shall be the fruit of your womb, the fruit of your ground, the increase of your cattle and the issue of your flock.

19 Cursed shall you be when you come

$\mathcal{B}$lessings

MONDAY

Scripture Reading
for Today:
Deuteronomy 28.1–6

Verse for Today:
Deuteronomy 28.6

In A Celtic Way of Prayer Esther de Waal includes several journey blessings spoken by mothers as a son or daughter in the Western Isles was leaving home.

And then comes this most lovely blessing of all, that from a mother to her children. It is full of warmth and tenderness, and shows her most natural desire for the protection and presence of God in their lives.

The joy of God in thy face,
　Joy to all who see thee,
The circle of God around thy neck,
　　Angels of God shielding thee,
　　Angels of God shielding thee.
Joy of night and day be thine,
Joy of sun and moon be thine,
Joy of men and women be thine,
　　Each land and sea thou goest,
　　Each land and sea thou goest.

Be every season happy for thee,
Be every season bright for thee,
Be every season glad for thee,
　　And the Son of Mary Virgin at peace with thee,
　　The Son of Mary Virgin at peace with thee.
Be thine the compassing of the God of life,
Be thine the compassing of the Christ of love,
Be thine the compassing of the Spirit of Grace,
To befriend thee and to aid thee,
Thou beloved one of my heart.

—ESTHER DE WAAL

Go to page 225 for your next devotional reading.

in, and cursed shall you be when you go out.

20 The LORD will send upon you disaster, panic, and frustration in everything you attempt to do, until you are destroyed and perish quickly, on account of the evil of your deeds, because you have forsaken me. 21The LORD will make the pestilence cling to you until it has consumed you off the land that you are entering to possess. 22The LORD will afflict you with consumption, fever, inflammation, with fiery heat and drought, and with blight and mildew; they shall pursue you until you perish. 23The sky over your head shall be bronze, and the earth under you iron. 24The LORD will change the rain of your land into powder, and only dust shall come down upon you from the sky until you are destroyed.

25 The LORD will cause you to be defeated before your enemies; you shall go out against them one way and flee before them seven ways. You shall become an object of horror to all the kingdoms of the earth. 26Your corpses shall be food for every bird of the air and animal of the earth, and there shall be no one to frighten them away. 27The LORD will afflict you with the boils of Egypt, with ulcers, scurvy, and itch, of which you cannot be healed. 28The LORD will afflict you with madness, blindness, and confusion of mind; 29you shall grope about at noon as blind people grope in darkness, but you shall be unable to find your way; and you shall be continually abused and robbed, without anyone to help. 30You shall become engaged to a woman, but another man shall lie with her. You shall build a house, but not live in it. You shall plant a vineyard, but not enjoy its fruit. 31Your ox shall be butchered before your eyes, but you shall not eat of it. Your donkey shall be stolen in front of you, and shall not be restored to you. Your sheep shall be given to your enemies, without anyone to help you. 32Your sons and daughters shall be given to another people, while you look on; you will strain your eyes looking for them all day but be powerless to do anything. 33A people whom you do not know shall eat up the fruit of your ground and of all your labors; you shall be continually abused and crushed, 34and driven mad by the sight that your eyes shall see. 35The LORD will strike you on the knees and on the legs with grievous boils of which you can-

not be healed, from the sole of your foot to the crown of your head. 36The LORD will bring you, and the king whom you set over you, to a nation that neither you nor your ancestors have known, where you shall serve other gods, of wood and stone. 37You shall become an object of horror, a proverb, and a byword among all the peoples where the LORD will lead you.

38 You shall carry much seed into the field but shall gather little in, for the locust shall consume it. 39You shall plant vineyards and dress them, but you shall neither drink the wine nor gather the grapes, for the worm shall eat them. 40You shall have olive trees throughout all your territory, but you shall not anoint yourself with the oil, for your olives shall drop off. 41You shall have sons and daughters, but they shall not remain yours, for they shall go into captivity. 42All your trees and the fruit of your ground the cicada shall take over. 43Aliens residing among you shall ascend above you higher and higher, while you shall descend lower and lower. 44They shall lend to you but you shall not lend to them; they shall be the head and you shall be the tail.

45 All these curses shall come upon you, pursuing and overtaking you until you are destroyed, because you did not obey the LORD your God, by observing the commandments and the decrees that he commanded you. 46They shall be among you and your descendants as a sign and a portent forever.

47 Because you did not serve the LORD your God joyfully and with gladness of heart for the abundance of everything, 48therefore you shall serve your enemies whom the LORD will send against you, in hunger and thirst, in nakedness and lack of everything. He will put an iron yoke on your neck until he has destroyed you. 49The LORD will bring a nation from far away, from the end of the earth, to swoop down on you like an eagle, a nation whose language you do not understand, 50a grim-faced nation showing no respect to the old or favor to the young. 51It shall consume the fruit of your livestock and the fruit of your ground until you are destroyed, leaving you neither grain, wine, and oil, nor the increase of your cattle and the issue of your flock, until it has made you perish. 52It shall besiege you in all your towns until your high and fortified walls, in which you trusted, come down

throughout your land; it shall besiege you in all your towns throughout the land that the LORD your God has given you. 53In the desperate straits to which the enemy siege reduces you, you will eat the fruit of your womb, the flesh of your own sons and daughters whom the LORD your God has given you. 54Even the most refined and gentle of men among you will begrudge food to his own brother, to the wife whom he embraces, and to the last of his remaining children, 55giving to none of them any of the flesh of his children whom he is eating, because nothing else remains to him, in the desperate straits to which the enemy siege will reduce you in all your towns. 56She who is the most refined and gentle among you, so gentle and refined that she does not venture to set the sole of her foot on the ground, will begrudge food to the husband whom she embraces, to her own son, and to her own daughter, 57begrudging even the afterbirth that comes out from between her thighs, and the children that she bears, because she is eating them in secret for lack of anything else, in the desperate straits to which the enemy siege will reduce you in your towns.

58 If you do not diligently observe all the words of this law that are written in this book, fearing this glorious and awesome name, the LORD your God, 59then the LORD will overwhelm both you and your offspring with severe and lasting afflictions and grievous and lasting maladies. 60He will bring back upon you all the diseases of Egypt, of which you were in dread, and they shall cling to you. 61Every other malady and affliction, even though not recorded in the book of this law, the LORD will inflict on you until you are destroyed. 62Although once you were as numerous as the stars in heaven, you shall be left few in number, because you did not obey the LORD your God. 63And just as the LORD took delight in making you prosperous and numerous, so the LORD will take delight in bringing you to ruin and destruction; you shall be plucked off the land that you are entering to possess. 64The LORD will scatter you among all peoples, from one end of the earth to the other; and there you shall serve other gods, of wood and stone, which neither you nor your ancestors have known. 65Among those nations you shall find no ease, no resting place for the sole of your foot.

There the LORD will give you a trembling heart, failing eyes, and a languishing spirit. 66Your life shall hang in doubt before you; night and day you shall be in dread, with no assurance of your life. 67In the morning you shall say, "If only it were evening!" and at evening you shall say, "If only it were morning!"—because of the dread that your heart shall feel and the sights that your eyes shall see. 68The LORD will bring you back in ships to Egypt, by a route that I promised you would never see again; and there you shall offer yourselves for sale to your enemies as male and female slaves, but there will be no buyer.

29 8These are the words of the covenant that the LORD commanded Moses to make with the Israelites in the land of Moab, in addition to the covenant that he had made with them at Horeb.

The Covenant Renewed in Moab

2hMoses summoned all Israel and said to them: You have seen all that the LORD did before your eyes in the land of Egypt, to Pharaoh and to all his servants and to all his land, 3the great trials that your eyes saw, the signs, and those great wonders. 4But to this day the LORD has not given you a mind to understand, or eyes to see, or ears to hear. 5I have led you forty years in the wilderness. The clothes on your back have not worn out, and the sandals on your feet have not worn out; 6you have not eaten bread, and you have not drunk wine or strong drink—so that you may know that I am the LORD your God. 7When you came to this place, King Sihon of Heshbon and King Og of Bashan came out against us for battle, but we defeated them. 8We took their land and gave it as an inheritance to the Reubenites, the Gadites, and the half-tribe of Manasseh. 9Therefore diligently observe the words of this covenant, in order that you may succeed[i] in everything that you do.

10 You stand assembled today, all of you, before the LORD your God—the leaders of your tribes,[j] your elders, and your officials, all the men of Israel, 11your children, your women, and the aliens who are in your camp, both those who cut your wood and those who draw your water— 12to enter into the covenant of the LORD your God, sworn by an oath, which the

g Ch 28.69 in Heb *h* Ch 29.1 in Heb *i* Or *deal wisely* *j* Gk Syr: Heb *your leaders, your tribes*

Lord your God is making with you today; [13]in order that he may establish you today as his people, and that he may be your God, as he promised you and as he swore to your ancestors, to Abraham, to Isaac, and to Jacob. [14]I am making this covenant, sworn by an oath, not only with you who stand here with us today before the Lord our God, [15]but also with those who are not here with us today. [16]You know how we lived in the land of Egypt, and how we came through the midst of the nations through which you passed. [17]You have seen their detestable things, the filthy idols of wood and stone, of silver and gold, that were among them. [18]It may be that there is among you a man or woman, or a family or tribe, whose heart is already turning away from the Lord our God to serve the gods of those nations. It may be that there is among you a root sprouting poisonous and bitter growth. [19]All who hear the words of this oath and bless themselves, thinking in their hearts, "We are safe even though we go our own stubborn ways" (thus bringing disaster on moist and dry alike)[k]— [20]the Lord will be unwilling to pardon them, for the Lord's anger and passion will smoke against them. All the curses written in this book will descend on them, and the Lord will blot out their names from under heaven. [21]The Lord will single them out from all the tribes of Israel for calamity, in accordance with all the curses of the covenant written in this book of the law. [22]The next generation, your children who rise up after you, as well as the foreigner who comes from a distant country, will see the devastation of that land and the afflictions with which the Lord has afflicted it— [23]all its soil burned out by sulfur and salt, nothing planted, nothing sprouting, unable to support any vegetation, like the destruction of Sodom and Gomorrah, Admah and Zeboiim, which the Lord destroyed in his fierce anger— [24]they and indeed all the nations will wonder, "Why has the Lord done thus to this land? What caused this great display of anger?" [25]They will conclude, "It is because they abandoned the covenant of the Lord, the God of their ancestors, which he made with them when he brought them out of the land of Egypt. [26]They turned and served other gods, worshiping them, gods whom they had not known and whom he had not allotted to them; [27]so the anger of the Lord was kindled against that land, bringing on it every curse written in this book. [28]The Lord uprooted them from their land in anger, fury, and great wrath, and cast them into another land, as is now the case." [29]The secret things belong to the Lord our God, but the revealed things belong to us and to our children forever, to observe all the words of this law.

God's Fidelity Assured

30 When all these things have happened to you, the blessings and the curses that I have set before you, if you call them to mind among all the nations where the Lord your God has driven you, [2]and return to the Lord your God, and you and your children obey him with all your heart and with all your soul, just as I am commanding you today, [3]then the Lord your God will restore your fortunes and have compassion on you, gathering you again from all the peoples among whom the Lord your God has scattered you. [4]Even if you are exiled to the ends of the world,[l] from there the Lord your God will gather you, and from there he will bring you back. [5]The Lord your God will bring you into the land that your ancestors possessed, and you will possess it; he will make you more prosperous and numerous than your ancestors.

6 Moreover, the Lord your God will circumcise your heart and the heart of your descendants, so that you will love the Lord your God with all your heart and with all your soul, in order that you may live. [7]The Lord your God will put all these curses on your enemies and on the adversaries who took advantage of you. [8]Then you shall again obey the Lord, observing all his commandments that I am commanding you today, [9]and the Lord your God will make you abundantly prosperous in all your undertakings, in the fruit of your body, in the fruit of your livestock, and in the fruit of your soil. For the Lord will again take delight in prospering you, just as he delighted in prospering your ancestors, [10]when you obey the Lord your God by observing his commandments and decrees that are written in this book of the law, because you turn to the Lord your God with all your heart and with all your soul.

k Meaning of Heb uncertain   l Heb of heaven

Exhortation to Choose Life

11 Surely, this commandment that I am commanding you today is not too hard for you, nor is it too far away. 12It is not in heaven, that you should say, "Who will go up to heaven for us, and get it for us so that we may hear it and observe it?" 13Neither is it beyond the sea, that you should say, "Who will cross to the other side of the sea for us, and get it for us so that we may hear it and observe it?" 14No, the word is very near to you; it is in your mouth and in your heart for you to observe.

15 See, I have set before you today life and prosperity, death and adversity. 16If you obey the commandments of the LORD your God[m] that I am commanding you today, by loving the LORD your God, walking in his ways, and observing his commandments, decrees, and ordinances, then you shall live and become numerous, and the LORD your God will bless you in the land that you are entering to possess. 17But if your heart turns away and you do not hear, but are led astray to bow down to other gods and serve them, 18I declare to you today that you shall perish; you shall not live long in the land that you are crossing the Jordan to enter and possess. 19I call heaven and earth to witness against you today that I have set before you life and death, blessings and curses. Choose life so that you and your descendants may live, 20loving the LORD your God, obeying him, and holding fast to him; for that means life to you and length of days, so that you may live in the land that the LORD swore to give to your ancestors, to Abraham, to Isaac, and to Jacob.

Joshua Becomes Moses' Successor

31 When Moses had finished speaking all[n] these words to all Israel, 2he said to them: "I am now one hundred twenty years old. I am no longer able to get about, and the LORD has told me, 'You shall not cross over this Jordan.' 3The LORD your God himself will cross over before you. He will destroy these nations before you, and you shall dispossess them. Joshua also will cross over before you, as the LORD promised. 4The LORD will do to them as he did to Sihon and Og, the kings of the Amorites, and to their land, when he destroyed them. 5The LORD will give them over to you and you shall deal with them in full accord with the command that I have given to you. 6Be strong and bold; have no fear or dread of them, because it is the LORD your God who goes with you; he will not fail you or forsake you."

7 Then Moses summoned Joshua and said to him in the sight of all Israel: "Be strong and bold, for you are the one who will go with this people into the land that the LORD has sworn to their ancestors to give them; and you will put them in possession of it. 8It is the LORD who goes before you. He will be with you; he will not fail you or forsake you. Do not fear or be dismayed."

The Law to Be Read Every Seventh Year

9 Then Moses wrote down this law, and gave it to the priests, the sons of Levi, who carried the ark of the covenant of the LORD, and to all the elders of Israel. 10Moses commanded them: "Every seventh year, in the scheduled year of remission, during the festival of booths,[o] 11when all Israel comes to appear before the LORD your God at the place that he will choose, you shall read this law before all Israel in their hearing. 12Assemble the people—men, women, and children, as well as the aliens residing in your towns—so that they may hear and learn to fear the LORD your God and to observe diligently all the words of this law, 13and so that their children, who have not known it, may hear and learn to fear the LORD your God, as long as you live in the land that you are crossing over the Jordan to possess."

Moses and Joshua Receive God's Charge

14 The LORD said to Moses, "Your time to die is near; call Joshua and present yourselves in the tent of meeting, so that I may commission him." So Moses and Joshua went and presented themselves in the tent of meeting, 15and the LORD appeared at the tent in a pillar of cloud; the pillar of cloud stood at the entrance to the tent.

16 The LORD said to Moses, "Soon you will lie down with your ancestors. Then this people will begin to prostitute themselves to the foreign gods in their midst, the gods of the land into which they are

m Gk: Heb lacks *If you obey the commandments of the LORD your God*   n Q Ms Gk: MT *Moses went and spoke*   o Or *tabernacles;* Heb *succoth*

going; they will forsake me, breaking my covenant that I have made with them. ¹⁷My anger will be kindled against them in that day. I will forsake them and hide my face from them; they will become easy prey, and many terrible troubles will come upon them. In that day they will say, 'Have not these troubles come upon us because our God is not in our midst?' ¹⁸On that day I will surely hide my face on account of all the evil they have done by turning to other gods. ¹⁹Now therefore write this song, and teach it to the Israelites; put it in their mouths, in order that this song may be a witness for me against the Israelites. ²⁰For when I have brought them into the land flowing with milk and honey, which I promised on oath to their ancestors, and they have eaten their fill and grown fat, they will turn to other gods and serve them, despising me and breaking my covenant. ²¹And when many terrible troubles come upon them, this song will confront them as a witness, because it will not be lost from the mouths of their descendants. For I know what they are inclined to do even now, before I have brought them into the land that I promised them on oath." ²²That very day Moses wrote this song and taught it to the Israelites.

23 Then the LORD commissioned Joshua son of Nun and said, "Be strong and bold, for you shall bring the Israelites into the land that I promised them; I will be with you."

24 When Moses had finished writing down in a book the words of this law to the very end, ²⁵Moses commanded the Levites who carried the ark of the covenant of the LORD, saying, ²⁶"Take this book of the law and put it beside the ark of the covenant of the LORD your God; let it remain there as a witness against you. ²⁷For I know well how rebellious and stubborn you are. If you already have been so rebellious toward the LORD while I am still alive among you, how much more after my death! ²⁸Assemble to me all the elders of your tribes and your officials, so that I may recite these words in their hearing and call heaven and earth to witness against them. ²⁹For I know that after my death you will surely act corruptly, turning aside from the way that I have commanded you. In time to come trouble will befall you, because you will do what is evil in the sight of the LORD, provoking him to anger through the work of your hands."

The Song of Moses

30 Then Moses recited the words of this song, to the very end, in the hearing of the whole assembly of Israel:

32 Give ear, O heavens, and I will speak;
 let the earth hear the words of my mouth.
² May my teaching drop like the rain,
 my speech condense like the dew;
like gentle rain on grass,
 like showers on new growth.
³ For I will proclaim the name of the LORD;
 ascribe greatness to our God!

⁴ The Rock, his work is perfect,
 and all his ways are just.
A faithful God, without deceit,
 just and upright is he;
⁵ yet his degenerate children have dealt falsely with him, *p*
 a perverse and crooked generation.
⁶ Do you thus repay the LORD,
 O foolish and senseless people?
Is not he your father, who created you,
 who made you and established you?
⁷ Remember the days of old,
 consider the years long past;
ask your father, and he will inform you;
 your elders, and they will tell you.
⁸ When the Most High*q* apportioned the nations,
 when he divided humankind,
he fixed the boundaries of the peoples
 according to the number of the gods;*r*
⁹ the LORD's own portion was his people,
 Jacob his allotted share.

¹⁰ He sustained*s* him in a desert land,
 in a howling wilderness waste;
he shielded him, cared for him,
 guarded him as the apple of his eye.

p Meaning of Heb uncertain   *q* Traditional rendering of Heb *Elyon*   *r* Q Ms Compare Gk Tg: MT *the Israelites*   *s* Sam Gk Compare Tg: MT *found*

11 As an eagle stirs up its nest,
    and hovers over its young;
  as it spreads its wings, takes them
      up,
    and bears them aloft on its
      pinions,
12 the LORD alone guided him;
    no foreign god was with him.
13 He set him atop the heights of the
      land,
    and fed him with*t* produce of
      the field;
  he nursed him with honey from the
      crags,
    with oil from flinty rock;
14 curds from the herd, and milk from
      the flock,
    with fat of lambs and rams;
  Bashan bulls and goats,
    together with the choicest wheat—
    you drank fine wine from the
      blood of grapes.
15 Jacob ate his fill;*u*
    Jeshurun grew fat, and kicked.
    You grew fat, bloated, and gorged!
  He abandoned God who made him,
    and scoffed at the Rock of his
      salvation.
16 They made him jealous with strange
      gods,
    with abhorrent things they
      provoked him.
17 They sacrificed to demons, not God,
    to deities they had never known,
  to new ones recently arrived,
    whom your ancestors had not
      feared.
18 You were unmindful of the Rock
    that bore you;*v*
    you forgot the God who gave you
      birth.

19 The LORD saw it, and was jealous;*w*
    he spurned*x* his sons and
      daughters.
20 He said: I will hide my face from
      them,
    I will see what their end will be;
  for they are a perverse generation,
    children in whom there is no
      faithfulness.
21 They made me jealous with what is
      no god,
    provoked me with their idols.
  So I will make them jealous with
    what is no people,
    provoke them with a foolish
      nation.

22 For a fire is kindled by my anger,
    and burns to the depths of Sheol;
  it devours the earth and its increase,
    and sets on fire the foundations of
      the mountains.
23 I will heap disasters upon them,
    spend my arrows against them:
24 wasting hunger,
    burning consumption,
    bitter pestilence.
  The teeth of beasts I will send
    against them,
    with venom of things crawling in
      the dust.
25 In the street the sword shall bereave,
    and in the chambers terror,
  for young man and woman alike,
    nursing child and old gray head.
26 I thought to scatter them*y*
    and blot out the memory of them
      from humankind;
27 but I feared provocation by the
      enemy,
    for their adversaries might
      misunderstand
  and say, "Our hand is triumphant;
    it was not the LORD who did all
      this."

28 They are a nation void of sense;
    there is no understanding in
      them.
29 If they were wise, they would
      understand this;
    they would discern what the end
      would be.
30 How could one have routed a
      thousand,
    and two put a myriad to flight,
  unless their Rock had sold them,
    the LORD had given them up?
31 Indeed their rock is not like our
      Rock;
    our enemies are fools.*y*
32 Their vine comes from the vinestock
      of Sodom,
    from the vineyards of Gomorrah;
  their grapes are grapes of poison,
    their clusters are bitter;
33 their wine is the poison of serpents,
    the cruel venom of asps.

---

t Sam Gk Syr Tg: MT *he ate*   *u* Q Mss Sam Gk:
MT lacks *Jacob ate his fill*   *v* Or *that begot you*
w Q Mss Gk: MT lacks *was jealous*   *x* Cn: Heb *he
spurned because of provocation*   *y* Gk: Meaning of
Heb uncertain

34 Is not this laid up in store with me,
     sealed up in my treasuries?
35 Vengeance is mine, and recompense,
     for the time when their foot shall
          slip;
   because the day of their calamity is
          at hand,
     their doom comes swiftly.

36 Indeed the LORD will vindicate his
          people,
     have compassion on his servants,
   when he sees that their power is
          gone,
     neither bond nor free remaining.
37 Then he will say: Where are their
          gods,
     the rock in which they took
          refuge,
38 who ate the fat of their sacrifices,
     and drank the wine of their
          libations?
   Let them rise up and help you,
     let them be your protection!

39 See now that I, even I, am he;
     there is no god besides me.
   I kill and I make alive;
     I wound and I heal;
     and no one can deliver from my
          hand.
40 For I lift up my hand to heaven,
     and swear: As I live forever,
41 when I whet my flashing sword,
     and my hand takes hold on
          judgment;
   I will take vengeance on my
          adversaries,
     and will repay those who hate me.
42 I will make my arrows drunk with
          blood,
     and my sword shall devour
          flesh—
   with the blood of the slain and the
          captives,
     from the long-haired enemy.

43 Praise, O heavens,[z] his people,
     worship him, all you gods![a]
   For he will avenge the blood of his
          children,[b]
     and take vengeance on his
          adversaries;
   he will repay those who hate him,[a]
     and cleanse the land for his
          people.[c]
44 Moses came and recited all the
words of this song in the hearing of the

people, he and Joshua[d] son of Nun.
45When Moses had finished reciting all
these words to all Israel, 46he said to
them: "Take to heart all the words that I
am giving in witness against you today;
give them as a command to your children,
so that they may diligently observe all the
words of this law. 47This is no trifling
matter for you, but rather your very life;
through it you may live long in the land
that you are crossing over the Jordan to
possess."

Moses' Death Foretold

48 On that very day the LORD addressed
Moses as follows: 49"Ascend this mountain of the Abarim, Mount Nebo, which is
in the land of Moab, across from Jericho,
and view the land of Canaan, which I am
giving to the Israelites for a possession;
50you shall die there on the mountain that
you ascend and shall be gathered to your
kin, as your brother Aaron died on Mount
Hor and was gathered to his kin; 51be-
cause both of you broke faith with me
among the Israelites at the waters of
Meribath-kadesh in the wilderness of Zin,
by failing to maintain my holiness among
the Israelites. 52Although you may view
the land from a distance, you shall not
enter it—the land that I am giving to the
Israelites."

Moses' Final Blessing on Israel

33 This is the blessing with which
Moses, the man of God, blessed
the Israelites before his death. 2He said:
   The LORD came from Sinai,
     and dawned from Seir upon us;[e]
   he shone forth from Mount Paran.
   With him were myriads of holy
          ones;[f]
     at his right, a host of his own.[g]
3 Indeed, O favorite among[h] peoples,
     all his holy ones were in your
          charge;
   they marched at your heels,
     accepted direction from you.
4 Moses charged us with the law,

z Q Ms Gk: MT *nations*   a Q Ms Gk: MT lacks
this line   b Q Ms Gk: MT *his servants*   c Q Ms
Sam Gk Vg: MT *his land his people*   d Sam Gk
Syr Vg: MT *Hoshea*   e Gk Syr Vg Compare Tg:
Heb *upon them*   f Cn Compare Gk Sam Syr Vg:
MT *He came from Ribeboth-kodesh*,   g Cn
Compare Gk: meaning of Heb uncertain   h Or
O lover of the

as a possession for the assembly
of Jacob.
5 There arose a king in Jeshurun,
when the leaders of the people
assembled—
the united tribes of Israel.

6 May Reuben live, and not die out,
even though his numbers are few.

7 And this he said of Judah:
O LORD, give heed to Judah,
and bring him to his people;
strengthen his hands for him,[i]
and be a help against his
adversaries.

8 And of Levi he said:
Give to Levi[j] your Thummim,
and your Urim to your loyal one,
whom you tested at Massah,
with whom you contended at the
waters of Meribah;
9 who said of his father and mother,
"I regard them not";
he ignored his kin,
and did not acknowledge his
children.
For they observed your word,
and kept your covenant.
10 They teach Jacob your ordinances,
and Israel your law;
they place incense before you,
and whole burnt offerings on your
altar.
11 Bless, O LORD, his substance,
and accept the work of his hands;
crush the loins of his adversaries,
of those that hate him, so that
they do not rise again.

12 Of Benjamin he said:
The beloved of the LORD rests in
safety—
the High God[k] surrounds him all
day long—
the beloved[l] rests between his
shoulders.

13 And of Joseph he said:
Blessed by the LORD be his land,
with the choice gifts of heaven
above,
and of the deep that lies beneath;
14 with the choice fruits of the sun,
and the rich yield of the months;
15 with the finest produce of the
ancient mountains,

and the abundance of the
everlasting hills;
16 with the choice gifts of the earth and
its fullness,
and the favor of the one who
dwells on Sinai.[m]
Let these come on the head of
Joseph,
on the brow of the prince among
his brothers.
17 A firstborn[n] bull—majesty is his!
His horns are the horns of a wild
ox;
with them he gores the peoples,
driving them to[o] the ends of the
earth;
such are the myriads of Ephraim,
such the thousands of Manasseh.

18 And of Zebulun he said:
Rejoice, Zebulun, in your going out;
and Issachar, in your tents.
19 They call peoples to the mountain;
there they offer the right sacrifices;
for they suck the affluence of the
seas
and the hidden treasures of the
sand.

20 And of Gad he said:
Blessed be the enlargement of Gad!
Gad lives like a lion;
he tears at arm and scalp.
21 He chose the best for himself,
for there a commander's allotment
was reserved;
he came at the head of the people,
he executed the justice of the
LORD,
and his ordinances for Israel.

22 And of Dan he said:
Dan is a lion's whelp
that leaps forth from Bashan.

23 And of Naphtali he said:
O Naphtali, sated with favor,
full of the blessing of the LORD,
possess the west and the south.

24 And of Asher he said:
Most blessed of sons be Asher;

i Cn: Heb *with his hands he contended*   j Q Ms
Gk: MT lacks *Give to Levi*   k Heb *above him*
l Heb *he*   m Cn: Heb *in the bush*   n Q Ms Gk
Syr Vg: MT *His firstborn*   o Cn: Heb *the peoples,
together*

may he be the favorite of his
brothers,
and may he dip his foot in oil.
25 Your bars are iron and bronze;
and as your days, so is your
strength.

26 There is none like God, O Jeshurun,
who rides through the heavens to
your help,
majestic through the skies.
27 He subdues the ancient gods, *p*
shatters*q* the forces of old;*r*
he drove out the enemy before you,
and said, "Destroy!"
28 So Israel lives in safety,
untroubled is Jacob's abode*s*
in a land of grain and wine,
where the heavens drop down
dew.
29 Happy are you, O Israel! Who is like
you,
a people saved by the LORD,
the shield of your help,
and the sword of your triumph!
Your enemies shall come fawning to
you,
and you shall tread on their
backs.

Moses Dies and Is Buried in the Land of Moab

34 Then Moses went up from the plains of Moab to Mount Nebo, to the top of Pisgah, which is opposite Jericho, and the LORD showed him the whole land: Gilead as far as Dan, 2all Naphtali, the land of Ephraim and Manasseh, all the land of Judah as far as the Western Sea, 3the Negeb, and the Plain—that is, the valley of Jericho, the city of palm trees—as far as Zoar. 4The LORD said to him, "This is the land of which I swore to Abraham, to Isaac, and to Jacob, saying, 'I will give it to your descendants'; I have let you see it with your eyes, but you shall not cross over there." 5Then Moses, the servant of the LORD, died there in the land of Moab, at the LORD's command. 6He was buried in a valley in the land of Moab, opposite Beth-peor, but no one knows his burial place to this day. 7Moses was one hundred twenty years old when he died; his sight was unimpaired and his vigor had not abated. 8The Israelites wept for Moses in the plains of Moab thirty days; then the period of mourning for Moses was ended.

9 Joshua son of Nun was full of the spirit of wisdom, because Moses had laid his hands on him; and the Israelites obeyed him, doing as the LORD had commanded Moses.

10 Never since has there arisen a prophet in Israel like Moses, whom the LORD knew face to face. 11He was unequaled for all the signs and wonders that the LORD sent him to perform in the land of Egypt, against Pharaoh and all his servants and his entire land, 12and for all the mighty deeds and all the terrifying displays of power that Moses performed in the sight of all Israel.

p Or *The eternal God is a dwelling place*   q Cn:
Heb *from underneath*   r Or *the everlasting arms*
s Or *fountain*

Joshua

Though Moses led the Israelites out of Egypt, he was unable to lead them into the promised land. That honor was reserved for his military aide, Joshua, whose name is the same as Jesus, both of which mean "the LORD is salvation."

Just as the waters of the sea had miraculously parted 40 years earlier to allow the Israelites to escape their Egyptian pursuers, the book of Joshua describes how the waters of the Jordan River parted in order to enable the Israelites to cross over. Only now, after their years in the wilderness, they have become the pursuers rather than the pursued.

Joshua is a book that describes the conquest of the promised land. It begins with the story of Rahab, the prostitute from Jericho who survived the destruction of her city. It ends with the death of Joshua.

Though we may shudder at some of its grisly details, we can read the book of Joshua with the knowledge that it represents a far larger reality. Today, the church is not involved in physical warfare but in a profound spiritual battle. The conquest of the promised land by Joshua and the Israelites points to the eventual spiritual conquest of the entire world by Jesus and his followers. Then as now, faith and obedience are essential weapons for our struggle.

God's Commission to Joshua

1 After the death of Moses the servant of the LORD, the LORD spoke to Joshua son of Nun, Moses' assistant, saying, 2 "My servant Moses is dead. Now proceed to cross the Jordan, you and all this people, into the land that I am giving to them, to the Israelites. 3 Every place that the sole of your foot will tread upon I have given to you, as I promised to Moses. 4 From the wilderness and the Lebanon as far as the great river, the river Euphrates, all the land of the Hittites, to the Great Sea in the west shall be your territory. 5 No one shall be able to stand against you all the days of your life. As I was with Moses, so I will be with you; I will not fail you or forsake you. 6 Be strong and courageous; for you shall put this people in possession of the land that I swore to their ancestors to give them. 7 Only be strong and very courageous, being careful to act in accordance with all the law that my servant Moses commanded you; do not turn

from it to the right hand or to the left, so that you may be successful wherever you go. 8This book of the law shall not depart out of your mouth; you shall meditate on it day and night, so that you may be careful to act in accordance with all that is written in it. For then you shall make your way prosperous, and then you shall be successful. 9I hereby command you: Be strong and courageous; do not be frightened or dismayed, for the LORD your God is with you wherever you go."

Preparations for the Invasion

10 Then Joshua commanded the officers of the people, 11"Pass through the camp, and command the people: 'Prepare your provisions; for in three days you are to cross over the Jordan, to go in to take possession of the land that the LORD your God gives you to possess.' "

12 To the Reubenites, the Gadites, and the half-tribe of Manasseh Joshua said, 13"Remember the word that Moses the servant of the LORD commanded you, saying, 'The LORD your God is providing you

When I Was Afraid

TUESDAY

Scripture Reading for Today: *Joshua 1.1–9*

Verse for Today: *Joshua 1.9*

One day about two months into my grueling chemotherapy, I came as near to despair as I have ever been. That evening when I journaled, I asked, "What am I afraid of?" I wrote: "I am afraid of dying. I'm afraid of living."

"What am I most afraid of?" I wrote, "I'm most afraid there is no God." My answer surprised me. I had assumed that I was most afraid of dying, but I realized that was not true. If there is a God, I reasoned, even death would be less frightening.

If there is a God, what would I want God to do in this situation? I wondered. *I would want God to hold me, to comfort me, to tell me that I am loved and will be all right,* I thought. At this particular moment I had one of the most profound experiences of my life. With a rush of feeling, I thought of my husband. He came home from work every day and gave me the shot that was necessary to elevate my white blood count. Although never comfortable with the procedure, my husband learned to do it.

Before administering the shot, he would dance with me in our dining room. It was the only moment of the day when I came close to relaxing. I felt safe and secure in his arms.

As I thought of my husband, I suddenly realized that God had been there all along, intimately close to me through my husband. When I had stopped praying in my usual way, God found another way to reach me. Five years later, this realization still brings tears of wonder to my eyes. God had not abandoned me but had found a way to be with me. This was the God in whom I had believed in the past, a faithful God filled with goodness and gentle compassion. When I was afraid, I needed the protective presence of another. God provided that for me through my husband.

—*FLORETTA MILLER CALMEYN*

Go to page 231 for your next devotional reading.

a place of rest, and will give you this land.' ¹⁴Your wives, your little ones, and your livestock shall remain in the land that Moses gave you beyond the Jordan. But all the warriors among you shall cross over armed before your kindred and shall help them, ¹⁵until the LORD gives rest to your kindred as well as to you, and they too take possession of the land that the LORD your God is giving them. Then you shall return to your own land and take possession of it, the land that Moses the servant of the LORD gave you beyond the Jordan to the east."

16 They answered Joshua: "All that you have commanded us we will do, and wherever you send us we will go. ¹⁷Just as we obeyed Moses in all things, so we will obey you. Only may the LORD your God be with you, as he was with Moses! ¹⁸Whoever rebels against your orders and disobeys your words, whatever you command, shall be put to death. Only be strong and courageous."

Spies Sent to Jericho

2 Then Joshua son of Nun sent two men secretly from Shittim as spies, saying, "Go, view the land, especially Jericho." So they went, and entered the house of a prostitute whose name was Rahab, and spent the night there. ²The king of Jericho was told, "Some Israelites have come here tonight to search out the land." ³Then the king of Jericho sent orders to Rahab, "Bring out the men who have come to you, who entered your house, for they have come only to search out the whole land." ⁴But the woman took the two men and hid them. Then she said, "True, the men came to me, but I did not know where they came from. ⁵And when it was time to close the gate at dark, the men went out. Where the men went I do not know. Pursue them quickly, for you can overtake them." ⁶She had, however, brought them up to the roof and hidden them with the stalks of flax that she had laid out on the roof. ⁷So the men pursued them on the way to the Jordan as far as the fords. As soon as the pursuers had gone out, the gate was shut.

8 Before they went to sleep, she came up to them on the roof ⁹and said to the men: "I know that the LORD has given you the land, and that dread of you has fallen on us, and that all the inhabitants of the land melt in fear before you. ¹⁰For we have heard how the LORD dried up the water of the Red Sea[a] before you when you came out of Egypt, and what you did to the two kings of the Amorites that were beyond the Jordan, to Sihon and Og, whom you utterly destroyed. ¹¹As soon as we heard it, our hearts melted, and there was no courage left in any of us because of you. The LORD your God is indeed God in heaven above and on earth below. ¹²Now then, since I have dealt kindly with you, swear to me by the LORD that you in turn will deal kindly with my family. Give me a sign of good faith ¹³that you will spare my father and mother, my brothers and sisters, and all who belong to them, and deliver our lives from death." ¹⁴The men said to her, "Our life for yours! If you do not tell this business of ours, then we will deal kindly and faithfully with you when the LORD gives us the land."

15 Then she let them down by a rope through the window, for her house was on the outer side of the city wall and she resided within the wall itself. ¹⁶She said to them, "Go toward the hill country, so that the pursuers may not come upon you. Hide yourselves there three days, until the pursuers have returned; then afterward you may go your way." ¹⁷The men said to her, "We will be released from this oath that you have made us swear to you ¹⁸if we invade the land and you do not tie this crimson cord in the window through which you let us down, and you do not gather into your house your father and mother, your brothers, and all your family. ¹⁹If any of you go out of the doors of your house into the street, they shall be responsible for their own death, and we shall be innocent; but if a hand is laid upon any who are with you in the house, we shall bear the responsibility for their death. ²⁰But if you tell this business of ours, then we shall be released from this oath that you made us swear to you." ²¹She said, "According to your words, so be it." She sent them away and they departed. Then she tied the crimson cord in the window.

22 They departed and went into the hill country and stayed there three days, until the pursuers returned. The pursuers had searched all along the way and found nothing. ²³Then the two men came down again from the hill country. They crossed

---

a Or *Sea of Reeds*

over, came to Joshua son of Nun, and told him all that had happened to them. ²⁴They said to Joshua, "Truly the Lord has given all the land into our hands; moreover all the inhabitants of the land melt in fear before us."

Israel Crosses the Jordan

3 Early in the morning Joshua rose and set out from Shittim with all the Israelites, and they came to the Jordan. They camped there before crossing over. ²At the end of three days the officers went through the camp ³and commanded the people, "When you see the ark of the covenant of the Lord your God being carried by the levitical priests, then you shall set out from your place. Follow it, ⁴so that you may know the way you should go, for you have not passed this way before. Yet there shall be a space between you and it, a distance of about two thousand cubits; do not come any nearer to it." ⁵Then Joshua said to the people, "Sanctify yourselves; for tomorrow the Lord will do wonders among you." ⁶To the priests Joshua said, "Take up the ark of the covenant, and pass on in front of the people." So they took up the ark of the covenant and went in front of the people.

7 The Lord said to Joshua, "This day I will begin to exalt you in the sight of all Israel, so that they may know that I will be with you as I was with Moses. ⁸You are the one who shall command the priests who bear the ark of the covenant, 'When you come to the edge of the waters of the Jordan, you shall stand still in the Jordan.' " ⁹Joshua then said to the Israelites, "Draw near and hear the words of the Lord your God." ¹⁰Joshua said, "By this you shall know that among you is the living God who without fail will drive out from before you the Canaanites, Hittites, Hivites, Perizzites, Girgashites, Amorites, and Jebusites: ¹¹the ark of the covenant of the Lord of all the earth is going to pass before you into the Jordan. ¹²So now select twelve men from the tribes of Israel, one from each tribe. ¹³When the soles of the feet of the priests who bear the ark of the Lord, the Lord of all the earth, rest in the waters of the Jordan, the waters of the Jordan flowing from above shall be cut off; they shall stand in a single heap."

14 When the people set out from their tents to cross over the Jordan, the priests bearing the ark of the covenant were in front of the people. ¹⁵Now the Jordan overflows all its banks throughout the time of harvest. So when those who bore the ark had come to the Jordan, and the feet of the priests bearing the ark were dipped in the edge of the water, ¹⁶the waters flowing from above stood still, rising up in a single heap far off at Adam, the city that is beside Zarethan, while those flowing toward the sea of the Arabah, the Dead Sea,ᵇ were wholly cut off. Then the people crossed over opposite Jericho. ¹⁷While all Israel were crossing over on dry ground, the priests who bore the ark of the covenant of the Lord stood on dry ground in the middle of the Jordan, until the entire nation finished crossing over the Jordan.

Twelve Stones Set Up at Gilgal

4 When the entire nation had finished crossing over the Jordan, the Lord said to Joshua: ²"Select twelve men from the people, one from each tribe, ³and command them, 'Take twelve stones from here out of the middle of the Jordan, from the place where the priests' feet stood, carry them over with you, and lay them down in the place where you camp tonight.' " ⁴Then Joshua summoned the twelve men from the Israelites, whom he had appointed, one from each tribe. ⁵Joshua said to them, "Pass on before the ark of the Lord your God into the middle of the Jordan, and each of you take up a stone on his shoulder, one for each of the tribes of the Israelites, ⁶so that this may be a sign among you. When your children ask in time to come, 'What do those stones mean to you?' ⁷then you shall tell them that the waters of the Jordan were cut off in front of the ark of the covenant of the Lord. When it crossed over the Jordan, the waters of the Jordan were cut off. So these stones shall be to the Israelites a memorial forever."

8 The Israelites did as Joshua commanded. They took up twelve stones out of the middle of the Jordan, according to the number of the tribes of the Israelites, as the Lord told Joshua, carried them over with them to the place where they camped, and laid them down there. ⁹(Joshua set up twelve stones in the middle of the Jordan, in the place where the feet of the priests bearing the ark of the

ᵇ Heb *Salt Sea*

covenant had stood; and they are there to this day.)

10 The priests who bore the ark remained standing in the middle of the Jordan, until everything was finished that the LORD commanded Joshua to tell the people, according to all that Moses had commanded Joshua. The people crossed over in haste. ¹¹As soon as all the people had finished crossing over, the ark of the LORD, and the priests, crossed over in front of the people. ¹²The Reubenites, the Gadites, and the half-tribe of Manasseh crossed over armed before the Israelites, as Moses had ordered them. ¹³About forty thousand armed for war crossed over before the LORD to the plains of Jericho for battle.

14 On that day the LORD exalted Joshua in the sight of all Israel; and they stood in awe of him, as they had stood in awe of Moses, all the days of his life.

15 The LORD said to Joshua, ¹⁶"Command the priests who bear the ark of the covenant,c to come up out of the Jordan." ¹⁷Joshua therefore commanded the priests, "Come up out of the Jordan." ¹⁸When the priests bearing the ark of the covenant of the LORD came up from the middle of the Jordan, and the soles of the priests' feet touched dry ground, the waters of the Jordan returned to their place and overflowed all its banks, as before.

19 The people came up out of the Jordan on the tenth day of the first month, and they camped in Gilgal on the east border of Jericho. ²⁰Those twelve stones, which they had taken out of the Jordan, Joshua set up in Gilgal, ²¹saying to the Israelites, "When your children ask their parents in time to come, 'What do these stones mean?' ²²then you shall let your children know, 'Israel crossed over the Jordan here on dry ground.' ²³For the LORD your God dried up the waters of the Jordan for you until you crossed over, as the LORD your God did to the Red Sea,d which he dried up for us until we crossed over, ²⁴so that all the peoples of the earth may know that the hand of the LORD is mighty, and so that you may fear the LORD your God forever."

The New Generation Circumcised

5 When all the kings of the Amorites beyond the Jordan to the west, and all the kings of the Canaanites by the sea, heard that the LORD had dried up the waters of the Jordan for the Israelites until they had crossed over, their hearts melted, and there was no longer any spirit in them, because of the Israelites.

2 At that time the LORD said to Joshua, "Make flint knives and circumcise the Israelites a second time." ³So Joshua made flint knives, and circumcised the Israelites at Gibeath-haaraloth.e ⁴This is the reason why Joshua circumcised them: all the males of the people who came out of Egypt, all the warriors, had died during the journey through the wilderness after they had come out of Egypt. ⁵Although all the people who came out had been circumcised, yet all the people born on the journey through the wilderness after they had come out of Egypt had not been circumcised. ⁶For the Israelites traveled forty years in the wilderness, until all the nation, the warriors who came out of Egypt, perished, not having listened to the voice of the LORD. To them the LORD swore that he would not let them see the land that he had sworn to their ancestors to give us, a land flowing with milk and honey. ⁷So it was their children, whom he raised up in their place, that Joshua circumcised; for they were uncircumcised, because they had not been circumcised on the way.

8 When the circumcising of all the nation was done, they remained in their places in the camp until they were healed. ⁹The LORD said to Joshua, "Today I have rolled away from you the disgrace of Egypt." And so that place is called Gilgalf to this day.

The Passover at Gilgal

10 While the Israelites were camped in Gilgal they kept the passover in the evening on the fourteenth day of the month in the plains of Jericho. ¹¹On the day after the passover, on that very day, they ate the produce of the land, unleavened cakes and parched grain. ¹²The manna ceased on the day they ate the produce of the land, and the Israelites no longer had manna; they ate the crops of the land of Canaan that year.

Joshua's Vision

13 Once when Joshua was by Jericho, he looked up and saw a man standing be-

c Or *treaty*, or *testimony*; Heb *eduth*   d Or *Sea of Reeds*   e That is *the Hill of the Foreskins*
f Related to Heb *galal* to roll

fore him with a drawn sword in his hand. Joshua went to him and said to him, "Are you one of us, or one of our adversaries?" [14]He replied, "Neither; but as commander of the army of the LORD I have now come." And Joshua fell on his face to the earth and worshiped, and he said to him, "What do you command your servant, my lord?" [15]The commander of the army of the LORD said to Joshua, "Remove the sandals from your feet, for the place where you stand is holy." And Joshua did so.

Jericho Taken and Destroyed

6 Now Jericho was shut up inside and out because of the Israelites; no one came out and no one went in. [2]The LORD said to Joshua, "See, I have handed Jericho over to you, along with its king and soldiers. [3]You shall march around the city, all the warriors circling the city once. Thus you shall do for six days, [4]with seven priests bearing seven trumpets of rams' horns before the ark. On the seventh day you shall march around the city seven times, the priests blowing the trumpets. [5]When they make a long blast with the ram's horn, as soon as you hear the sound of the trumpet, then all the people shall shout with a great shout; and the wall of the city will fall down flat, and all the people shall charge straight ahead." [6]So Joshua son of Nun summoned the priests and said to them, "Take up the ark of the covenant, and have seven priests carry seven trumpets of rams' horns in front of the ark of the LORD." [7]To the people he said, "Go forward and march around the city; have the armed men pass on before the ark of the LORD."

8 As Joshua had commanded the people, the seven priests carrying the seven trumpets of rams' horns before the LORD went forward, blowing the trumpets, with the ark of the covenant of the LORD following them. [9]And the armed men went before the priests who blew the trumpets; the rear guard came after the ark, while the trumpets blew continually. [10]To the people Joshua gave this command: "You shall not shout or let your voice be heard, nor shall you utter a word, until the day I tell you to shout. Then you shall shout." [11]So the ark of the LORD went around the city, circling it once; and they came into the camp, and spent the night in the camp.

12 Then Joshua rose early in the morning, and the priests took up the ark of the LORD. [13]The seven priests carrying the seven trumpets of rams' horns before the ark of the LORD passed on, blowing the trumpets continually. The armed men went before them, and the rear guard came after the ark of the LORD, while the trumpets blew continually. [14]On the second day they marched around the city once and then returned to the camp. They did this for six days.

15 On the seventh day they rose early, at dawn, and marched around the city in the same manner seven times. It was only on that day that they marched around the city seven times. [16]And at the seventh time, when the priests had blown the trumpets, Joshua said to the people, "Shout! For the LORD has given you the city. [17]The city and all that is in it shall be devoted to the LORD for destruction. Only Rahab the prostitute and all who are with her in her house shall live because she hid the messengers we sent. [18]As for you, keep away from the things devoted to destruction, so as not to covet[g] and take any of the devoted things and make the camp of Israel an object for destruction, bringing trouble upon it. [19]But all silver and gold, and vessels of bronze and iron, are sacred to the LORD; they shall go into the treasury of the LORD." [20]So the people shouted, and the trumpets were blown. As soon as the people heard the sound of the trumpets, they raised a great shout, and the wall fell down flat; so the people charged straight ahead into the city and captured it. [21]Then they devoted to destruction by the edge of the sword all in the city, both men and women, young and old, oxen, sheep, and donkeys.

22 Joshua said to the two men who had spied out the land, "Go into the prostitute's house, and bring the woman out of it and all who belong to her, as you swore to her." [23]So the young men who had been spies went in and brought Rahab out, along with her father, her mother, her brothers, and all who belonged to her—they brought all her kindred out—and set them outside the camp of Israel. [24]They burned down the city, and everything in it; only the silver and gold, and the vessels of bronze and iron, they put into the treasury of the house of the LORD. [25]But Rahab the prostitute, with her fami-

g Gk: Heb *devote to destruction* Compare 7.21

ly and all who belonged to her, Joshua spared. Her family*ʰ* has lived in Israel ever since. For she hid the messengers whom Joshua sent to spy out Jericho.

26 Joshua then pronounced this oath, saying,

"Cursed before the LORD be anyone
  who tries
  to build this city—this Jericho!
At the cost of his firstborn he shall
  lay its foundation,
and at the cost of his youngest he
  shall set up its gates!"

27 So the LORD was with Joshua; and his fame was in all the land.

The Sin of Achan and Its Punishment

7 But the Israelites broke faith in regard to the devoted things: Achan son of Carmi son of Zabdi son of Zerah, of the tribe of Judah, took some of the devoted things; and the anger of the LORD burned against the Israelites.

2 Joshua sent men from Jericho to Ai, which is near Beth-aven, east of Bethel, and said to them, "Go up and spy out the land." And the men went up and spied out Ai. 3Then they returned to Joshua and said to him, "Not all the people need go up; about two or three thousand men should go up and attack Ai. Since they are so few, do not make the whole people toil up there." 4So about three thousand of the people went up there; and they fled before the men of Ai. 5The men of Ai killed about thirty-six of them, chasing them from outside the gate as far as Shebarim and killing them on the slope. The hearts of the people melted and turned to water.

6 Then Joshua tore his clothes, and fell to the ground on his face before the ark of the LORD until the evening, he and the elders of Israel; and they put dust on their heads. 7Joshua said, "Ah, Lord GOD! Why have you brought this people across the Jordan at all, to hand us over to the Amorites so as to destroy us? Would that we had been content to settle beyond the Jordan! 8O Lord, what can I say, now that Israel has turned their backs to their enemies! 9The Canaanites and all the inhabitants of the land will hear of it, and surround us, and cut off our name from the earth. Then what will you do for your great name?"

10 The LORD said to Joshua, "Stand up! Why have you fallen upon your face? 11Is-

rael has sinned; they have transgressed my covenant that I imposed on them. They have taken some of the devoted things; they have stolen, they have acted deceitfully, and they have put them among their own belongings. 12Therefore the Israelites are unable to stand before their enemies; they turn their backs to their enemies, because they have become a thing devoted for destruction themselves. I will be with you no more, unless you destroy the devoted things from among you. 13Proceed to sanctify the people, and say, 'Sanctify yourselves for tomorrow; for thus says the LORD, the God of Israel, "There are devoted things among you, O Israel; you will be unable to stand before your enemies until you take away the devoted things from among you." 14In the morning therefore you shall come forward tribe by tribe. The tribe that the LORD takes shall come near by clans, the clan that the LORD takes shall come near by households, and the household that the LORD takes shall come near one by one. 15And the one who is taken as having the devoted things shall be burned with fire, together with all that he has, for having transgressed the covenant of the LORD, and for having done an outrageous thing in Israel.' "

16 So Joshua rose early in the morning, and brought Israel near tribe by tribe, and the tribe of Judah was taken. 17He brought near the clans of Judah, and the clan of the Zerahites was taken; and he brought near the clan of the Zerahites, family by family,*ⁱ* and Zabdi was taken. 18And he brought near his household one by one, and Achan son of Carmi son of Zabdi son of Zerah, of the tribe of Judah, was taken. 19Then Joshua said to Achan, "My son, give glory to the LORD God of Israel and make confession to him. Tell me now what you have done; do not hide it from me." 20And Achan answered Joshua, "It is true; I am the one who sinned against the LORD God of Israel. This is what I did: 21when I saw among the spoil a beautiful mantle from Shinar, and two hundred shekels of silver, and a bar of gold weighing fifty shekels, then I coveted them and took them. They now lie hidden in the ground inside my tent, with the silver underneath."

22 So Joshua sent messengers, and they

ʰ Heb *She*   *ⁱ* Mss Syr: MT *man by man*

ran to the tent; and there it was, hidden in his tent with the silver underneath. ²³They took them out of the tent and brought them to Joshua and all the Israelites; and they spread them out before the LORD. ²⁴Then Joshua and all Israel with him took Achan son of Zerah, with the silver, the mantle, and the bar of gold, with his sons and daughters, with his oxen, donkeys, and sheep, and his tent and all that he had; and they brought them up to the Valley of Achor. ²⁵Joshua said, "Why did you bring trouble on us? The LORD is bringing trouble on you today." And all Israel stoned him to death; they burned them with fire, cast stones on them, ²⁶and raised over him a great heap of stones that remains to this day. Then the LORD turned from his burning anger. Therefore that place to this day is called the Valley of Achor. *ʲ*

Ai Captured by a Stratagem and Destroyed

8 Then the LORD said to Joshua, "Do not fear or be dismayed; take all the fighting men with you, and go up now to Ai. See, I have handed over to you the king of Ai with his people, his city, and his land. ²You shall do to Ai and its king as you did to Jericho and its king; only its spoil and its livestock you may take as booty for yourselves. Set an ambush against the city, behind it."

3 So Joshua and all the fighting men set out to go up against Ai. Joshua chose thirty thousand warriors and sent them out by night ⁴with the command, "You shall lie in ambush against the city, behind it; do not go very far from the city, but all of you stay alert. ⁵I and all the people who are with me will approach the

ʲ That is Trouble

Ten-Cent Treasures

Scripture Reading
for Today:
Joshua 7.11–23

Verse for Today:
Joshua 7.21

I sigh and look about me at last year's acquisitions—the silver bowl that didn't polish up good enough to grace the dining table but looks elegant with my English ivy growing out of it, the only-slightly-unbalanced coatrack that stands up straight and handsome since I wedged it in the hall corner, the old washday boiler painted black that was just right to hold logs next to the fireplace.

Yes, I know. It's a *madness*, a craving. I should kick the habit and give up garages. But even now, in the clean white snow of winter, I long for a dark dirty garage with a *sale* sign on it!

Dear Lord, why do we always yearn for more? My house is full of ten-cent treasures, so why do I have the itchy-finger virus, always looking for more? My closet is full of clothes (some that fit, some that don't), so why do I always think one more outfit might make me look ten pounds thinner? Forgive my love of shopping, my need to change things around, my plotting and planning to do something different. Maybe it's a sign, Lord, of my yearning for you. In always searching, maybe it is you I am searching for. My need to change the house may be a symbol of my inner need to change myself. My need to add to my possessions may be a result of my need to possess you more. Help me sort out my priorities, Lord. Help me empty my life a bit, so I will have more time for prayer and more room to be filled by thoughts of you.

—BERNADETTE MCCARVER SNYDER

Go to page 248 for your next devotional reading.

city. When they come out against us, as before, we shall flee from them. ⁶They will come out after us until we have drawn them away from the city; for they will say, 'They are fleeing from us, as before.' While we flee from them, ⁷you shall rise up from the ambush and seize the city; for the LORD your God will give it into your hand. ⁸And when you have taken the city, you shall set the city on fire, doing as the LORD has ordered; see, I have commanded you." ⁹So Joshua sent them out; and they went to the place of ambush, and lay between Bethel and Ai, to the west of Ai; but Joshua spent that night in the camp.ᵏ

10 In the morning Joshua rose early and mustered the people, and went up, with the elders of Israel, before the people to Ai. ¹¹All the fighting men who were with him went up, and drew near before the city, and camped on the north side of Ai, with a ravine between them and Ai. ¹²Taking about five thousand men, he set them in ambush between Bethel and Ai, to the west of the city. ¹³So they stationed the forces, the main encampment that was north of the city and its rear guard west of the city. But Joshua spent that night in the valley. ¹⁴When the king of Ai saw this, he and all his people, the inhabitants of the city, hurried out early in the morning to the meeting place facing the Arabah to meet Israel in battle; but he did not know that there was an ambush against him behind the city. ¹⁵And Joshua and all Israel made a pretense of being beaten before them, and fled in the direction of the wilderness. ¹⁶So all the people who were in the city were called together to pursue them, and as they pursued Joshua they were drawn away from the city. ¹⁷There was not a man left in Ai or Bethel who did not go out after Israel; they left the city open, and pursued Israel.

18 Then the LORD said to Joshua, "Stretch out the sword that is in your hand toward Ai; for I will give it into your hand." And Joshua stretched out the sword that was in his hand toward the city. ¹⁹As soon as he stretched out his hand, the troops in ambush rose quickly out of their place and rushed forward. They entered the city, took it, and at once set the city on fire. ²⁰So when the men of Ai looked back, the smoke of the city was rising to the sky. They had no power to flee this way or that, for the people who fled to the wilderness turned back against the pursuers.

²¹When Joshua and all Israel saw that the ambush had taken the city and that the smoke of the city was rising, then they turned back and struck down the men of Ai. ²²And the others came out from the city against them; so they were surrounded by Israelites, some on one side, and some on the other; and Israel struck them down until no one was left who survived or escaped. ²³But the king of Ai was taken alive and brought to Joshua.

24 When Israel had finished slaughtering all the inhabitants of Ai in the open wilderness where they pursued them, and when all of them to the very last had fallen by the edge of the sword, all Israel returned to Ai, and attacked it with the edge of the sword. ²⁵The total of those who fell that day, both men and women, was twelve thousand—all the people of Ai. ²⁶For Joshua did not draw back his hand, with which he stretched out the sword, until he had utterly destroyed all the inhabitants of Ai. ²⁷Only the livestock and the spoil of that city Israel took as their booty, according to the word of the LORD that he had issued to Joshua. ²⁸So Joshua burned Ai, and made it forever a heap of ruins, as it is to this day. ²⁹And he hanged the king of Ai on a tree until evening; and at sunset Joshua commanded, and they took his body down from the tree, threw it down at the entrance of the gate of the city, and raised over it a great heap of stones, which stands there to this day.

Joshua Renews the Covenant

30 Then Joshua built on Mount Ebal an altar to the LORD, the God of Israel, ³¹just as Moses the servant of the LORD had commanded the Israelites, as it is written in the book of the law of Moses, "an altar of unhewnˡ stones, on which no iron tool has been used"; and they offered on it burnt offerings to the LORD, and sacrificed offerings of well-being. ³²And there, in the presence of the Israelites, Joshuaᵐ wrote on the stones a copy of the law of Moses, which he had written. ³³All Israel, alien as well as citizen, with their elders and officers and their judges, stood on opposite sides of the ark in front of the levitical priests who carried the ark of the covenant of the LORD, half of them in front of Mount Gerizim and half of them in front of Mount Ebal, as Moses the servant of the

ᵏ Heb *among the people*   ˡ Heb *whole*   ᵐ Heb *he*

LORD had commanded at the first, that they should bless the people of Israel. 34And afterward he read all the words of the law, blessings and curses, according to all that is written in the book of the law. 35There was not a word of all that Moses commanded that Joshua did not read before all the assembly of Israel, and the women, and the little ones, and the aliens who resided among them.

The Gibeonites Save Themselves by Trickery

9 Now when all the kings who were beyond the Jordan in the hill country and in the lowland all along the coast of the Great Sea toward Lebanon—the Hittites, the Amorites, the Canaanites, the Perizzites, the Hivites, and the Jebusites— heard of this, 2they gathered together with one accord to fight Joshua and Israel.

3 But when the inhabitants of Gibeon heard what Joshua had done to Jericho and to Ai, 4they on their part acted with cunning: they went and prepared provisions,*n* and took worn-out sacks for their donkeys, and wineskins, worn-out and torn and mended, 5with worn-out, patched sandals on their feet, and worn-out clothes; and all their provisions were dry and moldy. 6They went to Joshua in the camp at Gilgal, and said to him and to the Israelites, "We have come from a far country; so now make a treaty with us." 7But the Israelites said to the Hivites, "Perhaps you live among us; then how can we make a treaty with you?" 8They said to Joshua, "We are your servants." And Joshua said to them, "Who are you? And where do you come from?" 9They said to him, "Your servants have come from a very far country, because of the name of the LORD your God; for we have heard a report of him, of all that he did in Egypt, 10and of all that he did to the two kings of the Amorites who were beyond the Jordan, King Sihon of Heshbon, and King Og of Bashan who lived in Ashtaroth. 11So our elders and all the inhabitants of our country said to us, 'Take provisions in your hand for the journey; go to meet them, and say to them, "We are your servants; come now, make a treaty with us."' 12Here is our bread; it was still warm when we took it from our houses as our food for the journey, on the day we set out to come to you, but now, see, it is dry and moldy; 13these wineskins were new when we filled them, and see, they are burst;

and these garments and sandals of ours are worn out from the very long journey." 14So the leaders*o* partook of their provisions, and did not ask direction from the LORD. 15And Joshua made peace with them, guaranteeing their lives by a treaty; and the leaders of the congregation swore an oath to them.

16 But when three days had passed after they had made a treaty with them, they heard that they were their neighbors and were living among them. 17So the Israelites set out and reached their cities on the third day. Now their cities were Gibeon, Chephirah, Beeroth, and Kiriath-jearim. 18But the Israelites did not attack them, because the leaders of the congregation had sworn to them by the LORD, the God of Israel. Then all the congregation murmured against the leaders. 19But all the leaders said to all the congregation, "We have sworn to them by the LORD, the God of Israel, and now we must not touch them. 20This is what we will do to them: We will let them live, so that wrath may not come upon us, because of the oath that we swore to them." 21The leaders said to them, "Let them live." So they became hewers of wood and drawers of water for all the congregation, as the leaders had decided concerning them.

22 Joshua summoned them, and said to them, "Why did you deceive us, saying, 'We are very far from you,' while in fact you are living among us? 23Now therefore you are cursed, and some of you shall always be slaves, hewers of wood and drawers of water for the house of my God." 24They answered Joshua, "Because it was told to your servants for a certainty that the LORD your God had commanded his servant Moses to give you all the land, and to destroy all the inhabitants of the land before you; so we were in great fear for our lives because of you, and did this thing. 25And now we are in your hand: do as it seems good and right in your sight to do to us." 26This is what he did for them: he saved them from the Israelites; and they did not kill them. 27But on that day Joshua made them hewers of wood and drawers of water for the congregation and for the altar of the LORD, to continue to this day, in the place that he should choose.

n Cn: Meaning of Heb uncertain   o Gk: Heb men

The Sun Stands Still

10 When King Adoni-zedek of Jerusalem heard how Joshua had tak-
en Ai, and had utterly destroyed it, doing
to Ai and its king as he had done to Jericho and its king, and how the inhabitants
of Gibeon had made peace with Israel and
were among them, 2he[p] became greatly
frightened, because Gibeon was a large
city, like one of the royal cities, and was
larger than Ai, and all its men were warriors. 3So King Adoni-zedek of Jerusalem
sent a message to King Hoham of Hebron,
to King Piram of Jarmuth, to King Japhia
of Lachish, and to King Debir of Eglon,
saying, 4"Come up and help me, and let
us attack Gibeon; for it has made peace
with Joshua and with the Israelites." 5Then
the five kings of the Amorites—the king of
Jerusalem, the king of Hebron, the king of
Jarmuth, the king of Lachish, and the king
of Eglon—gathered their forces, and went
up with all their armies and camped
against Gibeon, and made war against it.
6 And the Gibeonites sent to Joshua at
the camp in Gilgal, saying, "Do not abandon your servants; come up to us quickly,
and save us, and help us; for all the kings
of the Amorites who live in the hill country are gathered against us." 7So Joshua
went up from Gilgal, he and all the fighting force with him, all the mighty warriors. 8The LORD said to Joshua, "Do not
fear them, for I have handed them over to
you; not one of them shall stand before
you." 9So Joshua came upon them suddenly, having marched up all night from Gilgal. 10And the LORD threw them into a
panic before Israel, who inflicted a great
slaughter on them at Gibeon, chased
them by the way of the ascent of Beth-
horon, and struck them down as far as
Azekah and Makkedah. 11As they fled before Israel, while they were going down
the slope of Beth-horon, the LORD threw
down huge stones from heaven on them
as far as Azekah, and they died; there were
more who died because of the hailstones
than the Israelites killed with the sword.
12 On the day when the LORD gave the
Amorites over to the Israelites, Joshua
spoke to the LORD; and he said in the sight
of Israel,
"Sun, stand still at Gibeon,
and Moon, in the valley of
Aijalon."
13 And the sun stood still, and the
moon stopped,
until the nation took vengeance
on their enemies.
Is this not written in the Book of Jashar?
The sun stopped in midheaven, and did
not hurry to set for about a whole day.
14There has been no day like it before or
since, when the LORD heeded a human
voice; for the LORD fought for Israel.
15 Then Joshua returned, and all Israel
with him, to the camp at Gilgal.

Five Kings Defeated

16 Meanwhile, these five kings fled
and hid themselves in the cave at Makkedah. 17And it was told Joshua, "The five
kings have been found, hidden in the cave
at Makkedah." 18Joshua said, "Roll large
stones against the mouth of the cave, and
set men by it to guard them; 19but do not
stay there yourselves; pursue your enemies, and attack them from the rear. Do
not let them enter their towns, for the
LORD your God has given them into your
hand." 20When Joshua and the Israelites
had finished inflicting a very great slaughter on them, until they were wiped out,
and when the survivors had entered into
the fortified towns, 21all the people returned safe to Joshua in the camp at Makkedah; no one dared to speak[q] against
any of the Israelites.
22 Then Joshua said, "Open the
mouth of the cave, and bring those five
kings out to me from the cave." 23They did
so, and brought the five kings out to him
from the cave, the king of Jerusalem, the
king of Hebron, the king of Jarmuth, the
king of Lachish, and the king of Eglon.
24When they brought the kings out to
Joshua, Joshua summoned all the Israelites, and said to the chiefs of the warriors
who had gone with him, "Come near, put
your feet on the necks of these kings." Then
they came near and put their feet on their
necks. 25And Joshua said to them, "Do
not be afraid or dismayed; be strong and
courageous; for thus the LORD will do to all
the enemies against whom you fight." 26Af-
terward Joshua struck them down and put
them to death, and he hung them on five
trees. And they hung on the trees until
evening. 27At sunset Joshua commanded,
and they took them down from the trees
and threw them into the cave where they

[p] Heb *they* [q] Heb *moved his tongue*

had hidden themselves; they set large stones against the mouth of the cave, which remain to this very day.

28 Joshua took Makkedah on that day, and struck it and its king with the edge of the sword; he utterly destroyed every person in it; he left no one remaining. And he did to the king of Makkedah as he had done to the king of Jericho.

29 Then Joshua passed on from Makkedah, and all Israel with him, to Libnah, and fought against Libnah. ³⁰The LORD gave it also and its king into the hand of Israel; and he struck it with the edge of the sword, and every person in it; he left no one remaining in it; and he did to its king as he had done to the king of Jericho.

31 Next Joshua passed on from Libnah, and all Israel with him, to Lachish, and laid siege to it, and assaulted it. ³²The LORD gave Lachish into the hand of Israel, and he took it on the second day, and struck it with the edge of the sword, and every person in it, as he had done to Libnah.

33 Then King Horam of Gezer came up to help Lachish; and Joshua struck him and his people, leaving him no survivors.

34 From Lachish Joshua passed on with all Israel to Eglon; and they laid siege to it, and assaulted it; ³⁵and they took it that day, and struck it with the edge of the sword; and every person in it he utterly destroyed that day, as he had done to Lachish.

36 Then Joshua went up with all Israel from Eglon to Hebron; they assaulted it, ³⁷and took it, and struck it with the edge of the sword, and its king and its towns, and every person in it; he left no one remaining, just as he had done to Eglon, and utterly destroyed it with every person in it.

38 Then Joshua, with all Israel, turned back to Debir and assaulted it, ³⁹and he took it with its king and all its towns; they struck them with the edge of the sword, and utterly destroyed every person in it; he left no one remaining; just as he had done to Hebron, and, as he had done to Libnah and its king, so he did to Debir and its king.

40 So Joshua defeated the whole land, the hill country and the Negeb and the lowland and the slopes, and all their kings; he left no one remaining, but utterly destroyed all that breathed, as the LORD God of Israel commanded. ⁴¹And Joshua defeated them from Kadesh-barnea to Gaza, and all the country of Goshen, as far as Gibeon. ⁴²Joshua took all these kings and their land at one time, because the LORD God of Israel fought for Israel. ⁴³Then Joshua returned, and all Israel with him, to the camp at Gilgal.

The United Kings of Northern Canaan Defeated

11 When King Jabin of Hazor heard of this, he sent to King Jobab of Madon, to the king of Shimron, to the king of Achshaph, ²and to the kings who were in the northern hill country, and in the Arabah south of Chinneroth, and in the lowland, and in Naphoth-dor on the west, ³to the Canaanites in the east and the west, the Amorites, the Hittites, the Perizzites, and the Jebusites in the hill country, and the Hivites under Hermon in the land of Mizpah. ⁴They came out, with all their troops, a great army, in number like the sand on the seashore, with very many horses and chariots. ⁵All these kings joined their forces, and came and camped together at the waters of Merom, to fight with Israel.

6 And the LORD said to Joshua, "Do not be afraid of them, for tomorrow at this time I will hand over all of them, slain, to Israel; you shall hamstring their horses, and burn their chariots with fire." ⁷So Joshua came suddenly upon them with all his fighting force, by the waters of Merom, and fell upon them. ⁸And the LORD handed them over to Israel, who attacked them and chased them as far as Great Sidon and Misrephoth-maim, and eastward as far as the valley of Mizpeh. They struck them down, until they had left no one remaining. ⁹And Joshua did to them as the LORD commanded him; he hamstrung their horses, and burned their chariots with fire.

10 Joshua turned back at that time, and took Hazor, and struck its king down with the sword. Before that time Hazor was the head of all those kingdoms. ¹¹And they put to the sword all who were in it, utterly destroying them; there was no one left who breathed, and he burned Hazor with fire. ¹²And all the towns of those kings, and all their kings, Joshua took, and struck them with the edge of the sword, utterly destroying them, as Moses the servant of the LORD had commanded. ¹³But Israel burned none of the towns that

stood on mounds except Hazor, which Joshua did burn. [14]All the spoil of these towns, and the livestock, the Israelites took for their booty; but all the people they struck down with the edge of the sword, until they had destroyed them, and they did not leave any who breathed. [15]As the LORD had commanded his servant Moses, so Moses commanded Joshua, and so Joshua did; he left nothing undone of all that the LORD had commanded Moses.

Summary of Joshua's Conquests

16 So Joshua took all that land: the hill country and all the Negeb and all the land of Goshen and the lowland and the Arabah and the hill country of Israel and its lowland, [17]from Mount Halak, which rises toward Seir, as far as Baal-gad in the valley of Lebanon below Mount Hermon. He took all their kings, struck them down, and put them to death. [18]Joshua made war a long time with all those kings. [19]There was not a town that made peace with the Israelites, except the Hivites, the inhabitants of Gibeon; all were taken in battle. [20]For it was the LORD's doing to harden their hearts so that they would come against Israel in battle, in order that they might be utterly destroyed, and might receive no mercy, but be exterminated, just as the LORD had commanded Moses.

21 At that time Joshua came and wiped out the Anakim from the hill country, from Hebron, from Debir, from Anab, and from all the hill country of Judah, and from all the hill country of Israel; Joshua utterly destroyed them with their towns. [22]None of the Anakim was left in the land of the Israelites; some remained only in Gaza, in Gath, and in Ashdod. [23]So Joshua took the whole land, according to all that the LORD had spoken to Moses; and Joshua gave it for an inheritance to Israel according to their tribal allotments. And the land had rest from war.

The Kings Conquered by Moses

12 Now these are the kings of the land, whom the Israelites defeated, whose land they occupied beyond the Jordan toward the east, from the Wadi Arnon to Mount Hermon, with all the Arabah eastward: [2]King Sihon of the Amorites who lived at Heshbon, and ruled from Aroer, which is on the edge of the Wadi Arnon, and from the middle of

the valley as far as the river Jabbok, the boundary of the Ammonites, that is, half of Gilead, [3]and the Arabah to the Sea of Chinneroth eastward, and in the direction of Beth-jeshimoth, to the sea of the Arabah, the Dead Sea,[r] southward to the foot of the slopes of Pisgah; [4]and King Og[s] of Bashan, one of the last of the Rephaim, who lived at Ashtaroth and at Edrei [5]and ruled over Mount Hermon and Salecah and all Bashan to the boundary of the Geshurites and the Maacathites, and over half of Gilead to the boundary of King Sihon of Heshbon. [6]Moses, the servant of the LORD, and the Israelites defeated them; and Moses the servant of the LORD gave their land for a possession to the Reubenites and the Gadites and the half-tribe of Manasseh.

The Kings Conquered by Joshua

7 The following are the kings of the land whom Joshua and the Israelites defeated on the west side of the Jordan, from Baal-gad in the valley of Lebanon to Mount Halak, that rises toward Seir (and Joshua gave their land to the tribes of Israel as a possession according to their allotments, [8]in the hill country, in the lowland, in the Arabah, in the slopes, in the wilderness, and in the Negeb, the land of the Hittites, Amorites, Canaanites, Perizzites, Hivites, and Jebusites):

[9] the king of Jericho	one
the king of Ai, which is next to Bethel	one
[10] the king of Jerusalem	one
the king of Hebron	one
[11] the king of Jarmuth	one
the king of Lachish	one
[12] the king of Eglon	one
the king of Gezer	one
[13] the king of Debir	one
the king of Geder	one
[14] the king of Hormah	one
the king of Arad	one
[15] the king of Libnah	one
the king of Adullam	one
[16] the king of Makkedah	one
the king of Bethel	one
[17] the king of Tappuah	one
the king of Hepher	one
[18] the king of Aphek	one
the king of Lasharon	one
[19] the king of Madon	one

r Heb *Salt Sea*   s Gk: Heb *the boundary of King Og*

the king of Hazor	one
20 the king of Shimron-meron	one
the king of Achshaph	one
21 the king of Taanach	one
the king of Megiddo	one
22 the king of Kedesh	one
the king of Jokneam in Carmel	one
23 the king of Dor in Naphath-dor	one
the king of Goiim in Galilee,^{t}	one
24 the king of Tirzah	one

thirty-one kings in all.

The Parts of Canaan Still Unconquered

13 Now Joshua was old and advanced in years; and the LORD said to him, "You are old and advanced in years, and very much of the land still remains to be possessed. ²This is the land that still remains: all the regions of the Philistines, and all those of the Geshurites ³(from the Shihor, which is east of Egypt, northward to the boundary of Ekron, it is reckoned as Canaanite; there are five rulers of the Philistines, those of Gaza, Ashdod, Ashkelon, Gath, and Ekron), and those of the Avvim ⁴in the south; all the land of the Canaanites, and Mearah that belongs to the Sidonians, to Aphek, to the boundary of the Amorites, ⁵and the land of the Gebalites, and all Lebanon, toward the east, from Baal-gad below Mount Hermon to Lebo-hamath, ⁶all the inhabitants of the hill country from Lebanon to Misrephoth-maim, even all the Sidonians. I will myself drive them out from before the Israelites; only allot the land to Israel for an inheritance, as I have commanded you. ⁷Now therefore divide this land for an inheritance to the nine tribes and the half-tribe of Manasseh."

The Territory East of the Jordan

8 With the other half-tribe of Manasseh^u the Reubenites and the Gadites received their inheritance, which Moses gave them, beyond the Jordan eastward, as Moses the servant of the LORD gave them: ⁹from Aroer, which is on the edge of the Wadi Arnon, and the town that is in the middle of the valley, and all the tableland from^v Medeba as far as Dibon; ¹⁰and all the cities of King Sihon of the Amorites, who reigned in Heshbon, as far as the boundary of the Ammonites; ¹¹and Gilead, and the region of the Geshurites and Maacathites, and all Mount Hermon, and all Bashan to Salecah; ¹²all the kingdom of Og in Bashan, who reigned in

Ashtaroth and in Edrei (he alone was left of the survivors of the Rephaim); these Moses had defeated and driven out. ¹³Yet the Israelites did not drive out the Geshurites or the Maacathites; but Geshur and Maacath live within Israel to this day.

14 To the tribe of Levi alone Moses gave no inheritance; the offerings by fire to the LORD God of Israel are their inheritance, as he said to them.

The Territory of Reuben

15 Moses gave an inheritance to the tribe of the Reubenites according to their clans. ¹⁶Their territory was from Aroer, which is on the edge of the Wadi Arnon, and the town that is in the middle of the valley, and all the tableland by Medeba; ¹⁷with Heshbon, and all its towns that are in the tableland; Dibon, and Bamoth-baal, and Beth-baal-meon, ¹⁸and Jahaz, and Kedemoth, and Mephaath, ¹⁹and Kiriathaim, and Sibmah, and Zereth-shahar on the hill of the valley, ²⁰and Beth-peor, and the slopes of Pisgah, and Beth-jeshimoth, ²¹that is, all the towns of the tableland, and all the kingdom of King Sihon of the Amorites, who reigned in Heshbon, whom Moses defeated with the leaders of Midian, Evi and Rekem and Zur and Hur and Reba, as princes of Sihon, who lived in the land. ²²Along with the rest of those they put to death, the Israelites also put to the sword Balaam son of Beor, who practiced divination. ²³And the border of the Reubenites was the Jordan and its banks. This was the inheritance of the Reubenites according to their families, with their towns and villages.

The Territory of Gad

24 Moses gave an inheritance also to the tribe of the Gadites, according to their families. ²⁵Their territory was Jazer, and all the towns of Gilead, and half the land of the Ammonites, to Aroer, which is east of Rabbah, ²⁶and from Heshbon to Ramath-mizpeh and Betonim, and from Mahanaim to the territory of Debir,^{w} ²⁷and in the valley Beth-haram, Beth-nimrah, Succoth, and Zaphon, the rest of the kingdom of King Sihon of Heshbon, the Jordan and its banks, as far as the lower end of the Sea of Chinnereth, eastward

^{t} Gk: Heb *Gilgal* ^{u} Cn: Heb *With it*
^{v} Compare Gk: Heb lacks *from* ^{w} Gk Syr Vg:
Heb *Lidebir*

beyond the Jordan. ²⁸This is the inheritance of the Gadites according to their clans, with their towns and villages.

The Territory of the Half-Tribe of Manasseh (East)

29 Moses gave an inheritance to the half-tribe of Manasseh; it was allotted to the half-tribe of the Manassites according to their families. ³⁰Their territory extended from Mahanaim, through all Bashan, the whole kingdom of King Og of Bashan, and all the settlements of Jair, which are in Bashan, sixty towns, ³¹and half of Gilead, and Ashtaroth, and Edrei, the towns of the kingdom of Og in Bashan; these were allotted to the people of Machir son of Manasseh according to their clans—for half the Machirites.

32 These are the inheritances that Moses distributed in the plains of Moab, beyond the Jordan east of Jericho. ³³But to the tribe of Levi Moses gave no inheritance; the LORD God of Israel is their inheritance, as he said to them.

The Distribution of Territory West of the Jordan

14 These are the inheritances that the Israelites received in the land of Canaan, which the priest Eleazar, and Joshua son of Nun, and the heads of the families of the tribes of the Israelites distributed to them. ²Their inheritance was by lot, as the LORD had commanded Moses for the nine and one-half tribes. ³For Moses had given an inheritance to the two and one-half tribes beyond the Jordan; but to the Levites he gave no inheritance among them. ⁴For the people of Joseph were two tribes, Manasseh and Ephraim; and no portion was given to the Levites in the land, but only towns to live in, with their pasture lands for their flocks and herds. ⁵The Israelites did as the LORD commanded Moses; they allotted the land.

Hebron Allotted to Caleb

6 Then the people of Judah came to Joshua at Gilgal; and Caleb son of Jephunneh the Kenizzite said to him, "You know what the LORD said to Moses the man of God in Kadesh-barnea concerning you and me. ⁷I was forty years old when Moses the servant of the LORD sent me from Kadesh-barnea to spy out the land; and I brought him an honest report. ⁸But my companions who went up with me made the heart of the people melt; yet I wholeheartedly followed the LORD my God. ⁹And Moses swore on that day, saying, 'Surely the land on which your foot has trodden shall be an inheritance for you and your children forever, because you have wholeheartedly followed the LORD my God.' ¹⁰And now, as you see, the LORD has kept me alive, as he said, these forty-five years since the time that the LORD spoke this word to Moses, while Israel was journeying through the wilderness; and here I am today, eighty-five years old. ¹¹I am still as strong today as I was on the day that Moses sent me; my strength now is as my strength was then, for war, and for going and coming. ¹²So now give me this hill country of which the LORD spoke on that day; for you heard on that day how the Anakim were there, with great fortified cities; it may be that the LORD will be with me, and I shall drive them out, as the LORD said."

13 Then Joshua blessed him, and gave Hebron to Caleb son of Jephunneh for an inheritance. ¹⁴So Hebron became the inheritance of Caleb son of Jephunneh the Kenizzite to this day, because he wholeheartedly followed the LORD, the God of Israel. ¹⁵Now the name of Hebron formerly was Kiriath-arba;^x this Arba was^y the greatest man among the Anakim. And the land had rest from war.

The Territory of Judah

15 The lot for the tribe of the people of Judah according to their families reached southward to the boundary of Edom, to the wilderness of Zin at the farthest south. ²And their south boundary ran from the end of the Dead Sea,^z from the bay that faces southward; ³it goes out southward of the ascent of Akrabbim, passes along to Zin, and goes up south of Kadesh-barnea, along by Hezron, up to Addar, makes a turn to Karka, ⁴passes along to Azmon, goes out by the Wadi of Egypt, and comes to its end at the sea. This shall be your south boundary. ⁵And the east boundary is the Dead Sea,^z to the mouth of the Jordan. And the boundary on the north side runs from the bay of the sea at the mouth of the Jordan; ⁶and the boundary goes up to Beth-hoglah, and passes along north of Beth-arabah; and

---

^x That is *the city of Arba*   ^y Heb lacks *this Arba was*   ^z Heb *Salt Sea*

the boundary goes up to the Stone of Bohan, Reuben's son; 7and the boundary
goes up to Debir from the Valley of Achor,
and so northward, turning toward Gilgal,
which is opposite the ascent of Adummim, which is on the south side of the
valley; and the boundary passes along to
the waters of En-shemesh, and ends at En-
rogel; 8then the boundary goes up by the
valley of the son of Hinnom at the southern slope of the Jebusites (that is, Jerusalem); and the boundary goes up to the top
of the mountain that lies over against the
valley of Hinnom, on the west, at the
northern end of the valley of Rephaim;
9then the boundary extends from the top
of the mountain to the spring of the Waters of Nephtoah, and from there to the
towns of Mount Ephron; then the boundary bends around to Baalah (that is,
Kiriath-jearim); 10and the boundary cir-
cles west of Baalah to Mount Seir, passes
along to the northern slope of Mount Jea-
rim (that is, Chesalon), and goes down to
Beth-shemesh, and passes along by Timnah; 11the boundary goes out to the slope
of the hill north of Ekron, then the
boundary bends around to Shikkeron,
and passes along to Mount Baalah, and
goes out to Jabneel; then the boundary
comes to an end at the sea. 12And the west
boundary was the Mediterranean with its
coast. This is the boundary surrounding
the people of Judah according to their
families.

Caleb Occupies His Portion

13 According to the commandment of
the Lord to Joshua, he gave to Caleb son
of Jephunneh a portion among the people
of Judah, Kiriath-arba,*a* that is, Hebron
(Arba was the father of Anak). 14And Caleb drove out from there the three sons of
Anak: Sheshai, Ahiman, and Talmai, the
descendants of Anak. 15From there he
went up against the inhabitants of Debir;
now the name of Debir formerly was
Kiriath-sepher. 16And Caleb said, "Whoever attacks Kiriath-sepher and takes it, to
him I will give my daughter Achsah as
wife." 17Othniel son of Kenaz, the brother
of Caleb, took it; and he gave him his
daughter Achsah as wife. 18When she
came to him, she urged him to ask her
father for a field. As she dismounted from
her donkey, Caleb said to her, "What do
you wish?" 19She said to him, "Give me a
present; since you have set me in the land

of the Negeb, give me springs of water as
well." So Caleb gave her the upper springs
and the lower springs.

The Towns of Judah

20 This is the inheritance of the tribe of
the people of Judah according to their
families. 21The towns belonging to the
tribe of the people of Judah in the extreme south, toward the boundary of
Edom, were Kabzeel, Eder, Jagur, 22Kinah,
Dimonah, Adadah, 23Kedesh, Hazor, Ith-
nan, 24Ziph, Telem, Bealoth, 25Hazor-
hadattah, Kerioth-hezron (that is, Hazor),
26Amam, Shema, Moladah, 27Hazar-
gaddah, Heshmon, Beth-pelet, 28Hazar-
shual, Beer-sheba, Biziothiah, 29Baalah,
Iim, Ezem, 30Eltolad, Chesil, Hormah,
31Ziklag, Madmannah, Sansannah, 32Le-
baoth, Shilhim, Ain, and Rimmon: in all,
twenty-nine towns, with their villages.

33 And in the lowland, Eshtaol, Zorah,
Ashnah, 34Zanoah, En-gannim, Tappuah,
Enam, 35Jarmuth, Adullam, Socoh, Aze-
kah, 36Shaaraim, Adithaim, Gederah,
Gederothaim: fourteen towns with their
villages.

37 Zenan, Hadashah, Migdal-gad,
38Dilan, Mizpeh, Jokthe-el, 39Lachish,
Bozkath, Eglon, 40Cabbon, Lahmam,
Chitlish, 41Gederoth, Beth-dagon, Naamah, and Makkedah: sixteen towns with
their villages.

42 Libnah, Ether, Ashan, 43Iphtah,
Ashnah, Nezib, 44Keilah, Achzib, and Mareshah: nine towns with their villages.

45 Ekron, with its dependencies and its
villages; 46from Ekron to the sea, all that
were near Ashdod, with their villages.

47 Ashdod, its towns and its villages;
Gaza, its towns and its villages; to the
Wadi of Egypt, and the Great Sea with its
coast.

48 And in the hill country, Shamir, Jattir, Socoh, 49Dannah, Kiriath-sannah
(that is, Debir), 50Anab, Eshtemoh, Anim,
51Goshen, Holon, and Giloh: eleven
towns with their villages.

52 Arab, Dumah, Eshan, 53Janim,
Beth-tappuah, Aphekah, 54Humtah,
Kiriath-arba (that is, Hebron), and Zior:
nine towns with their villages.

55 Maon, Carmel, Ziph, Juttah, 56Jezre-
el, Jokdeam, Zanoah, 57Kain, Gibeah, and
Timnah: ten towns with their villages.

58 Halhul, Beth-zur, Gedor, 59Maa-

---

a That is the city of Arba

rath, Beth-anoth, and Eltekon: six towns with their villages.

60 Kiriath-baal (that is, Kiriath-jearim) and Rabbah: two towns with their villages.

61 In the wilderness, Beth-arabah, Middin, Secacah, 62Nibshan, the City of Salt, and En-gedi: six towns with their villages.

63 But the people of Judah could not drive out the Jebusites, the inhabitants of Jerusalem; so the Jebusites live with the people of Judah in Jerusalem to this day.

The Territory of Ephraim

16 The allotment of the Josephites went from the Jordan by Jericho, east of the waters of Jericho, into the wilderness, going up from Jericho into the hill country to Bethel; 2then going from Bethel to Luz, it passes along to Ataroth, the territory of the Archites; 3then it goes down westward to the territory of the Japhletites, as far as the territory of Lower Beth-horon, then to Gezer, and it ends at the sea.

4 The Josephites—Manasseh and Ephraim—received their inheritance.

5 The territory of the Ephraimites by their families was as follows: the boundary of their inheritance on the east was Ataroth-addar as far as Upper Beth-horon, 6and the boundary goes from there to the sea; on the north is Michmethath; then on the east the boundary makes a turn toward Taanath-shiloh, and passes along beyond it on the east to Janoah, 7then it goes down from Janoah to Ataroth and to Naarah, and touches Jericho, ending at the Jordan. 8From Tappuah the boundary goes westward to the Wadi Kanah, and ends at the sea. Such is the inheritance of the tribe of the Ephraimites by their families, 9together with the towns that were set apart for the Ephraimites within the inheritance of the Manassites, all those towns with their villages. 10They did not, however, drive out the Canaanites who lived in Gezer: so the Canaanites have lived within Ephraim to this day but have been made to do forced labor.

The Other Half-Tribe of Manasseh (West)

17 Then allotment was made to the tribe of Manasseh, for he was the firstborn of Joseph. To Machir the firstborn of Manasseh, the father of Gilead, were allotted Gilead and Bashan, because he was a warrior. 2And allotments were made to the rest of the tribe of Manasseh, by their families, Abiezer, Helek, Asriel, Shechem, Hepher, and Shemida; these were the male descendants of Manasseh son of Joseph, by their families.

3 Now Zelophehad son of Hepher son of Gilead son of Machir son of Manasseh had no sons, but only daughters; and these are the names of his daughters: Mahlah, Noah, Hoglah, Milcah, and Tirzah. 4They came before the priest Eleazar and Joshua son of Nun and the leaders, and said, "The LORD commanded Moses to give us an inheritance along with our male kin." So according to the commandment of the LORD he gave them an inheritance among the kinsmen of their father. 5Thus there fell to Manasseh ten portions, besides the land of Gilead and Bashan, which is on the other side of the Jordan, 6because the daughters of Manasseh received an inheritance along with his sons. The land of Gilead was allotted to the rest of the Manassites.

7 The territory of Manasseh reached from Asher to Michmethath, which is east of Shechem; then the boundary goes along southward to the inhabitants of En-tappuah. 8The land of Tappuah belonged to Manasseh, but the town of Tappuah on the boundary of Manasseh belonged to the Ephraimites. 9Then the boundary went down to the Wadi Kanah. The towns here, to the south of the wadi, among the towns of Manasseh, belong to Ephraim. Then the boundary of Manasseh goes along the north side of the wadi and ends at the sea. 10The land to the south is Ephraim's and that to the north is Manasseh's, with the sea forming its boundary; on the north Asher is reached, and on the east Issachar. 11Within Issachar and Asher, Manasseh had Beth-shean and its villages, Ibleam and its villages, the inhabitants of Dor and its villages, the inhabitants of En-dor and its villages, the inhabitants of Taanach and its villages, and the inhabitants of Megiddo and its villages (the third is Naphath).*b* 12Yet the Manassites could not take possession of those towns; but the Canaanites continued to live in that land. 13But when the Israelites grew strong, they put the Canaanites to forced labor, but did not utterly drive them out.

b Meaning of Heb uncertain

The Tribe of Joseph Protests

14 The tribe of Joseph spoke to Joshua, saying, "Why have you given me but one lot and one portion as an inheritance, since we are a numerous people, whom all along the LORD has blessed?" 15And Joshua said to them, "If you are a numerous people, go up to the forest, and clear ground there for yourselves in the land of the Perizzites and the Rephaim, since the hill country of Ephraim is too narrow for you." 16The tribe of Joseph said, "The hill country is not enough for us; yet all the Canaanites who live in the plain have chariots of iron, both those in Beth-shean and its villages and those in the Valley of Jezreel." 17Then Joshua said to the house of Joseph, to Ephraim and Manasseh, "You are indeed a numerous people, and have great power; you shall not have one lot only, 18but the hill country shall be yours, for though it is a forest, you shall clear it and possess it to its farthest borders; for you shall drive out the Canaanites, though they have chariots of iron, and though they are strong."

The Territories of the Remaining Tribes

18 Then the whole congregation of the Israelites assembled at Shiloh, and set up the tent of meeting there. The land lay subdued before them.

2 There remained among the Israelites seven tribes whose inheritance had not yet been apportioned. 3So Joshua said to the Israelites, "How long will you be slack about going in and taking possession of the land that the LORD, the God of your ancestors, has given you? 4Provide three men from each tribe, and I will send them out that they may begin to go throughout the land, writing a description of it with a view to their inheritances. Then come back to me. 5They shall divide it into seven portions, Judah continuing in its territory on the south, and the house of Joseph in their territory on the north. 6You shall describe the land in seven divisions and bring the description here to me; and I will cast lots for you here before the LORD our God. 7The Levites have no portion among you, for the priesthood of the LORD is their heritage; and Gad and Reuben and the half-tribe of Manasseh have received their inheritance beyond the Jordan eastward, which Moses the servant of the LORD gave them."

8 So the men started on their way; and Joshua charged those who went to write the description of the land, saying, "Go throughout the land and write a description of it, and come back to me; and I will cast lots for you here before the LORD in Shiloh." 9So the men went and traversed the land and set down in a book a description of it by towns in seven divisions; then they came back to Joshua in the camp at Shiloh, 10and Joshua cast lots for them in Shiloh before the LORD; and there Joshua apportioned the land to the Israelites, to each a portion.

The Territory of Benjamin

11 The lot of the tribe of Benjamin according to its families came up, and the territory allotted to it fell between the tribe of Judah and the tribe of Joseph. 12On the north side their boundary began at the Jordan; then the boundary goes up to the slope of Jericho on the north, then up through the hill country westward; and it ends at the wilderness of Beth-aven. 13From there the boundary passes along southward in the direction of Luz, to the slope of Luz (that is, Bethel), then the boundary goes down to Ataroth-addar, on the mountain that lies south of Lower Beth-horon. 14Then the boundary goes in another direction, turning on the western side southward from the mountain that lies to the south, opposite Beth-horon, and it ends at Kiriath-baal (that is, Kiriath-jearim), a town belonging to the tribe of Judah. This forms the western side. 15The southern side begins at the outskirts of Kiriath-jearim; and the boundary goes from there to Ephron,*c* to the spring of the Waters of Nephtoah; 16then the boundary goes down to the border of the mountain that overlooks the valley of the son of Hinnom, which is at the north end of the valley of Rephaim; and it then goes down the valley of Hinnom, south of the slope of the Jebusites, and downward to En-rogel; 17then it bends in a northerly direction going on to En-shemesh, and from there goes to Geliloth, which is opposite the ascent of Adummim; then it goes down to the Stone of Bohan, Reuben's son; 18and passing on to the north of the slope of Beth-arabah*d* it goes down to the Arabah;

c Cn See 15.9. Heb *westward* *d* Gk: Heb *to the slope over against the Arabah*

[19]then the boundary passes on to the north of the slope of Beth-hoglah; and the boundary ends at the northern bay of the Dead Sea,[e] at the south end of the Jordan: this is the southern border. [20]The Jordan forms its boundary on the eastern side. This is the inheritance of the tribe of Benjamin, according to its families, boundary by boundary all around.

21 Now the towns of the tribe of Benjamin according to their families were Jericho, Beth-hoglah, Emek-keziz, [22]Beth-arabah, Zemaraim, Bethel, [23]Avvim, Parah, Ophrah, [24]Chephar-ammoni, Ophni, and Geba—twelve towns with their villages: [25]Gibeon, Ramah, Beeroth, [26]Mizpeh, Chephirah, Mozah, [27]Rekem, Irpeel, Taralah, [28]Zela, Haeleph, Jebus[f] (that is, Jerusalem), Gibeah[g] and Kiriath-jearim[h]—fourteen towns with their villages. This is the inheritance of the tribe of Benjamin according to its families.

The Territory of Simeon

19 The second lot came out for Simeon, for the tribe of Simeon, according to its families; its inheritance lay within the inheritance of the tribe of Judah. [2]It had for its inheritance Beer-sheba, Sheba, Moladah, [3]Hazar-shual, Balah, Ezem, [4]Eltolad, Bethul, Hormah, [5]Ziklag, Beth-marcaboth, Hazar-susah, [6]Beth-lebaoth, and Sharuhen—thirteen towns with their villages; [7]Ain, Rimmon, Ether, and Ashan—four towns with their villages; [8]together with all the villages all around these towns as far as Baalath-beer, Ramah of the Negeb. This was the inheritance of the tribe of Simeon according to its families. [9]The inheritance of the tribe of Simeon formed part of the territory of Judah; because the portion of the tribe of Judah was too large for them, the tribe of Simeon obtained an inheritance within their inheritance.

The Territory of Zebulun

10 The third lot came up for the tribe of Zebulun, according to its families. The boundary of its inheritance reached as far as Sarid; [11]then its boundary goes up westward, and on to Maralah, and touches Dabbesheth, then the wadi that is east of Jokneam; [12]from Sarid it goes in the other direction eastward toward the sunrise to the boundary of Chisloth-tabor; from there it goes to Daberath, then up to Japhia; [13]from there it passes along on the east toward the sunrise to Gath-hepher, to Eth-kazin, and going on to Rimmon it bends toward Neah; [14]then on the north the boundary makes a turn to Hannathon, and it ends at the valley of Iphtah-el; [15]and Kattath, Nahalal, Shimron, Idalah, and Bethlehem—twelve towns with their villages. [16]This is the inheritance of the tribe of Zebulun, according to its families—these towns with their villages.

The Territory of Issachar

17 The fourth lot came out for Issachar, for the tribe of Issachar, according to its families. [18]Its territory included Jezreel, Chesulloth, Shunem, [19]Hapharaim, Shion, Anaharath, [20]Rabbith, Kishion, Ebez, [21]Remeth, En-gannim, En-haddah, Beth-pazzez; [22]the boundary also touches Tabor, Shahazumah, and Beth-shemesh, and its boundary ends at the Jordan—sixteen towns with their villages. [23]This is the inheritance of the tribe of Issachar, according to its families—the towns with their villages.

The Territory of Asher

24 The fifth lot came out for the tribe of Asher according to its families. [25]Its boundary included Helkath, Hali, Beten, Achshaph, [26]Allammelech, Amad, and Mishal; on the west it touches Carmel and Shihor-libnath, [27]then it turns eastward, goes to Beth-dagon, and touches Zebulun and the valley of Iphtah-el northward to Beth-emek and Neiel; then it continues in the north to Cabul, [28]Ebron, Rehob, Hammon, Kanah, as far as Great Sidon; [29]then the boundary turns to Ramah, reaching to the fortified city of Tyre; then the boundary turns to Hosah, and it ends at the sea; Mahalab,[i] Achzib, [30]Ummah, Aphek, and Rehob—twenty-two towns with their villages. [31]This is the inheritance of the tribe of Asher according to its families—these towns with their villages.

The Territory of Naphtali

32 The sixth lot came out for Naphtali, for the tribe of Naphtali, according to its families. [33]And its boundary ran from Heleph, from the oak in Zaanannim, and Adami-nekeb, and Jabneel, as far as Lakkum; and it ended at the Jordan;

---

e Heb *Salt Sea*   *f* Gk Syr Vg: Heb *the Jebusite*
g Heb *Gibeath*   *h* Gk: Heb *Kiriath*   *i* Cn
Compare Gk: Heb *Mehebel*

³⁴then the boundary turns westward to Aznoth-tabor, and goes from there to Hukkok, touching Zebulun at the south, and Asher on the west, and Judah on the east at the Jordan. ³⁵The fortified towns are Ziddim, Zer, Hammath, Rakkath, Chinnereth, ³⁶Adamah, Ramah, Hazor, ³⁷Kedesh, Edrei, En-hazor, ³⁸Iron, Migdal-el, Horem, Beth-anath, and Beth-shemesh—nineteen towns with their villages. ³⁹This is the inheritance of the tribe of Naphtali according to its families—the towns with their villages.

The Territory of Dan

40 The seventh lot came out for the tribe of Dan, according to its families. ⁴¹The territory of its inheritance included Zorah, Eshtaol, Ir-shemesh, ⁴²Shaalabbin, Aijalon, Ithlah, ⁴³Elon, Timnah, Ekron, ⁴⁴Eltekeh, Gibbethon, Baalath, ⁴⁵Jehud, Bene-berak, Gath-rimmon, ⁴⁶Me-jarkon, and Rakkon at the border opposite Joppa. ⁴⁷When the territory of the Danites was lost to them, the Danites went up and fought against Leshem, and after capturing it and putting it to the sword, they took possession of it and settled in it, calling Leshem, Dan, after their ancestor Dan. ⁴⁸This is the inheritance of the tribe of Dan, according to their families—these towns with their villages.

Joshua's Inheritance

49 When they had finished distributing the several territories of the land as inheritances, the Israelites gave an inheritance among them to Joshua son of Nun. ⁵⁰By command of the LORD they gave him the town that he asked for, Timnath-serah in the hill country of Ephraim; he rebuilt the town, and settled in it.

51 These are the inheritances that the priest Eleazar and Joshua son of Nun and the heads of the families of the tribes of the Israelites distributed by lot at Shiloh before the LORD, at the entrance of the tent of meeting. So they finished dividing the land.

The Cities of Refuge

20 Then the LORD spoke to Joshua, saying, ²"Say to the Israelites, 'Appoint the cities of refuge, of which I spoke to you through Moses, ³so that anyone who kills a person without intent or by mistake may flee there; they shall be for you a refuge from the avenger of blood. ⁴The slayer shall flee to one of these cities and shall stand at the entrance of the gate of the city, and explain the case to the elders of that city; then the fugitive shall be taken into the city, and given a place, and shall remain with them. ⁵And if the avenger of blood is in pursuit, they shall not give up the slayer, because the neighbor was killed by mistake, there having been no enmity between them before. ⁶The slayer shall remain in that city until there is a trial before the congregation, until the death of the one who is high priest at the time: then the slayer may return home, to the town in which the deed was done.' "

7 So they set apart Kedesh in Galilee in the hill country of Naphtali, and Shechem in the hill country of Ephraim, and Kiriath-arba (that is, Hebron) in the hill country of Judah. ⁸And beyond the Jordan east of Jericho, they appointed Bezer in the wilderness on the tableland, from the tribe of Reuben, and Ramoth in Gilead, from the tribe of Gad, and Golan in Bashan, from the tribe of Manasseh. ⁹These were the cities designated for all the Israelites, and for the aliens residing among them, that anyone who killed a person without intent could flee there, so as not to die by the hand of the avenger of blood, until there was a trial before the congregation.

Cities Allotted to the Levites

21 Then the heads of the families of the Levites came to the priest Eleazar and to Joshua son of Nun and to the heads of the families of the tribes of the Israelites; ²they said to them at Shiloh in the land of Canaan, "The LORD commanded through Moses that we be given towns to live in, along with their pasture lands for our livestock." ³So by command of the LORD the Israelites gave to the Levites the following towns and pasture lands out of their inheritance.

4 The lot came out for the families of the Kohathites. So those Levites who were descendants of Aaron the priest received by lot thirteen towns from the tribes of Judah, Simeon, and Benjamin.

5 The rest of the Kohathites received by lot ten towns from the families of the tribe of Ephraim, from the tribe of Dan, and the half-tribe of Manasseh.

6 The Gershonites received by lot thirteen towns from the families of the tribe

of Issachar, from the tribe of Asher, from the tribe of Naphtali, and from the half-tribe of Manasseh in Bashan.

7 The Merarites according to their families received twelve towns from the tribe of Reuben, the tribe of Gad, and the tribe of Zebulun.

8 These towns and their pasture lands the Israelites gave by lot to the Levites, as the LORD had commanded through Moses.

9 Out of the tribe of Judah and the tribe of Simeon they gave the following towns mentioned by name, 10which went to the descendants of Aaron, one of the families of the Kohathites who belonged to the Levites, since the lot fell to them first. 11They gave them Kiriath-arba (Arba being the father of Anak), that is Hebron, in the hill country of Judah, along with the pasture lands around it. 12But the fields of the town and its villages had been given to Caleb son of Jephunneh as his holding.

13 To the descendants of Aaron the priest they gave Hebron, the city of refuge for the slayer, with its pasture lands, Libnah with its pasture lands, 14Jattir with its pasture lands, Eshtemoa with its pasture lands, 15Holon with its pasture lands, Debir with its pasture lands, 16Ain with its pasture lands, Juttah with its pasture lands, and Beth-shemesh with its pasture lands—nine towns out of these two tribes. 17Out of the tribe of Benjamin: Gibeon with its pasture lands, Geba with its pasture lands, 18Anathoth with its pasture lands, and Almon with its pasture lands—four towns. 19The towns of the descendants of Aaron—the priests—were thirteen in all, with their pasture lands.

20 As to the rest of the Kohathites belonging to the Kohathite families of the Levites, the towns allotted to them were out of the tribe of Ephraim. 21To them were given Shechem, the city of refuge for the slayer, with its pasture lands in the hill country of Ephraim, Gezer with its pasture lands, 22Kibzaim with its pasture lands, and Beth-horon with its pasture lands—four towns. 23Out of the tribe of Dan: Elteke with its pasture lands, Gibbethon with its pasture lands, 24Aijalon with its pasture lands, Gath-rimmon with its pasture lands—four towns. 25Out of the half-tribe of Manasseh: Taanach with its pasture lands, and Gath-rimmon with its pasture lands—two towns. 26The towns of the families of the rest of the Kohathites were ten in all, with their pasture lands.

27 To the Gershonites, one of the families of the Levites, were given out of the half-tribe of Manasseh, Golan in Bashan with its pasture lands, the city of refuge for the slayer, and Beeshterah with its pasture lands—two towns. 28Out of the tribe of Issachar: Kishion with its pasture lands, Daberath with its pasture lands, 29Jarmuth with its pasture lands, En-gannim with its pasture lands—four towns. 30Out of the tribe of Asher: Mishal with its pasture lands, Abdon with its pasture lands, 31Helkath with its pasture lands, and Rehob with its pasture lands—four towns. 32Out of the tribe of Naphtali: Kedesh in Galilee with its pasture lands, the city of refuge for the slayer, Hammoth-dor with its pasture lands, and Kartan with its pasture lands—three towns. 33The towns of the several families of the Gershonites were in all thirteen, with their pasture lands.

34 To the rest of the Levites—the Merarite families—were given out of the tribe of Zebulun: Jokneam with its pasture lands, Kartah with its pasture lands, 35Dimnah with its pasture lands, Nahalal with its pasture lands—four towns. 36Out of the tribe of Reuben: Bezer with its pasture lands, Jahzah with its pasture lands, 37Kedemoth with its pasture lands, and Mephaath with its pasture lands—four towns. 38Out of the tribe of Gad: Ramoth in Gilead with its pasture lands, the city of refuge for the slayer, Mahanaim with its pasture lands, 39Heshbon with its pasture lands, Jazer with its pasture lands—four towns in all. 40As for the towns of the several Merarite families, that is, the remainder of the families of the Levites, those allotted to them were twelve in all.

41 The towns of the Levites within the holdings of the Israelites were in all forty-eight towns with their pasture lands. 42Each of these towns had its pasture lands around it; so it was with all these towns.

43 Thus the LORD gave to Israel all the land that he swore to their ancestors that he would give them; and having taken possession of it, they settled there. 44And the LORD gave them rest on every side just as he had sworn to their ancestors; not one of all their enemies had withstood them, for the LORD had given all their enemies into their hands. 45Not one of all the

good promises that the LORD had made to the house of Israel had failed; all came to pass.

The Eastern Tribes Return to Their Territory

22 Then Joshua summoned the Reubenites, the Gadites, and the half-tribe of Manasseh, ²and said to them, "You have observed all that Moses the servant of the LORD commanded you, and have obeyed me in all that I have commanded you; ³you have not forsaken your kindred these many days, down to this day, but have been careful to keep the charge of the LORD your God. ⁴And now the LORD your God has given rest to your kindred, as he promised them; therefore turn and go to your tents in the land where your possession lies, which Moses the servant of the LORD gave you on the other side of the Jordan. ⁵Take good care to observe the commandment and instruction that Moses the servant of the LORD commanded you, to love the LORD your God, to walk in all his ways, to keep his commandments, and to hold fast to him, and to serve him with all your heart and with all your soul." ⁶So Joshua blessed them and sent them away, and they went to their tents.

7 Now to the one half of the tribe of Manasseh Moses had given a possession in Bashan; but to the other half Joshua had given a possession beside their fellow Israelites in the land west of the Jordan. And when Joshua sent them away to their tents and blessed them, ⁸he said to them, "Go back to your tents with much wealth, and with very much livestock, with silver, gold, bronze, and iron, and with a great quantity of clothing; divide the spoil of your enemies with your kindred." ⁹So the Reubenites and the Gadites and the half-tribe of Manasseh returned home, parting from the Israelites at Shiloh, which is in the land of Canaan, to go to the land of Gilead, their own land of which they had taken possession by command of the LORD through Moses.

A Memorial Altar East of the Jordan

10 When they came to the region ʲ near the Jordan that lies in the land of Canaan, the Reubenites and the Gadites and the half-tribe of Manasseh built there an altar by the Jordan, an altar of great size. ¹¹The Israelites heard that the Reubenites and the Gadites and the half-tribe

of Manasseh had built an altar at the frontier of the land of Canaan, in the region ᵏ near the Jordan, on the side that belongs to the Israelites. ¹²And when the people of Israel heard of it, the whole assembly of the Israelites gathered at Shiloh, to make war against them.

13 Then the Israelites sent the priest Phinehas son of Eleazar to the Reubenites and the Gadites and the half-tribe of Manasseh, in the land of Gilead, ¹⁴and with him ten chiefs, one from each of the tribal families of Israel, every one of them the head of a family among the clans of Israel. ¹⁵They came to the Reubenites, the Gadites, and the half-tribe of Manasseh, in the land of Gilead, and they said to them, ¹⁶"Thus says the whole congregation of the LORD, 'What is this treachery that you have committed against the God of Israel in turning away today from following the LORD, by building yourselves an altar today in rebellion against the LORD? ¹⁷Have we not had enough of the sin at Peor from which even yet we have not cleansed ourselves, and for which a plague came upon the congregation of the LORD, ¹⁸that you must turn away today from following the LORD! If you rebel against the LORD today, he will be angry with the whole congregation of Israel tomorrow. ¹⁹But now, if your land is unclean, cross over into the LORD's land where the LORD's tabernacle now stands, and take for yourselves a possession among us; only do not rebel against the LORD, or rebel against us ˡ by building yourselves an altar other than the altar of the LORD our God. ²⁰Did not Achan son of Zerah break faith in the matter of the devoted things, and wrath fell upon all the congregation of Israel? And he did not perish alone for his iniquity!' "

21 Then the Reubenites, the Gadites, and the half-tribe of Manasseh said in answer to the heads of the families of Israel, ²²"The LORD, God of gods! The LORD, God of gods! He knows; and let Israel itself know! If it was in rebellion or in breach of faith toward the LORD, do not spare us today ²³for building an altar to turn away from following the LORD; or if we did so to offer burnt offerings or grain offerings or offerings of well-being on it, may the LORD himself take vengeance. ²⁴No! We did it from fear that in time to come your chil-

---

ʲ Or to Geliloth   ᵏ Or at Geliloth   ˡ Or make rebels of us

dren might say to our children, 'What have you to do with the LORD, the God of Israel? 25For the LORD has made the Jordan a boundary between us and you, you Reubenites and Gadites; you have no portion in the LORD.' So your children might make our children cease to worship the LORD. 26Therefore we said, 'Let us now build an altar, not for burnt offering, nor for sacrifice, 27but to be a witness between us and you, and between the generations after us, that we do perform the service of the LORD in his presence with our burnt offerings and sacrifices and offerings of well-being; so that your children may never say to our children in time to come, "You have no portion in the LORD." ' 28And we thought, If this should be said to us or to our descendants in time to come, we could say, 'Look at this copy of the altar of the LORD, which our ancestors made, not for burnt offerings, nor for sacrifice, but to be a witness between us and you.' 29Far be it from us that we should rebel against the LORD, and turn away this day from following the LORD by building an altar for burnt offering, grain offering, or sacrifice, other than the altar of the LORD our God that stands before his tabernacle!"

30 When the priest Phinehas and the chiefs of the congregation, the heads of the families of Israel who were with him, heard the words that the Reubenites and the Gadites and the Manassites spoke, they were satisfied. 31The priest Phinehas son of Eleazar said to the Reubenites and the Gadites and the Manassites, "Today we know that the LORD is among us, because you have not committed this treachery against the LORD; now you have saved the Israelites from the hand of the LORD."

32 Then the priest Phinehas son of Eleazar and the chiefs returned from the Reubenites and the Gadites in the land of Gilead to the land of Canaan, to the Israelites, and brought back word to them. 33The report pleased the Israelites; and the Israelites blessed God and spoke no more of making war against them, to destroy the land where the Reubenites and the Gadites were settled. 34The Reubenites and the Gadites called the altar Witness;*m* "For," said they, "it is a witness between us that the LORD is God."

Joshua Exhorts the People

23 A long time afterward, when the LORD had given rest to Israel from all their enemies all around, and Joshua was old and well advanced in years, 2Joshua summoned all Israel, their elders and heads, their judges and officers, and said to them, "I am now old and well advanced in years; 3and you have seen all that the LORD your God has done to all these nations for your sake, for it is the LORD your God who has fought for you. 4I have allotted to you as an inheritance for your tribes those nations that remain, along with all the nations that I have already cut off, from the Jordan to the Great Sea in the west. 5The LORD your God will push them back before you, and drive them out of your sight; and you shall possess their land, as the LORD your God promised you. 6Therefore be very steadfast to observe and do all that is written in the book of the law of Moses, turning aside from it neither to the right nor to the left, 7so that you may not be mixed with these nations left here among you, or make mention of the names of their gods, or swear by them, or serve them, or bow yourselves down to them, 8but hold fast to the LORD your God, as you have done to this day. 9For the LORD has driven out before you great and strong nations; and as for you, no one has been able to withstand you to this day. 10One of you puts to flight a thousand, since it is the LORD your God who fights for you, as he promised you. 11Be very careful, therefore, to love the LORD your God. 12For if you turn back, and join the survivors of these nations left here among you, and intermarry with them, so that you marry their women and they yours, 13know assuredly that the LORD your God will not continue to drive out these nations before you; but they shall be a snare and a trap for you, a scourge on your sides, and thorns in your eyes, until you perish from this good land that the LORD your God has given you.

14 "And now I am about to go the way of all the earth, and you know in your hearts and souls, all of you, that not one thing has failed of all the good things that the LORD your God promised concerning you; all have come to pass for you, not one of them has failed. 15But just as all the good things that the LORD your God promised concerning you have been fulfilled for you, so the LORD will bring upon you all the bad things, until he has destroyed

---

m Cn Compare Syr: Heb lacks *Witness*

you from this good land that the LORD your God has given you. [16]If you transgress the covenant of the LORD your God, which he enjoined on you, and go and serve other gods and bow down to them, then the anger of the LORD will be kindled against you, and you shall perish quickly from the good land that he has given to you."

The Tribes Renew the Covenant

24 Then Joshua gathered all the tribes of Israel to Shechem, and summoned the elders, the heads, the judges, and the officers of Israel; and they presented themselves before God. [2]And Joshua said to all the people, "Thus says the LORD, the God of Israel: Long ago your ancestors—Terah and his sons Abraham and Nahor—lived beyond the Euphrates and served other gods. [3]Then I took your father Abraham from beyond the River and led him through all the land of Canaan and made his offspring many. I gave him Isaac; [4]and to Isaac I gave Jacob and Esau. I gave Esau the hill country of Seir to possess, but Jacob and his children went down to Egypt. [5]Then I sent Moses and Aaron, and I plagued Egypt with what I did in its midst; and afterwards I brought you out. [6]When I brought your ancestors out of Egypt, you came to the sea; and the Egyptians pursued your ancestors with chariots and horsemen to the Red Sea.[n] [7]When they cried out to the LORD, he put darkness between you and the Egyptians, and made the sea come upon them and cover them; and your eyes saw what I did to Egypt. Afterwards you lived in the wilderness a long time. [8]Then I brought you to the land of the Amorites, who lived on the other side of the Jordan; they fought with you, and I handed them over to you, and you took possession of their land, and I destroyed them before you. [9]Then King Balak son of Zippor of Moab, set out to fight against Israel. He sent and invited Balaam son of Beor to curse you, [10]but I would not listen to Balaam; therefore he blessed you; so I rescued you out of his hand. [11]When you went over the Jordan and came to Jericho, the citizens of Jericho fought against you, and also the Amorites, the Perizzites, the Canaanites, the Hittites, the Girgashites, the Hivites, and the Jebusites; and I handed them over to you. [12]I sent the hornet[o] ahead of you,

which drove out before you the two kings of the Amorites; it was not by your sword or by your bow. [13]I gave you a land on which you had not labored, and towns that you had not built, and you live in them; you eat the fruit of vineyards and oliveyards that you did not plant.

14 "Now therefore revere the LORD, and serve him in sincerity and in faithfulness; put away the gods that your ancestors served beyond the River and in Egypt, and serve the LORD. [15]Now if you are unwilling to serve the LORD, choose this day whom you will serve, whether the gods your ancestors served in the region beyond the River or the gods of the Amorites in whose land you are living; but as for me and my household, we will serve the LORD."

16 Then the people answered, "Far be it from us that we should forsake the LORD to serve other gods; [17]for it is the LORD our God who brought us and our ancestors up from the land of Egypt, out of the house of slavery, and who did those great signs in our sight. He protected us along all the way that we went, and among all the peoples through whom we passed; [18]and the LORD drove out before us all the peoples, the Amorites who lived in the land. Therefore we also will serve the LORD, for he is our God."

19 But Joshua said to the people, "You cannot serve the LORD, for he is a holy God. He is a jealous God; he will not forgive your transgressions or your sins. [20]If you forsake the LORD and serve foreign gods, then he will turn and do you harm, and consume you, after having done you good." [21]And the people said to Joshua, "No, we will serve the LORD!" [22]Then Joshua said to the people, "You are witnesses against yourselves that you have chosen the LORD, to serve him." And they said, "We are witnesses." [23]He said, "Then put away the foreign gods that are among you, and incline your hearts to the LORD, the God of Israel." [24]The people said to Joshua, "The LORD our God we will serve, and him we will obey." [25]So Joshua made a covenant with the people that day, and made statutes and ordinances for them at Shechem. [26]Joshua wrote these words in the book of the law of God; and he took a large stone, and set it up there under the oak in the

---

n Or *Sea of Reeds*   *o* Meaning of Heb uncertain

sanctuary of the LORD. [27]Joshua said to all the people, "See, this stone shall be a witness against us; for it has heard all the words of the LORD that he spoke to us; therefore it shall be a witness against you, if you deal falsely with your God." [28]So Joshua sent the people away to their inheritances.

Death of Joshua and Eleazar

29 After these things Joshua son of Nun, the servant of the LORD, died, being

*C*onversion

Raïssa Maritain was born into a Jewish family in Russia in 1883, her husband, Jacques, into a Protestant family in France a year earlier. They met as university students in the heady intellectual milieu of turn-of-the-century Paris and made a pact to commit suicide together if, within a year, they had not discovered the meaning of life. Through the influence of the philosopher Henri Bergson and especially of the writer Léon Bloy, the couple made their way into the Catholic Church—but only after sober assessment of the cost of conversion.

To ask for Baptism was also to accept separation from the world that we knew in order to enter into a world unknown: It was, we thought, to give up our simple and common liberty in order to undertake the conquest of spiritual liberty, so beautiful and so real among the saints, but placed too high, we thought, ever to be attained.

It meant the acceptance of separation—for how long a time?—from our parents and the comrades of our youth whose lack of understanding we thought would be total (and indeed it was in many cases)—but then too the goodness of God was to hold many surprises for us. Finally we already felt like the "filth of the world" when we thought of the disapproval of those we loved. Jacques remained, despite everything, so persuaded by the errors of the "philosophers," that he thought that in becoming Catholic he would have utterly to forswear the intellectual life.

While the spectacle alone of the sanctity, and that of the beauty of Catholic doctrine had occupied our thoughts, we had been happy in heart and mind, and our admiration had grown by leaps and bounds. Now that we were preparing ourselves to enter among those whom the world hates as it hates Christ, we suffered, Jacques and I, a kind of agony. This lasted for about two months. Once, during those months, I heard in my sleep these words, said to me with a certain impatience: "You are forever seeking what you must do. You have only to love God and serve him with all your heart."

—*RAÏSSA MARITAIN*

Go to page 258 for your next devotional reading.

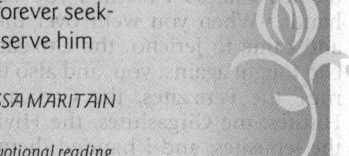

one hundred ten years old. [30]They buried him in his own inheritance at Timnathserah, which is in the hill country of Ephraim, north of Mount Gaash.

31 Israel served the LORD all the days of Joshua, and all the days of the elders who outlived Joshua and had known all the work that the LORD did for Israel.

32 The bones of Joseph, which the Israelites had brought up from Egypt, were buried at Shechem, in the portion of ground that Jacob had bought from the children of Hamor, the father of Shechem, for one hundred pieces of money;[p] it became an inheritance of the descendants of Joseph.

33 Eleazar son of Aaron died; and they buried him at Gibeah, the town of his son Phinehas, which had been given him in the hill country of Ephraim.

[p] Heb *one hundred qesitah*

Judges

The book of Judges recounts the stories, sometimes quite strange, of 12 tribal heroes who arose in Israel during the period after the death of Joshua and before the institution of the monarchy. The most memorable of the 12 judges mentioned in the book include Deborah, Gideon, and Samson. Also memorable is Samson's paramour Delilah, whose beguiling charms led to his downfall.

Strictly speaking, the judges were not simply magistrates (some may not have been magistrates at all), but charismatic military leaders sent by God to rescue the people in time of danger. Though Joshua had conquered much of Canaan, the Israelites had failed to drive out all the land's inhabitants. As a result, Canaanite worship customs had corrupted the Israelites and led to their moral and political decline. Over and over, Israel would sin, falling into idolatry, and then repent. Then God would graciously raise up a judge to deliver them. But as the cycle of disobedience repeated itself, the nation grew progressively weaker. The last line of the book of Judges sums up the situation, saying: "In those days there was no king in Israel; all the people did what was right in their own eyes."

Israel's Failure to Complete the Conquest of Canaan

1 After the death of Joshua, the Israelites inquired of the LORD, "Who shall go up first for us against the Canaanites, to fight against them?" ²The LORD said, "Judah shall go up. I hereby give the land into his hand." ³Judah said to his brother Simeon, "Come up with me into the territory allotted to me, that we may fight against the Canaanites; then I too will go with you into the territory allotted to you." So Simeon went with him. ⁴Then Judah went up and the LORD gave the Canaanites and the Perizzites into their hand; and they defeated ten thousand of them at Bezek. ⁵They came upon Adoni-bezek at Bezek, and fought against him, and defeated the Canaanites and the Perizzites. ⁶Adoni-bezek fled; but they pursued him, and caught him, and cut off his thumbs and big toes. ⁷Adoni-bezek said, "Seventy kings with their thumbs and big toes cut off used to pick up scraps under my table; as I have done, so God has paid me back." They brought him to Jerusalem, and he died there.

8 Then the people of Judah fought against Jerusalem and took it. They put it to the sword and set the city on fire. ⁹Af-

terward the people of Judah went down to fight against the Canaanites who lived in the hill country, in the Negeb, and in the lowland. 10Judah went against the Canaanites who lived in Hebron (the name of Hebron was formerly Kiriath-arba); and they defeated Sheshai and Ahiman and Talmai.

11 From there they went against the inhabitants of Debir (the name of Debir was formerly Kiriath-sepher). 12Then Caleb said, "Whoever attacks Kiriath-sepher and takes it, I will give him my daughter Achsah as wife." 13And Othniel son of Kenaz, Caleb's younger brother, took it; and he gave him his daughter Achsah as wife. 14When she came to him, she urged him to ask her father for a field. As she dismounted from her donkey, Caleb said to her, "What do you wish?" 15She said to him, "Give me a present; since you have set me in the land of the Negeb, give me also Gulloth-mayim."*a* So Caleb gave her Upper Gulloth and Lower Gulloth.

16 The descendants of Hobab*b* the Kenite, Moses' father-in-law, went up with the people of Judah from the city of palms into the wilderness of Judah, which lies in the Negeb near Arad. Then they went and settled with the Amalekites.*c* 17Judah went with his brother Simeon, and they defeated the Canaanites who inhabited Zephath, and devoted it to destruction. So the city was called Hormah. 18Judah took Gaza with its territory, Ashkelon with its territory, and Ekron with its territory. 19The LORD was with Judah, and he took possession of the hill country, but could not drive out the inhabitants of the plain, because they had chariots of iron. 20Hebron was given to Caleb, as Moses had said; and he drove out from it the three sons of Anak. 21But the Benjaminites did not drive out the Jebusites who lived in Jerusalem; so the Jebusites have lived in Jerusalem among the Benjaminites to this day.

22 The house of Joseph also went up against Bethel; and the LORD was with them. 23The house of Joseph sent out spies to Bethel (the name of the city was formerly Luz). 24When the spies saw a man coming out of the city, they said to him, "Show us the way into the city, and we will deal kindly with you." 25So he showed them the way into the city; and they put the city to the sword, but they let the man and all his family go. 26So the

man went to the land of the Hittites and built a city, and named it Luz; that is its name to this day.

27 Manasseh did not drive out the inhabitants of Beth-shean and its villages, or Taanach and its villages, or the inhabitants of Dor and its villages, or the inhabitants of Ibleam and its villages, or the inhabitants of Megiddo and its villages; but the Canaanites continued to live in that land. 28When Israel grew strong, they put the Canaanites to forced labor, but did not in fact drive them out.

29 And Ephraim did not drive out the Canaanites who lived in Gezer; but the Canaanites lived among them in Gezer.

30 Zebulun did not drive out the inhabitants of Kitron, or the inhabitants of Nahalol; but the Canaanites lived among them, and became subject to forced labor.

31 Asher did not drive out the inhabitants of Acco, or the inhabitants of Sidon, or of Ahlab, or of Achzib, or of Helbah, or of Aphik, or of Rehob; 32but the Asherites lived among the Canaanites, the inhabitants of the land; for they did not drive them out.

33 Naphtali did not drive out the inhabitants of Beth-shemesh, or the inhabitants of Beth-anath, but lived among the Canaanites, the inhabitants of the land; nevertheless the inhabitants of Beth-shemesh and of Beth-anath became subject to forced labor for them.

34 The Amorites pressed the Danites back into the hill country; they did not allow them to come down to the plain. 35The Amorites continued to live in Har-heres, in Aijalon, and in Shaalbim, but the hand of the house of Joseph rested heavily on them, and they became subject to forced labor. 36The border of the Amorites ran from the ascent of Akrabbim, from Sela and upward.

Israel's Disobedience

2 Now the angel of the LORD went up from Gilgal to Bochim, and said, "I brought you up from Egypt, and brought you into the land that I had promised to your ancestors. I said, 'I will never break my covenant with you. 2For your part, do not make a covenant with the inhabitants of this land; tear down their altars.' But you have not obeyed my command. See

---

a That is *Basins of Water*   *b* Gk: Heb lacks *Hobab*
c See 1 Sam 15.6: Heb *people*

what you have done! ³So now I say, I will not drive them out before you; but they shall become adversaries*d* to you, and their gods shall be a snare to you." ⁴When the angel of the LORD spoke these words to all the Israelites, the people lifted up their voices and wept. ⁵So they named that place Bochim,*e* and there they sacrificed to the LORD.

Death of Joshua

6 When Joshua dismissed the people, the Israelites all went to their own inheritances to take possession of the land. ⁷The people worshiped the LORD all the days of Joshua, and all the days of the elders who outlived Joshua, who had seen all the great work that the LORD had done for Israel. ⁸Joshua son of Nun, the servant of the LORD, died at the age of one hundred ten years. ⁹So they buried him within the bounds of his inheritance in Timnath-heres, in the hill country of Ephraim, north of Mount Gaash. ¹⁰Moreover, that whole generation was gathered to their ancestors, and another generation grew up after them, who did not know the LORD or the work that he had done for Israel.

Israel's Unfaithfulness

11 Then the Israelites did what was evil in the sight of the LORD and worshiped the Baals; ¹²and they abandoned the LORD, the God of their ancestors, who had brought them out of the land of Egypt; they followed other gods, from among the gods of the peoples who were all around them, and bowed down to them; and they provoked the LORD to anger. ¹³They abandoned the LORD, and worshiped Baal and the Astartes. ¹⁴So the anger of the LORD was kindled against Israel, and he gave them over to plunderers who plundered them, and he sold them into the power of their enemies all around, so that they could no longer withstand their enemies. ¹⁵Whenever they marched out, the hand of the LORD was against them to bring misfortune, as the LORD had warned them and sworn to them; and they were in great distress.

16 Then the LORD raised up judges, who delivered them out of the power of those who plundered them. ¹⁷Yet they did not listen even to their judges; for they lusted after other gods and bowed down to them. They soon turned aside from the way in which their ancestors had walked, who had obeyed the commandments of the LORD; they did not follow their example. ¹⁸Whenever the LORD raised up judges for them, the LORD was with the judge, and he delivered them from the hand of their enemies all the days of the judge; for the LORD would be moved to pity by their groaning because of those who persecuted and oppressed them. ¹⁹But whenever the judge died, they would relapse and behave worse than their ancestors, following other gods, worshiping them and bowing down to them. They would not drop any of their practices or their stubborn ways. ²⁰So the anger of the LORD was kindled against Israel; and he said, "Because this people have transgressed my covenant that I commanded their ancestors, and have not obeyed my voice, ²¹I will no longer drive out before them any of the nations that Joshua left when he died." ²²In order to test Israel, whether or not they would take care to walk in the way of the LORD as their ancestors did, ²³the LORD had left those nations, not driving them out at once, and had not handed them over to Joshua.

Nations Remaining in the Land

3 Now these are the nations that the LORD left to test all those in Israel who had no experience of any war in Canaan ²(it was only that successive generations of Israelites might know war, to teach those who had no experience of it before): ³the five lords of the Philistines, and all the Canaanites, and the Sidonians, and the Hivites who lived on Mount Lebanon, from Mount Baal-hermon as far as Lebo-hamath. ⁴They were for the testing of Israel, to know whether Israel would obey the commandments of the LORD, which he commanded their ancestors by Moses. ⁵So the Israelites lived among the Canaanites, the Hittites, the Amorites, the Perizzites, the Hivites, and the Jebusites; ⁶and they took their daughters as wives for themselves, and their own daughters they gave to their sons; and they worshiped their gods.

Othniel

7 The Israelites did what was evil in the sight of the LORD, forgetting the LORD their God, and worshiping the Baals and the

d OL Vg Compare Gk: Heb *sides* *e* That is *Weepers*

Asherahs. [8]Therefore the anger of the LORD was kindled against Israel, and he sold them into the hand of King Cushan-rishathaim of Aram-naharaim; and the Israelites served Cushan-rishathaim eight years. [9]But when the Israelites cried out to the LORD, the LORD raised up a deliverer for the Israelites, who delivered them, Othniel son of Kenaz, Caleb's younger brother. [10]The spirit of the LORD came upon him, and he judged Israel; he went out to war, and the LORD gave King Cushan-rishathaim of Aram into his hand; and his hand prevailed over Cushan-rishathaim. [11]So the land had rest forty years. Then Othniel son of Kenaz died.

Ehud

12 The Israelites again did what was evil in the sight of the LORD; and the LORD strengthened King Eglon of Moab against Israel, because they had done what was evil in the sight of the LORD. [13]In alliance with the Ammonites and the Amalekites, he went and defeated Israel; and they took possession of the city of palms. [14]So the Israelites served King Eglon of Moab eighteen years.

15 But when the Israelites cried out to the LORD, the LORD raised up for them a deliverer, Ehud son of Gera, the Benjaminite, a left-handed man. The Israelites sent tribute by him to King Eglon of Moab. [16]Ehud made for himself a sword with two edges, a cubit in length; and he fastened it on his right thigh under his clothes. [17]Then he presented the tribute to King Eglon of Moab. Now Eglon was a very fat man. [18]When Ehud had finished presenting the tribute, he sent the people who carried the tribute on their way. [19]But he himself turned back at the sculptured stones near Gilgal, and said, "I have a secret message for you, O king." So the king said,[f] "Silence!" and all his attendants went out from his presence. [20]Ehud came to him, while he was sitting alone in his cool roof chamber, and said, "I have a message from God for you." So he rose from his seat. [21]Then Ehud reached with his left hand, took the sword from his right thigh, and thrust it into Eglon's[g] belly; [22]the hilt also went in after the blade, and the fat closed over the blade, for he did not draw the sword out of his belly; and the dirt came out.[h] [23]Then Ehud went out into the vestibule,[i] and closed the doors of the roof chamber on him, and locked them.

24 After he had gone, the servants came. When they saw that the doors of the roof chamber were locked, they thought, "He must be relieving himself[j] in the cool chamber." [25]So they waited until they were embarrassed. When he still did not open the doors of the roof chamber, they took the key and opened them. There was their lord lying dead on the floor.

26 Ehud escaped while they delayed, and passed beyond the sculptured stones, and escaped to Seirah. [27]When he arrived, he sounded the trumpet in the hill country of Ephraim; and the Israelites went down with him from the hill country, having him at their head. [28]He said to them, "Follow after me; for the LORD has given your enemies the Moabites into your hand." So they went down after him, and seized the fords of the Jordan against the Moabites, and allowed no one to cross over. [29]At that time they killed about ten thousand of the Moabites, all strong, able-bodied men; no one escaped. [30]So Moab was subdued that day under the hand of Israel. And the land had rest eighty years.

Shamgar

31 After him came Shamgar son of Anath, who killed six hundred of the Philistines with an oxgoad. He too delivered Israel.

Deborah and Barak

4 The Israelites again did what was evil in the sight of the LORD, after Ehud died. [2]So the LORD sold them into the hand of King Jabin of Canaan, who reigned in Hazor; the commander of his army was Sisera, who lived in Harosheth-ha-goiim. [3]Then the Israelites cried out to the LORD for help; for he had nine hundred chariots of iron, and had oppressed the Israelites cruelly twenty years.

4 At that time Deborah, a prophetess, wife of Lappidoth, was judging Israel. [5]She used to sit under the palm of Deborah between Ramah and Bethel in the hill country of Ephraim; and the Israelites came up to her for judgment. [6]She sent and summoned Barak son of Abinoam from Kedesh in Naphtali, and said to him,

f Heb he said   g Heb his   h With Tg Vg:
Meaning of Heb uncertain   i Meaning of Heb
uncertain   j Heb covering his feet

"The LORD, the God of Israel, commands you, 'Go, take position at Mount Tabor, bringing ten thousand from the tribe of Naphtali and the tribe of Zebulun. 7I will draw out Sisera, the general of Jabin's army, to meet you by the Wadi Kishon with his chariots and his troops; and I will give him into your hand.' " 8Barak said to her, "If you will go with me, I will go; but if you will not go with me, I will not go." 9And she said, "I will surely go with you; nevertheless, the road on which you are going will not lead to your glory, for the LORD will sell Sisera into the hand of a woman." Then Deborah got up and went with Barak to Kedesh. 10Barak summoned Zebulun and Naphtali to Kedesh; and ten thousand warriors went up behind him; and Deborah went up with him.

11 Now Heber the Kenite had separated from the other Kenites,*k* that is, the descendants of Hobab the father-in-law of Moses, and had encamped as far away as Elon-bezaanannim, which is near Kedesh.

12 When Sisera was told that Barak son of Abinoam had gone up to Mount Tabor, 13Sisera called out all his chariots, nine hundred chariots of iron, and all the troops who were with him, from Harosheth-ha-goiim to the Wadi Kishon. 14Then Deborah said to Barak, "Up! For this is the day on which the LORD has given Sisera into your hand. The LORD is indeed going out before you." So Barak went down from Mount Tabor with ten thousand warriors following him. 15And the LORD threw Sisera and all his chariots and all his army into a panic*l* before Barak; Sisera got down from his chariot and fled away on foot, 16while Barak pursued the chariots and the army to Harosheth-ha-goiim. All the army of Sisera fell by the sword; no one was left.

17 Now Sisera had fled away on foot to the tent of Jael wife of Heber the Kenite; for there was peace between King Jabin of Hazor and the clan of Heber the Kenite. 18Jael came out to meet Sisera, and said to him, "Turn aside, my lord, turn aside to me; have no fear." So he turned aside to her into the tent, and she covered him with a rug. 19Then he said to her, "Please give me a little water to drink; for I am thirsty." So she opened a skin of milk and gave him a drink and covered him. 20He said to her, "Stand at the entrance of the tent, and if anybody comes and asks you,

'Is anyone here?' say, 'No.' " 21But Jael wife of Heber took a tent peg, and took a hammer in her hand, and went softly to him and drove the peg into his temple, until it went down into the ground—he was lying fast asleep from weariness—and he died. 22Then, as Barak came in pursuit of Sisera, Jael went out to meet him, and said to him, "Come, and I will show you the man whom you are seeking." So he went into her tent; and there was Sisera lying dead, with the tent peg in his temple.

23 So on that day God subdued King Jabin of Canaan before the Israelites. 24Then the hand of the Israelites bore harder and harder on King Jabin of Canaan, until they destroyed King Jabin of Canaan.

The Song of Deborah

5 Then Deborah and Barak son of Abinoam sang on that day, saying:
2 "When locks are long in Israel,
	when the people offer themselves
		willingly—
	bless*m* the LORD!

3 "Hear, O kings; give ear, O princes;
	to the LORD I will sing,
	I will make melody to the LORD,
		the God of Israel.

4 "LORD, when you went out from
		Seir,
	when you marched from the
		region of Edom,
	the earth trembled,
	and the heavens poured,
		the clouds indeed poured water.
5 The mountains quaked before the
		LORD, the One of Sinai,
	before the LORD, the God of Israel.

6 "In the days of Shamgar son of
		Anath,
	in the days of Jael, caravans
		ceased
	and travelers kept to the byways.
7 The peasantry prospered in Israel,
	they grew fat on plunder,
	because you arose, Deborah,
	arose as a mother in Israel.
8 When new gods were chosen,
	then war was in the gates.

k Heb *from the Kain*   *l* Heb adds *to the sword;* compare verse 16   *m* Or *You who offer yourselves willingly among the people, bless*

Was shield or spear to be seen
  among forty thousand in Israel?
9 My heart goes out to the
      commanders of Israel
  who offered themselves willingly
      among the people.
  Bless the LORD.

10 "Tell of it, you who ride on white
      donkeys,
  you who sit on rich carpets[n]
  and you who walk by the way.
11 To the sound of musicians[n] at the
      watering places,
  there they repeat the triumphs of
      the LORD,
  the triumphs of his peasantry in
      Israel.

  "Then down to the gates marched
      the people of the LORD.

12 "Awake, awake, Deborah!
      Awake, awake, utter a song!
  Arise, Barak, lead away your
      captives,
      O son of Abinoam.
13 Then down marched the remnant of
      the noble;
  the people of the LORD marched
      down for him[o] against the
      mighty.
14 From Ephraim they set out[p] into
      the valley,[q]
  following you, Benjamin, with
      your kin;
  from Machir marched down the
      commanders,
  and from Zebulun those who bear
      the marshal's staff;
15 the chiefs of Issachar came with
      Deborah,
  and Issachar faithful to Barak;
  into the valley they rushed out at
      his heels.
  Among the clans of Reuben
  there were great searchings of
      heart.
16 Why did you tarry among the
      sheepfolds,
  to hear the piping for the flocks?
  Among the clans of Reuben
  there were great searchings of
      heart.
17 Gilead stayed beyond the Jordan;
  and Dan, why did he abide with
      the ships?
  Asher sat still at the coast of the sea,

settling down by his landings.
18 Zebulun is a people that scorned
      death;
  Naphtali too, on the heights of
      the field.

19 "The kings came, they fought;
  then fought the kings of Canaan,
  at Taanach, by the waters of
      Megiddo;
  they got no spoils of silver.
20 The stars fought from heaven,
  from their courses they fought
      against Sisera.
21 The torrent Kishon swept them
      away,
  the onrushing torrent, the torrent
      Kishon.
  March on, my soul, with might!

22 "Then loud beat the horses' hoofs
  with the galloping, galloping of
      his steeds.

23 "Curse Meroz, says the angel of the
      LORD,
  curse bitterly its inhabitants,
  because they did not come to the
      help of the LORD,
  to the help of the LORD against the
      mighty.

24 "Most blessed of women be Jael,
  the wife of Heber the Kenite,
  of tent-dwelling women most
      blessed.
25 He asked water and she gave him
      milk,
  she brought him curds in a lordly
      bowl.
26 She put her hand to the tent peg
  and her right hand to the
      workmen's mallet;
  she struck Sisera a blow,
  she crushed his head,
  she shattered and pierced his
      temple.
27 He sank, he fell,
  he lay still at her feet;
  at her feet he sank, he fell;
  where he sank, there he fell dead.

28 "Out of the window she peered,

n Meaning of Heb uncertain   o Gk: Heb me
p Cn: Heb From Ephraim their root   q Gk: Heb in
Amalek

the mother of Sisera gazed[r]
    through the lattice:
'Why is his chariot so long in
    coming?
Why tarry the hoofbeats of his
    chariots?'
29 Her wisest ladies make answer,
    indeed, she answers the question
      herself:
30 'Are they not finding and dividing
    the spoil?—
A girl or two for every man;
spoil of dyed stuffs for Sisera,
    spoil of dyed stuffs embroidered,
two pieces of dyed work
    embroidered for my neck as
      spoil?'

31 "So perish all your enemies,
    O Lord!
But may your friends be like the
    sun as it rises in its might."

And the land had rest forty years.

The Midianite Oppression

6 The Israelites did what was evil in the sight of the Lord, and the Lord gave them into the hand of Midian seven years. 2The hand of Midian prevailed over Israel; and because of Midian the Israelites provided for themselves hiding places in the mountains, caves and strongholds. 3For whenever the Israelites put in seed, the Midianites and the Amalekites and the people of the east would come up against them. 4They would encamp against them and destroy the produce of the land, as far as the neighborhood of Gaza, and leave no sustenance in Israel, and no sheep or ox or donkey. 5For they and their livestock would come up, and they would even bring their tents, as thick as locusts; neither they nor their camels could be counted; so they wasted the land as they came in. 6Thus Israel was greatly impoverished because of Midian; and the Israelites cried out to the Lord for help.

7 When the Israelites cried to the Lord on account of the Midianites, 8the Lord sent a prophet to the Israelites; and he said to them, "Thus says the Lord, the God of Israel: I led you up from Egypt, and brought you out of the house of slavery; 9and I delivered you from the hand of the Egyptians, and from the hand of all who oppressed you, and drove them out before you, and gave you their land; 10and

I said to you, 'I am the Lord your God; you shall not pay reverence to the gods of the Amorites, in whose land you live.' But you have not given heed to my voice."

The Call of Gideon

11 Now the angel of the Lord came and sat under the oak at Ophrah, which belonged to Joash the Abiezrite, as his son Gideon was beating out wheat in the wine press, to hide it from the Midianites. 12The angel of the Lord appeared to him and said to him, "The Lord is with you, you mighty warrior." 13Gideon answered him, "But sir, if the Lord is with us, why then has all this happened to us? And where are all his wonderful deeds that our ancestors recounted to us, saying, 'Did not the Lord bring us up from Egypt?' But now the Lord has cast us off, and given us into the hand of Midian." 14Then the Lord turned to him and said, "Go in this might of yours and deliver Israel from the hand of Midian; I hereby commission you." 15He responded, "But sir, how can I deliver Israel? My clan is the weakest in Manasseh, and I am the least in my family." 16The Lord said to him, "But I will be with you, and you shall strike down the Midianites, every one of them." 17Then he said to him, "If now I have found favor with you, then show me a sign that it is you who speak with me. 18Do not depart from here until I come to you, and bring out my present, and set it before you." And he said, "I will stay until you return."

19 So Gideon went into his house and prepared a kid, and unleavened cakes from an ephah of flour; the meat he put in a basket, and the broth he put in a pot, and brought them to him under the oak and presented them. 20The angel of God said to him, "Take the meat and the unleavened cakes, and put them on this rock, and pour out the broth." And he did so. 21Then the angel of the Lord reached out the tip of the staff that was in his hand, and touched the meat and the unleavened cakes; and fire sprang up from the rock and consumed the meat and the unleavened cakes; and the angel of the Lord vanished from his sight. 22Then Gideon perceived that it was the angel of the Lord; and Gideon said, "Help me, Lord God! For I have seen the angel of the Lord face to face." 23But the Lord said to him,

r Gk Compare Tg: Heb *exclaimed*

"Peace be to you; do not fear, you shall not die." ²⁴Then Gideon built an altar there to the LORD, and called it, The LORD is peace. To this day it still stands at Ophrah, which belongs to the Abiezrites.

25 That night the LORD said to him, "Take your father's bull, the second bull seven years old, and pull down the altar of Baal that belongs to your father, and cut down the sacred poleˢ that is beside it; ²⁶and build an altar to the LORD your God on the top of the stronghold here, in proper order; then take the second bull, and offer it as a burnt offering with the wood of the sacred poleˢ that you shall cut down." ²⁷So Gideon took ten of his servants, and did as the LORD had told him; but because he was too afraid of his family and the townspeople to do it by day, he did it by night.

Gideon Destroys the Altar of Baal

28 When the townspeople rose early in the morning, the altar of Baal was broken down, and the sacred poleˢ beside it was cut down, and the second bull was offered on the altar that had been built. ²⁹So they said to one another, "Who has done this?" After searching and inquiring, they were told, "Gideon son of Joash did it." ³⁰Then the townspeople said to Joash, "Bring out your son, so that he may die, for he has pulled down the altar of Baal and cut down the sacred poleˢ beside it." ³¹But Joash said to all who were arrayed against him, "Will you contend for Baal? Or will you defend his cause? Whoever contends for him shall be put to death by morning. If he is a god, let him contend for himself, because his altar has been pulled down." ³²Therefore on that day Gideonᵗ was called Jerubbaal, that is to say, "Let Baal contend against him," because he pulled down his altar.

33 Then all the Midianites and the Amalekites and the people of the east came together, and crossing the Jordan they encamped in the Valley of Jezreel. ³⁴But the spirit of the LORD took possession of Gideon; and he sounded the trumpet, and the Abiezrites were called out to follow him. ³⁵He sent messengers throughout all Manasseh, and they too were called out to follow him. He also sent messengers to Asher, Zebulun, and Naphtali, and they went up to meet them.

The Sign of the Fleece

36 Then Gideon said to God, "In order to see whether you will deliver Israel by my hand, as you have said, ³⁷I am going to lay a fleece of wool on the threshing floor; if there is dew on the fleece alone, and it is dry on all the ground, then I shall know that you will deliver Israel by my hand, as you have said." ³⁸And it was so. When he rose early next morning and squeezed the fleece, he wrung enough dew from the fleece to fill a bowl with water. ³⁹Then Gideon said to God, "Do not let your anger burn against me, let me speak one more time; let me, please, make trial with the fleece just once more; let it be dry only on the fleece, and on all the ground let there be dew." ⁴⁰And God did so that night. It was dry on the fleece only, and on all the ground there was dew.

Gideon Surprises and Routes the Midianites

7 Then Jerubbaal (that is, Gideon) and all the troops that were with him rose early and encamped beside the spring of Harod; and the camp of Midian was north of them, belowᵘ the hill of Moreh, in the valley.

2 The LORD said to Gideon, "The troops with you are too many for me to give the Midianites into their hand. Israel would only take the credit away from me, saying, 'My own hand has delivered me.' ³Now therefore proclaim this in the hearing of the troops, 'Whoever is fearful and trembling, let him return home.' " Thus Gideon sifted them out;ᵛ twenty-two thousand returned, and ten thousand remained.

4 Then the LORD said to Gideon, "The troops are still too many; take them down to the water and I will sift them out for you there. When I say, 'This one shall go with you,' he shall go with you; and when I say, 'This one shall not go with you,' he shall not go." ⁵So he brought the troops down to the water; and the LORD said to Gideon, "All those who lap the water with their tongues, as a dog laps, you shall put to one side; all those who kneel down to drink, putting their hands to their mouths,ʷ you shall put to the other side." ⁶The number of those that lapped was three hundred; but all the rest of the

---

ˢ Heb *Asherah*   ᵗ Heb *he*   ᵘ Heb *from*   ᵛ Cn: Heb *home, and depart from Mount Gilead' "*
ʷ Heb places the words *putting their hands to their mouths* after the word *lapped* in verse 6

troops knelt down to drink water. ⁷Then the LORD said to Gideon, "With the three hundred that lapped I will deliver you, and give the Midianites into your hand. Let all the others go to their homes." ⁸So he took the jars of the troops from their hands,ˣ and their trumpets; and he sent all the rest of Israel back to their own tents, but retained the three hundred. The camp of Midian was below him in the valley.

9 That same night the LORD said to him, "Get up, attack the camp; for I have given it into your hand. ¹⁰But if you fear to attack, go down to the camp with your servant Purah; ¹¹and you shall hear what they say, and afterward your hands shall be strengthened to attack the camp." Then he went down with his servant Purah to the outposts of the armed men that were in the camp. ¹²The Midianites and the Amalekites and all the people of the east

lay along the valley as thick as locusts; and their camels were without number, countless as the sand on the seashore. ¹³When Gideon arrived, there was a man telling a dream to his comrade; and he said, "I had a dream, and in it a cake of barley bread tumbled into the camp of Midian, and came to the tent, and struck it so that it fell; it turned upside down, and the tent collapsed." ¹⁴And his comrade answered, "This is no other than the sword of Gideon son of Joash, a man of Israel; into his hand God has given Midian and all the army."

15 When Gideon heard the telling of the dream and its interpretation, he worshiped; and he returned to the camp of Israel, and said, "Get up; for the LORD has given the army of Midian into your hand."

x Cn: Heb *So the people took provisions in their hands*

*T*rusting

Scripture Reading for Today:
Judges 6.36–40

Verse for Today:
Judges 6.39

Do you realize that probably the greatest sign of faith in the world today is that little green left-turn arrow on stoplights?

Here you and your car sit at a red light, waiting. Ahead, on the other side of the street, you can see rows and rows of cars coming straight toward you. You know if even one of those cars smashed into you, it could dramatically change your present *and* your future. But the minute that little green arrow lights up, your foot is on the pedal and you go. You turn left, right across the path of those oncoming blobs of metal, exposing your broadside and *trusting* that everyone will follow the rules and stop before hitting you.

Dear Lord, forgive us for trusting a traffic signal more than we trust you. Every day you give us signals and directions much more important than that little green arrow, but we of little faith are afraid to follow your signs. Instead of putting our foot on the pedal to go, we hesitate, we wonder, we doubt.

It's hard, Lord. Today there are so many signs blinking at us from all directions. It's hard to know which ones to follow, hard to know which ones are really yours. Help us, Lord. Help us to know when to stop and when to go and which arrows point us in the way you want us to go.

—*BERNADETTE MCCARVER SNYDER*

Go to page 270 for your next devotional reading.

16After he divided the three hundred men into three companies, and put trumpets into the hands of all of them, and empty jars, with torches inside the jars, 17he said to them, "Look at me, and do the same; when I come to the outskirts of the camp, do as I do. 18When I blow the trumpet, I and all who are with me, then you also blow the trumpets around the whole camp, and shout, 'For the LORD and for Gideon!' "

19 So Gideon and the hundred who were with him came to the outskirts of the camp at the beginning of the middle watch, when they had just set the watch; and they blew the trumpets and smashed the jars that were in their hands. 20So the three companies blew the trumpets and broke the jars, holding in their left hands the torches, and in their right hands the trumpets to blow; and they cried, "A sword for the LORD and for Gideon!" 21Every man stood in his place all around the camp, and all the men in camp ran; they cried out and fled. 22When they blew the three hundred trumpets, the LORD set every man's sword against his fellow and against the army; and the army fled as far as Beth-shittah toward Zererah,y as far as the border of Abel-meholah, by Tabbath. 23And the men of Israel were called out from Naphtali and from Asher and from all Manasseh, and they pursued after the Midianites.

24 Then Gideon sent messengers throughout all the hill country of Ephraim, saying, "Come down against the Midianites and seize the waters against them, as far as Beth-barah, and also the Jordan." So all the men of Ephraim were called out, and they seized the waters as far as Beth-barah, and also the Jordan. 25They captured the two captains of Midian, Oreb and Zeeb; they killed Oreb at the rock of Oreb, and Zeeb they killed at the wine press of Zeeb, as they pursued the Midianites. They brought the heads of Oreb and Zeeb to Gideon beyond the Jordan.

Gideon's Triumph and Vengeance

8 Then the Ephraimites said to him, "What have you done to us, not to call us when you went to fight against the Midianites?" And they upbraided him violently. 2So he said to them, "What have I done now in comparison with you? Is not the gleaning of the grapes of Ephraim better than the vintage of Abiezer? 3God has

given into your hands the captains of Midian, Oreb and Zeeb; what have I been able to do in comparison with you?" When he said this, their anger against him subsided.

4 Then Gideon came to the Jordan and crossed over, he and the three hundred who were with him, exhausted and famished.z 5So he said to the people of Succoth, "Please give some loaves of bread to my followers, for they are exhausted, and I am pursuing Zebah and Zalmunna, the kings of Midian." 6But the officials of Succoth said, "Do you already have in your possession the hands of Zebah and Zalmunna, that we should give bread to your army?" 7Gideon replied, "Well then, when the LORD has given Zebah and Zalmunna into my hand, I will trample your flesh on the thorns of the wilderness and on briers." 8From there he went up to Penuel, and made the same request of them; and the people of Penuel answered him as the people of Succoth had answered. 9So he said to the people of Penuel, "When I come back victorious, I will break down this tower."

10 Now Zebah and Zalmunna were in Karkor with their army, about fifteen thousand men, all who were left of all the army of the people of the east; for one hundred twenty thousand men bearing arms had fallen. 11So Gideon went up by the caravan route east of Nobah and Jogbehah, and attacked the army; for the army was off its guard. 12Zebah and Zalmunna fled; and he pursued them and took the two kings of Midian, Zebah and Zalmunna, and threw all the army into a panic.

13 When Gideon son of Joash returned from the battle by the ascent of Heres, 14he caught a young man, one of the people of Succoth, and questioned him; and he listed for him the officials and elders of Succoth, seventy-seven people. 15Then he came to the people of Succoth, and said, "Here are Zebah and Zalmunna, about whom you taunted me, saying, 'Do you already have in your possession the hands of Zebah and Zalmunna, that we should give bread to your troops who are exhausted?' " 16So he took the elders of the city and he took thorns of the wilderness and briers and with them he trampleda

y Another reading is *Zeredah*   z Gk: Heb *pursuing*
a With verse 7, Compare Gk: Heb *he taught*

the people of Succoth. ¹⁷He also broke down the tower of Penuel, and killed the men of the city.

18 Then he said to Zebah and Zalmunna, "What about the men whom you killed at Tabor?" They answered, "As you are, so were they, every one of them; they resembled the sons of a king." ¹⁹And he replied, "They were my brothers, the sons of my mother; as the LORD lives, if you had saved them alive, I would not kill you." ²⁰So he said to Jether his firstborn, "Go kill them!" But the boy did not draw his sword, for he was afraid, because he was still a boy. ²¹Then Zebah and Zalmunna said, "You come and kill us; for as the man is, so is his strength." So Gideon proceeded to kill Zebah and Zalmunna; and he took the crescents that were on the necks of their camels.

Gideon's Idolatry

22 Then the Israelites said to Gideon, "Rule over us, you and your son and your grandson also; for you have delivered us out of the hand of Midian." ²³Gideon said to them, "I will not rule over you, and my son will not rule over you; the LORD will rule over you." ²⁴Then Gideon said to them, "Let me make a request of you; each of you give me an earring he has taken as booty." (For the enemy[b] had golden earrings, because they were Ishmaelites.) ²⁵"We will willingly give them," they answered. So they spread a garment, and each threw into it an earring he had taken as booty. ²⁶The weight of the golden earrings that he requested was one thousand seven hundred shekels of gold (apart from the crescents and the pendants and the purple garments worn by the kings of Midian, and the collars that were on the necks of their camels). ²⁷Gideon made an ephod of it and put it in his town, in Ophrah; and all Israel prostituted themselves to it there, and it became a snare to Gideon and to his family. ²⁸So Midian was subdued before the Israelites, and they lifted up their heads no more. So the land had rest forty years in the days of Gideon.

Death of Gideon

29 Jerubbaal son of Joash went to live in his own house. ³⁰Now Gideon had seventy sons, his own offspring, for he had many wives. ³¹His concubine who was in Shechem also bore him a son, and he named him Abimelech. ³²Then Gideon son of Joash died at a good old age, and was buried in the tomb of his father Joash at Ophrah of the Abiezrites.

33 As soon as Gideon died, the Israelites relapsed and prostituted themselves with the Baals, making Baal-berith their god. ³⁴The Israelites did not remember the LORD their God, who had rescued them from the hand of all their enemies on every side; ³⁵and they did not exhibit loyalty to the house of Jerubbaal (that is, Gideon) in return for all the good that he had done to Israel.

Abimelech Attempts to Establish a Monarchy

9 Now Abimelech son of Jerubbaal went to Shechem to his mother's kinsfolk and said to them and to the whole clan of his mother's family, ²"Say in the hearing of all the lords of Shechem, 'Which is better for you, that all seventy of the sons of Jerubbaal rule over you, or that one rule over you?' Remember also that I am your bone and your flesh." ³So his mother's kinsfolk spoke all these words on his behalf in the hearing of all the lords of Shechem; and their hearts inclined to follow Abimelech, for they said, "He is our brother." ⁴They gave him seventy pieces of silver out of the temple of Baal-berith with which Abimelech hired worthless and reckless fellows, who followed him. ⁵He went to his father's house at Ophrah, and killed his brothers the sons of Jerubbaal, seventy men, on one stone; but Jotham, the youngest son of Jerubbaal, survived, for he hid himself. ⁶Then all the lords of Shechem and all Beth-millo came together, and they went and made Abimelech king, by the oak of the pillar[c] at Shechem.

The Parable of the Trees

7 When it was told to Jotham, he went and stood on the top of Mount Gerizim, and cried aloud and said to them, "Listen to me, you lords of Shechem, so that God may listen to you.
8   The trees once went out
        to anoint a king over themselves.
    So they said to the olive tree,
        'Reign over us.'
9   The olive tree answered them,
        'Shall I stop producing my rich oil
            by which gods and mortals are
                honored,

b Heb they   c Cn: Meaning of Heb uncertain

and go to sway over the trees?'
10 Then the trees said to the fig tree,
   'You come and reign over us.'
11 But the fig tree answered them,
   'Shall I stop producing my
      sweetness
   and my delicious fruit,
   and go to sway over the trees?'
12 Then the trees said to the vine,
   'You come and reign over us.'
13 But the vine said to them,
   'Shall I stop producing my wine
      that cheers gods and mortals,
   and go to sway over the trees?'
14 So all the trees said to the bramble,
   'You come and reign over us.'
15 And the bramble said to the trees,
   'If in good faith you are anointing
      me king over you,
   then come and take refuge in
      my shade;
   but if not, let fire come out of the
      bramble
   and devour the cedars of
      Lebanon.'

16 "Now therefore, if you acted in good faith and honor when you made Abimelech king, and if you have dealt well with Jerubbaal and his house, and have done to him as his actions deserved— 17for my father fought for you, and risked his life, and rescued you from the hand of Midian; 18but you have risen up against my father's house this day, and have killed his sons, seventy men on one stone, and have made Abimelech, the son of his slave woman, king over the lords of Shechem, because he is your kinsman— 19if, I say, you have acted in good faith and honor with Jerubbaal and with his house this day, then rejoice in Abimelech, and let him also rejoice in you; 20but if not, let fire come out from Abimelech, and devour the lords of Shechem, and Beth-millo; and let fire come out from the lords of Shechem, and from Beth-millo, and devour Abimelech." 21Then Jotham ran away and fled, going to Beer, where he remained for fear of his brother Abimelech.

The Downfall of Abimelech

22 Abimelech ruled over Israel three years. 23But God sent an evil spirit between Abimelech and the lords of Shechem; and the lords of Shechem dealt treacherously with Abimelech. 24This happened so that the violence done to the seventy sons of Jerubbaal might be avenged[d] and their blood be laid on their brother Abimelech, who killed them, and on the lords of Shechem, who strengthened his hands to kill his brothers. 25So, out of hostility to him, the lords of Shechem set ambushes on the mountain tops. They robbed all who passed by them along that way; and it was reported to Abimelech.

26 When Gaal son of Ebed moved into Shechem with his kinsfolk, the lords of Shechem put confidence in him. 27They went out into the field and gathered the grapes from their vineyards, trod them, and celebrated. Then they went into the temple of their god, ate and drank, and ridiculed Abimelech. 28Gaal son of Ebed said, "Who is Abimelech, and who are we of Shechem, that we should serve him? Did not the son of Jerubbaal and Zebul his officer serve the men of Hamor father of Shechem? Why then should we serve him? 29If only this people were under my command! Then I would remove Abimelech; I would say[e] to him, 'Increase your army, and come out.' "

30 When Zebul the ruler of the city heard the words of Gaal son of Ebed, his anger was kindled. 31He sent messengers to Abimelech at Arumah,[f] saying, "Look, Gaal son of Ebed and his kinsfolk have come to Shechem, and they are stirring up[g] the city against you. 32Now therefore, go by night, you and the troops that are with you, and lie in wait in the fields. 33Then early in the morning, as soon as the sun rises, get up and rush on the city; and when he and the troops that are with him come out against you, you may deal with them as best you can."

34 So Abimelech and all the troops with him got up by night and lay in wait against Shechem in four companies. 35When Gaal son of Ebed went out and stood in the entrance of the gate of the city, Abimelech and the troops with him rose from the ambush. 36And when Gaal saw them, he said to Zebul, "Look, people are coming down from the mountain tops!" And Zebul said to him, "The shadows on the mountains look like people to you." 37Gaal spoke again and said, "Look, people are coming down from Tabburerez, and one company is coming from

d Heb might come   e Gk: Heb and he said   f Cn
See 9.41. Heb Tormah   g Cn: Heb are besieging

the direction of Elon-meonenim."[h] [38]Then Zebul said to him, "Where is your boast[i] now, you who said, 'Who is Abimelech, that we should serve him?' Are not these the troops you made light of? Go out now and fight with them." [39]So Gaal went out at the head of the lords of Shechem, and fought with Abimelech. [40]Abimelech chased him, and he fled before him. Many fell wounded, up to the entrance of the gate. [41]So Abimelech resided at Arumah; and Zebul drove out Gaal and his kinsfolk, so that they could not live on at Shechem.

42 On the following day the people went out into the fields. When Abimelech was told, [43]he took his troops and divided them into three companies, and lay in wait in the fields. When he looked and saw the people coming out of the city, he rose against them and killed them. [44]Abimelech and the company that was[j] with him rushed forward and stood at the entrance of the gate of the city, while the two companies rushed on all who were in the fields and killed them. [45]Abimelech fought against the city all that day; he took the city, and killed the people that were in it; and he razed the city and sowed it with salt.

46 When all the lords of the Tower of Shechem heard of it, they entered the stronghold of the temple of El-berith. [47]Abimelech was told that all the lords of the Tower of Shechem were gathered together. [48]So Abimelech went up to Mount Zalmon, he and all the troops that were with him. Abimelech took an ax in his hand, cut down a bundle of brushwood, and took it up and laid it on his shoulder. Then he said to the troops with him, "What you have seen me do, do quickly, as I have done." [49]So every one of the troops cut down a bundle and following Abimelech put it against the stronghold, and they set the stronghold on fire over them, so that all the people of the Tower of Shechem also died, about a thousand men and women.

50 Then Abimelech went to Thebez, and encamped against Thebez, and took it. [51]But there was a strong tower within the city, and all the men and women and all the lords of the city fled to it and shut themselves in; and they went to the roof of the tower. [52]Abimelech came to the tower, and fought against it, and came near to the entrance of the tower to burn it with fire. [53]But a certain woman threw an upper millstone on Abimelech's head, and crushed his skull. [54]Immediately he called to the young man who carried his armor and said to him, "Draw your sword and kill me, so people will not say about me, 'A woman killed him.' " So the young man thrust him through, and he died. [55]When the Israelites saw that Abimelech was dead, they all went home. [56]Thus God repaid Abimelech for the crime he committed against his father in killing his seventy brothers; [57]and God also made all the wickedness of the people of Shechem fall back on their heads, and on them came the curse of Jotham son of Jerubbaal.

Tola and Jair

10 After Abimelech, Tola son of Puah son of Dodo, a man of Issachar, who lived at Shamir in the hill country of Ephraim, rose to deliver Israel. [2]He judged Israel twenty-three years. Then he died, and was buried at Shamir.

3 After him came Jair the Gileadite, who judged Israel twenty-two years. [4]He had thirty sons who rode on thirty donkeys; and they had thirty towns, which are in the land of Gilead, and are called Havvoth-jair to this day. [5]Jair died, and was buried in Kamon.

Oppression by the Ammonites

6 The Israelites again did what was evil in the sight of the LORD, worshiping the Baals and the Astartes, the gods of Aram, the gods of Sidon, the gods of Moab, the gods of the Ammonites, and the gods of the Philistines. Thus they abandoned the LORD, and did not worship him. [7]So the anger of the LORD was kindled against Israel, and he sold them into the hand of the Philistines and into the hand of the Ammonites, [8]and they crushed and oppressed the Israelites that year. For eighteen years they oppressed all the Israelites that were beyond the Jordan in the land of the Amorites, which is in Gilead. [9]The Ammonites also crossed the Jordan to fight against Judah and against Benjamin and against the house of Ephraim; so that Israel was greatly distressed.

10 So the Israelites cried to the LORD, saying, "We have sinned against you, be-

---

h That is *Diviners' Oak*   i Heb *mouth*   j Vg and some Gk Mss: Heb *companies that were* cause we have abandoned our God and have worshiped the Baals." ¹¹And the LORD said to the Israelites, "Did I not deliver you*k* from the Egyptians and from the Amorites, from the Ammonites and from the Philistines? ¹²The Sidonians also, and the Amalekites, and the Maonites, oppressed you; and you cried to me, and I delivered you out of their hand. ¹³Yet you have abandoned me and worshiped other gods; therefore I will deliver you no more. ¹⁴Go and cry to the gods whom you have chosen; let them deliver you in the time of your distress." ¹⁵And the Israelites said to the LORD, "We have sinned; do to us whatever seems good to you; but deliver us this day!" ¹⁶So they put away the foreign gods from among them and worshiped the LORD; and he could no longer bear to see Israel suffer.

17 Then the Ammonites were called to arms, and they encamped in Gilead; and the Israelites came together, and they encamped at Mizpah. ¹⁸The commanders of the people of Gilead said to one another, "Who will begin the fight against the Ammonites? He shall be head over all the inhabitants of Gilead."

Jephthah

11 Now Jephthah the Gileadite, the son of a prostitute, was a mighty warrior. Gilead was the father of Jephthah. ²Gilead's wife also bore him sons; and when his wife's sons grew up, they drove Jephthah away, saying to him, "You shall not inherit anything in our father's house; for you are the son of another woman." ³Then Jephthah fled from his brothers and lived in the land of Tob. Outlaws collected around Jephthah and went raiding with him.

4 After a time the Ammonites made war against Israel. ⁵And when the Ammonites made war against Israel, the elders of Gilead went to bring Jephthah from the land of Tob. ⁶They said to Jephthah, "Come and be our commander, so that we may fight with the Ammonites." ⁷But Jephthah said to the elders of Gilead, "Are you not the very ones who rejected me and drove me out of my father's house? So why do you come to me now when you are in trouble?" ⁸The elders of Gilead said to Jephthah, "Nevertheless, we have now turned back to you, so that you may go with us and fight with the Ammonites, and become head over us,

over all the inhabitants of Gilead." ⁹Jephthah said to the elders of Gilead, "If you bring me home again to fight with the Ammonites, and the LORD gives them over to me, I will be your head." ¹⁰And the elders of Gilead said to Jephthah, "The LORD will be witness between us; we will surely do as you say." ¹¹So Jephthah went with the elders of Gilead, and the people made him head and commander over them; and Jephthah spoke all his words before the LORD at Mizpah.

12 Then Jephthah sent messengers to the king of the Ammonites and said, "What is there between you and me, that you have come to me to fight against my land?" ¹³The king of the Ammonites answered the messengers of Jephthah, "Because Israel, on coming from Egypt, took away my land from the Arnon to the Jabbok and to the Jordan; now therefore restore it peaceably." ¹⁴Once again Jephthah sent messengers to the king of the Ammonites ¹⁵and said to him: "Thus says Jephthah: Israel did not take away the land of Moab or the land of the Ammonites, ¹⁶but when they came up from Egypt, Israel went through the wilderness to the Red Sea*l* and came to Kadesh. ¹⁷Israel then sent messengers to the king of Edom, saying, 'Let us pass through your land'; but the king of Edom would not listen. They also sent to the king of Moab, but he would not consent. So Israel remained at Kadesh. ¹⁸Then they journeyed through the wilderness, went around the land of Edom and the land of Moab, arrived on the east side of the land of Moab, and camped on the other side of the Arnon. They did not enter the territory of Moab, for the Arnon was the boundary of Moab. ¹⁹Israel then sent messengers to King Sihon of the Amorites, king of Heshbon; and Israel said to him, 'Let us pass through your land to our country.' ²⁰But Sihon did not trust Israel to pass through his territory; so Sihon gathered all his people together, and encamped at Jahaz, and fought with Israel. ²¹Then the LORD, the God of Israel, gave Sihon and all his people into the hand of Israel, and they defeated them; so Israel occupied all the land of the Amorites, who inhabited that country. ²²They occupied all the territory of the Amorites from the Arnon to the

k Heb lacks *Did I not deliver you*   *l* Or *Sea of Reeds*

Jabbok and from the wilderness to the Jordan. [23]So now the LORD, the God of Israel, has conquered the Amorites for the benefit of his people Israel. Do you intend to take their place? [24]Should you not possess what your god Chemosh gives you to possess? And should we not be the ones to possess everything that the LORD our God has conquered for our benefit? [25]Now are you any better than King Balak son of Zippor of Moab? Did he ever enter into conflict with Israel, or did he ever go to war with them? [26]While Israel lived in Heshbon and its villages, and in Aroer and its villages, and in all the towns that are along the Arnon, three hundred years, why did you not recover them within that time? [27]It is not I who have sinned against you, but you are the one who does me wrong by making war on me. Let the LORD, who is judge, decide today for the Israelites or for the Ammonites." [28]But the king of the Ammonites did not heed the message that Jephthah sent him.

Jephthah's Vow

29 Then the spirit of the LORD came upon Jephthah, and he passed through Gilead and Manasseh. He passed on to Mizpah of Gilead, and from Mizpah of Gilead he passed on to the Ammonites. [30]And Jephthah made a vow to the LORD, and said, "If you will give the Ammonites into my hand, [31]then whoever comes out of the doors of my house to meet me, when I return victorious from the Ammonites, shall be the LORD's, to be offered up by me as a burnt offering." [32]So Jephthah crossed over to the Ammonites to fight against them; and the LORD gave them into his hand. [33]He inflicted a massive defeat on them from Aroer to the neighborhood of Minnith, twenty towns, and as far as Abel-keramim. So the Ammonites were subdued before the people of Israel.

Jephthah's Daughter

34 Then Jephthah came to his home at Mizpah; and there was his daughter coming out to meet him with timbrels and with dancing. She was his only child; he had no son or daughter except her. [35]When he saw her, he tore his clothes, and said, "Alas, my daughter! You have brought me very low; you have become the cause of great trouble to me. For I have opened my mouth to the LORD, and I can-

not take back my vow." [36]She said to him, "My father, if you have opened your mouth to the LORD, do to me according to what has gone out of your mouth, now that the LORD has given you vengeance against your enemies, the Ammonites." [37]And she said to her father, "Let this thing be done for me: Grant me two months, so that I may go and wander[m] on the mountains, and bewail my virginity, my companions and I." [38]"Go," he said and sent her away for two months. So she departed, she and her companions, and bewailed her virginity on the mountains. [39]At the end of two months, she returned to her father, who did with her according to the vow he had made. She had never slept with a man. So there arose an Israelite custom that [40]for four days every year the daughters of Israel would go out to lament the daughter of Jephthah the Gileadite.

Intertribal Dissension

12 The men of Ephraim were called to arms, and they crossed to Zaphon and said to Jephthah, "Why did you cross over to fight against the Ammonites, and did not call us to go with you? We will burn your house down over you!" [2]Jephthah said to them, "My people and I were engaged in conflict with the Ammonites who oppressed us[n] severely. But when I called you, you did not deliver me from their hand. [3]When I saw that you would not deliver me, I took my life in my hand, and crossed over against the Ammonites, and the LORD gave them into my hand. Why then have you come up to me this day, to fight against me?" [4]Then Jephthah gathered all the men of Gilead and fought with Ephraim; and the men of Gilead defeated Ephraim, because they said, "You are fugitives from Ephraim, you Gileadites—in the heart of Ephraim and Manasseh."[o] [5]Then the Gileadites took the fords of the Jordan against the Ephraimites. Whenever one of the fugitives of Ephraim said, "Let me go over," the men of Gilead would say to him, "Are you an Ephraimite?" When he said, "No," [6]they said to him, "Then say Shibboleth," and he said, "Sibboleth," for he could not pronounce it right. Then they seized him and

---

m Cn: Heb go down   n Gk OL, Syr H: Heb lacks *who oppressed us*   o Meaning of Heb uncertain: Gk omits *because . . . Manasseh*

killed him at the fords of the Jordan.
Forty-two thousand of the Ephraimites
fell at that time.

7 Jephthah judged Israel six years. Then
Jephthah the Gileadite died, and was buried in his town in Gilead. *p*

Ibzan, Elon, and Abdon

8 After him Ibzan of Bethlehem judged
Israel. 9He had thirty sons. He gave his
thirty daughters in marriage outside his
clan and brought in thirty young women
from outside for his sons. He judged Israel
seven years. 10Then Ibzan died, and was
buried at Bethlehem.

11 After him Elon the Zebulunite
judged Israel; and he judged Israel ten
years. 12Then Elon the Zebulunite died,
and was buried at Aijalon in the land of
Zebulun.

13 After him Abdon son of Hillel the
Pirathonite judged Israel. 14He had forty
sons and thirty grandsons, who rode on
seventy donkeys; he judged Israel eight
years. 15Then Abdon son of Hillel the Pirathonite died, and was buried at Pirathon
in the land of Ephraim, in the hill country
of the Amalekites.

The Birth of Samson

13 The Israelites again did what was
evil in the sight of the LORD, and
the LORD gave them into the hand of the
Philistines forty years.

2 There was a certain man of Zorah, of
the tribe of the Danites, whose name was
Manoah. His wife was barren, having
borne no children. 3And the angel of the
LORD appeared to the woman and said to
her, "Although you are barren, having
borne no children, you shall conceive and
bear a son. 4Now be careful not to drink
wine or strong drink, or to eat anything
unclean, 5for you shall conceive and bear
a son. No razor is to come on his head, for
the boy shall be a nazirite*q* to God from
birth. It is he who shall begin to deliver
Israel from the hand of the Philistines."
6Then the woman came and told her husband, "A man of God came to me, and his
appearance was like that of an angel*r* of
God, most awe-inspiring; I did not ask
him where he came from, and he did not
tell me his name; 7but he said to me, 'You
shall conceive and bear a son. So then
drink no wine or strong drink, and eat
nothing unclean, for the boy shall be a

nazirite*q* to God from birth to the day of
his death.' "

8 Then Manoah entreated the LORD,
and said, "O LORD, I pray, let the man of
God whom you sent come to us again and
teach us what we are to do concerning the
boy who will be born." 9God listened to
Manoah, and the angel of God came again
to the woman as she sat in the field; but
her husband Manoah was not with her.
10So the woman ran quickly and told her
husband, "The man who came to me the
other day has appeared to me." 11Manoah
got up and followed his wife, and came to
the man and said to him, "Are you the
man who spoke to this woman?" And he
said, "I am." 12Then Manoah said, "Now
when your words come true, what is to be
the boy's rule of life; what is he to do?"
13The angel of the LORD said to Manoah,
"Let the woman give heed to all that I said
to her. 14She may not eat of anything that
comes from the vine. She is not to drink
wine or strong drink, or eat any unclean
thing. She is to observe everything that I
commanded her."

15 Manoah said to the angel of the
LORD, "Allow us to detain you, and prepare a kid for you." 16The angel of the LORD
said to Manoah, "If you detain me, I will
not eat your food; but if you want to prepare a burnt offering, then offer it to the
LORD." (For Manoah did not know that he
was the angel of the LORD.) 17Then Manoah said to the angel of the LORD, "What is
your name, so that we may honor you
when your words come true?" 18But the angel of the LORD said to him, "Why do you
ask my name? It is too wonderful."

19 So Manoah took the kid with the
grain offering, and offered it on the rock
to the LORD, to him who works*s* wonders.*t* 20When the flame went up toward
heaven from the altar, the angel of the
LORD ascended in the flame of the altar
while Manoah and his wife looked on;
and they fell on their faces to the ground.
21The angel of the LORD did not appear
again to Manoah and his wife. Then Manoah realized that it was the angel of the
LORD. 22And Manoah said to his wife, "We
shall surely die, for we have seen God."
23But his wife said to him, "If the LORD

p Gk: Heb *in the towns of Gilead*   *q* That is *one
separated* or *one consecrated*   *r* Or *the angel*
s Gk Vg: Heb *and working*   *t* Heb *wonders, while
Manoah and his wife looked on*

had meant to kill us, he would not have accepted a burnt offering and a grain offering at our hands, or shown us all these things, or now announced to us such things as these."

24 The woman bore a son, and named him Samson. The boy grew, and the LORD blessed him. 25The spirit of the LORD began to stir him in Mahaneh-dan, between Zorah and Eshtaol.

Samson's Marriage

14 Once Samson went down to Timnah, and at Timnah he saw a Philistine woman. 2Then he came up, and told his father and mother, "I saw a Philistine woman at Timnah; now get her for me as my wife." 3But his father and mother said to him, "Is there not a woman among your kin, or among all our*u* peo-

ple, that you must go to take a wife from the uncircumcised Philistines?" But Samson said to his father, "Get her for me, because she pleases me." 4His father and mother did not know that this was from the LORD; for he was seeking a pretext to act against the Philistines. At that time the Philistines had dominion over Israel.

5 Then Samson went down with his father and mother to Timnah. When he came to the vineyards of Timnah, suddenly a young lion roared at him. 6The spirit of the LORD rushed on him, and he tore the lion apart barehanded as one might tear apart a kid. But he did not tell his father or his mother what he had done. 7Then he went down and talked with the woman, and she pleased Samson. 8After a

u Cn: Heb *my*

THE TRADITION

Purgatory

"We shall surely die, for we have seen God."
JUDGES 13.22

*P*urgatory makes sense.

Certainly the people of the Old Testament, who never used the word itself, felt the need for the process it refers to. They believed that because of the great divide between God's holiness and human sinfulness, no one could see God and live.

"We shall surely die, for we have seen God," said Samson's father after realizing the identity of the heavenly messenger who had announced his son's birth. "Woe is me! I am lost," Isaiah cried out when he had a vision of God enthroned. "I am a man of unclean lips, and I live among a people of unclean lips; yet my eyes have seen the King, the LORD of hosts!" (Isaiah 6.5). At Mount Sinai the Israelites were so overcome simply by *hearing* God that they begged Moses to be their go-between (see Deuteronomy 5.25).

With the incarnation, God became approachable in a way these people never could have imagined. But their basic instincts were

right. They knew themselves unfit for close dealings with God.

God invites us to a relationship of union with him. It is a "like Father, like child" calling: "Be perfect, therefore, as your heavenly Father is perfect" (Matthew 5.48). Like a vine being pruned, like gold being refined, we become purified so that we resemble Jesus more and more. If we cooperate with grace, the process is completed in this life. If not, there is purgatory.

Though we speak of being "in" it, purgatory is not so much a place as a purifying process. This process is symbolized in Scripture as a cleansing fire (1 Corinthians 3.15; 1 Peter 1.7), but it is a purification altogether different from the punishment of the damned. Souls in purgatory have the joy of knowing they will see God.

Purgatory not only makes sense, by giving us a chance to complete what we began on earth, it also reveals God's mercy.

while he returned to marry her, and he turned aside to see the carcass of the lion, and there was a swarm of bees in the body of the lion, and honey. 9He scraped it out into his hands, and went on, eating as he went. When he came to his father and mother, he gave some to them, and they ate it. But he did not tell them that he had taken the honey from the carcass of the lion.

10 His father went down to the woman, and Samson made a feast there as the young men were accustomed to do. 11When the people saw him, they brought thirty companions to be with him. 12Samson said to them, "Let me now put a riddle to you. If you can explain it to me within the seven days of the feast, and find it out, then I will give you thirty linen garments and thirty festal garments. 13But if you cannot explain it to me, then you shall give me thirty linen garments and thirty festal garments." So they said to him, "Ask your riddle; let us hear it." 14He said to them,

"Out of the eater came something
    to eat.
Out of the strong came something
    sweet."

But for three days they could not explain the riddle.

15 On the fourth*v* day they said to Samson's wife, "Coax your husband to explain the riddle to us, or we will burn you and your father's house with fire. Have you invited us here to impoverish us?" 16So Samson's wife wept before him, saying, "You hate me; you do not really love me. You have asked a riddle of my people, but you have not explained it to me." He said to her, "Look, I have not told my father or my mother. Why should I tell you?" 17She wept before him the seven days that their feast lasted; and because she nagged him, on the seventh day he told her. Then she explained the riddle to her people. 18The men of the town said to him on the seventh day before the sun went down,

"What is sweeter than honey?
What is stronger than a lion?"

And he said to them,

"If you had not plowed with my
    heifer,
you would not have found out my
    riddle."

19Then the spirit of the LORD rushed on him, and he went down to Ashkelon. He killed thirty men of the town, took their spoil, and gave the festal garments to those who had explained the riddle. In hot anger he went back to his father's house. 20And Samson's wife was given to his companion, who had been his best man.

Samson Defeats the Philistines

15 After a while, at the time of the wheat harvest, Samson went to visit his wife, bringing along a kid. He said, "I want to go into my wife's room." But her father would not allow him to go in. 2Her father said, "I was sure that you had rejected her; so I gave her to your companion. Is not her younger sister prettier than she? Why not take her instead?" 3Samson said to them, "This time, when I do mischief to the Philistines, I will be without blame." 4So Samson went and caught three hundred foxes, and took some torches; and he turned the foxes*w* tail to tail, and put a torch between each pair of tails. 5When he had set fire to the torches, he let the foxes go into the standing grain of the Philistines, and burned up the shocks and the standing grain, as well as the vineyards and*x* olive groves. 6Then the Philistines asked, "Who has done this?" And they said, "Samson, the son-in-law of the Timnite, because he has taken Samson's wife and given her to his companion." So the Philistines came up, and burned her and her father. 7Samson said to them, "If this is what you do, I swear I will not stop until I have taken revenge on you." 8He struck them down hip and thigh with great slaughter; and he went down and stayed in the cleft of the rock of Etam.

9 Then the Philistines came up and encamped in Judah, and made a raid on Lehi. 10The men of Judah said, "Why have you come up against us?" They said, "We have come up to bind Samson, to do to him as he did to us." 11Then three thousand men of Judah went down to the cleft of the rock of Etam, and they said to Samson, "Do you not know that the Philistines are rulers over us? What then have you done to us?" He replied, "As they did to me, so I have done to them." 12They said to him, "We have come down to bind you, so that we may give you into the hands of the Philistines." Samson answered them, "Swear to me that you your-

v Gk Syr: Heb *seventh*   *w* Heb *them*   *x* Gk Tg Vg: Heb lacks *and* selves will not attack me." [13]They said to him, "No, we will only bind you and give you into their hands; we will not kill you." So they bound him with two new ropes, and brought him up from the rock.

14 When he came to Lehi, the Philistines came shouting to meet him; and the spirit of the LORD rushed on him, and the ropes that were on his arms became like flax that has caught fire, and his bonds melted off his hands. [15]Then he found a fresh jawbone of a donkey, reached down and took it, and with it he killed a thousand men. [16]And Samson said,

"With the jawbone of a donkey,
heaps upon heaps,
with the jawbone of a donkey
I have slain a thousand men."

[17]When he had finished speaking, he threw away the jawbone; and that place was called Ramath-lehi.[y]

18 By then he was very thirsty, and he called on the LORD, saying, "You have granted this great victory by the hand of your servant. Am I now to die of thirst, and fall into the hands of the uncircumcised?" [19]So God split open the hollow place that is at Lehi, and water came from it. When he drank, his spirit returned, and he revived. Therefore it was named En-hakkore,[z] which is at Lehi to this day. [20]And he judged Israel in the days of the Philistines twenty years.

Samson and Delilah

16 Once Samson went to Gaza, where he saw a prostitute and went in to her. [2]The Gazites were told,[a] "Samson has come here." So they circled around and lay in wait for him all night at the city gate. They kept quiet all night, thinking, "Let us wait until the light of the morning; then we will kill him." [3]But Samson lay only until midnight. Then at midnight he rose up, took hold of the doors of the city gate and the two posts, pulled them up, bar and all, put them on his shoulders, and carried them to the top of the hill that is in front of Hebron.

4 After this he fell in love with a woman in the valley of Sorek, whose name was Delilah. [5]The lords of the Philistines came to her and said to her, "Coax him, and find out what makes his strength so great, and how we may overpower him, so that we may bind him in order to subdue him; and we will each give you eleven hundred pieces of silver." [6]So Delilah said to Samson, "Please tell me what makes your strength so great, and how you could be bound, so that one could subdue you." [7]Samson said to her, "If they bind me with seven fresh bowstrings that are not dried out, then I shall become weak, and be like anyone else." [8]Then the lords of the Philistines brought her seven fresh bowstrings that had not dried out, and she bound him with them. [9]While men were lying in wait in an inner chamber, she said to him, "The Philistines are upon you, Samson!" But he snapped the bowstrings, as a strand of fiber snaps when it touches the fire. So the secret of his strength was not known.

10 Then Delilah said to Samson, "You have mocked me and told me lies; please tell me how you could be bound." [11]He said to her, "If they bind me with new ropes that have not been used, then I shall become weak, and be like anyone else." [12]So Delilah took new ropes and bound him with them, and said to him, "The Philistines are upon you, Samson!" (The men lying in wait were in an inner chamber.) But he snapped the ropes off his arms like a thread.

13 Then Delilah said to Samson, "Until now you have mocked me and told me lies; tell me how you could be bound." He said to her, "If you weave the seven locks of my head with the web and make it tight with the pin, then I shall become weak, and be like anyone else." [14]So while he slept, Delilah took the seven locks of his head and wove them into the web,[b] and made them tight with the pin. Then she said to him, "The Philistines are upon you, Samson!" But he awoke from his sleep, and pulled away the pin, the loom, and the web.

15 Then she said to him, "How can you say, 'I love you,' when your heart is not with me? You have mocked me three times now and have not told me what makes your strength so great." [16]Finally, after she had nagged him with her words day after day, and pestered him, he was tired to death. [17]So he told her his whole secret, and said to her, "A razor has never come upon my head; for I have been a

y That is *The Hill of the Jawbone*   *z* That is *The Spring of the One who Called*   *a* Gk: Heb lacks *were told*   *b* Compare Gk: in verses 13–14, Heb lacks *and make it tight . . . into the web*

nazirite[c] to God from my mother's womb. If my head were shaved, then my strength would leave me; I would become weak, and be like anyone else."

18 When Delilah realized that he had told her his whole secret, she sent and called the lords of the Philistines, saying, "This time come up, for he has told his whole secret to me." Then the lords of the Philistines came up to her, and brought the money in their hands. [19]She let him fall asleep on her lap; and she called a man, and had him shave off the seven locks of his head. He began to weaken,[d] and his strength left him. [20]Then she said, "The Philistines are upon you, Samson!" When he awoke from his sleep, he thought, "I will go out as at other times, and shake myself free." But he did not know that the LORD had left him. [21]So the Philistines seized him and gouged out his eyes. They brought him down to Gaza and bound him with bronze shackles; and he ground at the mill in the prison. [22]But the hair of his head began to grow again after it had been shaved.

Samson's Death

23 Now the lords of the Philistines gathered to offer a great sacrifice to their god Dagon, and to rejoice; for they said, "Our god has given Samson our enemy into our hand." [24]When the people saw him, they praised their god; for they said, "Our god has given our enemy into our hand, the ravager of our country, who has killed many of us." [25]And when their hearts were merry, they said, "Call Samson, and let him entertain us." So they called Samson out of the prison, and he performed for them. They made him stand between the pillars; [26]and Samson said to the attendant who held him by the hand, "Let me feel the pillars on which the house rests, so that I may lean against them." [27]Now the house was full of men and women; all the lords of the Philistines were there, and on the roof there were about three thousand men and women, who looked on while Samson performed. 28 Then Samson called to the LORD and said, "Lord GOD, remember me and strengthen me only this once, O God, so that with this one act of revenge I may pay back the Philistines for my two eyes."[e] [29]And Samson grasped the two middle pillars on which the house rested, and he leaned his weight against them, his right

hand on the one and his left hand on the other. [30]Then Samson said, "Let me die with the Philistines." He strained with all his might; and the house fell on the lords and all the people who were in it. So those he killed at his death were more than those he had killed during his life. [31]Then his brothers and all his family came down and took him and brought him up and buried him between Zorah and Eshtaol in the tomb of his father Manoah. He had judged Israel twenty years.

Micah and the Levite

17 There was a man in the hill country of Ephraim whose name was Micah. [2]He said to his mother, "The eleven hundred pieces of silver that were taken from you, about which you uttered a curse, and even spoke it in my hearing,— that silver is in my possession; I took it; but now I will return it to you."[f] And his mother said, "May my son be blessed by the LORD!" [3]Then he returned the eleven hundred pieces of silver to his mother; and his mother said, "I consecrate the silver to the LORD from my hand for my son, to make an idol of cast metal." [4]So when he returned the money to his mother, his mother took two hundred pieces of silver, and gave it to the silversmith, who made it into an idol of cast metal; and it was in the house of Micah. [5]This man Micah had a shrine, and he made an ephod and teraphim, and installed one of his sons, who became his priest. [6]In those days there was no king in Israel; all the people did what was right in their own eyes.

7 Now there was a young man of Bethlehem in Judah, of the clan of Judah. He was a Levite residing there. [8]This man left the town of Bethlehem in Judah, to live wherever he could find a place. He came to the house of Micah in the hill country of Ephraim to carry on his work.[g] [9]Micah said to him, "From where do you come?" He replied, "I am a Levite of Bethlehem in Judah, and I am going to live wherever I can find a place." [10]Then Micah said to him, "Stay with me, and be to me a father and a priest, and I will give you ten pieces

---

[c] That is *one separated* or *one consecrated*
[d] Gk: Heb *She began to torment him*   [e] Or *so that I may be avenged upon the Philistines for one of my two eyes*   [f] The words *but now I will return it to you* are transposed from the end of verse 3 in Heb   [g] Or *Ephraim, continuing his journey*

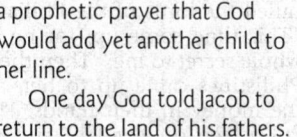

Rachel

Her Name Means "Ewe"

Read Genesis 29; 35.16–19

Was it better to have Jacob's love or to bear his children? Why did she even have to make such a choice? The questions battered Rachel, like wind slamming the same door again and again.

Leah had just given birth to her fourth son, Judah. In her joy she had shouted, "I will praise the LORD." Her firstborn son's name, Reuben, means "See, a son"; Simeon means, "he hears"; and Levi means, "he will become attached," as though Jacob could ever be attached to his plain wife! Rachel was sick to death of her sister's habit of naming her sons in ways that emphasized Rachel's own barrenness.

Years earlier, Rachel's father, Laban, had promised her to his nephew Jacob with the condition that the young man work for him for seven years. But when her wedding day arrived, Laban instructed Leah to disguise herself in Rachel's wedding garments. After dark he led his older daughter, covered by a veil, to Jacob's tent. As the first light crept across the tent floor, Jacob reached for Rachel only to find Leah at his side.

But soon Laban struck another bargain with Jacob, giving him Rachel in exchange for seven more years of labor. So the two sisters lived uneasily together, Leah's sons a grating reminder that Rachel, the second wife, was cheated still.

"Give me children, or I shall die!" she shouted at Jacob one day—as though he were God, able to create life (30.1). Finally, Rachel

THE STORY OF A WOMAN

Her Character: *Manipulated by her father, she had little say over her own life circumstances and relationships. But rather than dealing creatively with a difficult situation, she behaved like a victim who responded to sin with yet more sin, making things worse by competing with her sister.*
Her Tragedy: *That her rivalry with her sister led to family discord that continued to the next generation.*
Her Joy: *That her husband cherished her and would do whatever was in his power to make her happy.*

gave birth to a son, naming him Joseph, meaning "may he add"— a prophetic prayer that God would add yet another child to her line.

One day God told Jacob to return to the land of his fathers. More than 20 years before, Jacob had wrestled the blessing from Esau and had fled from his anger. Had the long years paid him back two-fold? Had Laban's treachery and the wrestling match between Rachel and Leah reminded him of his own struggles with his brother? Would God—and Esau—call it even?

As they made their way across the desert, Jacob faced his brother and the two reconciled. Soon after, however, Rachel struggled to give birth to a second son, the answer to her many prayers. Ironically, the woman who once said she would die unless she had children actually died giving birth. She named the child *Ben-oni,* "Son of my sorrow." But Jacob renamed him Benjamin, "Son of the right hand."

Like her husband, the beautiful Rachel was both schemer and victim. Tricked by her own father, she viewed her children as weapons in the struggle with her sister. But the lessons of treachery and competition were passed from generation to generation: Rachel's own son, Joseph, would be sold into slavery by his half-brothers, Leah's sons.

Yet through a remarkable set of twists and turns, Rachel's Joseph would one day rule Egypt, providing a refuge for his father and brothers in the midst of famine. Using people with mixed motives and confused desires (the only kind of people there are), God again revealed his grace and mercy, never forsaking his promise to be with his people.

Praying With Rachel

Then God remembered Rachel, and God heeded her and opened her womb.
—*Genesis 30.22*

Praise God: *Because he never for a moment forgets about us. He is present and attentive, aware of our deepest desires, even when we're certain he's lost track of us.*

Thank God: *That he alone is the Creator. Because of him, every human life is sacred.*

Confess: *That we sometimes use our children, our husbands, our homes, or even the size of our paychecks to compete with other women.*

Ask God: *To help you form deep and loyal friendships with other women so that you can know the joy that comes from being sisters in Christ.*

Lift Your Heart

Think of one woman you would like to get to know better in the next few months. Then pick up the phone and make a lunch date or invite her to a play, movie, or concert. Make sure you build in a little time to chat so you can begin to develop a relationship. One expert says it takes an average of three years to form a solid friendship. Don't waste another moment!

Father, forgive me for letting my identity rest on whose wife or mother I am or what kind of job I have. I don't want to view other women as my rivals but as potential friends and even soul mates. Please lead me to the friendships I desire and help me to be patient with the process.

Go to page 278 for your next devotional reading.

of silver a year, a set of clothes, and your living."[h] [11]The Levite agreed to stay with the man; and the young man became to him like one of his sons. [12]So Micah installed the Levite, and the young man became his priest, and was in the house of Micah. [13]Then Micah said, "Now I know that the LORD will prosper me, because the Levite has become my priest."

The Migration of Dan

18 In those days there was no king in Israel. And in those days the tribe of the Danites was seeking for itself a territory to live in; for until then no territory among the tribes of Israel had been allotted to them. [2]So the Danites sent five valiant men from the whole number of their clan, from Zorah and from Eshtaol, to spy out the land and to explore it; and they said to them, "Go, explore the land." When they came to the hill country of Ephraim, to the house of Micah, they stayed there. [3]While they were at Micah's house, they recognized the voice of the young Levite; so they went over and asked him, "Who brought you here? What are you doing in this place? What is your business here?" [4]He said to them, "Micah did such and such for me, and he hired me, and I have become his priest." [5]Then they said to him, "Inquire of God that we may know whether the mission we are undertaking will succeed." [6]The priest replied, "Go in peace. The mission you are on is under the eye of the LORD."

7 The five men went on, and when they came to Laish, they observed the people who were there living securely, after the manner of the Sidonians, quiet and unsuspecting, lacking[i] nothing on earth, and possessing wealth.[j] Furthermore, they were far from the Sidonians and had no dealings with Aram.[k] [8]When they came to their kinsfolk at Zorah and Eshtaol, they said to them, "What do you report?" [9]They said, "Come, let us go up against them; for we have seen the land, and it is very good. Will you do nothing? Do not be slow to go, but enter in and possess the land. [10]When you go, you will come to an unsuspecting people. The land is broad—God has indeed given it into your hands—a place where there is no lack of anything on earth."

11 Six hundred men of the Danite clan, armed with weapons of war, set out from Zorah and Eshtaol, [12]and went up and en-

camped at Kiriath-jearim in Judah. On this account that place is called Mahaneh-dan[l] to this day; it is west of Kiriath-jearim. [13]From there they passed on to the hill country of Ephraim, and came to the house of Micah.

14 Then the five men who had gone to spy out the land (that is, Laish) said to their comrades, "Do you know that in these buildings there are an ephod, teraphim, and an idol of cast metal? Now therefore consider what you will do." [15]So they turned in that direction and came to the house of the young Levite, at the home of Micah, and greeted him. [16]While the six hundred men of the Danites, armed with their weapons of war, stood by the entrance of the gate, [17]the five men who had gone to spy out the land proceeded to enter and take the idol of cast metal, the ephod, and the teraphim.[m] The priest was standing by the entrance of the gate with the six hundred men armed with weapons of war. [18]When the men went into Micah's house and took the idol of cast metal, the ephod, and the teraphim, the priest said to them, "What are you doing?" [19]They said to him, "Keep quiet! Put your hand over your mouth, and come with us, and be to us a father and a priest. Is it better for you to be priest to the house of one person, or to be priest to a tribe and clan in Israel?" [20]Then the priest accepted the offer. He took the ephod, the teraphim, and the idol, and went along with the people.

21 So they resumed their journey, putting the little ones, the livestock, and the goods in front of them. [22]When they were some distance from the home of Micah, the men who were in the houses near Micah's house were called out, and they overtook the Danites. [23]They shouted to the Danites, who turned around and said to Micah, "What is the matter that you come with such a company?" [24]He replied, "You take my gods that I made, and the priest, and go away, and what have I left? How then can you ask me, 'What is the matter?' " [25]And the Danites said to him, "You had better not let your voice be heard among us or else hot-tempered fel-

---

[h] Heb *living, and the Levite went*   [i] Cn Compare 18.10: Meaning of Heb uncertain   [j] Meaning of Heb uncertain   [k] Symmachus: Heb *with anyone*   [l] That is *Camp of Dan*   [m] Compare 17.4, 5; 18.14: Heb *teraphim and the cast metal*

lows will attack you, and you will lose your life and the lives of your household." 26Then the Danites went their way. When Micah saw that they were too strong for him, he turned and went back to his home.

The Danites Settle in Laish

27 The Danites, having taken what Micah had made, and the priest who belonged to him, came to Laish, to a people quiet and unsuspecting, put them to the sword, and burned down the city. 28There was no deliverer, because it was far from Sidon and they had no dealings with Aram.*n* It was in the valley that belongs to Beth-rehob. They rebuilt the city, and lived in it. 29They named the city Dan, after their ancestor Dan, who was born to Israel; but the name of the city was formerly Laish. 30Then the Danites set up the idol for themselves. Jonathan son of Gershom, son of Moses,*o* and his sons were priests to the tribe of the Danites until the time the land went into captivity. 31So they maintained as their own Micah's idol that he had made, as long as the house of God was at Shiloh.

The Levite's Concubine

19 In those days, when there was no king in Israel, a certain Levite, residing in the remote parts of the hill country of Ephraim, took to himself a concubine from Bethlehem in Judah. 2But his concubine became angry with*p* him, and she went away from him to her father's house at Bethlehem in Judah, and was there some four months. 3Then her husband set out after her, to speak tenderly to her and bring her back. He had with him his servant and a couple of donkeys. When he reached*q* her father's house, the girl's father saw him and came with joy to meet him. 4His father-in-law, the girl's father, made him stay, and he remained with him three days; so they ate and drank, and he*r* stayed there. 5On the fourth day they got up early in the morning, and he prepared to go; but the girl's father said to his son-in-law, "Fortify yourself with a bit of food, and after that you may go." 6So the two men sat and ate and drank together; and the girl's father said to the man, "Why not spend the night and enjoy yourself?" 7When the man got up to go, his father-in-law kept urging him until he spent the night there again.

8On the fifth day he got up early in the morning to leave; and the girl's father said, "Fortify yourself." So they lingered*s* until the day declined, and the two of them ate and drank.*t* 9When the man with his concubine and his servant got up to leave, his father-in-law, the girl's father, said to him, "Look, the day has worn on until it is almost evening. Spend the night. See, the day has drawn to a close. Spend the night here and enjoy yourself. Tomorrow you can get up early in the morning for your journey, and go home."

10 But the man would not spend the night; he got up and departed, and arrived opposite Jebus (that is, Jerusalem). He had with him a couple of saddled donkeys, and his concubine was with him. 11When they were near Jebus, the day was far spent, and the servant said to his master, "Come now, let us turn aside to this city of the Jebusites, and spend the night in it." 12But his master said to him, "We will not turn aside into a city of foreigners, who do not belong to the people of Israel; but we will continue on to Gibeah." 13Then he said to his servant, "Come, let us try to reach one of these places, and spend the night at Gibeah or at Ramah." 14So they passed on and went their way; and the sun went down on them near Gibeah, which belongs to Benjamin. 15They turned aside there, to go in and spend the night at Gibeah. He went in and sat down in the open square of the city, but no one took them in to spend the night.

16 Then at evening there was an old man coming from his work in the field. The man was from the hill country of Ephraim, and he was residing in Gibeah. (The people of the place were Benjaminites.) 17When the old man looked up and saw the wayfarer in the open square of the city, he said, "Where are you going and where do you come from?" 18He answered him, "We are passing from Bethlehem in Judah to the remote parts of the hill country of Ephraim, from which I come. I went to Bethlehem in Judah; and I am going to my home.*u* Nobody has offered to take

n Cn Compare verse 7: Heb *with anyone*
o Another reading is *son of Manasseh*   *p* Gk OL: Heb *prostituted herself against*   *q* Gk: Heb *she brought him to*   *r* Compare verse 7 and Gk: Heb *they*   *s* Cn: Heb *Linger*   *t* Gk: Heb lacks *and drank*   *u* Gk Compare 19.29. Heb *to the house of the LORD*

me in. ¹⁹We your servants have straw and fodder for our donkeys, with bread and wine for me and the woman and the young man along with us. We need nothing more." ²⁰The old man said, "Peace be to you. I will care for all your wants; only do not spend the night in the square." ²¹So he brought him into his house, and fed the donkeys; they washed their feet, and ate and drank.

Gibeah's Crime

22 While they were enjoying themselves, the men of the city, a perverse lot, surrounded the house, and started pounding on the door. They said to the old man, the master of the house, "Bring out the man who came into your house, so that we may have intercourse with him." ²³And the man, the master of the house, went out to them and said to them, "No, my brothers, do not act so wickedly. Since this man is my guest, do not do this vile thing. ²⁴Here are my virgin daughter and his concubine; let me bring them out now. Ravish them and do whatever you want to them; but against this man do not do such a vile thing." ²⁵But the men would not listen to him. So the man seized his concubine, and put her out to them. They wantonly raped her, and abused her all through the night until the morning. And as the dawn began to break, they let her go. ²⁶As morning appeared, the woman came and fell down at the door of the man's house where her master was, until it was light.

27 In the morning her master got up, opened the doors of the house, and when he went out to go on his way, there was his concubine lying at the door of the house, with her hands on the threshold. ²⁸"Get up," he said to her, "we are going." But there was no answer. Then he put her on the donkey; and the man set out for his home. ²⁹When he had entered his house, he took a knife, and grasping his concubine he cut her into twelve pieces, limb by limb, and sent her throughout all the territory of Israel. ³⁰Then he commanded the men whom he sent, saying, "Thus shall you say to all the Israelites, 'Has such a thing ever happened*v* since the day that the Israelites came up from the land of Egypt until this day? Consider it, take counsel, and speak out.' "

The Other Tribes Attack Benjamin

20 Then all the Israelites came out, from Dan to Beer-sheba, including the land of Gilead, and the congregation assembled in one body before the Lord at Mizpah. ²The chiefs of all the people, of all the tribes of Israel, presented themselves in the assembly of the people of God, four hundred thousand foot-soldiers bearing arms. ³(Now the Benjaminites heard that the people of Israel had gone up to Mizpah.) And the Israelites said, "Tell us, how did this criminal act come about?" ⁴The Levite, the husband of the woman who was murdered, answered, "I came to Gibeah that belongs to Benjamin, I and my concubine, to spend the night. ⁵The lords of Gibeah rose up against me, and surrounded the house at night. They intended to kill me, and they raped my concubine until she died. ⁶Then I took my concubine and cut her into pieces, and sent her throughout the whole extent of Israel's territory; for they have committed a vile outrage in Israel. ⁷So now, you Israelites, all of you, give your advice and counsel here."

8 All the people got up as one, saying, "We will not any of us go to our tents, nor will any of us return to our houses. ⁹But now this is what we will do to Gibeah: we will go up*w* against it by lot. ¹⁰We will take ten men of a hundred throughout all the tribes of Israel, and a hundred of a thousand, and a thousand of ten thousand, to bring provisions for the troops, who are going to repay*x* Gibeah of Benjamin for all the disgrace that they have done in Israel." ¹¹So all the men of Israel gathered against the city, united as one.

12 The tribes of Israel sent men through all the tribe of Benjamin, saying, "What crime is this that has been committed among you? ¹³Now then, hand over those scoundrels in Gibeah, so that we may put them to death, and purge the evil from Israel." But the Benjaminites would not listen to their kinsfolk, the Israelites. ¹⁴The Benjaminites came together out of the towns to Gibeah, to go out to battle against the Israelites. ¹⁵On that day the Benjaminites mustered twenty-six thousand armed men from their towns,

v Compare Gk: Heb ³⁰And all who saw it said, "Such a thing has not happened or been seen

w Gk: Heb lacks *we will go up*   *x* Compare Gk: Meaning of Heb uncertain besides the inhabitants of Gibeah. [16]Of all this force, there were seven hundred picked men who were left-handed; every one could sling a stone at a hair, and not miss. [17]And the Israelites, apart from Benjamin, mustered four hundred thousand armed men, all of them warriors.

18 The Israelites proceeded to go up to Bethel, where they inquired of God, "Which of us shall go up first to battle against the Benjaminites?" And the LORD answered, "Judah shall go up first."

19 Then the Israelites got up in the morning, and encamped against Gibeah. [20]The Israelites went out to battle against Benjamin; and the Israelites drew up the battle line against them at Gibeah. [21]The Benjaminites came out of Gibeah, and struck down on that day twenty-two thousand of the Israelites. [23][y] The Israelites went up and wept before the LORD until the evening; and they inquired of the LORD, "Shall we again draw near to battle against our kinsfolk the Benjaminites?" And the LORD said, "Go up against them." [22]The Israelites took courage, and again formed the battle line in the same place where they had formed it on the first day.

24 So the Israelites advanced against the Benjaminites the second day. [25]Benjamin moved out against them from Gibeah the second day, and struck down eighteen thousand of the Israelites, all of them armed men. [26]Then all the Israelites, the whole army, went back to Bethel and wept, sitting there before the LORD; they fasted that day until evening. Then they offered burnt offerings and sacrifices of well-being before the LORD. [27]And the Israelites inquired of the LORD (for the ark of the covenant of God was there in those days, [28]and Phinehas son of Eleazar, son of Aaron, ministered before it in those days), saying, "Shall we go out once more to battle against our kinsfolk the Benjaminites, or shall we desist?" The LORD answered, "Go up, for tomorrow I will give them into your hand."

29 So Israel stationed men in ambush around Gibeah. [30]Then the Israelites went up against the Benjaminites on the third day, and set themselves in array against Gibeah, as before. [31]When the Benjaminites went out against the army, they were drawn away from the city. As before they began to inflict casualties on the troops, along the main roads, one of which goes up to Bethel and the other to Gibeah, as well as in the open country, killing about thirty men of Israel. [32]The Benjaminites thought, "They are being routed before us, as previously." But the Israelites said, "Let us retreat and draw them away from the city toward the roads." [33]The main body of the Israelites drew back its battle line to Baal-tamar, while those Israelites who were in ambush rushed out of their place west[z] of Geba. [34]There came against Gibeah ten thousand picked men out of all Israel, and the battle was fierce. But the Benjaminites did not realize that disaster was close upon them.

35 The LORD defeated Benjamin before Israel; and the Israelites destroyed twenty-five thousand one hundred men of Benjamin that day, all of them armed.

36 Then the Benjaminites saw that they were defeated.[a]

The Israelites gave ground to Benjamin, because they trusted to the troops in ambush that they had stationed against Gibeah. [37]The troops in ambush rushed quickly upon Gibeah. Then they put the whole city to the sword. [38]Now the agreement between the main body of Israel and the men in ambush was that when they sent up a cloud of smoke out of the city [39]the main body of Israel should turn in battle. But Benjamin had begun to inflict casualties on the Israelites, killing about thirty of them; so they thought, "Surely they are defeated before us, as in the first battle." [40]But when the cloud, a column of smoke, began to rise out of the city, the Benjaminites looked behind them—and there was the whole city going up in smoke toward the sky! [41]Then the main body of Israel turned, and the Benjaminites were dismayed, for they saw that disaster was close upon them. [42]Therefore they turned away from the Israelites in the direction of the wilderness; but the battle overtook them, and those who came out of the city[b] were slaughtering them in between.[c] [43]Cutting down[d] the Benjaminites, they pursued them from Nohah[e] and trod them down as far as a place east of Gibeah. [44]Eighteen thousand Benjaminites fell, all of them courageous fighters. [45]When they

y Verses 22 and 23 are transposed   z Gk Vg:
Heb *in the plain*   a This sentence is continued
by verse 45.   b Compare Vg and some Gk Mss:
Heb *cities*   c Compare Syr: Meaning of Heb
uncertain   d Gk: Heb *Surrounding*   e Gk: Heb
pursued them at their resting place

turned and fled toward the wilderness to the rock of Rimmon, five thousand of them were cut down on the main roads, and they were pursued as far as Gidom, and two thousand of them were slain. ⁴⁶So all who fell that day of Benjamin were twenty-five thousand arms-bearing men, all of them courageous fighters. ⁴⁷But six hundred turned and fled toward the wilderness to the rock of Rimmon, and remained at the rock of Rimmon for four months. ⁴⁸Meanwhile, the Israelites turned back against the Benjaminites, and put them to the sword—the city, the people, the animals, and all that remained. Also the remaining towns they set on fire.

The Benjaminites Saved from Extinction

21 Now the Israelites had sworn at Mizpah, "No one of us shall give his daughter in marriage to Benjamin." ²And the people came to Bethel, and sat there until evening before God, and they lifted up their voices and wept bitterly. ³They said, "O LORD, the God of Israel, why has it come to pass that today there should be one tribe lacking in Israel?" ⁴On the next day, the people got up early, and built an altar there, and offered burnt offerings and sacrifices of well-being. ⁵Then the Israelites said, "Which of all the tribes of Israel did not come up in the assembly to the LORD?" For a solemn oath had been taken concerning whoever did not come up to the LORD to Mizpah, saying, "That one shall be put to death." ⁶But the Israelites had compassion for Benjamin their kin, and said, "One tribe is cut off from Israel this day. ⁷What shall we do for wives for those who are left, since we have sworn by the LORD that we will not give them any of our daughters as wives?"

8 Then they said, "Is there anyone from the tribes of Israel who did not come up to the LORD to Mizpah?" It turned out that no one from Jabesh-gilead had come to the camp, to the assembly. ⁹For when the roll was called among the people, not one of the inhabitants of Jabesh-gilead was there. ¹⁰So the congregation sent twelve thousand soldiers there and commanded them, "Go, put the inhabitants of Jabesh-gilead to the sword, including the women and the little ones. ¹¹This is what you shall do; every male and every woman that has lain with a male you shall devote to destruction." ¹²And they found among the inhabitants of Jabesh-gilead four hundred young virgins who had never slept with a man and brought them to the camp at Shiloh, which is in the land of Canaan.

13 Then the whole congregation sent word to the Benjaminites who were at the rock of Rimmon, and proclaimed peace to them. ¹⁴Benjamin returned at that time; and they gave them the women whom they had saved alive of the women of Jabesh-gilead; but they did not suffice for them.

15 The people had compassion on Benjamin because the LORD had made a breach in the tribes of Israel. ¹⁶So the elders of the congregation said, "What shall we do for wives for those who are left, since there are no women left in Benjamin?" ¹⁷And they said, "There must be heirs for the survivors of Benjamin, in order that a tribe may not be blotted out from Israel. ¹⁸Yet we cannot give any of our daughters to them as wives." For the Israelites had sworn, "Cursed be anyone who gives a wife to Benjamin." ¹⁹So they said, "Look, the yearly festival of the LORD is taking place at Shiloh, which is north of Bethel, on the east of the highway that goes up from Bethel to Shechem, and south of Lebonah." ²⁰And they instructed the Benjaminites, saying, "Go and lie in wait in the vineyards, ²¹and watch; when the young women of Shiloh come out to dance in the dances, then come out of the vineyards and each of you carry off a wife for himself from the young women of Shiloh, and go to the land of Benjamin. ²²Then if their fathers or their brothers come to complain to us, we will say to them, 'Be generous and allow us to have them; because we did not capture in battle a wife for each man. But neither did you incur guilt by giving your daughters to them.' " ²³The Benjaminites did so; they took wives for each of them from the dancers whom they abducted. Then they went and returned to their territory, and rebuilt the towns, and lived in them. ²⁴So the Israelites departed from there at that time by tribes and families, and they went out from there to their own territories.

25 In those days there was no king in Israel; all the people did what was right in their own eyes.

Ruth

The book of Ruth is one of only three books in the Bible in which a woman is featured as a central character. The other books are Esther and Judith. This short and wonderful narrative takes place in the time of the judges and provides a refreshing contrast to the stories contained in book of Judges. It also forms a bridge between the period of the judges and the period of Israel's first kings, Saul and David.

One of the central themes of Ruth is expressed by the Hebrew word *chesed*, meaning "loyalty." Ruth, a Moabite, showed extraordinary loyalty by leaving her homeland in order to follow her Jewish mother-in-law, Naomi, back to Bethlehem. In turn, God blessed Ruth by leading her to marry Boaz, an influential citizen of Bethlehem and Naomi's near relative. Ruth and Boaz became the great-grandparents of King David and ancestors of Jesus.

Like the stories of Tamar and of Rachel and Leah, the book of Ruth illustrates how God sometimes worked in unlikely ways to ensure the continuity of the family line of Christ, this time using an outsider and an elderly widow—two women who loved and cared for each other.

One of the most cherished verses in this book is spoken in Ruth 1.16: "Where you go, I will go; Where you lodge, I will lodge; your people shall be my people, and your God my God."

Elimelech's Family Goes to Moab

1 In the days when the judges ruled, there was a famine in the land, and a certain man of Bethlehem in Judah went to live in the country of Moab, he and his wife and two sons. ²The name of the man was Elimelech and the name of his wife Naomi, and the names of his two sons were Mahlon and Chilion; they were Ephrathites from Bethlehem in Judah. They went into the country of Moab and remained there. ³But Elimelech, the husband of Naomi, died, and she was left with her two sons. ⁴These took Moabite wives; the name of the one was Orpah and the name of the other Ruth. When they had lived there about ten years, ⁵both Mahlon and Chilion also died, so that the woman was left without her two sons and her husband.

Naomi and Her Moabite Daughters-in-Law

6 Then she started to return with her daughters-in-law from the country of

Moab, for she had heard in the country of Moab that the LORD had considered his people and given them food. ⁷So she set out from the place where she had been living, she and her two daughters-in-law, and they went on their way to go back to the land of Judah. ⁸But Naomi said to her two daughters-in-law, "Go back each of you to your mother's house. May the LORD deal kindly with you, as you have dealt with the dead and with me. ⁹The LORD grant that you may find security, each of you in the house of your husband." Then she kissed them, and they wept aloud.

¹⁰They said to her, "No, we will return with you to your people." ¹¹But Naomi said, "Turn back, my daughters, why will you go with me? Do I still have sons in my womb that they may become your husbands? ¹²Turn back, my daughters, go your way, for I am too old to have a husband. Even if I thought there was hope for me, even if I should have a husband to-night and bear sons, ¹³would you then wait until they were grown? Would you then refrain from marrying? No, my daughters, it has been far more bitter for me than for you, because the hand of the

Grieving

To a woman recently widowed:

A remark you made in your last letter echoes words that I found in one of Gabriel Marcel's plays: "Your death is my death." It is true that the moment we lose the beloved, something dies within us. And dying is both painful and fearful. When you say that you feel like a corpse, spiritually speaking, and resent being alive, "he" being dead, you are actually echoing the words of young Augustine writing about the death of his dearest friend: "I marveled more that I, his second self, could live when he was dead" (*Confessions* IV.6). And later, after he had become an ardent Christian, upon losing his beloved mother he wrote: "I closed her eyes, and a mighty sorrow welled up from the depths of my heart and overflowed into tears. At the same time, by a powerful command of my mind, my eyes drank up their source until it was dry. Most ill was it with me in such an agony!" (IX.12).

Death is and remains a great mystery. It is a moment of awesome aloneness in which I am cut off from the world I know so well. On the other hand, when I lose the person most beloved to me, I also undergo a death, a spiritual death that testifies to the depth of the bond that united us and to the depth of my sorrow.

If death is the separation of soul and body, is it surprising that I should experience some sort of death by being torn away from the person with whom I was one flesh? But the whole question of Christian widowhood hinges precisely on making of this dying a new source of life. "Unless a grain of wheat falls into the earth and dies, it remains just a single grain; but if it dies, it bears much fruit" (John 12.24).

—*ALICE VON HILDEBRAND*

MONDAY

Scripture Reading for Today:
Ruth 1

Verses for Today:
Ruth 1.20–21

Go to page 281 for your next devotional reading.

LORD has turned against me." [14]Then they wept aloud again. Orpah kissed her mother-in-law, but Ruth clung to her.

15 So she said, "See, your sister-in-law has gone back to her people and to her gods; return after your sister-in-law." [16]But Ruth said,

"Do not press me to leave you
    or to turn back from following
        you!
Where you go, I will go;
    where you lodge, I will lodge;
your people shall be my people,
    and your God my God.
[17] Where you die, I will die—
    there will I be buried.
May the LORD do thus and so to me,
    and more as well,
if even death parts me from you!"

[18]When Naomi saw that she was determined to go with her, she said no more to her.

19 So the two of them went on until they came to Bethlehem. When they came to Bethlehem, the whole town was stirred because of them; and the women said, "Is this Naomi?" [20]She said to them,

"Call me no longer Naomi,[a]
    call me Mara,[b]
    for the Almighty[c] has dealt
        bitterly with me.
[21] I went away full,
    but the LORD has brought me back
        empty;
why call me Naomi
    when the LORD has dealt harshly
        with[d] me,
    and the Almighty[c] has brought
        calamity upon me?"

22 So Naomi returned together with Ruth the Moabite, her daughter-in-law, who came back with her from the country of Moab. They came to Bethlehem at the beginning of the barley harvest.

Ruth Meets Boaz

2 Now Naomi had a kinsman on her husband's side, a prominent rich man, of the family of Elimelech, whose name was Boaz. [2]And Ruth the Moabite said to Naomi, "Let me go to the field and glean among the ears of grain, behind someone in whose sight I may find favor." She said to her, "Go, my daughter." [3]So she went. She came and gleaned in the field behind the reapers. As it happened, she came to the part of the field belonging to Boaz, who was of the family of Elime-

lech. [4]Just then Boaz came from Bethlehem. He said to the reapers, "The LORD be with you." They answered, "The LORD bless you." [5]Then Boaz said to his servant who was in charge of the reapers, "To whom does this young woman belong?" [6]The servant who was in charge of the reapers answered, "She is the Moabite who came back with Naomi from the country of Moab. [7]She said, 'Please, let me glean and gather among the sheaves behind the reapers.' So she came, and she has been on her feet from early this morning until now, without resting even for a moment."[e]

8 Then Boaz said to Ruth, "Now listen, my daughter, do not go to glean in another field or leave this one, but keep close to my young women. [9]Keep your eyes on the field that is being reaped, and follow behind them. I have ordered the young men not to bother you. If you get thirsty, go to the vessels and drink from what the young men have drawn." [10]Then she fell prostrate, with her face to the ground, and said to him, "Why have I found favor in your sight, that you should take notice of me, when I am a foreigner?" [11]But Boaz answered her, "All that you have done for your mother-in-law since the death of your husband has been fully told me, and how you left your father and mother and your native land and came to a people that you did not know before. [12]May the LORD reward you for your deeds, and may you have a full reward from the LORD, the God of Israel, under whose wings you have come for refuge!" [13]Then she said, "May I continue to find favor in your sight, my lord, for you have comforted me and spoken kindly to your servant, even though I am not one of your servants."

14 At mealtime Boaz said to her, "Come here, and eat some of this bread, and dip your morsel in the sour wine." So she sat beside the reapers, and he heaped up for her some parched grain. She ate until she was satisfied, and she had some left over. [15]When she got up to glean, Boaz instructed his young men, "Let her glean even among the standing sheaves, and do not reproach her. [16]You must also pull out some handfuls for her from the

---

[a] That is *Pleasant*   [b] That is *Bitter*   [c] Traditional rendering of Heb *Shaddai*   [d] Or *has testified against*   [e] Compare Gk Vg: Meaning of Heb uncertain

bundles, and leave them for her to glean, and do not rebuke her."

17 So she gleaned in the field until evening. Then she beat out what she had gleaned, and it was about an ephah of barley. 18She picked it up and came into the town, and her mother-in-law saw how much she had gleaned. Then she took out and gave her what was left over after she herself had been satisfied. 19Her mother-in-law said to her, "Where did you glean today? And where have you worked? Blessed be the man who took notice of you." So she told her mother-in-law with whom she had worked, and said, "The name of the man with whom I worked today is Boaz." 20Then Naomi said to her daughter-in-law, "Blessed be he by the LORD, whose kindness has not forsaken the living or the dead!" Naomi also said to her, "The man is a relative of ours, one of our nearest kin." f 21Then Ruth the Moabite said, "He even said to me, 'Stay close by my servants, until they have finished all my harvest.' " 22Naomi said to Ruth, her daughter-in-law, "It is better, my daughter, that you go out with his young women, otherwise you might be bothered in another field." 23So she stayed close to the young women of Boaz, gleaning until the end of the barley and wheat harvests; and she lived with her mother-in-law.

Ruth and Boaz at the Threshing Floor

3 Naomi her mother-in-law said to her, "My daughter, I need to seek some security for you, so that it may be well with you. 2Now here is our kinsman Boaz, with whose young women you have been working. See, he is winnowing barley tonight at the threshing floor. 3Now wash and anoint yourself, and put on your best clothes and go down to the threshing floor; but do not make yourself known to the man until he has finished eating and drinking. 4When he lies down, observe the place where he lies; then, go and uncover his feet and lie down; and he will tell you what to do." 5She said to her, "All that you tell me I will do."

6 So she went down to the threshing floor and did just as her mother-in-law had instructed her. 7When Boaz had eaten and drunk, and he was in a contented mood, he went to lie down at the end of the heap of grain. Then she came stealthily and uncovered his feet, and lay down. 8At midnight the man was startled, and

turned over, and there, lying at his feet, was a woman! 9He said, "Who are you?" And she answered, "I am Ruth, your servant; spread your cloak over your servant, for you are next-of-kin." f 10He said, "May you be blessed by the LORD, my daughter; this last instance of your loyalty is better than the first; you have not gone after young men, whether poor or rich. 11And now, my daughter, do not be afraid, I will do for you all that you ask, for all the assembly of my people know that you are a worthy woman. 12But now, though it is true that I am a near kinsman, there is another kinsman more closely related than I. 13Remain this night, and in the morning, if he will act as next-of-kin f for you, good; let him do it. If he is not willing to act as next-of-kin f for you, then, as the LORD lives, I will act as next-of-kin f for you. Lie down until the morning."

14 So she lay at his feet until morning, but got up before one person could recognize another; for he said, "It must not be known that the woman came to the threshing floor." 15Then he said, "Bring the cloak you are wearing and hold it out." So she held it, and he measured out six measures of barley, and put it on her back; then he went into the city. 16She came to her mother-in-law, who said, "How did things go with you, g my daughter?" Then she told her all that the man had done for her, 17saying, "He gave me these six measures of barley, for he said, 'Do not go back to your mother-in-law empty-handed.' " 18She replied, "Wait, my daughter, until you learn how the matter turns out, for the man will not rest, but will settle the matter today."

The Marriage of Boaz and Ruth

4 No sooner had Boaz gone up to the gate and sat down there than the next-of-kin, f of whom Boaz had spoken, came passing by. So Boaz said, "Come over, friend; sit down here." And he went over and sat down. 2Then Boaz took ten men of the elders of the city, and said, "Sit down here"; so they sat down. 3He then said to the next-of-kin, f "Naomi, who has come back from the country of Moab, is selling the parcel of land that belonged to our kinsman Elimelech. 4So I thought I would tell you of it, and say: Buy it in the

f Or one with the right to redeem   g Or "Who are you,

presence of those sitting here, and in the presence of the elders of my people. If you will redeem it, redeem it; but if you will not, tell me, so that I may know; for there is no one prior to you to redeem it, and I come after you." So he said, "I will redeem it." ⁵Then Boaz said, "The day you acquire

the field from the hand of Naomi, you are also acquiring Ruth[h] the Moabite, the widow of the dead man, to maintain the dead man's name on his inheritance." ⁶At

[h] OL Vg: Heb *from the hand of Naomi and from Ruth*

S*urrender*

TUESDAY

Scripture Reading
for Today:
Ruth 4.13–17

Verse for Today:
Ruth 4.15

Allow the questions that arise out of the story of Ruth to lead you to surrender even more deeply your whole being to God. Reflect upon the journey of Ruth by imagining yourself in a similar situation . . .

Your husband or a close friend is dead, gone—or the circumstances of your life have changed dramatically. You must face the rest of your life. Several choices lie before you. You can flee to the safety of the comfortable. Or you can choose the unknown, as did Ruth. When have you risked the unknown? What sacrifices did this entail? What did you leave behind?

The place you have come to is a place of hard work. You need to survive and to take care of the survival of others. For Ruth, this meant gathering the leftover grains in the field. It was a thankless job and she didn't fit in. When have you been in a situation [in which] mere survival occupied your every moment? When has taking care of another been a thankless task? What kept you going? When have you found yourself among strangers? How did you deal with the uncomfortable feelings of not being accepted?

Ruth obediently follows the detailed advice of Naomi in a plan to captivate her kinsman, Boaz. You have been in a situation where you are directed on how to act and what to wear in order to gain an advantage or perhaps even a husband as did Ruth. Duty challenges you to follow the customs of your family and culture in order to achieve something more. In what ways can you identify with Ruth? In your culture, what norms or customs do you need to obey? How does this feel? What have you gained by respecting the wishes of the elders in your family or your superiors on the job?

Finally, Ruth conceives and bears a child, who is the delight of Naomi. This son, Obed, was the father of Jesse, who was the father of David. How has your willingness to surrender led to new possibilities? When have you experienced the unexpected? What wondrous things has God wrought in you?

—*CAROL GURA*

Go to page 287 for your next devotional reading.

this, the next-of-kin[i] said, "I cannot redeem it for myself without damaging my own inheritance. Take my right of redemption yourself, for I cannot redeem it."

7 Now this was the custom in former times in Israel concerning redeeming and exchanging: to confirm a transaction, the one took off a sandal and gave it to the other; this was the manner of attesting in Israel. [8]So when the next-of-kin[i] said to Boaz, "Acquire it for yourself," he took off his sandal. [9]Then Boaz said to the elders and all the people, "Today you are witnesses that I have acquired from the hand of Naomi all that belonged to Elimelech and all that belonged to Chilion and Mahlon. [10]I have also acquired Ruth the Moabite, the wife of Mahlon, to be my wife, to maintain the dead man's name on his inheritance, in order that the name of the dead may not be cut off from his kindred and from the gate of his native place; today you are witnesses." [11]Then all the people who were at the gate, along with the elders, said, "We are witnesses. May the LORD make the woman who is coming into your house like Rachel and Leah, who together built up the house of Israel. May you produce children in Ephrathah and bestow a name in Bethlehem; [12]and, through the children that the LORD will give you by this young woman, may your house be like the house of Perez, whom Tamar bore to Judah."

The Genealogy of David

13 So Boaz took Ruth and she became his wife. When they came together, the LORD made her conceive, and she bore a son. [14]Then the women said to Naomi, "Blessed be the LORD, who has not left you this day without next-of-kin;[i] and may his name be renowned in Israel! [15]He shall be to you a restorer of life and a nourisher of your old age; for your daughter-in-law who loves you, who is more to you than seven sons, has borne him." [16]Then Naomi took the child and laid him in her bosom, and became his nurse. [17]The women of the neighborhood gave him a name, saying, "A son has been born to Naomi." They named him Obed; he became the father of Jesse, the father of David.

18 Now these are the descendants of Perez: Perez became the father of Hezron, [19]Hezron of Ram, Ram of Amminadab, [20]Amminadab of Nahshon, Nahshon of Salmon, [21]Salmon of Boaz, Boaz of Obed, [22]Obed of Jesse, and Jesse of David.

[i] Or *one with the right to redeem*

1 Samuel

Originally, this book of the Bible was part of a larger book that also contained 2 Samuel. First Samuel begins with the birth of Samuel, the last of the judges, and ends with the death of Saul, the first of the kings of Israel.

The opening chapter tells what is by now a familiar story in Scripture. After years of infertility, Hannah begs God for a child. Like Sarah and Rachel before her, Hannah becomes the mother of a son, Samuel, who will guide God's people at a turning point in their history.

A man of outstanding character, Samuel anoints Saul as Israel's first king. But Saul eventually disobeys God and ultimately dies for his unfaithfulness.

In addition to Hannah, 1 Samuel introduces the stories of several fascinating female characters: Michal, Saul's daughter and David's first wife; Abigail, who married a fool and then a king; and the woman of Endor, a medium who conjured up the dead and predicted Saul's demise.

First Samuel tells of the tremendous changes that took place in Israel between about 1050 and 1000 B.C. The stories of this book of the Bible highlight the important connection between the well being of a nation and the personal holiness of its leaders. It reminds us that God judges, not by outward appearance, but by what is in our hearts.

Samuel's Birth and Dedication

1 There was a certain man of Ramatha-im, a Zuphite*a* from the hill country of Ephraim, whose name was Elkanah son of Jeroham son of Elihu son of Tohu son of Zuph, an Ephraimite. ²He had two wives; the name of the one was Hannah, and the name of the other Peninnah. Peninnah had children, but Hannah had no children.

3 Now this man used to go up year by year from his town to worship and to sacrifice to the LORD of hosts at Shiloh, where the two sons of Eli, Hophni and Phinehas, were priests of the LORD. ⁴On the day when Elkanah sacrificed, he would give portions to his wife Peninnah and to all

a Compare Gk and 1 Chr 6.35-36: Heb *Ramathaim-zophim*

her sons and daughters; [5]but to Hannah he gave a double portion,[b] because he loved her, though the LORD had closed her womb. [6]Her rival used to provoke her severely, to irritate her, because the LORD had closed her womb. [7]So it went on year by year; as often as she went up to the house of the LORD, she used to provoke her. Therefore Hannah wept and would not eat. [8]Her husband Elkanah said to her, "Hannah, why do you weep? Why do you not eat? Why is your heart sad? Am I not more to you than ten sons?"

9 After they had eaten and drunk at Shiloh, Hannah rose and presented herself before the LORD.[c] Now Eli the priest was sitting on the seat beside the doorpost of the temple of the LORD. [10]She was deeply distressed and prayed to the LORD, and wept bitterly. [11]She made this vow: "O LORD of hosts, if only you will look on the misery of your servant, and remember me, and not forget your servant, but will give to your servant a male child, then I will set him before you as a nazirite[d] until the day of his death. He shall drink neither wine nor intoxicants,[e] and no razor shall touch his head."

12 As she continued praying before the LORD, Eli observed her mouth. [13]Hannah was praying silently; only her lips moved, but her voice was not heard; therefore Eli thought she was drunk. [14]So Eli said to her, "How long will you make a drunken spectacle of yourself? Put away your wine." [15]But Hannah answered, "No, my lord, I am a woman deeply troubled; I have drunk neither wine nor strong drink, but I have been pouring out my soul before the LORD. [16]Do not regard your servant as a worthless woman, for I have been speaking out of my great anxiety and vexation all this time." [17]Then Eli answered, "Go in peace; the God of Israel grant the petition you have made to him." [18]And she said, "Let your servant find favor in your sight." Then the woman went to her quarters,[f] ate and drank with her husband,[g] and her countenance was sad no longer.[h]

19 They rose early in the morning and worshiped before the LORD; then they went back to their house at Ramah. Elkanah knew his wife Hannah, and the LORD remembered her. [20]In due time Hannah conceived and bore a son. She named him Samuel, for she said, "I have asked him of the LORD."

21 The man Elkanah and all his household went up to offer to the LORD the yearly sacrifice, and to pay his vow. [22]But Hannah did not go up, for she said to her husband, "As soon as the child is weaned, I will bring him, that he may appear in the presence of the LORD, and remain there forever; I will offer him as a nazirite[d] for all time."[i] [23]Her husband Elkanah said to her, "Do what seems best to you, wait until you have weaned him; only—may the LORD establish his word."[j] So the woman remained and nursed her son, until she weaned him. [24]When she had weaned him, she took him up with her, along with a three-year-old bull,[k] an ephah of flour, and a skin of wine. She brought him to the house of the LORD at Shiloh; and the child was young. [25]Then they slaughtered the bull, and they brought the child to Eli. [26]And she said, "Oh, my lord! As you live, my lord, I am the woman who was standing here in your presence, praying to the LORD. [27]For this child I prayed; and the LORD has granted me the petition that I made to him. [28]Therefore I have lent him to the LORD; as long as he lives, he is given to the LORD."

She left him there for[l] the LORD.

Hannah's Prayer

2 Hannah prayed and said,
　"My heart exults in the LORD;
　　my strength is exalted in my
　　　God.[m]
　My mouth derides my enemies,
　　because I rejoice in my[n] victory.

2 "There is no Holy One like the
　　LORD,
　　no one besides you;
　　there is no Rock like our God.
3 Talk no more so very proudly,
　　let not arrogance come from your
　　　mouth;
　　for the LORD is a God of knowledge,

---

[b] Syr: Meaning of Heb uncertain　[c] Gk: Heb lacks *and presented herself before the LORD*　[d] That is *one separated* or *one consecrated*　[e] Cn Compare Gk Q Ms 1.22: MT *then I will give him to the LORD all the days of his life*　[f] Gk: Heb *went her way*　[g] Gk: Heb lacks *and drank with her husband*　[h] Gk: Meaning of Heb uncertain　[i] Cn Compare Q Ms: MT lacks *I will offer him as a nazirite for all time*　[j] MT: Q Ms Gk Compare Syr *that which goes out of your mouth*　[k] Q Ms Gk Syr: MT *three bulls*　[l] Gk (Compare Q Ms) and Gk at 2.11: MT *And he* (that is, Elkanah) *worshiped there before*　[m] Gk: Heb *the LORD*　[n] Q Ms: MT *your*

and by him actions are weighed.
4 The bows of the mighty are broken,
    but the feeble gird on strength.
5 Those who were full have hired
        themselves out for bread,
    but those who were hungry are fat
        with spoil.
The barren has borne seven,
    but she who has many children is
        forlorn.
6 The LORD kills and brings to life;
    he brings down to Sheol and
        raises up.
7 The LORD makes poor and makes
        rich;
    he brings low, he also exalts.
8 He raises up the poor from the dust;
    he lifts the needy from the ash
        heap,
to make them sit with princes
    and inherit a seat of honor.*o*
For the pillars of the earth are the
    LORD's,
    and on them he has set the world.

9 "He will guard the feet of his
        faithful ones,
    but the wicked shall be cut off in
        darkness;
    for not by might does one prevail.
10 The LORD! His adversaries shall be
        shattered;
    the Most High*p* will thunder in
        heaven.
The LORD will judge the ends of the
        earth;
    he will give strength to his king,
    and exalt the power of his
        anointed."

Eli's Wicked Sons

11 Then Elkanah went home to Ramah, while the boy remained to minister
to the LORD, in the presence of the priest
Eli.
12 Now the sons of Eli were scoundrels; they had no regard for the LORD 13or
for the duties of the priests to the people.
When anyone offered sacrifice, the priest's
servant would come, while the meat was
boiling, with a three-pronged fork in his
hand, 14and he would thrust it into the
pan, or kettle, or caldron, or pot; all that
the fork brought up the priest would take
for himself.*q* This is what they did at Shiloh to all the Israelites who came there.
15Moreover, before the fat was burned, the
priest's servant would come and say to the
one who was sacrificing, "Give meat for
the priest to roast; for he will not accept
boiled meat from you, but only raw."
16And if the man said to him, "Let them
burn the fat first, and then take whatever
you wish," he would say, "No, you must
give it now; if not, I will take it by force."
17Thus the sin of the young men was very
great in the sight of the LORD; for they
treated the offerings of the LORD with contempt.

The Child Samuel at Shiloh

18 Samuel was ministering before the
LORD, a boy wearing a linen ephod. 19His
mother used to make for him a little robe
and take it to him each year, when she
went up with her husband to offer the
yearly sacrifice. 20Then Eli would bless Elkanah and his wife, and say, "May the
LORD repay*r* you with children by this
woman for the gift that she made to*s* the
LORD"; and then they would return to their
home.
21 And*t* the LORD took note of Hannah; she conceived and bore three sons
and two daughters. And the boy Samuel
grew up in the presence of the LORD.

Prophecy against Eli's Household

22 Now Eli was very old. He heard all
that his sons were doing to all Israel, and
how they lay with the women who served
at the entrance to the tent of meeting.
23He said to them, "Why do you do such
things? For I hear of your evil dealings
from all these people. 24No, my sons; it is
not a good report that I hear the people of
the LORD spreading abroad. 25If one person sins against another, someone can intercede for the sinner with the LORD;*u* but
if someone sins against the LORD, who can
make intercession?" But they would not listen to the voice of their father; for it was
the will of the LORD to kill them.
26 Now the boy Samuel continued to
grow both in stature and in favor with the
LORD and with the people.
27 A man of God came to Eli and said
to him, "Thus the LORD has said, 'I revealed*v* myself to the family of your an-

---

o Gk (Compare Q Ms) adds *He grants the vow of
the one who vows, and blesses the years of the just*
p Cn Heb *against him he*   *q* Gk Syr Vg: Heb *with
it*   *r* Q Ms Gk: MT *give*   *s* Q Ms Gk: MT *for the
petition that she asked of*   *t* Q Ms Gk: MT *When*
u Gk Compare Q Ms: MT *another, God will mediate
for him*   *v* Gk Tg Syr: Heb *Did I reveal*

cestor in Egypt when they were slaves[w] to the house of Pharaoh. 28I chose him out of all the tribes of Israel to be my priest, to go up to my altar, to offer incense, to wear an ephod before me; and I gave to the family of your ancestor all my offerings by fire from the people of Israel. 29Why then look with greedy eye[x] at my sacrifices and my offerings that I commanded, and honor your sons more than me by fattening yourselves on the choicest parts of every offering of my people Israel?' 30Therefore the LORD the God of Israel declares: 'I promised that your family and the family of your ancestor should go in and out before me forever'; but now the LORD declares: 'Far be it from me; for those who honor me I will honor, and those who despise me shall be treated with contempt. 31See, a time is coming when I will cut off your strength and the strength of your ancestor's family, so that no one in your family will live to old age. 32Then in distress you will look with greedy eye[y] on all the prosperity that shall be bestowed upon Israel; and no one in your family shall ever live to old age. 33The only one of you whom I shall not cut off from my altar shall be spared to weep out his[z] eyes and grieve his[a] heart; all the members of your household shall die by the sword.[b] 34The fate of your two sons, Hophni and Phinehas, shall be the sign to you—both of them shall die on the same day. 35I will raise up for myself a faithful priest, who shall do according to what is in my heart and in my mind. I will build him a sure house, and he shall go in and out before my anointed one forever. 36Everyone who is left in your family shall come to implore him for a piece of silver or a loaf of bread, and shall say, Please put me in one of the priest's places, that I may eat a morsel of bread.' "

Samuel's Calling and Prophetic Activity

3 Now the boy Samuel was ministering to the LORD under Eli. The word of the LORD was rare in those days; visions were not widespread.

2 At that time Eli, whose eyesight had begun to grow dim so that he could not see, was lying down in his room; 3the lamp of God had not yet gone out, and Samuel was lying down in the temple of the LORD, where the ark of God was. 4Then the LORD called, "Samuel! Samuel!"[c] and he said, "Here I am!" 5and ran to Eli, and said, "Here I am, for you called me." But he said, "I did not call; lie down again." So he went and lay down. 6The LORD called again, "Samuel!" Samuel got up and went to Eli, and said, "Here I am, for you called me." But he said, "I did not call, my son; lie down again." 7Now Samuel did not yet know the LORD, and the word of the LORD had not yet been revealed to him. 8The LORD called Samuel again, a third time. And he got up and went to Eli, and said, "Here I am, for you called me." Then Eli perceived that the LORD was calling the boy. 9Therefore Eli said to Samuel, "Go, lie down; and if he calls you, you shall say, 'Speak, LORD, for your servant is listening.' " So Samuel went and lay down in his place.

10 Now the LORD came and stood there, calling as before, "Samuel! Samuel!" And Samuel said, "Speak, for your servant is listening." 11Then the LORD said to Samuel, "See, I am about to do something in Israel that will make both ears of anyone who hears of it tingle. 12On that day I will fulfill against Eli all that I have spoken concerning his house, from beginning to end. 13For I have told him that I am about to punish his house forever, for the iniquity that he knew, because his sons were blaspheming God,[d] and he did not restrain them. 14Therefore I swear to the house of Eli that the iniquity of Eli's house shall not be expiated by sacrifice or offering forever."

15 Samuel lay there until morning; then he opened the doors of the house of the LORD. Samuel was afraid to tell the vision to Eli. 16But Eli called Samuel and said, "Samuel, my son." He said, "Here I am." 17Eli said, "What was it that he told you? Do not hide it from me. May God do so to you and more also, if you hide anything from me of all that he told you." 18So Samuel told him everything and hid nothing from him. Then he said, "It is the LORD; let him do what seems good to him."

19 As Samuel grew up, the LORD was with him and let none of his words fall to the ground. 20And all Israel from Dan to Beer-sheba knew that Samuel was a trust-

---

w Q Ms Gk: MT lacks *slaves*　x Q Ms Gk: MT *then kick*　y Q Ms Gk: MT *will kick*　z Q Ms Gk: MT *your*　a Q Ms Gk: Heb *your*　b Q Ms See Gk: MT *die like mortals*　c Q Ms Gk See 3.10: MT *the LORD called Samuel*　d Another reading is *for themselves*

worthy prophet of the Lord. [21]The Lord continued to appear at Shiloh, for the Lord revealed himself to Samuel at Shiloh by the word of the Lord. [1]And the word of Samuel came to all Israel.

The Ark of God Captured

In those days the Philistines mustered for war against Israel,[e] and Israel went out to battle against them;[f] they encamped at Ebenezer, and the Philistines encamped at Aphek. [2]The Philistines drew up in line against Israel, and when the battle was joined,[g] Israel was defeated by the Philistines, who killed about four thousand men on the field of battle. [3]When the troops came to the camp, the elders of Israel said, "Why has the Lord put us to rout today before the Philistines? Let us bring the ark of the covenant of the Lord here from Shiloh, so that he may come among us and save us from the power of our enemies." [4]So the people sent to Shiloh, and brought from there the ark of the covenant of the Lord of hosts, who is enthroned on the cherubim. The two sons of Eli, Hophni and Phinehas, were

e Gk: Heb lacks *In those days the Philistines mustered for war against Israel*   f Gk: Heb *against the Philistines*   g Meaning of Heb uncertain

*P*ray and Listen

Scripture Reading for Today:
I Samuel 3.1–10

Verse for Today:
I Samuel 3.9

You've thoughtfully read the Scripture reading for the day. Now what? Let the Word sink into your whole being. Take the time to be present with God. Let him form you from what you have just read. Reply as Eli advised Samuel to respond: "Speak, Lord, for your servant is listening." Encounter your God, for he is waiting for you.

Start by stilling yourself. "Stop and consider the wondrous works of God" (Job 37.14). For some that may mean to close your eyes and take a few deep breaths. For others it may mean to focus your eyes on a holy object, a scene from your window, or whatever calms you. Be still and listen. Does a particular verse or scene from the reading come to mind? What insight into it, into God, or into yourself are you gaining?

Sometimes while meditating you may have so many distracting thoughts filling your head that you cannot focus on the reading or [on] God. If you have tried to clear your mind but cannot, perhaps God is telling you that it is time to simplify your life, to be single-minded on the things of the Lord. Or perhaps there is something going on in your life you need to take to him. Talk to him about your anxieties. The important thing is to take the time to be one-on-one with God. After you've had your say, be still, listen. Let God have his say.

There are other times when you've calmed yourself, thought of a verse or scene and nothing happens. There is nothing to distract you; you are calm, but you have no thoughts or insights. Be still, and cherish your oneness with God. People in love don't always have to converse. Their presence together is enough.

—*RENA DUFF*

Go to page 295 for your next devotional reading.

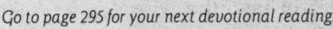

there with the ark of the covenant of God.

5 When the ark of the covenant of the LORD came into the camp, all Israel gave a mighty shout, so that the earth resounded. [6]When the Philistines heard the noise of the shouting, they said, "What does this great shouting in the camp of the Hebrews mean?" When they learned that the ark of the LORD had come to the camp, [7]the Philistines were afraid; for they said, "Gods have[h] come into the camp." They also said, "Woe to us! For nothing like this has happened before. [8]Woe to us! Who can deliver us from the power of these mighty gods? These are the gods who struck the Egyptians with every sort of plague in the wilderness. [9]Take courage, and be men, O Philistines, in order not to become slaves to the Hebrews as they have been to you; be men and fight."

10 So the Philistines fought; Israel was defeated, and they fled, everyone to his home. There was a very great slaughter, for there fell of Israel thirty thousand foot soldiers. [11]The ark of God was captured; and the two sons of Eli, Hophni and Phinehas, died.

Death of Eli

12 A man of Benjamin ran from the battle line, and came to Shiloh the same day, with his clothes torn and with earth upon his head. [13]When he arrived, Eli was sitting upon his seat by the road watching, for his heart trembled for the ark of God. When the man came into the city and told the news, all the city cried out. [14]When Eli heard the sound of the outcry, he said, "What is this uproar?" Then the man came quickly and told Eli. [15]Now Eli was ninety-eight years old and his eyes were set, so that he could not see. [16]The man said to Eli, "I have just come from the battle; I fled from the battle today." He said, "How did it go, my son?" [17]The messenger replied, "Israel has fled before the Philistines, and there has also been a great slaughter among the troops; your two sons also, Hophni and Phinehas, are dead, and the ark of God has been captured." [18]When he mentioned the ark of God, Eli[i] fell over backward from his seat by the side of the gate; and his neck was broken and he died, for he was an old man, and heavy. He had judged Israel forty years.

19 Now his daughter-in-law, the wife of Phinehas, was pregnant, about to give birth. When she heard the news that the ark of God was captured, and that her father-in-law and her husband were dead, she bowed and gave birth; for her labor pains overwhelmed her. [20]As she was about to die, the women attending her said to her, "Do not be afraid, for you have borne a son." But she did not answer or give heed. [21]She named the child Ichabod, meaning, "The glory has departed from Israel," because the ark of God had been captured and because of her father-in-law and her husband. [22]She said, "The glory has departed from Israel, for the ark of God has been captured."

The Philistines and the Ark

5 When the Philistines captured the ark of God, they brought it from Ebenezer to Ashdod; [2]then the Philistines took the ark of God and brought it into the house of Dagon and placed it beside Dagon. [3]When the people of Ashdod rose early the next day, there was Dagon, fallen on his face to the ground before the ark of the LORD. So they took Dagon and put him back in his place. [4]But when they rose early on the next morning, Dagon had fallen on his face to the ground before the ark of the LORD, and the head of Dagon and both his hands were lying cut off upon the threshold; only the trunk of[j] Dagon was left to him. [5]This is why the priests of Dagon and all who enter the house of Dagon do not step on the threshold of Dagon in Ashdod to this day.

6 The hand of the LORD was heavy upon the people of Ashdod, and he terrified and struck them with tumors, both in Ashdod and in its territory. [7]And when the inhabitants of Ashdod saw how things were, they said, "The ark of the God of Israel must not remain with us; for his hand is heavy on us and on our god Dagon." [8]So they sent and gathered together all the lords of the Philistines, and said, "What shall we do with the ark of the God of Israel?" The inhabitants of Gath replied, "Let the ark of God be moved on to us."[k] So they moved the ark of the God of Israel to Gath.[l] [9]But after they had brought it to Gath,[m] the hand of the LORD was

h Or *A god has*   *i* Heb *he*   *j* Heb lacks *the trunk of*   *k* Gk Compare Q Ms: MT *They answered, "Let the ark of the God of Israel be brought around to Gath."*   *l* Gk: Heb lacks *to Gath*   *m* Q Ms: MT lacks *to Gath*

against the city, causing a very great panic; he struck the inhabitants of the city, both young and old, so that tumors broke out on them. [10]So they sent the ark of the God of Israel[n] to Ekron. But when the ark of God came to Ekron, the people of Ekron cried out, "Why[o] have they brought around to us[p] the ark of the God of Israel to kill us[p] and our[q] people?" [11]They sent therefore and gathered together all the lords of the Philistines, and said, "Send away the ark of the God of Israel, and let it return to its own place, that it may not kill us and our people." For there was a deathly panic[r] throughout the whole city. The hand of God was very heavy there; [12]those who did not die were stricken with tumors, and the cry of the city went up to heaven.

The Ark Returned to Israel

6 The ark of the LORD was in the country of the Philistines seven months. [2]Then the Philistines called for the priests and the diviners and said, "What shall we do with the ark of the LORD? Tell us what we should send with it to its place." [3]They said, "If you send away the ark of the God of Israel, do not send it empty, but by all means return him a guilt offering. Then you will be healed and will be ransomed;[s] will not his hand then turn from you?" [4]And they said, "What is the guilt offering that we shall return to him?" They answered, "Five gold tumors and five gold mice, according to the number of the lords of the Philistines; for the same plague was upon all of you and upon your lords. [5]So you must make images of your tumors and images of your mice that ravage the land, and give glory to the God of Israel; perhaps he will lighten his hand on you and your gods and your land. [6]Why should you harden your hearts as the Egyptians and Pharaoh hardened their hearts? After he had made fools of them, did they not let the people go, and they departed? [7]Now then, get ready a new cart and two milch cows that have never borne a yoke, and yoke the cows to the cart, but take their calves home, away from them. [8]Take the ark of the LORD and place it on the cart, and put in a box at its side the figures of gold, which you are returning to him as a guilt offering. Then send it off, and let it go its way. [9]And watch; if it goes up on the way to its own land, to Beth-shemesh, then it is he who has done us

this great harm; but if not, then we shall know that it is not his hand that struck us; it happened to us by chance."

10 The men did so; they took two milch cows and yoked them to the cart, and shut up their calves at home. [11]They put the ark of the LORD on the cart, and the box with the gold mice and the images of their tumors. [12]The cows went straight in the direction of Beth-shemesh along one highway, lowing as they went; they turned neither to the right nor to the left, and the lords of the Philistines went after them as far as the border of Beth-shemesh.

13 Now the people of Beth-shemesh were reaping their wheat harvest in the valley. When they looked up and saw the ark, they went with rejoicing to meet it.[t] [14]The cart came into the field of Joshua of Beth-shemesh, and stopped there. A large stone was there; so they split up the wood of the cart and offered the cows as a burnt offering to the LORD. [15]The Levites took down the ark of the LORD and the box that was beside it, in which were the gold objects, and set them upon the large stone. Then the people of Beth-shemesh offered burnt offerings and presented sacrifices on that day to the LORD. [16]When the five lords of the Philistines saw it, they returned that day to Ekron.

17 These are the gold tumors, which the Philistines returned as a guilt offering to the LORD: one for Ashdod, one for Gaza, one for Ashkelon, one for Gath, one for Ekron; [18]also the gold mice, according to the number of all the cities of the Philistines belonging to the five lords, both fortified cities and unwalled villages. The great stone, beside which they set down the ark of the LORD, is a witness to this day in the field of Joshua of Beth-shemesh.

The Ark at Kiriath-jearim

19 The descendants of Jeconiah did not rejoice with the people of Beth-shemesh when they greeted[u] the ark of the LORD; and he killed seventy men of them.[v] The people mourned because the LORD had made a great slaughter among the people. [20]Then the people of Beth-

n Q Ms Gk: MT lacks of Israel   o Q Ms Gk: MT lacks Why   p Heb me   q Heb my   r Q Ms reads a panic from the LORD   s Q Ms Gk: MT and it will be known to you   t Gk: Heb rejoiced to see it   u Gk: Heb And he killed some of the people of Beth-shemesh, because they looked into   v Heb killed seventy men, fifty thousand men

shemesh said, "Who is able to stand before the LORD, this holy God? To whom shall he go so that we may be rid of him?" ²¹So they sent messengers to the inhabitants of Kiriath-jearim, saying, "The Philistines have returned the ark of the LORD.

7 Come down and take it up to you." ¹And the people of Kiriath-jearim came and took up the ark of the LORD, and brought it to the house of Abinadab on the hill. They consecrated his son, Eleazar, to have charge of the ark of the LORD.

2 From the day that the ark was lodged at Kiriath-jearim, a long time passed, some twenty years, and all the house of Israel lamentedʷ after the LORD.

Samuel as Judge

3 Then Samuel said to all the house of Israel, "If you are returning to the LORD with all your heart, then put away the foreign gods and the Astartes from among you. Direct your heart to the LORD, and serve him only, and he will deliver you out of the hand of the Philistines." ⁴So Israel put away the Baals and the Astartes, and they served the LORD only.

5 Then Samuel said, "Gather all Israel at Mizpah, and I will pray to the LORD for you." ⁶So they gathered at Mizpah, and drew water and poured it out before the LORD. They fasted that day, and said, "We have sinned against the LORD." And Samuel judged the people of Israel at Mizpah.

7 When the Philistines heard that the people of Israel had gathered at Mizpah, the lords of the Philistines went up against Israel. And when the people of Israel heard of it they were afraid of the Philistines. ⁸The people of Israel said to Samuel, "Do not cease to cry out to the LORD our God for us, and pray that he may save us from the hand of the Philistines." ⁹So Samuel took a sucking lamb and offered it as a whole burnt offering to the LORD; Samuel cried out to the LORD for Israel, and the LORD answered him. ¹⁰As Samuel was offering up the burnt offering, the Philistines drew near to attack Israel; but the LORD thundered with a mighty voice that day against the Philistines and threw them into confusion; and they were routed before Israel. ¹¹And the men of Israel went out of Mizpah and pursued the Philistines, and struck them down as far as beyond Beth-car.

12 Then Samuel took a stone and set it up between Mizpah and Jeshanah,ˣ and named it Ebenezer;ʸ for he said, "Thus far the LORD has helped us." ¹³So the Philistines were subdued and did not again enter the territory of Israel; the hand of the LORD was against the Philistines all the days of Samuel. ¹⁴The towns that the Philistines had taken from Israel were restored to Israel, from Ekron to Gath; and Israel recovered their territory from the hand of the Philistines. There was peace also between Israel and the Amorites.

15 Samuel judged Israel all the days of his life. ¹⁶He went on a circuit year by year to Bethel, Gilgal, and Mizpah; and he judged Israel in all these places. ¹⁷Then he would come back to Ramah, for his home was there; he administered justice there to Israel, and built there an altar to the LORD.

Israel Demands a King

8 When Samuel became old, he made his sons judges over Israel. ²The name of his firstborn son was Joel, and the name of his second, Abijah; they were judges in Beer-sheba. ³Yet his sons did not follow in his ways, but turned aside after gain; they took bribes and perverted justice.

4 Then all the elders of Israel gathered together and came to Samuel at Ramah, ⁵and said to him, "You are old and your sons do not follow in your ways; appoint for us, then, a king to govern us, like other nations." ⁶But the thing displeased Samuel when they said, "Give us a king to govern us." Samuel prayed to the LORD, ⁷and the LORD said to Samuel, "Listen to the voice of the people in all that they say to you; for they have not rejected you, but they have rejected me from being king over them. ⁸Just as they have done to me,ᶻ from the day I brought them up out of Egypt to this day, forsaking me and serving other gods, so also they are doing to you. ⁹Now then, listen to their voice; only—you shall solemnly warn them, and show them the ways of the king who shall reign over them."

10 So Samuel reported all the words of the LORD to the people who were asking him for a king. ¹¹He said, "These will be the ways of the king who will reign over you: he will take your sons and appoint them to his chariots and to be his horse-

w Meaning of Heb uncertain   *x* Gk Syr: Heb *Shen*   *y* That is *Stone of Help*   *z* Gk: Heb lacks *to me*

men, and to run before his chariots; 12and he will appoint for himself commanders of thousands and commanders of fifties, and some to plow his ground and to reap his harvest, and to make his implements of war and the equipment of his chariots. 13He will take your daughters to be perfumers and cooks and bakers. 14He will take the best of your fields and vineyards and olive orchards and give them to his courtiers. 15He will take one-tenth of your grain and of your vineyards and give it to his officers and his courtiers. 16He will take your male and female slaves, and the best of your cattle*a* and donkeys, and put them to his work. 17He will take one-tenth of your flocks, and you shall be his slaves. 18And in that day you will cry out because of your king, whom you have chosen for yourselves; but the LORD will not answer you in that day."

Israel's Request for a King Granted

19 But the people refused to listen to the voice of Samuel; they said, "No! but we are determined to have a king over us, 20so that we also may be like other nations, and that our king may govern us and go out before us and fight our battles." 21When Samuel had heard all the words of the people, he repeated them in the ears of the LORD. 22The LORD said to Samuel, "Listen to their voice and set a king over them." Samuel then said to the people of Israel, "Each of you return home."

Saul Chosen to Be King

9 There was a man of Benjamin whose name was Kish son of Abiel son of Zeror son of Becorath son of Aphiah, a Benjaminite, a man of wealth. 2He had a son whose name was Saul, a handsome young man. There was not a man among the people of Israel more handsome than he; he stood head and shoulders above everyone else.

3 Now the donkeys of Kish, Saul's father, had strayed. So Kish said to his son Saul, "Take one of the boys with you; go and look for the donkeys." 4He passed through the hill country of Ephraim and passed through the land of Shalishah, but they did not find them. And they passed through the land of Shaalim, but they were not there. Then he passed through the land of Benjamin, but they did not find them. 5 When they came to the land of Zuph,

Saul said to the boy who was with him, "Let us turn back, or my father will stop worrying about the donkeys and worry about us." 6But he said to him, "There is a man of God in this town; he is a man held in honor. Whatever he says always comes true. Let us go there now; perhaps he will tell us about the journey on which we have set out." 7Then Saul replied to the boy, "But if we go, what can we bring the man? For the bread in our sacks is gone, and there is no present to bring to the man of God. What have we?" 8The boy answered Saul again, "Here, I have with me a quarter shekel of silver; I will give it to the man of God, to tell us our way." 9(Formerly in Israel, anyone who went to inquire of God would say, "Come, let us go to the seer"; for the one who is now called a prophet was formerly called a seer.) 10Saul said to the boy, "Good; come, let us go." So they went to the town where the man of God was.

11 As they went up the hill to the town, they met some girls coming out to draw water, and said to them, "Is the seer here?" 12They answered, "Yes, there he is just ahead of you. Hurry; he has come just now to the town, because the people have a sacrifice today at the shrine. 13As soon as you enter the town, you will find him, before he goes up to the shrine to eat. For the people will not eat until he comes, since he must bless the sacrifice; afterward those eat who are invited. Now go up, for you will meet him immediately." 14So they went up to the town. As they were entering the town, they saw Samuel coming out toward them on his way up to the shrine.

15 Now the day before Saul came, the LORD had revealed to Samuel: 16"Tomorrow about this time I will send to you a man from the land of Benjamin, and you shall anoint him to be ruler over my people Israel. He shall save my people from the hand of the Philistines; for I have seen the suffering of*b* my people, because their outcry has come to me." 17When Samuel saw Saul, the LORD told him, "Here is the man of whom I spoke to you. He it is who shall rule over my people." 18Then Saul approached Samuel inside the gate, and said, "Tell me, please, where is the house of the seer?" 19Samuel an-

---

a Gk: Heb *young men*   *b* Gk: Heb lacks *the suffering of*

swered Saul, "I am the seer; go up before me to the shrine, for today you shall eat with me, and in the morning I will let you go and will tell you all that is on your mind. 20As for your donkeys that were lost three days ago, give no further thought to them, for they have been found. And on whom is all Israel's desire fixed, if not on you and on all your ancestral house?" 21Saul answered, "I am only a Benjaminite, from the least of the tribes of Israel, and my family is the humblest of all the families of the tribe of Benjamin. Why then have you spoken to me in this way?"

22 Then Samuel took Saul and his servant-boy and brought them into the hall, and gave them a place at the head of those who had been invited, of whom there were about thirty. 23And Samuel said to the cook, "Bring the portion I gave you, the one I asked you to put aside." 24The cook took up the thigh and what went with it*c* and set them before Saul. Samuel said, "See, what was kept is set before you. Eat; for it is set*d* before you at the appointed time, so that you might eat with the guests."*e*

So Saul ate with Samuel that day. 25When they came down from the shrine into the town, a bed was spread for Saul*f* on the roof, and he lay down to sleep.*g* 26Then at the break of dawn*h* Samuel called to Saul upon the roof, "Get up, so that I may send you on your way." Saul got up, and both he and Samuel went out into the street.

Samuel Anoints Saul

27 As they were going down to the outskirts of the town, Samuel said to Saul, "Tell the boy to go on before us, and when he has passed on, stop here yourself for a while, that I may make known to you the word of God." 10 1Samuel took a vial of oil and poured it on his head, and kissed him; he said, "The LORD has anointed you ruler over his people Israel. You shall reign over the people of the LORD and you will save them from the hand of their enemies all around. Now this shall be the sign to you that the LORD has anointed you ruler*i* over his heritage. 2When you depart from me today you will meet two men by Rachel's tomb in the territory of Benjamin at Zelzah; they will say to you, 'The donkeys that you went to seek are found, and now your father has stopped worrying about them and is wor-

rying about you, saying: What shall I do about my son?' 3Then you shall go on from there further and come to the oak of Tabor; three men going up to God at Bethel will meet you there, one carrying three kids, another carrying three loaves of bread, and another carrying a skin of wine. 4They will greet you and give you two loaves of bread, which you shall accept from them. 5After that you shall come to Gibeath-elohim,*j* at the place where the Philistine garrison is; there, as you come to the town, you will meet a band of prophets coming down from the shrine with harp, tambourine, flute, and lyre playing in front of them; they will be in a prophetic frenzy. 6Then the spirit of the LORD will possess you, and you will be in a prophetic frenzy along with them and be turned into a different person. 7Now when these signs meet you, do whatever you see fit to do, for God is with you. 8And you shall go down to Gilgal ahead of me; then I will come down to you to present burnt offerings and offer sacrifices of well-being. Seven days you shall wait, until I come to you and show you what you shall do."

Saul Prophesies

9 As he turned away to leave Samuel, God gave him another heart; and all these signs were fulfilled that day. 10When they were going from there*k* to Gibeah,*l* a band of prophets met him; and the spirit of God possessed him, and he fell into a prophetic frenzy along with them. 11When all who knew him before saw how he prophesied with the prophets, the people said to one another, "What has come over the son of Kish? Is Saul also among the prophets?" 12A man of the place answered, "And who is their father?" Therefore it became a proverb, "Is Saul also among the prophets?" 13When his prophetic frenzy had ended, he went home.*m*

14 Saul's uncle said to him and to the boy, "Where did you go?" And he replied,

c Meaning of Heb uncertain   *d* Q Ms Gk: MT *it was kept*   *e* Cn: Heb *it was kept for you, saying, I have invited the people*   *f* Gk: Heb *and he spoke with Saul*   *g* Gk: Heb lacks *and he lay down to sleep*   *h* Gk: Heb *and they arose early and at break of dawn*   *i* Gk: Heb lacks *over his people Israel. You shall . . . anointed you ruler*   *j* Or the Hill of God   *k* Gk: Heb *they came there*   *l* Or the hill   *m* Cn: Heb *he came to the shrine*

"To seek the donkeys; and when we saw they were not to be found, we went to Samuel." 15Saul's uncle said, "Tell me what Samuel said to you." 16Saul said to his uncle, "He told us that the donkeys had been found." But about the matter of the kingship, of which Samuel had spoken, he did not tell him anything.

Saul Proclaimed King

17 Samuel summoned the people to the LORD at Mizpah 18and said to them,[n] "Thus says the LORD, the God of Israel, 'I brought up Israel out of Egypt, and I rescued you from the hand of the Egyptians and from the hand of all the kingdoms that were oppressing you.' 19But today you have rejected your God, who saves you from all your calamities and your distresses; and you have said, 'No! but set a king over us.' Now therefore present yourselves before the LORD by your tribes and by your clans."

20 Then Samuel brought all the tribes of Israel near, and the tribe of Benjamin was taken by lot. 21He brought the tribe of Benjamin near by its families, and the family of the Matrites was taken by lot. Finally he brought the family of the Matrites near man by man,[o] and Saul the son of Kish was taken by lot. But when they sought him, he could not be found. 22So they inquired again of the LORD, "Did the man come here?"[p] and the LORD said, "See, he has hidden himself among the baggage." 23Then they ran and brought him from there. When he took his stand among the people, he was head and shoulders taller than any of them. 24Samuel said to all the people, "Do you see the one whom the LORD has chosen? There is no one like him among all the people." And all the people shouted, "Long live the king!"

25 Samuel told the people the rights and duties of the kingship; and he wrote them in a book and laid it up before the LORD. Then Samuel sent all the people back to their homes. 26Saul also went to his home at Gibeah, and with him went warriors whose hearts God had touched. 27But some worthless fellows said, "How can this man save us?" They despised him and brought him no present. But he held his peace.

Now Nahash, king of the Ammonites, had been grievously oppressing the Gadites and the Reubenites. He would gouge out the right eye of each of them and would not grant Israel a deliverer. No one was left of the Israelites across the Jordan whose right eye Nahash, king of the Ammonites, had not gouged out. But there were seven thousand men who had escaped from the Ammonites and had entered Jabesh-gilead.[q]

Saul Defeats the Ammonites

11 About a month later,[r] Nahash the Ammonite went up and besieged Jabesh-gilead; and all the men of Jabesh said to Nahash, "Make a treaty with us, and we will serve you." 2But Nahash the Ammonite said to them, "On this condition I will make a treaty with you, namely that I gouge out everyone's right eye, and thus put disgrace upon all Israel." 3The elders of Jabesh said to him, "Give us seven days' respite that we may send messengers through all the territory of Israel. Then, if there is no one to save us, we will give ourselves up to you." 4When the messengers came to Gibeah of Saul, they reported the matter in the hearing of the people; and all the people wept aloud.

5 Now Saul was coming from the field behind the oxen; and Saul said, "What is the matter with the people, that they are weeping?" So they told him the message from the inhabitants of Jabesh. 6And the spirit of God came upon Saul in power when he heard these words, and his anger was greatly kindled. 7He took a yoke of oxen, and cut them in pieces and sent them throughout all the territory of Israel by messengers, saying, "Whoever does not come out after Saul and Samuel, so shall it be done to his oxen!" Then the dread of the LORD fell upon the people, and they came out as one. 8When he mustered them at Bezek, those from Israel were three hundred thousand, and those from Judah seventy[s] thousand. 9They said to the messengers who had come, "Thus shall you say to the inhabitants of Jabesh-gilead: 'Tomorrow, by the time the sun is hot, you shall have deliverance.' " When the messengers came and told the

---

n Heb to the people of Israel   o Gk: Heb lacks Finally . . . man by man   p Gk: Heb Is there yet a man to come here?   q Ms Compare Josephus, Antiquities VI.v.1 (68-71): MT lacks Now Nahash . . . entered Jabesh-gilead.   r Q Ms Gk: MT lacks About a month later   s Q Ms Gk: MT thirty

inhabitants of Jabesh, they rejoiced. [10]So the inhabitants of Jabesh said, "Tomorrow we will give ourselves up to you, and you may do to us whatever seems good to you." [11]The next day Saul put the people in three companies. At the morning watch they came into the camp and cut down the Ammonites until the heat of the day; and those who survived were scattered, so that no two of them were left together.

12 The people said to Samuel, "Who is it that said, 'Shall Saul reign over us?' Give them to us so that we may put them to death." [13]But Saul said, "No one shall be put to death this day, for today the LORD has brought deliverance to Israel."

14 Samuel said to the people, "Come, let us go to Gilgal and there renew the kingship." [15]So all the people went to Gilgal, and there they made Saul king before the LORD in Gilgal. There they sacrificed offerings of well-being before the LORD, and there Saul and all the Israelites rejoiced greatly.

Samuel's Farewell Address

12 Samuel said to all Israel, "I have listened to you in all that you have said to me, and have set a king over you. [2]See, it is the king who leads you now; I am old and gray, but my sons are with you. I have led you from my youth until this day. [3]Here I am; testify against me before the LORD and before his anointed. Whose ox have I taken? Or whose donkey have I taken? Or whom have I defrauded? Whom have I oppressed? Or from whose hand have I taken a bribe to blind my eyes with it? Testify against me[t] and I will restore it to you." [4]They said, "You have not defrauded us or oppressed us or taken anything from the hand of anyone." [5]He said to them, "The LORD is witness against you, and his anointed is witness this day, that you have not found anything in my hand." And they said, "He is witness."

6 Samuel said to the people, "The LORD is witness, who[u] appointed Moses and Aaron and brought your ancestors up out of the land of Egypt. [7]Now therefore take your stand, so that I may enter into judgment with you before the LORD, and I will declare to you[v] all the saving deeds of the LORD that he performed for you and for your ancestors. [8]When Jacob went into Egypt and the Egyptians oppressed them,[w] then your ancestors cried to the LORD and the LORD sent Moses and Aaron, who brought forth your ancestors out of Egypt, and settled them in this place. [9]But they forgot the LORD their God; and he sold them into the hand of Sisera, commander of the army of King Jabin of[x] Hazor, and into the hand of the Philistines, and into the hand of the king of Moab; and they fought against them. [10]Then they cried to the LORD, and said, 'We have sinned, because we have forsaken the LORD, and have served the Baals and the Astartes; but now rescue us out of the hand of our enemies, and we will serve you.' [11]And the LORD sent Jerubbaal and Barak,[y] and Jephthah, and Samson,[z] and rescued you out of the hand of your enemies on every side; and you lived in safety. [12]But when you saw that King Nahash of the Ammonites came against you, you said to me, 'No, but a king shall reign over us,' though the LORD your God was your king. [13]See, here is the king whom you have chosen, for whom you have asked; see, the LORD has set a king over you. [14]If you will fear the LORD and serve him and heed his voice and not rebel against the commandment of the LORD, and if both you and the king who reigns over you will follow the LORD your God, it will be well; [15]but if you will not heed the voice of the LORD, but rebel against the commandment of the LORD, then the hand of the LORD will be against you and your king.[a] [16]Now therefore take your stand and see this great thing that the LORD will do before your eyes. [17]Is it not the wheat harvest today? I will call upon the LORD, that he may send thunder and rain; and you shall know and see that the wickedness that you have done in the sight of the LORD is great in demanding a king for yourselves." [18]So Samuel called upon the LORD, and the LORD sent thunder and rain that day; and all the people greatly feared the LORD and Samuel.

19 All the people said to Samuel, "Pray to the LORD your God for your servants, so that we may not die; for we have added to all our sins the evil of demanding a king for ourselves." [20]And Samuel said to the

---

[t] Gk: Heb lacks *Testify against me*   [u] Gk: Heb lacks *is witness, who*   [v] Gk: Heb lacks *and I will declare to you*   [w] Gk: Heb lacks *and the Egyptians oppressed them*   [x] Gk: Heb lacks *King Jabin of*   [y] Gk Syr: Heb *Bedan*   [z] Gk: Heb *Samuel*   [a] Gk: Heb *and your ancestors*

people, "Do not be afraid; you have done all this evil, yet do not turn aside from following the LORD, but serve the LORD with all your heart; ²¹and do not turn aside after useless things that cannot profit or save, for they are useless. ²²For the LORD will not cast away his people, for his great name's sake, because it has pleased the LORD to make you a people for himself. ²³Moreover as for me, far be it from me that I should sin against the LORD by ceasing to pray for you; and I will instruct you in the good and the right way. ²⁴Only fear the LORD, and serve him faithfully with all your heart; for consider what great things he has done for you. ²⁵But if you still do wickedly, you shall be swept away, both you and your king."

Saul's Unlawful Sacrifice

13 Saul was . . .ᵇ years old when he began to reign; and he reigned . . . and twoᶜ years over Israel.

2 Saul chose three thousand out of Israel; two thousand were with Saul in Michmash and the hill country of Bethel, and a thousand were with Jonathan in Gibeah of Benjamin; the rest of the people he sent home to their tents. ³Jonathan defeated the garrison of the Philistines that was at Geba; and the Philistines heard of it. And Saul blew the trumpet throughout all the land, saying, "Let the Hebrews hear!" ⁴When all Israel heard that Saul had defeated the garrison of the Philistines, and also that Israel had become odious to the Philistines, the people were called out to join Saul at Gilgal.

5 The Philistines mustered to fight with Israel, thirty thousand chariots, and six thousand horsemen, and troops like the sand on the seashore in multitude; they

ᵇ The number is lacking in the Heb text (the verse is lacking in the Septuagint). ᶜ *Two* is not the entire number; something has dropped out.

Control

THURSDAY

Scripture Reading for Today:
1 Samuel 13.5–14

Verse for Today:
1 Samuel 13.12

Anthony Bloom, the Orthodox archbishop, once told an interviewer, "The only question I ask is, 'What should I do at this particular moment?' I never ask myself what the result of an action will be—that is God's concern. All you can do is be at every single moment as true as you can with all the power in your being—and then leave it to God to use you, even despite yourself." I ponder these words, thinking how much I like to control outcomes. Last year, I got stuck on a steep ski run. "Let your skis go," called the ski instructor. "You'll be at the bottom in three turns." But I clung to where I was, afraid of losing control. Finally, fearfully, I made one turn . . . then another . . . then another . . . and the instructor was right. I reached the bottom. Without falling! Whatever I'm doing, can I release my insistence on controlling results and trust God to be with me, one turn in life after another?

—BARBARA BARTOCCI

Ask yourself: How do I tend to react to situations whose outcome I can't predict? Do I procrastinate, like Barbara Bartocci on the ski slopes? Am I like Saul, taking hasty action "in my anxiety" to make something happen?

Ask the Holy Spirit to help you learn to live in the present moment and to give you a trusting, obedient heart.

Go to page 301 for your next devotional reading.

came up and encamped at Michmash, to the east of Beth-aven. ⁶When the Israelites saw that they were in distress (for the troops were hard pressed), the people hid themselves in caves and in holes and in rocks and in tombs and in cisterns. ⁷Some Hebrews crossed the Jordan to the land of Gad and Gilead. Saul was still at Gilgal, and all the people followed him trembling.

8 He waited seven days, the time appointed by Samuel; but Samuel did not come to Gilgal, and the people began to slip away from Saul.ᵈ ⁹So Saul said, "Bring the burnt offering here to me, and the offerings of well-being." And he offered the burnt offering. ¹⁰As soon as he had finished offering the burnt offering, Samuel arrived; and Saul went out to meet him and salute him. ¹¹Samuel said, "What have you done?" Saul replied, "When I saw that the people were slipping away from me, and that you did not come within the days appointed, and that the Philistines were mustering at Michmash, ¹²I said, 'Now the Philistines will come down upon me at Gilgal, and I have not entreated the favor of the LORD'; so I forced myself, and offered the burnt offering." ¹³Samuel said to Saul, "You have done foolishly; you have not kept the commandment of the LORD your God, which he commanded you. The LORD would have established your kingdom over Israel forever, ¹⁴but now your kingdom will not continue; the LORD has sought out a man after his own heart; and the LORD has appointed him to be ruler over his people, because you have not kept what the LORD commanded you." ¹⁵And Samuel left and went on his way from Gilgal.ᵉ The rest of the people followed Saul to join the army; they went up from Gilgal toward Gibeah of Benjamin.ᶠ

Preparations for Battle

Saul counted the people who were present with him, about six hundred men. ¹⁶Saul, his son Jonathan, and the people who were present with them stayed in Geba of Benjamin; but the Philistines encamped at Michmash. ¹⁷And raiders came out of the camp of the Philistines in three companies; one company turned toward Ophrah, to the land of Shual, ¹⁸another company turned toward Beth-horon, and another company turned toward the

mountainᵍ that looks down upon the valley of Zeboim toward the wilderness.

19 Now there was no smith to be found throughout all the land of Israel; for the Philistines said, "The Hebrews must not make swords or spears for themselves"; ²⁰so all the Israelites went down to the Philistines to sharpen their plowshares, mattocks, axes, or sickles;ʰ ²¹The charge was two-thirds of a shekelⁱ for the plowshares and for the mattocks, and one-third of a shekel for sharpening the axes and for setting the goads.ʲ ²²So on the day of the battle neither sword nor spear was to be found in the possession of any of the people with Saul and Jonathan; but Saul and his son Jonathan had them.

Jonathan Surprises and Routs the Philistines

23 Now a garrison of the Philistines had gone out to the pass of Michmash.

14 ¹One day Jonathan son of Saul said to the young man who carried his armor, "Come, let us go over to the Philistine garrison on the other side." But he did not tell his father. ²Saul was staying in the outskirts of Gibeah under the pomegranate tree that is at Migron; the troops that were with him were about six hundred men, ³along with Ahijah son of Ahitub, Ichabod's brother, son of Phinehas son of Eli, the priest of the LORD in Shiloh, carrying an ephod. Now the people did not know that Jonathan had gone. ⁴In the pass,ᵏ by which Jonathan tried to go over to the Philistine garrison, there was a rocky crag on one side and a rocky crag on the other; the name of the one was Bozez, and the name of the other Seneh. ⁵One crag rose on the north in front of Michmash, and the other on the south in front of Geba.

6 Jonathan said to the young man who carried his armor, "Come, let us go over to the garrison of these uncircumcised; it may be that the LORD will act for us; for nothing can hinder the LORD from saving by many or by few." ⁷His armor-bearer said to him, "Do all that your mind inclines to.ˡ I am with you; as your mind is, so is mine."ᵐ ⁸Then Jonathan said,

ᵈ Heb him   ᵉ Gk: Heb *went up from Gilgal to Gibeah of Benjamin*   ᶠ Gk: Heb lacks *The rest . . . of Benjamin*   ᵍ Cn Compare Gk: Heb *toward the border*   ʰ Gk: Heb *plowshare*   ⁱ Heb *was a pim*   ʲ Cn: Meaning of Heb uncertain   ᵏ Heb *Between the passes*   ˡ Gk: Heb *Do all that is in your mind. Turn*   ᵐ Gk: Heb lacks *so is mine*

"Now we will cross over to those men and will show ourselves to them. 9If they say to us, 'Wait until we come to you,' then we will stand still in our place, and we will not go up to them. 10But if they say, 'Come up to us,' then we will go up; for the LORD has given them into our hand. That will be the sign for us." 11So both of them showed themselves to the garrison of the Philistines; and the Philistines said, "Look, Hebrews are coming out of the holes where they have hidden themselves." 12The men of the garrison hailed Jonathan and his armor-bearer, saying, "Come up to us, and we will show you something." Jonathan said to his armor-bearer, "Come up after me; for the LORD has given them into the hand of Israel." 13Then Jonathan climbed up on his hands and feet, with his armor-bearer following after him. The Philistines[n] fell before Jonathan, and his armor-bearer, coming after him, killed them. 14In that first slaughter Jonathan and his armor-bearer killed about twenty men within an area about half a furrow long in an acre[o] of land. 15There was a panic in the camp, in the field, and among all the people; the garrison and even the raiders trembled; the earth quaked; and it became a very great panic.

16 Saul's lookouts in Gibeah of Benjamin were watching as the multitude was surging back and forth.[p] 17Then Saul said to the troops that were with him, "Call the roll and see who has gone from us." When they had called the roll, Jonathan and his armor-bearer were not there. 18Saul said to Ahijah, "Bring the ark[q] of God here." For at that time the ark[q] of God went with the Israelites. 19While Saul was talking to the priest, the tumult in the camp of the Philistines increased more and more; and Saul said to the priest, "Withdraw your hand." 20Then Saul and all the people who were with him rallied and went into the battle; and every sword was against the other, so that there was very great confusion. 21Now the Hebrews who previously had been with the Philistines and had gone up with them into the camp turned and joined the Israelites who were with Saul and Jonathan. 22Likewise, when all the Israelites who had gone into hiding in the hill country of Ephraim heard that the Philistines were fleeing, they too followed closely after them in the

battle. 23So the LORD gave Israel the victory that day.

The battle passed beyond Beth-aven, and the troops with Saul numbered altogether about ten thousand men. The battle spread out over the hill country of Ephraim.

Saul's Rash Oath

24 Now Saul committed a very rash act on that day.[r] He had laid an oath on the troops, saying, "Cursed be anyone who eats food before it is evening and I have been avenged on my enemies." So none of the troops tasted food. 25All the troops[s] came upon a honeycomb; and there was honey on the ground. 26When the troops came upon the honeycomb, the honey was dripping out; but they did not put their hands to their mouths, for they feared the oath. 27But Jonathan had not heard his father charge the troops with the oath; so he extended the staff that was in his hand, and dipped the tip of it in the honeycomb, and put his hand to his mouth; and his eyes brightened. 28Then one of the soldiers said, "Your father strictly charged the troops with an oath, saying, 'Cursed be anyone who eats food this day.' And so the troops are faint." 29Then Jonathan said, "My father has troubled the land; see how my eyes have brightened because I tasted a little of this honey. 30How much better if today the troops had eaten freely of the spoil taken from their enemies; for now the slaughter among the Philistines has not been great."

31 After they had struck down the Philistines that day from Michmash to Aijalon, the troops were very faint; 32so the troops flew upon the spoil, and took sheep and oxen and calves, and slaughtered them on the ground; and the troops ate them with the blood. 33Then it was reported to Saul, "Look, the troops are sinning against the LORD by eating with the blood." And he said, "You have dealt treacherously; roll a large stone before me here."[t] 34Saul said, "Disperse yourselves among the troops, and say to them, 'Let all bring their oxen or their sheep, and slaughter them here, and eat; and do not sin against the LORD by eating with the

n Heb They   o Heb yoke   p Gk: Heb they went
and there   q Gk the ephod   r Gk: Heb The
Israelites were distressed that day   s Heb land
t Gk: Heb me this day

blood.' " So all of the troops brought their oxen with them that night, and slaughtered them there. ³⁵And Saul built an altar to the LORD; it was the first altar that he built to the LORD.

Jonathan in Danger of Death

36 Then Saul said, "Let us go down after the Philistines by night and despoil them until the morning light; let us not leave one of them." They said, "Do whatever seems good to you." But the priest said, "Let us draw near to God here." ³⁷So Saul inquired of God, "Shall I go down after the Philistines? Will you give them into the hand of Israel?" But he did not answer him that day. ³⁸Saul said, "Come here, all you leaders of the people; and let us find out how this sin has arisen today. ³⁹For as the LORD lives who saves Israel, even if it is in my son Jonathan, he shall surely die!" But there was no one among all the people who answered him. ⁴⁰He said to all Israel, "You shall be on one side, and I and my son Jonathan will be on the other side." The people said to Saul, "Do what seems good to you." ⁴¹Then Saul said, "O LORD God of Israel, why have you not answered your servant today? If this guilt is in me or in my son Jonathan, O LORD God of Israel, give Urim; but if this guilt is in your people Israel,ᵘ give Thummim." And Jonathan and Saul were indicated by the lot, but the people were cleared. ⁴²Then Saul said, "Cast the lot between me and my son Jonathan." And Jonathan was taken.

43 Then Saul said to Jonathan, "Tell me what you have done." Jonathan told him, "I tasted a little honey with the tip of the staff that was in my hand; here I am, I will die." ⁴⁴Saul said, "God do so to me and more also; you shall surely die, Jonathan!" ⁴⁵Then the people said to Saul, "Shall Jonathan die, who has accomplished this great victory in Israel? Far from it! As the LORD lives, not one hair of his head shall fall to the ground; for he has worked with God today." So the people ransomed Jonathan, and he did not die. ⁴⁶Then Saul withdrew from pursuing the Philistines; and the Philistines went to their own place.

Saul's Continuing Wars

47 When Saul had taken the kingship over Israel, he fought against all his enemies on every side—against Moab, against the Ammonites, against Edom, against the kings of Zobah, and against the Philistines; wherever he turned he routed them. ⁴⁸He did valiantly, and struck down the Amalekites, and rescued Israel out of the hands of those who plundered them.

49 Now the sons of Saul were Jonathan, Ishvi, and Malchishua; and the names of his two daughters were these: the name of the firstborn was Merab, and the name of the younger, Michal. ⁵⁰The name of Saul's wife was Ahinoam daughter of Ahimaaz. And the name of the commander of his army was Abner son of Ner, Saul's uncle; ⁵¹Kish was the father of Saul, and Ner the father of Abner was the son of Abiel.

52 There was hard fighting against the Philistines all the days of Saul; and when Saul saw any strong or valiant warrior, he took him into his service.

Saul Defeats the Amalekites but Spares Their King

15 Samuel said to Saul, "The LORD sent me to anoint you king over his people Israel; now therefore listen to the words of the LORD. ²Thus says the LORD of hosts, 'I will punish the Amalekites for what they did in opposing the Israelites when they came up out of Egypt. ³Now go and attack Amalek, and utterly destroy all that they have; do not spare them, but kill both man and woman, child and infant, ox and sheep, camel and donkey.' "

4 So Saul summoned the people, and numbered them in Telaim, two hundred thousand foot soldiers, and ten thousand soldiers of Judah. ⁵Saul came to the city of the Amalekites and lay in wait in the valley. ⁶Saul said to the Kenites, "Go! Leave! Withdraw from among the Amalekites, or I will destroy you with them; for you showed kindness to all the people of Israel when they came up out of Egypt." So the Kenites withdrew from the Amalekites. ⁷Saul defeated the Amalekites, from Havilah as far as Shur, which is east of Egypt. ⁸He took King Agag of the Amalekites alive, but utterly destroyed all the people with the edge of the sword. ⁹Saul and the people spared Agag, and the best of the sheep and of the cattle and of the fatlings, and the lambs, and all that was valuable, and would not utterly destroy them; all

---

ᵘ Vg Compare Gk: Heb ⁴¹*Saul said to the LORD, the God of Israel*

that was despised and worthless they utterly destroyed.

Saul Rejected as King

10 The word of the LORD came to Samuel: [11] "I regret that I made Saul king, for he has turned back from following me, and has not carried out my commands." Samuel was angry; and he cried out to the LORD all night. [12] Samuel rose early in the morning to meet Saul, and Samuel was told, "Saul went to Carmel, where he set up a monument for himself, and on returning he passed on down to Gilgal." [13] When Samuel came to Saul, Saul said to him, "May you be blessed by the LORD; I have carried out the command of the LORD." [14] But Samuel said, "What then is this bleating of sheep in my ears, and the lowing of cattle that I hear?" [15] Saul said, "They have brought them from the Amalekites; for the people spared the best of the sheep and the cattle, to sacrifice to the LORD your God; but the rest we have utterly destroyed." [16] Then Samuel said to Saul, "Stop! I will tell you what the LORD said to me last night." He replied, "Speak."

17 Samuel said, "Though you are little in your own eyes, are you not the head of the tribes of Israel? The LORD anointed you king over Israel. [18] And the LORD sent you on a mission, and said, 'Go, utterly destroy the sinners, the Amalekites, and fight against them until they are consumed.' [19] Why then did you not obey the voice of the LORD? Why did you swoop down on the spoil, and do what was evil in the sight of the LORD?" [20] Saul said to Samuel, "I have obeyed the voice of the LORD, I have gone on the mission on which the LORD sent me, I have brought Agag the king of Amalek, and I have utterly destroyed the Amalekites. [21] But from the spoil the people took sheep and cattle, the best of the things devoted to destruction, to sacrifice to the LORD your God in Gilgal." [22] And Samuel said,

"Has the LORD as great delight in
    burnt offerings and sacrifices,
    as in obedience to the voice of the
        LORD?
Surely, to obey is better than
        sacrifice,
    and to heed than the fat of rams.
[23] For rebellion is no less a sin than
        divination,
    and stubbornness is like iniquity
        and idolatry.

Because you have rejected the word
        of the LORD,
    he has also rejected you from
        being king."

24 Saul said to Samuel, "I have sinned; for I have transgressed the commandment of the LORD and your words, because I feared the people and obeyed their voice. [25] Now therefore, I pray, pardon my sin, and return with me, so that I may worship the LORD." [26] Samuel said to Saul, "I will not return with you; for you have rejected the word of the LORD, and the LORD has rejected you from being king over Israel." [27] As Samuel turned to go away, Saul caught hold of the hem of his robe, and it tore. [28] And Samuel said to him, "The LORD has torn the kingdom of Israel from you this very day, and has given it to a neighbor of yours, who is better than you. [29] Moreover the Glory of Israel will not recant[v] or change his mind; for he is not a mortal, that he should change his mind." [30] Then Saul[w] said, "I have sinned; yet honor me now before the elders of my people and before Israel, and return with me, so that I may worship the LORD your God." [31] So Samuel turned back after Saul; and Saul worshiped the LORD.

32 Then Samuel said, "Bring Agag king of the Amalekites here to me." And Agag came to him haltingly.[x] Agag said, "Surely this is the bitterness of death."[y] [33] But Samuel said,

"As your sword has made women
        childless,
    so your mother shall be childless
        among women."

And Samuel hewed Agag in pieces before the LORD in Gilgal.

34 Then Samuel went to Ramah; and Saul went up to his house in Gibeah of Saul. [35] Samuel did not see Saul again until the day of his death, but Samuel grieved over Saul. And the LORD was sorry that he had made Saul king over Israel.

David Anointed as King

16 The LORD said to Samuel, "How long will you grieve over Saul? I have rejected him from being king over Israel. Fill your horn with oil and set out; I will send you to Jesse the Bethlehemite, for I have provided for myself a king

v Q Ms Gk: MT *deceive*   w Heb *he*   x Cn
Compare Gk: Meaning of Heb uncertain
y Q Ms Gk: MT *Surely the bitterness of death is past*

among his sons." ²Samuel said, "How can I go? If Saul hears of it, he will kill me." And the LORD said, "Take a heifer with you, and say, 'I have come to sacrifice to the LORD.' ³Invite Jesse to the sacrifice, and I will show you what you shall do; and you shall anoint for me the one whom I name to you." ⁴Samuel did what the LORD commanded, and came to Bethlehem. The elders of the city came to meet him trembling, and said, "Do you come peaceably?" ⁵He said, "Peaceably; I have come to sacrifice to the LORD; sanctify yourselves and come with me to the sacrifice." And he sanctified Jesse and his sons and invited them to the sacrifice.

6 When they came, he looked on Eliab and thought, "Surely the LORD's anointed is now before the LORD."ᶻ ⁷But the LORD said to Samuel, "Do not look on his appearance or on the height of his stature, because I have rejected him; for the LORD does not see as mortals see; they look on the outward appearance, but the LORD looks on the heart." ⁸Then Jesse called Abinadab, and made him pass before Samuel. He said, "Neither has the LORD chosen this one." ⁹Then Jesse made Shammah pass by. And he said, "Neither has the LORD chosen this one." ¹⁰Jesse made seven of his sons pass before Samuel, and Samuel said to Jesse, "The LORD has not chosen any of these." ¹¹Samuel said to Jesse, "Are all your sons here?" And he said, "There remains yet the youngest, but he is keeping the sheep." And Samuel said to Jesse, "Send and bring him; for we will not sit down until he comes here." ¹²He sent and brought him in. Now he was ruddy, and had beautiful eyes, and was handsome. The LORD said, "Rise and anoint him; for this is the one." ¹³Then Samuel took the horn of oil, and anointed him in the presence of his brothers; and the spirit of the LORD came mightily upon David from that day forward. Samuel then set out and went to Ramah.

David Plays the Lyre for Saul

14 Now the spirit of the LORD departed from Saul, and an evil spirit from the LORD tormented him. ¹⁵And Saul's servants said to him, "See now, an evil spirit from God is tormenting you. ¹⁶Let our lord now command the servants who attend you to look for someone who is skillful in playing the lyre; and when the evil spirit from God is upon you, he will play it, and you

will feel better." ¹⁷So Saul said to his servants, "Provide for me someone who can play well, and bring him to me." ¹⁸One of the young men answered, "I have seen a son of Jesse the Bethlehemite who is skillful in playing, a man of valor, a warrior, prudent in speech, and a man of good presence; and the LORD is with him." ¹⁹So Saul sent messengers to Jesse, and said, "Send me your son David who is with the sheep." ²⁰Jesse took a donkey loaded with bread, a skin of wine, and a kid, and sent them by his son David to Saul. ²¹And David came to Saul, and entered his service. Saul loved him greatly, and he became his armor-bearer. ²²Saul sent to Jesse, saying, "Let David remain in my service, for he has found favor in my sight." ²³And whenever the evil spirit from God came upon Saul, David took the lyre and played it with his hand, and Saul would be relieved and feel better, and the evil spirit would depart from him.

David and Goliath

17 Now the Philistines gathered their armies for battle; they were gathered at Socoh, which belongs to Judah, and encamped between Socoh and Azekah, in Ephes-dammim. ²Saul and the Israelites gathered and encamped in the valley of Elah, and formed ranks against the Philistines. ³The Philistines stood on the mountain on the one side, and Israel stood on the mountain on the other side, with a valley between them. ⁴And there came out from the camp of the Philistines a champion named Goliath, of Gath, whose height was sixᵃ cubits and a span. ⁵He had a helmet of bronze on his head, and he was armed with a coat of mail; the weight of the coat was five thousand shekels of bronze. ⁶He had greaves of bronze on his legs and a javelin of bronze slung between his shoulders. ⁷The shaft of his spear was like a weaver's beam, and his spear's head weighed six hundred shekels of iron; and his shield-bearer went before him. ⁸He stood and shouted to the ranks of Israel, "Why have you come out to draw up for battle? Am I not a Philistine, and are you not servants of Saul? Choose a man for yourselves, and let him come down to me. ⁹If he is able to fight with me and kill me, then we will be your servants; but if I prevail against him and kill him,

ᶻ Heb *him*   ᵃ MT: Q Ms Gk *four*

then you shall be our servants and serve us." ¹⁰And the Philistine said, "Today I defy the ranks of Israel! Give me a man, that we may fight together." ¹¹When Saul and all Israel heard these words of the Philistine, they were dismayed and greatly afraid.

12 Now David was the son of an Ephrathite of Bethlehem in Judah, named Jesse, who had eight sons. In the days of Saul the man was already old and advanced in years.ᵇ ¹³The three eldest sons of Jesse had followed Saul to the battle; the names of his three sons who went to the battle

were Eliab the firstborn, and next to him Abinadab, and the third Shammah. ¹⁴David was the youngest; the three eldest followed Saul, ¹⁵but David went back and forth from Saul to feed his father's sheep at Bethlehem. ¹⁶For forty days the Philistine came forward and took his stand, morning and evening.

17 Jesse said to his son David, "Take for your brothers an ephah of this parched grain and these ten loaves, and carry them quickly to the camp to your brothers;

ᵇ Gk Syr: Heb *among men*

---

*P*laying It Safe

FRIDAY

Scripture Reading for Today:
1 Samuel 17.1–37

Verse for Today:
1 Samuel 17.33

"Watch out. Be careful. I wouldn't try that if I were you." Women may prefer to listen to such voices so that they won't be challenged to step out. Or we may choose to surround ourselves with other people who we know won't question us—people who will tell us what we hope to be true. Instead we need people who will challenge us to step out of the boat, to take risks.

I recently saw a cross-stitched wall plaque behind a woman's desk. It showed a cat stuck in a net, and it read, "It's easier to get into things than it is to get out." What a motto, I thought. It might as well have said, "Be careful, play it safe. Don't ever try anything new."

The call to fear, the call to be careful, is the call to waste a life, to bury one's talent in the ground. Remember that story? The landlord does not say to the one who buried the talent, "Hey, no problem. You got a bit nervous." Instead he calls the man worthless, wicked and lazy (Matthew 25.26–30) for being unwilling to take risks.

Jesus knew what it was to have people tell him to play it safe. When he told his disciples that he would go to Jerusalem and be killed, Peter offered excellent advice. Essentially he told Jesus to be careful and not to do anything dangerous. Jesus rebuked him: "Get behind me, Satan! . . . for you are setting your mind not on divine things but on human things" (Matthew 16.23).

We need to learn to say to those who tell us to play it safe, "Get behind me, Satan." That voice that tells us to be careful is the voice of the devil. The powers of evil love to freeze people by fear; they love to scare women so that over half of God's church can be paralyzed into passivity.

—*MARY ELLEN ASHCROFT*

Go to page 302 for your next devotional reading.

Leah

Her Name May Mean "Impatient" or "Wild Cow"

Her Character: *Capable of both strong and enduring love, she was a faithful mother and wife. Manipulated by her father into marrying Jacob before Rachel, she became jealous of her sister, with whom, it seems, she never reconciled.*
Her Sorrow: *That she lacked her sister's beauty and that her love for her husband was one-sided.*
Her Joy: *That she and Jacob had six sons and one daughter.*

Read Genesis 30.1–23; 35.16–19

"We buried Rachel today. But she is still alive. I catch glimpses of her yet in Jacob's broken heart, in dark-eyed Joseph and squalling little Benjamin, his favorite sons. I can hear my sister weeping loudly for the children she might have had, stubbornly refusing to be comforted. Yet who notices my tears? Should they flood the desert, no one would care.

"Reuben, Simeon, Levi, Judah, Issachar, Zebulun, Dinah, and then Gad and Asher by my maid—these are the children God has given me and I have given my Jacob. And still he loves her best. Should my husband and I live another hundred years, I will never be his only wife."

Contrary to what Leah might have felt, God had taken note of her sorrow. Knowing well that Jacob's heart was too cramped a space to shelter both Rachel and Leah, he made Leah a mother seven times, extending her influence in Jacob's household.

With each child Leah hoped to secure her husband's affection. Instead her disappointment grew. She felt the old curse once again: "Your desire shall be for your husband, and he shall rule over you" (Genesis 3.16).

Still, she thanked God each day for enabling her to bear Jacob's children. But children often cause a mother untold sorrow. Dinah, Leah's only daughter, was raped by a local prince upon the family's return to Jacob's homeland. Leah hardly knew how to comfort her. To make matters worse, her sons Levi and

Simeon avenged their sister by murdering a town full of people. Then Reuben disgraced himself by sleeping with his father's concubine Bilhah.

Hadn't God promised to protect them if they returned to this land of promise? How then could such things happen, Leah wondered? True, God had watched over them as they faced Esau and his four hundred men. But Leah's joy at the brothers' reunion was eclipsed by her sorrow at again being proved the lesser-loved wife. Jacob had made it plain enough by placing Rachel and her children last in their long caravan, giving them the best chance of escape should Esau turn violent.

But Jacob's love could not prevent Rachel from dying in childbirth. Leah, not Rachel, was destined to be his first and last wife. Alongside her husband, the father of Israel, she would be revered as a mother of Israel. In fact, the promise of a Savior was carried, not through Rachel's Joseph, but through Leah's Judah, whose descendants would include David, Israel's great king, and Jesus, the long-awaited Messiah. At the end of his life, Jacob was laid to rest next to his first wife Leah, rather than his favorite wife Rachel.

Rachel and Leah remind us that life is fraught with sorrow and peril, much of it caused by sin and selfishness. Both women suffered—each in her own way—the curse of Eve after she was expelled from her garden paradise. While Rachel died giving birth to a child, Leah experienced the anguish of loving a man who seemed indifferent to her. Yet both women became mothers in Israel, leaving their homeland to play essential roles in the story of God's great plan for his people.

Praying With Leah

When the LORD saw that Leah was unloved, he opened her womb; but Rachel was barren. Leah conceived and bore a son, and she named him Reuben; for she said, "Because the LORD has looked on my affliction; surely now my husband will love me."—*Genesis 29.31–32*

Praise God: *That though human beings often judge by outward appearances, God always sees the heart and judges accordingly.*

Offer Thanks: *That God is moved by our sorrow.*

Confess: *Your tendency to compare yourself with other women, judging them and yourself merely by appearances.*

Ask God: *To enable you to base your identity on your relationship with him rather than on what you see in the mirror.*

Lift Your Heart

Take five minutes a day this week to pay yourself a compliment by thanking God for making you the woman you are. Call to mind everything you like about yourself—your quirky sense of humor, your love of great literature, your compassion for other people, your curly hair, even the shape of your toes. Resist the temptation to think about what you don't like. (Imagine for a moment how God must feel when he hears us complaining about how he has made us.) Instead, decide now to honor him by your gratitude. At the end of the week, treat yourself to lunch with a friend or a leisurely *latte* at your favorite café in celebration of all the natural gifts with which God has blessed you.

Lord, I don't want to be critical of how you've put me together, relying on what others think of me for my sense of well-being. Make me a woman who is confident she is lovable, not because of any outward beauty, but because you have loved me from the moment you called me into being.

Go to page 305 for your next devotional reading.

18also take these ten cheeses to the commander of their thousand. See how your brothers fare, and bring some token from them."

19 Now Saul, and they, and all the men of Israel, were in the valley of Elah, fighting with the Philistines. 20David rose early in the morning, left the sheep with a keeper, took the provisions, and went as Jesse had commanded him. He came to the encampment as the army was going forth to the battle line, shouting the war cry. 21Israel and the Philistines drew up for battle, army against army. 22David left the things in charge of the keeper of the baggage, ran to the ranks, and went and greeted his brothers. 23As he talked with them, the champion, the Philistine of Gath, Goliath by name, came up out of the ranks of the Philistines, and spoke the same words as before. And David heard him.

24 All the Israelites, when they saw the man, fled from him and were very much afraid. 25The Israelites said, "Have you seen this man who has come up? Surely he has come up to defy Israel. The king will greatly enrich the man who kills him, and will give him his daughter and make his family free in Israel." 26David said to the men who stood by him, "What shall be done for the man who kills this Philistine, and takes away the reproach from Israel? For who is this uncircumcised Philistine that he should defy the armies of the living God?" 27The people answered him in the same way, "So shall it be done for the man who kills him."

28 His eldest brother Eliab heard him talking to the men; and Eliab's anger was kindled against David. He said, "Why have you come down? With whom have you left those few sheep in the wilderness? I know your presumption and the evil of your heart; for you have come down just to see the battle." 29David said, "What have I done now? It was only a question." 30He turned away from him toward another and spoke in the same way; and the people answered him again as before.

31 When the words that David spoke were heard, they repeated them before Saul; and he sent for him. 32David said to Saul, "Let no one's heart fail because of him; your servant will go and fight with this Philistine." 33Saul said to David, "You are not able to go against this Philistine to fight with him; for you are just a boy, and he has been a warrior from his youth." 34But David said to Saul, "Your servant used to keep sheep for his father; and whenever a lion or a bear came, and took a lamb from the flock, 35I went after it and struck it down, rescuing the lamb from its mouth; and if it turned against me, I would catch it by the jaw, strike it down, and kill it. 36Your servant has killed both lions and bears; and this uncircumcised Philistine shall be like one of them, since he has defied the armies of the living God." 37David said, "The LORD, who saved me from the paw of the lion and from the paw of the bear, will save me from the hand of this Philistine." So Saul said to David, "Go, and may the LORD be with you!"

38 Saul clothed David with his armor; he put a bronze helmet on his head and clothed him with a coat of mail. 39David strapped Saul's sword over the armor, and he tried in vain to walk, for he was not used to them. Then David said to Saul, "I cannot walk with these; for I am not used to them." So David removed them. 40Then he took his staff in his hand, and chose five smooth stones from the wadi, and put them in his shepherd's bag, in the pouch; his sling was in his hand, and he drew near to the Philistine.

41 The Philistine came on and drew near to David, with his shield-bearer in front of him. 42When the Philistine looked and saw David, he disdained him, for he was only a youth, ruddy and handsome in appearance. 43The Philistine said to David, "Am I a dog, that you come to me with sticks?" And the Philistine cursed David by his gods. 44The Philistine said to David, "Come to me, and I will give your flesh to the birds of the air and to the wild animals of the field." 45But David said to the Philistine, "You come to me with sword and spear and javelin; but I come to you in the name of the LORD of hosts, the God of the armies of Israel, whom you have defied. 46This very day the LORD will deliver you into my hand, and I will strike you down and cut off your head; and I will give the dead bodies of the Philistine army this very day to the birds of the air and to the wild animals of the earth, so that all the earth may know that there is a God in Israel, 47and that all this assembly may know that the LORD does not save by sword and spear; for the battle is the

LORD's and he will give you into our hand." 48 When the Philistine drew nearer to meet David, David ran quickly toward the battle line to meet the Philistine. ⁴⁹David put his hand in his bag, took out a stone, slung it, and struck the Philistine on his forehead; the stone sank into his fore-head, and he fell face down on the ground.

50 So David prevailed over the Philistine with a sling and a stone, striking down the Philistine and killing him; there was no sword in David's hand. ⁵¹Then David ran and stood over the Philistine; he

*S*truggles

MONDAY

Scripture Reading for Today: *1 Samuel 17.41–51*

Verse for Today: *1 Samuel 17.47*

Pitting David against Goliath would have been like sending a glid-er into battle with a Stealth Bomber. The boy with the slingshot didn't have a chance against a nine-foot colossus, sheathed in 125 pounds of bronze armor, toting a spear and a sword. But we all know that David got his man despite the odds.

The story of David and Goliath reveals much about our strug-gle with evil. For 40 days Goliath taunts King Saul and the Jews. Each day their fear increases as he grows larger and more hideous in their eyes. His threats weave a spell over the Israelites. He is like a spider toying with its prey.

Then David breaks upon the scene and exclaims with youthful indignation, "Who is this uncircumcised Philistine that he should defy the armies of the living God?" Was this courage on the boy's part or stupidity? Knowing the end of the story helps us to tell the difference.

A thousand years later, the story repeats itself, not far from where David fought Goliath. This time the battle takes place in the desert outside Jerusalem and the threatening giant is none other than the devil himself. In the Hebrew Scriptures, the devil is represented by figures like Goliath and Pharaoh, but in the Gospels he comes on the scene undisguised.

Like David, who stripped himself of Saul's protecting armor and sword, Jesus strips himself of bodily strength by fasting. David faced Goliath after 40 days of the giant's threats. Now Jesus meets Satan after 40 days in the desert. David battled Goliath with only a stone and a sling, while Jesus defeats Satan with only the Word of God.

Over and over the themes echo through Scripture and repeat themselves in the life of faith. God sends deliverance to his peo-ple, who are enslaved by sin and Satan. Weakness overcomes strength, humility defeats pride, faith confounds fear, light over-comes darkness. When hope appears to have vanished, victory breaks through. These are the paradoxes upon which faith rests and the life of grace unfolds.

—ANN SPANGLER

Go to page 331 for your next devotional reading.

grasped his sword, drew it out of its sheath, and killed him; then he cut off his head with it.

When the Philistines saw that their champion was dead, they fled. ⁵²The troops of Israel and Judah rose up with a shout and pursued the Philistines as far as Gath*ᶜ* and the gates of Ekron, so that the wounded Philistines fell on the way from Shaaraim as far as Gath and Ekron. ⁵³The Israelites came back from chasing the Philistines, and they plundered their camp. ⁵⁴David took the head of the Philistine and brought it to Jerusalem; but he put his armor in his tent.

55 When Saul saw David go out against the Philistine, he said to Abner, the commander of the army, "Abner, whose son is this young man?" Abner said, "As your soul lives, O king, I do not know." ⁵⁶The king said, "Inquire whose son the stripling is." ⁵⁷On David's return from killing the Philistine, Abner took him and brought him before Saul, with the head of the Philistine in his hand. ⁵⁸Saul said to him, "Whose son are you, young man?" And David answered, "I am the son of your servant Jesse the Bethlehemite."

Jonathan's Covenant with David

18 When David*ᵈ* had finished speaking to Saul, the soul of Jonathan was bound to the soul of David, and Jonathan loved him as his own soul. ²Saul took him that day and would not let him return to his father's house. ³Then Jonathan made a covenant with David, because he loved him as his own soul. ⁴Jonathan stripped himself of the robe that he was wearing, and gave it to David, and his armor, and even his sword and his bow and his belt. ⁵David went out and was successful wherever Saul sent him; as a result, Saul set him over the army. And all the people, even the servants of Saul, approved.

6 As they were coming home, when David returned from killing the Philistine, the women came out of all the towns of Israel, singing and dancing, to meet King Saul, with tambourines, with songs of joy, and with musical instruments.*ᵉ* ⁷And the women sang to one another as they made merry,

"Saul has killed his thousands,
  and David his ten thousands."

⁸Saul was very angry, for this saying displeased him. He said, "They have ascribed to David ten thousands, and to me they have ascribed thousands; what more can he have but the kingdom?" ⁹So Saul eyed David from that day on.

Saul Tries to Kill David

10 The next day an evil spirit from God rushed upon Saul, and he raved within his house, while David was playing the lyre, as he did day by day. Saul had his spear in his hand; ¹¹and Saul threw the spear, for he thought, "I will pin David to the wall." But David eluded him twice.

12 Saul was afraid of David, because the LORD was with him but had departed from Saul. ¹³So Saul removed him from his presence, and made him a commander of a thousand; and David marched out and came in, leading the army. ¹⁴David had success in all his undertakings; for the LORD was with him. ¹⁵When Saul saw that he had great success, he stood in awe of him. ¹⁶But all Israel and Judah loved David; for it was he who marched out and came in leading them.

David Marries Michal

17 Then Saul said to David, "Here is my elder daughter Merab; I will give her to you as a wife; only be valiant for me and fight the LORD's battles." For Saul thought, "I will not raise a hand against him; let the Philistines deal with him." ¹⁸David said to Saul, "Who am I and who are my kinsfolk, my father's family in Israel, that I should be son-in-law to the king?" ¹⁹But at the time when Saul's daughter Merab should have been given to David, she was given to Adriel the Meholathite as a wife.

20 Now Saul's daughter Michal loved David. Saul was told, and the thing pleased him. ²¹Saul thought, "Let me give her to him that she may be a snare for him and that the hand of the Philistines may be against him." Therefore Saul said to David a second time,*ᶠ* "You shall now be my son-in-law." ²²Saul commanded his servants, "Speak to David in private and say, 'See, the king is delighted with you, and all his servants love you; now then, become the king's son-in-law.'" ²³So Saul's servants reported these words to David in private. And David said, "Does it seem to you a little thing to become the

---

ᶜ Gk Syr: Heb *Gai*   *ᵈ* Heb *he*   *ᵉ* Or *triangles,* or *three-stringed instruments*   *ᶠ* Heb *by two*

king's son-in-law, seeing that I am a poor man and of no repute?" 24The servants of Saul told him, "This is what David said." 25Then Saul said, "Thus shall you say to David, 'The king desires no marriage present except a hundred foreskins of the Philistines, that he may be avenged on the king's enemies.' " Now Saul planned to make David fall by the hand of the Philistines. 26When his servants told David these words, David was well pleased to be the king's son-in-law. Before the time had expired, 27David rose and went, along with his men, and killed one hundredg of the Philistines; and David brought their foreskins, which were given in full number to the king, that he might become the king's son-in-law. Saul gave him his daughter Michal as a wife. 28But when Saul realized that the LORD was with David, and that Saul's daughter Michal loved him, 29Saul was still more afraid of David. So Saul was David's enemy from that time forward.

30 Then the commanders of the Philistines came out to battle; and as often as they came out, David had more success than all the servants of Saul, so that his fame became very great.

Jonathan Intercedes for David

19 Saul spoke with his son Jonathan and with all his servants about killing David. But Saul's son Jonathan took great delight in David. 2Jonathan told David, "My father Saul is trying to kill you; therefore be on guard tomorrow morning; stay in a secret place and hide yourself. 3I will go out and stand beside my father in the field where you are, and I will speak to my father about you; if I learn anything I will tell you." 4Jonathan spoke well of David to his father Saul, saying to him, "The king should not sin against his servant David, because he has not sinned against you, and because his deeds have been of good service to you; 5for he took his life in his hand when he attacked the Philistine, and the LORD brought about a great victory for all Israel. You saw it, and rejoiced; why then will you sin against an innocent person by killing David without cause?" 6Saul heeded the voice of Jonathan; Saul swore, "As the LORD lives, he shall not be put to death." 7So Jonathan called David and related all these things to him. Jonathan then

brought David to Saul, and he was in his presence as before.

Michal Helps David Escape from Saul

8 Again there was war, and David went out to fight the Philistines. He launched a heavy attack on them, so that they fled before him. 9Then an evil spirit from the LORD came upon Saul, as he sat in his house with his spear in his hand, while David was playing music. 10Saul sought to pin David to the wall with the spear; but he eluded Saul, so that he struck the spear into the wall. David fled and escaped that night.

11 Saul sent messengers to David's house to keep watch over him, planning to kill him in the morning. David's wife Michal told him, "If you do not save your life tonight, tomorrow you will be killed." 12So Michal let David down through the window; he fled away and escaped. 13Michal took an idolh and laid it on the bed; she put a neti of goats' hair on its head, and covered it with the clothes. 14When Saul sent messengers to take David, she said, "He is sick." 15Then Saul sent the messengers to see David for themselves. He said, "Bring him up to me in the bed, that I may kill him." 16When the messengers came in, the idolj was in the bed, with the coveringi of goats' hair on its head. 17Saul said to Michal, "Why have you deceived me like this, and let my enemy go, so that he has escaped?" Michal answered Saul, "He said to me, 'Let me go; why should I kill you?' "

David Joins Samuel in Ramah

18 Now David fled and escaped; he came to Samuel at Ramah, and told him all that Saul had done to him. He and Samuel went and settled at Naioth. 19Saul was told, "David is at Naioth in Ramah." 20Then Saul sent messengers to take David. When they saw the company of the prophets in a frenzy, with Samuel standing in charge ofi them, the spirit of God came upon the messengers of Saul, and they also fell into a prophetic frenzy. 21When Saul was told, he sent other messengers, and they also fell into a frenzy. Saul sent messengers again the third time, and they also fell into a frenzy. 22Then he

g Gk Compare 2 Sam 3.14: Heb *two hundred*   h Heb *took the teraphim*   i Meaning of Heb uncertain   j Heb *the teraphim*

himself went to Ramah. He came to the great well that is in Secu;[k] he asked, "Where are Samuel and David?" And someone said, "They are at Naioth in Ramah." 23He went there, toward Naioth in Ramah; and the spirit of God came upon him. As he was going, he fell into a prophetic frenzy, until he came to Naioth in Ramah. 24He too stripped off his clothes, and he too fell into a frenzy before Samuel. He lay naked all that day and all that night. Therefore it is said, "Is Saul also among the prophets?"

The Friendship of David and Jonathan

20 David fled from Naioth in Ramah. He came before Jonathan and said, "What have I done? What is my guilt? And what is my sin against your father that he is trying to take my life?" 2He said to him, "Far from it! You shall not die. My father does nothing either great or small without disclosing it to me; and why should my father hide this from me? Never!" 3But David also swore, "Your father knows well that you like me; and he thinks, 'Do not let Jonathan know this, or he will be grieved.' But truly, as the LORD lives and as you yourself live, there is but a step between me and death." 4Then Jonathan said to David, "Whatever you say, I will do for you." 5David said to Jonathan, "Tomorrow is the new moon, and I should not fail to sit with the king at the meal; but let me go, so that I may hide in the field until the third evening. 6If your father misses me at all, then say, 'David earnestly asked leave of me to run to Bethlehem his city; for there is a yearly sacrifice there for all the family.' 7If he says, 'Good!' it will be well with your servant; but if he is angry, then know that evil has been determined by him. 8Therefore deal kindly with your servant, for you have brought your servant into a sacred covenant[l] with you. But if there is guilt in me, kill me yourself; why should you bring me to your father?" 9Jonathan said, "Far be it from you! If I knew that it was decided by my father that evil should come upon you, would I not tell you?" 10Then David said to Jonathan, "Who will tell me if your father answers you harshly?" 11Jonathan replied to David, "Come, let us go out into the field." So they both went out into the field.

12 Jonathan said to David, "By the LORD, the God of Israel! When I have sounded out my father, about this time tomorrow, or on the third day, if he is well disposed toward David, shall I not then send and disclose it to you? 13But if my father intends to do you harm, the LORD do so to Jonathan, and more also, if I do not disclose it to you, and send you away, so that you may go in safety. May the LORD be with you, as he has been with my father. 14If I am still alive, show me the faithful love of the LORD; but if I die,[m] 15never cut off your faithful love from my house, even if the LORD were to cut off every one of the enemies of David from the face of the earth." 16Thus Jonathan made a covenant with the house of David, saying, "May the LORD seek out the enemies of David." 17Jonathan made David swear again by his love for him; for he loved him as he loved his own life.

18 Jonathan said to him, "Tomorrow is the new moon; you will be missed, because your place will be empty. 19On the day after tomorrow, you shall go a long way down; go to the place where you hid yourself earlier, and remain beside the stone there.[m] 20I will shoot three arrows to the side of it, as though I shot at a mark. 21Then I will send the boy, saying, 'Go, find the arrows.' If I say to the boy, 'Look, the arrows are on this side of you, collect them,' then you are to come, for, as the LORD lives, it is safe for you and there is no danger. 22But if I say to the young man, 'Look, the arrows are beyond you,' then go; for the LORD has sent you away. 23As for the matter about which you and I have spoken, the LORD is witness[n] between you and me forever."

24 So David hid himself in the field. When the new moon came, the king sat at the feast to eat. 25The king sat upon his seat, as at other times, upon the seat by the wall. Jonathan stood, while Abner sat by Saul's side; but David's place was empty.

26 Saul did not say anything that day; for he thought, "Something has befallen him; he is not clean, surely he is not clean." 27But on the second day, the day after the new moon, David's place was empty. And Saul said to his son Jonathan, "Why has the son of Jesse not come to the feast,

---

[k] Gk reads to the well of the threshing floor on the bare height   [l] Heb a covenant of the LORD   [m] Meaning of Heb uncertain   [n] Gk: Heb lacks witness

either yesterday or today?" 28Jonathan answered Saul, "David earnestly asked leave of me to go to Bethlehem; 29he said, 'Let me go; for our family is holding a sacrifice in the city, and my brother has commanded me to be there. So now, if I have found favor in your sight, let me get away, and see my brothers.' For this reason he has not come to the king's table."

30 Then Saul's anger was kindled against Jonathan. He said to him, "You son of a perverse, rebellious woman! Do I not know that you have chosen the son of Jesse to your own shame, and to the shame of your mother's nakedness? 31For as long as the son of Jesse lives upon the earth, neither you nor your kingdom shall be established. Now send and bring him to me, for he shall surely die." 32Then Jonathan answered his father Saul, "Why should he be put to death? What has he done?" 33But Saul threw his spear at him to strike him; so Jonathan knew that it was the decision of his father to put David to death. 34Jonathan rose from the table in fierce anger and ate no food on the second day of the month, for he was grieved for David, and because his father had disgraced him.

35 In the morning Jonathan went out into the field to the appointment with David, and with him was a little boy. 36He said to the boy, "Run and find the arrows that I shoot." As the boy ran, he shot an arrow beyond him. 37When the boy came to the place where Jonathan's arrow had fallen, Jonathan called after the boy and said, "Is the arrow not beyond you?" 38Jonathan called after the boy, "Hurry, be quick, do not linger." So Jonathan's boy gathered up the arrows and came to his master. 39But the boy knew nothing; only Jonathan and David knew the arrangement. 40Jonathan gave his weapons to the boy and said to him, "Go and carry them to the city." 41As soon as the boy had gone, David rose from beside the stone heap*o* and prostrated himself with his face to the ground. He bowed three times, and they kissed each other, and wept with each other; David wept the more. *p* 42Then Jonathan said to David, "Go in peace, since both of us have sworn in the name of the LORD, saying, 'The LORD shall be between me and you, and between my descendants and your descendants, forever.' " He got up and left; and Jonathan went into the city.*q*

David and the Holy Bread

21 *r*David came to Nob to the priest Ahimelech. Ahimelech came trembling to meet David, and said to him, "Why are you alone, and no one with you?" 2David said to the priest Ahimelech, "The king has charged me with a matter, and said to me, 'No one must know anything of the matter about which I send you, and with which I have charged you.' I have made an appointment*s* with the young men for such and such a place. 3Now then, what have you at hand? Give me five loaves of bread, or whatever is here." 4The priest answered David, "I have no ordinary bread at hand, only holy bread—provided that the young men have kept themselves from women." 5David answered the priest, "Indeed women have been kept from us as always when I go on an expedition; the vessels of the young men are holy even when it is a common journey; how much more today will their vessels be holy?" 6So the priest gave him the holy bread; for there was no bread there except the bread of the Presence, which is removed from before the LORD, to be replaced by hot bread on the day it is taken away.

7 Now a certain man of the servants of Saul was there that day, detained before the LORD; his name was Doeg the Edomite, the chief of Saul's shepherds.

8 David said to Ahimelech, "Is there no spear or sword here with you? I did not bring my sword or my weapons with me, because the king's business required haste." 9The priest said, "The sword of Goliath the Philistine, whom you killed in the valley of Elah, is here wrapped in a cloth behind the ephod; if you will take that, take it, for there is none here except that one." David said, "There is none like it; give it to me."

David Flees to Gath

10 David rose and fled that day from Saul; he went to King Achish of Gath. 11The servants of Achish said to him, "Is this not David the king of the land? Did they not sing to one another of him in dances,

o Gk: Heb *from beside the south*   *p* Vg: Meaning of Heb uncertain   *q* This sentence is 21.1 in Heb   *r* Ch 21.2 in Heb   *s* Q Ms Vg Compare Gk: Meaning of MT uncertain

'Saul has killed his thousands,
     and David his ten thousands'?"
12David took these words to heart and was
very much afraid of King Achish of Gath.
13So he changed his behavior before
them; he pretended to be mad when in
their presence.*t* He scratched marks on
the doors of the gate, and let his spittle
run down his beard. 14Achish said to his
servants, "Look, you see the man is mad;
why then have you brought him to me?
15Do I lack madmen, that you have
brought this fellow to play the madman
in my presence? Shall this fellow come
into my house?"

David and His Followers at Adullam

22 David left there and escaped to
the cave of Adullam; when his
brothers and all his father's house heard
of it, they went down there to him. 2Everyone who was in distress, and everyone
who was in debt, and everyone who was
discontented gathered to him; and he became captain over them. Those who were
with him numbered about four hundred.
3 David went from there to Mizpeh of
Moab. He said to the king of Moab,
"Please let my father and mother come*u*
to you, until I know what God will do for
me." 4He left them with the king of Moab,
and they stayed with him all the time that
David was in the stronghold. 5Then the
prophet Gad said to David, "Do not remain in the stronghold; leave, and go into
the land of Judah." So David left, and went
into the forest of Hereth.

Saul Slaughters the Priests at Nob

6 Saul heard that David and those who
were with him had been located. Saul was
sitting at Gibeah, under the tamarisk tree
on the height, with his spear in his hand,
and all his servants were standing around
him. 7Saul said to his servants who stood
around him, "Hear now, you Benjaminites; will the son of Jesse give every one of
you fields and vineyards, will he make
you all commanders of thousands and
commanders of hundreds? 8Is that why all
of you have conspired against me? No one
discloses to me when my son makes a
league with the son of Jesse, none of you
is sorry for me or discloses to me that my
son has stirred up my servant against me,
to lie in wait, as he is doing today." 9Doeg
the Edomite, who was in charge of Saul's
servants, answered, "I saw the son of Jesse

coming to Nob, to Ahimelech son of Ahitub; 10he inquired of the Lord for him,
gave him provisions, and gave him the
sword of Goliath the Philistine."

11 The king sent for the priest Ahimelech son of Ahitub and for all his father's
house, the priests who were at Nob; and
all of them came to the king. 12Saul said,
"Listen now, son of Ahitub." He answered,
"Here I am, my lord." 13Saul said to him,
"Why have you conspired against me, you
and the son of Jesse, by giving him bread
and a sword, and by inquiring of God for
him, so that he has risen against me, to lie
in wait, as he is doing today?"

14 Then Ahimelech answered the king,
"Who among all your servants is so faithful as David? He is the king's son-in-law,
and is quick*v* to do your bidding, and is
honored in your house. 15Is today the first
time that I have inquired of God for him?
By no means! Do not let the king impute
anything to his servant or to any member
of my father's house; for your servant has
known nothing of all this, much or little."
16The king said, "You shall surely die,
Ahimelech, you and all your father's
house." 17The king said to the guard who
stood around him, "Turn and kill the
priests of the Lord, because their hand
also is with David; they knew that he fled,
and did not disclose it to me." But the servants of the king would not raise their
hand to attack the priests of the Lord.
18Then the king said to Doeg, "You, Doeg,
turn and attack the priests." Doeg the
Edomite turned and attacked the priests;
on that day he killed eighty-five who wore
the linen ephod. 19Nob, the city of the
priests, he put to the sword; men and
women, children and infants, oxen, donkeys, and sheep, he put to the sword.

20 But one of the sons of Ahimelech
son of Ahitub, named Abiathar, escaped
and fled after David. 21Abiathar told David that Saul had killed the priests of the
Lord. 22David said to Abiathar, "I knew
on that day, when Doeg the Edomite was
there, that he would surely tell Saul. I am
responsible*w* for the lives of all your father's house. 23Stay with me, and do not
be afraid; for the one who seeks my life
seeks your life; you will be safe with me."

---

t Heb *in their hands*   *u* Syr Vg: Heb *come out*
v Heb *and turns aside*   *w* Gk Vg: Meaning of Heb
uncertain

David Saves the City of Keilah

23 Now they told David, "The Philistines are fighting against Keilah, and are robbing the threshing floors." ²David inquired of the LORD, "Shall I go and attack these Philistines?" The LORD said to David, "Go and attack the Philistines and save Keilah." ³But David's men said to him, "Look, we are afraid here in Judah; how much more then if we go to Keilah against the armies of the Philistines?" ⁴Then David inquired of the LORD again. The LORD answered him, "Yes, go down to Keilah; for I will give the Philistines into your hand." ⁵So David and his men went to Keilah, fought with the Philistines, brought away their livestock, and dealt them a heavy defeat. Thus David rescued the inhabitants of Keilah.

6 When Abiathar son of Ahimelech fled to David at Keilah, he came down with an ephod in his hand. ⁷Now it was told Saul that David had come to Keilah. And Saul said, "God has given[x] him into my hand; for he has shut himself in by entering a town that has gates and bars." ⁸Saul summoned all the people to war, to go down to Keilah, to besiege David and his men. ⁹When David learned that Saul was plotting evil against him, he said to the priest Abiathar, "Bring the ephod here." ¹⁰David said, "O LORD, the God of Israel, your servant has heard that Saul seeks to come to Keilah, to destroy the city on my account. ¹¹And now, will[y] Saul come down as your servant has heard? O LORD, the God of Israel, I beseech you, tell your servant." The LORD said, "He will come down." ¹²Then David said, "Will the men of Keilah surrender me and my men into the hand of Saul?" The LORD said, "They will surrender you." ¹³Then David and his men, who were about six hundred, set out and left Keilah; they wandered wherever they could go. When Saul was told that David had escaped from Keilah, he gave up the expedition. ¹⁴David remained in the strongholds in the wilderness, in the hill country of the Wilderness of Ziph. Saul sought him every day, but the LORD[z] did not give him into his hand.

David Eludes Saul in the Wilderness

15 David was in the Wilderness of Ziph at Horesh when he learned that[a] Saul had come out to seek his life. ¹⁶Saul's son Jonathan set out and came to David at Horesh; there he strengthened his hand through the LORD.[b] ¹⁷He said to him, "Do not be afraid; for the hand of my father Saul shall not find you; you shall be king over Israel, and I shall be second to you; my father Saul also knows that this is so." ¹⁸Then the two of them made a covenant before the LORD; David remained at Horesh, and Jonathan went home.

19 Then some Ziphites went up to Saul at Gibeah and said, "David is hiding among us in the strongholds of Horesh, on the hill of Hachilah, which is south of Jeshimon. ²⁰Now, O king, whenever you wish to come down, do so; and our part will be to surrender him into the king's hand." ²¹Saul said, "May you be blessed by the LORD for showing me compassion! ²²Go and make sure once more; find out exactly where he is, and who has seen him there; for I am told that he is very cunning. ²³Look around and learn all the hiding places where he lurks, and come back to me with sure information. Then I will go with you; and if he is in the land, I will search him out among all the thousands of Judah." ²⁴So they set out and went to Ziph ahead of Saul.

David and his men were in the wilderness of Maon, in the Arabah to the south of Jeshimon. ²⁵Saul and his men went to search for him. When David was told, he went down to the rock and stayed in the wilderness of Maon. When Saul heard that, he pursued David into the wilderness of Maon. ²⁶Saul went on one side of the mountain, and David and his men on the other side of the mountain. David was hurrying to get away from Saul, while Saul and his men were closing in on David and his men to capture them. ²⁷Then a messenger came to Saul, saying, "Hurry and come; for the Philistines have made a raid on the land." ²⁸So Saul stopped pursuing David, and went against the Philistines; therefore that place was called the Rock of Escape.[c] ²⁹[d] David then went up from there, and lived in the strongholds of En-gedi.

---

x Gk Tg: Heb *made a stranger of*   y Q Ms
Compare Gk: MT *Will the men of Keilah surrender me into his hand? Will*   z Q Ms Gk: MT *God*
a Or *saw that*   b Compare Q Ms Gk: MT *God*
c Or *Rock of Division;* meaning of Heb uncertain
d Ch 24.1 in Heb

David Spares Saul's Life

24 When Saul returned from following the Philistines, he was told, "David is in the wilderness of En-gedi." ²Then Saul took three thousand chosen men out of all Israel, and went to look for David and his men in the direction of the Rocks of the Wild Goats. ³He came to the sheepfolds beside the road, where there was a cave; and Saul went in to relieve himself.ᵉ Now David and his men were sitting in the innermost parts of the cave. ⁴The men of David said to him, "Here is the day of which the LORD said to you, 'I will give your enemy into your hand, and you shall do to him as it seems good to you.' " Then David went and stealthily cut off a corner of Saul's cloak. ⁵Afterward David was stricken to the heart because he had cut off a corner of Saul's cloak. ⁶He said to his men, "The LORD forbid that I should do this thing to my lord, the LORD's anointed, to raise my hand against him; for he is the LORD's anointed." ⁷So David scolded his men severely and did not permit them to attack Saul. Then Saul got up and left the cave, and went on his way.

8 Afterwards David also rose up and went out of the cave and called after Saul, "My lord the king!" When Saul looked behind him, David bowed with his face to the ground, and did obeisance. ⁹David said to Saul, "Why do you listen to the words of those who say, 'David seeks to do you harm'? ¹⁰This very day your eyes have seen how the LORD gave you into my hand in the cave; and some urged me to kill you, but I sparedᶠ you. I said, 'I will not raise my hand against my lord; for he is the LORD's anointed.' ¹¹See, my father, see the corner of your cloak in my hand; for by the fact that I cut off the corner of your cloak, and did not kill you, you may know for certain that there is no wrong or treason in my hands. I have not sinned against you, though you are hunting me to take my life. ¹²May the LORD judge between me and you! May the LORD avenge me on you; but my hand shall not be against you. ¹³As the ancient proverb says, 'Out of the wicked comes forth wickedness'; but my hand shall not be against you. ¹⁴Against whom has the king of Israel come out? Whom do you pursue? A dead dog? A single flea? ¹⁵May the LORD therefore be judge, and give sentence between

me and you. May he see to it, and plead my cause, and vindicate me against you."

16 When David had finished speaking these words to Saul, Saul said, "Is this your voice, my son David?" Saul lifted up his voice and wept. ¹⁷He said to David, "You are more righteous than I; for you have repaid me good, whereas I have repaid you evil. ¹⁸Today you have explained how you have dealt well with me, in that you did not kill me when the LORD put me into your hands. ¹⁹For who has ever found an enemy, and sent the enemy safely away? So may the LORD reward you with good for what you have done to me this day. ²⁰Now I know that you shall surely be king, and that the kingdom of Israel shall be established in your hand. ²¹Swear to me therefore by the LORD that you will not cut off my descendants after me, and that you will not wipe out my name from my father's house." ²²So David swore this to Saul. Then Saul went home; but David and his men went up to the stronghold.

Death of Samuel

25 Now Samuel died; and all Israel assembled and mourned for him. They buried him at his home in Ramah.

Then David got up and went down to the wilderness of Paran.

David and the Wife of Nabal

2 There was a man in Maon, whose property was in Carmel. The man was very rich; he had three thousand sheep and a thousand goats. He was shearing his sheep in Carmel. ³Now the name of the man was Nabal, and the name of his wife Abigail. The woman was clever and beautiful, but the man was surly and mean; he was a Calebite. ⁴David heard in the wilderness that Nabal was shearing his sheep. ⁵So David sent ten young men; and David said to the young men, "Go up to Carmel, and go to Nabal, and greet him in my name. ⁶Thus you shall salute him: 'Peace be to you, and peace be to your house, and peace be to all that you have. ⁷I hear that you have shearers; now your shepherds have been with us, and we did them no harm, and they missed nothing, all the time they were in Carmel. ⁸Ask your young men, and they will tell you. Therefore let my young men find favor in

---

ᵉ Heb *to cover his feet*   ᶠ Gk Syr Tg Vg: Heb *it (my eye) spared*

your sight; for we have come on a feast day. Please give whatever you have at hand to your servants and to your son David.' "

9 When David's young men came, they said all this to Nabal in the name of David; and then they waited. [10]But Nabal answered David's servants, "Who is David? Who is the son of Jesse? There are many servants today who are breaking away from their masters. [11]Shall I take my bread and my water and the meat that I have butchered for my shearers, and give it to men who come from I do not know where?" [12]So David's young men turned away, and came back and told him all this. [13]David said to his men, "Every man strap on his sword!" And every one of them strapped on his sword; David also strapped on his sword; and about four hundred men went up after David, while two hundred remained with the baggage.

14 But one of the young men told Abigail, Nabal's wife, "David sent messengers out of the wilderness to salute our master; and he shouted insults at them. [15]Yet the men were very good to us, and we suffered no harm, and we never missed anything when we were in the fields, as long as we were with them; [16]they were a wall to us both by night and by day, all the while we were with them keeping the sheep. [17]Now therefore know this and consider what you should do; for evil has been decided against our master and against all his house; he is so ill-natured that no one can speak to him."

18 Then Abigail hurried and took two hundred loaves, two skins of wine, five sheep ready dressed, five measures of parched grain, one hundred clusters of raisins, and two hundred cakes of figs. She loaded them on donkeys [19]and said to her young men, "Go on ahead of me; I am coming after you." But she did not tell her husband Nabal. [20]As she rode on the donkey and came down under cover of the mountain, David and his men came down toward her; and she met them. [21]Now David had said, "Surely it was in vain that I protected all that this fellow has in the wilderness, so that nothing was missed of all that belonged to him; but he has returned me evil for good. [22]God do so to David[g] and more also, if by morning I leave so much as one male of all who belong to him."

23 When Abigail saw David, she hur-

ried and alighted from the donkey, and fell before David on her face, bowing to the ground. [24]She fell at his feet and said, "Upon me alone, my lord, be the guilt; please let your servant speak in your ears, and hear the words of your servant. [25]My lord, do not take seriously this ill-natured fellow, Nabal; for as his name is, so is he; Nabal[h] is his name, and folly is with him; but I, your servant, did not see the young men of my lord, whom you sent.

26 "Now then, my lord, as the LORD lives, and as you yourself live, since the LORD has restrained you from bloodguilt and from taking vengeance with your own hand, now let your enemies and those who seek to do evil to my lord be like Nabal. [27]And now let this present that your servant has brought to my lord be given to the young men who follow my lord. [28]Please forgive the trespass of your servant; for the LORD will certainly make my lord a sure house, because my lord is fighting the battles of the LORD; and evil shall not be found in you so long as you live. [29]If anyone should rise up to pursue you and to seek your life, the life of my lord shall be bound in the bundle of the living under the care of the LORD your God; but the lives of your enemies he shall sling out as from the hollow of a sling. [30]When the LORD has done to my lord according to all the good that he has spoken concerning you, and has appointed you prince over Israel, [31]my lord shall have no cause of grief, or pangs of conscience, for having shed blood without cause or for having saved himself. And when the LORD has dealt well with my lord, then remember your servant."

32 David said to Abigail, "Blessed be the LORD, the God of Israel, who sent you to meet me today! [33]Blessed be your good sense, and blessed be you, who have kept me today from bloodguilt and from avenging myself by my own hand! [34]For as surely as the LORD the God of Israel lives, who has restrained me from hurting you, unless you had hurried and come to meet me, truly by morning there would not have been left to Nabal so much as one male." [35]Then David received from her hand what she had brought him; he said to her, "Go up to your house in peace;

g Gk Compare Syr: Heb the enemies of David
h That is Fool

see, I have heeded your voice, and I have granted your petition."

36 Abigail came to Nabal; he was holding a feast in his house, like the feast of a king. Nabal's heart was merry within him, for he was very drunk; so she told him nothing at all until the morning light. 37In the morning, when the wine had gone out of Nabal, his wife told him these things, and his heart died within him; he became like a stone. 38About ten days later the LORD struck Nabal, and he died.

39 When David heard that Nabal was dead, he said, "Blessed be the LORD who has judged the case of Nabal's insult to me, and has kept back his servant from evil; the LORD has returned the evildoing of Nabal upon his own head." Then David sent and wooed Abigail, to make her his wife. 40When David's servants came to Abigail at Carmel, they said to her, "David has sent us to you to take you to him as his wife." 41She rose and bowed down, with her face to the ground, and said, "Your servant is a slave to wash the feet of the servants of my lord." 42Abigail got up hurriedly and rode away on a donkey; her five maids attended her. She went after the messengers of David and became his wife.

43 David also married Ahinoam of Jezreel; both of them became his wives. 44Saul had given his daughter Michal, David's wife, to Palti son of Laish, who was from Gallim.

David Spares Saul's Life a Second Time

26 Then the Ziphites came to Saul at Gibeah, saying, "David is in hiding on the hill of Hachilah, which is opposite Jeshimon."[i] 2So Saul rose and went down to the Wilderness of Ziph, with three thousand chosen men of Israel, to seek David in the Wilderness of Ziph. 3Saul encamped on the hill of Hachilah, which is opposite Jeshimon[i] beside the road. But David remained in the wilderness. When he learned that Saul had come after him into the wilderness, 4David sent out spies, and learned that Saul had indeed arrived. 5Then David set out and came to the place where Saul had encamped; and David saw the place where Saul lay, with Abner son of Ner, the commander of his army. Saul was lying within the encampment, while the army was encamped around him.

6 Then David said to Ahimelech the Hittite, and to Joab's brother Abishai son of Zeruiah, "Who will go down with me into the camp to Saul?" Abishai said, "I will go down with you." 7So David and Abishai went to the army by night; there Saul lay sleeping within the encampment, with his spear stuck in the ground at his head; and Abner and the army lay around him. 8Abishai said to David, "God has given your enemy into your hand today; now therefore let me pin him to the ground with one stroke of the spear; I will not strike him twice." 9But David said to Abishai, "Do not destroy him; for who can raise his hand against the LORD's anointed, and be guiltless?" 10David said, "As the LORD lives, the LORD will strike him down; or his day will come to die; or he will go down into battle and perish. 11The LORD forbid that I should raise my hand against the LORD's anointed; but now take the spear that is at his head, and the water jar, and let us go." 12So David took the spear that was at Saul's head and the water jar, and they went away. No one saw it, or knew it, nor did anyone awake; for they were all asleep, because a deep sleep from the LORD had fallen upon them.

13 Then David went over to the other side, and stood on top of a hill far away, with a great distance between them. 14David called to the army and to Abner son of Ner, saying, "Abner! Will you not answer?" Then Abner replied, "Who are you that calls to the king?" 15David said to Abner, "Are you not a man? Who is like you in Israel? Why then have you not kept watch over your lord the king? For one of the people came in to destroy your lord the king. 16This thing that you have done is not good. As the LORD lives, you deserve to die, because you have not kept watch over your lord, the LORD's anointed. See now, where is the king's spear, or the water jar that was at his head?"

17 Saul recognized David's voice, and said, "Is this your voice, my son David?" David said, "It is my voice, my lord, O king." 18And he added, "Why does my lord pursue his servant? For what have I done? What guilt is on my hands? 19Now therefore let my lord the king hear the words of his servant. If it is the LORD who has stirred you up against me, may he accept an offering; but if it is mortals, may they be cursed before the LORD, for they

i *Or* opposite the wasteland

have driven me out today from my share in the heritage of the LORD, saying, 'Go, serve other gods.' 20Now therefore, do not let my blood fall to the ground, away from the presence of the LORD; for the king of Israel has come out to seek a single flea, like one who hunts a partridge in the mountains."

21 Then Saul said, "I have done wrong; come back, my son David, for I will never harm you again, because my life was precious in your sight today; I have been a fool, and have made a great mistake." 22David replied, "Here is the spear, O king! Let one of the young men come over and get it. 23The LORD rewards everyone for his righteousness and his faithfulness; for the LORD gave you into my hand today, but I would not raise my hand against the LORD's anointed. 24As your life was precious today in my sight, so may my life be precious in the sight of the LORD, and may he rescue me from all tribulation." 25Then Saul said to David, "Blessed be you, my son David! You will do many things and will succeed in them." So David went his way, and Saul returned to his place.

David Serves King Achish of Gath

27 David said in his heart, "I shall now perish one day by the hand of Saul; there is nothing better for me than to escape to the land of the Philistines; then Saul will despair of seeking me any longer within the borders of Israel, and I shall escape out of his hand." 2So David set out and went over, he and the six hundred men who were with him, to King Achish son of Maoch of Gath. 3David stayed with Achish at Gath, he and his troops, every man with his household, and David with his two wives, Ahinoam of Jezreel, and Abigail of Carmel, Nabal's widow. 4When Saul was told that David had fled to Gath, he no longer sought for him.

5 Then David said to Achish, "If I have found favor in your sight, let a place be given me in one of the country towns, so that I may live there; for why should your servant live in the royal city with you?" 6So that day Achish gave him Ziklag; therefore Ziklag has belonged to the kings of Judah to this day. 7The length of time that David lived in the country of the Philistines was one year and four months.

8 Now David and his men went up and made raids on the Geshurites, the Girzites, and the Amalekites; for these were the landed settlements from Telam[j] on the way to Shur and on to the land of Egypt. 9David struck the land, leaving neither man nor woman alive, but took away the sheep, the oxen, the donkeys, the camels, and the clothing, and came back to Achish. 10When Achish asked, "Against whom[k] have you made a raid today?" David would say, "Against the Negeb of Judah," or "Against the Negeb of the Jerahmeelites," or, "Against the Negeb of the Kenites." 11David left neither man nor woman alive to be brought back to Gath, thinking, "They might tell about us, and say, 'David has done so and so.' " Such was his practice all the time he lived in the country of the Philistines. 12Achish trusted David, thinking, "He has made himself utterly abhorrent to his people Israel; therefore he shall always be my servant."

28 In those days the Philistines gathered their forces for war, to fight against Israel. Achish said to David, "You know, of course, that you and your men are to go out with me in the army." 2David said to Achish, "Very well, then you shall know what your servant can do." Achish said to David, "Very well, I will make you my bodyguard for life."

Saul Consults a Medium

3 Now Samuel had died, and all Israel had mourned for him and buried him in Ramah, his own city. Saul had expelled the mediums and the wizards from the land. 4The Philistines assembled, and came and encamped at Shunem. Saul gathered all Israel, and they encamped at Gilboa. 5When Saul saw the army of the Philistines, he was afraid, and his heart trembled greatly. 6When Saul inquired of the LORD, the LORD did not answer him, not by dreams, or by Urim, or by prophets. 7Then Saul said to his servants, "Seek out for me a woman who is a medium, so that I may go to her and inquire of her." His servants said to him, "There is a medium at Endor."

8 So Saul disguised himself and put on other clothes and went there, he and two men with him. They came to the woman by night. And he said, "Consult a spirit for me, and bring up for me the one

j Compare Gk 15.4: Heb from of old   k Q Ms Gk Vg: MT lacks whom

whom I name to you." [9]The woman said to him, "Surely you know what Saul has done, how he has cut off the mediums and the wizards from the land. Why then are you laying a snare for my life to bring about my death?" [10]But Saul swore to her by the LORD, "As the LORD lives, no punishment shall come upon you for this thing." [11]Then the woman said, "Whom shall I bring up for you?" He answered, "Bring up Samuel for me." [12]When the woman saw Samuel, she cried out with a loud voice; and the woman said to Saul, "Why have you deceived me? You are Saul!" [13]The

king said to her, "Have no fear; what do you see?" The woman said to Saul, "I see a divine being[l] coming up out of the ground." [14]He said to her, "What is his appearance?" She said, "An old man is coming up; he is wrapped in a robe." So Saul knew that it was Samuel, and he bowed with his face to the ground, and did obeisance.

15 Then Samuel said to Saul, "Why have you disturbed me by bringing me up?" Saul answered, "I am in great distress,

[l] Or *a god;* or *gods*

THE TRADITION

Magic and Superstition

"Consult a spirit for me, and bring up for me the one whom I name to you."

I SAMUEL 28.8

King Saul is desperate. Enemy forces are advancing, his trusted prophet Samuel has died, and God is not giving him any clues about what to do. So Saul responds like any pagan of his day: He gets a medium to conjure up Samuel's spirit. Summoned from the dead, Samuel is not amused. Neither, apparently, is God.

For Saul is no pagan. He knows the Mosaic Law forbids magic and superstition (see Leviticus 19.31; 20.27; see also Deuteronomy 18.10–12). By his own order, mediums and fortune-tellers are supposed to have been driven from Israel (see 1 Samuel 28.3). So why does he do it?

What draws Saul to the medium of Endor and confirms his fate is his desire to know the future. Even today that same desire draws Christians to horoscopes, palm readings, tarot cards, and psychics. Divination, magic, sorcery, and occult practices—these expressions of superstition are offenses against the first commandment: You shall worship the Lord your God and him only shall you serve. "You will be like gods," they whisper—the same lie that seduced Adam and Eve (see

Genesis 3.5). Promising control over time, history, and even other people, such practices usurp the reverence and loving fear that we should direct to God alone.

Approaching pious practices as a mechanical means to an end—with no regard for the intentions of the heart—can become another form of superstition. Such self-seeking superstition can corrupt worship.

Send copies of this prayer to five people, and your intentions will be granted. This has never been known to fail.

Bury this statue upside down and your prayer will be answered.

Sometimes it's difficult to tell the difference between those who seek for magic and those who are truly devout. Each may exhibit the same behavior. Take two people wearing a cross, says psychologist Father Benedict Groeschel. "For one it is an informed devotion of piety and faith, and for the other it is simply magic." It is the attitude of the heart that makes all the difference.

The acid test: Am I trying to twist God's arm to get what *I* want? Or am I ready to trust and accept what *God* wants?

for the Philistines are warring against me, and God has turned away from me and answers me no more, either by prophets or by dreams; so I have summoned you to tell me what I should do." [16]Samuel said, "Why then do you ask me, since the LORD has turned from me and become your enemy? [17]The LORD has done to you just as he spoke by me; for the LORD has torn the kingdom out of your hand, and given it to your neighbor, David. [18]Because you did not obey the voice of the LORD, and did not carry out his fierce wrath against Amalek, therefore the LORD has done this thing to you today. [19]Moreover the LORD will give Israel along with you into the hands of the Philistines; and tomorrow you and your sons shall be with me; the LORD will also give the army of Israel into the hands of the Philistines."

20 Immediately Saul fell full length on the ground, filled with fear because of the words of Samuel; and there was no strength in him, for he had eaten nothing all day and all night. [21]The woman came to Saul, and when she saw that he was terrified, she said to him, "Your servant has listened to you; I have taken my life in my hand, and have listened to what you have said to me. [22]Now therefore, you also listen to your servant; let me set a morsel of bread before you. Eat, that you may have strength when you go on your way." [23]He refused, and said, "I will not eat." But his servants, together with the woman, urged him; and he listened to their words. So he got up from the ground and sat on the bed. [24]Now the woman had a fatted calf in the house. She quickly slaughtered it, and she took flour, kneaded it, and baked unleavened cakes. [25]She put them before Saul and his servants, and they ate. Then they rose and went away that night.

The Philistines Reject David

29 Now the Philistines gathered all their forces at Aphek, while the Israelites were encamped by the fountain that is in Jezreel. [2]As the lords of the Philistines were passing on by hundreds and by thousands, and David and his men were passing on in the rear with Achish, [3]the commanders of the Philistines said, "What are these Hebrews doing here?" Achish said to the commanders of the Philistines, "Is this not David, the servant of King Saul of Israel, who has been with

me now for days and years? Since he deserted to me I have found no fault in him to this day." [4]But the commanders of the Philistines were angry with him; and the commanders of the Philistines said to him, "Send the man back, so that he may return to the place that you have assigned to him; he shall not go down with us to battle, or else he may become an adversary to us in the battle. For how could this fellow reconcile himself to his lord? Would it not be with the heads of the men here? [5]Is this not David, of whom they sing to one another in dances,

'Saul has killed his thousands,
    and David his ten thousands'?"

6 Then Achish called David and said to him, "As the LORD lives, you have been honest, and to me it seems right that you should march out and in with me in the campaign; for I have found nothing wrong in you from the day of your coming to me until today. Nevertheless the lords do not approve of you. [7]So go back now; and go peaceably; do nothing to displease the lords of the Philistines." [8]David said to Achish, "But what have I done? What have you found in your servant from the day I entered your service until now, that I should not go and fight against the enemies of my lord the king?" [9]Achish replied to David, "I know that you are as blameless in my sight as an angel of God; nevertheless, the commanders of the Philistines have said, 'He shall not go up with us to the battle.' [10]Now then rise early in the morning, you and the servants of your lord who came with you, and go to the place that I appointed for you. As for the evil report, do not take it to heart, for you have done well before me.[m] Start early in the morning, and leave as soon as you have light." [11]So David set out with his men early in the morning, to return to the land of the Philistines. But the Philistines went up to Jezreel.

David Avenges the Destruction of Ziklag

30 Now when David and his men came to Ziklag on the third day, the Amalekites had made a raid on the Negeb and on Ziklag. They had attacked Ziklag, burned it down, [2]and taken captive the women and all[n] who were in it,

---

[m] Gk: Heb lacks *and go to the place . . . done well before me*   [n] Gk: Heb lacks *and all*

both small and great; they killed none of them, but carried them off, and went their way. ³When David and his men came to the city, they found it burned down, and their wives and sons and daughters taken captive. ⁴Then David and the people who were with him raised their voices and wept, until they had no more strength to weep. ⁵David's two wives also had been taken captive, Ahinoam of Jezreel, and Abigail the widow of Nabal of Carmel. ⁶David was in great danger; for the people spoke of stoning him, because all the people were bitter in spirit for their sons and daughters. But David strengthened himself in the LORD his God.

7 David said to the priest Abiathar son of Ahimelech, "Bring me the ephod." So Abiathar brought the ephod to David. ⁸David inquired of the LORD, "Shall I pursue this band? Shall I overtake them?" He answered him, "Pursue; for you shall surely overtake and shall surely rescue." ⁹So David set out, he and the six hundred men who were with him. They came to the Wadi Besor, where those stayed who were left behind. ¹⁰But David went on with the pursuit, he and four hundred men; two hundred stayed behind, too exhausted to cross the Wadi Besor.

11 In the open country they found an Egyptian, and brought him to David. They gave him bread and he ate; they gave him water to drink; ¹²they also gave him a piece of fig cake and two clusters of raisins. When he had eaten, his spirit revived; for he had not eaten bread or drunk water for three days and three nights. ¹³Then David said to him, "To whom do you belong? Where are you from?" He said, "I am a young man of Egypt, servant to an Amalekite. My master left me behind because I fell sick three days ago. ¹⁴We had made a raid on the Negeb of the Cherethites and on that which belongs to Judah and on the Negeb of Caleb; and we burned Ziklag down." ¹⁵David said to him, "Will you take me down to this raiding party?" He said, "Swear to me by God that you will not kill me, or hand me over to my master, and I will take you down to them."

16 When he had taken him down, they were spread out all over the ground, eating and drinking and dancing, because of the great amount of spoil they had taken from the land of the Philistines and from the land of Judah. ¹⁷David attacked them

from twilight until the evening of the next day. Not one of them escaped, except four hundred young men, who mounted camels and fled. ¹⁸David recovered all that the Amalekites had taken; and David rescued his two wives. ¹⁹Nothing was missing, whether small or great, sons or daughters, spoil or anything that had been taken; David brought back everything. ²⁰David also captured all the flocks and herds, which were driven ahead of the other cattle; people said, "This is David's spoil."

21 Then David came to the two hundred men who had been too exhausted to follow David, and who had been left at the Wadi Besor. They went out to meet David and to meet the people who were with him. When David drew near to the people he saluted them. ²²Then all the corrupt and worthless fellows among the men who had gone with David said, "Because they did not go with us, we will not give them any of the spoil that we have recovered, except that each man may take his wife and children, and leave." ²³But David said, "You shall not do so, my brothers, with what the LORD has given us; he has preserved us and handed over to us the raiding party that attacked us. ²⁴Who would listen to you in this matter? For the share of the one who goes down into the battle shall be the same as the share of the one who stays by the baggage; they shall share alike." ²⁵From that day forward he made it a statute and an ordinance for Israel; it continues to the present day.

26 When David came to Ziklag, he sent part of the spoil to his friends, the elders of Judah, saying, "Here is a present for you from the spoil of the enemies of the LORD"; ²⁷it was for those in Bethel, in Ramoth of the Negeb, in Jattir, ²⁸in Aroer, in Siphmoth, in Eshtemoa, ²⁹in Racal, in the towns of the Jerahmeelites, in the towns of the Kenites, ³⁰in Hormah, in Borashan, in Athach, ³¹in Hebron, all the places where David and his men had roamed.

The Death of Saul and His Sons

31 Now the Philistines fought against Israel; and the men of Israel fled before the Philistines, and many fell° on Mount Gilboa. ²The Philistines overtook Saul and his sons; and the Phil-

° Heb *and they fell slain*

istines killed Jonathan and Abinadab and Malchishua, the sons of Saul. ³The battle pressed hard upon Saul; the archers found him, and he was badly wounded by them. ⁴Then Saul said to his armor-bearer, "Draw your sword and thrust me through with it, so that these uncircumcised may not come and thrust me through, and make sport of me." But his armor-bearer was unwilling; for he was terrified. So Saul took his own sword and fell upon it. ⁵When his armor-bearer saw that Saul was dead, he also fell upon his sword and died with him. ⁶So Saul and his three sons and his armor-bearer and all his men died together on the same day. ⁷When the men of Israel who were on the other side of the valley and those beyond the Jordan saw that the men of Israel had fled and that Saul and his sons were dead, they forsook their towns and fled; and the Philistines came and occupied them.

8 The next day, when the Philistines came to strip the dead, they found Saul and his three sons fallen on Mount Gilboa. ⁹They cut off his head, stripped off his armor, and sent messengers throughout the land of the Philistines to carry the good news to the houses of their idols and to the people. ¹⁰They put his armor in the temple of Astarte;ᵖ and they fastened his body to the wall of Beth-shan. ¹¹But when the inhabitants of Jabesh-gilead heard what the Philistines had done to Saul, ¹²all the valiant men set out, traveled all night long, and took the body of Saul and the bodies of his sons from the wall of Beth-shan. They came to Jabesh and burned them there. ¹³Then they took their bones and buried them under the tamarisk tree in Jabesh, and fasted seven days.

ᵖ Heb plural

2 Samuel

While 1 Samuel relates the unforgettable story of young David's battle with the giant Goliath, 2 Samuel tells the story of David's reign as king after Saul's death. Establishing his capital at Jerusalem, David united the northern tribes of Israel with the southern tribe of Judah. During his lifetime and the life of his son Solomon, Israel enjoyed the only real Golden Age it had ever known.

But Israel's most beloved king sinned grievously by committing adultery with Bathsheba and then arranging for her husband's death. Though David's failures wreaked havoc on his family and on the nation of Israel, he was restored through repentance and God's mercy. Despite the tragedies that characterized the latter portion of David's reign, God promised to establish his house forever, helping to fuel Israel's longing for a Messiah.

In 2 Samuel we read of three women's stories as well: Bathsheba, Tamar the daughter of David, and Rizpah. Their lives are interwoven with some of Israel's most tragic moments. Still, throughout 2 Samuel we see God at work fulfilling his promises and showing mercy to the repentant of heart.

David Mourns for Saul and Jonathan

1 After the death of Saul, when David had returned from defeating the Amalekites, David remained two days in Ziklag. ²On the third day, a man came from Saul's camp, with his clothes torn and dirt on his head. When he came to David, he fell to the ground and did obeisance. ³David said to him, "Where have you come from?" He said to him, "I have escaped from the camp of Israel." ⁴David said to him, "How did things go? Tell me!" He answered, "The army fled from the battle, but also many of the army fell and died; and Saul and his son Jonathan also died."

⁵Then David asked the young man who was reporting to him, "How do you know that Saul and his son Jonathan died?" ⁶The young man reporting to him said, "I happened to be on Mount Gilboa; and there was Saul leaning on his spear, while the chariots and the horsemen drew close to him. ⁷When he looked behind him, he saw me, and called to me. I answered, 'Here sir.' ⁸And he said to me, 'Who are you?' I answered him, 'I am an Amalekite.' ⁹He said to me, 'Come, stand over me and kill me; for convulsions have seized me, and yet my life still lingers.' ¹⁰So I stood over him, and killed him, for I knew

that he could not live after he had fallen. I took the crown that was on his head and the armlet that was on his arm, and I have brought them here to my lord."

11 Then David took hold of his clothes and tore them; and all the men who were with him did the same. 12They mourned and wept, and fasted until evening for Saul and for his son Jonathan, and for the army of the LORD and for the house of Israel, because they had fallen by the sword. 13David said to the young man who had reported to him, "Where do you come from?" He answered, "I am the son of a resident alien, an Amalekite." 14David said to him, "Were you not afraid to lift your hand to destroy the LORD's anointed?" 15Then David called one of the young men and said, "Come here and strike him down." So he struck him down and he died. 16David said to him, "Your blood be on your head; for your own mouth has testified against you, saying, 'I have killed the LORD's anointed.'"

17 David intoned this lamentation over Saul and his son Jonathan. 18(He ordered that The Song of the Bow^a be taught to the people of Judah; it is written in the Book of Jashar.) He said:
19 Your glory, O Israel, lies slain upon
    your high places!
    How the mighty have fallen!
20 Tell it not in Gath,
    proclaim it not in the streets of
        Ashkelon;
    or the daughters of the Philistines
        will rejoice,
    the daughters of the
        uncircumcised will exult.

21 You mountains of Gilboa,
    let there be no dew or rain upon
        you,
    nor bounteous fields!^b
    For there the shield of the mighty
        was defiled,
    the shield of Saul, anointed with
        oil no more.

22 From the blood of the slain,
    from the fat of the mighty,
    the bow of Jonathan did not turn
        back,
    nor the sword of Saul return
        empty.

23 Saul and Jonathan, beloved and
        lovely!

In life and in death they were not
    divided;
they were swifter than eagles,
    they were stronger than lions.

24 O daughters of Israel, weep over
        Saul,
    who clothed you with crimson, in
        luxury,
    who put ornaments of gold on
        your apparel.

25 How the mighty have fallen
    in the midst of the battle!

Jonathan lies slain upon your high
    places.
26 I am distressed for you, my
        brother Jonathan;
    greatly beloved were you to me;
    your love to me was wonderful,
    passing the love of women.

27 How the mighty have fallen,
    and the weapons of war perished!

David Anointed King of Judah

2 After this David inquired of the LORD, "Shall I go up into any of the cities of Judah?" The LORD said to him, "Go up." David said, "To which shall I go up?" He said, "To Hebron." 2So David went up there, along with his two wives, Ahinoam of Jezreel, and Abigail the widow of Nabal of Carmel. 3David brought up the men who were with him, every one with his household; and they settled in the towns of Hebron. 4Then the people of Judah came, and there they anointed David king over the house of Judah.

When they told David, "It was the people of Jabesh-gilead who buried Saul," 5David sent messengers to the people of Jabesh-gilead, and said to them, "May you be blessed by the LORD, because you showed this loyalty to Saul your lord, and buried him! 6Now may the LORD show steadfast love and faithfulness to you! And I too will reward you because you have done this thing. 7Therefore let your hands be strong, and be valiant; for Saul your lord is dead, and the house of Judah has anointed me king over them."

^a Heb that The Bow   ^b Meaning of Heb uncertain

Ishbaal King of Israel

8 But Abner son of Ner, commander of Saul's army, had taken Ishbaal[c] son of Saul, and brought him over to Mahanaim. [9]He made him king over Gilead, the Ashurites, Jezreel, Ephraim, Benjamin, and over all Israel. [10]Ishbaal,[c] Saul's son, was forty years old when he began to reign over Israel, and he reigned two years. But the house of Judah followed David. [11]The time that David was king in Hebron over the house of Judah was seven years and six months.

The Battle of Gibeon

12 Abner son of Ner, and the servants of Ishbaal[c] son of Saul, went out from Mahanaim to Gibeon. [13]Joab son of Zeruiah, and the servants of David, went out and met them at the pool of Gibeon. One group sat on one side of the pool, while the other sat on the other side of the pool. [14]Abner said to Joab, "Let the young men come forward and have a contest before us." Joab said, "Let them come forward." [15]So they came forward and were counted as they passed by, twelve for Benjamin and Ishbaal[c] son of Saul, and twelve of the servants of David. [16]Each grasped his opponent by the head, and thrust his sword in his opponent's side; so they fell down together. Therefore that place was called Helkath-hazzurim,[d] which is at Gibeon. [17]The battle was very fierce that day; and Abner and the men of Israel were beaten by the servants of David.

18 The three sons of Zeruiah were there, Joab, Abishai, and Asahel. Now Asahel was as swift of foot as a wild gazelle. [19]Asahel pursued Abner, turning neither to the right nor to the left as he followed him. [20]Then Abner looked back and said, "Is it you, Asahel?" He answered, "Yes, it is." [21]Abner said to him, "Turn to your right or to your left, and seize one of the young men, and take his spoil." But Asahel would not turn away from following him. [22]Abner said again to Asahel, "Turn away from following me; why should I strike you to the ground? How then could I show my face to your brother Joab?" [23]But he refused to turn away. So Abner struck him in the stomach with the butt of his spear, so that the spear came out at his back. He fell there, and died where he lay. And all those who came to the place where Asahel had fallen and died, stood still.

24 But Joab and Abishai pursued Abner. As the sun was going down they came to the hill of Ammah, which lies before Giah on the way to the wilderness of Gibeon. [25]The Benjaminites rallied around Abner and formed a single band; they took their stand on the top of a hill. [26]Then Abner called to Joab, "Is the sword to keep devouring forever? Do you not know that the end will be bitter? How long will it be before you order your people to turn from the pursuit of their kinsmen?" [27]Joab said, "As God lives, if you had not spoken, the people would have continued to pursue their kinsmen, not stopping until morning." [28]Joab sounded the trumpet and all the people stopped; they no longer pursued Israel or engaged in battle any further.

29 Abner and his men traveled all that night through the Arabah; they crossed the Jordan, and, marching the whole forenoon,[e] they came to Mahanaim. [30]Joab returned from the pursuit of Abner; and when he had gathered all the people together, there were missing of David's servants nineteen men besides Asahel. [31]But the servants of David had killed of Benjamin three hundred sixty of Abner's men. [32]They took up Asahel and buried him in the tomb of his father, which was at Bethlehem. Joab and his men marched all night, and the day broke upon them at Hebron.

Abner Defects to David

3 There was a long war between the house of Saul and the house of David; David grew stronger and stronger, while the house of Saul became weaker and weaker.

2 Sons were born to David at Hebron: his firstborn was Amnon, of Ahinoam of Jezreel; [3]his second, Chileab, of Abigail the widow of Nabal of Carmel; the third, Absalom son of Maacah, daughter of King Talmai of Geshur; [4]the fourth, Adonijah son of Haggith; the fifth, Shephatiah son of Abital; [5]and the sixth, Ithream, of David's wife Eglah. These were born to David in Hebron.

6 While there was war between the

---

[c] Gk Compare 1 Chr 8.33; 9.39: Heb *Ish-bosheth*, "man of shame"   [d] That is *Field of Sword-edges*   [e] Meaning of Heb uncertain

house of Saul and the house of David, Abner was making himself strong in the house of Saul. 7Now Saul had a concubine whose name was Rizpah daughter of Aiah. And Ishbaal*f* said to Abner, "Why have you gone in to my father's concubine?" 8The words of Ishbaal*g* made Abner very angry; he said, "Am I a dog's head for Judah? Today I keep showing loyalty to the house of your father Saul, to his brothers, and to his friends, and have not given you into the hand of David; and yet you charge me now with a crime concerning this woman. 9So may God do to Abner and so may he add to it! For just what the LORD has sworn to David, that will I accomplish for him, 10to transfer the kingdom from the house of Saul, and set up the throne of David over Israel and over Judah, from Dan to Beer-sheba." 11And Ishbaal*f* could not answer Abner another word, because he feared him.

12 Abner sent messengers to David at Hebron,*h* saying, "To whom does the land belong? Make your covenant with me, and I will give you my support to bring all Israel over to you." 13He said, "Good; I will make a covenant with you. But one thing I require of you: you shall never appear in my presence unless you bring Saul's daughter Michal when you come to see me." 14Then David sent messengers to Saul's son Ishbaal,*i* saying, "Give me my wife Michal, to whom I became engaged at the price of one hundred foreskins of the Philistines." 15Ishbaal*i* sent and took her from her husband Paltiel the son of Laish. 16But her husband went with her, weeping as he walked behind her all the way to Bahurim. Then Abner said to him, "Go back home!" So he went back.

17 Abner sent word to the elders of Israel, saying, "For some time past you have been seeking David as king over you. 18Now then bring it about; for the LORD has promised David: Through my servant David I will save my people Israel from the hand of the Philistines, and from all their enemies." 19Abner also spoke directly to the Benjaminites; then Abner went to tell David at Hebron all that Israel and the whole house of Benjamin were ready to do.

20 When Abner came with twenty men to David at Hebron, David made a feast for Abner and the men who were with him. 21Abner said to David, "Let me go

and rally all Israel to my lord the king, in order that they may make a covenant with you, and that you may reign over all that your heart desires." So David dismissed Abner, and he went away in peace.

Abner Is Killed by Joab

22 Just then the servants of David arrived with Joab from a raid, bringing much spoil with them. But Abner was not with David at Hebron, for David*j* had dismissed him, and he had gone away in peace. 23When Joab and all the army that was with him came, it was told Joab, "Abner son of Ner came to the king, and he has dismissed him, and he has gone away in peace." 24Then Joab went to the king and said, "What have you done? Abner came to you; why did you dismiss him, so that he got away? 25You know that Abner son of Ner came to deceive you, and to learn your comings and goings and to learn all that you are doing."

26 When Joab came out from David's presence, he sent messengers after Abner, and they brought him back from the cistern of Sirah; but David did not know about it. 27When Abner returned to Hebron, Joab took him aside in the gateway to speak with him privately, and there he stabbed him in the stomach. So he died for shedding*k* the blood of Asahel, Joab's*l* brother. 28Afterward, when David heard of it, he said, "I and my kingdom are forever guiltless before the LORD for the blood of Abner son of Ner. 29May the guilt*m* fall on the head of Joab, and on all his father's house; and may the house of Joab never be without one who has a discharge, or who is leprous,*n* or who holds a spindle, or who falls by the sword, or who lacks food!" 30So Joab and his brother Abishai murdered Abner because he had killed their brother Asahel in the battle at Gibeon.

31 Then David said to Joab and to all the people who were with him, "Tear your clothes, and put on sackcloth, and mourn over Abner." And King David followed the bier. 32They buried Abner at Hebron. The king lifted up his voice and

f Heb *And he*   *g* Gk Compare 1 Chr 8.33; 9.39: Heb *Ish-bosheth,* "man of shame"   *h* Gk: Heb *where he was*   *i* Heb *Ish-bosheth*   *j* Heb *he* *k* Heb *lacks shedding*   *l* Heb *his*   *m* Heb *May it* *n* A term for several skin diseases; precise meaning uncertain

wept at the grave of Abner, and all the people wept. [33]The king lamented for Abner, saying,

"Should Abner die as a fool dies?
[34] Your hands were not bound,
    your feet were not fettered;
as one falls before the wicked
    you have fallen."

And all the people wept over him again. [35]Then all the people came to persuade David to eat something while it was still day; but David swore, saying, "So may God do to me, and more, if I taste bread or anything else before the sun goes down!" [36]All the people took notice of it, and it pleased them; just as everything the king did pleased all the people. [37]So all the people and all Israel understood that day that the king had no part in the killing of Abner son of Ner. [38]And the king said to his servants, "Do you not know that a prince and a great man has fallen this day in Israel? [39]Today I am powerless, even though anointed king; these men, the sons of Zeruiah, are too violent for me. The LORD pay back the one who does wickedly in accordance with his wickedness!"

Ishbaal Assassinated

4 When Saul's son Ishbaal[o] heard that Abner had died at Hebron, his courage failed, and all Israel was dismayed. [2]Saul's son had two captains of raiding bands; the name of the one was Baanah, and the name of the other Rechab. They were sons of Rimmon a Benjaminite from Beeroth—for Beeroth is considered to belong to Benjamin. [3](Now the people of Beeroth had fled to Gittaim and are there as resident aliens to this day).

4 Saul's son Jonathan had a son who was crippled in his feet. He was five years old when the news about Saul and Jonathan came from Jezreel. His nurse picked him up and fled; and, in her haste to flee, it happened that he fell and became lame. His name was Mephibosheth. [p]

5 Now the sons of Rimmon the Beerothite, Rechab and Baanah, set out, and about the heat of the day they came to the house of Ishbaal,[q] while he was taking his noonday rest. [6]They came inside the house as though to take wheat, and they struck him in the stomach; then Rechab and his brother Baanah escaped.[r] [7]Now they had come into the house while he was lying on his couch in his bedchamber; they attacked him, killed him, and

beheaded him. Then they took his head and traveled by way of the Arabah all night long. [8]They brought the head of Ishbaal[q] to David at Hebron and said to the king, "Here is the head of Ishbaal,[q] son of Saul, your enemy, who sought your life; the LORD has avenged my lord the king this day on Saul and on his offspring."

9 David answered Rechab and his brother Baanah, the sons of Rimmon the Beerothite, "As the LORD lives, who has redeemed my life out of every adversity, [10]when the one who told me, 'See, Saul is dead,' thought he was bringing good news, I seized him and killed him at Ziklag—this was the reward I gave him for his news. [11]How much more then, when wicked men have killed a righteous man on his bed in his own house! And now shall I not require his blood at your hand, and destroy you from the earth?" [12]So David commanded the young men, and they killed them; they cut off their hands and feet, and hung their bodies beside the pool at Hebron. But the head of Ishbaal[q] they took and buried in the tomb of Abner at Hebron.

David Anointed King of All Israel

5 Then all the tribes of Israel came to David at Hebron, and said, "Look, we are your bone and flesh. [2]For some time, while Saul was king over us, it was you who led out Israel and brought it in. The LORD said to you: It is you who shall be shepherd of my people Israel, you who shall be ruler over Israel." [3]So all the elders of Israel came to the king at Hebron; and King David made a covenant with them at Hebron before the LORD, and they anointed David king over Israel. [4]David was thirty years old when he began to reign, and he reigned forty years. [5]At Hebron he reigned over Judah seven years and six months; and at Jerusalem he reigned over all Israel and Judah thirty-three years.

Jerusalem Made Capital of the United Kingdom

6 The king and his men marched to Jerusalem against the Jebusites, the inhabitants of the land, who said to David, "You will not come in here, even the blind and the lame will turn you back"—thinking,

o Heb lacks Ishbaal   p In 1 Chr 8.34 and 9.40, Merib-baal   q Heb Ish-bosheth   r Meaning of Heb of verse 6 uncertain

"David cannot come in here." [7]Nevertheless David took the stronghold of Zion, which is now the city of David. [8]David had said on that day, "Whoever would strike down the Jebusites, let him get up the water shaft to attack the lame and the blind, those whom David hates."[s] Therefore it is said, "The blind and the lame shall not come into the house." [9]David occupied the stronghold, and named it the city of David. David built the city all around from the Millo inward. [10]And David became greater and greater, for the LORD, the God of hosts, was with him.

11 King Hiram of Tyre sent messengers to David, along with cedar trees, and carpenters and masons who built David a house. [12]David then perceived that the LORD had established him king over Israel, and that he had exalted his kingdom for the sake of his people Israel.

13 In Jerusalem, after he came from Hebron, David took more concubines and wives; and more sons and daughters were born to David. [14]These are the names of those who were born to him in Jerusalem: Shammua, Shobab, Nathan, Solomon, [15]Ibhar, Elishua, Nepheg, Japhia, [16]Elishama, Eliada, and Eliphelet.

Philistine Attack Repulsed

17 When the Philistines heard that David had been anointed king over Israel, all the Philistines went up in search of David; but David heard about it and went down to the stronghold. [18]Now the Philistines had come and spread out in the valley of Rephaim. [19]David inquired of the LORD, "Shall I go up against the Philistines? Will you give them into my hand?" The LORD said to David, "Go up; for I will certainly give the Philistines into your hand." [20]So David came to Baal-perazim, and David defeated them there. He said, "The LORD has burst forth against[t] my enemies before me, like a bursting flood." Therefore that place is called Baal-perazim.[u] [21]The Philistines abandoned their idols there, and David and his men carried them away.

22 Once again the Philistines came up, and were spread out in the valley of Rephaim. [23]When David inquired of the LORD, he said, "You shall not go up; go around to their rear, and come upon them opposite the balsam trees. [24]When you hear the sound of marching in the tops of the balsam trees, then be on the alert; for then

the LORD has gone out before you to strike down the army of the Philistines." [25]David did just as the LORD had commanded him; and he struck down the Philistines from Geba all the way to Gezer.

David Brings the Ark to Jerusalem

6 David again gathered all the chosen men of Israel, thirty thousand. [2]David and all the people with him set out and went from Baale-judah, to bring up from there the ark of God, which is called by the name of the LORD of hosts who is enthroned on the cherubim. [3]They carried the ark of God on a new cart, and brought it out of the house of Abinadab, which was on the hill. Uzzah and Ahio,[v] the sons of Abinadab, were driving the new cart [4]with the ark of God;[w] and Ahio[v] went in front of the ark. [5]David and all the house of Israel were dancing before the LORD with all their might, with songs[x] and lyres and harps and tambourines and castanets and cymbals.

6 When they came to the threshing floor of Nacon, Uzzah reached out his hand to the ark of God and took hold of it, for the oxen shook it. [7]The anger of the LORD was kindled against Uzzah; and God struck him there because he reached out his hand to the ark;[y] and he died there beside the ark of God. [8]David was angry because the LORD had burst forth with an outburst upon Uzzah; so that place is called Perez-uzzah,[z] to this day. [9]David was afraid of the LORD that day; he said, "How can the ark of the LORD come into my care?" [10]So David was unwilling to take the ark of the LORD into his care in the city of David; instead David took it to the house of Obed-edom the Gittite. [11]The ark of the LORD remained in the house of Obed-edom the Gittite three months; and the LORD blessed Obed-edom and all his household.

12 It was told King David, "The LORD has blessed the household of Obed-edom and all that belongs to him, because of the ark of God." So David went and brought up the ark of God from the house of

---

[s] Another reading is *those who hate David*   [t] Heb *paraz*   [u] That is *Lord of Bursting Forth*   [v] Or *and his brother*   [w] Compare Gk: Heb *and brought it out of the house of Abinadab, which was on the hill with the ark of God*   [x] Q Ms Gk 1 Chr 13.8: Heb *fir trees*   [y] 1 Chr 13.10 Compare Q Ms: Meaning of Heb uncertain   [z] That is *Bursting Out Against Uzzah*

Obed-edom to the city of David with rejoicing; 13and when those who bore the ark of the LORD had gone six paces, he sacrificed an ox and a fatling. 14David danced before the LORD with all his might; David was girded with a linen ephod. 15So David and all the house of Israel brought up the ark of the LORD with shouting, and with the sound of the trumpet.

16 As the ark of the LORD came into the city of David, Michal daughter of Saul looked out of the window, and saw King David leaping and dancing before the LORD; and she despised him in her heart.

17 They brought in the ark of the LORD, and set it in its place, inside the tent that David had pitched for it; and David offered burnt offerings and offerings of well-being before the LORD. 18When David had finished offering the burnt offerings and the offerings of well-being, he blessed the people in the name of the LORD of hosts, 19and distributed food among all the people, the whole multitude of Israel, both men and women, to each a cake of bread, a portion of meat,a and a cake of raisins. Then all the people went back to their homes.

20 David returned to bless his household. But Michal the daughter of Saul came out to meet David, and said, "How the king of Israel honored himself today, uncovering himself today before the eyes of his servants' maids, as any vulgar fellow might shamelessly uncover himself!" 21David said to Michal, "It was before the LORD, who chose me in place of your father and all his household, to appoint me as prince over Israel, the people of the LORD, that I have danced before the LORD. 22I will make myself yet more contemptible than this, and I will be abased in my own eyes; but by the maids of whom you have spoken, by them I shall be held in honor." 23And Michal the daughter of Saul had no child to the day of her death.

God's Covenant with David

7 Now when the king was settled in his house, and the LORD had given him rest from all his enemies around him, 2the king said to the prophet Nathan, "See now, I am living in a house of cedar, but the ark of God stays in a tent." 3Nathan said to the king, "Go, do all that you have in mind; for the LORD is with you."

4 But that same night the word of the LORD came to Nathan: 5Go and tell my servant David: Thus says the LORD: Are you the one to build me a house to live in? 6I have not lived in a house since the day I brought up the people of Israel from Egypt to this day, but I have been moving about in a tent and a tabernacle. 7Wherever I have moved about among all the people of Israel, did I ever speak a word with any of the tribal leadersb of Israel, whom I commanded to shepherd my people Israel, saying, "Why have you not built me a house of cedar?" 8Now therefore thus you shall say to my servant David: Thus says the LORD of hosts: I took you from the pasture, from following the sheep to be prince over my people Israel; 9and I have been with you wherever you went, and have cut off all your enemies from before you; and I will make for you a great name, like the name of the great ones of the earth. 10And I will appoint a place for my people Israel and will plant them, so that they may live in their own place, and be disturbed no more; and evildoers shall afflict them no more, as formerly, 11from the time that I appointed judges over my people Israel; and I will give you rest from all your enemies. Moreover the LORD declares to you that the LORD will make you a house. 12When your days are fulfilled and you lie down with your ancestors, I will raise up your offspring after you, who shall come forth from your body, and I will establish his kingdom. 13He shall build a house for my name, and I will establish the throne of his kingdom forever. 14I will be a father to him, and he shall be a son to me. When he commits iniquity, I will punish him with a rod such as mortals use, with blows inflicted by human beings. 15But I will not takec my steadfast love from him, as I took it from Saul, whom I put away from before you. 16Your house and your kingdom shall be made sure forever before me;d your throne shall be established forever. 17In accordance with all these words and with all this vision, Nathan spoke to David.

David's Prayer

18 Then King David went in and sat before the LORD, and said, "Who am I, O Lord GOD, and what is my house, that

---

a Vg: Meaning of Heb uncertain   b Or any of the tribes   c Gk Syr Vg 1 Chr 17.13: Heb shall not depart   d Gk Heb Mss: MT before you; Compare 2 Sam 7.26, 29

you have brought me thus far? [19]And yet this was a small thing in your eyes, O Lord GOD; you have spoken also of your servant's house for a great while to come. May this be instruction for the people,[e] O Lord GOD! [20]And what more can David say to you? For you know your servant, O Lord GOD! [21]Because of your promise, and according to your own heart, you have wrought all this greatness, so that your servant may know it. [22]Therefore you are great, O LORD God; for there is no one like you, and there is no God besides you, according to all that we have heard with our ears. [23]Who is like your people, like Israel? Is there another[f] nation on earth whose God went to redeem it as a people, and to make a name for himself, doing great and awesome things for them,[g] by driving out[h] before his people nations and their gods?[i] [24]And you established your people Israel for yourself to be your people forever; and you, O LORD, became their God. [25]And now, O LORD God, as for the word that you have spoken concerning your servant and concerning his house, confirm it forever; do as you have promised. [26]Thus your name will be magnified forever in the saying, 'The LORD of hosts is God over Israel'; and the house of your servant David will be established before you. [27]For you, O LORD of hosts, the God of Israel, have made this revelation to your servant, saying, 'I will build you a house'; therefore your servant has found courage to pray this prayer to you. [28]And now, O Lord GOD, you are God, and your words are true, and you have promised this good thing to your servant; [29]now therefore may it please you to bless the house of your servant, so that it may continue forever before you; for you, O Lord GOD, have spoken, and with your blessing shall the house of your servant be blessed forever."

David's Wars

8 Some time afterward, David attacked the Philistines and subdued them; David took Metheg-ammah out of the hand of the Philistines.

2 He also defeated the Moabites and, making them lie down on the ground, measured them off with a cord; he measured two lengths of cord for those who were to be put to death, and one length[j] for those who were to be spared. And the

Moabites became servants to David and brought tribute.

3 David also struck down King Hadadezer son of Rehob of Zobah, as he went to restore his monument[k] at the river Euphrates. [4]David took from him one thousand seven hundred horsemen, and twenty thousand foot soldiers. David hamstrung all the chariot horses, but left enough for a hundred chariots. [5]When the Arameans of Damascus came to help King Hadadezer of Zobah, David killed twenty-two thousand men of the Arameans. [6]Then David put garrisons among the Arameans of Damascus; and the Arameans became servants to David and brought tribute. The LORD gave victory to David wherever he went. [7]David took the gold shields that were carried by the servants of Hadadezer, and brought them to Jerusalem. [8]From Betah and from Berothai, towns of Hadadezer, King David took a great amount of bronze.

9 When King Toi of Hamath heard that David had defeated the whole army of Hadadezer, [10]Toi sent his son Joram to King David, to greet him and to congratulate him because he had fought against Hadadezer and defeated him. Now Hadadezer had often been at war with Toi. Joram brought with him articles of silver, gold, and bronze; [11]these also King David dedicated to the LORD, together with the silver and gold that he dedicated from all the nations he subdued, [12]from Edom, Moab, the Ammonites, the Philistines, Amalek, and from the spoil of King Hadadezer son of Rehob of Zobah.

13 David won a name for himself. When he returned, he killed eighteen thousand Edomites[l] in the Valley of Salt. [14]He put garrisons in Edom; throughout all Edom he put garrisons, and all the Edomites became David's servants. And the LORD gave victory to David wherever he went.

David's Officers

15 So David reigned over all Israel; and David administered justice and equity to all his people. [16]Joab son of Zeruiah was

e Meaning of Heb uncertain   f Gk: Heb *one*
g Heb *you*   h Gk 1 Chr 17.21: Heb *for your land*
i Cn: Heb *before your people, whom you redeemed for yourself from Egypt, nations and its gods*   j Heb *one full length*   k Compare 1 Sam 15.12 and 2 Sam 18.18   l Gk: Heb *returned from striking down eighteen thousand Arameans*

over the army; Jehoshaphat son of Ahilud was recorder; [17]Zadok son of Ahitub and Ahimelech son of Abiathar were priests; Seraiah was secretary; [18]Benaiah son of Jehoiada was over[m] the Cherethites and the Pelethites; and David's sons were priests.

David's Kindness to Mephibosheth

9 David asked, "Is there still anyone left of the house of Saul to whom I may show kindness for Jonathan's sake?" [2]Now there was a servant of the house of Saul whose name was Ziba, and he was summoned to David. The king said to him, "Are you Ziba?" And he said, "At your service!" [3]The king said, "Is there anyone remaining of the house of Saul to whom I may show the kindness of God?" Ziba said to the king, "There remains a son of Jonathan; he is crippled in his feet." [4]The king said to him, "Where is he?" Ziba said to the king, "He is in the house of Machir son of Ammiel, at Lo-debar." [5]Then King David sent and brought him from the house of Machir son of Ammiel, at Lo-debar. [6]Mephibosheth[n] son of Jonathan son of Saul came to David, and fell on his face and did obeisance. David said, "Mephibosheth!"[n] He answered, "I am your servant." [7]David said to him, "Do not be afraid, for I will show you kindness for the sake of your father Jonathan; I will restore to you all the land of your grandfather Saul, and you yourself shall eat at my table always." [8]He did obeisance and said, "What is your servant, that you should look upon a dead dog such as I?"

9 Then the king summoned Saul's servant Ziba, and said to him, "All that belonged to Saul and to all his house I have given to your master's grandson. [10]You and your sons and your servants shall till the land for him, and shall bring in the produce, so that your master's grandson may have food to eat; but your master's grandson Mephibosheth[n] shall always eat at my table." Now Ziba had fifteen sons and twenty servants. [11]Then Ziba said to the king, "According to all that my lord the king commands his servant, so your servant will do." Mephibosheth[n] ate at David's[o] table, like one of the king's sons. [12]Mephibosheth[n] had a young son whose name was Mica. And all who lived in Ziba's house became Mephibosheth's[p] servants. [13]Mephibosheth[n] lived in Jerusalem, for he always ate at the king's table. Now he was lame in both his feet.

The Ammonites and Arameans Are Defeated

10 Some time afterward, the king of the Ammonites died, and his son Hanun succeeded him. [2]David said, "I will deal loyally with Hanun son of Nahash, just as his father dealt loyally with me." So David sent envoys to console him concerning his father. When David's envoys came into the land of the Ammonites, [3]the princes of the Ammonites said to their lord Hanun, "Do you really think that David is honoring your father just because he has sent messengers with condolences to you? Has not David sent his envoys to you to search the city, to spy it out, and to overthrow it?" [4]So Hanun seized David's envoys, shaved off half the beard of each, cut off their garments in the middle at their hips, and sent them away. [5]When David was told, he sent to meet them, for the men were greatly ashamed. The king said, "Remain at Jericho until your beards have grown, and then return."

6 When the Ammonites saw that they had become odious to David, the Ammonites sent and hired the Arameans of Beth-rehob and the Arameans of Zobah, twenty thousand foot soldiers, as well as the king of Maacah, one thousand men, and the men of Tob, twelve thousand men. [7]When David heard of it, he sent Joab and all the army with the warriors. [8]The Ammonites came out and drew up in battle array at the entrance of the gate; but the Arameans of Zobah and of Rehob, and the men of Tob and Maacah, were by themselves in the open country.

9 When Joab saw that the battle was set against him both in front and in the rear, he chose some of the picked men of Israel, and arrayed them against the Arameans; [10]the rest of his men he put in the charge of his brother Abishai, and he arrayed them against the Ammonites. [11]He said, "If the Arameans are too strong for me, then you shall help me; but if the Ammonites are too strong for you, then I will come and help you. [12]Be strong, and let us be courageous for the sake of our people, and for the cities of our God; and may the LORD do what seems good to him." [13]So Joab and the people who were with him moved forward into battle against the Ara-

m Syr Tg Vg 20.23; 1 Chr 18.17: Heb lacks *was over*   n Or *Merib-baal*: See 4.4 note   o Gk: Heb *my*   p Or *Merib-baal's*: See 4.4 note

means; and they fled before him. 14When
the Ammonites saw that the Arameans
fled, they likewise fled before Abishai, and
entered the city. Then Joab returned from
fighting against the Ammonites, and came
to Jerusalem.

15 But when the Arameans saw that
they had been defeated by Israel, they
gathered themselves together. 16Hadade-
zer sent and brought out the Arameans
who were beyond the Euphrates; and they
came to Helam, with Shobach the commander of the army of Hadadezer at their
head. 17When it was told David, he gathered all Israel together, and crossed the
Jordan, and came to Helam. The Arameans arrayed themselves against David and
fought with him. 18The Arameans fled before Israel; and David killed of the Arameans seven hundred chariot teams, and forty thousand horsemen,*q* and wounded
Shobach the commander of their army, so
that he died there. 19When all the kings
who were servants of Hadadezer saw that
they had been defeated by Israel, they
made peace with Israel, and became subject to them. So the Arameans were afraid
to help the Ammonites any more.

David Commits Adultery with Bathsheba

11 In the spring of the year, the time
when kings go out to battle, Da-
vid sent Joab with his officers and all Israel with him; they ravaged the Ammonites,
and besieged Rabbah. But David remained at Jerusalem.

2 It happened, late one afternoon,
when David rose from his couch and was
walking about on the roof of the king's
house, that he saw from the roof a woman
bathing; the woman was very beautiful.
3David sent someone to inquire about the
woman. It was reported, "This is Bathsheba daughter of Eliam, the wife of Uriah
the Hittite." 4So David sent messengers to
get her, and she came to him, and he lay
with her. (Now she was purifying herself
after her period.) Then she returned to her
house. 5The woman conceived; and she
sent and told David, "I am pregnant."

6 So David sent word to Joab, "Send
me Uriah the Hittite." And Joab sent Uriah
to David. 7When Uriah came to him, David asked how Joab and the people fared,
and how the war was going. 8Then David
said to Uriah, "Go down to your house,
and wash your feet." Uriah went out of the
king's house, and there followed him a

present from the king. 9But Uriah slept at
the entrance of the king's house with all
the servants of his lord, and did not go
down to his house. 10When they told David, "Uriah did not go down to his house,"
David said to Uriah, "You have just come
from a journey. Why did you not go down
to your house?" 11Uriah said to David,
"The ark and Israel and Judah remain in
booths;*r* and my lord Joab and the servants of my lord are camping in the open
field; shall I then go to my house, to eat
and to drink, and to lie with my wife? As
you live, and as your soul lives, I will not
do such a thing." 12Then David said to Uriah, "Remain here today also, and tomorrow I will send you back." So Uriah remained in Jerusalem that day. On the next
day, 13David invited him to eat and drink
in his presence and made him drunk; and
in the evening he went out to lie on his
couch with the servants of his lord, but he
did not go down to his house.

David Has Uriah Killed

14 In the morning David wrote a letter
to Joab, and sent it by the hand of Uriah.
15In the letter he wrote, "Set Uriah in the
forefront of the hardest fighting, and then
draw back from him, so that he may be
struck down and die." 16As Joab was besieging the city, he assigned Uriah to the
place where he knew there were valiant
warriors. 17The men of the city came out
and fought with Joab; and some of the
servants of David among the people fell.
Uriah the Hittite was killed as well.
18Then Joab sent and told David all the
news about the fighting; 19and he instructed the messenger, "When you have finished telling the king all the news about
the fighting, 20then, if the king's anger
rises, and if he says to you, 'Why did you
go so near the city to fight? Did you not
know that they would shoot from the
wall? 21Who killed Abimelech son of Jerubbaal?*s* Did not a woman throw an upper millstone on him from the wall, so
that he died at Thebez? Why did you go so
near the wall?' then you shall say, 'Your
servant Uriah the Hittite is dead too.' "

22 So the messenger went, and came
and told David all that Joab had sent him
to tell. 23The messenger said to David,

---

q 1 Chr 19.18 and some Gk Mss read foot soldiers
r Or at Succoth   s Gk Syr Judg 7.1: Heb
Jerubbesheth

"The men gained an advantage over us, and came out against us in the field; but we drove them back to the entrance of the gate. 24Then the archers shot at your servants from the wall; some of the king's servants are dead; and your servant Uriah the Hittite is dead also." 25David said to the messenger, "Thus you shall say to Joab, 'Do not let this matter trouble you, for the sword devours now one and now another; press your attack on the city, and overthrow it.' And encourage him."

26 When the wife of Uriah heard that her husband was dead, she made lamentation for him. 27When the mourning was over, David sent and brought her to his house, and she became his wife, and bore him a son.

Nathan Condemns David

But the thing that David had done displeased the LORD, 12 1and the LORD sent Nathan to David. He came to him, and said to him, "There were two men in a certain city, the one rich and the other poor. 2The rich man had very many flocks and herds; 3but the poor man had nothing but one little ewe lamb, which he had bought. He brought it up, and it grew up with him and with his children; it used to eat of his meager fare, and drink from his cup, and lie in his bosom, and it was like a daughter to him. 4Now there came a traveler to the rich man, and he was loath to take one of his own flock or herd to prepare for the wayfarer who had come to him, but he took the poor man's lamb, and prepared that for the guest who had come to him." 5Then David's anger was greatly kindled against the man. He said to Nathan, "As the LORD lives, the man who has done this deserves to die; 6he shall restore the lamb fourfold, because he did this thing, and because he had no pity."

7 Nathan said to David, "You are the man! Thus says the LORD, the God of Israel: I anointed you king over Israel, and I rescued you from the hand of Saul; 8I gave you your master's house, and your master's wives into your bosom, and gave you the house of Israel and of Judah; and if that had been too little, I would have added as much more. 9Why have you despised the word of the LORD, to do what is evil in his sight? You have struck down Uriah the Hittite with the sword, and have taken his wife to be your wife, and have

killed him with the sword of the Ammonites. 10Now therefore the sword shall never depart from your house, for you have despised me, and have taken the wife of Uriah the Hittite to be your wife. 11Thus says the LORD: I will raise up trouble against you from within your own house; and I will take your wives before your eyes, and give them to your neighbor, and he shall lie with your wives in the sight of this very sun. 12For you did it secretly; but I will do this thing before all Israel, and before the sun." 13David said to Nathan, "I have sinned against the LORD." Nathan said to David, "Now the LORD has put away your sin; you shall not die. 14Nevertheless, because by this deed you have utterly scorned the LORD,*t* the child that is born to you shall die." 15Then Nathan went to his house.

Bathsheba's Child Dies

The LORD struck the child that Uriah's wife bore to David, and it became very ill. 16David therefore pleaded with God for the child; David fasted, and went in and lay all night on the ground. 17The elders of his house stood beside him, urging him to rise from the ground; but he would not, nor did he eat food with them. 18On the seventh day the child died. And the servants of David were afraid to tell him that the child was dead; for they said, "While the child was still alive, we spoke to him, and he did not listen to us; how then can we tell him the child is dead? He may do himself some harm." 19But when David saw that his servants were whispering together, he perceived that the child was dead; and David said to his servants, "Is the child dead?" They said, "He is dead."

20 Then David rose from the ground, washed, anointed himself, and changed his clothes. He went into the house of the LORD, and worshiped; he then went to his own house; and when he asked, they set food before him and he ate. 21Then his servants said to him, "What is this thing that you have done? You fasted and wept for the child while it was alive; but when the child died, you rose and ate food." 22He said, "While the child was still alive, I fasted and wept; for I said, 'Who knows? The LORD may be gracious to me, and the child may live.' 23But now he is dead; why

---

t Ancient scribal tradition: Compare 1 Sam 25.22 note: Heb *scorned the enemies of the LORD*

should I fast? Can I bring him back again? I shall go to him, but he will not return to me."

Solomon Is Born

24 Then David consoled his wife Bathsheba, and went to her, and lay with her; and she bore a son, and he named him Solomon. The LORD loved him, ²⁵and sent a message by the prophet Nathan; so he named him Jedidiah,ᵘ because of the LORD.

ᵘ That is *Beloved of the LORD*

TUESDAY

Scripture Reading
for Today:
2 Samuel 12.1–15

Verse for Today:
2 Samuel 12.13

Baptized With Truth

King David committed adultery with Bathsheba and then arranged for the death of her husband. But God sees David's sin and confronts him through the prophet Nathan.

If scripture is to become my teacher, I must put on each story like a robe to be worn, identifying with the characters, walking in their shoes, feeling with their hearts.

This lovely passage from the Old Testament has worn well in my soul, empowering me to look at the lies of my life. I am a David-figure longing for a prophet like Nathan to baptize me with the truth.

I carry the prophet Nathan
    in my heart.
I am challenged to the bone
    as David was challenged.
That man is you!
I hear it in the center
    of everything that feels in me.

I am the one
    who proclaims another's death sentence
    only to discover,
    the sentence is mine.
I have slaughtered other's lambs
    and saved my own.

Only one thing is necessary:
    conversion
    a change of heart.

I turn to Nathan
    and am baptized with truth.
That man is you!

—MACRINA WIEDERKEHR

Go to page 337 for your next devotional reading.

The Ammonites Crushed

26 Now Joab fought against Rabbah of the Ammonites, and took the royal city. [27]Joab sent messengers to David, and said, "I have fought against Rabbah; moreover, I have taken the water city. [28]Now, then, gather the rest of the people together, and encamp against the city, and take it; or I myself will take the city, and it will be called by my name." [29]So David gathered all the people together and went to Rabbah, and fought against it and took it. [30]He took the crown of Milcom[v] from his head; the weight of it was a talent of gold, and in it was a precious stone; and it was placed on David's head. He also brought forth the spoil of the city, a very great amount. [31]He brought out the people who were in it, and set them to work with saws and iron picks and iron axes, or sent them to the brickworks. Thus he did to all the cities of the Ammonites. Then David and all the people returned to Jerusalem.

Amnon and Tamar

13 Some time passed. David's son Absalom had a beautiful sister whose name was Tamar; and David's son Amnon fell in love with her. [2]Amnon was so tormented that he made himself ill because of his sister Tamar, for she was a virgin and it seemed impossible to Amnon to do anything to her. [3]But Amnon had a friend whose name was Jonadab, the son of David's brother Shimeah; and Jonadab was a very crafty man. [4]He said to him, "O son of the king, why are you so haggard morning after morning? Will you not tell me?" Amnon said to him, "I love Tamar, my brother Absalom's sister." [5]Jonadab said to him, "Lie down on your bed, and pretend to be ill; and when your father comes to see you, say to him, 'Let my sister Tamar come and give me something to eat, and prepare the food in my sight, so that I may see it and eat it from her hand.'" [6]So Amnon lay down, and pretended to be ill; and when the king came to see him, Amnon said to the king, "Please let my sister Tamar come and make a couple of cakes in my sight, so that I may eat from her hand."

7 Then David sent home to Tamar, saying, "Go to your brother Amnon's house, and prepare food for him." [8]So Tamar went to her brother Amnon's house, where he was lying down. She took dough, kneaded it, made cakes in his sight, and baked the cakes. [9]Then she took the pan and set them[w] out before him, but he refused to eat. Amnon said, "Send out everyone from me." So everyone went out from him. [10]Then Amnon said to Tamar, "Bring the food into the chamber, so that I may eat from your hand." So Tamar took the cakes she had made, and brought them into the chamber to Amnon her brother. [11]But when she brought them near him to eat, he took hold of her, and said to her, "Come, lie with me, my sister." [12]She answered him, "No, my brother, do not force me; for such a thing is not done in Israel; do not do anything so vile! [13]As for me, where could I carry my shame? And as for you, you would be as one of the scoundrels in Israel. Now therefore, I beg you, speak to the king; for he will not withhold me from you." [14]But he would not listen to her; and being stronger than she, he forced her and lay with her.

15 Then Amnon was seized with a very great loathing for her; indeed, his loathing was even greater than the lust he had felt for her. Amnon said to her, "Get out!" [16]But she said to him, "No, my brother;[x] for this wrong in sending me away is greater than the other that you did to me." But he would not listen to her. [17]He called the young man who served him and said, "Put this woman out of my presence, and bolt the door after her." [18](Now she was wearing a long robe with sleeves; for this is how the virgin daughters of the king were clothed in earlier times.[y]) So his servant put her out, and bolted the door after her. [19]But Tamar put ashes on her head, and tore the long robe that she was wearing; she put her hand on her head, and went away, crying aloud as she went.

20 Her brother Absalom said to her, "Has Amnon your brother been with you? Be quiet for now, my sister; he is your brother; do not take this to heart." So Tamar remained, a desolate woman, in her brother Absalom's house. [21]When King David heard of all these things, he became very angry, but he would not punish his son Amnon, because he loved him,

---

v Gk See 1 Kings 11.5, 33: Heb *their kings*
w Heb *and poured*   *x* Cn Compare Gk Vg:
Meaning of Heb uncertain   *y* Cn: Heb *were clothed in robes*

for he was his firstborn.[z] 22But Absalom spoke to Amnon neither good nor bad; for Absalom hated Amnon, because he had raped his sister Tamar.

Absalom Avenges the Violation of His Sister

23 After two full years Absalom had sheepshearers at Baal-hazor, which is near Ephraim, and Absalom invited all the king's sons. 24Absalom came to the king, and said, "Your servant has sheepshearers; will the king and his servants please go with your servant?" 25But the king said to Absalom, "No, my son, let us not all go, or else we will be burdensome to you." He pressed him, but he would not go but gave him his blessing. 26Then Absalom said, "If not, please let my brother Amnon go with us." The king said to him, "Why should he go with you?" 27But Absalom pressed him until he let Amnon and all the king's sons go with him. Absalom made a feast like a king's feast.[a] 28Then Absalom commanded his servants, "Watch when Amnon's heart is merry with wine, and when I say to you, 'Strike Amnon,' then kill him. Do not be afraid; have I not myself commanded you? Be courageous and valiant." 29So the servants of Absalom did to Amnon as Absalom had commanded. Then all the king's sons rose, and each mounted his mule and fled.

30 While they were on the way, the report came to David that Absalom had killed all the king's sons, and not one of them was left. 31The king rose, tore his garments, and lay on the ground; and all his servants who were standing by tore their garments. 32But Jonadab, the son of David's brother Shimeah, said, "Let not my lord suppose that they have killed all the young men the king's sons; Amnon alone is dead. This has been determined by Absalom from the day Amnon[b] raped his sister Tamar. 33Now therefore, do not let my lord the king take it to heart, as if all the king's sons were dead; for Amnon alone is dead."

34 But Absalom fled. When the young man who kept watch looked up, he saw many people coming from the Horonaim road[c] by the side of the mountain. 35Jonadab said to the king, "See, the king's sons have come; as your servant said, so it has come about." 36As soon as he had finished speaking, the king's sons arrived, and raised their voices and wept; and the king

and all his servants also wept very bitterly.

37 But Absalom fled, and went to Talmai son of Ammihud, king of Geshur. David mourned for his son day after day. 38Absalom, having fled to Geshur, stayed there three years. 39And the heart of[d] the king went out, yearning for Absalom; for he was now consoled over the death of Amnon.

Absalom Returns to Jerusalem

14 Now Joab son of Zeruiah perceived that the king's mind was on Absalom. 2Joab sent to Tekoa and brought from there a wise woman. He said to her, "Pretend to be a mourner; put on mourning garments, do not anoint yourself with oil, but behave like a woman who has been mourning many days for the dead. 3Go to the king and speak to him as follows." And Joab put the words into her mouth.

4 When the woman of Tekoa came to the king, she fell on her face to the ground and did obeisance, and said, "Help, O king!" 5The king asked her, "What is your trouble?" She answered, "Alas, I am a widow; my husband is dead. 6Your servant had two sons, and they fought with one another in the field; there was no one to part them, and one struck the other and killed him. 7Now the whole family has risen against your servant. They say, 'Give up the man who struck his brother, so that we may kill him for the life of his brother whom he murdered, even if we destroy the heir as well.' Thus they would quench my one remaining ember, and leave to my husband neither name nor remnant on the face of the earth."

8 Then the king said to the woman, "Go to your house, and I will give orders concerning you." 9The woman of Tekoa said to the king, "On me be the guilt, my lord the king, and on my father's house; let the king and his throne be guiltless." 10The king said, "If anyone says anything to you, bring him to me, and he shall never touch you again." 11Then she said, "Please, may the king keep the LORD your God in mind, so that the avenger of blood may kill no more, and my son not be de-

z Q Ms Gk: MT lacks *but he would not punish . . . firstborn*   a Gk Compare Q Ms: MT lacks *Absalom made a feast like a king's feast*   b Heb *he*
c Cn Compare Gk: Heb *the road behind him*
d Q Ms Gk: MT *And David*

stroyed." He said, "As the LORD lives, not one hair of your son shall fall to the ground."

12 Then the woman said, "Please let your servant speak a word to my lord the king." He said, "Speak." 13The woman said, "Why then have you planned such a thing against the people of God? For in giving this decision the king convicts himself, inasmuch as the king does not bring his banished one home again. 14We must all die; we are like water spilled on the ground, which cannot be gathered up. But God will not take away a life; he will devise plans so as not to keep an outcast banished forever from his presence.*e* 15Now I have come to say this to my lord the king because the people have made me afraid; your servant thought, 'I will speak to the king; it may be that the king will perform the request of his servant. 16For the king will hear, and deliver his servant from the hand of the man who would cut both me and my son off from the heritage of God.' 17Your servant thought, 'The word of my lord the king will set me at rest'; for my lord the king is like the angel of God, discerning good and evil. The LORD your God be with you!"

18 Then the king answered the woman, "Do not withhold from me anything I ask you." The woman said, "Let my lord the king speak." 19The king said, "Is the hand of Joab with you in all this?" The woman answered and said, "As surely as you live, my lord the king, one cannot turn right or left from anything that my lord the king has said. For it was your servant Joab who commanded me; it was he who put all these words into the mouth of your servant. 20In order to change the course of affairs your servant Joab did this. But my lord has wisdom like the wisdom of the angel of God to know all things that are on the earth."

21 Then the king said to Joab, "Very well, I grant this; go, bring back the young man Absalom." 22Joab prostrated himself with his face to the ground and did obeisance, and blessed the king; and Joab said, "Today your servant knows that I have found favor in your sight, my lord the king, in that the king has granted the request of his servant." 23So Joab set off, went to Geshur, and brought Absalom to Jerusalem. 24The king said, "Let him go to his own house; he is not to come into my presence." So Absalom went to his own

house, and did not come into the king's presence.

David Forgives Absalom

25 Now in all Israel there was no one to be praised so much for his beauty as Absalom; from the sole of his foot to the crown of his head there was no blemish in him. 26When he cut the hair of his head (for at the end of every year he used to cut it; when it was heavy on him, he cut it), he weighed the hair of his head, two hundred shekels by the king's weight. 27There were born to Absalom three sons, and one daughter whose name was Tamar; she was a beautiful woman.

28 So Absalom lived two full years in Jerusalem, without coming into the king's presence. 29Then Absalom sent for Joab to send him to the king; but Joab would not come to him. He sent a second time, but Joab would not come. 30Then he said to his servants, "Look, Joab's field is next to mine, and he has barley there; go and set it on fire." So Absalom's servants set the field on fire. 31Then Joab rose and went to Absalom at his house, and said to him, "Why have your servants set my field on fire?" 32Absalom answered Joab, "Look, I sent word to you: Come here, that I may send you to the king with the question, 'Why have I come from Geshur? It would be better for me to be there still.' Now let me go into the king's presence; if there is guilt in me, let him kill me!" 33Then Joab went to the king and told him; and he summoned Absalom. So he came to the king and prostrated himself with his face to the ground before the king; and the king kissed Absalom.

Absalom Usurps the Throne

15 After this Absalom got himself a chariot and horses, and fifty men to run ahead of him. 2Absalom used to rise early and stand beside the road into the gate; and when anyone brought a suit before the king for judgment, Absalom would call out and say, "From what city are you?" When the person said, "Your servant is of such and such a tribe in Israel," 3Absalom would say, "See, your claims are good and right; but there is no one deputed by the king to hear you." 4Absalom said moreover, "If only I were judge in the land! Then all who had a suit or

e Meaning of Heb uncertain

cause might come to me, and I would give them justice." [5]Whenever people came near to do obeisance to him, he would put out his hand and take hold of them, and kiss them. [6]Thus Absalom did to every Israelite who came to the king for judgment; so Absalom stole the hearts of the people of Israel.

7 At the end of four[f] years Absalom said to the king, "Please let me go to Hebron and pay the vow that I have made to the LORD. [8]For your servant made a vow while I lived at Geshur in Aram: If the LORD will indeed bring me back to Jerusalem, then I will worship the LORD in Hebron."[g] [9]The king said to him, "Go in peace." So he got up, and went to Hebron. [10]But Absalom sent secret messengers throughout all the tribes of Israel, saying, "As soon as you hear the sound of the trumpet, then shout: Absalom has become king at Hebron!" [11]Two hundred men from Jerusalem went with Absalom; they were invited guests, and they went in their innocence, knowing nothing of the matter. [12]While Absalom was offering the sacrifices, he sent for[h] Ahithophel the Gilonite, David's counselor, from his city Giloh. The conspiracy grew in strength, and the people with Absalom kept increasing.

David Flees from Jerusalem

13 A messenger came to David, saying, "The hearts of the Israelites have gone after Absalom." [14]Then David said to all his officials who were with him at Jerusalem, "Get up! Let us flee, or there will be no escape for us from Absalom. Hurry, or he will soon overtake us, and bring disaster down upon us, and attack the city with the edge of the sword." [15]The king's officials said to the king, "Your servants are ready to do whatever our lord the king decides." [16]So the king left, followed by all his household, except ten concubines whom he left behind to look after the house. [17]The king left, followed by all the people; and they stopped at the last house. [18]All his officials passed by him; and all the Cherethites, and all the Pelethites, and all the six hundred Gittites who had followed him from Gath, passed on before the king.

19 Then the king said to Ittai the Gittite, "Why are you also coming with us? Go back, and stay with the king; for you are a foreigner, and also an exile from your home. [20]You came only yesterday, and shall I today make you wander about with us, while I go wherever I can? Go back, and take your kinsfolk with you; and may the LORD show[i] steadfast love and faithfulness to you." [21]But Ittai answered the king, "As the LORD lives, and as my lord the king lives, wherever my lord the king may be, whether for death or for life, there also your servant will be." [22]David said to Ittai, "Go then, march on." So Ittai the Gittite marched on, with all his men and all the little ones who were with him. [23]The whole country wept aloud as all the people passed by; the king crossed the Wadi Kidron, and all the people moved on toward the wilderness.

24 Abiathar came up, and Zadok also, with all the Levites, carrying the ark of the covenant of God. They set down the ark of God, until the people had all passed out of the city. [25]Then the king said to Zadok, "Carry the ark of God back into the city. If I find favor in the eyes of the LORD, he will bring me back and let me see both it and the place where it stays. [26]But if he says, 'I take no pleasure in you,' here I am, let him do to me what seems good to him." [27]The king also said to the priest Zadok, "Look,[j] go back to the city in peace, you and Abiathar,[k] with your two sons, Ahimaaz your son, and Jonathan son of Abiathar. [28]See, I will wait at the fords of the wilderness until word comes from you to inform me." [29]So Zadok and Abiathar carried the ark of God back to Jerusalem, and they remained there.

30 But David went up the ascent of the Mount of Olives, weeping as he went, with his head covered and walking barefoot; and all the people who were with him covered their heads and went up, weeping as they went. [31]David was told that Ahithophel was among the conspirators with Absalom. And David said, "O LORD, I pray you, turn the counsel of Ahithophel into foolishness."

Hushai Becomes David's Spy

32 When David came to the summit, where God was worshiped, Hushai the Archite came to meet him with his coat torn and earth on his head. [33]David said to

---

f Gk Syr: Heb *forty*　　*g* Gk Mss: Heb lacks *in Hebron*　　*h* Or *he sent*　　*i* Gk Compare 2.6: Heb lacks *may the* LORD *show*　　*j* Gk: Heb *Are you a seer* or *Do you see?*　　*k* Cn: Heb lacks *and Abiathar*

him, "If you go on with me, you will be a burden to me. ³⁴But if you return to the city and say to Absalom, 'I will be your servant, O king; as I have been your father's servant in time past, so now I will be your servant,' then you will defeat for me the counsel of Ahithophel. ³⁵The priests Zadok and Abiathar will be with you there. So whatever you hear from the king's house, tell it to the priests Zadok and Abiathar. ³⁶Their two sons are with them there, Zadok's son Ahimaaz and Abiathar's son Jonathan; and by them you shall report to me everything you hear." ³⁷So Hushai, David's friend, came into the city, just as Absalom was entering Jerusalem.

David's Adversaries

16 When David had passed a little beyond the summit, Ziba the servant of Mephibosheth¹ met him, with a couple of donkeys saddled, carrying two hundred loaves of bread, one hundred bunches of raisins, one hundred of summer fruits, and one skin of wine. ²The king said to Ziba, "Why have you brought these?" Ziba answered, "The donkeys are for the king's household to ride, the bread and summer fruit for the young men to eat, and the wine is for those to drink who faint in the wilderness." ³The king said, "And where is your master's son?" Ziba said to the king, "He remains in Jerusalem; for he said, 'Today the house of Israel will give me back my grandfather's kingdom.'" ⁴Then the king said to Ziba, "All that belonged to Mephibosheth¹ is now yours." Ziba said, "I do obeisance; let me find favor in your sight, my lord the king."

Shimei Curses David

5 When King David came to Bahurim, a man of the family of the house of Saul came out whose name was Shimei son of Gera; he came out cursing. ⁶He threw stones at David and at all the servants of King David; now all the people and all the warriors were on his right and on his left. ⁷Shimei shouted while he cursed, "Out! Out! Murderer! Scoundrel! ⁸The LORD has avenged on all of you the blood of the house of Saul, in whose place you have reigned; and the LORD has given the kingdom into the hand of your son Absalom. See, disaster has overtaken you; for you are a man of blood."

9 Then Abishai son of Zeruiah said to the king, "Why should this dead dog curse my lord the king? Let me go over and take off his head." ¹⁰But the king said, "What have I to do with you, you sons of Zeruiah? If he is cursing because the LORD has said to him, 'Curse David,' who then shall say, 'Why have you done so?'" ¹¹David said to Abishai and to all his servants, "My own son seeks my life; how much more now may this Benjaminite! Let him alone, and let him curse; for the LORD has bidden him. ¹²It may be that the LORD will look on my distress,ᵐ and the LORD will repay me with good for this cursing of me today." ¹³So David and his men went on the road, while Shimei went along on the hillside opposite him and cursed as he went, throwing stones and flinging dust at him. ¹⁴The king and all the people who were with him arrived weary at the Jordan;ⁿ and there he refreshed himself.

The Counsel of Ahithophel

15 Now Absalom and all the Israelitesᵒ came to Jerusalem; Ahithophel was with him. ¹⁶When Hushai the Archite, David's friend, came to Absalom, Hushai said to Absalom, "Long live the king! Long live the king!" ¹⁷Absalom said to Hushai, "Is this your loyalty to your friend? Why did you not go with your friend?" ¹⁸Hushai said to Absalom, "No; but the one whom the LORD and this people and all the Israelites have chosen, his I will be, and with him I will remain. ¹⁹Moreover, whom should I serve? Should it not be his son? Just as I have served your father, so I will serve you."

20 Then Absalom said to Ahithophel, "Give us your counsel; what shall we do?" ²¹Ahithophel said to Absalom, "Go in to your father's concubines, the ones he has left to look after the house; and all Israel will hear that you have made yourself odious to your father, and the hands of all who are with you will be strengthened." ²²So they pitched a tent for Absalom upon the roof; and Absalom went in to his father's concubines in the sight of all Israel. ²³Now in those days the counsel that Ahithophel gave was as if one consulted the oracleᵖ of God; so all the counsel of

---

l Or *Merib-baal:* See 4.4 note   *m* Gk Vg: Heb *iniquity*   *n* Gk: Heb lacks *at the Jordan*   *o* Gk: Heb *all the people, the men of Israel*   *p* Heb *word*

Ahithophel was esteemed, both by David and by Absalom.

17 Moreover Ahithophel said to Absalom, "Let me choose twelve thousand men, and I will set out and pursue David tonight. [2]I will come upon him while he is weary and discouraged, and throw him into a panic; and all the people who are with him will flee. I will strike down only the king, [3]and I will bring all the people back to you as a bride comes home to her husband. You seek the life of only one man,[q] and all the people will be at peace." [4]The advice pleased Absalom and all the elders of Israel.

The Counsel of Hushai

5 Then Absalom said, "Call Hushai the Archite also, and let us hear too what he has to say." [6]When Hushai came to Absalom, Absalom said to him, "This is what Ahithophel has said; shall we do as he advises? If not, you tell us." [7]Then Hushai said to Absalom, "This time the counsel that Ahithophel has given is not good." [8]Hushai continued, "You know that your father and his men are warriors, and that they are enraged, like a bear robbed of her cubs in the field. Besides, your father is expert in war; he will not spend the night with the troops. [9]Even now he has hidden himself in one of the pits, or in some other place. And when some of our troops[r] fall at the first attack, whoever hears it will say, 'There has been a slaughter among the troops who follow Absalom.' [10]Then even the valiant warrior, whose heart is like the heart of a lion, will utterly melt with fear; for all Israel knows that your father is a warrior, and that those who are with him are valiant warriors. [11]But my counsel is that all Israel be gathered to

q Gk: Heb like the return of the whole (is) the man whom you seek   r Gk Mss: Heb some of them

---

Confusion

The longer we go on with life, the more mysterious, the more baffling it seems to most of us: and the more deeply we feel the need of being taught how to live. We go muddling on, secretly conscious that we are making a mess of it. Guides come forward to tell us this or that, yet always with an avoidance of the full mystery of our situation, seldom with any real sense of the richness of the material of life: and they all fail to be of much use to us when we come to the bad bits. The surface indications often mislead us. The tangle of new roads, bordered by important-looking factories and unhappy little trees, the arterial highways leading nowhere, the conflicting demands and directions which reach us from every side, only make our confusions worse. And at last we realize that only the Author of human life can teach us how to live human life, because he alone sees it in its eternal significance: and he does this by a disclosure that at first may seem strange and puzzling, but grows in beauty and meaning as we gaze at it, and which feeds, enlightens and supports us when we dare to take up the life that it reveals.

"Lord," said St. Thomas Aquinas, "set my life in order; making me to know what I ought to do and do it in the way that I should."

—*EVELYN UNDERHILL*

Go to page 344 for your next devotional reading.

you, from Dan to Beer-sheba, like the sand by the sea for multitude, and that you go to battle in person. 12So we shall come upon him in whatever place he may be found, and we shall light on him as the dew falls on the ground; and he will not survive, nor will any of those with him. 13If he withdraws into a city, then all Israel will bring ropes to that city, and we shall drag it into the valley, until not even a pebble is to be found there." 14Absalom and all the men of Israel said, "The counsel of Hushai the Archite is better than the counsel of Ahithophel." For the LORD had ordained to defeat the good counsel of Ahithophel, so that the LORD might bring ruin on Absalom.

Hushai Warns David to Escape

15 Then Hushai said to the priests Zadok and Abiathar, "Thus and so did Ahithophel counsel Absalom and the elders of Israel; and thus and so I have counseled. 16Therefore send quickly and tell David, 'Do not lodge tonight at the fords of the wilderness, but by all means cross over; otherwise the king and all the people who are with him will be swallowed up.' " 17Jonathan and Ahimaaz were waiting at En-rogel; a servant-girl used to go and tell them, and they would go and tell King David; for they could not risk being seen entering the city. 18But a boy saw them, and told Absalom; so both of them went away quickly, and came to the house of a man at Bahurim, who had a well in his courtyard; and they went down into it. 19The man's wife took a covering, stretched it over the well's mouth, and spread out grain on it; and nothing was known of it. 20When Absalom's servants came to the woman at the house, they said, "Where are Ahimaaz and Jonathan?" The woman said to them, "They have crossed over the brook*s* of water." And when they had searched and could not find them, they returned to Jerusalem.

21 After they had gone, the men came up out of the well, and went and told King David. They said to David, "Go and cross the water quickly; for thus and so has Ahithophel counseled against you." 22So David and all the people who were with him set out and crossed the Jordan; by daybreak not one was left who had not crossed the Jordan.

23 When Ahithophel saw that his counsel was not followed, he saddled his donkey and went off home to his own city. He set his house in order, and hanged himself; he died and was buried in the tomb of his father.

24 Then David came to Mahanaim, while Absalom crossed the Jordan with all the men of Israel. 25Now Absalom had set Amasa over the army in the place of Joab. Amasa was the son of a man named Ithra the Ishmaelite,*t* who had married Abigal daughter of Nahash, sister of Zeruiah, Joab's mother. 26The Israelites and Absalom encamped in the land of Gilead.

27 When David came to Mahanaim, Shobi son of Nahash from Rabbah of the Ammonites, and Machir son of Ammiel from Lo-debar, and Barzillai the Gileadite from Rogelim, 28brought beds, basins, and earthen vessels, wheat, barley, meal, parched grain, beans and lentils,*u* 29honey and curds, sheep, and cheese from the herd, for David and the people with him to eat; for they said, "The troops are hungry and weary and thirsty in the wilderness."

The Defeat and Death of Absalom

18 Then David mustered the men who were with him, and set over them commanders of thousands and commanders of hundreds. 2And David divided the army into three groups:*v* one third under the command of Joab, one third under the command of Abishai son of Zeruiah, Joab's brother, and one third under the command of Ittai the Gittite. The king said to the men, "I myself will also go out with you." 3But the men said, "You shall not go out. For if we flee, they will not care about us. If half of us die, they will not care about us. But you are worth ten thousand of us;*w* therefore it is better that you send us help from the city." 4The king said to them, "Whatever seems best to you I will do." So the king stood at the side of the gate, while all the army marched out by hundreds and by thousands. 5The king ordered Joab and Abishai and Ittai, saying, "Deal gently for my sake with the young man Absalom." And all the people heard when the king gave orders to all the commanders concerning Absalom.

s Meaning of Heb uncertain   *t* 1 Chr 2.17: Heb *Israelite*   *u* Heb *and lentils and parched grain*   *v* Gk: Heb *sent forth the army*   *w* Gk Vg Symmachus: Heb *for now there are ten thousand such as we*

6 So the army went out into the field against Israel; and the battle was fought in the forest of Ephraim. 7The men of Israel were defeated there by the servants of David, and the slaughter there was great on that day, twenty thousand men. 8The battle spread over the face of all the country; and the forest claimed more victims that day than the sword.

9 Absalom happened to meet the servants of David. Absalom was riding on his mule, and the mule went under the thick branches of a great oak. His head caught fast in the oak, and he was left hanging*x* between heaven and earth, while the mule that was under him went on. 10A man saw it, and told Joab, "I saw Absalom hanging in an oak." 11Joab said to the man who told him, "What, you saw him! Why then did you not strike him there to the ground? I would have been glad to give you ten pieces of silver and a belt." 12But the man said to Joab, "Even if I felt in my hand the weight of a thousand pieces of silver, I would not raise my hand against the king's son; for in our hearing the king commanded you and Abishai and Ittai, saying: For my sake protect the young man Absalom! 13On the other hand, if I had dealt treacherously against his life*y* (and there is nothing hidden from the king), then you yourself would have stood aloof." 14Joab said, "I will not waste time like this with you." He took three spears in his hand, and thrust them into the heart of Absalom, while he was still alive in the oak. 15And ten young men, Joab's armor-bearers, surrounded Absalom and struck him, and killed him.

16 Then Joab sounded the trumpet, and the troops came back from pursuing Israel, for Joab restrained the troops. 17They took Absalom, threw him into a great pit in the forest, and raised over him a very great heap of stones. Meanwhile all the Israelites fled to their homes. 18Now Absalom in his lifetime had taken and set up for himself a pillar that is in the King's Valley, for he said, "I have no son to keep my name in remembrance"; he called the pillar by his own name. It is called Absalom's Monument to this day.

David Hears of Absalom's Death

19 Then Ahimaaz son of Zadok said, "Let me run, and carry tidings to the king that the LORD has delivered him from the power of his enemies." 20Joab said to him,

"You are not to carry tidings today; you may carry tidings another day, but today you shall not do so, because the king's son is dead." 21Then Joab said to a Cushite, "Go, tell the king what you have seen." The Cushite bowed before Joab, and ran. 22Then Ahimaaz son of Zadok said again to Joab, "Come what may, let me also run after the Cushite." And Joab said, "Why will you run, my son, seeing that you have no reward*z* for the tidings?" 23"Come what may," he said, "I will run." So he said to him, "Run." Then Ahimaaz ran by the way of the Plain, and outran the Cushite.

24 Now David was sitting between the two gates. The sentinel went up to the roof of the gate by the wall, and when he looked up, he saw a man running alone. 25The sentinel shouted and told the king. The king said, "If he is alone, there are tidings in his mouth." He kept coming, and drew near. 26Then the sentinel saw another man running; and the sentinel called to the gatekeeper and said, "See, another man running alone!" The king said, "He also is bringing tidings." 27The sentinel said, "I think the running of the first one is like the running of Ahimaaz son of Zadok." The king said, "He is a good man, and comes with good tidings."

28 Then Ahimaaz cried out to the king, "All is well!" He prostrated himself before the king with his face to the ground, and said, "Blessed be the LORD your God, who has delivered up the men who raised their hand against my lord the king." 29The king said, "Is it well with the young man Absalom?" Ahimaaz answered, "When Joab sent your servant,*a* I saw a great tumult, but I do not know what it was." 30The king said, "Turn aside, and stand here." So he turned aside, and stood still.

31 Then the Cushite came; and the Cushite said, "Good tidings for my lord the king! For the LORD has vindicated you this day, delivering you from the power of all who rose up against you." 32The king said to the Cushite, "Is it well with the young man Absalom?" The Cushite answered, "May the enemies of my lord the king, and all who rise up to do you harm, be like that young man."

---

x Gk Syr Tg: Heb *was put*   *y* Another reading is *at the risk of my life*   *z* Meaning of Heb uncertain   *a* Heb *the king's servant, your servant*

David Mourns for Absalom

33[b]The king was deeply moved, and went up to the chamber over the gate, and wept; and as he went, he said, "O my son Absalom, my son, my son Absalom! Would I had died instead of you, O Absalom, my son, my son!"

19 It was told Joab, "The king is weeping and mourning for Absalom." 2So the victory that day was turned into mourning for all the troops; for the troops heard that day, "The king is grieving for his son." 3The troops stole into the city that day as soldiers steal in who are ashamed when they flee in battle. 4The king covered his face, and the king cried with a loud voice, "O my son Absalom, O Absalom, my son, my son!" 5Then Joab came into the house to the king, and said, "Today you have covered with shame the faces of all your officers who have saved your life today, and the lives of your sons and your daughters, and the lives of your wives and your concubines, 6for love of those who hate you and for hatred of those who love you. You have made it clear today that commanders and officers are nothing to you; for I perceive that if Absalom were alive and all of us were dead today, then you would be pleased. 7So go out at once and speak kindly to your servants; for I swear by the LORD, if you do not go, not a man will stay with you this night; and this will be worse for you than any disaster that has come upon you from your youth until now." 8Then the king got up and took his seat in the gate. The troops were all told, "See, the king is sitting in the gate"; and all the troops came before the king.

David Recalled to Jerusalem

Meanwhile, all the Israelites had fled to their homes. 9All the people were disputing throughout all the tribes of Israel, saying, "The king delivered us from the hand of our enemies, and saved us from the hand of the Philistines; and now he has fled out of the land because of Absalom. 10But Absalom, whom we anointed over us, is dead in battle. Now therefore why do you say nothing about bringing the king back?"

11 King David sent this message to the priests Zadok and Abiathar, "Say to the elders of Judah, 'Why should you be the last to bring the king back to his house?

The talk of all Israel has come to the king.[c] 12You are my kin, you are my bone and my flesh; why then should you be the last to bring back the king?' 13And say to Amasa, 'Are you not my bone and my flesh? So may God do to me, and more, if you are not the commander of my army from now on, in place of Joab.' " 14Amasa[d] swayed the hearts of all the people of Judah as one, and they sent word to the king, "Return, both you and all your servants." 15So the king came back to the Jordan; and Judah came to Gilgal to meet the king and to bring him over the Jordan.

16 Shimei son of Gera, the Benjaminite, from Bahurim, hurried to come down with the people of Judah to meet King David; 17with him were a thousand people from Benjamin. And Ziba, the servant of the house of Saul, with his fifteen sons and his twenty servants, rushed down to the Jordan ahead of the king, 18while the crossing was taking place,[e] to bring over the king's household, and to do his pleasure.

David's Mercy to Shimei

Shimei son of Gera fell down before the king, as he was about to cross the Jordan, 19and said to the king, "May my lord not hold me guilty or remember how your servant did wrong on the day my lord the king left Jerusalem; may the king not bear it in mind. 20For your servant knows that I have sinned; therefore, see, I have come this day, the first of all the house of Joseph to come down to meet my lord the king." 21Abishai son of Zeruiah answered, "Shall not Shimei be put to death for this, because he cursed the LORD's anointed?" 22But David said, "What have I to do with you, you sons of Zeruiah, that you should today become an adversary to me? Shall anyone be put to death in Israel this day? For do I not know that I am this day king over Israel?" 23The king said to Shimei, "You shall not die." And the king gave him his oath.

David and Mephibosheth Meet

24 Mephibosheth[f] grandson of Saul came down to meet the king; he had not taken care of his feet, or trimmed his

---

b Ch 19.1 in Heb   c Gk: Heb to the king, to his house   d Heb He   e Cn: Heb the ford crossed
f Or Merib-baal: See 4.4 note

beard, or washed his clothes, from the day the king left until the day he came back in safety. 25When he came from Jerusalem to meet the king, the king said to him, "Why did you not go with me, Mephibosheth?"*g* 26He answered, "My lord, O king, my servant deceived me; for your servant said to him, 'Saddle a donkey for me,'*h* so that I may ride on it and go with the king.' For your servant is lame. 27He has slandered your servant to my lord the king. But my lord the king is like the angel of God; do therefore what seems good to you. 28For all my father's house were doomed to death before my lord the king; but you set your servant among those who eat at your table. What further right have I, then, to appeal to the king?" 29The king said to him, "Why speak any more of your affairs? I have decided: you and Ziba shall divide the land." 30Mephibosheth*g* said to the king, "Let him take it all, since my lord the king has arrived home safely."

David's Kindness to Barzillai

31 Now Barzillai the Gileadite had come down from Rogelim; he went on with the king to the Jordan, to escort him over the Jordan. 32Barzillai was a very aged man, eighty years old. He had provided the king with food while he stayed at Mahanaim, for he was a very wealthy man. 33The king said to Barzillai, "Come over with me, and I will provide for you in Jerusalem at my side." 34But Barzillai said to the king, "How many years have I still to live, that I should go up with the king to Jerusalem? 35Today I am eighty years old; can I discern what is pleasant and what is not? Can your servant taste what he eats or what he drinks? Can I still listen to the voice of singing men and singing women? Why then should your servant be an added burden to my lord the king? 36Your servant will go a little way over the Jordan with the king. Why should the king recompense me with such a reward? 37Please let your servant return, so that I may die in my own town, near the graves of my father and my mother. But here is your servant Chimham; let him go over with my lord the king; and do for him whatever seems good to you." 38The king answered, "Chimham shall go over with me, and I will do for him whatever seems good to you; and all that you desire of me I will do for you." 39Then all the people crossed over the Jordan, and the king

crossed over; the king kissed Barzillai and blessed him, and he returned to his own home. 40The king went on to Gilgal, and Chimham went on with him; all the people of Judah, and also half the people of Israel, brought the king on his way.

41 Then all the people of Israel came to the king, and said to him, "Why have our kindred the people of Judah stolen you away, and brought the king and his household over the Jordan, and all David's men with him?" 42All the people of Judah answered the people of Israel, "Because the king is near of kin to us. Why then are you angry over this matter? Have we eaten at all at the king's expense? Or has he given us any gift?" 43But the people of Israel answered the people of Judah, "We have ten shares in the king, and in David also we have more than you. Why then did you despise us? Were we not the first to speak of bringing back our king?" But the words of the people of Judah were fiercer than the words of the people of Israel.

The Rebellion of Sheba

20 Now a scoundrel named Sheba son of Bichri, a Benjaminite, happened to be there. He sounded the trumpet and cried out,

"We have no portion in David,
no share in the son of Jesse!
Everyone to your tents, O Israel!"

2So all the people of Israel withdrew from David and followed Sheba son of Bichri; but the people of Judah followed their king steadfastly from the Jordan to Jerusalem.

3 David came to his house at Jerusalem; and the king took the ten concubines whom he had left to look after the house, and put them in a house under guard, and provided for them, but did not go in to them. So they were shut up until the day of their death, living as if in widowhood.

4 Then the king said to Amasa, "Call the men of Judah together to me within three days, and be here yourself." 5So Amasa went to summon Judah; but he delayed beyond the set time that had been appointed him. 6David said to Abishai, "Now Sheba son of Bichri will do us more harm than Absalom; take your lord's servants and pursue him, or he will find for-

g Or Merib-baal: See 4.4 note   h Gk Syr Vg: Heb said, 'I will saddle a donkey for myself

tified cities for himself, and escape from us." 7Joab's men went out after him, along with the Cherethites, the Pelethites, and all the warriors; they went out from Jerusalem to pursue Sheba son of Bichri. 8When they were at the large stone that is in Gibeon, Amasa came to meet them. Now Joab was wearing a soldier's garment and over it was a belt with a sword in its sheath fastened at his waist; as he went forward it fell out. 9Joab said to Amasa, "Is it well with you, my brother?" And Joab took Amasa by the beard with his right hand to kiss him. 10But Amasa did not notice the sword in Joab's hand; Joab struck him in the belly so that his entrails poured out on the ground, and he died. He did not strike a second blow.

Then Joab and his brother Abishai pursued Sheba son of Bichri. 11And one of Joab's men took his stand by Amasa, and said, "Whoever favors Joab, and whoever is for David, let him follow Joab." 12Amasa lay wallowing in his blood on the highway, and the man saw that all the people were stopping. Since he saw that all who came by him were stopping, he carried Amasa from the highway into a field, and threw a garment over him. 13Once he was removed from the highway, all the people went on after Joab to pursue Sheba son of Bichri.

14 Sheba*i* passed through all the tribes of Israel to Abel of Beth-maacah;*j* and all the Bichrites*k* assembled, and followed him inside. 15Joab's forces*l* came and besieged him in Abel of Beth-maacah; they threw up a siege ramp against the city, and it stood against the rampart. Joab's forces were battering the wall to break it down. 16Then a wise woman called from the city, "Listen! Listen! Tell Joab, 'Come here, I want to speak to you.' " 17He came near her; and the woman said, "Are you Joab?" He answered, "I am." Then she said to him, "Listen to the words of your servant." He answered, "I am listening." 18Then she said, "They used to say in the old days, 'Let them inquire at Abel'; and so they would settle a matter. 19I am one of those who are peaceable and faithful in Israel; you seek to destroy a city that is a mother in Israel; why will you swallow up the heritage of the LORD?" 20Joab answered, "Far be it from me, far be it, that I should swallow up or destroy! 21That is not the case! But a man of the hill country of Ephraim, called Sheba son

of Bichri, has lifted up his hand against King David; give him up alone, and I will withdraw from the city." The woman said to Joab, "His head shall be thrown over the wall to you." 22Then the woman went to all the people with her wise plan. And they cut off the head of Sheba son of Bichri, and threw it out to Joab. So he blew the trumpet, and they dispersed from the city, and all went to their homes, while Joab returned to Jerusalem to the king.

23 Now Joab was in command of all the army of Israel;*m* Benaiah son of Jehoiada was in command of the Cherethites and the Pelethites; 24Adoram was in charge of the forced labor; Jehoshaphat son of Ahilud was the recorder; 25Sheva was secretary; Zadok and Abiathar were priests; 26and Ira the Jairite was also David's priest.

David Avenges the Gibeonites

21 Now there was a famine in the days of David for three years, year after year; and David inquired of the LORD. The LORD said, "There is bloodguilt on Saul and on his house, because he put the Gibeonites to death." 2So the king called the Gibeonites and spoke to them. (Now the Gibeonites were not of the people of Israel, but of the remnant of the Amorites; although the people of Israel had sworn to spare them, Saul had tried to wipe them out in his zeal for the people of Israel and Judah.) 3David said to the Gibeonites, "What shall I do for you? How shall I make expiation, that you may bless the heritage of the LORD?" 4The Gibeonites said to him, "It is not a matter of silver or gold between us and Saul or his house; neither is it for us to put anyone to death in Israel." He said, "What do you say that I should do for you?" 5They said to the king, "The man who consumed us and planned to destroy us, so that we should have no place in all the territory of Israel— 6let seven of his sons be handed over to us, and we will impale them before the LORD at Gibeon on the mountain of the LORD."*n* The king said, "I will hand them over."

7 But the king spared Mephibosheth,*o*

the son of Saul's son Jonathan, because of
the oath of the LORD that was between
them, between David and Jonathan son of
Saul. [8]The king took the two sons of Rizpah daughter of Aiah, whom she bore to
Saul, Armoni and Mephibosheth;[p] and
the five sons of Merab[q] daughter of Saul,
whom she bore to Adriel son of Barzillai
the Meholathite; [9]he gave them into the
hands of the Gibeonites, and they impaled them on the mountain before the
LORD. The seven of them perished together. They were put to death in the first days
of harvest, at the beginning of barley harvest.

10 Then Rizpah the daughter of Aiah
took sackcloth, and spread it on a rock for
herself, from the beginning of harvest until rain fell on them from the heavens; she
did not allow the birds of the air to come
on the bodies[r] by day, or the wild animals by night. [11]When David was told
what Rizpah daughter of Aiah, the concubine of Saul, had done, [12]David went and
took the bones of Saul and the bones of
his son Jonathan from the people of
Jabesh-gilead, who had stolen them from
the public square of Beth-shan, where the
Philistines had hung them up, on the day
the Philistines killed Saul on Gilboa. [13]He
brought up from there the bones of Saul
and the bones of his son Jonathan; and
they gathered the bones of those who had
been impaled. [14]They buried the bones of
Saul and of his son Jonathan in the land
of Benjamin in Zela, in the tomb of his
father Kish; they did all that the king commanded. After that, God heeded supplications for the land.

Exploits of David's Men

15 The Philistines went to war again
with Israel, and David went down together with his servants. They fought against
the Philistines, and David grew weary.
[16]Ishbi-benob, one of the descendants of
the giants, whose spear weighed three
hundred shekels of bronze, and who was
fitted out with new weapons,[s] said he
would kill David. [17]But Abishai son of
Zeruiah came to his aid, and attacked the
Philistine and killed him. Then David's
men swore to him, "You shall not go out
with us to battle any longer, so that you
do not quench the lamp of Israel."

18 After this a battle took place with
the Philistines, at Gob; then Sibbecai the
Hushathite killed Saph, who was one of
the descendants of the giants. [19]Then
there was another battle with the Philistines at Gob; and Elhanan son of Jaare-
oregim, the Bethlehemite, killed Goliath
the Gittite, the shaft of whose spear was
like a weaver's beam. [20]There was again
war at Gath, where there was a man of
great size, who had six fingers on each
hand, and six toes on each foot, twenty-
four in number; he too was descended
from the giants. [21]When he taunted Israel,
Jonathan son of David's brother Shimei,
killed him. [22]These four were descended
from the giants in Gath; they fell by the
hands of David and his servants.

David's Song of Thanksgiving

22 David spoke to the LORD the
words of this song on the day
when the LORD delivered him from the
hand of all his enemies, and from the hand
of Saul. [2]He said:

The LORD is my rock, my fortress,
and my deliverer,
3 my God, my rock, in whom I take
refuge,
my shield and the horn of my
salvation,
my stronghold and my refuge,
my savior; you save me from
violence.
4 I call upon the LORD, who is worthy
to be praised,
and I am saved from my enemies.

5 For the waves of death encompassed
me,
the torrents of perdition assailed
me;
6 the cords of Sheol entangled me,
the snares of death confronted
me.

7 In my distress I called upon the
LORD;
to my God I called.
From his temple he heard my voice,
and my cry came to his ears.

8 Then the earth reeled and rocked;
the foundations of the heavens
trembled
and quaked, because he was
angry.

p Or *Merib-baal*: See 4.4 note q Two Heb Mss
Syr Compare Gk: MT *Michal* r Heb *them*
s Heb *was belted anew*

⁹ Smoke went up from his nostrils,
　and devouring fire from his
　　mouth;
　glowing coals flamed forth from
　　him.
¹⁰ He bowed the heavens, and came
　down;
　thick darkness was under his feet.
¹¹ He rode on a cherub, and flew;

he was seen upon the wings of
　the wind.
¹² He made darkness around him a
　canopy,
　thick clouds, a gathering of water.
¹³ Out of the brightness before him
　coals of fire flamed forth.
¹⁴ The LORD thundered from heaven;
　the Most High uttered his voice.

Thanks and Praise— Part of the Pattern

Scripture Reading
for Today:
2 Samuel 22.1–7

Verse for Today:
2 Samuel 22.4

I will have nothing to do with a God who cares only occasionally. I need a God who is with us always, everywhere, in the deepest depths as well as the highest heights. It is when things go wrong, when the good things do not happen, when our prayers seem to have been lost, that God is most present. We do not need the sheltering wings when things go smoothly. We are closest to God in the darkness, stumbling along blindly.

Yet even here I live with contradiction. Whenever anyone in the family is driving, I pray for a safe journey. And when I hear the car door slam and know that whoever it is is safely home, I breathe out, "Oh, God, thank you."

But I think there is a difference between offering a deep sigh of thanks and assuming that "the Lord was surely with me."

We need to say "Thank you" whenever possible, even if we are not able to reconcile the human creature's free will with the Maker's working out of the pattern. Thanks and praise are, I believe, some of the threads with which the pattern is woven.

There are many times when the idea that there is indeed a pattern seems absurd wishful thinking. Random events abound. There is much in life that seems meaningless. And then, when I can see no evidence of meaning, some glimpse is given which reveals the strange weaving of purposefulness and beauty.

The world of science lives fairly comfortable with paradox. We know that light is a wave, and also that light is a particle. The discoveries made in the infinitely small world of particle physics indicate randomness and chance, and I do not find it any more difficult to live with the paradox of a universe of randomness and chance and a universe of pattern and purpose than I do with light as a wave and light as a particle. Living with contradiction is nothing new to the human being.

—MADELEINE L'ENGLE

Go to page 354 for your next devotional reading.

15 He sent out arrows, and scattered
    them
    —lightning, and routed them.
16 Then the channels of the sea were
    seen,
      the foundations of the world were
      laid bare
at the rebuke of the LORD,
    at the blast of the breath of his
    nostrils.

17 He reached from on high, he
    took me,
    he drew me out of mighty waters.
18 He delivered me from my strong
    enemy,
    from those who hated me;
    for they were too mighty for me.
19 They came upon me in the day of
    my calamity,
    but the LORD was my stay.
20 He brought me out into a broad
    place;
    he delivered me, because he
    delighted in me.

21 The LORD rewarded me according to
    my righteousness;
    according to the cleanness of my
    hands he recompensed me.
22 For I have kept the ways of the LORD,
    and have not wickedly departed
    from my God.
23 For all his ordinances were before
    me,
    and from his statutes I did not
    turn aside.
24 I was blameless before him,
    and I kept myself from guilt.
25 Therefore the LORD has recompensed
    me according to my
    righteousness,
    according to my cleanness in his
    sight.

26 With the loyal you show yourself
    loyal;
    with the blameless you show
    yourself blameless;
27 with the pure you show yourself
    pure,
    and with the crooked you show
    yourself perverse.
28 You deliver a humble people,
    but your eyes are upon the
    haughty to bring them down.
29 Indeed, you are my lamp, O LORD,
    the LORD lightens my darkness.

30 By you I can crush a troop,
    and by my God I can leap over a
    wall.
31 This God—his way is perfect;
    the promise of the LORD proves
    true;
    he is a shield for all who take
    refuge in him.

32 For who is God, but the LORD?
    And who is a rock, except our
    God?
33 The God who has girded me with
    strength*t*
    has opened wide my path.*u*
34 He made my*v* feet like the feet of
    deer,
    and set me secure on the heights.
35 He trains my hands for war,
    so that my arms can bend a bow
    of bronze.
36 You have given me the shield of
    your salvation,
    and your help*w* has made me
    great.
37 You have made me stride freely,
    and my feet do not slip;
38 I pursued my enemies and destroyed
    them,
    and did not turn back until they
    were consumed.
39 I consumed them; I struck them
    down, so that they did not
    rise;
    they fell under my feet.
40 For you girded me with strength for
    the battle;
    you made my assailants sink
    under me.
41 You made my enemies turn their
    backs to me,
    those who hated me, and I
    destroyed them.
42 They looked, but there was no one
    to save them;
    they cried to the LORD, but he did
    not answer them.
43 I beat them fine like the dust of the
    earth,
    I crushed them and stamped them
    down like the mire of the
    streets.

t Q Ms Gk Syr Vg Compare Ps 18.32: MT *God is
my strong refuge*   *u* Meaning of Heb uncertain
v Another reading is *his*   *w* Q Ms: MT *your
answering*

44 You delivered me from strife with
    the peoples;*x*
  you kept me as the head of the
    nations;
  people whom I had not known
    served me.

45 Foreigners came cringing to me;
  as soon as they heard of me, they
    obeyed me.

46 Foreigners lost heart,
  and came trembling out of their
    strongholds.

47 The LORD lives! Blessed be my rock,
  and exalted be my God, the rock
    of my salvation,

48 the God who gave me vengeance
  and brought down peoples under
    me,

49 who brought me out from my
    enemies;
  you exalted me above my
    adversaries,
  you delivered me from the
    violent.

50 For this I will extol you, O LORD,
  among the nations,
  and sing praises to your name.

51 He is a tower of salvation for his
    king,
  and shows steadfast love to his
    anointed,
  to David and his descendants
    forever.

The Last Words of David

23 Now these are the last words of
David:
  The oracle of David, son of Jesse,
    the oracle of the man whom God
     exalted,*y*
  the anointed of the God of Jacob,
    the favorite of the Strong One of
    Israel:

2 The spirit of the LORD speaks
    through me,
  his word is upon my tongue.

3 The God of Israel has spoken,
  the Rock of Israel has said to me:
  One who rules over people justly,
  ruling in the fear of God,

4 is like the light of morning,
  like the sun rising on a cloudless
    morning,
  gleaming from the rain on the
    grassy land.

5 Is not my house like this with God?
  For he has made with me an
    everlasting covenant,
  ordered in all things and secure.
  Will he not cause to prosper
  all my help and my desire?

6 But the godless are*z* all like thorns
  that are thrown away;
  for they cannot be picked up with
    the hand;

7 to touch them one uses an iron bar
  or the shaft of a spear.
  And they are entirely consumed in
    fire on the spot.*a*

David's Mighty Men

8 These are the names of the warriors whom David had: Josheb-basshebeth a Tahchemonite; he was chief of the Three;*b* he wielded his spear*c* against eight hundred whom he killed at one time.

9 Next to him among the three warriors was Eleazar son of Dodo son of Ahohi. He was with David when they defied the Philistines who were gathered there for battle. The Israelites withdrew, 10but he stood his ground. He struck down the Philistines until his arm grew weary, though his hand clung to the sword. The LORD brought about a great victory that day. Then the people came back to him— but only to strip the dead.

11 Next to him was Shammah son of Agee, the Hararite. The Philistines gathered together at Lehi, where there was a plot of ground full of lentils; and the army fled from the Philistines. 12But he took his stand in the middle of the plot, defended it, and killed the Philistines; and the LORD brought about a great victory.

13 Towards the beginning of harvest three of the thirty*d* chiefs went down to join David at the cave of Adullam, while a band of Philistines was encamped in the valley of Rephaim. 14David was then in the stronghold; and the garrison of the Philistines was then at Bethlehem. 15David said longingly, "O that someone would give me water to drink from the well of Bethlehem that is by the gate!"

---

x Gk: Heb *from strife with my people*   *y* Q Ms: MT *who was raised on high*   *z* Heb *But worthlessness*   *a* Heb *in sitting*   *b* Gk Vg Compare 1 Chr 11.11: Meaning of Heb uncertain   *c* 1 Chr 11.11: Meaning of Heb uncertain   *d* Heb adds *head*

16Then the three warriors broke through the camp of the Philistines, drew water from the well of Bethlehem that was by the gate, and brought it to David. But he would not drink of it; he poured it out to the LORD, 17for he said, "The LORD forbid that I should do this. Can I drink the blood of the men who went at the risk of their lives?" Therefore he would not drink it. The three warriors did these things.

18 Now Abishai son of Zeruiah, the brother of Joab, was chief of the Thirty.*e* With his spear he fought against three hundred men and killed them, and won a name beside the Three. 19He was the most renowned of the Thirty,*f* and became their commander; but he did not attain to the Three.

20 Benaiah son of Jehoiada was a valiant warrior*g* from Kabzeel, a doer of great deeds; he struck down two sons of Ariel*h* of Moab. He also went down and killed a lion in a pit on a day when snow had fallen. 21And he killed an Egyptian, a handsome man. The Egyptian had a spear in his hand; but Benaiah went against him with a staff, snatched the spear out of the Egyptian's hand, and killed him with his own spear. 22Such were the things Benaiah son of Jehoiada did, and won a name beside the three warriors. 23He was renowned among the Thirty, but he did not attain to the Three. And David put him in charge of his bodyguard.

24 Among the Thirty were Asahel brother of Joab; Elhanan son of Dodo of Bethlehem; 25Shammah of Harod; Elika of Harod; 26Helez the Paltite; Ira son of Ikkesh of Tekoa; 27Abiezer of Anathoth; Mebunnai the Hushathite; 28Zalmon the Ahohite; Maharai of Netophah; 29Heleb son of Baanah of Netophah; Ittai son of Ribai of Gibeah of the Benjaminites; 30Benaiah of Pirathon; Hiddai of the torrents of Gaash; 31Abi-albon the Arbathite; Azmaveth of Bahurim; 32Eliahba of Shaalbon; the sons of Jashen: Jonathan 33son of*i* Shammah the Hararite; Ahiam son of Sharar the Hararite; 34Eliphelet son of Ahasbai of Maacah; Eliam son of Ahithophel the Gilonite; 35Hezro*j* of Carmel; Paarai the Arbite; 36Igal son of Nathan of Zobah; Bani the Gadite; 37Zelek the Ammonite; Naharai of Beeroth, the armorbearer of Joab son of Zeruiah; 38Ira the Ithrite; Gareb the Ithrite; 39Uriah the Hittite—thirty-seven in all.

David's Census of Israel and Judah

24 Again the anger of the LORD was kindled against Israel, and he incited David against them, saying, "Go, count the people of Israel and Judah." 2So the king said to Joab and the commanders of the army,*k* who were with him, "Go through all the tribes of Israel, from Dan to Beer-sheba, and take a census of the people, so that I may know how many there are." 3But Joab said to the king, "May the LORD your God increase the number of the people a hundredfold, while the eyes of my lord the king can still see it! But why does my lord the king want to do this?" 4But the king's word prevailed against Joab and the commanders of the army. So Joab and the commanders of the army went out from the presence of the king to take a census of the people of Israel. 5They crossed the Jordan, and began from*l* Aroer and from the city that is in the middle of the valley, toward Gad and on to Jazer. 6Then they came to Gilead, and to Kadesh in the land of the Hittites;*m* and they came to Dan, and from Dan*n* they went around to Sidon, 7and came to the fortress of Tyre and to all the cities of the Hivites and Canaanites; and they went out to the Negeb of Judah at Beer-sheba. 8So when they had gone through all the land, they came back to Jerusalem at the end of nine months and twenty days. 9Joab reported to the king the number of those who had been recorded: in Israel there were eight hundred thousand soldiers able to draw the sword, and those of Judah were five hundred thousand.

Judgment on David's Sin

10 But afterward, David was stricken to the heart because he had numbered the people. David said to the LORD, "I have sinned greatly in what I have done. But now, O LORD, I pray you, take away the guilt of your servant; for I have done very foolishly." 11When David rose in the morning, the word of the LORD came to the

e Two Heb Mss Syr: MT *Three*   *f* Syr Compare 1 Chr 11.25: Heb *Was he the most renowned of the Three?*   *g* Another reading is *the son of Ish-hai*   *h* Gk: Heb lacks *sons of*   *i* Gk: Heb lacks *son of*   *j* Another reading is *Hezrai*   *k* 1 Chr 21.2 Gk: Heb *to Joab the commander of the army*   *l* Gk Mss: Heb *encamped in Aroer south of*   *m* Gk: Heb *to the land of Tahtim-hodshi*   *n* Cn Compare Gk: Heb *they came to Dan-jaan and*

prophet Gad, David's seer, saying, [12]"Go and say to David: Thus says the LORD: Three things I offer[o] you; choose one of them, and I will do it to you." [13]So Gad came to David and told him; he asked him, "Shall three[p] years of famine come to you on your land? Or will you flee three months before your foes while they pursue you? Or shall there be three days' pestilence in your land? Now consider, and decide what answer I shall return to the one who sent me." [14]Then David said to Gad, "I am in great distress; let us fall into the hand of the LORD, for his mercy is great; but let me not fall into human hands."

15 So the LORD sent a pestilence on Israel from that morning until the appointed time; and seventy thousand of the people died, from Dan to Beer-sheba. [16]But when the angel stretched out his hand toward Jerusalem to destroy it, the LORD relented concerning the evil, and said to the angel who was bringing destruction among the people, "It is enough; now stay your hand." The angel of the LORD was then by the threshing floor of Araunah the Jebusite. [17]When David saw the angel who was destroying the people, he said to the LORD, "I alone have sinned, and I alone have done wickedly; but these sheep, what have they done? Let your hand, I pray, be against me and against my father's house."

David's Altar on the Threshing Floor

18 That day Gad came to David and said to him, "Go up and erect an altar to the LORD on the threshing floor of Araunah the Jebusite." [19]Following Gad's instructions, David went up, as the LORD had commanded. [20]When Araunah looked down, he saw the king and his servants coming toward him; and Araunah went out and prostrated himself before the king with his face to the ground. [21]Araunah said, "Why has my lord the king come to his servant?" David said, "To buy the threshing floor from you in order to build an altar to the LORD, so that the plague may be averted from the people." [22]Then Araunah said to David, "Let my lord the king take and offer up what seems good to him; here are the oxen for the burnt offering, and the threshing sledges and the yokes of the oxen for the wood. [23]All this, O king, Araunah gives to the king." And Araunah said to the king, "May the LORD your God respond favorably to you."

24 But the king said to Araunah, "No, but I will buy them from you for a price; I will not offer burnt offerings to the LORD my God that cost me nothing." So David bought the threshing floor and the oxen for fifty shekels of silver. [25]David built there an altar to the LORD, and offered burnt offerings and offerings of wellbeing. So the LORD answered his supplication for the land, and the plague was averted from Israel.

[o] Or *hold over*   [p] 1 Chr 21.12 Gk: Heb *seven*

1 Kings

First Kings begins with the death of King David (about 970 B.C.) and the accession of his son Solomon to the throne. This book describes an awesome scene: One night, God appeared to Solomon in a dream, inviting him to ask for whatever he desired. Rather than requesting power, riches, or a long life—items high on the wish lists of most kings—Solomon simply asked for wisdom. In addition to wisdom, God blessed him with riches and honor as well.

Solomon's legendary wisdom is emphasized by the story of the Queen of Sheba's encounter with him (10.1–13) as well as by the story of the two prostitutes, each of whom claimed to be the mother of the same child (3.16–28). Israel's most illustrious king, Solomon is also known for building the temple in Jerusalem, which provided a central sanctuary for worship. But Solomon had a fatal weakness—his love for women resulted in hundreds of marriages, many to foreign women whose pagan religions were imported to Israel. After Solomon's death, Israel split into two kingdoms, which were often at odds with each other and overrun by foreign powers.

The remainder of 1 Kings deals with the early history of the divided monarchy. The central theme of the book is that the fate of the nation was bound up with the fate of its kings. Faithfulness to God resulted in blessings, while unfaithfulness resulted in a multitude of evils, including division, strife, and foreign domination.

The Struggle for the Succession

1 King David was old and advanced in years; and although they covered him with clothes, he could not get warm. ²So his servants said to him, "Let a young virgin be sought for my lord the king, and let her wait on the king, and be his attendant; let her lie in your bosom, so that my lord the king may be warm." ³So they searched for a beautiful girl throughout all the territory of Israel, and found Abishag the Shunammite, and brought her to the king. ⁴The girl was very beautiful. She became the king's attendant and served him, but the king did not know her sexually.

5 Now Adonijah son of Haggith exalted himself, saying, "I will be king"; he prepared for himself chariots and horsemen,

and fifty men to run before him. 6His father had never at any time displeased him by asking, "Why have you done thus and so?" He was also a very handsome man, and he was born next after Absalom. 7He conferred with Joab son of Zeruiah and with the priest Abiathar, and they supported Adonijah. 8But the priest Zadok, and Benaiah son of Jehoiada, and the prophet Nathan, and Shimei, and Rei, and David's own warriors did not side with Adonijah.

9 Adonijah sacrificed sheep, oxen, and fatted cattle by the stone Zoheleth, which is beside En-rogel, and he invited all his brothers, the king's sons, and all the royal officials of Judah, 10but he did not invite the prophet Nathan or Benaiah or the warriors or his brother Solomon.

11 Then Nathan said to Bathsheba, Solomon's mother, "Have you not heard that Adonijah son of Haggith has become king and our lord David does not know it? 12Now therefore come, let me give you advice, so that you may save your own life and the life of your son Solomon. 13Go in at once to King David, and say to him, 'Did you not, my lord the king, swear to your servant, saying: Your son Solomon shall succeed me as king, and he shall sit on my throne? Why then is Adonijah king?' 14Then while you are still there speaking with the king, I will come in after you and confirm your words."

15 So Bathsheba went to the king in his room. The king was very old; Abishag the Shunammite was attending the king. 16Bathsheba bowed and did obeisance to the king, and the king said, "What do you wish?" 17She said to him, "My lord, you swore to your servant by the LORD your God, saying: Your son Solomon shall succeed me as king, and he shall sit on my throne. 18But now suddenly Adonijah has become king, though you, my lord the king, do not know it. 19He has sacrificed oxen, fatted cattle, and sheep in abundance, and has invited all the children of the king, the priest Abiathar, and Joab the commander of the army; but your servant Solomon he has not invited. 20But you, my lord the king—the eyes of all Israel are on you to tell them who shall sit on the throne of my lord the king after him. 21Otherwise it will come to pass, when my lord the king sleeps with his ancestors, that my son Solomon and I will be counted offenders."

22 While she was still speaking with the king, the prophet Nathan came in. 23The king was told, "Here is the prophet Nathan." When he came in before the king, he did obeisance to the king, with his face to the ground. 24Nathan said, "My lord the king, have you said, 'Adonijah shall succeed me as king, and he shall sit on my throne'? 25For today he has gone down and has sacrificed oxen, fatted cattle, and sheep in abundance, and has invited all the king's children, Joab the commander*a* of the army, and the priest Abiathar, who are now eating and drinking before him, and saying, 'Long live King Adonijah!' 26But he did not invite me, your servant, and the priest Zadok, and Benaiah son of Jehoiada, and your servant Solomon. 27Has this thing been brought about by my lord the king and you have not let your servants know who should sit on the throne of my lord the king after him?"

The Accession of Solomon

28 King David answered, "Summon Bathsheba to me." So she came into the king's presence, and stood before the king. 29The king swore, saying, "As the LORD lives, who has saved my life from every adversity, 30as I swore to you by the LORD, the God of Israel, 'Your son Solomon shall succeed me as king, and he shall sit on my throne in my place,' so will I do this day." 31Then Bathsheba bowed with her face to the ground, and did obeisance to the king, and said, "May my lord King David live forever!"

32 King David said, "Summon to me the priest Zadok, the prophet Nathan, and Benaiah son of Jehoiada." When they came before the king, 33the king said to them, "Take with you the servants of your lord, and have my son Solomon ride on my own mule, and bring him down to Gihon. 34There let the priest Zadok and the prophet Nathan anoint him king over Israel; then blow the trumpet, and say, 'Long live King Solomon!' 35You shall go up following him. Let him enter and sit on my throne; he shall be king in my place; for I have appointed him to be ruler over Israel and over Judah." 36Benaiah son of Jehoiada answered the king, "Amen! May the LORD, the God of my lord the king, so ordain. 37As the LORD has been with my lord the king, so may he be with

a Gk: Heb the commanders

Solomon, and make his throne greater than the throne of my lord King David."

38 So the priest Zadok, the prophet Nathan, and Benaiah son of Jehoiada, and the Cherethites and the Pelethites, went down and had Solomon ride on King David's mule, and led him to Gihon. ³⁹There the priest Zadok took the horn of oil from the tent and anointed Solomon. Then they blew the trumpet, and all the people said, "Long live King Solomon!" ⁴⁰And all the people went up following him, playing on pipes and rejoicing with great joy, so that the earth quaked at their noise.

41 Adonijah and all the guests who were with him heard it as they finished feasting. When Joab heard the sound of the trumpet, he said, "Why is the city in an uproar?" ⁴²While he was still speaking, Jonathan son of the priest Abiathar arrived. Adonijah said, "Come in, for you are a worthy man and surely you bring good news." ⁴³Jonathan answered Adonijah, "No, for our lord King David has made Solomon king; ⁴⁴the king has sent with him the priest Zadok, the prophet Nathan, and Benaiah son of Jehoiada, and the Cherethites and the Pelethites; and they had him ride on the king's mule; ⁴⁵the priest Zadok and the prophet Nathan have anointed him king at Gihon; and they have gone up from there rejoicing, so that the city is in an uproar. This is the noise that you heard. ⁴⁶Solomon now sits on the royal throne. ⁴⁷Moreover the king's servants came to congratulate our lord King David, saying, 'May God make the name of Solomon more famous than yours, and make his throne greater than your throne.' The king bowed in worship on the bed ⁴⁸and went on to pray thus, 'Blessed be the LORD, the God of Israel, who today has granted one of my offspring*b* to sit on my throne and permitted me to witness it.' "

49 Then all the guests of Adonijah got up trembling and went their own ways. ⁵⁰Adonijah, fearing Solomon, got up and went to grasp the horns of the altar. ⁵¹Solomon was informed, "Adonijah is afraid of King Solomon; see, he has laid hold of the horns of the altar, saying, 'Let King Solomon swear to me first that he will not kill his servant with the sword.' " ⁵²So Solomon responded, "If he proves to be a worthy man, not one of his hairs shall fall to the ground; but if wickedness is found in him, he shall die." ⁵³Then King Solo-

mon sent to have him brought down from the altar. He came to do obeisance to King Solomon; and Solomon said to him, "Go home."

David's Instruction to Solomon

2 When David's time to die drew near, he charged his son Solomon, saying: ²"I am about to go the way of all the earth. Be strong, be courageous, ³and keep the charge of the LORD your God, walking in his ways and keeping his statutes, his commandments, his ordinances, and his testimonies, as it is written in the law of Moses, so that you may prosper in all that you do and wherever you turn. ⁴Then the LORD will establish his word that he spoke concerning me: 'If your heirs take heed to their way, to walk before me in faithfulness with all their heart and with all their soul, there shall not fail you a successor on the throne of Israel.'

5 "Moreover you know also what Joab son of Zeruiah did to me, how he dealt with the two commanders of the armies of Israel, Abner son of Ner, and Amasa son of Jether, whom he murdered, retaliating in time of peace for blood that had been shed in war, and putting the blood of war on the belt around his waist, and on the sandals on his feet. ⁶Act therefore according to your wisdom, but do not let his gray head go down to Sheol in peace. ⁷Deal loyally, however, with the sons of Barzillai the Gileadite, and let them be among those who eat at your table; for with such loyalty they met me when I fled from your brother Absalom. ⁸There is also with you Shimei son of Gera, the Benjaminite from Bahurim, who cursed me with a terrible curse on the day when I went to Mahanaim; but when he came down to meet me at the Jordan, I swore to him by the LORD, 'I will not put you to death with the sword.' ⁹Therefore do not hold him guiltless, for you are a wise man; you will know what you ought to do to him, and you must bring his gray head down with blood to Sheol."

Death of David

10 Then David slept with his ancestors, and was buried in the city of David. ¹¹The time that David reigned over Israel was forty years; he reigned seven years in Hebron, and thirty-three years in Jerusalem.

b Gk: Heb *one*

¹²So Solomon sat on the throne of his father David; and his kingdom was firmly established.

Solomon Consolidates His Reign

13 Then Adonijah son of Haggith came to Bathsheba, Solomon's mother. She asked, "Do you come peaceably?" He said, "Peaceably." ¹⁴Then he said, "May I have a word with you?" She said, "Go on." ¹⁵He said, "You know that the kingdom was mine, and that all Israel expected me to reign; however, the kingdom has turned about and become my brother's, for it was his from the LORD. ¹⁶And now I have one request to make of you; do not refuse me." She said to him, "Go on." ¹⁷He said, "Please ask King Solomon—he will not refuse you—to give me Abishag the Shunammite as my wife." ¹⁸Bathsheba said, "Very well; I will speak to the king on your behalf."

19 So Bathsheba went to King Solomon, to speak to him on behalf of Adonijah. The king rose to meet her, and bowed down to her; then he sat on his throne, and had a throne brought for the king's mother, and she sat on his right. ²⁰Then she said, "I have one small request to make of you; do not refuse me." And the king said to her, "Make your request, my mother; for I will not refuse you." ²¹She said, "Let Abishag the Shunammite be given to your brother Adonijah as his wife." ²²King Solomon answered his mother, "And why do you ask Abishag the Shunammite for Adonijah? Ask for him the kingdom as well! For he is my elder brother; ask not only for him but also for the priest Abiathar and for Joab son of Zeruiah!" ²³Then King Solomon swore by the LORD, "So may God do to me, and more also, for Adonijah has devised this scheme at the risk of his life! ²⁴Now therefore as the LORD lives, who has established me and placed me on the throne of my father David, and who has made me a house as he promised, today Adonijah shall be put to death." ²⁵So King Solomon sent Benaiah son of Jehoiada; he struck him down, and he died.

26 The king said to the priest Abiathar, "Go to Anathoth, to your estate; for you deserve death. But I will not at this time put you to death, because you carried the ark of the Lord GOD before my father David, and because you shared in all the hardships my father endured." ²⁷So Solomon banished Abiathar from being priest to the LORD, thus fulfilling the word of the LORD that he had spoken concerning the house of Eli in Shiloh.

28 When the news came to Joab—for Joab had supported Adonijah though he had not supported Absalom—Joab fled to the tent of the LORD and grasped the horns of the altar. ²⁹When it was told King Solomon, "Joab has fled to the tent of the LORD and now is beside the altar," Solomon sent Benaiah son of Jehoiada, saying, "Go, strike him down." ³⁰So Benaiah came to the tent of the LORD and said to him, "The king commands, 'Come out.' " But he said, "No, I will die here." Then Benaiah brought the king word again, saying, "Thus said Joab, and thus he answered me." ³¹The king replied to him, "Do as he has said, strike him down and bury him; and thus take away from me and from my father's house the guilt for the blood that Joab shed without cause. ³²The LORD will bring back his bloody deeds on his own head, because, without the knowledge of my father David, he attacked and killed with the sword two men more righteous and better than himself, Abner son of Ner, commander of the army of Israel, and Amasa son of Jether, commander of the army of Judah. ³³So shall their blood come back on the head of Joab and on the head of his descendants forever; but to David, and to his descendants, and to his house, and to his throne, there shall be peace from the LORD forevermore." ³⁴Then Benaiah son of Jehoiada went up and struck him down and killed him; and he was buried at his own house near the wilderness. ³⁵The king put Benaiah son of Jehoiada over the army in his place, and the king put the priest Zadok in the place of Abiathar.

36 Then the king sent and summoned Shimei, and said to him, "Build yourself a house in Jerusalem, and live there, and do not go out from there to any place whatever. ³⁷For on the day you go out, and cross the Wadi Kidron, know for certain that you shall die; your blood shall be on your own head." ³⁸And Shimei said to the king, "The sentence is fair; as my lord the king has said, so will your servant do." So Shimei lived in Jerusalem many days.

39 But it happened at the end of three years that two of Shimei's slaves ran away to King Achish son of Maacah of Gath. When it was told Shimei, "Your slaves are

in Gath," ⁴⁰Shimei arose and saddled a donkey, and went to Achish in Gath, to search for his slaves; Shimei went and brought his slaves from Gath. ⁴¹When Solomon was told that Shimei had gone from Jerusalem to Gath and returned, ⁴²the king sent and summoned Shimei, and said to him, "Did I not make you swear by the LORD, and solemnly adjure you, saying, 'Know for certain that on the day you go out and go to any place whatever, you shall die'? And you said to me, 'The sentence is fair; I accept.' ⁴³Why then have you not kept your oath to the LORD and the commandment with which I charged you?" ⁴⁴The king also said to Shimei, "You know in your own heart all the evil that you did to my father David; so the LORD will bring back your evil on your own head. ⁴⁵But King Solomon shall be blessed, and the throne of David shall be established before the LORD forever." ⁴⁶Then the king commanded Benaiah son of Jehoiada; and he went out and struck him down, and he died.

So the kingdom was established in the hand of Solomon.

Solomon's Prayer for Wisdom

3 Solomon made a marriage alliance with Pharaoh king of Egypt; he took Pharaoh's daughter and brought her into the city of David, until he had finished building his own house and the house of the LORD and the wall around Jerusalem. ²The people were sacrificing at the high places, however, because no house had yet been built for the name of the LORD.

3 Solomon loved the LORD, walking in the statutes of his father David; only, he sacrificed and offered incense at the high places. ⁴The king went to Gibeon to sacrifice there, for that was the principal high place; Solomon used to offer a thousand burnt offerings on that altar. ⁵At Gibeon the LORD appeared to Solomon in a dream by night; and God said, "Ask what I should give you." ⁶And Solomon said, "You have shown great and steadfast love to your servant my father David, because he walked before you in faithfulness, in righteousness, and in uprightness of heart toward you; and you have kept for him this great and steadfast love, and have given him a son to sit on his throne today. ⁷And now, O LORD my God, you have made your servant king in place of my father David, although I am only a little

child; I do not know how to go out or come in. ⁸And your servant is in the midst of the people whom you have chosen, a great people, so numerous they cannot be numbered or counted. ⁹Give your servant therefore an understanding mind to govern your people, able to discern between good and evil; for who can govern this your great people?"

10 It pleased the Lord that Solomon had asked this. ¹¹God said to him, "Because you have asked this, and have not asked for yourself long life or riches, or for the life of your enemies, but have asked for yourself understanding to discern what is right, ¹²I now do according to your word. Indeed I give you a wise and discerning mind; no one like you has been before you and no one like you shall arise after you. ¹³I give you also what you have not asked, both riches and honor all your life; no other king shall compare with you. ¹⁴If you will walk in my ways, keeping my statutes and my commandments, as your father David walked, then I will lengthen your life."

15 Then Solomon awoke; it had been a dream. He came to Jerusalem where he stood before the ark of the covenant of the LORD. He offered up burnt offerings and offerings of well-being, and provided a feast for all his servants.

Solomon's Wisdom in Judgment

16 Later, two women who were prostitutes came to the king and stood before him. ¹⁷The one woman said, "Please, my lord, this woman and I live in the same house; and I gave birth while she was in the house. ¹⁸Then on the third day after I gave birth, this woman also gave birth. We were together; there was no one else with us in the house, only the two of us were in the house. ¹⁹Then this woman's son died in the night, because she lay on him. ²⁰She got up in the middle of the night and took my son from beside me while your servant slept. She laid him at her breast, and laid her dead son at my breast. ²¹When I rose in the morning to nurse my son, I saw that he was dead; but when I looked at him closely in the morning, clearly it was not the son I had borne." ²²But the other woman said, "No, the living son is mine, and the dead son is yours." The first said, "No, the dead son is yours, and the living son is mine." So they argued before the king.

23 Then the king said, "The one says, 'This is my son that is alive, and your son is dead'; while the other says, 'Not so! Your son is dead, and my son is the living one.' " 24So the king said, "Bring me a sword," and they brought a sword before the king. 25The king said, "Divide the living boy in two; then give half to the one, and half to the other." 26But the woman whose son was alive said to the king—because compassion for her son burned within her—"Please, my lord, give her the living boy; certainly do not kill him!" The other said, "It shall be neither mine nor yours; divide it." 27Then the king responded: "Give the first woman the living boy; do not kill him. She is his mother." 28All Israel heard of the judgment that the king had rendered; and they stood in awe of the king, because they perceived that the wisdom of God was in him, to execute justice.

Solomon's Administrative Officers

4 King Solomon was king over all Israel, 2and these were his high officials:

Children Are Precious

FRIDAY

Scripture Reading for Today:
1 Kings 3.16–28

Verse for Today:
1 Kings 3.26

I want to be an educated believer. I don't want to offer pat "Christian answers" to challenging conversations, thoughts, and experiences. I want to use "God's grid," to not be too quick with my opinion, but to allow Jesus to sift his truth through me on any given matter. I try to practice this daily in all areas, but one particular area comes to mind.

Realizing I wanted to learn more about the abortion issue in this country, I took a six-week course in the most important aspects of the issue. I have a tender heart for the unborn, and I knew just having an opinion wasn't enough. So I watched videos, listened to interviews, and read documents and statistics. The more educated I became, the more horrified I became.

Right after I completed the course, I performed a concert in Oregon. I spoke boldly that night, more strongly than ever before, on this particular topic. My spirit grieved within me. But then, as I climbed into bed that evening, I found myself wondering whether I had come off too strongly and offended people. Had I gone ahead of God? I asked the Lord to forgive me if I'd spoken out of turn.

Four years later, I returned to that same city. As I signed autographs and talked to as many people as were willing to wait, I noticed a young woman standing over to the side. After everyone left, she approached me. "Kathy," she said, "I had to wait to speak with you. You were here four years ago and spoke out for the unborn." As she spoke, a small child with bouncing blond hair ran to me and wrapped her tiny arms around my neck. "I was going to have an abortion that week," the woman went on. "I want to thank you for what you said that night. This is my little miracle," she finished, drawing the little girl close to her.

Oh, how I want to be about life—because God is about life.

—KATHY TROCCOLI

Go to page 358 for your next devotional reading.

Azariah son of Zadok was the priest; 3Eliphoreph and Ahijah sons of Shisha were secretaries; Jehoshaphat son of Ahilud was recorder; 4Benaiah son of Jehoiada was in command of the army; Zadok and Abiathar were priests; 5Azariah son of Nathan was over the officials; Zabud son of Nathan was priest and king's friend; 6Ahishar was in charge of the palace; and Adoniram son of Abda was in charge of the forced labor.

7 Solomon had twelve officials over all Israel, who provided food for the king and his household; each one had to make provision for one month in the year. 8These were their names: Ben-hur, in the hill country of Ephraim; 9Ben-deker, in Makaz, Shaalbim, Beth-shemesh, and Elon-beth-hanan; 10Ben-hesed, in Arubboth (to him belonged Socoh and all the land of Hepher); 11Ben-abinadab, in all Naphath-dor (he had Taphath, Solomon's daughter, as his wife); 12Baana son of Ahilud, in Taanach, Megiddo, and all Beth-shean, which is beside Zarethan below Jezreel, and from Beth-shean to Abel-meholah, as far as the other side of Jokmeam; 13Bengeber, in Ramoth-gilead (he had the villages of Jair son of Manasseh, which are in Gilead, and he had the region of Argob, which is in Bashan, sixty great cities with walls and bronze bars); 14Ahinadab son of Iddo, in Mahanaim; 15Ahimaaz, in Naphtali (he had taken Basemath, Solomon's daughter, as his wife); 16Baana son of Hushai, in Asher and Bealoth; 17Jehoshaphat son of Paruah, in Issachar; 18Shimei son of Ela, in Benjamin; 19Geber son of Uri, in the land of Gilead, the country of King Sihon of the Amorites and of King Og of Bashan. And there was one official in the land of Judah.

Magnificence of Solomon's Rule

20 Judah and Israel were as numerous as the sand by the sea; they ate and drank and were happy. 21cSolomon was sovereign over all the kingdoms from the Euphrates to the land of the Philistines, even to the border of Egypt; they brought tribute and served Solomon all the days of his life.

22 Solomon's provision for one day was thirty cors of choice flour, and sixty cors of meal, 23ten fat oxen, and twenty pasture-fed cattle, one hundred sheep, besides deer, gazelles, roebucks, and fatted fowl. 24For he had dominion over all the region west of the Euphrates from Tiphsah to Gaza, over all the kings west of the Euphrates; and he had peace on all sides. 25During Solomon's lifetime Judah and Israel lived in safety, from Dan even to Beer-sheba, all of them under their vines and fig trees. 26Solomon also had forty thousand stalls of horses for his chariots, and twelve thousand horsemen. 27Those officials supplied provisions for King Solomon and for all who came to King Solomon's table, each one in his month; they let nothing be lacking. 28They also brought to the required place barley and straw for the horses and swift steeds, each according to his charge.

Fame of Solomon's Wisdom

29 God gave Solomon very great wisdom, discernment, and breadth of understanding as vast as the sand on the seashore, 30so that Solomon's wisdom surpassed the wisdom of all the people of the east, and all the wisdom of Egypt. 31He was wiser than anyone else, wiser than Ethan the Ezrahite, and Heman, Calcol, and Darda, children of Mahol; his fame spread throughout all the surrounding nations. 32He composed three thousand proverbs, and his songs numbered a thousand and five. 33He would speak of trees, from the cedar that is in the Lebanon to the hyssop that grows in the wall; he would speak of animals, and birds, and reptiles, and fish. 34People came from all the nations to hear the wisdom of Solomon; they came from all the kings of the earth who had heard of his wisdom.

Preparations and Materials for the Temple

5 dNow King Hiram of Tyre sent his servants to Solomon, when he heard that they had anointed him king in place of his father; for Hiram had always been a friend to David. 2Solomon sent word to Hiram, saying, 3"You know that my father David could not build a house for the name of the LORD his God because of the warfare with which his enemies surrounded him, until the LORD put them under the soles of his feet.e 4But now the LORD my God has given me rest on every side; there is neither adversary nor misfortune. 5So I intend to build a house for the name of the LORD my God, as the LORD said to my

c Ch 5.1 in Heb   d Ch 5.15 in Heb   e Gk Tg Vg: Heb my feet or his feet father David, 'Your son, whom I will set on your throne in your place, shall build the house for my name.' ⁶Therefore command that cedars from the Lebanon be cut for me. My servants will join your servants, and I will give you whatever wages you set for your servants; for you know that there is no one among us who knows how to cut timber like the Sidonians."

7 When Hiram heard the words of Solomon, he rejoiced greatly, and said, "Blessed be the LORD today, who has given to David a wise son to be over this great people." ⁸Hiram sent word to Solomon, "I have heard the message that you have sent to me; I will fulfill all your needs in the matter of cedar and cypress timber. ⁹My servants shall bring it down to the sea from the Lebanon; I will make it into rafts to go by sea to the place you indicate. I will have them broken up there for you to take away. And you shall meet my needs by providing food for my household." ¹⁰So Hiram supplied Solomon's every need for timber of cedar and cypress. ¹¹Solomon in turn gave Hiram twenty thousand cors of wheat as food for his household, and twenty cors of fine oil. Solomon gave this to Hiram year by year. ¹²So the LORD gave Solomon wisdom, as he promised him. There was peace between Hiram and Solomon; and the two of them made a treaty.

13 King Solomon conscripted forced labor out of all Israel; the levy numbered thirty thousand men. ¹⁴He sent them to the Lebanon, ten thousand a month in shifts; they would be a month in the Lebanon and two months at home; Adoniram was in charge of the forced labor. ¹⁵Solomon also had seventy thousand laborers and eighty thousand stonecutters in the hill country, ¹⁶besides Solomon's three thousand three hundred supervisors who were over the work, having charge of the people who did the work. ¹⁷At the king's command, they quarried out great, costly stones in order to lay the foundation of the house with dressed stones. ¹⁸So Solomon's builders and Hiram's builders and the Gebalites did the stonecutting and prepared the timber and the stone to build the house.

Solomon Builds the Temple

6 In the four hundred eightieth year after the Israelites came out of the land of Egypt, in the fourth year of Solomon's reign over Israel, in the month of Ziv, which is the second month, he began to build the house of the LORD. ²The house that King Solomon built for the LORD was sixty cubits long, twenty cubits wide, and thirty cubits high. ³The vestibule in front of the nave of the house was twenty cubits wide, across the width of the house. Its depth was ten cubits in front of the house. ⁴For the house he made windows with recessed frames.ᶠ ⁵He also built a structure against the wall of the house, running around the walls of the house, both the nave and the inner sanctuary; and he made side chambers all around. ⁶The lowest storyᵍ was five cubits wide, the middle one was six cubits wide, and the third was seven cubits wide; for around the outside of the house he made offsets on the wall in order that the supporting beams should not be inserted into the walls of the house.

7 The house was built with stone finished at the quarry, so that neither hammer nor ax nor any tool of iron was heard in the temple while it was being built.

8 The entrance for the middle story was on the south side of the house: one went up by winding stairs to the middle story, and from the middle story to the third. ⁹So he built the house, and finished it; he roofed the house with beams and planks of cedar. ¹⁰He built the structure against the whole house, each storyʰ five cubits high, and it was joined to the house with timbers of cedar.

11 Now the word of the LORD came to Solomon, ¹²"Concerning this house that you are building, if you will walk in my statutes, obey my ordinances, and keep all my commandments by walking in them, then I will establish my promise with you, which I made to your father David. ¹³I will dwell among the children of Israel, and will not forsake my people Israel."

14 So Solomon built the house, and finished it. ¹⁵He lined the walls of the house on the inside with boards of cedar; from the floor of the house to the rafters of the ceiling, he covered them on the inside with wood; and he covered the floor of the house with boards of cypress. ¹⁶He built twenty cubits of the rear of the house with boards of cedar from the floor to the rafters, and he built this within as an inner sanctuary, as the most holy place. ¹⁷The

---

ᶠ Gk: Meaning of Heb uncertain   ᵍ Gk: Heb structure   ʰ Heb lacks each story

house, that is, the nave in front of the inner sanctuary, was forty cubits long. 18The cedar within the house had carvings of gourds and open flowers; all was cedar, no stone was seen. 19The inner sanctuary he prepared in the innermost part of the house, to set there the ark of the covenant of the LORD. 20The interior of the inner sanctuary was twenty cubits long, twenty cubits wide, and twenty cubits high; he overlaid it with pure gold. He also overlaid the altar with cedar.[i] 21Solomon overlaid the inside of the house with pure gold, then he drew chains of gold across, in front of the inner sanctuary, and overlaid it with gold. 22Next he overlaid the whole house with gold, in order that the whole house might be perfect; even the whole altar that belonged to the inner sanctuary he overlaid with gold.

The Furnishings of the Temple

23 In the inner sanctuary he made two cherubim of olivewood, each ten cubits high. 24Five cubits was the length of one wing of the cherub, and five cubits the length of the other wing of the cherub; it was ten cubits from the tip of one wing to the tip of the other. 25The other cherub also measured ten cubits; both cherubim had the same measure and the same form. 26The height of one cherub was ten cubits, and so was that of the other cherub. 27He put the cherubim in the innermost part of the house; the wings of the cherubim were spread out so that a wing of one was touching the one wall, and a wing of the other cherub was touching the other wall; their other wings toward the center of the house were touching wing to wing. 28He also overlaid the cherubim with gold.

29 He carved the walls of the house all around about with carved engravings of cherubim, palm trees, and open flowers, in the inner and outer rooms. 30The floor of the house he overlaid with gold, in the inner and outer rooms.

31 For the entrance to the inner sanctuary he made doors of olivewood; the lintel and the doorposts were five-sided.[i] 32He covered the two doors of olivewood with carvings of cherubim, palm trees, and open flowers; he overlaid them with gold, and spread gold on the cherubim and on the palm trees.

33 So also he made for the entrance to the nave doorposts of olivewood, four-sided each, 34and two doors of cypress wood; the two leaves of the one door were folding, and the two leaves of the other door were folding. 35He carved cherubim, palm trees, and open flowers, overlaying them with gold evenly applied upon the carved work. 36He built the inner court with three courses of dressed stone to one course of cedar beams.

37 In the fourth year the foundation of the house of the LORD was laid, in the month of Ziv. 38In the eleventh year, in the month of Bul, which is the eighth month, the house was finished in all its parts, and according to all its specifications. He was seven years in building it.

Solomon's Palace and Other Buildings

7 Solomon was building his own house thirteen years, and he finished his entire house.

2 He built the House of the Forest of the Lebanon one hundred cubits long, fifty cubits wide, and thirty cubits high, built on four rows of cedar pillars, with cedar beams on the pillars. 3It was roofed with cedar on the forty-five rafters, fifteen in each row, which were on the pillars. 4There were window frames in the three rows, facing each other in the three rows. 5All the doorways and doorposts had four-sided frames, opposite, facing each other in the three rows.

6 He made the Hall of Pillars fifty cubits long and thirty cubits wide. There was a porch in front with pillars, and a canopy in front of them.

7 He made the Hall of the Throne where he was to pronounce judgment, the Hall of Justice, covered with cedar from floor to floor.

8 His own house where he would reside, in the other court back of the hall, was of the same construction. Solomon also made a house like this hall for Pharaoh's daughter, whom he had taken in marriage.

9 All these were made of costly stones, cut according to measure, sawed with saws, back and front, from the foundation to the coping, and from outside to the great court. 10The foundation was of costly stones, huge stones, stones of eight and ten cubits. 11There were costly stones above, cut to measure, and cedarwood. 12The great court had three courses of dressed stone to one layer of cedar beams

[i] Meaning of Heb uncertain

Tamar, Daughter-in-Law of Judah

Her Name Means *"Date Tree"* or *"Palm Tree"*

Read Genesis 38; Matthew 1.3
Genealogies hardly make compelling reading. But even long lists of bewildering names can reveal interesting insights into God's plan. Take the genealogy in the first chapter of Matthew, for instance. It lists a grand total of 41 male ancestors of Jesus, beginning with Abraham, and a mere five female ancestors, three of whose stories (Tamar, Rahab, and Bathsheba) are colored by such distasteful details as incest, prostitution, adultery, and murder.

Jesus, it seems, had plenty of imperfect branches in his family tree and enough colorful characters to populate a modern romance novel. That women should be listed at all is surprising, let alone that four of the five got pregnant out of wedlock. In addition, four of the women were foreigners—non-Israelites.

Tamar was one of these—a foreigner who became pregnant by a man other than her husband. Years earlier, she had married the eldest son of Judah (the fourth child of Leah and Jacob). But her husband died and, in keeping with the custom of the day, Judah arranged for his second son to marry Tamar so that an heir could be provided for his eldest son. But this husband died also.

Already Judah had lost two sons, but to placate his daughter-in-law, he promised her his youngest and only remaining son, instructing her to return to her father's house until the boy was of marriageable age. But

Her Character: *Driven by one overwhelming need, she sacrificed her reputation, and nearly her life, to achieve her goals.*
Her Sorrow: *That the men in her life failed to keep their promises, leaving her a childless widow.*
Her Joy: *That her daring behavior resulted, not in ruin, but in the fulfillment of her hopes to have children.*

the years passed like a lazy river, and still there was no marriage.

One day, after Judah's wife had died, he set out for a place called Timnah. Hearing the news of his journey, Tamar covered herself with a veil and sat down beside the road to Timnah, passing herself off as a prostitute. That day Judah slept with her, leaving behind his personal seal and cord along with his staff in pledge of future payment.

About three months later, Judah learned of Tamar's pregnancy. Outraged, he ordered her burned to death. But before the sentence could be carried out, Tamar sent him a stunning message: " 'It was the owner of these who made me pregnant.' And she said, 'Take note, please, whose these are, the signet and the cord and the staff' " (verse 25).

The man who had so quickly passed judgment, little heeding his own tryst with a prostitute, was suddenly taken up short, saying: "She is more in the right than I, since I did not give her to my son Shelah" (verse 26).

Six months later, Tamar gave birth to twins. As with Jacob and Esau, the children struggled in her womb. A tiny hand came out and then disappeared, but not before being tied with a scarlet thread by the midwife. Then a small, slippery body emerged, but with no trace of the red thread. They named the first boy Perez (meaning "breach"). Then the little one with the ribbon around his wrist was born, and they named him Zerah (meaning "brightness" or "scarlet"). Perez was recognized as the firstborn. From his line would come King David and finally, hundreds of years later, Jesus of Nazareth.

God used Tamar's determination to ensure that the tribe of Judah would survive and one day bring forth the world's Messiah.

Praying With Tamar

And Judah [was] the father of Perez and Zerah by Tamar.—*Matthew 1.3*

Praise God: *That he allowed his own son to be so intimately linked with fallen human beings.*

Thank God: *That he can use everyone and everything to bring about a good result.*

Confess: *Any tendency you may have to judge others with a double standard, as Judah did Tamar.*

Ask God: *To take any desperation you may be feeling and replace it with hope, calling to mind Jeremiah 29.11: "For surely I know the plans I have for you, says the LORD, plans for your welfare and not for harm, to give you a future with hope."*

Lift Your Heart

If you've never sketched out your family tree, make an effort to trace your heritage, going back at least four or five generations—more if you have the time and energy. Ask older relatives to supply as much information as possible about your ancestors. Pay special attention to the women in your family tree. Take notes on everything you discover. Then transcribe all the information into a keepsake book that can be passed along to your own children. Include any photos and news clippings you can find.

Lord, you formed me in my mother's womb. You knew then what every single day of my life would be like. You saw the great things and the hard things, the joy and the sorrow. Right now I come before you with the situation (or the memory) with which I have not yet made peace. As I look back at painful circumstances, help me to realize that you were present even in the midst of them. And now, as I surrender them to you, help me to sense your healing presence in my life.

Go to page 366 for your next devotional reading.

all around; so had the inner court of the house of the LORD, and the vestibule of the house.

Products of Hiram the Bronzeworker

13 Now King Solomon invited and received Hiram from Tyre. [14]He was the son of a widow of the tribe of Naphtali, whose father, a man of Tyre, had been an artisan in bronze; he was full of skill, intelligence, and knowledge in working bronze. He came to King Solomon, and did all his work.

15 He cast two pillars of bronze. Eighteen cubits was the height of the one, and a cord of twelve cubits would encircle it; the second pillar was the same.[j] [16]He also made two capitals of molten bronze, to set on the tops of the pillars; the height of the one capital was five cubits, and the height of the other capital was five cubits. [17]There were nets of checker work with wreaths of chain work for the capitals on the tops of the pillars; seven[k] for the one capital, and seven[k] for the other capital. [18]He made the columns with two rows around each latticework to cover the capitals that were above the pomegranates; he did the same with the other capital. [19]Now the capitals that were on the tops of the pillars in the vestibule were of lily-work, four cubits high. [20]The capitals were on the two pillars and also above the rounded projection that was beside the latticework; there were two hundred pomegranates in rows all around; and so with the other capital. [21]He set up the pillars at the vestibule of the temple; he set up the pillar on the south and called it Jachin; and he set up the pillar on the north and called it Boaz. [22]On the tops of the pillars was lily-work. Thus the work of the pillars was finished.

23 Then he made the molten sea; it was round, ten cubits from brim to brim, and five cubits high. A line of thirty cubits would encircle it completely. [24]Under its brim were panels all around it, each of ten cubits, surrounding the sea; there were two rows of panels, cast when it was cast. [25]It stood on twelve oxen, three facing north, three facing west, three facing south, and three facing east; the sea was set on them. The hindquarters of each were toward the inside. [26]Its thickness was a handbreadth; its brim was made like the brim of a cup, like the flower of a lily; it held two thousand baths.[l]

27 He also made the ten stands of bronze; each stand was four cubits long, four cubits wide, and three cubits high. [28]This was the construction of the stands: they had borders; the borders were within the frames; [29]on the borders that were set in the frames were lions, oxen, and cherubim. On the frames, both above and below the lions and oxen, there were wreaths of beveled work. [30]Each stand had four bronze wheels and axles of bronze; at the four corners were supports for a basin. The supports were cast with wreaths at the side of each. [31]Its opening was within the crown whose height was one cubit; its opening was round, as a pedestal is made; it was a cubit and a half wide. At its opening there were carvings; its borders were four-sided, not round. [32]The four wheels were underneath the borders; the axles of the wheels were in the stands; and the height of a wheel was a cubit and a half. [33]The wheels were made like a chariot wheel; their axles, their rims, their spokes, and their hubs were all cast. [34]There were four supports at the four corners of each stand; the supports were of one piece with the stands. [35]On the top of the stand there was a round band half a cubit high; on the top of the stand, its stays and its borders were of one piece with it. [36]On the surfaces of its stays and on its borders he carved cherubim, lions, and palm trees, where each had space, with wreaths all around. [37]In this way he made the ten stands; all of them were cast alike, with the same size and the same form.

38 He made ten basins of bronze; each basin held forty baths,[l] each basin measured four cubits; there was a basin for each of the ten stands. [39]He set five of the stands on the south side of the house, and five on the north side of the house; he set the sea on the southeast corner of the house.

40 Hiram also made the pots, the shovels, and the basins. So Hiram finished all the work that he did for King Solomon on the house of the LORD: [41]the two pillars, the two bowls of the capitals that were on the tops of the pillars, the two latticeworks to cover the two bowls of the capitals that were on the tops of the pillars;

---

[j] Cn: Heb *and a cord of twelve cubits encircled the second pillar*; Compare Jer 52.21   [k] Heb: Gk *a net*   [l] A Heb measure of volume

42the four hundred pomegranates for the two latticeworks, two rows of pomegranates for each latticework, to cover the two bowls of the capitals that were on the pillars; 43the ten stands, the ten basins on the stands; 44the one sea, and the twelve oxen underneath the sea.

45 The pots, the shovels, and the basins, all these vessels that Hiram made for King Solomon for the house of the LORD were of burnished bronze. 46In the plain of the Jordan the king cast them, in the clay ground between Succoth and Zarethan. 47Solomon left all the vessels unweighed, because there were so many of them; the weight of the bronze was not determined.

48 So Solomon made all the vessels that were in the house of the LORD: the golden altar, the golden table for the bread of the Presence, 49the lampstands of pure gold, five on the south side and five on the north, in front of the inner sanctuary; the flowers, the lamps, and the tongs, of gold; 50the cups, snuffers, basins, dishes for incense, and firepans, of pure gold; the sockets for the doors of the innermost part of the house, the most holy place, and for the doors of the nave of the temple, of gold.

51 Thus all the work that King Solomon did on the house of the LORD was finished. Solomon brought in the things that his father David had dedicated, the silver, the gold, and the vessels, and stored them in the treasuries of the house of the LORD.

Dedication of the Temple

8 Then Solomon assembled the elders of Israel and all the heads of the tribes, the leaders of the ancestral houses of the Israelites, before King Solomon in Jerusalem, to bring up the ark of the covenant of the LORD out of the city of David, which is Zion. 2All the people of Israel assembled to King Solomon at the festival in the month Ethanim, which is the seventh month. 3And all the elders of Israel came, and the priests carried the ark. 4So they brought up the ark of the LORD, the tent of meeting, and all the holy vessels that were in the tent; the priests and the Levites brought them up. 5King Solomon and all the congregation of Israel, who had assembled before him, were with him before the ark, sacrificing so many sheep and oxen that they could not be counted

or numbered. 6Then the priests brought the ark of the covenant of the LORD to its place, in the inner sanctuary of the house, in the most holy place, underneath the wings of the cherubim. 7For the cherubim spread out their wings over the place of the ark, so that the cherubim made a covering above the ark and its poles. 8The poles were so long that the ends of the poles were seen from the holy place in front of the inner sanctuary; but they could not be seen from outside; they are there to this day. 9There was nothing in the ark except the two tablets of stone that Moses had placed there at Horeb, where the LORD made a covenant with the Israelites, when they came out of the land of Egypt. 10And when the priests came out of the holy place, a cloud filled the house of the LORD, 11so that the priests could not stand to minister because of the cloud; for the glory of the LORD filled the house of the LORD.

12 Then Solomon said,

"The LORD has said that he would
    dwell in thick darkness.
13 I have built you an exalted house,
    a place for you to dwell in
        forever."

Solomon's Speech

14 Then the king turned around and blessed all the assembly of Israel, while all the assembly of Israel stood. 15He said, "Blessed be the LORD, the God of Israel, who with his hand has fulfilled what he promised with his mouth to my father David, saying, 16'Since the day that I brought my people Israel out of Egypt, I have not chosen a city from any of the tribes of Israel in which to build a house, that my name might be there; but I chose David to be over my people Israel.' 17My father David had it in mind to build a house for the name of the LORD, the God of Israel. 18But the LORD said to my father David, 'You did well to consider building a house for my name; 19nevertheless you shall not build the house, but your son who shall be born to you shall build the house for my name.' 20Now the LORD has upheld the promise that he made; for I have risen in the place of my father David; I sit on the throne of Israel, as the LORD promised, and have built the house for the name of the LORD, the God of Israel. 21There I have provided a place for the ark, in which is the covenant of the LORD

that he made with our ancestors when he brought them out of the land of Egypt."

Solomon's Prayer of Dedication

22 Then Solomon stood before the altar of the LORD in the presence of all the assembly of Israel, and spread out his hands to heaven. 23He said, "O LORD, God of Israel, there is no God like you in heaven above or on earth beneath, keeping covenant and steadfast love for your servants who walk before you with all their heart, 24the covenant that you kept for your servant my father David as you declared to him; you promised with your mouth and have this day fulfilled with your hand. 25Therefore, O LORD, God of Israel, keep for your servant my father David that which you promised him, saying, 'There shall never fail you a successor before me to sit on the throne of Israel, if only your children look to their way, to walk before me as you have walked before me.' 26Therefore, O God of Israel, let your word be confirmed, which you promised to your servant my father David.

27 "But will God indeed dwell on the earth? Even heaven and the highest heaven cannot contain you, much less this house that I have built! 28Regard your servant's prayer and his plea, O LORD my God, heeding the cry and the prayer that your servant prays to you today; 29that your eyes may be open night and day toward this house, the place of which you said, 'My name shall be there,' that you may heed the prayer that your servant prays toward this place. 30Hear the plea of your servant and of your people Israel when they pray toward this place; O hear in heaven your dwelling place; heed and forgive.

31 "If someone sins against a neighbor and is given an oath to swear, and comes and swears before your altar in this house, 32then hear in heaven, and act, and judge your servants, condemning the guilty by bringing their conduct on their own head, and vindicating the righteous by rewarding them according to their righteousness.

33 "When your people Israel, having sinned against you, are defeated before an enemy but turn again to you, confess your name, pray and plead with you in this house, 34then hear in heaven, forgive the sin of your people Israel, and bring them again to the land that you gave to their ancestors.

35 "When heaven is shut up and there is no rain because they have sinned against you, and then they pray toward this place, confess your name, and turn from their sin, because you punish[m] them, 36then hear in heaven, and forgive the sin of your servants, your people Israel, when you teach them the good way in which they should walk; and grant rain on your land, which you have given to your people as an inheritance.

37 "If there is famine in the land, if there is plague, blight, mildew, locust, or caterpillar; if their enemy besieges them in any[n] of their cities; whatever plague, whatever sickness there is; 38whatever prayer, whatever plea there is from any individual or from all your people Israel, all knowing the afflictions of their own hearts so that they stretch out their hands toward this house; 39then hear in heaven your dwelling place, forgive, act, and render to all whose hearts you know—according to all their ways, for only you know what is in every human heart— 40so that they may fear you all the days that they live in the land that you gave to our ancestors.

41 "Likewise when a foreigner, who is not of your people Israel, comes from a distant land because of your name 42—for they shall hear of your great name, your mighty hand, and your outstretched arm—when a foreigner comes and prays toward this house, 43then hear in heaven your dwelling place, and do according to all that the foreigner calls to you, so that all the peoples of the earth may know your name and fear you, as do your people Israel, and so that they may know that your name has been invoked on this house that I have built.

44 "If your people go out to battle against their enemy, by whatever way you shall send them, and they pray to the LORD toward the city that you have chosen and the house that I have built for your name, 45then hear in heaven their prayer and their plea, and maintain their cause.

46 "If they sin against you—for there is no one who does not sin—and you are angry with them and give them to an enemy, so that they are carried away captive to the land of the enemy, far off or near; 47yet if they come to their senses in the land to which they have been taken cap-

---

[m] Or when you answer   [n] Gk Syr: Heb in the land

tive, and repent, and plead with you in the land of their captors, saying, 'We have sinned, and have done wrong; we have acted wickedly'; ⁴⁸if they repent with all their heart and soul in the land of their enemies, who took them captive, and pray to you toward their land, which you gave to their ancestors, the city that you have chosen, and the house that I have built for your name; ⁴⁹then hear in heaven your dwelling place their prayer and their plea, maintain their cause ⁵⁰and forgive your people who have sinned against you, and all their transgressions that they have committed against you; and grant them compassion in the sight of their captors, so that they may have compassion on them ⁵¹(for they are your people and heritage, which you brought out of Egypt, from the midst of the iron-smelter). ⁵²Let your eyes be open to the plea of your servant, and to the plea of your people Israel, listening to them whenever they call to you. ⁵³For you have separated them from among all the peoples of the earth, to be your heritage, just as you promised through Moses, your servant, when you brought our ancestors out of Egypt, O Lord GOD."

Solomon Blesses the Assembly

54 Now when Solomon finished offering all this prayer and this plea to the LORD, he arose from facing the altar of the LORD, where he had knelt with hands outstretched toward heaven; ⁵⁵he stood and blessed all the assembly of Israel with a loud voice:

56 "Blessed be the LORD, who has given rest to his people Israel according to all that he promised; not one word has failed of all his good promise, which he spoke through his servant Moses. ⁵⁷The LORD our God be with us, as he was with our ancestors; may he not leave us or abandon us, ⁵⁸but incline our hearts to him, to walk in all his ways, and to keep his commandments, his statutes, and his ordinances, which he commanded our ancestors. ⁵⁹Let these words of mine, with which I pleaded before the LORD, be near to the LORD our God day and night, and may he maintain the cause of his servant and the cause of his people Israel, as each day requires; ⁶⁰so that all the peoples of the earth may know that the LORD is God; there is no other. ⁶¹Therefore devote yourselves completely to the LORD our God, walking in his statutes and keeping his commandments, as at this day."

Solomon Offers Sacrifices

62 Then the king, and all Israel with him, offered sacrifice before the LORD. ⁶³Solomon offered as sacrifices of well-being to the LORD twenty-two thousand oxen and one hundred twenty thousand sheep. So the king and all the people of Israel dedicated the house of the LORD. ⁶⁴The same day the king consecrated the middle of the court that was in front of the house of the LORD; for there he offered the burnt offerings and the grain offerings and the fat pieces of the sacrifices of well-being, because the bronze altar that was before the LORD was too small to receive the burnt offerings and the grain offerings and the fat pieces of the sacrifices of well-being.

65 So Solomon held the festival at that time, and all Israel with him—a great assembly, people from Lebo-hamath to the Wadi of Egypt—before the LORD our God, seven days.ᵒ ⁶⁶On the eighth day he sent the people away; and they blessed the king, and went to their tents, joyful and in good spirits because of all the goodness that the LORD had shown to his servant David and to his people Israel.

God Appears Again to Solomon

9 When Solomon had finished building the house of the LORD and the king's house and all that Solomon desired to build, ²the LORD appeared to Solomon a second time, as he had appeared to him at Gibeon. ³The LORD said to him, "I have heard your prayer and your plea, which you made before me; I have consecrated this house that you have built, and put my name there forever; my eyes and my heart will be there for all time. ⁴As for you, if you will walk before me, as David your father walked, with integrity of heart and uprightness, doing according to all that I have commanded you, and keeping my statutes and my ordinances, ⁵then I will establish your royal throne over Israel forever, as I promised your father David, saying, 'There shall not fail you a successor on the throne of Israel.'

6 "If you turn aside from following me, you or your children, and do not keep

ᵒ Compare Gk: Heb seven days and seven days, fourteen days

my commandments and my statutes that I have set before you, but go and serve other gods and worship them, ⁷then I will cut Israel off from the land that I have given them; and the house that I have consecrated for my name I will cast out of my sight; and Israel will become a proverb and a taunt among all peoples. ⁸This house will become a heap of ruins;ᵖ everyone passing by it will be astonished, and will hiss; and they will say, 'Why has the LORD done such a thing to this land and to this house?' ⁹Then they will say, 'Because they have forsaken the LORD their God, who brought their ancestors out of the land of Egypt, and embraced other gods, worshiping them and serving them; therefore the LORD has brought this disaster upon them.' "

10 At the end of twenty years, in which Solomon had built the two houses, the house of the LORD and the king's house, ¹¹King Hiram of Tyre having supplied Solomon with cedar and cypress timber and gold, as much as he desired, King Solomon gave to Hiram twenty cities in the land of Galilee. ¹²But when Hiram came from Tyre to see the cities that Solomon had given him, they did not please him. ¹³Therefore he said, "What kind of cities are these that you have given me, my brother?" So they are called the land of Cabulᵠ to this day. ¹⁴But Hiram had sent to the king one hundred twenty talents of gold.

Other Acts of Solomon

15 This is the account of the forced labor that King Solomon conscripted to build the house of the LORD and his own house, the Millo and the wall of Jerusalem, Hazor, Megiddo, Gezer ¹⁶(Pharaoh king of Egypt had gone up and captured Gezer and burned it down, had killed the Canaanites who lived in the city, and had given it as dowry to his daughter, Solomon's wife; ¹⁷so Solomon rebuilt Gezer), Lower Beth-horon, ¹⁸Baalath, Tamar in the wilderness, within the land, ¹⁹as well as all of Solomon's storage cities, the cities for his chariots, the cities for his cavalry, and whatever Solomon desired to build, in Jerusalem, in Lebanon, and in all the land of his dominion. ²⁰All the people who were left of the Amorites, the Hittites, the Perizzites, the Hivites, and the Jebusites, who were not of the people of Israel— ²¹their descendants who were still left

in the land, whom the Israelites were unable to destroy completely—these Solomon conscripted for slave labor, and so they are to this day. ²²But of the Israelites Solomon made no slaves; they were the soldiers, they were his officials, his commanders, his captains, and the commanders of his chariotry and cavalry.

23 These were the chief officers who were over Solomon's work: five hundred fifty, who had charge of the people who carried on the work.

24 But Pharaoh's daughter went up from the city of David to her own house that Solomon had built for her; then he built the Millo.

25 Three times a year Solomon used to offer up burnt offerings and sacrifices of well-being on the altar that he built for the LORD, offering incenseʳ before the LORD. So he completed the house.

Solomon's Commercial Activity

26 King Solomon built a fleet of ships at Ezion-geber, which is near Eloth on the shore of the Red Sea,ˢ in the land of Edom. ²⁷Hiram sent his servants with the fleet, sailors who were familiar with the sea, together with the servants of Solomon. ²⁸They went to Ophir, and imported from there four hundred twenty talents of gold, which they delivered to King Solomon.

Visit of the Queen of Sheba

10 When the queen of Sheba heard of the fame of Solomon (fame due toᵗ the name of the LORD), she came to test him with hard questions. ²She came to Jerusalem with a very great retinue, with camels bearing spices, and very much gold, and precious stones; and when she came to Solomon, she told him all that was on her mind. ³Solomon answered all her questions; there was nothing hidden from the king that he could not explain to her. ⁴When the queen of Sheba had observed all the wisdom of Solomon, the house that he had built, ⁵the food of his table, the seating of his officials, and the attendance of his servants, their clothing, his valets, and his burnt offerings that he offered at the

ᵖ Syr Old Latin: Heb *will become high*   ᵠ Perhaps meaning *a land good for nothing*   ʳ Gk: Heb *offering incense with it that was*   ˢ Or *Sea of Reeds*   ᵗ Meaning of Heb uncertain

house of the LORD, there was no more spirit in her.

6 So she said to the king, "The report was true that I heard in my own land of your accomplishments and of your wisdom, 7but I did not believe the reports until I came and my own eyes had seen it. Not even half had been told me; your wisdom and prosperity far surpass the report that I had heard. 8Happy are your wives!u Happy are these your servants, who continually attend you and hear your wisdom! 9Blessed be the LORD your God, who has delighted in you and set you on the throne of Israel! Because the LORD loved Israel forever, he has made you king to execute justice and righteousness." 10Then she gave the king one hundred twenty talents of gold, a great quantity of spices, and precious stones; never again did spices come in such quantity as that which the queen of Sheba gave to King Solomon.

11 Moreover, the fleet of Hiram, which carried gold from Ophir, brought from Ophir a great quantity of almug wood and precious stones. 12From the almug wood the king made supports for the house of the LORD, and for the king's house, lyres also and harps for the singers; no such almug wood has come or been seen to this day.

13 Meanwhile King Solomon gave to the queen of Sheba every desire that she expressed, as well as what he gave her out of Solomon's royal bounty. Then she returned to her own land, with her servants.

14 The weight of gold that came to Solomon in one year was six hundred sixty-six talents of gold, 15besides that which came from the traders and from the business of the merchants, and from all the kings of Arabia and the governors of the land. 16King Solomon made two hundred large shields of beaten gold; six hundred shekels of gold went into each large shield. 17He made three hundred shields of beaten gold; three minas of gold went into each shield; and the king put them in the House of the Forest of Lebanon. 18The king also made a great ivory throne, and overlaid it with the finest gold. 19The throne had six steps. The top of the throne was rounded in the back, and on each side of the seat were arm rests and two lions standing beside the arm rests, 20while twelve lions were standing, one on each end of a step on the six steps. Nothing like

it was ever made in any kingdom. 21All King Solomon's drinking vessels were of gold, and all the vessels of the House of the Forest of Lebanon were of pure gold; none were of silver—it was not considered as anything in the days of Solomon. 22For the king had a fleet of ships of Tarshish at sea with the fleet of Hiram. Once every three years the fleet of ships of Tarshish used to come bringing gold, silver, ivory, apes, and peacocks.v

23 Thus King Solomon excelled all the kings of the earth in riches and in wisdom. 24The whole earth sought the presence of Solomon to hear his wisdom, which God had put into his mind. 25Every one of them brought a present, objects of silver and gold, garments, weaponry, spices, horses, and mules, so much year by year.

26 Solomon gathered together chariots and horses; he had fourteen hundred chariots and twelve thousand horses, which he stationed in the chariot cities and with the king in Jerusalem. 27The king made silver as common in Jerusalem as stones, and he made cedars as numerous as the sycamores of the Shephelah. 28Solomon's import of horses was from Egypt and Kue, and the king's traders received them from Kue at a price. 29A chariot could be imported from Egypt for six hundred shekels of silver, and a horse for one hundred fifty; so through the king's traders they were exported to all the kings of the Hittites and the kings of Aram.

Solomon's Errors

11 King Solomon loved many foreign women along with the daughter of Pharaoh: Moabite, Ammonite, Edomite, Sidonian, and Hittite women, 2from the nations concerning which the LORD had said to the Israelites, "You shall not enter into marriage with them, neither shall they with you; for they will surely incline your heart to follow their gods"; Solomon clung to these in love. 3Among his wives were seven hundred princesses and three hundred concubines; and his wives turned away his heart. 4For when Solomon was old, his wives turned away his heart after other gods; and his heart was not true to the LORD his God, as was the heart of his father David. 5For Solomon followed Astarte the goddess of the

u Gk Syr: Heb *men*   v Or *baboons*

Sidonians, and Milcom the abomination of the Ammonites. 6So Solomon did what was evil in the sight of the LORD, and did not completely follow the LORD, as his father David had done. 7Then Solomon built a high place for Chemosh the abom-ination of Moab, and for Molech the abomination of the Ammonites, on the mountain east of Jerusalem. 8He did the same for all his foreign wives, who offered incense and sacrificed to their gods.

Starting and Finishing

MONDAY

Scripture Reading for Today:
I Kings 11.1–10

Verse for Today:
I Kings 11.4

She was shy, plump, bookish—not a formula for social success at Suburban High. The trendsetters passed her by, no cool guys ever called.

Ten years later at the class reunion, it was a different story. She was poised and radiant, obviously successful. Pretty, too. "Who are you?" the guys wanted to know, flocking around. Funny how *they'd* changed. The once handsome one was looking a lot like his bald, beer-bellied father. Mr. "Most Popular" had a nervous twitch and seemed to be making a mess of his relationships.

Amazing, isn't it, how just about any class reunion can yield some good moral tales? *People don't necessarily turn out as you thought they would. Ugly ducklings grow into gracious swans. Good starts don't guarantee good finishes.*

The first book of Kings offers a "good start/bad finish" story that rivals any sobering tale you might bring back from a reunion. If ever anyone was "most likely to succeed," it was Solomon. Wealth, rank, good looks, a God-loving father—Solomon had it all. Best of all, he enjoyed God's special favor.

"Ask what I should give you," God offered when Solomon be-came king. Matchless wisdom was granted him, with matchless wealth thrown in (see I Kings 3.5–14).

But talk about dashed expectations! Despite the best of starts, Solomon went wrong—a victim of that classic spiritual disease, "God *and* . . ." Solomon "loved the LORD," *and* he loved his foreign wives too—enough to worship their gods. In the end, because "his heart was not true to the LORD," Solomon failed to realize the promise of his early years (I Kings 3.3; 11.4).

What can we learn from Solomon?

That front-runners, no matter how promising, won't stay the course if they don't put God first. That each of us—whether ugly duckling or "most likely to succeed"—must be eager, as Peter urges us, to make our "call and election" firm. "For in this way,"—and not by coasting on our gifts—"entry into the eternal kingdom of our Lord and Savior Jesus Christ will be richly provided for you" (2 Peter 1.10–11).

—*LOUISE PERROTTA*

Go to page 377 for your next devotional reading.

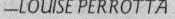

9 Then the LORD was angry with Solomon, because his heart had turned away from the LORD, the God of Israel, who had appeared to him twice, 10and had commanded him concerning this matter, that he should not follow other gods; but he did not observe what the LORD commanded. 11Therefore the LORD said to Solomon, "Since this has been your mind and you have not kept my covenant and my statutes that I have commanded you, I will surely tear the kingdom from you and give it to your servant. 12Yet for the sake of your father David I will not do it in your lifetime; I will tear it out of the hand of your son. 13I will not, however, tear away the entire kingdom; I will give one tribe to your son, for the sake of my servant David and for the sake of Jerusalem, which I have chosen."

Adversaries of Solomon

14 Then the LORD raised up an adversary against Solomon, Hadad the Edomite; he was of the royal house in Edom. 15For when David was in Edom, and Joab the commander of the army went up to bury the dead, he killed every male in Edom 16(for Joab and all Israel remained there six months, until he had eliminated every male in Edom); 17but Hadad fled to Egypt with some Edomites who were servants of his father. He was a young boy at that time. 18They set out from Midian and came to Paran; they took people with them from Paran and came to Egypt, to Pharaoh king of Egypt, who gave him a house, assigned him an allowance of food, and gave him land. 19Hadad found great favor in the sight of Pharaoh, so that he gave him his sister-in-law for a wife, the sister of Queen Tahpenes. 20The sister of Tahpenes gave birth by him to his son Genubath, whom Tahpenes weaned in Pharaoh's house; Genubath was in Pharaoh's house among the children of Pharaoh. 21When Hadad heard in Egypt that David slept with his ancestors and that Joab the commander of the army was dead, Hadad said to Pharaoh, "Let me depart, that I may go to my own country." 22But Pharaoh said to him, "What do you lack with me that you now seek to go to your own country?" And he said, "No, do let me go."

23 God raised up another adversary against Solomon,w Rezon son of Eliada, who had fled from his master, King Hadadezer of Zobah. 24He gathered followers around him and became leader of a marauding band, after the slaughter by David; they went to Damascus, settled there, and made him king in Damascus. 25He was an adversary of Israel all the days of Solomon, making trouble as Hadad did; he despised Israel and reigned over Aram.

Jeroboam's Rebellion

26 Jeroboam son of Nebat, an Ephraimite of Zeredah, a servant of Solomon, whose mother's name was Zeruah, a widow, rebelled against the king. 27The following was the reason he rebelled against the king. Solomon built the Millo, and closed up the gap in the wallx of the city of his father David. 28The man Jeroboam was very able, and when Solomon saw that the young man was industrious he gave him charge over all the forced labor of the house of Joseph. 29About that time, when Jeroboam was leaving Jerusalem, the prophet Ahijah the Shilonite found him on the road. Ahijah had clothed himself with a new garment. The two of them were alone in the open country 30when Ahijah laid hold of the new garment he was wearing and tore it into twelve pieces. 31He then said to Jeroboam: Take for yourself ten pieces; for thus says the LORD, the God of Israel, "See, I am about to tear the kingdom from the hand of Solomon, and will give you ten tribes. 32One tribe will remain his, for the sake of my servant David and for the sake of Jerusalem, the city that I have chosen out of all the tribes of Israel. 33This is because he hasy forsaken me, worshiped Astarte the goddess of the Sidonians, Chemosh the god of Moab, and Milcom the god of the Ammonites, and hasy not walked in my ways, doing what is right in my sight and keeping my statutes and my ordinances, as his father David did. 34Nevertheless I will not take the whole kingdom away from him but will make him ruler all the days of his life, for the sake of my servant David whom I chose and who did keep my commandments and my statutes; 35but I will take the kingdom away from his son and give it to you—that is, the ten tribes. 36Yet to his son I will give one tribe, so that my servant David may always have a lamp before me in Jerusalem, the city where I have

w Heb *him*   x Heb lacks *in the wall*   y Gk Syr Vg: Heb *they have* chosen to put my name. 37I will take you, and you shall reign over all that your soul desires; you shall be king over Israel. 38If you will listen to all that I command you, walk in my ways, and do what is right in my sight by keeping my statutes and my commandments, as David my servant did, I will be with you, and will build you an enduring house, as I built for David, and I will give Israel to you. 39For this reason I will punish the descendants of David, but not forever." 40Solomon sought therefore to kill Jeroboam; but Jeroboam promptly fled to Egypt, to King Shishak of Egypt, and remained in Egypt until the death of Solomon.

Death of Solomon

41 Now the rest of the acts of Solomon, all that he did as well as his wisdom, are they not written in the Book of the Acts of Solomon? 42The time that Solomon reigned in Jerusalem over all Israel was forty years. 43Solomon slept with his ancestors and was buried in the city of his father David; and his son Rehoboam succeeded him.

The Northern Tribes Secede

12 Rehoboam went to Shechem, for all Israel had come to Shechem to make him king. 2When Jeroboam son of Nebat heard of it (for he was still in Egypt, where he had fled from King Solomon), then Jeroboam returned from^z Egypt. 3And they sent and called him; and Jeroboam and all the assembly of Israel came and said to Rehoboam, 4"Your father made our yoke heavy. Now therefore lighten the hard service of your father and his heavy yoke that he placed on us, and we will serve you." 5He said to them, "Go away for three days, then come again to me." So the people went away.

6 Then King Rehoboam took counsel with the older men who had attended his father Solomon while he was still alive, saying, "How do you advise me to answer this people?" 7They answered him, "If you will be a servant to this people today and serve them, and speak good words to them when you answer them, then they will be your servants forever." 8But he disregarded the advice that the older men gave him, and consulted with the young men who had grown up with him and now attended him. 9He said to them, "What do you advise that we answer this

people who have said to me, 'Lighten the yoke that your father put on us'?" 10The young men who had grown up with him said to him, "Thus you should say to this people who spoke to you, 'Your father made our yoke heavy, but you must lighten it for us'; thus you should say to them, 'My little finger is thicker than my father's loins. 11Now, whereas my father laid on you a heavy yoke, I will add to your yoke. My father disciplined you with whips, but I will discipline you with scorpions.' "

12 So Jeroboam and all the people came to Rehoboam the third day, as the king had said, "Come to me again the third day." 13The king answered the people harshly. He disregarded the advice that the older men had given him 14and spoke to them according to the advice of the young men, "My father made your yoke heavy, but I will add to your yoke; my father disciplined you with whips, but I will discipline you with scorpions." 15So the king did not listen to the people, because it was a turn of affairs brought about by the LORD that he might fulfill his word, which the LORD had spoken by Ahijah the Shilonite to Jeroboam son of Nebat.

16 When all Israel saw that the king would not listen to them, the people answered the king,

"What share do we have in David?
　We have no inheritance in the son
　　of Jesse.
To your tents, O Israel!
　Look now to your own house,
　　O David."

So Israel went away to their tents. 17But Rehoboam reigned over the Israelites who were living in the towns of Judah. 18When King Rehoboam sent Adoram, who was taskmaster over the forced labor, all Israel stoned him to death. King Rehoboam then hurriedly mounted his chariot to flee to Jerusalem. 19So Israel has been in rebellion against the house of David to this day.

First Dynasty: Jeroboam Reigns over Israel

20 When all Israel heard that Jeroboam had returned, they sent and called him to the assembly and made him king over all Israel. There was no one who followed the house of David, except the tribe of Judah alone.

21 When Rehoboam came to Jerusa-

z Gk Vg Compare 2 Chr 10.2: Heb *lived in*

lem, he assembled all the house of Judah and the tribe of Benjamin, one hundred eighty thousand chosen troops to fight against the house of Israel, to restore the kingdom to Rehoboam son of Solomon. 22But the word of God came to Shemaiah the man of God: 23Say to King Rehoboam of Judah, son of Solomon, and to all the house of Judah and Benjamin, and to the rest of the people, 24"Thus says the LORD, You shall not go up or fight against your kindred the people of Israel. Let everyone go home, for this thing is from me." So they heeded the word of the LORD and went home again, according to the word of the LORD.

Jeroboam's Golden Calves

25 Then Jeroboam built Shechem in the hill country of Ephraim, and resided there; he went out from there and built Penuel. 26Then Jeroboam said to himself, "Now the kingdom may well revert to the house of David. 27If this people continues to go up to offer sacrifices in the house of the LORD at Jerusalem, the heart of this people will turn again to their master, King Rehoboam of Judah; they will kill me and return to King Rehoboam of Judah." 28So the king took counsel, and made two calves of gold. He said to the people,a "You have gone up to Jerusalem long enough. Here are your gods, O Israel, who brought you up out of the land of Egypt." 29He set one in Bethel, and the other he put in Dan. 30And this thing became a sin, for the people went to worship before the one at Bethel and before the other as far as Dan.b 31He also made housesc on high places, and appointed priests from among all the people, who were not Levites. 32Jeroboam appointed a festival on the fifteenth day of the eighth month like the festival that was in Judah, and he offered sacrifices on the altar; so he did in Bethel, sacrificing to the calves that he had made. And he placed in Bethel the priests of the high places that he had made. 33He went up to the altar that he had made in Bethel on the fifteenth day in the eighth month, in the month that he alone had devised; he appointed a festival for the people of Israel, and he went up to the altar to offer incense.

A Man of God from Judah

13 While Jeroboam was standing by the altar to offer incense, a man of God came out of Judah by the word of the LORD to Bethel 2and proclaimed against the altar by the word of the LORD, and said, "O altar, altar, thus says the LORD: 'A son shall be born to the house of David, Josiah by name; and he shall sacrifice on you the priests of the high places who offer incense on you, and human bones shall be burned on you.' " 3He gave a sign the same day, saying, "This is the sign that the LORD has spoken: 'The altar shall be torn down, and the ashes that are on it shall be poured out.' " 4When the king heard what the man of God cried out against the altar at Bethel, Jeroboam stretched out his hand from the altar, saying, "Seize him!" But the hand that he stretched out against him withered so that he could not draw it back to himself. 5The altar also was torn down, and the ashes poured out from the altar, according to the sign that the man of God had given by the word of the LORD. 6The king said to the man of God, "Entreat now the favor of the LORD your God, and pray for me, so that my hand may be restored to me." So the man of God entreated the LORD; and the king's hand was restored to him, and became as it was before. 7Then the king said to the man of God, "Come home with me and dine, and I will give you a gift." 8But the man of God said to the king, "If you give me half your kingdom, I will not go in with you; nor will I eat food or drink water in this place. 9For thus I was commanded by the word of the LORD: You shall not eat food, or drink water, or return by the way that you came." 10So he went another way, and did not return by the way that he had come to Bethel.

11 Now there lived an old prophet in Bethel. One of his sons came and told him all that the man of God had done that day in Bethel; the words also that he had spoken to the king, they told to their father. 12Their father said to them, "Which way did he go?" And his sons showed him the way that the man of God who came from Judah had gone. 13Then he said to his sons, "Saddle a donkey for me." So they saddled a donkey for him, and he mounted it. 14He went after the man of God, and found him sitting under an oak tree. He said to him, "Are you the

---

a Gk: Heb to them   b Compare Gk: Heb went to the one as far as Dan   c Gk Vg Compare 13.32: Heb a house

man of God who came from Judah?" He answered, "I am." ¹⁵Then he said to him, "Come home with me and eat some food." ¹⁶But he said, "I cannot return with you, or go in with you; nor will I eat food or drink water with you in this place; ¹⁷for it was said to me by the word of the LORD: You shall not eat food or drink water there, or return by the way that you came." ¹⁸Then the other*ᵈ* said to him, "I also am a prophet as you are, and an angel spoke to me by the word of the LORD: Bring him back with you into your house so that he may eat food and drink water." But he was deceiving him. ¹⁹Then the man of God*ᵈ* went back with him, and ate food and drank water in his house.

20 As they were sitting at the table, the word of the LORD came to the prophet who had brought him back; ²¹and he proclaimed to the man of God who came from Judah, "Thus says the LORD: Because you have disobeyed the word of the LORD, and have not kept the commandment that the LORD your God commanded you, ²²but have come back and have eaten food and drunk water in the place of which he said to you, 'Eat no food, and drink no water,' your body shall not come to your ancestral tomb." ²³After the man of God*ᵈ* had eaten food and had drunk, they saddled for him a donkey belonging to the prophet who had brought him back. ²⁴Then as he went away, a lion met him on the road and killed him. His body was thrown in the road, and the donkey stood beside it; the lion also stood beside the body. ²⁵People passed by and saw the body thrown in the road, with the lion standing by the body. And they came and told it in the town where the old prophet lived.

26 When the prophet who had brought him back from the way heard of it, he said, "It is the man of God who disobeyed the word of the LORD; therefore the LORD has given him to the lion, which has torn him and killed him according to the word that the LORD spoke to him." ²⁷Then he said to his sons, "Saddle a donkey for me." So they saddled one, ²⁸and he went and found the body thrown in the road, with the donkey and the lion standing beside the body. The lion had not eaten the body or attacked the donkey. ²⁹The prophet took up the body of the man of God, laid it on the donkey, and brought it back to the city,*ᵉ* to mourn and to bury

him. ³⁰He laid the body in his own grave; and they mourned over him, saying, "Alas, my brother!" ³¹After he had buried him, he said to his sons, "When I die, bury me in the grave in which the man of God is buried; lay my bones beside his bones. ³²For the saying that he proclaimed by the word of the LORD against the altar in Bethel, and against all the houses of the high places that are in the cities of Samaria, shall surely come to pass."

33 Even after this event Jeroboam did not turn from his evil way, but made priests for the high places again from among all the people; any who wanted to be priests he consecrated for the high places. ³⁴This matter became sin to the house of Jeroboam, so as to cut it off and to destroy it from the face of the earth.

Judgment on the House of Jeroboam

14 At that time Abijah son of Jeroboam fell sick. ²Jeroboam said to his wife, "Go, disguise yourself, so that it will not be known that you are the wife of Jeroboam, and go to Shiloh; for the prophet Ahijah is there, who said of me that I should be king over this people. ³Take with you ten loaves, some cakes, and a jar of honey, and go to him; he will tell you what shall happen to the child."

4 Jeroboam's wife did so; she set out and went to Shiloh, and came to the house of Ahijah. Now Ahijah could not see, for his eyes were dim because of his age. ⁵But the LORD said to Ahijah, "The wife of Jeroboam is coming to inquire of you concerning her son; for he is sick. Thus and thus you shall say to her."

When she came, she pretended to be another woman. ⁶But when Ahijah heard the sound of her feet, as she came in at the door, he said, "Come in, wife of Jeroboam; why do you pretend to be another? For I am charged with heavy tidings for you. ⁷Go, tell Jeroboam, 'Thus says the LORD, the God of Israel: Because I exalted you from among the people, made you leader over my people Israel, ⁸and tore the kingdom away from the house of David to give it to you; yet you have not been like my servant David, who kept my commandments and followed me with all his heart, doing only that which was right in

---

ᵈ Heb *he*   *ᵉ* Gk: Heb *he came to the town of the old prophet*

my sight, 9but you have done evil above all those who were before you and have gone and made for yourself other gods, and cast images, provoking me to anger, and have thrust me behind your back; 10therefore, I will bring evil upon the house of Jeroboam. I will cut off from Jeroboam every male, both bond and free in Israel, and will consume the house of Jeroboam, just as one burns up dung until it is all gone. 11Anyone belonging to Jeroboam who dies in the city, the dogs shall eat; and anyone who dies in the open country, the birds of the air shall eat; for the LORD has spoken.' 12Therefore set out, go to your house. When your feet enter the city, the child shall die. 13All Israel shall mourn for him and bury him; for he alone of Jeroboam's family shall come to the grave, because in him there is found something pleasing to the LORD, the God of Israel, in the house of Jeroboam. 14Moreover the LORD will raise up for himself a king over Israel, who shall cut off the house of Jeroboam today, even right now! *f*

15 "The LORD will strike Israel, as a reed is shaken in the water; he will root up Israel out of this good land that he gave to their ancestors, and scatter them beyond the Euphrates, because they have made their sacred poles, *g* provoking the LORD to anger. 16He will give Israel up because of the sins of Jeroboam, which he sinned and which he caused Israel to commit."

17 Then Jeroboam's wife got up and went away, and she came to Tirzah. As she came to the threshold of the house, the child died. 18All Israel buried him and mourned for him, according to the word of the LORD, which he spoke by his servant the prophet Ahijah.

Death of Jeroboam

19 Now the rest of the acts of Jeroboam, how he warred and how he reigned, are written in the Book of the Annals of the Kings of Israel. 20The time that Jeroboam reigned was twenty-two years; then he slept with his ancestors, and his son Nadab succeeded him.

Rehoboam Reigns over Judah

21 Now Rehoboam son of Solomon reigned in Judah. Rehoboam was forty-one years old when he began to reign, and he reigned seventeen years in Jerusalem, the city that the LORD had chosen out of all the tribes of Israel, to put his name there.

His mother's name was Naamah the Ammonite. 22Judah did what was evil in the sight of the LORD; they provoked him to jealousy with their sins that they committed, more than all that their ancestors had done. 23For they also built for themselves high places, pillars, and sacred poles *g* on every high hill and under every green tree; 24there were also male temple prostitutes in the land. They committed all the abominations of the nations that the LORD drove out before the people of Israel.

25 In the fifth year of King Rehoboam, King Shishak of Egypt came up against Jerusalem; 26he took away the treasures of the house of the LORD and the treasures of the king's house; he took everything. He also took away all the shields of gold that Solomon had made; 27so King Rehoboam made shields of bronze instead, and committed them to the hands of the officers of the guard, who kept the door of the king's house. 28As often as the king went into the house of the LORD, the guard carried them and brought them back to the guardroom.

29 Now the rest of the acts of Rehoboam, and all that he did, are they not written in the Book of the Annals of the Kings of Judah? 30There was war between Rehoboam and Jeroboam continually. 31Rehoboam slept with his ancestors and was buried with his ancestors in the city of David. His mother's name was Naamah the Ammonite. His son Abijam succeeded him.

Abijam Reigns over Judah: Idolatry and War

15 Now in the eighteenth year of King Jeroboam son of Nebat, Abijam began to reign over Judah. 2He reigned for three years in Jerusalem. His mother's name was Maacah daughter of Abishalom. 3He committed all the sins that his father did before him; his heart was not true to the LORD his God, like the heart of his father David. 4Nevertheless for David's sake the LORD his God gave him a lamp in Jerusalem, setting up his son after him, and establishing Jerusalem; 5because David did what was right in the sight of the LORD, and did not turn aside from anything that he commanded him all the days of his life, except in the matter of Uriah the Hittite. 6The war begun between Rehoboam and Jeroboam contin-

f Meaning of Heb uncertain   *g* Heb *Asherim*

ued all the days of his life. [7]The rest of the acts of Abijam, and all that he did, are they not written in the Book of the Annals of the Kings of Judah? There was war between Abijam and Jeroboam. [8]Abijam slept with his ancestors, and they buried him in the city of David. Then his son Asa succeeded him.

Asa Reigns over Judah

9 In the twentieth year of King Jeroboam of Israel, Asa began to reign over Judah; [10]he reigned forty-one years in Jerusalem. His mother's name was Maacah daughter of Abishalom. [11]Asa did what was right in the sight of the LORD, as his father David had done. [12]He put away the male temple prostitutes out of the land, and removed all the idols that his ancestors had made. [13]He also removed his mother Maacah from being queen mother, because she had made an abominable image for Asherah; Asa cut down her image and burned it at the Wadi Kidron. [14]But the high places were not taken away. Nevertheless the heart of Asa was true to the LORD all his days. [15]He brought into the house of the LORD the votive gifts of his father and his own votive gifts—silver, gold, and utensils.

Alliance with Aram against Israel

16 There was war between Asa and King Baasha of Israel all their days. [17]King Baasha of Israel went up against Judah, and built Ramah, to prevent anyone from going out or coming in to King Asa of Judah. [18]Then Asa took all the silver and the gold that were left in the treasures of the house of the LORD and the treasures of the king's house, and gave them into the hands of his servants. King Asa sent them to King Ben-hadad son of Tabrimmon son of Hezion of Aram, who resided in Damascus, saying, [19]"Let there be an alliance between me and you, like that between my father and your father: I am sending you a present of silver and gold; go, break your alliance with King Baasha of Israel, so that he may withdraw from me." [20]Ben-hadad listened to King Asa, and sent the commanders of his armies against the cities of Israel. He conquered Ijon, Dan, Abel-beth-maacah, and all Chinneroth, with all the land of Naphtali. [21]When Baasha heard of it, he stopped building Ramah and lived in Tirzah. [22]Then King Asa made a proclamation to all Judah, none

was exempt: they carried away the stones of Ramah and its timber, with which Baasha had been building; with them King Asa built Geba of Benjamin and Mizpah. [23]Now the rest of all the acts of Asa, all his power, all that he did, and the cities that he built, are they not written in the Book of the Annals of the Kings of Judah? But in his old age he was diseased in his feet. [24]Then Asa slept with his ancestors, and was buried with his ancestors in the city of his father David; his son Jehoshaphat succeeded him.

Nadab Reigns over Israel

25 Nadab son of Jeroboam began to reign over Israel in the second year of King Asa of Judah; he reigned over Israel two years. [26]He did what was evil in the sight of the LORD, walking in the way of his ancestor and in the sin that he caused Israel to commit.

27 Baasha son of Ahijah, of the house of Issachar, conspired against him; and Baasha struck him down at Gibbethon, which belonged to the Philistines; for Nadab and all Israel were laying siege to Gibbethon. [28]So Baasha killed Nadab[h] in the third year of King Asa of Judah, and succeeded him. [29]As soon as he was king, he killed all the house of Jeroboam; he left to the house of Jeroboam not one that breathed, until he had destroyed it, according to the word of the LORD that he spoke by his servant Ahijah the Shilonite— [30]because of the sins of Jeroboam that he committed and that he caused Israel to commit, and because of the anger to which he provoked the LORD, the God of Israel.

31 Now the rest of the acts of Nadab, and all that he did, are they not written in the Book of the Annals of the Kings of Israel? [32]There was war between Asa and King Baasha of Israel all their days.

Second Dynasty: Baasha Reigns over Israel

33 In the third year of King Asa of Judah, Baasha son of Ahijah began to reign over all Israel at Tirzah; he reigned twenty-four years. [34]He did what was evil in the sight of the LORD, walking in the way of Jeroboam and in the sin that he caused Israel to commit.

16 The word of the LORD came to Jehu son of Hanani against Baa-

[h] Heb *him*

sha, saying, 2"Since I exalted you out of the dust and made you leader over my people Israel, and you have walked in the way of Jeroboam, and have caused my people Israel to sin, provoking me to anger with their sins, 3therefore, I will consume Baasha and his house, and I will make your house like the house of Jeroboam son of Nebat. 4Anyone belonging to Baasha who dies in the city the dogs shall eat; and anyone of his who dies in the field the birds of the air shall eat."

5 Now the rest of the acts of Baasha, what he did, and his power, are they not written in the Book of the Annals of the Kings of Israel? 6Baasha slept with his ancestors, and was buried at Tirzah; and his son Elah succeeded him. 7Moreover the word of the LORD came by the prophet Jehu son of Hanani against Baasha and his house, both because of all the evil that he did in the sight of the LORD, provoking him to anger with the work of his hands, in being like the house of Jeroboam, and also because he destroyed it.

Elah Reigns over Israel

8 In the twenty-sixth year of King Asa of Judah, Elah son of Baasha began to reign over Israel in Tirzah; he reigned two years. 9But his servant Zimri, commander of half his chariots, conspired against him. When he was at Tirzah, drinking himself drunk in the house of Arza, who was in charge of the palace at Tirzah, 10Zimri came in and struck him down and killed him, in the twenty-seventh year of King Asa of Judah, and succeeded him.

11 When he began to reign, as soon as he had seated himself on his throne, he killed all the house of Baasha; he did not leave him a single male of his kindred or his friends. 12Thus Zimri destroyed all the house of Baasha, according to the word of the LORD, which he spoke against Baasha by the prophet Jehu— 13because of all the sins of Baasha and the sins of his son Elah that they committed, and that they caused Israel to commit, provoking the LORD God of Israel to anger with their idols. 14Now the rest of the acts of Elah, and all that he did, are they not written in the Book of the Annals of the Kings of Israel?

Third Dynasty: Zimri Reigns over Israel

15 In the twenty-seventh year of King Asa of Judah, Zimri reigned seven days in Tirzah. Now the troops were encamped against Gibbethon, which belonged to the Philistines, 16and the troops who were encamped heard it said, "Zimri has conspired, and he has killed the king"; therefore all Israel made Omri, the commander of the army, king over Israel that day in the camp. 17So Omri went up from Gibbethon, and all Israel with him, and they besieged Tirzah. 18When Zimri saw that the city was taken, he went into the citadel of the king's house; he burned down the king's house over himself with fire, and died— 19because of the sins that he committed, doing evil in the sight of the LORD, walking in the way of Jeroboam, and for the sin that he committed, causing Israel to sin. 20Now the rest of the acts of Zimri, and the conspiracy that he made, are they not written in the Book of the Annals of the Kings of Israel?

Fourth Dynasty: Omri Reigns over Israel

21 Then the people of Israel were divided into two parts; half of the people followed Tibni son of Ginath, to make him king, and half followed Omri. 22But the people who followed Omri overcame the people who followed Tibni son of Ginath; so Tibni died, and Omri became king. 23In the thirty-first year of King Asa of Judah, Omri began to reign over Israel; he reigned for twelve years, six of them in Tirzah.

Samaria the New Capital

24 He bought the hill of Samaria from Shemer for two talents of silver; he fortified the hill, and called the city that he built, Samaria, after the name of Shemer, the owner of the hill.

25 Omri did what was evil in the sight of the LORD; he did more evil than all who were before him. 26For he walked in all the way of Jeroboam son of Nebat, and in the sins that he caused Israel to commit, provoking the LORD, the God of Israel, to anger by their idols. 27Now the rest of the acts of Omri that he did, and the power that he showed, are they not written in the Book of the Annals of the Kings of Israel? 28Omri slept with his ancestors, and was buried in Samaria; his son Ahab succeeded him.

Ahab Reigns over Israel

29 In the thirty-eighth year of King Asa of Judah, Ahab son of Omri began to reign over Israel; Ahab son of Omri

reigned over Israel in Samaria twenty-two years. [30]Ahab son of Omri did evil in the sight of the LORD more than all who were before him.

Ahab Marries Jezebel and Worships Baal

31 And as if it had been a light thing for him to walk in the sins of Jeroboam son of Nebat, he took as his wife Jezebel daughter of King Ethbaal of the Sidonians, and went and served Baal, and worshiped him. [32]He erected an altar for Baal in the house of Baal, which he built in Samaria. [33]Ahab also made a sacred pole.[i] Ahab did more to provoke the anger of the LORD, the God of Israel, than had all the kings of Israel who were before him. [34]In his days Hiel of Bethel built Jericho; he laid its foundation at the cost of Abiram his firstborn, and set up its gates at the cost of his youngest son Segub, according to the word of the LORD, which he spoke by Joshua son of Nun.

Elijah Predicts a Drought

17 Now Elijah the Tishbite, of Tishbe[j] in Gilead, said to Ahab, "As the LORD the God of Israel lives, before whom I stand, there shall be neither dew nor rain these years, except by my word." [2]The word of the LORD came to him, saying, [3]"Go from here and turn eastward, and hide yourself by the Wadi Cherith, which is east of the Jordan. [4]You shall drink from the wadi, and I have commanded the ravens to feed you there." [5]So he went and did according to the word of the LORD; he went and lived by the Wadi Cherith, which is east of the Jordan. [6]The ravens brought him bread and meat in the morning, and bread and meat in the evening; and he drank from the wadi. [7]But after a while the wadi dried up, because there was no rain in the land.

The Widow of Zarephath

8 Then the word of the LORD came to him, saying, [9]"Go now to Zarephath, which belongs to Sidon, and live there; for I have commanded a widow there to feed you." [10]So he set out and went to Zarephath. When he came to the gate of the town, a widow was there gathering sticks; he called to her and said, "Bring me a little water in a vessel, so that I may drink." [11]As she was going to bring it, he called to her and said, "Bring me a morsel of bread in your hand." [12]But she said, "As the LORD your God lives, I have nothing baked, only a handful of meal in a jar, and a little oil in a jug; I am now gathering a couple of sticks, so that I may go home and prepare it for myself and my son, that we may eat it, and die." [13]Elijah said to her, "Do not be afraid; go and do as you have said; but first make me a little cake of it and bring it to me, and afterwards make something for yourself and your son. [14]For thus says the LORD the God of Israel: The jar of meal will not be emptied and the jug of oil will not fail until the day that the LORD sends rain on the earth." [15]She went and did as Elijah said, so that she as well as he and her household ate for many days. [16]The jar of meal was not emptied, neither did the jug of oil fail, according to the word of the LORD that he spoke by Elijah.

Elijah Revives the Widow's Son

17 After this the son of the woman, the mistress of the house, became ill; his illness was so severe that there was no breath left in him. [18]She then said to Elijah, "What have you against me, O man of God? You have come to me to bring my sin to remembrance, and to cause the death of my son!" [19]But he said to her, "Give me your son." He took him from her bosom, carried him up into the upper chamber where he was lodging, and laid him on his own bed. [20]He cried out to the LORD, "O LORD my God, have you brought calamity even upon the widow with whom I am staying, by killing her son?" [21]Then he stretched himself upon the child three times, and cried out to the LORD, "O LORD my God, let this child's life come into him again." [22]The LORD listened to the voice of Elijah; the life of the child came into him again, and he revived. [23]Elijah took the child, brought him down from the upper chamber into the house, and gave him to his mother; then Elijah said, "See, your son is alive." [24]So the woman said to Elijah, "Now I know that you are a man of God, and that the word of the LORD in your mouth is truth."

Elijah's Message to Ahab

18 After many days the word of the LORD came to Elijah, in the third year of the drought,[k] saying, "Go, present yourself to Ahab; I will send rain

---

i Heb Asherah   j Gk: Heb of the settlers   k Heb lacks of the drought on the earth." ²So Elijah went to present himself to Ahab. The famine was severe in Samaria. ³Ahab summoned Obadiah, who was in charge of the palace. (Now Obadiah revered the LORD greatly; ⁴when Jezebel was killing off the prophets of the LORD, Obadiah took a hundred prophets, hid them fifty to a cave, and provided them with bread and water.) ⁵Then Ahab said to Obadiah, "Go through the land to all the springs of water and to all the wadis; perhaps we may find grass to keep the horses and mules alive, and not lose some of the animals." ⁶So they divided the land between them to pass through it; Ahab went in one direction by himself, and Obadiah went in another direction by himself.

7 As Obadiah was on the way, Elijah met him; Obadiah recognized him, fell on his face, and said, "Is it you, my lord Elijah?" ⁸He answered him, "It is I. Go, tell your lord that Elijah is here." ⁹And he said, "How have I sinned, that you would hand your servant over to Ahab, to kill me? ¹⁰As the LORD your God lives, there is no nation or kingdom to which my lord has not sent to seek you; and when they would say,

THE TRADITION

Miracles

"The jar of meal will not be emptied and the jug of oil will not fail."

I KINGS 17.14

Does God exist?
What is God like?
Does God care about my troubles?

Even before such questions are laid to rest with the grace of faith, miracles point us to the answers and prepare our minds to accept the truth.

Not that we are always so accepting. Scripture offers many cautionary tales about people who rejected remarkable supernatural signs from God (see Exodus 7.8–13; John 11.46–53; Acts 16.16–24). Still, for those with eyes to see, miracles illuminate and invite belief in deeper realities. Beyond their very real, amazing externals, they have symbolic meaning. Miracles reveal the very nature of God.

The miracles of Elijah underline God's sovereignty—especially highlighted in the story of Elijah's contest with the pagan prophets. They also reveal God's compassion—as shown to "little people" like the starving widow and her son (see 1 Kings 17.17–24). But the best examples of "miracles with a message" are the ones Jesus worked. Astounding in themselves, they reveal his

mission and authenticate him as the Son of God.

Jesus heals lepers and the blind—a sign that he has come to cure spiritual blindness and the leprosy of sin. He feeds the multitudes—a sign that he himself is the Bread of Life. He calms and walks on the sea—a sign that he rules the universe. And in every miracle, Jesus shows a compassionate God who loves his people in a very personal way.

Still today our loving God uses miracles to draw us to himself. Take healings, for example, perhaps the more spectacular of these interventions. But on a smaller scale, too, God provides countless signs of his presence.

For one woman on chemotherapy, this assurance took the form of a Scripture verse she happened on "by chance" one morning, just after she realized that her hair was falling out: "Even the hairs of your head are all counted," she read and started to cry (Matthew 10.30). "I felt God's love so strongly at that moment, as I realized that he cares about every little aspect of my life."

Personal, everyday miracles like this may be the most persuasive of all.

'He is not here,' he would require an oath of the kingdom or nation, that they had not found you. ¹¹But now you say, 'Go, tell your lord that Elijah is here.' ¹²As soon as I have gone from you, the spirit of the Lord will carry you I know not where; so, when I come and tell Ahab and he cannot find you, he will kill me, although I your servant have revered the Lord from my youth. ¹³Has it not been told my lord what I did when Jezebel killed the prophets of the Lord, how I hid a hundred of the Lord's prophets fifty to a cave, and provided them with bread and water? ¹⁴Yet now you say, 'Go, tell your lord that Elijah is here'; he will surely kill me." ¹⁵Elijah said, "As the Lord of hosts lives, before whom I stand, I will surely show myself to him today." ¹⁶So Obadiah went to meet Ahab, and told him; and Ahab went to meet Elijah.

17 When Ahab saw Elijah, Ahab said to him, "Is it you, you troubler of Israel?" ¹⁸He answered, "I have not troubled Israel; but you have, and your father's house, because you have forsaken the commandments of the Lord and followed the Baals. ¹⁹Now therefore have all Israel assemble for me at Mount Carmel, with the four hundred fifty prophets of Baal and the four hundred prophets of Asherah, who eat at Jezebel's table."

Elijah's Triumph over the Priests of Baal

20 So Ahab sent to all the Israelites, and assembled the prophets at Mount Carmel. ²¹Elijah then came near to all the people, and said, "How long will you go limping with two different opinions? If the Lord is God, follow him; but if Baal, then follow him." The people did not answer him a word. ²²Then Elijah said to the people, "I, even I only, am left a prophet of the Lord; but Baal's prophets number four hundred fifty. ²³Let two bulls be given to us; let them choose one bull for themselves, cut it in pieces, and lay it on the wood, but put no fire to it; I will prepare the other bull and lay it on the wood, but put no fire to it. ²⁴Then you call on the name of your god and I will call on the name of the Lord; the god who answers by fire is indeed God." All the people answered, "Well spoken!" ²⁵Then Elijah said to the prophets of Baal, "Choose for yourselves one bull and prepare it first, for you

are many; then call on the name of your god, but put no fire to it." ²⁶So they took the bull that was given them, prepared it, and called on the name of Baal from morning until noon, crying, "O Baal, answer us!" But there was no voice, and no answer. They limped about the altar that they had made. ²⁷At noon Elijah mocked them, saying, "Cry aloud! Surely he is a god; either he is meditating, or he has wandered away, or he is on a journey, or perhaps he is asleep and must be awakened." ²⁸Then they cried aloud and, as was their custom, they cut themselves with swords and lances until the blood gushed out over them. ²⁹As midday passed, they raved on until the time of the offering of the oblation, but there was no voice, no answer, and no response.

30 Then Elijah said to all the people, "Come closer to me"; and all the people came closer to him. First he repaired the altar of the Lord that had been thrown down; ³¹Elijah took twelve stones, according to the number of the tribes of the sons of Jacob, to whom the word of the Lord came, saying, "Israel shall be your name"; ³²with the stones he built an altar in the name of the Lord. Then he made a trench around the altar, large enough to contain two measures of seed. ³³Next he put the wood in order, cut the bull in pieces, and laid it on the wood. He said, "Fill four jars with water and pour it on the burnt offering and on the wood." ³⁴Then he said, "Do it a second time"; and they did it a second time. Again he said, "Do it a third time"; and they did it a third time, ³⁵so that the water ran all around the altar, and filled the trench also with water.

36 At the time of the offering of the oblation, the prophet Elijah came near and said, "O Lord, God of Abraham, Isaac, and Israel, let it be known this day that you are God in Israel, that I am your servant, and that I have done all these things at your bidding. ³⁷Answer me, O Lord, answer me, so that this people may know that you, O Lord, are God, and that you have turned their hearts back." ³⁸Then the fire of the Lord fell and consumed the burnt offering, the wood, the stones, and the dust, and even licked up the water that was in the trench. ³⁹When all the people saw it, they fell on their faces and said, "The Lord indeed is God; the Lord indeed is God." ⁴⁰Elijah said to them, "Seize the prophets of Baal;

do not let one of them escape." Then they seized them; and Elijah brought them down to the Wadi Kishon, and killed them there.

The Drought Ends

41 Elijah said to Ahab, "Go up, eat and drink; for there is a sound of rushing rain." 42So Ahab went up to eat and to drink. Elijah went up to the top of Carmel; there he bowed himself down upon the earth and put his face between his knees. 43He said to his servant, "Go up now, look to-

ward the sea." He went up and looked, and said, "There is nothing." Then he said, "Go again seven times." 44At the seventh time he said, "Look, a little cloud no bigger than a person's hand is rising out of the sea." Then he said, "Go say to Ahab, 'Harness your chariot and go down before the rain stops you.'" 45In a little while the heavens grew black with clouds and wind; there was a heavy rain. Ahab rode off and went to Jezreel. 46But the hand of the LORD was on Elijah; he girded up his loins and ran in front of Ahab to the entrance of Jezreel.

Cherish the Truth

Scripture Reading for Today:
1 Kings 18.20–38

Verse for Today:
1 Kings 18.38

Nowadays we are suspicious of people who talk about "the truth," especially when it comes to moral matters or religious faith. Like many people, I dislike the way the truth can be twisted and used as a weapon to control others, especially by religious people. But I have discovered that without real truth, life has no meaning.

Elijah was one of history's most famous prophets, a man who risked his life in the service of truth. It happened one day on Mount Carmel, where Israel had gathered to witness one of the most lopsided contests in Biblical history. On one side ranged 450 prophets of the Canaanite god Baal. On the other was the lone figure of Elijah, prophet of the Lord.

The power of one against 450. It was indeed a lopsided contest. And Elijah held the advantage. After all, he had the One who created the universe on his side. How could he possibly lose?

Now, like then, truth is often an unpopular choice. The false prophets spoke words that the people welcomed. Elijah, on the other hand, spoke of judgment and repentance, words that most of us find unpleasant and distasteful. In a superficial sense, truth is often not nearly as attractive as falsehood. The latter often soothes our consciences and affirms the deceits of our hearts. It turns a blind eye to the worst distortions of our culture, calling the light darkness and the darkness light. It glibly chooses lust over love, convenience over life, and greed over generosity. It enslaves us to our passions and renders us blind and deaf to truth. If we are wise we will pray for the humility to see and embrace the truth, no matter how unpopular or unpalatable. For in the end, it is only the truth that has the power to set us free.

—ANN SPANGLER

Go to page 378 for your next devotional reading.

Elijah Flees from Jezebel

19 Ahab told Jezebel all that Elijah had done, and how he had killed all the prophets with the sword. ²Then Jezebel sent a messenger to Elijah, saying, "So may the gods do to me, and more also, if I do not make your life like the life of one of them by this time tomorrow." ³Then he was afraid; he got up and fled for his life, and came to Beer-sheba, which belongs to Judah; he left his servant there.

4 But he himself went a day's journey into the wilderness, and came and sat down under a solitary broom tree. He asked that he might die: "It is enough; now, O LORD, take away my life, for I am no better than my ancestors." ⁵Then he lay down under the broom tree and fell asleep. Suddenly an angel touched him and said to him, "Get up and eat." ⁶He looked, and there at his head was a cake baked on hot stones, and a jar of water. He ate and drank, and lay down again. ⁷The angel of the LORD came a second time, touched him, and said, "Get up and eat, otherwise the journey will be too much for you." ⁸He got up, and ate and drank; then he went in the strength of that food forty days and forty nights to Horeb the mount of God. ⁹At that place he came to a cave, and spent the night there.

Then the word of the LORD came to him, saying, "What are you doing here, Elijah?" ¹⁰He answered, "I have been very zealous for the LORD, the God of hosts; for the Israelites have forsaken your covenant, thrown down your altars, and killed your prophets with the sword. I alone am left,

*D*epression

WEDNESDAY

Scripture Reading for Today:
I Kings 19.1–8

Verse for Today:
I Kings 19.4

The trauma of depression is devastating. You become immobilized, unable to make decisions, uninterested, and unable to care about anything. You become terrorized because you are unable to communicate and unbearably lonely because you are not able to connect to other human beings. You become a frustration to friends and relatives who alternately empathize and criticize. They tell you to look up and see the sun and the trees. They don't know that for the person who has lost hope, albeit temporarily, there is no sun, there are no trees.

When the reaction to the blows of life is serious depression, it takes something close to a miracle to help melt the ice and get unstuck so as to go on with life, with hope, and find joy again. But it can be done, and once you are in the light again, life takes on a beauty you couldn't have imagined before.

When I think of the many times I have had to deal with pain and tragedy, I am also conscious of what I was supposed to learn from these shocks. Simply put, it is how to discern what is really important. And as for what really matters, I have learned it is only life and death.

Imagine, for example, if your child is in danger of death—and I have lost two sons—how little such things as furniture, a clean house, a job promotion, or a cranky relative matter. You become terribly conscious of how finite this world is and you reach out for what is lasting, the Eternal. You go to God.

—*ANTOINETTE BOSCO*

Go to page 388 for your next devotional reading.

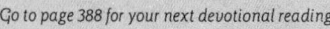

and they are seeking my life, to take it away."

Elijah Meets God at Horeb

11 He said, "Go out and stand on the mountain before the LORD, for the LORD is about to pass by." Now there was a great wind, so strong that it was splitting mountains and breaking rocks in pieces before the LORD, but the LORD was not in the wind; and after the wind an earthquake, but the LORD was not in the earthquake; 12and after the earthquake a fire, but the LORD was not in the fire; and after the fire a sound of sheer silence. 13When Elijah heard it, he wrapped his face in his mantle and went out and stood at the entrance of the cave. Then there came a voice to him that said, "What are you doing here, Elijah?" 14He answered, "I have been very zealous for the LORD, the God of hosts; for the Israelites have forsaken your covenant, thrown down your altars, and killed your prophets with the sword. I alone am left, and they are seeking my life, to take it away." 15Then the LORD said to him, "Go, return on your way to the wilderness of Damascus; when you arrive, you shall anoint Hazael as king over Aram. 16Also you shall anoint Jehu son of Nimshi as king over Israel; and you shall anoint Elisha son of Shaphat of Abel-meholah as prophet in your place. 17Whoever escapes from the sword of Hazael, Jehu shall kill; and whoever escapes from the sword of Jehu, Elisha shall kill. 18Yet I will leave seven thousand in Israel, all the knees that have not bowed to Baal, and every mouth that has not kissed him."

Elisha Becomes Elijah's Disciple

19 So he set out from there, and found Elisha son of Shaphat, who was plowing. There were twelve yoke of oxen ahead of him, and he was with the twelfth. Elijah passed by him and threw his mantle over him. 20He left the oxen, ran after Elijah, and said, "Let me kiss my father and my mother, and then I will follow you." Then Elijah*l* said to him, "Go back again; for what have I done to you?" 21He returned from following him, took the yoke of oxen, and slaughtered them; using the equipment from the oxen, he boiled their flesh, and gave it to the people, and they ate. Then he set out and followed Elijah, and became his servant.

Ahab's Wars with the Arameans

20 King Ben-hadad of Aram gathered all his army together; thirty-two kings were with him, along with horses and chariots. He marched against Samaria, laid siege to it, and attacked it. 2Then he sent messengers into the city to King Ahab of Israel, and said to him: "Thus says Ben-hadad: 3Your silver and gold are mine; your fairest wives and children also are mine." 4The king of Israel answered, "As you say, my lord, O king, I am yours, and all that I have." 5The messengers came again and said: "Thus says Ben-hadad: I sent to you, saying, 'Deliver to me your silver and gold, your wives and children'; 6nevertheless I will send my servants to you tomorrow about this time, and they shall search your house and the houses of your servants, and lay hands on whatever pleases them,*m* and take it away."

7 Then the king of Israel called all the elders of the land, and said, "Look now! See how this man is seeking trouble; for he sent to me for my wives, my children, my silver, and my gold; and I did not refuse him." 8Then all the elders and all the people said to him, "Do not listen or consent." 9So he said to the messengers of Ben-hadad, "Tell my lord the king: All that you first demanded of your servant I will do; but this thing I cannot do." The messengers left and brought him word again. 10Ben-hadad sent to him and said, "The gods do so to me, and more also, if the dust of Samaria will provide a handful for each of the people who follow me." 11The king of Israel answered, "Tell him: One who puts on armor should not brag like one who takes it off." 12When Ben-hadad heard this message—now he had been drinking with the kings in the booths—he said to his men, "Take your positions!" And they took their positions against the city.

Prophetic Opposition to Ahab

13 Then a certain prophet came up to King Ahab of Israel and said, "Thus says the LORD, Have you seen all this great multitude? Look, I will give it into your hand today; and you shall know that I am the LORD." 14Ahab said, "By whom?" He said, "Thus says the LORD, By the young men

---

l Heb *he*   *m* Gk Syr Vg: Heb *you*

who serve the district governors." Then he said, "Who shall begin the battle?" He answered, "You." [15]Then he mustered the young men who served the district governors, two hundred thirty-two; after them he mustered all the people of Israel, seven thousand.

16 They went out at noon, while Ben-hadad was drinking himself drunk in the booths, he and the thirty-two kings allied with him. [17]The young men who served the district governors went out first. Ben-hadad had sent out scouts,[n] and they reported to him, "Men have come out from Samaria." [18]He said, "If they have come out for peace, take them alive; if they have come out for war, take them alive."

19 But these had already come out of the city: the young men who served the district governors, and the army that followed them. [20]Each killed his man; the Arameans fled and Israel pursued them, but King Ben-hadad of Aram escaped on a horse with the cavalry. [21]The king of Israel went out, attacked the horses and chariots, and defeated the Arameans with a great slaughter.

22 Then the prophet approached the king of Israel and said to him, "Come, strengthen yourself, and consider well what you have to do; for in the spring the king of Aram will come up against you."

The Arameans Are Defeated

23 The servants of the king of Aram said to him, "Their gods are gods of the hills, and so they were stronger than we; but let us fight against them in the plain, and surely we shall be stronger than they. [24]Also do this: remove the kings, each from his post, and put commanders in place of them; [25]and muster an army like the army that you have lost, horse for horse, and chariot for chariot; then we will fight against them in the plain, and surely we shall be stronger than they." He heeded their voice, and did so.

26 In the spring Ben-hadad mustered the Arameans and went up to Aphek to fight against Israel. [27]After the Israelites had been mustered and provisioned, they went out to engage them; the people of Israel encamped opposite them like two little flocks of goats, while the Arameans filled the country. [28]A man of God approached and said to the king of Israel, "Thus says the LORD: Because the Arameans have said, 'The LORD is a god of the

hills but he is not a god of the valleys,' therefore I will give all this great multitude into your hand, and you shall know that I am the LORD." [29]They encamped opposite one another seven days. Then on the seventh day the battle began; the Israelites killed one hundred thousand Aramean foot soldiers in one day. [30]The rest fled into the city of Aphek; and the wall fell on twenty-seven thousand men that were left.

Ben-hadad also fled, and entered the city to hide. [31]His servants said to him, "Look, we have heard that the kings of the house of Israel are merciful kings; let us put sackcloth around our waists and ropes on our heads, and go out to the king of Israel; perhaps he will spare your life." [32]So they tied sackcloth around their waists, put ropes on their heads, went to the king of Israel, and said, "Your servant Ben-hadad says, 'Please let me live.' " And he said, "Is he still alive? He is my brother." [33]Now the men were watching for an omen; they quickly took it up from him and said, "Yes, Ben-hadad is your brother." Then he said, "Go and bring him." So Ben-hadad came out to him; and he had him come up into the chariot. [34]Ben-hadad[o] said to him, "I will restore the towns that my father took from your father; and you may establish bazaars for yourself in Damascus, as my father did in Samaria." The king of Israel responded,[p] "I will let you go on those terms." So he made a treaty with him and let him go.

A Prophet Condemns Ahab

35 At the command of the LORD a certain member of a company of prophets[q] said to another, "Strike me!" But the man refused to strike him. [36]Then he said to him, "Because you have not obeyed the voice of the LORD, as soon as you have left me, a lion will kill you." And when he had left him, a lion met him and killed him. [37]Then he found another man and said, "Strike me!" So the man hit him, striking and wounding him. [38]Then the prophet departed, and waited for the king along the road, disguising himself with a bandage over his eyes. [39]As the king passed by, he cried to the king and said, "Your servant went out into the thick of the bat-

n Heb lacks scouts   o Heb He   p Heb lacks The king of Israel responded   q Heb of the sons of the prophets tle; then a soldier turned and brought a man to me, and said, 'Guard this man; if he is missing, your life shall be given for his life, or else you shall pay a talent of silver.' 40While your servant was busy here and there, he was gone." The king of Israel said to him, "So shall your judgment be; you yourself have decided it." 41Then he quickly took the bandage away from his eyes. The king of Israel recognized him as one of the prophets. 42Then he said to him, "Thus says the LORD, 'Because you have let the man go whom I had devoted to destruction, therefore your life shall be for his life, and your people for his people.' " 43The king of Israel set out toward home, resentful and sullen, and came to Samaria.

Naboth's Vineyard

21 Later the following events took place: Naboth the Jezreelite had a vineyard in Jezreel, beside the palace of King Ahab of Samaria. 2And Ahab said to Naboth, "Give me your vineyard, so that I may have it for a vegetable garden, because it is near my house; I will give you a better vineyard for it; or, if it seems good to you, I will give you its value in money." 3But Naboth said to Ahab, "The LORD forbid that I should give you my ancestral inheritance." 4Ahab went home resentful and sullen because of what Naboth the Jezreelite had said to him; for he had said, "I will not give you my ancestral inheritance." He lay down on his bed, turned away his face, and would not eat.

5 His wife Jezebel came to him and said, "Why are you so depressed that you will not eat?" 6He said to her, "Because I spoke to Naboth the Jezreelite and said to him, 'Give me your vineyard for money; or else, if you prefer, I will give you another vineyard for it'; but he answered, 'I will not give you my vineyard.' " 7His wife Jezebel said to him, "Do you now govern Israel? Get up, eat some food, and be cheerful; I will give you the vineyard of Naboth the Jezreelite."

8 So she wrote letters in Ahab's name and sealed them with his seal; she sent the letters to the elders and the nobles who lived with Naboth in his city. 9She wrote in the letters, "Proclaim a fast, and seat Naboth at the head of the assembly; 10seat two scoundrels opposite him, and have them bring a charge against him, saying, 'You have cursed God and the king.' Then

take him out, and stone him to death." 11The men of his city, the elders and the nobles who lived in his city, did as Jezebel had sent word to them. Just as it was written in the letters that she had sent to them, 12they proclaimed a fast and seated Naboth at the head of the assembly. 13The two scoundrels came in and sat opposite him; and the scoundrels brought a charge against Naboth, in the presence of the people, saying, "Naboth cursed God and the king." So they took him outside the city, and stoned him to death. 14Then they sent to Jezebel, saying, "Naboth has been stoned; he is dead."

15 As soon as Jezebel heard that Naboth had been stoned and was dead, Jezebel said to Ahab, "Go, take possession of the vineyard of Naboth the Jezreelite, which he refused to give you for money; for Naboth is not alive, but dead." 16As soon as Ahab heard that Naboth was dead, Ahab set out to go down to the vineyard of Naboth the Jezreelite, to take possession of it.

Elijah Pronounces God's Sentence

17 Then the word of the LORD came to Elijah the Tishbite, saying: 18Go down to meet King Ahab of Israel, who rules*r* in Samaria; he is now in the vineyard of Naboth, where he has gone to take possession. 19You shall say to him, "Thus says the LORD: Have you killed, and also taken possession?" You shall say to him, "Thus says the LORD: In the place where dogs licked up the blood of Naboth, dogs will also lick up your blood."

20 Ahab said to Elijah, "Have you found me, O my enemy?" He answered, "I have found you. Because you have sold yourself to do what is evil in the sight of the LORD, 21I will bring disaster on you; I will consume you, and will cut off from Ahab every male, bond or free, in Israel; 22and I will make your house like the house of Jeroboam son of Nebat, and like the house of Baasha son of Ahijah, because you have provoked me to anger and have caused Israel to sin. 23Also concerning Jezebel the LORD said, 'The dogs shall eat Jezebel within the bounds of Jezreel.' 24Anyone belonging to Ahab who dies in the city the dogs shall eat; and anyone of his who dies in the open country the birds of the air shall eat."

r Heb *who is*

25 (Indeed, there was no one like Ahab, who sold himself to do what was evil in the sight of the LORD, urged on by his wife Jezebel. 26He acted most abominably in going after idols, as the Amorites had done, whom the LORD drove out before the Israelites.)

27 When Ahab heard those words, he tore his clothes and put sackcloth over his bare flesh; he fasted, lay in the sackcloth, and went about dejectedly. 28Then the word of the LORD came to Elijah the Tishbite: 29"Have you seen how Ahab has humbled himself before me? Because he has humbled himself before me, I will not bring the disaster in his days; but in his son's days I will bring the disaster on his house."

Joint Campaign with Judah against Aram

22 For three years Aram and Israel continued without war. 2But in the third year King Jehoshaphat of Judah came down to the king of Israel. 3The king of Israel said to his servants, "Do you know that Ramoth-gilead belongs to us, yet we are doing nothing to take it out of the hand of the king of Aram?" 4He said to Jehoshaphat, "Will you go with me to battle at Ramoth-gilead?" Jehoshaphat replied to the king of Israel, "I am as you are; my people are your people, my horses are your horses."

5 But Jehoshaphat also said to the king of Israel, "Inquire first for the word of the LORD." 6Then the king of Israel gathered the prophets together, about four hundred of them, and said to them, "Shall I go to battle against Ramoth-gilead, or shall I refrain?" They said, "Go up; for the LORD will give it into the hand of the king." 7But Jehoshaphat said, "Is there no other prophet of the LORD here of whom we may inquire?" 8The king of Israel said to Jehoshaphat, "There is still one other by whom we may inquire of the LORD, Micaiah son of Imlah; but I hate him, for he never prophesies anything favorable about me, but only disaster." Jehoshaphat said, "Let the king not say such a thing." 9Then the king of Israel summoned an officer and said, "Bring quickly Micaiah son of Imlah." 10Now the king of Israel and King Jehoshaphat of Judah were sitting on their thrones, arrayed in their robes, at the threshing floor at the entrance of the gate of Samaria; and all the prophets were prophesying before them. 11Zedekiah son of Chenaanah made for himself horns of iron, and he said, "Thus says the LORD: With these you shall gore the Arameans until they are destroyed." 12All the prophets were prophesying the same and saying, "Go up to Ramoth-gilead and triumph; the LORD will give it into the hand of the king."

Micaiah Predicts Failure

13 The messenger who had gone to summon Micaiah said to him, "Look, the words of the prophets with one accord are favorable to the king; let your word be like the word of one of them, and speak favorably." 14But Micaiah said, "As the LORD lives, whatever the LORD says to me, that I will speak."

15 When he had come to the king, the king said to him, "Micaiah, shall we go to Ramoth-gilead to battle, or shall we refrain?" He answered him, "Go up and triumph; the LORD will give it into the hand of the king." 16But the king said to him, "How many times must I make you swear to tell me nothing but the truth in the name of the LORD?" 17Then Micaiah[s] said, "I saw all Israel scattered on the mountains, like sheep that have no shepherd; and the LORD said, 'These have no master; let each one go home in peace.'" 18The king of Israel said to Jehoshaphat, "Did I not tell you that he would not prophesy anything favorable about me, but only disaster?"

19 Then Micaiah[s] said, "Therefore hear the word of the LORD: I saw the LORD sitting on his throne, with all the host of heaven standing beside him to the right and to the left of him. 20And the LORD said, 'Who will entice Ahab, so that he may go up and fall at Ramoth-gilead?' Then one said one thing, and another said another, 21until a spirit came forward and stood before the LORD, saying, 'I will entice him.' 22'How?' the LORD asked him. He replied, 'I will go out and be a lying spirit in the mouth of all his prophets.' Then the LORD[s] said, 'You are to entice him, and you shall succeed; go out and do it.' 23So you see, the LORD has put a lying spirit in the mouth of all these your prophets; the LORD has decreed disaster for you."

24 Then Zedekiah son of Chenaanah came up to Micaiah, slapped him on the

s Heb he

cheek, and said, "Which way did the spirit of the LORD pass from me to speak to you?" 25Micaiah replied, "You will find out on that day when you go in to hide in an inner chamber." 26The king of Israel then ordered, "Take Micaiah, and return him to Amon the governor of the city and to Joash the king's son, 27and say, 'Thus says the king: Put this fellow in prison, and feed him on reduced rations of bread and water until I come in peace.' " 28Micaiah said, "If you return in peace, the LORD has not spoken by me." And he said, "Hear, you peoples, all of you!"

Defeat and Death of Ahab

29 So the king of Israel and King Jehoshaphat of Judah went up to Ramoth-gilead. 30The king of Israel said to Jehoshaphat, "I will disguise myself and go into battle, but you wear your robes." So the king of Israel disguised himself and went into battle. 31Now the king of Aram had commanded the thirty-two captains of his chariots, "Fight with no one small or great, but only with the king of Israel." 32When the captains of the chariots saw Jehoshaphat, they said, "It is surely the king of Israel." So they turned to fight against him; and Jehoshaphat cried out. 33When the captains of the chariots saw that it was not the king of Israel, they turned back from pursuing him. 34But a certain man drew his bow and unknowingly struck the king of Israel between the scale armor and the breastplate; so he said to the driver of his chariot, "Turn around, and carry me out of the battle, for I am wounded." 35The battle grew hot that day, and the king was propped up in his chariot facing the Arameans, until at evening he died; the blood from the wound had flowed into the bottom of the chariot. 36Then about sunset a shout went through the army, "Every man to his city, and every man to his country!"

37 So the king died, and was brought to Samaria; they buried the king in Samaria. 38They washed the chariot by the pool of Samaria; the dogs licked up his blood, and the prostitutes washed themselves in it,ᵗ according to the word of the LORD that he had spoken. 39Now the rest of the acts of Ahab, and all that he did, and the ivory house that he built, and all the cities that he built, are they not written in the Book of the Annals of the Kings of Israel? 40So Ahab slept with his ancestors; and his son Ahaziah succeeded him.

Jehoshaphat Reigns over Judah

41 Jehoshaphat son of Asa began to reign over Judah in the fourth year of King Ahab of Israel. 42Jehoshaphat was thirty-five years old when he began to reign, and he reigned twenty-five years in Jerusalem. His mother's name was Azubah daughter of Shilhi. 43He walked in all the way of his father Asa; he did not turn aside from it, doing what was right in the sight of the LORD; yet the high places were not taken away, and the people still sacrificed and offered incense on the high places. 44Jehoshaphat also made peace with the king of Israel.

45 Now the rest of the acts of Jehoshaphat, and his power that he showed, and how he waged war, are they not written in the Book of the Annals of the Kings of Judah? 46The remnant of the male temple prostitutes who were still in the land in the days of his father Asa, he exterminated.

47 There was no king in Edom; a deputy was king. 48Jehoshaphat made ships of the Tarshish type to go to Ophir for gold; but they did not go, for the ships were wrecked at Ezion-geber. 49Then Ahaziah son of Ahab said to Jehoshaphat, "Let my servants go with your servants in the ships," but Jehoshaphat was not willing. 50Jehoshaphat slept with his ancestors and was buried with his ancestors in the city of his father David; his son Jehoram succeeded him.

Ahaziah Reigns over Israel

51 Ahaziah son of Ahab began to reign over Israel in Samaria in the seventeenth year of King Jehoshaphat of Judah; he reigned two years over Israel. 52He did what was evil in the sight of the LORD, and walked in the way of his father and mother, and in the way of Jeroboam son of Nebat, who caused Israel to sin. 53He served Baal and worshiped him; he provoked the LORD, the God of Israel, to anger, just as his father had done.

ᵗ Heb lacks in it

2 Kings

Second Kings begins by describing the exploits of two great prophets, Elijah and Elisha. The prophets were God's representatives, often called to speak out against corrupt rulers like Ahab and his wife, Jezebel, whom we meet in both 1 and 2 Kings. In addition to the evil Jezebel, who imported Baal worship into the northern kingdom of Israel, we meet Queen Athaliah, who murdered her own grandsons in order to claim the throne of the southern kingdom of Judah (chapter 11).

By way of contrast, 2 Kings also contains the refreshing stories of the Shunammite woman (4.8–37) and the prophetess Huldah (22.14–20).

Because 2 Kings traces two lines of kings, one in the northern kingdom of Israel and the other in the southern kingdom of Judah, it can make for confusing reading. Though both nations had their share of unfaithful kings, Judah fared better because some of its kings "did what was right in the sight of the LORD." Israel was finally crushed by Assyria in 722 B.C., and Judah was conquered by Babylon in 586 B.C.

Elijah Denounces Ahaziah

1 After the death of Ahab, Moab rebelled against Israel.

2 Ahaziah had fallen through the lattice in his upper chamber in Samaria, and lay injured; so he sent messengers, telling them, "Go, inquire of Baal-zebub, the god of Ekron, whether I shall recover from this injury." 3 But the angel of the LORD said to Elijah the Tishbite, "Get up, go to meet the messengers of the king of Samaria, and say to them, 'Is it because there is no God in Israel that you are going to inquire of Baal-zebub, the god of Ekron?' 4 Now therefore thus says the LORD, 'You shall not leave the bed to which you have gone, but you shall surely die.' " So Elijah went.

5 The messengers returned to the king, who said to them, "Why have you returned?" 6 They answered him, "There came a man to meet us, who said to us, 'Go back to the king who sent you, and say to him: Thus says the LORD: Is it because there is no God in Israel that you are sending to inquire of Baal-zebub, the god of Ekron? Therefore you shall not leave the bed to which you have gone, but shall surely die.' " 7 He said to them, "What sort of man was he who came to meet you and told you these things?" 8 They answered him, "A hairy man, with a leather belt around his waist." He said, "It is Elijah the Tishbite."

9 Then the king sent to him a captain

of fifty with his fifty men. He went up to Elijah, who was sitting on the top of a hill, and said to him, "O man of God, the king says, 'Come down.'" [10]But Elijah answered the captain of fifty, "If I am a man of God, let fire come down from heaven and consume you and your fifty." Then fire came down from heaven, and consumed him and his fifty.

11 Again the king sent to him another captain of fifty with his fifty. He went up[a] and said to him, "O man of God, this is the king's order: Come down quickly!" [12]But Elijah answered them, "If I am a man of God, let fire come down from heaven and consume you and your fifty." Then the fire of God came down from heaven and consumed him and his fifty.

13 Again the king sent the captain of a third fifty with his fifty. So the third captain of fifty went up, and came and fell on his knees before Elijah, and entreated him, "O man of God, please let my life, and the life of these fifty servants of yours, be precious in your sight. [14]Look, fire came down from heaven and consumed the two former captains of fifty men with their fifties; but now let my life be precious in your sight." [15]Then the angel of the LORD said to Elijah, "Go down with him; do not be afraid of him." So he set out and went down with him to the king, [16]and said to him, "Thus says the LORD: Because you have sent messengers to inquire of Baal-zebub, the god of Ekron,—is it because there is no God in Israel to inquire of his word?—therefore you shall not leave the bed to which you have gone, but you shall surely die."

Death of Ahaziah

17 So he died according to the word of the LORD that Elijah had spoken. His brother,[b] Jehoram succeeded him as king in the second year of King Jehoram son of Jehoshaphat of Judah, because Ahaziah had no son. [18]Now the rest of the acts of Ahaziah that he did, are they not written in the Book of the Annals of the Kings of Israel?

Elijah Ascends to Heaven

2 Now when the LORD was about to take Elijah up to heaven by a whirlwind, Elijah and Elisha were on their way from Gilgal. [2]Elijah said to Elisha, "Stay here; for the LORD has sent me as far as Bethel." But Elisha said, "As the LORD lives,

and as you yourself live, I will not leave you." So they went down to Bethel. [3]The company of prophets[c] who were in Bethel came out to Elisha, and said to him, "Do you know that today the LORD will take your master away from you?" And he said, "Yes, I know; keep silent."

4 Elijah said to him, "Elisha, stay here; for the LORD has sent me to Jericho." But he said, "As the LORD lives, and as you yourself live, I will not leave you." So they came to Jericho. [5]The company of prophets[c] who were at Jericho drew near to Elisha, and said to him, "Do you know that today the LORD will take your master away from you?" And he answered, "Yes, I know; be silent."

6 Then Elijah said to him, "Stay here; for the LORD has sent me to the Jordan." But he said, "As the LORD lives, and as you yourself live, I will not leave you." So the two of them went on. [7]Fifty men of the company of prophets[c] also went, and stood at some distance from them, as they both were standing by the Jordan. [8]Then Elijah took his mantle and rolled it up, and struck the water; the water was parted to the one side and to the other, until the two of them crossed on dry ground.

9 When they had crossed, Elijah said to Elisha, "Tell me what I may do for you, before I am taken from you." Elisha said, "Please let me inherit a double share of your spirit." [10]He responded, "You have asked a hard thing; yet, if you see me as I am being taken from you, it will be granted you; if not, it will not." [11]As they continued walking and talking, a chariot of fire and horses of fire separated the two of them, and Elijah ascended in a whirlwind into heaven. [12]Elisha kept watching and crying out, "Father, father! The chariots of Israel and its horsemen!" But when he could no longer see him, he grasped his own clothes and tore them in two pieces.

Elisha Succeeds Elijah

13 He picked up the mantle of Elijah that had fallen from him, and went back and stood on the bank of the Jordan. [14]He took the mantle of Elijah that had fallen from him, and struck the water, saying, "Where is the LORD, the God of Elijah?" When he had struck the water, the water

a Gk Compare verses 9, 13: Heb He answered
b Gk Syr: Heb lacks His brother   c Heb sons of the prophets

was parted to the one side and to the other, and Elisha went over.

15 When the company of prophets[d] who were at Jericho saw him at a distance, they declared, "The spirit of Elijah rests on Elisha." They came to meet him and bowed to the ground before him. 16They said to him, "See now, we have fifty strong men among your servants; please let them go and seek your master; it may be that the spirit of the LORD has caught him up and thrown him down on some mountain or into some valley." He responded, "No, do not send them." 17But when they urged him until he was ashamed, he said, "Send them." So they sent fifty men who searched for three days but did not find him. 18When they came back to him (he had remained at Jericho), he said to them, "Did I not say to you, Do not go?"

Elisha Performs Miracles

19 Now the people of the city said to Elisha, "The location of this city is good, as my lord sees; but the water is bad, and the land is unfruitful." 20He said, "Bring me a new bowl, and put salt in it." So they brought it to him. 21Then he went to the spring of water and threw the salt into it, and said, "Thus says the LORD, I have made this water wholesome; from now on neither death nor miscarriage shall come from it." 22So the water has been wholesome to this day, according to the word that Elisha spoke.

23 He went up from there to Bethel; and while he was going up on the way, some small boys came out of the city and jeered at him, saying, "Go away, baldhead! Go away, baldhead!" 24When he turned around and saw them, he cursed them in the name of the LORD. Then two she-bears came out of the woods and mauled forty-two of the boys. 25From there he went on to Mount Carmel, and then returned to Samaria.

Jehoram Reigns over Israel

3 In the eighteenth year of King Jehoshaphat of Judah, Jehoram son of Ahab became king over Israel in Samaria; he reigned twelve years. 2He did what was evil in the sight of the LORD, though not like his father and mother, for he removed the pillar of Baal that his father had made. 3Nevertheless he clung to the sin of Jeroboam son of Nebat, which he caused Israel to commit; he did not depart from it.

War with Moab

4 Now King Mesha of Moab was a sheep breeder, who used to deliver to the king of Israel one hundred thousand lambs, and the wool of one hundred thousand rams. 5But when Ahab died, the king of Moab rebelled against the king of Israel. 6So King Jehoram marched out of Samaria at that time and mustered all Israel. 7As he went he sent word to King Jehoshaphat of Judah, "The king of Moab has rebelled against me; will you go with me to battle against Moab?" He answered, "I will; I am with you, my people are your people, my horses are your horses." 8Then he asked, "By which way shall we march?" Jehoram answered, "By the way of the wilderness of Edom."

9 So the king of Israel, the king of Judah, and the king of Edom set out; and when they had made a roundabout march of seven days, there was no water for the army or for the animals that were with them. 10Then the king of Israel said, "Alas! The LORD has summoned us, three kings, only to be handed over to Moab." 11But Jehoshaphat said, "Is there no prophet of the LORD here, through whom we may inquire of the LORD?" Then one of the servants of the king of Israel answered, "Elisha son of Shaphat, who used to pour water on the hands of Elijah, is here." 12Jehoshaphat said, "The word of the LORD is with him." So the king of Israel and Jehoshaphat and the king of Edom went down to him.

13 Elisha said to the king of Israel, "What have I to do with you? Go to your father's prophets or to your mother's." But the king of Israel said to him, "No; it is the LORD who has summoned us, three kings, only to be handed over to Moab." 14Elisha said, "As the LORD of hosts lives, whom I serve, were it not that I have regard for King Jehoshaphat of Judah, I would give you neither a look nor a glance. 15But get me a musician." And then, while the musician was playing, the power of the LORD came on him. 16And he said, "Thus says the LORD, 'I will make this wadi full of pools.' 17For thus says the LORD, 'You shall see neither wind nor rain, but the wadi shall be filled with water, so

d Heb sons of the prophets

that you shall drink, you, your cattle, and your animals.' [18]This is only a trifle in the sight of the LORD, for he will also hand Moab over to you. [19]You shall conquer every fortified city and every choice city; every good tree you shall fell, all springs of water you shall stop up, and every good piece of land you shall ruin with stones." [20]The next day, about the time of the morning offering, suddenly water began to flow from the direction of Edom, until the country was filled with water.

21 When all the Moabites heard that the kings had come up to fight against them, all who were able to put on armor, from the youngest to the oldest, were called out and were drawn up at the frontier. [22]When they rose early in the morning, and the sun shone upon the water, the Moabites saw the water opposite them as red as blood. [23]They said, "This is blood; the kings must have fought together, and killed one another. Now then, Moab, to the spoil!" [24]But when they came to the camp of Israel, the Israelites rose up and attacked the Moabites, who fled before them; as they entered Moab they continued the attack.[e] [25]The cities they overturned, and on every good piece of land everyone threw a stone, until it was covered; every spring of water they stopped up, and every good tree they felled. Only at Kir-hareseth did the stone walls remain, until the slingers surrounded and attacked it. [26]When the king of Moab saw that the battle was going against him, he took with him seven hundred swordsmen to break through, opposite the king of Edom; but they could not. [27]Then he took his firstborn son who was to succeed him, and offered him as a burnt offering on the wall. And great wrath came upon Israel, so they withdrew from him and returned to their own land.

Elisha and the Widow's Oil

4 Now the wife of a member of the company of prophets[f] cried to Elisha, "Your servant my husband is dead; and you know that your servant feared the LORD, but a creditor has come to take my two children as slaves." [2]Elisha said to her, "What shall I do for you? Tell me, what do you have in the house?" She answered, "Your servant has nothing in the house, except a jar of oil." [3]He said, "Go outside, borrow vessels from all your neighbors, empty vessels and not just a few. [4]Then go

in, and shut the door behind you and your children, and start pouring into all these vessels; when each is full, set it aside." [5]So she left him and shut the door behind her and her children; they kept bringing vessels to her, and she kept pouring. [6]When the vessels were full, she said to her son, "Bring me another vessel." But he said to her, "There are no more." Then the oil stopped flowing. [7]She came and told the man of God, and he said, "Go sell the oil and pay your debts, and you and your children can live on the rest."

Elisha Raises the Shunammite's Son

8 One day Elisha was passing through Shunem, where a wealthy woman lived, who urged him to have a meal. So whenever he passed that way, he would stop there for a meal. [9]She said to her husband, "Look, I am sure that this man who regularly passes our way is a holy man of God. [10]Let us make a small roof chamber with walls, and put there for him a bed, a table, a chair, and a lamp, so that he can stay there whenever he comes to us."

11 One day when he came there, he went up to the chamber and lay down there. [12]He said to his servant Gehazi, "Call the Shunammite woman." When he had called her, she stood before him. [13]He said to him, "Say to her, Since you have taken all this trouble for us, what may be done for you? Would you have a word spoken on your behalf to the king or to the commander of the army?" She answered, "I live among my own people." [14]He said, "What then may be done for her?" Gehazi answered, "Well, she has no son, and her husband is old." [15]He said, "Call her." When he had called her, she stood at the door. [16]He said, "At this season, in due time, you shall embrace a son." She replied, "No, my lord, O man of God; do not deceive your servant."

17 The woman conceived and bore a son at that season, in due time, as Elisha had declared to her.

18 When the child was older, he went out one day to his father among the reapers. [19]He complained to his father, "Oh, my head, my head!" The father said to his servant, "Carry him to his mother." [20]He carried him and brought him to his mother; the child sat on her lap until noon, and

---

e Compare Gk Syr: Meaning of Heb uncertain
f Heb *the sons of the prophets*

he died. ²¹She went up and laid him on the bed of the man of God, closed the door on him, and left. ²²Then she called to her husband, and said, "Send me one of the servants and one of the donkeys, so that I may quickly go to the man of God and come back again." ²³He said, "Why go to him today? It is neither new moon nor sabbath." She said, "It will be all right." ²⁴Then she saddled the donkey and said to her servant, "Urge the animal on; do not hold back for me unless I tell you."

²⁵So she set out, and came to the man of God at Mount Carmel.

When the man of God saw her coming, he said to Gehazi his servant, "Look, there is the Shunammite woman; ²⁶run at once to meet her, and say to her, Are you all right? Is your husband all right? Is the child all right?" She answered, "It is all right." ²⁷When she came to the man of God at the mountain, she caught hold of his feet. Gehazi approached to push her away. But the man of God said, "Let her alone,

*W*e Are Needy

THURSDAY

Scripture Reading for Today:
2 Kings 4.1–7

Verse for Today:
2 Kings 4.2

I have never had the misfortune of being in debt up to my ears. The wolf has never stood howling at my door. And the bank has never threatened to repossess anything, not even my car. I have been greatly blessed, and I know it. But it is one thing to have money in the bank and another to have enough spiritual capital in your soul. The truth is that I often lack both the emotional and spiritual resources that seem so necessary to daily life—patience, time, perspective, energy, confidence, wisdom, understanding, forgiveness, faith, hope for the future. Perhaps you can identify with my list. Or maybe you have a list of your own.

But God can take what little we have and multiply it if we will ask and have faith. Elisha encouraged the widow to exercise her faith by requiring her to borrow as many jars as she could in which to store the oil. But when she went knocking on doors, she still had only a little oil in her possession. It was the same with Noah when God instructed him to make an ark. He had to build the boat before even a drop of water had fallen from the sky.

This doesn't mean that God will answer every one of our prayers precisely as we want him to if we will only have enough faith. He may assess our needs differently than we do, allowing some of them to go unmet or to wait awhile so that he can work out a deeper purpose in our lives.

Whatever the case, life goes much better with faith. If you feel that you have too little of this precious commodity, ask God to multiply it. And if you haven't already done so, pray for his Spirit to indwell you. Interestingly enough, oil is actually a symbol for the Holy Spirit. And it is the Spirit who gives us life, enabling us to have faith in a God who will meet our deepest needs, no matter how impossibly desperate we feel.

—ANN SPANGLER

Go to page 391 for your next devotional reading.

for she is in bitter distress; the LORD has hidden it from me and has not told me." ²⁸Then she said, "Did I ask my lord for a son? Did I not say, Do not mislead me?" ²⁹He said to Gehazi, "Gird up your loins, and take my staff in your hand, and go. If you meet anyone, give no greeting, and if anyone greets you, do not answer; and lay my staff on the face of the child." ³⁰Then the mother of the child said, "As the LORD lives, and as you yourself live, I will not leave without you." So he rose up and followed her. ³¹Gehazi went on ahead and laid the staff on the face of the child, but there was no sound or sign of life. He came back to meet him and told him, "The child has not awakened."

32 When Elisha came into the house, he saw the child lying dead on his bed. ³³So he went in and closed the door on the two of them, and prayed to the LORD. ³⁴Then he got up on the bed[g] and lay upon the child, putting his mouth upon his mouth, his eyes upon his eyes, and his hands upon his hands; and while he lay bent over him, the flesh of the child became warm. ³⁵He got down, walked once to and fro in the room, then got up again and bent over him; the child sneezed seven times, and the child opened his eyes. ³⁶Elisha[h] summoned Gehazi and said, "Call the Shunammite woman." So he called her. When she came to him, he said, "Take your son." ³⁷She came and fell at his feet, bowing to the ground; then she took her son and left.

Elisha Purifies the Pot of Stew

38 When Elisha returned to Gilgal, there was a famine in the land. As the company of prophets was[i] sitting before him, he said to his servant, "Put the large pot on, and make some stew for the company of prophets."[j] ³⁹One of them went out into the field to gather herbs; he found a wild vine and gathered from it a lapful of wild gourds, and came and cut them up into the pot of stew, not knowing what they were. ⁴⁰They served some for the men to eat. But while they were eating the stew, they cried out, "O man of God, there is death in the pot!" They could not eat it. ⁴¹He said, "Then bring some flour." He threw it into the pot, and said, "Serve the people and let them eat." And there was nothing harmful in the pot.

Elisha Feeds One Hundred Men

42 A man came from Baal-shalishah, bringing food from the first fruits to the man of God: twenty loaves of barley and fresh ears of grain in his sack. Elisha said, "Give it to the people and let them eat." ⁴³But his servant said, "How can I set this before a hundred people?" So he repeated, "Give it to the people and let them eat, for thus says the LORD, 'They shall eat and have some left.' " ⁴⁴He set it before them, they ate, and had some left, according to the word of the LORD.

The Healing of Naaman

5 Naaman, commander of the army of the king of Aram, was a great man and in high favor with his master, because by him the LORD had given victory to Aram. The man, though a mighty warrior, suffered from leprosy.[k] ²Now the Arameans on one of their raids had taken a young girl captive from the land of Israel, and she served Naaman's wife. ³She said to her mistress, "If only my lord were with the prophet who is in Samaria! He would cure him of his leprosy."[k] ⁴So Naaman[h] went in and told his lord just what the girl from the land of Israel had said. ⁵And the king of Aram said, "Go then, and I will send along a letter to the king of Israel."

He went, taking with him ten talents of silver, six thousand shekels of gold, and ten sets of garments. ⁶He brought the letter to the king of Israel, which read, "When this letter reaches you, know that I have sent to you my servant Naaman, that you may cure him of his leprosy."[k] ⁷When the king of Israel read the letter, he tore his clothes and said, "Am I God, to give death or life, that this man sends word to me to cure a man of his leprosy?[k] Just look and see how he is trying to pick a quarrel with me."

8 But when Elisha the man of God heard that the king of Israel had torn his clothes, he sent a message to the king, "Why have you torn your clothes? Let him come to me, that he may learn that there is a prophet in Israel." ⁹So Naaman came with his horses and chariots, and halted at the entrance of Elisha's house.

---

g Heb lacks *on the bed*   h Heb *he*   i Heb *sons of the prophets were*   j Heb *sons of the prophets*
k A term for several skin diseases; precise meaning uncertain

¹⁰Elisha sent a messenger to him, saying, "Go, wash in the Jordan seven times, and your flesh shall be restored and you shall be clean." ¹¹But Naaman became angry and went away, saying, "I thought that for me he would surely come out, and stand and call on the name of the LORD his God, and would wave his hand over the spot, and cure the leprosy!¹ ¹²Are not Ab-anaᵐ and Pharpar, the rivers of Damascus, better than all the waters of Israel? Could I not wash in them, and be clean?" He turned and went away in a rage. ¹³But his servants approached and said to him, "Father, if the prophet had commanded you to do something difficult, would you not have done it? How much more, when all he said to you was, 'Wash, and be clean'?" ¹⁴So he went down and immersed himself seven times in the Jordan, according to the word of the man of God; his flesh was restored like the flesh of a young boy, and he was clean.

15 Then he returned to the man of God, he and all his company; he came and stood before him and said, "Now I know that there is no God in all the earth except in Israel; please accept a present from your servant." ¹⁶But he said, "As the LORD lives, whom I serve, I will accept nothing!" He urged him to accept, but he refused. ¹⁷Then Naaman said, "If not, please let two mule-loads of earth be given to your servant; for your servant will no longer offer burnt offering or sacrifice to any god except the LORD. ¹⁸But may the LORD pardon your servant on one count: when my master goes into the house of Rimmon to worship there, leaning on my arm, and I bow down in the house of Rimmon, when I do bow down in the house of Rimmon, may the LORD pardon your servant on this one count." ¹⁹He said to him, "Go in peace."

Gehazi's Greed

But when Naaman had gone from him a short distance, ²⁰Gehazi, the servant of Elisha the man of God, thought, "My master has let that Aramean Naaman off too lightly by not accepting from him what he offered. As the LORD lives, I will run after him and get something out of him." ²¹So Gehazi went after Naaman. When Naaman saw someone running after him, he jumped down from the chariot to meet him and said, "Is everything all right?" ²²He replied, "Yes, but my master has sent me to say, 'Two members of a company of prophetsⁿ have just come to me from the hill country of Ephraim; please give them a talent of silver and two changes of clothing.' " ²³Naaman said, "Please accept two talents." He urged him, and tied up two talents of silver in two bags, with two changes of clothing, and gave them to two of his servants, who carried them in front of Gehazi.ᵒ ²⁴When he came to the citadel, he took the bagsᵖ from them, and stored them inside; he dismissed the men, and they left.

25 He went in and stood before his master; and Elisha said to him, "Where have you been, Gehazi?" He answered, "Your servant has not gone anywhere at all." ²⁶But he said to him, "Did I not go with you in spirit when someone left his chariot to meet you? Is this a time to accept money and to accept clothing, olive orchards and vineyards, sheep and oxen, and male and female slaves? ²⁷Therefore the leprosy¹ of Naaman shall cling to you, and to your descendants forever." So he left his presence leprous,¹ as white as snow.

The Miracle of the Ax Head

6 Now the company of prophetsⁿ said to Elisha, "As you see, the place where we live under your charge is too small for us. ²Let us go to the Jordan, and let us collect logs there, one for each of us, and build a place there for us to live." He answered, "Do so." ³Then one of them said, "Please come with your servants." And he answered, "I will." ⁴So he went with them. When they came to the Jordan, they cut down trees. ⁵But as one was felling a log, his ax head fell into the water; he cried out, "Alas, master! It was borrowed." ⁶Then the man of God said, "Where did it fall?" When he showed him the place, he cut off a stick, and threw it in there, and made the iron float. ⁷He said, "Pick it up." So he reached out his hand and took it.

The Aramean Attack Is Thwarted

8 Once when the king of Aram was at war with Israel, he took counsel with his officers. He said, "At such and such a

---

¹ A term for several skin diseases; precise meaning uncertain   ᵐ Another reading is Amana   ⁿ Heb sons of the prophets   ᵒ Heb him   ᵖ Heb lacks the bags

place shall be my camp." ⁹But the man of God sent word to the king of Israel, "Take care not to pass this place, because the Arameans are going down there." ¹⁰The king of Israel sent word to the place of which the man of God spoke. More than once or twice he warned such a place*q* so that it was on the alert.

11 The mind of the king of Aram was greatly perturbed because of this; he called his officers and said to them, "Now tell me who among us sides with the king of Israel?" ¹²Then one of his officers said, "No one, my lord king. It is Elisha, the prophet in Israel, who tells the king of Israel the words that you speak in your bedchamber." ¹³He said, "Go and find where he is; I will send and seize him." He was told, "He is in Dothan." ¹⁴So he sent horses and chariots there and a great army; they came by night, and surrounded the city.

15 When an attendant of the man of God rose early in the morning and went out, an army with horses and chariots was all around the city. His servant said, "Alas, master! What shall we do?" ¹⁶He replied, "Do not be afraid, for there are more with us than there are with them." ¹⁷Then Elisha

q Heb *warned it*

*E*yes of Faith

FRIDAY

Scripture Reading for Today:
2 Kings 6.8–17

Verse for Today:
2 Kings 6.17

Sometimes we feel surrounded by trouble and difficulty, beset on every side by problems of one kind or another. This was the case with Elisha on the morning when he and his servant woke up to find themselves surrounded by an army intent on capturing them. They were outgunned, outmanned, and outmaneuvered. It must have felt like the last stand of Butch Cassidy and the Sundance Kid. But it wasn't: God had planned a heavenly ambush to protect them.

Elisha's story tells us that some things can only be seen through the eyes of faith. But faith is something that does not come naturally to us. We want to taste, touch, and see for ourselves before we will believe.

A few years ago, a friend of mine was consumed by anxiety for her future. As she voiced her apprehensions, she said something that sums up our struggle to believe: "If I could only see what's going to happen, I could trust God for it." But the point of faith is that we need it *because* we can't see into the future.

My friend was making the same mistake I have often made. She was identifying faith with a certain kind of outcome. If things would work out as she hoped they would, then she would believe. But our faith will fail us if we tie it to a set of circumstances. It will become more like positive thinking than real faith. Instead, the faith that nourishes us involves trust in Someone rather than something—in the character of a God who is both loving and powerful enough to save us. God does not ask us to blindly trust him. Instead, he reveals himself through Scripture and through our own experiences to convince us that he is trustworthy.

—ANN SPANGLER

Go to page 398 for your next devotional reading.

prayed: "O LORD, please open his eyes that he may see." So the LORD opened the eyes of the servant, and he saw; the mountain was full of horses and chariots of fire all around Elisha. [18]When the Arameans[r] came down against him, Elisha prayed to the LORD, and said, "Strike this people, please, with blindness." So he struck them with blindness as Elisha had asked. [19]Elisha said to them, "This is not the way, and this is not the city; follow me, and I will bring you to the man whom you seek." And he led them to Samaria.

20 As soon as they entered Samaria, Elisha said, "O LORD, open the eyes of these men so that they may see." The LORD opened their eyes, and they saw that they were inside Samaria. [21]When the king of Israel saw them he said to Elisha, "Father, shall I kill them? Shall I kill them?" [22]He answered, "No! Did you capture with your sword and your bow those whom you want to kill? Set food and water before them so that they may eat and drink; and let them go to their master." [23]So he prepared for them a great feast; after they ate and drank, he sent them on their way, and they went to their master. And the Arameans no longer came raiding into the land of Israel.

Ben-hadad's Siege of Samaria

24 Some time later King Ben-hadad of Aram mustered his entire army; he marched against Samaria and laid siege to it. [25]As the siege continued, famine in Samaria became so great that a donkey's head was sold for eighty shekels of silver, and one-fourth of a kab of dove's dung for five shekels of silver. [26]Now as the king of Israel was walking on the city wall, a woman cried out to him, "Help, my lord king!" [27]He said, "No! Let the LORD help you. How can I help you? From the threshing floor or from the wine press?" [28]But then the king asked her, "What is your complaint?" She answered, "This woman said to me, 'Give up your son; we will eat him today, and we will eat my son tomorrow.' [29]So we cooked my son and ate him. The next day I said to her, 'Give up your son and we will eat him.' But she has hidden her son." [30]When the king heard the words of the woman he tore his clothes—now since he was walking on the city wall, the people could see that he had sackcloth on his body underneath— [31]and he said, "So may God do to me,

and more, if the head of Elisha son of Shaphat stays on his shoulders today." [32]So he dispatched a man from his presence.

Now Elisha was sitting in his house, and the elders were sitting with him. Before the messenger arrived, Elisha said to the elders, "Are you aware that this murderer has sent someone to take off my head? When the messenger comes, see that you shut the door and hold it closed against him. Is not the sound of his master's feet behind him?" [33]While he was still speaking with them, the king[s] came down to him and said, "This trouble is from the LORD! Why should I hope in the LORD any longer?" [1]But Elisha said, "Hear the word of the LORD: thus says the LORD, Tomorrow about this time a measure of choice meal shall be sold for a shekel, and two measures of barley for a shekel, at the gate of Samaria." [2]Then the captain on whose hand the king leaned said to the man of God, "Even if the LORD were to make windows in the sky, could such a thing happen?" But he said, "You shall see it with your own eyes, but you shall not eat from it."

The Arameans Flee

3 Now there were four leprous[t] men outside the city gate, who said to one another, "Why should we sit here until we die? [4]If we say, 'Let us enter the city,' the famine is in the city, and we shall die there; but if we sit here, we shall also die. Therefore, let us desert to the Aramean camp; if they spare our lives, we shall live; and if they kill us, we shall but die." [5]So they arose at twilight to go to the Aramean camp; but when they came to the edge of the Aramean camp, there was no one there at all. [6]For the Lord had caused the Aramean army to hear the sound of chariots, and of horses, the sound of a great army, so that they said to one another, "The king of Israel has hired the kings of the Hittites and the kings of Egypt to fight against us." [7]So they fled away in the twilight and abandoned their tents, their horses, and their donkeys leaving the camp just as it was, and fled for their lives. [8]When these leprous[t] men had come to the edge of the camp, they went into a tent, ate and drank, carried off silver, gold,

---

[r] Heb *they*   [s] See 7.2: Heb *messenger*   [t] A term for several skin diseases; precise meaning uncertain

and clothing, and went and hid them. Then they came back, entered another tent, carried off things from it, and went and hid them.

9 Then they said to one another, "What we are doing is wrong. This is a day of good news; if we are silent and wait until the morning light, we will be found guilty; therefore let us go and tell the king's household." 10So they came and called to the gatekeepers of the city, and told them, "We went to the Aramean camp, but there was no one to be seen or heard there, nothing but the horses tied, the donkeys tied, and the tents as they were." 11Then the gatekeepers called out and proclaimed it to the king's household. 12The king got up in the night, and said to his servants, "I will tell you what the Arameans have prepared against us. They know that we are starving; so they have left the camp to hide themselves in the open country, thinking, 'When they come out of the city, we shall take them alive and get into the city.' " 13One of his servants said, "Let some men take five of the remaining horses, since those left here will suffer the fate of the whole multitude of Israel that have perished already;u let us send and find out." 14So they took two mounted men, and the king sent them after the Aramean army, saying, "Go and find out." 15So they went after them as far as the Jordan; the whole way was littered with garments and equipment that the Arameans had thrown away in their haste. So the messengers returned, and told the king.

16 Then the people went out, and plundered the camp of the Arameans. So a measure of choice meal was sold for a shekel, and two measures of barley for a shekel, according to the word of the Lord. 17Now the king had appointed the captain on whose hand he leaned to have charge of the gate; the people trampled him to death in the gate, just as the man of God had said when the king came down to him. 18For when the man of God had said to the king, "Two measures of barley shall be sold for a shekel, and a measure of choice meal for a shekel, about this time tomorrow in the gate of Samaria," 19the captain had answered the man of God, "Even if the Lord were to make windows in the sky, could such a thing happen?" And he had answered, "You shall see it with your own eyes, but you shall not eat

from it." 20It did indeed happen to him; the people trampled him to death in the gate.

The Shunammite Woman's Land Restored

8 Now Elisha had said to the woman whose son he had restored to life, "Get up and go with your household, and settle wherever you can; for the Lord has called for a famine, and it will come on the land for seven years." 2So the woman got up and did according to the word of the man of God; she went with her household and settled in the land of the Philistines seven years. 3At the end of the seven years, when the woman returned from the land of the Philistines, she set out to appeal to the king for her house and her land. 4Now the king was talking with Gehazi the servant of the man of God, saying, "Tell me all the great things that Elisha has done." 5While he was telling the king how Elisha had restored a dead person to life, the woman whose son he had restored to life appealed to the king for her house and her land. Gehazi said, "My lord king, here is the woman, and here is her son whom Elisha restored to life." 6When the king questioned the woman, she told him. So the king appointed an official for her, saying, "Restore all that was hers, together with all the revenue of the fields from the day that she left the land until now."

Death of Ben-hadad

7 Elisha went to Damascus while King Ben-hadad of Aram was ill. When it was told him, "The man of God has come here," 8the king said to Hazael, "Take a present with you and go to meet the man of God. Inquire of the Lord through him, whether I shall recover from this illness." 9So Hazael went to meet him, taking a present with him, all kinds of goods of Damascus, forty camel loads. When he entered and stood before him, he said, "Your son King Ben-hadad of Aram has sent me to you, saying, 'Shall I recover from this illness?' " 10Elisha said to him, "Go, say to him, 'You shall certainly recover'; but the Lord has shown me that he shall certainly die." 11He fixed his gaze and stared at him, until he was ashamed. Then the man of God wept. 12Hazael asked, "Why does my lord weep?" He answered,

u Compare Gk Syr Vg: Meaning of Heb uncertain

"Because I know the evil that you will do to the people of Israel; you will set their fortresses on fire, you will kill their young men with the sword, dash in pieces their little ones, and rip up their pregnant women." 13Hazael said, "What is your servant, who is a mere dog, that he should do this great thing?" Elisha answered, "The LORD has shown me that you are to be king over Aram." 14Then he left Elisha, and went to his master Ben-hadad,ᵛ who said to him, "What did Elisha say to you?" And he answered, "He told me that you would certainly recover." 15But the next day he took the bed-cover and dipped it in water and spread it over the king's face, until he died. And Hazael succeeded him.

Jehoram Reigns over Judah

16 In the fifth year of King Joram son of Ahab of Israel,ʷ Jehoram son of King Jehoshaphat of Judah began to reign. 17He was thirty-two years old when he became king, and he reigned eight years in Jerusalem. 18He walked in the way of the kings of Israel, as the house of Ahab had done, for the daughter of Ahab was his wife. He did what was evil in the sight of the LORD. 19Yet the LORD would not destroy Judah, for the sake of his servant David, since he had promised to give a lamp to him and to his descendants forever.

20 In his days Edom revolted against the rule of Judah, and set up a king of their own. 21Then Joram crossed over to Zair with all his chariots. He set out by night and attacked the Edomites and their chariot commanders who had surrounded him;ˣ but his army fled home. 22So Edom has been in revolt against the rule of Judah to this day. Libnah also revolted at the same time. 23Now the rest of the acts of Joram, and all that he did, are they not written in the Book of the Annals of the Kings of Judah? 24So Joram slept with his ancestors, and was buried with them in the city of David; his son Ahaziah succeeded him.

Ahaziah Reigns over Judah

25 In the twelfth year of King Joram son of Ahab of Israel, Ahaziah son of King Jehoram of Judah began to reign. 26Ahaziah was twenty-two years old when he began to reign; he reigned one year in Jerusalem. His mother's name was Athaliah, a granddaughter of King Omri of Israel. 27He also walked in the way of the house of Ahab, doing what was evil in the sight of the LORD, as the house of Ahab had done, for he was son-in-law to the house of Ahab. 28 He went with Joram son of Ahab to wage war against King Hazael of Aram at Ramoth-gilead, where the Arameans wounded Joram. 29King Joram returned to be healed in Jezreel of the wounds that the Arameans had inflicted on him at Ramah, when he fought against King Hazael of Aram. King Ahaziah son of Jehoram of Judah went down to see Joram son of Ahab in Jezreel, because he was wounded.

Anointing of Jehu

9 Then the prophet Elisha called a member of the company of prophetsʸ and said to him, "Gird up your loins; take this flask of oil in your hand, and go to Ramoth-gilead. 2When you arrive, look there for Jehu son of Jehoshaphat, son of Nimshi; go in and get him to leave his companions, and take him into an inner chamber. 3Then take the flask of oil, pour it on his head, and say, 'Thus says the LORD: I anoint you king over Israel.' Then open the door and flee; do not linger."

4 So the young man, the young prophet, went to Ramoth-gilead. 5He arrived while the commanders of the army were in council, and he announced, "I have a message for you, commander." "For which one of us?" asked Jehu. "For you, commander." 6So Jehuᶻ got up and went inside; the young man poured the oil on his head, saying to him, "Thus says the LORD the God of Israel: I anoint you king over the people of the LORD, over Israel. 7You shall strike down the house of your master Ahab, so that I may avenge on Jezebel the blood of my servants the prophets, and the blood of all the servants of the LORD. 8For the whole house of Ahab shall perish; I will cut off from Ahab every male, bond or free, in Israel. 9I will make the house of Ahab like the house of Jeroboam son of Nebat, and like the house of Baasha son of Ahijah. 10The dogs shall eat Jezebel in the territory of Jezreel, and no one shall bury her." Then he opened the door and fled.

ᵛ Heb lacks Ben-hadad   ʷ Gk Syr: Heb adds Jehoshaphat being king of Judah,   ˣ Meaning of Heb uncertain   ʸ Heb sons of the prophets   ᶻ Heb he

11 When Jehu came back to his master's officers, they said to him, "Is everything all right? Why did that madman come to you?" He answered them, "You know the sort and how they babble." [12]They said, "Liar! Come on, tell us!" So he said, "This is just what he said to me: 'Thus says the LORD, I anoint you king over Israel.'" [13]Then hurriedly they all took their cloaks and spread them for him on the bare[a] steps; and they blew the trumpet, and proclaimed, "Jehu is king."

Joram of Israel Killed

14 Thus Jehu son of Jehoshaphat son of Nimshi conspired against Joram. Joram with all Israel had been on guard at Ramoth-gilead against King Hazael of Aram; [15]but King Joram had returned to be healed in Jezreel of the wounds that the Arameans had inflicted on him, when he fought against King Hazael of Aram. So Jehu said, "If this is your wish, then let no one slip out of the city to go and tell the news in Jezreel." [16]Then Jehu mounted his chariot and went to Jezreel, where Joram was lying ill. King Ahaziah of Judah had come down to visit Joram.

17 In Jezreel, the sentinel standing on the tower spied the company of Jehu arriving, and said, "I see a company." Joram said, "Take a horseman; send him to meet them, and let him say, 'Is it peace?'" [18]So the horseman went to meet him; he said, "Thus says the king, 'Is it peace?'" Jehu responded, "What have you to do with peace? Fall in behind me." The sentinel reported, saying, "The messenger reached them, but he is not coming back." [19]Then he sent out a second horseman, who came to them and said, "Thus says the king, 'Is it peace?'" Jehu answered, "What have you to do with peace? Fall in behind me." [20]Again the sentinel reported, "He reached them, but he is not coming back. It looks like the driving of Jehu son of Nimshi; for he drives like a maniac."

21 Joram said, "Get ready." And they got his chariot ready. Then King Joram of Israel and King Ahaziah of Judah set out, each in his chariot, and went to meet Jehu; they met him at the property of Naboth the Jezreelite. [22]When Joram saw Jehu, he said, "Is it peace, Jehu?" He answered, "What peace can there be, so long as the many whoredoms and sorceries of your mother Jezebel continue?" [23]Then Joram reined about and fled, saying to Aha-

ziah, "Treason, Ahaziah!" [24]Jehu drew his bow with all his strength, and shot Joram between the shoulders, so that the arrow pierced his heart; and he sank in his chariot. [25]Jehu said to his aide Bidkar, "Lift him out, and throw him on the plot of ground belonging to Naboth the Jezreelite; for remember, when you and I rode side by side behind his father Ahab how the LORD uttered this oracle against him: [26]'For the blood of Naboth and for the blood of his children that I saw yesterday, says the LORD, I swear I will repay you on this very plot of ground.' Now therefore lift him out and throw him on the plot of ground, in accordance with the word of the LORD."

Ahaziah of Judah Killed

27 When King Ahaziah of Judah saw this, he fled in the direction of Beth-haggan. Jehu pursued him, saying, "Shoot him also!" And they shot him[b] in the chariot at the ascent to Gur, which is by Ibleam. Then he fled to Megiddo, and died there. [28]His officers carried him in a chariot to Jerusalem, and buried him in his tomb with his ancestors in the city of David.

29 In the eleventh year of Joram son of Ahab, Ahaziah began to reign over Judah.

Jezebel's Violent Death

30 When Jehu came to Jezreel, Jezebel heard of it; she painted her eyes, and adorned her head, and looked out of the window. [31]As Jehu entered the gate, she said, "Is it peace, Zimri, murderer of your master?" [32]He looked up to the window and said, "Who is on my side? Who?" Two or three eunuchs looked out at him. [33]He said, "Throw her down." So they threw her down; some of her blood spattered on the wall and on the horses, which trampled on her. [34]Then he went in and ate and drank; he said, "See to that cursed woman and bury her; for she is a king's daughter." [35]But when they went to bury her, they found no more of her than the skull and the feet and the palms of her hands. [36]When they came back and told him, he said, "This is the word of the LORD, which he spoke by his servant Elijah the Tishbite, 'In the territory of Jezreel the dogs shall eat the flesh of Jezebel; [37]the corpse of

---

[a] Meaning of Heb uncertain   [b] Syr Vg Compare Gk: Heb lacks *and they shot him*

Jezebel shall be like dung on the field in the territory of Jezreel, so that no one can say, This is Jezebel.' "

Massacre of Ahab's Descendants

10 Now Ahab had seventy sons in Samaria. So Jehu wrote letters and sent them to Samaria, to the rulers of Jezreel,c to the elders, and to the guardians of the sons ofd Ahab, saying, 2"Since your master's sons are with you and you have at your disposal chariots and horses, a fortified city, and weapons, 3select the son of your master who is the best qualified, set him on his father's throne, and fight for your master's house." 4But they were utterly terrified and said, "Look, two kings could not withstand him; how then can we stand?" 5So the steward of the palace, and the governor of the city, along with the elders and the guardians, sent word to Jehu: "We are your servants; we will do anything you say. We will not make anyone king; do whatever you think right." 6Then he wrote them a second letter, saying, "If you are on my side, and if you are ready to obey me, take the heads of your master's sons and come to me at Jezreel tomorrow at this time." Now the king's sons, seventy persons, were with the leaders of the city, who were charged with their upbringing. 7When the letter reached them, they took the king's sons and killed them, seventy persons; they put their heads in baskets and sent them to him at Jezreel. 8When the messenger came and told him, "They have brought the heads of the king's sons," he said, "Lay them in two heaps at the entrance of the gate until the morning." 9Then in the morning when he went out, he stood and said to all the people, "You are innocent. It was I who conspired against my master and killed him; but who struck down all these? 10Know then that there shall fall to the earth nothing of the word of the LORD, which the LORD spoke concerning the house of Ahab; for the LORD has done what he said through his servant Elijah." 11So Jehu killed all who were left of the house of Ahab in Jezreel, all his leaders, close friends, and priests, until he left him no survivor.

12 Then he set out and went to Samaria. On the way, when he was at Beth-eked of the Shepherds, 13Jehu met relatives of King Ahaziah of Judah and said, "Who are you?" They answered, "We are kin of Ahaziah; we have come down to visit the royal princes and the sons of the queen mother." 14He said, "Take them alive." They took them alive, and slaughtered them at the pit of Beth-eked, forty-two in all; he spared none of them.

15 When he left there, he met Jehonadab son of Rechab coming to meet him; he greeted him, and said to him, "Is your heart as true to mine as mine is to yours?"e Jehonadab answered, "It is." Jehu said,f "If it is, give me your hand." So he gave him his hand. Jehu took him up with him into the chariot. 16He said, "Come with me, and see my zeal for the LORD." So heg had him ride in his chariot. 17When he came to Samaria, he killed all who were left to Ahab in Samaria, until he had wiped them out, according to the word of the LORD that he spoke to Elijah.

Slaughter of Worshipers of Baal

18 Then Jehu assembled all the people and said to them, "Ahab offered Baal small service; but Jehu will offer much more. 19Now therefore summon to me all the prophets of Baal, all his worshipers, and all his priests; let none be missing, for I have a great sacrifice to offer to Baal; whoever is missing shall not live." But Jehu was acting with cunning in order to destroy the worshipers of Baal. 20Jehu decreed, "Sanctify a solemn assembly for Baal." So they proclaimed it. 21Jehu sent word throughout all Israel; all the worshipers of Baal came, so that there was no one left who did not come. They entered the temple of Baal, until the temple of Baal was filled from wall to wall. 22He said to the keeper of the wardrobe, "Bring out the vestments for all the worshipers of Baal." So he brought out the vestments for them. 23Then Jehu entered the temple of Baal with Jehonadab son of Rechab; he said to the worshipers of Baal, "Search and see that there is no worshiper of the LORD here among you, but only worshipers of Baal." 24Then they proceeded to offer sacrifices and burnt offerings.

Now Jehu had stationed eighty men outside, saying, "Whoever allows any of those to escape whom I deliver into your hands shall forfeit his life." 25As soon as he

c Or of the city; Vg Compare Gk   d Gk: Heb lacks of the sons of   e Gk: Heb Is it right with your heart, as my heart is with your heart?   f Gk: Heb lacks Jehu said   g Gk Syr Tg: Heb they had finished presenting the burnt offering, Jehu said to the guards and to the officers, "Come in and kill them; let no one escape." So they put them to the sword. The guards and the officers threw them out, and then went into the citadel of the temple of Baal. 26They brought out the pillar*h* that was in the temple of Baal, and burned it. 27Then they demolished the pillar of Baal, and destroyed the temple of Baal, and made it a latrine to this day.

28 Thus Jehu wiped out Baal from Israel. 29But Jehu did not turn aside from the sins of Jeroboam son of Nebat, which he caused Israel to commit—the golden calves that were in Bethel and in Dan. 30The LORD said to Jehu, "Because you have done well in carrying out what I consider right, and in accordance with all that was in my heart have dealt with the house of Ahab, your sons of the fourth generation shall sit on the throne of Israel." 31But Jehu was not careful to follow the law of the LORD the God of Israel with all his heart; he did not turn from the sins of Jeroboam, which he caused Israel to commit.

Death of Jehu

32 In those days the LORD began to trim off parts of Israel. Hazael defeated them throughout the territory of Israel: 33from the Jordan eastward, all the land of Gilead, the Gadites, the Reubenites, and the Manassites, from Aroer, which is by the Wadi Arnon, that is, Gilead and Bashan. 34Now the rest of the acts of Jehu, all that he did, and all his power, are they not written in the Book of the Annals of the Kings of Israel? 35So Jehu slept with his ancestors, and they buried him in Samaria. His son Jehoahaz succeeded him. 36The time that Jehu reigned over Israel in Samaria was twenty-eight years.

Athaliah Reigns over Judah

11 Now when Athaliah, Ahaziah's mother, saw that her son was dead, she set about to destroy all the royal family. 2But Jehosheba, King Joram's daughter, Ahaziah's sister, took Joash son of Ahaziah, and stole him away from among the king's children who were about to be killed; she put*i* him and his nurse in a bedroom. Thus she*j* hid him from Athaliah, so that he was not killed; 3he remained with her six years, hidden

in the house of the LORD, while Athaliah reigned over the land.

Jehoiada Anoints the Child Joash

4 But in the seventh year Jehoiada summoned the captains of the Carites and of the guards and had them come to him in the house of the LORD. He made a covenant with them and put them under oath in the house of the LORD; then he showed them the king's son. 5He commanded them, "This is what you are to do: one-third of you, those who go off duty on the sabbath and guard the king's house 6(another third being at the gate Sur and a third at the gate behind the guards), shall guard the palace; 7and your two divisions that come on duty in force on the sabbath and guard the house of the LORD*k* 8shall surround the king, each with weapons in hand; and whoever approaches the ranks is to be killed. Be with the king in his comings and goings."

9 The captains did according to all that the priest Jehoiada commanded; each brought his men who were to go off duty on the sabbath, with those who were to come on duty on the sabbath, and came to the priest Jehoiada. 10The priest delivered to the captains the spears and shields that had been King David's, which were in the house of the LORD; 11the guards stood, every man with his weapons in his hand, from the south side of the house to the north side of the house, around the altar and the house, to guard the king on every side. 12Then he brought out the king's son, put the crown on him, and gave him the covenant;*l* they proclaimed him king, and anointed him; they clapped their hands and shouted, "Long live the king!"

Death of Athaliah

13 When Athaliah heard the noise of the guard and of the people, she went into the house of the LORD to the people; 14when she looked, there was the king standing by the pillar, according to custom, with the captains and the trumpeters beside the king, and all the people of the land rejoicing and blowing trumpets. Athaliah tore her clothes and cried, "Treason!

h Gk Vg Syr Tg: Heb *pillars*   *i* With 2 Chr 22.11: Heb lacks *she put*   *j* Gk Syr Vg Compare 2 Chr 22.11: Heb *they*   *k* Heb *the LORD to the king*   *l* Or *treaty* or *testimony*; Heb *eduth*

THE
STORY
OF A
WOMAN

Potiphar's
Wife

Her Character: *The wife of a prosperous and influential Egyptian, she was unfaithful and vindictive, ready to lie in order to protect herself and ruin an innocent man.*
Her Sorrow: *To be rebuffed by a slave.*

Read Genesis 39

We don't even know her name. She is merely presented as the spoiled wife of a prosperous Egyptian official, a Cleopatra wanna-be, determined to employ her charms to seduce the handsome young Hebrew slave, Joseph.

At the age of seventeen, Joseph had been sold into slavery by his half-brothers, the sons of Leah. The favorite child of Rachel and Jacob, he seems to have unwittingly done everything possible to ensure his brothers' enmity, even recounting a dream predicting that he, the younger son, would one day rule over them. Envious, the brothers faked his death and contemptuously sold him to Midianite traders en route to Egypt.

Potiphar, captain of Pharaoh's executioners, bought the young slave and eventually entrusted him with responsibility for his entire household. Even in his exile, everything Joseph touched prospered, and Potiphar couldn't help but notice.

But the captain of the guard wasn't the only Egyptian impressed by Joseph. His wife had taken special note as well. She made her desire plain enough by inviting Joseph to share her bed. The young slave must have surprised his wealthy mistress with his quick rebuff: "Look, with me here, my master has no concern about anything in the house, and he has put everything that he has in my hand. He is not greater in this house than I am, nor

has he kept back anything from me except yourself, because you are his wife. How then could I do this great wickedness, and sin against God?" (verses 8–9). From then on, Joseph did his best to avoid her.

But with little else to occupy her time and attention, Potiphar's wife simply waited for her next opportunity. It came when Joseph entered the house one day to attend to his duties. Alone with him, she caught hold of his cloak, whispering again, "Lie with me!" But Joseph fled from her, leaving his would-be seducer alone with her lust, furiously clutching his cloak in her fingers.

Fearing, perhaps, that Joseph would speak to Potiphar about what had happened, she wasted no time accusing him of attempted rape. When her husband heard the news, he was outraged, quickly consigning his favorite servant to prison.

The story of Joseph and how God blessed him even in his prison cell, eventually enabling him to become master of the nation he had entered as a slave, is well known to us. But we haven't a clue about Potiphar's wife. Whatever became of her? Did her husband suspect her duplicity? Is that why he merely confined Joseph to prison rather than executing him, as he had every right to do? Compared with Joseph, the story's protagonist, Potiphar's wife is a hollow woman, whose soul was steadily decaying through the corrosive power of lust and hate. Surrounded by luxury, she was yet spiritually impoverished. Empty of God, she was full of herself.

Praying in Light of the Story of Potiphar's Wife

Create in me a clean heart, O God, and put a new and right spirit within me.
—Psalm 51:10

Praise God: Because the pure in heart will see him.

Offer Thanks: That he invites us to enjoy an intimate relationship with himself rather than the empty pleasures this world offers.

Confess: Any tendency toward becoming emotionally or physically involved in an off-limits relationship.

Ask God: To help you break the habit of fantasizing about relationships you wish you had.

Lift Your Heart

We know what happened to Joseph after he was falsely accused, but we don't know anything about Potiphar's wife. Write a short account from your own imagination, entitled "Whatever Became of Potiphar's Wife?" You can give her a happy ending or a sad one, just make sure it's believable. Try to put yourself in the story. You could be Potiphar's wife, her mother, her maid, her little sister, or whatever character you dream up. Does anything occur to you as you ponder her story's conclusion?

Lord, I don't want my soul to feed on empty pleasures, to long for what belongs to someone else. Instead, increase my hunger for you and create in me a pure heart, one that you will find irresistibly beautiful.

Go to page 409 for your next devotional reading.

Treason!" [15]Then the priest Jehoiada commanded the captains who were set over the army, "Bring her out between the ranks, and kill with the sword anyone who follows her." For the priest said, "Let her not be killed in the house of the LORD." [16]So they laid hands on her; she went through the horses' entrance to the king's house, and there she was put to death.

17 Jehoiada made a covenant between the LORD and the king and people, that they should be the LORD's people; also between the king and the people. [18]Then all the people of the land went to the house of Baal, and tore it down; his altars and his images they broke in pieces, and they killed Mattan, the priest of Baal, before the altars. The priest posted guards over the house of the LORD. [19]He took the captains, the Carites, the guards, and all the people of the land; then they brought the king down from the house of the LORD, marching through the gate of the guards to the king's house. He took his seat on the throne of the kings. [20]So all the people of the land rejoiced; and the city was quiet after Athaliah had been killed with the sword at the king's house.

[21][m] Jehoash[n] was seven years old when he began to reign.

The Temple Repaired

12 In the seventh year of Jehu, Jehoash began to reign; he reigned forty years in Jerusalem. His mother's name was Zibiah of Beer-sheba. [2]Jehoash did what was right in the sight of the LORD all his days, because the priest Jehoiada instructed him. [3]Nevertheless the high places were not taken away; the people continued to sacrifice and make offerings on the high places.

4 Jehoash said to the priests, "All the money offered as sacred donations that is brought into the house of the LORD, the money for which each person is assessed—the money from the assessment of persons—and the money from the voluntary offerings brought into the house of the LORD, [5]let the priests receive from each of the donors; and let them repair the house wherever any need of repairs is discovered." [6]But by the twenty-third year of King Jehoash the priests had made no repairs on the house. [7]Therefore King Jehoash summoned the priest Jehoiada with the other priests and said to them, "Why are you not repairing the house? Now

therefore do not accept any more money from your donors but hand it over for the repair of the house." [8]So the priests agreed that they would neither accept more money from the people nor repair the house.

9 Then the priest Jehoiada took a chest, made a hole in its lid, and set it beside the altar on the right side as one entered the house of the LORD; the priests who guarded the threshold put in it all the money that was brought into the house of the LORD. [10]Whenever they saw that there was a great deal of money in the chest, the king's secretary and the high priest went up, counted the money that was found in the house of the LORD, and tied it up in bags. [11]They would give the money that was weighed out into the hands of the workers who had the oversight of the house of the LORD; then they paid it out to the carpenters and the builders who worked on the house of the LORD, [12]to the masons and the stonecutters, as well as to buy timber and quarried stone for making repairs on the house of the LORD, as well as for any outlay for repairs of the house. [13]But for the house of the LORD no basins of silver, snuffers, bowls, trumpets, or any vessels of gold, or of silver, were made from the money that was brought into the house of the LORD, [14]for that was given to the workers who were repairing the house of the LORD with it. [15]They did not ask an accounting from those into whose hand they delivered the money to pay out to the workers, for they dealt honestly. [16]The money from the guilt offerings and the money from the sin offerings was not brought into the house of the LORD; it belonged to the priests.

Hazael Threatens Jerusalem

17 At that time King Hazael of Aram went up, fought against Gath, and took it. But when Hazael set his face to go up against Jerusalem, [18]King Jehoash of Judah took all the votive gifts that Jehoshaphat, Jehoram, and Ahaziah, his ancestors, the kings of Judah, had dedicated, as well as his own votive gifts, all the gold that was found in the treasuries of the house of the LORD and of the king's house, and sent these to King Hazael of Aram. Then Hazael withdrew from Jerusalem.

[m] Ch 12.1 in Heb   [n] Another spelling is *Joash;* see verse 19

Death of Joash

19 Now the rest of the acts of Joash, and all that he did, are they not written in the Book of the Annals of the Kings of Judah? 20His servants arose, devised a conspiracy, and killed Joash in the house of Millo, on the way that goes down to Silla. 21It was Jozacar son of Shimeath and Jehozabad son of Shomer, his servants, who struck him down, so that he died. He was buried with his ancestors in the city of David; then his son Amaziah succeeded him.

Jehoahaz Reigns over Israel

13 In the twenty-third year of King Joash son of Ahaziah of Judah, Jehoahaz son of Jehu began to reign over Israel in Samaria; he reigned seventeen years. 2He did what was evil in the sight of the LORD, and followed the sins of Jeroboam son of Nebat, which he caused Israel to sin; he did not depart from them. 3The anger of the LORD was kindled against Israel, so that he gave them repeatedly into the hand of King Hazael of Aram, then into the hand of Ben-hadad son of Hazael. 4But Jehoahaz entreated the LORD, and the LORD heeded him; for he saw the oppression of Israel, how the king of Aram oppressed them. 5Therefore the LORD gave Israel a savior, so that they escaped from the hand of the Arameans; and the people of Israel lived in their homes as formerly. 6Nevertheless they did not depart from the sins of the house of Jeroboam, which he caused Israel to sin, but walked⁰ in them; the sacred poleᵖ also remained in Samaria. 7So Jehoahaz was left with an army of not more than fifty horsemen, ten chariots and ten thousand footmen; for the king of Aram had destroyed them and made them like the dust at threshing. 8Now the rest of the acts of Jehoahaz and all that he did, including his might, are they not written in the Book of the Annals of the Kings of Israel? 9So Jehoahaz slept with his ancestors, and they buried him in Samaria; then his son Joash succeeded him.

Jehoash Reigns over Israel

10 In the thirty-seventh year of King Joash of Judah, Jehoash son of Jehoahaz began to reign over Israel in Samaria; he reigned sixteen years. 11He also did what was evil in the sight of the LORD; he did not depart from all the sins of Jeroboam son of Nebat, which he caused Israel to sin, but he walked in them. 12Now the rest of the acts of Joash, and all that he did, as well as the might with which he fought against King Amaziah of Judah, are they not written in the Book of the Annals of the Kings of Israel? 13So Joash slept with his ancestors, and Jeroboam sat upon his throne; Joash was buried in Samaria with the kings of Israel.

Death of Elisha

14 Now when Elisha had fallen sick with the illness of which he was to die, King Joash of Israel went down to him, and wept before him, crying, "My father, my father! The chariots of Israel and its horsemen!" 15Elisha said to him, "Take a bow and arrows"; so he took a bow and arrows. 16Then he said to the king of Israel, "Draw the bow"; and he drew it. Elisha laid his hands on the king's hands. 17Then he said, "Open the window eastward"; and he opened it. Elisha said, "Shoot"; and he shot. Then he said, "The LORD's arrow of victory, the arrow of victory over Aram! For you shall fight the Arameans in Aphek until you have made an end of them." 18He continued, "Take the arrows"; and he took them. He said to the king of Israel, "Strike the ground with them"; he struck three times, and stopped. 19Then the man of God was angry with him, and said, "You should have struck five or six times; then you would have struck down Aram until you had made an end of it, but now you will strike down Aram only three times."

20 So Elisha died, and they buried him. Now bands of Moabites used to invade the land in the spring of the year. 21As a man was being buried, a marauding band was seen and the man was thrown into the grave of Elisha; as soon as the man touched the bones of Elisha, he came to life and stood on his feet.

Israel Recaptures Cities from Aram

22 Now King Hazael of Aram oppressed Israel all the days of Jehoahaz. 23But the LORD was gracious to them and had compassion on them; he turned toward them, because of his covenant with Abraham, Isaac, and Jacob, and would not destroy them; nor has he banished them from his presence until now.

⁰ Gk Syr Tg Vg: Heb *he walked*   ᵖ Heb *Asherah*

24 When King Hazael of Aram died, his son Ben-hadad succeeded him. 25 Then Jehoash son of Jehoahaz took again from Ben-hadad son of Hazael the towns that he had taken from his father Jehoahaz in war. Three times Joash defeated him and recovered the towns of Israel.

Amaziah Reigns over Judah

14 In the second year of King Joash son of Joahaz of Israel, King Amaziah son of Joash of Judah, began to reign. 2 He was twenty-five years old when he began to reign, and he reigned twenty-nine years in Jerusalem. His mother's name was Jehoaddin of Jerusalem. 3 He did what was right in the sight of the LORD, yet not like his ancestor David; in all things he did as his father Joash had done. 4 But the high places were not removed; the people still sacrificed and made offerings on the high places. 5 As soon as the royal power was firmly in his hand he killed his servants who had murdered his father the king. 6 But he did not put to death the children of the murderers; according to what is written in the book of the law of Moses, where the LORD commanded, "The parents shall not be put to death for the children, or the children be put to death for the parents; but all shall be put to death for their own sins."

7 He killed ten thousand Edomites in the Valley of Salt and took Sela by storm; he called it Jokthe-el, which is its name to this day.

8 Then Amaziah sent messengers to King Jehoash son of Jehoahaz, son of Jehu, of Israel, saying, "Come, let us look one another in the face." 9 King Jehoash of Israel sent word to King Amaziah of Judah, "A thornbush on Lebanon sent to a cedar on Lebanon, saying, 'Give your daughter to my son for a wife'; but a wild animal of Lebanon passed by and trampled down the thornbush. 10 You have indeed defeated Edom, and your heart has lifted you up. Be content with your glory, and stay at home; for why should you provoke trouble so that you fall, you and Judah with you?"

11 But Amaziah would not listen. So King Jehoash of Israel went up; he and King Amaziah of Judah faced one another in battle at Beth-shemesh, which belongs to Judah. 12 Judah was defeated by Israel; everyone fled home. 13 King Jehoash of Israel captured King Amaziah of Judah son of Jehoash, son of Ahaziah, at Beth-shemesh; he came to Jerusalem, and broke down the wall of Jerusalem from the Ephraim Gate to the Corner Gate, a distance of four hundred cubits. 14 He seized all the gold and silver, and all the vessels that were found in the house of the LORD and in the treasuries of the king's house, as well as hostages; then he returned to Samaria.

15 Now the rest of the acts that Jehoash did, his might, and how he fought with King Amaziah of Judah, are they not written in the Book of the Annals of the Kings of Israel? 16 Jehoash slept with his ancestors, and was buried in Samaria with the kings of Israel; then his son Jeroboam succeeded him.

17 King Amaziah son of Joash of Judah lived fifteen years after the death of King Jehoash son of Jehoahaz of Israel. 18 Now the rest of the deeds of Amaziah, are they not written in the Book of the Annals of the Kings of Judah? 19 They made a conspiracy against him in Jerusalem, and he fled to Lachish. But they sent after him to Lachish, and killed him there. 20 They brought him on horses; he was buried in Jerusalem with his ancestors in the city of David. 21 All the people of Judah took Azariah, who was sixteen years old, and made him king to succeed his father Amaziah. 22 He rebuilt Elath and restored it to Judah, after King Amaziah[q] slept with his ancestors.

Jeroboam II Reigns over Israel

23 In the fifteenth year of King Amaziah son of Joash of Judah, King Jeroboam son of Joash of Israel began to reign in Samaria; he reigned forty-one years. 24 He did what was evil in the sight of the LORD; he did not depart from all the sins of Jeroboam son of Nebat, which he caused Israel to sin. 25 He restored the border of Israel from Lebo-hamath as far as the Sea of the Arabah, according to the word of the LORD, the God of Israel, which he spoke by his servant Jonah son of Amittai, the prophet, who was from Gath-hepher. 26 For the LORD saw that the distress of Israel was very bitter; there was no one left, bond or free, and no one to help Israel. 27 But the LORD had not said that he would blot out the name of Israel from under heaven, so

q Heb the king

he saved them by the hand of Jeroboam son of Joash.

28 Now the rest of the acts of Jeroboam, and all that he did, and his might, how he fought, and how he recovered for Israel Damascus and Hamath, which had belonged to Judah, are they not written in the Book of the Annals of the Kings of Israel? 29Jeroboam slept with his ancestors, the kings of Israel; his son Zechariah succeeded him.

Azariah Reigns over Judah

15 In the twenty-seventh year of King Jeroboam of Israel King Azariah son of Amaziah of Judah began to reign. 2He was sixteen years old when he began to reign, and he reigned fifty-two years in Jerusalem. His mother's name was Jecoliah of Jerusalem. 3He did what was right in the sight of the LORD, just as his father Amaziah had done. 4Nevertheless the high places were not taken away; the people still sacrificed and made offerings on the high places. 5The LORD struck the king, so that he was leprousʳ to the day of his death, and lived in a separate house. Jotham the king's son was in charge of the palace, governing the people of the land. 6Now the rest of the acts of Azariah, and all that he did, are they not written in the Book of the Annals of the Kings of Judah? 7Azariah slept with his ancestors; they buried him with his ancestors in the city of David; his son Jotham succeeded him.

Zechariah Reigns over Israel

8 In the thirty-eighth year of King Azariah of Judah, Zechariah son of Jeroboam reigned over Israel in Samaria six months. 9He did what was evil in the sight of the LORD, as his ancestors had done. He did not depart from the sins of Jeroboam son of Nebat, which he caused Israel to sin. 10Shallum son of Jabesh conspired against him, and struck him down in public and killed him, and reigned in place of him. 11Now the rest of the deeds of Zechariah are written in the Book of the Annals of the Kings of Israel. 12This was the promise of the LORD that he gave to Jehu, "Your sons shall sit on the throne of Israel to the fourth generation." And so it happened.

Shallum Reigns over Israel

13 Shallum son of Jabesh began to reign in the thirty-ninth year of King Uzzi-ah of Judah; he reigned one month in Samaria. 14Then Menahem son of Gadi came up from Tirzah and came to Samaria; he struck down Shallum son of Jabesh in Samaria and killed him; he reigned in place of him. 15Now the rest of the deeds of Shallum, including the conspiracy that he made, are written in the Book of the Annals of the Kings of Israel. 16At that time Menahem sacked Tiphsah, all who were in it and its territory from Tirzah on; because they did not open it to him, he sacked it. He ripped open all the pregnant women in it.

Menahem Reigns over Israel

17 In the thirty-ninth year of King Azariah of Judah, Menahem son of Gadi began to reign over Israel; he reigned ten years in Samaria. 18He did what was evil in the sight of the LORD; he did not depart all his days from any of the sins of Jeroboam son of Nebat, which he caused Israel to sin. 19King Pul of Assyria came against the land; Menahem gave Pul a thousand talents of silver, so that he might help him confirm his hold on the royal power. 20Menahem exacted the money from Israel, that is, from all the wealthy, fifty shekels of silver from each one, to give to the king of Assyria. So the king of Assyria turned back, and did not stay there in the land. 21Now the rest of the deeds of Menahem, and all that he did, are they not written in the Book of the Annals of the Kings of Israel? 22Menahem slept with his ancestors, and his son Pekahiah succeeded him.

Pekahiah Reigns over Israel

23 In the fiftieth year of King Azariah of Judah, Pekahiah son of Menahem began to reign over Israel in Samaria; he reigned two years. 24He did what was evil in the sight of the LORD; he did not turn away from the sins of Jeroboam son of Nebat, which he caused Israel to sin. 25Pekah son of Remaliah, his captain, conspired against him with fifty of the Gileadites, and attacked him in Samaria, in the citadel of the palace along with Argob and Arieh; he killed him, and reigned in place of him. 26Now the rest of the deeds of Pekahiah, and all that he did, are written in the Book of the Annals of the Kings of Israel.

ʳ A term for several skin diseases; precise meaning uncertain

Pekah Reigns over Israel

27 In the fifty-second year of King Aza-riah of Judah, Pekah son of Remaliah be-gan to reign over Israel in Samaria; he reigned twenty years. 28He did what was evil in the sight of the LORD; he did not depart from the sins of Jeroboam son of Nebat, which he caused Israel to sin.

29 In the days of King Pekah of Israel, King Tiglath-pileser of Assyria came and captured Ijon, Abel-beth-maacah, Janoah, Kedesh, Hazor, Gilead, and Galilee, all the land of Naphtali; and he carried the peo-ple captive to Assyria. 30Then Hoshea son of Elah made a conspiracy against Pekah son of Remaliah, attacked him, and killed him; he reigned in place of him, in the twentieth year of Jotham son of Uzziah. 31Now the rest of the acts of Pekah, and all that he did, are written in the Book of the Annals of the Kings of Israel.

Jotham Reigns over Judah

32 In the second year of King Pekah son of Remaliah of Israel, King Jotham son of Uzziah of Judah began to reign. 33He was twenty-five years old when he began to reign and reigned sixteen years in Jerusalem. His mother's name was Jerusha daughter of Zadok. 34He did what was right in the sight of the LORD, just as his father Uzziah had done. 35Nevertheless the high places were not removed; the people still sacrificed and made offerings on the high places. He built the upper gate of the house of the LORD. 36Now the rest of the acts of Jotham, and all that he did, are they not written in the Book of the Annals of the Kings of Judah? 37In those days the LORD began to send King Rezin of Aram and Pekah son of Remaliah against Judah. 38Jotham slept with his ancestors, and was buried with his ancestors in the city of David, his ancestor; his son Ahaz succeed-ed him.

Ahaz Reigns over Judah

16 In the seventeenth year of Pekah son of Remaliah, King Ahaz son of Jotham of Judah began to reign. 2Ahaz was twenty years old when he began to reign; he reigned sixteen years in Jerusa-lem. He did not do what was right in the sight of the LORD his God, as his ancestor David had done, 3but he walked in the way of the kings of Israel. He even made his son pass through fire, according to the abominable practices of the nations whom the LORD drove out before the peo-ple of Israel. 4He sacrificed and made offerings on the high places, on the hills, and under every green tree.

5 Then King Rezin of Aram and King Pekah son of Remaliah of Israel came up to wage war on Jerusalem; they besieged Ahaz but could not conquer him. 6At that time the king of Edom*s* recovered Elath for Edom,*t* and drove the Judeans from Elath; and the Edomites came to Elath, where they live to this day. 7Ahaz sent messengers to King Tiglath-pileser of As-syria, saying, "I am your servant and your son. Come up, and rescue me from the hand of the king of Aram and from the hand of the king of Israel, who are attack-ing me." 8Ahaz also took the silver and gold found in the house of the LORD and in the treasures of the king's house, and sent a present to the king of Assyria. 9The king of Assyria listened to him; the king of Assyria marched up against Da-mascus, and took it, carrying its people captive to Kir; then he killed Rezin.

10 When King Ahaz went to Damascus to meet King Tiglath-pileser of Assyria, he saw the altar that was at Damascus. King Ahaz sent to the priest Uriah a model of the altar, and its pattern, exact in all its details. 11The priest Uriah built the altar; in accordance with all that King Ahaz had sent from Damascus, just so did the priest Uriah build it, before King Ahaz arrived from Damascus. 12When the king came from Damascus, the king viewed the altar. Then the king drew near to the altar, went up on it, 13and offered his burnt offering and his grain offering, poured his drink offering, and dashed the blood of his offerings of well-being against the altar. 14The bronze altar that was before the LORD he removed from the front of the house, from the place between his altar and the house of the LORD, and put it on the north side of his altar. 15King Ahaz commanded the priest Uriah, saying, "Upon the great altar offer the morning burnt offering, and the evening grain offering, and the king's burnt offering, and his grain offering, with the burnt offering of all the people of the land, their grain offering, and their drink offering; then dash against it all the blood of the burnt offering, and all the blood of the

s Cn: Heb *King Rezin of Aram*   *t* Cn: Heb *Aram*

sacrifice; but the bronze altar shall be for me to inquire by." [16]The priest Uriah did everything that King Ahaz commanded.

17 Then King Ahaz cut off the frames of the stands, and removed the laver from them; he removed the sea from the bronze oxen that were under it, and put it on a pediment of stone. [18]The covered portal for use on the sabbath that had been built inside the palace, and the outer entrance for the king he removed from[u] the house of the LORD. He did this because of the king of Assyria. [19]Now the rest of the acts of Ahaz that he did, are they not written in the Book of the Annals of the Kings of Judah? [20]Ahaz slept with his ancestors, and was buried with his ancestors in the city of David; his son Hezekiah succeeded him.

Hoshea Reigns over Israel

17 In the twelfth year of King Ahaz of Judah, Hoshea son of Elah began to reign in Samaria over Israel; he reigned nine years. [2]He did what was evil in the sight of the LORD, yet not like the kings of Israel who were before him. [3]King Shalmaneser of Assyria came up against him; Hoshea became his vassal, and paid him tribute. [4]But the king of Assyria found treachery in Hoshea; for he had sent messengers to King So of Egypt, and offered no tribute to the king of Assyria, as he had done year by year; therefore the king of Assyria confined him and imprisoned him.

Israel Carried Captive to Assyria

5 Then the king of Assyria invaded all the land and came to Samaria; for three years he besieged it. [6]In the ninth year of Hoshea the king of Assyria captured Samaria; he carried the Israelites away to Assyria. He placed them in Halah, on the Habor, the river of Gozan, and in the cities of the Medes.

7 This occurred because the people of Israel had sinned against the LORD their God, who had brought them up out of the land of Egypt from under the hand of Pharaoh king of Egypt. They had worshiped other gods [8]and walked in the customs of the nations whom the LORD drove out before the people of Israel, and in the customs that the kings of Israel had introduced.[v] [9]The people of Israel secretly did things that were not right against the LORD their God. They built for themselves high places at all their towns, from watchtower to fortified city; [10]they set up for themselves pillars and sacred poles[w] on every high hill and under every green tree; [11]there they made offerings on all the high places, as the nations did whom the LORD carried away before them. They did wicked things, provoking the LORD to anger; [12]they served idols, of which the LORD had said to them, "You shall not do this." [13]Yet the LORD warned Israel and Judah by every prophet and every seer, saying, "Turn from your evil ways and keep my commandments and my statutes, in accordance with all the law that I commanded your ancestors and that I sent to you by my servants the prophets." [14]They would not listen but were stubborn, as their ancestors had been, who did not believe in the LORD their God. [15]They despised his statutes, and his covenant that he made with their ancestors, and the warnings that he gave them. They went after false idols and became false; they followed the nations that were around them, concerning whom the LORD had commanded them that they should not do as they did. [16]They rejected all the commandments of the LORD their God and made for themselves cast images of two calves; they made a sacred pole,[x] worshiped all the host of heaven, and served Baal. [17]They made their sons and their daughters pass through fire; they used divination and augury; and they sold themselves to do evil in the sight of the LORD, provoking him to anger. [18]Therefore the LORD was very angry with Israel and removed them out of his sight; none was left but the tribe of Judah alone.

19 Judah also did not keep the commandments of the LORD their God but walked in the customs that Israel had introduced. [20]The LORD rejected all the descendants of Israel; he punished them and gave them into the hand of plunderers, until he had banished them from his presence.

21 When he had torn Israel from the house of David, they made Jeroboam son of Nebat king. Jeroboam drove Israel from following the LORD and made them commit great sin. [22]The people of Israel continued in all the sins that Jeroboam committed; they did not depart from them

u Cn: Heb lacks *from*   v Meaning of Heb uncertain   w Heb *Asherim*   x Heb *Asherah*

23until the LORD removed Israel out of his sight, as he had foretold through all his servants the prophets. So Israel was exiled from their own land to Assyria until this day.

Assyria Resettles Samaria

24 The king of Assyria brought people from Babylon, Cuthah, Avva, Hamath, and Sepharvaim, and placed them in the cities of Samaria in place of the people of Israel; they took possession of Samaria, and settled in its cities. 25When they first settled there, they did not worship the LORD; therefore the LORD sent lions among them, which killed some of them. 26So the king of Assyria was told, "The nations that you have carried away and placed in the cities of Samaria do not know the law of the god of the land; therefore he has sent lions among them; they are killing them, because they do not know the law of the god of the land." 27Then the king of Assyria commanded, "Send there one of the priests whom you carried away from there; let himy go and live there, and teach them the law of the god of the land." 28So one of the priests whom they had carried away from Samaria came and lived in Bethel; he taught them how they should worship the LORD.

29 But every nation still made gods of its own and put them in the shrines of the high places that the people of Samaria had made, every nation in the cities in which they lived; 30the people of Babylon made Succoth-benoth, the people of Cuth made Nergal, the people of Hamath made Ashima; 31the Avvites made Nibhaz and Tartak; the Sepharvites burned their children in the fire to Adrammelech and Anammelech, the gods of Sepharvaim. 32They also worshiped the LORD and appointed from among themselves all sorts of people as priests of the high places, who sacrificed for them in the shrines of the high places. 33So they worshiped the LORD but also served their own gods, after the manner of the nations from among whom they had been carried away. 34To this day they continue to practice their former customs.

They do not worship the LORD and they do not follow the statutes or the ordinances or the law or the commandment that the LORD commanded the children of Jacob, whom he named Israel. 35The LORD had made a covenant with them and com-manded them, "You shall not worship other gods or bow yourselves to them or serve them or sacrifice to them, 36but you shall worship the LORD, who brought you out of the land of Egypt with great power and with an outstretched arm; you shall bow yourselves to him, and to him you shall sacrifice. 37The statutes and the ordinances and the law and the commandment that he wrote for you, you shall always be careful to observe. You shall not worship other gods; 38you shall not forget the covenant that I have made with you. You shall not worship other gods, 39but you shall worship the LORD your God; he will deliver you out of the hand of all your enemies." 40They would not listen, however, but they continued to practice their former custom.

41 So these nations worshiped the LORD, but also served their carved images; to this day their children and their children's children continue to do as their ancestors did.

Hezekiah's Reign over Judah

18 In the third year of King Hoshea son of Elah of Israel, Hezekiah son of King Ahaz of Judah began to reign. 2He was twenty-five years old when he began to reign; he reigned twenty-nine years in Jerusalem. His mother's name was Abi daughter of Zechariah. 3He did what was right in the sight of the LORD just as his ancestor David had done. 4He removed the high places, broke down the pillars, and cut down the sacred pole.z He broke in pieces the bronze serpent that Moses had made, for until those days the people of Israel had made offerings to it; it was called Nehushtan. 5He trusted in the LORD the God of Israel; so that there was no one like him among all the kings of Judah after him, or among those who were before him. 6For he held fast to the LORD; he did not depart from following him but kept the commandments that the LORD commanded Moses. 7The LORD was with him; wherever he went, he prospered. He rebelled against the king of Assyria and would not serve him. 8He attacked the Philistines as far as Gaza and its territory, from watchtower to fortified city.

9 In the fourth year of King Hezekiah, which was the seventh year of King Ho-

y Syr Vg: Heb *them*   z Heb *Asherah*

shea son of Elah of Israel, King Shalmaneser of Assyria came up against Samaria, besieged it, [10]and at the end of three years, took it. In the sixth year of Hezekiah, which was the ninth year of King Hoshea of Israel, Samaria was taken. [11]The king of Assyria carried the Israelites away to Assyria, settled them in Halah, on the Habor, the river of Gozan, and in the cities of the Medes, [12]because they did not obey the voice of the LORD their God but transgressed his covenant—all that Moses the servant of the LORD had commanded; they neither listened nor obeyed.

Sennacherib Invades Judah

13 In the fourteenth year of King Hezekiah, King Sennacherib of Assyria came up against all the fortified cities of Judah and captured them. [14]King Hezekiah of Judah sent to the king of Assyria at Lachish, saying, "I have done wrong; withdraw from me; whatever you impose on me I will bear." The king of Assyria demanded of King Hezekiah of Judah three hundred talents of silver and thirty talents of gold. [15]Hezekiah gave him all the silver that was found in the house of the LORD and in the treasuries of the king's house. [16]At that time Hezekiah stripped the gold from the doors of the temple of the LORD, and from the doorposts that King Hezekiah of Judah had overlaid and gave it to the king of Assyria. [17]The king of Assyria sent the Tartan, the Rabsaris, and the Rabshakeh with a great army from Lachish to King Hezekiah at Jerusalem. They went up and came to Jerusalem. When they arrived, they came and stood by the conduit of the upper pool, which is on the highway to the Fuller's Field. [18]When they called for the king, there came out to them Eliakim son of Hilkiah, who was in charge of the palace, and Shebnah the secretary, and Joah son of Asaph, the recorder.

19 The Rabshakeh said to them, "Say to Hezekiah: Thus says the great king, the king of Assyria: On what do you base this confidence of yours? [20]Do you think that mere words are strategy and power for war? On whom do you now rely, that you have rebelled against me? [21]See, you are relying now on Egypt, that broken reed of a staff, which will pierce the hand of anyone who leans on it. Such is Pharaoh king of Egypt to all who rely on him. [22]But if you say to me, 'We rely on the LORD our God,' is it not he whose high places and altars Hezekiah has removed, saying to Judah and to Jerusalem, 'You shall worship before this altar in Jerusalem'? [23]Come now, make a wager with my master the king of Assyria: I will give you two thousand horses, if you are able on your part to set riders on them. [24]How then can you repulse a single captain among the least of my master's servants, when you rely on Egypt for chariots and for horsemen? [25]Moreover, is it without the LORD that I have come up against this place to destroy it? The LORD said to me, Go up against this land, and destroy it."

26 Then Eliakim son of Hilkiah, and Shebnah, and Joah said to the Rabshakeh, "Please speak to your servants in the Aramaic language, for we understand it; do not speak to us in the language of Judah within the hearing of the people who are on the wall." [27]But the Rabshakeh said to them, "Has my master sent me to speak these words to your master and to you, and not to the people sitting on the wall, who are doomed with you to eat their own dung and to drink their own urine?"

28 Then the Rabshakeh stood and called out in a loud voice in the language of Judah, "Hear the word of the great king, the king of Assyria! [29]Thus says the king: 'Do not let Hezekiah deceive you, for he will not be able to deliver you out of my hand. [30]Do not let Hezekiah make you rely on the LORD by saying, The LORD will surely deliver us, and this city will not be given into the hand of the king of Assyria.' [31]Do not listen to Hezekiah; for thus says the king of Assyria: 'Make your peace with me and come out to me; then every one of you will eat from your own vine and your own fig tree, and drink water from your own cistern, [32]until I come and take you away to a land like your own land, a land of grain and wine, a land of bread and vineyards, a land of olive oil and honey, that you may live and not die. Do not listen to Hezekiah when he misleads you by saying, The LORD will deliver us. [33]Has any of the gods of the nations ever delivered its land out of the hand of the king of Assyria? [34]Where are the gods of Hamath and Arpad? Where are the gods of Sepharvaim, Hena, and Ivvah? Have they delivered Samaria out of my hand? [35]Who among all the gods of the countries have delivered their countries out of my hand, that the LORD should deliver Jerusalem out of my hand?' "

36 But the people were silent and answered him not a word, for the king's command was, "Do not answer him." 37Then Eliakim son of Hilkiah, who was in charge of the palace, and Shebna the secretary, and Joah son of Asaph, the recorder, came to Hezekiah with their clothes torn and told him the words of the Rabshakeh.

Hezekiah Consults Isaiah

19 When King Hezekiah heard it, he tore his clothes, covered himself with sackcloth, and went into the house of the LORD. 2And he sent Eliakim, who was in charge of the palace, and Shebna the secretary, and the senior priests, covered with sackcloth, to the prophet Isaiah son of Amoz. 3They said to him, "Thus says Hezekiah, This day is a day of distress, of rebuke, and of disgrace; children have come to the birth, and there is no strength to bring them forth. 4It may be that the LORD your God heard all the words of the Rabshakeh, whom his master the king of Assyria has sent to mock the living God, and will rebuke the words that the LORD your God has heard; therefore lift up your prayer for the remnant that is left." 5When the servants of King Hezekiah came to Isaiah, 6Isaiah said to them, "Say to your master, 'Thus says the LORD: Do not be afraid because of the words that you have heard, with which the servants of the king of Assyria have reviled me. 7I myself will put a spirit in him, so that he shall hear a rumor and return to his own land; I will cause him to fall by the sword in his own land.' "

Sennacherib's Threat

8 The Rabshakeh returned, and found the king of Assyria fighting against Libnah; for he had heard that the king had left Lachish. 9When the king[a] heard concerning King Tirhakah of Ethiopia,[b] "See, he has set out to fight against you," he sent messengers again to Hezekiah, saying, 10"Thus shall you speak to King Hezekiah of Judah: Do not let your God on whom you rely deceive you by promising that Jerusalem will not be given into the hand of the king of Assyria. 11See, you have heard what the kings of Assyria have done to all lands, destroying them utterly. Shall you be delivered? 12Have the gods of the nations delivered them, the nations that my predecessors destroyed, Gozan, Haran, Rezeph, and the people of Eden who were in Telassar? 13Where is the king of Hamath, the king of Arpad, the king of the city of Sepharvaim, the king of Hena, or the king of Ivvah?"

Hezekiah's Prayer

14 Hezekiah received the letter from the hand of the messengers and read it; then Hezekiah went up to the house of the LORD and spread it before the LORD. 15And Hezekiah prayed before the LORD, and said: "O LORD the God of Israel, who are enthroned above the cherubim, you are God, you alone, of all the kingdoms of the earth; you have made heaven and earth. 16Incline your ear, O LORD, and hear; open your eyes, O LORD, and see; hear the words of Sennacherib, which he has sent to mock the living God. 17Truly, O LORD, the kings of Assyria have laid waste the nations and their lands, 18and have hurled their gods into the fire, though they were no gods but the work of human hands—wood and stone—and so they were destroyed. 19So now, O LORD our God, save us, I pray you, from his hand, so that all the kingdoms of the earth may know that you, O LORD, are God alone."

20 Then Isaiah son of Amoz sent to Hezekiah, saying, "Thus says the LORD, the God of Israel: I have heard your prayer to me about King Sennacherib of Assyria. 21This is the word that the LORD has spoken concerning him:

She despises you, she scorns you—
    virgin daughter Zion;
she tosses her head—behind your
        back,
    daughter Jerusalem.

22 "Whom have you mocked and
        reviled?
    Against whom have you raised
        your voice
    and haughtily lifted your eyes?
    Against the Holy One of Israel!
23 By your messengers you have
        mocked the Lord,
    and you have said, 'With my
        many chariots
    I have gone up the heights of the
        mountains,

---

a Heb *he*   b Or *Nubia*; Heb *Cush*

to the far recesses of Lebanon;
I felled its tallest cedars,
   its choicest cypresses;
I entered its farthest retreat,
   its densest forest.
24 I dug wells
   and drank foreign waters,
I dried up with the sole of my
     foot
   all the streams of Egypt.'

25 "Have you not heard
   that I determined it long ago?

I planned from days of old
   what now I bring to pass,
that you should make fortified
    cities
   crash into heaps of ruins,
26 while their inhabitants, shorn of
    strength,
   are dismayed and confounded;
they have become like plants of the
    field
   and like tender grass,
like grass on the housetops,
   blighted before it is grown.

MONDAY

Scripture Reading
for Today:
2 Kings 19.14–19

Verse for Today:
2 Kings 19.19

The Prayer That God Cannot Refuse

Intercessory prayer, or prayer of petition, is a frequent part of my single life, especially when I bring before the Lord, in addition to my needs, those of family members, friends, colleagues and students. In prayers of intercession we unite our will to God's and in faith and trust ask humbly for all that we need. This prayer is impossible without faith, for it begins where reason and natural means to accomplish human ends cease to be effective.

   I sometimes call this my peasant prayer—a prayer God cannot refuse to answer in some way because it is uttered with no sophistication, only pure faith. I believe that if I ask, I shall receive; that if I seek, I shall find; that if I knock, the door shall be opened to me (see Matthew 7.7–8). This prayer touches the heart of God because it is uttered in desperation. Like the tax collector, we beseech God's mercy (see Luke 18.13). Like the centurion, we know that we are not worthy to receive the Lord, but that if he says so, our soul, his servant, shall be healed (see Luke 7.6–7).

   When all human means are exhausted, when we witness the futility of our own efforts, we turn to God for mercy, for healing, for the fulfillment of physical and spiritual needs. This prayer acknowledges what we singles often feel: that God alone can satisfy our heart's desire. It is when we are powerless, vulnerable and out of control that God can work most freely in our lives. We allow God to be God because we have been reduced to nothing. Sometimes this prayer is composed of only one word: Help! We pray full of confidence that God always responds to human desperation. He does not scorn the broken, contrite heart (see Psalm 51.17).

—SUSAN MUTO

Go to page 418 for your next devotional reading.

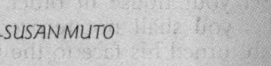

27 "But I know your rising[c] and your
        sitting,
    your going out and coming in,
    and your raging against me.
28 Because you have raged against me
    and your arrogance has come to
        my ears,
    I will put my hook in your nose
    and my bit in your mouth;
    I will turn you back on the way
    by which you came.

29 "And this shall be the sign for you:
This year you shall eat what grows of itself, and in the second year what springs
from that; then in the third year sow, reap,
plant vineyards, and eat their fruit. 30The
surviving remnant of the house of Judah
shall again take root downward, and bear
fruit upward; 31for from Jerusalem a remnant shall go out, and from Mount Zion a
band of survivors. The zeal of the LORD of
hosts will do this.

32 "Therefore thus says the LORD concerning the king of Assyria: He shall not
come into this city, shoot an arrow there,
come before it with a shield, or cast up a
siege ramp against it. 33By the way that he
came, by the same he shall return; he shall
not come into this city, says the LORD.
34For I will defend this city to save it, for
my own sake and for the sake of my servant David."

Sennacherib's Defeat and Death

35 That very night the angel of the LORD
set out and struck down one hundred
eighty-five thousand in the camp of the
Assyrians; when morning dawned, they
were all dead bodies. 36Then King Sennacherib of Assyria left, went home, and
lived at Nineveh. 37As he was worshiping
in the house of his god Nisroch, his sons
Adrammelech and Sharezer killed him
with the sword, and they escaped into the
land of Ararat. His son Esar-haddon succeeded him.

Hezekiah's Illness

20 In those days Hezekiah became
sick and was at the point of death.
The prophet Isaiah son of Amoz came
to him, and said to him, "Thus says the
LORD: Set your house in order, for you
shall die; you shall not recover." 2Then
Hezekiah turned his face to the wall and
prayed to the LORD: 3"Remember now,
O LORD, I implore you, how I have walked

before you in faithfulness with a whole
heart, and have done what is good in your
sight." Hezekiah wept bitterly. 4Before Isaiah had gone out of the middle court, the
word of the LORD came to him: 5"Turn
back, and say to Hezekiah prince of my
people, Thus says the LORD, the God of
your ancestor David: I have heard your
prayer, I have seen your tears; indeed, I
will heal you; on the third day you shall
go up to the house of the LORD. 6I will add
fifteen years to your life. I will deliver you
and this city out of the hand of the king of
Assyria; I will defend this city for my own
sake and for my servant David's sake."
7Then Isaiah said, "Bring a lump of figs.
Let them take it and apply it to the boil, so
that he may recover."

8 Hezekiah said to Isaiah, "What shall
be the sign that the LORD will heal me, and
that I shall go up to the house of the LORD
on the third day?" 9Isaiah said, "This is the
sign to you from the LORD, that the LORD
will do the thing that he has promised:
the shadow has now advanced ten intervals; shall it retreat ten intervals?" 10Heze-
kiah answered, "It is normal for the shadow to lengthen ten intervals; rather let the
shadow retreat ten intervals." 11The prophet Isaiah cried to the LORD; and he brought
the shadow back the ten intervals, by
which the sun[d] had declined on the dial
of Ahaz.

Envoys from Babylon

12 At that time King Merodach-
baladan son of Baladan of Babylon sent
envoys with letters and a present to Hezekiah, for he had heard that Hezekiah had
been sick. 13Hezekiah welcomed them;[e]
he showed them all his treasure house,
the silver, the gold, the spices, the precious oil, his armory, all that was found in
his storehouses; there was nothing in his
house or in all his realm that Hezekiah
did not show them. 14Then the prophet
Isaiah came to King Hezekiah, and said
to him, "What did these men say? From
where did they come to you?" Hezekiah
answered, "They have come from a far
country, from Babylon." 15He said, "What
have they seen in your house?" Hezekiah
answered, "They have seen all that is in

c Gk Compare Isa 37.27 Q Ms: MT lacks *rising*
d Syr See Isa 38.8 and Tg: Heb *it*   e Gk Vg Syr:
Heb *When Hezekiah heard about them*

my house; there is nothing in my store-houses that I did not show them."

16 Then Isaiah said to Hezekiah, "Hear the word of the LORD: ¹⁷Days are coming when all that is in your house, and that which your ancestors have stored up until this day, shall be carried to Babylon; nothing shall be left, says the LORD. ¹⁸Some of your own sons who are born to you shall be taken away; they shall be eunuchs in the palace of the king of Babylon." ¹⁹Then Hezekiah said to Isaiah, "The word of the LORD that you have spoken is good." For he thought, "Why not, if there will be peace and security in my days?"

Death of Hezekiah

20 The rest of the deeds of Hezekiah, all his power, how he made the pool and the conduit and brought water into the city, are they not written in the Book of the Annals of the Kings of Judah? ²¹Hezekiah slept with his ancestors; and his son Manasseh succeeded him.

Manasseh Reigns over Judah

21 Manasseh was twelve years old when he began to reign; he reigned fifty-five years in Jerusalem. His mother's name was Hephzibah. ²He did what was evil in the sight of the LORD, following the abominable practices of the nations that the LORD drove out before the people of Israel. ³For he rebuilt the high places that his father Hezekiah had destroyed; he erected altars for Baal, made a sacred pole,ᶠ as King Ahab of Israel had done, worshiped all the host of heaven, and served them. ⁴He built altars in the house of the LORD, of which the LORD had said, "In Jerusalem I will put my name." ⁵He built altars for all the host of heaven in the two courts of the house of the LORD. ⁶He made his son pass through fire; he practiced soothsaying and augury, and dealt with mediums and with wizards. He did much evil in the sight of the LORD, provoking him to anger. ⁷The carved image of Asherah that he had made he set in the house of which the LORD said to David and to his son Solomon, "In this house, and in Jerusalem, which I have chosen out of all the tribes of Israel, I will put my name forever; ⁸I will not cause the feet of Israel to wander any more out of the land that I gave to their ancestors, if only they will be careful to do according to all that

I have commanded them, and according to all the law that my servant Moses commanded them." ⁹But they did not listen; Manasseh misled them to do more evil than the nations had done that the LORD destroyed before the people of Israel.

10 The LORD said by his servants the prophets, ¹¹"Because King Manasseh of Judah has committed these abominations, has done things more wicked than all that the Amorites did, who were before him, and has caused Judah also to sin with his idols; ¹²therefore thus says the LORD, the God of Israel, I am bringing upon Jerusalem and Judah such evil that the ears of everyone who hears of it will tingle. ¹³I will stretch over Jerusalem the measuring line for Samaria, and the plummet for the house of Ahab; I will wipe Jerusalem as one wipes a dish, wiping it and turning it upside down. ¹⁴I will cast off the remnant of my heritage, and give them into the hand of their enemies; they shall become a prey and a spoil to all their enemies, ¹⁵because they have done what is evil in my sight and have provoked me to anger, since the day their ancestors came out of Egypt, even to this day."

16 Moreover Manasseh shed very much innocent blood, until he had filled Jerusalem from one end to another, besides the sin that he caused Judah to sin so that they did what was evil in the sight of the LORD.

17 Now the rest of the acts of Manasseh, all that he did, and the sin that he committed, are they not written in the Book of the Annals of the Kings of Judah? ¹⁸Manasseh slept with his ancestors, and was buried in the garden of his house, in the garden of Uzza. His son Amon succeeded him.

Amon Reigns over Judah

19 Amon was twenty-two years old when he began to reign; he reigned two years in Jerusalem. His mother's name was Meshullemeth daughter of Haruz of Jotbah. ²⁰He did what was evil in the sight of the LORD, as his father Manasseh had done. ²¹He walked in all the way in which his father walked, served the idols that his father served, and worshiped them; ²²he abandoned the LORD, the God of his ancestors, and did not walk in the way of the LORD. ²³The servants of Amon conspired

ᶠ Heb *Asherah*

against him, and killed the king in his house. 24But the people of the land killed all those who had conspired against King Amon, and the people of the land made his son Josiah king in place of him. 25Now the rest of the acts of Amon that he did, are they not written in the Book of the Annals of the Kings of Judah? 26He was buried in his tomb in the garden of Uzza; then his son Josiah succeeded him.

Josiah Reigns over Judah

22 Josiah was eight years old when he began to reign; he reigned thirty-one years in Jerusalem. His mother's name was Jedidah daughter of Adaiah of Bozkath. 2He did what was right in the sight of the LORD, and walked in all the way of his father David; he did not turn aside to the right or to the left.

Hilkiah Finds the Book of the Law

3 In the eighteenth year of King Josiah, the king sent Shaphan son of Azaliah, son of Meshullam, the secretary, to the house of the LORD, saying, 4"Go up to the high priest Hilkiah, and have him count the entire sum of the money that has been brought into the house of the LORD, which the keepers of the threshold have collected from the people; 5let it be given into the hand of the workers who have the oversight of the house of the LORD; let them give it to the workers who are at the house of the LORD, repairing the house, 6that is, to the carpenters, to the builders, to the masons; and let them use it to buy timber and quarried stone to repair the house. 7But no accounting shall be asked from them for the money that is delivered into their hand, for they deal honestly."

8 The high priest Hilkiah said to Shaphan the secretary, "I have found the book of the law in the house of the LORD." When Hilkiah gave the book to Shaphan, he read it. 9Then Shaphan the secretary came to the king, and reported to the king, "Your servants have emptied out the money that was found in the house, and have delivered it into the hand of the workers who have oversight of the house of the LORD." 10Shaphan the secretary informed the king, "The priest Hilkiah has given me a book." Shaphan then read it aloud to the king.

11 When the king heard the words of the book of the law, he tore his clothes. 12Then the king commanded the priest Hilkiah, Ahikam son of Shaphan, Achbor son of Micaiah, Shaphan the secretary, and the king's servant Asaiah, saying, 13"Go, inquire of the LORD for me, for the people, and for all Judah, concerning the words of this book that has been found; for great is the wrath of the LORD that is kindled against us, because our ancestors did not obey the words of this book, to do according to all that is written concerning us."

14 So the priest Hilkiah, Ahikam, Achbor, Shaphan, and Asaiah went to the prophetess Huldah the wife of Shallum son of Tikvah, son of Harhas, keeper of the wardrobe; she resided in Jerusalem in the Second Quarter, where they consulted her. 15She declared to them, "Thus says the LORD, the God of Israel: Tell the man who sent you to me, 16Thus says the LORD, I will indeed bring disaster on this place and on its inhabitants—all the words of the book that the king of Judah has read. 17Because they have abandoned me and have made offerings to other gods, so that they have provoked me to anger with all the work of their hands, therefore my wrath will be kindled against this place, and it will not be quenched. 18But as to the king of Judah, who sent you to inquire of the LORD, thus shall you say to him, Thus says the LORD, the God of Israel: Regarding the words that you have heard, 19because your heart was penitent, and you humbled yourself before the LORD, when you heard how I spoke against this place, and against its inhabitants, that they should become a desolation and a curse, and because you have torn your clothes and wept before me, I also have heard you, says the LORD. 20Therefore, I will gather you to your ancestors, and you shall be gathered to your grave in peace; your eyes shall not see all the disaster that I will bring on this place." They took the message back to the king.

Josiah's Reformation

23 Then the king directed that all the elders of Judah and Jerusalem should be gathered to him. 2The king went up to the house of the LORD, and with him went all the people of Judah, all the inhabitants of Jerusalem, the priests, the prophets, and all the people, both small and great; he read in their hearing all the words of the book of the covenant that had been found in the house of the

LORD. 3The king stood by the pillar and made a covenant before the LORD, to follow the LORD, keeping his commandments, his decrees, and his statutes, with all his heart and all his soul, to perform the words of this covenant that were written in this book. All the people joined in the covenant.

4 The king commanded the high priest Hilkiah, the priests of the second order, and the guardians of the threshold, to bring out of the temple of the LORD all the vessels made for Baal, for Asherah, and for all the host of heaven; he burned them outside Jerusalem in the fields of the Kidron, and carried their ashes to Bethel. 5He deposed the idolatrous priests whom the kings of Judah had ordained to make offerings in the high places at the cities of Judah and around Jerusalem; those also who made offerings to Baal, to the sun, the moon, the constellations, and all the host of the heavens. 6He brought out the image of*g* Asherah from the house of the LORD, outside Jerusalem, to the Wadi Kidron, burned it at the Wadi Kidron, beat it to dust and threw the dust of it upon the graves of the common people. 7He broke down the houses of the male temple prostitutes that were in the house of the LORD, where the women did weaving for Asherah. 8He brought all the priests out of the towns of Judah, and defiled the high places where the priests had made offerings, from Geba to Beer-sheba; he broke down the high places of the gates that were at the entrance of the gate of Joshua the governor of the city, which were on the left at the gate of the city. 9The priests of the high places, however, did not come up to the altar of the LORD in Jerusalem, but ate unleavened bread among their kindred. 10He defiled Topheth, which is in the valley of Ben-hinnom, so that no one would make a son or a daughter pass through fire as an offering to Molech. 11He removed the horses that the kings of Judah had dedicated to the sun, at the entrance to the house of the LORD, by the chamber of the eunuch Nathan-melech, which was in the precincts;*h* then he burned the chariots of the sun with fire. 12The altars on the roof of the upper chamber of Ahaz, which the kings of Judah had made, and the altars that Manasseh had made in the two courts of the house of the LORD, he pulled down from there and broke in pieces, and threw the

rubble into the Wadi Kidron. 13The king defiled the high places that were east of Jerusalem, to the south of the Mount of Destruction, which King Solomon of Israel had built for Astarte the abomination of the Sidonians, for Chemosh the abomination of Moab, and for Milcom the abomination of the Ammonites. 14He broke the pillars in pieces, cut down the sacred poles,*i* and covered the sites with human bones.

15 Moreover, the altar at Bethel, the high place erected by Jeroboam son of Nebat, who caused Israel to sin—he pulled down that altar along with the high place. He burned the high place, crushing it to dust; he also burned the sacred pole.*j* 16As Josiah turned, he saw the tombs there on the mount; and he sent and took the bones out of the tombs, and burned them on the altar, and defiled it, according to the word of the LORD that the man of God proclaimed,*k* when Jeroboam stood by the altar at the festival; he turned and looked up at the tomb of the man of God who had predicted these things. 17Then he said, "What is that monument that I see?" The people of the city told him, "It is the tomb of the man of God who came from Judah and predicted these things that you have done against the altar at Bethel." 18He said, "Let him rest; let no one move his bones." So they let his bones alone, with the bones of the prophet who came out of Samaria. 19Moreover, Josiah removed all the shrines of the high places that were in the towns of Samaria, which kings of Israel had made, provoking the LORD to anger; he did to them just as he had done at Bethel. 20He slaughtered on the altars all the priests of the high places who were there, and burned human bones on them. Then he returned to Jerusalem.

The Passover Celebrated

21 The king commanded all the people, "Keep the passover to the LORD your God as prescribed in this book of the covenant." 22No such passover had been kept since the days of the judges who judged Israel, even during all the days of the kings of Israel and of the kings of Judah; 23but in the eighteenth year of King Josiah this

g Heb lacks *image of*   *h* Meaning of Heb uncertain   *i* Heb *Asherim*   *j* Heb *Asherah*
k Gk: Heb *proclaimed, who had predicted these things*

passover was kept to the LORD in Jerusalem.

24 Moreover Josiah put away the mediums, wizards, teraphim,[1] idols, and all the abominations that were seen in the land of Judah and in Jerusalem, so that he established the words of the law that were written in the book that the priest Hilkiah had found in the house of the LORD. 25 Before him there was no king like him, who turned to the LORD with all his heart, with all his soul, and with all his might, according to all the law of Moses; nor did any like him arise after him.

26 Still the LORD did not turn from the fierceness of his great wrath, by which his anger was kindled against Judah, because of all the provocations with which Manasseh had provoked him. 27 The LORD said, "I will remove Judah also out of my sight, as I have removed Israel; and I will reject this city that I have chosen, Jerusalem, and the house of which I said, My name shall be there."

Josiah Dies in Battle

28 Now the rest of the acts of Josiah, and all that he did, are they not written in the Book of the Annals of the Kings of Judah? 29 In his days Pharaoh Neco king of Egypt went up to the king of Assyria to the river Euphrates. King Josiah went to meet him; but when Pharaoh Neco met him at Megiddo, he killed him. 30 His servants carried him dead in a chariot from Megiddo, brought him to Jerusalem, and buried him in his own tomb. The people of the land took Jehoahaz son of Josiah, anointed him, and made him king in place of his father.

Reign and Captivity of Jehoahaz

31 Jehoahaz was twenty-three years old when he began to reign; he reigned three months in Jerusalem. His mother's name was Hamutal daughter of Jeremiah of Libnah. 32 He did what was evil in the sight of the LORD, just as his ancestors had done. 33 Pharaoh Neco confined him at Riblah in the land of Hamath, so that he might not reign in Jerusalem, and imposed tribute on the land of one hundred talents of silver and a talent of gold. 34 Pharaoh Neco made Eliakim son of Josiah king in place of his father Josiah, and changed his name to Jehoiakim. But he took Jehoahaz away; he came to Egypt, and died there. 35 Jehoiakim gave the silver and the gold to Pharaoh, but he taxed the land in order to meet Pharaoh's demand for money. He exacted the silver and the gold from the people of the land, from all according to their assessment, to give it to Pharaoh Neco.

Jehoiakim Reigns over Judah

36 Jehoiakim was twenty-five years old when he began to reign; he reigned eleven years in Jerusalem. His mother's name was Zebidah daughter of Pedaiah of Rumah. 37 He did what was evil in the sight of the LORD, just as all his ancestors had done.

Judah Overrun by Enemies

24 In his days King Nebuchadnezzar of Babylon came up; Jehoiakim became his servant for three years; then he turned and rebelled against him. 2 The LORD sent against him bands of the Chaldeans, bands of the Arameans, bands of the Moabites, and bands of the Ammonites; he sent them against Judah to destroy it, according to the word of the LORD that he spoke by his servants the prophets. 3 Surely this came upon Judah at the command of the LORD, to remove them out of his sight, for the sins of Manasseh, for all that he had committed, 4 and also for the innocent blood that he had shed; for he filled Jerusalem with innocent blood, and the LORD was not willing to pardon. 5 Now the rest of the deeds of Jehoiakim, and all that he did, are they not written in the Book of the Annals of the Kings of Judah? 6 So Jehoiakim slept with his ancestors; then his son Jehoiachin succeeded him. 7 The king of Egypt did not come again out of his land, for the king of Babylon had taken over all that belonged to the king of Egypt from the Wadi of Egypt to the River Euphrates.

Reign and Captivity of Jehoiachin

8 Jehoiachin was eighteen years old when he began to reign; he reigned three months in Jerusalem. His mother's name was Nehushta daughter of Elnathan of Jerusalem. 9 He did what was evil in the sight of the LORD, just as his father had done.

10 At that time the servants of King Nebuchadnezzar of Babylon came up to Jerusalem, and the city was besieged.

[1] Or household gods

11King Nebuchadnezzar of Babylon came to the city, while his servants were besieging it; 12King Jehoiachin of Judah gave himself up to the king of Babylon, himself, his mother, his servants, his officers, and his palace officials. The king of Babylon took him prisoner in the eighth year of his reign.

Capture of Jerusalem

13 He carried off all the treasures of the house of the Lord, and the treasures of the king's house; he cut in pieces all the vessels of gold in the temple of the Lord, which King Solomon of Israel had made, all this as the Lord had foretold. 14He carried away all Jerusalem, all the officials, all the warriors, ten thousand captives, all the artisans and the smiths; no one remained, except the poorest people of the land. 15He carried away Jehoiachin to Babylon; the king's mother, the king's wives, his officials, and the elite of the land, he took into captivity from Jerusalem to Babylon. 16The king of Babylon brought captive to Babylon all the men of valor, seven thousand, the artisans and the smiths, one thousand, all of them strong and fit for war. 17The king of Babylon made Mattaniah, Jehoiachin's uncle, king in his place, and changed his name to Zedekiah.

Zedekiah Reigns over Judah

18 Zedekiah was twenty-one years old when he began to reign; he reigned eleven years in Jerusalem. His mother's name was Hamutal daughter of Jeremiah of Libnah. 19He did what was evil in the sight of the Lord, just as Jehoiakim had done. 20Indeed, Jerusalem and Judah so angered the Lord that he expelled them from his presence.

The Fall and Captivity of Judah

25 Zedekiah rebelled against the king of Babylon. 1And in the ninth year of his reign, in the tenth month, on the tenth day of the month, King Nebuchadnezzar of Babylon came with all his army against Jerusalem, and laid siege to it; they built siegeworks against it all around. 2So the city was besieged until the eleventh year of King Zedekiah. 3On the ninth day of the fourth month the famine became so severe in the city that there was no food for the people of the land. 4Then a breach was made in the city wall;m the king with all the soldiers fledn by night

by the way of the gate between the two walls, by the king's garden, though the Chaldeans were all around the city. They went in the direction of the Arabah. 5But the army of the Chaldeans pursued the king, and overtook him in the plains of Jericho; all his army was scattered, deserting him. 6Then they captured the king and brought him up to the king of Babylon at Riblah, who passed sentence on him. 7They slaughtered the sons of Zedekiah before his eyes, then put out the eyes of Zedekiah; they bound him in fetters and took him to Babylon.

8 In the fifth month, on the seventh day of the month—which was the nineteenth year of King Nebuchadnezzar, king of Babylon—Nebuzaradan, the captain of the bodyguard, a servant of the king of Babylon, came to Jerusalem. 9He burned the house of the Lord, the king's house, and all the houses of Jerusalem; every great house he burned down. 10All the army of the Chaldeans who were with the captain of the guard broke down the walls around Jerusalem. 11Nebuzaradan the captain of the guard carried into exile the rest of the people who were left in the city and the deserters who had defected to the king of Babylon—all the rest of the population. 12But the captain of the guard left some of the poorest people of the land to be vinedressers and tillers of the soil.

13 The bronze pillars that were in the house of the Lord, as well as the stands and the bronze sea that were in the house of the Lord, the Chaldeans broke in pieces, and carried the bronze to Babylon. 14They took away the pots, the shovels, the snuffers, the dishes for incense, and all the bronze vessels used in the temple service, 15as well as the firepans and the basins. What was made of gold the captain of the guard took away for the gold, and what was made of silver, for the silver. 16As for the two pillars, the one sea, and the stands, which Solomon had made for the house of the Lord, the bronze of all these vessels was beyond weighing. 17The height of the one pillar was eighteen cubits, and on it was a bronze capital; the height of the capital was three cubits; latticework and pomegranates, all of bronze, were on the capital all around. The second pillar had the same, with the latticework.

m Heb lacks *wall*   n Gk Compare Jer 39.4; 52.7: Heb lacks *the king* and lacks *fled*

18 The captain of the guard took the chief priest Seraiah, the second priest Zephaniah, and the three guardians of the threshold; 19from the city he took an officer who had been in command of the soldiers, and five men of the king's council who were found in the city; the secretary who was the commander of the army who mustered the people of the land; and sixty men of the people of the land who were found in the city. 20Nebuzaradan the captain of the guard took them, and brought them to the king of Babylon at Riblah. 21The king of Babylon struck them down and put them to death at Riblah in the land of Hamath. So Judah went into exile out of its land.

Gedaliah Made Governor of Judah

22 He appointed Gedaliah son of Ahikam son of Shaphan as governor over the people who remained in the land of Judah, whom King Nebuchadnezzar of Babylon had left. 23Now when all the captains of the forces and their men heard that the king of Babylon had appointed Gedaliah as governor, they came with their men to Gedaliah at Mizpah, namely, Ishmael son of Nethaniah, Johanan son of Kareah, Seraiah son of Tanhumeth the Netophathite, and Jaazaniah son of the Maacathite. 24Gedaliah swore to them and their

men, saying, "Do not be afraid because of the Chaldean officials; live in the land, serve the king of Babylon, and it shall be well with you." 25But in the seventh month, Ishmael son of Nethaniah son of Elishama, of the royal family, came with ten men; they struck down Gedaliah so that he died, along with the Judeans and Chaldeans who were with him at Mizpah. 26Then all the people, high and low,o and the captains of the forces set out and went to Egypt; for they were afraid of the Chaldeans.

Jehoiachin Released from Prison

27 In the thirty-seventh year of the exile of King Jehoiachin of Judah, in the twelfth month, on the twenty-seventh day of the month, King Evil-merodach of Babylon, in the year that he began to reign, released King Jehoiachin of Judah from prison; 28he spoke kindly to him, · and gave him a seat above the other seats of the kings who were with him in Babylon. 29So Jehoiachin put aside his prison clothes. Every day of his life he dined regularly in the king's presence. 30For his allowance, a regular allowance was given him by the king, a portion every day, as long as he lived.

o Or young and old

1 Chronicles

First and Second Chronicles (originally one book) cover much of the same territory as 1 and 2 Samuel and 1 and 2 Kings, only from a different point of view. The Chronicler, who possibly was Ezra, offers a more priestly point of view, focusing primarily on the temple and worship. Even the portrait of King David in 1 Chronicles is primarily concerned with his role as a religious leader rather than with his military conquests.

The first nine chapters consist of a lengthy genealogy, beginning with Adam and ending with Saul and also including those who returned to Jerusalem after exile in Babylon. Though such an approach hardly makes for fascinating bedtime reading, it reinforces the understanding that God is inexorably involved in human history and in the history of his people in particular. This account was probably written in order to encourage exiled Jews (at the end of the fifth century B.C.) who had returned to a Jerusalem in ruins. The Chronicler was reminding them that faithfulness is the key to future blessings.

The rest of the book retells the story of David, directing attention to the ark of the covenant and describing the way worship was to be conducted. First Chronicles ends with the death of King David.

What does Chronicles have to do with us today? As believers we, too, belong to God's people. The sacred history contained in these books is part of our own sacred history.

From Adam to Abraham

1 Adam, Seth, Enosh; ²Kenan, Mahalalel, Jared; ³Enoch, Methuselah, Lamech; ⁴Noah, Shem, Ham, and Japheth.

5 The descendants of Japheth: Gomer, Magog, Madai, Javan, Tubal, Meshech, and Tiras. ⁶The descendants of Gomer: Ashkenaz, Diphath,*a* and Togarmah.

⁷The descendants of Javan: Elishah, Tarshish, Kittim, and Rodanim.*b*

8 The descendants of Ham: Cush, Egypt, Put, and Canaan. ⁹The descendants of Cush: Seba, Havilah, Sabta, Raama, and

a Gen 10.3 Ripath; See Gk Vg   *b* Gen 10.4 *Dodanim;* See Syr Vg

Sabteca. The descendants of Raamah: She-ba and Dedan. [10]Cush became the father of Nimrod; he was the first to be a mighty one on the earth.

11 Egypt became the father of Ludim, Anamim, Lehabim, Naphtuhim, [12]Pathru-sim, Casluhim, and Caphtorim, from whom the Philistines come.[c]

13 Canaan became the father of Sidon his firstborn, and Heth, [14]and the Jebu-sites, the Amorites, the Girgashites, [15]the Hivites, the Arkites, the Sinites, [16]the Ar-vadites, the Zemarites, and the Hamath-ites.

17 The descendants of Shem: Elam, As-shur, Arpachshad, Lud, Aram, Uz, Hul, Gether, and Meshech.[d] [18]Arpachshad be-came the father of Shelah; and Shelah be-

[c] Heb *Casluhim, from which the Philistines come, Caphtorim*; See Am 9.7, Jer 47.4   [d] *Mash* in Gen 10.23

TUESDAY

God's Children

Scripture Reading for Today:
I Chronicles I.I–16

The books of 1 and 2 Chronicles have a perplexing beginning: a list of names nine chapters long! The reader might well ask, "Who *are* these people? And what in the world do they have to do with me?"

Verses for Today:
I Chronicles 3.I–4

These opening chapters provide a genealogy of the human family, beginning with the first human being, Adam, and his sons (1.1). Next the Chronicler lists the children of the man called "Israel" (who was also named Jacob [2.1]), and chapters 2 to 8 tell who their descendants were. All Hebrew people are called chil-dren of Israel, and so these chapters name the ancestors of the original readers of these books.

Chapter 3 introduces the reader to David, greatest of the kings of Israel, and his family (verses 1–4). Then chapters 4 and 5 look backwards several generations to tell about the people of Judah, who came from one of Israel's sons. Judah gave his name to the territory around the city of Jerusalem, David's royal city. This is where the original readers lived. Chapter 6 tells about the priests of Israel and the Levites, the progeny of Israel's son Levi, who have special duties in the temple.

The Chronicler begins with these rather daunting lists to as-sure the Jews of his day that they are included in the promises that God made to their forebears.

How does all this relate to us? Through Jesus, Israel becomes our ancestor as well: the Lord has "grafted" us onto the tree of Israel (see Romans 11.11–24). The history of Israel has become our history; God's promises to Israel now include us! Therefore we can learn about our own place in the scheme of salvation by read-ing the books of Chronicles. We can learn from the triumphs of our ancestors in the Lord, and we can take warning from their tragic mistakes. By knowing our spiritual roots, we can learn how to walk more closely in the ways of the Lord.

—*CECILE GRAY*

Go to page 444 for your next devotional reading.

came the father of Eber. [19]To Eber were born two sons: the name of the one was Peleg (for in his days the earth was divided), and the name of his brother Joktan. [20]Joktan became the father of Almodad, Sheleph, Hazarmaveth, Jerah, [21]Hadoram, Uzal, Diklah, [22]Ebal, Abimael, Sheba, [23]Ophir, Havilah, and Jobab; all these were the descendants of Joktan.

24 Shem, Arpachshad, Shelah; [25]Eber, Peleg, Reu; [26]Serug, Nahor, Terah; [27]Abram, that is, Abraham.

From Abraham to Jacob

28 The sons of Abraham: Isaac and Ishmael. [29]These are their genealogies: the firstborn of Ishmael, Nebaioth; and Kedar, Adbeel, Mibsam, [30]Mishma, Dumah, Massa, Hadad, Tema, [31]Jetur, Naphish, and Kedemah. These are the sons of Ishmael. [32]The sons of Keturah, Abraham's concubine: she bore Zimran, Jokshan, Medan, Midian, Ishbak, and Shuah. The sons of Jokshan: Sheba and Dedan. [33]The sons of Midian: Ephah, Epher, Hanoch, Abida, and Eldaah. All these were the descendants of Keturah.

34 Abraham became the father of Isaac. The sons of Isaac: Esau and Israel. [35]The sons of Esau: Eliphaz, Reuel, Jeush, Jalam, and Korah. [36]The sons of Eliphaz: Teman, Omar, Zephi, Gatam, Kenaz, Timna, and Amalek. [37]The sons of Reuel: Nahath, Zerah, Shammah, and Mizzah.

38 The sons of Seir: Lotan, Shobal, Zibeon, Anah, Dishon, Ezer, and Dishan. [39]The sons of Lotan: Hori and Homam; and Lotan's sister was Timna. [40]The sons of Shobal: Alian, Manahath, Ebal, Shephi, and Onam. The sons of Zibeon: Aiah and Anah. [41]The sons of Anah: Dishon. The sons of Dishon: Hamran, Eshban, Ithran, and Cheran. [42]The sons of Ezer: Bilhan, Zaavan, and Jaakan.[e] The sons of Dishan:[f] Uz and Aran.

43 These are the kings who reigned in the land of Edom before any king reigned over the Israelites: Bela son of Beor, whose city was called Dinhabah. [44]When Bela died, Jobab son of Zerah of Bozrah succeeded him. [45]When Jobab died, Husham of the land of the Temanites succeeded him. [46]When Husham died, Hadad son of Bedad, who defeated Midian in the country of Moab, succeeded him; and the name of his city was Avith. [47]When Hadad died, Samlah of Masrekah succeeded him. [48]When Samlah died, Shaul[g] of Reho-

both on the Euphrates succeeded him. [49]When Shaul[g] died, Baal-hanan son of Achbor succeeded him. [50]When Baal-hanan died, Hadad succeeded him; the name of his city was Pai, and his wife's name Mehetabel daughter of Matred, daughter of Me-zahab. [51]And Hadad died.

The clans[h] of Edom were: clans[h] Timna, Aliah,[i] Jetheth, [52]Oholibamah, Elah, Pinon, [53]Kenaz, Teman, Mibzar, [54]Magdiel, and Iram; these are the clans[h] of Edom.

The Sons of Israel and the Descendants of Judah

2 These are the sons of Israel: Reuben, Simeon, Levi, Judah, Issachar, Zebulun, [2]Dan, Joseph, Benjamin, Naphtali, Gad, and Asher. [3]The sons of Judah: Er, Onan, and Shelah; these three the Canaanite woman Bath-shua bore to him. Now Er, Judah's firstborn, was wicked in the sight of the LORD, and he put him to death. [4]His daughter-in-law Tamar also bore him Perez and Zerah. Judah had five sons in all.

5 The sons of Perez: Hezron and Hamul. [6]The sons of Zerah: Zimri, Ethan, Heman, Calcol, and Dara,[j] five in all. [7]The sons of Carmi: Achar, the troubler of Israel, who transgressed in the matter of the devoted thing; [8]and Ethan's son was Azariah.

9 The sons of Hezron, who were born to him: Jerahmeel, Ram, and Chelubai. [10]Ram became the father of Amminadab, and Amminadab became the father of Nahshon, prince of the sons of Judah. [11]Nahshon became the father of Salma, Salma of Boaz, [12]Boaz of Obed, Obed of Jesse. [13]Jesse became the father of Eliab his firstborn, Abinadab the second, Shimea the third, [14]Nethanel the fourth, Raddai the fifth, [15]Ozem the sixth, David the seventh; [16]and their sisters were Zeruiah and Abigail. The sons of Zeruiah: Abishai, Joab, and Asahel, three. [17]Abigail bore Amasa, and the father of Amasa was Jether the Ishmaelite.

18 Caleb son of Hezron had children by his wife Azubah, and by Jerioth; these were her sons: Jesher, Shobab, and Ardon. [19]When Azubah died, Caleb married Eph-

---

e Or *and Akan*; See Gen 36.27   *f* See 1.38: Heb *Dishon*   *g* Or *Saul*   *h* Or *chiefs*   *i* Or *Alvah*; See Gen 36.40   *j* Or *Darda*; Compare Syr Tg some Gk Mss; See 1 Kings 4.31

rath, who bore him Hur. ²⁰Hur became the father of Uri, and Uri became the father of Bezalel.

21 Afterward Hezron went in to the daughter of Machir father of Gilead, whom he married when he was sixty years old; and she bore him Segub; ²²and Segub became the father of Jair, who had twenty-three towns in the land of Gilead. ²³But Geshur and Aram took from them Havvoth-jair, Kenath and its villages, sixty towns. All these were descendants of Machir, father of Gilead. ²⁴After the death of Hezron, in Caleb-ephrathah, Abijah wife of Hezron bore him Ashhur, father of Tekoa.

25 The sons of Jerahmeel, the firstborn of Hezron: Ram his firstborn, Bunah, Oren, Ozem, and Ahijah. ²⁶Jerahmeel also had another wife, whose name was Atarah; she was the mother of Onam. ²⁷The sons of Ram, the firstborn of Jerahmeel: Maaz, Jamin, and Eker. ²⁸The sons of Onam: Shammai and Jada. The sons of Shammai: Nadab and Abishur. ²⁹The name of Abishur's wife was Abihail, and she bore him Ahban and Molid. ³⁰The sons of Nadab: Seled and Appaim; and Seled died childless. ³¹The son^k of Appaim: Ishi. The son^k of Ishi: Sheshan. The son^k of Sheshan: Ahlai. ³²The sons of Jada, Shammai's brother: Jether and Jonathan; and Jether died childless. ³³The sons of Jonathan: Peleth and Zaza. These were the descendants of Jerahmeel. ³⁴Now Sheshan had no sons, only daughters; but Sheshan had an Egyptian slave, whose name was Jarha. ³⁵So Sheshan gave his daughter in marriage to his slave Jarha; and she bore him Attai. ³⁶Attai became the father of Nathan, and Nathan of Zabad. ³⁷Zabad became the father of Ephlal, and Ephlal of Obed. ³⁸Obed became the father of Jehu, and Jehu of Azariah. ³⁹Azariah became the father of Helez, and Helez of Eleasah. ⁴⁰Eleasah became the father of Sismai, and Sismai of Shallum. ⁴¹Shallum became the father of Jekamiah, and Jekamiah of Elishama.

42 The sons of Caleb brother of Jerahmeel: Mesha^l his firstborn, who was father of Ziph. The sons of Mareshah father of Hebron. ⁴³The sons of Hebron: Korah, Tappuah, Rekem, and Shema. ⁴⁴Shema became father of Raham, father of Jorkeam; and Rekem became the father of Shammai. ⁴⁵The son of Shammai: Maon; and Maon was the father of Beth-zur.

⁴⁶Ephah also, Caleb's concubine, bore Haran, Moza, and Gazez; and Haran became the father of Gazez. ⁴⁷The sons of Jahdai: Regem, Jotham, Geshan, Pelet, Ephah, and Shaaph. ⁴⁸Maacah, Caleb's concubine, bore Sheber and Tirhanah. ⁴⁹She also bore Shaaph father of Madmannah, Sheva father of Machbenah and father of Gibea; and the daughter of Caleb was Achsah. ⁵⁰These were the descendants of Caleb.

The sons^m of Hur the firstborn of Ephrathah: Shobal father of Kiriath-jearim, ⁵¹Salma father of Bethlehem, and Hareph father of Beth-gader. ⁵²Shobal father of Kiriath-jearim had other sons: Haroeh, half of the Menuhoth. ⁵³And the families of Kiriath-jearim: the Ithrites, the Puthites, the Shumathites, and the Mishraites; from these came the Zorathites and the Eshtaolites. ⁵⁴The sons of Salma: Bethlehem, the Netophathites, Atroth-beth-joab, and half of the Manahathites, the Zorites. ⁵⁵The families also of the scribes that lived at Jabez: the Tirathites, the Shimeathites, and the Sucathites. These are the Kenites who came from Hammath, father of the house of Rechab.

Descendants of David and Solomon

3 These are the sons of David who were born to him in Hebron: the firstborn Amnon, by Ahinoam the Jezreelite; the second Daniel, by Abigail the Carmelite; ²the third Absalom, son of Maacah, daughter of King Talmai of Geshur; the fourth Adonijah, son of Haggith; ³the fifth Shephatiah, by Abital; the sixth Ithream, by his wife Eglah; ⁴six were born to him in Hebron, where he reigned for seven years and six months. And he reigned thirty-three years in Jerusalem. ⁵These were born to him in Jerusalem: Shimea, Shobab, Nathan, and Solomon, four by Bath-shua, daughter of Ammiel; ⁶then Ibhar, Elishama, Eliphelet, ⁷Nogah, Nepheg, Japhia, ⁸Elishama, Eliada, and Eliphelet, nine. ⁹All these were David's sons, besides the sons of the concubines; and Tamar was their sister.

10 The descendants of Solomon: Rehoboam, Abijah his son, Asa his son, Jehoshaphat his son, ¹¹Joram his son, Ahaziah his son, Joash his son, ¹²Amaziah his son, Azariah his son, Jotham his son, ¹³Ahaz

---

^k Heb *sons*   ^l Gk reads *Mareshah*   ^m Gk Vg:
Heb *son*

his son, Hezekiah his son, Manasseh his son, [14]Amon his son, Josiah his son. [15]The sons of Josiah: Johanan the firstborn, the second Jehoiakim, the third Zedekiah, the fourth Shallum. [16]The descendants of Jehoiakim: Jeconiah his son, Zedekiah his son; [17]and the sons of Jeconiah, the captive: Shealtiel his son, [18]Malchiram, Pedaiah, Shenazzar, Jekamiah, Hoshama, and Nedabiah; [19]The sons of Pedaiah: Zerubbabel and Shimei; and the sons of Zerubbabel: Meshullam and Hananiah, and Shelomith was their sister; [20]and Hashubah, Ohel, Berechiah, Hasadiah, and Jushab-hesed, five. [21]The sons of Hananiah: Pelatiah and Jeshaiah, his son[n] Rephaiah, his son[n] Arnan, his son[n] Obadiah, his son[n] Shecaniah. [22]The son[o] of Shecaniah: Shemaiah. And the sons of Shemaiah: Hattush, Igal, Bariah, Neariah, and Shaphat, six. [23]The sons of Neariah: Elioenai, Hizkiah, and Azrikam, three. [24]The sons of Elioenai: Hodaviah, Eliashib, Pelaiah, Akkub, Johanan, Delaiah, and Anani, seven.

Descendants of Judah

4 The sons of Judah: Perez, Hezron, Carmi, Hur, and Shobal. [2]Reaiah son of Shobal became the father of Jahath, and Jahath became the father of Ahumai and Lahad. These were the families of the Zorathites. [3]These were the sons[p] of Etam: Jezreel, Ishma, and Idbash; and the name of their sister was Hazzelelponi, [4]and Penuel was the father of Gedor, and Ezer the father of Hushah. These were the sons of Hur, the firstborn of Ephrathah, the father of Bethlehem. [5]Ashhur father of Tekoa had two wives, Helah and Naarah; [6]Naarah bore him Ahuzzam, Hepher, Temeni, and Haahashtari.[q] These were the sons of Naarah. [7]The sons of Helah: Zereth, Izhar,[r] and Ethnan. [8]Koz became the father of Anub, Zobebah, and the families of Aharhel son of Harum. [9]Jabez was honored more than his brothers; and his mother named him Jabez, saying, "Because I bore him in pain." [10]Jabez called on the God of Israel, saying, "Oh that you would bless me and enlarge my border, and that your hand might be with me, and that you would keep me from hurt and harm!" And God granted what he asked. [11]Chelub the brother of Shuhah became the father of Mehir, who was the father of Eshton. [12]Eshton became the father of Beth-rapha, Paseah, and Tehinnah

the father of Ir-nahash. These are the men of Recah. [13]The sons of Kenaz: Othniel and Seraiah; and the sons of Othniel: Hathath and Meonothai.[s] [14]Meonothai became the father of Ophrah; and Seraiah became the father of Joab father of Ge-harashim,[t] so-called because they were artisans. [15]The sons of Caleb son of Jephunneh: Iru, Elah, and Naam; and the son[o] of Elah: Kenaz. [16]The sons of Jehallelel: Ziph, Ziphah, Tiria, and Asarel. [17]The sons of Ezrah: Jether, Mered, Epher, and Jalon. These are the sons of Bithiah, daughter of Pharaoh, whom Mered married;[u] and she conceived and bore[v] Miriam, Shammai, and Ishbah father of Eshtemoa. [18]And his Judean wife bore Jered father of Gedor, Heber father of Soco, and Jekuthiel father of Zanoah. [19]The sons of the wife of Hodiah, the sister of Naham, were the fathers of Keilah the Garmite and Eshtemoa the Maacathite. [20]The sons of Shimon: Amnon, Rinnah, Ben-hanan, and Tilon. The sons of Ishi: Zoheth and Ben-zoheth. [21]The sons of Shelah son of Judah: Er father of Lecah, Laadah father of Mareshah, and the families of the guild of linen workers at Beth-ashbea; [22]and Jokim, and the men of Cozeba, and Joash, and Saraph, who married into Moab but returned to Lehem[w] (now the records[x] are ancient). [23]These were the potters and inhabitants of Netaim and Gederah; they lived there with the king in his service.

Descendants of Simeon

24 The sons of Simeon: Nemuel, Jamin, Jarib, Zerah, Shaul;[y] [25]Shallum was his son, Mibsam his son, Mishma his son. [26]The sons of Mishma: Hammuel his son, Zaccur his son, Shimei his son. [27]Shimei had sixteen sons and six daughters; but his brothers did not have many children, nor did all their family multiply like the Judeans. [28]They lived in Beer-sheba, Moladah, Hazar-shual, [29]Bilhah, Ezem, Tolad, [30]Bethuel, Hormah, Ziklag, [31]Bethmarcaboth, Hazar-susim, Beth-biri, and Shaaraim. These were their towns until David became king. [32]And their villages

---

n Gk Compare Syr Vg: Heb *sons of*   o Heb *sons*
p Gk Compare Vg: Heb *the father*   q Or *Ahashtari*
r Another reading is *Zohar*   s Gk Vg: Heb lacks
and Meonothai   t That is *Valley of artisans*
u The clause: *These are . . . married* is transposed
from verse 18   v Heb lacks *and bore*   w Vg
Compare Gk: Heb *and Jashubi-lahem*   x Or
matters   y Or *Saul*

were Etam, Ain, Rimmon, Tochen, and Ashan, five towns, ³³along with all their villages that were around these towns as far as Baal. These were their settlements. And they kept a genealogical record.

34 Meshobab, Jamlech, Joshah son of Amaziah, ³⁵Joel, Jehu son of Joshibiah son of Seraiah son of Asiel, ³⁶Elioenai, Jaakobah, Jeshohaiah, Asaiah, Adiel, Jesimiel, Benaiah, ³⁷Ziza son of Shiphi son of Allon son of Jedaiah son of Shimri son of Shemaiah— ³⁸these mentioned by name were leaders in their families, and their clans increased greatly. ³⁹They journeyed to the entrance of Gedor, to the east side of the valley, to seek pasture for their flocks, ⁴⁰where they found rich, good pasture, and the land was very broad, quiet, and peaceful; for the former inhabitants there belonged to Ham. ⁴¹These, registered by name, came in the days of King Hezekiah of Judah, and attacked their tents and the Meunim who were found there, and exterminated them to this day, and settled in their place, because there was pasture there for their flocks. ⁴²And some of them, five hundred men of the Simeonites, went to Mount Seir, having as their leaders Pelatiah, Neariah, Rephaiah, and Uzziel, sons of Ishi; ⁴³they destroyed the remnant of the Amalekites that had escaped, and they have lived there to this day.

Descendants of Reuben

5 The sons of Reuben the firstborn of Israel. (He was the firstborn, but because he defiled his father's bed his birthright was given to the sons of Joseph son of Israel, so that he is not enrolled in the genealogy according to the birthright; ²though Judah became prominent among his brothers and a ruler came from him, yet the birthright belonged to Joseph.) ³The sons of Reuben, the firstborn of Israel: Hanoch, Pallu, Hezron, and Carmi. ⁴The sons of Joel: Shemaiah his son, Gog his son, Shimei his son, ⁵Micah his son, Reaiah his son, Baal his son, ⁶Beerah his son, whom King Tilgath-pilneser of Assyria carried away into exile; he was a chieftain of the Reubenites. ⁷And his kindred by their families, when the genealogy of their generations was reckoned: the chief, Jeiel, and Zechariah, ⁸and Bela son of Azaz, son of Shema, son of Joel, who lived in Aroer, as far as Nebo and Baal-meon. ⁹He also lived to the east as far as the

beginning of the desert this side of the Euphrates, because their cattle had multiplied in the land of Gilead. ¹⁰And in the days of Saul they made war on the Hagrites, who fell by their hand; and they lived in their tents throughout all the region east of Gilead.

Descendants of Gad

11 The sons of Gad lived beside them in the land of Bashan as far as Salecah: ¹²Joel the chief, Shapham the second, Janai, and Shaphat in Bashan. ¹³And their kindred according to their clans: Michael, Meshullam, Sheba, Jorai, Jacan, Zia, and Eber, seven. ¹⁴These were the sons of Abihail son of Huri, son of Jaroah, son of Gilead, son of Michael, son of Jeshishai, son of Jahdo, son of Buz; ¹⁵Ahi son of Abdiel, son of Guni, was chief in their clan; ¹⁶and they lived in Gilead, in Bashan and in its towns, and in all the pasture lands of Sharon to their limits. ¹⁷All of these were enrolled by genealogies in the days of King Jotham of Judah, and in the days of King Jeroboam of Israel.

18 The Reubenites, the Gadites, and the half-tribe of Manasseh had valiant warriors, who carried shield and sword, and drew the bow, expert in war, fortyfour thousand seven hundred sixty, ready for service. ¹⁹They made war on the Hagrites, Jetur, Naphish, and Nodab; ²⁰and when they received help against them, the Hagrites and all who were with them were given into their hands, for they cried to God in the battle, and he granted their entreaty because they trusted in him. ²¹They captured their livestock: fifty thousand of their camels, two hundred fifty thousand sheep, two thousand donkeys, and one hundred thousand captives. ²²Many fell slain, because the war was of God. And they lived in their territory until the exile.

The Half-Tribe of Manasseh

23 The members of the half-tribe of Manasseh lived in the land; they were very numerous from Bashan to Baal-hermon, Senir, and Mount Hermon. ²⁴These were the heads of their clans: Epher,ᶻ Ishi, Eliel, Azriel, Jeremiah, Hodaviah, and Jahdiel, mighty warriors, famous men, heads of their clans. ²⁵But they transgressed against the God of their ancestors, and prostituted

ᶻ Gk Vg: Heb *and Epher*

themselves to the gods of the peoples of the land, whom God had destroyed before them. ²⁶So the God of Israel stirred up the spirit of King Pul of Assyria, the spirit of King Tilgath-pilneser of Assyria, and he carried them away, namely, the Reubenites, the Gadites, and the half-tribe of Manasseh, and brought them to Halah, Habor, Hara, and the river Gozan, to this day.

Descendants of Levi

6 ᵃThe sons of Levi: Gershom,ᵇ Kohath, and Merari. ²The sons of Kohath: Amram, Izhar, Hebron, and Uzziel. ³The children of Amram: Aaron, Moses, and Miriam. The sons of Aaron: Nadab, Abihu, Eleazar, and Ithamar. ⁴Eleazar became the father of Phinehas, Phinehas of Abishua, ⁵Abishua of Bukki, Bukki of Uzzi, ⁶Uzzi of Zerahiah, Zerahiah of Meraioth, ⁷Meraioth of Amariah, Amariah of Ahitub, ⁸Ahitub of Zadok, Zadok of Ahimaaz, ⁹Ahimaaz of Azariah, Azariah of Johanan, ¹⁰and Johanan of Azariah (it was he who served as priest in the house that Solomon built in Jerusalem). ¹¹Azariah became the father of Amariah, Amariah of Ahitub, ¹²Ahitub of Zadok, Zadok of Shallum, ¹³Shallum of Hilkiah, Hilkiah of Azariah, ¹⁴Azariah of Seraiah, Seraiah of Jehozadak; ¹⁵and Jehozadak went into exile when the Lord sent Judah and Jerusalem into exile by the hand of Nebuchadnezzar.

16ᶜThe sons of Levi: Gershom, Kohath, and Merari. ¹⁷These are the names of the sons of Gershom: Libni and Shimei. ¹⁸The sons of Kohath: Amram, Izhar, Hebron, and Uzziel. ¹⁹The sons of Merari: Mahli and Mushi. These are the clans of the Levites according to their ancestry. ²⁰Of Gershom: Libni his son, Jahath his son, Zimmah his son, ²¹Joah his son, Iddo his son, Zerah his son, Jeatherai his son. ²²The sons of Kohath: Amminadab his son, Korah his son, Assir his son, ²³Elkanah his son, Ebiasaph his son, Assir his son, ²⁴Tahath his son, Uriel his son, Uzziah his son, and Shaul his son. ²⁵The sons of Elkanah: Amasai and Ahimoth, ²⁶Elkanah his son, Zophai his son, Nahath his son, ²⁷Eliab his son, Jeroham his son, Elkanah his son. ²⁸The sons of Samuel: Joelᵈ his firstborn, the second Abijah.ᵉ ²⁹The sons of Merari: Mahli, Libni his son, Shimei his son, Uzzah his son, ³⁰Shimea

his son, Haggiah his son, and Asaiah his son.

Musicians Appointed by David

31 These are the men whom David put in charge of the service of song in the house of the Lord, after the ark came to rest there. ³²They ministered with song before the tabernacle of the tent of meeting, until Solomon had built the house of the Lord in Jerusalem; and they performed their service in due order. ³³These are the men who served; and their sons were: Of the Kohathites: Heman, the singer, son of Joel, son of Samuel, ³⁴son of Elkanah, son of Jeroham, son of Eliel, son of Toah, ³⁵son of Zuph, son of Elkanah, son of Mahath, son of Amasai, ³⁶son of Elkanah, son of Joel, son of Azariah, son of Zephaniah, ³⁷son of Tahath, son of Assir, son of Ebiasaph, son of Korah, ³⁸son of Izhar, son of Kohath, son of Levi, son of Israel; ³⁹and his brother Asaph, who stood on his right, namely, Asaph son of Berechiah, son of Shimea, ⁴⁰son of Michael, son of Baaseiah, son of Malchijah, ⁴¹son of Ethni, son of Zerah, son of Adaiah, ⁴²son of Ethan, son of Zimmah, son of Shimei, ⁴³son of Jahath, son of Gershom, son of Levi. ⁴⁴On the left were their kindred the sons of Merari: Ethan son of Kishi, son of Abdi, son of Malluch, ⁴⁵son of Hashabiah, son of Amaziah, son of Hilkiah, ⁴⁶son of Amzi, son of Bani, son of Shemer, ⁴⁷son of Mahli, son of Mushi, son of Merari, son of Levi; ⁴⁸and their kindred the Levites were appointed for all the service of the tabernacle of the house of God.

49 But Aaron and his sons made offerings on the altar of burnt offering and on the altar of incense, doing all the work of the most holy place, to make atonement for Israel, according to all that Moses the servant of God had commanded. ⁵⁰These are the sons of Aaron: Eleazar his son, Phinehas his son, Abishua his son, ⁵¹Bukki his son, Uzzi his son, Zerahiah his son, ⁵²Meraioth his son, Amariah his son, Ahitub his son, ⁵³Zadok his son, Ahimaaz his son.

ᵃ Ch 5.27 in Heb   ᵇ Heb *Gershon,* variant of *Gershom;* See 6.16   ᶜ Ch 6.1 in Heb   ᵈ Gk Syr Compare verse 33 and 1 Sam 8.2: Heb lacks *Joel* ᵉ Heb reads *Vashni, and Abijah* for *the second Abijah,* taking *the second* as a proper name

Settlements of the Levites

54 These are their dwelling places according to their settlements within their borders: to the sons of Aaron of the families of Kohathites—for the lot fell to them first— ⁵⁵to them they gave Hebron in the land of Judah and its surrounding pasture lands, ⁵⁶but the fields of the city and its villages they gave to Caleb son of Jephunneh. ⁵⁷To the sons of Aaron they gave the cities of refuge: Hebron, Libnah with its pasture lands, Jattir, Eshtemoa with its pasture lands, ⁵⁸Hilen*f* with its pasture lands, Debir with its pasture lands, ⁵⁹Ashan with its pasture lands, and Beth-shemesh with its pasture lands. ⁶⁰From the tribe of Benjamin, Geba with its pasture lands, Alemeth with its pasture lands, and Anathoth with its pasture lands. All their towns throughout their families were thirteen.

61 To the rest of the Kohathites were given by lot out of the family of the tribe, out of the half-tribe, the half of Manasseh, ten towns. ⁶²To the Gershomites according to their families were allotted thirteen towns out of the tribes of Issachar, Asher, Naphtali, and Manasseh in Bashan. ⁶³To the Merarites according to their families were allotted twelve towns out of the tribes of Reuben, Gad, and Zebulun. ⁶⁴So the people of Israel gave the Levites the towns with their pasture lands. ⁶⁵They also gave them by lot out of the tribes of Judah, Simeon, and Benjamin these towns that are mentioned by name.

66 And some of the families of the sons of Kohath had towns of their territory out of the tribe of Ephraim. ⁶⁷They were given the cities of refuge: Shechem with its pasture lands in the hill country of Ephraim, Gezer with its pasture lands, ⁶⁸Jokmeam with its pasture lands, Beth-horon with its pasture lands, ⁶⁹Aijalon with its pasture lands, Gath-rimmon with its pasture lands; ⁷⁰and out of the half-tribe of Manasseh, Aner with its pasture lands, and Bileam with its pasture lands, for the rest of the families of the Kohathites.

71 To the Gershomites: out of the half-tribe of Manasseh: Golan in Bashan with its pasture lands and Ashtaroth with its pasture lands; ⁷²and out of the tribe of Issachar: Kedesh with its pasture lands, Daberath*g* with its pasture lands, ⁷³Ramoth with its pasture lands, and Anem with its pasture lands; ⁷⁴out of the tribe of Asher: Mashal with its pasture lands, Abdon with its pasture lands, ⁷⁵Hukok with its pasture lands, and Rehob with its pasture lands; ⁷⁶and out of the tribe of Naphtali: Kedesh in Galilee with its pasture lands, Hammon with its pasture lands, and Kiriathaim with its pasture lands. ⁷⁷To the rest of the Merarites out of the tribe of Zebulun: Rimmono with its pasture lands, Tabor with its pasture lands, ⁷⁸and across the Jordan from Jericho, on the east side of the Jordan, out of the tribe of Reuben: Bezer in the steppe with its pasture lands, Jahzah with its pasture lands, ⁷⁹Kedemoth with its pasture lands, and Mephaath with its pasture lands; ⁸⁰and out of the tribe of Gad: Ramoth in Gilead with its pasture lands, Mahanaim with its pasture lands, ⁸¹Heshbon with its pasture lands, and Jazer with its pasture lands.

Descendants of Issachar

7 The sons*h* of Issachar: Tola, Puah, Jashub, and Shimron, four. ²The sons of Tola: Uzzi, Rephaiah, Jeriel, Jahmai, Ibsam, and Shemuel, heads of their ancestral houses, namely of Tola, mighty warriors of their generations, their number in the days of David being twenty-two thousand six hundred. ³The son*i* of Uzzi: Izrahiah. And the sons of Izrahiah: Michael, Obadiah, Joel, and Isshiah, five, all of them chiefs; ⁴and along with them, by their generations, according to their ancestral houses, were units of the fighting force, thirty-six thousand, for they had many wives and sons. ⁵Their kindred belonging to all the families of Issachar were in all eighty-seven thousand mighty warriors, enrolled by genealogy.

Descendants of Benjamin

6 The sons of Benjamin: Bela, Becher, and Jediael, three. ⁷The sons of Bela: Ezbon, Uzzi, Uzziel, Jerimoth, and Iri, five, heads of ancestral houses, mighty warriors; and their enrollment by genealogies was twenty-two thousand thirty-four. ⁸The sons of Becher: Zemirah, Joash, Eliezer, Elioenai, Omri, Jeremoth, Abijah, Anathoth, and Alemeth. All these were the sons of Becher; ⁹and their enrollment by genealogies, according to their genera-

---

f Other readings *Hilez, Holon*; See Josh 21.15
g Or *Dobrath*   *h* Syr Compare Vg: Heb *And to the sons*   *i* Heb *sons*

tions, as heads of their ancestral houses, mighty warriors, was twenty thousand two hundred. [10]The sons of Jediael: Bilhan. And the sons of Bilhan: Jeush, Benjamin, Ehud, Chenaanah, Zethan, Tarshish, and Ahishahar. [11]All these were the sons of Jediael according to the heads of their ancestral houses, mighty warriors, seventeen thousand two hundred, ready for service in war. [12]And Shuppim and Huppim were the sons of Ir, Hushim the son[j] of Aher.

Descendants of Naphtali

13 The descendants of Naphtali: Jahziel, Guni, Jezer, and Shallum, the descendants of Bilhah.

Descendants of Manasseh

14 The sons of Manasseh: Asriel, whom his Aramean concubine bore; she bore Machir the father of Gilead. [15]And Machir took a wife for Huppim and for Shuppim. The name of his sister was Maacah. And the name of the second was Zelophehad; and Zelophehad had daughters. [16]Maacah the wife of Machir bore a son, and she named him Peresh; the name of his brother was Sheresh; and his sons were Ulam and Rekem. [17]The son[j] of Ulam: Bedan. These were the sons of Gilead son of Machir, son of Manasseh. [18]And his sister Hammolecheth bore Ishhod, Abiezer, and Mahlah. [19]The sons of Shemida were Ahian, Shechem, Likhi, and Aniam.

Descendants of Ephraim

20 The sons of Ephraim: Shuthelah, and Bered his son, Tahath his son, Eleadah his son, Tahath his son, [21]Zabad his son, Shuthelah his son, and Ezer and Elead. Now the people of Gath, who were born in the land, killed them, because they came down to raid their cattle. [22]And their father Ephraim mourned many days, and his brothers came to comfort him. [23]Ephraim[k] went in to his wife, and she conceived and bore a son; and he named him Beriah, because disaster[l] had befallen his house. [24]His daughter was Sheerah, who built both Lower and Upper Bethhoron, and Uzzen-sheerah. [25]Rephah was his son, Resheph his son, Telah his son, Tahan his son, [26]Ladan his son, Ammihud his son, Elishama his son, [27]Nun[m] his son, Joshua his son. [28]Their possessions and settlements were Bethel and its towns,

and eastward Naaran, and westward Gezer and its towns, Shechem and its towns, as far as Ayyah and its towns; [29]also along the borders of the Manassites, Beth-shean and its towns, Taanach and its towns, Megiddo and its towns, Dor and its towns. In these lived the sons of Joseph son of Israel.

Descendants of Asher

30 The sons of Asher: Imnah, Ishvah, Ishvi, Beriah, and their sister Serah. [31]The sons of Beriah: Heber and Malchiel, who was the father of Birzaith. [32]Heber became the father of Japhlet, Shomer, Hotham, and their sister Shua. [33]The sons of Japhlet: Pasach, Bimhal, and Ashvath. These are the sons of Japhlet. [34]The sons of Shemer: Ahi, Rohgah, Hubbah, and Aram. [35]The sons of Helem[n] his brother: Zophah, Imna, Shelesh, and Amal. [36]The sons of Zophah: Suah, Harnepher, Shual, Beri, Imrah, [37]Bezer, Hod, Shamma, Shilshah, Ithran, and Beera. [38]The sons of Jether: Jephunneh, Pispa, and Ara. [39]The sons of Ulla: Arah, Hanniel, and Rizia. [40]All of these were men of Asher, heads of ancestral houses, select mighty warriors, chief of the princes. Their number enrolled by genealogies, for service in war, was twenty-six thousand men.

Descendants of Benjamin

8 Benjamin became the father of Bela his firstborn, Ashbel the second, Aharah the third, [2]Nohah the fourth, and Rapha the fifth. [3]And Bela had sons: Addar, Gera, Abihud,[o] [4]Abishua, Naaman, Ahoah, [5]Gera, Shephuphan, and Huram. [6]These are the sons of Ehud (they were heads of ancestral houses of the inhabitants of Geba, and they were carried into exile to Manahath): [7]Naaman,[p] Ahijah, and Gera, that is, Heglam,[q] who became the father of Uzza and Ahihud. [8]And Shaharaim had sons in the country of Moab after he had sent away his wives Hushim and Baara. [9]He had sons by his wife Hodesh: Jobab, Zibia, Mesha, Malcam, [10]Jeuz, Sachia, and Mirmah. These were his sons, heads of ancestral houses. [11]He also had sons by Hushim: Abitub and Elpaal. [12]The sons of Elpaal: Eber, Misham,

---

j Heb *sons*   *k* Heb *He*   *l* Heb *beraah*   *m* Here spelled *Non*; see Ex 33.11   *n* Or *Hotham*; see 7.32   *o* Or *father of Ehud*; see 8.6   *p* Heb *and Naaman*   *q* Or *he carried them into exile*

and Shemed, who built Ono and Lod with its towns, 13and Beriah and Shema (they were heads of ancestral houses of the inhabitants of Aijalon, who put to flight the inhabitants of Gath); 14and Ahio, Shashak, and Jeremoth. 15Zebadiah, Arad, Eder, 16Michael, Ishpah, and Joha were sons of Beriah. 17Zebadiah, Meshullam, Hizki, Heber, 18Ishmerai, Izliah, and Jobab were the sons of Elpaal. 19Jakim, Zichri, Zabdi, 20Elienai, Zillethai, Eliel, 21Adaiah, Beraiah, and Shimrath were the sons of Shimei. 22Ishpan, Eber, Eliel, 23Abdon, Zichri, Hanan, 24Hananiah, Elam, Anthothijah, 25Iphdeiah, and Penuel were the sons of Shashak. 26Shamsherai, Shehariah, Athaliah, 27Jaareshiah, Elijah, and Zichri were the sons of Jeroham. 28These were the heads of ancestral houses, according to their generations, chiefs. These lived in Jerusalem.

29 Jeiel*r* the father of Gibeon lived in Gibeon, and the name of his wife was Maacah. 30His firstborn son: Abdon, then Zur, Kish, Baal,*s* Nadab, 31Gedor, Ahio, Zecher, 32and Mikloth, who became the father of Shimeah. Now these also lived opposite their kindred in Jerusalem, with their kindred. 33Ner became the father of Kish, Kish of Saul,*t* Saul*t* of Jonathan, Malchishua, Abinadab, and Esh-baal; 34and the son of Jonathan was Meribbaal; and Merib-baal became the father of Micah. 35The sons of Micah: Pithon, Melech, Tarea, and Ahaz. 36Ahaz became the father of Jehoaddah; and Jehoaddah became the father of Alemeth, Azmaveth, and Zimri; Zimri became the father of Moza. 37Moza became the father of Binea; Raphah was his son, Eleasah his son, Azel his son. 38Azel had six sons, and these are their names: Azrikam, Bocheru, Ishmael, Sheariah, Obadiah, and Hanan; all these were the sons of Azel. 39The sons of his brother Eshek: Ulam his firstborn, Jeush the second, and Eliphelet the third. 40The sons of Ulam were mighty warriors, archers, having many children and grandchildren, one hundred fifty. All these were Benjaminites.

9 So all Israel was enrolled by genealogies; and these are written in the Book of the Kings of Israel. And Judah was taken into exile in Babylon because of their unfaithfulness. 2Now the first to live again in their possessions in their towns were Israelites, priests, Levites, and temple servants.

Inhabitants of Jerusalem after the Exile

3 And some of the people of Judah, Benjamin, Ephraim, and Manasseh lived in Jerusalem: 4Uthai son of Ammihud, son of Omri, son of Imri, son of Bani, from the sons of Perez son of Judah. 5And of the Shilonites: Asaiah the firstborn, and his sons. 6Of the sons of Zerah: Jeuel and their kin, six hundred ninety. 7Of the Benjaminites: Sallu son of Meshullam, son of Hodaviah, son of Hassenuah, 8Ibneiah son of Jeroham, Elah son of Uzzi, son of Michri, and Meshullam son of Shephatiah, son of Reuel, son of Ibnijah; 9and their kindred according to their generations, nine hundred fifty-six. All these were heads of families according to their ancestral houses.

Priestly Families

10 Of the priests: Jedaiah, Jehoiarib, Jachin, 11and Azariah son of Hilkiah, son of Meshullam, son of Zadok, son of Meraioth, son of Ahitub, the chief officer of the house of God; 12and Adaiah son of Jeroham, son of Pashhur, son of Malchijah, and Maasai son of Adiel, son of Jahzerah, son of Meshullam, son of Meshillemith, son of Immer; 13besides their kindred, heads of their ancestral houses, one thousand seven hundred sixty, qualified for the work of the service of the house of God.

Levitical Families

14 Of the Levites: Shemaiah son of Hasshub, son of Azrikam, son of Hashabiah, of the sons of Merari; 15and Bakbakkar, Heresh, Galal, and Mattaniah son of Mica, son of Zichri, son of Asaph; 16and Obadiah son of Shemaiah, son of Galal, son of Jeduthun, and Berechiah son of Asa, son of Elkanah, who lived in the villages of the Netophathites.

17 The gatekeepers were: Shallum, Akkub, Talmon, Ahiman; and their kindred Shallum was the chief, 18stationed previously in the king's gate on the east side. These were the gatekeepers of the camp of the Levites. 19Shallum son of Kore, son of Ebiasaph, son of Korah, and his kindred of his ancestral house, the Korahites, were in charge of the work of the service, guardians of the thresholds of the tent, as their

---

r Compare 9.35: Heb lacks *Jeiel*　　*s* Gk Ms adds *Ner*; Compare 8.33 and 9.36　　*t* Or *Shaul*

ancestors had been in charge of the camp of the LORD, guardians of the entrance. 20And Phinehas son of Eleazar was chief over them in former times; the LORD was with him. 21Zechariah son of Meshelemiah was gatekeeper at the entrance of the tent of meeting. 22All these, who were chosen as gatekeepers at the thresholds, were two hundred twelve. They were enrolled by genealogies in their villages. David and the seer Samuel established them in their office of trust. 23So they and their descendants were in charge of the gates of the house of the LORD, that is, the house of the tent, as guards. 24The gatekeepers were on the four sides, east, west, north, and south; 25and their kindred who were in their villages were obliged to come in every seven days, in turn, to be with them; 26for the four chief gatekeepers, who were Levites, were in charge of the chambers and the treasures of the house of God. 27And they would spend the night near the house of God; for on them lay the duty of watching, and they had charge of opening it every morning.

28 Some of them had charge of the utensils of service, for they were required to count them when they were brought in and taken out. 29Others of them were appointed over the furniture, and over all the holy utensils, also over the choice flour, the wine, the oil, the incense, and the spices. 30Others, of the sons of the priests, prepared the mixing of the spices, 31and Mattithiah, one of the Levites, the firstborn of Shallum the Korahite, was in charge of making the flat cakes. 32Also some of their kindred of the Kohathites had charge of the rows of bread, to prepare them for each sabbath.

33 Now these are the singers, the heads of ancestral houses of the Levites, living in the chambers of the temple free from other service, for they were on duty day and night. 34These were heads of ancestral houses of the Levites, according to their generations; these leaders lived in Jerusalem.

The Family of King Saul

35 In Gibeon lived the father of Gibeon, Jeiel, and the name of his wife was Maacah. 36His firstborn son was Abdon, then Zur, Kish, Baal, Ner, Nadab, 37Gedor, Ahio, Zechariah, and Mikloth; 38and Mikloth became the father of Shimeam; and these also lived opposite their kindred in Jerusalem, with their kindred. 39Ner became the father of Kish, Kish of Saul, Saul of Jonathan, Malchishua, Abinadab, and Esh-baal; 40and the son of Jonathan was Merib-baal; and Merib-baal became the father of Micah. 41The sons of Micah: Pithon, Melech, Tahrea, and Ahaz;u 42and Ahaz became the father of Jarah, and Jarah of Alemeth, Azmaveth, and Zimri; and Zimri became the father of Moza. 43Moza became the father of Binea; and Rephaiah was his son, Eleasah his son, Azel his son. 44Azel had six sons, and these are their names: Azrikam, Bocheru, Ishmael, Sheariah, Obadiah, and Hanan; these were the sons of Azel.

Death of Saul and His Sons

10 Now the Philistines fought against Israel; and the men of Israel fled before the Philistines, and fell slain on Mount Gilboa. 2The Philistines overtook Saul and his sons; and the Philistines killed Jonathan and Abinadab and Malchishua, sons of Saul. 3The battle pressed hard on Saul; and the archers found him, and he was wounded by the archers. 4Then Saul said to his armor-bearer, "Draw your sword, and thrust me through with it, so that these uncircumcised may not come and make sport of me." But his armor-bearer was unwilling, for he was terrified. So Saul took his own sword and fell on it. 5When his armor-bearer saw that Saul was dead, he also fell on his sword and died. 6Thus Saul died; he and his three sons and all his house died together. 7When all the men of Israel who were in the valley saw that the armyv had fled and that Saul and his sons were dead, they abandoned their towns and fled; and the Philistines came and occupied them.

8 The next day when the Philistines came to strip the dead, they found Saul and his sons fallen on Mount Gilboa. 9They stripped him and took his head and his armor, and sent messengers throughout the land of the Philistines to carry the good news to their idols and to the people. 10They put his armor in the temple of their gods, and fastened his head in the temple of Dagon. 11But when all Jabesh-gilead heard everything that the Philistines had done to Saul, 12all the valiant

u Compare 8.35: Heb lacks and Ahaz   v Heb they

warriors got up and took away the body of Saul and the bodies of his sons, and brought them to Jabesh. Then they buried their bones under the oak in Jabesh, and fasted seven days.

13 So Saul died for his unfaithfulness; he was unfaithful to the LORD in that he did not keep the command of the LORD; moreover, he had consulted a medium, seeking guidance, 14and did not seek guidance from the LORD. Therefore the LORD *w* put him to death and turned the kingdom over to David son of Jesse.

David Anointed King of All Israel

11 Then all Israel gathered together to David at Hebron and said, "See, we are your bone and flesh. 2For some time now, even while Saul was king, it was you who commanded the army of Israel. The LORD your God said to you: It is you who shall be shepherd of my people Israel, you who shall be ruler over my people Israel." 3So all the elders of Israel came to the king at Hebron, and David made a covenant with them at Hebron before the LORD. And they anointed David king over Israel, according to the word of the LORD by Samuel.

Jerusalem Captured

4 David and all Israel marched to Jerusalem, that is Jebus, where the Jebusites were, the inhabitants of the land. 5The inhabitants of Jebus said to David, "You will not come in here." Nevertheless David took the stronghold of Zion, now the city of David. 6David had said, "Whoever attacks the Jebusites first shall be chief and commander." And Joab son of Zeruiah went up first, so he became chief. 7David resided in the stronghold; therefore it was called the city of David. 8He built the city all around, from the Millo in complete circuit; and Joab repaired the rest of the city. 9And David became greater and greater, for the LORD of hosts was with him.

David's Mighty Men and Their Exploits

10 Now these are the chiefs of David's warriors, who gave him strong support in his kingdom, together with all Israel, to make him king, according to the word of the LORD concerning Israel. 11This is an account of David's mighty warriors: Jashobeam, son of Hachmoni,*x* was chief of the Three;*y* he wielded his spear against three hundred whom he killed at one time.

12 And next to him among the three warriors was Eleazar son of Dodo, the Ahohite. 13He was with David at Pasdammim when the Philistines were gathered there for battle. There was a plot of ground full of barley. Now the people had fled from the Philistines, 14but he and David took their stand in the middle of the plot, defended it, and killed the Philistines; and the LORD saved them by a great victory.

15 Three of the thirty chiefs went down to the rock to David at the cave of Adullam, while the army of Philistines was encamped in the valley of Rephaim. 16David was then in the stronghold; and the garrison of the Philistines was then at Bethlehem. 17David said longingly, "O that someone would give me water to drink from the well of Bethlehem that is by the gate!" 18Then the Three broke through the camp of the Philistines, and drew water from the well of Bethlehem that was by the gate, and they brought it to David. But David would not drink of it; he poured it out to the LORD, 19and said, "My God forbid that I should do this. Can I drink the blood of these men? For at the risk of their lives they brought it." Therefore he would not drink it. The three warriors did these things.

20 Now Abishai,*z* the brother of Joab, was chief of the Thirty.*a* With his spear he fought against three hundred and killed them, and won a name beside the Three. 21He was the most renowned*b* of the Thirty,*a* and became their commander; but he did not attain to the Three.

22 Benaiah son of Jehoiada was a valiant man*c* of Kabzeel, a doer of great deeds; he struck down two sons of*d* Ariel of Moab. He also went down and killed a lion in a pit on a day when snow had fallen. 23And he killed an Egyptian, a man of great stature, five cubits tall. The Egyptian had in his hand a spear like a weaver's beam; but Benaiah went against him with a staff, snatched the spear out of the Egyptian's hand, and killed him with his own

w Heb *he*   *x* Or *a Hachmonite*   *y* Compare
2 Sam 23.8: Heb *Thirty* or *captains*   *z* Gk Vg Tg
Compare 2 Sam 23.18: Heb *Abishai*   *a* Syr: Heb
Three   *b* Compare 2 Sam 23.19: Heb *more
renowned among the two*   *c* Syr: Heb *the son of
a valiant man*   *d* See 2 Sam 23.20: Heb lacks
sons of

spear. [24]Such were the things Benaiah son of Jehoiada did, and he won a name beside the three warriors. [25]He was renowned among the Thirty, but he did not attain to the Three. And David put him in charge of his bodyguard.

[26] The warriors of the armies were Asahel brother of Joab, Elhanan son of Dodo of Bethlehem, [27]Shammoth of Harod,[e] Helez the Pelonite, [28]Ira son of Ikkesh of Tekoa, Abiezer of Anathoth, [29]Sibbecai the Hushathite, Ilai the Ahohite, [30]Maharai of Netophah, Heled son of Baanah of Netophah, [31]Ithai son of Ribai of Gibeah of the Benjaminites, Benaiah of Pirathon, [32]Hurai of the wadis of Gaash, Abiel the Arbathite, [33]Azmaveth of Baharum, Eliahba of Shaalbon, [34]Hashem[f] the Gizonite, Jonathan son of Shagee the Hararite, [35]Ahiam son of Sachar the Hararite, Eliphal son of Ur, [36]Hepher the Mecherathite, Ahijah the Pelonite, [37]Hezro of Carmel, Naarai son of Ezbai, [38]Joel the brother of Nathan, Mibhar son of Hagri, [39]Zelek the Ammonite, Naharai of Beeroth, the armor-bearer of Joab son of Zeruiah, [40]Ira the Ithrite, Gareb the Ithrite, [41]Uriah the Hittite, Zabad son of Ahlai, [42]Adina son of Shiza the Reubenite, a leader of the Reubenites, and thirty with him, [43]Hanan son of Maacah, and Joshaphat the Mithnite, [44]Uzzia the Ashterathite, Shama and Jeiel sons of Hotham the Aroerite, [45]Jediael son of Shimri, and his brother Joha the Tizite, [46]Eliel the Mahavite, and Jeribai and Joshaviah sons of Elnaam, and Ithmah the Moabite, [47]Eliel, and Obed, and Jaasiel the Mezobaite.

David's Followers in the Wilderness

12 The following are those who came to David at Ziklag, while he could not move about freely because of Saul son of Kish; they were among the mighty warriors who helped him in war. [2]They were archers, and could shoot arrows and sling stones with either the right hand or the left; they were Benjaminites, Saul's kindred. [3]The chief was Ahiezer, then Joash, both sons of Shemaah of Gibeah; also Jeziel and Pelet sons of Azmaveth; Beracah, Jehu of Anathoth, [4]Ishmaiah of Gibeon, a warrior among the Thirty and a leader over the Thirty; Jeremiah,[g] Jahaziel, Johanan, Jozabad of Gederah, [5]Eluzai,[h] Jerimoth, Bealiah, Shemariah, Shephatiah the Haruphite; [6]Elkanah, Isshiah, Azarel, Joezer, and Jashobeam, the

Korahites; [7]and Joelah and Zebadiah, sons of Jeroham of Gedor.

[8] From the Gadites there went over to David at the stronghold in the wilderness mighty and experienced warriors, expert with shield and spear, whose faces were like the faces of lions, and who were swift as gazelles on the mountains: [9]Ezer the chief, Obadiah second, Eliab third, [10]Mishmannah fourth, Jeremiah fifth, [11]Attai sixth, Eliel seventh, [12]Johanan eighth, Elzabad ninth, [13]Jeremiah tenth, Machbannai eleventh. [14]These Gadites were officers of the army, the least equal to a hundred and the greatest to a thousand. [15]These are the men who crossed the Jordan in the first month, when it was overflowing all its banks, and put to flight all those in the valleys, to the east and to the west.

[16] Some Benjaminites and Judahites came to the stronghold to David. [17]David went out to meet them and said to them, "If you have come to me in friendship, to help me, then my heart will be knit to you; but if you have come to betray me to my adversaries, though my hands have done no wrong, then may the God of our ancestors see and give judgment." [18]Then the spirit came upon Amasai, chief of the Thirty, and he said,

"We are yours, O David;
   and with you, O son of Jesse!
Peace, peace to you,
   and peace to the one who helps
   you!
For your God is the one who
   helps you."

Then David received them, and made them officers of his troops.

[19] Some of the Manassites deserted to David when he came with the Philistines for the battle against Saul. (Yet he did not help them, for the rulers of the Philistines took counsel and sent him away, saying, "He will desert to his master Saul at the cost of our heads.") [20]As he went to Ziklag these Manassites deserted to him: Adnah, Jozabad, Jediael, Michael, Jozabad, Elihu, and Zillethai, chiefs of the thousands in Manasseh. [21]They helped David against

---

e Compare 2 Sam 23.25: Heb *the Harorite*
f Compare Gk and 2 Sam 23.32: Heb *the sons of Hashem*   g Heb verse 5   h Heb verse 6

the band of raiders,[i] for they were all warriors and commanders in the army. 22Indeed from day to day people kept coming to David to help him, until there was a great army, like an army of God.

David's Army at Hebron

23 These are the numbers of the divisions of the armed troops who came to David in Hebron to turn the kingdom of Saul over to him, according to the word of the LORD. 24The people of Judah bearing shield and spear numbered six thousand eight hundred armed troops. 25Of the Simeonites, mighty warriors, seven thousand one hundred. 26Of the Levites four thousand six hundred. 27Jehoiada, leader of the house of Aaron, and with him three thousand seven hundred. 28Zadok, a young warrior, and twenty-two commanders from his own ancestral house. 29Of the Benjaminites, the kindred of Saul, three thousand, of whom the majority had continued to keep their allegiance to the house of Saul. 30Of the Ephraimites, twenty thousand eight hundred, mighty warriors, notables in their ancestral houses. 31Of the half-tribe of Manasseh, eighteen thousand, who were expressly named to come and make David king. 32Of Issachar, those who had understanding of the times, to know what Israel ought to do, two hundred chiefs, and all their kindred under their command. 33Of Zebulun, fifty thousand seasoned troops, equipped for battle with all the weapons of war, to help David[j] with singleness of purpose. 34Of Naphtali, a thousand commanders, with whom there were thirty-seven thousand armed with shield and spear. 35Of the Danites, twenty-eight thousand six hundred equipped for battle. 36Of Asher, forty thousand seasoned troops ready for battle. 37Of the Reubenites and Gadites and the half-tribe of Manasseh from beyond the Jordan, one hundred twenty thousand armed with all the weapons of war.

38 All these, warriors arrayed in battle order, came to Hebron with full intent to make David king over all Israel; likewise all the rest of Israel were of a single mind to make David king. 39They were there with David for three days, eating and drinking, for their kindred had provided for them. 40And also their neighbors, from as far away as Issachar and Zebulun and Naphtali, came bringing food on donkeys, camels, mules, and oxen—abundant provisions of meal, cakes of figs, clusters of raisins, wine, oil, oxen, and sheep, for there was joy in Israel.

The Ark Brought from Kiriath-jearim

13 David consulted with the commanders of the thousands and of the hundreds, with every leader. 2David said to the whole assembly of Israel, "If it seems good to you, and if it is the will of the LORD our God, let us send abroad to our kindred who remain in all the land of Israel, including the priests and Levites in the cities that have pasture lands, that they may come together to us. 3Then let us bring again the ark of our God to us; for we did not turn to it in the days of Saul." 4The whole assembly agreed to do so, for the thing pleased all the people.

5 So David assembled all Israel from the Shihor of Egypt to Lebo-hamath, to bring the ark of God from Kiriath-jearim. 6And David and all Israel went up to Baalah, that is, to Kiriath-jearim, which belongs to Judah, to bring up from there the ark of God, the LORD, who is enthroned on the cherubim, which is called by his[k] name. 7They carried the ark of God on a new cart, from the house of Abinadab, and Uzzah and Ahio[l] were driving the cart. 8David and all Israel were dancing before God with all their might, with song and lyres and harps and tambourines and cymbals and trumpets.

9 When they came to the threshing floor of Chidon, Uzzah put out his hand to hold the ark, for the oxen shook it. 10The anger of the LORD was kindled against Uzzah; he struck him down because he put out his hand to the ark; and he died there before God. 11David was angry because the LORD had burst out against Uzzah; so that place is called Perez-uzzah[m] to this day. 12David was afraid of God that day; he said, "How can I bring the ark of God into my care?" 13So David did not take the ark into his care into the city of David; he took it instead to the house of Obed-edom the Gittite. 14The ark of God remained with the household of Obed-edom in his house three months, and the LORD blessed the household of Obed-edom and all that he had.

---

[i] Or as officers of his troops   [j] Gk: Heb lacks David   [k] Heb lacks his   [l] Or and his brother   [m] That is Bursting Out Against Uzzah

David Established at Jerusalem

14 King Hiram of Tyre sent messengers to David, along with cedar logs, and masons and carpenters to build a house for him. ²David then perceived that the LORD had established him as king over Israel, and that his kingdom was highly exalted for the sake of his people Israel.

3 David took more wives in Jerusalem, and David became the father of more sons and daughters. ⁴These are the names of the children whom he had in Jerusalem: Shammua, Shobab, and Nathan; Solomon, ⁵Ibhar, Elishua, and Elpelet; ⁶Nogah, Nepheg, and Japhia; ⁷Elishama, Beeliada, and Eliphelet.

Defeat of the Philistines

8 When the Philistines heard that David had been anointed king over all Israel, all the Philistines went up in search of David; and David heard of it and went out against them. ⁹Now the Philistines had come and made a raid in the valley of Rephaim. ¹⁰David inquired of God, "Shall I go up against the Philistines? Will you give them into my hand?" The LORD said to him, "Go up, and I will give them into your hand." ¹¹So he went up to Baalperazim, and David defeated them there. David said, "God has burst out*ⁿ* against my enemies by my hand, like a bursting flood." Therefore that place is called Baalperazim.*ᵒ* ¹²They abandoned their gods there, and at David's command they were burned.

13 Once again the Philistines made a raid in the valley. ¹⁴When David again inquired of God, God said to him, "You shall not go up after them; go around and come on them opposite the balsam trees. ¹⁵When you hear the sound of marching in the tops of the balsam trees, then go out to battle; for God has gone out before you to strike down the army of the Philistines." ¹⁶David did as God had commanded him, and they struck down the Philistine army from Gibeon to Gezer. ¹⁷The fame of David went out into all lands, and the LORD brought the fear of him on all nations.

The Ark Brought to Jerusalem

15 David*ᵖ* built houses for himself in the city of David, and he prepared a place for the ark of God and pitched a tent for it. ²Then David commanded that no one but the Levites were to carry the ark of God, for the LORD had chosen them to carry the ark of the LORD and to minister to him forever. ³David assembled all Israel in Jerusalem to bring up the ark of the LORD to its place, which he had prepared for it. ⁴Then David gathered together the descendants of Aaron and the Levites: ⁵of the sons of Kohath, Uriel the chief, with one hundred twenty of his kindred; ⁶of the sons of Merari, Asaiah the chief, with two hundred twenty of his kindred; ⁷of the sons of Gershom, Joel the chief, with one hundred thirty of his kindred; ⁸of the sons of Elizaphan, Shemaiah the chief, with two hundred of his kindred; ⁹of the sons of Hebron, Eliel the chief, with eighty of his kindred; ¹⁰of the sons of Uzziel, Amminadab the chief, with one hundred twelve of his kindred.

11 David summoned the priests Zadok and Abiathar, and the Levites Uriel, Asaiah, Joel, Shemaiah, Eliel, and Amminadab. ¹²He said to them, "You are the heads of families of the Levites; sanctify yourselves, you and your kindred, so that you may bring up the ark of the LORD, the God of Israel, to the place that I have prepared for it. ¹³Because you did not carry it the first time,* q* the LORD our God burst out against us, because we did not give it proper care." ¹⁴So the priests and the Levites sanctified themselves to bring up the ark of the LORD, the God of Israel. ¹⁵And the Levites carried the ark of God on their shoulders with the poles, as Moses had commanded according to the word of the LORD.

16 David also commanded the chiefs of the Levites to appoint their kindred as the singers to play on musical instruments, on harps and lyres and cymbals, to raise loud sounds of joy. ¹⁷So the Levites appointed Heman son of Joel; and of his kindred Asaph son of Berechiah; and of the sons of Merari, their kindred, Ethan son of Kushaiah; ¹⁸and with them their kindred of the second order, Zechariah, Jaaziel, Shemiramoth, Jehiel, Unni, Eliab, Benaiah, Maaseiah, Mattithiah, Eliphelehu, and Mikneiah, and the gatekeepers Obed-edom and Jeiel. ¹⁹The singers Heman, Asaph, and Ethan were to sound bronze cymbals; ²⁰Zechariah, Aziel, She-

miramoth, Jehiel, Unni, Eliab, Maaseiah, and Benaiah were to play harps according to Alamoth; [21]but Mattithiah, Eliphelehu, Mikneiah, Obed-edom, Jeiel, and Azaziah were to lead with lyres according to the Sheminith. [22]Chenaniah, leader of the Levites in music, was to direct the music, for he understood it. [23]Berechiah and Elkanah were to be gatekeepers for the ark. [24]Shebaniah, Joshaphat, Nethanel, Amasai, Zechariah, Benaiah, and Eliezer, the priests, were to blow the trumpets before the ark of God. Obed-edom and Jehiah also were to be gatekeepers for the ark.

25 So David and the elders of Israel, and the commanders of the thousands, went to bring up the ark of the covenant of the LORD from the house of Obed-edom with rejoicing. [26]And because God helped the Levites who were carrying the ark of the covenant of the LORD, they sacrificed seven bulls and seven rams. [27]David was clothed with a robe of fine linen, as also were all the Levites who were carrying the ark, and the singers, and Chenaniah the leader of the music of the singers; and David wore a linen ephod. [28]So all Israel brought up the ark of the covenant of the LORD with shouting, to the sound of the horn, trumpets, and cymbals, and made loud music on harps and lyres.

29 As the ark of the covenant of the LORD came to the city of David, Michal daughter of Saul looked out of the window, and saw King David leaping and dancing; and she despised him in her heart.

The Ark Placed in the Tent

16 They brought in the ark of God, and set it inside the tent that David had pitched for it; and they offered burnt offerings and offerings of well-being before God. [2]When David had finished offering the burnt offerings and the offerings of well-being, he blessed the people in the name of the LORD; [3]and he distributed to every person in Israel—man and woman alike—to each a loaf of bread, a portion of meat,[r] and a cake of raisins.

4 He appointed certain of the Levites as ministers before the ark of the LORD, to invoke, to thank, and to praise the LORD, the God of Israel. [5]Asaph was the chief, and second to him Zechariah, Jeiel, Shemiramoth, Jehiel, Mattithiah, Eliab, Benaiah, Obed-edom, and Jeiel, with harps and lyres; Asaph was to sound the cymbals, [6]and the priests Benaiah and Jahaziel were to blow trumpets regularly, before the ark of the covenant of God.

David's Psalm of Thanksgiving

7 Then on that day David first appointed the singing of praises to the LORD by Asaph and his kindred.

8 O give thanks to the LORD, call on
    his name,
  make known his deeds among the
    peoples.
9 Sing to him, sing praises to him,
  tell of all his wonderful works.
10 Glory in his holy name;
  let the hearts of those who seek
    the LORD rejoice.
11 Seek the LORD and his strength,
  seek his presence continually.
12 Remember the wonderful works he
    has done,
  his miracles, and the judgments
    he uttered,
13 O offspring of his servant Israel,[s]
  children of Jacob, his chosen
    ones.

14 He is the LORD our God;
  his judgments are in all the earth.
15 Remember his covenant forever,
  the word that he commanded, for
    a thousand generations,
16 the covenant that he made with
    Abraham,
  his sworn promise to Isaac,
17 which he confirmed to Jacob as a
    statute,
  to Israel as an everlasting
    covenant,
18 saying, "To you I will give the land
    of Canaan
  as your portion for an inheritance."

19 When they were few in number,
  of little account, and strangers in
    the land,[t]
20 wandering from nation to nation,
  from one kingdom to another
    people,
21 he allowed no one to oppress them;
  he rebuked kings on their account,

---

r Compare Gk Syr Vg: Meaning of Heb uncertain
s Another reading is *Abraham* (compare Ps 105.6)
t Heb *in it*

22 saying, "Do not touch my anointed
　　ones;
　　do my prophets no harm."

23 Sing to the LORD, all the earth.
　　Tell of his salvation from day to
　　day.
24 Declare his glory among the nations,
　　his marvelous works among all
　　the peoples.
25 For great is the LORD, and greatly to
　　be praised;
　　he is to be revered above all gods.
26 For all the gods of the peoples are
　　idols,

but the LORD made the heavens.
27 Honor and majesty are before
　　him;
　　strength and joy are in his place.

28 Ascribe to the LORD, O families of
　　the peoples,
　　ascribe to the LORD glory and
　　strength.
29 Ascribe to the LORD the glory due his
　　name;
　　bring an offering, and come
　　before him.
　　Worship the LORD in holy splendor;
30 　　tremble before him, all the earth.

THE TRADITION

Special Blessings

*When David had finished offering the burnt offerings and the offerings
of well-being, he blessed the people in the name of the LORD.*

1 CHRONICLES 16.2

A *little girl brings her pet rabbit to
church for the blessing of animals on the
feast of Saint Francis.*

*A family invites the parish priest over to
bless their new home.*

*Parish religious education teachers kick
off the school year by gathering for a special
blessing.*

*Two college students in a fast-food
restaurant make the sign of the cross and
say grace before digging into their hamburg-
ers and fries.*

Special blessings are a part of Catholic life.
They are holy words through which God enters our everyday world and helps us use his
gifts in the spirit of the gospel.

Some of these prayers can be said by any
of us, while others are reserved for bishops,
priests, or deacons. But all of them are "let it
happen" statements that originate with God
and are spoken on his behalf. God himself pronounced the first blessings—over birds and
sea creatures, Adam and Eve, Noah and his
sons (see Genesis 1.22, 28; 9.1). He taught

Aaron, Israel's first high priest, to bless the
people in his name (see Numbers 6.22–26).
The New Testament shows Jesus blessing
children, food, and followers.

Because blessings come from God, they
really do something. Like a key in the igni-
tion, they activate a special kind of power:
Food is made holy, catechists are commissioned, homes and religious articles are dedicated to God's service, and animals are put
under special protection.

Through the words of every blessing, we
are reminded that God is the source of life
and of every good thing. Even as we ask God
to sanctify what we offer, we acknowledge
that the offering itself is something he has
blessed us with.

The blessings of Scripture and the Church
also give us a glimpse into God's hopes for us.
Without addressing the specifics of "what
does God want for my life?" they leave no
doubt that God intends only goodness. Blessings verbalize a loving God's desire for his
children's welfare. They are God's wishes
made audible.

The world is firmly established; it
  shall never be moved.
31 Let the heavens be glad, and let the
    earth rejoice,
  and let them say among the
    nations, "The LORD is king!"
32 Let the sea roar, and all that fills it;
  let the field exult, and everything
    in it.
33 Then shall the trees of the forest
    sing for joy
  before the LORD, for he comes to
    judge the earth.
34 O give thanks to the LORD, for he is
    good;
  for his steadfast love endures
    forever.

35 Say also:
  "Save us, O God of our salvation,
    and gather and rescue us from
      among the nations,
  that we may give thanks to your
    holy name,
  and glory in your praise.
36 Blessed be the LORD, the God of
    Israel,
  from everlasting to everlasting."
Then all the people said "Amen!" and
praised the LORD.

Regular Worship Maintained

37 David left Asaph and his kinsfolk
there before the ark of the covenant of the
LORD to minister regularly before the ark as
each day required, 38and also Obed-edom
and his*u* sixty-eight kinsfolk; while
Obed-edom son of Jeduthun and Hosah
were to be gatekeepers. 39And he left the
priest Zadok and his kindred the priests
before the tabernacle of the LORD in the
high place that was at Gibeon, 40to offer
burnt offerings to the LORD on the altar of
burnt offering regularly, morning and evening, according to all that is written in the
law of the LORD that he commanded Israel.
41With them were Heman and Jeduthun,
and the rest of those chosen and expressly
named to render thanks to the LORD, for
his steadfast love endures forever. 42He-
man and Jeduthun had with them trumpets and cymbals for the music, and instruments for sacred song. The sons of
Jeduthun were appointed to the gate.
43 Then all the people departed to
their homes, and David went home to
bless his household.

God's Covenant with David

17 Now when David settled in his
house, David said to the prophet
Nathan, "I am living in a house of cedar,
but the ark of the covenant of the LORD is
under a tent." 2Nathan said to David, "Do
all that you have in mind, for God is with
you."

3 But that same night the word of the
LORD came to Nathan, saying: 4Go and tell
my servant David: Thus says the LORD: You
shall not build me a house to live in. 5For
I have not lived in a house since the day I
brought out Israel to this very day, but I
have lived in a tent and a tabernacle.*v*
6Wherever I have moved about among all
Israel, did I ever speak a word with any of
the judges of Israel, whom I commanded
to shepherd my people, saying, Why have
you not built me a house of cedar? 7Now
therefore thus you shall say to my servant
David: Thus says the LORD of hosts: I took
you from the pasture, from following the
sheep, to be ruler over my people Israel;
8and I have been with you wherever you
went, and have cut off all your enemies
before you; and I will make for you a
name, like the name of the great ones of
the earth. 9I will appoint a place for my
people Israel, and will plant them, so that
they may live in their own place, and be
disturbed no more; and evildoers shall
wear them down no more, as they did
formerly, 10from the time that I appointed
judges over my people Israel; and I will
subdue all your enemies.

Moreover I declare to you that the LORD
will build you a house. 11When your days
are fulfilled to go to be with your ancestors, I will raise up your offspring after
you, one of your own sons, and I will establish his kingdom. 12He shall build a
house for me, and I will establish his
throne forever. 13I will be a father to him,
and he shall be a son to me. I will not take
my steadfast love from him, as I took it
from him who was before you, 14but I will
confirm him in my house and in my kingdom forever, and his throne shall be established forever. 15In accordance with all
these words and all this vision, Nathan
spoke to David.

---

u Gk Syr Vg: Heb *their*   *v* Gk 2 Sam 7.6: Heb *but
I have been from tent to tent and from tabernacle*

David's Prayer

16 Then King David went in and sat before the Lord, and said, "Who am I, O Lord God, and what is my house, that you have brought me thus far? 17And even this was a small thing in your sight, O God; you have also spoken of your servant's house for a great while to come. You regard me as someone of high rank,[w] O Lord God! 18And what more can David say to you for honoring your servant? You know your servant. 19For your servant's sake, O Lord, and according to your own heart, you have done all these great deeds, making known all these great things. 20There is no one like you, O Lord, and there is no God besides you, according to all that we have heard with our ears. 21Who is like your people Israel, one nation on the earth whom God went to redeem to be his people, making for yourself a name for great and terrible things, in driving out nations before your people whom you redeemed from Egypt? 22And you made your people Israel to be your people forever; and you, O Lord, became their God.

23 "And now, O Lord, as for the word that you have spoken concerning your servant and concerning his house, let it be established forever, and do as you have promised. 24Thus your name will be established and magnified forever in the saying, 'The Lord of hosts, the God of Israel, is Israel's God'; and the house of your servant David will be established in your presence. 25For you, my God, have revealed to your servant that you will build a house for him; therefore your servant has found it possible to pray before you. 26And now, O Lord, you are God, and you have promised this good thing to your servant; 27therefore may it please you to bless the house of your servant, that it may continue forever before you. For you, O Lord, have blessed and are blessed[x] forever."

David's Kingdom Established and Extended

18 Some time afterward, David attacked the Philistines and subdued them; he took Gath and its villages from the Philistines.

2 He defeated Moab, and the Moabites became subject to David and brought tribute.

3 David also struck down King Hadadezer of Zobah, toward Hamath,[w] as he went to set up a monument at the river Euphrates. 4David took from him one thousand chariots, seven thousand cavalry, and twenty thousand foot soldiers. David hamstrung all the chariot horses, but left one hundred of them. 5When the Arameans of Damascus came to help King Hadadezer of Zobah, David killed twenty-two thousand Arameans. 6Then David put garrisons[y] in Aram of Damascus; and the Arameans became subject to David, and brought tribute. The Lord gave victory to David wherever he went. 7David took the gold shields that were carried by the servants of Hadadezer, and brought them to Jerusalem. 8From Tibhath and from Cun, cities of Hadadezer, David took a vast quantity of bronze; with it Solomon made the bronze sea and the pillars and the vessels of bronze.

9 When King Tou of Hamath heard that David had defeated the whole army of King Hadadezer of Zobah, 10he sent his son Hadoram to King David, to greet him and to congratulate him, because he had fought against Hadadezer and defeated him. Now Hadadezer had often been at war with Tou. He sent all sorts of articles of gold, of silver, and of bronze; 11these also King David dedicated to the Lord, together with the silver and gold that he had carried off from all the nations, from Edom, Moab, the Ammonites, the Philistines, and Amalek.

12 Abishai son of Zeruiah killed eighteen thousand Edomites in the Valley of Salt. 13He put garrisons in Edom; and all the Edomites became subject to David. And the Lord gave victory to David wherever he went.

David's Administration

14 So David reigned over all Israel; and he administered justice and equity to all his people. 15Joab son of Zeruiah was over the army; Jehoshaphat son of Ahilud was recorder; 16Zadok son of Ahitub and Ahimelech son of Abiathar were priests; Shavsha was secretary; 17Benaiah son of Jehoiada was over the Cherethites and the Pelethites; and David's sons were the chief officials in the service of the king.

---

w Meaning of Heb uncertain   x Or *and it is blessed*   y Gk Vg 2 Sam 8.6 Compare Syr: Heb lacks *garrisons*

Defeat of the Ammonites and Arameans

19 Some time afterward, King Nahash of the Ammonites died, and his son succeeded him. ²David said, "I will deal loyally with Hanun son of Nahash, for his father dealt loyally with me." So David sent messengers to console him concerning his father. When David's servants came to Hanun in the land of the Ammonites, to console him, ³the officials of the Ammonites said to Hanun, "Do you think, because David has sent consolers to you, that he is honoring your father? Have not his servants come to you to search and to overthrow and to spy out the land?" ⁴So Hanun seized David's servants, shaved them, cut off their garments in the middle at their hips, and sent them away; ⁵and they departed. When David was told about the men, he sent messengers to them, for they felt greatly humiliated. The king said, "Remain at Jericho until your beards have grown, and then return."

6 When the Ammonites saw that they had made themselves odious to David, Hanun and the Ammonites sent a thousand talents of silver to hire chariots and cavalry from Mesopotamia, from Aram-maacah and from Zobah. ⁷They hired thirty-two thousand chariots and the king of Maacah with his army, who came and camped before Medeba. And the Ammonites were mustered from their cities and came to battle. ⁸When David heard of it, he sent Joab and all the army of the warriors. ⁹The Ammonites came out and drew up in battle array at the entrance of the city, and the kings who had come were by themselves in the open country.

10 When Joab saw that the line of battle was set against him both in front and in the rear, he chose some of the picked men of Israel and arrayed them against the Arameans; ¹¹the rest of his troops he put in the charge of his brother Abishai, and they were arrayed against the Ammonites. ¹²He said, "If the Arameans are too strong for me, then you shall help me; but if the Ammonites are too strong for you, then I will help you. ¹³Be strong, and let us be courageous for our people and for the cities of our God; and may the LORD do what seems good to him." ¹⁴So Joab and the troops who were with him advanced toward the Arameans for battle; and they fled before him. ¹⁵When the Am-

monites saw that the Arameans fled, they likewise fled before Abishai, Joab's brother, and entered the city. Then Joab came to Jerusalem.

16 But when the Arameans saw that they had been defeated by Israel, they sent messengers and brought out the Arameans who were beyond the Euphrates, with Shophach the commander of the army of Hadadezer at their head. ¹⁷When David was informed, he gathered all Israel together, crossed the Jordan, came to them, and drew up his forces against them. When David set the battle in array against the Arameans, they fought with him. ¹⁸The Arameans fled before Israel; and David killed seven thousand Aramean charioteers and forty thousand foot soldiers, and also killed Shophach the commander of their army. ¹⁹When the servants of Hadadezer saw that they had been defeated by Israel, they made peace with David, and became subject to him. So the Arameans were not willing to help the Ammonites any more.

Siege and Capture of Rabbah

20 In the spring of the year, the time when kings go out to battle, Joab led out the army, ravaged the country of the Ammonites, and came and besieged Rabbah. But David remained at Jerusalem. Joab attacked Rabbah, and overthrew it. ²David took the crown of Milcom^z from his head; he found that it weighed a talent of gold, and in it was a precious stone; and it was placed on David's head. He also brought out the booty of the city, a very great amount. ³He brought out the people who were in it, and set them to work^a with saws and iron picks and axes.^b Thus David did to all the cities of the Ammonites. Then David and all the people returned to Jerusalem.

Exploits against the Philistines

4 After this, war broke out with the Philistines at Gezer; then Sibbecai the Hushathite killed Sippai, who was one of the descendants of the giants; and the Philistines were subdued. ⁵Again there was war with the Philistines; and Elhanan son of Jair killed Lahmi the brother of Goliath the Gittite, the shaft of whose spear was

---

z Gk Vg See 1 Kings 11.5, 33: MT *of their king*
a Compare 2 Sam 12.31: Heb *and he sawed*
b Compare 2 Sam 12.31: Heb *saws*

like a weaver's beam. ⁶Again there was war at Gath, where there was a man of great size, who had six fingers on each hand, and six toes on each foot, twenty-four in number; he also was descended from the giants. ⁷When he taunted Israel, Jonathan son of Shimea, David's brother, killed him. ⁸These were descended from the giants in Gath; they fell by the hand of David and his servants.

The Census and Plague

21 Satan stood up against Israel, and incited David to count the people of Israel. ²So David said to Joab and the commanders of the army, "Go, number Israel, from Beer-sheba to Dan, and bring me a report, so that I may know their number." ³But Joab said, "May the LORD increase the number of his people a hundredfold! Are they not, my lord the king, all of them my lord's servants? Why then should my lord require this? Why should he bring guilt on Israel?" ⁴But the king's word prevailed against Joab. So Joab departed and went throughout all Israel, and came back to Jerusalem. ⁵Joab gave the total count of the people to David. In all Israel there were one million one hundred thousand men who drew the sword, and in Judah four hundred seventy thousand who drew the sword. ⁶But he did not include Levi and Benjamin in the numbering, for the king's command was abhorrent to Joab.

7 But God was displeased with this thing, and he struck Israel. ⁸David said to God, "I have sinned greatly in that I have done this thing. But now, I pray you, take away the guilt of your servant; for I have done very foolishly." ⁹The LORD spoke to Gad, David's seer, saying, ¹⁰"Go and say to David, 'Thus says the LORD: Three things I offer you; choose one of them, so that I may do it to you.' " ¹¹So Gad came to David and said to him, "Thus says the LORD, 'Take your choice: ¹²either three years of famine; or three months of devastation by your foes, while the sword of your enemies overtakes you; or three days of the sword of the LORD, pestilence on the land, and the angel of the LORD destroying throughout all the territory of Israel.' Now decide what answer I shall return to the one who sent me." ¹³Then David said to Gad, "I am in great distress; let me fall into the hand of the LORD, for his mercy is very great; but let me not fall into human hands."

14 So the LORD sent a pestilence on Israel; and seventy thousand persons fell in Israel. ¹⁵And God sent an angel to Jerusalem to destroy it; but when he was about to destroy it, the LORD took note and relented concerning the calamity; he said to the destroying angel, "Enough! Stay your hand." The angel of the LORD was then standing by the threshing floor of Ornan the Jebusite. ¹⁶David looked up and saw the angel of the LORD standing between earth and heaven, and in his hand a drawn sword stretched out over Jerusalem. Then David and the elders, clothed in sackcloth, fell on their faces. ¹⁷And David said to God, "Was it not I who gave the command to count the people? It is I who have sinned and done very wickedly. But these sheep, what have they done? Let your hand, I pray, O LORD my God, be against me and against my father's house; but do not let your people be plagued!"

David's Altar and Sacrifice

18 Then the angel of the LORD commanded Gad to tell David that he should go up and erect an altar to the LORD on the threshing floor of Ornan the Jebusite. ¹⁹So David went up following Gad's instructions, which he had spoken in the name of the LORD. ²⁰Ornan turned and saw the angel; and while his four sons who were with him hid themselves, Ornan continued to thresh wheat. ²¹As David came to Ornan, Ornan looked and saw David; he went out from the threshing floor, and did obeisance to David with his face to the ground. ²²David said to Ornan, "Give me the site of the threshing floor that I may build on it an altar to the LORD—give it to me at its full price—so that the plague may be averted from the people." ²³Then Ornan said to David, "Take it; and let my lord the king do what seems good to him; see, I present the oxen for burnt offerings, and the threshing sledges for the wood, and the wheat for a grain offering. I give it all." ²⁴But King David said to Ornan, "No; I will buy them for the full price. I will not take for the LORD what is yours, nor offer burnt offerings that cost me nothing." ²⁵So David paid Ornan six hundred shekels of gold by weight for the site. ²⁶David built there an altar to the LORD and presented burnt offerings and offerings of well-being. He called upon the LORD, and he

answered him with fire from heaven on the altar of burnt offering. 27Then the LORD commanded the angel, and he put his sword back into its sheath.

The Place Chosen for the Temple

28 At that time, when David saw that the LORD had answered him at the threshing floor of Ornan the Jebusite, he made his sacrifices there. 29For the tabernacle of the LORD, which Moses had made in the wilderness, and the altar of burnt offering were at that time in the high place at Gibeon; 30but David could not go before it to inquire of God, for he was afraid of the sword of the angel of the LORD. 22 1Then David said, "Here shall be the house of the LORD God and here the altar of burnt offering for Israel."

David Prepares to Build the Temple

2 David gave orders to gather together the aliens who were residing in the land of Israel, and he set stonecutters to prepare dressed stones for building the house of God. 3David also provided great stores of iron for nails for the doors of the gates and for clamps, as well as bronze in quantities beyond weighing, 4and cedar logs without number—for the Sidonians and Tyrians brought great quantities of cedar to David. 5For David said, "My son Solomon is young and inexperienced, and the house that is to be built for the LORD must be exceedingly magnificent, famous and glorified throughout all lands; I will therefore make preparation for it." So David provided materials in great quantity before his death.

David's Charge to Solomon and the Leaders

6 Then he called for his son Solomon and charged him to build a house for the LORD, the God of Israel. 7David said to Solomon, "My son, I had planned to build a house to the name of the LORD my God. 8But the word of the LORD came to me, saying, 'You have shed much blood and have waged great wars; you shall not build a house to my name, because you have shed so much blood in my sight on the earth. 9See, a son shall be born to you; he shall be a man of peace. I will give him peace from all his enemies on every side; for his name shall be Solomon,c and I will give peaced and quiet to Israel in his days. 10He shall build a house for my name. He shall be a son to me, and I will

be a father to him, and I will establish his royal throne in Israel forever.' 11Now, my son, the LORD be with you, so that you may succeed in building the house of the LORD your God, as he has spoken concerning you. 12Only, may the LORD grant you discretion and understanding, so that when he gives you charge over Israel you may keep the law of the LORD your God. 13Then you will prosper if you are careful to observe the statutes and the ordinances that the LORD commanded Moses for Israel. Be strong and of good courage. Do not be afraid or dismayed. 14With great pains I have provided for the house of the LORD one hundred thousand talents of gold, one million talents of silver, and bronze and iron beyond weighing, for there is so much of it; timber and stone too I have provided. To these you must add more. 15You have an abundance of workers: stonecutters, masons, carpenters, and all kinds of artisans without number, skilled in working 16gold, silver, bronze, and iron. Now begin the work, and the LORD be with you."

17 David also commanded all the leaders of Israel to help his son Solomon, saying, 18"Is not the LORD your God with you? Has he not given you peace on every side? For he has delivered the inhabitants of the land into my hand; and the land is subdued before the LORD and his people. 19Now set your mind and heart to seek the LORD your God. Go and build the sanctuary of the LORD God so that the ark of the covenant of the LORD and the holy vessels of God may be brought into a house built for the name of the LORD."

Families of the Levites and Their Functions

23 When David was old and full of days, he made his son Solomon king over Israel.

2 David assembled all the leaders of Israel and the priests and the Levites. 3The Levites, thirty years old and upward, were counted, and the total was thirty-eight thousand. 4"Twenty-four thousand of these," David said, "shall have charge of the work in the house of the LORD, six thousand shall be officers and judges, 5four thousand gatekeepers, and four thousand shall offer praises to the LORD with the instruments that I have made for praise." 6And David organized them in di-

c Heb Shelomoh   d Heb shalom

visions corresponding to the sons of Levi: Gershon,[e] Kohath, and Merari.

7 The sons of Gershon[f] were Ladan and Shimei. [8]The sons of Ladan: Jehiel the chief, Zetham, and Joel, three. [9]The sons of Shimei: Shelomoth, Haziel, and Haran, three. These were the heads of families of Ladan. [10]And the sons of Shimei: Jahath, Zina, Jeush, and Beriah. These four were the sons of Shimei. [11]Jahath was the chief, and Zizah the second; but Jeush and Beriah did not have many sons, so they were enrolled as a single family.

12 The sons of Kohath: Amram, Izhar, Hebron, and Uzziel, four. [13]The sons of Amram: Aaron and Moses. Aaron was set apart to consecrate the most holy things, so that he and his sons forever should make offerings before the LORD, and minister to him and pronounce blessings in his name forever; [14]but as for Moses the man of God, his sons were to be reckoned among the tribe of Levi. [15]The sons of Moses: Gershom and Eliezer. [16]The sons of Gershom: Shebuel the chief. [17]The sons of Eliezer: Rehabiah the chief; Eliezer had no other sons, but the sons of Rehabiah were very numerous. [18]The sons of Izhar: Shelomith the chief. [19]The sons of Hebron: Jeriah the chief, Amariah the second, Jahaziel the third, and Jekameam the fourth. [20]The sons of Uzziel: Micah the chief and Isshiah the second.

21 The sons of Merari: Mahli and Mushi. The sons of Mahli: Eleazar and Kish. [22]Eleazar died having no sons, but only daughters; their kindred, the sons of Kish, married them. [23]The sons of Mushi: Mahli, Eder, and Jeremoth, three.

24 These were the sons of Levi by their ancestral houses, the heads of families as they were enrolled according to the number of the names of the individuals from twenty years old and upward who were to do the work for the service of the house of the LORD. [25]For David said, "The LORD, the God of Israel, has given rest to his people; and he resides in Jerusalem forever. [26]And so the Levites no longer need to carry the tabernacle or any of the things for its service"— [27]for according to the last words of David these were the number of the Levites from twenty years old and upward— [28]"but their duty shall be to assist the descendants of Aaron for the service of the house of the LORD, having the care of the courts and the chambers, the cleansing of all that is holy, and any work for the ser-

vice of the house of God; [29]to assist also with the rows of bread, the choice flour for the grain offering, the wafers of unleavened bread, the baked offering, the offering mixed with oil, and all measures of quantity or size. [30]And they shall stand every morning, thanking and praising the LORD, and likewise at evening, [31]and whenever burnt offerings are offered to the LORD on sabbaths, new moons, and appointed festivals, according to the number required of them, regularly before the LORD. [32]Thus they shall keep charge of the tent of meeting and the sanctuary, and shall attend the descendants of Aaron, their kindred, for the service of the house of the LORD."

Divisions of the Priests

24 The divisions of the descendants of Aaron were these. The sons of Aaron: Nadab, Abihu, Eleazar, and Ithamar. [2]But Nadab and Abihu died before their father, and had no sons; so Eleazar and Ithamar became the priests. [3]Along with Zadok of the sons of Eleazar, and Ahimelech of the sons of Ithamar, David organized them according to the appointed duties in their service. [4]Since more chief men were found among the sons of Eleazar than among the sons of Ithamar, they organized them under sixteen heads of ancestral houses of the sons of Eleazar, and eight of the sons of Ithamar. [5]They organized them by lot, all alike, for there were officers of the sanctuary and officers of God among both the sons of Eleazar and the sons of Ithamar. [6]The scribe Shemaiah son of Nethanel, a Levite, recorded them in the presence of the king, and the officers, and Zadok the priest, and Ahimelech son of Abiathar, and the heads of ancestral houses of the priests and of the Levites; one ancestral house being chosen for Eleazar and one chosen for Ithamar.

7 The first lot fell to Jehoiarib, the second to Jedaiah, [8]the third to Harim, the fourth to Seorim, [9]the fifth to Malchijah, the sixth to Mijamin, [10]the seventh to Hakkoz, the eighth to Abijah, [11]the ninth to Jeshua, the tenth to Shecaniah, [12]the eleventh to Eliashib, the twelfth to Jakim, [13]the thirteenth to Huppah, the fourteenth to Jeshebeab, [14]the fifteenth to Bilgah, the sixteenth to Immer, [15]the seven-

e Or *Gershom*; See 1 Chr 6.1, note, and 23.15
f Vg Compare Gk Syr: Heb *to the Gershonite*

teenth to Hezir, the eighteenth to Happizzez, [16]the nineteenth to Pethahiah, the twentieth to Jehezkel, [17]the twenty-first to Jachin, the twenty-second to Gamul, [18]the twenty-third to Delaiah, the twenty-fourth to Maaziah. [19]These had as their appointed duty in their service to enter the house of the LORD according to the procedure established for them by their ancestor Aaron, as the LORD God of Israel had commanded him.

Other Levites

20 And of the rest of the sons of Levi: of the sons of Amram, Shubael; of the sons of Shubael, Jehdeiah. [21]Of Rehabiah: of the sons of Rehabiah, Isshiah the chief. [22]Of the Izharites, Shelomoth; of the sons of Shelomoth, Jahath. [23]The sons of Hebron: [g] Jeriah the chief,[h] Amariah the second, Jahaziel the third, Jekameam the fourth. [24]The sons of Uzziel, Micah; of the sons of Micah, Shamir. [25]The brother of Micah, Isshiah; of the sons of Isshiah, Zechariah. [26]The sons of Merari: Mahli and Mushi. The sons of Jaaziah: Beno.[i] [27]The sons of Merari: of Jaaziah, Beno,[i] Shoham, Zaccur, and Ibri. [28]Of Mahli: Eleazar, who had no sons. [29]Of Kish, the sons of Kish: Jerahmeel. [30]The sons of Mushi: Mahli, Eder, and Jerimoth. These were the sons of the Levites according to their ancestral houses. [31]These also cast lots corresponding to their kindred, the descendants of Aaron, in the presence of King David, Zadok, Ahimelech, and the heads of ancestral houses of the priests and of the Levites, the chief as well as the youngest brother.

The Temple Musicians

25 David and the officers of the army also set apart for the service the sons of Asaph, and of Heman, and of Jeduthun, who should prophesy with lyres, harps, and cymbals. The list of those who did the work and of their duties was: [2]Of the sons of Asaph: Zaccur, Joseph, Nethaniah, and Asarelah, sons of Asaph, under the direction of Asaph, who prophesied under the direction of the king. [3]Of Jeduthun, the sons of Jeduthun: Gedaliah, Zeri, Jeshaiah, Shimei,[j] Hashabiah, and Mattithiah, six, under the direction of their father Jeduthun, who prophesied with the lyre in thanksgiving and praise to the LORD. [4]Of Heman, the sons of Heman: Bukkiah, Mattaniah, Uzziel, Shebuel, and Jerimoth, Hananiah, Hanani, Eliathah, Giddalti, and Romamti-ezer, Joshbekashah, Mallothi, Hothir, Mahazioth. [5]All these were the sons of Heman the king's seer, according to the promise of God to exalt him; for God had given Heman fourteen sons and three daughters. [6]They were all under the direction of their father for the music in the house of the LORD with cymbals, harps, and lyres for the service of the house of God. Asaph, Jeduthun, and Heman were under the order of the king. [7]They and their kindred, who were trained in singing to the LORD, all of whom were skillful, numbered two hundred eighty-eight. [8]And they cast lots for their duties, small and great, teacher and pupil alike.

9 The first lot fell for Asaph to Joseph; the second to Gedaliah, to him and his brothers and his sons, twelve; [10]the third to Zaccur, his sons and his brothers, twelve; [11]the fourth to Izri, his sons and his brothers, twelve; [12]the fifth to Nethaniah, his sons and his brothers, twelve; [13]the sixth to Bukkiah, his sons and his brothers, twelve; [14]the seventh to Jesarelah,[k] his sons and his brothers, twelve; [15]the eighth to Jeshaiah, his sons and his brothers, twelve; [16]the ninth to Mattaniah, his sons and his brothers, twelve; [17]the tenth to Shimei, his sons and his brothers, twelve; [18]the eleventh to Azarel, his sons and his brothers, twelve; [19]the twelfth to Hashabiah, his sons and his brothers, twelve; [20]to the thirteenth, Shubael, his sons and his brothers, twelve; [21]to the fourteenth, Mattithiah, his sons and his brothers, twelve; [22]to the fifteenth, to Jeremoth, his sons and his brothers, twelve; [23]to the sixteenth, to Hananiah, his sons and his brothers, twelve; [24]to the seventeenth, to Joshbekashah, his sons and his brothers, twelve; [25]to the eighteenth, to Hanani, his sons and his brothers, twelve; [26]to the nineteenth, to Mallothi, his sons and his brothers, twelve; [27]to the twentieth, to Eliathah, his sons and his brothers, twelve; [28]to the twenty-first, to Hothir, his sons and his brothers, twelve; [29]to the twenty-second, to Giddalti, his sons and his brothers, twelve; [30]to the twenty-third, to Mahazioth, his sons and his brothers, twelve; [31]to the twenty-fourth, to

g See 23.19: Heb lacks *Hebron*   h See 23.19: Heb lacks *the chief*   i Or *his son*: Meaning of Heb uncertain   j One Ms: Gk: MT lacks *Shimei*   k Or *Asarelah*; see 25.2

Romamti-ezer, his sons and his brothers, twelve.

The Gatekeepers

26 As for the divisions of the gatekeepers: of the Korahites, Meshelemiah son of Kore, of the sons of Asaph. [2]Meshelemiah had sons: Zechariah the firstborn, Jediael the second, Zebadiah the third, Jathniel the fourth, [3]Elam the fifth, Jehohanan the sixth, Eliehoenai the seventh. [4]Obed-edom had sons: Shemaiah the firstborn, Jehozabad the second, Joah the third, Sachar the fourth, Nethanel the fifth, [5]Ammiel the sixth, Issachar the seventh, Peullethai the eighth; for God blessed him. [6]Also to his son Shemaiah sons were born who exercised authority in their ancestral houses, for they were men of great ability. [7]The sons of Shemaiah: Othni, Rephael, Obed, and Elzabad, whose brothers were able men, Elihu and Semachiah. [8]All these, sons of Obed-edom with their sons and brothers, were able men qualified for the service; sixty-two of Obed-edom. [9]Meshelemiah had sons and brothers, able men, eighteen. [10]Hosah, of the sons of Merari, had sons: Shimri the chief (for though he was not the firstborn, his father made him chief), [11]Hilkiah the second, Tebaliah the third, Zechariah the fourth: all the sons and brothers of Hosah totaled thirteen.

12 These divisions of the gatekeepers, corresponding to their leaders, had duties, just as their kindred did, ministering in the house of the LORD; [13]and they cast lots by ancestral houses, small and great alike, for their gates. [14]The lot for the east fell to Shelemiah. They cast lots also for his son Zechariah, a prudent counselor, and his lot came out for the north. [15]Obed-edom's came out for the south, and to his sons was allotted the storehouse. [16]For Shuppim and Hosah it came out for the west, at the gate of Shallecheth on the ascending road. Guard corresponded to guard. [17]On the east there were six Levites each day,[l] on the north four each day, on the south four each day, as well as two and two at the storehouse; [18]and for the colonnade[m] on the west there were four at the road and two at the colonnade.[m] [19]These were the divisions of the gatekeepers among the Korahites and the sons of Merari.

The Treasurers, Officers, and Judges

20 And of the Levites, Ahijah had charge of the treasuries of the house of God and the treasuries of the dedicated gifts. [21]The sons of Ladan, the sons of the Gershonites belonging to Ladan, the heads of families belonging to Ladan the Gershonite: Jehieli.[n]

22 The sons of Jehieli, Zetham and his brother Joel, were in charge of the treasuries of the house of the LORD. [23]Of the Amramites, the Izharites, the Hebronites, and the Uzzielites: [24]Shebuel son of Gershom, son of Moses, was chief officer in charge of the treasuries. [25]His brothers: from Eliezer were his son Rehabiah, his son Jeshaiah, his son Joram, his son Zichri, and his son Shelomoth. [26]This Shelomoth and his brothers were in charge of all the treasuries of the dedicated gifts that King David, and the heads of families, and the officers of the thousands and the hundreds, and the commanders of the army, had dedicated. [27]From booty won in battles they dedicated gifts for the maintenance of the house of the LORD. [28]Also all that Samuel the seer, and Saul son of Kish, and Abner son of Ner, and Joab son of Zeruiah had dedicated—all dedicated gifts were in the care of Shelomoth[o] and his brothers.

29 Of the Izharites, Chenaniah and his sons were appointed to outside duties for Israel, as officers and judges. [30]Of the Hebronites, Hashabiah and his brothers, one thousand seven hundred men of ability, had the oversight of Israel west of the Jordan for all the work of the LORD and for the service of the king. [31]Of the Hebronites, Jerijah was chief of the Hebronites. (In the fortieth year of David's reign search was made, of whatever genealogy or family, and men of great ability among them were found at Jazer in Gilead.) [32]King David appointed him and his brothers, two thousand seven hundred men of ability, heads of families, to have the oversight of the Reubenites, the Gadites, and the half-tribe of the Manassites for everything pertaining to God and for the affairs of the king.

The Military Divisions

27 This is the list of the people of Israel, the heads of families, the

---

[l] Gk: Heb lacks *each day*   [m] Heb *parbar*: meaning uncertain   [n] The Hebrew text of verse 21 is confused   [o] Gk Compare 26.28: Heb *Shelomith*

commanders of the thousands and the hundreds, and their officers who served the king in all matters concerning the divisions that came and went, month after month throughout the year, each division numbering twenty-four thousand:

2 Jashobeam son of Zabdiel was in charge of the first division in the first month; in his division were twenty-four thousand. ³He was a descendant of Perez, and was chief of all the commanders of the army for the first month. ⁴Dodai the Ahohite was in charge of the division of the second month; Mikloth was the chief officer of his division. In his division were twenty-four thousand. ⁵The third commander, for the third month, was Benaiah son of the priest Jehoiada, as chief; in his division were twenty-four thousand. ⁶This is the Benaiah who was a mighty man of the Thirty and in command of the Thirty; his son Ammizabad was in charge of his division.ᴾ ⁷Asahel brother of Joab was fourth, for the fourth month, and his son Zebadiah after him; in his division were twenty-four thousand. ⁸The fifth commander, for the fifth month, was Shamhuth, the Izrahite; in his division were twenty-four thousand. ⁹Sixth, for the sixth month, was Ira son of Ikkesh the Tekoite; in his division were twenty-four thousand. ¹⁰Seventh, for the seventh month, was Helez the Pelonite, of the Ephraimites; in his division were twenty-four thousand. ¹¹Eighth, for the eighth month, was Sibbecai the Hushathite, of the Zerahites; in his division were twenty-four thousand. ¹²Ninth, for the ninth month, was Abiezer of Anathoth, a Benjaminite; in his division were twenty-four thousand. ¹³Tenth, for the tenth month, was Maharai of Netophah, of the Zerahites; in his division were twenty-four thousand. ¹⁴Eleventh, for the eleventh month, was Benaiah of Pirathon, of the Ephraimites; in his division were twenty-four thousand. ¹⁵Twelfth, for the twelfth month, was Heldai the Netophathite, of Othniel; in his division were twenty-four thousand.

Leaders of Tribes

16 Over the tribes of Israel, for the Reubenites, Eliezer son of Zichri was chief officer; for the Simeonites, Shephatiah son of Maacah; ¹⁷for Levi, Hashabiah son of Kemuel; for Aaron, Zadok; ¹⁸for Judah, Elihu, one of David's brothers; for Issachar, Omri son of Michael; ¹⁹for Zebulun, Ishmaiah son of Obadiah; for Naphtali, Jerimoth son of Azriel; ²⁰for the Ephraimites, Hoshea son of Azaziah; for the half-tribe of Manasseh, Joel son of Pedaiah; ²¹for the half-tribe of Manasseh in Gilead, Iddo son of Zechariah; for Benjamin, Jaasiel son of Abner; ²²for Dan, Azarel son of Jeroham. These were the leaders of the tribes of Israel. ²³David did not count those below twenty years of age, for the LORD had promised to make Israel as numerous as the stars of heaven. ²⁴Joab son of Zeruiah began to count them, but did not finish; yet wrath came upon Israel for this, and the number was not entered into the account of the Annals of King David.

Other Civic Officials

25 Over the king's treasuries was Azmaveth son of Adiel. Over the treasuries in the country, in the cities, in the villages and in the towers, was Jonathan son of Uzziah. ²⁶Over those who did the work of the field, tilling the soil, was Ezri son of Chelub. ²⁷Over the vineyards was Shimei the Ramathite. Over the produce of the vineyards for the wine cellars was Zabdi the Shiphmite. ²⁸Over the olive and sycamore trees in the Shephelah was Baal-hanan the Gederite. Over the stores of oil was Joash. ²⁹Over the herds that pastured in Sharon was Shitrai the Sharonite. Over the herds in the valleys was Shaphat son of Adlai. ³⁰Over the camels was Obil the Ishmaelite. Over the donkeys was Jehdeiah the Meronothite. Over the flocks was Jaziz the Hagrite. ³¹All these were stewards of King David's property.

32 Jonathan, David's uncle, was a counselor, being a man of understanding and a scribe; Jehiel son of Hachmoni attended the king's sons. ³³Ahithophel was the king's counselor, and Hushai the Archite was the king's friend. ³⁴After Ahithophel came Jehoiada son of Benaiah, and Abiathar. Joab was commander of the king's army.

Solomon Instructed to Build the Temple

28 David assembled at Jerusalem all the officials of Israel, the officials of the tribes, the officers of the divisions that served the king, the commanders of the thousands, the commanders of the hundreds, the stewards of all the property

ᴾ Gk Vg: Heb *Ammizabad was his division*

and cattle of the king and his sons, together with the palace officials, the mighty warriors, and all the warriors. 2Then King David rose to his feet and said: "Hear me, my brothers and my people. I had planned to build a house of rest for the ark of the covenant of the LORD, for the footstool of our God; and I made preparations for building. 3But God said to me, 'You shall not build a house for my name, for you are a warrior and have shed blood.' 4Yet the LORD God of Israel chose me from all my ancestral house to be king over Israel forever; for he chose Judah as leader, and in the house of Judah my father's house, and among my father's sons he took delight in making me king over all Israel. 5And of all my sons, for the LORD has given me many, he has chosen my son Solomon to sit upon the throne of the kingdom of the LORD over Israel. 6He said to me, 'It is your son Solomon who shall build my house and my courts, for I have chosen him to be a son to me, and I will be a father to him. 7I will establish his kingdom forever if he continues resolute in keeping my commandments and my ordinances, as he is today.' 8Now therefore in the sight of all Israel, the assembly of the LORD, and in the hearing of our God, observe and search out all the commandments of the LORD your God; that you may possess this good land, and leave it for an inheritance to your children after you forever.

9 "And you, my son Solomon, know the God of your father, and serve him with single mind and willing heart; for the LORD searches every mind, and understands every plan and thought. If you seek him, he will be found by you; but if you forsake him, he will abandon you forever. 10Take heed now, for the LORD has chosen you to build a house as the sanctuary; be strong, and act."

11 Then David gave his son Solomon the plan of the vestibule of the temple, and of its houses, its treasuries, its upper rooms, and its inner chambers, and of the room for the mercy seat;q 12and the plan of all that he had in mind: for the courts of the house of the LORD, all the surrounding chambers, the treasuries of the house of God, and the treasuries for dedicated gifts; 13for the divisions of the priests and of the Levites, and all the work of the service in the house of the LORD; for all the vessels for the service in the house of the LORD, 14the weight of gold for all golden vessels for each service, the weight of silver vessels for each service, 15the weight of the golden lampstands and their lamps, the weight of gold for each lampstand and its lamps, the weight of silver for a lampstand and its lamps, according to the use of each in the service, 16the weight of gold for each table for the rows of bread, the silver for the silver tables, 17and pure gold for the forks, the basins, and the cups; for the golden bowls and the weight of each; for the silver bowls and the weight of each; 18for the altar of incense made of refined gold, and its weight; also his plan for the golden chariot of the cherubim that spread their wings and covered the ark of the covenant of the LORD.

19 "All this, in writing at the LORD's direction, he made clear to me—the plan of all the works."

20 David said further to his son Solomon, "Be strong and of good courage, and act. Do not be afraid or dismayed; for the LORD God, my God, is with you. He will not fail you or forsake you, until all the work for the service of the house of the LORD is finished. 21Here are the divisions of the priests and the Levites for all the service of the house of God; and with you in all the work will be every volunteer who has skill for any kind of service; also the officers and all the people will be wholly at your command."

Offerings for Building the Temple

29 King David said to the whole assembly, "My son Solomon, whom alone God has chosen, is young and inexperienced, and the work is great; for the templer will not be for mortals but for the LORD God. 2So I have provided for the house of my God, so far as I was able, the gold for the things of gold, the silver for the things of silver, and the bronze for the things of bronze, the iron for the things of iron, and wood for the things of wood, besides great quantities of onyx and stones for setting, antimony, colored stones, all sorts of precious stones, and marble in abundance. 3Moreover, in addition to all that I have provided for the holy house, I have a treasure of my own of gold and silver, and because of my devotion to the house of my God I give it to the house of my God: 4three

q Or *the cover*   r Heb *fortress*

thousand talents of gold, of the gold of Ophir, and seven thousand talents of refined silver, for overlaying the walls of the house, ⁵and for all the work to be done by artisans, gold for the things of gold and silver for the things of silver. Who then will offer willingly, consecrating themselves today to the LORD?"

6 Then the leaders of ancestral houses made their freewill offerings, as did also the leaders of the tribes, the commanders of the thousands and of the hundreds, and the officers over the king's work. ⁷They gave for the service of the house of God five thousand talents and ten thousand darics of gold, ten thousand talents of silver, eighteen thousand talents of bronze, and one hundred thousand tal-

Prayer in Our Bones

WEDNESDAY

Scripture Reading for Today:
1 Chronicles 29.10–19

Verses for Today:
1 Chronicles 29.10–13

The presence of prayers in the books of Chronicles demonstrates the Chronicler's conviction of the importance of prayer. Traditional prayers are used in new situations and modified to fit a new context. New prayers are created based on learned phrases. Throughout there is a conviction that prayer has an effect on the lives of individuals and the people as a whole.

Old prayers in new contexts: 1 Chronicles 16.8–36. The prayer is a collage of psalms, woven together to form a single hymn of thanksgiving.

New prayers out of old: 1 Chronicles 29.10–19. [The books of] Chronicles' last report of David before his death is a prayer on the occasion of the people's making offerings for the temple to be built by Solomon. The prayer is original, but it is created out of many phrases from the tradition.

We too know many traditional prayers. How do the staples of our tradition—Our Father and Hail Mary—change with the context in which we pray them? How do the ancient prayers of the Eucharistic celebration speak to our own needs? What does it mean to us now to say, "Deliver us, Lord, from every evil, and grant us peace in our day"?

The prayers we know, the prayers in our bones, also teach us how to compose our own prayers. How many table blessings are created from remembered phrases? How often are children blessed with phrases treasured by their parents? A woman told me once of trying to pray Psalm 23 with her daughter who was dying. She couldn't remember the whole psalm so she just created a prayer about the beauty and peace of heaven from all the descriptions she could remember.

Finally, [the books of] Chronicles teach us that prayer makes a difference. Prayer really does change our situation. God hears and answers our prayer. The books of Chronicles teach us how to pray.

—IRENE NOWELL, O.S.B.

Go to page 447 for your next devotional reading.

ents of iron. [8]Whoever had precious stones gave them to the treasury of the house of the LORD, into the care of Jehiel the Gershonite. [9]Then the people rejoiced because these had given willingly, for with single mind they had offered freely to the LORD; King David also rejoiced greatly.

David's Praise to God

10 Then David blessed the LORD in the presence of all the assembly; David said: "Blessed are you, O LORD, the God of our ancestor Israel, forever and ever. [11]Yours, O LORD, are the greatness, the power, the glory, the victory, and the majesty; for all that is in the heavens and on the earth is yours; yours is the kingdom, O LORD, and you are exalted as head above all. [12]Riches and honor come from you, and you rule over all. In your hand are power and might; and it is in your hand to make great and to give strength to all. [13]And now, our God, we give thanks to you and praise your glorious name.

14 "But who am I, and what is my people, that we should be able to make this freewill offering? For all things come from you, and of your own have we given you. [15]For we are aliens and transients before you, as were all our ancestors; our days on the earth are like a shadow, and there is no hope. [16]O LORD our God, all this abundance that we have provided for building you a house for your holy name comes from your hand and is all your own. [17]I know, my God, that you search the heart, and take pleasure in uprightness; in the uprightness of my heart I have freely offered all these things, and now I have seen your people, who are present here, offering freely and joyously to you. [18]O LORD, the God of Abraham, Isaac, and Israel, our ancestors, keep forever such purposes and thoughts in the hearts of your people, and direct their hearts toward you. [19]Grant to my son Solomon that with single mind he may keep your commandments, your decrees, and your statutes, performing all of

them, and that he may build the temple[s] for which I have made provision."

20 Then David said to the whole assembly, "Bless the LORD your God." And all the assembly blessed the LORD, the God of their ancestors, and bowed their heads and prostrated themselves before the LORD and the king. [21]On the next day they offered sacrifices and burnt offerings to the LORD, a thousand bulls, a thousand rams, and a thousand lambs, with their libations, and sacrifices in abundance for all Israel; [22]and they ate and drank before the LORD on that day with great joy.

Solomon Anointed King

They made David's son Solomon king a second time; they anointed him as the LORD's prince, and Zadok as priest. [23]Then Solomon sat on the throne of the LORD, succeeding his father David as king; he prospered, and all Israel obeyed him. [24]All the leaders and the mighty warriors, and also all the sons of King David, pledged their allegiance to King Solomon. [25]The LORD highly exalted Solomon in the sight of all Israel, and bestowed upon him such royal majesty as had not been on any king before him in Israel.

Summary of David's Reign

26 Thus David son of Jesse reigned over all Israel. [27]The period that he reigned over Israel was forty years; he reigned seven years in Hebron, and thirty-three years in Jerusalem. [28]He died in a good old age, full of days, riches, and honor; and his son Solomon succeeded him. [29]Now the acts of King David, from first to last, are written in the records of the seer Samuel, and in the records of the prophet Nathan, and in the records of the seer Gad, [30]with accounts of all his rule and his might and of the events that befell him and Israel and all the kingdoms of the earth.

s Heb *fortress*

2 Chronicles

Second Chronicles begins by focusing on Solomon's work of building a magnificent temple in Jerusalem. After describing Israel's division into northern and southern kingdoms following the death of Solomon, the Chronicler virtually ignores the history of the northern kings in order to focus on the kings of Judah, judging the merit of their reigns only by whether they supported the temple and its worship. By so doing, he treated the northern kingdom of Israel as schismatic and emphasized the importance of the Davidic line, ruling from Judah, with Jerusalem as the center of worship for all Jews.

The last chapter quickly describes the fall of Jerusalem, the destruction of Solomon's temple, and the exile of the Jews to Babylon and then ends with Cyrus, the king of Persia, making provision for the Jews to return to Jerusalem (538 B.C.) in order to rebuild the temple that was destroyed.

Centuries later, we are reminded that the liturgy of worship, so painstakingly described in Chronicles, foreshadowed the liturgy of the Eucharist that is the heart of our worship today.

Solomon Requests Wisdom

1 Solomon son of David established himself in his kingdom; the LORD his God was with him and made him exceedingly great.

2 Solomon summoned all Israel, the commanders of the thousands and of the hundreds, the judges, and all the leaders of all Israel, the heads of families. ³Then Solomon, and the whole assembly with him, went to the high place that was at Gibeon; for God's tent of meeting, which Moses the servant of the LORD had made in the wilderness, was there. ⁴(But David had brought the ark of God up from Kiriath-jearim to the place that David had pre-

pared for it; for he had pitched a tent for it in Jerusalem.) ⁵Moreover the bronze altar that Bezalel son of Uri, son of Hur, had made, was there in front of the tabernacle of the LORD. And Solomon and the assembly inquired at it. ⁶Solomon went up there to the bronze altar before the LORD, which was at the tent of meeting, and offered a thousand burnt offerings on it.

7 That night God appeared to Solomon, and said to him, "Ask what I should give you." ⁸Solomon said to God, "You have shown great and steadfast love to my father David, and have made me succeed him as king. ⁹O LORD God, let your promise to my father David now be fulfilled,

for you have made me king over a people as numerous as the dust of the earth. [10]Give me now wisdom and knowledge to go out and come in before this people, for who can rule this great people of yours?" [11]God answered Solomon, "Because this was in your heart, and you have not asked for possessions, wealth, honor, or the life of those who hate you, and have not even asked for long life, but have asked for wisdom and knowledge for yourself that you may rule my people over whom I have made you king, [12]wisdom and knowledge are granted to you. I will also give you riches, possessions, and honor, such as

none of the kings had who were before you, and none after you shall have the like." [13]So Solomon came from[a] the high place at Gibeon, from the tent of meeting, to Jerusalem. And he reigned over Israel.

Solomon's Military and Commercial Activity

14 Solomon gathered together chariots and horses; he had fourteen hundred chariots and twelve thousand horses, which he stationed in the chariot cities

[a] Gk Vg: Heb *to*

Gift of Wisdom

THURSDAY

Scripture Reading for Today:
2 Chronicles 1.7–12

Verse for Today:
2 Chronicles 1.10

In the epistle of James (1.5) we are told to pray for wisdom. "If any of you is lacking in wisdom, ask God, who gives to all generously and ungrudgingly, and it will be given you."

I had prayed for the gift of wisdom since I was seven years old, at the time of my confirmation, right through to that day, and I found I had no wisdom. So, I began consciously to pray for wisdom, still not understanding what it was.

One day, I was at work helping a patient prepare for her examination by the doctor. She was relating to me all her different problems. As we talked, I tried to point out to her certain things about her concerns. At the end of the conversation, when she was ready for the doctor, I said to her, "Okay. God bless you." And she said to me, "Thank you, Mrs. Bleasdell, for all the wisdom you have shared."

I said, "Wisdom? I don't know that I gave you any wisdom. In fact, I'm always praying for wisdom, but I am not sure that I have any." She said, "I would have you know that in the last twenty minutes when you spoke to me, all I heard was wisdom."

I left the room laughing, but perplexed. As I got outside the room, I said to the Lord, "Jesus, I've prayed so much for wisdom, and I don't know that I have it. But she said that all she heard was wisdom."

Immediately, in my spirit, I heard the Lord come right back:

"Wisdom? I am Wisdom! Wisdom is not something that you acquire and carry around on your back in a knapsack. No, I am the source of all wisdom, and when you are in me and I am in you, I release it to you moment by moment as you need it. I give you my wisdom so you may be able to deal with things wisely."

—*BABSIE BLEASDELL*

Go to page 453 for your next devotional reading.

and with the king in Jerusalem. [15]The king made silver and gold as common in Jerusalem as stone, and he made cedar as plentiful as the sycamore of the Shephelah. [16]Solomon's horses were imported from Egypt and Kue; the king's traders received them from Kue at the prevailing price. [17]They imported from Egypt, and then exported, a chariot for six hundred shekels of silver, and a horse for one hundred fifty; so through them these were exported to all the kings of the Hittites and the kings of Aram.

Preparations for Building the Temple

2 [b]Solomon decided to build a temple for the name of the LORD, and a royal palace for himself. [2c]Solomon conscripted seventy thousand laborers and eighty thousand stonecutters in the hill country, with three thousand six hundred to oversee them.

Alliance with Huram of Tyre

3 Solomon sent word to King Huram of Tyre: "Once you dealt with my father David and sent him cedar to build himself a house to live in. [4]I am now about to build a house for the name of the LORD my God and dedicate it to him for offering fragrant incense before him, and for the regular offering of the rows of bread, and for burnt offerings morning and evening, on the sabbaths and the new moons and the appointed festivals of the LORD our God, as ordained forever for Israel. [5]The house that I am about to build will be great, for our God is greater than other gods. [6]But who is able to build him a house, since heaven, even highest heaven, cannot contain him? Who am I to build a house for him, except as a place to make offerings before him? [7]So now send me an artisan skilled to work in gold, silver, bronze, and iron, and in purple, crimson, and blue fabrics, trained also in engraving, to join the skilled workers who are with me in Judah and Jerusalem, whom my father David provided. [8]Send me also cedar, cypress, and algum timber from Lebanon, for I know that your servants are skilled in cutting Lebanon timber. My servants will work with your servants [9]to prepare timber for me in abundance, for the house I am about to build will be great and wonderful. [10]I will provide for your servants, those who cut the timber, twenty thousand cors of crushed wheat, twenty

thousand cors of barley, twenty thousand baths[d] of wine, and twenty thousand baths of oil."

11 Then King Huram of Tyre answered in a letter that he sent to Solomon, "Because the LORD loves his people he has made you king over them." [12]Huram also said, "Blessed be the LORD God of Israel, who made heaven and earth, who has given King David a wise son, endowed with discretion and understanding, who will build a temple for the LORD, and a royal palace for himself.

13 "I have dispatched Huram-abi, a skilled artisan, endowed with understanding, [14]the son of one of the Danite women, his father a Tyrian. He is trained to work in gold, silver, bronze, iron, stone, and wood, and in purple, blue, and crimson fabrics and fine linen, and to do all sorts of engraving and execute any design that may be assigned him, with your artisans, the artisans of my lord, your father David. [15]Now, as for the wheat, barley, oil, and wine, of which my lord has spoken, let him send them to his servants. [16]We will cut whatever timber you need from Lebanon, and bring it to you as rafts by sea to Joppa; you will take it up to Jerusalem."

17 Then Solomon took a census of all the aliens who were residing in the land of Israel, after the census that his father David had taken; and there were found to be one hundred fifty-three thousand six hundred. [18]Seventy thousand of them he assigned as laborers, eighty thousand as stonecutters in the hill country, and three thousand six hundred as overseers to make the people work.

Solomon Builds the Temple

3 Solomon began to build the house of the LORD in Jerusalem on Mount Moriah, where the LORD had appeared to his father David, at the place that David had designated, on the threshing floor of Ornan the Jebusite. [2]He began to build on the second day of the second month of the fourth year of his reign. [3]These are Solomon's measurements[e] for building the house of God: the length, in cubits of the old standard, was sixty cubits, and the width twenty cubits. [4]The vestibule in

b Ch 1.18 in Heb   c Ch 2.1 in Heb   d A Hebrew measure of volume   e Syr: Heb foundations front of the nave of the house was twenty cubits long, across the width of the house;*f* and its height was one hundred twenty cubits. He overlaid it on the inside with pure gold. 5The nave he lined with cypress, covered it with fine gold, and made palms and chains on it. 6He adorned the house with settings of precious stones. The gold was gold from Parvaim. 7So he lined the house with gold— its beams, its thresholds, its walls, and its doors; and he carved cherubim on the walls.

8 He made the most holy place; its length, corresponding to the width of the house, was twenty cubits, and its width was twenty cubits; he overlaid it with six hundred talents of fine gold. 9The weight of the nails was fifty shekels of gold. He overlaid the upper chambers with gold.

10 In the most holy place he made two carved cherubim and overlaid *g* them with gold. 11The wings of the cherubim together extended twenty cubits: one wing of the one, five cubits long, touched the wall of the house, and its other wing, five cubits long, touched the wing of the other cherub; 12and of this cherub, one wing, five cubits long, touched the wall of the house, and the other wing, also five cubits long, was joined to the wing of the first cherub. 13The wings of these cherubim extended twenty cubits; the cherubim*h* stood on their feet, facing the nave. 14And Solomon*i* made the curtain of blue and purple and crimson fabrics and fine linen, and worked cherubim into it.

15 In front of the house he made two pillars thirty-five cubits high, with a capital of five cubits on the top of each. 16He made encircling*j* chains and put them on the tops of the pillars; and he made one hundred pomegranates, and put them on the chains. 17He set up the pillars in front of the temple, one on the right, the other on the left; the one on the right he called Jachin, and the one on the left, Boaz.

Furnishings of the Temple

4 He made an altar of bronze, twenty cubits long, twenty cubits wide, and ten cubits high. 2Then he made the molten sea; it was round, ten cubits from rim to rim, and five cubits high. A line of thirty cubits would encircle it completely. 3Under it were panels all around, each of ten cubits, surrounding the sea; there were two rows of panels, cast when it was cast. 4It stood on twelve oxen, three facing north, three facing west, three facing south, and three facing east; the sea was set on them. The hindquarters of each were toward the inside. 5Its thickness was a handbreadth; its rim was made like the rim of a cup, like the flower of a lily; it held three thousand baths.*k* 6He also made ten basins in which to wash, and set five on the right side, and five on the left. In these they were to rinse what was used for the burnt offering. The sea was for the priests to wash in.

7 He made ten golden lampstands as prescribed, and set them in the temple, five on the south side and five on the north. 8He also made ten tables and placed them in the temple, five on the right side and five on the left. And he made one hundred basins of gold. 9He made the court of the priests, and the great court, and doors for the court; he overlaid their doors with bronze. 10He set the sea at the southeast corner of the house.

11 And Huram made the pots, the shovels, and the basins. Thus Huram finished the work that he did for King Solomon on the house of God: 12the two pillars, the bowls, and the two capitals on the top of the pillars; and the two latticeworks to cover the two bowls of the capitals that were on the top of the pillars; 13the four hundred pomegranates for the two latticeworks, two rows of pomegranates for each latticework, to cover the two bowls of the capitals that were on the pillars. 14He made the stands, the basins on the stands, 15the one sea, and the twelve oxen underneath it. 16The pots, the shovels, the forks, and all the equipment for these Huram-abi made of burnished bronze for King Solomon for the house of the LORD. 17In the plain of the Jordan the king cast them, in the clay ground between Succoth and Zeredah. 18Solomon made all these things in great quantities, so that the weight of the bronze was not determined.

19 So Solomon made all the things that were in the house of God: the golden altar, the tables for the bread of the Pres-

---

f Compare 1 Kings 6.3: Meaning of Heb uncertain
g Heb *they overlaid*   *h* Heb *they*   *i* Heb *he*
j Cn: Heb *in the inner sanctuary*   *k* A Hebrew measure of volume

ence, 20the lampstands and their lamps of pure gold to burn before the inner sanctuary, as prescribed; 21the flowers, the lamps, and the tongs, of purest gold; 22the snuffers, basins, ladles, and firepans, of pure gold. As for the entrance to the temple: the inner doors to the most holy place and the doors of the nave of the temple were of gold.

5 Thus all the work that Solomon did for the house of the LORD was finished. Solomon brought in the things that his father David had dedicated, and stored the silver, the gold, and all the vessels in the treasuries of the house of God.

The Ark Brought into the Temple

2 Then Solomon assembled the elders of Israel and all the heads of the tribes, the leaders of the ancestral houses of the people of Israel, in Jerusalem, to bring up the ark of the covenant of the LORD out of the city of David, which is Zion. 3And all the Israelites assembled before the king at the festival that is in the seventh month. 4And all the elders of Israel came, and the Levites carried the ark. 5So they brought up the ark, the tent of meeting, and all the holy vessels that were in the tent; the priests and the Levites brought them up. 6King Solomon and all the congregation of Israel, who had assembled before him, were before the ark, sacrificing so many sheep and oxen that they could not be numbered or counted. 7Then the priests brought the ark of the covenant of the LORD to its place, in the inner sanctuary of the house, in the most holy place, underneath the wings of the cherubim. 8For the cherubim spread out their wings over the place of the ark, so that the cherubim made a covering above the ark and its poles. 9The poles were so long that the ends of the poles were seen from the holy place in front of the inner sanctuary; but they could not be seen from outside; they are there to this day. 10There was nothing in the ark except the two tablets that Moses put there at Horeb, where the LORD made a covenant*l* with the people of Israel after they came out of Egypt.

11 Now when the priests came out of the holy place (for all the priests who were present had sanctified themselves, without regard to their divisions), 12all the levitical singers, Asaph, Heman, and Jeduthun, their sons and kindred, arrayed in fine linen, with cymbals, harps, and lyres,

stood east of the altar with one hundred twenty priests who were trumpeters. 13It was the duty of the trumpeters and singers to make themselves heard in unison in praise and thanksgiving to the LORD, and when the song was raised, with trumpets and cymbals and other musical instruments, in praise to the LORD,

"For he is good,
　for his steadfast love endures
　　forever,"

the house, the house of the LORD, was filled with a cloud, 14so that the priests could not stand to minister because of the cloud; for the glory of the LORD filled the house of God.

Dedication of the Temple

6 Then Solomon said, "The LORD has said that he would reside in thick darkness. 2I have built you an exalted house, a place for you to reside in forever."

3 Then the king turned around and blessed all the assembly of Israel, while all the assembly of Israel stood. 4And he said, "Blessed be the LORD, the God of Israel, who with his hand has fulfilled what he promised with his mouth to my father David, saying, 5'Since the day that I brought my people out of the land of Egypt, I have not chosen a city from any of the tribes of Israel in which to build a house, so that my name might be there, and I chose no one as ruler over my people Israel; 6but I have chosen Jerusalem in order that my name may be there, and I have chosen David to be over my people Israel.' 7My father David had it in mind to build a house for the name of the LORD, the God of Israel. 8But the LORD said to my father David, 'You did well to consider building a house for my name; 9nevertheless you shall not build the house, but your son who shall be born to you shall build the house for my name.' 10Now the LORD has fulfilled his promise that he made; for I have succeeded my father David, and sit on the throne of Israel, as the LORD promised, and have built the house for the name of the LORD, the God of Israel. 11There I have set the ark, in which is the covenant of the LORD that he made with the people of Israel."

Solomon's Prayer of Dedication

12 Then Solomon*m* stood before the

---

l Heb lacks *a covenant*　　*m* Heb *he*

altar of the LORD in the presence of the whole assembly of Israel, and spread out his hands. ¹³Solomon had made a bronze platform five cubits long, five cubits wide, and three cubits high, and had set it in the court; and he stood on it. Then he knelt on his knees in the presence of the whole assembly of Israel, and spread out his hands toward heaven. ¹⁴He said, "O LORD, God of Israel, there is no God like you, in heaven or on earth, keeping covenant in steadfast love with your servants who walk before you with all their heart— ¹⁵you who have kept for your servant, my father David, what you promised to him. Indeed, you promised with your mouth and this day have fulfilled with your hand. ¹⁶Therefore, O LORD, God of Israel, keep for your servant, my father David, that which you promised him, saying, 'There shall never fail you a successor before me to sit on the throne of Israel, if only your children keep to their way, to walk in my law as you have walked before me.' ¹⁷Therefore, O LORD, God of Israel, let your word be confirmed, which you promised to your servant David.

18 "But will God indeed reside with mortals on earth? Even heaven and the highest heaven cannot contain you, how much less this house that I have built! ¹⁹Regard your servant's prayer and his plea, O LORD my God, heeding the cry and the prayer that your servant prays to you. ²⁰May your eyes be open day and night toward this house, the place where you promised to set your name, and may you heed the prayer that your servant prays toward this place. ²¹And hear the plea of your servant and of your people Israel, when they pray toward this place; may you hear from heaven your dwelling place; hear and forgive.

22 "If someone sins against another and is required to take an oath and comes and swears before your altar in this house, ²³may you hear from heaven, and act, and judge your servants, repaying the guilty by bringing their conduct on their own head, and vindicating those who are in the right by rewarding them in accordance with their righteousness.

24 "When your people Israel, having sinned against you, are defeated before an enemy but turn again to you, confess your name, pray and plead with you in this house, ²⁵may you hear from heaven, and forgive the sin of your people Israel, and

bring them again to the land that you gave to them and to their ancestors.

26 "When heaven is shut up and there is no rain because they have sinned against you, and then they pray toward this place, confess your name, and turn from their sin, because you punish them, ²⁷may you hear in heaven, forgive the sin of your servants, your people Israel, when you teach them the good way in which they should walk; and send down rain upon your land, which you have given to your people as an inheritance.

28 "If there is famine in the land, if there is plague, blight, mildew, locust, or caterpillar; if their enemies besiege them in any of the settlements of the lands; whatever suffering, whatever sickness there is; ²⁹whatever prayer, whatever plea from any individual or from all your people Israel, all knowing their own suffering and their own sorrows so that they stretch out their hands toward this house; ³⁰may you hear from heaven, your dwelling place, forgive, and render to all whose heart you know, according to all their ways, for only you know the human heart. ³¹Thus may they fear you and walk in your ways all the days that they live in the land that you gave to our ancestors.

32 "Likewise when foreigners, who are not of your people Israel, come from a distant land because of your great name, and your mighty hand, and your outstretched arm, when they come and pray toward this house, ³³may you hear from heaven your dwelling place, and do whatever the foreigners ask of you, in order that all the peoples of the earth may know your name and fear you, as do your people Israel, and that they may know that your name has been invoked on this house that I have built.

34 "If your people go out to battle against their enemies, by whatever way you shall send them, and they pray to you toward this city that you have chosen and the house that I have built for your name, ³⁵then hear from heaven their prayer and their plea, and maintain their cause.

36 "If they sin against you—for there is no one who does not sin—and you are angry with them and give them to an enemy, so that they are carried away captive to a land far or near; ³⁷then if they come to their senses in the land to which they have been taken captive, and repent, and plead with you in the land of their captivi-

ty, saying, 'We have sinned, and have done wrong; we have acted wickedly'; [38]if they repent with all their heart and soul in the land of their captivity, to which they were taken captive, and pray toward their land, which you gave to their ancestors, the city that you have chosen, and the house that I have built for your name, [39]then hear from heaven your dwelling place their prayer and their pleas, maintain their cause and forgive your people who have sinned against you. [40]Now, O my God, let your eyes be open and your ears attentive to prayer from this place.

[41] "Now rise up, O LORD God, and go
    to your resting place,
    you and the ark of your might.
Let your priests, O LORD God, be
    clothed with salvation,
    and let your faithful rejoice in
    your goodness.
[42] O LORD God, do not reject your
    anointed one.
    Remember your steadfast love for
    your servant David."

Solomon Dedicates the Temple

7 When Solomon had ended his prayer, fire came down from heaven and consumed the burnt offering and the sacrifices; and the glory of the LORD filled the temple. [2]The priests could not enter the house of the LORD, because the glory of the LORD filled the LORD's house. [3]When all the people of Israel saw the fire come down and the glory of the LORD on the temple, they bowed down on the pavement with their faces to the ground, and worshiped and gave thanks to the LORD, saying,

"For he is good,
    for his steadfast love endures
    forever."

[4] Then the king and all the people offered sacrifice before the LORD. [5]King Solomon offered as a sacrifice twenty-two thousand oxen and one hundred twenty thousand sheep. So the king and all the people dedicated the house of God. [6]The priests stood at their posts; the Levites also, with the instruments for music to the LORD that King David had made for giving thanks to the LORD—for his steadfast love endures forever—whenever David offered praises by their ministry. Opposite them the priests sounded trumpets; and all Israel stood.

[7] Solomon consecrated the middle of the court that was in front of the house of the LORD; for there he offered the burnt offerings and the fat of the offerings of well-being because the bronze altar Solomon had made could not hold the burnt offering and the grain offering and the fat parts.

[8] At that time Solomon held the festival for seven days, and all Israel with him, a very great congregation, from Lebo-hamath to the Wadi of Egypt. [9]On the eighth day they held a solemn assembly; for they had observed the dedication of the altar seven days and the festival seven days. [10]On the twenty-third day of the seventh month he sent the people away to their homes, joyful and in good spirits because of the goodness that the LORD had shown to David and to Solomon and to his people Israel.

[11] Thus Solomon finished the house of the LORD and the king's house; all that Solomon had planned to do in the house of the LORD and in his own house he successfully accomplished.

God's Second Appearance to Solomon

[12] Then the LORD appeared to Solomon in the night and said to him: "I have heard your prayer, and have chosen this place for myself as a house of sacrifice. [13]When I shut up the heavens so that there is no rain, or command the locust to devour the land, or send pestilence among my people, [14]if my people who are called by my name humble themselves, pray, seek my face, and turn from their wicked ways, then I will hear from heaven, and will forgive their sin and heal their land. [15]Now my eyes will be open and my ears attentive to the prayer that is made in this place. [16]For now I have chosen and consecrated this house so that my name may be there forever; my eyes and my heart will be there for all time. [17]As for you, if you walk before me, as your father David walked, doing according to all that I have commanded you and keeping my statutes and my ordinances, [18]then I will establish your royal throne, as I made covenant with your father David saying, 'You shall never lack a successor to rule over Israel.'

[19] "But if you[n] turn aside and forsake my statutes and my commandments that

[n] The word you in this verse is plural

I have set before you, and go and serve other gods and worship them, ²⁰then I will pluck you° up from the land that I have given you;° and this house, which I have consecrated for my name, I will cast out of my sight, and will make it a proverb and a byword among all peoples. ²¹And regarding this house, now exalted, everyone passing by will be astonished, and say, 'Why has the LORD done such a thing to this land and to this house?' ²²Then they will say, 'Because they abandoned the LORD the God of their ancestors who brought them out of the land of Egypt, and they adopted other gods, and worshiped them and served them; therefore he has brought all this calamity upon them.'"

Various Activities of Solomon

8 At the end of twenty years, during which Solomon had built the house

° Heb *them*

Paradise Within

FRIDAY

Scripture Reading
for Today:
2 Chronicles 7.1–6

Verse for Today:
2 Chronicles 7.2

The glory of the Lord fell on Solomon's temple with great power and splendor. That same glory lives in us, says Saint Teresa of Avila, as she urges us to pay attention to the "interior castle," the temple of God within.

Consider our soul to be like a castle made entirely out of a diamond or of very clear crystal in which there are many rooms, just as in heaven there are many dwelling places (see John 14.2). For in reflecting upon it carefully, Sisters, we realize that the soul of the just person is nothing else but a paradise where the Lord says he finds his delight (see Proverbs 8.31). So then what do you think that abode will be like where a King so powerful, so wise, so pure, so full of all good things takes his delight? I don't find anything comparable to the magnificent beauty of a soul and its marvelous capacity. Indeed, our intellects, however keen, can hardly comprehend it, just as they cannot comprehend God.

It is a shame and unfortunate that through our own fault we don't understand ourselves or know who we are. Wouldn't it show great ignorance, my daughters, if someone, when asked who he was, didn't know, and didn't know his father or mother or from what country he came? Well now, if this would be so extremely stupid, we are incomparably more so when we do not strive to know who we are, but limit ourselves to considering only roughly these bodies. Because we have heard and because faith tells us so, we know we have souls. But we seldom consider the precious things that can be found in this soul, or who dwells within it, or its high value. Consequently, little effort is made to preserve its beauty. All our attention is taken up with the plainness of the diamond's setting or the outer wall of the castle; that is, with these bodies of ours.

—SAINT TERESA OF AVILA

Go to page 460 for your next devotional reading.

of the LORD and his own house, ²Solomon rebuilt the cities that Huram had given to him, and settled the people of Israel in them.

3 Solomon went to Hamath-zobah, and captured it. ⁴He built Tadmor in the wilderness and all the storage towns that he built in Hamath. ⁵He also built Upper Beth-horon and Lower Beth-horon, fortified cities, with walls, gates, and bars, ⁶and Baalath, as well as all Solomon's storage towns, and all the towns for his chariots, the towns for his cavalry, and whatever Solomon desired to build, in Jerusalem, in Lebanon, and in all the land of his dominion. ⁷All the people who were left of the Hittites, the Amorites, the Perizzites, the Hivites, and the Jebusites, who were not of Israel, ⁸from their descendants who were still left in the land, whom the people of Israel had not destroyed—these Solomon conscripted for forced labor, as is still the case today. ⁹But of the people of Israel Solomon made no slaves for his work; they were soldiers, and his officers, the commanders of his chariotry and cavalry. ¹⁰These were the chief officers of King Solomon, two hundred fifty of them, who exercised authority over the people.

11 Solomon brought Pharaoh's daughter from the city of David to the house that he had built for her, for he said, "My wife shall not live in the house of King David of Israel, for the places to which the ark of the LORD has come are holy."

12 Then Solomon offered up burnt offerings to the LORD on the altar of the LORD that he had built in front of the vestibule, ¹³as the duty of each day required, offering according to the commandment of Moses for the sabbaths, the new moons, and the three annual festivals—the festival of unleavened bread, the festival of weeks, and the festival of booths. ¹⁴According to the ordinance of his father David, he appointed the divisions of the priests for their service, and the Levites for their offices of praise and ministry alongside the priests as the duty of each day required, and the gatekeepers in their divisions for the several gates; for so David the man of God had commanded. ¹⁵They did not turn away from what the king had commanded the priests and Levites regarding anything at all, or regarding the treasuries.

16 Thus all the work of Solomon was accomplished from ᵖ the day the foundation of the house of the LORD was laid until the house of the LORD was finished completely.

17 Then Solomon went to Ezion-geber and Eloth on the shore of the sea, in the land of Edom. ¹⁸Huram sent him, in the care of his servants, ships and servants familiar with the sea. They went to Ophir, together with the servants of Solomon, and imported from there four hundred fifty talents of gold and brought it to King Solomon.

Visit of the Queen of Sheba

9 When the queen of Sheba heard of the fame of Solomon, she came to Jerusalem to test him with hard questions, having a very great retinue and camels bearing spices and very much gold and precious stones. When she came to Solomon, she discussed with him all that was on her mind. ²Solomon answered all her questions; there was nothing hidden from Solomon that he could not explain to her. ³When the queen of Sheba had observed the wisdom of Solomon, the house that he had built, ⁴the food of his table, the seating of his officials, and the attendance of his servants, and their clothing, his valets, and their clothing, and his burnt offeringsᑫ that he offered at the house of the LORD, there was no more spirit left in her.

5 So she said to the king, "The report was true that I heard in my own land of your accomplishments and of your wisdom, ⁶but I did not believe theʳ reports until I came and my own eyes saw it. Not even half of the greatness of your wisdom had been told to me; you far surpass the report that I had heard. ⁷Happy are your people! Happy are these your servants, who continually attend you and hear your wisdom! ⁸Blessed be the LORD your God, who has delighted in you and set you on his throne as king for the LORD your God. Because your God loved Israel and would establish them forever, he has made you king over them, that you may execute justice and righteousness." ⁹Then she gave the king one hundred twenty talents of gold, a very great quantity of spices, and precious stones: there were no spices such as

those that the queen of Sheba gave to King Solomon.

10 Moreover the servants of Huram and the servants of Solomon who brought gold from Ophir brought algum wood and precious stones. [11]From the algum wood, the king made steps[s] for the house of the LORD and for the king's house, lyres also and harps for the singers; there never was seen the like of them before in the land of Judah.

12 Meanwhile King Solomon granted the queen of Sheba every desire that she expressed, well beyond what she had brought to the king. Then she returned to her own land, with her servants.

Solomon's Great Wealth

13 The weight of gold that came to Solomon in one year was six hundred sixty-six talents of gold, [14]besides that which the traders and merchants brought; and all the kings of Arabia and the governors of the land brought gold and silver to Solomon. [15]King Solomon made two hundred large shields of beaten gold; six hundred shekels of beaten gold went into each large shield. [16]He made three hundred shields of beaten gold; three hundred shekels of gold went into each shield; and the king put them in the House of the Forest of Lebanon. [17]The king also made a great ivory throne, and overlaid it with pure gold. [18]The throne had six steps and a footstool of gold, which were attached to the throne, and on each side of the seat were arm rests and two lions standing beside the arm rests, [19]while twelve lions were standing, one on each end of a step on the six steps. The like of it was never made in any kingdom. [20]All King Solomon's drinking vessels were of gold, and all the vessels of the House of the Forest of Lebanon were of pure gold; silver was not considered as anything in the days of Solomon. [21]For the king's ships went to Tarshish with the servants of Huram; once every three years the ships of Tarshish used to come bringing gold, silver, ivory, apes, and peacocks.[t]

22 Thus King Solomon excelled all the kings of the earth in riches and in wisdom. [23]All the kings of the earth sought the presence of Solomon to hear his wisdom, which God had put into his mind. [24]Every one of them brought a present, objects of silver and gold, garments, weap-

onry, spices, horses, and mules, so much year by year. [25]Solomon had four thousand stalls for horses and chariots, and twelve thousand horses, which he stationed in the chariot cities and with the king in Jerusalem. [26]He ruled over all the kings from the Euphrates to the land of the Philistines, and to the border of Egypt. [27]The king made silver as common in Jerusalem as stone, and cedar as plentiful as the sycamore of the Shephelah. [28]Horses were imported for Solomon from Egypt and from all lands.

Death of Solomon

29 Now the rest of the acts of Solomon, from first to last, are they not written in the history of the prophet Nathan, and in the prophecy of Ahijah the Shilonite, and in the visions of the seer Iddo concerning Jeroboam son of Nebat? [30]Solomon reigned in Jerusalem over all Israel forty years. [31]Solomon slept with his ancestors and was buried in the city of his father David; and his son Rehoboam succeeded him.

The Revolt against Rehoboam

10 Rehoboam went to Shechem, for all Israel had come to Shechem to make him king. [2]When Jeroboam son of Nebat heard of it (for he was in Egypt, where he had fled from King Solomon), then Jeroboam returned from Egypt. [3]They sent and called him; and Jeroboam and all Israel came and said to Rehoboam, [4]"Your father made our yoke heavy. Now therefore lighten the hard service of your father and his heavy yoke that he placed on us, and we will serve you." [5]He said to them, "Come to me again in three days." So the people went away.

6 Then King Rehoboam took counsel with the older men who had attended his father Solomon while he was still alive, saying, "How do you advise me to answer this people?" [7]They answered him, "If you will be kind to this people and please them, and speak good words to them, then they will be your servants forever." [8]But he rejected the advice that the older men gave him, and consulted the young men who had grown up with him and now attended him. [9]He said to them, "What do you advise that we answer this

[s] Gk Vg: Meaning of Heb uncertain   [t] Or baboons

people who have said to me, 'Lighten the yoke that your father put on us'?" [10]The young men who had grown up with him said to him, "Thus should you speak to the people who said to you, 'Your father made our yoke heavy, but you must lighten it for us'; tell them, 'My little finger is thicker than my father's loins. [11]Now, whereas my father laid on you a heavy yoke, I will add to your yoke. My father disciplined you with whips, but I will discipline you with scorpions.' "

12 So Jeroboam and all the people came to Rehoboam the third day, as the king had said, "Come to me again the third day." [13]The king answered them harshly. King Rehoboam rejected the advice of the older men; [14]he spoke to them in accordance with the advice of the young men, "My father made your yoke heavy, but I will add to it; my father disciplined you with whips, but I will discipline you with scorpions." [15]So the king did not listen to the people, because it was a turn of affairs brought about by God so that the LORD might fulfill his word, which he had spoken by Ahijah the Shilonite to Jeroboam son of Nebat.

16 When all Israel saw that the king would not listen to them, the people answered the king,

"What share do we have in David?
We have no inheritance in the son
of Jesse.
Each of you to your tents, O Israel!
Look now to your own house,
O David."

So all Israel departed to their tents. [17]But Rehoboam reigned over the people of Israel who were living in the cities of Judah. [18]When King Rehoboam sent Hadoram, who was taskmaster over the forced labor, the people of Israel stoned him to death. King Rehoboam hurriedly mounted his chariot to flee to Jerusalem. [19]So Israel has been in rebellion against the house of David to this day.

Judah and Benjamin Fortified

11 When Rehoboam came to Jerusalem, he assembled one hundred eighty thousand chosen troops of the house of Judah and Benjamin to fight against Israel, to restore the kingdom to Rehoboam. [2]But the word of the LORD came to Shemaiah the man of God: [3]Say to King Rehoboam of Judah, son of Solomon, and to all Israel in Judah and Benja-

min, [4]"Thus says the LORD: You shall not go up or fight against your kindred. Let everyone return home, for this thing is from me." So they heeded the word of the LORD and turned back from the expedition against Jeroboam.

5 Rehoboam resided in Jerusalem, and he built cities for defense in Judah. [6]He built up Bethlehem, Etam, Tekoa, [7]Bethzur, Soco, Adullam, [8]Gath, Mareshah, Ziph, [9]Adoraim, Lachish, Azekah, [10]Zorah, Aijalon, and Hebron, fortified cities that are in Judah and in Benjamin. [11]He made the fortresses strong, and put commanders in them, and stores of food, oil, and wine. [12]He also put large shields and spears in all the cities, and made them very strong. So he held Judah and Benjamin.

Priests and Levites Support Rehoboam

13 The priests and the Levites who were in all Israel presented themselves to him from all their territories. [14]The Levites had left their common lands and their holdings and had come to Judah and Jerusalem, because Jeroboam and his sons had prevented them from serving as priests of the LORD, [15]and had appointed his own priests for the high places, and for the goat-demons, and for the calves that he had made. [16]Those who had set their hearts to seek the LORD God of Israel came after them from all the tribes of Israel to Jerusalem to sacrifice to the LORD, the God of their ancestors. [17]They strengthened the kingdom of Judah, and for three years they made Rehoboam son of Solomon secure, for they walked for three years in the way of David and Solomon.

Rehoboam's Marriages

18 Rehoboam took as his wife Mahalath daughter of Jerimoth son of David, and of Abihail daughter of Eliab son of Jesse. [19]She bore him sons: Jeush, Shemariah, and Zaham. [20]After her he took Maacah daughter of Absalom, who bore him Abijah, Attai, Ziza, and Shelomith. [21]Rehoboam loved Maacah daughter of Absalom more than all his other wives and concubines (he took eighteen wives and sixty concubines, and became the father of twenty-eight sons and sixty daughters). [22]Rehoboam appointed Abijah son of Maacah as chief prince among his brothers, for he intended to make him king. [23]He dealt wisely, and distributed some of his

sons through all the districts of Judah and Benjamin, in all the fortified cities; he gave them abundant provisions, and found many wives for them.

Egypt Attacks Judah

12 When the rule of Rehoboam was established and he grew strong, he abandoned the law of the LORD, he and all Israel with him. ²In the fifth year of King Rehoboam, because they had been unfaithful to the LORD, King Shishak of Egypt came up against Jerusalem ³with twelve hundred chariots and sixty thousand cavalry. A countless army came with him from Egypt—Libyans, Sukkiim, and Ethiopians.ᵘ ⁴He took the fortified cities of Judah and came as far as Jerusalem. ⁵Then the prophet Shemaiah came to Rehoboam and to the officers of Judah, who had gathered at Jerusalem because of Shishak, and said to them, "Thus says the LORD: You abandoned me, so I have abandoned you to the hand of Shishak." ⁶Then the officers of Israel and the king humbled themselves and said, "The LORD is in the right." ⁷When the LORD saw that they humbled themselves, the word of the LORD came to Shemaiah, saying: "They have humbled themselves; I will not destroy them, but I will grant them some deliverance, and my wrath shall not be poured out on Jerusalem by the hand of Shishak. ⁸Nevertheless they shall be his servants, so that they may know the difference between serving me and serving the kingdoms of other lands."

9 So King Shishak of Egypt came up against Jerusalem; he took away the treasures of the house of the LORD and the treasures of the king's house; he took everything. He also took away the shields of gold that Solomon had made; ¹⁰but King Rehoboam made in place of them shields of bronze, and committed them to the hands of the officers of the guard, who kept the door of the king's house. ¹¹Whenever the king went into the house of the LORD, the guard would come along bearing them, and would then bring them back to the guardroom. ¹²Because he humbled himself the wrath of the LORD turned from him, so as not to destroy them completely; moreover, conditions were good in Judah.

Death of Rehoboam

13 So King Rehoboam established himself in Jerusalem and reigned. Rehoboam was forty-one years old when he began to reign; he reigned seventeen years in Jerusalem, the city that the LORD had chosen out of all the tribes of Israel to put his name there. His mother's name was Naamah the Ammonite. ¹⁴He did evil, for he did not set his heart to seek the LORD.

15 Now the acts of Rehoboam, from first to last, are they not written in the records of the prophet Shemaiah and of the seer Iddo, recorded by genealogy? There were continual wars between Rehoboam and Jeroboam. ¹⁶Rehoboam slept with his ancestors and was buried in the city of David; and his son Abijah succeeded him.

Abijah Reigns over Judah

13 In the eighteenth year of King Jeroboam, Abijah began to reign over Judah. ²He reigned for three years in Jerusalem. His mother's name was Micaiah daughter of Uriel of Gibeah.

Now there was war between Abijah and Jeroboam. ³Abijah engaged in battle, having an army of valiant warriors, four hundred thousand picked men; and Jeroboam drew up his line of battle against him with eight hundred thousand picked mighty warriors. ⁴Then Abijah stood on the slope of Mount Zemaraim that is in the hill country of Ephraim, and said, "Listen to me, Jeroboam and all Israel! ⁵Do you not know that the LORD God of Israel gave the kingship over Israel forever to David and his sons by a covenant of salt? ⁶Yet Jeroboam son of Nebat, a servant of Solomon son of David, rose up and rebelled against his lord; ⁷and certain worthless scoundrels gathered around him and defied Rehoboam son of Solomon, when Rehoboam was young and irresolute and could not withstand them.

8 "And now you think that you can withstand the kingdom of the LORD in the hand of the sons of David, because you are a great multitude and have with you the golden calves that Jeroboam made as gods for you. ⁹Have you not driven out the priests of the LORD, the descendants of Aaron, and the Levites, and made priests for yourselves like the peoples of other lands? Whoever comes to be consecrated with a young bull or seven rams becomes a priest of what are no gods. ¹⁰But as for

ᵘ Or *Nubians;* Heb *Cushites*

us, the LORD is our God, and we have not abandoned him. We have priests ministering to the LORD who are descendants of Aaron, and Levites for their service. [11] They offer to the LORD every morning and every evening burnt offerings and fragrant incense, set out the rows of bread on the table of pure gold, and care for the golden lampstand so that its lamps may burn every evening; for we keep the charge of the LORD our God, but you have abandoned him. [12] See, God is with us at our head, and his priests have their battle trumpets to sound the call to battle against you. O Israelites, do not fight against the LORD, the God of your ancestors; for you cannot succeed."

13 Jeroboam had sent an ambush around to come on them from behind; thus his troops[v] were in front of Judah, and the ambush was behind them. [14] When Judah turned, the battle was in front of them and behind them. They cried out to the LORD, and the priests blew the trumpets. [15] Then the people of Judah raised the battle shout. And when the people of Judah shouted, God defeated Jeroboam and all Israel before Abijah and Judah. [16] The Israelites fled before Judah, and God gave them into their hands. [17] Abijah and his army defeated them with great slaughter; five hundred thousand picked men of Israel fell slain. [18] Thus the Israelites were subdued at that time, and the people of Judah prevailed, because they relied on the LORD, the God of their ancestors. [19] Abijah pursued Jeroboam, and took cities from him: Bethel with its villages and Jeshanah with its villages and Ephron[w] with its villages. [20] Jeroboam did not recover his power in the days of Abijah; the LORD struck him down, and he died. [21] But Abijah grew strong. He took fourteen wives, and became the father of twenty-two sons and sixteen daughters. [22] The rest of the acts of Abijah, his behavior and his deeds, are written in the story of the prophet Iddo.

Asa Reigns

14 [x] So Abijah slept with his ancestors, and they buried him in the city of David. His son Asa succeeded him. In his days the land had rest for ten years. [2] [y] Asa did what was good and right in the sight of the LORD his God. [3] He took away the foreign altars and the high places, broke down the pillars, hewed down the sacred poles,[z] [4] and commanded Judah to seek the LORD, the God of their ancestors, and to keep the law and the commandment. [5] He also removed from all the cities of Judah the high places and the incense altars. And the kingdom had rest under him. [6] He built fortified cities in Judah while the land had rest. He had no war in those years, for the LORD gave him peace. [7] He said to Judah, "Let us build these cities, and surround them with walls and towers, gates and bars; the land is still ours because we have sought the LORD our God; we have sought him, and he has given us peace on every side." So they built and prospered. [8] Asa had an army of three hundred thousand from Judah, armed with large shields and spears, and two hundred eighty thousand troops from Benjamin who carried shields and drew bows; all these were mighty warriors.

Ethiopian Invasion Repulsed

9 Zerah the Ethiopian[a] came out against them with an army of a million men and three hundred chariots, and came as far as Mareshah. [10] Asa went out to meet him, and they drew up their lines of battle in the valley of Zephathah at Mareshah. [11] Asa cried to the LORD his God, "O LORD, there is no difference for you between helping the mighty and the weak. Help us, O LORD our God, for we rely on you, and in your name we have come against this multitude. O LORD, you are our God; let no mortal prevail against you." [12] So the LORD defeated the Ethiopians[b] before Asa and before Judah, and the Ethiopians[b] fled. [13] Asa and the army with him pursued them as far as Gerar, and the Ethiopians[b] fell until no one remained alive; for they were broken before the LORD and his army. The people of Judah[c] carried away a great quantity of booty. [14] They defeated all the cities around Gerar, for the fear of the LORD was on them. They plundered all the cities; for there was much plunder in them. [15] They also attacked the tents of those who had livestock,[d] and carried away sheep and goats in abundance, and camels. Then they returned to Jerusalem.

---

v Heb *they*   w Another reading is *Ephrain*   x Ch 13.23 in Heb   y Ch 14.1 in Heb   z Heb *Asherim*   a Or *Nubian*; Heb *Cushite*   b Or *Nubians*; Heb *Cushites*   c Heb *They*   d Meaning of Heb uncertain

15 The spirit of God came upon Azariah son of Oded. [2]He went out to meet Asa and said to him, "Hear me, Asa, and all Judah and Benjamin: The LORD is with you, while you are with him. If you seek him, he will be found by you, but if you abandon him, he will abandon you. [3]For a long time Israel was without the true God, and without a teaching priest, and without law; [4]but when in their distress they turned to the LORD, the God of Israel, and sought him, he was found by them. [5]In those times it was not safe for anyone to go or come, for great disturbances afflicted all the inhabitants of the lands. [6]They were broken in pieces, nation against nation and city against city, for God troubled them with every sort of distress. [7]But you, take courage! Do not let your hands be weak, for your work shall be rewarded."

8 When Asa heard these words, the prophecy of Azariah son of Oded,[e] he took courage, and put away the abominable idols from all the land of Judah and Benjamin and from the towns that he had taken in the hill country of Ephraim. He repaired the altar of the LORD that was in front of the vestibule of the house of the LORD.[f] [9]He gathered all Judah and Benjamin, and those from Ephraim, Manasseh, and Simeon who were residing as aliens with them, for great numbers had deserted to him from Israel when they saw that the LORD his God was with him. [10]They were gathered at Jerusalem in the third month of the fifteenth year of the reign of Asa. [11]They sacrificed to the LORD on that day, from the booty that they had brought, seven hundred oxen and seven thousand sheep. [12]They entered into a covenant to seek the LORD, the God of their ancestors, with all their heart and with all their soul. [13]Whoever would not seek the LORD, the God of Israel, should be put to death, whether young or old, man or woman. [14]They took an oath to the LORD with a loud voice, and with shouting, and with trumpets, and with horns. [15]All Judah rejoiced over the oath; for they had sworn with all their heart, and had sought him with their whole desire, and he was found by them, and the LORD gave them rest all around.

16 King Asa even removed his mother Maacah from being queen mother because she had made an abominable image for Asherah. Asa cut down her image,

crushed it, and burned it at the Wadi Kidron. [17]But the high places were not taken out of Israel. Nevertheless the heart of Asa was true all his days. [18]He brought into the house of God the votive gifts of his father and his own votive gifts—silver, gold, and utensils. [19]And there was no more war until the thirty-fifth year of the reign of Asa.

Alliance with Aram Condemned

16 In the thirty-sixth year of the reign of Asa, King Baasha of Israel went up against Judah, and built Ramah, to prevent anyone from going out or coming into the territory of[g] King Asa of Judah. [2]Then Asa took silver and gold from the treasures of the house of the LORD and the king's house, and sent them to King Ben-hadad of Aram, who resided in Damascus, saying, [3]"Let there be an alliance between me and you, like that between my father and your father; I am sending to you silver and gold; go, break your alliance with King Baasha of Israel, so that he may withdraw from me." [4]Ben-hadad listened to King Asa, and sent the commanders of his armies against the cities of Israel. They conquered Ijon, Dan, Abel-maim, and all the store-cities of Naphtali. [5]When Baasha heard of it, he stopped building Ramah, and let his work cease. [6]Then King Asa brought all Judah, and they carried away the stones of Ramah and its timber, with which Baasha had been building, and with them he built up Geba and Mizpah.

7 At that time the seer Hanani came to King Asa of Judah, and said to him, "Because you relied on the king of Aram, and did not rely on the LORD your God, the army of the king of Aram has escaped you. [8]Were not the Ethiopians[h] and the Libyans a huge army with exceedingly many chariots and cavalry? Yet because you relied on the LORD, he gave them into your hand. [9]For the eyes of the LORD range throughout the entire earth, to strengthen those whose heart is true to him. You have done foolishly in this; for from now on you will have wars." [10]Then Asa was angry with the seer, and put him in the stocks, in prison, for he was in a rage with him

e Compare Syr Vg: Heb *the prophecy, the prophet Obed*   f Heb *the vestibule of the LORD*   g Heb lacks *the territory of*   h Or *Nubians*; Heb *Cushites*

Jochebed

Her Name Means "The Lord Is Glory"

Her Character: *Her fierce love for her son, coupled with her faith, enabled her to act heroically in the midst of great oppression.*
Her Sorrow: *To live in bondage as a slave.*
Her Joy: *That God not only preserved the son she surrendered to him but also that he restored her child to her.*

Read Exodus 2.1–10

Three hundred years after the death of the patriarch Joseph, a boy was born in Egypt, his lusty cries muffled by a woman's sobs.

Slave though she was, she was yet a Levite, a woman who belonged to the God of Abraham and Sarah, of Isaac and Rebekah, of Jacob, Rachel, and Leah. She knew the stories. She believed the promises. Hadn't her people already grown as numerous as the sand of the sea, just as God said they would?

Too numerous, she knew, to ease the many fears of the pharaohs, who worried the Israelites might one day betray the nation from within. So the rulers had tightened their grip, finally enslaving the Hebrews, until one pharaoh's paranoia produced the monstrous command to murder every male child of the slaves. But the Israelite midwives feared God more than the king and refused to follow his orders of execution, excusing themselves by claiming that Hebrew women were stronger than Egyptian women, giving birth before the midwives even arrived.

So Pharaoh commanded his soldiers to find every newborn male and drown him in the waters of the Nile. Jochebed could hear the screams as children were torn from their mothers' arms. Her own arms tightened around her baby as he slept peacefully against her breast. This one, she vowed, would never be fed to the Egyptian river god. She and her husband Amram would pray. They would plan. And they would trust God.

For three months, as long as she dared, she hid the infant, managing to keep Miriam and three-year-old Aaron quiet about their new baby brother. Finally, she acted on an idea that had been growing in her mind. Pharaoh had commanded her to consign her son to the Nile River. All right then. Her own hands would put him into the water.

Remembering how God had spared the child Isaac, she bent down and laid her son in a basket of papyrus, waterproofed with tar and pitch. Then, with a whispered prayer and a last caress, she wiped her eyes, begging God to preserve her baby from the crocodiles that swarmed the river.

Still she could not bear to watch as he drifted away from her. Instead, young Miriam kept vigil, following at a distance to see what would become of him.

Soon Pharaoh's daughter arrived at the riverbank. Spotting the basket among the reeds, she sent her slave girl to fetch it. As soon as she beheld the brown-eyed baby, she loved him. The river had brought her a child whom she would cherish as her own. She could not save all the innocent children, but she could spare one mother's son.

Was she surprised when a young slave girl, Miriam, approached, asking whether she could go after a Hebrew woman to nurse the baby for her? Did she suspect the truth when Jochebed gathered the boy in her arms, this time as his nursemaid?

Whatever was in the mind of the royal princess, she named the child Moses, saying "I drew him out of the water" (verse 10). For the next 40 years, she educated him, a prince in the courts of Pharaoh himself.

Two women—a slave and a princess—preserved the life of Israel's future deliverer.

Praying With Jochebed

When she could hide him no longer she got a papyrus basket for him, and plastered it with bitumen and pitch; she put the child in it and placed it among the reeds on the bank of the river.—*Exodus 2:3*

Praise God: *That even the worst enemies we encounter are weak compared to him.*

Offer Thanks: *For God's power to save.*

Confess: *Any failure to trust God for the lives of your children.*

Ask God: *To help you be an encouragement to another mother who is concerned about her children's well-being.*

Lift Your Heart

Find a mother, perhaps a teenage mom or a friend who is having difficulty with her own children right now. Put together a gift basket for her, filled with small gifts such as a scented candle, dried fruit, and some small cards inscribed with encouraging Scripture verses. Tell her you will be praying for each of her children by name every day for the next couple of months. Don't expect her to confide in you, but if she does, cherish what she tells you by keeping it confidential and letting it shape your prayers.

Father, thank you for the gift and calling of motherhood. Help me to remember that my love for my children is merely a reflection of your own love for them. With that in mind, give me grace to surrender my anxiety. Replace it with a sense of trust and calm as I learn to depend on you for everything.

Go to page 483 for your next devotional reading.

because of this. And Asa inflicted cruelties on some of the people at the same time.

Asa's Disease and Death

11 The acts of Asa, from first to last, are written in the Book of the Kings of Judah and Israel. 12In the thirty-ninth year of his reign Asa was diseased in his feet, and his disease became severe; yet even in his disease he did not seek the LORD, but sought help from physicians. 13Then Asa slept with his ancestors, dying in the forty-first year of his reign. 14They buried him in the tomb that he had hewn out for himself in the city of David. They laid him on a bier that had been filled with various kinds of spices prepared by the perfumer's art; and they made a very great fire in his honor.

Jehoshaphat's Reign

17 His son Jehoshaphat succeeded him, and strengthened himself against Israel. 2He placed forces in all the fortified cities of Judah, and set garrisons in the land of Judah, and in the cities of Ephraim that his father Asa had taken. 3The LORD was with Jehoshaphat, because he walked in the earlier ways of his father;*i* he did not seek the Baals, 4but sought the God of his father and walked in his commandments, and not according to the ways of Israel. 5Therefore the LORD established the kingdom in his hand. All Judah brought tribute to Jehoshaphat, and he had great riches and honor. 6His heart was courageous in the ways of the LORD; and furthermore he removed the high places and the sacred poles*j* from Judah.

7 In the third year of his reign he sent his officials, Ben-hail, Obadiah, Zechariah, Nethanel, and Micaiah, to teach in the cities of Judah. 8With them were the Levites, Shemaiah, Nethaniah, Zebadiah, Asahel, Shemiramoth, Jehonathan, Adonijah, Tobijah, and Tob-adonijah; and with these Levites, the priests Elishama and Jehoram. 9They taught in Judah, having the book of the law of the LORD with them; they went around through all the cities of Judah and taught among the people.

10 The fear of the LORD fell on all the kingdoms of the lands around Judah, and they did not make war against Jehoshaphat. 11Some of the Philistines brought Jehoshaphat presents, and silver for tribute; and the Arabs also brought him seven thousand seven hundred rams and seven thousand seven hundred male goats. 12Jehoshaphat grew steadily greater. He built fortresses and storage cities in Judah. 13He carried out great works in the cities of Judah. He had soldiers, mighty warriors, in Jerusalem. 14This was the muster of them by ancestral houses: Of Judah, the commanders of the thousands: Adnah the commander, with three hundred thousand mighty warriors, 15and next to him Jehohanan the commander, with two hundred eighty thousand, 16and next to him Amasiah son of Zichri, a volunteer for the service of the LORD, with two hundred thousand mighty warriors. 17Of Benjamin: Eliada, a mighty warrior, with two hundred thousand armed with bow and shield, 18and next to him Jehozabad with one hundred eighty thousand armed for war. 19These were in the service of the king, besides those whom the king had placed in the fortified cities throughout all Judah.

Micaiah Predicts Failure

18 Now Jehoshaphat had great riches and honor; and he made a marriage alliance with Ahab. 2After some years he went down to Ahab in Samaria. Ahab slaughtered an abundance of sheep and oxen for him and for the people who were with him, and induced him to go up against Ramoth-gilead. 3King Ahab of Israel said to King Jehoshaphat of Judah, "Will you go with me to Ramoth-gilead?" He answered him, "I am with you, my people are your people. We will be with you in the war."

4 But Jehoshaphat also said to the king of Israel, "Inquire first for the word of the LORD." 5Then the king of Israel gathered the prophets together, four hundred of them, and said to them, "Shall we go to battle against Ramoth-gilead, or shall I refrain?" They said, "Go up; for God will give it into the hand of the king." 6But Jehoshaphat said, "Is there no other prophet of the LORD here of whom we may inquire?" 7The king of Israel said to Jehoshaphat, "There is still one other by whom we may inquire of the LORD, Micaiah son of Imlah; but I hate him, for he never prophesies anything favorable about me, but only disaster." Jehoshaphat said, "Let the king not say such a thing." 8Then the king of Israel

---

i Another reading is *his father David*   *j* Heb *Asherim*

summoned an officer and said, "Bring quickly Micaiah son of Imlah." 9Now the king of Israel and King Jehoshaphat of Judah were sitting on their thrones, arrayed in their robes; and they were sitting at the threshing floor at the entrance of the gate of Samaria; and all the prophets were prophesying before them. 10Zedekiah son of Chenaanah made for himself horns of iron, and he said, "Thus says the LORD: With these you shall gore the Arameans until they are destroyed." 11All the prophets were prophesying the same and saying, "Go up to Ramoth-gilead and triumph; the LORD will give it into the hand of the king."

12 The messenger who had gone to summon Micaiah said to him, "Look, the words of the prophets with one accord are favorable to the king; let your word be like the word of one of them, and speak favorably." 13But Micaiah said, "As the LORD lives, whatever my God says, that I will speak."

14 When he had come to the king, the king said to him, "Micaiah, shall we go to Ramoth-gilead to battle, or shall I refrain?" He answered, "Go up and triumph; they will be given into your hand." 15But the king said to him, "How many times must I make you swear to tell me nothing but the truth in the name of the LORD?" 16Then Micaiah*k* said, "I saw all Israel scattered on the mountains, like sheep without a shepherd; and the LORD said, 'These have no master; let each one go home in peace.' " 17The king of Israel said to Jehoshaphat, "Did I not tell you that he would not prophesy anything favorable about me, but only disaster?"

18 Then Micaiah*k* said, "Therefore hear the word of the LORD: I saw the LORD sitting on his throne, with all the host of heaven standing to the right and to the left of him. 19And the LORD said, 'Who will entice King Ahab of Israel, so that he may go up and fall at Ramoth-gilead?' Then one said one thing, and another said another, 20until a spirit came forward and stood before the LORD, saying, 'I will entice him.' The LORD asked him, 'How?' 21He replied, 'I will go out and be a lying spirit in the mouth of all his prophets.' Then the LORD*k* said, 'You are to entice him, and you shall succeed; go out and do it.' 22So you see, the LORD has put a lying spirit in the mouth of these your prophets; the LORD has decreed disaster for you."

23 Then Zedekiah son of Chenaanah came up to Micaiah, slapped him on the cheek, and said, "Which way did the spirit of the LORD pass from me to speak to you?" 24Micaiah replied, "You will find out on that day when you go in to hide in an inner chamber." 25The king of Israel then ordered, "Take Micaiah, and return him to Amon the governor of the city and to Joash the king's son; 26and say, 'Thus says the king: Put this fellow in prison, and feed him on reduced rations of bread and water until I return in peace.' " 27Micaiah said, "If you return in peace, the LORD has not spoken by me." And he said, "Hear, you peoples, all of you!"

Defeat and Death of Ahab

28 So the king of Israel and King Jehoshaphat of Judah went up to Ramoth-gilead. 29The king of Israel said to Jehoshaphat, "I will disguise myself and go into battle, but you wear your robes." So the king of Israel disguised himself, and they went into battle. 30Now the king of Aram had commanded the captains of his chariots, "Fight with no one small or great, but only with the king of Israel." 31When the captains of the chariots saw Jehoshaphat, they said, "It is the king of Israel." So they turned to fight against him; and Jehoshaphat cried out, and the LORD helped him. God drew them away from him, 32for when the captains of the chariots saw that it was not the king of Israel, they turned back from pursuing him. 33But a certain man drew his bow and unknowingly struck the king of Israel between the scale armor and the breastplate; so he said to the driver of his chariot, "Turn around, and carry me out of the battle, for I am wounded." 34The battle grew hot that day, and the king of Israel propped himself up in his chariot facing the Arameans until evening; then at sunset he died.

19 King Jehoshaphat of Judah returned in safety to his house in Jerusalem. 2Jehu son of Hanani the seer went out to meet him and said to King Jehoshaphat, "Should you help the wicked and love those who hate the LORD? Because of this, wrath has gone out against you from the LORD. 3Nevertheless, some good is found in you, for you destroyed the sacred poles*l* out of the land, and have set your heart to seek God."

k Heb *he*   *l* Heb *Asheroth*

The Reforms of Jehoshaphat

4 Jehoshaphat resided at Jerusalem; then he went out again among the people, from Beer-sheba to the hill country of Ephraim, and brought them back to the LORD, the God of their ancestors. 5He appointed judges in the land in all the fortified cities of Judah, city by city, 6and said to the judges, "Consider what you are doing, for you judge not on behalf of human beings but on the LORD's behalf; he is with you in giving judgment. 7Now, let the fear of the LORD be upon you; take care what you do, for there is no perversion of justice with the LORD our God, or partiality, or taking of bribes."

8 Moreover in Jerusalem Jehoshaphat appointed certain Levites and priests and heads of families of Israel, to give judgment for the LORD and to decide disputed cases. They had their seat at Jerusalem. 9He charged them: "This is how you shall act: in the fear of the LORD, in faithfulness, and with your whole heart; 10whenever a case comes to you from your kindred who live in their cities, concerning bloodshed, law or commandment, statutes or ordinances, then you shall instruct them, so that they may not incur guilt before the LORD and wrath may not come on you and your kindred. Do so, and you will not incur guilt. 11See, Amariah the chief priest is over you in all matters of the LORD; and Zebadiah son of Ishmael, the governor of the house of Judah, in all the king's matters; and the Levites will serve you as officers. Deal courageously, and may the LORD be with the good!"

Invasion from the East

20 After this the Moabites and Ammonites, and with them some of the Meunites,*m* came against Jehoshaphat for battle. 2Messengers*n* came and told Jehoshaphat, "A great multitude is coming against you from Edom,*o* from beyond the sea; already they are at Hazazon-tamar" (that is, En-gedi). 3Jehoshaphat was afraid; he set himself to seek the LORD, and proclaimed a fast throughout all Judah. 4Judah assembled to seek help from the LORD; from all the towns of Judah they came to seek the LORD.

Jehoshaphat's Prayer and Victory

5 Jehoshaphat stood in the assembly of Judah and Jerusalem, in the house of the LORD, before the new court, 6and said, "O LORD, God of our ancestors, are you not God in heaven? Do you not rule over all the kingdoms of the nations? In your hand are power and might, so that no one is able to withstand you. 7Did you not, O our God, drive out the inhabitants of this land before your people Israel, and give it forever to the descendants of your friend Abraham? 8They have lived in it, and in it have built you a sanctuary for your name, saying, 9'If disaster comes upon us, the sword, judgment,*p* or pestilence, or famine, we will stand before this house, and before you, for your name is in this house, and cry to you in our distress, and you will hear and save.' 10See now, the people of Ammon, Moab, and Mount Seir, whom you would not let Israel invade when they came from the land of Egypt, and whom they avoided and did not destroy— 11they reward us by coming to drive us out of your possession that you have given us to inherit. 12O our God, will you not execute judgment upon them? For we are powerless against this great multitude that is coming against us. We do not know what to do, but our eyes are on you."

13 Meanwhile all Judah stood before the LORD, with their little ones, their wives, and their children. 14Then the spirit of the LORD came upon Jahaziel son of Zechariah, son of Benaiah, son of Jeiel, son of Mattaniah, a Levite of the sons of Asaph, in the middle of the assembly. 15He said, "Listen, all Judah and inhabitants of Jerusalem, and King Jehoshaphat: Thus says the LORD to you: 'Do not fear or be dismayed at this great multitude; for the battle is not yours but God's. 16Tomorrow go down against them; they will come up by the ascent of Ziz; you will find them at the end of the valley, before the wilderness of Jeruel. 17This battle is not for you to fight; take your position, stand still, and see the victory of the LORD on your behalf, O Judah and Jerusalem.' Do not fear or be dismayed; tomorrow go out against them, and the LORD will be with you."

18 Then Jehoshaphat bowed down with his face to the ground, and all Judah and the inhabitants of Jerusalem fell down before the LORD, worshiping the LORD. 19And the Levites, of the Kohathites

---

m Compare 26.7: Heb *Ammonites*   *n* Heb *They*
o One Ms: MT *Aram*   *p* Or *the sword of judgment*

and the Korahites, stood up to praise the LORD, the God of Israel, with a very loud voice.

20 They rose early in the morning and went out into the wilderness of Tekoa; and as they went out, Jehoshaphat stood and said, "Listen to me, O Judah and inhabitants of Jerusalem! Believe in the LORD your God and you will be established; believe his prophets." ²¹When he had taken counsel with the people, he appointed those who were to sing to the LORD and praise him in holy splendor, as they went before the army, saying,
"Give thanks to the LORD,
　for his steadfast love endures
　　forever."
²²As they began to sing and praise, the LORD set an ambush against the Ammonites, Moab, and Mount Seir, who had come against Judah, so that they were routed. ²³For the Ammonites and Moab attacked the inhabitants of Mount Seir, destroying them utterly; and when they had made an end of the inhabitants of Seir, they all helped to destroy one another.

24 When Judah came to the watchtower of the wilderness, they looked toward the multitude; they were corpses lying on the ground; no one had escaped. ²⁵When Jehoshaphat and his people came to take the booty from them, they found livestock*q* in great numbers, goods, clothing, and precious things, which they took for themselves until they could carry no more. They spent three days taking the booty, because of its abundance. ²⁶On the fourth day they assembled in the Valley of Beracah, for there they blessed the LORD; therefore that place has been called the Valley of Beracah*r* to this day. ²⁷Then all the people of Judah and Jerusalem, with Jehoshaphat at their head, returned to Jerusalem with joy, for the LORD had enabled them to rejoice over their enemies. ²⁸They came to Jerusalem, with harps and lyres and trumpets, to the house of the LORD. ²⁹The fear of God came on all the kingdoms of the countries when they heard that the LORD had fought against the enemies of Israel. ³⁰And the realm of Jehoshaphat was quiet, for his God gave him rest all around.

The End of Jehoshaphat's Reign

31 So Jehoshaphat reigned over Judah. He was thirty-five years old when he be-

gan to reign; he reigned twenty-five years in Jerusalem. His mother's name was Azubah daughter of Shilhi. ³²He walked in the way of his father Asa and did not turn aside from it, doing what was right in the sight of the LORD. ³³Yet the high places were not removed; the people had not yet set their hearts upon the God of their ancestors.

34 Now the rest of the acts of Jehoshaphat, from first to last, are written in the Annals of Jehu son of Hanani, which are recorded in the Book of the Kings of Israel.

35 After this King Jehoshaphat of Judah joined with King Ahaziah of Israel, who did wickedly. ³⁶He joined him in building ships to go to Tarshish; they built the ships in Ezion-geber. ³⁷Then Eliezer son of Dodavahu of Mareshah prophesied against Jehoshaphat, saying, "Because you have joined with Ahaziah, the LORD will destroy what you have made." And the ships were wrecked and were not able to go to Tarshish.

Jehoram's Reign

21 Jehoshaphat slept with his ancestors and was buried with his ancestors in the city of David; his son Jehoram succeeded him. ²He had brothers, the sons of Jehoshaphat: Azariah, Jehiel, Zechariah, Azariah, Michael, and Shephatiah; all these were the sons of King Jehoshaphat of Judah.*s* ³Their father gave them many gifts, of silver, gold, and valuable possessions, together with fortified cities in Judah; but he gave the kingdom to Jehoram, because he was the firstborn. ⁴When Jehoram had ascended the throne of his father and was established, he put all his brothers to the sword, and also some of the officials of Israel. ⁵Jehoram was thirty-two years old when he began to reign; he reigned eight years in Jerusalem. ⁶He walked in the way of the kings of Israel, as the house of Ahab had done; for the daughter of Ahab was his wife. He did what was evil in the sight of the LORD. ⁷Yet the LORD would not destroy the house of David because of the covenant that he had made with David, and since he had promised to give a lamp to him and to his descendants forever.

q Gk: Heb *among them*　*r* That is *Blessing*　*s* Gk Syr: Heb *Israel*

Revolt of Edom

8 In his days Edom revolted against the rule of Judah and set up a king of their own. ⁹Then Jehoram crossed over with his commanders and all his chariots. He set out by night and attacked the Edomites, who had surrounded him and his chariot commanders. ¹⁰So Edom has been in revolt against the rule of Judah to this day. At that time Libnah also revolted against his rule, because he had forsaken the Lord, the God of his ancestors.

Elijah's Letter

11 Moreover he made high places in the hill country of Judah, and led the inhabitants of Jerusalem into unfaithfulness, and made Judah go astray. ¹²A letter came to him from the prophet Elijah, saying: "Thus says the Lord, the God of your father David: Because you have not walked in the ways of your father Jehoshaphat or in the ways of King Asa of Judah, ¹³but have walked in the way of the kings of Israel, and have led Judah and the inhabitants of Jerusalem into unfaithfulness, as the house of Ahab led Israel into unfaithfulness, and because you also have killed your brothers, members of your father's house, who were better than yourself, ¹⁴see, the Lord will bring a great plague on your people, your children, your wives, and all your possessions, ¹⁵and you yourself will have a severe sickness with a disease of your bowels, until your bowels come out, day after day, because of the disease."

16 The Lord aroused against Jehoram the anger of the Philistines and of the Arabs who are near the Ethiopians.ᵗ ¹⁷They came up against Judah, invaded it, and carried away all the possessions they found that belonged to the king's house, along with his sons and his wives, so that no son was left to him except Jehoahaz, his youngest son.

Disease and Death of Jehoram

18 After all this the Lord struck him in his bowels with an incurable disease. ¹⁹In course of time, at the end of two years, his bowels came out because of the disease, and he died in great agony. His people made no fire in his honor, like the fires made for his ancestors. ²⁰He was thirty-two years old when he began to reign; he reigned eight years in Jerusalem. He departed with no one's regret. They buried him in the city of David, but not in the tombs of the kings.

Ahaziah's Reign

22 The inhabitants of Jerusalem made his youngest son Ahaziah king as his successor; for the troops who came with the Arabs to the camp had killed all the older sons. So Ahaziah son of Jehoram reigned as king of Judah. ²Ahaziah was forty-two years old when he began to reign; he reigned one year in Jerusalem. His mother's name was Athaliah, a granddaughter of Omri. ³He also walked in the ways of the house of Ahab, for his mother was his counselor in doing wickedly. ⁴He did what was evil in the sight of the Lord, as the house of Ahab had done; for after the death of his father they were his counselors, to his ruin. ⁵He even followed their advice, and went with Jehoram son of King Ahab of Israel to make war against King Hazael of Aram at Ramoth-gilead. The Arameans wounded Joram, ⁶and he returned to be healed in Jezreel of the wounds that he had received at Ramah, when he fought King Hazael of Aram. And Ahaziah son of King Jehoram of Judah went down to see Joram son of Ahab in Jezreel, because he was sick.

7 But it was ordained by God that the downfall of Ahaziah should come about through his going to visit Joram. For when he came there he went out with Jehoram to meet Jehu son of Nimshi, whom the Lord had anointed to destroy the house of Ahab. ⁸When Jehu was executing judgment on the house of Ahab, he met the officials of Judah and the sons of Ahaziah's brothers, who attended Ahaziah, and he killed them. ⁹He searched for Ahaziah, who was captured while hiding in Samaria and was brought to Jehu, and put to death. They buried him, for they said, "He is the grandson of Jehoshaphat, who sought the Lord with all his heart." And the house of Ahaziah had no one able to rule the kingdom.

Athaliah Seizes the Throne

10 Now when Athaliah, Ahaziah's mother, saw that her son was dead, she set about to destroy all the royal family of the house of Judah. ¹¹But Jehoshabeath, the king's daughter, took Joash son of Ahazi-

ᵗ Or *Nubians*; Heb *Cushites*

ah, and stole him away from among the king's children who were about to be killed; she put him and his nurse in a bedroom. Thus Jehoshabeath, daughter of King Jehoram and wife of the priest Jehoiada—because she was a sister of Ahaziah—hid him from Athaliah, so that she did not kill him; 12he remained with them six years, hidden in the house of God, while Athaliah reigned over the land.

23 But in the seventh year Jehoiada took courage, and entered into a compact with the commanders of the hundreds, Azariah son of Jeroham, Ishmael son of Jehohanan, Azariah son of Obed, Maaseiah son of Adaiah, and Elishaphat son of Zichri. 2They went around through Judah and gathered the Levites from all the towns of Judah, and the heads of families of Israel, and they came to Jerusalem. 3Then the whole assembly made a covenant with the king in the house of God. Jehoiadau said to them, "Here is the king's son! Let him reign, as the LORD promised concerning the sons of David. 4This is what you are to do: one-third of you, priests and Levites, who come on duty on the sabbath, shall be gatekeepers, 5one-third shall be at the king's house, and one-third at the Gate of the Foundation; and all the people shall be in the courts of the house of the LORD. 6Do not let anyone enter the house of the LORD except the priests and ministering Levites; they may enter, for they are holy, but all the otherv people shall observe the instructions of the LORD. 7The Levites shall surround the king, each with his weapons in his hand; and whoever enters the house shall be killed. Stay with the king in his comings and goings."

Joash Crowned King

8 The Levites and all Judah did according to all that the priest Jehoiada commanded; each brought his men, who were to come on duty on the sabbath, with those who were to go off duty on the sabbath; for the priest Jehoiada did not dismiss the divisions. 9The priest Jehoiada delivered to the captains the spears and the large and small shields that had been King David's, which were in the house of God; 10and he set all the people as a guard for the king, everyone with weapon in hand, from the south side of the house to the north side of the house, around the altar and the house. 11Then he brought

out the king's son, put the crown on him, and gave him the covenant;w they proclaimed him king, and Jehoiada and his sons anointed him; and they shouted, "Long live the king!"

Athaliah Murdered

12 When Athaliah heard the noise of the people running and praising the king, she went into the house of the LORD to the people; 13and when she looked, there was the king standing by his pillar at the entrance, and the captains and the trumpeters beside the king, and all the people of the land rejoicing and blowing trumpets, and the singers with their musical instruments leading in the celebration. Athaliah tore her clothes, and cried, "Treason! Treason!" 14Then the priest Jehoiada brought out the captains who were set over the army, saying to them, "Bring her out between the ranks; anyone who follows her is to be put to the sword." For the priest said, "Do not put her to death in the house of the LORD." 15So they laid hands on her; she went into the entrance of the Horse Gate of the king's house, and there they put her to death.

16 Jehoiada made a covenant between himself and all the people and the king that they should be the LORD's people. 17Then all the people went to the house of Baal, and tore it down; his altars and his images they broke in pieces, and they killed Mattan, the priest of Baal, in front of the altars. 18Jehoiada assigned the care of the house of the LORD to the levitical priests whom David had organized to be in charge of the house of the LORD, to offer burnt offerings to the LORD, as it is written in the law of Moses, with rejoicing and with singing, according to the order of David. 19He stationed the gatekeepers at the gates of the house of the LORD so that no one should enter who was in any way unclean. 20And he took the captains, the nobles, the governors of the people, and all the people of the land, and they brought the king down from the house of the LORD, marching through the upper gate to the king's house. They set the king on the royal throne. 21So all the people of the land rejoiced, and the city was quiet after Athaliah had been killed with the sword.

u Heb He   v Heb lacks other   w Or treaty, or testimony; Heb eduth

Joash Repairs the Temple

24 Joash was seven years old when he began to reign; he reigned forty years in Jerusalem; his mother's name was Zibiah of Beer-sheba. ²Joash did what was right in the sight of the LORD all the days of the priest Jehoiada. ³Jehoiada got two wives for him, and he became the father of sons and daughters.

4 Some time afterward Joash decided to restore the house of the LORD. ⁵He assembled the priests and the Levites and said to them, "Go out to the cities of Judah and gather money from all Israel to repair the house of your God, year by year; and see that you act quickly." But the Levites did not act quickly. ⁶So the king summoned Jehoiada the chief, and said to him, "Why have you not required the Levites to bring in from Judah and Jerusalem the tax levied by Moses, the servant of the LORD, onˣ the congregation of Israel for the tent of the covenant?"ʸ ⁷For the children of Athaliah, that wicked woman, had broken into the house of God, and had even used all the dedicated things of the house of the LORD for the Baals.

8 So the king gave command, and they made a chest, and set it outside the gate of the house of the LORD. ⁹A proclamation was made throughout Judah and Jerusalem to bring in for the LORD the tax that Moses the servant of God laid on Israel in the wilderness. ¹⁰All the leaders and all the people rejoiced and brought their tax and dropped it into the chest until it was full. ¹¹Whenever the chest was brought to the king's officers by the Levites, when they saw that there was a large amount of money in it, the king's secretary and the officer of the chief priest would come and empty the chest and take it and return it to its place. So they did day after day, and collected money in abundance. ¹²The king and Jehoiada gave it to those who had charge of the work of the house of the LORD, and they hired masons and carpenters to restore the house of the LORD, and also workers in iron and bronze to repair the house of the LORD. ¹³So those who were engaged in the work labored, and the repairing went forward at their hands, and they restored the house of God to its proper condition and strengthened it. ¹⁴When they had finished, they brought the rest of the money to the king and Jehoiada, and with it were made utensils for the house of the LORD, utensils for the service and for the burnt offerings, and ladles, and vessels of gold and silver. They offered burnt offerings in the house of the LORD regularly all the days of Jehoiada.

Apostasy of Joash

15 But Jehoiada grew old and full of days, and died; he was one hundred thirty years old at his death. ¹⁶And they buried him in the city of David among the kings, because he had done good in Israel, and for God and his house.

17 Now after the death of Jehoiada the officials of Judah came and did obeisance to the king; then the king listened to them. ¹⁸They abandoned the house of the LORD, the God of their ancestors, and served the sacred polesᶻ and the idols. And wrath came upon Judah and Jerusalem for this guilt of theirs. ¹⁹Yet he sent prophets among them to bring them back to the LORD; they testified against them, but they would not listen.

20 Then the spirit of God took possession ofᵃ Zechariah son of the priest Jehoiada; he stood above the people and said to them, "Thus says God: Why do you transgress the commandments of the LORD, so that you cannot prosper? Because you have forsaken the LORD, he has also forsaken you." ²¹But they conspired against him, and by command of the king they stoned him to death in the court of the house of the LORD. ²²King Joash did not remember the kindness that Jehoiada, Zechariah's father, had shown him, but killed his son. As he was dying, he said, "May the LORD see and avenge!"

Death of Joash

23 At the end of the year the army of Aram came up against Joash. They came to Judah and Jerusalem, and destroyed all the officials of the people from among them, and sent all the booty they took to the king of Damascus. ²⁴Although the army of Aram had come with few men, the LORD delivered into their hand a very great army, because they had abandoned the LORD, the God of their ancestors. Thus they executed judgment on Joash.

25 When they had withdrawn, leaving him severely wounded, his servants con-

---

ˣ Compare Vg: Heb *and*   ʸ Or *treaty*, or *testimony*; Heb *eduth*   ᶻ Heb *Asherim*   ᵃ Heb *clothed itself with*

spired against him because of the blood of the son[b] of the priest Jehoiada, and they killed him on his bed. So he died; and they buried him in the city of David, but they did not bury him in the tombs of the kings. [26]Those who conspired against him were Zabad son of Shimeath the Ammonite, and Jehozabad son of Shimrith the Moabite. [27]Accounts of his sons, and of the many oracles against him, and of the rebuilding[c] of the house of God are written in the Commentary on the Book of the Kings. And his son Amaziah succeeded him.

Reign of Amaziah

25 Amaziah was twenty-five years old when he began to reign, and he reigned twenty-nine years in Jerusalem. His mother's name was Jehoaddan of Jerusalem. [2]He did what was right in the sight of the LORD, yet not with a true heart. [3]As soon as the royal power was firmly in his hand he killed his servants who had murdered his father the king. [4]But he did not put their children to death, according to what is written in the law, in the book of Moses, where the LORD commanded, "The parents shall not be put to death for the children, or the children be put to death for the parents; but all shall be put to death for their own sins."

Slaughter of the Edomites

5 Amaziah assembled the people of Judah, and set them by ancestral houses under commanders of the thousands and of the hundreds for all Judah and Benjamin. He mustered those twenty years old and upward, and found that they were three hundred thousand picked troops fit for war, able to handle spear and shield. [6]He also hired one hundred thousand mighty warriors from Israel for one hundred talents of silver. [7]But a man of God came to him and said, "O king, do not let the army of Israel go with you, for the LORD is not with Israel—all these Ephraimites. [8]Rather, go by yourself and act; be strong in battle, or God will fling you down before the enemy; for God has power to help or to overthrow." [9]Amaziah said to the man of God, "But what shall we do about the hundred talents that I have given to the army of Israel?" The man of God answered, "The LORD is able to give you much more than this." [10]Then Amaziah discharged the army that had come to him

from Ephraim, letting them go home again. But they became very angry with Judah, and returned home in fierce anger. [11]Amaziah took courage, and led out his people; he went to the Valley of Salt, and struck down ten thousand men of Seir. [12]The people of Judah captured another ten thousand alive, took them to the top of Sela, and threw them down from the top of Sela, so that all of them were dashed to pieces. [13]But the men of the army whom Amaziah sent back, not letting them go with him to battle, fell on the cities of Judah from Samaria to Beth-horon; they killed three thousand people in them, and took much booty.

14 Now after Amaziah came from the slaughter of the Edomites, he brought the gods of the people of Seir, set them up as his gods, and worshiped them, making offerings to them. [15]The LORD was angry with Amaziah and sent to him a prophet, who said to him, "Why have you resorted to a people's gods who could not deliver their own people from your hand?" [16]But as he was speaking the king[d] said to him, "Have we made you a royal counselor? Stop! Why should you be put to death?" So the prophet stopped, but said, "I know that God has determined to destroy you, because you have done this and have not listened to my advice."

Israel Defeats Judah

17 Then King Amaziah of Judah took counsel and sent to King Joash son of Jehoahaz son of Jehu of Israel, saying, "Come, let us look one another in the face." [18]King Joash of Israel sent word to King Amaziah of Judah, "A thornbush on Lebanon sent to a cedar on Lebanon, saying, 'Give your daughter to my son for a wife'; but a wild animal of Lebanon passed by and trampled down the thornbush. [19]You say, 'See, I have defeated Edom,' and your heart has lifted you up in boastfulness. Now stay at home; why should you provoke trouble so that you fall, you and Judah with you?" [20]But Amaziah would not listen—it was God's doing, in order to hand them over, because they had sought the gods of Edom. [21]So King Joash of Israel went up; he and King Amaziah of Judah faced one another in battle at Beth-shemesh, which belongs to Judah. [22]Judah was defeated by

b Gk Vg: Heb *sons*   c Heb *founding*   d Heb *he*

Israel; everyone fled home. ²³King Joash of Israel captured King Amaziah of Judah, son of Joash, son of Ahaziah, at Beth-shemesh; he brought him to Jerusalem, and broke down the wall of Jerusalem from the Ephraim Gate to the Corner Gate, a distance of four hundred cubits. ²⁴He seized all the gold and silver, and all the vessels that were found in the house of God, and Obed-edom with them; he seized also the treasuries of the king's house, also hostages; then he returned to Samaria.

Death of Amaziah

25 King Amaziah son of Joash of Judah, lived fifteen years after the death of King Joash son of Jehoahaz of Israel. ²⁶Now the rest of the deeds of Amaziah, from first to last, are they not written in the Book of the Kings of Judah and Israel? ²⁷From the time that Amaziah turned away from the LORD they made a conspiracy against him in Jerusalem, and he fled to Lachish. But they sent after him to Lachish, and killed him there. ²⁸They brought him back on horses; he was buried with his ancestors in the city of David.

Reign of Uzziah

26 Then all the people of Judah took Uzziah, who was sixteen years old, and made him king to succeed his father Amaziah. ²He rebuilt Eloth and restored it to Judah, after the king slept with his ancestors. ³Uzziah was sixteen years old when he began to reign, and he reigned fifty-two years in Jerusalem. His mother's name was Jecoliah of Jerusalem. ⁴He did what was right in the sight of the LORD, just as his father Amaziah had done. ⁵He set himself to seek God in the days of Zechariah, who instructed him in the fear of God; and as long as he sought the LORD, God made him prosper.

6 He went out and made war against the Philistines, and broke down the wall of Gath and the wall of Jabneh and the wall of Ashdod; he built cities in the territory of Ashdod and elsewhere among the Philistines. ⁷God helped him against the Philistines, against the Arabs who lived in Gur-baal, and against the Meunites. ⁸The Ammonites paid tribute to Uzziah, and his fame spread even to the border of Egypt, for he became very strong. ⁹Moreover Uzziah built towers in Jerusalem at the Corner Gate, at the Valley Gate, and at the Angle, and fortified them. ¹⁰He built towers in the wilderness and hewed out many cisterns, for he had large herds, both in the Shephelah and in the plain, and he had farmers and vinedressers in the hills and in the fertile lands, for he loved the soil. ¹¹Moreover Uzziah had an army of soldiers, fit for war, in divisions according to the numbers in the muster made by the secretary Jeiel and the officer Maaseiah, under the direction of Hananiah, one of the king's commanders. ¹²The whole number of the heads of ancestral houses of mighty warriors was two thousand six hundred. ¹³Under their command was an army of three hundred seven thousand five hundred, who could make war with mighty power, to help the king against the enemy. ¹⁴Uzziah provided for all the army the shields, spears, helmets, coats of mail, bows, and stones for slinging. ¹⁵In Jerusalem he set up machines, invented by skilled workers, on the towers and the corners for shooting arrows and large stones. And his fame spread far, for he was marvelously helped until he became strong.

Pride and Apostasy

16 But when he had become strong he grew proud, to his destruction. For he was false to the LORD his God, and entered the temple of the LORD to make offering on the altar of incense. ¹⁷But the priest Azariah went in after him, with eighty priests of the LORD who were men of valor; ¹⁸they withstood King Uzziah, and said to him, "It is not for you, Uzziah, to make offering to the LORD, but for the priests the descendants of Aaron, who are consecrated to make offering. Go out of the sanctuary; for you have done wrong, and it will bring you no honor from the LORD God." ¹⁹Then Uzziah was angry. Now he had a censer in his hand to make offering, and when he became angry with the priests a leprous*ᵉ* disease broke out on his forehead, in the presence of the priests in the house of the LORD, by the altar of incense. ²⁰When the chief priest Azariah, and all the priests, looked at him, he was leprous*ᵉ* in his forehead. They hurried him out, and he himself hurried to get out, because the LORD had struck him. ²¹King Uzziah was leprous*ᵉ* to the day of his death, and be-

ᵉ A term for several skin diseases; precise meaning uncertain

ing leprous f lived in a separate house, for he was excluded from the house of the LORD. His son Jotham was in charge of the palace of the king, governing the people of the land.

22 Now the rest of the acts of Uzziah, from first to last, the prophet Isaiah son of Amoz wrote. 23Uzziah slept with his ancestors; they buried him near his ancestors in the burial field that belonged to the kings, for they said, "He is leprous." f His son Jotham succeeded him.

Reign of Jotham

27 Jotham was twenty-five years old when he began to reign; he reigned sixteen years in Jerusalem. His mother's name was Jerushah daughter of Zadok. 2He did what was right in the sight of the LORD just as his father Uzziah had done—only he did not invade the temple of the LORD. But the people still followed corrupt practices. 3He built the upper gate of the house of the LORD, and did extensive building on the wall of Ophel. 4Moreover he built cities in the hill country of Judah, and forts and towers on the wooded hills. 5He fought with the king of the Ammonites and prevailed against them. The Ammonites gave him that year one hundred talents of silver, ten thousand cors of wheat and ten thousand of barley. The Ammonites paid him the same amount in the second and the third years. 6So Jotham became strong because he ordered his ways before the LORD his God. 7Now the rest of the acts of Jotham, and all his wars and his ways, are written in the Book of the Kings of Israel and Judah. 8He was twenty-five years old when he began to reign; he reigned sixteen years in Jerusalem. 9Jotham slept with his ancestors, and they buried him in the city of David; and his son Ahaz succeeded him.

Reign of Ahaz

28 Ahaz was twenty years old when he began to reign; he reigned sixteen years in Jerusalem. He did not do what was right in the sight of the LORD, as his ancestor David had done, 2but he walked in the ways of the kings of Israel. He even made cast images for the Baals; 3and he made offerings in the valley of the son of Hinnom, and made his sons pass through fire, according to the abominable practices of the nations whom the LORD drove out before the people of Israel. 4He

sacrificed and made offerings on the high places, on the hills, and under every green tree.

Aram and Israel Defeat Judah

5 Therefore the LORD his God gave him into the hand of the king of Aram, who defeated him and took captive a great number of his people and brought them to Damascus. He was also given into the hand of the king of Israel, who defeated him with great slaughter. 6Pekah son of Remaliah killed one hundred twenty thousand in Judah in one day, all of them valiant warriors, because they had abandoned the LORD, the God of their ancestors. 7And Zichri, a mighty warrior of Ephraim, killed the king's son Maaseiah, Azrikam the commander of the palace, and Elkanah the next in authority to the king.

Intervention of Oded

8 The people of Israel took captive two hundred thousand of their kin, women, sons, and daughters; they also took much booty from them and brought the booty to Samaria. 9But a prophet of the LORD was there, whose name was Oded; he went out to meet the army that came to Samaria, and said to them, "Because the LORD, the God of your ancestors, was angry with Judah, he gave them into your hand, but you have killed them in a rage that has reached up to heaven. 10Now you intend to subjugate the people of Judah and Jerusalem, male and female, as your slaves. But what have you except sins against the LORD your God? 11Now hear me, and send back the captives whom you have taken from your kindred, for the fierce wrath of the LORD is upon you." 12Moreover, certain chiefs of the Ephraimites, Azariah son of Johanan, Berechiah son of Meshillemoth, Jehizkiah son of Shallum, and Amasa son of Hadlai, stood up against those who were coming from the war, 13and said to them, "You shall not bring the captives in here, for you propose to bring on us guilt against the LORD in addition to our present sins and guilt. For our guilt is already great, and there is fierce wrath against Israel." 14So the warriors left the captives and the booty before the officials and all the assembly. 15Then those who were men-

---

f A term for several skin diseases; precise meaning uncertain

tioned by name got up and took the captives, and with the booty they clothed all that were naked among them; they clothed them, gave them sandals, provided them with food and drink, and anointed them; and carrying all the feeble among them on donkeys, they brought them to their kindred at Jericho, the city of palm trees. Then they returned to Samaria.

Assyria Refuses to Help Judah

16 At that time King Ahaz sent to the king*g* of Assyria for help. 17For the Edomites had again invaded and defeated Judah, and carried away captives. 18And the Philistines had made raids on the cities in the Shephelah and the Negeb of Judah, and had taken Beth-shemesh, Aijalon, Gederoth, Soco with its villages, Timnah with its villages, and Gimzo with its villages; and they settled there. 19For the LORD brought Judah low because of King Ahaz of Israel, for he had behaved without restraint in Judah and had been faithless to the LORD. 20So King Tilgath-pilneser of Assyria came against him, and oppressed him instead of strengthening him. 21For Ahaz plundered the house of the LORD and the houses of the king and of the officials, and gave tribute to the king of Assyria; but it did not help him.

Apostasy and Death of Ahaz

22 In the time of his distress he became yet more faithless to the LORD—this same King Ahaz. 23For he sacrificed to the gods of Damascus, which had defeated him, and said, "Because the gods of the kings of Aram helped them, I will sacrifice to them so that they may help me." But they were the ruin of him, and of all Israel. 24Ahaz gathered together the utensils of the house of God, and cut in pieces the utensils of the house of God. He shut up the doors of the house of the LORD and made himself altars in every corner of Jerusalem. 25In every city of Judah he made high places to make offerings to other gods, provoking to anger the LORD, the God of his ancestors. 26Now the rest of his acts and all his ways, from first to last, are written in the Book of the Kings of Judah and Israel. 27Ahaz slept with his ancestors, and they buried him in the city, in Jerusalem; but they did not bring him into the tombs of the kings of Israel. His son Hezekiah succeeded him.

Reign of Hezekiah

29 Hezekiah began to reign when he was twenty-five years old; he reigned twenty-nine years in Jerusalem. His mother's name was Abijah daughter of Zechariah. 2He did what was right in the sight of the LORD, just as his ancestor David had done.

The Temple Cleansed

3 In the first year of his reign, in the first month, he opened the doors of the house of the LORD and repaired them. 4He brought in the priests and the Levites and assembled them in the square on the east. 5He said to them, "Listen to me, Levites! Sanctify yourselves, and sanctify the house of the LORD, the God of your ancestors, and carry out the filth from the holy place. 6For our ancestors have been unfaithful and have done what was evil in the sight of the LORD our God; they have forsaken him, and have turned away their faces from the dwelling of the LORD, and turned their backs. 7They also shut the doors of the vestibule and put out the lamps, and have not offered incense or made burnt offerings in the holy place to the God of Israel. 8Therefore the wrath of the LORD came upon Judah and Jerusalem, and he has made them an object of horror, of astonishment, and of hissing, as you see with your own eyes. 9Our fathers have fallen by the sword and our sons and our daughters and our wives are in captivity for this. 10Now it is in my heart to make a covenant with the LORD, the God of Israel, so that his fierce anger may turn away from us. 11My sons, do not now be negligent, for the LORD has chosen you to stand in his presence to minister to him, and to be his ministers and make offerings to him."

12 Then the Levites arose, Mahath son of Amasai, and Joel son of Azariah, of the sons of the Kohathites; and of the sons of Merari, Kish son of Abdi, and Azariah son of Jehallelel; and of the Gershonites, Joah son of Zimmah, and Eden son of Joah; 13and of the sons of Elizaphan, Shimri and Jeuel; and of the sons of Asaph, Zechariah and Mattaniah; 14and of the sons of Heman, Jehuel and Shimei; and of the sons of Jeduthun, Shemaiah and Uzziel. 15They gathered their brothers, sanctified

g Gk Syr Vg Compare 2 Kings 16.7: Heb *kings*

themselves, and went in as the king had commanded, by the words of the LORD, to cleanse the house of the LORD. [16]The priests went into the inner part of the house of the LORD to cleanse it, and they brought out all the unclean things that they found in the temple of the LORD into the court of the house of the LORD; and the Levites took them and carried them out to the Wadi Kidron. [17]They began to sanctify on the first day of the first month, and on the eighth day of the month they came to the vestibule of the LORD; then for eight days they sanctified the house of the LORD, and on the sixteenth day of the first month they finished. [18]Then they went inside to King Hezekiah and said, "We have cleansed all the house of the LORD, the altar of burnt offering and all its utensils, and the table for the rows of bread and all its utensils. [19]All the utensils that King Ahaz repudiated during his reign when he was faithless, we have made ready and sanctified; see, they are in front of the altar of the LORD."

Temple Worship Restored

20 Then King Hezekiah rose early, assembled the officials of the city, and went up to the house of the LORD. [21]They brought seven bulls, seven rams, seven lambs, and seven male goats for a sin offering for the kingdom and for the sanctuary and for Judah. He commanded the priests the descendants of Aaron to offer them on the altar of the LORD. [22]So they slaughtered the bulls, and the priests received the blood and dashed it against the altar; they slaughtered the rams and their blood was dashed against the altar; they also slaughtered the lambs and their blood was dashed against the altar. [23]Then the male goats for the sin offering were brought to the king and the assembly; they laid their hands on them, [24]and the priests slaughtered them and made a sin offering with their blood at the altar, to make atonement for all Israel. For the king commanded that the burnt offering and the sin offering should be made for all Israel.

25 He stationed the Levites in the house of the LORD with cymbals, harps, and lyres, according to the commandment of David and of Gad the king's seer and of the prophet Nathan, for the commandment was from the LORD through his prophets. [26]The Levites stood with the in-

struments of David, and the priests with the trumpets. [27]Then Hezekiah commanded that the burnt offering be offered on the altar. When the burnt offering began, the song to the LORD began also, and the trumpets, accompanied by the instruments of King David of Israel. [28]The whole assembly worshiped, the singers sang, and the trumpeters sounded; all this continued until the burnt offering was finished. [29]When the offering was finished, the king and all who were present with him bowed down and worshiped. [30]King Hezekiah and the officials commanded the Levites to sing praises to the LORD with the words of David and of the seer Asaph. They sang praises with gladness, and they bowed down and worshiped.

31 Then Hezekiah said, "You have now consecrated yourselves to the LORD; come near, bring sacrifices and thank offerings to the house of the LORD." The assembly brought sacrifices and thank offerings; and all who were of a willing heart brought burnt offerings. [32]The number of the burnt offerings that the assembly brought was seventy bulls, one hundred rams, and two hundred lambs; all these were for a burnt offering to the LORD. [33]The consecrated offerings were six hundred bulls and three thousand sheep. [34]But the priests were too few and could not skin all the burnt offerings, so, until other priests had sanctified themselves, their kindred, the Levites, helped them until the work was finished—for the Levites were more conscientious[h] than the priests in sanctifying themselves. [35]Besides the great number of burnt offerings there was the fat of the offerings of well-being, and there were the drink offerings for the burnt offerings. Thus the service of the house of the LORD was restored. [36]And Hezekiah and all the people rejoiced because of what God had done for the people; for the thing had come about suddenly.

The Great Passover

30 Hezekiah sent word to all Israel and Judah, and wrote letters also to Ephraim and Manasseh, that they should come to the house of the LORD at Jerusalem, to keep the passover to the LORD the God of Israel. [2]For the king and his officials and all the assembly in Jerusa-

h Heb *upright in heart*

lem had taken counsel to keep the passover in the second month ³(for they could not keep it at its proper time because the priests had not sanctified themselves in sufficient number, nor had the people assembled in Jerusalem). ⁴The plan seemed right to the king and all the assembly. ⁵So they decreed to make a proclamation throughout all Israel, from Beer-sheba to Dan, that the people should come and keep the passover to the LORD the God of Israel, at Jerusalem; for they had not kept it in great numbers as prescribed. ⁶So couriers went throughout all Israel and Judah with letters from the king and his officials, as the king had commanded, saying, "O people of Israel, return to the LORD, the God of Abraham, Isaac, and Israel, so that he may turn again to the remnant of you who have escaped from the hand of the kings of Assyria. ⁷Do not be like your ancestors and your kindred, who were faithless to the LORD God of their ancestors, so that he made them a desolation, as you see. ⁸Do not now be stiff-necked as your ancestors were, but yield yourselves to the LORD and come to his sanctuary, which he has sanctified forever, and serve the LORD your God, so that his fierce anger may turn away from you. ⁹For as you return to the LORD, your kindred and your children will find compassion with their captors, and return to this land. For the LORD your God is gracious and merciful, and will not turn away his face from you, if you return to him."

10 So the couriers went from city to city through the country of Ephraim and Manasseh, and as far as Zebulun; but they laughed them to scorn, and mocked them. ¹¹Only a few from Asher, Manasseh, and Zebulun humbled themselves and came to Jerusalem. ¹²The hand of God was also on Judah to give them one heart to do what the king and the officials commanded by the word of the LORD.

13 Many people came together in Jerusalem to keep the festival of unleavened bread in the second month, a very large assembly. ¹⁴They set to work and removed the altars that were in Jerusalem, and all the altars for offering incense they took away and threw into the Wadi Kidron. ¹⁵They slaughtered the passover lamb on the fourteenth day of the second month. The priests and the Levites were ashamed, and they sanctified themselves and brought burnt offerings into the house of

the LORD. ¹⁶They took their accustomed posts according to the law of Moses the man of God; the priests dashed the blood that they received[i] from the hands of the Levites. ¹⁷For there were many in the assembly who had not sanctified themselves; therefore the Levites had to slaughter the passover lamb for everyone who was not clean, to make it holy to the LORD. ¹⁸For a multitude of the people, many of them from Ephraim, Manasseh, Issachar, and Zebulun, had not cleansed themselves, yet they ate the passover otherwise than as prescribed. But Hezekiah prayed for them, saying, "The good LORD pardon all ¹⁹who set their hearts to seek God, the LORD the God of their ancestors, even though not in accordance with the sanctuary's rules of cleanness." ²⁰The LORD heard Hezekiah, and healed the people. ²¹The people of Israel who were present at Jerusalem kept the festival of unleavened bread seven days with great gladness; and the Levites and the priests praised the LORD day by day, accompanied by loud instruments for the LORD. ²²Hezekiah spoke encouragingly to all the Levites who showed good skill in the service of the LORD. So the people ate the food of the festival for seven days, sacrificing offerings of well-being and giving thanks to the LORD the God of their ancestors.

23 Then the whole assembly agreed together to keep the festival for another seven days; so they kept it for another seven days with gladness. ²⁴For King Hezekiah of Judah gave the assembly a thousand bulls and seven thousand sheep for offerings, and the officials gave the assembly a thousand bulls and ten thousand sheep. The priests sanctified themselves in great numbers. ²⁵The whole assembly of Judah, the priests and the Levites, and the whole assembly that came out of Israel, and the resident aliens who came out of the land of Israel, and the resident aliens who lived in Judah, rejoiced. ²⁶There was great joy in Jerusalem, for since the time of Solomon son of King David of Israel there had been nothing like this in Jerusalem. ²⁷Then the priests and the Levites stood up and blessed the people, and their voice was heard; their prayer came to his holy dwelling in heaven.

---

i Heb lacks *that they received*

Pagan Shrines Destroyed

31 Now when all this was finished, all Israel who were present went out to the cities of Judah and broke down the pillars, hewed down the sacred poles,[j] and pulled down the high places and the altars throughout all Judah and Benjamin, and in Ephraim and Manasseh, until they had destroyed them all. Then all the people of Israel returned to their cities, all to their individual properties.

2 Hezekiah appointed the divisions of the priests and of the Levites, division by division, everyone according to his service, the priests and the Levites, for burnt offerings and offerings of well-being, to minister in the gates of the camp of the LORD and to give thanks and praise. 3The contribution of the king from his own possessions was for the burnt offerings: the burnt offerings of morning and evening, and the burnt offerings for the sabbaths, the new moons, and the appointed festivals, as it is written in the law of the LORD. 4He commanded the people who lived in Jerusalem to give the portion due to the priests and the Levites, so that they might devote themselves to the law of the LORD. 5As soon as the word spread, the people of Israel gave in abundance the first fruits of grain, wine, oil, honey, and of all the produce of the field; and they brought in abundantly the tithe of everything. 6The people of Israel and Judah who lived in the cities of Judah also brought in the tithe of cattle and sheep, and the tithe of the dedicated things that had been consecrated to the LORD their God, and laid them in heaps. 7In the third month they began to pile up the heaps, and finished them in the seventh month. 8When Hezekiah and the officials came and saw the heaps, they blessed the LORD and his people Israel. 9Hezekiah questioned the priests and the Levites about the heaps. 10The chief priest Azariah, who was of the house of Zadok, answered him, "Since they began to bring the contributions into the house of the LORD, we have had enough to eat and have plenty to spare; for the LORD has blessed his people, so that we have this great supply left over."

Reorganization of Priests and Levites

11 Then Hezekiah commanded them to prepare store-chambers in the house of the LORD; and they prepared them. 12Faithfully they brought in the contributions, the tithes and the dedicated things. The chief officer in charge of them was Conaniah the Levite, with his brother Shimei as second; 13while Jehiel, Azaziah, Nahath, Asahel, Jerimoth, Jozabad, Eliel, Ismachiah, Mahath, and Benaiah were overseers assisting Conaniah and his brother Shimei, by the appointment of King Hezekiah and of Azariah the chief officer of the house of God. 14Kore son of Imnah the Levite, keeper of the east gate, was in charge of the freewill offerings to God, to apportion the contribution reserved for the LORD and the most holy offerings. 15Eden, Miniamin, Jeshua, Shemaiah, Amariah, and Shecaniah were faithfully assisting him in the cities of the priests, to distribute the portions to their kindred, old and young alike, by divisions, 16except those enrolled by genealogy, males from three years old and upwards, all who entered the house of the LORD as the duty of each day required, for their service according to their offices, by their divisions. 17The enrollment of the priests was according to their ancestral houses; that of the Levites from twenty years old and upwards was according to their offices, by their divisions. 18The priests were enrolled with all their little children, their wives, their sons, and their daughters, the whole multitude; for they were faithful in keeping themselves holy. 19And for the descendants of Aaron, the priests, who were in the fields of common land belonging to their towns, town by town, the people designated by name were to distribute portions to every male among the priests and to everyone among the Levites who was enrolled.

20 Hezekiah did this throughout all Judah; he did what was good and right and faithful before the LORD his God. 21And every work that he undertook in the service of the house of God, and in accordance with the law and the commandments, to seek his God, he did with all his heart; and he prospered.

Sennacherib's Invasion

32 After these things and these acts of faithfulness, King Sennacherib of Assyria came and invaded Judah and encamped against the fortified cities, thinking to win them for himself. 2When

j Heb Asherim

Hezekiah saw that Sennacherib had come and intended to fight against Jerusalem, [3]he planned with his officers and his warriors to stop the flow of the springs that were outside the city; and they helped him. [4]A great many people were gathered, and they stopped all the springs and the wadi that flowed through the land, saying, "Why should the Assyrian kings come and find water in abundance?" [5]Hezekiah[k] set to work resolutely and built up the entire wall that was broken down, and raised towers on it,[l] and outside it he built another wall; he also strengthened the Millo in the city of David, and made weapons and shields in abundance. [6]He appointed combat commanders over the people, and gathered them together to him in the square at the gate of the city and spoke encouragingly to them, saying, [7]"Be strong and of good courage. Do not be afraid or dismayed before the king of Assyria and all the horde that is with him; for there is one greater with us than with him. [8]With him is an arm of flesh; but with us is the LORD our God, to help us and to fight our battles." The people were encouraged by the words of King Hezekiah of Judah.

[9] After this, while King Sennacherib of Assyria was at Lachish with all his forces, he sent his servants to Jerusalem to King Hezekiah of Judah and to all the people of Judah that were in Jerusalem, saying, [10]"Thus says King Sennacherib of Assyria: On what are you relying, that you undergo the siege of Jerusalem? [11]Is not Hezekiah misleading you, handing you over to die by famine and by thirst, when he tells you, 'The LORD our God will save us from the hand of the king of Assyria'? [12]Was it not this same Hezekiah who took away his high places and his altars and commanded Judah and Jerusalem, saying, 'Before one altar you shall worship, and upon it you shall make your offerings'? [13]Do you not know what I and my ancestors have done to all the peoples of other lands? Were the gods of the nations of those lands at all able to save their lands out of my hand? [14]Who among all the gods of those nations that my ancestors utterly destroyed was able to save his people from my hand, that your God should be able to save you from my hand? [15]Now therefore do not let Hezekiah deceive you or mislead you in this fashion, and do not believe him, for no god of any nation or kingdom has been able to save his people from my hand or from the hand of my ancestors. How much less will your God save you out of my hand!"

16 His servants said still more against the Lord GOD and against his servant Hezekiah. [17]He also wrote letters to throw contempt on the LORD the God of Israel and to speak against him, saying, "Just as the gods of the nations in other lands did not rescue their people from my hands, so the God of Hezekiah will not rescue his people from my hand." [18]They shouted it with a loud voice in the language of Judah to the people of Jerusalem who were on the wall, to frighten and terrify them, in order that they might take the city. [19]They spoke of the God of Jerusalem as if he were like the gods of the peoples of the earth, which are the work of human hands.

Sennacherib's Defeat and Death

20 Then King Hezekiah and the prophet Isaiah son of Amoz prayed because of this and cried to heaven. [21]And the LORD sent an angel who cut off all the mighty warriors and commanders and officers in the camp of the king of Assyria. So he returned in disgrace to his own land. When he came into the house of his god, some of his own sons struck him down there with the sword. [22]So the LORD saved Hezekiah and the inhabitants of Jerusalem from the hand of King Sennacherib of Assyria and from the hand of all his enemies; he gave them rest[m] on every side. [23]Many brought gifts to the LORD in Jerusalem and precious things to King Hezekiah of Judah, so that he was exalted in the sight of all nations from that time onward.

Hezekiah's Sickness

24 In those days Hezekiah became sick and was at the point of death. He prayed to the LORD, and he answered him and gave him a sign. [25]But Hezekiah did not respond according to the benefit done to him, for his heart was proud. Therefore wrath came upon him and upon Judah and Jerusalem. [26]Then Hezekiah humbled himself for the pride of his heart, both he and the inhabitants of Jerusalem, so that

---

[k] Heb *He*   [l] Vg: Heb *and raised on the towers*
[m] Gk Vg: Heb *guided them*

the wrath of the Lord did not come upon them in the days of Hezekiah.

Hezekiah's Prosperity and Achievements

27 Hezekiah had very great riches and honor; and he made for himself treasuries for silver, for gold, for precious stones, for spices, for shields, and for all kinds of costly objects; 28storehouses also for the yield of grain, wine, and oil; and stalls for all kinds of cattle, and sheepfolds.[n] 29He likewise provided cities for himself, and flocks and herds in abundance; for God had given him very great possessions. 30This same Hezekiah closed the upper outlet of the waters of Gihon and directed them down to the west side of the city of David. Hezekiah prospered in all his works. 31So also in the matter of the envoys of the officials of Babylon, who had been sent to him to inquire about the sign that had been done in the land, God left him to himself, in order to test him and to know all that was in his heart.

32 Now the rest of the acts of Hezekiah, and his good deeds, are written in the vision of the prophet Isaiah son of Amoz in the Book of the Kings of Judah and Israel. 33Hezekiah slept with his ancestors, and they buried him on the ascent to the tombs of the descendants of David; and all Judah and the inhabitants of Jerusalem did him honor at his death. His son Manasseh succeeded him.

Reign of Manasseh

33 Manasseh was twelve years old when he began to reign; he reigned fifty-five years in Jerusalem. 2He did what was evil in the sight of the Lord, according to the abominable practices of the nations whom the Lord drove out before the people of Israel. 3For he rebuilt the high places that his father Hezekiah had pulled down, and erected altars to the Baals, made sacred poles,[o] worshiped all the host of heaven, and served them. 4He built altars in the house of the Lord, of which the Lord had said, "In Jerusalem shall my name be forever." 5He built altars for all the host of heaven in the two courts of the house of the Lord. 6He made his son pass through fire in the valley of the son of Hinnom, practiced soothsaying and augury and sorcery, and dealt with mediums and with wizards. He did much evil in the sight of the Lord, provoking him to anger. 7The carved image of the idol that he had made he set in the house of God, of which God said to David and to his son Solomon, "In this house, and in Jerusalem, which I have chosen out of all the tribes of Israel, I will put my name forever; 8I will never again remove the feet of Israel from the land that I appointed for your ancestors, if only they will be careful to do all that I have commanded them, all the law, the statutes, and the ordinances given through Moses." 9Manasseh misled Judah and the inhabitants of Jerusalem, so that they did more evil than the nations whom the Lord had destroyed before the people of Israel.

Manasseh Restored after Repentance

10 The Lord spoke to Manasseh and to his people, but they gave no heed. 11Therefore the Lord brought against them the commanders of the army of the king of Assyria, who took Manasseh captive in manacles, bound him with fetters, and brought him to Babylon. 12While he was in distress he entreated the favor of the Lord his God and humbled himself greatly before the God of his ancestors. 13He prayed to him, and God received his entreaty, heard his plea, and restored him again to Jerusalem and to his kingdom. Then Manasseh knew that the Lord indeed was God.

14 Afterward he built an outer wall for the city of David west of Gihon, in the valley, reaching the entrance at the Fish Gate; he carried it around Ophel, and raised it to a very great height. He also put commanders of the army in all the fortified cities in Judah. 15He took away the foreign gods and the idol from the house of the Lord, and all the altars that he had built on the mountain of the house of the Lord and in Jerusalem, and he threw them out of the city. 16He also restored the altar of the Lord and offered on it sacrifices of well-being and of thanksgiving; and he commanded Judah to serve the Lord the God of Israel. 17The people, however, still sacrificed at the high places, but only to the Lord their God.

Death of Manasseh

18 Now the rest of the acts of Manasseh, his prayer to his God, and the words of the seers who spoke to him in the name of the Lord God of Israel, these are in the

[n] Gk Vg: Heb *flocks for folds*　[o] Heb *Asheroth*

Annals of the Kings of Israel. ¹⁹His prayer, and how God received his entreaty, all his sin and his faithlessness, the sites on which he built high places and set up the sacred poles*p* and the images, before he humbled himself, these are written in the records of the seers.*q* ²⁰So Manasseh slept with his ancestors, and they buried him in his house. His son Amon succeeded him.

Amon's Reign and Death

21 Amon was twenty-two years old when he began to reign; he reigned two years in Jerusalem. ²²He did what was evil in the sight of the LORD, as his father Manasseh had done. Amon sacrificed to all the images that his father Manasseh had made, and served them. ²³He did not humble himself before the LORD, as his father Manasseh had humbled himself, but this Amon incurred more and more guilt. ²⁴His servants conspired against him and killed him in his house. ²⁵But the people of the land killed all those who had conspired against King Amon; and the people of the land made his son Josiah king to succeed him.

Reign of Josiah

34 Josiah was eight years old when he began to reign; he reigned thirty-one years in Jerusalem. ²He did what was right in the sight of the LORD, and walked in the ways of his ancestor David; he did not turn aside to the right or to the left. ³For in the eighth year of his reign, while he was still a boy, he began to seek the God of his ancestor David, and in the twelfth year he began to purge Judah and Jerusalem of the high places, the sacred poles,*p* and the carved and the cast images. ⁴In his presence they pulled down the altars of the Baals; he demolished the incense altars that stood above them. He broke down the sacred poles*p* and the carved and the cast images; he made dust of them and scattered it over the graves of those who had sacrificed to them. ⁵He also burned the bones of the priests on their altars, and purged Judah and Jerusalem. ⁶In the towns of Manasseh, Ephraim, and Simeon, and as far as Naphtali, in their ruins*r* all around, ⁷he broke down the altars, beat the sacred poles*p* and the images into powder, and demolished all the incense altars throughout all the land of Israel. Then he returned to Jerusalem.

Discovery of the Book of the Law

8 In the eighteenth year of his reign, when he had purged the land and the house, he sent Shaphan son of Azaliah, Maaseiah the governor of the city, and Joah son of Joahaz, the recorder, to repair the house of the LORD his God. ⁹They came to the high priest Hilkiah and delivered the money that had been brought into the house of God, which the Levites, the keepers of the threshold, had collected from Manasseh and Ephraim and from all the remnant of Israel and from all Judah and Benjamin and from the inhabitants of Jerusalem. ¹⁰They delivered it to the workers who had the oversight of the house of the LORD, and the workers who were working in the house of the LORD gave it for repairing and restoring the house. ¹¹They gave it to the carpenters and the builders to buy quarried stone, and timber for binders, and beams for the buildings that the kings of Judah had let go to ruin. ¹²The people did the work faithfully. Over them were appointed the Levites Jahath and Obadiah, of the sons of Merari, along with Zechariah and Meshullam, of the sons of the Kohathites, to have oversight. Other Levites, all skillful with instruments of music, ¹³were over the burden bearers and directed all who did work in every kind of service; and some of the Levites were scribes, and officials, and gatekeepers.

14 While they were bringing out the money that had been brought into the house of the LORD, the priest Hilkiah found the book of the law of the LORD given through Moses. ¹⁵Hilkiah said to the secretary Shaphan, "I have found the book of the law in the house of the LORD"; and Hilkiah gave the book to Shaphan. ¹⁶Shaphan brought the book to the king, and further reported to the king, "All that was committed to your servants they are doing. ¹⁷They have emptied out the money that was found in the house of the LORD and have delivered it into the hand of the overseers and the workers." ¹⁸The secretary Shaphan informed the king, "The priest Hilkiah has given me a book." Shaphan then read it aloud to the king.

19 When the king heard the words of the law he tore his clothes. ²⁰Then the

---

p Heb *Asherim*   *q* One Ms Gk: MT *of Hozai*
r Meaning of Heb uncertain

king commanded Hilkiah, Ahikam son of Shaphan, Abdon son of Micah, the secretary Shaphan, and the king's servant Asaiah: ²¹"Go, inquire of the LORD for me and for those who are left in Israel and in Judah, concerning the words of the book that has been found; for the wrath of the LORD that is poured out on us is great, because our ancestors did not keep the word of the LORD, to act in accordance with all that is written in this book."

The Prophet Huldah Consulted

22 So Hilkiah and those whom the king had sent went to the prophet Huldah, the wife of Shallum son of Tokhath son of Hasrah, keeper of the wardrobe (who lived in Jerusalem in the Second Quarter) and spoke to her to that effect. ²³She declared to them, "Thus says the LORD, the God of Israel: Tell the man who sent you to me, ²⁴Thus says the LORD: I will indeed bring disaster upon this place and upon its inhabitants, all the curses that are written in the book that was read before the king of Judah. ²⁵Because they have forsaken me and have made offerings to other gods, so that they have provoked me to anger with all the works of their hands, my wrath will be poured out on this place and will not be quenched. ²⁶But as to the king of Judah, who sent you to inquire of the LORD, thus shall you say to him: Thus says the LORD, the God of Israel: Regarding the words that you have heard, ²⁷because your heart was penitent and you humbled yourself before God when you heard his words against this place and its inhabitants, and you have humbled yourself before me, and have torn your clothes and wept before me, I also have heard you, says the LORD. ²⁸I will gather you to your ancestors and you shall be gathered to your grave in peace; your eyes shall not see all the disaster that I will bring on this place and its inhabitants." They took the message back to the king.

The Covenant Renewed

29 Then the king sent word and gathered together all the elders of Judah and Jerusalem. ³⁰The king went up to the house of the LORD, with all the people of Judah, the inhabitants of Jerusalem, the priests and the Levites, all the people both great and small; he read in their hearing all the words of the book of the covenant that had been found in the house of the LORD. ³¹The king stood in his place and made a covenant before the LORD, to follow the LORD, keeping his commandments, his decrees, and his statutes, with all his heart and all his soul, to perform the words of the covenant that were written in this book. ³²Then he made all who were present in Jerusalem and in Benjamin pledge themselves to it. And the inhabitants of Jerusalem acted according to the covenant of God, the God of their ancestors. ³³Josiah took away all the abominations from all the territory that belonged to the people of Israel, and made all who were in Israel worship the LORD their God. All his days they did not turn away from following the LORD the God of their ancestors.

Celebration of the Passover

35 Josiah kept a passover to the LORD in Jerusalem; they slaughtered the passover lamb on the fourteenth day of the first month. ²He appointed the priests to their offices and encouraged them in the service of the house of the LORD. ³He said to the Levites who taught all Israel and who were holy to the LORD, "Put the holy ark in the house that Solomon son of David, king of Israel, built; you need no longer carry it on your shoulders. Now serve the LORD your God and his people Israel. ⁴Make preparations by your ancestral houses by your divisions, following the written directions of King David of Israel and the written directions of his son Solomon. ⁵Take position in the holy place according to the groupings of the ancestral houses of your kindred the people, and let there be Levites for each division of an ancestral house.ˢ ⁶Slaughter the passover lamb, sanctify yourselves, and on behalf of your kindred make preparations, acting according to the word of the LORD by Moses."

7 Then Josiah contributed to the people, as passover offerings for all that were present, lambs and kids from the flock to the number of thirty thousand, and three thousand bulls; these were from the king's possessions. ⁸His officials contributed willingly to the people, to the priests, and to the Levites. Hilkiah, Zechariah, and Jehiel, the chief officers of the house of

ˢ Meaning of Heb uncertain

God, gave to the priests for the passover offerings two thousand six hundred lambs and kids and three hundred bulls. 9Conaniah also, and his brothers Shemaiah and Nethanel, and Hashabiah and Jeiel and Jozabad, the chiefs of the Levites, gave to the Levites for the passover offerings five thousand lambs and kids and five hundred bulls.

10 When the service had been prepared for, the priests stood in their place, and the Levites in their divisions according to the king's command. 11They slaughtered the passover lamb, and the priests dashed the blood that they received[t] from them, while the Levites did the skinning. 12They set aside the burnt offerings so that they might distribute them according to the groupings of the ancestral houses of the people, to offer to the LORD, as it is written in the book of Moses. And they did the same with the bulls. 13They roasted the passover lamb with fire according to the ordinance; and they boiled the holy offerings in pots, in caldrons, and in pans, and carried them quickly to all the people. 14Afterward they made preparations for themselves and for the priests, because the priests the descendants of Aaron were occupied in offering the burnt offerings and the fat parts until night; so the Levites made preparations for themselves and for the priests, the descendants of Aaron. 15The singers, the descendants of Asaph, were in their place according to the command of David, and Asaph, and Heman, and the king's seer Jeduthun. The gatekeepers were at each gate; they did not need to interrupt their service, for their kindred the Levites made preparations for them.

16 So all the service of the LORD was prepared that day, to keep the passover and to offer burnt offerings on the altar of the LORD, according to the command of King Josiah. 17The people of Israel who were present kept the passover at that time, and the festival of unleavened bread seven days. 18No passover like it had been kept in Israel since the days of the prophet Samuel; none of the kings of Israel had kept such a passover as was kept by Josiah, by the priests and the Levites, by all Judah and Israel who were present, and by the inhabitants of Jerusalem. 19In the eighteenth year of the reign of Josiah this passover was kept.

Defeat by Pharaoh Neco and Death of Josiah

20 After all this, when Josiah had set the temple in order, King Neco of Egypt went up to fight at Carchemish on the Euphrates, and Josiah went out against him. 21But Neco[u] sent envoys to him, saying, "What have I to do with you, king of Judah? I am not coming against you today, but against the house with which I am at war; and God has commanded me to hurry. Cease opposing God, who is with me, so that he will not destroy you." 22But Josiah would not turn away from him, but disguised himself in order to fight with him. He did not listen to the words of Neco from the mouth of God, but joined battle in the plain of Megiddo. 23The archers shot King Josiah; and the king said to his servants, "Take me away, for I am badly wounded." 24So his servants took him out of the chariot and carried him in his second chariot[v] and brought him to Jerusalem. There he died, and was buried in the tombs of his ancestors. All Judah and Jerusalem mourned for Josiah. 25Jeremiah also uttered a lament for Josiah, and all the singing men and singing women have spoken of Josiah in their laments to this day. They made these a custom in Israel; they are recorded in the Laments. 26Now the rest of the acts of Josiah and his faithful deeds in accordance with what is written in the law of the LORD, 27and his acts, first and last, are written in the Book of the Kings of Israel and Judah.

Reign of Jehoahaz

36 The people of the land took Jehoahaz son of Josiah and made him king to succeed his father in Jerusalem. 2Jehoahaz was twenty-three years old when he began to reign; he reigned three months in Jerusalem. 3Then the king of Egypt deposed him in Jerusalem and laid on the land a tribute of one hundred talents of silver and one talent of gold. 4The king of Egypt made his brother Eliakim king over Judah and Jerusalem, and changed his name to Jehoiakim; but Neco took his brother Jehoahaz and carried him to Egypt.

---

t Heb lacks *that they received*   u Heb *he*   v Or *the chariot of his deputy*

Reign and Captivity of Jehoiakim

5 Jehoiakim was twenty-five years old when he began to reign; he reigned eleven years in Jerusalem. He did what was evil in the sight of the LORD his God. 6Against him King Nebuchadnezzar of Babylon came up, and bound him with fetters to take him to Babylon. 7Nebuchadnezzar also carried some of the vessels of the house of the LORD to Babylon and put them in his palace in Babylon. 8Now the rest of the acts of Jehoiakim, and the abominations that he did, and what was found against him, are written in the Book of the Kings of Israel and Judah; and his son Jehoiachin succeeded him.

Reign and Captivity of Jehoiachin

9 Jehoiachin was eight years old when he began to reign; he reigned three months and ten days in Jerusalem. He did what was evil in the sight of the LORD. 10In the spring of the year King Nebuchadnezzar sent and brought him to Babylon, along with the precious vessels of the house of the LORD, and made his brother Zedekiah king over Judah and Jerusalem.

Reign of Zedekiah

11 Zedekiah was twenty-one years old when he began to reign; he reigned eleven years in Jerusalem. 12He did what was evil in the sight of the LORD his God. He did not humble himself before the prophet Jeremiah who spoke from the mouth of the LORD. 13He also rebelled against King Nebuchadnezzar, who had made him swear by God; he stiffened his neck and hardened his heart against turning to the LORD, the God of Israel. 14All the leading priests and the people also were exceedingly unfaithful, following all the abominations of the nations; and they polluted the house of the LORD that he had consecrated in Jerusalem.

The Fall of Jerusalem

15 The LORD, the God of their ancestors, sent persistently to them by his messengers, because he had compassion on his people and on his dwelling place; 16but they kept mocking the messengers of God, despising his words, and scoffing at his prophets, until the wrath of the LORD against his people became so great that there was no remedy.

17 Therefore he brought up against them the king of the Chaldeans, who killed their youths with the sword in the house of their sanctuary, and had no compassion on young man or young woman, the aged or the feeble; he gave them all into his hand. 18All the vessels of the house of God, large and small, and the treasures of the house of the LORD, and the treasures of the king and of his officials, all these he brought to Babylon. 19They burned the house of God, broke down the wall of Jerusalem, burned all its palaces with fire, and destroyed all its precious vessels. 20He took into exile in Babylon those who had escaped from the sword, and they became servants to him and to his sons until the establishment of the kingdom of Persia, 21to fulfill the word of the LORD by the mouth of Jeremiah, until the land had made up for its sabbaths. All the days that it lay desolate it kept sabbath, to fulfill seventy years.

Cyrus Proclaims Liberty for the Exiles

22 In the first year of King Cyrus of Persia, in fulfillment of the word of the LORD spoken by Jeremiah, the LORD stirred up the spirit of King Cyrus of Persia so that he sent a herald throughout all his kingdom and also declared in a written edict: 23"Thus says King Cyrus of Persia: The LORD, the God of heaven, has given me all the kingdoms of the earth, and he has charged me to build him a house at Jerusalem, which is in Judah. Whoever is among you of all his people, may the LORD his God be with him! Let him go up."

Ezra

The book of Ezra, along with the book of Nehemiah, tells the story of the second exodus, in which Jews exiled to Babylon returned to Jerusalem in order to rebuild the temple and the city. Life for the Jews of Babylon (present-day Iraq) was fairly comfortable, and it is no surprise that only a small percentage returned to Jerusalem, located 900 miles to the southwest.

Most of the Jews who migrated to Jerusalem had been born in Babylon and must have been shocked to see how devastated and overgrown their holy city had become. This period of return and rebuilding, known as the restoration, was critical in the history of the Jews. Even though the temple was rebuilt by 515 B.C., there was no guarantee this small band of Jews would be able to survive the effects of the exile and rebuild their life as a people.

Thanks to Ezra, a priest and scribe, who urged the people to follow the Mosaic Law and to repudiate marriages to foreign women who were leading the people into worship of idols, the Jews regained their identity as a spiritual community, unique in the history of the world. Their survival at this critical juncture depended more on spiritual than political leadership.

The book of Ezra reminds us of our own need for restoration and of the importance of putting our relationship with God first in our lives.

End of the Babylonian Captivity

1 In the first year of King Cyrus of Persia, in order that the word of the LORD by the mouth of Jeremiah might be accomplished, the LORD stirred up the spirit of King Cyrus of Persia so that he sent a herald throughout all his kingdom, and also in a written edict declared:

2 "Thus says King Cyrus of Persia: The LORD, the God of heaven, has given me all the kingdoms of the earth, and he has charged me to build him a house at Jerusalem in Judah. ³Any of those among you who are of his people—may their God be with them!—are now permitted to go up to Jerusalem in Judah, and rebuild the house of the LORD, the God of Israel—he is the God who is in Jerusalem; ⁴and let all survivors, in whatever place they reside, be assisted by the people of their place

with silver and gold, with goods and with animals, besides freewill offerings for the house of God in Jerusalem."

5 The heads of the families of Judah and Benjamin, and the priests and the Levites—everyone whose spirit God had stirred—got ready to go up and rebuild the house of the LORD in Jerusalem. 6All their neighbors aided them with silver vessels, with gold, with goods, with animals, and with valuable gifts, besides all that was freely offered. 7King Cyrus himself brought out the vessels of the house of the LORD that Nebuchadnezzar had carried away from Jerusalem and placed in the house of his gods. 8King Cyrus of Persia had them released into the charge of Mithredath the treasurer, who counted them out to Sheshbazzar the prince of Ju-

dah. 9And this was the inventory: gold basins, thirty; silver basins, one thousand; knives,*a* twenty-nine; 10gold bowls, thirty; other silver bowls, four hundred ten; other vessels, one thousand; 11the total of the gold and silver vessels was five thousand four hundred. All these Sheshbazzar brought up, when the exiles were brought up from Babylonia to Jerusalem.

List of the Returned Exiles

2 Now these were the people of the province who came from those captive exiles whom King Nebuchadnezzar of Babylon had carried captive to Babylonia; they returned to Jerusalem and Judah, all

a Vg: Meaning of Heb uncertain

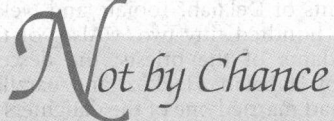

Not by Chance

MONDAY

Scripture Reading for Today:
Ezra 1

Verse for Today:
Ezra 1.2

Where is God when nations collide and governments rise and fall? Is he really in control of the events of history, or do things happen by chance?

The Jews who had been exiled to Babylon must have asked questions like these during the time of their captivity. But then, quickly and with astounding ease, once-mighty Babylon fell to the armies of the Persian king, Cyrus. Through the actions of this unlikely instrument, a pagan ruler, God reversed a seemingly hopeless situation and advanced his plan for the restoration of Israel.

It may not always seem so, but God is still using and orchestrating all kinds of events to fulfill his purposes today. Whether on the world scene or on the smaller stage of our individual lives, we can trust that God is always in control.

I saw in truth that God does all things. And I saw that nothing happens by chance, but by the far-sighted wisdom of God. If it seems like chance to us, it is because we are blind and blinkered.

The things planned before the world began come upon us suddenly, so that in our blindness we say that they are chance. But God knows better. Constantly and lovingly he brings all that happens to its best end.

All that is done is well done, for it is done by God.

When a soul holds onto God in trust—whether in seeking him or contemplating him—this is the highest worship it can bring.

—JULIAN OF NORWICH

Go to page 494 for your next devotional reading.

to their own towns. [2]They came with Zerubbabel, Jeshua, Nehemiah, Seraiah, Reelaiah, Mordecai, Bilshan, Mispar, Bigvai, Rehum, and Baanah.

The number of the Israelite people: [3]the descendants of Parosh, two thousand one hundred seventy-two. [4]Of Shephatiah, three hundred seventy-two. [5]Of Arah, seven hundred seventy-five. [6]Of Pahath-moab, namely the descendants of Jeshua and Joab, two thousand eight hundred twelve. [7]Of Elam, one thousand two hundred fifty-four. [8]Of Zattu, nine hundred forty-five. [9]Of Zaccai, seven hundred sixty. [10]Of Bani, six hundred forty-two. [11]Of Bebai, six hundred twenty-three. [12]Of Azgad, one thousand two hundred twenty-two. [13]Of Adonikam, six hundred sixty-six. [14]Of Bigvai, two thousand fifty-six. [15]Of Adin, four hundred fifty-four. [16]Of Ater, namely of Hezekiah, ninety-eight. [17]Of Bezai, three hundred twenty-three. [18]Of Jorah, one hundred twelve. [19]Of Hashum, two hundred twenty-three. [20]Of Gibbar, ninety-five. [21]Of Bethlehem, one hundred twenty-three. [22]The people of Netophah, fifty-six. [23]Of Anathoth, one hundred twenty-eight. [24]The descendants of Azmaveth, forty-two. [25]Of Kiriatharim, Chephirah, and Beeroth, seven hundred forty-three. [26]Of Ramah and Geba, six hundred twenty-one. [27]The people of Michmas, one hundred twenty-two. [28]Of Bethel and Ai, two hundred twenty-three. [29]The descendants of Nebo, fifty-two. [30]Of Magbish, one hundred fifty-six. [31]Of the other Elam, one thousand two hundred fifty-four. [32]Of Harim, three hundred twenty. [33]Of Lod, Hadid, and Ono, seven hundred twenty-five. [34]Of Jericho, three hundred forty-five. [35]Of Senaah, three thousand six hundred thirty.

36 The priests: the descendants of Jedaiah, of the house of Jeshua, nine hundred seventy-three. [37]Of Immer, one thousand fifty-two. [38]Of Pashhur, one thousand two hundred forty-seven. [39]Of Harim, one thousand seventeen.

40 The Levites: the descendants of Jeshua and Kadmiel, of the descendants of Hodaviah, seventy-four. [41]The singers: the descendants of Asaph, one hundred twenty-eight. [42]The descendants of the gatekeepers: of Shallum, of Ater, of Talmon, of Akkub, of Hatita, and of Shobai, in all one hundred thirty-nine.

43 The temple servants: the descendants of Ziha, Hasupha, Tabbaoth, [44]Keros, Siaha, Padon, [45]Lebanah, Hagabah, Akkub, [46]Hagab, Shamlai, Hanan, [47]Giddel, Gahar, Reaiah, [48]Rezin, Nekoda, Gazzam, [49]Uzza, Paseah, Besai, [50]Asnah, Meunim, Nephisim, [51]Bakbuk, Hakupha, Harhur, [52]Bazluth, Mehida, Harsha, [53]Barkos, Sisera, Temah, [54]Neziah, and Hatipha.

55 The descendants of Solomon's servants: Sotai, Hassophereth, Peruda, [56]Jaalah, Darkon, Giddel, [57]Shephatiah, Hattil, Pochereth-hazzebaim, and Ami.

58 All the temple servants and the descendants of Solomon's servants were three hundred ninety-two.

59 The following were those who came up from Tel-melah, Tel-harsha, Cherub, Addan, and Immer, though they could not prove their families or their descent, whether they belonged to Israel: [60]the descendants of Delaiah, Tobiah, and Nekoda, six hundred fifty-two. [61]Also, of the descendants of the priests: the descendants of Habaiah, Hakkoz, and Barzillai (who had married one of the daughters of Barzillai the Gileadite, and was called by their name). [62]These looked for their entries in the genealogical records, but they were not found there, and so they were excluded from the priesthood as unclean; [63]the governor told them that they were not to partake of the most holy food, until there should be a priest to consult Urim and Thummim.

64 The whole assembly together was forty-two thousand three hundred sixty, [65]besides their male and female servants, of whom there were seven thousand three hundred thirty-seven; and they had two hundred male and female singers. [66]They had seven hundred thirty-six horses, two hundred forty-five mules, [67]four hundred thirty-five camels, and six thousand seven hundred twenty donkeys.

68 As soon as they came to the house of the LORD in Jerusalem, some of the heads of families made freewill offerings for the house of God, to erect it on its site. [69]According to their resources they gave to the building fund sixty-one thousand darics of gold, five thousand minas of silver, and one hundred priestly robes.

70 The priests, the Levites, and some of the people lived in Jerusalem and its vicinity;[b] and the singers, the gatekeepers, and

_b_ 1 Esdras 5.46: Heb lacks _lived in Jerusalem and its vicinity_ the temple servants lived in their towns, and all Israel in their towns.

Worship Restored at Jerusalem

3 When the seventh month came, and the Israelites were in the towns, the people gathered together in Jerusalem. [2]Then Jeshua son of Jozadak, with his fellow priests, and Zerubbabel son of Shealtiel with his kin set out to build the altar of the God of Israel, to offer burnt offerings on it, as prescribed in the law of Moses the man of God. [3]They set up the altar on its foundation, because they were in dread of the neighboring peoples, and they offered burnt offerings upon it to the LORD, morning and evening. [4]And they kept the festival of booths,[c] as prescribed, and offered the daily burnt offerings by number according to the ordinance, as required for each day, [5]and after that the regular burnt offerings, the offerings at the new moon and at all the sacred festivals of the LORD, and the offerings of everyone who made a freewill offering to the LORD. [6]From the first day of the seventh month they began to offer burnt offerings to the LORD. But the foundation of the temple of the LORD was not yet laid. [7]So they gave money to the masons and the carpenters, and food, drink, and oil to the Sidonians and the Tyrians to bring cedar trees from Lebanon to the sea, to Joppa, according to the grant that they had from King Cyrus of Persia.

Foundation Laid for the Temple

8 In the second year after their arrival at the house of God at Jerusalem, in the second month, Zerubbabel son of Shealtiel and Jeshua son of Jozadak made a beginning, together with the rest of their people, the priests and the Levites and all who had come to Jerusalem from the captivity. They appointed the Levites, from twenty years old and upward, to have the oversight of the work on the house of the LORD. [9]And Jeshua with his sons and his kin, and Kadmiel and his sons, Binnui and Hodaviah[d] along with the sons of Henadad, the Levites, their sons and kin, together took charge of the workers in the house of God.

10 When the builders laid the foundation of the temple of the LORD, the priests in their vestments were stationed to praise the LORD with trumpets, and the Levites, the sons of Asaph, with cymbals, according to the directions of King David of Israel; [11]and they sang responsively, praising and giving thanks to the LORD,

"For he is good,
    for his steadfast love endures forever
        toward Israel."

And all the people responded with a great shout when they praised the LORD, because the foundation of the house of the LORD was laid. [12]But many of the priests and Levites and heads of families, old people who had seen the first house on its foundations, wept with a loud voice when they saw this house, though many shouted aloud for joy, [13]so that the people could not distinguish the sound of the joyful shout from the sound of the people's weeping, for the people shouted so loudly that the sound was heard far away.

Resistance to Rebuilding the Temple

4 When the adversaries of Judah and Benjamin heard that the returned exiles were building a temple to the LORD, the God of Israel, [2]they approached Zerubbabel and the heads of families and said to them, "Let us build with you, for we worship your God as you do, and we have been sacrificing to him ever since the days of King Esar-haddon of Assyria who brought us here." [3]But Zerubbabel, Jeshua, and the rest of the heads of families in Israel said to them, "You shall have no part with us in building a house to our God; but we alone will build to the LORD, the God of Israel, as King Cyrus of Persia has commanded us."

4 Then the people of the land discouraged the people of Judah, and made them afraid to build, [5]and they bribed officials to frustrate their plan throughout the reign of King Cyrus of Persia and until the reign of King Darius of Persia.

Rebuilding of Jerusalem Opposed

6 In the reign of Ahasuerus, in his accession year, they wrote an accusation against the inhabitants of Judah and Jerusalem.

7 And in the days of Artaxerxes, Bishlam and Mithredath and Tabeel and the rest of their associates wrote to King Artaxerxes of Persia; the letter was written in

---

c Or tabernacles; Heb succoth   d Compare 2.40;
Neh 7.43; 1 Esdras 5.58: Heb sons of Judah

Aramaic and translated.*e* 8Rehum the royal deputy and Shimshai the scribe wrote a letter against Jerusalem to King Artaxerxes as follows 9(then Rehum the royal deputy, Shimshai the scribe, and the rest of their associates, the judges, the envoys, the officials, the Persians, the people of Erech, the Babylonians, the people of Susa, that is, the Elamites, 10and the rest of the nations whom the great and noble Osnappar deported and settled in the cities of Samaria and in the rest of the province Beyond the River wrote—and now 11this is a copy of the letter that they sent):

"To King Artaxerxes: Your servants, the people of the province Beyond the River, send greeting. And now 12may it be known to the king that the Jews who came up from you to us have gone to Jerusalem. They are rebuilding that rebellious and wicked city; they are finishing the walls and repairing the foundations. 13Now may it be known to the king that, if this city is rebuilt and the walls finished, they will not pay tribute, custom, or toll, and the royal revenue will be reduced. 14Now because we share the salt of the palace and it is not fitting for us to witness the king's dishonor, therefore we send and inform the king, 15so that a search may be made in the annals of your ancestors. You will discover in the annals that this is a rebellious city, hurtful to kings and provinces, and that sedition was stirred up in it from long ago. On that account this city was laid waste. 16We make known to the king that, if this city is rebuilt and its walls finished, you will then have no possession in the province Beyond the River."

17 The king sent an answer: "To Rehum the royal deputy and Shimshai the scribe and the rest of their associates who live in Samaria and in the rest of the province Beyond the River, greeting. And now 18the letter that you sent to us has been read in translation before me. 19So I made a decree, and someone searched and discovered that this city has risen against kings from long ago, and that rebellion and sedition have been made in it. 20Jerusalem has had mighty kings who ruled over the whole province Beyond the River, to whom tribute, custom, and toll were paid. 21Therefore issue an order that these people be made to cease, and that this city not be rebuilt, until I make a decree. 22Moreover, take care not to be slack in

this matter; why should damage grow to the hurt of the king?"

23 Then when the copy of King Artaxerxes' letter was read before Rehum and the scribe Shimshai and their associates, they hurried to the Jews in Jerusalem and by force and power made them cease. 24At that time the work on the house of God in Jerusalem stopped and was discontinued until the second year of the reign of King Darius of Persia.

Restoration of the Temple Resumed

5 Now the prophets, Haggai*f* and Zechariah son of Iddo, prophesied to the Jews who were in Judah and Jerusalem, in the name of the God of Israel who was over them. 2Then Zerubbabel son of Shealtiel and Jeshua son of Jozadak set out to rebuild the house of God in Jerusalem; and with them were the prophets of God, helping them.

3 At the same time Tattenai the governor of the province Beyond the River and Shethar-bozenai and their associates came to them and spoke to them thus, "Who gave you a decree to build this house and to finish this structure?" 4They*g* also asked them this, "What are the names of the men who are building this building?" 5But the eye of their God was upon the elders of the Jews, and they did not stop them until a report reached Darius and then answer was returned by letter in reply to it.

6 The copy of the letter that Tattenai the governor of the province Beyond the River and Shethar-bozenai and his associates the envoys who were in the province Beyond the River sent to King Darius; 7they sent him a report, in which was written as follows: "To Darius the king, all peace! 8May it be known to the king that we went to the province of Judah, to the house of the great God. It is being built of hewn stone, and timber is laid in the walls; this work is being done diligently and prospers in their hands. 9Then we spoke to those elders and asked them, 'Who gave you a decree to build this house and to finish this structure?' 10We also asked them their names, for your information, so that we might write down

e Heb adds *in Aramaic,* indicating that 4.8-6.18 is in Aramaic. Another interpretation is *The letter was written in the Aramaic script and set forth in the Aramaic language   f* Aram adds *the prophet   g* Gk Syr: Aram *We*

the names of the men at their head. ¹¹This was their reply to us: 'We are the servants of the God of heaven and earth, and we are rebuilding the house that was built many years ago, which a great king of Israel built and finished. ¹²But because our ancestors had angered the God of heaven, he gave them into the hand of King Nebuchadnezzar of Babylon, the Chaldean, who destroyed this house and carried away the people to Babylonia. ¹³However, King Cyrus of Babylon, in the first year of his reign, made a decree that this house of God should be rebuilt. ¹⁴Moreover, the gold and silver vessels of the house of God, which Nebuchadnezzar had taken out of the temple in Jerusalem and had brought into the temple of Babylon, these King Cyrus took out of the temple of Babylon, and they were delivered to a man named Sheshbazzar, whom he had made governor. ¹⁵He said to him, "Take these vessels; go and put them in the temple in Jerusalem, and let the house of God be rebuilt on its site." ¹⁶Then this Sheshbazzar came and laid the foundations of the house of God in Jerusalem; and from that time until now it has been under construction, and it is not yet finished.' ¹⁷And now, if it seems good to the king, have a search made in the royal archives there in Babylon, to see whether a decree was issued by King Cyrus for the rebuilding of this house of God in Jerusalem. Let the king send us his pleasure in this matter."

The Decree of Darius

6 Then King Darius made a decree, and they searched the archives where the documents were stored in Babylon. ²But it was in Ecbatana, the capital in the province of Media, that a scroll was found on which this was written: "A record. ³In the first year of his reign, King Cyrus issued a decree: Concerning the house of God at Jerusalem, let the house be rebuilt, the place where sacrifices are offered and burnt offerings are brought;ʰ its height shall be sixty cubits and its width sixty cubits, ⁴with three courses of hewn stones and one course of timber; let the cost be paid from the royal treasury. ⁵Moreover, let the gold and silver vessels of the house of God, which Nebuchadnezzar took out of the temple in Jerusalem and brought to Babylon, be restored and brought back to the temple in Jerusalem, each to its place; you shall put them in the house of God."

6 "Now you, Tattenai, governor of the province Beyond the River, Shethar-bozenai, and you, their associates, the envoys in the province Beyond the River, keep away; ⁷let the work on this house of God alone; let the governor of the Jews and the elders of the Jews rebuild this house of God on its site. ⁸Moreover I make a decree regarding what you shall do for these elders of the Jews for the rebuilding of this house of God: the cost is to be paid to these people, in full and without delay, from the royal revenue, the tribute of the province Beyond the River. ⁹Whatever is needed—young bulls, rams, or sheep for burnt offerings to the God of heaven, wheat, salt, wine, or oil, as the priests in Jerusalem require—let that be given to them day by day without fail, ¹⁰so that they may offer pleasing sacrifices to the God of heaven, and pray for the life of the king and his children. ¹¹Furthermore I decree that if anyone alters this edict, a beam shall be pulled out of the house of the perpetrator, who then shall be impaled on it. The house shall be made a dunghill. ¹²May the God who has established his name there overthrow any king or people that shall put forth a hand to alter this, or to destroy this house of God in Jerusalem. I, Darius, make a decree; let it be done with all diligence."

Completion and Dedication of the Temple

13 Then, according to the word sent by King Darius, Tattenai, the governor of the province Beyond the River, Shethar-bozenai, and their associates did with all diligence what King Darius had ordered. ¹⁴So the elders of the Jews built and prospered, through the prophesying of the prophet Haggai and Zechariah son of Iddo. They finished their building by command of the God of Israel and by decree of Cyrus, Darius, and King Artaxerxes of Persia; ¹⁵and this house was finished on the third day of the month of Adar, in the sixth year of the reign of King Darius.

16 The people of Israel, the priests and the Levites, and the rest of the returned exiles, celebrated the dedication of this house of God with joy. ¹⁷They offered at the dedication of this house of God one hundred bulls, two hundred rams, four hundred lambs, and as a sin offering for all Israel, twelve male goats, according to

ʰ Meaning of Aram uncertain

the number of the tribes of Israel. [18]Then they set the priests in their divisions and the Levites in their courses for the service of God at Jerusalem, as it is written in the book of Moses.

The Passover Celebrated

[19] On the fourteenth day of the first month the returned exiles kept the passover. [20]For both the priests and the Levites had purified themselves; all of them were clean. So they killed the passover lamb for all the returned exiles, for their fellow priests, and for themselves. [21]It was eaten by the people of Israel who had returned from exile, and also by all who had joined them and separated themselves from the pollutions of the nations of the land to worship the LORD, the God of Israel. [22]With joy they celebrated the festival of unleavened bread seven days; for the LORD had made them joyful, and had turned the heart of the king of Assyria to them, so that he aided them in the work on the house of God, the God of Israel.

The Coming and Work of Ezra

7 After this, in the reign of King Artaxerxes of Persia, Ezra son of Seraiah, son of Azariah, son of Hilkiah, [2]son of Shallum, son of Zadok, son of Ahitub, [3]son of Amariah, son of Azariah, son of Meraioth, [4]son of Zerahiah, son of Uzzi, son of Bukki, [5]son of Abishua, son of Phinehas, son of Eleazar, son of the chief priest Aaron— [6]this Ezra went up from Babylonia. He was a scribe skilled in the law of Moses that the LORD the God of Israel had given; and the king granted him all that he asked, for the hand of the LORD his God was upon him.

[7] Some of the people of Israel, and some of the priests and Levites, the singers and gatekeepers, and the temple servants also went up to Jerusalem, in the seventh year of King Artaxerxes. [8]They came to Jerusalem in the fifth month, which was in the seventh year of the king. [9]On the first day of the first month the journey up from Babylon was begun, and on the first day of the fifth month he came to Jerusalem, for the gracious hand of his God was upon him. [10]For Ezra had set his heart to study the law of the LORD, and to do it, and to teach the statutes and ordinances in Israel.

The Letter of Artaxerxes to Ezra

[11] This is a copy of the letter that King Artaxerxes gave to the priest Ezra, the scribe, a scholar of the text of the commandments of the LORD and his statutes for Israel: [12]"Artaxerxes, king of kings, to the priest Ezra, the scribe of the law of the God of heaven: Peace.[i] And now [13]I decree that any of the people of Israel or their priests or Levites in my kingdom who freely offers to go to Jerusalem may go with you. [14]For you are sent by the king and his seven counselors to make inquiries about Judah and Jerusalem according to the law of your God, which is in your hand, [15]and also to convey the silver and gold that the king and his counselors have freely offered to the God of Israel, whose dwelling is in Jerusalem, [16]with all the silver and gold that you shall find in the whole province of Babylonia, and with the freewill offerings of the people and the priests, given willingly for the house of their God in Jerusalem. [17]With this money, then, you shall with all diligence buy bulls, rams, and lambs, and their grain offerings and their drink offerings, and you shall offer them on the altar of the house of your God in Jerusalem. [18]Whatever seems good to you and your colleagues to do with the rest of the silver and gold, you may do, according to the will of your God. [19]The vessels that have been given you for the service of the house of your God, you shall deliver before the God of Jerusalem. [20]And whatever else is required for the house of your God, which you are responsible for providing, you may provide out of the king's treasury.

[21] "I, King Artaxerxes, decree to all the treasurers in the province Beyond the River: Whatever the priest Ezra, the scribe of the law of the God of heaven, requires of you, let it be done with all diligence, [22]up to one hundred talents of silver, one hundred cors of wheat, one hundred baths[j] of wine, one hundred baths[j] of oil, and unlimited salt. [23]Whatever is commanded by the God of heaven, let it be done with zeal for the house of the God of heaven, or wrath will come upon the realm of the king and his heirs. [24]We also notify you that it shall not be lawful to impose trib-

i Syr Vg 1 Esdras 8.9: Aram *Perfect*   *j* A Heb measure of volume ute, custom, or toll on any of the priests, the Levites, the singers, the doorkeepers, the temple servants, or other servants of this house of God.

25 "And you, Ezra, according to the God-given wisdom you possess, appoint magistrates and judges who may judge all the people in the province Beyond the River who know the laws of your God; and you shall teach those who do not know them. 26All who will not obey the law of your God and the law of the king, let judgment be strictly executed on them, whether for death or for banishment or for confiscation of their goods or for imprisonment."

27 Blessed be the LORD, the God of our ancestors, who put such a thing as this into the heart of the king to glorify the house of the LORD in Jerusalem, 28and who extended to me steadfast love before the king and his counselors, and before all the king's mighty officers. I took courage, for the hand of the LORD my God was upon me, and I gathered leaders from Israel to go up with me.

Heads of Families Who Returned with Ezra

8 These are their family heads, and this is the genealogy of those who went up with me from Babylonia, in the reign of King Artaxerxes: 2Of the descendants of Phinehas, Gershom. Of Ithamar, Daniel. Of David, Hattush, 3of the descendants of Shecaniah. Of Parosh, Zechariah, with whom were registered one hundred fifty males. 4Of the descendants of Pahath-moab, Eliehoenai son of Zerahiah, and with him two hundred males. 5Of the descendants of Zattu,k Shecaniah son of Jahaziel, and with him three hundred males. 6Of the descendants of Adin, Ebed son of Jonathan, and with him fifty males. 7Of the descendants of Elam, Jeshaiah son of Athaliah, and with him seventy males. 8Of the descendants of Shephatiah, Zebadiah son of Michael, and with him eighty males. 9Of the descendants of Joab, Obadiah son of Jehiel, and with him two hundred eighteen males. 10Of the descendants of Bani,l Shelomith son of Josiphiah, and with him one hundred sixty males. 11Of the descendants of Bebai, Zechariah son of Bebai, and with him twenty-eight males. 12Of the descendants of Azgad, Johanan son of Hakkatan, and with him one hundred ten males. 13Of the descendants of Adonikam, those who came later,

their names being Eliphelet, Jeuel, and Shemaiah, and with them sixty males. 14Of the descendants of Bigvai, Uthai and Zaccur, and with them seventy males.

Servants for the Temple

15 I gathered them by the river that runs to Ahava, and there we camped three days. As I reviewed the people and the priests, I found there none of the descendants of Levi. 16Then I sent for Eliezer, Ariel, Shemaiah, Elnathan, Jarib, Elnathan, Nathan, Zechariah, and Meshullam, who were leaders, and for Joiarib and Elnathan, who were wise, 17and sent them to Iddo, the leader at the place called Casiphia, telling them what to say to Iddo and his colleagues the temple servants at Casiphia, namely, to send us ministers for the house of our God. 18Since the gracious hand of our God was upon us, they brought us a man of discretion, of the descendants of Mahli son of Levi son of Israel, namely Sherebiah, with his sons and kin, eighteen; 19also Hashabiah with him Jeshaiah of the descendants of Merari, with his kin and their sons, twenty; 20besides two hundred twenty of the temple servants, whom David and his officials had set apart to attend the Levites. These were all mentioned by name.

Fasting and Prayer for Protection

21 Then I proclaimed a fast there, at the river Ahava, that we might deny ourselvesm before our God, to seek from him a safe journey for ourselves, our children, and all our possessions. 22For I was ashamed to ask the king for a band of soldiers and cavalry to protect us against the enemy on our way, since we had told the king that the hand of our God is gracious to all who seek him, but his power and his wrath are against all who forsake him. 23So we fasted and petitioned our God for this, and he listened to our entreaty.

Gifts for the Temple

24 Then I set apart twelve of the leading priests: Sherebiah, Hashabiah, and ten of their kin with them. 25And I weighed out to them the silver and the gold and the vessels, the offering for the house of our God that the king, his counselors, his

k Gk 1 Esdras 8.32: Heb lacks of Zattu   l Gk
1 Esdras 8.36: Heb lacks Bani   m Or might fast

lords, and all Israel there present had offered; [26]I weighed out into their hand six hundred fifty talents of silver, and one hundred silver vessels worth . . . talents,[n] and one hundred talents of gold, [27]twenty gold bowls worth a thousand darics, and two vessels of fine polished bronze as precious as gold. [28]And I said to them, "You are holy to the LORD, and the vessels are holy; and the silver and the gold are a freewill offering to the LORD, the God of your ancestors. [29]Guard them and keep them until you weigh them before the chief priests and the Levites and the heads of families in Israel at Jerusalem, within the chambers of the house of the LORD." [30]So the priests and the Levites took over the silver, the gold, and the vessels as they were weighed out, to bring them to Jerusalem, to the house of our God.

The Return to Jerusalem

31 Then we left the river Ahava on the twelfth day of the first month, to go to Jerusalem; the hand of our God was upon us, and he delivered us from the hand of the enemy and from ambushes along the way. [32]We came to Jerusalem and remained there three days. [33]On the fourth day, within the house of our God, the silver, the gold, and the vessels were weighed into the hands of the priest Meremoth son of Uriah, and with him was Eleazar son of Phinehas, and with them were the Levites, Jozabad son of Jeshua and Noadiah son of Binnui. [34]The total was counted and weighed, and the weight of everything was recorded.

35 At that time those who had come from captivity, the returned exiles, offered burnt offerings to the God of Israel, twelve bulls for all Israel, ninety-six rams, seventy-seven lambs, and as a sin offering twelve male goats; all this was a burnt offering to the LORD. [36]They also delivered the king's commissions to the king's satraps and to the governors of the province Beyond the River; and they supported the people and the house of God.

Denunciation of Mixed Marriages

9 After these things had been done, the officials approached me and said, "The people of Israel, the priests, and the Levites have not separated themselves from the peoples of the lands with their abominations, from the Canaanites, the Hittites, the Perizzites, the Jebusites, the Ammonites, the Moabites, the Egyptians, and the Amorites. [2]For they have taken some of their daughters as wives for themselves and for their sons. Thus the holy seed has mixed itself with the peoples of the lands, and in this faithlessness the officials and leaders have led the way." [3]When I heard this, I tore my garment and my mantle, and pulled hair from my head and beard, and sat appalled. [4]Then all who trembled at the words of the God of Israel, because of the faithlessness of the returned exiles, gathered around me while I sat appalled until the evening sacrifice.

Ezra's Prayer

5 At the evening sacrifice I got up from my fasting, with my garments and my mantle torn, and fell on my knees, spread out my hands to the LORD my God, [6]and said,

"O my God, I am too ashamed and embarrassed to lift my face to you, my God, for our iniquities have risen higher than our heads, and our guilt has mounted up to the heavens. [7]From the days of our ancestors to this day we have been deep in guilt, and for our iniquities we, our kings, and our priests have been handed over to the kings of the lands, to the sword, to captivity, to plundering, and to utter shame, as is now the case. [8]But now for a brief moment favor has been shown by the LORD our God, who has left us a remnant, and given us a stake in his holy place, in order that he[o] may brighten our eyes and grant us a little sustenance in our slavery. [9]For we are slaves; yet our God has not forsaken us in our slavery, but has extended to us his steadfast love before the kings of Persia, to give us new life to set up the house of our God, to repair its ruins, and to give us a wall in Judea and Jerusalem.

10 "And now, our God, what shall we say after this? For we have forsaken your commandments, [11]which you commanded by your servants the prophets, saying, 'The land that you are entering to possess is a land unclean with the pollutions of the peoples of the lands, with their abominations. They have filled it from end to end with their uncleanness. [12]Therefore do not give your daughters to their sons, neither take their daughters for your sons,

---

[n] The number of talents is lacking   [o] Heb *our God*

and never seek their peace or prosperity,
so that you may be strong and eat the
good of the land and leave it for an inheritance to your children forever.' 13After all
that has come upon us for our evil deeds
and for our great guilt, seeing that you,
our God, have punished us less than our
iniquities deserved and have given us such
a remnant as this, 14shall we break your
commandments again and intermarry
with the peoples who practice these
abominations? Would you not be angry
with us until you destroy us without remnant or survivor? 15O LORD, God of Israel,
you are just, but we have escaped as a
remnant, as is now the case. Here we are
before you in our guilt, though no one
can face you because of this."

The People's Response

10 While Ezra prayed and made confession, weeping and throwing
himself down before the house of God, a
very great assembly of men, women, and
children gathered to him out of Israel; the
people also wept bitterly. 2Shecaniah son
of Jehiel, of the descendants of Elam, addressed Ezra, saying, "We have broken
faith with our God and have married foreign women from the peoples of the land,
but even now there is hope for Israel in
spite of this. 3So now let us make a covenant with our God to send away all these
wives and their children, according to the
counsel of my lord and of those who
tremble at the commandment of our God;
and let it be done according to the law.
4Take action, for it is your duty, and we
are with you; be strong, and do it." 5Then
Ezra stood up and made the leading
priests, the Levites, and all Israel swear
that they would do as had been said. So
they swore.

Foreign Wives and Their Children Rejected

6 Then Ezra withdrew from before the
house of God, and went to the chamber
of Jehohanan son of Eliashib, where he
spent the night.[p] He did not eat bread or
drink water, for he was mourning over the
faithlessness of the exiles. 7They made a
proclamation throughout Judah and Jerusalem to all the returned exiles that they
should assemble at Jerusalem, 8and that if
any did not come within three days, by
order of the officials and the elders all
their property should be forfeited, and
they themselves banned from the congregation of the exiles.

9 Then all the people of Judah and
Benjamin assembled at Jerusalem within
the three days; it was the ninth month, on
the twentieth day of the month. All the
people sat in the open square before the
house of God, trembling because of this
matter and because of the heavy rain.
10Then Ezra the priest stood up and said
to them, "You have trespassed and married foreign women, and so increased the
guilt of Israel. 11Now make confession to
the LORD the God of your ancestors, and
do his will; separate yourselves from the
peoples of the land and from the foreign
wives." 12Then all the assembly answered
with a loud voice, "It is so; we must do as
you have said. 13But the people are many,
and it is a time of heavy rain; we cannot
stand in the open. Nor is this a task for
one day or for two, for many of us have
transgressed in this matter. 14Let our officials represent the whole assembly, and
let all in our towns who have taken foreign wives come at appointed times, and
with them the elders and judges of every
town, until the fierce wrath of our God on
this account is averted from us." 15Only
Jonathan son of Asahel and Jahzeiah son
of Tikvah opposed this, and Meshullam
and Shabbethai the Levites supported
them.

16 Then the returned exiles did so. Ezra
the priest selected men,[q] heads of families, according to their families, each of
them designated by name. On the first
day of the tenth month they sat down to
examine the matter. 17By the first day of
the first month they had come to the end
of all the men who had married foreign
women.

18 There were found of the descendants of the priests who had married foreign women, of the descendants of Jeshua
son of Jozadak and his brothers: Maaseiah, Eliezer, Jarib, and Gedaliah. 19They
pledged themselves to send away their
wives, and their guilt offering was a ram of
the flock for their guilt. 20Of the descendants of Immer: Hanani and Zebadiah.
21Of the descendants of Harim: Maaseiah,
Elijah, Shemaiah, Jehiel, and Uzziah. 22Of
the descendants of Pashhur: Elioenai, Ma-

[p] 1 Esdras 9.2: Heb *where he went*
[q] 1 Esdras 9.16: Syr: Heb *And there were selected Ezra,*

aseiah, Ishmael, Nethanel, Jozabad, and Elasah.

23 Of the Levites: Jozabad, Shimei, Kelaiah (that is, Kelita), Pethahiah, Judah, and Eliezer. 24 Of the singers: Eliashib. Of the gatekeepers: Shallum, Telem, and Uri.

25 And of Israel: of the descendants of Parosh: Ramiah, Izziah, Malchijah, Mijamin, Eleazar, Hashabiah,ʳ and Benaiah. 26 Of the descendants of Elam: Mattaniah, Zechariah, Jehiel, Abdi, Jeremoth, and Elijah. 27 Of the descendants of Zattu: Elioenai, Eliashib, Mattaniah, Jeremoth, Zabad, and Aziza. 28 Of the descendants of Bebai: Jehohanan, Hananiah, Zabbai, and Athlai. 29 Of the descendants of Bani: Meshullam, Malluch, Adaiah, Jashub, Sheal, and Jeremoth. 30 Of the descendants of Pahath-moab: Adna, Chelal, Benaiah, Maaseiah, Mattaniah, Bezalel, Binnui, and Manasseh. 31 Of the descendants of Harim: Eliezer, Isshijah, Malchijah, Shema-

iah, Shimeon, 32 Benjamin, Malluch, and Shemariah. 33 Of the descendants of Hashum: Mattenai, Mattattah, Zabad, Eliphelet, Jeremai, Manasseh, and Shimei. 34 Of the descendants of Bani: Maadai, Amram, Uel, 35 Benaiah, Bedeiah, Cheluhi, 36 Vaniah, Meremoth, Eliashib, 37 Mattaniah, Mattenai, and Jaasu. 38 Of the descendants of Binnui:ˢ Shimei, 39 Shelemiah, Nathan, Adaiah, 40 Machnadebai, Shashai, Sharai, 41 Azarel, Shelemiah, Shemariah, 42 Shallum, Amariah, and Joseph. 43 Of the descendants of Nebo: Jeiel, Mattithiah, Zabad, Zebina, Jaddai, Joel, and Benaiah. 44 All these had married foreign women, and they sent them away with their children.ᵗ

ʳ 1 Esdras 9.26 Gk: Heb *Malchijah*   ˢ Gk: Heb *Bani, Binnui*   ᵗ 1 Esdras 9.36; meaning of Heb uncertain

Nehemiah

Nehemiah was a cupbearer (a court official who tasted the king's wine to prevent him from being poisoned) to Artaxerxes, king of Persia. After receiving permission to return to Jerusalem to act as governor of Judah, Nehemiah organized the work of rebuilding the city walls and instituted important administrative reforms.

Chapter four tells the remarkable story of how Nehemiah rebuilt the walls of Jerusalem despite strong external opposition by organizing the people to work with one hand while holding a weapon in the other. The walls were completed in just 52 days, a sign to Israel's enemies that God was still with his chosen people.

Much of the book is cast as Nehemiah's personal memoir, the last lines of which read: "Thus I cleansed them from everything foreign, and I established the duties of the priests and Levites, each in his work; and I provided for the wood offering, at appointed times, and for the first fruits. Remember me, O my God, for good" (13.30–31).

Nehemiah was a layman whose practical gifts were devoted to rebuilding Jerusalem. He had already achieved a position of worldly influence in Persia when he heeded God's call to go to Jerusalem and influence the Jews as a spiritual people.

Nehemiah Prays for His People

1 The words of Nehemiah son of Hacaliah. In the month of Chislev, in the twentieth year, while I was in Susa the capital, ²one of my brothers, Hanani, came with certain men from Judah; and I asked them about the Jews that survived, those who had escaped the captivity, and about Jerusalem. ³They replied, "The survivors there in the province who escaped captivity are in great trouble and shame; the wall of Jerusalem is broken down, and its gates have been destroyed by fire."

4 When I heard these words I sat down and wept, and mourned for days, fasting and praying before the God of heaven. ⁵I said, "O LORD God of heaven, the great and awesome God who keeps covenant and steadfast love with those who love him and keep his commandments; ⁶let your ear be attentive and your eyes open to hear the prayer of your servant that I now pray before you day and night for your servants, the people of Israel, confessing the sins of the people of Israel, which we have sinned against you. Both I

and my family have sinned. ⁷We have offended you deeply, failing to keep the commandments, the statutes, and the ordinances that you commanded your servant Moses. ⁸Remember the word that you commanded your servant Moses, 'If you are unfaithful, I will scatter you among the peoples; ⁹but if you return to me and keep my commandments and do them, though your outcasts are under the farthest skies, I will gather them from there and bring them to the place at which I have chosen to establish my name.' ¹⁰They are your servants and your people, whom you redeemed by your great power and your strong hand. ¹¹O Lord, let your ear be attentive to the prayer of your servant, and to the prayer of your servants who delight in revering your name. Give success to your servant today, and grant him mercy in the sight of this man!"

At the time, I was cupbearer to the king.

Nehemiah Sent to Judah

2 In the month of Nisan, in the twentieth year of King Artaxerxes, when wine was served him, I carried the wine and gave it to the king. Now, I had never been sad in his presence before. ²So the king said to me, "Why is your face sad, since you are not sick? This can only be

"*Forgive Us*"

TUESDAY

Scripture Reading
for Today:
Nehemiah 1.4–11

Verse for Today:
Nehemiah 1.6

"The sacrifice acceptable to God is a broken spirit" (Psalm 51.17).

Pope John Paul II has publicly shown such "contrite spirit" in the name of the Catholic Church by admitting church faults at least 94 times. Luigi Accatoli has written of it in his book, *When a Pope Asks Forgiveness: The Mea Culpas of John Paul II.*

Some Catholics have objected: "Why admit wrongdoing to Native Americans of North and South America, to Protestants, to Jews, even to admit the wrongful condemnation of Galileo Galilei?"

I can answer for myself. In *National Geographic* I saw a photo of the pope weeping at the point of debarkation for Africans sold into slavery. For me that was an emotional moment, an act of reconciliation, a freeing from some of the bitterness I have felt for my suffering slave ancestors. At the same time, it also freed me from some of the resentfulness toward my own Catholic Church, which segregated me for the first 30 years of my life.

In preparation for the year 2000, the pope has called on the church to purify itself and acknowledge past mistakes. I think King David would approve of purifying the past to meet the new millennium with a "clean heart . . . [and] a new and right spirit" (Psalm 51.10).

Being sorry for our sins and faults—individually and collectively—we can realize that we were born into this human condition. But we can and must take responsibility for and accept the consequences of our sins and ask for God's cleansing renewal. We can promise to change our lives for the better and henceforth give good example.

—*HARRIET GILLUM ROBINET*

Go to page 501 for your next devotional reading.

sadness of the heart." Then I was very much afraid. [3]I said to the king, "May the king live forever! Why should my face not be sad, when the city, the place of my ancestors' graves, lies waste, and its gates have been destroyed by fire?" [4]Then the king said to me, "What do you request?" So I prayed to the God of heaven. [5]Then I said to the king, "If it pleases the king, and if your servant has found favor with you, I ask that you send me to Judah, to the city of my ancestors' graves, so that I may rebuild it." [6]The king said to me (the queen also was sitting beside him), "How long will you be gone, and when will you return?" So it pleased the king to send me, and I set him a date. [7]Then I said to the king, "If it pleases the king, let letters be given me to the governors of the province Beyond the River, that they may grant me passage until I arrive in Judah; [8]and a letter to Asaph, the keeper of the king's forest, directing him to give me timber to make beams for the gates of the temple fortress, and for the wall of the city, and for the house that I shall occupy." And the king granted me what I asked, for the gracious hand of my God was upon me.

9 Then I came to the governors of the province Beyond the River, and gave them the king's letters. Now the king had sent officers of the army and cavalry with me. [10]When Sanballat the Horonite and Tobiah the Ammonite official heard this, it displeased them greatly that someone had come to seek the welfare of the people of Israel.

Nehemiah's Inspection of the Walls

11 So I came to Jerusalem and was there for three days. [12]Then I got up during the night, I and a few men with me; I told no one what my God had put into my heart to do for Jerusalem. The only animal I took was the animal I rode. [13]I went out by night by the Valley Gate past the Dragon's Spring and to the Dung Gate, and I inspected the walls of Jerusalem that had been broken down and its gates that had been destroyed by fire. [14]Then I went on to the Fountain Gate and to the King's Pool; but there was no place for the animal I was riding to continue. [15]So I went up by way of the valley by night and inspected the wall. Then I turned back and entered by the Valley Gate, and so returned. [16]The officials did not know where I had gone or what I was doing; I had not yet told the Jews, the priests, the nobles, the officials, and the rest that were to do the work.

Decision to Restore the Walls

17 Then I said to them, "You see the trouble we are in, how Jerusalem lies in ruins with its gates burned. Come, let us rebuild the wall of Jerusalem, so that we may no longer suffer disgrace." [18]I told them that the hand of my God had been gracious upon me, and also the words that the king had spoken to me. Then they said, "Let us start building!" So they committed themselves to the common good. [19]But when Sanballat the Horonite and Tobiah the Ammonite official, and Geshem the Arab heard of it, they mocked and ridiculed us, saying, "What is this that you are doing? Are you rebelling against the king?" [20]Then I replied to them, "The God of heaven is the one who will give us success, and we his servants are going to start building; but you have no share or claim or historic right in Jerusalem."

Organization of the Work

3 Then the high priest Eliashib set to work with his fellow priests and rebuilt the Sheep Gate. They consecrated it and set up its doors; they consecrated it as far as the Tower of the Hundred and as far as the Tower of Hananel. [2]And the men of Jericho built next to him. And next to them[a] Zaccur son of Imri built.

3 The sons of Hassenaah built the Fish Gate; they laid its beams and set up its doors, its bolts, and its bars. [4]Next to them Meremoth son of Uriah son of Hakkoz made repairs. Next to them Meshullam son of Berechiah son of Meshezabel made repairs. Next to them Zadok son of Baana made repairs. [5]Next to them the Tekoites made repairs; but their nobles would not put their shoulders to the work of their Lord.[b]

6 Joiada son of Paseah and Meshullam son of Besodeiah repaired the Old Gate; they laid its beams and set up its doors, its bolts, and its bars. [7]Next to them repairs were made by Melatiah the Gibeonite and Jadon the Meronothite—the men of Gibe-

---

a Heb *him*   *b* Or *lords*

on and of Mizpah—who were under the jurisdiction of[c] the governor of the province Beyond the River. [8]Next to them Uzziel son of Harhaiah, one of the goldsmiths, made repairs. Next to him Hananiah, one of the perfumers, made repairs; and they restored Jerusalem as far as the Broad Wall. [9]Next to them Rephaiah son of Hur, ruler of half the district of[d] Jerusalem, made repairs. [10]Next to them Jedaiah son of Harumaph made repairs opposite his house; and next to him Hattush son of Hashabneiah made repairs. [11]Malchijah son of Harim and Hasshub son of Pahath-moab repaired another section and the Tower of the Ovens. [12]Next to him Shallum son of Hallohesh, ruler of half the district of[d] Jerusalem, made repairs, he and his daughters.

13 Hanun and the inhabitants of Zanoah repaired the Valley Gate; they rebuilt it and set up its doors, its bolts, and its bars, and repaired a thousand cubits of the wall, as far as the Dung Gate.

14 Malchijah son of Rechab, ruler of the district of[e] Beth-haccherem, repaired the Dung Gate; he rebuilt it and set up its doors, its bolts, and its bars.

15 And Shallum son of Col-hozeh, ruler of the district of[e] Mizpah, repaired the Fountain Gate; he rebuilt it and covered it and set up its doors, its bolts, and its bars; and he built the wall of the Pool of Shelah of the king's garden, as far as the stairs that go down from the City of David. [16]After him Nehemiah son of Azbuk, ruler of half the district of[d] Beth-zur, repaired from a point opposite the graves of David, as far as the artificial pool and the house of the warriors. [17]After him the Levites made re-

[c] Meaning of Heb uncertain   [d] Or *supervisor of half the portion assigned to*   [e] Or *supervisor of the portion assigned to*

THE TRADITION

Vocation

Next to them Meremoth . . . made repairs. Next to them Meshullam . . . made repairs. Next to them Zadok . . . Next to them the Tekoites . . .

NEHEMIAH 3.4–5

"Let somebody else do it."

What if the Israelites returned from exile in Babylon had reacted this way when Nehemiah mobilized them to rebuild Jerusalem's walls? "I have other things to do," they could have said. And they did have other things to do. The city's destruction, followed by decades of neglect, had left homes, fields, and every area of their lives in need of serious attention. "Too controversial," they could have said. Neighboring officials and bigwigs who saw the city as their turf wanted it unprotected, and they opposed rebuilding the walls with mockery, threats, and other demoralizing tactics.

Though some of those summoned by Nehemiah hung back (see verse 5), most responded and took responsibility for their assigned part of the wall. The workers' roster is somewhat dull reading, though there are highlights (verse 12, for example, where Shallum's daughters wrestle stones into place alongside the guys). But the list makes the point that each family's contribution was vital. Just one gap makes a city wall totally useless!

Taking our place of service as members of the Church is in some ways like working together on a city wall. Each of us has gifts and abilities. Each is called to make a unique contribution. The work may be hidden, humble, routine. Sometimes it does not seem to amount to much. Still, in ways that we may or may not see, our service is crucial to God's plan of salvation for the world.

"Let somebody else run the soup kitchen. Let somebody else teach CCD . . . visit the sick . . . do prison ministry . . . head that committee . . . do clean-up . . ."

What part of the wall are we leaving unattended?

pairs: Rehum son of Bani; next to him Hashabiah, ruler of half the district of*f* Keilah, made repairs for his district. 18After him their kin made repairs: Binnui,*g* son of Henadad, ruler of half the district of*f* Keilah; 19next to him Ezer son of Jeshua, ruler*h* of Mizpah, repaired another section opposite the ascent to the armory at the Angle. 20After him Baruch son of Zabbai repaired another section from the Angle to the door of the house of the high priest Eliashib. 21After him Meremoth son of Uriah son of Hakkoz repaired another section from the door of the house of Eliashib to the end of the house of Eliashib. 22After him the priests, the men of the surrounding area, made repairs. 23After them Benjamin and Hasshub made repairs opposite their house. After them Azariah son of Maaseiah son of Ananiah made repairs beside his own house. 24After him Binnui son of Henadad repaired another section, from the house of Azariah to the Angle and to the corner. 25Palal son of Uzai repaired opposite the Angle and the tower projecting from the upper house of the king at the court of the guard. After him Pedaiah son of Parosh 26and the temple servants living*i* on Ophel made repairs up to a point opposite the Water Gate on the east and the projecting tower. 27After him the Tekoites repaired another section opposite the great projecting tower as far as the wall of Ophel.

28 Above the Horse Gate the priests made repairs, each one opposite his own house. 29After them Zadok son of Immer made repairs opposite his own house. After him Shemaiah son of Shecaniah, the keeper of the East Gate, made repairs. 30After him Hananiah son of Shelemiah and Hanun sixth son of Zalaph repaired another section. After him Meshullam son of Berechiah made repairs opposite his living quarters. 31After him Malchijah, one of the goldsmiths, made repairs as far as the house of the temple servants and of the merchants, opposite the Muster Gate,*j* and to the upper room of the corner. 32And between the upper room of the corner and the Sheep Gate the goldsmiths and the merchants made repairs.

Hostile Plots Thwarted

4 *k*Now when Sanballat heard that we were building the wall, he was angry and greatly enraged, and he mocked the Jews. 2He said in the presence of his asso-

ciates and of the army of Samaria, "What are these feeble Jews doing? Will they restore things? Will they sacrifice? Will they finish it in a day? Will they revive the stones out of the heaps of rubbish—and burned ones at that?" 3Tobiah the Ammonite was beside him, and he said, "That stone wall they are building—any fox going up on it would break it down!" 4Hear, O our God, for we are despised; turn their taunt back on their own heads, and give them over as plunder in a land of captivity. 5Do not cover their guilt, and do not let their sin be blotted out from your sight; for they have hurled insults in the face of the builders.

6 So we rebuilt the wall, and all the wall was joined together to half its height; for the people had a mind to work.

7*l* But when Sanballat and Tobiah and the Arabs and the Ammonites and the Ashdodites heard that the repairing of the walls of Jerusalem was going forward and the gaps were beginning to be closed, they were very angry, 8and all plotted together to come and fight against Jerusalem and to cause confusion in it. 9So we prayed to our God, and set a guard as a protection against them day and night.

10 But Judah said, "The strength of the burden bearers is failing, and there is too much rubbish so that we are unable to work on the wall." 11And our enemies said, "They will not know or see anything before we come upon them and kill them and stop the work." 12When the Jews who lived near them came, they said to us ten times, "From all the places where they live*m* they will come up against us."*n* 13So in the lowest parts of the space behind the wall, in open places, I stationed the people according to their families,*o* with their swords, their spears, and their bows. 14After I looked these things over, I stood up and said to the nobles and the officials and the rest of the people, "Do not be afraid of them. Remember the Lord, who is great and awesome, and fight for your kin, your sons, your daughters, your wives, and your homes."

15 When our enemies heard that their

f Or *supervisor of half the portion assigned to*   *g* Gk Syr Compare verse 24, 10.9: Heb *Bavvai*   *h* Or *supervisor*   *i* Cn: Heb *were living*   *j* Or *Hammiphkad Gate*   *k* Ch 3.33 in Heb   *l* Ch 4.1 in Heb   *m* Cn: Heb *you return*   *n* Compare Gk Syr: Meaning of Heb uncertain   *o* Meaning of Heb uncertain

plot was known to us, and that God had frustrated it, we all returned to the wall, each to his work. [16]From that day on, half of my servants worked on construction, and half held the spears, shields, bows, and body-armor; and the leaders posted themselves behind the whole house of Judah, [17]who were building the wall. The burden bearers carried their loads in such a way that each labored on the work with one hand and with the other held a weapon. [18]And each of the builders had his sword strapped at his side while he built. The man who sounded the trumpet was beside me. [19]And I said to the nobles, the officials, and the rest of the people, "The work is great and widely spread out, and we are separated far from one another on the wall. [20]Rally to us wherever you hear the sound of the trumpet. Our God will fight for us."

21 So we labored at the work, and half of them held the spears from break of dawn until the stars came out. [22]I also said to the people at that time, "Let every man and his servant pass the night inside Jerusalem, so that they may be a guard for us by night and may labor by day." [23]So neither I nor my brothers nor my servants nor the men of the guard who followed me ever took off our clothes; each kept his weapon in his right hand. *p*

Nehemiah Deals with Oppression

5 Now there was a great outcry of the people and of their wives against their Jewish kin. [2]For there were those who said, "With our sons and our daughters, we are many; we must get grain, so that we may eat and stay alive." [3]There were also those who said, "We are having to pledge our fields, our vineyards, and our houses in order to get grain during the famine." [4]And there were those who said, "We are having to borrow money on our fields and vineyards to pay the king's tax. [5]Now our flesh is the same as that of our kindred; our children are the same as their children; and yet we are forcing our sons and daughters to be slaves, and some of our daughters have been ravished; we are powerless, and our fields and vineyards now belong to others."

6 I was very angry when I heard their outcry and these complaints. [7]After thinking it over, I brought charges against the nobles and the officials; I said to them, "You are all taking interest from your own

people." And I called a great assembly to deal with them, [8]and said to them, "As far as we were able, we have bought back our Jewish kindred who had been sold to other nations; but now you are selling your own kin, who must then be bought back by us!" They were silent, and could not find a word to say. [9]So I said, "The thing that you are doing is not good. Should you not walk in the fear of our God, to prevent the taunts of the nations our enemies? [10]Moreover I and my brothers and my servants are lending them money and grain. Let us stop this taking of interest. [11]Restore to them, this very day, their fields, their vineyards, their olive orchards, and their houses, and the interest on money, grain, wine, and oil that you have been exacting from them." [12]Then they said, "We will restore everything and demand nothing more from them. We will do as you say." And I called the priests, and made them take an oath to do as they had promised. [13]I also shook out the fold of my garment and said, "So may God shake out everyone from house and from property who does not perform this promise. Thus may they be shaken out and emptied." And all the assembly said, "Amen," and praised the LORD. And the people did as they had promised.

The Generosity of Nehemiah

14 Moreover from the time that I was appointed to be their governor in the land of Judah, from the twentieth year to the thirty-second year of King Artaxerxes, twelve years, neither I nor my brothers ate the food allowance of the governor. [15]The former governors who were before me laid heavy burdens on the people, and took food and wine from them, besides forty shekels of silver. Even their servants lorded it over the people. But I did not do so, because of the fear of God. [16]Indeed, I devoted myself to the work on this wall, and acquired no land; and all my servants were gathered there for the work. [17]Moreover there were at my table one hundred fifty people, Jews and officials, besides those who came to us from the nations around us. [18]Now that which was prepared for one day was one ox and six choice sheep; also fowls were prepared for me, and every ten days skins of wine in abundance; yet with all this I did not de-

p Cn: Heb each his weapon the water

mand the food allowance of the governor, because of the heavy burden of labor on the people. [19]Remember for my good, O my God, all that I have done for this people.

Intrigues of Enemies Foiled

6 Now when it was reported to Sanballat and Tobiah and to Geshem the Arab and to the rest of our enemies that I had built the wall and that there was no gap left in it (though up to that time I had not set up the doors in the gates), [2]Sanballat and Geshem sent to me, saying, "Come and let us meet together in one of the villages in the plain of Ono." But they intended to do me harm. [3]So I sent messengers to them, saying, "I am doing a great work and I cannot come down. Why should the work stop while I leave it to come down to you?" [4]They sent to me four times in this way, and I answered them in the same manner. [5]In the same way Sanballat for the fifth time sent his servant to me with an open letter in his hand. [6]In it was written, "It is reported among the nations—and Geshem[q] also says it—that you and the Jews intend to rebel; that is why you are building the wall; and according to this report you wish to become their king. [7]You have also set up prophets to proclaim in Jerusalem concerning you, 'There is a king in Judah!' And now it will be reported to the king according to these words. So come, therefore, and let us confer together." [8]Then I sent to him, saying, "No such things as you say have been done; you are inventing them out of your own mind" [9]—for they all wanted to frighten us, thinking, "Their hands will drop from the work, and it will not be done." But now, O God, strengthen my hands.

10 One day when I went into the house of Shemaiah son of Delaiah son of Mehetabel, who was confined to his house, he said, "Let us meet together in the house of God, within the temple, and let us close the doors of the temple, for they are coming to kill you; indeed, tonight they are coming to kill you." [11]But I said, "Should a man like me run away? Would a man like me go into the temple to save his life? I will not go in!" [12]Then I perceived and saw that God had not sent him at all, but he had pronounced the prophecy against me because Tobiah and Sanballat had hired him. [13]He was hired for this purpose, to intimidate me and

make me sin by acting in this way, and so they could give me a bad name, in order to taunt me. [14]Remember Tobiah and Sanballat, O my God, according to these things that they did, and also the prophetess Noadiah and the rest of the prophets who wanted to make me afraid.

The Wall Completed

15 So the wall was finished on the twenty-fifth day of the month Elul, in fifty-two days. [16]And when all our enemies heard of it, all the nations around us were afraid[r] and fell greatly in their own esteem; for they perceived that this work had been accomplished with the help of our God. [17]Moreover in those days the nobles of Judah sent many letters to Tobiah, and Tobiah's letters came to them. [18]For many in Judah were bound by oath to him, because he was the son-in-law of Shecaniah son of Arah: and his son Jehohanan had married the daughter of Meshullam son of Berechiah. [19]Also they spoke of his good deeds in my presence, and reported my words to him. And Tobiah sent letters to intimidate me.

7 Now when the wall had been built and I had set up the doors, and the gatekeepers, the singers, and the Levites had been appointed, [2]I gave my brother Hanani charge over Jerusalem, along with Hananiah the commander of the citadel—for he was a faithful man and feared God more than many. [3]And I said to them, "The gates of Jerusalem are not to be opened until the sun is hot; while the gatekeepers[s] are still standing guard, let them shut and bar the doors. Appoint guards from among the inhabitants of Jerusalem, some at their watch posts, and others before their own houses." [4]The city was wide and large, but the people within it were few and no houses had been built.

Lists of the Returned Exiles

5 Then my God put it into my mind to assemble the nobles and the officials and the people to be enrolled by genealogy. And I found the book of the genealogy of those who were the first to come back, and I found the following written in it:

6 These are the people of the province who came up out of the captivity of those exiles whom King Nebuchadnezzar of

q Heb Gashmu   r Another reading is saw
s Heb while they

Babylon had carried into exile; they re- turned to Jerusalem and Judah, each to his town. 7They came with Zerubbabel, Jesh- ua, Nehemiah, Azariah, Raamiah, Naha- mani, Mordecai, Bilshan, Mispereth, Big- vai, Nehum, Baanah.

The number of the Israelite people: 8the descendants of Parosh, two thousand one hundred seventy-two. 9Of Shephatiah, three hundred seventy-two. 10Of Arah, six hundred fifty-two. 11Of Pahath-moab, namely the descendants of Jeshua and Joab, two thousand eight hundred eigh- teen. 12Of Elam, one thousand two hun- dred fifty-four. 13Of Zattu, eight hundred forty-five. 14Of Zaccai, seven hundred six- ty. 15Of Binnui, six hundred forty-eight. 16Of Bebai, six hundred twenty-eight. 17Of Azgad, two thousand three hundred twenty-two. 18Of Adonikam, six hun- dred sixty-seven. 19Of Bigvai, two thou- sand sixty-seven. 20Of Adin, six hundred fifty-five. 21Of Ater, namely of Heze- kiah, ninety-eight. 22Of Hashum, three hundred twenty-eight. 23Of Bezai, three hundred twenty-four. 24Of Hariph, one hundred twelve. 25Of Gibeon, ninety-five. 26The people of Bethlehem and Netophah, one hundred eighty-eight. 27Of Anathoth, one hundred twenty- eight. 28Of Beth-azmaveth, forty-two. 29Of Kiriath-jearim, Chephirah, and Bee- roth, seven hundred forty-three. 30Of Ra- mah and Geba, six hundred twenty-one. 31Of Michmas, one hundred twenty-two. 32Of Bethel and Ai, one hundred twenty- three. 33Of the other Nebo, fifty-two. 34The descendants of the other Elam, one thousand two hundred fifty-four. 35Of Harim, three hundred twenty. 36Of Jeri- cho, three hundred forty-five. 37Of Lod, Hadid, and Ono, seven hundred twenty- one. 38Of Senaah, three thousand nine hundred thirty.

39 The priests: the descendants of Jeda- iah, namely the house of Jeshua, nine hundred seventy-three. 40Of Immer, one thousand fifty-two. 41Of Pashhur, one thousand two hundred forty-seven. 42Of Harim, one thousand seventeen.

43 The Levites: the descendants of Jesh- ua, namely of Kadmiel of the descendants of Hodevah, seventy-four. 44The singers: the descendants of Asaph, one hundred forty-eight. 45The gatekeepers: the descen- dants of Shallum, of Ater, of Talmon, of Akkub, of Hatita, of Shobai, one hundred thirty-eight.

46 The temple servants: the descen- dants of Ziha, of Hasupha, of Tabbaoth, 47of Keros, of Sia, of Padon, 48of Lebana, of Hagaba, of Shalmai, 49of Hanan, of Giddel, of Gahar, 50of Reaiah, of Rezin, of Nekoda, 51of Gazzam, of Uzza, of Paseah, 52of Besai, of Meunim, of Nephushesim, 53of Bakbuk, of Hakupha, of Harhur, 54of Bazlith, of Mehida, of Harsha, 55of Bar- kos, of Sisera, of Temah, 56of Neziah, of Hatipha.

57 The descendants of Solomon's ser- vants: of Sotai, of Sophereth, of Perida, 58of Jaala, of Darkon, of Giddel, 59of Shephatiah, of Hattil, of Pochereth- hazzebaim, of Amon.

60 All the temple servants and the de- scendants of Solomon's servants were three hundred ninety-two.

61 The following were those who came up from Tel-melah, Tel-harsha, Cherub, Addon, and Immer, but they could not prove their ancestral houses or their de- scent, whether they belonged to Israel: 62the descendants of Delaiah, of Tobiah, of Nekoda, six hundred forty-two. 63Also, of the priests: the descendants of Hoba- iah, of Hakkoz, of Barzillai (who had mar- ried one of the daughters of Barzillai the Gileadite and was called by their name). 64These sought their registration among those enrolled in the genealogies, but it was not found there, so they were exclud- ed from the priesthood as unclean; 65the governor told them that they were not to partake of the most holy food, until a priest with Urim and Thummim should come.

66 The whole assembly together was forty-two thousand three hundred sixty, 67besides their male and female slaves, of whom there were seven thousand three hundred thirty-seven; and they had two hundred forty-five singers, male and fe- male. 68They had seven hundred thirty-six horses, two hundred forty-five mules,[t] 69four hundred thirty-five camels, and six thousand seven hundred twenty donkeys.

70 Now some of the heads of ancestral houses contributed to the work. The gov- ernor gave to the treasury one thousand darics of gold, fifty basins, and five hun- dred thirty priestly robes. 71And some of

---

t Ezra 2.66 and the margins of some Hebrew Mss: MT lacks *They had . . . forty-five mules*

the heads of ancestral houses gave into the building fund twenty thousand darics of gold and two thousand two hundred minas of silver. 72And what the rest of the people gave was twenty thousand darics of gold, two thousand minas of silver, and sixty-seven priestly robes.

73 So the priests, the Levites, the gatekeepers, the singers, some of the people, the temple servants, and all Israel settled in their towns.

Ezra Summons the People to Obey the Law

When the seventh month came—the people of Israel being settled in their towns— 8 1all the people gathered together into the square before the Wa-

---

Celebrate!

"*Go your way, eat the fat and drink sweet wine ... for this day is holy to our* LORD" *(Nehemiah 8.10).* Surely, this call to celebrate a holy day with feasting is one of Scripture's most welcome commands! The Israelites who received it had just been brought to tearful repentance by a public reading of Scripture, No matter, said their leaders: because it was the first day of the seventh month—the festival of Booths, or Tabernacles—celebration was in order.

For us, as for the Israelites, rich foods and sweet drinks are an appropriate response to holy days. And says Ann Ball, author of Catholic Traditions in Cooking, our celebrations of the feasts of the Church year will be enhanced as we learn to mark them with the specific foods that are traditionally associated with each one.

I strongly believe that it is important to pass tradition and heritage to one's children. For this very reason I baked bread, canned tomatoes, and made jelly with my children. Today we buy these items at the grocery store and do not make them at home on a regular basis. My children, however, understand the specialness of the homemade products. Today, they can feel a closeness to their ancestors who had no handy supermarket just down the street.

One day when we were making bread, a friend of my son's dropped by. He asked what we were doing. On being told we were baking bread, he refused to believe that it could be made at home! He extended his visit until the bread was done to see if we were "fooling" him. I found this sad as well as funny.

Just as the making of wild plum, crabapple, or mayhaw jelly is a part of my children's East Texas heritage, so too are the traditional foods for the feasts of the Church a part of their Catholic heritage. The taste of mince pie may be the same for believer and non-believer, but it receives its Catholic flavor when we recall that the spices are symbolic of the gifts of the Magi—and that it was originally baked in a shape to recall the manger of our Lord.

—ANN BALL

WEDNESDAY

Scripture Reading for Today:
Nehemiah 8.1–10

Verse for Today:
Nehemiah 8.10

Go to page 508 for your next devotional reading.

ter Gate. They told the scribe Ezra to bring the book of the law of Moses, which the LORD had given to Israel. ²Accordingly, the priest Ezra brought the law before the assembly, both men and women and all who could hear with understanding. This was on the first day of the seventh month. ³He read from it facing the square before the Water Gate from early morning until midday, in the presence of the men and the women and those who could understand; and the ears of all the people were attentive to the book of the law. ⁴The scribe Ezra stood on a wooden platform that had been made for the purpose; and beside him stood Mattithiah, Shema, Anaiah, Uriah, Hilkiah, and Maaseiah on his right hand; and Pedaiah, Mishael, Malchijah, Hashum, Hash-baddanah, Zechariah, and Meshullam on his left hand. ⁵And Ezra opened the book in the sight of all the people, for he was standing above all the people; and when he opened it, all the people stood up. ⁶Then Ezra blessed the LORD, the great God, and all the people answered, "Amen, Amen," lifting up their hands. Then they bowed their heads and worshiped the LORD with their faces to the ground. ⁷Also Jeshua, Bani, Sherebiah, Jamin, Akkub, Shabbethai, Hodiah, Maaseiah, Kelita, Azariah, Jozabad, Hanan, Pelaiah, the Levites,ᵘ helped the people to understand the law, while the people remained in their places. ⁸So they read from the book, from the law of God, with interpretation. They gave the sense, so that the people understood the reading.

9 And Nehemiah, who was the governor, and Ezra the priest and scribe, and the Levites who taught the people said to all the people, "This day is holy to the LORD your God; do not mourn or weep." For all the people wept when they heard the words of the law. ¹⁰Then he said to them, "Go your way, eat the fat and drink sweet wine and send portions of them to those for whom nothing is prepared, for this day is holy to our LORD; and do not be grieved, for the joy of the LORD is your strength." ¹¹So the Levites stilled all the people, saying, "Be quiet, for this day is holy; do not be grieved." ¹²And all the people went their way to eat and drink and to send portions and to make great rejoicing, because they had understood the words that were declared to them.

The Festival of Booths Celebrated

13 On the second day the heads of ancestral houses of all the people, with the priests and the Levites, came together to the scribe Ezra in order to study the words of the law. ¹⁴And they found it written in the law, which the LORD had commanded by Moses, that the people of Israel should live in boothsᵛ during the festival of the seventh month, ¹⁵and that they should publish and proclaim in all their towns and in Jerusalem as follows, "Go out to the hills and bring branches of olive, wild olive, myrtle, palm, and other leafy trees to make booths,ᵛ as it is written." ¹⁶So the people went out and brought them, and made boothsᵛ for themselves, each on the roofs of their houses, and in their courts and in the courts of the house of God, and in the square at the Water Gate and in the square at the Gate of Ephraim. ¹⁷And all the assembly of those who had returned from the captivity made boothsᵛ and lived in them; for from the days of Jeshua son of Nun to that day the people of Israel had not done so. And there was very great rejoicing. ¹⁸And day by day, from the first day to the last day, he read from the book of the law of God. They kept the festival seven days; and on the eighth day there was a solemn assembly, according to the ordinance.

National Confession

9 Now on the twenty-fourth day of this month the people of Israel were assembled with fasting and in sackcloth, and with earth on their heads.ʷ ²Then those of Israelite descent separated themselves from all foreigners, and stood and confessed their sins and the iniquities of their ancestors. ³They stood up in their place and read from the book of the law of the LORD their God for a fourth part of the day, and for another fourth they made confession and worshiped the LORD their God. ⁴Then Jeshua, Bani, Kadmiel, Shebaniah, Bunni, Sherebiah, Bani, and Chenani stood on the stairs of the Levites and cried out with a loud voice to the LORD their God. ⁵Then the Levites, Jeshua, Kadmiel, Bani, Hashabneiah, Sherebiah, Hodiah, Shebaniah, and Pethahiah, said, "Stand up and bless the LORD your God

---

u 1 Esdras 9.48 Vg: Heb *and the Levites*   v Or *tabernacles*; Heb *succoth*   w Heb *on them*

from everlasting to everlasting. Blessed be your glorious name, which is exalted above all blessing and praise."

6 And Ezra said:*x* "You are the LORD, you alone; you have made heaven, the heaven of heavens, with all their host, the earth and all that is on it, the seas and all that is in them. To all of them you give life, and the host of heaven worships you. ⁷You are the LORD, the God who chose Abram and brought him out of Ur of the Chaldeans and gave him the name Abraham; ⁸and you found his heart faithful before you, and made with him a covenant to give to his descendants the land of the Canaanite, the Hittite, the Amorite, the Perizzite, the Jebusite, and the Girgashite; and you have fulfilled your promise, for you are righteous.

9 "And you saw the distress of our ancestors in Egypt and heard their cry at the Red Sea.*y* ¹⁰You performed signs and wonders against Pharaoh and all his servants and all the people of his land, for you knew that they acted insolently against our ancestors. You made a name for yourself, which remains to this day. ¹¹And you divided the sea before them, so that they passed through the sea on dry land, but you threw their pursuers into the depths, like a stone into mighty waters. ¹²Moreover, you led them by day with a pillar of cloud, and by night with a pillar of fire, to give them light on the way in which they should go. ¹³You came down also upon Mount Sinai, and spoke with them from heaven, and gave them right ordinances and true laws, good statutes and commandments, ¹⁴and you made known your holy sabbath to them and gave them commandments and statutes and a law through your servant Moses. ¹⁵For their hunger you gave them bread from heaven, and for their thirst you brought water for them out of the rock, and you told them to go in to possess the land that you swore to give them.

16 "But they and our ancestors acted presumptuously and stiffened their necks and did not obey your commandments; ¹⁷they refused to obey, and were not mindful of the wonders that you performed among them; but they stiffened their necks and determined to return to their slavery in Egypt. But you are a God ready to forgive, gracious and merciful, slow to anger and abounding in steadfast love, and you did not forsake them.

¹⁸Even when they had cast an image of a calf for themselves and said, 'This is your God who brought you up out of Egypt,' and had committed great blasphemies, ¹⁹you in your great mercies did not forsake them in the wilderness; the pillar of cloud that led them in the way did not leave them by day, nor the pillar of fire by night that gave them light on the way by which they should go. ²⁰You gave your good spirit to instruct them, and did not withhold your manna from their mouths, and gave them water for their thirst. ²¹Forty years you sustained them in the wilderness so that they lacked nothing; their clothes did not wear out and their feet did not swell. ²²And you gave them kingdoms and peoples, and allotted to them every corner,*z* so they took possession of the land of King Sihon of Heshbon and the land of King Og of Bashan. ²³You multiplied their descendants like the stars of heaven, and brought them into the land that you had told their ancestors to enter and possess. ²⁴So the descendants went in and possessed the land, and you subdued before them the inhabitants of the land, the Canaanites, and gave them into their hands, with their kings and the peoples of the land, to do with them as they pleased. ²⁵And they captured fortress cities and a rich land, and took possession of houses filled with all sorts of goods, hewn cisterns, vineyards, olive orchards, and fruit trees in abundance; so they ate, and were filled and became fat, and delighted themselves in your great goodness.

26 "Nevertheless they were disobedient and rebelled against you and cast your law behind their backs and killed your prophets, who had warned them in order to turn them back to you, and they committed great blasphemies. ²⁷Therefore you gave them into the hands of their enemies, who made them suffer. Then in the time of their suffering they cried out to you and you heard them from heaven, and according to your great mercies you gave them saviors who saved them from the hands of their enemies. ²⁸But after they had rest, they again did evil before you, and you abandoned them to the hands of their enemies, so that they had dominion over them; yet when they turned and cried to you, you heard from

x Gk: Heb lacks *And Ezra said*   *y* Or *Sea of Reeds*
z Meaning of Heb uncertain

heaven, and many times you rescued them according to your mercies. 29And you warned them in order to turn them back to your law. Yet they acted presumptuously and did not obey your commandments, but sinned against your ordinances, by the observance of which a person shall live. They turned a stubborn shoulder and stiffened their neck and would not obey. 30Many years you were patient with them, and warned them by your spirit through your prophets; yet they would not listen. Therefore you handed them over to the peoples of the lands. 31Nevertheless, in your great mercies you did not make an end of them or forsake them, for you are a gracious and merciful God.

32 "Now therefore, our God—the great and mighty and awesome God, keeping covenant and steadfast love—do not treat lightly all the hardship that has come upon us, upon our kings, our officials, our priests, our prophets, our ancestors, and all your people, since the time of the kings of Assyria until today. 33You have been just in all that has come upon us, for you have dealt faithfully and we have acted wickedly; 34our kings, our officials, our priests, and our ancestors have not kept your law or heeded the commandments and the warnings that you gave them. 35Even in their own kingdom, and in the great goodness you bestowed on them, and in the large and rich land that you set before them, they did not serve you and did not turn from their wicked works. 36Here we are, slaves to this day—slaves in the land that you gave to our ancestors to enjoy its fruit and its good gifts. 37Its rich yield goes to the kings whom you have set over us because of our sins; they have power also over our bodies and over our livestock at their pleasure, and we are in great distress."

Those Who Signed the Covenant

38ª Because of all this we make a firm agreement in writing, and on that sealed document are inscribed the names of our officials, our Levites, and our priests.

10ᵇ Upon the sealed document are the names of Nehemiah the governor, son of Hacaliah, and Zedekiah; 2Seraiah, Azariah, Jeremiah, 3Pashhur, Amariah, Malchijah, 4Hattush, Shebaniah, Malluch, 5Harim, Meremoth, Obadiah, 6Daniel, Ginnethon, Baruch, 7Meshullam,

Abijah, Mijamin, 8Maaziah, Bilgai, Shemaiah; these are the priests. 9And the Levites: Jeshua son of Azaniah, Binnui of the sons of Henadad, Kadmiel; 10and their associates, Shebaniah, Hodiah, Kelita, Pelaiah, Hanan, 11Mica, Rehob, Hashabiah, 12Zaccur, Sherebiah, Shebaniah, 13Hodiah, Bani, Beninu. 14The leaders of the people: Parosh, Pahath-moab, Elam, Zattu, Bani, 15Bunni, Azgad, Bebai, 16Adonijah, Bigvai, Adin, 17Ater, Hezekiah, Azzur, 18Hodiah, Hashum, Bezai, 19Hariph, Anathoth, Nebai, 20Magpiash, Meshullam, Hezir, 21Meshezabel, Zadok, Jaddua, 22Pelatiah, Hanan, Anaiah, 23Hoshea, Hananiah, Hasshub, 24Hallohesh, Pilha, Shobek, 25Rehum, Hashabnah, Maaseiah, 26Ahiah, Hanan, Anan, 27Malluch, Harim, and Baanah.

Summary of the Covenant

28 The rest of the people, the priests, the Levites, the gatekeepers, the singers, the temple servants, and all who have separated themselves from the peoples of the lands to adhere to the law of God, their wives, their sons, their daughters, all who have knowledge and understanding, 29join with their kin, their nobles, and enter into a curse and an oath to walk in God's law, which was given by Moses the servant of God, and to observe and do all the commandments of the LORD our Lord and his ordinances and his statutes. 30We will not give our daughters to the peoples of the land or take their daughters for our sons; 31and if the peoples of the land bring in merchandise or any grain on the sabbath day to sell, we will not buy it from them on the sabbath or on a holy day; and we will forego the crops of the seventh year and the exaction of every debt.

32 We also lay on ourselves the obligation to charge ourselves yearly one-third of a shekel for the service of the house of our God: 33for the rows of bread, the regular grain offering, the regular burnt offering, the sabbaths, the new moons, the appointed festivals, the sacred donations, and the sin offerings to make atonement for Israel, and for all the work of the house of our God. 34We have also cast lots among the priests, the Levites, and the people, for the wood offering, to bring it into the house of our God, by ancestral

houses, at appointed times, year by year, to burn on the altar of the LORD our God, as it is written in the law. 35We obligate ourselves to bring the first fruits of our soil and the first fruits of all fruit of every tree, year by year, to the house of the LORD; 36also to bring to the house of our God, to the priests who minister in the house of our God, the firstborn of our sons and of our livestock, as it is written in the law, and the firstlings of our herds and of our flocks; 37and to bring the first of our dough, and our contributions, the fruit of every tree, the wine and the oil, to the priests, to the chambers of the house of our God; and to bring to the Levites the tithes from our soil, for it is the Levites who collect the tithes in all our rural towns. 38And the priest, the descendant of Aaron, shall be with the Levites when the Levites receive the tithes; and the Levites shall bring up a tithe of the tithes to the house of our God, to the chambers of the storehouse. 39For the people of Israel and the sons of Levi shall bring the contribution of grain, wine, and oil to the storerooms where the vessels of the sanctuary are, and where the priests that minister, and the gatekeepers and the singers are. We will not neglect the house of our God.

Population of the City Increased

11 Now the leaders of the people lived in Jerusalem; and the rest of the people cast lots to bring one out of ten to live in the holy city Jerusalem, while nine-tenths remained in the other towns. 2And the people blessed all those who willingly offered to live in Jerusalem.

3 These are the leaders of the province who lived in Jerusalem; but in the towns of Judah all lived on their property in their towns: Israel, the priests, the Levites, the temple servants, and the descendants of Solomon's servants. 4And in Jerusalem lived some of the Judahites and of the Benjaminites. Of the Judahites: Athaiah son of Uzziah son of Zechariah son of Amariah son of Shephatiah son of Mahalalel, of the descendants of Perez; 5and Maaseiah son of Baruch son of Col-hozeh son of Hazaiah son of Adaiah son of Joiarib son of Zechariah son of the Shilonite. 6All the descendants of Perez who lived in Jerusalem were four hundred sixty-eight valiant warriors.

7 And these are the Benjaminites: Sallu son of Meshullam son of Joed son of Pe-

daiah son of Kolaiah son of Maaseiah son of Ithiel son of Jeshaiah. 8And his brothersc Gabbai, Sallai: nine hundred twenty-eight. 9Joel son of Zichri was their overseer; and Judah son of Hassenuah was second in charge of the city.

10 Of the priests: Jedaiah son of Joiarib, Jachin, 11Seraiah son of Hilkiah son of Meshullam son of Zadok son of Meraioth son of Ahitub, officer of the house of God, 12and their associates who did the work of the house, eight hundred twenty-two; and Adaiah son of Jeroham son of Pelaliah son of Amzi son of Zechariah son of Pashhur son of Malchijah, 13and his associates, heads of ancestral houses, two hundred forty-two; and Amashsai son of Azarel son of Ahzai son of Meshillemoth son of Immer, 14and their associates, valiant warriors, one hundred twenty-eight; their overseer was Zabdiel son of Haggedolim.

15 And of the Levites: Shemaiah son of Hasshub son of Azrikam son of Hashabiah son of Bunni; 16and Shabbethai and Jozabad, of the leaders of the Levites, who were over the outside work of the house of God; 17and Mattaniah son of Mica son of Zabdi son of Asaph, who was the leader to begin the thanksgiving in prayer, and Bakbukiah, the second among his associates; and Abda son of Shammua son of Galal son of Jeduthun. 18All the Levites in the holy city were two hundred eighty-four.

19 The gatekeepers, Akkub, Talmon and their associates, who kept watch at the gates, were one hundred seventy-two. 20And the rest of Israel, and of the priests and the Levites, were in all the towns of Judah, all of them in their inheritance. 21But the temple servants lived on Ophel; and Ziha and Gishpa were over the temple servants.

22 The overseer of the Levites in Jerusalem was Uzzi son of Bani son of Hashabiah son of Mattaniah son of Mica, of the descendants of Asaph, the singers, in charge of the work of the house of God. 23For there was a command from the king concerning them, and a settled provision for the singers, as was required every day. 24And Pethahiah son of Meshezabel, of the descendants of Zerah son of Judah, was at the king's hand in all matters concerning the people.

c Gk Mss: Heb *And after him*

Villages outside Jerusalem

25 And as for the villages, with their fields, some of the people of Judah lived in Kiriath-arba and its villages, and in Dibon and its villages, and in Jekabzeel and its villages, 26and in Jeshua and in Moladah and Beth-pelet, 27in Hazar-shual, in Beer-sheba and its villages, 28in Ziklag, in Meconah and its villages, 29in Enrimmon, in Zorah, in Jarmuth, 30Zanoah, Adullam, and their villages, Lachish and its fields, and Azekah and its villages. So they camped from Beer-sheba to the valley of Hinnom. 31The people of Benjamin also lived from Geba onward, at Michmash, Aija, Bethel and its villages, 32Anathoth, Nob, Ananiah, 33Hazor, Ramah, Gittaim, 34Hadid, Zeboim, Neballat, 35Lod, and Ono, the valley of artisans. 36And certain divisions of the Levites in Judah were joined to Benjamin.

A List of Priests and Levites

12 These are the priests and the Levites who came up with Zerubbabel son of Shealtiel, and Jeshua: Seraiah, Jeremiah, Ezra, 2Amariah, Malluch, Hattush, 3Shecaniah, Rehum, Meremoth, 4Iddo, Ginnethoi, Abijah, 5Mijamin, Maadiah, Bilgah, 6Shemaiah, Joiarib, Jedaiah, 7Sallu, Amok, Hilkiah, Jedaiah. These were the leaders of the priests and of their associates in the days of Jeshua.

8 And the Levites: Jeshua, Binnui, Kadmiel, Sherebiah, Judah, and Mattaniah, who with his associates was in charge of the songs of thanksgiving. 9And Bakbukiah and Unno their associates stood opposite them in the service. 10Jeshua was the father of Joiakim, Joiakim the father of Eliashib, Eliashib the father of Joiada, 11Joiada the father of Jonathan, and Jonathan the father of Jaddua.

12 In the days of Joiakim the priests, heads of ancestral houses, were: of Seraiah, Meraiah; of Jeremiah, Hananiah; 13of Ezra, Meshullam; of Amariah, Jehohanan; 14of Malluchi, Jonathan; of Shebaniah, Joseph; 15of Harim, Adna; of Meraioth, Helkai; 16of Iddo, Zechariah; of Ginnethon, Meshullam; 17of Abijah, Zichri; of Miniamin, of Moadiah, Piltai; 18of Bilgah, Shammua; of Shemaiah, Jehonathan; 19of Joiarib, Mattenai; of Jedaiah, Uzzi; 20of Sallai, Kallai; of Amok, Eber; 21of Hilkiah, Hashabiah; of Jedaiah, Nethanel.

22 As for the Levites, in the days of Eliashib, Joiada, Johanan, and Jaddua, there were recorded the heads of ancestral houses; also the priests until the reign of Darius the Persian. 23The Levites, heads of ancestral houses, were recorded in the Book of the Annals until the days of Johanan son of Eliashib. 24And the leaders of the Levites: Hashabiah, Sherebiah, and Jeshua son of Kadmiel, with their associates over against them, to praise and to give thanks, according to the commandment of David the man of God, section opposite to section. 25Mattaniah, Bakbukiah, Obadiah, Meshullam, Talmon, and Akkub were gatekeepers standing guard at the storehouses of the gates. 26These were in the days of Joiakim son of Jeshua son of Jozadak, and in the days of the governor Nehemiah and of the priest Ezra, the scribe.

Dedication of the City Wall

27 Now at the dedication of the wall of Jerusalem they sought out the Levites in all their places, to bring them to Jerusalem to celebrate the dedication with rejoicing, with thanksgivings and with singing, with cymbals, harps, and lyres. 28The companies of the singers gathered together from the circuit around Jerusalem and from the villages of the Netophathites; 29also from Beth-gilgal and from the region of Geba and Azmaveth; for the singers had built for themselves villages around Jerusalem. 30And the priests and the Levites purified themselves; and they purified the people and the gates and the wall.

31 Then I brought the leaders of Judah up onto the wall, and appointed two great companies that gave thanks and went in procession. One went to the right on the wall to the Dung Gate; 32and after them went Hoshaiah and half the officials of Judah, 33and Azariah, Ezra, Meshullam, 34Judah, Benjamin, Shemaiah, and Jeremiah, 35and some of the young priests with trumpets: Zechariah son of Jonathan son of Shemaiah son of Mattaniah son of Micaiah son of Zaccur son of Asaph; 36and his kindred, Shemaiah, Azarel, Milalai, Gilalai, Maai, Nethanel, Judah, and Hanani, with the musical instruments of David the man of God; and the scribe Ezra went in front of them. 37At the Fountain Gate, in front of them, they went straight up by the stairs of the city of David, at the ascent of the wall, above the house of David, to the Water Gate on the east.

38 The other company of those who gave thanks went to the left,[d] and I followed them with half of the people on the wall, above the Tower of the Ovens, to the Broad Wall, 39and above the Gate of Ephraim, and by the Old Gate, and by the Fish Gate and the Tower of Hananel and the Tower of the Hundred, to the Sheep Gate; and they came to a halt at the Gate of the Guard. 40So both companies of those who gave thanks stood in the house of God, and I and half of the officials with me; 41and the priests Eliakim, Maaseiah, Miniamin, Micaiah, Elioenai, Zechariah, and Hananiah, with trumpets; 42and Maaseiah, Shemaiah, Eleazar, Uzzi, Jehohanan, Malchijah, Elam, and Ezer. And the singers sang with Jezrahiah as their leader. 43They offered great sacrifices that day and rejoiced, for God had made them rejoice with great joy; the women and children also rejoiced. The joy of Jerusalem was heard far away.

Temple Responsibilities

44 On that day men were appointed over the chambers for the stores, the contributions, the first fruits, and the tithes, to gather into them the portions required by the law for the priests and for the Levites from the fields belonging to the towns; for Judah rejoiced over the priests and the Levites who ministered. 45They performed the service of their God and the service of purification, as did the singers and the gatekeepers, according to the command of David and his son Solomon. 46For in the days of David and Asaph long ago there was a leader of the singers, and there were songs of praise and thanksgiving to God. 47In the days of Zerubbabel and in the days of Nehemiah all Israel gave the daily portions for the singers and the gatekeepers. They set apart that which was for the Levites; and the Levites set apart that which was for the descendants of Aaron.

Foreigners Separated from Israel

13 On that day they read from the book of Moses in the hearing of the people; and in it was found written that no Ammonite or Moabite should ever enter the assembly of God, 2because they did not meet the Israelites with bread and water, but hired Balaam against them to curse them—yet our God turned the curse into a blessing. 3When the people heard the law, they separated from Israel all those of foreign descent.

The Reforms of Nehemiah

4 Now before this, the priest Eliashib, who was appointed over the chambers of the house of our God, and who was related to Tobiah, 5prepared for Tobiah a large room where they had previously put the grain offering, the frankincense, the vessels, and the tithes of grain, wine, and oil, which were given by commandment to the Levites, singers, and gatekeepers, and the contributions for the priests. 6While this was taking place I was not in Jerusalem, for in the thirty-second year of King Artaxerxes of Babylon I went to the king. After some time I asked leave of the king 7and returned to Jerusalem. I then discovered the wrong that Eliashib had done on behalf of Tobiah, preparing a room for him in the courts of the house of God. 8And I was very angry, and I threw all the household furniture of Tobiah out of the room. 9Then I gave orders and they cleansed the chambers, and I brought back the vessels of the house of God, with the grain offering and the frankincense.

10 I also found out that the portions of the Levites had not been given to them; so that the Levites and the singers, who had conducted the service, had gone back to their fields. 11So I remonstrated with the officials and said, "Why is the house of God forsaken?" And I gathered them together and set them in their stations. 12Then all Judah brought the tithe of the grain, wine, and oil into the storehouses. 13And I appointed as treasurers over the storehouses the priest Shelemiah, the scribe Zadok, and Pedaiah of the Levites, and as their assistant Hanan son of Zaccur son of Mattaniah, for they were considered faithful; and their duty was to distribute to their associates. 14Remember me, O my God, concerning this, and do not wipe out my good deeds that I have done for the house of my God and for his service.

Sabbath Reforms Begun

15 In those days I saw in Judah people treading wine presses on the sabbath, and bringing in heaps of grain and loading them on donkeys; and also wine, grapes,

d Cn: Heb *opposite*

figs, and all kinds of burdens, which they brought into Jerusalem on the sabbath day; and I warned them at that time against selling food. [16]Tyrians also, who lived in the city, brought in fish and all kinds of merchandise and sold them on the sabbath to the people of Judah, and in Jerusalem. [17]Then I remonstrated with the nobles of Judah and said to them, "What is this evil thing that you are doing, profaning the sabbath day? [18]Did not your ancestors act in this way, and did not our God bring all this disaster on us and on this city? Yet you bring more wrath on Israel by profaning the sabbath."

19 When it began to be dark at the gates of Jerusalem before the sabbath, I commanded that the doors should be shut and gave orders that they should not be opened until after the sabbath. And I set some of my servants over the gates, to prevent any burden from being brought in on the sabbath day. [20]Then the merchants and sellers of all kinds of merchandise spent the night outside Jerusalem once or twice. [21]But I warned them and said to them, "Why do you spend the night in front of the wall? If you do so again, I will lay hands on you." From that time on they did not come on the sabbath. [22]And I commanded the Levites that they should purify themselves and come and guard the gates, to keep the sabbath day holy. Remember this also in my favor,

To Do List

THURSDAY

Scripture Reading
for Today:
Nehemiah 13.9–14

Verse for Today:
Nehemiah 13.14

✓ Bake 30 cupcakes for Gina's class party

✓ Check office e-mails

✓ Schedule tetanus shot for Joe and Becca

✓ Have van brakes checked

✓ Prepare presentation to parish finance committee

✓ Return overdue videos and library books

✓ Send Gemma belated birthday card—tomorrow

✓ Clean out refrigerator

✓ Angel costume for Katie's school play

✓ Make time to PRAY!!!!

✓ Exercise!

"Remember me, O my God, concerning this, and do not wipe out my good deeds that I have done for the house of my God and for his service" (Nehemiah 13.14).

—LOUISE PERROTTA

Go to page 519 for your next devotional reading.

O my God, and spare me according to the greatness of your steadfast love.

Mixed Marriages Condemned

23 In those days also I saw Jews who had married women of Ashdod, Ammon, and Moab; 24and half of their children spoke the language of Ashdod, and they could not speak the language of Judah, but spoke the language of various peoples. 25And I contended with them and cursed them and beat some of them and pulled out their hair; and I made them take an oath in the name of God, saying, "You shall not give your daughters to their sons, or take their daughters for your sons or for yourselves. 26Did not King Solomon of Israel sin on account of such women? Among the many nations there was no king like him, and he was beloved by his God, and God made him king over all Israel; nevertheless, foreign women made even him to sin. 27Shall we then listen to you and do all this great evil and act treacherously against our God by marrying foreign women?"

28 And one of the sons of Jehoiada, son of the high priest Eliashib, was the son-in-law of Sanballat the Horonite; I chased him away from me. 29Remember them, O my God, because they have defiled the priesthood, the covenant of the priests and the Levites.

30 Thus I cleansed them from everything foreign, and I established the duties of the priests and Levites, each in his work; 31and I provided for the wood offering, at appointed times, and for the first fruits. Remember me, O my God, for good.

Tobit

Tobit is one of the Deuterocanonical books of Scripture. These books were circulated in Greek and used by the early church and were included in the canon of Scripture by the Council of Trent in 1546. Protestants do not consider them canonical, which explains why Protestant Bibles have only 66 books while Catholic Bibles have 73.

Set in Nineveh, the capital of Assyria, the book is named after a Jew who had been exiled from his native land. The unfortunate Tobit had become blind and so sent his son Tobias to Media in order to bring back money that he had deposited there. Tobias is accompanied by an angel in disguise, Raphael, who guides him on his journey and helps him win the lovely Sarah, a woman whose husbands had been killed by a demon on the night of each of her weddings. Raphael instructs Tobias how to get rid of the demon and free Sarah to marry him.

Though placed with the historical books, the book of Tobit is probably an inspired religious novel, whose themes of prayer, spiritual warfare, and God's healing power are still relevant for Catholics today.

1 This book tells the story of Tobit son of Tobiel son of Hananiel son of Aduel son of Gabael son of Raphael son of Raguel of the descendants[a] of Asiel, of the tribe of Naphtali, 2who in the days of King Shalmaneser[b] of the Assyrians was taken into captivity from Thisbe, which is to the south of Kedesh Naphtali in Upper Galilee, above Asher toward the west, and north of Phogor.

Tobit's Youth and Virtuous Life

3 I, Tobit, walked in the ways of truth and righteousness all the days of my life. I performed many acts of charity for my kindred and my people who had gone with me in exile to Nineveh in the land of the Assyrians. 4When I was in my own country, in the land of Israel, while I was still a young man, the whole tribe of my ancestor Naphtali deserted the house of David and Jerusalem. This city had been chosen from among all the tribes of Israel, where all the tribes of Israel should offer sacrifice and where the temple, the dwelling of God, had been consecrated and established for all generations forever.

5 All my kindred and our ancestral house of Naphtali sacrificed to the calf[c] that King Jeroboam of Israel had erected in Dan and on all the mountains of Galilee. 6But I alone went often to Jerusalem

a Other ancient authorities lack *of Raphael son of Raguel of the descendants*   b Gk *Enemessaros*
c Other ancient authorities read *heifer*

for the festivals, as it is prescribed for all Israel by an everlasting decree. I would hurry off to Jerusalem with the first fruits of the crops and the firstlings of the flock, the tithes of the cattle, and the first shearings of the sheep. 7I would give these to the priests, the sons of Aaron, at the altar; likewise the tenth of the grain, wine, olive oil, pomegranates, figs, and the rest of the fruits to the sons of Levi who ministered at Jerusalem. Also for six years I would save up a second tenth in money and go and distribute it in Jerusalem. 8A third tenth*d* I would give to the orphans and widows and to the converts who had attached themselves to Israel. I would bring it and give it to them in the third year, and we would eat it according to the ordinance decreed concerning it in the law of Moses and according to the instructions of Deborah, the mother of my father Tobiel,*e* for my father had died and left me an orphan. 9When I became a man I married a woman,*f* a member of our own family, and by her I became the father of a son whom I named Tobias.

Taken Captive to Nineveh

10 After I was carried away captive to Assyria and came as a captive to Nineveh, everyone of my kindred and my people ate the food of the Gentiles, 11but I kept myself from eating the food of the Gentiles. 12Because I was mindful of God with all my heart, 13the Most High gave me favor and good standing with Shalmaneser,*g* and I used to buy everything he needed. 14Until his death I used to go into Media, and buy for him there. While in the country of Media I left bags of silver worth ten talents in trust with Gabael, the brother of Gabri. 15But when Shalmaneser*g* died, and his son Sennacherib reigned in his place, the highways into Media became unsafe and I could no longer go there.

Courage in Burying the Dead

16 In the days of Shalmaneser*g* I performed many acts of charity to my kindred, those of my tribe. 17I would give my food to the hungry and my clothing to the naked; and if I saw the dead body of any of my people thrown out behind the wall of Nineveh, I would bury it. 18I also buried any whom King Sennacherib put to death when he came fleeing from Judea in those days of judgment that the king of

heaven executed upon him because of his blasphemies. For in his anger he put to death many Israelites; but I would secretly remove the bodies and bury them. So when Sennacherib looked for them he could not find them. 19Then one of the Ninevites went and informed the king about me, that I was burying them; so I hid myself. But when I realized that the king knew about me and that I was being searched for to be put to death, I was afraid and ran away. 20Then all my property was confiscated; nothing was left to me that was not taken into the royal treasury except my wife Anna and my son Tobias.

21 But not forty*h* days passed before two of Sennacherib's*i* sons killed him, and they fled to the mountains of Ararat, and his son Esar-haddon*j* reigned after him. He appointed Ahikar, the son of my brother Hanael*k* over all the accounts of his kingdom, and he had authority over the entire administration. 22Ahikar interceded for me, and I returned to Nineveh. Now Ahikar was chief cupbearer, keeper of the signet, and in charge of administration of the accounts under King Sennacherib of Assyria; so Esar-haddon*j* reappointed him. He was my nephew and so a close relative.

2 Then during the reign of Esar-haddon*j* I returned home, and my wife Anna and my son Tobias were restored to me. At our festival of Pentecost, which is the sacred festival of weeks, a good dinner was prepared for me and I reclined to eat. 2When the table was set for me and an abundance of food placed before me, I said to my son Tobias, "Go, my child, and bring whatever poor person you may find of our people among the exiles in Nineveh, who is wholeheartedly mindful of God,*l* and he shall eat together with me. I will wait for you, until you come back." 3So Tobias went to look for some poor person of our people. When he had returned he said, "Father!" And I replied, "Here I am, my child." Then he went on to say, "Look, father, one of our own people has been murdered and thrown

---

d A third tenth added from other ancient authorities   *e* Lat: Gk *Hananiel*   *f* Other ancient authorities add *Anna*   *g* Gk *Enemessaros*   *h* Other ancient authorities read either *forty-five* or *fifty*   *i* Gk *his*   *j* Gk *Sacherdonos*   *k* Other authorities read *Hananael*   *l* Lat: Gk *wholeheartedly mindful*

into the market place, and now he lies there strangled." ⁴Then I sprang up, left the dinner before even tasting it, and removed the body^m from the square^n and laid it^m in one of the rooms until sunset when I might bury it.^m ⁵When I returned, I washed myself and ate my food in sorrow. ⁶Then I remembered the prophecy of Amos, how he said against Bethel,^o

"Your festivals shall be turned
    into mourning,
and all your songs into
    lamentation."
And I wept.

Tobit Becomes Blind

7 When the sun had set, I went and dug a grave and buried him. ⁸And my neighbors laughed and said, "Is he still not afraid? He has already been hunted down to be put to death for doing this, and he ran away; yet here he is again burying the dead!" ⁹That same night I washed myself and went into my courtyard and slept by the wall of the courtyard; and my face was uncovered because of the heat. ¹⁰I did not know that there were sparrows on the wall; their fresh droppings fell into my eyes and produced white films. I went to physicians to be healed, but the more they treated me with ointments the more my vision was obscured by the white films, until I became completely blind. For four years I remained unable to see. All my kindred were sorry for me, and Ahikar took care of me for two years before he went to Elymais.

Tobit's Wife Earns Their Livelihood

11 At that time, also, my wife Anna earned money at women's work. ¹²She used to send what she made to the owners and they would pay wages to her. One day, the seventh of Dystrus, when she cut off a piece she had woven and sent it to the owners, they paid her full wages and also gave her a young goat for a meal. ¹³When she returned to me, the goat began to bleat. So I called her and said, "Where did you get this goat? It is surely not stolen, is it? Return it to the owners; for we have no right to eat anything stolen." ¹⁴But she said to me, "It was given to me as a gift in addition to my wages." But I did not believe her, and told her to return it to the owners. I became flushed with anger against her over this. Then she replied to me, "Where are your acts of charity? Where are your righteous deeds? These things are known about you!" ^p

Tobit's Prayer

3 Then with much grief and anguish of heart I wept, and with groaning began to pray:
2 "You are righteous, O Lord,
    and all your deeds are just;
all your ways are mercy and truth;
    you judge the world.^q
3 And now, O Lord, remember me
    and look favorably upon me.
Do not punish me for my sins
    and for my unwitting offenses
    and those that my ancestors
        committed before you.
They sinned against you,
4   and disobeyed your
        commandments.
So you gave us over to plunder,
    exile, and death,
to become the talk, the byword,
    and an object of reproach
among all the nations among
    whom you have dispersed us.
5 And now your many judgments are
        true
    in exacting penalty from me for
        my sins.
For we have not kept your
        commandments
    and have not walked in
        accordance with truth before
        you.
6 So now deal with me as you will;
    command my spirit to be taken
        from me,
    so that I may be released from the
        face of the earth and become
        dust.
For it is better for me to die than to
        live,
    because I have had to listen to
        undeserved insults,
    and great is the sorrow within me.
Command, O Lord, that I be
    released from this distress;
release me to go to the eternal
        home,
    and do not, O Lord, turn your
        face away from me.

---

^m Gk him   ^n Other ancient authorities lack from the square   ^o Other ancient authorities read against Bethlehem   ^p Or to you; Gk with you   ^q Other ancient authorities read you render true and righteous judgment forever

For it is better for me to die
  than to see so much distress in
    my life
  and to listen to insults."

Sarah Falsely Accused

7 On the same day, at Ecbatana in Media, it also happened that Sarah, the daughter of Raguel, was reproached by one of her father's maids. 8For she had been married to seven husbands, and the wicked demon Asmodeus had killed each of them before they had been with her as is customary for wives. So the maid said to her, "You are the one who kills[r] your husbands! See, you have already been married to seven husbands and have not borne the name of[s] a single one of them. 9Why do you beat us? Because your husbands are dead? Go with them! May we never see a son or daughter of yours!"

Sarah's Prayer for Death

10 On that day she was grieved in spirit and wept. When she had gone up to her father's upper room, she intended to hang herself. But she thought it over and said, "Never shall they reproach my father, saying to him, 'You had only one beloved daughter but she hanged herself because of her distress.' And I shall bring my father in his old age down in sorrow to Hades. It is better for me not to hang myself, but to pray the Lord that I may die and not listen to these reproaches anymore." 11At that same time, with hands outstretched toward the window, she prayed and said,

  "Blessed are you, merciful God!
  Blessed is your name forever;
    let all your works praise you
      forever.
12 And now, Lord,[t] I turn my face to
      you,
  and raise my eyes toward you.
13 Command that I be released from
      the earth
  and not listen to such reproaches
      any more.
14 You know, O Master, that I am
      innocent
  of any defilement with a man,
15 and that I have not disgraced my
      name
  or the name of my father in the
      land of my exile.
  I am my father's only child;

he has no other child to be his
      heir;
  and he has no close relative or other
      kindred
  for whom I should keep myself as
      wife.
  Already seven husbands of mine
      have died.
  Why should I still live?
  But if it is not pleasing to you,
    O Lord, to take my life,
  hear me in my disgrace."

An Answer to Prayer

16 At that very moment, the prayers of both of them were heard in the glorious presence of God. 17So Raphael was sent to heal both of them: Tobit, by removing the white films from his eyes, so that he might see God's light with his eyes; and Sarah, daughter of Raguel, by giving her in marriage to Tobias son of Tobit, and by setting her free from the wicked demon Asmodeus. For Tobias was entitled to have her before all others who had desired to marry her. At the same time that Tobit returned from the courtyard into his house, Sarah daughter of Raguel came down from her upper room.

Tobit Gives Instructions to His Son

4 That same day Tobit remembered the money that he had left in trust with Gabael at Rages in Media, 2and he said to himself, "Now I have asked for death. Why do I not call my son Tobias and explain to him about the money before I die?" 3Then he called his son Tobias, and when he came to him he said, "My son, when I die,[u] give me a proper burial. Honor your mother and do not abandon her all the days of her life. Do whatever pleases her, and do not grieve her in anything. 4Remember her, my son, because she faced many dangers for you while you were in her womb. And when she dies, bury her beside me in the same grave.

5 "Revere the Lord all your days, my son, and refuse to sin or to transgress his commandments. Live uprightly all the days of your life, and do not walk in the ways of wrongdoing; 6for those who act in accordance with truth will prosper in all

---

r Other ancient authorities read *strangles*
s Other ancient authorities read *have had no
benefit from*   t Other ancient authorities lack
Lord   u Lat

their activities. To all those who practice righteousness[v] [7]give alms from your possessions, and do not let your eye begrudge the gift when you make it. Do not turn your face away from anyone who is poor, and the face of God will not be turned away from you. [8]If you have many possessions, make your gift from them in proportion; if few, do not be afraid to give according to the little you have. [9]So you will be laying up a good treasure for yourself against the day of necessity. [10]For almsgiving delivers from death and keeps you from going into the Darkness. [11]Indeed, almsgiving, for all who practice it, is an excellent offering in the presence of the Most High.

[12] "Beware, my son, of every kind of fornication. First of all, marry a woman from among the descendants of your ancestors; do not marry a foreign woman, who is not of your father's tribe; for we are the descendants of the prophets. Remember, my son, that Noah, Abraham, Isaac, and Jacob, our ancestors of old, all took wives from among their kindred. They were blessed in their children, and their posterity will inherit the land. [13]So now, my son, love your kindred, and in your heart do not disdain your kindred, the sons and daughters of your people, by refusing to take a wife for yourself from among them. For in pride there is ruin and great confusion. And in idleness there is loss and dire poverty, because idleness is the mother of famine.

[14] "Do not keep over until the next day the wages of those who work for you, but pay them at once. If you serve God you will receive payment. Watch yourself, my son, in everything you do, and discipline yourself in all your conduct. [15]And what you hate, do not do to anyone. Do not drink wine to excess or let drunkenness go with you on your way. [16]Give some of your food to the hungry, and some of your clothing to the naked. Give all your surplus as alms, and do not let your eye begrudge your giving of alms. [17]Place your bread on the grave of the righteous, but give none to sinners. [18]Seek advice from any wise person and do not despise any useful counsel. [19]At all times bless the Lord God, and ask him that your ways may be made straight and that all your paths and plans may prosper. For none of the nations has understanding, but the Lord himself will give them good

counsel; but if he chooses otherwise, he casts down to deepest Hades. So now, my child, remember these commandments, and do not let them be erased from your heart.

Money Left in Trust with Gabael

[20] "And now, my son, let me explain to you that I left ten talents of silver in trust with Gabael son of Gabrias, at Rages in Media. [21]Do not be afraid, my son, because we have become poor. You have great wealth if you fear God and flee from every sin and do what is good in the sight of the Lord your God."

The Angel Raphael

5 Then Tobias answered his father Tobit, "I will do everything that you have commanded me, father; [2]but how can I obtain the money[w] from him, since he does not know me and I do not know him? What evidence[x] am I to give him so that he will recognize and trust me, and give me the money? Also, I do not know the roads to Media, or how to get there." [3]Then Tobit answered his son Tobias, "He gave me his bond and I gave him my bond. I[y] divided his in two; we each took one part, and I put one with the money. And now twenty years have passed since I left this money in trust. So now, my son, find yourself a trustworthy man to go with you, and we will pay him wages until you return. But get back the money from Gabael."[z]

[4] So Tobias went out to look for a man to go with him to Media, someone who was acquainted with the way. He went out and found the angel Raphael standing in front of him; but he did not perceive that he was an angel of God. [5]Tobias[a] said to him, "Where do you come from, young man?" "From your kindred, the Israelites," he replied, "and I have come here to work." Then Tobias[b] said to him, "Do you know the way to go to Media?" [6]"Yes," he replied, "I have been there many times; I am acquainted with it and know all the roads. I have often traveled to Media, and would stay with our kinsman

---

[v] The text of codex Sinaiticus goes directly from verse 6 to verse 19, reading *To those who practice righteousness* [19]*the Lord will give good counsel.* In order to fill the lacuna verses 7 to 18 are derived from other ancient authorities   [w] Gk *it*   [x] Gk *sign*   [y] Other authorities read *He*   [z] Gk *from him*   [a] Gk *He*   [b] Gk *he*

Gabael who lives in Rages of Media. It is a journey of two days from Ecbatana to Rages; for it lies in a mountainous area, while Ecbatana is in the middle of the plain." [7]Then Tobias said to him, "Wait for me, young man, until I go in and tell my father; for I do need you to travel with me, and I will pay you your wages." [8]He replied, "All right, I will wait; but do not take too long."

9 So Tobias[c] went in to tell his father Tobit and said to him, "I have just found a man who is one of our own Israelite kindred!" He replied, "Call the man in, my son, so that I may learn about his family and to what tribe he belongs, and whether he is trustworthy enough to go with you."

10 Then Tobias went out and called him, and said, "Young man, my father is calling for you." So he went in to him, and Tobit greeted him first. He replied, "Joyous greetings to you!" But Tobit retorted, "What joy is left for me any more? I am a man without eyesight; I cannot see the

c Gk he

THE TRADITION

Angels

He went out and found the angel Raphael standing in front of him.
TOBIT 5.4

Only "thirty-something" years ago, a prominent Catholic theologian explained that modern people tend to be scandalized by the Catholic belief in angels because these creatures are outside our scientific sphere of experience. Were this theologian to browse the spirituality section of almost any bookstore today, he would find it mysteriously "touched by an angel."

Angel power, angel miracles, oracles, energy, magic, therapy, letters, answers . . . angels with urchins, aliens, and elves . . . how to attract angels, use them for channeling, harness their energy, find them within, learn angel-speak . . . For many people now, the difficulty about angels is not disbelief but a readiness to believe just about anything!

Why this fascination with the angelic world? One explanation is that it taps into a widespread interest in the supernatural without raising uncomfortable issues like conversion and commitment to Christ.

But angels cannot be considered apart from God. They are beings who have made a wholehearted choice for God and who rejoice to serve his plan by acting as his servants and messengers. In a special way, angels accompany Jesus and belong to him: At the end of time, Scripture tells us, "The Son of Man is to come with his angels" (Matthew 16.27).

Excepting the fallen angels, every angel in the Bible is portrayed serving God and his plan. A random sampling: Raphael is sent to guide Tobiah (Tobit 5). Gabriel announces two momentous births (Luke 1.11–13, 26–31). Michael and his angels fight God's enemies (Revelation 12.7). Unnamed angels save Isaac (Genesis 22.11), assist the prophet Elijah (1 Kings 19.5), appear to shepherds (Luke 2.8–14), attend Jesus (Matthew 4.11; Luke 22.43), and unlock prison doors (Acts 12.7). Hosts of angels offer unceasing praise (Revelation 5.11).

Some of the current literature conveys the impression that, with the right technique, you can get angels to respond to your wishes—almost like pets with supernatural powers. This attitude demonstrates incredible naïveté about what angels are like and whose servants they are.

Angels are pure spirits—intelligent, powerful, and sometimes fearsome to behold. The amazing thing is that, at *God's* command, these glorious creatures do serve us! As Thomas Aquinas said, "The angels work together for the benefit of us all."

light of heaven, but I lie in darkness like the dead who no longer see the light. Although still alive, I am among the dead. I hear people but I cannot see them." But the young man*d* said, "Take courage; the time is near for God to heal you; take courage." Then Tobit said to him, "My son Tobias wishes to go to Media. Can you accompany him and guide him? I will pay your wages, brother." He answered, "I can go with him and I know all the roads, for I have often gone to Media and have crossed all its plains, and I am familiar with its mountains and all of its roads."

11 Then Tobit*d* said to him, "Brother, of what family are you and from what tribe? Tell me, brother." 12He replied, "Why do you need to know my tribe?" But Tobit*d* said, "I want to be sure, brother, whose son you are and what your name is." 13He replied, "I am Azariah, the son of the great Hananiah, one of your relatives." 14Then Tobit said to him, "Welcome! God save you, brother. Do not feel bitter toward me, brother, because I wanted to be sure about your ancestry. It turns out that you are a kinsman, and of good and noble lineage. For I knew Hananiah and Nathan,*e* the two sons of Shemeliah,*f* and they used to go with me to Jerusalem and worshiped with me there, and were not led astray. Your kindred are good people; you come of good stock. Hearty welcome!"

15 Then he added, "I will pay you a drachma a day as wages, as well as expenses for yourself and my son. So go with my son, 16and*g* I will add something to your wages." Raphael*h* answered, "I will go with him; so do not fear. We shall leave in good health and return to you in good health, because the way is safe." 17So Tobit*d* said to him, "Blessings be upon you, brother."

Then he called his son and said to him, "Son, prepare supplies for the journey and set out with your brother. May God in heaven bring you safely there and return you in good health to me; and may his angel, my son, accompany you both for your safety."

Before he went out to start his journey, he kissed his father and mother. Tobit then said to him, "Have a safe journey."

18 But his mother*i* began to weep, and said to Tobit, "Why is it that you have sent my child away? Is he not the staff of our hand as he goes in and out before us?

19Do not heap money upon money, but let it be a ransom for our child. 20For the life that is given to us by the Lord is enough for us." 21Tobit*h* said to her, "Do not worry; our child will leave in good health and return to us in good health. Your eyes will see him on the day when he returns to you in good health. Say no more! Do not fear for them, my sister. 22For a good angel will accompany him; his journey will be successful, and he will come back in good health." 1So she stopped weeping.

Journey to Rages

The young man went out and the angel went with him; 2and the dog came out with him and went along with them. So they both journeyed along, and when the first night overtook them they camped by the Tigris river. 3Then the young man went down to wash his feet in the Tigris river. Suddenly a large fish leaped up from the water and tried to swallow the young man's foot, and he cried out. 4But the angel said to the young man, "Catch hold of the fish and hang on to it!" So the young man grasped the fish and drew it up on the land. 5Then the angel said to him, "Cut open the fish and take out its gall, heart, and liver. Keep them with you, but throw away the intestines. For its gall, heart, and liver are useful as medicine." 6So after cutting open the fish the young man gathered together the gall, heart, and liver; then he roasted and ate some of the fish, and kept some to be salted.

The two continued on their way together until they were near Media.*j* 7Then the young man questioned the angel and said to him, "Brother Azariah, what medicinal value is there in the fish's heart and liver, and in the gall?" 8He replied, "As for the fish's heart and liver, you must burn them to make a smoke in the presence of a man or woman afflicted by a demon or evil spirit, and every affliction will flee away and never remain with that person any longer. 9And as for the gall, anoint a person's eyes where white films have appeared on them; blow upon them, upon

d Gk *he*　　*e* Other ancient authorities read *Jathan* or *Nathaniah*　　*f* Other ancient authorities read *Shemaiah*　　*g* Other ancient authorities add *when you return safely*　　*h* Gk *He*　　*i* Other ancient authorities add *Anna*　　*j* Other ancient authorities read *Ecbatana*

the white films, and the eyes[k] will be healed."

Raphael's Instructions

10 When he entered Media and already was approaching Ecbatana,[l] [11]Raphael said to the young man, "Brother Tobias." "Here I am," he answered. Then Raphael[m] said to him, "We must stay this night in the home of Raguel. He is your relative, and he has a daughter named Sarah. [12]He has no male heir and no daughter except Sarah only, and you, as next of kin to her, have before all other men a hereditary claim on her. Also it is right for you to inherit her father's possessions. Moreover, the girl is sensible, brave, and very beautiful, and her father is a good man." [13]He continued, "You have every right to take her in marriage. So listen to me, brother; tonight I will speak to her father about the girl, so that we may take her to be your bride. When we return from Rages we will celebrate her marriage. For I know that Raguel can by no means keep her from you or promise her to another man without incurring the penalty of death according to the decree of the book of Moses. Indeed he knows that you, rather than any other man, are entitled to marry his daughter. So now listen to me, brother, and tonight we shall speak concerning the girl and arrange her engagement to you. And when we return from Rages we will take her and bring her back with us to your house."

14 Then Tobias said in answer to Raphael, "Brother Azariah, I have heard that she already has been married to seven husbands and that they died in the bridal chamber. On the night when they went in to her, they would die. I have heard people saying that it was a demon that killed them. [15]It does not harm her, but it kills anyone who desires to approach her. So now, since I am the only son my father has, I am afraid that I may die and bring my father's and mother's life down to their grave, grieving for me—and they have no other son to bury them."

16 But Raphael[m] said to him, "Do you not remember your father's orders when he commanded you to take a wife from your father's house? Now listen to me, brother, and say no more about this demon. Take her. I know that this very night she will be given to you in marriage. [17]When you enter the bridal chamber,

take some of the fish's liver and heart, and put them on the embers of the incense. An odor will be given off; [18]the demon will smell it and flee, and will never be seen near her any more. Now when you are about to go to bed with her, both of you must first stand up and pray, imploring the Lord of heaven that mercy and safety may be granted to you. Do not be afraid, for she was set apart for you before the world was made. You will save her, and she will go with you. I presume that you will have children by her, and they will be as brothers to you. Now say no more!" When Tobias heard the words of Raphael and learned that she was his kinswoman,[n] related through his father's lineage, he loved her very much, and his heart was drawn to her.

Arrival at Home of Raguel

7 Now when they[o] entered Ecbatana, Tobias[m] said to him, "Brother Azariah, take me straight to our brother Raguel." So he took him to Raguel's house, where they found him sitting beside the courtyard door. They greeted him first, and he replied, "Joyous greetings, brothers; welcome and good health!" Then he brought them into his house. [2]He said to his wife Edna, "How much the young man resembles my kinsman Tobit!" [3]Then Edna questioned them, saying, "Where are you from, brothers?" They answered, "We belong to the descendants of Naphtali who are exiles in Nineveh." [4]She said to them, "Do you know our kinsman Tobit?" And they replied, "Yes, we know him." Then she asked them, "Is he[p] in good health?" [5]They replied, "He is alive and in good health." And Tobias added, "He is my father!" [6]At that Raguel jumped up and kissed him and wept. [7]He also spoke to him as follows, "Blessings on you, my child, son of a good and noble father![q] O most miserable of calamities that such an upright and beneficent man has become blind!" He then embraced his kinsman Tobias and wept. [8]His wife Edna also wept for him, and their daughter Sarah likewise wept. [9]Then Raguel[m] slaughtered

---

k Gk *they* l Other ancient authorities read *Rages* m Gk *he* n Gk *sister* o Other ancient authorities read *he* p Other ancient authorities add *alive and* q Other ancient authorities add *When he heard that Tobit had lost his sight, he was stricken with grief and wept. Then he said,*

a ram from the flock and received them very warmly.

Marriage of Tobias and Sarah

When they had bathed and washed themselves and had reclined to dine, Tobias said to Raphael, "Brother Azariah, ask Raguel to give me my kinswoman[r] Sarah." ¹⁰But Raguel overheard it and said to the lad, "Eat and drink, and be merry tonight. For no one except you, brother, has the right to marry my daughter Sarah. Likewise I am not at liberty to give her to any other man than yourself, because you are my nearest relative. But let me explain to you the true situation more fully, my child. ¹¹I have given her to seven men of our kinsmen, and all died on the night when they went in to her. But now, my child, eat and drink, and the Lord will act on behalf of you both." But Tobias said, "I will neither eat nor drink anything until you settle the things that pertain to me." So Raguel said, "I will do so. She is given to you in accordance with the decree in the book of Moses, and it has been decreed from heaven that she be given to you. Take your kinswoman;[r] from now on you are her brother and she is your sister. She is given to you from today and forever. May the Lord of heaven, my child, guide and prosper you both this night and grant you mercy and peace." ¹²Then Raguel summoned his daughter Sarah. When she came to him he took her by the hand and gave her to Tobias,[s] saying, "Take her to be your wife in accordance with the law and decree written in the book of Moses. Take her and bring her safely to your father. And may the God of heaven prosper your journey with his peace." ¹³Then he called her mother and told her to bring writing material; and he wrote out a copy of a marriage contract, to the effect that he gave her to him as wife according to the decree of the law of Moses. ¹⁴Then they began to eat and drink.

15 Raguel called his wife Edna and said to her, "Sister, get the other room ready, and take her there." ¹⁶So she went and made the bed in the room as he had told her, and brought Sarah[t] there. She wept for her daughter.[t] Then, wiping away the tears,[u] she said to her, "Take courage, my daughter; the Lord of heaven grant you joy[v] in place of your sorrow. Take courage, my daughter." Then she went out.

Tobias Routs the Demon

8 When they had finished eating and drinking they wanted to retire; so they took the young man and brought him into the bedroom. ²Then Tobias remembered the words of Raphael, and he took the fish's liver and heart out of the bag where he had them and put them on the embers of the incense. ³The odor of the fish so repelled the demon that he fled to the remotest parts[w] of Egypt. But Raphael followed him, and at once bound him there hand and foot.

4 When the parents[x] had gone out and shut the door of the room, Tobias got out of bed and said to Sarah,[t] "Sister, get up, and let us pray and implore our Lord that he grant us mercy and safety." ⁵So she got up, and they began to pray and implore that they might be kept safe. Tobias[y] began by saying,

"Blessed are you, O God of our
    ancestors,
and blessed is your name in all
    generations forever.
Let the heavens and the whole
    creation bless you forever.
⁶ You made Adam, and for him you
    made his wife Eve
as a helper and support.
From the two of them the human
    race has sprung.
You said, 'It is not good that the
    man should be alone;
let us make a helper for him like
    himself.'
⁷ I now am taking this kinswoman of
    mine,
not because of lust,
but with sincerity.
Grant that she and I may find mercy
and that we may grow old
    together."

⁸And they both said, "Amen, Amen." ⁹Then they went to sleep for the night.

But Raguel arose and called his servants to him, and they went and dug a grave, ¹⁰for he said, "It is possible that he will die and we will become an object of ridicule and derision." ¹¹When they had finished digging the grave, Raguel went into his house and called his wife, ¹²saying, "Send one of the maids and have her go in to see if he is alive. But if he is dead, let us bury him without anyone knowing it." [13]So they sent the maid, lit a lamp, and opened the door; and she went in and found them sound asleep together. [14]Then the maid came out and informed them that he was alive and that nothing was wrong. [15]So they blessed the God of heaven, and Raguel[z] said,

"Blessed are you, O God, with every
      pure blessing;
let all your chosen ones bless
      you.[a]
Let them bless you forever.
[16] Blessed are you because you have
      made me glad.
It has not turned out as I
      expected,

but you have dealt with us
      according to your great
      mercy.
[17] Blessed are you because you had
      compassion
on two only children.
Be merciful to them, O Master, and
      keep them safe;
bring their lives to fulfillment
      in happiness and mercy."
[18]Then he ordered his servants to fill in the grave before daybreak.

Wedding Feast

19 After this he asked his wife to bake

[z] Gk *they*   [a] Other ancient authorities lack this line

*S*acred Marriage

In the von Trapp family, anyone who became engaged read the book of Tobit with their spouse-to-be during the week before the wedding. Each couple was strongly encouraged to begin their married life with prayer, as Sarah and Tobiah do in chapter 8, and to see it as a high call to holiness.

I have always deplored the fact that there is a tendency among certain writers and theologians to put a stigma on the married state in its relation to holiness. These people seem to regret that certain saints were married; if they could hush it up, they no doubt would. But there is no getting around it: there was a Saint Catherine of Genoa, a Saint Monica and a Saint Elizabeth of Hungary, a great Saint Louis of France, and the excellent family man, Saint Thomas More, to mention only a few among many, many others. I feel that the Church has placed these great heroic figures in the forefront of the canonized saints in order to assure us that sanctity is not incompatible with married life. And how absurd such a thought would be!

Only if we see marriage as a great sacrament, the symbol of the relationship between Christ and the Church, between the soul and God during all eternity, only then chastity becomes meaningful as a sacrifice, when marriage is given up voluntarily by our priests and religious. What good would it be to offer up something second-rate, something we shouldn't want anyhow? Again, how absurd!

—*MARIA VON TRAPP*

FRIDAY

Scripture Reading
for Today:
Tobit 8.5–8

Verse for Today:
Tobit 8.6

Go to page 522 for your next devotional reading.

many loaves of bread; and he went out to the herd and brought two steers and four rams and ordered them to be slaughtered. So they began to make preparations. 20Then he called for Tobias and swore on oath to him in these words:[b] "You shall not leave here for fourteen days, but shall stay here eating and drinking with me; and you shall cheer up my daughter, who has been depressed. 21Take at once half of what I own and return in safety to your father; the other half will be yours when my wife and I die. Take courage, my child. I am your father and Edna is your mother, and we belong to you as well as to your wife[c] now and forever. Take courage, my child."

The Money Recovered

9 Then Tobias called Raphael and said to him, 2"Brother Azariah, take four servants and two camels with you and travel to Rages. Go to the home of Gabael, give him the bond, get the money, and then bring him with you to the wedding celebration. 4For you know that my father must be counting the days, and if I delay even one day I will upset him very much. 3You are witness to the oath Raguel has sworn, and I cannot violate his oath."[d] 5So Raphael with the four servants and two camels went to Rages in Media and stayed with Gabael. Raphael[e] gave him the bond and informed him that Tobit's son Tobias had married and was inviting him to the wedding celebration. So Gabael[f] got up and counted out to him the money bags, with their seals intact; then they loaded them on the camels.[g] 6In the morning they both got up early and went to the wedding celebration. When they came into Raguel's house they found Tobias reclining at table. He sprang up and greeted Gabael,[h] who wept and blessed him with the words, "Good and noble son of a father good and noble, upright and generous! May the Lord grant the blessing of heaven to you and your wife, and to your wife's father and mother. Blessed be God, for I see in Tobias the very image of my cousin Tobit."

Anxiety of the Parents

10 Now, day by day, Tobit kept counting how many days Tobias[f] would need for going and for returning. And when the days had passed and his son did not appear, 2he said, "Is it possible that he has been detained? Or that Gabael has died, and there is no one to give him the money?" 3And he began to worry. 4His wife Anna said, "My child has perished and is no longer among the living." And she began to weep and mourn for her son, saying, 5"Woe to me, my child, the light of my eyes, that I let you make the journey." 6But Tobit kept saying to her, "Be quiet and stop worrying, my dear;[c] he is all right. Probably something unexpected has happened there. The man who went with him is trustworthy and is one of our own kin. Do not grieve for him, my dear;[c] he will soon be here." 7She answered him, "Be quiet yourself! Stop trying to deceive me! My child has perished." She would rush out every day and watch the road her son had taken, and would heed no one.[i] When the sun had set she would go in and mourn and weep all night long, getting no sleep at all.

Tobias and Sarah Start for Home

Now when the fourteen days of the wedding celebration had ended that Raguel had sworn to observe for his daughter, Tobias came to him and said, "Send me back, for I know that my father and mother do not believe that they will see me again. So I beg of you, father, to let me go so that I may return to my own father. I have already explained to you how I left him." 8But Raguel said to Tobias, "Stay, my child, stay with me; I will send messengers to your father Tobit and they will inform him about you." 9But he said, "No! I beg you to send me back to my father." 10So Raguel promptly gave Tobias his wife Sarah, as well as half of all his property: male and female slaves, oxen and sheep, donkeys and camels, clothing, money, and household goods. 11Then he saw them safely off; he embraced Tobias[h] and said, "Farewell, my child; have a safe journey. The Lord of heaven prosper you and your wife Sarah, and may I see children of yours before I die." 12Then he kissed his daughter Sarah and said to her, "My daughter, honor your father-in-law and your mother-in-law,[j] since from now on

---

[b] Other ancient authorities read *Tobias and said to him* [c] Gk *sister* [d] In other ancient authorities verse 3 precedes verse 4 [e] Gk *He* [f] Gk *he* [g] Other ancient authorities lack *on the camels* [h] Gk *him* [i] Other ancient authorities read *and she would eat nothing* [j] Other ancient authorities lack parts of *Then . . . mother-in-law*

they are as much your parents as those who gave you birth. Go in peace, daughter, and may I hear a good report about you as long as I live." Then he bade them farewell and let them go. Then Edna said to Tobias, "My child and dear brother, the Lord of heaven bring you back safely, and may I live long enough to see children of you and of my daughter Sarah before I die. In the sight of the Lord I entrust my daughter to you; do nothing to grieve her all the days of your life. Go in peace, my child. From now on I am your mother and Sarah is your beloved wife.[k] May we all prosper together all the days of our lives." Then she kissed them both and saw them safely off. 13Tobias parted from Raguel with happiness and joy, praising the Lord of heaven and earth, King over all, because he had made his journey a success. Finally, he blessed Raguel and his wife Edna, and said, "I have been commanded by the Lord to honor you all the days of my life."[l]

Homeward Journey

11 When they came near to Kaserin, which is opposite Nineveh, Raphael said, 2"You are aware of how we left your father. 3Let us run ahead of your wife and prepare the house while they are still on the way." 4As they went on together Raphael[m] said to him, "Have the gall ready." And the dog[n] went along behind them.

5 Meanwhile Anna sat looking intently down the road by which her son would come. 6When she caught sight of him coming, she said to his father, "Look, your son is coming, and the man who went with him!"

Tobit's Sight Restored

7 Raphael said to Tobias, before he had approached his father, "I know that his eyes will be opened. 8Smear the gall of the fish on his eyes; the medicine will make the white films shrink and peel off from his eyes, and your father will regain his sight and see the light."

9 Then Anna ran up to her son and threw her arms around him, saying, "Now that I have seen you, my child, I am ready to die." And she wept. 10Then Tobit got up and came stumbling out through the courtyard door. Tobias went up to him, 11with the gall of the fish in his hand, and holding him firmly, he blew into his eyes, saying, "Take courage, father." With this he applied the medicine on his eyes, 12and it made them smart.[l] 13Next, with both his hands he peeled off the white films from the corners of his eyes. Then Tobit[m] saw his son and[o] threw his arms around him, 14and he wept and said to him, "I see you, my son, the light of my eyes!" Then he said,

"Blessed be God,
  and blessed be his great name,
  and blessed be all his holy angels.
May his holy name be blessed[p]
  throughout all the ages.
15 Though he afflicted me,
  he has had mercy upon me.[q]
  Now I see my son Tobias!"

So Tobit went in rejoicing and praising God at the top of his voice. Tobias reported to his father that his journey had been successful, that he had brought the money, that he had married Raguel's daughter Sarah, and that she was, indeed, on her way there, very near to the gate of Nineveh.

16 Then Tobit, rejoicing and praising God, went out to meet his daughter-in-law at the gate of Nineveh. When the people of Nineveh saw him coming, walking along in full vigor and with no one leading him, they were amazed. 17Before them all, Tobit acknowledged that God had been merciful to him and had restored his sight. When Tobit met Sarah the wife of his son Tobias, he blessed her saying, "Come in, my daughter, and welcome. Blessed be your God who has brought you to us, my daughter. Blessed be your father and your mother, blessed be my son Tobias, and blessed be you, my daughter. Come in now to your home, and welcome, with blessing and joy. Come in, my daughter." So on that day there was rejoicing among all the Jews who were in Nineveh. 18Ahikar and his nephew Nadab were also present to share Tobit's joy. With merriment they celebrated Tobias's wedding feast for seven days, and many gifts were given to him.[r]

k Gk *sister*   *l* Lat: Meaning of Gk uncertain
m Gk *he*   *n* Codex Sinaiticus reads *And the Lord*
o Other ancient authorities lack *saw his son and*
p Codex Sinaiticus reads *May his great name be upon us and blessed be all the angels*   *q* Lat: Gk lacks this line   *r* Other ancient authorities lack parts of this sentence

Miriam

Her Name May Mean
"Bitterness"

**Read Exodus 15.20–21
and Numbers 12.1–15**

"Seven days I must stay outside the camp of my people, an old woman, fenced in by memories of what has been.

"How could I forget our years in Egypt, the cries of the mothers whose children were murdered or the moans of our brothers as they worked themselves to death? I have only to shut my eyes and see—the wall of water, the soldiers chasing us through the sea, the sounds of their noisy drowning, and finally the silence and the peace. How we praised God for casting our enemies into the deep waters, certain we would never see them again.

"But we did see them again—our enemies, though not the Egyptians. Ingratitude stalked us. Fear kept us from entering the land of promise.

"Time and again Moses and Aaron and I encouraged the people to stand firm, to have faith, to obey God. But there came a day when Aaron and I could stand with our brother no longer. Instead we spoke against him and his Cushite wife.

"But the Lord who speaks also heard our complaint and summoned the three of us to stand before him at the tent of meeting. He addressed us with terrible words.

"When the cloud of his presence finally lifted, I was a leper. I could see the horror on every face turned toward me. Aaron begged Moses to forgive us both. And Moses cried out to the Lord to heal me.

THE STORY OF A WOMAN

Her Character: *Even as a young girl, she showed fortitude and wisdom. A leader of God's people at a crucial moment in history, she led the celebration after crossing the Red Sea and spoke God's Word to his people, sharing their 40-year journey through the wilderness.*
Her Sorrow: *That she was struck with leprosy for pride and insubordination and was denied entry into the promised land.*
Her Joy: *To have played an instrumental role in leading God's people.*

"Now I see that my enemies were not merely buried in the sea nor in the hearts of an obstinate people, but in my own heart as well. Still, God has let me live, and I believe he will heal me. Though he brings grief, he will yet show compassion. One thing I know, he has thrown my pride into the sea and for that I will also sing his praises."

Though Scripture doesn't reveal Miriam's thoughts or the attitude of her heart after she was chastened for standing against Moses, it is not unreasonable to think she would have repented during the seven days of her banishment.

Perhaps Miriam, and the nation itself, needed a shocking rebuke in order to recognize the seriousness of a sin that threatened the unity of all God's people.

The last we hear of Miriam is that she died and was buried in Kadesh Barnea, not all that far from where Hagar, another slave woman, had encountered an angel in the wilderness so many years earlier. Like her brothers Moses and Aaron, Miriam died shortly before the Israelites ended their 40 years of wandering in the wilderness. She too was prevented from entering the promised land.

Yet, like them, she is one of the great heroes of our faith. As a young girl, she helped to save the infant Moses, Israel's future deliverer. Herself a prophetess, she exhorted and encouraged God's people and led the singing of one of the first psalms ever recorded in Scripture. Strong though she was, she sinned against God and suffered a punishment designed to bring her to repentance.

Praying With Miriam

"Sing to the LORD, for he has triumphed gloriously; horse and rider he has thrown into the sea."—*Exodus 15:21*

Praise God: *That he disciplines those he loves, every daughter who belongs to him.*

Thank God: *That his anger lasts for a moment but his favor, forever.*

Confess: *Any arrogance that may have crept into your heart, especially as it relates to your role at church or at work.*

Ask God: *To help you remember that discipline is an expression of his love for his children.*

Lift Your Heart

If a woman like Miriam could act in a way so displeasing to God, certainly we, too, are capable of sinning, no matter what we have done for him in the past. Take time this week to do a little honest soul-searching. If you discover anything displeasing to God, ask for forgiveness. Don't just whisper a quick prayer and be done with it. Instead, express your sincere repentance by taking advantage of the Sacrament of Reconciliation. After confessing your sins, consider driving to the nearest river, lake, or pond. Collect a few small stones and then deliberately throw each stone into the water, remembering Miriam's song of praise. Thank God for delivering you just as he delivered the Israelites from Pharaoh's pursuing army.

Father, thank you for the times you've brought me up short, loved me enough to discipline me. Help me to be quick to repent, to see my sin so that you needn't discipline me any further. Then let me experience the joy that comes from receiving your forgiveness.

Go to page 524 for your next devotional reading.

Raphael's Wages

12 When the wedding celebration was ended, Tobit called his son Tobias and said to him, "My child, see to paying the wages of the man who went with you, and give him a bonus as well." [2]He replied, "Father, how much shall I pay him? It would do no harm to give him half of the possessions brought back with me. [3]For he has led me back to you safely, he cured my wife, he brought the money back with me, and he healed you. How much extra shall I give him as a bonus?" [4]Tobit said, "He deserves, my child, to receive half of all that he brought back." [5]So Tobias[s] called him and said, "Take for your wages half of all that you brought back, and farewell."

Raphael's Exhortation

6 Then Raphael[s] called the two of them privately and said to them, "Bless God and acknowledge him in the presence of all the living for the good things he has done for you. Bless and sing praise to his name. With fitting honor declare to all people the deeds[t] of God. Do not be slow to acknowledge him. [7]It is good to conceal the secret of a king, but to acknowledge and reveal the works of God, and with fitting honor to acknowledge him. Do good and evil will not overtake you. [8]Prayer with fasting[u] is good, but better than both is almsgiving with righteousness. A little with righteousness is better than wealth with wrongdoing.[v] It is better to give alms than to lay up gold. [9]For almsgiving saves from death and purges away every sin. Those who give alms will enjoy a full life, [10]but those who commit sin and do wrong are their own worst enemies.

Raphael Discloses His Identity

11 "I will now declare the whole truth to you and will conceal nothing from you. Already I have declared it to you when I said, 'It is good to conceal the secret of a king, but to reveal with due honor the works of God.' [12]So now when you and Sarah prayed, it was I who brought and read[w] the record of your prayer before the glory of the Lord, and likewise whenever you would bury the dead. [13]And that time when you did not hesitate to get up and leave your dinner to go and bury the dead, [14]I was sent to you to test you. And at the same time God sent me to heal you and Sarah your daughter-in-law. [15]I am Ra-

---

[s] Gk he   [t] Gk words; other ancient authorities read words of the deeds   [u] Codex Sinaiticus with sincerity   [v] Lat   [w] Lat: Gk lacks and read

---

MONDAY

Take Angels Seriously

Scripture Reading for Today:
Tobit 12.11–22

Verse for Today:
Tobit 12.22

I believe in angels; guardian angels; the angels who came to Gideon and told a shy, not very brave young man that he was a man of valour who was going to free his people; the angels who came to Jesus in the agony of the Garden. And, what is less comforting, avenging angels, destroying angels, angels who come bringing terror when any part of God's creation becomes too rebellious, too full of pride to remember that they are God's creatures. And, most fearful of all, fallen angels, angels who have left God and followed Lucifer, and daily offer us their seductive and reasonable temptations. If we read the Bible, and if what we read has anything to do with what we believe, then we have no choice but to take angels seriously; and most artists do, from Milton to Doré to Shakespeare.

—MADELEINE L'ENGLE

Go to page 535 for your next devotional reading.

phael, one of the seven angels who stand ready and enter before the glory of the Lord."

16 The two of them were shaken; they fell face down, for they were afraid. 17But he said to them, "Do not be afraid; peace be with you. Bless God forevermore. 18As for me, when I was with you, I was not acting on my own will, but by the will of God. Bless him each and every day; sing his praises. 19Although you were watching me, I really did not eat or drink anything—but what you saw was a vision. 20So now get up from the ground,*x* and acknowledge God. See, I am ascending to him who sent me. Write down all these things that have happened to you." And he ascended. 21Then they stood up, and could see him no more. 22They kept blessing God and singing his praises, and they acknowledged God for these marvelous deeds of his, when an angel of God had appeared to them.

Tobit's Thanksgiving to God

13 Then Tobit*y* said:
"Blessed be God who lives forever,
　because his kingdom*z* lasts throughout all ages.
2 For he afflicts, and he shows mercy;
　he leads down to Hades in the lowest regions of the earth,
　and he brings up from the great abyss,*a*
　and there is nothing that can escape his hand.
3 Acknowledge him before the nations, O children of Israel;
　for he has scattered you among them.
4 　He has shown you his greatness even there.
Exalt him in the presence of every living being,
　because he is our Lord and he is our God;
　he is our Father and he is God forever.
5 He will afflict*b* you for your iniquities,
　but he will again show mercy on all of you.
He will gather you from all the nations
　among whom you have been scattered.

6 If you turn to him with all your heart and with all your soul,
　to do what is true before him,
then he will turn to you
　and will no longer hide his face from you.
So now see what he has done for you;
　acknowledge him at the top of your voice.
Bless the Lord of righteousness,
　and exalt the King of the ages.*c*
In the land of my exile I acknowledge him,
　and show his power and majesty to a nation of sinners:
'Turn back, you sinners, and do what is right before him;
　perhaps he may look with favor upon you and show you mercy.'
7 As for me, I exalt my God,
　and my soul rejoices in the King of heaven.
8 Let all people speak of his majesty,
　and acknowledge him in Jerusalem.
9 O Jerusalem, the holy city,
　he afflicted*d* you for the deeds of your hands,*e*
　but will again have mercy on the children of the righteous.
10 Acknowledge the Lord, for he is good,*f*
　and bless the King of the ages,
　so that his tent*g* may be rebuilt in you in joy.
May he cheer all those within you who are captives,
　and love all those within you who are distressed,
　to all generations forever.
11 A bright light will shine to all the ends of the earth;
　many nations will come to you from far away,

x Other ancient authorities read *now bless the Lord on earth*　　*y* Gk *he*　　*z* Other ancient authorities read *forever, and his kingdom*　　*a* Gk *from destruction*　　*b* Other ancient authorities read *He afflicted*　　*c* The lacuna in codex Sinaiticus, verses 6b to 10a, is filled in from other ancient authorities　　*d* Other ancient authorities read *will afflict*　　*e* Other ancient authorities read *your children*　　*f* Other ancient authorities read *Lord worthily*　　*g* Or *tabernacle*

the inhabitants of the remotest parts
of the earth to your holy
name,
bearing gifts in their hands for the
King of heaven.
Generation after generation will give
joyful praise in you;
the name of the chosen city will
endure forever.

12 Cursed are all who speak a harsh
word against you;
cursed are all who conquer you
and pull down your walls,
all who overthrow your towers
and set your homes on fire.
But blessed forever will be all who
revere you.[h]

13 Go, then, and rejoice over the
children of the righteous,
for they will be gathered together
and will praise the Lord of the
ages.

14 Happy are those who love you,
and happy are those who rejoice
in your prosperity.
Happy also are all people who
grieve with you
because of your afflictions;
for they will rejoice with you
and witness all your glory forever.

15 My soul blesses[i] the Lord, the great
King!

16 For Jerusalem will be built[j] as
his house for all ages.
How happy I will be if a remnant of
my descendants should
survive
to see your glory and acknowledge
the King of heaven.
The gates of Jerusalem will be built
with sapphire and emerald,
and all your walls with precious
stones.
The towers of Jerusalem will be built
with gold,
and their battlements with pure
gold.
The streets of Jerusalem will be
paved
with ruby and with stones of
Ophir.

17 The gates of Jerusalem will sing
hymns of joy,
and all her houses will cry,
'Hallelujah!
Blessed be the God of Israel!'
and the blessed will bless the holy
name forever and ever."

Tobit's Final Counsel

14 So ended Tobit's words of praise.
2 Tobit[k] died in peace when he
was one hundred twelve years old, and
was buried with great honor in Nineveh.
He was sixty-two[l] years old when he lost
his eyesight, and after regaining it he lived
in prosperity, giving alms and continually
blessing God and acknowledging God's
majesty.

3 When he was about to die, he called
his son Tobias and the seven sons of Tobias[m] and gave this command: "My son,
take your children 4and hurry off to Media, for I believe the word of God that
Nahum spoke about Nineveh, that all
these things will take place and overtake
Assyria and Nineveh. Indeed, everything
that was spoken by the prophets of Israel,
whom God sent, will occur. None of all
their words will fail, but all will come true
at their appointed times. So it will be safer
in Media than in Assyria and Babylon. For
I know and believe that whatever God has
said will be fulfilled and will come true;
not a single word of the prophecies will
fail. All of our kindred, inhabitants of the
land of Israel, will be scattered and taken
as captives from the good land; and the
whole land of Israel will be desolate, even
Samaria and Jerusalem will be desolate.
And the temple of God in it will be
burned to the ground, and it will be desolate for a while.[n]

5 "But God will again have mercy on
them, and God will bring them back into
the land of Israel; and they will rebuild
the temple of God, but not like the first
one until the period when the times of
fulfillment shall come. After this they all
will return from their exile and will rebuild Jerusalem in splendor; and in it the
temple of God will be rebuilt, just as the
prophets of Israel have said concerning it.
6Then the nations in the whole world will
all be converted and worship God in
truth. They will all abandon their idols,
which deceitfully have led them into their
error; 7and in righteousness they will
praise the eternal God. All the Israelites

h Other ancient authorities read *who build you up*
i Or *O my soul, bless*   j Other ancient authorities
add *for a city*   k Gk *He*   l Other ancient
authorities read *fifty-eight*   m Lat: Gk lacks *and
the seven sons of Tobias*   n Lat: Other ancient
authorities read *of God will be in distress and will
be burned for a while*

who are saved in those days and are truly mindful of God will be gathered together; they will go to Jerusalem and live in safety forever in the land of Abraham, and it will be given over to them. Those who sincerely love God will rejoice, but those who commit sin and injustice will vanish from all the earth. 8,9So now, my children, I command you, serve God faithfully and do what is pleasing in his sight. Your children are also to be commanded to do what is right and to give alms, and to be mindful of God and to bless his name at all times with sincerity and with all their strength. So now, my son, leave Nineveh; do not remain here. 10On whatever day you bury your mother beside me, do not stay overnight within the confines of the city. For I see that there is much wickedness within it, and that much deceit is practiced within it, while the people are without shame. See, my son, what Nadab did to Ahikar who had reared him. Was he not, while still alive, brought down into the earth? For God repaid him to his face for this shameful treatment. Ahikar came out into the light, but Nadab went into the eternal darkness, because he tried to kill Ahikar. Because he gave alms, Ahikar[o] escaped the fatal trap that Nadab had set for him, but Nadab fell into it himself, and was destroyed. 11So now, my children, see what almsgiving accomplishes, and what injustice does—it brings death! But now my breath fails me."

Death of Tobit and Anna

Then they laid him on his bed, and he died; and he received an honorable funeral. 12When Tobias's mother died, he buried her beside his father. Then he and his wife and children[p] returned to Media and settled in Ecbatana with Raguel his father-in-law. 13He treated his parents-in-law[q] with great respect in their old age, and buried them in Ecbatana of Media. He inherited both the property of Raguel and that of his father Tobit. 14He died highly respected at the age of one hundred seventeen[r] years. 15Before he died he heard[s] of the destruction of Nineveh, and he saw its prisoners being led into Media, those whom King Cyaxares[t] of Media had taken captive. Tobias[u] praised God for all he had done to the people of Nineveh and Assyria; before he died he rejoiced over Nineveh, and he blessed the Lord God forever and ever. Amen.[v]

o Gk *he*; other ancient authorities read *Manasses*
p Codex Sinaiticus lacks *and children* q Gk *them*
r Other authorities read other numbers s Codex Sinaiticus reads *saw and heard* t Cn: Codex Sinaiticus *Ahikar*; other ancient authorities read *Nebuchadnezzar and Ahasuerus* u Gk *He*
v Other ancient authorities lack *Amen*

Judith

One of only three books of the Bible named after a woman (the others are Ruth and Esther), Judith contains the dramatic story of how God delivered his people through the courage and faith of a woman, Judith, whose name means "Jewess." Though the story of Judith is not considered historical, it emphasizes God's faithfulness and his ability to overcome Israel's enemies by virtue of just one person's faith.

Holofernes, commander-in-chief of Nebuchadnezzar's armies, besieged Bethulia for 34 days, cutting off its water supply. Just when the Jews were ready to surrender to the Assyrians, the pious widow Judith counseled them to stand fast. After praying and fasting, she courageously made her way into Holofernes' camp, charmed him with her beauty, and cut off his head while he was in a drunken stupor.

The character of Judith may be considered a foreshadowing of Mary, the new Eve whose offspring will crush the head of the serpent (Genesis 3.15). Judith 15.9–10, marvelous words of praise for Judith, are often applied to Mary in the liturgy: "You are the glory of Jerusalem, you are the great boast of Israel, you are the great pride of our nation! You have done all this with your own hand; you have done great good to Israel, and God is well pleased with it."

Arphaxad Fortifies Ecbatana

1 It was the twelfth year of the reign of Nebuchadnezzar, who ruled over the Assyrians in the great city of Nineveh. In those days Arphaxad ruled over the Medes in Ecbatana. [2] He built walls around Ecbatana with hewn stones three cubits thick and six cubits long; he made the walls seventy cubits high and fifty cubits wide. [3] At its gates he raised towers one hundred cubits high and sixty cubits wide at the foundations. [4] He made its gates seventy cubits high and forty cubits wide to allow his armies to march out in force and his infantry to form their ranks. [5] Then King Nebuchadnezzar made war against King Arphaxad in the great plain that is on the borders of Ragau. [6] There rallied to him all the people of the hill country and all those who lived along the Euphrates, the Tigris, and the Hydaspes, and, on the plain, Arioch, king of the Elymeans. Thus, many nations joined the forces of the Chaldeans.[a]

a Syr: Gk *Cheleoudites*

Nebuchadnezzar Issues Ultimatum

7 Then Nebuchadnezzar, king of the Assyrians, sent messengers to all who lived in Persia and to all who lived in the west, those who lived in Cilicia and Damascus, Lebanon and Antilebanon, and all who lived along the seacoast, 8and those among the nations of Carmel and Gilead, and Upper Galilee and the great plain of Esdraelon, 9and all who were in Samaria and its towns, and beyond the Jordan as far as Jerusalem and Bethany and Chelous and Kadesh and the river of Egypt, and Tahpanhes and Raamses and the whole land of Goshen, 10even beyond Tanis and Memphis, and all who lived in Egypt as far as the borders of Ethiopia. 11But all who lived in the whole region disregarded the summons of Nebuchadnezzar, king of the Assyrians, and refused to join him in the war; for they were not afraid of him, but regarded him as only one man.*b* So they sent back his messengers empty-handed and in disgrace.

12 Then Nebuchadnezzar became very angry with this whole region, and swore by his throne and kingdom that he would take revenge on the whole territory of Cilicia and Damascus and Syria, that he would kill with his sword also all the inhabitants of the land of Moab, and the people of Ammon, and all Judea, and every one in Egypt, as far as the coasts of the two seas.

Arphaxad Is Defeated

13 In the seventeenth year he led his forces against King Arphaxad and defeated him in battle, overthrowing the whole army of Arphaxad and all his cavalry and all his chariots. 14Thus he took possession of his towns and came to Ecbatana, captured its towers, plundered its markets, and turned its glory into disgrace. 15He captured Arphaxad in the mountains of Ragau and struck him down with his spears, thus destroying him once and for all. 16Then he returned to Nineveh, he and all his combined forces, a vast body of troops; and there he and his forces rested and feasted for one hundred twenty days.

The Expedition against the West

2 In the eighteenth year, on the twenty-second day of the first month, there was talk in the palace of Nebuchadnezzar, king of the Assyrians, about carrying out his revenge on the whole region, just as he had said. 2He summoned all his ministers and all his nobles and set before them his secret plan and recounted fully, with his own lips, all the wickedness of the region.*c* 3They decided that every one who had not obeyed his command should be destroyed.

4 When he had completed his plan, Nebuchadnezzar, king of the Assyrians, called Holofernes, the chief general of his army, second only to himself, and said to him, 5"Thus says the Great King, the lord of the whole earth: Leave my presence and take with you men confident in their strength, one hundred twenty thousand foot soldiers and twelve thousand cavalry. 6March out against all the land to the west, because they disobeyed my orders. 7Tell them to prepare earth and water, for I am coming against them in my anger, and will cover the whole face of the earth with the feet of my troops, to whom I will hand them over to be plundered. 8Their wounded shall fill their ravines and gullies, and the swelling river shall be filled with their dead. 9I will lead them away captive to the ends of the whole earth. 10You shall go and seize all their territory for me in advance. They must yield themselves to you, and you shall hold them for me until the day of their punishment. 11But to those who resist show no mercy, but hand them over to slaughter and plunder throughout your whole region. 12For as I live, and by the power of my kingdom, what I have spoken I will accomplish by my own hand. 13And you—take care not to transgress any of your lord's commands, but carry them out exactly as I have ordered you; do it without delay."

Campaign of Holofernes

14 So Holofernes left the presence of his lord, and summoned all the commanders, generals, and officers of the Assyrian army. 15He mustered the picked troops by divisions as his lord had ordered him to do, one hundred twenty thousand of them, together with twelve thousand archers on horseback, 16and he organized them as a great army is marshaled for a campaign. 17He took along a vast number of camels and donkeys and mules for transport, and innumerable

b Or *a man*   *c* Meaning of Gk uncertain

sheep and oxen and goats for food; [18]also ample rations for everyone, and a huge amount of gold and silver from the royal palace.

19 Then he set out with his whole army, to go ahead of King Nebuchadnezzar and to cover the whole face of the earth to the west with their chariots and cavalry and picked foot soldiers. [20]Along with them went a mixed crowd like a swarm of locusts, like the dust[d] of the earth—a multitude that could not be counted.

21 They marched for three days from Nineveh to the plain of Bectileth, and camped opposite Bectileth near the mountain that is to the north of Upper Cilicia. [22]From there Holofernes[e] took his whole army, the infantry, cavalry, and chariots, and went up into the hill country. [23]He ravaged Put and Lud, and plundered all the Rassisites and the Ishmaelites on the border of the desert, south of the country of the Chelleans. [24]Then he followed[f] the Euphrates and passed through Mesopotamia and destroyed all the fortified towns along the brook Abron, as far as the sea. [25]He also seized the territory of Cilicia, and killed everyone who resisted him. Then he came to the southern borders of Japheth, facing Arabia. [26]He surrounded all the Midianites, and burned their tents and plundered their sheepfolds. [27]Then he went down into the plain of Damascus during the wheat harvest, and burned all their fields and destroyed their flocks and herds and sacked their towns and ravaged their lands and put all their young men to the sword.

28 So fear and dread of him fell upon all the people who lived along the seacoast, at Sidon and Tyre, and those who lived in Sur and Ocina and all who lived in Jamnia. Those who lived in Azotus and Ascalon feared him greatly.

Entreaties for Peace

3 They therefore sent messengers to him to sue for peace in these words: [2]"We, the servants of Nebuchadnezzar, the Great King, lie prostrate before you. Do with us whatever you will. [3]See, our buildings and all our land and all our wheat fields and our flocks and herds and all our encampments[g] lie before you; do with them as you please. [4]Our towns and their inhabitants are also your slaves; come and deal with them as you see fit."

5 The men came to Holofernes and told him all this. [6]Then he went down to the seacoast with his army and stationed garrisons in the fortified towns and took picked men from them as auxiliaries. [7]These people and all in the countryside welcomed him with garlands and dances and tambourines. [8]Yet he demolished all their shrines[h] and cut down their sacred groves; for he had been commissioned to destroy all the gods of the land, so that all nations should worship Nebuchadnezzar alone, and that all their dialects and tribes should call upon him as a god.

9 Then he came toward Esdraelon, near Dothan, facing the great ridge of Judea; [10]he camped between Geba and Scythopolis, and remained for a whole month in order to collect all the supplies for his army.

Judea on the Alert

4 When the Israelites living in Judea heard of everything that Holofernes, the general of Nebuchadnezzar, the king of the Assyrians, had done to the nations, and how he had plundered and destroyed all their temples, [2]they were therefore greatly terrified at his approach; they were alarmed both for Jerusalem and for the temple of the Lord their God. [3]For they had only recently returned from exile, and all the people of Judea had just now gathered together, and the sacred vessels and the altar and the temple had been consecrated after their profanation. [4]So they sent word to every district of Samaria, and to Kona, Beth-horon, Belmain, and Jericho, and to Choba and Aesora, and the valley of Salem. [5]They immediately seized all the high hilltops and fortified the villages on them and stored up food in preparation for war—since their fields had recently been harvested.

6 The high priest, Joakim, who was in Jerusalem at the time, wrote to the people of Bethulia and Betomesthaim, which faces Esdraelon opposite the plain near Dothan, [7]ordering them to seize the mountain passes, since by them Judea could be invaded; and it would be easy to stop any who tried to enter, for the approach was narrow, wide enough for only two at a time to pass.

---

d Gk *sand*   *e* Gk *he*   *f* Or *crossed*   *g* Gk *all the sheepfolds of our tents*   *h* Syr: Gk *borders*

Prayer and Penance

8 So the Israelites did as they had been ordered by the high priest Joakim and the senate of the whole people of Israel, in session at Jerusalem. 9And every man of Israel cried out to God with great fervor, and they humbled themselves with much fasting. 10They and their wives and their children and their cattle and every resident alien and hired laborer and purchased slave—they all put sackcloth around their waists. 11And all the Israelite men, women, and children living at Jerusalem prostrated themselves before the temple and put ashes on their heads and spread out their sackcloth before the Lord. 12They even draped the altar with sackcloth and cried out in unison, praying fervently to the God of Israel not to allow their infants to be carried off and their wives to be taken as booty, and the towns they had inherited to be destroyed, and the sanctuary to be profaned and desecrated to the malicious joy of the Gentiles.

13 The Lord heard their prayers and had regard for their distress; for the people fasted many days throughout Judea and in Jerusalem before the sanctuary of the Lord Almighty. 14The high priest Joakim and all the priests who stood before the Lord and ministered to the Lord, with sackcloth around their loins, offered the daily burnt offerings, the votive offerings, and freewill offerings of the people. 15With ashes on their turbans, they cried out to the Lord with all their might to look with favor on the whole house of Israel.

Council against the Israelites

5 It was reported to Holofernes, the general of the Assyrian army, that the people of Israel had prepared for war and had closed the mountain passes and fortified all the high hilltops and set up barricades in the plains. 2In great anger he called together all the princes of Moab and the commanders of Ammon and all the governors of the coastland, 3and said to them, "Tell me, you Canaanites, what people is this that lives in the hill country? What towns do they inhabit? How large is their army, and in what does their power and strength consist? Who rules over them as king and leads their army? 4And why have they alone, of all who live in the west, refused to come out and meet me?"

Achior's Report

5 Then Achior, the leader of all the Ammonites, said to him, "May my lord please listen to a report from the mouth of your servant, and I will tell you the truth about this people that lives in the mountain district near you. No falsehood shall come from your servant's mouth. 6These people are descended from the Chaldeans. 7At one time they lived in Mesopotamia, because they did not wish to follow the gods of their ancestors who were in Chaldea. 8Since they had abandoned the ways of their ancestors, and worshiped the God of heaven, the God they had come to know, their ancestors[i] drove them out from the presence of their gods. So they fled to Mesopotamia, and lived there for a long time. 9Then their God commanded them to leave the place where they were living and go to the land of Canaan. There they settled, and grew very prosperous in gold and silver and very much livestock. 10When a famine spread over the land of Canaan they went down to Egypt and lived there as long as they had food. There they became so great a multitude that their race could not be counted. 11So the king of Egypt became hostile to them; he exploited them and forced them to make bricks. 12They cried out to their God, and he afflicted the whole land of Egypt with incurable plagues. So the Egyptians drove them out of their sight. 13Then God dried up the Red Sea before them, 14and he led them by the way of Sinai and Kadesh-barnea. They drove out all the people of the desert, 15and took up residence in the land of the Amorites, and by their might destroyed all the inhabitants of Heshbon; and crossing over the Jordan they took possession of all the hill country. 16They drove out before them the Canaanites, the Perizzites, the Jebusites, the Shechemites, and all the Gergesites, and lived there a long time.

17 "As long as they did not sin against their God they prospered, for the God who hates iniquity is with them. 18But when they departed from the way he had prescribed for them, they were utterly defeated in many battles and were led away captive to a foreign land. The temple of their God was razed to the ground, and

i Gk *they*

their towns were occupied by their enemies. [19]But now they have returned to
their God, and have come back from the
places where they were scattered, and
have occupied Jerusalem, where their
sanctuary is, and have settled in the hill
country, because it was uninhabited.

20 "So now, my master and lord, if
there is any oversight in this people and
they sin against their God and we find out
their offense, then we can go up and defeat them. [21]But if they are not a guilty
nation, then let my lord pass them by; for
their Lord and God will defend them, and
we shall become the laughingstock of the
whole world."

22 When Achior had finished saying
these things, all the people standing
around the tent began to complain; Holofernes' officers and all the inhabitants of
the seacoast and Moab insisted that he
should be cut to pieces. [23]They said, "We
are not afraid of the Israelites; they are a
people with no strength or power for
making war. [24]Therefore let us go ahead,
Lord Holofernes, and your vast army will
swallow them up."

Achior Handed over to the Israelites

6 When the disturbance made by the
people outside the council had died
down, Holofernes, the commander of the
Assyrian army, said to Achior[j] in the
presence of all the foreign contingents:

2 "Who are you, Achior and you mercenaries of Ephraim, to prophesy among
us as you have done today and tell us not
to make war against the people of Israel
because their God will defend them?
What god is there except Nebuchadnezzar? He will send his forces and destroy
them from the face of the earth. Their God
will not save them; [3]we the king's[k] servants will destroy them as one man. They
cannot resist the might of our cavalry. [4]We
will overwhelm them;[l] their mountains
will be drunk with their blood, and their
fields will be full of their dead. Not even
their footprints will survive our attack;
they will utterly perish. So says King Nebuchadnezzar, lord of the whole earth. For
he has spoken; none of his words shall be
in vain.

5 "As for you, Achior, you Ammonite
mercenary, you have said these words in a
moment of perversity; you shall not see
my face again from this day until I take
revenge on this race that came out of

Egypt. [6]Then at my return the sword of my
army and the spear[m] of my servants shall
pierce your sides, and you shall fall
among their wounded. [7]Now my slaves
are going to take you back into the hill
country and put you in one of the towns
beside the passes. [8]You will not die until
you perish along with them. [9]If you really
hope in your heart that they will not be
taken, then do not look downcast! I have
spoken, and none of my words shall fail
to come true."

10 Then Holofernes ordered his slaves,
who waited on him in his tent, to seize
Achior and take him away to Bethulia and
hand him over to the Israelites. [11]So the
slaves took him and led him out of the
camp into the plain, and from the plain
they went up into the hill country and
came to the springs below Bethulia.
[12]When the men of the town saw them,[n]
they seized their weapons and ran out of
the town to the top of the hill, and all the
slingers kept them from coming up by
throwing stones at them. [13]So having tak-
en shelter below the hill, they bound
Achior and left him lying at the foot of the
hill, and returned to their master.

14 Then the Israelites came down from
their town and found him; they untied
him and brought him into Bethulia and
placed him before the magistrates of their
town, [15]who in those days were Uzziah
son of Micah, of the tribe of Simeon, and
Chabris son of Gothoniel, and Charmis
son of Melchiel. [16]They called together all
the elders of the town, and all their young
men and women ran to the assembly.
They set Achior in the midst of all their
people, and Uzziah questioned him about
what had happened. [17]He answered and
told them what had taken place at the
council of Holofernes, and all that he had
said in the presence of the Assyrian leaders, and all that Holofernes had boasted
he would do against the house of Israel.
[18]Then the people fell down and worshiped God, and cried out:

19 "O Lord God of heaven, see their
arrogance, and have pity on our people in
their humiliation, and look kindly today
on the faces of those who are consecrated
to you."

---

j Other ancient authorities add *and to all the
Moabites* *k* Gk *his* *l* Other ancient authorities
add *with it* *m* Lat Syr: Gk *people* *n* Other
ancient authorities add *on the top of the hill*

20 Then they reassured Achior, and praised him highly. ²¹Uzziah took him from the assembly to his own house and gave a banquet for the elders; and all that night they called on the God of Israel for help.

The Campaign against Bethulia

7 The next day Holofernes ordered his whole army, and all the allies who had joined him, to break camp and move against Bethulia, and to seize the passes up into the hill country and make war on the Israelites. ²So all their warriors marched off that day; their fighting forces numbered one hundred seventy thousand infantry and twelve thousand cavalry, not counting the baggage and the foot soldiers handling it, a very great multitude. ³They encamped in the valley near Bethulia, beside the spring, and they spread out in breadth over Dothan as far as Balbaim and in length from Bethulia to Cyamon, which faces Esdraelon.

4 When the Israelites saw their vast numbers, they were greatly terrified and said to one another, "They will now strip clean the whole land; neither the high mountains nor the valleys nor the hills will bear their weight." ⁵Yet they all seized their weapons, and when they had kindled fires on their towers, they remained on guard all that night.

6 On the second day Holofernes led out all his cavalry in full view of the Israelites in Bethulia. ⁷He reconnoitered the approaches to their town, and visited the springs that supplied their water; he seized them and set guards of soldiers over them, and then returned to his army.

8 Then all the chieftains of the Edomites and all the leaders of the Moabites and the commanders of the coastland came to him and said, ⁹"Listen to what we have to say, my lord, and your army will suffer no losses. ¹⁰This people, the Israelites, do not rely on their spears but on the height of the mountains where they live, for it is not easy to reach the tops of their mountains. ¹¹Therefore, my lord, do not fight against them in regular formation, and not a man of your army will fall. ¹²Remain in your camp, and keep all the men in your forces with you; let your servants take possession of the spring of water that flows from the foot of the mountain, ¹³for this is where all the people of Bethulia get their water. So thirst will destroy them, and they will surrender their town. Meanwhile, we and our people will go up to the tops of the nearby mountains and camp there to keep watch to see that no one gets out of the town. ¹⁴They and their wives and children will waste away with famine, and before the sword reaches them they will be strewn about in the streets where they live. ¹⁵Thus you will pay them back with evil, because they rebelled and did not receive you peaceably."

16 These words pleased Holofernes and all his attendants, and he gave orders to do as they had said. ¹⁷So the army of the Ammonites moved forward, together with five thousand Assyrians, and they encamped in the valley and seized the water supply and the springs of the Israelites. ¹⁸And the Edomites and Ammonites went up and encamped in the hill country opposite Dothan; and they sent some of their men toward the south and the east, toward Egrebeh, which is near Chusi beside the Wadi Mochmur. The rest of the Assyrian army encamped in the plain, and covered the whole face of the land. Their tents and supply trains spread out in great number, and they formed a vast multitude.

The Distress of the Israelites

19 The Israelites then cried out to the Lord their God, for their courage failed, because all their enemies had surrounded them, and there was no way of escape from them. ²⁰The whole Assyrian army, their infantry, chariots, and cavalry, surrounded them for thirty-four days, until all the water containers of every inhabitant of Bethulia were empty; ²¹their cisterns were going dry, and on no day did they have enough water to drink, for their drinking water was rationed. ²²Their children were listless, and the women and young men fainted from thirst and were collapsing in the streets of the town and in the gateways; they no longer had any strength.

23 Then all the people, the young men, the women, and the children, gathered around Uzziah and the rulers of the town and cried out with a loud voice, and said before all the elders, ²⁴"Let God judge between you and us! You have done us a great injury in not making peace with the Assyrians. ²⁵For now we have no one to help us; God has sold us into their hands, to be strewn before them in thirst and ex-

haustion. 26Now summon them and surrender the whole town as booty to the army of Holofernes and to all his forces. 27For it would be better for us to be captured by them.*o* We shall indeed become slaves, but our lives will be spared, and we shall not witness our little ones dying before our eyes, and our wives and children drawing their last breath. 28We call to witness against you heaven and earth and our God, the Lord of our ancestors, who punishes us for our sins and the sins of our ancestors; do today the things that we have described!"

29 Then great and general lamentation arose throughout the assembly, and they cried out to the Lord God with a loud voice. 30But Uzziah said to them, "Courage, my brothers and sisters!*p* Let us hold out for five days more; by that time the Lord our God will turn his mercy to us again, for he will not forsake us utterly. 31But if these days pass by, and no help comes for us, I will do as you say."

32 Then he dismissed the people to their various posts, and they went up on the walls and towers of their town. The women and children he sent home. In the town they were in great misery.

The Character of Judith

8 Now in those days Judith heard about these things: she was the daughter of Merari son of Ox son of Joseph son of Oziel son of Elkiah son of Ananias son of Gideon son of Raphain son of Ahitub son of Elijah son of Hilkiah son of Eliab son of Nathanael son of Salamiel son of Sarasadai son of Israel. 2Her husband Manasseh, who belonged to her tribe and family, had died during the barley harvest. 3For as he stood overseeing those who were binding sheaves in the field, he was overcome by the burning heat, and took to his bed and died in his town Bethulia. So they buried him with his ancestors in the field between Dothan and Balamon. 4Judith remained as a widow for three years and four months 5at home where she set up a tent for herself on the roof of her house. She put sackcloth around her waist and dressed in widow's clothing. 6She fasted all the days of her widowhood, except the day before the sabbath and the sabbath itself, the day before the new moon and the day of the new moon, and the festivals and days of rejoicing of the house of Israel. 7She was

beautiful in appearance, and was very lovely to behold. Her husband Manasseh had left her gold and silver, men and women slaves, livestock, and fields; and she maintained this estate. 8No one spoke ill of her, for she feared God with great devotion.

Judith and the Elders

9 When Judith heard the harsh words spoken by the people against the ruler, because they were faint for lack of water, and when she heard all that Uzziah said to them, and how he promised them under oath to surrender the town to the Assyrians after five days, 10she sent her maid, who was in charge of all she possessed, to summon Uzziah and*q* Chabris and Charmis, the elders of her town. 11They came to her, and she said to them:

"Listen to me, rulers of the people of Bethulia! What you have said to the people today is not right; you have even sworn and pronounced this oath between God and you, promising to surrender the town to our enemies unless the Lord turns and helps us within so many days. 12Who are you to put God to the test today, and to set yourselves up in the place of*r* God in human affairs? 13You are putting the Lord Almighty to the test, but you will never learn anything! 14You cannot plumb the depths of the human heart or understand the workings of the human mind; how do you expect to search out God, who made all these things, and find out his mind or comprehend his thought? No, my brothers, do not anger the Lord our God. 15For if he does not choose to help us within these five days, he has power to protect us within any time he pleases, or even to destroy us in the presence of our enemies. 16Do not try to bind the purposes of the Lord our God; for God is not like a human being, to be threatened, or like a mere mortal, to be won over by pleading. 17Therefore, while we wait for his deliverance, let us call upon him to help us, and he will hear our voice, if it pleases him.

18 "For never in our generation, nor in these present days, has there been any tribe or family or people or town of ours

o Other ancient authorities add *than to die of thirst*
p Gk *Courage, brothers*   *q* Other ancient authorities lack *Uzziah and* (see verses 28 and 35)
r Or *above*

that worships gods made with hands, as was done in days gone by. [19]That was why our ancestors were handed over to the sword and to pillage, and so they suffered a great catastrophe before our enemies. [20]But we know no other god but him, and so we hope that he will not disdain us or any of our nation. [21]For if we are captured, all Judea will be captured and our sanctuary will be plundered; and he will make us pay for its desecration with our blood. [22]The slaughter of our kindred and the captivity of the land and the desolation of our inheritance—all this he will

True Power

TUESDAY

Scripture Reading for Today:
Judith 8.9–35

Verses for Today:
Judith 8.32–33

The book of Judith illustrates for every age the source and availability of true power. The story is set in two panels, the first describing apparent power and the second illustrating real power.

In the first panel (chapters 1—7), there is a description of Nebuchadnezzar. Everything about him is drawn larger than life. [He] seems to be invincible, "lord of all the whole earth" (2.5). Another group of people, who seem to be wielders of power, is encountered in the first panel—the Israelite men, especially the elders. [They] know the source of real power, but in the crucial moment they fail to believe in it.

The second panel begins in chapter 8 with the introduction of the widow Judith. She is introduced with a description of her fidelity to God, the source of her strength and her gifts (8.4–8). Judith understands real power, and her confidence in its effectiveness never falters.

Judith makes preparation for her task as the instrument of God's victory. Her primary preparation is prayer. Her attitude of prayer demonstrates her faith in the absolute supremacy of God. However, [it] is not a statement of weakness but a request to be filled with the power of God. Judith's subsequent activity is the preparation of the weapons given her by God. She will not win the victory with horses and chariots but rather with beauty and wit, gifts from the God in whose power she acts.

Judith stands as companion to other women of God: women who look not to themselves for power and strength, but who place their trust completely in God; women who are strong enough in faith to allow God to be free and strong enough to wait for God's good time; women who cannot be defeated by despair. This is the model, the strong and faithful woman of God, which the author of the book of Judith presents to the Jewish people, threatened by world powers and bearing the weight of persecution. This same model may well give courage and direction to our own age, besieged by the arms race and threatened by nuclear destruction.

—IRENE NOWELL, O.S.B.

Go to page 538 for your next devotional reading.

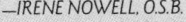

bring on our heads among the Gentiles, wherever we serve as slaves; and we shall be an offense and a disgrace in the eyes of those who acquire us. 23For our slavery will not bring us into favor, but the Lord our God will turn it to dishonor.

24 "Therefore, my brothers, let us set an example for our kindred, for their lives depend upon us, and the sanctuary—both the temple and the altar—rests upon us. 25In spite of everything let us give thanks to the Lord our God, who is putting us to the test as he did our ancestors. 26Remember what he did with Abraham, and how he tested Isaac, and what happened to Jacob in Syrian Mesopotamia, while he was tending the sheep of Laban, his mother's brother. 27For he has not tried us with fire, as he did them, to search their hearts, nor has he taken vengeance on us; but the Lord scourges those who are close to him in order to admonish them."

28 Then Uzziah said to her, "All that you have said was spoken out of a true heart, and there is no one who can deny your words. 29Today is not the first time your wisdom has been shown, but from the beginning of your life all the people have recognized your understanding, for your heart's disposition is right. 30But the people were so thirsty that they compelled us to do for them what we have promised, and made us take an oath that we cannot break. 31Now since you are a God-fearing woman, pray for us, so that the Lord may send us rain to fill our cisterns. Then we will no longer feel faint from thirst."

32 Then Judith said to them, "Listen to me. I am about to do something that will go down through all generations of our descendants. 33Stand at the town gate tonight so that I may go out with my maid; and within the days after which you have promised to surrender the town to our enemies, the Lord will deliver Israel by my hand. 34Only, do not try to find out what I am doing; for I will not tell you until I have finished what I am about to do."

35 Uzziah and the rulers said to her, "Go in peace, and may the Lord God go before you, to take vengeance on our enemies." 36So they returned from the tent and went to their posts.

The Prayer of Judith

9 Then Judith prostrated herself, put ashes on her head, and uncovered the sackcloth she was wearing. At the very time when the evening incense was being offered in the house of God in Jerusalem, Judith cried out to the Lord with a loud voice, and said,

2 "O Lord God of my ancestor Simeon, to whom you gave a sword to take revenge on those strangers who had torn off a virgin's clothing[s] to defile her, and exposed her thighs to put her to shame, and polluted her womb to disgrace her; for you said, 'It shall not be done'—yet they did it; 3so you gave up their rulers to be killed, and their bed, which was ashamed of the deceit they had practiced, was stained with blood, and you struck down slaves along with princes, and princes on their thrones. 4You gave up their wives for booty and their daughters to captivity, and all their booty to be divided among your beloved children who burned with zeal for you and abhorred the pollution of their blood and called on you for help. O God, my God, hear me also, a widow.

5 "For you have done these things and those that went before and those that followed. You have designed the things that are now, and those that are to come. What you had in mind has happened; 6the things you decided on presented themselves and said, 'Here we are!' For all your ways are prepared in advance, and your judgment is with foreknowledge.

7 "Here now are the Assyrians, a greatly increased force, priding themselves in their horses and riders, boasting in the strength of their foot soldiers, and trusting in shield and spear, in bow and sling. They do not know that you are the Lord who crushes wars; the Lord is your name. 8Break their strength by your might, and bring down their power in your anger; for they intend to defile your sanctuary, and to pollute the tabernacle where your glorious name resides, and to break off the horns[t] of your altar with the sword. 9Look at their pride, and send your wrath upon their heads. Give to me, a widow, the strong hand to do what I plan. 10By the deceit of my lips strike down the slave with the prince and the prince with his servant; crush their arrogance by the hand of a woman.

11 "For your strength does not depend on numbers, nor your might on the powerful. But you are the God of the lowly,

---

[s] Cn: Gk *loosed her womb*   [t] Syr: Gk *horn*

helper of the oppressed, upholder of the weak, protector of the forsaken, savior of those without hope. ¹²Please, please, God of my father, God of the heritage of Israel, Lord of heaven and earth, Creator of the waters, King of all your creation, hear my prayer! ¹³Make my deceitful words bring wound and bruise on those who have planned cruel things against your covenant, and against your sacred house, and against Mount Zion, and against the house your children possess. ¹⁴Let your whole nation and every tribe know and understand that you are God, the God of all power and might, and that there is no other who protects the people of Israel but you alone!"

Judith Prepares to Go to Holofernes

10 When Judithᵘ had stopped crying out to the God of Israel, and had ended all these words, ²she rose from where she lay prostrate. She called her maid and went down into the house where she lived on sabbaths and on her festal days. ³She removed the sackcloth she had been wearing, took off her widow's garments, bathed her body with water, and anointed herself with precious ointment. She combed her hair, put on a tiara, and dressed herself in the festive attire that she used to wear while her husband Manasseh was living. ⁴She put sandals on her feet, and put on her anklets, bracelets, rings, earrings, and all her other jewelry. Thus she made herself very beautiful, to entice the eyes of all the men who might see her. ⁵She gave her maid a skin of wine and a flask of oil, and filled a bag with roasted grain, dried fig cakes, and fine bread;ᵛ then she wrapped up all her dishes and gave them to her to carry.

6 Then they went out to the town gate of Bethulia and found Uzziah standing there with the elders of the town, Chabris and Charmis. ⁷When they saw her transformed in appearance and dressed differently, they were very greatly astounded at her beauty and said to her, ⁸"May the God of our ancestors grant you favor and fulfill your plans, so that the people of Israel may glory and Jerusalem may be exalted." She bowed down to God.

9 Then she said to them, "Order the gate of the town to be opened for me so that I may go out and accomplish the things you have just said to me." So they ordered the young men to open the gate for her, as she requested. ¹⁰When they had done this, Judith went out, accompanied by her maid. The men of the town watched her until she had gone down the mountain and passed through the valley, where they lost sight of her.

Judith Is Captured

11 As the womenʷ were going straight on through the valley, an Assyrian patrol met her ¹²and took her into custody. They asked her, "To what people do you belong, and where are you coming from, and where are you going?" She replied, "I am a daughter of the Hebrews, but I am fleeing from them, for they are about to be handed over to you to be devoured. ¹³I am on my way to see Holofernes the commander of your army, to give him a true report; I will show him a way by which he can go and capture all the hill country without losing one of his men, captured or slain."

14 When the men heard her words, and observed her face—she was in their eyes marvelously beautiful—they said to her, ¹⁵"You have saved your life by hurrying down to see our lord. Go at once to his tent; some of us will escort you and hand you over to him. ¹⁶When you stand before him, have no fear in your heart, but tell him what you have just said, and he will treat you well."

17 They chose from their number a hundred men to accompany her and her maid, and they brought them to the tent of Holofernes. ¹⁸There was great excitement in the whole camp, for her arrival was reported from tent to tent. They came and gathered around her as she stood outside the tent of Holofernes, waiting until they told him about her. ¹⁹They marveled at her beauty and admired the Israelites, judging them by her. They said to one another, "Who can despise these people, who have women like this among them? It is not wise to leave one of their men alive, for if we let them go they will be able to beguile the whole world!"

Judith Is Brought before Holofernes

20 Then the guards of Holofernes and all his servants came out and led her into the tent. ²¹Holofernes was resting on his

ᵘ Gk *she*   ᵛ Other ancient authorities add *and cheese*   ʷ Gk *they* bed under a canopy that was woven with purple and gold, emeralds and other precious stones. ²²When they told him of her, he came to the front of the tent, with silver lamps carried before him. ²³When Judith came into the presence of Holofernes*ˣ* and his servants, they all marveled at the beauty of her face. She prostrated herself and did obeisance to him, but his slaves raised her up.

11 Then Holofernes said to her, "Take courage, woman, and do not be afraid in your heart, for I have never hurt anyone who chose to serve Nebuchadnezzar, king of all the earth. ²Even now, if your people who live in the hill country had not slighted me, I would never have lifted my spear against them. They

ˣ Gk *him*

*S*he Won

Perpetua was one of five Christians martyred in A.D. 203 in Carthage, Africa, by being thrown to wild animals in an amphitheater.

WEDNESDAY

Scripture Reading for Today:
Judith 10.1–10

Verse for Today:
Judith 10.9

The day before we were to fight the beasts, I had a vision of Pomponius the deacon knocking loudly at the prison door. I opened the door and went out to see him. He said to me, "Perpetua, we are waiting for you. Come." He then held my hand as we passed through rough and rocky country. Breathing heavily and in pain, we finally arrived at an amphitheater. Pomponius led me into the middle of the arena. Then he said, "Do not be afraid, for I am with you now and suffer with you." He then left, and I saw a large crowd of people looking on with anticipation. I knew that I was condemned to fight the beasts.

Then I was stripped and changed into a man. My supporters began to rub me with oil as is done before combat. I saw the Egyptian opposite me rolling in the sand. Then a wondrously tall man who rose higher than the top of the amphitheater came forward. He said, "If this Egyptian conquers Perpetua, he shall kill her with the sword. If she conquers him, she shall receive this bough." Then he departed.

We approached each other and used our fists. My adversary tried to catch hold of my feet, but I kept striking his face with my heels. I began to strike him in a way that no earthly being could. I then caught hold of his head and he fell on his face. I walked on his head and all the people began to shout. My supporters started to sing psalms. Then I came forward to receive the bough from the trainer. He kissed me and said to me, "Peace be with you, my daughter." I began to walk triumphantly to the Gate of Life. I awoke.

Then I understood that I would be fighting not with the beasts but with the devil. I knew the victory was to be mine, however.

—*SAINT PERPETUA*

Go to page 543 for your next devotional reading.

have brought this on themselves. ³But now tell me why you have fled from them and have come over to us. In any event, you have come to safety. Take courage! You will live tonight and ever after. ⁴No one will hurt you. Rather, all will treat you well, as they do the servants of my lord King Nebuchadnezzar."

Judith Explains Her Presence

5 Judith answered him, "Accept the words of your slave, and let your servant speak in your presence. I will say nothing false to my lord this night. ⁶If you follow out the words of your servant, God will accomplish something through you, and my lord will not fail to achieve his purposes. ⁷By the life of Nebuchadnezzar, king of the whole earth, and by the power of him who has sent you to direct every living being! Not only do human beings serve him because of you, but also the animals of the field and the cattle and the birds of the air will live, because of your power, under Nebuchadnezzar and all his house. ⁸For we have heard of your wisdom and skill, and it is reported throughout the whole world that you alone are the best in the whole kingdom, the most informed and the most astounding in military strategy.

9 "Now as for Achior's speech in your council, we have heard his words, for the people of Bethulia spared him and he told them all he had said to you. ¹⁰Therefore, lord and master, do not disregard what he said, but keep it in your mind, for it is true. Indeed our nation cannot be punished, nor can the sword prevail against them, unless they sin against their God.

11 "But now, in order that my lord may not be defeated and his purpose frustrated, death will fall upon them, for a sin has overtaken them by which they are about to provoke their God to anger when they do what is wrong. ¹²Since their food supply is exhausted and their water has almost given out, they have planned to kill their livestock and have determined to use all that God by his laws has forbidden them to eat. ¹³They have decided to consume the first fruits of the grain and the tithes of the wine and oil, which they had consecrated and set aside for the priests who minister in the presence of our God in Jerusalem—things it is not lawful for any of the people even to touch with their hands. ¹⁴Since even the people in Jerusa-

lem have been doing this, they have sent messengers there in order to bring back permission from the council of the elders. ¹⁵When the response reaches them and they act upon it, on that very day they will be handed over to you to be destroyed.

16 "So when I, your slave, learned all this, I fled from them. God has sent me to accomplish with you things that will astonish the whole world wherever people shall hear about them. ¹⁷Your servant is indeed God-fearing and serves the God of heaven night and day. So, my lord, I will remain with you; but every night your servant will go out into the valley and pray to God. He will tell me when they have committed their sins. ¹⁸Then I will come and tell you, so that you may go out with your whole army, and not one of them will be able to withstand you. ¹⁹Then I will lead you through Judea, until you come to Jerusalem; there I will set your throne.ʸ You will drive them like sheep that have no shepherd, and no dog will so much as growl at you. For this was told me to give me foreknowledge; it was announced to me, and I was sent to tell you."

20 Her words pleased Holofernes and all his servants. They marveled at her wisdom and said, ²¹"No other woman from one end of the earth to the other looks so beautiful or speaks so wisely!" ²²Then Holofernes said to her, "God has done well to send you ahead of the people, to strengthen our hands and bring destruction on those who have despised my lord. ²³You are not only beautiful in appearance, but wise in speech. If you do as you have said, your God shall be my God, and you shall live in the palace of King Nebuchadnezzar and be renowned throughout the whole world."

Judith as a Guest of Holofernes

12 Then he commanded them to bring her in where his silver dinnerware was kept, and ordered them to set a table for her with some of his own delicacies, and with some of his own wine to drink. ²But Judith said, "I cannot partake of them, or it will be an offense; but I will have enough with the things I brought with me." ³Holofernes said to her, "If your supply runs out, where can we get you more of the same? For none of your people are here with us." ⁴Judith replied, "As

ʸ Or *chariot*

surely as you live, my lord, your servant will not use up the supplies I have with me before the Lord carries out by my hand what he has determined."

5 Then the servants of Holofernes brought her into the tent, and she slept until midnight. Toward the morning watch she got up [6]and sent this message to Holofernes: "Let my lord now give orders to allow your servant to go out and pray." [7]So Holofernes commanded his guards not to hinder her. She remained in the camp three days. She went out each night to the valley of Bethulia, and bathed at the spring in the camp.[z] [8]After bathing, she prayed the Lord God of Israel to direct her way for the triumph of his[a] people. [9]Then she returned purified and stayed in the tent until she ate her food toward evening.

Judith Attends Holofernes' Banquet

10 On the fourth day Holofernes held a banquet for his personal attendants only, and did not invite any of his officers. [11]He said to Bagoas, the eunuch who had charge of his personal affairs, "Go and persuade the Hebrew woman who is in your care to join us and to eat and drink with us. [12]For it would be a disgrace if we let such a woman go without having intercourse with her. If we do not seduce her, she will laugh at us."

13 So Bagoas left the presence of Holofernes, and approached her and said, "Let this pretty girl not hesitate to come to my lord to be honored in his presence, and to enjoy drinking wine with us, and to become today like one of the Assyrian women who serve in the palace of Nebuchadnezzar." [14]Judith replied, "Who am I to refuse my lord? Whatever pleases him I will do at once, and it will be a joy to me until the day of my death." [15]So she proceeded to dress herself in all her woman's finery. Her maid went ahead and spread for her on the ground before Holofernes the lambskins she had received from Bagoas for her daily use in reclining.

16 Then Judith came in and lay down. Holofernes' heart was ravished with her and his passion was aroused, for he had been waiting for an opportunity to seduce her from the day he first saw her. [17]So Holofernes said to her, "Have a drink and be merry with us!" [18]Judith said, "I will gladly drink, my lord, because today is the greatest day in my whole life." [19]Then she took what her maid had prepared and ate and drank before him. [20]Holofernes was greatly pleased with her, and drank a great quantity of wine, much more than he had ever drunk in any one day since he was born.

Judith Beheads Holofernes

13 When evening came, his slaves quickly withdrew. Bagoas closed the tent from outside and shut out the attendants from his master's presence. They went to bed, for they all were weary because the banquet had lasted so long. [2]But Judith was left alone in the tent, with Holofernes stretched out on his bed, for he was dead drunk.

3 Now Judith had told her maid to stand outside the bedchamber and to wait for her to come out, as she did on the other days; for she said she would be going out for her prayers. She had said the same thing to Bagoas. [4]So everyone went out, and no one, either small or great, was left in the bedchamber. Then Judith, standing beside his bed, said in her heart, "O Lord God of all might, look in this hour on the work of my hands for the exaltation of Jerusalem. [5]Now indeed is the time to help your heritage and to carry out my design to destroy the enemies who have risen up against us."

6 She went up to the bedpost near Holofernes' head, and took down his sword that hung there. [7]She came close to his bed, took hold of the hair of his head, and said, "Give me strength today, O Lord God of Israel!" [8]Then she struck his neck twice with all her might, and cut off his head. [9]Next she rolled his body off the bed and pulled down the canopy from the posts. Soon afterward she went out and gave Holofernes' head to her maid, [10]who placed it in her food bag.

Judith Returns to Bethulia

Then the two of them went out together, as they were accustomed to do for prayer. They passed through the camp, circled around the valley, and went up the mountain to Bethulia, and came to its gates. [11]From a distance Judith called out to the sentries at the gates, "Open, open the gate! God, our God, is with us, still showing his power in Israel and his

---

z Other ancient authorities lack *in the camp*
a Other ancient authorities read *her*

strength against our enemies, as he has done today!"

12 When the people of her town heard her voice, they hurried down to the town gate and summoned the elders of the town. ¹³They all ran together, both small and great, for it seemed unbelievable that she had returned. They opened the gate and welcomed them. Then they lit a fire to give light, and gathered around them. ¹⁴Then she said to them with a loud voice, "Praise God, O praise him! Praise God, who has not withdrawn his mercy from the house of Israel, but has destroyed our enemies by my hand this very night!"

15 Then she pulled the head out of the bag and showed it to them, and said, "See here, the head of Holofernes, the commander of the Assyrian army, and here is the canopy beneath which he lay in his drunken stupor. The Lord has struck him down by the hand of a woman. ¹⁶As the Lord lives, who has protected me in the way I went, I swear that it was my face that seduced him to his destruction, and that he committed no sin with me, to defile and shame me."

17 All the people were greatly astonished. They bowed down and worshiped God, and said with one accord, "Blessed are you our God, who have this day humiliated the enemies of your people."

18 Then Uzziah said to her, "O daughter, you are blessed by the Most High God above all other women on earth; and blessed be the Lord God, who created the heavens and the earth, who has guided you to cut off the head of the leader of our enemies. ¹⁹Your praise[b] will never depart from the hearts of those who remember the power of God. ²⁰May God grant this to be a perpetual honor to you, and may he reward you with blessings, because you risked your own life when our nation was brought low, and you averted our ruin, walking in the straight path before our God." And all the people said, "Amen. Amen."

Judith's Counsel

14 Then Judith said to them, "Listen to me, my friends. Take this head and hang it upon the parapet of your wall. ²As soon as day breaks and the sun rises on the earth, each of you take up your weapons, and let every able-bodied man go out of the town; set a captain over them, as if you were going down to the plain against the Assyrian outpost; only do not go down. ³Then they will seize their arms and go into the camp and rouse the officers of the Assyrian army. They will rush into the tent of Holofernes and will not find him. Then panic will come over them, and they will flee before you. ⁴Then you and all who live within the borders of Israel will pursue them and cut them down in their tracks. ⁵But before you do all this, bring Achior the Ammonite to me so that he may see and recognize the man who despised the house of Israel and sent him to us as if to his death."

6 So they summoned Achior from the house of Uzziah. When he came and saw the head of Holofernes in the hand of one of the men in the assembly of the people, he fell down on his face in a faint. ⁷When they raised him up he threw himself at Judith's feet, and did obeisance to her, and said, "Blessed are you in every tent of Judah! In every nation those who hear your name will be alarmed. ⁸Now tell me what you have done during these days."

So Judith told him in the presence of the people all that she had done, from the day she left until the moment she began speaking to them. ⁹When she had finished, the people raised a great shout and made a joyful noise in their town. ¹⁰When Achior saw all that the God of Israel had done, he believed firmly in God. So he was circumcised, and joined the house of Israel, remaining so to this day.

Holofernes' Death Is Discovered

11 As soon as it was dawn they hung the head of Holofernes on the wall. Then they all took their weapons, and they went out in companies to the mountain passes. ¹²When the Assyrians saw them they sent word to their commanders, who then went to the generals and the captains and to all their other officers. ¹³They came to Holofernes' tent and said to the steward in charge of all his personal affairs, "Wake up our lord, for the slaves have been so bold as to come down against us to give battle, to their utter destruction."

14 So Bagoas went in and knocked at the entry of the tent, for he supposed that he was sleeping with Judith. ¹⁵But when no one answered, he opened it and went into the bedchamber and found him sprawled on the floor dead, with his head

---

b Other ancient authorities read hope

missing. [16]He cried out with a loud voice and wept and groaned and shouted, and tore his clothes. [17]Then he went to the tent where Judith had stayed, and when he did not find her, he rushed out to the people and shouted, [18]"The slaves have tricked us! One Hebrew woman has brought disgrace on the house of King Nebuchadnezzar. Look, Holofernes is lying on the ground, and his head is missing!"

19 When the leaders of the Assyrian army heard this, they tore their tunics and were greatly dismayed, and their loud cries and shouts rose up throughout the camp.

The Assyrians Flee in Panic

15 When the men in the tents heard it, they were amazed at what had happened. [2]Overcome with fear and trembling, they did not wait for one another, but with one impulse all rushed out and fled by every path across the plain and through the hill country. [3]Those who had camped in the hills around Bethulia also took to flight. Then the Israelites, everyone that was a soldier, rushed out upon them. [4]Uzziah sent men to Betomasthaim[c] and Choba and Kola, and to all the frontiers of Israel, to tell what had taken place and to urge all to rush out upon the enemy to destroy them. [5]When the Israelites heard it, with one accord they fell upon the enemy,[d] and cut them down as far as Choba. Those in Jerusalem and all the hill country also came, for they were told what had happened in the camp of the enemy. The men in Gilead and in Galilee outflanked them with great slaughter, even beyond Damascus and its borders. [6]The rest of the people of Bethulia fell upon the Assyrian camp and plundered it, acquiring great riches. [7]And the Israelites, when they returned from the slaughter, took possession of what remained. Even the villages and towns in the hill country and in the plain got a great amount of booty, since there was a vast quantity of it.

The Israelites Celebrate Their Victory

8 Then the high priest Joakim and the elders of the Israelites who lived in Jerusalem came to witness the good things that the Lord had done for Israel, and to see Judith and to wish her well. [9]When they met her, they all blessed her with one accord and said to her, "You are the glory of Jerusalem, you are the great boast of Israel, you are the great pride of our nation! [10]You have done all this with your own hand; you have done great good to Israel, and God is well pleased with it. May the Almighty Lord bless you forever!" And all the people said, "Amen."

11 All the people plundered the camp for thirty days. They gave Judith the tent of Holofernes and all his silver dinnerware, his beds, his bowls, and all his furniture. She took them and loaded her mules and hitched up her carts and piled the things on them.

12 All the women of Israel gathered to see her, and blessed her, and some of them performed a dance in her honor. She took ivy-wreathed wands in her hands and distributed them to the women who were with her; [13]and she and those who were with her crowned themselves with olive wreaths. She went before all the people in the dance, leading all the women, while all the men of Israel followed, bearing their arms and wearing garlands and singing hymns.

Judith Offers Her Hymn of Praise

14 Judith began this thanksgiving before all Israel, and all the people loudly sang this song of praise. [1]And Judith said,

16 Begin a song to my God with tambourines,
sing to my Lord with cymbals.
Raise to him a new psalm;[e]
exalt him, and call upon his name.
[2] For the Lord is a God who crushes wars;
he sets up his camp among his people;
he delivered me from the hands of my pursuers.
[3] The Assyrian came down from the mountains of the north;
he came with myriads of his warriors;
their numbers blocked up the wadis, and their cavalry covered the hills.

---

c Other ancient authorities add and Bebai   *d Gk them*   *e Other ancient authorities read a psalm and praise*

⁴ He boasted that he would burn up
        my territory,
    and kill my young men with the
        sword,
  and dash my infants to the ground,
    and seize my children as booty,
    and take my virgins as spoil.

⁵ But the Lord Almighty has foiled
        them
    by the hand of a woman.ᶠ
⁶ For their mighty one did not fall by
        the hands of the young men,
    nor did the sons of the Titans
        strike him down,
    nor did tall giants set upon him;
  but Judith daughter of Merari
    with the beauty of her
        countenance undid him.

⁷ For she put away her widow's
        clothing
    to exalt the oppressed in Israel.
  She anointed her face with perfume;
⁸   she fastened her hair with a tiara
    and put on a linen gown to
        beguile him.
⁹ Her sandal ravished his eyes,
    her beauty captivated his mind,
    and the sword severed his neck!
¹⁰ The Persians trembled at her
        boldness,
    the Medes were daunted at her
        daring.

¹¹ Then my oppressed people shouted;

ᶠ Other ancient authorities add *he has confounded them*

THURSDAY

Scripture Reading
for Today:
Judith 16.1–12

Verse for Today:
Judith 16.2

God Uses the Weak

Hymns of praise are a recurring feature of Jewish victory celebrations. This particular hymn is similar to the song offered by
Deborah following the death of Sisera (see Judges 5). Here a new
hymn is announced, as it is in [the book of] Judges. Mountains
quake, a woman overcomes the enemy, and God punishes an oppressor (compare Judith 16.1, 5–9, 15, 17 and Judges 5.3–5, 24–31).
The authors of both books make the same point: God uses the
weak and the powerless to come to the aid of his faithful people.

The author of Judith also intends to recall the victory song of
Moses following the exodus from Egypt (see Exodus 15). This
event was the defining moment in Israelite history, the model for
every deliverance and every victory to follow. Judith's triumph
over the Assyrians marks another exodus, another journey from
oppression to freedom, from darkness to light.

God often uses unlikely events and people to accomplish his
plan. Who would have expected a widow, acting alone, to dis-
mantle the Assyrian army? Who would have expected a carpenter, dying on a cross, to smash the army of evil?

It is not likely that God would call any of us to so heroic a gesture as the single-handed destruction of an army. But he does call
each of us to the sort of heroism that frees us to take a stand for
the truth, no matter what the consequences might be.

The book of Judith affirms that God works in mysterious
ways, using those wholly surrendered to him.

—CINDY CAVNAR

Go to page 551 for your next devotional reading.

my weak people cried out,[g] and
the enemy[h] trembled;
they lifted up their voices, and the
enemy[h] were turned back.
12 Sons of slave-girls pierced them
through
and wounded them like the
children of fugitives;
they perished before the army of
my Lord.

13 I will sing to my God a new song:
O Lord, you are great and glorious,
wonderful in strength, invincible.
14 Let all your creatures serve you,
for you spoke, and they were made.
You sent forth your spirit,[i] and it
formed them;[j]
there is none that can resist your
voice.
15 For the mountains shall be shaken
to their foundations with the
waters;
before your glance the rocks shall
melt like wax.
But to those who fear you
you show mercy.
16 For every sacrifice as a fragrant
offering is a small thing,
and the fat of all whole burnt
offerings to you is a very little
thing;
but whoever fears the Lord is great
forever.

17 Woe to the nations that rise up
against my people!
The Lord Almighty will take
vengeance on them in the day
of judgment;
he will send fire and worms into
their flesh;
they shall weep in pain forever.

18 When they arrived at Jerusalem, they worshiped God. As soon as the people were purified, they offered their burnt offerings, their freewill offerings, and their gifts. 19Judith also dedicated to God all the possessions of Holofernes, which the people had given her; and the canopy that she had taken for herself from his bedchamber she gave as a votive offering. 20For three months the people continued feasting in Jerusalem before the sanctuary, and Judith remained with them.

The Renown and Death of Judith

21 After this they all returned home to their own inheritances. Judith went to Bethulia, and remained on her estate. For the rest of her life she was honored throughout the whole country. 22Many desired to marry her, but she gave herself to no man all the days of her life after her husband Manasseh died and was gathered to his people. 23She became more and more famous, and grew old in her husband's house, reaching the age of one hundred five. She set her maid free. She died in Bethulia, and they buried her in the cave of her husband Manasseh; 24and the house of Israel mourned her for seven days. Before she died she distributed her property to all those who were next of kin to her husband Manasseh, and to her own nearest kindred. 25No one ever again spread terror among the Israelites during the lifetime of Judith, or for a long time after her death.

g Other ancient authorities read *feared*   h Gk
they   i Or *breath*   j Other ancient authorities
read *they were created*

Esther

The book of Esther relates one of the most marvelous stories contained in the Bible, featuring Esther, a Jewish orphan who becomes a queen; her pious uncle Mordecai; an evil vizier named Haman; and a Persian king, Ahasuerus (Xerxes). While Haman plots to annihilate the Jews of Persia in a single day, God is at work plotting a series of stunning reversals that will be brought about through the agency of prayer and the courage of his servants Esther and Mordecai. The events described in Esther are celebrated annually in the Jewish feast of Purim (meaning "lots" because Haman cast lots to determine what day to destroy the Jews).

The book of Esther is made up of two parts: the shorter Hebrew text and a longer Greek version, containing 107 additional verses. The Greek additions are indicated as such by the letters A–F. Though the shorter Hebrew version never mentions God, his providential guidance is at work throughout the story.

Anyone who has ever felt threatened and alone, with an impossible burden to bear, will find solace in Esther's prayer: "O God, whose might is over all, hear the voice of the despairing, and save us from the hands of evildoers. And save me from my fear!" (14.19).

ADDITION A

Mordecai's Dream

11[a] [2]In the second year of the reign of Ahasuerus the Great, on the first day of Nisan, Mordecai son of Jair son of Shimei[b] son of Kish, of the tribe of Benjamin, had a dream. [3]He was a Jew living in the city of Susa, a great man, serving in the court of the king. [4]He was one of the captives whom King Nebuchadnezzar of Babylon had brought from Jerusalem with King Jeconiah of Judah. And this was his dream: [5]Noises[c] and confusion, thunders and earthquake, tumult on the earth! [6]Then two great dragons came forward, both ready to fight, and they roared terribly. [7]At their roaring every nation prepared for war, to fight against the righteous nation. [8]It was a day of darkness and gloom, of tribulation and distress, affliction and great tumult on the earth!

a Chapters 11.2—12.6 correspond to chapter A 1-17 in some translations.   b Gk Semeios   c Or Voices

9And the whole righteous nation was troubled; they feared the evils that threatened them,[d] and were ready to perish. 10Then they cried out to God; and at their outcry, as though from a tiny spring, there came a great river, with abundant water; 11light came, and the sun rose, and the lowly were exalted and devoured those held in honor.

12 Mordecai saw in this dream what God had determined to do, and after he awoke he had it on his mind, seeking all day to understand it in every detail.

A Plot against the King

12 Now Mordecai took his rest in the courtyard with Bigthan and Teresh, the two eunuchs of the king who kept watch in the courtyard. 2He overheard their conversation and inquired into their purposes, and learned that they were preparing to lay hands on King Ahasuerus; and he informed the king concerning them. 3Then the king examined the two eunuchs, and after they had confessed it, they were led away to execution. 4The king made a permanent record of these things, and Mordecai wrote an account of them. 5And the king ordered Mordecai to serve in the court, and rewarded him for these things. 6But Haman son of Hammedatha the Agagite, who was in great honor with the king, determined to injure Mordecai and his people because of the two eunuchs of the king.

END OF ADDITION A

King Ahasuerus Deposes Queen Vashti

1 This happened in the days of Ahasuerus, the same Ahasuerus who ruled over one hundred twenty-seven provinces from India to Ethiopia.[e] 2In those days when King Ahasuerus sat on his royal throne in the citadel of Susa, 3in the third year of his reign, he gave a banquet for all his officials and ministers. The army of Persia and Media and the nobles and governors of the provinces were present, 4while he displayed the great wealth of his kingdom and the splendor and pomp of his majesty for many days, one hundred eighty days in all.

5 When these days were completed, the king gave for all the people present in the citadel of Susa, both great and small, a banquet lasting for seven days, in the court of the garden of the king's palace. 6There were white cotton curtains and blue hangings tied with cords of fine linen and purple to silver rings[f] and marble pillars. There were couches of gold and silver on a mosaic pavement of porphyry, marble, mother-of-pearl, and colored stones. 7Drinks were served in golden goblets, goblets of different kinds, and the royal wine was lavished according to the bounty of the king. 8Drinking was by flagons, without restraint; for the king had given orders to all the officials of his palace to do as each one desired. 9Furthermore, Queen Vashti gave a banquet for the women in the palace of King Ahasuerus.

10 On the seventh day, when the king was merry with wine, he commanded Mehuman, Biztha, Harbona, Bigtha and Abagtha, Zethar and Carkas, the seven eunuchs who attended him, 11to bring Queen Vashti before the king, wearing the royal crown, in order to show the peoples and the officials her beauty; for she was fair to behold. 12But Queen Vashti refused to come at the king's command conveyed by the eunuchs. At this the king was enraged, and his anger burned within him.

13 Then the king consulted the sages who knew the laws[g] (for this was the king's procedure toward all who were versed in law and custom, 14and those next to him were Carshena, Shethar, Admatha, Tarshish, Meres, Marsena, and Memucan, the seven officials of Persia and Media, who had access to the king, and sat first in the kingdom): 15"According to the law, what is to be done to Queen Vashti because she has not performed the command of King Ahasuerus conveyed by the eunuchs?" 16Then Memucan said in the presence of the king and the officials, "Not only has Queen Vashti done wrong to the king, but also to all the officials and all the peoples who are in all the provinces of King Ahasuerus. 17For this deed of the queen will be made known to all women, causing them to look with contempt on their husbands, since they will say, 'King Ahasuerus commanded Queen Vashti to be brought before him, and she did not come.' 18This very day the noble ladies of Persia and Media who have

---

[d] Gk *their own evils*   [e] Or *Nubia*; Heb *Cush*
[f] Or *rods*   [g] Cn: Heb *times*

heard of the queen's behavior will rebel against[h] the king's officials, and there will be no end of contempt and wrath! [19]If it pleases the king, let a royal order go out from him, and let it be written among the laws of the Persians and the Medes so that it may not be altered, that Vashti is never again to come before King Ahasuerus; and let the king give her royal position to another who is better than she. [20]So when the decree made by the king is proclaimed throughout all his kingdom, vast as it is, all women will give honor to their husbands, high and low alike."

21 This advice pleased the king and the officials, and the king did as Memucan proposed; [22]he sent letters to all the royal provinces, to every province in its own script and to every people in its own language, declaring that every man should be master in his own house.[i]

Esther Becomes Queen

2 After these things, when the anger of King Ahasuerus had abated, he remembered Vashti and what she had done and what had been decreed against her. [2]Then the king's servants who attended him said, "Let beautiful young virgins be sought out for the king. [3]And let the king appoint commissioners in all the provinces of his kingdom to gather all the beautiful young virgins to the harem in the citadel of Susa under custody of Hegai, the king's eunuch, who is in charge of the women; let their cosmetic treatments be given them. [4]And let the girl who pleases the king be queen instead of Vashti." This pleased the king, and he did so.

5 Now there was a Jew in the citadel of Susa whose name was Mordecai son of Jair son of Shimei son of Kish, a Benjaminite. [6]Kish[j] had been carried away from Jerusalem among the captives carried away with King Jeconiah of Judah, whom King Nebuchadnezzar of Babylon had carried away. [7]Mordecai[k] had brought up Hadassah, that is Esther, his cousin, for she had neither father nor mother; the girl was fair and beautiful, and when her father and her mother died, Mordecai adopted her as his own daughter. [8]So when the king's order and his edict were proclaimed, and when many young women were gathered in the citadel of Susa in custody of Hegai, Esther also was taken into the king's palace and put in custody of Hegai, who had charge

of the women. [9]The girl pleased him and won his favor, and he quickly provided her with her cosmetic treatments and her portion of food, and with seven chosen maids from the king's palace, and advanced her and her maids to the best place in the harem. [10]Esther did not reveal her people or kindred, for Mordecai had charged her not to tell. [11]Every day Mordecai would walk around in front of the court of the harem, to learn how Esther was and how she fared.

12 The turn came for each girl to go in to King Ahasuerus, after being twelve months under the regulations for the women, since this was the regular period of their cosmetic treatment, six months with oil of myrrh and six months with perfumes and cosmetics for women. [13]When the girl went in to the king she was given whatever she asked for to take with her from the harem to the king's palace. [14]In the evening she went in; then in the morning she came back to the second harem in custody of Shaashgaz, the king's eunuch, who was in charge of the concubines; she did not go in to the king again, unless the king delighted in her and she was summoned by name.

15 When the turn came for Esther daughter of Abihail the uncle of Mordecai, who had adopted her as his own daughter, to go in to the king, she asked for nothing except what Hegai the king's eunuch, who had charge of the women, advised. Now Esther was admired by all who saw her. [16]When Esther was taken to King Ahasuerus in his royal palace in the tenth month, which is the month of Tebeth, in the seventh year of his reign, [17]the king loved Esther more than all the other women; of all the virgins she won his favor and devotion, so that he set the royal crown on her head and made her queen instead of Vashti. [18]Then the king gave a great banquet to all his officials and ministers— "Esther's banquet." He also granted a holiday[l] to the provinces, and gave gifts with royal liberality.

Mordecai Discovers a Plot

19 When the virgins were being gathered together,[m] Mordecai was sitting at

---

h Cn: Heb *will tell*   i Heb adds *and speak according to the language of his people*   j Heb *a Benjaminite* 6*who*   k Heb *He*   l Or *an amnesty*   m Heb adds *a second time*

the king's gate. [20]Now Esther had not revealed her kindred or her people, as Mordecai had charged her; for Esther obeyed Mordecai just as when she was brought up by him. [21]In those days, while Mordecai was sitting at the king's gate, Bigthan and Teresh, two of the king's eunuchs, who guarded the threshold, became angry and conspired to assassinate[n] King Ahasuerus. [22]But the matter came to the knowledge of Mordecai, and he told it to Queen Esther, and Esther told the king in the name of Mordecai. [23]When the affair was investigated and found to be so, both the men were hanged on the gallows. It was recorded in the book of the annals in the presence of the king.

Haman Undertakes to Destroy the Jews

3 After these things King Ahasuerus promoted Haman son of Hammedatha the Agagite, and advanced him and set his seat above all the officials who were with him. [2]And all the king's servants who were at the king's gate bowed down and did obeisance to Haman; for the king had so commanded concerning him. But Mordecai did not bow down or do obeisance. [3]Then the king's servants who were at the king's gate said to Mordecai, "Why do you disobey the king's command?" [4]When they spoke to him day after day and he would not listen to them, they told Haman, in order to see whether Mordecai's words would avail; for he had told them that he was a Jew. [5]When Haman saw that Mordecai did not bow down or do obeisance to him, Haman was infuriated. [6]But he thought it beneath him to lay hands on Mordecai alone. So, having been told who Mordecai's people were, Haman plotted to destroy all the Jews, the people of Mordecai, throughout the whole kingdom of Ahasuerus.

[7] In the first month, which is the month of Nisan, in the twelfth year of King Ahasuerus, they cast Pur—which means "the lot"—before Haman for the day and for the month, and the lot fell on the thirteenth day[o] of the twelfth month, which is the month of Adar. [8]Then Haman said to King Ahasuerus, "There is a certain people scattered and separated among the peoples in all the provinces of your kingdom; their laws are different from those of every other people, and they do not keep the king's laws, so that it is not appropriate for the king to tolerate them. [9]If it pleases the king, let a decree be issued for their destruction, and I will pay ten thousand talents of silver into the hands of those who have charge of the king's business, so that they may put it into the king's treasuries." [10]So the king took his signet ring from his hand and gave it to Haman son of Hammedatha the Agagite, the enemy of the Jews. [11]The king said to Haman, "The money is given to you, and the people as well, to do with them as it seems good to you."

[12] Then the king's secretaries were summoned on the thirteenth day of the first month, and an edict, according to all that Haman commanded, was written to the king's satraps and to the governors over all the provinces and to the officials of all the peoples, to every province in its own script and every people in its own language; it was written in the name of King Ahasuerus and sealed with the king's ring. [13]Letters were sent by couriers to all the king's provinces, giving orders to destroy, to kill, and to annihilate all Jews, young and old, women and children, in one day, the thirteenth day of the twelfth month, which is the month of Adar, and to plunder their goods.

Addition B

The King's Letter

13 [p] This is a copy of the letter: "The Great King, Ahasuerus, writes the following to the governors of the hundred twenty-seven provinces from India to Ethiopia and to the officials under them:

[2] "Having become ruler of many nations and master of the whole world (not elated with presumption of authority but always acting reasonably and with kindness), I have determined to settle the lives of my subjects in lasting tranquility and, in order to make my kingdom peaceable and open to travel throughout all its extent, to restore the peace desired by all people.

[3] "When I asked my counselors how this might be accomplished, Haman—

---

[n] Heb *to lay hands on*   [o] Cn Compare Gk and verse 13 below: Heb *the twelfth month*
[p] Chapter 13.1-7 corresponds to chapter B 1-7 in some translations.

who excels among us in sound judgment, and is distinguished for his unchanging goodwill and steadfast fidelity, and has attained the second place in the kingdom— [4]pointed out to us that among all the nations in the world there is scattered a certain hostile people, who have laws contrary to those of every nation and continually disregard the ordinances of kings, so that the unifying of the kingdom that we honorably intend cannot be brought about. [5]We understand that this people, and it alone, stands constantly in opposition to every nation, perversely following a strange manner of life and laws, and is ill-disposed to our government, doing all the harm they can so that our kingdom may not attain stability.

6 "Therefore we have decreed that those indicated to you in the letters written by Haman, who is in charge of affairs and is our second father, shall all—wives and children included—be utterly destroyed by the swords of their enemies, without pity or restraint, on the fourteenth day of the twelfth month, Adar, of this present year, [7]so that those who have long been hostile and remain so may in a single day go down in violence to Hades, and leave our government completely secure and untroubled hereafter."

END OF ADDITION B

———————————————

3 [14]A copy of the document was to be issued as a decree in every province by proclamation, calling on all the peoples to be ready for that day. [15]The couriers went quickly by order of the king, and the decree was issued in the citadel of Susa. The king and Haman sat down to drink; but the city of Susa was thrown into confusion.

Esther Agrees to Help the Jews

4 When Mordecai learned all that had been done, Mordecai tore his clothes and put on sackcloth and ashes, and went through the city, wailing with a loud and bitter cry; [2]he went up to the entrance of the king's gate, for no one might enter the king's gate clothed with sackcloth. [3]In every province, wherever the king's command and his decree came, there was great mourning among the Jews, with fast-

ing and weeping and lamenting, and most of them lay in sackcloth and ashes.

4 When Esther's maids and her eunuchs came and told her, the queen was deeply distressed; she sent garments to clothe Mordecai, so that he might take off his sackcloth; but he would not accept them. [5]Then Esther called for Hathach, one of the king's eunuchs, who had been appointed to attend her, and ordered him to go to Mordecai to learn what was happening and why. [6]Hathach went out to Mordecai in the open square of the city in front of the king's gate, [7]and Mordecai told him all that had happened to him, and the exact sum of money that Haman had promised to pay into the king's treasuries for the destruction of the Jews. [8]Mordecai also gave him a copy of the written decree issued in Susa for their destruction, that he might show it to Esther, explain it to her, and charge her to go to the king to make supplication to him and entreat him for her people.

9 Hathach went and told Esther what Mordecai had said. [10]Then Esther spoke to Hathach and gave him a message for Mordecai, saying, [11]"All the king's servants and the people of the king's provinces know that if any man or woman goes to the king inside the inner court without being called, there is but one law—all alike are to be put to death. Only if the king holds out the golden scepter to someone, may that person live. I myself have not been called to come in to the king for thirty days." [12]When they told Mordecai what Esther had said, [13]Mordecai told them to reply to Esther, "Do not think that in the king's palace you will escape any more than all the other Jews. [14]For if you keep silence at such a time as this, relief and deliverance will rise for the Jews from another quarter, but you and your father's family will perish. Who knows? Perhaps you have come to royal dignity for just such a time as this." [15]Then Esther said in reply to Mordecai, [16]"Go, gather all the Jews to be found in Susa, and hold a fast on my behalf, and neither eat nor drink for three days, night or day. I and my maids will also fast as you do. After that I will go to the king, though it is against the law; and if I perish, I perish." [17]Mordecai then went away and did everything as Esther had ordered him.

ADDITION C

Mordecai's Prayer

13 [8q] Then Mordecai[r] prayed to the Lord, calling to remembrance all the works of the Lord.

9 He said, "O Lord, Lord, you rule as King over all things, for the universe is in your power and there is no one who can oppose you when it is your will to save Israel, [10]for you have made heaven and earth and every wonderful thing under heaven. [11]You are Lord of all, and there is no one who can resist you, the Lord. [12]You know all things; you know, O Lord, that it was not in insolence or pride or for any love of glory that I did this, and refused to bow down to this proud Haman; [13]for I would have been willing to kiss the soles of his feet to save Israel! [14]But I did this so that I might not set human glory above the glory of God, and I will not bow down to anyone but you, who are my Lord; and I will not do these things in pride. [15]And now, O Lord God and King, God of Abraham, spare your people; for the eyes of our foes are upon us[s] to annihilate us, and they desire to destroy the inheritance that has been yours from the beginning. [16]Do not neglect your portion, which you redeemed for yourself out of the land of Egypt. [17]Hear my prayer, and have mercy upon your inheritance; turn our mourning into feasting that we may live and sing praise to your name, O Lord; do not destroy the lips[t] of those who praise you."

18 And all Israel cried out mightily, for their death was before their eyes.

Esther's Prayer

14 Then Queen Esther, seized with deadly anxiety, fled to the Lord. [2]She took off her splendid apparel and put on the garments of distress and mourning, and instead of costly perfumes she covered her head with ashes and dung, and she utterly humbled her body; every part that she loved to adorn she covered with her tangled hair. [3]She prayed to the Lord God of Israel, and said: "O my Lord, you only are our king; help me, who am alone and have no helper but you, [4]for my danger is in my hand. [5]Ever since I was born I have heard in the tribe of my family that you, O Lord, took Israel out of all the nations, and our ancestors from among all their forebears, for an everlasting inheritance, and that you did for them all that you promised. [6]And now we have sinned before you, and you have handed us over to our enemies [7]because we glorified their gods. You are righteous, O Lord! [8]And now they are not satisfied that we are in bitter slavery, but they have covenanted with their idols [9]to abolish what your mouth has ordained, and to destroy your inheritance, to stop the mouths of those who praise you and to quench your altar and the glory of your house, [10]to open the mouths of the nations for the praise of vain idols, and to magnify forever a mortal king.

11 "O Lord, do not surrender your scepter to what has no being; and do not let them laugh at our downfall; but turn their plan against them, and make an example of him who began this against us. [12]Remember, O Lord; make yourself known in this time of our affliction, and give me courage, O King of the gods and Master of all dominion! [13]Put eloquent speech in my mouth before the lion, and turn his heart to hate the man who is fighting against us, so that there may be an end of him and those who agree with him. [14]But save us by your hand, and help me, who am alone and have no helper but you, O Lord. [15]You have knowledge of all things, and you know that I hate the splendor of the wicked and abhor the bed of the uncircumcised and of any alien. [16]You know my necessity—that I abhor the sign of my proud position, which is upon my head on days when I appear in public. I abhor it like a filthy rag, and I do not wear it on the days when I am at leisure. [17]And your servant has not eaten at Haman's table, and I have not honored the king's feast or drunk the wine of libations. [18]Your servant has had no joy since the day that I was brought here until now, except in you, O Lord God of Abraham. [19]O God, whose might is over all, hear the voice of the despairing, and save us from the hands of evildoers. And save me from my fear!"

END OF ADDITION C

---

[q] Chapters 13.8—15.16 correspond to chapters C 1-30 and D 1-16 in some translations.   [r] Gk *he*   [s] Gk *for they are eying us*   [t] Gk *mouth*

ADDITION D

Esther Is Received by the King

15 On the third day, when she ended her prayer, she took off the garments in which she had worshiped, and arrayed herself in splendid attire. ²Then, majestically adorned, after invoking the aid of the all-seeing God and Savior, she took two maids with her; ³on one she leaned gently for support, ⁴while the other followed, carrying her train. ⁵She was radiant with perfect beauty, and she looked happy, as if beloved, but her heart was frozen with fear. ⁶When she had gone through all the doors, she stood before the king. He was seated on his royal throne, clothed in the full array of his majesty, all covered with gold and precious stones. He was most terrifying.

7 Lifting his face, flushed with splendor, he looked at her in fierce anger. The queen faltered, and turned pale and faint, and collapsed on the head of the maid

Fear

The word "fear" is mentioned in Scripture so many times that you would think it was another name for being human. Think of all the types of fear: fear of one's own death and the death of loved ones; fear of violence; fear of losing a job; fear of illness; fear of losing the love of those upon whom you are most dependent; fear of making a fool of oneself; fear of the loss of God's love through sin or of the fatal consequences of the sins of loved ones; fear of losing one's faith; and finally that most difficult fear to overcome, a free-floating anxiety without known cause.

Steps in overcoming fear through trust in Christ:

Admit the extent of your fear in prayer to God, crying out from the depths for courage. Repeat the words of Jesus: "My Father, if it is possible, let this cup pass from me; yet not what I want but what you want" (Matthew 26.39).

Renew your faith, perhaps by reciting the Creed, to remember that what you fear to lose is less valuable than God himself and eternal life where you will find what you might seem to lose on earth.

Cry out to Christ to help you in your fear, picturing his hand reaching out to you on the waves of fear, as he did with Saint Peter.

Instead of spending time analyzing your fears, seek times of peaceful interior prayer, preferably before the Blessed Sacrament. You might repeat often the words of Jesus on the cross, "Father, into your hands I commend my spirit" (Luke 23.46).

To prevent fear from overpowering you to the extent of paralyzing your will to do what would otherwise be good, ask Christ to give you a conviction that you are never alone and that he will be with you at the exact time of your feared future trial.

—*RONDA DE SOLA CHERVIN*

Go to page 552 for your next devotional reading.

FRIDAY

Scripture Reading for Today:
Esther 14.1–19

Verse for Today:
Esther 14.19

Rahab

Her Name Means "Storm," "Arrogance," "Broad," or "Spacious"

THE STORY OF A WOMAN

Her Character: *She was wise as well as clever. She saw judgment coming and was able to devise an escape plan for herself and her family. As soon as she heard what God had done for the Israelites, she cast her lot with his people, risking her life in an act of faith.*
Her Sorrow: *To see her own people destroyed and her city demolished.*
Her Joy: *That God had given her, a prostitute and a foreigner, the opportunity to know him and belong to his people.*

Read Joshua 2.1–21; 6.17–25

Jericho may be the world's oldest city. Established nearly six thousand years before Miriam and Moses completed their desert wanderings, its ancient ruins can be found just 17 miles northeast of Jerusalem. Gateway to Canaan, it was also the home of a prostitute named Rahab, whose house nestled snugly into its thick surrounding walls.

As well as entertaining locals, Rahab welcomed guests from various caravans whose routes crisscrossed Jericho. Men from all over the East brought news of a swarm of people encamped east of the Jordan River. Rahab heard marvelous stories about the exploits of their God: How he had dried up the Red Sea so they could escape their Egyptian slave masters; how he had trained and toughened the Israelites for 40 years in the desert.

Before long, two Israelite spies made their way to Rahab's house, where she hid them beneath stalks of flax drying on the roof. Later, when she received a message from the king of Jericho, inquiring about the spies, Rahab lied in order to save them: "True, the men came to me, but I did not know where they came from. And when it was time to close the gate at dark, the men went out. Where the men went I do not know. Pursue them quickly, for you can overtake them" (2.4–5).

As soon as the king's men left, she hurried to the roof, warning her guests: "I know that the LORD has given you the land, and that dread of you has fallen on us, and that all the inhabitants of the land melt in fear before you ... The LORD your God is indeed God in heaven above and on earth below. Now then, since I have dealt kindly with you, swear to me by the LORD that you in turn will deal kindly with my family. Give me a sign of good faith that you will spare my father and mother, my brothers and sisters, and all who belong to them, and deliver our lives from death" (2.9, 11–13).

Quickly, the two men handed her a scarlet cord, instructing Rahab to tie it in the window on the side of the house built into the city wall. Their people, they promised, would see it and spare everyone inside. With that they slipped out the window and scrambled down the city walls.

Later, Rahab watched from her window as the Israelites gathered around the city. Her eyes followed the curious scene: Seven priests were carrying an ark, followed by thousands of men, and they all were marching around the city walls. The spectacle repeated itself for the next five days. Then, as the sun rose on the seventh day, she watched as they marched several times around Jericho. As they completed their seventh turn, Rahab heard the ram's horn and a thunderous cry of voices. Suddenly the city walls collapsed. The invading army killed everyone inside, sparing only Rahab and her family.

A prostitute and a foreigner, Rahab is the only woman singled out by name and commended for her faith as part of the great cloud of witnesses mentioned in the book of Hebrews. Her own people destroyed, Rahab left everything behind and joined the Israelites, eventually becoming an ancestor of King David and one of Jesus' ancestors as well.

Praying With Rahab

"I know that the LORD has given you the land, and that dread of you has fallen on us, and that all the inhabitants of the land melt in fear before you . . . The LORD your God is indeed God in heaven above and on earth below. Now then, since I have dealt kindly with you, swear to me by the LORD that you in turn will deal kindly with my family. Give me a sign of good faith that you will spare my father and mother, my brothers and sisters, and all who belong to them, and deliver our lives from death."—Joshua 2.9, 11–13

Praise God: For giving women key roles in his plan of salvation.

Offer Thanks: That no one, including yourself, is beyond the reach of grace.

Confess: Your unwillingness to take risks in order to follow God.

Ask God: To increase your awe of him.

Lift Your Heart

The scarlet cord that saved Rahab and her family reminds us of the red blood of Jesus, who still saves us today, and of Isaiah's words, "Though your sins are like scarlet, they shall be like snow" (Isaiah 1.18). This week, use a small red ribbon as a bookmark or tie a scarlet ribbon around the pot of a favorite plant to remind yourself of the vital importance of living by faith. Each time you notice your scarlet cord, let it remind you of the lengths Jesus went to in order to save you. Your life and the vitality of your relationship with God depend on faith.

Father, I praise you for the wonderful and unexpected ways you have acted in my life. Let the knowledge of your faithfulness increase my courage to take the risks that faith demands.

Go to page 556 for your next devotional reading.

who went in front of her. [8]Then God changed the spirit of the king to gentleness, and in alarm he sprang from his throne and took her in his arms until she came to herself. He comforted her with soothing words, and said to her, [9]"What is it, Esther? I am your husband.[u] Take courage; [10]You shall not die, for our law applies only to our subjects.[v] Come near."

11 Then he raised the golden scepter and touched her neck with it; [12]he embraced her, and said, "Speak to me." [13]She said to him, "I saw you, my lord, like an angel of God, and my heart was shaken with fear at your glory. [14]For you are wonderful, my lord, and your countenance is full of grace." [15]And while she was speaking, she fainted and fell. [16]Then the king was agitated, and all his servants tried to comfort her.

END OF ADDITION D

Esther's Banquet

5 [w][3]The king said to her, "What is it, Queen Esther? What is your request? It shall be given you, even to the half of my kingdom." [4]Then Esther said, "If it pleases the king, let the king and Haman come today to a banquet that I have prepared for the king." [5]Then the king said, "Bring Haman quickly, so that we may do as Esther desires." So the king and Haman came to the banquet that Esther had prepared. [6]While they were drinking wine, the king said to Esther, "What is your petition? It shall be granted you. And what is your request? Even to the half of my kingdom, it shall be fulfilled." [7]Then Esther said, "This is my petition and request: [8]If I have won the king's favor, and if it pleases the king to grant my petition and fulfill my request, let the king and Haman come tomorrow to the banquet that I will prepare for them, and then I will do as the king has said."

Haman Plans to Have Mordecai Hanged

9 Haman went out that day happy and in good spirits. But when Haman saw Mordecai in the king's gate, and observed that he neither rose nor trembled before him, he was infuriated with Mordecai; [10]nevertheless Haman restrained himself and went home. Then he sent and called for his friends and his wife Zeresh, [11]and

Haman recounted to them the splendor of his riches, the number of his sons, all the promotions with which the king had honored him, and how he had advanced him above the officials and the ministers of the king. [12]Haman added, "Even Queen Esther let no one but myself come with the king to the banquet that she prepared. Tomorrow also I am invited by her, together with the king. [13]Yet all this does me no good so long as I see the Jew Mordecai sitting at the king's gate." [14]Then his wife Zeresh and all his friends said to him, "Let a gallows fifty cubits high be made, and in the morning tell the king to have Mordecai hanged on it; then go with the king to the banquet in good spirits." This advice pleased Haman, and he had the gallows made.

The King Honors Mordecai

6 On that night the king could not sleep, and he gave orders to bring the book of records, the annals, and they were read to the king. [2]It was found written how Mordecai had told about Bigthana and Teresh, two of the king's eunuchs, who guarded the threshold, and who had conspired to assassinate[x] King Ahasuerus. [3]Then the king said, "What honor or distinction has been bestowed on Mordecai for this?" The king's servants who attended him said, "Nothing has been done for him." [4]The king said, "Who is in the court?" Now Haman had just entered the outer court of the king's palace to speak to the king about having Mordecai hanged on the gallows that he had prepared for him. [5]So the king's servants told him, "Haman is there, standing in the court." The king said, "Let him come in." [6]So Haman came in, and the king said to him, "What shall be done for the man whom the king wishes to honor?" Haman said to himself, "Whom would the king wish to honor more than me?" [7]So Haman said to the king, "For the man whom the king wishes to honor, [8]let royal robes be brought, which the king has worn, and a horse that the king has ridden, with a royal crown on its head. [9]Let the robes and the horse be handed over to one of the king's most noble officials; let him[y] robe the man whom the king wishes to honor,

---

u Gk *brother*   *v* Meaning of Gk uncertain   *w* In Greek, Chapter D replaces verses 1 and 2 in Hebrew.   *x* Heb *to lay hands on*   *y* Heb *them*

and let him[z] conduct the man on horseback through the open square of the city, proclaiming before him: 'Thus shall it be done for the man whom the king wishes to honor.' " [10]Then the king said to Haman, "Quickly, take the robes and the horse, as you have said, and do so to the Jew Mordecai who sits at the king's gate. Leave out nothing that you have mentioned." [11]So Haman took the robes and the horse and robed Mordecai and led him riding through the open square of the city, proclaiming, "Thus shall it be done for the man whom the king wishes to honor."

12 Then Mordecai returned to the king's gate, but Haman hurried to his house, mourning and with his head covered. [13]When Haman told his wife Zeresh and all his friends everything that had happened to him, his advisers and his wife Zeresh said to him, "If Mordecai, before whom your downfall has begun, is of the Jewish people, you will not prevail against him, but will surely fall before him."

Haman's Downfall and Mordecai's Advancement

14 While they were still talking with him, the king's eunuchs arrived and hurried Haman off to the banquet that Esther had prepared. [1]So the king and Haman went in to feast with Queen Esther. [2]On the second day, as they were drinking wine, the king again said to Esther, "What is your petition, Queen Esther? It shall be granted you. And what is your request? Even to the half of my kingdom, it shall be fulfilled." [3]Then Queen Esther answered, "If I have won your favor, O king, and if it pleases the king, let my life be given me—that is my petition—and the lives of my people—that is my request. [4]For we have been sold, I and my people, to be destroyed, to be killed, and to be annihilated. If we had been sold merely as slaves, men and women, I would have held my peace; but no enemy can compensate for this damage to the king."[a] [5]Then King Ahasuerus said to Queen Esther, "Who is he, and where is he, who has presumed to do this?" [6]Esther said, "A foe and enemy, this wicked Haman!" Then Haman was terrified before the king and the queen. [7]The king rose from the feast in wrath and went into the

palace garden, but Haman stayed to beg his life from Queen Esther, for he saw that the king had determined to destroy him. [8]When the king returned from the palace garden to the banquet hall, Haman had thrown himself on the couch where Esther was reclining; and the king said, "Will he even assault the queen in my own house?" As the words left the mouth of the king, they covered Haman's face. [9]Then Harbona, one of the eunuchs in attendance on the king, said, "Look, the very gallows that Haman has prepared for Mordecai, whose word saved the king, stands at Haman's house, fifty cubits high." And the king said, "Hang him on that." [10]So they hanged Haman on the gallows that he had prepared for Mordecai. Then the anger of the king abated.

8 [1]On that day King Ahasuerus gave to Queen Esther the house of Haman, the enemy of the Jews; and Mordecai came before the king, for Esther had told what he was to her. [2]Then the king took off his signet ring, which he had taken from Haman, and gave it to Mordecai. So Esther set Mordecai over the house of Haman.

Esther Saves the Jews

3 Then Esther spoke again to the king; she fell at his feet, weeping and pleading with him to avert the evil design of Haman the Agagite and the plot that he had devised against the Jews. [4]The king held out the golden scepter to Esther, [5]and Esther rose and stood before the king. She said, "If it pleases the king, and if I have won his favor, and if the thing seems right before the king, and I have his approval, let an order be written to revoke the letters devised by Haman son of Hammedatha the Agagite, which he wrote giving orders to destroy the Jews who are in all the provinces of the king. [6]For how can I bear to see the calamity that is coming on my people? Or how can I bear to see the destruction of my kindred?" [7]Then King Ahasuerus said to Queen Esther and to the Jew Mordecai, "See, I have given Esther the house of Haman, and they have hanged him on the gallows, because he plotted to lay hands on the Jews. [8]You may write as you please with regard to the

z Heb *them*   a Meaning of Heb uncertain

Jews, in the name of the king, and seal it with the king's ring; for an edict written in the name of the king and sealed with the king's ring cannot be revoked."

9 The king's secretaries were summoned at that time, in the third month, which is the month of Sivan, on the twenty-third day; and an edict was written, according to all that Mordecai commanded, to the Jews and to the satraps and the governors and the officials of the provinces from India to Ethiopia,[b] one hundred twenty-seven provinces, to every province in its own script and to every people in its own language, and also to the Jews in their script and their language. [10]He wrote letters in the name of King Ahasuerus, sealed them with the king's ring, and sent them by mounted couriers riding on fast steeds bred from the royal herd.[c] [11]By these letters the king allowed the Jews who were in every city to assemble and defend their lives, to destroy, to kill, and to annihilate any armed force of any people or province that might attack them, with their children and women, and to plunder their goods [12]on a single day throughout all the provinces of King Ahasuerus, on the thirteenth day of the twelfth month, which is the month of Adar.

[b] Or *Nubia*; Heb *Cush* [c] Meaning of Heb uncertain

MONDAY

Scripture Reading for Today:
Esther 7.1–4

Verse for Today:
Esther 7.3

Intercession

In a letter to her confessor, the mystic Catherine of Siena left a vivid account of her intercessory prayer for the Church and of the spiritual warfare that accompanied it.

It seemed to me as if my soul were parted from my body. I could not move the tongue or any member of it, any more than a body quite dead. Then I let the body stay just as it was; and the intellect was fixed on the abyss of the Trinity. Memory was full of recollection of the need of Holy Church and of all the Christian people; and I cried before [God's] face, and demanded divine help with assurance, offering to him my desires, and constraining him by the blood of the Lamb and the pains that had been borne. And so eager was the demand that it seemed to me sure that he would not deny that petition. Then I asked for all you others, praying him that he would fulfill in you his will and my desires. Then I asked that he would save me from eternal condemnation.

The presence of the Humble Lamb came before my soul, saying: "Fear not: for I will fulfill thy desires, and those of my other servants."

[Then] the room appeared full of devils; they began to wage another battle, the most terrible that I ever had. "God, listen for my help! Lord, haste thee to help me!" Two nights and two days passed in these tempests.

In this way, and many others, which I cannot tell, my life is consumed and shed for this sweet Bride. I pray the Divine Goodness soon to let me see the redemption of his people.

—*SAINT CATHERINE OF SIENA*

Go to page 562 for your next devotional reading.

ADDITION E

The Decree of Ahasuerus

16^d The following is a copy of this letter:

"The Great King, Ahasuerus, to the governors of the provinces from India to Ethiopia, one hundred twenty-seven provinces, and to those who are loyal to our government, greetings.

2 "Many people, the more they are honored with the most generous kindness of their benefactors, the more proud do they become, ³and not only seek to injure our subjects, but in their inability to stand prosperity, they even undertake to scheme against their own benefactors. ⁴They not only take away thankfulness from others, but, carried away by the boasts of those who know nothing of goodness, they even assume that they will escape the evil-hating justice of God, who always sees everything. ⁵And often many of those who are set in places of authority have been made in part responsible for the shedding of innocent blood, and have been involved in irremediable calamities, by the persuasion of friends who have been entrusted with the administration of public affairs, ⁶when these persons by the false trickery of their evil natures beguile the sincere goodwill of their sovereigns.

7 "What has been wickedly accomplished through the pestilent behavior of those who exercise authority unworthily can be seen, not so much from the more ancient records that we hand on, as from investigation of matters close at hand.^e ⁸In the future we will take care to render our kingdom quiet and peaceable for all, ⁹by changing our methods and always judging what comes before our eyes with more equitable consideration. ¹⁰For Haman son of Hammedatha, a Macedonian (really an alien to the Persian blood, and quite devoid of our kindliness), having become our guest, ¹¹enjoyed so fully the goodwill that we have for every nation that he was called our father and was continually bowed down to by all as the person second to the royal throne. ¹²But, unable to restrain his arrogance, he undertook to deprive us of our kingdom and our life,^f ¹³and with intricate craft and deceit asked for the destruction of Mordecai, our savior and perpetual benefactor, and of Esther, the blameless partner of our kingdom, together with their whole nation. ¹⁴He thought that by these methods he would catch us undefended and would transfer the kingdom of the Persians to the Macedonians.

15 "But we find that the Jews, who were consigned to annihilation by this thrice-accursed man, are not evildoers, but are governed by most righteous laws ¹⁶and are children of the living God, most high, most mighty,^g who has directed the kingdom both for us and for our ancestors in the most excellent order.

17 "You will therefore do well not to put in execution the letters sent by Haman son of Hammedatha, ¹⁸since he, the one who did these things, has been hanged at the gate of Susa with all his household— for God, who rules over all things, has speedily inflicted on him the punishment that he deserved.

19 "Therefore post a copy of this letter publicly in every place, and permit the Jews to live under their own laws. ²⁰And give them reinforcements, so that on the thirteenth day of the twelfth month, Adar, on that very day, they may defend themselves against those who attack them at the time of oppression. ²¹For God, who rules over all things, has made this day to be a joy for his chosen people instead of a day of destruction for them.

22 "Therefore you shall observe this with all good cheer as a notable day among your commemorative festivals, ²³so that both now and hereafter it may represent deliverance for you^h and the loyal Persians, but that it may be a reminder of destruction for those who plot against us.

24 "Every city and country, without exception, that does not act accordingly shall be destroyed in wrath with spear and fire. It shall be made not only impassable for human beings, but also most hateful to wild animals and birds for all time."

END OF ADDITION E

---

^d Chapter 16.1-24 corresponds to chapter E 1-24 in some translations.   ^e Gk *matters beside* (your) *feet*   ^f Gk *our spirit*   ^g Gk *greatest*   ^h Other ancient authorities read *for us*

8 13A copy of the writ was to be issued as a decree in every province and published to all peoples, and the Jews were to be ready on that day to take revenge on their enemies. 14So the couriers, mounted on their swift royal steeds, hurried out, urged by the king's command. The decree was issued in the citadel of Susa.

15 Then Mordecai went out from the presence of the king, wearing royal robes of blue and white, with a great golden crown and a mantle of fine linen and purple, while the city of Susa shouted and rejoiced. 16For the Jews there was light and gladness, joy and honor. 17In every province and in every city, wherever the king's command and his edict came, there was gladness and joy among the Jews, a festival and a holiday. Furthermore, many of the peoples of the country professed to be Jews, because the fear of the Jews had fallen upon them.

Destruction of the Enemies of the Jews

9 Now in the twelfth month, which is the month of Adar, on the thirteenth day, when the king's command and edict were about to be executed, on the very day when the enemies of the Jews hoped to gain power over them, but which had been changed to a day when the Jews would gain power over their foes, 2the Jews gathered in their cities throughout all the provinces of King Ahasuerus to lay hands on those who had sought their ruin; and no one could withstand them, because the fear of them had fallen upon all peoples. 3All the officials of the provinces, the satraps and the governors, and the royal officials were supporting the Jews, because the fear of Mordecai had fallen upon them. 4For Mordecai was powerful in the king's house, and his fame spread throughout all the provinces as the man Mordecai grew more and more powerful. 5So the Jews struck down all their enemies with the sword, slaughtering, and destroying them, and did as they pleased to those who hated them. 6In the citadel of Susa the Jews killed and destroyed five hundred people. 7They killed Parshandatha, Dalphon, Aspatha, 8Poratha, Adalia, Aridatha, 9Parmashta, Arisai, Aridai, Vaizatha, 10the ten sons of Haman son of Hammedatha, the enemy of the Jews; but they did not touch the plunder.

11 That very day the number of those killed in the citadel of Susa was reported to the king. 12The king said to Queen Esther, "In the citadel of Susa the Jews have killed five hundred people and also the ten sons of Haman. What have they done in the rest of the king's provinces? Now what is your petition? It shall be granted you. And what further is your request? It shall be fulfilled." 13Esther said, "If it pleases the king, let the Jews who are in Susa be allowed tomorrow also to do according to this day's edict, and let the ten sons of Haman be hanged on the gallows." 14So the king commanded this to be done; a decree was issued in Susa, and the ten sons of Haman were hanged. 15The Jews who were in Susa gathered also on the fourteenth day of the month of Adar and they killed three hundred persons in Susa; but they did not touch the plunder.

16 Now the other Jews who were in the king's provinces also gathered to defend their lives, and gained relief from their enemies, and killed seventy-five thousand of those who hated them; but they laid no hands on the plunder. 17This was on the thirteenth day of the month of Adar, and on the fourteenth day they rested and made that a day of feasting and gladness.

The Feast of Purim Inaugurated

18 But the Jews who were in Susa gathered on the thirteenth day and on the fourteenth, and rested on the fifteenth day, making that a day of feasting and gladness. 19Therefore the Jews of the villages, who live in the open towns, hold the fourteenth day of the month of Adar as a day for gladness and feasting, a holiday on which they send gifts of food to one another.

20 Mordecai recorded these things, and sent letters to all the Jews who were in all the provinces of King Ahasuerus, both near and far, 21enjoining them that they should keep the fourteenth day of the month Adar and also the fifteenth day of the same month, year by year, 22as the days on which the Jews gained relief from their enemies, and as the month that had been turned for them from sorrow into gladness and from mourning into a holiday; that they should make them days of feasting and gladness, days for sending gifts of food to one another and presents to the poor. 23So the Jews adopted as a custom what they had begun to do, as Mordecai had written to them.

24 Haman son of Hammedatha the Agagite, the enemy of all the Jews, had plotted against the Jews to destroy them, and had cast Pur—that is "the lot"—to crush and destroy them; 25but when Esther came before the king, he gave orders in writing that the wicked plot that he had devised against the Jews should come upon his own head, and that he and his sons should be hanged on the gallows. 26Therefore these days are called Purim, from the word Pur. Thus because of all that was written in this letter, and of what they had faced in this matter, and of what had happened to them, 27the Jews established and accepted as a custom for themselves and their descendants and all who joined them, that without fail they would continue to observe these two days every year, as it was written and at the time appointed. 28These days should be remembered and kept throughout every generation, in every family, province, and city; and these days of Purim should never fall into disuse among the Jews, nor should the commemoration of these days cease among their descendants.

29 Queen Esther daughter of Abihail, along with the Jew Mordecai, gave full written authority, confirming this second letter about Purim. 30Letters were sent wishing peace and security to all the Jews, to the one hundred twenty-seven provinces of the kingdom of Ahasuerus, 31giving orders that these days of Purim should be observed at their appointed seasons, as the Jew Mordecai and Queen Esther enjoined on the Jews, just as they had laid down for themselves and for their descendants regulations concerning their fasts and their lamentations. 32The command of Queen Esther fixed these practices of Purim, and it was recorded in writing.

10 King Ahasuerus laid tribute on the land and on the islands of the sea. 2All the acts of his power and might, and the full account of the high honor of Mordecai, to which the king advanced him, are they not written in the annals of the kings of Media and Persia? 3For Mordecai the Jew was next in rank to King Ahasuerus, and he was powerful among the Jews and popular with his many kindred, for he sought the good of his people

and interceded for the welfare of all his descendants.

ADDITION F

Mordecai's Dream Fulfilled

4*i* And Mordecai said, "These things have come from God; 5for I remember the dream that I had concerning these matters, and none of them has failed to be fulfilled. 6There was the little spring that became a river, and there was light and sun and abundant water—the river is Esther, whom the king married and made queen. 7The two dragons are Haman and myself. 8The nations are those that gathered to destroy the name of the Jews. 9And my nation, this is Israel, who cried out to God and was saved. The Lord has saved his people; the Lord has rescued us from all these evils; God has done great signs and wonders, wonders that have never happened among the nations. 10For this purpose he made two lots, one for the people of God and one for all the nations, 11and these two lots came to the hour and moment and day of decision before God and among all the nations. 12And God remembered his people and vindicated his inheritance. 13So they will observe these days in the month of Adar, on the fourteenth and fifteenth*j* of that month, with an assembly and joy and gladness before God, from generation to generation forever among his people Israel."

Postscript

11 1In the fourth year of the reign of Ptolemy and Cleopatra, Dositheus, who said that he was a priest and a Levite,*k* and his son Ptolemy brought to Egypt*l* the preceding Letter about Purim, which they said was authentic and had been translated by Lysimachus son of Ptolemy, one of the residents of Jerusalem.

END OF ADDITION F

---

i Chapter 10.4-13 and 11.1 correspond to chapter F 1-11 in some translations.   *j* Other ancient authorities lack *and fifteenth*   *k* Or *priest, and Levitas*   *l* Cn: Gk *brought in*

1 Maccabees

First Maccabees covers the period from about 175–134 B.C., a time in which the Jews faced tremendous pressure to abandon their own forms of worship in order to adopt Hellenistic culture and worship. The name *Maccabee* probably means "hammer" and is the name of the family that led the revolt against Antiochus Epiphanes, the Syrian ruler who plundered the temple, burned the books of the Old Testament, forbade circumcision, and sacrificed a pig on the altar of the temple—all in an attempt to eradicate Jewish culture and worship.

Many of the Jews adopted the customs of their pagan overlords willingly enough. But a priest named Mattathias refused to forsake his faith and instead rallied the people against their persecutors. He and his followers fled to the mountains to carry on their revolt.

First Maccabees tells, with historical accuracy, of the revolt and the guerilla warfare conducted by Mattathias and his sons: Judas, Jonathan, and Simon, all of whom died violent deaths. After Simon finally established the independence of Judea, he was assassinated and then succeeded by his son, John Hyrcanus.

Were it not for God acting through the fierce loyalty of the Maccabees, the Jews might have lost their identity and become like the pagan peoples around them. Though the battle is less obvious, we are reminded of our need to remain faithful when we face cultural pressures that threaten to suffocate our faith.

Alexander the Great

1 After Alexander son of Philip, the Macedonian, who came from the land of Kittim, had defeated[a] King Darius of the Persians and the Medes, he succeeded him as king. (He had previously become king of Greece.) ²He fought many battles, conquered strongholds, and put to death the kings of the earth. ³He advanced to the ends of the earth, and plundered many nations. When the earth became quiet before him, he was exalted, and his heart was lifted up. ⁴He gathered a very strong army and ruled over countries, nations, and princes, and they became tributary to him.

a Gk adds *and he defeated*

5 After this he fell sick and perceived that he was dying. 6So he summoned his most honored officers, who had been brought up with him from youth, and divided his kingdom among them while he was still alive. 7And after Alexander had reigned twelve years, he died.

8 Then his officers began to rule, each in his own place. 9They all put on crowns after his death, and so did their descendants after them for many years; and they caused many evils on the earth.

Antiochus Epiphanes and Renegade Jews

10 From them came forth a sinful root, Antiochus Epiphanes, son of King Antiochus; he had been a hostage in Rome. He began to reign in the one hundred thirty-seventh year of the kingdom of the Greeks.[b]

11 In those days certain renegades came out from Israel and misled many, saying, "Let us go and make a covenant with the Gentiles around us, for since we separated from them many disasters have come upon us." 12This proposal pleased them, 13and some of the people eagerly went to the king, who authorized them to observe the ordinances of the Gentiles. 14So they built a gymnasium in Jerusalem, according to Gentile custom, 15and removed the marks of circumcision, and abandoned the holy covenant. They joined with the Gentiles and sold themselves to do evil.

Antiochus in Egypt

16 When Antiochus saw that his kingdom was established, he determined to become king of the land of Egypt, in order that he might reign over both kingdoms. 17So he invaded Egypt with a strong force, with chariots and elephants and cavalry and with a large fleet. 18He engaged King Ptolemy of Egypt in battle, and Ptolemy turned and fled before him, and many were wounded and fell. 19They captured the fortified cities in the land of Egypt, and he plundered the land of Egypt.

Persecution of the Jews

20 After subduing Egypt, Antiochus returned in the one hundred forty-third year.[c] He went up against Israel and came to Jerusalem with a strong force. 21He arrogantly entered the sanctuary and took the golden altar, the lampstand for the light, and all its utensils. 22He took

also the table for the bread of the Presence, the cups for drink offerings, the bowls, the golden censers, the curtain, the crowns, and the gold decoration on the front of the temple; he stripped it all off. 23He took the silver and the gold, and the costly vessels; he took also the hidden treasures that he found. 24Taking them all, he went into his own land.

He shed much blood,
 and spoke with great arrogance.
25 Israel mourned deeply in every
  community,
26 rulers and elders groaned,
 young women and young men
  became faint,
 the beauty of the women faded.
27 Every bridegroom took up the
  lament;
 she who sat in the bridal chamber
  was mourning.
28 Even the land trembled for its
  inhabitants,
 and all the house of Jacob was
  clothed with shame.

The Occupation of Jerusalem

29 Two years later the king sent to the cities of Judah a chief collector of tribute, and he came to Jerusalem with a large force. 30Deceitfully he spoke peaceable words to them, and they believed him; but he suddenly fell upon the city, dealt it a severe blow, and destroyed many people of Israel. 31He plundered the city, burned it with fire, and tore down its houses and its surrounding walls. 32They took captive the women and children, and seized the livestock. 33Then they fortified the city of David with a great strong wall and strong towers, and it became their citadel. 34They stationed there a sinful people, men who were renegades. These strengthened their position; 35they stored up arms and food, and collecting the spoils of Jerusalem they stored them there, and became a great menace,
36 for the citadel[d] became an ambush
  against the sanctuary,
 an evil adversary of Israel at all
  times.
37 On every side of the sanctuary they
  shed innocent blood;
 they even defiled the sanctuary.
38 Because of them the residents of
  Jerusalem fled;

b 175 B.C. c 169 B.C. d Gk it

she became a dwelling of
   strangers;
she became strange to her offspring,
   and her children forsook her.
39 Her sanctuary became desolate like a
      desert;
   her feasts were turned into
      mourning,
   her sabbaths into a reproach,
   her honor into contempt.
40 Her dishonor now grew as great as
      her glory;
   her exaltation was turned into
      mourning.

Installation of Gentile Cults

41 Then the king wrote to his whole
kingdom that all should be one people,
42and that all should give up their particular customs. 43All the Gentiles accepted
the command of the king. Many even
from Israel gladly adopted his religion;
they sacrificed to idols and profaned the
sabbath. 44And the king sent letters by
messengers to Jerusalem and the towns of
Judah; he directed them to follow customs strange to the land, 45to forbid burnt
offerings and sacrifices and drink offerings
in the sanctuary, to profane sabbaths and
festivals, 46to defile the sanctuary and the
priests, 47to build altars and sacred precincts and shrines for idols, to sacrifice
swine and other unclean animals, 48and
to leave their sons uncircumcised. They
were to make themselves abominable by
everything unclean and profane, 49so that
they would forget the law and change all
the ordinances. 50He added,*e* "And whoever does not obey the command of the
king shall die."

51 In such words he wrote to his whole
kingdom. He appointed inspectors over
all the people and commanded the towns
of Judah to offer sacrifice, town by town.
52Many of the people, everyone who forsook the law, joined them, and they did

e Gk lacks *He added*

Hidden Martyrdoms

TUESDAY

Scripture Reading
for Today:
I Maccabees 1.41–50

Verse for Today:
I Maccabees 1.50

We are all waiting for great opportunities to show heroism, letting countless opportunities go by to enlarge our hearts, increase
our faith, and show our love for our fellows, and so for him. We are
living in this world and must make choices now, choices which
may mean the sacrifice of our lives in the future, but for now our
goods, our reputation even.

We are trying to spread the gospel of peace. And in doing this
we are accounted fools, and it is the folly of the Cross in the eyes
of an unbelieving world.

Martyrdom is not [always] gallantly standing before a firing
squad. Usually it is the losing of a job because of not taking a loyalty oath, or buying a war bond, or paying a tax. Martyrdom is
small, hidden, misunderstood. Or if it is a bloody martyrdom, it is
the cry in the dark, the terror, the shame, the loneliness, nobody
to hear, nobody to suffer with, let alone to save.

But we proclaim our faith. Christ has died for us. Adam and Eve
fell, and as Julian of Norwich wrote, the worst has already happened and been repaired. It is [Christ's] dying, not the killing in
wars, which will save the world.

—DOROTHY DAY

Go to page 588 for your next devotional reading.

evil in the land; ⁵³they drove Israel into hiding in every place of refuge they had.

54 Now on the fifteenth day of Chislev, in the one hundred forty-fifth year,ᶠ they erected a desolating sacrilege on the altar of burnt offering. They also built altars in the surrounding towns of Judah, ⁵⁵and offered incense at the doors of the houses and in the streets. ⁵⁶The books of the law that they found they tore to pieces and burned with fire. ⁵⁷Anyone found possessing the book of the covenant, or anyone who adhered to the law, was condemned to death by decree of the king. ⁵⁸They kept using violence against Israel, against those who were found month after month in the towns. ⁵⁹On the twenty-fifth day of the month they offered sacrifice on the altar that was on top of the altar of burnt offering. ⁶⁰According to the decree, they put to death the women who had their children circumcised, ⁶¹and their families and those who circumcised them; and they hung the infants from their mothers' necks.

62 But many in Israel stood firm and were resolved in their hearts not to eat unclean food. ⁶³They chose to die rather than to be defiled by food or to profane the holy covenant; and they did die. ⁶⁴Very great wrath came upon Israel.

Mattathias and His Sons

2 In those days Mattathias son of John son of Simeon, a priest of the family of Joarib, moved from Jerusalem and settled in Modein. ²He had five sons, John surnamed Gaddi, ³Simon called Thassi, ⁴Judas called Maccabeus, ⁵Eleazar called Avaran, and Jonathan called Apphus. ⁶He saw the blasphemies being committed in Judah and Jerusalem, ⁷and said,

"Alas! Why was I born to see this,
    the ruin of my people, the ruin of
        the holy city,
and to live there when it was given
        over to the enemy,
    the sanctuary given over to aliens?
⁸ Her temple has become like a
        person without honor;ᵍ
⁹   her glorious vessels have been
        carried into exile.
Her infants have been killed in her
        streets,
    her youths by the sword of the
        foe.
¹⁰ What nation has not inherited her
        palacesʰ

and has not seized her spoils?
¹¹ All her adornment has been taken
        away;
    no longer free, she has become a
        slave.
¹² And see, our holy place, our beauty,
        and our glory have been laid
        waste;
    the Gentiles have profaned them.
¹³   Why should we live any longer?"

14 Then Mattathias and his sons tore their clothes, put on sackcloth, and mourned greatly.

Pagan Worship Refused

15 The king's officers who were enforcing the apostasy came to the town of Modein to make them offer sacrifice. ¹⁶Many from Israel came to them; and Mattathias and his sons were assembled. ¹⁷Then the king's officers spoke to Mattathias as follows: "You are a leader, honored and great in this town, and supported by sons and brothers. ¹⁸Now be the first to come and do what the king commands, as all the Gentiles and the people of Judah and those that are left in Jerusalem have done. Then you and your sons will be numbered among the Friends of the king, and you and your sons will be honored with silver and gold and many gifts."

19 But Mattathias answered and said in a loud voice: "Even if all the nations that live under the rule of the king obey him, and have chosen to obey his commandments, everyone of them abandoning the religion of their ancestors, ²⁰I and my sons and my brothers will continue to live by the covenant of our ancestors. ²¹Far be it from us to desert the law and the ordinances. ²²We will not obey the king's words by turning aside from our religion to the right hand or to the left."

23 When he had finished speaking these words, a Jew came forward in the sight of all to offer sacrifice on the altar in Modein, according to the king's command. ²⁴When Mattathias saw it, he burned with zeal and his heart was stirred. He gave vent to righteous anger; he ran and killed him on the altar. ²⁵At the same time he killed the king's officer who was forcing them to sacrifice, and he tore down the altar. ²⁶Thus he burned with

---

ᶠ 167 B.C.   ᵍ Meaning of Gk uncertain   ʰ Other ancient authorities read *has not had a part in her kingdom*

zeal for the law, just as Phinehas did against Zimri son of Salu.

27 Then Mattathias cried out in the town with a loud voice, saying: "Let every one who is zealous for the law and supports the covenant come out with me!" 28Then he and his sons fled to the hills and left all that they had in the town.

29 At that time many who were seeking righteousness and justice went down to the wilderness to live there, 30they, their sons, their wives, and their livestock, because troubles pressed heavily upon them. 31And it was reported to the king's officers, and to the troops in Jerusalem the city of David, that those who had rejected the king's command had gone down to the hiding places in the wilderness. 32Many pursued them, and overtook them; they encamped opposite them and prepared for battle against them on the sabbath day. 33They said to them, "Enough of this! Come out and do what the king commands, and you will live." 34But they said, "We will not come out, nor will we do what the king commands and so profane the sabbath day." 35Then the enemy[i] quickly attacked them. 36But they did not answer them or hurl a stone at them or block up their hiding places, 37for they said, "Let us all die in our innocence; heaven and earth testify for us that you are killing us unjustly." 38So they attacked them on the sabbath, and they died, with their wives and children and livestock, to the number of a thousand persons.

39 When Mattathias and his friends learned of it, they mourned for them deeply. 40And all said to their neighbors: "If we all do as our kindred have done and refuse to fight with the Gentiles for our lives and for our ordinances, they will quickly destroy us from the earth." 41So they made this decision that day: "Let us fight against anyone who comes to attack us on the sabbath day; let us not all die as our kindred died in their hiding places."

Counter-Attack

42 Then there united with them a company of Hasideans, mighty warriors of Israel, all who offered themselves willingly for the law. 43And all who became fugitives to escape their troubles joined them and reinforced them. 44They organized an army, and struck down sinners in their anger and renegades in their wrath; the survivors fled to the Gentiles for safety. 45And Mattathias and his friends went around and tore down the altars; 46they forcibly circumcised all the uncircumcised boys that they found within the borders of Israel. 47They hunted down the arrogant, and the work prospered in their hands. 48They rescued the law out of the hands of the Gentiles and kings, and they never let the sinner gain the upper hand.

The Last Words of Mattathias

49 Now the days drew near for Mattathias to die, and he said to his sons: "Arrogance and scorn have now become strong; it is a time of ruin and furious anger. 50Now, my children, show zeal for the law, and give your lives for the covenant of our ancestors.

51 "Remember the deeds of the ancestors, which they did in their generations; and you will receive great honor and an everlasting name. 52Was not Abraham found faithful when tested, and it was reckoned to him as righteousness? 53Joseph in the time of his distress kept the commandment, and became lord of Egypt. 54Phinehas our ancestor, because he was deeply zealous, received the covenant of everlasting priesthood. 55Joshua, because he fulfilled the command, became a judge in Israel. 56Caleb, because he testified in the assembly, received an inheritance in the land. 57David, because he was merciful, inherited the throne of the kingdom forever. 58Elijah, because of great zeal for the law, was taken up into heaven. 59Hananiah, Azariah, and Mishael believed and were saved from the flame. 60Daniel, because of his innocence, was delivered from the mouth of the lions.

61 "And so observe, from generation to generation, that none of those who put their trust in him will lack strength. 62Do not fear the words of sinners, for their splendor will turn into dung and worms. 63Today they will be exalted, but tomorrow they will not be found, because they will have returned to the dust, and their plans will have perished. 64My children, be courageous and grow strong in the law, for by it you will gain honor.

65 "Here is your brother Simeon who, I know, is wise in counsel; always listen to him; he shall be your father. 66Judas Mac-

i Gk they

cabeus has been a mighty warrior from his youth; he shall command the army for you and fight the battle against the peoples.[j] 67You shall rally around you all who observe the law, and avenge the wrong done to your people. 68Pay back the Gentiles in full, and obey the commands of the law."

69 Then he blessed them, and was gathered to his ancestors. 70He died in the one hundred forty-sixth year[k] and was buried in the tomb of his ancestors at Modein. And all Israel mourned for him with great lamentation.

The Early Victories of Judas

3 Then his son Judas, who was called Maccabeus, took command in his place. 2All his brothers and all who had joined his father helped him; they gladly fought for Israel.

3 He extended the glory of his people.
Like a giant he put on his
breastplate;
he bound on his armor of war and
waged battles,
protecting the camp by his sword.
4 He was like a lion in his deeds,
like a lion's cub roaring for prey.
5 He searched out and pursued those
who broke the law;
he burned those who troubled his
people.
6 Lawbreakers shrank back for fear of
him;
all the evildoers were confounded;
and deliverance prospered by his
hand.
7 He embittered many kings,
but he made Jacob glad by his
deeds,
and his memory is blessed forever.
8 He went through the cities of Judah;
he destroyed the ungodly out of
the land;[l]
thus he turned away wrath from
Israel.
9 He was renowned to the ends of the
earth;
he gathered in those who were
perishing.

10 Apollonius now gathered together Gentiles and a large force from Samaria to fight against Israel. 11When Judas learned of it, he went out to meet him, and he defeated and killed him. Many were wounded and fell, and the rest fled. 12Then they seized their spoils; and Judas

took the sword of Apollonius, and used it in battle the rest of his life.

13 When Seron, the commander of the Syrian army, heard that Judas had gathered a large company, including a body of faithful soldiers who stayed with him and went out to battle, 14he said, "I will make a name for myself and win honor in the kingdom. I will make war on Judas and his companions, who scorn the king's command." 15Once again a strong army of godless men went up with him to help him, to take vengeance on the Israelites.

16 When he approached the ascent of Beth-horon, Judas went out to meet him with a small company. 17But when they saw the army coming to meet them, they said to Judas, "How can we, few as we are, fight against so great and so strong a multitude? And we are faint, for we have eaten nothing today." 18Judas replied, "It is easy for many to be hemmed in by few, for in the sight of Heaven there is no difference between saving by many or by few. 19It is not on the size of the army that victory in battle depends, but strength comes from Heaven. 20They come against us in great insolence and lawlessness to destroy us and our wives and our children, and to despoil us; 21but we fight for our lives and our laws. 22He himself will crush them before us; as for you, do not be afraid of them."

23 When he finished speaking, he rushed suddenly against Seron and his army, and they were crushed before him. 24They pursued them[m] down the descent of Beth-horon to the plain; eight hundred of them fell, and the rest fled into the land of the Philistines. 25Then Judas and his brothers began to be feared, and terror fell on the Gentiles all around them. 26His fame reached the king, and the Gentiles talked of the battles of Judas.

The Policy of Antiochus

27 When King Antiochus heard these reports, he was greatly angered; and he sent and gathered all the forces of his kingdom, a very strong army. 28He opened his coffers and gave a year's pay to his forces, and ordered them to be ready for any need. 29Then he saw that the money in the treasury was exhausted, and that the revenues from the country were small

j Or *of the people*   k 166 B.C.   l Gk *it*   m Other ancient authorities read *him*

because of the dissension and disaster that he had caused in the land by abolishing the laws that had existed from the earliest days. ³⁰He feared that he might not have such funds as he had before for his expenses and for the gifts that he used to give more lavishly than preceding kings. ³¹He was greatly perplexed in mind; then he determined to go to Persia and collect the revenues from those regions and raise a large fund.

32 He left Lysias, a distinguished man of royal lineage, in charge of the king's affairs from the river Euphrates to the borders of Egypt. ³³Lysias was also to take care of his son Antiochus until he returned. ³⁴And he turned over to Lysias[n] half of his forces and the elephants, and gave him orders about all that he wanted done. As for the residents of Judea and Jerusalem, ³⁵Lysias was to send a force against them to wipe out and destroy the strength of Israel and the remnant of Jerusalem; he was to banish the memory of them from the place, ³⁶settle aliens in all their territory, and distribute their land by lot. ³⁷Then the king took the remaining half of his forces and left Antioch his capital in the one hundred and forty-seventh year.[o] He crossed the Euphrates river and went through the upper provinces.

Preparations for Battle

38 Lysias chose Ptolemy son of Dorymenes, and Nicanor and Gorgias, able men among the Friends of the king, ³⁹and sent with them forty thousand infantry and seven thousand cavalry to go into the land of Judah and destroy it, as the king had commanded. ⁴⁰So they set out with their entire force, and when they arrived they encamped near Emmaus in the plain. ⁴¹When the traders of the region heard what was said to them, they took silver and gold in immense amounts, and fetters,[p] and went to the camp to get the Israelites for slaves. And forces from Syria and the land of the Philistines joined with them.

42 Now Judas and his brothers saw that misfortunes had increased and that the forces were encamped in their territory. They also learned what the king had commanded to do to the people to cause their final destruction. ⁴³But they said to one another, "Let us restore the ruins of our people, and fight for our people and the sanctuary." ⁴⁴So the congregation assembled to be ready for battle, and to pray and ask for mercy and compassion.

⁴⁵ Jerusalem was uninhabited like a
wilderness;
    not one of her children went in or
    out.
The sanctuary was trampled down,
    and aliens held the citadel;
    it was a lodging place for the
    Gentiles.
Joy was taken from Jacob;
    the flute and the harp ceased to
    play.

46 Then they gathered together and went to Mizpah, opposite Jerusalem, because Israel formerly had a place of prayer in Mizpah. ⁴⁷They fasted that day, put on sackcloth and sprinkled ashes on their heads, and tore their clothes. ⁴⁸And they opened the book of the law to inquire into those matters about which the Gentiles consulted the likenesses of their gods. ⁴⁹They also brought the vestments of the priesthood and the first fruits and the tithes, and they stirred up the nazirites[q] who had completed their days; ⁵⁰and they cried aloud to Heaven, saying,

"What shall we do with these?
    Where shall we take them?
⁵¹ Your sanctuary is trampled down
        and profaned,
    and your priests mourn in
        humiliation.
⁵² Here the Gentiles are assembled
        against us to destroy us;
    you know what they plot against
        us.
⁵³ How will we be able to withstand
        them,
    if you do not help us?"

54 Then they sounded the trumpets and gave a loud shout. ⁵⁵After this Judas appointed leaders of the people, in charge of thousands and hundreds and fifties and tens. ⁵⁶Those who were building houses, or were about to be married, or were planting a vineyard, or were fainthearted, he told to go home again, according to the law. ⁵⁷Then the army marched out and encamped to the south of Emmaus.

58 And Judas said, "Arm yourselves and be courageous. Be ready early in the morning to fight with these Gentiles who have assembled against us to destroy us

---

[n] Gk *him*   [o] 165 B.C.   [p] Syr: Gk Mss, Vg *slaves*
[q] That is *those separated* or *those consecrated*

and our sanctuary. 59It is better for us to die in battle than to see the misfortunes of our nation and of the sanctuary. 60But as his will in heaven may be, so shall he do."

The Battle at Emmaus

4 Now Gorgias took five thousand infantry and one thousand picked cavalry, and this division moved out by night 2to fall upon the camp of the Jews and attack them suddenly. Men from the citadel were his guides. 3But Judas heard of it, and he and his warriors moved out to attack the king's force in Emmaus 4while the division was still absent from the camp. 5When Gorgias entered the camp of Judas by night, he found no one there, so he looked for them in the hills, because he said, "These men are running away from us."

6 At daybreak Judas appeared in the plain with three thousand men, but they did not have armor and swords such as they desired. 7And they saw the camp of the Gentiles, strong and fortified, with cavalry all around it; and these men were trained in war. 8But Judas said to those who were with him, "Do not fear their numbers or be afraid when they charge. 9Remember how our ancestors were saved at the Red Sea, when Pharaoh with his forces pursued them. 10And now, let us cry to Heaven, to see whether he will favor us and remember his covenant with our ancestors and crush this army before us today. 11Then all the Gentiles will know that there is one who redeems and saves Israel."

12 When the foreigners looked up and saw them coming against them, 13they went out from their camp to battle. Then the men with Judas blew their trumpets 14and engaged in battle. The Gentiles were crushed, and fled into the plain, 15and all those in the rear fell by the sword. They pursued them to Gazara, and to the plains of Idumea, and to Azotus and Jamnia; and three thousand of them fell. 16Then Judas and his force turned back from pursuing them, 17and he said to the people, "Do not be greedy for plunder, for there is a battle before us; 18Gorgias and his force are near us in the hills. But stand now against our enemies and fight them, and afterward seize the plunder boldly."

19 Just as Judas was finishing this speech, a detachment appeared, coming out of the hills. 20They saw that their army[r] had been put to flight, and that the Jews[r] were burning the camp, for the smoke that was seen showed what had happened. 21When they perceived this, they were greatly frightened, and when they also saw the army of Judas drawn up in the plain for battle, 22they all fled into the land of the Philistines. 23Then Judas returned to plunder the camp, and they seized a great amount of gold and silver, and cloth dyed blue and sea purple, and great riches. 24On their return they sang hymns and praises to Heaven—"For he is good, for his mercy endures forever." 25Thus Israel had a great deliverance that day.

First Campaign of Lysias

26 Those of the foreigners who escaped went and reported to Lysias all that had happened. 27When he heard it, he was perplexed and discouraged, for things had not happened to Israel as he had intended, nor had they turned out as the king had ordered. 28But the next year he mustered sixty thousand picked infantry and five thousand cavalry to subdue them. 29They came into Idumea and encamped at Beth-zur, and Judas met them with ten thousand men.

30 When he saw that their army was strong, he prayed, saying, "Blessed are you, O Savior of Israel, who crushed the attack of the mighty warrior by the hand of your servant David, and gave the camp of the Philistines into the hands of Jonathan son of Saul, and of the man who carried his armor. 31Hem in this army by the hand of your people Israel, and let them be ashamed of their troops and their cavalry. 32Fill them with cowardice; melt the boldness of their strength; let them tremble in their destruction. 33Strike them down with the sword of those who love you, and let all who know your name praise you with hymns."

34 Then both sides attacked, and there fell of the army of Lysias five thousand men; they fell in action.[s] 35When Lysias saw the rout of his troops and observed the boldness that inspired those of Judas, and how ready they were either to live or to die nobly, he withdrew to Antioch and enlisted mercenaries in order to invade Judea again with an even larger army.

[r] Gk they   [s] Or and some fell on the opposite side

Cleansing and Dedication of the Temple

36 Then Judas and his brothers said, "See, our enemies are crushed; let us go up to cleanse the sanctuary and dedicate it." 37So all the army assembled and went up to Mount Zion. 38There they saw the sanctuary desolate, the altar profaned, and the gates burned. In the courts they saw bushes sprung up as in a thicket, or as on one of the mountains. They saw also the chambers of the priests in ruins. 39Then they tore their clothes and mourned with great lamentation; they sprinkled themselves with ashes 40and fell face down on the ground. And when the signal was given with the trumpets, they cried out to Heaven.

41 Then Judas detailed men to fight against those in the citadel until he had cleansed the sanctuary. 42He chose blameless priests devoted to the law, 43and they cleansed the sanctuary and removed the defiled stones to an unclean place. 44They deliberated what to do about the altar of burnt offering, which had been profaned. 45And they thought it best to tear it down, so that it would not be a lasting shame to them that the Gentiles had defiled it. So they tore down the altar, 46and stored the stones in a convenient place on the temple hill until a prophet should come to tell what to do with them. 47Then they took unhewn[t] stones, as the law directs, and built a new altar like the former one. 48They also rebuilt the sanctuary and the interior of the temple, and consecrated the courts. 49They made new holy vessels, and brought the lampstand, the altar of incense, and the table into the temple. 50Then they offered incense on the altar and lit the lamps on the lampstand, and these gave light in the temple. 51They placed the bread on the table and hung up the curtains. Thus they finished all the work they had undertaken.

52 Early in the morning on the twenty-fifth day of the ninth month, which is the month of Chislev, in the one hundred forty-eighth year,[u] 53they rose and offered sacrifice, as the law directs, on the new altar of burnt offering that they had built. 54At the very season and on the very day that the Gentiles had profaned it, it was dedicated with songs and harps and lutes and cymbals. 55All the people fell on their faces and worshiped and blessed Heaven, who had prospered them. 56So

they celebrated the dedication of the altar for eight days, and joyfully offered burnt offerings; they offered a sacrifice of well-being and a thanksgiving offering. 57They decorated the front of the temple with golden crowns and small shields; they restored the gates and the chambers for the priests, and fitted them with doors. 58There was very great joy among the people, and the disgrace brought by the Gentiles was removed.

59 Then Judas and his brothers and all the assembly of Israel determined that every year at that season the days of dedication of the altar should be observed with joy and gladness for eight days, beginning with the twenty-fifth day of the month of Chislev.

60 At that time they fortified Mount Zion with high walls and strong towers all around, to keep the Gentiles from coming and trampling them down as they had done before. 61Judas[v] stationed a garrison there to guard it; he also fortified Beth-zur to guard it, so that the people might have a stronghold that faced Idumea.

Wars with Neighboring Peoples

5 When the Gentiles all around heard that the altar had been rebuilt and the sanctuary dedicated as it was before, they became very angry, 2and they determined to destroy the descendants of Jacob who lived among them. So they began to kill and destroy among the people. 3But Judas made war on the descendants of Esau in Idumea, at Akrabattene, because they kept lying in wait for Israel. He dealt them a heavy blow and humbled them and despoiled them. 4He also remembered the wickedness of the sons of Baean, who were a trap and a snare to the people and ambushed them on the highways. 5They were shut up by him in their[w] towers; and he encamped against them, vowed their complete destruction, and burned with fire their towers and all who were in them. 6Then he crossed over to attack the Ammonites, where he found a strong band and many people, with Timothy as their leader. 7He engaged in many battles with them, and they were crushed before him; he struck them down. 8He also took Jazer and its villages; then he returned to Judea.

t Gk *whole*   *u* 164 B.C.   *v* Gk *He*   *w* Gk *her*

Liberation of Galilean Jews

9 Now the Gentiles in Gilead gathered together against the Israelites who lived in their territory, and planned to destroy them. But they fled to the stronghold of Dathema, 10and sent to Judas and his brothers a letter that said, "The Gentiles around us have gathered together to destroy us. 11They are preparing to come and capture the stronghold to which we have fled, and Timothy is leading their forces. 12Now then, come and rescue us from their hands, for many of us have fallen, 13and all our kindred who were in the land of Tob have been killed; the enemy*x* have captured their wives and children and goods, and have destroyed about a thousand persons there."

14 While the letter was still being read, other messengers, with their garments torn, came from Galilee and made a similar report; 15they said that the people of Ptolemais and Tyre and Sidon, and all Galilee of the Gentiles,*y* had gathered together against them "to annihilate us." 16When Judas and the people heard these messages, a great assembly was called to determine what they should do for their kindred who were in distress and were being attacked by enemies.*z* 17Then Judas said to his brother Simon, "Choose your men and go and rescue your kindred in Galilee; Jonathan my brother and I will go to Gilead." 18But he left Joseph, son of Zechariah, and Azariah, a leader of the people, with the rest of the forces, in Judea to guard it; 19and he gave them this command, "Take charge of this people, but do not engage in battle with the Gentiles until we return." 20Then three thousand men were assigned to Simon to go to Galilee, and eight thousand to Judas for Gilead.

21 So Simon went to Galilee and fought many battles against the Gentiles, and the Gentiles were crushed before him. 22He pursued them to the gate of Ptolemais; as many as three thousand of the Gentiles fell, and he despoiled them. 23Then he took the Jews*a* of Galilee and Arbatta, with their wives and children, and all they possessed, and led them to Judea with great rejoicing.

Judas and Jonathan in Gilead

24 Judas Maccabeus and his brother Jonathan crossed the Jordan and made three days' journey into the wilderness. 25They encountered the Nabateans, who met them peaceably and told them all that had happened to their kindred in Gilead: 26"Many of them have been shut up in Bozrah and Bosor, in Alema and Chaspho, Maked and Carnaim"—all these towns were strong and large— 27"and some have been shut up in the other towns of Gilead; the enemy*x* are getting ready to attack the strongholds tomorrow and capture and destroy all these people in a single day."

28 Then Judas and his army quickly turned back by the wilderness road to Bozrah; and he took the town, and killed every male by the edge of the sword; then he seized all its spoils and burned it with fire. 29He left the place at night, and they went all the way to the stronghold of Dathema.*b* 30At dawn they looked out and saw a large company, which could not be counted, carrying ladders and engines of war to capture the stronghold, and attacking the Jews within.*c* 31So Judas saw that the battle had begun and that the cry of the town went up to Heaven, with trumpets and loud shouts, 32and he said to the men of his forces, "Fight today for your kindred!" 33Then he came up behind them in three companies, who sounded their trumpets and cried aloud in prayer. 34And when the army of Timothy realized that it was Maccabeus, they fled before him, and he dealt them a heavy blow. As many as eight thousand of them fell that day.

35 Next he turned aside to Maapha,*d* and fought against it and took it; and he killed every male in it, plundered it, and burned it with fire. 36From there he marched on and took Chaspho, Maked, and Bosor, and the other towns of Gilead.

37 After these things Timothy gathered another army and encamped opposite Raphon, on the other side of the stream. 38Judas sent men to spy out the camp, and they reported to him, "All the Gentiles around us have gathered to him; it is a very large force. 39They also have hired Arabs to help them, and they are encamped across the stream, ready to come

---

x Gk *they*   *y* Gk *aliens*   *z* Gk *them*   *a* Gk *those*
b Gk lacks *of Dathema.* See verse 9   *c* Gk *and they were attacking them*   *d* Other ancient authorities read *Alema*

and fight against you." And Judas went to meet them.

40 Now as Judas and his army drew near to the stream of water, Timothy said to the officers of his forces, "If he crosses over to us first, we will not be able to resist him, for he will surely defeat us. 41But if he shows fear and camps on the other side of the river, we will cross over to him and defeat him." 42When Judas approached the stream of water, he stationed the officers*e* of the army at the stream and gave them this command, "Permit no one to encamp, but make them all enter the battle." 43Then he crossed over against them first, and the whole army followed him. All the Gentiles were defeated before him, and they threw away their arms and fled into the sacred precincts at Carnaim. 44But he took the town and burned the sacred precincts with fire, together with all who were in them. Thus Carnaim was conquered; they could stand before Judas no longer.

The Return to Jerusalem

45 Then Judas gathered together all the Israelites in Gilead, the small and the great, with their wives and children and goods, a very large company, to go to the land of Judah. 46So they came to Ephron. This was a large and very strong town on the road, and they could not go around it to the right or to the left; they had to go through it. 47But the people of the town shut them out and blocked up the gates with stones. 48 Judas sent them this friendly message, "Let us pass through your land to get to our land. No one will do you harm; we will simply pass by on foot." But they refused to open to him. 49Then Judas ordered proclamation to be made to the army that all should encamp where they were. 50So the men of the forces encamped, and he fought against the town all that day and all the night, and the town was delivered into his hands. 51He destroyed every male by the edge of the sword, and razed and plundered the town. Then he passed through the town over the bodies of the dead.

52 Then they crossed the Jordan into the large plain before Beth-shan. 53Judas kept rallying the laggards and encouraging the people all the way until he came to the land of Judah. 54So they went up to Mount Zion with joy and gladness, and offered burnt offerings, because they had returned in safety; not one of them had fallen.

Joseph and Azariah Defeated

55 Now while Judas and Jonathan were in Gilead and their*f* brother Simon was in Galilee before Ptolemais, 56Joseph son of Zechariah, and Azariah, the commanders of the forces, heard of their brave deeds and of the heroic war they had fought. 57So they said, "Let us also make a name for ourselves; let us go and make war on the Gentiles around us." 58So they issued orders to the men of the forces that were with them and marched against Jamnia. 59Gorgias and his men came out of the town to meet them in battle. 60Then Joseph and Azariah were routed, and were pursued to the borders of Judea; as many as two thousand of the people of Israel fell that day. 61Thus the people suffered a great rout because, thinking to do a brave deed, they did not listen to Judas and his brothers. 62But they did not belong to the family of those men through whom deliverance was given to Israel.

63 The man Judas and his brothers were greatly honored in all Israel and among all the Gentiles, wherever their name was heard. 64People gathered to them and praised them.

Success at Hebron and Philistia

65 Then Judas and his brothers went out and fought the descendants of Esau in the land to the south. He struck Hebron and its villages and tore down its strongholds and burned its towers on all sides. 66Then he marched off to go into the land of the Philistines, and passed through Marisa.*g* 67On that day some priests, who wished to do a brave deed, fell in battle, for they went out to battle unwisely. 68But Judas turned aside to Azotus in the land of the Philistines; he tore down their altars, and the carved images of their gods he burned with fire; he plundered the towns and returned to the land of Judah.

The Last Days of Antiochus Epiphanes

6 King Antiochus was going through the upper provinces when he heard that Elymais in Persia was a city famed for its wealth in silver and gold. 2Its temple

---

e Or *scribes*   *f* Gk *his*   *g* Other ancient authorities read *Samaria*

was very rich, containing golden shields, breastplates, and weapons left there by Alexander son of Philip, the Macedonian king who first reigned over the Greeks. [3]So he came and tried to take the city and plunder it, but he could not because his plan had become known to the citizens [4]and they withstood him in battle. So he fled and in great disappointment left there to return to Babylon.

5 Then someone came to him in Persia and reported that the armies that had gone into the land of Judah had been routed; [6]that Lysias had gone first with a strong force, but had turned and fled before the Jews;[h] that the Jews[i] had grown strong from the arms, supplies, and abundant spoils that they had taken from the armies they had cut down; [7]that they had torn down the abomination that he had erected on the altar in Jerusalem; and that they had surrounded the sanctuary with high walls as before, and also Beth-zur, his town.

8 When the king heard this news, he was astounded and badly shaken. He took to his bed and became sick from disappointment, because things had not turned out for him as he had planned. [9]He lay there for many days, because deep disappointment continually gripped him, and he realized that he was dying. [10]So he called all his Friends and said to them, "Sleep has departed from my eyes and I am downhearted with worry. [11]I said to myself, 'To what distress I have come! And into what a great flood I now am plunged! For I was kind and beloved in my power.' [12]But now I remember the wrong I did in Jerusalem. I seized all its vessels of silver and gold, and I sent to destroy the inhabitants of Judah without good reason. [13]I know that it is because of this that these misfortunes have come upon me; here I am, perishing of bitter disappointment in a strange land."

14 Then he called for Philip, one of his Friends, and made him ruler over all his kingdom. [15]He gave him the crown and his robe and the signet, so that he might guide his son Antiochus and bring him up to be king. [16]Thus King Antiochus died there in the one hundred forty-ninth year.[j] [17]When Lysias learned that the king was dead, he set up Antiochus the king's[k] son to reign. Lysias[l] had brought him up from boyhood; he named him Eupator.

Renewed Attacks from Syria

18 Meanwhile the garrison in the citadel kept hemming Israel in around the sanctuary. They were trying in every way to harm them and strengthen the Gentiles. [19]Judas therefore resolved to destroy them, and assembled all the people to besiege them. [20]They gathered together and besieged the citadel[m] in the one hundred fiftieth year;[n] and he built siege towers and other engines of war. [21]But some of the garrison escaped from the siege and some of the ungodly Israelites joined them. [22]They went to the king and said, "How long will you fail to do justice and to avenge our kindred? [23]We were happy to serve your father, to live by what he said, and to follow his commands. [24]For this reason the sons of our people besieged the citadel[o] and became hostile to us; moreover, they have put to death as many of us as they have caught, and they have seized our inheritances. [25]It is not against us alone that they have stretched out their hands; they have also attacked all the lands on their borders. [26]And see, today they have encamped against the citadel in Jerusalem to take it; they have fortified both the sanctuary and Beth-zur; [27]unless you quickly prevent them, they will do still greater things, and you will not be able to stop them."

28 The king was enraged when he heard this. He assembled all his Friends, the commanders of his forces and those in authority.[p] [29]Mercenary forces also came to him from other kingdoms and from islands of the seas. [30]The number of his forces was one hundred thousand foot soldiers, twenty thousand horsemen, and thirty-two elephants accustomed to war. [31]They came through Idumea and encamped against Beth-zur, and for many days they fought and built engines of war; but the Jews[i] sallied out and burned these with fire, and fought courageously.

The Battle at Beth-zechariah

32 Then Judas marched away from the citadel and encamped at Beth-zechariah, opposite the camp of the king. [33]Early in the morning the king set out and took his army by a forced march along the road to Beth-zechariah, and his troops made

h Gk them   i Gk they   j 163 B.C.   k Gk his
l Gk He   m Gk it   n 162 B.C.   o Meaning of
Gk uncertain   p Gk those over the reins

ready for battle and sounded their trumpets. [34]They offered the elephants the juice of grapes and mulberries, to arouse them for battle. [35]They distributed the animals among the phalanxes; with each elephant they stationed a thousand men armed with coats of mail, and with brass helmets on their heads; and five hundred picked horsemen were assigned to each beast. [36]These took their position beforehand wherever the animal was; wherever it went, they went with it, and they never left it. [37]On the elephants[q] were wooden towers, strong and covered; they were fastened on each animal by special harness, and on each were four[r] armed men who fought from there, and also its Indian driver. [38]The rest of the cavalry were stationed on either side, on the two flanks of the army, to harass the enemy while being themselves protected by the phalanxes. [39]When the sun shone on the shields of gold and brass, the hills were ablaze with them and gleamed like flaming torches.

40 Now a part of the king's army was spread out on the high hills, and some troops were on the plain, and they advanced steadily and in good order. [41]All who heard the noise made by their multitude, by the marching of the multitude and the clanking of their arms, trembled, for the army was very large and strong. [42]But Judas and his army advanced to the battle, and six hundred of the king's army fell. [43]Now Eleazar, called Avaran, saw that one of the animals was equipped with royal armor. It was taller than all the others, and he supposed that the king was on it. [44]So he gave his life to save his people and to win for himself an everlasting name. [45]He courageously ran into the midst of the phalanx to reach it; he killed men right and left, and they parted before him on both sides. [46]He got under the elephant, stabbed it from beneath, and killed it; but it fell to the ground upon him and he died. [47]When the Jews[s] saw the royal might and the fierce attack of the forces, they turned away in flight.

The Siege of the Temple

48 The soldiers of the king's army went up to Jerusalem against them, and the king encamped in Judea and at Mount Zion. [49]He made peace with the people of Beth-zur, and they evacuated the town because they had no provisions there to withstand a siege, since it was a sabbatical year for the land. [50]So the king took Beth-zur and stationed a guard there to hold it. [51]Then he encamped before the sanctuary for many days. He set up siege towers, engines of war to throw fire and stones, machines to shoot arrows, and catapults. [52]The Jews[s] also made engines of war to match theirs, and fought for many days. [53]But they had no food in storage,[t] because it was the seventh year; those who had found safety in Judea from the Gentiles had consumed the last of the stores. [54]Only a few men were left in the sanctuary; the rest scattered to their own homes, for the famine proved too much for them.

Syria Offers Terms

55 Then Lysias heard that Philip, whom King Antiochus while still living had appointed to bring up his son Antiochus to be king, [56]had returned from Persia and Media with the forces that had gone with the king, and that he was trying to seize control of the government. [57]So he quickly gave orders to withdraw, and said to the king, to the commanders of the forces, and to the troops, "Daily we grow weaker, our food supply is scant, the place against which we are fighting is strong, and the affairs of the kingdom press urgently on us. [58]Now then let us come to terms with these people, and make peace with them and with all their nation. [59]Let us agree to let them live by their laws as they did before; for it was on account of their laws that we abolished that they became angry and did all these things."

60 The speech pleased the king and the commanders, and he sent to the Jews[q] an offer of peace, and they accepted it. [61]So the king and the commanders gave them their oath. On these conditions the Jews[s] evacuated the stronghold. [62]But when the king entered Mount Zion and saw what a strong fortress the place was, he broke the oath he had sworn and gave orders to tear down the wall all around. [63]Then he set off in haste and returned to Antioch. He found Philip in control of the city, but he fought against him, and took the city by force.

[q] Gk *them* [r] Cn: Some authorities read *thirty*; others *thirty-two* [s] Gk *they* [t] Other ancient authorities read *in the sanctuary*

Expedition of Bacchides and Alcimus

7 In the one hundred fifty-first year[u] Demetrius son of Seleucus set out from Rome, sailed with a few men to a town by the sea, and there began to reign. [2]As he was entering the royal palace of his ancestors, the army seized Antiochus and Lysias to bring them to him. [3]But when this act became known to him, he said, "Do not let me see their faces!" [4]So the army killed them, and Demetrius took his seat on the throne of his kingdom.

5 Then there came to him all the renegade and godless men of Israel; they were led by Alcimus, who wanted to be high priest. [6]They brought to the king this accusation against the people: "Judas and his brothers have destroyed all your Friends, and have driven us out of our land. [7]Now then send a man whom you trust; let him go and see all the ruin that Judas[v] has brought on us and on the land of the king, and let him punish them and all who help them."

8 So the king chose Bacchides, one of the king's Friends, governor of the province Beyond the River; he was a great man in the kingdom and was faithful to the king. [9]He sent him, and with him he sent the ungodly Alcimus, whom he made high priest; and he commanded him to take vengeance on the Israelites. [10]So they marched away and came with a large force into the land of Judah; and he sent messengers to Judas and his brothers with peaceable but treacherous words. [11]But they paid no attention to their words, for they saw that they had come with a large force.

12 Then a group of scribes appeared in a body before Alcimus and Bacchides to ask for just terms. [13]The Hasideans were first among the Israelites to seek peace from them, [14]for they said, "A priest of the line of Aaron has come with the army, and he will not harm us." [15]Alcimus[w] spoke peaceable words to them and swore this oath to them, "We will not seek to injure you or your friends." [16]So they trusted him; but he seized sixty of them and killed them in one day, in accordance with the word that was written,

[17] "The flesh of your faithful ones and
    their blood
  they poured out all around
    Jerusalem,

and there was no one to bury
    them."

[18]Then the fear and dread of them fell on all the people, for they said, "There is no truth or justice in them, for they have violated the agreement and the oath that they swore."

19 Then Bacchides withdrew from Jerusalem and encamped in Beth-zaith. And he sent and seized many of the men who had deserted to him,[x] and some of the people, and killed them and threw them into a great pit. [20]He placed Alcimus in charge of the country and left with him a force to help him; then Bacchides went back to the king.

21 Alcimus struggled to maintain his high priesthood, [22]and all who were troubling their people joined him. They gained control of the land of Judah and did great damage in Israel. [23]And Judas saw all the wrongs that Alcimus and those with him had done among the Israelites; it was more than the Gentiles had done. [24]So Judas[v] went out into all the surrounding parts of Judea, taking vengeance on those who had deserted and preventing those in the city[y] from going out into the country. [25]When Alcimus saw that Judas and those with him had grown strong, and realized that he could not withstand them, he returned to the king and brought malicious charges against them.

Nicanor in Judea

26 Then the king sent Nicanor, one of his honored princes, who hated and detested Israel, and he commanded him to destroy the people. [27]So Nicanor came to Jerusalem with a large force, and treacherously sent to Judas and his brothers this peaceable message, [28]"Let there be no fighting between you and me; I shall come with a few men to see you face to face in peace."

29 So he came to Judas, and they greeted one another peaceably; but the enemy were preparing to kidnap Judas. [30]It became known to Judas that Nicanor[v] had come to him with treacherous intent, and he was afraid of him and would not meet him again. [31]When Nicanor learned that his plan had been disclosed, he went out to meet Judas in battle near Caphar-

u 161 B.C.   v Gk he   w Gk He   x Or many of his men who had deserted   y Gk and they were prevented

salama. ³²About five hundred of the army of Nicanor fell, and the rest^z fled into the city of David.

Nicanor Threatens the Temple

33 After these events Nicanor went up to Mount Zion. Some of the priests from the sanctuary and some of the elders of the people came out to greet him peaceably and to show him the burnt offering that was being offered for the king. ³⁴But he mocked them and derided them and defiled them and spoke arrogantly, ³⁵and in anger he swore this oath, "Unless Judas and his army are delivered into my hands this time, then if I return safely I will burn up this house." And he went out in great anger. ³⁶At this the priests went in and stood before the altar and the temple; they wept and said,

³⁷ "You chose this house to be called
　　by your name,
　　and to be for your people a house
　　　of prayer and supplication.
³⁸ Take vengeance on this man and on
　　his army,
　　and let them fall by the sword;
　　remember their blasphemies,
　　and let them live no longer."

The Death of Nicanor

39 Now Nicanor went out from Jerusalem and encamped in Beth-horon, and the Syrian army joined him. ⁴⁰Judas encamped in Adasa with three thousand men. Then Judas prayed and said, ⁴¹"When the messengers from the king spoke blasphemy, your angel went out and struck down one hundred eighty-five thousand of the Assyrians.^a ⁴²So also crush this army before us today; let the rest learn that Nicanor^b has spoken wickedly against the sanctuary, and judge him according to this wickedness."

43 So the armies met in battle on the thirteenth day of the month of Adar. The army of Nicanor was crushed, and he himself was the first to fall in the battle. ⁴⁴When his army saw that Nicanor had fallen, they threw down their arms and fled. ⁴⁵The Jews^z pursued them a day's journey, from Adasa as far as Gazara, and as they followed they kept sounding the battle call on the trumpets. ⁴⁶People came out of all the surrounding villages of Judea, and they outflanked the enemy^c and drove them back to their pursuers,^d so that they all fell by the sword; not even

one of them was left. ⁴⁷Then the Jews^z seized the spoils and the plunder; they cut off Nicanor's head and the right hand that he had so arrogantly stretched out, and brought them and displayed them just outside Jerusalem. ⁴⁸The people rejoiced greatly and celebrated that day as a day of great gladness. ⁴⁹They decreed that this day should be celebrated each year on the thirteenth day of Adar. ⁵⁰So the land of Judah had rest for a few days.

A Eulogy of the Romans

8 Now Judas heard of the fame of the Romans, that they were very strong and were well-disposed toward all who made an alliance with them, that they pledged friendship to those who came to them, ²and that they were very strong. He had been told of their wars and of the brave deeds that they were doing among the Gauls, how they had defeated them and forced them to pay tribute, ³and what they had done in the land of Spain to get control of the silver and gold mines there, ⁴and how they had gained control of the whole region by their planning and patience, even though the place was far distant from them. They also subdued the kings who came against them from the ends of the earth, until they crushed them and inflicted great disaster on them; the rest paid them tribute every year. ⁵They had crushed in battle and conquered Philip, and King Perseus of the Macedonians,^e and the others who rose up against them. ⁶They also had defeated Antiochus the Great, king of Asia, who went to fight against them with one hundred twenty elephants and with cavalry and chariots and a very large army. He was crushed by them; ⁷they took him alive and decreed that he and those who would reign after him should pay a heavy tribute and give hostages and surrender some of their best provinces, ⁸the countries of India, Media, and Lydia. These they took from him and gave to King Eumenes. ⁹The Greeks planned to come and destroy them, ¹⁰but this became known to them, and they sent a general against the Greeks^c and attacked them. Many of them were wounded and fell, and the Romans^z took captive their wives and children; they plundered them, conquered the land, tore

z Gk they　　a Gk of them　　b Gk he　　c Gk them
d Gk these　　e Or Kittim

down their strongholds, and enslaved them to this day. ¹¹The remaining kingdoms and islands, as many as ever opposed them, they destroyed and enslaved; ¹²but with their friends and those who rely on them they have kept friendship. They have subdued kings far and near, and as many as have heard of their fame have feared them. ¹³Those whom they wish to help and to make kings, they make kings, and those whom they wish they depose; and they have been greatly exalted. ¹⁴Yet for all this not one of them has put on a crown or worn purple as a mark of pride, ¹⁵but they have built for themselves a senate chamber, and every day three hundred twenty senators constantly deliberate concerning the people, to govern them well. ¹⁶They trust one man each year to rule over them and to control all their land; they all heed the one man, and there is no envy or jealousy among them.

An Alliance with Rome

17 So Judas chose Eupolemus son of John son of Accos, and Jason son of Eleazar, and sent them to Rome to establish friendship and alliance, ¹⁸and to free themselves from the yoke; for they saw that the kingdom of the Greeks was enslaving Israel completely. ¹⁹They went to Rome, a very long journey; and they entered the senate chamber and spoke as follows: ²⁰"Judas, who is also called Maccabeus, and his brothers and the people of the Jews have sent us to you to establish alliance and peace with you, so that we may be enrolled as your allies and friends." ²¹The proposal pleased them, ²²and this is a copy of the letter that they wrote in reply, on bronze tablets, and sent to Jerusalem to remain with them there as a memorial of peace and alliance:

23 "May all go well with the Romans and with the nation of the Jews at sea and on land forever, and may sword and enemy be far from them. ²⁴If war comes first to Rome or to any of their allies in all their dominion, ²⁵the nation of the Jews shall act as their allies wholeheartedly, as the occasion may indicate to them. ²⁶To the enemy that makes war they shall not give or supply grain, arms, money, or ships, just as Rome has decided; and they shall keep their obligations without receiving any return. ²⁷In the same way, if war comes first to the nation of the Jews, the Romans shall willingly act as their allies, as the occasion may indicate to them. ²⁸And to their enemies there shall not be given grain, arms, money, or ships, just as Rome has decided; and they shall keep these obligations and do so without deceit. ²⁹Thus on these terms the Romans make a treaty with the Jewish people. ³⁰If after these terms are in effect both parties shall determine to add or delete anything, they shall do so at their discretion, and any addition or deletion that they may make shall be valid.

31 "Concerning the wrongs that King Demetrius is doing to them, we have written to him as follows, 'Why have you made your yoke heavy on our friends and allies the Jews? ³²If now they appeal again for help against you, we will defend their rights and fight you on sea and on land.' "

Bacchides Returns to Judea

9 When Demetrius heard that Nicanor and his army had fallen in battle, he sent Bacchides and Alcimus into the land of Judah a second time, and with them the right wing of the army. ²They went by the road that leads to Gilgal and encamped against Mesaloth in Arbela, and they took it and killed many people. ³In the first month of the one hundred fifty-second year*f* they encamped against Jerusalem; ⁴then they marched off and went to Berea with twenty thousand foot soldiers and two thousand cavalry.

5 Now Judas was encamped in Elasa, and with him were three thousand picked men. ⁶When they saw the huge number of the enemy forces, they were greatly frightened, and many slipped away from the camp, until no more than eight hundred of them were left.

7 When Judas saw that his army had slipped away and the battle was imminent, he was crushed in spirit, for he had no time to assemble them. ⁸He became faint, but he said to those who were left, "Let us get up and go against our enemies. We may have the strength to fight them." ⁹But they tried to dissuade him, saying, "We do not have the strength. Let us rather save our own lives now, and let us come back with our kindred and fight them; we are too few." ¹⁰But Judas said, "Far be it from us to do such a thing as to flee from them. If our time has come, let

f 160 B.C.

us die bravely for our kindred, and leave no cause to question our honor."

The Last Battle of Judas

11 Then the army of Bacchides[g] marched out from the camp and took its stand for the encounter. The cavalry was divided into two companies, and the slingers and the archers went ahead of the army, as did all the chief warriors. 12Bacchides was on the right wing. Flanked by the two companies, the phalanx advanced to the sound of the trumpets; and the men with Judas also blew their trumpets. 13The earth was shaken by the noise of the armies, and the battle raged from morning until evening.

14 Judas saw that Bacchides and the strength of his army were on the right; then all the stouthearted men went with him, 15and they crushed the right wing, and he pursued them as far as Mount Azotus. 16When those on the left wing saw that the right wing was crushed, they turned and followed close behind Judas and his men. 17The battle became desperate, and many on both sides were wounded and fell. 18Judas also fell, and the rest fled.

19 Then Jonathan and Simon took their brother Judas and buried him in the tomb of their ancestors at Modein, 20and wept for him. All Israel made great lamentation for him; they mourned many days and said,

21 "How is the mighty fallen,
        the savior of Israel!"

22Now the rest of the acts of Judas, and his wars and the brave deeds that he did, and his greatness, have not been recorded, but they were very many.

Jonathan Succeeds Judas

23 After the death of Judas, the renegades emerged in all parts of Israel; all the wrongdoers reappeared. 24In those days a very great famine occurred, and the country went over to their side. 25Bacchides chose the godless and put them in charge of the country. 26They made inquiry and searched for the friends of Judas, and brought them to Bacchides, who took vengeance on them and made sport of them. 27So there was great distress in Israel, such as had not been since the time that prophets ceased to appear among them.

28 Then all the friends of Judas assembled and said to Jonathan, 29"Since the death of your brother Judas there has been no one like him to go against our enemies and Bacchides, and to deal with those of our nation who hate us. 30Now therefore we have chosen you today to take his place as our ruler and leader, to fight our battle." 31So Jonathan accepted the leadership at that time in place of his brother Judas.

The Campaigns of Jonathan

32 When Bacchides learned of this, he tried to kill him. 33But Jonathan and his brother Simon and all who were with him heard of it, and they fled into the wilderness of Tekoa and camped by the water of the pool of Asphar. 34Bacchides found this out on the sabbath day, and he with all his army crossed the Jordan.

35 So Jonathan[h] sent his brother as leader of the multitude and begged the Nabateans, who were his friends, for permission to store with them the great amount of baggage that they had. 36But the family of Jambri from Medeba came out and seized John and all that he had, and left with it.

37 After these things it was reported to Jonathan and his brother Simon, "The family of Jambri are celebrating a great wedding, and are conducting the bride, a daughter of one of the great nobles of Canaan, from Nadabath with a large escort." 38Remembering how their brother John had been killed, they went up and hid under cover of the mountain. 39They looked out and saw a tumultuous procession with a great amount of baggage; and the bridegroom came out with his friends and his brothers to meet them with tambourines and musicians and many weapons. 40Then they rushed on them from the ambush and began killing them. Many were wounded and fell, and the rest fled to the mountain; and the Jews[i] took all their goods. 41So the wedding was turned into mourning and the voice of their musicians into a funeral dirge. 42After they had fully avenged the blood of their brother, they returned to the marshes of the Jordan.

43 When Bacchides heard of this, he came with a large force on the sabbath day to the banks of the Jordan. 44And Jonathan said to those with him, "Let us get

up now and fight for our lives, for today things are not as they were before. ⁴⁵For look! the battle is in front of us and behind us; the water of the Jordan is on this side and on that, with marsh and thicket; there is no place to turn. ⁴⁶Cry out now to Heaven that you may be delivered from the hands of our enemies." ⁴⁷So the battle began, and Jonathan stretched out his hand to strike Bacchides, but he eluded him and went to the rear. ⁴⁸Then Jonathan and the men with him leaped into the Jordan and swam across to the other side, and the enemy*ʲ* did not cross the Jordan to attack them. ⁴⁹And about one thousand of Bacchides' men fell that day.

Bacchides Builds Fortifications

50 Then Bacchides*ᵏ* returned to Jerusalem and built strong cities in Judea: the fortress in Jericho, and Emmaus, and Beth-horon, and Bethel, and Timnath, and*ˡ* Pharathon, and Tephon, with high walls and gates and bars. ⁵¹And he placed garrisons in them to harass Israel. ⁵²He also fortified the town of Beth-zur, and Gazara, and the citadel, and in them he put troops and stores of food. ⁵³And he took the sons of the leading men of the land as hostages and put them under guard in the citadel at Jerusalem.

54 In the one hundred and fifty-third year,*ᵐ* in the second month, Alcimus gave orders to tear down the wall of the inner court of the sanctuary. He tore down the work of the prophets! ⁵⁵But he only began to tear it down, for at that time Alcimus was stricken and his work was hindered; his mouth was stopped and he was paralyzed, so that he could no longer say a word or give commands concerning his house. ⁵⁶And Alcimus died at that time in great agony. ⁵⁷When Bacchides saw that Alcimus was dead, he returned to the king, and the land of Judah had rest for two years.

The End of the War

58 Then all the lawless plotted and said, "See! Jonathan and his men are living in quiet and confidence. So now let us bring Bacchides back, and he will capture them all in one night." ⁵⁹And they went and consulted with him. ⁶⁰He started to come with a large force, and secretly sent letters to all his allies in Judea, telling them to seize Jonathan and his men; but they were unable to do it, because their plan became known. ⁶¹And Jonathan's men*ʲ* seized about fifty of the men of the country who were leaders in this treachery, and killed them.

62 Then Jonathan with his men, and Simon, withdrew to Bethbasi in the wilderness; he rebuilt the parts of it that had been demolished, and they fortified it. ⁶³When Bacchides learned of this, he assembled all his forces, and sent orders to the men of Judea. ⁶⁴Then he came and encamped against Bethbasi; he fought against it for many days and made machines of war.

65 But Jonathan left his brother Simon in the town, while he went out into the country; and he went with only a few men. ⁶⁶He struck down Odomera and his kindred and the people of Phasiron in their tents. ⁶⁷Then he*ⁿ* began to attack and went into battle with his forces; and Simon and his men sallied out from the town and set fire to the machines of war. ⁶⁸They fought with Bacchides, and he was crushed by them. They pressed him very hard, for his plan and his expedition had been in vain. ⁶⁹So he was very angry at the renegades who had counseled him to come into the country, and he killed many of them. Then he decided to go back to his own land.

70 When Jonathan learned of this, he sent ambassadors to him to make peace with him and obtain release of the captives. ⁷¹He agreed, and did as he said; and he swore to Jonathan*ᵒ* that he would not try to harm him as long as he lived. ⁷²He restored to him the captives whom he had taken previously from the land of Judah; then he turned and went back to his own land, and did not come again into their territory. ⁷³Thus the sword ceased from Israel. Jonathan settled in Michmash and began to judge the people; and he destroyed the godless out of Israel.

Revolt of Alexander Epiphanes

10 In the one hundred sixtieth year*ᵖ* Alexander Epiphanes, son of Antiochus, landed and occupied Ptolemais. They welcomed him, and there he began to reign. ²When King Demetrius heard of it, he assembled a very large army and marched out to meet him in battle. ³De-

---

ʲ Gk *they*   ᵏ Gk *he*   ˡ Some authorities omit *and*   ᵐ 159 B.C.   ⁿ Other ancient authorities read *they*   ᵒ Gk *him*   ᵖ 152 B.C.

metrius sent Jonathan a letter in peaceable words to honor him; ⁴for he said to himself, "Let us act first to make peace with him*q* before he makes peace with Alexander against us, ⁵for he will remember all the wrongs that we did to him and to his brothers and his nation." ⁶So Demetrius*r* gave him authority to recruit troops, to equip them with arms, and to become his ally; and he commanded that the hostages in the citadel should be released to him.

7 Then Jonathan came to Jerusalem and read the letter in the hearing of all the people and of those in the citadel. ⁸They were greatly alarmed when they heard that the king had given him authority to recruit troops. ⁹But those in the citadel released the hostages to Jonathan, and he returned them to their parents.

10 And Jonathan took up residence in Jerusalem and began to rebuild and restore the city. ¹¹He directed those who were doing the work to build the walls and encircle Mount Zion with squared stones, for better fortification; and they did so.

12 Then the foreigners who were in the strongholds that Bacchides had built fled; ¹³all of them left their places and went back to their own lands. ¹⁴Only in Bethzur did some remain who had forsaken the law and the commandments, for it served as a place of refuge.

15 Now King Alexander heard of all the promises that Demetrius had sent to Jonathan, and he heard of the battles that Jonathan*r* and his brothers had fought, of the brave deeds that they had done, and of the troubles that they had endured. ¹⁶So he said, "Shall we find another such man? Come now, we will make him our friend and ally." ¹⁷And he wrote a letter and sent it to him, in the following words:

Jonathan Becomes High Priest

18 "King Alexander to his brother Jonathan, greetings. ¹⁹We have heard about you, that you are a mighty warrior and worthy to be our friend. ²⁰And so we have appointed you today to be the high priest of your nation; you are to be called the king's Friend and you are to take our side and keep friendship with us." He also sent him a purple robe and a golden crown.

21 So Jonathan put on the sacred vestments in the seventh month of the one hundred sixtieth year,*s* at the festival of booths,*t* and he recruited troops and

equipped them with arms in abundance. ²²When Demetrius heard of these things he was distressed and said, ²³"What is this that we have done? Alexander has gotten ahead of us in forming a friendship with the Jews to strengthen himself. ²⁴I also will write them words of encouragement and promise them honor and gifts, so that I may have their help." ²⁵So he sent a message to them in the following words:

A Letter from Demetrius to Jonathan

"King Demetrius to the nation of the Jews, greetings. ²⁶Since you have kept your agreement with us and have continued your friendship with us, and have not sided with our enemies, we have heard of it and rejoiced. ²⁷Now continue still to keep faith with us, and we will repay you with good for what you do for us. ²⁸We will grant you many immunities and give you gifts.

29 "I now free you and exempt all the Jews from payment of tribute and salt tax and crown levies, ³⁰and instead of collecting the third of the grain and the half of the fruit of the trees that I should receive, I release them from this day and henceforth. I will not collect them from the land of Judah or from the three districts added to it from Samaria and Galilee, from this day and for all time. ³¹Jerusalem and its environs, its tithes and its revenues, shall be holy and free from tax. ³²I release also my control of the citadel in Jerusalem and give it to the high priest, so that he may station in it men of his own choice to guard it. ³³And everyone of the Jews taken as a captive from the land of Judah into any part of my kingdom, I set free without payment; and let all officials cancel also the taxes on their livestock.

34 "All the festivals and sabbaths and new moons and appointed days, and the three days before a festival and the three after a festival—let them all be days of immunity and release for all the Jews who are in my kingdom. ³⁵No one shall have authority to exact anything from them or annoy any of them about any matter.

36 "Let Jews be enrolled in the king's forces to the number of thirty thousand men, and let the maintenance be given them that is due to all the forces of the king. ³⁷Let some of them be stationed in

q Gk them   *r* Gk he   *s* 152 B.C.   *t* Or tabernacles

the great strongholds of the king, and let some of them be put in positions of trust in the kingdom. Let their officers and leaders be of their own number, and let them live by their own laws, just as the king has commanded in the land of Judah.

38 "As for the three districts that have been added to Judea from the country of Samaria, let them be annexed to Judea so that they may be considered to be under one ruler and obey no other authority than the high priest. 39Ptolemais and the land adjoining it I have given as a gift to the sanctuary in Jerusalem, to meet the necessary expenses of the sanctuary. 40I also grant fifteen thousand shekels of silver yearly out of the king's revenues from appropriate places. 41And all the additional funds that the government officials have not paid as they did in the first years,*u* they shall give from now on for the service of the temple.*v* 42Moreover, the five thousand shekels of silver that my officials*w* have received every year from the income of the services of the temple, this too is canceled, because it belongs to the priests who minister there. 43And all who take refuge at the temple in Jerusalem, or in any of its precincts, because they owe money to the king or are in debt, let them be released and receive back all their property in my kingdom.

44 "Let the cost of rebuilding and restoring the structures of the sanctuary be paid from the revenues of the king. 45And let the cost of rebuilding the walls of Jerusalem and fortifying it all around, and the cost of rebuilding the walls in Judea, also be paid from the revenues of the king."

Death of Demetrius

46 When Jonathan and the people heard these words, they did not believe or accept them, because they remembered the great wrongs that Demetrius*x* had done in Israel and how much he had oppressed them. 47They favored Alexander, because he had been the first to speak peaceable words to them, and they remained his allies all his days.

48 Now King Alexander assembled large forces and encamped opposite Demetrius. 49The two kings met in battle, and the army of Demetrius fled, and Alexander*y* pursued him and defeated them. 50He pressed the battle strongly until the sun set, and on that day Demetrius fell.

Treaty of Ptolemy and Alexander

51 Then Alexander sent ambassadors to Ptolemy king of Egypt with the following message: 52"Since I have returned to my kingdom and have taken my seat on the throne of my ancestors, and established my rule—for I crushed Demetrius and gained control of our country; 53I met him in battle, and he and his army were crushed by us, and we have taken our seat on the throne of his kingdom— 54now therefore let us establish friendship with one another; give me now your daughter as my wife, and I will become your son-in-law, and will make gifts to you and to her in keeping with your position."

55 Ptolemy the king replied and said, "Happy was the day on which you returned to the land of your ancestors and took your seat on the throne of their kingdom. 56And now I will do for you as you wrote, but meet me at Ptolemais, so that we may see one another, and I will become your father-in-law, as you have said."

57 So Ptolemy set out from Egypt, he and his daughter Cleopatra, and came to Ptolemais in the one hundred sixty-second year.*z* 58King Alexander met him, and Ptolemy*x* gave him his daughter Cleopatra in marriage, and celebrated her wedding at Ptolemais with great pomp, as kings do.

59 Then King Alexander wrote to Jonathan to come and meet him. 60So he went with pomp to Ptolemais and met the two kings; he gave them and their Friends silver and gold and many gifts, and found favor with them. 61A group of malcontents from Israel, renegades, gathered together against him to accuse him; but the king paid no attention to them. 62The king gave orders to take off Jonathan's garments and to clothe him in purple, and they did so. 63The king also seated him at his side; and he said to his officers, "Go out with him into the middle of the city and proclaim that no one is to bring charges against him about any matter, and let no one annoy him for any reason." 64When his accusers saw the honor that was paid him, in accord with the proclamation, and saw him clothed in purple, they all fled. 65Thus the king honored him

---

u Meaning of Gk uncertain   v Gk house   w Gk they   x Gk he   y Other ancient authorities read Alexander fled, and Demetrius   z 150 B.C.

and enrolled him among his chief[a] Friends, and made him general and governor of the province. [66]And Jonathan returned to Jerusalem in peace and gladness.

Apollonius Is Defeated by Jonathan

[67] In the one hundred sixty-fifth year[b] Demetrius son of Demetrius came from Crete to the land of his ancestors. [68]When King Alexander heard of it, he was greatly distressed and returned to Antioch. [69]And Demetrius appointed Apollonius the governor of Coelesyria, and he assembled a large force and encamped against Jamnia. Then he sent the following message to the high priest Jonathan:

[70] "You are the only one to rise up against us, and I have fallen into ridicule and disgrace because of you. Why do you assume authority against us in the hill country? [71]If you now have confidence in your forces, come down to the plain to meet us, and let us match strength with each other there, for I have with me the power of the cities. [72]Ask and learn who I am and who the others are that are helping us. People will tell you that you cannot stand before us, for your ancestors were twice put to flight in their own land. [73]And now you will not be able to withstand my cavalry and such an army in the plain, where there is no stone or pebble, or place to flee."

[74] When Jonathan heard the words of Apollonius, his spirit was aroused. He chose ten thousand men and set out from Jerusalem, and his brother Simon met him to help him. [75]He encamped before Joppa, but the people of the city closed its gates, for Apollonius had a garrison in Joppa. [76]So they fought against it, and the people of the city became afraid and opened the gates, and Jonathan gained possession of Joppa.

[77] When Apollonius heard of it, he mustered three thousand cavalry and a large army, and went to Azotus as though he were going farther. At the same time he advanced into the plain, for he had a large troop of cavalry and put confidence in it. [78]Jonathan[c] pursued him to Azotus, and the armies engaged in battle. [79]Now Apollonius had secretly left a thousand cavalry behind them. [80]Jonathan learned that there was an ambush behind him, for they surrounded his army and shot arrows at his men from early morning until late

afternoon. [81]But his men stood fast, as Jonathan had commanded, and the enemy's[d] horses grew tired.

[82] Then Simon brought forward his force and engaged the phalanx in battle (for the cavalry was exhausted); they were overwhelmed by him and fled, [83]and the cavalry was dispersed in the plain. They fled to Azotus and entered Beth-dagon, the temple of their idol, for safety. [84]But Jonathan burned Azotus and the surrounding towns and plundered them; and the temple of Dagon, and those who had taken refuge in it, he burned with fire. [85]The number of those who fell by the sword, with those burned alive, came to eight thousand.

[86] Then Jonathan left there and encamped against Askalon, and the people of the city came out to meet him with great pomp.

[87] He and those with him then returned to Jerusalem with a large amount of booty. [88]When King Alexander heard of these things, he honored Jonathan still more; [89]and he sent to him a golden buckle, such as it is the custom to give to the King's Kinsmen. He also gave him Ekron and all its environs as his possession.

Ptolemy Invades Syria

11 Then the king of Egypt gathered great forces, like the sand by the seashore, and many ships; and he tried to get possession of Alexander's kingdom by trickery and add it to his own kingdom. [2]He set out for Syria with peaceable words, and the people of the towns opened their gates to him and went to meet him, for King Alexander had commanded them to meet him, since he was Alexander's[e] father-in-law. [3]But when Ptolemy entered the towns he stationed forces as a garrison in each town.

[4] When he[f] approached Azotus, they showed him the burnt-out temple of Dagon, and Azotus and its suburbs destroyed, and the corpses lying about, and the charred bodies of those whom Jonathan[c] had burned in the war, for they had piled them in heaps along his route. [5]They also told the king what Jonathan had done, to throw blame on him; but the king kept silent. [6]Jonathan met the king at Joppa with pomp, and they greeted one

---

a Gk first   *b* 147 B.C.   *c* Gk he   *d* Gk their
e Gk his   *f* Other ancient authorities read they

another and spent the night there. [7]And Jonathan went with the king as far as the river called Eleutherus; then he returned to Jerusalem.

8 So King Ptolemy gained control of the coastal cities as far as Seleucia by the sea, and he kept devising wicked designs against Alexander. [9]He sent envoys to King Demetrius, saying, "Come, let us make a covenant with each other, and I will give you in marriage my daughter who was Alexander's wife, and you shall reign over your father's kingdom. [10]I now regret that I gave him my daughter, for he has tried to kill me." [11]He threw blame on Alexander[g] because he coveted his kingdom. [12]So he took his daughter away from him and gave her to Demetrius. He was estranged from Alexander, and their enmity became manifest.

13 Then Ptolemy entered Antioch and put on the crown of Asia. Thus he put two crowns on his head, the crown of Egypt and that of Asia. [14]Now King Alexander was in Cilicia at that time, because the people of that region were in revolt. [15]When Alexander heard of it, he came against him in battle. Ptolemy marched out and met him with a strong force, and put him to flight. [16]So Alexander fled into Arabia to find protection there, and King Ptolemy was triumphant. [17]Zabdiel the Arab cut off the head of Alexander and sent it to Ptolemy. [18]But King Ptolemy died three days later, and his troops in the strongholds were killed by the inhabitants of the strongholds. [19]So Demetrius became king in the one hundred sixty-seventh year.[h]

Jonathan's Diplomacy

20 In those days Jonathan assembled the Judeans to attack the citadel in Jerusalem, and he built many engines of war to use against it. [21]But certain renegades who hated their nation went to the king and reported to him that Jonathan was besieging the citadel. [22]When he heard this he was angry, and as soon as he heard it he set out and came to Ptolemais; and he wrote Jonathan not to continue the siege, but to meet him for a conference at Ptolemais as quickly as possible.

23 When Jonathan heard this, he gave orders to continue the siege. He chose some of the elders of Israel and some of the priests, and put himself in danger, [24]for he went to the king at Ptolemais,

taking silver and gold and clothing and numerous other gifts. And he won his favor. [25]Although certain renegades of his nation kept making complaints against him, [26]the king treated him as his predecessors had treated him; he exalted him in the presence of all his Friends. [27]He confirmed him in the high priesthood and in as many other honors as he had formerly had, and caused him to be reckoned among his chief[i] Friends. [28]Then Jonathan asked the king to free Judea and the three districts of Samaria[j] from tribute, and promised him three hundred talents. [29]The king consented, and wrote a letter to Jonathan about all these things; its contents were as follows:

30 "King Demetrius to his brother Jonathan and to the nation of the Jews, greetings. [31]This copy of the letter that we wrote concerning you to our kinsman Lasthenes we have written to you also, so that you may know what it says. [32]'King Demetrius to his father Lasthenes, greetings. [33]We have determined to do good to the nation of the Jews, who are our friends and fulfill their obligations to us, because of the goodwill they show toward us. [34]We have confirmed as their possession both the territory of Judea and the three districts of Aphairema and Lydda and Rathamin; the latter, with all the region bordering them, were added to Judea from Samaria. To all those who offer sacrifice in Jerusalem we have granted release from[k] the royal taxes that the king formerly received from them each year, from the crops of the land and the fruit of the trees. [35]And the other payments henceforth due to us of the tithes, and the taxes due to us, and the salt pits and the crown taxes due to us—from all these we shall grant them release. [36]And not one of these grants shall be canceled from this time on forever. [37]Now therefore take care to make a copy of this, and let it be given to Jonathan and put up in a conspicuous place on the holy mountain.' "

The Intrigue of Trypho

38 When King Demetrius saw that the land was quiet before him and that there was no opposition to him, he dismissed all his troops, all of them to their own

---

g Gk *him*   *h* 145 B.C.   *i* Gk *first*   *j* Cn: Gk *the three districts and Samaria*   *k* Or *Samaria, for all those who offer sacrifice in Jerusalem, in place of*

homes, except the foreign troops that he had recruited from the islands of the nations. So all the troops who had served under his predecessors hated him. ³⁹A certain Trypho had formerly been one of Alexander's supporters; he saw that all the troops were grumbling against Demetrius. So he went to Imalkue the Arab, who was bringing up Antiochus, the young son of Alexander, ⁴⁰and insistently urged him to hand Antiochus*[l]* over to him, to become king in place of his father. He also reported to Imalkue*[l]* what Demetrius had done and told of the hatred that the troops of Demetrius*[m]* had for him; and he stayed there many days.

41 Now Jonathan sent to King Demetrius the request that he remove the troops of the citadel from Jerusalem, and the troops in the strongholds; for they kept fighting against Israel. ⁴²And Demetrius sent this message back to Jonathan: "Not only will I do these things for you and your nation, but I will confer great honor on you and your nation, if I find an opportunity. ⁴³Now then you will do well to send me men who will help me, for all my troops have revolted." ⁴⁴So Jonathan sent three thousand stalwart men to him at Antioch, and when they came to the king, the king rejoiced at their arrival.

45 Then the people of the city assembled within the city, to the number of a hundred and twenty thousand, and they wanted to kill the king. ⁴⁶But the king fled into the palace. Then the people of the city seized the main streets of the city and began to fight. ⁴⁷So the king called the Jews to his aid, and they all rallied around him and then spread out through the city; and they killed on that day about one hundred thousand. ⁴⁸They set fire to the city and seized a large amount of spoil on that day, and saved the king. ⁴⁹When the people of the city saw that the Jews had gained control of the city as they pleased, their courage failed and they cried out to the king with this entreaty: ⁵⁰"Grant us peace, and make the Jews stop fighting against us and our city." ⁵¹And they threw down their arms and made peace. So the Jews gained glory in the sight of the king and of all the people in his kingdom, and they returned to Jerusalem with a large amount of spoil.

52 So King Demetrius sat on the throne of his kingdom, and the land was quiet before him. ⁵³But he broke his word

about all that he had promised; he became estranged from Jonathan and did not repay the favors that Jonathan*[n]* had done him, but treated him very harshly.

Trypho Seizes Power

54 After this Trypho returned, and with him the young boy Antiochus who began to reign and put on the crown. ⁵⁵All the troops that Demetrius had discharged gathered around him; they fought against Demetrius,*[l]* and he fled and was routed. ⁵⁶Trypho captured the elephants*[o]* and gained control of Antioch. ⁵⁷Then the young Antiochus wrote to Jonathan, saying, "I confirm you in the high priesthood and set you over the four districts and make you one of the king's Friends." ⁵⁸He also sent him gold plates and a table service, and granted him the right to drink from gold cups and dress in purple and wear a gold buckle. ⁵⁹He appointed Jonathan's*[p]* brother Simon governor from the Ladder of Tyre to the borders of Egypt.

Campaigns of Jonathan and Simon

60 Then Jonathan set out and traveled beyond the river and among the towns, and all the army of Syria gathered to him as allies. When he came to Askalon, the people of the city met him and paid him honor. ⁶¹From there he went to Gaza, but the people of Gaza shut him out. So he besieged it and burned its suburbs with fire and plundered them. ⁶²Then the people of Gaza pleaded with Jonathan, and he made peace with them, and took the sons of their rulers as hostages and sent them to Jerusalem. And he passed through the country as far as Damascus.

63 Then Jonathan heard that the officers of Demetrius had come to Kadesh in Galilee with a large army, intending to remove him from office. ⁶⁴He went to meet them, but left his brother Simon in the country. ⁶⁵Simon encamped before Bethzur and fought against it for many days and hemmed it in. ⁶⁶Then they asked him to grant them terms of peace, and he did so. He removed them from there, took possession of the town, and set a garrison over it.

67 Jonathan and his army encamped by the waters of Gennesaret. Early in the morning they marched to the plain of Ha-

[l] Gk him   *[m]* Gk his troops   *[n]* Gk he   *[o]* Gk
animals   *[p]* Gk his

zor, 68and there in the plain the army of
the foreigners met him; they had set an
ambush against him in the mountains,
but they themselves met him face to face.
69Then the men in ambush emerged from
their places and joined battle. 70All the
men with Jonathan fled; not one of them
was left except Mattathias son of Absalom
and Judas son of Chalphi, commanders of
the forces of the army. 71Jonathan tore his
clothes, put dust on his head, and prayed.
72Then he turned back to the battle
against the enemy*q* and routed them,
and they fled. 73When his men who were
fleeing saw this, they returned to him and
joined him in the pursuit as far as Kadesh,
to their camp, and there they encamped.
74As many as three thousand of the foreigners fell that day. And Jonathan returned to Jerusalem.

Alliances with Rome and Sparta

12 Now when Jonathan saw that the
time was favorable for him, he
chose men and sent them to Rome to confirm and renew the friendship with them.
2He also sent letters to the same effect to
the Spartans and to other places. 3So they
went to Rome and entered the senate
chamber and said, "The high priest Jonathan and the Jewish nation have sent us to
renew the former friendship and alliance
with them." 4And the Romans*r* gave them
letters to the people in every place, asking
them to provide for the envoys*q* safe conduct to the land of Judah.

5 This is a copy of the letter that Jonathan wrote to the Spartans: 6"The high
priest Jonathan, the senate of the nation,
the priests, and the rest of the Jewish people to their brothers the Spartans, greetings. 7Already in time past a letter was
sent to the high priest Onias from Arius,*s*
who was king among you, stating that you
are our brothers, as the appended copy
shows. 8Onias welcomed the envoy with
honor, and received the letter, which contained a clear declaration of alliance and
friendship. 9Therefore, though we have no
need of these things, since we have as encouragement the holy books that are in
our hands, 10we have undertaken to send
to renew our family ties and friendship
with you, so that we may not become estranged from you, for considerable time
has passed since you sent your letter to us.
11We therefore remember you constantly
on every occasion, both at our festivals

and on other appropriate days, at the sacrifices that we offer and in our prayers, as
it is right and proper to remember brothers. 12And we rejoice in your glory. 13But
as for ourselves, many trials and many
wars have encircled us; the kings around
us have waged war against us. 14We were
unwilling to annoy you and our other allies and friends with these wars, 15for we
have the help that comes from Heaven for
our aid, and so we were delivered from
our enemies, and our enemies were humbled. 16We therefore have chosen Numenius son of Antiochus and Antipater son
of Jason, and have sent them to Rome to
renew our former friendship and alliance
with them. 17We have commanded them
to go also to you and greet you and deliver
to you this letter from us concerning the
renewal of our family ties. 18And now
please send us a reply to this."

19 This is a copy of the letter that they
sent to Onias: 20"King Arius of the Spartans, to the high priest Onias, greetings.
21It has been found in writing concerning
the Spartans and the Jews that they are
brothers and are of the family of Abraham. 22And now that we have learned
this, please write us concerning your welfare; 23we on our part write to you that
your livestock and your property belong
to us, and ours belong to you. We therefore command that our envoys*r* report to
you accordingly."

Further Campaigns of Jonathan and Simon

24 Now Jonathan heard that the commanders of Demetrius had returned, with
a larger force than before, to wage war
against him. 25So he marched away from
Jerusalem and met them in the region of
Hamath, for he gave them no opportunity
to invade his own country. 26He sent spies
to their camp, and they returned and reported to him that the enemy*r* were being drawn up in formation to attack the
Jews*q* by night. 27So when the sun had
set, Jonathan commanded his troops to
be alert and to keep their arms at hand so
as to be ready all night for battle, and
he stationed outposts around the camp.
28When the enemy heard that Jonathan
and his troops were prepared for battle,
they were afraid and were terrified at
heart; so they kindled fires in their camp

q Gk them   *r* Gk they   *s* Vg Compare verse 20:
Gk *Darius*

and withdrew.*ᵗ* ²⁹But Jonathan and his troops did not know it until morning, for they saw the fires burning. ³⁰Then Jonathan pursued them, but he did not overtake them, for they had crossed the Eleutherus river. ³¹So Jonathan turned aside against the Arabs who are called Zabadeans, and he crushed them and plundered them. ³²Then he broke camp and went to Damascus, and marched through all that region.

33 Simon also went out and marched through the country as far as Askalon and the neighboring strongholds. He turned aside to Joppa and took it by surprise, ³⁴for he had heard that they were ready to hand over the stronghold to those whom Demetrius had sent. And he stationed a garrison there to guard it.

35 When Jonathan returned he convened the elders of the people and planned with them to build strongholds in Judea, ³⁶to build the walls of Jerusalem still higher, and to erect a high barrier between the citadel and the city to separate it from the city, in order to isolate it so that its garrison*ᵘ* could neither buy nor sell. ³⁷So they gathered together to rebuild the city; part of the wall on the valley to the east had fallen, and he repaired the section called Chaphenatha. ³⁸Simon also built Adida in the Shephelah; he fortified it and installed gates with bolts.

Trypho Captures Jonathan

39 Then Trypho attempted to become king in Asia and put on the crown, and to raise his hand against King Antiochus. ⁴⁰He feared that Jonathan might not permit him to do so, but might make war on him, so he kept seeking to seize and kill him, and he marched out and came to Beth-shan. ⁴¹Jonathan went out to meet him with forty thousand picked warriors, and he came to Beth-shan. ⁴²When Trypho saw that he had come with a large army, he was afraid to raise his hand against him. ⁴³So he received him with honor and commended him to all his Friends, and he gave him gifts and commanded his Friends and his troops to obey him as they would himself. ⁴⁴Then he said to Jonathan, "Why have you put all these people to so much trouble when we are not at war? ⁴⁵Dismiss them now to their homes and choose for yourself a few men to stay with you, and come with me to Ptolemais. I will hand it over to you as

well as the other strongholds and the remaining troops and all the officials, and will turn around and go home. For that is why I am here."

46 Jonathan*ᵛ* trusted him and did as he said; he sent away the troops, and they returned to the land of Judah. ⁴⁷He kept with himself three thousand men, two thousand of whom he left in Galilee, while one thousand accompanied him. ⁴⁸But when Jonathan entered Ptolemais, the people of Ptolemais closed the gates and seized him, and they killed with the sword all who had entered with him.

49 Then Trypho sent troops and cavalry into Galilee and the Great Plain to destroy all Jonathan's soldiers. ⁵⁰But they realized that Jonathan had been seized and had perished along with his men, and they encouraged one another and kept marching in close formation, ready for battle. ⁵¹When their pursuers saw that they would fight for their lives, they turned back. ⁵²So they all reached the land of Judah safely, and they mourned for Jonathan and his companions and were in great fear; and all Israel mourned deeply. ⁵³All the nations around them tried to destroy them, for they said, "They have no leader or helper. Now therefore let us make war on them and blot out the memory of them from humankind."

Simon Takes Command

13 Simon heard that Trypho had assembled a large army to invade the land of Judah and destroy it, ²and he saw that the people were trembling with fear. So he went up to Jerusalem, and gathering the people together ³he encouraged them, saying to them, "You yourselves know what great things my brothers and I and the house of my father have done for the laws and the sanctuary; you know also the wars and the difficulties that my brothers and I have seen. ⁴By reason of this all my brothers have perished for the sake of Israel, and I alone am left. ⁵And now, far be it from me to spare my life in any time of distress, for I am not better than my brothers. ⁶But I will avenge my nation and the sanctuary and your wives and children, for all the nations have gathered together out of hatred to destroy us."

ᵗ Other ancient authorities omit and withdrew
ᵘ Gk they   ᵛ Gk he

7 The spirit of the people was rekindled when they heard these words, 8and they answered in a loud voice, "You are our leader in place of Judas and your brother Jonathan. 9Fight our battles, and all that you say to us we will do." 10So he assembled all the warriors and hurried to complete the walls of Jerusalem, and he fortified it on every side. 11He sent Jonathan son of Absalom to Joppa, and with him a considerable army; he drove out its occupants and remained there.

Deceit and Treachery of Trypho

12 Then Trypho left Ptolemais with a large army to invade the land of Judah, and Jonathan was with him under guard. 13Simon encamped in Adida, facing the plain. 14Trypho learned that Simon had risen up in place of his brother Jonathan, and that he was about to join battle with him, so he sent envoys to him and said, 15"It is for the money that your brother Jonathan owed the royal treasury, in connection with the offices he held, that we are detaining him. 16Send now one hundred talents of silver and two of his sons as hostages, so that when released he will not revolt against us, and we will release him."

17 Simon knew that they were speaking deceitfully to him, but he sent to get the money and the sons, so that he would not arouse great hostility among the people, who might say, 18"It was because Simon[w] did not send him the money and the sons, that Jonathan[x] perished." 19So he sent the sons and the hundred talents, but Trypho[x] broke his word and did not release Jonathan.

20 After this Trypho came to invade the country and destroy it, and he circled around by the way to Adora. But Simon and his army kept marching along opposite him to every place he went. 21Now the men in the citadel kept sending envoys to Trypho urging him to come to them by way of the wilderness and to send them food. 22So Trypho got all his cavalry ready to go, but that night a very heavy snow fell, and he did not go because of the snow. He marched off and went into the land of Gilead. 23When he approached Baskama, he killed Jonathan, and he was buried there. 24Then Trypho turned and went back to his own land.

Jonathan's Tomb

25 Simon sent and took the bones of his brother Jonathan, and buried him in Modein, the city of his ancestors. 26All Israel bewailed him with great lamentation, and mourned for him many days. 27And Simon built a monument over the tomb of his father and his brothers; he made it high so that it might be seen, with polished stone at the front and back. 28He also erected seven pyramids, opposite one another, for his father and mother and four brothers. 29For the pyramids[y] he devised an elaborate setting, erecting about them great columns, and on the columns he put suits of armor for a permanent memorial, and beside the suits of armor he carved ships, so that they could be seen by all who sail the sea. 30This is the tomb that he built in Modein; it remains to this day.

Judea Gains Independence

31 Trypho dealt treacherously with the young King Antiochus; he killed him 32and became king in his place, putting on the crown of Asia; and he brought great calamity on the land. 33But Simon built up the strongholds of Judea and walled them all around, with high towers and great walls and gates and bolts, and he stored food in the strongholds. 34Simon also chose emissaries and sent them to King Demetrius with a request to grant relief to the country, for all that Trypho did was to plunder. 35King Demetrius sent him a favorable reply to this request, and wrote him a letter as follows, 36"King Demetrius to Simon, the high priest and friend of kings, and to the elders and nation of the Jews, greetings. 37We have received the gold crown and the palm branch that you[z] sent, and we are ready to make a general peace with you and to write to our officials to grant you release from tribute. 38All the grants that we have made to you remain valid, and let the strongholds that you have built be your possession. 39We pardon any errors and offenses committed to this day, and cancel the crown tax that you owe; and whatever other tax has been collected in Jerusalem shall be collected no longer. 40And if any of you are qualified to be enrolled in

our bodyguard,[a] let them be enrolled, and let there be peace between us."

41 In the one hundred seventieth year[b] the yoke of the Gentiles was removed from Israel, [42]and the people began to write in their documents and contracts, "In the first year of Simon the great high priest and commander and leader of the Jews."

The Capture of Gazara by Simon

43 In those days Simon[c] encamped against Gazara[d] and surrounded it with troops. He made a siege engine, brought it up to the city, and battered and captured one tower. [44]The men in the siege engine leaped out into the city, and a great tumult arose in the city. [45]The men in the city, with their wives and children, went up on the wall with their clothes torn, and they cried out with a loud voice, asking Simon to make peace with them; [46]they said, "Do not treat us according to our wicked acts but according to your mercy." [47]So Simon reached an agreement with them and stopped fighting against them. But he expelled them from the city and cleansed the houses in which the idols were located, and then entered it with hymns and praise. [48]He removed all uncleanness from it, and settled in it those who observed the law. He also strengthened its fortifications and built in it a house for himself.

Simon Regains the Citadel at Jerusalem

49 Those who were in the citadel at Jerusalem were prevented from going in and out to buy and sell in the country. So they were very hungry, and many of them perished from famine. [50]Then they cried to Simon to make peace with them, and he did so. But he expelled them from there and cleansed the citadel from its pollutions. [51]On the twenty-third day of the second month, in the one hundred seventy-first year,[e] the Jews[f] entered it with praise and palm branches, and with harps and cymbals and stringed instruments, and with hymns and songs, because a great enemy had been crushed and removed from Israel. [52]Simon[g] decreed that every year they should celebrate this day with rejoicing. He strengthened the fortifications of the temple hill alongside the citadel, and he and his men lived there. [53]Simon saw that his son John had reached manhood, and so he made him commander of all the forces; and he lived at Gazara.

Capture of Demetrius

14 In the one hundred seventy-second year[h] King Demetrius assembled his forces and marched into Media to obtain help, so that he could make war against Trypho. [2]When King Arsaces of Persia and Media heard that Demetrius had invaded his territory, he sent one of his generals to take him alive. [3]The general[g] went and defeated the army of Demetrius, and seized him and took him to Arsaces, who put him under guard.

Eulogy of Simon

4 The land[i] had rest all the days of
   Simon.
  He sought the good of his nation;
his rule was pleasing to them,
  as was the honor shown him, all
   his days.
5 To crown all his honors he took
   Joppa for a harbor,
  and opened a way to the isles of
   the sea.
6 He extended the borders of his
   nation,
  and gained full control of the
   country.
7 He gathered a host of captives;
  he ruled over Gazara and Beth-zur
    and the citadel,
and he removed its uncleanness
   from it;
  and there was none to oppose
   him.
8 They tilled their land in peace;
  the ground gave its increase,
  and the trees of the plains their
   fruit.
9 Old men sat in the streets;
  they all talked together of good
   things,
  and the youths put on splendid
   military attire.
10 He supplied the towns with food,
  and furnished them with the
   means of defense,
  until his renown spread to the
   ends of the earth.
11 He established peace in the land,
  and Israel rejoiced with great joy.

---

a Or court   b 142 B.C.   c Gk he   d Cn: Gk Gaza   e 141 B.C.   f Gk they   g Gk He   h 140 B.C.   i Other ancient authorities add of Judah

12 All the people sat under their own
        vines and fig trees,
    and there was none to make them
        afraid.
13 No one was left in the land to fight
        them,
    and the kings were crushed in
        those days.
14 He gave help to all the humble
        among his people;
    he sought out the law,
    and did away with all the
        renegades and outlaws.
15 He made the sanctuary glorious,
    and added to the vessels of the
        sanctuary.

Diplomacy with Rome and Sparta

16 It was heard in Rome, and as far
away as Sparta, that Jonathan had died,
and they were deeply grieved. 17When
they heard that his brother Simon had become high priest in his stead, and that he
was ruling over the country and the towns
in it, 18they wrote to him on bronze tablets to renew with him the friendship and
alliance that they had established with his
brothers Judas and Jonathan. 19And these
were read before the assembly in Jerusalem.

20 This is a copy of the letter that the
Spartans sent:

"The rulers and the city of the Spartans
to the high priest Simon and to the elders
and the priests and the rest of the Jewish
people, our brothers, greetings. 21The envoys who were sent to our people have
told us about your glory and honor, and
we rejoiced at their coming. 22We have
recorded what they said in our public decrees, as follows, 'Numenius son of Antiochus and Antipater son of Jason, envoys of
the Jews, have come to us to renew their
friendship with us. 23It has pleased our
people to receive these men with honor
and to put a copy of their words in the
public archives, so that the people of the
Spartans may have a record of them. And
they have sent a copy of this to the high
priest Simon.' "

24 After this Simon sent Numenius to
Rome with a large gold shield weighing
one thousand minas, to confirm the alliance with the Romans.*j*

Official Honors for Simon

25 When the people heard these things
they said, "How shall we thank Simon

and his sons? 26For he and his brothers
and the house of his father have stood
firm; they have fought and repulsed Israel's enemies and established its freedom."
27So they made a record on bronze tablets
and put it on pillars on Mount Zion.

This is a copy of what they wrote: "On
the eighteenth day of Elul, in the one hundred seventy-second year,*k* which is the
third year of the great high priest Simon,
28in Asaramel,*l* in the great assembly of
the priests and the people and the rulers
of the nation and the elders of the country, the following was proclaimed to us:

29 "Since wars often occurred in the
country, Simon son of Mattathias, a priest
of the sons*m* of Joarib, and his brothers,
exposed themselves to danger and resisted
the enemies of their nation, in order that
their sanctuary and the law might be preserved; and they brought great glory to
their nation. 30Jonathan rallied the*n* nation, became their high priest, and was
gathered to his people. 31When their enemies decided to invade their country and
lay hands on their sanctuary, 32then Simon rose up and fought for his nation.
He spent great sums of his own money; he
armed the soldiers of his nation and paid
them wages. 33He fortified the towns of
Judea, and Beth-zur on the borders of Judea, where formerly the arms of the enemy had been stored, and he placed there
a garrison of Jews. 34He also fortified Joppa, which is by the sea, and Gazara, which
is on the borders of Azotus, where the enemy formerly lived. He settled Jews there,
and provided in those towns*j* whatever
was necessary for their restoration.

35 "The people saw Simon's faithfulness*o* and the glory that he had resolved
to win for his nation, and they made him
their leader and high priest, because he
had done all these things and because of
the justice and loyalty that he had maintained toward his nation. He sought in
every way to exalt his people. 36In his days
things prospered in his hands, so that the
Gentiles were put out of the*n* country, as
were also those in the city of David in
Jerusalem, who had built themselves a cit-

---

j Gk *them*   *k* 140 B.C.   *l* This word resembles
the Hebrew words for *the court of the people of
God* or *the prince of the people of God*   *m* Meaning
of Gk uncertain   *n* Gk *their*   *o* Other ancient
authorities read *conduct*

adel from which they used to sally forth and defile the environs of the sanctuary, doing great damage to its purity. [37]He settled Jews in it and fortified it for the safety of the country and of the city, and built the walls of Jerusalem higher.

38 "In view of these things King Demetrius confirmed him in the high priesthood, [39]made him one of his Friends, and

paid him high honors. [40]For he had heard that the Jews were addressed by the Romans as friends and allies and brothers, and that the Romans[p] had received the envoys of Simon with honor.

41 "The Jews and their priests have resolved that Simon should be their leader

[p] Gk they

WEDNESDAY

Scripture Reading for Today:
1 Maccabees 14.25–35

Verse for Today:
1 Maccabees 14.26

Stand and Fight

From Esther de Waal's commentary on the Rule of St. Benedict:

True stability is fruitful. To be standing as still as a dead tree stump is quite wrong. There is the danger of inertia taking over, so that even if I am physically present, I am not alive, awake. I think of Christ turning to the disciples in the garden and asking them to stay awake to support him, and one another, during the struggle, to fight sleep and the forces of darkness. They failed him, as so often I fail through laziness, weakness, carelessness, and, perhaps most insidious of all, sheer inertia.

The image of fighting, fighting the forces of darkness, further enriches the concept of stability. Benedict was a true Roman and the resonance of *stare*, "to stand," would carry military connotations for him, as does that passage in Ephesians 6.13: "Therefore take up the whole armor of God, so that you may be able to withstand on that evil day, and having done everything, to stand firm." By standing still I find where the real battle has to be fought, not the least with the forces within. Maturity comes from facing what has to be faced and not running away from all the dark and murky elements that lie in wait to attack us.

What this asks is the ability to hang on, to endure, even when there does not seem much prospect of the end of the road. It means holding on against the odds, being willing to keep on keeping on. This is a sort of constancy that does not become either discouraged or cynical in the face of anxiety, boredom. Refusing to give up because I am in it for the long haul brings an entirely different perspective. In the end I am brought back, of course, to Christ himself and to his example, the willingness to endure faithfully and with patience, *patientia*, reminding me that this means both waiting and suffering.

What makes this possible? The faithfulness of God. My stability is possible in the end because of the certain, guaranteed, steadfastness of God.

—ESTHER DE WAAL

Go to page 601 for your next devotional reading.

and high priest forever, until a trustworthy prophet should arise, ⁴²and that he should be governor over them and that he should take charge of the sanctuary and appoint officials over its tasks and over the country and the weapons and the strongholds, and that he should take charge of the sanctuary, ⁴³and that he should be obeyed by all, and that all contracts in the country should be written in his name, and that he should be clothed in purple and wear gold.

44 "None of the people or priests shall be permitted to nullify any of these decisions or to oppose what he says, or to convene an assembly in the country without his permission, or to be clothed in purple or put on a gold buckle. ⁴⁵Whoever acts contrary to these decisions or rejects any of them shall be liable to punishment."

46 All the people agreed to grant Simon the right to act in accordance with these decisions. ⁴⁷So Simon accepted and agreed to be high priest, to be commander and ethnarch of the Jews and priests, and to be protector of them all.*q* ⁴⁸And they gave orders to inscribe this decree on bronze tablets, to put them up in a conspicuous place in the precincts of the sanctuary, ⁴⁹and to deposit copies of them in the treasury, so that Simon and his sons might have them.

Letter of Antiochus VII

15 Antiochus, son of King Demetrius, sent a letter from the islands of the sea to Simon, the priest and ethnarch of the Jews, and to all the nation; ²its contents were as follows: "King Antiochus to Simon the high priest and ethnarch and to the nation of the Jews, greetings. ³Whereas certain scoundrels have gained control of the kingdom of our ancestors, and I intend to lay claim to the kingdom so that I may restore it as it formerly was, and have recruited a host of mercenary troops and have equipped warships, ⁴and intend to make a landing in the country so that I may proceed against those who have destroyed our country and those who have devastated many cities in my kingdom, ⁵now therefore I confirm to you all the tax remissions that the kings before me have granted you, and a release from all the other payments from which they have released you. ⁶I permit you to mint your own coinage as money

for your country, ⁷and I grant freedom to Jerusalem and the sanctuary. All the weapons that you have prepared and the strongholds that you have built and now hold shall remain yours. ⁸Every debt you owe to the royal treasury and any such future debts shall be canceled for you from henceforth and for all time. ⁹When we gain control of our kingdom, we will bestow great honor on you and your nation and the temple, so that your glory will become manifest in all the earth."

10 In the one hundred seventy-fourth year*r* Antiochus set out and invaded the land of his ancestors. All the troops rallied to him, so that there were only a few with Trypho. ¹¹Antiochus pursued him, and Trypho*s* came in his flight to Dor, which is by the sea; ¹²for he knew that troubles had converged on him, and his troops had deserted him. ¹³So Antiochus encamped against Dor, and with him were one hundred twenty thousand warriors and eight thousand cavalry. ¹⁴He surrounded the town, and the ships joined battle from the sea; he pressed the town hard from land and sea, and permitted no one to leave or enter it.

Rome Supports the Jews

15 Then Numenius and his companions arrived from Rome, with letters to the kings and countries, in which the following was written: ¹⁶"Lucius, consul of the Romans, to King Ptolemy, greetings. ¹⁷The envoys of the Jews have come to us as our friends and allies to renew our ancient friendship and alliance. They had been sent by the high priest Simon and by the Jewish people ¹⁸and have brought a gold shield weighing one thousand minas. ¹⁹We therefore have decided to write to the kings and countries that they should not seek their harm or make war against them and their cities and their country, or make alliance with those who war against them. ²⁰And it has seemed good to us to accept the shield from them. ²¹Therefore if any scoundrels have fled to you from their country, hand them over to the high priest Simon, so that he may punish them according to their law."

22 The consul*t* wrote the same thing to King Demetrius and to Attalus and Ariarathes and Arsaces, ²³and to all the coun-

---

q Or to preside over them all   *r 138 B.C.*   *s Gk he*
t Gk He

tries, and to Sampsames,[u] and to the Spartans, and to Delos, and to Myndos, and to Sicyon, and to Caria, and to Samos, and to Pamphylia, and to Lycia, and to Halicarnassus, and to Rhodes, and to Phaselis, and to Cos, and to Side, and to Aradus and Gortyna and Cnidus and Cyprus and Cyrene. [24]They also sent a copy of these things to the high priest Simon.

Antiochus VII Threatens Simon

25 King Antiochus besieged Dor for the second time, continually throwing his forces against it and making engines of war; and he shut Trypho up and kept him from going out or in. [26]And Simon sent to Antiochus[v] two thousand picked troops, to fight for him, and silver and gold and a large amount of military equipment. [27]But he refused to receive them, and broke all the agreements he formerly had made with Simon, and became estranged from him. [28]He sent to him Athenobius, one of his Friends, to confer with him, saying, "You hold control of Joppa and Gazara and the citadel in Jerusalem; they are cities of my kingdom. [29]You have devastated their territory, you have done great damage in the land, and you have taken possession of many places in my kingdom. [30]Now then, hand over the cities that you have seized and the tribute money of the places that you have conquered outside the borders of Judea; [31]or else pay me five hundred talents of silver for the destruction that you have caused and five hundred talents more for the tribute money of the cities. Otherwise we will come and make war on you."

32 So Athenobius, the king's Friend, came to Jerusalem, and when he saw the splendor of Simon, and the sideboard with its gold and silver plate, and his great magnificence, he was amazed. When he reported to him the king's message, [33]Simon said to him in reply: "We have neither taken foreign land nor seized foreign property, but only the inheritance of our ancestors, which at one time had been unjustly taken by our enemies. [34]Now that we have the opportunity, we are firmly holding the inheritance of our ancestors. [35]As for Joppa and Gazara, which you demand, they were causing great damage among the people and to our land; for them we will give you one hundred talents."

Athenobius[w] did not answer him a word, [36]but returned in wrath to the king and reported to him these words, and also the splendor of Simon and all that he had seen. And the king was very angry.

Victory over Cendebeus

37 Meanwhile Trypho embarked on a ship and escaped to Orthosia. [38]Then the king made Cendebeus commander-in-chief of the coastal country, and gave him troops of infantry and cavalry. [39]He commanded him to encamp against Judea, to build up Kedron and fortify its gates, and to make war on the people; but the king pursued Trypho. [40]So Cendebeus came to Jamnia and began to provoke the people and invade Judea and take the people captive and kill them. [41]He built up Kedron and stationed horsemen and troops there, so that they might go out and make raids along the highways of Judea, as the king had ordered him.

16 John went up from Gazara and reported to his father Simon what Cendebeus had done. [2]And Simon called in his two eldest sons Judas and John, and said to them: "My brothers and I and my father's house have fought the wars of Israel from our youth until this day, and things have prospered in our hands so that we have delivered Israel many times. [3]But now I have grown old, and you by Heaven's[x] mercy are mature in years. Take my place and my brother's, and go out and fight for our nation, and may the help that comes from Heaven be with you."

4 So John[y] chose out of the country twenty thousand warriors and cavalry, and they marched against Cendebeus and camped for the night in Modein. [5]Early in the morning they started out and marched into the plain, where a large force of infantry and cavalry was coming to meet them; and a stream lay between them. [6]Then he and his army lined up against them. He saw that the soldiers were afraid to cross the stream, so he crossed over first; and when his troops saw him, they crossed over after him. [7]Then he divided the army and placed the cavalry in the center of the infantry, for the cavalry of the enemy were very numerous. [8]They sounded the trumpets, and Cendebeus and his army were put to flight; many of

[u] The name is uncertain   [v] Gk *him*   [w] Gk *He*   [x] Gk *his*   [y] Other ancient authorities read *he*

them fell wounded and the rest fled into the stronghold. [9]At that time Judas the brother of John was wounded, but John pursued them until Cendebeus[z] reached Kedron, which he had built. [10]They also fled into the towers that were in the fields of Azotus, and John[z] burned it with fire, and about two thousand of them fell. He then returned to Judea safely.

Murder of Simon and His Sons

[11] Now Ptolemy son of Abubus had been appointed governor over the plain of Jericho; he had a large store of silver and gold, [12]for he was son-in-law of the high priest. [13]His heart was lifted up; he determined to get control of the country, and made treacherous plans against Simon and his sons, to do away with them. [14]Now Simon was visiting the towns of the country and attending to their needs, and he went down to Jericho with his sons Mattathias and Judas, in the one hundred seventy-seventh year,[a] in the eleventh month, which is the month of Shebat. [15]The son of Abubus received them treacherously in the little stronghold called Dok, which he had built; he gave them a great banquet, and hid men there. [16]When Simon and his sons were drunk, Ptolemy and his men rose up, took their weapons, rushed in against Simon in the banquet hall and killed him and his two sons, as well as some of his servants. [17]So he committed an act of great treachery and returned evil for good.

John Succeeds Simon

[18] Then Ptolemy wrote a report about these things and sent it to the king, asking him to send troops to aid him and to turn over to him the towns and the country. [19]He sent other troops to Gazara to do away with John; he sent letters to the captains asking them to come to him so that he might give them silver and gold and gifts; [20]and he sent other troops to take possession of Jerusalem and the temple hill. [21]But someone ran ahead and reported to John at Gazara that his father and brothers had perished, and that "he has sent men to kill you also." [22]When he heard this, he was greatly shocked; he seized the men who came to destroy him and killed them, for he had found out that they were seeking to destroy him.

[23] The rest of the acts of John and his wars and the brave deeds that he did, and the building of the walls that he completed, and his achievements, [24]are written in the annals of his high priesthood, from the time that he became high priest after his father.

[z] Gk *he*　　[a] 134 B.C.

2 Maccabees

Despite its title, 2 Maccabees is not a sequel to 1 Maccabees, though there is some overlap. Written by a different author, its purpose was to provide a theological interpretation of the period.

Second Maccabees contains the earliest stories that glorify martyrdom. The most vivid of these is contained in chapter 7, which tells the grisly but inspiring story of the martyrdom of a mother and her seven sons.

Second Maccabees 12.38–45 is a particularly fascinating passage because it documents the Jewish practice of praying for the dead at least a hundred years before the time of Christ. For the Catholic Church, it forms the Scriptural basis for the doctrine of purgatory and praying for the dead.

Furthermore, this book recounts a dream of Judas Maccabeus in which the high priest Onias and the prophet Jeremiah appear in heaven praying for Judas and the Jews (15.12–16)—reminding us of our belief in the intercession of the saints.

Second Maccabees challenges us to review our commitment to God—how far would we go in defending and maintaining our faith in the midst of powerful opposition? Do we really believe that God will remain faithful even in the worst of times? Do we really believe paradise awaits the faithful?

A Letter to the Jews in Egypt

1 The Jews in Jerusalem and those in the land of Judea,
To their Jewish kindred in Egypt,
Greetings and true peace.

2 May God do good to you, and may he remember his covenant with Abraham and Isaac and Jacob, his faithful servants. [3]May he give you all a heart to worship him and to do his will with a strong heart and a willing spirit. [4]May he open your heart to his law and his commandments, and may he bring peace. [5]May he hear your prayers and be reconciled to you, and may he not forsake you in time of evil. [6]We are now praying for you here.

7 In the reign of Demetrius, in the one hundred sixty-ninth year,[a] we Jews wrote

a 143 B.C.

to you, in the critical distress that came upon us in those years after Jason and his company revolted from the holy land and the kingdom [8]and burned the gate and shed innocent blood. We prayed to the Lord and were heard, and we offered sacrifice and grain offering, and we lit the lamps and set out the loaves. [9]And now see that you keep the festival of booths in the month of Chislev, in the one hundred eighty-eighth year.[b]

A Letter to Aristobulus

10 The people of Jerusalem and of Judea and the senate and Judas,

To Aristobulus, who is of the family of the anointed priests, teacher of King Ptolemy, and to the Jews in Egypt,

Greetings and good health.

11 Having been saved by God out of grave dangers we thank him greatly for taking our side against the king,[c] [12]for he drove out those who fought against the holy city. [13]When the leader reached Persia with a force that seemed irresistible, they were cut to pieces in the temple of Nanea by a deception employed by the priests of the goddess[d] Nanea. [14]On the pretext of intending to marry her, Antiochus came to the place together with his Friends, to secure most of its treasures as a dowry. [15]When the priests of the temple of Nanea had set out the treasures and Antiochus had come with a few men inside the wall of the sacred precinct, they closed the temple as soon as he entered it. [16]Opening a secret door in the ceiling, they threw stones and struck down the leader and his men; they dismembered them and cut off their heads and threw them to the people outside. [17]Blessed in every way be our God, who has brought judgment on those who have behaved impiously.

Fire Consumes Nehemiah's Sacrifice

18 Since on the twenty-fifth day of Chislev we shall celebrate the purification of the temple, we thought it necessary to notify you, in order that you also may celebrate the festival of booths and the festival of the fire given when Nehemiah, who built the temple and the altar, offered sacrifices.

19 For when our ancestors were being led captive to Persia, the pious priests of that time took some of the fire of the altar and secretly hid it in the hollow of a dry cistern, where they took such precautions that the place was unknown to anyone. [20]But after many years had passed, when it pleased God, Nehemiah, having been commissioned by the king of Persia, sent the descendants of the priests who had hidden the fire to get it. And when they reported to us that they had not found fire but only a thick liquid, he ordered them to dip it out and bring it. [21]When the materials for the sacrifices were presented, Nehemiah ordered the priests to sprinkle the liquid on the wood and on the things laid upon it. [22]When this had been done and some time had passed, and when the sun, which had been clouded over, shone out, a great fire blazed up, so that all marveled. [23]And while the sacrifice was being consumed, the priests offered prayer—the priests and everyone. Jonathan led, and the rest responded, as did Nehemiah. [24]The prayer was to this effect:

"O Lord, Lord God, Creator of all things, you are awe-inspiring and strong and just and merciful, you alone are king and are kind, [25]you alone are bountiful, you alone are just and almighty and eternal. You rescue Israel from every evil; you chose the ancestors and consecrated them. [26]Accept this sacrifice on behalf of all your people Israel and preserve your portion and make it holy. [27]Gather together our scattered people, set free those who are slaves among the Gentiles, look on those who are rejected and despised, and let the Gentiles know that you are our God. [28]Punish those who oppress and are insolent with pride. [29]Plant your people in your holy place, as Moses promised."

30 Then the priests sang the hymns. [31]After the materials of the sacrifice had been consumed, Nehemiah ordered that the liquid that was left should be poured on large stones. [32]When this was done, a flame blazed up; but when the light from the altar shone back, it went out. [33]When this matter became known, and it was reported to the king of the Persians that, in the place where the exiled priests had hidden the fire, the liquid had appeared with which Nehemiah and his associates had burned the materials of the sacrifice, [34]the king investigated the matter, and enclosed the place and made it sacred. [35]And with those persons whom the king favored he

---

[b] 124 B.C.   [c] Cn: Gk as those who array themselves against a king   [d] Gk lacks the goddess

exchanged many excellent gifts. [36]Nehemiah and his associates called this "nephthar," which means purification, but by most people it is called naphtha.[e]

Jeremiah Hides the Tent, Ark, and Altar

2 One finds in the records that the prophet Jeremiah ordered those who were being deported to take some of the fire, as has been mentioned, [2]and that the prophet, after giving them the law, instructed those who were being deported not to forget the commandments of the Lord, or to be led astray in their thoughts on seeing the gold and silver statues and their adornment. [3]And with other similar words he exhorted them that the law should not depart from their hearts.

[4] It was also in the same document that the prophet, having received an oracle, ordered that the tent and the ark should follow with him, and that he went out to the mountain where Moses had gone up and had seen the inheritance of God. [5]Jeremiah came and found a cave-dwelling, and he brought there the tent and the ark and the altar of incense; then he sealed up the entrance. [6]Some of those who followed him came up intending to mark the way, but could not find it. [7]When Jeremiah learned of it, he rebuked them and declared: "The place shall remain unknown until God gathers his people together again and shows his mercy. [8]Then the Lord will disclose these things, and the glory of the Lord and the cloud will appear, as they were shown in the case of Moses, and as Solomon asked that the place should be specially consecrated."

[9] It was also made clear that being possessed of wisdom Solomon[f] offered sacrifice for the dedication and completion of the temple. [10]Just as Moses prayed to the Lord, and fire came down from heaven and consumed the sacrifices, so also Solomon prayed, and the fire came down and consumed the whole burnt offerings. [11]And Moses said, "They were consumed because the sin offering had not been eaten." [12]Likewise Solomon also kept the eight days.

[13] The same things are reported in the records and in the memoirs of Nehemiah, and also that he founded a library and collected the books about the kings and prophets, and the writings of David, and letters of kings about votive offerings. [14]In the same way Judas also collected all the books that had been lost on account of the war that had come upon us, and they are in our possession. [15]So if you have need of them, send people to get them for you.

[16] Since, therefore, we are about to celebrate the purification, we write to you. Will you therefore please keep the days? [17]It is God who has saved all his people, and has returned the inheritance to all, and the kingship and the priesthood and the consecration, [18]as he promised through the law. We have hope in God that he will soon have mercy on us and will gather us from everywhere under heaven into his holy place, for he has rescued us from great evils and has purified the place.

The Compiler's Preface

[19] The story of Judas Maccabeus and his brothers, and the purification of the great temple, and the dedication of the altar, [20]and further the wars against Antiochus Epiphanes and his son Eupator, [21]and the appearances that came from heaven to those who fought bravely for Judaism, so that though few in number they seized the whole land and pursued the barbarian hordes, [22]and regained possession of the temple famous throughout the world, and liberated the city, and re-established the laws that were about to be abolished, while the Lord with great kindness became gracious to them— [23]all this, which has been set forth by Jason of Cyrene in five volumes, we shall attempt to condense into a single book. [24]For considering the flood of statistics involved and the difficulty there is for those who wish to enter upon the narratives of history because of the mass of material, [25]we have aimed to please those who wish to read, to make it easy for those who are inclined to memorize, and to profit all readers. [26]For us who have undertaken the toil of abbreviating, it is no light matter but calls for sweat and loss of sleep, [27]just as it is not easy for one who prepares a banquet and seeks the benefit of others. Nevertheless, to secure the gratitude of many we will gladly endure the uncomfortable toil, [28]leaving the responsibility for exact details to the compiler, while devoting our effort to arriving at the outlines of the condensation. [29]For as the master builder

e Gk nephthai   f Gk he

of a new house must be concerned with the whole construction, while the one who undertakes its painting and decoration has to consider only what is suitable for its adornment, such in my judgment is the case with us. 30It is the duty of the original historian to occupy the ground, to discuss matters from every side, and to take trouble with details, 31but the one who recasts the narrative should be allowed to strive for brevity of expression and to forego exhaustive treatment. 32At this point therefore let us begin our narrative, without adding any more to what has already been said; for it would be foolish to lengthen the preface while cutting short the history itself.

Arrival of Heliodorus in Jerusalem

3 While the holy city was inhabited in unbroken peace and the laws were strictly observed because of the piety of the high priest Onias and his hatred of wickedness, 2it came about that the kings themselves honored the place and glorified the temple with the finest presents, 3even to the extent that King Seleucus of Asia defrayed from his own revenues all the expenses connected with the service of the sacrifices.

4 But a man named Simon, of the tribe of Benjamin, who had been made captain of the temple, had a disagreement with the high priest about the administration of the city market. 5Since he could not prevail over Onias, he went to Apollonius of Tarsus,g who at that time was governor of Coelesyria and Phoenicia, 6and reported to him that the treasury in Jerusalem was full of untold sums of money, so that the amount of the funds could not be reckoned, and that they did not belong to the account of the sacrifices, but that it was possible for them to fall under the control of the king. 7When Apollonius met the king, he told him of the money about which he had been informed. The kingh chose Heliodorus, who was in charge of his affairs, and sent him with commands to effect the removal of the reported wealth. 8Heliodorus at once set out on his journey, ostensibly to make a tour of inspection of the cities of Coelesyria and Phoenicia, but in fact to carry out the king's purpose.

9 When he had arrived at Jerusalem and had been kindly welcomed by the high priest ofi the city, he told about the disclosure that had been made and stated why he had come, and he inquired whether this really was the situation. 10The high priest explained that there were some deposits belonging to widows and orphans, 11and also some money of Hyrcanus son of Tobias, a man of very prominent position, and that it totaled in all four hundred talents of silver and two hundred of gold. To such an extent the impious Simon had misrepresented the facts. 12And he said that it was utterly impossible that wrong should be done to those people who had trusted in the holiness of the place and in the sanctity and inviolability of the temple that is honored throughout the whole world.

Heliodorus Plans to Rob the Temple

13 But Heliodorus, because of the orders he had from the king, said that this money must in any case be confiscated for the king's treasury. 14So he set a day and went in to direct the inspection of these funds.

There was no little distress throughout the whole city. 15The priests prostrated themselves before the altar in their priestly vestments and called toward heaven upon him who had given the law about deposits, that he should keep them safe for those who had deposited them. 16To see the appearance of the high priest was to be wounded at heart, for his face and the change in his color disclosed the anguish of his soul. 17For terror and bodily trembling had come over the man, which plainly showed to those who looked at him the pain lodged in his heart. 18People also hurried out of their houses in crowds to make a general supplication because the holy place was about to be brought into dishonor. 19Women, girded with sackcloth under their breasts, thronged the streets. Some of the young women who were kept indoors ran together to the gates, and some to the walls, while others peered out of the windows. 20And holding up their hands to heaven, they all made supplication. 21There was something pitiable in the prostration of the whole populace and the anxiety of the high priest in his great anguish.

g Gk *Apollonius son of Tharseas*   h Gk *He*
i Other ancient authorities read *and*

The Lord Protects His Temple

22 While they were calling upon the Almighty Lord that he would keep what had been entrusted safe and secure for those who had entrusted it, 23Heliodorus went on with what had been decided. 24But when he arrived at the treasury with his bodyguard, then and there the Sovereign of spirits and of all authority caused so great a manifestation that all who had been so bold as to accompany him were astounded by the power of God, and became faint with terror. 25For there appeared to them a magnificently caparisoned horse, with a rider of frightening mien; it rushed furiously at Heliodorus and struck at him with its front hoofs. Its rider was seen to have armor and weapons of gold. 26Two young men also appeared to him, remarkably strong, gloriously beautiful and splendidly dressed, who stood on either side of him and flogged him continuously, inflicting many blows on him. 27When he suddenly fell to the ground and deep darkness came over him, his men took him up, put him on a stretcher, 28and carried him away—this man who had just entered the aforesaid treasury with a great retinue and all his bodyguard but was now unable to help himself. They recognized clearly the sovereign power of God.

Onias Prays for Heliodorus

29 While he lay prostrate, speechless because of the divine intervention and deprived of any hope of recovery, 30they praised the Lord who had acted marvelously for his own place. And the temple, which a little while before was full of fear and disturbance, was filled with joy and gladness, now that the Almighty Lord had appeared.

31 Some of Heliodorus's friends quickly begged Onias to call upon the Most High to grant life to one who was lying quite at his last breath. 32So the high priest, fearing that the king might get the notion that some foul play had been perpetrated by the Jews with regard to Heliodorus, offered sacrifice for the man's recovery. 33While the high priest was making an atonement, the same young men appeared again to Heliodorus dressed in the same clothing, and they stood and said, "Be very grateful to the high priest Onias, since for his sake the Lord has granted you your life. 34And see that you, who have been flogged by heaven, report to all people the majestic power of God." Having said this they vanished.

The Conversion of Heliodorus

35 Then Heliodorus offered sacrifice to the Lord and made very great vows to the Savior of his life, and having bidden Onias farewell, he marched off with his forces to the king. 36He bore testimony to all concerning the deeds of the supreme God, which he had seen with his own eyes. 37When the king asked Heliodorus what sort of person would be suitable to send on another mission to Jerusalem, he replied, 38"If you have any enemy or plotter against your government, send him there, for you will get him back thoroughly flogged, if he survives at all; for there is certainly some power of God about the place. 39For he who has his dwelling in heaven watches over that place himself and brings it aid, and he strikes and destroys those who come to do it injury." 40This was the outcome of the episode of Heliodorus and the protection of the treasury.

Simon Accuses Onias

4 The previously mentioned Simon, who had informed about the money against*j* his own country, slandered Onias, saying that it was he who had incited Heliodorus and had been the real cause of the misfortune. 2He dared to designate as a plotter against the government the man who was the benefactor of the city, the protector of his compatriots, and a zealot for the laws. 3When his hatred progressed to such a degree that even murders were committed by one of Simon's approved agents, 4Onias recognized that the rivalry was serious and that Apollonius son of Menestheus,*k* and governor of Coelesyria and Phoenicia, was intensifying the malice of Simon. 5So he appealed to the king, not accusing his compatriots but having in view the welfare, both public and private, of all the people. 6For he saw that without the king's attention public affairs could not again reach a peaceful settlement, and that Simon would not stop his folly.

---

j Gk *and*   *k* Vg Compare verse 21: Meaning of Gk uncertain

Jason's Reforms

7 When Seleucus died and Antiochus, who was called Epiphanes, succeeded to the kingdom, Jason the brother of Onias obtained the high priesthood by corruption, [8]promising the king at an interview[l] three hundred sixty talents of silver, and from another source of revenue eighty talents. [9]In addition to this he promised to pay one hundred fifty more if permission were given to establish by his authority a gymnasium and a body of youth for it, and to enroll the people of Jerusalem as citizens of Antioch. [10]When the king assented and Jason[m] came to office, he at once shifted his compatriots over to the Greek way of life.

11 He set aside the existing royal concessions to the Jews, secured through John the father of Eupolemus, who went on the mission to establish friendship and alliance with the Romans; and he destroyed the lawful ways of living and introduced new customs contrary to the law. [12]He took delight in establishing a gymnasium right under the citadel, and he induced the noblest of the young men to wear the Greek hat. [13]There was such an extreme of Hellenization and increase in the adoption of foreign ways because of the surpassing wickedness of Jason, who was ungodly and no true[n] high priest, [14]that the priests were no longer intent upon their service at the altar. Despising the sanctuary and neglecting the sacrifices, they hurried to take part in the unlawful proceedings in the wrestling arena after the signal for the discus-throwing, [15]disdaining the honors prized by their ancestors and putting the highest value upon Greek forms of prestige. [16]For this reason heavy disaster overtook them, and those whose ways of living they admired and wished to imitate completely became their enemies and punished them. [17]It is no light thing to show irreverence to the divine laws—a fact that later events will make clear.

Jason Introduces Greek Customs

18 When the quadrennial games were being held at Tyre and the king was present, [19]the vile Jason sent envoys, chosen as being Antiochian citizens from Jerusalem, to carry three hundred silver drachmas for the sacrifice to Hercules. Those who carried the money, however, thought best not to use it for sacrifice, because that was inappropriate, but to expend it for another purpose. [20]So this money was intended by the sender for the sacrifice to Hercules, but by the decision of its carriers it was applied to the construction of triremes.

21 When Apollonius son of Menestheus was sent to Egypt for the coronation[o] of Philometor as king, Antiochus learned that Philometor[m] had become hostile to his government, and he took measures for his own security. Therefore upon arriving at Joppa he proceeded to Jerusalem. [22]He was welcomed magnificently by Jason and the city, and ushered in with a blaze of torches and with shouts. Then he marched his army into Phoenicia.

Menelaus Becomes High Priest

23 After a period of three years Jason sent Menelaus, the brother of the previously mentioned Simon, to carry the money to the king and to complete the records of essential business. [24]But he, when presented to the king, extolled him with an air of authority, and secured the high priesthood for himself, outbidding Jason by three hundred talents of silver. [25]After receiving the king's orders he returned, possessing no qualification for the high priesthood, but having the hot temper of a cruel tyrant and the rage of a savage wild beast. [26]So Jason, who after supplanting his own brother was supplanted by another man, was driven as a fugitive into the land of Ammon. [27]Although Menelaus continued to hold the office, he did not pay regularly any of the money promised to the king. [28]When Sostratus the captain of the citadel kept requesting payment—for the collection of the revenue was his responsibility—the two of them were summoned by the king on account of this issue. [29]Menelaus left his own brother Lysimachus as deputy in the high priesthood, while Sostratus left Crates, the commander of the Cyprian troops.

The Murder of Onias

30 While such was the state of affairs, it happened that the people of Tarsus and of Mallus revolted because their cities had been given as a present to Antiochis, the

---

l Or *by a petition*   *m* Gk *he*   *n* Gk lacks *true*
o Meaning of Gk uncertain

king's concubine. 31So the king went hurriedly to settle the trouble, leaving Andronicus, a man of high rank, to act as his
deputy. 32But Menelaus, thinking he had
obtained a suitable opportunity, stole
some of the gold vessels of the temple and
gave them to Andronicus; other vessels, as
it happened, he had sold to Tyre and the
neighboring cities. 33When Onias became
fully aware of these acts, he publicly exposed them, having first withdrawn to a
place of sanctuary at Daphne near Antioch. 34Therefore Menelaus, taking Andronicus aside, urged him to kill Onias. Andronicus[p] came to Onias, and resorting
to treachery, offered him sworn pledges
and gave him his right hand; he persuaded him, though still suspicious, to come
out from the place of sanctuary; then,
with no regard for justice, he immediately
put him out of the way.

Andronicus Is Punished

35 For this reason not only Jews, but
many also of other nations, were grieved
and displeased at the unjust murder of the
man. 36When the king returned from the
region of Cilicia, the Jews in the city[q] appealed to him with regard to the unreasonable murder of Onias, and the Greeks
shared their hatred of the crime. 37There-
fore Antiochus was grieved at heart and
filled with pity, and wept because of the
moderation and good conduct of the deceased. 38Inflamed with anger, he immediately stripped off the purple robe from
Andronicus, tore off his clothes, and led
him around the whole city to that very
place where he had committed the outrage against Onias, and there he dispatched the bloodthirsty fellow. The Lord
thus repaid him with the punishment he
deserved.

Unpopularity of Lysimachus and Menelaus

39 When many acts of sacrilege had
been committed in the city by Lysimachus
with the connivance of Menelaus, and
when report of them had spread abroad,
the populace gathered against Lysimachus, because many of the gold vessels
had already been stolen. 40Since the
crowds were becoming aroused and filled
with anger, Lysimachus armed about
three thousand men and launched an unjust attack, under the leadership of a certain Auranus, a man advanced in years
and no less advanced in folly. 41But when
the Jews[r] became aware that Lysimachus
was attacking them, some picked up
stones, some blocks of wood, and others
took handfuls of the ashes that were lying
around, and threw them in wild confusion at Lysimachus and his men. 42As a
result, they wounded many of them, and
killed some, and put all the rest to flight;
the temple robber himself they killed
close by the treasury.

43 Charges were brought against
Menelaus about this incident. 44When the
king came to Tyre, three men sent by the
senate presented the case before him.
45But Menelaus, already as good as beat-
en, promised a substantial bribe to Ptolemy son of Dorymenes to win over the
king. 46Therefore Ptolemy, taking the king
aside into a colonnade as if for refreshment, induced the king to change his
mind. 47Menelaus, the cause of all the
trouble, he acquitted of the charges
against him, while he sentenced to death
those unfortunate men, who would have
been freed uncondemned if they had
pleaded even before Scythians. 48And so
those who had spoken for the city and the
villages[s] and the holy vessels quickly suffered the unjust penalty. 49Therefore even
the Tyrians, showing their hatred of the
crime, provided magnificently for their
funeral. 50But Menelaus, because of the
greed of those in power, remained in office, growing in wickedness, having become the chief plotter against his compatriots.

Jason Tries to Regain Control

5 About this time Antiochus made his
second invasion of Egypt. 2And it
happened that, for almost forty days,
there appeared over all the city golden-
clad cavalry charging through the air, in
companies fully armed with lances and
drawn swords— 3troops of cavalry drawn
up, attacks and counterattacks made on
this side and on that, brandishing of
shields, massing of spears, hurling of missiles, the flash of golden trappings, and
armor of all kinds. 4Therefore everyone
prayed that the apparition might prove to
have been a good omen.

5 When a false rumor arose that Antiochus was dead, Jason took no fewer than
a thousand men and suddenly made an

[p] Gk *He* [q] Or *in each city* [r] Gk *they* [s] Other
ancient authorities read *the people*

assault on the city. When the troops on the wall had been forced back and at last the city was being taken, Menelaus took refuge in the citadel. ⁶But Jason kept relentlessly slaughtering his compatriots, not realizing that success at the cost of one's kindred is the greatest misfortune, but imagining that he was setting up trophies of victory over enemies and not over compatriots. ⁷He did not, however, gain control of the government; in the end he got only disgrace from his conspiracy, and fled again into the country of the Ammonites. ⁸Finally he met a miserable end. Accused[t] before Aretas the ruler of the Arabs, fleeing from city to city, pursued by everyone, hated as a rebel against the laws, and abhorred as the executioner of his country and his compatriots, he was cast ashore in Egypt. ⁹There he who had driven many from their own country into exile died in exile, having embarked to go to the Lacedaemonians in hope of finding protection because of their kinship. ¹⁰He who had cast out many to lie unburied had no one to mourn for him; he had no funeral of any sort and no place in the tomb of his ancestors.

11 When news of what had happened reached the king, he took it to mean that Judea was in revolt. So, raging inwardly, he left Egypt and took the city by storm. ¹²He commanded his soldiers to cut down relentlessly everyone they met and to kill those who went into their houses. ¹³Then there was massacre of young and old, destruction of boys, women, and children, and slaughter of young girls and infants. ¹⁴Within the total of three days eighty thousand were destroyed, forty thousand in hand-to-hand fighting, and as many were sold into slavery as were killed.

Pillage of the Temple

15 Not content with this, Antiochus[u] dared to enter the most holy temple in all the world, guided by Menelaus, who had become a traitor both to the laws and to his country. ¹⁶He took the holy vessels with his polluted hands, and swept away with profane hands the votive offerings that other kings had made to enhance the glory and honor of the place. ¹⁷Antiochus was elated in spirit, and did not perceive that the Lord was angered for a little while because of the sins of those who lived in the city, and that this was the reason he was disregarding the holy place. ¹⁸But if it

had not happened that they were involved in many sins, this man would have been flogged and turned back from his rash act as soon as he came forward, just as Heliodorus had been, whom King Seleucus sent to inspect the treasury. ¹⁹But the Lord did not choose the nation for the sake of the holy place, but the place for the sake of the nation. ²⁰Therefore the place itself shared in the misfortunes that befell the nation and afterward participated in its benefits; and what was forsaken in the wrath of the Almighty was restored again in all its glory when the great Lord became reconciled.

21 So Antiochus carried off eighteen hundred talents from the temple, and hurried away to Antioch, thinking in his arrogance that he could sail on the land and walk on the sea, because his mind was elated. ²²He left governors to oppress the people: at Jerusalem, Philip, by birth a Phrygian and in character more barbarous than the man who appointed him; ²³and at Gerizim, Andronicus; and besides these Menelaus, who lorded it over his compatriots worse than the others did. In his malice toward the Jewish citizens,[v] ²⁴Antiochus[u] sent Apollonius, the captain of the Mysians, with an army of twenty-two thousand, and commanded him to kill all the grown men and to sell the women and boys as slaves. ²⁵When this man arrived in Jerusalem, he pretended to be peaceably disposed and waited until the holy sabbath day; then, finding the Jews not at work, he ordered his troops to parade under arms. ²⁶He put to the sword all those who came out to see them, then rushed into the city with his armed warriors and killed great numbers of people.

27 But Judas Maccabeus, with about nine others, got away to the wilderness, and kept himself and his companions alive in the mountains as wild animals do; they continued to live on what grew wild, so that they might not share in the defilement.

The Suppression of Judaism

6 Not long after this, the king sent an Athenian[w] senator[x] to compel the Jews to forsake the laws of their ancestors

---

[t] Cn: Gk *Imprisoned*   [u] Gk *he*   [v] Or *worse than the others did in his malice toward the Jewish citizens*   [w] Other ancient authorities read *Antiochian*   [x] Or *Geron an Athenian*

and no longer to live by the laws of God; ²also to pollute the temple in Jerusalem and to call it the temple of Olympian Zeus, and to call the one in Gerizim the temple of Zeus-the-Friend-of-Strangers, as did the people who lived in that place.

3 Harsh and utterly grievous was the onslaught of evil. ⁴For the temple was filled with debauchery and reveling by the Gentiles, who dallied with prostitutes and had intercourse with women within the sacred precincts, and besides brought in things for sacrifice that were unfit. ⁵The altar was covered with abominable offerings that were forbidden by the laws. ⁶People could neither keep the sabbath, nor observe the festivals of their ancestors, nor so much as confess themselves to be Jews.

7 On the monthly celebration of the king's birthday, the Jews *y* were taken, under bitter constraint, to partake of the sacrifices; and when a festival of Dionysus was celebrated, they were compelled to wear wreaths of ivy and to walk in the procession in honor of Dionysus. ⁸At the suggestion of the people of Ptolemais *z* a decree was issued to the neighboring Greek cities that they should adopt the same policy toward the Jews and make them partake of the sacrifices, ⁹and should kill those who did not choose to change over to Greek customs. One could see, therefore, the misery that had come upon them. ¹⁰For example, two women were brought in for having circumcised their children. They publicly paraded them around the city, with their babies hanging at their breasts, and then hurled them down headlong from the wall. ¹¹Others who had assembled in the caves nearby, in order to observe the seventh day secretly, were betrayed to Philip and were all burned together, because their piety kept them from defending themselves, in view of their regard for that most holy day.

Providential Significance of the Persecution

12 Now I urge those who read this book not to be depressed by such calamities, but to recognize that these punishments were designed not to destroy but to discipline our people. ¹³In fact, it is a sign of great kindness not to let the impious alone for long, but to punish them immediately. ¹⁴For in the case of the other nations the Lord waits patiently to punish them until they have reached the full measure of their sins; but he does not deal in this way with us, ¹⁵in order that he may not take vengeance on us afterward when our sins have reached their height. ¹⁶Therefore he never withdraws his mercy from us. Although he disciplines us with calamities, he does not forsake his own people. ¹⁷Let what we have said serve as a reminder; we must go on briefly with the story.

The Martyrdom of Eleazar

18 Eleazar, one of the scribes in high position, a man now advanced in age and of noble presence, was being forced to open his mouth to eat swine's flesh. ¹⁹But he, welcoming death with honor rather than life with pollution, went up to the rack of his own accord, spitting out the flesh, ²⁰as all ought to go who have the courage to refuse things that it is not right to taste, even for the natural love of life.

21 Those who were in charge of that unlawful sacrifice took the man aside because of their long acquaintance with him, and privately urged him to bring meat of his own providing, proper for him to use, and to pretend that he was eating the flesh of the sacrificial meal that had been commanded by the king, ²²so that by doing this he might be saved from death, and be treated kindly on account of his old friendship with them. ²³But making a high resolve, worthy of his years and the dignity of his old age and the gray hairs that he had reached with distinction and his excellent life even from childhood, and moreover according to the holy God-given law, he declared himself quickly, telling them to send him to Hades.

24 "Such pretense is not worthy of our time of life," he said, "for many of the young might suppose that Eleazar in his ninetieth year had gone over to an alien religion, ²⁵and through my pretense, for the sake of living a brief moment longer, they would be led astray because of me, while I defile and disgrace my old age. ²⁶Even if for the present I would avoid the punishment of mortals, yet whether I live or die I will not escape the hands of the Almighty. ²⁷Therefore, by bravely giving up my life now, I will show myself worthy

y Gk *they*   *z* Cn: Gk *suggestion of the Ptolemies* (or *of Ptolemy*)

of my old age ²⁸and leave to the young a noble example of how to die a good death willingly and nobly for the revered and holy laws."

When he had said this, he went^a at once to the rack. ²⁹Those who a little before had acted toward him with goodwill now changed to ill will, because the words he had uttered were in their opinion sheer madness.^b ³⁰When he was about to die under the blows, he groaned aloud and

said: "It is clear to the Lord in his holy knowledge that, though I might have been saved from death, I am enduring terrible sufferings in my body under this beating, but in my soul I am glad to suffer these things because I fear him."

31 So in this way he died, leaving in his death an example of nobility and a me-

a Other ancient authorities read *was dragged*
b Meaning of Gk uncertain

THURSDAY

*L*ove Makes Everything Easy

Scripture Reading for Today:
2 Maccabees 6.18–31

Verse for Today:
2 Maccabees 6.30

Nijole Sadunaite, a Lithuanian Catholic, was arrested by the Soviet KGB for circulating and reproducing an underground newspaper, The Chronicle of the Lithuanian Catholic Church. During her 1975 trial, she spoke out fearlessly against the "physical and spiritual tyranny" of the Communist regime. "Every day your crimes are bringing you closer to the dust-heap of history," she told her accusers. This is an excerpt from her final statement to the court. Nijole Sadunaite was sentenced to three years in a Siberian labor camp and three years of exile.

This is the happiest day of my life. I'm being tried because I love our people and desire the truth. Loving men is the greatest love and fighting for their rights is the most beautiful love song. May it echo in everyone's heart and never stop! I'm privileged; my fate is an honorable one: Not only have I fought for human rights and justice, but I'm being punished for doing so. My sentence will be my triumph! I will gladly lose my freedom for the freedom of others, and I'm willing to die so that others may live.

Today I'm standing on the side of Eternal Truth—Jesus Christ— and I recall his fourth beatitude: "Blessed are those who hunger and thirst for righteousness, for they will be filled." How can I fail to be happy when Almighty God has shown that light triumphs over darkness and truth over lies and falsehood! In order to bring this about, I'm willing not only to be imprisoned, but also to die.

Yesterday you were surprised that I was in such good spirits at such a tragic hour of my life. This proves that my heart is burning with love for all people, since only love makes everything seem easy! We have to condemn evil as harshly as possible, but we must love men, even if they are wrong. And we can learn to do this in the school of Jesus Christ, who is our Way, our Truth and our Life. May your kingdom, Jesus, come into every soul!

—NIJOLE SADUNAITE

Go to page 615 for your next devotional reading.

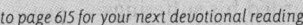

morial of courage, not only to the young but to the great body of his nation.

The Martyrdom of Seven Brothers

7 It happened also that seven brothers and their mother were arrested and were being compelled by the king, under torture with whips and thongs, to partake of unlawful swine's flesh. ²One of them, acting as their spokesman, said, "What do you intend to ask and learn from us? For we are ready to die rather than transgress the laws of our ancestors."

3 The king fell into a rage, and gave orders to have pans and caldrons heated. ⁴These were heated immediately, and he commanded that the tongue of their spokesman be cut out and that they scalp him and cut off his hands and feet, while the rest of the brothers and the mother looked on. ⁵When he was utterly helpless, the king*c* ordered them to take him to the fire, still breathing, and to fry him in a pan. The smoke from the pan spread widely, but the brothers*d* and their mother encouraged one another to die nobly, saying, ⁶"The Lord God is watching over us and in truth has compassion on us, as Moses declared in his song that bore witness against the people to their faces, when he said, 'And he will have compassion on his servants.' "*e*

7 After the first brother had died in this way, they brought forward the second for their sport. They tore off the skin of his head with the hair, and asked him, "Will you eat rather than have your body punished limb by limb?" ⁸He replied in the language of his ancestors and said to them, "No." Therefore he in turn underwent tortures as the first brother had done. ⁹And when he was at his last breath, he said, "You accursed wretch, you dismiss us from this present life, but the King of the universe will raise us up to an everlasting renewal of life, because we have died for his laws."

10 After him, the third was the victim of their sport. When it was demanded, he quickly put out his tongue and courageously stretched forth his hands, ¹¹and said nobly, "I got these from Heaven, and because of his laws I disdain them, and from him I hope to get them back again." ¹²As a result the king himself and those with him were astonished at the young man's spirit, for he regarded his sufferings as nothing.

13 After he too had died, they maltreated and tortured the fourth in the same way. ¹⁴When he was near death, he said, "One cannot but choose to die at the hands of mortals and to cherish the hope God gives of being raised again by him. But for you there will be no resurrection to life!"

15 Next they brought forward the fifth and maltreated him. ¹⁶But he looked at the king,*f* and said, "Because you have authority among mortals, though you also are mortal, you do what you please. But do not think that God has forsaken our people. ¹⁷Keep on, and see how his mighty power will torture you and your descendants!"

18 After him they brought forward the sixth. And when he was about to die, he said, "Do not deceive yourself in vain. For we are suffering these things on our own account, because of our sins against our own God. Therefore*g* astounding things have happened. ¹⁹But do not think that you will go unpunished for having tried to fight against God!"

20 The mother was especially admirable and worthy of honorable memory. Although she saw her seven sons perish within a single day, she bore it with good courage because of her hope in the Lord. ²¹She encouraged each of them in the language of their ancestors. Filled with a noble spirit, she reinforced her woman's reasoning with a man's courage, and said to them, ²²"I do not know how you came into being in my womb. It was not I who gave you life and breath, nor I who set in order the elements within each of you. ²³Therefore the Creator of the world, who shaped the beginning of humankind and devised the origin of all things, will in his mercy give life and breath back to you again, since you now forget yourselves for the sake of his laws."

24 Antiochus felt that he was being treated with contempt, and he was suspicious of her reproachful tone. The youngest brother being still alive, Antiochus*c* not only appealed to him in words, but promised with oaths that he would make him rich and enviable if he would turn from the ways of his ancestors, and that he would take him for his Friend and entrust him with public affairs. ²⁵Since the

---

c Gk *he*　　*d* Gk *they*　　*e* Gk *slaves*　　*f* Gk *at him*
g Lat: Other ancient authorities lack *Therefore*

young man would not listen to him at all, the king called the mother to him and urged her to advise the youth to save himself. [26]After much urging on his part, she undertook to persuade her son. [27]But, leaning close to him, she spoke in their native language as follows, deriding the cruel tyrant: "My son, have pity on me. I carried you nine months in my womb, and nursed you for three years, and have reared you and brought you up to this point in your life, and have taken care of you.[h] [28]I beg you, my child, to look at the heaven and the earth and see everything that is in them, and recognize that God did not make them out of things that existed.[i] And in the same way the human race came into being. [29]Do not fear this butcher, but prove worthy of your brothers. Accept death, so that in God's mercy I may get you back again along with your brothers."

30 While she was still speaking, the young man said, "What are you[j] waiting for? I will not obey the king's command, but I obey the command of the law that was given to our ancestors through Moses. [31]But you,[k] who have contrived all sorts of evil against the Hebrews, will certainly not escape the hands of God. [32]For we are suffering because of our own sins. [33]And if our living Lord is angry for a little while, to rebuke and discipline us, he will again be reconciled with his own servants.[l] [34]But you, unholy wretch, you most defiled of all mortals, do not be elated in vain and puffed up by uncertain hopes, when you raise your hand against the children of heaven. [35]You have not yet escaped the judgment of the almighty, all-seeing God. [36]For our brothers after enduring a brief suffering have drunk[m] of ever-flowing life, under God's covenant; but you, by the judgment of God, will receive just punishment for your arrogance. [37]I, like my brothers, give up body and life for the laws of our ancestors, appealing to God to show mercy soon to our nation and by trials and plagues to make you confess that he alone is God, [38]and through me and my brothers to bring to an end the wrath of the Almighty that has justly fallen on our whole nation."

39 The king fell into a rage, and handled him worse than the others, being exasperated at his scorn. [40]So he died in his integrity, putting his whole trust in the Lord.

41 Last of all, the mother died, after her sons.

42 Let this be enough, then, about the eating of sacrifices and the extreme tortures.

The Revolt of Judas Maccabeus

8 Meanwhile Judas, who was also called Maccabeus, and his companions secretly entered the villages and summoned their kindred and enlisted those who had continued in the Jewish faith, and so they gathered about six thousand. [2]They implored the Lord to look upon the people who were oppressed by all; and to have pity on the temple that had been profaned by the godless; [3]to have mercy on the city that was being destroyed and about to be leveled to the ground; to hearken to the blood that cried out to him; [4]to remember also the lawless destruction of the innocent babies and the blasphemies committed against his name; and to show his hatred of evil.

5 As soon as Maccabeus got his army organized, the Gentiles could not withstand him, for the wrath of the Lord had turned to mercy. [6]Coming without warning, he would set fire to towns and villages. He captured strategic positions and put to flight not a few of the enemy. [7]He found the nights most advantageous for such attacks. And talk of his valor spread everywhere.

8 When Philip saw that the man was gaining ground little by little, and that he was pushing ahead with more frequent successes, he wrote to Ptolemy, the governor of Coelesyria and Phoenicia, to come to the aid of the king's government. [9]Then Ptolemy[n] promptly appointed Nicanor son of Patroclus, one of the king's chief[o] Friends, and sent him, in command of no fewer than twenty thousand Gentiles of all nations, to wipe out the whole race of Judea. He associated with him Gorgias, a general and a man of experience in military service. [10]Nicanor determined to make up for the king the tribute due to the Romans, two thousand talents, by selling the captured Jews into slavery. [11]So he immediately sent to the towns on the sea-

[h] Or *have borne the burden of your education*   [i] Or *God made them out of things that did not exist*   [j] The Gk here for *you* is plural   [k] The Gk here for *you* is singular   [l] Gk *slaves*   [m] Cn: Gk *fallen*   [n] Gk *he*   [o] Gk *one of the first*

coast, inviting them to buy Jewish slaves and promising to hand over ninety slaves for a talent, not expecting the judgment from the Almighty that was about to overtake him.

Preparation for Battle

12 Word came to Judas concerning Nicanor's invasion; and when he told his companions of the arrival of the army, 13those who were cowardly and distrustful of God's justice ran off and got away. 14Others sold all their remaining property, and at the same time implored the Lord to rescue those who had been sold by the ungodly Nicanor before he ever met them, 15if not for their own sake, then for the sake of the covenants made with their ancestors, and because he had called them by his holy and glorious name. 16But Maccabeus gathered his forces together, to the number six thousand, and exhorted them not to be frightened by the enemy and not to fear the great multitude of Gentiles who were wickedly coming against them, but to fight nobly, 17keeping before their eyes the lawless outrage that the Gentiles*p* had committed against the holy place, and the torture of the derided city, and besides, the overthrow of their ancestral way of life. 18"For they trust to arms and acts of daring," he said, "but we trust in the Almighty God, who is able with a single nod to strike down those who are coming against us, and even, if necessary, the whole world."

19 Moreover, he told them of the occasions when help came to their ancestors; how, in the time of Sennacherib, when one hundred eighty-five thousand perished, 20and the time of the battle against the Galatians that took place in Babylonia, when eight thousand Jews*q* fought along with four thousand Macedonians; yet when the Macedonians were hard pressed, the eight thousand, by the help that came to them from heaven, destroyed one hundred twenty thousand Galatians*r* and took a great amount of booty.

Judas Defeats Nicanor

21 With these words he filled them with courage and made them ready to die for their laws and their country; then he divided his army into four parts. 22He appointed his brothers also, Simon and Joseph and Jonathan, each to command a division, putting fifteen hundred men under each. 23Besides, he appointed Eleazar to read aloud*s* from the holy book, and gave the watchword, "The help of God"; then, leading the first division himself, he joined battle with Nicanor.

24 With the Almighty as their ally, they killed more than nine thousand of the enemy, and wounded and disabled most of Nicanor's army, and forced them all to flee. 25They captured the money of those who had come to buy them as slaves. After pursuing them for some distance, they were obliged to return because the hour was late. 26It was the day before the sabbath, and for that reason they did not continue their pursuit. 27When they had collected the arms of the enemy and stripped them of their spoils, they kept the sabbath, giving great praise and thanks to the Lord, who had preserved them for that day and allotted it to them as the beginning of mercy. 28After the sabbath they gave some of the spoils to those who had been tortured and to the widows and orphans, and distributed the rest among themselves and their children. 29When they had done this, they made common supplication and implored the merciful Lord to be wholly reconciled with his servants.*t*

Judas Defeats Timothy and Bacchides

30 In encounters with the forces of Timothy and Bacchides they killed more than twenty thousand of them and got possession of some exceedingly high strongholds, and they divided a very large amount of plunder, giving to those who had been tortured and to the orphans and widows, and also to the aged, shares equal to their own. 31They collected the arms of the enemy,*u* and carefully stored all of them in strategic places; the rest of the spoils they carried to Jerusalem. 32They killed the commander of Timothy's forces, a most wicked man, and one who had greatly troubled the Jews. 33While they were celebrating the victory in the city of their ancestors, they burned those who had set fire to the sacred gates, Callisthenes and some others, who had fled into one little house; so these received the proper reward for their impiety.*s* 34 The thrice-accursed Nicanor, who

p Gk they   q Gk lacks Jews   r Gk lacks Galatians
s Meaning of Gk uncertain   t Gk slaves   u Gk
their arms

had brought the thousand merchants to buy the Jews, 35having been humbled with the help of the Lord by opponents whom he regarded as of the least account, took off his splendid uniform and made his way alone like a runaway slave across the country until he reached Antioch, having succeeded chiefly in the destruction of his own army! 36So he who had undertaken to secure tribute for the Romans by the capture of the people of Jerusalem proclaimed that the Jews had a Defender, and that therefore the Jews were invulnerable, because they followed the laws ordained by him.

The Last Campaign of Antiochus Epiphanes

9 About that time, as it happened, Antiochus had retreated in disorder from the region of Persia. 2He had entered the city called Persepolis and attempted to rob the temples and control the city. Therefore the people rushed to the rescue with arms, and Antiochus and his army were defeated,*v* with the result that Antiochus was put to flight by the inhabitants and beat a shameful retreat. 3While he was in Ecbatana, news came to him of what had happened to Nicanor and the forces of Timothy. 4Transported with rage, he conceived the idea of turning upon the Jews the injury done by those who had put him to flight; so he ordered his charioteer to drive without stopping until he completed the journey. But the judgment of heaven rode with him! For in his arrogance he said, "When I get there I will make Jerusalem a cemetery of Jews."

5 But the all-seeing Lord, the God of Israel, struck him with an incurable and invisible blow. As soon as he stopped speaking he was seized with a pain in his bowels, for which there was no relief, and with sharp internal tortures— 6and that very justly, for he had tortured the bowels of others with many and strange inflictions. 7Yet he did not in any way stop his insolence, but was even more filled with arrogance, breathing fire in his rage against the Jews, and giving orders to drive even faster. And so it came about that he fell out of his chariot as it was rushing along, and the fall was so hard as to torture every limb of his body. 8Thus he who only a little while before had thought in his superhuman arrogance that he could command the waves of the sea, and had imagined that he could weigh the

high mountains in a balance, was brought down to earth and carried in a litter, making the power of God manifest to all. 9And so the ungodly man's body swarmed with worms, and while he was still living in anguish and pain, his flesh rotted away, and because of the stench the whole army felt revulsion at his decay. 10Because of his intolerable stench no one was able to carry the man who a little while before had thought that he could touch the stars of heaven. 11Then it was that, broken in spirit, he began to lose much of his arrogance and to come to his senses under the scourge of God, for he was tortured with pain every moment. 12And when he could not endure his own stench, he uttered these words, "It is right to be subject to God; mortals should not think that they are equal to God."*w*

Antiochus Makes a Promise to God

13 Then the abominable fellow made a vow to the Lord, who would no longer have mercy on him, stating 14that the holy city, which he was hurrying to level to the ground and to make a cemetery, he was now declaring to be free; 15and the Jews, whom he had not considered worth burying but had planned to throw out with their children for the wild animals and for the birds to eat, he would make, all of them, equal to citizens of Athens; 16and the holy sanctuary, which he had formerly plundered, he would adorn with the finest offerings; and all the holy vessels he would give back, many times over; and the expenses incurred for the sacrifices he would provide from his own revenues; 17and in addition to all this he also would become a Jew and would visit every inhabited place to proclaim the power of God. 18But when his sufferings did not in any way abate, for the judgment of God had justly come upon him, he gave up all hope for himself and wrote to the Jews the following letter, in the form of a supplication. This was its content:

Antiochus's Letter and Death

19 "To his worthy Jewish citizens, Antiochus their king and general sends hearty greetings and good wishes for their health and prosperity. 20If you and your children are well and your affairs are as

v Gk they were defeated   w Or not think thoughts proper only to God

you wish, I am glad. As my hope is in heaven, [21]I remember with affection your esteem and goodwill. On my way back from the region of Persia I suffered an annoying illness, and I have deemed it necessary to take thought for the general security of all. [22]I do not despair of my condition, for I have good hope of recovering from my illness, [23]but I observed that my father, on the occasions when he made expeditions into the upper country, appointed his successor, [24]so that, if anything unexpected happened or any unwelcome news came, the people throughout the realm would not be troubled, for they would know to whom the government was left. [25]Moreover, I understand how the princes along the borders and the neighbors of my kingdom keep watching for opportunities and waiting to see what will happen. So I have appointed my son Antiochus to be king, whom I have often entrusted and commended to most of you when I hurried off to the upper provinces; and I have written to him what is written here. [26]I therefore urge and beg you to remember the public and private services rendered to you and to maintain your present goodwill, each of you, toward me and my son. [27]For I am sure that he will follow my policy and will treat you with moderation and kindness."

[28] So the murderer and blasphemer, having endured the more intense suffering, such as he had inflicted on others, came to the end of his life by a most pitiable fate, among the mountains in a strange land. [29]And Philip, one of his courtiers, took his body home; then, fearing the son of Antiochus, he withdrew to Ptolemy Philometor in Egypt.

Purification of the Temple

10 Now Maccabeus and his followers, the Lord leading them on, recovered the temple and the city; [2]they tore down the altars that had been built in the public square by the foreigners, and also destroyed the sacred precincts. [3]They purified the sanctuary, and made another altar of sacrifice; then, striking fire out of flint, they offered sacrifices, after a lapse of two years, and they offered incense and lighted lamps and set out the bread of the Presence. [4]When they had done this, they fell prostrate and implored the Lord that they might never again fall into such misfortunes, but that, if they should ever sin, they might be disciplined by him with forbearance and not be handed over to blasphemous and barbarous nations. [5]It happened that on the same day on which the sanctuary had been profaned by the foreigners, the purification of the sanctuary took place, that is, on the twenty-fifth day of the same month, which was Chislev. [6]They celebrated it for eight days with rejoicing, in the manner of the festival of booths, remembering how not long before, during the festival of booths, they had been wandering in the mountains and caves like wild animals. [7]Therefore, carrying ivy-wreathed wands and beautiful branches and also fronds of palm, they offered hymns of thanksgiving to him who had given success to the purifying of his own holy place. [8]They decreed by public edict, ratified by vote, that the whole nation of the Jews should observe these days every year.

[9] Such then was the end of Antiochus, who was called Epiphanes.

Accession of Antiochus Eupator

[10] Now we will tell what took place under Antiochus Eupator, who was the son of that ungodly man, and will give a brief summary of the principal calamities of the wars. [11]This man, when he succeeded to the kingdom, appointed one Lysias to have charge of the government and to be chief governor of Coelesyria and Phoenicia. [12]Ptolemy, who was called Macron, took the lead in showing justice to the Jews because of the wrong that had been done to them, and attempted to maintain peaceful relations with them. [13]As a result he was accused before Eupator by the king's Friends. He heard himself called a traitor at every turn, because he had abandoned Cyprus, which Philometor had entrusted to him, and had gone over to Antiochus Epiphanes. Unable to command the respect due his office,[x] he took poison and ended his life.

Campaign in Idumea

[14] When Gorgias became governor of the region, he maintained a force of mercenaries, and at every turn kept attacking the Jews. [15]Besides this, the Idumeans, who had control of important strongholds, were harassing the Jews; they received those who were banished from Je-

[x] Cn: Meaning of Gk uncertain

rusalem, and endeavored to keep up the war. [16]But Maccabeus and his forces, after making solemn supplication and imploring God to fight on their side, rushed to the strongholds of the Idumeans. [17]Attacking them vigorously, they gained possession of the places, and beat off all who fought upon the wall, and slaughtered those whom they encountered, killing no fewer than twenty thousand.

18 When at least nine thousand took refuge in two very strong towers well equipped to withstand a siege, [19]Maccabeus left Simon and Joseph, and also Zacchaeus and his troops, a force sufficient to besiege them; and he himself set off for places where he was more urgently needed. [20]But those with Simon, who were money-hungry, were bribed by some of those who were in the towers, and on receiving seventy thousand drachmas let some of them slip away. [21]When word of what had happened came to Maccabeus, he gathered the leaders of the people, and accused these men of having sold their kindred for money by setting their enemies free to fight against them. [22]Then he killed these men who had turned traitor, and immediately captured the two towers. [23]Having success at arms in everything he undertook, he destroyed more than twenty thousand in the two strongholds.

Judas Defeats Timothy

24 Now Timothy, who had been defeated by the Jews before, gathered a tremendous force of mercenaries and collected the cavalry from Asia in no small number. He came on, intending to take Judea by storm. [25]As he drew near, Maccabeus and his men sprinkled dust on their heads and girded their loins with sackcloth, in supplication to God. [26]Falling upon the steps before the altar, they implored him to be gracious to them and to be an enemy to their enemies and an adversary to their adversaries, as the law declares. [27]And rising from their prayer they took up their arms and advanced a considerable distance from the city; and when they came near the enemy they halted. [28]Just as dawn was breaking, the two armies joined battle, the one having as pledge of success and victory not only their valor but also their reliance on the Lord, while the other made rage their leader in the fight.

29 When the battle became fierce, there appeared to the enemy from heaven five resplendent men on horses with golden bridles, and they were leading the Jews. [30]Two of them took Maccabeus between them, and shielding him with their own armor and weapons, they kept him from being wounded. They showered arrows and thunderbolts on the enemy, so that, confused and blinded, they were thrown into disorder and cut to pieces. [31]Twenty thousand five hundred were slaughtered, besides six hundred cavalry.

32 Timothy himself fled to a stronghold called Gazara, especially well garrisoned, where Chaereas was commander. [33]Then Maccabeus and his men were glad, and they besieged the fort for four days. [34]The men within, relying on the strength of the place, kept blaspheming terribly and uttering wicked words. [35]But at dawn of the fifth day, twenty young men in the army of Maccabeus, fired with anger because of the blasphemies, bravely stormed the wall and with savage fury cut down everyone they met. [36]Others who came up in the same way wheeled around against the defenders and set fire to the towers; they kindled fires and burned the blasphemers alive. Others broke open the gates and let in the rest of the force, and they occupied the city. [37]They killed Timothy, who was hiding in a cistern, and his brother Chaereas, and Apollophanes. [38]When they had accomplished these things, with hymns and thanksgivings they blessed the Lord who shows great kindness to Israel and gives them the victory.

Lysias Besieges Beth-zur

11 Very soon after this, Lysias, the king's guardian and kinsman, who was in charge of the government, being vexed at what had happened, [2]gathered about eighty thousand infantry and all his cavalry and came against the Jews. He intended to make the city a home for Greeks, [3]and to levy tribute on the temple as he did on the sacred places of the other nations, and to put up the high priesthood for sale every year. [4]He took no account whatever of the power of God, but was elated with his ten thousands of infantry, and his thousands of cavalry, and his eighty elephants. [5]Invading Judea, he approached Beth-zur, which was a forti-

fied place about five stadia*y* from Jerusalem, and pressed it hard.

6 When Maccabeus and his men got word that Lysias*z* was besieging the strongholds, they and all the people, with lamentations and tears, prayed the Lord to send a good angel to save Israel. 7Maccabeus himself was the first to take up arms, and he urged the others to risk their lives with him to aid their kindred. Then they eagerly rushed off together. 8And there, while they were still near Jerusalem, a horseman appeared at their head, clothed in white and brandishing weapons of gold. 9And together they all praised the merciful God, and were strengthened in heart, ready to assail not only humans but the wildest animals or walls of iron. 10They advanced in battle order, having their heavenly ally, for the Lord had mercy on them. 11They hurled themselves like lions against the enemy, and laid low eleven thousand of them and sixteen hundred cavalry, and forced all the rest to flee. 12Most of them got away stripped and wounded, and Lysias himself escaped by disgraceful flight.

Lysias Makes Peace with the Jews

13 As he was not without intelligence, he pondered over the defeat that had befallen him, and realized that the Hebrews were invincible because the mighty God fought on their side. So he sent to them 14and persuaded them to settle everything on just terms, promising that he would persuade the king, constraining him to be their friend.*y* 15Maccabeus, having regard for the common good, agreed to all that Lysias urged. For the king granted every request in behalf of the Jews which Maccabeus delivered to Lysias in writing.

16 The letter written to the Jews by Lysias was to this effect:

"Lysias to the people of the Jews, greetings. 17John and Absalom, who were sent by you, have delivered your signed communication and have asked about the matters indicated in it. 18I have informed the king of everything that needed to be brought before him, and he has agreed to what was possible. 19If you will maintain your goodwill toward the government, I will endeavor in the future to help promote your welfare. 20And concerning such matters and their details, I have ordered these men and my representatives to confer with you. 21Farewell. The one hun-

dred forty-eighth year,*a* Dioscorinthius twenty-fourth."

22 The king's letter ran thus:

"King Antiochus to his brother Lysias, greetings. 23Now that our father has gone on to the gods, we desire that the subjects of the kingdom be undisturbed in caring for their own affairs. 24We have heard that the Jews do not consent to our father's change to Greek customs, but prefer their own way of living and ask that their own customs be allowed them. 25Accordingly, since we choose that this nation also should be free from disturbance, our decision is that their temple be restored to them and that they shall live according to the customs of their ancestors. 26You will do well, therefore, to send word to them and give them pledges of friendship, so that they may know our policy and be of good cheer and go on happily in the conduct of their own affairs."

27 To the nation the king's letter was as follows:

"King Antiochus to the senate of the Jews and to the other Jews, greetings. 28If you are well, it is as we desire. We also are in good health. 29Menelaus has informed us that you wish to return home and look after your own affairs. 30Therefore those who go home by the thirtieth of Xanthicus will have our pledge of friendship and full permission 31for the Jews to enjoy their own food and laws, just as formerly, and none of them shall be molested in any way for what may have been done in ignorance. 32And I have also sent Menelaus to encourage you. 33Farewell. The one hundred forty-eighth year,*a* Xanthicus fifteenth."

34 The Romans also sent them a letter, which read thus:

"Quintus Memmius and Titus Manius, envoys of the Romans, to the people of the Jews, greetings. 35With regard to what Lysias the kinsman of the king has granted you, we also give consent. 36But as to the matters that he decided are to be referred to the king, as soon as you have considered them, send some one promptly so that we may make proposals appropriate for you. For we are on our way to Antioch. 37Therefore make haste and send messengers so that we may have your judgment. 38Farewell. The one hundred forty-eighth year,*a* Xanthicus fifteenth."

---

y Meaning of Gk uncertain   *z* Gk *he*   *a* 164 B.C.

Incidents at Joppa and Jamnia

12 When this agreement had been reached, Lysias returned to the king, and the Jews went about their farming.

2 But some of the governors in various places, Timothy and Apollonius son of Gennaeus, as well as Hieronymus and Demophon, and in addition to these Nicanor the governor of Cyprus, would not let them live quietly and in peace. ³And the people of Joppa did so ungodly a deed as this: they invited the Jews who lived among them, with their wives and children, on boats that they had provided, as though there were no ill will to the Jews;*b* ⁴and this was done by public vote of the city. When they accepted, because they wished to live peaceably and suspected nothing, the people of Joppa*c* took them out to sea and drowned them, at least two hundred. ⁵When Judas heard of the cruelty visited on his compatriots, he gave orders to his men ⁶and, calling upon God, the righteous judge, attacked the murderers of his kindred. He set fire to the harbor by night, burned the boats, and massacred those who had taken refuge there. ⁷Then, because the city's gates were closed, he withdrew, intending to come again and root out the whole community of Joppa. ⁸But learning that the people in Jamnia meant in the same way to wipe out the Jews who were living among them, ⁹he attacked the Jamnites by night and set fire to the harbor and the fleet, so that the glow of the light was seen in Jerusalem, thirty miles*d* distant.

The Campaign in Gilead

10 When they had gone more than a mile*e* from there, on their march against Timothy, at least five thousand Arabs with five hundred cavalry attacked them. ¹¹After a hard fight, Judas and his companions, with God's help, were victorious. The defeated nomads begged Judas to grant them pledges of friendship, promising to give him livestock and to help his people*f* in all other ways. ¹²Judas, realizing that they might indeed be useful in many ways, agreed to make peace with them; and after receiving his pledges they went back to their tents.

13 He also attacked a certain town that was strongly fortified with earthworks*g* and walls, and inhabited by all sorts of

Gentiles. Its name was Caspin. ¹⁴Those who were within, relying on the strength of the walls and on their supply of provisions, behaved most insolently toward Judas and his men, railing at them and even blaspheming and saying unholy things. ¹⁵But Judas and his men, calling upon the great Sovereign of the world, who without battering rams or engines of war overthrew Jericho in the days of Joshua, rushed furiously upon the walls. ¹⁶They took the town by the will of God, and slaughtered untold numbers, so that the adjoining lake, a quarter of a mile*h* wide, appeared to be running over with blood.

Judas Defeats Timothy's Army

17 When they had gone ninety-five miles*i* from there, they came to Charax, to the Jews who are called Toubiani. ¹⁸They did not find Timothy in that region, for he had by then left there without accomplishing anything, though in one place he had left a very strong garrison. ¹⁹Dositheus and Sosipater, who were captains under Maccabeus, marched out and destroyed those whom Timothy had left in the stronghold, more than ten thousand men. ²⁰But Maccabeus arranged his army in divisions, set men*f* in command of the divisions, and hurried after Timothy, who had with him one hundred twenty thousand infantry and two thousand five hundred cavalry. ²¹When Timothy learned of the approach of Judas, he sent off the women and the children and also the baggage to a place called Carnaim; for that place was hard to besiege and difficult of access because of the narrowness of all the approaches. ²²But when Judas's first division appeared, terror and fear came over the enemy at the manifestation to them of him who sees all things. In their flight they rushed headlong in every direction, so that often they were injured by their own men and pierced by the points of their own swords. ²³Judas pressed the pursuit with the utmost vigor, putting the sinners to the sword, and destroyed as many as thirty thousand.

24 Timothy himself fell into the hands of Dositheus and Sosipater and their men. With great guile he begged them to let

b Gk to them *c* Gk they *d* Gk two hundred forty stadia *e* Gk nine stadia *f* Gk them *g* Meaning of Gk uncertain *h* Gk two stadia *i* Gk seven hundred fifty stadia

him go in safety, because he held the parents of most of them, and the brothers of some, to whom no consideration would be shown. 25And when with many words he had confirmed his solemn promise to restore them unharmed, they let him go, for the sake of saving their kindred.

Judas Wins Other Victories

26 Then Judas[j] marched against Carnaim and the temple of Atargatis, and slaughtered twenty-five thousand people. 27After the rout and destruction of these, he marched also against Ephron, a fortified town where Lysias lived with multitudes of people of all nationalities.[k] Stalwart young men took their stand before the walls and made a vigorous defense; and great stores of war engines and missiles were there. 28But the Jews[l] called upon the Sovereign who with power shatters the might of his enemies, and they got the town into their hands, and killed as many as twenty-five thousand of those who were in it.

29 Setting out from there, they hastened to Scythopolis, which is seventy-five miles[m] from Jerusalem. 30But when the Jews who lived there bore witness to the goodwill that the people of Scythopolis had shown them and their kind treatment of them in times of misfortune, 31they thanked them and exhorted them to be well disposed to their race in the future also. Then they went up to Jerusalem, as the festival of weeks was close at hand.

Judas Defeats Gorgias

32 After the festival called Pentecost, they hurried against Gorgias, the governor of Idumea, 33who came out with three thousand infantry and four hundred cavalry. 34When they joined battle, it happened that a few of the Jews fell. 35But a certain Dositheus, one of Bacenor's men, who was on horseback and was a strong man, caught hold of Gorgias, and grasping his cloak was dragging him off by main strength, wishing to take the accursed man alive, when one of the Thracian cavalry bore down on him and cut off his arm; so Gorgias escaped and reached Marisa.

36 As Esdris and his men had been fighting for a long time and were weary, Judas called upon the Lord to show himself their ally and leader in the battle. 37In the language of their ancestors he raised the battle cry, with hymns; then he charged against Gorgias's troops when they were not expecting it, and put them to flight.

Prayers for Those Killed in Battle

38 Then Judas assembled his army and went to the city of Adullam. As the seventh day was coming on, they purified themselves according to the custom, and kept the sabbath there.

39 On the next day, as had now become necessary, Judas and his men went to take up the bodies of the fallen and to bring them back to lie with their kindred in the sepulchres of their ancestors. 40Then under the tunic of each one of the dead they found sacred tokens of the idols of Jamnia, which the law forbids the Jews to wear. And it became clear to all that this was the reason these men had fallen. 41So they all blessed the ways of the Lord, the righteous judge, who reveals the things that are hidden; 42and they turned to supplication, praying that the sin that had been committed might be wholly blotted out. The noble Judas exhorted the people to keep themselves free from sin, for they had seen with their own eyes what had happened as the result of the sin of those who had fallen. 43He also took up a collection, man by man, to the amount of two thousand drachmas of silver, and sent it to Jerusalem to provide for a sin offering. In doing this he acted very well and honorably, taking account of the resurrection. 44For if he were not expecting that those who had fallen would rise again, it would have been superfluous and foolish to pray for the dead. 45But if he was looking to the splendid reward that is laid up for those who fall asleep in godliness, it was a holy and pious thought. Therefore he made atonement for the dead, so that they might be delivered from their sin.

Menelaus Is Put to Death

13 In the one hundred forty-ninth year[n] word came to Judas and his men that Antiochus Eupator was coming with a great army against Judea, 2and with him Lysias, his guardian, who had charge of the government. Each of them had a Greek force of one hundred ten

---

[j] Gk he   [k] Meaning of Gk uncertain   [l] Gk they
[m] Gk six hundred stadia   [n] 163 B.C.

thousand infantry, five thousand three hundred cavalry, twenty-two elephants, and three hundred chariots armed with scythes.

3 Menelaus also joined them and with utter hypocrisy urged Antiochus on, not for the sake of his country's welfare, but because he thought that he would be established in office. 4But the King of kings aroused the anger of Antiochus against the scoundrel; and when Lysias informed him that this man was to blame for all the trouble, he ordered them to take him to Beroea and to put him to death by the method that is customary in that place. 5For there is a tower there, fifty cubits high, full of ashes, and it has a rim run-

ning around it that on all sides inclines precipitously into the ashes. 6There they all push to destruction anyone guilty of sacrilege or notorious for other crimes. 7By such a fate it came about that Menelaus the lawbreaker died, without even burial in the earth. 8And this was eminently just; because he had committed many sins against the altar whose fire and ashes were holy, he met his death in ashes.

A Battle Near the City of Modein

9 The king with barbarous arrogance was coming to show the Jews things far worse than those that had been done*o* in

o Or the worst of the things that had been done

THE
TRADITION

Praying for the Dead

Therefore he made atonement for the dead,
so that they might be delivered from their sin.
2 MACCABEES 12.45

Do Catholics maintain a connection with the dead?

Well, yes. But not by conjuring up spirits or attending seances or consulting mediums. All of these things are clearly forbidden as rebellious attempts to seize power and knowledge that belong to God alone.

Perhaps it would be more accurate to say that Catholics see themselves in *communion* with the dead—that is, with those who have died in Christ. We communicate not by trying to send messages but by offering spiritual goods—prayers, almsgiving, and works of penance—to help those who are undergoing the final purification process we call purgatory.

Just as families help each other out in times of difficulty, members of the body of Christ share what they have with each other. It is a bit like the early Christian community, that held everything in common and distributed its goods so that no one would suffer need (see Acts 4.32, 34–35). In the larger body of Christ, we experience this exchange with our fellow pilgrims on earth, and also

with the souls in purgatory and the saints in heaven. The family ties established through Baptism are stronger than death!

The earliest Scriptural reference to praying for the dead is in 2 Maccabees 12.43–46, which is often read at funeral masses. It praises the Jewish leader Judas Maccabeus for offering atoning prayers and sacrifices on behalf of some of his soldiers who had died in battle wearing pagan charms—a sinful practice.

From the beginning the Church has honored the memory of the dead and offered prayers for them. Brief versions of these appear on Christian tombs dating back to the first century. They ask God to bless the dead with eternal life, rest, peace, and light. Every November 2, on the Feast of All Souls, we too request these blessings for those who have fallen asleep in Christ.

All year round, praying for the dead is an important service to the body of Christ. And so, as Saint John Chrysostom urges us, "Let us not hesitate to help those who have died and to offer our prayers for them."

his father's time. [10]But when Judas heard of this, he ordered the people to call upon the Lord day and night, now if ever to help those who were on the point of being deprived of the law and their country and the holy temple, [11]and not to let the people who had just begun to revive fall into the hands of the blasphemous Gentiles. [12]When they had all joined in the same petition and had implored the merciful Lord with weeping and fasting and lying prostrate for three days without ceasing, Judas exhorted them and ordered them to stand ready.

13 After consulting privately with the elders, he determined to march out and decide the matter by the help of God before the king's army could enter Judea and get possession of the city. [14]So, committing the decision to the Creator of the world and exhorting his troops to fight bravely to the death for the laws, temple, city, country, and commonwealth, he pitched his camp near Modein. [15]He gave his troops the watchword, "God's victory," and with a picked force of the bravest young men, he attacked the king's pavilion at night and killed as many as two thousand men in the camp. He stabbed[p] the leading elephant and its rider. [16]In the end they filled the camp with terror and confusion and withdrew in triumph. [17]This happened, just as day was dawning, because the Lord's help protected him.

Antiochus Makes a Treaty with the Jews

18 The king, having had a taste of the daring of the Jews, tried strategy in attacking their positions. [19]He advanced against Beth-zur, a strong fortress of the Jews, was turned back, attacked again,[q] and was defeated. [20]Judas sent in to the garrison whatever was necessary. [21]But Rhodocus, a man from the ranks of the Jews, gave secret information to the enemy; he was sought for, caught, and put in prison. [22]The king negotiated a second time with the people in Beth-zur, gave pledges, received theirs, withdrew, attacked Judas and his men, was defeated; [23]he got word that Philip, who had been left in charge of the government, had revolted in Antioch; he was dismayed, called in the Jews, yielded and swore to observe all their rights, settled with them and offered sacrifice, honored the sanctuary and showed generosity to the holy place. [24]He received Maccabeus, left Hegemonides as governor from Ptolemais to Gerar, [25]and went to Ptolemais. The people of Ptolemais were indignant over the treaty; in fact they were so angry that they wanted to annul its terms.[p] [26]Lysias took the public platform, made the best possible defense, convinced them, appeased them, gained their goodwill, and set out for Antioch. This is how the king's attack and withdrawal turned out.

Alcimus Speaks against Judas

14 Three years later, word came to Judas and his men that Demetrius son of Seleucus had sailed into the harbor of Tripolis with a strong army and a fleet, [2]and had taken possession of the country, having made away with Antiochus and his guardian Lysias.

3 Now a certain Alcimus, who had formerly been high priest but had willfully defiled himself in the times of separation,[r] realized that there was no way for him to be safe or to have access again to the holy altar, [4]and went to King Demetrius in about the one hundred fifty-first year,[s] presenting to him a crown of gold and a palm, and besides these some of the customary olive branches from the temple. During that day he kept quiet. [5]But he found an opportunity that furthered his mad purpose when he was invited by Demetrius to a meeting of the council and was asked about the attitude and intentions of the Jews. He answered:

6 "Those of the Jews who are called Hasideans, whose leader is Judas Maccabeus, are keeping up war and stirring up sedition, and will not let the kingdom attain tranquility. [7]Therefore I have laid aside my ancestral glory—I mean the high priesthood—and have now come here, [8]first because I am genuinely concerned for the interests of the king, and second because I have regard also for my compatriots. For through the folly of those whom I have mentioned our whole nation is now in no small misfortune. [9]Since you are acquainted, O king, with the details of this matter, may it please you to take thought for our country and our hard-pressed nation with the gracious kindness that you show to all. [10]For as long as Judas lives, it is impossible for the

---

[p] Meaning of Gk uncertain   [q] Or faltered
[r] Other ancient authorities read of mixing
[s] 161 B.C.

government to find peace." [11]When he had said this, the rest of the king's Friends,[t] who were hostile to Judas, quickly inflamed Demetrius still more. [12]He immediately chose Nicanor, who had been in command of the elephants, appointed him governor of Judea, and sent him off [13]with orders to kill Judas and scatter his troops, and to install Alcimus as high priest of the great[u] temple. [14]And the Gentiles throughout Judea, who had fled before[v] Judas, flocked to join Nicanor, thinking that the misfortunes and calamities of the Jews would mean prosperity for themselves.

Nicanor Makes Friends with Judas

15 When the Jews[w] heard of Nicanor's coming and the gathering of the Gentiles, they sprinkled dust on their heads and prayed to him who established his own people forever and always upholds his own heritage by manifesting himself. [16]At the command of the leader, they[x] set out from there immediately and engaged them in battle at a village called Dessau.[v] [17]Simon, the brother of Judas, had encountered Nicanor, but had been temporarily[y] checked because of the sudden consternation created by the enemy.

18 Nevertheless Nicanor, hearing of the valor of Judas and his troops and their courage in battle for their country, shrank from deciding the issue by bloodshed. [19]Therefore he sent Posidonius, Theodotus, and Mattathias to give and receive pledges of friendship. [20]When the terms had been fully considered, and the leader had informed the people, and it had appeared that they were of one mind, they agreed to the covenant. [21]The leaders[z] set a day on which to meet by themselves. A chariot came forward from each army; seats of honor were set in place; [22]Judas posted armed men in readiness at key places to prevent sudden treachery on the part of the enemy; so they duly held the consultation.

23 Nicanor stayed on in Jerusalem and did nothing out of the way, but dismissed the flocks of people that had gathered. [24]And he kept Judas always in his presence; he was warmly attached to the man. [25]He urged him to marry and have children; so Judas[x] married, settled down, and shared the common life.

Nicanor Turns against Judas

26 But when Alcimus noticed their goodwill for one another, he took the covenant that had been made and went to Demetrius. He told him that Nicanor was disloyal to the government, since he had appointed that conspirator against the kingdom, Judas, to be his successor. [27]The king became excited and, provoked by the false accusations of that depraved man, wrote to Nicanor, stating that he was displeased with the covenant and commanding him to send Maccabeus to Antioch as a prisoner without delay.

28 When this message came to Nicanor, he was troubled and grieved that he had to annul their agreement when the man had done no wrong. [29]Since it was not possible to oppose the king, he watched for an opportunity to accomplish this by a stratagem. [30]But Maccabeus, noticing that Nicanor was more austere in his dealings with him and was meeting him more rudely than had been his custom, concluded that this austerity did not spring from the best motives. So he gathered not a few of his men, and went into hiding from Nicanor. [31]When the latter became aware that he had been cleverly outwitted by the man, he went to the great[u] and holy temple while the priests were offering the customary sacrifices, and commanded them to hand the man over. [32]When they declared on oath that they did not know where the man was whom he wanted, [33]he stretched out his right hand toward the sanctuary, and swore this oath: "If you do not hand Judas over to me as a prisoner, I will level this shrine of God to the ground and tear down the altar, and build here a splendid temple to Dionysus."

34 Having said this, he went away. Then the priests stretched out their hands toward heaven and called upon the constant Defender of our nation, in these words: [35]"O Lord of all, though you have need of nothing, you were pleased that there should be a temple for your habitation among us; [36]so now, O holy One, Lord of all holiness, keep undefiled forever this house that has been so recently purified."

---

[t] Gk of the Friends   [u] Gk greatest   [v] Meaning of Gk uncertain   [w] Gk they   [x] Gk he   [y] Other ancient authorities read slowly   [z] Gk They

Razis Dies for His Country

37 A certain Razis, one of the elders of Jerusalem, was denounced to Nicanor as a man who loved his compatriots and was very well thought of and for his goodwill was called father of the Jews. ³⁸In former times, when there was no mingling with the Gentiles, he had been accused of Judaism, and he had most zealously risked body and life for Judaism. ³⁹Nicanor, wishing to exhibit the enmity that he had for the Jews, sent more than five hundred soldiers to arrest him; ⁴⁰for he thought that by arresting[a] him he would do them an injury. ⁴¹When the troops were about to capture the tower and were forcing the door of the courtyard, they ordered that fire be brought and the doors burned. Being surrounded, Razis[b] fell upon his own sword, ⁴²preferring to die nobly rather than to fall into the hands of sinners and suffer outrages unworthy of his noble birth. ⁴³But in the heat of the struggle he did not hit exactly, and the crowd was now rushing in through the doors. He courageously ran up on the wall, and bravely threw himself down into the crowd. ⁴⁴But as they quickly drew back, a space opened and he fell in the middle of the empty space. ⁴⁵Still alive and aflame with anger, he rose, and though his blood gushed forth and his wounds were severe he ran through the crowd; and standing upon a steep rock, ⁴⁶with his blood now completely drained from him, he tore out his entrails, took them in both hands and hurled them at the crowd, calling upon the Lord of life and spirit to give them back to him again. This was the manner of his death.

Nicanor's Arrogance

15 When Nicanor heard that Judas and his troops were in the region of Samaria, he made plans to attack them with complete safety on the day of rest. ²When the Jews who were compelled to follow him said, "Do not destroy so savagely and barbarously, but show respect for the day that he who sees all things has honored and hallowed above other days," ³the thrice-accursed wretch asked if there were a sovereign in heaven who had commanded the keeping of the sabbath day. ⁴When they declared, "It is the living Lord himself, the Sovereign in heaven, who or-dered us to observe the seventh day," ⁵he replied, "But I am a sovereign also, on earth, and I command you to take up arms and finish the king's business." Nevertheless, he did not succeed in carrying out his abominable design.

Judas Prepares the Jews for Battle

6 This Nicanor in his utter boastfulness and arrogance had determined to erect a public monument of victory over Judas and his forces. ⁷But Maccabeus did not cease to trust with all confidence that he would get help from the Lord. ⁸He exhorted his troops not to fear the attack of the Gentiles, but to keep in mind the former times when help had come to them from heaven, and so to look for the victory that the Almighty would give them. ⁹Encouraging them from the law and the prophets, and reminding them also of the struggles they had won, he made them the more eager. ¹⁰When he had aroused their courage, he issued his orders, at the same time pointing out the perfidy of the Gentiles and their violation of oaths. ¹¹He armed each of them not so much with confidence in shields and spears as with the inspiration of brave words, and he cheered them all by relating a dream, a sort of vision,[a] which was worthy of belief.

12 What he saw was this: Onias, who had been high priest, a noble and good man, of modest bearing and gentle manner, one who spoke fittingly and had been trained from childhood in all that belongs to excellence, was praying with out-stretched hands for the whole body of the Jews. ¹³Then in the same fashion another appeared, distinguished by his gray hair and dignity, and of marvelous majesty and authority. ¹⁴And Onias spoke, saying, "This is a man who loves the family of Israel and prays much for the people and the holy city—Jeremiah, the prophet of God." ¹⁵Jeremiah stretched out his right hand and gave to Judas a golden sword, and as he gave it he addressed him thus: ¹⁶"Take this holy sword, a gift from God, with which you will strike down your adversaries."

17 Encouraged by the words of Judas, so noble and so effective in arousing valor

---

[a] Meaning of Gk uncertain   [b] Gk *he*

and awaking courage in the souls of the young, they determined not to carry on a campaign[c] but to attack bravely, and to decide the matter by fighting hand to hand with all courage, because the city and the sanctuary and the temple were in danger. [18]Their concern for wives and children, and also for brothers and sisters[d] and relatives, lay upon them less heavily; their greatest and first fear was for the consecrated sanctuary. [19]And those who had to remain in the city were in no little distress, being anxious over the encounter in the open country.

The Defeat and Death of Nicanor

[20] When all were now looking forward to the coming issue, and the enemy was already close at hand with their army drawn up for battle, the elephants[e] strategically stationed and the cavalry deployed on the flanks, [21]Maccabeus, observing the masses that were in front of him and the varied supply of arms and the savagery of the elephants, stretched out his hands toward heaven and called upon

[c] Or *to remain in camp*   [d] Gk for *brothers*   [e] Gk *animals*

Do Your Best

FRIDAY

Scripture Reading for Today:
2 Maccabees 15.37–39

Verse for Today:
2 Maccabees 15.38

Today we are not content with little achievements, with small beginnings. We should look to Saint Theresa, the Little Flower, to walk her little way, her way of love. We should look to Saint Teresa of Avila, who was not content to be like those people who proceeded with the pace of hens about God's business, but like those people who on their own account were greatly daring in what they wished to do for God. It is we ourselves that we have to think about, no one else. That is the way the saints worked. They paid attention to what they were doing, and if others were attracted to them by their enterprise, why, well and good. But they looked to themselves first of all.

"Whatever your hand finds to do, do with your might" (Ecclesiastes 9.10). After all, God is with us. It shows too much conceit to trust to ourselves, to be discouraged at what we ourselves can accomplish. It is lacking in faith in God to be discouraged. After all, we are going to proceed with his help. We offer him what we are going to do. If he wishes it to prosper, it will. We must depend solely on him. Work as though everything depended on ourselves, and pray as though everything depended on God, as Saint Ignatius says.

I suppose it is a grace not to be able to have time to take or derive satisfaction in the work we are doing. In what time I have, my impulse is to self-criticism and examination of conscience, and I am constantly humiliated at my own imperfections and at my halting progress. Perhaps I deceive myself here, too, and excuse my lack of recollection. But I do know how small I am and how little I can do, and I beg you, Lord, to help me, for I cannot help myself.

—DOROTHY DAY

Go to page 618 for your next devotional reading.

the Lord who works wonders; for he knew that it is not by arms, but as the Lord[f] decides, that he gains the victory for those who deserve it. [22]He called upon him in these words: "O Lord, you sent your angel in the time of King Hezekiah of Judea, and he killed fully one hundred eighty-five thousand in the camp of Sennacherib. [23]So now, O Sovereign of the heavens, send a good angel to spread terror and trembling before us. [24]By the might of your arm may these blasphemers who come against your holy people be struck down." With these words he ended his prayer.

25 Nicanor and his troops advanced with trumpets and battle songs, [26]but Judas and his troops met the enemy in battle with invocations to God and prayers. [27]So, fighting with their hands and praying to God in their hearts, they laid low at least thirty-five thousand, and were greatly gladdened by God's manifestation.

28 When the action was over and they were returning with joy, they recognized Nicanor, lying dead, in full armor. [29]Then there was shouting and tumult, and they blessed the Sovereign Lord in the language of their ancestors. [30]Then the man who was ever in body and soul the defender of his people, the man who maintained his youthful goodwill toward his compatriots, ordered them to cut off Nicanor's head and arm and carry them to Jerusalem. [31]When he arrived there and had called his compatriots together and stationed the priests before the altar, he sent for those who were in the citadel. [32]He showed them the vile Nicanor's head and that profane man's arm, which had been boastfully stretched out against the holy house of the Almighty. [33]He cut out the tongue of the ungodly Nicanor and said that he would feed it piecemeal to the birds and would hang up these rewards of his folly opposite the sanctuary. [34]And they all, looking to heaven, blessed the Lord who had manifested himself, saying, "Blessed is he who has kept his own place undefiled!" [35]Judas[g] hung Nicanor's head from the citadel, a clear and conspicuous sign to everyone of the help of the Lord. [36]And they all decreed by public vote never to let this day go unobserved, but to celebrate the thirteenth day of the twelfth month—which is called Adar in the Aramaic language—the day before Mordecai's day.

37 This, then, is how matters turned out with Nicanor, and from that time the city has been in the possession of the Hebrews. So I will here end my story.

The Compiler's Epilogue

38 If it is well told and to the point, that is what I myself desired; if it is poorly done and mediocre, that was the best I could do. [39]For just as it is harmful to drink wine alone, or, again, to drink water alone, while wine mixed with water is sweet and delicious and enhances one's enjoyment, so also the style of the story delights the ears of those who read the work. And here will be the end.

f Gk *he*   *g* Gk *He*

Job

The book of Job is a literary masterpiece that probes the age-old problem of suffering. The book begins with God and Satan talking in heaven. God points out his servant, Job, praising him as a righteous and God-fearing man. But Satan merely accuses Job of being a fair-weather friend of God: "Stretch out your hand now, and touch all that he has, and he will curse you to your face" (1.11). Thus begin Job's sorrows. In rapid succession, he loses everything—children, possessions, even his health.

Job is thrust into a terrible kind of internal darkness, unable to find answers to his many questions. His wife is no help, advising him to curse God because of his misfortunes. His three friends only add to his suffering by concluding that Job must not be the good man he appears to be. But Job asserts his innocence. Despairing of life, he pleads with God to answer him.

God finally reveals himself to Job, but instead of answering his many questions, God challenges Job to consider God's mighty works.

In the end, God rebukes Job's three friends for speaking falsely and blesses Job doubly for his sufferings. Though God does not satisfy Job's questions, he reveals himself to Job in a way that satisfies him in the deepest possible way.

Job's story offers profound hope to anyone who is suffering. When you think you can't endure any more difficulty, read Job and pray for a deeper experience of God.

Job and His Family

1 There was once a man in the land of Uz whose name was Job. That man was blameless and upright, one who feared God and turned away from evil. ²There were born to him seven sons and three daughters. ³He had seven thousand sheep, three thousand camels, five hun-dred yoke of oxen, five hundred donkeys, and very many servants; so that this man was the greatest of all the people of the east. ⁴His sons used to go and hold feasts in one another's houses in turn; and they would send and invite their three sisters to eat and drink with them. ⁵And when the feast days had run their course, Job would

Deborah

Her Name Means "Honey Bee"

Her Character: *Her vision of the world was shaped, not by the political situation of her day, but by her relationship with God. Though women in the ancient world did not usually become political leaders, she was exactly the leader Israel needed. A prophetess and judge who heard God and believed him, her courage inspired the people.*

Her Sorrow: *That her people had sunk into despair because of their idolatry.*

Her Joy: *That God turned the enemy's strength on its head, giving power to the weak and blessing the land with peace for 40 years.*

Read Judges 4.1–16

Jericho, gateway to Canaan, had lain in ruins for two hundred years. From there, the Israelites had swept across the country like a swarm of locusts. But the native Canaanite peoples had somehow managed to survive, and like well-rooted weeds, their idolatry spread until it began to strangle Israel's faith.

Now the slaves-turned-warriors were once again underdogs, oppressed for 20 years by a coalition of Canaanite rulers, whose chief warrior was Sisera. His nine hundred iron-plated chariots terrified the poorly armed people of Israel, threatening to sweep over them with invincible force. Small wonder no one challenged him.

Sisera must have felt smugly secure, especially since Israel was now led by a woman. But his military calculations failed to account for one key variable—the strategic power of that woman's faith. Deborah was a prophetess who held court under a palm tree several miles northwest of Jericho. Though much of Israel was divided and dispirited, she refused to lose heart.

She summoned Barak, an Israelite from the north and told him plainly: "The LORD, the God of Israel, commands you, 'Go, take position at Mount Tabor, bringing ten thousand from the tribe of Naphtali and the tribe of Zebulun. I will draw out Sisera, the general of Jabin's army, to meet you by the Wadi Kishon with his chariots and his troops; and I will give him into your hand'" (verses 6–7).

But Barak was terrified of Sisera, and he refused to comply unless one condition was met: Deborah must accompany him. She would be his talisman on the day of battle. But she told him that as a result of his lack of faith in God alone: "I will surely go with you; nevertheless, the road on which you are going will not lead to your glory, for the LORD will sell Sisera into the hand of a woman" (verse 9).

Hearing of the plot, Sisera led his troops and chariots to Wadi Kishon, a dry riverbed, determined to crush the uprising. But his strength turned against him as rain flooded the valley. Suddenly nine hundred iron chariots became a huge liability. No matter how furiously the soldiers flogged their horses, urging them onward, the oozing mud held them fast, making them easy targets for Barak's troops, who killed every man but Sisera.

Once again, God had heard his people's cries and sent a deliverer—this time a woman whose faith overwhelmed their fear. On their day of victory, Deborah and Barak sang this song: "When the people offer themselves willingly—bless the LORD! ... The peasantry prospered in Israel, they grew fat on plunder, because you arose, Deborah, arose as a mother in Israel ... Then down to the gates marched the people of the LORD" (5.2, 7, 11).

Indeed, a mother in Israel had arisen, a woman whose strong faith gave birth to hope and freedom and a peace that lasted 40 years. Like an ancient Joan of Arc, Deborah arose and called the people to battle, leading them out of idolatry and restoring their dignity as God's chosen ones.

Praying With Deborah

"Hear, O kings; give ear, O princes; to the LORD I will sing, I will make melody to the LORD, the God of Israel."—Judges 5.3

Praise God: For speaking clearly to his people.

Offer Thanks: That God gives prophets to the church, women as well as men.

Confess: Anything that makes you reluctant to listen for God's voice.

Ask God: To help you discern his voice.

Lift Your Heart

It's difficult, even unpleasant, to listen to two pieces of music at once. Likewise, it's hard to listen to God's voice if at the same time you are listening to voices of confusion, discouragement, and condemnation. Deborah's peace and confidence as a leader stemmed in part from her ability to hear God clearly. This week ask the Holy Spirit to help you distinguish God's voice from all the background noise. Ask for grace to discipline your thoughts in order to hear God more clearly. As you pray, put on some quiet background music, favorite hymns or classical music, to remind you to tune in to the one Voice worth listening to.

Lord, I want to hear your voice. Help me to recognize and resist all the phony voices that masquerade as yours. Make me a woman who both listens to and speaks your word.

Go to page 621 for your next devotional reading.

send and sanctify them, and he would rise early in the morning and offer burnt offerings according to the number of them all; for Job said, "It may be that my children have sinned, and cursed God in their hearts." This is what Job always did.

Attack on Job's Character

6 One day the heavenly beings[a] came to present themselves before the Lord, and Satan[b] also came among them. 7The Lord said to Satan,[b] "Where have you come from?" Satan[b] answered the Lord, "From going to and fro on the earth, and from walking up and down on it." 8The Lord said to Satan,[b] "Have you considered my servant Job? There is no one like him on the earth, a blameless and upright man who fears God and turns away from evil." 9Then Satan[b] answered the Lord, "Does Job fear God for nothing? 10Have you not put a fence around him and his house and all that he has, on every side? You have blessed the work of his hands, and his possessions have increased in the land. 11But stretch out your hand now, and touch all that he has, and he will curse you to your face." 12The Lord said to Satan,[b] "Very well, all that he has is in your power; only do not stretch out your hand against him!" So Satan[b] went out from the presence of the Lord.

Job Loses Property and Children

13 One day when his sons and daughters were eating and drinking wine in the eldest brother's house, 14a messenger came to Job and said, "The oxen were plowing and the donkeys were feeding beside them, 15and the Sabeans fell on them and carried them off, and killed the servants with the edge of the sword; I alone have escaped to tell you." 16While he was still speaking, another came and said, "The fire of God fell from heaven and burned up the sheep and the servants, and consumed them; I alone have escaped to tell you." 17While he was still speaking, another came and said, "The Chaldeans formed three columns, made a raid on the camels and carried them off, and killed the servants with the edge of the sword; I alone have escaped to tell you." 18While he was still speaking, another came and said, "Your sons and daughters were eating and drinking wine in their eldest brother's house, 19and suddenly a great wind came across the desert, struck the four corners

of the house, and it fell on the young people, and they are dead; I alone have escaped to tell you."

20 Then Job arose, tore his robe, shaved his head, and fell on the ground and worshiped. 21He said, "Naked I came from my mother's womb, and naked shall I return there; the Lord gave, and the Lord has taken away; blessed be the name of the Lord."

22 In all this Job did not sin or charge God with wrongdoing.

Attack on Job's Health

2 One day the heavenly beings[a] came to present themselves before the Lord, and Satan[b] also came among them to present himself before the Lord. 2The Lord said to Satan,[b] "Where have you come from?" Satan[c] answered the Lord, "From going to and fro on the earth, and from walking up and down on it." 3The Lord said to Satan,[b] "Have you considered my servant Job? There is no one like him on the earth, a blameless and upright man who fears God and turns away from evil. He still persists in his integrity, although you incited me against him, to destroy him for no reason." 4Then Satan[b] answered the Lord, "Skin for skin! All that people have they will give to save their lives.[d] 5But stretch out your hand now and touch his bone and his flesh, and he will curse you to your face." 6The Lord said to Satan,[b] "Very well, he is in your power; only spare his life."

7 So Satan[b] went out from the presence of the Lord, and inflicted loathsome sores on Job from the sole of his foot to the crown of his head. 8Job[e] took a potsherd with which to scrape himself, and sat among the ashes.

9 Then his wife said to him, "Do you still persist in your integrity? Curse[f] God, and die." 10But he said to her, "You speak as any foolish woman would speak. Shall we receive the good at the hand of God, and not receive the bad?" In all this Job did not sin with his lips.

Job's Three Friends

11 Now when Job's three friends heard of all these troubles that had come upon

---

a Heb *sons of God*   *b* Or *the Accuser;* Heb *ha-satan*   *c* Or *The Accuser;* Heb *ha-satan*   *d* Or *All that the man has he will give for his life*   *e* Heb *He*   *f* Heb *Bless*

him, each of them set out from his home—Eliphaz the Temanite, Bildad the Shuhite, and Zophar the Naamathite. They met together to go and console and comfort him. [12]When they saw him from a distance, they did not recognize him, and they raised their voices and wept aloud; they tore their robes and threw dust in the air upon their heads. [13]They sat with him on the ground seven days and seven nights, and no one spoke a word to him, for they saw that his suffering was very great.

Job Curses the Day He Was Born

3 After this Job opened his mouth and cursed the day of his birth. [2]Job said:

[3] "Let the day perish in which I was
      born,
  and the night that said,
  'A man-child is conceived.'
[4] Let that day be darkness!

May God above not seek it,
  or light shine on it.
[5] Let gloom and deep darkness claim
      it.
  Let clouds settle upon it;
  let the blackness of the day terrify
      it.
[6] That night—let thick darkness seize
      it!
  let it not rejoice among the days
      of the year;
  let it not come into the number
      of the months.
[7] Yes, let that night be barren;
  let no joyful cry be heard[g] in it.
[8] Let those curse it who curse the
      Sea,[h]
  those who are skilled to rouse up
      Leviathan.
[9] Let the stars of its dawn be dark;

g Heb come   h Cn: Heb day

Giving Hands

MONDAY

Scripture Reading
for Today:
Job 2.1–10

Verse for Today:
Job 2.10

To trust God means that we must know that whatever comes to us comes from his hand. If we do not see that sorrow comes from his hand and cannot get the comfort of his love from it, it may be because we do not acknowledge our joys as his gifts. If we felt grateful for our food, for the sunlight, for our work, our homes, for those we love, if we were conscious that these were all given by God, we should have formed a clear enough idea of his love to know him; we should know him well enough to know, because we know him, that he does not want us to suffer, but allows it because there is good for us in it. To resist, to be bitter, to say it is no use, all increases the pain. To accept it gratefully from God eases the pain.

Now, is there a way in which a busy person could practice this growing trust without having to meditate all day long? Yes, it is very simple. Make a mental picture of two huge giving hands, God's hands, and every so often in the day or night, stop for a moment and think: "At this moment, God is handing me all I have, my life—" and so on, mentioning all that you are conscious of. It may be at some moments you will realize what a lot of obvious good God is giving you still; at other times it will help you to understand that the trials you suffer also come from his hands.

—CARYLL HOUSELANDER

Go to page 628 for your next devotional reading.

let it hope for light, but have
none;
may it not see the eyelids of the
morning—
10 because it did not shut the doors of
my mother's womb,
and hide trouble from my eyes.

11 "Why did I not die at birth,
come forth from the womb and
expire?
12 Why were there knees to receive me,
or breasts for me to suck?
13 Now I would be lying down and
quiet;
I would be asleep; then I would
be at rest
14 with kings and counselors of the
earth
who rebuild ruins for themselves,
15 or with princes who have gold,
who fill their houses with silver.
16 Or why was I not buried like a
stillborn child,
like an infant that never sees the
light?
17 There the wicked cease from
troubling,
and there the weary are at rest.
18 There the prisoners are at ease
together;
they do not hear the voice of the
taskmaster.
19 The small and the great are there,
and the slaves are free from their
masters.

20 "Why is light given to one in
misery,
and life to the bitter in soul,
21 who long for death, but it does not
come,
and dig for it more than for
hidden treasures;
22 who rejoice exceedingly,
and are glad when they find the
grave?
23 Why is light given to one who
cannot see the way,
whom God has fenced in?
24 For my sighing comes like[i] my
bread,
and my groanings are poured out
like water.
25 Truly the thing that I fear comes
upon me,
and what I dread befalls me.

26 I am not at ease, nor am I quiet;
I have no rest; but trouble comes."

Eliphaz Speaks: Job Has Sinned

4 Then Eliphaz the Temanite answered:
2 "If one ventures a word with
you, will you be offended?
But who can keep from speaking?
3 See, you have instructed many;
you have strengthened the weak
hands.
4 Your words have supported those
who were stumbling,
and you have made firm the
feeble knees.
5 But now it has come to you, and
you are impatient;
it touches you, and you are
dismayed.
6 Is not your fear of God your
confidence,
and the integrity of your ways
your hope?

7 "Think now, who that was innocent
ever perished?
Or where were the upright cut
off?
8 As I have seen, those who plow
iniquity
and sow trouble reap the same.
9 By the breath of God they perish,
and by the blast of his anger they
are consumed.
10 The roar of the lion, the voice of the
fierce lion,
and the teeth of the young lions
are broken.
11 The strong lion perishes for lack of
prey,
and the whelps of the lioness are
scattered.

12 "Now a word came stealing to me,
my ear received the whisper of it.
13 Amid thoughts from visions of the
night,
when deep sleep falls on mortals,
14 dread came upon me, and
trembling,
which made all my bones shake.
15 A spirit glided past my face;
the hair of my flesh bristled.
16 It stood still,
but I could not discern its
appearance.

i Heb *before*

A form was before my eyes;
    there was silence, then I heard a
        voice:
17 'Can mortals be righteous before[j]
        God?
    Can human beings be pure
        before[j] their Maker?
18 Even in his servants he puts no trust,
    and his angels he charges with
        error;
19 how much more those who live in
        houses of clay,
    whose foundation is in the dust,
    who are crushed like a moth.
20 Between morning and evening they
        are destroyed;
    they perish forever without any
        regarding it.
21 Their tent-cord is plucked up within
        them,
    and they die devoid of wisdom.'

Job Is Corrected by God

5 "Call now; is there anyone who
        will answer you?
    To which of the holy ones will you
        turn?
2 Surely vexation kills the fool,
    and jealousy slays the simple.
3 I have seen fools taking root,
    but suddenly I cursed their
        dwelling.
4 Their children are far from safety,
    they are crushed in the gate,
    and there is no one to deliver
        them.
5 The hungry eat their harvest,
    and they take it even out of the
        thorns;[k]
    and the thirsty[l] pant after their
        wealth.
6 For misery does not come from the
        earth,
    nor does trouble sprout from the
        ground;
7 but human beings are born to
        trouble
    just as sparks[m] fly upward.

8 "As for me, I would seek God,
    and to God I would commit my
        cause.
9 He does great things and
        unsearchable,
    marvelous things without number.
10 He gives rain on the earth
    and sends waters on the fields;
11 he sets on high those who are lowly,

and those who mourn are lifted to
        safety.
12 He frustrates the devices of the
        crafty,
    so that their hands achieve no
        success.
13 He takes the wise in their own
        craftiness;
    and the schemes of the wily are
        brought to a quick end.
14 They meet with darkness in the
        daytime,
    and grope at noonday as in the
        night.
15 But he saves the needy from the
        sword of their mouth,
    from the hand of the mighty.
16 So the poor have hope,
    and injustice shuts its mouth.

17 "How happy is the one whom God
        reproves;
    therefore do not despise the
        discipline of the Almighty.[n]
18 For he wounds, but he binds up;
    he strikes, but his hands heal.
19 He will deliver you from six
        troubles;
    in seven no harm shall touch you.
20 In famine he will redeem you from
        death,
    and in war from the power of the
        sword.
21 You shall be hidden from the
        scourge of the tongue,
    and shall not fear destruction
        when it comes.
22 At destruction and famine you shall
        laugh,
    and shall not fear the wild
        animals of the earth.
23 For you shall be in league with the
        stones of the field,
    and the wild animals shall be at
        peace with you.
24 You shall know that your tent is
        safe,
    you shall inspect your fold and
        miss nothing.
25 You shall know that your
        descendants will be many,
    and your offspring like the grass
        of the earth.

---

j Or *more than*   *k* Meaning of Heb uncertain
l Aquila Symmachus Syr Vg: Heb *snare*   *m* Or
birds; Heb *sons of Resheph*   *n* Traditional
rendering of Heb *Shaddai*

26 You shall come to your grave in ripe
old age,
   as a shock of grain comes up to
      the threshing floor in its
      season.
27 See, we have searched this out; it is
true.
   Hear, and know it for yourself."

Job Replies: My Complaint Is Just

6 Then Job answered:
2 "O that my vexation were
weighed,
   and all my calamity laid in the
      balances!
3 For then it would be heavier than
      the sand of the sea;
   therefore my words have been
      rash.
4 For the arrows of the Almighty*o* are
in me;
   my spirit drinks their poison;
   the terrors of God are arrayed
      against me.
5 Does the wild ass bray over its grass,
   or the ox low over its fodder?
6 Can that which is tasteless be eaten
      without salt,
   or is there any flavor in the juice
      of mallows? *p*
7 My appetite refuses to touch them;
   they are like food that is
      loathsome to me. *p*

8 "O that I might have my request,
   and that God would grant my
      desire;
9 that it would please God to crush
me,
   that he would let loose his hand
      and cut me off!
10 This would be my consolation;
   I would even exult*p* in
      unrelenting pain;
   for I have not denied the words of
      the Holy One.
11 What is my strength, that I should
wait?
   And what is my end, that I should
      be patient?
12 Is my strength the strength of stones,
   or is my flesh bronze?
13 In truth I have no help in me,
   and any resource is driven from
      me.

14 "Those who withhold*q* kindness
      from a friend

forsake the fear of the Almighty.*o*
15 My companions are treacherous like
      a torrent-bed,
   like freshets that pass away,
16 that run dark with ice,
   turbid with melting snow.
17 In time of heat they disappear;
   when it is hot, they vanish from
      their place.
18 The caravans turn aside from their
      course;
   they go up into the waste, and
      perish.
19 The caravans of Tema look,
   the travelers of Sheba hope.
20 They are disappointed because they
      were confident;
   they come there and are
      confounded.
21 Such you have now become to
      me;*r*
   you see my calamity, and are
      afraid.
22 Have I said, 'Make me a gift'?
   Or, 'From your wealth offer a
      bribe for me'?
23 Or, 'Save me from an opponent's
      hand'?
   Or, 'Ransom me from the hand of
      oppressors'?

24 "Teach me, and I will be silent;
   make me understand how I have
      gone wrong.
25 How forceful are honest words!
   But your reproof, what does it
      reprove?
26 Do you think that you can reprove
      words,
   as if the speech of the desperate
      were wind?
27 You would even cast lots over the
      orphan,
   and bargain over your friend.

28 "But now, be pleased to look at me;
   for I will not lie to your face.
29 Turn, I pray, let no wrong be done.
   Turn now, my vindication is at
      stake.
30 Is there any wrong on my tongue?
   Cannot my taste discern calamity?

o Traditional rendering of Heb *Shaddai*
p Meaning of Heb uncertain   *q* Syr Vg Compare
Tg: Meaning of Heb uncertain   *r* Cn Compare
Gk Syr: Meaning of Heb uncertain

Job: My Suffering Is without End

7 "Do not human beings have a hard
        service on earth,
      and are not their days like the
        days of a laborer?
2 Like a slave who longs for the
        shadow,
      and like laborers who look for
        their wages,
3 so I am allotted months of
        emptiness,
      and nights of misery are
        apportioned to me.
4 When I lie down I say, 'When shall
        I rise?'
      But the night is long,
      and I am full of tossing until
        dawn.
5 My flesh is clothed with worms and
        dirt;
      my skin hardens, then breaks out
        again.
6 My days are swifter than a weaver's
        shuttle,
      and come to their end without
        hope.[s]

7 "Remember that my life is a breath;
      my eye will never again see good.
8 The eye that beholds me will see me
        no more;
      while your eyes are upon me, I
        shall be gone.
9 As the cloud fades and vanishes,
      so those who go down to Sheol
        do not come up;
10 they return no more to their houses,
      nor do their places know them
        any more.

11 "Therefore I will not restrain my
        mouth;
      I will speak in the anguish of my
        spirit;
      I will complain in the bitterness
        of my soul.
12 Am I the Sea, or the Dragon,
      that you set a guard over me?
13 When I say, 'My bed will comfort
        me,
      my couch will ease my
        complaint,'
14 then you scare me with dreams
      and terrify me with visions,
15 so that I would choose strangling
      and death rather than this body.

16 I loathe my life; I would not live
        forever.
      Let me alone, for my days are a
        breath.
17 What are human beings, that you
        make so much of them,
      that you set your mind on them,
18 visit them every morning,
      test them every moment?
19 Will you not look away from me for
        a while,
      let me alone until I swallow my
        spittle?
20 If I sin, what do I do to you, you
        watcher of humanity?
      Why have you made me your
        target?
      Why have I become a burden to
        you?
21 Why do you not pardon my
        transgression
      and take away my iniquity?
      For now I shall lie in the earth;
      you will seek me, but I shall not
        be."

Bildad Speaks: Job Should Repent

8 Then Bildad the Shuhite answered:
2 "How long will you say these
        things,
      and the words of your mouth be a
        great wind?
3 Does God pervert justice?
      Or does the Almighty[t] pervert
        the right?
4 If your children sinned against him,
      he delivered them into the power
        of their transgression.
5 If you will seek God
      and make supplication to the
        Almighty,[t]
6 if you are pure and upright,
      surely then he will rouse himself
        for you
      and restore to you your rightful
        place.
7 Though your beginning was small,
      your latter days will be very great.

8 "For inquire now of bygone
        generations,
      and consider what their ancestors
        have found;
9 for we are but of yesterday, and we
        know nothing,

---

[s] Or *as the thread runs out*   [t] Traditional
rendering of Heb *Shaddai*

for our days on earth are but a
shadow.
10 Will they not teach you and tell you
and utter words out of their
understanding?

11 "Can papyrus grow where there is
no marsh?
Can reeds flourish where there is
no water?
12 While yet in flower and not cut
down,
they wither before any other
plant.
13 Such are the paths of all who forget
God;
the hope of the godless shall
perish.
14 Their confidence is gossamer,
a spider's house their trust.
15 If one leans against its house, it will
not stand;
if one lays hold of it, it will not
endure.
16 The wicked thrive^u before the sun,
and their shoots spread over the
garden.
17 Their roots twine around the
stoneheap;
they live among the rocks.^v
18 If they are destroyed from their
place,
then it will deny them, saying, 'I
have never seen you.'
19 See, these are their happy ways,^w
and out of the earth still others
will spring.

20 "See, God will not reject a blameless
person,
nor take the hand of evildoers.
21 He will yet fill your mouth with
laughter,
and your lips with shouts of joy.
22 Those who hate you will be clothed
with shame,
and the tent of the wicked will be
no more."

Job Replies: There Is No Mediator

9 Then Job answered:
2 "Indeed I know that this is so;
but how can a mortal be just
before God?
3 If one wished to contend with him,
one could not answer him once in
a thousand.

4 He is wise in heart, and mighty in
strength
—who has resisted him, and
succeeded?—
5 he who removes mountains, and
they do not know it,
when he overturns them in his
anger;
6 who shakes the earth out of its
place,
and its pillars tremble;
7 who commands the sun, and it does
not rise;
who seals up the stars;
8 who alone stretched out the heavens
and trampled the waves of the
Sea;^x
9 who made the Bear and Orion,
the Pleiades and the chambers of
the south;
10 who does great things beyond
understanding,
and marvelous things without
number.
11 Look, he passes by me, and I do not
see him;
he moves on, but I do not
perceive him.
12 He snatches away; who can stop
him?
Who will say to him, 'What are
you doing?'

13 "God will not turn back his anger;
the helpers of Rahab bowed
beneath him.
14 How then can I answer him,
choosing my words with him?
15 Though I am innocent, I cannot
answer him;
I must appeal for mercy to my
accuser.^y
16 If I summoned him and he
answered me,
I do not believe that he would
listen to my voice.
17 For he crushes me with a tempest,
and multiplies my wounds
without cause;
18 he will not let me get my breath,
but fills me with bitterness.
19 If it is a contest of strength, he is the
strong one!

u Heb *He thrives*   v Gk Vg: Meaning of Heb
uncertain   w Meaning of Heb uncertain   x Or
trampled the back of the sea dragon   y Or *for my
right*

If it is a matter of justice, who can
    summon him?[z]
20 Though I am innocent, my own
    mouth would condemn me;
    though I am blameless, he would
    prove me perverse.
21 I am blameless; I do not know
    myself;
    I loathe my life.
22 It is all one; therefore I say,
    he destroys both the blameless
    and the wicked.
23 When disaster brings sudden death,
    he mocks at the calamity[a] of the
    innocent.
24 The earth is given into the hand of
    the wicked;
    he covers the eyes of its judges—
    if it is not he, who then is it?

25 "My days are swifter than a runner;
    they flee away, they see no good.
26 They go by like skiffs of reed,
    like an eagle swooping on the
    prey.
27 If I say, 'I will forget my complaint;
    I will put off my sad countenance
    and be of good cheer,'
28 I become afraid of all my suffering,
    for I know you will not hold me
    innocent.
29 I shall be condemned;
    why then do I labor in vain?
30 If I wash myself with soap
    and cleanse my hands with lye,
31 yet you will plunge me into filth,
    and my own clothes will abhor
    me.
32 For he is not a mortal, as I am, that
    I might answer him,
    that we should come to trial
    together.
33 There is no umpire[b] between us,
    who might lay his hand on us
    both.
34 If he would take his rod away from
    me,
    and not let dread of him terrify
    me,
35 then I would speak without fear of
    him,
    for I know I am not what I am
    thought to be.[c]

Job: I Loathe My Life

10 "I loathe my life;
    I will give free utterance to my
    complaint;

    I will speak in the bitterness of
    my soul.
2 I will say to God, Do not condemn
    me;
    let me know why you contend
    against me.
3 Does it seem good to you to
    oppress,
    to despise the work of your hands
    and favor the schemes of the
    wicked?
4 Do you have eyes of flesh?
    Do you see as humans see?
5 Are your days like the days of
    mortals,
    or your years like human years,
6 that you seek out my iniquity
    and search for my sin,
7 although you know that I am not
    guilty,
    and there is no one to deliver out
    of your hand?
8 Your hands fashioned and made me;
    and now you turn and destroy
    me.[d]
9 Remember that you fashioned me
    like clay;
    and will you turn me to dust
    again?
10 Did you not pour me out like milk
    and curdle me like cheese?
11 You clothed me with skin and flesh,
    and knit me together with bones
    and sinews.
12 You have granted me life and
    steadfast love,
    and your care has preserved my
    spirit.
13 Yet these things you hid in your
    heart;
    I know that this was your
    purpose.
14 If I sin, you watch me,
    and do not acquit me of my
    iniquity.
15 If I am wicked, woe to me!
    If I am righteous, I cannot lift up
    my head,
    for I am filled with disgrace
    and look upon my affliction.

[z] Compare Gk: Heb *me*   [a] Meaning of Heb
uncertain   [b] Another reading is *Would that there
were an umpire*   [c] Cn: Heb *for I am not so in
myself*   [d] Cn Compare Gk Syr: Heb *made me
together all around, and you destroy me*

16 Bold as a lion you hunt me;
    you repeat your exploits against
        me.
17 You renew your witnesses against
        me,
    and increase your vexation toward
        me;
    you bring fresh troops against
        me.*e*

18 "Why did you bring me forth from
        the womb?
    Would that I had died before any
        eye had seen me,
19 and were as though I had not been,

e Cn Compare Gk: Heb *toward me; changes and a
troop are with me*

TUESDAY

Scripture Reading
for Today:
Job 10.1–8

Verse for Today:
Job 10.2

Why, Lord?

[When my son] was about six years old, he had a million questions and I had answers for all of them.

And then he began to grow in age and wisdom.

In normal, everyday conversations, he started to slip in such
questions as: "Why does breaking the sound barrier make a
noise? How does a quartz watch work? What do you think of the
theory of thermonuclear plasma turbulence?"

When I had to start answering, "Well, I never really thought
about that before"—or—"I don't know the answer," he looked at
me in wonder. "What happened to you? You used to be so smart."

*Dear Lord, when I was younger and asked you, "Why, Lord,
WHY?" your answers always satisfied me. I was secure. God was
good. God knew everything and answered all my questions and
needs. Like my son, I basked in my Father's omniscience.*

*Then I began to grow in my "faith experience." My questions
got harder, and it seemed your answers were more vague. I asked,
"Why is life unfair? Why do we have to have war? Why do people have to suffer? Why do some seem to have more problems
than others? Why did the garbage disposal back up the day I
was having the bridge party? Why, Lord, why?"*

*Unlike my son's mother, you, my Father, have all the answers,
even to the questions I will never be smart enough to ask. You
even give the answers to me sometimes. But I don't always understand them or I don't like them, so I keep asking over again,
hoping that I will hear an answer that suits me better next time.
Forgive my arrogance, Lord.*

*I know the growing pains are necessary. I know I have to keep
wondering and searching and asking if I am to grow toward a
mature faith. Forgive my yearning for the old security. Help me to
enjoy the journey and the never-ending discovery of your dimensions and delights.*

—*BERNADETTE McCARVER SNYDER*

Go to page 652 for your next devotional reading.

carried from the womb to the
grave.

20 Are not the days of my life few? *f*
Let me alone, that I may find a
little comfort*g*
21 before I go, never to return,
to the land of gloom and deep
darkness,
22 the land of gloom*h* and chaos,
where light is like darkness."

Zophar Speaks: Job's Guilt Deserves Punishment

11 Then Zophar the Naamathite answered:
2 "Should a multitude of words go
unanswered,
and should one full of talk be
vindicated?
3 Should your babble put others to
silence,
and when you mock, shall no one
shame you?
4 For you say, 'My conduct*i* is pure,
and I am clean in God's*j* sight.'
5 But O that God would speak,
and open his lips to you,
6 and that he would tell you the
secrets of wisdom!
For wisdom is many-sided.*k*
Know then that God exacts of you
less than your guilt deserves.

7 "Can you find out the deep things
of God?
Can you find out the limit of the
Almighty?*l*
8 It is higher than heaven*m*—what can
you do?
Deeper than Sheol—what can you
know?
9 Its measure is longer than the earth,
and broader than the sea.
10 If he passes through, and imprisons,
and assembles for judgment, who
can hinder him?
11 For he knows those who are
worthless;
when he sees iniquity, will he not
consider it?
12 But a stupid person will get
understanding,
when a wild ass is born human.*k*

13 "If you direct your heart rightly,
you will stretch out your hands
toward him.

14 If iniquity is in your hand, put it far
away,
and do not let wickedness reside
in your tents.
15 Surely then you will lift up your face
without blemish;
you will be secure, and will not
fear.
16 You will forget your misery;
you will remember it as waters
that have passed away.
17 And your life will be brighter than
the noonday;
its darkness will be like the
morning.
18 And you will have confidence,
because there is hope;
you will be protected*n* and take
your rest in safety.
19 You will lie down, and no one will
make you afraid;
many will entreat your favor.
20 But the eyes of the wicked will fail;
all way of escape will be lost to
them,
and their hope is to breathe their
last."

Job Replies: I Am a Laughingstock

12 Then Job answered:
2 "No doubt you are the
people,
and wisdom will die with you.
3 But I have understanding as well as
you;
I am not inferior to you.
Who does not know such things
as these?
4 I am a laughingstock to my friends;
I, who called upon God and he
answered me,
a just and blameless man, I am a
laughingstock.
5 Those at ease have contempt for
misfortune,*k*
but it is ready for those whose
feet are unstable.
6 The tents of robbers are at peace,
and those who provoke God are
secure,

f Cn Compare Gk Syr: Heb *Are not my days few?
Let him cease!*   *g* Heb *that I may brighten up a
little*   *h* Heb *gloom as darkness, deep darkness*
i Gk: Heb *teaching*   *j* Heb *your*   *k* Meaning of
Heb uncertain   *l* Traditional rendering of Heb
Shaddai   *m* Heb *The heights of heaven*   *n* Or *you
will look around*

who bring their god in their
hands.*o*

7 "But ask the animals, and they will
teach you;
the birds of the air, and they will
tell you;

8 ask the plants of the earth, *p* and
they will teach you;
and the fish of the sea will declare
to you.

9 Who among all these does not know
that the hand of the LORD has
done this?

10 In his hand is the life of every living
thing
and the breath of every human
being.

11 Does not the ear test words
as the palate tastes food?

12 Is wisdom with the aged,
and understanding in length of
days?

13 "With God*q* are wisdom and
strength;
he has counsel and understanding.

14 If he tears down, no one can
rebuild;
if he shuts someone in, no one
can open up.

15 If he withholds the waters, they dry
up;
if he sends them out, they
overwhelm the land.

16 With him are strength and wisdom;
the deceived and the deceiver are
his.

17 He leads counselors away stripped,
and makes fools of judges.

18 He looses the sash of kings,
and binds a waistcloth on their
loins.

19 He leads priests away stripped,
and overthrows the mighty.

20 He deprives of speech those who are
trusted,
and takes away the discernment of
the elders.

21 He pours contempt on princes,
and looses the belt of the strong.

22 He uncovers the deeps out of
darkness,
and brings deep darkness to light.

23 He makes nations great, then
destroys them;
he enlarges nations, then leads
them away.

24 He strips understanding from the
leaders*r* of the earth,
and makes them wander in a
pathless waste.

25 They grope in the dark without light;
he makes them stagger like a
drunkard.

13 "Look, my eye has seen all this,
my ear has heard and
understood it.

2 What you know, I also know;
I am not inferior to you.

3 But I would speak to the
Almighty,*s*
and I desire to argue my case with
God.

4 As for you, you whitewash with lies;
all of you are worthless
physicians.

5 If you would only keep silent,
that would be your wisdom!

6 Hear now my reasoning,
and listen to the pleadings of my
lips.

7 Will you speak falsely for God,
and speak deceitfully for him?

8 Will you show partiality toward him,
will you plead the case for God?

9 Will it be well with you when he
searches you out?
Or can you deceive him, as one
person deceives another?

10 He will surely rebuke you
if in secret you show partiality.

11 Will not his majesty terrify you,
and the dread of him fall upon
you?

12 Your maxims are proverbs of ashes,
your defenses are defenses of clay.

13 "Let me have silence, and I will
speak,
and let come on me what may.

14 I will take my flesh in my teeth,
and put my life in my hand.*t*

15 See, he will kill me; I have no
hope;*u*
but I will defend my ways to his
face.

16 This will be my salvation,

---

o Or *whom God brought forth by his hand;* Meaning
of Heb uncertain　　*p* Or *speak to the earth*
q Heb *him*　　*r* Heb adds *of the people*
s Traditional rendering of Heb *Shaddai*
t Gk: Heb *Why should I take . . . in my hand?*
u Or *Though he kill me, yet I will trust in him*

that the godless shall not come
before him.

17 Listen carefully to my words,
and let my declaration be in your
ears.

18 I have indeed prepared my case;
I know that I shall be vindicated.

19 Who is there that will contend with
me?
For then I would be silent and
die.

Job's Despondent Prayer

20 Only grant two things to me,
then I will not hide myself from
your face:

21 withdraw your hand far from me,
and do not let dread of you terrify
me.

22 Then call, and I will answer;
or let me speak, and you reply to
me.

23 How many are my iniquities and my
sins?
Make me know my transgression
and my sin.

24 Why do you hide your face,
and count me as your enemy?

25 Will you frighten a windblown leaf
and pursue dry chaff?

26 For you write bitter things against
me,
and make me reap[v] the iniquities
of my youth.

27 You put my feet in the stocks,
and watch all my paths;
you set a bound to the soles of
my feet.

28 One wastes away like a rotten thing,
like a garment that is moth-eaten.

14 "A mortal, born of woman, few
of days and full of trouble,

2 comes up like a flower and
withers,
flees like a shadow and does not
last.

3 Do you fix your eyes on such a one?
Do you bring me into judgment
with you?

4 Who can bring a clean thing out of
an unclean?
No one can.

5 Since their days are determined,
and the number of their months
is known to you,
and you have appointed the
bounds that they cannot pass,

6 look away from them, and desist,[w]
that they may enjoy, like laborers,
their days.

7 "For there is hope for a tree,
if it is cut down, that it will
sprout again,
and that its shoots will not cease.

8 Though its root grows old in the
earth,
and its stump dies in the ground,

9 yet at the scent of water it will bud
and put forth branches like a
young plant.

10 But mortals die, and are laid low;
humans expire, and where are
they?

11 As waters fail from a lake,
and a river wastes away and dries
up,

12 so mortals lie down and do not rise
again;
until the heavens are no more,
they will not awake
or be roused out of their sleep.

13 O that you would hide me in Sheol,
that you would conceal me until
your wrath is past,
that you would appoint me a set
time, and remember me!

14 If mortals die, will they live again?
All the days of my service I would
wait
until my release should come.

15 You would call, and I would answer
you;
you would long for the work of
your hands.

16 For then you would not[x] number
my steps,
you would not keep watch over
my sin;

17 my transgression would be sealed up
in a bag,
and you would cover over my
iniquity.

18 "But the mountain falls and
crumbles away,
and the rock is removed from its
place;

19 the waters wear away the stones;
the torrents wash away the soil of
the earth;

v Heb inherit   w Cn: Heb that they may desist
x Syr: Heb lacks not

so you destroy the hope of
   mortals.
20 You prevail forever against them,
      and they pass away;
   you change their countenance,
      and send them away.
21 Their children come to honor, and
      they do not know it;
   they are brought low, and it goes
      unnoticed.
22 They feel only the pain of their own
      bodies,
   and mourn only for themselves."

Eliphaz Speaks: Job Undermines Religion

15 Then Eliphaz the Temanite an-
      swered:
2 "Should the wise answer with windy
      knowledge,
   and fill themselves with the east
      wind?
3 Should they argue in unprofitable
      talk,
   or in words with which they can
      do no good?
4 But you are doing away with the
      fear of God,
   and hindering meditation before
      God.
5 For your iniquity teaches your
      mouth,
   and you choose the tongue of the
      crafty.
6 Your own mouth condemns you,
      and not I;
   your own lips testify against you.

7 "Are you the firstborn of the human
      race?
   Were you brought forth before the
      hills?
8 Have you listened in the council of
      God?
   And do you limit wisdom to
      yourself?
9 What do you know that we do not
      know?
   What do you understand that is
      not clear to us?
10 The gray-haired and the aged are on
      our side,
   those older than your father.
11 Are the consolations of God too
      small for you,
   or the word that deals gently with
      you?
12 Why does your heart carry you away,
   and why do your eyes flash, y

13 so that you turn your spirit against
      God,
   and let such words go out of your
      mouth?
14 What are mortals, that they can be
      clean?
   Or those born of woman, that
      they can be righteous?
15 God puts no trust even in his holy
      ones,
   and the heavens are not clean in
      his sight;
16 how much less one who is
      abominable and corrupt,
   one who drinks iniquity like
      water!

17 "I will show you; listen to me;
   what I have seen I will declare—
18 what sages have told,
   and their ancestors have not
      hidden,
19 to whom alone the land was given,
   and no stranger passed among
      them.
20 The wicked writhe in pain all their
      days,
   through all the years that are laid
      up for the ruthless.
21 Terrifying sounds are in their ears;
   in prosperity the destroyer will
      come upon them.
22 They despair of returning from
      darkness,
   and they are destined for the
      sword.
23 They wander abroad for bread,
      saying, 'Where is it?'
   They know that a day of darkness
      is ready at hand;
24 distress and anguish terrify them;
   they prevail against them, like a
      king prepared for battle.
25 Because they stretched out their
      hands against God,
   and bid defiance to the
      Almighty, z
26 running stubbornly against him
   with a thick-bossed shield;
27 because they have covered their faces
      with their fat,
   and gathered fat upon their loins,
28 they will live in desolate cities,
   in houses that no one should
      inhabit,

y Meaning of Heb uncertain   z Traditional
rendering of Heb *Shaddai*

houses destined to become heaps
     of ruins;
29 they will not be rich, and their
     wealth will not endure,
     nor will they strike root in the
     earth;*a*
30 they will not escape from darkness;
     the flame will dry up their shoots,
     and their blossom*b* will be swept
     away*c* by the wind.
31 Let them not trust in emptiness,
     deceiving themselves;
     for emptiness will be their
     recompense.
32 It will be paid in full before their
     time,
     and their branch will not be
     green.
33 They will shake off their unripe
     grape, like the vine,
     and cast off their blossoms, like
     the olive tree.
34 For the company of the godless is
     barren,
     and fire consumes the tents of
     bribery.
35 They conceive mischief and bring
     forth evil
     and their heart prepares deceit."

Job Reaffirms His Innocence

16 Then Job answered:
2 "I have heard many such
     things;
     miserable comforters are you all.
3 Have windy words no limit?
     Or what provokes you that you
     keep on talking?
4 I also could talk as you do,
     if you were in my place;
     I could join words together against
     you,
     and shake my head at you.
5 I could encourage you with my
     mouth,
     and the solace of my lips would
     assuage your pain.

6 "If I speak, my pain is not assuaged,
     and if I forbear, how much of it
     leaves me?
7 Surely now God has worn me out;
     he has*d* made desolate all my
     company.
8 And he has*d* shriveled me up,
     which is a witness against me;

my leanness has risen up against
     me,
     and it testifies to my face.
9 He has torn me in his wrath, and
     hated me;
     he has gnashed his teeth at me;
     my adversary sharpens his eyes
     against me.
10 They have gaped at me with their
     mouths;
     they have struck me insolently on
     the cheek;
     they mass themselves together
     against me.
11 God gives me up to the ungodly,
     and casts me into the hands of
     the wicked.
12 I was at ease, and he broke me in
     two;
     he seized me by the neck and
     dashed me to pieces;
     he set me up as his target;
13   his archers surround me.
     He slashes open my kidneys, and
     shows no mercy;
     he pours out my gall on the
     ground.
14 He bursts upon me again and again;
     he rushes at me like a warrior.
15 I have sewed sackcloth upon my
     skin,
     and have laid my strength in the
     dust.
16 My face is red with weeping,
     and deep darkness is on my
     eyelids,
17 though there is no violence in my
     hands,
     and my prayer is pure.

18 "O earth, do not cover my blood;
     let my outcry find no resting
     place.
19 Even now, in fact, my witness is in
     heaven,
     and he that vouches for me is on
     high.
20 My friends scorn me;
     my eye pours out tears to God,
21 that he would maintain the right of
     a mortal with God,
     as*e* one does for a neighbor.

a Vg: Meaning of Heb uncertain   *b* Gk: Heb
mouth   *c* Cn: Heb *will depart*   *d* Heb *you have*
e Syr Vg Tg: Heb *and*

22 For when a few years have come,
   I shall go the way from which I
      shall not return.

Job Prays for Relief

17 My spirit is broken, my days are
   extinct,
   the grave is ready for me.
2 Surely there are mockers around me,
   and my eye dwells on their
      provocation.

3 "Lay down a pledge for me with
      yourself;
   who is there that will give surety
      for me?
4 Since you have closed their minds to
      understanding,
   therefore you will not let them
      triumph.
5 Those who denounce friends for
      reward—
   the eyes of their children will fail.

6 "He has made me a byword of the
      peoples,
   and I am one before whom
      people spit.
7 My eye has grown dim from grief,
   and all my members are like a
      shadow.
8 The upright are appalled at this,
   and the innocent stir themselves
      up against the godless.
9 Yet the righteous hold to their way,
   and they that have clean hands
      grow stronger and stronger.
10 But you, come back now, all of you,
   and I shall not find a sensible
      person among you.
11 My days are past, my plans are
      broken off,
   the desires of my heart.
12 They make night into day;
   'The light,' they say, 'is near to
      the darkness.'*f*
13 If I look for Sheol as my house,
   if I spread my couch in darkness,
14 if I say to the Pit, 'You are my
      father,'
   and to the worm, 'My mother,' or
      'My sister,'
15 where then is my hope?
   Who will see my hope?
16 Will it go down to the bars of
      Sheol?
   Shall we descend together into the
      dust?"

Bildad Speaks: God Punishes the Wicked

18 Then Bildad the Shuhite answered:
2 "How long will you hunt for words?
   Consider, and then we shall
      speak.
3 Why are we counted as cattle?
   Why are we stupid in your sight?
4 You who tear yourself in your
      anger—
   shall the earth be forsaken
      because of you,
   or the rock be removed out of its
      place?

5 "Surely the light of the wicked is
      put out,
   and the flame of their fire does
      not shine.
6 The light is dark in their tent,
   and the lamp above them is put
      out.
7 Their strong steps are shortened,
   and their own schemes throw
      them down.
8 For they are thrust into a net by
      their own feet,
   and they walk into a pitfall.
9 A trap seizes them by the heel;
   a snare lays hold of them.
10 A rope is hid for them in the
      ground,
   a trap for them in the path.
11 Terrors frighten them on every side,
   and chase them at their heels.
12 Their strength is consumed by
      hunger,*g*
   and calamity is ready for their
      stumbling.
13 By disease their skin is consumed,*h*
   the firstborn of Death consumes
      their limbs.
14 They are torn from the tent in which
      they trusted,
   and are brought to the king of
      terrors.
15 In their tents nothing remains;
   sulfur is scattered upon their
      habitations.
16 Their roots dry up beneath,
   and their branches wither above.
17 Their memory perishes from the
      earth,

---

f Meaning of Heb uncertain   *g* Or *Disaster is
hungry for them*   *h* Cn: Heb *It consumes the limbs
of his skin*

and they have no name in the
street.
18 They are thrust from light into
darkness,
and driven out of the world.
19 They have no offspring or
descendant among their
people,
and no survivor where they used
to live.
20 They of the west are appalled at
their fate,
and horror seizes those of the
east.
21 Surely such are the dwellings of the
ungodly,
such is the place of those who do
not know God."

Job Replies: I Know That My Redeemer Lives

19 Then Job answered:
2 "How long will you torment
me,
and break me in pieces with
words?
3 These ten times you have cast
reproach upon me;
are you not ashamed to wrong
me?
4 And even if it is true that I have
erred,
my error remains with me.
5 If indeed you magnify yourselves
against me,
and make my humiliation an
argument against me,
6 know then that God has put me in
the wrong,
and closed his net around me.
7 Even when I cry out, 'Violence!' I
am not answered;
I call aloud, but there is no
justice.
8 He has walled up my way so that I
cannot pass,
and he has set darkness upon my
paths.
9 He has stripped my glory from me,
and taken the crown from my
head.
10 He breaks me down on every side,
and I am gone,
he has uprooted my hope like a
tree.
11 He has kindled his wrath against
me,
and counts me as his adversary.

12 His troops come on together;
they have thrown up siegeworks*i*
against me,
and encamp around my tent.

13 "He has put my family far from me,
and my acquaintances are wholly
estranged from me.
14 My relatives and my close friends
have failed me;
15 the guests in my house have
forgotten me;
my serving girls count me as a
stranger;
I have become an alien in their
eyes.
16 I call to my servant, but he gives me
no answer;
I must myself plead with him.
17 My breath is repulsive to my wife;
I am loathsome to my own
family.
18 Even young children despise me;
when I rise, they talk against me.
19 All my intimate friends abhor me,
and those whom I loved have
turned against me.
20 My bones cling to my skin and to
my flesh,
and I have escaped by the skin of
my teeth.
21 Have pity on me, have pity on me,
O you my friends,
for the hand of God has touched
me!
22 Why do you, like God, pursue me,
never satisfied with my flesh?

23 "O that my words were written
down!
O that they were inscribed in a
book!
24 O that with an iron pen and with
lead
they were engraved on a rock
forever!
25 For I know that my Redeemer*j*
lives,
and that at the last he*k* will stand
upon the earth;*l*
26 and after my skin has been thus
destroyed,
then in*m* my flesh I shall see
God,*n*

i Cn: Heb *their way*   *j* Or *Vindicator*   *k* Or *that
he the Last*   *l* Heb *dust*   *m* Or *without*
n Meaning of Heb of this verse uncertain

27 whom I shall see on my side,[o]
and my eyes shall behold, and not another.
My heart faints within me!
28 If you say, 'How we will persecute him!'
and, 'The root of the matter is found in him';
29 be afraid of the sword,
for wrath brings the punishment of the sword,
so that you may know there is a judgment."

Zophar Speaks: Wickedness Receives Just Retribution

20 Then Zophar the Naamathite answered:
2 "Pay attention! My thoughts urge me to answer,
because of the agitation within me.
3 I hear censure that insults me,
and a spirit beyond my understanding answers me.
4 Do you not know this from of old,
ever since mortals were placed on earth,
5 that the exulting of the wicked is short,
and the joy of the godless is but for a moment?
6 Even though they mount up high as the heavens,
and their head reaches to the clouds,
7 they will perish forever like their own dung;
those who have seen them will say, 'Where are they?'
8 They will fly away like a dream, and not be found;
they will be chased away like a vision of the night.
9 The eye that saw them will see them no more,
nor will their place behold them any longer.
10 Their children will seek the favor of the poor,
and their hands will give back their wealth.
11 Their bodies, once full of youth,
will lie down in the dust with them.

12 "Though wickedness is sweet in their mouth,
though they hide it under their tongues,
13 though they are loath to let it go,
and hold it in their mouths,
14 yet their food is turned in their stomachs;
it is the venom of asps within them.
15 They swallow down riches and vomit them up again;
God casts them out of their bellies.
16 They will suck the poison of asps;
the tongue of a viper will kill them.
17 They will not look on the rivers,
the streams flowing with honey and curds.
18 They will give back the fruit of their toil,
and will not swallow it down;
from the profit of their trading
they will get no enjoyment.
19 For they have crushed and abandoned the poor,
they have seized a house that they did not build.

20 "They knew no quiet in their bellies;
in their greed they let nothing escape.
21 There was nothing left after they had eaten;
therefore their prosperity will not endure.
22 In full sufficiency they will be in distress;
all the force of misery will come upon them.
23 To fill their belly to the full
God[p] will send his fierce anger into them,
and rain it upon them as their food.[q]
24 They will flee from an iron weapon;
a bronze arrow will strike them through.
25 It is drawn forth and comes out of their body,
and the glittering point comes out of their gall;
terrors come upon them.
26 Utter darkness is laid up for their treasures;

[o] Or *for myself* [p] Heb *he* [q] Cn: Meaning of Heb uncertain

a fire fanned by no one will
    devour them;
what is left in their tent will be
    consumed.
27 The heavens will reveal their
    iniquity,
and the earth will rise up against
    them.
28 The possessions of their house will
    be carried away,
dragged off in the day of God's*r*
    wrath.
29 This is the portion of the wicked
    from God,
the heritage decreed for them by
    God."

Job Replies: The Wicked Often Go Unpunished

21 Then Job answered:
2 "Listen carefully to my
    words,
and let this be your consolation.
3 Bear with me, and I will speak;
    then after I have spoken, mock
    on.
4 As for me, is my complaint
    addressed to mortals?
Why should I not be impatient?
5 Look at me, and be appalled,
    and lay your hand upon your
    mouth.
6 When I think of it I am dismayed,
    and shuddering seizes my flesh.
7 Why do the wicked live on,
    reach old age, and grow mighty in
    power?
8 Their children are established in
    their presence,
and their offspring before their
    eyes.
9 Their houses are safe from fear,
    and no rod of God is upon them.
10 Their bull breeds without fail;
    their cow calves and never
    miscarries.
11 They send out their little ones like a
    flock,
and their children dance around.
12 They sing to the tambourine and the
    lyre,
and rejoice to the sound of the
    pipe.
13 They spend their days in prosperity,
    and in peace they go down to
    Sheol.
14 They say to God, 'Leave us alone!

We do not desire to know your
    ways.
15 What is the Almighty,*s* that we
    should serve him?
And what profit do we get if we
    pray to him?'
16 Is not their prosperity indeed their
    own achievement?*t*
The plans of the wicked are
    repugnant to me.

17 "How often is the lamp of the
    wicked put out?
How often does calamity come
    upon them?
How often does God*u* distribute
    pains in his anger?
18 How often are they like straw before
    the wind,
and like chaff that the storm
    carries away?
19 You say, 'God stores up their
    iniquity for their children.'
Let it be paid back to them, so
    that they may know it.
20 Let their own eyes see their
    destruction,
and let them drink of the wrath of
    the Almighty.*s*
21 For what do they care for their
    household after them,
when the number of their months
    is cut off?
22 Will any teach God knowledge,
    seeing that he judges those that
    are on high?
23 One dies in full prosperity,
    being wholly at ease and secure,
24 his loins full of milk
    and the marrow of his bones
    moist.
25 Another dies in bitterness of soul,
    never having tasted of good.
26 They lie down alike in the dust,
    and the worms cover them.

27 "Oh, I know your thoughts,
    and your schemes to wrong me.
28 For you say, 'Where is the house of
    the prince?
Where is the tent in which the
    wicked lived?'
29 Have you not asked those who
    travel the roads,

r Heb *his*   *s* Traditional rendering of Heb
Shaddai   *t* Heb *in their hand*   *u* Heb *he*

and do you not accept their
  testimony,
30 that the wicked are spared in the
  day of calamity,
  and are rescued in the day of
  wrath?
31 Who declares their way to their face,
  and who repays them for what
  they have done?
32 When they are carried to the grave,
  a watch is kept over their tomb.
33 The clods of the valley are sweet to
  them;
  everyone will follow after,
  and those who went before are
  innumerable.
34 How then will you comfort me with
  empty nothings?
  There is nothing left of your
  answers but falsehood."

Eliphaz Speaks: Job's Wickedness Is Great

22 Then Eliphaz the Temanite answered:
2 "Can a mortal be of use to God?
  Can even the wisest be of service
  to him?
3 Is it any pleasure to the Almighty[v]
  if you are righteous,
  or is it gain to him if you make
  your ways blameless?
4 Is it for your piety that he reproves
  you,
  and enters into judgment with
  you?
5 Is not your wickedness great?
  There is no end to your iniquities.
6 For you have exacted pledges from
  your family for no reason,
  and stripped the naked of their
  clothing.
7 You have given no water to the
  weary to drink,
  and you have withheld bread
  from the hungry.
8 The powerful possess the land,
  and the favored live in it.
9 You have sent widows away
  empty-handed,
  and the arms of the orphans you
  have crushed.[w]
10 Therefore snares are around you,
  and sudden terror overwhelms
  you,
11 or darkness so that you cannot see;
  a flood of water covers you.

12 "Is not God high in the heavens?

See the highest stars, how lofty
  they are!
13 Therefore you say, 'What does God
  know?
  Can he judge through the deep
  darkness?
14 Thick clouds enwrap him, so that he
  does not see,
  and he walks on the dome of
  heaven.'
15 Will you keep to the old way
  that the wicked have trod?
16 They were snatched away before
  their time;
  their foundation was washed away
  by a flood.
17 They said to God, 'Leave us alone,'
  and 'What can the Almighty[v] do
  to us?'[x]
18 Yet he filled their houses with good
  things—
  but the plans of the wicked are
  repugnant to me.
19 The righteous see it and are glad;
  the innocent laugh them to scorn,
20 saying, 'Surely our adversaries are
  cut off,
  and what they left, the fire has
  consumed.'

21 "Agree with God,[y] and be at peace;
  in this way good will come to
  you.
22 Receive instruction from his mouth,
  and lay up his words in your
  heart.
23 If you return to the Almighty,[v] you
  will be restored,
  if you remove unrighteousness
  from your tents,
24 if you treat gold like dust,
  and gold of Ophir like the stones
  of the torrent-bed,
25 and if the Almighty[v] is your gold
  and your precious silver,
26 then you will delight yourself in the
  Almighty,[v]
  and lift up your face to God.
27 You will pray to him, and he will
  hear you,
  and you will pay your vows.
28 You will decide on a matter, and it
  will be established for you,
  and light will shine on your ways.

---

[v] Traditional rendering of Heb *Shaddai*   [w] Gk
Syr Tg Vg: Heb *were crushed*   [x] Gk Syr: Heb *them*
[y] Heb *him*

29 When others are humiliated, you say
   it is pride;
   for he saves the humble.
30 He will deliver even those who are
   guilty;
   they will escape because of the
   cleanness of your hands."*z*

Job Replies: My Complaint Is Bitter

23 Then Job answered:
2 "Today also my complaint
   is bitter;*a*
   his*b* hand is heavy despite my
   groaning.
3 Oh, that I knew where I might find
   him,
   that I might come even to his
   dwelling!
4 I would lay my case before him,
   and fill my mouth with
   arguments.
5 I would learn what he would answer
   me,
   and understand what he would
   say to me.
6 Would he contend with me in the
   greatness of his power?
   No; but he would give heed to
   me.
7 There an upright person could
   reason with him,
   and I should be acquitted forever
   by my judge.

8 "If I go forward, he is not there;
   or backward, I cannot perceive
   him;
9 on the left he hides, and I cannot
   behold him;
   I turn*c* to the right, but I cannot
   see him.
10 But he knows the way that I take;
   when he has tested me, I shall
   come out like gold.
11 My foot has held fast to his steps;
   I have kept his way and have not
   turned aside.
12 I have not departed from the
   commandment of his lips;
   I have treasured in*d* my bosom
   the words of his mouth.
13 But he stands alone and who can
   dissuade him?
   What he desires, that he does.
14 For he will complete what he
   appoints for me;
   and many such things are in his
   mind.

15 Therefore I am terrified at his
   presence;
   when I consider, I am in dread of
   him.
16 God has made my heart faint;
   the Almighty*e* has terrified me;
17 If only I could vanish in darkness,
   and thick darkness would cover
   my face!*f*

Job Complains of Violence on the Earth

24 "Why are times not kept by the
   Almighty,*e*
   and why do those who know him
   never see his days?
2 The wicked*g* remove landmarks;
   they seize flocks and pasture
   them.
3 They drive away the donkey of the
   orphan;
   they take the widow's ox for a
   pledge.
4 They thrust the needy off the road;
   the poor of the earth all hide
   themselves.
5 Like wild asses in the desert
   they go out to their toil,
   scavenging in the wasteland
   food for their young.
6 They reap in a field not their own
   and they glean in the vineyard of
   the wicked.
7 They lie all night naked, without
   clothing,
   and have no covering in the cold.
8 They are wet with the rain of the
   mountains,
   and cling to the rock for want of
   shelter.

9 "There are those who snatch the
   orphan child from the breast,
   and take as a pledge the infant of
   the poor.
10 They go about naked, without
   clothing;
   though hungry, they carry the
   sheaves;
11 between their terraces*z* they press
   out oil;

---

z Meaning of Heb uncertain   *a* Syr Vg Tg: Heb
rebellious   *b* Gk Syr: Heb *my*   *c* Syr Vg: Heb *he
turns*   *d* Gk Vg: Heb *from*   *e* Traditional
rendering of Heb *Shaddai*   *f* Or *But I am not
destroyed by the darkness; he has concealed the thick
darkness from me*   *g* Gk: Heb *they*

they tread the wine presses, but
suffer thirst.
12 From the city the dying groan,
and the throat of the wounded
cries for help;
yet God pays no attention to their
prayer.

13 "There are those who rebel against
the light,
who are not acquainted with its
ways,
and do not stay in its paths.
14 The murderer rises at dusk
to kill the poor and needy,
and in the night is like a thief.
15 The eye of the adulterer also waits
for the twilight,
saying, 'No eye will see me';
and he disguises his face.
16 In the dark they dig through houses;
by day they shut themselves up;
they do not know the light.
17 For deep darkness is morning to all
of them;
for they are friends with the
terrors of deep darkness.

18 "Swift are they on the face of the
waters;
their portion in the land is cursed;
no treader turns toward their
vineyards.
19 Drought and heat snatch away the
snow waters;
so does Sheol those who have
sinned.
20 The womb forgets them;
the worm finds them sweet;
they are no longer remembered;
so wickedness is broken like a
tree.

21 "They harm^h the childless woman,
and do no good to the widow.
22 Yet God^i prolongs the life of the
mighty by his power;
they rise up when they despair of
life.
23 He gives them security, and they are
supported;
his eyes are upon their ways.
24 They are exalted a little while, and
then are gone;
they wither and fade like the
mallow;^j
they are cut off like the heads of
grain.

25 If it is not so, who will prove me a
liar,
and show that there is nothing in
what I say?"

Bildad Speaks: How Can a Mortal Be Righteous Before God?

25 Then Bildad the Shuhite answered:
2 "Dominion and fear are with
God;^k
he makes peace in his high
heaven.
3 Is there any number to his armies?
Upon whom does his light not
arise?
4 How then can a mortal be righteous
before God?
How can one born of woman be
pure?
5 If even the moon is not bright
and the stars are not pure in his
sight,
6 how much less a mortal, who is a
maggot,
and a human being, who is a
worm!"

Job Replies: God's Majesty Is Unsearchable

26 Then Job answered:
2 "How you have helped one
who has no power!
How you have assisted the arm
that has no strength!
3 How you have counseled one who
has no wisdom,
and given much good advice!
4 With whose help have you uttered
words,
and whose spirit has come forth
from you?
5 The shades below tremble,
the waters and their inhabitants.
6 Sheol is naked before God,
and Abaddon has no covering.
7 He stretches out Zaphon^l over the
void,
and hangs the earth upon
nothing.
8 He binds up the waters in his thick
clouds,
and the cloud is not torn open by
them.
9 He covers the face of the full moon,

---

h Gk Tg: Heb *feed on* or *associate with*   *i* Heb *he*
j Gk: Heb *like all others*   *k* Heb *him*   *l* Or
the North

and spreads over it his cloud.
10 He has described a circle on the face
      of the waters,
    at the boundary between light and
      darkness.
11 The pillars of heaven tremble,
    and are astounded at his rebuke.
12 By his power he stilled the Sea;
    by his understanding he struck
      down Rahab.
13 By his wind the heavens were made
      fair;
    his hand pierced the fleeing
      serpent.
14 These are indeed but the outskirts of
      his ways;
    and how small a whisper do we
      hear of him!
    But the thunder of his power who
      can understand?"

Job Maintains His Integrity

27 Job again took up his discourse
      and said:
2 "As God lives, who has taken away
      my right,
    and the Almighty,*m* who has
      made my soul bitter,
3 as long as my breath is in me
    and the spirit of God is in my
      nostrils,
4 my lips will not speak falsehood,
    and my tongue will not utter
      deceit.
5 Far be it from me to say that you
      are right;
    until I die I will not put away my
      integrity from me.
6 I hold fast my righteousness, and
      will not let it go;
    my heart does not reproach me
      for any of my days.

7 "May my enemy be like the wicked,
    and may my opponent be like the
      unrighteous.
8 For what is the hope of the godless
      when God cuts them off,
    when God takes away their lives?
9 Will God hear their cry
    when trouble comes upon them?
10 Will they take delight in the
      Almighty?*m*
    Will they call upon God at all
      times?
11 I will teach you concerning the hand
      of God;

that which is with the Almighty*m*
    I will not conceal.
12 All of you have seen it yourselves;
    why then have you become
      altogether vain?

13 "This is the portion of the wicked
      with God,
    and the heritage that oppressors
      receive from the Almighty:*m*
14 If their children are multiplied, it is
      for the sword;
    and their offspring have not
      enough to eat.
15 Those who survive them the
      pestilence buries,
    and their widows make no
      lamentation.
16 Though they heap up silver like
      dust,
    and pile up clothing like clay—
17 they may pile it up, but the just will
      wear it,
    and the innocent will divide the
      silver.
18 They build their houses like nests,
    like booths made by sentinels of
      the vineyard.
19 They go to bed with wealth, but will
      do so no more;
    they open their eyes, and it is
      gone.
20 Terrors overtake them like a flood;
    in the night a whirlwind carries
      them off.
21 The east wind lifts them up and they
      are gone;
    it sweeps them out of their place.
22 It*n* hurls at them without pity;
    they flee from its*o* power in
      headlong flight.
23 It*n* claps its*o* hands at them,
    and hisses at them from its*o*
      place.

Interlude: Where Wisdom Is Found

28 "Surely there is a mine for
      silver,
    and a place for gold to be refined.
2 Iron is taken out of the earth,
    and copper is smelted from ore.
3 Miners put*p* an end to darkness,
    and search out to the farthest
      bound

m Traditional rendering of Heb *Shaddai*   *n* Or
He (that is God)   *o* Or *his*   *p* Heb *He puts*

the ore in gloom and deep
　　darkness.
4 They open shafts in a valley away
　　from human habitation;
　they are forgotten by travelers,
　they sway suspended, remote from
　　people.
5 As for the earth, out of it comes
　　bread;
　but underneath it is turned up as
　　by fire.
6 Its stones are the place of
　　sapphires,*q*
　and its dust contains gold.

7 "That path no bird of prey knows,
　and the falcon's eye has not seen
　　it.
8 The proud wild animals have not
　　trodden it;
　the lion has not passed over it.

9 "They put their hand to the flinty
　　rock,
　and overturn mountains by the
　　roots.
10 They cut out channels in the rocks,
　and their eyes see every precious
　　thing.
11 The sources of the rivers they
　　probe;*r*
　hidden things they bring to light.

12 "But where shall wisdom be found?
　And where is the place of
　　understanding?
13 Mortals do not know the way to
　　it,*s*
　and it is not found in the land of
　　the living.
14 The deep says, 'It is not in me,'
　and the sea says, 'It is not with
　　me.'
15 It cannot be gotten for gold,
　and silver cannot be weighed out
　　as its price.
16 It cannot be valued in the gold of
　　Ophir,
　in precious onyx or sapphire.*q*
17 Gold and glass cannot equal it,
　nor can it be exchanged for jewels
　　of fine gold.
18 No mention shall be made of coral
　　or of crystal;
　the price of wisdom is above
　　pearls.

19 The chrysolite of Ethiopia*t* cannot
　　compare with it,
　nor can it be valued in pure gold.

20 "Where then does wisdom come
　　from?
　And where is the place of
　　understanding?
21 It is hidden from the eyes of all
　　living,
　and concealed from the birds of
　　the air.
22 Abaddon and Death say,
　'We have heard a rumor of it with
　　our ears.'

23 "God understands the way to it,
　and he knows its place.
24 For he looks to the ends of the
　　earth,
　and sees everything under the
　　heavens.
25 When he gave to the wind its
　　weight,
　and apportioned out the waters by
　　measure;
26 when he made a decree for the rain,
　and a way for the thunderbolt;
27 then he saw it and declared it;
　he established it, and searched it
　　out.
28 And he said to humankind,
　'Truly, the fear of the Lord, that is
　　wisdom;
　and to depart from evil is
　　understanding.' "

Job Finishes His Defense

29 Job again took up his discourse
　　and said:
2 "O that I were as in the months of
　　old,
　as in the days when God watched
　　over me;
3 when his lamp shone over my head,
　and by his light I walked through
　　darkness;
4 when I was in my prime,
　when the friendship of God was
　　upon my tent;
5 when the Almighty*u* was still with
　　me,
　when my children were around
　　me;

q Or *lapis lazuli*　　*r* Gk Vg: Heb *bind*　　*s* Gk: Heb
its price　　*t* Or *Nubia*; Heb *Cush*　　*u* Traditional
rendering of Heb *Shaddai*

6 when my steps were washed with
  milk,
  and the rock poured out for me
  streams of oil!
7 When I went out to the gate of the
  city,
  when I took my seat in the
  square,
8 the young men saw me and
  withdrew,
  and the aged rose up and stood;
9 the nobles refrained from talking,
  and laid their hands on their
  mouths;
10 the voices of princes were hushed,
  and their tongues stuck to the
  roof of their mouths.
11 When the ear heard, it commended
  me,
  and when the eye saw, it
  approved;
12 because I delivered the poor who
  cried,
  and the orphan who had no
  helper.
13 The blessing of the wretched came
  upon me,
  and I caused the widow's heart to
  sing for joy.
14 I put on righteousness, and it
  clothed me;
  my justice was like a robe and a
  turban.
15 I was eyes to the blind,
  and feet to the lame.
16 I was a father to the needy,
  and I championed the cause of
  the stranger.
17 I broke the fangs of the unrighteous,
  and made them drop their prey
  from their teeth.
18 Then I thought, 'I shall die in my
  nest,
  and I shall multiply my days like
  the phoenix;*v*
19 my roots spread out to the waters,
  with the dew all night on my
  branches;
20 my glory was fresh with me,
  and my bow ever new in my
  hand.'

21 "They listened to me, and waited,
  and kept silence for my counsel.
22 After I spoke they did not speak
  again,
  and my word dropped upon them
  like dew.*w*

23 They waited for me as for the rain;
  they opened their mouths as for
  the spring rain.
24 I smiled on them when they had no
  confidence;
  and the light of my countenance
  they did not extinguish.*x*
25 I chose their way, and sat as chief,
  and I lived like a king among his
  troops,
  like one who comforts mourners.

30 "But now they make sport of
    me,
  those who are younger than I,
  whose fathers I would have
  disdained
  to set with the dogs of my flock.
2 What could I gain from the strength
  of their hands?
  All their vigor is gone.
3 Through want and hard hunger
  they gnaw the dry and desolate
  ground,
4 they pick mallow and the leaves of
  bushes,
  and to warm themselves the roots
  of broom.
5 They are driven out from society;
  people shout after them as after a
  thief.
6 In the gullies of wadis they must
  live,
  in holes in the ground, and in the
  rocks.
7 Among the bushes they bray;
  under the nettles they huddle
  together.
8 A senseless, disreputable brood,
  they have been whipped out of
  the land.

9 "And now they mock me in song;
  I am a byword to them.
10 They abhor me, they keep aloof
  from me;
  they do not hesitate to spit at the
  sight of me.
11 Because God has loosed my
  bowstring and humbled me,
  they have cast off restraint in my
  presence.
12 On my right hand the rabble rise
  up;
  they send me sprawling,

---

v Or *like sand*   *w* Heb lacks *like dew*
x Meaning of Heb uncertain

and build roads for my ruin.
¹³ They break up my path,
    they promote my calamity;
    no one restrains[y] them.
¹⁴ As through a wide breach they
      come;
    amid the crash they roll on.
¹⁵ Terrors are turned upon me;
    my honor is pursued as by the
      wind,
    and my prosperity has passed
      away like a cloud.

¹⁶ "And now my soul is poured out
      within me;
    days of affliction have taken hold
      of me.
¹⁷ The night racks my bones,
    and the pain that gnaws me takes
      no rest.
¹⁸ With violence he seizes my
      garment;[z]
    he grasps me by[a] the collar of
      my tunic.
¹⁹ He has cast me into the mire,
    and I have become like dust and
      ashes.
²⁰ I cry to you and you do not answer
      me;
    I stand, and you merely look at
      me.
²¹ You have turned cruel to me;
    with the might of your hand you
      persecute me.
²² You lift me up on the wind, you
      make me ride on it,
    and you toss me about in the roar
      of the storm.
²³ I know that you will bring me to
      death,
    and to the house appointed for all
      living.

²⁴ "Surely one does not turn against
      the needy,[b]
    when in disaster they cry for
      help.[c]
²⁵ Did I not weep for those whose day
      was hard?
    Was not my soul grieved for the
      poor?
²⁶ But when I looked for good, evil
      came;
    and when I waited for light,
      darkness came.
²⁷ My inward parts are in turmoil, and
    are never still;

days of affliction come to meet
      me.
²⁸ I go about in sunless gloom;
    I stand up in the assembly and cry
      for help.
²⁹ I am a brother of jackals,
    and a companion of ostriches.
³⁰ My skin turns black and falls from
      me,
    and my bones burn with heat.
³¹ My lyre is turned to mourning,
    and my pipe to the voice of those
      who weep.

31 "I have made a covenant with
      my eyes;
    how then could I look upon a
      virgin?
² What would be my portion from
      God above,
    and my heritage from the
      Almighty[d] on high?
³ Does not calamity befall the
      unrighteous,
    and disaster the workers of
      iniquity?
⁴ Does he not see my ways,
    and number all my steps?

⁵ "If I have walked with falsehood,
    and my foot has hurried to
      deceit—
⁶ let me be weighed in a just balance,
    and let God know my integrity!—
⁷ if my step has turned aside from the
      way,
    and my heart has followed my
      eyes,
    and if any spot has clung to my
      hands;
⁸ then let me sow, and another eat;
    and let what grows for me be
      rooted out.

⁹ "If my heart has been enticed by a
      woman,
    and I have lain in wait at my
      neighbor's door;
¹⁰ then let my wife grind for another,
    and let other men kneel over her.
¹¹ For that would be a heinous crime;
    that would be a criminal offense;

---

[y] Cn: Heb *helps*   [z] Gk: Heb *my garment is
disfigured*   [a] Heb *like*   [b] Heb *ruin*   [c] Cn:
Meaning of Heb uncertain   [d] Traditional
rendering of Heb *Shaddai*

12 for that would be a fire consuming
    down to Abaddon,
  and it would burn to the root all
    my harvest.

13 "If I have rejected the cause of my
    male or female slaves,
  when they brought a complaint
    against me;
14 what then shall I do when God rises
    up?
  When he makes inquiry, what
    shall I answer him?
15 Did not he who made me in the
    womb make them?
  And did not one fashion us in the
    womb?

16 "If I have withheld anything that
    the poor desired,
  or have caused the eyes of the
    widow to fail,
17 or have eaten my morsel alone,
    and the orphan has not eaten
    from it—
18 for from my youth I reared the
    orphan*e* like a father,
  and from my mother's womb I
    guided the widow*f*—
19 if I have seen anyone perish for lack
    of clothing,
  or a poor person without
    covering,
20 whose loins have not blessed me,
    and who was not warmed with
    the fleece of my sheep;
21 if I have raised my hand against the
    orphan,
  because I saw I had supporters at
    the gate;
22 then let my shoulder blade fall from
    my shoulder,
  and let my arm be broken from
    its socket.
23 For I was in terror of calamity from
    God,
  and I could not have faced his
    majesty.

24 "If I have made gold my trust,
    or called fine gold my confidence;
25 if I have rejoiced because my wealth
    was great,
  or because my hand had gotten
    much;
26 if I have looked at the sun*g* when it
    shone,
  or the moon moving in splendor,

27 and my heart has been secretly
    enticed,
  and my mouth has kissed my
    hand;
28 this also would be an iniquity to be
    punished by the judges,
  for I should have been false to
    God above.

29 "If I have rejoiced at the ruin of
    those who hated me,
  or exulted when evil overtook
    them—
30 I have not let my mouth sin
    by asking for their lives with a
    curse—
31 if those of my tent ever said,
    'O that we might be sated with
    his flesh!'*h*—
32 the stranger has not lodged in the
    street;
  I have opened my doors to the
    traveler—
33 if I have concealed my transgressions
    as others do,*i*
  by hiding my iniquity in my
    bosom,
34 because I stood in great fear of the
    multitude,
  and the contempt of families
    terrified me,
  so that I kept silence, and did not
    go out of doors—
35 O that I had one to hear me!
  (Here is my signature! Let the
    Almighty*j* answer me!)
  O, that I had the indictment
    written by my adversary!
36 Surely I would carry it on my
    shoulder;
  I would bind it on me like a
    crown;
37 I would give him an account of all
    my steps;
  like a prince I would approach
    him.

38 "If my land has cried out against
    me,
  and its furrows have wept
    together;
39 if I have eaten its yield without
    payment,

e Heb *him*   *f* Heb *her*   *g* Heb *the light*
h Meaning of Heb uncertain   *i* Or *as Adam did*
j Traditional rendering of Heb *Shaddai*

and caused the death of its
owners;

40 let thorns grow instead of wheat,
and foul weeds instead of barley."

The words of Job are ended.

Elihu Rebukes Job's Friends

32 So these three men ceased to answer Job, because he was righteous in his own eyes. ²Then Elihu son of Barachel the Buzite, of the family of Ram, became angry. He was angry at Job because he justified himself rather than God; ³he was angry also at Job's three friends because they had found no answer, though they had declared Job to be in the wrong.ᵏ ⁴Now Elihu had waited to speak to Job, because they were older than he. ⁵But when Elihu saw that there was no answer in the mouths of these three men, he became angry.

6 Elihu son of Barachel the Buzite answered:

"I am young in years,
and you are aged;
therefore I was timid and afraid
to declare my opinion to you.

7 I said, 'Let days speak,
and many years teach wisdom.'

8 But truly it is the spirit in a mortal,
the breath of the Almighty,ˡ that
makes for understanding.

9 It is not the oldᵐ that are wise,
nor the aged that understand what
is right.

10 Therefore I say, 'Listen to me;
let me also declare my opinion.'

11 "See, I waited for your words,
I listened for your wise sayings,
while you searched out what to
say.

12 I gave you my attention,
but there was in fact no one that
confuted Job,
no one among you that answered
his words.

13 Yet do not say, 'We have found
wisdom;
God may vanquish him, not a
human.'

14 He has not directed his words
against me,
and I will not answer him with
your speeches.

15 "They are dismayed, they answer no
more;
they have not a word to say.

16 And am I to wait, because they do
not speak,
because they stand there, and
answer no more?

17 I also will give my answer;
I also will declare my opinion.

18 For I am full of words;
the spirit within me constrains
me.

19 My heart is indeed like wine that
has no vent;
like new wineskins, it is ready to
burst.

20 I must speak, so that I may find
relief;
I must open my lips and answer.

21 I will not show partiality to any
person
or use flattery toward anyone.

22 For I do not know how to flatter—
or my Maker would soon put an
end to me!

Elihu Rebukes Job

33 "But now, hear my speech,
O Job,
and listen to all my words.

2 See, I open my mouth;
the tongue in my mouth speaks.

3 My words declare the uprightness of
my heart,
and what my lips know they
speak sincerely.

4 The spirit of God has made me,
and the breath of the Almightyˡ
gives me life.

5 Answer me, if you can;
set your words in order before me;
take your stand.

6 See, before God I am as you are;
I too was formed from a piece of
clay.

7 No fear of me need terrify you;
my pressure will not be heavy on
you.

8 "Surely, you have spoken in my
hearing,
and I have heard the sound of
your words.

ᵏ Another ancient tradition reads *answer, and had
put God in the wrong*   ˡ Traditional rendering of
Heb *Shaddai*   ᵐ Gk Syr Vg: Heb *many*

9 You say, 'I am clean, without
transgression;
I am pure, and there is no
iniquity in me.
10 Look, he finds occasions against me,
he counts me as his enemy;
11 he puts my feet in the stocks,
and watches all my paths.'

12 "But in this you are not right. I will
answer you:
God is greater than any mortal.
13 Why do you contend against him,
saying, 'He will answer none of
my[n] words'?
14 For God speaks in one way,
and in two, though people do not
perceive it.
15 In a dream, in a vision of the night,
when deep sleep falls on mortals,
while they slumber on their beds,
16 then he opens their ears,
and terrifies them with warnings,
17 that he may turn them aside from
their deeds,
and keep them from pride,
18 to spare their souls from the Pit,
their lives from traversing the
River.
19 They are also chastened with pain
upon their beds,
and with continual strife in their
bones,
20 so that their lives loathe bread,
and their appetites dainty food.
21 Their flesh is so wasted away that it
cannot be seen;
and their bones, once invisible,
now stick out.
22 Their souls draw near the Pit,
and their lives to those who bring
death.
23 Then, if there should be for one of
them an angel,
a mediator, one of a thousand,
one who declares a person
upright,
24 and he is gracious to that person,
and says,
'Deliver him from going down
into the Pit;
I have found a ransom;
25 let his flesh become fresh with
youth;
let him return to the days of his
youthful vigor';
26 then he prays to God, and is
accepted by him,

he comes into his presence with
joy,
and God[o] repays him for his
righteousness.
27 That person sings to others and
says,
'I sinned, and perverted what was
right,
and it was not paid back to me.
28 He has redeemed my soul from
going down to the Pit,
and my life shall see the light.'
29 "God indeed does all these things,
twice, three times, with mortals,
30 to bring back their souls from the
Pit,
so that they may see the light of
life.[p]
31 Pay heed, Job, listen to me;
be silent, and I will speak.
32 If you have anything to say, answer
me;
speak, for I desire to justify you.
33 If not, listen to me;
be silent, and I will teach you
wisdom."

Elihu Proclaims God's Justice

34 Then Elihu continued and said:
2 "Hear my words, you wise
men,
and give ear to me, you who
know;
3 for the ear tests words
as the palate tastes food.
4 Let us choose what is right;
let us determine among ourselves
what is good.
5 For Job has said, 'I am innocent,
and God has taken away my right;
6 in spite of being right I am counted
a liar;
my wound is incurable, though I
am without transgression.'
7 Who is there like Job,
who drinks up scoffing like water,
8 who goes in company with evildoers
and walks with the wicked?
9 For he has said, 'It profits one
nothing
to take delight in God.'

10 "Therefore, hear me, you who have
sense,

---

[n] Compare Gk: Heb *his*   [o] Heb *he*   [p] Syr: Heb
to be lighted with the light of life

far be it from God that he should
do wickedness,
and from the Almighty[q] that he
should do wrong.
11 For according to their deeds he will
repay them,
and according to their ways he
will make it befall them.
12 Of a truth, God will not do
wickedly,
and the Almighty[q] will not
pervert justice.
13 Who gave him charge over the earth
and who laid on him[r] the whole
world?
14 If he should take back his spirit[s] to
himself,
and gather to himself his breath,
15 all flesh would perish together,
and all mortals return to dust.

16 "If you have understanding, hear
this;
listen to what I say.
17 Shall one who hates justice govern?
Will you condemn one who is
righteous and mighty,
18 who says to a king, 'You scoundrel!'
and to princes, 'You wicked
men!';
19 who shows no partiality to nobles,
nor regards the rich more than the
poor,
for they are all the work of his
hands?
20 In a moment they die;
at midnight the people are shaken
and pass away,
and the mighty are taken away by
no human hand.
21 "For his eyes are upon the ways of
mortals,
and he sees all their steps.
22 There is no gloom or deep darkness
where evildoers may hide
themselves.
23 For he has not appointed a time[t]
for anyone
to go before God in judgment.
24 He shatters the mighty without
investigation,
and sets others in their place.
25 Thus, knowing their works,
he overturns them in the night,
and they are crushed.
26 He strikes them for their wickedness
while others look on,

27 because they turned aside from
following him,
and had no regard for any of his
ways,
28 so that they caused the cry of the
poor to come to him,
and he heard the cry of the
afflicted—
29 When he is quiet, who can
condemn?
When he hides his face, who can
behold him,
whether it be a nation or an
individual?—
30 so that the godless should not reign,
or those who ensnare the people.

31 "For has anyone said to God,
'I have endured punishment; I
will not offend any more;
32 teach me what I do not see;
if I have done iniquity, I will do it
no more'?
33 Will he then pay back to suit you,
because you reject it?
For you must choose, and not I;
therefore declare what you
know.[u]
34 Those who have sense will say to
me,
and the wise who hear me will
say,
35 'Job speaks without knowledge,
his words are without insight.'
36 Would that Job were tried to the
limit,
because his answers are those of
the wicked.
37 For he adds rebellion to his sin;
he claps his hands among us,
and multiplies his words against
God."

Elihu Condemns Self-Righteousness

35 Elihu continued and said:
2 "Do you think this to be
just?
You say, 'I am in the right before
God.'
3 If you ask, 'What advantage have I?
How am I better off than if I had
sinned?'
4 I will answer you

---

[q] Traditional rendering of Heb *Shaddai*   [r] Heb
lacks *on him*   [s] Heb *his heart his spirit*   [t] Cn:
Heb *yet*   [u] Meaning of Heb of verses 29-33
uncertain

and your friends with you.

5 Look at the heavens and see;
    observe the clouds, which are
        higher than you.
6 If you have sinned, what do you
        accomplish against him?
    And if your transgressions are
        multiplied, what do you do
        to him?
7 If you are righteous, what do you
        give to him;
    or what does he receive from your
        hand?
8 Your wickedness affects others like
        you,
    and your righteousness, other
        human beings.

9 "Because of the multitude of
        oppressions people cry out;
    they call for help because of the
        arm of the mighty.
10 But no one says, 'Where is God my
        Maker,
    who gives strength in the night,
11 who teaches us more than the
        animals of the earth,
    and makes us wiser than the birds
        of the air?'
12 There they cry out, but he does not
        answer,
    because of the pride of evildoers.
13 Surely God does not hear an empty
        cry,
    nor does the Almighty*v* regard it.
14 How much less when you say that
        you do not see him,
    that the case is before him, and
        you are waiting for him!
15 And now, because his anger does
        not punish,
    and he does not greatly heed
        transgression,*w*
16 Job opens his mouth in empty talk,
    he multiplies words without
        knowledge."

Elihu Exalts God's Goodness

36 Elihu continued and said:
2 "Bear with me a little, and I
        will show you,
    for I have yet something to say on
        God's behalf.
3 I will bring my knowledge from far
        away,
    and ascribe righteousness to my
        Maker.
4 For truly my words are not false;

one who is perfect in knowledge
    is with you.

5 "Surely God is mighty and does not
        despise any;
    he is mighty in strength of
        understanding.
6 He does not keep the wicked alive,
    but gives the afflicted their right.
7 He does not withdraw his eyes from
        the righteous,
    but with kings on the throne
    he sets them forever, and they are
        exalted.
8 And if they are bound in fetters
    and caught in the cords of
        affliction,
9 then he declares to them their work
    and their transgressions, that they
        are behaving arrogantly.
10 He opens their ears to instruction,
    and commands that they return
        from iniquity.
11 If they listen, and serve him,
    they complete their days in
        prosperity,
    and their years in pleasantness.
12 But if they do not listen, they shall
        perish by the sword,
    and die without knowledge.

13 "The godless in heart cherish anger;
    they do not cry for help when he
        binds them.
14 They die in their youth,
    and their life ends in shame.*x*
15 He delivers the afflicted by their
        affliction,
    and opens their ear by adversity.
16 He also allured you out of distress
    into a broad place where there
        was no constraint,
    and what was set on your table
        was full of fatness.

17 "But you are obsessed with the case
        of the wicked;
    judgment and justice seize you.
18 Beware that wrath does not entice
        you into scoffing,
    and do not let the greatness of the
        ransom turn you aside.

---

v Traditional rendering of Heb *Shaddai*
w Theodotion Symmachus Compare Vg: Meaning
of Heb uncertain   *x* Heb *ends among the temple
prostitutes*

19 Will your cry avail to keep you from
          distress,
       or will all the force of your
          strength?
20 Do not long for the night,
       when peoples are cut off in their
          place.
21 Beware! Do not turn to iniquity;
       because of that you have been
          tried by affliction.
22 See, God is exalted in his power;
       who is a teacher like him?
23 Who has prescribed for him his way,
       or who can say, 'You have done
          wrong'?

Elihu Proclaims God's Majesty

24 "Remember to extol his work,
       of which mortals have sung.
25 All people have looked on it;
       everyone watches it from far away.
26 Surely God is great, and we do not
          know him;
       the number of his years is
          unsearchable.
27 For he draws up the drops of water;
       he distills *y* his mist in rain,
28 which the skies pour down
       and drop upon mortals
          abundantly.
29 Can anyone understand the
          spreading of the clouds,
       the thunderings of his pavilion?
30 See, he scatters his lightning around
          him
       and covers the roots of the sea.
31 For by these he governs peoples;
       he gives food in abundance.
32 He covers his hands with the
          lightning,
       and commands it to strike the
          mark.
33 Its crashing*z* tells about him;
       he is jealous*z* with anger against
          iniquity.

37 "At this also my heart trembles,
       and leaps out of its place.
2 Listen, listen to the thunder of his
          voice
       and the rumbling that comes from
          his mouth.
3 Under the whole heaven he lets it
          loose,
       and his lightning to the corners of
          the earth.
4 After it his voice roars;

he thunders with his majestic
          voice
       and he does not restrain the
          lightnings*a* when his voice is
          heard.
5 God thunders wondrously with his
          voice;
       he does great things that we
          cannot comprehend.
6 For to the snow he says, 'Fall on the
          earth';
       and the shower of rain, his heavy
          shower of rain,
7 serves as a sign on everyone's hand,
       so that all whom he has made
          may know it.*b*
8 Then the animals go into their lairs
       and remain in their dens.
9 From its chamber comes the
          whirlwind,
       and cold from the scattering
          winds.
10 By the breath of God ice is given,
       and the broad waters are frozen
          fast.
11 He loads the thick cloud with
          moisture;
       the clouds scatter his lightning.
12 They turn round and round by his
          guidance,
       to accomplish all that he
          commands them
       on the face of the habitable
          world.
13 Whether for correction, or for his
          land,
       or for love, he causes it to
          happen.

14 "Hear this, O Job;
       stop and consider the wondrous
          works of God.
15 Do you know how God lays his
          command upon them,
       and causes the lightning of his
          cloud to shine?
16 Do you know the balancings of the
          clouds,
       the wondrous works of the one
          whose knowledge is perfect,
17 you whose garments are hot
       when the earth is still because of
          the south wind?

y Cn: Heb *they distill*   *z* Meaning of Heb
uncertain   *a* Heb *them*   *b* Meaning of Heb of
verse 7 uncertain

18 Can you, like him, spread out the
   skies,
   hard as a molten mirror?
19 Teach us what we shall say to him;
   we cannot draw up our case
   because of darkness.
20 Should he be told that I want to
   speak?
   Did anyone ever wish to be
   swallowed up?
21 Now, no one can look on the light
   when it is bright in the skies,
   when the wind has passed and
   cleared them.
22 Out of the north comes golden
   splendor;
   around God is awesome majesty.
23 The Almighty[c]—we cannot find
   him;
   he is great in power and justice,
   and abundant righteousness he
   will not violate.
24 Therefore mortals fear him;
   he does not regard any who are
   wise in their own conceit."

The LORD Answers Job

38 Then the LORD answered Job out
   of the whirlwind:
2 "Who is this that darkens counsel
   by words without knowledge?
3 Gird up your loins like a man,
   I will question you, and you shall
   declare to me.

4 "Where were you when I laid the
   foundation of the earth?
   Tell me, if you have
   understanding.
5 Who determined its measurements—
   surely you know!
   Or who stretched the line upon it?
6 On what were its bases sunk,
   or who laid its cornerstone
7 when the morning stars sang
   together
   and all the heavenly beings[d]
   shouted for joy?

8 "Or who shut in the sea with doors
   when it burst out from the
   womb?—
9 when I made the clouds its garment,
   and thick darkness its swaddling
   band,

10 and prescribed bounds for it,
   and set bars and doors,
11 and said, 'Thus far shall you come,
   and no farther,
   and here shall your proud waves
   be stopped'?

12 "Have you commanded the
   morning since your days
   began,
   and caused the dawn to know its
   place,
13 so that it might take hold of the
   skirts of the earth,
   and the wicked be shaken out of
   it?
14 It is changed like clay under the
   seal,
   and it is dyed[e] like a garment.
15 Light is withheld from the wicked,
   and their uplifted arm is broken.

16 "Have you entered into the springs
   of the sea,
   or walked in the recesses of the
   deep?
17 Have the gates of death been
   revealed to you,
   or have you seen the gates of deep
   darkness?
18 Have you comprehended the
   expanse of the earth?
   Declare, if you know all this.

19 "Where is the way to the dwelling
   of light,
   and where is the place of
   darkness,
20 that you may take it to its territory
   and that you may discern the
   paths to its home?
21 Surely you know, for you were born
   then,
   and the number of your days is
   great!

22 "Have you entered the storehouses
   of the snow,
   or have you seen the storehouses
   of the hail,
23 which I have reserved for the time of
   trouble,
   for the day of battle and war?
24 What is the way to the place where
   the light is distributed,

---

c Traditional rendering of Heb *Shaddai*   d Heb
sons of God   e Cn: Heb *and they stand forth*

or where the east wind is scattered
upon the earth?

25 "Who has cut a channel for the
torrents of rain,
and a way for the thunderbolt,
26 to bring rain on a land where no
one lives,

on the desert, which is empty of
human life,
27 to satisfy the waste and desolate
land,
and to make the ground put forth
grass?

28 "Has the rain a father,

WEDNESDAY

Scripture Reading
for Today:
Job 38.1–7, 31–33

Verse for Today:
Job 38.31

The Mystery of God

The only God who seems to me to be worth believing in is impossible for mortal man to understand, and therefore he teaches us through this impossible.

But we rebel against the impossible. I sense a wish in some professional religion-mongers to make [the understanding of God] comprehensible to the naked intellect, domesticate him so that he's easy to believe in. Every century the Church makes a fresh attempt to make Christianity acceptable. But an acceptable Christianity is not Christian; a comprehensible God is no more than an idol.

I don't want that kind of God.

What kind of God, then?

One time, when I was little more than a baby, I was taken to visit my grandmother, who was living in a cottage on a nearly uninhabited stretch of beach in northern Florida. All I remember of this visit is being picked up from my crib in what seemed the middle of the night and carried from my bedroom and out of doors, where I had my first look at the stars.

It must have been an unusually clear and beautiful night for someone to have said, "Let's wake the baby and show her the stars." The night sky, the constant rolling of breakers against the shore, the stupendous light of the stars, all made an indelible impression on me. I was intuitively aware not only of a beauty I had never seen before but also that the world was far greater than the protected limits of the small child's world which was all that I had known thus far. I had a total, if not very conscious, moment of revelation; I saw creation bursting the bounds of daily restriction and stretching out from dimension to dimension, beyond any human comprehension.

I had been taught to say my prayers at night: Our Father, and a long string of God-blesses, and it was that first showing of the galaxies which gave me an awareness that the God I spoke to at bedtime was extraordinary and not just a bigger and better combination of the grownup powers of my mother and father.

—MADELEINE L'ENGLE

Go to page 656 for your next devotional reading.

or who has begotten the drops of
dew?

29 From whose womb did the ice come
forth,
and who has given birth to the
hoarfrost of heaven?

30 The waters become hard like stone,
and the face of the deep is frozen.

31 "Can you bind the chains of the
Pleiades,
or loose the cords of Orion?

32 Can you lead forth the Mazzaroth in
their season,
or can you guide the Bear with its
children?

33 Do you know the ordinances of the
heavens?
Can you establish their rule on
the earth?

34 "Can you lift up your voice to the
clouds,
so that a flood of waters may
cover you?

35 Can you send forth lightnings, so
that they may go
and say to you, 'Here we are'?

36 Who has put wisdom in the inward
parts, f
or given understanding to the
mind? f

37 Who has the wisdom to number the
clouds?
Or who can tilt the waterskins of
the heavens,

38 when the dust runs into a mass
and the clods cling together?

39 "Can you hunt the prey for the lion,
or satisfy the appetite of the
young lions,

40 when they crouch in their dens,
or lie in wait in their covert?

41 Who provides for the raven its prey,
when its young ones cry to God,
and wander about for lack of
food?

39 "Do you know when the
mountain goats give birth?
Do you observe the calving of the
deer?

2 Can you number the months that
they fulfill,
and do you know the time when
they give birth,

3 when they crouch to give birth to
their offspring,

and are delivered of their young?

4 Their young ones become strong,
they grow up in the open;
they go forth, and do not return
to them.

5 "Who has let the wild ass go free?
Who has loosed the bonds of the
swift ass,

6 to which I have given the steppe for
its home,
the salt land for its dwelling
place?

7 It scorns the tumult of the city;
it does not hear the shouts of the
driver.

8 It ranges the mountains as its
pasture,
and it searches after every green
thing.

9 "Is the wild ox willing to serve you?
Will it spend the night at your
crib?

10 Can you tie it in the furrow with
ropes,
or will it harrow the valleys after
you?

11 Will you depend on it because its
strength is great,
and will you hand over your labor
to it?

12 Do you have faith in it that it will
return,
and bring your grain to your
threshing floor? g

13 "The ostrich's wings flap wildly,
though its pinions lack
plumage. f

14 For it leaves its eggs to the earth,
and lets them be warmed on the
ground,

15 forgetting that a foot may crush
them,
and that a wild animal may
trample them.

16 It deals cruelly with its young, as if
they were not its own;
though its labor should be in
vain, yet it has no fear;

17 because God has made it forget
wisdom,
and given it no share in
understanding.

f Meaning of Heb uncertain   g Heb your grain
and your threshing floor

18 When it spreads its plumes aloft,[h]
   it laughs at the horse and its rider.

19 "Do you give the horse its might?
   Do you clothe its neck with
      mane?
20 Do you make it leap like the locust?
   Its majestic snorting is terrible.
21 It paws[i] violently, exults mightily;
   it goes out to meet the weapons.
22 It laughs at fear, and is not
      dismayed;
   it does not turn back from the
      sword.
23 Upon it rattle the quiver,
   the flashing spear, and the javelin.
24 With fierceness and rage it swallows
      the ground;
   it cannot stand still at the sound
      of the trumpet.
25 When the trumpet sounds, it says
      'Aha!'
   From a distance it smells the
      battle,
   the thunder of the captains, and
      the shouting.

26 "Is it by your wisdom that the hawk
      soars,
   and spreads its wings toward the
      south?
27 Is it at your command that the eagle
      mounts up
   and makes its nest on high?
28 It lives on the rock and makes its
      home
   in the fastness of the rocky crag.
29 From there it spies the prey;
   its eyes see it from far away.
30 Its young ones suck up blood;
   and where the slain are, there it is."

40
And the LORD said to Job:
2 "Shall a faultfinder contend
   with the Almighty?[j]
Anyone who argues with God
   must respond."

Job's Response to God

3 Then Job answered the LORD:
4 "See, I am of small account; what
      shall I answer you?
   I lay my hand on my mouth.
5 I have spoken once, and I will not
      answer;
   twice, but will proceed no further."

God's Challenge to Job

6 Then the LORD answered Job out of
the whirlwind:
7 "Gird up your loins like a man;
   I will question you, and you
      declare to me.
8 Will you even put me in the wrong?
   Will you condemn me that you
      may be justified?
9 Have you an arm like God,
   and can you thunder with a voice
      like his?

10 "Deck yourself with majesty and
      dignity;
   clothe yourself with glory and
      splendor.
11 Pour out the overflowings of your
      anger,
   and look on all who are proud,
      and abase them.
12 Look on all who are proud, and
      bring them low;
   tread down the wicked where they
      stand.
13 Hide them all in the dust together;
   bind their faces in the world
      below.[k]
14 Then I will also acknowledge to you
   that your own right hand can give
      you victory.

15 "Look at Behemoth,
   which I made just as I made you;
   it eats grass like an ox.
16 Its strength is in its loins,
   and its power in the muscles of its
      belly.
17 It makes its tail stiff like a cedar;
   the sinews of its thighs are knit
      together.
18 Its bones are tubes of bronze,
   its limbs like bars of iron.

19 "It is the first of the great acts of
      God—
   only its Maker can approach it
      with the sword.
20 For the mountains yield food for it
   where all the wild animals play.
21 Under the lotus plants it lies,
   in the covert of the reeds and in
      the marsh.
22 The lotus trees cover it for shade;

---

h Meaning of Heb uncertain   i Gk Syr Vg: Heb
they dig   j Traditional rendering of Heb *Shaddai*
k Heb *the hidden place*

the willows of the wadi surround
  it.
23 Even if the river is turbulent, it is
      not frightened;
    it is confident though Jordan
      rushes against its mouth.
24 Can one take it with hooks[l]
    or pierce its nose with a snare?

41 [m] "Can you draw out Leviathan[n]
      with a fishhook,
    or press down its tongue with a
      cord?
2 Can you put a rope in its nose,
    or pierce its jaw with a hook?
3 Will it make many supplications to
      you?
    Will it speak soft words to you?
4 Will it make a covenant with you
      to be taken as your servant
      forever?
5 Will you play with it as with a bird,
    or will you put it on leash for
      your girls?
6 Will traders bargain over it?
    Will they divide it up among the
      merchants?
7 Can you fill its skin with harpoons,
    or its head with fishing spears?
8 Lay hands on it;
    think of the battle; you will not
      do it again!
9[o] Any hope of capturing it[p] will be
      disappointed;
    were not even the gods[q]
      overwhelmed at the sight of
      it?
10 No one is so fierce as to dare to stir
      it up.
    Who can stand before it?[r]
11 Who can confront it[r] and be
      safe?[s]
    —under the whole heaven,
      who?[t]

12 "I will not keep silence concerning
      its limbs,
    or its mighty strength, or its
      splendid frame.
13 Who can strip off its outer garment?
    Who can penetrate its double coat
      of mail?[u]
14 Who can open the doors of its face?
    There is terror all around its teeth.
15 Its back[v] is made of shields in
      rows,
    shut up closely as with a seal.
16 One is so near to another

that no air can come between
  them.
17 They are joined one to another;
    they clasp each other and cannot
      be separated.
18 Its sneezes flash forth light,
    and its eyes are like the eyelids of
      the dawn.
19 From its mouth go flaming torches;
    sparks of fire leap out.
20 Out of its nostrils comes smoke,
    as from a boiling pot and burning
      rushes.
21 Its breath kindles coals,
    and a flame comes out of its
      mouth.
22 In its neck abides strength,
    and terror dances before it.
23 The folds of its flesh cling together;
    it is firmly cast and immovable.
24 Its heart is as hard as stone,
    as hard as the lower millstone.
25 When it raises itself up the gods are
      afraid;
    at the crashing they are beside
      themselves.
26 Though the sword reaches it, it does
      not avail,
    nor does the spear, the dart, or
      the javelin.
27 It counts iron as straw,
    and bronze as rotten wood.
28 The arrow cannot make it flee;
    slingstones, for it, are turned to
      chaff.
29 Clubs are counted as chaff;
    it laughs at the rattle of javelins.
30 Its underparts are like sharp
      potsherds;
    it spreads itself like a threshing
      sledge on the mire.
31 It makes the deep boil like a pot;
    it makes the sea like a pot of
      ointment.
32 It leaves a shining wake behind it;
    one would think the deep to be
      white-haired.
33 On earth it has no equal,
    a creature without fear.
34 It surveys everything that is lofty;
    it is king over all that are proud."

[l] Cn: Heb *in his eyes*   [m] Ch 40.25 in Heb
[n] Or *the crocodile*   [o] Ch 41.1 in Heb   [p] Heb *of
it*   [q] Cn Compare Symmachus Syr: Heb *one is*
[r] Heb *me*   [s] Gk: Heb *that I shall repay*   [t] Heb
to me   [u] Gk: Heb *bridle*   [v] Cn Compare Gk Vg:
Heb *pride*

Job Is Humbled and Satisfied

42 Then Job answered the LORD:
2 "I know that you can do all
things,
  and that no purpose of yours can
be thwarted.

3 'Who is this that hides counsel
without knowledge?'
Therefore I have uttered what I did
not understand,
  things too wonderful for me,
which I did not know.

THURSDAY

Scripture Reading
for Today:
Job 42.1–6

Verse for Today:
Job 42.5

Lost in Wonder

Job questions. He theologizes. He wishes he hadn't been born. He
wonders why he, a good and righteous man, should have received
this from God. God's answer to Job is on a wholly different plane.
It is like Beethoven's Ode to Joy (with full chorus and orchestra)
sweeping away the sound of chopsticks (fingered by a child on an
out-of-tune piano).

His answer to Job is essentially, "I AM." "I AM: Know me, experience me, love me, worship me."

So the book of Job becomes for us not only an intriguing exploration of theodicy (the study of the problem of evil) or the
case study of a man who lost it all, or even an intriguing book that
raises questions we all wonder about. It compels us to check our
priorities.

Our possessions, our families, our jobs, our health give us a
sense of control, and they also seem all-important. We forget that
they require our stewardship, but are not who we are. Many voices tell us that what we drive, what we wear, where we live, or our
career—[that] these are what make us who we are. We need to
begin to find ourselves instead in "loving God with all our heart,
soul, mind, and strength" and in knowing him.

When we experience God in the love of the community, we
see what's truly important. When we experience God in the
Eucharist or in silence, we can begin to "know him." When we experience God in worship, our lives slip into perspective. When
we are "lost in wonder, love, and praise," we can loose our hold on
some things which are less important.

People sometimes say, "When I get to heaven, I'm going to
ask God about . . ."

We all have questions and things we don't understand, but I
don't expect there to be a big line in heaven stretching from the
throne of God and around the pearly gates with people waiting to
ask their questions.

After all his theological questioning, Job listens and begins to
know God. Basically Job says, "I see that I didn't understand at all."

—MARY ELLEN ASHCROFT

Go to page 662 for your next devotional reading.

4 'Hear, and I will speak;
  I will question you, and you
    declare to me.'
5 I had heard of you by the hearing
    of the ear,
  but now my eye sees you;
6 therefore I despise myself,
  and repent in dust and
    ashes."

Job's Friends Are Humiliated

7 After the LORD had spoken these words to Job, the LORD said to Eliphaz the Temanite: "My wrath is kindled against you and against your two friends; for you have not spoken of me what is right, as my servant Job has. 8Now therefore take seven bulls and seven rams, and go to my servant Job, and offer up for yourselves a burnt offering; and my servant Job shall pray for you, for I will accept his prayer not to deal with you according to your folly; for you have not spoken of me what is right, as my servant Job has done." 9So Eliphaz the Temanite and Bildad the Shuhite and Zophar the Naamathite went and did what the LORD had told them; and the LORD accepted Job's prayer.

Job's Fortunes Are Restored Twofold

10 And the LORD restored the fortunes of Job when he had prayed for his friends; and the LORD gave Job twice as much as he had before. 11Then there came to him all his brothers and sisters and all who had known him before, and they ate bread with him in his house; they showed him sympathy and comforted him for all the evil that the LORD had brought upon him; and each of them gave him a piece of money*w* and a gold ring. 12The LORD blessed the latter days of Job more than his beginning; and he had fourteen thousand sheep, six thousand camels, a thousand yoke of oxen, and a thousand donkeys. 13He also had seven sons and three daughters. 14He named the first Jemimah, the second Keziah, and the third Kerenhappuch. 15In all the land there were no women so beautiful as Job's daughters; and their father gave them an inheritance along with their brothers. 16After this Job lived one hundred and forty years, and saw his children, and his children's children, four generations. 17And Job died, old and full of days.

w Heb *a qesitah*

Psalms

The book of Psalms has been called the prayer book of God's people. It contains 150 songs expressing lament, praise, thanksgiving, blessing, anger, repentance, petition, and adoration. In ancient times, many of the psalms were used in the temple liturgy. Composed over a period of many centuries by various authors, including King David, the psalms are addressed directly to God. Jesus himself quoted the first verse of Psalm 22 when he was dying on the cross (Mark 15.34): "My God, my God, why have you forsaken me?"

The Liturgy of the Hours provides a way for Catholics to pray the Psalter over a four-week period. Additionally, the psalms are included in the lectionary of the church, with a different psalm read each day at Mass. But whether you pray the psalms based on the Liturgy of the Hours, hear them at Mass, or simply read them on a regular basis, these ancient prayers will add great depth to your prayer life. Even the so-called "cursing psalms" (like Psalm 58) can be prayed, not against human enemies but against spiritual enemies—"For our struggle is not against enemies of blood and flesh, but against the rulers, against the authorities, against the cosmic powers of this present darkness, against the spiritual forces of evil in the heavenly places" (Ephesians 6.12).

BOOK I
(Psalms 1–41)

Psalm 1

The Two Ways

1 Happy are those
   who do not follow the advice of
      the wicked,
   or take the path that sinners tread,
      or sit in the seat of scoffers;

2 but their delight is in the law
      of the LORD,
   and on his law they meditate
      day and night.
3 They are like trees
      planted by streams of water,
   which yield their fruit in its
      season,
   and their leaves do not wither.
   In all that they do, they prosper.

4 The wicked are not so,

but are like chaff that the wind
    drives away.
5 Therefore the wicked will not stand
    in the judgment,
    nor sinners in the congregation of
    the righteous;
6 for the Lord watches over the way of
    the righteous,
    but the way of the wicked will
    perish.

Psalm 2

God's Promise to His Anointed

1 Why do the nations conspire,
    and the peoples plot in vain?
2 The kings of the earth set
    themselves,
    and the rulers take counsel
    together,
    against the Lord and his anointed,
    saying,
3 "Let us burst their bonds asunder,
    and cast their cords from us."

4 He who sits in the heavens laughs;
    the Lord has them in derision.
5 Then he will speak to them in his
    wrath,
    and terrify them in his fury,
    saying,
6 "I have set my king on Zion, my
    holy hill."

7 I will tell of the decree of the Lord:
    He said to me, "You are my son;
    today I have begotten you.
8 Ask of me, and I will make the
    nations your heritage,
    and the ends of the earth your
    possession.
9 You shall break them with a rod of
    iron,
    and dash them in pieces like a
    potter's vessel."

10 Now therefore, O kings, be wise;
    be warned, O rulers of the earth.
11 Serve the Lord with fear,
    with trembling 12kiss his feet,*a*
    or he will be angry, and you will
    perish in the way;
    for his wrath is quickly kindled.

Happy are all who take refuge
    in him.

Psalm 3

Trust in God under Adversity

A Psalm of David, when he fled from
his son Absalom.

1 O Lord, how many are my foes!
    Many are rising against me;
2 many are saying to me,
    "There is no help for you*b* in
    God."   *Selah*

3 But you, O Lord, are a shield around
    me,
    my glory, and the one who lifts
    up my head.
4 I cry aloud to the Lord,
    and he answers me from his
    holy hill.   *Selah*

5 I lie down and sleep;
    I wake again, for the Lord sustains
    me.
6 I am not afraid of ten thousands of
    people
    who have set themselves against
    me all around.

7 Rise up, O Lord!
    Deliver me, O my God!
For you strike all my enemies on the
    cheek;
    you break the teeth of the wicked.

8 Deliverance belongs to the Lord;
    may your blessing be on your
    people!   *Selah*

Psalm 4

Confident Plea for Deliverance
from Enemies

To the leader: with stringed instruments.
A Psalm of David.

1 Answer me when I call, O God of
    my right!
    You gave me room when I was in
    distress.
    Be gracious to me, and hear my
    prayer.

2 How long, you people, shall my
    honor suffer shame?
    How long will you love vain
    words, and seek after lies?
        Selah

a Cn: Meaning of Heb of verses 11b and 12a is
uncertain   *b* Syr: Heb *him*

³ But know that the LORD has set apart
　　the faithful for himself;
　　the LORD hears when I call to him.

⁴ When you are disturbed,ᶜ do not
　　sin;
　　ponder it on your beds, and be
　　　silent.   *Selah*
⁵ Offer right sacrifices,
　　and put your trust in the LORD.

⁶ There are many who say, "O that we
　　might see some good!
　　Let the light of your face shine on
　　us, O LORD!"
⁷ You have put gladness in my heart
　　more than when their grain and
　　wine abound.

⁸ I will both lie down and sleep in
　　peace;
　　for you alone, O LORD, make me
　　lie down in safety.

Psalm 5

Trust in God for Deliverance from Enemies

To the leader: for the flutes. A Psalm
of David.

¹ Give ear to my words, O LORD;
　　give heed to my sighing.
² Listen to the sound of my cry,
　　my King and my God,
　　for to you I pray.
³ O LORD, in the morning you hear my
　　voice;
　　in the morning I plead my case to
　　you, and watch.

⁴ For you are not a God who delights
　　in wickedness;
　　evil will not sojourn with you.
⁵ The boastful will not stand before
　　your eyes;
　　you hate all evildoers.
⁶ You destroy those who speak lies;
　　the LORD abhors the bloodthirsty
　　and deceitful.

⁷ But I, through the abundance of
　　your steadfast love,
　　will enter your house,
　　I will bow down toward your holy
　　temple
　　in awe of you.
⁸ Lead me, O LORD, in your
　　righteousness

because of my enemies;
　　make your way straight before me.

⁹ For there is no truth in their
　　mouths;
　　their hearts are destruction;
　　their throats are open graves;
　　they flatter with their tongues.
¹⁰ Make them bear their guilt, O God;
　　let them fall by their own
　　counsels;
　　because of their many transgressions
　　cast them out,
　　for they have rebelled against you.

¹¹ But let all who take refuge in you
　　rejoice;
　　let them ever sing for joy.
　　Spread your protection over them,
　　so that those who love your name
　　may exult in you.
¹² For you bless the righteous, O LORD;
　　you cover them with favor as with
　　a shield.

Psalm 6

Prayer for Recovery from Grave Illness

To the leader: with stringed instruments;
according to The Sheminith.
A Psalm of David.

¹ O LORD, do not rebuke me in your
　　anger,
　　or discipline me in your wrath.
² Be gracious to me, O LORD, for I am
　　languishing;
　　O LORD, heal me, for my bones
　　are shaking with terror.
³ My soul also is struck with terror,
　　while you, O LORD—how long?

⁴ Turn, O LORD, save my life;
　　deliver me for the sake of your
　　steadfast love.
⁵ For in death there is no
　　remembrance of you;
　　in Sheol who can give you praise?

⁶ I am weary with my moaning;
　　every night I flood my bed with
　　tears;
　　I drench my couch with my
　　weeping.
⁷ My eyes waste away because of grief;
　　they grow weak because of all
　　my foes.

ᶜ Or *are angry*

8 Depart from me, all you workers
　　of evil,
　　for the LORD has heard the sound
　　　of my weeping.
9 The LORD has heard my supplication;
　　the LORD accepts my prayer.
10 All my enemies shall be ashamed
　　and struck with terror;
　　they shall turn back, and in a
　　　moment be put to shame.

Psalm 7

Plea for Help against Persecutors

A Shiggaion of David, which he sang to
the LORD concerning Cush, a Benjaminite.

1 O LORD my God, in you I take
　　refuge;
　　save me from all my pursuers, and
　　　deliver me,
2 or like a lion they will tear me apart;
　　they will drag me away, with no
　　　one to rescue.

3 O LORD my God, if I have done this,
　　if there is wrong in my hands,
4 if I have repaid my ally with harm
　　or plundered my foe without
　　　cause,
5 then let the enemy pursue and
　　overtake me,
　　trample my life to the ground,
　　and lay my soul in the dust.　　*Selah*

6 Rise up, O LORD, in your anger;
　　lift yourself up against the fury of
　　　my enemies;
　　awake, O my God;*d* you have
　　　appointed a judgment.
7 Let the assembly of the peoples be
　　gathered around you,
　　and over it take your seat*e* on
　　　high.
8 The LORD judges the peoples;
　　judge me, O LORD, according to
　　　my righteousness
　　and according to the integrity that
　　　is in me.

9 O let the evil of the wicked come to
　　an end,
　　but establish the righteous,
　　you who test the minds and hearts,
　　O righteous God.
10 God is my shield,
　　who saves the upright in heart.
11 God is a righteous judge,

and a God who has indignation
　　every day.
12 If one does not repent, God*f* will
　　whet his sword;
　　he has bent and strung his bow;
13 he has prepared his deadly weapons,
　　making his arrows fiery shafts.
14 See how they conceive evil,
　　and are pregnant with mischief,
　　and bring forth lies.
15 They make a pit, digging it out,
　　and fall into the hole that they
　　　have made.
16 Their mischief returns upon their
　　own heads,
　　and on their own heads their
　　　violence descends.

17 I will give to the LORD the thanks
　　due to his righteousness,
　　and sing praise to the name of the
　　　LORD, the Most High.

Psalm 8

Divine Majesty and Human Dignity

To the leader: according to The Gittith.
A Psalm of David.

1 O LORD, our Sovereign,
　　how majestic is your name in all
　　　the earth!

You have set your glory above the
　　heavens.
2 Out of the mouths of babes and
　　infants
you have founded a bulwark because
　　of your foes,
　　to silence the enemy and the
　　　avenger.

3 When I look at your heavens, the
　　work of your fingers,
　　the moon and the stars that you
　　　have established;
4 what are human beings that you are
　　mindful of them,
　　mortals*g* that you care for them?

5 Yet you have made them a little
　　lower than God,*h*
　　and crowned them with glory and
　　　honor.

d Or *awake for me*　　*e* Cn: Heb *return*　　*f* Heb *he*
g Heb *ben adam*, lit. *son of man*　　*h* Or *than the
divine beings* or *angels*: Heb *elohim*

6 You have given them dominion over
        the works of your hands;
    you have put all things under
        their feet,
7 all sheep and oxen,
        and also the beasts of the
            field,
8 the birds of the air, and the fish
        of the sea,
    whatever passes along the paths
        of the seas.

9 O LORD, our Sovereign,
    how majestic is your name in all
        the earth!

Psalm 9

God's Power and Justice

To the leader: according to Muth-labben.
A Psalm of David.

1 I will give thanks to the LORD with
        my whole heart;
    I will tell of all your wonderful
        deeds.
2 I will be glad and exult in you;
    I will sing praise to your name,
        O Most High.

3 When my enemies turned back,

FRIDAY

Scripture Reading
for Today:
Psalm 8

Verses for Today:
Psalm 8.3–4

*A*wesome Prayers

On a nature walk our guide pointed out a beautiful mighty oak
tree. It had stood there for over 500 years. The branches that sheltered our group from the sun had shaded the first European settlers to reach American shores. As my son put it, that was an
"awesome" thought.

The psalter is "awesome" in much the same way. It was Psalm
8.3 that first brought this book of Scripture alive for me: "I look at
your heavens . . ." Century after century, God's faithful have looked
at the sky and responded with these words. Jesus himself probably recited this psalm on a clear, warm night.

I longed to be able to pray these words too, as I took an
evening walk or sat on the porch after the children were in bed.
Three years ago I began to memorize the psalms. I have limited
study time, and my progress is slow, but I've worked through the
first half of the psalter, sometimes learning the entire psalm,
sometimes just a verse or two. My humble efforts have brought
me unexpected joy and peace.

I marvel at the psalms' timelessness and universality. As I recite a verse, I wonder if holy monks are uttering the same words
in a monastery on the other side of the world. If I awake at night, I
think of a nursing mother cradling her infant at 3:00 A.M.; together
we pray Psalm 131. When I turn to the psalms of lament, I pray
with those who are sick, hungry, or grieving.

Jesus lived in a culture two thousand years [ago] and half a
globe away, yet the psalms were part of his life, as they are part of
ours. It is comforting to imagine him at prayer with us, joining us
in words that transcend time.

—SANDY MAYRAND

Go to page 664 for your next devotional reading.

they stumbled and perished before
   you.
4 For you have maintained my just
   cause;
   you have sat on the throne giving
      righteous judgment.

5 You have rebuked the nations, you
   have destroyed the wicked;
   you have blotted out their name
      forever and ever.
6 The enemies have vanished in
   everlasting ruins;
   their cities you have rooted out;
   the very memory of them has
      perished.

7 But the LORD sits enthroned forever,
   he has established his throne for
      judgment.
8 He judges the world with
   righteousness;
   he judges the peoples with equity.

9 The LORD is a stronghold for the
   oppressed,
   a stronghold in times of trouble.
10 And those who know your name put
   their trust in you,
   for you, O LORD, have not
      forsaken those who seek you.

11 Sing praises to the LORD, who dwells
   in Zion.
   Declare his deeds among the
      peoples.
12 For he who avenges blood is
   mindful of them;
   he does not forget the cry of the
      afflicted.

13 Be gracious to me, O LORD.
   See what I suffer from those who
      hate me;
   you are the one who lifts me up
      from the gates of death,
14 so that I may recount all your
   praises,
   and, in the gates of daughter Zion,
   rejoice in your deliverance.

15 The nations have sunk in the pit
   that they made;
   in the net that they hid has their
      own foot been caught.
16 The LORD has made himself known,
   he has executed judgment;

the wicked are snared in the work
   of their own hands.
          Higgaion. Selah

17 The wicked shall depart to Sheol,
   all the nations that forget God.

18 For the needy shall not always be
   forgotten,
   nor the hope of the poor perish
      forever.

19 Rise up, O LORD! Do not let mortals
   prevail;
   let the nations be judged before
      you.
20 Put them in fear, O LORD;
   let the nations know that they are
      only human.   *Selah*

Psalm 10

Prayer for Deliverance from Enemies

1 Why, O LORD, do you stand far off?
   Why do you hide yourself in
      times of trouble?
2 In arrogance the wicked persecute
   the poor—
   let them be caught in the schemes
      they have devised.

3 For the wicked boast of the desires
   of their heart,
   those greedy for gain curse and
      renounce the LORD.
4 In the pride of their countenance the
   wicked say, "God will not
      seek it out";
   all their thoughts are, "There is
      no God."

5 Their ways prosper at all times;
   your judgments are on high, out
      of their sight;
   as for their foes, they scoff at
      them.
6 They think in their heart, "We shall
   not be moved;
   throughout all generations we
      shall not meet adversity."

7 Their mouths are filled with cursing
   and deceit and oppression;
   under their tongues are mischief
      and iniquity.
8 They sit in ambush in the villages;
   in hiding places they murder the
      innocent.

THE STORY OF A WOMAN

Jael

Her Name Means *"A Wild or Mountain Goat"*

Her Character: *Decisive and courageous, she seized the opportunity to slay an enemy of God's people.*
Her Joy: *To be lauded by Deborah and Barak for her part in a decisive victory.*

Read Judges 4.17–24

Jael had heard rumors of war. She and her husband Heber were Kenites, members of a nomadic tribe whose survival depended on its ability to stay clear of local disputes. Her husband had made his peace with the Canaanites, despite his descent from Hobab, Moses' brother-in-law. The ancient ties no longer seemed expedient.

Jael watched uneasily through the flaps of her tent as clouds swept the blue from the sky and rain fell, like a giant shroud covering the horizon. Sisera, she knew, had marched to Tabor. But what good were iron chariots in a flooded valley, she wondered? The Israelites were poorly armed with little chance of prevailing. Still, she remembered the stories of Moses and the people he had led across the wilderness. Had their God been asleep these many years?

The sight of a man running, then stumbling toward her interrupted her thoughts. A soldier fleeing? Was he Israelite or Canaanite? His identity might reveal the way the winds of battle were blowing. She went out to meet him, surprised to find that Sisera himself was approaching.

"Turn aside, my lord, turn aside to me; have no fear," she welcomed him.

"Please give me a little water to drink; for I am thirsty," he said. Instead Jael opened a skin of milk, gave him a drink, and covered him.

"Stand at the entrance of the tent," he said to her, "and if anybody comes and asks you, 'Is anyone here?' say, 'No.'"

As soon as Sisera fell into an exhausted sleep, Jael picked up a tent peg and hammer. Her arm was steady, her aim sure. Hadn't she been in charge of the tents all these years? Quickly, she thrust the peg through his temple and into the ground. Like a piece of canvas fixed in place, Sisera, the great general, lay dead, slain by a woman's hand, just as Deborah had prophesied to Barak.

Was Jael a hero, an opportunist, or merely a treacherous woman? It is difficult to know. Perhaps she believed in Israel's God. Perhaps she merely wanted to curry favor with the day's clear winners. Certainly Barak and Deborah approved of her, singing: "Most blessed of women be Jael, the wife of Heber the Kenite, of tent-dwelling women most blessed . . . She put her hand to the tent peg and her right hand to the workmen's mallet; she struck Sisera a blow, she crushed his head, she shattered and pierced his temple . . . at her feet he sank, he fell; where he sank, there he fell dead. So perish all your enemies, O LORD! But may your friends be like the sun as it rises in its might" (5.24, 26–27, 31).

Jael's treachery and Deborah's gloating strike us as bloodthirsty, all the more so because we don't usually attribute such behavior to women. But by the standards of ancient warfare, both were heroes. Decisive and courageous, they were women who helped God's people at a critical moment in history.

Praying With Jael

Most blessed of women be Jael . . . she struck Sisera a blow, she crushed his head . . . at her feet he sank, he fell.—*Judges 5.24, 26–27*

Praise God: For defeating the enemies of our soul.
Offer Thanks: That we can be instruments of deliverance.
Confess: Any tendency toward passivity in your struggle against sin and Satan.
Ask God: To give you wisdom and discernment.

Lift Your Heart

Ephesians 6 talks about the importance of putting on the full armor of God in order to successfully engage in battle. Take some time for a wardrobe check. Here's a quick checklist for the well-dressed spiritual warrior:

The Belt of Truth (verse 14)—have any small dishonesties crept into your life?

The Breastplate of Righteousness (verse 14)—are you cooperating with grace to become more Christlike?

The Shoes of the Gospel of Peace (verse 15)—the gospel reconciles us to God and others. Are you willing to receive it, live by it and share it?

The Shield of Faith (verse 16)—Do you really believe God is as loving or as powerful as he says?

The Helmet of Salvation (verse 17)—Salvation is a gift. But like any gift, it has to be received.

The Sword of the Spirit (verse 17)—Reading and praying through Scripture helps us take the offensive.

Lord, help me to be ready so that at any moment I am equipped to stand against the enemy and even deal a decisive blow in the battle. Give me courage, discernment, and wisdom and help me to stay close to you in the midst of the fray.

Go to page 671 for your next devotional reading.

Their eyes stealthily watch for the
   helpless;
9   they lurk in secret like a lion in its
      covert;
   they lurk that they may seize the
      poor;
   they seize the poor and drag them
      off in their net.

10 They stoop, they crouch,
   and the helpless fall by their
      might.
11 They think in their heart, "God has
      forgotten,
   he has hidden his face, he will
      never see it."

12 Rise up, O LORD; O God, lift up your
      hand;
   do not forget the oppressed.
13 Why do the wicked renounce God,
   and say in their hearts, "You will
      not call us to account"?

14 But you do see! Indeed you note
      trouble and grief,
   that you may take it into your
      hands;
   the helpless commit themselves
      to you;
   you have been the helper of the
      orphan.

15 Break the arm of the wicked and
      evildoers;
   seek out their wickedness until
      you find none.
16 The LORD is king forever and ever;
   the nations shall perish from his
      land.

17 O LORD, you will hear the desire of
      the meek;
   you will strengthen their heart,
   you will incline your ear
18 to do justice for the orphan and the
      oppressed,
   so that those from earth may
      strike terror no more. *i*

Psalm 11

Song of Trust in God

To the leader. Of David.

1 In the LORD I take refuge; how can
   you say to me,

"Flee like a bird to the
   mountains; *j*
2 for look, the wicked bend the bow,
   they have fitted their arrow to the
      string,
   to shoot in the dark at the upright
      in heart.
3 If the foundations are destroyed,
   what can the righteous do?"

4 The LORD is in his holy temple;
   the LORD's throne is in heaven.
   His eyes behold, his gaze
      examines humankind.
5 The LORD tests the righteous and the
      wicked,
   and his soul hates the lover of
      violence.
6 On the wicked he will rain coals of
      fire and sulfur;
   a scorching wind shall be the
      portion of their cup.
7 For the LORD is righteous;
   he loves righteous deeds;
   the upright shall behold his face.

Psalm 12

Plea for Help in Evil Times

To the leader: according to The
Sheminith. A Psalm of David.

1 Help, O LORD, for there is no longer
      anyone who is godly;
   the faithful have disappeared from
      humankind.
2 They utter lies to each other;
   with flattering lips and a double
      heart they speak.

3 May the LORD cut off all flattering
      lips,
   the tongue that makes great
      boasts,
4 those who say, "With our tongues
      we will prevail;
   our lips are our own—who is our
      master?"

5 "Because the poor are despoiled,
      because the needy groan,
   I will now rise up," says the LORD;
   "I will place them in the safety
      for which they long."
6 The promises of the LORD are
      promises that are pure,

*i Meaning of Heb uncertain   j Gk Syr Jerome
Tg: Heb flee to your mountain, O bird*

silver refined in a furnace on the
    ground,
  purified seven times.

7 You, O L ORD, will protect us;
    you will guard us from this
    generation forever.
8 On every side the wicked prowl,
    as vileness is exalted among
    humankind.

Psalm 13

Prayer for Deliverance from Enemies

To the leader. A Psalm of David.

1 How long, O L ORD? Will you forget
    me forever?
  How long will you hide your face
    from me?
2 How long must I bear pain*k* in my
    soul,
  and have sorrow in my heart all
    day long?
  How long shall my enemy be
    exalted over me?

3 Consider and answer me, O L ORD
    my God!
  Give light to my eyes, or I will
    sleep the sleep of death,
4 and my enemy will say, "I have
    prevailed";
  my foes will rejoice because I am
    shaken.

5 But I trusted in your steadfast love;
    my heart shall rejoice in your
    salvation.
6 I will sing to the L ORD,
    because he has dealt bountifully
    with me.

Psalm 14

Denunciation of Godlessness

To the leader. Of David.

1 Fools say in their hearts, "There is
    no God."
  They are corrupt, they do
    abominable deeds;
  there is no one who does good.

2 The L ORD looks down from heaven
    on humankind
  to see if there are any who are
    wise,
  who seek after God.

3 They have all gone astray, they are
    all alike perverse;
  there is no one who does good,
    no, not one.

4 Have they no knowledge, all the
    evildoers
  who eat up my people as they eat
    bread,
  and do not call upon the L ORD?

5 There they shall be in great terror,
    for God is with the company of
    the righteous.
6 You would confound the plans of
    the poor,
  but the L ORD is their refuge.

7 O that deliverance for Israel would
    come from Zion!
  When the L ORD restores the
    fortunes of his people,
  Jacob will rejoice; Israel will be
    glad.

Psalm 15

Who Shall Abide in God's Sanctuary?

A Psalm of David.

1 O L ORD, who may abide in your
    tent?
  Who may dwell on your holy hill?

2 Those who walk blamelessly, and do
    what is right,
  and speak the truth from their
    heart;
3 who do not slander with their
    tongue,
  and do no evil to their friends,
  nor take up a reproach against
    their neighbors;
4 in whose eyes the wicked are
    despised,
  but who honor those who fear the
    L ORD;
  who stand by their oath even to
    their hurt;
5 who do not lend money at interest,
  and do not take a bribe against
    the innocent.

Those who do these things shall
    never be moved.

k Syr: Heb hold counsels

Psalm 16

Song of Trust and Security in God

A Miktam of David.

1 Protect me, O God, for in you I take
    refuge.
2 I say to the LORD, "You are my Lord;
    I have no good apart from you."[l]

3 As for the holy ones in the land,
        they are the noble,
    in whom is all my delight.

4 Those who choose another god
        multiply their sorrows;[m]
    their drink offerings of blood I
        will not pour out
    or take their names upon my lips.

5 The LORD is my chosen portion and
        my cup;
    you hold my lot.
6 The boundary lines have fallen for
        me in pleasant places;
    I have a goodly heritage.

7 I bless the LORD who gives me
        counsel;
    in the night also my heart
        instructs me.
8 I keep the LORD always before me;
    because he is at my right hand, I
        shall not be moved.

9 Therefore my heart is glad, and my
        soul rejoices;
    my body also rests secure.
10 For you do not give me up to Sheol,
    or let your faithful one see the Pit.

11 You show me the path of life.
    In your presence there is fullness
        of joy;
    in your right hand are pleasures
        forevermore.

Psalm 17

Prayer for Deliverance from Persecutors

A Prayer of David.

1 Hear a just cause, O LORD; attend to
        my cry;
    give ear to my prayer from lips
        free of deceit.
2 From you let my vindication come;
    let your eyes see the right.

3 If you try my heart, if you visit me
        by night,
    if you test me, you will find no
        wickedness in me;
    my mouth does not transgress.
4 As for what others do, by the word
        of your lips
    I have avoided the ways of the
        violent.
5 My steps have held fast to your
        paths;
    my feet have not slipped.

6 I call upon you, for you will answer
        me, O God;
    incline your ear to me, hear my
        words.
7 Wondrously show your steadfast
        love,
    O savior of those who seek refuge
    from their adversaries at your right
        hand.

8 Guard me as the apple of the eye;
    hide me in the shadow of your
        wings,
9 from the wicked who despoil me,
    my deadly enemies who
        surround me.
10 They close their hearts to pity;
    with their mouths they speak
        arrogantly.
11 They track me down;[n] now they
        surround me;
    they set their eyes to cast me to
        the ground.
12 They are like a lion eager to tear,
    like a young lion lurking in
        ambush.

13 Rise up, O LORD, confront them,
        overthrow them!
    By your sword deliver my life
        from the wicked,
14 from mortals—by your hand,
        O LORD—
    from mortals whose portion in
        life is in this world.
May their bellies be filled with what
        you have stored up for them;
    may their children have more
        than enough;
    may they leave something over to
        their little ones.

---

[l] Jerome Tg: Meaning of Heb uncertain   [m] Cn:
Meaning of Heb uncertain   [n] One Ms Compare
Syr: MT *Our steps*

15 As for me, I shall behold your face
    in righteousness;
   when I awake I shall be satisfied,
    beholding your likeness.

Psalm 18

Royal Thanksgiving for Victory

To the leader. A Psalm of David the
servant of the LORD, who addressed the
words of this song to the LORD on the day
when the LORD delivered him from the
hand of all his enemies, and from the
hand of Saul. He said:

1 I love you, O LORD, my strength.
2 The LORD is my rock, my fortress,
    and my deliverer,
   my God, my rock in whom I take
    refuge,
   my shield, and the horn of my
    salvation, my stronghold.
3 I call upon the LORD, who is worthy
    to be praised,
   so I shall be saved from my
    enemies.

4 The cords of death encompassed me;
   the torrents of perdition
    assailed me;
5 the cords of Sheol entangled me;
   the snares of death confronted
    me.

6 In my distress I called upon the
    LORD;
   to my God I cried for help.
   From his temple he heard my voice,
   and my cry to him reached his
    ears.

7 Then the earth reeled and rocked;
   the foundations also of the
    mountains trembled
   and quaked, because he was
    angry.
8 Smoke went up from his nostrils,
   and devouring fire from his
    mouth;
   glowing coals flamed forth from
    him.
9 He bowed the heavens, and came
    down;
   thick darkness was under his feet.
10 He rode on a cherub, and flew;
   he came swiftly upon the wings of
    the wind.
11 He made darkness his covering
    around him,

his canopy thick clouds dark with
    water.
12 Out of the brightness before him
   there broke through his clouds
   hailstones and coals of fire.
13 The LORD also thundered in the
    heavens,
   and the Most High uttered his
    voice.[o]
14 And he sent out his arrows, and
    scattered them;
   he flashed forth lightnings, and
    routed them.
15 Then the channels of the sea were
    seen,
   and the foundations of the world
    were laid bare
   at your rebuke, O LORD,
   at the blast of the breath of your
    nostrils.

16 He reached down from on high, he
    took me;
   he drew me out of mighty waters.
17 He delivered me from my strong
    enemy,
   and from those who hated me;
   for they were too mighty for me.
18 They confronted me in the day of
    my calamity;
   but the LORD was my support.
19 He brought me out into a broad
    place;
   he delivered me, because he
    delighted in me.

20 The LORD rewarded me according to
    my righteousness;
   according to the cleanness of my
    hands he recompensed me.
21 For I have kept the ways of the LORD,
   and have not wickedly departed
    from my God.
22 For all his ordinances were before
    me,
   and his statutes I did not put
    away from me.
23 I was blameless before him,
   and I kept myself from guilt.
24 Therefore the LORD has recompensed
    me according to my
    righteousness,
   according to the cleanness of my
    hands in his sight.

o Gk See 2 Sam 22.14: Heb adds *hailstones and
coals of fire*

25 With the loyal you show yourself
loyal;
   with the blameless you show
yourself blameless;
26 with the pure you show yourself
pure;
   and with the crooked you show
yourself perverse;
27 For you deliver a humble people,
   but the haughty eyes you bring
down.
28 It is you who light my lamp;
   the LORD, my God, lights up my
darkness.
29 By you I can crush a troop,
   and by my God I can leap over a
wall.
30 This God—his way is perfect;
   the promise of the LORD proves
true;
   he is a shield for all who take
refuge in him.

31 For who is God except the LORD?
   And who is a rock besides our
God?—
32 the God who girded me with
strength,
   and made my way safe.
33 He made my feet like the feet of a
deer,
   and set me secure on the heights.
34 He trains my hands for war,
   so that my arms can bend a bow
of bronze.
35 You have given me the shield of
your salvation,
   and your right hand has
supported me;
   your help[p] has made me great.
36 You gave me a wide place for my
steps under me,
   and my feet did not slip.
37 I pursued my enemies and overtook
them;
   and did not turn back until they
were consumed.
38 I struck them down, so that they
were not able to rise;
   they fell under my feet.
39 For you girded me with strength for
the battle;
   you made my assailants sink
under me.
40 You made my enemies turn their
backs to me,
   and those who hated me I
destroyed.

41 They cried for help, but there was
no one to save them;
   they cried to the LORD, but he did
not answer them.
42 I beat them fine, like dust before the
wind;
   I cast them out like the mire of
the streets.

43 You delivered me from strife with
the peoples;[q]
   you made me head of the nations;
   people whom I had not known
served me.
44 As soon as they heard of me they
obeyed me;
   foreigners came cringing to me.
45 Foreigners lost heart,
   and came trembling out of their
strongholds.

46 The LORD lives! Blessed be my rock,
   and exalted be the God of my
salvation,
47 the God who gave me vengeance
   and subdued peoples under me;
48 who delivered me from my enemies;
indeed, you exalted me above my
adversaries;
   you delivered me from the
violent.

49 For this I will extol you, O LORD,
among the nations,
   and sing praises to your name.
50 Great triumphs he gives to his king,
   and shows steadfast love to his
anointed,
   to David and his descendants
forever.

Psalm 19

God's Glory in Creation and the Law

To the leader. A Psalm of David.

1 The heavens are telling the glory of
God;
   and the firmament[r] proclaims
his handiwork.
2 Day to day pours forth speech,
   and night to night declares
knowledge.
3 There is no speech, nor are there
words;
   their voice is not heard;

---

p Or *gentleness*   *q* Gk Tg: Heb *people*   *r* Or *dome*

4 yet their voice[s] goes out through all
    the earth,
    and their words to the end of the
      world.

In the heavens[t] he has set a tent
    for the sun,
5 which comes out like a bridegroom
    from his wedding canopy,
    and like a strong man runs its
      course with joy.
6 Its rising is from the end of the
    heavens,
    and its circuit to the end of them;
    and nothing is hid from its heat.

7 The law of the LORD is perfect,
    reviving the soul;
the decrees of the LORD are sure,
    making wise the simple;
8 the precepts of the LORD are right,
    rejoicing the heart;
the commandment of the LORD is
    clear,
    enlightening the eyes;
9 the fear of the LORD is pure,

enduring forever;
the ordinances of the LORD are true
    and righteous altogether.
10 More to be desired are they than
    gold,
    even much fine gold;
sweeter also than honey,
    and drippings of the honeycomb.

11 Moreover by them is your servant
    warned;
    in keeping them there is great
      reward.
12 But who can detect their errors?
    Clear me from hidden faults.
13 Keep back your servant also from
    the insolent;[u]
    do not let them have dominion
      over me.
Then I shall be blameless,
    and innocent of great
      transgression.

[s] Gk Jerome Compare Syr: Heb *line*   [t] Heb
In them   [u] Or *from proud thoughts*

*S*ecret *Sins*

MONDAY

Scripture Reading
for Today:
Psalm 19

Verse for Today:
Psalm 19.12

Much as we want to know ourselves, we do not really know ourselves. Do we really want to see ourselves as God sees us, or even
as our fellow human beings see us? Could we bear it, weak as we
are?

    You know that feeling of contentment in which we sometimes
go about, clothed in it, as it were, like a garment, content with the
world and with ourselves. We are ourselves and we would be no
one else. We are glad that God made us as we are and we would
not have had him make us like anyone else. According to the
weather, our state of health, we have moods of purely animal happiness and contentment. We do not want to be given that clear
inward vision which discloses to us our most secret faults.

    In the psalms there is that prayer, "Clear me from hidden
faults." We do not really know how much pride and self-love we
have until someone whom we respect or love suddenly turns
against us. Then some sudden affront, some sudden offense we
take, reveals to us in all its glaring distinctness our self-love, and
we are ashamed.

—DOROTHY DAY

Go to page 673 for your next devotional reading.

14 Let the words of my mouth and the
 meditation of my heart
be acceptable to you,
 O LORD, my rock and my
 redeemer.

Psalm 20

Prayer for Victory

To the leader. A Psalm of David.

1 The LORD answer you in the day of
 trouble!
The name of the God of Jacob
 protect you!
2 May he send you help from the
 sanctuary,
and give you support from Zion.
3 May he remember all your offerings,
 and regard with favor your burnt
 sacrifices.   *Selah*

4 May he grant you your heart's desire,
 and fulfill all your plans.
5 May we shout for joy over your
 victory,
and in the name of our God set
 up our banners.
May the LORD fulfill all your
 petitions.

6 Now I know that the LORD will help
 his anointed;
he will answer him from his holy
 heaven
with mighty victories by his right
 hand.
7 Some take pride in chariots, and
 some in horses,
but our pride is in the name of
 the LORD our God.
8 They will collapse and fall,
 but we shall rise and stand
 upright.

9 Give victory to the king, O LORD;
 answer us when we call.[v]

Psalm 21

Thanksgiving for Victory

To the leader. A Psalm of David.

1 In your strength the king rejoices,
 O LORD,
and in your help how greatly he
 exults!
2 You have given him his heart's
 desire,

and have not withheld the request
 of his lips.   *Selah*
3 For you meet him with rich
 blessings;
you set a crown of fine gold on
 his head.
4 He asked you for life; you gave it to
 him—
length of days forever and ever.
5 His glory is great through your help;
 splendor and majesty you bestow
 on him.
6 You bestow on him blessings
 forever;
you make him glad with the joy
 of your presence.
7 For the king trusts in the LORD,
 and through the steadfast love of
 the Most High he shall not
 be moved.

8 Your hand will find out all your
 enemies;
your right hand will find out
 those who hate you.
9 You will make them like a fiery
 furnace
when you appear.
The LORD will swallow them up in
 his wrath,
and fire will consume them.
10 You will destroy their offspring from
 the earth,
and their children from among
 humankind.
11 If they plan evil against you,
 if they devise mischief, they will
 not succeed.
12 For you will put them to flight;
 you will aim at their faces with
 your bows.

13 Be exalted, O LORD, in your strength!
 We will sing and praise your
 power.

Psalm 22

*Plea for Deliverance from Suffering
and Hostility*

To the leader: according to The Deer
 of the Dawn. A Psalm of David.

1 My God, my God, why have you
 forsaken me?

---

v Gk: Heb *give victory, O LORD; let the King answer
us when we call*

Why are you so far from helping me, from the words of my groaning?
2 O my God, I cry by day, but you do not answer;
and by night, but find no rest.

3 Yet you are holy,
enthroned on the praises of Israel.
4 In you our ancestors trusted;
they trusted, and you delivered them.

5 To you they cried, and were saved;
in you they trusted, and were not put to shame.

6 But I am a worm, and not human;
scorned by others, and despised by the people.
7 All who see me mock at me;
they make mouths at me, they shake their heads;
8 "Commit your cause to the LORD; let him deliver—

Scripture Reading for Today:
Psalm 22

Verse for Today:
Psalm 22.1

Abandoned

The anguished cry of Jesus from the cross—the first verse of Psalm 22—resounds across the centuries to fill our own hearts with almost unbearable grief. How is it that the Son of God, the one who breathed life into creation, was apparently conquered by death and abandoned by his Father?

Is this love, we ask? Jesus himself assured us that no earthly father would give a stone to a son who asked for bread. Yet wasn't his heavenly Father giving Jesus precisely that—a silence so stony hard as to seem like complete abandonment? Couldn't God have broken the terrifying silence with a word of encouragement?

Sometimes we too feel this seemingly heartless absence of God in our lives. Where is he when a child dies, when we lose a job, suffer the pain of divorce, or feel betrayed by a fellow believer? On a larger scale, where was God when the Jews were gassed at Auschwitz? Where is he today when thousands are slaughtered in Bosnia and hundreds of thousands in Rwanda?

Nailed to a cross, suffering a horrible death, Jesus did not deny his feeling of abandonment. His cry was an honest one. At the same time, he affirmed with utter certainty his faith in the Father's goodness and in the purpose of his plan. For in repeating the first verse of Psalm 22, Jesus was calling forth the words of the entire psalm. "You who fear the LORD, praise him! All you offspring of Jacob, glorify him; . . . For [God] . . . heard when I cried to him" (verses 23–24). If we stop with the first verse of Psalm 22, we fail to plumb the depths of Christ's faith in his Father even in the midst of his suffering.

Perhaps you are facing some kind of death in your life. It may be the death of a dream or the death of a relationship or the very real death of someone you love. Remember to pray all of Psalm 22, not just the first line, for God hears you when you cry to him.

—ANN SPANGLER

Go to page 675 for your next devotional reading.

let him rescue the one in whom
 he delights!"

9 Yet it was you who took me from
 the womb;
 you kept me safe on my mother's
 breast.
10 On you I was cast from my birth,
 and since my mother bore me you
 have been my God.
11 Do not be far from me,
 for trouble is near
 and there is no one to help.

12 Many bulls encircle me,
 strong bulls of Bashan surround
 me;
13 they open wide their mouths at me,
 like a ravening and roaring lion.

14 I am poured out like water,
 and all my bones are out of joint;
 my heart is like wax;
 it is melted within my breast;
15 my mouth[w] is dried up like a
 potsherd,
 and my tongue sticks to my jaws;
 you lay me in the dust of death.

16 For dogs are all around me;
 a company of evildoers
 encircles me.
 My hands and feet have shriveled;[x]
17 I can count all my bones.
 They stare and gloat over me;
18 they divide my clothes among
 themselves,
 and for my clothing they cast lots.

19 But you, O LORD, do not be far
 away!
 O my help, come quickly to
 my aid!
20 Deliver my soul from the sword,
 my life[y] from the power of the
 dog!
21 Save me from the mouth of the
 lion!

 From the horns of the wild oxen
 you have rescued[z] me.
22 I will tell of your name to my
 brothers and sisters;[a]
 in the midst of the congregation I
 will praise you:
23 You who fear the LORD, praise him!
 All you offspring of Jacob, glorify
 him;

stand in awe of him, all you
 offspring of Israel!
24 For he did not despise or abhor
 the affliction of the afflicted;
 he did not hide his face from me,[b]
 but heard when I[c] cried to him.

25 From you comes my praise in the
 great congregation;
 my vows I will pay before those
 who fear him.
26 The poor[d] shall eat and be satisfied;
 those who seek him shall praise
 the LORD.
 May your hearts live forever!

27 All the ends of the earth shall
 remember
 and turn to the LORD;
 and all the families of the nations
 shall worship before him.[e]
28 For dominion belongs to the LORD,
 and he rules over the nations.

29 To him,[f] indeed, shall all who
 sleep in[g] the earth bow
 down;
 before him shall bow all who go
 down to the dust,
 and I shall live for him.[h]
30 Posterity will serve him;
 future generations will be told
 about the Lord,
31 and[i] proclaim his deliverance to a
 people yet unborn,
 saying that he has done it.

Psalm 23

The Divine Shepherd

A Psalm of David.

1 The LORD is my shepherd, I shall not
 want.
2 He makes me lie down in green
 pastures;
 he leads me beside still waters;[j]
3 he restores my soul.[k]

---

w Cn: Heb *strength* x Meaning of Heb uncertain
y Heb *my only one* z Heb *answered* a Or
kindred b Heb *him* c Heb *he* d Or *afflicted*
e Gk Syr Jerome: Heb *you* f Cn: Heb *They
have eaten and* g Cn: Heb *all the fat ones*
h Compare Gk Syr Vg: Heb *and he who cannot keep
himself alive* i Compare Gk: Heb *it will be told
about the Lord to the generation,* 31*they will come
and* j Heb *waters of rest* k Or *life*

He leads me in right paths[l]
  for his name's sake.

4 Even though I walk through the
      darkest valley,[m]
  I fear no evil;
for you are with me;
  your rod and your staff—
  they comfort me.

5 You prepare a table before me
  in the presence of my enemies;
you anoint my head with oil;
  my cup overflows.
6 Surely[n] goodness and mercy[o] shall
  follow me

all the days of my life,
and I shall dwell in the house of the
  LORD
my whole life long. [p]

Psalm 24

Entrance into the Temple

Of David. A Psalm.

1 The earth is the LORD's and all that is
  in it,

---

[l] Or *paths of righteousness*   [m] Or *the valley of the shadow of death*   [n] Or *Only*   [o] Or *kindness*   [p] Heb *for length of days*

WEDNESDAY

Scripture Reading
for Today:
Psalm 23

Verse for Today:
Psalm 23.1

*P*erfect Peace

I am in the travel business and often meet people who are uncomfortable with flying. I have a solution. Whenever I am worried, I say the 23rd psalm. This truly gives me "the peace of God, which surpasses all understanding" (Philippians 4.7).

My most dramatic experience of this was on a recent flight to Dallas, Texas. Shortly after departure the pilot announced that bad storms were ahead and that he would try to avoid them. Soon lightning was flashing, thunder was crashing, and the plane was really being tossed about. I closed my eyes and concentrated on Psalm 23:

"Even though I walk [or fly] through the darkest valley, I fear no evil; for you are with me." Once again I verified that if you say this—and believe it with your whole heart—fear does go away!

Next thing I knew, we were on the ground. I bumped into the captain as I deplaned and joked about the rough ride. "Hope I didn't scare you," he said. And that's when I learned how rough the ride had been. We had almost landed in Dallas when the pilot was told to pull up and head for Austin. Then, while doing this, he was instructed to return and land immediately, as tornadoes had been sighted. Apparently, this abrupt shifting of direction caused quite a disturbance in the cabin!

But guess what? I had missed it all. The Lord in his kindness had put me to sleep—he *must* have, as I knew nothing about any of this! What could have been a very fearful experience was nothing more than a quick snooze. I trusted God, and he took care of the situation and took away my fear!

Thank you, Lord, for the wonderful peace of Psalm 23.

—*HAZEL MILLER*

Go to page 678 for your next devotional reading.

the world, and those who live in
it;
2 for he has founded it on the seas,
and established it on the rivers.

3 Who shall ascend the hill of the
LORD?
And who shall stand in his holy
place?
4 Those who have clean hands and
pure hearts,
who do not lift up their souls to
what is false,
and do not swear deceitfully.
5 They will receive blessing from the
LORD,
and vindication from the God of
their salvation.
6 Such is the company of those who
seek him,
who seek the face of the God of
Jacob.*q*   *Selah*

7 Lift up your heads, O gates!
and be lifted up, O ancient doors!
that the King of glory may
come in.
8 Who is the King of glory?
The LORD, strong and mighty,
the LORD, mighty in battle.
9 Lift up your heads, O gates!
and be lifted up, O ancient doors!
that the King of glory may
come in.
10 Who is this King of glory?
The LORD of hosts,
he is the King of glory.   *Selah*

Psalm 25

Prayer for Guidance and for Deliverance

Of David.

1 To you, O LORD, I lift up my soul.
2 O my God, in you I trust;
do not let me be put to shame;
do not let my enemies exult
over me.
3 Do not let those who wait for you
be put to shame;
let them be ashamed who are
wantonly treacherous.

4 Make me to know your ways,
O LORD;
teach me your paths.
5 Lead me in your truth, and teach
me,

for you are the God of my
salvation;
for you I wait all day long.

6 Be mindful of your mercy, O LORD,
and of your steadfast love,
for they have been from of old.
7 Do not remember the sins of my
youth or my transgressions;
according to your steadfast love
remember me,
for your goodness' sake, O LORD!

8 Good and upright is the LORD;
therefore he instructs sinners in
the way.
9 He leads the humble in what is
right,
and teaches the humble his way.
10 All the paths of the LORD are
steadfast love and
faithfulness,
for those who keep his covenant
and his decrees.

11 For your name's sake, O LORD,
pardon my guilt, for it is great.
12 Who are they that fear the LORD?
He will teach them the way that
they should choose.

13 They will abide in prosperity,
and their children shall possess
the land.
14 The friendship of the LORD is for
those who fear him,
and he makes his covenant known
to them.
15 My eyes are ever toward the LORD,
for he will pluck my feet out of
the net.

16 Turn to me and be gracious to me,
for I am lonely and afflicted.
17 Relieve the troubles of my heart,
and bring me*r* out of my distress.
18 Consider my affliction and my
trouble,
and forgive all my sins.

19 Consider how many are my foes,
and with what violent hatred they
hate me.
20 O guard my life, and deliver me;

*q Gk Syr: Heb your face, O Jacob   r Or The
troubles of my heart are enlarged; bring me*

do not let me be put to shame,
   for I take refuge in you.
21 May integrity and uprightness
   preserve me,
   for I wait for you.

22 Redeem Israel, O God,
   out of all its troubles.

Psalm 26

Plea for Justice and Declaration of Righteousness

Of David.

1 Vindicate me, O LORD,
   for I have walked in my integrity,
   and I have trusted in the LORD
     without wavering.
2 Prove me, O LORD, and try me;
   test my heart and mind.
3 For your steadfast love is before my
     eyes,
   and I walk in faithfulness to
     you.*s*

4 I do not sit with the worthless,
   nor do I consort with hypocrites;
5 I hate the company of evildoers,
   and will not sit with the wicked.

6 I wash my hands in innocence,
   and go around your altar, O LORD,
7 singing aloud a song of
     thanksgiving,
   and telling all your wondrous
     deeds.

8 O LORD, I love the house in which
     you dwell,
   and the place where your glory
     abides.
9 Do not sweep me away with sinners,
   nor my life with the bloodthirsty,
10 those in whose hands are evil
     devices,
   and whose right hands are full of
     bribes.

11 But as for me, I walk in my
     integrity;
   redeem me, and be gracious
     to me.
12 My foot stands on level ground;
   in the great congregation I will
     bless the LORD.

Psalm 27

Triumphant Song of Confidence

Of David.

1 The LORD is my light and my
     salvation;
   whom shall I fear?
The LORD is the stronghold*t* of my
     life;
   of whom shall I be afraid?

2 When evildoers assail me
   to devour my flesh—
my adversaries and foes—
   they shall stumble and fall.

3 Though an army encamp against me,
   my heart shall not fear;
though war rise up against me,
   yet I will be confident.

4 One thing I asked of the LORD,
   that will I seek after:
to live in the house of the LORD
   all the days of my life,
to behold the beauty of the LORD,
   and to inquire in his temple.

5 For he will hide me in his shelter
   in the day of trouble;
he will conceal me under the cover
     of his tent;
   he will set me high on a rock.

6 Now my head is lifted up
   above my enemies all around me,
and I will offer in his tent
   sacrifices with shouts of joy;
I will sing and make melody to the
     LORD.

7 Hear, O LORD, when I cry aloud,
   be gracious to me and answer me!
8 "Come," my heart says, "seek his
     face!"
   Your face, LORD, do I seek.
9   Do not hide your face from me.

Do not turn your servant away in
     anger,
   you who have been my help.
Do not cast me off, do not
     forsake me,
   O God of my salvation!

s Or in your faithfulness   *t Or refuge*

¹⁰ If my father and mother forsake me,
   the LORD will take me up.

¹¹ Teach me your way, O LORD,
   and lead me on a level path
   because of my enemies.
¹² Do not give me up to the will of
       my adversaries,
   for false witnesses have risen
       against me,
   and they are breathing out violence.

¹³ I believe that I shall see the
   goodness of the LORD

in the land of the living.
¹⁴ Wait for the LORD;
   be strong, and let your heart take
       courage;
   wait for the LORD!

Psalm 28

Prayer for Help and Thanksgiving for It

Of David.

¹ To you, O LORD, I call;
   my rock, do not refuse to hear me,
   for if you are silent to me,

Seeking His Face

THURSDAY

Scripture Reading
for Today:
Psalm 27.7–14

Verse for Today:
Psalm 27.8

I have at least one child whom I can usually discipline with merely a frown. She knows me so well and cares so much that if a wrinkle appears on my brow her tears begin. So sensitive to my delight or displeasure is this child, that I must be careful to visibly express my joy as well as my grief. I am reminded of the psalmist's prayer: "Hear, O LORD, when I cry aloud . . . Your face, LORD, do I seek. Do not hide your face from me."

My daughter's love for me puts me to shame when compared with my love for the Lord. He rarely hides his face from us, yet until very recently I had a highly-developed escape pattern, turning away whenever I sensed that the Lord was about to get a furrowed brow because of me. I have hidden my face from him.

Averting the eyes because I am not worthy to look upon the face of God and live is one kind of response. But to run away internally or, worse, to cease praying for a period of time because I only want to see the Lord smiling at me is self-centered. The only corrective is to look upon the bloody, agonized face of Christ crucified and accept in those eyes of pain neither disgust nor approval, but only salvation and love beyond comprehension.

To focus on the face of the Lord may mean that we need to bear his reproof, but even more it means we can see what delights him. We can begin to understand and enter into a whole new way of being which seeks only to please the beloved of our souls.

C. S. Lewis has put it this way: "In the end that Face which is the delight or the terror of the universe must be turned upon each of us either with one expression or with the other, either conferring glory inexpressible or inflicting shame that can never be cured or disguised" (*The Weight of Glory*). Said that way, I would rather face him now while there is still time to change.

—DOROTHY RANAGHAN

Go to page 688 for your next devotional reading.

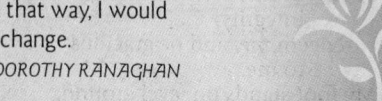

I shall be like those who go down
  to the Pit.
2 Hear the voice of my supplication,
    as I cry to you for help,
  as I lift up my hands
    toward your most holy
      sanctuary.*u*

3 Do not drag me away with the
    wicked,
  with those who are workers
    of evil,
  who speak peace with their
    neighbors,
  while mischief is in their hearts.
4 Repay them according to their work,
    and according to the evil of their
      deeds;
  repay them according to the work of
    their hands;
  render them their due reward.
5 Because they do not regard the
    works of the LORD,
  or the work of his hands,
  he will break them down and build
    them up no more.

6 Blessed be the LORD,
    for he has heard the sound of my
      pleadings.
7 The LORD is my strength and my
    shield;
  in him my heart trusts;
  so I am helped, and my heart exults,
    and with my song I give thanks to
      him.

8 The LORD is the strength of his
    people;
  he is the saving refuge of his
    anointed.
9 O save your people, and bless your
    heritage;
  be their shepherd, and carry them
    forever.

Psalm 29

The Voice of God in a Great Storm

A Psalm of David.

1 Ascribe to the LORD, O heavenly
    beings,*v*
  ascribe to the LORD glory and
    strength.
2 Ascribe to the LORD the glory of his
    name;

worship the LORD in holy
  splendor.

3 The voice of the LORD is over the
    waters;
  the God of glory thunders,
  the LORD, over mighty waters.
4 The voice of the LORD is powerful;
  the voice of the LORD is full of
    majesty.

5 The voice of the LORD breaks the
    cedars;
  the LORD breaks the cedars of
    Lebanon.
6 He makes Lebanon skip like a calf,
  and Sirion like a young wild ox.

7 The voice of the LORD flashes forth
    flames of fire.
8 The voice of the LORD shakes the
    wilderness;
  the LORD shakes the wilderness of
    Kadesh.

9 The voice of the LORD causes the
    oaks to whirl,*w*
  and strips the forest bare;
  and in his temple all say, "Glory!"

10 The LORD sits enthroned over the
    flood;
  the LORD sits enthroned as king
    forever.
11 May the LORD give strength to his
    people!
  May the LORD bless his people
    with peace!

Psalm 30

*Thanksgiving for Recovery
from Grave Illness*

A Psalm. A Song at the dedication of the
temple. Of David.

1 I will extol you, O LORD, for you
    have drawn me up,
  and did not let my foes rejoice
    over me.
2 O LORD my God, I cried to you for
    help,
  and you have healed me.
3 O LORD, you brought up my soul
    from Sheol,

u Heb *your innermost sanctuary*   *v* Heb *sons of
gods*   *w* Or *causes the deer to calve*

restored me to life from among
those gone down to the Pit.*x*

4 Sing praises to the LORD, O you his
faithful ones,
and give thanks to his holy name.
5 For his anger is but for a moment;
his favor is for a lifetime.
Weeping may linger for the night,
but joy comes with the morning.

6 As for me, I said in my prosperity,
"I shall never be moved."
7 By your favor, O LORD,
you had established me as a
strong mountain;
you hid your face;
I was dismayed.

8 To you, O LORD, I cried,
and to the LORD I made
supplication:
9 "What profit is there in my death,
if I go down to the Pit?
Will the dust praise you?
Will it tell of your faithfulness?
10 Hear, O LORD, and be gracious to
me!
O LORD, be my helper!"

11 You have turned my mourning into
dancing;
you have taken off my sackcloth
and clothed me with joy,
12 so that my soul *y* may praise you
and not be silent.
O LORD my God, I will give thanks
to you forever.

Psalm 31

*Prayer and Praise for Deliverance
from Enemies*

To the leader. A Psalm of David.

1 In you, O LORD, I seek refuge;
do not let me ever be put to
shame;
in your righteousness deliver me.
2 Incline your ear to me;
rescue me speedily.
Be a rock of refuge for me,
a strong fortress to save me.

3 You are indeed my rock and my
fortress;
for your name's sake lead me and
guide me,

4 take me out of the net that is
hidden for me,
for you are my refuge.
5 Into your hand I commit my spirit;
you have redeemed me, O LORD,
faithful God.

6 You hate *z* those who pay regard to
worthless idols,
but I trust in the LORD.
7 I will exult and rejoice in your
steadfast love,
because you have seen my
affliction;
you have taken heed of my
adversities,
8 and have not delivered me into the
hand of the enemy;
you have set my feet in a broad
place.

9 Be gracious to me, O LORD, for I am
in distress;
my eye wastes away from grief,
my soul and body also.
10 For my life is spent with sorrow,
and my years with sighing;
my strength fails because of my
misery, *a*
and my bones waste away.

11 I am the scorn of all my adversaries,
a horror *b* to my neighbors,
an object of dread to my
acquaintances;
those who see me in the street
flee from me.
12 I have passed out of mind like one
who is dead;
I have become like a broken
vessel.
13 For I hear the whispering of many—
terror all around!—
as they scheme together against me,
as they plot to take my life.

14 But I trust in you, O LORD;
I say, "You are my God."
15 My times are in your hand;
deliver me from the hand of my
enemies and persecutors.
16 Let your face shine upon your
servant;

*x Or that I should not go down to the Pit   y Heb
that glory   z One Heb Ms Gk Syr Jerome: MT I
hate   a Gk Syr: Heb my iniquity   b Cn:
Heb exceedingly*

save me in your steadfast love.
17 Do not let me be put to shame,
    O Lord,
    for I call on you;
let the wicked be put to shame;
    let them go dumbfounded to
        Sheol.
18 Let the lying lips be stilled
    that speak insolently against the
        righteous
    with pride and contempt.

19 O how abundant is your goodness
    that you have laid up for those
        who fear you,
and accomplished for those who
        take refuge in you,
    in the sight of everyone!
20 In the shelter of your presence you
        hide them
    from human plots;
you hold them safe under your
        shelter
    from contentious tongues.

21 Blessed be the Lord,
    for he has wondrously shown his
        steadfast love to me
    when I was beset as a city under
        siege.
22 I had said in my alarm,
    "I am driven far*c* from your
        sight."
But you heard my supplications
    when I cried out to you for help.

23 Love the Lord, all you his saints.
    The Lord preserves the faithful,
    but abundantly repays the one
        who acts haughtily.
24 Be strong, and let your heart take
        courage,
    all you who wait for the Lord.

Psalm 32

The Joy of Forgiveness

Of David. A Maskil.

1 Happy are those whose transgression
        is forgiven,
    whose sin is covered.
2 Happy are those to whom the Lord
        imputes no iniquity,
    and in whose spirit there is no
        deceit.

3 While I kept silence, my body
        wasted away
    through my groaning all day long.
4 For day and night your hand was
        heavy upon me;
    my strength was dried up*d* as by
        the heat of summer.   *Selah*

5 Then I acknowledged my sin to you,
    and I did not hide my iniquity;
I said, "I will confess my
        transgressions to the Lord,"
    and you forgave the guilt of
        my sin.   *Selah*

6 Therefore let all who are faithful
    offer prayer to you;
at a time of distress,*e* the rush of
        mighty waters
    shall not reach them.
7 You are a hiding place for me;
    you preserve me from trouble;
    you surround me with glad cries
        of deliverance.   *Selah*

8 I will instruct you and teach you the
        way you should go;
    I will counsel you with my eye
        upon you.
9 Do not be like a horse or a mule,
        without understanding,
    whose temper must be curbed
        with bit and bridle,
    else it will not stay near you.

10 Many are the torments of the
        wicked,
    but steadfast love surrounds those
        who trust in the Lord.
11 Be glad in the Lord and rejoice,
        O righteous,
    and shout for joy, all you upright
        in heart.

Psalm 33

The Greatness and Goodness of God

1 Rejoice in the Lord, O you
        righteous.
    Praise befits the upright.
2 Praise the Lord with the lyre;
    make melody to him with the
        harp of ten strings.
3 Sing to him a new song;

c Another reading is *cut off*   *d* Meaning of Heb
uncertain   *e* Cn: Heb *at a time of finding only*

play skillfully on the strings, with
loud shouts.

4 For the word of the LORD is upright,
and all his work is done in
faithfulness.
5 He loves righteousness and justice;
the earth is full of the steadfast
love of the LORD.

6 By the word of the LORD the heavens
were made,
and all their host by the breath of
his mouth.
7 He gathered the waters of the sea as
in a bottle;
he put the deeps in storehouses.

8 Let all the earth fear the LORD;
let all the inhabitants of the world
stand in awe of him.
9 For he spoke, and it came to be;
he commanded, and it stood firm.

10 The LORD brings the counsel of the
nations to nothing;
he frustrates the plans of the
peoples.
11 The counsel of the LORD stands
forever,
the thoughts of his heart to all
generations.
12 Happy is the nation whose God is
the LORD,

THE TRADITION

Reconciliation

I said, "I will confess my transgressions to the LORD,"
and you forgave the guilt of my sin.
PSALM 32.5

"*Adam*, why did you eat that forbidden fruit?"

"It wasn't my fault, God. Eve gave it to me."

"Wendy, did you put that big dent in the garage door?"

"Who, me? I don't know a thing about it."

It's hard to admit the truth when you've done something wrong. And if you do, it's hard to repent sincerely. "Sorry," you mutter and then carry on as before, eager to forget the whole thing.

It isn't that easy. Saint Peter put his finger on why when he told one offender, "You did not lie to us but to God" (Acts 5.4). Though there are degrees of wrongdoing—everything from deliberately embracing evil to not-so-deliberate faults and weaknesses—every sin is an offense against God. Sin can separate us from God forever. At the very least, it diminishes our sharing in Christ's life and damages our relationships with members of his body.

The sacrament of Reconciliation helps us to take sin seriously. Any person-to-person admission of guilt can be an incentive to honesty. But when the person we confess to is Christ, there are no limits to the possibilities of conversion!

God alone can forgive sin. But on the evening of his resurrection, Jesus entrusted this power to his chosen representatives. "If you forgive the sins of any, they are forgiven them," he said (John 20.23).

Because the priest has received this power and is authorized to act as a special instrument of grace, what goes on in the confessional is a meeting with Jesus. In the person of the priest, Jesus hears our admission of sin, receives our expression of sorrow, and extends his healing forgiveness.

"I absolve you in the name of the Father, and of the Son, and of the Holy Spirit." What relief and freedom these words bring! And how happy are we who have Jesus' *personal* assurance that our "transgression is forgiven" and our "sin is covered"! (Psalm 32.1).

the people whom he has chosen
    as his heritage.

13 The LORD looks down from heaven;
    he sees all humankind.
14 From where he sits enthroned he
        watches
    all the inhabitants of the earth—
15 he who fashions the hearts of
        them all,
    and observes all their deeds.
16 A king is not saved by his great
        army;
    a warrior is not delivered by his
        great strength.
17 The war horse is a vain hope for
        victory,
    and by its great might it cannot
        save.

18 Truly the eye of the LORD is on those
        who fear him,
    on those who hope in his
        steadfast love,
19 to deliver their soul from death,
    and to keep them alive in famine.

20 Our soul waits for the LORD;
    he is our help and shield.
21 Our heart is glad in him,
    because we trust in his holy name.
22 Let your steadfast love, O LORD, be
        upon us,
    even as we hope in you.

Psalm 34

Praise for Deliverance from Trouble

Of David, when he feigned madness
before Abimelech, so that he drove him
out, and he went away.

1 I will bless the LORD at all times;
    his praise shall continually be in
        my mouth.
2 My soul makes its boast in the LORD;
    let the humble hear and be glad.
3 O magnify the LORD with me,
    and let us exalt his name together.

4 I sought the LORD, and he answered
        me,
    and delivered me from all my
        fears.
5 Look to him, and be radiant;
    so your*f* faces shall never be
        ashamed.
6 This poor soul cried, and was heard
        by the LORD,

and was saved from every trouble.
7 The angel of the LORD encamps
    around those who fear him, and
        delivers them.
8 O taste and see that the LORD is
        good;
    happy are those who take refuge
        in him.
9 O fear the LORD, you his holy ones,
    for those who fear him have no
        want.
10 The young lions suffer want and
        hunger,
    but those who seek the LORD lack
        no good thing.

11 Come, O children, listen to me;
    I will teach you the fear of the
        LORD.
12 Which of you desires life,
    and covets many days to enjoy
        good?
13 Keep your tongue from evil,
    and your lips from speaking
        deceit.
14 Depart from evil, and do good;
    seek peace, and pursue it.

15 The eyes of the LORD are on the
        righteous,
    and his ears are open to their cry.
16 The face of the LORD is against
        evildoers,
    to cut off the remembrance of
        them from the earth.
17 When the righteous cry for help, the
        LORD hears,
    and rescues them from all their
        troubles.
18 The LORD is near to the
        brokenhearted,
    and saves the crushed in spirit.

19 Many are the afflictions of the
        righteous,
    but the LORD rescues them from
        them all.
20 He keeps all their bones;
    not one of them will be broken.
21 Evil brings death to the wicked,
    and those who hate the righteous
        will be condemned.
22 The LORD redeems the life of his
        servants;
    none of those who take refuge in
        him will be condemned.

f Gk Syr Jerome: Heb *their*

Psalm 35

Prayer for Deliverance from Enemies

Of David.

1 Contend, O LORD, with those who
     contend with me;
   fight against those who fight
     against me!
2 Take hold of shield and buckler,
   and rise up to help me!
3 Draw the spear and javelin
     against my pursuers;
   say to my soul,
     "I am your salvation."

4 Let them be put to shame and
     dishonor
   who seek after my life.
   Let them be turned back and
     confounded
   who devise evil against me.
5 Let them be like chaff before the
     wind,
   with the angel of the LORD driving
     them on.
6 Let their way be dark and slippery,
   with the angel of the LORD
     pursuing them.

7 For without cause they hid their
     net*g* for me;
   without cause they dug a pit*h* for
     my life.
8 Let ruin come on them unawares.
   And let the net that they hid ensnare
     them;
   let them fall in it—to their ruin.

9 Then my soul shall rejoice in the
     LORD,
   exulting in his deliverance.
10 All my bones shall say,
   "O LORD, who is like you?
   You deliver the weak
     from those too strong for them,
     the weak and needy from those
       who despoil them."

11 Malicious witnesses rise up;
   they ask me about things I do not
     know.
12 They repay me evil for good;
   my soul is forlorn.
13 But as for me, when they were sick,
   I wore sackcloth;
   I afflicted myself with fasting.

I prayed with head bowed*i* on my
     bosom,
14 as though I grieved for a friend or
     a brother;
   I went about as one who laments
     for a mother,
   bowed down and in mourning.

15 But at my stumbling they gathered
     in glee,
   they gathered together against me;
   ruffians whom I did not know
     tore at me without ceasing;
16 they impiously mocked more and
     more,*j*
   gnashing at me with their teeth.

17 How long, O LORD, will you look
     on?
   Rescue me from their ravages,
   my life from the lions!
18 Then I will thank you in the great
     congregation;
   in the mighty throng I will
     praise you.

19 Do not let my treacherous enemies
     rejoice over me,
   or those who hate me without
     cause wink the eye.
20 For they do not speak peace,
   but they conceive deceitful words
     against those who are quiet in the
       land.
21 They open wide their mouths
     against me;
   they say, "Aha, Aha,
     our eyes have seen it."

22 You have seen, O LORD; do not be
     silent!
   O Lord, do not be far from me!
23 Wake up! Bestir yourself for my
     defense,
   for my cause, my God and my
     Lord!
24 Vindicate me, O LORD, my God,
     according to your righteousness,
   and do not let them rejoice
     over me.
25 Do not let them say to themselves,
   "Aha, we have our heart's desire."

---

g Heb *a pit, their net*   *h* The word *pit* is
transposed from the preceding line   *i* Or *My
prayer turned back*   *j* Cn Compare Gk: Heb *like
the profanest of mockers of a cake*

Do not let them say, "We have
swallowed you[k] up."

26 Let all those who rejoice at my
calamity
be put to shame and confusion;
let those who exalt themselves
against me
be clothed with shame and
dishonor.

27 Let those who desire my vindication
shout for joy and be glad,
and say evermore,
"Great is the LORD,
who delights in the welfare of his
servant."
28 Then my tongue shall tell of your
righteousness
and of your praise all day long.

Psalm 36

Human Wickedness and Divine Goodness

To the leader. Of David, the servant
of the LORD.

1 Transgression speaks to the wicked
deep in their hearts;
there is no fear of God
before their eyes.
2 For they flatter themselves in their
own eyes
that their iniquity cannot be
found out and hated.
3 The words of their mouths are
mischief and deceit;
they have ceased to act wisely and
do good.
4 They plot mischief while on their
beds;
they are set on a way that is
not good;
they do not reject evil.

5 Your steadfast love, O LORD, extends
to the heavens,
your faithfulness to the clouds.
6 Your righteousness is like the mighty
mountains,
your judgments are like the great
deep;
you save humans and animals
alike, O LORD.

7 How precious is your steadfast love,
O God!
All people may take refuge in the
shadow of your wings.

8 They feast on the abundance of your
house,
and you give them drink from the
river of your delights.
9 For with you is the fountain of life;
in your light we see light.

10 O continue your steadfast love to
those who know you,
and your salvation to the upright
of heart!
11 Do not let the foot of the arrogant
tread on me,
or the hand of the wicked drive
me away.
12 There the evildoers lie prostrate;
they are thrust down, unable
to rise.

Psalm 37

Exhortation to Patience and Trust

Of David.

1 Do not fret because of the wicked;
do not be envious of wrongdoers,
2 for they will soon fade like the grass,
and wither like the green herb.

3 Trust in the LORD, and do good;
so you will live in the land, and
enjoy security.
4 Take delight in the LORD,
and he will give you the desires of
your heart.

5 Commit your way to the LORD;
trust in him, and he will act.
6 He will make your vindication shine
like the light,
and the justice of your cause like
the noonday.

7 Be still before the LORD, and wait
patiently for him;
do not fret over those who
prosper in their way,
over those who carry out evil
devices.

8 Refrain from anger, and forsake
wrath.
Do not fret—it leads only to evil.
9 For the wicked shall be cut off,
but those who wait for the LORD
shall inherit the land.

k Heb *him*

10 Yet a little while, and the wicked
　　will be no more;
　　　though you look diligently for
　　　　their place, they will not
　　　　be there.
11 But the meek shall inherit the land,
　　and delight themselves in
　　　abundant prosperity.

12 The wicked plot against the
　　righteous,
　　and gnash their teeth at them;
13 but the LORD laughs at the wicked,
　　for he sees that their day is
　　　coming.

14 The wicked draw the sword and
　　bend their bows
　　　to bring down the poor and
　　　　needy,
　　　to kill those who walk uprightly;
15 their sword shall enter their own
　　heart,
　　　and their bows shall be broken.

16 Better is a little that the righteous
　　person has
　　　than the abundance of many
　　　　wicked.
17 For the arms of the wicked shall be
　　broken,
　　　but the LORD upholds the
　　　　righteous.

18 The LORD knows the days of the
　　blameless,
　　　and their heritage will abide
　　　　forever;
19 they are not put to shame in evil
　　times,
　　　in the days of famine they have
　　　　abundance.

20 But the wicked perish,
　　and the enemies of the LORD are
　　　like the glory of the pastures;
　　they vanish—like smoke they
　　　vanish away.

21 The wicked borrow, and do not pay
　　back,
　　　but the righteous are generous
　　　　and keep giving;
22 for those blessed by the LORD shall
　　inherit the land,
　　　but those cursed by him shall be
　　　　cut off.

23 Our steps*l* are made firm by the
　　LORD,
　　　when he delights in our*m* way;
24 though we stumble,*n* we*o* shall not
　　fall headlong,
　　　for the LORD holds us*p* by the
　　　　hand.

25 I have been young, and now am
　　old,
　　　yet I have not seen the righteous
　　　　forsaken
　　　or their children begging bread.
26 They are ever giving liberally and
　　lending,
　　　and their children become a
　　　　blessing.

27 Depart from evil, and do good;
　　so you shall abide forever.
28 For the LORD loves justice;
　　he will not forsake his faithful
　　　ones.

　　The righteous shall be kept safe
　　　forever,
　　　but the children of the wicked
　　　　shall be cut off.
29 The righteous shall inherit the land,
　　and live in it forever.

30 The mouths of the righteous utter
　　wisdom,
　　　and their tongues speak justice.
31 The law of their God is in their
　　hearts;
　　　their steps do not slip.

32 The wicked watch for the righteous,
　　and seek to kill them.
33 The LORD will not abandon them to
　　their power,
　　　or let them be condemned when
　　　　they are brought to trial.

34 Wait for the LORD, and keep to his
　　way,
　　　and he will exalt you to inherit
　　　　the land;
　　　you will look on the destruction
　　　　of the wicked.

35 I have seen the wicked oppressing,

l Heb *A man's steps*　　*m* Heb *his*　　*n* Heb *he stumbles*　　*o* Heb *he*　　*p* Heb *him*

and towering like a cedar of
    Lebanon.*q*
36 Again I*r* passed by, and they were
    no more;
    though I sought them, they could
    not be found.

37 Mark the blameless, and behold the
    upright,
    for there is posterity for the
    peaceable.
38 But transgressors shall be altogether
    destroyed;
    the posterity of the wicked shall
    be cut off.

39 The salvation of the righteous is
    from the LORD;
    he is their refuge in the time of
    trouble.
40 The LORD helps them and rescues
    them;
    he rescues them from the wicked,
    and saves them,
    because they take refuge in him.

Psalm 38

A Penitent Sufferer's Plea for Healing

A Psalm of David, for the
memorial offering.

1 O LORD, do not rebuke me in your
    anger,
    or discipline me in your wrath.
2 For your arrows have sunk into me,
    and your hand has come down
    on me.

3 There is no soundness in my flesh
    because of your indignation;
    there is no health in my bones
    because of my sin.
4 For my iniquities have gone over my
    head;
    they weigh like a burden too
    heavy for me.

5 My wounds grow foul and fester
    because of my foolishness;
6 I am utterly bowed down and
    prostrate;
    all day long I go around
    mourning.
7 For my loins are filled with burning,
    and there is no soundness in my
    flesh.
8 I am utterly spent and crushed;

I groan because of the tumult of
    my heart.

9 O Lord, all my longing is known
    to you;
    my sighing is not hidden from
    you.
10 My heart throbs, my strength
    fails me;
    as for the light of my eyes—it also
    has gone from me.
11 My friends and companions stand
    aloof from my affliction,
    and my neighbors stand far off.

12 Those who seek my life lay their
    snares;
    those who seek to hurt me speak
    of ruin,
    and meditate treachery all day
    long.

13 But I am like the deaf, I do not
    hear;
    like the mute, who cannot speak.
14 Truly, I am like one who does not
    hear,
    and in whose mouth is no retort.

15 But it is for you, O LORD, that I wait;
    it is you, O Lord my God, who
    will answer.
16 For I pray, "Only do not let them
    rejoice over me,
    those who boast against me when
    my foot slips."

17 For I am ready to fall,
    and my pain is ever with me.
18 I confess my iniquity;
    I am sorry for my sin.
19 Those who are my foes without
    cause*s* are mighty,
    and many are those who hate me
    wrongfully.
20 Those who render me evil for good
    are my adversaries because I
    follow after good.

21 Do not forsake me, O LORD;
    O my God, do not be far from
    me;
22 make haste to help me,
    O Lord, my salvation.

q Gk: Meaning of Heb uncertain   *r* Gk Syr
Jerome: Heb *he*   *s* Q Ms: MT *my living foes*

Psalm 39

Prayer for Wisdom and Forgiveness

To the leader: to Jeduthun. A Psalm
of David.

1 I said, "I will guard my ways
     that I may not sin with my
          tongue;
   I will keep a muzzle on my
          mouth
     as long as the wicked are
          in my presence."
2 I was silent and still;
     I held my peace to no avail;
   my distress grew worse,
3   my heart became hot within
          me.
   While I mused, the fire burned;
     then I spoke with my tongue:

4 "LORD, let me know my end,
   and what is the measure of my
          days;
     let me know how fleeting my life is.
5 You have made my days a few
          handbreadths,
     and my lifetime is as nothing in
          your sight.
   Surely everyone stands as a mere
          breath.   *Selah*
6   Surely everyone goes about like a
          shadow.
   Surely for nothing they are in
          turmoil;
     they heap up, and do not know
          who will gather.

7 "And now, O Lord, what do I wait
          for?
     My hope is in you.
8 Deliver me from all my
          transgressions.

Silence

FRIDAY

Scripture Reading
for Today:
Psalm 38.9–22

Verse for Today:
Psalm 38.13

Silence is God's special instrument. He uses it like a harpist reaches for heavenly chords to say things to us that are beyond words.

I remember a priest telling me of an experience he had with a severely ill parishioner who had been hospitalized for some time. When he met her, she was inconsolable. Ever since she had been admitted for care, she had been unable to pray. This was an immense shock to her, for all of her life she had been a believer in daily prayer.

The priest visited her regularly and offered what help he could, but her inability to pray persisted. Finally, he asked her to tell him as clearly as possible how she prayed. She said she mainly talked to God. Now, when she tried to do so, she became choked up, angry, disgusted with life. The priest advised her to try saying nothing to the Lord, simply to remain silent, as Jesus did before his accusers. Suddenly the lady started weeping. It was as if his words had taken from her the burden of having to talk to God. She could be quiet in his presence. She could allow her pent-up emotions to gush out in silence, without trying to analyze what she was feeling. It was impossible to understand fully all that he was asking of her anyway, so why not be still and listen? Only silence proved to be an empty enough space to contain her feelings about life and pending death.

—SUSAN MUTO

Go to page 690 for your next devotional reading.

Do not make me the scorn of the
    fool.
9 I am silent; I do not open my
    mouth,
    for it is you who have done it.
10 Remove your stroke from me;
    I am worn down by the blows[t]
      of your hand.

11 "You chastise mortals
    in punishment for sin,
    consuming like a moth what is dear
      to them;
    surely everyone is a mere breath.
                 Selah

12 "Hear my prayer, O LORD,
    and give ear to my cry;
    do not hold your peace at my
      tears.
    For I am your passing guest,
      an alien, like all my forebears.
13 Turn your gaze away from me, that I
      may smile again,
    before I depart and am no more."

Psalm 40

*Thanksgiving for Deliverance and Prayer
for Help*

To the leader. Of David. A Psalm.

1 I waited patiently for the LORD;
    he inclined to me and heard
      my cry.
2 He drew me up from the desolate
      pit,[u]
    out of the miry bog,
    and set my feet upon a rock,
      making my steps secure.
3 He put a new song in my mouth,
    a song of praise to our God.
    Many will see and fear,
      and put their trust in the LORD.

4 Happy are those who make
    the LORD their trust,
    who do not turn to the proud,
      to those who go astray after false
        gods.
5 You have multiplied, O LORD my
      God,
    your wondrous deeds and your
      thoughts toward us;
    none can compare with you.
    Were I to proclaim and tell of them,
      they would be more than can be
        counted.

6 Sacrifice and offering you do not
      desire,
    but you have given me an open
      ear.[v]
    Burnt offering and sin offering
      you have not required.
7 Then I said, "Here I am;
    in the scroll of the book it is
      written of me.[w]
8 I delight to do your will, O my God;
    your law is within my heart."

9 I have told the glad news of
      deliverance
    in the great congregation;
    see, I have not restrained my lips,
      as you know, O LORD.
10 I have not hidden your saving help
      within my heart,
    I have spoken of your faithfulness
      and your salvation;
    I have not concealed your steadfast
      love and your faithfulness
    from the great congregation.

11 Do not, O LORD, withhold
    your mercy from me;
    let your steadfast love and your
      faithfulness
    keep me safe forever.
12 For evils have encompassed me
      without number;
    my iniquities have overtaken me,
      until I cannot see;
    they are more than the hairs of my
      head,
    and my heart fails me.

13 Be pleased, O LORD, to deliver me;
    O LORD, make haste to help me.
14 Let all those be put to shame and
      confusion
    who seek to snatch away my life;
    let those be turned back and
      brought to dishonor
    who desire my hurt.
15 Let those be appalled because of
      their shame
    who say to me, "Aha, Aha!"

16 But may all who seek you
    rejoice and be glad in you;
    may those who love your salvation

---

t Heb *hostility*   *u* Cn: Heb *pit of tumult*   *v* Heb
ears you have dug for me   *w* Meaning of Heb
uncertain

THE STORY OF A WOMAN

Delilah

Her Name Means "Dainty One"

Her Character: *She used her beauty to betray her lover and enrich herself. Her nationality is unknown.*

Her Sorrow: *That Samson lied to her, making her look foolish on three different occasions.*

Her Triumph: *That she overpowered one of history's most powerful men, handing him over to his enemy, the Philistines.*

Read Judges 16.4–22

Her teeth gleamed white in the dusky light, as a smile parted lips as soft and red as a scarlet ribbon. Earrings glinted gold as she threw back her head and laughed out loud. Fortune had come knocking on her door that day. No lover had ever paid Delilah so well as Samson would.

The Philistine kings hated the longhaired strongman who had set their fields afire and slain a thousand of their countrymen. Each had offered Delilah an incredible sum for betraying him.

But her efforts to discover the secret of his strength at first met with failure. Like a man toying with a kitten, Samson tricked Delilah three times with crazy stories about how he could be captured. Finally Delilah confronted him, "How can you say, 'I love you,' when your heart is not with me?" (verse 15). Worn down by her nagging, Samson gave in.

"A razor has never come upon my head," he confided, "for I have been a nazirite to God from my mother's womb. If my head were shaved, then my strength would leave me; I would become weak, and be like anyone else" (verse 17). Before his birth, an angel had forbidden Samson's mother to cut his hair. He was to be consecrated to God. Though Samson was a strong man, he was unable to subdue his own tempestuous nature. So he gave away the secret to please his lover.

Sensing she had heard the truth at last, Delilah cut his hair while he was sleeping.

Samson awoke unable to resist his Philistine captors, who gouged out his eyes. Imprisoned in Gaza, he spent his days performing women's work: grinding grain.

That's the last we hear of the lovely, treacherous, and now wealthy Delilah, but not the last we hear of her lover. Slowly Samson's hair began to grow back, first a short cap to warm his head and then a cover for his ears. What harm could a blind man do them, the Philistines must have reasoned?

One day they held a great celebration in honor of Dagon, god of the harvest, for delivering Samson into their hands. They brought Samson out of prison, gloating over their once-mighty enemy, oblivious to their danger. But when Samson stood among the pillars of their temple, he prayed: "Lord GOD, remember me and strengthen me only this once, O God, so that with this one act of revenge I may pay back the Philistines for my two eyes" (verse 28). Then he braced himself against the two central pillars of the temple and pushed. The roof buckled and collapsed, and Samson and his enemies were buried together under its rubble. By his death he killed more Philistines than he had in life.

The strange story of Samson and Delilah is hardly edifying. It's tempting to conclude that the selfish, ill-disciplined Samson had finally met his match in the greedy Delilah. If anything, Delilah's role in this sordid tale assures us that God will use anything and anyone to accomplish his purpose. Even our sin. Even our enemies. Our deliverance is purely a matter of grace. But how much better if we become people whose inner strengths match our outer strengths, enabling us to live out the role God intends, assured of his pleasure.

Praying in Light of the Story of Delilah

Then she said to him, "How can you say, 'I love you,' when your heart is not with me? You have mocked me three times now and have not told me what makes your strength so great." Finally, after she had nagged him with her words day after day, and pestered him, he was tired to death. —Judges 16:15–16

Praise God: *That he is sovereign, able to use our most tangled relationships to achieve his purposes.*

Offer Thanks: *For calling you to be devoted to him, set apart in a special way.*

Confess: *Any tendency to manipulate others.*

Ask God: *To help you surrender any unhealthy relationship to him. Take whatever steps God is calling you to take.*

Lift Your Heart

Take inventory of your most important relationships. Have you formed any unhealthy dependencies? Is a spouse or boyfriend leading you away from God rather than closer to him? Have you made compromises that diminish your desire for God? If so, find a trusted friend or counselor to confide in. Pray together about the best course of action and then follow it. Be faithful to marital commitments but find a way to restore your spiritual passion. Right now, take time to write God a letter. Tell him how much you long to be connected to him. Don't be afraid to wear your heart on your sleeve—God is looking for men and women who love him more than they love their own lives.

Lord, you know all the struggles of my heart. You created me in such a way that no one but you can fully satisfy my longings. Yet you also know how easily I am fooled, believing that flesh and blood relationships hold the key to all my needs. Forgive me for the times I've put my relationship with

_____ *above my relationship with you.*

Go to page 694 for your next devotional reading.

say continually, "Great is the
Lord!"

¹⁷ As for me, I am poor and needy,
but the Lord takes thought for me.
You are my help and my deliverer;
do not delay, O my God.

Psalm 41

Assurance of God's Help and a Plea for Healing

To the leader. A Psalm of David.

¹ Happy are those who consider the
poor;ˣ

the Lord delivers them in the day
of trouble.
² The Lord protects them and keeps
them alive;
they are called happy in the land.
You do not give them up to the
will of their enemies.
³ The Lord sustains them on their
sickbed;
in their illness you heal all their
infirmities.ʸ

⁴ As for me, I said, "O Lord, be
gracious to me;

x Or weak   y Heb you change all his bed

THE
TRADITION

The Liturgy of the Hours

Be pleased, O Lord, to deliver me;
O Lord, make haste to help me.
PSALM 40.13

Every day many Catholics join
priests and religious leaders the world over in
regular times of prayer that open with verse
13 of Psalm 40: "Be pleased, O Lord, to deliver
me; O Lord, make haste to help me." In groups
if possible, in song or chant if possible, they
sanctify the day by offering the official prayer
of the Church, the Liturgy of the Hours.

Like "the Jesus prayer" (see page 1279)
but more formally, the Divine Office, as it is
sometimes called, provides a way to "pray
without ceasing" (1 Thessalonians 5.17). It
continues the practice of the first Christians
who met daily at the Jerusalem temple to participate in sacrifices and services (see Acts
2.42, 46; 3.1). They soon developed their own
cycle of prayer, which the monastic movement later took up and refined.

Even if your lifestyle does not permit four
or more prayer breaks a day, you are encouraged to join in the Liturgy of the Hours by focusing on one or both of its "hinges," the
prayers of morning and evening. In them you
will find canticles, readings, and prayers—

especially prayers from the Bible's great collection, the book of Psalms.

Psalms are the backbone of the Divine
Office, and to pray them day after day is to
discover a treasure. Expressing the range of
human emotions, they provide "as you go"
training in the honesty with God that nourishes faith.

"The psalms demand engagement, they
ask you to read them with your whole self,"
comments Kathleen Norris, a Presbyterian
poet who encountered the Liturgy of the
Hours at a Benedictine monastery. "To your
surprise, you find that the psalms do not deny
your true feelings but allow you to reflect on
them, right in front of God and everyone."

Jesus prayed the psalms during his earthly life (see, for example, Mark 14.27; 15.34). In
the Liturgy of the Hours, he prays them still.
When we join in, as Vatican II explained
(*Constitution on the Sacred Liturgy*, 84), we
offer "the very prayer that Christ himself
together with his body addresses to the
Father."

heal me, for I have sinned against
   you."
5 My enemies wonder in malice
   when I will die, and my name
     perish.
6 And when they come to see me,
   they utter empty words,
   while their hearts gather mischief;
   when they go out, they tell it
     abroad.
7 All who hate me whisper together
   about me;
   they imagine the worst for me.

8 They think that a deadly thing has
   fastened on me,
   that I will not rise again from
   where I lie.
9 Even my bosom friend in whom I
   trusted,
   who ate of my bread, has lifted
   the heel against me.
10 But you, O LORD, be gracious to me,
   and raise me up, that I may repay
   them.

11 By this I know that you are pleased
   with me;
   because my enemy has not
   triumphed over me.
12 But you have upheld me because of
   my integrity,
   and set me in your presence
   forever.

13 Blessed be the LORD, the God of
   Israel,
   from everlasting to everlasting.
     Amen and Amen.

BOOK II
(Psalms 42–72)

Psalm 42

Longing for God and His Help in Distress

To the leader. A Maskil of the Korahites.

1 As a deer longs for flowing streams,
   so my soul longs for you, O God.
2 My soul thirsts for God,
   for the living God.
When shall I come and behold
   the face of God?
3 My tears have been my food
   day and night,

while people say to me continually,
   "Where is your God?"

4 These things I remember,
   as I pour out my soul:
how I went with the throng,[z]
   and led them in procession to the
   house of God,
with glad shouts and songs of
   thanksgiving,
   a multitude keeping festival.
5 Why are you cast down, O my soul,
   and why are you disquieted
   within me?
Hope in God; for I shall again praise
   him,
   my help 6and my God.

My soul is cast down within me;
   therefore I remember you
from the land of Jordan and of
   Hermon,
   from Mount Mizar.
7 Deep calls to deep
   at the thunder of your cataracts;
all your waves and your billows
   have gone over me.
8 By day the LORD commands his
   steadfast love,
   and at night his song is with me,
   a prayer to the God of my life.
9 I say to God, my rock,
   "Why have you forgotten me?
Why must I walk about mournfully
   because the enemy oppresses me?"
10 As with a deadly wound in my
   body,
   my adversaries taunt me,
while they say to me continually,
   "Where is your God?"

11 Why are you cast down, O my soul,
   and why are you disquieted
   within me?
Hope in God; for I shall again praise
   him,
   my help and my God.

Psalm 43

Prayer to God in Time of Trouble

1 Vindicate me, O God, and defend
   my cause
   against an ungodly people;

z Meaning of Heb uncertain

from those who are deceitful and
unjust
deliver me!

2 For you are the God in whom I take
refuge;
why have you cast me off?
Why must I walk about mournfully
because of the oppression of the
enemy?

3 O send out your light and your
truth;
let them lead me;
let them bring me to your holy hill
and to your dwelling.

4 Then I will go to the altar of God,
to God my exceeding joy;
and I will praise you with the harp,
O God, my God.

5 Why are you cast down, O my soul,
and why are you disquieted
within me?

Hope in God; for I shall again praise
him,
my help and my God.

Psalm 44

National Lament and Prayer for Help

To the leader. Of the Korahites. A Maskil.

1 We have heard with our ears,
O God,
our ancestors have told us,
what deeds you performed in their
days,
in the days of old:

2 you with your own hand drove out
the nations,
but them you planted;
you afflicted the peoples,
but them you set free;

3 for not by their own sword did they
win the land,
nor did their own arm give them
victory;

Gift of Light

I was walking out a great loneliness in my life one night. As I moved along the wooded path, I saw a bright light in the distance. I quietly drew closer and saw that it was only one tiny firefly. It was just a small fragile frame that was giving forth such brightness! The lone firefly then joined the dance of a hundred fireflies as I walked in the late dusk. All across the vast meadow, far into the woods, their little lights danced and brought me a sense of bondedness. They were like a silent symphony, a gift to my lonely spirit. Like Christmas tree lights without the strings to mar their freedom, the fireflies held vigil with me. They danced for the earth, giving light to its darkness, and I thought they danced for me, a pure and simple gift of beauty in the night.

In our darkest hour, it is often the smallest spark that brings us the gift of light, be it ever so frail a flicker. It is the moment of simple grace in a softly spoken word, a letter from a friend, an unexpected phone call, a warm touch from a loved one, or even, a glance at the earth in its moment of hope. God has blessed our spirits with his own fireflies. They are small and fragile, but they fly in our dark woods and their little, beaming lights seem brilliant in our need.

—JOYCE RUPP

MONDAY

Scripture Reading
for Today:
Psalm 43

Verse for Today:
Psalm 43.3

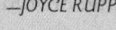

Go to page 697 for your next devotional reading.

but your right hand, and your arm,
   and the light of your countenance,
   for you delighted in them.

4 You are my King and my God;
   you command*ᵃ* victories for
      Jacob.
5 Through you we push down our
      foes;
   through your name we tread
      down our assailants.
6 For not in my bow do I trust,
   nor can my sword save me.
7 But you have saved us from our
      foes,
   and have put to confusion those
      who hate us.
8 In God we have boasted continually,
   and we will give thanks to your
      name forever.   *Selah*

9 Yet you have rejected us and abased
      us,
   and have not gone out with our
      armies.
10 You made us turn back from
      the foe,
   and our enemies have gotten
      spoil.
11 You have made us like sheep for
      slaughter,
   and have scattered us among
      the nations.
12 You have sold your people for a
      trifle,
   demanding no high price for
      them.

13 You have made us the taunt of our
      neighbors,
   the derision and scorn of those
      around us.
14 You have made us a byword among
      the nations,
   a laughingstock*ᵇ* among the
      peoples.
15 All day long my disgrace is before
      me,
   and shame has covered my face
16 at the words of the taunters and
      revilers,
   at the sight of the enemy and the
      avenger.

17 All this has come upon us,
   yet we have not forgotten you,
   or been false to your covenant.
18 Our heart has not turned back,

nor have our steps departed from
      your way,
19 yet you have broken us in the haunt
      of jackals,
   and covered us with deep
      darkness.

20 If we had forgotten the name of our
      God,
   or spread out our hands to a
      strange god,
21 would not God discover this?
   For he knows the secrets of the
      heart.
22 Because of you we are being killed
      all day long,
   and accounted as sheep for the
      slaughter.

23 Rouse yourself! Why do you sleep,
      O Lord?
   Awake, do not cast us off forever!
24 Why do you hide your face?
   Why do you forget our affliction
      and oppression?
25 For we sink down to the dust;
   our bodies cling to the ground.
26 Rise up, come to our help.
   Redeem us for the sake of your
      steadfast love.

Psalm 45

Ode for a Royal Wedding

To the leader: according to Lilies.
Of the Korahites. A Maskil. A love song.

1 My heart overflows with a goodly
      theme;
   I address my verses to the king;
   my tongue is like the pen of a
      ready scribe.

2 You are the most handsome of men;
   grace is poured upon your lips;
   therefore God has blessed you
      forever.
3 Gird your sword on your thigh,
      O mighty one,
   in your glory and majesty.

4 In your majesty ride on victoriously
      for the cause of truth and to
      defend*ᶜ* the right;

ᵃ Gk Syr: Heb *You are my King, O God; command*
ᵇ Heb *a shaking of the head*   *ᶜ* Cn: Heb *and the
meekness of*

let your right hand teach you
    dread deeds.
5 Your arrows are sharp
    in the heart of the king's enemies;
    the peoples fall under you.

6 Your throne, O God,[d] endures
    forever and ever.
    Your royal scepter is a scepter of
        equity;
7 you love righteousness and hate
    wickedness.
Therefore God, your God, has
    anointed you
with the oil of gladness beyond
    your companions;
8 your robes are all fragrant with
    myrrh and aloes and cassia.
From ivory palaces stringed
    instruments make you glad;
9 daughters of kings are among your
    ladies of honor;
    at your right hand stands the
        queen in gold of Ophir.

10 Hear, O daughter, consider and
    incline your ear;
forget your people and your
    father's house,
11 and the king will desire your
    beauty.
Since he is your lord, bow to
    him;
12 the people[e] of Tyre will seek
    your favor with gifts,
the richest of the people 13with
    all kinds of wealth.

The princess is decked in her
    chamber with gold-woven
    robes;[f]
14 in many-colored robes she is led
    to the king;
behind her the virgins, her
    companions, follow.
15 With joy and gladness they are
    led along
    as they enter the palace of the
        king.

16 In the place of ancestors you,
    O king,[g] shall have sons;
you will make them princes in all
    the earth.
17 I will cause your name to be
    celebrated in all generations;

therefore the peoples will praise
    you forever and ever.

Psalm 46

God's Defense of His City and People

To the leader. Of the Korahites.
According to Alamoth. A Song.

1 God is our refuge and strength,
    a very present[h] help in trouble.
2 Therefore we will not fear, though
    the earth should change,
    though the mountains shake in
        the heart of the sea;
3 though its waters roar and foam,
    though the mountains tremble
        with its tumult.   *Selah*

4 There is a river whose streams make
    glad the city of God,
    the holy habitation of the
        Most High.
5 God is in the midst of the city;[i] it
    shall not be moved;
God will help it when the
    morning dawns.
6 The nations are in an uproar, the
    kingdoms totter;
he utters his voice, the earth
    melts.
7 The LORD of hosts is with us;
    the God of Jacob is our refuge.[j]
        Selah

8 Come, behold the works of the
    LORD;
see what desolations he has
    brought on the earth.
9 He makes wars cease to the end of
    the earth;
he breaks the bow, and shatters
    the spear;
he burns the shields with fire.
10 "Be still, and know that I am God!
    I am exalted among the nations,
    I am exalted in the earth."
11 The LORD of hosts is with us;
    the God of Jacob is our refuge.[j]
        Selah

---

d Or *Your throne is a throne of God, it*   e Heb
daughter   f Or *people.* 13*All glorious is the princess
within, gold embroidery is her clothing*   g Heb
lacks *O king*   h Or *well proved*   i Heb *of it*
j Or *fortress*

Psalm 47

God's Rule over the Nations

To the leader. Of the Korahites. A Psalm.

¹ Clap your hands, all you peoples;
    shout to God with loud songs
        of joy.
² For the LORD, the Most High, is
        awesome,
    a great king over all the earth.
³ He subdued peoples under us,
and nations under our feet.
⁴ He chose our heritage for us,
    the pride of Jacob whom he loves.
                                              Selah

⁵ God has gone up with a shout,
    the LORD with the sound of a
        trumpet.
⁶ Sing praises to God, sing praises;
    sing praises to our King, sing
        praises.

Be Still

TUESDAY

Scripture Reading
for Today:
Psalm 46

Verse for Today:
Psalm 46.10

As I lay my head on the pillow one Sunday evening, I made the mistake of rehearsing the week ahead. All my anxieties about work came flooding in. I shut my eyes and prayed, admitting that I didn't know what to do and asking God's help. The dream that followed was anything but restful, but I believe it was an answer to prayer.

I dreamed I had agreed to fill in as a last-minute speaker at a women's luncheon at a local church. As soon as I said yes, I panicked: with only twenty minutes to prepare, I hadn't the slightest idea what I would say to the two hundred women who would attend. I took off running, looking for a quiet room in which to gather my thoughts, and soon found myself sprinting across the top of a piano. As I glanced down, I noticed a piece of sheet music resting on the piano, entitled "Be Still, and Know that I Am God." Suddenly, it dawned on me—I had been given the text of my talk!

I began frantically working out the meaning of this verse. What exactly did it mean to "be still"? I had been anxious and angry and anything but still. And what about the "God" part? Had I been playing "God" by trying to handle everything on my own? Trying to make sure everything worked out smoothly? In my dream, the insights were coming so rapidly. As the luncheon was about to begin, I woke up.

When I opened my eyes, I realized that the message "Be Still, and Know that I Am God" was meant for me, not for the women in my dream. God was trying to get through to me about my own anxiety. I was running too fast, doing too much, trying to take charge of things that were outside my control. I needed to stop saying yes to the impossible demands I placed on myself, to slow down and learn to be still, letting God be God in every situation in my life.

—ANN SPANGLER

Go to page 700 for your next devotional reading.

7 For God is the king of all the earth;
  sing praises with a psalm.*k*

8 God is king over the nations;
  God sits on his holy throne.
9 The princes of the peoples gather
  as the people of the God of
  Abraham.
For the shields of the earth belong
  to God;
he is highly exalted.

Psalm 48

The Glory and Strength of Zion

A Song. A Psalm of the Korahites.

1 Great is the LORD and greatly to be
  praised
  in the city of our God.
His holy mountain, 2beautiful in
  elevation,
  is the joy of all the earth,
Mount Zion, in the far north,
  the city of the great King.
3 Within its citadels God
  has shown himself a sure defense.

4 Then the kings assembled,
  they came on together.
5 As soon as they saw it, they were
  astounded;
  they were in panic, they took to
  flight;
6 trembling took hold of them there,
  pains as of a woman in labor,
7 as when an east wind shatters
  the ships of Tarshish.
8 As we have heard, so have we seen
  in the city of the LORD of hosts,
in the city of our God,
  which God establishes forever.
                                    Selah

9 We ponder your steadfast love,
  O God,
  in the midst of your temple.
10 Your name, O God, like your praise,
  reaches to the ends of the earth.
Your right hand is filled with
  victory.
11   Let Mount Zion be glad,
let the towns*l* of Judah rejoice
  because of your judgments.

12 Walk about Zion, go all around it,
  count its towers,
13 consider well its ramparts;

go through its citadels,
that you may tell the next
  generation
14   that this is God,
our God forever and ever.
  He will be our guide forever.

Psalm 49

The Folly of Trust in Riches

To the leader. Of the Korahites. A Psalm.

1 Hear this, all you peoples;
  give ear, all inhabitants of the
  world,
2 both low and high,
  rich and poor together.
3 My mouth shall speak wisdom;
  the meditation of my heart shall
  be understanding.
4 I will incline my ear to a proverb;
  I will solve my riddle to the music
  of the harp.

5 Why should I fear in times of
  trouble,
  when the iniquity of my
  persecutors surrounds me,
6 those who trust in their wealth
  and boast of the abundance of
  their riches?
7 Truly, no ransom avails for one's
  life,*m*
  there is no price one can give to
  God for it.
8 For the ransom of life is costly,
  and can never suffice,
9 that one should live on forever
  and never see the grave.*n*

10 When we look at the wise, they die;
  fool and dolt perish together
  and leave their wealth to others.
11 Their graves*o* are their homes
  forever,
  their dwelling places to all
  generations,
  though they named lands their
  own.
12 Mortals cannot abide in their pomp;
  they are like the animals that
  perish.

13 Such is the fate of the foolhardy,

k Heb *Maskil*   *l* Heb *daughters*   *m* Another
reading is *no one can ransom a brother*   *n* Heb *the
pit*   *o* Gk Syr Compare Tg: Heb *their inward*
(thought)

the end of those _p_ who are
   pleased with their lot.   _Selah_

14 Like sheep they are appointed for
   Sheol;
   Death shall be their shepherd;
straight to the grave they descend, _q_
   and their form shall waste away;
   Sheol shall be their home. _r_
15 But God will ransom my soul from
   the power of Sheol,
   for he will receive me.   _Selah_

16 Do not be afraid when some
   become rich,
   when the wealth of their houses
   increases.
17 For when they die they will carry
   nothing away;
   their wealth will not go down
   after them.
18 Though in their lifetime they count
   themselves happy
   —for you are praised when you
   do well for yourself—
19 they _s_ will go to the company of
   their ancestors,
   who will never again see the light.
20 Mortals cannot abide in their pomp;
   they are like the animals that
   perish.

Psalm 50

The Acceptable Sacrifice

A Psalm of Asaph.

1 The mighty one, God the LORD,
   speaks and summons the earth
   from the rising of the sun to its
   setting.
2 Out of Zion, the perfection of
   beauty,
   God shines forth.

3 Our God comes and does not keep
   silence,
   before him is a devouring fire,
   and a mighty tempest all around
   him.
4 He calls to the heavens above
   and to the earth, that he may
   judge his people:
5 "Gather to me my faithful ones,
   who made a covenant with me by
   sacrifice!"
6 The heavens declare his
   righteousness,
   for God himself is judge.   _Selah_

7 "Hear, O my people, and I will
   speak,
   O Israel, I will testify against you.
   I am God, your God.
8 Not for your sacrifices do I rebuke
   you;
   your burnt offerings are
   continually before me.
9 I will not accept a bull from your
   house,
   or goats from your folds.
10 For every wild animal of the forest is
   mine,
   the cattle on a thousand hills.
11 I know all the birds of the air, _t_
   and all that moves in the field is
   mine.

12 "If I were hungry, I would not tell
   you,
   for the world and all that is in it
   is mine.
13 Do I eat the flesh of bulls,
   or drink the blood of goats?
14 Offer to God a sacrifice of
   thanksgiving, _u_
   and pay your vows to the
   Most High.
15 Call on me in the day of trouble;
   I will deliver you, and you shall
   glorify me."

16 But to the wicked God says:
   "What right have you to recite my
   statutes,
   or take my covenant on your lips?
17 For you hate discipline,
   and you cast my words behind
   you.
18 You make friends with a thief when
   you see one,
   and you keep company with
   adulterers.

19 "You give your mouth free rein
   for evil,
   and your tongue frames deceit.
20 You sit and speak against your kin;
   you slander your own mother's
   child.

_p_ Tg: Heb _after them_   _q_ Cn: Heb _the upright
shall have dominion over them in the morning_
_r_ Meaning of Heb uncertain   _s_ Cn: Heb _you_
_t_ Gk Syr Tg: Heb _mountains_   _u_ Or _make
thanksgiving your sacrifice to God_

21 These things you have done and I
        have been silent;
   you thought that I was one just
        like yourself.
   But now I rebuke you, and lay the
        charge before you.

22 "Mark this, then, you who forget
        God,
   or I will tear you apart, and there
        will be no one to deliver.
23 Those who bring thanksgiving as
        their sacrifice honor me;
   to those who go the right way*v*
   I will show the salvation of God."

v Heb who set a way

Psalm 51

Prayer for Cleansing and Pardon

To the leader. A Psalm of David, when
the prophet Nathan came to him, after he
had gone in to Bathsheba.

1 Have mercy on me, O God,
        according to your steadfast love;
   according to your abundant mercy
        blot out my transgressions.
2 Wash me thoroughly from my
        iniquity,
   and cleanse me from my sin.

What He Loves in Us

WEDNESDAY

Scripture Reading
for Today:
Psalm 51

Verse for Today:
Psalm 51.3

The condition of the Christian after conversion—or "in" conversion—is not a state of blissful equanimity. It is a state of tension
between the human self and the ideal Christian yet to be. A
Christian is a person always in the process of becoming, of turning, and there are places in his journey which may be filled with
dryness and despair.

   This insight—that conversion is a lifetime of continuous turning—need not discourage us, however.

   When we first come to the Lord, we try to hide behind our
pretenses, to be some other person that we think we are supposed to be. But the more we get to know him, the more we discover that he has created us to be ourselves. And we discover this
not all at once, but little by little. Like patients at the first therapy
session, we blurt out to the Lord everything we have done that is
hateful to ourselves, everything we hate ourselves for, fully expecting to be able to shock him. The Lord retains his composure.
His compassion is inexhaustible.

   When we begin to experience that forgiveness personally, it
no longer seems to matter that he offers it to the whole world; for
each of us knows that the Lord is giving it "just" to him [or her].
In this encounter we become aware of the wonder of individuality. God has made me; I am unique, even with all my faults I am
worthwhile; this kind of self-discovery is strengthening and
restoring; loving the Lord makes it possible to love ourselves in
ways that are constructive and healthy. We grow to know ourselves better in the light he pours into our lives; we come to see
what it is that he loves in us, how pleasing we are to him.

—EMILIE GRIFFIN

Go to page 710 for your next devotional reading.

3 For I know my transgressions,
　　and my sin is ever before me.
4 Against you, you alone, have I
　　　sinned,
　　　and done what is evil in your
　　　　sight,
　　so that you are justified in your
　　　sentence
　　　and blameless when you pass
　　　　judgment.
5 Indeed, I was born guilty,
　　a sinner when my mother
　　　conceived me.

6 You desire truth in the inward
　　being;[w]
　　therefore teach me wisdom in my
　　　secret heart.
7 Purge me with hyssop, and I shall
　　　be clean;
　　wash me, and I shall be whiter
　　　than snow.
8 Let me hear joy and gladness;
　　let the bones that you have
　　　crushed rejoice.
9 Hide your face from my sins,
　　and blot out all my iniquities.

10 Create in me a clean heart, O God,
　　and put a new and right[x] spirit
　　　within me.
11 Do not cast me away from your
　　　presence,
　　and do not take your holy spirit
　　　from me.
12 Restore to me the joy of your
　　　salvation,
　　and sustain in me a willing[y]
　　　spirit.

13 Then I will teach transgressors your
　　　ways,
　　and sinners will return to you.
14 Deliver me from bloodshed, O God,
　　O God of my salvation,
　　and my tongue will sing aloud of
　　　your deliverance.

15 O Lord, open my lips,
　　and my mouth will declare your
　　　praise.
16 For you have no delight in sacrifice;
　　if I were to give a burnt offering,
　　　you would not be pleased.
17 The sacrifice acceptable to God[z] is
　　　a broken spirit;
　　a broken and contrite heart,
　　　O God, you will not despise.

18 Do good to Zion in your good
　　　pleasure;
　　rebuild the walls of Jerusalem,
19 then you will delight in right
　　　sacrifices,
　　in burnt offerings and whole
　　　burnt offerings;
　　then bulls will be offered on your
　　　altar.

Psalm 52

Judgment on the Deceitful

To the leader. A Maskil of David, when
Doeg the Edomite came to Saul and said
to him, "David has come to the house
of Ahimelech."

1 Why do you boast, O mighty one,
　　of mischief done against the
　　　godly?[a]
　　All day long [2]you are plotting
　　　destruction.
　　Your tongue is like a sharp razor,
　　　you worker of treachery.
3 You love evil more than good,
　　and lying more than speaking the
　　　truth.   *Selah*
4 You love all words that devour,
　　O deceitful tongue.

5 But God will break you down
　　　forever;
　　he will snatch and tear you from
　　　your tent;
　　he will uproot you from the land
　　　of the living.   *Selah*
6 The righteous will see, and fear,
　　and will laugh at the evildoer,[b]
　　　saying,
7 "See the one who would not take
　　　refuge in God,
　　but trusted in abundant riches,
　　　and sought refuge in wealth!"[c]

8 But I am like a green olive tree
　　in the house of God.
　　I trust in the steadfast love of God
　　　forever and ever.
9 I will thank you forever,
　　because of what you have done.
　　In the presence of the faithful
　　I will proclaim[d] your name, for it
　　　is good.

w Meaning of Heb uncertain   x Or *steadfast*
y Or *generous*   z Or *My sacrifice, O God,*   a Cn
Compare Syr: Heb *the kindness of God*   b Heb
him   c Syr Tg: Heb *in his destruction*   d Cn:
Heb *wait for*

Psalm 53

Denunciation of Godlessness

To the leader: according to Mahalath.
A Maskil of David.

1 Fools say in their hearts, "There is
   no God."
   They are corrupt, they commit
      abominable acts;
   there is no one who does good.

2 God looks down from heaven on
      humankind
   to see if there are any who are
      wise,
   who seek after God.

3 They have all fallen away, they are
      all alike perverse;
   there is no one who does good,
   no, not one.

4 Have they no knowledge, those
      evildoers,
   who eat up my people as they eat
      bread,
   and do not call upon God?

5 There they shall be in great terror,
   in terror such as has not been.
   For God will scatter the bones of the
      ungodly;[e]
   they will be put to shame,[f] for
      God has rejected them.

6 O that deliverance for Israel would
      come from Zion!
   When God restores the fortunes of
      his people,
   Jacob will rejoice; Israel will be
      glad.

Psalm 54

Prayer for Vindication

To the leader: with stringed instruments.
A Maskil of David, when the Ziphites
went and told Saul, "David is in hiding
among us."

1 Save me, O God, by your name,
   and vindicate me by your might.

2 Hear my prayer, O God;
   give ear to the words of my
      mouth.

3 For the insolent have risen
      against me,
   the ruthless seek my life;

they do not set God before them.
                              Selah

4 But surely, God is my helper;
   the Lord is the upholder of[g] my
      life.

5 He will repay my enemies for their
      evil.
   In your faithfulness, put an end to
      them.

6 With a freewill offering I will
      sacrifice to you;
   I will give thanks to your name,
      O LORD, for it is good.

7 For he has delivered me from every
      trouble,
   and my eye has looked in
      triumph on my enemies.

Psalm 55

Complaint about a Friend's Treachery

To the leader: with stringed instruments.
A Maskil of David.

1 Give ear to my prayer, O God;
   do not hide yourself from my
      supplication.

2 Attend to me, and answer me;
   I am troubled in my complaint.
   I am distraught 3by the noise of the
      enemy,
   because of the clamor of the
      wicked.
   For they bring[h] trouble upon me,
   and in anger they cherish enmity
      against me.

4 My heart is in anguish within me,
   the terrors of death have fallen
      upon me.

5 Fear and trembling come upon me,
   and horror overwhelms me.

6 And I say, "O that I had wings like
      a dove!
   I would fly away and be at rest;

7 truly, I would flee far away;
   I would lodge in the wilderness;
                              Selah

8 I would hurry to find a shelter for
      myself

[e] Cn Compare Gk Syr: Heb *him who encamps
against you*   [f] Gk: Heb *you have put (them) to
shame*   [g] Gk Syr Jerome: Heb *is of those who
uphold* or *is with those who uphold*   [h] Cn
Compare Gk: Heb *they cause to totter*

from the raging wind and
   tempest."

9 Confuse, O Lord, confound their
      speech;
   for I see violence and strife in the
      city.
10 Day and night they go around it
      on its walls,
   and iniquity and trouble are
      within it;
11   ruin is in its midst;
   oppression and fraud
      do not depart from its
         marketplace.

12 It is not enemies who taunt me—
   I could bear that;
   it is not adversaries who deal
      insolently with me—
   I could hide from them.
13 But it is you, my equal,
   my companion, my familiar
      friend,
14 with whom I kept pleasant
      company;
   we walked in the house of God
      with the throng.
15 Let death come upon them;
   let them go down alive to Sheol;
   for evil is in their homes and in
      their hearts.

16 But I call upon God,
   and the Lord will save me.
17 Evening and morning and at noon
   I utter my complaint and moan,
   and he will hear my voice.
18 He will redeem me unharmed
   from the battle that I wage,
   for many are arrayed against me.
19 God, who is enthroned from of old,
                                    Selah
   will hear, and will humble them—
   because they do not change,
   and do not fear God.

20 My companion laid hands on a
      friend
   and violated a covenant with
      me*i*
21 with speech smoother than butter,
   but with a heart set on war;
   with words that were softer than oil,
   but in fact were drawn swords.

22 Cast your burden *j* on the Lord,
   and he will sustain you;

he will never permit
   the righteous to be moved.

23 But you, O God, will cast them
      down
   into the lowest pit;
   the bloodthirsty and treacherous
      shall not live out half their days.
   But I will trust in you.

Psalm 56

Trust in God under Persecution

To the leader: according to The Dove
on Far-off Terebinths. Of David.
A Miktam, when the Philistines seized
      him in Gath.

1 Be gracious to me, O God, for
      people trample on me;
   all day long foes oppress me;
2 my enemies trample on me all day
      long,
   for many fight against me.
   O Most High, 3when I am afraid,
   I put my trust in you.
4 In God, whose word I praise,
   in God I trust; I am not afraid;
   what can flesh do to me?

5 All day long they seek to injure my
      cause;
   all their thoughts are against me
      for evil.
6 They stir up strife, they lurk,
   they watch my steps.
   As they hoped to have my life,
7   so repay*k* them for their crime;
   in wrath cast down the peoples,
      O God!

8 You have kept count of my tossings;
   put my tears in your bottle.
   Are they not in your record?
9 Then my enemies will retreat
   in the day when I call.
   This I know, that*l* God is for me.
10 In God, whose word I praise,
   in the Lord, whose word I praise,
11 in God I trust; I am not afraid.
   What can a mere mortal do to
      me?

12 My vows to you I must perform,
      O God;

i Heb lacks *with me*   *j* Or *Cast what he has given
you*   *k* Cn: Heb *rescue*   *l* Or *because*

I will render thank offerings
to you.
13 For you have delivered my soul
from death,
and my feet from falling,
so that I may walk before God
in the light of life.

Psalm 57

Praise and Assurance under Persecution

To the leader: Do Not Destroy. Of David.
A Miktam, when he fled from Saul,
in the cave.

1 Be merciful to me, O God, be
merciful to me,
for in you my soul takes refuge;
in the shadow of your wings I will
take refuge,
until the destroying storms
pass by.
2 I cry to God Most High,
to God who fulfills his purpose
for me.
3 He will send from heaven and
save me,
he will put to shame those who
trample on me.   *Selah*
God will send forth his steadfast
love and his faithfulness.

4 I lie down among lions
that greedily devour[m] human
prey;
their teeth are spears and arrows,
their tongues sharp swords.

5 Be exalted, O God, above the
heavens.
Let your glory be over all the
earth.

6 They set a net for my steps;
my soul was bowed down.
They dug a pit in my path,
but they have fallen into it
themselves.   *Selah*
7 My heart is steadfast, O God,
my heart is steadfast.
I will sing and make melody.
8   Awake, my soul!
Awake, O harp and lyre!
I will awake the dawn.
9 I will give thanks to you, O Lord,
among the peoples;
I will sing praises to you among
the nations.

10 For your steadfast love is as high as
the heavens;
your faithfulness extends to the
clouds.

11 Be exalted, O God, above the
heavens.
Let your glory be over all the
earth.

Psalm 58

Prayer for Vengeance

To the leader: Do Not Destroy. Of David.
A Miktam.

1 Do you indeed decree what is right,
you gods?[n]
Do you judge people fairly?
2 No, in your hearts you devise
wrongs;
your hands deal out violence on
earth.

3 The wicked go astray from the
womb;
they err from their birth, speaking
lies.
4 They have venom like the venom of
a serpent,
like the deaf adder that stops
its ear,
5 so that it does not hear the voice of
charmers
or of the cunning enchanter.

6 O God, break the teeth in their
mouths;
tear out the fangs of the young
lions, O LORD!
7 Let them vanish like water that runs
away;
like grass let them be trodden
down[o] and wither.
8 Let them be like the snail that
dissolves into slime;
like the untimely birth that never
sees the sun.
9 Sooner than your pots can feel the
heat of thorns,
whether green or ablaze, may he
sweep them away!

10 The righteous will rejoice when they
see vengeance done;

m Cn: Heb *are aflame for*   *n* Or *mighty lords*
o Cn: Meaning of Heb uncertain

they will bathe their feet in the
    blood of the wicked.
11 People will say, "Surely there is a
    reward for the righteous;
    surely there is a God who judges
    on earth."

Psalm 59

Prayer for Deliverance from Enemies

To the leader: Do Not Destroy. Of David.
A Miktam, when Saul ordered his house
to be watched in order to kill him.

1 Deliver me from my enemies, O my
    God;
    protect me from those who rise
    up against me.
2 Deliver me from those who work
    evil;
    from the bloodthirsty save me.

3 Even now they lie in wait for my
    life;
    the mighty stir up strife against
    me.
For no transgression or sin of mine,
    O LORD,
4   for no fault of mine, they run and
    make ready.

Rouse yourself, come to my help
    and see!
5   You, LORD God of hosts, are God
    of Israel.
Awake to punish all the nations;
    spare none of those who
    treacherously plot evil.   *Selah*

6 Each evening they come back,
    howling like dogs
    and prowling about the city.
7 There they are, bellowing with their
    mouths,
    with sharp words *p* on their lips—
    for "Who," they think,*q* "will hear
    us?"

8 But you laugh at them, O LORD;
    you hold all the nations in
    derision.
9 O my strength, I will watch for you;
    for you, O God, are my fortress.
10 My God in his steadfast love will
    meet me;
    my God will let me look in
    triumph on my enemies.

11 Do not kill them, or my people may
    forget;
    make them totter by your power,
    and bring them down,
    O Lord, our shield.
12 For the sin of their mouths, the
    words of their lips,
    let them be trapped in their pride.
For the cursing and lies that they
    utter,
13   consume them in wrath;
    consume them until they are no
    more.
Then it will be known to the ends of
    the earth
    that God rules over Jacob.   *Selah*

14 Each evening they come back,
    howling like dogs
    and prowling about the city.
15 They roam about for food,
    and growl if they do not get
    their fill.

16 But I will sing of your might;
    I will sing aloud of your steadfast
    love in the morning.
For you have been a fortress for me
    and a refuge in the day of my
    distress.
17 O my strength, I will sing praises to
    you,
    for you, O God, are my fortress,
    the God who shows me steadfast
    love.

Psalm 60

Prayer for National Victory after Defeat

To the leader: according to the Lily
of the Covenant. A Miktam of David;
for instruction; when he struggled
with Aram-naharaim and with
Aram-zobah, and when Joab on his
return killed twelve thousand Edomites
in the Valley of Salt.

1 O God, you have rejected us, broken
    our defenses;
    you have been angry; now
    restore us!
2 You have caused the land to quake;
    you have torn it open;
    repair the cracks in it, for it is
    tottering.
3 You have made your people suffer
    hard things;

p Heb *with swords*   *q* Heb lacks *they think*

you have given us wine to drink
that made us reel.

4 You have set up a banner for those
who fear you,
to rally to it out of bowshot.[r]

Selah

5 Give victory with your right hand,
and answer us,[s]
so that those whom you love may
be rescued.

6 God has promised in his
sanctuary:[t]
"With exultation I will divide up
Shechem,
and portion out the Vale of
Succoth.

7 Gilead is mine, and Manasseh is
mine;
Ephraim is my helmet;
Judah is my scepter.

8 Moab is my washbasin;
on Edom I hurl my shoe;
over Philistia I shout in triumph."

9 Who will bring me to the fortified
city?
Who will lead me to Edom?

10 Have you not rejected us, O God?
You do not go out, O God, with
our armies.

11 O grant us help against the foe,
for human help is worthless.

12 With God we shall do valiantly;
it is he who will tread down our
foes.

Psalm 61

Assurance of God's Protection

To the leader: with stringed instruments.
Of David.

1 Hear my cry, O God;
listen to my prayer.

2 From the end of the earth I call
to you,
when my heart is faint.

Lead me to the rock
that is higher than I;

3 for you are my refuge,
a strong tower against the enemy.

4 Let me abide in your tent forever,
find refuge under the shelter of
your wings.

Selah

5 For you, O God, have heard my
vows;
you have given me the heritage of
those who fear your name.

6 Prolong the life of the king;
may his years endure to all
generations!

7 May he be enthroned forever
before God;
appoint steadfast love and
faithfulness to watch
over him!

8 So I will always sing praises to your
name,
as I pay my vows day after day.

Psalm 62

Song of Trust in God Alone

To the leader: according to Jeduthun.
A Psalm of David.

1 For God alone my soul waits in
silence;
from him comes my salvation.

2 He alone is my rock and my
salvation,
my fortress; I shall never be
shaken.

3 How long will you assail a person,
will you batter your victim, all
of you,
as you would a leaning wall, a
tottering fence?

4 Their only plan is to bring down a
person of prominence.
They take pleasure in falsehood;
they bless with their mouths,
but inwardly they curse.

Selah

5 For God alone my soul waits in
silence,
for my hope is from him.

6 He alone is my rock and my
salvation,
my fortress; I shall not be shaken.

7 On God rests my deliverance and
my honor;
my mighty rock, my refuge is in
God.

8 Trust in him at all times, O people;

---

r Gk Syr Jerome: Heb *because of the truth*
s Another reading is *me* t Or *by his holiness*

pour out your heart before him;
God is a refuge for us.   *Selah*

9 Those of low estate are but a breath,
   those of high estate are a
       delusion;
   in the balances they go up;
   they are together lighter than a
       breath.
10 Put no confidence in extortion,
   and set no vain hopes on robbery;
   if riches increase, do not set your
       heart on them.

11 Once God has spoken;
   twice have I heard this:
   that power belongs to God,
12   and steadfast love belongs to you,
       O Lord.
   For you repay to all
       according to their work.

Psalm 63

Comfort and Assurance in God's Presence

A Psalm of David, when he was
in the Wilderness of Judah.

1 O God, you are my God, I seek you,
   my soul thirsts for you;
   my flesh faints for you,
       as in a dry and weary land where
       there is no water.
2 So I have looked upon you in the
       sanctuary,
   beholding your power and glory.
3 Because your steadfast love is better
       than life,
   my lips will praise you.
4 So I will bless you as long as I live;
   I will lift up my hands and call
       on your name.

5 My soul is satisfied as with a rich
       feast,*u*
   and my mouth praises you with
       joyful lips
6 when I think of you on my bed,
   and meditate on you in the
       watches of the night;
7 for you have been my help,
   and in the shadow of your wings I
       sing for joy.
8 My soul clings to you;
   your right hand upholds me.

9 But those who seek to destroy
       my life

shall go down into the depths of
       the earth;
10 they shall be given over to the
       power of the sword,
   they shall be prey for jackals.
11 But the king shall rejoice in God;
   all who swear by him shall exult,
   for the mouths of liars will be
       stopped.

Psalm 64

Prayer for Protection from Enemies

To the leader. A Psalm of David.

1 Hear my voice, O God, in my
       complaint;
   preserve my life from the dread
       enemy.
2 Hide me from the secret plots of the
       wicked,
   from the scheming of evildoers,
3 who whet their tongues like swords,
   who aim bitter words like arrows,
4 shooting from ambush at the
       blameless;
   they shoot suddenly and without
       fear.
5 They hold fast to their evil purpose;
   they talk of laying snares secretly,
   thinking, "Who can see us?*v*
6   Who can search out our crimes?*w*
   We have thought out a cunningly
       conceived plot."
   For the human heart and mind
       are deep.

7 But God will shoot his arrow at
       them;
   they will be wounded suddenly.
8 Because of their tongue he will bring
       them to ruin;*x*
   all who see them will shake with
       horror.
9 Then everyone will fear;
   they will tell what God has
       brought about,
   and ponder what he has done.

10 Let the righteous rejoice in the LORD
   and take refuge in him.
   Let all the upright in heart glory.

u Heb *with fat and fatness*   *v* Syr: Heb *them*
w Cn: Heb *They search out crimes*   *x* Cn: Heb
*They will bring him to ruin, their tongue being
against them*

Psalm 65

Thanksgiving for Earth's Bounty

To the leader. A Psalm of David. A Song.

1 Praise is due to you,
  O God, in Zion;
  and to you shall vows be performed,
2   O you who answer prayer!
  To you all flesh shall come.
3 When deeds of iniquity overwhelm
    us,
  you forgive our transgressions.
4 Happy are those whom you choose
    and bring near
  to live in your courts.
  We shall be satisfied with the
    goodness of your house,
    your holy temple.

5 By awesome deeds you answer us
    with deliverance,
  O God of our salvation;
  you are the hope of all the ends of
    the earth
  and of the farthest seas.
6 By your *y* strength you established
    the mountains;
  you are girded with might.
7 You silence the roaring of the seas,
  the roaring of their waves,
  the tumult of the peoples.
8 Those who live at earth's farthest
    bounds are awed by your
    signs;
  you make the gateways of the
    morning and the evening
    shout for joy.

9 You visit the earth and water it,
  you greatly enrich it;
  the river of God is full of water;
  you provide the people with grain,
  for so you have prepared it.
10 You water its furrows abundantly,
  settling its ridges,
  softening it with showers,
  and blessing its growth.
11 You crown the year with your
    bounty;
  your wagon tracks overflow with
    richness.
12 The pastures of the wilderness
    overflow,
  the hills gird themselves with joy,
13 the meadows clothe themselves with
    flocks,

the valleys deck themselves with
    grain,
they shout and sing together for
    joy.

Psalm 66

Praise for God's Goodness to Israel

To the leader. A Song. A Psalm.

1 Make a joyful noise to God, all the
    earth;
2   sing the glory of his name;
  give to him glorious praise.
3 Say to God, "How awesome are
    your deeds!
  Because of your great power, your
    enemies cringe before you.
4 All the earth worships you;
  they sing praises to you,
  sing praises to your name."   *Selah*

5 Come and see what God has done:
  he is awesome in his deeds
    among mortals.
6 He turned the sea into dry land;
  they passed through the river
    on foot.
There we rejoiced in him,
7 who rules by his might forever,
  whose eyes keep watch on the
    nations—
  let the rebellious not exalt
    themselves.   *Selah*

8 Bless our God, O peoples,
  let the sound of his praise be
    heard,
9 who has kept us among the living,
  and has not let our feet slip.
10 For you, O God, have tested us;
  you have tried us as silver is tried.
11 You brought us into the net;
  you laid burdens on our backs;
12 you let people ride over our heads;
  we went through fire and through
    water;
  yet you have brought us out to a
    spacious place.*z*

13 I will come into your house with
    burnt offerings;
  I will pay you my vows,
14 those that my lips uttered
  and my mouth promised when I
    was in trouble.

y Gk Jerome: Heb *his*   *z* Cn Compare Gk Syr
Jerome Tg: Heb *to a saturation*

15 I will offer to you burnt offerings of
    fatlings,
    with the smoke of the sacrifice of
      rams;
    I will make an offering of bulls and
      goats.   *Selah*

16 Come and hear, all you who fear
    God,
    and I will tell what he has done
      for me.
17 I cried aloud to him,
    and he was extolled with my
      tongue.
18 If I had cherished iniquity in my
    heart,
    the Lord would not have listened.
19 But truly God has listened;
    he has given heed to the words of
      my prayer.

20 Blessed be God,
    because he has not rejected my
      prayer
    or removed his steadfast love from
      me.

Psalm 67

The Nations Called to Praise God

To the leader: with stringed instruments.
A Psalm. A Song.

1 May God be gracious to us and bless
    us
    and make his face to shine upon
      us,   *Selah*
2 that your way may be known upon
    earth,
    your saving power among all
      nations.
3 Let the peoples praise you, O God;
    let all the peoples praise you.

4 Let the nations be glad and sing
    for joy,
    for you judge the peoples with
      equity
    and guide the nations upon earth.
      Selah
5 Let the peoples praise you, O God;
    let all the peoples praise you.

6 The earth has yielded its increase;
    God, our God, has blessed us.
7 May God continue to bless us;
    let all the ends of the earth revere
      him.

Psalm 68

Praise and Thanksgiving

To the leader. Of David. A Psalm. A Song.

1 Let God rise up, let his enemies be
    scattered;
    let those who hate him flee before
      him.
2 As smoke is driven away, so drive
    them away;
    as wax melts before the fire,
    let the wicked perish before God.
3 But let the righteous be joyful;
    let them exult before God;
    let them be jubilant with joy.

4 Sing to God, sing praises to his
    name;
    lift up a song to him who rides
      upon the clouds[a]—
    his name is the LORD—
    be exultant before him.

5 Father of orphans and protector of
    widows
    is God in his holy habitation.
6 God gives the desolate a home to
    live in;
    he leads out the prisoners to
      prosperity,
    but the rebellious live in a
      parched land.

7 O God, when you went out before
    your people,
    when you marched through the
      wilderness,   *Selah*
8 the earth quaked, the heavens
    poured down rain
    at the presence of God, the God
      of Sinai,
    at the presence of God, the God
      of Israel.
9 Rain in abundance, O God, you
    showered abroad;
    you restored your heritage when it
      languished;
10 your flock found a dwelling in it;
    in your goodness, O God, you
      provided for the needy.

11 The Lord gives the command;
    great is the company of those[b]
      who bore the tidings:

a Or *cast up a highway for him who rides through the
deserts*   b Or *company of the women*

12 "The kings of the armies, they
        flee, they flee!"
   The women at home divide the
        spoil,
13   though they stay among the
        sheepfolds—
   the wings of a dove covered with
        silver,
   its pinions with green gold.
14 When the Almighty[c] scattered kings
        there,
   snow fell on Zalmon.

15 O mighty mountain, mountain of
        Bashan;

   O many-peaked mountain,
        mountain of Bashan!
16 Why do you look with envy,
        O many-peaked mountain,
   at the mount that God desired
        for his abode,
   where the LORD will reside
        forever?

17 With mighty chariotry, twice ten
        thousand,
   thousands upon thousands,

[c] Traditional rendering of Heb *Shaddai*

THURSDAY

Scripture Reading
for Today:
Psalm 68.1–16

Verse for Today:
Psalm 68.1

*L*et God Rise Up

From a letter written by Elizabeth Seton to an Italian friend in March 1805, just after Elizabeth was received into the Catholic Church and had made her First Communion:

At last Amabilia—at last—*God is mine and I am his.* Now let all go its round. *I have received him.* The awful impressions of the evening before, fears of not having done all to prepare, and yet even then transports of confidence and hope in his goodness.

My God, to the last breath of life will I not remember this night of watching for morning dawn—the fearful beating heart so pressing to be gone—the long walk to town, but every step counted nearer that street—then nearer that tabernacle, then nearer the moment he would enter the poor, poor little dwelling so all his own.

And when he did—the first thought I remember was, "Let God rise up, let his enemies be scattered." For it seemed to me my King had come to take his throne, and instead of the humble, tender welcome I had expected to give him, it was but a triumph of joy and gladness that the deliverer was come, and my defense and shield and strength and salvation made mine for this world and the next.

Now then all the excesses of my heart found their play, and it danced with fervor, perhaps almost with as much as the royal Prophet's before his ark, for I was far richer than he and more honored than he ever could be. So far, truly I feel all the powers of my soul held fast by him who came with so much majesty to take possession of this little poor Kingdom.

—*SAINT ELIZABETH ANN SETON*

Go to page 714 for your next devotional reading.

the Lord came from Sinai into the
holy place.*d*

18 You ascended the high mount,
leading captives in your train
and receiving gifts from people,
even from those who rebel against
the LORD God's abiding there.

19 Blessed be the Lord,
who daily bears us up;
God is our salvation.   *Selah*

20 Our God is a God of salvation,
and to GOD, the Lord, belongs
escape from death.

21 But God will shatter the heads of his
enemies,
the hairy crown of those who
walk in their guilty ways.

22 The Lord said,
"I will bring them back from Bashan,
I will bring them back from the
depths of the sea,

23 so that you may bathe*e* your feet in
blood,
so that the tongues of your dogs
may have their share from the
foe."

24 Your solemn processions are seen, *f*
O God,
the processions of my God, my
King, into the sanctuary—

25 the singers in front, the musicians
last,
between them girls playing
tambourines:

26 "Bless God in the great
congregation,
the LORD, O you who are of
Israel's fountain!"

27 There is Benjamin, the least of them,
in the lead,
the princes of Judah in a body,
the princes of Zebulun, the
princes of Naphtali.

28 Summon your might, O God;
show your strength, O God, as
you have done for us before.

29 Because of your temple at Jerusalem
kings bear gifts to you.

30 Rebuke the wild animals that live
among the reeds,
the herd of bulls with the calves
of the peoples.
Trample*g* under foot those who lust
after tribute;
scatter the peoples who delight in
war.*h*

31 Let bronze be brought from Egypt;
let Ethiopia*i* hasten to stretch out
its hands to God.

32 Sing to God, O kingdoms of the
earth;
sing praises to the Lord,   *Selah*

33 O rider in the heavens, the ancient
heavens;
listen, he sends out his voice, his
mighty voice.

34 Ascribe power to God,
whose majesty is over Israel;
and whose power is in the skies.

35 Awesome is God in his*j* sanctuary,
the God of Israel;
he gives power and strength to his
people.

Blessed be God!

Psalm 69

Prayer for Deliverance from Persecution

To the leader: according to Lilies.
Of David.

1 Save me, O God,
for the waters have come up to
my neck.

2 I sink in deep mire,
where there is no foothold;
I have come into deep waters,
and the flood sweeps over me.

3 I am weary with my crying;
my throat is parched.
My eyes grow dim
with waiting for my God.

4 More in number than the hairs of
my head
are those who hate me without
cause;
many are those who would destroy
me,
my enemies who accuse me
falsely.
What I did not steal
must I now restore?

5 O God, you know my folly;
the wrongs I have done are not
hidden from you.

d Cn: Heb *The Lord among them Sinai in the holy*
(place)   *e* Gk Syr Tg: Heb *shatter*   *f* Or *have been
seen   g* Cn: Heb *Trampling   h* Meaning of Heb
of verse 30 is uncertain   *i* Or *Nubia;* Heb *Cush
j* Gk: Heb *from your*

⁶ Do not let those who hope in you
      be put to shame because of
      me,
   O Lord GOD of hosts;
  do not let those who seek you be
      dishonored because of me,
   O God of Israel.
⁷ It is for your sake that I have borne
      reproach,
   that shame has covered my face.
⁸ I have become a stranger to my
      kindred,
   an alien to my mother's children.

⁹ It is zeal for your house that has
      consumed me;
   the insults of those who insult
      you have fallen on me.
¹⁰ When I humbled my soul with
      fasting,ᵏ
   they insulted me for doing so.
¹¹ When I made sackcloth my clothing,
   I became a byword to them.
¹² I am the subject of gossip for those
      who sit in the gate,
   and the drunkards make songs
      about me.

¹³ But as for me, my prayer is to you,
      O LORD.
   At an acceptable time, O God,
   in the abundance of your steadfast
      love, answer me.
  With your faithful help ¹⁴rescue me
      from sinking in the mire;
  let me be delivered from my
      enemies
   and from the deep waters.
¹⁵ Do not let the flood sweep over
      me,
   or the deep swallow me up,
   or the Pit close its mouth
      over me.

¹⁶ Answer me, O LORD, for your
      steadfast love is good;
   according to your abundant
      mercy, turn to me.
¹⁷ Do not hide your face from your
      servant,
   for I am in distress—make haste
      to answer me.
¹⁸ Draw near to me, redeem me,
   set me free because of my
      enemies.

¹⁹ You know the insults I receive,

   and my shame and dishonor;
   my foes are all known to you.
²⁰ Insults have broken my heart,
   so that I am in despair.
  I looked for pity, but there was
      none;
   and for comforters, but I found
      none.
²¹ They gave me poison for food,
   and for my thirst they gave me
      vinegar to drink.

²² Let their table be a trap for them,
   a snare for their allies.
²³ Let their eyes be darkened so that
      they cannot see,
   and make their loins tremble
      continually.
²⁴ Pour out your indignation upon
      them,
   and let your burning anger
      overtake them.
²⁵ May their camp be a desolation;
   let no one live in their tents.
²⁶ For they persecute those whom you
      have struck down,
   and those whom you have
      wounded, they attack still
      more.ˡ
²⁷ Add guilt to their guilt;
   may they have no acquittal from
      you.
²⁸ Let them be blotted out of the book
      of the living;
   let them not be enrolled among
      the righteous.
²⁹ But I am lowly and in pain;
   let your salvation, O God, protect
      me.

³⁰ I will praise the name of God with a
      song;
   I will magnify him with
      thanksgiving.
³¹ This will please the LORD more than
      an ox
   or a bull with horns and hoofs.
³² Let the oppressed see it and be
      glad;
   you who seek God, let your hearts
      revive.

ᵏ Gk Syr: Heb *I wept, with fasting my soul,* or *I
made my soul mourn with fasting*   ˡ Gk Syr: Heb
recount the pain of

³³ For the LORD hears the needy,
　　and does not despise his own that
　　　are in bonds.

³⁴ Let heaven and earth praise him,
　　the seas and everything that
　　　moves in them.
³⁵ For God will save Zion
　　and rebuild the cities of Judah;
　and his servants shall live*ᵐ* there
　　　and possess it;
³⁶　the children of his servants shall
　　　inherit it,
　and those who love his name
　　　shall live in it.

Psalm 70

Prayer for Deliverance from Enemies

*To the leader. Of David, for the
memorial offering.*

¹ Be pleased, O God, to deliver me.
　　O LORD, make haste to help me!
² Let those be put to shame and
　　　confusion
　　who seek my life.
　Let those be turned back and
　　　brought to dishonor
　　who desire to hurt me.

m Syr: Heb and they shall live

THE

TRADITION

Enemies

*Pour out your indignation upon them,
and let your burning anger overtake them.*

PSALM 69.24

Discovering the angry passages of the psalms is like accidentally putting our hand on a hot burner or a scorching iron. We flinch when beautiful prayers suddenly blaze with anger, even malice. Psalm 69 begins with petition and repentance and continues with frightful curses on "my foes" (verses 23–29). The seventh penitential psalm makes a vengeful and seemingly irrational appeal to God: "In your steadfast love cut off my enemies, and destroy all my adversaries" (143.12). The poignant lament of Psalm 137 ends by pronouncing a horrifying "blessing" on murderers of Babylonian children: "Happy shall they be who take your little ones and dash them against the rock!" (verse 9).

These and other vindictive statements leave us squirming and puzzled. Their gleeful portrayal of enemy defeat is radically at odds with Jesus' teaching to love and forgive. How should we deal with these blasts of fury?

Over the centuries Christians have taken various approaches. The simplest is avoidance. As the revised Liturgy of the Hours does, we can just skip over the offending verses. Or we might consider the following traditional ways to adapt the psalmists' hatred of their enemies:

Saint Augustine and others suggested that we direct such verses against the enemy within—that is, the personal defects, evil desires, and vices that keep us from God. Against enemies like these, it is always appropriate to pray, "Smash them! Destroy them! Obliterate them!"

The One who told us to love our enemies called Satan a lying murderer (see John 8.44) and gave up his life "to destroy the works of the devil" (1 John 3.8). The wrath of the angry psalms is well directed when it targets spiritual enemies who oppose God and seek our destruction.

Saint Jerome noted that God's strategy toward human beings who oppose him is to destroy them as enemies by leading them to repentance and making them his friends. Taking Jerome's lead, we can use the "destroy my enemies" psalms to pray that God would give the grace of conversion to those who still reject him.

³ Let those who say, "Aha, Aha!"
　　turn back because of their shame.

⁴ Let all who seek you
　　rejoice and be glad in you.
　Let those who love your salvation
　　say evermore, "God is great!"
⁵ But I am poor and needy;
　　hasten to me, O God!
　You are my help and my deliverer;
　　O LORD, do not delay!

Psalm 71

Prayer for Lifelong Protection and Help

¹ In you, O LORD, I take refuge;
　　let me never be put to shame.
² In your righteousness deliver me and
　　rescue me;

　　incline your ear to me and
　　　save me.
³ Be to me a rock of refuge,
　　a strong fortress,ⁿ to save
　　　me,
　for you are my rock and
　　my fortress.

⁴ Rescue me, O my God, from the
　　hand of the wicked,
　from the grasp of the unjust and
　　cruel.
⁵ For you, O Lord, are my hope,
　　my trust, O LORD, from my
　　　youth.
⁶ Upon you I have leaned from
　　my birth;

ⁿ Gk Compare 31.3: Heb *to come continually you
have commanded*

"*I Know You Love Me*"

FRIDAY

Scripture Reading
for Today:
Psalm 71.1–19

Verses for Today:
Psalm 71.17–19

I asked a very old and holy confessor what one must do to be holy in old age. "What do you expect to do throughout eternity?" he inquired.

"To adore God, I hope."

"Begin now," he counseled, and added, "and be like a little child."

I think of that when I see some elderly persons. Going into the chapel at the Home the other day, I noted a frail, blue-eyed, old lady wrapped in a pretty light blue shawl. Her wheel chair was drawn up behind the Sisters who were reciting the office. She did not seem to be engaged in any special form of prayer herself. I recalled little Aunt Lucy, who used to say after she grew old, that she sat before the Blessed Sacrament telling our Lord not only that she loved him, but also that she knew that he loved her. Perhaps some such thoughts were in this old lady's mind. Jesus, whose delight is to be with the children of men, doubtless has great joy in the visits of those who have been his through long years.

Were I perfectly recollected in church, I would not observe the aged adorers as I do. But, just as I watch the antics of the school-children and altar boys and smile with our Lord, asking him to make saints of the culprits, so I ask help for his old, old friends who tell him of their love.

—MARY HOPE

Go to page 718 for your next devotional reading.

it was you who took me from my
   mother's womb.
My praise is continually of you.

7 I have been like a portent to many,
   but you are my strong refuge.
8 My mouth is filled with your praise,
   and with your glory all day long.
9 Do not cast me off in the time of
      old age;
   do not forsake me when my
      strength is spent.
10 For my enemies speak concerning
      me,
   and those who watch for my life
      consult together.
11 They say, "Pursue and seize that
      person
   whom God has forsaken,
   for there is no one to deliver."

12 O God, do not be far from me;
   O my God, make haste to
      help me!
13 Let my accusers be put to shame
      and consumed;
   let those who seek to hurt me
      be covered with scorn and
      disgrace.
14 But I will hope continually,
   and will praise you yet more and
      more.
15 My mouth will tell of your righteous
      acts,
   of your deeds of salvation all day
      long,
   though their number is past my
      knowledge.
16 I will come praising the mighty
      deeds of the Lord GOD,
   I will praise your righteousness,
      yours alone.

17 O God, from my youth you have
      taught me,
   and I still proclaim your
      wondrous deeds.
18 So even to old age and gray hairs,
   O God, do not forsake me,
   until I proclaim your might
      to all the generations to come.*o*
Your power 19and your
      righteousness, O God,
   reach the high heavens.

You who have done great things,
   O God, who is like you?

20 You who have made me see many
      troubles and calamities
   will revive me again;
from the depths of the earth
   you will bring me up again.
21 You will increase my honor,
   and comfort me once again.

22 I will also praise you with the harp
      for your faithfulness, O my God;
   I will sing praises to you with the
      lyre,
   O Holy One of Israel.
23 My lips will shout for joy
      when I sing praises to you;
   my soul also, which you have
      rescued.
24 All day long my tongue will talk of
      your righteous help,
   for those who tried to do me harm
      have been put to shame, and
      disgraced.

Psalm 72

*Prayer for Guidance and Support
for the King*

Of Solomon.

1 Give the king your justice, O God,
   and your righteousness to a king's
      son.
2 May he judge your people with
      righteousness,
   and your poor with justice.
3 May the mountains yield prosperity
      for the people,
   and the hills, in righteousness.
4 May he defend the cause of the poor
      of the people,
   give deliverance to the needy,
   and crush the oppressor.

5 May he live *p* while the sun endures,
   and as long as the moon,
      throughout all generations.
6 May he be like rain that falls on the
      mown grass,
   like showers that water the earth.
7 In his days may righteousness
      flourish
   and peace abound, until the
      moon is no more.

8 May he have dominion from sea to
      sea,

o Gk Compare Syr: Heb *to a generation, to all that
come*   *p* Gk: Heb *may they fear you*

and from the River to the ends of
the earth.
9 May his foes*q* bow down before
him,
and his enemies lick the dust.
10 May the kings of Tarshish and of the
isles
render him tribute,
may the kings of Sheba and Seba
bring gifts.
11 May all kings fall down before him,
all nations give him service.

12 For he delivers the needy when they
call,
the poor and those who have no
helper.
13 He has pity on the weak and the
needy,
and saves the lives of the needy.
14 From oppression and violence he
redeems their life;
and precious is their blood in his
sight.

15 Long may he live!
May gold of Sheba be given to
him.
May prayer be made for him
continually,
and blessings invoked for him all
day long.
16 May there be abundance of grain in
the land;
may it wave on the tops of the
mountains;
may its fruit be like Lebanon;
and may people blossom in the
cities
like the grass of the field.
17 May his name endure forever,
his fame continue as long as the
sun.
May all nations be blessed in him;*r*
may they pronounce him happy.

18 Blessed be the LORD, the God of
Israel,
who alone does wondrous things.
19 Blessed be his glorious name forever;
may his glory fill the whole earth.
Amen and Amen.

20 The prayers of David son of Jesse are
ended.

BOOK III
(Psalms 73–89)

Psalm 73

Plea for Relief from Oppressors
A Psalm of Asaph.

1 Truly God is good to the upright,*s*
to those who are pure in heart.
2 But as for me, my feet had almost
stumbled;
my steps had nearly slipped.
3 For I was envious of the arrogant;
I saw the prosperity of the wicked.

4 For they have no pain;
their bodies are sound and sleek.
5 They are not in trouble as others are;
they are not plagued like other
people.
6 Therefore pride is their necklace;
violence covers them like a
garment.
7 Their eyes swell out with fatness;
their hearts overflow with follies.
8 They scoff and speak with malice;
loftily they threaten oppression.
9 They set their mouths against
heaven,
and their tongues range over the
earth.

10 Therefore the people turn and praise
them,*t*
and find no fault in them.*u*
11 And they say, "How can God know?
Is there knowledge in the
Most High?"
12 Such are the wicked;
always at ease, they increase in
riches.
13 All in vain I have kept my heart
clean
and washed my hands in
innocence.
14 For all day long I have been
plagued,
and am punished every morning.

15 If I had said, "I will talk on in this
way,"
I would have been untrue to the
circle of your children.

q Cn: Heb *those who live in the wilderness*   *r* Or
bless themselves by him   *s* Or *good to Israel*
t Cn: Heb *his people return here*   *u* Cn: Heb
abundant waters are drained by them

16 But when I thought how to
        understand this,
    it seemed to me a wearisome task,
17 until I went into the sanctuary
        of God;
    then I perceived their end.
18 Truly you set them in slippery
        places;
    you make them fall to ruin.
19 How they are destroyed in a
        moment,
    swept away utterly by terrors!
20 They are*v* like a dream when one
        awakes;
    on awaking you despise their
        phantoms.

21 When my soul was embittered,
    when I was pricked in heart,
22 I was stupid and ignorant;
    I was like a brute beast toward
        you.
23 Nevertheless I am continually
        with you;
    you hold my right hand.
24 You guide me with your counsel,
    and afterward you will receive me
        with honor.*w*
25 Whom have I in heaven but you?
    And there is nothing on earth that
        I desire other than you.
26 My flesh and my heart may fail,
    but God is the strength*x* of my
        heart and my portion forever.

27 Indeed, those who are far from you
        will perish;
    you put an end to those who are
        false to you.
28 But for me it is good to be near
        God;
    I have made the Lord GOD my
        refuge,
    to tell of all your works.

Psalm 74

*Plea for Help in Time of National
Humiliation*

A Maskil of Asaph.

1 O God, why do you cast us off
        forever?
    Why does your anger smoke
        against the sheep of your
        pasture?
2 Remember your congregation, which
        you acquired long ago,

which you redeemed to be the
        tribe of your heritage.
    Remember Mount Zion, where
        you came to dwell.
3 Direct your steps to the perpetual
        ruins;
    the enemy has destroyed
        everything in the sanctuary.

4 Your foes have roared within your
        holy place;
    they set up their emblems there.
5 At the upper entrance they hacked
    the wooden trellis with axes.*y*
6 And then, with hatchets and
        hammers,
    they smashed all its carved work.
7 They set your sanctuary on fire;
    they desecrated the dwelling place
        of your name,
    bringing it to the ground.
8 They said to themselves, "We will
        utterly subdue them";
    they burned all the meeting places
        of God in the land.

9 We do not see our emblems;
    there is no longer any prophet,
    and there is no one among us
        who knows how long.
10 How long, O God, is the foe to
        scoff?
    Is the enemy to revile your name
        forever?
11 Why do you hold back your hand;
    why do you keep your hand in*z*
        your bosom?

12 Yet God my King is from of old,
    working salvation in the earth.
13 You divided the sea by your might;
    you broke the heads of the
        dragons in the waters.
14 You crushed the heads of Leviathan;
    you gave him as food*a* for the
        creatures of the wilderness.
15 You cut openings for springs and
        torrents;
    you dried up ever-flowing streams.
16 Yours is the day, yours also the
        night;
    you established the luminaries*b*
        and the sun.

---

v Cn: Heb *Lord*   *w* Or *to glory*   *x* Heb *rock*
y Cn Compare Gk Syr: Meaning of Heb uncertain
z Cn: Heb *do you consume your right hand from*
a Heb *food for the people*   *b* Or *moon;* Heb *light*

Naomi

Her Name Means *"My Joy"* or
"Pleasant"

Read Ruth 1

She stood like an old tree twisted against the sky. The wind that swept the hillside blew through her as though her body were hollow. Naomi could not remember what it felt like to be full, to feel secure. Though she could see for miles from her vantage point high on the road that led from Moab to Judah, she could glimpse nothing at all of her future. Instead, her thoughts were fixed on the past.

Ten years before, she and Elimelech had lived happily in Bethlehem. But the city whose name meant "house of bread" suddenly had none, so they migrated to the highlands of Moab to escape the famine. But Elimelech had died and her two sons had married Moabite women. Then she suffered the worst grief a mother could—outliving her own children.

Now Ruth and Orpah, her daughters-in-law, were the only kin she had left in Moab. She felt their widowhood as a double grief, loving them tenderly. Together they had cried and comforted each other, finally deciding to leave Moab for Bethlehem. But once on the road, Naomi's misgivings outran her craving for companionship. It wasn't right for young women to forsake their families and friends for so uncertain a future.

"Turn back, my daughters, why will you go with me? Do I still have sons in my womb

THE STORY OF A WOMAN

Her Character: *Suffering a three-fold tragedy, she refused to hide her sorrow or bitterness. Believing in God's sovereignty, she attributed her suffering to his will. But her fixation on circumstances, both past and present, led to hopelessness. A kind and loving mother-in-law, she inspired unusual love and loyalty in her daughters-in-law.*

Her Sorrow: *To have lost a husband and two sons in a foreign land, far from family and friends.*

Her Joy: *To have returned safely to Bethlehem with her daughter-in-law Ruth, who would eventually rekindle her happiness and hope.*

that they may become your husbands? Turn back, my daughters, go your way, for I am too old to have a husband. Even if I thought there was hope for me, even if I should have a husband tonight and bear sons, would you then wait until they were grown?" (verses 11–13).

The three women embraced, tears streaking their cheeks. Then Orpah kissed her mother-in-law good-bye. But Ruth clutched Naomi and whispered fiercely, "Where you go, I will go; where you lodge, I will lodge; your people shall be my people, and your God my God. Where you die, I will die—there will I be buried" (verses 16–17).

The old woman's stubbornness was no match for the younger woman's love. And so Naomi and Ruth continued on to Bethlehem. After so long an absence, Naomi's return created a great commotion in the town, and all the women welcomed her, saying, "Is this Naomi?" (verse 19).

"Call me no longer Naomi," she told them, "call me Mara [meaning 'Bitter'], for the Almighty has dealt bitterly with me. I went away full, but the LORD has brought me back empty" (verses 20–21).

Naomi's grief made it difficult for her to see beyond her circumstances. Like many of us, she may have felt her tragedies were meant as punishment for her sins. Yet had she known the blessings yet in store, she might not have felt bitter. Though she couldn't know it, she was just beginning a new episode in her life's story. Her future was full of hope.

Praying With Naomi

"Where you go, I will go; where you lodge, I will lodge; your people shall be my people, and your God my God. Where you die, I will die—there will I be buried."—*Ruth 1.16–17*

Praise God: *For creating us with the power to form deep and lasting friendships.*

Offer Thanks: *For the variety of friends God has given you.*

Confess: *Your tendency to be too busy to pay attention to your friends or too preoccupied with your own concerns to take time for theirs.*

Ask God: *To make you a more loyal and loving friend.*

Lift Your Heart

Think about someone you used to be especially close to. Perhaps time or distance has eroded the friendship. Wax nostalgic as you recall the great meals, the oddball jokes, the late night conversations, or the crazy adventures you shared. Wouldn't it be great to have that person back in your life? Pick up the phone or write a letter to renew the friendship. If the other person seems willing, invest some energy rebuilding the relationship in the year ahead. Let your memories form a foundation for your friendship but don't stop there. Get busy making new ones. If she's nearby, have her over for a meal or a fancy dessert. If not, exchange family photos. Stay in touch by e-mail. If you can afford to, you can even meet halfway for a weekend excursion.

Lord, thank you for the blessing of friends who, by sharing their lives with us, double our joy and halve our sorrows. Help me to cherish the friends you've given me and to become the kind of friend others will cherish: a woman who listens, encourages, and keeps confidences; a woman who knows how to laugh and how to cry, who is loyal, forgiving, and loving.

Go to page 731 for your next devotional reading.

17 You have fixed all the bounds of the
   earth;
      you made summer and winter.

18 Remember this, O LORD, how the
   enemy scoffs,
      and an impious people reviles
      your name.
19 Do not deliver the soul of your dove
   to the wild animals;
      do not forget the life of your poor
      forever.

20 Have regard for your*c* covenant,
      for the dark places of the land are
      full of the haunts of violence.
21 Do not let the downtrodden be put
   to shame;
      let the poor and needy praise your
      name.
22 Rise up, O God, plead your cause;
      remember how the impious scoff
      at you all day long.
23 Do not forget the clamor of your
   foes,
      the uproar of your adversaries that
      goes up continually.

Psalm 75

Thanksgiving for God's Wondrous Deeds

To the leader: Do Not Destroy. A Psalm
of Asaph. A Song.

1 We give thanks to you, O God;
      we give thanks; your name is near.
   People tell of your wondrous deeds.

2 At the set time that I appoint
      I will judge with equity.
3 When the earth totters, with all its
   inhabitants,
      it is I who keep its pillars steady.
                                   Selah
4 I say to the boastful, "Do not boast,"
      and to the wicked, "Do not lift
      up your horn;
5 do not lift up your horn on high,
      or speak with insolent neck."

6 For not from the east or from
   the west
      and not from the wilderness
      comes lifting up;
7 but it is God who executes
   judgment,
      putting down one and lifting up
      another.

8 For in the hand of the LORD there is
   a cup
      with foaming wine, well mixed;
   he will pour a draught from it,
      and all the wicked of the earth
      shall drain it down to the dregs.
9 But I will rejoice*d* forever;
      I will sing praises to the God of
      Jacob.

10 All the horns of the wicked I will cut
   off,
      but the horns of the righteous
      shall be exalted.

Psalm 76

Israel's God—Judge of All the Earth

To the leader: with stringed instruments.
A Psalm of Asaph. A Song.

1 In Judah God is known,
      his name is great in Israel.
2 His abode has been established in
   Salem,
      his dwelling place in Zion.
3 There he broke the flashing arrows,
      the shield, the sword, and the
      weapons of war.   *Selah*

4 Glorious are you, more majestic
      than the everlasting mountains.*e*
5 The stouthearted were stripped of
      their spoil;
      they sank into sleep;
   none of the troops
      was able to lift a hand.
6 At your rebuke, O God of Jacob,
      both rider and horse lay stunned.

7 But you indeed are awesome!
      Who can stand before you
      when once your anger is roused?
8 From the heavens you uttered
      judgment;
      the earth feared and was still
9 when God rose up to establish
      judgment,
      to save all the oppressed of the
      earth.   *Selah*

10 Human wrath serves only to
      praise you,
      when you bind the last bit of
      your*f* wrath around you.

c Gk Syr: Heb *the*   *d* Gk: Heb *declare*
e Gk: Heb *the mountains of prey*   *f* Heb lacks *your*

11 Make vows to the LORD your God,
    and perform them;
  let all who are around him bring
    gifts
  to the one who is awesome,
12 who cuts off the spirit of princes,
  who inspires fear in the kings of
    the earth.

Psalm 77

God's Mighty Deeds Recalled

To the leader: according to Jeduthun.
Of Asaph. A Psalm.

1 I cry aloud to God,
  aloud to God, that he may
    hear me.
2 In the day of my trouble I seek
    the Lord;
  in the night my hand is stretched
    out without wearying;
  my soul refuses to be comforted.
3 I think of God, and I moan;
  I meditate, and my spirit faints.
                                        Selah

4 You keep my eyelids from closing;
  I am so troubled that I cannot
    speak.
5 I consider the days of old,
  and remember the years of long
    ago.
6 I commune *g* with my heart in the
    night;
  I meditate and search my spirit: *h*
7 "Will the Lord spurn forever,
  and never again be favorable?
8 Has his steadfast love ceased forever?
  Are his promises at an end for all
    time?
9 Has God forgotten to be gracious?
  Has he in anger shut up his
    compassion?"   *Selah*
10 And I say, "It is my grief
  that the right hand of the Most
    High has changed."

11 I will call to mind the deeds of the
    LORD;
  I will remember your wonders
    of old.
12 I will meditate on all your work,
  and muse on your mighty deeds.
13 Your way, O God, is holy.
  What god is so great as our God?
14 You are the God who works
    wonders;

  you have displayed your might
    among the peoples.
15 With your strong arm you redeemed
    your people,
  the descendants of Jacob and
    Joseph.   *Selah*

16 When the waters saw you, O God,
  when the waters saw you, they
    were afraid;
  the very deep trembled.
17 The clouds poured out water;
  the skies thundered;
  your arrows flashed on every side.
18 The crash of your thunder was in
    the whirlwind;
  your lightnings lit up the world;
  the earth trembled and shook.
19 Your way was through the sea,
  your path, through the mighty
    waters;
  yet your footprints were unseen.
20 You led your people like a flock
  by the hand of Moses and Aaron.

Psalm 78

God's Goodness and Israel's Ingratitude

A Maskil of Asaph.

1 Give ear, O my people, to my
    teaching;
  incline your ears to the words of
    my mouth.
2 I will open my mouth in a parable;
  I will utter dark sayings from
    of old,
3 things that we have heard and
    known,
  that our ancestors have told us.
4 We will not hide them from their
    children;
  we will tell to the coming
    generation
  the glorious deeds of the LORD, and
    his might,
  and the wonders that he has
    done.

5 He established a decree in Jacob,
  and appointed a law in Israel,
  which he commanded our ancestors
  to teach to their children;
6 that the next generation might know
    them,
  the children yet unborn,

g Gk Syr: Heb *My music*   *h* Syr Jerome: Heb *my
spirit searches*

and rise up and tell them to their
     children,
7   so that they should set their hope
         in God,
     and not forget the works of God,
         but keep his commandments;
8   and that they should not be like
         their ancestors,
     a stubborn and rebellious
         generation,
     a generation whose heart was not
         steadfast,
     whose spirit was not faithful
         to God.

9   The Ephraimites, armed with[i] the
         bow,
     turned back on the day of battle.
10 They did not keep God's covenant,
     but refused to walk according to
         his law.
11 They forgot what he had done,
     and the miracles that he had
         shown them.
12 In the sight of their ancestors he
         worked marvels
     in the land of Egypt, in the fields
         of Zoan.
13 He divided the sea and let them
         pass through it,
     and made the waters stand like
         a heap.
14 In the daytime he led them with
         a cloud,
     and all night long with a fiery
         light.
15 He split rocks open in the
         wilderness,
     and gave them drink abundantly
         as from the deep.
16 He made streams come out of the
         rock,
     and caused waters to flow down
         like rivers.

17 Yet they sinned still more against
         him,
     rebelling against the Most High in
         the desert.
18 They tested God in their heart
     by demanding the food they
         craved.
19 They spoke against God, saying,
     "Can God spread a table in the
         wilderness?
20 Even though he struck the rock so
         that water gushed out
     and torrents overflowed,

can he also give bread,
     or provide meat for his people?"

21 Therefore, when the LORD heard, he
         was full of rage;
     a fire was kindled against Jacob,
         his anger mounted against Israel,
22 because they had no faith in God,
     and did not trust his saving
         power.
23 Yet he commanded the skies above,
     and opened the doors of heaven;
24 he rained down on them manna
         to eat,
     and gave them the grain of
         heaven.
25 Mortals ate of the bread of angels;
     he sent them food in abundance.
26 He caused the east wind to blow in
         the heavens,
     and by his power he led out the
         south wind;
27 he rained flesh upon them like dust,
     winged birds like the sand of the
         seas;
28 he let them fall within their camp,
     all around their dwellings.
29 And they ate and were well filled,
     for he gave them what they
         craved.
30 But before they had satisfied their
         craving,
     while the food was still in their
         mouths,
31 the anger of God rose against them
     and he killed the strongest of
         them,
     and laid low the flower of Israel.

32 In spite of all this they still sinned;
     they did not believe in his
         wonders.
33 So he made their days vanish like a
         breath,
     and their years in terror.
34 When he killed them, they sought
         for him;
     they repented and sought God
         earnestly.
35 They remembered that God was
         their rock,
     the Most High God their
         redeemer.
36 But they flattered him with their
         mouths;

---

i Heb *armed with shooting*

they lied to him with their
    tongues.
37 Their heart was not steadfast toward
    him;
    they were not true to his
        covenant.
38 Yet he, being compassionate,
    forgave their iniquity,
    and did not destroy them;
  often he restrained his anger,
    and did not stir up all his wrath.
39 He remembered that they were but
    flesh,
    a wind that passes and does not
        come again.
40 How often they rebelled against him
    in the wilderness
    and grieved him in the desert!
41 They tested God again and again,
    and provoked the Holy One of
        Israel.
42 They did not keep in mind his
    power,
    or the day when he redeemed
        them from the foe;
43 when he displayed his signs in
    Egypt,
    and his miracles in the fields of
        Zoan.
44 He turned their rivers to blood,
    so that they could not drink of
        their streams.
45 He sent among them swarms of
    flies, which devoured them,
    and frogs, which destroyed them.
46 He gave their crops to the caterpillar,
    and the fruit of their labor to the
        locust.
47 He destroyed their vines with hail,
    and their sycamores with frost.
48 He gave over their cattle to the hail,
    and their flocks to thunderbolts.
49 He let loose on them his fierce
    anger,
    wrath, indignation, and distress,
    a company of destroying angels.
50 He made a path for his anger;
    he did not spare them from death,
    but gave their lives over to the
        plague.
51 He struck all the firstborn in Egypt,
    the first issue of their strength in
        the tents of Ham.
52 Then he led out his people like
    sheep,
    and guided them in the wilderness
        like a flock.

53 He led them in safety, so that they
    were not afraid;
    but the sea overwhelmed their
        enemies.
54 And he brought them to his holy
    hill,
    to the mountain that his right
        hand had won.
55 He drove out nations before them;
    he apportioned them for a
        possession
    and settled the tribes of Israel in
        their tents.

56 Yet they tested the Most High God,
    and rebelled against him.
    They did not observe his decrees,
57 but turned away and were faithless
    like their ancestors;
    they twisted like a treacherous
        bow.
58 For they provoked him to anger
    with their high places;
    they moved him to jealousy with
        their idols.
59 When God heard, he was full of
    wrath,
    and he utterly rejected Israel.
60 He abandoned his dwelling at
    Shiloh,
    the tent where he dwelt among
        mortals,
61 and delivered his power to captivity,
    his glory to the hand of the foe.
62 He gave his people to the sword,
    and vented his wrath on his
        heritage.
63 Fire devoured their young men,
    and their girls had no marriage
        song.
64 Their priests fell by the sword,
    and their widows made no
        lamentation.
65 Then the Lord awoke as from sleep,
    like a warrior shouting because of
        wine.
66 He put his adversaries to rout;
    he put them to everlasting
        disgrace.
67 He rejected the tent of Joseph,
    he did not choose the tribe of
        Ephraim;
68 but he chose the tribe of Judah,
    Mount Zion, which he loves.
69 He built his sanctuary like the high
    heavens,

like the earth, which he has
founded forever.
70 He chose his servant David,
and took him from the
sheepfolds;
71 from tending the nursing ewes he
brought him
to be the shepherd of his people
Jacob,
of Israel, his inheritance.
72 With upright heart he tended them,
and guided them with skillful
hand.

Psalm 79

Plea for Mercy for Jerusalem

A Psalm of Asaph.

1 O God, the nations have come into
your inheritance;
they have defiled your holy
temple;
they have laid Jerusalem in ruins.
2 They have given the bodies of your
servants
to the birds of the air for food,
the flesh of your faithful to the
wild animals of the earth.
3 They have poured out their blood
like water
all around Jerusalem,
and there was no one to bury
them.
4 We have become a taunt to our
neighbors,
mocked and derided by those
around us.

5 How long, O LORD? Will you be
angry forever?
Will your jealous wrath burn like
fire?
6 Pour out your anger on the nations
that do not know you,
and on the kingdoms
that do not call on your name.
7 For they have devoured Jacob
and laid waste his habitation.

8 Do not remember against us the
iniquities of our ancestors;
let your compassion come
speedily to meet us,
for we are brought very low.
9 Help us, O God of our salvation,
for the glory of your name;
deliver us, and forgive our sins,

for your name's sake.
10 Why should the nations say,
"Where is their God?"
Let the avenging of the outpoured
blood of your servants
be known among the nations
before our eyes.
11 Let the groans of the prisoners come
before you;
according to your great power
preserve those doomed to die.
12 Return sevenfold into the bosom of
our neighbors
the taunts with which they
taunted you, O Lord!
13 Then we your people, the flock of
your pasture,
will give thanks to you forever;
from generation to generation we
will recount your praise.

Psalm 80

Prayer for Israel's Restoration

To the leader: on Lilies, a Covenant.
Of Asaph. A Psalm.

1 Give ear, O Shepherd of Israel,
you who lead Joseph like a flock!
You who are enthroned upon the
cherubim, shine forth
2 before Ephraim and Benjamin and
Manasseh.
Stir up your might,
and come to save us!

3 Restore us, O God;
let your face shine, that we may
be saved.

4 O LORD God of hosts,
how long will you be angry with
your people's prayers?
5 You have fed them with the bread of
tears,
and given them tears to drink in
full measure.
6 You make us the scorn *j* of our
neighbors;
our enemies laugh among
themselves.

7 Restore us, O God of hosts;
let your face shine, that we may
be saved.

j Syr: Heb *strife*

8 You brought a vine out of Egypt;
    you drove out the nations and
      planted it.
9 You cleared the ground for it;
    it took deep root and filled the
      land.
10 The mountains were covered with its
      shade,
    the mighty cedars with its
      branches;
11 it sent out its branches to the sea,
    and its shoots to the River.
12 Why then have you broken down its
      walls,
    so that all who pass along the way
      pluck its fruit?
13 The boar from the forest ravages it,
    and all that move in the field feed
      on it.

14 Turn again, O God of hosts;
    look down from heaven, and see;
  have regard for this vine,
15   the stock that your right hand
      planted.[k]
16 They have burned it with fire, they
      have cut it down;[l]
    may they perish at the rebuke of
      your countenance.
17 But let your hand be upon the one
      at your right hand,
    the one whom you made strong
      for yourself.
18 Then we will never turn back from
      you;
    give us life, and we will call on
      your name.

19 Restore us, O LORD God of hosts;
    let your face shine, that we may
      be saved.

Psalm 81

God's Appeal to Stubborn Israel

To the leader: according to The Gittith.
Of Asaph.

1 Sing aloud to God our strength;
    shout for joy to the God of Jacob.
2 Raise a song, sound the tambourine,
    the sweet lyre with the harp.
3 Blow the trumpet at the new moon,
    at the full moon, on our
      festal day.
4 For it is a statute for Israel,
    an ordinance of the God of Jacob.

5 He made it a decree in Joseph,
    when he went out over[m] the land
      of Egypt.

I hear a voice I had not known:
6 "I relieved your[n] shoulder of the
      burden;
    your[n] hands were freed from the
      basket.
7 In distress you called, and I rescued
      you;
    I answered you in the secret place
      of thunder;
    I tested you at the waters of
      Meribah.   *Selah*
8 Hear, O my people, while I
      admonish you;
    O Israel, if you would but listen
      to me!
9 There shall be no strange god
      among you;
    you shall not bow down to a
      foreign god.
10 I am the LORD your God,
    who brought you up out of the
      land of Egypt.
    Open your mouth wide and I will
      fill it.

11 "But my people did not listen to my
      voice;
    Israel would not submit to me.
12 So I gave them over to their
      stubborn hearts,
    to follow their own counsels.
13 O that my people would listen
      to me,
    that Israel would walk in my
      ways!
14 Then I would quickly subdue their
      enemies,
    and turn my hand against their
      foes.
15 Those who hate the LORD would
      cringe before him,
    and their doom would last
      forever.
16 I would feed you[o] with the finest of
      the wheat,
    and with honey from the rock I
      would satisfy you."

---

k Heb adds from verse 17 *and upon the one whom*
you made strong for yourself   l Cn: Heb *it is cut*
down   m Or *against*   n Heb *his*   o Cn
Compare verse 16b: Heb *he would feed him*

Psalm 82

A Plea for Justice

A Psalm of Asaph.

1 God has taken his place in the
    divine council;
  in the midst of the gods he holds
    judgment:
2 "How long will you judge unjustly
    and show partiality to the wicked?
                                    Selah
3 Give justice to the weak and the
    orphan;
  maintain the right of the lowly
    and the destitute.
4 Rescue the weak and the needy;
    deliver them from the hand of the
    wicked."

5 They have neither knowledge nor
    understanding,
  they walk around in darkness;
  all the foundations of the earth
    are shaken.

6 I say, "You are gods,
    children of the Most High, all
    of you;
7 nevertheless, you shall die like
    mortals,
  and fall like any prince." *p*

8 Rise up, O God, judge the earth;
    for all the nations belong to you!

Psalm 83

Prayer for Judgment on Israel's Foes

A Song. A Psalm of Asaph.

1 O God, do not keep silence;
    do not hold your peace or be still,
    O God!
2 Even now your enemies are in
    tumult;
  those who hate you have raised
    their heads.
3 They lay crafty plans against your
    people;
  they consult together against those
    you protect.
4 They say, "Come, let us wipe them
    out as a nation;
  let the name of Israel be
    remembered no more."
5 They conspire with one accord;
  against you they make a
    covenant—

6 the tents of Edom and the
    Ishmaelites,
  Moab and the Hagrites,
7 Gebal and Ammon and Amalek,
  Philistia with the inhabitants of
    Tyre;
8 Assyria also has joined them;
  they are the strong arm of the
    children of Lot.   *Selah*

9 Do to them as you did to Midian,
    as to Sisera and Jabin at the Wadi
    Kishon,
10 who were destroyed at En-dor,
  who became dung for the ground.
11 Make their nobles like Oreb and
    Zeeb,
  all their princes like Zebah and
    Zalmunna,
12 who said, "Let us take the pastures
    of God
  for our own possession."

13 O my God, make them like whirling
    dust,*q*
  like chaff before the wind.
14 As fire consumes the forest,
    as the flame sets the mountains
    ablaze,
15 so pursue them with your tempest
    and terrify them with your
    hurricane.
16 Fill their faces with shame,
    so that they may seek your name,
    O LORD.
17 Let them be put to shame and
    dismayed forever;
  let them perish in disgrace.
18 Let them know that you alone,
    whose name is the LORD,
  are the Most High over all the
    earth.

Psalm 84

The Joy of Worship in the Temple

To the leader: according to The Gittith.
Of the Korahites. A Psalm.

1 How lovely is your dwelling place,
    O LORD of hosts!
2 My soul longs, indeed it faints
    for the courts of the LORD;
  my heart and my flesh sing for joy
    to the living God.

*p Or fall as one man, O princes   q Or a
tumbleweed*

3 Even the sparrow finds a home,
    and the swallow a nest for herself,
    where she may lay her young,
  at your altars, O LORD of hosts,
    my King and my God.
4 Happy are those who live in your
      house,
    ever singing your praise.   *Selah*

5 Happy are those whose strength is
      in you,
    in whose heart are the highways
      to Zion.[r]
6 As they go through the valley of
      Baca
    they make it a place of springs;
    the early rain also covers it with
      pools.
7 They go from strength to strength;
    the God of gods will be seen
      in Zion.

8 O LORD God of hosts, hear my
      prayer;
    give ear, O God of Jacob!   *Selah*
9 Behold our shield, O God;
    look on the face of your anointed.

10 For a day in your courts is better
      than a thousand elsewhere.
    I would rather be a doorkeeper in
      the house of my God
    than live in the tents of
      wickedness.
11 For the LORD God is a sun and
      shield;
    he bestows favor and honor.
    No good thing does the LORD
      withhold
    from those who walk uprightly.
12 O LORD of hosts,
    happy is everyone who trusts
      in you.

Psalm 85

Prayer for the Restoration of God's Favor

To the leader. Of the Korahites. A Psalm.

1 LORD, you were favorable to your
      land;
    you restored the fortunes of Jacob.
2 You forgave the iniquity of your
      people;
    you pardoned all their sin.   *Selah*
3 You withdrew all your wrath;
    you turned from your hot anger.

4 Restore us again, O God of our
      salvation,
    and put away your indignation
      toward us.
5 Will you be angry with us forever?
    Will you prolong your anger to all
      generations?
6 Will you not revive us again,
    so that your people may rejoice
      in you?
7 Show us your steadfast love, O LORD,
    and grant us your salvation.

8 Let me hear what God the LORD will
      speak,
    for he will speak peace to his
      people,
    to his faithful, to those who turn
      to him in their hearts.[s]
9 Surely his salvation is at hand for
      those who fear him,
    that his glory may dwell in our
      land.

10 Steadfast love and faithfulness
      will meet;
    righteousness and peace will kiss
      each other.
11 Faithfulness will spring up from the
      ground,
    and righteousness will look down
      from the sky.
12 The LORD will give what is good,
    and our land will yield its
      increase.
13 Righteousness will go before him,
    and will make a path for his
      steps.

Psalm 86

Supplication for Help against Enemies

A Prayer of David.

1 Incline your ear, O LORD, and answer
      me,
    for I am poor and needy.
2 Preserve my life, for I am devoted to
      you;
    save your servant who trusts
      in you.
  You are my God; 3be gracious to
      me, O Lord,
    for to you do I cry all day long.

r Heb lacks *to Zion*   s Gk: Heb *but let them not*
turn back to folly

4 Gladden the soul of your servant,
   for to you, O Lord, I lift up my
      soul.
5 For you, O Lord, are good and
      forgiving,
   abounding in steadfast love to all
      who call on you.
6 Give ear, O LORD, to my prayer;
   listen to my cry of supplication.
7 In the day of my trouble I call
      on you,
   for you will answer me.

8 There is none like you among the
      gods, O Lord,
   nor are there any works like
      yours.
9 All the nations you have made
      shall come
   and bow down before you,
      O Lord,
   and shall glorify your name.
10 For you are great and do wondrous
      things;
   you alone are God.
11 Teach me your way, O LORD,
   that I may walk in your truth;
   give me an undivided heart to
      revere your name.
12 I give thanks to you, O Lord my
      God, with my whole heart,
   and I will glorify your name
      forever.
13 For great is your steadfast love
      toward me;
   you have delivered my soul from
      the depths of Sheol.

14 O God, the insolent rise up against
      me;
   a band of ruffians seeks my life,
   and they do not set you before
      them.
15 But you, O Lord, are a God merciful
      and gracious,
   slow to anger and abounding in
      steadfast love and
      faithfulness.
16 Turn to me and be gracious to me;
   give your strength to your servant;
   save the child of your serving
      girl.
17 Show me a sign of your favor,
   so that those who hate me may
      see it and be put to shame,
   because you, LORD, have helped
      me and comforted me.

Psalm 87

The Joy of Living in Zion

Of the Korahites. A Psalm. A Song.

1 On the holy mount stands the city
      he founded;
2   the LORD loves the gates of Zion
   more than all the dwellings of
      Jacob.
3 Glorious things are spoken of you,
      O city of God.   Selah

4 Among those who know me I
      mention Rahab and Babylon;
   Philistia too, and Tyre, with
      Ethiopia[t]—
   "This one was born there," they
      say.
5 And of Zion it shall be said,
   "This one and that one were born
      in it";
   for the Most High himself will
      establish it.
6 The LORD records, as he registers the
      peoples,
   "This one was born there."   Selah

7 Singers and dancers alike say,
   "All my springs are in you."

Psalm 88

Prayer for Help in Despondency

A Song. A Psalm of the Korahites.
To the leader: according to Mahalath
Leannoth. A Maskil of Heman
the Ezrahite.

1 O LORD, God of my salvation,
   when, at night, I cry out in your
      presence,
2 let my prayer come before you;
   incline your ear to my cry.

3 For my soul is full of troubles,
   and my life draws near to Sheol.
4 I am counted among those who go
      down to the Pit;
   I am like those who have no help,
5 like those forsaken among the dead,
   like the slain that lie in the grave,
   like those whom you remember
      no more,
   for they are cut off from your
      hand.

t Or *Nubia;* Heb *Cush*

6 You have put me in the depths of
  the Pit,
    in the regions dark and deep.
7 Your wrath lies heavy upon me,
    and you overwhelm me with all
      your waves.   *Selah*

8 You have caused my companions to
    shun me;
    you have made me a thing of
      horror to them.
  I am shut in so that I cannot escape;
9   my eye grows dim through
      sorrow.
  Every day I call on you, O LORD;
    I spread out my hands to you.
10 Do you work wonders for the dead?
    Do the shades rise up to praise
      you?   *Selah*
11 Is your steadfast love declared in the
      grave,
    or your faithfulness in Abaddon?
12 Are your wonders known in the
      darkness,
    or your saving help in the land of
      forgetfulness?

13 But I, O LORD, cry out to you;
    in the morning my prayer comes
      before you.
14 O LORD, why do you cast me off?
    Why do you hide your face from
      me?
15 Wretched and close to death from
      my youth up,
    I suffer your terrors; I am
      desperate.[u]
16 Your wrath has swept over me;
    your dread assaults destroy me.
17 They surround me like a flood all
      day long;
    from all sides they close in on me.
18 You have caused friend and
      neighbor to shun me;
    my companions are in darkness.

Psalm 89

God's Covenant with David

A Maskil of Ethan the Ezrahite.

1 I will sing of your steadfast love,
    O LORD,[v] forever;
    with my mouth I will proclaim
      your faithfulness to all
      generations.
2 I declare that your steadfast love is
      established forever;

your faithfulness is as firm as the
  heavens.

3 You said, "I have made a covenant
    with my chosen one,
    I have sworn to my servant David:
4 'I will establish your descendants
      forever,
    and build your throne for all
      generations.' "   *Selah*

5 Let the heavens praise your wonders,
    O LORD,
    your faithfulness in the assembly
      of the holy ones.
6 For who in the skies can be
      compared to the LORD?
    Who among the heavenly beings
      is like the LORD,
7 a God feared in the council of the
      holy ones,
    great and awesome[w] above all
      that are around him?
8 O LORD God of hosts,
    who is as mighty as you, O LORD?
    Your faithfulness surrounds you.
9 You rule the raging of the sea;
    when its waves rise, you still
      them.
10 You crushed Rahab like a carcass;
    you scattered your enemies with
      your mighty arm.
11 The heavens are yours, the earth also
      is yours;
    the world and all that is in it—
      you have founded them.
12 The north and the south[x]—you
      created them;
    Tabor and Hermon joyously praise
      your name.
13 You have a mighty arm;
    strong is your hand, high your
      right hand.
14 Righteousness and justice are the
      foundation of your throne;
    steadfast love and faithfulness go
      before you.
15 Happy are the people who know the
      festal shout,
    who walk, O LORD, in the light of
      your countenance;
16 they exult in your name all day
      long,

u Meaning of Heb uncertain   v Gk: Heb *the
steadfast love of the LORD*   w Gk Syr: Heb *greatly
awesome*   x Or *Zaphon and Yamin*

and extol ʸ your righteousness.
17 For you are the glory of their
     strength;
     by your favor our horn is exalted.
18 For our shield belongs to the LORD,
     our king to the Holy One of
     Israel.

19 Then you spoke in a vision to your
     faithful one, and said:
     "I have set the crown ᶻ on one
     who is mighty,
     I have exalted one chosen from
     the people.
20 I have found my servant David;
     with my holy oil I have anointed
     him;
21 my hand shall always remain with
     him;
     my arm also shall strengthen him.
22 The enemy shall not outwit him,
     the wicked shall not humble him.
23 I will crush his foes before him
     and strike down those who hate
     him.
24 My faithfulness and steadfast love
     shall be with him;
     and in my name his horn shall be
     exalted.
25 I will set his hand on the sea
     and his right hand on the rivers.
26 He shall cry to me, 'You are my
     Father,
     my God, and the Rock of my
     salvation!'
27 I will make him the firstborn,
     the highest of the kings of the
     earth.
28 Forever I will keep my steadfast love
     for him,
     and my covenant with him will
     stand firm.
29 I will establish his line forever,
     and his throne as long as the
     heavens endure.
30 If his children forsake my law
     and do not walk according to my
     ordinances,
31 if they violate my statutes
     and do not keep my
     commandments,
32 then I will punish their transgression
     with the rod
     and their iniquity with scourges;
33 but I will not remove from him my
     steadfast love,
     or be false to my faithfulness.
34 I will not violate my covenant,

or alter the word that went forth
     from my lips.
35 Once and for all I have sworn by
     my holiness;
     I will not lie to David.
36 His line shall continue forever,
     and his throne endure before me
     like the sun.
37 It shall be established forever like
     the moon,
     an enduring witness in the skies."
                              Selah

38 But now you have spurned and
     rejected him;
     you are full of wrath against your
     anointed.
39 You have renounced the covenant
     with your servant;
     you have defiled his crown in
     the dust.
40 You have broken through all
     his walls;
     you have laid his strongholds
     in ruins.
41 All who pass by plunder him;
     he has become the scorn of his
     neighbors.
42 You have exalted the right hand of
     his foes;
     you have made all his enemies
     rejoice.
43 Moreover, you have turned back the
     edge of his sword,
     and you have not supported him
     in battle.
44 You have removed the scepter from
     his hand, ᵃ
     and hurled his throne to the
     ground.
45 You have cut short the days of his
     youth;
     you have covered him with
     shame.   Selah

46 How long, O LORD? Will you hide
     yourself forever?
     How long will your wrath burn
     like fire?
47 Remember how short my time is— ᵇ
     for what vanity you have created
     all mortals!

y Cn: Heb *are exalted in*   z Cn: Heb *help*   a Cn:
Heb *removed his cleanness*   b Meaning of Heb
uncertain

48 Who can live and never see death?
  Who can escape the power of
    Sheol?   *Selah*

49 Lord, where is your steadfast love of
    old,
  which by your faithfulness you
    swore to David?
50 Remember, O Lord, how your
    servant is taunted;
  how I bear in my bosom the
    insults of the peoples,[c]
51 with which your enemies taunt,
    O Lord,
  with which they taunted the
    footsteps of your anointed.

52 Blessed be the Lord forever.
    Amen and Amen.

BOOK IV
(Psalms 90–106)

Psalm 90

God's Eternity and Human Frailty

A Prayer of Moses, the man of God.

1 Lord, you have been our dwelling
    place[d]

[c] Cn: Heb *bosom all of many peoples*   [d] Another reading is *our refuge*

"*Where Are You, God?*"

I clasp the newspaper to my heart like a Bible. I weep over the tragedy of human life. My candle flickers in the darkness of the night. I am trying for an hour of vigil for my dear broken world.

God, I feel angry. This morning, with Psalm 102, I prayed, "The children of your servants shall live secure." So many people who serve you do not dwell secure, and neither do their children. I glance again at the paper. I see the poverty, the wars, the enslavement of the human person. I see, in many instances, the injustice people have to suffer simply because they are trying to serve you. I see the immense helplessness that so many people experience in the face of unjust systems. And I say to you, "What's happening to their prayers, God? Are you using their prayers for a carpet in heaven? These people need for you to lean down from heaven. It is enough! It is enough, God!"

In the shadows of this dark night, I seem to see God leaning from heaven again. This time God comes not as a tiny, helpless child but as a sorrowing, desperate parent, and God repeats to the human race my own agonizing cry, "It is enough! How long must I wait for you to put on the mind of Christ? How long must I wait for you to live in my image? What are you doing with the prayers of your brothers and sisters? Are you making them into plush carpets for your own feet to rest on?"

I've never been very good at feasting on the daily newspaper. It turns bitter in my mouth. And yet, this is my world. This face of suffering I must embrace as a part of my responsibility. I clasp the newspaper to my heart and ask once again in the stillness of the night, "What are we doing to the image of God in one another?"

—*MACRINA WIEDERKEHR*

Go to page 735 for your next devotional reading.

MONDAY

Scripture Reading
for Today:
Psalm 89.46–52

Verses for Today:
Psalm 89.46–47

in all generations.

2 Before the mountains were brought
    forth,
  or ever you had formed the earth
    and the world,
  from everlasting to everlasting you
    are God.

3 You turn us*e* back to dust,
  and say, "Turn back, you mortals."
4 For a thousand years in your sight
  are like yesterday when it is past,
  or like a watch in the night.

5 You sweep them away; they are like
    a dream,
  like grass that is renewed in the
    morning;
6 in the morning it flourishes and is
    renewed;
  in the evening it fades and
    withers.

7 For we are consumed by your anger;
  by your wrath we are
    overwhelmed.
8 You have set our iniquities
    before you,
  our secret sins in the light of your
    countenance.

9 For all our days pass away under
    your wrath;
  our years come to an end*f* like
    a sigh.
10 The days of our life are seventy
    years,
  or perhaps eighty, if we are strong;
  even then their span*g* is only toil
    and trouble;
  they are soon gone, and we fly
    away.

11 Who considers the power of your
    anger?
  Your wrath is as great as the fear
    that is due you.
12 So teach us to count our days
  that we may gain a wise heart.

13 Turn, O LORD! How long?
  Have compassion on your
    servants!
14 Satisfy us in the morning with your
    steadfast love,
  so that we may rejoice and be
    glad all our days.

15 Make us glad as many days as you
    have afflicted us,
  and as many years as we have
    seen evil.
16 Let your work be manifest to your
    servants,
  and your glorious power to their
    children.
17 Let the favor of the Lord our God be
    upon us,
  and prosper for us the work of
    our hands—
  O prosper the work of our hands!

Psalm 91

Assurance of God's Protection

1 You who live in the shelter of the
    Most High,
  who abide in the shadow of the
    Almighty,*h*
2 will say to the LORD, "My refuge and
    my fortress;
  my God, in whom I trust."
3 For he will deliver you from the
    snare of the fowler
  and from the deadly pestilence;
4 he will cover you with his pinions,
  and under his wings you will find
    refuge;
  his faithfulness is a shield and
    buckler.
5 You will not fear the terror of the
    night,
  or the arrow that flies by day,
6 or the pestilence that stalks in
    darkness,
  or the destruction that wastes at
    noonday.

7 A thousand may fall at your side,
  ten thousand at your right hand,
  but it will not come near you.
8 You will only look with your eyes
  and see the punishment of the
    wicked.

9 Because you have made the LORD
    your refuge,*i*
  the Most High your dwelling
    place,

---

e Heb *humankind*   *f* Syr: Heb *we bring our years to
an end*   *g* Cn Compare Gk Syr Jerome Tg: Heb
pride   *h* Traditional rendering of Heb *Shaddai*
i Cn: Heb *Because you, LORD, are my refuge; you
have made*

10 no evil shall befall you,
    no scourge come near your tent.

11 For he will command his angels
    concerning you
    to guard you in all your ways.
12 On their hands they will bear
    you up,
    so that you will not dash your
    foot against a stone.
13 You will tread on the lion and the
    adder,
    the young lion and the serpent
    you will trample under foot.

14 Those who love me, I will deliver;
    I will protect those who know my
    name.
15 When they call to me, I will answer
    them;
    I will be with them in trouble,
    I will rescue them and honor
    them.
16 With long life I will satisfy them,
    and show them my salvation.

Psalm 92

Thanksgiving for Vindication

A Psalm. A Song for the Sabbath Day.

1 It is good to give thanks to the LORD,
    to sing praises to your name,
    O Most High;
2 to declare your steadfast love in the
    morning,
    and your faithfulness by night,
3 to the music of the lute and the
    harp,
    to the melody of the lyre.
4 For you, O LORD, have made me glad
    by your work;
    at the works of your hands I sing
    for joy.

5 How great are your works, O LORD!
    Your thoughts are very deep!
6 The dullard cannot know,
    the stupid cannot understand this:
7 though the wicked sprout like grass
    and all evildoers flourish,
    they are doomed to destruction
    forever,
8 but you, O LORD, are on high
    forever.
9 For your enemies, O LORD,
    for your enemies shall perish;
    all evildoers shall be scattered.

10 But you have exalted my horn like
    that of the wild ox;
    you have poured over me[j]
    fresh oil.
11 My eyes have seen the downfall of
    my enemies;
    my ears have heard the doom of
    my evil assailants.

12 The righteous flourish like the palm
    tree,
    and grow like a cedar in Lebanon.
13 They are planted in the house of the
    LORD;
    they flourish in the courts of our
    God.
14 In old age they still produce fruit;
    they are always green and full
    of sap,
15 showing that the LORD is upright;
    he is my rock, and there is no
    unrighteousness in him.

Psalm 93

The Majesty of God's Rule

1 The LORD is king, he is robed in
    majesty;
    the LORD is robed, he is girded
    with strength.
He has established the world; it
    shall never be moved;
2 your throne is established from
    of old;
    you are from everlasting.

3 The floods have lifted up, O LORD,
    the floods have lifted up their
    voice;
    the floods lift up their roaring.
4 More majestic than the thunders of
    mighty waters,
    more majestic than the waves[k] of
    the sea,
    majestic on high is the LORD!

5 Your decrees are very sure;
    holiness befits your house,
    O LORD, forevermore.

Psalm 94

God the Avenger of the Righteous

1 O LORD, you God of vengeance,

---

j Syr: Meaning of Heb uncertain   *k* Cn: Heb
majestic are the waves

you God of vengeance, shine
forth!
2 Rise up, O judge of the earth;
give to the proud what they
deserve!
3 O LORD, how long shall the wicked,
how long shall the wicked exult?

4 They pour out their arrogant words;
all the evildoers boast.
5 They crush your people, O LORD,
and afflict your heritage.
6 They kill the widow and the
stranger,
they murder the orphan,
7 and they say, "The LORD does
not see;
the God of Jacob does not
perceive."

8 Understand, O dullest of the people;
fools, when will you be wise?
9 He who planted the ear, does he not
hear?
He who formed the eye, does he
not see?
10 He who disciplines the nations,
he who teaches knowledge to
humankind,
does he not chastise?
11 The LORD knows our thoughts,[1]
that they are but an empty breath.

12 Happy are those whom you
discipline, O LORD,
and whom you teach out of
your law,
13 giving them respite from days of
trouble,
until a pit is dug for the wicked.
14 For the LORD will not forsake his
people;
he will not abandon his heritage;
15 for justice will return to the
righteous,
and all the upright in heart will
follow it.

16 Who rises up for me against the
wicked?
Who stands up for me against
evildoers?
17 If the LORD had not been my help,
my soul would soon have lived in
the land of silence.
18 When I thought, "My foot is
slipping,"

your steadfast love, O LORD, held
me up.
19 When the cares of my heart are
many,
your consolations cheer my soul.
20 Can wicked rulers be allied
with you,
those who contrive mischief by
statute?
21 They band together against the life
of the righteous,
and condemn the innocent to
death.
22 But the LORD has become my
stronghold,
and my God the rock of my
refuge.
23 He will repay them for their iniquity
and wipe them out for their
wickedness;
the LORD our God will wipe
them out.

Psalm 95

A Call to Worship and Obedience

1 O come, let us sing to the LORD;
let us make a joyful noise to the
rock of our salvation!
2 Let us come into his presence with
thanksgiving;
let us make a joyful noise to him
with songs of praise!
3 For the LORD is a great God,
and a great King above all gods.
4 In his hand are the depths of the
earth;
the heights of the mountains are
his also.
5 The sea is his, for he made it,
and the dry land, which his hands
have formed.

6 O come, let us worship and bow
down,
let us kneel before the LORD,
our Maker!
7 For he is our God,
and we are the people of his
pasture,
and the sheep of his hand.

O that today you would listen to his
voice!
8 Do not harden your hearts, as at
Meribah,

---

[1] Heb *the thoughts of humankind*

as on the day at Massah in the
wilderness,
⁹ when your ancestors tested me,
and put me to the proof, though
they had seen my work.
¹⁰ For forty years I loathed that
generation
and said, "They are a people
whose hearts go astray,
and they do not regard my ways."
¹¹ Therefore in my anger I swore,
"They shall not enter my rest."

Psalm 96

Praise to God Who Comes in Judgment

¹ O sing to the LORD a new song;
sing to the LORD, all the earth.
² Sing to the LORD, bless his name;
tell of his salvation from day
to day.
³ Declare his glory among the nations,
his marvelous works among all
the peoples.
⁴ For great is the LORD, and greatly to
be praised;
he is to be revered above all gods.
⁵ For all the gods of the peoples are
idols,
but the LORD made the heavens.
⁶ Honor and majesty are before him;

strength and beauty are in his
sanctuary.

⁷ Ascribe to the LORD, O families of
the peoples,
ascribe to the LORD glory and
strength.
⁸ Ascribe to the LORD the glory due his
name;
bring an offering, and come into
his courts.
⁹ Worship the LORD in holy splendor;
tremble before him, all the earth.

¹⁰ Say among the nations, "The LORD is
king!
The world is firmly established; it
shall never be moved.
He will judge the peoples with
equity."
¹¹ Let the heavens be glad, and let the
earth rejoice;
let the sea roar, and all that
fills it;
¹² let the field exult, and everything
in it.
Then shall all the trees of the forest
sing for joy
¹³ before the LORD; for he is coming,
for he is coming to judge the
earth.

*P*raise

There are so many ways of praying, so many ways of addressing God: in repentance, in petition, in intercession. But in the end we were made to praise our Creator. Gratitude puts everything into a different perspective. It prevents me from taking anything for granted. It helps me to live my life awake, alert to those good gifts that I am given, in a state of mindfulness or awareness. Then, when I look at the world with eyes of wonder, I discover, rather to my chagrin, that it is often only too easy to drift and become neglectful, lazy, forgetful of gratefulness.

I enjoy that line of W. H. Auden, "Practice the scales of rejoicing," because of its suggestion that it really is hard work and needs discipline. I might rewrite those familiar words "pray without ceasing" so that they become "praise without ceasing," giving thanks to my Creator for all the good gifts in my life.

—*ESTHER DE WAAL*

Go to page 739 for your next devotional reading.

TUESDAY

Scripture Reading
for Today:
Psalm 95

Verse for Today:
Psalm 95.2

He will judge the world with
righteousness,
and the peoples with his truth.

Psalm 97

The Glory of God's Reign

1 The LORD is king! Let the earth
rejoice;
let the many coastlands be glad!
2 Clouds and thick darkness are all
around him;
righteousness and justice are the
foundation of his throne.
3 Fire goes before him,
and consumes his adversaries on
every side.
4 His lightnings light up the world;
the earth sees and trembles.
5 The mountains melt like wax before
the LORD,
before the Lord of all the earth.

6 The heavens proclaim his
righteousness;
and all the peoples behold his
glory.
7 All worshipers of images are put
to shame,
those who make their boast in
worthless idols;
all gods bow down before him.
8 Zion hears and is glad,
and the towns[m] of Judah rejoice,
because of your judgments,
O God.
9 For you, O LORD, are most high over
all the earth;
you are exalted far above all gods.

10 The LORD loves those who hate[n]
evil;
he guards the lives of his faithful;
he rescues them from the hand of
the wicked.
11 Light dawns[o] for the righteous,
and joy for the upright in heart.
12 Rejoice in the LORD, O you
righteous,
and give thanks to his holy name!

Psalm 98

Praise the Judge of the World

A Psalm.

1 O sing to the LORD a new song,
for he has done marvelous things.

His right hand and his holy arm
have gotten him victory.
2 The LORD has made known his
victory;
he has revealed his vindication in
the sight of the nations.
3 He has remembered his steadfast
love and faithfulness
to the house of Israel.
All the ends of the earth have seen
the victory of our God.

4 Make a joyful noise to the LORD, all
the earth;
break forth into joyous song and
sing praises.
5 Sing praises to the LORD with the
lyre,
with the lyre and the sound of
melody.
6 With trumpets and the sound of the
horn
make a joyful noise before the
King, the LORD.

7 Let the sea roar, and all that fills it;
the world and those who live
in it.
8 Let the floods clap their hands;
let the hills sing together for joy
9 at the presence of the LORD, for he is
coming
to judge the earth.
He will judge the world with
righteousness,
and the peoples with equity.

Psalm 99

Praise to God for His Holiness

1 The LORD is king; let the peoples
tremble!
He sits enthroned upon the
cherubim; let the earth
quake!
2 The LORD is great in Zion;
he is exalted over all the peoples.
3 Let them praise your great and
awesome name.
Holy is he!
4 Mighty King, [p] lover of justice,

---

m Heb *daughters*   n Cn: Heb *You who love the
LORD hate*   o Gk Syr Jerome: Heb *is sown*   p Cn:
Heb *And a king's strength*

you have established equity;
you have executed justice
and righteousness in Jacob.
5 Extol the LORD our God;
worship at his footstool.
Holy is he!

6 Moses and Aaron were among his
priests,
Samuel also was among those
who called on his name.
They cried to the LORD, and he
answered them.
7 He spoke to them in the pillar of
cloud;
they kept his decrees,
and the statutes that he gave
them.

8 O LORD our God, you answered
them;
you were a forgiving God to
them,
but an avenger of their
wrongdoings.
9 Extol the LORD our God,
and worship at his holy
mountain;
for the LORD our God is holy.

Psalm 100

All Lands Summoned to Praise God

A Psalm of thanksgiving.

1 Make a joyful noise to the LORD, all
the earth.
2   Worship the LORD with gladness;
come into his presence with
singing.

3 Know that the LORD is God.
It is he that made us, and we are
his;*q*
we are his people, and the sheep
of his pasture.

4 Enter his gates with thanksgiving,
and his courts with praise.
Give thanks to him, bless his
name.

5 For the LORD is good;
his steadfast love endures forever,
and his faithfulness to all
generations.

Psalm 101

A Sovereign's Pledge of Integrity and Justice

Of David. A Psalm.

1 I will sing of loyalty and of justice;
to you, O LORD, I will sing.
2 I will study the way that is
blameless.
When shall I attain it?

I will walk with integrity of heart
within my house;
3 I will not set before my eyes
anything that is base.

I hate the work of those who
fall away;
it shall not cling to me.
4 Perverseness of heart shall be far
from me;
I will know nothing of evil.

5 One who secretly slanders a
neighbor
I will destroy.
A haughty look and an arrogant
heart
I will not tolerate.

6 I will look with favor on the faithful
in the land,
so that they may live with me;
whoever walks in the way that is
blameless
shall minister to me.

7 No one who practices deceit
shall remain in my house;
no one who utters lies
shall continue in my presence.

8 Morning by morning I will destroy
all the wicked in the land,
cutting off all evildoers
from the city of the LORD.

Psalm 102

Prayer to the Eternal King for Help

A prayer of one afflicted, when faint and
pleading before the LORD.

1 Hear my prayer, O LORD;
let my cry come to you.
2 Do not hide your face from me
in the day of my distress.

q Another reading is *and not we ourselves*

Incline your ear to me;
  answer me speedily in the day
    when I call.

3 For my days pass away like smoke,
  and my bones burn like a furnace.
4 My heart is stricken and withered
    like grass;
  I am too wasted to eat my bread.
5 Because of my loud groaning
  my bones cling to my skin.
6 I am like an owl of the wilderness,
  like a little owl of the waste
    places.
7 I lie awake;
  I am like a lonely bird on the
    housetop.
8 All day long my enemies taunt me;
  those who deride me use my
    name for a curse.
9 For I eat ashes like bread,
  and mingle tears with my drink,
10 because of your indignation and
    anger;
  for you have lifted me up and
    thrown me aside.
11 My days are like an evening shadow;
  I wither away like grass.

12 But you, O Lord, are enthroned
    forever;
  your name endures to all
    generations.
13 You will rise up and have
    compassion on Zion,
  for it is time to favor it;
  the appointed time has come.
14 For your servants hold its stones
    dear,
  and have pity on its dust.
15 The nations will fear the name of
    the Lord,
  and all the kings of the earth your
    glory.
16 For the Lord will build up Zion;
  he will appear in his glory.
17 He will regard the prayer of the
    destitute,
  and will not despise their prayer.

18 Let this be recorded for a generation
    to come,
  so that a people yet unborn may
    praise the Lord:
19 that he looked down from his holy
    height,
  from heaven the Lord looked at
    the earth,

20 to hear the groans of the prisoners,
  to set free those who were
    doomed to die;
21 so that the name of the Lord may be
    declared in Zion,
  and his praise in Jerusalem,
22 when peoples gather together,
  and kingdoms, to worship the
    Lord.

23 He has broken my strength in
    midcourse;
  he has shortened my days.
24 "O my God," I say, "do not take
    me away
  at the midpoint of my life,
you whose years endure
  throughout all generations."

25 Long ago you laid the foundation of
    the earth,
  and the heavens are the work of
    your hands.
26 They will perish, but you endure;
  they will all wear out like a
    garment.
You change them like clothing, and
    they pass away;
27 but you are the same, and your
    years have no end.
28 The children of your servants shall
    live secure;
  their offspring shall be established
    in your presence.

Psalm 103

Thanksgiving for God's Goodness

Of David.

1 Bless the Lord, O my soul,
  and all that is within me,
  bless his holy name.
2 Bless the Lord, O my soul,
  and do not forget all his
    benefits—
3 who forgives all your iniquity,
  who heals all your diseases,
4 who redeems your life from the Pit,
  who crowns you with steadfast
    love and mercy,
5 who satisfies you with good as long
    as you live[r]
  so that your youth is renewed like
    the eagle's.

r Meaning of Heb uncertain

6 The LORD works vindication
   and justice for all who are
      oppressed.
7 He made known his ways to Moses,
   his acts to the people of Israel.
8 The LORD is merciful and gracious,
   slow to anger and abounding in
      steadfast love.
9 He will not always accuse,
   nor will he keep his anger forever.
10 He does not deal with us according
   to our sins,

nor repay us according to our
   iniquities.
11 For as the heavens are high above
   the earth,
      so great is his steadfast love
         toward those who fear
            him;
12 as far as the east is from the west,
   so far he removes our
      transgressions from us.
13 As a father has compassion for his
   children,

*F*resh Mercy

WEDNESDAY

Scripture Reading
for Today:
Psalm 103.1–13

Verses for Today:
Psalm 103.11–12

There are often times in my travels when I do not have to rush to
a plane to show up somewhere at an appropriate time. Some days
I'll have to drive to arrive at the next city on time, [setting] my
alarm at what feels like the middle of the night to leave at a de-
cent hour in the morning. Surprisingly these times on the road are
some of my most precious.

I may be in New England on a cool, crisp fall day, when the
leaves are parading their colors. Some days may take me through
the Midwest during summer, where farmland stretches way beyond what I can see, and old houses seem painted on the landscape in just the right places as the sun awakens and gently
touches the earth with rays of splendor. I could be somewhere on
the West Coast, or way down south or on one of the islands
where I can hear all sorts of beautiful sounds from a vast array of
birds as they dance over waters touched by light so magnificent
it looks as if someone had dropped thousands of diamonds from
the sky.

These scenes are endless in my mind. All of them produce the
same experience for me—a sense of newness, freshness, peaceful-
ness, stillness, calm—another day, another start. Untouched, clean,
ready to experience all that life has to offer once again. I am constantly reminded of the faithfulness of God and that his mercies
are new every morning. What I was yesterday, what I felt yesterday, what I did yesterday is covered by his grace. He remembers it
no more. He throws it as far as the east is from the west—as I turn,
as I repent, as I offer him my sins, my failures, and even the consequences of my choices. There is so much beauty to the morning,
and there is so much beauty in a heart filled with the certainty
that the Lord has once again come to fill, restore, and heal.

His steadfast love never ceases. His mercies never end.

—KATHY TROCCOLI

Go to page 742 for your next devotional reading.

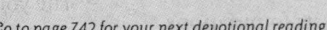

so the LORD has compassion for
those who fear him.
14 For he knows how we were made;
he remembers that we are dust.

15 As for mortals, their days are like
grass;
they flourish like a flower of the
field;
16 for the wind passes over it, and it is
gone,
and its place knows it no more.
17 But the steadfast love of the LORD is
from everlasting to everlasting
on those who fear him,
and his righteousness to children's
children,
18 to those who keep his covenant
and remember to do his
commandments.

19 The LORD has established his throne
in the heavens,
and his kingdom rules over all.
20 Bless the LORD, O you his angels,
you mighty ones who do his
bidding,
obedient to his spoken word.
21 Bless the LORD, all his hosts,
his ministers that do his will.
22 Bless the LORD, all his works,
in all places of his dominion.
Bless the LORD, O my soul.

Psalm 104

God the Creator and Provider

1 Bless the LORD, O my soul.
O LORD my God, you are very
great.
You are clothed with honor and
majesty,
2 wrapped in light as with a
garment.
You stretch out the heavens like
a tent,
3 you set the beams of your^s
chambers on the waters,
you make the clouds your^s chariot,
you ride on the wings of the
wind,
4 you make the winds your^s
messengers,
fire and flame your^s ministers.

5 You set the earth on its foundations,
so that it shall never be shaken.

6 You cover it with the deep as with a
garment;
the waters stood above the
mountains.
7 At your rebuke they flee;
at the sound of your thunder they
take to flight.
8 They rose up to the mountains, ran
down to the valleys
to the place that you appointed
for them.
9 You set a boundary that they may
not pass,
so that they might not again cover
the earth.

10 You make springs gush forth in the
valleys;
they flow between the hills,
11 giving drink to every wild animal;
the wild asses quench their thirst.
12 By the streams^t the birds of the air
have their habitation;
they sing among the branches.
13 From your lofty abode you water the
mountains;
the earth is satisfied with the fruit
of your work.

14 You cause the grass to grow for the
cattle,
and plants for people to use,^{u}
to bring forth food from the earth,
15 and wine to gladden the human
heart,
oil to make the face shine,
and bread to strengthen the
human heart.
16 The trees of the LORD are watered
abundantly,
the cedars of Lebanon that he
planted.
17 In them the birds build their nests;
the stork has its home in the fir
trees.
18 The high mountains are for the wild
goats;
the rocks are a refuge for the
coneys.
19 You have made the moon to mark
the seasons;
the sun knows its time for setting.
20 You make darkness, and it is night,
when all the animals of the forest
come creeping out.
21 The young lions roar for their prey,

^{s} Heb *his* ^{t} Heb *By them* ^{u} Or *to cultivate*

seeking their food from God.
22 When the sun rises, they withdraw
   and lie down in their dens.
23 People go out to their work
   and to their labor until the
      evening.

24 O Lord, how manifold are your
      works!
   In wisdom you have made
      them all;
   the earth is full of your creatures.
25 Yonder is the sea, great and wide,
   creeping things innumerable are
      there,
   living things both small and great.
26 There go the ships,
   and Leviathan that you formed
      to sport in it.

27 These all look to you
   to give them their food in due
      season;
28 when you give to them, they gather
      it up;
   when you open your hand, they
      are filled with good things.
29 When you hide your face, they are
      dismayed;
   when you take away their breath,
      they die
   and return to their dust.
30 When you send forth your spirit,[v]
      they are created;
   and you renew the face of the
      ground.

31 May the glory of the Lord endure
      forever;
   may the Lord rejoice in his
      works—
32 who looks on the earth and it
      trembles,
   who touches the mountains and
      they smoke.
33 I will sing to the Lord as long as
      I live;
   I will sing praise to my God while
      I have being.
34 May my meditation be pleasing
      to him,
   for I rejoice in the Lord.
35 Let sinners be consumed from the
      earth,
   and let the wicked be no more.
   Bless the Lord, O my soul.
   Praise the Lord!

Psalm 105

God's Faithfulness to Israel

1 O give thanks to the Lord, call on
      his name,
   make known his deeds among the
      peoples.
2 Sing to him, sing praises to him;
   tell of all his wonderful works.
3 Glory in his holy name;
   let the hearts of those who seek
      the Lord rejoice.
4 Seek the Lord and his strength;
   seek his presence continually.
5 Remember the wonderful works he
      has done,
   his miracles, and the judgments
      he has uttered,
6 O offspring of his servant
      Abraham,[w]
   children of Jacob, his chosen
      ones.

7 He is the Lord our God;
   his judgments are in all the earth.
8 He is mindful of his covenant
      forever,
   of the word that he commanded,
      for a thousand generations,
9 the covenant that he made with
      Abraham,
   his sworn promise to Isaac,
10 which he confirmed to Jacob as a
      statute,
   to Israel as an everlasting
      covenant,
11 saying, "To you I will give the land
      of Canaan
   as your portion for an inheritance."

12 When they were few in number,
   of little account, and strangers
      in it,
13 wandering from nation to nation,
   from one kingdom to another
      people,
14 he allowed no one to oppress them;
   he rebuked kings on their account,
15 saying, "Do not touch my anointed
      ones;
   do my prophets no harm."

16 When he summoned famine against
      the land,
   and broke every staff of bread,

v Or *your breath*   *w* Another reading is *Israel*
(compare 1 Chr 16.13)

¹⁷ he had sent a man ahead of them,
　　Joseph, who was sold as a slave.
¹⁸ His feet were hurt with fetters,
　　his neck was put in a collar of
　　　iron;
¹⁹ until what he had said came to pass,
　　the word of the LORD kept testing
　　　him.
²⁰ The king sent and released him;
　　the ruler of the peoples set
　　　him free.
²¹ He made him lord of his house,
　　and ruler of all his possessions,

²² to instruct ˣ his officials at his
　　pleasure,
　　and to teach his elders wisdom.
²³ Then Israel came to Egypt;
　　Jacob lived as an alien in the land
　　　of Ham.
²⁴ And the LORD made his people very
　　fruitful,
　　and made them stronger than
　　their foes,

ˣ Gk Syr Jerome: Heb *to bind*

*S*hare *Your Story,* *Share Your Love*

THURSDAY

Scripture Reading
for Today:
Psalm 105.1–6

Verse for Today:
Psalm 105.2

You and I together have been called to be ambassadors of Christ
Jesus in the world (see 2 Corinthians 5.20). And what could be a
more glorious call than to proclaim the marvelous truth of our salvation? Why, then, do we resist?

"I don't know enough." Even if we do not have Scripture passages memorized, even if we do not feel as knowledgeable about
our faith as we'd like, each of us *does* know about our own experience with Jesus Christ. A most effective way to evangelize is simply to share our story.

Sharing our own personal stories of God's action in our lives
simply means we tell others about what God has done for us—*his
wonderful deeds*—and how he called us out of the darkness of ignorance and sin and into his marvelous light of grace and knowledge.

In a television program we produced on evangelization, our
guest shared with us an easy and efficient way to share our story.
He suggested that we divide it into three parts: *I Was, He Did, I
Am.* First, we tell others about the way we were before we entered into relationship with Jesus or called on him for help. Then,
we share with them about the moment of conversion that occurred in our lives, or a moment of grace that helped us in the
midst of a struggle. Finally we outline the ways in which we have
been touched, changed, healed by knowing Jesus in a personal
way and being open to the grace he longs to give us.

Sharing our personal stories is effective evangelization. It is
non-threatening, irrefutable, and engaging. It is one way we can all
share our love of God.

—*JOHNETTE BENKOVIC*

Go to page 747 for your next devotional reading.

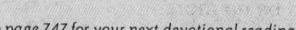

25 whose hearts he then turned to hate
his people,
to deal craftily with his servants.

26 He sent his servant Moses,
and Aaron whom he had chosen.
27 They performed his signs among
them,
and miracles in the land of Ham.
28 He sent darkness, and made the
land dark;
they rebelled[y] against his words.
29 He turned their waters into blood,
and caused their fish to die.
30 Their land swarmed with frogs,
even in the chambers of their
kings.
31 He spoke, and there came swarms of
flies,
and gnats throughout their
country.
32 He gave them hail for rain,
and lightning that flashed through
their land.
33 He struck their vines and fig trees,
and shattered the trees of their
country.
34 He spoke, and the locusts came,
and young locusts without
number;
35 they devoured all the vegetation in
their land,
and ate up the fruit of their
ground.
36 He struck down all the firstborn in
their land,
the first issue of all their strength.

37 Then he brought Israel[z] out with
silver and gold,
and there was no one among their
tribes who stumbled.
38 Egypt was glad when they departed,
for dread of them had fallen
upon it.
39 He spread a cloud for a covering,
and fire to give light by night.
40 They asked, and he brought quails,
and gave them food from heaven
in abundance.
41 He opened the rock, and water
gushed out;
it flowed through the desert like a
river.
42 For he remembered his holy
promise,
and Abraham, his servant.

43 So he brought his people out
with joy,
his chosen ones with singing.
44 He gave them the lands of the
nations,
and they took possession of the
wealth of the peoples,
45 that they might keep his statutes
and observe his laws.
Praise the LORD!

Psalm 106

A Confession of Israel's Sins

1 Praise the LORD!
O give thanks to the LORD, for he
is good;
for his steadfast love endures
forever.
2 Who can utter the mighty doings of
the LORD,
or declare all his praise?
3 Happy are those who observe
justice,
who do righteousness at all times.

4 Remember me, O LORD, when you
show favor to your people;
help me when you deliver them;
5 that I may see the prosperity of your
chosen ones,
that I may rejoice in the gladness
of your nation,
that I may glory in your heritage.

6 Both we and our ancestors have
sinned;
we have committed iniquity, have
done wickedly.
7 Our ancestors, when they were in
Egypt,
did not consider your wonderful
works;
they did not remember the
abundance of your steadfast
love,
but rebelled against the Most
High[a] at the Red Sea.[b]
8 Yet he saved them for his name's
sake,
so that he might make known his
mighty power.
9 He rebuked the Red Sea,[b] and it
became dry;

y Cn Compare Gk Syr: Heb *they did not rebel*
z Heb *them*   a Cn Compare 78.17, 56: Heb
rebelled at the sea   b Or *Sea of Reeds*

he led them through the deep as
  through a desert.
10 So he saved them from the hand of
  the foe,
  and delivered them from the hand
  of the enemy.
11 The waters covered their adversaries;
  not one of them was left.
12 Then they believed his words;
  they sang his praise.

13 But they soon forgot his works;
  they did not wait for his counsel.
14 But they had a wanton craving in
  the wilderness,
  and put God to the test in the
  desert;
15 he gave them what they asked,
  but sent a wasting disease among
  them.

16 They were jealous of Moses in
  the camp,
  and of Aaron, the holy one of
  the LORD.
17 The earth opened and swallowed
  up Dathan,
  and covered the faction of
  Abiram.
18 Fire also broke out in their
  company;
  the flame burned up the wicked.

19 They made a calf at Horeb
  and worshiped a cast image.
20 They exchanged the glory of God*c*
  for the image of an ox that eats
  grass.
21 They forgot God, their Savior,
  who had done great things in
  Egypt,
22 wondrous works in the land of
  Ham,
  and awesome deeds by the
  Red Sea.*d*
23 Therefore he said he would destroy
  them—
  had not Moses, his chosen one,
  stood in the breach before him,
  to turn away his wrath from
  destroying them.

24 Then they despised the pleasant
  land,
  having no faith in his promise.
25 They grumbled in their tents,
  and did not obey the voice of
  the LORD.

26 Therefore he raised his hand and
  swore to them
  that he would make them fall in
  the wilderness,
27 and would disperse*e* their
  descendants among the
  nations,
  scattering them over the lands.

28 Then they attached themselves to the
  Baal of Peor,
  and ate sacrifices offered to
  the dead;
29 they provoked the LORD to anger
  with their deeds,
  and a plague broke out among
  them.
30 Then Phinehas stood up and
  interceded,
  and the plague was stopped.
31 And that has been reckoned to him
  as righteousness
  from generation to generation
  forever.

32 They angered the LORD*f* at the
  waters of Meribah,
  and it went ill with Moses on
  their account;
33 for they made his spirit bitter,
  and he spoke words that were
  rash.

34 They did not destroy the peoples,
  as the LORD commanded them,
35 but they mingled with the nations
  and learned to do as they did.
36 They served their idols,
  which became a snare to them.
37 They sacrificed their sons
  and their daughters to the
  demons;
38 they poured out innocent blood,
  the blood of their sons and
  daughters,
  whom they sacrificed to the idols of
  Canaan;
  and the land was polluted with
  blood.
39 Thus they became unclean by their
  acts,
  and prostituted themselves in their
  doings.

c Compare Gk Mss: Heb *exchanged their glory*
d Or *Sea of Reeds*   *e* Syr Compare Ezek 20.23:
Heb *cause to fall*   *f* Heb *him*

40 Then the anger of the LORD was
    kindled against his people,
    and he abhorred his heritage;
41 he gave them into the hand of the
    nations,
    so that those who hated them
    ruled over them.
42 Their enemies oppressed them,
    and they were brought into
    subjection under their power.
43 Many times he delivered them,
    but they were rebellious in their
    purposes,
    and were brought low through
    their iniquity.
44 Nevertheless he regarded their
    distress
    when he heard their cry.
45 For their sake he remembered his
    covenant,
    and showed compassion according
    to the abundance of his
    steadfast love.
46 He caused them to be pitied
    by all who held them captive.

47 Save us, O LORD our God,
    and gather us from among the
    nations,
    that we may give thanks to your
    holy name
    and glory in your praise.

48 Blessed be the LORD, the God of
    Israel,
    from everlasting to everlasting.
    And let all the people say, "Amen."
    Praise the LORD!

BOOK V

(Psalms 107–150)

Psalm 107

*Thanksgiving for Deliverance from Many
Troubles*

1 O give thanks to the LORD, for he is
    good;
    for his steadfast love endures
    forever.
2 Let the redeemed of the LORD say so,
    those he redeemed from trouble
3 and gathered in from the lands,
    from the east and from the west,
    from the north and from the
    south. *g*

4 Some wandered in desert wastes,
    finding no way to an inhabited
    town;
5 hungry and thirsty,
    their soul fainted within them.
6 Then they cried to the LORD in their
    trouble,
    and he delivered them from their
    distress;
7 he led them by a straight way,
    until they reached an inhabited
    town.
8 Let them thank the LORD for his
    steadfast love,
    for his wonderful works to
    humankind.
9 For he satisfies the thirsty,
    and the hungry he fills with good
    things.

10 Some sat in darkness and in gloom,
    prisoners in misery and in irons,
11 for they had rebelled against the
    words of God,
    and spurned the counsel of the
    Most High.
12 Their hearts were bowed down with
    hard labor;
    they fell down, with no one
    to help.
13 Then they cried to the LORD in their
    trouble,
    and he saved them from their
    distress;
14 he brought them out of darkness
    and gloom,
    and broke their bonds asunder.
15 Let them thank the LORD for his
    steadfast love,
    for his wonderful works to
    humankind.
16 For he shatters the doors of bronze,
    and cuts in two the bars of iron.

17 Some were sick*h* through their
    sinful ways,
    and because of their iniquities
    endured affliction;
18 they loathed any kind of food,
    and they drew near to the gates of
    death.
19 Then they cried to the LORD in their
    trouble,
    and he saved them from their
    distress;

g Cn: Heb *sea*   *h* Cn: Heb *fools*

20 he sent out his word and healed
them,
   and delivered them from
   destruction.
21 Let them thank the LORD for his
steadfast love,
   for his wonderful works to
   humankind.
22 And let them offer thanksgiving
sacrifices,
   and tell of his deeds with songs of
   joy.

23 Some went down to the sea in ships,
   doing business on the mighty
   waters;
24 they saw the deeds of the LORD,
   his wondrous works in the deep.
25 For he commanded and raised the
stormy wind,
   which lifted up the waves of
   the sea.
26 They mounted up to heaven, they
went down to the depths;
   their courage melted away in their
   calamity;
27 they reeled and staggered like
drunkards,
   and were at their wits' end.
28 Then they cried to the LORD in their
trouble,
   and he brought them out from
   their distress;
29 he made the storm be still,
   and the waves of the sea were
   hushed.
30 Then they were glad because they
had quiet,
   and he brought them to their
   desired haven.
31 Let them thank the LORD for his
steadfast love,
   for his wonderful works to
   humankind.
32 Let them extol him in the
congregation of the people,
   and praise him in the assembly of
   the elders.

33 He turns rivers into a desert,
   springs of water into thirsty
   ground,
34 a fruitful land into a salty waste,
   because of the wickedness of its
   inhabitants.
35 He turns a desert into pools of
water,

a parched land into springs of
   water.
36 And there he lets the hungry live,
   and they establish a town to
   live in;
37 they sow fields, and plant vineyards,
   and get a fruitful yield.
38 By his blessing they multiply greatly,
   and he does not let their cattle
   decrease.

39 When they are diminished and
brought low
   through oppression, trouble,
   and sorrow,
40 he pours contempt on princes
   and makes them wander in
   trackless wastes;
41 but he raises up the needy out of
distress,
   and makes their families like
   flocks.
42 The upright see it and are glad;
   and all wickedness stops its
   mouth.
43 Let those who are wise give heed to
these things,
   and consider the steadfast love of
   the LORD.

Psalm 108

Praise and Prayer for Victory

A Song. A Psalm of David.

1 My heart is steadfast, O God, my
heart is steadfast;[i]
   I will sing and make melody.
   Awake, my soul![j]
2 Awake, O harp and lyre!
   I will awake the dawn.
3 I will give thanks to you, O LORD,
among the peoples,
   and I will sing praises to you
   among the nations.
4 For your steadfast love is higher
than the heavens,
   and your faithfulness reaches to
   the clouds.

5 Be exalted, O God, above the
heavens,
   and let your glory be over all the
   earth.
6 Give victory with your right hand,
   and answer me,

i Heb Mss Gk Syr: MT lacks *my heart is steadfast*
j Compare 57.8: Heb *also my soul*

so that those whom you love may
be rescued.

7 God has promised in his
sanctuary:[k]
"With exultation I will divide up
Shechem,
and portion out the Vale of
Succoth.
8 Gilead is mine; Manasseh is mine;
Ephraim is my helmet;
Judah is my scepter.
9 Moab is my washbasin;

on Edom I hurl my shoe;
over Philistia I shout in triumph."

10 Who will bring me to the fortified
city?
Who will lead me to Edom?
11 Have you not rejected us, O God?
You do not go out, O God, with
our armies.
12 O grant us help against the foe,
for human help is worthless.

k Or by his holiness

Sing Your Prayers

FRIDAY

Scripture Reading
for Today:
Psalm 108.1–6

Verses for Today:
Psalm 108.1–2

Have you ever noticed that time seems to pass more quickly—and enjoyably!—on the family vacation if you sing together with your kids during the long car ride? Or that hikers reach the last bend in the long trail with more ease when they sing a rousing hiking tune? Singing can lift the heart and spirits when the journey gets tough and zeal for the final stretch of the road flags, and many songs have been written to do just that.

Like tired vacationers and weary hikers know, singing on life's pilgrimage can sustain you and give you new heart. Psalms and hymns can renew your energy for the way ahead, and help you to "lift your drooping hands and strengthen your weak knees" (Hebrews 12.12). They also help keep your vision focused on your destination. An Advent responsory in the Liturgy of the Hours describes this well: "We are Christ's pilgrim people, journeying until we reach our homeland, singing on the way as we eagerly expect the fulfillment of our hope, for if one hopes, even though his tongue is still, he is singing always in his heart."

While most of us know that singing hymns and psalms at Mass brings us more consciously into the presence of God and aids our worship, probably only a few of us make a practice of singing in our own times of personal prayer. When I began to sing some of my favorite songs during my morning prayer at home or while driving to work, my spiritual life was revived. Why not try it yourself?

Choose hymns and songs whose words reflect and express to the Lord what is in your heart, as well as ones that help you to praise him. And don't worry if you can't carry a tune—you are singing for God's ears only, and he loves to listen to you! As Saint Augustine wrote, "He who sings prays twice."

—JEANNE KUN

Go to page 750 for your next devotional reading.

13 With God we shall do valiantly;
   it is he who will tread down
   our foes.

Psalm 109

Prayer for Vindication and Vengeance

To the leader. Of David. A Psalm.

1 Do not be silent, O God of my
   praise.
2 For wicked and deceitful mouths are
   opened against me,
   speaking against me with lying
   tongues.
3 They beset me with words of hate,
   and attack me without cause.
4 In return for my love they
   accuse me,
   even while I make prayer for
   them.[l]
5 So they reward me evil for good,
   and hatred for my love.

6 They say,[m] "Appoint a wicked man
   against him;
   let an accuser stand on his right.
7 When he is tried, let him be found
   guilty;
   let his prayer be counted as sin.
8 May his days be few;
   may another seize his position.
9 May his children be orphans,
   and his wife a widow.
10 May his children wander about
   and beg;
   may they be driven out of[n] the
   ruins they inhabit.
11 May the creditor seize all that
   he has;
   may strangers plunder the fruits of
   his toil.
12 May there be no one to do him a
   kindness,
   nor anyone to pity his orphaned
   children.
13 May his posterity be cut off;
   may his name be blotted out in
   the second generation.
14 May the iniquity of his father[o] be
   remembered before the LORD,
   and do not let the sin of his
   mother be blotted out.
15 Let them be before the LORD
   continually,
   and may his[p] memory be cut off
   from the earth.

16 For he did not remember to show
   kindness,
   but pursued the poor and needy
   and the brokenhearted to their
   death.
17 He loved to curse; let curses come
   on him.
   He did not like blessing; may it
   be far from him.
18 He clothed himself with cursing as
   his coat,
   may it soak into his body like
   water,
   like oil into his bones.
19 May it be like a garment that he
   wraps around himself,
   like a belt that he wears every day."

20 May that be the reward of my
   accusers from the LORD,
   of those who speak evil against
   my life.
21 But you, O LORD my Lord,
   act on my behalf for your name's
   sake;
   because your steadfast love is
   good, deliver me.
22 For I am poor and needy,
   and my heart is pierced
   within me.
23 I am gone like a shadow at evening;
   I am shaken off like a locust.
24 My knees are weak through fasting;
   my body has become gaunt.
25 I am an object of scorn to my
   accusers;
   when they see me, they shake
   their heads.

26 Help me, O LORD my God!
   Save me according to your
   steadfast love.
27 Let them know that this is your
   hand;
   you, O LORD, have done it.
28 Let them curse, but you will bless.
   Let my assailants be put to
   shame;[q] may your servant be
   glad.
29 May my accusers be clothed with
   dishonor;
   may they be wrapped in their own
   shame as in a mantle.

l Syr: Heb *I prayer*   *m* Heb lacks *They say*
n Gk: Heb *and seek*   *o* Cn: Heb *fathers*
p Gk: Heb *their*   *q* Gk: Heb *They have risen up
and have been put to shame*

30 With my mouth I will give great
        thanks to the LORD;
    I will praise him in the midst of
        the throng.
31 For he stands at the right hand of
        the needy,
    to save them from those who
        would condemn them to
        death.

Psalm 110

Assurance of Victory for God's Priest-King

Of David. A Psalm.

1 The LORD says to my lord,
    "Sit at my right hand
  until I make your enemies your
        footstool."

2 The LORD sends out from Zion
        your mighty scepter.
    Rule in the midst of your foes.
3 Your people will offer themselves
        willingly
    on the day you lead your forces
        on the holy mountains.[r]
  From the womb of the morning,
    like dew, your youth[s] will come
        to you.
4 The LORD has sworn and will not
        change his mind,
    "You are a priest forever
        according to the order of
        Melchizedek."[t]

5 The Lord is at your right hand;
    he will shatter kings on the day of
        his wrath.
6 He will execute judgment among the
        nations,
    filling them with corpses;
  he will shatter heads
    over the wide earth.
7 He will drink from the stream by
        the path;
    therefore he will lift up his head.

Psalm 111

Praise for God's Wonderful Works

1 Praise the LORD!
  I will give thanks to the LORD with
        my whole heart,
    in the company of the upright, in
        the congregation.
2 Great are the works of the LORD,

studied by all who delight
        in them.
3 Full of honor and majesty is
        his work,
    and his righteousness endures
        forever.
4 He has gained renown by his
        wonderful deeds;
    the LORD is gracious and merciful.
5 He provides food for those who fear
        him;
    he is ever mindful of his
        covenant.
6 He has shown his people the power
        of his works,
    in giving them the heritage of the
        nations.
7 The works of his hands are faithful
        and just;
    all his precepts are trustworthy.
8 They are established forever and
        ever,
    to be performed with faithfulness
        and uprightness.
9 He sent redemption to his people;
    he has commanded his covenant
        forever.
  Holy and awesome is his name.
10 The fear of the LORD is the beginning
        of wisdom;
    all those who practice it[u] have a
        good understanding.
    His praise endures forever.

Psalm 112

Blessings of the Righteous

1 Praise the LORD!
  Happy are those who fear
        the LORD,
    who greatly delight in his
        commandments.
2 Their descendants will be mighty in
        the land;
    the generation of the upright will
        be blessed.
3 Wealth and riches are in their
        houses,
    and their righteousness endures
        forever.
4 They rise in the darkness as a light
        for the upright;
    they are gracious, merciful, and
        righteous.

r Another reading is *in holy splendor*   s Cn: Heb
the dew of your youth   t Or *forever, a rightful king
by my edict*   u Gk Syr: Heb *them*

Ruth

Her Name Means "Friendship"

Her Character: *Generous, loyal, and loving, she was strong and serene, able to take unusual risks, dealing actively with the consequences.*
Her Sorrow: *To have lost her husband, homeland, and family.*
Her Joy: *To discover firsthand the generous, loyal, and loving nature of God, as he provided her with a husband, a son, and a home to call her own.*

Read Ruth 2—4

It was harvest time in Israel when Boaz first laid eyes on the young woman. The sun painted the fields a tawny gold as workers swung their sickles in even rhythms through the standing grain. According to Israel's law and custom, the poor had the right to gather whatever the harvesters missed.

Ruth toiled quickly and efficiently, he noticed, stuffing grain into a coarse sack slung across her shoulder. Strands of black hair escaped her head covering, softly framing olive-colored skin, still smooth despite the sun. She rested, but only for a moment, her eyes wary for any sign of trouble from the men working the fields. Gleaning was rough work and dangerous, especially for an attractive young foreigner.

Everyone in Bethlehem had been talking about his relative Naomi and her unexpected return. Ruth, he knew, had come with her. He had heard of their shared tragedy and the extraordinary loyalty the younger had displayed toward the older. A man could wish for such a friend as Ruth had been to Naomi.

One evening he and the other men were winnowing barley on the threshing floor. After he had finished eating and drinking, he lay down under the stars at the far end of the grain pile. With so many men to guard the harvest, robbers wouldn't dare approach. But in the middle of the night he woke with a start, realizing that someone had dared. To his surprise, he discovered the intruder was neither a robber nor a man, but a woman, who lay at his feet, and she, too, was awake.

"I am Ruth, your servant," she whispered, "spread your cloak over your servant, for you are next-of-kin" (3.9).

He could hardly believe her words. The young woman had risked her reputation by lying down with him. Quickly he covered her, saying, "May you be blessed by the LORD, my daughter; this last instance of your loyalty is better than the first; you have not gone after young men, whether poor or rich. And now, my daughter, do not be afraid, I will do for you all that you ask" (verses 10—11).

Soon after, Boaz and Ruth were married, and God blessed them with a son, whom they named Obed.

Pulling Ruth close to him, Boaz watched one day as Naomi held her grandson to her breast. Surrounded by the other women of Bethlehem, she looked young again, more like the woman he remembered when her husband, Elimelech, had been alive. He watched as she closed her eyes, listening to the women's prayer regarding the child: "Blessed be the LORD, who has not left you this day without next-of-kin; and may his name be renowned in Israel! He shall be to you a restorer of life and a nourisher of your old age; for your daughter-in-law who loves you, who is more to you than seven sons, has borne him" (4.14–15).

Yes, he thought, his Ruth was better than seven sons. Boaz felt strong and young again. But even he couldn't have realized how greatly God had blessed him in the person of Ruth. For their son Obed would be the father of Jesse and Jesse, the father of David. In addition to being King David's great-grandparents, both Boaz and Ruth are mentioned in the genealogy of Jesus Christ.

Praying With Ruth

"Blessed be the LORD, who has not left you this day without next-of-kin; and may his name be renowned in Israel! He shall be to you a restorer of life and a nourisher of your old age; for your daughter-in-law who loves you, who is more to you than seven sons, has borne him."—Ruth 4:14–15

Praise God: *That he provides for those who have no one to provide for them.*

Offer Thanks: *For the way God has used other women to provide for you.*

Confess: *Any tendency to compete with other women.*

Ask God: *To help you appreciate your own mother and mother-in-law and to give you a vision for the power of two women, linked by love and faith.*

Lift Your Heart

It's easy to assume that the important women in our lives know how much we cherish them. But Mother's Day cards and friendship cards, nice as they are to get and give, don't really do the trick. We also need to verbalize our love sincerely and regularly. Don't wait until Mother's Day to treat your mother, mother-in-law, or an older friend to tea or a leisurely lunch. Tell her just how much you care about her. (Make sure you take time beforehand to think about all her wonderful qualities. Take notes so that you can be specific.) You might even buy a small blank book and record all the ways she's blessed you. Decorate each page with colorful stickers or stencils. Package it with scented soap and bath salts and give it as a keepsake she can treasure.

Father, I thank you for the women who have played such an important role in my life. Please bless each one in a special way today and help me find ways to express to them my love and gratitude.

Go to page 759 for your next devotional reading.

5 It is well with those who deal
      generously and lend,
   who conduct their affairs with
      justice.
6 For the righteous will never
      be moved;
   they will be remembered forever.
7 They are not afraid of evil tidings;
   their hearts are firm, secure in the
      LORD.
8 Their hearts are steady, they will not
      be afraid;
   in the end they will look in
      triumph on their foes.
9 They have distributed freely, they
      have given to the poor;
   their righteousness endures
      forever;
   their horn is exalted in honor.
10 The wicked see it and are angry;
   they gnash their teeth and melt
      away;
   the desire of the wicked comes
      to nothing.

Psalm 113

God the Helper of the Needy

1 Praise the LORD!
   Praise, O servants of the LORD;
      praise the name of the LORD.

2 Blessed be the name of the LORD
      from this time on and
      forevermore.
3 From the rising of the sun to its
      setting
   the name of the LORD is to be
      praised.
4 The LORD is high above all nations,
   and his glory above the heavens.

5 Who is like the LORD our God,
   who is seated on high,
6 who looks far down
   on the heavens and the earth?
7 He raises the poor from the dust,
   and lifts the needy from the ash
      heap,
8 to make them sit with princes,
   with the princes of his people.
9 He gives the barren woman a home,
   making her the joyous mother of
      children.
   Praise the LORD!

Psalm 114

God's Wonders at the Exodus

1 When Israel went out from Egypt,
   the house of Jacob from a people
      of strange language,
2 Judah became God's[v] sanctuary,
   Israel his dominion.

3 The sea looked and fled;
   Jordan turned back.
4 The mountains skipped like rams,
   the hills like lambs.

5 Why is it, O sea, that you flee?
   O Jordan, that you turn back?
6 O mountains, that you skip like
      rams?
   O hills, like lambs?

7 Tremble, O earth, at the presence of
      the LORD,
   at the presence of the God of
      Jacob,
8 who turns the rock into a pool of
      water,
   the flint into a spring of water.

Psalm 115

The Impotence of Idols and the Greatness
of God

1 Not to us, O LORD, not to us, but to
      your name give glory,
   for the sake of your steadfast love
      and your faithfulness.
2 Why should the nations say,
   "Where is their God?"

3 Our God is in the heavens;
   he does whatever he pleases.
4 Their idols are silver and gold,
   the work of human hands.
5 They have mouths, but do not
      speak;
   eyes, but do not see.
6 They have ears, but do not hear;
   noses, but do not smell.
7 They have hands, but do not feel;
   feet, but do not walk;
   they make no sound in their
      throats.
8 Those who make them are like
      them;
   so are all who trust in them.

v Heb *his*

9 O Israel, trust in the LORD!
  He is their help and their shield.
10 O house of Aaron, trust in the LORD!
  He is their help and their shield.
11 You who fear the LORD, trust in
    the LORD!
  He is their help and their shield.

12 The LORD has been mindful of us; he
    will bless us;
  he will bless the house of Israel;
  he will bless the house of Aaron;
13 he will bless those who fear the
    LORD,
  both small and great.

14 May the LORD give you increase,
  both you and your children.
15 May you be blessed by the LORD,
  who made heaven and earth.

16 The heavens are the LORD's heavens,
  but the earth he has given to
    human beings.
17 The dead do not praise the LORD,
  nor do any that go down into
    silence.
18 But we will bless the LORD
  from this time on and
    forevermore.
Praise the LORD!

Psalm 116

Thanksgiving for Recovery from Illness

1 I love the LORD, because he has
    heard
  my voice and my supplications.
2 Because he inclined his ear to me,
  therefore I will call on him as
    long as I live.
3 The snares of death encompassed
    me;
  the pangs of Sheol laid hold
    on me;
  I suffered distress and anguish.
4 Then I called on the name of
    the LORD:
  "O LORD, I pray, save my life!"

5 Gracious is the LORD, and righteous;
  our God is merciful.
6 The LORD protects the simple;
  when I was brought low, he saved
    me.
7 Return, O my soul, to your rest,
  for the LORD has dealt bountifully
    with you.

8 For you have delivered my soul
    from death,
  my eyes from tears,
  my feet from stumbling.
9 I walk before the LORD
  in the land of the living.
10 I kept my faith, even when I said,
  "I am greatly afflicted";
11 I said in my consternation,
  "Everyone is a liar."

12 What shall I return to the LORD
  for all his bounty to me?
13 I will lift up the cup of salvation
  and call on the name of the LORD,
14 I will pay my vows to the LORD
  in the presence of all his people.
15 Precious in the sight of the LORD
  is the death of his faithful ones.
16 O LORD, I am your servant;
  I am your servant, the child of
    your serving girl.
  You have loosed my bonds.
17 I will offer to you a thanksgiving
    sacrifice
  and call on the name of the LORD.
18 I will pay my vows to the LORD
  in the presence of all his people,
19 in the courts of the house of
    the LORD,
  in your midst, O Jerusalem.
Praise the LORD!

Psalm 117

Universal Call to Worship

1 Praise the LORD, all you nations!
  Extol him, all you peoples!
2 For great is his steadfast love toward
    us,
  and the faithfulness of the LORD
    endures forever.
Praise the LORD!

Psalm 118

A Song of Victory

1 O give thanks to the LORD, for he is
    good;
  his steadfast love endures forever!

2 Let Israel say,
  "His steadfast love endures
    forever."
3 Let the house of Aaron say,
  "His steadfast love endures
    forever."
4 Let those who fear the LORD say,

"His steadfast love endures
   forever."

5 Out of my distress I called on the
      LORD;
   the LORD answered me and set me
      in a broad place.
6 With the LORD on my side I do
      not fear.
   What can mortals do to me?
7 The LORD is on my side to help me;
   I shall look in triumph on those
      who hate me.
8 It is better to take refuge in the LORD
   than to put confidence in mortals.
9 It is better to take refuge in the LORD
   than to put confidence in princes.

10 All nations surrounded me;
   in the name of the LORD I cut
      them off!
11 They surrounded me, surrounded
      me on every side;
   in the name of the LORD I cut
      them off!
12 They surrounded me like bees;
   they blazed[w] like a fire of thorns;
   in the name of the LORD I cut
      them off!
13 I was pushed hard,[x] so that I was
      falling,
   but the LORD helped me.
14 The LORD is my strength and my
      might;
   he has become my salvation.

15 There are glad songs of victory in
      the tents of the righteous:
   "The right hand of the LORD does
      valiantly;
16   the right hand of the LORD is
      exalted;
   the right hand of the LORD does
      valiantly."
17 I shall not die, but I shall live,
   and recount the deeds of the LORD.
18 The LORD has punished me severely,
   but he did not give me over to
      death.

19 Open to me the gates of
      righteousness,
   that I may enter through them
   and give thanks to the LORD.

20 This is the gate of the LORD;
   the righteous shall enter
      through it.

21 I thank you that you have answered
      me
   and have become my salvation.
22 The stone that the builders rejected
   has become the chief cornerstone.
23 This is the LORD's doing;
   it is marvelous in our eyes.
24 This is the day that the LORD has
      made;
   let us rejoice and be glad in it.[y]
25 Save us, we beseech you, O LORD!
   O LORD, we beseech you, give us
      success!

26 Blessed is the one who comes in the
      name of the LORD.[z]
   We bless you from the house of
      the LORD.
27 The LORD is God,
   and he has given us light.
   Bind the festal procession with
      branches,
   up to the horns of the altar.[a]

28 You are my God, and I will give
      thanks to you;
   you are my God, I will extol you.

29 O give thanks to the LORD, for he is
      good,
   for his steadfast love endures
      forever.

Psalm 119

The Glories of God's Law

1 Happy are those whose way is
      blameless,
   who walk in the law of the LORD.
2 Happy are those who keep his
      decrees,
   who seek him with their whole
      heart,
3 who also do no wrong,
   but walk in his ways.
4 You have commanded your precepts
   to be kept diligently.
5 O that my ways may be steadfast
   in keeping your statutes!
6 Then I shall not be put to shame,
   having my eyes fixed on all your
      commandments.

---

w Gk: Heb *were extinguished*   *x* Gk Syr Jerome:
Heb *You pushed me hard*   *y* Or *in him*   *z* Or
Blessed in the name of the LORD *is the one who comes*
a Meaning of Heb uncertain

7 I will praise you with an upright
   heart,
     when I learn your righteous
     ordinances.
8 I will observe your statutes;
   do not utterly forsake me.

9 How can young people keep their
   way pure?
     By guarding it according to your
     word.
10 With my whole heart I seek you;
   do not let me stray from your
   commandments.
11 I treasure your word in my heart,
   so that I may not sin against you.
12 Blessed are you, O LORD;
   teach me your statutes.
13 With my lips I declare
   all the ordinances of your mouth.
14 I delight in the way of your decrees
   as much as in all riches.
15 I will meditate on your precepts,
   and fix my eyes on your ways.
16 I will delight in your statutes;
   I will not forget your word.

17 Deal bountifully with your servant,
   so that I may live and observe
   your word.
18 Open my eyes, so that I may behold
   wondrous things out of your law.
19 I live as an alien in the land;
   do not hide your commandments
   from me.
20 My soul is consumed with longing
   for your ordinances at all times.
21 You rebuke the insolent, accursed
   ones,
     who wander from your
     commandments;
22 take away from me their scorn and
   contempt,
     for I have kept your decrees.
23 Even though princes sit plotting
   against me,
     your servant will meditate on your
     statutes.
24 Your decrees are my delight,
   they are my counselors.

25 My soul clings to the dust;
   revive me according to your word.
26 When I told of my ways, you
   answered me;
     teach me your statutes.
27 Make me understand the way of
   your precepts,

and I will meditate on your
wondrous works.
28 My soul melts away for sorrow;
   strengthen me according to your
   word.
29 Put false ways far from me;
   and graciously teach me your law.
30 I have chosen the way of
   faithfulness;
     I set your ordinances before me.
31 I cling to your decrees, O LORD;
   let me not be put to shame.
32 I run the way of your
   commandments,
     for you enlarge my understanding.

33 Teach me, O LORD, the way of your
   statutes,
     and I will observe it to the end.
34 Give me understanding, that I may
   keep your law
     and observe it with my whole
     heart.
35 Lead me in the path of your
   commandments,
     for I delight in it.
36 Turn my heart to your decrees,
   and not to selfish gain.
37 Turn my eyes from looking at
   vanities;
     give me life in your ways.
38 Confirm to your servant your
   promise,
     which is for those who fear you.
39 Turn away the disgrace that I dread,
   for your ordinances are good.
40 See, I have longed for your precepts;
   in your righteousness give me life.

41 Let your steadfast love come to me,
   O LORD,
     your salvation according to your
     promise.
42 Then I shall have an answer for
   those who taunt me,
     for I trust in your word.
43 Do not take the word of truth
   utterly out of my mouth,
     for my hope is in your
     ordinances.
44 I will keep your law continually,
   forever and ever.
45 I shall walk at liberty,
   for I have sought your precepts.
46 I will also speak of your decrees
   before kings,
     and shall not be put to shame;

47 I find my delight in your
     commandments,
   because I love them.
48 I revere your commandments, which
     I love,
   and I will meditate on your
     statutes.

49 Remember your word to your
     servant,
   in which you have made
     me hope.
50 This is my comfort in my distress,
   that your promise gives me life.
51 The arrogant utterly deride me,
   but I do not turn away from
     your law.
52 When I think of your ordinances
     from of old,
   I take comfort, O LORD.
53 Hot indignation seizes me because
     of the wicked,
   those who forsake your law.
54 Your statutes have been my songs
   wherever I make my home.
55 I remember your name in the night,
     O LORD,
   and keep your law.
56 This blessing has fallen to me,
   for I have kept your precepts.

57 The LORD is my portion;
   I promise to keep your words.
58 I implore your favor with all my
     heart;
   be gracious to me according to
     your promise.
59 When I think of your ways,
   I turn my feet to your decrees;
60 I hurry and do not delay
   to keep your commandments.
61 Though the cords of the wicked
     ensnare me,
   I do not forget your law.
62 At midnight I rise to praise you,
   because of your righteous
     ordinances.
63 I am a companion of all who fear
     you,
   of those who keep your precepts.
64 The earth, O LORD, is full of your
     steadfast love;
   teach me your statutes.

65 You have dealt well with your
     servant,
   O LORD, according to your word.

66 Teach me good judgment and
     knowledge,
   for I believe in your
     commandments.
67 Before I was humbled I went astray,
   but now I keep your word.
68 You are good and do good;
   teach me your statutes.
69 The arrogant smear me with lies,
   but with my whole heart I keep
     your precepts.
70 Their hearts are fat and gross,
   but I delight in your law.
71 It is good for me that I was
     humbled,
   so that I might learn your statutes.
72 The law of your mouth is better
     to me
   than thousands of gold and silver
     pieces.

73 Your hands have made and
     fashioned me;
   give me understanding that I may
     learn your commandments.
74 Those who fear you shall see me
     and rejoice,
   because I have hoped in your
     word.
75 I know, O LORD, that your judgments
     are right,
   and that in faithfulness you have
     humbled me.
76 Let your steadfast love become my
     comfort
   according to your promise to your
     servant.
77 Let your mercy come to me, that I
     may live;
   for your law is my delight.
78 Let the arrogant be put to shame,
   because they have subverted me
     with guile;
   as for me, I will meditate on your
     precepts.
79 Let those who fear you turn to me,
   so that they may know your
     decrees.
80 May my heart be blameless in your
     statutes,
   so that I may not be put to
     shame.

81 My soul languishes for your
     salvation;
   I hope in your word.
82 My eyes fail with watching for your
     promise;

I ask, "When will you comfort
  me?"
83 For I have become like a wineskin in
    the smoke,
  yet I have not forgotten your
    statutes.
84 How long must your servant endure?
  When will you judge those who
    persecute me?
85 The arrogant have dug pitfalls
    for me;
  they flout your law.
86 All your commandments are
    enduring;
  I am persecuted without cause;
    help me!
87 They have almost made an end of
    me on earth;
  but I have not forsaken your
    precepts.
88 In your steadfast love spare my life,
  so that I may keep the decrees of
    your mouth.

89 The LORD exists forever;
  your word is firmly fixed in
    heaven.
90 Your faithfulness endures to all
    generations;
  you have established the earth,
    and it stands fast.
91 By your appointment they stand
    today,
  for all things are your servants.
92 If your law had not been my
    delight,
  I would have perished in my
    misery.
93 I will never forget your precepts,
  for by them you have given
    me life.
94 I am yours; save me,
  for I have sought your precepts.
95 The wicked lie in wait to
    destroy me,
  but I consider your decrees.
96 I have seen a limit to all perfection,
  but your commandment is
    exceedingly broad.

97 Oh, how I love your law!
  It is my meditation all day long.
98 Your commandment makes me
    wiser than my enemies,
  for it is always with me.
99 I have more understanding than all
    my teachers,

for your decrees are my
  meditation.
100 I understand more than the aged,
  for I keep your precepts.
101 I hold back my feet from every evil
    way,
  in order to keep your word.
102 I do not turn away from your
    ordinances,
  for you have taught me.
103 How sweet are your words to my
    taste,
  sweeter than honey to my
    mouth!
104 Through your precepts I get
    understanding;
  therefore I hate every false way.

105 Your word is a lamp to my feet
  and a light to my path.
106 I have sworn an oath and
    confirmed it,
  to observe your righteous
    ordinances.
107 I am severely afflicted;
  give me life, O LORD, according to
    your word.
108 Accept my offerings of praise,
    O LORD,
  and teach me your ordinances.
109 I hold my life in my hand
    continually,
  but I do not forget your law.
110 The wicked have laid a snare
    for me,
  but I do not stray from your
    precepts.
111 Your decrees are my heritage
    forever;
  they are the joy of my heart.
112 I incline my heart to perform your
    statutes
  forever, to the end.

113 I hate the double-minded,
  but I love your law.
114 You are my hiding place and my
    shield;
  I hope in your word.
115 Go away from me, you evildoers,
  that I may keep the
    commandments of my God.
116 Uphold me according to your
    promise, that I may live,
  and let me not be put to shame
    in my hope.
117 Hold me up, that I may be safe

and have regard for your statutes
continually.

118 You spurn all who go astray from
your statutes;
for their cunning is in vain.

119 All the wicked of the earth you
count as dross;
therefore I love your decrees.

120 My flesh trembles for fear of you,
and I am afraid of your
judgments.

121 I have done what is just and right;
do not leave me to my
oppressors.

122 Guarantee your servant's well-being;
do not let the godless oppress
me.

123 My eyes fail from watching for your
salvation,
and for the fulfillment of your
righteous promise.

124 Deal with your servant according to
your steadfast love,
and teach me your statutes.

125 I am your servant; give me
understanding,
so that I may know your decrees.

126 It is time for the LORD to act,
for your law has been broken.

127 Truly I love your commandments
more than gold, more than
fine gold.

128 Truly I direct my steps by all your
precepts;*b*
I hate every false way.

129 Your decrees are wonderful;
therefore my soul keeps them.

130 The unfolding of your words gives
light;
it imparts understanding to the
simple.

131 With open mouth I pant,
because I long for your
commandments.

132 Turn to me and be gracious to me,
as is your custom toward those
who love your name.

133 Keep my steps steady according to
your promise,
and never let iniquity have
dominion over me.

134 Redeem me from human
oppression,
that I may keep your precepts.

135 Make your face shine upon your
servant,
and teach me your statutes.

136 My eyes shed streams of tears
because your law is not kept.

137 You are righteous, O LORD,
and your judgments are right.

138 You have appointed your decrees in
righteousness
and in all faithfulness.

139 My zeal consumes me
because my foes forget your
words.

140 Your promise is well tried,
and your servant loves it.

141 I am small and despised,
yet I do not forget your precepts.

142 Your righteousness is an everlasting
righteousness,
and your law is the truth.

143 Trouble and anguish have come
upon me,
but your commandments are my
delight.

144 Your decrees are righteous forever;
give me understanding that I may
live.

145 With my whole heart I cry; answer
me, O LORD.
I will keep your statutes.

146 I cry to you; save me,
that I may observe your decrees.

147 I rise before dawn and cry for help;
I put my hope in your words.

148 My eyes are awake before each
watch of the night,
that I may meditate on your
promise.

149 In your steadfast love hear my
voice;
O LORD, in your justice preserve
my life.

150 Those who persecute me with evil
purpose draw near;
they are far from your law.

151 Yet you are near, O LORD,
and all your commandments
are true.

152 Long ago I learned from your
decrees
that you have established them
forever.

153 Look on my misery and rescue me,
for I do not forget your law.

154 Plead my cause and redeem me;

b Gk Jerome: Meaning of Heb uncertain

give me life according to your
   promise.
¹⁵⁵ Salvation is far from the wicked,
   for they do not seek your
   statutes.
¹⁵⁶ Great is your mercy, O LORD;
   give me life according to your
   justice.
¹⁵⁷ Many are my persecutors and my
   adversaries,
   yet I do not swerve from your
   decrees.
¹⁵⁸ I look at the faithless with disgust,
   because they do not keep your
   commands.
¹⁵⁹ Consider how I love your precepts;
   preserve my life according to your
   steadfast love.
¹⁶⁰ The sum of your word is truth;
   and every one of your righteous
   ordinances endures forever.

¹⁶¹ Princes persecute me without cause,
   but my heart stands in awe of
   your words.
¹⁶² I rejoice at your word
   like one who finds great spoil.
¹⁶³ I hate and abhor falsehood,
   but I love your law.
¹⁶⁴ Seven times a day I praise you
   for your righteous ordinances.
¹⁶⁵ Great peace have those who love
   your law;

nothing can make them stumble.
¹⁶⁶ I hope for your salvation, O LORD,
   and I fulfill your commandments.
¹⁶⁷ My soul keeps your decrees;
   I love them exceedingly.
¹⁶⁸ I keep your precepts and decrees,
   for all my ways are before you.

¹⁶⁹ Let my cry come before you,
   O LORD;
   give me understanding according
   to your word.
¹⁷⁰ Let my supplication come before
   you;
   deliver me according to your
   promise.
¹⁷¹ My lips will pour forth praise,
   because you teach me your
   statutes.
¹⁷² My tongue will sing of your
   promise,
   for all your commandments are
   right.
¹⁷³ Let your hand be ready to help me,
   for I have chosen your precepts.
¹⁷⁴ I long for your salvation, O LORD,
   and your law is my delight.
¹⁷⁵ Let me live that I may praise you,
   and let your ordinances help me.
¹⁷⁶ I have gone astray like a lost sheep;
   seek out your servant,
   for I do not forget your
   commandments.

The Light That Conquers

MONDAY

Scripture Reading
for Today:
Psalm 119.169–176

Verse for Today:
Psalm 119.169

Discernment is that light which dissolves all darkness, dissipates ignorance, and seasons every virtue and virtuous deed. It has a prudence that cannot be deceived, a strength that is invincible, a constancy right up to the end, reaching as it does from heaven to earth, that is, from the knowledge of me to the knowledge of one-self, from love of me to love of one's neighbors.

   Discernment's truly humble prudence evades every devilish and creaturely snare, and with unarmed hand—that is, through suffering—it overcomes the devil and the flesh. By this gentle glorious light the soul sees and rightly despises her own weakness; and by so making a fool of herself she gains mastery of the world, treading it underfoot with her love, scorning it as worthless.

   —*SAINT CATHERINE OF SIENA*

Go to page 762 for your next devotional reading.

Psalm 120

Prayer for Deliverance from Slanderers

A Song of Ascents.

1 In my distress I cry to the LORD,
    that he may answer me:
2 "Deliver me, O LORD,
    from lying lips,
    from a deceitful tongue."

3 What shall be given to you?
    And what more shall be done
        to you,
    you deceitful tongue?
4 A warrior's sharp arrows,
    with glowing coals of the broom
        tree!

5 Woe is me, that I am an alien in
        Meshech,
    that I must live among the tents
        of Kedar.
6 Too long have I had my dwelling
    among those who hate peace.
7 I am for peace;
    but when I speak,
    they are for war.

Psalm 121

Assurance of God's Protection

A Song of Ascents.

1 I lift up my eyes to the hills—
    from where will my help come?
2 My help comes from the LORD,
    who made heaven and earth.

3 He will not let your foot be moved;
    he who keeps you will not
        slumber.
4 He who keeps Israel
    will neither slumber nor sleep.

5 The LORD is your keeper;
    the LORD is your shade at your
        right hand.
6 The sun shall not strike you by day,
    nor the moon by night.

7 The LORD will keep you from all evil;
    he will keep your life.
8 The LORD will keep
    your going out and your
        coming in
    from this time on and
        forevermore.

Psalm 122

Song of Praise and Prayer for Jerusalem

A Song of Ascents. Of David.

1 I was glad when they said to me,
    "Let us go to the house of the
        LORD!"
2 Our feet are standing
    within your gates, O Jerusalem.

3 Jerusalem—built as a city
    that is bound firmly together.
4 To it the tribes go up,
    the tribes of the LORD,
    as was decreed for Israel,
    to give thanks to the name of
        the LORD.
5 For there the thrones for judgment
        were set up,
    the thrones of the house of David.

6 Pray for the peace of Jerusalem:
    "May they prosper who love you.
7 Peace be within your walls,
    and security within your towers."
8 For the sake of my relatives and
        friends
    I will say, "Peace be within you."
9 For the sake of the house of the
        LORD our God,
    I will seek your good.

Psalm 123

Supplication for Mercy

A Song of Ascents.

1 To you I lift up my eyes,
    O you who are enthroned in the
        heavens!
2 As the eyes of servants
    look to the hand of their master,
as the eyes of a maid
    to the hand of her mistress,
so our eyes look to the LORD
        our God,
    until he has mercy upon us.

3 Have mercy upon us, O LORD, have
        mercy upon us,
    for we have had more than
        enough of contempt.
4 Our soul has had more than its fill
    of the scorn of those who are
        at ease,
    of the contempt of the proud.

Psalm 124

Thanksgiving for Israel's Deliverance

A Song of Ascents. Of David.

1 If it had not been the LORD who was
     on our side
   —let Israel now say—
2 if it had not been the LORD who was
     on our side,
   when our enemies attacked us,
3 then they would have swallowed us
     up alive,
   when their anger was kindled
     against us;
4 then the flood would have swept us
     away,
   the torrent would have gone
     over us;
5 then over us would have gone
   the raging waters.

6 Blessed be the LORD,
   who has not given us
   as prey to their teeth.
7 We have escaped like a bird
   from the snare of the fowlers;
   the snare is broken,
   and we have escaped.

8 Our help is in the name of the LORD,
   who made heaven and earth.

Psalm 125

The Security of God's People

A Song of Ascents.

1 Those who trust in the LORD are like
     Mount Zion,
   which cannot be moved, but
     abides forever.
2 As the mountains surround
     Jerusalem,
   so the LORD surrounds his people,
   from this time on and
     forevermore.
3 For the scepter of wickedness shall
     not rest
   on the land allotted to the
     righteous,
   so that the righteous might not
     stretch out
   their hands to do wrong.
4 Do good, O LORD, to those who are
     good,
   and to those who are upright in
     their hearts.

5 But those who turn aside to their
     own crooked ways
   the LORD will lead away with
     evildoers.
   Peace be upon Israel!

Psalm 126

A Harvest of Joy

A Song of Ascents.

1 When the LORD restored the fortunes
     of Zion,*c*
   we were like those who dream.
2 Then our mouth was filled with
     laughter,
   and our tongue with shouts
     of joy;
   then it was said among the nations,
   "The LORD has done great things
     for them."
3 The LORD has done great things
     for us,
   and we rejoiced.

4 Restore our fortunes, O LORD,
   like the watercourses in the
     Negeb.
5 May those who sow in tears
   reap with shouts of joy.
6 Those who go out weeping,
   bearing the seed for sowing,
   shall come home with shouts of joy,
   carrying their sheaves.

Psalm 127

God's Blessings in the Home

A Song of Ascents. Of Solomon.

1 Unless the LORD builds the house,
   those who build it labor in vain.
   Unless the LORD guards the city,
   the guard keeps watch in vain.
2 It is in vain that you rise up early
   and go late to rest,
   eating the bread of anxious toil;
   for he gives sleep to his beloved.*d*

3 Sons are indeed a heritage from
     the LORD,
   the fruit of the womb a reward.
4 Like arrows in the hand of a warrior
   are the sons of one's youth.
5 Happy is the man who has
   his quiver full of them.

c Or brought back those who returned to Zion   *d Or
for he provides for his beloved during sleep*

He shall not be put to shame
  when he speaks with his enemies
    in the gate.

Psalm 128

The Happy Home of the Faithful

A Song of Ascents.

¹ Happy is everyone who fears the
    LORD,
  who walks in his ways.

² You shall eat the fruit of the labor
    of your hands;
  you shall be happy, and it shall
    go well with you.

³ Your wife will be like a fruitful vine
    within your house;
  your children will be like olive
    shoots
  around your table.
⁴ Thus shall the man be blessed
  who fears the LORD.

Harsh Prayers?

When I found out what kinds of things were being sold by pornographers, it frightened me, but it also made me angry. Particularly horrifying to me is the so-called "kiddie pornography."

When I hear about things like this, my first reaction is to cry out, "Lord, crush these evildoers. Destroy them!"

But is that how God wants me to pray? Of course not. When I turn to the Lord in prayer, it is not as judge and executioner but as intercessor. So I began to pray like this: "Have mercy on *us* sinners, O Lord our God. All of us have sinned. Send your Spirit on your faithful so that we can go out and do what we need to do to overcome evil."

It is true that committed Christians must do whatever we can in practical terms to work against evil. Nevertheless, when we come to prayer we are to come humbly, as sinners ourselves, begging God's mercy on all.

I still want to see all the pornographic businesses and abortion clinics closed. I want to see drug abuse and violence cease. I want to see the downfall of dictators who persecute their people and terrorists who take the lives of the innocent.

But how much more powerful it would be if the people who run abortion clinics and pornography businesses had a change of heart because of the prayers of Christians who love them. What a witness it would be if we heard them say publicly, "I am closing my business because I belong to Jesus. I have repented. I don't want to be involved in this wicked business anymore."

I believe that it is God's will that we pray in this way. He doesn't want anyone to be lost. He wants to extend his mercy to all who will call on his name.

—*ANN SHIELDS*

TUESDAY

Scripture Reading
for Today:
Psalm 125

Verse for Today:
Psalm 125.4

Go to page 764 for your next devotional reading.

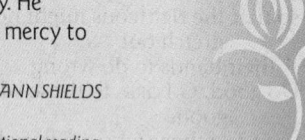

5 The LORD bless you from Zion.
   May you see the prosperity of
      Jerusalem
   all the days of your life.
6 May you see your children's
      children.
   Peace be upon Israel!

Psalm 129

Prayer for the Downfall of Israel's Enemies

A Song of Ascents.

1 "Often have they attacked me from
      my youth"
   —let Israel now say—
2 "often have they attacked me from
      my youth,
   yet they have not prevailed against
      me.
3 The plowers plowed on my back;
   they made their furrows long."
4 The LORD is righteous;
   he has cut the cords of the
      wicked.
5 May all who hate Zion
   be put to shame and turned
      backward.
6 Let them be like the grass on the
      housetops
   that withers before it grows up,
7 with which reapers do not fill their
      hands
   or binders of sheaves their arms,
8 while those who pass by do not say,
   "The blessing of the LORD be upon
      you!
   We bless you in the name of the
      LORD!"

Psalm 130

Waiting for Divine Redemption

A Song of Ascents.

1 Out of the depths I cry to you,
   O LORD.
2   Lord, hear my voice!
   Let your ears be attentive
      to the voice of my supplications!

3 If you, O LORD, should mark
      iniquities,
   Lord, who could stand?
4 But there is forgiveness with you,
   so that you may be revered.

5 I wait for the LORD, my soul waits,
   and in his word I hope;

6 my soul waits for the Lord
   more than those who watch for
      the morning,
   more than those who watch for
      the morning.

7 O Israel, hope in the LORD!
   For with the LORD there is steadfast
      love,
   and with him is great power to
      redeem.
8 It is he who will redeem Israel
   from all its iniquities.

Psalm 131

Song of Quiet Trust

A Song of Ascents. Of David.

1 O LORD, my heart is not lifted up,
   my eyes are not raised too high;
   I do not occupy myself with things
   too great and too marvelous
      for me.
2 But I have calmed and quieted
      my soul,
   like a weaned child with its
      mother;
   my soul is like the weaned child
      that is with me.*e*

3 O Israel, hope in the LORD
   from this time on and
      forevermore.

Psalm 132

The Eternal Dwelling of God in Zion

A Song of Ascents.

1 O LORD, remember in David's favor
   all the hardships he endured;
2 how he swore to the LORD
   and vowed to the Mighty One of
      Jacob,
3 "I will not enter my house
   or get into my bed;
4 I will not give sleep to my eyes
   or slumber to my eyelids,
5 until I find a place for the LORD,
   a dwelling place for the Mighty
      One of Jacob."

6 We heard of it in Ephrathah;
   we found it in the fields of Jaar.
7 "Let us go to his dwelling place;
   let us worship at his footstool."

e Or my soul within me is like a weaned child

8 Rise up, O LORD, and go to your
    resting place,
  you and the ark of your might.
9 Let your priests be clothed with
    righteousness,
  and let your faithful shout for joy.
10 For your servant David's sake
  do not turn away the face of your
    anointed one.

11 The LORD swore to David a sure
    oath
  from which he will not turn
    back:
"One of the sons of your body
  I will set on your throne.
12 If your sons keep my covenant
  and my decrees that I shall teach
    them,
  their sons also, forevermore,
    shall sit on your throne."

13 For the LORD has chosen Zion;
  he has desired it for his
    habitation:
14 "This is my resting place forever;
  here I will reside, for I have
    desired it.
15 I will abundantly bless its
    provisions;
  I will satisfy its poor with bread.
16 Its priests I will clothe with
    salvation,
  and its faithful will shout for
    joy.
17 There I will cause a horn to sprout
    up for David;
  I have prepared a lamp for my
    anointed one.
18 His enemies I will clothe with
    disgrace,
  but on him, his crown will
    gleam."

Waiting

WEDNESDAY

Scripture Reading
for Today:
Psalm 130

Verse for Today:
Psalm 130.5

Human life is full of waiting: people wait for trains, buses and
planes; they stand in queues at shops; they sit nervously in den-
tists' waiting rooms; they wait in anguish for news of a lost loved
one. They wait for the slow process of healing to take its time;
they wait for the birth of a child. Waiting can be very different in
these different situations, according to our attitude. In an age of
"instant" products any delay can be viewed as purely negative, for
"time is money." Yet some things cannot be skimped or hurried;
we have to let them take the time they need. You can't make the
grass grow by pulling it.

    Faith [is sometimes] a breakthrough, the leap towards the invi-
tation of the Lover. But it is not like that all the time. In between
those obviously creative moments, faith can demand long, patient
waiting, when nothing seems to be happening, and this is just as
necessary to growth. We sometimes have to go on doing the
small, ordinary things while we wait for God, as Mary did while
she waited for the birth of Jesus; we have to wait for his moment,
and wait for his work to ripen in ourselves. It may sometimes be
more fruitful in the end if we live with a lingering question, and
grow slowly towards wisdom, than if we find a quick answer
partly dictated by our own desires. The waiting changes us,
schools us, teaches us to know God.

—*MARIA BOULDING*

Go to page 765 for your next devotional reading.

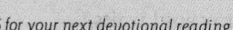

Psalm 133

The Blessedness of Unity

A Song of Ascents.

1 How very good and pleasant it is
   when kindred live together in
      unity!
2 It is like the precious oil on the
      head,
   running down upon the beard,
on the beard of Aaron,
   running down over the collar of
      his robes.

3 It is like the dew of Hermon,
   which falls on the mountains of
      Zion.
For there the LORD ordained his
      blessing,
   life forevermore.

Psalm 134

Praise in the Night

A Song of Ascents.

1 Come, bless the LORD, all you
   servants of the LORD,

A Mother's Liturgy of Hours

Scripture Reading
for Today:
Psalm 134

Verse for Today:
Psalm 134.1

The house is quiet except for the stirring of a baby. Her mother does not need to look at the clock. She knows it is time for the 2:00 A.M. feeding. Rousing herself from the warm cocoon of blankets, she shuffles into the nursery. Deftly, her hands scoop the infant from its crib. Talking in quiet, mother tones, she soothes the child while changing her diaper and replacing the little terry sleeper.

Smells of sweet baby breath and soft skin fill the mother's nostrils as she settles into the living-room rocker to nurse her child. The early-morning feeding isn't always so peaceful. Sometimes the baby is demanding and fussy. But always there are a few quiet moments when the child begins to suckle. The mother rocks gently and gazes out the window into the night.

In monasteries the world over monks and sisters rise early for Matins. As a child, I was instructed never to speak to a priest if he had his head bowed over his prayer book. I might interrupt his praying the Divine Office. It seemed very mysterious to me.

It isn't mysterious anymore. Mothers, too, pray a liturgy of hours. Their Matins are the 2:00 A.M. feedings; the hours, morning prayer and making breakfast and getting children off to school. Vespers are preparing meals and saying grace before them. Compline is bedtime stories and prayers. In homes everywhere, mothers rise together and give of themselves to nourish the new life God has created with them. In the evenings they gather their children and help them close their day with peace and with God.

In middle-class homes, in grass huts, in homeless shelters, in adobe buildings, in ghettos and cities and farmhouses, the mothers pray Matins and Compline with their babes.

—MARY VAN BALEN HOLT

Go to page 772 for your next devotional reading.

who stand by night in the house
of the LORD!
2 Lift up your hands to the holy place,
and bless the LORD.

3 May the LORD, maker of heaven and
earth,
bless you from Zion.

Psalm 135

Praise for God's Goodness and Might

1 Praise the LORD!
Praise the name of the LORD;
give praise, O servants of the LORD,
2 you that stand in the house of
the LORD,
in the courts of the house of
our God.
3 Praise the LORD, for the LORD is good;
sing to his name, for he is
gracious.
4 For the LORD has chosen Jacob for
himself,
Israel as his own possession.

5 For I know that the LORD is great;
our Lord is above all gods.
6 Whatever the LORD pleases he does,
in heaven and on earth,
in the seas and all deeps.
7 He it is who makes the clouds rise
at the end of the earth;
he makes lightnings for the rain
and brings out the wind from his
storehouses.

8 He it was who struck down the
firstborn of Egypt,
both human beings and animals;
9 he sent signs and wonders
into your midst, O Egypt,
against Pharaoh and all his
servants.
10 He struck down many nations
and killed mighty kings—
11 Sihon, king of the Amorites,
and Og, king of Bashan,
and all the kingdoms of Canaan—
12 and gave their land as a heritage,
a heritage to his people Israel.

13 Your name, O LORD, endures forever,
your renown, O LORD, throughout
all ages.
14 For the LORD will vindicate his
people,

and have compassion on his
servants.

15 The idols of the nations are silver
and gold,
the work of human hands.
16 They have mouths, but they do not
speak;
they have eyes, but they do
not see;
17 they have ears, but they do not hear,
and there is no breath in their
mouths.
18 Those who make them
and all who trust them
shall become like them.

19 O house of Israel, bless the LORD!
O house of Aaron, bless the LORD!
20 O house of Levi, bless the LORD!
You that fear the LORD, bless
the LORD!
21 Blessed be the LORD from Zion,
he who resides in Jerusalem.
Praise the LORD!

Psalm 136

God's Work in Creation and in History

1 O give thanks to the LORD, for he is
good,
for his steadfast love endures
forever.
2 O give thanks to the God of gods,
for his steadfast love endures
forever.
3 O give thanks to the Lord of lords,
for his steadfast love endures
forever;

4 who alone does great wonders,
for his steadfast love endures
forever;
5 who by understanding made the
heavens,
for his steadfast love endures
forever;
6 who spread out the earth on the
waters,
for his steadfast love endures
forever;
7 who made the great lights,
for his steadfast love endures
forever;
8 the sun to rule over the day,
for his steadfast love endures
forever;

9 the moon and stars to rule over
the night,
for his steadfast love endures
forever;
10 who struck Egypt through their
firstborn,
for his steadfast love endures
forever;
11 and brought Israel out from among
them,
for his steadfast love endures
forever;
12 with a strong hand and an
outstretched arm,
for his steadfast love endures
forever;
13 who divided the Red Sea *f* in two,
for his steadfast love endures
forever;
14 and made Israel pass through the
midst of it,
for his steadfast love endures
forever;
15 but overthrew Pharaoh and his army
in the Red Sea, *f*
for his steadfast love endures
forever;
16 who led his people through the
wilderness,
for his steadfast love endures
forever;
17 who struck down great kings,
for his steadfast love endures
forever;
18 and killed famous kings,
for his steadfast love endures
forever;
19 Sihon, king of the Amorites,
for his steadfast love endures
forever;
20 and Og, king of Bashan,
for his steadfast love endures
forever;
21 and gave their land as a heritage,
for his steadfast love endures
forever;
22 a heritage to his servant Israel,
for his steadfast love endures
forever.

23 It is he who remembered us in our
low estate,
for his steadfast love endures
forever;
24 and rescued us from our foes,
for his steadfast love endures
forever;

25 who gives food to all flesh,
for his steadfast love endures
forever.

26 O give thanks to the God of heaven,
for his steadfast love endures
forever.

Psalm 137

Lament over the Destruction of Jerusalem

1 By the rivers of Babylon—
there we sat down and there
we wept
when we remembered Zion.
2 On the willows *g* there
we hung up our harps.
3 For there our captors
asked us for songs,
and our tormentors asked for mirth,
saying,
"Sing us one of the songs of
Zion!"

4 How could we sing the LORD's song
in a foreign land?
5 If I forget you, O Jerusalem,
let my right hand wither!
6 Let my tongue cling to the roof of
my mouth,
if I do not remember you,
if I do not set Jerusalem
above my highest joy.

7 Remember, O LORD, against the
Edomites
the day of Jerusalem's fall,
how they said, "Tear it down! Tear
it down!
Down to its foundations!"
8 O daughter Babylon, you
devastator! *h*
Happy shall they be who pay
you back
what you have done to us!
9 Happy shall they be who take your
little ones
and dash them against the rock!

Psalm 138

Thanksgiving and Praise

Of David.

1 I give you thanks, O LORD, with my
whole heart;

*f Or Sea of Reeds   g Or poplars   h Or you who
are devastated*

before the gods I sing your praise;
2 I bow down toward your holy
temple
and give thanks to your name for
your steadfast love and your
faithfulness;
for you have exalted your name
and your word
above everything.[i]
3 On the day I called, you answered
me,
you increased my strength of
soul.[j]

4 All the kings of the earth shall praise
you, O LORD,
for they have heard the words of
your mouth.
5 They shall sing of the ways of the
LORD,
for great is the glory of the LORD.
6 For though the LORD is high, he
regards the lowly;
but the haughty he perceives from
far away.

7 Though I walk in the midst of
trouble,
you preserve me against the wrath
of my enemies;
you stretch out your hand,
and your right hand delivers me.
8 The LORD will fulfill his purpose
for me;
your steadfast love, O LORD,
endures forever.
Do not forsake the work of your
hands.

Psalm 139

The Inescapable God

To the leader. Of David. A Psalm.

1 O LORD, you have searched me and
known me.
2 You know when I sit down and
when I rise up;
you discern my thoughts from
far away.
3 You search out my path and my
lying down,
and are acquainted with all
my ways.
4 Even before a word is on my
tongue,

O LORD, you know it completely.
5 You hem me in, behind and before,
and lay your hand upon me.
6 Such knowledge is too wonderful for
me;
it is so high that I cannot attain it.

7 Where can I go from your spirit?
Or where can I flee from your
presence?
8 If I ascend to heaven, you are there;
if I make my bed in Sheol, you
are there.
9 If I take the wings of the morning
and settle at the farthest limits of
the sea,
10 even there your hand shall lead me,
and your right hand shall hold
me fast.
11 If I say, "Surely the darkness shall
cover me,
and the light around me become
night,"
12 even the darkness is not dark to
you;
the night is as bright as the day,
for darkness is as light to you.

13 For it was you who formed my
inward parts;
you knit me together in my
mother's womb.
14 I praise you, for I am fearfully and
wonderfully made.
Wonderful are your works;
that I know very well.
15 My frame was not hidden from
you,
when I was being made in secret,
intricately woven in the depths of
the earth.
16 Your eyes beheld my unformed
substance.
In your book were written
all the days that were formed
for me,
when none of them as yet existed.
17 How weighty to me are your
thoughts, O God!
How vast is the sum of them!
18 I try to count them—they are more
than the sand;

---

i Cn: Heb *you have exalted your word above all your
name* j Syr Compare Gk Tg: Heb *you made me
arrogant in my soul with strength*

I come to the end[k]—I am still
with you.

19 O that you would kill the wicked,
O God,
and that the bloodthirsty would
depart from me—
20 those who speak of you maliciously,
and lift themselves up against you
for evil![l]
21 Do I not hate those who hate you,
O LORD?
And do I not loathe those who
rise up against you?

22 I hate them with perfect hatred;
I count them my enemies.
23 Search me, O God, and know my
heart;
test me and know my thoughts.
24 See if there is any wicked[m] way
in me,
and lead me in the way
everlasting.[n]

k Or *I awake*   l Cn: Meaning of Heb uncertain
m Heb *hurtful*   n Or *the ancient way.* Compare
Jer 6.16

THE

T R A D I T I O N

Unborn Life

*For it was you who formed my inward parts . . .
My frame was not hidden from you.*

PSALM 139.13, 15

"I'll never know what her first word
would have been . . . whether she would have
looked like me . . . what our relationship
would have been like . . . what she might
have done in her life."

Women who have had abortions and suffer bitter regrets over what might have been
are often caught in a downward spiral of
black despair. *What have I done? There is no
forgiveness for me.* But Scripture says the exact opposite: "The LORD is merciful and gracious . . . He does not deal with us according
to our sins" (Psalm 103.8, 10). Women who
seek forgiveness from the God of unfailing
love will surely find it—and will also find
help to deal with the anguish that is an inescapable fruit of abortion.

This anguish is no small thing, because
abortion is no small thing. The decision, often made hastily and under duress, is irrevocable; there is no way back. Like a rosebud
nipped before it can bloom and display
its beauty, new life has been snuffed out,
and the world has been deprived of . . .
what?

God knows.

From the instant of conception, the child
in the womb is in a relationship with God.
Hidden to everyone else, the child is cherished by its Creator, who lovingly and "wonderfully" fashions it (Psalm 139.13–16). Each
unborn child's death is first and foremost
God's loss.

Like all violations of the fifth commandment, "You shall not murder" (Exodus 20.13),
abortion opposes God's creative action. It
ends one phase of his special relationship
with a human being who is sacred, called
into existence by God as a unique person
made in his image and likeness. The relationship continues, but not in the way God originally intended.

This child should have been born . . .
should have had a chance to grow, to become
aware of God's love, to choose and respond.
Love reciprocated and returned wholeheartedly, love overflowing back to God and to his
people in a life of joyful service—this was
part of God's call to the child.

Human beings grieve over someone they
never got to know. God grieves over someone he knows intimately. What has the
world lost in losing an unborn child? God
sees—and grieves.

Psalm 140

Prayer for Deliverance from Enemies

To the leader. A Psalm of David.

1 Deliver me, O LORD, from evildoers;
   protect me from those who are
      violent,
2 who plan evil things in their minds
   and stir up wars continually.
3 They make their tongue sharp as a
      snake's,
   and under their lips is the venom
      of vipers.   *Selah*

4 Guard me, O LORD, from the hands
      of the wicked;
   protect me from the violent
   who have planned my downfall.
5 The arrogant have hidden a trap for
      me,
   and with cords they have spread a
      net,*o*
   along the road they have set
      snares for me.   *Selah*

6 I say to the LORD, "You are my God;
   give ear, O LORD, to the voice
      of my supplications."
7 O LORD, my Lord, my strong
      deliverer,
   you have covered my head in
      the day of battle.
8 Do not grant, O LORD, the desires of
      the wicked;
   do not further their evil plot. *p*
                              Selah

9 Those who surround me lift up their
      heads;*q*
   let the mischief of their lips
      overwhelm them!
10 Let burning coals fall on them!
   Let them be flung into pits, no
      more to rise!
11 Do not let the slanderer be
      established in the land;
   let evil speedily hunt down the
      violent!

12 I know that the LORD maintains the
      cause of the needy,
   and executes justice for the poor.
13 Surely the righteous shall give
      thanks to your name;
   the upright shall live in your
      presence.

Psalm 141

Prayer for Preservation from Evil

A Psalm of David.

1 I call upon you, O LORD; come
      quickly to me;
   give ear to my voice when I call to
      you.
2 Let my prayer be counted as incense
      before you,
   and the lifting up of my hands as
      an evening sacrifice.

3 Set a guard over my mouth, O LORD;
   keep watch over the door of
      my lips.
4 Do not turn my heart to any evil,
   to busy myself with wicked deeds
   in company with those who work
      iniquity;
   do not let me eat of their
      delicacies.

5 Let the righteous strike me;
   let the faithful correct me.
   Never let the oil of the wicked
      anoint my head,*r*
   for my prayer is continually*s*
      against their wicked deeds.
6 When they are given over to those
      who shall condemn them,
   then they shall learn that my
      words were pleasant.
7 Like a rock that one breaks apart
      and shatters on the land,
   so shall their bones be strewn at
      the mouth of Sheol.*t*

8 But my eyes are turned toward you,
      O GOD, my Lord;
   in you I seek refuge; do not leave
      me defenseless.
9 Keep me from the trap that they
      have laid for me,
   and from the snares of evildoers.
10 Let the wicked fall into their
      own nets,
   while I alone escape.

o Or *they have spread cords as a net*   *p* Heb adds
they are exalted   *q* Cn Compare Gk: Heb *those
who surround me are uplifted in head*; Heb divides
verses 8 and 9 differently   *r* Gk: Meaning of
Heb uncertain   *s* Cn: Heb *for continually and my
prayer*   *t* Meaning of Heb of verses 5-7 is
uncertain

Psalm 142

Prayer for Deliverance from Persecutors

A Maskil of David. When he was in the
cave. A Prayer.

1 With my voice I cry to the LORD;
    with my voice I make supplication
        to the LORD.
2 I pour out my complaint before
        him;
    I tell my trouble before him.
3 When my spirit is faint,
    you know my way.

In the path where I walk
    they have hidden a trap for me.
4 Look on my right hand and see—
    there is no one who takes notice
        of me;
no refuge remains to me;
    no one cares for me.

5 I cry to you, O LORD;
    I say, "You are my refuge,
    my portion in the land of the
        living."
6 Give heed to my cry,
    for I am brought very low.

Save me from my persecutors,
    for they are too strong for me.
7 Bring me out of prison,
    so that I may give thanks to your
        name.
The righteous will surround me,
    for you will deal bountifully
        with me.

Psalm 143

Prayer for Deliverance from Enemies

A Psalm of David.

1 Hear my prayer, O LORD;
    give ear to my supplications in
        your faithfulness;
    answer me in your righteousness.
2 Do not enter into judgment with
        your servant,
    for no one living is righteous
        before you.

3 For the enemy has pursued me,
    crushing my life to the ground,
    making me sit in darkness like
        those long dead.
4 Therefore my spirit faints within me;
    my heart within me is appalled.

5 I remember the days of old,
    I think about all your deeds,
    I meditate on the works of your
        hands.
6 I stretch out my hands to you;
    my soul thirsts for you like a
        parched land.   *Selah*

7 Answer me quickly, O LORD;
    my spirit fails.
Do not hide your face from me,
    or I shall be like those who go
        down to the Pit.
8 Let me hear of your steadfast love in
        the morning,
    for in you I put my trust.
Teach me the way I should go,
    for to you I lift up my soul.

9 Save me, O LORD, from my enemies;
    I have fled to you for refuge.*u*
10 Teach me to do your will,
    for you are my God.
Let your good spirit lead me
    on a level path.

11 For your name's sake, O LORD,
    preserve my life.
In your righteousness bring me
    out of trouble.
12 In your steadfast love cut off my
        enemies,
    and destroy all my adversaries,
    for I am your servant.

Psalm 144

*Prayer for National Deliverance
and Security*

Of David.

1 Blessed be the LORD, my rock,
    who trains my hands for war, and
        my fingers for battle;
2 my rock*v* and my fortress,
    my stronghold and my deliverer,
    my shield, in whom I take refuge,
    who subdues the peoples*w*
        under me.

3 O LORD, what are human beings that
        you regard them,
    or mortals that you think of
        them?

u One Heb Ms Gk: MT *to you I have hidden*
v With 18.2 and 2 Sam 22.2: Heb *my steadfast love*
w Heb Mss Syr Aquila Jerome: MT *my people*

4 They are like a breath;
    their days are like a passing
      shadow.

5 Bow your heavens, O LORD, and
     come down;
    touch the mountains so that they
      smoke.
6 Make the lightning flash and scatter
     them;
    send out your arrows and rout
     them.
7 Stretch out your hand from on high;
    set me free and rescue me from
      the mighty waters,
    from the hand of aliens,
8 whose mouths speak lies,
    and whose right hands are false.

9 I will sing a new song to you,
     O God;
    upon a ten-stringed harp I will
      play to you,
10 the one who gives victory to kings,
    who rescues his servant David.
11 Rescue me from the cruel sword,
    and deliver me from the hand of
      aliens,
    whose mouths speak lies,
    and whose right hands are false.

12 May our sons in their youth
    be like plants full grown,
    our daughters like corner pillars,
    cut for the building of a palace.
13 May our barns be filled,
    with produce of every kind;

Divine Absence

FRIDAY

Scripture Reading
for Today:
Psalm 143

Verse for Today:
Psalm 143.6

Like thirsty ground I am yearning for you, but you do not come. I
feel angry because of this Divine Absence.

It is the story of my life. I neglect you for days. But I expect
you to be here like morning sunshine when I remember you again.
Yes, there are times when my heart becomes numb with getting
used to you, so numb that it feels like a great void. Then I blame
you for your absence. All this week I have felt smothered by your
disappearance. If the truth be known, it is I who have become too
casual about you, God. I let the fire that you are escape my notice.
I let the wonder in me die. There is nothing more deadly than getting used to the Beloved.

You were long in coming today, my God. I expected you to be
present in glory at the snap of my fingers, at the longing of my
heart, even though I've kept you safely in heaven for days. Today
when I began to look for you, I came to realize that I was no
longer in the habit of searching for you in deep places.

*O God of tender mercies, I know I've kept you at arm's length.
I've kept you safe in heaven. But heaven has leaned down to the
earth and I've been touched anew. Like thirsty ground I long for
you. Forgive my casualness about your Love. Forgive my shallow
life. I am finished with shallowness. I used to pray that I be saved
from eternal death, but now I pray to be saved from shallow living. Eternal death? Shallow living? Is there a difference? O God,
deliver me from shallow living!*

—MACRINA WIEDERKEHR

Go to page 774 for your next devotional reading.

may our sheep increase by
     thousands,
  by tens of thousands in our fields,
14   and may our cattle be heavy with
     young.
  May there be no breach in the
     walls,^x no exile,
  and no cry of distress in our
     streets.

15 Happy are the people to whom such
     blessings fall;
  happy are the people whose God
     is the LORD.

Psalm 145

The Greatness and the Goodness of God

Praise. Of David.

1 I will extol you, my God and King,
  and bless your name forever
     and ever.
2 Every day I will bless you,
  and praise your name forever
     and ever.
3 Great is the LORD, and greatly to be
     praised;
  his greatness is unsearchable.

4 One generation shall laud your
     works to another,
  and shall declare your mighty acts.
5 On the glorious splendor of your
     majesty,
  and on your wondrous works, I
     will meditate.
6 The might of your awesome deeds
     shall be proclaimed,
  and I will declare your greatness.
7 They shall celebrate the fame of your
     abundant goodness,
  and shall sing aloud of your
     righteousness.

8 The LORD is gracious and merciful,
  slow to anger and abounding in
     steadfast love.
9 The LORD is good to all,
  and his compassion is over all
     that he has made.

10 All your works shall give thanks to
     you, O LORD,
  and all your faithful shall
     bless you.
11 They shall speak of the glory of your
     kingdom,

and tell of your power,
12 to make known to all people your^y
     mighty deeds,
  and the glorious splendor of
     your^z kingdom.
13 Your kingdom is an everlasting
     kingdom,
  and your dominion endures
     throughout all generations.

The LORD is faithful in all his words,
  and gracious in all his deeds.^a
14 The LORD upholds all who are
     falling,
  and raises up all who are bowed
     down.
15 The eyes of all look to you,
  and you give them their food in
     due season.
16 You open your hand,
  satisfying the desire of every living
     thing.
17 The LORD is just in all his ways,
  and kind in all his doings.
18 The LORD is near to all who call
     on him,
  to all who call on him in truth.
19 He fulfills the desire of all who
     fear him;
  he also hears their cry, and saves
     them.
20 The LORD watches over all who
     love him,
  but all the wicked he will destroy.

21 My mouth will speak the praise of
     the LORD,
  and all flesh will bless his holy
     name forever and ever.

Psalm 146

Praise for God's Help

1 Praise the LORD!
  Praise the LORD, O my soul!
2 I will praise the LORD as long as
     I live;
  I will sing praises to my God all
     my life long.

3 Do not put your trust in princes,
  in mortals, in whom there is no
     help.

x Heb lacks *in the walls*   y Gk Jerome Syr: Heb
his   z Heb *his*   a These two lines supplied by
Q Ms Gk Syr

THE
STORY
OF A
WOMAN

Hannah

Her Name Means *"Graciousness"*
or *"Favor"*

Her Character: *Provoked by another woman's malice, she refused to respond in kind. Instead she poured out her hurt and sorrow to God, allowing him to vindicate her.*
Her Sorrow: *To be taunted and misunderstood.*
Her Joy: *To proclaim God's power and goodness, his habit of raising the lowly and humbling the proud.*

Read I Samuel 1.1—2.11

It was only 15 miles, but every year the journey from Ramah to Shiloh, to worship at the tabernacle, the tent of God's dwelling, seemed longer. At home Hannah found ways to avoid her husband's second wife, but once in Shiloh there was no escaping her taunts. Hannah felt like a leaky tent in a driving rain, unable to defend herself against the harsh weather of the other woman's heart.

Even Elkanah's arm around her provided no shelter. "Hannah, why do you weep? Why do you not eat? Why is your heart sad? Am I not more to you than ten sons?" (1.8).

How could Hannah make him understand that even the best of men could not erase a woman's longing for children? His attempt at comforting her only heightened her sense of isolation.

She stood for a long time at the tabernacle weeping and praying. Her shoulders shook and her lips moved without making a sound, as her heart poured out its grief, begging God for a son whom she would dedicate to him all the days of his life.

The priest Eli watched Hannah as she prayed, thinking her drunk. He was used to people coming to Shiloh to celebrate the feasts, eating and drinking more than they should. So he interrupted her silent prayer with a rebuke: "How long will you make a drunken spectacle of yourself? Put away your wine" (verse 14).

"No, my lord," Hannah defended herself, "I am a woman deeply troubled; I have drunk neither wine nor strong drink, but I have been pouring out my soul before the LORD" (verse 15). So Eli blessed her and sent her on her way.

Early the next morning, Hannah and Elkanah returned to their home in Ramah, where Hannah conceived. Soon she held a tiny son against her breast, Samuel, the child she had dedicated to God. After he was weaned, she would take him to Eli at Shiloh. Like Jochebed placing the child Moses into the waters of the Nile as though into God's own hands, she would surrender her child to the priest's care. Eventually Hannah's boy would become a prophet and Israel's last judge as well as a priest. His hands would anoint both Saul and David as Israel's first kings.

Like Sarah and Rachel, Hannah grieved over the children she couldn't have. But unlike them, she took her anguish directly to God. Misunderstood by both her husband and her priest, she could easily have turned her sorrow on herself or others, becoming angry and vindictive. Instead, her great prayer, echoed nearly a thousand years later by Mary's Magnificat, expresses her praise: "My heart exults in the LORD; my strength is exalted in my God. My mouth derides my enemies, because I rejoice in my victory. There is no Holy One like the LORD, no one besides you; there is no Rock like our God" (2.1–2).

For a time, Hannah suffered the harsh climate of another's heart. But instead of allowing herself to descend into pity or spite, she poured out her troubles to God. And God graciously heard her.

Praying With Hannah

"If only you will look on the misery of your servant, and remember me, and not forget your servant, but will give to your servant a male child, then I will set him before you as a nazirite until the day of his death."—*1 Samuel 1.11*

Praise God: *For he knows your heart.*
Offer Thanks: *For prayers already answered.*
Confess: *Your tendency to pour out your heart to everyone but God, making him a last, rather than first, resort.*
Ask God: *To give you the grace to trust his strength more than you trust your own.*

Lift Your Heart

One way to build your confidence in God's willingness to hear and answer your prayers is to form a habit of remembrance. It's so easy to forget everything he's already done for you by being preoccupied with what you want him to do right here, right now. By forgetting his blessings, you form a habit of ingratitude. By frequently recalling and thanking God for what he's done, you build a habit of gratitude that will also deepen your trust in God. Find a beautiful notebook or a lovely scrapbook that can become your Remembrance Book. Write down ways that God has answered your prayers. Recall how his answer sometimes took you by surprise—it was so ingenious, so creative. Keep special letters, photos of loved ones, or newspaper clippings—anything that reminds you of how God has answered you in the past. Let your Remembrance Book be a tangible way to keep God's faithfulness in the forefront of your heart.

Father, you've answered small prayers and big prayers, evening prayers and morning prayers, soft prayers and loud prayers, anxious prayers and peaceful prayers. May my own prayers become less selfish and frantic and more calm and trusting with each day that passes.

Go to page 780 for your next devotional reading.

4 When their breath departs, they
      return to the earth;
    on that very day their plans
      perish.

5 Happy are those whose help is the
      God of Jacob,
    whose hope is in the LORD their
      God,
6 who made heaven and earth,
    the sea, and all that is in them;
  who keeps faith forever;
7 who executes justice for the
      oppressed;
    who gives food to the hungry.

  The LORD sets the prisoners free;
8   the LORD opens the eyes of
      the blind.
  The LORD lifts up those who are
      bowed down;
    the LORD loves the righteous.
9 The LORD watches over the strangers;
    he upholds the orphan and the
      widow,
    but the way of the wicked he
      brings to ruin.

10 The LORD will reign forever,
     your God, O Zion, for all
       generations.
   Praise the LORD!

Psalm 147

Praise for God's Care for Jerusalem

1 Praise the LORD!
  How good it is to sing praises to our
      God;
    for he is gracious, and a song of
      praise is fitting.
2 The LORD builds up Jerusalem;
    he gathers the outcasts of Israel.
3 He heals the brokenhearted,
    and binds up their wounds.
4 He determines the number of
      the stars;
    he gives to all of them their
      names.
5 Great is our Lord, and abundant
      in power;
    his understanding is beyond
      measure.
6 The LORD lifts up the downtrodden;
    he casts the wicked to the ground.

7 Sing to the LORD with thanksgiving;
    make melody to our God on
      the lyre.
8 He covers the heavens with clouds,
    prepares rain for the earth,
    makes grass grow on the hills.
9 He gives to the animals their food,
    and to the young ravens when
      they cry.
10 His delight is not in the strength of
      the horse,
    nor his pleasure in the speed of
      a runner;[b]
11 but the LORD takes pleasure in those
      who fear him,
    in those who hope in his steadfast
      love.

12 Praise the LORD, O Jerusalem!
     Praise your God, O Zion!
13 For he strengthens the bars of
      your gates;
    he blesses your children within
      you.
14 He grants peace[c] within your
      borders;
    he fills you with the finest of
      wheat.
15 He sends out his command to the
      earth;
    his word runs swiftly.
16 He gives snow like wool;
    he scatters frost like ashes.
17 He hurls down hail like crumbs—
    who can stand before his cold?
18 He sends out his word, and melts
      them;
    he makes his wind blow, and the
      waters flow.
19 He declares his word to Jacob,
    his statutes and ordinances to
      Israel.
20 He has not dealt thus with any other
      nation;
    they do not know his ordinances.
  Praise the LORD!

Psalm 148

Praise for God's Universal Glory

1 Praise the LORD!
  Praise the LORD from the heavens;
    praise him in the heights!
2 Praise him, all his angels;
    praise him, all his host!

b Heb *legs of a person*   c Or *prosperity*

³ Praise him, sun and moon;
 praise him, all you shining stars!
⁴ Praise him, you highest heavens,
 and you waters above the
 heavens!

⁵ Let them praise the name of
 the LORD,
 for he commanded and they
 were created.
⁶ He established them forever
 and ever;
 he fixed their bounds, which
 cannot be passed.^d

⁷ Praise the LORD from the earth,
 you sea monsters and all deeps,
⁸ fire and hail, snow and frost,
 stormy wind fulfilling his
 command!

⁹ Mountains and all hills,
 fruit trees and all cedars!
¹⁰ Wild animals and all cattle,
 creeping things and flying birds!

¹¹ Kings of the earth and all peoples,
 princes and all rulers of the earth!
¹² Young men and women alike,
 old and young together!

¹³ Let them praise the name of
 the LORD,
 for his name alone is exalted;
 his glory is above earth and
 heaven.
¹⁴ He has raised up a horn for his
 people,
 praise for all his faithful,

^d Or *he set a law that cannot pass away*

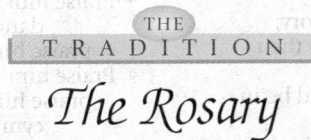

The Rosary

Praise him for his mighty deeds!
PSALM 150.2

Some people consider the rosary a peripheral devotion that detracts from the basics of the faith.

Just the reverse is true. The rosary is a user-friendly prayer; its simplicity plunges us into the heart of Scripture and the Christian mystery. While not an essential part of the Church's public prayer, the rosary focuses on the essentials of our faith. "An epitome of the whole gospel," Pope Paul VI called it.

The rosary's main prayer concerns the central event of salvation history, the incarnation. "Greetings, favored one! The Lord is with you . . . Blessed are you among women!" (Luke 1.28, 42). With the angel Gabriel we acknowledge Mary as mother of the Redeemer; with Elizabeth, we congratulate her for wholeheartedly saying "yes" to God.

The rhythm of Hail Marys draws us to meditate on realities that transform us as we ponder them. In the presence of Mary, who treasured God's Word in her heart (Luke 2.19,

51), we reflect on the events of Jesus' life. The joyful mysteries point us to his coming, the sorrowful mysteries to his suffering and dying, and the glorious mysteries to his triumph over death.

Less obvious, but just as real as its New Testament connection, is the rosary's link with the Bible's great book of prayer, the Psalms. The rosary probably originated in ninth-century Ireland when lay people who could not read but who wanted to imitate the monks' practice of praying the 150 psalms were advised to pray 150 Our Fathers instead. The devotion evolved and took many forms, with the one most familiar to us appearing in the fifteenth century. The whole rosary—all 15 mysteries—includes 150 Hail Marys.

Like the psalms, which call us to remember and proclaim God's works, the rosary is a repeated recalling and declaring of what God has done to save us. Essentially, it helps us to meditate on the life of Jesus.

for the people of Israel who are
close to him.
Praise the LORD!

Psalm 149

Praise for God's Goodness to Israel

1 Praise the LORD!
Sing to the LORD a new song,
his praise in the assembly of the
faithful.
2 Let Israel be glad in its Maker;
let the children of Zion rejoice in
their King.
3 Let them praise his name with
dancing,
making melody to him with
tambourine and lyre.
4 For the LORD takes pleasure in
his people;
he adorns the humble with
victory.
5 Let the faithful exult in glory;
let them sing for joy on their
couches.
6 Let the high praises of God be in
their throats
and two-edged swords in their
hands,
7 to execute vengeance on the nations
and punishment on the peoples,
8 to bind their kings with fetters

and their nobles with chains
of iron,
9 to execute on them the judgment
decreed.
This is glory for all his faithful
ones.
Praise the LORD!

Psalm 150

Praise for God's Surpassing Greatness

1 Praise the LORD!
Praise God in his sanctuary;
praise him in his mighty
firmament![e]
2 Praise him for his mighty deeds;
praise him according to his
surpassing greatness!

3 Praise him with trumpet sound;
praise him with lute and harp!
4 Praise him with tambourine and
dance;
praise him with strings and pipe!
5 Praise him with clanging cymbals;
praise him with loud clashing
cymbals!
6 Let everything that breathes praise
the LORD!
Praise the LORD!

e Or *dome*

Proverbs

The book of Proverbs is a collection of wisdom sayings composed over the course of centuries; it may have been edited into its current form in the fifth century B.C. One of its most beautiful passages is found in Proverbs 8.22–36 in which wisdom is personified. This book offers tried and true wisdom for living a good and happy life.

Proverbs is best read in bits and pieces rather than straight through. Though it is primarily cast as advice to the young, its sayings can guide even the oldest among us. Here's a sampling of Proverbs' down-to-earth advice:

A soft answer turns away wrath, but a harsh word stirs up anger.
(15.1)

A cheerful heart is a good medicine, but a downcast spirit dries up the bones.
(17.22)

A capable wife who can find? She is far more precious than jewels ... Strength and dignity are her clothing, and she laughs at the time to come.
(31.10, 25)

1 The proverbs of Solomon son of David, king of Israel:

Prologue

2 For learning about wisdom and instruction,
   for understanding words of insight,
3 for gaining instruction in wise dealing,
   righteousness, justice, and equity;
4 to teach shrewdness to the simple,
   knowledge and prudence to the young—
5 let the wise also hear and gain in learning,
   and the discerning acquire skill,
6 to understand a proverb and a figure,
   the words of the wise and their riddles.

7 The fear of the LORD is the beginning of knowledge;

fools despise wisdom and
    instruction.

Warnings against Evil Companions

8 Hear, my child, your father's
    instruction,
    and do not reject your mother's
       teaching;
9 for they are a fair garland for your
      head,
    and pendants for your neck.
10 My child, if sinners entice you,
    do not consent.

11 If they say, "Come with us, let us lie
    in wait for blood;
    let us wantonly ambush the
      innocent;
12 like Sheol let us swallow them alive
    and whole, like those who go
      down to the Pit.
13 We shall find all kinds of costly
      things;
    we shall fill our houses with
      booty.
14 Throw in your lot among us;
    we will all have one purse"—

Awe

MONDAY

Scripture Reading
for Today:
Proverbs 1.1–7

Verse for Today:
Proverbs 1.7

Fear of the Lord is deep reverence for God and for his Word. It is
the kind of reverence that enables us to respect the laws of God,
not just acknowledge that God and his laws exist.

Fear of the Lord goes hand in hand with knowledge and love of
the Lord. How can we come face to face with a God who has no
beginning and no end—who needs nothing and no one, but still
creates out of love—and not feel such a deep reverence and awe?

God is awesome, in the truest meaning of that word. When
we encounter God, we can only stand in awe. "Awe" means the
ability to inspire dread and the mingling of dread, veneration and
wonder. Awesome is a word used too loosely today.

We might say, "This celebrity is awesome." But he isn't, is he?
He doesn't inspire dread. He may inspire false veneration and wonder—but he has no power in himself to inspire them. He cannot
make anything at all from nothing. Every note he plays, every lyric
he sings, every line he recites is all done with gifts given him by
God. Likewise, we cannot call awesome that new video game or
the latest action movie.

But God is indeed awesome! He always was, is now, and always will be. He alone is unchanging. One God, mighty God, awesome God, holy God, Triune God. He made all things from nothing.
He willed the universe to be and it was. He willed us to be and we
are. Now, that is awesome—and I stand in wonder before my
mighty God. I stand in awe. I stand with fear and trembling before
such a power that could simply will me out of existence. And I
stand in veneration and in love for he has chosen to make me, to
give me not only life, but his Spirit as well. He has chosen to let
me know him, to love him, and to serve him. He has called me to
eternal happiness.

—*BABSIE BLEASDELL*

Go to page 782 for your next devotional reading.

15 my child, do not walk in their way,
    keep your foot from their paths;
16 for their feet run to evil,
    and they hurry to shed blood.
17 For in vain is the net baited
    while the bird is looking on;
18 yet they lie in wait—to kill
    themselves!
    and set an ambush—for their own
    lives!
19 Such is the end*a* of all who are
    greedy for gain;
    it takes away the life of its
    possessors.

The Call of Wisdom

20 Wisdom cries out in the street;
    in the squares she raises her voice.
21 At the busiest corner she cries out;
    at the entrance of the city gates
    she speaks:
22 "How long, O simple ones, will you
    love being simple?
    How long will scoffers delight in
    their scoffing
    and fools hate knowledge?
23 Give heed to my reproof;
    I will pour out my thoughts to you;
    I will make my words known
    to you.
24 Because I have called and you
    refused,
    have stretched out my hand and
    no one heeded,
25 and because you have ignored all
    my counsel
    and would have none of my
    reproof,
26 I also will laugh at your calamity;
    I will mock when panic strikes
    you,
27 when panic strikes you like a storm,
    and your calamity comes like a
    whirlwind,
    when distress and anguish come
    upon you.
28 Then they will call upon me, but I
    will not answer;
    they will seek me diligently, but
    will not find me.
29 Because they hated knowledge
    and did not choose the fear of the
    LORD,
30 would have none of my counsel,
    and despised all my reproof,
31 therefore they shall eat the fruit of
    their way

and be sated with their own
    devices.
32 For waywardness kills the simple,
    and the complacency of fools
    destroys them;
33 but those who listen to me will be
    secure
    and will live at ease, without
    dread of disaster."

The Value of Wisdom

2 My child, if you accept my words
    and treasure up my
    commandments within you,
2 making your ear attentive to wisdom
    and inclining your heart to
    understanding;
3 if you indeed cry out for insight,
    and raise your voice for
    understanding;
4 if you seek it like silver,
    and search for it as for hidden
    treasures—
5 then you will understand the fear of
    the LORD
    and find the knowledge of God.
6 For the LORD gives wisdom;
    from his mouth come knowledge
    and understanding;
7 he stores up sound wisdom for the
    upright;
    he is a shield to those who walk
    blamelessly,
8 guarding the paths of justice
    and preserving the way of his
    faithful ones.
9 Then you will understand
    righteousness and justice
    and equity, every good path;
10 for wisdom will come into your
    heart,
    and knowledge will be pleasant to
    your soul;
11 prudence will watch over you;
    and understanding will guard you.
12 It will save you from the way of evil,
    from those who speak perversely,
13 who forsake the paths of uprightness
    to walk in the ways of darkness,
14 who rejoice in doing evil
    and delight in the perverseness
    of evil;
15 those whose paths are crooked,
    and who are devious in their
    ways.

a Gk: Heb *are the ways*

16 You will be saved from the loose[b]
    woman,
    from the adulteress with her
      smooth words,
17 who forsakes the partner of her
    youth
    and forgets her sacred covenant;
18 for her way[c] leads down to death,
    and her paths to the shades;
19 those who go to her never come
    back,
    nor do they regain the paths
      of life.

20 Therefore walk in the way of the
    good,
    and keep to the paths of the
      just.
21 For the upright will abide in the
    land,
    and the innocent will remain
      in it;
22 but the wicked will be cut off from
    the land,
    and the treacherous will be rooted
      out of it.

Admonition to Trust and Honor God

3 My child, do not forget my
    teaching,
    but let your heart keep my
      commandments;
2 for length of days and years of life
    and abundant welfare they will
      give you.

3 Do not let loyalty and faithfulness
    forsake you;
    bind them around your neck,
    write them on the tablet of your
      heart.
4 So you will find favor and good
    repute
    in the sight of God and of people.

5 Trust in the LORD with all your heart,
    and do not rely on your own
      insight.
6 In all your ways acknowledge him,

b Heb *strange*   *c* Cn: Heb *house*

Money Doesn't Equal Serenity

TUESDAY

Scripture Reading
for Today:
Proverbs 3.5–10

Verses for Today:
Proverbs 3.9–10

Twenty years ago, I worried a lot about money. Or rather, the lack of it. My husband was out of work, our family's financial future depended on me, and I felt burdened by the responsibility. "If I had more money, my worries would be over," I complained to my friend Don. He raised an eyebrow. "Don't put your faith in your bank balance, Barb. 'Where your treasure is, there your heart will be also.'" He showed me an interesting statistic. While personal consumption has doubled in forty years, the percentage of people satisfied with life remains the same—about thirty-three percent. If having more "things" doesn't guarantee more happiness, what does?

    Don encouraged me to start tithing as a way to focus on all I do have, rather than what I don't have. He pointed to Proverbs 3.9–10 where King Solomon says, "Honor the LORD with your substance and with the first fruits of all your produce; then your barns will be filled with plenty, and your vats will be bursting with wine." I was scared when I wrote my first tithing check, but gradually, I've learned that it's true: When you give, you receive, and your needs will be met. Just don't expect a direct payback.

—*BARBARA BARTOCCI*

Go to page 791 for your next devotional reading.

and he will make straight your
paths.
7 Do not be wise in your own eyes;
fear the LORD, and turn away from
evil.
8 It will be a healing for your flesh
and a refreshment for your body.

9 Honor the LORD with your substance
and with the first fruits of all your
produce;
10 then your barns will be filled with
plenty,
and your vats will be bursting
with wine.

11 My child, do not despise the LORD's
discipline
or be weary of his reproof,
12 for the LORD reproves the one he
loves,
as a father the son in whom he
delights.

The True Wealth

13 Happy are those who find wisdom,
and those who get understanding,
14 for her income is better than silver,
and her revenue better than gold.
15 She is more precious than jewels,
and nothing you desire can
compare with her.
16 Long life is in her right hand;
in her left hand are riches and
honor.
17 Her ways are ways of pleasantness,
and all her paths are peace.
18 She is a tree of life to those who lay
hold of her;
those who hold her fast are called
happy.

God's Wisdom in Creation

19 The LORD by wisdom founded the
earth;
by understanding he established
the heavens;
20 by his knowledge the deeps broke
open,
and the clouds drop down the
dew.

The True Security

21 My child, do not let these escape
from your sight:
keep sound wisdom and
prudence,
22 and they will be life for your soul

and adornment for your neck.
23 Then you will walk on your way
securely
and your foot will not stumble.
24 If you sit down,*d* you will not be
afraid;
when you lie down, your sleep
will be sweet.
25 Do not be afraid of sudden panic,
or of the storm that strikes the
wicked;
26 for the LORD will be your confidence
and will keep your foot from
being caught.

27 Do not withhold good from those
to whom it is due,*e*
when it is in your power to do it.
28 Do not say to your neighbor, "Go,
and come again,
tomorrow I will give it"—when you
have it with you.
29 Do not plan harm against your
neighbor
who lives trustingly beside you.
30 Do not quarrel with anyone without
cause,
when no harm has been done
to you.
31 Do not envy the violent
and do not choose any of their
ways;
32 for the perverse are an abomination
to the LORD,
but the upright are in his
confidence.
33 The LORD's curse is on the house of
the wicked,
but he blesses the abode of the
righteous.
34 Toward the scorners he is scornful,
but to the humble he shows favor.
35 The wise will inherit honor,
but stubborn fools, disgrace.

Parental Advice

4 Listen, children, to a father's
instruction,
and be attentive, that you may
gain *f* insight;
2 for I give you good precepts:
do not forsake my teaching.
3 When I was a son with my father,
tender, and my mother's favorite,
4 he taught me, and said to me,

d Gk: Heb *lie down*   *e* Heb *from its owners*
f Heb *know*

"Let your heart hold fast my words;
keep my commandments,
and live.

5 Get wisdom; get insight: do not
forget, nor turn away
from the words of my mouth.

6 Do not forsake her, and she will
keep you;
love her, and she will guard you.

7 The beginning of wisdom is this:
Get wisdom,
and whatever else you get, get
insight.

8 Prize her highly, and she will
exalt you;
she will honor you if you
embrace her.

9 She will place on your head a fair
garland;
she will bestow on you a beautiful
crown."

Admonition to Keep to the Right Path

10 Hear, my child, and accept my
words,
that the years of your life may
be many.

11 I have taught you the way of
wisdom;
I have led you in the paths of
uprightness.

12 When you walk, your step will not
be hampered;
and if you run, you will not
stumble.

13 Keep hold of instruction; do not
let go;
guard her, for she is your life.

14 Do not enter the path of the wicked,
and do not walk in the way of
evildoers.

15 Avoid it; do not go on it;
turn away from it and pass on.

16 For they cannot sleep unless they
have done wrong;
they are robbed of sleep unless
they have made someone
stumble.

17 For they eat the bread of wickedness
and drink the wine of violence.

18 But the path of the righteous is like
the light of dawn,
which shines brighter and brighter
until full day.

19 The way of the wicked is like deep
darkness;
they do not know what they
stumble over.

20 My child, be attentive to my words;
incline your ear to my sayings.

21 Do not let them escape from
your sight;
keep them within your heart.

22 For they are life to those who
find them,
and healing to all their flesh.

23 Keep your heart with all vigilance,
for from it flow the springs of life.

24 Put away from you crooked speech,
and put devious talk far from you.

25 Let your eyes look directly forward,
and your gaze be straight
before you.

26 Keep straight the path of your feet,
and all your ways will be sure.

27 Do not swerve to the right or to
the left;
turn your foot away from evil.

Warning against Impurity and Infidelity

5 My child, be attentive to my
wisdom;
incline your ear to my
understanding,

2 so that you may hold on to
prudence,
and your lips may guard
knowledge.

3 For the lips of a loose *g* woman drip
honey,
and her speech is smoother
than oil;

4 but in the end she is bitter as
wormwood,
sharp as a two-edged sword.

5 Her feet go down to death;
her steps follow the path to Sheol.

6 She does not keep straight to the
path of life;
her ways wander, and she does
not know it.

7 And now, my child,*h* listen to me,
and do not depart from the words
of my mouth.

8 Keep your way far from her,
and do not go near the door of
her house;

9 or you will give your honor to
others,
and your years to the merciless,

10 and strangers will take their fill of
your wealth,

g Heb *strange*   *h* Gk Vg: Heb *children*

and your labors will go to the
house of an alien;
11 and at the end of your life you will
groan,
when your flesh and body are
consumed,
12 and you say, "Oh, how I hated
discipline,
and my heart despised reproof!
13 I did not listen to the voice of my
teachers
or incline my ear to my
instructors.
14 Now I am at the point of utter ruin
in the public assembly."

15 Drink water from your own cistern,
flowing water from your own
well.
16 Should your springs be scattered
abroad,
streams of water in the streets?
17 Let them be for yourself alone,
and not for sharing with strangers.
18 Let your fountain be blessed,
and rejoice in the wife of your
youth,
19 a lovely deer, a graceful doe.
May her breasts satisfy you at all
times;
may you be intoxicated always by
her love.
20 Why should you be intoxicated, my
son, by another woman
and embrace the bosom of an
adulteress?
21 For human ways are under the eyes
of the LORD,
and he examines all their paths.
22 The iniquities of the wicked ensnare
them,
and they are caught in the toils of
their sin.
23 They die for lack of discipline,
and because of their great folly
they are lost.

Practical Admonitions

6 My child, if you have given your
pledge to your neighbor,
if you have bound yourself to
another,[i]
2 you are snared by the utterance of
your lips,[j]
caught by the words of your
mouth.
3 So do this, my child, and save
yourself,

for you have come into your
neighbor's power:
go, hurry,[k] and plead with your
neighbor.
4 Give your eyes no sleep
and your eyelids no slumber;
5 save yourself like a gazelle from the
hunter,[l]
like a bird from the hand of the
fowler.

6 Go to the ant, you lazybones;
consider its ways, and be wise.
7 Without having any chief
or officer or ruler,
8 it prepares its food in summer,
and gathers its sustenance in
harvest.
9 How long will you lie there,
O lazybones?
When will you rise from your
sleep?
10 A little sleep, a little slumber,
a little folding of the hands
to rest,
11 and poverty will come upon you
like a robber,
and want, like an armed warrior.

12 A scoundrel and a villain
goes around with crooked speech,
13 winking the eyes, shuffling the feet,
pointing the fingers,
14 with perverted mind devising evil,
continually sowing discord;
15 on such a one calamity will descend
suddenly;
in a moment, damage beyond
repair.

16 There are six things that the LORD
hates,
seven that are an abomination
to him:
17 haughty eyes, a lying tongue,
and hands that shed innocent
blood,
18 a heart that devises wicked plans,
feet that hurry to run to evil,
19 a lying witness who testifies falsely,
and one who sows discord in a
family.

---

i Or *a stranger*   *j* Cn Compare Gk Syr: Heb *the
words of your mouth*   *k* Or *humble yourself*   *l* Cn:
Heb *from the hand*

20 My child, keep your father's
commandment,
and do not forsake your mother's
teaching.
21 Bind them upon your heart always;
tie them around your neck.
22 When you walk, they[m] will
lead you;
when you lie down, they[m] will
watch over you;
and when you awake, they[m] will
talk with you.
23 For the commandment is a lamp
and the teaching a light,
and the reproofs of discipline are
the way of life,
24 to preserve you from the wife of
another,[n]
from the smooth tongue of the
adulteress.
25 Do not desire her beauty in your
heart,
and do not let her capture you
with her eyelashes;
26 for a prostitute's fee is only a loaf of
bread,[o]
but the wife of another stalks a
man's very life.
27 Can fire be carried in the bosom
without burning one's clothes?
28 Or can one walk on hot coals
without scorching the feet?
29 So is he who sleeps with his
neighbor's wife;
no one who touches her will go
unpunished.
30 Thieves are not despised who
steal only
to satisfy their appetite when they
are hungry.
31 Yet if they are caught, they will pay
sevenfold;
they will forfeit all the goods of
their house.
32 But he who commits adultery has
no sense;
he who does it destroys himself.
33 He will get wounds and dishonor,
and his disgrace will not be wiped
away.
34 For jealousy arouses a husband's
fury,
and he shows no restraint when
he takes revenge.
35 He will accept no compensation,
and refuses a bribe no matter how
great.

The False Attractions of Adultery

7 My child, keep my words
and store up my commandments
with you;
2 keep my commandments and live,
keep my teachings as the apple of
your eye;
3 bind them on your fingers,
write them on the tablet of your
heart.
4 Say to wisdom, "You are my sister,"
and call insight your intimate
friend,
5 that they may keep you from the
loose[p] woman,
from the adulteress with her
smooth words.

6 For at the window of my house
I looked out through my lattice,
7 and I saw among the simple ones,
I observed among the youths,
a young man without sense,
8 passing along the street near her
corner,
taking the road to her house
9 in the twilight, in the evening,
at the time of night and darkness.

10 Then a woman comes toward him,
decked out like a prostitute, wily
of heart.[q]
11 She is loud and wayward;
her feet do not stay at home;
12 now in the street, now in the
squares,
and at every corner she lies
in wait.
13 She seizes him and kisses him,
and with impudent face she says
to him:
14 "I had to offer sacrifices,
and today I have paid my vows;
15 so now I have come out to
meet you,
to seek you eagerly, and I have
found you!
16 I have decked my couch with
coverings,
colored spreads of Egyptian linen;
17 I have perfumed my bed with
myrrh,
aloes, and cinnamon.

m Heb it   n Gk: MT the evil woman   o Cn
Compare Gk Syr Vg Tg: Heb for because of a harlot
to a piece of bread   p Heb strange   q Meaning of
Heb uncertain

18 Come, let us take our fill of love
        until morning;
    let us delight ourselves with love.
19 For my husband is not at home;
        he has gone on a long journey.
20 He took a bag of money with him;
        he will not come home until full
        moon."

21 With much seductive speech she
        persuades him;
    with her smooth talk she
        compels him.
22 Right away he follows her,
        and goes like an ox to the
        slaughter,
    or bounds like a stag toward
        the trap[r]
23   until an arrow pierces its entrails.
    He is like a bird rushing into a
        snare,
        not knowing that it will cost him
        his life.

24 And now, my children, listen to me,
        and be attentive to the words of
        my mouth.
25 Do not let your hearts turn aside to
        her ways;
    do not stray into her paths.
26 For many are those she has laid low,
        and numerous are her victims.
27 Her house is the way to Sheol,
        going down to the chambers of
        death.

The Gifts of Wisdom

8 Does not wisdom call,
        and does not understanding raise
        her voice?
2 On the heights, beside the way,
        at the crossroads she takes her
        stand;
3 beside the gates in front of the
        town,
    at the entrance of the portals she
        cries out:
4 "To you, O people, I call,
        and my cry is to all that live.
5 O simple ones, learn prudence;
        acquire intelligence, you who lack
        it.
6 Hear, for I will speak noble things,
        and from my lips will come what
        is right;
7 for my mouth will utter truth;
        wickedness is an abomination to
        my lips.

8 All the words of my mouth are
        righteous;
    there is nothing twisted or
        crooked in them.
9 They are all straight to one who
        understands
    and right to those who find
        knowledge.
10 Take my instruction instead of silver,
        and knowledge rather than choice
        gold;
11 for wisdom is better than jewels,
        and all that you may desire
        cannot compare with her.
12 I, wisdom, live with prudence,[s]
        and I attain knowledge and
        discretion.
13 The fear of the LORD is hatred of evil.
    Pride and arrogance and the way
        of evil
        and perverted speech I hate.
14 I have good advice and sound
        wisdom;
    I have insight, I have strength.
15 By me kings reign,
        and rulers decree what is just;
16 by me rulers rule,
        and nobles, all who govern
        rightly.
17 I love those who love me,
        and those who seek me diligently
        find me.
18 Riches and honor are with me,
        enduring wealth and prosperity.
19 My fruit is better than gold, even
        fine gold,
        and my yield than choice silver.
20 I walk in the way of righteousness,
        along the paths of justice,
21 endowing with wealth those who
        love me,
        and filling their treasuries.

Wisdom's Part in Creation

22 The LORD created me at the
        beginning[t] of his work,[u]
    the first of his acts of long ago.
23 Ages ago I was set up,
        at the first, before the beginning
        of the earth.
24 When there were no depths I was
        brought forth,
    when there were no springs
        abounding with water.

_____

[r] Cn Compare Gk: Meaning of Heb uncertain
[s] Meaning of Heb uncertain   [t] Or *me as the
beginning*   [u] Heb *way*

25 Before the mountains had been
     shaped,
   before the hills, I was brought
     forth—
26 when he had not yet made earth
     and fields,[v]
   or the world's first bits of soil.
27 When he established the heavens, I
     was there,
   when he drew a circle on the face
     of the deep,
28 when he made firm the skies above,
   when he established the fountains
     of the deep,
29 when he assigned to the sea its
     limit,
   so that the waters might not
     transgress his command,
   when he marked out the
     foundations of the earth,
30   then I was beside him, like a
     master worker;[w]
   and I was daily his[x] delight,
     rejoicing before him always,
31 rejoicing in his inhabited world
   and delighting in the human race.

32 "And now, my children, listen to
     me:
   happy are those who keep
     my ways.
33 Hear instruction and be wise,
   and do not neglect it.
34 Happy is the one who listens to me,
   watching daily at my gates,
     waiting beside my doors.
35 For whoever finds me finds life
   and obtains favor from the LORD;
36 but those who miss me injure
     themselves;
   all who hate me love death."

Wisdom's Feast

9 Wisdom has built her house,
   she has hewn her seven pillars.
2 She has slaughtered her animals, she
     has mixed her wine,
   she has also set her table.
3 She has sent out her servant-girls,
     she calls
   from the highest places in
     the town,
4 "You that are simple, turn in here!"
   To those without sense she says,
5 "Come, eat of my bread
   and drink of the wine I have
     mixed.

6 Lay aside immaturity,[y] and live,
   and walk in the[y] way of insight."

General Maxims

7 Whoever corrects a scoffer wins
     abuse;
   whoever rebukes the wicked
     gets hurt.
8 A scoffer who is rebuked will only
     hate you;
   the wise, when rebuked, will
     love you.
9 Give instruction[z] to the wise, and
   they will become wiser still;
   teach the righteous and they will
     gain in learning.
10 The fear of the LORD is the beginning
     of wisdom,
   and the knowledge of the Holy
     One is insight.
11 For by me your days will be
     multiplied,
   and years will be added to your
     life.
12 If you are wise, you are wise for
     yourself;
   if you scoff, you alone will bear it.

Folly's Invitation and Promise

13 The foolish woman is loud;
   she is ignorant and knows
     nothing.
14 She sits at the door of her house,
   on a seat at the high places of the
     town,
15 calling to those who pass by,
   who are going straight on their
     way,
16 "You who are simple, turn in here!"
   And to those without sense she
     says,
17 "Stolen water is sweet,
   and bread eaten in secret is
     pleasant."
18 But they do not know that the
     dead[a] are there,
   that her guests are in the depths
     of Sheol.

Wise Sayings of Solomon

10 The proverbs of Solomon.

A wise child makes a glad father,

---

v Meaning of Heb uncertain   w Another reading
is *little child*   x Gk: Heb lacks *his*   y Or
simpleness   z Heb lacks *instruction*   a Heb
shades

but a foolish child is a mother's
   grief.
2 Treasures gained by wickedness do
      not profit,
   but righteousness delivers from
      death.
3 The LORD does not let the righteous
      go hungry,
   but he thwarts the craving of the
      wicked.
4 A slack hand causes poverty,
   but the hand of the diligent
      makes rich.
5 A child who gathers in summer is
      prudent,
   but a child who sleeps in harvest
      brings shame.
6 Blessings are on the head of the
      righteous,
   but the mouth of the wicked
      conceals violence.
7 The memory of the righteous is a
      blessing,
   but the name of the wicked
      will rot.
8 The wise of heart will heed
      commandments,
   but a babbling fool will come
      to ruin.
9 Whoever walks in integrity walks
      securely,
   but whoever follows perverse ways
      will be found out.
10 Whoever winks the eye causes
      trouble,
   but the one who rebukes boldly
      makes peace.*b*
11 The mouth of the righteous is a
      fountain of life,
   but the mouth of the wicked
      conceals violence.
12 Hatred stirs up strife,
   but love covers all offenses.
13 On the lips of one who has
      understanding wisdom
      is found,
   but a rod is for the back of one
      who lacks sense.
14 The wise lay up knowledge,
   but the babbling of a fool brings
      ruin near.
15 The wealth of the rich is their
      fortress;
   the poverty of the poor is their
      ruin.
16 The wage of the righteous leads
      to life,
   the gain of the wicked to sin.

17 Whoever heeds instruction is on the
      path to life,
   but one who rejects a rebuke goes
      astray.
18 Lying lips conceal hatred,
   and whoever utters slander is
      a fool.
19 When words are many, transgression
      is not lacking,
   but the prudent are restrained in
      speech.
20 The tongue of the righteous is choice
      silver;
   the mind of the wicked is of
      little worth.
21 The lips of the righteous feed many,
   but fools die for lack of sense.
22 The blessing of the LORD makes rich,
   and he adds no sorrow with it.*c*
23 Doing wrong is like sport to a fool,
   but wise conduct is pleasure to a
      person of understanding.
24 What the wicked dread will come
      upon them,
   but the desire of the righteous will
      be granted.
25 When the tempest passes, the wicked
      are no more,
   but the righteous are established
      forever.
26 Like vinegar to the teeth, and smoke
      to the eyes,
   so are the lazy to their employers.
27 The fear of the LORD prolongs life,
   but the years of the wicked will be
      short.
28 The hope of the righteous ends in
      gladness,
   but the expectation of the wicked
      comes to nothing.
29 The way of the LORD is a stronghold
      for the upright,
   but destruction for evildoers.
30 The righteous will never be removed,
   but the wicked will not remain in
      the land.
31 The mouth of the righteous brings
      forth wisdom,
   but the perverse tongue will be
      cut off.
32 The lips of the righteous know what
      is acceptable,
   but the mouth of the wicked what
      is perverse.

b Gk: Heb *but a babbling fool will come to ruin*
c Or *and toil adds nothing to it*

11

A false balance is an
abomination to the LORD,
but an accurate weight is his
delight.

2 When pride comes, then comes
disgrace;
but wisdom is with the humble.

3 The integrity of the upright guides
them,
but the crookedness of the
treacherous destroys them.

4 Riches do not profit in the day
of wrath,
but righteousness delivers from
death.

5 The righteousness of the blameless
keeps their ways straight,
but the wicked fall by their own
wickedness.

6 The righteousness of the upright
saves them,
but the treacherous are taken
captive by their schemes.

7 When the wicked die, their hope
perishes,
and the expectation of the godless
comes to nothing.

8 The righteous are delivered from
trouble,
and the wicked get into it instead.

9 With their mouths the godless
would destroy their
neighbors,
but by knowledge the righteous
are delivered.

10 When it goes well with the
righteous, the city rejoices;
and when the wicked perish, there
is jubilation.

11 By the blessing of the upright a city
is exalted,
but it is overthrown by the mouth
of the wicked.

12 Whoever belittles another lacks
sense,
but an intelligent person remains
silent.

13 A gossip goes about telling secrets,
but one who is trustworthy in
spirit keeps a confidence.

14 Where there is no guidance, a
nation*d* falls,
but in an abundance of
counselors there is safety.

15 To guarantee loans for a stranger
brings trouble,
but there is safety in refusing
to do so.

16 A gracious woman gets honor,
but she who hates virtue is
covered with shame.*e*
The timid become destitute,*f*
but the aggressive gain riches.

17 Those who are kind reward
themselves,
but the cruel do themselves harm.

18 The wicked earn no real gain,
but those who sow righteousness
get a true reward.

19 Whoever is steadfast in righteousness
will live,
but whoever pursues evil will die.

20 Crooked minds are an abomination
to the LORD,
but those of blameless ways are
his delight.

21 Be assured, the wicked will not go
unpunished,
but those who are righteous will
escape.

22 Like a gold ring in a pig's snout
is a beautiful woman without
good sense.

23 The desire of the righteous ends
only in good;
the expectation of the wicked in
wrath.

24 Some give freely, yet grow all the
richer;
others withhold what is due, and
only suffer want.

25 A generous person will be enriched,
and one who gives water will
get water.

26 The people curse those who hold
back grain,
but a blessing is on the head of
those who sell it.

27 Whoever diligently seeks good seeks
favor,
but evil comes to the one who
searches for it.

28 Those who trust in their riches will
wither,*g*
but the righteous will flourish like
green leaves.

29 Those who trouble their households
will inherit wind,
and the fool will be servant to the
wise.

---

d Or *an army*   *e* Compare Gk Syr: Heb lacks *but
she . . . shame*   *f* Gk: Heb lacks *The timid . . .
destitute*   *g* Cn: Heb *fall*

30 The fruit of the righteous is a tree of
   life,
   but violence[h] takes lives away.
31 If the righteous are repaid on earth,
   how much more the wicked and
   the sinner!

12 Whoever loves discipline loves
   knowledge,
   but those who hate to be rebuked
   are stupid.
2 The good obtain favor from the
   LORD,
   but those who devise evil he
   condemns.
3 No one finds security by wickedness,
   but the root of the righteous will
   never be moved.
4 A good wife is the crown of her
   husband,
   but she who brings shame is like
   rottenness in his bones.
5 The thoughts of the righteous
   are just;
   the advice of the wicked is
   treacherous.
6 The words of the wicked are a
   deadly ambush,
   but the speech of the upright
   delivers them.

7 The wicked are overthrown and are
   no more,
   but the house of the righteous
   will stand.
8 One is commended for good sense,
   but a perverse mind is despised.
9 Better to be despised and have a
   servant,
   than to be self-important and lack
   food.
10 The righteous know the needs of
   their animals,
   but the mercy of the wicked is
   cruel.
11 Those who till their land will have
   plenty of food,
   but those who follow worthless
   pursuits have no sense.
12 The wicked covet the proceeds of
   wickedness,[i]
   but the root of the righteous bears
   fruit.
13 The evil are ensnared by the
   transgression of their lips,
   but the righteous escape from
   trouble.

h Cn Compare Gk Syr: Heb *a wise man*   i Or
covet the catch of the wicked

Criticism

WEDNESDAY

Scripture Reading
for Today:
Proverbs 12.1, 15–19

Verse for Today:
Proverbs 12.1

It is such a burden to always need to be right. I remember with
some amusement my difficulty in being wrong as a child. If anyone told me that something was wrong, like my shoe was untied
or a button was in the wrong buttonhole, I would simply say, "I
like it like that." Then when no one was looking I would set
things right.

The things that are sometimes wrong in my life have gone far
beyond untied shoes and unbuttoned buttons, but the memory of
my insistent "I like it like that" lingers with me and makes me
smile. I have come to realize that, "no, I don't like it like that!" I
don't like that stubborn streak in me that insists on being right.
Needing to be right all the time comes out of my insecurity. As I
mature, that need to be right diminishes.

Mistakes can be such friends. They rough up my smooth
edges, convincing me that I don't need to be perfect to be loved.
What a freedom to be able to say, "I was wrong"!

—*MACRINA WIEDERKEHR*

Go to page 795 for your next devotional reading.

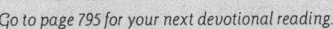

14 From the fruit of the mouth one is
      filled with good things,
    and manual labor has its reward.
15 Fools think their own way is right,
    but the wise listen to advice.
16 Fools show their anger at once,
    but the prudent ignore an insult.
17 Whoever speaks the truth gives
      honest evidence,
    but a false witness speaks
      deceitfully.
18 Rash words are like sword thrusts,
    but the tongue of the wise brings
      healing.
19 Truthful lips endure forever,
    but a lying tongue lasts only a
      moment.
20 Deceit is in the mind of those who
      plan evil,
    but those who counsel peace
      have joy.
21 No harm happens to the righteous,
    but the wicked are filled with
      trouble.
22 Lying lips are an abomination to the
      LORD,
    but those who act faithfully are
      his delight.
23 One who is clever conceals
      knowledge,
    but the mind of a fool *j*
      broadcasts folly.
24 The hand of the diligent will rule,
    while the lazy will be put to
      forced labor.
25 Anxiety weighs down the human
      heart,
    but a good word cheers it up.
26 The righteous gives good advice
      to friends, *k*
    but the way of the wicked leads
      astray.
27 The lazy do not roast *l* their game,
    but the diligent obtain precious
      wealth. *l*
28 In the path of righteousness there is
      life,
    in walking its path there is no
      death.

13 A wise child loves discipline, *m*
    but a scoffer does not listen to
      rebuke.
2 From the fruit of their words good
      persons eat good things,
    but the desire of the treacherous is
      for wrongdoing.
3 Those who guard their mouths
      preserve their lives;

those who open wide their lips
      come to ruin.
4 The appetite of the lazy craves, and
      gets nothing,
    while the appetite of the diligent
      is richly supplied.
5 The righteous hate falsehood,
    but the wicked act shamefully and
      disgracefully.
6 Righteousness guards one whose
      way is upright,
    but sin overthrows the wicked.
7 Some pretend to be rich, yet have
      nothing;
    others pretend to be poor, yet
      have great wealth.
8 Wealth is a ransom for a person's
      life,
    but the poor get no threats.
9 The light of the righteous rejoices,
    but the lamp of the wicked
      goes out.
10 By insolence the heedless make
      strife,
    but wisdom is with those who
      take advice.
11 Wealth hastily gotten *n* will dwindle,
    but those who gather little by
      little will increase it.
12 Hope deferred makes the heart sick,
    but a desire fulfilled is a tree
      of life.
13 Those who despise the word bring
      destruction on themselves,
    but those who respect the
      commandment will be
      rewarded.
14 The teaching of the wise is a
      fountain of life,
    so that one may avoid the snares
      of death.
15 Good sense wins favor,
    but the way of the faithless is
      their ruin. *o*
16 The clever do all things intelligently,
    but the fool displays folly.
17 A bad messenger brings trouble,
    but a faithful envoy, healing.
18 Poverty and disgrace are for the one
      who ignores instruction,
    but one who heeds reproof is
      honored.

j Heb *the heart of fools*   *k* Syr: Meaning of Heb
uncertain   *l* Meaning of Heb uncertain   *m* Cn:
Heb *A wise child the discipline of his father*   *n* Gk
Vg: Heb *from vanity*   *o* Cn Compare Gk Syr Vg
Tg: Heb *is enduring*

19 A desire realized is sweet to the soul,
   but to turn away from evil is an
      abomination to fools.
20 Whoever walks with the wise
      becomes wise,
   but the companion of fools suffers
      harm.
21 Misfortune pursues sinners,
   but prosperity rewards the
      righteous.
22 The good leave an inheritance to
      their children's children,
   but the sinner's wealth is laid up
      for the righteous.
23 The field of the poor may yield
      much food,
   but it is swept away through
      injustice.
24 Those who spare the rod hate their
      children,
   but those who love them are
      diligent to discipline them.
25 The righteous have enough to satisfy
      their appetite,
   but the belly of the wicked is
      empty.

14 The wise woman *p* builds her
      house,
   but the foolish tears it down with
      her own hands.
2 Those who walk uprightly fear the
      LORD,
   but one who is devious in
      conduct despises him.
3 The talk of fools is a rod for their
      backs,*q*
   but the lips of the wise preserve
      them.
4 Where there are no oxen, there is no
      grain;
   abundant crops come by the
      strength of the ox.
5 A faithful witness does not lie,
   but a false witness breathes
      out lies.
6 A scoffer seeks wisdom in vain,
   but knowledge is easy for one
      who understands.
7 Leave the presence of a fool,
   for there you do not find words of
      knowledge.
8 It is the wisdom of the clever to
      understand where they go,
   but the folly of fools misleads.
9 Fools mock at the guilt offering,*r*
   but the upright enjoy God's favor.
10 The heart knows its own bitterness,
   and no stranger shares its joy.

11 The house of the wicked is
      destroyed,
   but the tent of the upright
      flourishes.
12 There is a way that seems right to a
      person,
   but its end is the way to death.*s*
13 Even in laughter the heart is sad,
   and the end of joy is grief.
14 The perverse get what their ways
      deserve,
   and the good, what their deeds
      deserve.*t*
15 The simple believe everything,
   but the clever consider their steps.
16 The wise are cautious and turn away
      from evil,
   but the fool throws off restraint
      and is careless.
17 One who is quick-tempered acts
      foolishly,
   and the schemer is hated.
18 The simple are adorned with*u* folly,
   but the clever are crowned with
      knowledge.
19 The evil bow down before the good,
   the wicked at the gates of the
      righteous.
20 The poor are disliked even by their
      neighbors,
   but the rich have many friends.
21 Those who despise their neighbors
      are sinners,
   but happy are those who are kind
      to the poor.
22 Do they not err that plan evil?
   Those who plan good find loyalty
      and faithfulness.
23 In all toil there is profit,
   but mere talk leads only
      to poverty.
24 The crown of the wise is their
      wisdom,*v*
   but folly is the garland*w* of fools.
25 A truthful witness saves lives,
   but one who utters lies is a
      betrayer.
26 In the fear of the LORD one has
      strong confidence,
   and one's children will have a
      refuge.

p Heb *Wisdom of women*   *q* Cn: Heb *a rod of
pride*   *r* Meaning of Heb uncertain   *s* Heb *ways
of death*   *t* Cn: Heb *from upon him*   *u* Or *inherit*
v Cn Compare Gk: Heb *riches*   *w* Cn: Heb *is the
folly*

27 The fear of the LORD is a fountain of
    life,
        so that one may avoid the snares
        of death.
28 The glory of a king is a multitude of
    people;
        without people a prince is ruined.
29 Whoever is slow to anger has great
    understanding,
        but one who has a hasty temper
        exalts folly.
30 A tranquil mind gives life to
    the flesh,
        but passion makes the bones rot.
31 Those who oppress the poor insult
    their Maker,
        but those who are kind to the
        needy honor him.
32 The wicked are overthrown by their
    evildoing,
        but the righteous find a refuge in
        their integrity.*x*
33 Wisdom is at home in the mind of
    one who has understanding,
        but it is not*y* known in the heart
        of fools.
34 Righteousness exalts a nation,
        but sin is a reproach to any
        people.
35 A servant who deals wisely has the
    king's favor,
        but his wrath falls on one who
        acts shamefully.

15 A soft answer turns away wrath,
    but a harsh word stirs up anger.
2 The tongue of the wise dispenses
    knowledge,*z*
        but the mouths of fools pour
        out folly.
3 The eyes of the LORD are in every
    place,
        keeping watch on the evil and the
        good.
4 A gentle tongue is a tree of life,
        but perverseness in it breaks the
        spirit.
5 A fool despises a parent's
    instruction,
        but the one who heeds
        admonition is prudent.
6 In the house of the righteous there
    is much treasure,
        but trouble befalls the income of
        the wicked.
7 The lips of the wise spread
    knowledge;
        not so the minds of fools.

8 The sacrifice of the wicked is an
    abomination to the LORD,
        but the prayer of the upright is his
        delight.
9 The way of the wicked is an
    abomination to the LORD,
        but he loves the one who pursues
        righteousness.
10 There is severe discipline for one
    who forsakes the way,
        but one who hates a rebuke
        will die.
11 Sheol and Abaddon lie open before
    the LORD,
        how much more human hearts!
12 Scoffers do not like to be rebuked;
        they will not go to the wise.
13 A glad heart makes a cheerful
    countenance,
        but by sorrow of heart the spirit is
        broken.
14 The mind of one who has
    understanding seeks
    knowledge,
        but the mouths of fools feed
        on folly.
15 All the days of the poor are hard,
        but a cheerful heart has a
        continual feast.
16 Better is a little with the fear of the
    LORD
        than great treasure and trouble
        with it.
17 Better is a dinner of vegetables
    where love is
        than a fatted ox and hatred
        with it.
18 Those who are hot-tempered stir up
    strife,
        but those who are slow to anger
        calm contention.
19 The way of the lazy is overgrown
    with thorns,
        but the path of the upright is a
        level highway.
20 A wise child makes a glad father,
        but the foolish despise their
        mothers.
21 Folly is a joy to one who has no
    sense,
        but a person of understanding
        walks straight ahead.
22 Without counsel, plans go wrong,
        but with many advisers they
        succeed.

x Gk Syr: Heb *in their death*   *y* Gk Syr: Heb *lacks
not*   *z* Cn: Heb *makes knowledge good*

23 To make an apt answer is a joy to
   anyone,
   and a word in season, how good
   it is!
24 For the wise the path of life leads
   upward,
   in order to avoid Sheol below.

25 The LORD tears down the house of
   the proud,
   but maintains the widow's
   boundaries.
26 Evil plans are an abomination to the
   LORD,
   but gracious words are pure.

The Power of Kindness

THURSDAY

Scripture Reading
for Today:
Proverbs 15.1–7

Verse for Today:
Proverbs 15.1

I was delighted to find out that Karin, my friend from college days, was coming to visit. How wonderful it would be to see her again and to meet her new husband!

My husband, Al, and I decided to take our friends to one of the finest restaurants in town for the occasion. It was a place known for its excellent food, elegant decor, and courteous service.

Imagine my disappointment when we were greeted halfheartedly at the entrance to the restaurant. After waiting for a table, we were seated in a busy corner of a room that looked like a waiting room. But the worst part of it all was the waiter. The man was downright rude.

At first I was embarrassed and then angry at the treatment we were receiving. I was ready to ask for another table, when Karin caught my eye. "It's all right," she said softly.

What happened in the next hour or so was a marvel to behold. Each time this gruff waiter appeared, Karin smiled at him sweetly and said something kind. She went out of her way to compliment him even in the midst of his unwilling service. Instead of allowing his rude manner to spoil our joy, she seemed bent on drawing him into the celebration. By the end of the meal Karin had so completely won him over that he seemed like a different man. Before we left he picked a fresh flower from the table nearby and handed it to her.

"How did you manage to change that waiter, Karin?" I asked as we left.

Her answer came from the scriptures: "A soft answer turns away wrath, but a harsh word stirs up anger."

What a lesson I learned from my friend that day! When it would have been so easy to take offense, Karin chose instead to respond with kindness. That kindness did calm wrath (mine!). It touched hearts, made a new friend, and added to the joy of our celebration. The glory of God was revealed because one person chose to be kind.

—PATTI GALLAGHER MANSFIELD

Go to page 803 for your next devotional reading.

27 Those who are greedy for unjust
gain make trouble for their
households,
but those who hate bribes
will live.
28 The mind of the righteous ponders
how to answer,
but the mouth of the wicked
pours out evil.
29 The LORD is far from the wicked,
but he hears the prayer of the
righteous.
30 The light of the eyes rejoices the
heart,
and good news refreshes the body.
31 The ear that heeds wholesome
admonition
will lodge among the wise.
32 Those who ignore instruction
despise themselves,
but those who heed admonition
gain understanding.
33 The fear of the LORD is instruction in
wisdom,
and humility goes before honor.

16 The plans of the mind belong to
mortals,
but the answer of the tongue is
from the LORD.
2 All one's ways may be pure in one's
own eyes,
but the LORD weighs the spirit.
3 Commit your work to the LORD,
and your plans will be
established.
4 The LORD has made everything for its
purpose,
even the wicked for the day of
trouble.
5 All those who are arrogant are an
abomination to the LORD;
be assured, they will not go
unpunished.
6 By loyalty and faithfulness iniquity
is atoned for,
and by the fear of the LORD one
avoids evil.
7 When the ways of people please
the LORD,
he causes even their enemies to be
at peace with them.
8 Better is a little with righteousness
than large income with injustice.
9 The human mind plans the way,
but the LORD directs the steps.
10 Inspired decisions are on the lips of
a king;

his mouth does not sin in
judgment.
11 Honest balances and scales are
the LORD's;
all the weights in the bag are
his work.
12 It is an abomination to kings to
do evil,
for the throne is established by
righteousness.
13 Righteous lips are the delight of
a king,
and he loves those who speak
what is right.
14 A king's wrath is a messenger
of death,
and whoever is wise will
appease it.
15 In the light of a king's face there
is life,
and his favor is like the clouds
that bring the spring rain.
16 How much better to get wisdom
than gold!
To get understanding is to be
chosen rather than silver.
17 The highway of the upright
avoids evil;
those who guard their way
preserve their lives.
18 Pride goes before destruction,
and a haughty spirit before a fall.
19 It is better to be of a lowly spirit
among the poor
than to divide the spoil with
the proud.
20 Those who are attentive to a matter
will prosper,
and happy are those who trust in
the LORD.
21 The wise of heart is called
perceptive,
and pleasant speech increases
persuasiveness.
22 Wisdom is a fountain of life to one
who has it,
but folly is the punishment of
fools.
23 The mind of the wise makes their
speech judicious,
and adds persuasiveness to
their lips.
24 Pleasant words are like a
honeycomb,
sweetness to the soul and health
to the body.
25 Sometimes there is a way that seems
to be right,

but in the end it is the way
    to death.
26 The appetite of workers works for
    them;
    their hunger urges them on.
27 Scoundrels concoct evil,
    and their speech is like a
    scorching fire.
28 A perverse person spreads strife,
    and a whisperer separates close
    friends.
29 The violent entice their neighbors,
    and lead them in a way that is
    not good.
30 One who winks the eyes plans[a]
    perverse things;
    one who compresses the lips
    brings evil to pass.
31 Gray hair is a crown of glory;
    it is gained in a righteous life.
32 One who is slow to anger is better
    than the mighty,
    and one whose temper is
    controlled than one who
    captures a city.
33 The lot is cast into the lap,
    but the decision is the LORD's
    alone.

17 Better is a dry morsel with quiet
    than a house full of feasting
    with strife.
2 A slave who deals wisely will rule
    over a child who acts
    shamefully,
    and will share the inheritance as
    one of the family.
3 The crucible is for silver, and the
    furnace is for gold,
    but the LORD tests the heart.
4 An evildoer listens to wicked lips;
    and a liar gives heed to a
    mischievous tongue.
5 Those who mock the poor insult
    their Maker;
    those who are glad at calamity
    will not go unpunished.
6 Grandchildren are the crown of
    the aged,
    and the glory of children is their
    parents.
7 Fine speech is not becoming to
    a fool;
    still less is false speech to a
    ruler.[b]
8 A bribe is like a magic stone in the
    eyes of those who give it;
    wherever they turn they prosper.

9 One who forgives an affront fosters
    friendship,
    but one who dwells on disputes
    will alienate a friend.
10 A rebuke strikes deeper into a
    discerning person
    than a hundred blows into a fool.
11 Evil people seek only rebellion,
    but a cruel messenger will be sent
    against them.
12 Better to meet a she-bear robbed of
    its cubs
    than to confront a fool immersed
    in folly.
13 Evil will not depart from the house
    of one who returns evil for good.
14 The beginning of strife is like letting
    out water;
    so stop before the quarrel
    breaks out.
15 One who justifies the wicked and
    one who condemns the
    righteous
    are both alike an abomination to
    the LORD.
16 Why should fools have a price
    in hand
    to buy wisdom, when they have
    no mind to learn?
17 A friend loves at all times,
    and kinsfolk are born to share
    adversity.
18 It is senseless to give a pledge,
    to become surety for a neighbor.
19 One who loves transgression
    loves strife;
    one who builds a high threshold
    invites broken bones.
20 The crooked of mind do not
    prosper,
    and the perverse of tongue fall
    into calamity.
21 The one who begets a fool gets
    trouble;
    the parent of a fool has no joy.
22 A cheerful heart is a good medicine,
    but a downcast spirit dries up
    the bones.
23 The wicked accept a concealed bribe
    to pervert the ways of justice.
24 The discerning person looks to
    wisdom,
    but the eyes of a fool to the ends
    of the earth.
25 Foolish children are a grief to their
    father

---

a Gk Syr Vg Tg: Heb *to plan*   b Or *a noble person*

and bitterness to her who
bore them.
26 To impose a fine on the innocent is
not right,
or to flog the noble for their
integrity.
27 One who spares words is
knowledgeable;
one who is cool in spirit has
understanding.
28 Even fools who keep silent are
considered wise;
when they close their lips, they
are deemed intelligent.

18 The one who lives alone is
self-indulgent,
showing contempt for all who
have sound judgment.c
2 A fool takes no pleasure in
understanding,
but only in expressing personal
opinion.
3 When wickedness comes, contempt
comes also;
and with dishonor comes disgrace.
4 The words of the mouth are deep
waters;
the fountain of wisdom is a
gushing stream.
5 It is not right to be partial to
the guilty,
or to subvert the innocent in
judgment.
6 A fool's lips bring strife,
and a fool's mouth invites a
flogging.
7 The mouths of fools are their ruin,
and their lips a snare to
themselves.
8 The words of a whisperer are like
delicious morsels;
they go down into the inner parts
of the body.
9 One who is slack in work
is close kin to a vandal.
10 The name of the LORD is a strong
tower;
the righteous run into it and
are safe.
11 The wealth of the rich is their strong
city;
in their imagination it is like a
high wall.
12 Before destruction one's heart is
haughty,
but humility goes before honor.
13 If one gives answer before hearing,
it is folly and shame.

14 The human spirit will endure
sickness;
but a broken spirit—who
can bear?
15 An intelligent mind acquires
knowledge,
and the ear of the wise seeks
knowledge.
16 A gift opens doors;
it gives access to the great.
17 The one who first states a case seems
right,
until the other comes and
cross-examines.
18 Casting the lot puts an end to
disputes
and decides between powerful
contenders.
19 An ally offended is stronger than
a city;d
such quarreling is like the bars of
a castle.
20 From the fruit of the mouth one's
stomach is satisfied;
the yield of the lips brings
satisfaction.
21 Death and life are in the power of
the tongue,
and those who love it will eat
its fruits.
22 He who finds a wife finds a
good thing,
and obtains favor from the LORD.
23 The poor use entreaties,
but the rich answer roughly.
24 Somee friends play at friendshipf
but a true friend sticks closer than
one's nearest kin.

19 Better the poor walking in
integrity
than one perverse of speech who
is a fool.
2 Desire without knowledge is
not good,
and one who moves too hurriedly
misses the way.
3 One's own folly leads to ruin,
yet the heart rages against
the LORD.
4 Wealth brings many friends,
but the poor are left friendless.
5 A false witness will not go
unpunished,

c Meaning of Heb uncertain   d Gk Syr Vg Tg:
Meaning of Heb uncertain   e Syr Tg: Heb A
man of   f Cn Compare Syr Vg Tg: Meaning of
Heb uncertain

and a liar will not escape.

6 Many seek the favor of the generous,
  and everyone is a friend to a giver
    of gifts.

7 If the poor are hated even by their
    kin,
  how much more are they shunned
    by their friends!
  When they call after them, they are
    not there. *g*

8 To get wisdom is to love oneself;
  to keep understanding is
    to prosper.

9 A false witness will not go
    unpunished,
  and the liar will perish.

10 It is not fitting for a fool to live
    in luxury,
  much less for a slave to rule over
    princes.

11 Those with good sense are slow
    to anger,
  and it is their glory to overlook an
    offense.

12 A king's anger is like the growling of
    a lion,
  but his favor is like dew on
    the grass.

13 A stupid child is ruin to a father,
  and a wife's quarreling is a
    continual dripping of rain.

14 House and wealth are inherited from
    parents,
  but a prudent wife is from
    the LORD.

15 Laziness brings on deep sleep;
  an idle person will suffer hunger.

16 Those who keep the commandment
    will live;
  those who are heedless of their
    ways will die.

17 Whoever is kind to the poor lends
    to the LORD,
  and will be repaid in full.

18 Discipline your children while there
    is hope;
  do not set your heart on their
    destruction.

19 A violent tempered person will pay
    the penalty;
  if you effect a rescue, you will
    only have to do it again. *g*

20 Listen to advice and accept
    instruction,
  that you may gain wisdom for the
    future.

21 The human mind may devise
    many plans,

but it is the purpose of the LORD
  that will be established.

22 What is desirable in a person
    is loyalty,
  and it is better to be poor than
    a liar.

23 The fear of the LORD is life indeed;
  filled with it one rests secure
  and suffers no harm.

24 The lazy person buries a hand in the
    dish,
  and will not even bring it back to
    the mouth.

25 Strike a scoffer, and the simple will
    learn prudence;
  reprove the intelligent, and they
    will gain knowledge.

26 Those who do violence to their
    father and chase away their
    mother
  are children who cause shame and
    bring reproach.

27 Cease straying, my child, from the
    words of knowledge,
  in order that you may hear
    instruction.

28 A worthless witness mocks at justice,
  and the mouth of the wicked
    devours iniquity.

29 Condemnation is ready for scoffers,
  and flogging for the backs of
    fools.

20 Wine is a mocker, strong drink a
    brawler,
  and whoever is led astray by it is
    not wise.

2 The dread anger of a king is like the
    growling of a lion;
  anyone who provokes him to
    anger forfeits life itself.

3 It is honorable to refrain from strife,
  but every fool is quick to quarrel.

4 The lazy person does not plow
    in season;
  harvest comes, and there is
    nothing to be found.

5 The purposes in the human mind
    are like deep water,
  but the intelligent will draw them
    out.

6 Many proclaim themselves loyal,
  but who can find one worthy
    of trust?

7 The righteous walk in integrity—
  happy are the children who follow
    them!

g Meaning of Heb uncertain

8 A king who sits on the throne of
  judgment
   winnows all evil with his eyes.
9 Who can say, "I have made my
   heart clean;
   I am pure from my sin"?
10 Diverse weights and diverse
   measures
   are both alike an abomination to
   the LORD.
11 Even children make themselves
   known by their acts,
   by whether what they do is pure
   and right.
12 The hearing ear and the seeing eye—
   the LORD has made them both.
13 Do not love sleep, or else you will
   come to poverty;

open your eyes, and you will have
   plenty of bread.
14 "Bad, bad," says the buyer,
   then goes away and boasts.
15 There is gold, and abundance of
   costly stones;
   but the lips informed by
   knowledge are a
   precious jewel.
16 Take the garment of one who has
   given surety for a stranger;
   seize the pledge given as surety for
   foreigners.
17 Bread gained by deceit is sweet,
   but afterward the mouth will be
   full of gravel.
18 Plans are established by
   taking advice;

THE TRADITION

Almsgiving

Whoever is kind to the poor lends to the LORD.
PROVERBS 19.17

Who is the world's greatest philan-
thropist?

The best answer is "God." He is the
supreme lover of humanity, the almsgiver par
excellence.

God is the source of every good thing.
All the wonders of the cosmos, every person's treasury of joys, abilities, and relationships . . . the list of God's "alms" unfurls into
infinity.

None of God's gifts is substandard, like
the tattered clothing and no-brand canned
goods we sometimes donate to charity. In
fact, one gift is so precious that it eclipses all
the rest. Paul spoke of this gift as the "surpassing value of knowing Christ Jesus my
Lord" and "the power of his resurrection"
(Philippians 3.7–11).

God lavishes his gifts on us, who are
poor in ourselves and have no claim to them.
His generosity sets the standard. "You received without payment; give without payment," Jesus tells the apostles—and us

(Matthew 10.8). Almsgiving is every Christian's commission.

Whatever form our almsgiving takes, we
are to offer it as mercy. In fact, New Testament Greek makes an explicit connection between alms and mercy: The word for the first
is derived from the word for the second.
When the crippled beggar at the temple gate
pleads for alms—that is, mercy—Peter offers
what he has: not silver or gold, but a stunning
expression of God's mercy (see Acts 3.1–10).

While few of us feel equipped to heal
people who are disabled, few of us can plead
inability to offer more ordinary alms of money or goods. Almsgiving is one of the charitable actions we call the "corporal works of
mercy."

Above all, almsgiving is a matter of giving
love—a love that sees beyond its immediate
recipient—to the Lord (see Proverbs 19.17).
Distressingly disguised in the needy, as
Mother Teresa liked to say, it is Jesus who so-
licits our mercy.

wage war by following wise
   guidance.
19 A gossip reveals secrets;
   therefore do not associate with a
      babbler.
20 If you curse father or mother,
   your lamp will go out in utter
      darkness.
21 An estate quickly acquired in the
      beginning
   will not be blessed in the end.
22 Do not say, "I will repay evil";
   wait for the LORD, and he will help
      you.
23 Differing weights are an
      abomination to the LORD,
   and false scales are not good.
24 All our steps are ordered by the
      LORD;
   how then can we understand our
      own ways?
25 It is a snare for one to say rashly,
      "It is holy,"
   and begin to reflect only after
      making a vow.
26 A wise king winnows the wicked,
   and drives the wheel over them.
27 The human spirit is the lamp of the
      LORD,
   searching every inmost part.
28 Loyalty and faithfulness preserve the
      king,
   and his throne is upheld by
      righteousness.*h*
29 The glory of youths is their strength,
   but the beauty of the aged is their
      gray hair.
30 Blows that wound cleanse away evil;
   beatings make clean the innermost
      parts.

21 The king's heart is a stream of
      water in the hand of
      the LORD;
   he turns it wherever he will.
2 All deeds are right in the sight of the
      doer,
   but the LORD weighs the heart.
3 To do righteousness and justice
   is more acceptable to the LORD
      than sacrifice.
4 Haughty eyes and a proud heart—
   the lamp of the wicked—are sin.
5 The plans of the diligent lead surely
      to abundance,
   but everyone who is hasty comes
      only to want.
6 The getting of treasures by a lying
      tongue

is a fleeting vapor and a snare*i*
   of death.
7 The violence of the wicked will
      sweep them away,
   because they refuse to do what
      is just.
8 The way of the guilty is crooked,
   but the conduct of the pure
      is right.
9 It is better to live in a corner of the
      housetop
   than in a house shared with a
      contentious wife.
10 The souls of the wicked desire evil;
   their neighbors find no mercy in
      their eyes.
11 When a scoffer is punished, the
      simple become wiser;
   when the wise are instructed, they
      increase in knowledge.
12 The Righteous One observes the
      house of the wicked;
   he casts the wicked down to ruin.
13 If you close your ear to the cry of
      the poor,
   you will cry out and not be heard.
14 A gift in secret averts anger;
   and a concealed bribe in the
      bosom, strong wrath.
15 When justice is done, it is a joy to
      the righteous,
   but dismay to evildoers.
16 Whoever wanders from the way of
      understanding
   will rest in the assembly of
      the dead.
17 Whoever loves pleasure will suffer
      want;
   whoever loves wine and oil will
      not be rich.
18 The wicked is a ransom for the
      righteous,
   and the faithless for the upright.
19 It is better to live in a desert land
   than with a contentious and
      fretful wife.
20 Precious treasure remains*j* in the
      house of the wise,
   but the fool devours it.
21 Whoever pursues righteousness and
      kindness
   will find life*k* and honor.
22 One wise person went up against a
      city of warriors

h Gk: Heb *loyalty*   *i* Gk: Heb *seekers*   *j* Gk: Heb
and oil   *k* Gk: Heb *life and righteousness*

and brought down the stronghold
in which they trusted.
23 To watch over mouth and tongue
is to keep out of trouble.
24 The proud, haughty person, named
"Scoffer,"
acts with arrogant pride.
25 The craving of the lazy person
is fatal,
for lazy hands refuse to labor.
26 All day long the wicked covet,[l]
but the righteous give and do not
hold back.
27 The sacrifice of the wicked is an
abomination;
how much more when brought
with evil intent.
28 A false witness will perish,
but a good listener will testify
successfully.
29 The wicked put on a bold face,
but the upright give thought to[m]
their ways.
30 No wisdom, no understanding, no
counsel,
can avail against the LORD.
31 The horse is made ready for the day
of battle,
but the victory belongs to
the LORD.

22 A good name is to be chosen
rather than great riches,
and favor is better than silver
or gold.
2 The rich and the poor have this in
common:
the LORD is the maker of them all.
3 The clever see danger and hide;
but the simple go on, and suffer
for it.
4 The reward for humility and fear of
the LORD
is riches and honor and life.
5 Thorns and snares are in the way of
the perverse;
the cautious will keep far from
them.
6 Train children in the right way,
and when old, they will not stray.
7 The rich rule over the poor,
and the borrower is the slave of
the lender.
8 Whoever sows injustice will reap
calamity,
and the rod of anger will fail.
9 Those who are generous are blessed,
for they share their bread with the
poor.

10 Drive out a scoffer, and strife
goes out;
quarreling and abuse will cease.
11 Those who love a pure heart and are
gracious in speech
will have the king as a friend.
12 The eyes of the LORD keep watch
over knowledge,
but he overthrows the words of
the faithless.
13 The lazy person says, "There is a
lion outside!
I shall be killed in the streets!"
14 The mouth of a loose[n] woman is a
deep pit;
he with whom the LORD is angry
falls into it.
15 Folly is bound up in the heart of
a boy,
but the rod of discipline drives it
far away.
16 Oppressing the poor in order to
enrich oneself,
and giving to the rich, will lead
only to loss.

Sayings of the Wise

17 The words of the wise:

Incline your ear and hear my
words,[o]
and apply your mind to my
teaching;
18 for it will be pleasant if you keep
them within you,
if all of them are ready on
your lips.
19 So that your trust may be in
the LORD,
I have made them known to you
today—yes, to you.
20 Have I not written for you thirty
sayings
of admonition and knowledge,
21 to show you what is right and true,
so that you may give a true
answer to those who
sent you?

22 Do not rob the poor because they
are poor,
or crush the afflicted at the gate;
23 for the LORD pleads their cause

---

l Gk: Heb *all day long one covets covetously*
m Another reading is *establish*　　*n* Heb *strange*
o Cn Compare Gk: Heb *Incline your ear, and hear
the words of the wise*

and despoils of life those who
   despoil them.
²⁴ Make no friends with those given to
   anger,
   and do not associate with
   hotheads,
²⁵ or you may learn their ways
   and entangle yourself in a snare.
²⁶ Do not be one of those who give
   pledges,
   who become surety for debts.
²⁷ If you have nothing with which
   to pay,

why should your bed be taken
   from under you?
²⁸ Do not remove the ancient
   landmark
   that your ancestors set up.
²⁹ Do you see those who are skillful in
   their work?
   They will serve kings;
   they will not serve common
   people.

23 When you sit down to eat with
   a ruler,

An Understanding Heart

FRIDAY

Scripture Reading
for Today:
Proverbs 22.1–6

Verses for Today:
Proverbs 22.6

Once one of my sons came home from school, and I knew instantly that something was wrong. I ventured a question, "What's
wrong, Mike?" and his quick answer, "Nothing," told me that indeed something was amiss. If it wasn't, I knew him well enough
to know that he would have looked up questioningly and asked,
"Nothing. Why?" His abrupt "Nothing" also told me not to meddle, so I didn't.

But a while later, when he was ready to talk about it, he came
and told me he had been the last one chosen that day for football.
Remember how painful that was? You stood there praying silently
to be chosen and as the list got lower and lower, your stomach
cramps got stronger and stronger. And there was an ultimate in-
dignity. If you were really bad, as I was in baseball, even when you
were the last one chosen, once in a while the team would ask, "Do
we have to take her?"

So when Mike told me he had been the last one chosen, primarily because he was short then and the game was football, I
knew how he felt. "That's a terrible feeling," I said, "standing there
and watching everyone else get picked."

His head snapped up. It never occurred to him that a parent
could have been the last one chosen. He asked a lot of questions,
shifting the attention from his pain to my experiences as a child.
After a while, he ate a couple of bananas and went out to play.

So often we parents neglect to share with our children our
past—and present—feelings of being inadequate, awkward, ugly,
not loved, or not treated fairly. Unless we share ourselves with
them, they think we've come full-blown to adulthood, never once
doubting ourselves. They're much more likely to communicate
their feelings to us if they know we experience such feelings, too.

—*DOLORES CURRAN*

Go to page 808 for your next devotional reading.

observe carefully what[p] is
  before you,
2 and put a knife to your throat
  if you have a big appetite.
3 Do not desire the ruler's[q] delicacies,
  for they are deceptive food.
4 Do not wear yourself out to get rich;
  be wise enough to desist.
5 When your eyes light upon it,
    it is gone;
  for suddenly it takes wings to
    itself,
  flying like an eagle toward heaven.
6 Do not eat the bread of the stingy;
  do not desire their delicacies;
7 for like a hair in the throat, so
    are they.[r]
  "Eat and drink!" they say to you;
  but they do not mean it.
8 You will vomit up the little you
    have eaten,
  and you will waste your pleasant
    words.
9 Do not speak in the hearing of
    a fool,
  who will only despise the wisdom
    of your words.
10 Do not remove an ancient landmark
  or encroach on the fields of
    orphans,
11 for their redeemer is strong;
  he will plead their cause
    against you.
12 Apply your mind to instruction
  and your ear to words of
    knowledge.
13 Do not withhold discipline from
    your children;
  if you beat them with a rod, they
    will not die.
14 If you beat them with the rod,
  you will save their lives from
    Sheol.
15 My child, if your heart is wise,
  my heart too will be glad.
16 My soul will rejoice
  when your lips speak what
    is right.
17 Do not let your heart envy sinners,
  but always continue in the fear of
    the LORD.
18 Surely there is a future,
  and your hope will not be cut off.

19 Hear, my child, and be wise,
  and direct your mind in the way.
20 Do not be among winebibbers,

or among gluttonous eaters
    of meat;
21 for the drunkard and the glutton
  will come to poverty,
  and drowsiness will clothe them
    with rags.

22 Listen to your father who begot you,
  and do not despise your mother
    when she is old.
23 Buy truth, and do not sell it;
  buy wisdom, instruction, and
    understanding.
24 The father of the righteous will
    greatly rejoice;
  he who begets a wise son will be
    glad in him.
25 Let your father and mother be glad;
  let her who bore you rejoice.

26 My child, give me your heart,
  and let your eyes observe[s] my
    ways.
27 For a prostitute is a deep pit;
  an adulteress[t] is a narrow well.
28 She lies in wait like a robber
  and increases the number of the
    faithless.

29 Who has woe? Who has sorrow?
  Who has strife? Who has
    complaining?
  Who has wounds without cause?
  Who has redness of eyes?
30 Those who linger late over wine,
  those who keep trying
    mixed wines.
31 Do not look at wine when it is red,
  when it sparkles in the cup
  and goes down smoothly.
32 At the last it bites like a serpent,
  and stings like an adder.
33 Your eyes will see strange things,
  and your mind utter perverse
    things.
34 You will be like one who lies down
    in the midst of the sea,
  like one who lies on the top of
    a mast.[r]
35 "They struck me," you will say,[u]
  "but I was not hurt;
  they beat me, but I did not feel it.
  When shall I awake?

p Or who   q Heb his   r Meaning of Heb
uncertain   s Another reading is delight in
t Heb an alien woman   u Gk Syr Vg Tg: Heb
lacks you will say

I will seek another drink."

24
Do not envy the wicked,
nor desire to be with them;
2 for their minds devise violence,
and their lips talk of mischief.

3 By wisdom a house is built,
and by understanding it is
established;
4 by knowledge the rooms are filled
with all precious and pleasant
riches.
5 Wise warriors are mightier than
strong ones,*v*
and those who have knowledge
than those who have strength;
6 for by wise guidance you can wage
your war,
and in abundance of counselors
there is victory.
7 Wisdom is too high for fools;
in the gate they do not open
their mouths.

8 Whoever plans to do evil
will be called a mischief-maker.
9 The devising of folly is sin,
and the scoffer is an abomination
to all.

10 If you faint in the day of adversity,
your strength being small;
11 if you hold back from rescuing those
taken away to death,
those who go staggering to the
slaughter;
12 if you say, "Look, we did not
know this" —
does not he who weighs the heart
perceive it?
Does not he who keeps watch over
your soul know it?
And will he not repay all
according to their deeds?

13 My child, eat honey, for it is good,
and the drippings of the
honeycomb are sweet to
your taste.
14 Know that wisdom is such to
your soul;
if you find it, you will find a
future,
and your hope will not be cut off.

15 Do not lie in wait like an outlaw
against the home of the
righteous;

do no violence to the place where
the righteous live;
16 for though they fall seven times,
they will rise again;
but the wicked are overthrown by
calamity.

17 Do not rejoice when your enemies
fall,
and do not let your heart be glad
when they stumble,
18 or else the LORD will see it and be
displeased,
and turn away his anger
from them.

19 Do not fret because of evildoers.
Do not envy the wicked;
20 for the evil have no future;
the lamp of the wicked will
go out.

21 My child, fear the LORD and the king,
and do not disobey either of
them;*w*
22 for disaster comes from them
suddenly,
and who knows the ruin that both
can bring?

Further Sayings of the Wise

23 These also are sayings of the wise:

Partiality in judging is not good.
24 Whoever says to the wicked, "You
are innocent,"
will be cursed by peoples,
abhorred by nations;
25 but those who rebuke the wicked
will have delight,
and a good blessing will come
upon them.
26 One who gives an honest answer
gives a kiss on the lips.

27 Prepare your work outside,
get everything ready for you in the
field;
and after that build your house.

28 Do not be a witness against your
neighbor without cause,
and do not deceive with your lips.
29 Do not say, "I will do to others as
they have done to me;

v Gk Compare Syr Tg: Heb *A wise man is strength*
w Gk: Heb *do not associate with those who change*

I will pay them back for what they
have done."

30 I passed by the field of one who was
lazy,
by the vineyard of a stupid
person;
31 and see, it was all overgrown with
thorns;
the ground was covered with
nettles,
and its stone wall was broken
down.
32 Then I saw and considered it;
I looked and received instruction.
33 A little sleep, a little slumber,
a little folding of the hands
to rest,
34 and poverty will come upon you
like a robber,
and want, like an armed warrior.

Further Wise Sayings of Solomon

25 These are other proverbs of Solomon that the officials of King
Hezekiah of Judah copied.

2 It is the glory of God to conceal
things,
but the glory of kings is to search
things out.
3 Like the heavens for height, like the
earth for depth,
so the mind of kings is
unsearchable.
4 Take away the dross from the silver,
and the smith has material for
a vessel;
5 take away the wicked from the
presence of the king,
and his throne will be established
in righteousness.
6 Do not put yourself forward in the
king's presence
or stand in the place of the great;
7 for it is better to be told, "Come
up here,"
than to be put lower in the
presence of a noble.

What your eyes have seen
8 do not hastily bring into court;
for[x] what will you do in the end,
when your neighbor puts you to
shame?
9 Argue your case with your neighbor
directly,

and do not disclose another's
secret;
10 or else someone who hears you will
bring shame upon you,
and your ill repute will have
no end.

11 A word fitly spoken
is like apples of gold in a setting
of silver.
12 Like a gold ring or an ornament
of gold
is a wise rebuke to a listening ear.
13 Like the cold of snow in the time
of harvest
are faithful messengers to those
who send them;
they refresh the spirit of their
masters.
14 Like clouds and wind without rain
is one who boasts of a gift never
given.
15 With patience a ruler may be
persuaded,
and a soft tongue can break
bones.
16 If you have found honey, eat only
enough for you,
or else, having too much, you will
vomit it.
17 Let your foot be seldom in your
neighbor's house,
otherwise the neighbor will
become weary of you and
hate you.
18 Like a war club, a sword, or a sharp
arrow
is one who bears false witness
against a neighbor.
19 Like a bad tooth or a lame foot
is trust in a faithless person in
time of trouble.
20 Like vinegar on a wound[y]
is one who sings songs to a heavy
heart.
Like a moth in clothing or a worm
in wood,
sorrow gnaws at the human
heart.[z]
21 If your enemies are hungry, give
them bread to eat;
and if they are thirsty, give them
water to drink;

x Cn: Heb *or else*   *y* Gk: Heb *Like one who takes
off a garment on a cold day, like vinegar on lye*
z Gk Syr Tg: Heb lacks *Like a moth . . . human
heart*

22 for you will heap coals of fire on
     their heads,
  and the Lord will reward you.
23 The north wind produces rain,
  and a backbiting tongue, angry
     looks.
24 It is better to live in a corner of the
     housetop
  than in a house shared with a
     contentious wife.
25 Like cold water to a thirsty soul,
  so is good news from a far
     country.
26 Like a muddied spring or a polluted
     fountain
  are the righteous who give way
     before the wicked.
27 It is not good to eat much honey,
  or to seek honor on top of honor.
28 Like a city breached, without walls,
  is one who lacks self-control.

26 Like snow in summer or rain in
     harvest,
  so honor is not fitting for a fool.
2 Like a sparrow in its flitting, like a
     swallow in its flying,
  an undeserved curse goes
     nowhere.
3 A whip for the horse, a bridle for
     the donkey,
  and a rod for the back of fools.
4 Do not answer fools according to
     their folly,
  or you will be a fool yourself.
5 Answer fools according to their folly,
  or they will be wise in their
     own eyes.
6 It is like cutting off one's foot and
     drinking down violence,
  to send a message by a fool.
7 The legs of a disabled person hang
     limp;
  so does a proverb in the mouth of
     a fool.
8 It is like binding a stone in a sling
  to give honor to a fool.
9 Like a thornbush brandished by the
     hand of a drunkard
  is a proverb in the mouth of
     a fool.
10 Like an archer who wounds
     everybody
  is one who hires a passing fool or
     drunkard.*a*
11 Like a dog that returns to its vomit
  is a fool who reverts to his folly.
12 Do you see persons wise in their
     own eyes?

There is more hope for fools than
     for them.
13 The lazy person says, "There is a
     lion in the road!
  There is a lion in the streets!"
14 As a door turns on its hinges,
  so does a lazy person in bed.
15 The lazy person buries a hand in the
     dish,
  and is too tired to bring it back to
     the mouth.
16 The lazy person is wiser in
     self-esteem
  than seven who can answer
     discreetly.
17 Like somebody who takes a passing
     dog by the ears
  is one who meddles in the quarrel
     of another.
18 Like a maniac who shoots deadly
     firebrands and arrows,
19 so is one who deceives a neighbor
  and says, "I am only joking!"
20 For lack of wood the fire goes out,
  and where there is no whisperer,
     quarreling ceases.
21 As charcoal is to hot embers and
     wood to fire,
  so is a quarrelsome person for
     kindling strife.
22 The words of a whisperer are like
     delicious morsels;
  they go down into the inner parts
     of the body.
23 Like the glaze*b* covering an earthen
     vessel
  are smooth*c* lips with an
     evil heart.
24 An enemy dissembles in speaking
  while harboring deceit within;
25 when an enemy speaks graciously,
     do not believe it,
  for there are seven abominations
     concealed within;
26 though hatred is covered with guile,
  the enemy's wickedness will be
     exposed in the assembly.
27 Whoever digs a pit will fall into it,
  and a stone will come back on the
     one who starts it rolling.
28 A lying tongue hates its victims,
  and a flattering mouth works ruin.

27 Do not boast about tomorrow,
  for you do not know what a
     day may bring.

---

a Meaning of Heb uncertain *b* Cn: Heb *silver of
dross* *c* Gk: Heb *burning*

Michal

Her Name Means "Who Is Like God?"

Read I Samuel 18.20–29; 19.11–17

Scene One: Michal stretched herself across the window's edge. Leaning out as far as she dared, she watched as David ran through the night shadows. Even if her father the king pursued with an army, she was confident he would not catch her husband.

She had loved the shepherd boy since the day he had calmed Saul's troubled soul with his harp playing. After he defeated the hideous Goliath with only a sling and a stone, all Israel fell in love with him. She turned from the window, grateful for the chance to have aided her husband's escape.

Discovering David's disappearance, Saul confronted his daughter: "Why have you deceived me like this, and let my enemy go, so that he has escaped?" (19.17).

Michal lowered her eyes and replied, "He said to me, 'Let me go; why should I kill you?' " (verse 17). She held her breath, certain her father would never swallow so bold a lie.

Scene Two: (Nine years or more have passed.) Michal glanced out the window, arms folded tightly against her breast, observing the scene below. King David had entered Jerusalem, leaping and dancing as the ark of the covenant was carried into Jerusalem (see 2 Samuel 6.16). He looked, she thought, more like a romping goat than a great king.

From then on, silence spread like thickening ice between them. The queen ended her days alone, with neither children nor family to warm her.

Twice, Michal stood at a window observ-

Her Character: *A woman of strong emotions, she was unable to control the important circumstances of her life. Forcibly separated from two husbands, she lost her father and her brother, who were savaged by their enemies.*

Her Sorrow: *That she was ensnared in the drawn-out battle between Saul and David.*

Her Joy: *She enjoyed a passionate, though short-lived, love for David.*

ing David. In the first scene, Scripture paints her as David's wife but in the second, as Saul's daughter. In fact, her attitude is so changed that we feel perplexed, watching her as she watches David. We need to find a corridor connecting the two windows, a passageway that led somehow from love to scorn.

Michal may have expected her separation from David to be a short one, her idealism forging a happy ending to their fairy tale love. Was she shocked when her father punished her by marrying her to another man (see I Samuel 25.44)? Did her bitterness grow during David's long absence? Had she finally made peace with her new husband only to be torn from him when David demanded her back after Saul's death?

Perhaps Michal realized she had always been someone else's pawn, a mere woman manipulated by powerful men. First her own father used her, promising her to David in hopes she would prove a snare to him. Finally, one of her brothers handed her back to David after Saul's death, further legitimizing David's claim to the throne. A princess, then a queen, she was still a slave.

Michal's story is tragic. Throughout the difficult circumstances of her life, we see little evidence of a faith to sustain her. Instead, she is tossed back and forth, her heart left to draw its own bitter conclusions. In the last scene with David, we see a woman blind with scorn.

The story of Michal seems to indicate that she grew to be more like Saul than David. As such, she reminds us that even victims have choices. No matter how much we've been sinned against, we still have the power to choose the attitude of our heart.

Praying With Michal

Now Saul's daughter Michal loved David. Saul was told, and the thing pleased him. Saul thought, "Let me give her to him that she may be a snare for him and that the hand of the Philistines may be against him." —*1 Samuel 18.20–21*

As the ark of the LORD came into the city of David, Michal daughter of Saul looked out of the window, and saw King David leaping and dancing before the LORD; and she despised him in her heart. —*2 Samuel 6.16*

Praise God: *Because he is the same, yesterday, today, and forever.*

Offer Thanks: *That God gives us the freedom to choose how we will respond to him.*

Confess: *Allowing skepticism or cynicism to infiltrate your faith.*

Ask God: *To increase your awe of him.*

Lift Your Heart

David was so exuberant that he danced in public as a way of worshiping God. You may not be quite ready to take your joy to the streets, but you can loosen up a bit by raising your hands in prayer, visiting a church whose worship style is a little outside your comfort zone, or just dancing and singing along with a praise and worship tape when no one else is home. Go ahead. Enjoy yourself in God's presence! If he's not worth getting excited about, who is?

"Make a joyful noise to God, all the earth; sing the glory of his name; give to him glorious praise. Say to God, 'How awesome are your deeds! Because of your great power, your enemies cringe before you. All the earth worships you; they sing praises to you, sing praises to your name'" (Psalm 66.1–4).

Go to page 818 for your next devotional reading.

2 Let another praise you, and not your
        own mouth—
     a stranger, and not your own lips.
3 A stone is heavy, and sand is
        weighty,
     but a fool's provocation is heavier
        than both.
4 Wrath is cruel, anger is
        overwhelming,
     but who is able to stand before
        jealousy?
5 Better is open rebuke
     than hidden love.
6 Well meant are the wounds a friend
        inflicts,
     but profuse are the kisses of an
        enemy.
7 The sated appetite spurns honey,
     but to a ravenous appetite even
        the bitter is sweet.
8 Like a bird that strays from its nest
     is one who strays from home.
9 Perfume and incense make the heart
        glad,
     but the soul is torn by trouble.*d*
10 Do not forsake your friend or the
        friend of your parent;
     do not go to the house of your
        kindred in the day of your
        calamity.
     Better is a neighbor who is nearby
        than kindred who are far away.
11 Be wise, my child, and make my
        heart glad,
     so that I may answer whoever
        reproaches me.
12 The clever see danger and hide;
     but the simple go on, and suffer
        for it.
13 Take the garment of one who has
        given surety for a stranger;
     seize the pledge given as surety for
        foreigners.*e*
14 Whoever blesses a neighbor with a
        loud voice,
     rising early in the morning,
     will be counted as cursing.
15 A continual dripping on a rainy day
     and a contentious wife are alike;
16 to restrain her is to restrain the wind
     or to grasp oil in the right hand.*f*
17 Iron sharpens iron,
     and one person sharpens the
        wits*g* of another.
18 Anyone who tends a fig tree will eat
        its fruit,
     and anyone who takes care of a
        master will be honored.

19 Just as water reflects the face,
     so one human heart reflects
        another.
20 Sheol and Abaddon are never
        satisfied,
     and human eyes are never
        satisfied.
21 The crucible is for silver, and the
        furnace is for gold,
     so a person is tested*h* by being
        praised.
22 Crush a fool in a mortar with a
        pestle
     along with crushed grain,
     but the folly will not be
        driven out.

23 Know well the condition of
        your flocks,
     and give attention to your herds;
24 for riches do not last forever,
     nor a crown for all generations.
25 When the grass is gone, and new
        growth appears,
     and the herbage of the mountains
        is gathered,
26 the lambs will provide your
        clothing,
     and the goats the price of a field;
27 there will be enough goats' milk for
        your food,
     for the food of your household
     and nourishment for your
        servant-girls.

28 The wicked flee when no one
        pursues,
     but the righteous are as bold as
        a lion.
2 When a land rebels
     it has many rulers;
     but with an intelligent ruler
        there is lasting order.*f*
3 A ruler*i* who oppresses the poor
     is a beating rain that leaves
        no food.
4 Those who forsake the law praise
        the wicked,
     but those who keep the law
        struggle against them.
5 The evil do not understand justice,
     but those who seek the LORD
        understand it completely.

d Gk: Heb *the sweetness of a friend is better than
one's own counsel*   *e* Vg and 20.16: Heb *for a
foreign woman*   *f* Meaning of Heb uncertain
g Heb *face*   *h* Heb lacks *is tested*   *i* Cn: Heb *A
poor person*

6 Better to be poor and walk in
        integrity
    than to be crooked in one's ways
        even though rich.
7 Those who keep the law are wise
        children,
    but companions of gluttons
        shame their parents.
8 One who augments wealth by
        exorbitant interest
    gathers it for another who is kind
        to the poor.
9 When one will not listen to the
        law,
    even one's prayers are an
        abomination.
10 Those who mislead the upright into
        evil ways
    will fall into pits of their own
        making,
    but the blameless will have a
        goodly inheritance.
11 The rich is wise in self-esteem,
    but an intelligent poor person sees
        through the pose.
12 When the righteous triumph, there
        is great glory,
    but when the wicked prevail,
        people go into hiding.
13 No one who conceals transgressions
        will prosper,
    but one who confesses and
        forsakes them will obtain
        mercy.
14 Happy is the one who is never
        without fear,
    but one who is hard-hearted will
        fall into calamity.
15 Like a roaring lion or a charging
        bear
    is a wicked ruler over a poor
        people.
16 A ruler who lacks understanding is a
        cruel oppressor;
    but one who hates unjust gain
        will enjoy a long life.
17 If someone is burdened with the
        blood of another,
    let that killer be a fugitive
        until death;
    let no one offer assistance.
18 One who walks in integrity will
        be safe,
    but whoever follows crooked ways
        will fall into the Pit. *j*
19 Anyone who tills the land will have
        plenty of bread,

    but one who follows worthless
        pursuits will have plenty
        of poverty.
20 The faithful will abound with
        blessings,
    but one who is in a hurry to be
        rich will not go unpunished.
21 To show partiality is not good—
    yet for a piece of bread a person
        may do wrong.
22 The miser is in a hurry to get rich
    and does not know that loss is
        sure to come.
23 Whoever rebukes a person will
        afterward find more favor
    than one who flatters with
        the tongue.
24 Anyone who robs father or mother
    and says, "That is no crime,"
    is partner to a thug.
25 The greedy person stirs up strife,
    but whoever trusts in the LORD will
        be enriched.
26 Those who trust in their own wits
        are fools;
    but those who walk in wisdom
        come through safely.
27 Whoever gives to the poor will lack
        nothing,
    but one who turns a blind eye
        will get many a curse.
28 When the wicked prevail, people go
        into hiding;
    but when they perish, the
        righteous increase.

29 One who is often reproved, yet
        remains stubborn,
    will suddenly be broken beyond
        healing.
2 When the righteous are in authority,
        the people rejoice;
    but when the wicked rule, the
        people groan.
3 A child who loves wisdom makes a
        parent glad,
    but to keep company with
        prostitutes is to squander
        one's substance.
4 By justice a king gives stability to the
        land,
    but one who makes heavy
        exactions ruins it.
5 Whoever flatters a neighbor
    is spreading a net for the
        neighbor's feet.

j Syr: Heb *fall all at once*

6 In the transgression of the evil there
　　is a snare,
　　but the righteous sing and rejoice.
7 The righteous know the rights of the
　　poor;
　　the wicked have no such
　　understanding.
8 Scoffers set a city aflame,
　　but the wise turn away wrath.
9 If the wise go to law with fools,
　　there is ranting and ridicule
　　without relief.
10 The bloodthirsty hate the blameless,
　　and they seek the life of the
　　upright.
11 A fool gives full vent to anger,
　　but the wise quietly holds it back.
12 If a ruler listens to falsehood,
　　all his officials will be wicked.
13 The poor and the oppressor have
　　this in common:
　　the LORD gives light to the eyes of
　　both.
14 If a king judges the poor with
　　equity,
　　his throne will be established
　　forever.
15 The rod and reproof give wisdom,
　　but a mother is disgraced by a
　　neglected child.
16 When the wicked are in authority,
　　transgression increases,
　　but the righteous will look upon
　　their downfall.
17 Discipline your children, and they
　　will give you rest;
　　they will give delight to your
　　heart.
18 Where there is no prophecy, the
　　people cast off restraint,
　　but happy are those who keep
　　the law.
19 By mere words servants are not
　　disciplined,
　　for though they understand, they
　　will not give heed.
20 Do you see someone who is hasty
　　in speech?
　　There is more hope for a fool
　　than for anyone like that.
21 A slave pampered from childhood
　　will come to a bad end.[k]
22 One given to anger stirs up strife,
　　and the hothead causes much
　　transgression.
23 A person's pride will bring
　　humiliation,

but one who is lowly in spirit will
　　obtain honor.
24 To be a partner of a thief is to hate
　　one's own life;
　　one hears the victim's curse, but
　　discloses nothing.[l]
25 The fear of others[m] lays a snare,
　　but one who trusts in the LORD
　　is secure.
26 Many seek the favor of a ruler,
　　but it is from the LORD that one
　　gets justice.
27 The unjust are an abomination to
　　the righteous,
　　but the upright are an
　　abomination to the wicked.

Sayings of Agur

30 The words of Agur son of Jakeh.
　　An oracle.

Thus says the man: I am weary,
　　O God,
　　I am weary, O God. How can I
　　prevail?[n]
2 Surely I am too stupid to be human;
　　I do not have human
　　understanding.
3 I have not learned wisdom,
　　nor have I knowledge of the
　　holy ones.[o]
4 Who has ascended to heaven and
　　come down?
　　Who has gathered the wind in the
　　hollow of the hand?
　　Who has wrapped up the waters in a
　　garment?
　　Who has established all the ends
　　of the earth?
　　What is the person's name?
　　And what is the name of the
　　person's child?
　　Surely you know!

5 Every word of God proves true;
　　he is a shield to those who take
　　refuge in him.
6 Do not add to his words,
　　or else he will rebuke you, and
　　you will be found a liar.

7 Two things I ask of you;
　　do not deny them to me before
　　I die:

k Vg: Meaning of Heb uncertain　　l Meaning of
Heb uncertain　　m Or *human fear*　　n Or *I am
spent.* Meaning of Heb uncertain　　o Or *Holy One*

8 Remove far from me falsehood and
      lying;
    give me neither poverty nor riches;
    feed me with the food that I need,
9 or I shall be full, and deny you,
    and say, "Who is the LORD?"
    or I shall be poor, and steal,
    and profane the name of my God.

10 Do not slander a servant to a
      master,
    or the servant will curse you, and
      you will be held guilty.

11 There are those who curse their
      fathers
    and do not bless their mothers.
12 There are those who are pure in
      their own eyes
    yet are not cleansed of their
      filthiness.
13 There are those—how lofty are their
      eyes,
    how high their eyelids lift!—
14 there are those whose teeth are
      swords,
    whose teeth are knives,
    to devour the poor from off the
      earth,
    the needy from among mortals.

15 The leech *p* has two daughters;
    "Give, give," they cry.
    Three things are never satisfied;
    four never say, "Enough":
16 Sheol, the barren womb,
    the earth ever thirsty for water,
    and the fire that never says,
      "Enough." *p*

17 The eye that mocks a father
    and scorns to obey a mother
    will be pecked out by the ravens of
      the valley
    and eaten by the vultures.

18 Three things are too wonderful
      for me;
    four I do not understand:
19 the way of an eagle in the sky,
    the way of a snake on a rock,
    the way of a ship on the high seas,
    and the way of a man with a girl.

20 This is the way of an adulteress:
    she eats, and wipes her mouth,
    and says, "I have done no wrong."

21 Under three things the earth
      trembles;
    under four it cannot bear up:
22 a slave when he becomes king,
    and a fool when glutted
      with food;
23 an unloved woman when she gets
      a husband,
    and a maid when she succeeds her
      mistress.

24 Four things on earth are small,
    yet they are exceedingly wise:
25 the ants are a people without
      strength,
    yet they provide their food in
      the summer;
26 the badgers are a people without
      power,
    yet they make their homes in
      the rocks;
27 the locusts have no king,
    yet all of them march in rank;
28 the lizard*q* can be grasped in
      the hand,
    yet it is found in kings' palaces.

29 Three things are stately in their
      stride;
    four are stately in their gait:
30 the lion, which is mightiest among
      wild animals
    and does not turn back
      before any;
31 the strutting rooster,*r* the he-goat,
    and a king striding before *p*
      his people.

32 If you have been foolish, exalting
      yourself,
    or if you have been devising evil,
    put your hand on your mouth.
33 For as pressing milk produces curds,
    and pressing the nose produces
      blood,
    so pressing anger produces strife.

The Teaching of King Lemuel's Mother

31 The words of King Lemuel. An or-
    acle that his mother taught him:

2 No, my son! No, son of my womb!
    No, son of my vows!
3 Do not give your strength to
      women,

---

p Meaning of Heb uncertain   *q* Or *spider*   *r* Gk
Syr Tg Compare Vg: Meaning of Heb uncertain

your ways to those who destroy
    kings.
4 It is not for kings, O Lemuel,
    it is not for kings to drink wine,
    or for rulers to desire*s* strong
        drink;
5 or else they will drink and forget
        what has been decreed,
    and will pervert the rights of all
        the afflicted.
6 Give strong drink to one who is
        perishing,
    and wine to those in bitter
        distress;
7 let them drink and forget their
        poverty,
    and remember their misery
        no more.
8 Speak out for those who cannot
        speak,
    for the rights of all the destitute.*t*
9 Speak out, judge righteously,
    defend the rights of the poor
        and needy.

Ode to a Capable Wife

10 A capable wife who can find?
    She is far more precious than
        jewels.
11 The heart of her husband trusts
        in her,
    and he will have no lack of gain.
12 She does him good, and not harm,
    all the days of her life.
13 She seeks wool and flax,
    and works with willing hands.
14 She is like the ships of the
        merchant,
    she brings her food from far away.
15 She rises while it is still night
    and provides food for her
        household
    and tasks for her servant-girls.
16 She considers a field and buys it;
    with the fruit of her hands she
        plants a vineyard.
17 She girds herself with strength,
    and makes her arms strong.
18 She perceives that her merchandise
        is profitable.

Her lamp does not go out
    at night.
19 She puts her hands to the distaff,
    and her hands hold the spindle.
20 She opens her hand to the poor,
    and reaches out her hands to
        the needy.
21 She is not afraid for her household
        when it snows,
    for all her household are clothed
        in crimson.
22 She makes herself coverings;
    her clothing is fine linen and
        purple.
23 Her husband is known in the
        city gates,
    taking his seat among the elders
        of the land.
24 She makes linen garments and sells
        them;
    she supplies the merchant with
        sashes.
25 Strength and dignity are her
        clothing,
    and she laughs at the time
        to come.
26 She opens her mouth with wisdom,
    and the teaching of kindness is on
        her tongue.
27 She looks well to the ways of her
        household,
    and does not eat the bread of
        idleness.
28 Her children rise up and call her
        happy;
    her husband too, and he
        praises her:
29 "Many women have done
        excellently,
    but you surpass them all."
30 Charm is deceitful, and beauty
        is vain,
    but a woman who fears the LORD
        is to be praised.
31 Give her a share in the fruit of her
        hands,
    and let her works praise her in the
        city gates.

s Cn: Heb *where*   *t* Heb *all children of passing
away*

Ecclesiastes

Ecclesiastes won't be popular with anyone determined to view life through rose-colored glasses. This is not a book to read when you're feeling depressed. Written by a philosopher who refers to himself as the "Teacher," Ecclesiastes begins and ends with the words: "Vanity of vanities! All is vanity." (The epilogue, apparently written by another author, supplies a more satisfying ending to the book.)

The Teacher lays out his arguments regarding the futility of life by describing how he has searched for meaning everywhere: by pursuing wisdom, pleasure, riches, power, and hard work. But in the end, these prove empty because the wise and the foolish, the rich and the poor, the diligent and the slacker all meet the same end. Whatever gains have been made during their brief time on earth vanish at the moment of death.

Ecclesiastes poses the hard questions of life that any honest person must ask. Does life ultimately have meaning? What are we to make of a world in which the good suffer while those who do evil often seem to thrive? Without an understanding of eternal life, many of us may feel compelled to agree with the pessimistic conclusions of Ecclesiastes. Fortunately, we read this important book of the Bible in light of the entire Bible, especially in light of the great revelation we have received in the New Testament regarding the saving work of Christ.

Reflections of a Royal Philosopher

1 The words of the Teacher,[a] the son of David, king in Jerusalem.
2 Vanity of vanities, says the
   Teacher,[a]
   vanity of vanities! All is vanity.
3 What do people gain from all
      the toil
   at which they toil under the sun?

4 A generation goes, and a generation
      comes,
   but the earth remains forever.
5 The sun rises and the sun
      goes down,
   and hurries to the place where
      it rises.

---

a Heb *Qoheleth*, traditionally rendered *Preacher*

6 The wind blows to the south,
   and goes around to the north;
  round and round goes the wind,
   and on its circuits the wind
    returns.
7 All streams run to the sea,
   but the sea is not full;
  to the place where the streams flow,
   there they continue to flow.
8 All things*b* are wearisome;
   more than one can express;
  the eye is not satisfied with seeing,
   or the ear filled with hearing.
9 What has been is what will be,
   and what has been done is what
    will be done;
  there is nothing new under
    the sun.
10 Is there a thing of which it is said,
   "See, this is new"?
  It has already been,
   in the ages before us.
11 The people of long ago are not
    remembered,
   nor will there be any
    remembrance
  of people yet to come
   by those who come after them.

The Futility of Seeking Wisdom

12 I, the Teacher,*c* when king over Israel in Jerusalem, 13applied my mind to seek and to search out by wisdom all that is done under heaven; it is an unhappy business that God has given to human beings to be busy with. 14I saw all the deeds that are done under the sun; and see, all is vanity and a chasing after wind.*d*
15 What is crooked cannot be made
    straight,
   and what is lacking cannot
    be counted.

16 I said to myself, "I have acquired great wisdom, surpassing all who were over Jerusalem before me; and my mind has had great experience of wisdom and knowledge." 17And I applied my mind to know wisdom and to know madness and folly. I perceived that this also is but a chasing after wind.*d*
18 For in much wisdom is much
    vexation,
   and those who increase knowledge
    increase sorrow.

The Futility of Self-Indulgence

2 I said to myself, "Come now, I will make a test of pleasure; enjoy your-self." But again, this also was vanity. 2I said of laughter, "It is mad," and of pleasure, "What use is it?" 3I searched with my mind how to cheer my body with wine—my mind still guiding me with wisdom—and how to lay hold on folly, until I might see what was good for mortals to do under heaven during the few days of their life. 4I made great works; I built houses and planted vineyards for myself; 5I made myself gardens and parks, and planted in them all kinds of fruit trees. 6I made myself pools from which to water the forest of growing trees. 7I bought male and female slaves, and had slaves who were born in my house; I also had great possessions of herds and flocks, more than any who had been before me in Jerusalem. 8I also gathered for myself silver and gold and the treasure of kings and of the provinces; I got singers, both men and women, and delights of the flesh, and many concubines.*e*

9 So I became great and surpassed all who were before me in Jerusalem; also my wisdom remained with me. 10Whatever my eyes desired I did not keep from them; I kept my heart from no pleasure, for my heart found pleasure in all my toil, and this was my reward for all my toil. 11Then I considered all that my hands had done and the toil I had spent in doing it, and again, all was vanity and a chasing after wind,*d* and there was nothing to be gained under the sun.

Wisdom and Joy Given
to One Who Pleases God

12 So I turned to consider wisdom and madness and folly; for what can the one do who comes after the king? Only what has already been done. 13Then I saw that wisdom excels folly as light excels darkness.
14 The wise have eyes in their head,
   but fools walk in darkness.

Yet I perceived that the same fate befalls all of them. 15Then I said to myself, "What happens to the fool will happen to me also; why then have I been so very wise?" And I said to myself that this also is vanity. 16For there is no enduring remembrance of the wise or of fools, seeing that in the days to come all will have been

b Or *words*   *c* Heb *Qoheleth,* traditionally rendered *Preacher*   *d* Or *a feeding on wind.* See Hos 12.1   *e* Meaning of Heb uncertain

long forgotten. How can the wise die just like fools? [17]So I hated life, because what is done under the sun was grievous to me; for all is vanity and a chasing after wind. [f]

18 I hated all my toil in which I had toiled under the sun, seeing that I must leave it to those who come after me [19]—and who knows whether they will be wise or foolish? Yet they will be master of all for which I toiled and used my wisdom under the sun. This also is vanity. [20]So I turned and gave my heart up to despair concerning all the toil of my labors under the sun, [21]because sometimes one who has toiled with wisdom and knowledge and skill must leave all to be enjoyed by another who did not toil for it. This also is vanity and a great evil. [22]What do mortals get from all the toil and strain with which they toil under the sun? [23]For all their days are full of pain, and their work is a vexation; even at night their minds do not rest. This also is vanity.

24 There is nothing better for mortals than to eat and drink, and find enjoyment in their toil. This also, I saw, is from the hand of God; [25]for apart from him[g] who can eat or who can have enjoyment? [26]For to the one who pleases him God gives wisdom and knowledge and joy; but to the sinner he gives the work of gathering and heaping, only to give to one who pleases God. This also is vanity and a chasing after wind. [f]

Everything Has Its Time

3 For everything there is a season, and a time for every matter under heaven:
[2] a time to be born, and a time to die;
a time to plant, and a time to pluck up what is planted;
[3] a time to kill, and a time to heal;
a time to break down, and a time to build up;
[4] a time to weep, and a time to laugh;
a time to mourn, and a time to dance;
[5] a time to throw away stones, and a time to gather stones together;
a time to embrace, and a time to refrain from embracing;
[6] a time to seek, and a time to lose;
a time to keep, and a time to throw away;
[7] a time to tear, and a time to sew;

a time to keep silence, and a time to speak;
[8] a time to love, and a time to hate;
a time for war, and a time for peace.

The God-Given Task

9 What gain have the workers from their toil? [10]I have seen the business that God has given to everyone to be busy with. [11]He has made everything suitable for its time; moreover he has put a sense of past and future into their minds, yet they cannot find out what God has done from the beginning to the end. [12]I know that there is nothing better for them than to be happy and enjoy themselves as long as they live; [13]moreover, it is God's gift that all should eat and drink and take pleasure in all their toil. [14]I know that whatever God does endures forever; nothing can be added to it, nor anything taken from it; God has done this, so that all should stand in awe before him. [15]That which is, already has been; that which is to be, already is; and God seeks out what has gone by.[h]

Judgment and the Future Belong to God

16 Moreover I saw under the sun that in the place of justice, wickedness was there, and in the place of righteousness, wickedness was there as well. [17]I said in my heart, God will judge the righteous and the wicked, for he has appointed a time for every matter, and for every work. [18]I said in my heart with regard to human beings that God is testing them to show that they are but animals. [19]For the fate of humans and the fate of animals is the same; as one dies, so dies the other. They all have the same breath, and humans have no advantage over the animals; for all is vanity. [20]All go to one place; all are from the dust, and all turn to dust again. [21]Who knows whether the human spirit goes upward and the spirit of animals goes downward to the earth? [22]So I saw that there is nothing better than that all should enjoy their work, for that is their lot; who can bring them to see what will be after them?

4 Again I saw all the oppressions that are practiced under the sun. Look, the tears of the oppressed—with no one to

---

[f] Or *a feeding on wind.* See Hos 12.1   [g] Gk Syr:
Heb *apart from me*   [h] Heb *what is pursued*

comfort them! On the side of their oppressors there was power—with no one to
comfort them. ²And I thought the dead,
who have already died, more fortunate
than the living, who are still alive; ³but
better than both is the one who has not
yet been, and has not seen the evil deeds
that are done under the sun.

4 Then I saw that all toil and all skill in
work come from one person's envy of another. This also is vanity and a chasing
after wind.*ⁱ*

⁵ Fools fold their hands
  and consume their own flesh.

⁶ Better is a handful with quiet
  than two handfuls with toil,
  and a chasing after wind.*ⁱ*

7 Again, I saw vanity under the sun:
⁸the case of solitary individuals, without
sons or brothers; yet there is no end to all
their toil, and their eyes are never satisfied
with riches. "For whom am I toiling," they
ask, "and depriving myself of pleasure?"
This also is vanity and an unhappy business.

ⁱ Or a feeding on wind. See Hos 12.1

---

*S*easons

MONDAY

Scripture Reading
for Today:
Ecclesiastes 3.1–8

Verse for Today:
Ecclesiastes 3.1

Those of us who live in northern climates have grown used to
the simple joys of seasonal life. Each season has its trials and glories. The liturgy of the church reflects that wisdom. Feasting, parties, and even weddings are discouraged in Lent. But we never fast
after Easter. The bridegroom is with us in a special way. There is
clearly "a time to weep, and a time to laugh; a time to mourn, and
a time to dance" (Ecclesiastes 3.4).

Yet it was not until I started advising a few women about how
to live on a schedule that I found out what seasonal reality could
mean for me personally. I am a believer in schedules. They help
bring peace to a hectic day and enable us to utilize our time well.
We begin to find that there can be "a time for every matter under
heaven." But a couple of my friends, who like me had several small
children, were finding that even with guidance and a good schedule it was hard to find time for everything.

Then one of them overheard me lamenting the lack of time for
a beloved project one day and said, "I guess it's not the season of
your life for that. But it may come again." It was as if flashcubes
went off in my brain. "A time to keep, and a time to throw away"
(Ecclesiastes 3.6). I didn't have to do it all *now.* In fact, the will of
God for me did not include everything I willed to do.

I shared my newfound freedom with my friends. One of those
women discovered it was not the season of her life to sew at all.
Financial considerations became less important than needed time
and so, painfully, she had to give it up "for a season." For another
woman it was writing Christmas cards and baking dozens and
dozens of cookies. Celebration of Christmas in peace had to pre-
clude those projects.

Seasons change and so must we. Turn, turn, turn—to the Lord.

—DOROTHY RANAGHAN

Go to page 821 for your next devotional reading.

The Value of a Friend

9 Two are better than one, because they have a good reward for their toil. [10]For if they fall, one will lift up the other; but woe to one who is alone and falls and does not have another to help. [11]Again, if two lie together, they keep warm; but how can one keep warm alone? [12]And though one might prevail against another, two will withstand one. A threefold cord is not quickly broken.

13 Better is a poor but wise youth than an old but foolish king, who will no longer take advice. [14]One can indeed come out of prison to reign, even though born poor in the kingdom. [15]I saw all the living who, moving about under the sun, follow that[j] youth who replaced the king;[k] [16]there was no end to all those people whom he led. Yet those who come later will not rejoice in him. Surely this also is vanity and a chasing after wind.[l]

Reverence, Humility, and Contentment

5 [m]Guard your steps when you go to the house of God; to draw near to listen is better than the sacrifice offered by fools; for they do not know how to keep from doing evil.[n] [2o]Never be rash with your mouth, nor let your heart be quick to utter a word before God, for God is in heaven, and you upon earth; therefore let your words be few.

3 For dreams come with many cares, and a fool's voice with many words.

4 When you make a vow to God, do not delay fulfilling it; for he has no pleasure in fools. Fulfill what you vow. [5]It is better that you should not vow than that you should vow and not fulfill it. [6]Do not let your mouth lead you into sin, and do not say before the messenger that it was a mistake; why should God be angry at your words, and destroy the work of your hands?

7 With many dreams come vanities and a multitude of words;[p] but fear God.

8 If you see in a province the oppres- of the poor and the violation of jus- nd right, do not be amazed at the for the high official is watched by r, and there are yet higher ones 9But all things considered, this e for a land: a king for a

money will not be sat-

isfied with money; nor the lover of wealth, with gain. This also is vanity.

11 When goods increase, those who eat them increase; and what gain has their owner but to see them with his eyes?

12 Sweet is the sleep of laborers, whether they eat little or much; but the surfeit of the rich will not let them sleep.

13 There is a grievous ill that I have seen under the sun: riches were kept by their owners to their hurt, [14]and those riches were lost in a bad venture; though they are parents of children, they have nothing in their hands. [15]As they came from their mother's womb, so they shall go again, naked as they came; they shall take nothing for their toil, which they may carry away with their hands. [16]This also is a grievous ill: just as they came, so shall they go; and what gain do they have from toiling for the wind? [17]Besides, all their days they eat in darkness, in much vexation and sickness and resentment.

18 This is what I have seen to be good: it is fitting to eat and drink and find enjoyment in all the toil with which one toils under the sun the few days of the life God gives us; for this is our lot. [19]Likewise all to whom God gives wealth and possessions and whom he enables to enjoy them, and to accept their lot and find enjoyment in their toil—this is the gift of God. [20]For they will scarcely brood over the days of their lives, because God keeps them occupied with the joy of their hearts.

The Frustration of Desires

6 There is an evil that I have seen under the sun, and it lies heavy upon humankind: [2]those to whom God gives wealth, possessions, and honor, so that they lack nothing of all that they desire, yet God does not enable them to enjoy these things, but a stranger enjoys them. This is vanity; it is a grievous ill. [3]A man may beget a hundred children, and live many years; but however many are the days of his years, if he does not enjoy life's good things, or has no burial, I say that a stillborn child is better off than he. [4]For it comes into vanity and goes into darkness, and in darkness its name is covered; [5]moreover it has not seen the sun or

j Heb *the second*   k Heb *him*   l Or *a feeding on wind*. See Hos 12.1   m Ch 4.17 in Heb   n Cn: Heb *they do not know how to do evil*   o Ch 5.1 in Heb   p Meaning of Heb uncertain

known anything; yet it finds rest rather than he. 6Even though he should live a thousand years twice over, yet enjoy no good—do not all go to one place?

7 All human toil is for the mouth, yet the appetite is not satisfied. 8For what advantage have the wise over fools? And what do the poor have who know how to conduct themselves before the living? 9Better is the sight of the eyes than the wandering of desire; this also is vanity and a chasing after wind.*q*

10 Whatever has come to be has already been named, and it is known what human beings are, and that they are not able to dispute with those who are stronger. 11The more words, the more vanity, so how is one the better? 12For who knows what is good for mortals while they live the few days of their vain life, which they pass like a shadow? For who can tell them what will be after them under the sun?

A Disillusioned View of Life

7 A good name is better than
  precious ointment,
    and the day of death, than the
      day of birth.
2 It is better to go to the house of
    mourning
      than to go to the house of
        feasting;
  for this is the end of everyone,
    and the living will lay it to heart.
3 Sorrow is better than laughter,
    for by sadness of countenance the
      heart is made glad.
4 The heart of the wise is in the house
    of mourning;
      but the heart of fools is in the
        house of mirth.
5 It is better to hear the rebuke of the
    wise
      than to hear the song of fools.
6 For like the crackling of thorns
    under a pot,
      so is the laughter of fools;
        this also is vanity.
7 Surely oppression makes the wise
    foolish,
      and a bribe corrupts the heart.
8 Better is the end of a thing than its
    beginning;
      the patient in spirit are better than
        the proud in spirit.
9 Do not be quick to anger,

  for anger lodges in the bosom
    of fools.
10 Do not say, "Why were the former
    days better than these?"
      For it is not from wisdom that
        you ask this.
11 Wisdom is as good as an
    inheritance,
      an advantage to those who see the
        sun.
12 For the protection of wisdom is like
    the protection of money,
      and the advantage of knowledge is
        that wisdom gives life to the
          one who possesses it.
13 Consider the work of God;
    who can make straight what he
      has made crooked?

14 In the day of prosperity be joyful, and in the day of adversity consider; God has made the one as well as the other, so that mortals may not find out anything that will come after them.

The Riddles of Life

15 In my vain life I have seen everything; there are righteous people who perish in their righteousness, and there are wicked people who prolong their life in their evildoing. 16Do not be too righteous, and do not act too wise; why should you destroy yourself? 17Do not be too wicked, and do not be a fool; why should you die before your time? 18It is good that you should take hold of the one, without letting go of the other; for the one who fears God shall succeed with both.

19 Wisdom gives strength to the wise more than ten rulers that are in a city.

20 Surely there is no one on earth so righteous as to do good without ever sinning.

21 Do not give heed to everything that people say, or you may hear your servant cursing you; 22your heart knows that many times you have yourself cursed others.

23 All this I have tested by wisdom; said, "I will be wise," but it was far fr me. 24That which is, is far off, and d very deep; who can find it out? 25I t my mind to know and to search o to seek wisdom and the sum of and to know that wickedness that foolishness is madn

q Or a feeding on wind. See H

more bitter than death the woman who is a trap, whose heart is snares and nets, whose hands are fetters; one who pleases God escapes her, but the sinner is taken by her. ²⁷See, this is what I found, says the Teacher,ʳ adding one thing to another to find the sum, ²⁸which my mind has sought repeatedly, but I have not found. One man among a thousand I found, but a woman among all these I have not found. ²⁹See, this alone I found, that God made human beings straightforward, but they have devised many schemes.

Obey the King and Enjoy Yourself

8 Who is like the wise man?
And who knows the interpretation of a thing?
Wisdom makes one's face shine,

and the hardness of one's countenance is changed.

2 Keepˢ the king's command because of your sacred oath. ³Do not be terrified; go from his presence, do not delay when the matter is unpleasant, for he does whatever he pleases. ⁴For the word of the king is powerful, and who can say to him, "What are you doing?" ⁵Whoever obeys a command will meet no harm, and the wise mind will know the time and way. ⁶For every matter has its time and way, although the troubles of mortals lie heavy upon them. ⁷Indeed, they do not know what is to be, for who can tell them how it will be? ⁸No one has power over the

---

ʳ Qoheleth, traditionally rendered Preacher   ˢ Heb I keep

Lofty Daydreams

TUESDAY

Scripture Reading for Today:
Ecclesiastes 7.5–9

Verse for Today:
Ecclesiastes 7.8

Let us make no mistake. God is not pleased with wonderful daydreams: How much we would suffer for him, how patiently we would endure everything if he would only send us something really great and glorious. If we pray for such things, our prayer may often be heard, though in a very unexpected manner. Here I am, praying: "Please, Lord, send me suffering, that I may further your kingdom by it." In the midst of it, I would greet my friends with a heavenly smile that would show them how deeply united I am to God, and would bring them all closer to him.

Next morning I get the answer. The bacon comes up rather cold and tough. I rage interiorly, being prevented from making a scene only by the thought that the maid might give notice. Next thing, of course, I miss the bus and consequently push an old lady aside in order to get the next one. And, finally, to fill up the cup, my secretary has rung up the office that she is down with flu and cannot come. And here I am, with double the day's work on my hands; and my temper is such that no one dares come near me for the next 24 hours.

Well, is not this an answer to prayer? "You silly child," the Lord seems to say, "here you are dreaming about your heroic patience in terrible sufferings—and now you cannot even muster sufficient patience to endure a few tiny pin-pricks with equanimity. Learn first to bear the ordinary little trials of everyday life for love of me, and then you may perhaps be given something greater to endure."

—HILDA GRAEF

Go to page 824 for your next devotional reading.

wind[t] to restrain the wind,[t] or power over the day of death; there is no discharge from the battle, nor does wickedness deliver those who practice it. [9]All this I observed, applying my mind to all that is done under the sun, while one person exercises authority over another to the other's hurt.

God's Ways Are Inscrutable

10 Then I saw the wicked buried; they used to go in and out of the holy place, and were praised in the city where they had done such things.[u] This also is vanity. [11]Because sentence against an evil deed is not executed speedily, the human heart is fully set to do evil. [12]Though sinners do evil a hundred times and prolong their lives, yet I know that it will be well with those who fear God, because they stand in fear before him, [13]but it will not be well with the wicked, neither will they prolong their days like a shadow, because they do not stand in fear before God.

14 There is a vanity that takes place on earth, that there are righteous people who are treated according to the conduct of the wicked, and there are wicked people who are treated according to the conduct of the righteous. I said that this also is vanity. [15]So I commend enjoyment, for there is nothing better for people under the sun than to eat, and drink, and enjoy themselves, for this will go with them in their toil through the days of life that God gives them under the sun.

16 When I applied my mind to know wisdom, and to see the business that is done on earth, how one's eyes see sleep neither day nor night, [17]then I saw all the work of God, that no one can find out what is happening under the sun. However much they may toil in seeking, they will not find it out; even though those who are wise claim to know, they cannot find it out.

Take Life as It Comes

9 All this I laid to heart, examining it all, how the righteous and the wise and their deeds are in the hand of God; whether it is love or hate one does not know. Everything that confronts them [2]is vanity,[v] since the same fate comes to all, to the righteous and the wicked, to the good and the evil,[w] to the clean and the unclean, to those who sacrifice and those who do not sacrifice. As are the good, so are the sinners; those who swear are like those who shun an oath. [3]This is an evil in all that happens under the sun, that the same fate comes to everyone. Moreover, the hearts of all are full of evil; madness is in their hearts while they live, and after that they go to the dead. [4]But whoever is joined with all the living has hope, for a living dog is better than a dead lion. [5]The living know that they will die, but the dead know nothing; they have no more reward, and even the memory of them is lost. [6]Their love and their hate and their envy have already perished; never again will they have any share in all that happens under the sun.

7 Go, eat your bread with enjoyment, and drink your wine with a merry heart; for God has long ago approved what you do. [8]Let your garments always be white; do not let oil be lacking on your head. [9]Enjoy life with the wife whom you love, all the days of your vain life that are given you under the sun, because that is your portion in life and in your toil at which you toil under the sun. [10]Whatever your hand finds to do, do with your might; for there is no work or thought or knowledge or wisdom in Sheol, to which you are going.

11 Again I saw that under the sun the race is not to the swift, nor the battle to the strong, nor bread to the wise, nor riches to the intelligent, nor favor to the skillful; but time and chance happen to them all. [12]For no one can anticipate the time of disaster. Like fish taken in a cruel net, and like birds caught in a snare, so mortals are snared at a time of calamity, when it suddenly falls upon them.

Wisdom Superior to Folly

13 I have also seen this example of wisdom under the sun, and it seemed great to me. [14]There was a little city with few people in it. A great king came against it and besieged it, building great siegeworks against it. [15]Now there was found in it a poor wise man, and he by his wisdom delivered the city. Yet no one remembered that poor man. [16]So I said, "Wisdom is better than might; yet the poor man's wis-

[t] Or *breath*   [u] Meaning of Heb uncertain   [v] Syr Compare Gk: Heb *Everything that confronts them* [2]*is everything*   [w] Gk Syr Vg: Heb lacks *and the evil*

dom is despised, and his words are not heeded."
17 The quiet words of the wise are
     more to be heeded
  than the shouting of a ruler
     among fools.
18 Wisdom is better than weapons
     of war,
  but one bungler destroys much
     good.

Miscellaneous Observations

10 Dead flies make the perfumer's
     ointment give off a foul odor;
  so a little folly outweighs wisdom
     and honor.
2 The heart of the wise inclines to the
     right,
  but the heart of a fool to the left.
3 Even when fools walk on the road,
     they lack sense,
  and show to everyone that they
     are fools.
4 If the anger of the ruler rises against
     you, do not leave your post,
  for calmness will undo great
     offenses.

5 There is an evil that I have seen under the sun, as great an error as if it proceeded from the ruler: 6folly is set in many high places, and the rich sit in a low place. 7I have seen slaves on horseback, and princes walking on foot like slaves.
8 Whoever digs a pit will fall into it;
  and whoever breaks through a
     wall will be bitten by a snake.
9 Whoever quarries stones will be hurt
     by them;
  and whoever splits logs will be
     endangered by them.
10 If the iron is blunt, and one does
     not whet the edge,
  then more strength must be
     exerted;
  but wisdom helps one to succeed.
11 If the snake bites before it is
     charmed,
  there is no advantage in a
     charmer.

12 Words spoken by the wise bring
     them favor,
  but the lips of fools consume
     them.
13 The words of their mouths begin in
     foolishness,
  and their talk ends in wicked
     madness;

14 yet fools talk on and on.
  No one knows what is to happen,
  and who can tell anyone what the
     future holds?
15 The toil of fools wears them out,
  for they do not even know the
     way to town.

16 Alas for you, O land, when your
     king is a servant,ˣ
  and your princes feast in the
     morning!
17 Happy are you, O land, when your
     king is a nobleman,
  and your princes feast at the
     proper time—
  for strength, and not for
     drunkenness!
18 Through sloth the roof sinks in,
  and through indolence the house
     leaks.
19 Feasts are made for laughter;
  wine gladdens life,
  and money meets every need.
20 Do not curse the king, even in your
     thoughts,
  or curse the rich, even in your
     bedroom;
  for a bird of the air may carry
     your voice,
  or some winged creature tell
     the matter.

The Value of Diligence

11 Send out your bread upon the
     waters,
  for after many days you will get it
     back.
2 Divide your means seven ways, or
     even eight,
  for you do not know what disaster
     may happen on earth.
3 When clouds are full,
  they empty rain on the earth;
  whether a tree falls to the south or
     to the north,
  in the place where the tree falls,
     there it will lie.
4 Whoever observes the wind will
     not sow;
  and whoever regards the clouds
     will not reap.

5 Just as you do not know how the breath comes to the bones in the mother's womb, so you do not know the work of God, who makes everything.

ˣ Or *a child*

6 In the morning sow your seed, and at evening do not let your hands be idle; for you do not know which will prosper, this or that, or whether both alike will be good.

Youth and Old Age

7 Light is sweet, and it is pleasant for the eyes to see the sun.

8 Even those who live many years should rejoice in them all; yet let them remember that the days of darkness will be many. All that comes is vanity.

9 Rejoice, young man, while you are young, and let your heart cheer you in the days of your youth. Follow the inclination of your heart and the desire of your eyes, but know that for all these things God will bring you into judgment.

10 Banish anxiety from your mind, and put away pain from your body; for youth and the dawn of life are vanity.

12 Remember your creator in the days of your youth, before the days of trouble come, and the years draw near when you will say, "I have no pleasure in them"; 2before the sun and the light and the moon and the stars are darkened and the clouds return with y the rain; 3in the day when the guards of the house tremble, and the strong men are bent, and the women who grind cease working because they are few, and those who look through the windows see dimly; 4when the doors on the street are shut, and the sound of the grinding is low, and one rises up at the sound of a bird, and all the daughters of song are brought low; 5when

y Or after; Heb 'ahar

WEDNESDAY

Scripture Reading for Today:
Ecclesiastes 11.3–6

Verse for Today:
Ecclesiastes 11.6

God's Beauty

Who is a gardener? He is a person who prays to God in the beauty of flowers. He is a painter of the Lord. A musician of God. A poet of the Almighty. He is a writer of music in the colors and plants called flowers.

No one, be he saint or sinner, atheist or Communist, can pass a flower garden without stopping. In India and Japan, the raising of flowers has reached the proportions of an art beyond our western understanding. A man's soul, a whole nation's soul, is expressed in a garden. The tulips of Holland were originally planted for beauty and not for profit.

Who is a flower gardener? He is an utterly dedicated person. Flowers are his life. He knows each one tenderly, knows the ways and habits, the likes and dislikes of each one.

But [a gardener] is more. He is someone who gives beauty to others—not just ordinary beauty, but God's beauty. And if he did not know God before he became interested in flowers, he will come to know him very soon if he perseveres in his growing and tending of flowers.

Who is a flower gardener? He is a person who sooner or later falls utterly in love with God. No one can approach flowers reverently (you must, you know, otherwise they will not grow for you!) without silently shouting his love for God. He who grows flowers gives God to man and by God is possessed.

—CATHERINE DOHERTY

Go to page 827 for your next devotional reading.

one is afraid of heights, and terrors are in the road; the almond tree blossoms, the grasshopper drags itself along[z] and desire fails; because all must go to their eternal home, and the mourners will go about the streets; [6]before the silver cord is snapped,[a] and the golden bowl is broken, and the pitcher is broken at the fountain, and the wheel broken at the cistern, [7]and the dust returns to the earth as it was, and the breath[b] returns to God who gave it. [8]Vanity of vanities, says the Teacher;[c] all is vanity.

Epilogue

9 Besides being wise, the Teacher[c] also taught the people knowledge, weighing and studying and arranging many proverbs. [10]The Teacher[c] sought to find pleasing words, and he wrote words of truth plainly.

11 The sayings of the wise are like goads, and like nails firmly fixed are the collected sayings that are given by one shepherd.[d] [12]Of anything beyond these, my child, beware. Of making many books there is no end, and much study is a weariness of the flesh.

13 The end of the matter; all has been heard. Fear God, and keep his commandments; for that is the whole duty of everyone. [14]For God will bring every deed into judgment, including[e] every secret thing, whether good or evil.

z Or *is a burden*   a Syr Vg Compare Gk: Heb *is removed*   b Or *the spirit*   c *Qoheleth,* traditionally rendered *Preacher*   d Meaning of Heb uncertain   e Or *into the judgment on*

The *Song* of *Solomon*

Also known as the Song of Songs (meaning "the greatest of songs"), this book is unlike any other in the Bible. Full of erotic imagery, it is a richly woven work that captures the various passions and tensions of love. Speakers and scenes shift so rapidly that it can be difficult to tell who is speaking and what is going on. No wonder there have been so many different interpretations of this book.

The Jews believed the Song of Solomon was not primarily about individual lovers but about God's love for his people Israel. Christians initially read it as a parable of Christ's love for the church and later, with St. Bernard, as a parable of his love for the individual soul. It is also possible to view this collection of love songs more literally, as an expression of human love in its most ideal form. However you interpret it, this beautifully written book of the Bible, mysterious as it is, touches our longing to love and be loved.

1 The Song of Songs, which is Solomon's.

Colloquy of Bride and Friends

2 Let him kiss me with the kisses of
  his mouth!
For your love is better than wine,
3 your anointing oils are fragrant,
your name is perfume poured out;
  therefore the maidens love you.
4 Draw me after you, let us make
  haste.
 The king has brought me into his
  chambers.
We will exult and rejoice in you;
 we will extol your love more
  than wine;
  rightly do they love you.

5 I am black and beautiful,
O daughters of Jerusalem,
 like the tents of Kedar,
 like the curtains of Solomon.
6 Do not gaze at me because I am
  dark,
 because the sun has gazed on me.
My mother's sons were angry
  with me;
 they made me keeper of the
  vineyards,
 but my own vineyard I have
  not kept!
7 Tell me, you whom my soul loves,
 where you pasture your flock,
 where you make it lie down
  at noon;
for why should I be like one who
  is veiled
 beside the flocks of your
  companions?

8 If you do not know,
  O fairest among women,
follow the tracks of the flock,
  and pasture your kids
  beside the shepherds' tents.

Colloquy of Bridegroom, Friends,
and Bride

9 I compare you, my love,
  to a mare among Pharaoh's
  chariots.

10 Your cheeks are comely with
   ornaments,
   your neck with strings of jewels.
11 We will make you ornaments
   of gold,
   studded with silver.

12 While the king was on his couch,
   my nard gave forth its fragrance.
13 My beloved is to me a bag of myrrh
   that lies between my breasts.

The Man in My Life

THURSDAY

Scripture Reading
for Today:
Song of Solomon
1.2–4

Verse for Today:
Song of Solomon 1.2

On Nantucket Island, off the coast of Massachusetts, it was a cloudy, windy day. Cobblestones lined the main street, and small shops and restaurants were attached together with old-fashioned elegance. As I passed them, I knew each had a story to tell. I couldn't help but feel in every sense Nantucket's romantic atmosphere; I felt its embrace, and I longed to share it with someone I loved.

As I returned to the inn where I was spending the night, I felt that deep familiar longing. I thought how much I would love to be strongly but gently held. I tearfully expressed my feelings, and God listened. "You alone can fill me with the peace and comfort I need right now." There was a long silence, then my voice broke through the quiet. "I realize you were right beside me today. *You* put me in an environment I loved, and my desire to be in love was met in a very unique way. In a way I hadn't expected. *You,* Jesus, are the man in my life. You've been here all along. *You* are my beloved. *You* are the One I have betrothed my life to. You've granted me this day and the sweetness of your presence."

As I listened to myself pray, I was reminded of my covenant with him—intimacy with him. Marriage or not, Jesus will always be my bridegroom. Always be my first love. I realized that we had a memory-making day together and that he had lavishly given me many of the kinds of things I cherish. I truly am in the midst of a love affair that will last for all eternity.

You are his bride. You are his love. "I am my beloved's, and his desire is for me" (Song of Solomon 7.10). Don't ever forget the place you have with Jesus. It is a place that is reserved for you and you alone. You are so deeply loved. Walk arm and arm with him today. Your eternal escort. Your faithful bridegroom. He will never let you go.

—*KATHY TROCCOLI*

Go to page 831 for your next devotional reading.

14 My beloved is to me a cluster of
     henna blossoms
   in the vineyards of En-gedi.

15 Ah, you are beautiful, my love;
   ah, you are beautiful;
   your eyes are doves.
16 Ah, you are beautiful, my beloved,
   truly lovely.
   Our couch is green;
17   the beams of our house are cedar,
   our rafters*a* are pine.

2 I am a rose*b* of Sharon,
   a lily of the valleys.

2 As a lily among brambles,
   so is my love among maidens.

3 As an apple tree among the trees of
   the wood,
   so is my beloved among young
   men.
   With great delight I sat in his
   shadow,
   and his fruit was sweet to
   my taste.
4 He brought me to the banqueting
   house,
   and his intention toward me
   was love.
5 Sustain me with raisins,
   refresh me with apples;
   for I am faint with love.
6 O that his left hand were under my
   head,
   and that his right hand embraced
   me!
7 I adjure you, O daughters of
   Jerusalem,
   by the gazelles or the wild does:
   do not stir up or awaken love
   until it is ready!

Springtime Rhapsody

8 The voice of my beloved!
   Look, he comes,
   leaping upon the mountains,
   bounding over the hills.
9 My beloved is like a gazelle
   or a young stag.
   Look, there he stands
   behind our wall,
   gazing in at the windows,
   looking through the lattice.
10 My beloved speaks and says to me:
   "Arise, my love, my fair one,
   and come away;

11 for now the winter is past,
   the rain is over and gone.
12 The flowers appear on the earth;
   the time of singing has come,
   and the voice of the turtledove
   is heard in our land.
13 The fig tree puts forth its figs,
   and the vines are in blossom;
   they give forth fragrance.
   Arise, my love, my fair one,
   and come away.
14 O my dove, in the clefts of the rock,
   in the covert of the cliff,
   let me see your face,
   let me hear your voice;
   for your voice is sweet,
   and your face is lovely.
15 Catch us the foxes,
   the little foxes,
   that ruin the vineyards—
   for our vineyards are in blossom."

16 My beloved is mine and I am his;
   he pastures his flock among the
   lilies.
17 Until the day breathes
   and the shadows flee,
   turn, my beloved, be like a gazelle
   or a young stag on the cleft
   mountains.*c*

Love's Dream

3 Upon my bed at night
   I sought him whom my soul
   loves;
   I sought him, but found him not;
   I called him, but he gave no
   answer.*d*
2 "I will rise now and go about
   the city,
   in the streets and in the squares;
   I will seek him whom my soul
   loves."
   I sought him, but found him not.
3 The sentinels found me,
   as they went about in the city.
   "Have you seen him whom my soul
   loves?"
4 Scarcely had I passed them,
   when I found him whom my soul
   loves.
   I held him, and would not let
   him go

a Meaning of Heb uncertain   *b* Heb *crocus*
c Or *on the mountains of Bether*; meaning of Heb
uncertain   *d* Gk: Heb lacks this line

until I brought him into my
    mother's house,
and into the chamber of her that
    conceived me.
5 I adjure you, O daughters of
    Jerusalem,
by the gazelles or the wild does:
do not stir up or awaken love
    until it is ready!

The Groom and His Party Approach

6 What is that coming up from the
    wilderness,
like a column of smoke,

perfumed with myrrh and
    frankincense,
with all the fragrant powders of
    the merchant?
7 Look, it is the litter of Solomon!
Around it are sixty mighty men
    of the mighty men of Israel,
8 all equipped with swords
    and expert in war,
each with his sword at his thigh
    because of alarms by night.
9 King Solomon made himself a
    palanquin
from the wood of Lebanon.

THE TRADITION

Marriage

He brought me to the banqueting house,
and his intention toward me was love.

Song of Solomon 2.4

She hates scraping ice off the windshield. He tries to get to it first ...

    He likes his eggs fried so hard they bounce. She trains herself to fix them that way ...

    She's a morning person. He's not, but he makes an effort at cheerfulness ... He finds certain social occasions painful. She doesn't insist ...

    He's heard her jokes a million times, but he's still her most appreciative audience ...

You probably know married couples who are heroically keeping their promise to love in bad times as well as good—in financial hardship and family emergencies, under the shadow of Alzheimer's or cancer. But do you notice too how, all along, happily married couples express their love for one another in countless little attentions?

    In big ways and small, marriage always calls a man and a woman to self-giving love of each other and of their children. But when spouses base their marriage on Jesus Christ, their covenant becomes a sacrament with an even deeper call: They are to model Christ's

redemptive love. They themselves become sacred signs of how Christ relates to the Church. Indeed, as Saint Paul muses, "This is a great mystery" (see Ephesians 5.28–32).

    Amazing enough that Jesus is the Church's bridegroom. The theme is developed in Scripture, though gradually, by prophets such as Hosea and in the Song of Solomon's lyrical description of married love. But no less amazing is the bridegroom's call to every Christian couple. In a symbolic but real way, every married couple—even Steve and Jane down the street—are to make visible the mystery of Christ's love for the Church. Just as Saint Paul says of evangelism, we might ask, "Who is sufficient for these things?" (2 Corinthians 2.16).

    This is where sacramental grace comes in. Without the life and power of the Holy Spirit, husband and wife are helpless to fulfill their high calling. With it, though, they will find all they need—faith, perseverance, and deepening love for every challenge of married life.

    Even for frying eggs tennis-ball hard and for *not* rolling eyes at tired, old jokes.

10 He made its posts of silver,
      its back of gold, its seat of purple;
    its interior was inlaid with love.*
      Daughters of Jerusalem,
11   come out.
    Look, O daughters of Zion,
      at King Solomon,
    at the crown with which his mother
      crowned him
      on the day of his wedding,
      on the day of the gladness of
        his heart.

The Bride's Beauty Extolled

4 How beautiful you are, my love,
      how very beautiful!
    Your eyes are doves
      behind your veil.
    Your hair is like a flock of goats,
      moving down the slopes of
        Gilead.
2 Your teeth are like a flock of
      shorn ewes
      that have come up from the
        washing,
    all of which bear twins,
      and not one among them is
        bereaved.
3 Your lips are like a crimson thread,
      and your mouth is lovely.
    Your cheeks are like halves of a
        pomegranate
      behind your veil.
4 Your neck is like the tower of David,
      built in courses;
    on it hang a thousand bucklers,
      all of them shields of warriors.
5 Your two breasts are like two fawns,
      twins of a gazelle,
      that feed among the lilies.
6 Until the day breathes
      and the shadows flee,
    I will hasten to the mountain of
        myrrh
      and the hill of frankincense.
7 You are altogether beautiful,
        my love;
      there is no flaw in you.
8 Come with me from Lebanon,
        my bride;
      come with me from Lebanon.
    Depart *f* from the peak of Amana,
      from the peak of Senir and
        Hermon,
    from the dens of lions,
      from the mountains of leopards.

9 You have ravished my heart, my
        sister, my bride,
      you have ravished my heart with a
        glance of your eyes,
      with one jewel of your necklace.
10 How sweet is your love, my sister,
        my bride!
      how much better is your love than
        wine,
      and the fragrance of your oils
        than any spice!
11 Your lips distill nectar, my bride;
      honey and milk are under your
        tongue;
      the scent of your garments is like
        the scent of Lebanon.
12 A garden locked is my sister,
        my bride,
      a garden locked, a fountain sealed.
13 Your channel* is an orchard of
        pomegranates
      with all choicest fruits,
      henna with nard,
14 nard and saffron, calamus and
        cinnamon,
      with all trees of frankincense,
    myrrh and aloes,
      with all chief spices—
15 a garden fountain, a well of living
        water,
      and flowing streams from
        Lebanon.

16 Awake, O north wind,
      and come, O south wind!
    Blow upon my garden
      that its fragrance may be wafted
        abroad.
    Let my beloved come to his garden,
      and eat its choicest fruits.

5 I come to my garden, my sister,
        my bride;
      I gather my myrrh with my spice,
      I eat my honeycomb with my
        honey,
      I drink my wine with my milk.

    Eat, friends, drink,
      and be drunk with love.

Another Dream

2 I slept, but my heart was awake.
    Listen! my beloved is knocking.
    "Open to me, my sister, my love,
      my dove, my perfect one;

e Meaning of Heb uncertain   f Or Look

for my head is wet with dew,
　my locks with the drops of the
　　night."

3 I had put off my garment;
　how could I put it on again?
I had bathed my feet;
　how could I soil them?
4 My beloved thrust his hand into the
　　opening,
　and my inmost being yearned
　　for him.
5 I arose to open to my beloved,
　and my hands dripped with
　　myrrh,
my fingers with liquid myrrh,
　upon the handles of the bolt.
6 I opened to my beloved,
　but my beloved had turned and
　　was gone.
My soul failed me when he spoke.
I sought him, but did not find him;
　I called him, but he gave
　　no answer.
7 Making their rounds in the city
　the sentinels found me;
they beat me, they wounded me,
　they took away my mantle,
　those sentinels of the walls.
8 I adjure you, O daughters of
　　Jerusalem,
　if you find my beloved,

tell him this:
　I am faint with love.

Colloquy of Friends and Bride

9 What is your beloved more than
　　another beloved,
　O fairest among women?
What is your beloved more than
　　another beloved,
　that you thus adjure us?

10 My beloved is all radiant and ruddy,
　distinguished among ten
　　thousand.
11 His head is the finest gold;
　his locks are wavy,
　　black as a raven.
12 His eyes are like doves
　beside springs of water,
bathed in milk,
　fitly set. *g*
13 His cheeks are like beds of spices,
　yielding fragrance.
His lips are lilies,
　distilling liquid myrrh.
14 His arms are rounded gold,
　set with jewels.
His body is ivory work, *g*
　encrusted with sapphires. *h*
15 His legs are alabaster columns,

g Meaning of Heb uncertain　　*h* Heb *lapis lazuli*

The Nature of Things

The fish will never drown within the tide,
Nor birds fall from the air on which they ride.
The flame will not corrode or blacken gold,
For fire burns it pure and clean,
Gives it a shining colour.
To all his creatures God has granted
To live according to their nature.
How then could I deny my breath and bone?
In all things I submit to God alone,
Who is my father by nature,
Who is my brother by his humanhood,
Who is my bridegroom by his love,
And from the outset I am all his own.

—*SAINT MECHTILD OF MAGDEBURG*

FRIDAY

Scripture Reading
for Today:
*Song of Solomon
6.1–3*

Verse for Today:
Song of Solomon 6.3

Go to page 832 for your next devotional reading.

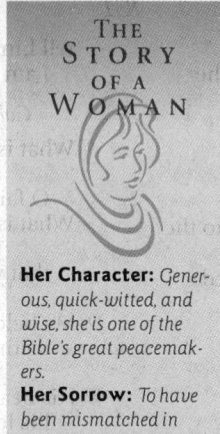

THE STORY OF A WOMAN

Abigail

Her Name Means
"My Father Is Joy"

Her Character: *Generous, quick-witted, and wise, she is one of the Bible's great peacemakers.*

Her Sorrow: *To have been mismatched in marriage to her first husband.*

Her Joy: *That God used her to save lives, eventually making her the wife of David.*

Read I Samuel 25.2–42

Abigail had heard nothing but good of David. Since his arrival with six hundred men, marauders had not troubled her husband Nabal's livestock, and his flocks prospered as a result.

But the news turned sour soon enough. It happened when David sent ten men to ask for provisions. Nabal, who had grown richer by the day, thanks to David, nearly spit in their faces. Rich though he was, he foolishly insulted the region's most powerful man.

Learning what had happened, Abigail loaded a caravan of donkeys with gifts of food for David and his men. As soon as she saw him, she fell to the ground at his feet, making one of the longest speeches by a woman recorded in the Bible.

"Upon me alone, my lord, be the guilt; please let your servant speak in your ears, and hear the words of your servant. My lord, do not take seriously this ill-natured fellow, Nabal; for as his name is, so is he; Nabal is his name, and folly is with him . . . since the LORD has restrained you from bloodguilt and from taking vengeance with your own hand . . . the life of my lord shall be bound in the bundle of the living under the care of the LORD your God; but the lives of your enemies he shall sling out as from the hollow of a sling" (verses 24–26, 29).

These last words, of course, reminded David of his success against the giant Goliath, erasing his anger and enabling his reply: "Blessed be your good sense, and blessed be you, who have kept me today from blood-

guilt and from avenging myself by my own hand! For as surely as the LORD the God of Israel lives, who has restrained me from hurting you, unless you had hurried and come to meet me, truly by morning there would not have been left to Nabal so much as one male" (verses 33–34).

After her encounter with David, Abigail went to Carmel, where Nabal had been shearing his sheep and celebrating his good fortune. She waited until morning, when he was sober, to tell him what had happened. As soon as Nabal heard the news, his heart failed. Ten days later he was dead.

Arrogance, greed, and selfishness had conspired to rob Nabal of any good sense he might once have possessed. Thinking himself a great man when he was only a small one, he lost everything.

Abigail was his opposite, a woman whose humility, faith, generosity, intelligence, and honesty made her wise. Rather than putting others at risk by an ungoverned tongue, her gracious words saved lives.

Then David asked Abigail to be his wife. She accepted, becoming David's third wife and eventually mother to his second son, Kileab.

Abigail was a woman who rose above her circumstances to change the course of events. Perhaps her marriage was actually the catalyst for her character, helping her to cultivate contrasting virtues to Nabal's vices. Though Scripture doesn't offer details, it is logical to suppose she was a good wife. Even her entreaty to David was the act of a faithful wife. Through her quick-witted action, she spared her husband's life and goods. It was God, not Abigail or David, who paid Nabal back for his arrogance and greed.

Praying With Abigail

"Blessed be the LORD, the God of Israel, who sent you to meet me today! Blessed be your good sense, and blessed be you, who have kept me today from bloodguilt and from avenging myself by my own hand!"—1 Samuel 25.32–33

Praise God: For calling you to be a peacemaker in your family, neighborhood, and world.

Offer Thanks: That God knows every challenge facing your marriage.

Confess: Any bitterness you may have harbored about your own marriage.

Ask God: To use your relationship with your husband to strengthen your character and increase your faith.

Lift Your Heart

If you haven't yet made a commitment to pray daily for your husband, do so today. Set aside a few minutes to surrender your marriage to God, specifically asking him to bless your spouse. Try to refrain from focusing on your laundry list of complaints and instead pray for the needs you know he has. Ask God to shape your relationship and use it for his purposes. Relinquish any desire you may have to control your husband, and ask God to work in his life. For help in forming the habit, try reading *Praying God's Will for My Husband* by Lee Roberts or *Praying for Your Unbelieving Husband* by Michael and Diane Fanstone.

Father, I ask you to bless my husband in every facet of his life—
his health
his work
his relationship with our children
our relationship together
and his relationship to you.
Let nothing and no one, including myself, hinder your work.

Go to page 835 for your next devotional reading.

set upon bases of gold.
His appearance is like Lebanon,
    choice as the cedars.
16 His speech is most sweet,
    and he is altogether desirable.
This is my beloved and this is
        my friend,
    O daughters of Jerusalem.

6 Where has your beloved gone,
    O fairest among women?
Which way has your beloved turned,
    that we may seek him with you?

2 My beloved has gone down to his
        garden,
    to the beds of spices,
to pasture his flock in the gardens,
    and to gather lilies.
3 I am my beloved's and my beloved
        is mine;
    he pastures his flock among the
        lilies.

The Bride's Matchless Beauty

4 You are beautiful as Tirzah, my love,
    comely as Jerusalem,
    terrible as an army with banners.
5 Turn away your eyes from me,
    for they overwhelm me!
Your hair is like a flock of goats,
    moving down the slopes of
        Gilead.
6 Your teeth are like a flock of ewes,
    that have come up from the
        washing;
all of them bear twins,
    and not one among them is
        bereaved.
7 Your cheeks are like halves of a
        pomegranate
    behind your veil.
8 There are sixty queens and eighty
        concubines,
    and maidens without number.
9 My dove, my perfect one, is the only
        one,
    the darling of her mother,
    flawless to her that bore her.
The maidens saw her and called her
        happy;
    the queens and concubines also,
        and they praised her.
10 "Who is this that looks forth like
        the dawn,
    fair as the moon, bright as
        the sun,
    terrible as an army with banners?"

11 I went down to the nut orchard,
    to look at the blossoms of the
        valley,
to see whether the vines had
        budded,
    whether the pomegranates were in
        bloom.
12 Before I was aware, my fancy set me
    in a chariot beside my prince.[i]

13 jReturn, return, O Shulammite!
    Return, return, that we may look
        upon you.

Why should you look upon the
        Shulammite,
    as upon a dance before two
        armies?[k]

Expressions of Praise

7 How graceful are your feet in
        sandals,
    O queenly maiden!
Your rounded thighs are like jewels,
    the work of a master hand.
2 Your navel is a rounded bowl
    that never lacks mixed wine.
Your belly is a heap of wheat,
    encircled with lilies.
3 Your two breasts are like two fawns,
    twins of a gazelle.
4 Your neck is like an ivory tower.
Your eyes are pools in Heshbon,
    by the gate of Bath-rabbim.
Your nose is like a tower of
        Lebanon,
    overlooking Damascus.
5 Your head crowns you like Carmel,
    and your flowing locks are like
        purple;
    a king is held captive in the
        tresses.[l]

6 How fair and pleasant you are,
    O loved one, delectable maiden![m]
7 You are stately[n] as a palm tree,
    and your breasts are like its
        clusters.
8 I say I will climb the palm tree
    and lay hold of its branches.
O may your breasts be like clusters
        of the vine,

i Cn: Meaning of Heb uncertain   j Ch 7.1 in
Heb   k Or *dance of Mahanaim*   l Meaning of
Heb uncertain   m Syr: Heb *in delights*   n Heb
This your stature is

and the scent of your breath like
apples,

9 and your kisses*o* like the best wine
that goes down *p* smoothly,
gliding over lips and teeth.*q*

10 I am my beloved's,
and his desire is for me.
11 Come, my beloved,
let us go forth into the fields,
and lodge in the villages;
12 let us go out early to the vineyards,
and see whether the vines have
budded,
whether the grape blossoms have
opened
and the pomegranates are
in bloom.
There I will give you my love.
13 The mandrakes give forth fragrance,
and over our doors are all choice
fruits,
new as well as old,
which I have laid up for you,
O my beloved.

8 O that you were like a brother
to me,
who nursed at my mother's
breast!
If I met you outside, I would
kiss you,
and no one would despise me.
2 I would lead you and bring you
into the house of my mother,
and into the chamber of the one
who bore me.*r*
I would give you spiced wine
to drink,
the juice of my pomegranates.
3 O that his left hand were under
my head,
and that his right hand embraced
me!
4 I adjure you, O daughters of
Jerusalem,
do not stir up or awaken love
until it is ready!

o Heb *palate*   *p* Heb *down for my lover*   *q* Gk
Syr Vg: Heb *lips of sleepers*   *r* Gk Syr: Heb *my
mother; she* (or *you*) *will teach me*

*T*rue Love

I have never been able to understand how people who do not believe in God, who do not believe in the immortality of the soul, who do not believe that love is stronger than death can bear the loss of the people they love most. But perhaps the real question is: Can one truly, fully, completely love when one is convinced that the beloved is made exclusively of flesh and bones destined to rot under the earth? Is not the very capacity for true, full love essentially related to our love for the Holy One whom Saint John defines as Love? I personally think that great loves are possible independent of Christian revelation; but they are crippled, tragic loves, for they can never live up to love's sublime requirements.

Someone very dear to me was engaged to an atheist who was convinced that death has the last word. One day she exclaimed in despair, "But if this is so, Willy, how can you truly love me?" Clearly, love is very different from a physical attraction. It is the perception of an inner beauty which through its very glow promises to transcend time and space. If this transcendence is sheer illusion, how can one truly love?

—*ALICE VON HILDEBRAND*

MONDAY

Scripture Reading
for Today:
*Song of Solomon
8.5–7*

Verse for Today:
Song of Solomon 8.6

Go to page 840 for your next devotional reading.

Homecoming

5 Who is that coming up from the
    wilderness,
    leaning upon her beloved?

Under the apple tree I awakened
    you.
There your mother was in labor with
    you;
    there she who bore you was in
    labor.

6 Set me as a seal upon your heart,
    as a seal upon your arm;
for love is strong as death,
    passion fierce as the grave.
Its flashes are flashes of fire,
    a raging flame.
7 Many waters cannot quench love,
    neither can floods drown it.
If one offered for love
    all the wealth of one's house,
    it would be utterly scorned.

8 We have a little sister,
    and she has no breasts.
What shall we do for our sister,
    on the day when she is
    spoken for?
9 If she is a wall,
    we will build upon her a
    battlement of silver;

but if she is a door,
    we will enclose her with boards of
    cedar.
10 I was a wall,
    and my breasts were like towers;
then I was in his eyes
    as one who brings⁵ peace.
11 Solomon had a vineyard at
    Baal-hamon;
    he entrusted the vineyard to
    keepers;
    each one was to bring for its fruit
    a thousand pieces of silver.
12 My vineyard, my very own, is
    for myself;
you, O Solomon, may have the
    thousand,
and the keepers of the fruit two
    hundred!

13 O you who dwell in the gardens,
    my companions are listening for
    your voice;
    let me hear it.

14 Make haste, my beloved,
    and be like a gazelle
or a young stag
    upon the mountains of spices!

⁵ Or *finds*

The *Wisdom* of *Solomon*

Though the author speaks in the name of King Solomon (a common literary device, not an attempt at forgery), an unknown writer composed this book in Greek. He was probably a Jew living in Alexandria, during a time in which there were more Jews in Egypt than in Palestine.

Wherever they lived in the last few centuries before Christ, the Jewish people were under great pressures to abandon their own religious beliefs and cultural identity in favor of the pagan practices of a Hellenistic civilization. The writer retells the Exodus story, emphasizing God's provision for the Israelites and his punishment of the Egyptians—a reminder to his readers that they should resist the temptation to abandon their traditions in favor of the Greek ideas dominant in Egypt.

This book affirms God's goodness and offers the clearest presentation on eternal life found in the Old Testament.

Exhortation to Uprightness

1 Love righteousness, you rulers of
the earth,
think of the Lord in goodness
and seek him with sincerity of
heart;
2 because he is found by those who
do not put him to the test,
and manifests himself to those who
do not distrust him.
3 For perverse thoughts separate
people from God,
and when his power is tested, it
exposes the foolish;
4 because wisdom will not enter a
deceitful soul,
or dwell in a body enslaved to sin.
5 For a holy and disciplined spirit will
flee from deceit,
and will leave foolish thoughts
behind,

and will be ashamed at the
approach of unrighteousness.
6 For wisdom is a kindly spirit,
but will not free blasphemers from
the guilt of their words;
because God is witness of their
inmost feelings,
and a true observer of their hearts,
and a hearer of their tongues.
7 Because the spirit of the Lord has
filled the world,
and that which holds all things
together knows what is said,
8 therefore those who utter
unrighteous things will not
escape notice,
and justice, when it punishes, will
not pass them by.
9 For inquiry will be made into the
counsels of the ungodly,

and a report of their words will
come to the Lord,
to convict them of their lawless
deeds;
10 because a jealous ear hears all
things,
and the sound of grumbling does
not go unheard.
11 Beware then of useless grumbling,
and keep your tongue from slander;
because no secret word is without
result,*a*
and a lying mouth destroys the soul.

12 Do not invite death by the error of
your life,
or bring on destruction by the works
of your hands;
13 because God did not make death,
and he does not delight in the death
of the living.
14 For he created all things so that they
might exist;
the generative forces*b* of the world
are wholesome,
and there is no destructive poison in
them,
and the dominion*c* of Hades is not
on earth.
15 For righteousness is immortal.

Life as the Ungodly See It

16 But the ungodly by their words and
deeds summoned death;*d*
considering him a friend, they pined
away
and made a covenant with him,
because they are fit to belong to his
company.

2 For they reasoned unsoundly,
saying to themselves,
"Short and sorrowful is our life,
and there is no remedy when a life
comes to its end,
and no one has been known to
return from Hades.
2 For we were born by mere chance,
and hereafter we shall be as though
we had never been,
for the breath in our nostrils is
smoke,
and reason is a spark kindled by the
beating of our hearts;
3 when it is extinguished, the body
will turn to ashes,

and the spirit will dissolve like
empty air.
4 Our name will be forgotten in time,
and no one will remember our
works;
our life will pass away like the traces
of a cloud,
and be scattered like mist
that is chased by the rays of the sun
and overcome by its heat.
5 For our allotted time is the passing
of a shadow,
and there is no return from our
death,
because it is sealed up and no one
turns back.

6 "Come, therefore, let us enjoy the
good things that exist,
and make use of the creation to the
full as in youth.
7 Let us take our fill of costly wine
and perfumes,
and let no flower of spring pass us
by.
8 Let us crown ourselves with
rosebuds before they wither.
9 Let none of us fail to share in our
revelry;
everywhere let us leave signs of
enjoyment,
because this is our portion, and this
our lot.
10 Let us oppress the righteous poor
man;
let us not spare the widow
or regard the gray hairs of the aged.
11 But let our might be our law of
right,
for what is weak proves itself to be
useless.

12 "Let us lie in wait for the righteous
man,
because he is inconvenient to us and
opposes our actions;
he reproaches us for sins against the
law,
and accuses us of sins against our
training.
13 He professes to have knowledge of
God,
and calls himself a child*e* of the
Lord.

---

a Or *will go unpunished*　　*b* Or *the creatures*　　*c* Or *palace*　　*d* Gk *him*　　*e* Or *servant*

14 He became to us a reproof of our
     thoughts;
15 the very sight of him is a burden to
     us,
   because his manner of life is unlike
     that of others,
   and his ways are strange.
16 We are considered by him as
     something base,
   and he avoids our ways as unclean;
   he calls the last end of the righteous
     happy,
   and boasts that God is his father.
17 Let us see if his words are true,
   and let us test what will happen at
     the end of his life;
18 for if the righteous man is God's
     child, he will help him,
   and will deliver him from the hand
     of his adversaries.
19 Let us test him with insult and
     torture,
   so that we may find out how gentle
     he is,
   and make trial of his forbearance.
20 Let us condemn him to a shameful
     death,
   for, according to what he says, he
     will be protected."

Error of the Wicked

21 Thus they reasoned, but they were
     led astray,
   for their wickedness blinded them,
22 and they did not know the secret
     purposes of God,
   nor hoped for the wages of holiness,
   nor discerned the prize for blameless
     souls;
23 for God created us for incorruption,
   and made us in the image of his
     own eternity,*f*
24 but through the devil's envy death
     entered the world,
   and those who belong to his
     company experience it.

The Destiny of the Righteous

3 But the souls of the righteous are in
     the hand of God,
   and no torment will ever touch
     them.
2 In the eyes of the foolish they
     seemed to have died,
   and their departure was thought to
     be a disaster,
3 and their going from us to be their
     destruction;

but they are at peace.
4 For though in the sight of others
     they were punished,
   their hope is full of immortality.
5 Having been disciplined a little, they
     will receive great good,
   because God tested them and found
     them worthy of himself;
6 like gold in the furnace he tried
     them,
   and like a sacrificial burnt offering
     he accepted them.
7 In the time of their visitation they
     will shine forth,
   and will run like sparks through the
     stubble.
8 They will govern nations and rule
     over peoples,
   and the Lord will reign over them
     forever.
9 Those who trust in him will
     understand truth,
   and the faithful will abide with him
     in love,
   because grace and mercy are upon
     his holy ones,
   and he watches over his elect. *g*

The Destiny of the Ungodly

10 But the ungodly will be punished as
     their reasoning deserves,
   those who disregarded the
     righteous*h*
   and rebelled against the Lord;
11 for those who despise wisdom and
     instruction are miserable.
   Their hope is vain, their labors are
     unprofitable,
   and their works are useless.
12 Their wives are foolish, and their
     children evil;
13 their offspring are accursed.

On Childlessness

For blessed is the barren woman
     who is undefiled,
   who has not entered into a sinful
     union;
   she will have fruit when God
     examines souls.
14 Blessed also is the eunuch whose
     hands have done no lawless
     deed,

*f Other ancient authorities read nature   g Text of
this line uncertain; omitted by some ancient
authorities. Compare 4.15   h Or what is right*

and who has not devised wicked
things against the Lord;
for special favor will be shown him
for his faithfulness,
and a place of great delight in the
temple of the Lord.
15 For the fruit of good labors is
renowned,
and the root of understanding does
not fail.
16 But children of adulterers will not
come to maturity,
and the offspring of an unlawful
union will perish.
17 Even if they live long they will be
held of no account,
and finally their old age will be
without honor.
18 If they die young, they will have no
hope
and no consolation on the day of
judgment.
19 For the end of an unrighteous
generation is grievous.

4 Better than this is childlessness with
virtue,

for in the memory of virtue[i] is
immortality,
because it is known both by God
and by mortals.
2 When it is present, people imitate[j]
it,
and they long for it when it has
gone;
throughout all time it marches,
crowned in triumph,
victor in the contest for prizes that
are undefiled.
3 But the prolific brood of the
ungodly will be of no use,
and none of their illegitimate
seedlings will strike a deep
root
or take a firm hold.
4 For even if they put forth boughs for
a while,
standing insecurely they will be
shaken by the wind,
and by the violence of the winds
they will be uprooted.

i Gk *it*   j Other ancient authorities read *honor*

TUESDAY

Motherhood

Scripture Reading
for Today:
*Wisdom of Solomon
3.13–15; 4.1*

Verse for Today:
*Wisdom of Solomon
4.1*

I feel very deeply that every woman is born to be a mother. But it
is a great mistake to limit this mission to biological maternity.
Great and noble as the latter is, it is an incarnation of something
much deeper: a sharing of one's very life; an ardent desire to give
oneself to others; a willingness to suffer so that another may live.
This is why women are ideal nurses; this is why Saint Edith
Stein—a Jewish convert who died in a concentration camp—char-
acterizes women as those who "cherish, guard, protect, nourish
and advance growth" in keeping with their "natural, maternal
yearning." There is a spiritual motherhood: an openness of one's
heart to whatever is helpless, feeble, or needy.

A woman's vocation is to love and to nurture. Understanding
this, we can see that abortion is the crime par excellence of our
decadent and sad century. Not only does it sin against God,
against the Child Jesus, against the sacredness of human life, but it
kills one of the most noble and tender qualities rooted in the female heart: the vocation to protect what is weak.

—*ALICE VON HILDEBRAND*

Go to page 843 for your next devotional reading.

5 The branches will be broken off
    before they come to maturity,
and their fruit will be useless,
    not ripe enough to eat, and good for
        nothing.
6 For children born of unlawful
        unions
    are witnesses of evil against their
        parents when God examines
        them.[k]
7 But the righteous, though they die
        early, will be at rest.
8 For old age is not honored for
        length of time,
    or measured by number of years;
9 but understanding is gray hair for
        anyone,
    and a blameless life is ripe old age.

10 There were some who pleased God
        and were loved by him,
    and while living among sinners were
        taken up.
11 They were caught up so that evil
        might not change their
        understanding
    or guile deceive their souls.
12 For the fascination of wickedness
        obscures what is good,
    and roving desire perverts the
        innocent mind.
13 Being perfected in a short time, they
        fulfilled long years;
14 for their souls were pleasing to the
        Lord,
    therefore he took them quickly from
        the midst of wickedness.
15 Yet the peoples saw and did not
        understand,
    or take such a thing to heart,
    that God's grace and mercy are with
        his elect,
    and that he watches over his holy
        ones.

The Triumph of the Righteous

16 The righteous who have died will
        condemn the ungodly who
        are living,
    and youth that is quickly perfected[l]
        will condemn the prolonged
        old age of the unrighteous.
17 For they will see the end of the wise,
    and will not understand what the
        Lord purposed for them,
    and for what he kept them safe.
18 The unrighteous[m] will see, and will
        have contempt for them,

but the Lord will laugh them to
    scorn.
After this they will become
    dishonored corpses,
    and an outrage among the dead
        forever;
19 because he will dash them
        speechless to the ground,
    and shake them from the
        foundations;
they will be left utterly dry and
        barren,
    and they will suffer anguish,
    and the memory of them will
        perish.

The Final Judgment

20 They will come with dread when
        their sins are reckoned up,
    and their lawless deeds will convict
        them to their face.

5 Then the righteous will stand with
        great confidence
in the presence of those who have
        oppressed them
    and those who make light of their
        labors.
2 When the unrighteous[n] see them,
        they will be shaken with
        dreadful fear,
    and they will be amazed at the
        unexpected salvation of the
        righteous.
3 They will speak to one another in
        repentance,
    and in anguish of spirit they will
        groan, and say,
4 "These are persons whom we once
        held in derision
    and made a byword of reproach—
        fools that we were!
We thought that their lives were
        madness
    and that their end was without
        honor.
5 Why have they been numbered
        among the children of God?
    And why is their lot among the
        saints?
6 So it was we who strayed from the
        way of truth,
    and the light of righteousness did
        not shine on us,
    and the sun did not rise upon us.

---

k Gk *at their examination*   l Or *ended*   m Gk
They   n Gk *they*

7 We took our fill of the paths of
> lawlessness and destruction,
and we journeyed through trackless
> deserts,
but the way of the Lord we have not
> known.
8 What has our arrogance profited us?
And what good has our boasted
> wealth brought us?

9 "All those things have vanished like
> a shadow,
and like a rumor that passes by;
10 like a ship that sails through the
> billowy water,
and when it has passed no trace can
> be found,
no track of its keel in the waves;
11 or as, when a bird flies through the
> air,
no evidence of its passage is found;
the light air, lashed by the beat of
> its pinions
and pierced by the force of its
> rushing flight,
is traversed by the movement of its
> wings,
and afterward no sign of its coming
> is found there;
12 or as, when an arrow is shot at a
> target,
the air, thus divided, comes together
> at once,
so that no one knows its pathway.
13 So we also, as soon as we were
> born, ceased to be,
and we had no sign of virtue to
> show,
but were consumed in our
> wickedness."
14 Because the hope of the ungodly is
> like thistledown*o* carried by
> the wind,
and like a light frost *p* driven away
> by a storm;
it is dispersed like smoke before the
> wind,
and it passes like the remembrance
> of a guest who stays but a
> day.

The Reward of the Righteous

15 But the righteous live forever,
and their reward is with the Lord;
the Most High takes care of them.
16 Therefore they will receive a glorious
> crown

and a beautiful diadem from the
> hand of the Lord,
because with his right hand he will
> cover them,
and with his arm he will shield
> them.
17 The Lord*q* will take his zeal as his
> whole armor,
and will arm all creation to repel*r*
> his enemies;
18 he will put on righteousness as a
> breastplate,
and wear impartial justice as a
> helmet;
19 he will take holiness as an invincible
> shield,
20 and sharpen stern wrath for a sword,
and creation will join with him to
> fight against his frenzied foes.
21 Shafts of lightning will fly with true
> aim,
and will leap from the clouds to the
> target, as from a well-drawn
> bow,
22 and hailstones full of wrath will be
> hurled as from a catapult;
the water of the sea will rage against
> them,
and rivers will relentlessly
> overwhelm them;
23 a mighty wind will rise against
> them,
and like a tempest it will winnow
> them away.
Lawlessness will lay waste the whole
> earth,
and evildoing will overturn the
> thrones of rulers.

Kings Should Seek Wisdom

6 Listen therefore, O kings, and
> understand;
learn, O judges of the ends of the
> earth.
2 Give ear, you that rule over
> multitudes,
and boast of many nations.
3 For your dominion was given you
> from the Lord,
and your sovereignty from the Most
> High;

---

o Other ancient authorities read *dust*   *p* Other
ancient authorities read *spider's web*   *q* Gk He
r Or *punish*

he will search out your works and
inquire into your plans.

⁴ Because as servants of his kingdom
you did not rule rightly,
or keep the law,
or walk according to the purpose of
God,

⁵ he will come upon you terribly and
swiftly,
because severe judgment falls on
those in high places.

⁶ For the lowliest may be pardoned in
mercy,
but the mighty will be mightily
tested.

⁷ For the Lord of all will not stand in
awe of anyone,
or show deference to greatness;
because he himself made both small
and great,
and he takes thought for all alike.

⁸ But a strict inquiry is in store for the
mighty.

⁹ To you then, O monarchs, my words
are directed,
so that you may learn wisdom and
not transgress.

¹⁰ For they will be made holy who
observe holy things in
holiness,

and those who have been taught
them will find a defense.

¹¹ Therefore set your desire on my
words;
long for them, and you will be
instructed.

Description of Wisdom

¹² Wisdom is radiant and unfading,
and she is easily discerned by those
who love her,
and is found by those who seek
her.

¹³ She hastens to make herself known
to those who desire her.

¹⁴ One who rises early to seek her will
have no difficulty,
for she will be found sitting at the
gate.

¹⁵ To fix one's thought on her is
perfect understanding,
and one who is vigilant on her
account will soon be free
from care,

¹⁶ because she goes about seeking
those worthy of her,
and she graciously appears to them
in their paths,
and meets them in every thought.

The Spirit, Part I

Excerpts from the diary of a humble Mexican housewife and mystic who kept a journal of Jesus' words to her.

February 19, 1911: There exists a hidden treasure, a treasure remaining unexploited and in no ways appreciated at its true worth, which is nevertheless that which is the greatest in heaven and earth: the Holy Spirit. The world of souls itself does not know him as it should. He is the Light of intellects and the Fire that enkindles hearts. If there is indifference, coldness, weakness, and so many other evils, which afflict the spiritual world and even my Church, it is because recourse is not had to the Holy Spirit.

His mission in heaven, his life, his being, is Love.

On earth, his mission consists in leading souls toward this heart of Love, which is God. With him, there is possessed all that can be desired.

—*CONCEPCIÓN CABRERA DE ARMIDA*

Go to page 845 for your next devotional reading.

WEDNESDAY

Scripture Reading
for Today:
*Wisdom of Solomon
6.12–16*

Verse for Today:
*Wisdom of Solomon
6.12*

17 The beginning of wisdom[s] is the
　　most sincere desire for
　　instruction,
　and concern for instruction is love
　　of her,
18 and love of her is the keeping of her
　　laws,
　and giving heed to her laws is
　　assurance of immortality,
19 and immortality brings one near to
　　God;
20 so the desire for wisdom leads to a
　　kingdom.

21 Therefore if you delight in thrones
　　and scepters, O monarchs
　　over the peoples,
　honor wisdom, so that you may
　　reign forever.
22 I will tell you what wisdom is and
　　how she came to be,
　and I will hide no secrets from you,
　but I will trace her course from the
　　beginning of creation,
　and make knowledge of her clear,
　and I will not pass by the truth;
23 nor will I travel in the company of
　　sickly envy,
　for envy[t] does not associate with
　　wisdom.
24 The multitude of the wise is the
　　salvation of the world,
　and a sensible king is the stability of
　　any people.
25 Therefore be instructed by my
　　words, and you will profit.

Solomon Like Other Mortals

7 I also am mortal, like everyone else,
　　a descendant of the first-formed
　　child of earth;
　and in the womb of a mother I was
　　molded into flesh,
2 within the period of ten months,
　　compacted with blood,
　from the seed of a man and the
　　pleasure of marriage.
3 And when I was born, I began to
　　breathe the common air,
　and fell upon the kindred earth;
　my first sound was a cry, as is true
　　of all.
4 I was nursed with care in swaddling
　　cloths.
5 For no king has had a different
　　beginning of existence;
6 there is for all one entrance into life,
　　and one way out.

Solomon's Respect for Wisdom

7 Therefore I prayed, and
　　understanding was given me;
　I called on God, and the spirit of
　　wisdom came to me.
8 I preferred her to scepters and
　　thrones,
　and I accounted wealth as nothing
　　in comparison with her.
9 Neither did I liken to her any
　　priceless gem,
　because all gold is but a little sand
　　in her sight,
　and silver will be accounted as clay
　　before her.
10 I loved her more than health and
　　beauty,
　and I chose to have her rather than
　　light,
　because her radiance never ceases.
11 All good things came to me along
　　with her,
　and in her hands uncounted wealth.
12 I rejoiced in them all, because
　　wisdom leads them;
　but I did not know that she was
　　their mother.
13 I learned without guile and I impart
　　without grudging;
　I do not hide her wealth,
14 for it is an unfailing treasure for
　　mortals;
　those who get it obtain friendship
　　with God,
　commended for the gifts that come
　　from instruction.

Solomon Prays for Wisdom

15 May God grant me to speak with
　　judgment,
　and to have thoughts worthy of
　　what I have received;
　for he is the guide even of wisdom
　　and the corrector of the wise.
16 For both we and our words are in
　　his hand,
　as are all understanding and skill in
　　crafts.
17 For it is he who gave me unerring
　　knowledge of what exists,
　to know the structure of the world
　　and the activity of the
　　elements;
18 the beginning and end and middle
　　of times,

s Gk *Her beginning*　　t Gk *this*

the alternations of the solstices and
     the changes of the seasons,
19 the cycles of the year and the
     constellations of the stars,
20 the natures of animals and the
     tempers of wild animals,
   the powers of spirits[u] and the
     thoughts of human beings,
   the varieties of plants and the virtues
     of roots;
21 I learned both what is secret and
     what is manifest,
22 for wisdom, the fashioner of all
     things, taught me.

The Nature of Wisdom

There is in her a spirit that is
     intelligent, holy,
unique, manifold, subtle,
mobile, clear, unpolluted,
distinct, invulnerable, loving the
     good, keen,
irresistible, 23beneficent, humane,
steadfast, sure, free from anxiety,
all-powerful, overseeing all,
and penetrating through all spirits
that are intelligent, pure, and
     altogether subtle.
24 For wisdom is more mobile than
     any motion;

because of her pureness she pervades
     and penetrates all things.
25 For she is a breath of the power of
     God,
and a pure emanation of the glory
     of the Almighty;
therefore nothing defiled gains
     entrance into her.
26 For she is a reflection of eternal
     light,
a spotless mirror of the working of
     God,
and an image of his goodness.
27 Although she is but one, she can do
     all things,
and while remaining in herself, she
     renews all things;
in every generation she passes into
     holy souls
and makes them friends of God, and
     prophets;
28 for God loves nothing so much as
     the person who lives with
     wisdom.
29 She is more beautiful than the sun,
and excels every constellation of the
     stars.
Compared with the light she is
     found to be superior,
30 for it is succeeded by the night,

[u] Or *winds*

THURSDAY

Scripture Reading
for Today:
*Wisdom of Solomon
7.7–12*

Verse for Today:
*Wisdom of Solomon
7.11*

The Spirit, Part II

Some souls think that the Holy Spirit is very far away, far, far, up
above. Actually he is, we might say, the divine Person who is
most closely present to the creature. He accompanies him everywhere. He penetrates him with himself. He calls him; he protects
him. He makes of him his living temple. He defends him. He helps
him. He guards him from all his enemies. He is closer to him than
his own soul. All the good a soul accomplishes, it carries out under his inspiration, in his light, by his grace and his help. And yet,
he is not invoked, he is not thanked for his direct and intimate action in each soul. If you invoke the Father, if you love him, it is
through the Holy Spirit. If you love me ardently, if you know me, if
you serve me, if you imitate me, if you make yourself but one
with my wishes and with my heart, it is through the Holy Spirit.

—*CONCEPCIÓN CABRERA DE ARMIDA*

Go to page 849 for your next devotional reading.

but against wisdom evil does not
prevail.

8 She reaches mightily from one end
of the earth to the other,
and she orders all things well.

Solomon's Love for Wisdom

2 I loved her and sought her from my
youth;
I desired to take her for my bride,
and became enamored of her
beauty.
3 She glorifies her noble birth by
living with God,
and the Lord of all loves her.
4 For she is an initiate in the
knowledge of God,
and an associate in his works.
5 If riches are a desirable possession in
life,
what is richer than wisdom, the
active cause of all things?
6 And if understanding is effective,
who more than she is fashioner of
what exists?
7 And if anyone loves righteousness,
her labors are virtues;
for she teaches self-control and
prudence,
justice and courage;
nothing in life is more profitable for
mortals than these.
8 And if anyone longs for wide
experience,
she knows the things of old, and
infers the things to come;
she understands turns of speech and
the solutions of riddles;
she has foreknowledge of signs and
wonders
and of the outcome of seasons and
times.

Wisdom Indispensible to Rulers

9 Therefore I determined to take her
to live with me,
knowing that she would give me
good counsel
and encouragement in cares and
grief.
10 Because of her I shall have glory
among the multitudes
and honor in the presence of the
elders, though I am young.
11 I shall be found keen in judgment,
and in the sight of rulers I shall be
admired.

12 When I am silent they will wait for
me,
and when I speak they will give
heed;
if I speak at greater length,
they will put their hands on their
mouths.
13 Because of her I shall have
immortality,
and leave an everlasting
remembrance to those who
come after me.
14 I shall govern peoples,
and nations will be subject to me;
15 dread monarchs will be afraid of me
when they hear of me;
among the people I shall show
myself capable, and
courageous in war.
16 When I enter my house, I shall find
rest with her;
for companionship with her has no
bitterness,
and life with her has no pain, but
gladness and joy.
17 When I considered these things
inwardly,
and pondered in my heart
that in kinship with wisdom there is
immortality,
18 and in friendship with her, pure
delight,
and in the labors of her hands,
unfailing wealth,
and in the experience of her
company, understanding,
and renown in sharing her words,
I went about seeking how to get her
for myself.
19 As a child I was naturally gifted,
and a good soul fell to my lot;
20 or rather, being good, I entered an
undefiled body.
21 But I perceived that I would not
possess wisdom unless God
gave her to me—
and it was a mark of insight to
know whose gift she was—
so I appealed to the Lord and
implored him,
and with my whole heart I said:

Solomon's Prayer for Wisdom

9 "O God of my ancestors and Lord
of mercy,
who have made all things by your
word,

2 and by your wisdom have formed
    humankind
  to have dominion over the creatures
    you have made,
3 and rule the world in holiness and
    righteousness,
  and pronounce judgment in
    uprightness of soul,
4 give me the wisdom that sits by
    your throne,
  and do not reject me from among
    your servants.
5 For I am your servant[v] the son of
    your serving girl,
  a man who is weak and short-lived,
  with little understanding of
    judgment and laws;
6 for even one who is perfect among
    human beings
  will be regarded as nothing without
    the wisdom that comes from
    you.
7 You have chosen me to be king of
    your people
  and to be judge over your sons and
    daughters.
8 You have given command to build a
    temple on your holy
    mountain,
  and an altar in the city of your
    habitation,
  a copy of the holy tent that you
    prepared from the beginning.
9 With you is wisdom, she who knows
    your works
  and was present when you made the
    world;
  she understands what is pleasing in
    your sight
  and what is right according to your
    commandments.
10 Send her forth from the holy
    heavens,
  and from the throne of your glory
    send her,
  that she may labor at my side,
  and that I may learn what is
    pleasing to you.
11 For she knows and understands all
    things,
  and she will guide me wisely in my
    actions
  and guard me with her glory.
12 Then my works will be acceptable,
  and I shall judge your people justly,
  and shall be worthy of the throne[w]
    of my father.

13 For who can learn the counsel of
    God?
  Or who can discern what the Lord
    wills?
14 For the reasoning of mortals is
    worthless,
  and our designs are likely to fail;
15 for a perishable body weighs down
    the soul,
  and this earthy tent burdens the
    thoughtful[x] mind.
16 We can hardly guess at what is on
    earth,
  and what is at hand we find with
    labor;
  but who has traced out what is in
    the heavens?
17 Who has learned your counsel,
  unless you have given wisdom
  and sent your holy spirit from on
    high?
18 And thus the paths of those on earth
    were set right,
  and people were taught what pleases
    you,
  and were saved by wisdom."

The Work of Wisdom from Adam to Moses

10 Wisdom[y] protected the
    first-formed father of the
    world, when he alone had
    been created;
  she delivered him from his
    transgression,
2 and gave him strength to rule all
    things.
3 But when an unrighteous man
    departed from her in his
    anger,
  he perished because in rage he killed
    his brother.
4 When the earth was flooded because
    of him, wisdom again saved
    it,
  steering the righteous man by a
    paltry piece of wood.

5 Wisdom[y] also, when the nations in
    wicked agreement had been
    put to confusion,
  recognized the righteous man and
    preserved him blameless
    before God,
  and kept him strong in the face of
    his compassion for his child.

v Gk *slave*   *w* Gk *thrones*   *x* Or *anxious*
y Gk *She*

6 Wisdom[z] rescued a righteous man
    when the ungodly were
    perishing;
he escaped the fire that descended
    on the Five Cities.[a]
7 Evidence of their wickedness still
    remains:
a continually smoking wasteland,
plants bearing fruit that does not
    ripen,
and a pillar of salt standing as a
    monument to an unbelieving
    soul.
8 For because they passed wisdom by,
they not only were hindered from
    recognizing the good,
but also left for humankind a
    reminder of their folly,
so that their failures could never go
    unnoticed.

9 Wisdom rescued from troubles those
    who served her.
10 When a righteous man fled from his
    brother's wrath,
she guided him on straight paths;
she showed him the kingdom of
    God,
and gave him knowledge of holy
    things;
she prospered him in his labors,
and increased the fruit of his toil.
11 When his oppressors were covetous,
she stood by him and made him
    rich.
12 She protected him from his enemies,
and kept him safe from those who
    lay in wait for him;
in his arduous contest she gave him
    the victory,
so that he might learn that godliness
    is more powerful than
    anything else.

13 When a righteous man was sold,
    wisdom[b] did not desert him,
but delivered him from sin.
She descended with him into the
    dungeon,
14 and when he was in prison she did
    not leave him,
until she brought him the scepter of
    a kingdom
and authority over his masters.
Those who accused him she showed
    to be false,
and she gave him everlasting honor.

Wisdom Led the Israelites out of Egypt

15 A holy people and blameless race
wisdom delivered from a nation of
    oppressors.
16 She entered the soul of a servant of
    the Lord,
and withstood dread kings with
    wonders and signs.
17 She gave to holy people the reward
    of their labors;
she guided them along a marvelous
    way,
and became a shelter to them by
    day,
and a starry flame through the night.
18 She brought them over the Red Sea,
and led them through deep waters;
19 but she drowned their enemies,
and cast them up from the depth of
    the sea.
20 Therefore the righteous plundered
    the ungodly;
they sang hymns, O Lord, to your
    holy name,
and praised with one accord your
    defending hand;
21 for wisdom opened the mouths of
    those who were mute,
and made the tongues of infants
    speak clearly.

Wisdom Led the Israelites through the Desert

11 Wisdom[z] prospered their works
    by the hand of a holy
    prophet.
2 They journeyed through an
    uninhabited wilderness,
and pitched their tents in untrodden
    places.
3 They withstood their enemies and
    fought off their foes.
4 When they were thirsty, they called
    upon you,
and water was given them out of
    flinty rock,
and from hard stone a remedy for
    their thirst.
5 For through the very things by
    which their enemies were
    punished,
they themselves received benefit in
    their need.

z Gk She   a Or on Pentapolis   b Gk she

6 Instead of the fountain of an
    ever-flowing river,
  stirred up and defiled with blood
7 in rebuke for the decree to kill the
    infants,
  you gave them abundant water
    unexpectedly,
8 showing by their thirst at that
    time
  how you punished their enemies.
9 For when they were tried, though
    they were being disciplined in
    mercy,
  they learned how the ungodly were
    tormented when judged in
    wrath.
10 For you tested them as a parent[c]
    does in warning,
  but you examined the ungodly[d] as
    a stern king does in
    condemnation.
11 Whether absent or present, they
    were equally distressed,
12 for a twofold grief possessed them,
  and a groaning at the memory of
    what had occurred.
13 For when they heard that through
    their own punishments
  the righteous[e] had received benefit,
    they perceived it was the
    Lord's doing.

14 For though they had mockingly
    rejected him who long before
    had been cast out and
    exposed,
  at the end of the events they
    marveled at him,
  when they felt thirst in a different
    way from the righteous.

Punishment of the Wicked

15 In return for their foolish and
    wicked thoughts,
  which led them astray to worship
    irrational serpents and
    worthless animals,
  you sent upon them a multitude of
    irrational creatures to punish
    them,
16 so that they might learn that one is
    punished by the very things
    by which one sins.
17 For your all-powerful hand,
  which created the world out of
    formless matter,
  did not lack the means to send
    upon them a multitude of
    bears, or bold lions,
18 or newly-created unknown beasts
    full of rage,

c Gk a father   d Gk those   e Gk they

---

*B*ecause God Loves It

He showed me a little thing, the size of a hazelnut, in the palm of
my hand, and it was as round as a ball. I looked at it with my
mind's eye and I thought, "What can this be?" An answer came,
"It is all that is made." I marveled that it could last, for I thought it
might have crumbled to nothing, it was so small. And the answer
came into my mind, "It lasts and ever shall because God loves it."
And all things have being through the love of God.

   In this little thing I saw three truths. The first is that God
made it. The second is that God loves it. The third is that God
looks after it.

   What is he indeed that is maker and lover and keeper? I cannot
find words to tell. For until I am one with him, I can never have
true rest nor peace. I can never know it until I am held so close to
him that there is nothing in between.

—*JULIAN OF NORWICH*

Go to page 852 for your next devotional reading.

FRIDAY

Scripture Reading
for Today:
*Wisdom of Solomon
11.17–26*

Verse for Today:
*Wisdom of Solomon
11.24*

or such as breathe out fiery breath,
or belch forth a thick pall of smoke,
or flash terrible sparks from their
eyes;
19 not only could the harm they did
destroy people,*f*
but the mere sight of them could
kill by fright.
20 Even apart from these, people*g*
could fall at a single breath
when pursued by justice
and scattered by the breath of your
power.
But you have arranged all things by
measure and number and
weight.

God Is Powerful and Merciful

21 For it is always in your power to
show great strength,
and who can withstand the might of
your arm?
22 Because the whole world before you
is like a speck that tips the
scales,
and like a drop of morning dew that
falls on the ground.
23 But you are merciful to all, for you
can do all things,
and you overlook people's sins, so
that they may repent.
24 For you love all things that exist,
and detest none of the things that
you have made,
for you would not have made
anything if you had hated it.
25 How would anything have endured
if you had not willed it?
Or how would anything not called
forth by you have been
preserved?
26 You spare all things, for they are
yours, O Lord, you who love
the living.

12 For your immortal spirit is in all
things.
2 Therefore you correct little by little
those who trespass,
and you remind and warn them of
the things through which they
sin,
so that they may be freed from
wickedness and put their trust
in you, O Lord.

The Sins of the Canaanites

3 Those who lived long ago in your
holy land

4 you hated for their detestable
practices,
their works of sorcery and unholy
rites,
5 their merciless slaughter*h* of
children,
and their sacrificial feasting on
human flesh and blood.
These initiates from the midst of a
heathen cult,*i*
6 these parents who murder helpless
lives,
you willed to destroy by the hands
of our ancestors,
7 so that the land most precious of all
to you
might receive a worthy colony of the
servants*j* of God.
8 But even these you spared, since
they were but mortals,
and sent wasps*k* as forerunners of
your army
to destroy them little by little,
9 though you were not unable to give
the ungodly into the hands of
the righteous in battle,
or to destroy them at one blow by
dread wild animals or your
stern word.
10 But judging them little by little you
gave them an opportunity to
repent,
though you were not unaware that
their origin*l* was evil
and their wickedness inborn,
and that their way of thinking
would never change.
11 For they were an accursed race from
the beginning,
and it was not through fear of
anyone that you left them
unpunished for their sins.

God Is Sovereign

12 For who will say, "What have you
done?"
or will resist your judgment?
Who will accuse you for the
destruction of nations that
you made?
Or who will come before you to
plead as an advocate for the
unrighteous?

f Gk *them*   *g* Gk *they*   *h* Gk *slaughterers*
i Meaning of Gk uncertain   *j* Or *children*   *k* Or
hornets   *l* Or *nature*

13 For neither is there any god besides
you, whose care is for all
people,[m]
to whom you should prove that you
have not judged unjustly;

14 nor can any king or monarch
confront you about those
whom you have punished.

15 You are righteous and you rule all
things righteously,
deeming it alien to your power
to condemn anyone who does not
deserve to be punished.

16 For your strength is the source of
righteousness,
and your sovereignty over all causes
you to spare all.

17 For you show your strength when
people doubt the
completeness of your power,
and you rebuke any insolence
among those who know it.[n]

18 Although you are sovereign in
strength, you judge with
mildness,
and with great forbearance you
govern us;
for you have power to act whenever
you choose.

God's Lessons for Israel

19 Through such works you have taught
your people
that the righteous must be kind,
and you have filled your children
with good hope,
because you give repentance for sins.

20 For if you punished with such great
care and indulgence[o]
the enemies of your servants[p] and
those deserving of death,
granting them time and opportunity
to give up their wickedness,

21 with what strictness you have judged
your children,
to whose ancestors you gave oaths
and covenants full of good
promises!

22 So while chastening us you scourge
our enemies ten thousand
times more,
so that, when we judge, we may
meditate upon your
goodness,
and when we are judged, we may
expect mercy.

The Punishment of the Egyptians

23 Therefore those who lived
unrighteously, in a life of
folly,
you tormented through their own
abominations.

24 For they went far astray on the paths
of error,
accepting as gods those animals that
even their enemies[q]
despised;
they were deceived like foolish
infants.

25 Therefore, as though to children
who cannot reason,
you sent your judgment to mock
them.

26 But those who have not heeded the
warning of mild rebukes
will experience the deserved
judgment of God.

27 For when in their suffering they
became incensed
at those creatures that they had
thought to be gods, being
punished by means of them,
they saw and recognized as the true
God the one whom they had
before refused to know.
Therefore the utmost condemnation
came upon them.

The Foolishness of Nature Worship

13 For all people who were
ignorant of God were foolish
by nature;
and they were unable from the good
things that are seen to know
the one who exists,
nor did they recognize the artisan
while paying heed to his
works;

2 but they supposed that either fire or
wind or swift air,
or the circle of the stars, or turbulent
water,
or the luminaries of heaven were the
gods that rule the world.

3 If through delight in the beauty of
these things people assumed
them to be gods,
let them know how much better
than these is their Lord,

---

m Or *all things*   n Meaning of Gk uncertain
o Other ancient authorities lack *and indulgence;*
others read *and entreaty*   p Or *children*
q Gk *they*

Woman of Endor

**THE
STORY
OF A
WOMAN**

Her Character: *Compassionate to Saul on the eve of his death, she exercised power by acting as a medium.*
Her Sorrow: *To have delivered a hopeless message to Israel's king.*

Read I Samuel 28.3–25

It was a night for frightening apparitions. Squinting through the open doorway, the woman stiffened, retreating a step. A face loomed before her, floating on its own like a full, white moon in the outer darkness. Before she could close the door, she felt fingers gripping her wrist.

"Consult a spirit for me," the voice insisted, "and bring up for me the one whom I name to you."

A large man pushed through the door. She could feel fear enter as he swept past her and sat down.

"Surely you know what Saul has done, how he has cut off the mediums and the wizards from the land. Why then are you laying a snare for my life to bring about my death?" she asked.

"As the LORD lives, no punishment shall come upon you for this," he swore. "Bring up Samuel for me."

So the woman sat down and yielded herself, making her soul a bridge for the dead to walk across.

Suddenly she screamed, "Why have you deceived me? You are Saul!"

The king calmed her, saying, "Have no fear; what do you see?"

"An old man is coming up; he is wrapped in a robe."

Samuel said to Saul, "Why have you disturbed me by bringing me up?"

"I am in great distress," Saul replied, "for the Philistines are warring against me, and God has turned away from me and answers me no more, either by prophets or by dreams;

so I have summoned you to tell me what I should do."

Samuel said, "The LORD has done to you just as he spoke by me; for the LORD has torn the kingdom out of your hand, and given it to your neighbor, David . . . tomorrow you and your sons shall be with me; the LORD will also give the army of Israel into the hands of the Philistines."

The woman shuddered, the message delivered. Little wonder the king had seemed so desolate. Fear had crushed the life out of his once-strong face, hollowing the eyes, etching deep lines across cheeks and forehead. Kindly, she served what may have been Saul's last meal. The next day he was dead.

The woman of Endor is a strange character, steeped in the occult, yet kind and motherly in her attitude toward the tormented king. For some reason, God allowed her to call up the prophet Samuel even though necromancy (conjuring spirits for the purpose of knowing or influencing future events) was strictly forbidden in Israel.

Perhaps she had become a medium because women in those days had so little power. Or perhaps it seemed an outlet for her helpful nature. But by yielding her soul to spirits, she was abusing herself in the deepest possible way, distorting her dignity as a person for the sake of obtaining power.

That night the woman of Endor looked into the eyes of the most powerful man in Israel and saw the terror there. Did the vision shake her? Did her encounter with a true prophet cause her to forsake her trade? We have no idea what became of her. Sadly, her meeting with Saul marks one of the lowest moments in the life of Israel's first king, revealing his disintegration as a man whose future was destroyed by disobedience.

Praying in Light of the Story of the Woman of Endor

"Do not turn to mediums or wizards; do not seek them out, to be defiled by them: I am the LORD your God."—*Leviticus 19.31*

Praise God: *That he protects us against evil.*

Offer Thanks: *That God doesn't hide himself from those who love and follow him.*

Confess: *Any dealings you may have had with the occult: using tarot cards, consulting horoscopes, visiting fortune-tellers, or reading occultic books.*

Ask God: *To cleanse and free you from any ill effect of your contact with the occult.*

Lift Your Heart

Sometimes we expose ourselves to the occult naïvely—reading horoscopes in the daily paper, consulting a medium on a whim or thinking tarot cards is simply an innocent game. At other times, our interest is more serious, based on a desire for knowledge, healing, or power over others and ourselves. If you have ever dabbled in the occult, now is the time to come clean before God. Express your sorrow and your resolve to follow God by removing from your home anything remotely related to the occult. Confess your involvement and ask a priest or a mature Christian friend to pray with you as you seek God's protection.

Father, forgive me for my involvement in the occult. I want nothing whatever to do with the realm of evil. Draw me out of the darkness and into the light of your presence. Free me from any lingering effects of my involvement and help me to trust you completely for my future.

Go to page 867 for your next devotional reading.

for the author of beauty created
them.

⁴ And if people^r were amazed at
their power and working,
let them perceive from them
how much more powerful is the one
who formed them.

⁵ For from the greatness and beauty of
created things
comes a corresponding perception of
their Creator.

⁶ Yet these people are little to be
blamed,
for perhaps they go astray
while seeking God and desiring to
find him.

⁷ For while they live among his works,
they keep searching,
and they trust in what they see,
because the things that are
seen are beautiful.

⁸ Yet again, not even they are to be
excused;

⁹ for if they had the power to know
so much
that they could investigate the
world,
how did they fail to find sooner the
Lord of these things?

The Foolishness of Idolatry

¹⁰ But miserable, with their hopes set
on dead things, are those
who give the name "gods" to the
works of human hands,
gold and silver fashioned with skill,
and likenesses of animals,
or a useless stone, the work of an
ancient hand.

¹¹ A skilled woodcutter may saw down
a tree easy to handle
and skillfully strip off all its bark,
and then with pleasing
workmanship
make a useful vessel that serves life's
needs,

¹² and burn the cast-off pieces of his
work
to prepare his food, and eat his fill.

¹³ But a cast-off piece from among
them, useful for nothing,
a stick crooked and full of knots,
he takes and carves with care in his
leisure,
and shapes it with skill gained in
idleness;^s
he forms it in the likeness of a
human being,

¹⁴ or makes it like some worthless
animal,
giving it a coat of red paint and
coloring its surface red
and covering every blemish in it
with paint;

¹⁵ then he makes a suitable niche for
it,
and sets it in the wall, and fastens it
there with iron.

¹⁶ He takes thought for it, so that it
may not fall,
because he knows that it cannot
help itself,
for it is only an image and has need
of help.

¹⁷ When he prays about possessions
and his marriage and
children,
he is not ashamed to address a
lifeless thing.

¹⁸ For health he appeals to a thing that
is weak;
for life he prays to a thing that is
dead;
for aid he entreats a thing that is
utterly inexperienced;
for a prosperous journey, a thing
that cannot take a step;

¹⁹ for money-making and work and
success with his hands
he asks strength of a thing whose
hands have no strength.

Folly of a Navigator Praying to an Idol

14 Again, one preparing to sail and
about to voyage over raging
waves
calls upon a piece of wood more
fragile than the ship that
carries him.

² For it was desire for gain that
planned that vessel,
and wisdom was the artisan who
built it;

³ but it is your providence, O Father,
that steers its course,
because you have given it a path in
the sea,
and a safe way through the waves,

⁴ showing that you can save from
every danger,
so that even a person who lacks skill
may put to sea.

---

^r Gk *they*   ^s Other ancient authorities read *with
intelligent skill*

5 It is your will that works of your
wisdom should not be
without effect;
therefore people trust their lives
even to the smallest piece of
wood,
and passing through the billows on
a raft they come safely to
land.
6 For even in the beginning, when
arrogant giants were
perishing,
the hope of the world took refuge
on a raft,
and guided by your hand left to the
world the seed of a new
generation.
7 For blessed is the wood by which
righteousness comes.

8 But the idol made with hands is
accursed, and so is the one
who made it—
he for having made it, and the
perishable thing because it
was named a god.
9 For equally hateful to God are the
ungodly and their
ungodliness;
10 for what was done will be punished
together with the one who
did it.
11 Therefore there will be a visitation
also upon the heathen idols,
because, though part of what God
created, they became an
abomination,
snares for human souls
and a trap for the feet of the foolish.

The Origin and Evils of Idolatry

12 For the idea of making idols was the
beginning of fornication,
and the invention of them was the
corruption of life;
13 for they did not exist from the
beginning,
nor will they last forever.
14 For through human vanity they
entered the world,
and therefore their speedy end has
been planned.

15 For a father, consumed with grief at
an untimely bereavement,
made an image of his child, who
had been suddenly taken
from him;

he now honored as a god what was
once a dead human being,
and handed on to his dependents
secret rites and initiations.
16 Then the ungodly custom, grown
strong with time, was kept as
a law,
and at the command of monarchs
carved images were
worshiped.
17 When people could not honor
monarchs[t] in their presence,
since they lived at a distance,
they imagined their appearance far
away,
and made a visible image of the
king whom they honored,
so that by their zeal they might
flatter the absent one as
though present.

18 Then the ambition of the artisan
impelled
even those who did not know the
king to intensify their
worship.
19 For he, perhaps wishing to please
his ruler,
skillfully forced the likeness to take
more beautiful form,
20 and the multitude, attracted by the
charm of his work,
now regarded as an object of
worship the one whom
shortly before they had
honored as a human being.
21 And this became a hidden trap for
humankind,
because people, in bondage to
misfortune or to royal
authority,
bestowed on objects of stone or
wood the name that ought
not to be shared.

22 Then it was not enough for them to
err about the knowledge of
God,
but though living in great strife due
to ignorance,
they call such great evils peace.
23 For whether they kill children in
their initiations, or celebrate
secret mysteries,
or hold frenzied revels with strange
customs,

t Gk them

24 they no longer keep either their lives
          or their marriages pure,
     but they either treacherously kill one
          another, or grieve one
          another by adultery,
25 and all is a raging riot of blood and
          murder, theft and deceit,
          corruption, faithlessness,
          tumult, perjury,
26 confusion over what is good,
          forgetfulness of favors,
     defiling of souls, sexual perversion,
     disorder in marriages, adultery, and
          debauchery.
27 For the worship of idols not to be
          named
     is the beginning and cause and end
          of every evil.
28 For their worshipers[u] either rave in
          exultation,
     or prophesy lies, or live
          unrighteously, or readily
          commit perjury;
29 for because they trust in lifeless idols
     they swear wicked oaths and expect
          to suffer no harm.
30 But just penalties will overtake them
          on two counts:
     because they thought wrongly about
          God in devoting themselves
          to idols,
     and because in deceit they swore
          unrighteously through
          contempt for holiness.
31 For it is not the power of the things
          by which people swear,[v]
     but the just penalty for those who
          sin,
     that always pursues the transgression
          of the unrighteous.

Benefits of Worshiping the True God

15 But you, our God, are kind and
          true,
     patient, and ruling all things[w] in
          mercy.
2 For even if we sin we are yours,
          knowing your power;
     but we will not sin, because we
          know that you acknowledge
          us as yours.
3 For to know you is complete
          righteousness,
     and to know your power is the root
          of immortality.
4 For neither has the evil intent of
          human art misled us,
     nor the fruitless toil of painters,

a figure stained with varied colors,
5 whose appearance arouses yearning
          in fools,
     so that they desire[x] the lifeless form
          of a dead image.
6 Lovers of evil things and fit for such
          objects of hope[y]
     are those who either make or desire
          or worship them.

The Foolishness of Worshiping Clay Idols

7 A potter kneads the soft earth
     and laboriously molds each vessel
          for our service,
     fashioning out of the same clay
     both the vessels that serve clean uses
     and those for contrary uses, making
          all alike;
     but which shall be the use of each
          of them
     the worker in clay decides.
8 With misspent toil, these workers
          form a futile god from the
          same clay—
     these mortals who were made of
          earth a short time before
     and after a little while go to the
          earth from which all mortals
          are taken,
     when the time comes to return the
          souls that were borrowed.
9 But the workers are not concerned
          that mortals are destined to
          die
     or that their life is brief,
     but they compete with workers in
          gold and silver,
     and imitate workers in copper;
     and they count it a glorious thing to
          mold counterfeit gods.
10 Their heart is ashes, their hope is
          cheaper than dirt,
     and their lives are of less worth than
          clay,
11 because they failed to know the one
          who formed them
     and inspired them with active souls
     and breathed a living spirit into
          them.
12 But they considered our existence an
          idle game,
     and life a festival held for profit,

u Gk *they*   v Or *of the oaths people swear*   w Or
ruling the universe   x Gk *and he desires*   y Gk
such hopes

for they say one must get money
      however one can, even by
      base means.

13 For these persons, more than all
      others, know that they sin
   when they make from earthy matter
      fragile vessels and carved
      images.

14 But most foolish, and more
      miserable than an infant,
   are all the enemies who oppressed
      your people.

15 For they thought that all their
      heathen idols were gods,
   though these have neither the use of
      their eyes to see with,
   nor nostrils with which to draw
      breath,
   nor ears with which to hear,
   nor fingers to feel with,
   and their feet are of no use for
      walking.

16 For a human being made them,
   and one whose spirit is borrowed
      formed them;
   for none can form gods that are like
      themselves.

17 People are mortal, and what they
      make with lawless hands is
      dead;
   for they are better than the objects
      they worship,
   since[z] they have life, but the
      idols[a] never had.

Serpents in the Desert

18 Moreover, they worship even the
      most hateful animals,
   which are worse than all others
      when judged by their lack of
      intelligence;

19 and even as animals they are not so
      beautiful in appearance that
      one would desire them,
   but they have escaped both the
      praise of God and his
      blessing.

16 Therefore those people[b] were
      deservedly punished through
      such creatures,
   and were tormented by a multitude
      of animals.

2 Instead of this punishment you
      showed kindness to your
      people,
   and you prepared quails to eat,

a delicacy to satisfy the desire of
      appetite;

3 in order that those people, when
      they desired food,
   might lose the least remnant of
      appetite[c]
   because of the odious creatures sent
      to them,
   while your people,[b] after suffering
      want a short time,
   might partake of delicacies.

4 For it was necessary that upon those
      oppressors inescapable want
      should come,
   while to these others it was merely
      shown how their enemies
      were being tormented.

5 For when the terrible rage of wild
      animals came upon your
      people[d]
   and they were being destroyed by
      the bites of writhing serpents,
   your wrath did not continue to the
      end;

6 they were troubled for a little while
      as a warning,
   and received a symbol of deliverance
      to remind them of your law's
      command.

7 For the one who turned toward it
      was saved, not by the thing
      that was beheld,
   but by you, the Savior of all.

8 And by this also you convinced our
      enemies
   that it is you who deliver from every
      evil.

9 For they were killed by the bites of
      locusts and flies,
   and no healing was found for them,
   because they deserved to be
      punished by such things.

10 But your children were not
      conquered even by the fangs
      of venomous serpents,
   for your mercy came to their help
      and healed them.

11 To remind them of your oracles they
      were bitten,
   and then were quickly delivered,
   so that they would not fall into deep
      forgetfulness

---

z Other ancient authorities read *of which*   a Gk
but they   b Gk *they*   c Gk *loathed the necessary
appetite*   d Gk *them*

and become unresponsive[e] to your
kindness.

12 For neither herb nor poultice cured
them,
but it was your word, O Lord, that
heals all people.

13 For you have power over life and
death;
you lead mortals down to the gates
of Hades and back again.

14 A person in wickedness kills
another,
but cannot bring back the departed
spirit,
or set free the imprisoned soul.

Disastrous Storms Strike Egypt

15 To escape from your hand is
impossible;

16 for the ungodly, refusing to know
you,
were flogged by the strength of your
arm,
pursued by unusual rains and hail
and relentless storms,
and utterly consumed by fire.

17 For—most incredible of all—in
water, which quenches all
things,
the fire had still greater effect,
for the universe defends the
righteous.

18 At one time the flame was
restrained,
so that it might not consume the
creatures sent against the
ungodly,
but that seeing this they might know
that they were being pursued by the
judgment of God;

19 and at another time even in the
midst of water it burned
more intensely than fire,
to destroy the crops of the
unrighteous land.

The Israelites Receive Manna

20 Instead of these things you gave
your people food of angels,
and without their toil you supplied
them from heaven with bread
ready to eat,
providing every pleasure and suited
to every taste.

21 For your sustenance manifested your
sweetness toward your
children;

and the bread, ministering[f] to the
desire of the one who took it,
was changed to suit everyone's
liking.

22 Snow and ice withstood fire without
melting,
so that they might know that the
crops of their enemies
were being destroyed by the fire that
blazed in the hail
and flashed in the showers of rain;

23 whereas the fire,[g] in order that the
righteous might be fed,
even forgot its native power.

24 For creation, serving you who made
it,
exerts itself to punish the
unrighteous,
and in kindness relaxes on behalf of
those who trust in you.

25 Therefore at that time also, changed
into all forms,
it served your all-nourishing bounty,
according to the desire of those who
had need,[h]

26 so that your children, whom you
loved, O Lord, might learn
that it is not the production of crops
that feeds humankind
but that your word sustains those
who trust in you.

27 For what was not destroyed by fire
was melted when simply warmed by
a fleeting ray of the sun,

28 to make it known that one must rise
before the sun to give you
thanks,
and must pray to you at the
dawning of the light;

29 for the hope of an ungrateful person
will melt like wintry frost,
and flow away like waste water.

Terror Strikes the Egyptians at Night

17 Great are your judgments and
hard to describe;
therefore uninstructed souls have
gone astray.

2 For when lawless people supposed
that they held the holy nation
in their power,

---

e Meaning of Gk uncertain   f Gk and it,
ministering   g Gk this   h Or who made
supplication

they themselves lay as captives of
　　darkness and prisoners of
　　long night,
shut in under their roofs, exiles from
　　eternal providence.
3 For thinking that in their secret sins
　　they were unobserved
behind a dark curtain of
　　forgetfulness,
they were scattered, terribly[i]
　　alarmed,
and appalled by specters.
4 For not even the inner chamber that
　　held them protected them
　　from fear,
but terrifying sounds rang out
　　around them,
and dismal phantoms with gloomy
　　faces appeared.
5 And no power of fire was able to
　　give light,
nor did the brilliant flames of the
　　stars
avail to illumine that hateful night.
6 Nothing was shining through to
　　them
except a dreadful, self-kindled fire,
and in terror they deemed the things
　　that they saw
to be worse than that unseen
　　appearance.
7 The delusions of their magic art lay
　　humbled,
and their boasted wisdom was
　　scornfully rebuked.
8 For those who promised to drive off
　　the fears and disorders of a
　　sick soul
were sick themselves with ridiculous
　　fear.
9 For even if nothing disturbing
　　frightened them,
yet, scared by the passing of wild
　　animals and the hissing of
　　snakes
10 they perished in trembling fear,
refusing to look even at the air,
　　though it nowhere could be
　　avoided.
11 For wickedness is a cowardly thing,
　　condemned by its own
　　testimony;[j]
distressed by conscience, it has
　　always exaggerated[k] the
　　difficulties.
12 For fear is nothing but a giving up
　　of the helps that come from
　　reason;

13 and hope, defeated by this inward
　　weakness,
prefers ignorance of what causes the
　　torment.
14 But throughout the night, which was
　　really powerless
and which came upon them from
　　the recesses of powerless
　　Hades,
they all slept the same sleep,
15 and now were driven by monstrous
　　specters,
and now were paralyzed by their
　　souls' surrender;
for sudden and unexpected fear
　　overwhelmed them.
16 And whoever was there fell down,
and thus was kept shut up in a
　　prison not made of iron;
17 for whether they were farmers or
　　shepherds
or workers who toiled in the
　　wilderness,
they were seized, and endured the
　　inescapable fate;
for with one chain of darkness they
　　all were bound.
18 Whether there came a whistling
　　wind,
or a melodious sound of birds in
　　wide-spreading branches,
or the rhythm of violently rushing
　　water,
19 or the harsh crash of rocks hurled
　　down,
or the unseen running of leaping
　　animals,
or the sound of the most savage
　　roaring beasts,
or an echo thrown back from a
　　hollow of the mountains,
it paralyzed them with terror.
20 For the whole world was illumined
　　with brilliant light,
and went about its work
　　unhindered,
21 while over those people alone heavy
　　night was spread,
an image of the darkness that was
　　destined to receive them;
but still heavier than darkness were
　　they to themselves.

---

i Other ancient authorities read unobserved, they
were darkened behind a dark curtain of forgetfulness,
terribly *j Meaning of Gk uncertain* *k Other*
ancient authorities read anticipated

Light Shines on the Israelites

18 But for your holy ones there
was very great light.
Their enemies[l] heard their voices
but did not see their forms,
and counted them happy for not
having suffered,

2 and were thankful that your holy
ones,[m] though previously
wronged, were doing them no
injury;
and they begged their pardon for
having been at variance with
them.[m]

3 Therefore you provided a flaming
pillar of fire
as a guide for your people's[n]
unknown journey,
and a harmless sun for their glorious
wandering.

4 For their enemies[o] deserved to be
deprived of light and
imprisoned in darkness,
those who had kept your children
imprisoned,

---

l Gk *They*   *m* Meaning of Gk uncertain   *n* Gk
their   *o* Gk *those persons*

THE TRADITION

Hell

They were seized, and endured the inescapable fate;
for with one chain of darkness they all were bound.

WISDOM 17.17

*D*ante pictured hell not as a fire but as a barren pit of ice. The French writer Sartre saw it as a group of nasty people trapped in a room with no exits. Jesus spoke of hell as a prison and torture chamber, outer darkness, and unquenchable fire (see Matthew 5.25–26, 29; 8.12; Mark 9.43).

Many people today do not picture hell at all, for they do not believe that it exists. But the fact that Jesus insisted on the reality of eternal punishment is one strong reason for believing in its existence. "Let us face the facts," said British writer Dorothy Sayers. "The doctrine of hell is not 'medieval': It is Christ's . . . One cannot get rid of it without tearing the New Testament to tatters." Besides, if everything is going to turn out the same for all of us no matter how we live, if Mother Teresa and Adolf Hitler are going to break bread together at the heavenly banquet, why struggle to grow in virtue? Without the possibility of heaven and hell, our life choices are meaningless.

Like heaven, hell defies description. What we do know of it indicates a state of unending suffering, the worst of which is being forever unable to enjoy the goal for which we were created. On earth, as Saint Augustine said, our hearts are unhappy and restless until they rest in God. In hell, where choosing God is no longer possible, restlessness becomes unfathomable anguish.

No one can penetrate the mental state of those in hell, but with some imagination, you can get a pretty strong whiff of hell from chapter 17 of the book of Wisdom. It is a dramatic re-creation of how the Egyptians experienced one of the seven plagues that God worked to free Israel. Read with hell in mind, it is quite evocative.

Thought provoking, too. Though we usually think of hell mainly in terms of its physical torments, it is mental anguish that stands out here. The Egyptians—*read, the damned*—are trembling and terrified, mocked and jeered, paralyzed, powerless, sick at heart, more burdensome to themselves than the oppressive darkness, which is a sign of their separation from God, who is light.

"Enter through the narrow gate," Jesus tells us (Matthew 7.13). Thinking about hell once in a while can help us resolve to do just that.

through whom the imperishable
light of the law was to be
given to the world.

The Death of the Egyptian Firstborn

5 When they had resolved to kill the
infants of your holy ones,
and one child had been abandoned
and rescued,
you in punishment took away a
multitude of their children;
and you destroyed them all together
by a mighty flood.
6 That night was made known
beforehand to our ancestors,
so that they might rejoice in sure
knowledge of the oaths in
which they trusted.
7 The deliverance of the righteous and
the destruction of their
enemies
were expected by your people.
8 For by the same means by which
you punished our enemies
you called us to yourself and
glorified us.
9 For in secret the holy children of
good people offered sacrifices,
and with one accord agreed to the
divine law,
so that the saints would share alike
the same things,
both blessings and dangers;
and already they were singing the
praises of the ancestors. *p*
10 But the discordant cry of their
enemies echoed back,
and their piteous lament for their
children was spread abroad.
11 The slave was punished with the
same penalty as the master,
and the commoner suffered the
same loss as the king;
12 and they all together, by the one
form*q* of death,
had corpses too many to count.
For the living were not sufficient
even to bury them,
since in one instant their most
valued children had been
destroyed.
13 For though they had disbelieved
everything because of their
magic arts,
yet, when their firstborn were
destroyed, they acknowledged
your people to be God's
child.

14 For while gentle silence enveloped
all things,
and night in its swift course was
now half gone,
15 your all-powerful word leaped from
heaven, from the royal
throne,
into the midst of the land that was
doomed,
a stern warrior
16 carrying the sharp sword of your
authentic command,
and stood and filled all things with
death,
and touched heaven while standing
on the earth.
17 Then at once apparitions in dreadful
dreams greatly troubled them,
and unexpected fears assailed them;
18 and one here and another there,
hurled down half dead,
made known why they were dying;
19 for the dreams that disturbed them
forewarned them of this,
so that they might not perish
without knowing why they
suffered.

Threat of Annihilation in the Desert

20 The experience of death touched
also the righteous,
and a plague came upon the
multitude in the desert,
but the wrath did not long continue.
21 For a blameless man was quick to
act as their champion;
he brought forward the shield of his
ministry,
prayer and propitiation by incense;
he withstood the anger and put an
end to the disaster,
showing that he was your servant.
22 He conquered the wrath*r* not by
strength of body,
not by force of arms,
but by his word he subdued the
avenger,
appealing to the oaths and
covenants given to our
ancestors.
23 For when the dead had already
fallen on one another in
heaps,

p Other ancient authorities read dangers, the
ancestors already leading the songs of praise   *q Gk*
name   *r Cn: Gk* multitude

he intervened and held back the
wrath,
and cut off its way to the living.
24 For on his long robe the whole
world was depicted,
and the glories of the ancestors were
engraved on the four rows of
stones,
and your majesty was on the diadem
upon his head.
25 To these the destroyer yielded, these
he*s* feared;
for merely to test the wrath was
enough.

The Red Sea

19 But the ungodly were assailed to
the end by pitiless anger,
for God*t* knew in advance even
their future actions:
2 how, though they themselves had
permitted*u* your people to
depart
and hastily sent them out,
they would change their minds and
pursue them.
3 For while they were still engaged in
mourning,
and were lamenting at the graves of
their dead,
they reached another foolish
decision,
and pursued as fugitives those
whom they had begged and
compelled to leave.
4 For the fate they deserved drew
them on to this end,
and made them forget what had
happened,
in order that they might fill up the
punishment that their
torments still lacked,
5 and that your people might
experience*v* an incredible
journey,
but they themselves might meet a
strange death.

God Guides and Protects His People

6 For the whole creation in its nature
was fashioned anew,
complying with your commands,
so that your children*w* might be
kept unharmed.
7 The cloud was seen overshadowing
the camp,
and dry land emerging where water
had stood before,

an unhindered way out of the Red
Sea,
and a grassy plain out of the raging
waves,
8 where those protected by your hand
passed through as one nation,
after gazing on marvelous wonders.
9 For they ranged like horses,
and leaped like lambs,
praising you, O Lord, who delivered
them.
10 For they still recalled the events of
their sojourn,
how instead of producing animals
the earth brought forth gnats,
and instead of fish the river spewed
out vast numbers of frogs.
11 Afterward they saw also a new
kind*x* of birds,
when desire led them to ask for
luxurious food;
12 for, to give them relief, quails came
up from the sea.

The Punishment of the Egyptians

13 The punishments did not come
upon the sinners
without prior signs in the violence
of thunder,
for they justly suffered because of
their wicked acts;
for they practiced a more bitter
hatred of strangers.
14 Others had refused to receive
strangers when they came to
them,
but these made slaves of guests who
were their benefactors.
15 And not only so—but, while
punishment of some sort will
come upon the former
for having received strangers with
hostility,
16 the latter, having first received them
with festal celebrations,
afterward afflicted with terrible
sufferings
those who had already shared the
same rights.
17 They were stricken also with loss of
sight—
just as were those at the door of the
righteous man—

---

s Other ancient authorities read *they*   *t* Gk *he*
u Other ancient authorities read *had changed their
minds to permit*   *v* Other ancient authorities read
accomplish   *w* Or *servants*   *x* Or *production*

when, surrounded by yawning
      darkness,
all of them tried to find the way
      through their own doors.

A New Harmony in Nature

18 For the elements changed *y* places
      with one another,
as on a harp the notes vary the
      nature of the rhythm,
while each note remains the same.*z*
This may be clearly inferred from
      the sight of what took place.
19 For land animals were transformed
      into water creatures,
and creatures that swim moved over
      to the land.
20 Fire even in water retained its
      normal power,

and water forgot its fire-quenching
      nature.
21 Flames, on the contrary, failed to
      consume
the flesh of perishable creatures that
      walked among them,
nor did they melt*a* the crystalline,
      quick-melting kind of
      heavenly food.

Conclusion

22 For in everything, O Lord, you have
      exalted and glorified your
      people,
and you have not neglected to help
      them at all times and in all
      places.

y Gk *changing*   *z* Meaning of Gk uncertain
a Cn: Gk *nor could be melted*

Sirach *(Ecclesiasticus)*

The book of Sirach is named after its author, Jesus, son of Eleazar, son of Sirach. Ben Sira, as he is generally known, was a sage who lived in Jerusalem and wrote this book in Hebrew between 200 and 175 B.C. Though the foreword is not considered part of the inspired text, it describes how Ben Sira's grandson translated it into Greek sometime after 132 B.C. Not part of the Hebrew or Protestant Bible, the Catholic church considers it part of the canon and has used it extensively in the liturgy. The title, *Ecclesiasticus,* refers to its use as the "Church Book."

Sirach echoes the book of Proverbs for its practical wisdom on such topics as humility, friendship, speech, family life, sickness, and health. In various places, Ben Sira espouses negative views of women, ascribing to Eve (unlike Paul, who reserves the honor to Adam) the beginnings of sin and death.

There are many wonderful statements of practical advice in Sirach, including these:

Pleasant speech multiplies friends.

(6.5)

Do not argue with the loud of mouth, and do not heap wood on their fire.

(8.3)

Healthy sleep depends on moderate eating ... The distress of sleeplessness and of nausea and colic are with the glutton.

(31.20)

THE PROLOGUE

Many great teachings have been given to us through the Law and the Prophets and the others[a] that followed them, and for these we should praise Israel for instruction and wisdom. Now, those who read the scriptures must not only themselves understand them, but must also as lovers of learning be able through the spoken and written word to help the outsiders. So my grandfather Jesus, who had devoted himself especially to the reading of the Law and the Prophets and the other books of our ancestors, and had acquired considerable proficiency in them, was himself also led to write something per-

a Or *other books*

taining to instruction and wisdom, so that by becoming familiar also with his book[b] those who love learning might make even greater progress in living according to the law.

You are invited therefore to read it with goodwill and attention, and to be indulgent in cases where, despite our diligent labor in translating, we may seem to have rendered some phrases imperfectly. For what was originally expressed in Hebrew does not have exactly the same sense when translated into another language. Not only this book, but even the Law itself, the Prophecies, and the rest of the books differ not a little when read in the original.

When I came to Egypt in the thirty-eighth year of the reign of Euergetes and stayed for some time, I found opportunity for no little instruction.[c] It seemed highly necessary that I should myself devote some diligence and labor to the translation of this book. During that time I have applied my skill day and night to complete and publish the book for those living abroad who wished to gain learning and are disposed to live according to the law.

In Praise of Wisdom

1 All wisdom is from the Lord,
  and with him it remains forever.
2 The sand of the sea, the drops of
    rain,
  and the days of eternity—who can
    count them?
3 The height of heaven, the breadth of
    the earth,
  the abyss, and wisdom[d]—who
    can search them out?
4 Wisdom was created before all other
    things,
  and prudent understanding from
    eternity.[e]
6 The root of wisdom—to whom has
    it been revealed?
  Her subtleties—who knows
    them?[f]
8 There is but one who is wise, greatly
    to be feared,
  seated upon his throne—the Lord.
9 It is he who created her;
  he saw her and took her measure;
  he poured her out upon all his
    works,
10 upon all the living according to his
    gift;

he lavished her upon those who
    love him.[g]

Fear of the Lord Is True Wisdom

11 The fear of the Lord is glory and
    exultation,
  and gladness and a crown of
    rejoicing.
12 The fear of the Lord delights the
    heart,
  and gives gladness and joy and
    long life.[h]
13 Those who fear the Lord will have a
    happy end;
  on the day of their death they will
    be blessed.

14 To fear the Lord is the beginning of
    wisdom;
  she is created with the faithful in
    the womb.
15 She made[i] among human beings
    an eternal foundation,
  and among their descendants she
    will abide faithfully.
16 To fear the Lord is fullness of
    wisdom;
  she inebriates mortals with her
    fruits;
17 she fills their[j] whole house with
    desirable goods,
  and their[j] storehouses with her
    produce.
18 The fear of the Lord is the crown of
    wisdom,
  making peace and perfect health
    to flourish.[k]
19 She rained down knowledge and
    discerning comprehension,
  and she heightened the glory of
    those who held her fast.

---

[b] Gk *with these things*   [c] Other ancient authorities read *I found a copy affording no little instruction*   [d] Other ancient authorities read *the depth of the abyss*   [e] Other ancient authorities add as verse 5, *The source of wisdom is God's word in the highest heaven, and her ways are the eternal commandments.*   [f] Other ancient authorities add as verse 7, *The knowledge of wisdom—to whom was it manifested? And her abundant experience—who has understood it?*   [g] Other ancient authorities add *Love of the Lord is glorious wisdom; to those to whom he appears he apportions her, that they may see him.*   [h] Other ancient authorities add *The fear of the Lord is a gift from the Lord; also for love he makes firm paths.*   [i] Gk *made as a nest*   [j] Other ancient authorities read *her*   [k] Other ancient authorities add *Both are gifts of God for peace; glory opens out for those who love him. He saw her and took her measure.*

20 To fear the Lord is the root of
wisdom,
and her branches are long life.^{l}

22 Unjust anger cannot be justified,
for anger tips the scale to one's
ruin.
23 Those who are patient stay calm
until the right moment,
and then cheerfulness comes back
to them.
24 They hold back their words until the
right moment;
then the lips of many tell of their
good sense.

25 In the treasuries of wisdom are wise
sayings,
but godliness is an abomination
to a sinner.
26 If you desire wisdom, keep the
commandments,
and the Lord will lavish her upon
you.
27 For the fear of the Lord is wisdom
and discipline,
fidelity and humility are his
delight.

28 Do not disobey the fear of the Lord;
do not approach him with a
divided mind.
29 Do not be a hypocrite before others,
and keep watch over your lips.
30 Do not exalt yourself, or you may
fall
and bring dishonor upon yourself.
The Lord will reveal your secrets
and overthrow you before the
whole congregation,
because you did not come in the
fear of the Lord,
and your heart was full of deceit.

Duties toward God

2 My child, when you come to serve
the Lord,
prepare yourself for testing.^{m}
2 Set your heart right and be steadfast,
and do not be impetuous in time
of calamity.
3 Cling to him and do not depart,
so that your last days may be
prosperous.
4 Accept whatever befalls you,
and in times of humiliation be
patient.
5 For gold is tested in the fire,

and those found acceptable, in the
furnace of humiliation.^{n}
6 Trust in him, and he will help you;
make your ways straight, and
hope in him.

7 You who fear the Lord, wait for his
mercy;
do not stray, or else you may fall.
8 You who fear the Lord, trust in him,
and your reward will not be lost.
9 You who fear the Lord, hope for
good things,
for lasting joy and mercy.^{o}
10 Consider the generations of old and
see:
has anyone trusted in the Lord
and been disappointed?
Or has anyone persevered in the fear
of the Lord ^{p} and been
forsaken?
Or has anyone called upon him
and been neglected?
11 For the Lord is compassionate and
merciful;
he forgives sins and saves in time
of distress.

12 Woe to timid hearts and to slack
hands,
and to the sinner who walks a
double path!
13 Woe to the fainthearted who have
no trust!
Therefore they will have no
shelter.
14 Woe to you who have lost your
nerve!
What will you do when the Lord's
reckoning comes?

15 Those who fear the Lord do not
disobey his words,
and those who love him keep his
ways.
16 Those who fear the Lord seek to
please him,
and those who love him are filled
with his law.
17 Those who fear the Lord prepare
their hearts,

---

^{l} Other ancient authorities add as verse 21, *The
fear of the Lord drives away sins; and where it abides,
it will turn away all anger.* ^{m} Or *trials* ^{n} Other
ancient authorities add *in sickness and poverty put
your trust in him* ^{o} Other ancient authorities
add *For his reward is an everlasting gift with joy.*
^{p} Gk *of him*

and humble themselves before
him.
18 Let us fall into the hands of the
Lord,
but not into the hands of mortals;
for equal to his majesty is his mercy,
and equal to his name are his
works.[q]

Duties toward Parents

3 Listen to me your father,
O children;
act accordingly, that you may be
kept in safety.
2 For the Lord honors a father above
his children,
and he confirms a mother's right
over her children.
3 Those who honor their father atone
for sins,
4 and those who respect their
mother are like those who lay
up treasure.
5 Those who honor their father will
have joy in their own
children,
and when they pray they will be
heard.
6 Those who respect their father will
have long life,

[q] Syr: Gk lacks this line

MONDAY

Scripture Reading for Today:
Sirach 3.1–16

Verses for Today:
Sirach 3.12–13

My Mother and I

We sit there, my mother and I, across a kitchen table full of nicks and scratches put there years ago by my brothers and sisters and me. The talk is about her friends, my children, and who will bring what to Thanksgiving dinner at the farm.

My mind wanders. I think of my mother as a young wife and mother of five. She steadied my hand as I learned to maneuver cereal from bowl to mouth. Now I look at her fine, white hair, her thickly veined hands, and wonder that this is the same woman. My stomach knots up and a rush of sadness sweeps over me. I want her back, her hair more pepper than salt, her skin smooth and young.

She is tired from planning and preparations for the big dinner. Her hand quivers and tea spills on the table.

"I'll get it, Mom."

I slide out of the chair and hurry to the sink for the dishcloth. I hate to watch her getting old. Or thinking of life without her.

My young mother has grown through the middle years and into old age. One day she will be with you, Lord. Somewhere, but not here. Letting go of my mother and trusting her to you is not always gracefully done. Sometimes I want to grab time and turn it back, or at least hold it still.

I cannot imagine life without her. Yet, sometimes I lack patience to deal with the effects advancing years have had on her. Help me see past the aging body to the spirit that remains vibrant and eager to be a part of my life. Lord, help us both embrace this season of life with trust as well as love.

—MARY VAN BALEN HOLT

Go to page 871 for your next devotional reading.

and those who honor[r] their
mother obey the Lord;
7 they will serve their parents as
their masters.[s]
8 Honor your father by word and
deed,
that his blessing may come upon
you.
9 For a father's blessing strengthens
the houses of the children,
but a mother's curse uproots their
foundations.
10 Do not glorify yourself by
dishonoring your father,
for your father's dishonor is no
glory to you.
11 The glory of one's father is one's
own glory,
and it is a disgrace for children
not to respect their mother.

12 My child, help your father in his old
age,
and do not grieve him as long as
he lives;
13 even if his mind fails, be patient
with him;
because you have all your faculties
do not despise him.
14 For kindness to a father will not be
forgotten,
and will be credited to you against
your sins;
15 in the day of your distress it will be
remembered in your favor;
like frost in fair weather, your sins
will melt away.
16 Whoever forsakes a father is like a
blasphemer,
and whoever angers a mother is
cursed by the Lord.

Humility

17 My child, perform your tasks with
humility;[t]
then you will be loved by those
whom God accepts.
18 The greater you are, the more you
must humble yourself;
so you will find favor in the sight
of the Lord.[u]
20 For great is the might of the Lord;
but by the humble he is glorified.
21 Neither seek what is too difficult for
you,
nor investigate what is beyond
your power.

22 Reflect upon what you have been
commanded,
for what is hidden is not your
concern.
23 Do not meddle in matters that are
beyond you,
for more than you can understand
has been shown you.
24 For their conceit has led many
astray,
and wrong opinion has impaired
their judgment.

25 Without eyes there is no light;
without knowledge there is no
wisdom.[v]
26 A stubborn mind will fare badly at
the end,
and whoever loves danger will
perish in it.
27 A stubborn mind will be burdened
by troubles,
and the sinner adds sin to sins.
28 When calamity befalls the proud,
there is no healing,
for an evil plant has taken root in
him.
29 The mind of the intelligent
appreciates proverbs,
and an attentive ear is the desire
of the wise.

Alms for the Poor

30 As water extinguishes a blazing fire,
so almsgiving atones for sin.
31 Those who repay favors give thought
to the future;
when they fall they will find
support.

Duties toward the Poor and the Oppressed

4 My child, do not cheat the poor of
their living,
and do not keep needy eyes
waiting.
2 Do not grieve the hungry,
or anger one in need.
3 Do not add to the troubles of the
desperate,
or delay giving to the needy.
4 Do not reject a suppliant in distress,

---

[r] Heb: Other ancient authorities read *comfort*
[s] In other ancient authorities this line is preceded
by *Those who fear the Lord honor their father,*
[t] Heb: Gk *meekness*   [u] Other ancient authorities
add as verse 19, *Many are lofty and renowned, but
to the humble he reveals his secrets.*   [v] Heb: Other
ancient authorities lack verse 25

or turn your face away from the poor.

5 Do not avert your eye from the needy,
and give no one reason to curse you;

6 for if in bitterness of soul some should curse you,
their Creator will hear their prayer.

7 Endear yourself to the congregation;
bow your head low to the great.

8 Give a hearing to the poor,
and return their greeting politely.

9 Rescue the oppressed from the oppressor;
and do not be hesitant in giving a verdict.

10 Be a father to orphans,
and be like a husband to their mother;
you will then be like a son of the Most High,
and he will love you more than does your mother.

The Rewards of Wisdom

11 Wisdom teaches[w] her children
and gives help to those who seek her.

12 Whoever loves her loves life,
and those who seek her from early morning are filled with joy.

13 Whoever holds her fast inherits glory,
and the Lord blesses the place she[x] enters.

14 Those who serve her minister to the Holy One;
the Lord loves those who love her.

15 Those who obey her will judge the nations,
and all who listen to her will live secure.

16 If they remain faithful, they will inherit her;
their descendants will also obtain her.

17 For at first she will walk with them on tortuous paths;
she will bring fear and dread upon them,
and will torment them by her discipline
until she trusts them, [y]
and she will test them with her ordinances.

18 Then she will come straight back to them again and gladden them,
and will reveal her secrets to them.

19 If they go astray she will forsake them,
and hand them over to their ruin.

20 Watch for the opportune time, and beware of evil,
and do not be ashamed to be yourself.

21 For there is a shame that leads to sin,
and there is a shame that is glory and favor.

22 Do not show partiality, to your own harm,
or deference, to your downfall.

23 Do not refrain from speaking at the proper moment,[z]
and do not hide your wisdom.[a]

24 For wisdom becomes known through speech,
and education through the words of the tongue.

25 Never speak against the truth,
but be ashamed of your ignorance.

26 Do not be ashamed to confess your sins,
and do not try to stop the current of a river.

27 Do not subject yourself to a fool,
or show partiality to a ruler.

28 Fight to the death for truth,
and the Lord God will fight for you.

29 Do not be reckless in your speech,
or sluggish and remiss in your deeds.

30 Do not be like a lion in your home,
or suspicious of your servants.

31 Do not let your hand be stretched out to receive
and closed when it is time to give.

Precepts for Everyday Living

5 Do not rely on your wealth,
or say, "I have enough."

w Heb Syr: Gk *exalts*   x Or *he*   y Or *until they remain faithful in their heart*   z Heb: Gk *at a time of salvation*   a So some Gk Mss and Heb Syr Lat: Other Gk Mss lack *and do not hide your wisdom*

² Do not follow your inclination and
strength
in pursuing the desires of your
heart.
³ Do not say, "Who can have power
over me?"
for the Lord will surely punish
you.
⁴ Do not say, "I sinned, yet what has
happened to me?"
for the Lord is slow to anger.
⁵ Do not be so confident of
forgiveness[b]
that you add sin to sin.
⁶ Do not say, "His mercy is great,
he will forgive[c] the multitude of
my sins,"
for both mercy and wrath are with
him,
and his anger will rest on sinners.
⁷ Do not delay to turn back to the
Lord,
and do not postpone it from day
to day;
for suddenly the wrath of the Lord
will come upon you,
and at the time of punishment
you will perish.
⁸ Do not depend on dishonest wealth,
for it will not benefit you on the
day of calamity.

⁹ Do not winnow in every wind,
or follow every path.[d]
¹⁰ Stand firm for what you know,
and let your speech be consistent.
¹¹ Be quick to hear,
but deliberate in answering.
¹² If you know what to say, answer
your neighbor;
but if not, put your hand over
your mouth.

¹³ Honor and dishonor come from
speaking,
and the tongue of mortals may be
their downfall.
¹⁴ Do not be called double-tongued[e]
and do not lay traps with your
tongue;
for shame comes to the thief,
and severe condemnation to the
double-tongued.
¹⁵ In great and small matters cause no
harm,[f]

6 ¹ and do not become an enemy
instead of a friend;

for a bad name incurs shame and
reproach;
so it is with the double-tongued
sinner.

² Do not fall into the grip of
passion,[g]
or you may be torn apart as by a
bull.[h]
³ Your leaves will be devoured and
your fruit destroyed,
and you will be left like a
withered tree.
⁴ Evil passion destroys those who
have it,
and makes them the laughingstock
of their enemies.

Friendship, False and True

⁵ Pleasant speech multiplies friends,
and a gracious tongue multiplies
courtesies.
⁶ Let those who are friendly with you
be many,
but let your advisers be one in a
thousand.
⁷ When you gain friends, gain them
through testing,
and do not trust them hastily.
⁸ For there are friends who are such
when it suits them,
but they will not stand by you in
time of trouble.
⁹ And there are friends who change
into enemies,
and tell of the quarrel to your
disgrace.
¹⁰ And there are friends who sit at your
table,
but they will not stand by you in
time of trouble.
¹¹ When you are prosperous, they
become your second self,
and lord it over your servants;
¹² but if you are brought low, they
turn against you,
and hide themselves from you.
¹³ Keep away from your enemies,
and be on guard with your
friends.

b Heb: Gk *atonement*   *c* Heb: Gk *he* (or *it*) *will
atone for*   *d* Gk adds *so it is with the
double-tongued sinner* (see 6.1)   *e* Heb: Gk *a
slanderer*   *f* Heb Syr: Gk *be ignorant*
g Heb: Meaning of Gk uncertain   *h* Meaning of
Gk uncertain

14 Faithful friends are a sturdy shelter:
    whoever finds one has found a
    treasure.
15 Faithful friends are beyond price;
    no amount can balance their
    worth.
16 Faithful friends are life-saving
    medicine;
    and those who fear the Lord will
    find them.
17 Those who fear the Lord direct their
    friendship aright,
    for as they are, so are their
    neighbors also.

Blessings of Wisdom

18 My child, from your youth choose
    discipline,
    and when you have gray hair you
    will still find wisdom.
19 Come to her like one who plows
    and sows,
    and wait for her good harvest.
    For when you cultivate her you will
    toil but little,
    and soon you will eat of her
    produce.
20 She seems very harsh to the
    undisciplined;

Friends

Sometimes I call a friend when my spirit or body needs support: a child is struggling, bronchitis strikes, a relationship is strained. And friends come. They sit at the end of my bed or a telephone line and listen.

Friends bring wisdom, memories, and more questions. They hug us and cry at our predicaments.

Friends are responsible for each other. My friend Eileen can always be counted on to deliver her steaming pot of homemade chicken soup, fragrant with tomato, rice, potato, and onion. The food deliveries go both ways. Each one of us has gifts to offer as well as needs to be filled.

Because openness creates vulnerability, friends can also be a source of pain, separation, loss, and misunderstanding. Mary, Martha, Lazarus, and Jesus knew that side of friendship as well. They shared concern for Jesus' work. Lazarus's illness and death made his sisters wonder why Jesus had not been there to cure him. Lazarus's death moved Jesus to weep, and his own suffering and death left his friends anguished.

Anyone who is a friend, anyone who has a friend, knows that the relationship intensifies life's experiences and emotions. Friendship is a blessing. It is a gift. At a time when schedules and technologies can work against establishing and maintaining such relationships, friendships are worth the effort they require.

Saint Thomas Aquinas said that nothing on earth is more prized than true friendship. Jesus chose to be part of a web of friends while he walked the earth and shared our human existence. He continues to desire true friendship with each one of us. Our own friends are a reflection of that desire.

—*MARY VAN BALEN HOLT*

TUESDAY

Scripture Reading
for Today:
Sirach 6.5–17

Verse for Today:
Sirach 6.15

Go to page 876 for your next devotional reading.

fools cannot remain with her.

21 She will be like a heavy stone to test
them,
and they will not delay in casting
her aside.

22 For wisdom is like her name;
she is not readily perceived by
many.

23 Listen, my child, and accept my
judgment;
do not reject my counsel.

24 Put your feet into her fetters,
and your neck into her collar.

25 Bend your shoulders and carry her,
and do not fret under her bonds.

26 Come to her with all your soul,
and keep her ways with all your
might.

27 Search out and seek, and she will
become known to you;
and when you get hold of her, do
not let her go.

28 For at last you will find the rest she
gives,
and she will be changed into joy
for you.

29 Then her fetters will become for you
a strong defense,
and her collar a glorious robe.

30 Her yoke*i* is a golden ornament,
and her bonds a purple cord.

31 You will wear her like a glorious
robe,
and put her on like a splendid
crown.*j*

32 If you are willing, my child, you can
be disciplined,
and if you apply yourself you will
become clever.

33 If you love to listen you will gain
knowledge,
and if you pay attention you will
become wise.

34 Stand in the company of the elders.
Who is wise? Attach yourself to
such a one.

35 Be ready to listen to every godly
discourse,
and let no wise proverbs escape
you.

36 If you see an intelligent person, rise
early to visit him;
let your foot wear out his
doorstep.

37 Reflect on the statutes of the Lord,

and meditate at all times on his
commandments.
It is he who will give insight to*k*
your mind,
and your desire for wisdom will
be granted.

Miscellaneous Advice

7 Do no evil, and evil will never
overtake you.

2 Stay away from wrong, and it will
turn away from you.

3 Do*l* not sow in the furrows of
injustice,
and you will not reap a sevenfold
crop.

4 Do not seek from the Lord high
office,
or the seat of honor from the
king.

5 Do not assert your righteousness
before the Lord,
or display your wisdom before the
king.

6 Do not seek to become a judge,
or you may be unable to root out
injustice;
you may be partial to the powerful,
and so mar your integrity.

7 Commit no offense against the
public,
and do not disgrace yourself
among the people.

8 Do not commit a sin twice;
not even for one will you go
unpunished.

9 Do not say, "He will consider the
great number of my gifts,
and when I make an offering to
the Most High God, he will
accept it."

10 Do not grow weary when you pray;
do not neglect to give alms.

11 Do not ridicule a person who is
embittered in spirit,
for there is One who humbles and
exalts.

12 Do not devise*m* a lie against your
brother,
or do the same to a friend.

13 Refuse to utter any lie,

---

i Heb: Gk *Upon her*   *j* Heb: Gk *crown of gladness*
k Heb: Gk *will confirm*   *l* Gk *My child, do*
m Heb: Gk *plow*

for it is a habit that results in no
good.

14 Do not babble in the assembly of
the elders,
and do not repeat yourself when
you pray.

15 Do not hate hard labor
or farm work, which was created
by the Most High.

16 Do not enroll in the ranks of
sinners;
remember that retribution does
not delay.

17 Humble yourself to the utmost,
for the punishment of the
ungodly is fire and worms.[n]

Relations with Others

18 Do not exchange a friend for
money,
or a real brother for the gold of
Ophir.

19 Do not dismiss[o] a wise and good
wife,
for her charm is worth more than
gold.

20 Do not abuse slaves who work
faithfully,
or hired laborers who devote
themselves to their task.

21 Let your soul love intelligent
slaves;[p]
do not withhold from them their
freedom.

22 Do you have cattle? Look after them;
if they are profitable to you, keep
them.

23 Do you have children? Discipline
them,
and make them obedient[q] from
their youth.

24 Do you have daughters? Be
concerned for their chastity,[r]
and do not show yourself too
indulgent with them.

25 Give a daughter in marriage, and
you complete a great task;
but give her to a sensible man.

26 Do you have a wife who pleases
you?[s] Do not divorce her;
but do not trust yourself to one
whom you detest.

27 With all your heart honor your
father,

and do not forget the birth pangs
of your mother.

28 Remember that it was of your
parents[t] you were born;
how can you repay what they
have given to you?

29 With all your soul fear the Lord,
and revere his priests.

30 With all your might love your
Maker,
and do not neglect his ministers.

31 Fear the Lord and honor the priest,
and give him his portion, as you
have been commanded:
the first fruits, the guilt offering, the
gift of the shoulders,
the sacrifice of sanctification, and
the first fruits of the holy
things.

32 Stretch out your hand to the poor,
so that your blessing may be
complete.

33 Give graciously to all the living;
do not withhold kindness even
from the dead.

34 Do not avoid those who weep,
but mourn with those who
mourn.

35 Do not hesitate to visit the sick,
because for such deeds you will
be loved.

36 In all you do, remember the end of
your life,
and then you will never sin.

Prudence and Common Sense

8 Do not contend with the powerful,
or you may fall into their hands.

2 Do not quarrel with the rich,
in case their resources outweigh
yours;
for gold has ruined many,
and has perverted the minds of
kings.

3 Do not argue with the loud of
mouth,
and do not heap wood on their
fire.

4 Do not make fun of one who is
ill-bred,

n Heb for the expectation of mortals is worms
o Heb: Gk deprive yourself of   p Heb Love a wise
slave as yourself   q Gk bend their necks   r Gk
body   s Heb Syr lack who pleases you   t Gk them

or your ancestors may be insulted.
5 Do not reproach one who is turning
away from sin;
  remember that we all deserve
  punishment.
6 Do not disdain one who is old,
  for some of us are also growing
  old.
7 Do not rejoice over anyone's death;
  remember that we must all die.

8 Do not slight the discourse of the
sages,
  but busy yourself with their
  maxims;
because from them you will learn
  discipline
  and how to serve princes.
9 Do not ignore the discourse of the
aged,
  for they themselves learned from
  their parents;*u*
from them you learn how to
  understand
  and to give an answer when the
  need arises.

10 Do not kindle the coals of sinners,
  or you may be burned in their
  flaming fire.
11 Do not let the insolent bring you to
your feet,
  or they may lie in ambush against
  your words.
12 Do not lend to one who is stronger
than you;
  but if you do lend anything,
  count it as a loss.
13 Do not give surety beyond your
means;
  but if you give surety, be prepared
  to pay.

14 Do not go to law against a judge,
  for the decision will favor him
  because of his standing.
15 Do not go traveling with the
reckless,
  or they will be burdensome to
  you;
for they will act as they please,
  and through their folly you will
  perish with them.
16 Do not pick a fight with the
quick-tempered,
  and do not journey with them
  through lonely country,

because bloodshed means nothing
  to them,
  and where no help is at hand,
  they will strike you down.
17 Do not consult with fools,
  for they cannot keep a secret.
18 In the presence of strangers do
  nothing that is to be kept
  secret,
  for you do not know what they
  will divulge.*v*
19 Do not reveal your thoughts to
anyone,
  or you may drive away your
  happiness.*w*

Advice Concerning Women

9 Do not be jealous of the wife of
your bosom,
  or you will teach her an evil
  lesson to your own hurt.
2 Do not give yourself to a woman
  and let her trample down your
  strength.
3 Do not go near a loose woman,
  or you will fall into her snares.
4 Do not dally with a singing girl,
  or you will be caught by her
  tricks.
5 Do not look intently at a virgin,
  or you may stumble and incur
  penalties for her.
6 Do not give yourself to prostitutes,
  or you may lose your inheritance.
7 Do not look around in the streets of
a city,
  or wander about in its deserted
  sections.
8 Turn away your eyes from a shapely
woman,
  and do not gaze at beauty
  belonging to another;
many have been seduced by a
  woman's beauty,
  and by it passion is kindled like a
  fire.
9 Never dine with another man's wife,
  or revel with her at wine;
or your heart may turn aside to her,
  and in blood*x* you may be
  plunged into destruction.

Choice of Friends

10 Do not abandon old friends,

u Or *ancestors*   *v* Or *it will bring forth*   *w* Heb:
Gk *and let him not return a favor to you*   *x* Heb:
Gk *by your spirit*

for new ones cannot equal them.
A new friend is like new wine;
  when it has aged, you can drink it
  with pleasure.

11 Do not envy the success of sinners,
  for you do not know what their
  end will be like.
12 Do not delight in what pleases the
  ungodly;
  remember that they will not be
  held guiltless all their lives.

13 Keep far from those who have
  power to kill,
  and you will not be haunted by
  the fear of death.
But if you approach them, make no
  misstep,
  or they may rob you of your life.
Know that you are stepping among
  snares,
  and that you are walking on the
  city battlements.

14 As much as you can, aim to know
  your neighbors,
  and consult with the wise.
15 Let your conversation be with
  intelligent people,
  and let all your discussion be
  about the law of the Most
  High.
16 Let the righteous be your dinner
  companions,
  and let your glory be in the fear
  of the Lord.

Concerning Rulers

17 A work is praised for the skill of the
  artisan;
  so a people's leader is proved wise
  by his words.
18 The loud of mouth are feared in
  their city,
  and the one who is reckless in
  speech is hated.

10 A wise magistrate educates his
  people,
  and the rule of an intelligent
  person is well ordered.
2 As the people's judge is, so are his
  officials;
  as the ruler of the city is, so are
  all its inhabitants.
3 An undisciplined king ruins his
  people,

but a city becomes fit to live in
  through the understanding of
  its rulers.
4 The government of the earth is in
  the hand of the Lord,
  and over it he will raise up the
  right leader for the time.
5 Human success is in the hand of the
  Lord,
  and it is he who confers honor
  upon the lawgiver. *y*

The Sin of Pride

6 Do not get angry with your neighbor
  for every injury,
  and do not resort to acts of
  insolence.
7 Arrogance is hateful to the Lord and
  to mortals,
  and injustice is outrageous to
  both.
8 Sovereignty passes from nation to
  nation
  on account of injustice and
  insolence and wealth. *z*
9 How can dust and ashes be proud?
  Even in life the human body
  decays. *a*
10 A long illness baffles the
  physician; *b*
  the king of today will die
  tomorrow.
11 For when one is dead
  he inherits maggots and vermin *c*
  and worms.
12 The beginning of human pride is to
  forsake the Lord;
  the heart has withdrawn from its
  Maker.
13 For the beginning of pride is sin,
  and the one who clings to it
  pours out abominations.
Therefore the Lord brings upon
  them unheard-of calamities,
  and destroys them completely.
14 The Lord overthrows the thrones of
  rulers,
  and enthrones the lowly in their
  place.
15 The Lord plucks up the roots of the
  nations, *d*

y Heb: Gk *scribe*   *z* Other ancient authorities add
here or after verse 9a, *Nothing is more wicked than
one who loves money, for such a person puts his own
soul up for sale.*   *a* Heb: Meaning of Gk
uncertain   *b* Heb Lat: Meaning of Gk uncertain
c Heb: Gk *wild animals*   *d* Other ancient
authorities read *proud nations*

and plants the humble in their
place.
16 The Lord lays waste the lands of the
nations,
and destroys them to the
foundations of the earth.
17 He removes some of them and
destroys them,
and erases the memory of them
from the earth.
18 Pride was not created for human
beings,
or violent anger for those born of
women.

Persons Deserving Honor

19 Whose offspring are worthy of
honor?
Human offspring.
Whose offspring are worthy of
honor?
Those who fear the Lord.
Whose offspring are unworthy of
honor?
Human offspring.
Whose offspring are unworthy of
honor?

Those who break the
commandments.
20 Among family members their leader
is worthy of honor,
but those who fear the Lord are
worthy of honor in his
eyes.*e*
22 The rich, and the eminent, and the
poor—
their glory is the fear of the Lord.
23 It is not right to despise one who is
intelligent but poor,
and it is not proper to honor one
who is sinful.
24 The prince and the judge and the
ruler are honored,
but none of them is greater than
the one who fears the Lord.
25 Free citizens will serve a wise
servant,
and an intelligent person will not
complain.

*e Other ancient authorities add as verse 21, The
fear of the Lord is the beginning of acceptance;
obduracy and pride are the beginning of rejection.*

WEDNESDAY

Scripture Reading
for Today:
Sirach 10.6–18

Verse for Today:
Sirach 10.13

Antidotes to Pride

It is our emptiness and lowliness that God needs and not our plen-
itude. These are a few of the ways we can practice humility:
Speak as little as possible of oneself.
Mind one's own business.
Avoid curiosity.
Do not want to manage other people's affairs.
Accept contradiction and correction cheerfully.
Pass over the mistakes of others.
Accept blame when innocent.
Yield to the will of others.
Accept insults and injuries.
Accept being slighted, forgotten, and disliked.
Be kind and gentle even under provocation.
Do not seek to be specially loved and admired.
Never stand on one's dignity.
Yield in discussion even though one is right.
Choose always the hardest.

—*MOTHER TERESA OF CALCUTTA*

Go to page 886 for your next devotional reading.

Concerning Humility

26 Do not make a display of your
       wisdom when you do your
       work,
    and do not boast when you are in
       need.
27 Better is the worker who has goods
       in plenty
    than the boaster who lacks bread.

28 My child, honor yourself with
       humility,
    and give yourself the esteem you
       deserve.
29 Who will acquit those who
       condemn ƒ themselves?
    And who will honor those who
       dishonor themselves? ᵍ
30 The poor are honored for their
       knowledge,
    while the rich are honored for
       their wealth.
31 One who is honored in poverty,
       how much more in wealth!
    And one dishonored in wealth,
       how much more in poverty!

The Deceptiveness of Appearances

11 The wisdom of the humble lifts
       their heads high,
    and seats them among the great.
2 Do not praise individuals for their
       good looks,
    or loathe anyone because of
       appearance alone.
3 The bee is small among flying
       creatures,
    but what it produces is the best of
       sweet things.
4 Do not boast about wearing fine
       clothes,
    and do not exalt yourself when
       you are honored;
    for the works of the Lord are
       wonderful,
    and his works are concealed from
       humankind.
5 Many kings have had to sit on the
       ground,
    but one who was never thought of
       has worn a crown.
6 Many rulers have been utterly
       disgraced,
    and the honored have been
       handed over to others.

Deliberation and Caution

7 Do not find fault before you
       investigate;
    examine first, and then criticize.
8 Do not answer before you listen,
    and do not interrupt when
       another is speaking.
9 Do not argue about a matter that
       does not concern you,
    and do not sit with sinners when
       they judge a case.

10 My child, do not busy yourself with
       many matters;
    if you multiply activities, you will
       not be held blameless.
    If you pursue, you will not overtake,
    and by fleeing you will not
       escape.
11 There are those who work and
       struggle and hurry,
    but are so much the more in
       want.
12 There are others who are slow and
       need help,
    who lack strength and abound in
       poverty;
    but the eyes of the Lord look kindly
       upon them;
    he lifts them out of their lowly
       condition
13 and raises up their heads
    to the amazement of the many.

14 Good things and bad, life and
       death,
    poverty and wealth, come from
       the Lord.ʰ
17 The Lord's gift remains with the
       devout,
    and his favor brings lasting
       success.
18 One becomes rich through diligence
       and self-denial,
    and the reward allotted to him is
       this:
19 when he says, "I have found rest,
       and now I shall feast on my
       goods!"

ƒ Heb: Gk sin against   ᵍ Heb Lat: Gk their own
life   ʰ Other ancient authorities add as verses 15
and 16, 15Wisdom, understanding, and knowledge
of the law come from the Lord; affection and the
ways of good works come from him. 16Error and
darkness were created with sinners; evil grows old
with those who take pride in malice.

he does not know how long it will
be
until he leaves them to others and
dies.

20 Stand by your agreement and attend
to it,
and grow old in your work.
21 Do not wonder at the works of a
sinner,
but trust in the Lord and keep at
your job;
for it is easy in the sight of the Lord
to make the poor rich suddenly,
in an instant.
22 The blessing of the Lord is[i] the
reward of the pious,
and quickly God causes his
blessing to flourish.
23 Do not say, "What do I need,
and what further benefit can be
mine?"
24 Do not say, "I have enough,
and what harm can come to me
now?"
25 In the day of prosperity, adversity is
forgotten,
and in the day of adversity,
prosperity is not remembered.
26 For it is easy for the Lord on the day
of death
to reward individuals according to
their conduct.
27 An hour's misery makes one forget
past delights,
and at the close of one's life one's
deeds are revealed.
28 Call no one happy before his death;
by how he ends, a person
becomes known.[j]

Care in Choosing Friends

29 Do not invite everyone into your
home,
for many are the tricks of the
crafty.
30 Like a decoy partridge in a cage, so
is the mind of the proud,
and like spies they observe your
weakness;[k]
31 for they lie in wait, turning good
into evil,
and to worthy actions they attach
blame.
32 From a spark many coals are
kindled,
and a sinner lies in wait to shed
blood.

33 Beware of scoundrels, for they devise
evil,
and they may ruin your reputation
forever.
34 Receive strangers into your home
and they will stir up trouble
for you,
and will make you a stranger to
your own family.

12 If you do good, know to whom
you do it,
and you will be thanked for your
good deeds.
2 Do good to the devout, and you will
be repaid—
if not by them, certainly by the
Most High.
3 No good comes to one who persists
in evil
or to one who does not give alms.
4 Give to the devout, but do not help
the sinner.
5 Do good to the humble, but do
not give to the ungodly;
hold back their bread, and do not
give it to them,
for by means of it they might
subdue you;
then you will receive twice as much
evil
for all the good you have done to
them.
6 For the Most High also hates sinners
and will inflict punishment on the
ungodly.[l]
7 Give to the one who is good, but do
not help the sinner.
8 A friend is not known[m] in
prosperity,
nor is an enemy hidden in
adversity.
9 One's enemies are friendly[n] when
one prospers,
but in adversity even one's friend
disappears.
10 Never trust your enemy,
for like corrosion in copper, so is
his wickedness.
11 Even if he humbles himself and
walks bowed down,

i Heb: Gk is in   j Heb: Gk and through his
children a person becomes known   k Heb: Gk
downfall   l Other ancient authorities add and he
is keeping them for the day of their punishment
m Other ancient authorities read punished
n Heb: Gk grieved

take care to be on your guard
  against him.
Be to him like one who polishes a
  mirror,
  to be sure it does not become
  completely tarnished.
12 Do not put him next to you,
  or he may overthrow you and take
  your place.
Do not let him sit at your right
  hand,
  or else he may try to take your
  own seat,
and at last you will realize the truth
  of my words,
  and be stung by what I have said.

13 Who pities a snake charmer when he
  is bitten,
  or all those who go near wild
  animals?
14 So no one pities a person who
  associates with a sinner
  and becomes involved in the
  other's sins.
15 He stands by you for a while,
  but if you falter, he will not be
  there.
16 An enemy speaks sweetly with his
  lips,
  but in his heart he plans to throw
  you into a pit;
an enemy may have tears in his
  eyes,
  but if he finds an opportunity he
  will never have enough of
  your blood.
17 If evil comes upon you, you will
  find him there ahead of you;
  pretending to help, he will trip
  you up.
18 Then he will shake his head, and
  clap his hands,
  and whisper much, and show his
  true face.

Caution Regarding Associates

13 Whoever touches pitch gets
  dirty,
  and whoever associates with a
  proud person becomes like
  him.
2 Do not lift a weight too heavy for
  you,
  or associate with one mightier and
  richer than you.

How can the clay pot associate with
  the iron kettle?
  The pot will strike against it and
  be smashed.
3 A rich person does wrong, and even
  adds insults;
  a poor person suffers wrong, and
  must add apologies.
4 A rich person*o* will exploit you if
  you can be of use to him,
  but if you are in need he will
  abandon you.
5 If you own something, he will live
  with you;
  he will drain your resources
  without a qualm.
6 When he needs you he will deceive
  you,
  and will smile at you and
  encourage you;
  he will speak to you kindly and
  say, "What do you need?"
7 He will embarrass you with his
  delicacies,
  until he has drained you two or
  three times,
  and finally he will laugh at you.
Should he see you afterwards, he
  will pass you by
  and shake his head at you.

8 Take care not to be led astray
  and humiliated when you are
  enjoying yourself. *p*
9 When an influential person invites
  you, be reserved,
  and he will invite you more
  insistently.
10 Do not be forward, or you may be
  rebuffed;
  do not stand aloof, or you will be
  forgotten.
11 Do not try to treat him as an equal,
  or trust his lengthy conversations;
  for he will test you by prolonged
  talk,
  and while he smiles he will be
  examining you.
12 Cruel are those who do not keep
  your secrets;
  they will not spare you harm or
  imprisonment.
13 Be on your guard and very careful,

---

o Gk *He*   *p* Other ancient authorities read *in
your folly*

for you are walking about with
your own downfall.[q]

15 Every creature loves its like,
and every person the neighbor.
16 All living beings associate with their
own kind,
and people stick close to those
like themselves.
17 What does a wolf have in common
with a lamb?
No more has a sinner with the
devout.
18 What peace is there between a hyena
and a dog?
And what peace between the rich
and the poor?
19 Wild asses in the wilderness are the
prey of lions;
likewise the poor are feeding
grounds for the rich.
20 Humility is an abomination to the
proud;
likewise the poor are an
abomination to the rich.

21 When the rich person totters, he is
supported by friends,
but when the humble[r] falls, he is
pushed away even by friends.
22 If the rich person slips, many come
to the rescue;
he speaks unseemly words, but
they justify him.
If the humble person slips, they
even criticize him;
he talks sense, but is not given a
hearing.
23 The rich person speaks and all are
silent;
they extol to the clouds what he
says.
The poor person speaks and they
say, "Who is this fellow?"
And should he stumble, they even
push him down.
24 Riches are good if they are free from
sin;
poverty is evil only in the opinion
of the ungodly.

25 The heart changes the countenance,
either for good or for evil.[s]
26 The sign of a happy heart is a
cheerful face,
but to devise proverbs requires
painful thinking.

14 Happy are those who do not
blunder with their lips,
and need not suffer remorse for
sin.
2 Happy are those whose hearts do
not condemn them,
and who have not given up their
hope.

Responsible Use of Wealth

3 Riches are inappropriate for a
small-minded person;
and of what use is wealth to a
miser?
4 What he denies himself he collects
for others;
and others will live in luxury on
his goods.
5 If one is mean to himself, to whom
will he be generous?
He will not enjoy his own riches.
6 No one is worse than one who is
grudging to himself;
this is the punishment for his
meanness.
7 If ever he does good, it is by
mistake;
and in the end he reveals his
meanness.
8 The miser is an evil person;
he turns away and disregards
people.
9 The eye of the greedy person is not
satisfied with his share;
greedy injustice withers the soul.
10 A miser begrudges bread,
and it is lacking at his table.

11 My child, treat yourself well,
according to your means,
and present worthy offerings to
the Lord.
12 Remember that death does not tarry,
and the decree[t] of Hades has not
been shown to you.
13 Do good to friends before you die,
and reach out and give to them as
much as you can.
14 Do not deprive yourself of a day's
enjoyment;

q Other ancient authorities add as verse 14, *When
you hear these things in your sleep, wake up! During
all your life love the Lord, and call on him for your
salvation.* r Other ancient authorities read *poor*
s Other ancient authorities add *and a glad heart
makes a cheerful countenance* t Heb Syr: Gk
covenant

do not let your share of desired
good pass by you.

15 Will you not leave the fruit of your
labors to another,
and what you acquired by toil to
be divided by lot?

16 Give, and take, and indulge yourself,
because in Hades one cannot look
for luxury.

17 All living beings become old like a
garment,
for the decree[u] from of old is,
"You must die!"

18 Like abundant leaves on a spreading
tree
that sheds some and puts forth
others,
so are the generations of flesh and
blood:
one dies and another is born.

19 Every work decays and ceases to
exist,
and the one who made it will
pass away with it.

The Happiness of Seeking Wisdom

20 Happy is the person who meditates
on[v] wisdom
and reasons intelligently,

21 who[w] reflects in his heart on her
ways
and ponders her secrets,

22 pursuing her like a hunter,
and lying in wait on her paths;

23 who peers through her windows
and listens at her doors;

24 who camps near her house
and fastens his tent peg to her
walls;

25 who pitches his tent near her,
and so occupies an excellent
lodging place;

26 who places his children under her
shelter,
and lodges under her boughs;

27 who is sheltered by her from the
heat,
and dwells in the midst of her
glory.

15 Whoever fears the Lord will do
this,
and whoever holds to the law will
obtain wisdom.[x]

2 She will come to meet him like a
mother,
and like a young bride she will
welcome him.

3 She will feed him with the bread of
learning,
and give him the water of wisdom
to drink.

4 He will lean on her and not fall,
and he will rely on her and not
be put to shame.

5 She will exalt him above his
neighbors,
and will open his mouth in the
midst of the assembly.

6 He will find gladness and a crown
of rejoicing,
and will inherit an everlasting
name.

7 The foolish will not obtain her,
and sinners will not see her.

8 She is far from arrogance,
and liars will never think of her.

9 Praise is unseemly on the lips of a
sinner,
for it has not been sent from the
Lord.

10 For in wisdom must praise be
uttered,
and the Lord will make it prosper.

Freedom of Choice

11 Do not say, "It was the Lord's doing
that I fell away";
for he does not do[y] what he
hates.

12 Do not say, "It was he who led me
astray";
for he has no need of the sinful.

13 The Lord hates all abominations;
such things are not loved by those
who fear him.

14 It was he who created humankind in
the beginning,
and he left them in the power of
their own free choice.

15 If you choose, you can keep the
commandments,
and to act faithfully is a matter of
your own choice.

16 He has placed before you fire and
water;
stretch out your hand for
whichever you choose.

17 Before each person are life and
death,

---

u Heb: Gk *covenant*   v Other ancient authorities
read *dies in*   w The structure adopted in
verses 21–27 follows the Heb   x Gk *her*
y Heb: Gk *you ought not to do*

and whichever one chooses will
be given.
¹⁸ For great is the wisdom of the Lord;
he is mighty in power and sees
everything;
¹⁹ his eyes are on those who fear him,
and he knows every human
action.
²⁰ He has not commanded anyone to
be wicked,
and he has not given anyone
permission to sin.

God's Punishment of Sinners

16 Do not desire a multitude of
worthlessᶻ children,
and do not rejoice in ungodly
offspring.
² If they multiply, do not rejoice in
them,
unless the fear of the Lord is in
them.
³ Do not trust in their survival,
or rely on their numbers;ᵃ
for one can be better than a
thousand,
and to die childless is better than
to have ungodly children.
⁴ For through one intelligent person a
city can be filled with people,
but through a clan of outlaws it
becomes desolate.

⁵ Many such things my eye has seen,
and my ear has heard things more
striking than these.
⁶ In an assembly of sinners a fire is
kindled,
and in a disobedient nation wrath
blazes up.
⁷ He did not forgive the ancient giants
who revolted in their might.
⁸ He did not spare the neighbors of
Lot,
whom he loathed on account of
their arrogance.
⁹ He showed no pity on the doomed
nation,
on those dispossessed because of
their sins;ᵇ
¹⁰ or on the six hundred thousand foot
soldiers
who assembled in their
stubbornness.ᶜ
¹¹ Even if there were only one
stiff-necked person,
it would be a wonder if he
remained unpunished.

For mercy and wrath are with the
Lord;ᵈ
he is mighty to forgive—but he
also pours out wrath.
¹² Great as is his mercy, so also is his
chastisement;
he judges a person according to
his or her deeds.
¹³ The sinner will not escape with
plunder,
and the patience of the godly will
not be frustrated.
¹⁴ He makes room for every act of
mercy;
everyone receives in accordance
with his or her deeds.ᵉ

¹⁷ Do not say, "I am hidden from the
Lord,
and who from on high has me in
mind?
Among so many people I am
unknown,
for what am I in a boundless
creation?
¹⁸ Lo, heaven and the highest heaven,
the abyss and the earth, tremble at
his visitation!ᶠ
¹⁹ The very mountains and the
foundations of the earth
quiver and quake when he looks
upon them.
²⁰ But no human mind can grasp this,
and who can comprehend his
ways?
²¹ Like a tempest that no one can see,
so most of his works are
concealed.ᵍ
²² Who is to announce his acts of
justice?

ᶻ Heb: Gk *unprofitable*   ᵃ Other ancient
authorities add *For you will groan in untimely
mourning, and will know of their sudden end.*
ᵇ Other ancient authorities add *All these things he
did to the hard-hearted nations, and by the multitude
of his holy ones he was not appeased.*   ᶜ Other
ancient authorities add *Chastising, showing mercy,
striking, healing, the Lord persisted in mercy and
discipline.*   ᵈ Gk *him*   ᵉ Other ancient
authorities add ¹⁵*The Lord hardened Pharaoh so
that he did not recognize him, in order that his works
might be known under heaven.* ¹⁶*His mercy is
manifest to the whole of creation, and he divided his
light and darkness with a plumb line.*   ᶠ Other
ancient authorities add *The whole world past and
present is in his will.*   ᵍ Meaning of Gk uncertain:
Heb Syr *If I sin, no eye can see me, and if I am
disloyal in all secret, who is to know?*

Or who can await them? For his
   decree[h] is far off."[i]

23 Such are the thoughts of one devoid
      of understanding;
   a senseless and misguided person
      thinks foolishly.

God's Wisdom Seen in Creation

24 Listen to me, my child, and acquire
      knowledge,
   and pay close attention to my
      words.
25 I will impart discipline precisely[j]
   and declare knowledge accurately.

26 When the Lord created[k] his works
      from the beginning,
   and, in making them, determined
      their boundaries,
27 he arranged his works in an eternal
      order,
   and their dominion[l] for all
      generations.
   They neither hunger nor grow weary,
   and they do not abandon their
      tasks.
28 They do not crowd one another,
   and they never disobey his word.
29 Then the Lord looked upon the
      earth,
   and filled it with his good things.
30 With all kinds of living beings he
      covered its surface,
   and into it they must return.

17 The Lord created human beings
      out of earth,
   and makes them return to it
      again.
2 He gave them a fixed number of
      days,
   but granted them authority over
      everything on the earth.[m]
3 He endowed them with strength like
      his own,[n]
   and made them in his own image.
4 He put the fear of them[o] in all
      living beings,
   and gave them dominion over
      beasts and birds.[p]
6 Discretion and tongue and eyes,
   ears and a mind for thinking he
      gave them.
7 He filled them with knowledge and
      understanding,
   and showed them good and evil.
8 He put the fear of him into[q] their
      hearts

to show them the majesty of his
   works.[r]
10 And they will praise his holy name,
9   to proclaim the grandeur of his
      works.
11 He bestowed knowledge upon them,
   and allotted to them the law of
      life.[s]
12 He established with them an eternal
      covenant,
   and revealed to them his decrees.
13 Their eyes saw his glorious majesty,
   and their ears heard the glory of
      his voice.
14 He said to them, "Beware of all evil."
   And he gave commandment to
      each of them concerning the
      neighbor.
15 Their ways are always known to
      him;
   they will not be hid from his
      eyes.[t]
17 He appointed a ruler for every
      nation,
   but Israel is the Lord's own
      portion.[u]
19 All their works are as clear as the
      sun before him,
   and his eyes are ever upon their
      ways.
20 Their iniquities are not hidden from
      him,
   and all their sins are before the
      Lord.[v]
22 One's almsgiving is like a signet ring
      with the Lord,[w]

h Heb the decree: Gk the covenant   i Other
ancient authorities add and a scrutiny for all comes
at the end   j Gk by weight   k Heb: Gk judged
l Or elements   m Lat: Gk it   n Lat: Gk proper to
them   o Syr: Gk him   p Other ancient
authorities add as verse 5, They obtained the use of
the five faculties of the Lord; as sixth he distributed to
them the gift of mind, and as seventh, reason, the
interpreter of one's faculties.   q Other ancient
authorities read He set his eye upon   r Other
ancient authorities add and he gave them to boast
of his marvels forever   s Other ancient authorities
add so that they may know that they who are alive
now are mortal   t Other ancient authorities add
16Their ways from youth tend toward evil, and they
are unable to make for themselves hearts of flesh in
place of their stony hearts. 17For in the division of the
nations of the whole earth, he appointed   u Other
ancient authorities add as verse 18, whom, being
his firstborn, he brings up with discipline, and
allotting to him the light of his love, he does not
neglect him.   v Other ancient authorities add as
verse 21, But the Lord, who is gracious and knows
how they are formed, has neither left them nor
abandoned them, but has spared them.   w Gk him

and he will keep a person's
kindness like the apple of his
eye.*

23 Afterward he will rise up and repay
them,
and he will bring their
recompense on their heads.

24 Yet to those who repent he grants a
return,
and he encourages those who are
losing hope.

A Call to Repentance

25 Turn back to the Lord and forsake
your sins;
pray in his presence and lessen
your offense.

26 Return to the Most High and turn
away from iniquity, *y*
and hate intensely what he
abhors.

27 Who will sing praises to the Most
High in Hades
in place of the living who give
thanks?

28 From the dead, as from one who
does not exist, thanksgiving
has ceased;
those who are alive and well sing
the Lord's praises.

29 How great is the mercy of the Lord,
and his forgiveness for those who
return to him!

30 For not everything is within human
capability,
since human beings are not
immortal.

31 What is brighter than the sun? Yet it
can be eclipsed.
So flesh and blood devise evil.

32 He marshals the host of the height
of heaven;
but all human beings are dust and
ashes.

The Majesty of God

18 He who lives forever created the
whole universe;

2 the Lord alone is just.*z*

4 To none has he given power to
proclaim his works;
and who can search out his
mighty deeds?

5 Who can measure his majestic
power?
And who can fully recount his
mercies?

6 It is not possible to diminish or
increase them,
nor is it possible to fathom the
wonders of the Lord.

7 When human beings have finished,
they are just beginning,
and when they stop, they are still
perplexed.

8 What are human beings, and of
what use are they?
What is good in them, and what
is evil?

9 The number of days in their life is
great if they reach one
hundred years.*a*

10 Like a drop of water from the sea
and a grain of sand,
so are a few years among the days
of eternity.

11 That is why the Lord is patient with
them
and pours out his mercy upon
them.

12 He sees and recognizes that their
end is miserable;
therefore he grants them
forgiveness all the more.

13 The compassion of human beings is
for their neighbors,
but the compassion of the Lord is
for every living thing.
He rebukes and trains and teaches
them,
and turns them back, as a
shepherd his flock.

14 He has compassion on those who
accept his discipline
and who are eager for his
precepts.

The Right Spirit in Giving Alms

15 My child, do not mix reproach with
your good deeds,
or spoil your gift by harsh words.

16 Does not the dew give relief from
the scorching heat?
So a word is better than a gift.

---

x Other ancient authorities add *apportioning
repentance to his sons and daughters*   *y* Other
ancient authorities add *for he will lead you out of
darkness to the light of health.*   *z* Other ancient
authorities add *and there is no other beside him;* 3*he
steers the world with the span of his hand, and all
things obey his will; for he is king of all things by his
power, separating among them the holy things from
the profane.*   *a* Other ancient authorities add *but
the death of each one is beyond the calculation of all*

¹⁷ Indeed, does not a word surpass a
        good gift?
    Both are to be found in a gracious
        person.
¹⁸ A fool is ungracious and abusive,
    and the gift of a grudging giver
        makes the eyes dim.

The Need of Reflection and Self-control

¹⁹ Before you speak, learn;
    and before you fall ill, take care of
        your health.
²⁰ Before judgment comes, examine
        yourself;
    and at the time of scrutiny you
        will find forgiveness.
²¹ Before falling ill, humble yourself;
    and when you have sinned,
        repent.
²² Let nothing hinder you from paying
        a vow promptly,
    and do not wait until death to be
        released from it.
²³ Before making a vow, prepare
        yourself;
    do not be like one who puts the
        Lord to the test.
²⁴ Think of his wrath on the day of
        death,
    and of the moment of vengeance
        when he turns away his face.
²⁵ In the time of plenty think of the
        time of hunger;
    in days of wealth think of poverty
        and need.
²⁶ From morning to evening conditions
        change;
    all things move swiftly before the
        Lord.

²⁷ One who is wise is cautious in
        everything;
    when sin is all around, one guards
        against wrongdoing.
²⁸ Every intelligent person knows
        wisdom,
    and praises the one who finds her.
²⁹ Those who are skilled in words
        become wise themselves,
    and pour forth apt proverbs.ᵇ

Self-Control ᶜ

³⁰ Do not follow your base desires,
    but restrain your appetites.
³¹ If you allow your soul to take
        pleasure in base desire,

it will make you the laughingstock
        of your enemies.
³² Do not revel in great luxury,
    or you may become impoverished
        by its expense.
³³ Do not become a beggar by feasting
        with borrowed money,
    when you have nothing in your
        purse.ᵈ

19 The one who does thisᵉ will
        not become rich;
    one who despises small things
        will fail little by little.
² Wine and women lead intelligent
        men astray,
    and the man who consorts with
        prostitutes is reckless.
³ Decay and worms will take
        possession of him,
    and the reckless person will be
        snatched away.

Against Loose Talk

⁴ One who trusts others too quickly
        has a shallow mind,
    and one who sins does wrong to
        himself.
⁵ One who rejoices in wickednessᶠ
        will be condemned, ᵍ
⁶   but one who hates gossip has less
        evil.
⁷ Never repeat a conversation,
    and you will lose nothing at all.
⁸ With friend or foe do not report it,
    and unless it would be a sin for
        you, do not reveal it;
⁹ for someone may have heard you
        and watched you,
    and in time will hate you.
¹⁰ Have you heard something? Let it
        die with you.
    Be brave, it will not make you
        burst!
¹¹ Having heard something, the fool
        suffers birth pangs
    like a woman in labor with a
        child.

ᵇ Other ancient authorities add *Better is confidence
in the one Lord than clinging with a dead heart to a
dead one.*   ᶜ This heading is included in the Gk
text.   ᵈ Other ancient authorities add *for you will
be plotting against your own life*   ᵉ Heb: Gk A
worker who is a drunkard   ᶠ Other ancient
authorities read *heart*   ᵍ Other ancient
authorities add *but one who withstands pleasures
crowns his life.* ⁶*One who controls the tongue will live
without strife,*

¹² Like an arrow stuck in a person's
　　thigh,
　　so is gossip inside a fool.

¹³ Question a friend; perhaps he did
　　not do it;
　　or if he did, so that he may not
　　do it again.

¹⁴ Question a neighbor; perhaps he did
　　not say it;
　　or if he said it, so that he may not
　　repeat it.

¹⁵ Question a friend, for often it is
　　slander;
　　so do not believe everything you
　　hear.

*W*atching Our Words

THURSDAY

Scripture Reading
for Today:
Sirach 19.5–17

Verse for Today:
Sirach 19.9

Perhaps you will say we have prayers enough? It may be so. In my
own case, unfortunately, I must confess that a little extra prayer
such as I am going to propose would be very useful. Here is the
proposal:

That once daily we should pray:

"Set a watch, O Lord, before my mouth, and a door of prudence
around my lips; that my heart incline not to evil words . . ."

"Our Father. Hail Mary."

The object, of course, will be to seek supernatural grace to enable us to take better care of our tongues than most of us are in
the habit of doing. So that we may get out of the way of talking
so much about our neighbors, may refrain from passing on everything we know for certain and a great deal of which we know
nothing at all for certain, may be content to see a rumor fly past
our door without asking it to come in so that we too may have a
look at it.

And then we ought to read the good old Epistle of Saint James.
As you know, what he says about the tongue is in the third chapter (see James 3.1–12).

I do not mean that we ought literally to start up as though bitten whenever anybody begins: "Have you heard about Mrs. So-
and-So?" crossing ourselves like semaphores and snatching at a
book or a rosary. But there is one thing we must remember: We
have all grown up in a state of society in which everyone more or
less has a passion for chatting about other people's intimate affairs.

This does not mean that we are to condemn ourselves to silence like Trappists. But our aim should be rather to err on the
side of renunciation. We in our part of the world are like people
who have ruined their digestions by too much and too rich food,
and we ought to diet ourselves for the rest of our lives; it takes so
little to bring on an attack of our old malady—loquacity.

—*SIGRID UNDSET*

Go to page 909 for your next devotional reading.

16 A person may make a slip without
  intending it.
    Who has not sinned with his
    tongue?
17 Question your neighbor before you
  threaten him;
    and let the law of the Most High
    take its course.*h*

True and False Wisdom

20 The whole of wisdom is fear of the
  Lord,
    and in all wisdom there is the
    fulfillment of the law.*i*
22 The knowledge of wickedness is not
  wisdom,
    nor is there prudence in the
    counsel of sinners.
23 There is a cleverness that is
  detestable,
    and there is a fool who merely
    lacks wisdom.
24 Better are the God-fearing who lack
  understanding
    than the highly intelligent who
    transgress the law.
25 There is a cleverness that is exact but
  unjust,
    and there are people who abuse
    favors to gain a verdict.
26 There is the villain bowed down in
  mourning,
    but inwardly he is full of deceit.
27 He hides his face and pretends not
  to hear,
    but when no one notices, he will
    take advantage of you.
28 Even if lack of strength keeps him
  from sinning,
    he will nevertheless do evil when
    he finds the opportunity.
29 A person is known by his
  appearance,
    and a sensible person is known
    when first met, face to face.
30 A person's attire and hearty laughter,
    and the way he walks, show what
    he is.

Silence and Speech

20 There is a rebuke that is
  untimely,
    and there is the person who is
    wise enough to keep silent.
2 How much better it is to rebuke
    than to fume!
3 And the one who admits his fault
    will be kept from failure.

4 Like a eunuch lusting to violate a
  girl
    is the person who does right
    under compulsion.
5 Some people keep silent and are
    thought to be wise,
    while others are detested for being
    talkative.
6 Some people keep silent because
    they have nothing to say,
    while others keep silent because
    they know when to speak.
7 The wise remain silent until the
    right moment,
    but a boasting fool misses the
    right moment.
8 Whoever talks too much is detested,
    and whoever pretends to authority
    is hated.*j*

Paradoxes

9 There may be good fortune for a
    person in adversity,
    and a windfall may result in a
    loss.
10 There is the gift that profits you
    nothing,
    and the gift to be paid back
    double.
11 There are losses for the sake of glory,
    and there are some who have
    raised their heads from
    humble circumstances.
12 Some buy much for little,
    but pay for it seven times over.
13 The wise make themselves beloved
    by only few words,*k*
    but the courtesies of fools are
    wasted.
14 A fool's gift will profit you
    nothing,*l*
    for he looks for recompense
    sevenfold.*m*

---

h Other ancient authorities add *and do not be
angry.* *18The fear of the Lord is the beginning of
acceptance, and wisdom obtains his love.* *19The
knowledge of the Lord's commandments is life-giving
discipline; and those who do what is pleasing to him
enjoy the fruit of the tree of immortality.*   *i* Other
ancient authorities add *and the knowledge of his
omnipotence.* *21When a slave says to his master, "I
will not act as you wish," even if later he does it, he
angers the one who supports him.*   *j* Other ancient
authorities add *How good it is to show repentance
when you are reproved, for so you will escape
deliberate sin!*   *k* Heb: Gk *by words*   *l* Other
ancient authorities add *so it is with the envious who
give under compulsion*   *m* Syr: Gk *he has many eyes
instead of one*

15 He gives little and upbraids much;
　　he opens his mouth like a town
　　　crier.
　Today he lends and tomorrow he
　　asks it back;
　　such a one is hateful to God and
　　　humans.[n]
16 The fool says, "I have no friends,
　　and I get no thanks for my good
　　　deeds.
　Those who eat my bread are
　　evil-tongued."
17 How many will ridicule him, and
　　how often![o]

Inappropriate Speech

18 A slip on the pavement is better
　　than a slip of the tongue;
　　the downfall of the wicked will
　　　occur just as speedily.
19 A coarse person is like an
　　inappropriate story,
　　continually on the lips of the
　　　ignorant.
20 A proverb from a fool's lips will be
　　rejected,
　　for he does not tell it at the
　　　proper time.

21 One may be prevented from sinning
　　by poverty;
　　so when he rests he feels no
　　　remorse.
22 One may lose his life through
　　shame,
　　or lose it because of human
　　　respect.[p]
23 Another out of shame makes
　　promises to a friend,
　　and so makes an enemy for
　　　nothing.

Lying

24 A lie is an ugly blot on a person;
　　it is continually on the lips of the
　　　ignorant.
25 A thief is preferable to a habitual
　　liar,
　　but the lot of both is ruin.
26 A liar's way leads to disgrace,
　　and his shame is ever with him.

Proverbial Sayings [q]

27 The wise person advances himself by
　　his words,
　　and one who is sensible pleases
　　　the great.

28 Those who cultivate the soil heap up
　　their harvest,
　　and those who please the great
　　　atone for injustice.
29 Favors and gifts blind the eyes of the
　　wise;
　　like a muzzle on the mouth they
　　　stop reproofs.
30 Hidden wisdom and unseen
　　treasure,
　　of what value is either?
31 Better are those who hide their folly
　　than those who hide their
　　　wisdom.[r]

Various Sins

21 Have you sinned, my child? Do
　　so no more,
　　but ask forgiveness for your past
　　　sins.
2 Flee from sin as from a snake;
　　for if you approach sin, it will bite
　　　you.
　Its teeth are lion's teeth,
　　and can destroy human lives.
3 All lawlessness is like a two-edged
　　sword;
　　there is no healing for the wound
　　　it inflicts.

4 Panic and insolence will waste away
　　riches;
　　thus the house of the proud will
　　　be laid waste.[s]
5 The prayer of the poor goes from
　　their lips to the ears of
　　　God,[t]
　and his judgment comes speedily.
6 Those who hate reproof walk in the
　　sinner's steps,
　　but those who fear the Lord
　　　repent in their heart.
7 The mighty in speech are widely
　　known;
　　when they slip, the sensible
　　　person knows it.

[n] Other ancient authorities lack *to God and
humans*　[o] Other ancient authorities add *for he
has not honestly received what he has, and what he
does not have is unimportant to him*　[p] Other
ancient authorities read *his foolish look*　[q] This
heading is included in the Gk text.　[r] Other
ancient authorities add *32Unwearied endurance in
seeking the Lord is better than a masterless charioteer
of one's own life.*　[s] Other ancient authorities
read *uprooted*　[t] Gk *his ears*

8 Whoever builds his house with other
  people's money
    is like one who gathers stones for
    his burial mound.[u]
9 An assembly of the wicked is like a
  bundle of tow,
    and their end is a blazing fire.
10 The way of sinners is paved with
  smooth stones,
    but at its end is the pit of Hades.

Wisdom and Foolishness

11 Whoever keeps the law controls his
  thoughts,
    and the fulfillment of the fear of
    the Lord is wisdom.
12 The one who is not clever cannot be
  taught,
    but there is a cleverness that
    increases bitterness.
13 The knowledge of the wise will
  increase like a flood,
    and their counsel like a life-giving
    spring.
14 The mind[v] of a fool is like a
  broken jar;
    it can hold no knowledge.

15 When an intelligent person hears a
  wise saying,
    he praises it and adds to it;
  when a fool[w] hears it, he laughs
    at[x] it
    and throws it behind his back.
16 A fool's chatter is like a burden on a
  journey,
    but delight is found in the speech
    of the intelligent.
17 The utterance of a sensible person is
  sought in the assembly,
    and they ponder his words in
    their minds.

18 Like a house in ruins is wisdom to a
  fool,
    and to the ignorant, knowledge is
    talk that has no meaning.
19 To a senseless person education is
  fetters on his feet,
    and like manacles on his right
    hand.
20 A fool raises his voice when he
  laughs,
    but the wise[y] smile quietly.
21 To the sensible person education is
  like a golden ornament,
    and like a bracelet on the right
    arm.

22 The foot of a fool rushes into a
  house,
    but an experienced person waits
    respectfully outside.
23 A boor peers into the house from
  the door,
    but a cultivated person remains
    outside.
24 It is ill-mannered for a person to
  listen at a door;
    the discreet would be grieved by
    the disgrace.

25 The lips of babblers speak of what is
  not their concern,[z]
    but the words of the prudent are
    weighed in the balance.
26 The mind of fools is in their mouth,
    but the mouth of the wise is in[a]
    their mind.
27 When an ungodly person curses an
  adversary,[b]
    he curses himself.
28 A whisperer degrades himself
    and is hated in his neighborhood.

The Idler

22 The idler is like a filthy stone,
    and every one hisses at his
    disgrace.
2 The idler is like the filth of
  dunghills;
    anyone that picks it up will shake
    it off his hand.

Degenerate Children

3 It is a disgrace to be the father of an
  undisciplined son,
    and the birth of a daughter is a
    loss.
4 A sensible daughter obtains a
  husband of her own,
    but one who acts shamefully is a
    grief to her father.
5 An impudent daughter disgraces
  father and husband,
    and is despised by both.
6 Like music in time of mourning is
  ill-timed conversation,

u Other ancient authorities read *for the winter*
v Syr Lat: Gk *entrails*   w Syr: Gk *reveler*
x Syr: Gk *dislikes*   y Syr Lat: Gk *clever*   z Other
ancient authorities read *of strangers speak of these
things*   a Other ancient authorities omit *in*
b Or *curses Satan*

but a thrashing and discipline are
at all times wisdom.[c]

Wisdom and Folly

9 Whoever teaches a fool is like one
who glues potsherds together,
or who rouses a sleeper from deep
slumber.
10 Whoever tells a story to a fool tells
it to a drowsy man;
and at the end he will say, "What
is it?"
11 Weep for the dead, for he has left
the light behind;
and weep for the fool, for he has
left intelligence behind.
Weep less bitterly for the dead, for
he is at rest;
but the life of the fool is worse
than death.
12 Mourning for the dead lasts seven
days,
but for the foolish or the ungodly
it lasts all the days of their
lives.

13 Do not talk much with a senseless
person
or visit an unintelligent person.[d]
Stay clear of him, or you may have
trouble,
and be spattered when he shakes
himself off.
Avoid him and you will find rest,
and you will never be wearied by
his lack of sense.
14 What is heavier than lead?
And what is its name except
"Fool"?
15 Sand, salt, and a piece of iron
are easier to bear than a stupid
person.

16 A wooden beam firmly bonded into
a building
is not loosened by an earthquake;
so the mind firmly resolved after
due reflection
will not be afraid in a crisis.
17 A mind settled on an intelligent
thought
is like stucco decoration that
makes a wall smooth.
18 Fences[e] set on a high place
will not stand firm against the
wind;
so a timid mind with a fool's resolve
will not stand firm against any
fear.

The Preservation of Friendship

19 One who pricks the eye brings tears,
and one who pricks the heart
makes clear its feelings.
20 One who throws a stone at birds
scares them away,
and one who reviles a friend
destroys a friendship.
21 Even if you draw your sword against
a friend,
do not despair, for there is a way
back.
22 If you open your mouth against
your friend,
do not worry, for reconciliation is
possible.
But as for reviling, arrogance,
disclosure of secrets, or a
treacherous blow—
in these cases any friend will take
to flight.

23 Gain the trust of your neighbor in
his poverty,
so that you may rejoice with him
in his prosperity.
Stand by him in time of distress,
so that you may share with him
in his inheritance.[f]
24 The vapor and smoke of the furnace
precede the fire;
so insults precede bloodshed.
25 I am not ashamed to shelter a
friend,
and I will not hide from him.
26 But if harm should come to me
because of him,
whoever hears of it will beware of
him.

A Prayer for Help against Sinning

27 Who will set a guard over my
mouth,
and an effective seal upon my
lips,

---

c Other ancient authorities add 7Children who are
brought up in a good life, conceal the lowly birth of
their parents. 8Children who are disdainfully and
boorishly haughty stain the nobility of their kindred.
d Other ancient authorities add For being without
sense he will despise everything about you   e Other
ancient authorities read Pebbles   f Other ancient
authorities add For one should not always despise
restricted circumstances, or admire a rich person who
is stupid.

so that I may not fall because of
them,
and my tongue may not destroy
me?

23

O Lord, Father and Master of
my life,
do not abandon me to their
designs,
and do not let me fall because of
them!

2 Who will set whips over my
thoughts,
and the discipline of wisdom over
my mind,
so as not to spare me in my errors,
and not overlook my g sins?

3 Otherwise my mistakes may be
multiplied,
and my sins may abound,
and I may fall before my adversaries,
and my enemy may rejoice over
me.h

4 O Lord, Father and God of my life,
do not give me haughty eyes,

5 and remove evil desire from me.

6 Let neither gluttony nor lust
overcome me,
and do not give me over to
shameless passion.

DISCIPLINE OF THE TONGUE i

7 Listen, my children, to instruction
concerning the mouth;
the one who observes it will never
be caught.

8 Sinners are overtaken through their
lips;
by them the reviler and the
arrogant are tripped up.

9 Do not accustom your mouth to
oaths,
nor habitually utter the name of
the Holy One;

10 for as a servant who is constantly
under scrutiny
will not lack bruises,
so also the person who always
swears and utters the Name
will never be cleansed j from sin.

11 The one who swears many oaths is
full of iniquity,
and the scourge will not leave his
house.
If he swears in error, his sin remains
on him,
and if he disregards it, he sins
doubly;

if he swears a false oath, he will not
be justified,
for his house will be filled with
calamities.

Foul Language

12 There is a manner of speaking
comparable to death;k
may it never be found in the
inheritance of Jacob!
Such conduct will be far from the
godly,
and they will not wallow in sins.

13 Do not accustom your mouth to
coarse, foul language,
for it involves sinful speech.

14 Remember your father and mother
when you sit among the great,
or you may forget yourself in their
presence,
and behave like a fool through
bad habit;
then you will wish that you had
never been born,
and you will curse the day of your
birth.

15 Those who are accustomed to using
abusive language
will never become disciplined as
long as they live.

Concerning Sexual Sins

16 Two kinds of individuals multiply
sins,
and a third incurs wrath.
Hot passion that blazes like a fire
will not be quenched until it
burns itself out;
one who commits fornication with
his near of kin
will never cease until the fire
burns him up.

17 To a fornicator all bread is sweet;
he will never weary until he dies.

18 The one who sins against his
marriage bed
says to himself, "Who can see
me?
Darkness surrounds me, the walls
hide me,
and no one sees me. Why should
I worry?

g Gk *their*   h Other ancient authorities add *From
them the hope of your mercy is remote*   i This
heading is included in the Gk text.   j Syr *be free*
k Other ancient authorities read *clothed about with
death*

The Most High will not remember
sins."

19 His fear is confined to human eyes
and he does not realize that the
eyes of the Lord
are ten thousand times brighter
than the sun;
they look upon every aspect of
human behavior
and see into hidden corners.

20 Before the universe was created, it
was known to him,
and so it is since its completion.

21 This man will be punished in the
streets of the city,
and where he least suspects it, he
will be seized.

22 So it is with a woman who leaves
her husband
and presents him with an heir by
another man.

23 For first of all, she has disobeyed the
law of the Most High;
second, she has committed an
offense against her husband;
and third, through her fornication
she has committed adultery
and brought forth children by
another man.

24 She herself will be brought before
the assembly,
and her punishment will extend
to her children.

25 Her children will not take root,
and her branches will not bear
fruit.

26 She will leave behind an accursed
memory
and her disgrace will never be
blotted out.

27 Those who survive her will recognize
that nothing is better than the fear
of the Lord,
and nothing sweeter than to heed
the commandments of the
Lord.[l]

The Praise of Wisdom [m]

24 Wisdom praises herself,
and tells of her glory in the
midst of her people.

2 In the assembly of the Most High
she opens her mouth,
and in the presence of his hosts
she tells of her glory:

3 "I came forth from the mouth of
the Most High,
and covered the earth like a mist.

4 I dwelt in the highest heavens,
and my throne was in a pillar of
cloud.

5 Alone I compassed the vault of
heaven
and traversed the depths of the
abyss.

6 Over waves of the sea, over all the
earth,
and over every people and nation
I have held sway.[n]

7 Among all these I sought a resting
place;
in whose territory should I abide?

8 "Then the Creator of all things gave
me a command,
and my Creator chose the place
for my tent.
He said, 'Make your dwelling in
Jacob,
and in Israel receive your
inheritance.'

9 Before the ages, in the beginning, he
created me,
and for all the ages I shall not
cease to be.

10 In the holy tent I ministered before
him,
and so I was established in Zion.

11 Thus in the beloved city he gave me
a resting place,
and in Jerusalem was my domain.

12 I took root in an honored people,
in the portion of the Lord, his
heritage.

13 "I grew tall like a cedar in Lebanon,
and like a cypress on the heights
of Hermon.

14 I grew tall like a palm tree in
En-gedi,[o]
and like rosebushes in Jericho;
like a fair olive tree in the field,
and like a plane tree beside
water[p] I grew tall.

15 Like cassia and camel's thorn I gave
forth perfume,

[l] Other ancient authorities add as verse 28, *It is a
great honor to follow God, and to be received by him
is long life.*   [m] This heading is included in the
Gk text.   [n] Other ancient authorities read *I have
acquired a possession*   [o] Other ancient authorities
read *on the beaches*   [p] Other ancient authorities
omit *beside water*

and like choice myrrh I spread my
        fragrance,
like galbanum, onycha, and stacte,
        and like the odor of incense in
        the tent.
16 Like a terebinth I spread out my
        branches,
        and my branches are glorious and
        graceful.
17 Like the vine I bud forth delights,
        and my blossoms become glorious
        and abundant fruit.*q*

19 "Come to me, you who desire me,
        and eat your fill of my fruits.
20 For the memory of me is sweeter
        than honey,
        and the possession of me sweeter
        than the honeycomb.
21 Those who eat of me will hunger for
        more,
        and those who drink of me will
        thirst for more.
22 Whoever obeys me will not be put
        to shame,
        and those who work with me will
        not sin."

Wisdom and the Law

23 All this is the book of the covenant
        of the Most High God,
        the law that Moses commanded
        us
        as an inheritance for the
        congregations of Jacob.*r*
25 It overflows, like the Pishon, with
        wisdom,
        and like the Tigris at the time of
        the first fruits.
26 It runs over, like the Euphrates, with
        understanding,
        and like the Jordan at harvest
        time.
27 It pours forth instruction like the
        Nile,*s*
        like the Gihon at the time of
        vintage.
28 The first man did not know
        wisdom*t* fully,
        nor will the last one fathom her.
29 For her thoughts are more abundant
        than the sea,
        and her counsel deeper than the
        great abyss.

30 As for me, I was like a canal from a
        river,
        like a water channel into a garden.

31 I said, "I will water my garden
        and drench my flower-beds."
        And lo, my canal became a river,
        and my river a sea.
32 I will again make instruction shine
        forth like the dawn,
        and I will make it clear from far
        away.
33 I will again pour out teaching like
        prophecy,
        and leave it to all future
        generations.
34 Observe that I have not labored for
        myself alone,
        but for all who seek wisdom.*t*

Those Who Are Worthy of Praise

25 I take pleasure in three things,
        and they are beautiful in the
        sight of God and of
        mortals:*u*
agreement among brothers and
        sisters, friendship among
        neighbors,
        and a wife and a husband who
        live in harmony.
2 I hate three kinds of people,
        and I loathe their manner of life:
a pauper who boasts, a rich person
        who lies,
        and an old fool who commits
        adultery.

3 If you gathered nothing in your
        youth,
        how can you find anything in
        your old age?
4 How attractive is sound judgment in
        the gray-haired,
        and for the aged to possess good
        counsel!
5 How attractive is wisdom in the
        aged,
        and understanding and counsel in
        the venerable!
6 Rich experience is the crown of the
        aged,

*q Other ancient authorities add as verse 18, I am
the mother of beautiful love, of fear, of knowledge,
and of holy hope; being eternal, I am given to all my
children, to those who are named by him.   r Other
ancient authorities add as verse 24, "Do not cease
to be strong in the Lord, cling to him so that he may
strengthen you; the Lord Almighty alone is God, and
besides him there is no savior."   s Syr: Gk It makes
instruction shine forth like light   t Gk her   u Syr
Lat: Gk In three things I was beautiful and I stood in
beauty before the Lord and mortals.*

and their boast is the fear of the
Lord.

7 I can think of nine whom I would
call blessed,
and a tenth my tongue proclaims:
a man who can rejoice in his
children;
a man who lives to see the
downfall of his foes.
8 Happy the man who lives with a
sensible wife,
and the one who does not plow
with ox and ass together.*v*
Happy is the one who does not sin
with the tongue,
and the one who has not served
an inferior.
9 Happy is the one who finds a
friend,*w*
and the one who speaks to
attentive listeners.
10 How great is the one who finds
wisdom!
But none is superior to the one
who fears the Lord.
11 Fear of the Lord surpasses
everything;
to whom can we compare the one
who has it?*x*

Some Extreme Forms of Evil

13 Any wound, but not a wound of the
heart!
Any wickedness, but not the
wickedness of a woman!
14 Any suffering, but not suffering from
those who hate!
And any vengeance, but not the
vengeance of enemies!
15 There is no venom*y* worse than a
snake's venom,*y*
and no anger worse than a
woman's*z* wrath.

The Evil of a Wicked Woman

16 I would rather live with a lion and a
dragon
than live with an evil woman.
17 A woman's wickedness changes her
appearance,
and darkens her face like that of a
bear.
18 Her husband sits*a* among the
neighbors,
and he cannot help sighing*b*
bitterly.

19 Any iniquity is small compared to a
woman's iniquity;
may a sinner's lot befall her!
20 A sandy ascent for the feet of the
aged—
such is a garrulous wife to a quiet
husband.
21 Do not be ensnared by a woman's
beauty,
and do not desire a woman for
her possessions.*c*
22 There is wrath and impudence and
great disgrace
when a wife supports her
husband.
23 Dejected mind, gloomy face,
and wounded heart come from an
evil wife.
Drooping hands and weak knees
come from the wife who does not
make her husband happy.
24 From a woman sin had its
beginning,
and because of her we all die.
25 Allow no outlet to water,
and no boldness of speech to an
evil wife.
26 If she does not go as you direct,
separate her from yourself.

The Joy of a Good Wife

26 Happy is the husband of a good
wife;
the number of his days will be
doubled.
2 A loyal wife brings joy to her
husband,
and he will complete his years in
peace.
3 A good wife is a great blessing;
she will be granted among the
blessings of the man who
fears the Lord.
4 Whether rich or poor, his heart is
content,
and at all times his face is
cheerful.

---

v Heb Syr: Gk lacks *and the one who does not plow
with ox and ass together*   *w* Lat Syr: Gk *good sense*
x Other ancient authorities add as verse 12, *The
fear of the Lord is the beginning of love for him, and
faith is the beginning of clinging to him.*   *y* Syr: Gk
head   *z* Other ancient authorities read *an
enemy's*   *a* Heb Syr: Gk *loses heart*   *b* Other
ancient authorities read *and listening he sighs*
c Heb Syr: Other Gk authorities read *for her beauty*

The Worst of Evils: A Wicked Wife

5 Of three things my heart is
  frightened,
  and of a fourth I am in great
   fear:[d]
  Slander in the city, the gathering of
   a mob,
   and false accusation—all these are
    worse than death.
6 But it is heartache and sorrow when
   a wife is jealous of a rival,
   and a tongue-lashing makes it
    known to all.
7 A bad wife is a chafing yoke;
  taking hold of her is like grasping
   a scorpion.
8 A drunken wife arouses great anger;
  she cannot hide her shame.
9 The haughty stare betrays an
   unchaste wife;
  her eyelids give her away.

10 Keep strict watch over a headstrong
   daughter,
  or else, when she finds liberty, she
   will make use of it.
11 Be on guard against her impudent
   eye,
  and do not be surprised if she
   sins against you.
12 As a thirsty traveler opens his mouth
   and drinks from any water near
   him,
  so she will sit in front of every tent
   peg
   and open her quiver to the arrow.

The Blessing of a Good Wife

13 A wife's charm delights her husband,
  and her skill puts flesh on his
   bones.
14 A silent wife is a gift from the Lord,
  and nothing is so precious as her
   self-discipline.
15 A modest wife adds charm to charm,
  and no scales can weigh the value
   of her chastity.
16 Like the sun rising in the heights of
   the Lord,
  so is the beauty of a good wife in
   her well-ordered home.
17 Like the shining lamp on the holy
   lampstand,
  so is a beautiful face on a stately
   figure.
18 Like golden pillars on silver bases,
  so are shapely legs and steadfast
   feet.

Other ancient authorities add
verses 19–27:

19 *My child, keep sound the bloom of your*
  youth,
  and do not give your strength to
  strangers.
20 *Seek a fertile field within the whole*
  plain,
  and sow it with your own seed,
  trusting in your fine stock.
21 *So your offspring will prosper,*
  and, having confidence in their good
  descent, will grow great.
22 *A prostitute is regarded as spittle,*
  and a married woman as a tower of
  death to her lovers.
23 *A godless wife is given as a portion to a*
  lawless man,
  but a pious wife is given to the man
  who fears the Lord.
24 *A shameless woman constantly acts*
  disgracefully,
  but a modest daughter will even be
  embarrassed before her husband.
25 *A headstrong wife is regarded as a dog,*
  but one who has a sense of shame
  will fear the Lord.
26 *A wife honoring her husband will seem*
  wise to all,
  but if she dishonors him in her pride
  she will be known to all as
  ungodly.
  Happy is the husband of a good wife;
  for the number of his years will be
  doubled.
27 *A loud-voiced and garrulous wife is like*
  a trumpet sounding the charge,
  and every person like this lives in the
  anarchy of war.

Three Depressing Things

28 At two things my heart is grieved,
  and because of a third anger
   comes over me:
  a warrior in want through poverty,
  intelligent men who are treated
   contemptuously,
  and a man who turns back from
   righteousness to sin—

d Syr: Meaning of Gk uncertain

the Lord will prepare him for the sword!

The Temptations of Commerce

29 A merchant can hardly keep from wrongdoing,
nor is a tradesman innocent of sin.

27 Many have committed sin for gain,[e]
and those who seek to get rich will avert their eyes.

2 As a stake is driven firmly into a fissure between stones,
so sin is wedged in between selling and buying.

3 If a person is not steadfast in the fear of the Lord,
his house will be quickly overthrown.

Tests in Life

4 When a sieve is shaken, the refuse appears;
so do a person's faults when he speaks.

5 The kiln tests the potter's vessels;
so the test of a person is in his conversation.

6 Its fruit discloses the cultivation of a tree;
so a person's speech discloses the cultivation of his mind.

7 Do not praise anyone before he speaks,
for this is the way people are tested.

Reward and Retribution

8 If you pursue justice, you will attain it
and wear it like a glorious robe.

9 Birds roost with their own kind,
so honesty comes home to those who practice it.

10 A lion lies in wait for prey;
so does sin for evildoers.

Varieties of Speech

11 The conversation of the godly is always wise,
but the fool changes like the moon.

12 Among stupid people limit your time,
but among thoughtful people linger on.

13 The talk of fools is offensive,
and their laughter is wantonly sinful.

14 Their cursing and swearing make one's hair stand on end,
and their quarrels make others stop their ears.

15 The strife of the proud leads to bloodshed,
and their abuse is grievous to hear.

Betraying Secrets

16 Whoever betrays secrets destroys confidence,
and will never find a congenial friend.

17 Love your friend and keep faith with him;
but if you betray his secrets, do not follow after him.

18 For as a person destroys his enemy,
so you have destroyed the friendship of your neighbor.

19 And as you allow a bird to escape from your hand,
so you have let your neighbor go, and will not catch him again.

20 Do not go after him, for he is too far off,
and has escaped like a gazelle from a snare.

21 For a wound may be bandaged,
and there is reconciliation after abuse,
but whoever has betrayed secrets is without hope.

Hypocrisy and Retribution

22 Whoever winks the eye plots mischief,
and those who know him will keep their distance.

23 In your presence his mouth is all sweetness,
and he admires your words;
but later he will twist his speech
and with your own words he will trip you up.

24 I have hated many things, but him above all;
even the Lord hates him.

25 Whoever throws a stone straight up throws it on his own head,
and a treacherous blow opens up many wounds.

26 Whoever digs a pit will fall into it,

e Other ancient authorities read *a trifle*

and whoever sets a snare will be
caught in it.
27 If a person does evil, it will roll back
upon him,
and he will not know where it
came from.
28 Mockery and abuse issue from the
proud,
but vengeance lies in wait for
them like a lion.
29 Those who rejoice in the fall of the
godly will be caught in a
snare,
and pain will consume them
before their death.

Anger and Vengeance

30 Anger and wrath, these also are
abominations,
yet a sinner holds on to them.

28 The vengeful will face the Lord's
vengeance,
for he keeps a strict account of *f*
their sins.
2 Forgive your neighbor the wrong he
has done,
and then your sins will be
pardoned when you pray.
3 Does anyone harbor anger against
another,
and expect healing from the Lord?
4 If one has no mercy toward another
like himself,
can he then seek pardon for his
own sins?
5 If a mere mortal harbors wrath,
who will make an atoning
sacrifice for his sins?
6 Remember the end of your life, and
set enmity aside;
remember corruption and death,
and be true to the
commandments.
7 Remember the commandments, and
do not be angry with your
neighbor;
remember the covenant of the
Most High, and overlook
faults.

8 Refrain from strife, and your sins
will be fewer;
for the hot-tempered kindle strife,
9 and the sinner disrupts friendships
and sows discord among those
who are at peace.
10 In proportion to the fuel, so will the
fire burn,

and in proportion to the
obstinacy, so will strife
increase; *g*
in proportion to a person's strength
will be his anger,
and in proportion to his wealth
he will increase his wrath.
11 A hasty quarrel kindles a fire,
and a hasty dispute sheds blood.

The Evil Tongue

12 If you blow on a spark, it will glow;
if you spit on it, it will be put
out;
yet both come out of your mouth.
13 Curse the gossips and the
double-tongued,
for they destroy the peace of
many.
14 Slander*h* has shaken many,
and scattered them from nation to
nation;
it has destroyed strong cities,
and overturned the houses of the
great.
15 Slander*h* has driven virtuous
women from their homes,
and deprived them of the fruit of
their toil.
16 Those who pay heed to slander*i*
will not find rest,
nor will they settle down in peace.
17 The blow of a whip raises a welt,
but a blow of the tongue crushes
the bones.
18 Many have fallen by the edge of the
sword,
but not as many as have fallen
because of the tongue.
19 Happy is the one who is protected
from it,
who has not been exposed to its
anger,
who has not borne its yoke,
and has not been bound with its
fetters.
20 For its yoke is a yoke of iron,
and its fetters are fetters of bronze;
21 its death is an evil death,
and Hades is preferable to it.
22 It has no power over the godly;
they will not be burned in its
flame.

*f Other ancient authorities read for he firmly
establishes   g Other ancient authorities read burn
h Gk A third tongue   i Gk it*

23 Those who forsake the Lord will fall
     into its power;
  it will burn among them and will
     not be put out.
  It will be sent out against them like
     a lion;
  like a leopard it will mangle them.
24a As you fence in your property with
     thorns,
25b   so make a door and a bolt for
     your mouth.
24b As you lock up your silver and
     gold,
25a   so make balances and scales for
     your words.
26 Take care not to err with your
     tongue, *j*
  and fall victim to one lying in
     wait.

On Lending and Borrowing

29 The merciful lend to their
         neighbors;
  by holding out a helping hand
     they keep the
     commandments.
2 Lend to your neighbor in his time of
     need;
  repay your neighbor when a loan
     falls due.
3 Keep your promise and be honest
     with him,
  and on every occasion you will
     find what you need.
4 Many regard a loan as a windfall,
  and cause trouble to those who
     help them.
5 One kisses another's hands until he
     gets a loan,
  and is deferential in speaking of
     his neighbor's money;
  but at the time for repayment he
     delays,
  and pays back with empty
     promises,
  and finds fault with the time.
6 If he can pay, his creditor*k* will
     hardly get back half,
  and will regard that as a windfall.
  If he cannot pay, the borrower*k* has
     robbed the other of his
     money,
  and he has needlessly made him
     an enemy;
  he will repay him with curses and
     reproaches,
  and instead of glory will repay
     him with dishonor.

7 Many refuse to lend, not because of
     meanness,
  but from fear*l* of being
     defrauded needlessly.

8 Nevertheless, be patient with
     someone in humble
     circumstances,
  and do not keep him waiting for
     your alms.
9 Help the poor for the
     commandment's sake,
  and in their need do not send
     them away empty-handed.
10 Lose your silver for the sake of a
     brother or a friend,
  and do not let it rust under a
     stone and be lost.
11 Lay up your treasure according to
     the commandments of the
     Most High,
  and it will profit you more than
     gold.
12 Store up almsgiving in your treasury,
  and it will rescue you from every
     disaster;
13 better than a stout shield and a
     sturdy spear,
  it will fight for you against the
     enemy.

On Guaranteeing Debts

14 A good person will be surety for his
     neighbor,
  but the one who has lost all sense
     of shame will fail him.
15 Do not forget the kindness of your
     guarantor,
  for he has given his life for you.
16 A sinner wastes the property of his
     guarantor,
17   and the ungrateful person
     abandons his rescuer.
18 Being surety has ruined many who
     were prosperous,
  and has tossed them about like
     waves of the sea;
  it has driven the influential into
     exile,
  and they have wandered among
     foreign nations.
19 The sinner comes to grief through
     surety;

j Gk *with it*   *k* Gk *he*   *l* Other ancient
authorities read *many refuse to lend, therefore,
because of such meanness; they are afraid*

his pursuit of gain involves him in
  lawsuits.
20 Assist your neighbor to the best of
  your ability,
    but be careful not to fall yourself.

Home and Hospitality

21 The necessities of life are water,
  bread, and clothing,
    and also a house to assure
    privacy.
22 Better is the life of the poor under
  their own crude roof
    than sumptuous food in the
    house of others.
23 Be content with little or much,
    and you will hear no reproach for
    being a guest.*m*
24 It is a miserable life to go from
  house to house;
    as a guest you should not open
    your mouth;
25 you will play the host and provide
    drink without being thanked,
    and besides this you will hear
    rude words like these:
26 "Come here, stranger, prepare the
    table;
    let me eat what you have there."
27 "Be off, stranger, for an honored
    guest is here;
    my brother has come for a visit,
    and I need the guest-room."
28 It is hard for a sensible person to
  bear
    scolding about lodging*n* and the
    insults of the moneylender.

Concerning Children *o*

30 He who loves his son will whip
    him often,
    so that he may rejoice at the way
    he turns out.
2 He who disciplines his son will
    profit by him,
    and will boast of him among
    acquaintances.
3 He who teaches his son will make
    his enemies envious,
    and will glory in him among his
    friends.
4 When the father dies he will not
    seem to be dead,
    for he has left behind him one
    like himself,
5 whom in his life he looked upon
    with joy

and at death, without grief.
6 He has left behind him an avenger
    against his enemies,
    and one to repay the kindness of
    his friends.
7 Whoever spoils his son will bind up
    his wounds,
    and will suffer heartache at every
    cry.
8 An unbroken horse turns out
    stubborn,
    and an unchecked son turns out
    headstrong.
9 Pamper a child, and he will terrorize
    you;
    play with him, and he will grieve
    you.
10 Do not laugh with him, or you will
    have sorrow with him,
    and in the end you will gnash
    your teeth.
11 Give him no freedom in his youth,
    and do not ignore his errors.
12 Bow down his neck in his youth, *p*
    and beat his sides while he is
    young,
    or else he will become stubborn and
    disobey you,
    and you will have sorrow of soul
    from him.*q*
13 Discipline your son and make his
    yoke heavy,*r*
    so that you may not be offended
    by his shamelessness.

14 Better off poor, healthy, and fit
    than rich and afflicted in body.
15 Health and fitness are better than
    any gold,
    and a robust body than countless
    riches.
16 There is no wealth better than health
    of body,
    and no gladness above joy of
    heart.
17 Death is better than a life of misery,
    and eternal sleep*s* than chronic
    sickness.

---

m Lat: Gk *reproach from your family*; other ancient
authorities lack this line   *n* Or *scolding from the
household*   *o* This heading is included in the Gk
text.   *p* Other ancient authorities lack this line
and the preceding line   *q* Other ancient
authorities lack this line   *r* Heb: Gk *take pains
with him*   *s* Other ancient authorities lack *eternal
sleep*

CONCERNING FOODS [t]

18 Good things poured out upon a
   mouth that is closed
   are like offerings of food placed
      upon a grave.

19 Of what use to an idol is a sacrifice?
   For it can neither eat nor smell.
   So is the one punished by the Lord;

20 he sees with his eyes and groans
   as a eunuch groans when
      embracing a girl. [u]

21 Do not give yourself over to sorrow,
   and do not distress yourself
      deliberately.

22 A joyful heart is life itself,
   and rejoicing lengthens one's life
      span.

23 Indulge yourself [v] and take comfort,
   and remove sorrow far from you,
   for sorrow has destroyed many,
   and no advantage ever comes
      from it.

24 Jealousy and anger shorten life,
   and anxiety brings on premature
      old age.

25 Those who are cheerful and merry at
      table
   will benefit from their food.

Right Attitude toward Riches

31 Wakefulness over wealth wastes
      away one's flesh,
   and anxiety about it drives away
      sleep.

2 Wakeful anxiety prevents slumber,
   and a severe illness carries off
      sleep. [w]

3 The rich person toils to amass a
      fortune,
   and when he rests he fills himself
      with his dainties.

4 The poor person toils to make a
      meager living,
   and if ever he rests he becomes
      needy.

5 One who loves gold will not be
      justified;
   one who pursues money will be
      led astray [x] by it.

6 Many have come to ruin because of
      gold,
   and their destruction has met
      them face to face.

7 It is a stumbling block to those who
      are avid for it,

and every fool will be taken
   captive by it.

8 Blessed is the rich person who is
      found blameless,
   and who does not go after gold.

9 Who is he, that we may praise him?
   For he has done wonders among
      his people.

10 Who has been tested by it and been
      found perfect?
   Let it be for him a ground for
      boasting.
   Who has had the power to
      transgress and did not
      transgress,
   and to do evil and did not do it?

11 His prosperity will be established, [y]
   and the assembly will proclaim
      his acts of charity.

Table Etiquette

12 Are you seated at the table of the
      great? [z]
   Do not be greedy at it,
   and do not say, "How much food
      there is here!"

13 Remember that a greedy eye is a bad
      thing.
   What has been created more
      greedy than the eye?
   Therefore it sheds tears for any
      reason.

14 Do not reach out your hand for
      everything you see,
   and do not crowd your
      neighbor [a] at the dish.

15 Judge your neighbor's feelings by
      your own,
   and in every matter be thoughtful.

16 Eat what is set before you like a well
      brought-up person, [b]
   and do not chew greedily, or you
      will give offense.

17 Be the first to stop, as befits good
      manners,
   and do not be insatiable, or you
      will give offense.

---

t This heading is included in the Gk text; other
ancient authorities place the heading before
verse 16   u Other ancient authorities add *So is
the person who does right under compulsion*
v Other ancient authorities read *Beguile yourself*
w Other ancient authorities read *sleep carries off a
severe illness*   x Heb Syr: Gk *pursues destruction
will be filled*   y Other ancient authorities add
because of this   z Heb Syr: Gk *at a great table*
a Gk *him*   b Heb: Gk *like a human being*

18 If you are seated among many
        persons,
    do not help yourself[c] before they
        do.
19 How ample a little is for a
        well-disciplined person!
    He does not breathe heavily when
        in bed.
20 Healthy sleep depends on moderate
        eating;
    he rises early, and feels fit.
    The distress of sleeplessness and of
        nausea
    and colic are with the glutton.
21 If you are overstuffed with food,
    get up to vomit, and you will
        have relief.
22 Listen to me, my child, and do not
        disregard me,
    and in the end you will appreciate
        my words.
    In everything you do be moderate,[d]
    and no sickness will overtake you.
23 People bless the one who is liberal
        with food,
    and their testimony to his
        generosity is trustworthy.
24 The city complains of the one who
        is stingy with food,
    and their testimony to his
        stinginess is accurate.

Temperance in Drinking Wine

25 Do not try to prove your strength by
        wine-drinking,
    for wine has destroyed many.
26 As the furnace tests the work of the
        smith,[e]
    so wine tests hearts when the
        insolent quarrel.
27 Wine is very life to human beings
        if taken in moderation.
    What is life to one who is without
        wine?
    It has been created to make
        people happy.
28 Wine drunk at the proper time and
        in moderation
    is rejoicing of heart and gladness
        of soul.
29 Wine drunk to excess leads to
        bitterness of spirit,
    to quarrels and stumbling.
30 Drunkenness increases the anger of a
        fool to his own hurt,
    reducing his strength and adding
        wounds.

31 Do not reprove your neighbor at a
        banquet of wine,
    and do not despise him in his
        merrymaking;
    speak no word of reproach to him,
    and do not distress him by
        making demands of him.

Etiquette at a Banquet

32 If they make you master of the
        feast, do not exalt yourself;
    be among them as one of their
        number.
    Take care of them first and then sit
        down;
2   when you have fulfilled all your
        duties, take your place,
    so that you may be merry along
        with them
    and receive a wreath for your
        excellent leadership.

3 Speak, you who are older, for it is
        your right,
    but with accurate knowledge, and
        do not interrupt the music.
4 Where there is entertainment, do not
        pour out talk;
    do not display your cleverness at
        the wrong time.
5 A ruby seal in a setting of gold
    is a concert of music at a banquet
        of wine.
6 A seal of emerald in a rich setting of
        gold
    is the melody of music with good
        wine.

7 Speak, you who are young, if you
        are obliged to,
    but no more than twice, and only
        if asked.
8 Be brief; say much in few words;
    be as one who knows and can
        still hold his tongue.
9 Among the great do not act as their
        equal;
    and when another is speaking, do
        not babble.

10 Lightning travels ahead of the
        thunder,
    and approval goes before one who
        is modest.

---

[c] Gk reach out your hand   [d] Heb Syr: Gk
industrious   [e] Heb: Gk tests the hardening of steel
by dipping

11 Leave in good time and do not be
the last;
go home quickly and do not
linger.
12 Amuse yourself there to your heart's
content,
but do not sin through proud
speech.
13 But above all bless your Maker,
who fills you with his good gifts.

The Providence of God

14 The one who seeks God *f* will
accept his discipline,
and those who rise early to seek
him *g* will find favor.
15 The one who seeks the law will be
filled with it,
but the hypocrite will stumble at
it.
16 Those who fear the Lord will form
true judgments,
and they will kindle righteous
deeds like a light.
17 The sinner will shun reproof,
and will find a decision according
to his liking.

18 A sensible person will not overlook
a thoughtful suggestion;
an insolent *h* and proud person
will not be deterred by fear. *i*
19 Do nothing without deliberation,
but when you have acted, do not
regret it.
20 Do not go on a path full of hazards,
and do not stumble at an obstacle
twice. *j*
21 Do not be overconfident on a
smooth *k* road,
22 and give good heed to your
paths. *l*
23 Guard *m* yourself in every act,
for this is the keeping of the
commandments.
24 The one who keeps the law preserves
himself, *n*
and the one who trusts the Lord
will not suffer loss.

33 No evil will befall the one who
fears the Lord,
but in trials such a one will be
rescued again and again.
2 The wise will not hate the law,
but the one who is hypocritical
about it is like a boat in a
storm.

3 The sensible person will trust in the
law;
for such a one the law is as
dependable as a divine oracle.

4 Prepare what to say, and then you
will be listened to;
draw upon your training, and give
your answer.
5 The heart of a fool is like a cart
wheel,
and his thoughts like a turning
axle.
6 A mocking friend is like a stallion
that neighs no matter who the
rider is.

Differences in Nature and in Humankind

7 Why is one day more important
than another,
when all the daylight in the year
is from the sun?
8 By the Lord's wisdom they were
distinguished,
and he appointed the different
seasons and festivals.
9 Some days he exalted and hallowed,
and some he made ordinary days.
10 All human beings come from the
ground,
and humankind *o* was created out
of the dust.
11 In the fullness of his knowledge the
Lord distinguished them
and appointed their different
ways.
12 Some he blessed and exalted,
and some he made holy and
brought near to himself;
but some he cursed and brought
low,
and turned them out of their
place.
13 Like clay in the hand of the potter,
to be molded as he pleases,
so all are in the hand of their
Maker,
to be given whatever he decides.

---

f Heb: Gk *who fears the Lord* *g* Other ancient
authorities lack *to seek him* *h* Heb: Gk *alien*
i Meaning of Gk uncertain. Other ancient
authorities add *and after acting, with him, without
deliberation* *j* Heb: Gk *stumble on stony ground*
k Or *an unexplored* *l* Heb Syr: Gk *and beware of
your children* *m* Heb Syr: Gk *Trust* *n* Heb: Gk
who believes the law heeds the commandments
o Heb: Gk *Adam*

14 Good is the opposite of evil,
    and life the opposite of death;
    so the sinner is the opposite of
        the godly.
15 Look at all the works of the Most
        High;
    they come in pairs, one the
        opposite of the other.

16 Now I was the last to keep vigil;
    I was like a gleaner following the
        grape-pickers;
17 by the blessing of the Lord I arrived
        first,
    and like a grape-picker I filled my
        wine press.
18 Consider that I have not labored for
        myself alone,
    but for all who seek instruction.
19 Hear me, you who are great among
        the people,
    and you leaders of the
        congregation, pay heed!

The Advantage of Independence

20 To son or wife, to brother or friend,
    do not give power over yourself,
        as long as you live;
    and do not give your property to
        another,
    in case you change your mind and
        must ask for it.
21 While you are still alive and have
        breath in you,
    do not let anyone take your place.
22 For it is better that your children
        should ask from you
    than that you should look to the
        hand of your children.
23 Excel in all that you do;
    bring no stain upon your honor.
24 At the time when you end the days
        of your life,
    in the hour of death, distribute
        your inheritance.

The Treatment of Slaves

25 Fodder and a stick and burdens for a
        donkey;
    bread and discipline and work for
        a slave.
26 Set your slave to work, and you will
        find rest;
    leave his hands idle, and he will
        seek liberty.
27 Yoke and thong will bow the neck,
    and for a wicked slave there are
        racks and tortures.

28 Put him to work, in order that he
        may not be idle,
29   for idleness teaches much evil.
30 Set him to work, as is fitting for
        him,
    and if he does not obey, make his
        fetters heavy.
    Do not be overbearing toward
        anyone,
    and do nothing unjust.

31 If you have but one slave, treat him
        like yourself,
    because you have bought him
        with blood.
    If you have but one slave, treat him
        like a brother,
    for you will need him as you need
        your life.
32 If you ill-treat him, and he leaves
        you and runs away,
33   which way will you go to seek
        him?

Dreams Mean Nothing

34 The senseless have vain and
    false hopes,
    and dreams give wings to fools.
2 As one who catches at a shadow and
        pursues the wind,
    so is anyone who believes in *p*
        dreams.
3 What is seen in dreams is but a
        reflection,
    the likeness of a face looking at
        itself.
4 From an unclean thing what can be
        clean?
    And from something false what
        can be true?
5 Divinations and omens and dreams
        are unreal,
    and like a woman in labor, the
        mind has fantasies.
6 Unless they are sent by intervention
        from the Most High,
    pay no attention to them.
7 For dreams have deceived many,
    and those who put their hope in
        them have perished.
8 Without such deceptions the law
        will be fulfilled,
    and wisdom is complete in the
        mouth of the faithful.

p Syr: Gk *pays heed to*

Experience as a Teacher

9 An educated[q] person knows many
    things,
   and one with much experience
    knows what he is talking
    about.
10 An inexperienced person knows few
    things,
11   but he that has traveled acquires
    much cleverness.
12 I have seen many things in my
    travels,
   and I understand more than I can
    express.
13 I have often been in danger of
    death,
   but have escaped because of these
    experiences.

Fear the Lord

14 The spirit of those who fear the Lord
    will live,
15   for their hope is in him who saves
    them.
16 Those who fear the Lord will not be
    timid,
   or play the coward, for he is their
    hope.
17 Happy is the soul that fears the
    Lord!
18   To whom does he look? And who
    is his support?
19 The eyes of the Lord are on those
    who love him,
   a mighty shield and strong
    support,
   a shelter from scorching wind and a
    shade from noonday sun,
   a guard against stumbling and a
    help against falling.
20 He lifts up the soul and makes the
    eyes sparkle;
   he gives health and life and
    blessing.

Offering Sacrifices

21 If one sacrifices ill-gotten goods, the
    offering is blemished;[r]
22   the gifts[s] of the lawless are not
    acceptable.
23 The Most High is not pleased with
    the offerings of the ungodly,
   nor for a multitude of sacrifices
    does he forgive sins.
24 Like one who kills a son before his
    father's eyes

is the person who offers a sacrifice
    from the property of the
    poor.
25 The bread of the needy is the life of
    the poor;
   whoever deprives them of it is a
    murderer.
26 To take away a neighbor's living is
    to commit murder;
27   to deprive an employee of wages
    is to shed blood.

28 When one builds and another tears
    down,
   what do they gain but hard work?
29 When one prays and another curses,
   to whose voice will the Lord
    listen?
30 If one washes after touching a
    corpse, and touches it again,
   what has been gained by washing?
31 So if one fasts for his sins,
   and goes again and does the same
    things,
   who will listen to his prayer?
   And what has he gained by
    humbling himself?

The Law and Sacrifices

35 The one who keeps the law
    makes many offerings;
2   one who heeds the
    commandments makes an
    offering of well-being.
3 The one who returns a kindness
    offers choice flour,
4   and one who gives alms sacrifices
    a thank offering.
5 To keep from wickedness is pleasing
    to the Lord,
   and to forsake unrighteousness is
    an atonement.
6 Do not appear before the Lord
    empty-handed,
7   for all that you offer is in
    fulfillment of the
    commandment.
8 The offering of the righteous
    enriches the altar,
   and its pleasing odor rises before
    the Most High.
9 The sacrifice of the righteous is
    acceptable,
   and it will never be forgotten.

---

q Other ancient authorities read *A traveled*
r Other ancient authorities read *is made in mockery*
s Other ancient authorities read *mockeries*

10 Be generous when you worship the
     Lord,
     and do not stint the first fruits of
          your hands.
11 With every gift show a cheerful face,
     and dedicate your tithe with
          gladness.
12 Give to the Most High as he has
          given to you,
     and as generously as you can
          afford.
13 For the Lord is the one who repays,
     and he will repay you sevenfold.

Divine Justice

14 Do not offer him a bribe, for he will
          not accept it;
15 and do not rely on a dishonest
          sacrifice;
     for the Lord is the judge,
     and with him there is no
          partiality.
16 He will not show partiality to the
          poor;
     but he will listen to the prayer of
          one who is wronged.
17 He will not ignore the supplication
          of the orphan,
     or the widow when she pours out
          her complaint.
18 Do not the tears of the widow run
          down her cheek
19 as she cries out against the one
          who causes them to fall?
20 The one whose service is pleasing to
          the Lord will be accepted,
     and his prayer will reach to the
          clouds.
21 The prayer of the humble pierces the
          clouds,
     and it will not rest until it reaches
          its goal;
     it will not desist until the Most High
          responds
22 and does justice for the righteous,
     and executes judgment.
     Indeed, the Lord will not delay,
     and like a warrior*t* will not be
          patient
     until he crushes the loins of the
          unmerciful
23 and repays vengeance on the
          nations;
     until he destroys the multitude of
          the insolent,
     and breaks the scepters of the
          unrighteous;

24 until he repays mortals according to
          their deeds,
     and the works of all according to
          their thoughts;
25 until he judges the case of his
          people
     and makes them rejoice in his
          mercy.
26 His mercy is as welcome in time of
          distress
     as clouds of rain in time of
          drought.

A Prayer for God's People

36 Have mercy upon us, O God*u*
          of all,
2   and put all the nations in fear of
          you.
3 Lift up your hand against foreign
          nations
     and let them see your might.
4 As you have used us to show your
          holiness to them,
     so use them to show your glory to
          us.
5 Then they will know,*v* as we have
          known,
     that there is no God but you,
          O Lord.
6 Give new signs, and work other
          wonders;
7   make your hand and right arm
          glorious.
8 Rouse your anger and pour out your
          wrath;
9   destroy the adversary and wipe
          out the enemy.
10 Hasten the day, and remember the
          appointed time,*w*
     and let people recount your
          mighty deeds.
11 Let survivors be consumed in the
          fiery wrath,
     and may those who harm your
          people meet destruction.
12 Crush the heads of hostile rulers
     who say, "There is no one but
          ourselves."
13 Gather all the tribes of Jacob,*x*
16   and give them their inheritance, as
          at the beginning.

*t Heb: Gk and with them   u Heb: Gk O Master,
the God   v Heb: Gk And let them know you
w Other ancient authorities read remember your
oath   x Owing to a dislocation in the Greek Mss
of Sirach, the verse numbers 14 and 15 are not
used in chapter 36, though no text is missing.*

17 Have mercy, O Lord, on the people
    called by your name,
  on Israel, whom you have
    named *y* your firstborn,
18 Have pity on the city of your
    sanctuary, *z*
  Jerusalem, the place of your
    dwelling. *a*
19 Fill Zion with your majesty, *b*
  and your temple *c* with your
    glory.
20 Bear witness to those whom you
    created in the beginning,
  and fulfill the prophecies spoken
    in your name.
21 Reward those who wait for you
  and let your prophets be found
    trustworthy.
22 Hear, O Lord, the prayer of your
    servants, according to your
    goodwill toward *d* your
    people,
  and all who are on the earth will
    know
    that you are the Lord, the God of
    the ages.

Concerning Discrimination

23 The stomach will take any food,
  yet one food is better than
    another.
24 As the palate tastes the kinds of
    game,
  so an intelligent mind detects false
    words.
25 A perverse mind will cause grief,
  but a person with experience will
    pay him back.
26 A woman will accept any man as a
    husband,
  but one girl is preferable to
    another.
27 A woman's beauty lights up a man's
    face,
  and there is nothing he desires
    more.
28 If kindness and humility mark her
    speech,
  her husband is more fortunate
    than other men.
29 He who acquires a wife gets his best
    possession, *e*
  a helper fit for him and a pillar of
    support. *f*
30 Where there is no fence, the
    property will be plundered;

and where there is no wife, a man
  will become a fugitive and a
  wanderer. *g*
31 For who will trust a nimble robber
  that skips from city to city?
  So who will trust a man that has no
    nest,
  but lodges wherever night
    overtakes him?

False Friends

37 Every friend says, "I too am a
    friend";
  but some friends are friends only
    in name.
2 Is it not a sorrow like that for death
    itself
  when a dear friend turns into an
    enemy?
3 O inclination to evil, why were you
    formed
  to cover the land with deceit?
4 Some companions rejoice in the
    happiness of a friend,
  but in time of trouble they are
    against him.
5 Some companions help a friend for
    their stomachs' sake,
  yet in battle they will carry his
    shield.
6 Do not forget a friend during the
    battle, *h*
  and do not be unmindful of him
    when you distribute your
    spoils. *i*

Caution in Taking Advice

7 All counselors praise the counsel
    they give,
  but some give counsel in their
    own interest.
8 Be wary of a counselor,
  and learn first what is his interest,
  for he will take thought for
    himself.
  He may cast the lot against you
9   and tell you, "Your way is good,"
  and then stand aside to see what
    happens to you.

y Other ancient authorities read *you have likened to*
z Or *on your holy city*   *a* Heb: Gk *your rest*
b Heb Syr: Gk *the celebration of your wondrous deeds*
c Heb Syr: Gk Lat *people*   *d* Heb and two Gk
witnesses: Lat and most Gk witnesses read
according to the blessing of Aaron for   *e* Heb: Gk
enters upon a possession   *f* Heb: Gk *rest*
g Heb: Gk *wander about and sigh*   *h* Heb: Gk *in
your heart*   *i* Heb: Gk *him in your wealth*

¹⁰ Do not consult the one who regards
  you with suspicion;
 hide your intentions from those
  who are jealous of you.
¹¹ Do not consult with a woman about
  her rival
 or with a coward about war,
with a merchant about business
 or with a buyer about selling,
with a miser about generosity *j*
 or with the merciless about
  kindness,
with an idler about any work
 or with a seasonal laborer about
  completing his work,
with a lazy servant about a big
  task—
 pay no attention to any advice
  they give.

¹² But associate with a godly person
  whom you know to be a keeper of
  the commandments,
 who is like-minded with yourself,
  and who will grieve with you if
  you fail.
¹³ And heed*k* the counsel of your own
  heart,
 for no one is more faithful to you
  than it is.
¹⁴ For our own mind sometimes keeps
  us better informed
 than seven sentinels sitting high
  on a watchtower.
¹⁵ But above all pray to the Most High
  that he may direct your way in
  truth.

j Heb: Gk *gratitude* *k* Heb: Gk *establish*

THE TRADITION

Spiritual Direction

All counselors praise the counsel they give,
but some give counsel in their own interest.
SIRACH 37.7

"**D**o you seriously wish to travel the road to devotion?" asks Saint Francis de Sales in his *Introduction to the Devout Life*. If so, then find a faithful friend who gives good spiritual counsel. "This is the most important of all words of advice."

How many would-be disciples of Christ have lost their way to him because they followed their own misguided lights? How many more have given up any attempt at holiness because they grew discouraged and confused? How many have suffered the painful consequences of incompetent spiritual guides?

Saint Teresa of Avila, who appreciated some spiritual directors but suffered at the hands of others, always stressed the benefits of these holy friendships as aids to prayer—provided the guide was wise, prudent, and virtuous. She and the author of Sirach would have agreed about what type of person to

avoid: the naïve and inexperienced, the self-interested, the unmerciful, the irreligious. "Choose carefully!" they would advise us.

Catholics looking for spiritual direction usually begin by seeking out a priest or a lay person with formal training in the area. But the Holy Spirit gives the necessary gifts to other people too (see I Corinthians 12.4–11). Sometimes God leads one person to another, as with Saul and Ananias (Acts 9.10–19).

What do we do until the right guide turns up? Sirach has some words of advice here, too. Listen to your conscience, and "above all pray to the Most High that he may direct your way in truth" (37.13, 15). Especially, we might add, get to know the best Counselor of all, the Holy Spirit.

And of course, when you do find that wise and prudent friend, don't hesitate. "Rise early to visit him," Sirach urges, "let your foot wear out his doorstep" (6.36).

True and False Wisdom

16 Discussion is the beginning of every
      work,
   and counsel precedes every
      undertaking.
17 The mind is the root of all conduct;
18   it sprouts four branches,[l]
   good and evil, life and death;
   and it is the tongue that
      continually rules them.
19 Some people may be clever enough
      to teach many,
   and yet be useless to themselves.
20 A skillful speaker may be hated;
   he will be destitute of all food,
21 for the Lord has withheld the gift of
      charm,
   since he is lacking in all wisdom.
22 If a person is wise to his own
      advantage,
   the fruits of his good sense will be
      praiseworthy.[m]
23 A wise person instructs his own
      people,
   and the fruits of his good sense
      will endure.
24 A wise person will have praise
      heaped upon him,
   and all who see him will call him
      happy.
25 The days of a person's life are
      numbered,
   but the days of Israel are without
      number.
26 One who is wise among his people
      will inherit honor,[n]
   and his name will live forever.

Concerning Moderation

27 My child, test yourself while you
      live;
   see what is bad for you and do
      not give in to it.
28 For not everything is good for
      everyone,
   and no one enjoys everything.
29 Do not be greedy for every delicacy,
   and do not eat without restraint;
30 for overeating brings sickness,
   and gluttony leads to nausea.
31 Many have died of gluttony,
   but the one who guards against it
      prolongs his life.

Concerning Physicians and Health

38 Honor physicians for their
      services,

for the Lord created them;
2 for their gift of healing comes from
      the Most High,
   and they are rewarded by the
      king.
3 The skill of physicians makes them
      distinguished,
   and in the presence of the great
      they are admired.
4 The Lord created medicines out of
      the earth,
   and the sensible will not despise
      them.
5 Was not water made sweet with a
      tree
   in order that its[o] power might be
      known?
6 And he gave skill to human beings
   that he[p] might be glorified in his
      marvelous works.
7 By them the physician[q] heals and
      takes away pain;
8   the pharmacist makes a mixture
      from them.
   God's[r] works will never be
      finished;
   and from him health[s] spreads
      over all the earth.

9 My child, when you are ill, do not
      delay,
   but pray to the Lord, and he will
      heal you.
10 Give up your faults and direct your
      hands rightly,
   and cleanse your heart from all
      sin.
11 Offer a sweet-smelling sacrifice, and
      a memorial portion of choice
      flour,
   and pour oil on your offering, as
      much as you can afford.[t]
12 Then give the physician his place,
      for the Lord created him;
   do not let him leave you, for you
      need him.
13 There may come a time when
      recovery lies in the hands of
      physicians,[u]
14   for they too pray to the Lord

---

[l] Heb: Gk As a clue to changes of heart four kinds of
destiny appear   [m] Other ancient witnesses read
trustworthy   [n] Other ancient authorities read
confidence   [o] Or his   [p] Or they   [q] Heb: Gk he
[r] Gk His   [s] Or peace   [t] Heb: Lat lacks as much
as you can afford; Meaning of Gk uncertain
[u] Gk in their hands

that he grant them success in
   diagnosis[v]
and in healing, for the sake of
   preserving life.
15 He who sins against his Maker,
   will be defiant toward the
   physician.[w]

On Mourning for the Dead

16 My child, let your tears fall for the
   dead,
   and as one in great pain begin the
      lament.
   Lay out the body with due
      ceremony,
   and do not neglect the burial.
17 Let your weeping be bitter and your
   wailing fervent;
   make your mourning worthy of
      the departed,
   for one day, or two, to avoid
      criticism;
   then be comforted for your grief.
18 For grief may result in death,
   and a sorrowful heart saps one's
      strength.

19 When a person is taken away,
   sorrow is over;
   but the life of the poor weighs
      down the heart.
20 Do not give your heart to grief;
   drive it away, and remember your
      own end.
21 Do not forget, there is no coming
      back;
   you do the dead[x] no good, and
      you injure yourself.
22 Remember his[y] fate, for yours is
      like it;
   yesterday it was his,[z] and today it
      is yours.
23 When the dead is at rest, let his
   remembrance rest too,
   and be comforted for him when
      his spirit has departed.

Trades and Crafts

24 The wisdom of the scribe depends
   on the opportunity of leisure;

v Heb: Gk *rest*　　w Heb: Gk *may he fall into the
hands of the physician*　　x Gk *him*　　y Heb: Gk *my*
z Heb: Gk *mine*

Healing

As in all things in life, God expects us to do our part when it comes to our health. He wants us to take good care of ourselves at all times, which means seeking proper medical care when we fall ill. Also, he wants us to heed the warnings of clergy of all religions to beware of charlatans who masquerade as "healers" and prey on the ill and the weak in order to enrich themselves. Such con artists, motivated not by love of God and a desire to help others, but by greed and selfishness, should be shunned.

When we are ill, of course we should pray. But we must always keep in mind that prayer isn't a magic formula for good health. Sometimes, no matter how sincerely we pray, how diligently we cooperate with physicians, however good and kind and blameless we are, recovery does not happen. At such times we must walk in faith, with prayer itself as a blessing, a way of bringing peace to ourselves and those around us. God's reasons may not be immediately apparent, but we can always be sure that he knows what he's doing—and will never abandon us.

—*JOAN WESTER ANDERSON*

FRIDAY

Scripture Reading
for Today:
Sirach 38.1–15

Verses for Today:
Sirach 38.9, 12

Go to page 924 for your next devotional reading.

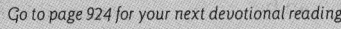

only the one who has little
  business can become wise.
25 How can one become wise who
  handles the plow,
    and who glories in the shaft of a
    goad,
  who drives oxen and is occupied
  with their work,
    and whose talk is about bulls?
26 He sets his heart on plowing
  furrows,
    and he is careful about fodder for
    the heifers.
27 So it is with every artisan and master
  artisan
    who labors by night as well as by
    day;
  those who cut the signets of seals,
    each is diligent in making a great
    variety;
  they set their heart on painting a
    lifelike image,
    and they are careful to finish their
    work.
28 So it is with the smith, sitting by the
  anvil,
    intent on his iron-work;
  the breath of the fire melts his flesh,
    and he struggles with the heat of
    the furnace;
  the sound of the hammer deafens
    his ears,[a]
    and his eyes are on the pattern of
    the object.
  He sets his heart on finishing his
    handiwork,
    and he is careful to complete its
    decoration.
29 So it is with the potter sitting at his
  work
    and turning the wheel with his
    feet;
  he is always deeply concerned over
    his products,
    and he produces them in quantity.
30 He molds the clay with his arm
    and makes it pliable with his feet;
  he sets his heart to finish the
    glazing,
    and he takes care in firing[b] the
    kiln.

31 All these rely on their hands,
    and all are skillful in their own
    work.
32 Without them no city can be
  inhabited,

and wherever they live, they will
  not go hungry.[c]
Yet they are not sought out for the
  council of the people,[d]
33   nor do they attain eminence in
    the public assembly.
They do not sit in the judge's seat,
  nor do they understand the
    decisions of the courts;
they cannot expound discipline or
  judgment,
    and they are not found among the
    rulers.[e]
34 But they maintain the fabric of the
  world,
    and their concern is for[f] the
    exercise of their trade.

The Activity of the Scribe

How different the one who devotes
  himself
to the study of the law of the
  Most High!

39 He seeks out the wisdom of all
  the ancients,
    and is concerned with prophecies;
2   he preserves the sayings of the
    famous
    and penetrates the subtleties of
    parables;
3   he seeks out the hidden meanings of
    proverbs
    and is at home with the
    obscurities of parables.
4 He serves among the great
    and appears before rulers;
  he travels in foreign lands
    and learns what is good and evil
    in the human lot.
5 He sets his heart to rise early
    to seek the Lord who made him,
    and to petition the Most High;
  he opens his mouth in prayer
    and asks pardon for his sins.

6 If the great Lord is willing,
    he will be filled with the spirit of
    understanding;
  he will pour forth words of wisdom
    of his own
    and give thanks to the Lord in
    prayer.

---

[a] Cn: Gk *renews his ear*   [b] Cn: Gk *cleaning*
[c] Syr: Gk *and people can neither live nor walk there*
[d] Most ancient authorities lack this line   [e] Cn:
Gk *among parables*   [f] Syr: Gk *prayer is in*

7 The Lord g will direct his counsel
    and knowledge,
    as he meditates on his mysteries.
8 He will show the wisdom of what
    he has learned,
    and will glory in the law of the
    Lord's covenant.
9 Many will praise his understanding;
    it will never be blotted out.
    His memory will not disappear,
    and his name will live through all
    generations.
10 Nations will speak of his wisdom,
    and the congregation will
    proclaim his praise.
11 If he lives long, he will leave a name
    greater than a thousand,
    and if he goes to rest, it is
    enough h for him.

A Hymn of Praise to God

12 I have more on my mind to express;
    I am full like the full moon.
13 Listen to me, my faithful children,
    and blossom
    like a rose growing by a stream of
    water.
14 Send out fragrance like incense,
    and put forth blossoms like a lily.
    Scatter the fragrance, and sing a
    hymn of praise;
    bless the Lord for all his works.
15 Ascribe majesty to his name
    and give thanks to him with
    praise,
    with songs on your lips, and with
    harps;
    this is what you shall say in
    thanksgiving:

16 "All the works of the Lord are very
    good,
    and whatever he commands will
    be done at the appointed
    time.
17 No one can say, 'What is this?' or
    'Why is that?'—
    for at the appointed time all such
    questions will be answered.
    At his word the waters stood in a
    heap,
    and the reservoirs of water at the
    word of his mouth.
18 When he commands, his every
    purpose is fulfilled,
    and none can limit his saving
    power.
19 The works of all are before him,

and nothing can be hidden from
    his eyes.
20 From the beginning to the end of
    time he can see everything,
    and nothing is too marvelous for
    him.
21 No one can say, 'What is this?' or
    'Why is that?'—
    for everything has been created for
    its own purpose.

22 "His blessing covers the dry land
    like a river,
    and drenches it like a flood.
23 But his wrath drives out the nations,
    as when he turned a watered land
    into salt.
24 To the faithful his ways are straight,
    but full of pitfalls for the wicked.
25 From the beginning good things
    were created for the good,
    but for sinners good things and
    bad. i
26 The basic necessities of human life
    are water and fire and iron and
    salt
    and wheat flour and milk and
    honey,
    the blood of the grape and oil
    and clothing.
27 All these are good for the godly,
    but for sinners they turn into
    evils.

28 "There are winds created for
    vengeance,
    and in their anger they can
    dislodge mountains; j
    on the day of reckoning they will
    pour out their strength
    and calm the anger of their
    Maker.
29 Fire and hail and famine and
    pestilence,
    all these have been created for
    vengeance;
30 the fangs of wild animals and
    scorpions and vipers,
    and the sword that punishes the
    ungodly with destruction.
31 They take delight in doing his
    bidding,
    always ready for his service on
    earth;

g Gk *He himself*   h Cn: Meaning of Gk uncertain
i Heb Lat: Gk *sinners bad things*   j Heb Syr: Gk
can scourge mightily

and when their time comes they
　　never disobey his command."

32 So from the beginning I have been
　　convinced of all this
　　and have thought it out and left it
　　in writing:
33 All the works of the Lord are good,
　　and he will supply every need in
　　its time.
34 No one can say, "This is not as
　　good as that,"
　　for everything proves good in its
　　appointed time.
35 So now sing praise with all your
　　heart and voice,
　　and bless the name of the Lord.

Human Wretchedness

40 Hard work was created for
　　everyone,
　　and a heavy yoke is laid on the
　　children of Adam,
　　from the day they come forth from
　　their mother's womb
　　until the day they return to[k] the
　　mother of all the living.[l]
2 Perplexities and fear of heart are
　　theirs,
　　and anxious thought of the day of
　　their death.
3 From the one who sits on a
　　splendid throne
　　to the one who grovels in dust
　　and ashes,
4 from the one who wears purple and
　　a crown
　　to the one who is clothed in
　　burlap,
5 there is anger and envy and trouble
　　and unrest,
　　and fear of death, and fury and
　　strife.
　And when one rests upon his bed,
　　his sleep at night confuses his
　　mind.
6 He gets little or no rest;
　　he struggles in his sleep as he did
　　by day.[m]
　He is troubled by the visions of his
　　mind
　　like one who has escaped from
　　the battlefield.
7 At the moment he reaches safety he
　　wakes up,
　　astonished that his fears were
　　groundless.
8 To all creatures, human and animal,

but to sinners seven times more,
9 come death and bloodshed and
　　strife and sword,
　　calamities and famine and ruin
　　and plague.
10 All these were created for the
　　wicked,
　　and on their account the flood
　　came.
11 All that is of earth returns to earth,
　　and what is from above returns
　　above.[n]

Injustice Will Not Prosper

12 All bribery and injustice will be
　　blotted out,
　　but good faith will last forever.
13 The wealth of the unjust will dry up
　　like a river,
　　and crash like a loud clap of
　　thunder in a storm.
14 As a generous person has cause to
　　rejoice,
　　so lawbreakers will utterly fail.
15 The children of the ungodly put out
　　few branches;
　　they are unhealthy roots on sheer
　　rock.
16 The reeds by any water or river bank
　　are plucked up before any grass;
17 but kindness is like a garden of
　　blessings,
　　and almsgiving endures forever.

The Joys of Life

18 Wealth and wages make life sweet,[o]
　　but better than either is finding a
　　treasure.
19 Children and the building of a city
　　establish one's name,
　　but better than either is the one
　　who finds wisdom.
　Cattle and orchards make one
　　prosperous;[p]
　　but a blameless wife is accounted
　　better than either.
20 Wine and music gladden the heart,
　　but the love of friends[q] is better
　　than either.
21 The flute and the harp make sweet
　　melody,

---

k Other Gk and Lat authorities read *are buried in*
l Heb: Gk *of all*　　m Arm: Meaning of Gk
uncertain　　n Heb Syr: Gk Lat *from the waters
returns to the sea*　　o Heb: Gk *Life is sweet for the
self-reliant worker*　　p Heb Syr: Gk lacks *but better
. . . prosperous*　　q Heb: Gk *wisdom*

but a pleasant voice is better than
either.
22 The eye desires grace and beauty,
but the green shoots of grain
more than either.
23 A friend or companion is always
welcome,
but a sensible wife[r] is better than
either.
24 Kindred and helpers are for a time
of trouble,
but almsgiving rescues better than
either.
25 Gold and silver make one stand
firm,
but good counsel is esteemed
more than either.
26 Riches and strength build up
confidence,
but the fear of the Lord is better
than either.
There is no want in the fear of the
Lord,
and with it there is no need to
seek for help.
27 The fear of the Lord is like a garden
of blessing,
and covers a person better than
any glory.

The Disgrace of Begging

28 My child, do not lead the life of a
beggar;
it is better to die than to beg.
29 When one looks to the table of
another,
one's way of life cannot be
considered a life.
One loses self-respect with another
person's food,
but one who is intelligent and
well instructed guards against
that.
30 In the mouth of the shameless
begging is sweet,
but it kindles a fire inside him.

Concerning Death

41

O death, how bitter is the
thought of you
to the one at peace among
possessions,
who has nothing to worry about
and is prosperous in
everything,
and still is vigorous enough to
enjoy food!

2 O death, how welcome is your
sentence
to one who is needy and failing in
strength,
worn down by age and anxious
about everything;
to one who is contrary, and has
lost all patience!
3 Do not fear death's decree for you;
remember those who went before
you and those who will come
after.
4 This is the Lord's decree for all flesh;
why then should you reject the
will of the Most High?
Whether life lasts for ten years or a
hundred or a thousand,
there are no questions asked in
Hades.

The Fate of the Wicked

5 The children of sinners are
abominable children,
and they frequent the haunts of
the ungodly.
6 The inheritance of the children of
sinners will perish,
and on their offspring will be a
perpetual disgrace.
7 Children will blame an ungodly
father,
for they suffer disgrace because of
him.
8 Woe to you, the ungodly,
who have forsaken the law of the
Most High God!
9 If you have children, calamity will
be theirs;
you will beget them only for
groaning.
When you stumble, there is lasting
joy;[s]
and when you die, a curse is your
lot.
10 Whatever comes from earth returns
to earth;
so the ungodly go from curse to
destruction.

11 The human body is a fleeting thing,
but a virtuous name will never be
blotted out.[t]

r Heb Compare Syr: Gk *wife with her husband*
s Heb: Meaning of Gk uncertain   t Heb: Gk
*People grieve over the death of the body, but the bad
name of sinners will be blotted out*

12 Have regard for your name, since it
　　will outlive you
　longer than a thousand hoards of
　　gold.
13 The days of a good life are
　　numbered,
　but a good name lasts forever.

14 My children, be true to your training
　　and be at peace;
　hidden wisdom and unseen
　　treasure—
　of what value is either?

A Series of Contrasts

15 Better are those who hide their folly
　　than those who hide their
　　wisdom.
16 Therefore show respect for my
　　words;
　for it is not good to feel shame in
　　every circumstance,
　nor is every kind of abashment to
　　be approved.u

17 Be ashamed of sexual immorality,
　　before your father or mother;
　and of a lie, before a prince or a
　　ruler;
18 of a crime, before a judge or
　　magistrate;
　and of a breach of the law, before
　　the congregation and the
　　people;
　of unjust dealing, before your
　　partner or your friend;
19 　and of theft, in the place where
　　you live.
　Be ashamed of breaking an oath or
　　agreement,v
　and of leaning on your elbow at
　　meals;
　of surliness in receiving or giving,
20 　and of silence, before those who
　　greet you;
　of looking at a prostitute,
21 　and of rejecting the appeal of a
　　relative;
　of taking away someone's portion or
　　gift,
　and of gazing at another man's
　　wife;
22 of meddling with his servant-girl—
　　and do not approach her bed;
　of abusive words, before friends—
　　and do not be insulting after
　　making a gift.

42 Be ashamed of repeating what
　　you hear,
　and of betraying secrets.
　Then you will show proper shame,
　　and will find favor with everyone.

Of the following things do not be
　　ashamed,
　and do not sin to save face:
2 Do not be ashamed of the law of
　　the Most High and his
　　covenant,
　and of rendering judgment to
　　acquit the ungodly;
3 of keeping accounts with a partner
　　or with traveling companions,
　and of dividing the inheritance of
　　friends;
4 of accuracy with scales and weights,
　　and of acquiring much or little;
5 of profit from dealing with
　　merchants,
　and of frequent disciplining of
　　children,
　and of drawing blood from the
　　back of a wicked slave.
6 Where there is an untrustworthy
　　wife, a seal is a good thing;
　and where there are many hands,
　　lock things up.
7 When you make a deposit, be sure it
　　is counted and weighed,
　and when you give or receive, put
　　it all in writing.
8 Do not be ashamed to correct the
　　stupid or foolish
　or the aged who are guilty of
　　sexual immorality.
　Then you will show your sound
　　training,
　and will be approved by all.

Daughters and Fathers

9 A daughter is a secret anxiety to her
　　father,
　and worry over her robs him of
　　sleep;
　when she is young, for fear she may
　　not marry,
　or if married, for fear she may be
　　disliked;
10 while a virgin, for fear she may be
　　seduced

u Heb: Gk and not everything is confidently esteemed
by everyone　　v Heb: Gk before the truth of God and
the covenant

and become pregnant in her
father's house;
or having a husband, for fear she
may go astray,
or, though married, for fear she
may be barren.

11 Keep strict watch over a headstrong
daughter,
or she may make you a
laughingstock to your
enemies,
a byword in the city and the
assembly of[w] the people,
and put you to shame in public
gatherings.[x]
See that there is no lattice in her
room,
no spot that overlooks the
approaches to the house.[y]

12 Do not let her parade her beauty
before any man,
or spend her time among married
women;[w]

13 for from garments comes the moth,
and from a woman comes
woman's wickedness.

14 Better is the wickedness of a man
than a woman who does
good;
it is woman who brings shame
and disgrace.

The Works of God in Nature

15 I will now call to mind the works of
the Lord,
and will declare what I have seen.
By the word of the Lord his works
are made;
and all his creatures do his will.[z]

16 The sun looks down on everything
with its light,
and the work of the Lord is full of
his glory.

17 The Lord has not empowered even
his holy ones
to recount all his marvelous
works,
which the Lord the Almighty has
established
so that the universe may stand
firm in his glory.

18 He searches out the abyss and the
human heart;
he understands their innermost
secrets.
For the Most High knows all that
may be known;

he sees from of old the things that
are to come.[a]

19 He discloses what has been and
what is to be,
and he reveals the traces of
hidden things.

20 No thought escapes him,
and nothing is hidden from him.

21 He has set in order the splendors of
his wisdom;
he is from all eternity one and the
same.
Nothing can be added or taken
away,
and he needs no one to be his
counselor.

22 How desirable are all his works,
and how sparkling they are to
see![b]

23 All these things live and remain
forever;
each creature is preserved to meet
a particular need.[c]

24 All things come in pairs, one
opposite the other,
and he has made nothing
incomplete.

25 Each supplements the virtues of the
other.
Who could ever tire of seeing his
glory?

The Splendor of the Sun

43 The pride of the higher realms is
the clear vault of the sky,
as glorious to behold as the sight
of the heavens.

2 The sun, when it appears, proclaims
as it rises
what a marvelous instrument it is,
the work of the Most High.

3 At noon it parches the land,
and who can withstand its
burning heat?

4 A man tending[d] a furnace works in
burning heat,
but three times as hot is the sun
scorching the mountains;
it breathes out fiery vapors,
and its bright rays blind the eyes.

5 Great is the Lord who made it;

w Heb: Meaning of Gk uncertain   x Heb: Gk to
shame before the great multitude   y Heb: Gk lacks
See . . . house   z Syr Compare Heb: most Gk
witnesses lack and all . . . will   a Heb: Gk he sees
the sign(s) of the age   b Meaning of Gk uncertain
c Heb: Gk forever for every need, and all are obedient
d Other ancient authorities read blowing upon

at his orders it hurries on its
course.

The Splendor of the Moon

6 It is the moon that marks the
changing seasons,[e]
governing the times, their
everlasting sign.
7 From the moon comes the sign for
festal days,
a light that wanes when it
completes its course.
8 The new moon, as its name suggests,
renews itself;[f]
how marvelous it is in this
change,
a beacon to the hosts on high,
shining in the vault of the
heavens!

The Glory of the Stars and the Rainbow

9 The glory of the stars is the beauty
of heaven,
a glittering array in the heights of
the Lord.
10 On the orders of the Holy One they
stand in their appointed
places;
they never relax in their watches.
11 Look at the rainbow, and praise him
who made it;
it is exceedingly beautiful in its
brightness.
12 It encircles the sky with its glorious
arc;
the hands of the Most High have
stretched it out.

The Marvels of Nature

13 By his command he sends the
driving snow
and speeds the lightnings of his
judgment.
14 Therefore the storehouses are
opened,
and the clouds fly out like birds.
15 In his majesty he gives the clouds
their strength,
and the hailstones are broken in
pieces.
17a The voice of his thunder rebukes
the earth;
16 when he appears, the mountains
shake.
At his will the south wind blows;
17b so do the storm from the north
and the whirlwind.

He scatters the snow like birds flying
down,
and its descent is like locusts
alighting.
18 The eye is dazzled by the beauty of
its whiteness,
and the mind is amazed as it falls.
19 He pours frost over the earth like
salt,
and icicles form like pointed
thorns.
20 The cold north wind blows,
and ice freezes on the water;
it settles on every pool of water,
and the water puts it on like a
breastplate.
21 He consumes the mountains and
burns up the wilderness,
and withers the tender grass like
fire.
22 A mist quickly heals all things;
the falling dew gives refreshment
from the heat.

23 By his plan he stilled the deep
and planted islands in it.
24 Those who sail the sea tell of its
dangers,
and we marvel at what we hear.
25 In it are strange and marvelous
creatures,
all kinds of living things, and
huge sea-monsters.
26 Because of him each of his
messengers succeeds,
and by his word all things hold
together.

27 We could say more but could never
say enough;
let the final word be: "He is the
all."
28 Where can we find the strength to
praise him?
For he is greater than all his
works.
29 Awesome is the Lord and very great,
and marvelous is his power.
30 Glorify the Lord and exalt him as
much as you can,
for he surpasses even that.
When you exalt him, summon all
your strength,
and do not grow weary, for you
cannot praise him enough.

e Heb: Meaning of Gk uncertain   f Heb: Gk The
month is named after the moon

31 Who has seen him and can describe
      him?
   Or who can extol him as he
      is?
32 Many things greater than these lie
      hidden,
   for I *g* have seen but few of his
      works.
33 For the Lord has made all things,
   and to the godly he has given
      wisdom.

HYMN IN HONOR OF OUR ANCESTORS *h*

44

Let us now sing the praises of
   famous men,
   our ancestors in their generations.
2 The Lord apportioned to them*i*
   great glory,
   his majesty from the beginning.
3 There were those who ruled in their
   kingdoms,

and made a name for themselves
   by their valor;
those who gave counsel because they
   were intelligent;
those who spoke in prophetic
   oracles;
4 those who led the people by their
   counsels
   and by their knowledge of the
      people's lore;
   they were wise in their words of
      instruction;
5 those who composed musical tunes,
   or put verses in writing;
6 rich men endowed with resources,
   living peacefully in their homes—
7 all these were honored in their
      generations,
   and were the pride of their times.

g Heb: Gk *we*   *h* This title is included in the Gk
text.   *i* Heb: Gk *created*

THE TRADITION

The Saints

Let us now sing the praises of famous men, our ancestors.
SIRACH 44.1

And famous women. And sometimes famous children.

Chapters 44 to 50 of the book of Sirach are a walk through a hall of fame featuring 12 types of heroes from Israel's history. The lineup has its limitations—the absence of women, for example. Still, it is an admirable presentation of role models chosen to inspire Sirach's first readers, who lived at a time when pagan Greek culture was luring many Jews away from their ancestral beliefs.

Likewise, the letter to the Hebrews presents the faith of the Old Testament saints in a long litany (chapter 11). The example of this great "cloud of witnesses" (12.1) was invoked to strengthen Jewish Christians who were being pressured to abandon faith in Jesus.

Looking at the saints—those who have died in union with Christ, and especially those whose heroic virtue the Church has officially recognized—should have the same

tonic effect on us. Examples who draw us "to the Father through Christ," as Vatican II explained (*Dogmatic Constitution on the Church*, 49–51), the saints in all their diversity represent countless inspired, concrete approaches to the question "WWJD?" As we ask, "What would Jesus do?" in our place, we find direction by considering what his servants have done in similar seasons and circumstances of life.

Even better, because these servants live on in the same body of Christ as we do, they relate to us in a brotherly and sisterly way. The saints understand our struggles. Because they are intimately connected to God, intercession is their special role of service; they stand ready to intercede for our needs and the needs of the entire world.

So let us praise these godly men and women and imitate them. And by all means, let us get to know them.

8 Some of them have left behind a
   name,
   so that others declare their praise.
9 But of others there is no memory;
   they have perished as though they
     had never existed;
   they have become as though they
     had never been born,
   they and their children after them.
10 But these also were godly men,
   whose righteous deeds have not
     been forgotten;
11 their wealth will remain with their
     descendants,
   and their inheritance with their
     children's children.[j]
12 Their descendants stand by the
     covenants;
   their children also, for their sake.
13 Their offspring will continue forever,
   and their glory will never be
     blotted out.
14 Their bodies are buried in peace,
   but their name lives on generation
     after generation.
15 The assembly declares[k] their
     wisdom,
   and the congregation proclaims
     their praise.

Enoch

16 Enoch pleased the Lord and was
     taken up,
   an example of repentance to all
     generations.

Noah

17 Noah was found perfect and
     righteous;
   in the time of wrath he kept the
     race alive;[l]
   therefore a remnant was left on the
     earth
   when the flood came.
18 Everlasting covenants were made
     with him
   that all flesh should never again
     be blotted out by a flood.

Abraham

19 Abraham was the great father of a
     multitude of nations,
   and no one has been found like
     him in glory.
20 He kept the law of the Most High,
   and entered into a covenant with
     him;
   he certified the covenant in his flesh,

and when he was tested he proved
   faithful.
21 Therefore the Lord[m] assured him
     with an oath
   that the nations would be blessed
     through his offspring;
   that he would make him as
     numerous as the dust of the
     earth,
   and exalt his offspring like the
     stars,
   and give them an inheritance from
     sea to sea
   and from the Euphrates[n] to the
     ends of the earth.

Isaac and Jacob

22 To Isaac also he gave the same
     assurance
   for the sake of his father
     Abraham.
   The blessing of all people and the
     covenant
23 he made to rest on the head of
     Jacob;
   he acknowledged him with his
     blessings,
   and gave him his inheritance;
   he divided his portions,
   and distributed them among
     twelve tribes.

Moses

From his descendants the Lord[m]
   brought forth a godly man,
   who found favor in the sight of
     all

45 1and was beloved by God and
     people,
   Moses, whose memory is blessed.
2 He made him equal in glory to the
     holy ones,
   and made him great, to the terror
     of his enemies.
3 By his words he performed swift
     miracles;[o]
   the Lord[m] glorified him in the
     presence of kings.
   He gave him commandments for his
     people,
   and revealed to him his glory.
4 For his faithfulness and meekness he
     consecrated him,

j Heb Compare Lat Syr: Meaning of Gk uncertain
k Heb: Gk *Peoples declare*   l Heb: Gk *was taken in
exchange*   m Gk *he*   n Syr: Heb Gk *River*
o Heb: Gk *caused signs to cease*

choosing him out of all
    humankind.
5 He allowed him to hear his voice,
    and led him into the dark cloud,
and gave him the commandments
    face to face,
    the law of life and knowledge,
so that he might teach Jacob the
    covenant,
    and Israel his decrees.

Aaron

6 He exalted Aaron, a holy man like
    Moses *p*
    who was his brother, of the tribe
    of Levi.
7 He made an everlasting covenant
    with him,
    and gave him the priesthood of
    the people.
He blessed him with stateliness,
    and put a glorious robe on him.
8 He clothed him in perfect splendor,
    and strengthened him with the
    symbols of authority,
    the linen undergarments, the long
    robe, and the ephod.
9 And he encircled him with
    pomegranates,
    with many golden bells all
    around,
to send forth a sound as he walked,
    to make their ringing heard in the
    temple
    as a reminder to his people;
10 with the sacred vestment, of gold
    and violet
    and purple, the work of an
    embroiderer;
with the oracle of judgment, Urim
    and Thummim;
11 with twisted crimson, the work of
    an artisan;
with precious stones engraved like
    seals,
    in a setting of gold, the work of a
    jeweler,
to commemorate in engraved letters
    each of the tribes of Israel;
12 with a gold crown upon his turban,
    inscribed like a seal with
    "Holiness,"
a distinction to be prized, the work
    of an expert,
    a delight to the eyes, richly
    adorned.
13 Before him such beautiful things did
    not exist.

No outsider ever put them on,
    but only his sons
    and his descendants in perpetuity.
14 His sacrifices shall be wholly burned
    twice every day continually.
15 Moses ordained him,
    and anointed him with holy oil;
it was an everlasting covenant for
    him
    and for his descendants as long as
    the heavens endure,
to minister to the Lord *p* and serve
    as priest
    and bless his people in his name.
16 He chose him out of all the living
    to offer sacrifice to the Lord,
incense and a pleasing odor as a
    memorial portion,
    to make atonement for the *q*
    people.
17 In his commandments he gave him
    authority and statutes and *r*
    judgments,
to teach Jacob the testimonies,
    and to enlighten Israel with his
    law.
18 Outsiders conspired against him,
    and envied him in the wilderness,
Dathan and Abiram and their
    followers
    and the company of Korah, in
    wrath and anger.
19 The Lord saw it and was not
    pleased,
    and in the heat of his anger they
    were destroyed;
he performed wonders against them
    to consume them in flaming fire.
20 He added glory to Aaron
    and gave him a heritage;
he allotted to him the best of the
    first fruits,
    and prepared bread of first fruits
    in abundance;
21 for they eat the sacrifices of the
    Lord,
    which he gave to him and his
    descendants.
22 But in the land of the people he has
    no inheritance,
    and he has no portion among the
    people;
    for the Lord *s* himself is his *t*
    portion and inheritance.

p Gk *him*   *q* Other ancient authorities read *his* or
your   *r* Heb: Gk *authority in covenants of*   *s* Gk
he   *t* Other ancient authorities read *your*

Phinehas

23 Phinehas son of Eleazar ranks third
   in glory
   for being zealous in the fear of
      the Lord,
   and standing firm, when the people
      turned away,
   in the noble courage of his soul;
   and he made atonement for Israel.
24 Therefore a covenant of friendship
      was established with him,
   that he should be leader of the
      sanctuary and of his people,
   that he and his descendants should
      have
   the dignity of the priesthood
      forever.
25 Just as a covenant was established
      with David
   son of Jesse of the tribe of Judah,
   that the king's heritage passes only
      from son to son,
   so the heritage of Aaron is for his
      descendants alone.

26 And now bless the Lord
   who has crowned you with
      glory.*u*
   May the Lord*v* grant you wisdom of
      mind
   to judge his people with justice,
   so that their prosperity may not
      vanish,
   and that their glory may endure
      through all their generations.

Joshua and Caleb

46 Joshua son of Nun was mighty
   in war,
   and was the successor of Moses in
      the prophetic office.
   He became, as his name implies,
   a great savior of God's*w* elect,
   to take vengeance on the enemies
      that rose against them,
   so that he might give Israel its
      inheritance.
2 How glorious he was when he lifted
      his hands
   and brandished his sword against
      the cities!
3 Who before him ever stood so firm?
   For he waged the wars of the
      Lord.
4 Was it not through him that the sun
      stood still

and one day became as long as
   two?
5 He called upon the Most High, the
      Mighty One,
   when enemies pressed him on
      every side,
   and the great Lord answered him
   with hailstones of mighty power.
6 He overwhelmed that nation in
      battle,
   and on the slope he destroyed his
      opponents,
   so that the nations might know his
      armament,
   that he was fighting in the sight of
      the Lord;
   for he was a devoted follower of
      the Mighty One.
7 And in the days of Moses he proved
      his loyalty,
   he and Caleb son of Jephunneh:
   they opposed the congregation,*x*
   restrained the people from sin,
   and stilled their wicked
      grumbling.
8 And these two alone were spared
   out of six hundred thousand
      infantry,
   to lead the people*y* into their
      inheritance,
   the land flowing with milk and
      honey.
9 The Lord gave Caleb strength,
   which remained with him in his
      old age,
   so that he went up to the hill
      country,
   and his children obtained it for an
      inheritance,
10 so that all the Israelites might see
   how good it is to follow the Lord.

The Judges

11 The judges also, with their respective
      names,
   whose hearts did not fall into
      idolatry
   and who did not turn away from the
      Lord—
   may their memory be blessed!
12 May their bones send forth new life
   from where they lie,

---

u Heb: Gk lacks *And . . . glory*   *v* Gk he   *w* Gk
his   *x* Other ancient authorities read *the enemy*
y Gk *them*

and may the names of those who
have been honored
live again in their children!

13 Samuel was beloved by his Lord;
a prophet of the Lord, he
established the kingdom
and anointed rulers over his
people.
14 By the law of the Lord he judged the
congregation,
and the Lord watched over Jacob.
15 By his faithfulness he was proved to
be a prophet,
and by his words he became
known as a trustworthy seer.
16 He called upon the Lord, the Mighty
One,
when his enemies pressed him on
every side,
and he offered in sacrifice a
suckling lamb.
17 Then the Lord thundered from
heaven,
and made his voice heard with a
mighty sound;
18 he subdued the leaders of the
enemy*z*
and all the rulers of the
Philistines.
19 Before the time of his eternal sleep,
Samuel*a* bore witness before the
Lord and his anointed:
"No property, not so much as a pair
of shoes,
have I taken from anyone!"
And no one accused him.
20 Even after he had fallen asleep, he
prophesied
and made known to the king his
death,
and lifted up his voice from the
ground
in prophecy, to blot out the
wickedness of the people.

Nathan

47 After him Nathan rose up
to prophesy in the days of
David.

David

2 As the fat is set apart from the
offering of well-being,
so David was set apart from the
Israelites.
3 He played with lions as though they
were young goats,

and with bears as though they
were lambs of the flock.
4 In his youth did he not kill a giant,
and take away the people's
disgrace,
when he whirled the stone in the
sling
and struck down the boasting
Goliath?
5 For he called on the Lord, the Most
High,
and he gave strength to his right
arm
to strike down a mighty warrior,
and to exalt the power*b* of his
people.
6 So they glorified him for the tens of
thousands he conquered,
and praised him for the blessings
bestowed by the Lord,
when the glorious diadem was
given to him.
7 For he wiped out his enemies on
every side,
and annihilated his adversaries the
Philistines;
he crushed their power*b* to our
own day.
8 In all that he did he gave thanks
to the Holy One, the Most High,
proclaiming his glory;
he sang praise with all his heart,
and he loved his Maker.
9 He placed singers before the altar,
to make sweet melody with their
voices.*c*
10 He gave beauty to the festivals,
and arranged their times
throughout the year,*d*
while they praised God's*e* holy
name,
and the sanctuary resounded from
early morning.
11 The Lord took away his sins,
and exalted his power*b* forever;
he gave him a covenant of kingship
and a glorious throne in Israel.

Solomon

12 After him a wise son rose up
who because of him lived in
security:*f*
13 Solomon reigned in an age of peace,

z Heb: Gk *leaders of the people of Tyre*   a Gk *he*
b Gk *horn*   c Other ancient authorities add *and
daily they sing his praises*   d Gk *to completion*
e Gk *his*   f Heb: Gk *in a broad place*

because God made all his borders
   tranquil,
so that he might build a house in
      his name
   and provide a sanctuary to stand
      forever.
14 How wise you were when you were
      young!
   You overflowed like the Nile*g*
      with understanding.
15 Your influence spread throughout
      the earth,
   and you filled it with proverbs
      having deep meaning.
16 Your fame reached to far-off islands,
   and you were loved for your
      peaceful reign.
17 Your songs, proverbs, and parables,
   and the answers you gave
      astounded the nations.
18 In the name of the Lord God,
   who is called the God of Israel,
you gathered gold like tin
   and amassed silver like lead.
19 But you brought in women to lie at
      your side,
   and through your body you were
      brought into subjection.
20 You stained your honor,
   and defiled your family line,
so that you brought wrath upon
      your children,
   and they were grieved*h* at your
      folly,
21 because the sovereignty was divided
   and a rebel kingdom arose out of
      Ephraim.
22 But the Lord will never give up his
      mercy,
   or cause any of his works to
      perish;
he will never blot out the
      descendants of his chosen
      one,
   or destroy the family line of him
      who loved him.
So he gave a remnant to Jacob,
   and to David a root from his own
      family.

Rehoboam and Jeroboam

23 Solomon rested with his ancestors,
   and left behind him one of his
      sons,
broad in*i* folly and lacking in
      sense,
   Rehoboam, whose policy drove
      the people to revolt.

Then Jeroboam son of Nebat led
      Israel into sin
   and started Ephraim on its sinful
      ways.
24 Their sins increased more and more,
   until they were exiled from their
      land.
25 For they sought out every kind of
      wickedness,
   until vengeance came upon them.

Elijah

48 Then Elijah arose, a prophet like
      fire,
   and his word burned like a torch.
2 He brought a famine upon them,
   and by his zeal he made them few
      in number.
3 By the word of the Lord he shut up
      the heavens,
   and also three times brought
      down fire.
4 How glorious you were, Elijah, in
      your wondrous deeds!
   Whose glory is equal to yours?
5 You raised a corpse from death
   and from Hades, by the word of
      the Most High.
6 You sent kings down to destruction,
   and famous men, from their
      sickbeds.
7 You heard rebuke at Sinai
   and judgments of vengeance at
      Horeb.
8 You anointed kings to inflict
      retribution,
   and prophets to succeed you.*j*
9 You were taken up by a whirlwind
      of fire,
   in a chariot with horses of fire.
10 At the appointed time, it is written,
      you are destined*k*
   to calm the wrath of God before it
      breaks out in fury,
   to turn the hearts of parents to their
      children,
   and to restore the tribes of Jacob.
11 Happy are those who saw you
   and were adorned*l* with your
      love!
   For we also shall surely live.*m*

---

g Heb: Gk *a river*   *h* Other ancient authorities
read *I was grieved*   *i* Heb (with a play on the
name Rehoboam) Syr: Gk *the people's*
j Heb: Gk *him*   *k* Heb: Gk *are for reproofs*
l Other ancient authorities read *and have died*
m Text and meaning of Gk uncertain

Elisha

12 When Elijah was enveloped in the
    whirlwind,
      Elisha was filled with his spirit.
  He performed twice as many signs,
      and marvels with every utterance
      of his mouth.[n]
  Never in his lifetime did he tremble
      before any ruler,
      nor could anyone intimidate him
      at all.
13 Nothing was too hard for him,
      and when he was dead, his body
      prophesied.
14 In his life he did wonders,
      and in death his deeds were
      marvelous.

15 Despite all this the people did not
    repent,
      nor did they forsake their sins,
  until they were carried off as
      plunder from their land,
      and were scattered over all the
      earth.
  The people were left very few in
      number,
      but with a ruler from the house of
      David.
16 Some of them did what was right,
      but others sinned more and more.

Hezekiah

17 Hezekiah fortified his city,
      and brought water into its midst;
  he tunneled the rock with iron tools,
      and built cisterns for the water.
18 In his days Sennacherib invaded the
    country;
      he sent his commander[o] and
      departed;
  he shook his fist against Zion,
      and made great boasts in his
      arrogance.
19 Then their hearts were shaken and
    their hands trembled,
      and they were in anguish, like
      women in labor.
20 But they called upon the Lord who
    is merciful,
      spreading out their hands toward
      him.
  The Holy One quickly heard them
      from heaven,
      and delivered them through
      Isaiah.

21 The Lord[p] struck down the camp of
    the Assyrians,
      and his angel wiped them out.
22 For Hezekiah did what was pleasing
    to the Lord,
      and he kept firmly to the ways of
      his ancestor David,
  as he was commanded by the
      prophet Isaiah,
      who was great and trustworthy in
      his visions.

Isaiah

23 In Isaiah's[q] days the sun went
    backward,
      and he prolonged the life of the
      king.
24 By his dauntless spirit he saw the
    future,
      and comforted the mourners in
      Zion.
25 He revealed what was to occur to
    the end of time,
      and the hidden things before they
      happened.

Josiah and Other Worthies

49 The name[r] of Josiah is like
      blended incense
  prepared by the skill of the
      perfumer;
  his memory[s] is as sweet as honey
      to every mouth,
      and like music at a banquet of
      wine.
2 He did what was right by reforming
    the people,
      and removing the wicked
      abominations.
3 He kept his heart fixed on the Lord;
      in lawless times he made
      godliness prevail.

4 Except for David and Hezekiah and
    Josiah,
      all of them were great sinners,
  for they abandoned the law of the
      Most High;
      the kings of Judah came to an
      end.
5 They[t] gave their power to others,
      and their glory to a foreign
      nation,

---

n Heb: Gk lacks *He performed . . . mouth*   *o* Other
ancient authorities add *from Lachish*   *p* Gk *He*
q Gk *his*   *r* Heb: Gk *memory*   *s* Heb: Gk *it*
t Heb *He*

THE STORY OF A WOMAN

Bathsheba

Her Name Means *"The Seventh Daughter"* or *"The Daughter of an Oath"*

Read 2 Samuel 11

Bathsheba squeezed the sponge, moving it across her body in even rhythms as though to calm the restless cadence of her thoughts. Normally, she looked forward to the ritual bath marking the end of her monthly period, but tonight the water soothed her skin without refreshing her spirit.

She should be glad for the cool breeze. For a lush harvest. But spring, the season of armies and battles, could also yield its crop of sorrows. Though her husband Uriah was a seasoned soldier, she still worried, wishing she could fall asleep in his arms. But he was camped with the king's army some 40 miles northeast of Jerusalem.

Her Character: *Her beauty made her victim to a king's desire. Though it is difficult to discern her true character, she seems to have found the courage to endure tragedy, winning the king's confidence and eventually securing the kingdom for her son Solomon.*

Her Sorrow: *To have been molested by a supposedly godly man who then had her husband killed in battle, and to have suffered the loss of her son.*

Her Joy: *To have given birth to five sons, one of whom became the king of Israel after David's death.*

David rose from his bed, unable to sleep. Pacing across the palace roof, he gazed at the city below. In the half-light he noticed the figure of a young woman, bathing in the garden below him. He leaned against the outer edge of the roof for a closer view. Wet hair curling languidly against skin white as lamb's wool. Breasts like rounded apples. He reached as though to steal a touch. Unaware of his gaze, she toweled herself dry and then stepped into the house. He waited and watched, but even the king could not see through walls.

So David made inquiries and discovered that the vision had a name: She was Bathsheba, the wife of one of his soldiers, Uriah the

Hittite. He sent for her and she became pregnant with his child.

Fearing discovery, the king ordered Uriah home from battle. But the soldier surprised him by refusing to spend the night with his wife out of loyalty to the army. Even David's efforts to get him drunk did not weaken Uriah's resolve. So the king arranged for Uriah to be assigned to the front line of battle where he was sure to die.

Then David claimed Bathsheba as his wife, her child as his own.

David's lust for Bathsheba marked the beginning of his long decline. Though God forgave him, he still suffered the consequences of his wrongdoing. His sin was a whirlpool that dragged others into its swirling path. Despite David's pleading, God allowed the son he had conceived with Bathsheba to die from an illness.

But why did Bathsheba have to suffer? Though the story gives us little insight into her true character, it is hardly likely that Bathsheba was in a position to refuse the king, whose power was absolute. Why then have so many people painted her as a seductress? Perhaps Bathsheba's innocence is too painful to face. That a good person can suffer such tragedies, especially at the hands of a godly person, appalls us.

Perhaps some comfort can be drawn from the words of Psalm 22, part of which Jesus quoted from the cross. This psalm affirms the truth that no matter how evil the circumstances, it remains true that God never disdains our suffering, never hides his face from us, but always listens to our cries for help.

Praying With Bathsheba

"You are the man! Thus says the LORD, the God of Israel: I anointed you king over Israel, and I rescued you from the hand of Saul; I gave you your master's house, and your master's wives into your bosom, and gave you the house of Israel and of Judah ... Why have you despised the word of the LORD, to do what is evil in his sight? You have struck down Uriah the Hittite with the sword, and have taken his wife to be your wife."—2 Samuel 12.7–9

Praise God: *That he is quick to note the suffering of the afflicted.*

Offer Thanks: *That God calls the powerful to abide by the same moral standards as the weak.*

Confess: *Any lack of forgiveness you may have toward someone who has taken advantage of you.*

Ask God: *To restore your confidence and to free you from any tendency to take on the mindset of a victim.*

Lift Your Heart

In our culture, many of us are especially vulnerable to sexual abuse. If you have suffered abuse, don't bury your feelings, absorbing the shame and guilt that belong to the abuser. Instead, find other women who have endured similar abuse and gone on to lead fruitful and significant lives. Determine that you will not let someone else's sin ruin your life. If you've never been abused, you probably know someone who has—a daughter, friend, or acquaintance. Do whatever you can to help that person and pray that God will restore her hope.

Father, forgiveness is so hard sometimes. I want justice, not mercy. Please help me to begin the process of forgiveness by letting go of my desire for revenge. Every time I start wishing something negative on those who've hurt me, help me to pray a blessing on their behalf instead.

Go to page 936 for your next devotional reading.

6 who set fire to the chosen city of the
     sanctuary,
   and made its streets desolate,
   as Jeremiah had foretold.[u]

7 For they had mistreated him,
   who even in the womb had been
     consecrated a prophet,
   to pluck up and ruin and destroy,
   and likewise to build and to
     plant.

8 It was Ezekiel who saw the vision of
     glory,
   which God[v] showed him above
     the chariot of the cherubim.

9 For God[w] also mentioned Job
   who held fast to all the ways of
     justice.[x]

10 May the bones of the Twelve
     Prophets
   send forth new life from where
     they lie,
   for they comforted the people of
     Jacob
   and delivered them with confident
     hope.

11 How shall we magnify Zerubbabel?
   He was like a signet ring on the
     right hand,
12 and so was Jeshua son of Jozadak;
   in their days they built the house
   and raised a temple[y] holy to the
     Lord,
   destined for everlasting glory.

13 The memory of Nehemiah also is
     lasting;
   he raised our fallen walls,
   and set up gates and bars,
   and rebuilt our ruined houses.

Retrospect

14 Few have[z] ever been created on
     earth like Enoch,
   for he was taken up from the
     earth.
15 Nor was anyone ever born like
     Joseph;[a]
   even his bones were cared for.
16 Shem and Seth and Enosh were
     honored,[b]
   but above every other created
     living being was Adam.

Simon Son of Onias

50 The leader of his brothers and
     the pride of his people[c]

was the high priest, Simon son of
     Onias,
   who in his life repaired the house,
   and in his time fortified the
     temple.
2 He laid the foundations for the high
     double walls,
   the high retaining walls for the
     temple enclosure.
3 In his days a water cistern was
     dug,[d]
   a reservoir like the sea in
     circumference.
4 He considered how to save his
     people from ruin,
   and fortified the city against siege.
5 How glorious he was, surrounded by
     the people,
   as he came out of the house of
     the curtain.
6 Like the morning star among the
     clouds,
   like the full moon at the festal
     season;[d]
7 like the sun shining on the temple
     of the Most High,
   like the rainbow gleaming in
     splendid clouds;
8 like roses in the days of first fruits,
   like lilies by a spring of water,
   like a green shoot on Lebanon on
     a summer day;
9 like fire and incense in the censer,
   like a vessel of hammered gold
   studded with all kinds of precious
     stones;
10 like an olive tree laden with fruit,
   and like a cypress towering in the
     clouds.
11 When he put on his glorious robe
   and clothed himself in perfect
     splendor,
   when he went up to the holy altar,
   he made the court of the
     sanctuary glorious.

12 When he received the portions from
     the hands of the priests,
   as he stood by the hearth of the
     altar

---

u Gk by the hand of Jeremiah   v Gk He   w Gk he
x Heb Compare Syr: Meaning of Gk uncertain
y Other ancient authorities read people   z Heb
Syr: Gk No one has   a Heb Syr: Gk adds the
leader of his brothers, the support of the people
b Heb: Gk Shem and Seth were honored by people
c Heb Syr: Gk lacks this line. Compare 49.15
d Heb: Meaning of Gk uncertain

with a garland of brothers around
him,
he was like a young cedar on
Lebanon
surrounded by the trunks of palm
trees.

13 All the sons of Aaron in their
splendor
held the Lord's offering in their
hands
before the whole congregation of
Israel.

14 Finishing the service at the altars,[e]
and arranging the offering to the
Most High, the Almighty,

15 he held out his hand for the cup
and poured a drink offering of the
blood of the grape;
he poured it out at the foot of the
altar,
a pleasing odor to the Most High,
the king of all.

16 Then the sons of Aaron shouted;
they blew their trumpets of
hammered metal;
they sounded a mighty fanfare
as a reminder before the Most
High.

17 Then all the people together quickly
fell to the ground on their faces
to worship their Lord,
the Almighty, God Most High.

18 Then the singers praised him with
their voices
in sweet and full-toned melody.[f]

19 And the people of the Lord Most
High offered
their prayers before the Merciful
One,
until the order of worship of the
Lord was ended,
and they completed his ritual.

20 Then Simon[g] came down and
raised his hands
over the whole congregation of
Israelites,
to pronounce the blessing of the
Lord with his lips,
and to glory in his name;

21 and they bowed down in worship a
second time,
to receive the blessing from the
Most High.

A Benediction

22 And now bless the God of all,

who everywhere works great
wonders,
who fosters our growth from birth,
and deals with us according to his
mercy.

23 May he give us[h] gladness of heart,
and may there be peace in our[i]
days
in Israel, as in the days of old.

24 May he entrust to us his mercy,
and may he deliver us in our[j]
days!

Epilogue

25 Two nations my soul detests,
and the third is not even a
people:

26 Those who live in Seir,[k] and the
Philistines,
and the foolish people that live in
Shechem.

27 Instruction in understanding and
knowledge
I have written in this book,
Jesus son of Eleazar son of Sirach[l]
of Jerusalem,
whose mind poured forth
wisdom.

28 Happy are those who concern
themselves with these things,
and those who lay them to heart
will become wise.

29 For if they put them into practice,
they will be equal to
anything,
for the fear[m] of the Lord is their
path.

PRAYER OF JESUS SON OF SIRACH [n]

51 I give you thanks, O Lord and
King,
and praise you, O God my Savior.
I give thanks to your name,

2 for you have been my protector
and helper

---

e Other ancient authorities read *altar*   *f* Other
ancient authorities read *in sweet melody throughout
the house*   *g* Gk *he*   *h* Other ancient authorities
read *you*   *i* Other ancient authorities read *your*
j Other ancient authorities read *his*   *k* Heb
Compare Lat: Gk *on the mountain of Samaria*
l Heb: Meaning of Gk uncertain   *m* Heb: Other
ancient authorities read *light*   *n* This title is
included in the Gk text.

and have delivered me from
   destruction
   and from the trap laid by a
      slanderous tongue,
   from lips that fabricate lies.
In the face of my adversaries
   you have been my helper ³and
      delivered me,
   in the greatness of your mercy and
      of your name,
   from grinding teeth about to devour
      me,
   from the hand of those seeking
      my life,
   from the many troubles I endured,
⁴ from choking fire on every side,
   and from the midst of fire that I
      had not kindled,
⁵ from the deep belly of Hades,
   from an unclean tongue and lying
      words—
⁶   the slander of an unrighteous
      tongue to the king.
   My soul drew near to death,
      and my life was on the brink of
         Hades below.
⁷ They surrounded me on every side,
   and there was no one to help
      me;
   I looked for human assistance,
      and there was none.
⁸ Then I remembered your mercy,
      O Lord,
   and your kindness° from of old,
   for you rescue those who wait for
      you
   and save them from the hand of
      their enemies.
⁹ And I sent up my prayer from the
      earth,
   and begged for rescue from death.
¹⁰ I cried out, "Lord, you are my
      Father; ᵖ
   do not forsake me in the days of
      trouble,
   when there is no help against the
      proud.
¹¹ I will praise your name continually,
   and will sing hymns of
      thanksgiving."
   My prayer was heard,
¹²   for you saved me from destruction
   and rescued me in time of
      trouble.
   For this reason I thank you and
      praise you,
   and I bless the name of the Lord.

Heb adds:

Give thanks to the LORD, for he is good,
   for his mercy endures forever;

Give thanks to the God of praises,
   for his mercy endures forever;

Give thanks to the guardian of Israel,
   for his mercy endures forever;

Give thanks to him who formed all
      things,
   for his mercy endures forever;

Give thanks to the redeemer of Israel,
   for his mercy endures forever;

Give thanks to him who gathers the
      dispersed of Israel,
   for his mercy endures forever;

Give thanks to him who rebuilt his city
      and his sanctuary,
   for his mercy endures forever;

Give thanks to him who makes a horn
      to sprout for the house of David,
   for his mercy endures forever;

Give thanks to him who has chosen the
      sons of Zadok to be priests,
   for his mercy endures forever;

Give thanks to the shield of Abraham,
   for his mercy endures forever;

Give thanks to the rock of Isaac,
   for his mercy endures forever;

Give thanks to the mighty one of Jacob,
   for his mercy endures forever;

Give thanks to him who has chosen
      Zion,
   for his mercy endures forever;

Give thanks to the King of the kings of
      kings,
   for his mercy endures forever;

He has raised up a horn for his people,
   praise for all his loyal ones.

° Other ancient authorities read *work*   ᵖ Heb: Gk
the Father of my lord

For the children of Israel, the people
    close to him.
Praise the LORD!

Autobiographical Poem on Wisdom

13 While I was still young, before I
    went on my travels,
  I sought wisdom openly in my
    prayer.
14 Before the temple I asked for her,
  and I will search for her until the
    end.
15 From the first blossom to the
    ripening grape
  my heart delighted in her;
  my foot walked on the straight path;
  from my youth I followed her
    steps.
16 I inclined my ear a little and
    received her,
  and I found for myself much
    instruction.
17 I made progress in her;
  to him who gives wisdom I will
    give glory.
18 For I resolved to live according to
    wisdom,*q*
  and I was zealous for the good,
  and I shall never be disappointed.
19 My soul grappled with wisdom,*q*
  and in my conduct I was strict;*r*

  I spread out my hands to the
    heavens,
  and lamented my ignorance of
    her.
20 I directed my soul to her,
  and in purity I found her.

  With her I gained understanding
    from the first;

  therefore I will never be forsaken.
21 My heart was stirred to seek her;
  therefore I have gained a prize
    possession.
22 The Lord gave me my tongue as a
    reward,
  and I will praise him with it.
23 Draw near to me, you who are
    uneducated,
  and lodge in the house of
    instruction.
24 Why do you say you are lacking in
    these things,*s*
  and why do you endure such great
    thirst?
25 I opened my mouth and said,
  Acquire wisdom*t* for yourselves
    without money.
26 Put your neck under her*u* yoke,
  and let your souls receive
    instruction;
  it is to be found close by.
27 See with your own eyes that I have
    labored but little
  and found for myself much
    serenity.
28 Hear but a little of my instruction,
  and through me you will acquire
    silver and gold.*v*
29 May your soul rejoice in God's*w*
    mercy,
  and may you never be ashamed to
    praise him.
30 Do your work in good time,
  and in his own time God*x* will
    give you your reward.

*q Gk her   r Meaning of Gk uncertain   s Cn
Compare Heb Syr: Meaning of Gk uncertain
t Heb: Gk lacks wisdom   u Heb: other ancient
authorities read the   v Syr Compare Heb: Gk
Get instruction with a large sum of silver, and you
will gain by it much gold.   w Gk his   x Gk he*

Isaiah

If you have ever listened to Handel's *Messiah*, you are already on familiar terms with this book because many of the lines of this famous ora-
torio come straight from Isaiah. Modern scholars believe Isaiah is the
work of two or three different writers. But whether the prophet Isaiah
wrote every word or whether someone else contributed to the book
need not affect our belief in its divine inspiration.

Isaiah was one of the greatest prophets of the Old Testament, active in Jerusalem from 742–686 B.C. During Isaiah's lifetime, the northern kingdom of Israel fell to Assyria, while the southern kingdom of
Judah was threatened by external enemies, including Assyria, with
whom Judah formed an ill-advised alliance.

Isaiah 1–39 contain the prophet's impassioned calls for repentance,
in which he also stresses the need for continual dependence on God
rather than on worldly powers.

Chapters 40–66 focus on the hope of deliverance from exile and on
the restoration of Jerusalem. They contain poignant passages regarding
the "suffering servant," prophetic descriptions of the suffering and glorification of Christ that would take place hundreds of years later. In
fact, Isaiah contains so many Messianic prophecies that it has sometimes been referred to as "the gospel within the Old Testament" (see
2.2–4; 9.1, 6; 40.3–5; 42.1–4, 6–7; 53 for just a few examples of these).

1 The vision of Isaiah son of Amoz,
which he saw concerning Judah and
Jerusalem in the days of Uzziah, Jotham,
Ahaz, and Hezekiah, kings of Judah.

The Wickedness of Judah

2 Hear, O heavens, and listen,
    O earth;
for the LORD has spoken:
I reared children and brought
    them up,
    but they have rebelled against me.
3 The ox knows its owner,
    and the donkey its master's crib;
but Israel does not know,
    my people do not understand.

4 Ah, sinful nation,
    people laden with iniquity,
offspring who do evil,
    children who deal corruptly,
who have forsaken the LORD,

who have despised the Holy One
 of Israel,
who are utterly estranged!

5 Why do you seek further beatings?
 Why do you continue to rebel?
The whole head is sick,
 and the whole heart faint.
6 From the sole of the foot even to
  the head,
 there is no soundness in it,
but bruises and sores
 and bleeding wounds;
they have not been drained, or
  bound up,
 or softened with oil.

7 Your country lies desolate,
 your cities are burned with fire;
in your very presence
 aliens devour your land;
 it is desolate, as overthrown by
  foreigners.
8 And daughter Zion is left
 like a booth in a vineyard,
like a shelter in a cucumber field,
 like a besieged city.
9 If the LORD of hosts
 had not left us a few survivors,
we would have been like Sodom,
 and become like Gomorrah.

10 Hear the word of the LORD,
 you rulers of Sodom!
Listen to the teaching of our God,
 you people of Gomorrah!
11 What to me is the multitude of your
  sacrifices?
 says the LORD;
I have had enough of burnt offerings
 of rams
 and the fat of fed beasts;
I do not delight in the blood
 of bulls,
 or of lambs, or of goats.

12 When you come to appear
  before me,*a*
 who asked this from your hand?
 Trample my courts no more;
13 bringing offerings is futile;
 incense is an abomination to me.
New moon and sabbath and calling
 of convocation—
 I cannot endure solemn
  assemblies with iniquity.
14 Your new moons and your
  appointed festivals

my soul hates;
they have become a burden to me,
 I am weary of bearing them.
15 When you stretch out your hands,
 I will hide my eyes from you;
even though you make many
  prayers,
 I will not listen;
 your hands are full of blood.
16 Wash yourselves; make yourselves
  clean;
 remove the evil of your doings
 from before my eyes;
cease to do evil,
17 learn to do good;
seek justice,
 rescue the oppressed,
defend the orphan,
 plead for the widow.

18 Come now, let us argue it out,
 says the LORD:
though your sins are like scarlet,
 they shall be like snow;
though they are red like crimson,
 they shall become like wool.
19 If you are willing and obedient,
 you shall eat the good of the land;
20 but if you refuse and rebel,
 you shall be devoured by the
  sword;
 for the mouth of the LORD has
  spoken.

The Degenerate City

21 How the faithful city
 has become a whore!
 She that was full of justice,
righteousness lodged in her—
 but now murderers!
22 Your silver has become dross,
 your wine is mixed with water.
23 Your princes are rebels
 and companions of thieves.
Everyone loves a bribe
 and runs after gifts.
They do not defend the orphan,
 and the widow's cause does not
  come before them.

24 Therefore says the Sovereign, the
 LORD of hosts, the Mighty
 One of Israel:
Ah, I will pour out my wrath on my
  enemies,
 and avenge myself on my foes!

a Or see my face

25 I will turn my hand against you;
  I will smelt away your dross as
    with lye
  and remove all your alloy.
26 And I will restore your judges as at
    the first,
  and your counselors as at the
    beginning.
  Afterward you shall be called the
    city of righteousness,
  the faithful city.

27 Zion shall be redeemed by justice,
  and those in her who repent, by
    righteousness.
28 But rebels and sinners shall be
    destroyed together,
  and those who forsake the LORD
    shall be consumed.
29 For you shall be ashamed of
    the oaks
  in which you delighted;
  and you shall blush for the gardens
    that you have chosen.
30 For you shall be like an oak
    whose leaf withers,
  and like a garden without water.
31 The strong shall become like tinder,
  and their work*b* like a spark;
  they and their work shall burn
    together,
  with no one to quench them.

The Future House of God

2 The word that Isaiah son of Amoz
  saw concerning Judah and Jerusalem.

2 In days to come
  the mountain of the LORD's house
  shall be established as the highest of
    the mountains,
  and shall be raised above
    the hills;
  all the nations shall stream to it.
3   Many peoples shall come and say,
  "Come, let us go up to the
    mountain of the LORD,
  to the house of the God of Jacob;
  that he may teach us his ways
    and that we may walk in his
      paths."
  For out of Zion shall go forth
    instruction,
  and the word of the LORD from
    Jerusalem.
4 He shall judge between the nations,
  and shall arbitrate for many
    peoples;

they shall beat their swords into
    plowshares,
  and their spears into pruning
    hooks;
  nation shall not lift up sword
    against nation,
  neither shall they learn war
    any more.

Judgment Pronounced on Arrogance

5 O house of Jacob,
  come, let us walk
  in the light of the LORD!
6 For you have forsaken the ways of*c*
    your people,
  O house of Jacob.
  Indeed they are full of diviners*d*
    from the east
  and of soothsayers like the
    Philistines,
  and they clasp hands with
    foreigners.
7 Their land is filled with silver
    and gold,
  and there is no end to their
    treasures;
  their land is filled with horses,
  and there is no end to their
    chariots.
8 Their land is filled with idols;
  they bow down to the work of
    their hands,
  to what their own fingers
    have made.
9 And so people are humbled,
  and everyone is brought low—
  do not forgive them!
10 Enter into the rock,
  and hide in the dust
  from the terror of the LORD,
  and from the glory of his majesty.
11 The haughty eyes of people shall be
    brought low,
  and the pride of everyone shall be
    humbled;
  and the LORD alone will be exalted
    on that day.
12 For the LORD of hosts has a day
  against all that is proud and lofty,
  against all that is lifted up
    and high;*e*
13 against all the cedars of Lebanon,
  lofty and lifted up;

b Or *its makers*   *c* Heb lacks *the ways of*   *d* Cn:
Heb lacks *of diviners*   *e* Cn Compare Gk: Heb
low

and against all the oaks of
    Bashan;
14 against all the high mountains,
    and against all the lofty hills;
15 against every high tower,
    and against every fortified wall;
16 against all the ships of Tarshish,
    and against all the beautiful
    craft. *f*
17 The haughtiness of people shall be
    humbled,
    and the pride of everyone shall be
    brought low;
    and the LORD alone will be exalted
    on that day.
18 The idols shall utterly pass away.
19 Enter the caves of the rocks
    and the holes of the ground,
from the terror of the LORD,
    and from the glory of his majesty,
    when he rises to terrify the earth.
20 On that day people will throw away
    to the moles and to the bats
their idols of silver and their idols of
    gold,
    which they made for themselves
    to worship,
21 to enter the caverns of the rocks
    and the clefts in the crags,
from the terror of the LORD,
    and from the glory of his majesty,
    when he rises to terrify the earth.
22 Turn away from mortals,
    who have only breath in their
    nostrils,
    for of what account are they?

3 For now the Sovereign, the LORD
    of hosts,
    is taking away from Jerusalem and
    from Judah
support and staff—
    all support of bread,
    and all support of water—
2 warrior and soldier,
    judge and prophet,
    diviner and elder,
3 captain of fifty
    and dignitary,
    counselor and skillful magician
    and expert enchanter.
4 And I will make boys their princes,
    and babes shall rule over them.
5 The people will be oppressed,
    everyone by another
    and everyone by a neighbor;
the youth will be insolent to
    the elder,
    and the base to the honorable.

6 Someone will even seize a relative,
    a member of the clan, saying,
"You have a cloak;
    you shall be our leader,
and this heap of ruins
    shall be under your rule."
7 But the other will cry out on that
    day, saying,
"I will not be a healer;
    in my house there is neither bread
    nor cloak;
you shall not make me
    leader of the people."
8 For Jerusalem has stumbled
    and Judah has fallen,
because their speech and their deeds
    are against the LORD,
    defying his glorious presence.
9 The look on their faces bears witness
    against them;
    they proclaim their sin like
    Sodom,
    they do not hide it.
Woe to them!
    For they have brought evil on
    themselves.
10 Tell the innocent how fortunate they
    are,
    for they shall eat the fruit of their
    labors.
11 Woe to the guilty! How unfortunate
    they are,
    for what their hands have done
    shall be done to them.
12 My people—children are their
    oppressors,
    and women rule over them.
O my people, your leaders mislead
    you,
    and confuse the course of your
    paths.
13 The LORD rises to argue his case;
    he stands to judge the peoples.
14 The LORD enters into judgment
    with the elders and princes of his
    people:
It is you who have devoured the
    vineyard;
    the spoil of the poor is in your
    houses.
15 What do you mean by crushing my
    people,
    by grinding the face of the poor?
    says the Lord GOD of hosts.

f Compare Gk: Meaning of Heb uncertain

16 The LORD said:
Because the daughters of Zion are
      haughty
   and walk with outstretched necks,
   glancing wantonly with their eyes,
mincing along as they go,
   tinkling with their feet;
17 the Lord will afflict with scabs
   the heads of the daughters of
      Zion,
   and the LORD will lay bare their
      secret parts.

18 In that day the Lord will take away
the finery of the anklets, the headbands,
and the crescents; 19the pendants, the
bracelets, and the scarfs; 20the headdresses, the armlets, the sashes, the perfume boxes, and the amulets; 21the signet
rings and nose rings; 22the festal robes, the
mantles, the cloaks, and the handbags;
23the garments of gauze, the linen garments, the turbans, and the veils.
24 Instead of perfume there will be a
      stench;
   and instead of a sash, a rope;
and instead of well-set hair,
      baldness;
   and instead of a rich robe, a
      binding of sackcloth;
   instead of beauty, shame. *8*
25 Your men shall fall by the sword
   and your warriors in battle.
26 And her gates shall lament and
      mourn;
   ravaged, she shall sit upon the
      ground.

4 Seven women shall take hold of one
man in that day, saying,
"We will eat our own bread and
      wear our own clothes;
just let us be called by your name;
   take away our disgrace."

The Future Glory of the Survivors in Zion

2 On that day the branch of the LORD
shall be beautiful and glorious, and the
fruit of the land shall be the pride and
glory of the survivors of Israel. 3Whoever
is left in Zion and remains in Jerusalem
will be called holy, everyone who has
been recorded for life in Jerusalem, 4once
the Lord has washed away the filth of the
daughters of Zion and cleansed the blood-
stains of Jerusalem from its midst by a
spirit of judgment and by a spirit of burning. 5Then the LORD will create over the
whole site of Mount Zion and over its

places of assembly a cloud by day and
smoke and the shining of a flaming fire by
night. Indeed over all the glory there will
be a canopy. 6It will serve as a pavilion, a
shade by day from the heat, and a refuge
and a shelter from the storm and rain.

The Song of the Unfruitful Vineyard

5 Let me sing for my beloved
   my love-song concerning his
      vineyard:
My beloved had a vineyard
   on a very fertile hill.
2 He dug it and cleared it of stones,
   and planted it with choice vines;
he built a watchtower in the midst
   of it,
   and hewed out a wine vat in it;
he expected it to yield grapes,
   but it yielded wild grapes.

3 And now, inhabitants of Jerusalem
   and people of Judah,
judge between me
   and my vineyard.
4 What more was there to do for my
      vineyard
   that I have not done in it?
When I expected it to yield grapes,
   why did it yield wild grapes?

5 And now I will tell you
   what I will do to my vineyard.
I will remove its hedge,
   and it shall be devoured;
I will break down its wall,
   and it shall be trampled down.
6 I will make it a waste;
   it shall not be pruned or hoed,
   and it shall be overgrown with
      briers and thorns;
I will also command the clouds
   that they rain no rain upon it.

7 For the vineyard of the LORD of hosts
   is the house of Israel,
and the people of Judah
   are his pleasant planting;
he expected justice,
   but saw bloodshed;
righteousness,
   but heard a cry!

Social Injustice Denounced

8 Ah, you who join house to house,
   who add field to field,

8 Q Ms: MT lacks *shame*

until there is room for no one
  but you,
and you are left to live alone
  in the midst of the land!
9 The LORD of hosts has sworn in my
    hearing:
  Surely many houses shall be
    desolate,
  large and beautiful houses,
    without inhabitant.
10 For ten acres of vineyard shall yield
    but one bath,
  and a homer of seed shall yield a
    mere ephah.*h*

11 Ah, you who rise early in the
    morning
  in pursuit of strong drink,
  who linger in the evening
    to be inflamed by wine,
12 whose feasts consist of lyre and
    harp,
  tambourine and flute and wine,
  but who do not regard the deeds of
    the LORD,
  or see the work of his hands!
13 Therefore my people go into exile
    without knowledge;
  their nobles are dying of hunger,
    and their multitude is parched
    with thirst.
14 Therefore Sheol has enlarged its
    appetite
  and opened its mouth beyond
    measure;
  the nobility of Jerusalem*i* and her
    multitude go down,
  her throng and all who exult
    in her.
15 People are bowed down, everyone is
    brought low,
  and the eyes of the haughty are
    humbled.
16 But the LORD of hosts is exalted
    by justice,
  and the Holy God shows himself
    holy by righteousness.
17 Then the lambs shall graze as in
    their pasture,
  fatlings and kids*j* shall feed
    among the ruins.

18 Ah, you who drag iniquity along
    with cords of falsehood,
  who drag sin along as with cart
    ropes,

19 who say, "Let him make haste,
    let him speed his work
    that we may see it;
  let the plan of the Holy One of
      Israel hasten to fulfillment,
    that we may know it!"
20 Ah, you who call evil good
    and good evil,
  who put darkness for light
    and light for darkness,
  who put bitter for sweet
    and sweet for bitter!
21 Ah, you who are wise in your
    own eyes,
  and shrewd in your own sight!
22 Ah, you who are heroes in drinking
    wine
  and valiant at mixing drink,
23 who acquit the guilty for a bribe,
    and deprive the innocent of their
    rights!

Foreign Invasion Predicted

24 Therefore, as the tongue of fire
    devours the stubble,
  and as dry grass sinks down in the
    flame,
  so their root will become rotten,
    and their blossom go up like dust;
  for they have rejected the instruction
      of the LORD of hosts,
  and have despised the word of the
      Holy One of Israel.

25 Therefore the anger of the LORD was
    kindled against his people,
  and he stretched out his hand
    against them and struck
    them;
  the mountains quaked,
  and their corpses were like refuse
    in the streets.
  For all this his anger has not turned
    away,
  and his hand is stretched out still.

26 He will raise a signal for a nation far
    away,
  and whistle for a people at the
    ends of the earth;
  Here they come, swiftly, speedily!
27 None of them is weary, none
    stumbles,

h The Heb *bath, homer,* and *ephah* are measures of
quantity   *i* Heb *her nobility*   *j* Cn Compare
Gk: Heb *aliens*

none slumbers or sleeps,
not a loincloth is loose,
not a sandal-thong broken;

28 their arrows are sharp,
all their bows bent,
their horses' hoofs seem like flint,
and their wheels like the
whirlwind.

29 Their roaring is like a lion,
like young lions they roar;
they growl and seize their prey,
they carry it off, and no one
can rescue.

30 They will roar over it on that
day,
like the roaring of the sea.
And if one look to the land—
only darkness and distress;
and the light grows dark with
clouds.

A Vision of God in the Temple

6 In the year that King Uzziah died, I saw the Lord sitting on a throne, high and lofty; and the hem of his robe filled the temple. ²Seraphs were in attendance above him; each had six wings: with two they covered their faces, and with two they covered their feet, and with two they flew. ³And one called to another and said:

"Holy, holy, holy is the LORD of
hosts;
the whole earth is full of his glory."

⁴The pivots*ᵏ* on the thresholds shook at the voices of those who called, and the house filled with smoke. ⁵And I said: "Woe is me! I am lost, for I am a man of unclean lips, and I live among a people of

ᵏ Meaning of Heb uncertain

MONDAY

Scripture Reading
for Today:
Isaiah 6.1–8

Verses for Today:
Isaiah 6.6–7

*O*ne Loving Soul Sets Another on Fire

The seraphs are some of the more exotic angels described in the Bible. They are associated with the fire of the altar, perhaps because they reflect God's holiness. I like to think that they burn with love for God. The picture that Isaiah paints is of a royal court in which the King is accompanied by a magnificent retinue of supernatural attendants.

It is good to read such passages in Scripture, though they seem so strange. As flesh and blood creatures, it is often difficult for us to paint a very compelling picture of heaven. Partly because of this, we lose our sense of reverence, trying to tame God for our purposes. We disregard his greatness, presume on his goodness, and sometimes try to manipulate him. And though the God of the universe beckons, calling us into his presence, we are sometimes simply too busy to come.

Augustine says that "one loving soul sets another on fire." Perhaps that's what the seraphim can do for us. They can show by example what it means to live in the presence of God.

Quiet your heart, for a moment, and imagine the scene in heaven. Ask God to give you a glimpse of his majesty. Beg him to purify your soul. Sing his praises and then cover your face and bow before him. Let him touch you with his own fiery love.

—ANN SPANGLER

Go to page 938 for your next devotional reading.

unclean lips; yet my eyes have seen the King, the LORD of hosts!"

6 Then one of the seraphs flew to me, holding a live coal that had been taken from the altar with a pair of tongs. 7The seraph*l* touched my mouth with it and said: "Now that this has touched your lips, your guilt has departed and your sin is blotted out." 8Then I heard the voice of the Lord saying, "Whom shall I send, and who will go for us?" And I said, "Here am I; send me!" 9And he said, "Go and say to this people:

'Keep listening, but do not
          comprehend;
keep looking, but do not
          understand.'

10 Make the mind of this people dull,
          and stop their ears,
          and shut their eyes,
so that they may not look with their
          eyes,
          and listen with their ears,
and comprehend with their minds,
          and turn and be healed."

11 Then I said, "How long, O Lord?"
          And he said:
"Until cities lie waste
          without inhabitant,
and houses without people,
          and the land is utterly desolate;

12 until the LORD sends everyone
          far away,
          and vast is the emptiness in the
          midst of the land.

13 Even if a tenth part remain in it,
          it will be burned again,
like a terebinth or an oak
          whose stump remains standing
          when it is felled."*m*
The holy seed is its stump.

Isaiah Reassures King Ahaz

7 In the days of Ahaz son of Jotham son of Uzziah, king of Judah, King Rezin of Aram and King Pekah son of Remaliah of Israel went up to attack Jerusalem, but could not mount an attack against it. 2When the house of David heard that Aram had allied itself with Ephraim, the heart of Ahaz*n* and the heart of his people shook as the trees of the forest shake before the wind.

3 Then the LORD said to Isaiah, Go out to meet Ahaz, you and your son Shearjashub,*o* at the end of the conduit of the upper pool on the highway to the Fuller's Field, 4and say to him, Take heed, be quiet, do not fear, and do not let your heart be faint because of these two smoldering stumps of firebrands, because of the fierce anger of Rezin and Aram and the son of Remaliah. 5Because Aram—with Ephraim and the son of Remaliah—has plotted evil against you, saying, 6Let us go up against Judah and cut off Jerusalem*p* and conquer it for ourselves and make the son of Tabeel king in it; 7therefore thus says the Lord GOD:

It shall not stand,
          and it shall not come to pass.

8 For the head of Aram is Damascus,
          and the head of Damascus is
          Rezin.
(Within sixty-five years Ephraim will be shattered, no longer a people.)

9 The head of Ephraim is Samaria,
          and the head of Samaria is the
          son of Remaliah.
If you do not stand firm in faith,
          you shall not stand at all.

Isaiah Gives Ahaz the Sign of Immanuel

10 Again the LORD spoke to Ahaz, saying, 11Ask a sign of the LORD your God; let it be deep as Sheol or high as heaven. 12But Ahaz said, I will not ask, and I will not put the LORD to the test. 13Then Isaiah*q* said: "Hear then, O house of David! Is it too little for you to weary mortals, that you weary my God also? 14Therefore the Lord himself will give you a sign. Look, the young woman*r* is with child and shall bear a son, and shall name him Immanuel.*s* 15He shall eat curds and honey by the time he knows how to refuse the evil and choose the good. 16For before the child knows how to refuse the evil and choose the good, the land before whose two kings you are in dread will be deserted. 17The LORD will bring on you and on your people and on your ancestral house such days as have not come since the day that Ephraim departed from Judah—the king of Assyria."

18 On that day the LORD will whistle for the fly that is at the sources of the streams of Egypt, and for the bee that is in the land of Assyria. 19And they will all come and settle in the steep ravines, and

---

l Heb *He*   *m* Meaning of Heb uncertain   *n* Heb
his heart   *o* That is *A remnant shall return*
p Heb *cut it off*   *q* Heb *he*   *r* Gk *the virgin*
s That is *God is with us*

in the clefts of the rocks, and on all the thornbushes, and on all the pastures.

20 On that day the Lord will shave with a razor hired beyond the River—with the king of Assyria—the head and the hair of the feet, and it will take off the beard as well.

21 On that day one will keep alive a young cow and two sheep, 22and will eat curds because of the abundance of milk that they give; for everyone that is left in the land shall eat curds and honey.

23 On that day every place where there used to be a thousand vines, worth a thousand shekels of silver, will become briers and thorns. 24With bow and arrows one will go there, for all the land will be briers and thorns; 25and as for all the hills that used to be hoed with a hoe, you will not go there for fear of briers and thorns; but they will become a place where cattle are let loose and where sheep tread.

Isaiah's Son a Sign of the Assyrian Invasion

8 Then the LORD said to me, Take a large tablet and write on it in common characters, "Belonging to Maher-

How Unreasonable of God!

Einstein wrote that anyone who is not lost in rapturous awe and amazement at the power and glory of the mind behind the universe is as good as a burned-out candle.

Think of the power in our own sun, which is constantly bursting with hydrogen explosions. The very violence of our sun is what makes our green and pleasant earth. But how could all this power, power beyond our puny comprehension, willingly limit itself to the form of a tiny baby, growing up like any child, walking the dusty roads, being bitten by flies, feeling the heat of the sun, simply being one of us? That is awesome beyond explanation. That bursts the bounds of any kind of reasonableness. What a totally unreasonable thing for God to do! What a totally loving thing for God to do! Would'st thou witten thy Lord's meaning in these things? "Wit it well. Love was his meaning."

Love that was willing to come, to share, to eat and drink and laugh and talk. To walk away from his friends and those who had come to be healed and to go into the hills to be alone with God, to be refilled with the power of love. To be recognized as who he was by the demons, but not by scribes and Pharisees. To be betrayed, abandoned by friends. To weep, as we all at times must weep. To cry out in anguish, My God, my God, why have you forsaken me?

And then, knowing that despite the seeming failure of his mission, he had finished the work he came to do, Jesus gave it up, all of it.

Into your hands, O God, I commend my spirit.
Into your hands. Into total love.
Amen.

—MADELEINE L'ENGLE

Go to page 940 for your next devotional reading.

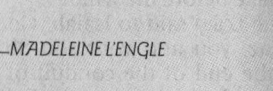

shalal-hash-baz,"[t] [2]and have it attested[u] for me by reliable witnesses, the priest Uriah and Zechariah son of Jeberechiah. [3]And I went to the prophetess, and she conceived and bore a son. Then the LORD said to me, Name him Maher-shalal-hash-baz; [4]for before the child knows how to call "My father" or "My mother," the wealth of Damascus and the spoil of Samaria will be carried away by the king of Assyria.

5 The LORD spoke to me again: [6]Because this people has refused the waters of Shiloah that flow gently, and melt in fear before[v] Rezin and the son of Remaliah; [7]therefore, the Lord is bringing up against it the mighty flood waters of the River, the king of Assyria and all his glory; it will rise above all its channels and overflow all its banks; [8]it will sweep on into Judah as a flood, and, pouring over, it will reach up to the neck; and its outspread wings will fill the breadth of your land, O Immanuel.

[9] Band together, you peoples, and be
         dismayed;
   listen, all you far countries;
   gird yourselves and be dismayed;
     gird yourselves and be dismayed!
[10] Take counsel together, but it shall be
         brought to naught;
   speak a word, but it will not
         stand,
     for God is with us.[w]

11 For the LORD spoke thus to me while his hand was strong upon me, and warned me not to walk in the way of this people, saying: [12]Do not call conspiracy all that this people calls conspiracy, and do not fear what it fears, or be in dread. [13]But the LORD of hosts, him you shall regard as holy; let him be your fear, and let him be your dread. [14]He will become a sanctuary, a stone one strikes against; for both houses of Israel he will become a rock one stumbles over—a trap and a snare for the inhabitants of Jerusalem. [15]And many among them shall stumble; they shall fall and be broken; they shall be snared and taken.

Disciples of Isaiah

16 Bind up the testimony, seal the teaching among my disciples. [17]I will wait for the LORD, who is hiding his face from the house of Jacob, and I will hope in him. [18]See, I and the children whom the LORD has given me are signs and portents in Israel from the LORD of hosts, who dwells on Mount Zion. [19]Now if people say to you, "Consult the ghosts and the familiar spirits that chirp and mutter; should not a people consult their gods, the dead on behalf of the living, [20]for teaching and for instruction?" surely, those who speak like this will have no dawn! [21]They will pass through the land,[x] greatly distressed and hungry; when they are hungry, they will be enraged and will curse[y] their king and their gods. They will turn their faces upward, [22]or they will look to the earth, but will see only distress and darkness, the gloom of anguish; and they will be thrust into thick darkness.[z]

The Righteous Reign of the Coming King

9 [a]But there will be no gloom for those who were in anguish. In the former time he brought into contempt the land of Zebulun and the land of Naphtali, but in the latter time he will make glorious the way of the sea, the land beyond the Jordan, Galilee of the nations.
[2][b]The people who walked in darkness
         have seen a great light;
   those who lived in a land of deep
         darkness—
     on them light has shined.
[3] You have multiplied the nation,
         you have increased its joy;
   they rejoice before you
     as with joy at the harvest,
     as people exult when dividing
         plunder.
[4] For the yoke of their burden,
     and the bar across their shoulders,
     the rod of their oppressor,
   you have broken as on the day of
         Midian.
[5] For all the boots of the tramping
         warriors
     and all the garments rolled in
         blood
   shall be burned as fuel for
         the fire.
[6] For a child has been born for us,
     a son given to us;
   authority rests upon his shoulders;
     and he is named

[t] That is *The spoil speeds, the prey hastens*   [u] Q Ms
Gk Syr: MT *and I caused to be attested*   [v] Cn:
Meaning of Heb uncertain   [w] Heb *immanu el*
[x] Heb *it*   [y] Or *curse by*   [z] Meaning of Heb
uncertain   [a] Ch 8.23 in Heb   [b] Ch 9.1 in Heb

Wonderful Counselor, Mighty God,
Everlasting Father, Prince of Peace.
7 His authority shall grow continually,
and there shall be endless peace
for the throne of David and his
kingdom.
He will establish and uphold it
with justice and with righteousness
from this time onward and
forevermore.
The zeal of the LORD of hosts will do
this.

Judgment on Arrogance and Oppression

8 The Lord sent a word against Jacob,
and it fell on Israel;
9 and all the people knew it—
Ephraim and the inhabitants of
Samaria—
but in pride and arrogance of
heart they said:
10 "The bricks have fallen,
but we will build with dressed
stones;
the sycamores have been cut down,

but we will put cedars in their
place."
11 So the LORD raised adversaries[c]
against them,
and stirred up their enemies,
12 the Arameans on the east and the
Philistines on the west,
and they devoured Israel with
open mouth.
For all this his anger has not turned
away;
his hand is stretched out still.

13 The people did not turn to him who
struck them,
or seek the LORD of hosts.
14 So the LORD cut off from Israel head
and tail,
palm branch and reed in one
day—
15 elders and dignitaries are the head,
and prophets who teach lies are
the tail;

c Cn: Heb the adversaries of Rezin

Unto Us a Son Is Given

WEDNESDAY

Scripture Reading
for Today:
Isaiah 9.1–6

Verse for Today:
Isaiah 9.6

Given, not lent,
And not withdrawn—once sent,
This Infant of mankind, this One,
Is still the little welcome Son.

New every year,
New born and newly dear,
He comes with tidings, and a song,
The ages long, the ages long;

Even as the cold
Keen winter grows not old,
As childhood is so fresh, foreseen,
And spring in the familiar green—

Sudden as sweet
Come the expected feet.
All joy is young, and new all art,
And He, too, Whom we have by heart.

—ALICE MEYNELL

Go to page 965 for your next devotional reading.

16 for those who led this people led
    them astray,
    and those who were led by them
      were left in confusion.
17 That is why the Lord did not have
    pity on[d] their young people,
    or compassion on their orphans
      and widows;
for everyone was godless and an
    evildoer,
    and every mouth spoke folly.
For all this his anger has not turned
    away;
    his hand is stretched out still.

18 For wickedness burned like a fire,
    consuming briers and thorns;
it kindled the thickets of the forest,
    and they swirled upward in a
      column of smoke.
19 Through the wrath of the LORD of
    hosts
    the land was burned,
and the people became like fuel for
    the fire;
    no one spared another.
20 They gorged on the right, but still
    were hungry,
    and they devoured on the left, but
      were not satisfied;
they devoured the flesh of their own
    kindred;[e]
21 Manasseh devoured Ephraim, and
    Ephraim Manasseh,
    and together they were against
      Judah.
For all this his anger has not turned
    away;
    his hand is stretched out still.

10 Ah, you who make iniquitous
    decrees,
    who write oppressive statutes,
2 to turn aside the needy from justice
    and to rob the poor of my people
      of their right,
that widows may be your spoil,
    and that you may make the
      orphans your prey!
3 What will you do on the day of
    punishment,
    in the calamity that will come
      from far away?
To whom will you flee for help,
    and where will you leave your
      wealth,
4 so as not to crouch among the
    prisoners

or fall among the slain?
For all this his anger has not turned
    away;
    his hand is stretched out still.

Arrogant Assyria Also Judged

5 Ah, Assyria, the rod of my anger—
    the club in their hands is my fury!
6 Against a godless nation I send him,
    and against the people of my
      wrath I command him,
to take spoil and seize plunder,
    and to tread them down like the
      mire of the streets.
7 But this is not what he intends,
    nor does he have this in mind;
but it is in his heart to destroy,
    and to cut off nations not a few.
8 For he says:
"Are not my commanders all kings?
9 Is not Calno like Carchemish?
    Is not Hamath like Arpad?
    Is not Samaria like Damascus?
10 As my hand has reached to the
    kingdoms of the idols
    whose images were greater than
      those of Jerusalem and
      Samaria,
11 shall I not do to Jerusalem and
    her idols
    what I have done to Samaria and
      her images?"

12 When the Lord has finished all his work on Mount Zion and on Jerusalem, he[f] will punish the arrogant boasting of the king of Assyria and his haughty pride. 13 For he says:
"By the strength of my hand I have
    done it,
    and by my wisdom, for I have
      understanding;
I have removed the boundaries of
    peoples,
    and have plundered their
      treasures;
like a bull I have brought down
    those who sat on thrones.
14 My hand has found, like a nest,
    the wealth of the peoples;
and as one gathers eggs that have
    been forsaken,
so I have gathered all the earth;
    and there was none that moved a
      wing,
    or opened its mouth, or chirped."

d Q Ms: MT *rejoice over*   e Or *arm*   f Heb *I*

15 Shall the ax vaunt itself over the one
  who wields it,
    or the saw magnify itself against
    the one who handles it?
  As if a rod should raise the one who
  lifts it up,
    or as if a staff should lift the one
    who is not wood!
16 Therefore the Sovereign, the Lord of
  hosts,
    will send wasting sickness among
    his stout warriors,
  and under his glory a burning will
  be kindled,
    like the burning of fire.
17 The light of Israel will become a fire,
    and his Holy One a flame;
  and it will burn and devour
    his thorns and briers in one day.
18 The glory of his forest and his
  fruitful land
    the Lord will destroy, both soul
    and body,
    and it will be as when an invalid
    wastes away.
19 The remnant of the trees of his
  forest will be so few
    that a child can write them down.

The Repentant Remnant of Israel

20 On that day the remnant of Israel
and the survivors of the house of Jacob
will no more lean on the one who struck
them, but will lean on the Lord, the Holy
One of Israel, in truth. 21A remnant will
return, the remnant of Jacob, to the
mighty God. 22For though your people Israel were like the sand of the sea, only a
remnant of them will return. Destruction
is decreed, overflowing with righteousness. 23For the Lord God of hosts will
make a full end, as decreed, in all the
earth. g

24 Therefore thus says the Lord God of
hosts: O my people, who live in Zion, do
not be afraid of the Assyrians when they
beat you with a rod and lift up their staff
against you as the Egyptians did. 25For
in a very little while my indignation will
come to an end, and my anger will be
directed to their destruction. 26The Lord of
hosts will wield a whip against them, as
when he struck Midian at the rock of
Oreb; his staff will be over the sea, and he
will lift it as he did in Egypt. 27On that day
his burden will be removed from your
shoulder, and his yoke will be destroyed
from your neck.

He has gone up from Rimmon,h
28   he has come to Aiath;
  he has passed through Migron,
    at Michmash he stores his
    baggage;
29 they have crossed over the pass,
    at Geba they lodge for the night;
  Ramah trembles,
    Gibeah of Saul has fled.
30 Cry aloud, O daughter Gallim!
    Listen, O Laishah!
    Answer her, O Anathoth!
31 Madmenah is in flight,
    the inhabitants of Gebim flee
    for safety.
32 This very day he will halt at Nob,
    he will shake his fist
    at the mount of daughter Zion,
    the hill of Jerusalem.

33 Look, the Sovereign, the Lord
    of hosts,
    will lop the boughs with terrifying
    power;
  the tallest trees will be cut down,
    and the lofty will be brought low.
34 He will hack down the thickets of
    the forest with an ax,
    and Lebanon with its majestic
    treesi will fall.

The Peaceful Kingdom

11 A shoot shall come out from the
    stump of Jesse,
  and a branch shall grow out of his
  roots.
2 The spirit of the Lord shall rest
    on him,
    the spirit of wisdom and
    understanding,
    the spirit of counsel and might,
    the spirit of knowledge and the
    fear of the Lord.
3 His delight shall be in the fear of
    the Lord.

  He shall not judge by what his
    eyes see,
    or decide by what his ears hear;
4 but with righteousness he shall
    judge the poor,
    and decide with equity for the
    meek of the earth;

---

g Or *land* h Cn: Heb *and his yoke from your neck,
and a yoke will be destroyed because of fatness*
i Cn Compare Gk Vg: Heb *with a majestic one*

he shall strike the earth with the rod
    of his mouth,
and with the breath of his lips he
    shall kill the wicked.
5 Righteousness shall be the belt
    around his waist,
and faithfulness the belt around
    his loins.

6 The wolf shall live with the lamb,
    the leopard shall lie down with
      the kid,
the calf and the lion and the fatling
    together,
and a little child shall lead them.
7 The cow and the bear shall graze,
    their young shall lie down
      together;

and the lion shall eat straw like
    the ox.
8 The nursing child shall play over the
    hole of the asp,
and the weaned child shall put its
    hand on the adder's den.
9 They will not hurt or destroy
    on all my holy mountain;
for the earth will be full of the
    knowledge of the LORD
    as the waters cover the sea.

Return of the Remnant of Israel and Judah

10 On that day the root of Jesse shall stand as a signal to the peoples; the nations shall inquire of him, and his dwelling shall be glorious.

11 On that day the Lord will extend his

THE TRADITION

Confirmation

The spirit of the LORD shall rest on him.
ISAIAH 11.2

"It's a gift," people said of Mozart, who composed his first symphony at age ten.

"It's a gift," people say of someone with a photographic memory or a personality so winning it can coax a smile from the grumpy or a generous contribution from the stingy.

Unearned, unsought, unmerited. "It's a gift."

Amazingly, the greatest free gift of all is available to all. This is the Holy Spirit, *the* gift of God, according to Jesus (see John 4.10). Received for the first time in Baptism, the Spirit comes to us in a special way in the sacrament of Confirmation.

"God anointed Jesus of Nazareth with the Holy Spirit and with power" (Acts 10.38). In Confirmation we are anointed with chrism and receive an outpouring of the Spirit and an increase of baptismal grace that gives us new power to witness to Christ even in the face of opposition. Receiving the Spirit is like being given a set of nestled boxes within a box—but one that has no end. This Gift

comes bearing gifts so numerous and diverse that they could never be counted and classified! Traditionally, we speak of them as "the seven gifts of the Holy Spirit," the number derived from Isaiah's list (see 11.2–3), because seven is the Biblical number that symbolizes fullness; however, this is best read as a shorthand indicator that the Spirit dispenses gifts without measure.

Some of the Spirit's gifts equip us for specific tasks, great or small. Some, like healing and miracles, are extraordinary signs of God's power and action and pack an evangelistic punch. The classic gifts associated with Confirmation—wisdom, understanding, knowledge, counsel, fortitude, piety, and fear of the Lord—are directed to our personal growth in holiness. Characteristics of Jesus, these seven gifts are a way to "put on Christ" and experience his life from the inside.

Confirmation is a privileged moment for meeting the Holy Spirit as our soul's greatest guide.

Truly, it's a gift.

hand yet a second time to recover the remnant that is left of his people, from Assyria, from Egypt, from Pathros, from Ethiopia, *j* from Elam, from Shinar, from Hamath, and from the coastlands of the sea.

12 He will raise a signal for the nations,
and will assemble the outcasts of
Israel,
and gather the dispersed of Judah
from the four corners of the earth.
13 The jealousy of Ephraim shall
depart,
the hostility of Judah shall be
cut off;
Ephraim shall not be jealous of
Judah,
and Judah shall not be hostile
towards Ephraim.
14 But they shall swoop down on the
backs of the Philistines in the
west,
together they shall plunder the
people of the east.
They shall put forth their hand
against Edom and Moab,
and the Ammonites shall
obey them.
15 And the LORD will utterly destroy
the tongue of the sea of Egypt;
and will wave his hand over
the River
with his scorching wind;
and will split it into seven channels,
and make a way to cross on foot;
16 so there shall be a highway from
Assyria
for the remnant that is left of
his people,
as there was for Israel
when they came up from the land
of Egypt.

Thanksgiving and Praise

12 You will say in that day:
I will give thanks to you,
O LORD,
for though you were angry
with me,
your anger turned away,
and you comforted me.

2 Surely God is my salvation;
I will trust, and will not be afraid,
for the LORD GOD *k* is my strength
and my might;
he has become my salvation.

3 With joy you will draw water from
the wells of salvation. 4And you will say in
that day:
Give thanks to the LORD,
call on his name;
make known his deeds among the
nations;
proclaim that his name is exalted.

5 Sing praises to the LORD, for he has
done gloriously;
let this be known*l* in all the
earth.
6 Shout aloud and sing for joy,
O royal*m* Zion,
for great in your midst is the Holy
One of Israel.

Proclamation against Babylon

13 The oracle concerning Babylon
that Isaiah son of Amoz saw.

2 On a bare hill raise a signal,
cry aloud to them;
wave the hand for them to enter
the gates of the nobles.
3 I myself have commanded my
consecrated ones,
have summoned my warriors, my
proudly exulting ones,
to execute my anger.

4 Listen, a tumult on the mountains
as of a great multitude!
Listen, an uproar of kingdoms,
of nations gathering together!
The LORD of hosts is mustering
an army for battle.
5 They come from a distant land,
from the end of the heavens,
the LORD and the weapons of his
indignation,
to destroy the whole earth.

6 Wail, for the day of the LORD is near;
it will come like destruction from
the Almighty!*n*
7 Therefore all hands will be feeble,
and every human heart will melt,
8 and they will be dismayed.
Pangs and agony will seize them;
they will be in anguish like a
woman in labor.

j Or *Nubia*; Heb *Cush*   *k* Heb *for Yah, the* LORD
l Or *this is made known*   *m* Or *O inhabitant of*
n Traditional rendering of Heb *Shaddai*

They will look aghast at one
    another;
  their faces will be aflame.
⁹ See, the day of the LORD comes,
    cruel, with wrath and fierce anger,
  to make the earth a desolation,
    and to destroy its sinners from it.
¹⁰ For the stars of the heavens and
    their constellations
  will not give their light;
  the sun will be dark at its rising,
    and the moon will not shed
      its light.
¹¹ I will punish the world for its evil,
    and the wicked for their iniquity;
  I will put an end to the pride of
    the arrogant,
  and lay low the insolence of
    tyrants.
¹² I will make mortals more rare than
    fine gold,
  and humans than the gold of
    Ophir.
¹³ Therefore I will make the heavens
    tremble,
  and the earth will be shaken out
    of its place,
  at the wrath of the LORD of hosts
    in the day of his fierce anger.
¹⁴ Like a hunted gazelle,
    or like sheep with no one to
      gather them,
  all will turn to their own people,
    and all will flee to their
      own lands.
¹⁵ Whoever is found will be thrust
    through,
  and whoever is caught will fall by
    the sword.
¹⁶ Their infants will be dashed
    to pieces
  before their eyes;
  their houses will be plundered,
    and their wives ravished.
¹⁷ See, I am stirring up the Medes
    against them,
  who have no regard for silver
    and do not delight in gold.
¹⁸ Their bows will slaughter the young
    men;
  they will have no mercy on the
    fruit of the womb;
  their eyes will not pity children.
¹⁹ And Babylon, the glory of kingdoms,
    the splendor and pride of the
      Chaldeans,
  will be like Sodom and Gomorrah
    when God overthrew them.

²⁰ It will never be inhabited
    or lived in for all generations;
  Arabs will not pitch their tents there,
    shepherds will not make their
      flocks lie down there.
²¹ But wild animals will lie
    down there,
  and its houses will be full of
    howling creatures;
  there ostriches will live,
    and there goat-demons will dance.
²² Hyenas will cry in its towers,
    and jackals in the pleasant
      palaces;
  its time is close at hand,
    and its days will not be
      prolonged.

Restoration of Judah

14 But the LORD will have compassion on Jacob and will again choose Israel, and will set them in their own land; and aliens will join them and attach themselves to the house of Jacob. ²And the nations will take them and bring them to their place, and the house of Israel will possess the nations*ᵒ* as male and female slaves in the LORD's land; they will take captive those who were their captors, and rule over those who oppressed them.

Downfall of the King of Babylon

3 When the LORD has given you rest from your pain and turmoil and the hard service with which you were made to serve, ⁴you will take up this taunt against the king of Babylon:
  How the oppressor has ceased!
    How his insolence *ᵖ* has ceased!
⁵ The LORD has broken the staff of the
    wicked,
  the scepter of rulers,
⁶ that struck down the peoples
    in wrath
  with unceasing blows,
  that ruled the nations in anger
    with unrelenting persecution.
⁷ The whole earth is at rest and quiet;
    they break forth into singing.
⁸ The cypresses exult over you,
    the cedars of Lebanon, saying,
  "Since you were laid low,
    no one comes to cut us down."
⁹ Sheol beneath is stirred up
    to meet you when you come;

ᵒ Heb *them*   *ᵖ* Q Ms Compare Gk Syr Vg:
Meaning of MT uncertain

it rouses the shades to greet you,
    all who were leaders of the earth;
it raises from their thrones
    all who were kings of the nations.
10 All of them will speak
    and say to you:
"You too have become as weak
        as we!
You have become like us!"
11 Your pomp is brought down
        to Sheol,
    and the sound of your harps;
maggots are the bed beneath you,
    and worms are your covering.

12 How you are fallen from heaven,
    O Day Star, son of Dawn!
How you are cut down to the
        ground,
    you who laid the nations low!
13 You said in your heart,
    "I will ascend to heaven;
I will raise my throne
    above the stars of God;
I will sit on the mount of assembly
    on the heights of Zaphon;*q*
14 I will ascend to the tops of the
        clouds,
    I will make myself like the
        Most High."
15 But you are brought down to Sheol,
    to the depths of the Pit.
16 Those who see you will stare at you,
    and ponder over you:
"Is this the man who made the
        earth tremble,
    who shook kingdoms,
17 who made the world like a desert
    and overthrew its cities,
    who would not let his prisoners
        go home?"
18 All the kings of the nations lie
    in glory,
    each in his own tomb;
19 but you are cast out, away from
        your grave,
    like loathsome carrion,*r*
clothed with the dead, those pierced
        by the sword,
    who go down to the stones of
        the Pit,
    like a corpse trampled underfoot.
20 You will not be joined with them
    in burial,
    because you have destroyed
        your land,
    you have killed your people.

May the descendants of evildoers
    nevermore be named!
21 Prepare slaughter for his sons
    because of the guilt of their
        father.*s*
Let them never rise to possess
        the earth
    or cover the face of the world
        with cities.

22 I will rise up against them, says the
Lord of hosts, and will cut off from Babylon name and remnant, offspring and
posterity, says the Lord. 23And I will make
it a possession of the hedgehog, and pools
of water, and I will sweep it with the
broom of destruction, says the Lord of
hosts.

An Oracle concerning Assyria

24 The Lord of hosts has sworn:
As I have designed,
    so shall it be;
and as I have planned,
    so shall it come to pass:
25 I will break the Assyrian in my land,
    and on my mountains trample
        him under foot;
his yoke shall be removed
        from them,
    and his burden from their
        shoulders.
26 This is the plan that is planned
    concerning the whole earth;
and this is the hand that is stretched
        out
    over all the nations.
27 For the Lord of hosts has planned,
    and who will annul it?
His hand is stretched out,
    and who will turn it back?

An Oracle concerning Philistia

28In the year that King Ahaz died this oracle came:

29 Do not rejoice, all you Philistines,
    that the rod that struck you
        is broken,
for from the root of the snake will
        come forth an adder,
    and its fruit will be a flying
        fiery serpent.
30 The firstborn of the poor will graze,

q Or *assembly in the far north*   *r* Cn Compare Gk:
Heb *like a loathed branch*   *s* Syr Compare Gk:
Heb *fathers*

and the needy lie down in safety;
but I will make your root die
    of famine,
and your remnant I[t] will kill.
31 Wail, O gate; cry, O city;
    melt in fear, O Philistia, all
    of you!
For smoke comes out of the north,
    and there is no straggler in
    its ranks.

32 What will one answer the
    messengers of the nation?
"The LORD has founded Zion,
    and the needy among his people
    will find refuge in her."

An Oracle concerning Moab

15 An oracle concerning Moab.

Because Ar is laid waste in a night,
    Moab is undone;
because Kir is laid waste in a night,
    Moab is undone.
2 Dibon[u] has gone up to the temple,
    to the high places to weep;
over Nebo and over Medeba
    Moab wails.
On every head is baldness,
    every beard is shorn;
3 in the streets they bind on sackcloth;
    on the housetops and in the
      squares
    everyone wails and melts in tears.
4 Heshbon and Elealeh cry out,
    their voices are heard as far
    as Jahaz;
therefore the loins of Moab quiver;[v]
    his soul trembles.
5 My heart cries out for Moab;
    his fugitives flee to Zoar,
    to Eglath-shelishiyah.
For at the ascent of Luhith
    they go up weeping;
on the road to Horonaim
    they raise a cry of destruction;
6 the waters of Nimrim
    are a desolation;
the grass is withered, the new
      growth fails,
    the verdure is no more.
7 Therefore the abundance they
      have gained
    and what they have laid up
they carry away
    over the Wadi of the Willows.
8 For a cry has gone
    around the land of Moab;

the wailing reaches to Eglaim,
    the wailing reaches to Beer-elim.
9 For the waters of Dibon[w] are full
    of blood;
yet I will bring upon Dibon[w]
    even more—
a lion for those of Moab
    who escape,
for the remnant of the land.

16 Send lambs
    to the ruler of the land,
from Sela, by way of the desert,
    to the mount of daughter Zion.
2 Like fluttering birds,
    like scattered nestlings,
so are the daughters of Moab
    at the fords of the Arnon.
3 "Give counsel,
    grant justice;
make your shade like night
    at the height of noon;
hide the outcasts,
    do not betray the fugitive;
4 let the outcasts of Moab
    settle among you;
be a refuge to them
    from the destroyer."

When the oppressor is no more,
    and destruction has ceased,
and marauders have vanished from
      the land,
5 then a throne shall be established in
      steadfast love
    in the tent of David,
    and on it shall sit in faithfulness
a ruler who seeks justice
    and is swift to do what is right.

6 We have heard of the pride of Moab
    —how proud he is!—
of his arrogance, his pride, and his
      insolence;
    his boasts are false.
7 Therefore let Moab wail,
    let everyone wail for Moab.
Mourn, utterly stricken,
    for the raisin cakes of
    Kir-hareseth.

8 For the fields of Heshbon languish,
    and the vines of Sibmah,
whose clusters once made drunk

---

t Q Ms Vg: MT *he*   u Cn: Heb *the house and
Dibon*   v Cn Compare Gk Syr: Heb *the armed
men of Moab cry aloud*   w Q Ms Vg Compare Syr:
MT *Dimon*

the lords of the nations,
reached to Jazer
and strayed to the desert;
their shoots once spread abroad
and crossed over the sea.
9 Therefore I weep with the weeping
of Jazer
for the vines of Sibmah;
I drench you with my tears,
O Heshbon and Elealeh;
for the shout over your fruit harvest
and your grain harvest has ceased.
10 Joy and gladness are taken away
from the fruitful field;
and in the vineyards no songs
are sung,
no shouts are raised;
no treader treads out wine in
the presses;
the vintage-shout is hushed.*x*
11 Therefore my heart throbs like a
harp for Moab,
and my very soul for Kir-heres.

12 When Moab presents himself, when he wearies himself upon the high place, when he comes to his sanctuary to pray, he will not prevail.

13 This was the word that the LORD spoke concerning Moab in the past. 14But now the LORD says, In three years, like the years of a hired worker, the glory of Moab will be brought into contempt, in spite of all its great multitude; and those who survive will be very few and feeble.

An Oracle concerning Damascus

17

An oracle concerning Damascus.

See, Damascus will cease to be
a city,
and will become a heap of ruins.
2 Her towns will be deserted forever;*y*
they will be places for flocks,
which will lie down, and no one
will make them afraid.
3 The fortress will disappear from
Ephraim,
and the kingdom from Damascus;
and the remnant of Aram will be
like the glory of the children
of Israel,
says the LORD of hosts.

4 On that day
the glory of Jacob will be
brought low,
and the fat of his flesh will
grow lean.

5 And it shall be as when reapers
gather standing grain
and their arms harvest the ears,
and as when one gleans the ears
of grain
in the Valley of Rephaim.
6 Gleanings will be left in it,
as when an olive tree is beaten—
two or three berries
in the top of the highest bough,
four or five
on the branches of a fruit tree,
says the LORD God of Israel.

7 On that day people will regard their Maker, and their eyes will look to the Holy One of Israel; 8they will not have regard for the altars, the work of their hands, and they will not look to what their own fingers have made, either the sacred poles*z* or the altars of incense.

9 On that day their strong cities will be like the deserted places of the Hivites and the Amorites,*a* which they deserted because of the children of Israel, and there will be desolation.

10 For you have forgotten the God of
your salvation,
and have not remembered the
Rock of your refuge;
therefore, though you plant pleasant
plants
and set out slips of an alien god,
11 though you make them grow on the
day that you plant them,
and make them blossom in the
morning that you sow;
yet the harvest will flee away
in a day of grief and incurable
pain.

12 Ah, the thunder of many peoples,
they thunder like the thundering
of the sea!
Ah, the roar of nations,
they roar like the roaring of
mighty waters!
13 The nations roar like the roaring of
many waters,
but he will rebuke them, and they
will flee far away,

---

x Gk: Heb *I have hushed*   *y* Cn Compare Gk: Heb *the cities of Aroer are deserted*   *z* Heb *Asherim*   *a* Cn Compare Gk: Heb *places of the wood and the highest bough*

chased like chaff on the mountains
before the wind
and whirling dust before the
storm.
14 At evening time, lo, terror!
Before morning, they are no more.
This is the fate of those who
despoil us,
and the lot of those who
plunder us.

An Oracle concerning Ethiopia

18 Ah, land of whirring wings
beyond the rivers of Ethiopia,[b]
2 sending ambassadors by the Nile
in vessels of papyrus on the
waters!
Go, you swift messengers,
to a nation tall and smooth,
to a people feared near and far,
a nation mighty and conquering,
whose land the rivers divide.

3 All you inhabitants of the world,
you who live on the earth,
when a signal is raised on the
mountains, look!
When a trumpet is blown, listen!
4 For thus the LORD said to me:
I will quietly look from my dwelling
like clear heat in sunshine,
like a cloud of dew in the heat
of harvest.
5 For before the harvest, when the
blossom is over
and the flower becomes a ripening
grape,
he will cut off the shoots with
pruning hooks,
and the spreading branches he
will hew away.
6 They shall all be left
to the birds of prey of the
mountains
and to the animals of the earth.
And the birds of prey will summer
on them,
and all the animals of the earth
will winter on them.

7 At that time gifts will be brought to
the LORD of hosts from[c] a people tall and
smooth, from a people feared near and
far, a nation mighty and conquering,
whose land the rivers divide, to Mount
Zion, the place of the name of the LORD of
hosts.

An Oracle concerning Egypt

19 An oracle concerning Egypt.

See, the LORD is riding on a
swift cloud
and comes to Egypt;
the idols of Egypt will tremble at his
presence,
and the heart of the Egyptians will
melt within them.
2 I will stir up Egyptians against
Egyptians,
and they will fight, one against
the other,
neighbor against neighbor,
city against city, kingdom against
kingdom;
3 the spirit of the Egyptians within
them will be emptied out,
and I will confound their plans;
they will consult the idols and the
spirits of the dead
and the ghosts and the familiar
spirits;
4 I will deliver the Egyptians
into the hand of a hard master;
a fierce king will rule over them,
says the Sovereign, the LORD
of hosts.

5 The waters of the Nile will be
dried up,
and the river will be parched
and dry;
6 its canals will become foul,
and the branches of Egypt's Nile
will diminish and dry up,
reeds and rushes will rot away.
7 There will be bare places by
the Nile,
on the brink of the Nile;
and all that is sown by the Nile will
dry up,
be driven away, and be no more.
8 Those who fish will mourn,
all who cast hooks in the Nile will
lament,
and those who spread nets on the
water will languish.
9 The workers in flax will be in
despair,
and the carders and those at the
loom will grow pale.
10 Its weavers will be dismayed,

b Or *Nubia*; Heb *Cush*   c Q Ms Gk Vg: MT *of*

and all who work for wages will
be grieved.

11 The princes of Zoan are utterly
foolish;
the wise counselors of Pharaoh
give stupid counsel.
How can you say to Pharaoh,
"I am one of the sages,
a descendant of ancient kings"?
12 Where now are your sages?
Let them tell you and make
known
what the LORD of hosts has
planned against Egypt.
13 The princes of Zoan have become
fools,
and the princes of Memphis
are deluded;
those who are the cornerstones of its
tribes
have led Egypt astray.
14 The LORD has poured into them[d]
a spirit of confusion;
and they have made Egypt stagger in
all its doings
as a drunkard staggers around
in vomit.
15 Neither head nor tail, palm branch
or reed,
will be able to do anything for
Egypt.

16 On that day the Egyptians will be
like women, and tremble with fear before
the hand that the LORD of hosts raises
against them. 17And the land of Judah will
become a terror to the Egyptians; everyone to whom it is mentioned will fear because of the plan that the LORD of hosts is
planning against them.

Egypt, Assyria, and Israel Blessed

18 On that day there will be five cities
in the land of Egypt that speak the language of Canaan and swear allegiance to
the LORD of hosts. One of these will be
called the City of the Sun.

19 On that day there will be an altar to
the LORD in the center of the land of Egypt,
and a pillar to the LORD at its border. 20It
will be a sign and a witness to the LORD of
hosts in the land of Egypt; when they cry
to the LORD because of oppressors, he will
send them a savior, and will defend and
deliver them. 21The LORD will make himself known to the Egyptians; and the
Egyptians will know the LORD on that day,
and will worship with sacrifice and burnt
offering, and they will make vows to the
LORD and perform them. 22The LORD will
strike Egypt, striking and healing; they
will return to the LORD, and he will listen
to their supplications and heal them.

23 On that day there will be a highway
from Egypt to Assyria, and the Assyrian
will come into Egypt, and the Egyptian
into Assyria, and the Egyptians will worship with the Assyrians.

24 On that day Israel will be the third
with Egypt and Assyria, a blessing in the
midst of the earth, 25whom the LORD of
hosts has blessed, saying, "Blessed be
Egypt my people, and Assyria the work of
my hands, and Israel my heritage."

Isaiah Dramatizes the Conquest of Egypt and Ethiopia

20 In the year that the commander-
in-chief, who was sent by King
Sargon of Assyria, came to Ashdod and
fought against it and took it— 2at that
time the LORD had spoken to Isaiah son of
Amoz, saying, "Go, and loose the sackcloth from your loins and take your sandals off your feet," and he had done so,
walking naked and barefoot. 3Then the
LORD said, "Just as my servant Isaiah has
walked naked and barefoot for three years
as a sign and a portent against Egypt and
Ethiopia,[e] 4so shall the king of Assyria
lead away the Egyptians as captives and
the Ethiopians[f] as exiles, both the young
and the old, naked and barefoot, with
buttocks uncovered, to the shame of
Egypt. 5And they shall be dismayed and
confounded because of Ethiopia[e] their
hope and of Egypt their boast. 6In that day
the inhabitants of this coastland will say,
'See, this is what has happened to those in
whom we hoped and to whom we fled for
help and deliverance from the king of Assyria! And we, how shall we escape?' "

Oracles concerning Babylon, Edom, and Arabia

21 The oracle concerning the wilderness of the sea.

As whirlwinds in the Negeb
sweep on,
it comes from the desert,
from a terrible land.

[d] Gk Compare Tg: Heb *it*   [e] Or *Nubia*; Heb *Cush*
[f] Or *Nubians*; Heb *Cushites*

2 A stern vision is told to me;
   the betrayer betrays,
   and the destroyer destroys.
Go up, O Elam,
   lay siege, O Media;
all the sighing she has caused
   I bring to an end.
3 Therefore my loins are filled
       with anguish;
   pangs have seized me,
   like the pangs of a woman
       in labor;
I am bowed down so that I
       cannot hear,
I am dismayed so that I
       cannot see.
4 My mind reels, horror has
       appalled me;
   the twilight I longed for
   has been turned for me into
       trembling.
5 They prepare the table,
   they spread the rugs,
   they eat, they drink.
Rise up, commanders,
   oil the shield!
6 For thus the Lord said to me:
"Go, post a lookout,
   let him announce what he sees.
7 When he sees riders, horsemen
       in pairs,
   riders on donkeys, riders
       on camels,
   let him listen diligently,
       very diligently."
8 Then the watcher *g* called out:
"Upon a watchtower I stand,
       O Lord,
   continually by day,
and at my post I am stationed
   throughout the night.
9 Look, there they come, riders,
   horsemen in pairs!"
Then he responded,
   "Fallen, fallen is Babylon;
and all the images of her gods
   lie shattered on the ground."
10 O my threshed and winnowed one,
   what I have heard from the LORD
       of hosts,
   the God of Israel, I announce
       to you.

11 The oracle concerning Dumah.

One is calling to me from Seir,
   "Sentinel, what of the night?
   Sentinel, what of the night?"

12 The sentinel says:
"Morning comes, and also the night.
   If you will inquire, inquire;
   come back again."

13 The oracle concerning the desert plain.

In the scrub of the desert plain you
       will lodge,
   O caravans of Dedanites.
14 Bring water to the thirsty,
   meet the fugitive with bread,
   O inhabitants of the land
       of Tema.
15 For they have fled from the swords,
   from the drawn sword,
from the bent bow,
   and from the stress of battle.

16 For thus the Lord said to me: Within a year, according to the years of a hired worker, all the glory of Kedar will come to an end; 17and the remaining bows of Kedar's warriors will be few; for the LORD, the God of Israel, has spoken.

A Warning of Destruction of Jerusalem

22 The oracle concerning the valley of vision.

What do you mean that you have
       gone up,
   all of you, to the housetops,
2 you that are full of shoutings,
   tumultuous city, exultant town?
Your slain are not slain by
       the sword,
   nor are they dead in battle.
3 Your rulers have all fled together;
   they were captured without the
       use of a bow.*h*
All of you who were found were
       captured,
   though they had fled far away.*i*
4 Therefore I said:
Look away from me,
   let me weep bitter tears;
do not try to comfort me
   for the destruction of my
       beloved people.

5 For the Lord GOD of hosts has a day
   of tumult and trampling and
       confusion
   in the valley of vision,

---

g Q Ms: MT *a lion*   *h* Or *without their bows*
i Gk Syr Vg: Heb *fled from far away*

a battering down of walls
and a cry for help to the
mountains.
6 Elam bore the quiver
with chariots and cavalry,[j]
and Kir uncovered the shield.
7 Your choicest valleys were full of
chariots,
and the cavalry took their stand at
the gates.
8 He has taken away the covering
of Judah.

On that day you looked to the weapons of the House of the Forest, 9and you saw that there were many breaches in the city of David, and you collected the waters of the lower pool. 10You counted the houses of Jerusalem, and you broke down the houses to fortify the wall. 11You made a reservoir between the two walls for the water of the old pool. But you did not look to him who did it, or have regard for him who planned it long ago.

12 In that day the Lord GOD of hosts
called to weeping and mourning,
to baldness and putting on
sackcloth;
13 but instead there was joy and
festivity,
killing oxen and slaughtering
sheep,
eating meat and drinking wine.
"Let us eat and drink,
for tomorrow we die."
14 The LORD of hosts has revealed
himself in my ears:
Surely this iniquity will not be
forgiven you until you die,
says the Lord GOD of hosts.

Denunciation of Self-Seeking Officials

15 Thus says the Lord GOD of hosts: Come, go to this steward, to Shebna, who is master of the household, and say to him: 16What right do you have here? Who are your relatives here, that you have cut out a tomb here for yourself, cutting a tomb on the height, and carving a habitation for yourself in the rock? 17The LORD is about to hurl you away violently, my fellow. He will seize firm hold on you, 18whirl you round and round, and throw you like a ball into a wide land; there you shall die, and there your splendid chariots shall lie, O you disgrace to your master's house! 19I will thrust you from your of-

fice, and you will be pulled down from your post.

20 On that day I will call my servant Eliakim son of Hilkiah, 21and will clothe him with your robe and bind your sash on him. I will commit your authority to his hand, and he shall be a father to the inhabitants of Jerusalem and to the house of Judah. 22I will place on his shoulder the key of the house of David; he shall open, and no one shall shut; he shall shut, and no one shall open. 23I will fasten him like a peg in a secure place, and he will become a throne of honor to his ancestral house. 24And they will hang on him the whole weight of his ancestral house, the offspring and issue, every small vessel, from the cups to all the flagons. 25On that day, says the LORD of hosts, the peg that was fastened in a secure place will give way; it will be cut down and fall, and the load that was on it will perish, for the LORD has spoken.

An Oracle concerning Tyre

23 The oracle concerning Tyre.

Wail, O ships of Tarshish,
for your fortress is destroyed.[k]
When they came in from Cyprus
they learned of it.
2 Be still, O inhabitants of the coast,
O merchants of Sidon,
your messengers crossed over
the sea[l]
3 and were on the mighty waters;
your revenue was the grain of
Shihor,
the harvest of the Nile;
you were the merchant of the
nations.
4 Be ashamed, O Sidon, for the sea
has spoken,
the fortress of the sea, saying:
"I have neither labored nor given
birth,
I have neither reared young men
nor brought up young women."
5 When the report comes to Egypt,
they will be in anguish over the
report about Tyre.
6 Cross over to Tarshish—
wail, O inhabitants of the coast!

j Meaning of Heb uncertain   k Cn Compare
verse 14: Heb *for it is destroyed, without houses*
l Q Ms: MT *crossing over the sea, they replenished
you*

7 Is this your exultant city
  whose origin is from days of old,
whose feet carried her
  to settle far away?
8 Who has planned this
  against Tyre, the bestower
    of crowns,
whose merchants were princes,
  whose traders were the honored of
    the earth?
9 The LORD of hosts has planned it—
  to defile the pride of all glory,
  to shame all the honored of the
    earth.
10 Cross over to your own land,
  O ships of[m] Tarshish;
  this is a harbor[n] no more.
11 He has stretched out his hand over
    the sea,
  he has shaken the kingdoms;
the LORD has given command
    concerning Canaan
  to destroy its fortresses.
12 He said:
  You will exult no longer,
  O oppressed virgin daughter
    Sidon;
  rise, cross over to Cyprus—
  even there you will have no rest.

13 Look at the land of the Chaldeans!
This is the people; it was not Assyria. They
destined Tyre for wild animals. They erected their siege towers, they tore down her
palaces, they made her a ruin.[o]
14 Wail, O ships of Tarshish,
  for your fortress is destroyed.
15From that day Tyre will be forgotten for
seventy years, the lifetime of one king. At
the end of seventy years, it will happen to
Tyre as in the song about the prostitute:
16 Take a harp,
  go about the city,
  you forgotten prostitute!
  Make sweet melody,
  sing many songs,
  that you may be remembered.
17At the end of seventy years, the LORD will
visit Tyre, and she will return to her trade,
and will prostitute herself with all the
kingdoms of the world on the face of the
earth. 18Her merchandise and her wages
will be dedicated to the LORD; her profits[p]
will not be stored or hoarded, but her
merchandise will supply abundant food
and fine clothing for those who live in the
presence of the LORD.

Impending Judgment on the Earth

24 Now the LORD is about to lay
    waste the earth and make
    it desolate,
  and he will twist its surface and
    scatter its inhabitants.
2 And it shall be, as with the people,
    so with the priest;
  as with the slave, so with his
    master;
  as with the maid, so with her
    mistress;
  as with the buyer, so with the seller;
  as with the lender, so with the
    borrower;
  as with the creditor, so with
    the debtor.
3 The earth shall be utterly laid waste
    and utterly despoiled;
  for the LORD has spoken this word.

4 The earth dries up and withers,
  the world languishes and withers;
  the heavens languish together with
    the earth.
5 The earth lies polluted
  under its inhabitants;
for they have transgressed laws,
  violated the statutes,
  broken the everlasting covenant.
6 Therefore a curse devours the earth,
  and its inhabitants suffer for their
    guilt;
therefore the inhabitants of the earth
    dwindled,
  and few people are left.
7 The wine dries up,
  the vine languishes,
  all the merry-hearted sigh.
8 The mirth of the timbrels is stilled,
  the noise of the jubilant
    has ceased,
  the mirth of the lyre is stilled.
9 No longer do they drink wine with
    singing;
  strong drink is bitter to those who
    drink it.
10 The city of chaos is broken down,
  every house is shut up so that no
    one can enter.
11 There is an outcry in the streets for
    lack of wine;
  all joy has reached its eventide;

m Cn Compare Gk: Heb *like the Nile, daughter*
n Cn: Heb *restraint*   o Meaning of Heb uncertain
p Heb *it*

the gladness of the earth is
banished.
12 Desolation is left in the city,
the gates are battered into ruins.
13 For thus it shall be on the earth
and among the nations,
as when an olive tree is beaten,
as at the gleaning when the grape
harvest is ended.

14 They lift up their voices, they sing
for joy;
they shout from the west over the
majesty of the LORD.
15 Therefore in the east give glory to
the LORD;
in the coastlands of the sea glorify
the name of the LORD, the
God of Israel.
16 From the ends of the earth we hear
songs of praise,
of glory to the Righteous One.
But I say, I pine away,
I pine away. Woe is me!
For the treacherous deal
treacherously,
the treacherous deal very
treacherously.

17 Terror, and the pit, and the snare
are upon you, O inhabitant of the
earth!
18 Whoever flees at the sound of
the terror
shall fall into the pit;
and whoever climbs out of the pit
shall be caught in the snare.
For the windows of heaven are
opened,
and the foundations of the earth
tremble.
19 The earth is utterly broken,
the earth is torn asunder,
the earth is violently shaken.
20 The earth staggers like a drunkard,
it sways like a hut;
its transgression lies heavy upon it,
and it falls, and will not
rise again.

21 On that day the LORD will punish
the host of heaven in heaven,
and on earth the kings of
the earth.
22 They will be gathered together
like prisoners in a pit;
they will be shut up in a prison,

and after many days they will be
punished.
23 Then the moon will be abashed,
and the sun ashamed;
for the LORD of hosts will reign
on Mount Zion and in Jerusalem,
and before his elders he will
manifest his glory.

Praise for Deliverance from Oppression

25 O LORD, you are my God;
I will exalt you, I will praise
your name;
for you have done wonderful things,
plans formed of old, faithful
and sure.
2 For you have made the city a heap,
the fortified city a ruin;
the palace of aliens is a city
no more,
it will never be rebuilt.
3 Therefore strong peoples will glorify
you;
cities of ruthless nations will
fear you.
4 For you have been a refuge to
the poor,
a refuge to the needy in their
distress,
a shelter from the rainstorm and a
shade from the heat.
When the blast of the ruthless was
like a winter rainstorm,
5 the noise of aliens like heat in a
dry place,
you subdued the heat with the
shade of clouds;
the song of the ruthless
was stilled.

6 On this mountain the LORD of hosts
will make for all peoples
a feast of rich food, a feast of
well-aged wines,
of rich food filled with marrow, of
well-aged wines strained
clear.
7 And he will destroy on this
mountain
the shroud that is cast over all
peoples,
the sheet that is spread over all
nations;
8 he will swallow up death forever.
Then the Lord GOD will wipe away
the tears from all faces,

and the disgrace of his people he
   will take away from all
   the earth,
for the LORD has spoken.
9 It will be said on that day,
   Lo, this is our God; we have
      waited for him, so that he
      might save us.
   This is the LORD for whom we
      have waited;
   let us be glad and rejoice in his
      salvation.
10 For the hand of the LORD will rest on
   this mountain.

The Moabites shall be trodden down
   in their place
   as straw is trodden down in a
      dung-pit.
11 Though they spread out their hands
   in the midst of it,
   as swimmers spread out their
      hands to swim,
   their pride will be laid low despite
      the struggle*q* of their hands.
12 The high fortifications of his walls
   will be brought down,
   laid low, cast to the ground, even
      to the dust.

Judah's Song of Victory

26 On that day this song will be sung
in the land of Judah:
We have a strong city;
   he sets up victory
   like walls and bulwarks.
2 Open the gates,
   so that the righteous nation that
      keeps faith
   may enter in.
3 Those of steadfast mind you keep
   in peace—
   in peace because they trust in you.
4 Trust in the LORD forever,
   for in the LORD GOD *r*
   you have an everlasting rock.
5 For he has brought low
   the inhabitants of the height;
   the lofty city he lays low.
He lays it low to the ground,
   casts it to the dust.
6 The foot tramples it,
   the feet of the poor,
   the steps of the needy.

7 The way of the righteous is level;
   O Just One, you make smooth the
      path of the righteous.

8 In the path of your judgments,
   O LORD, we wait for you;
your name and your renown
   are the soul's desire.
9 My soul yearns for you in the night,
   my spirit within me earnestly
      seeks you.
For when your judgments are in the
   earth,
   the inhabitants of the world learn
      righteousness.
10 If favor is shown to the wicked,
   they do not learn righteousness;
in the land of uprightness they deal
   perversely
   and do not see the majesty of
      the LORD.
11 O LORD, your hand is lifted up,
   but they do not see it.
Let them see your zeal for your
      people, and be ashamed.
   Let the fire for your adversaries
      consume them.
12 O LORD, you will ordain peace
   for us,
   for indeed, all that we have done,
      you have done for us.
13 O LORD our God,
   other lords besides you have ruled
      over us,
   but we acknowledge your
      name alone.
14 The dead do not live;
   shades do not rise—
because you have punished and
      destroyed them,
   and wiped out all memory
      of them.
15 But you have increased the nation,
   O LORD,
   you have increased the nation;
      you are glorified;
   you have enlarged all the borders
      of the land.

16 O LORD, in distress they sought you,
   they poured out a prayer*q*
   when your chastening was
      on them.
17 Like a woman with child,
   who writhes and cries out in
      her pangs
   when she is near her time,
so were we because of you, O LORD;
18   we were with child, we writhed,

q Meaning of Heb uncertain   *r Heb in Yah,*
the LORD

but we gave birth only to wind.
We have won no victories on earth,
and no one is born to inhabit
the world.
19 Your dead shall live, their corpses[s]
shall rise.
O dwellers in the dust, awake and
sing for joy!
For your dew is a radiant dew,
and the earth will give birth to
those long dead.[t]

20 Come, my people, enter your
chambers,
and shut your doors behind you;
hide yourselves for a little while
until the wrath is past.
21 For the LORD comes out from
his place
to punish the inhabitants of the
earth for their iniquity;
the earth will disclose the blood
shed on it,
and will no longer cover its slain.

Israel's Redemption

27 On that day the LORD with his cruel and great and strong sword will punish Leviathan the fleeing serpent, Leviathan the twisting serpent, and he will kill the dragon that is in the sea.

2 On that day:
A pleasant vineyard, sing about it!
3 I, the LORD, am its keeper;
every moment I water it.
I guard it night and day
so that no one can harm it;
4 I have no wrath.
If it gives me thorns and briers,
I will march to battle against it.
I will burn it up.
5 Or else let it cling to me for
protection,
let it make peace with me,
let it make peace with me.

6 In days to come[u] Jacob shall
take root,
Israel shall blossom and put
forth shoots,
and fill the whole world
with fruit.

7 Has he struck them down as he
struck down those who struck
them?

Or have they been killed as their
killers were killed?
8 By expulsion,[v] by exile you
struggled against them;
with his fierce blast he removed
them in the day of the
east wind.
9 Therefore by this the guilt of Jacob
will be expiated,
and this will be the full fruit of
the removal of his sin:
when he makes all the stones of the
altars
like chalkstones crushed to pieces,
no sacred poles[w] or incense altars
will remain standing.
10 For the fortified city is solitary,
a habitation deserted and
forsaken, like the wilderness;
the calves graze there,
there they lie down, and strip its
branches.
11 When its boughs are dry, they
are broken;
women come and make a fire
of them.
For this is a people without
understanding;
therefore he that made them will
not have compassion
on them,
he that formed them will show
them no favor.

12 On that day the LORD will thresh from the channel of the Euphrates to the Wadi of Egypt, and you will be gathered one by one, O people of Israel. 13 And on that day a great trumpet will be blown, and those who were lost in the land of Assyria and those who were driven out to the land of Egypt will come and worship the LORD on the holy mountain at Jerusalem.

Judgment on Corrupt Rulers, Priests, and Prophets

28 Ah, the proud garland of the drunkards of Ephraim,
and the fading flower of its
glorious beauty,
which is on the head of those
bloated with rich food, of
those overcome with wine!

[s] Cn Compare Syr Tg: Heb *my corpse*   [t] Heb *to the shades*   [u] Heb *Those to come*   [v] Meaning of Heb uncertain   [w] Heb *Asherim*

2 See, the Lord has one who is mighty
    and strong;
  like a storm of hail, a destroying
      tempest,
  like a storm of mighty, overflowing
      waters;
  with his hand he will hurl them
      down to the earth.
3 Trampled under foot will be
    the proud garland of the
      drunkards of Ephraim.
4 And the fading flower of its glorious
    beauty,
  which is on the head of those
      bloated with rich food,
  will be like a first-ripe fig before the
      summer;
  whoever sees it, eats it up
      as soon as it comes to hand.

5 In that day the Lord of hosts will be
    a garland of glory,
  and a diadem of beauty, to the
      remnant of his people;
6 and a spirit of justice to the one
    who sits in judgment,
  and strength to those who turn
      back the battle at the gate.

7 These also reel with wine
    and stagger with strong drink;
  the priest and the prophet reel with
      strong drink,
  they are confused with wine,
    they stagger with strong drink;
  they err in vision,
    they stumble in giving judgment.
8 All tables are covered with
    filthy vomit;
  no place is clean.

9 "Whom will he teach knowledge,
    and to whom will he explain
      the message?
  Those who are weaned from milk,
    those taken from the breast?
10 For it is precept upon precept,
      precept upon precept,
    line upon line, line upon line,
      here a little, there a little."ˣ

11 Truly, with stammering lip
    and with alien tongue
  he will speak to this people,
12   to whom he has said,
  "This is rest;
    give rest to the weary;
  and this is repose";

yet they would not hear.
13 Therefore the word of the Lord will
      be to them,
    "Precept upon precept, precept
      upon precept,
  line upon line, line upon line,
    here a little, there a little;"ˣ
  in order that they may go, and fall
      backward,
    and be broken, and snared,
      and taken.

14 Therefore hear the word of the Lord,
      you scoffers
  who rule this people in Jerusalem.
15 Because you have said, "We have
      made a covenant with death,
    and with Sheol we have an
      agreement;
  when the overwhelming scourge
      passes through
    it will not come to us;
  for we have made lies our refuge,
    and in falsehood we have taken
      shelter";
16 therefore thus says the Lord God,
  See, I am laying in Zion a
      foundation stone,
    a tested stone,
  a precious cornerstone, a sure
      foundation:
    "One who trusts will not panic."
17 And I will make justice the line,
    and righteousness the plummet;
  hail will sweep away the refuge
      of lies,
    and waters will overwhelm the
      shelter.
18 Then your covenant with death will
      be annulled,
    and your agreement with Sheol
      will not stand;
  when the overwhelming scourge
      passes through
    you will be beaten down by it.
19 As often as it passes through, it will
      take you;
  for morning by morning it will
      pass through,
    by day and by night;
  and it will be sheer terror to
      understand the message.
20 For the bed is too short to stretch
      oneself on it,
    and the covering too narrow to
      wrap oneself in it.

ˣ Meaning of Heb of this verse uncertain

21 For the LORD will rise up as on
Mount Perazim,
  he will rage as in the valley of
  Gibeon
to do his deed—strange is his
  deed!—
  and to work his work—alien is his
  work!
22 Now therefore do not scoff,
  or your bonds will be made
  stronger;
for I have heard a decree of
  destruction
  from the Lord GOD of hosts upon
  the whole land.

23 Listen, and hear my voice;
  Pay attention, and hear my
  speech.
24 Do those who plow for sowing plow
  continually?
  Do they continually open and
  harrow their ground?
25 When they have leveled its surface,
  do they not scatter dill, sow
  cummin,
and plant wheat in rows
  and barley in its proper place,
  and spelt as the border?
26 For they are well instructed;
  their God teaches them.

27 Dill is not threshed with a threshing
  sledge,
  nor is a cart wheel rolled over
  cummin;
but dill is beaten out with a stick,
  and cummin with a rod.
28 Grain is crushed for bread,
  but one does not thresh it forever;
one drives the cart wheel and horses
  over it,
  but does not pulverize it.
29 This also comes from the LORD
  of hosts;
  he is wonderful in counsel,
  and excellent in wisdom.

The Siege of Jerusalem

29 Ah, Ariel, Ariel,
  the city where David
  encamped!
Add year to year;
  let the festivals run their round.
2 Yet I will distress Ariel,
  and there shall be moaning and
  lamentation,

and Jerusalem *y* shall be to me
  like an Ariel.*z*
3 And like David*a* I will encamp
  against you;
  I will besiege you with towers
  and raise siegeworks against you.
4 Then deep from the earth you
  shall speak,
  from low in the dust your words
  shall come;
your voice shall come from the
  ground like the voice of
  a ghost,
  and your speech shall whisper out
  of the dust.

5 But the multitude of your foes*b*
  shall be like small dust,
  and the multitude of tyrants like
  flying chaff.
And in an instant, suddenly,
6   you will be visited by the LORD
  of hosts
with thunder and earthquake and
  great noise,
  with whirlwind and tempest, and
  the flame of a devouring fire.
7 And the multitude of all the nations
  that fight against Ariel,
  all that fight against her and her
  stronghold, and who
  distress her,
  shall be like a dream, a vision
  of the night.
8 Just as when a hungry person
  dreams of eating
  and wakes up still hungry,
or a thirsty person dreams of
  drinking
  and wakes up faint, still thirsty,
so shall the multitude of all the
  nations be
  that fight against Mount Zion.

9 Stupefy yourselves and be in a
  stupor,
  blind yourselves and be blind!
Be drunk, but not from wine;
  stagger, but not from strong
  drink!
10 For the LORD has poured out
  upon you
  a spirit of deep sleep;

y Heb *she* *z* Probable meaning, *altar hearth*;
compare Ezek 43.15 *a* Gk: Meaning of Heb
uncertain *b* Cn: Heb *strangers*

he has closed your eyes, you
     prophets,
and covered your heads, you seers.

11 The vision of all this has become for
you like the words of a sealed document.
If it is given to those who can read, with
the command, "Read this," they say, "We
cannot, for it is sealed." 12And if it is given
to those who cannot read, saying, "Read
this," they say, "We cannot read."

13 The Lord said:
Because these people draw near with
     their mouths
and honor me with their lips,
     while their hearts are far from me,
and their worship of me is a human
     commandment learned
     by rote;
14 so I will again do
     amazing things with this people,
     shocking and amazing.
The wisdom of their wise shall
     perish,
     and the discernment of the
          discerning shall be hidden.

15 Ha! You who hide a plan too deep
     for the LORD,
     whose deeds are in the dark,
     and who say, "Who sees us? Who
          knows us?"
16 You turn things upside down!
     Shall the potter be regarded as the
          clay?
     Shall the thing made say of its
          maker,
     "He did not make me";
     or the thing formed say of the one
          who formed it,
     "He has no understanding"?

Hope for the Future

17 Shall not Lebanon in a very little
     while
     become a fruitful field,
     and the fruitful field be regarded
          as a forest?
18 On that day the deaf shall hear
     the words of a scroll,
     and out of their gloom and darkness
     the eyes of the blind shall see.
19 The meek shall obtain fresh joy in
     the LORD,
     and the neediest people shall exult
          in the Holy One of Israel.
20 For the tyrant shall be no more,
     and the scoffer shall cease to be;

all those alert to do evil shall be
     cut off—
21 those who cause a person to lose a
     lawsuit,
     who set a trap for the arbiter in
          the gate,
     and without grounds deny justice
          to the one in the right.

22 Therefore thus says the LORD, who
redeemed Abraham, concerning the
house of Jacob:
No longer shall Jacob be ashamed,
     no longer shall his face grow pale.
23 For when he sees his children,
     the work of my hands, in
          his midst,
     they will sanctify my name;
they will sanctify the Holy One of
     Jacob,
     and will stand in awe of the God
          of Israel.
24 And those who err in spirit will
     come to understanding,
     and those who grumble will
          accept instruction.

The Futility of Reliance on Egypt

30 Oh, rebellious children, says the
     LORD,
who carry out a plan, but not mine;
who make an alliance, but against
     my will,
     adding sin to sin;
2 who set out to go down to Egypt
     without asking for my counsel,
to take refuge in the protection of
     Pharaoh,
     and to seek shelter in the shadow
          of Egypt;
3 Therefore the protection of Pharaoh
     shall become your shame,
     and the shelter in the shadow of
          Egypt your humiliation.
4 For though his officials are at Zoan
     and his envoys reach Hanes,
5 everyone comes to shame
     through a people that cannot
          profit them,
     that brings neither help nor profit,
     but shame and disgrace.

6 An oracle concerning the animals of
the Negeb.
Through a land of trouble and
     distress,

of lioness and roaring[c] lion,
  of viper and flying serpent,
they carry their riches on the backs
      of donkeys,
  and their treasures on the humps
      of camels,
  to a people that cannot profit
      them.
7 For Egypt's help is worthless and
      empty,
  therefore I have called her,
      "Rahab who sits still."[d]

A Rebellious People

8 Go now, write it before them on
      a tablet,
  and inscribe it in a book,
so that it may be for the time
      to come
  as a witness forever.
9 For they are a rebellious people,
      faithless children,
  children who will not hear
      the instruction of the LORD;
10 who say to the seers, "Do not see";
  and to the prophets, "Do not
      prophesy to us what is right;
speak to us smooth things,
  prophesy illusions,
11 leave the way, turn aside from
      the path,
  let us hear no more about the
      Holy One of Israel."
12 Therefore thus says the Holy One of
      Israel:
Because you reject this word,
  and put your trust in oppression
      and deceit,
  and rely on them;
13 therefore this iniquity shall become
      for you
  like a break in a high wall,
      bulging out, and about to
      collapse,
  whose crash comes suddenly, in
      an instant;
14 its breaking is like that of a potter's
      vessel
  that is smashed so ruthlessly
that among its fragments not a sherd
      is found
  for taking fire from the hearth,
  or dipping water out of the
      cistern.

15 For thus said the Lord GOD, the
      Holy One of Israel:

In returning and rest you shall
      be saved;
  in quietness and in trust shall be
      your strength.
But you refused [16]and said,
  "No! We will flee upon horses" —
      therefore you shall flee!
and, "We will ride upon swift
      steeds" —
  therefore your pursuers shall be
      swift!
17 A thousand shall flee at the threat of
      one,
  at the threat of five you shall flee,
until you are left
  like a flagstaff on the top of
      a mountain,
  like a signal on a hill.

God's Promise to Zion

18 Therefore the LORD waits to be
      gracious to you;
  therefore he will rise up to show
      mercy to you.
For the LORD is a God of justice;
  blessed are all those who wait for
      him.

19 Truly, O people in Zion, inhabitants of Jerusalem, you shall weep no more. He will surely be gracious to you at the sound of your cry; when he hears it, he will answer you. [20]Though the Lord may give you the bread of adversity and the water of affliction, yet your Teacher will not hide himself any more, but your eyes shall see your Teacher. [21]And when you turn to the right or when you turn to the left, your ears shall hear a word behind you, saying, "This is the way; walk in it." [22]Then you will defile your silver-covered idols and your gold-plated images. You will scatter them like filthy rags; you will say to them, "Away with you!"

23 He will give rain for the seed with which you sow the ground, and grain, the produce of the ground, which will be rich and plenteous. On that day your cattle will graze in broad pastures; [24]and the oxen and donkeys that till the ground will eat silage, which has been winnowed with shovel and fork. [25]On every lofty mountain and every high hill there will be brooks running with water—on a day of the great slaughter, when the towers fall. [26]Moreover the light of the moon will be

---

[c] Cn: Heb from them   [d] Meaning of Heb
uncertain

like the light of the sun, and the light of the sun will be sevenfold, like the light of seven days, on the day when the LORD binds up the injuries of his people, and heals the wounds inflicted by his blow.

Judgment on Assyria

27 See, the name of the LORD comes
        from far away,
    burning with his anger, and in
        thick rising smoke;*e*
    his lips are full of indignation,
        and his tongue is like a devouring
            fire;
28 his breath is like an overflowing
        stream
        that reaches up to the neck—
    to sift the nations with the sieve of
        destruction,
        and to place on the jaws of the
            peoples a bridle that leads
            them astray.

29 You shall have a song as in the night when a holy festival is kept; and gladness of heart, as when one sets out to the sound of the flute to go to the mountain of the LORD, to the Rock of Israel. 30And the LORD will cause his majestic voice to be heard and the descending blow of his arm to be seen, in furious anger and a flame of devouring fire, with a cloudburst and tempest and hailstones. 31The Assyrian will be terror-stricken at the voice of the LORD, when he strikes with his rod. 32And every stroke of the staff of punishment that the LORD lays upon him will be to the sound of timbrels and lyres; battling with brandished arm he will fight with him. 33For his burning place*f* has long been prepared; truly it is made ready for the king, *g* its pyre made deep and wide, with fire and wood in abundance; the breath of the LORD, like a stream of sulfur, kindles it.

Alliance with Egypt Is Futile

31 Alas for those who go down to
        Egypt for help
    and who rely on horses,
    who trust in chariots because they
        are many
    and in horsemen because they are
        very strong,
    but do not look to the Holy One
        of Israel
    or consult the LORD!
2 Yet he too is wise and brings
        disaster;

he does not call back his words,
    but will rise against the house of the
        evildoers,
    and against the helpers of those
        who work iniquity.
3 The Egyptians are human, and
        not God;
    their horses are flesh, and
        not spirit.
When the LORD stretches out
        his hand,
    the helper will stumble, and the
        one helped will fall,
    and they will all perish together.

4 For thus the LORD said to me,
As a lion or a young lion growls
        over its prey,
    and—when a band of shepherds is
        called out against it—
is not terrified by their shouting
    or daunted at their noise,
so the LORD of hosts will come down
    to fight upon Mount Zion and
        upon its hill.
5 Like birds hovering overhead, so the
        LORD of hosts
    will protect Jerusalem;
he will protect and deliver it,
    he will spare and rescue it.

6 Turn back to him whom you*h* have deeply betrayed, O people of Israel. 7For on that day all of you shall throw away your idols of silver and idols of gold, which your hands have sinfully made for you.
8 "Then the Assyrian shall fall by a
        sword, not of mortals;
    and a sword, not of humans, shall
        devour him;
he shall flee from the sword,
    and his young men shall be put
        to forced labor.
9 His rock shall pass away in terror,
    and his officers desert the
        standard in panic,"
says the LORD, whose fire is in Zion,
    and whose furnace is in Jerusalem.

Government with Justice Predicted

32 See, a king will reign in
        righteousness,
    and princes will rule with justice.

e Meaning of Heb uncertain   *f* Or *Topheth*
g Or *Molech*   *h* Heb *they*

2 Each will be like a hiding place from
the wind,
a covert from the tempest,
like streams of water in a dry place,
like the shade of a great rock in a
weary land.
3 Then the eyes of those who have
sight will not be closed,
and the ears of those who have
hearing will listen.
4 The minds of the rash will have
good judgment,
and the tongues of stammerers
will speak readily and
distinctly.
5 A fool will no longer be called
noble,
nor a villain said to be honorable.
6 For fools speak folly,
and their minds plot iniquity:
to practice ungodliness,
to utter error concerning the LORD,
to leave the craving of the hungry
unsatisfied,
and to deprive the thirsty of drink.
7 The villainies of villains are evil;
they devise wicked devices
to ruin the poor with lying words,
even when the plea of the needy
is right.
8 But those who are noble plan noble
things,
and by noble things they stand.

Complacent Women Warned of Disaster

9 Rise up, you women who are at
ease, hear my voice;
you complacent daughters, listen
to my speech.
10 In little more than a year
you will shudder, you complacent
ones;
for the vintage will fail,
the fruit harvest will not come.
11 Tremble, you women who are
at ease,
shudder, you complacent ones;
strip, and make yourselves bare,
and put sackcloth on your loins.
12 Beat your breasts for the pleasant
fields,
for the fruitful vine,
13 for the soil of my people
growing up in thorns and briers;
yes, for all the joyous houses
in the jubilant city.
14 For the palace will be forsaken,
the populous city deserted;

the hill and the watchtower
will become dens forever,
the joy of wild asses,
a pasture for flocks;
15 until a spirit from on high is poured
out on us,
and the wilderness becomes a
fruitful field,
and the fruitful field is deemed
a forest.

The Peace of God's Reign

16 Then justice will dwell in the
wilderness,
and righteousness abide in the
fruitful field.
17 The effect of righteousness will
be peace,
and the result of righteousness,
quietness and trust forever.
18 My people will abide in a peaceful
habitation,
in secure dwellings, and in quiet
resting places.
19 The forest will disappear
completely,[i]
and the city will be utterly
laid low.
20 Happy will you be who sow beside
every stream,
who let the ox and the donkey
range freely.

A Prophecy of Deliverance from Foes

33 Ah, you destroyer,
who yourself have not been
destroyed;
you treacherous one,
with whom no one has dealt
treacherously!
When you have ceased to destroy,
you will be destroyed;
and when you have stopped dealing
treacherously,
you will be dealt with
treacherously.

2 O LORD, be gracious to us; we wait
for you.
Be our arm every morning,
our salvation in the time of
trouble.
3 At the sound of tumult, peoples
fled;

---

i Cn: Heb *And it will hail when the forest comes
down*

before your majesty, nations
    scattered.
4 Spoil was gathered as the caterpillar
    gathers;
    as locusts leap, they leaped *j*
    upon it.
5 The LORD is exalted, he dwells
    on high;
    he filled Zion with justice and
    righteousness;
6 he will be the stability of your
    times,
    abundance of salvation, wisdom,
    and knowledge;
    the fear of the LORD is Zion's
    treasure.*k*

7 Listen! the valiant *j* cry in the
    streets;
    the envoys of peace weep bitterly.
8 The highways are deserted,
    travelers have quit the road.
    The treaty is broken,
    its oaths *l* are despised,
    its obligation *m* is disregarded.
9 The land mourns and languishes;
    Lebanon is confounded and
    withers away;
    Sharon is like a desert;
    and Bashan and Carmel shake off
    their leaves.

10 "Now I will arise," says the LORD,
    "now I will lift myself up;
    now I will be exalted.
11 You conceive chaff, you bring
    forth stubble;
    your breath is a fire that will
    consume you.
12 And the peoples will be as if burned
    to lime,
    like thorns cut down, that are
    burned in the fire."

13 Hear, you who are far away, what I
    have done;
    and you who are near,
    acknowledge my might.
14 The sinners in Zion are afraid;
    trembling has seized the godless:
    "Who among us can live with the
    devouring fire?
    Who among us can live with
    everlasting flames?"
15 Those who walk righteously and
    speak uprightly,
    who despise the gain of
    oppression,

who wave away a bribe instead of
    accepting it,
    who stop their ears from hearing
    of bloodshed
    and shut their eyes from looking
    on evil,
16 they will live on the heights;
    their refuge will be the fortresses
    of rocks;
    their food will be supplied, their
    water assured.

The Land of the Majestic King

17 Your eyes will see the king in his
    beauty;
    they will behold a land that
    stretches far away.
18 Your mind will muse on the terror:
    "Where is the one who counted?
    Where is the one who weighed
    the tribute?
    Where is the one who counted the
    towers?"
19 No longer will you see the insolent
    people,
    the people of an obscure speech
    that you cannot comprehend,
    stammering in a language that
    you cannot understand.
20 Look on Zion, the city of our
    appointed festivals!
    Your eyes will see Jerusalem,
    a quiet habitation, an immovable
    tent,
    whose stakes will never be
    pulled up,
    and none of whose ropes will
    be broken.
21 But there the LORD in majesty will be
    for us
    a place of broad rivers and
    streams,
    where no galley with oars can go,
    nor stately ship can pass.
22 For the LORD is our judge, the LORD is
    our ruler,
    the LORD is our king; he will
    save us.

23 Your rigging hangs loose;
    it cannot hold the mast firm in its
    place,
    or keep the sail spread out.

j Meaning of Heb uncertain   *k* Heb *his treasure*;
meaning of Heb uncertain   *l* Q Ms: MT *cities*
m Or *everyone*

Then prey and spoil in abundance
will be divided;
even the lame will fall to
plundering.
24 And no inhabitant will say, "I am
sick";
the people who live there will be
forgiven their iniquity.

Judgment on the Nations

34 Draw near, O nations, to hear;
O peoples, give heed!
Let the earth hear, and all that fills
it;
the world, and all that comes
from it.
2 For the LORD is enraged against all
the nations,
and furious against all their
hordes;
he has doomed them, has given
them over for slaughter.
3 Their slain shall be cast out,
and the stench of their corpses
shall rise;
the mountains shall flow with
their blood.
4 All the host of heaven shall rot
away,
and the skies roll up like a scroll.
All their host shall wither
like a leaf withering on a vine,
or fruit withering on a fig tree.
5 When my sword has drunk its fill in
the heavens,
lo, it will descend upon Edom,
upon the people I have doomed
to judgment.
6 The LORD has a sword; it is sated
with blood,
it is gorged with fat,
with the blood of lambs and
goats,
with the fat of the kidneys
of rams.
For the LORD has a sacrifice in
Bozrah,
a great slaughter in the land
of Edom.
7 Wild oxen shall fall with them,
and young steers with the
mighty bulls.
Their land shall be soaked with
blood,
and their soil made rich with fat.

8 For the LORD has a day of vengeance,
a year of vindication by Zion's
cause.[n]
9 And the streams of Edom[o] shall be
turned into pitch,
and her soil into sulfur;
her land shall become burning
pitch.
10 Night and day it shall not be
quenched;
its smoke shall go up forever.
From generation to generation it
shall lie waste;
no one shall pass through it
forever and ever.
11 But the hawk[p] and the hedgehog[p]
shall possess it;
the owl[p] and the raven shall live
in it.
He shall stretch the line of
confusion over it,
and the plummet of chaos over[q]
its nobles.
12 They shall name it No Kingdom
There,
and all its princes shall be
nothing.
13 Thorns shall grow over its
strongholds,
nettles and thistles in its fortresses.
It shall be the haunt of jackals,
an abode for ostriches.
14 Wildcats shall meet with hyenas,
goat-demons shall call to
each other;
there too Lilith shall repose,
and find a place to rest.
15 There shall the owl nest
and lay and hatch and brood in
its shadow;
there too the buzzards shall gather,
each one with its mate.
16 Seek and read from the book of
the LORD:
Not one of these shall be missing;
none shall be without its mate.
For the mouth of the LORD has
commanded,
and his spirit has gathered them.
17 He has cast the lot for them,
his hand has portioned it out to
them with the line;
they shall possess it forever,
from generation to generation
they shall live in it.

n Or of recompense by Zion's defender   o Heb her
streams   p Identification uncertain   q Heb lacks
over

The Return of the Redeemed to Zion

35 The wilderness and the dry land
          shall be glad,
    the desert shall rejoice and
          blossom;
    like the crocus ²it shall blossom
          abundantly,
    and rejoice with joy and singing.
    The glory of Lebanon shall be given
          to it,
    the majesty of Carmel and
          Sharon.

They shall see the glory of the LORD,
    the majesty of our God.

³ Strengthen the weak hands,
    and make firm the feeble knees.
⁴ Say to those who are of a fearful
          heart,
    "Be strong, do not fear!
Here is your God.
    He will come with vengeance,
with terrible recompense.
    He will come and save you."

Simple Encouragement

THURSDAY

Scripture Reading
for Today:
Isaiah 35.3–10

Verse for Today:
Isaiah 35.4

How frequently we fail to offer an encouraging word, to extend a verbal reassurance of our care, to compliment and build up, or to express our gratitude, concern, or appreciation. This graciousness of speech is aptly described in Proverbs: "A word in season, how good it is" (15.23), and "A word fitly spoken is like apples of gold in a setting of silver" (25.11).

More often our failure is due to negligence, awkwardness, or self-centeredness than to deliberate selfishness or malicious intent. One example illustrates this point and shows how significant an impact this omission can have.

One of the women in our parish had a miscarriage. Afterwards, other women skirted around this event, as if ignoring it had happened. They even refrained from asking her about it. They failed to express sympathy or concern, or to acknowledge that she might appreciate prayer, emotional support, or the opportunity to talk about it.

Some of these women were trying to be sensitive to her needs, thinking it might be hard for her if they brought up her miscarriage. Others were more conscious of their own ineptness and couldn't reach out past themselves. But the effect was that she received none of the simple, life-giving kindness that might have flowed from them.

Isaiah wrote: "The Lord GOD has given me the tongue of a teacher, that I may know how to sustain the weary with a word" (50.4). And A. L. Waring prayed, "I ask thee for a thoughtful love / Through constant watchings wise ... And a heart at leisure from itself / To soothe and sympathize." Sometimes it only takes a heartfelt word to communicate love, a moment taken from our time to compliment someone on a job well done, a simple expression of encouragement to bring life and joy to others.

—JEANNE KUN

Go to page 972 for your next devotional reading.

5 Then the eyes of the blind shall
 be opened,
 and the ears of the deaf
  unstopped;
6 then the lame shall leap like a
 deer,
 and the tongue of the speechless
  sing for joy.
For waters shall break forth in the
 wilderness,
 and streams in the desert;
7 the burning sand shall become
 a pool,
 and the thirsty ground springs
  of water;
the haunt of jackals shall become
 a swamp,[r]
 the grass shall become reeds and
  rushes.

8 A highway shall be there,
 and it shall be called the
  Holy Way;
the unclean shall not travel on it,[s]
 but it shall be for God's people;[t]
 no traveler, not even fools, shall
  go astray.
9 No lion shall be there,
 nor shall any ravenous beast come
  up on it;
they shall not be found there,
 but the redeemed shall walk there.
10 And the ransomed of the LORD shall
 return,
 and come to Zion with singing;
everlasting joy shall be upon their
 heads;
 they shall obtain joy and gladness,
 and sorrow and sighing shall
  flee away.

Sennacherib Threatens Jerusalem

36 In the fourteenth year of King
Hezekiah, King Sennacherib of
Assyria came up against all the fortified
cities of Judah and captured them. ²The
king of Assyria sent the Rabshakeh from
Lachish to King Hezekiah at Jerusalem,
with a great army. He stood by the conduit of the upper pool on the highway to
the Fuller's Field. ³And there came out to
him Eliakim son of Hilkiah, who was in
charge of the palace, and Shebna the secretary, and Joah son of Asaph, the recorder.

4 The Rabshakeh said to them, "Say to
Hezekiah: Thus says the great king, the
king of Assyria: On what do you base this
confidence of yours? ⁵Do you think that
mere words are strategy and power for
war? On whom do you now rely, that you
have rebelled against me? ⁶See, you are
relying on Egypt, that broken reed of a
staff, which will pierce the hand of anyone who leans on it. Such is Pharaoh king
of Egypt to all who rely on him. ⁷But if
you say to me, 'We rely on the LORD our
God,' is it not he whose high places and
altars Hezekiah has removed, saying to Judah and to Jerusalem, 'You shall worship
before this altar'? ⁸Come now, make a wager with my master the king of Assyria: I
will give you two thousand horses, if you
are able on your part to set riders on them.
⁹How then can you repulse a single captain among the least of my master's servants, when you rely on Egypt for chariots
and for horsemen? ¹⁰Moreover, is it without the LORD that I have come up against
this land to destroy it? The LORD said to
me, Go up against this land, and destroy it."

11 Then Eliakim, Shebna, and Joah
said to the Rabshakeh, "Please speak to
your servants in Aramaic, for we understand it; do not speak to us in the language of Judah within the hearing of the
people who are on the wall." ¹²But the
Rabshakeh said, "Has my master sent me
to speak these words to your master and
to you, and not to the people sitting on
the wall, who are doomed with you to
eat their own dung and drink their own
urine?"

13 Then the Rabshakeh stood and
called out in a loud voice in the language
of Judah, "Hear the words of the great
king, the king of Assyria! ¹⁴Thus says the
king: 'Do not let Hezekiah deceive you,
for he will not be able to deliver you. ¹⁵Do
not let Hezekiah make you rely on the
LORD by saying, The LORD will surely deliver us; this city will not be given into the
hand of the king of Assyria.' ¹⁶Do not listen to Hezekiah; for thus says the king of
Assyria: 'Make your peace with me and
come out to me; then everyone of you will
eat from your own vine and your own fig
tree and drink water from your own cistern, ¹⁷until I come and take you away to
a land like your own land, a land of grain

---

r Cn: Heb *in the haunt of jackals is her resting place*
s Or *pass it by*   t Cn: Heb *for them*

and wine, a land of bread and vineyards. [18]Do not let Hezekiah mislead you by saying, The LORD will save us. Has any of the gods of the nations saved their land out of the hand of the king of Assyria? [19]Where are the gods of Hamath and Arpad? Where are the gods of Sepharvaim? Have they delivered Samaria out of my hand? [20]Who among all the gods of these countries have saved their countries out of my hand, that the LORD should save Jerusalem out of my hand?' "

21 But they were silent and answered him not a word, for the king's command was, "Do not answer him." [22]Then Eliakim son of Hilkiah, who was in charge of the palace, and Shebna the secretary, and Joah son of Asaph, the recorder, came to Hezekiah with their clothes torn, and told him the words of the Rabshakeh.

Hezekiah Consults Isaiah

37 When King Hezekiah heard it, he tore his clothes, covered himself with sackcloth, and went into the house of the LORD. [2]And he sent Eliakim, who was in charge of the palace, and Shebna the secretary, and the senior priests, covered with sackcloth, to the prophet Isaiah son of Amoz. [3]They said to him, "Thus says Hezekiah, This day is a day of distress, of rebuke, and of disgrace; children have come to the birth, and there is no strength to bring them forth. [4]It may be that the LORD your God heard the words of the Rabshakeh, whom his master the king of Assyria has sent to mock the living God, and will rebuke the words that the LORD your God has heard; therefore lift up your prayer for the remnant that is left."

5 When the servants of King Hezekiah came to Isaiah, [6]Isaiah said to them, "Say to your master, 'Thus says the LORD: Do not be afraid because of the words that you have heard, with which the servants of the king of Assyria have reviled me. [7]I myself will put a spirit in him, so that he shall hear a rumor, and return to his own land; I will cause him to fall by the sword in his own land.' "

8 The Rabshakeh returned, and found the king of Assyria fighting against Libnah; for he had heard that the king had left Lachish. [9]Now the king[u] heard concerning King Tirhakah of Ethiopia,[v] "He has set out to fight against you." When he heard it, he sent messengers to Hezekiah, saying, [10]"Thus shall you speak to King Hezekiah of Judah: Do not let your God on whom you rely deceive you by promising that Jerusalem will not be given into the hand of the king of Assyria. [11]See, you have heard what the kings of Assyria have done to all lands, destroying them utterly. Shall you be delivered? [12]Have the gods of the nations delivered them, the nations that my predecessors destroyed, Gozan, Haran, Rezeph, and the people of Eden who were in Telassar? [13]Where is the king of Hamath, the king of Arpad, the king of the city of Sepharvaim, the king of Hena, or the king of Ivvah?"

Hezekiah's Prayer

14 Hezekiah received the letter from the hand of the messengers and read it; then Hezekiah went up to the house of the LORD and spread it before the LORD. [15]And Hezekiah prayed to the LORD, saying: [16]"O LORD of hosts, God of Israel, who are enthroned above the cherubim, you are God, you alone, of all the kingdoms of the earth; you have made heaven and earth. [17]Incline your ear, O LORD, and hear; open your eyes, O LORD, and see; hear all the words of Sennacherib, which he has sent to mock the living God. [18]Truly, O LORD, the kings of Assyria have laid waste all the nations and their lands, [19]and have hurled their gods into the fire, though they were no gods, but the work of human hands—wood and stone—and so they were destroyed. [20]So now, O LORD our God, save us from his hand, so that all the kingdoms of the earth may know that you alone are the LORD."

21 Then Isaiah son of Amoz sent to Hezekiah, saying: "Thus says the LORD, the God of Israel: Because you have prayed to me concerning King Sennacherib of Assyria, [22]this is the word that the LORD has spoken concerning him:

She despises you, she scorns you—
  virgin daughter Zion;
she tosses her head—behind
    your back,
  daughter Jerusalem.

23 "Whom have you mocked and
    reviled?
  Against whom have you raised
    your voice
and haughtily lifted your eyes?
  Against the Holy One of Israel!

u Heb he   v Or Nubia; Heb Cush

24 By your servants you have mocked
         the Lord,
      and you have said, 'With my
         many chariots
   I have gone up the heights of the
         mountains,
      to the far recesses of Lebanon;
   I felled its tallest cedars,
      its choicest cypresses;
   I came to its remotest height,
      its densest forest.
25 I dug wells
      and drank waters,
   I dried up with the sole of my foot
      all the streams of Egypt.'

26 "Have you not heard
      that I determined it long ago?
   I planned from days of old
      what now I bring to pass,
   that you should make fortified cities
      crash into heaps of ruins,
27 while their inhabitants, shorn of
         strength,
      are dismayed and confounded;
   they have become like plants of
         the field
      and like tender grass,
   like grass on the housetops,
      blighted*w* before it is grown.

28 "I know your rising up*x* and your
         sitting down,
      your going out and coming in,
      and your raging against me.
29 Because you have raged against me
      and your arrogance has come to
         my ears,
   I will put my hook in your nose
      and my bit in your mouth;
   I will turn you back on the way
      by which you came.

30 "And this shall be the sign for you:
This year eat what grows of itself, and in
the second year what springs from that;
then in the third year sow, reap, plant
vineyards, and eat their fruit. 31The surviving remnant of the house of Judah shall
again take root downward, and bear fruit
upward; 32for from Jerusalem a remnant
shall go out, and from Mount Zion a band
of survivors. The zeal of the LORD of hosts
will do this.

33 "Therefore thus says the LORD concerning the king of Assyria: He shall not
come into this city, shoot an arrow there,
come before it with a shield, or cast up a

siege ramp against it. 34By the way that he
came, by the same he shall return; he shall
not come into this city, says the LORD.
35For I will defend this city to save it, for
my own sake and for the sake of my servant David."

Sennacherib's Defeat and Death

36 Then the angel of the LORD set out
and struck down one hundred eighty-five
thousand in the camp of the Assyrians;
when morning dawned, they were all
dead bodies. 37Then King Sennacherib of
Assyria left, went home, and lived at Nineveh. 38As he was worshiping in the house
of his god Nisroch, his sons Adrammelech
and Sharezer killed him with the sword,
and they escaped into the land of Ararat.
His son Esar-haddon succeeded him.

Hezekiah's Illness

38 In those days Hezekiah became
    sick and was at the point of death.
The prophet Isaiah son of Amoz came
to him, and said to him, "Thus says the
LORD: Set your house in order, for you
shall die; you shall not recover." 2Then
Hezekiah turned his face to the wall, and
prayed to the LORD: 3"Remember now,
O LORD, I implore you, how I have walked
before you in faithfulness with a whole
heart, and have done what is good in your
sight." And Hezekiah wept bitterly.

4 Then the word of the LORD came to
Isaiah: 5"Go and say to Hezekiah, Thus
says the LORD, the God of your ancestor
David: I have heard your prayer, I have
seen your tears; I will add fifteen years to
your life. 6I will deliver you and this city
out of the hand of the king of Assyria, and
defend this city.

7 "This is the sign to you from the
LORD, that the LORD will do this thing that
he has promised: 8See, I will make the
shadow cast by the declining sun on
the dial of Ahaz turn back ten steps."
So the sun turned back on the dial the
ten steps by which it had declined. *y*

9 A writing of King Hezekiah of Judah,
after he had been sick and had recovered
from his sickness:
10 I said: In the noontide of my days
      I must depart;
   I am consigned to the gates of Sheol

---

w With 2 Kings 19.26: Heb *field*   *x* Q Ms Gk: MT
lacks *your rising up*   *y* Meaning of Heb uncertain

for the rest of my years.

11 I said, I shall not see the LORD
in the land of the living;
I shall look upon mortals no more
among the inhabitants of
the world.

12 My dwelling is plucked up and
removed from me
like a shepherd's tent;
like a weaver I have rolled up
my life;
he cuts me off from the loom;
from day to night you bring me to
an end;[z]

13 I cry for help[a] until morning;
like a lion he breaks all my bones;
from day to night you bring me
to an end.[z]

14 Like a swallow or a crane[z] I
clamor,
I moan like a dove.
My eyes are weary with looking
upward.
O Lord, I am oppressed; be my
security!

15 But what can I say? For he has
spoken to me,
and he himself has done it.
All my sleep has fled[b]
because of the bitterness of
my soul.

16 O Lord, by these things people live,
and in all these is the life of
my spirit.[z]
Oh, restore me to health and
make me live!

17 Surely it was for my welfare
that I had great bitterness;
but you have held back[c] my life
from the pit of destruction,
for you have cast all my sins
behind your back.

18 For Sheol cannot thank you,
death cannot praise you;
those who go down to the Pit
cannot hope
for your faithfulness.

19 The living, the living, they
thank you,
as I do this day;
fathers make known to children
your faithfulness.

20 The LORD will save me,
and we will sing to stringed
instruments[d]

all the days of our lives,
at the house of the LORD.

21 Now Isaiah had said, "Let them take a lump of figs, and apply it to the boil, so that he may recover." 22Hezekiah also had said, "What is the sign that I shall go up to the house of the LORD?"

Envoys from Babylon Welcomed

39 At that time King Merodach-baladan son of Baladan of Babylon sent envoys with letters and a present to Hezekiah, for he heard that he had been sick and had recovered. 2Hezekiah welcomed them; he showed them his treasure house, the silver, the gold, the spices, the precious oil, his whole armory, all that was found in his storehouses. There was nothing in his house or in all his realm that Hezekiah did not show them. 3Then the prophet Isaiah came to King Hezekiah and said to him, "What did these men say? From where did they come to you?" Hezekiah answered, "They have come to me from a far country, from Babylon." 4He said, "What have they seen in your house?" Hezekiah answered, "They have seen all that is in my house; there is nothing in my storehouses that I did not show them."

5 Then Isaiah said to Hezekiah, "Hear the word of the LORD of hosts: 6Days are coming when all that is in your house, and that which your ancestors have stored up until this day, shall be carried to Babylon; nothing shall be left, says the LORD. 7Some of your own sons who are born to you shall be taken away; they shall be eunuchs in the palace of the king of Babylon." 8Then Hezekiah said to Isaiah, "The word of the LORD that you have spoken is good." For he thought, "There will be peace and security in my days."

God's People Are Comforted

40 Comfort, O comfort my people,
says your God.
2 Speak tenderly to Jerusalem,
and cry to her
that she has served her term,
that her penalty is paid,

---

z Meaning of Heb uncertain   a Cn: Meaning of Heb uncertain   b Cn Compare Syr: Heb *I will walk slowly all my years*   c Cn Compare Gk Vg: Heb *loved*   d Heb *my stringed instruments*

that she has received from the LORD's
    hand
    double for all her sins.

3 A voice cries out:
  "In the wilderness prepare the way
    of the LORD,
    make straight in the desert a
      highway for our God.
4 Every valley shall be lifted up,
    and every mountain and hill be
      made low;
  the uneven ground shall become
    level,
    and the rough places a plain.
5 Then the glory of the LORD shall
    be revealed,
    and all people shall see it
      together,
  for the mouth of the LORD has
    spoken."

6 A voice says, "Cry out!"
  And I said, "What shall I cry?"
  All people are grass,
    their constancy is like the flower
      of the field.
7 The grass withers, the flower fades,
    when the breath of the LORD
      blows upon it;
  surely the people are grass.
8 The grass withers, the flower fades;
    but the word of our God will
      stand forever.
9 Get you up to a high mountain,
    O Zion, herald of good tidings;*e*
  lift up your voice with strength,
    O Jerusalem, herald of good
      tidings,*f*
    lift it up, do not fear;
  say to the cities of Judah,
    "Here is your God!"
10 See, the Lord GOD comes with
    might,
    and his arm rules for him;
  his reward is with him,
    and his recompense before him.
11 He will feed his flock like a
    shepherd;
    he will gather the lambs in
      his arms,
  and carry them in his bosom,
    and gently lead the mother sheep.

12 Who has measured the waters in the
    hollow of his hand
    and marked off the heavens with
      a span,

enclosed the dust of the earth in
    a measure,
    and weighed the mountains
      in scales
    and the hills in a balance?
13 Who has directed the spirit of
    the LORD,
    or as his counselor has instructed
      him?
14 Whom did he consult for his
    enlightenment,
    and who taught him the path of
      justice?
  Who taught him knowledge,
    and showed him the way of
      understanding?
15 Even the nations are like a drop
    from a bucket,
    and are accounted as dust on
      the scales;
  see, he takes up the isles like fine
    dust.
16 Lebanon would not provide fuel
    enough,
    nor are its animals enough for a
      burnt offering.
17 All the nations are as nothing before
    him;
    they are accounted by him as less
      than nothing and emptiness.

18 To whom then will you liken God,
    or what likeness compare
      with him?
19 An idol? —A workman casts it,
    and a goldsmith overlays it
      with gold,
    and casts for it silver chains.
20 As a gift one chooses mulberry
    wood*g*
    —wood that will not rot—
  then seeks out a skilled artisan
    to set up an image that will
      not topple.

21 Have you not known? Have you
    not heard?
    Has it not been told you from the
      beginning?
  Have you not understood from
      the foundations of the earth?
22 It is he who sits above the circle of
    the earth,

e Or *O herald of good tidings to Zion*   *f* Or
O herald of good tidings to Jerusalem   *g* Meaning
of Heb uncertain

and its inhabitants are like
　　grasshoppers;
who stretches out the heavens like a
　　curtain,
　　and spreads them like a tent to
　　　live in;
23 who brings princes to naught,
　　and makes the rulers of the earth
　　　as nothing.

24 Scarcely are they planted, scarcely
　　　sown,
　　scarcely has their stem taken root
　　　in the earth,
when he blows upon them, and they
　　wither,
　　and the tempest carries them off
　　　like stubble.

25 To whom then will you compare
　　　me,
　　or who is my equal? says the Holy
　　　One.
26 Lift up your eyes on high and see:
　　Who created these?
He who brings out their host and
　　numbers them,
　　calling them all by name;
because he is great in strength,
　　mighty in power,
　　not one is missing.

27 Why do you say, O Jacob,
　　and speak, O Israel,
"My way is hidden from the LORD,
　　and my right is disregarded by my
　　　God"?
28 Have you not known? Have you
　　　not heard?
The LORD is the everlasting God,
　　the Creator of the ends of
　　　the earth.
He does not faint or grow weary;
　　his understanding is unsearchable.
29 He gives power to the faint,
　　and strengthens the powerless.
30 Even youths will faint and be weary,
　　and the young will fall exhausted;
31 but those who wait for the LORD
　　　shall renew their strength,
　　they shall mount up with wings
　　　like eagles,
they shall run and not be weary,
　　they shall walk and not faint.

Israel Assured of God's Help

41 Listen to me in silence,
　　O coastlands;
let the peoples renew their
　　strength;
let them approach, then let
　　them speak;
　　let us together draw near for
　　　judgment.

2 Who has roused a victor from
　　the east,
　　summoned him to his service?
He delivers up nations to him,
　　and tramples kings under foot;
he makes them like dust with
　　his sword,
　　like driven stubble with his bow.
3 He pursues them and passes
　　on safely,
　　scarcely touching the path with
　　　his feet.
4 Who has performed and done this,
　　calling the generations from the
　　　beginning?
I, the LORD, am first,
　　and will be with the last.
5 The coastlands have seen and
　　are afraid,
　　the ends of the earth tremble;
　　they have drawn near and come.
6 Each one helps the other,
　　saying to one another, "Take
　　　courage!"
7 The artisan encourages the
　　goldsmith,
　　and the one who smooths with
　　　the hammer encourages the
　　　one who strikes the anvil,
saying of the soldering, "It is good";
　　and they fasten it with nails so
　　　that it cannot be moved.
8 But you, Israel, my servant,
　　Jacob, whom I have chosen,
　　the offspring of Abraham,
　　　my friend;
9 you whom I took from the ends of
　　　the earth,
　　and called from its farthest
　　　corners,
saying to you, "You are my servant,
　　I have chosen you and not cast
　　　you off";
10 do not fear, for I am with you,
　　do not be afraid, for I am your
　　　God;
I will strengthen you, I will help
　　you,
　　I will uphold you with my
　　　victorious right hand.

Hope

FRIDAY

Scripture Reading
for Today:
Isaiah 40.27–31

Verse for Today:
Isaiah 40.31

Take time alone and in silence today to reflect on the gift of hope, which has been freely given to you at Baptism. Pray this prayer often during the day, asking God to rekindle and enlarge this gift of hope.

God, you are like a mother hen, gathering her chicks, watching over them with loving care. Help me to place my hope in your promise to care for and watch over me and those I love.

God, you promise to raise me up on the wings of an eagle. Lift me out of this fog of depression and loneliness which covers me with the fear that I might lose my way. I place my hope in your power to raise me and draw me to your breast.

God, you are [like] the baker woman who knows the miraculous capacity of yeast to raise a whole loaf of bread. I hope in this same miraculous power of your Spirit to penetrate my whole being and fill me with an enthusiasm for life and love. I place my entire hope in your mysterious ways of kneading the yeast of your Spirit into my entire family, my faith community, and even this world.

God, you are the forgiving parent who embraces the sinful child even before the words of apology are uttered. I place my hope in your unending mercy as I acknowledge my sinfulness. I desire the hope to trust that even before I can offer my sorrow for the sins of my life you have forgiven, healed and set me free.

God, you are the potter who continues to shape and mold me. Grant me hope enough to surrender to your providential plan for my life. I give you my life, placing my feeble hope in the knowledge that your ways are better than I can imagine.

God, you are the bridegroom who calls me like a lover and companion. Increase my hope that you delight in me, love me unconditionally and have made me for goodness.

God of Mary, Mother of Sorrows, Woman of Hope, even in the impossible, foster a deeper sense of hope in me. Amen.

—CAROL GURA

Go to page 976 for your next devotional reading.

11 Yes, all who are incensed
          against you
    shall be ashamed and disgraced;
    those who strive against you
        shall be as nothing and
            shall perish.
12 You shall seek those who contend
          with you,
    but you shall not find them;
    those who war against you
        shall be as nothing at all.
13 For I, the LORD your God,
    hold your right hand;
    it is I who say to you, "Do not fear,
    I will help you."

14 Do not fear, you worm Jacob,
    you insect[h] Israel!
    I will help you, says the LORD;
        your Redeemer is the Holy One of
            Israel.
15 Now, I will make of you a threshing
          sledge,
    sharp, new, and having teeth;
    you shall thresh the mountains and
          crush them,
        and you shall make the hills
            like chaff.
16 You shall winnow them and the
          wind shall carry them away,
    and the tempest shall scatter
          them.
    Then you shall rejoice in the LORD;
        in the Holy One of Israel you
            shall glory.

17 When the poor and needy seek
          water,
    and there is none,
    and their tongue is parched
          with thirst,
    I the LORD will answer them,
        I the God of Israel will not
            forsake them.
18 I will open rivers on the bare
          heights,[i]
    and fountains in the midst of
          the valleys;
    I will make the wilderness a pool
          of water,
    and the dry land springs of water.
19 I will put in the wilderness
          the cedar,
        the acacia, the myrtle, and
            the olive;
    I will set in the desert the cypress,
        the plane and the pine together,
20 so that all may see and know,

all may consider and understand,
    that the hand of the LORD has
          done this,
        the Holy One of Israel has created
            it.

The Futility of Idols

21 Set forth your case, says the LORD;
    bring your proofs, says the King of
          Jacob.
22 Let them bring them, and tell us
          what is to happen.
    Tell us the former things, what they
          are,
        so that we may consider them,
    and that we may know their
          outcome;
        or declare to us the things
            to come.
23 Tell us what is to come hereafter,
        that we may know that you
            are gods;
    do good, or do harm,
        that we may be afraid and
            terrified.
24 You, indeed, are nothing
        and your work is nothing at all;
    whoever chooses you is an
          abomination.

25 I stirred up one from the north, and
          he has come,
    from the rising of the sun he was
          summoned by name.[j]
    He shall trample[k] on rulers as on
          mortar,
        as the potter treads clay.
26 Who declared it from the beginning,
        so that we might know,
    and beforehand, so that we might
          say, "He is right"?
    There was no one who declared it,
        none who proclaimed,
    none who heard your words.
27 I first have declared it to Zion,[l]
        and I give to Jerusalem a herald of
            good tidings.
28 But when I look there is no one;
        among these there is no counselor
    who, when I ask, gives an answer.
29 No, they are all a delusion;
        their works are nothing;
    their images are empty wind.

---

h Syr: Heb *men of*   i Or *trails*   j Cn Compare
Q Ms Gk: MT *and he shall call on my name*
k Cn: Heb *come*   l Cn: Heb *First to Zion—Behold,
behold them*

The Servant, a Light to the Nations

42 Here is my servant, whom I
uphold,
my chosen, in whom my soul
delights;
I have put my spirit upon him;
he will bring forth justice to the
nations.
2 He will not cry or lift up his voice,
or make it heard in the street;
3 a bruised reed he will not break,
and a dimly burning wick he will
not quench;
he will faithfully bring forth
justice.
4 He will not grow faint or be crushed
until he has established justice in
the earth;
and the coastlands wait for his
teaching.

5 Thus says God, the LORD,
who created the heavens and
stretched them out,
who spread out the earth and
what comes from it,
who gives breath to the people upon
it
and spirit to those who walk in it:
6 I am the LORD, I have called you in
righteousness,
I have taken you by the hand and
kept you;
I have given you as a covenant to
the people,[m]
a light to the nations,
7 to open the eyes that are blind,
to bring out the prisoners from the
dungeon,
from the prison those who sit in
darkness.
8 I am the LORD, that is my name;
my glory I give to no other,
nor my praise to idols.
9 See, the former things have come
to pass,
and new things I now declare;
before they spring forth,
I tell you of them.

A Hymn of Praise

10 Sing to the LORD a new song,
his praise from the end of the
earth!
Let the sea roar[n] and all that fills it,
the coastlands and their
inhabitants.

11 Let the desert and its towns lift up
their voice,
the villages that Kedar inhabits;
let the inhabitants of Sela sing
for joy,
let them shout from the tops of
the mountains.
12 Let them give glory to the LORD,
and declare his praise in the
coastlands.
13 The LORD goes forth like a soldier,
like a warrior he stirs up his fury;
he cries out, he shouts aloud,
he shows himself mighty against
his foes.

14 For a long time I have held my
peace,
I have kept still and restrained
myself;
now I will cry out like a woman
in labor,
I will gasp and pant.
15 I will lay waste mountains and hills,
and dry up all their herbage;
I will turn the rivers into islands,
and dry up the pools.
16 I will lead the blind
by a road they do not know,
by paths they have not known
I will guide them.
I will turn the darkness before them
into light,
the rough places into level
ground.
These are the things I will do,
and I will not forsake them.
17 They shall be turned back and
utterly put to shame—
those who trust in carved images,
who say to cast images,
"You are our gods."

18 Listen, you that are deaf;
and you that are blind, look up
and see!
19 Who is blind but my servant,
or deaf like my messenger whom I
send?
Who is blind like my dedicated one,
or blind like the servant of
the LORD?
20 He sees many things, but does[o] not
observe them;

---

m Meaning of Heb uncertain   n Cn Compare Ps
96.11; 98.7: Heb *Those who go down to the sea*
o Heb *You see many things but do*

his ears are open, but he does
    not hear.

Israel's Disobedience

21 The LORD was pleased, for the sake
    of his righteousness,
    to magnify his teaching and make
      it glorious.
22 But this is a people robbed and
    plundered,
    all of them are trapped in holes
    and hidden in prisons;
they have become a prey with no
    one to rescue,
    a spoil with no one to say,
    "Restore!"
23 Who among you will give heed
    to this,
    who will attend and listen for the
      time to come?
24 Who gave up Jacob to the spoiler,
    and Israel to the robbers?
Was it not the LORD, against whom
    we have sinned,
    in whose ways they would
      not walk,
    and whose law they would
      not obey?
25 So he poured upon him the heat of
    his anger
    and the fury of war;
it set him on fire all around, but he
    did not understand;
    it burned him, but he did not
      take it to heart.

Restoration and Protection Promised

43 But now thus says the LORD,
    he who created you, O Jacob,
he who formed you, O Israel:
Do not fear, for I have redeemed
    you;
    I have called you by name, you
      are mine.
2 When you pass through the waters, I
    will be with you;
    and through the rivers, they shall
      not overwhelm you;
when you walk through fire you
      shall not be burned,
    and the flame shall not
      consume you.
3 For I am the LORD your God,
    the Holy One of Israel, your
      Savior.
I give Egypt as your ransom,
    Ethiopia p and Seba in exchange
      for you.

4 Because you are precious in
    my sight,
    and honored, and I love you,
I give people in return for you,
    nations in exchange for your life.
5 Do not fear, for I am with you;
    I will bring your offspring from
      the east,
    and from the west I will
      gather you;
6 I will say to the north, "Give
    them up,"
    and to the south, "Do not
      withhold;
bring my sons from far away
    and my daughters from the end of
      the earth—
7 everyone who is called by my name,
    whom I created for my glory,
    whom I formed and made."

8 Bring forth the people who are
    blind, yet have eyes,
    who are deaf, yet have ears!
9 Let all the nations gather together,
    and let the peoples assemble.
Who among them declared this,
    and foretold to us the former
      things?
Let them bring their witnesses to
    justify them,
    and let them hear and say, "It
      is true."
10 You are my witnesses, says the LORD,
    and my servant whom I have
      chosen,
so that you may know and
      believe me
    and understand that I am he.
Before me no god was formed,
    nor shall there be any after me.
11 I, I am the LORD,
    and besides me there is no savior.
12 I declared and saved and
    proclaimed,
    when there was no strange god
      among you;
    and you are my witnesses, says
      the LORD.
13 I am God, and also henceforth I
    am He;
    there is no one who can deliver
      from my hand;
    I work and who can hinder it?

14 Thus says the LORD,

p Or Nubia; Heb Cush

Tamar, the Daughter of David

Her Name Means *"Date Tree"* or *"Palm Tree"*

THE
STORY
OF A
WOMAN

Her Character: *She shared her father David's good looks. Young and innocent, she was naïve to the danger that threatened from her own family.*
Her Sorrow: *That her half-brother saw her only as an object for his lust, destroying her future as a result, and that her father the king did nothing to protect her.*

Read 2 Samuel 13.1–22

David's daughter Tamar was a knockout. No doubt she was destined for a marriage that would strengthen the king's political alliances. Though not under lock and key, she probably lived a rather protected life. But all the precautions in the world couldn't save her from the danger that threatened from David's inner circle.

Amnon was David's heir. As the king's eldest, he was used to getting his way. But lately he'd grown despondent. Something was bothering him, chasing away his sleep, gnawing at his heart.

One day, Jonadab, David's nephew and Amnon's cousin, asked him: "O son of the king, why are you so haggard morning after morning? Will you not tell me?"

Amnon confided in his friend, saying, "I love Tamar, my brother Absalom's sister."

"Lie down on your bed, and pretend to be ill," Jonadab shrewdly advised, "and when your father comes to see you, say to him, 'Let my sister Tamar come and give me something to eat.'"

So David, concerned for his son, sent his daughter into a trap that would ruin her life. Feigning illness, Amnon asked his half-sister to enter his bedroom and feed him. But as soon as Tamar did, he grabbed her, begging, "Come, lie with me, my sister."

"No, my brother, do not force me; for such a thing is not done in Israel; do not do anything so vile! As for me, where could I carry my shame? And as for you, you would be as one of the scoundrels in Israel." But Amnon forced himself on her. As soon as the storm of his passion died down, he threw Tamar out of his house, as though she, not he, were the guilty one. The young girl tore her robes, throwing ashes on her head and weeping loudly. When her brother Absalom found her, he hushed her, saying, "Be quiet for now, my sister; he is your brother; do not take this to heart." But Absalom took it to heart, hating Amnon for what he had done.

Though David was furious when he heard the news, he did nothing to punish Amnon. Did he favor his son over his daughter, thinking her hurt a small matter? Or was his moral authority so compromised by his own past—his lust for Bathsheba—that he simply couldn't bring himself to confront his eldest son?

Whatever the case, Absalom did not share his father's complacency. Instead, he bided his time, waiting for an opportunity for vengeance. Two years later, he murdered his half-brother Amnon.

First rape, then murder. David's household was devastated, not by barbarians outside the gate, but by those inside his own family. The prophecy Nathan had delivered after Uriah's death must have haunted David: "Now therefore the sword shall never depart from your house" (12.10). The father's lust was mirrored by the son's—the father's violence, by one son's murder of the other.

Tamar, unprotected by her father, betrayed by her own brother, lived in Absalom's house as a desolate woman, without the possibility of marriage or children. Thus a chain of sin wove its way through David's family, enslaving the innocent along with the guilty.

Praying With Tamar

You who have made me see many troubles and calamities will revive me again;
from the depths of the earth you will bring me up again. You will increase my
honor, and comfort me once again.—*Psalm 71.20–21*

Praise God: For giving us a hope rooted, not in the events of
this life, but in eternity.
Offer Thanks: That God has the power to restore our hope.
Confess: Any despair about your life.
Ask God: To show you that he really does care about you.

Lift Your Heart

Whether we suffer from sexual abuse, the loss of a loved one, divorce, sickness, or financial reverses, we can sometimes feel hopeless about the future.
But anyone who belongs to God will not be consigned to a hopeless end. Even
if you have difficulty believing this, pray for the grace to *want* to believe it. As
a small gesture expressing your desire, plant a bulb garden in the fall. This simple act will affirm your belief that, even after the harshest winter, spring will
come again, with its profusion of colors and new life. If fall is still far away, buy
a colorful bouquet to grace your bedside table for the week ahead and a copy
of Judy Couchman's beautiful book, *A Garden of Promise.* Just reading her practical and graceful insights about gardening will make you glad.

 *Father, plant something new in my life, a sprig of hope that will set me on
a new course. Help me to live in the present, spending my emotional energies
on this moment rather than squandering them on regrets about the past or
anxieties about the future.*

Go to page 989 for your next devotional reading.

your Redeemer, the Holy One
   of Israel:
For your sake I will send to Babylon
   and break down all the bars,
   and the shouting of the Chaldeans
    will be turned to
    lamentation.*q*

15 I am the LORD, your Holy One,
   the Creator of Israel, your King.
16 Thus says the LORD,
   who makes a way in the sea,
   a path in the mighty waters,
17 who brings out chariot and horse,
   army and warrior;
they lie down, they cannot rise,
   they are extinguished, quenched
    like a wick:
18 Do not remember the former things,
   or consider the things of old.
19 I am about to do a new thing;
   now it springs forth, do you not
    perceive it?
I will make a way in the wilderness
   and rivers in the desert.
20 The wild animals will honor me,
   the jackals and the ostriches;
for I give water in the wilderness,
   rivers in the desert,
to give drink to my chosen people,
21   the people whom I formed
    for myself
so that they might declare my praise.

22 Yet you did not call upon me,
   O Jacob;
but you have been weary of me,
   O Israel!
23 You have not brought me your
    sheep for burnt offerings,
   or honored me with your
    sacrifices.
I have not burdened you with
    offerings,
   or wearied you with frankincense.
24 You have not bought me sweet cane
    with money,
   or satisfied me with the fat of
    your sacrifices.
But you have burdened me with
    your sins;
   you have wearied me with your
    iniquities.

25 I, I am He
   who blots out your transgressions
    for my own sake,
   and I will not remember
    your sins.

26 Accuse me, let us go to trial;
   set forth your case, so that you
    may be proved right.
27 Your first ancestor sinned,
   and your interpreters transgressed
    against me.
28 Therefore I profaned the princes of
    the sanctuary,
   I delivered Jacob to utter
    destruction,
   and Israel to reviling.

God's Blessing on Israel

44 But now hear, O Jacob
    my servant,
   Israel whom I have chosen!
2 Thus says the LORD who made you,
   who formed you in the womb
    and will help you:
Do not fear, O Jacob my servant,
   Jeshurun whom I have chosen.
3 For I will pour water on the
    thirsty land,
   and streams on the dry ground;
I will pour my spirit upon your
    descendants,
   and my blessing on your
    offspring.
4 They shall spring up like a green
    tamarisk,
   like willows by flowing streams.
5 This one will say, "I am the LORD's,"
   another will be called by the
    name of Jacob,
yet another will write on the hand,
    "The LORD's,"
   and adopt the name of Israel.

6 Thus says the LORD, the King
    of Israel,
   and his Redeemer, the LORD
    of hosts:
I am the first and I am the last;
   besides me there is no god.
7 Who is like me? Let them
    proclaim it,
   let them declare and set it forth
    before me.
Who has announced from of old the
    things to come?*r*
   Let them tell us*s* what is yet
    to be.
8 Do not fear, or be afraid;

---

q Meaning of Heb uncertain   *r* Cn: Heb *from my placing an eternal people and things to come*   *s* Tg: Heb *them*

have I not told you from of old
　　and declared it?
You are my witnesses!
Is there any god besides me?
　　There is no other rock; I know not
　　　　one.

The Absurdity of Idol Worship

9 All who make idols are nothing, and
the things they delight in do not profit;
their witnesses neither see nor know. And
so they will be put to shame. 10Who
would fashion a god or cast an image that
can do no good? 11Look, all its devotees
shall be put to shame; the artisans too are
merely human. Let them all assemble, let
them stand up; they shall be terrified, they
shall all be put to shame.

12 The ironsmith fashions it*t* and
works it over the coals, shaping it with
hammers, and forging it with his strong
arm; he becomes hungry and his strength
fails, he drinks no water and is faint. 13The
carpenter stretches a line, marks it out
with a stylus, fashions it with planes, and
marks it with a compass; he makes it in
human form, with human beauty, to be
set up in a shrine. 14He cuts down cedars
or chooses a holm tree or an oak and lets
it grow strong among the trees of the forest. He plants a cedar and the rain nourishes it. 15Then it can be used as fuel. Part
of it he takes and warms himself; he kindles a fire and bakes bread. Then he
makes a god and worships it, makes it a
carved image and bows down before it.
16Half of it he burns in the fire; over this
half he roasts meat, eats it and is satisfied.
He also warms himself and says, "Ah, I
am warm, I can feel the fire!" 17The rest of
it he makes into a god, his idol, bows
down to it and worships it; he prays to it
and says, "Save me, for you are my god!"

18 They do not know, nor do they
comprehend; for their eyes are shut, so
that they cannot see, and their minds as
well, so that they cannot understand.
19No one considers, nor is there knowledge or discernment to say, "Half of it I
burned in the fire; I also baked bread on
its coals, I roasted meat and have eaten.
Now shall I make the rest of it an abomination? Shall I fall down before a block of
wood?" 20He feeds on ashes; a deluded
mind has led him astray, and he cannot
save himself or say, "Is not this thing in
my right hand a fraud?"

Israel Is Not Forgotten

21 Remember these things, O Jacob,
　　and Israel, for you are my servant;
I formed you, you are my servant;
　　O Israel, you will not be forgotten
　　　　by me.
22 I have swept away your
　　　　transgressions like a cloud,
　　and your sins like mist;
return to me, for I have redeemed
　　you.

23 Sing, O heavens, for the LORD has
　　　　done it;
　　shout, O depths of the earth;
break forth into singing,
　　O mountains,
O forest, and every tree in it!
For the LORD has redeemed Jacob,
　　and will be glorified in Israel.

24 Thus says the LORD, your Redeemer,
　　who formed you in the womb:
I am the LORD, who made all
　　　　things,
　　who alone stretched out the
　　　　heavens,
　　who by myself spread out
　　　　the earth;
25 who frustrates the omens of liars,
　　and makes fools of diviners;
who turns back the wise,
　　and makes their knowledge
　　　　foolish;
26 who confirms the word of his
　　　　servant,
　　and fulfills the prediction of his
　　　　messengers;
who says of Jerusalem, "It shall be
　　　　inhabited,"
　　and of the cities of Judah, "They
　　　　shall be rebuilt,
　　and I will raise up their ruins";
27 who says to the deep, "Be dry—
　　I will dry up your rivers";
28 who says of Cyrus, "He is my
　　　　shepherd,
　　and he shall carry out all my
　　　　purpose";
　　and who says of Jerusalem, "It shall
　　　　be rebuilt,"
　　and of the temple, "Your
　　　　foundation shall be laid."

t Cn: Heb *an ax*

Cyrus, God's Instrument

45 Thus says the LORD to his anointed, to Cyrus,
whose right hand I have grasped
to subdue nations before him
and strip kings of their robes,
to open doors before him—
and the gates shall not be closed:
2 I will go before you
and level the mountains,[u]
I will break in pieces the doors
of bronze
and cut through the bars of iron,
3 I will give you the treasures of
darkness
and riches hidden in secret places,
so that you may know that it is I,
the LORD,
the God of Israel, who call you by
your name.
4 For the sake of my servant Jacob,
and Israel my chosen,
I call you by your name,
I surname you, though you do
not know me.
5 I am the LORD, and there is no other;
besides me there is no god.
I arm you, though you do not
know me,
6 so that they may know, from the
rising of the sun
and from the west, that there is
no one besides me;
I am the LORD, and there is
no other.
7 I form light and create darkness,
I make weal and create woe;
I the LORD do all these things.

8 Shower, O heavens, from above,
and let the skies rain down
righteousness;
let the earth open, that salvation
may spring up,[v]
and let it cause righteousness to
sprout up also;
I the LORD have created it.

9 Woe to you who strive with your
Maker,
earthen vessels with the potter![w]
Does the clay say to the one who
fashions it, "What are you
making"?
or "Your work has no handles"?
10 Woe to anyone who says to a father,
"What are you begetting?"

or to a woman, "With what are
you in labor?"
11 Thus says the LORD,
the Holy One of Israel, and its
Maker:
Will you question me[x] about my
children,
or command me concerning the
work of my hands?
12 I made the earth,
and created humankind upon it;
it was my hands that stretched out
the heavens,
and I commanded all their host.
13 I have aroused Cyrus[y] in
righteousness,
and I will make all his paths
straight;
he shall build my city
and set my exiles free,
not for price or reward,
says the LORD of hosts.
14 Thus says the LORD:
The wealth of Egypt and the
merchandise of Ethiopia,[z]
and the Sabeans, tall of stature,
shall come over to you and
be yours,
they shall follow you;
they shall come over in chains
and bow down to you.
They will make supplication to you,
saying,
"God is with you alone, and there
is no other;
there is no god besides him."
15 Truly, you are a God who hides
himself,
O God of Israel, the Savior.
16 All of them are put to shame and
confounded,
the makers of idols go in
confusion together.
17 But Israel is saved by the LORD
with everlasting salvation;
you shall not be put to shame or
confounded
to all eternity.

18 For thus says the LORD,
who created the heavens
(he is God!),

u Q Ms Gk: MT *the swellings*
they may bring forth salvation   w Cn: Heb *with the*
potterds, or *with the potters*   x Cn: Heb *Ask me*
of things to come   y Heb *him*   z Or *Nubia*; Heb
Cush

who formed the earth and made it
    (he established it;
he did not create it a chaos,
    he formed it to be inhabited!):
I am the LORD, and there is no other.
19 I did not speak in secret,
    in a land of darkness;
I did not say to the offspring
    of Jacob,
    "Seek me in chaos."
I the LORD speak the truth,
    I declare what is right.

Idols Cannot Save Babylon

20 Assemble yourselves and come
    together,
    draw near, you survivors of the
    nations!
They have no knowledge—
    those who carry about their
    wooden idols,
and keep on praying to a god
    that cannot save.
21 Declare and present your case;
    let them take counsel together!
Who told this long ago?
    Who declared it of old?
Was it not I, the LORD?
    There is no other god besides me,
a righteous God and a Savior;
    there is no one besides me.

22 Turn to me and be saved,
    all the ends of the earth!
    For I am God, and there is
    no other.
23 By myself I have sworn,
    from my mouth has gone forth in
    righteousness
a word that shall not return:
"To me every knee shall bow,
    every tongue shall swear."

24 Only in the LORD, it shall be said
    of me,
    are righteousness and strength;
all who were incensed against him
    shall come to him and be
    ashamed.
25 In the LORD all the offspring of Israel
    shall triumph and glory.

46 Bel bows down, Nebo stoops,
    their idols are on beasts
    and cattle;
these things you carry are loaded
    as burdens on weary animals.

2 They stoop, they bow down
    together;
    they cannot save the burden,
    but themselves go into captivity.

3 Listen to me, O house of Jacob,
    all the remnant of the house of
    Israel,
who have been borne by me from
    your birth,
    carried from the womb;
4 even to your old age I am he,
    even when you turn gray I will
    carry you.
I have made, and I will bear;
    I will carry and will save.

5 To whom will you liken me and
    make me equal,
    and compare me, as though we
    were alike?
6 Those who lavish gold from the
    purse,
    and weigh out silver in the
    scales—
they hire a goldsmith, who makes it
    into a god;
    then they fall down and worship!
7 They lift it to their shoulders, they
    carry it,
    they set it in its place, and it
    stands there;
    it cannot move from its place.
If one cries out to it, it does
    not answer
    or save anyone from trouble.

8 Remember this and consider,[a]
    recall it to mind, you
    transgressors,
9   remember the former things
    of old;
for I am God, and there is no other;
    I am God, and there is no one
    like me,
10 declaring the end from the
    beginning
    and from ancient times things not
    yet done,
saying, "My purpose shall stand,
    and I will fulfill my intention,"
11 calling a bird of prey from the east,
    the man for my purpose from a
    far country.

---

a Meaning of Heb uncertain

I have spoken, and I will bring it
    to pass;
I have planned, and I will do it.

12 Listen to me, you stubborn of
    heart,
  you who are far from deliverance:
13 I bring near my deliverance, it is not
    far off,
  and my salvation will not tarry;
I will put salvation in Zion,
  for Israel my glory.

The Humiliation of Babylon

47 Come down and sit in the dust,
    virgin daughter Babylon!
Sit on the ground without a throne,
  daughter Chaldea!
For you shall no more be called
  tender and delicate.
2 Take the millstones and grind meal,
  remove your veil,
strip off your robe, uncover
    your legs,
  pass through the rivers.
3 Your nakedness shall be uncovered,
  and your shame shall be seen.
I will take vengeance,
  and I will spare no one.
4 Our Redeemer—the LORD of hosts is
    his name—
  is the Holy One of Israel.

5 Sit in silence, and go into darkness,
  daughter Chaldea!
For you shall no more be called
  the mistress of kingdoms.
6 I was angry with my people,
  I profaned my heritage;
I gave them into your hand,
  you showed them no mercy;
on the aged you made your yoke
  exceedingly heavy.
7 You said, "I shall be mistress
    forever,"
  so that you did not lay these
    things to heart
  or remember their end.

8 Now therefore hear this, you lover
    of pleasures,
  who sit securely,
who say in your heart,
  "I am, and there is no one
    besides me;
I shall not sit as a widow
  or know the loss of children"—

9 both these things shall come
    upon you
  in a moment, in one day:
the loss of children and widowhood
  shall come upon you in full
    measure,
in spite of your many sorceries
  and the great power of your
    enchantments.

10 You felt secure in your wickedness;
  you said, "No one sees me."
Your wisdom and your knowledge
  led you astray,
and you said in your heart,
  "I am, and there is no one
    besides me."
11 But evil shall come upon you,
  which you cannot charm away;
disaster shall fall upon you,
  which you will not be able to
    ward off;
and ruin shall come on you
    suddenly,
  of which you know nothing.

12 Stand fast in your enchantments
  and your many sorceries,
  with which you have labored from
    your youth;
perhaps you may be able to succeed,
  perhaps you may inspire terror.
13 You are wearied with your many
    consultations;
  let those who study[b] the heavens
stand up and save you,
  those who gaze at the stars,
and at each new moon predict
  what[c] shall befall you.

14 See, they are like stubble,
  the fire consumes them;
they cannot deliver themselves
  from the power of the flame.
No coal for warming oneself is this,
  no fire to sit before!
15 Such to you are those with whom
    you have labored,
  who have trafficked with you from
    your youth;
they all wander about in their
    own paths;
  there is no one to save you.

b Meaning of Heb uncertain   *c* Gk Syr Compare
Vg: Heb *from what*

God the Creator and Redeemer

48

Hear this, O house of Jacob,
who are called by the name of
Israel,
and who came forth from the
loins*d* of Judah;
who swear by the name of the LORD,
and invoke the God of Israel,
but not in truth or right.
2 For they call themselves after the
holy city,
and lean on the God of Israel;
the LORD of hosts is his name.

3 The former things I declared
long ago,
they went out from my mouth
and I made them known;
then suddenly I did them and
they came to pass.
4 Because I know that you are
obstinate,
and your neck is an iron sinew
and your forehead brass,
5 I declared them to you from
long ago,
before they came to pass I
announced them to you,
so that you would not say, "My idol
did them,
my carved image and my cast
image commanded them."

6 You have heard; now see all this;
and will you not declare it?
From this time forward I make you
hear new things,
hidden things that you have not
known.
7 They are created now, not long ago;
before today you have never heard
of them,
so that you could not say, "I
already knew them."
8 You have never heard, you have
never known,
from of old your ear has not been
opened.
For I knew that you would deal very
treacherously,
and that from birth you were
called a rebel.

9 For my name's sake I defer my
anger,
for the sake of my praise I restrain
it for you,

so that I may not cut you off.
10 See, I have refined you, but not
like*e* silver;
I have tested you in the furnace of
adversity.
11 For my own sake, for my own sake,
I do it,
for why should my name*f* be
profaned?
My glory I will not give to
another.

12 Listen to me, O Jacob,
and Israel, whom I called:
I am He; I am the first,
and I am the last.
13 My hand laid the foundation of
the earth,
and my right hand spread out
the heavens;
when I summon them,
they stand at attention.

14 Assemble, all of you, and hear!
Who among them has declared
these things?
The LORD loves him;
he shall perform his purpose on
Babylon,
and his arm shall be against the
Chaldeans.
15 I, even I, have spoken and
called him,
I have brought him, and he will
prosper in his way.
16 Draw near to me, hear this!
From the beginning I have not
spoken in secret,
from the time it came to be I have
been there.
And now the Lord GOD has sent me
and his spirit.

17 Thus says the LORD,
your Redeemer, the Holy One
of Israel:
I am the LORD your God,
who teaches you for your
own good,
who leads you in the way you
should go.
18 O that you had paid attention to my
commandments!
Then your prosperity would have
been like a river,

---

d Cn: Heb *waters*   *e* Cn: Heb *with*   *f* Gk Old
Latin: Heb *for why should it*

and your success like the waves of
    the sea;
19 your offspring would have been like
    the sand,
    and your descendants like its
        grains;
    their name would never be cut off
    or destroyed from before me.

20 Go out from Babylon, flee from
    Chaldea,
    declare this with a shout of joy,
        proclaim it,
    send it forth to the end of the earth;
    say, "The LORD has redeemed his
        servant Jacob!"
21 They did not thirst when he led
    them through the deserts;
    he made water flow for them
        from the rock;
    he split open the rock and the
        water gushed out.

22 "There is no peace," says the LORD,
    "for the wicked."

The Servant's Mission

49 Listen to me, O coastlands,
    pay attention, you peoples
        from far away!
The LORD called me before I
    was born,
    while I was in my mother's womb
    he named me.
2 He made my mouth like a sharp
    sword,
    in the shadow of his hand he
    hid me;
he made me a polished arrow,
    in his quiver he hid me away.
3 And he said to me, "You are my
    servant,
    Israel, in whom I will be glorified."
4 But I said, "I have labored in vain,
    I have spent my strength for
        nothing and vanity;
    yet surely my cause is with the LORD,
    and my reward with my God."

5 And now the LORD says,
    who formed me in the womb to
        be his servant,
    to bring Jacob back to him,
    and that Israel might be gathered
        to him,
    for I am honored in the sight of
        the LORD,

and my God has become my
    strength—
6 he says,
    "It is too light a thing that you
        should be my servant
    to raise up the tribes of Jacob
    and to restore the survivors of
        Israel;
I will give you as a light to the
    nations,
    that my salvation may reach to
        the end of the earth."

7 Thus says the LORD,
    the Redeemer of Israel and his
        Holy One,
to one deeply despised, abhorred by
    the nations,
    the slave of rulers,
"Kings shall see and stand up,
    princes, and they shall prostrate
        themselves,
because of the LORD, who is faithful,
    the Holy One of Israel, who has
        chosen you."

Zion's Children to Be Brought Home

8 Thus says the LORD:
In a time of favor I have answered
    you,
    on a day of salvation I have
        helped you;
I have kept you and given you
    as a covenant to the people, g
to establish the land,
    to apportion the desolate
        heritages;
9 saying to the prisoners, "Come out,"
    to those who are in darkness,
        "Show yourselves."
They shall feed along the ways,
    on all the bare heightsʰ shall be
        their pasture;
10 they shall not hunger or thirst,
    neither scorching wind nor sun
        shall strike them down,
    for he who has pity on them will
        lead them,
    and by springs of water will guide
        them.
11 And I will turn all my mountains
    into a road,
    and my highways shall be
        raised up.
12 Lo, these shall come from far away,

g Meaning of Heb uncertain   h Or the trails

and lo, these from the north and
from the west,
and these from the land of
Syene.[i]

13 Sing for joy, O heavens, and exult,
O earth;
break forth, O mountains, into
singing!
For the LORD has comforted his
people,
and will have compassion on his
suffering ones.

14 But Zion said, "The LORD has
forsaken me,
my Lord has forgotten me."
15 Can a woman forget her nursing
child,
or show no compassion for the
child of her womb?
Even these may forget,
yet I will not forget you.
16 See, I have inscribed you on the
palms of my hands;
your walls are continually
before me.
17 Your builders outdo your
destroyers,[j]
and those who laid you waste go
away from you.
18 Lift up your eyes all around and see;
they all gather, they come to you.
As I live, says the LORD,
you shall put all of them on like
an ornament,
and like a bride you shall bind
them on.

19 Surely your waste and your desolate
places
and your devastated land—
surely now you will be too crowded
for your inhabitants,
and those who swallowed you up
will be far away.
20 The children born in the time of
your bereavement
will yet say in your hearing:
"The place is too crowded for me;
make room for me to settle."
21 Then you will say in your heart,
"Who has borne me these?
I was bereaved and barren,
exiled and put away—
so who has reared these?
I was left all alone—

where then have these come
from?"

22 Thus says the Lord GOD:
I will soon lift up my hand to the
nations,
and raise my signal to the
peoples;
and they shall bring your sons in
their bosom,
and your daughters shall be
carried on their shoulders.
23 Kings shall be your foster fathers,
and their queens your nursing
mothers.
With their faces to the ground they
shall bow down to you,
and lick the dust of your feet.
Then you will know that I am the
LORD;
those who wait for me shall not
be put to shame.

24 Can the prey be taken from the
mighty,
or the captives of a tyrant[k] be
rescued?
25 But thus says the LORD:
Even the captives of the mighty shall
be taken,
and the prey of the tyrant be
rescued;
for I will contend with those who
contend with you,
and I will save your children.
26 I will make your oppressors eat their
own flesh,
and they shall be drunk with their
own blood as with wine.
Then all flesh shall know
that I am the LORD your Savior,
and your Redeemer, the Mighty
One of Jacob.

50 Thus says the LORD:
Where is your mother's bill of
divorce
with which I put her away?
Or which of my creditors is it
to whom I have sold you?
No, because of your sins you
were sold,
and for your transgressions your
mother was put away.

---

[i] Q Ms: MT *Sinim*   [j] Or *Your children come
swiftly; your destroyers*   [k] Q Ms Syr Vg: MT *of a
righteous person*

2 Why was no one there when I came?
  Why did no one answer when I
    called?
  Is my hand shortened, that it cannot
    redeem?
    Or have I no power to deliver?
  By my rebuke I dry up the sea,
    I make the rivers a desert;
  their fish stink for lack of water,
    and die of thirst.*l*
3 I clothe the heavens with blackness,
    and make sackcloth their covering.

The Servant's Humiliation and Vindication

4 The Lord GOD has given me
    the tongue of a teacher,*m*
  that I may know how to sustain
    the weary with a word.
  Morning by morning he wakens—
    wakens my ear
  to listen as those who are taught.
5 The Lord GOD has opened my ear,
    and I was not rebellious,
    I did not turn backward.
6 I gave my back to those who
    struck me,
  and my cheeks to those who
    pulled out the beard;
  I did not hide my face
    from insult and spitting.

7 The Lord GOD helps me;
    therefore I have not been
      disgraced;
  therefore I have set my face
    like flint,
  and I know that I shall not be put
    to shame;
8   he who vindicates me is near.
  Who will contend with me?
    Let us stand up together.
  Who are my adversaries?
    Let them confront me.
9 It is the Lord GOD who helps me;
    who will declare me guilty?
  All of them will wear out like a
    garment;
    the moth will eat them up.

10 Who among you fears the LORD
    and obeys the voice of his servant,
  who walks in darkness
    and has no light,
  yet trusts in the name of the LORD
    and relies upon his God?
11 But all of you are kindlers of fire,
    lighters of firebrands.*n*
  Walk in the flame of your fire,

and among the brands that you
    have kindled!
This is what you shall have from my
    hand:
  you shall lie down in torment.

Blessings in Store for God's People

51 Listen to me, you that pursue
    righteousness,
  you that seek the LORD.
  Look to the rock from which you
    were hewn,
    and to the quarry from which
    you were dug.
2 Look to Abraham your father
    and to Sarah who bore you;
  for he was but one when I called
    him,
    but I blessed him and made
    him many.
3 For the LORD will comfort Zion;
    he will comfort all her waste
      places,
  and will make her wilderness
    like Eden,
    her desert like the garden of
    the LORD;
  joy and gladness will be found
    in her,
    thanksgiving and the voice
    of song.

4 Listen to me, my people,
    and give heed to me, my nation;
  for a teaching will go out from me,
    and my justice for a light to
    the peoples.
5 I will bring near my deliverance
    swiftly,
    my salvation has gone out
  and my arms will rule the
    peoples;
  the coastlands wait for me,
    and for my arm they hope.
6 Lift up your eyes to the heavens,
    and look at the earth beneath;
  for the heavens will vanish like
    smoke,
    the earth will wear out like a
    garment,
  and those who live on it will die
    like gnats;*o*
  but my salvation will be forever,

*l Or die on the thirsty ground   m Cn: Heb of those
who are taught   n Syr: Heb you gird yourselves with
firebrands   o Or in like manner*

and my deliverance will never
 be ended.

7 Listen to me, you who know
  righteousness,
   you people who have my teaching
    in your hearts;
  do not fear the reproach of others,
   and do not be dismayed when
    they revile you.
8 For the moth will eat them up like a
  garment,
   and the worm will eat them
    like wool;
  but my deliverance will be forever,
   and my salvation to all
    generations.

9 Awake, awake, put on strength,
  O arm of the LORD!
  Awake, as in days of old,
   the generations of long ago!
  Was it not you who cut Rahab in
   pieces,
   who pierced the dragon?
10 Was it not you who dried up
   the sea,
   the waters of the great deep;
  who made the depths of the sea
   a way
  for the redeemed to cross over?
11 So the ransomed of the LORD shall
   return,
   and come to Zion with singing;
  everlasting joy shall be upon their
   heads;
  they shall obtain joy and gladness,
   and sorrow and sighing shall
    flee away.

12 I, I am he who comforts you;
   why then are you afraid of a mere
    mortal who must die,
   a human being who fades like
    grass?
13 You have forgotten the LORD, your
   Maker,
   who stretched out the heavens
   and laid the foundations of
    the earth.
  You fear continually all day long
   because of the fury of the
    oppressor,
  who is bent on destruction.
   But where is the fury of the
    oppressor?
14 The oppressed shall speedily be
   released;

they shall not die and go down to
  the Pit,
  nor shall they lack bread.
15 For I am the LORD your God,
   who stirs up the sea so that its
    waves roar—
   the LORD of hosts is his name.
16 I have put my words in your mouth,
   and hidden you in the shadow of
    my hand,
  stretching out *p* the heavens
   and laying the foundations of
    the earth,
   and saying to Zion, "You are my
    people."

17 Rouse yourself, rouse yourself!
   Stand up, O Jerusalem,
  you who have drunk at the hand of
   the LORD
   the cup of his wrath,
  who have drunk to the dregs
   the bowl of staggering.
18 There is no one to guide her
   among all the children she
    has borne;
  there is no one to take her by
   the hand
   among all the children she has
    brought up.
19 These two things have befallen you
   —who will grieve with you?—
  devastation and destruction, famine
   and sword—
   who will comfort you?*q*
20 Your children have fainted,
   they lie at the head of every street
   like an antelope in a net;
  they are full of the wrath of
   the LORD,
   the rebuke of your God.

21 Therefore hear this, you who are
   wounded,*r*
   who are drunk, but not with wine:
22 Thus says your Sovereign, the LORD,
   your God who pleads the cause of
    his people:
  See, I have taken from your hand
   the cup of staggering;
  you shall drink no more
   from the bowl of my wrath.
23 And I will put it into the hand of
   your tormentors,
   who have said to you,

---

p Syr: Heb *planting*   *q* Q Ms Gk Syr Vg: MT *how
may I comfort you?*   *r* Or *humbled*

"Bow down, that we may walk
on you";
and you have made your back like
the ground
and like the street for them to
walk on.

Let Zion Rejoice

52 Awake, awake,
put on your strength, O Zion!
Put on your beautiful garments,
O Jerusalem, the holy city;
for the uncircumcised and the
unclean
shall enter you no more.
2 Shake yourself from the dust,
rise up,
O captive[s] Jerusalem;
loose the bonds from your neck,
O captive daughter Zion!

3 For thus says the LORD: You were sold for nothing, and you shall be redeemed without money. 4For thus says the Lord GOD: Long ago, my people went down into Egypt to reside there as aliens; the Assyrian, too, has oppressed them without cause. 5Now therefore what am I doing here, says the LORD, seeing that my people are taken away without cause? Their rulers howl, says the LORD, and continually, all day long, my name is despised. 6Therefore my people shall know my name; therefore in that day they shall know that it is I who speak; here am I.

7 How beautiful upon the mountains
are the feet of the messenger who
announces peace,
who brings good news,
who announces salvation,
who says to Zion, "Your God
reigns."
8 Listen! Your sentinels lift up
their voices,
together they sing for joy;
for in plain sight they see
the return of the LORD to Zion.
9 Break forth together into singing,
you ruins of Jerusalem;
for the LORD has comforted his
people,
he has redeemed Jerusalem.
10 The LORD has bared his holy arm
before the eyes of all the nations;
and all the ends of the earth
shall see
the salvation of our God.

11 Depart, depart, go out from there!
Touch no unclean thing;
go out from the midst of it, purify
yourselves,
you who carry the vessels of
the LORD.
12 For you shall not go out in haste,
and you shall not go in flight;
for the LORD will go before you,
and the God of Israel will be your
rear guard.

The Suffering Servant

13 See, my servant shall prosper;
he shall be exalted and lifted up,
and shall be very high.
14 Just as there were many who were
astonished at him[t]
—so marred was his appearance,
beyond human semblance,
and his form beyond that of
mortals—
15 so he shall startle[u] many nations;
kings shall shut their mouths
because of him;
for that which had not been told
them they shall see,
and that which they had not
heard they shall contemplate.

53 Who has believed what we have
heard?
And to whom has the arm of the
LORD been revealed?
2 For he grew up before him like a
young plant,
and like a root out of dry ground;
he had no form or majesty that we
should look at him,
nothing in his appearance that we
should desire him.
3 He was despised and rejected
by others;
a man of suffering[v] and
acquainted with infirmity;
and as one from whom others hide
their faces[w]
he was despised, and we held him
of no account.

4 Surely he has borne our infirmities
and carried our diseases;
yet we accounted him stricken,
struck down by God, and afflicted.

---

s Cn: Heb *rise up, sit*   t Syr Tg: Heb *you*
u Meaning of Heb uncertain   v Or *a man of*
sorrows   w Or *as one who hides his face from us*

5 But he was wounded for our
        transgressions,
    crushed for our iniquities;
upon him was the punishment that
        made us whole,
    and by his bruises we are healed.
6 All we like sheep have gone astray;
    we have all turned to our
        own way,
and the LORD has laid on him
    the iniquity of us all.

7 He was oppressed, and he was
        afflicted,
    yet he did not open his mouth;
like a lamb that is led to the
        slaughter,
    and like a sheep that before its
        shearers is silent,
    so he did not open his mouth.
8 By a perversion of justice he was
        taken away.
    Who could have imagined his
        future?
For he was cut off from the land of
        the living,
    stricken for the transgression of
        my people.
9 They made his grave with the wicked

and his tomb[x] with the rich,[y]
    although he had done no violence,
    and there was no deceit in
        his mouth.

10 Yet it was the will of the LORD to
        crush him with pain.[z]
When you make his life an offering
        for sin,[a]
    he shall see his offspring, and
        shall prolong his days;
through him the will of the LORD
        shall prosper.
11   Out of his anguish he shall
            see light;[b]
    he shall find satisfaction through his
        knowledge.
    The righteous one,[c] my servant,
        shall make many righteous,
    and he shall bear their iniquities.
12 Therefore I will allot him a portion
        with the great,
    and he shall divide the spoil with
        the strong;

x Q Ms: MT *and in his death*   y Cn: Heb *with a*
rich person   z Or *by disease;* meaning of Heb
uncertain   a Meaning of Heb uncertain
b Q Mss: MT lacks *light*   c Or *and he shall find*
satisfaction. Through his knowledge, the righteous one

$\mathcal{M}$an of Suffering

MONDAY

Scripture Reading
for Today:
Isaiah 53.1–6

Verse for Today:
Isaiah 53.5

We would simply die if we did not fix our gaze on you. We see
you brought to a complete standstill as you cry out from the
cross in absolute inactivity, in a living death. You hurled all your
fire upon the earth as you turned cold, and finishing your life
there, you flung infinite, endless life into us, who live it now with
elation.

    We want nothing more than to see ourselves like you, at least
a little, joining our pain to yours and offering it to the Father.

    So that we might possess the light, you lost your sight.

    To acquire union for us, you experienced separation from the
Father.

    So that we might have wisdom, you made yourself ignorance.

    To clothe us in innocence, you became sin.

    So that God might be present in us, you felt him far away
from you.

—*CHIARA LUBICH*

Go to page 990 for your next devotional reading.

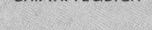

because he poured out himself
    to death,
and was numbered with the
    transgressors;
yet he bore the sin of many,
    and made intercession for the
        transgressors.

The Eternal Covenant of Peace

54 Sing, O barren one who did
        not bear;
burst into song and shout,
    you who have not been in labor!
For the children of the desolate
        woman will be more
    than the children of her that is
        married, says the LORD.
² Enlarge the site of your tent,

and let the curtains of your
        habitations be stretched out;
do not hold back; lengthen
        your cords
    and strengthen your stakes.
³ For you will spread out to the right
        and to the left,
    and your descendants will possess
        the nations
    and will settle the desolate towns.

⁴ Do not fear, for you will not be
        ashamed;
    do not be discouraged, for you
        will not suffer disgrace;
    for you will forget the shame of
        your youth,

Feelings of Inadequacy

TUESDAY

Scripture Reading
for Today:
Isaiah 54.1–8

Verses for Today:
Isaiah 54.4–5

Guilt is an action word—it's about the things I do that offend God, other people, or myself. The Holy Spirit comes into my heart, convicting me of these wrongs, inviting me to repentance and behavioral changes. When I am guilty of a transgression, something can be done about it.

But the accusatory words I was hearing in my head were not convicting me of specific sins that I could confess and receive forgiveness for. These words made me feel like a complete waste. They were condemning me by saying, "You're no good. You never do anything right. Your salvation is lost." The light finally dawned: I was dealing with shame. Shame is an excruciatingly internal experience of exposure. It gives rise to feelings of being unprotected, naked, and ugly.

This explained my inability to overcome the inner voices. I was approaching them in the wrong way. I was trying to repent for my feelings of being flawed. Guilt is about breaking rules. It says, "I made a mistake," and the proper response is, "I'm sorry." Shame is about feeling bad, and it says, "I am a mistake." The proper response is to get out from under it.

The one who redeemed me has already freed me from the chains of self-loathing. "Jesus . . . for the sake of the joy that was set before him endured the cross, disregarding its shame, and has taken his seat at the right hand of the throne of God" (Hebrews 12.2). I can invite God to heal the roots of shame within me as I come to recognize and resolve this hold on my life.

—BARBARA LEAHY SHLEMON

Go to page 992 for your next devotional reading.

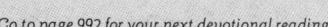

and the disgrace of your
   widowhood you will
   remember no more.
5 For your Maker is your husband,
   the LORD of hosts is his name;
the Holy One of Israel is your
   Redeemer,
   the God of the whole earth he
   is called.
6 For the LORD has called you
   like a wife forsaken and grieved in
   spirit,
like the wife of a man's youth when
   she is cast off,
   says your God.
7 For a brief moment I abandoned
   you,
   but with great compassion I will
   gather you.
8 In overflowing wrath for a moment
   I hid my face from you,
but with everlasting love I will have
   compassion on you,
   says the LORD, your Redeemer.

9 This is like the days of Noah to me:
   Just as I swore that the waters
   of Noah
   would never again go over
   the earth,
so I have sworn that I will not be
   angry with you
   and will not rebuke you.
10 For the mountains may depart
   and the hills be removed,
but my steadfast love shall not
   depart from you,
   and my covenant of peace shall
   not be removed,
   says the LORD, who has
   compassion on you.

11 O afflicted one, storm-tossed, and
   not comforted,
   I am about to set your stones in
   antimony,
   and lay your foundations with
   sapphires.[d]
12 I will make your pinnacles of rubies,
   your gates of jewels,
   and all your wall of precious
   stones.
13 All your children shall be taught by
   the LORD,
   and great shall be the prosperity
   of your children.
14 In righteousness you shall be
   established;

you shall be far from oppression,
   for you shall not fear;
   and from terror, for it shall not
   come near you.
15 If anyone stirs up strife,
   it is not from me;
whoever stirs up strife with you
   shall fall because of you.
16 See it is I who have created
   the smith
   who blows the fire of coals,
   and produces a weapon fit for
   its purpose;
I have also created the ravager
   to destroy.
17   No weapon that is fashioned
      against you shall prosper,
   and you shall confute every
      tongue that rises against you
      in judgment.
This is the heritage of the servants of
   the LORD
   and their vindication from me,
   says the LORD.

An Invitation to Abundant Life

55 Ho, everyone who thirsts,
   come to the waters;
and you that have no money,
   come, buy and eat!
Come, buy wine and milk
   without money and without price.
2 Why do you spend your money for
      that which is not bread,
   and your labor for that which
      does not satisfy?
Listen carefully to me, and eat what
   is good,
   and delight yourselves in
   rich food.
3 Incline your ear, and come to me;
   listen, so that you may live.
I will make with you an everlasting
   covenant,
   my steadfast, sure love for David.
4 See, I made him a witness to
      the peoples,
   a leader and commander for
      the peoples.
5 See, you shall call nations that you
      do not know,
   and nations that do not know you
      shall run to you,
because of the LORD your God, the
      Holy One of Israel,
   for he has glorified you.

d Or *lapis lazuli*

⁶ Seek the LORD while he may
be found,
call upon him while he is
near;
⁷ let the wicked forsake their way,
and the unrighteous their
thoughts;
let them return to the LORD, that he
may have mercy on them,
and to our God, for he will
abundantly pardon.

⁸ For my thoughts are not your
thoughts,
nor are your ways my ways, says
the LORD.
⁹ For as the heavens are higher than
the earth,
so are my ways higher than
your ways
and my thoughts than your
thoughts.

¹⁰ For as the rain and the snow come
down from heaven,
and do not return there until they
have watered the earth,

making it bring forth and sprout,
giving seed to the sower and
bread to the eater,
¹¹ so shall my word be that goes out
from my mouth;
it shall not return to me empty,
but it shall accomplish that which I
purpose,
and succeed in the thing for
which I sent it.

¹² For you shall go out in joy,
and be led back in peace;
the mountains and the hills
before you
shall burst into song,
and all the trees of the field shall
clap their hands.
¹³ Instead of the thorn shall come up
the cypress;
instead of the brier shall come up
the myrtle;
and it shall be to the LORD for a
memorial,
for an everlasting sign that shall
not be cut off.

*L*iving Water

Oh, how many times do I recall the living water that the Lord told the Samaritan woman about! And so I am very fond of that gospel passage. Thus it is, indeed, that from the time I was a little child, without understanding this good as I do now, I often begged the Lord to give me the water. I always carried with me a painting of this episode of the Lord at the well, with the words, inscribed: *Domine, da mihi aquam.* "Lord, give me water."

O compassionate and loving Lord of my soul! You likewise say: Come to me all who thirst, for I will give you drink.

O Life, who gives life to all! Do not deny me this sweetest water that you promise to those who want it. I want it, Lord, and I beg for it, and I come to you. Don't hide yourself, Lord, from me, since you know my need and that this water is the true medicine for a soul wounded with love of you. O living founts from the wounds of my God, how you have flowed with great abundance for our sustenance, and how surely he who strives to sustain himself with this divine liqueur will advance in the midst of the dangers of this life.

—*SAINT TERESA OF AVILA*

Scripture Reading
for Today:
Isaiah 55.1–7

Verse for Today:
Isaiah 55.1

Go to page 998 for your next devotional reading.

The Covenant Extended to All Who Obey

56 Thus says the LORD:
Maintain justice, and do what
is right,
for soon my salvation will come,
and my deliverance be revealed.

2 Happy is the mortal who does this,
the one who holds it fast,
who keeps the sabbath, not
profaning it,
and refrains from doing any evil.

3 Do not let the foreigner joined to
the LORD say,
"The LORD will surely separate me
from his people";
and do not let the eunuch say,
"I am just a dry tree."
4 For thus says the LORD:
To the eunuchs who keep my
sabbaths,
who choose the things that
please me
and hold fast my covenant,
5 I will give, in my house and within
my walls,
a monument and a name
better than sons and daughters;
I will give them an everlasting name
that shall not be cut off.

6 And the foreigners who join
themselves to the LORD,
to minister to him, to love the
name of the LORD,
and to be his servants,
all who keep the sabbath, and do
not profane it,
and hold fast my covenant—
7 these I will bring to my holy
mountain,
and make them joyful in my
house of prayer;
their burnt offerings and their
sacrifices
will be accepted on my altar;
for my house shall be called a house
of prayer
for all peoples.
8 Thus says the Lord GOD,
who gathers the outcasts of Israel,
I will gather others to them
besides those already gathered.e

The Corruption of Israel's Rulers

9 All you wild animals,

all you wild animals in the forest,
come to devour!
10 Israel'sf sentinels are blind,
they are all without knowledge;
they are all silent dogs
that cannot bark;
dreaming, lying down,
loving to slumber.
11 The dogs have a mighty appetite;
they never have enough.
The shepherds also have no
understanding;
they have all turned to their
own way,
to their own gain, one and all.
12 "Come," they say, "let usg get wine;
let us fill ourselves with
strong drink.
And tomorrow will be like today,
great beyond measure."

Israel's Futile Idolatry

57 The righteous perish,
and no one takes it to heart;
the devout are taken away,
while no one understands.
For the righteous are taken away
from calamity,
2 and they enter into peace;
those who walk uprightly
will rest on their couches.
3 But as for you, come here,
you children of a sorceress,
you offspring of an adulterer and
a whore.h
4 Whom are you mocking?
Against whom do you open your
mouth wide
and stick out your tongue?
Are you not children of
transgression,
the offspring of deceit—
5 you that burn with lust among
the oaks,
under every green tree;
you that slaughter your children in
the valleys,
under the clefts of the rocks?
6 Among the smooth stones of the
valley is your portion;
they, they, are your lot;
to them you have poured out a
drink offering,
you have brought a grain offering.

---

e Heb *besides his gathered ones*   f Heb *His*
g Q Ms Syr Vg Tg: MT *me*   h Heb *an adulterer
and she plays the whore*

Shall I be appeased for these
    things?

7 Upon a high and lofty mountain
    you have set your bed,
    and there you went up to offer
        sacrifice.

8 Behind the door and the doorpost
    you have set up your symbol;
for, in deserting me,[i] you have
    uncovered your bed,
    you have gone up to it,
    you have made it wide;
and you have made a bargain for
    yourself with them,
    you have loved their bed,
    you have gazed on their
        nakedness.[j]

9 You journeyed to Molech[k] with oil,
    and multiplied your perfumes;
you sent your envoys far away,
    and sent down even to Sheol.

10 You grew weary from your many
        wanderings,
    but you did not say, "It is useless."
You found your desire rekindled,
    and so you did not weaken.

11 Whom did you dread and fear
    so that you lied,
and did not remember me
    or give me a thought?
Have I not kept silent and closed my
    eyes,[l]
    and so you do not fear me?

12 I will concede your righteousness
        and your works,
    but they will not help you.

13 When you cry out, let your
        collection of idols deliver
        you!
The wind will carry them off,
    a breath will take them away.
But whoever takes refuge in me shall
        possess the land
    and inherit my holy mountain.

A Promise of Help and Healing

14 It shall be said,
    "Build up, build up, prepare
        the way,
    remove every obstruction from my
        people's way."

15 For thus says the high and lofty one
    who inhabits eternity, whose
        name is Holy:
I dwell in the high and holy place,
    and also with those who are
        contrite and humble in spirit,
to revive the spirit of the humble,
    and to revive the heart of the
        contrite.

16 For I will not continually accuse,
    nor will I always be angry;
for then the spirits would grow faint
        before me,
    even the souls that I have made.

17 Because of their wicked covetousness
        I was angry;
    I struck them, I hid and was
        angry;
    but they kept turning back to their
        own ways.

18 I have seen their ways, but I will
        heal them;
    I will lead them and repay them
        with comfort,
    creating for their mourners the
        fruit of the lips.[l]

19 Peace, peace, to the far and the near,
        says the LORD;
    and I will heal them.

20 But the wicked are like the
        tossing sea
    that cannot keep still;
    its waters toss up mire and mud.

21 There is no peace, says my God, for
        the wicked.

False and True Worship

58 Shout out, do not hold back!
    Lift up your voice like a
        trumpet!
Announce to my people their
        rebellion,
    to the house of Jacob their sins.

2 Yet day after day they seek me
    and delight to know my ways,
as if they were a nation that
        practiced righteousness
    and did not forsake the ordinance
        of their God;
they ask of me righteous judgments,
    they delight to draw near to God.

3 "Why do we fast, but you do
        not see?
    Why humble ourselves, but you
        do not notice?"
Look, you serve your own interest
        on your fast day,
    and oppress all your workers.

---

i Meaning of Heb uncertain   *j* Or *their phallus;*
Heb *the hand*   *k* Or *the king*   *l* Gk Vg: Heb
silent even for a long time

⁴ Look, you fast only to quarrel and
        to fight
    and to strike with a wicked fist.
Such fasting as you do today
    will not make your voice heard on
        high.
⁵ Is such the fast that I choose,
    a day to humble oneself?
Is it to bow down the head like a
        bulrush,
    and to lie in sackcloth and ashes?
Will you call this a fast,
    a day acceptable to the LORD?

⁶ Is not this the fast that I choose:

to loose the bonds of injustice,
    to undo the thongs of the
        yoke,
to let the oppressed go free,
    and to break every yoke?
⁷ Is it not to share your bread with
        the hungry,
    and bring the homeless poor into
        your house;
when you see the naked, to
        cover them,
    and not to hide yourself from
        your own kin?
⁸ Then your light shall break forth like
        the dawn,

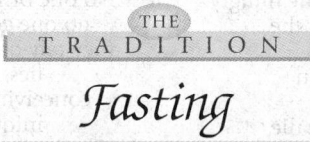

THE TRADITION

Fasting

Is not this the fast that I choose?
ISAIAH 58.6

*I*n our weight-obsessed culture, "Why am I doing this?" is always a good question to ask before fasting. If you take time to reflect and answer it honestly, you might be surprised.

"Because I'm too fat" is the most obvious sign of the "fasting for self-improvement" error.

"Because I've lost control, and I need to discipline myself" might represent a healthy desire to curb bodily appetites. Then again, if it expresses a view of the body as wayward and evil, it is the stuff of which eating disorders are made.

"Because I'm supposed to" suggests an overly routine, even mechanical approach.

A better answer focuses on fasting as self-emptying—detaching ourselves from some good things in order to focus on higher ones. Fasting helps open us to a deeper relationship with God and links us with the concerns of others.

Concern for others is certainly what Isaiah had in mind in his great prophecy on fasting that we hear at Mass on the Friday after Ash Wednesday (Isaiah 58.1–9). In it God reproaches his people for going through the

motions of repentance without giving up their self-centeredness and oppression of the helpless. Where is their love for him? Where is their love for their neighbors?

Why don't you notice how we're putting ourselves out? the Israelites demand (verse 3). God retorts, *Why don't you translate your pious-looking practices into deeds of justice and mercy?* And he proceeds to describe acceptable fasting in terms of works of mercy (verses 5–7).

This "social justice" approach situates fasting in a broader context than we may be used to. Elsewhere too, though, Scripture presents fasting as part of a holy trio of penitential practices, along with prayer and almsgiving (see Tobit 12.8; Matthew 6.1–18). Church writers from the beginning have done the same.

One of them, the fifth-century Doctor of the Church, Peter Chrysologus, said: "Fasting is the soul of prayer, mercy [almsgiving] is the lifeblood of fasting. Let no one try to separate them . . . So if you pray, fast; if you fast, show mercy."

Food for thought as you ask yourself, "Why fast?"

and your healing shall spring
up quickly;
your vindicator[m] shall go
before you,
the glory of the LORD shall be your
rear guard.
9 Then you shall call, and the LORD
will answer;
you shall cry for help, and he will
say, Here I am.

If you remove the yoke from
among you,
the pointing of the finger, the
speaking of evil,
10 if you offer your food to the hungry
and satisfy the needs of the
afflicted,
then your light shall rise in
the darkness
and your gloom be like the
noonday.
11 The LORD will guide you continually,
and satisfy your needs in parched
places,
and make your bones strong;
and you shall be like a watered
garden,
like a spring of water,
whose waters never fail.
12 Your ancient ruins shall be rebuilt;
you shall raise up the foundations
of many generations;
you shall be called the repairer of
the breach,
the restorer of streets to live in.

13 If you refrain from trampling the
sabbath,
from pursuing your own interests
on my holy day;
if you call the sabbath a delight
and the holy day of the LORD
honorable;
if you honor it, not going your
own ways,
serving your own interests, or
pursuing your own affairs;[n]
14 then you shall take delight in
the LORD,
and I will make you ride upon the
heights of the earth;
I will feed you with the heritage of
your ancestor Jacob,
for the mouth of the LORD has
spoken.

Injustice and Oppression to Be Punished

59 See, the LORD's hand is not too
short to save,
nor his ear too dull to hear.
2 Rather, your iniquities have been
barriers
between you and your God,
and your sins have hidden his face
from you
so that he does not hear.
3 For your hands are defiled
with blood,
and your fingers with iniquity;
your lips have spoken lies,
your tongue mutters wickedness.
4 No one brings suit justly,
no one goes to law honestly;
they rely on empty pleas, they speak
lies,
conceiving mischief and begetting
iniquity.
5 They hatch adders' eggs,
and weave the spider's web;
whoever eats their eggs dies,
and the crushed egg hatches out a
viper.
6 Their webs cannot serve as clothing;
they cannot cover themselves with
what they make.
Their works are works of iniquity,
and deeds of violence are in their
hands.
7 Their feet run to evil,
and they rush to shed innocent
blood;
their thoughts are thoughts
of iniquity,
desolation and destruction are in
their highways.
8 The way of peace they do not know,
and there is no justice in
their paths.
Their roads they have made crooked;
no one who walks in them knows
peace.

9 Therefore justice is far from us,
and righteousness does not
reach us;
we wait for light, and lo! there is
darkness;
and for brightness, but we walk in
gloom.
10 We grope like the blind along
a wall,

m Or vindication   n Heb or speaking words

groping like those who have
no eyes;
we stumble at noon as in the
twilight,
among the vigorous[o] as though
we were dead.
11 We all growl like bears;
like doves we moan mournfully.
We wait for justice, but there is
none;
for salvation, but it is far from us.
12 For our transgressions before you are
many,
and our sins testify against us.
Our transgressions indeed are
with us,
and we know our iniquities:
13 transgressing, and denying the LORD,
and turning away from following
our God,
talking oppression and revolt,
conceiving lying words and
uttering them from the heart.
14 Justice is turned back,
and righteousness stands at a
distance;
for truth stumbles in the public
square,
and uprightness cannot enter.
15 Truth is lacking,
and whoever turns from evil is
despoiled.

The LORD saw it, and it displeased
him
that there was no justice.
16 He saw that there was no one,
and was appalled that there was
no one to intervene;
so his own arm brought him victory,
and his righteousness upheld him.
17 He put on righteousness like a
breastplate,
and a helmet of salvation on
his head;
he put on garments of vengeance for
clothing,
and wrapped himself in fury as in
a mantle.
18 According to their deeds, so will
he repay;
wrath to his adversaries, requital
to his enemies;
to the coastlands he will render
requital.
19 So those in the west shall fear the
name of the LORD,
and those in the east, his glory;

for he will come like a pent-up
stream
that the wind of the LORD
drives on.
20 And he will come to Zion as
Redeemer,
to those in Jacob who turn from
transgression, says the LORD.
21 And as for me, this is my covenant with
them, says the LORD: my spirit that is upon
you, and my words that I have put in
your mouth, shall not depart out of your
mouth, or out of the mouths of your children, or out of the mouths of your children's children, says the LORD, from now
on and forever.

The Ingathering of the Dispersed

60 Arise, shine; for your light
has come,
and the glory of the LORD has
risen upon you.
2 For darkness shall cover the earth,
and thick darkness the peoples;
but the LORD will arise upon you,
and his glory will appear
over you.
3 Nations shall come to your light,
and kings to the brightness of
your dawn.

4 Lift up your eyes and look around;
they all gather together, they come
to you;
your sons shall come from far away,
and your daughters shall be
carried on their nurses' arms.
5 Then you shall see and be radiant;
your heart shall thrill and
rejoice,[p]
because the abundance of the sea
shall be brought to you,
the wealth of the nations shall
come to you.
6 A multitude of camels shall
cover you,
the young camels of Midian and
Ephah;
all those from Sheba shall come.
They shall bring gold and
frankincense,
and shall proclaim the praise of
the LORD.
7 All the flocks of Kedar shall be
gathered to you,

o Meaning of Heb uncertain   p Heb *be enlarged*

the rams of Nebaioth shall
  minister to you;
they shall be acceptable on my altar,
  and I will glorify my glorious
    house.

8 Who are these that fly like a cloud,
  and like doves to their windows?
9 For the coastlands shall wait for me,
  the ships of Tarshish first,
to bring your children from far
    away,
  their silver and gold with them,
for the name of the LORD your God,
  and for the Holy One of Israel,

because he has glorified you.
10 Foreigners shall build up your
    walls,
  and their kings shall minister
    to you;
for in my wrath I struck you down,
  but in my favor I have had mercy
    on you.
11 Your gates shall always be open;
  day and night they shall not
    be shut,
so that nations shall bring you their
    wealth,
  with their kings led in procession.
12 For the nation and kingdom

THURSDAY

Scripture Reading
for Today:
Isaiah 60.1–7

Verse for Today:
Isaiah 60.1

Called to Be Light

When I was little, I was afraid of the dark. But what especially struck terror in my heart every night were the car lights that appeared on my bedroom wall. Since our house sat at the bottom of a hill on a curve, headlights zoomed across my bedroom wall as each car went by. Lying in the dark and seeing these lights flashing by on the wall convinced me that aliens had landed and invasion was imminent.

We laugh at childish fears of the dark and flashing lights. But deep down, I bet we'd all rather go down into the basement or up to the attic with the lights on. Perhaps we don't see aliens in every dark room. But we are the people who dwell in darkness and who make fear our home.

But Light is given to us. Fear no longer need be our home. In the first reading for the feast of the Epiphany, the revelation of our God, we hear, "Arise, shine; for your light has come, and the glory of the LORD has risen upon you." He who was born before the Daystar is born of our flesh, the Light of the World! This is the mystery we celebrate ... Epiphany, when God reveals to all nations the depths of his love poured out in his Son, Christ Jesus.

Epiphany is nothing less than the call to be Light, to reveal to one another the face of Christ Jesus in our day-to-day dealings and by the words with which we weave our lives.

The Light now dwells within us. We no longer are the people who dwell in darkness. We have received the Light so that we might become Light. Though we journey in darkness, we keep our eyes on the Light who leads us: Christ Jesus, the splendor of the Eternal Father.

—CORA LOMBARDO, A.S.C.J.

Go to page 1005 for your next devotional reading.

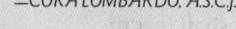

that will not serve you shall
    perish;
those nations shall be utterly
    laid waste.
13 The glory of Lebanon shall come
    to you,
the cypress, the plane, and
    the pine,
to beautify the place of my
    sanctuary;
and I will glorify where my
    feet rest.
14 The descendants of those who
    oppressed you
shall come bending low to you,
and all who despised you
    shall bow down at your feet;
they shall call you the City of
    the LORD,
    the Zion of the Holy One of
    Israel.
15 Whereas you have been forsaken
    and hated,
    with no one passing through,
I will make you majestic forever,
    a joy from age to age.
16 You shall suck the milk of nations,
    you shall suck the breasts
    of kings;
and you shall know that I, the LORD,
    am your Savior
    and your Redeemer, the Mighty
    One of Jacob.

17 Instead of bronze I will bring gold,
    instead of iron I will bring silver;
instead of wood, bronze,
    instead of stones, iron.
I will appoint Peace as your overseer
    and Righteousness as your
    taskmaster.
18 Violence shall no more be heard in
    your land,
    devastation or destruction within
    your borders;
you shall call your walls Salvation,
    and your gates Praise.

God the Glory of Zion

19 The sun shall no longer be
    your light by day,
nor for brightness shall the moon
    give light to you by night;*q*
but the LORD will be your everlasting
    light,
    and your God will be your glory.
20 Your sun shall no more go down,
    or your moon withdraw itself;

for the LORD will be your everlasting
    light,
    and your days of mourning shall
    be ended.
21 Your people shall all be righteous;
    they shall possess the land forever.
They are the shoot that I planted,
    the work of my hands,
    so that I might be glorified.
22 The least of them shall become
    a clan,
    and the smallest one a mighty
    nation;
I am the LORD;
    in its time I will accomplish
    it quickly.

The Good News of Deliverance

61 The spirit of the Lord GOD is
    upon me,
because the LORD has anointed me;
he has sent me to bring good news
    to the oppressed,
    to bind up the brokenhearted,
to proclaim liberty to the captives,
    and release to the prisoners;
2 to proclaim the year of the
    LORD's favor,
    and the day of vengeance of
    our God;
    to comfort all who mourn;
3 to provide for those who mourn in
    Zion—
    to give them a garland instead
    of ashes,
the oil of gladness instead of
    mourning,
    the mantle of praise instead of a
    faint spirit.
They will be called oaks of
    righteousness,
    the planting of the LORD, to
    display his glory.
4 They shall build up the ancient
    ruins,
    they shall raise up the former
    devastations;
they shall repair the ruined cities,
    the devastations of many
    generations.

5 Strangers shall stand and feed
    your flocks,
    foreigners shall till your land and
    dress your vines;

q Q Ms Gk Old Latin Tg: MT lacks *by night*

6 but you shall be called priests of the
 LORD,
  you shall be named ministers of
   our God;
  you shall enjoy the wealth of
   the nations,
  and in their riches you shall glory.
7 Because their[r] shame was double,
  and dishonor was proclaimed as
   their lot,
  therefore they shall possess a double
   portion;
  everlasting joy shall be theirs.

8 For I the LORD love justice,
  I hate robbery and wrongdoing;[s]
  I will faithfully give them their
   recompense,
  and I will make an everlasting
   covenant with them.
9 Their descendants shall be known
   among the nations,
  and their offspring among the
   peoples;
  all who see them shall acknowledge
  that they are a people whom the
   LORD has blessed.
10 I will greatly rejoice in the LORD,
  my whole being shall exult in
   my God;
  for he has clothed me with the
   garments of salvation,
  he has covered me with the robe
   of righteousness,
  as a bridegroom decks himself with
   a garland,
  and as a bride adorns herself with
   her jewels.
11 For as the earth brings forth its
   shoots,
  and as a garden causes what is
   sown in it to spring up,
  so the Lord GOD will cause
   righteousness and praise
  to spring up before all the
   nations.

The Vindication and Salvation of Zion

62 For Zion's sake I will not keep
   silent,
  and for Jerusalem's sake I will not
   rest,
  until her vindication shines out like
   the dawn,
  and her salvation like a burning
   torch.
2 The nations shall see your
   vindication,
  and all the kings your glory;
  and you shall be called by a
   new name
  that the mouth of the LORD
   will give.
3 You shall be a crown of beauty in
   the hand of the LORD,
  and a royal diadem in the hand of
   your God.
4 You shall no more be termed
   Forsaken,[t]
  and your land shall no more be
   termed Desolate;[u]
  but you shall be called My Delight
   Is in Her,[v]
  and your land Married;[w]
  for the LORD delights in you,
  and your land shall be married.
5 For as a young man marries a young
   woman,
  so shall your builder[x] marry you,
  and as the bridegroom rejoices over
   the bride,
  so shall your God rejoice
   over you.
6 Upon your walls, O Jerusalem,
  I have posted sentinels;
  all day and all night
   they shall never be silent.
  You who remind the LORD,
   take no rest,
7 and give him no rest
  until he establishes Jerusalem
  and makes it renowned
   throughout the earth.
8 The LORD has sworn by his
   right hand
  and by his mighty arm:
  I will not again give your grain
   to be food for your enemies,
  and foreigners shall not drink
   the wine
  for which you have labored;
9 but those who garner it shall eat it
   and praise the LORD,
  and those who gather it shall
   drink it
  in my holy courts.

10 Go through, go through the gates,
   prepare the way for the people;
  build up, build up the highway,
   clear it of stones,
  lift up an ensign over the peoples.

---

r Heb *your*   s Or *robbery with a burnt offering*
t Heb *Azubah*   u Heb *Shemamah*   v Heb
Hephzibah   w Heb *Beulah*   x Cn: Heb *your sons*

11 The LORD has proclaimed
    to the end of the earth:
Say to daughter Zion,
    "See, your salvation comes;
his reward is with him,
    and his recompense before him."
12 They shall be called, "The
        Holy People,
    The Redeemed of the LORD";
and you shall be called,
        "Sought Out,
    A City Not Forsaken."

Vengeance on Edom

63 "Who is this that comes from
        Edom,
    from Bozrah in garments stained
        crimson?
Who is this so splendidly robed,
    marching in his great might?"

"It is I, announcing vindication,
    mighty to save."

2 "Why are your robes red,
    and your garments like theirs who
        tread the wine press?"

3 "I have trodden the wine press
        alone,
    and from the peoples no one was
        with me;
I trod them in my anger
    and trampled them in my wrath;
their juice spattered on my
        garments,
    and stained all my robes.
4 For the day of vengeance was in my
        heart,
    and the year for my redeeming
        work had come.
5 I looked, but there was no helper;
    I stared, but there was no one to
        sustain me;
so my own arm brought me victory,
    and my wrath sustained me.
6 I trampled down peoples in my
        anger,
    I crushed them in my wrath,
and I poured out their lifeblood
    on the earth."

God's Mercy Remembered

7 I will recount the gracious deeds of
        the LORD,
    the praiseworthy acts of the LORD,
because of all that the LORD has
        done for us,

and the great favor to the house
        of Israel
that he has shown them according
        to his mercy,
    according to the abundance of his
        steadfast love.
8 For he said, "Surely they are
        my people,
    children who will not deal falsely";
and he became their savior
9   in all their distress.
It was no messenger*y* or angel
    but his presence that saved
        them;*z*
in his love and in his pity he
        redeemed them;
    he lifted them up and carried
        them all the days of old.

10 But they rebelled
    and grieved his holy spirit;
therefore he became their enemy;
    he himself fought against them.
11 Then they*a* remembered the days of
        old,
    of Moses his servant.*b*
Where is the one who brought them
        up out of the sea
    with the shepherds of his flock?
Where is the one who put
        within them
    his holy spirit,
12 who caused his glorious arm
    to march at the right hand
        of Moses,
who divided the waters before them
    to make for himself an everlasting
        name,
13   who led them through the depths?
Like a horse in the desert,
    they did not stumble.
14 Like cattle that go down into
        the valley,
    the spirit of the LORD gave
        them rest.
Thus you led your people,
    to make for yourself a glorious
        name.

A Prayer of Penitence

15 Look down from heaven and see,
    from your holy and glorious
        habitation.

---

y Gk: Heb *anguish*   *z* Or *savior.* *9In all their
distress he was distressed; the angel of his presence
saved them;*   *a* Heb *he*   *b* Cn: Heb *his people*

Where are your zeal and your
　　might?
　　The yearning of your heart and
　　　your compassion?
　　They are withheld from me.
16 For you are our father,
　　though Abraham does not
　　　know us
　　and Israel does not acknowledge
　　　us;
　　you, O Lord, are our father;
　　our Redeemer from of old is
　　　your name.
17 Why, O Lord, do you make us stray
　　from your ways
　　and harden our heart, so that we
　　　do not fear you?
　　Turn back for the sake of your
　　　servants,
　　for the sake of the tribes that are
　　　your heritage.
18 Your holy people took possession
　　for a little while;
　　but now our adversaries have
　　　trampled down your
　　　sanctuary.
19 We have long been like those whom
　　you do not rule,
　　like those not called by your
　　　name.

64 O that you would tear open the
　　heavens and come down,
　　so that the mountains would
　　　quake at your presence—
2 c as when fire kindles brushwood
　　and the fire causes water to boil—
　　to make your name known to your
　　　adversaries,
　　so that the nations might tremble
　　　at your presence!
3 When you did awesome deeds that
　　we did not expect,
　　you came down, the mountains
　　　quaked at your presence.
4 From ages past no one has heard,
　　no ear has perceived,
　　no eye has seen any God besides
　　　you,
　　who works for those who wait
　　　for him.
5 You meet those who gladly do right,
　　those who remember you in
　　　your ways.
　　But you were angry, and we sinned;
　　because you hid yourself we
　　　transgressed. d

6 We have all become like one who is
　　unclean,
　　and all our righteous deeds are
　　　like a filthy cloth.
　　We all fade like a leaf,
　　and our iniquities, like the wind,
　　　take us away.
7 There is no one who calls on
　　your name,
　　or attempts to take hold of you;
　　for you have hidden your face
　　　from us,
　　and have delivered e us into the
　　　hand of our iniquity.
8 Yet, O Lord, you are our Father;
　　we are the clay, and you are
　　　our potter;
　　we are all the work of your hand.
9 Do not be exceedingly angry,
　　　O Lord,
　　and do not remember iniquity
　　　forever.
　　Now consider, we are all your
　　　people.
10 Your holy cities have become a
　　wilderness,
　　Zion has become a wilderness,
　　Jerusalem a desolation.
11 Our holy and beautiful house,
　　where our ancestors praised you,
　　has been burned by fire,
　　and all our pleasant places have
　　　become ruins.
12 After all this, will you restrain
　　　yourself, O Lord?
　　Will you keep silent, and punish
　　　us so severely?

The Righteousness of God's Judgment

65 I was ready to be sought out by
　　those who did not ask,
　　to be found by those who did not
　　　seek me.
　　I said, "Here I am, here I am,"
　　to a nation that did not call on
　　　my name.
2 I held out my hands all day long
　　to a rebellious people,
　　who walk in a way that is not good,
　　　following their own devices;
3 a people who provoke me
　　to my face continually,
　　sacrificing in gardens
　　and offering incense on bricks;
4 who sit inside tombs,

c Ch 64.1 in Heb　　d Meaning of Heb uncertain
e Gk Syr Old Latin Tg: Heb *melted*

and spend the night in secret
    places;
who eat swine's flesh,
    with broth of abominable things
    in their vessels;
5 who say, "Keep to yourself,
    do not come near me, for I am
    too holy for you."
These are a smoke in my nostrils,
    a fire that burns all day long.
6 See, it is written before me:
    I will not keep silent, but I will
    repay;
I will indeed repay into their laps
7   their f iniquities and their f
    ancestors' iniquities together,
                says the LORD;
because they offered incense on the
    mountains
    and reviled me on the hills,
I will measure into their laps
    full payment for their actions.
8 Thus says the LORD:
As the wine is found in the cluster,
    and they say, "Do not destroy it,
    for there is a blessing in it,"
so I will do for my servants' sake,
    and not destroy them all.
9 I will bring forth descendants g from
    Jacob,
    and from Judah inheritors h of my
    mountains;
my chosen shall inherit it,
    and my servants shall settle there.
10 Sharon shall become a pasture
    for flocks,
    and the Valley of Achor a place
    for herds to lie down,
    for my people who have
    sought me.
11 But you who forsake the LORD,
    who forget my holy mountain,
who set a table for Fortune
    and fill cups of mixed wine for
    Destiny;
12 I will destine you to the sword,
    and all of you shall bow down to
    the slaughter;
because, when I called, you did
    not answer,
    when I spoke, you did not listen,
but you did what was evil in
    my sight,
    and chose what I did not
    delight in.
13 Therefore thus says the Lord GOD:
My servants shall eat,
    but you shall be hungry;

my servants shall drink,
    but you shall be thirsty;
my servants shall rejoice,
    but you shall be put to shame;
14 my servants shall sing for gladness
    of heart,
    but you shall cry out for pain
    of heart,
    and shall wail for anguish
    of spirit.
15 You shall leave your name to my
    chosen to use as a curse,
    and the Lord GOD will put you
    to death;
but to his servants he will give a
    different name.
16 Then whoever invokes a blessing in
    the land
    shall bless by the God of
    faithfulness,
and whoever takes an oath in
    the land
    shall swear by the God of
    faithfulness;
because the former troubles are
    forgotten
    and are hidden from my sight.

The Glorious New Creation

17 For I am about to create new
    heavens
    and a new earth;
the former things shall not be
    remembered
    or come to mind.
18 But be glad and rejoice forever
    in what I am creating;
for I am about to create Jerusalem as
    a joy,
    and its people as a delight.
19 I will rejoice in Jerusalem,
    and delight in my people;
no more shall the sound of weeping
    be heard in it,
    or the cry of distress.
20 No more shall there be in it
    an infant that lives but a few days,
    or an old person who does not
    live out a lifetime;
for one who dies at a hundred years
    will be considered a youth,
    and one who falls short of a
    hundred will be considered
    accursed.

f Gk Syr: Heb *your*   g Or *a descendant*   h Or *an
inheritor*

21 They shall build houses and inhabit
        them;
    they shall plant vineyards and eat
        their fruit.
22 They shall not build and another
        inhabit;
    they shall not plant and
        another eat;
    for like the days of a tree shall the
        days of my people be,
    and my chosen shall long enjoy
        the work of their hands.
23 They shall not labor in vain,
    or bear children for calamity;[i]
    for they shall be offspring blessed by
        the LORD—
    and their descendants as well.
24 Before they call I will answer,
    while they are yet speaking I
        will hear.
25 The wolf and the lamb shall feed
        together,
    the lion shall eat straw like the ox;
    but the serpent—its food shall
        be dust!
    They shall not hurt or destroy
    on all my holy mountain,
                        says the LORD.

The Worship God Demands

66 Thus says the LORD:
    Heaven is my throne
    and the earth is my footstool;
    what is the house that you would
        build for me,
    and what is my resting place?
2 All these things my hand has made,
    and so all these things
        are mine, [j]
                        says the LORD.
    But this is the one to whom I will
        look,
    to the humble and contrite
        in spirit,
    who trembles at my word.

3 Whoever slaughters an ox is like one
        who kills a human being;
    whoever sacrifices a lamb, like one
        who breaks a dog's neck;
    whoever presents a grain offering,
        like one who offers swine's
        blood;[k]
    whoever makes a memorial
        offering of frankincense, like
        one who blesses an idol.

These have chosen their own ways,
    and in their abominations they
        take delight;
4 I also will choose to mock[l] them,
    and bring upon them what
        they fear;
    because, when I called, no one
        answered,
    when I spoke, they did not listen;
    but they did what was evil in
        my sight,
    and chose what did not
        please me.

The LORD Vindicates Zion

5 Hear the word of the LORD,
    you who tremble at his word:
    Your own people who hate you
    and reject you for my name's sake
    have said, "Let the LORD be glorified,
        so that we may see your joy";
    but it is they who shall be put
        to shame.

6 Listen, an uproar from the city!
    A voice from the temple!
    The voice of the LORD,
        dealing retribution to his enemies!

7 Before she was in labor
        she gave birth;
    before her pain came upon her
        she delivered a son.
8 Who has heard of such a thing?
    Who has seen such things?
    Shall a land be born in one day?
        Shall a nation be delivered in one
        moment?
    Yet as soon as Zion was in labor
        she delivered her children.
9 Shall I open the womb and not
        deliver?
        says the LORD;
    shall I, the one who delivers, shut
        the womb?
        says your God.

10 Rejoice with Jerusalem, and be glad
        for her,
    all you who love her;
    rejoice with her in joy,
    all you who mourn over her—

i Or sudden terror   j Gk Syr: Heb these things
came to be   k Meaning of Heb uncertain   l Or
to punish

11 that you may nurse and be satisfied
    from her consoling breast;
  that you may drink deeply with
    delight
    from her glorious bosom.

12 For thus says the LORD:
  I will extend prosperity to her like a
    river,
    and the wealth of the nations like
      an overflowing stream;
  and you shall nurse and be carried
    on her arm,

and dandled on her knees.
13 As a mother comforts her child,
    so I will comfort you;
  you shall be comforted in
    Jerusalem.

The Reign and Indignation of God

14 You shall see, and your heart shall
    rejoice;
  your bodies[m] shall flourish like
    the grass;

[m] Heb *bones*

FRIDAY

Scripture Reading
for Today:
Isaiah 66.10–13

Verse for Today:
Isaiah 66.13

Like a Loving Mother

A number of years ago, a mission organization in Africa printed a calendar as a fundraising effort. It contained photos depicting everyday life in the mission community. One photo showed a woman working hard at basketmaking, but a Westerner's eye was drawn, not to that work, but to her toddler son standing next to her as she sat on the ground. He was standing there, nursing at her exposed breast the way toddlers in our part of the world often walk around with a bottle. Even though they don't really need the milk, both the African child and the Western toddler are seeking the comfort of a moment with a familiar method of nurturing.

This kind of mothering was the norm in the West until this century, and it still is in much of the Third World. It would have been the familiar context for this reading from Isaiah.

The message of comfort conveyed by this image would have been easily understood and welcomed as a metaphor for God's nurturing and restorative love. The reign of God is presented here in the image of the nursing mother. God as a nursing mother: "You shall nurse and be carried on her arm, and dandled on her knees. As a mother comforts her child, so I will comfort you" (66.12–13).

When our zeal for the task outstrips our abilities and we collapse, like a toddler, in a tantrum of frustration, our God, like a loving Mother, scoops us up, hugs and cuddles us, and gives us the nurturing we need to be refreshed and joyful. It is in this loving relationship that the reign of God becomes fully realized. This is the fulfillment of the reign of God at last: When our words fail, when our best laid plans collapse, when the fulfillment of the dream seems completely lost—God loves us, nurtures us, restores us. The reign of God becomes reality in the union of God and humanity in loving embrace.

—KATHLEEN SPEARS HOPKINS

Go to page 1010 for your next devotional reading.

and it shall be known that the hand
of the LORD is with his
servants,
and his indignation is against
his enemies.
15 For the LORD will come in fire,
and his chariots like the
whirlwind,
to pay back his anger in fury,
and his rebuke in flames of fire.
16 For by fire will the LORD execute
judgment,
and by his sword, on all flesh;
and those slain by the LORD shall
be many.

17 Those who sanctify and purify themselves to go into the gardens, following the one in the center, eating the flesh of pigs, vermin, and rodents, shall come to an end together, says the LORD.

18 For I know*n* their works and their thoughts, and I am*o* coming to gather all nations and tongues; and they shall come and shall see my glory, 19and I will set a sign among them. From them I will send survivors to the nations, to Tarshish, Put,*p* and Lud—which draw the bow—to Tubal and Javan, to the coastlands far away that have not heard of my fame or seen my glory; and they shall declare my glory among the nations. 20They shall bring all your kindred from all the nations as an offering to the LORD, on horses, and in chariots, and in litters, and on mules, and on dromedaries, to my holy mountain Jerusalem, says the LORD, just as the Israelites bring a grain offering in a clean vessel to the house of the LORD. 21And I will also take some of them as priests and as Levites, says the LORD.

22 For as the new heavens and the new
earth,
which I will make,
shall remain before me, says
the LORD;
so shall your descendants and
your name remain.
23 From new moon to new moon,
and from sabbath to sabbath,
all flesh shall come to worship
before me,
says the LORD.

24 And they shall go out and look at the dead bodies of the people who have rebelled against me; for their worm shall not die, their fire shall not be quenched, and they shall be an abhorrence to all flesh.

n Gk Syr: Heb lacks *know*   *o* Gk Syr Vg Tg: Heb *it is*   *p* Gk: Heb *Pul*

Jeremiah

Perhaps Jesus was thinking of the prophet Jeremiah when he spoke scathingly to the Pharisees, likening them to their forebears who had murdered God's prophets. For tradition holds that Jeremiah was murdered by his own people after being forced into exile in Egypt.

Jeremiah was mocked, scourged, imprisoned, arrested as a traitor, and then thrown into a muddy cistern in Jerusalem and left to die before being rescued by an Ethiopian eunuch. Even his relatives plotted against him. The prophet became so despondent that he seemed at times to despair of life. Still, he could not stop speaking God's word: "If I say, 'I will not mention him, or speak any more in his name,' then within me there is something like a burning fire shut up in my bones" (20.9).

Jeremiah was born into a priestly family about 650 B.C., a few years after Isaiah's ministry had ended, in a town just north of Jerusalem. He received his prophetic calling when he was just a boy, and God told him to remain celibate because of the tragedy that would eventually overtake parents and their children. His message was primarily concerned with the fall of Judah and its eventual restoration. Known as the "weeping prophet," he warned of the calamity that would result from Judah's unfaithfulness. But his message was also one of great hope and comfort (31.3–4): "I have loved you with an everlasting love; therefore I have continued my faithfulness to you. Again I will build you, and you shall be built, O virgin Israel!"

1 The words of Jeremiah son of Hilkiah, of the priests who were in Anathoth in the land of Benjamin, ²to whom the word of the LORD came in the days of King Josiah son of Amon of Judah, in the thirteenth year of his reign. ³It came also in the days of King Jehoiakim son of Josiah of Judah, and until the end of the elev-

enth year of King Zedekiah son of Josiah of Judah, until the captivity of Jerusalem in the fifth month.

Jeremiah's Call and Commission

4 Now the word of the LORD came to me saying,

5 "Before I formed you in the womb I
knew you,
and before you were born I
consecrated you;
I appointed you a prophet to the
nations."
6Then I said, "Ah, Lord GOD! Truly I do
not know how to speak, for I am only a
boy." 7But the LORD said to me,
"Do not say, 'I am only a boy';
for you shall go to all to whom I
send you,
and you shall speak whatever I
command you.
8 Do not be afraid of them,
for I am with you to deliver you,
says the LORD."
9Then the LORD put out his hand and
touched my mouth; and the LORD said
to me,
"Now I have put my words in your
mouth.
10 See, today I appoint you over
nations and over kingdoms,
to pluck up and to pull down,
to destroy and to overthrow,
to build and to plant."

11 The word of the LORD came to me,
saying, "Jeremiah, what do you see?" And
I said, "I see a branch of an almond
tree."*a* 12Then the LORD said to me, "You
have seen well, for I am watching*b* over
my word to perform it." 13The word of the
LORD came to me a second time, saying,
"What do you see?" And I said, "I see a
boiling pot, tilted away from the north."

14 Then the LORD said to me: Out of
the north disaster shall break out on all
the inhabitants of the land. 15For now I
am calling all the tribes of the kingdoms
of the north, says the LORD; and they shall
come and all of them shall set their
thrones at the entrance of the gates of Jerusalem, against all its surrounding walls
and against all the cities of Judah. 16And I
will utter my judgments against them, for
all their wickedness in forsaking me; they
have made offerings to other gods, and
worshiped the works of their own hands.
17But you, gird up your loins; stand up
and tell them everything that I command
you. Do not break down before them, or
I will break you before them. 18And I for
my part have made you today a fortified
city, an iron pillar, and a bronze wall,
against the whole land—against the kings
of Judah, its princes, its priests, and the
people of the land. 19They will fight

against you; but they shall not prevail
against you, for I am with you, says the
LORD, to deliver you.

God Pleads with Israel to Repent

2 The word of the LORD came to me,
saying: 2Go and proclaim in the hearing of Jerusalem, Thus says the LORD:
I remember the devotion of your
youth,
your love as a bride,
how you followed me in the
wilderness,
in a land not sown.
3 Israel was holy to the LORD,
the first fruits of his harvest.
All who ate of it were held guilty;
disaster came upon them,
says the LORD.

4 Hear the word of the LORD, O house
of Jacob, and all the families of the house
of Israel. 5Thus says the LORD:
What wrong did your ancestors find
in me
that they went far from me,
and went after worthless things, and
became worthless themselves?
6 They did not say, "Where is
the LORD
who brought us up from the land
of Egypt,
who led us in the wilderness,
in a land of deserts and pits,
in a land of drought and deep
darkness,
in a land that no one passes
through,
where no one lives?"
7 I brought you into a plentiful land
to eat its fruits and its good
things.
But when you entered you defiled
my land,
and made my heritage an
abomination.
8 The priests did not say, "Where is
the LORD?"
Those who handle the law did not
know me;
the rulers*c* transgressed against me;
the prophets prophesied by Baal,
and went after things that do
not profit.

a Heb shaqed   *b* Heb shoqed   *c* Heb shepherds

⁹ Therefore once more I accuse you,
                        says the LORD,
    and I accuse your children's
        children.
¹⁰ Cross to the coasts of Cyprus
        and look,
    send to Kedar and examine with
        care;
    see if there has ever been such
        a thing.
¹¹ Has a nation changed its gods,
        even though they are no gods?
    But my people have changed
        their glory
    for something that does not
        profit.
¹² Be appalled, O heavens, at this,
    be shocked, be utterly desolate,
                        says the LORD,
¹³ for my people have committed
        two evils:
    they have forsaken me,
    the fountain of living water,
        and dug out cisterns for
            themselves,
    cracked cisterns
        that can hold no water.

¹⁴ Is Israel a slave? Is he a homeborn
        servant?
    Why then has he become
        plunder?
¹⁵ The lions have roared against him,
        they have roared loudly.
    They have made his land a waste;
        his cities are in ruins, without
            inhabitant.
¹⁶ Moreover, the people of Memphis
        and Tahpanhes
    have broken the crown of
        your head.
¹⁷ Have you not brought this upon
        yourself
    by forsaking the LORD your God,
        while he led you in the way?
¹⁸ What then do you gain by going
        to Egypt,
    to drink the waters of the Nile?
    Or what do you gain by going to
        Assyria,
    to drink the waters of the
        Euphrates?
¹⁹ Your wickedness will punish you,
        and your apostasies will
            convict you.
    Know and see that it is evil
        and bitter

for you to forsake the LORD
        your God;
    the fear of me is not in you,
        says the Lord GOD of hosts.

²⁰ For long ago you broke your yoke
        and burst your bonds,
    and you said, "I will not serve!"
    On every high hill
        and under every green tree
    you sprawled and played
        the whore.
²¹ Yet I planted you as a choice vine,
        from the purest stock.
    How then did you turn degenerate
        and become a wild vine?
²² Though you wash yourself with lye
        and use much soap,
    the stain of your guilt is still
        before me,
                        says the Lord GOD.
²³ How can you say, "I am not defiled,
        I have not gone after the Baals"?
    Look at your way in the valley;
        know what you have done—
    a restive young camel interlacing her
        tracks,
²⁴   a wild ass at home in the
            wilderness,
    in her heat sniffing the wind!
        Who can restrain her lust?
    None who seek her need weary
        themselves;
    in her month they will find her.
²⁵ Keep your feet from going unshod
        and your throat from thirst.
    But you said, "It is hopeless,
        for I have loved strangers,
        and after them I will go."

²⁶ As a thief is shamed when caught,
        so the house of Israel shall be
            shamed—
    they, their kings, their officials,
        their priests, and their prophets,
²⁷ who say to a tree, "You are
        my father,"
    and to a stone, "You gave
        me birth."
    For they have turned their backs
        to me,
        and not their faces.
    But in the time of their trouble they
        say,
    "Come and save us!"
²⁸ But where are your gods
        that you made for yourself?
    Let them come, if they can save you,

Rizpah

Her Name Means "A Hot Stone or Coal"

Read 2 Samuel 21.8–14

One day a rabbi stood on a hill overlooking a certain city. The rabbi watched in horror as a band of cossacks on horseback suddenly attacked the town, killing innocent men, women, and children. Some of the slaughtered were his own disciples. Looking up to heaven, the rabbi exclaimed, "Oh, if only I were God." An astonished student, standing nearby, asked, "But, Master, if you were God, what would you do differently?" The rabbi replied, "If I were God I would do nothing differently. If I were God, I would understand."

One day a woman stood on a hill in Israel and watched the execution of seven men. Her grief was sharp, for among the dead were her two sons. Executed for their father's crime, their bodies were left to rot on the hillside, despite a law requiring burial by sunset. Perhaps Rizpah, too, wished she were God. Maybe then she would understand the "why" of what she had just seen.

It is not hard to imagine her suffering. To watch as her body convulses in sorrow. To see her pound a fist against her breast to beat away the grief. When will she turn away from the gruesome spectacle, we wonder. But instead of fleeing the scene, she faces it, drawing close to bloodied bodies she once had cradled in her arms. Then she spreads sackcloth on a rock and sits down. She will not move except to beat off birds of prey by day and jackals by night. Her vigil will last for

Her Character: *As a concubine in the king's court, she became the mother of Armoni and Mephibosheth. Though a woman with few rights and little power, she displayed great courage and loyalty after the death of her sons.*
Her Sorrow: *That her only sons were executed and their bodies dishonored because of their father's crime.*
Her Joy: *That the bodies of her sons were finally given an honorable burial.*

several months—from mid-April to early October. Rizpah will not bury her grief as long as the bodies of her sons remain unburied.

Joshua had promised to live in peace with the Gibeonites, but Saul had murdered many of them during his reign, attempting to annihilate them. As a result of Saul's oath-breaking, Israel suffered a famine for three years running. In retribution, the Gibeonites had asked David for seven of Saul's male offspring. David surrendered Saul's two sons by Rizpah and five grandsons by Saul's daughter Merab. Blood was spilt for blood.

Scripture doesn't say whether Rizpah's sons shared their father's guilt. But like all mothers whose children have perished by violence, Rizpah must have understood the terrible link between sin and death. One person's sin is a cancer that spreads. By refusing to hide her grief, by living out her anguish in public, she gave meaning to her sons' deaths, making the entire nation face the evil of what had happened.

Finally came the rains. Finally the king's heart was touched. Hearing of Rizpah's loyalty and courage, David ordered the remains of the executed to be buried.

Rizpah's actions caused the people to look at the cost of sin. Like many women in ancient cultures, she had few rights and little power. But her persistent courage gave meaning to her sons' deaths and helped a nation deal with the sin of its leader. Her story is tragic; her response memorable. Perhaps because of her, other mothers in Israel were spared, at least for a time, a similar grief.

Praying With Rizpah

Then Rizpah the daughter of Aiah took sackcloth, and spread it on a rock for herself, from the beginning of harvest until rain fell on them from the heavens; she did not allow the birds of the air to come on the bodies by day, or the wild animals by night.—2 Samuel 21.10

Praise God: For giving mothers the power to love their children so fiercely.

Offer Thanks: For the way other women have stood by you.

Confess: Any tendency to back off rather than confront important moral issues with love and courage.

Ask God: To stretch your love beyond your own family circle so that it becomes a force that shapes the world around you.

Lift Your Heart

Mothers are often their children's line of first defense. How tragic when children never experience the power of a mother's protecting love. So many abused children shuffle through our social system with tragic results. So many unborn children perish quietly, with no one to mourn their passing. We cannot save all the motherless children, but we can reach out to one at a time. Pray about whether you could become a big sister to a young girl in need. Go out of your way to make a neglected child feel welcome in your home. Speak out against the forces in our culture that devalue human life. Lend your voices to those that clamor for peace in our world. Do what you can where you can. Let your love be fierce and strong. Don't back off.

Father, thank you for the protecting, persistent love of women in my life. I know your own love better because of how they love me. Help me become a spiritual mother to those you bring into my life. Make me willing to do what it takes to love them fiercely and well.

Go to page 1019 for your next devotional reading.

in your time of trouble;
for you have as many gods
as you have towns, O Judah.

29 Why do you complain against me?
    You have all rebelled against me,
                        says the LORD.
30 In vain I have struck down
        your children;
    they accepted no correction.
    Your own sword devoured your
        prophets
    like a ravening lion.
31 And you, O generation, behold the
        word of the LORD![d]
    Have I been a wilderness to Israel,
        or a land of thick darkness?
    Why then do my people say, "We
        are free,
    we will come to you no more"?
32 Can a girl forget her ornaments,
        or a bride her attire?
    Yet my people have forgotten me,
        days without number.

33 How well you direct your course
        to seek lovers!
    So that even to wicked women
        you have taught your ways.
34 Also on your skirts is found
        the lifeblood of the innocent
        poor,
    though you did not catch them
        breaking in.
    Yet in spite of all these things[d]
35 you say, "I am innocent;
        surely his anger has turned
        from me."
    Now I am bringing you to judgment
        for saying, "I have not sinned."
36 How lightly you gad about,
        changing your ways!
    You shall be put to shame by Egypt
        as you were put to shame
        by Assyria.
37 From there also you will come away
        with your hands on your head;
    for the LORD has rejected those in
        whom you trust,
    and you will not prosper through
        them.

Unfaithful Israel

3 If[e] a man divorces his wife
    and she goes from him
    and becomes another man's wife,
        will he return to her?

Would not such a land be greatly
        polluted?
    You have played the whore with
        many lovers;
    and would you return to me?
                        says the LORD.
2 Look up to the bare heights,[f]
        and see!
    Where have you not been
        lain with?
    By the waysides you have sat waiting
        for lovers,
    like a nomad in the wilderness.
    You have polluted the land
        with your whoring and
        wickedness.
3 Therefore the showers have been
        withheld,
    and the spring rain has not come;
    yet you have the forehead of
        a whore,
    you refuse to be ashamed.
4 Have you not just now called to me,
    "My Father, you are the friend of
        my youth—
5 will he be angry forever,
        will he be indignant to the end?"
    This is how you have spoken,
        but you have done all the evil
        that you could.

A Call to Repentance

6 The LORD said to me in the days of
King Josiah: Have you seen what she did,
that faithless one, Israel, how she went up
on every high hill and under every green
tree, and played the whore there? 7And I
thought, "After she has done all this she
will return to me"; but she did not return,
and her false sister Judah saw it. 8She[g]
saw that for all the adulteries of that faithless one, Israel, I had sent her away with a
decree of divorce; yet her false sister Judah
did not fear, but she too went and played
the whore. 9Because she took her whoredom so lightly, she polluted the land,
committing adultery with stone and tree.
10Yet for all this her false sister Judah did
not return to me with her whole heart, but
only in pretense, says the LORD.

11 Then the LORD said to me: Faithless
Israel has shown herself less guilty than
false Judah. 12Go, and proclaim these
words toward the north, and say:

---

d Meaning of Heb uncertain   e Q Ms Gk Syr:
MT Saying, If   f Or the trails   g Q Ms Gk Mss
Syr: MT I

Return, faithless Israel,
　　　　　　says the LORD.
I will not look on you in anger,
　for I am merciful,
　　　　　　says the LORD;
I will not be angry forever.
13 Only acknowledge your guilt,
　that you have rebelled against the
　　　　LORD your God,
　and scattered your favors among
　　　　　strangers under every
　　　　　green tree,
　and have not obeyed my voice,
　　　　　　says the LORD.
14 Return, O faithless children,
　　　　　　says the LORD,
　for I am your master;
I will take you, one from a city and
　　　　　two from a family,
　and I will bring you to Zion.

15 I will give you shepherds after my
own heart, who will feed you with knowledge and understanding. 16And when you
have multiplied and increased in the land,
in those days, says the LORD, they shall no
longer say, "The ark of the covenant of
the LORD." It shall not come to mind, or be
remembered, or missed; nor shall another
one be made. 17At that time Jerusalem
shall be called the throne of the LORD, and
all nations shall gather to it, to the presence of the LORD in Jerusalem, and they
shall no longer stubbornly follow their
own evil will. 18In those days the house of
Judah shall join the house of Israel, and
together they shall come from the land of
the north to the land that I gave your ancestors for a heritage.

19 I thought
　　how I would set you among
　　　　my children,
　and give you a pleasant land,
　　the most beautiful heritage of all
　　　　the nations.
And I thought you would call me,
　　My Father,
　and would not turn from
　　　following me.
20 Instead, as a faithless wife leaves her
　　　husband,
　so you have been faithless to me,
　　O house of Israel,
　　　　　　says the LORD.

21 A voice on the bare heights[h]
　is heard,

the plaintive weeping of Israel's
　　children,
because they have perverted
　　their way,
they have forgotten the LORD their
　　God:
22 Return, O faithless children,
　I will heal your faithlessness.

"Here we come to you;
　for you are the LORD our God.
23 Truly the hills are[i] a delusion,
　the orgies on the mountains.
Truly in the LORD our God
　is the salvation of Israel.

24 "But from our youth the shameful
thing has devoured all for which our ancestors had labored, their flocks and their
herds, their sons and their daughters.
25Let us lie down in our shame, and let
our dishonor cover us; for we have sinned
against the LORD our God, we and our ancestors, from our youth even to this day;
and we have not obeyed the voice of the
LORD our God."

4 If you return, O Israel,
　　　　　　says the LORD,
　if you return to me,
　if you remove your abominations
　　　from my presence,
　　and do not waver,
2 and if you swear, "As the LORD lives!"
　in truth, in justice, and in
　　　uprightness,
　then nations shall be blessed[j]
　　by him,
　and by him they shall boast.

3 For thus says the LORD to the people
of Judah and to the inhabitants of Jerusalem:
Break up your fallow ground,
　and do not sow among thorns.
4 Circumcise yourselves to the LORD,
　remove the foreskin of your
　　hearts,
　O people of Judah and
　　inhabitants of Jerusalem,
　or else my wrath will go forth
　　like fire,
　and burn with no one to
　　quench it,
　because of the evil of your doings.

h Or the trails　i Gk Syr Vg: Heb Truly from the
hills is　j Or shall bless themselves

Invasion and Desolation of Judah Threatened

5 Declare in Judah, and proclaim in Jerusalem, and say:

Blow the trumpet through the land;
    shout aloud[k] and say,
"Gather together, and let us go
    into the fortified cities!"
6 Raise a standard toward Zion,
    flee for safety, do not delay,
for I am bringing evil from the
        north,
    and a great destruction.
7 A lion has gone up from its thicket,
    a destroyer of nations has set out;
    he has gone out from his place
to make your land a waste;
    your cities will be ruins
    without inhabitant.
8 Because of this put on sackcloth,
    lament and wail:
"The fierce anger of the LORD
    has not turned away from us."

9 On that day, says the LORD, courage shall fail the king and the officials; the priests shall be appalled and the prophets astounded. 10 Then I said, "Ah, Lord GOD, how utterly you have deceived this people and Jerusalem, saying, 'It shall be well with you,' even while the sword is at the throat!"

11 At that time it will be said to this people and to Jerusalem: A hot wind comes from me out of the bare heights[l] in the desert toward my poor people, not to winnow or cleanse— 12 a wind too strong for that. Now it is I who speak in judgment against them.
13 Look! He comes up like clouds,
    his chariots like the whirlwind;
his horses are swifter than eagles—
    woe to us, for we are ruined!
14 O Jerusalem, wash your heart clean
        of wickedness
    so that you may be saved.
How long shall your evil schemes
    lodge within you?
15 For a voice declares from Dan
    and proclaims disaster from
        Mount Ephraim.
16 Tell the nations, "Here they are!"
    Proclaim against Jerusalem,
"Besiegers come from a distant land;
    they shout against the cities of
        Judah.
17 They have closed in around her like
        watchers of a field,
    because she has rebelled
        against me,
                                    says the LORD.
18 Your ways and your doings
    have brought this upon you.
This is your doom; how bitter it is!
    It has reached your very heart."

Sorrow for a Doomed Nation

19 My anguish, my anguish! I writhe in
        pain!
    Oh, the walls of my heart!
My heart is beating wildly;
    I cannot keep silent;
for I[m] hear the sound of the
        trumpet,
    the alarm of war.
20 Disaster overtakes disaster,
    the whole land is laid waste.
Suddenly my tents are destroyed,
    my curtains in a moment.
21 How long must I see the standard,
    and hear the sound of the
        trumpet?
22 "For my people are foolish,
    they do not know me;
they are stupid children,
    they have no understanding.
They are skilled in doing evil,
    but do not know how to do good."

23 I looked on the earth, and lo, it was
        waste and void;
    and to the heavens, and they had
        no light.
24 I looked on the mountains, and lo,
        they were quaking,
    and all the hills moved to and fro.
25 I looked, and lo, there was no one
        at all,
    and all the birds of the air
        had fled.
26 I looked, and lo, the fruitful land
        was a desert,
    and all its cities were laid in ruins
    before the LORD, before his fierce
        anger.

27 For thus says the LORD: The whole land shall be a desolation; yet I will not make a full end.
28 Because of this the earth shall
        mourn,

---

k Or shout, take your weapons: Heb shout, fill (your hand)   l Or the trails   m Another reading is for you, O my soul,

and the heavens above grow
  black;
for I have spoken, I have purposed;
  I have not relented nor will I turn
    back.

29 At the noise of horseman and archer
  every town takes to flight;
  they enter thickets; they climb
    among rocks;
  all the towns are forsaken,
    and no one lives in them.
30 And you, O desolate one,
  what do you mean that you dress in
    crimson,
    that you deck yourself with
      ornaments of gold,
    that you enlarge your eyes with
      paint?
  In vain you beautify yourself.
    Your lovers despise you;
    they seek your life.
31 For I heard a cry as of a woman
    in labor,
  anguish as of one bringing forth
    her first child,
  the cry of daughter Zion gasping for
    breath,
    stretching out her hands,
  "Woe is me! I am fainting before
    killers!"

The Utter Corruption of God's People

5 Run to and fro through the streets
    of Jerusalem,
  look around and take note!
Search its squares and see
  if you can find one person
who acts justly
  and seeks truth—
so that I may pardon Jerusalem.*n*
2 Although they say, "As the LORD
    lives,"
  yet they swear falsely.
3 O LORD, do your eyes not look
    for truth?
You have struck them,
  but they felt no anguish;
you have consumed them,
  but they refused to take
    correction.
They have made their faces harder
    than rock;
  they have refused to turn back.

4 Then I said, "These are only
    the poor,
  they have no sense;

for they do not know the way of
    the LORD,
  the law of their God.
5 Let me go to the rich*o*
  and speak to them;
surely they know the way of
    the LORD,
  the law of their God."
But they all alike had broken
    the yoke,
  they had burst the bonds.

6 Therefore a lion from the forest shall
    kill them,
  a wolf from the desert shall
    destroy them.
A leopard is watching against
    their cities;
  everyone who goes out of them
    shall be torn in pieces—
because their transgressions
    are many,
  their apostasies are great.

7 How can I pardon you?
  Your children have forsaken me,
  and have sworn by those who are
    no gods.
When I fed them to the full,
  they committed adultery
  and trooped to the houses of
    prostitutes.
8 They were well-fed lusty stallions,
  each neighing for his neighbor's
    wife.
9 Shall I not punish them for these
    things?
                    says the LORD;
  and shall I not bring retribution
  on a nation such as this?

10 Go up through her vine-rows
    and destroy,
  but do not make a full end;
strip away her branches,
  for they are not the LORD's.
11 For the house of Israel and the
    house of Judah
  have been utterly faithless to me,
                    says the LORD.
12 They have spoken falsely of
    the LORD,
  and have said, "He will do
    nothing.
No evil will come upon us,

n Heb *it*   *o* Or *the great*

and we shall not see sword or
famine."
13 The prophets are nothing but wind,
for the word is not in them.
Thus shall it be done to them!

14 Therefore thus says the LORD, the
God of hosts:
Because they p have spoken
this word,
I am now making my words in your
mouth a fire,
and this people wood, and the
fire shall devour them.
15 I am going to bring upon you
a nation from far away, O house
of Israel,
          says the LORD.
It is an enduring nation,
it is an ancient nation,
a nation whose language you do
not know,
nor can you understand what they
say.
16 Their quiver is like an open tomb;
all of them are mighty warriors.
17 They shall eat up your harvest and
your food;
they shall eat up your sons and
your daughters;
they shall eat up your flocks and
your herds;
they shall eat up your vines and
your fig trees;
they shall destroy with the sword
your fortified cities in which
you trust.

18 But even in those days, says the
LORD, I will not make a full end of you.
19 And when your people say, "Why has
the LORD our God done all these things to
us?" you shall say to them, "As you have
forsaken me and served foreign gods in
your land, so you shall serve strangers in a
land that is not yours."

20 Declare this in the house of Jacob,
proclaim it in Judah:
21 Hear this, O foolish and senseless
people,
who have eyes, but do not see,
who have ears, but do not hear.
22 Do you not fear me? says the LORD;
Do you not tremble before me?
I placed the sand as a boundary for
the sea,

a perpetual barrier that it cannot
pass;
though the waves toss, they cannot
prevail,
though they roar, they cannot pass
over it.
23 But this people has a stubborn and
rebellious heart;
they have turned aside and
gone away.
24 They do not say in their hearts,
"Let us fear the LORD our God,
who gives the rain in its season,
the autumn rain and the
spring rain,
and keeps for us
the weeks appointed for the
harvest."
25 Your iniquities have turned
these away,
and your sins have deprived you
of good.
26 For scoundrels are found among
my people;
they take over the goods of others.
Like fowlers they set a trap; q
they catch human beings.
27 Like a cage full of birds,
their houses are full of treachery;
therefore they have become great
and rich,
28   they have grown fat and sleek.
They know no limits in deeds of
wickedness;
they do not judge with justice
the cause of the orphan, to make
it prosper,
and they do not defend the rights
of the needy.
29 Shall I not punish them for these
things?
          says the LORD,
and shall I not bring retribution
on a nation such as this?

30 An appalling and horrible thing
has happened in the land:
31 the prophets prophesy falsely,
and the priests rule as the
prophets direct; r
my people love to have it so,
but what will you do when the
end comes?

p Heb you   q Meaning of Heb uncertain   r Or
rule by their own authority

The Imminence and Horror of the Invasion

6 Flee for safety, O children of
        Benjamin,
    from the midst of Jerusalem!
Blow the trumpet in Tekoa,
    and raise a signal on
        Beth-haccherem;
for evil looms out of the north,
    and great destruction.
² I have likened daughter Zion
    to the loveliest pasture.ˢ
³ Shepherds with their flocks shall
        come against her.
    They shall pitch their tents around
        her;
    they shall pasture, all in
        their places.
⁴ "Prepare war against her;
    up, and let us attack at noon!"
"Woe to us, for the day declines,
    the shadows of evening lengthen!"
⁵ "Up, and let us attack by night,
    and destroy her palaces!"
⁶ For thus says the LORD of hosts:
Cut down her trees;
    cast up a siege ramp against
        Jerusalem.
This is the city that must be
    punished;ᵗ
    there is nothing but oppression
        within her.
⁷ As a well keeps its water fresh,
    so she keeps fresh her wickedness;
violence and destruction are heard
        within her;
    sickness and wounds are ever
        before me.
⁸ Take warning, O Jerusalem,
    or I shall turn from you in
        disgust,
and make you a desolation,
    an uninhabited land.

⁹ Thus says the LORD of hosts:
Gleanᵘ thoroughly as a vine
    the remnant of Israel;
like a grape-gatherer, pass your hand
        again
    over its branches.

¹⁰ To whom shall I speak and give
        warning,
    that they may hear?
See, their ears are closed,ᵛ
    they cannot listen.
The word of the LORD is to them an
    object of scorn;

they take no pleasure in it.
¹¹ But I am full of the wrath of
        the LORD;
    I am weary of holding it in.

Pour it out on the children in
        the street,
    and on the gatherings of young
        men as well;
both husband and wife shall
        be taken,
    the old folk and the very aged.
¹² Their houses shall be turned over to
        others,
    their fields and wives together;
for I will stretch out my hand
        against the inhabitants of
        the land,
                    says the LORD.

¹³ For from the least to the greatest
        of them,
    everyone is greedy for unjust gain;
and from prophet to priest,
    everyone deals falsely.
¹⁴ They have treated the wound of my
        people carelessly,
    saying, "Peace, peace,"
    when there is no peace.
¹⁵ They acted shamefully, they
        committed abomination;
    yet they were not ashamed,
    they did not know how to blush.
Therefore they shall fall among
        those who fall;
    at the time that I punish them,
        they shall be overthrown,
                    says the LORD.

¹⁶ Thus says the LORD:
Stand at the crossroads, and look,
    and ask for the ancient paths,
where the good way lies; and walk
        in it,
    and find rest for your souls.
But they said, "We will not walk
        in it."
¹⁷ Also I raised up sentinels for you:
    "Give heed to the sound of the
        trumpet!"
But they said, "We will not give
        heed."
¹⁸ Therefore hear, O nations,
    and know, O congregation, what
        will happen to them.

ˢ Or I *will destroy daughter Zion, the loveliest pasture*
ᵗ Or *the city of license*   ᵘ Cn: Heb *They shall glean*
ᵛ Heb *are uncircumcised*

19 Hear, O earth; I am going to bring
  disaster on this people,
    the fruit of their schemes,
  because they have not given heed to
    my words;
    and as for my teaching, they have
      rejected it.
20 Of what use to me is frankincense
    that comes from Sheba,
  or sweet cane from a distant land?
  Your burnt offerings are not
    acceptable,
    nor are your sacrifices pleasing
      to me.
21 Therefore thus says the LORD:
  See, I am laying before this people
    stumbling blocks against which
      they shall stumble;
  parents and children together,
    neighbor and friend shall perish.

22 Thus says the LORD:
  See, a people is coming from the
    land of the north,
    a great nation is stirring from the
      farthest parts of the earth.
23 They grasp the bow and the javelin,
    they are cruel and have no mercy,
    their sound is like the roaring sea;
  they ride on horses,
    equipped like a warrior for battle,
    against you, O daughter Zion!

24 "We have heard news of them,
    our hands fall helpless;
  anguish has taken hold of us,
    pain as of a woman in labor.
25 Do not go out into the field,
    or walk on the road;
  for the enemy has a sword,
    terror is on every side."

26 O my poor people, put on
    sackcloth,
    and roll in ashes;
  make mourning as for an only child,
    most bitter lamentation:
  for suddenly the destroyer
    will come upon us.

27 I have made you a tester and a
    refiner[w] among my people
  so that you may know and test
    their ways.
28 They are all stubbornly rebellious,
    going about with slanders;
  they are bronze and iron,
    all of them act corruptly.

29 The bellows blow fiercely,
    the lead is consumed by the fire;
  in vain the refining goes on,
    for the wicked are not removed.
30 They are called "rejected silver,"
    for the LORD has rejected them.

Jeremiah Proclaims God's Judgment on the Nation

7 The word that came to Jeremiah from the LORD: 2Stand in the gate of the LORD's house, and proclaim there this word, and say, Hear the word of the LORD, all you people of Judah, you that enter these gates to worship the LORD. 3Thus says the LORD of hosts, the God of Israel: Amend your ways and your doings, and let me dwell with you[x] in this place. 4Do not trust in these deceptive words: "This is[y] the temple of the LORD, the temple of the LORD, the temple of the LORD."

5 For if you truly amend your ways and your doings, if you truly act justly one with another, 6if you do not oppress the alien, the orphan, and the widow, or shed innocent blood in this place, and if you do not go after other gods to your own hurt, 7then I will dwell with you in this place, in the land that I gave of old to your ancestors forever and ever.

8 Here you are, trusting in deceptive words to no avail. 9Will you steal, murder, commit adultery, swear falsely, make offerings to Baal, and go after other gods that you have not known, 10and then come and stand before me in this house, which is called by my name, and say, "We are safe!"—only to go on doing all these abominations? 11Has this house, which is called by my name, become a den of robbers in your sight? You know, I too am watching, says the LORD. 12Go now to my place that was in Shiloh, where I made my name dwell at first, and see what I did to it for the wickedness of my people Israel. 13And now, because you have done all these things, says the LORD, and when I spoke to you persistently, you did not listen, and when I called you, you did not answer, 14therefore I will do to the house that is called by my name, in which you trust, and to the place that I gave to you and to your ancestors, just what I did to Shiloh. 15And I will cast you out of my

---

w Or a fortress   x Or and I will let you dwell
y Heb They are

sight, just as I cast out all your kinsfolk, all the offspring of Ephraim.

The People's Disobedience

16 As for you, do not pray for this people, do not raise a cry or prayer on their behalf, and do not intercede with me, for I will not hear you. ¹⁷Do you not see what they are doing in the towns of Judah and in the streets of Jerusalem? ¹⁸The children gather wood, the fathers kindle fire, and the women knead dough, to make cakes for the queen of heaven; and they pour out drink offerings to other gods, to pro-

Scripture Reading for Today:
Jeremiah 7.1–7

Verses for Today:
Jeremiah 7.5–7

Remember the Needy

Prophets like Jeremiah never stop being gadflies. Today, some 2500 years after he pricked the conscience of his fellow Israelites, he pricks ours too. "Reform your ways! Deal justly with your neighbor! Remember the needy!"

Jeremiah had little success with his first audience, who were mired in complacency and took false security in their identity as God's chosen people. But with God's grace, his words can spur us to conversion and compassion, and help us move from lip service to real service. Youth ministers Lisa and Steve Walker offer some practical suggestions about how to point children in the same direction.

We constantly model ideals that are more *caught* than *taught*. Children will see the importance of compassion when their parents live it.

Parents can reap great benefits by serving alongside their children. Here are some suggestions:

Spring clean for a shut-in.

Write Christmas cards to senior citizens without family.

Make Easter baskets for people living alone.

Visit or sing Christmas carols at a nursing home.

Volunteer to work on a parish service project.

Become a big brother or big sister to a needy child or parish newcomer.

Babysit during church services.

Put up Christmas decorations for shut-ins or senior citizens.

Participate in a day or week of service (cleaning, repairing or building) in an impoverished area.

Drop off clothes or blankets to the local homeless center.

Organize a canned goods drive for a local service center.

Work with organizations such as Habitat for Humanity.

Join a local walk for hunger.

Help with Special Olympics for handicapped youth.

Teach disadvantaged children how to read and write.

—*LISA AND STEVE WALKER*

Go to page 1025 for your next devotional reading.

voke me to anger. ¹⁹Is it I whom they provoke? says the LORD. Is it not themselves, to their own hurt? ²⁰Therefore thus says the Lord GOD: My anger and my wrath shall be poured out on this place, on human beings and animals, on the trees of the field and the fruit of the ground; it will burn and not be quenched.

21 Thus says the LORD of hosts, the God of Israel: Add your burnt offerings to your sacrifices, and eat the flesh. ²²For in the day that I brought your ancestors out of the land of Egypt, I did not speak to them or command them concerning burnt offerings and sacrifices. ²³But this command I gave them, "Obey my voice, and I will be your God, and you shall be my people; and walk only in the way that I command you, so that it may be well with you." ²⁴Yet they did not obey or incline their ear, but, in the stubbornness of their evil will, they walked in their own counsels, and looked backward rather than forward. ²⁵From the day that your ancestors came out of the land of Egypt until this day, I have persistently sent all my servants the prophets to them, day after day; ²⁶yet they did not listen to me, or pay attention, but they stiffened their necks. They did worse than their ancestors did.

27 So you shall speak all these words to them, but they will not listen to you. You shall call to them, but they will not answer you. ²⁸You shall say to them: This is the nation that did not obey the voice of the LORD their God, and did not accept discipline; truth has perished; it is cut off from their lips.

²⁹ Cut off your hair and throw it away;
   raise a lamentation on the bare
      heights,ᶻ
  for the LORD has rejected and
      forsaken
   the generation that provoked
      his wrath.

30 For the people of Judah have done evil in my sight, says the LORD; they have set their abominations in the house that is called by my name, defiling it. ³¹And they go on building the high placeᵃ of Topheth, which is in the valley of the son of Hinnom, to burn their sons and their daughters in the fire—which I did not command, nor did it come into my mind. ³²Therefore, the days are surely coming, says the LORD, when it will no more be called Topheth, or the valley of the son of Hinnom, but the valley of Slaughter: for

they will bury in Topheth until there is no more room. ³³The corpses of this people will be food for the birds of the air, and for the animals of the earth; and no one will frighten them away. ³⁴And I will bring to an end the sound of mirth and gladness, the voice of the bride and bridegroom in the cities of Judah and in the streets of Jerusalem; for the land shall become a waste.

8 At that time, says the LORD, the bones of the kings of Judah, the bones of its officials, the bones of the priests, the bones of the prophets, and the bones of the inhabitants of Jerusalem shall be brought out of their tombs; ²and they shall be spread before the sun and the moon and all the host of heaven, which they have loved and served, which they have followed, and which they have inquired of and worshiped; and they shall not be gathered or buried; they shall be like dung on the surface of the ground. ³Death shall be preferred to life by all the remnant that remains of this evil family in all the places where I have driven them, says the LORD of hosts.

The Blind Perversity of the Whole Nation

⁴ You shall say to them, Thus says the
    LORD:
  When people fall, do they not get
     up again?
   If they go astray, do they not turn
     back?
⁵ Why then has this peopleᵇ turned
    away
   in perpetual backsliding?
  They have held fast to deceit,
   they have refused to return.
⁶ I have given heed and listened,
   but they do not speak honestly;
  no one repents of wickedness,
   saying, "What have I done!"
  All of them turn to their own
    course,
   like a horse plunging headlong
    into battle.
⁷ Even the stork in the heavens
    knows its times;
  and the turtledove, swallow, and
    craneᶜ
   observe the time of their coming;

ᶻ Or *the trails*   ᵃ Gk Tg: Heb *high places*   ᵇ One Ms Gk: MT *this people, Jerusalem,*   ᶜ Meaning of Heb uncertain

but my people do not know
    the ordinance of the Lord.

8 How can you say, "We are wise,
    and the law of the Lord is with us,"
when, in fact, the false pen of
      the scribes
    has made it into a lie?
9 The wise shall be put to shame,
    they shall be dismayed and taken;
since they have rejected the word
    of the Lord,
    what wisdom is in them?
10 Therefore I will give their wives
      to others
    and their fields to conquerors,
because from the least to the greatest
    everyone is greedy for unjust gain;
from prophet to priest
    everyone deals falsely.
11 They have treated the wound of my
      people carelessly,
    saying, "Peace, peace,"
    when there is no peace.
12 They acted shamefully, they
      committed abomination;
yet they were not at all ashamed,
    they did not know how to blush.
Therefore they shall fall among
      those who fall;
    at the time when I punish them,
    they shall be overthrown,
           says the Lord.
13 When I wanted to gather them, says
    the Lord,
there are^d no grapes on the vine,
    nor figs on the fig tree;
even the leaves are withered,
    and what I gave them has passed
      away from them.^e

14 Why do we sit still?
Gather together, let us go into the
      fortified cities
    and perish there;
for the Lord our God has doomed
      us to perish,
    and has given us poisoned water
      to drink,
because we have sinned against
    the Lord.
15 We look for peace, but find no
      good,
    for a time of healing, but there is
      terror instead.

16 The snorting of their horses is heard
    from Dan;

at the sound of the neighing of
    their stallions
the whole land quakes.
They come and devour the land and
    all that fills it,
    the city and those who live in it.
17 See, I am letting snakes loose among
    you,
    adders that cannot be charmed,
    and they shall bite you,
           says the Lord.

The Prophet Mourns for the People

18 My joy is gone, grief is upon me,
    my heart is sick.
19 Hark, the cry of my poor people
    from far and wide in the land:
"Is the Lord not in Zion?
    Is her King not in her?"
("Why have they provoked me to
      anger with their images,
    with their foreign idols?")
20 "The harvest is past, the summer
      is ended,
    and we are not saved."
21 For the hurt of my poor people I am
      hurt,
    I mourn, and dismay has taken
      hold of me.

22 Is there no balm in Gilead?
    Is there no physician there?
Why then has the health of my poor
      people
    not been restored?
9 ^f O that my head were a spring of
      water,
    and my eyes a fountain of tears,
so that I might weep day and night
    for the slain of my poor people!
2 ^g O that I had in the desert
    a traveler's lodging place,
that I might leave my people
    and go away from them!
For they are all adulterers,
    a band of traitors.
3 They bend their tongues like bows;
    they have grown strong in the
      land for falsehood, and not
      for truth;
for they proceed from evil to evil,
    and they do not know me, says
      the Lord.

---

^d Or *I will make an end of them, says the Lord.*
There are   ^e Meaning of Heb uncertain   ^f Ch
8.23 in Heb   ^g Ch 9.1 in Heb

4 Beware of your neighbors,
  and put no trust in any of
     your kin;*h*
  for all your kin*i* are supplanters,
     and every neighbor goes around
        like a slanderer.
5 They all deceive their neighbors,
     and no one speaks the truth;
  they have taught their tongues to
     speak lies;
  they commit iniquity and are too
     weary to repent.*j*
6 Oppression upon oppression,
     deceit*k* upon deceit!
  They refuse to know me, says
     the LORD.

7 Therefore thus says the LORD of
     hosts:
  I will now refine and test them,
     for what else can I do with my
        sinful people?*l*
8 Their tongue is a deadly arrow;
     it speaks deceit through the
        mouth.
  They all speak friendly words to
     their neighbors,
  but inwardly are planning to lay
     an ambush.
9 Shall I not punish them for these
     things? says the LORD;
  and shall I not bring retribution
     on a nation such as this?

10 Take up*m* weeping and wailing for
      the mountains,
   and a lamentation for the pastures
      of the wilderness,
   because they are laid waste so that
      no one passes through,
   and the lowing of cattle is not
      heard;
   both the birds of the air and the
      animals
   have fled and are gone.
11 I will make Jerusalem a heap
      of ruins,
   a lair of jackals;
   and I will make the towns of Judah
      a desolation,
      without inhabitant.

12 Who is wise enough to understand
this? To whom has the mouth of the LORD
spoken, so that they may declare it?
Why is the land ruined and laid waste
like a wilderness, so that no one passes
through? 13And the LORD says: Because

they have forsaken my law that I set before them, and have not obeyed my voice,
or walked in accordance with it, 14but
have stubbornly followed their own
hearts and have gone after the Baals, as
their ancestors taught them. 15Therefore
thus says the LORD of hosts, the God of
Israel: I am feeding this people with
wormwood, and giving them poisonous
water to drink. 16I will scatter them
among nations that neither they nor their
ancestors have known; and I will send the
sword after them, until I have consumed
them.

The People Mourn in Judgment

17 Thus says the LORD of hosts:
   Consider, and call for the mourning
      women to come;
   send for the skilled women
      to come;
18 let them quickly raise a dirge
      over us,
   so that our eyes may run down
      with tears,
   and our eyelids flow with water.
19 For a sound of wailing is heard from
      Zion:
   "How we are ruined!
   We are utterly shamed,
   because we have left the land,
      because they have cast down our
         dwellings."

20 Hear, O women, the word of
      the LORD,
   and let your ears receive the word
      of his mouth;
   teach to your daughters a dirge,
      and each to her neighbor
         a lament.
21 "Death has come up into our
      windows,
   it has entered our palaces,
   to cut off the children from
      the streets
   and the young men from
      the squares."
22 Speak! Thus says the LORD:
   "Human corpses shall fall
      like dung upon the open field,

h Heb *in a brother*   *i* Heb *for every brother*   *j* Cn
Compare Gk: Heb *they weary themselves with
iniquity.* *6Your dwelling*   *k* Cn: Heb *Your dwelling
in the midst of deceit*   *l* Or *my poor people*   *m* Gk
Syr: Heb *I will take up*

like sheaves behind the reaper,
  and no one shall gather them."

23 Thus says the LORD: Do not let the
wise boast in their wisdom, do not let the
mighty boast in their might, do not let
the wealthy boast in their wealth; 24but
let those who boast boast in this, that
they understand and know me, that I am
the LORD; I act with steadfast love, justice,
and righteousness in the earth, for in
these things I delight, says the LORD.

25 The days are surely coming, says the
LORD, when I will attend to all those who
are circumcised only in the foreskin:
26Egypt, Judah, Edom, the Ammonites,
Moab, and all those with shaven temples
who live in the desert. For all these nations are uncircumcised, and all the house
of Israel is uncircumcised in heart.

Idolatry Has Brought Ruin on Israel

10 Hear the word that the LORD
speaks to you, O house of Israel.
2Thus says the LORD:
  Do not learn the way of the nations,
    or be dismayed at the signs of the
      heavens;
    for the nations are dismayed
      at them.
3 For the customs of the peoples
    are false:
  a tree from the forest is cut down,
    and worked with an ax by the
      hands of an artisan;
4 people deck it with silver and gold;
    they fasten it with hammer
      and nails
    so that it cannot move.
5 Their idolsn are like scarecrows in a
    cucumber field,
  and they cannot speak;
  they have to be carried,
    for they cannot walk.
  Do not be afraid of them,
    for they cannot do evil,
    nor is it in them to do good.

6 There is none like you, O LORD;
    you are great, and your name is
      great in might.
7 Who would not fear you, O King of
      the nations?
  For that is your due;
  among all the wise ones of the
      nations
    and in all their kingdoms
      there is no one like you.

8 They are both stupid and foolish;
    the instruction given by idols
    is no better than wood!o
9 Beaten silver is brought from
      Tarshish,
    and gold from Uphaz.
  They are the work of the artisan and
      of the hands of the
      goldsmith;
    their clothing is blue and purple;
    they are all the product of skilled
      workers.
10 But the LORD is the true God;
    he is the living God and the
      everlasting King.
  At his wrath the earth quakes,
    and the nations cannot endure his
      indignation.

11 Thus shall you say to them: The
gods who did not make the heavens and
the earth shall perish from the earth
and from under the heavens. p

12 It is he who made the earth by
      his power,
    who established the world by
      his wisdom,
    and by his understanding
      stretched out the heavens.
13 When he utters his voice, there is a
      tumult of waters in the
      heavens,
    and he makes the mist rise from
      the ends of the earth.
  He makes lightnings for the rain,
    and he brings out the wind from
      his storehouses.
14 Everyone is stupid and without
      knowledge;
    goldsmiths are all put to shame
      by their idols;
    for their images are false,
    and there is no breath in them.
15 They are worthless, a work of
      delusion;
    at the time of their punishment
      they shall perish.
16 Not like these is the LORD,q the
      portion of Jacob,
    for he is the one who formed
      all things,

---

n Heb *They*   o Meaning of Heb uncertain
p This verse is in Aramaic   q Heb lacks *the LORD*

and Israel is the tribe of his
　　inheritance;
the LORD of hosts is his name.

The Coming Exile

17 Gather up your bundle from the
　　ground,
　　O you who live under siege!
18 For thus says the LORD:
　I am going to sling out the
　　　inhabitants of the land
　　at this time,
　and I will bring distress on them,
　　so that they shall feel it.

19 Woe is me because of my hurt!
　　My wound is severe.
　But I said, "Truly this is my
　　　punishment,
　　and I must bear it."
20 My tent is destroyed,
　　and all my cords are broken;
　my children have gone from me,
　　and they are no more;
　there is no one to spread my tent
　　　again,
　　and to set up my curtains.
21 For the shepherds are stupid,
　　and do not inquire of the LORD;
　therefore they have not prospered,
　　and all their flock is scattered.

22 Hear, a noise! Listen, it is coming—
　　a great commotion from the land
　　　of the north
　to make the cities of Judah a
　　　desolation,
　　a lair of jackals.

23 I know, O LORD, that the way of
　　　human beings is not in
　　　their control,
　　that mortals as they walk cannot
　　　direct their steps.
24 Correct me, O LORD, but in
　　　just measure;
　　not in your anger, or you will
　　　bring me to nothing.

25 Pour out your wrath on the nations
　　　that do not know you,
　and on the peoples that do not
　　　call on your name;
　for they have devoured Jacob;
　　they have devoured him and
　　　consumed him,
　　and have laid waste his
　　　habitation.

Israel and Judah Have Broken the Covenant

11 The word that came to Jeremiah from the LORD: 2Hear the words of this covenant, and speak to the people of Judah and the inhabitants of Jerusalem. 3You shall say to them, Thus says the LORD, the God of Israel: Cursed be anyone who does not heed the words of this covenant, 4which I commanded your ancestors when I brought them out of the land of Egypt, from the iron-smelter, saying, Listen to my voice, and do all that I command you. So shall you be my people, and I will be your God, 5that I may perform the oath that I swore to your ancestors, to give them a land flowing with milk and honey, as at this day. Then I answered, "So be it, LORD."

6 And the LORD said to me: Proclaim all these words in the cities of Judah, and in the streets of Jerusalem: Hear the words of this covenant and do them. 7For I solemnly warned your ancestors when I brought them up out of the land of Egypt, warning them persistently, even to this day, saying, Obey my voice. 8Yet they did not obey or incline their ear, but everyone walked in the stubbornness of an evil will. So I brought upon them all the words of this covenant, which I commanded them to do, but they did not.

9 And the LORD said to me: Conspiracy exists among the people of Judah and the inhabitants of Jerusalem. 10They have turned back to the iniquities of their ancestors of old, who refused to heed my words; they have gone after other gods to serve them; the house of Israel and the house of Judah have broken the covenant that I made with their ancestors. 11Therefore, thus says the LORD, assuredly I am going to bring disaster upon them that they cannot escape; though they cry out to me, I will not listen to them. 12Then the cities of Judah and the inhabitants of Jerusalem will go and cry out to the gods to whom they make offerings, but they will never save them in the time of their trouble. 13For your gods have become as many as your towns, O Judah; and as many as the streets of Jerusalem are the altars to shame you have set up, altars to make offerings to Baal.

14 As for you, do not pray for this people, or lift up a cry or prayer on their behalf, for I will not listen when they call to me in the time of their trouble. 15What

right has my beloved in my house, when she has done vile deeds? Can vows[r] and sacrificial flesh avert your doom? Can you then exult? [16]The LORD once called you, "A green olive tree, fair with goodly fruit"; but with the roar of a great tempest he will set fire to it, and its branches will be consumed. [17]The LORD of hosts, who planted you, has pronounced evil against you, because of the evil that the house of Israel and the house of Judah have done, provoking me to anger by making offerings to Baal.

Jeremiah's Life Threatened

[18] It was the LORD who made it known
    to me, and I knew;

then you showed me their
    evil deeds.
[19] But I was like a gentle lamb
    led to the slaughter.
And I did not know it was
    against me
    that they devised schemes, saying,
"Let us destroy the tree with
    its fruit,
    let us cut him off from the land
    of the living,
    so that his name will no longer be
    remembered!"
[20] But you, O LORD of hosts, who judge
    righteously,

r Gk: Heb *Can many*

"Let Me Live Until I Die"

Scripture Reading
for Today:
Jeremiah 10.23–24

Verse for Today:
Jeremiah 10.23

When I first found out I had cancer, I didn't know what to pray for. I didn't know if I should pray for healing or life or death. Then, I found peace in praying for what my folks call "God's perfect will." As it evolved, my prayer has become, "Lord, let me live until I die." By that I mean I want to live, love and serve fully until death comes. If that prayer is answered, if I am able to live until I die, how long really doesn't matter. Whether it's just a few months or a few years is really immaterial.

I grew up with people who believed you could serve the Lord from a sickbed or a deathbed. The great commandment is to love the Lord your God with your whole heart, your whole soul, your whole mind, and all your strength. As long as I have my mental facility, I want to keep on loving. I want to keep on serving. That's what I hope to be about.

My illness has helped me to realize how fragile our hold on life is. I always thought I was going to live to be an old woman, like my mother and my father and all the other old people I knew and was close to when I was a child. But I no longer think that. My time isn't long. Now, I just want to find ways to make the most of the time I have left.

I try to keep myself open to people and to laughter and to love and to have faith. I try each day to see God's will. I pray, "Oh Jesus, I surrender." I pray, "Father, take this cross away. Not my will, but thy will be done." I console myself with the old Negro spiritual: "Sooner will be done the troubles of this world. I'm going home to live with God."

—*SISTER THEA BOWMAN*

Go to page 1036 for your next devotional reading.

who try the heart and the mind,
    let me see your retribution upon
        them,
    for to you I have committed
        my cause.

21 Therefore thus says the Lord concerning the people of Anathoth, who seek your life, and say, "You shall not prophesy in the name of the Lord, or you will die by our hand"— 22therefore thus says the Lord of hosts: I am going to punish them; the young men shall die by the sword; their sons and their daughters shall die by famine; 23and not even a remnant shall be left of them. For I will bring disaster upon the people of Anathoth, the year of their punishment.

Jeremiah Complains to God

12 You will be in the right, O Lord,
    when I lay charges against you;
  but let me put my case to you.
Why does the way of the guilty
        prosper?
  Why do all who are treacherous
        thrive?
2 You plant them, and they take root;
    they grow and bring forth fruit;
you are near in their mouths
    yet far from their hearts.
3 But you, O Lord, know me;
    You see me and test me—my
        heart is with you.
Pull them out like sheep for the
        slaughter,
  and set them apart for the day
        of slaughter.
4 How long will the land mourn,
    and the grass of every field
        wither?
For the wickedness of those who live
        in it
  the animals and the birds are
        swept away,
  and because people said, "He is
        blind to our ways."[s]

God Replies to Jeremiah

5 If you have raced with foot-runners
    and they have wearied you,
  how will you compete with
        horses?
And if in a safe land you fall down,
    how will you fare in the thickets
        of the Jordan?
6 For even your kinsfolk and your
        own family,

even they have dealt treacherously
        with you;
  they are in full cry after you;
do not believe them,
    though they speak friendly words
        to you.

7 I have forsaken my house,
    I have abandoned my heritage;
I have given the beloved of my heart
    into the hands of her enemies.
8 My heritage has become to me
    like a lion in the forest;
she has lifted up her voice
        against me—
  therefore I hate her.
9 Is the hyena greedy[t] for my
        heritage at my command?
  Are the birds of prey all
        around her?
Go, assemble all the wild animals;
    bring them to devour her.
10 Many shepherds have destroyed
        my vineyard,
  they have trampled down
        my portion,
they have made my pleasant portion
    a desolate wilderness.
11 They have made it a desolation;
    desolate, it mourns to me.
The whole land is made desolate,
    but no one lays it to heart.
12 Upon all the bare heights[u] in
        the desert
    spoilers have come;
for the sword of the Lord devours
    from one end of the land to
        the other;
    no one shall be safe.
13 They have sown wheat and have
        reaped thorns,
  they have tired themselves out but
        profit nothing.
They shall be ashamed of their[v]
        harvests
  because of the fierce anger of
        the Lord.

14 Thus says the Lord concerning all my evil neighbors who touch the heritage that I have given my people Israel to inherit: I am about to pluck them up from their land, and I will pluck up the house of Judah from among them. 15And after I have plucked them up, I will again have

---

[s] Gk: Heb *to our future*   [t] Cn: Heb *Is the hyena,
the bird of prey*   [u] Or *the trails*   [v] Heb *your*

compassion on them, and I will bring them again to their heritage and to their land, everyone of them. 16And then, if they will diligently learn the ways of my people, to swear by my name, "As the LORD lives," as they taught my people to swear by Baal, then they shall be built up in the midst of my people. 17But if any nation will not listen, then I will completely uproot it and destroy it, says the LORD.

The Linen Loincloth

13 Thus said the LORD to me, "Go and buy yourself a linen loincloth, and put it on your loins, but do not dip it in water." 2So I bought a loincloth according to the word of the LORD, and put it on my loins. 3And the word of the LORD came to me a second time, saying, 4"Take the loincloth that you bought and are wearing, and go now to the Euphrates,*w* and hide it there in a cleft of the rock." 5So I went, and hid it by the Euphrates,*x* as the LORD commanded me. 6And after many days the LORD said to me, "Go now to the Euphrates,*w* and take from there the loincloth that I commanded you to hide there." 7Then I went to the Euphrates,*w* and dug, and I took the loincloth from the place where I had hidden it. But now the loincloth was ruined; it was good for nothing.

8 Then the word of the LORD came to me: 9Thus says the LORD: Just so I will ruin the pride of Judah and the great pride of Jerusalem. 10This evil people, who refuse to hear my words, who stubbornly follow their own will and have gone after other gods to serve them and worship them, shall be like this loincloth, which is good for nothing. 11For as the loincloth clings to one's loins, so I made the whole house of Israel and the whole house of Judah cling to me, says the LORD, in order that they might be for me a people, a name, a praise, and a glory. But they would not listen.

Symbol of the Wine-Jars

12 You shall speak to them this word: Thus says the LORD, the God of Israel: Every wine-jar should be filled with wine. And they will say to you, "Do you think we do not know that every wine-jar should be filled with wine?" 13Then you shall say to them: Thus says the LORD: I am about to fill all the inhabitants of this land—the kings who sit on David's throne, the priests, the prophets, and all the inhabitants of Jerusalem—with drunkenness. 14And I will dash them one against another, parents and children together, says the LORD. I will not pity or spare or have compassion when I destroy them.

Exile Threatened

15 Hear and give ear; do not be
  haughty,
  for the LORD has spoken.
16 Give glory to the LORD your God
  before he brings darkness,
and before your feet stumble
  on the mountains at twilight;
while you look for light,
  he turns it into gloom
  and makes it deep darkness.
17 But if you will not listen,
  my soul will weep in secret for
    your pride;
my eyes will weep bitterly and run
    down with tears,
  because the LORD's flock has been
    taken captive.

18 Say to the king and the queen
    mother:
  "Take a lowly seat,
for your beautiful crown
  has come down from your head."*y*
19 The towns of the Negeb are shut up
  with no one to open them;
all Judah is taken into exile,
  wholly taken into exile.

20 Lift up your eyes and see
  those who come from the north.
Where is the flock that was
    given you,
  your beautiful flock?
21 What will you say when they set as
    head over you
  those whom you have trained
  to be your allies?
Will not pangs take hold of you,
  like those of a woman in labor?
22 And if you say in your heart,
  "Why have these things come
    upon me?"
it is for the greatness of your
    iniquity
  that your skirts are lifted up,

---

w Or *to Parah*; Heb *perath*   *x* Or *by Parah*; Heb *perath*   *y* Gk Syr Vg: Meaning of Heb uncertain

and you are violated.

23 Can Ethiopians[z] change their skin
     or leopards their spots?
   Then also you can do good
     who are accustomed to do evil.
24 I will scatter you[a] like chaff
     driven by the wind from
       the desert.
25 This is your lot,
     the portion I have measured out
       to you, says the LORD,
   because you have forgotten me
     and trusted in lies.
26 I myself will lift up your skirts over
       your face,
     and your shame will be seen.
27 I have seen your abominations,
     your adulteries and neighings,
       your shameless prostitutions
   on the hills of the countryside.
   Woe to you, O Jerusalem!
     How long will it be
   before you are made clean?

The Great Drought

14 The word of the LORD that came to
   Jeremiah concerning the drought:
2 Judah mourns
     and her gates languish;
   they lie in gloom on the ground,
     and the cry of Jerusalem goes up.
3 Her nobles send their servants
       for water;
     they come to the cisterns,
   they find no water,
     they return with their
       vessels empty.
   They are ashamed and dismayed
     and cover their heads,
4 because the ground is cracked.
   Because there has been no rain on
       the land
   the farmers are dismayed;
     they cover their heads.
5 Even the doe in the field forsakes
       her newborn fawn
     because there is no grass.
6 The wild asses stand on the bare
       heights,[b]
   they pant for air like jackals;
   their eyes fail
     because there is no herbage.

7 Although our iniquities testify
       against us,
     act, O LORD, for your name's sake;
   our apostasies indeed are many,
     and we have sinned against you.

8 O hope of Israel,
     its savior in time of trouble,
   why should you be like a stranger in
       the land,
     like a traveler turning aside for the
       night?
9 Why should you be like someone
       confused,
     like a mighty warrior who cannot
       give help?
   Yet you, O LORD, are in the midst of
       us,
     and we are called by your name;
   do not forsake us!

10 Thus says the LORD concerning
       this people:
   Truly they have loved to wander,
     they have not restrained their feet;
   therefore the LORD does not
       accept them,
     now he will remember their
       iniquity
     and punish their sins.

11 The LORD said to me: Do not pray
for the welfare of this people. 12Although
they fast, I do not hear their cry, and although they offer burnt offering and grain
offering, I do not accept them; but by the
sword, by famine, and by pestilence I consume them.

Denunciation of Lying Prophets

13 Then I said: "Ah, Lord GOD! Here
are the prophets saying to them, 'You
shall not see the sword, nor shall you have
famine, but I will give you true peace in
this place.'" 14And the LORD said to me:
The prophets are prophesying lies in my
name; I did not send them, nor did I command them or speak to them. They are
prophesying to you a lying vision, worthless divination, and the deceit of their
own minds. 15Therefore thus says the LORD
concerning the prophets who prophesy in
my name though I did not send them,
and who say, "Sword and famine shall
not come on this land": By sword and famine those prophets shall be consumed.
16And the people to whom they prophesy
shall be thrown out into the streets of
Jerusalem, victims of famine and sword.
There shall be no one to bury them—
themselves, their wives, their sons, and

z Or Nubians; Heb Cushites   a Heb them   b Or
the trails

their daughters. For I will pour out their wickedness upon them.

17 You shall say to them this word:
Let my eyes run down with tears
        night and day,
    and let them not cease,
for the virgin daughter—my
        people—is struck down with
        a crushing blow,
    with a very grievous wound.
18 If I go out into the field,
    look—those killed by the sword!
And if I enter the city,
    look—those sick with*c* famine!
For both prophet and priest ply their
        trade throughout the land,
    and have no knowledge.

The People Plead for Mercy

19 Have you completely rejected Judah?
        Does your heart loathe Zion?
Why have you struck us down
    so that there is no healing for us?
We look for peace, but find no
        good;
    for a time of healing, but there is
        terror instead.
20 We acknowledge our wickedness,
        O LORD,
    the iniquity of our ancestors,
    for we have sinned against you.
21 Do not spurn us, for your name's
        sake;
    do not dishonor your glorious
        throne;
    remember and do not break your
        covenant with us.
22 Can any idols of the nations
        bring rain?
    Or can the heavens give showers?
Is it not you, O LORD our God?
    We set our hope on you,
    for it is you who do all this.

Punishment Is Inevitable

15 Then the LORD said to me: Though Moses and Samuel stood before me, yet my heart would not turn toward this people. Send them out of my sight, and let them go! 2And when they say to you, "Where shall we go?" you shall say to them: Thus says the LORD:
Those destined for pestilence, to
        pestilence,
    and those destined for the sword,
        to the sword;

those destined for famine, to
        famine,
    and those destined for captivity,
        to captivity.
3And I will appoint over them four kinds of destroyers, says the LORD: the sword to kill, the dogs to drag away, and the birds of the air and the wild animals of the earth to devour and destroy. 4I will make them a horror to all the kingdoms of the earth because of what King Manasseh son of Hezekiah of Judah did in Jerusalem.

5 Who will have pity on you,
        O Jerusalem,
    or who will bemoan you?
Who will turn aside
    to ask about your welfare?
6 You have rejected me, says the LORD,
        you are going backward;
so I have stretched out my hand
        against you and destroyed
        you—
    I am weary of relenting.
7 I have winnowed them with a
        winnowing fork
    in the gates of the land;
I have bereaved them, I have
        destroyed my people;
    they did not turn from their ways.
8 Their widows became more
        numerous
    than the sand of the seas;
I have brought against the mothers
        of youths
    a destroyer at noonday;
I have made anguish and terror
    fall upon her suddenly.
9 She who bore seven has languished;
        she has swooned away;
her sun went down while it was
        yet day;
    she has been shamed and
        disgraced.
And the rest of them I will give to
        the sword
    before their enemies,
                    says the LORD.

Jeremiah Complains Again and Is Reassured

10 Woe is me, my mother, that you ever bore me, a man of strife and contention to the whole land! I have not lent, nor have I borrowed, yet all of them curse

---

c Heb look—the sicknesses of

me. [11]The LORD said: Surely I have intervened in your life[d] for good, surely I have imposed enemies on you in a time of trouble and in a time of distress.[e] [12]Can iron and bronze break iron from the north?

13 Your wealth and your treasures I will give as plunder, without price, for all your sins, throughout all your territory. [14]I will make you serve your enemies in a land that you do not know, for in my anger a fire is kindled that shall burn forever.
[15] O LORD, you know;

> remember me and visit me,
> and bring down retribution for
> me on my persecutors.

In your forbearance do not take
> me away;
> know that on your account I
> suffer insult.

16 Your words were found, and I
> ate them,
> and your words became to me
> a joy
> and the delight of my heart;
> for I am called by your name,
> O LORD, God of hosts.

17 I did not sit in the company of
> merrymakers,

---

[d] Heb *intervened with you*   [e] Meaning of Heb uncertain

THE TRADITION

Praying the Scriptures

Your words were found, and I ate them, and your words became to me a joy and the delight of my heart.

JEREMIAH 15.16

Reading the Bible without responding to it in prayer is like reducing great paintings to their subjects: "That's a haystack; that's a sunflower; that's a ballerina …" It's like reading a love letter for its factual content without any regard for tone, nuance, and underlying messages. It's the difference between popping food pellets and enjoying every luscious morsel at a sumptuous banquet.

Scripture—like art, love letters, and good food—is meant to be savored. No one had to explain that to the prophet Jeremiah. God's Word was his life and delight—not just a source of information about God, but contact with God himself.

If your reaction to Scripture falls short of Jeremiah's, you might explore the time-tested approach called, in Latin, *lectio divina*. Developed by the early monks, this "divine reading" (or "divinely inspired reading") of God's Word is prayerful lingering over a particular text. It has three basic elements that can combine in various ways:

Reading. You choose a short passage from Scripture and read it slowly, reflectively. You might read it aloud. You might read it several times. You might memorize it. The point is to give it your whole attention, as you would to some succulent morsel you were lifting to your lips.

Thinking. You "chew" on this tasty morsel, turning it over in your mind and heart as you consider its various meanings and apply it to yourself. There is a time for studying the historical background of the text, but this is not it. You are trying to engage the Scripture in a personal way. "What I'm reading is written to *me*," you might remind yourself as you meditate.

Praying. Using the Scripture passage as your starting point, talk to Jesus. This heart-to-heart conversation is the goal of your reading and thinking. By this step, what could otherwise be a mere intellectual exercise becomes a personal encounter with God.

Praying the Scriptures in this way is not a technique. If you practice it regularly, it becomes a way of life that will transform all of your life.

nor did I rejoice;
under the weight of your hand I
    sat alone,
for you had filled me with
    indignation.
18 Why is my pain unceasing,
    my wound incurable,
    refusing to be healed?
Truly, you are to me like a deceitful
    brook,
    like waters that fail.

19 Therefore thus says the LORD:
If you turn back, I will take
    you back,
    and you shall stand before me.
If you utter what is precious, and
    not what is worthless,
    you shall serve as my mouth.
It is they who will turn to you,
    not you who will turn to them.
20 And I will make you to this people
    a fortified wall of bronze;
they will fight against you,
    but they shall not prevail
        over you,
for I am with you
    to save you and deliver you,
                    says the LORD.
21 I will deliver you out of the hand of
        the wicked,
    and redeem you from the grasp of
        the ruthless.

Jeremiah's Celibacy and Message

16 The word of the LORD came to me: 2You shall not take a wife, nor shall you have sons or daughters in this place. 3For thus says the LORD concerning the sons and daughters who are born in this place, and concerning the mothers who bear them and the fathers who beget them in this land: 4They shall die of deadly diseases. They shall not be lamented, nor shall they be buried; they shall become like dung on the surface of the ground. They shall perish by the sword and by famine, and their dead bodies shall become food for the birds of the air and for the wild animals of the earth.

5 For thus says the LORD: Do not enter the house of mourning, or go to lament, or bemoan them; for I have taken away my peace from this people, says the LORD, my steadfast love and mercy. 6Both great and small shall die in this land; they shall not be buried, and no one shall lament for them; there shall be no gashing, no shaving of the head for them. 7No one shall break bread*f* for the mourner, to offer comfort for the dead; nor shall anyone give them the cup of consolation to drink for their fathers or their mothers. 8You shall not go into the house of feasting to sit with them, to eat and drink. 9For thus says the LORD of hosts, the God of Israel: I am going to banish from this place, in your days and before your eyes, the voice of mirth and the voice of gladness, the voice of the bridegroom and the voice of the bride.

10 And when you tell this people all these words, and they say to you, "Why has the LORD pronounced all this great evil against us? What is our iniquity? What is the sin that we have committed against the LORD our God?" 11then you shall say to them: It is because your ancestors have forsaken me, says the LORD, and have gone after other gods and have served and worshiped them, and have forsaken me and have not kept my law; 12and because you have behaved worse than your ancestors, for here you are, every one of you, following your stubborn evil will, refusing to listen to me. 13Therefore I will hurl you out of this land into a land that neither you nor your ancestors have known, and there you shall serve other gods day and night, for I will show you no favor.

God Will Restore Israel

14 Therefore, the days are surely coming, says the LORD, when it shall no longer be said, "As the LORD lives who brought the people of Israel up out of the land of Egypt," 15but "As the LORD lives who brought the people of Israel up out of the land of the north and out of all the lands where he had driven them." For I will bring them back to their own land that I gave to their ancestors.

16 I am now sending for many fishermen, says the LORD, and they shall catch them; and afterward I will send for many hunters, and they shall hunt them from every mountain and every hill, and out of the clefts of the rocks. 17For my eyes are on all their ways; they are not hidden from my presence, nor is their iniquity concealed from my sight. 18And*g* I will doubly repay their iniquity and their sin, because they have polluted my land with

---

f Two Mss Gk: MT *break for them*   *g* Gk: Heb
And first

the carcasses of their detestable idols, and have filled my inheritance with their abominations.

19 O LORD, my strength and my
  stronghold,
  my refuge in the day of trouble,
to you shall the nations come
  from the ends of the earth
  and say:
Our ancestors have inherited
  nothing but lies,
  worthless things in which there is
  no profit.
20 Can mortals make for themselves
  gods?
  Such are no gods!

21 "Therefore I am surely going to teach them, this time I am going to teach them my power and my might, and they shall know that my name is the LORD."

Judah's Sin and Punishment

17 The sin of Judah is written with an iron pen; with a diamond point it is engraved on the tablet of their hearts, and on the horns of their altars, 2while their children remember their altars and their sacred poles,[h] beside every green tree, and on the high hills, 3on the mountains in the open country. Your wealth and all your treasures I will give for spoil as the price of your sin[i] throughout all your territory. 4By your own act you shall lose the heritage that I gave you, and I will make you serve your enemies in a land that you do not know, for in my anger a fire is kindled[j] that shall burn forever.

5 Thus says the LORD:
  Cursed are those who trust in
  mere mortals
  and make mere flesh their
  strength,
  whose hearts turn away from
  the LORD.
6 They shall be like a shrub in
  the desert,
  and shall not see when relief
  comes.
They shall live in the parched places
  of the wilderness,
  in an uninhabited salt land.

7 Blessed are those who trust in
  the LORD,

whose trust is the LORD.
8 They shall be like a tree planted
  by water,
  sending out its roots by
  the stream.
It shall not fear when heat comes,
  and its leaves shall stay green;
in the year of drought it is
  not anxious,
  and it does not cease to bear fruit.

9 The heart is devious above all else;
  it is perverse—
  who can understand it?
10 I the LORD test the mind
  and search the heart,
  to give to all according to
  their ways,
  according to the fruit of
  their doings.

11 Like the partridge hatching what
  it did not lay,
  so are all who amass wealth
  unjustly;
in mid-life it will leave them,
  and at their end they will prove to
  be fools.

12 O glorious throne, exalted from the
  beginning,
  shrine of our sanctuary!
13 O hope of Israel! O LORD!
  All who forsake you shall be put
  to shame;
those who turn away from you[k]
  shall be recorded in the
  underworld,[l]
for they have forsaken the
  fountain of living water,
  the LORD.

Jeremiah Prays for Vindication

14 Heal me, O LORD, and I shall
  be healed;
  save me, and I shall be saved;
  for you are my praise.
15 See how they say to me,
  "Where is the word of the LORD?
  Let it come!"
16 But I have not run away from being
  a shepherd[m] in your service,
  nor have I desired the fatal day.

---

h Heb *Asherim*   i Cn: Heb *spoil your high places for sin*   j Two Mss Theodotion: *you kindled*   k Heb *me*   l Or *in the earth*   m Meaning of Heb uncertain

You know what came from my lips;
  it was before your face.
17 Do not become a terror to me;
  you are my refuge in the day
    of disaster;
18 Let my persecutors be shamed,
  but do not let me be shamed;
  let them be dismayed,
  but do not let me be dismayed;
  bring on them the day of disaster;
  destroy them with double
    destruction!

Hallow the Sabbath Day

19 Thus said the LORD to me: Go and stand in the People's Gate, by which the kings of Judah enter and by which they go out, and in all the gates of Jerusalem, 20and say to them: Hear the word of the LORD, you kings of Judah, and all Judah, and all the inhabitants of Jerusalem, who enter by these gates. 21Thus says the LORD: For the sake of your lives, take care that you do not bear a burden on the sabbath day or bring it in by the gates of Jerusalem. 22And do not carry a burden out of your houses on the sabbath or do any work, but keep the sabbath day holy, as I commanded your ancestors. 23Yet they did not listen or incline their ear; they stiffened their necks and would not hear or receive instruction.

24 But if you listen to me, says the LORD, and bring in no burden by the gates of this city on the sabbath day, but keep the sabbath day holy and do no work on it, 25then there shall enter by the gates of this city kings*n* who sit on the throne of David, riding in chariots and on horses, they and their officials, the people of Judah and the inhabitants of Jerusalem; and this city shall be inhabited forever. 26And people shall come from the towns of Judah and the places around Jerusalem, from the land of Benjamin, from the Shephelah, from the hill country, and from the Negeb, bringing burnt offerings and sacrifices, grain offerings and frankincense, and bringing thank offerings to the house of the LORD. 27But if you do not listen to me, to keep the sabbath day holy, and to carry in no burden through the gates of Jerusalem on the sabbath day, then I will kindle a fire in its gates; it shall devour the palaces of Jerusalem and shall not be quenched.

The Potter and the Clay

18 The word that came to Jeremiah from the LORD: 2"Come, go down to the potter's house, and there I will let you hear my words." 3So I went down to the potter's house, and there he was working at his wheel. 4The vessel he was making of clay was spoiled in the potter's hand, and he reworked it into another vessel, as seemed good to him.

5 Then the word of the LORD came to me: 6Can I not do with you, O house of Israel, just as this potter has done? says the LORD. Just like the clay in the potter's hand, so are you in my hand, O house of Israel. 7At one moment I may declare concerning a nation or a kingdom, that I will pluck up and break down and destroy it, 8but if that nation, concerning which I have spoken, turns from its evil, I will change my mind about the disaster that I intended to bring on it. 9And at another moment I may declare concerning a nation or a kingdom that I will build and plant it, 10but if it does evil in my sight, not listening to my voice, then I will change my mind about the good that I had intended to do to it. 11Now, therefore, say to the people of Judah and the inhabitants of Jerusalem: Thus says the LORD: Look, I am a potter shaping evil against you and devising a plan against you. Turn now, all of you from your evil way, and amend your ways and your doings.

Israel's Stubborn Idolatry

12 But they say, "It is no use! We will follow our own plans, and each of us will act according to the stubbornness of our evil will."

13 Therefore thus says the LORD:
  Ask among the nations:
    Who has heard the like of this?
  The virgin Israel has done
    a most horrible thing.
14 Does the snow of Lebanon leave
    the crags of Sirion?*o*
  Do the mountain*p* waters
      run dry,*q*
    the cold flowing streams?
15 But my people have forgotten me,
    they burn offerings to a delusion;

---

n Cn: Heb *kings and officials*   *o* Cn: Heb *of the field*   *p* Cn: Heb *foreign*   *q* Cn: Heb *Are . . . plucked up?*

they have stumbled[r] in their ways,
　　in the ancient roads,
and have gone into bypaths,
　　not the highway,
16 making their land a horror,
　　a thing to be hissed at forever.
All who pass by it are horrified
　　and shake their heads.
17 Like the wind from the east,
　　I will scatter them before
　　　　the enemy.
I will show them my back, not
　　my face,
　　in the day of their calamity.

A Plot against Jeremiah

18 Then they said, "Come, let us make plots against Jeremiah—for instruction shall not perish from the priest, nor counsel from the wise, nor the word from the prophet. Come, let us bring charges against him,[s] and let us not heed any of his words."

19 Give heed to me, O Lord,
　　and listen to what my adversaries
　　　　say!
20 Is evil a recompense for good?
　　Yet they have dug a pit for
　　　　my life.
Remember how I stood before you
　　to speak good for them,
　　to turn away your wrath
　　　　from them.
21 Therefore give their children over to
　　　　famine;
　　hurl them out to the power of
　　　　the sword,
let their wives become childless and
　　widowed.
May their men meet death by
　　pestilence,
　　their youths be slain by the sword
　　　　in battle.
22 May a cry be heard from their
　　　　houses,
　　when you bring the marauder
　　　　suddenly upon them!
For they have dug a pit to catch me,
　　and laid snares for my feet.
23 Yet you, O Lord, know
　　all their plotting to kill me.
Do not forgive their iniquity,
　　do not blot out their sin from
　　　　your sight.
Let them be tripped up before you;
　　deal with them while you are
　　　　angry.

The Broken Earthenware Jug

19 Thus said the Lord: Go and buy a potter's earthenware jug. Take with you[t] some of the elders of the people and some of the senior priests, 2and go out to the valley of the son of Hinnom at the entry of the Potsherd Gate, and proclaim there the words that I tell you. 3You shall say: Hear the word of the Lord, O kings of Judah and inhabitants of Jerusalem. Thus says the Lord of hosts, the God of Israel: I am going to bring such disaster upon this place that the ears of everyone who hears of it will tingle. 4Because the people have forsaken me, and have profaned this place by making offerings in it to other gods whom neither they nor their ancestors nor the kings of Judah have known, and because they have filled this place with the blood of the innocent, 5and gone on building the high places of Baal to burn their children in the fire as burnt offerings to Baal, which I did not command or decree, nor did it enter my mind; 6therefore the days are surely coming, says the Lord, when this place shall no more be called Topheth, or the valley of the son of Hinnom, but the valley of Slaughter. 7And in this place I will make void the plans of Judah and Jerusalem, and will make them fall by the sword before their enemies, and by the hand of those who seek their life. I will give their dead bodies for food to the birds of the air and to the wild animals of the earth. 8And I will make this city a horror, a thing to be hissed at; everyone who passes by it will be horrified and will hiss because of all its disasters. 9And I will make them eat the flesh of their sons and the flesh of their daughters, and all shall eat the flesh of their neighbors in the siege, and in the distress with which their enemies and those who seek their life afflict them.

10 Then you shall break the jug in the sight of those who go with you, 11and shall say to them: Thus says the Lord of hosts: So will I break this people and this city, as one breaks a potter's vessel, so that it can never be mended. In Topheth they shall bury until there is no more room to bury. 12Thus will I do to this place, says the Lord, and to its inhabitants, making this city like Topheth. 13And the houses of

---

r Gk Syr Vg: Heb *they made them stumble*   s Heb *strike him with the tongue*   t Syr Tg Compare Gk: Heb lacks *take with you*

Jerusalem and the houses of the kings of Judah shall be defiled like the place of Topheth—all the houses upon whose roofs offerings have been made to the whole host of heaven, and libations have been poured out to other gods.

14 When Jeremiah came from Topheth, where the LORD had sent him to prophesy, he stood in the court of the LORD's house and said to all the people: 15Thus says the LORD of hosts, the God of Israel: I am now bringing upon this city and upon all its towns all the disaster that I have pronounced against it, because they have stiffened their necks, refusing to hear my words.

Jeremiah Persecuted by Pashhur

20 Now the priest Pashhur son of Immer, who was chief officer in the house of the LORD, heard Jeremiah prophesying these things. 2Then Pashhur struck the prophet Jeremiah, and put him in the stocks that were in the upper Benjamin Gate of the house of the LORD. 3The next morning when Pashhur released Jeremiah from the stocks, Jeremiah said to him, The LORD has named you not Pashhur but "Terror-all-around." 4For thus says the LORD: I am making you a terror to yourself and to all your friends; and they shall fall by the sword of their enemies while you look on. And I will give all Judah into the hand of the king of Babylon; he shall carry them captive to Babylon, and shall kill them with the sword. 5I will give all the wealth of this city, all its gains, all its prized belongings, and all the treasures of the kings of Judah into the hand of their enemies, who shall plunder them, and seize them, and carry them to Babylon. 6And you, Pashhur, and all who live in your house, shall go into captivity, and to Babylon you shall go; there you shall die, and there you shall be buried, you and all your friends, to whom you have prophesied falsely.

Jeremiah Denounces His Persecutors

7 O LORD, you have enticed me,
   and I was enticed;
you have overpowered me,
   and you have prevailed.
I have become a laughingstock all
   day long;
everyone mocks me.
8 For whenever I speak, I must
   cry out,

I must shout, "Violence and
   destruction!"
For the word of the LORD has
   become for me
a reproach and derision all
   day long.
9 If I say, "I will not mention him,
   or speak any more in his name,"
then within me there is something
   like a burning fire
shut up in my bones;
I am weary with holding it in,
   and I cannot.
10 For I hear many whispering:
   "Terror is all around!
Denounce him! Let us denounce
   him!"
   All my close friends
   are watching for me to stumble.
"Perhaps he can be enticed,
   and we can prevail against him,
   and take our revenge on him."
11 But the LORD is with me like a dread
   warrior;
   therefore my persecutors will
   stumble,
   and they will not prevail.
They will be greatly shamed,
   for they will not succeed.
Their eternal dishonor
   will never be forgotten.
12 O LORD of hosts, you test the
   righteous,
   you see the heart and the mind;
let me see your retribution
   upon them,
   for to you I have committed
   my cause.

13 Sing to the LORD;
   praise the LORD!
For he has delivered the life of
   the needy
   from the hands of evildoers.

14 Cursed be the day
   on which I was born!
The day when my mother bore me,
   let it not be blessed!
15 Cursed be the man
   who brought the news to my
   father, saying,
"A child is born to you, a son,"
   making him very glad.
16 Let that man be like the cities
   that the LORD overthrew
   without pity;
let him hear a cry in the morning

and an alarm at noon,

17 because he did not kill me in
    the womb;
so my mother would have been
    my grave,
and her womb forever great.
18 Why did I come forth from
    the womb
    to see toil and sorrow,
and spend my days in shame?

Jerusalem Will Fall to Nebuchadrezzar

21 This is the word that came to Jeremiah from the LORD, when King Zedekiah sent to him Pashhur son of Malchiah and the priest Zephaniah son of Maaseiah, saying, 2"Please inquire of the LORD on our behalf, for King Nebuchadrezzar of Babylon is making war against us; perhaps the LORD will perform a won-

Having It Out With God

A few months after this loss of my grandmother, I had my first major fight with God. During one of the many hours I spent alone in my room daydreaming, reading, just missing her, I began voicing a vague promise to live my life in tune with the forming power on which "Nunny" based her faith. What I was not prepared to accept were the demands such an assent might mean. Though I played it cool with the other girls in the eighth grade, I knew inside that I was different, if nothing else, more reflective—a tendency I strove mightily to hide. So I giggled, even if I did not find the boys' jokes particularly funny. I confessed to the girls' room crowd my first crush on E., an acknowledged "totally cool" guy, who wore a black leather jacket and once walked me home from school.

On the surface I was pretty popular, but inside I knew I was being prompted to another level of awareness. But of what? Of whom? I wondered if others my age ever thought as much about things like life and death as I did.

One day I decided to have it out with God. I vented my anger and confusion. I wanted God to answer the great questions or to leave me alone. I wanted out of the pact I had made at the time of grandmother's death, the promise to be faithful—whatever that might mean. I was suffering from a feeling of inner solitude, pretending to conform to peer notions of fun when I really felt fragmented. I was conscious of being beckoned to I knew not where, and I was afraid.

I remember walking to the end of our yard and begging God to leave me alone, to let me be like everyone else. I did not want to take the road less traveled or dance to a different drummer. When the venting ceased, I felt drained of emotion but strangely at peace. It was as if God had confirmed my feelings by allowing me to be exactly who and where I was.

—SUSAN MUTO

Scripture Reading
for Today:
Jeremiah 20.7–13

Verse for Today:
Jeremiah 20.7

Go to page 1045 for your next devotional reading.

derful deed for us, as he has often done, and will make him withdraw from us."

3 Then Jeremiah said to them: ⁴Thus you shall say to Zedekiah: Thus says the LORD, the God of Israel: I am going to turn back the weapons of war that are in your hands and with which you are fighting against the king of Babylon and against the Chaldeans who are besieging you outside the walls; and I will bring them together into the center of this city. ⁵I myself will fight against you with outstretched hand and mighty arm, in anger, in fury, and in great wrath. ⁶And I will strike down the inhabitants of this city, both human beings and animals; they shall die of a great pestilence. ⁷Afterward, says the LORD, I will give King Zedekiah of Judah, and his servants, and the people in this city—those who survive the pestilence, sword, and famine—into the hands of King Nebuchadrezzar of Babylon, into the hands of their enemies, into the hands of those who seek their lives. He shall strike them down with the edge of the sword; he shall not pity them, or spare them, or have compassion.

8 And to this people you shall say: Thus says the LORD: See, I am setting before you the way of life and the way of death. ⁹Those who stay in this city shall die by the sword, by famine, and by pestilence; but those who go out and surrender to the Chaldeans who are besieging you shall live and shall have their lives as a prize of war. ¹⁰For I have set my face against this city for evil and not for good, says the LORD: it shall be given into the hands of the king of Babylon, and he shall burn it with fire.

Message to the House of David

11 To the house of the king of Judah say: Hear the word of the LORD, ¹²O house of David! Thus says the LORD:

Execute justice in the morning,
    and deliver from the hand of the
        oppressor
    anyone who has been robbed,
or else my wrath will go forth
        like fire,
    and burn, with no one to
        quench it,
    because of your evil doings.

¹³ See, I am against you, O inhabitant
    of the valley,

O rock of the plain,
                                    says the LORD;
you who say, "Who can come down
        against us,
    or who can enter our places
        of refuge?"
¹⁴ I will punish you according to the
        fruit of your doings,
                                    says the LORD;
    I will kindle a fire in its forest,
    and it shall devour all that is
        around it.

Exhortation to Repent

22 Thus says the LORD: Go down to the house of the king of Judah, and speak there this word, ²and say: Hear the word of the LORD, O King of Judah sitting on the throne of David—you, and your servants, and your people who enter these gates. ³Thus says the LORD: Act with justice and righteousness, and deliver from the hand of the oppressor anyone who has been robbed. And do no wrong or violence to the alien, the orphan, and the widow, or shed innocent blood in this place. ⁴For if you will indeed obey this word, then through the gates of this house shall enter kings who sit on the throne of David, riding in chariots and on horses, they, and their servants, and their people. ⁵But if you will not heed these words, I swear by myself, says the LORD, that this house shall become a desolation. ⁶For thus says the LORD concerning the house of the king of Judah:

You are like Gilead to me,
    like the summit of Lebanon;
but I swear that I will make you
        a desert,
    an uninhabited city.ᵘ
⁷ I will prepare destroyers against you,
    all with their weapons;
they shall cut down your choicest
        cedars
    and cast them into the fire.

8 And many nations will pass by this city, and all of them will say one to another, "Why has the LORD dealt in this way with that great city?" ⁹And they will answer, "Because they abandoned the covenant of the LORD their God, and worshiped other gods and served them."

¹⁰ Do not weep for him who is dead,
    nor bemoan him;

─────────────
ᵘ Cn: Heb *uninhabited cities*

weep rather for him who goes away,
  for he shall return no more
  to see his native land.

Message to the Sons of Josiah

11 For thus says the LORD concerning Shallum son of King Josiah of Judah, who succeeded his father Josiah, and who went away from this place: He shall return here no more, 12but in the place where they have carried him captive he shall die, and he shall never see this land again.

13 Woe to him who builds his house
      by unrighteousness,
    and his upper rooms by injustice;
  who makes his neighbors work for
      nothing,
    and does not give them their
      wages;
14 who says, "I will build myself a
      spacious house
    with large upper rooms,"
  and who cuts out windows for it,
    paneling it with cedar,
    and painting it with vermilion.
15 Are you a king
    because you compete in cedar?
  Did not your father eat and drink
    and do justice and righteousness?
    Then it was well with him.
16 He judged the cause of the poor
      and needy;
    then it was well.
  Is not this to know me?
    says the LORD.
17 But your eyes and heart
    are only on your dishonest gain,
  for shedding innocent blood,
    and for practicing oppression and
      violence.
18 Therefore thus says the LORD concerning King Jehoiakim son of Josiah of Judah:
  They shall not lament for him,
      saying,
    "Alas, my brother!" or "Alas,
      sister!"
  They shall not lament for him,
      saying,
    "Alas, lord!" or "Alas, his majesty!"
19 With the burial of a donkey he shall
      be buried—
    dragged off and thrown out
      beyond the gates of
      Jerusalem.

20 Go up to Lebanon, and cry out,

and lift up your voice in Bashan;
  cry out from Abarim,
    for all your lovers are crushed.
21 I spoke to you in your prosperity,
    but you said, "I will not listen."
  This has been your way from
      your youth,
    for you have not obeyed
      my voice.
22 The wind shall shepherd all your
      shepherds,
    and your lovers shall go into
      captivity;
  then you will be ashamed and
      dismayed
    because of all your wickedness.
23 O inhabitant of Lebanon,
    nested among the cedars,
  how you will groan*v* when pangs
      come upon you,
    pain as of a woman in labor!

Judgment on Coniah (Jehoiachin)

24 As I live, says the LORD, even if King Coniah son of Jehoiakim of Judah were the signet ring on my right hand, even from there I would tear you off 25and give you into the hands of those who seek your life, into the hands of those of whom you are afraid, even into the hands of King Nebuchadrezzar of Babylon and into the hands of the Chaldeans. 26I will hurl you and the mother who bore you into another country, where you were not born, and there you shall die. 27But they shall not return to the land to which they long to return.
28 Is this man Coniah a despised
      broken pot,
    a vessel no one wants?
  Why are he and his offspring hurled
      out
    and cast away in a land that they
      do not know?
29 O land, land, land,
    hear the word of the LORD!
30 Thus says the LORD:
  Record this man as childless,
    a man who shall not succeed in
      his days;
  for none of his offspring shall
      succeed
    in sitting on the throne of David,
    and ruling again in Judah.

---

v Gk Vg Syr: Heb *will be pitied*

Restoration after Exile

23 Woe to the shepherds who destroy and scatter the sheep of my pasture! says the LORD. ²Therefore thus says the LORD, the God of Israel, concerning the shepherds who shepherd my people: It is you who have scattered my flock, and have driven them away, and you have not attended to them. So I will attend to you for your evil doings, says the LORD. ³Then I myself will gather the remnant of my flock out of all the lands where I have driven them, and I will bring them back to their fold, and they shall be fruitful and multiply. ⁴I will raise up shepherds over them who will shepherd them, and they shall not fear any longer, or be dismayed, nor shall any be missing, says the LORD.

The Righteous Branch of David

5 The days are surely coming, says the LORD, when I will raise up for David a righteous Branch, and he shall reign as king and deal wisely, and shall execute justice and righteousness in the land. ⁶In his days Judah will be saved and Israel will live in safety. And this is the name by which he will be called: "The LORD is our righteousness."

7 Therefore, the days are surely coming, says the LORD, when it shall no longer be said, "As the LORD lives who brought the people of Israel up out of the land of Egypt," ⁸but "As the LORD lives who brought out and led the offspring of the house of Israel out of the land of the north and out of all the lands where he*ʷ* had driven them." Then they shall live in their own land.

False Prophets of Hope Denounced

9 Concerning the prophets:
My heart is crushed within me,
    all my bones shake;
I have become like a drunkard,
    like one overcome by wine,
because of the LORD
    and because of his holy words.
¹⁰ For the land is full of adulterers;
    because of the curse the land
      mourns,
    and the pastures of the wilderness
      are dried up.
Their course has been evil,
    and their might is not right.
¹¹ Both prophet and priest are ungodly;

even in my house I have found
    their wickedness,
               says the LORD.
¹² Therefore their way shall be to them
    like slippery paths in the darkness,
    into which they shall be driven
      and fall;
for I will bring disaster upon them
    in the year of their punishment,
               says the LORD.
¹³ In the prophets of Samaria
    I saw a disgusting thing:
they prophesied by Baal
    and led my people Israel astray.
¹⁴ But in the prophets of Jerusalem
    I have seen a more shocking
      thing:
they commit adultery and walk
    in lies;
    they strengthen the hands of
      evildoers,
so that no one turns from
    wickedness;
all of them have become like Sodom
    to me,
    and its inhabitants like Gomorrah.
¹⁵ Therefore thus says the LORD of hosts
    concerning the prophets:
"I am going to make them eat
    wormwood,
    and give them poisoned water
      to drink;
for from the prophets of Jerusalem
    ungodliness has spread
      throughout the land."

16 Thus says the LORD of hosts: Do not listen to the words of the prophets who prophesy to you; they are deluding you. They speak visions of their own minds, not from the mouth of the LORD. ¹⁷They keep saying to those who despise the word of the LORD, "It shall be well with you"; and to all who stubbornly follow their own stubborn hearts, they say, "No calamity shall come upon you."

¹⁸ For who has stood in the council of
    the LORD
    so as to see and to hear his word?
    Who has given heed to his word
      so as to proclaim it?
¹⁹ Look, the storm of the LORD!
    Wrath has gone forth,
    a whirling tempest;

w Gk: Heb *I*

it will burst upon the head of
the wicked.
20 The anger of the LORD will not
turn back
until he has executed and
accomplished
the intents of his mind.
In the latter days you will
understand it clearly.

21 I did not send the prophets,
yet they ran;
I did not speak to them,
yet they prophesied.
22 But if they had stood in my council,
then they would have proclaimed
my words to my people,
and they would have turned them
from their evil way,
and from the evil of their doings.

23 Am I a God near by, says the LORD,
and not a God far off? 24Who can hide in
secret places so that I cannot see them?
says the LORD. Do I not fill heaven and
earth? says the LORD. 25I have heard what
the prophets have said who prophesy lies
in my name, saying, "I have dreamed, I
have dreamed!" 26How long? Will the
hearts of the prophets ever turn back—
those who prophesy lies, and who prophesy the deceit of their own heart? 27They
plan to make my people forget my name
by their dreams that they tell one another,
just as their ancestors forgot my name for
Baal. 28Let the prophet who has a dream
tell the dream, but let the one who has my
word speak my word faithfully. What has
straw in common with wheat? says the
LORD. 29Is not my word like fire, says the
LORD, and like a hammer that breaks a
rock in pieces? 30See, therefore, I am
against the prophets, says the LORD, who
steal my words from one another. 31See, I
am against the prophets, says the LORD,
who use their own tongues and say, "Says
the LORD." 32See, I am against those who
prophesy lying dreams, says the LORD, and
who tell them, and who lead my people
astray by their lies and their recklessness,
when I did not send them or appoint
them; so they do not profit this people at
all, says the LORD.

33 When this people, or a prophet, or a
priest asks you, "What is the burden of
the LORD?" you shall say to them, "You are
the burden,^{x} and I will cast you off, says
the LORD." 34And as for the prophet, priest,

or the people who say, "The burden of the
LORD," I will punish them and their households. 35Thus shall you say to one another, among yourselves, "What has the LORD
answered?" or "What has the LORD spoken?"
36But "the burden of the LORD" you shall
mention no more, for the burden is everyone's own word, and so you pervert the
words of the living God, the LORD of hosts,
our God. 37Thus you shall ask the prophet, "What has the LORD answered you?" or
"What has the LORD spoken?" 38But if you
say, "the burden of the LORD," thus says the
LORD: Because you have said these words,
"the burden of the LORD," when I sent to
you, saying, You shall not say, "the burden of the LORD," 39therefore, I will surely
lift you up^y and cast you away from my
presence, you and the city that I gave to
you and your ancestors. 40And I will bring
upon you everlasting disgrace and perpetual shame, which shall not be forgotten.

The Good and the Bad Figs

24 The LORD showed me two baskets
of figs placed before the temple of
the LORD. This was after King Nebuchadrezzar of Babylon had taken into exile
from Jerusalem King Jeconiah son of Jehoiakim of Judah, together with the officials of Judah, the artisans, and the
smiths, and had brought them to Babylon. 2One basket had very good figs, like
first-ripe figs, but the other basket had
very bad figs, so bad that they could not
be eaten. 3And the LORD said to me, "What
do you see, Jeremiah?" I said, "Figs, the
good figs very good, and the bad figs very
bad, so bad that they cannot be eaten."

4 Then the word of the LORD came to
me: 5Thus says the LORD, the God of Israel:
Like these good figs, so I will regard as
good the exiles from Judah, whom I have
sent away from this place to the land of
the Chaldeans. 6I will set my eyes upon
them for good, and I will bring them back
to this land. I will build them up, and not
tear them down; I will plant them, and
not pluck them up. 7I will give them a
heart to know that I am the LORD; and they
shall be my people and I will be their
God, for they shall return to me with their
whole heart.

8 But thus says the LORD: Like the bad
figs that are so bad they cannot be eaten,

---

x Gk Vg: Heb *What burden* y Heb Mss Gk Vg:
MT *forget you*

so will I treat King Zedekiah of Judah, his officials, the remnant of Jerusalem who remain in this land, and those who live in the land of Egypt. ⁹I will make them a horror, an evil thing, to all the kingdoms of the earth—a disgrace, a byword, a taunt, and a curse in all the places where I shall drive them. ¹⁰And I will send sword, famine, and pestilence upon them, until they are utterly destroyed from the land that I gave to them and their ancestors.

The Babylonian Captivity Foretold

25 The word that came to Jeremiah concerning all the people of Judah, in the fourth year of King Jehoiakim son of Josiah of Judah (that was the first year of King Nebuchadrezzar of Babylon), ²which the prophet Jeremiah spoke to all the people of Judah and all the inhabitants of Jerusalem: ³For twenty-three years, from the thirteenth year of King Josiah son of Amon of Judah, to this day, the word of the LORD has come to me, and I have spoken persistently to you, but you have not listened. ⁴And though the LORD persistently sent you all his servants the prophets, you have neither listened nor inclined your ears to hear ⁵when they said, "Turn now, everyone of you, from your evil way and wicked doings, and you will remain upon the land that the LORD has given to you and your ancestors from of old and forever; ⁶do not go after other gods to serve and worship them, and do not provoke me to anger with the work of your hands. Then I will do you no harm." ⁷Yet you did not listen to me, says the LORD, and so you have provoked me to anger with the work of your hands to your own harm.

8 Therefore thus says the LORD of hosts: Because you have not obeyed my words, ⁹I am going to send for all the tribes of the north, says the LORD, even for King Nebuchadrezzar of Babylon, my servant, and I will bring them against this land and its inhabitants, and against all these nations around; I will utterly destroy them, and make them an object of horror and of hissing, and an everlasting disgrace.ᶻ ¹⁰And I will banish from them the sound of mirth and the sound of gladness, the voice of the bridegroom and the voice of the bride, the sound of the millstones and the light of the lamp. ¹¹This whole land shall become a ruin and a waste, and these nations shall serve the king of Babylon seventy years. ¹²Then after seventy years are completed, I will punish the king of Babylon and that nation, the land of the Chaldeans, for their iniquity, says the LORD, making the land an everlasting waste. ¹³I will bring upon that land all the words that I have uttered against it, everything written in this book, which Jeremiah prophesied against all the nations. ¹⁴For many nations and great kings shall make slaves of them also; and I will repay them according to their deeds and the work of their hands.

The Cup of God's Wrath

15 For thus the LORD, the God of Israel, said to me: Take from my hand this cup of the wine of wrath, and make all the nations to whom I send you drink it. ¹⁶They shall drink and stagger and go out of their minds because of the sword that I am sending among them.

17 So I took the cup from the LORD's hand, and made all the nations to whom the LORD sent me drink it: ¹⁸Jerusalem and the towns of Judah, its kings and officials, to make them a desolation and a waste, an object of hissing and of cursing, as they are today; ¹⁹Pharaoh king of Egypt, his servants, his officials, and all his people; ²⁰all the mixed people;ᵃ all the kings of the land of Uz; all the kings of the land of the Philistines—Ashkelon, Gaza, Ekron, and the remnant of Ashdod; ²¹Edom, Moab, and the Ammonites; ²²all the kings of Tyre, all the kings of Sidon, and the kings of the coastland across the sea; ²³Dedan, Tema, Buz, and all who have shaven temples; ²⁴all the kings of Arabia and all the kings of the mixed peoplesᵃ that live in the desert; ²⁵all the kings of Zimri, all the kings of Elam, and all the kings of Media; ²⁶all the kings of the north, far and near, one after another, and all the kingdoms of the world that are on the face of the earth. And after them the king of Sheshachᵇ shall drink.

27 Then you shall say to them, Thus says the LORD of hosts, the God of Israel: Drink, get drunk and vomit, fall and rise no more, because of the sword that I am sending among you.

28 And if they refuse to accept the cup

ᶻ Gk Compare Syr: Heb *and everlasting desolations* ᵃ Meaning of Heb uncertain   ᵇ *Sheshach* is a cryptogram for *Babel*, Babylon

from your hand to drink, then you shall say to them: Thus says the LORD of hosts: You must drink! 29See, I am beginning to bring disaster on the city that is called by my name, and how can you possibly avoid punishment? You shall not go unpunished, for I am summoning a sword against all the inhabitants of the earth, says the LORD of hosts.

30 You, therefore, shall prophesy against them all these words, and say to them:

The LORD will roar from on high,
   and from his holy habitation utter
    his voice;
he will roar mightily against
   his fold,
  and shout, like those who tread
    grapes,
  against all the inhabitants of
    the earth.
31 The clamor will resound to the ends
   of the earth,
  for the LORD has an indictment
    against the nations;
  he is entering into judgment with all
    flesh,
  and the guilty he will put to
    the sword,
              says the LORD.

32 Thus says the LORD of hosts:
  See, disaster is spreading
   from nation to nation,
  and a great tempest is stirring
   from the farthest parts of
    the earth!
33 Those slain by the LORD on that day shall extend from one end of the earth to the other. They shall not be lamented, or gathered, or buried; they shall become dung on the surface of the ground.
34 Wail, you shepherds, and cry out;
  roll in ashes, you lords of
   the flock,
  for the days of your slaughter have
   come—and your
    dispersions,*c*
  and you shall fall like a
   choice vessel.
35 Flight shall fail the shepherds,
  and there shall be no escape for
   the lords of the flock.
36 Hark! the cry of the shepherds,
  and the wail of the lords of
   the flock!
For the LORD is despoiling their
   pasture,

37 and the peaceful folds are
   devastated,
  because of the fierce anger of
   the LORD.
38 Like a lion he has left his covert;
   for their land has become a waste
  because of the cruel sword,
   and because of his fierce anger.

Jeremiah's Prophecies in the Temple

26 At the beginning of the reign of King Jehoiakim son of Josiah of Judah, this word came from the LORD: 2Thus says the LORD: Stand in the court of the LORD's house, and speak to all the cities of Judah that come to worship in the house of the LORD; speak to them all the words that I command you; do not hold back a word. 3It may be that they will listen, all of them, and will turn from their evil way, that I may change my mind about the disaster that I intend to bring on them because of their evil doings. 4You shall say to them: Thus says the LORD: If you will not listen to me, to walk in my law that I have set before you, 5and to heed the words of my servants the prophets whom I send to you urgently—though you have not heeded— 6then I will make this house like Shiloh, and I will make this city a curse for all the nations of the earth.

7 The priests and the prophets and all the people heard Jeremiah speaking these words in the house of the LORD. 8And when Jeremiah had finished speaking all that the LORD had commanded him to speak to all the people, then the priests and the prophets and all the people laid hold of him, saying, "You shall die! 9Why have you prophesied in the name of the LORD, saying, 'This house shall be like Shiloh, and this city shall be desolate, without inhabitant'?" And all the people gathered around Jeremiah in the house of the LORD.

10 When the officials of Judah heard these things, they came up from the king's house to the house of the LORD and took their seat in the entry of the New Gate of the house of the LORD. 11Then the priests and the prophets said to the officials and to all the people, "This man deserves the sentence of death because he has prophesied against this city, as you have heard with your own ears."

c Meaning of Heb uncertain

12 Then Jeremiah spoke to all the officials and all the people, saying, "It is the LORD who sent me to prophesy against this house and this city all the words you have heard. 13Now therefore amend your ways and your doings, and obey the voice of the LORD your God, and the LORD will change his mind about the disaster that he has pronounced against you. 14But as for me, here I am in your hands. Do with me as seems good and right to you. 15Only know for certain that if you put me to death, you will be bringing innocent blood upon yourselves and upon this city and its inhabitants, for in truth the LORD sent me to you to speak all these words in your ears."

16 Then the officials and all the people said to the priests and the prophets, "This man does not deserve the sentence of death, for he has spoken to us in the name of the LORD our God." 17And some of the elders of the land arose and said to all the assembled people, 18"Micah of Moresheth, who prophesied during the days of King Hezekiah of Judah, said to all the people of Judah: 'Thus says the LORD of hosts,

Zion shall be plowed as a field;
Jerusalem shall become a heap
of ruins,
and the mountain of the house a
wooded height.'

19Did King Hezekiah of Judah and all Judah actually put him to death? Did he not fear the LORD and entreat the favor of the LORD, and did not the LORD change his mind about the disaster that he had pronounced against them? But we are about to bring great disaster on ourselves!"

20 There was another man prophesying in the name of the LORD, Uriah son of Shemaiah from Kiriath-jearim. He prophesied against this city and against this land in words exactly like those of Jeremiah. 21And when King Jehoiakim, with all his warriors and all the officials, heard his words, the king sought to put him to death; but when Uriah heard of it, he was afraid and fled and escaped to Egypt. 22Then King Jehoiakim sent*d* Elnathan son of Achbor and men with him to Egypt, 23and they took Uriah from Egypt and brought him to King Jehoiakim, who struck him down with the sword and threw his dead body into the burial place of the common people.

24 But the hand of Ahikam son of Shaphan was with Jeremiah so that he was not given over into the hands of the people to be put to death.

The Sign of the Yoke

27 In the beginning of the reign of King Zedekiah*e* son of Josiah of Judah, this word came to Jeremiah from the LORD. 2Thus the LORD said to me: Make yourself a yoke of straps and bars, and put them on your neck. 3Send word*f* to the king of Edom, the king of Moab, the king of the Ammonites, the king of Tyre, and the king of Sidon by the hand of the envoys who have come to Jerusalem to King Zedekiah of Judah. 4Give them this charge for their masters: Thus says the LORD of hosts, the God of Israel: This is what you shall say to your masters: 5It is I who by my great power and my outstretched arm have made the earth, with the people and animals that are on the earth, and I give it to whomever I please. 6Now I have given all these lands into the hand of King Nebuchadnezzar of Babylon, my servant, and I have given him even the wild animals of the field to serve him. 7All the nations shall serve him and his son and his grandson, until the time of his own land comes; then many nations and great kings shall make him their slave.

8 But if any nation or kingdom will not serve this king, Nebuchadnezzar of Babylon, and put its neck under the yoke of the king of Babylon, then I will punish that nation with the sword, with famine, and with pestilence, says the LORD, until I have completed its*g* destruction by his hand. 9You, therefore, must not listen to your prophets, your diviners, your dreamers,*h* your soothsayers, or your sorcerers, who are saying to you, "You shall not serve the king of Babylon." 10For they are prophesying a lie to you, with the result that you will be removed far from your land; I will drive you out, and you will perish. 11But any nation that will bring its neck under the yoke of the king of Babylon and serve him, I will leave on its own land, says the LORD, to till it and live there.

12 I spoke to King Zedekiah of Judah in the same way: Bring your necks under the yoke of the king of Babylon, and serve him and his people, and live. 13Why

d Heb adds *men to Egypt*   *e* Another reading is *Jehoiakim*   *f* Cn: Heb *send them*   *g* Heb *their*   *h* Gk Syr Vg: Heb *dreams*

should you and your people die by the
sword, by famine, and by pestilence, as
the Lord has spoken concerning any nation that will not serve the king of Babylon? 14Do not listen to the words of the
prophets who are telling you not to serve
the king of Babylon, for they are prophesying a lie to you. 15I have not sent them,
says the Lord, but they are prophesying
falsely in my name, with the result that I
will drive you out and you will perish, you
and the prophets who are prophesying to
you.

16 Then I spoke to the priests and to all
this people, saying, Thus says the Lord: Do
not listen to the words of your prophets
who are prophesying to you, saying, "The
vessels of the Lord's house will soon be
brought back from Babylon," for they are
prophesying a lie to you. 17Do not listen
to them; serve the king of Babylon and
live. Why should this city become a desolation? 18If indeed they are prophets, and
if the word of the Lord is with them, then
let them intercede with the Lord of hosts,
that the vessels left in the house of the
Lord, in the house of the king of Judah,
and in Jerusalem may not go to Babylon.
19For thus says the Lord of hosts concerning the pillars, the sea, the stands, and the
rest of the vessels that are left in this city,
20which King Nebuchadnezzar of Babylon
did not take away when he took into exile
from Jerusalem to Babylon King Jeconiah
son of Jehoiakim of Judah, and all the
nobles of Judah and Jerusalem— 21thus
says the Lord of hosts, the God of Israel,
concerning the vessels left in the house of
the Lord, in the house of the king of Judah, and in Jerusalem: 22They shall be carried to Babylon, and there they shall stay,
until the day when I give attention to
them, says the Lord. Then I will bring
them up and restore them to this place.

Hananiah Opposes Jeremiah and Dies

28 In that same year, at the beginning of the reign of King Zedekiah of Judah, in the fifth month of the
fourth year, the prophet Hananiah son of
Azzur, from Gibeon, spoke to me in the
house of the Lord, in the presence of the
priests and all the people, saying, 2"Thus
says the Lord of hosts, the God of Israel: I
have broken the yoke of the king of Babylon. 3Within two years I will bring back
to this place all the vessels of the Lord's
house, which King Nebuchadnezzar of

Babylon took away from this place and
carried to Babylon. 4I will also bring back
to this place King Jeconiah son of Jehoiakim of Judah, and all the exiles from Judah who went to Babylon, says the Lord,
for I will break the yoke of the king of
Babylon."

5 Then the prophet Jeremiah spoke to
the prophet Hananiah in the presence of
the priests and all the people who were
standing in the house of the Lord; 6and
the prophet Jeremiah said, "Amen! May
the Lord do so; may the Lord fulfill the
words that you have prophesied, and
bring back to this place from Babylon the
vessels of the house of the Lord, and all
the exiles. 7But listen now to this word
that I speak in your hearing and in the
hearing of all the people. 8The prophets
who preceded you and me from ancient
times prophesied war, famine, and pestilence against many countries and great
kingdoms. 9As for the prophet who
prophesies peace, when the word of that
prophet comes true, then it will be known
that the Lord has truly sent the prophet."

10 Then the prophet Hananiah took
the yoke from the neck of the prophet
Jeremiah, and broke it. 11And Hananiah
spoke in the presence of all the people,
saying, "Thus says the Lord: This is how I
will break the yoke of King Nebuchadnezzar of Babylon from the neck of all the
nations within two years." At this, the
prophet Jeremiah went his way.

12 Sometime after the prophet Hananiah had broken the yoke from the neck
of the prophet Jeremiah, the word of the
Lord came to Jeremiah: 13Go, tell Hananiah, Thus says the Lord: You have broken
wooden bars only to forge iron bars in
place of them! 14For thus says the Lord of
hosts, the God of Israel: I have put an iron
yoke on the neck of all these nations so
that they may serve King Nebuchadnezzar
of Babylon, and they shall indeed serve
him; I have even given him the wild animals. 15And the prophet Jeremiah said to
the prophet Hananiah, "Listen, Hananiah, the Lord has not sent you, and you
made this people trust in a lie. 16Therefore
thus says the Lord: I am going to send you
off the face of the earth. Within this year
you will be dead, because you have spoken rebellion against the Lord."

17 In that same year, in the seventh
month, the prophet Hananiah died.

Jeremiah's Letter to the Exiles in Babylon

29 These are the words of the letter that the prophet Jeremiah sent from Jerusalem to the remaining elders among the exiles, and to the priests, the prophets, and all the people, whom Nebuchadnezzar had taken into exile from Jerusalem to Babylon. ²This was after King Jeconiah, and the queen mother, the court officials, the leaders of Judah and Jerusalem, the artisans, and the smiths had departed from Jerusalem. ³The letter was sent by the hand of Elasah son of Shaphan and Gemariah son of Hilkiah, whom King Zedekiah of Judah sent to Babylon to King Nebuchadnezzar of Babylon. It said: ⁴Thus says the LORD of hosts, the God of Israel, to all the exiles whom I have sent into exile from Jerusalem to Babylon: ⁵Build houses and live in them; plant gardens and eat what they produce. ⁶Take wives and have sons and daughters; take wives for your sons, and give your daughters in marriage, that they may bear sons and daughters; multiply there, and do not decrease. ⁷But seek the welfare of the city where I have sent you into exile, and pray to the LORD on its behalf, for in its welfare you will find your welfare. ⁸For thus says the LORD of hosts, the God of Israel: Do not let the prophets and the diviners who are among you deceive you, and do not listen to the dreams that they dream,ⁱ ⁹for it is a lie that they are prophesying to you in my name; I did not send them, says the LORD.

10 For thus says the LORD: Only when Babylon's seventy years are completed will I visit you, and I will fulfill to you my promise and bring you back to this place. ¹¹For surely I know the plans I have for you, says the LORD, plans for your welfare and not for harm, to give you a future with hope. ¹²Then when you call upon me and come and pray to me, I will hear you. ¹³When you search for me, you will find me; if you seek me with all your heart, ¹⁴I will let you find me, says the LORD, and I will restore your fortunes and gather you from all the nations and all the places where I have driven you, says the LORD,

ⁱ Cn: Heb *your dreams that you cause to dream*

With All Your Heart

THURSDAY

Scripture Reading for Today:
Jeremiah 29.10–14

Verses for Today:
Jeremiah 29.13–14

Once there was a teacher who took a seeker to a river and held him underwater until he nearly drowned. As the seeker came up gasping, the teacher said, "When you want God as much as you wanted air, he will surely come to you."

The prophet Jeremiah had a similar experience. After years of obedient response to his prophetic call, he begged God for fulfillment of his own being and that of his people. God said, "If you seek me with all your heart, I will let you find me." Seeking God is not a casual matter. Seeking God is a wholehearted affair, or it brings no results.

Still, persistence is not aimed to persuade God. He needs no persuading. We are urged to persist because of the effect persistence has in ourselves. If we persevere in wanting God, we will want him more. If we persist in our practice of the way Jesus taught us to live, we will become stronger, more prepared to receive him and to keep him. If we keep asking for God's presence, we will open a place for him within ourselves.

—*MARILYN GUSTIN*

Go to page 1050 for your next devotional reading.

and I will bring you back to the place from which I sent you into exile.

15 Because you have said, "The LORD has raised up prophets for us in Babylon,"— ¹⁶Thus says the LORD concerning the king who sits on the throne of David, and concerning all the people who live in this city, your kinsfolk who did not go out with you into exile: ¹⁷Thus says the LORD of hosts, I am going to let loose on them sword, famine, and pestilence, and I will make them like rotten figs that are so bad they cannot be eaten. ¹⁸I will pursue them with the sword, with famine, and with pestilence, and will make them a horror to all the kingdoms of the earth, to be an object of cursing, and horror, and hissing, and a derision among all the nations where I have driven them, ¹⁹because they did not heed my words, says the LORD, when I persistently sent to you my servants the prophets, but they[j] would not listen, says the LORD. ²⁰But now, all you exiles whom I sent away from Jerusalem to Babylon, hear the word of the LORD: ²¹Thus says the LORD of hosts, the God of Israel, concerning Ahab son of Kolaiah and Zedekiah son of Maaseiah, who are prophesying a lie to you in my name: I am going to deliver them into the hand of King Nebuchadrezzar of Babylon, and he shall kill them before your eyes. ²²And on account of them this curse shall be used by all the exiles from Judah in Babylon: "The LORD make you like Zedekiah and Ahab, whom the king of Babylon roasted in the fire," ²³because they have perpetrated outrage in Israel and have committed adultery with their neighbors' wives, and have spoken in my name lying words that I did not command them; I am the one who knows and bears witness, says the LORD.

The Letter of Shemaiah

24 To Shemaiah of Nehelam you shall say: ²⁵Thus says the LORD of hosts, the God of Israel: In your own name you sent a letter to all the people who are in Jerusalem, and to the priest Zephaniah son of Maaseiah, and to all the priests, saying, ²⁶The LORD himself has made you priest instead of the priest Jehoiada, so that there may be officers in the house of the LORD to control any madman who plays the prophet, to put him in the stocks and the collar. ²⁷So now why have you not rebuked Jeremiah of Anathoth who plays the prophet for you? ²⁸For he has actually sent to us in Babylon, saying, "It will be a long time; build houses and live in them, and plant gardens and eat what they produce."

29 The priest Zephaniah read this letter in the hearing of the prophet Jeremiah. ³⁰Then the word of the LORD came to Jeremiah: ³¹Send to all the exiles, saying, Thus says the LORD concerning Shemaiah of Nehelam: Because Shemaiah has prophesied to you, though I did not send him, and has led you to trust in a lie, ³²therefore thus says the LORD: I am going to punish Shemaiah of Nehelam and his descendants; he shall not have anyone living among this people to see[k] the good that I am going to do to my people, says the LORD, for he has spoken rebellion against the LORD.

Restoration Promised for Israel and Judah

30 The word that came to Jeremiah from the LORD: ²Thus says the LORD, the God of Israel: Write in a book all the words that I have spoken to you. ³For the days are surely coming, says the LORD, when I will restore the fortunes of my people, Israel and Judah, says the LORD, and I will bring them back to the land that I gave to their ancestors and they shall take possession of it.

4 These are the words that the LORD spoke concerning Israel and Judah:

5 Thus says the LORD:
We have heard a cry of panic,
   of terror, and no peace.
6 Ask now, and see,
   can a man bear a child?
Why then do I see every man
   with his hands on his loins like a
      woman in labor?
   Why has every face turned pale?
7 Alas! that day is so great
   there is none like it;
it is a time of distress for Jacob;
   yet he shall be rescued from it.

8 On that day, says the LORD of hosts, I will break the yoke from off his[l] neck, and I will burst his[l] bonds, and strangers shall no more make a servant of him. ⁹But they shall serve the LORD their God and David their king, whom I will raise up for them.

j Syr: Heb *you* k Gk: Heb *and he shall not see*
l Cn: Heb *your*

10 But as for you, have no fear, my
        servant Jacob, says the LORD,
    and do not be dismayed, O Israel;
for I am going to save you from
        far away,
    and your offspring from the land
        of their captivity.
Jacob shall return and have quiet
        and ease,
    and no one shall make him
        afraid.
11 For I am with you, says the LORD, to
        save you;
    I will make an end of all the nations
        among which I scattered you,
    but of you I will not make
        an end.
I will chastise you in just measure,
    and I will by no means leave you
        unpunished.

12 For thus says the LORD:
Your hurt is incurable,
    your wound is grievous.
13 There is no one to uphold your
        cause,
    no medicine for your wound,
    no healing for you.
14 All your lovers have forgotten you;
        they care nothing for you;
    for I have dealt you the blow of
        an enemy,
        the punishment of a merciless foe,
because your guilt is great,
        because your sins are so
        numerous.
15 Why do you cry out over your hurt?
    Your pain is incurable.
Because your guilt is great,
        because your sins are so
        numerous,
    I have done these things to you.
16 Therefore all who devour you shall
        be devoured,
    and all your foes, everyone of
        them, shall go into captivity;
those who plunder you shall be
        plundered,
    and all who prey on you I will
        make a prey.
17 For I will restore health to you,
    and your wounds I will heal,
                        says the LORD,
because they have called you
        an outcast:
    "It is Zion; no one cares for her!"

18 Thus says the LORD:

I am going to restore the fortunes of
        the tents of Jacob,
    and have compassion on his
        dwellings;
the city shall be rebuilt upon its
        mound,
    and the citadel set on its
        rightful site.
19 Out of them shall come
        thanksgiving,
    and the sound of merrymakers.
I will make them many, and they
        shall not be few;
    I will make them honored, and
        they shall not be disdained.
20 Their children shall be as of old,
    their congregation shall be
        established before me;
    and I will punish all who oppress
        them.
21 Their prince shall be one of
        their own,
    their ruler shall come from their
        midst;
I will bring him near, and he shall
        approach me,
    for who would otherwise dare to
        approach me?
                        says the LORD.
22 And you shall be my people,
    and I will be your God.

23 Look, the storm of the LORD!
    Wrath has gone forth,
a whirling[m] tempest;
    it will burst upon the head of
        the wicked.
24 The fierce anger of the LORD will not
        turn back
    until he has executed and
        accomplished
    the intents of his mind.
In the latter days you will
    understand this.

The Joyful Return of the Exiles

31 At that time, says the LORD, I will
        be the God of all the families of
Israel, and they shall be my people.
2 Thus says the LORD:
The people who survived the sword
    found grace in the wilderness;
when Israel sought for rest,
3   the LORD appeared to him[n] from
            far away.[o]

---

m One Ms: Meaning of MT uncertain
n Gk: Heb me   o Or to him long ago

I have loved you with an everlasting
love;
therefore I have continued my
faithfulness to you.
4 Again I will build you, and you shall
be built,
O virgin Israel!
Again you shall take*p* your
tambourines,
and go forth in the dance of the
merrymakers.
5 Again you shall plant vineyards
on the mountains of Samaria;
the planters shall plant,
and shall enjoy the fruit.
6 For there shall be a day when
sentinels will call
in the hill country of Ephraim:
"Come, let us go up to Zion,
to the LORD our God."

7 For thus says the LORD:
Sing aloud with gladness for Jacob,
and raise shouts for the chief of
the nations;
proclaim, give praise, and say,
"Save, O LORD, your people,
the remnant of Israel."
8 See, I am going to bring them from
the land of the north,
and gather them from the farthest
parts of the earth,
among them the blind and
the lame,
those with child and those in
labor, together;
a great company, they shall return
here.
9 With weeping they shall come,
and with consolations*q* I will
lead them back,
I will let them walk by brooks of
water,
in a straight path in which they
shall not stumble;
for I have become a father to Israel,
and Ephraim is my firstborn.

10 Hear the word of the LORD,
O nations,
and declare it in the coastlands far
away;
say, "He who scattered Israel will
gather him,
and will keep him as a shepherd a
flock."
11 For the LORD has ransomed Jacob,

and has redeemed him from
hands too strong for him.
12 They shall come and sing aloud on
the height of Zion,
and they shall be radiant over the
goodness of the LORD,
over the grain, the wine, and the oil,
and over the young of the flock
and the herd;
their life shall become like a watered
garden,
and they shall never languish
again.
13 Then shall the young women rejoice
in the dance,
and the young men and the old
shall be merry.
I will turn their mourning into joy,
I will comfort them, and give
them gladness for sorrow.
14 I will give the priests their fill of
fatness,
and my people shall be satisfied
with my bounty,
                                    says the LORD.

15 Thus says the LORD:
A voice is heard in Ramah,
lamentation and bitter weeping.
Rachel is weeping for her children;
she refuses to be comforted for
her children,
because they are no more.
16 Thus says the LORD:
Keep your voice from weeping,
and your eyes from tears;
for there is a reward for your work,
                                    says the LORD:
they shall come back from the
land of the enemy;
17 there is hope for your future,
                                    says the LORD:
your children shall come back to
their own country.

18 Indeed I heard Ephraim pleading:
"You disciplined me, and I took the
discipline;
I was like a calf untrained.
Bring me back, let me come back,
for you are the LORD my God.
19 For after I had turned away I
repented;
and after I was discovered, I struck
my thigh;

p Or *adorn yourself with*   *q* Gk Compare Vg Tg:
Heb *supplications*

I was ashamed, and I was dismayed
    because I bore the disgrace of my
    youth."
20 Is Ephraim my dear son?
    Is he the child I delight in?
As often as I speak against him,
    I still remember him.
Therefore I am deeply moved
    for him;
    I will surely have mercy on him,
                    says the LORD.

21 Set up road markers for yourself,
    make yourself signposts;
consider well the highway,
    the road by which you went.
Return, O virgin Israel,
    return to these your cities.
22 How long will you waver,
    O faithless daughter?
For the LORD has created a new thing
    on the earth:
    a woman encompasses*r* a man.

23 Thus says the LORD of hosts, the God
of Israel: Once more they shall use these
words in the land of Judah and in its
towns when I restore their fortunes:
    "The LORD bless you, O abode of
        righteousness,
    O holy hill!"
24And Judah and all its towns shall live
there together, and the farmers and those
who wander*s* with their flocks.
25 I will satisfy the weary,
    and all who are faint I will
        replenish.
26 Thereupon I awoke and looked, and
my sleep was pleasant to me.

Individual Retribution

27 The days are surely coming, says the
LORD, when I will sow the house of Israel
and the house of Judah with the seed of
humans and the seed of animals. 28And
just as I have watched over them to pluck
up and break down, to overthrow, destroy, and bring evil, so I will watch over
them to build and to plant, says the LORD.
29In those days they shall no longer say:
    "The parents have eaten sour grapes,
        and the children's teeth are set on
        edge."
30But all shall die for their own sins; the
teeth of everyone who eats sour grapes
shall be set on edge.

A New Covenant

31 The days are surely coming, says the
LORD, when I will make a new covenant
with the house of Israel and the house of
Judah. 32It will not be like the covenant
that I made with their ancestors when I
took them by the hand to bring them out
of the land of Egypt—a covenant that they
broke, though I was their husband,*t* says
the LORD. 33But this is the covenant that I
will make with the house of Israel after
those days, says the LORD: I will put my
law within them, and I will write it on
their hearts; and I will be their God, and
they shall be my people. 34No longer shall
they teach one another, or say to each
other, "Know the LORD," for they shall all
know me, from the least of them to the
greatest, says the LORD; for I will forgive
their iniquity, and remember their sin no
more.

35 Thus says the LORD,
    who gives the sun for light by day
        and the fixed order of the moon
            and the stars for light
            by night,
    who stirs up the sea so that its
            waves roar—
        the LORD of hosts is his name:
36 If this fixed order were ever to cease
        from my presence, says the LORD,
    then also the offspring of Israel
            would cease
        to be a nation before me forever.

37 Thus says the LORD:
If the heavens above can be
        measured,
    and the foundations of the earth
        below can be explored,
    then I will reject all the offspring
        of Israel
    because of all they have done,
                    says the LORD.

Jerusalem to Be Enlarged

38 The days are surely coming, says the
LORD, when the city shall be rebuilt for
the LORD from the tower of Hananel to the
Corner Gate. 39And the measuring line
shall go out farther, straight to the hill
Gareb, and shall then turn to Goah. 40The
whole valley of the dead bodies and the

r Meaning of Heb uncertain   *s* Cn Compare Syr
Vg Tg: Heb *and they shall wander*   *t* Or *master*

ashes, and all the fields as far as the Wadi Kidron, to the corner of the Horse Gate toward the east, shall be sacred to the LORD. It shall never again be uprooted or overthrown.

Jeremiah Buys a Field During the Siege

32 The word that came to Jeremiah from the LORD in the tenth year of King Zedekiah of Judah, which was the eighteenth year of Nebuchadrezzar. ²At that time the army of the king of Babylon was besieging Jerusalem, and the prophet Jeremiah was confined in the court of the guard that was in the palace of the king of Judah, ³where King Zedekiah of Judah had confined him. Zedekiah had said, "Why do you prophesy and say: Thus says the LORD: I am going to give this city into the hand of the king of Babylon, and he shall take it; ⁴King Zedekiah of Judah shall not escape out of the hands of the Chaldeans, but shall surely be given into the hands of the king of Babylon, and shall speak with him face to face and see him eye to eye; ⁵and he shall take Zedekiah to Babylon, and there he shall remain until I attend to him, says the LORD; though you fight against the Chaldeans, you shall not succeed?"

6 Jeremiah said, The word of the LORD came to me: ⁷Hanamel son of your uncle Shallum is going to come to you and say, "Buy my field that is at Anathoth, for the right of redemption by purchase is yours." ⁸Then my cousin Hanamel came to me in

FRIDAY

Scripture Reading for Today:
Jeremiah 31.31–34

Verses for Today:
Jeremiah 31.33–34

Give Me a Pure Love

O my God, let me walk in the way of love which knows not how to seek self in anything whatsoever. Let this love wholly possess my soul and heart, which, I beseech you, may live and move only in, and out of, a pure and sincere love to you. Oh! that your pure love were so grounded and established in my heart that I might sigh and pant without ceasing after you. O sight to be wished, desired, and longed for, because once to have seen you is to have learned all things!

Nothing can bring us to this sight but love. But what love must it be? Not a sensible love only, a childish love, a love which seeks itself more than the Beloved. No, it must be an ardent love, a pure love, a courageous love, a love of charity, a humble love, and a constant love, not worn out with labors, nor daunted with any difficulties.

O Lord, give this love into my soul, that I may never more live nor breathe but out of a most pure love of you, my All and only Good. Let me love you for yourself, and nothing else but in and for you. Let me love nothing instead of you, for to give all for love is a most sweet bargain. Let your love work in me and by me, and let me love you as you would be loved by me. I cannot tell how much love I would have of you, because I would love you beyond all that can be imagined or desired by me.

Be in this, as in all other things, my chooser for me, for you are my only choice, most dear to me. The more I shall love you, the more will my soul desire you, and desire to suffer for you.

—DAME GERTRUDE MORE

Go to page 1054 for your next devotional reading.

the court of the guard, in accordance with the word of the LORD, and said to me, "Buy my field that is at Anathoth in the land of Benjamin, for the right of possession and redemption is yours; buy it for yourself." Then I knew that this was the word of the LORD.

9 And I bought the field at Anathoth from my cousin Hanamel, and weighed out the money to him, seventeen shekels of silver. 10I signed the deed, sealed it, got witnesses, and weighed the money on scales. 11Then I took the sealed deed of purchase, containing the terms and conditions, and the open copy; 12and I gave the deed of purchase to Baruch son of Neriah son of Mahseiah, in the presence of my cousin Hanamel, in the presence of the witnesses who signed the deed of purchase, and in the presence of all the Judeans who were sitting in the court of the guard. 13In their presence I charged Baruch, saying, 14Thus says the LORD of hosts, the God of Israel: Take these deeds, both this sealed deed of purchase and this open deed, and put them in an earthenware jar, in order that they may last for a long time. 15For thus says the LORD of hosts, the God of Israel: Houses and fields and vineyards shall again be bought in this land.

Jeremiah Prays for Understanding

16 After I had given the deed of purchase to Baruch son of Neriah, I prayed to the LORD, saying: 17Ah Lord GOD! It is you who made the heavens and the earth by your great power and by your outstretched arm! Nothing is too hard for you. 18You show steadfast love to the thousandth generation,*u* but repay the guilt of parents into the laps of their children after them, O great and mighty God whose name is the LORD of hosts, 19great in counsel and mighty in deed; whose eyes are open to all the ways of mortals, rewarding all according to their ways and according to the fruit of their doings. 20You showed signs and wonders in the land of Egypt, and to this day in Israel and among all humankind, and have made yourself a name that continues to this very day. 21You brought your people Israel out of the land of Egypt with signs and wonders, with a strong hand and outstretched arm, and with great terror; 22and you gave them this land, which you swore to their ancestors to give them, a land flowing with milk and honey; 23and they entered and

took possession of it. But they did not obey your voice or follow your law; of all you commanded them to do, they did nothing. Therefore you have made all these disasters come upon them. 24See, the siege ramps have been cast up against the city to take it, and the city, faced with sword, famine, and pestilence, has been given into the hands of the Chaldeans who are fighting against it. What you spoke has happened, as you yourself can see. 25Yet you, O Lord GOD, have said to me, "Buy the field for money and get witnesses"—though the city has been given into the hands of the Chaldeans.

God's Assurance of the People's Return

26 The word of the LORD came to Jeremiah: 27See, I am the LORD, the God of all flesh; is anything too hard for me? 28Therefore, thus says the LORD: I am going to give this city into the hands of the Chaldeans and into the hand of King Nebuchadrezzar of Babylon, and he shall take it. 29The Chaldeans who are fighting against this city shall come, set it on fire, and burn it, with the houses on whose roofs offerings have been made to Baal and libations have been poured out to other gods, to provoke me to anger. 30For the people of Israel and the people of Judah have done nothing but evil in my sight from their youth; the people of Israel have done nothing but provoke me to anger by the work of their hands, says the LORD. 31This city has aroused my anger and wrath, from the day it was built until this day, so that I will remove it from my sight 32because of all the evil of the people of Israel and the people of Judah that they did to provoke me to anger—they, their kings and their officials, their priests and their prophets, the citizens of Judah and the inhabitants of Jerusalem. 33They have turned their backs to me, not their faces; though I have taught them persistently, they would not listen and accept correction. 34They set up their abominations in the house that bears my name, and defiled it. 35They built the high places of Baal in the valley of the son of Hinnom, to offer up their sons and daughters to Molech, though I did not command them, nor did it enter my mind that they should do this abomination, causing Judah to sin.

u Or to thousands

36 Now therefore thus says the LORD, the God of Israel, concerning this city of which you say, "It is being given into the hand of the king of Babylon by the sword, by famine, and by pestilence": 37See, I am going to gather them from all the lands to which I drove them in my anger and my wrath and in great indignation; I will bring them back to this place, and I will settle them in safety. 38They shall be my people, and I will be their God. 39I will give them one heart and one way, that they may fear me for all time, for their own good and the good of their children after them. 40I will make an everlasting covenant with them, never to draw back from doing good to them; and I will put the fear of me in their hearts, so that they may not turn from me. 41I will rejoice in doing good to them, and I will plant them in this land in faithfulness, with all my heart and all my soul.

42 For thus says the LORD: Just as I have brought all this great disaster upon this people, so I will bring upon them all the good fortune that I now promise them. 43Fields shall be bought in this land of which you are saying, It is a desolation, without human beings or animals; it has been given into the hands of the Chaldeans. 44Fields shall be bought for money, and deeds shall be signed and sealed and witnessed, in the land of Benjamin, in the places around Jerusalem, and in the cities of Judah, of the hill country, of the Shephelah, and of the Negeb; for I will restore their fortunes, says the LORD.

Healing after Punishment

33 The word of the LORD came to Jeremiah a second time, while he was still confined in the court of the guard: 2Thus says the LORD who made the earth,[v] the LORD who formed it to establish it—the LORD is his name: 3Call to me and I will answer you, and will tell you great and hidden things that you have not known. 4For thus says the LORD, the God of Israel, concerning the houses of this city and the houses of the kings of Judah that were torn down to make a defense against the siege ramps and before the sword:[w] 5The Chaldeans are coming in to fight[x] and to fill them with the dead bodies of those whom I shall strike down in my anger and my wrath, for I have hidden my face from this city because of all their wickedness. 6I am going to bring it recov-

ery and healing; I will heal them and reveal to them abundance[w] of prosperity and security. 7I will restore the fortunes of Judah and the fortunes of Israel, and rebuild them as they were at first. 8I will cleanse them from all the guilt of their sin against me, and I will forgive all the guilt of their sin and rebellion against me. 9And this city[y] shall be to me a name of joy, a praise and a glory before all the nations of the earth who shall hear of all the good that I do for them; they shall fear and tremble because of all the good and all the prosperity I provide for it.

10 Thus says the LORD: In this place of which you say, "It is a waste without human beings or animals," in the towns of Judah and the streets of Jerusalem that are desolate, without inhabitants, human or animal, there shall once more be heard 11the voice of mirth and the voice of gladness, the voice of the bridegroom and the voice of the bride, the voices of those who sing, as they bring thank offerings to the house of the LORD:

"Give thanks to the LORD of hosts,
 for the LORD is good,
  for his steadfast love endures
   forever!"

For I will restore the fortunes of the land as at first, says the LORD.

12 Thus says the LORD of hosts: In this place that is waste, without human beings or animals, and in all its towns there shall again be pasture for shepherds resting their flocks. 13In the towns of the hill country, of the Shephelah, and of the Negeb, in the land of Benjamin, the places around Jerusalem, and in the towns of Judah, flocks shall again pass under the hands of the one who counts them, says the LORD.

The Righteous Branch and the Covenant with David

14 The days are surely coming, says the LORD, when I will fulfill the promise I made to the house of Israel and the house of Judah. 15In those days and at that time I will cause a righteous Branch to spring up for David; and he shall execute justice and righteousness in the land. 16In those days Judah will be saved and Jerusalem will live in safety. And this is the name by

---

v Gk: Heb *it*   w Meaning of Heb uncertain
x Cn: Heb *They are coming in to fight against the Chaldeans*   y Heb *And it*

which it will be called: "The LORD is our righteousness."

17 For thus says the LORD: David shall never lack a man to sit on the throne of the house of Israel, 18and the levitical priests shall never lack a man in my presence to offer burnt offerings, to make grain offerings, and to make sacrifices for all time.

19 The word of the LORD came to Jeremiah: 20Thus says the LORD: If any of you could break my covenant with the day and my covenant with the night, so that day and night would not come at their appointed time, 21only then could my covenant with my servant David be broken, so that he would not have a son to reign on his throne, and my covenant with my ministers the Levites. 22Just as the host of heaven cannot be numbered and the sands of the sea cannot be measured, so I will increase the offspring of my servant David, and the Levites who minister to me.

23 The word of the LORD came to Jeremiah: 24Have you not observed how these people say, "The two families that the LORD chose have been rejected by him," and how they hold my people in such contempt that they no longer regard them as a nation? 25Thus says the LORD: Only if I had not established my covenant with day and night and the ordinances of heaven and earth, 26would I reject the offspring of Jacob and of my servant David and not choose any of his descendants as rulers over the offspring of Abraham, Isaac, and Jacob. For I will restore their fortunes, and will have mercy upon them.

Death in Captivity Predicted for Zedekiah

34 The word that came to Jeremiah from the LORD, when King Nebuchadrezzar of Babylon and all his army and all the kingdoms of the earth and all the peoples under his dominion were fighting against Jerusalem and all its cities: 2Thus says the LORD, the God of Israel: Go and speak to King Zedekiah of Judah and say to him: Thus says the LORD: I am going to give this city into the hand of the king of Babylon, and he shall burn it with fire. 3And you yourself shall not escape from his hand, but shall surely be captured and handed over to him; you shall see the king of Babylon eye to eye and speak with him face to face; and you shall go to Babylon. 4Yet hear the word of the LORD, O King

Zedekiah of Judah! Thus says the LORD concerning you: You shall not die by the sword; 5you shall die in peace. And as spices were burned[z] for your ancestors, the earlier kings who preceded you, so they shall burn spices[a] for you and lament for you, saying, "Alas, lord!" For I have spoken the word, says the LORD.

6 Then the prophet Jeremiah spoke all these words to Zedekiah king of Judah, in Jerusalem, 7when the army of the king of Babylon was fighting against Jerusalem and against all the cities of Judah that were left, Lachish and Azekah; for these were the only fortified cities of Judah that remained.

Treacherous Treatment of Slaves

8 The word that came to Jeremiah from the LORD, after King Zedekiah had made a covenant with all the people in Jerusalem to make a proclamation of liberty to them— 9that all should set free their Hebrew slaves, male and female, so that no one should hold another Judean in slavery. 10And they obeyed, all the officials and all the people who had entered into the covenant that all would set free their slaves, male or female, so that they would not be enslaved again; they obeyed and set them free. 11But afterward they turned around and took back the male and female slaves they had set free, and brought them again into subjection as slaves. 12The word of the LORD came to Jeremiah from the LORD: 13Thus says the LORD, the God of Israel: I myself made a covenant with your ancestors when I brought them out of the land of Egypt, out of the house of slavery, saying, 14"Every seventh year each of you must set free any Hebrews who have been sold to you and have served you six years; you must set them free from your service." But your ancestors did not listen to me or incline their ears to me. 15You yourselves recently repented and did what was right in my sight by proclaiming liberty to one another, and you made a covenant before me in the house that is called by my name; 16but then you turned around and profaned my name when each of you took back your male and female slaves, whom you had set free according to their desire, and you brought them again into subjection to be your slaves. 17Therefore, thus says the

---

z Heb *as there was burning*   a Heb *shall burn*

The Queen of Sheba

Read I Kings 10.1–13

Sheba was a fragrant land, famous for its perfumes and spices. Located on the southwestern tip of Arabia, bordering the Red Sea, it traded precious commodities such as gold, frankincense, and myrrh to kingdoms in Africa, India, and the Mediterranean. Little wonder that passing caravans brought news of the wide world to Sheba's queen.

Her Character:
Though a pagan queen, she prized wisdom above power. She appears to have been intellectually gifted, with a good head for business and diplomacy.

Her Joy: *That her quest for wisdom was rewarded beyond her expectations.*

Lately she had heard marvelous stories of Solomon, the son of Bathsheba and David, now Israel's third king. Some said he was the wisest man alive.

The queen smiled as she recalled the tale of the two prostitutes. Both had claimed to be mother of the same infant. How could the king possibly know who was telling the truth and who a lie? But Solomon merely ordered the baby cut in half, to be divided equally between the two women. He knew the real mother would relinquish her rights rather than let her child perish.

The queen had also heard of the fabulous temple and palace Solomon had built in Jerusalem. Such a ruler, she realized, would have little trouble controlling the international trade routes crisscrossing his kingdom.

Though Jerusalem lay fifteen hundred miles to the north, the queen was determined to see for herself whether Solomon measured up to even half the tales told of him. Perhaps she could also establish a trade agreement with Israel that would ensure Sheba's future prosperity. So she assembled a caravan of camels and loaded them with precious spices, gems, and a mere four-and-a-

half tons of gold. Her entrance into Jerusalem would have created an unforgettable spectacle, adding to Solomon's growing fame.

Day after day, the queen pounded Solomon with hard questions. But nothing was too difficult for him to explain. She finally exclaimed:

The report was true that I heard in my own land of your accomplishments and of your wisdom, but I did not believe the reports until I came and my own eyes had seen it. Not even half had been told me; your wisdom and prosperity far surpass the report that I had heard . . . Happy are these your servants, who continually attend you and hear your wisdom! Blessed be the LORD your God, who has delighted in you and set you on the throne of Israel!

(10.6–9)

Then the queen gave Solomon all the gold and spices she had brought with her, perhaps foreshadowing the Magi's gift of gold, frankincense, and myrrh to the Christ Child nearly a thousand years later.

Jesus himself referred to the queen of Sheba when he replied to the Pharisees who demanded from him a miraculous sign: "The queen of the South will rise up at the judgment with this generation and condemn it, because she came from the ends of the earth to listen to the wisdom of Solomon, and see, something greater than Solomon is here!" (Matthew 12.42).

Though queen of a pagan nation, she was drawn to the wisdom of God. She made an arduous and dangerous journey in order to meet the world's wisest man. Surely she must have thought the price worth paying.

Praying With the Queen of Sheba

"Happy are these your servants, who continually attend you and hear your wisdom! Blessed be the LORD your God, who has delighted in you and set you on the throne of Israel! Because the LORD loved Israel forever, he has made you king to execute justice and righteousness."—1 Kings 10.8–9

Praise God: *For his wisdom working through others.*

Offer Thanks: *That true wisdom has nothing to do with intellectual ability but everything to do with humble dependence on God.*

Confess: *Any laziness that keeps you from searching out God's wisdom for your own life.*

Ask God: *To pour out wisdom on leaders in the church and in the government, so that his ways are honored.*

Lift Your Heart

Think about the gifts the queen of Sheba lavished on Solomon—the perfume, spices, precious stones, and gold—as tangible acknowledgement of his greatness. Yet Solomon was only a man. What can you lavish on the One who is far greater than any person? You can be generous with your praise, telling God everything you love about him. You can be generous with your time, going out of your way to help those in need. You can be generous with your trust, acting and praying in a way that shows your confidence in God's goodness and power. You can be generous with your money, giving what you can from your small hoard. This week, don't be stingy. Think of at least one extravagant way to express your awe and affection for God.

Jesus, everything I've heard about you is true, but I didn't believe it until you showed yourself to me. Then I realized I hadn't been told the half of it. Your wisdom, mercy, power, and kindness exceed everything I've ever heard.

Go to page 1065 for your next devotional reading.

LORD: You have not obeyed me by granting a release to your neighbors and friends; I am going to grant a release to you, says the LORD—a release to the sword, to pestilence, and to famine. I will make you a horror to all the kingdoms of the earth. 18And those who transgressed my covenant and did not keep the terms of the covenant that they made before me, I will make like[b] the calf when they cut it in two and passed between its parts: 19the officials of Judah, the officials of Jerusalem, the eunuchs, the priests, and all the people of the land who passed between the parts of the calf 20shall be handed over to their enemies and to those who seek their lives. Their corpses shall become food for the birds of the air and the wild animals of the earth. 21And as for King Zedekiah of Judah and his officials, I will hand them over to their enemies and to those who seek their lives, to the army of the king of Babylon, which has withdrawn from you. 22I am going to command, says the LORD, and will bring them back to this city; and they will fight against it, and take it, and burn it with fire. The towns of Judah I will make a desolation without inhabitant.

The Rechabites Commended

35 The word that came to Jeremiah from the LORD in the days of King Jehoiakim son of Josiah of Judah: 2Go to the house of the Rechabites, and speak with them, and bring them to the house of the LORD, into one of the chambers; then offer them wine to drink. 3So I took Jaazaniah son of Jeremiah son of Habazziniah, and his brothers, and all his sons, and the whole house of the Rechabites. 4I brought them to the house of the LORD into the chamber of the sons of Hanan son of Igdaliah, the man of God, which was near the chamber of the officials, above the chamber of Maaseiah son of Shallum, keeper of the threshold. 5Then I set before the Rechabites pitchers full of wine, and cups; and I said to them, "Have some wine." 6But they answered, "We will drink no wine, for our ancestor Jonadab son of Rechab commanded us, 'You shall never drink wine, neither you nor your children; 7nor shall you ever build a house, or sow seed; nor shall you plant a vineyard, or even own one; but you shall live in tents all your days, that you may live many days in the land where you re-side.' 8We have obeyed the charge of our ancestor Jonadab son of Rechab in all that he commanded us, to drink no wine all our days, ourselves, our wives, our sons, or our daughters, 9and not to build houses to live in. We have no vineyard or field or seed; 10but we have lived in tents, and have obeyed and done all that our ancestor Jonadab commanded us. 11But when King Nebuchadrezzar of Babylon came up against the land, we said, 'Come, and let us go to Jerusalem for fear of the army of the Chaldeans and the army of the Arameans.' That is why we are living in Jerusalem."

12 Then the word of the LORD came to Jeremiah: 13Thus says the LORD of hosts, the God of Israel: Go and say to the people of Judah and the inhabitants of Jerusalem, Can you not learn a lesson and obey my words? says the LORD. 14The command has been carried out that Jonadab son of Rechab gave to his descendants to drink no wine; and they drink none to this day, for they have obeyed their ancestor's command. But I myself have spoken to you persistently, and you have not obeyed me. 15I have sent to you all my servants the prophets, sending them persistently, saying, "Turn now everyone of you from your evil way, and amend your doings, and do not go after other gods to serve them, and then you shall live in the land that I gave to you and your ancestors." But you did not incline your ear or obey me. 16The descendants of Jonadab son of Rechab have carried out the command that their ancestor gave them, but this people has not obeyed me. 17Therefore, thus says the LORD, the God of hosts, the God of Israel: I am going to bring on Judah and on all the inhabitants of Jerusalem every disaster that I have pronounced against them; because I have spoken to them and they have not listened, I have called to them and they have not answered.

18 But to the house of the Rechabites Jeremiah said: Thus says the LORD of hosts, the God of Israel: Because you have obeyed the command of your ancestor Jonadab, and kept all his precepts, and done all that he commanded you, 19therefore thus says the LORD of hosts, the God of Israel: Jonadab son of Rechab shall not lack a descendant to stand before me for all time.

b Cn: Heb lacks like

The Scroll Read in the Temple

36 In the fourth year of King Jehoiakim son of Josiah of Judah, this word came to Jeremiah from the LORD: ²Take a scroll and write on it all the words that I have spoken to you against Israel and Judah and all the nations, from the day I spoke to you, from the days of Josiah until today. ³It may be that when the house of Judah hears of all the disasters that I intend to do to them, all of them may turn from their evil ways, so that I may forgive their iniquity and their sin.

4 Then Jeremiah called Baruch son of Neriah, and Baruch wrote on a scroll at Jeremiah's dictation all the words of the LORD that he had spoken to him. ⁵And Jeremiah ordered Baruch, saying, "I am prevented from entering the house of the LORD; ⁶so you go yourself, and on a fast day in the hearing of the people in the LORD's house you shall read the words of the LORD from the scroll that you have written at my dictation. You shall read them also in the hearing of all the people of Judah who come up from their towns. ⁷It may be that their plea will come before the LORD, and that all of them will turn from their evil ways, for great is the anger and wrath that the LORD has pronounced against this people." ⁸And Baruch son of Neriah did all that the prophet Jeremiah ordered him about reading from the scroll the words of the LORD in the LORD's house.

9 In the fifth year of King Jehoiakim son of Josiah of Judah, in the ninth month, all the people in Jerusalem and all the people who came from the towns of Judah to Jerusalem proclaimed a fast before the LORD. ¹⁰Then, in the hearing of all the people, Baruch read the words of Jeremiah from the scroll, in the house of the LORD, in the chamber of Gemariah son of Shaphan the secretary, which was in the upper court, at the entry of the New Gate of the LORD's house.

The Scroll Read in the Palace

11 When Micaiah son of Gemariah son of Shaphan heard all the words of the LORD from the scroll, ¹²he went down to the king's house, into the secretary's chamber; and all the officials were sitting there: Elishama the secretary, Delaiah son of Shemaiah, Elnathan son of Achbor, Gemariah son of Shaphan, Zedekiah son of Hananiah, and all the officials. ¹³And Micaiah told them all the words that he had heard, when Baruch read the scroll in the hearing of the people. ¹⁴Then all the officials sent Jehudi son of Nethaniah son of Shelemiah son of Cushi to say to Baruch, "Bring the scroll that you read in the hearing of the people, and come." So Baruch son of Neriah took the scroll in his hand and came to them. ¹⁵And they said to him, "Sit down and read it to us." So Baruch read it to them. ¹⁶When they heard all the words, they turned to one another in alarm, and said to Baruch, "We certainly must report all these words to the king." ¹⁷Then they questioned Baruch, "Tell us now, how did you write all these words? Was it at his dictation?" ¹⁸Baruch answered them, "He dictated all these words to me, and I wrote them with ink on the scroll." ¹⁹Then the officials said to Baruch, "Go and hide, you and Jeremiah, and let no one know where you are."

Jehoiakim Burns the Scroll

20 Leaving the scroll in the chamber of Elishama the secretary, they went to the court of the king; and they reported all the words to the king. ²¹Then the king sent Jehudi to get the scroll, and he took it from the chamber of Elishama the secretary; and Jehudi read it to the king and all the officials who stood beside the king. ²²Now the king was sitting in his winter apartment (it was the ninth month), and there was a fire burning in the brazier before him. ²³As Jehudi read three or four columns, the king*c* would cut them off with a penknife and throw them into the fire in the brazier, until the entire scroll was consumed in the fire that was in the brazier. ²⁴Yet neither the king, nor any of his servants who heard all these words, was alarmed, nor did they tear their garments. ²⁵Even when Elnathan and Delaiah and Gemariah urged the king not to burn the scroll, he would not listen to them. ²⁶And the king commanded Jerahmeel the king's son and Seraiah son of Azriel and Shelemiah son of Abdeel to arrest the secretary Baruch and the prophet Jeremiah. But the LORD hid them.

Jeremiah Dictates Another

27 Now, after the king had burned the scroll with the words that Baruch wrote at Jeremiah's dictation, the word of the LORD

c Heb he

came to Jeremiah: 28Take another scroll and write on it all the former words that were in the first scroll, which King Jehoiakim of Judah has burned. 29And concerning King Jehoiakim of Judah you shall say: Thus says the LORD, You have dared to burn this scroll, saying, Why have you written in it that the king of Babylon will certainly come and destroy this land, and will cut off from it human beings and animals? 30Therefore thus says the LORD concerning King Jehoiakim of Judah: He shall have no one to sit upon the throne of David, and his dead body shall be cast out to the heat by day and the frost by night. 31And I will punish him and his offspring and his servants for their iniquity; I will bring on them, and on the inhabitants of Jerusalem, and on the people of Judah, all the disasters with which I have threatened them—but they would not listen.

32 Then Jeremiah took another scroll and gave it to the secretary Baruch son of Neriah, who wrote on it at Jeremiah's dictation all the words of the scroll that King Jehoiakim of Judah had burned in the fire; and many similar words were added to them.

Zedekiah's Vain Hope

37 Zedekiah son of Josiah, whom King Nebuchadrezzar of Babylon made king in the land of Judah, succeeded Coniah son of Jehoiakim. 2But neither he nor his servants nor the people of the land listened to the words of the LORD that he spoke through the prophet Jeremiah.

3 King Zedekiah sent Jehucal son of Shelemiah and the priest Zephaniah son of Maaseiah to the prophet Jeremiah saying, "Please pray for us to the LORD our God." 4Now Jeremiah was still going in and out among the people, for he had not yet been put in prison. 5Meanwhile, the army of Pharaoh had come out of Egypt; and when the Chaldeans who were besieging Jerusalem heard news of them, they withdrew from Jerusalem.

6 Then the word of the LORD came to the prophet Jeremiah: 7Thus says the LORD, God of Israel: This is what the two of you shall say to the king of Judah, who sent you to me to inquire of me: Pharaoh's army, which set out to help you, is going to return to its own land, to Egypt. 8And the Chaldeans shall return and fight against this city; they shall take it and burn it with fire. 9Thus says the LORD: Do not deceive yourselves, saying, "The Chaldeans will surely go away from us," for they will not go away. 10Even if you defeated the whole army of Chaldeans who are fighting against you, and there remained of them only wounded men in their tents, they would rise up and burn this city with fire.

Jeremiah Is Imprisoned

11 Now when the Chaldean army had withdrawn from Jerusalem at the approach of Pharaoh's army, 12Jeremiah set out from Jerusalem to go to the land of Benjamin to receive his share of property*d* among the people there. 13When he reached the Benjamin Gate, a sentinel there named Irijah son of Shelemiah son of Hananiah arrested the prophet Jeremiah saying, "You are deserting to the Chaldeans." 14And Jeremiah said, "That is a lie; I am not deserting to the Chaldeans." But Irijah would not listen to him, and arrested Jeremiah and brought him to the officials. 15The officials were enraged at Jeremiah, and they beat him and imprisoned him in the house of the secretary Jonathan, for it had been made a prison. 16Thus Jeremiah was put in the cistern house, in the cells, and remained there many days.

17 Then King Zedekiah sent for him, and received him. The king questioned him secretly in his house, and said, "Is there any word from the LORD?" Jeremiah said, "There is!" Then he said, "You shall be handed over to the king of Babylon." 18Jeremiah also said to King Zedekiah, "What wrong have I done to you or your servants or this people, that you have put me in prison? 19Where are your prophets who prophesied to you, saying, 'The king of Babylon will not come against you and against this land'? 20Now please hear me, my lord king: be good enough to listen to my plea, and do not send me back to the house of the secretary Jonathan to die there." 21So King Zedekiah gave orders, and they committed Jeremiah to the court of the guard; and a loaf of bread was given him daily from the bakers' street, until all the bread of the city was gone. So Jeremiah remained in the court of the guard.

d Meaning of Heb uncertain

Jeremiah in the Cistern

38 Now Shephatiah son of Mattan, Gedaliah son of Pashhur, Jucal son of Shelemiah, and Pashhur son of Malchiah heard the words that Jeremiah was saying to all the people, ²Thus says the LORD, Those who stay in this city shall die by the sword, by famine, and by pestilence; but those who go out to the Chaldeans shall live; they shall have their lives as a prize of war, and live. ³Thus says the LORD, This city shall surely be handed over to the army of the king of Babylon and be taken. ⁴Then the officials said to the king, "This man ought to be put to death, because he is discouraging the soldiers who are left in this city, and all the people, by speaking such words to them. For this man is not seeking the welfare of this people, but their harm." ⁵King Zedekiah said, "Here he is; he is in your hands; for the king is powerless against you." ⁶So they took Jeremiah and threw him into the cistern of Malchiah, the king's son, which was in the court of the guard, letting Jeremiah down by ropes. Now there was no water in the cistern, but only mud, and Jeremiah sank in the mud.

Jeremiah Is Rescued by Ebed-melech

7 Ebed-melech the Ethiopian,ᵉ a eunuch in the king's house, heard that they had put Jeremiah into the cistern. The king happened to be sitting at the Benjamin Gate, ⁸So Ebed-melech left the king's house and spoke to the king, ⁹"My lord king, these men have acted wickedly in all they did to the prophet Jeremiah by throwing him into the cistern to die there of hunger, for there is no bread left in the city." ¹⁰Then the king commanded Ebed-melech the Ethiopian,ᵉ "Take three men with you from here, and pull the prophet Jeremiah up from the cistern before he dies." ¹¹So Ebed-melech took the men with him and went to the house of the king, to a wardrobe ofᶠ the storehouse, and took from there old rags and worn-out clothes, which he let down to Jeremiah in the cistern by ropes. ¹²Then Ebed-melech the Ethiopianᵉ said to Jeremiah, "Just put the rags and clothes between your armpits and the ropes." Jeremiah did so. ¹³Then they drew Jeremiah up by the ropes and pulled him out of the cistern. And Jeremiah remained in the court of the guard.

Zedekiah Consults Jeremiah Again

14 King Zedekiah sent for the prophet Jeremiah and received him at the third entrance of the temple of the LORD. The king said to Jeremiah, "I have something to ask you; do not hide anything from me." ¹⁵Jeremiah said to Zedekiah, "If I tell you, you will put me to death, will you not? And if I give you advice, you will not listen to me." ¹⁶So King Zedekiah swore an oath in secret to Jeremiah, "As the LORD lives, who gave us our lives, I will not put you to death or hand you over to these men who seek your life."

17 Then Jeremiah said to Zedekiah, "Thus says the LORD, the God of hosts, the God of Israel, If you will only surrender to the officials of the king of Babylon, then your life shall be spared, and this city shall not be burned with fire, and you and your house shall live. ¹⁸But if you do not surrender to the officials of the king of Babylon, then this city shall be handed over to the Chaldeans, and they shall burn it with fire, and you yourself shall not escape from their hand." ¹⁹King Zedekiah said to Jeremiah, "I am afraid of the Judeans who have deserted to the Chaldeans, for I might be handed over to them and they would abuse me." ²⁰Jeremiah said, "That will not happen. Just obey the voice of the LORD in what I say to you, and it shall go well with you, and your life shall be spared. ²¹But if you are determined not to surrender, this is what the LORD has shown me— ²²a vision of all the women remaining in the house of the king of Judah being led out to the officials of the king of Babylon and saying,

'Your trusted friends have
    seduced you
  and have overcome you;
 Now that your feet are stuck in
    the mud,
  they desert you.'

²³All your wives and your children shall be led out to the Chaldeans, and you yourself shall not escape from their hand, but shall be seized by the king of Babylon; and this city shall be burned with fire."

24 Then Zedekiah said to Jeremiah, "Do not let anyone else know of this conversation, or you will die. ²⁵If the officials should hear that I have spoken with you,

---

ᵉ Or *Nubian*; Heb *Cushite*   ᶠ Cn: Heb *to under*

and they should come and say to you,
'Just tell us what you said to the king; do
not conceal it from us, or we will put you
to death. What did the king say to you?'
²⁶then you shall say to them, 'I was presenting my plea to the king not to send
me back to the house of Jonathan to die
there.'" ²⁷All the officials did come to Jeremiah and questioned him; and he answered them in the very words the king
had commanded. So they stopped questioning him, for the conversation had not
been overheard. ²⁸And Jeremiah remained
in the court of the guard until the day that
Jerusalem was taken.

The Fall of Jerusalem

39 In the ninth year of King Zedekiah of Judah, in the tenth month,
King Nebuchadrezzar of Babylon and all
his army came against Jerusalem and besieged it; ²in the eleventh year of Zedekiah, in the fourth month, on the ninth day
of the month, a breach was made in the
city. ³When Jerusalem was taken, ᵍ all the
officials of the king of Babylon came and
sat in the middle gate: Nergal-sharezer,
Samgar-nebo, Sarsechim the Rabsaris,
Nergal-sharezer the Rabmag, with all the
rest of the officials of the king of Babylon.
⁴When King Zedekiah of Judah and all the
soldiers saw them, they fled, going out of
the city at night by way of the king's garden through the gate between the two
walls; and they went toward the Arabah.
⁵But the army of the Chaldeans pursued
them, and overtook Zedekiah in the
plains of Jericho; and when they had tak-
en him, they brought him up to King Nebuchadrezzar of Babylon, at Riblah, in the
land of Hamath; and he passed sentence
on him. ⁶The king of Babylon slaughtered
the sons of Zedekiah at Riblah before his
eyes; also the king of Babylon slaughtered
all the nobles of Judah. ⁷He put out the
eyes of Zedekiah, and bound him in fetters to take him to Babylon. ⁸The Chaldeans burned the king's house and the
houses of the people, and broke down the
walls of Jerusalem. ⁹Then Nebuzaradan
the captain of the guard exiled to Babylon
the rest of the people who were left in the
city, those who had deserted to him, and
the people who remained. ¹⁰Nebuzaradan
the captain of the guard left in the land
of Judah some of the poor people who
owned nothing, and gave them vineyards
and fields at the same time.

Jeremiah, Set Free, Remembers Ebed-melech

11 King Nebuchadrezzar of Babylon
gave command concerning Jeremiah
through Nebuzaradan, the captain of the
guard, saying, ¹²"Take him, look after him
well and do him no harm, but deal with
him as he may ask you." ¹³So Nebuzaradan
the captain of the guard, Nebushazban
the Rabsaris, Nergal-sharezer the Rabmag,
and all the chief officers of the king of
Babylon sent ¹⁴and took Jeremiah from
the court of the guard. They entrusted him
to Gedaliah son of Ahikam son of Shaphan to be brought home. So he stayed
with his own people.

15 The word of the LORD came to Jeremiah while he was confined in the court
of the guard: ¹⁶Go and say to Ebed-
melech the Ethiopian:ʰ Thus says the
LORD of hosts, the God of Israel: I am going to fulfill my words against this city for
evil and not for good, and they shall be
accomplished in your presence on that
day. ¹⁷But I will save you on that day, says
the LORD, and you shall not be handed
over to those whom you dread. ¹⁸For I
will surely save you, and you shall not fall
by the sword; but you shall have your life
as a prize of war, because you have trusted
in me, says the LORD.

Jeremiah with Gedaliah the Governor

40 The word that came to Jeremiah
from the LORD after Nebuzaradan
the captain of the guard had let him go
from Ramah, when he took him bound in
fetters along with all the captives of Jerusalem and Judah who were being exiled to
Babylon. ²The captain of the guard took
Jeremiah and said to him, "The LORD your
God threatened this place with this disaster; ³and now the LORD has brought it
about, and has done as he said, because
all of you sinned against the LORD and did
not obey his voice. Therefore this thing
has come upon you. ⁴Now look, I have
just released you today from the fetters on
your hands. If you wish to come with me
to Babylon, come, and I will take good
care of you; but if you do not wish to
come with me to Babylon, you need not
come. See, the whole land is before you;
go wherever you think it good and right to
go. ⁵If you remain,ⁱ then return to Geda-

ᵍ This clause has been transposed from 38.28
ʰ Or Nubian; Heb Cushite   ⁱ Syr: Meaning of
Heb uncertain

liah son of Ahikam son of Shaphan, whom the king of Babylon appointed governor of the towns of Judah, and stay with him among the people; or go wherever you think it right to go." So the captain of the guard gave him an allowance of food and a present, and let him go. 6Then Jeremiah went to Gedaliah son of Ahikam at Mizpah, and stayed with him among the people who were left in the land.

7 When all the leaders of the forces in the open country and their troops heard that the king of Babylon had appointed Gedaliah son of Ahikam governor in the land, and had committed to him men, women, and children, those of the poorest of the land who had not been taken into exile to Babylon, 8they went to Gedaliah at Mizpah—Ishmael son of Nethaniah, Johanan son of Kareah, Seraiah son of Tanhumeth, the sons of Ephai the Netophathite, Jezaniah son of the Maacathite, they and their troops. 9Gedaliah son of Ahikam son of Shaphan swore to them and their troops, saying, "Do not be afraid to serve the Chaldeans. Stay in the land and serve the king of Babylon, and it shall go well with you. 10As for me, I am staying at Mizpah to represent you before the Chaldeans who come to us; but as for you, gather wine and summer fruits and oil, and store them in your vessels, and live in the towns that you have taken over." 11Likewise, when all the Judeans who were in Moab and among the Ammonites and in Edom and in other lands heard that the king of Babylon had left a remnant in Judah and had appointed Gedaliah son of Ahikam son of Shaphan as governor over them, 12then all the Judeans returned from all the places to which they had been scattered and came to the land of Judah, to Gedaliah at Mizpah; and they gathered wine and summer fruits in great abundance.

13 Now Johanan son of Kareah and all the leaders of the forces in the open country came to Gedaliah at Mizpah 14and said to him, "Are you at all aware that Baalis king of the Ammonites has sent Ishmael son of Nethaniah to take your life?" But Gedaliah son of Ahikam would not believe them. 15Then Johanan son of Kareah spoke secretly to Gedaliah at Mizpah, "Please let me go and kill Ishmael son of Nethaniah, and no one else will know. Why should he take your life, so that all

the Judeans who are gathered around you would be scattered, and the remnant of Judah would perish?" 16But Gedaliah son of Ahikam said to Johanan son of Kareah, "Do not do such a thing, for you are telling a lie about Ishmael."

Insurrection against Gedaliah

41 In the seventh month, Ishmael son of Nethaniah son of Elishama, of the royal family, one of the chief officers of the king, came with ten men to Gedaliah son of Ahikam, at Mizpah. As they ate bread together there at Mizpah, 2Ishmael son of Nethaniah and the ten men with him got up and struck down Gedaliah son of Ahikam son of Shaphan with the sword and killed him, because the king of Babylon had appointed him governor in the land. 3Ishmael also killed all the Judeans who were with Gedaliah at Mizpah, and the Chaldean soldiers who happened to be there.

4 On the day after the murder of Gedaliah, before anyone knew of it, 5eighty men arrived from Shechem and Shiloh and Samaria, with their beards shaved and their clothes torn, and their bodies gashed, bringing grain offerings and incense to present at the temple of the LORD. 6And Ishmael son of Nethaniah came out from Mizpah to meet them, weeping as he came. As he met them, he said to them, "Come to Gedaliah son of Ahikam." 7When they reached the middle of the city, Ishmael son of Nethaniah and the men with him slaughtered them, and threw them^j into a cistern. 8But there were ten men among them who said to Ishmael, "Do not kill us, for we have stores of wheat, barley, oil, and honey hidden in the fields." So he refrained, and did not kill them along with their companions.

9 Now the cistern into which Ishmael had thrown all the bodies of the men whom he had struck down was the large cistern^k that King Asa had made for defense against King Baasha of Israel; Ishmael son of Nethaniah filled that cistern with those whom he had killed. 10Then Ishmael took captive all the rest of the people who were in Mizpah, the king's daughters and all the people who were left at Miz-

---

j Syr: Heb lacks *and threw them*; compare verse 9
k Gk: Heb *whom he had killed by the hand of Gedaliah*

pah, whom Nebuzaradan, the captain of the guard, had committed to Gedaliah son of Ahikam. Ishmael son of Nethaniah took them captive and set out to cross over to the Ammonites.

11 But when Johanan son of Kareah and all the leaders of the forces with him heard of all the crimes that Ishmael son of Nethaniah had done, [12]they took all their men and went to fight against Ishmael son of Nethaniah. They came upon him at the great pool that is in Gibeon. [13]And when all the people who were with Ishmael saw Johanan son of Kareah and all the leaders of the forces with him, they were glad. [14]So all the people whom Ishmael had carried away captive from Mizpah turned around and came back, and went to Johanan son of Kareah. [15]But Ishmael son of Nethaniah escaped from Johanan with eight men, and went to the Ammonites. [16]Then Johanan son of Kareah and all the leaders of the forces with him took all the rest of the people whom Ishmael son of Nethaniah had carried away captive[l] from Mizpah after he had slain Gedaliah son of Ahikam—soldiers, women, children, and eunuchs, whom Johanan brought back from Gibeon.[m] [17]And they set out, and stopped at Geruth Chimham near Bethlehem, intending to go to Egypt [18]because of the Chaldeans; for they were afraid of them, because Ishmael son of Nethaniah had killed Gedaliah son of Ahikam, whom the king of Babylon had made governor over the land.

Jeremiah Advises Survivors Not to Migrate

42 Then all the commanders of the forces, and Johanan son of Kareah and Azariah[n] son of Hoshaiah, and all the people from the least to the greatest, approached [2]the prophet Jeremiah and said, "Be good enough to listen to our plea, and pray to the LORD your God for us—for all this remnant. For there are only a few of us left out of many, as your eyes can see. [3]Let the LORD your God show us where we should go and what we should do." [4]The prophet Jeremiah said to them, "Very well: I am going to pray to the LORD your God as you request, and whatever the LORD answers you I will tell you; I will keep nothing back from you." [5]They in their turn said to Jeremiah, "May the LORD be a true and faithful witness against us if we do not act according to everything that the LORD your God sends

us through you. [6]Whether it is good or bad, we will obey the voice of the LORD our God to whom we are sending you, in order that it may go well with us when we obey the voice of the LORD our God."

7 At the end of ten days the word of the LORD came to Jeremiah. [8]Then he summoned Johanan son of Kareah and all the commanders of the forces who were with him, and all the people from the least to the greatest, [9]and said to them, "Thus says the LORD, the God of Israel, to whom you sent me to present your plea before him: [10]If you will only remain in this land, then I will build you up and not pull you down; I will plant you, and not pluck you up; for I am sorry for the disaster that I have brought upon you. [11]Do not be afraid of the king of Babylon, as you have been; do not be afraid of him, says the LORD, for I am with you, to save you and to rescue you from his hand. [12]I will grant you mercy, and he will have mercy on you and restore you to your native soil. [13]But if you continue to say, 'We will not stay in this land,' thus disobeying the voice of the LORD your God [14]and saying, 'No, we will go to the land of Egypt, where we shall not see war, or hear the sound of the trumpet, or be hungry for bread, and there we will stay,' [15]then hear the word of the LORD, O remnant of Judah. Thus says the LORD of hosts, the God of Israel: If you are determined to enter Egypt and go to settle there, [16]then the sword that you fear shall overtake you there, in the land of Egypt; and the famine that you dread shall follow close after you into Egypt; and there you shall die. [17]All the people who have determined to go to Egypt to settle there shall die by the sword, by famine, and by pestilence; they shall have no remnant or survivor from the disaster that I am bringing upon them.

18 "For thus says the LORD of hosts, the God of Israel: Just as my anger and my wrath were poured out on the inhabitants of Jerusalem, so my wrath will be poured out on you when you go to Egypt. You shall become an object of execration and horror, of cursing and ridicule. You shall see this place no more. [19]The LORD has said to you, O remnant of Judah, Do not go to Egypt. Be well aware that I have

---

[l] Cn: Heb *whom he recovered from Ishmael son of Nethaniah*   [m] Meaning of Heb uncertain
[n] Gk: Heb *Jezaniah*

warned you today 20that you have made a
fatal mistake. For you yourselves sent me
to the LORD your God, saying, 'Pray for us
to the LORD our God, and whatever the
LORD our God says, tell us and we will do
it.' 21So I have told you today, but you
have not obeyed the voice of the LORD
your God in anything that he sent me to
tell you. 22Be well aware, then, that you
shall die by the sword, by famine, and by
pestilence in the place where you desire to
go and settle."

Taken to Egypt, Jeremiah Warns of Judgment

43 When Jeremiah finished speaking
to all the people all these words
of the LORD their God, with which the LORD
their God had sent him to them, 2Azariah
son of Hoshaiah and Johanan son of Kareah and all the other insolent men said
to Jeremiah, "You are telling a lie. The
LORD our God did not send you to say, 'Do
not go to Egypt to settle there'; 3but Baruch son of Neriah is inciting you against
us, to hand us over to the Chaldeans, in
order that they may kill us or take us into
exile in Babylon." 4So Johanan son of Kareah and all the commanders of the forces
and all the people did not obey the voice
of the LORD, to stay in the land of Judah.
5But Johanan son of Kareah and all the
commanders of the forces took all the
remnant of Judah who had returned to
settle in the land of Judah from all the
nations to which they had been driven—
6the men, the women, the children, the
princesses, and everyone whom Nebuzaradan the captain of the guard had left with
Gedaliah son of Ahikam son of Shaphan;
also the prophet Jeremiah and Baruch son
of Neriah. 7And they came into the land
of Egypt, for they did not obey the voice
of the LORD. And they arrived at Tahpanhes.

8 Then the word of the LORD came to
Jeremiah in Tahpanhes: 9Take some large
stones in your hands, and bury them in
the clay pavement[o] that is at the entrance
to Pharaoh's palace in Tahpanhes. Let the
Judeans see you do it, 10and say to them,
Thus says the LORD of hosts, the God of
Israel: I am going to send and take my
servant King Nebuchadrezzar of Babylon,
and he[p] will set his throne above these
stones that I have buried, and he will
spread his royal canopy over them. 11He
shall come and ravage the land of Egypt,
giving

those who are destined for
pestilence, to pestilence,
and those who are destined for
captivity, to captivity,
and those who are destined for
the sword, to the sword.

12He[q] shall kindle a fire in the temples of
the gods of Egypt; and he shall burn them
and carry them away captive; and he shall
pick clean the land of Egypt, as a shepherd
picks his cloak clean of vermin; and he
shall depart from there safely. 13He shall
break the obelisks of Heliopolis, which is
in the land of Egypt; and the temples of
the gods of Egypt he shall burn with fire.

Denunciation of Persistent Idolatry

44 The word that came to Jeremiah
for all the Judeans living in the
land of Egypt, at Migdol, at Tahpanhes,
at Memphis, and in the land of Pathros,
2Thus says the LORD of hosts, the God of
Israel: You yourselves have seen all the disaster that I have brought on Jerusalem
and on all the towns of Judah. Look at
them; today they are a desolation, without
an inhabitant in them, 3because of the
wickedness that they committed, provoking me to anger, in that they went to make
offerings and serve other gods that they
had not known, neither they, nor you, nor
your ancestors. 4Yet I persistently sent to
you all my servants the prophets, saying,
"I beg you not to do this abominable
thing that I hate!" 5But they did not listen
or incline their ear, to turn from their
wickedness and make no offerings to other gods. 6So my wrath and my anger were
poured out and kindled in the towns of
Judah and in the streets of Jerusalem; and
they became a waste and a desolation, as
they still are today. 7And now thus says
the LORD God of hosts, the God of Israel:
Why are you doing such great harm to
yourselves, to cut off man and woman,
child and infant, from the midst of Judah,
leaving yourselves without a remnant?
8Why do you provoke me to anger with
the works of your hands, making offerings
to other gods in the land of Egypt where
you have come to settle? Will you be cut

[o] Meaning of Heb uncertain [p] Gk Syr: Heb *I*
[q] Gk Syr Vg: Heb *I*

off and become an object of cursing and ridicule among all the nations of the earth? ⁹Have you forgotten the crimes of your ancestors, of the kings of Judah, of their' wives, your own crimes and those of your wives, which they committed in the land of Judah and in the streets of Jerusalem? ¹⁰They have shown no contrition or fear to this day, nor have they walked in my law and my statutes that I set before you and before your ancestors.

11 Therefore thus says the LORD of hosts, the God of Israel: I am determined to bring disaster on you, to bring all Judah to an end. ¹²I will take the remnant of Judah who are determined to come to the land of Egypt to settle, and they shall perish, everyone; in the land of Egypt they shall fall; by the sword and by famine they shall perish; from the least to the greatest, they shall die by the sword and by famine; and they shall become an object of execration and horror, of cursing and ridicule. ¹³I will punish those who live in the land of Egypt, as I have punished Jerusalem, with the sword, with famine, and with pestilence, ¹⁴so that none of the remnant of Judah who have come to settle in the land of Egypt shall escape or survive or return to the land of Judah. Although they long to go back to live there, they shall not go back, except some fugitives.

15 Then all the men who were aware that their wives had been making offerings to other gods, and all the women who stood by, a great assembly, all the people who lived in Pathros in the land of Egypt, answered Jeremiah: ¹⁶"As for the word that you have spoken to us in the name of the LORD, we are not going to listen to you. ¹⁷Instead, we will do everything that we have vowed, make offerings to the queen of heaven and pour out libations to her, just as we and our ancestors, our kings and our officials, used to do in the towns of Judah and in the streets of Jerusalem. We used to have plenty of food, and prospered, and saw no misfortune. ¹⁸But from the time we stopped making offerings to the queen of heaven and pouring out libations to her, we have lacked everything and have perished by the sword and by famine." ¹⁹And the women said,ˢ "Indeed we will go on making offerings to the queen of heaven and pouring out libations to her; do you think that we made cakes for her, marked with her image, and poured out libations

to her without our husbands' being involved?"

20 Then Jeremiah said to all the people, men and women, all the people who were giving him this answer: ²¹"As for the offerings that you made in the towns of Judah and in the streets of Jerusalem, you and your ancestors, your kings and your officials, and the people of the land, did not the LORD remember them? Did it not come into his mind? ²²The LORD could no longer bear the sight of your evil doings, the abominations that you committed; therefore your land became a desolation and a waste and a curse, without inhabitant, as it is to this day. ²³It is because you burned offerings, and because you sinned against the LORD and did not obey the voice of the LORD or walk in his law and in his statutes and in his decrees, that this disaster has befallen you, as is still evident today."

24 Jeremiah said to all the people and all the women, "Hear the word of the LORD, all you Judeans who are in the land of Egypt, ²⁵Thus says the LORD of hosts, the God of Israel: You and your wives have accomplished in deeds what you declared in words, saying, 'We are determined to perform the vows that we have made, to make offerings to the queen of heaven and to pour out libations to her.' By all means, keep your vows and make your libations! ²⁶Therefore hear the word of the LORD, all you Judeans who live in the land of Egypt: Lo, I swear by my great name, says the LORD, that my name shall no longer be pronounced on the lips of any of the people of Judah in all the land of Egypt, saying, 'As the Lord GOD lives.' ²⁷I am going to watch over them for harm and not for good; all the people of Judah who are in the land of Egypt shall perish by the sword and by famine, until not one is left. ²⁸And those who escape the sword shall return from the land of Egypt to the land of Judah, few in number; and all the remnant of Judah, who have come to the land of Egypt to settle, shall know whose words will stand, mine or theirs! ²⁹This shall be the sign to you, says the LORD, that I am going to punish you in this place, in order that you may know that my words against you will surely be carried out: ³⁰Thus says the LORD, I am going

to give Pharaoh Hophra, king of Egypt, into the hands of his enemies, those who seek his life, just as I gave King Zedekiah of Judah into the hand of King Nebuchadrezzar of Babylon, his enemy who sought his life."

A Word of Comfort to Baruch

45 The word that the prophet Jeremiah spoke to Baruch son of Neriah, when he wrote these words in a scroll at the dictation of Jeremiah, in the fourth year of King Jehoiakim son of Josiah of Judah: ²Thus says the LORD, the God of Israel, to you, O Baruch: ³You said, "Woe is me! The LORD has added sorrow to my pain; I am weary with my groaning, and I find no rest." ⁴Thus you shall say to him, "Thus says the LORD: I am going to break down what I have built, and pluck up what I have planted—that is, the whole land. ⁵And you, do you seek great things for yourself? Do not seek them; for I am going to bring disaster upon all flesh, says the LORD; but I will give you your life as a prize of war in every place to which you may go."

Judgment on Egypt

46 The word of the LORD that came to the prophet Jeremiah concerning the nations.

2 Concerning Egypt, about the army of Pharaoh Neco, king of Egypt, which was by the river Euphrates at Carchemish and which King Nebuchadrezzar of Babylon defeated in the fourth year of King Jehoiakim son of Josiah of Judah:

³ Prepare buckler and shield,
    and advance for battle!
⁴ Harness the horses;
    mount the steeds!
  Take your stations with your
        helmets,
    whet your lances,
    put on your coats of mail!
⁵ Why do I see them terrified?
    They have fallen back;
  their warriors are beaten down,
    and have fled in haste.
  They do not look back—
    terror is all around!
                          says the LORD.
⁶ The swift cannot flee away,
    nor can the warrior escape;

Little Things

Always be faithful in little things, for in them our strength lies. To God nothing is little. He cannot make anything small; they are infinite. Practice fidelity in the least things, not for their own sake, but for the sake of the great thing that is the will of God, and which I respect greatly.

Do not pursue spectacular deeds. We must deliberately renounce all desires to see the fruit of our labor, doing all we can as best we can, leaving the rest in the hands of God. What matters is the gift of your self, the degree of love that you put into each one of your actions.

Do not allow yourselves to be disheartened by any failure as long as you have done your best. Neither glory in your success, but refer all to God in deepest thankfulness.

If you are discouraged, it is a sign of pride because it shows you trust in your own powers. Never bother about people's opinions. Be humble and you will never be disturbed. The Lord has willed me here where I am. He will offer a solution.

—MOTHER TERESA OF CALCUTTA

Scripture Reading for Today:
Jeremiah 45.1–5

Verse for Today:
Jeremiah 45.5

Go to page 1080 for your next devotional reading.

in the north by the river Euphrates
  they have stumbled and fallen.

7 Who is this, rising like the Nile,
  like rivers whose waters surge?
8 Egypt rises like the Nile,
  like rivers whose waters surge.
It said, Let me rise, let me cover the
  earth,
  let me destroy cities and their
    inhabitants.
9 Advance, O horses,
  and dash madly, O chariots!
Let the warriors go forth:
  Ethiopia[t] and Put who carry
    the shield,
  the Ludim, who draw[u] the bow.
10 That day is the day of the Lord GOD
    of hosts,
  a day of retribution,
  to gain vindication from his foes.
The sword shall devour and
    be sated,
  and drink its fill of their blood.
For the Lord GOD of hosts holds
    a sacrifice
  in the land of the north by the
    river Euphrates.
11 Go up to Gilead, and take balm,
  O virgin daughter Egypt!
In vain you have used many
    medicines;
  there is no healing for you.
12 The nations have heard of
    your shame,
  and the earth is full of your cry;
for warrior has stumbled against
    warrior;
  both have fallen together.

Babylonia Will Strike Egypt

13 The word that the LORD spoke to the
prophet Jeremiah about the coming of
King Nebuchadrezzar of Babylon to attack
the land of Egypt:

14 Declare in Egypt, and proclaim
    in Migdol;
  proclaim in Memphis and
    Tahpanhes;
Say, "Take your stations and
    be ready,
  for the sword shall devour those
    around you."
15 Why has Apis fled?[v]
  Why did your bull not stand?
  —because the LORD thrust
    him down.
16 Your multitude stumbled[w] and fell,

and one said to another,[x]
"Come, let us go back to our
    own people
  and to the land of our birth,
  because of the destroying sword."
17 Give Pharaoh, king of Egypt,
    the name
  "Braggart who missed his chance."

18 As I live, says the King,
  whose name is the LORD of hosts,
one is coming
  like Tabor among the mountains,
  and like Carmel by the sea.
19 Pack your bags for exile,
  sheltered daughter Egypt!
For Memphis shall become a waste,
  a ruin, without inhabitant.

20 A beautiful heifer is Egypt—
  a gadfly from the north lights
    upon her.
21 Even her mercenaries in her midst
  are like fatted calves;
they too have turned and fled
    together,
  they did not stand;
for the day of their calamity has
    come upon them,
  the time of their punishment.

22 She makes a sound like a snake
    gliding away;
  for her enemies march in force,
and come against her with axes,
  like those who fell trees.
23 They shall cut down her forest,
                   says the LORD,
  though it is impenetrable,
because they are more numerous
    than locusts;
  they are without number.
24 Daughter Egypt shall be put
    to shame;
  she shall be handed over to a
    people from the north.

25 The LORD of hosts, the God of Israel,
said: See, I am bringing punishment upon
Amon of Thebes, and Pharaoh, and Egypt
and her gods and her kings, upon Pharaoh and those who trust in him. 26I will
hand them over to those who seek their

---

[t] Or *Nubia;* Heb *Cush*   [u] Cn: Heb *who grasp, who
draw*   [v] Gk: Heb *Why was it swept away*
[w] Gk: Meaning of Heb uncertain   [x] Gk: Heb *and
fell one to another and they said*

life, to King Nebuchadrezzar of Babylon
and his officers. Afterward Egypt shall be
inhabited as in the days of old, says the
LORD.

God Will Save Israel

27 But as for you, have no fear, my
        servant Jacob,
    and do not be dismayed, O Israel;
  for I am going to save you from
        far away,
    and your offspring from the land
        of their captivity.
  Jacob shall return and have quiet
        and ease,
    and no one shall make him
        afraid.
28 As for you, have no fear, my servant
        Jacob,
                    says the LORD,
    for I am with you.
  I will make an end of all the nations
    among which I have banished
        you,
    but I will not make an end
        of you!
  I will chastise you in just measure,
    and I will by no means leave you
        unpunished.

Judgment on the Philistines

47 The word of the LORD that came to
      the prophet Jeremiah concerning
the Philistines, before Pharaoh attacked
Gaza:

2 Thus says the LORD:
    See, waters are rising out of
        the north
      and shall become an overflowing
        torrent;
    they shall overflow the land and all
        that fills it,
      the city and those who live in it.
    People shall cry out,
      and all the inhabitants of the land
        shall wail.
3 At the noise of the stamping of the
        hoofs of his stallions,
      at the clatter of his chariots, at the
        rumbling of their wheels,
    parents do not turn back for
        children,
      so feeble are their hands,
4 because of the day that is coming
      to destroy all the Philistines,
    to cut off from Tyre and Sidon
      every helper that remains.

For the LORD is destroying the
        Philistines,
    the remnant of the coastland
        of Caphtor.
5 Baldness has come upon Gaza,
      Ashkelon is silenced.
    O remnant of their power! *ʸ*
      How long will you gash
        yourselves?
6 Ah, sword of the LORD!
      How long until you are quiet?
    Put yourself into your scabbard,
      rest and be still!
7 How can it*ᶻ* be quiet,
      when the LORD has given it
        an order?
    Against Ashkelon and against the
        seashore—
      there he has appointed it.

Judgment on Moab

48 Concerning Moab.

Thus says the LORD of hosts, the God of
Israel:
    Alas for Nebo, it is laid waste!
      Kiriathaim is put to shame, it
        is taken;
    the fortress is put to shame and
        broken down;
2   the renown of Moab is no more.
    In Heshbon they planned evil
        against her:
      "Come, let us cut her off from
        being a nation!"
    You also, O Madmen, shall be
        brought to silence;*ᵃ*
      the sword shall pursue you.

3 Hark! a cry from Horonaim,
      "Desolation and great destruction!"
4 "Moab is destroyed!"
      her little ones cry out.
5 For at the ascent of Luhith
      they go*ᵇ* up weeping bitterly;
    for at the descent of Horonaim
      they have heard the distressing cry
        of anguish.
6 Flee! Save yourselves!
      Be like a wild ass*ᶜ* in the desert!

ʸ Gk: Heb *their valley*   *ᶻ* Gk Vg: Heb *you*   *ᵃ* The
place-name *Madmen* sounds like the Hebrew verb
to be silent   *ᵇ* Cn: Heb *he goes*   *ᶜ* Gk Aquila:
Heb *like Aroer*

7 Surely, because you trusted in your
    strongholds*d* and your
    treasures,
  you also shall be taken;
Chemosh shall go out into exile,
    with his priests and his
    attendants.
8 The destroyer shall come upon every
    town,
  and no town shall escape;
the valley shall perish,
  and the plain shall be destroyed,
  as the LORD has spoken.

9 Set aside salt for Moab,
  for she will surely fall;
  her towns shall become a
    desolation,
  with no inhabitant in them.

10 Accursed is the one who is slack in
doing the work of the LORD; and accursed
is the one who keeps back the sword from
bloodshed.

11 Moab has been at ease from his
    youth,
  settled like wine*e* on its dregs;
he has not been emptied from vessel
    to vessel,
  nor has he gone into exile;
therefore his flavor has remained
  and his aroma is unspoiled.

12 Therefore, the time is surely coming, says the LORD, when I shall send to
him decanters to decant him, and empty
his vessels, and break his*f* jars in pieces.
13Then Moab shall be ashamed of Chemosh, as the house of Israel was ashamed
of Bethel, their confidence.

14 How can you say, "We are heroes
    and mighty warriors"?
15 The destroyer of Moab and his
    towns has come up,
  and the choicest of his young men
    have gone down to slaughter,
  says the King, whose name is the
    LORD of hosts.
16 The calamity of Moab is near
    at hand
  and his doom approaches swiftly.
17 Mourn over him, all you his
    neighbors,
  and all who know his name;
  say, "How the mighty scepter is
    broken,
  the glorious staff!"

18 Come down from glory,
  and sit on the parched ground,
  enthroned daughter Dibon!
For the destroyer of Moab has come
    up against you;
  he has destroyed your
    strongholds.
19 Stand by the road and watch,
  you inhabitant of Aroer!
Ask the man fleeing and the woman
    escaping;
  say, "What has happened?"
20 Moab is put to shame, for it is
    broken down;
  wail and cry!
Tell it by the Arnon,
  that Moab is laid waste.

21 Judgment has come upon the tableland, upon Holon, and Jahzah, and
Mephaath, 22and Dibon, and Nebo,
and Beth-diblathaim, 23and Kiriathaim,
and Beth-gamul, and Beth-meon, 24and
Kerioth, and Bozrah, and all the towns of
the land of Moab, far and near. 25The
horn of Moab is cut off, and his arm is
broken, says the LORD.
26 Make him drunk, because he magnified himself against the LORD; let Moab
wallow in his vomit; he too shall become
a laughingstock. 27Israel was a laughingstock for you, though he was not caught
among thieves; but whenever you spoke
of him you shook your head!

28 Leave the towns, and live on
    the rock,
  O inhabitants of Moab!
Be like the dove that nests
  on the sides of the mouth of
    a gorge.
29 We have heard of the pride of
    Moab—
  he is very proud—
of his loftiness, his pride, and his
    arrogance,
  and the haughtiness of his heart.
30 I myself know his insolence, says the
    LORD;
  his boasts are false,
  his deeds are false.
31 Therefore I wail for Moab;
  I cry out for all Moab;
  for the people of Kir-heres I
    mourn.

d Gk: Heb *works*   *e* Heb lacks *like wine*   *f* Gk
Aquila: Heb *their*

32 More than for Jazer I weep for you,
    O vine of Sibmah!
Your branches crossed over the sea,
    reached as far as Jazer; *g*
upon your summer fruits and
    your vintage
    the destroyer has fallen.
33 Gladness and joy have been
    taken away
    from the fruitful land of Moab;
I have stopped the wine from the
    wine presses;
    no one treads them with shouts of
    joy;
    the shouting is not the shout
    of joy.

34 Heshbon and Elealeh cry out;*h* as far as Jahaz they utter their voice, from Zoar to Horonaim and Eglath-shelishiyah. For even the waters of Nimrim have become desolate. 35And I will bring to an end in Moab, says the LORD, those who offer sacrifice at a high place and make offerings to their gods. 36Therefore my heart moans for Moab like a flute, and my heart moans like a flute for the people of Kir-heres; for the riches they gained have perished.

37 For every head is shaved and every beard cut off; on all the hands there are gashes, and on the loins sackcloth. 38On all the housetops of Moab and in the squares there is nothing but lamentation; for I have broken Moab like a vessel that no one wants, says the LORD. 39How it is broken! How they wail! How Moab has turned his back in shame! So Moab has become a derision and a horror to all his neighbors.

40 For thus says the LORD:
    Look, he shall swoop down like
        an eagle,
    and spread his wings against
        Moab;
41 the towns*i* shall be taken
    and the strongholds seized.
The hearts of the warriors of Moab,
    on that day,
    shall be like the heart of a woman
    in labor.
42 Moab shall be destroyed as a people,
    because he magnified himself
    against the LORD.
43 Terror, pit, and trap
    are before you, O inhabitants
    of Moab!
             says the LORD.

44 Everyone who flees from the terror
    shall fall into the pit,
and everyone who climbs out of
    the pit
    shall be caught in the trap.
For I will bring these things*j*
    upon Moab
    in the year of their punishment,
             says the LORD.

45 In the shadow of Heshbon
    fugitives stop exhausted;
for a fire has gone out from
    Heshbon,
    a flame from the house of Sihon;
it has destroyed the forehead
    of Moab,
    the scalp of the people of
    tumult.*k*
46 Woe to you, O Moab!
    The people of Chemosh have
        perished,
for your sons have been taken
    captive,
    and your daughters into captivity.
47 Yet I will restore the fortunes
    of Moab
    in the latter days, says the LORD.
Thus far is the judgment on Moab.

Judgment on the Ammonites

49 Concerning the Ammonites.

Thus says the LORD:
    Has Israel no sons?
    Has he no heir?
    Why then has Milcom dispossessed
        Gad,
    and his people settled in its
        towns?
2 Therefore, the time is surely coming,
    says the LORD,
when I will sound the battle alarm
    against Rabbah of the Ammonites;
it shall become a desolate mound,
    and its villages shall be burned
        with fire;
then Israel shall dispossess those
    who dispossessed him,
    says the LORD.

3 Wail, O Heshbon, for Ai is laid
    waste!

g Two Mss and Isa 16.8: MT *the sea of Jazer*
h Cn: Heb *From the cry of Heshbon to Elealeh*
i Or *Kerioth*   *j* Gk Syr: Heb *bring upon it*
k Or *of Shaon*

Cry out, O daughters[l] of
    Rabbah!
Put on sackcloth,
    lament, and slash yourselves with
      whips![m]
For Milcom shall go into exile,
    with his priests and his
      attendants.
4 Why do you boast in your strength?
    Your strength is ebbing,
  O faithless daughter.
    You trusted in your treasures,
      saying,
    "Who will attack me?"
5 I am going to bring terror upon you,
    says the Lord GOD of hosts,
    from all your neighbors,
  and you will be scattered, each
      headlong,
    with no one to gather the
      fugitives.

6 But afterward I will restore the fortunes of the Ammonites, says the LORD.

Judgment on Edom

7 Concerning Edom.

Thus says the LORD of hosts:
  Is there no longer wisdom in
    Teman?
    Has counsel perished from
      the prudent?
    Has their wisdom vanished?
8 Flee, turn back, get down low,
    inhabitants of Dedan!
  For I will bring the calamity of Esau
    upon him,
    the time when I punish him.
9 If grape-gatherers came to you,
    would they not leave gleanings?
  If thieves came by night,
    even they would pillage only what
      they wanted.
10 But as for me, I have stripped
    Esau bare,
  I have uncovered his hiding
      places,
  and he is not able to conceal
      himself.
  His offspring are destroyed,
    his kinsfolk
  and his neighbors; and he is
      no more.
11 Leave your orphans, I will keep
    them alive;
    and let your widows trust in me.

12 For thus says the LORD: If those who do not deserve to drink the cup still have to drink it, shall you be the one to go unpunished? You shall not go unpunished; you must drink it. 13For by myself I have sworn, says the LORD, that Bozrah shall become an object of horror and ridicule, a waste, and an object of cursing; and all her towns shall be perpetual wastes.

14 I have heard tidings from the LORD,
    and a messenger has been sent
      among the nations:
  "Gather yourselves together and
      come against her,
    and rise up for battle!"
15 For I will make you least among the
    nations,
    despised by humankind.
16 The terror you inspire
    and the pride of your heart have
      deceived you,
  you who live in the clefts of
      the rock,[n]
    who hold the height of the hill.
  Although you make your nest as
      high as the eagle's,
    from there I will bring you down,
          says the LORD.

17 Edom shall become an object of horror; everyone who passes by it will be horrified and will hiss because of all its disasters. 18As when Sodom and Gomorrah and their neighbors were overthrown, says the LORD, no one shall live there, nor shall anyone settle in it. 19Like a lion coming up from the thickets of the Jordan against a perennial pasture, I will suddenly chase Edom[o] away from it; and I will appoint over it whomever I choose.[p] For who is like me? Who can summon me? Who is the shepherd who can stand before me? 20Therefore hear the plan that the LORD has made against Edom and the purposes that he has formed against the inhabitants of Teman: Surely the little ones of the flock shall be dragged away; surely their fold shall be appalled at their fate. 21At the sound of their fall the earth shall tremble; the sound of their cry shall be heard at the Red Sea.[q] 22Look, he shall mount up and swoop down like an eagle, and spread his wings against Bozrah, and the heart of the warriors of Edom in that

---

[l] Or *villages*   [m] Cn: Meaning of Heb uncertain
[n] Or *of Sela*   [o] Heb *him*   [p] Or *and I will single out the choicest of his rams*: Meaning of Heb uncertain   [q] Or *Sea of Reeds*

day shall be like the heart of a woman in labor.

Judgment on Damascus

23 Concerning Damascus.

Hamath and Arpad are confounded,
　for they have heard bad news;
they melt in fear, they are troubled
　　like the sea*r*
　that cannot be quiet.
24 Damascus has become feeble, she
　　turned to flee,
　and panic seized her;
anguish and sorrows have taken
　　hold of her,
　as of a woman in labor.
25 How the famous city is forsaken,*s*
　the joyful town!*t*
26 Therefore her young men shall fall
　　in her squares,
　and all her soldiers shall be
　　destroyed in that day,
　　　says the LORD of hosts.
27 And I will kindle a fire at the wall of
　　Damascus,
　and it shall devour the
　　strongholds of Ben-hadad.

Judgment on Kedar and Hazor

28 Concerning Kedar and the kingdoms of Hazor that King Nebuchadrezzar of Babylon defeated.

Thus says the LORD:
Rise up, advance against Kedar!
　Destroy the people of the east!
29 Take their tents and their flocks,
　their curtains and all their goods;
carry off their camels for yourselves,
　and a cry shall go up: "Terror is
　　all around!"
30 Flee, wander far away, hide in
　　deep places,
　O inhabitants of Hazor!
　　　says the LORD.
For King Nebuchadrezzar of Babylon
　has made a plan against you
　and formed a purpose against
　　you.

31 Rise up, advance against a nation at
　　ease,
　that lives secure,
　　　says the LORD,
that has no gates or bars,
　that lives alone.
32 Their camels shall become booty,

their herds of cattle a spoil.
I will scatter to every wind
　those who have shaven temples,
and I will bring calamity
　against them from every side,
　　　says the LORD.
33 Hazor shall become a lair of jackals,
　an everlasting waste;
no one shall live there,
　nor shall anyone settle in it.

Judgment on Elam

34 The word of the LORD that came to the prophet Jeremiah concerning Elam, at the beginning of the reign of King Zedekiah of Judah.

35 Thus says the LORD of hosts: I am going to break the bow of Elam, the mainstay of their might; 36and I will bring upon Elam the four winds from the four quarters of heaven; and I will scatter them to all these winds, and there shall be no nation to which the exiles from Elam shall not come. 37I will terrify Elam before their enemies, and before those who seek their life; I will bring disaster upon them, my fierce anger, says the LORD. I will send the sword after them, until I have consumed them; 38and I will set my throne in Elam, and destroy their king and officials, says the LORD.

39 But in the latter days I will restore the fortunes of Elam, says the LORD.

Judgment on Babylon

50 The word that the LORD spoke concerning Babylon, concerning the land of the Chaldeans, by the prophet Jeremiah:
2 Declare among the nations
　　　and proclaim,
　set up a banner and proclaim,
　do not conceal it, say:
Babylon is taken,
　Bel is put to shame,
　Merodach is dismayed.
Her images are put to shame,
　her idols are dismayed.

3 For out of the north a nation has come up against her; it shall make her land a desolation, and no one shall live in it; both human beings and animals shall flee away.

4 In those days and in that time, says

---

r Cn: Heb *there is trouble in the sea*　　*s* Vg: Heb *is not forsaken*　　*t* Syr Vg Tg: Heb *the town of my joy*

the LORD, the people of Israel shall come,
they and the people of Judah together;
they shall come weeping as they seek the
LORD their God. 5They shall ask the way
to Zion, with faces turned toward it, and
they shall come and join*u* themselves to
the LORD by an everlasting covenant that
will never be forgotten.

6 My people have been lost sheep;
their shepherds have led them astray,
turning them away on the mountains;
from mountain to hill they have gone,
they have forgotten their fold. 7All who
found them have devoured them, and
their enemies have said, "We are not
guilty, because they have sinned against
the LORD, the true pasture, the LORD, the
hope of their ancestors."

8 Flee from Babylon, and go out of the
land of the Chaldeans, and be like male
goats leading the flock. 9For I am going to
stir up and bring against Babylon a company of great nations from the land of the
north; and they shall array themselves
against her; from there she shall be taken.
Their arrows are like the arrows of a
skilled warrior who does not return
empty-handed. 10Chaldea shall be plundered; all who plunder her shall be sated,
says the LORD.

11 Though you rejoice, though
      you exult,
  O plunderers of my heritage,
though you frisk about like a heifer
      on the grass,
  and neigh like stallions,
12 your mother shall be utterly shamed,
      and she who bore you shall
      be disgraced.
  Lo, she shall be the last of the
      nations,
  a wilderness, dry land, and
      a desert.
13 Because of the wrath of the LORD she
      shall not be inhabited,
  but shall be an utter desolation;
everyone who passes by Babylon
      shall be appalled
  and hiss because of all her
      wounds.
14 Take up your positions around
      Babylon,
  all you that bend the bow;
shoot at her, spare no arrows,

  for she has sinned against
      the LORD.
15 Raise a shout against her from
      all sides,
  "She has surrendered;
her bulwarks have fallen,
  her walls are thrown down."
For this is the vengeance of
      the LORD:
  take vengeance on her,
  do to her as she has done.
16 Cut off from Babylon the sower,
  and the wielder of the sickle in
      time of harvest;
because of the destroying sword
  all of them shall return to their
      own people,
  and all of them shall flee to their
      own land.

17 Israel is a hunted sheep driven away
by lions. First the king of Assyria devoured
it, and now at the end King Nebuchadrezzar of Babylon has gnawed its bones.
18Therefore, thus says the LORD of hosts,
the God of Israel: I am going to punish the
king of Babylon and his land, as I punished the king of Assyria. 19I will restore
Israel to its pasture, and it shall feed on
Carmel and in Bashan, and on the hills of
Ephraim and in Gilead its hunger shall be
satisfied. 20In those days and at that time,
says the LORD, the iniquity of Israel shall
be sought, and there shall be none; and
the sins of Judah, and none shall be
found; for I will pardon the remnant that
I have spared.

21 Go up to the land of Merathaim;*v*
      go up against her,
  and attack the inhabitants of
      Pekod*w*
  and utterly destroy the last
      of them,*x*
                    says the LORD;
  do all that I have commanded
      you.
22 The noise of battle is in the land,
      and great destruction!
23 How the hammer of the whole earth
      is cut down and broken!
How Babylon has become
      a horror among the nations!

---

u Gk: Heb *toward it. Come! They shall join*
v Or *of Double Rebellion*   *w* Or *of Punishment*
x Tg: Heb *destroy after them*

24 You set a snare for yourself and you
      were caught, O Babylon,
   but you did not know it;
   you were discovered and seized,
      because you challenged the LORD.
25 The LORD has opened his armory,
      and brought out the weapons of
         his wrath,
   for the Lord GOD of hosts has a task
      to do
   in the land of the Chaldeans.
26 Come against her from every
      quarter;
      open her granaries;
   pile her up like heaps of grain, and
      destroy her utterly;
      let nothing be left of her.
27 Kill all her bulls,
      let them go down to the slaughter.
   Alas for them, their day has come,
      the time of their punishment!

28 Listen! Fugitives and refugees from
the land of Babylon are coming to declare
in Zion the vengeance of the LORD our
God, vengeance for his temple.

29 Summon archers against Babylon,
all who bend the bow. Encamp all around
her; let no one escape. Repay her according to her deeds; just as she has done, do
to her—for she has arrogantly defied the
LORD, the Holy One of Israel. 30Therefore
her young men shall fall in her squares,
and all her soldiers shall be destroyed on
that day, says the LORD.

31 I am against you, O arrogant one,
      says the Lord GOD of hosts;
   for your day has come,
      the time when I will punish you.
32 The arrogant one shall stumble
      and fall,
      with no one to raise him up,
   and I will kindle a fire in his cities,
      and it will devour everything
         around him.

33 Thus says the LORD of hosts: The
people of Israel are oppressed, and so too
are the people of Judah; all their captors
have held them fast and refuse to let them
go. 34Their Redeemer is strong; the LORD of
hosts is his name. He will surely plead
their cause, that he may give rest to the
earth, but unrest to the inhabitants of
Babylon.

35 A sword against the Chaldeans, says
      the LORD,
   and against the inhabitants of
      Babylon,
   and against her officials and
      her sages!
36 A sword against the diviners,
      so that they may become fools!
   A sword against her warriors,
      so that they may be destroyed!
37 A sword against her[y] horses and
      against her[y] chariots,
   and against all the foreign troops
      in her midst,
      so that they may become women!
   A sword against all her treasures,
      that they may be plundered!
38 A drought[z] against her waters,
      that they may be dried up!
   For it is a land of images,
      and they go mad over idols.

39 Therefore wild animals shall live
with hyenas in Babylon,[a] and ostriches
shall never again be peopled, or inhabited for all generations.
40As when God overthrew Sodom and Go-
morrah and their neighbors, says the
LORD, so no one shall live there, nor shall
anyone settle in her.

41 Look, a people is coming from
      the north;
   a mighty nation and many kings
   are stirring from the farthest parts
      of the earth.
42 They wield bow and spear,
      they are cruel and have no mercy.
   The sound of them is like the
      roaring sea;
   they ride upon horses,
   set in array as a warrior for battle,
      against you, O daughter Babylon!

43 The king of Babylon heard news
      of them,
   and his hands fell helpless;
   anguish seized him,
   pain like that of a woman
      in labor.

44 Like a lion coming up from the
thickets of the Jordan against a perennial
pasture, I will suddenly chase them away
from her; and I will appoint over her

y Cn: Heb his   z Another reading is A sword
a Heb lacks in Babylon

whomever I choose.*b* For who is like me?
Who can summon me? Who is the shepherd who can stand before me? 45There-
fore hear the plan that the LORD has made
against Babylon, and the purposes that he
has formed against the land of the Chaldeans: Surely the little ones of the flock
shall be dragged away; surely their*c* fold
shall be appalled at their fate. 46At the
sound of the capture of Babylon the earth
shall tremble, and her cry shall be heard
among the nations.

51 Thus says the LORD:
I am going to stir up a
destructive wind*d*
against Babylon
and against the inhabitants of
Leb-qamai;*e*
2 and I will send winnowers to
Babylon,
and they shall winnow her.
They shall empty her land
when they come against her from
every side
on the day of trouble.
3 Let not the archer bend his bow,
and let him not array himself in
his coat of mail.
Do not spare her young men;
utterly destroy her entire army.
4 They shall fall down slain in the
land of the Chaldeans,
and wounded in her streets.
5 Israel and Judah have not been
forsaken
by their God, the LORD of hosts,
though their land is full of guilt
before the Holy One of Israel.

6 Flee from the midst of Babylon,
save your lives, each of you!
Do not perish because of her guilt,
for this is the time of the LORD's
vengeance;
he is repaying her what is due.
7 Babylon was a golden cup in the
LORD's hand,
making all the earth drunken;
the nations drank of her wine,
and so the nations went mad.
8 Suddenly Babylon has fallen and
is shattered;
wail for her!
Bring balm for her wound;
perhaps she may be healed.
9 We tried to heal Babylon,
but she could not be healed.

Forsake her, and let each of us go
to our own country;
for her judgment has reached up
to heaven
and has been lifted up even to the
skies.
10 The LORD has brought forth our
vindication;
come, let us declare in Zion
the work of the LORD our God.

11 Sharpen the arrows!
Fill the quivers!
The LORD has stirred up the spirit of the
kings of the Medes, because his purpose
concerning Babylon is to destroy it, for
that is the vengeance of the LORD, vengeance for his temple.
12 Raise a standard against the walls of
Babylon;
make the watch strong;
post sentinels;
prepare the ambushes;
for the LORD has both planned
and done
what he spoke concerning the
inhabitants of Babylon.
13 You who live by mighty waters,
rich in treasures,
your end has come,
the thread of your life is cut.
14 The LORD of hosts has sworn
by himself:
Surely I will fill you with troops like
a swarm of locusts,
and they shall raise a shout of
victory over you.

15 It is he who made the earth by
his power,
who established the world by
his wisdom,
and by his understanding stretched
out the heavens.
16 When he utters his voice there is a
tumult of waters in the
heavens,
and he makes the mist rise from
the ends of the earth.
He makes lightnings for the rain,
and he brings out the wind from
his storehouses.

*b Or and I will single out the choicest of her rams:
Meaning of Heb uncertain   c Syr Gk Tg
Compare 49.20: Heb lacks their   d Or stir up the
spirit of a destroyer   e Leb-qamai is a cryptogram
for Kasdim, Chaldea*

¹⁷ Everyone is stupid and without
        knowledge;
    goldsmiths are all put to shame
        by their idols;
    for their images are false,
        and there is no breath in them.
¹⁸ They are worthless, a work of
        delusion;
    at the time of their punishment
        they shall perish.
¹⁹ Not like these is the LORD, *f* the
        portion of Jacob,
    for he is the one who formed
        all things,
    and Israel is the tribe of his
        inheritance;
    the LORD of hosts is his name.

Israel the Creator's Instrument

²⁰ You are my war club, my weapon of
        battle:
    with you I smash nations;
    with you I destroy kingdoms;
²¹ with you I smash the horse and
        its rider;
    with you I smash the chariot and
        the charioteer;
²² with you I smash man and woman;
    with you I smash the old man
        and the boy;
    with you I smash the young man
        and the girl;
²³   with you I smash shepherds and
        their flocks;
    with you I smash farmers and
        their teams;
    with you I smash governors and
        deputies.

The Doom of Babylon

24 I will repay Babylon and all the inhabitants of Chaldea before your very eyes
for all the wrong that they have done in
Zion, says the LORD.

²⁵ I am against you, O destroying
        mountain,
                        says the LORD,
    that destroys the whole earth;
    I will stretch out my hand
        against you,
    and roll you down from the crags,
    and make you a burned-out
        mountain.
²⁶ No stone shall be taken from you
        for a corner
    and no stone for a foundation,

    but you shall be a perpetual waste,
        says the LORD.

²⁷ Raise a standard in the land,
    blow the trumpet among the
        nations;
    prepare the nations for war
        against her,
    summon against her the
        kingdoms,
        Ararat, Minni, and Ashkenaz;
    appoint a marshal against her,
    bring up horses like bristling
        locusts.
²⁸ Prepare the nations for war
        against her,
    the kings of the Medes, with their
        governors and deputies,
    and every land under their
        dominion.
²⁹ The land trembles and writhes,
    for the LORD's purposes against
        Babylon stand,
    to make the land of Babylon a
        desolation,
    without inhabitant.
³⁰ The warriors of Babylon have given
        up fighting,
    they remain in their strongholds;
    their strength has failed,
    they have become women;
    her buildings are set on fire,
    her bars are broken.
³¹ One runner runs to meet another,
    and one messenger to meet
        another,
    to tell the king of Babylon
    that his city is taken from end
        to end:
³² the fords have been seized,
    the marshes have been burned
        with fire,
    and the soldiers are in panic.
³³ For thus says the LORD of hosts, the
        God of Israel:
    Daughter Babylon is like a threshing
        floor
    at the time when it is trodden;
    yet a little while
    and the time of her harvest
        will come.

³⁴ "King Nebuchadrezzar of Babylon
        has devoured me,
    he has crushed me;
    he has made me an empty vessel,

f Heb lacks the LORD

he has swallowed me like
    a monster;
he has filled his belly with my
    delicacies,
he has spewed me out.
35 May my torn flesh be avenged on
    Babylon,"
    the inhabitants of Zion shall say.
"May my blood be avenged on the
    inhabitants of Chaldea,"
Jerusalem shall say.
36 Therefore thus says the LORD:
I am going to defend your cause
    and take vengeance for you.
I will dry up her sea
    and make her fountain dry;
37 and Babylon shall become a heap
    of ruins,
    a den of jackals,
an object of horror and of hissing,
    without inhabitant.

38 Like lions they shall roar together;
    they shall growl like lions'
    whelps.
39 When they are inflamed, I will set
    out their drink
    and make them drunk, until they
    become merry
and then sleep a perpetual sleep
    and never wake, says the LORD.
40 I will bring them down like lambs
    to the slaughter,
    like rams and goats.

41 How Sheshach g is taken,
    the pride of the whole earth
    seized!
How Babylon has become
    an object of horror among the
    nations!
42 The sea has risen over Babylon;
    she has been covered by its
    tumultuous waves.
43 Her cities have become an object
    of horror,
    a land of drought and a desert,
a land in which no one lives,
    and through which no mortal
    passes.
44 I will punish Bel in Babylon,
    and make him disgorge what he
    has swallowed.
The nations shall no longer stream
    to him;
    the wall of Babylon has fallen.

45 Come out of her, my people!

Save your lives, each of you,
    from the fierce anger of the LORD!
46 Do not be fainthearted or fearful
    at the rumors heard in the land—
one year one rumor comes,
    the next year another,
rumors of violence in the land
    and of ruler against ruler.

47 Assuredly, the days are coming
    when I will punish the images
    of Babylon;
her whole land shall be put to
    shame,
    and all her slain shall fall in
    her midst.
48 Then the heavens and the earth,
    and all that is in them,
shall shout for joy over Babylon;
    for the destroyers shall come
    against them out of
    the north,
    says the LORD.
49 Babylon must fall for the slain of
    Israel,
    as the slain of all the earth have
    fallen because of Babylon.

50 You survivors of the sword,
    go, do not linger!
Remember the LORD in a distant
    land,
    and let Jerusalem come into your
    mind:
51 We are put to shame, for we have
    heard insults;
    dishonor has covered our face,
for aliens have come
    into the holy places of the
    LORD's house.

52 Therefore the time is surely coming,
    says the LORD,
    when I will punish her idols,
and through all her land
    the wounded shall groan.
53 Though Babylon should mount up
    to heaven,
    and though she should fortify her
    strong height,
from me destroyers would come
    upon her,
    says the LORD.

54 Listen!—a cry from Babylon!

g *Sheshach* is a cryptogram for *Babel*, Babylon

A great crashing from the land of
   the Chaldeans!
55 For the LORD is laying Babylon waste,
   and stilling her loud clamor.
Their waves roar like mighty waters,
   the sound of their clamor
     resounds;
56 for a destroyer has come against her,
   against Babylon;
her warriors are taken,
   their bows are broken;
for the LORD is a God of recompense,
   he will repay in full.
57 I will make her officials and her
     sages drunk,
   also her governors, her deputies,
     and her warriors;
they shall sleep a perpetual sleep
   and never wake,
   says the King, whose name is the
     LORD of hosts.

58 Thus says the LORD of hosts:
The broad wall of Babylon
   shall be leveled to the ground,
and her high gates
   shall be burned with fire.
The peoples exhaust themselves for
     nothing,
   and the nations weary themselves
     only for fire.[h]

Jeremiah's Command to Seraiah

59 The word that the prophet Jeremiah
commanded Seraiah son of Neriah son of
Mahseiah, when he went with King Zedekiah of Judah to Babylon, in the fourth
year of his reign. Seraiah was the quarter-
master. 60 Jeremiah wrote in a[i] scroll all
the disasters that would come on Babylon, all these words that are written concerning Babylon. 61 And Jeremiah said to
Seraiah: "When you come to Babylon, see
that you read all these words, 62 and say,
'O LORD, you yourself threatened to destroy this place so that neither human beings nor animals shall live in it, and it
shall be desolate forever.' 63 When you finish reading this scroll, tie a stone to it, and
throw it into the middle of the Euphrates,
64 and say, 'Thus shall Babylon sink, to rise
no more, because of the disasters that I
am bringing on her.'"[j]
Thus far are the words of Jeremiah.

The Destruction of Jerusalem Reviewed

52 Zedekiah was twenty-one years
old when he began to reign; he
reigned eleven years in Jerusalem. His
mother's name was Hamutal daughter of
Jeremiah of Libnah. 2 He did what was evil
in the sight of the LORD, just as Jehoiakim
had done. 3 Indeed, Jerusalem and Judah
so angered the LORD that he expelled them
from his presence.

Zedekiah rebelled against the king of
Babylon. 4 And in the ninth year of his
reign, in the tenth month, on the tenth
day of the month, King Nebuchadrezzar
of Babylon came with all his army against
Jerusalem, and they laid siege to it; they
built siegeworks against it all around. 5 So
the city was besieged until the eleventh
year of King Zedekiah. 6 On the ninth day
of the fourth month the famine became
so severe in the city that there was no food
for the people of the land. 7 Then a breach
was made in the city wall;[k] and all the
soldiers fled and went out from the city by
night by the way of the gate between the
two walls, by the king's garden, though
the Chaldeans were all around the city.
They went in the direction of the Arabah.
8 But the army of the Chaldeans pursued
the king, and overtook Zedekiah in the
plains of Jericho; and all his army was
scattered, deserting him. 9 Then they captured the king, and brought him up to the
king of Babylon at Riblah in the land of
Hamath, and he passed sentence on him.
10 The king of Babylon killed the sons of
Zedekiah before his eyes, and also killed
all the officers of Judah at Riblah. 11 He
put out the eyes of Zedekiah, and bound
him in fetters, and the king of Babylon
took him to Babylon, and put him in prison until the day of his death.

12 In the fifth month, on the tenth day
of the month—which was the nineteenth
year of King Nebuchadrezzar, king of Babylon—Nebuzaradan the captain of the
bodyguard who served the king of Babylon, entered Jerusalem. 13 He burned the
house of the LORD, the king's house, and
all the houses of Jerusalem; every great
house he burned down. 14 All the army of
the Chaldeans, who were with the captain
of the guard, broke down all the walls
around Jerusalem. 15 Nebuzaradan the
captain of the guard carried into exile
some of the poorest of the people and the

h Gk Syr Compare Hab 2.13: Heb *and the nations
for fire, and they are weary*   i Or *one
on her. And they shall weary themselves*   j Gk: Heb
   k Heb
lacks *wall*

rest of the people who were left in the city and the deserters who had defected to the king of Babylon, together with the rest of the artisans. [16]But Nebuzaradan the captain of the guard left some of the poorest people of the land to be vinedressers and tillers of the soil.

17 The pillars of bronze that were in the house of the LORD, and the stands and the bronze sea that were in the house of the LORD, the Chaldeans broke in pieces, and carried all the bronze to Babylon. [18]They took away the pots, the shovels, the snuffers, the basins, the ladles, and all the vessels of bronze used in the temple service. [19]The captain of the guard took away the small bowls also, the firepans, the basins, the pots, the lampstands, the ladles, and the bowls for libation, both those of gold and those of silver. [20]As for the two pillars, the one sea, the twelve bronze bulls that were under the sea, and the stands,[i] which King Solomon had made for the house of the LORD, the bronze of all these vessels was beyond weighing. [21]As for the pillars, the height of the one pillar was eighteen cubits, its circumference was twelve cubits; it was hollow and its thickness was four fingers. [22]Upon it was a capital of bronze; the height of the capital was five cubits; latticework and pomegranates, all of bronze, encircled the top of the capital. And the second pillar had the same, with pomegranates. [23]There were ninety-six pomegranates on the sides; all the pomegranates encircling the latticework numbered one hundred.

24 The captain of the guard took the chief priest Seraiah, the second priest Zephaniah, and the three guardians of the threshold; [25]and from the city he took an officer who had been in command of the soldiers, and seven men of the king's council who were found in the city; the secretary of the commander of the army who mustered the people of the land; and sixty men of the people of the land who were found inside the city. [26]Then Nebuzaradan the captain of the guard took them, and brought them to the king of Babylon at Riblah. [27]And the king of Babylon struck them down, and put them to death at Riblah in the land of Hamath. So Judah went into exile out of its land.

28 This is the number of the people whom Nebuchadrezzar took into exile: in the seventh year, three thousand twenty-three Judeans; [29]in the eighteenth year of Nebuchadrezzar he took into exile from Jerusalem eight hundred thirty-two persons; [30]in the twenty-third year of Nebuchadrezzar, Nebuzaradan the captain of the guard took into exile of the Judeans seven hundred forty-five persons; all the persons were four thousand six hundred.

Jehoiachin Favored in Captivity

31 In the thirty-seventh year of the exile of King Jehoiachin of Judah, in the twelfth month, on the twenty-fifth day of the month, King Evil-merodach of Babylon, in the year he began to reign, showed favor to King Jehoiachin of Judah and brought him out of prison; [32]he spoke kindly to him, and gave him a seat above the seats of the other kings who were with him in Babylon. [33]So Jehoiachin put aside his prison clothes, and every day of his life he dined regularly at the king's table. [34]For his allowance, a regular daily allowance was given him by the king of Babylon, as long as he lived, up to the day of his death.

---

[i] Cn: Heb *that were under the stands*

Lamentations

Lamentations could also be entitled "Grief from A to Z" because it is a collection of five poems that lament the destruction of Jerusalem and its temple by the Babylonians in 587 B.C. The poems are constructed as acrostics—each verse begins with one of the 22 letters of the Hebrew alphabet in alphabetic sequence. It's as though the poet decided to explore Judah's terrible loss and the reasons for its punishment from beginning to end, from A to Z.

The first verse of Lamentations compares Jerusalem, not to God's bride, but to a widow in mourning. She weeps bitterly. Her lovers have left her, and her closest friends have become enemies. God has punished her unfaithfulness. But her grief is tinged with hope. Lamentations 3.22–24 proclaims: "The steadfast love of the LORD never ceases, his mercies never come to an end; they are new every morning; great is your faithfulness. 'The LORD is my portion,' says my soul, 'therefore I will hope in him.'"

The Deserted City

1 How lonely sits the city
    that once was full of people!
How like a widow she has become,
    she that was great among the
        nations!
She that was a princess among the
        provinces
    has become a vassal.

2 She weeps bitterly in the night,
    with tears on her cheeks;
among all her lovers
    she has no one to comfort her;
all her friends have dealt
        treacherously with her,
    they have become her enemies.

3 Judah has gone into exile with
        suffering
    and hard servitude;
she lives now among the nations,
    and finds no resting place;
her pursuers have all overtaken her
    in the midst of her distress.

4 The roads to Zion mourn,
    for no one comes to the festivals;
all her gates are desolate,
    her priests groan;
her young girls grieve,[a]
    and her lot is bitter.

a Meaning of Heb uncertain

5 Her foes have become the masters,
  her enemies prosper,
because the LORD has made
    her suffer
  for the multitude of her
    transgressions;
her children have gone away,
  captives before the foe.

6 From daughter Zion has departed
  all her majesty.

Her princes have become like
    stags
  that find no pasture;
they fled without strength
  before the pursuer.

7 Jerusalem remembers,
  in the days of her affliction and
    wandering,
all the precious things
  that were hers in days of old.

Comfort in Sorrow

Scripture Reading
for Today:
Lamentations 1.1–4

Verse for Today:
Lamentations 1.2

Compassionate friend,
in the Garden of Olives you cried,
"My soul is sorrowful
to the point of death" (see Matthew 26.38).
You are no stranger to grief.
My heart too is overcome with sadness.
I mourn for the loss
of the love relationship
with my former spouse.
I cry for the shattered dreams.
My heart aches when contemplating
the unrealized hopes and uncompleted plans
that are no longer possible.
Broken promises
and betrayal of trust
bring agony into my heart.
Sometimes the pain is so overwhelming
I no longer want to live.
The words of Psalm 6 echo within me,
"I have no strength left . . .
my bones are in torment . . .
I am worn out with groaning,
every night I drench my pillow
and soak my bed with tears;
my eye is wasted with grief."

Lord, comfort me in my sorrow.
Let me feel your gentle arms
surrounding my tired body.
Give me your strength so I may continue
the passage through this time of sadness.

—BARBARA LEAHY SHLEMON

Go to page 1084 for your next devotional reading.

When her people fell into the hand
    of the foe,
and there was no one to help her,
the foe looked on mocking
    over her downfall.

8 Jerusalem sinned grievously,
    so she has become a mockery;
all who honored her despise her,
    for they have seen her nakedness;
she herself groans,
    and turns her face away.

9 Her uncleanness was in her skirts;
    she took no thought of her future;
her downfall was appalling,
    with none to comfort her.
"O LORD, look at my affliction,
    for the enemy has triumphed!"

10 Enemies have stretched out
    their hands
    over all her precious things;
she has even seen the nations
    invade her sanctuary,
those whom you forbade
    to enter your congregation.

11 All her people groan
    as they search for bread;
they trade their treasures for food
    to revive their strength.
Look, O LORD, and see
    how worthless I have become.

12 Is it nothing to you,[b] all you who
    pass by?
    Look and see
if there is any sorrow like my
    sorrow,
    which was brought upon me,
which the LORD inflicted
    on the day of his fierce anger.

13 From on high he sent fire;
    it went deep into my bones;
he spread a net for my feet;
    he turned me back;
he has left me stunned,
    faint all day long.

14 My transgressions were bound[b] into
    a yoke;
    by his hand they were fastened
    together;
they weigh on my neck,
    sapping my strength;
the Lord handed me over
    to those whom I cannot
    withstand.

15 The LORD has rejected
    all my warriors in the midst
    of me;
he proclaimed a time against me
    to crush my young men;
the Lord has trodden as in a
    wine press
    the virgin daughter Judah.

16 For these things I weep;
    my eyes flow with tears;
for a comforter is far from me,
    one to revive my courage;
my children are desolate,
    for the enemy has prevailed.

17 Zion stretches out her hands,
    but there is no one to
    comfort her;
the LORD has commanded against
    Jacob
    that his neighbors should become
    his foes;
Jerusalem has become
    a filthy thing among them.

18 The LORD is in the right,
    for I have rebelled against
    his word;
but hear, all you peoples,
    and behold my suffering;
my young women and young men
    have gone into captivity.

19 I called to my lovers
    but they deceived me;
my priests and elders
    perished in the city
while seeking food
    to revive their strength.

20 See, O LORD, how distressed I am;
    my stomach churns,
my heart is wrung within me,
    because I have been very
    rebellious.
In the street the sword bereaves;
    in the house it is like death.

21 They heard how I was groaning,
    with no one to comfort me.
All my enemies heard of my trouble;

b Meaning of Heb uncertain

they are glad that you have done
    it.
Bring on the day you have
    announced,
    and let them be as I am.

22 Let all their evil doing come
      before you;
    and deal with them
as you have dealt with me
    because of all my transgressions;
for my groans are many
    and my heart is faint.

God's Warnings Fulfilled

2 How the Lord in his anger
    has humiliated[c] daughter Zion!
He has thrown down from heaven
      to earth
    the splendor of Israel;
he has not remembered his footstool
    in the day of his anger.

2 The Lord has destroyed without
      mercy
    all the dwellings of Jacob;
in his wrath he has broken down
    the strongholds of daughter Judah;
he has brought down to the ground
      in dishonor
    the kingdom and its rulers.

3 He has cut down in fierce anger
    all the might of Israel;
he has withdrawn his right hand
      from them
    in the face of the enemy;
he has burned like a flaming fire
      in Jacob,
    consuming all around.

4 He has bent his bow like an enemy,
    with his right hand set like a foe;
he has killed all in whom we
      took pride
    in the tent of daughter Zion;
he has poured out his fury like fire.

5 The Lord has become like an enemy;
    he has destroyed Israel.
He has destroyed all its palaces,
    laid in ruins its strongholds,
and multiplied in daughter Judah
    mourning and lamentation.

6 He has broken down his booth like
      a garden,
    he has destroyed his tabernacle;

the LORD has abolished in Zion
    festival and sabbath,
and in his fierce indignation has
      spurned
    king and priest.

7 The Lord has scorned his altar,
    disowned his sanctuary;
he has delivered into the hand of
      the enemy
    the walls of her palaces;
a clamor was raised in the house of
      the LORD
    as on a day of festival.

8 The LORD determined to lay in ruins
    the wall of daughter Zion;
he stretched the line;
    he did not withhold his hand
      from destroying;
he caused rampart and wall
      to lament;
    they languish together.

9 Her gates have sunk into
      the ground;
he has ruined and broken
      her bars;
her king and princes are among
      the nations;
    guidance is no more,
and her prophets obtain
    no vision from the LORD.

10 The elders of daughter Zion
    sit on the ground in silence;
they have thrown dust on
      their heads
    and put on sackcloth;
the young girls of Jerusalem
    have bowed their heads to
      the ground.

11 My eyes are spent with weeping;
    my stomach churns;
my bile is poured out on the ground
    because of the destruction of
      my people,
because infants and babes faint
    in the streets of the city.

12 They cry to their mothers,
    "Where is bread and wine?"
as they faint like the wounded
    in the streets of the city,

c Meaning of Heb uncertain

as their life is poured out
   on their mothers' bosom.

13 What can I say for you, to what
     compare you,
   O daughter Jerusalem?
To what can I liken you, that I may
     comfort you,
   O virgin daughter Zion?
For vast as the sea is your ruin;
   who can heal you?

14 Your prophets have seen for you
   false and deceptive visions;
they have not exposed your iniquity
   to restore your fortunes,
but have seen oracles for you
   that are false and misleading.

15 All who pass along the way
   clap their hands at you;
they hiss and wag their heads
   at daughter Jerusalem;
"Is this the city that was called
   the perfection of beauty,
   the joy of all the earth?"

16 All your enemies
   open their mouths against you;
they hiss, they gnash their teeth,
   they cry: "We have devoured her!
Ah, this is the day we longed for;
   at last we have seen it!"

17 The LORD has done what he
     purposed,
   he has carried out his threat;
as he ordained long ago,
   he has demolished without pity;
he has made the enemy rejoice
     over you,
   and exalted the might of
     your foes.

18 Cry aloud[d] to the Lord!
   O wall of daughter Zion!
Let tears stream down like a torrent
   day and night!
Give yourself no rest,
   your eyes no respite!

19 Arise, cry out in the night,
   at the beginning of the watches!
Pour out your heart like water
   before the presence of the Lord!
Lift your hands to him
   for the lives of your children,

who faint for hunger
   at the head of every street.

20 Look, O LORD, and consider!
   To whom have you done this?
Should women eat their offspring,
   the children they have borne?
Should priest and prophet be killed
   in the sanctuary of the Lord?

21 The young and the old are lying
   on the ground in the streets;
my young women and my
     young men
   have fallen by the sword;
in the day of your anger you have
     killed them,
   slaughtering without mercy.

22 You invited my enemies from
     all around
   as if for a day of festival;
and on the day of the anger of
     the LORD
   no one escaped or survived;
those whom I bore and reared
   my enemy has destroyed.

God's Steadfast Love Endures

3 I am one who has seen affliction
   under the rod of God's[e] wrath;
2 he has driven and brought me
   into darkness without any light;
3 against me alone he turns his hand,
   again and again, all day long.

4 He has made my flesh and my skin
     waste away,
   and broken my bones;
5 he has besieged and enveloped me
   with bitterness and tribulation;
6 he has made me sit in darkness
   like the dead of long ago.

7 He has walled me about so that I
     cannot escape;
   he has put heavy chains on me;
8 though I call and cry for help,
   he shuts out my prayer;
9 he has blocked my ways with hewn
     stones,
   he has made my paths crooked.

10 He is a bear lying in wait for me,
   a lion in hiding;

d Cn: Heb *Their heart cried*   e Heb *his*

11 he led me off my way and tore me
   to pieces;
   he has made me desolate;
12 he bent his bow and set me
   as a mark for his arrow.
13 He shot into my vitals
   the arrows of his quiver;
14 I have become the laughingstock
   of all my people,
   the object of their taunt-songs all
   day long.

15 He has filled me with bitterness,
   he has sated me with wormwood.
16 He has made my teeth grind
   on gravel,
   and made me cower in ashes;
17 my soul is bereft of peace;
   I have forgotten what
   happiness is;
18 so I say, "Gone is my glory,
   and all that I had hoped for from
   the LORD."

God, Hold My Hand

WEDNESDAY

Scripture Reading
for Today:
*Lamentations
3.16–33*

Verse for Today:
Lamentations 3.24

The phone rang, and our lives were changed forever. It is difficult to tell this story. As I write, it is just six months since our only grandson—year-and-a-half-old Paul, the joy of our family, the fourth generation of Paul Vogels—died at the hands of a babysitter.

Rushing to Children's Hospital and watching our precious baby, grandpa's "Little Buddy," on life support, seeing our son and daughter-in-law in anguish our whole family in disbelief—Paul died three days later. We were all around his bed praying. Robin, his mom, held him as he died. Paul, his dad, cried with his head on Robin's shoulder.

Late that night, I sat alone and wondered how and why this had happened. My Bible lay where I had left it three days before. I opened it to Lamentations 3. Now I could really understand the author's suffering. My whole family was broken and tired beyond anything we had ever known. Why had God allowed this? It was too awful to see Paul and Robin's grief, to conceive of life without their only child. Verse 18: "Gone is my glory, and all that I had hoped for from the LORD"; our line of Pauls was gone. Verse 20: "My soul . . . is bowed down."

But verses 21 to 24 offered hope—and they seemed to be for us too. Surely the Lord knew of our grief and was at our side. He was holding out a hand to me, a promise, some hope.

I have held onto this promise. The pain of loss will never go away, but the Lord is at our side. Verse 24 has become my daily prayer, reminding me to hope in God and take one day at a time, strengthening me to console others. In this hard journey, Lamentations 3 has indeed been the very hand of God holding ours.

—*BARBARA VOGEL*

Go to page 1090 for your next devotional reading.

¹⁹ The thought of my affliction and my
        homelessness
      is wormwood and gall!
²⁰ My soul continually thinks of it
      and is bowed down within me.
²¹ But this I call to mind,
      and therefore I have hope:

²² The steadfast love of the LORD never
        ceases, *f*
      his mercies never come to an end;
²³ they are new every morning;
      great is your faithfulness.
²⁴ "The LORD is my portion," says
        my soul,
      "therefore I will hope in him."

²⁵ The LORD is good to those who
        wait for him,
      to the soul that seeks him.
²⁶ It is good that one should wait
        quietly
      for the salvation of the LORD.
²⁷ It is good for one to bear
      the yoke in youth,
²⁸ to sit alone in silence
      when the Lord has imposed it,
²⁹ to put one's mouth to the dust
      (there may yet be hope),
³⁰ to give one's cheek to the smiter,
      and be filled with insults.

³¹ For the Lord will not
      reject forever.
³² Although he causes grief, he will
        have compassion
      according to the abundance of his
        steadfast love;
³³ for he does not willingly afflict
      or grieve anyone.

³⁴ When all the prisoners of the land
      are crushed under foot,
³⁵ when human rights are perverted
      in the presence of the Most High,
³⁶ when one's case is subverted
      —does the Lord not see it?

³⁷ Who can command and have
        it done,
      if the Lord has not ordained it?
³⁸ Is it not from the mouth of the
        Most High
      that good and bad come?
³⁹ Why should any who draw breath
        complain
      about the punishment of
        their sins?

⁴⁰ Let us test and examine our
        ways,
      and return to the LORD.
⁴¹ Let us lift up our hearts as well as
        our hands
      to God in heaven.
⁴² We have transgressed and rebelled,
      and you have not forgiven.

⁴³ You have wrapped yourself with
        anger and pursued us,
      killing without pity;
⁴⁴ you have wrapped yourself with
        a cloud
      so that no prayer can pass
        through.
⁴⁵ You have made us filth and rubbish
      among the peoples.

⁴⁶ All our enemies
      have opened their mouths against
        us;
⁴⁷ panic and pitfall have come
        upon us,
      devastation and destruction.
⁴⁸ My eyes flow with rivers of tears
      because of the destruction of
        my people.

⁴⁹ My eyes will flow without ceasing,
        without respite,
⁵⁰ until the LORD from heaven
      looks down and sees.
⁵¹ My eyes cause me grief
      at the fate of all the young
        women in my city.

⁵² Those who were my enemies
        without cause
      have hunted me like a bird;
⁵³ they flung me alive into a pit
      and hurled stones on me;
⁵⁴ water closed over my head;
      I said, "I am lost."

⁵⁵ I called on your name, O LORD,
      from the depths of the pit;
⁵⁶ you heard my plea, "Do not close
        your ear
      to my cry for help, but give
        me relief!"
⁵⁷ You came near when I called
        on you;
      you said, "Do not fear!"

f Syr Tg: Heb LORD, *we are not cut off*

58 You have taken up my cause,
O Lord,
you have redeemed my life.
59 You have seen the wrong done to
me, O Lord;
judge my cause.
60 You have seen all their malice,
all their plots against me.

61 You have heard their taunts,
O Lord,
all their plots against me.
62 The whispers and murmurs of my
assailants
are against me all day long.
63 Whether they sit or rise—see,
I am the object of their
taunt-songs.

64 Pay them back for their deeds,
O Lord,
according to the work of their
hands!
65 Give them anguish of heart;
your curse be on them!
66 Pursue them in anger and
destroy them
from under the Lord's heavens.

The Punishment of Zion

4 How the gold has grown dim,
how the pure gold is changed!
The sacred stones lie scattered
at the head of every street.

2 The precious children of Zion,
worth their weight in fine gold—
how they are reckoned as
earthen pots,
the work of a potter's hands!

3 Even the jackals offer the breast
and nurse their young,
but my people has become cruel,
like the ostriches in the
wilderness.

4 The tongue of the infant sticks
to the roof of its mouth for thirst;
the children beg for food,
but no one gives them anything.

5 Those who feasted on delicacies
perish in the streets;
those who were brought up
in purple
cling to ash heaps.

6 For the chastisement g of my people
has been greater
than the punishmenth of Sodom,
which was overthrown in a moment,
though no hand was laid on it. i

7 Her princes were purer than snow,
whiter than milk;
their bodies were more ruddy
than coral,
their hairi like sapphire. j

8 Now their visage is blacker
than soot;
they are not recognized in
the streets.
Their skin has shriveled on
their bones;
it has become as dry as wood.

9 Happier were those pierced by
the sword
than those pierced by hunger,
whose life drains away, deprived
of the produce of the field.

10 The hands of compassionate
women
have boiled their own children;
they became their food
in the destruction of my people.

11 The Lord gave full vent to his
wrath;
he poured out his hot anger,
and kindled a fire in Zion
that consumed its foundations.

12 The kings of the earth did
not believe,
nor did any of the inhabitants
of the world,
that foe or enemy could enter
the gates of Jerusalem.

13 It was for the sins of her prophets
and the iniquities of her priests,
who shed the blood of the
righteous
in the midst of her.

14 Blindly they wandered through
the streets,
so defiled with blood

g Or *iniquity*   h Or *sin*   i Meaning of Heb
uncertain   j Or *lapis lazuli*

that no one was able
   to touch their garments.

15 "Away! Unclean!" people shouted
    at them;
"Away! Away! Do not touch!"
So they became fugitives and
    wanderers;
   it was said among the nations,
   "They shall stay here no longer."

16 The LORD himself has scattered them,
   he will regard them no more;
no honor was shown to the priests,
   no favor to the elders.

17 Our eyes failed, ever watching
   vainly for help;
we were watching eagerly
   for a nation that could not save.

18 They dogged our steps
    so that we could not walk in
     our streets;
our end drew near; our days were
    numbered;
   for our end had come.

19 Our pursuers were swifter
    than the eagles in the heavens;
they chased us on the mountains,
    they lay in wait for us in the
     wilderness.

20 The LORD's anointed, the breath of
    our life,
   was taken in their pits—
the one of whom we said, "Under
    his shadow
   we shall live among the nations."

21 Rejoice and be glad, O daughter
    Edom,
   you that live in the land of Uz;
but to you also the cup shall pass;
    you shall become drunk and strip
     yourself bare.

22 The punishment of your iniquity,
    O daughter Zion, is
    accomplished,
   he will keep you in exile
    no longer;
but your iniquity, O daughter Edom,
    he will punish,
   he will uncover your sins.

A Plea for Mercy

5 Remember, O LORD, what has
   befallen us;
   look, and see our disgrace!
2 Our inheritance has been turned
    over to strangers,
   our homes to aliens.
3 We have become orphans, fatherless;
   our mothers are like widows.
4 We must pay for the water we drink;
   the wood we get must be bought.
5 With a yoke[k] on our necks we are
    hard driven;
   we are weary, we are given
    no rest.
6 We have made a pact with[l] Egypt
    and Assyria,
   to get enough bread.
7 Our ancestors sinned; they are
    no more,
   and we bear their iniquities.
8 Slaves rule over us;
   there is no one to deliver us from
    their hand.
9 We get our bread at the peril of
    our lives,
   because of the sword in the
    wilderness.
10 Our skin is black as an oven
   from the scorching heat of famine.
11 Women are raped in Zion,
   virgins in the towns of Judah.
12 Princes are hung up by their hands;
   no respect is shown to the elders.
13 Young men are compelled to grind,
    and boys stagger under loads
    of wood.
14 The old men have left the city
    gate,
   the young men their music.
15 The joy of our hearts has ceased;
    our dancing has been turned
    to mourning.
16 The crown has fallen from our
    head;
   woe to us, for we have sinned!
17 Because of this our hearts are sick,
    because of these things our eyes
    have grown dim:
18 because of Mount Zion, which
    lies desolate;
   jackals prowl over it.

19 But you, O LORD, reign forever;

---

k Symmachus: Heb lacks *With a yoke*   *l* Heb
have given the hand to

your throne endures to all
generations.
20 Why have you forgotten us
completely?
Why have you forsaken us these
many days?

21 Restore us to yourself, O LORD, that
we may be restored;
renew our days as of old—
22 unless you have utterly rejected us,
and are angry with us beyond
measure.

Baruch

Baruch was the secretary of the prophet Jeremiah. Though the opening lines ascribe the book to him as though he were writing from his exile in Babylon (Chaldea), there are varying opinions about who wrote it and when. In any case, Baruch is composed of five very different sections.

The first section opens with the Jews of Babylon weeping, fasting, and sending money to the high priest in Jerusalem so that an offering can be prepared on their behalf. They acknowledge their sins openly, admitting that God is in the right. Jerusalem and the temple are in ruins because the people have failed to keep his law. The next sections contain a poem praising the Law of Moses, a lament for Jerusalem, a song of hope for its restoration, and a letter ascribed to Jeremiah warning the Jews once again about the perils of idolatry.

Over and over, the pattern repeats itself. The people and their leaders sin. God sends a prophet to bring them back. If they fail to listen, they eventually suffer the consequences of their unfaithfulness. God is patient, but judgment will not be delayed forever. Baruch acknowledges that both punishment and restoration come from the hand of the Almighty.

Baruch and the Jews in Babylon

1 These are the words of the book that Baruch son of Neriah son of Mahseiah son of Zedekiah son of Hasadiah son of Hilkiah wrote in Babylon, ²in the fifth year, on the seventh day of the month, at the time when the Chaldeans took Jerusalem and burned it with fire.

3 Baruch read the words of this book to Jeconiah son of Jehoiakim, king of Judah, and to all the people who came to hear the book, ⁴and to the nobles and the princes, and to the elders, and to all the people, small and great, all who lived in Babylon by the river Sud.

5 Then they wept, and fasted, and prayed before the Lord; ⁶they collected as much money as each could give, ⁷and sent it to Jerusalem to the high priest*a* Jehoiakim son of Hilkiah son of Shallum, and to the priests, and to all the people who were present with him in Jerusalem. ⁸At the same time, on the tenth day of Sivan, Baruch*b* took the vessels of the house of the

a Gk *the priest*   *b* Gk *he*

Lord, which had been carried away from the temple, to return them to the land of Judah—the silver vessels that Zedekiah son of Josiah, king of Judah, had made, [9]after King Nebuchadnezzar of Babylon had carried away from Jerusalem Jeconiah and the princes and the prisoners and the nobles and the people of the land, and brought them to Babylon.

A Letter to Jerusalem

10 They said: Here we send you money; so buy with the money burnt offerings and sin offerings and incense, and prepare a grain offering, and offer them on the altar of the Lord our God; [11]and pray for the life of King Nebuchadnezzar of Babylon, and for the life of his son Belshazzar, so that their days on earth may be like the days of heaven. [12]The Lord will give us strength, and light to our eyes; we shall live under the protection[c] of King Nebuchadnezzar of Babylon, and under the protection of his son Belshazzar, and we shall serve them many days and find favor in their sight. [13]Pray also for us to the Lord our God, for we have sinned against the Lord our God, and to this day the anger of the Lord and his wrath have not turned away from us. [14]And you shall read aloud this scroll that we are sending you, to

c Gk in the shadow

THURSDAY

Scripture Reading for Today:
Baruch 1.13–22

Verse for Today:
Baruch 1.18

"Please Forgive Me"

I often ask why people don't go to confession today more than they do. It can't be that we're sinning less. Can we have lost our appreciation for the sacrament of reconciliation because we no longer realize how terrible sin is? Is it that we no longer appreciate the suffering and death of Jesus, that he died for us? Do we no longer realize that all we have to do, to claim the benefits of his suffering, is to confess our sins and to rely on his mercy?

When we go to confession, we realize that we fell, but Jesus forgives us. That's the beauty of our good and compassionate God. As Saint Paul says, "While we still were sinners Christ died for us" (Romans 5.8).

One of my favorite stories in Scripture is about Peter saying to Jesus, "Even though all become deserters, I will not . . . I will not deny you" (Mark 14.29, 31). Jesus who knows us so well was able to say to him, "Before the cock crows twice, you will deny me three times."

It is true that Peter denied the Lord, but when the Lord looked at him, he repented and wept bitterly for his sin (see Mark 14.72). The difference between Peter and Judas was Peter's ability to say, "Well, I sinned and denied my Master, but he has forgiven me." Judas couldn't forgive himself and couldn't accept God's forgiveness.

We must not allow guilt to beat us to the ground. It must not lead us into discouragement or depression. We have to keep humbling ourselves and saying, "Jesus, I did it again; please forgive me" and then to get up and keep going.

—BRIEGE MCKENNA, O.S.C.

Go to page 1092 for your next devotional reading.

make your confession in the house of the Lord on the days of the festivals and at appointed seasons.

Confession of Sins

15 And you shall say: The Lord our God is in the right, but there is open shame on us today, on the people of Judah, on the inhabitants of Jerusalem, 16and on our kings, our rulers, our priests, our prophets, and our ancestors, 17because we have sinned before the Lord. 18We have disobeyed him, and have not heeded the voice of the Lord our God, to walk in the statutes of the Lord that he set before us. 19From the time when the Lord brought our ancestors out of the land of Egypt until today, we have been disobedient to the Lord our God, and we have been negligent, in not heeding his voice. 20So to this day there have clung to us the calamities and the curse that the Lord declared through his servant Moses at the time when he brought our ancestors out of the land of Egypt to give to us a land flowing with milk and honey. 21We did not listen to the voice of the Lord our God in all the words of the prophets whom he sent to us, 22but all of us followed the intent of our own wicked hearts by serving other gods and doing what is evil in the sight of the Lord our God.

2 So the Lord carried out the threat he spoke against us: against our judges who ruled Israel, and against our kings and our rulers and the people of Israel and Judah. 2Under the whole heaven there has not been done the like of what he has done in Jerusalem, in accordance with the threats that were*d* written in the law of Moses. 3Some of us ate the flesh of their sons and others the flesh of their daughters. 4He made them subject to all the kingdoms around us, to be an object of scorn and a desolation among all the surrounding peoples, where the Lord has scattered them. 5They were brought down and not raised up, because our nation*e* sinned against the Lord our God, in not heeding his voice.

6 The Lord our God is in the right, but there is open shame on us and our ancestors this very day. 7All those calamities with which the Lord threatened us have come upon us. 8Yet we have not entreated the favor of the Lord by turning away, each of us, from the thoughts of our wick-

ed hearts. 9And the Lord has kept the calamities ready, and the Lord has brought them upon us, for the Lord is just in all the works that he has commanded us to do. 10Yet we have not obeyed his voice, to walk in the statutes of the Lord that he set before us.

Prayer for Deliverance

11 And now, O Lord God of Israel, who brought your people out of the land of Egypt with a mighty hand and with signs and wonders and with great power and outstretched arm, and made yourself a name that continues to this day, 12we have sinned, we have been ungodly, we have done wrong, O Lord our God, against all your ordinances. 13Let your anger turn away from us, for we are left, few in number, among the nations where you have scattered us. 14Hear, O Lord, our prayer and our supplication, and for your own sake deliver us, and grant us favor in the sight of those who have carried us into exile; 15so that all the earth may know that you are the Lord our God, for Israel and his descendants are called by your name.

16 O Lord, look down from your holy dwelling, and consider us. Incline your ear, O Lord, and hear; 17open your eyes, O Lord, and see, for the dead who are in Hades, whose spirit has been taken from their bodies, will not ascribe glory or justice to the Lord; 18but the person who is deeply grieved, who walks bowed and feeble, with failing eyes and famished soul, will declare your glory and righteousness, O Lord.

19 For it is not because of any righteous deeds of our ancestors or our kings that we bring before you our prayer for mercy, O Lord our God. 20For you have sent your anger and your wrath upon us, as you declared by your servants the prophets, saying: 21Thus says the Lord: Bend your shoulders and serve the king of Babylon, and you will remain in the land that I gave to your ancestors. 22But if you will not obey the voice of the Lord and will not serve the king of Babylon, 23I will make to cease from the towns of Judah and from the region around Jerusalem the voice of mirth and the voice of gladness, the voice of the bridegroom and the voice of the bride, and the whole land will be a desolation without inhabitants.

---

d Gk in accordance with what is   *e Gk because we*

24 But we did not obey your voice, to serve the king of Babylon; and you have carried out your threats, which you spoke by your servants the prophets, that the bones of our kings and the bones of our ancestors would be brought out of their resting place; 25and indeed they have been thrown out to the heat of day and the frost of night. They perished in great misery, by famine and sword and pestilence. 26And the house that is called by your name you have made as it is today, because of the wickedness of the house of Israel and the house of Judah.

God's Promise Recalled

27 Yet you have dealt with us, O Lord our God, in all your kindness and in all your great compassion, 28as you spoke by your servant Moses on the day when you commanded him to write your law in the presence of the people of Israel, saying, 29"If you will not obey my voice, this very

Mercy

FRIDAY

Scripture Reading for Today:
Baruch 2.27–35

Verse for Today:
Baruch 2.32

Céline Martin, sister of Saint Thérèse of Lisieux, had plenty of time to put her sister's "little way" to God into practice: she died at 89, after 64 years of religious life in the same Carmelite monastery as Thérèse and her other sisters. Longing for heaven, Céline learned deep trust and surrender as she praised God year after year in the "land of exile" (see Baruch 2.32).

I take as my own this passage from a prayer of Saint Thomas Aquinas: "At distant intervals, Lord, you draw me out of my lethargy, but alas! They are only passing visits. I do not know if you love me, or if I love you. I do not even know if I live by faith! I find only infidelity in myself, only random beginnings, only fruitless sacrifices and yet, I long for you."

Oh! yes, I too, but I am not discouraged; and for many years I have taken comfort in this verse of Psalm 63, which we recite each Sunday at Lauds: "O God, you are my God, I seek you, my soul thirsts for you; my flesh faints for you, as in a dry and weary land where there is no water. So I have looked upon you in the sanctuary, beholding your power and glory. Because your steadfast love is better than life, my lips will praise you."

I feel this so deeply that, in my imperfection, although I regret it, I thrill with happiness at the thought that God's mercy is better than life. Perfection, the possession of virtues, spiritual consolations, I call "life"; and "death" is the state in which I now am, in that dry, weary land without water, a state that does not prevent me, however, from approaching God with assurance, as if I were perfect, because I know it, I feel it: His "steadfast love is better than life." Yes, I rely only on God's mercy and on his compassion; I want to arouse his compassion by my poverty, for I know that is how I will have gained all.

—CÉLINE MARTIN

Go to page 1108 for your next devotional reading.

great multitude will surely turn into a small number among the nations, where I will scatter them. ³⁰For I know that they will not obey me, for they are a stiff-necked people. But in the land of their exile they will come to themselves ³¹and know that I am the Lord their God. I will give them a heart that obeys and ears that hear; ³²they will praise me in the land of their exile, and will remember my name ³³and turn from their stubbornness and their wicked deeds; for they will remember the ways of their ancestors, who sinned before the Lord. ³⁴I will bring them again into the land that I swore to give to their ancestors, to Abraham, Isaac, and Jacob, and they will rule over it; and I will increase them, and they will not be diminished. ³⁵I will make an everlasting covenant with them to be their God and they shall be my people; and I will never again remove my people Israel from the land that I have given them."

3 O Lord Almighty, God of Israel, the soul in anguish and the wearied spirit cry out to you. ²Hear, O Lord, and have mercy, for we have sinned before you. ³For you are enthroned forever, and we are perishing forever. ⁴O Lord Almighty, God of Israel, hear now the prayer of the people*f* of Israel, the children of those who sinned before you, who did not heed the voice of the Lord their God, so that calamities have clung to us. ⁵Do not remember the iniquities of our ancestors, but in this crisis remember your power and your name. ⁶For you are the Lord our God, and it is you, O Lord, whom we will praise. ⁷For you have put the fear of you in our hearts so that we would call upon your name; and we will praise you in our exile, for we have put away from our hearts all the iniquity of our ancestors who sinned against you. ⁸See, we are today in our exile where you have scattered us, to be reproached and cursed and punished for all the iniquities of our ancestors, who forsook the Lord our God.

In Praise of Wisdom

⁹ Hear the commandments of life,
     O Israel;
   give ear, and learn wisdom!
¹⁰ Why is it, O Israel, why is it that
       you are in the land of your
       enemies,
   that you are growing old in a
       foreign country,

that you are defiled with the dead,
¹¹   that you are counted among those
         in Hades?
¹² You have forsaken the fountain of
       wisdom.
¹³ If you had walked in the way of
       God,
   you would be living in peace
       forever.
¹⁴ Learn where there is wisdom,
   where there is strength,
   where there is understanding,
so that you may at the same time
       discern
   where there is length of days, and
       life,
   where there is light for the eyes,
       and peace.

¹⁵ Who has found her place?
   And who has entered her
       storehouses?
¹⁶ Where are the rulers of the nations,
   and those who lorded it over the
       animals on earth;
¹⁷ those who made sport of the birds
       of the air,
   and who hoarded up silver and
       gold
in which people trust,
   and there is no end to their
       getting;
¹⁸ those who schemed to get silver,
       and were anxious,
   but there is no trace of their
       works?
¹⁹ They have vanished and gone down
       to Hades,
   and others have arisen in their
       place.
²⁰ Later generations have seen the light
       of day,
   and have lived upon the earth;
but they have not learned the way to
       knowledge,
   nor understood her paths,
   nor laid hold of her.
²¹ Their descendants have strayed far
       from her*g* way.
²² She has not been heard of in
       Canaan,
   or seen in Teman;
²³ the descendants of Hagar, who seek
       for understanding on the
       earth,

_f_ Gk *dead*   _g_ Other ancient authorities read *their*

the merchants of Merran and
Teman,
the story-tellers and the seekers
for understanding,
have not learned the way to
wisdom,
or given thought to her paths.

24 O Israel, how great is the house of
God,
how vast the territory that he
possesses!
25 It is great and has no bounds;
it is high and immeasurable.
26 The giants were born there, who
were famous of old,
great in stature, expert in war.
27 God did not choose them,
or give them the way to
knowledge;
28 so they perished because they had
no wisdom,
they perished through their folly.

29 Who has gone up into heaven, and
taken her,
and brought her down from the
clouds?
30 Who has gone over the sea, and
found her,
and will buy her for pure gold?
31 No one knows the way to her,
or is concerned about the path to
her.
32 But the one who knows all things
knows her,
he found her by his
understanding.
The one who prepared the earth for
all time
filled it with four-footed creatures;
33 the one who sends forth the light,
and it goes;
he called it, and it obeyed him,
trembling;
34 the stars shone in their watches, and
were glad;
he called them, and they said,
"Here we are!"
They shone with gladness for him
who made them.
35 This is our God;
no other can be compared to
him.
36 He found the whole way to
knowledge,
and gave her to his servant Jacob
and to Israel, whom he loved.

37 Afterward she appeared on earth
and lived with humankind.

4 She is the book of the
commandments of God,
the law that endures forever.
All who hold her fast will live,
and those who forsake her will
die.
2 Turn, O Jacob, and take her;
walk toward the shining of her
light.
3 Do not give your glory to another,
or your advantages to an alien
people.
4 Happy are we, O Israel,
for we know what is pleasing to God.

Encouragement for Israel

5 Take courage, my people,
who perpetuate Israel's name!
6 It was not for destruction
that you were sold to the nations,
but you were handed over to your
enemies
because you angered God.
7 For you provoked the one who
made you
by sacrificing to demons and not
to God.
8 You forgot the everlasting God, who
brought you up,
and you grieved Jerusalem, who
reared you.
9 For she saw the wrath that came
upon you from God,
and she said:
Listen, you neighbors of Zion,
God has brought great sorrow
upon me;
10 for I have seen the exile of my sons
and daughters,
which the Everlasting brought
upon them.
11 With joy I nurtured them,
but I sent them away with
weeping and sorrow.
12 Let no one rejoice over me, a widow
and bereaved of many;
I was left desolate because of the
sins of my children,
because they turned away from
the law of God.
13 They had no regard for his statutes;
they did not walk in the ways of
God's commandments,
or tread the paths his
righteousness showed them.

14 Let the neighbors of Zion come;
      remember the capture of my sons
         and daughters,
      which the Everlasting brought
         upon them.
15 For he brought a distant nation
         against them,
      a nation ruthless and of a strange
         language,
   which had no respect for the aged
      and no pity for a child.
16 They led away the widow's beloved
         sons,
      and bereaved the lonely woman
         of her daughters.

17 But I, how can I help you?
18 For he who brought these calamities
         upon you
      will deliver you from the hand of
         your enemies.
19 Go, my children, go;
      for I have been left desolate.
20 I have taken off the robe of peace
      and put on sackcloth for my
         supplication;
      I will cry to the Everlasting all my
         days.

21 Take courage, my children, cry to
         God,
      and he will deliver you from the
         power and hand of the
         enemy.
22 For I have put my hope in the
         Everlasting to save you,
      and joy has come to me from the
         Holy One,
   because of the mercy that will soon
      come to you
      from your everlasting savior.*h*
23 For I sent you out with sorrow and
         weeping,
      but God will give you back to me
         with joy and gladness forever.
24 For as the neighbors of Zion have
         now seen your capture,
      so they soon will see your
         salvation by God,
   which will come to you with great
      glory
      and with the splendor of the
         Everlasting.
25 My children, endure with patience
         the wrath that has come
         upon you from God.
      Your enemy has overtaken you,

but you will soon see their
         destruction
      and will tread upon their necks.
26 My pampered children have traveled
         rough roads;
      they were taken away like a flock
         carried off by the enemy.

27 Take courage, my children, and cry
         to God,
      for you will be remembered by
         the one who brought this
         upon you.
28 For just as you were disposed to go
         astray from God,
      return with tenfold zeal to seek
         him.
29 For the one who brought these
         calamities upon you
      will bring you everlasting joy with
         your salvation.

Jerusalem Is Assured of Help

30 Take courage, O Jerusalem,
      for the one who named you will
         comfort you.
31 Wretched will be those who
         mistreated you
      and who rejoiced at your fall.
32 Wretched will be the cities that your
         children served as slaves;
      wretched will be the city that
         received your offspring.
33 For just as she rejoiced at your fall
         and was glad for your ruin,
      so she will be grieved at her own
         desolation.
34 I will take away her pride in her
         great population,
      and her insolence will be turned
         to grief.
35 For fire will come upon her from
         the Everlasting for many days,
      and for a long time she will be
         inhabited by demons.

36 Look toward the east, O Jerusalem,
      and see the joy that is coming to
         you from God.
37 Look, your children are coming,
         whom you sent away;
      they are coming, gathered from
         east and west,
   at the word of the Holy One,
      rejoicing in the glory of God.

h Or from the Everlasting, your savior

5 Take off the garment of your
sorrow and affliction,
O Jerusalem,
and put on forever the beauty of
the glory from God.
² Put on the robe of the righteousness
that comes from God;
put on your head the diadem of
the glory of the Everlasting;
³ for God will show your splendor
everywhere under heaven.
⁴ For God will give you evermore the
name,
"Righteous Peace, Godly Glory."

⁵ Arise, O Jerusalem, stand upon the
height;
look toward the east,

and see your children gathered from
west and east
at the word of the Holy One,
rejoicing that God has
remembered them.
⁶ For they went out from you on foot,
led away by their enemies;
but God will bring them back to
you,
carried in glory, as on a royal
throne.
⁷ For God has ordered that every high
mountain and the everlasting
hills be made low
and the valleys filled up, to make
level ground,
so that Israel may walk safely in
the glory of God.

THE TRADITION

Advent

Arise, O Jerusalem, stand upon the height . . .
and see the joy that is coming to you from God.
BARUCH 5.5; 4.36

W hen we enter into Advent, the
Church's four-week preparation for Christmas,
we are stepping into a long line of horizon-
watchers. The first ones were Old Testament
prophets such as Baruch who kept vigil for
the fulfillment of God's promise to restore his
people and establish his reign on earth. John
the Baptist, the last and greatest prophet,
was standing watch when that long-awaited
moment arrived. In words that recall Baruch
and others, John proclaimed the arrival, or
"advent," of God's kingdom and of the Messiah who would usher it in (see Luke 3.4–6).

Christ's coming changed everything, but
still God's people are on the watch. In Advent
our vigilance and expectation take on a keen-
er edge. Aiming our spiritual binoculars toward the past, we join with the men and
women of old who waited for the Savior
with eager longing. Looking to the future, we
prepare our hearts to welcome that Savior
again—not just at Christmas, but when he returns in glory. Christ has come; Christ will

come again—this is the true spirit of Advent.

Those of us who would rather watch at
the manger than listen for the final trumpet
should pay special attention to the Old Testament readings in the Advent liturgy. Like
the composite verse (above) from Baruch,
which appears as the Communion antiphon
for the second Sunday of Advent, they sound
exultant themes of joy and restoration, of
God's gathering in the poor and oppressed.

Jesus began this work at his first coming;
he will complete it at his second. The King
will establish his perfect reign, and there we
will be wrapped in justice and splendor,
raised up in glory, led in joy (see Baruch
5.1–9).

Advent is a season for learning to thrill at
our destiny and for longing that all humanity
might share it. Fundamentally, it is not about
buying Christmas gifts and decorating the
house. In Advent we prepare ourselves. We
live in hope as we do what we can to bring
God's kingdom into our world.

⁸ The woods and every fragrant tree
    have shaded Israel at God's
      command.
⁹ For God will lead Israel with joy,
    in the light of his glory,
    with the mercy and righteousness
      that come from him.

The Letter of Jeremiah

6 *i* A copy of a letter that Jeremiah sent to those who were to be taken to Babylon as exiles by the king of the Babylonians, to give them the message that God had commanded him.

The People Face a Long Captivity

2 Because of the sins that you have committed before God, you will be taken to Babylon as exiles by Nebuchadnezzar, king of the Babylonians. ³Therefore when you have come to Babylon you will remain there for many years, for a long time, up to seven generations; after that I will bring you away from there in peace. ⁴Now in Babylon you will see gods made of silver and gold and wood, which people carry on their shoulders, and which cause the heathen to fear. ⁵So beware of becoming at all like the foreigners or of letting fear for these gods*j* possess you ⁶when you see the multitude before and behind them worshiping them. But say in your heart, "It is you, O Lord, whom we must worship." ⁷For my angel is with you, and he is watching over your lives.

The Helplessness of Idols

8 Their tongues are smoothed by the carpenter, and they themselves are overlaid with gold and silver; but they are false and cannot speak. ⁹People*k* take gold and make crowns for the heads of their gods, as they might for a girl who loves ornaments. ¹⁰Sometimes the priests secretly take gold and silver from their gods and spend it on themselves, ¹¹or even give some of it to the prostitutes on the terrace. They deck their gods*l* out with garments like human beings—these gods of silver and gold and wood ¹²that cannot save themselves from rust and corrosion. When they have been dressed in purple robes, ¹³their faces are wiped because of the dust from the temple, which is thick upon them. ¹⁴One of them holds a scepter, like a district judge, but is unable to destroy anyone who offends it. ¹⁵Another has a dagger in its right hand, and an ax,

but cannot defend itself from war and robbers. ¹⁶From this it is evident that they are not gods; so do not fear them.

17 For just as someone's dish is useless when it is broken, ¹⁸so are their gods when they have been set up in the temples. Their eyes are full of the dust raised by the feet of those who enter. And just as the gates are shut on every side against anyone who has offended a king, as though under sentence of death, so the priests make their temples secure with doors and locks and bars, in order that they may not be plundered by robbers. ¹⁹They light more lamps for them than they light for themselves, though their gods*m* can see none of them. ²⁰They are*n* just like a beam of the temple, but their hearts, it is said, are eaten away when crawling creatures from the earth devour them and their robes. They do not notice ²¹when their faces have been blackened by the smoke of the temple. ²²Bats, swallows, and birds alight on their bodies and heads; and so do cats. ²³From this you will know that they are not gods; so do not fear them.

24 As for the gold that they wear for beauty—it*o* will not shine unless someone wipes off the tarnish; for even when they were being cast, they did not feel it. ²⁵They are bought without regard to cost, but there is no breath in them. ²⁶Having no feet, they are carried on the shoulders of others, revealing to humankind their worthlessness. And those who serve them are put to shame ²⁷because, if any of these gods falls*p* to the ground, they themselves must pick it up. If anyone sets it upright, it cannot move itself; and if it is tipped over, it cannot straighten itself. Gifts are placed before them just as before the dead. ²⁸The priests sell the sacrifices that are offered to these gods*q* and use the money themselves. Likewise their wives preserve some of the meat*r* with salt, but give none to the poor or helpless. ²⁹Sacrifices to them may even be touched by women in their periods or at child-

---

i The King James Version (like the Latin Vulgate) prints The Letter of Jeremiah as Chapter 6 of the Book of Baruch, and the chapter and verse numbers are here retained. In the Greek Septuagint, the Letter is separated from Baruch by the Book of Lamentations.   *j* Gk for them
k Gk They   *l* Gk them   *m* Gk they   *n* Gk It is
o Lat Syr: Gk *they*   *p* Gk *if they fall*   *q* Gk
to them   *r* Gk *of them*

birth. Since you know by these things that they are not gods, do not fear them.

30 For how can they be called gods? Women serve meals for gods of silver and gold and wood; [31]and in their temples the priests sit with their clothes torn, their heads and beards shaved, and their heads uncovered. [32]They howl and shout before their gods as some do at a funeral banquet. [33]The priests take some of the clothing of their gods[s] to clothe their wives and children. [34]Whether one does evil to them or good, they will not be able to repay it. They cannot set up a king or depose one. [35]Likewise they are not able to give either wealth or money; if one makes a vow to them and does not keep it, they will not require it. [36]They cannot save anyone from death or rescue the weak from the strong. [37]They cannot restore sight to the blind; they cannot rescue one who is in distress. [38]They cannot take pity on a widow or do good to an orphan. [39]These things that are made of wood and overlaid with gold and silver are like stones from the mountain, and those who serve them will be put to shame. [40]Why then must anyone think that they are gods, or call them gods?

The Foolishness of Worshiping Idols

Besides, even the Chaldeans themselves dishonor them; for when they see someone who cannot speak, they bring Bel and pray that the mute may speak, as though Bel[t] were able to understand! [41]Yet they themselves cannot perceive this and abandon them, for they have no sense. [42]And the women, with cords around them, sit along the passageways, burning bran for incense. [43]When one of them is led off by one of the passers-by and is taken to bed by him, she derides the woman next to her, because she was not as attractive as herself and her cord was not broken. [44]Whatever is done for these idols[u] is false. Why then must anyone think that they are gods, or call them gods?

45 They are made by carpenters and goldsmiths; they can be nothing but what the artisans wish them to be. [46]Those who make them will certainly not live very long themselves; [47]how then can the things that are made by them be gods? They have left only lies and reproach for those who come after. [48]For when war or calamity comes upon them, the priests consult together as to where they can hide themselves and their gods.[u] [49]How then can one fail to see that these are not gods, for they cannot save themselves from war or calamity? [50]Since they are made of wood and overlaid with gold and silver, it will afterward be known that they are false. [51]It will be manifest to all the nations and kings that they are not gods but the work of human hands, and that there is no work of God in them. [52]Who then can fail to know that they are not gods?[v]

53 For they cannot set up a king over a country or give rain to people. [54]They cannot judge their own cause or deliver one who is wronged, for they have no power; [55]they are like crows between heaven and earth. When fire breaks out in a temple of wooden gods overlaid with gold or silver, their priests will flee and escape, but the gods[w] will be burned up like timbers. [56]Besides, they can offer no resistance to king or enemy. Why then must anyone admit or think that they are gods?

57 Gods made of wood and overlaid with silver and gold are unable to save themselves from thieves or robbers. [58]Anyone who can will strip them of their gold and silver and of the robes they wear, and go off with this booty, and they will not be able to help themselves. [59]So it is better to be a king who shows his courage, or a household utensil that serves its owner's need, than to be these false gods; better even the door of a house that protects its contents, than these false gods; better also a wooden pillar in a palace, than these false gods.

60 For sun and moon and stars are bright, and when sent to do a service, they are obedient. [61]So also the lightning, when it flashes, is widely seen; and the wind likewise blows in every land. [62]When God commands the clouds to go over the whole world, they carry out his command. [63]And the fire sent from above to consume mountains and woods does what it is ordered. But these idols[x] are not to be compared with them in appearance or power. [64]Therefore one must not think that they are gods, nor call them gods, for they are not able either to decide a case or to do good to anyone. [65]Since you know then that they are not gods, do not fear them.

---

[s] Gk some of their clothing   [t] Gk he   [u] Gk them
[v] Meaning of Gk uncertain   [w] Gk they   [x] Gk these things

66 They can neither curse nor bless kings; 67they cannot show signs in the heavens for the nations, or shine like the sun or give light like the moon. 68The wild animals are better than they are, for they can flee to shelter and help themselves. 69So we have no evidence whatever that they are gods; therefore do not fear them.

70 Like a scarecrow in a cucumber bed, which guards nothing, so are their gods of wood, overlaid with gold and silver. 71In the same way, their gods of wood, over-laid with gold and silver, are like a thorn-bush in a garden on which every bird perches; or like a corpse thrown out in the darkness. 72From the purple and linen*y* that rot upon them you will know that they are not gods; and they will finally be consumed themselves, and be a reproach in the land. 73Better, therefore, is someone upright who has no idols; such a person will be far above reproach.

y Cn: Gk *marble*, Syr *silk*

Ezekiel

The book of Ezekiel, full of marvelous supernatural visions that both terrify and fascinate, reminds us of Revelation, the last book of the New Testament. The prophet Ezekiel is known for his sense of the majesty of God and for his dramatic prophetic gestures. He builds a model of Jerusalem under siege and then lies on his left side for 390 days and on his right side for an additional 40 days (see chapter 4). He shaves all the hair from his face and head, burning and scattering it (see chapter 5). Ezekiel delivers his prophecies as though to people who are deaf, who will not hear unless the word is spoken twice—first through actions and then through words.

Ezekiel prophesied in Babylon, where he and thousands of other Israelites were taken captive in 597 B.C. The first to prophesy outside Palestine, he warned the exiles about the coming destruction of Jerusalem and its temple, an event that took place in 587 B.C. when Nebuchadnezzar crushed a revolt by Zedekiah, Judah's last king. Once Jerusalem lay in ruins, Ezekiel's message dramatically altered, becoming hopeful as he envisioned a restored temple and a new Israel.

Ezekiel is a prophet whose message was designed to reshape the hearts of God's people in exile, keeping alive the promise of their eventual return to Jerusalem. Though the glory of the Lord had departed the temple, his word had not left his people without hope.

The Vision of the Chariot

1 In the thirtieth year, in the fourth month, on the fifth day of the month, as I was among the exiles by the river Chebar, the heavens were opened, and I saw visions of God. ²On the fifth day of the month (it was the fifth year of the exile of King Jehoiachin), ³the word of the LORD came to the priest Ezekiel son of Buzi, in the land of the Chaldeans by the river Chebar; and the hand of the LORD was on him there.

4 As I looked, a stormy wind came out of the north: a great cloud with brightness around it and fire flashing forth continually, and in the middle of the fire, something like gleaming amber. ⁵In the middle of it was something like four living creatures. This was their appearance: they were of human form. ⁶Each had four

faces, and each of them had four wings. 7Their legs were straight, and the soles of their feet were like the sole of a calf's foot; and they sparkled like burnished bronze. 8Under their wings on their four sides they had human hands. And the four had their faces and their wings thus: 9their wings touched one another; each of them moved straight ahead, without turning as they moved. 10As for the appearance of their faces: the four had the face of a human being, the face of a lion on the right side, the face of an ox on the left side, and the face of an eagle; 11such were their faces. Their wings were spread out above; each creature had two wings, each of which touched the wing of another, while two covered their bodies. 12Each moved straight ahead; wherever the spirit would go, they went, without turning as they went. 13In the middle of*a* the living creatures there was something that looked like burning coals of fire, like torches moving to and fro among the living creatures; the fire was bright, and lightning issued from the fire. 14The living creatures darted to and fro, like a flash of lightning.

15 As I looked at the living creatures, I saw a wheel on the earth beside the living creatures, one for each of the four of them.*b* 16As for the appearance of the wheels and their construction: their appearance was like the gleaming of beryl; and the four had the same form, their construction being something like a wheel within a wheel. 17When they moved, they moved in any of the four directions without veering as they moved. 18Their rims were tall and awesome, for the rims of all four were full of eyes all around. 19When the living creatures moved, the wheels moved beside them; and when the living creatures rose from the earth, the wheels rose. 20Wherever the spirit would go, they went, and the wheels rose along with them; for the spirit of the living creatures was in the wheels. 21When they moved, the others moved; when they stopped, the others stopped; and when they rose from the earth, the wheels rose along with them; for the spirit of the living creatures was in the wheels.

22 Over the heads of the living creatures there was something like a dome, shining like crystal,*c* spread out above their heads. 23Under the dome their wings were stretched out straight, one toward another; and each of the creatures had two wings covering its body. 24When they moved, I heard the sound of their wings like the sound of mighty waters, like the thunder of the Almighty,*d* a sound of tumult like the sound of an army; when they stopped, they let down their wings. 25And there came a voice from above the dome over their heads; when they stopped, they let down their wings.

26 And above the dome over their heads there was something like a throne, in appearance like sapphire;*e* and seated above the likeness of a throne was something that seemed like a human form. 27Upward from what appeared like the loins I saw something like gleaming amber, something that looked like fire enclosed all around; and downward from what looked like the loins I saw something that looked like fire, and there was a splendor all around. 28Like the bow in a cloud on a rainy day, such was the appearance of the splendor all around. This was the appearance of the likeness of the glory of the LORD.

When I saw it, I fell on my face, and I heard the voice of someone speaking.

The Vision of the Scroll

2 He said to me: O mortal,*f* stand up on your feet, and I will speak with you. 2And when he spoke to me, a spirit entered into me and set me on my feet; and I heard him speaking to me. 3He said to me, Mortal, I am sending you to the people of Israel, to a nation*g* of rebels who have rebelled against me; they and their ancestors have transgressed against me to this very day. 4The descendants are impudent and stubborn. I am sending you to them, and you shall say to them, "Thus says the Lord GOD." 5Whether they hear or refuse to hear (for they are a rebellious house), they shall know that there has been a prophet among them. 6And you, O mortal, do not be afraid of them, and do not be afraid of their words, though briers and thorns surround you and you live among scorpions; do not be afraid of their words, and do not be dismayed at their looks, for they are a rebel-

a Gk OL: Heb *And the appearance of*   *b* Heb *of their faces*   *c* Gk: Heb *like the awesome crystal*   *d* Traditional rendering of Heb *Shaddai*   *e* Or *lapis lazuli*   *f* Or *son of man;* Heb *ben adam* (and so throughout the book when Ezekiel is addressed)   *g* Syr: Heb *to nations*

lious house. [7]You shall speak my words to them, whether they hear or refuse to hear; for they are a rebellious house.

8 But you, mortal, hear what I say to you; do not be rebellious like that rebellious house; open your mouth and eat what I give you. [9]I looked, and a hand was stretched out to me, and a written scroll was in it. [10]He spread it before me; it had writing on the front and on the back, and written on it were words of lamentation and mourning and woe.

3 He said to me, O mortal, eat what is offered to you; eat this scroll, and go, speak to the house of Israel. [2]So I opened my mouth, and he gave me the scroll to eat. [3]He said to me, Mortal, eat this scroll that I give you and fill your stomach with it. Then I ate it; and in my mouth it was as sweet as honey.

4 He said to me: Mortal, go to the house of Israel and speak my very words to them. [5]For you are not sent to a people of obscure speech and difficult language, but to the house of Israel— [6]not to many peoples of obscure speech and difficult language, whose words you cannot understand. Surely, if I sent you to them, they would listen to you. [7]But the house of Israel will not listen to you, for they are not willing to listen to me; because all the house of Israel have a hard forehead and a stubborn heart. [8]See, I have made your face hard against their faces, and your forehead hard against their foreheads. [9]Like the hardest stone, harder than flint, I have made your forehead; do not fear them or be dismayed at their looks, for they are a rebellious house. [10]He said to me: Mortal, all my words that I shall speak to you receive in your heart and hear with your ears; [11]then go to the exiles, to your people, and speak to them. Say to them, "Thus says the Lord GOD"; whether they hear or refuse to hear.

Ezekiel at the River Chebar

12 Then the spirit lifted me up, and as the glory of the LORD rose[h] from its place, I heard behind me the sound of loud rumbling; [13]it was the sound of the wings of the living creatures brushing against one another, and the sound of the wheels beside them, that sounded like a loud rumbling. [14]The spirit lifted me up and bore me away; I went in bitterness in the heat of my spirit, the hand of the LORD being strong upon me. [15]I came to the exiles at

Tel-abib, who lived by the river Chebar.[i] And I sat there among them, stunned, for seven days.

16 At the end of seven days, the word of the LORD came to me: [17]Mortal, I have made you a sentinel for the house of Israel; whenever you hear a word from my mouth, you shall give them warning from me. [18]If I say to the wicked, "You shall surely die," and you give them no warning, or speak to warn the wicked from their wicked way, in order to save their life, those wicked persons shall die for their iniquity; but their blood I will require at your hand. [19]But if you warn the wicked, and they do not turn from their wickedness, or from their wicked way, they shall die for their iniquity; but you will have saved your life. [20]Again, if the righteous turn from their righteousness and commit iniquity, and I lay a stumbling block before them, they shall die; because you have not warned them, they shall die for their sin, and their righteous deeds that they have done shall not be remembered; but their blood I will require at your hand. [21]If, however, you warn the righteous not to sin, and they do not sin, they shall surely live, because they took warning; and you will have saved your life.

Ezekiel Isolated and Silenced

22 Then the hand of the LORD was upon me there; and he said to me, Rise up, go out into the valley, and there I will speak with you. [23]So I rose up and went out into the valley; and the glory of the LORD stood there, like the glory that I had seen by the river Chebar; and I fell on my face. [24]The spirit entered into me, and set me on my feet; and he spoke with me and said to me: Go, shut yourself inside your house. [25]As for you, mortal, cords shall be placed on you, and you shall be bound with them, so that you cannot go out among the people; [26]and I will make your tongue cling to the roof of your mouth, so that you shall be speechless and unable to reprove them; for they are a rebellious house. [27]But when I speak with you, I will open your mouth, and you shall say to them, "Thus says the Lord GOD"; let those who will hear, hear; and let those who

---

h Cn: Heb *and blessed be the glory of the LORD*
i Two Mss Syr: Heb *Chebar, and to where they lived.* Another reading is *Chebar, and I sat where they sat*

refuse to hear, refuse; for they are a rebellious house.

The Siege of Jerusalem Portrayed

4 And you, O mortal, take a brick and set it before you. On it portray a city, Jerusalem; ²and put siegeworks against it, and build a siege wall against it, and cast up a ramp against it; set camps also against it, and plant battering rams against it all around. ³Then take an iron plate and place it as an iron wall between you and the city; set your face toward it, and let it be in a state of siege, and press the siege against it. This is a sign for the house of Israel.

4 Then lie on your left side, and place the punishment of the house of Israel upon it; you shall bear their punishment for the number of the days that you lie there. ⁵For I assign to you a number of days, three hundred ninety days, equal to the number of the years of their punishment; and so you shall bear the punishment of the house of Israel. ⁶When you have completed these, you shall lie down a second time, but on your right side, and bear the punishment of the house of Judah; forty days I assign you, one day for each year. ⁷You shall set your face toward the siege of Jerusalem, and with your arm bared you shall prophesy against it. ⁸See, I am putting cords on you so that you cannot turn from one side to the other until you have completed the days of your siege.

9 And you, take wheat and barley, beans and lentils, millet and spelt; put them into one vessel, and make bread for yourself. During the number of days that you lie on your side, three hundred ninety days, you shall eat it. ¹⁰The food that you eat shall be twenty shekels a day by weight; at fixed times you shall eat it. ¹¹And you shall drink water by measure, one-sixth of a hin; at fixed times you shall drink. ¹²You shall eat it as a barley-cake, baking it in their sight on human dung. ¹³The Lord said, "Thus shall the people of Israel eat their bread, unclean, among the nations to which I will drive them." ¹⁴Then I said, "Ah Lord God! I have never defiled myself; from my youth up until now I have never eaten what died of itself or was torn by animals, nor has carrion flesh come into my mouth." ¹⁵Then he said to me, "See, I will let you have cow's dung

instead of human dung, on which you may prepare your bread."

16 Then he said to me, Mortal, I am going to break the staff of bread in Jerusalem; they shall eat bread by weight and with fearfulness; and they shall drink water by measure and in dismay. ¹⁷Lacking bread and water, they will look at one another in dismay, and waste away under their punishment.

A Sword against Jerusalem

5 And you, O mortal, take a sharp sword; use it as a barber's razor and run it over your head and your beard; then take balances for weighing, and divide the hair. ²One third of the hair you shall burn in the fire inside the city, when the days of the siege are completed; one third you shall take and strike with the sword all around the city;ʲ and one third you shall scatter to the wind, and I will unsheathe the sword after them. ³Then you shall take from these a small number, and bind them in the skirts of your robe. ⁴From these, again, you shall take some, throw them into the fire and burn them up; from there a fire will come out against all the house of Israel.

5 Thus says the Lord God: This is Jerusalem; I have set her in the center of the nations, with countries all around her. ⁶But she has rebelled against my ordinances and my statutes, becoming more wicked than the nations and the countries all around her, rejecting my ordinances and not following my statutes. ⁷Therefore thus says the Lord God: Because you are more turbulent than the nations that are all around you, and have not followed my statutes or kept my ordinances, but have acted according to the ordinances of the nations that are all around you; ⁸therefore thus says the Lord God: I, I myself, am coming against you; I will execute judgments among you in the sight of the nations. ⁹And because of all your abominations, I will do to you what I have never yet done, and the like of which I will never do again. ¹⁰Surely, parents shall eat their children in your midst, and children shall eat their parents; I will execute judgments on you, and any of you who survive I will scatter to every wind. ¹¹Therefore, as I live, says the Lord God, surely, because you have defiled my sanctuary with all

ʲ Heb *it*

your detestable things and with all your abominations—therefore I will cut you down;[k] my eye will not spare, and I will have no pity. [12]One third of you shall die of pestilence or be consumed by famine among you; one third shall fall by the sword around you; and one third I will scatter to every wind and will unsheathe the sword after them.

13 My anger shall spend itself, and I will vent my fury on them and satisfy myself; and they shall know that I, the LORD, have spoken in my jealousy, when I spend my fury on them. [14]Moreover I will make you a desolation and an object of mocking among the nations around you, in the sight of all that pass by. [15]You shall be[l] a mockery and a taunt, a warning and a horror, to the nations around you, when I execute judgments on you in anger and fury, and with furious punishments—I, the LORD, have spoken— [16]when I loose against you[m] my deadly arrows of famine, arrows for destruction, which I will let loose to destroy you, and when I bring more and more famine upon you, and break your staff of bread. [17]I will send famine and wild animals against you, and they will rob you of your children; pestilence and bloodshed shall pass through you; and I will bring the sword upon you. I, the LORD, have spoken.

Judgment on Idolatrous Israel

6 The word of the LORD came to me: [2]O mortal, set your face toward the mountains of Israel, and prophesy against them, [3]and say, You mountains of Israel, hear the word of the Lord GOD! Thus says the Lord GOD to the mountains and the hills, to the ravines and the valleys: I, I myself will bring a sword upon you, and I will destroy your high places. [4]Your altars shall become desolate, and your incense stands shall be broken; and I will throw down your slain in front of your idols. [5]I will lay the corpses of the people of Israel in front of their idols; and I will scatter your bones around your altars. [6]Wherever you live, your towns shall be waste and your high places ruined, so that your altars will be waste and ruined,[n] your idols broken and destroyed, your incense stands cut down, and your works wiped out. [7]The slain shall fall in your midst; then you shall know that I am the LORD.

8 But I will spare some. Some of you shall escape the sword among the nations and be scattered through the countries. [9]Those of you who escape shall remember me among the nations where they are carried captive, how I was crushed by their wanton heart that turned away from me, and their wanton eyes that turned after their idols. Then they will be loathsome in their own sight for the evils that they have committed, for all their abominations. [10]And they shall know that I am the LORD; I did not threaten in vain to bring this disaster upon them.

11 Thus says the Lord GOD: Clap your hands and stamp your foot, and say, Alas for all the vile abominations of the house of Israel! For they shall fall by the sword, by famine, and by pestilence. [12]Those far off shall die of pestilence; those nearby shall fall by the sword; and any who are left and are spared shall die of famine. Thus I will spend my fury upon them. [13]And you shall know that I am the LORD, when their slain lie among their idols around their altars, on every high hill, on all the mountain tops, under every green tree, and under every leafy oak, wherever they offered pleasing odor to all their idols. [14]I will stretch out my hand against them, and make the land desolate and waste, throughout all their settlements, from the wilderness to Riblah.[o] Then they shall know that I am the LORD.

Impending Disaster

7 The word of the LORD came to me: [2]You, O mortal, thus says the Lord GOD to the land of Israel:
An end! The end has come
    upon the four corners of the land.
[3] Now the end is upon you,
    I will let loose my anger
        upon you;
    I will judge you according to
        your ways,
    I will punish you for all your
        abominations.
[4] My eye will not spare you, I will
        have no pity.
    I will punish you for your ways,
        while your abominations are
            among you.
Then you shall know that I am the LORD.

---

[k] Another reading is *I will withdraw*   [l] Gk Syr Vg Tg: Heb *It shall be*   [m] Heb *them*   [n] Syr Vg Tg: Heb *and be made guilty*   [o] Another reading is *Diblah*

5 Thus says the Lord GOD:
Disaster after disaster! See, it comes.
6   An end has come, the end
        has come.
It has awakened against you; see,
        it comes!
7 Your doom *p* has come to you,
    O inhabitant of the land.
The time has come, the day
    is near—
    of tumult, not of reveling on the
        mountains.
8 Soon now I will pour out my wrath
        upon you;
    I will spend my anger against you.
I will judge you according to
        your ways,
    and punish you for all your
        abominations.
9 My eye will not spare; I will have no
        pity.
    I will punish you according to
        your ways,
    while your abominations are
        among you.
Then you shall know that it is I the LORD
who strike.
10 See, the day! See, it comes!
    Your doom *p* has gone out.
The rod has blossomed, pride has
        budded.
11   Violence has grown into a rod
        of wickedness.
    None of them shall remain,
        not their abundance, not their
            wealth;
        no pre-eminence among them. *p*
12 The time has come, the day
        draws near;
    let not the buyer rejoice, nor the
        seller mourn,
    for wrath is upon all their
        multitude.
13 For the sellers shall not return to what
has been sold as long as they remain alive.
For the vision concerns all their multitude; it shall not be revoked. Because of
their iniquity, they cannot maintain their
lives. *p*
14 They have blown the horn and
        made everything ready;
    but no one goes to battle,
    for my wrath is upon all their
        multitude.
15 The sword is outside, pestilence and
        famine are inside;
    those in the field die by
        the sword;

those in the city—famine and
        pestilence devour them.
16 If any survivors escape,
    they shall be found on the
        mountains
    like doves of the valleys,
    all of them moaning over
        their iniquity.
17 All hands shall grow feeble,
    all knees turn to water.
18 They shall put on sackcloth,
    horror shall cover them.
Shame shall be on all faces,
    baldness on all their heads.
19 They shall fling their silver into the
        streets,
    their gold shall be treated as
        unclean.
Their silver and gold cannot save them on
the day of the wrath of the LORD. They
shall not satisfy their hunger or fill their
stomachs with it. For it was the stumbling
block of their iniquity. 20 From their *q*
beautiful ornament, in which they took
pride, they made their abominable images, their detestable things; therefore I
will make of it an unclean thing to them.
21 I will hand it over to strangers
        as booty,
    to the wicked of the earth
        as plunder;
    they shall profane it.
22 I will avert my face from them,
    so that they may profane my
        treasured *r* place;
    the violent shall enter it,
    they shall profane it.
23 Make a chain! *p*
For the land is full of bloody crimes;
    the city is full of violence.
24 I will bring the worst of the nations
    to take possession of their houses.
I will put an end to the arrogance of
        the strong,
    and their holy places shall be
        profaned.
25 When anguish comes, they will seek
        peace,
    but there shall be none.
26 Disaster comes upon disaster,
    rumor follows rumor;
    they shall keep seeking a vision
        from the prophet;
    instruction shall perish from
        the priest,

p Meaning of Heb uncertain   *q* Syr Symmachus:
Heb *its*   *r* Or *secret*

and counsel from the elders.
27 The king shall mourn,
    the prince shall be wrapped
      in despair,
    and the hands of the people of
      the land shall tremble.
According to their way I will deal
    with them;
    according to their own judgments
      I will judge them.
And they shall know that I am the LORD.

Abominations in the Temple

8 In the sixth year, in the sixth month, on the fifth day of the month, as I sat in my house, with the elders of Judah sitting before me, the hand of the Lord GOD fell upon me there. 2I looked, and there was a figure that looked like a human being;*s* below what appeared to be its loins it was fire, and above the loins it was like the appearance of brightness, like gleaming amber. 3It stretched out the form of a hand, and took me by a lock of my head; and the spirit lifted me up between earth and heaven, and brought me in visions of God to Jerusalem, to the entrance of the gateway of the inner court that faces north, to the seat of the image of jealousy, which provokes to jealousy. 4And the glory of the God of Israel was there, like the vision that I had seen in the valley.

5 Then God*t* said to me, "O mortal, lift up your eyes now in the direction of the north." So I lifted up my eyes toward the north, and there, north of the altar gate, in the entrance, was this image of jealousy. 6He said to me, "Mortal, do you see what they are doing, the great abominations that the house of Israel are committing here, to drive me far from my sanctuary? Yet you will see still greater abominations."

7 And he brought me to the entrance of the court; I looked, and there was a hole in the wall. 8Then he said to me, "Mortal, dig through the wall"; and when I dug through the wall, there was an entrance. 9He said to me, "Go in, and see the vile abominations that they are committing here." 10So I went in and looked; there, portrayed on the wall all around, were all kinds of creeping things, and loathsome animals, and all the idols of the house of Israel. 11Before them stood seventy of the elders of the house of Israel, with Jaazaniah son of Shaphan standing among them. Each had his censer in his hand, and the fragrant cloud of incense was ascending. 12Then he said to me, "Mortal, have you seen what the elders of the house of Israel are doing in the dark, each in his room of images? For they say, 'The LORD does not see us, the LORD has forsaken the land.' " 13He said also to me, "You will see still greater abominations that they are committing."

14 Then he brought me to the entrance of the north gate of the house of the LORD; women were sitting there weeping for Tammuz. 15Then he said to me, "Have you seen this, O mortal? You will see still greater abominations than these."

16 And he brought me into the inner court of the house of the LORD; there, at the entrance of the temple of the LORD, between the porch and the altar, were about twenty-five men, with their backs to the temple of the LORD, and their faces toward the east, prostrating themselves to the sun toward the east. 17Then he said to me, "Have you seen this, O mortal? Is it not bad enough that the house of Judah commits the abominations done here? Must they fill the land with violence, and provoke my anger still further? See, they are putting the branch to their nose! 18Therefore I will act in wrath; my eye will not spare, nor will I have pity; and though they cry in my hearing with a loud voice, I will not listen to them."

The Slaughter of the Idolaters

9 Then he cried in my hearing with a loud voice, saying, "Draw near, you executioners of the city, each with his destroying weapon in his hand." 2And six men came from the direction of the upper gate, which faces north, each with his weapon for slaughter in his hand; among them was a man clothed in linen, with a writing case at his side. They went in and stood beside the bronze altar.

3 Now the glory of the God of Israel had gone up from the cherub on which it rested to the threshold of the house. The LORD called to the man clothed in linen, who had the writing case at his side; 4and said to him, "Go through the city, through Jerusalem, and put a mark on the foreheads of those who sigh and groan over all the abominations that are committed in it." 5To the others he said in my hearing, "Pass through the city after him,

s Gk: Heb *like fire*   *t* Heb *he*

and kill; your eye shall not spare, and you shall show no pity. ⁶Cut down old men, young men and young women, little children and women, but touch no one who has the mark. And begin at my sanctuary." So they began with the elders who were in front of the house. ⁷Then he said to them, "Defile the house, and fill the courts with the slain. Go!" So they went out and killed in the city. ⁸While they were killing, and I was left alone, I fell prostrate on my face and cried out, "Ah Lord GOD! will you destroy all who remain of Israel as you pour out your wrath upon Jerusalem?" ⁹He said to me, "The guilt of the house of Israel and Judah is exceedingly great; the land is full of bloodshed and the city full of perversity; for they say, 'The LORD has forsaken the land, and the LORD does not see.' ¹⁰As for me, my eye will not spare, nor will I have pity, but I will bring down their deeds upon their heads."

11 Then the man clothed in linen, with the writing case at his side, brought back word, saying, "I have done as you commanded me."

God's Glory Leaves Jerusalem

10 Then I looked, and above the dome that was over the heads of the cherubim there appeared above them something like a sapphire,ᵘ in form resembling a throne. ²He said to the man clothed in linen, "Go within the wheelwork underneath the cherubim; fill your hands with burning coals from among the cherubim, and scatter them over the city." He went in as I looked on. ³Now the cherubim were standing on the south side of the house when the man went in; and a cloud filled the inner court. ⁴Then the glory of the LORD rose up from the cherub to the threshold of the house; the house was filled with the cloud, and the court was full of the brightness of the glory of the LORD. ⁵The sound of the wings of the cherubim was heard as far as the outer court, like the voice of God Almightyᵛ when he speaks.

6 When he commanded the man clothed in linen, "Take fire from within the wheelwork, from among the cherubim," he went in and stood beside a wheel. ⁷And a cherub stretched out his hand from among the cherubim to the fire that was among the cherubim, took some of it and put it into the hands of the man clothed in linen, who took it and went

out. ⁸The cherubim appeared to have the form of a human hand under their wings.

9 I looked, and there were four wheels beside the cherubim, one beside each cherub; and the appearance of the wheels was like gleaming beryl. ¹⁰And as for their appearance, the four looked alike, something like a wheel within a wheel. ¹¹When they moved, they moved in any of the four directions without veering as they moved; but in whatever direction the front wheel faced, the others followed without veering as they moved. ¹²Their entire body, their rims, their spokes, their wings, and the wheels—the wheels of the four of them—were full of eyes all around. ¹³As for the wheels, they were called in my hearing "the wheelwork." ¹⁴Each one had four faces: the first face was that of the cherub, the second face was that of a human being, the third that of a lion, and the fourth that of an eagle.

15 The cherubim rose up. These were the living creatures that I saw by the river Chebar. ¹⁶When the cherubim moved, the wheels moved beside them; and when the cherubim lifted up their wings to rise up from the earth, the wheels at their side did not veer. ¹⁷When they stopped, the others stopped, and when they rose up, the others rose up with them; for the spirit of the living creatures was in them.

18 Then the glory of the LORD went out from the threshold of the house and stopped above the cherubim. ¹⁹The cherubim lifted up their wings and rose up from the earth in my sight as they went out with the wheels beside them. They stopped at the entrance of the east gate of the house of the LORD; and the glory of the God of Israel was above them.

20 These were the living creatures that I saw underneath the God of Israel by the river Chebar; and I knew that they were cherubim. ²¹Each had four faces, each four wings, and underneath their wings something like human hands. ²²As for what their faces were like, they were the same faces whose appearance I had seen by the river Chebar. Each one moved straight ahead.

Judgment on Wicked Counselors

11 The spirit lifted me up and brought me to the east gate of the

ᵘ Or *lapis lazuli*   ᵛ Traditional rendering of Heb *El Shaddai*

THE STORY OF A WOMAN

Jezebel

Her Name Means, "Where Is the Prince?"

Her Character: *A religious woman, she spread idolatry throughout Israel. Powerful, cunning, and arrogant, she actively opposed God, even in the face of indisputable proofs of his sovereignty.*
Her Triumph: *To have enhanced her own power at the expense of others.*
Her Tragedy: *Her arrogance led to a shameful death.*

Read I Kings 16.29–33; 18.1—19.2; 21.1–25; 2 Kings 9

Jezebel was a Phoenician princess, married to King Ahab, who reigned in Israel 100 years after David's death and 60 years after Israel split into northern and southern kingdoms.

A woman of great conviction and unwavering devotion, her ardent worship was directed, not to the God of Israel, but to the pagan fertility god, Baal, thought to control the rain and hence the harvest. So determined was she to convert Israel to her own religion that she hunted down and killed every prophet of God she could lay hands on, replacing them with 850 of her own.

The prophet Elijah had earlier warned King Ahab that Israel's God would punish the nation's idolatry with a lengthy drought, showing that it was God not Baal who was in charge. After three-and-a-half years of drought and famine, Elijah challenged Jezebel's prophets to a lopsided contest—850 to 1. After performing a miracle, Elijah rallied the people and slaughtered every last one of the false prophets.

Enraged, the queen sent a messenger to Elijah, vowing to kill him. But he fled south, beyond her grasp. To the queen's great annoyance, the pesky prophet showed up again one day to confront King Ahab:

Because you have sold yourself to do what is evil in the sight of the LORD, I will bring disaster on you; I will consume you,

and will cut off from Ahab every male, bond or free, in Israel. Also concerning Jezebel the LORD said, "The dogs shall eat Jezebel within the bounds of Jezreel."
(I Kings 21.20–21, 23)

Jezebel survived her husband by at least ten years. Finally, a man called Jehu came riding into town one day to carry out the last half of Elijah's prophecy.

Tough as nails, Jezebel stood proudly at an upper window of her palace. With painted eyes and perfectly coifed hair, she looked every inch the queen. Never one to back away from a fight, Jezebel shouted at Jehu, but he simply ignored her, challenging her servants to throw her out the window. Her blood spattered the walls of the palace as horses trampled her underfoot and a pack of dogs finished the job.

Like helium escaping a balloon, Jezebel's anger, threats, and dire warnings instantly disappeared. A powerful figure while she lived, hardly anything of her remained just shortly after her death. Paired with Israel's worst king, she was the nation's worst queen and one of the Bible's most infamous women.

Jezebel's story highlights the fact that God is just, as well as loving. Judgment is sometimes hard to think about, but in Jezebel's case we almost cheer her demise. For we know that to tolerate murder, idolatry, and the host of evils she presided over is not a sign of love but is itself evil. In fact, Jezebel had years in which to avail herself of God's mercy. But despite obvious miracles and repeated warnings, she was a woman who chose instead to harden her heart and suffer the consequences.

Praying in Light of the Story of Jezebel

Who considers the power of your anger? Your wrath is as great as the fear that is due you. So teach us to count our days that we may gain a wise heart.
—Psalm 90:11–12

Praise God: That he does not allow evil to go unpunished.
Offer Thanks: For justice, even when it seems delayed.
Confess: Any tendency to take God's mercy for granted.
Ask God: To give you a healthy fear of offending him.

Lift Your Heart

Had Jezebel thought more about her inevitable end, her story may have been remarkably different. As much as we like to pretend we're never going to die, it's healthy to consider our own demise from time to time. Doing so humbles us, strips away our illusions, reminds us we are creatures answerable to a Creator. Take 30 minutes to imagine your last day on earth. Who do you want to spend it with? What kind of memories do you want to leave behind? Do you have any lingering regrets, any unfinished business, any unfulfilled dreams? Ask God to guide you through this exercise. Let him show you what in your life can be affirmed and celebrated and what still needs to be transformed by his grace. Then tell him you're willing to do whatever it takes to become the woman he wants you to be.

Lord, I don't want to fear you for the wrong reasons but for the right ones— to stand in awe because of who you are. Gracious God, let me never make light of your justice or your power. Instead, let me live in a way that honors you. For you are Wonderful Counselor, Mighty God, Everlasting Father, Prince of Peace.

Go to page 1123 for your next devotional reading.

house of the LORD, which faces east. There, at the entrance of the gateway, were twenty-five men; among them I saw Jaazaniah son of Azzur, and Pelatiah son of Benaiah, officials of the people. 2He said to me, "Mortal, these are the men who devise iniquity and who give wicked counsel in this city; 3they say, 'The time is not near to build houses; this city is the pot, and we are the meat.' 4Therefore prophesy against them; prophesy, O mortal."

5 Then the spirit of the LORD fell upon me, and he said to me, "Say, Thus says the LORD: This is what you think, O house of Israel; I know the things that come into your mind. 6You have killed many in this city, and have filled its streets with the slain. 7Therefore thus says the Lord GOD: The slain whom you have placed within it are the meat, and this city is the pot; but you shall be taken out of it. 8You have feared the sword; and I will bring the sword upon you, says the Lord GOD. 9I will take you out of it and give you over to the hands of foreigners, and execute judgments upon you. 10You shall fall by the sword; I will judge you at the border of Israel. And you shall know that I am the LORD. 11This city shall not be your pot, and you shall not be the meat inside it; I will judge you at the border of Israel. 12Then you shall know that I am the LORD, whose statutes you have not followed, and whose ordinances you have not kept, but you have acted according to the ordinances of the nations that are around you."

13 Now, while I was prophesying, Pelatiah son of Benaiah died. Then I fell down on my face, cried with a loud voice, and said, "Ah Lord GOD! will you make a full end of the remnant of Israel?"

God Will Restore Israel

14 Then the word of the LORD came to me: 15Mortal, your kinsfolk, your own kin, your fellow exiles,w the whole house of Israel, all of them, are those of whom the inhabitants of Jerusalem have said, "They have gone far from the LORD; to us this land is given for a possession." 16Therefore say: Thus says the Lord GOD: Though I removed them far away among the nations, and though I scattered them among the countries, yet I have been a sanctuary to them for a little whilex in the countries where they have gone. 17Therefore say: Thus says the Lord GOD: I

will gather you from the peoples, and assemble you out of the countries where you have been scattered, and I will give you the land of Israel. 18When they come there, they will remove from it all its detestable things and all its abominations. 19I will give them oney heart, and put a new spirit within them; I will remove the heart of stone from their flesh and give them a heart of flesh, 20so that they may follow my statutes and keep my ordinances and obey them. Then they shall be my people, and I will be their God. 21But as for those whose heart goes after their detestable things and their abominations,z I will bring their deeds upon their own heads, says the Lord GOD.

22 Then the cherubim lifted up their wings, with the wheels beside them; and the glory of the God of Israel was above them. 23And the glory of the LORD ascended from the middle of the city, and stopped on the mountain east of the city. 24The spirit lifted me up and brought me in a vision by the spirit of God into Chaldea, to the exiles. Then the vision that I had seen left me. 25And I told the exiles all the things that the LORD had shown me.

Judah's Captivity Portrayed

12 The word of the LORD came to me: 2Mortal, you are living in the midst of a rebellious house, who have eyes to see but do not see, who have ears to hear but do not hear; 3for they are a rebellious house. Therefore, mortal, prepare for yourself an exile's baggage, and go into exile by day in their sight; you shall go like an exile from your place to another place in their sight. Perhaps they will understand, though they are a rebellious house. 4You shall bring out your baggage by day in their sight, as baggage for exile; and you shall go out yourself at evening in their sight, as those do who go into exile. 5Dig through the wall in their sight, and carry the baggage through it. 6In their sight you shall lift the baggage on your shoulder, and carry it out in the dark; you shall cover your face, so that you may not see the land; for I have made you a sign for the house of Israel.

7 I did just as I was commanded. I

---

w Gk Syr: Heb *people of your kindred*   x Or *to some extent*   y Another reading is *a new*   z Cn: Heb *And to the heart of their detestable things and their abominations their heart goes* brought out my baggage by day, as baggage for exile, and in the evening I dug through the wall with my own hands; I brought it out in the dark, carrying it on my shoulder in their sight.

8 In the morning the word of the LORD came to me: ⁹Mortal, has not the house of Israel, the rebellious house, said to you, "What are you doing?" ¹⁰Say to them, "Thus says the Lord GOD: This oracle concerns the prince in Jerusalem and all the house of Israel in it." ¹¹Say, "I am a sign for you: as I have done, so shall it be done to them; they shall go into exile, into captivity." ¹²And the prince who is among them shall lift his baggage on his shoulder in the dark, and shall go out; he*ᵃ* shall dig through the wall and carry it through; he shall cover his face, so that he may not see the land with his eyes. ¹³I will spread my net over him, and he shall be caught in my snare; and I will bring him to Babylon, the land of the Chaldeans, yet he shall not see it; and he shall die there. ¹⁴I will scatter to every wind all who are around him, his helpers and all his troops; and I will unsheathe the sword behind them. ¹⁵And they shall know that I am the LORD, when I disperse them among the nations and scatter them through the countries. ¹⁶But I will let a few of them escape from the sword, from famine and pestilence, so that they may tell of all their abominations among the nations where they go; then they shall know that I am the LORD.

Judgment Not Postponed

17 The word of the LORD came to me: ¹⁸Mortal, eat your bread with quaking, and drink your water with trembling and with fearfulness; ¹⁹and say to the people of the land, Thus says the Lord GOD concerning the inhabitants of Jerusalem in the land of Israel: They shall eat their bread with fearfulness, and drink their water in dismay, because their land shall be stripped of all it contains, on account of the violence of all those who live in it. ²⁰The inhabited cities shall be laid waste, and the land shall become a desolation; and you shall know that I am the LORD.

21 The word of the LORD came to me: ²²Mortal, what is this proverb of yours about the land of Israel, which says, "The days are prolonged, and every vision comes to nothing"? ²³Tell them therefore, "Thus says the Lord GOD: I will put an end to this proverb, and they shall use it no more as a proverb in Israel." But say to them, The days are near, and the fulfillment of every vision. ²⁴For there shall no longer be any false vision or flattering divination within the house of Israel. ²⁵But I the LORD will speak the word that I speak, and it will be fulfilled. It will no longer be delayed; but in your days, O rebellious house, I will speak the word and fulfill it, says the Lord GOD.

26 The word of the LORD came to me: ²⁷Mortal, the house of Israel is saying, "The vision that he sees is for many years ahead; he prophesies for distant times." ²⁸Therefore say to them, Thus says the Lord GOD: None of my words will be delayed any longer, but the word that I speak will be fulfilled, says the Lord GOD.

False Prophets Condemned

13 The word of the LORD came to me: ²Mortal, prophesy against the prophets of Israel who are prophesying; say to those who prophesy out of their own imagination: "Hear the word of the LORD!" ³Thus says the Lord GOD, Alas for the senseless prophets who follow their own spirit, and have seen nothing! ⁴Your prophets have been like jackals among ruins, O Israel. ⁵You have not gone up into the breaches, or repaired a wall for the house of Israel, so that it might stand in battle on the day of the LORD. ⁶They have envisioned falsehood and lying divination; they say, "Says the LORD," when the LORD has not sent them, and yet they wait for the fulfillment of their word! ⁷Have you not seen a false vision or uttered a lying divination, when you have said, "Says the LORD," even though I did not speak?

8 Therefore thus says the Lord GOD: Because you have uttered falsehood and envisioned lies, I am against you, says the Lord GOD. ⁹My hand will be against the prophets who see false visions and utter lying divinations; they shall not be in the council of my people, nor be enrolled in the register of the house of Israel, nor shall they enter the land of Israel; and you shall know that I am the Lord GOD. ¹⁰Because, in truth, because they have misled my people, saying, "Peace," when there is no peace; and because, when the people build a wall, these prophets*ᵇ*

ᵃ Gk Syr: Heb they   ᵇ Heb they

smear whitewash on it. 11Say to those who smear whitewash on it that it shall fall. There will be a deluge of rain,*c* great hailstones will fall, and a stormy wind will break out. 12When the wall falls, will it not be said to you, "Where is the whitewash you smeared on it?" 13Therefore thus says the Lord God: In my wrath I will make a stormy wind break out, and in my anger there shall be a deluge of rain, and hailstones in wrath to destroy it. 14I will break down the wall that you have smeared with whitewash, and bring it to the ground, so that its foundation will be laid bare; when it falls, you shall perish within it; and you shall know that I am the Lord. 15Thus I will spend my wrath upon the wall, and upon those who have smeared it with whitewash; and I will say to you, The wall is no more, nor those who smeared it— 16the prophets of Israel who prophesied concerning Jerusalem and saw visions of peace for it, when there was no peace, says the Lord God.

17 As for you, mortal, set your face against the daughters of your people, who prophesy out of their own imagination; prophesy against them 18and say, Thus says the Lord God: Woe to the women who sew bands on all wrists, and make veils for the heads of persons of every height, in the hunt for human lives! Will you hunt down lives among my people, and maintain your own lives? 19You have profaned me among my people for handfuls of barley and for pieces of bread, putting to death persons who should not die and keeping alive persons who should not live, by your lies to my people, who listen to lies.

20 Therefore thus says the Lord God: I am against your bands with which you hunt lives;*d* I will tear them from your arms, and let the lives go free, the lives that you hunt down like birds. 21I will tear off your veils, and save my people from your hands; they shall no longer be prey in your hands; and you shall know that I am the Lord. 22Because you have disheartened the righteous falsely, although I have not disheartened them, and you have encouraged the wicked not to turn from their wicked way and save their lives; 23therefore you shall no longer see false visions or practice divination; I will save my people from your hand. Then you will know that I am the Lord.

God's Judgments Justified

14 Certain elders of Israel came to me and sat down before me. 2And the word of the Lord came to me: 3Mortal, these men have taken their idols into their hearts, and placed their iniquity as a stumbling block before them; shall I let myself be consulted by them? 4Therefore speak to them, and say to them, Thus says the Lord God: Any of those of the house of Israel who take their idols into their hearts and place their iniquity as a stumbling block before them, and yet come to the prophet—I the Lord will answer those who come with the multitude of their idols, 5in order that I may take hold of the hearts of the house of Israel, all of whom are estranged from me through their idols.

6 Therefore say to the house of Israel, Thus says the Lord God: Repent and turn away from your idols; and turn away your faces from all your abominations. 7For any of those of the house of Israel, or of the aliens who reside in Israel, who separate themselves from me, taking their idols into their hearts and placing their iniquity as a stumbling block before them, and yet come to a prophet to inquire of me by him, I the Lord will answer them myself. 8I will set my face against them; I will make them a sign and a byword and cut them off from the midst of my people; and you shall know that I am the Lord.

9 If a prophet is deceived and speaks a word, I, the Lord, have deceived that prophet, and I will stretch out my hand against him, and will destroy him from the midst of my people Israel. 10And they shall bear their punishment—the punishment of the inquirer and the punishment of the prophet shall be the same— 11so that the house of Israel may no longer go astray from me, nor defile themselves any more with all their transgressions. Then they shall be my people, and I will be their God, says the Lord God.

12 The word of the Lord came to me: 13Mortal, when a land sins against me by acting faithlessly, and I stretch out my hand against it, and break its staff of bread and send famine upon it, and cut off from it human beings and animals, 14even if Noah, Daniel,*e* and Job, these three, were

---

c Heb *rain and you*   *d* Gk Syr: Heb *lives for birds*
e Or, as otherwise read, *Danel*

in it, they would save only their own lives by their righteousness, says the Lord GOD. ¹⁵If I send wild animals through the land to ravage it, so that it is made desolate, and no one may pass through because of the animals; ¹⁶even if these three men were in it, as I live, says the Lord GOD, they would save neither sons nor daughters; they alone would be saved, but the land would be desolate. ¹⁷Or if I bring a sword upon that land and say, "Let a sword pass through the land," and I cut off human beings and animals from it; ¹⁸though these three men were in it, as I live, says the Lord GOD, they would save neither sons nor daughters, but they alone would be saved. ¹⁹Or if I send a pestilence into that land, and pour out my wrath upon it with blood, to cut off humans and animals from it; ²⁰even if Noah, Daniel,ᶠ and Job were in it, as I live, says the Lord GOD, they would save neither son nor daughter; they would save only their own lives by their righteousness.

21 For thus says the Lord GOD: How much more when I send upon Jerusalem my four deadly acts of judgment, sword, famine, wild animals, and pestilence, to cut off humans and animals from it! ²²Yet, survivors shall be left in it, sons and daughters who will be brought out; they will come out to you. When you see their ways and their deeds, you will be consoled for the evil that I have brought upon Jerusalem, for all that I have brought upon it. ²³They shall console you, when you see their ways and their deeds; and you shall know that it was not without cause that I did all that I have done in it, says the Lord GOD.

The Useless Vine

15 The word of the LORD came to me: ² O mortal, how does the
wood of the vine surpass all
other wood—
the vine branch that is among the
trees of the forest?
³ Is wood taken from it to make
anything?
Does one take a peg from it on
which to hang any object?
⁴ It is put in the fire for fuel;
when the fire has consumed both
ends of it
and the middle of it is charred,
is it useful for anything?

⁵ When it was whole it was used for
nothing;
how much less—when the fire has
consumed it,
and it is charred—
can it ever be used for anything!

6 Therefore thus says the Lord GOD: Like the wood of the vine among the trees of the forest, which I have given to the fire for fuel, so I will give up the inhabitants of Jerusalem. ⁷I will set my face against them; although they escape from the fire, the fire shall still consume them; and you shall know that I am the LORD, when I set my face against them. ⁸And I will make the land desolate, because they have acted faithlessly, says the Lord GOD.

God's Faithless Bride

16 The word of the LORD came to me: ²Mortal, make known to Jerusalem her abominations, ³and say, Thus says the Lord GOD to Jerusalem: Your origin and your birth were in the land of the Canaanites; your father was an Amorite, and your mother a Hittite. ⁴As for your birth, on the day you were born your navel cord was not cut, nor were you washed with water to cleanse you, nor rubbed with salt, nor wrapped in cloths. ⁵No eye pitied you, to do any of these things for you out of compassion for you; but you were thrown out in the open field, for you were abhorred on the day you were born.

6 I passed by you, and saw you flailing about in your blood. As you lay in your blood, I said to you, "Live! ⁷and grow upᵍ like a plant of the field." You grew up and became tall and arrived at full womanhood;ʰ your breasts were formed, and your hair had grown; yet you were naked and bare.

8 I passed by you again and looked on you; you were at the age for love. I spread the edge of my cloak over you, and covered your nakedness: I pledged myself to you and entered into a covenant with you, says the Lord GOD, and you became mine. ⁹Then I bathed you with water and washed off the blood from you, and anointed you with oil. ¹⁰I clothed you with embroidered cloth and with sandals of fine leather; I bound you in fine linen and covered you with rich fabric.ⁱ ¹¹I

---

f Or, as otherwise read, *Danel*   g Gk Syr: Heb
Live! I made you a myriad   h Cn: Heb *ornament
of ornaments*   i Meaning of Heb uncertain

adorned you with ornaments: I put bracelets on your arms, a chain on your neck,
12a ring on your nose, earrings in your
ears, and a beautiful crown upon your
head. 13You were adorned with gold and
silver, while your clothing was of fine lin-
en, rich fabric,*j* and embroidered cloth.
You had choice flour and honey and oil
for food. You grew exceedingly beautiful,
fit to be a queen. 14Your fame spread
among the nations on account of your
beauty, for it was perfect because of my
splendor that I had bestowed on you, says
the Lord GOD.

15 But you trusted in your beauty, and
played the whore because of your fame,
and lavished your whorings on any
passer-by.*k* 16You took some of your garments, and made for yourself colorful
shrines, and on them played the whore;
nothing like this has ever been or ever
shall be.*j* 17You also took your beautiful
jewels of my gold and my silver that I had
given you, and made for yourself male images, and with them played the whore;
18and you took your embroidered garments to cover them, and set my oil and
my incense before them. 19Also my bread
that I gave you—I fed you with choice
flour and oil and honey—you set it before
them as a pleasing odor; and so it was,
says the Lord GOD. 20You took your sons
and your daughters, whom you had borne
to me, and these you sacrificed to them to
be devoured. As if your whorings were not
enough! 21You slaughtered my children
and delivered them up as an offering to
them. 22And in all your abominations and
your whorings you did not remember the
days of your youth, when you were naked
and bare, flailing about in your blood.

23 After all your wickedness (woe, woe
to you! says the Lord GOD), 24you built
yourself a platform and made yourself a
lofty place in every square; 25at the head
of every street you built your lofty place
and prostituted your beauty, offering
yourself to every passer-by, and multiplying your whoring. 26You played the whore
with the Egyptians, your lustful neighbors, multiplying your whoring, to provoke me to anger. 27Therefore I stretched
out my hand against you, reduced your
rations, and gave you up to the will of
your enemies, the daughters of the Philistines, who were ashamed of your lewd behavior. 28You played the whore with the
Assyrians, because you were insatiable;

you played the whore with them, and still
you were not satisfied. 29You multiplied
your whoring with Chaldea, the land of
merchants; and even with this you were
not satisfied.

30 How sick is your heart, says the
Lord GOD, that you did all these things,
the deeds of a brazen whore; 31building
your platform at the head of every street,
and making your lofty place in every
square! Yet you were not like a whore,
because you scorned payment. 32Adulter-
ous wife, who receives strangers instead
of her husband! 33Gifts are given to all
whores; but you gave your gifts to all your
lovers, bribing them to come to you from
all around for your whorings. 34So you
were different from other women in your
whorings: no one solicited you to play the
whore; and you gave payment, while no
payment was given to you; you were different.

35 Therefore, O whore, hear the word
of the LORD: 36Thus says the Lord GOD, Because your lust was poured out and your
nakedness uncovered in your whoring
with your lovers, and because of all your
abominable idols, and because of the
blood of your children that you gave to
them, 37therefore, I will gather all your
lovers, with whom you took pleasure, all
those you loved and all those you hated;
I will gather them against you from all
around, and will uncover your nakedness
to them, so that they may see all your
nakedness. 38I will judge you as women
who commit adultery and shed blood are
judged, and bring blood upon you in
wrath and jealousy. 39I will deliver you
into their hands, and they shall throw
down your platform and break down your
lofty places; they shall strip you of your
clothes and take your beautiful objects
and leave you naked and bare. 40They
shall bring up a mob against you, and
they shall stone you and cut you to pieces
with their swords. 41They shall burn your
houses and execute judgments on you in
the sight of many women; I will stop you
from playing the whore, and you shall
also make no more payments. 42So I will
satisfy my fury on you, and my jealousy
shall turn away from you; I will be calm,
and will be angry no longer. 43Because
you have not remembered the days of

---

j Meaning of Heb uncertain   *k* Heb adds *let it
be his*

your youth, but have enraged me with all these things; therefore, I have returned your deeds upon your head, says the Lord God.

Have you not committed lewdness beyond all your abominations? 44See, everyone who uses proverbs will use this proverb about you, "Like mother, like daughter." 45You are the daughter of your mother, who loathed her husband and her children; and you are the sister of your sisters, who loathed their husbands and their children. Your mother was a Hittite and your father an Amorite. 46Your elder sister is Samaria, who lived with her daughters to the north of you; and your younger sister, who lived to the south of you, is Sodom with her daughters. 47You not only followed their ways, and acted according to their abominations; within a very little time you were more corrupt than they in all your ways. 48As I live, says the Lord God, your sister Sodom and her daughters have not done as you and your daughters have done. 49This was the guilt of your sister Sodom: she and her daughters had pride, excess of food, and prosperous ease, but did not aid the poor and needy. 50They were haughty, and did abominable things before me; therefore I removed them when I saw it. 51Samaria has not committed half your sins; you have committed more abominations than they, and have made your sisters appear righteous by all the abominations that you have committed. 52Bear your disgrace, you also, for you have brought about for your sisters a more favorable judgment; because of your sins in which you acted more abominably than they, they are more in the right than you. So be ashamed, you also, and bear your disgrace, for you have made your sisters appear righteous.

53 I will restore their fortunes, the fortunes of Sodom and her daughters and the fortunes of Samaria and her daughters, and I will restore your own fortunes along with theirs, 54in order that you may bear your disgrace and be ashamed of all that you have done, becoming a consolation to them. 55As for your sisters, Sodom and her daughters shall return to their former state, Samaria and her daughters shall return to their former state, and you and your daughters shall return to your former state. 56Was not your sister Sodom a byword in your mouth in the day of your pride, 57before your wickedness was uncovered? Now you are a mockery to the daughters of Aram[l] and all her neighbors, and to the daughters of the Philistines, those all around who despise you. 58You must bear the penalty of your lewdness and your abominations, says the Lord.

An Everlasting Covenant

59 Yes, thus says the Lord God: I will deal with you as you have done, you who have despised the oath, breaking the covenant; 60yet I will remember my covenant with you in the days of your youth, and I will establish with you an everlasting covenant. 61Then you will remember your ways, and be ashamed when I[m] take your sisters, both your elder and your younger, and give them to you as daughters, but not on account of my[n] covenant with you. 62I will establish my covenant with you, and you shall know that I am the Lord, 63in order that you may remember and be confounded, and never open your mouth again because of your shame, when I forgive you all that you have done, says the Lord God.

The Two Eagles and the Vine

17 The word of the Lord came to me: 2O mortal, propound a riddle, and speak an allegory to the house of Israel. 3Say: Thus says the Lord God:

A great eagle, with great wings and
    long pinions,
  rich in plumage of many colors,
    came to the Lebanon.
He took the top of the cedar,
4   broke off its topmost shoot;
he carried it to a land of trade,
    set it in a city of merchants.
5 Then he took a seed from the land,
    placed it in fertile soil;
a plant[o] by abundant waters,
    he set it like a willow twig.
6 It sprouted and became a vine
    spreading out, but low;
its branches turned toward him,
    its roots remained where it stood.
So it became a vine;
    it brought forth branches,
    put forth foliage.

7 There was another great eagle,

---

l Another reading is *Edom*   *m* Syr: Heb *you*
n Heb lacks *my*   *o* Meaning of Heb uncertain

with great wings and much
plumage.
And see! This vine stretched out
its roots toward him;
it shot out its branches toward him,
so that he might water it.
From the bed where it was planted
8 it was transplanted
to good soil by abundant waters,
so that it might produce branches
and bear fruit
and become a noble vine.
⁹Say: Thus says the Lord GOD:
Will it prosper?
Will he not pull up its roots,
cause its fruit to rot *p* and wither,
its fresh sprouting leaves to fade?
No strong arm or mighty army will
be needed
to pull it from its roots.
¹⁰ When it is transplanted, will
it thrive?
When the east wind strikes it,
will it not utterly wither,
wither on the bed where it grew?

11 Then the word of the LORD came to me: ¹²Say now to the rebellious house: Do you not know what these things mean? Tell them: The king of Babylon came to Jerusalem, took its king and its officials, and brought them back with him to Babylon. ¹³He took one of the royal offspring and made a covenant with him, putting him under oath (he had taken away the chief men of the land), ¹⁴so that the kingdom might be humble and not lift itself up, and that by keeping his covenant it might stand. ¹⁵But he rebelled against him by sending ambassadors to Egypt, in order that they might give him horses and a large army. Will he succeed? Can one escape who does such things? Can he break the covenant and yet escape? ¹⁶As I live, says the Lord GOD, surely in the place where the king resides who made him king, whose oath he despised, and whose covenant with him he broke—in Babylon he shall die. ¹⁷Pharaoh with his mighty army and great company will not help him in war, when ramps are cast up and siege walls built to cut off many lives. ¹⁸Because he despised the oath and broke the covenant, because he gave his hand and yet did all these things, he shall not escape. ¹⁹Therefore thus says the Lord GOD: As I live, I will surely return upon his head my oath that he despised, and my covenant that he broke. ²⁰I will spread my net over him, and he shall be caught in my snare; I will bring him to Babylon and enter into judgment with him there for the treason he has committed against me. ²¹All the pick*q* of his troops shall fall by the sword, and the survivors shall be scattered to every wind; and you shall know that I, the LORD, have spoken.

Israel Exalted at Last

22 Thus says the Lord GOD:
I myself will take a sprig
from the lofty top of a cedar;
I will set it out.
I will break off a tender one
from the topmost of its
young twigs;
I myself will plant it
on a high and lofty mountain.
23 On the mountain height of Israel
I will plant it,
in order that it may produce boughs
and bear fruit,
and become a noble cedar.
Under it every kind of bird will live;
in the shade of its branches
will nest
winged creatures of every kind.
24 All the trees of the field shall know
that I am the LORD.
I bring low the high tree,
I make high the low tree;
I dry up the green tree
and make the dry tree flourish.
I the LORD have spoken;
I will accomplish it.

Individual Retribution

18 The word of the LORD came to me: ²What do you mean by repeating this proverb concerning the land of Israel, "The parents have eaten sour grapes, and the children's teeth are set on edge"? ³As I live, says the Lord GOD, this proverb shall no more be used by you in Israel. ⁴Know that all lives are mine; the life of the parent as well as the life of the child is mine: it is only the person who sins that shall die.

5 If a man is righteous and does what is lawful and right— ⁶if he does not eat upon the mountains or lift up his eyes to the idols of the house of Israel, does not defile his neighbor's wife or approach a woman during her menstrual period,

p Meaning of Heb uncertain *q* Another reading is *fugitives*

[7]does not oppress anyone, but restores to the debtor his pledge, commits no robbery, gives his bread to the hungry and covers the naked with a garment, [8]does not take advance or accrued interest, withholds his hand from iniquity, executes true justice between contending parties, [9]follows my statutes, and is careful to observe my ordinances, acting faithfully—such a one is righteous; he shall surely live, says the Lord GOD.

10 If he has a son who is violent, a shedder of blood, [11]who does any of these things (though his father[r] does none of them), who eats upon the mountains, defiles his neighbor's wife, [12]oppresses the poor and needy, commits robbery, does not restore the pledge, lifts up his eyes to the idols, commits abomination, [13]takes advance or accrued interest; shall he then live? He shall not. He has done all these abominable things; he shall surely die; his blood shall be upon himself.

14 But if this man has a son who sees all the sins that his father has done, considers, and does not do likewise, [15]who does not eat upon the mountains or lift up his eyes to the idols of the house of Israel, does not defile his neighbor's wife, [16]does not wrong anyone, exacts no pledge, commits no robbery, but gives his bread to the hungry and covers the naked with a garment, [17]withholds his hand from iniquity,[s] takes no advance or accrued interest, observes my ordinances, and follows my statutes; he shall not die for his father's iniquity; he shall surely live. [18]As for his father, because he practiced extortion, robbed his brother, and did what is not good among his people, he dies for his iniquity.

19 Yet you say, "Why should not the son suffer for the iniquity of the father?" When the son has done what is lawful and right, and has been careful to observe all my statutes, he shall surely live. [20]The person who sins shall die. A child shall not suffer for the iniquity of a parent, nor a parent suffer for the iniquity of a child; the righteousness of the righteous shall be his own, and the wickedness of the wicked shall be his own.

21 But if the wicked turn away from all their sins that they have committed and keep all my statutes and do what is lawful and right, they shall surely live; they shall not die. [22]None of the transgressions that they have committed shall be remembered against them; for the righteousness that they have done they shall live. [23]Have I any pleasure in the death of the wicked, says the Lord GOD, and not rather that they should turn from their ways and live? [24]But when the righteous turn away from their righteousness and commit iniquity and do the same abominable things that the wicked do, shall they live? None of the righteous deeds that they have done shall be remembered; for the treachery of which they are guilty and the sin they have committed, they shall die.

25 Yet you say, "The way of the Lord is unfair." Hear now, O house of Israel: Is my way unfair? Is it not your ways that are unfair? [26]When the righteous turn away from their righteousness and commit iniquity, they shall die for it; for the iniquity that they have committed they shall die. [27]Again, when the wicked turn away from the wickedness they have committed and do what is lawful and right, they shall save their life. [28]Because they considered and turned away from all the transgressions that they had committed, they shall surely live; they shall not die. [29]Yet the house of Israel says, "The way of the Lord is unfair." O house of Israel, are my ways unfair? Is it not your ways that are unfair?

30 Therefore I will judge you, O house of Israel, all of you according to your ways, says the Lord GOD. Repent and turn from all your transgressions; otherwise iniquity will be your ruin.[t] [31]Cast away from you all the transgressions that you have committed against me, and get yourselves a new heart and a new spirit! Why will you die, O house of Israel? [32]For I have no pleasure in the death of anyone, says the Lord GOD. Turn, then, and live.

Israel Degraded

19 As for you, raise up a lamentation for the princes of Israel, [2]and say:
What a lioness was your mother
    among lions!
She lay down among young lions,
    rearing her cubs.
3 She raised up one of her cubs;
    he became a young lion,
and he learned to catch prey;
    he devoured humans.
4 The nations sounded an alarm
    against him;

---

r Heb *he*   s Gk: Heb *the poor*   t Or *so that they shall not be a stumbling block of iniquity to you*

he was caught in their pit;
and they brought him with hooks
   to the land of Egypt.
5 When she saw that she was
   thwarted,
   that her hope was lost,
she took another of her cubs
   and made him a young lion.
6 He prowled among the lions;
   he became a young lion,
and he learned to catch prey;
   he devoured people.
7 And he ravaged their strongholds,[u]
   and laid waste their towns;
the land was appalled, and all in it,
   at the sound of his roaring.
8 The nations set upon him
   from the provinces all around;
they spread their net over him;
   he was caught in their pit.
9 With hooks they put him in a cage,
   and brought him to the king
     of Babylon;
they brought him into custody,
so that his voice should be heard
   no more
   on the mountains of Israel.
10 Your mother was like a vine in
   a vineyard[v]
   transplanted by the water,
fruitful and full of branches
   from abundant water.
11 Its strongest stem became
   a ruler's scepter;[w]
it towered aloft
   among the thick boughs;
it stood out in its height
   with its mass of branches.
12 But it was plucked up in fury,
   cast down to the ground;
the east wind dried it up;
   its fruit was stripped off,
its strong stem was withered;
   the fire consumed it.
13 Now it is transplanted into
   the wilderness,
   into a dry and thirsty land.
14 And fire has gone out from its stem,
   has consumed its branches
     and fruit,
so that there remains in it no strong
   stem,
   no scepter for ruling.

This is a lamentation, and it is used as a lamentation.

Israel's Continuing Rebellion

20 In the seventh year, in the fifth month, on the tenth day of the month, certain elders of Israel came to consult the LORD, and sat down before me. 2And the word of the LORD came to me: 3Mortal, speak to the elders of Israel, and say to them: Thus says the Lord GOD: Why are you coming? To consult me? As I live, says the Lord GOD, I will not be consulted by you. 4Will you judge them, mortal, will you judge them? Then let them know the abominations of their ancestors, 5and say to them: Thus says the Lord GOD: On the day when I chose Israel, I swore to the offspring of the house of Jacob—making myself known to them in the land of Egypt—I swore to them, saying, I am the LORD your God. 6On that day I swore to them that I would bring them out of the land of Egypt into a land that I had searched out for them, a land flowing with milk and honey, the most glorious of all lands. 7And I said to them, Cast away the detestable things your eyes feast on, every one of you, and do not defile yourselves with the idols of Egypt; I am the LORD your God. 8But they rebelled against me and would not listen to me; not one of them cast away the detestable things their eyes feasted on, nor did they forsake the idols of Egypt.

Then I thought I would pour out my wrath upon them and spend my anger against them in the midst of the land of Egypt. 9But I acted for the sake of my name, that it should not be profaned in the sight of the nations among whom they lived, in whose sight I made myself known to them in bringing them out of the land of Egypt. 10So I led them out of the land of Egypt and brought them into the wilderness. 11I gave them my statutes and showed them my ordinances, by whose observance everyone shall live. 12Moreover I gave them my sabbaths, as a sign between me and them, so that they might know that I the LORD sanctify them. 13But the house of Israel rebelled against me in the wilderness; they did not observe my statutes but rejected my ordinances, by whose observance everyone shall live; and my sabbaths they greatly profaned. Then I thought I would pour out my

[u] Heb *his widows*   [v] Cn: Heb *in your blood*
[w] Heb *Its strongest stems became rulers' scepters*

wrath upon them in the wilderness, to make an end of them. 14But I acted for the sake of my name, so that it should not be profaned in the sight of the nations, in whose sight I had brought them out. 15Moreover I swore to them in the wilderness that I would not bring them into the land that I had given them, a land flowing with milk and honey, the most glorious of all lands, 16because they rejected my ordinances and did not observe my statutes, and profaned my sabbaths; for their heart went after their idols. 17Nevertheless my eye spared them, and I did not destroy them or make an end of them in the wilderness.

18 I said to their children in the wilderness, Do not follow the statutes of your parents, nor observe their ordinances, nor defile yourselves with their idols. 19I the LORD am your God; follow my statutes, and be careful to observe my ordinances, 20and hallow my sabbaths that they may be a sign between me and you, so that you may know that I the LORD am your God. 21But the children rebelled against me; they did not follow my statutes, and were not careful to observe my ordinances, by whose observance everyone shall live; they profaned my sabbaths.

Then I thought I would pour out my wrath upon them and spend my anger against them in the wilderness. 22But I withheld my hand, and acted for the sake of my name, so that it should not be profaned in the sight of the nations, in whose sight I had brought them out. 23Moreover I swore to them in the wilderness that I would scatter them among the nations and disperse them through the countries, 24because they had not executed my ordinances, but had rejected my statutes and profaned my sabbaths, and their eyes were set on their ancestors' idols. 25Moreover I gave them statutes that were not good and ordinances by which they could not live. 26I defiled them through their very gifts, in their offering up all their firstborn, in order that I might horrify them, so that they might know that I am the LORD.

27 Therefore, mortal, speak to the house of Israel and say to them, Thus says the Lord GOD: In this again your ancestors blasphemed me, by dealing treacherously with me. 28For when I had brought them into the land that I swore to give them, then wherever they saw any high hill or any leafy tree, there they offered their sacrifices and presented the provocation of their offering; there they sent up their pleasing odors, and there they poured out their drink offerings. 29(I said to them, What is the high place to which you go? So it is called Bamahˣ to this day.) 30Therefore say to the house of Israel, Thus says the Lord GOD: Will you defile yourselves after the manner of your ancestors and go astray after their detestable things? 31When you offer your gifts and make your children pass through the fire, you defile yourselves with all your idols to this day. And shall I be consulted by you, O house of Israel? As I live, says the Lord GOD, I will not be consulted by you.

32 What is in your mind shall never happen—the thought, "Let us be like the nations, like the tribes of the countries, and worship wood and stone."

God Will Restore Israel

33 As I live, says the Lord GOD, surely with a mighty hand and an outstretched arm, and with wrath poured out, I will be king over you. 34I will bring you out from the peoples and gather you out of the countries where you are scattered, with a mighty hand and an outstretched arm, and with wrath poured out; 35and I will bring you into the wilderness of the peoples, and there I will enter into judgment with you face to face. 36As I entered into judgment with your ancestors in the wilderness of the land of Egypt, so I will enter into judgment with you, says the Lord GOD. 37I will make you pass under the staff, and will bring you within the bond of the covenant. 38I will purge out the rebels among you, and those who transgress against me; I will bring them out of the land where they reside as aliens, but they shall not enter the land of Israel. Then you shall know that I am the LORD.

39 As for you, O house of Israel, thus says the Lord GOD: Go serve your idols, everyone of you now and hereafter, if you will not listen to me; but my holy name you shall no more profane with your gifts and your idols.

40 For on my holy mountain, the mountain height of Israel, says the Lord GOD, there all the house of Israel, all of them, shall serve me in the land; there I will accept them, and there I will require

ˣ That is *High Place*

your contributions and the choicest of your gifts, with all your sacred things. [41]As a pleasing odor I will accept you, when I bring you out from the peoples, and gather you out of the countries where you have been scattered; and I will manifest my holiness among you in the sight of the nations. [42]You shall know that I am the LORD, when I bring you into the land of Israel, the country that I swore to give to your ancestors. [43]There you shall remember your ways and all the deeds by which you have polluted yourselves; and you shall loathe yourselves for all the evils that you have committed. [44]And you shall know that I am the LORD, when I deal with you for my name's sake, not according to your evil ways, or corrupt deeds, O house of Israel, says the Lord GOD.

A Prophecy against the Negeb

45 [y]The word of the LORD came to me: [46]Mortal, set your face toward the south, preach against the south, and prophesy against the forest land in the Negeb; [47]say to the forest of the Negeb, Hear the word of the LORD: Thus says the Lord GOD, I will kindle a fire in you, and it shall devour every green tree in you and every dry tree; the blazing flame shall not be quenched, and all faces from south to north shall be scorched by it. [48]All flesh shall see that I the LORD have kindled it; it shall not be quenched. [49]Then I said, "Ah Lord GOD! they are saying of me, 'Is he not a maker of allegories?'"

The Drawn Sword of God

21 [z] The word of the LORD came to me: [2]Mortal, set your face toward Jerusalem and preach against the sanctuaries; prophesy against the land of Israel [3]and say to the land of Israel, Thus says the LORD: I am coming against you, and will draw my sword out of its sheath, and will cut off from you both righteous and wicked. [4]Because I will cut off from you both righteous and wicked, therefore my sword shall go out of its sheath against all flesh from south to north; [5]and all flesh shall know that I the LORD have drawn my sword out of its sheath; it shall not be sheathed again. [6]Moan therefore, mortal; moan with breaking heart and bitter grief before their eyes. [7]And when they say to you, "Why do you moan?" you shall say, "Because of the news that has come. Every heart will melt and all hands will be feeble, every spirit will faint and all knees will turn to water. See, it comes and it will be fulfilled," says the Lord GOD.

8 And the word of the LORD came to me: [9]Mortal, prophesy and say: Thus says the Lord; Say:

A sword, a sword is sharpened,
　　it is also polished;
[10] it is sharpened for slaughter,
　　honed to flash like lightning!
How can we make merry?
　　You have despised the rod,
　　and all discipline.[a]
[11] The sword[b] is given to be polished,
　　to be grasped in the hand;
it is sharpened, the sword is
　　polished,
　　to be placed in the slayer's hand.
[12] Cry and wail, O mortal,
　　for it is against my people;
it is against all Israel's princes;
　　they are thrown to the sword,
　　together with my people.
　　Ah! Strike the thigh!

[13]For consider: What! If you despise the rod, will it not happen?[a] says the Lord GOD.

[14] And you, mortal, prophesy;
　　strike hand to hand.
Let the sword fall twice, thrice;
　　it is a sword for killing.
A sword for great slaughter—
　　it surrounds them;
[15] therefore hearts melt
　　and many stumble.
At all their gates I have set
　　the point[a] of the sword.
Ah! It is made for flashing,
　　it is polished[c] for slaughter.
[16] Attack to the right!
　　Engage to the left!
　　—wherever your edge is directed.
[17] I too will strike hand to hand,
　　I will satisfy my fury;
　　I the LORD have spoken.

18 The word of the LORD came to me: [19]Mortal, mark out two roads for the sword of the king of Babylon to come; both of them shall issue from the same land. And make a signpost, make it for a fork in the road leading to a city; [20]mark out the road for the sword to come to Rabbah of the Ammonites or to Judah and to[d] Jerusalem the fortified. [21]For the

---

[y] Ch 21.1 in Heb　　[z] Ch 21.6 in Heb
[a] Meaning of Heb uncertain　[b] Heb It　[c] Tg: Heb *wrapped up*　[d] Gk Syr: Heb *Judah in*

king of Babylon stands at the parting of the way, at the fork in the two roads, to use divination; he shakes the arrows, he consults the teraphim,*e* he inspects the liver. 22Into his right hand comes the lot for Jerusalem, to set battering rams, to call out for slaughter, for raising the battle cry, to set battering rams against the gates, to cast up ramps, to build siege towers. 23But to them it will seem like a false divination; they have sworn solemn oaths; but he brings their guilt to remembrance, bringing about their capture.

24 Therefore thus says the Lord GOD: Because you have brought your guilt to remembrance, in that your transgressions are uncovered, so that in all your deeds your sins appear—because you have come to remembrance, you shall be taken in hand.*f*

25 As for you, vile, wicked prince
        of Israel,
    you whose day has come,
        the time of final punishment,
26 thus says the Lord GOD:
    Remove the turban, take off
        the crown;
    things shall not remain as
        they are.
    Exalt that which is low,
        abase that which is high.
27 A ruin, a ruin, a ruin—
        I will make it!
    (Such has never occurred.)
    Until he comes whose right it is;
        to him I will give it.

28 As for you, mortal, prophesy, and say, Thus says the Lord GOD concerning the Ammonites, and concerning their reproach; say:
    A sword, a sword! Drawn for
        slaughter,
        polished to consume,*g* to flash
            like lightning.
29 Offering false visions for you,
        divining lies for you,
    they place you over the necks
        of the vile, wicked ones—
    those whose day has come,
        the time of final punishment.
30 Return it to its sheath!
    In the place where you were created,
        in the land of your origin,
    I will judge you.
31 I will pour out my indignation upon
        you,
    with the fire of my wrath
    I will blow upon you.

    I will deliver you into brutish hands,
        those skillful to destroy.
32 You shall be fuel for the fire,
        your blood shall enter the earth;
    you shall be remembered no more,
        for I the LORD have spoken.

The Bloody City

22 The word of the LORD came to me: 2You, mortal, will you judge, will you judge the bloody city? Then declare to it all its abominable deeds. 3You shall say, Thus says the Lord GOD: A city! Shedding blood within itself; its time has come; making its idols, defiling itself. 4You have become guilty by the blood that you have shed, and defiled by the idols that you have made; you have brought your day near, the appointed time of your years has come. Therefore I have made you a disgrace before the nations, and a mockery to all the countries. 5Those who are near and those who are far from you will mock you, you infamous one, full of tumult.

6 The princes of Israel in you, everyone according to his power, have been bent on shedding blood. 7Father and mother are treated with contempt in you; the alien residing within you suffers extortion; the orphan and the widow are wronged in you. 8You have despised my holy things, and profaned my sabbaths. 9In you are those who slander to shed blood, those in you who eat upon the mountains, who commit lewdness in your midst. 10In you they uncover their fathers' nakedness; in you they violate women in their menstrual periods. 11One commits abomination with his neighbor's wife; another lewdly defiles his daughter-in-law; another in you defiles his sister, his father's daughter. 12In you, they take bribes to shed blood; you take both advance interest and accrued interest, and make gain of your neighbors by extortion; and you have forgotten me, says the Lord GOD.

13 See, I strike my hands together at the dishonest gain you have made, and at the blood that has been shed within you. 14Can your courage endure, or can your hands remain strong in the days when I shall deal with you? I the LORD have spoken, and I will do it. 15I will scatter you among the nations and disperse you through the countries, and I will purge

e Or *the household gods*   *f* Or *be taken captive*
g Cn: Heb *to contain*

your filthiness out of you. ¹⁶And I^h shall be profaned through you in the sight of the nations; and you shall know that I am the LORD.

17 The word of the LORD came to me: ¹⁸Mortal, the house of Israel has become dross to me; all of them, silver,ⁱ bronze, tin, iron, and lead. In the smelter they have become dross. ¹⁹Therefore thus says the Lord GOD: Because you have all become dross, I will gather you into the midst of Jerusalem. ²⁰As one gathers silver, bronze, iron, lead, and tin into a smelter, to blow the fire upon them in order to melt them; so I will gather you in my anger and in my wrath, and I will put you in and melt you. ²¹I will gather you and blow upon you with the fire of my wrath, and you shall be melted within it. ²²As silver is melted in a smelter, so you shall be melted in it; and you shall know that I the LORD have poured out my wrath upon you.

23 The word of the LORD came to me: ²⁴Mortal, say to it: You are a land that is not cleansed, not rained upon in the day of indignation. ²⁵Its princes^j within it are like a roaring lion tearing the prey; they have devoured human lives; they have taken treasure and precious things; they have made many widows within it. ²⁶Its priests have done violence to my teaching and have profaned my holy things; they have made no distinction between the holy and the common, neither have they taught the difference between the unclean and the clean, and they have disregarded my sabbaths, so that I am profaned among them. ²⁷Its officials within it are like wolves tearing the prey, shedding blood, destroying lives to get dishonest gain. ²⁸Its prophets have smeared whitewash on their behalf, seeing false visions and divining lies for them, saying, "Thus says the Lord GOD," when the LORD has not spoken. ²⁹The people of the land have practiced extortion and committed robbery; they have oppressed the poor and needy, and have extorted from the alien without redress. ³⁰And I sought for anyone among them who would repair the wall and stand in the breach before me on behalf of the land, so that I would not destroy it; but I found no one. ³¹Therefore I have poured out my indignation upon them; I have consumed them with the fire of my wrath; I have returned their conduct upon their heads, says the Lord GOD.

Oholah and Oholibah

23 The word of the LORD came to me: ²Mortal, there were two women, the daughters of one mother; ³they played the whore in Egypt; they played the whore in their youth; their breasts were caressed there, and their virgin bosoms were fondled. ⁴Oholah was the name of the elder and Oholibah the name of her sister. They became mine, and they bore sons and daughters. As for their names, Oholah is Samaria, and Oholibah is Jerusalem.

5 Oholah played the whore while she was mine; she lusted after her lovers the Assyrians, warriors^k ⁶clothed in blue, governors and commanders, all of them handsome young men, mounted horsemen. ⁷She bestowed her favors upon them, the choicest men of Assyria all of them; and she defiled herself with all the idols of everyone for whom she lusted. ⁸She did not give up her whorings that she had practiced since Egypt; for in her youth men had lain with her and fondled her virgin bosom and poured out their lust upon her. ⁹Therefore I delivered her into the hands of her lovers, into the hands of the Assyrians, for whom she lusted. ¹⁰These uncovered her nakedness; they seized her sons and her daughters; and they killed her with the sword. Judgment was executed upon her, and she became a byword among women.

11 Her sister Oholibah saw this, yet she was more corrupt than she in her lusting and in her whorings, which were worse than those of her sister. ¹²She lusted after the Assyrians, governors and commanders, warriors^k clothed in full armor, mounted horsemen, all of them handsome young men. ¹³And I saw that she was defiled; they both took the same way. ¹⁴But she carried her whorings further; she saw male figures carved on the wall, images of the Chaldeans portrayed in vermilion, ¹⁵with belts around their waists, with flowing turbans on their heads, all of them looking like officers—a picture of Babylonians whose native land was Chaldea. ¹⁶When she saw them she lusted after them, and sent messengers to them in Chaldea. ¹⁷And the Babylonians came to

---

^h Gk Syr Vg: Heb *you*   ⁱ Transposed from the end of the verse; compare verse 20   ^j Gk: Heb *indignation.* 25*A conspiracy of its prophets*   ^k Meaning of Heb uncertain

her into the bed of love, and they defiled her with their lust; and after she defiled herself with them, she turned from them in disgust. ¹⁸When she carried on her whorings so openly and flaunted her nakedness, I turned in disgust from her, as I had turned from her sister. ¹⁹Yet she increased her whorings, remembering the days of her youth, when she played the whore in the land of Egypt ²⁰and lusted after her paramours there, whose members were like those of donkeys, and whose emission was like that of stallions. ²¹Thus you longed for the lewdness of your youth, when the Egyptians[l] fondled

---

l Two Mss: MT *from Egypt*

MONDAY

Scripture Reading for Today:
Ezekiel 22.23–31

Verse for Today:
Ezekiel 22.30

Called to Intercede

We are to intercede for the needs of the world. Sometimes our intercession will be for a special intention or individual, a family member or friend. Perhaps at other times it will be for a personal need we are experiencing—a disability or an illness, difficulties with our spouse or children, financial trouble, problems at work. At still other times, our intercession will be for the broader community in which we live—our neighborhood or school district; our city or state; our nation; an end to abortion, euthanasia, and infanticide; shelter for the homeless. Whatever the need or intention, when we stand before the throne of God, we will do much to aid humanity and to be the healers of the world.

It was because of Mary's "yes" to God that salvation entered the world and to each of us was given the pledge of redemptive grace. If we are to be mediators of redemptive grace in our world today, we too must say "yes" to the call.

In Ezekiel 22 God lists for the prophet the many crimes of Jerusalem: sexual promiscuity, usury, a disregard for the dignity of the human person, godlessness, and murder. But then God says something to Ezekiel that should set us on the edge of our seats. [In verse 30] he is saying that even though he sees the lack of morality in a nation, even though he sees man's inhumanity to man, even though a country may be godless, even though bloodshed may characterize a culture, if there is someone who is standing in the gap, who is making intercession, who is pleading before him to save that people, that culture, that nation, then his wrath can be held back.

If this is the case over situations so devastating and sinful, then surely this same God of mercy will show kindness and love to the many petitions we bring to him. Only one thing is required—individuals who are willing to accept the mission. God is looking for people today to stand in the gap and make intercession for the needs of the world. Are we willing to say "yes" as did Mary, our spiritual Mother? Will we accept the mission?

—JOHNETTE BENKOVIC

Go to page 1139 for your next devotional reading.

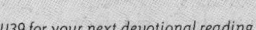

your bosom and caressed[m] your young breasts.

22 Therefore, O Oholibah, thus says the Lord GOD: I will rouse against you your lovers from whom you turned in disgust, and I will bring them against you from every side: 23the Babylonians and all the Chaldeans, Pekod and Shoa and Koa, and all the Assyrians with them, handsome young men, governors and commanders all of them, officers and warriors,[n] all of them riding on horses. 24They shall come against you from the north[o] with chariots and wagons and a host of peoples; they shall set themselves against you on every side with buckler, shield, and helmet, and I will commit the judgment to them, and they shall judge you according to their ordinances. 25I will direct my indignation against you, in order that they may deal with you in fury. They shall cut off your nose and your ears, and your survivors shall fall by the sword. They shall seize your sons and your daughters, and your survivors shall be devoured by fire. 26They shall also strip you of your clothes and take away your fine jewels. 27So I will put an end to your lewdness and your whoring brought from the land of Egypt; you shall not long for them, or remember Egypt any more. 28For thus says the Lord GOD: I will deliver you into the hands of those whom you hate, into the hands of those from whom you turned in disgust; 29and they shall deal with you in hatred, and take away all the fruit of your labor, and leave you naked and bare, and the nakedness of your whorings shall be exposed. Your lewdness and your whorings 30have brought this upon you, because you played the whore with the nations, and polluted yourself with their idols. 31You have gone the way of your sister; therefore I will give her cup into your hand. 32Thus says the Lord GOD:

You shall drink your sister's cup,
    deep and wide;
you shall be scorned and derided,
    it holds so much.
33 You shall be filled with drunkenness
        and sorrow.

A cup of horror and desolation
    is the cup of your sister Samaria;
34 you shall drink it and drain it out,
    and gnaw its sherds,
    and tear out your breasts;

for I have spoken, says the Lord GOD. 35Therefore thus says the Lord GOD: Be-cause you have forgotten me and cast me behind your back, therefore bear the consequences of your lewdness and whorings.

36 The LORD said to me: Mortal, will you judge Oholah and Oholibah? Then declare to them their abominable deeds. 37For they have committed adultery, and blood is on their hands; with their idols they have committed adultery; and they have even offered up to them for food the children whom they had borne to me. 38Moreover this they have done to me: they have defiled my sanctuary on the same day and profaned my sabbaths. 39For when they had slaughtered their children for their idols, on the same day they came into my sanctuary to profane it. This is what they did in my house.

40 They even sent for men to come from far away, to whom a messenger was sent, and they came. For them you bathed yourself, painted your eyes, and decked yourself with ornaments; 41you sat on a stately couch, with a table spread before it on which you had placed my incense and my oil. 42The sound of a raucous multitude was around her, with many of the rabble brought in drunken from the wilderness; and they put bracelets on the arms[p] of the women, and beautiful crowns upon their heads.

43 Then I said, Ah, she is worn out with adulteries, but they carry on their sexual acts with her. 44For they have gone in to her, as one goes in to a whore. Thus they went in to Oholah and to Oholibah, wanton women. 45But righteous judges shall declare them guilty of adultery and of bloodshed; because they are adulteresses and blood is on their hands.

46 For thus says the Lord GOD: Bring up an assembly against them, and make them an object of terror and of plunder. 47The assembly shall stone them and with their swords they shall cut them down; they shall kill their sons and their daughters, and burn up their houses. 48Thus will I put an end to lewdness in the land, so that all women may take warning and not commit lewdness as you have done. 49They shall repay you for your lewdness, and you shall bear the penalty for your

---

m Cn: Heb for the sake of   n Compare verses 6 and 12: Heb officers and called ones
o Gk: Meaning of Heb uncertain   p Heb hands

sinful idolatry; and you shall know that I am the Lord GOD.

The Boiling Pot

24 In the ninth year, in the tenth month, on the tenth day of the month, the word of the LORD came to me: ²Mortal, write down the name of this day, this very day. The king of Babylon has laid siege to Jerusalem this very day. ³And utter an allegory to the rebellious house and say to them, Thus says the Lord GOD:

Set on the pot, set it on,
  pour in water also;
⁴ put in it the pieces,
  all the good pieces, the thigh and
    the shoulder;
  fill it with choice bones.
⁵ Take the choicest one of the flock,
  pile the logs*q* under it;
  boil its pieces,*r*
  seethe*s* also its bones in it.

6 Therefore thus says the Lord GOD:
Woe to the bloody city,
  the pot whose rust is in it,
  whose rust has not gone out of it!
Empty it piece by piece,
  making no choice at all.*t*
7 For the blood she shed is inside it;
  she placed it on a bare rock;
  she did not pour it out on the
    ground,
  to cover it with earth.
8 To rouse my wrath, to take
    vengeance,
  I have placed the blood she shed
  on a bare rock,
  so that it may not be covered.
9Therefore thus says the Lord GOD:
Woe to the bloody city!
  I will even make the pile great.
10 Heap up the logs, kindle the fire;
  boil the meat well, mix in
    the spices,
  let the bones be burned.
11 Stand it empty upon the coals,
  so that it may become hot, its
    copper glow,
  its filth melt in it, its rust
    be consumed.
12 In vain I have wearied myself;*u*
  its thick rust does not depart.
  To the fire with its rust!*v*
13 Yet, when I cleansed you in your
    filthy lewdness,
  you did not become clean from
    your filth;

you shall not again be cleansed
  until I have satisfied my fury
    upon you.
¹⁴I the LORD have spoken; the time is coming, I will act. I will not refrain, I will not spare, I will not relent. According to your ways and your doings I will judge you, says the Lord GOD.

Ezekiel's Bereavement

15 The word of the LORD came to me: ¹⁶Mortal, with one blow I am about to take away from you the delight of your eyes; yet you shall not mourn or weep, nor shall your tears run down. ¹⁷Sigh, but not aloud; make no mourning for the dead. Bind on your turban, and put your sandals on your feet; do not cover your upper lip or eat the bread of mourners.*w* ¹⁸So I spoke to the people in the morning, and at evening my wife died. And on the next morning I did as I was commanded.

19 Then the people said to me, "Will you not tell us what these things mean for us, that you are acting this way?" ²⁰Then I said to them: The word of the LORD came to me: ²¹Say to the house of Israel, Thus says the Lord GOD: I will profane my sanctuary, the pride of your power, the delight of your eyes, and your heart's desire; and your sons and your daughters whom you left behind shall fall by the sword. ²²And you shall do as I have done; you shall not cover your upper lip or eat the bread of mourners.*w* ²³Your turbans shall be on your heads and your sandals on your feet; you shall not mourn or weep, but you shall pine away in your iniquities and groan to one another. ²⁴Thus Ezekiel shall be a sign to you; you shall do just as he has done. When this comes, then you shall know that I am the Lord GOD.

25 And you, mortal, on the day when I take from them their stronghold, their joy and glory, the delight of their eyes and their heart's affection, and also*x* their sons and their daughters, ²⁶on that day, one who has escaped will come to you to report to you the news. ²⁷On that day your mouth shall be opened to the one who has escaped, and you shall speak and no longer be silent. So you shall be a sign

---

q Compare verse 10: Heb *the bones*   *r* Two Mss:
Heb *its boilings*   *s* Cn: Heb *its bones seethe*
t Heb *piece, no lot has fallen on it*   *u* Cn: Meaning
of Heb uncertain   *v* Meaning of Heb uncertain
w Vg Tg: Heb *of men*   *x* Heb lacks *and also*

to them; and they shall know that I am the Lord.

Proclamation against Ammon

25 The word of the Lord came to me: ²Mortal, set your face toward the Ammonites and prophesy against them. ³Say to the Ammonites, Hear the word of the Lord God: Thus says the Lord God, Because you said, "Aha!" over my sanctuary when it was profaned, and over the land of Israel when it was made desolate, and over the house of Judah when it went into exile; ⁴therefore I am handing you over to the people of the east for a possession. They shall set their encampments among you and pitch their tents in your midst; they shall eat your fruit, and they shall drink your milk. ⁵I will make Rabbah a pasture for camels and Ammon a fold for flocks. Then you shall know that I am the Lord. ⁶For thus says the Lord God: Because you have clapped your hands and stamped your feet and rejoiced with all the malice within you against the land of Israel, ⁷therefore I have stretched out my hand against you, and will hand you over as plunder to the nations. I will cut you off from the peoples and will make you perish out of the countries; I will destroy you. Then you shall know that I am the Lord.

Proclamation against Moab

8 Thus says the Lord God: Because Moab ʸ said, The house of Judah is like all the other nations, ⁹therefore I will lay open the flank of Moab from the towns ᶻ on its frontier, the glory of the country, Beth-jeshimoth, Baal-meon, and Kiriathaim. ¹⁰I will give it along with Ammon to the people of the east as a possession. Thus Ammon shall be remembered no more among the nations, ¹¹and I will execute judgments upon Moab. Then they shall know that I am the Lord.

Proclamation against Edom

12 Thus says the Lord God: Because Edom acted revengefully against the house of Judah and has grievously offended in taking vengeance upon them, ¹³therefore thus says the Lord God, I will stretch out my hand against Edom, and cut off from it humans and animals, and I will make it desolate; from Teman even to Dedan they shall fall by the sword. ¹⁴I will lay my vengeance upon Edom by the

hand of my people Israel; and they shall act in Edom according to my anger and according to my wrath; and they shall know my vengeance, says the Lord God.

Proclamation against Philistia

15 Thus says the Lord God: Because with unending hostilities the Philistines acted in vengeance, and with malice of heart took revenge in destruction; ¹⁶therefore thus says the Lord God, I will stretch out my hand against the Philistines, cut off the Cherethites, and destroy the rest of the seacoast. ¹⁷I will execute great vengeance on them with wrathful punishments. Then they shall know that I am the Lord, when I lay my vengeance on them.

Proclamation against Tyre

26 In the eleventh year, on the first day of the month, the word of the Lord came to me: ²Mortal, because Tyre said concerning Jerusalem,

"Aha, broken is the gateway of
    the peoples;
it has swung open to me;
I shall be replenished,
    now that it is wasted,"
³therefore, thus says the Lord God:
  See, I am against you, O Tyre!
  I will hurl many nations
    against you,
  as the sea hurls its waves.
⁴ They shall destroy the walls of Tyre
    and break down its towers.
  I will scrape its soil from it
    and make it a bare rock.
⁵ It shall become, in the midst of the
    sea,
  a place for spreading nets.
I have spoken, says the Lord God.
  It shall become plunder for
    the nations,
⁶   and its daughter-towns in
      the country
  shall be killed by the sword.
Then they shall know that I am the Lord.

7 For thus says the Lord God: I will bring against Tyre from the north King Nebuchadrezzar of Babylon, king of kings, together with horses, chariots, cavalry, and a great and powerful army. ⁸ Your daughter-towns in the country he shall put to the sword.

ʸ Gk Old Latin: Heb *Moab and Seir*   ᶻ Heb *towns from its towns*

He shall set up a siege wall
    against you,
    cast up a ramp against you,
    and raise a roof of shields
      against you.
9 He shall direct the shock of his
      battering rams against
      your walls
    and break down your towers
      with his axes.
10 His horses shall be so many
    that their dust shall cover you.
At the noise of cavalry, wheels,
      and chariots
    your very walls shall shake,
    when he enters your gates
      like those entering a breached city.
11 With the hoofs of his horses
    he shall trample all your streets.
He shall put your people to
      the sword,
    and your strong pillars shall fall
      to the ground.
12 They will plunder your riches
    and loot your merchandise;
they shall break down your walls
    and destroy your fine houses.
Your stones and timber and soil
    they shall cast into the water.
13 I will silence the music of
      your songs;
    the sound of your lyres shall be
      heard no more.
14 I will make you a bare rock;
    you shall be a place for
      spreading nets.
You shall never again be rebuilt,
    for I the LORD have spoken,
    says the Lord GOD.

15 Thus says the Lord GOD to Tyre: Shall not the coastlands shake at the sound of your fall, when the wounded groan, when slaughter goes on within you? 16Then all the princes of the sea shall step down from their thrones; they shall remove their robes and strip off their embroidered garments. They shall clothe themselves with trembling, and shall sit on the ground; they shall tremble every moment, and be appalled at you. 17And they shall raise a lamentation over you, and say to you:

How you have vanished*a* from
      the seas,
  O city renowned,
once mighty on the sea,
    you and your inhabitants,*b*
who imposed your*c* terror

on all the mainland!*d*
18 Now the coastlands tremble
    on the day of your fall;
the coastlands by the sea
    are dismayed at your passing.

19 For thus says the Lord GOD: When I make you a city laid waste, like cities that are not inhabited, when I bring up the deep over you, and the great waters cover you, 20then I will thrust you down with those who descend into the Pit, to the people of long ago, and I will make you live in the world below, among primeval ruins, with those who go down to the Pit, so that you will not be inhabited or have a place*e* in the land of the living. 21I will bring you to a dreadful end, and you shall be no more; though sought for, you will never be found again, says the Lord GOD.

Lamentation over Tyre

27 The word of the LORD came to me: 2Now you, mortal, raise a lamentation over Tyre, 3and say to Tyre, which sits at the entrance to the sea, merchant of the peoples on many coastlands, Thus says the Lord GOD:

O Tyre, you have said,
  "I am perfect in beauty."
4 Your borders are in the heart of the
      seas;
    your builders made perfect
      your beauty.
5 They made all your planks
    of fir trees from Senir;
they took a cedar from Lebanon
    to make a mast for you.
6 From oaks of Bashan
    they made your oars;
they made your deck of pines*f*
    from the coasts of Cyprus,
    inlaid with ivory.
7 Of fine embroidered linen
      from Egypt
  was your sail,
    serving as your ensign;
blue and purple from the coasts
      of Elishah
  was your awning.
8 The inhabitants of Sidon and Arvad
    were your rowers;

---

a Gk OL Aquila: Heb *have vanished, O inhabited one,*   *b* Heb *it and its inhabitants*   *c* Heb *their*   *d* Cn: Heb *its inhabitants*   *e* Gk: Heb *I will give beauty*   *f* Or *boxwood*

skilled men of Zemer[g] were
 within you,
 they were your pilots.
9 The elders of Gebal and its artisans
  were within you,
 caulking your seams;
all the ships of the sea with their
  mariners were within you,
 to barter for your wares.
10 Paras[h] and Lud and Put
 were in your army,
 your mighty warriors;
they hung shield and helmet in you;
 they gave you splendor.
11 Men of Arvad and Helech[i]
 were on your walls all around;
 men of Gamad were at
  your towers.
They hung their quivers all around
  your walls;
 they made perfect your beauty.

12 Tarshish did business with you out of the abundance of your great wealth; silver, iron, tin, and lead they exchanged for your wares. [13]Javan, Tubal, and Meshech traded with you; they exchanged human beings and vessels of bronze for your merchandise. [14]Beth-togarmah exchanged for your wares horses, war horses, and mules. [15]The Rhodians[j] traded with you; many coastlands were your own special markets; they brought you in payment ivory tusks and ebony. [16]Edom[k] did business with you because of your abundant goods; they exchanged for your wares turquoise, purple, embroidered work, fine linen, coral, and rubies. [17]Judah and the land of Israel traded with you; they exchanged for your merchandise wheat from Minnith, millet,[l] honey, oil, and balm. [18]Damascus traded with you for your abundant goods—because of your great wealth of every kind—wine of Helbon, and white wool. [19]Vedan and Javan from Uzal[l] entered into trade for your wares; wrought iron, cassia, and sweet cane were bartered for your merchandise. [20]Dedan traded with you in saddlecloths for riding. [21]Arabia and all the princes of Kedar were your favored dealers in lambs, rams, and goats; in these they did business with you. [22]The merchants of Sheba and Raamah traded with you; they exchanged for your wares the best of all kinds of spices, and all precious stones, and gold. [23]Haran, Canneh, Eden, the merchants of Sheba, Asshur, and Chilmad traded with you. [24]These traded with you in choice garments, in clothes of blue and embroidered work, and in carpets of colored material, bound with cords and made secure; in these they traded with you.[m] [25]The ships of Tarshish traveled for you in your trade.

So you were filled and heavily laden
 in the heart of the seas.
26 Your rowers have brought you
 into the high seas.
The east wind has wrecked you
 in the heart of the seas.
27 Your riches, your wares, your
  merchandise,
 your mariners and your pilots,
 your caulkers, your dealers in
  merchandise,
 and all your warriors within you,
with all the company
 that is with you,
sink into the heart of the seas
 on the day of your ruin.
28 At the sound of the cry of
  your pilots
 the countryside shakes,
29 and down from their ships
 come all that handle the oar.
The mariners and all the pilots
 of the sea
 stand on the shore
30 and wail aloud over you,
 and cry bitterly.
They throw dust on their heads
 and wallow in ashes;
31 they make themselves bald for you,
 and put on sackcloth,
and they weep over you in bitterness
 of soul,
 with bitter mourning.
32 In their wailing they raise a
  lamentation for you,
 and lament over you:
"Who was ever destroyed[n] like Tyre
 in the midst of the sea?
33 When your wares came from
  the seas,
 you satisfied many peoples;
with your abundant wealth and
  merchandise
 you enriched the kings of
  the earth.
34 Now you are wrecked by the seas,
 in the depths of the waters;

---

g Cn Compare Gen 10.18: Heb *your skilled men,
O Tyre*   h Or *Persia*   i Or *and your army*
j Gk: Heb *The Dedanites*   k Another reading is
Aram   l Meaning of Heb uncertain   m Cn:
Heb *in your market*   n Tg Vg: Heb *like silence*

your merchandise and all your crew
have sunk with you.
35 All the inhabitants of the coastlands
are appalled at you;
and their kings are horribly afraid,
their faces are convulsed.
36 The merchants among the peoples
hiss at you;
you have come to a dreadful end
and shall be no more forever."

Proclamation against the King of Tyre

28 The word of the LORD came to me:
2Mortal, say to the prince of Tyre,
Thus says the Lord GOD:
Because your heart is proud
and you have said, "I am a god;
I sit in the seat of the gods,
in the heart of the seas,"
yet you are but a mortal, and
no god,
though you compare your mind
with the mind of a god.
3 You are indeed wiser than Daniel;[o]
no secret is hidden from you;
4 by your wisdom and your
understanding
you have amassed wealth
for yourself,
and have gathered gold and silver
into your treasuries.
5 By your great wisdom in trade
you have increased your wealth,
and your heart has become proud
in your wealth.
6 Therefore thus says the Lord GOD:
Because you compare your mind
with the mind of a god,
7 therefore, I will bring strangers
against you,
the most terrible of the nations;
they shall draw their swords against
the beauty of your wisdom
and defile your splendor.
8 They shall thrust you down to
the Pit,
and you shall die a violent death
in the heart of the seas.
9 Will you still say, "I am a god,"
in the presence of those who
kill you,
though you are but a mortal, and no
god,
in the hands of those who
wound you?
10 You shall die the death of the
uncircumcised
by the hand of foreigners;
for I have spoken, says the
Lord GOD.

Lamentation over the King of Tyre

11 Moreover the word of the LORD
came to me: 12Mortal, raise a lamentation
over the king of Tyre, and say to him, Thus
says the Lord GOD:
You were the signet of perfection,[p]
full of wisdom and perfect in
beauty.
13 You were in Eden, the garden
of God;
every precious stone was your
covering,
carnelian, chrysolite, and
moonstone,
beryl, onyx, and jasper,
sapphire,[q] turquoise, and emerald;
and worked in gold were your
settings
and your engravings.[p]
On the day that you were created
they were prepared.
14 With an anointed cherub as
guardian I placed you;[p]
you were on the holy mountain
of God;
you walked among the stones
of fire.
15 You were blameless in your ways
from the day that you were
created,
until iniquity was found in you.
16 In the abundance of your trade
you were filled with violence, and
you sinned;
so I cast you as a profane thing from
the mountain of God,
and the guardian cherub drove
you out
from among the stones of fire.
17 Your heart was proud because of
your beauty;
you corrupted your wisdom for
the sake of your splendor.
I cast you to the ground;
I exposed you before kings,
to feast their eyes on you.
18 By the multitude of your iniquities,
in the unrighteousness of
your trade,
you profaned your sanctuaries.
So I brought out fire from
within you;

[o] Or, as otherwise read, *Danel* [p] Meaning of Heb uncertain [q] Or *lapis lazuli*

it consumed you,
and I turned you to ashes on
the earth
in the sight of all who saw you.
¹⁹ All who know you among the
peoples
are appalled at you;
you have come to a dreadful end
and shall be no more forever.

Proclamation against Sidon

20 The word of the LORD came to me:
²¹Mortal, set your face toward Sidon, and
prophesy against it, ²²and say, Thus says
the Lord GOD:
I am against you, O Sidon,
and I will gain glory in your
midst.
They shall know that I am the LORD
when I execute judgments in it,
and manifest my holiness in it;
²³ for I will send pestilence into it,
and bloodshed into its streets;
and the dead shall fall in its midst,
by the sword that is against it on
every side.
And they shall know that I am
the LORD.
24 The house of Israel shall no longer
find a pricking brier or a piercing thorn
among all their neighbors who have treated them with contempt. And they shall
know that I am the Lord GOD.

Future Blessing for Israel

25 Thus says the Lord GOD: When I
gather the house of Israel from the peoples among whom they are scattered, and
manifest my holiness in them in the sight
of the nations, then they shall settle on
their own soil that I gave to my servant
Jacob. ²⁶They shall live in safety in it, and
shall build houses and plant vineyards.
They shall live in safety, when I execute
judgments upon all their neighbors who
have treated them with contempt. And
they shall know that I am the LORD their
God.

Proclamation against Egypt

29 In the tenth year, in the tenth
month, on the twelfth day of the
month, the word of the LORD came to me:
²Mortal, set your face against Pharaoh
king of Egypt, and prophesy against him
and against all Egypt; ³speak, and say,
Thus says the Lord GOD:
I am against you,

Pharaoh king of Egypt,
the great dragon sprawling
in the midst of its channels,
saying, "My Nile is my own;
I made it for myself."
⁴ I will put hooks in your jaws,
and make the fish of your
channels stick to your scales.
I will draw you up from your
channels,
with all the fish of your channels
sticking to your scales.
⁵ I will fling you into the wilderness,
you and all the fish of your
channels;
you shall fall in the open field,
and not be gathered and buried.
To the animals of the earth and to
the birds of the air
I have given you as food.
⁶ Then all the inhabitants of Egypt
shall know
that I am the LORD
because you^r were a staff of reed
to the house of Israel;
⁷ when they grasped you with the
hand, you broke,
and tore all their shoulders;
and when they leaned on you,
you broke,
and made all their legs
unsteady.^s

8 Therefore, thus says the Lord GOD: I
will bring a sword upon you, and will cut
off from you human being and animal;
⁹and the land of Egypt shall be a desolation and a waste. Then they shall know
that I am the LORD.

Because you^t said, "The Nile is mine,
and I made it," ¹⁰therefore, I am against
you, and against your channels, and I will
make the land of Egypt an utter waste and
desolation, from Migdol to Syene, as far as
the border of Ethiopia.^u ¹¹No human
foot shall pass through it, and no animal
foot shall pass through it; it shall be uninhabited forty years. ¹²I will make the land
of Egypt a desolation among desolated
countries; and her cities shall be a desolation forty years among cities that are laid
waste. I will scatter the Egyptians among
the nations, and disperse them among the
countries.

13 Further, thus says the Lord GOD: At
the end of forty years I will gather the

^r Gk Syr Vg: Heb *they*   ^s Syr: Heb *stand*   ^t Gk
Syr Vg: Heb *he*   ^u Or *Nubia;* Heb *Cush*

Egyptians from the peoples among whom they were scattered; [14]and I will restore the fortunes of Egypt, and bring them back to the land of Pathros, the land of their origin; and there they shall be a lowly kingdom. [15]It shall be the most lowly of the kingdoms, and never again exalt itself above the nations; and I will make them so small that they will never again rule over the nations. [16]The Egyptians[v] shall never again be the reliance of the house of Israel; they will recall their iniquity, when they turned to them for aid. Then they shall know that I am the Lord GOD.

Babylonia Will Plunder Egypt

17 In the twenty-seventh year, in the first month, on the first day of the month, the word of the LORD came to me: [18]Mortal, King Nebuchadrezzar of Babylon made his army labor hard against Tyre; every head was made bald and every shoulder was rubbed bare; yet neither he nor his army got anything from Tyre to pay for the labor that he had expended against it. [19]Therefore thus says the Lord GOD: I will give the land of Egypt to King Nebuchadrezzar of Babylon; and he shall carry off its wealth and despoil it and plunder it; and it shall be the wages for his army. [20]I have given him the land of Egypt as his payment for which he labored, because they worked for me, says the Lord GOD.

21 On that day I will cause a horn to sprout up for the house of Israel, and I will open your lips among them. Then they shall know that I am the LORD.

Lamentation for Egypt

30 The word of the LORD came to me: [2]Mortal, prophesy, and say, Thus says the Lord GOD:
Wail, "Alas for the day!"
3   For a day is near,
      the day of the LORD is near;
    it will be a day of clouds,
      a time of doom[w] for the nations.
4   A sword shall come upon Egypt,
      and anguish shall be in
          Ethiopia,[x]
    when the slain fall in Egypt,
      and its wealth is carried away,
      and its foundations are
          torn down.
[5]Ethiopia,[x] and Put, and Lud, and all Arabia, and Libya,[y] and the people of the

allied land[z] shall fall with them by the sword.

6   Thus says the LORD:
    Those who support Egypt shall fall,
      and its proud might shall
          come down;
    from Migdol to Syene
      they shall fall within it by
          the sword,
    says the Lord GOD.
7   They shall be desolated among other
          desolated countries,
      and their cities shall lie among
          cities laid waste.
8   Then they shall know that I am
          the LORD,
      when I have set fire to Egypt,
      and all who help it are broken.

9 On that day, messengers shall go out from me in ships to terrify the unsuspecting Ethiopians;[a] and anguish shall come upon them on the day of Egypt's doom;[b] for it is coming!

10 Thus says the Lord GOD:
    I will put an end to the hordes
          of Egypt,
      by the hand of King
          Nebuchadrezzar of Babylon.
11 He and his people with him, the
          most terrible of the nations,
      shall be brought in to destroy
          the land;
    and they shall draw their swords
          against Egypt,
      and fill the land with the slain.
12 I will dry up the channels,
      and will sell the land into the
          hand of evildoers;
    I will bring desolation upon the
          land and everything in it
      by the hand of foreigners;
    I the LORD have spoken.

13 Thus says the Lord GOD:
    I will destroy the idols
      and put an end to the images
          in Memphis;
    there shall no longer be a prince in
          the land of Egypt;
    so I will put fear in the land
          of Egypt.

---

v Heb It   w Heb lacks of doom   x Or Nubia;
Heb Cush   y Compare Gk Syr Vg: Heb Cub
z Meaning of Heb uncertain   a Or Nubians; Heb
Cush   b Heb the day of Egypt

14 I will make Pathros a desolation,
 and will set fire to Zoan,
 and will execute acts of judgment
  on Thebes.
15 I will pour my wrath upon
  Pelusium,
 the stronghold of Egypt,
 and cut off the hordes of Thebes.
16 I will set fire to Egypt;
 Pelusium shall be in great agony;
Thebes shall be breached,
 and Memphis face adversaries
  by day.
17 The young men of On and of
  Pi-beseth shall fall by
  the sword;
 and the cities themselves*c* shall
  go into captivity.
18 At Tehaphnehes the day shall
  be dark,
 when I break there the dominion
  of Egypt,
 and its proud might shall come to
  an end;
 the city*d* shall be covered by
  a cloud,
 and its daughter-towns shall go
  into captivity.
19 Thus I will execute acts of judgment
  on Egypt.
 Then they shall know that I am
  the LORD.

Proclamation against Pharaoh

20 In the eleventh year, in the first month, on the seventh day of the month, the word of the LORD came to me: 21Mortal, I have broken the arm of Pharaoh king of Egypt; it has not been bound up for healing or wrapped with a bandage, so that it may become strong to wield the sword. 22Therefore thus says the Lord GOD: I am against Pharaoh king of Egypt, and will break his arms, both the strong arm and the one that was broken; and I will make the sword fall from his hand. 23I will scatter the Egyptians among the nations, and disperse them throughout the lands. 24I will strengthen the arms of the king of Babylon, and put my sword in his hand; but I will break the arms of Pharaoh, and he will groan before him with the groans of one mortally wounded. 25I will strengthen the arms of the king of Babylon, but the arms of Pharaoh shall fall. And they shall know that I am the LORD, when I put my sword into the hand of the king of Babylon. He shall stretch it

out against the land of Egypt, 26and I will scatter the Egyptians among the nations and disperse them throughout the countries. Then they shall know that I am the LORD.

The Lofty Cedar

31 In the eleventh year, in the third month, on the first day of the month, the word of the LORD came to me: 2Mortal, say to Pharaoh king of Egypt and to his hordes:

Whom are you like in your
  greatness?
3 Consider Assyria, a cedar
   of Lebanon,
with fair branches and forest shade,
 and of great height,
 its top among the clouds.*e*
4 The waters nourished it,
 the deep made it grow tall,
making its rivers flow*f*
 around the place it was planted,
sending forth its streams
 to all the trees of the field.
5 So it towered high
 above all the trees of the field;
its boughs grew large
 and its branches long,
 from abundant water in its shoots.
6 All the birds of the air
 made their nests in its boughs;
under its branches all the animals of
  the field
 gave birth to their young;
and in its shade
 all great nations lived.
7 It was beautiful in its greatness,
 in the length of its branches;
for its roots went down
 to abundant water.
8 The cedars in the garden of God
   could not rival it,
 nor the fir trees equal its boughs;
the plane trees were as nothing
  compared with its branches;
no tree in the garden of God
 was like it in beauty.
9 I made it beautiful
 with its mass of branches,
the envy of all the trees of Eden
 that were in the garden of God.

10 Therefore thus says the Lord GOD: Because it*g* towered high and set its top

---

c Heb *and they*   *d* Heb *she*   *e* Gk: Heb *thick boughs*   *f* Gk: Heb *rivers going*   *g* Syr Vg: Heb *you* among the clouds,[h] and its heart was proud of its height, [11]I gave it into the hand of the prince of the nations; he has dealt with it as its wickedness deserves. I have cast it out. [12]Foreigners from the most terrible of the nations have cut it down and left it. On the mountains and in all the valleys its branches have fallen, and its boughs lie broken in all the watercourses of the land; and all the peoples of the earth went away from its shade and left it.

[13] On its fallen trunk settle
    all the birds of the air,
and among its boughs lodge
    all the wild animals.

[14]All this is in order that no trees by the waters may grow to lofty height or set their tops among the clouds,[h] and that no trees that drink water may reach up to them in height.

For all of them are handed over
        to death,
    to the world below;
along with all mortals,
    with those who go down to
        the Pit.

[15] Thus says the Lord God: On the day it went down to Sheol I closed the deep over it and covered it; I restrained its rivers, and its mighty waters were checked. I clothed Lebanon in gloom for it, and all the trees of the field fainted because of it. [16]I made the nations quake at the sound of its fall, when I cast it down to Sheol with those who go down to the Pit; and all the trees of Eden, the choice and best of Lebanon, all that were well watered, were consoled in the world below. [17]They also went down to Sheol with it, to those killed by the sword, along with its allies,[i] those who lived in its shade among the nations.

[18] Which among the trees of Eden was like you in glory and in greatness? Now you shall be brought down with the trees of Eden to the world below; you shall lie among the uncircumcised, with those who are killed by the sword. This is Pharaoh and all his horde, says the Lord God.

Lamentation over Pharaoh and Egypt

32 In the twelfth year, in the twelfth month, on the first day of the month, the word of the Lord came to me: [2]Mortal, raise a lamentation over Pharaoh king of Egypt, and say to him:

You consider yourself a lion among
        the nations,
    but you are like a dragon in
        the seas;
you thrash about in your streams,
    trouble the water with your feet,
    and foul your[j] streams.

[3] Thus says the Lord God:
    In an assembly of many peoples
        I will throw my net over you;
    and I[k] will haul you up in
        my dragnet.
[4] I will throw you on the ground,
        on the open field I will fling you,
    and will cause all the birds of the air
        to settle on you,
    and I will let the wild animals of
        the whole earth gorge
        themselves with you.
[5] I will strew your flesh on the
        mountains,
    and fill the valleys with your
        carcass.[l]
[6] I will drench the land with your
        flowing blood
    up to the mountains,
    and the watercourses will be filled
        with you.
[7] When I blot you out, I will cover the
        heavens,
    and make their stars dark;
    I will cover the sun with a cloud,
        and the moon shall not give
        its light.
[8] All the shining lights of the heavens
        I will darken above you,
    and put darkness on your land,
                    says the Lord God.
[9] I will trouble the hearts of many
        peoples,
    as I carry you captive[m] among the
        nations,
    into countries you have not
        known.
[10] I will make many peoples appalled
        at you;
    their kings shall shudder because
        of you.
    When I brandish my sword before
        them,
    they shall tremble every moment
    for their lives, each one of them,
        on the day of your downfall.
[11] For thus says the Lord God:

---

h Gk: Heb *thick boughs*   i Heb *its arms*   j Heb *their*   k Gk Vg: Heb *they*   l Symmachus Syr Vg: Heb *your height*   m Gk: Heb *bring your destruction*

The sword of the king of Babylon
    shall come against you.
12 I will cause your hordes to fall
    by the swords of mighty ones,
  all of them most terrible among
    the nations.
They shall bring to ruin the pride of
    Egypt,
  and all its hordes shall perish.
13 I will destroy all its livestock
    from beside abundant waters;
  and no human foot shall trouble
    them any more,
  nor shall the hoofs of cattle
    trouble them.
14 Then I will make their waters clear,
    and cause their streams to run like
    oil, says the Lord God.
15 When I make the land of Egypt
    desolate
  and when the land is stripped of
    all that fills it,
  when I strike down all who live in
    it,
  then they shall know that I am
    the Lord.
16 This is a lamentation; it shall
    be chanted.
  The women of the nations shall
    chant it.
Over Egypt and all its hordes they
    shall chant it,
  says the Lord God.

Dirge over Egypt

17 In the twelfth year, in the first
month,[n] on the fifteenth day of the
month, the word of the Lord came to me:
18 Mortal, wail over the hordes
    of Egypt,
  and send them down,
with Egypt[o] and the daughters of
    majestic nations,
  to the world below,
  with those who go down to
    the Pit.
19 "Whom do you surpass in beauty?
    Go down! Be laid to rest with the
    uncircumcised!"
20They shall fall among those who are
killed by the sword. Egypt[p] has been
handed over to the sword; carry away
both it and its hordes. 21The mighty chiefs
shall speak of them, with their helpers,
out of the midst of Sheol: "They have
come down, they lie still, the uncircumcised, killed by the sword."
22 Assyria is there, and all its company,

their graves all around it, all of them
killed, fallen by the sword. 23Their graves
are set in the uttermost parts of the Pit. Its
company is all around its grave, all of
them killed, fallen by the sword, who
spread terror in the land of the living.

24 Elam is there, and all its hordes
around its grave; all of them killed, fallen
by the sword, who went down uncircumcised into the world below, who spread
terror in the land of the living. They bear
their shame with those who go down to
the Pit. 25They have made Elam[o] a bed
among the slain with all its hordes, their
graves all around it, all of them uncircumcised, killed by the sword; for terror of
them was spread in the land of the living,
and they bear their shame with those who
go down to the Pit; they are placed among
the slain.

26 Meshech and Tubal are there, and
all their multitude, their graves all around
them, all of them uncircumcised, killed by
the sword; for they spread terror in the
land of the living. 27And they do not lie
with the fallen warriors of long ago[q] who
went down to Sheol with their weapons of
war, whose swords were laid under their
heads, and whose shields[r] are upon their
bones; for the terror of the warriors was in
the land of the living. 28So you shall be
broken and lie among the uncircumcised,
with those who are killed by the sword.

29 Edom is there, its kings and all its
princes, who for all their might are laid
with those who are killed by the sword;
they lie with the uncircumcised, with
those who go down to the Pit.

30 The princes of the north are there,
all of them, and all the Sidonians, who
have gone down in shame with the slain,
for all the terror that they caused by their
might; they lie uncircumcised with those
who are killed by the sword, and bear
their shame with those who go down to
the Pit.

31 When Pharaoh sees them, he will be
consoled for all his hordes—Pharaoh and
all his army, killed by the sword, says the
Lord God. 32For he[s] spread terror in the
land of the living; therefore he shall be
laid to rest among the uncircumcised,
with those who are slain by the sword—

n Gk: Heb lacks in the first month   o Heb
it   p Heb It   q Gk Old Latin: Heb of the
uncircumcised   r Cn: Heb iniquities
s Cn: Heb I

Pharaoh and all his multitude, says the Lord GOD.

Ezekiel Israel's Sentry

33 The word of the LORD came to me: [2]O Mortal, speak to your people and say to them, If I bring the sword upon a land, and the people of the land take one of their number as their sentinel; [3]and if the sentinel sees the sword coming upon the land and blows the trumpet and warns the people; [4]then if any who hear the sound of the trumpet do not take warning, and the sword comes and takes them away, their blood shall be upon their own heads. [5]They heard the sound of the trumpet and did not take warning; their blood shall be upon themselves. But if they had taken warning, they would have saved their lives. [6]But if the sentinel sees the sword coming and does not blow the trumpet, so that the people are not warned, and the sword comes and takes any of them, they are taken away in their iniquity, but their blood I will require at the sentinel's hand.

7 So you, mortal, I have made a sentinel for the house of Israel; whenever you hear a word from my mouth, you shall give them warning from me. [8]If I say to the wicked, "O wicked ones, you shall surely die," and you do not speak to warn the wicked to turn from their ways, the wicked shall die in their iniquity, but their blood I will require at your hand. [9]But if you warn the wicked to turn from their ways, and they do not turn from their ways, the wicked shall die in their iniquity, but you will have saved your life.

God's Justice and Mercy

10 Now you, mortal, say to the house of Israel, Thus you have said: "Our transgressions and our sins weigh upon us, and we waste away because of them; how then can we live?" [11]Say to them, As I live, says the Lord GOD, I have no pleasure in the death of the wicked, but that the wicked turn from their ways and live; turn back, turn back from your evil ways; for why will you die, O house of Israel? [12]And you, mortal, say to your people, The righteousness of the righteous shall not save them when they transgress; and as for the wickedness of the wicked, it shall not make them stumble when they turn from their wickedness; and the righteous shall not be able to live by their righteousness[t]

when they sin. [13]Though I say to the righteous that they shall surely live, yet if they trust in their righteousness and commit iniquity, none of their righteous deeds shall be remembered; but in the iniquity that they have committed they shall die. [14]Again, though I say to the wicked, "You shall surely die," yet if they turn from their sin and do what is lawful and right— [15]if the wicked restore the pledge, give back what they have taken by robbery, and walk in the statutes of life, committing no iniquity—they shall surely live, they shall not die. [16]None of the sins that they have committed shall be remembered against them; they have done what is lawful and right, they shall surely live.

17 Yet your people say, "The way of the Lord is not just," when it is their own way that is not just. [18]When the righteous turn from their righteousness, and commit iniquity, they shall die for it.[u] [19]And when the wicked turn from their wickedness, and do what is lawful and right, they shall live by it.[u] [20]Yet you say, "The way of the Lord is not just." O house of Israel, I will judge all of you according to your ways!

The Fall of Jerusalem

21 In the twelfth year of our exile, in the tenth month, on the fifth day of the month, someone who had escaped from Jerusalem came to me and said, "The city has fallen." [22]Now the hand of the LORD had been upon me the evening before the fugitive came; but he had opened my mouth by the time the fugitive came to me in the morning; so my mouth was opened, and I was no longer unable to speak.

The Survivors in Judah

23 The word of the LORD came to me: [24]Mortal, the inhabitants of these waste places in the land of Israel keep saying, "Abraham was only one man, yet he got possession of the land; but we are many; the land is surely given us to possess." [25]Therefore say to them, Thus says the Lord GOD: You eat flesh with the blood, and lift up your eyes to your idols, and shed blood; shall you then possess the land? [26]You depend on your swords, you commit abominations, and each of you defiles his neighbor's wife; shall you then

t Heb *by it*   *u* Heb *them*

possess the land? [27]Say this to them, Thus says the Lord GOD: As I live, surely those who are in the waste places shall fall by the sword; and those who are in the open field I will give to the wild animals to be devoured; and those who are in strongholds and in caves shall die by pestilence. [28]I will make the land a desolation and a waste, and its proud might shall come to an end; and the mountains of Israel shall be so desolate that no one will pass through. [29]Then they shall know that I am the LORD, when I have made the land a desolation and a waste because of all their abominations that they have committed.

30 As for you, mortal, your people who talk together about you by the walls, and at the doors of the houses, say to one another, each to a neighbor, "Come and hear what the word is that comes from the LORD." [31]They come to you as people come, and they sit before you as my people, and they hear your words, but they will not obey them. For flattery is on their lips, but their heart is set on their gain. [32]To them you are like a singer of love songs,[v] one who has a beautiful voice and plays well on an instrument; they hear what you say, but they will not do it. [33]When this comes—and come it will!—then they shall know that a prophet has been among them.

Israel's False Shepherds

34 The word of the LORD came to me: [2]Mortal, prophesy against the shepherds of Israel: prophesy, and say to them—to the shepherds: Thus says the Lord GOD: Ah, you shepherds of Israel who have been feeding yourselves! Should not shepherds feed the sheep? [3]You eat the fat, you clothe yourselves with the wool, you slaughter the fatlings; but you do not feed the sheep. [4]You have not strengthened the weak, you have not healed the sick, you have not bound up the injured, you have not brought back the strayed, you have not sought the lost, but with force and harshness you have ruled them. [5]So they were scattered, because there was no shepherd; and scattered, they became food for all the wild animals. [6]My sheep were scattered, they wandered over all the mountains and on every high hill; my sheep were scattered over all the face of the earth, with no one to search or seek for them.

7 Therefore, you shepherds, hear the word of the LORD: [8]As I live, says the Lord GOD, because my sheep have become a prey, and my sheep have become food for all the wild animals, since there was no shepherd; and because my shepherds have not searched for my sheep, but the shepherds have fed themselves, and have not fed my sheep; [9]therefore, you shepherds, hear the word of the LORD: [10]Thus says the Lord GOD, I am against the shepherds; and I will demand my sheep at their hand, and put a stop to their feeding the sheep; no longer shall the shepherds feed themselves. I will rescue my sheep from their mouths, so that they may not be food for them.

God, the True Shepherd

11 For thus says the Lord GOD: I myself will search for my sheep, and will seek them out. [12]As shepherds seek out their flocks when they are among their scattered sheep, so I will seek out my sheep. I will rescue them from all the places to which they have been scattered on a day of clouds and thick darkness. [13]I will bring them out from the peoples and gather them from the countries, and will bring them into their own land; and I will feed them on the mountains of Israel, by the watercourses, and in all the inhabited parts of the land. [14]I will feed them with good pasture, and the mountain heights of Israel shall be their pasture; there they shall lie down in good grazing land, and they shall feed on rich pasture on the mountains of Israel. [15]I myself will be the shepherd of my sheep, and I will make them lie down, says the Lord GOD. [16]I will seek the lost, and I will bring back the strayed, and I will bind up the injured, and I will strengthen the weak, but the fat and the strong I will destroy. I will feed them with justice.

17 As for you, my flock, thus says the Lord GOD: I shall judge between sheep and sheep, between rams and goats: [18]Is it not enough for you to feed on the good pasture, but you must tread down with your feet the rest of your pasture? When you drink of clear water, must you foul the rest with your feet? [19]And must my sheep eat what you have trodden with your feet, and drink what you have fouled with your feet?

20 Therefore, thus says the Lord GOD to

[v] Cn: Heb *like a love song*

them: I myself will judge between the fat sheep and the lean sheep. [21]Because you pushed with flank and shoulder, and butted at all the weak animals with your horns until you scattered them far and wide, [22]I will save my flock, and they shall no longer be ravaged; and I will judge between sheep and sheep.

23 I will set up over them one shepherd, my servant David, and he shall feed them: he shall feed them and be their shepherd. [24]And I, the LORD, will be their God, and my servant David shall be prince among them; I, the LORD, have spoken.

25 I will make with them a covenant of peace and banish wild animals from the land, so that they may live in the wild and sleep in the woods securely. [26]I will make them and the region around my hill a blessing; and I will send down the showers in their season; they shall be showers of blessing. [27]The trees of the field shall yield their fruit, and the earth shall yield its increase. They shall be secure on their soil; and they shall know that I am the LORD, when I break the bars of their yoke, and save them from the hands of those who enslaved them. [28]They shall no more be plunder for the nations, nor shall the animals of the land devour them; they shall live in safety, and no one shall make them afraid. [29]I will provide for them a splendid vegetation so that they shall no more be consumed with hunger in the land, and no longer suffer the insults of the nations. [30]They shall know that I, the LORD their God, am with them, and that they, the house of Israel, are my people, says the Lord GOD. [31]You are my sheep, the sheep of my pasture[w] and I am your God, says the Lord GOD.

Judgment on Mount Seir

35 The word of the LORD came to me: [2]Mortal, set your face against Mount Seir, and prophesy against it, [3]and say to it, Thus says the Lord GOD:

I am against you, Mount Seir;
    I stretch out my hand against you
    to make you a desolation and
        a waste.
[4] I lay your towns in ruins;
    you shall become a desolation,
    and you shall know that I am
        the LORD.

[5]Because you cherished an ancient enmity, and gave over the people of Israel to the power of the sword at the time of their calamity, at the time of their final punishment; [6]therefore, as I live, says the Lord GOD, I will prepare you for blood, and blood shall pursue you; since you did not hate bloodshed, bloodshed shall pursue you. [7]I will make Mount Seir a waste and a desolation; and I will cut off from it all who come and go. [8]I will fill its mountains with the slain; on your hills and in your valleys and in all your watercourses those killed with the sword shall fall. [9]I will make you a perpetual desolation, and your cities shall never be inhabited. Then you shall know that I am the LORD.

10 Because you said, "These two nations and these two countries shall be mine, and we will take possession of them,"—although the LORD was there— [11]therefore, as I live, says the Lord GOD, I will deal with you according to the anger and envy that you showed because of your hatred against them; and I will make myself known among you,[x] when I judge you. [12]You shall know that I, the LORD, have heard all the abusive speech that you uttered against the mountains of Israel, saying, "They are laid desolate, they are given us to devour." [13]And you magnified yourselves against me with your mouth, and multiplied your words against me; I heard it. [14]Thus says the Lord GOD: As the whole earth rejoices, I will make you desolate. [15]As you rejoiced over the inheritance of the house of Israel, because it was desolate, so I will deal with you; you shall be desolate, Mount Seir, and all Edom, all of it. Then they shall know that I am the LORD.

Blessing on Israel

36 And you, mortal, prophesy to the mountains of Israel, and say: O mountains of Israel, hear the word of the LORD. [2]Thus says the Lord GOD: Because the enemy said of you, "Aha!" and, "The ancient heights have become our possession," [3]therefore prophesy, and say: Thus says the Lord GOD: Because they made you desolate indeed, and crushed you from all sides, so that you became the possession of the rest of the nations, and you became an object of gossip and slander among the people; [4]therefore, O mountains of Israel, hear the word of

w Gk OL: Heb *pasture, you are people*   *x* Gk: Heb *them* the Lord GOD: Thus says the Lord GOD to the mountains and the hills, the watercourses and the valleys, the desolate wastes and the deserted towns, which have become a source of plunder and an object of derision to the rest of the nations all around; 5therefore thus says the Lord GOD: I am speaking in my hot jealousy against the rest of the nations, and against all Edom, who, with wholehearted joy and utter contempt, took my land as their possession, because of its pasture, to plunder it. 6Therefore prophesy concerning the land of Israel, and say to the mountains and hills, to the watercourses and valleys, Thus says the Lord GOD: I am speaking in my jealous wrath, because you have suffered the insults of the nations; 7therefore thus says the Lord GOD: I swear that the nations that are all around you shall themselves suffer insults.

8 But you, O mountains of Israel, shall shoot out your branches, and yield your fruit to my people Israel; for they shall soon come home. 9See now, I am for you; I will turn to you, and you shall be tilled and sown; 10and I will multiply your population, the whole house of Israel, all of it; the towns shall be inhabited and the waste places rebuilt; 11and I will multiply human beings and animals upon you. They shall increase and be fruitful; and I will cause you to be inhabited as in your former times, and will do more good to you than ever before. Then you shall know that I am the LORD. 12I will lead people upon you—my people Israel—and they shall possess you, and you shall be their inheritance. No longer shall you bereave them of children.

13 Thus says the Lord GOD: Because they say to you, "You devour people, and you bereave your nation of children," 14therefore you shall no longer devour people and no longer bereave your nation of children, says the Lord GOD; 15and no longer will I let you hear the insults of the nations, no longer shall you bear the disgrace of the peoples; and no longer shall you cause your nation to stumble, says the Lord GOD.

The Renewal of Israel

16 The word of the LORD came to me: 17Mortal, when the house of Israel lived on their own soil, they defiled it with their ways and their deeds; their conduct in my sight was like the uncleanness of a woman in her menstrual period. 18So I poured out my wrath upon them for the blood that they had shed upon the land, and for the idols with which they had defiled it. 19I scattered them among the nations, and they were dispersed through the countries; in accordance with their conduct and their deeds I judged them. 20But when they came to the nations, wherever they came, they profaned my holy name, in that it was said of them, "These are the people of the LORD, and yet they had to go out of his land." 21But I had concern for my holy name, which the house of Israel had profaned among the nations to which they came.

22 Therefore say to the house of Israel, Thus says the Lord GOD: It is not for your sake, O house of Israel, that I am about to act, but for the sake of my holy name, which you have profaned among the nations to which you came. 23I will sanctify my great name, which has been profaned among the nations, and which you have profaned among them; and the nations shall know that I am the LORD, says the Lord GOD, when through you I display my holiness before their eyes. 24I will take you from the nations, and gather you from all the countries, and bring you into your own land. 25I will sprinkle clean water upon you, and you shall be clean from all your uncleannesses, and from all your idols I will cleanse you. 26A new heart I will give you, and a new spirit I will put within you; and I will remove from your body the heart of stone and give you a heart of flesh. 27I will put my spirit within you, and make you follow my statutes and be careful to observe my ordinances. 28Then you shall live in the land that I gave to your ancestors; and you shall be my people, and I will be your God. 29I will save you from all your uncleannesses, and I will summon the grain and make it abundant and lay no famine upon you. 30I will make the fruit of the tree and the produce of the field abundant, so that you may never again suffer the disgrace of famine among the nations. 31Then you shall remember your evil ways, and your dealings that were not good; and you shall loathe yourselves for your iniquities and your abominable deeds. 32It is not for your sake that I will act, says the Lord GOD; let that be known to you. Be ashamed and dismayed for your ways, O house of Israel.

33 Thus says the Lord God: On the day that I cleanse you from all your iniquities, I will cause the towns to be inhabited, and the waste places shall be rebuilt. 34The land that was desolate shall be tilled, instead of being the desolation that it was in the sight of all who passed by. 35And they will say, "This land that was desolate has become like the garden of Eden; and the waste and desolate and ruined towns are now inhabited and fortified." 36Then the nations that are left all around you shall know that I, the Lord, have rebuilt the ruined places, and replanted that which was desolate; I, the Lord, have spoken, and I will do it.

37 Thus says the Lord God: I will also let the house of Israel ask me to do this for them: to increase their population like a flock. 38Like the flock for sacrifices,*ʸ* like the flock at Jerusalem during her appointed festivals, so shall the ruined towns be filled with flocks of people. Then they shall know that I am the Lord.

The Valley of Dry Bones

37 The hand of the Lord came upon me, and he brought me out by the spirit of the Lord and set me down in the middle of a valley; it was full of bones. 2He led me all around them; there were very many lying in the valley, and they were very dry. 3He said to me, "Mortal, can these bones live?" I answered, "O Lord God, you know." 4Then he said to me, "Prophesy to these bones, and say to them: O dry bones, hear the word of the Lord. 5Thus says the Lord God to these bones: I will cause breath*ᶻ* to enter you, and you shall live. 6I will lay sinews on you, and will cause flesh to come upon you, and cover you with skin, and put

ʸ Heb flock of holy things   ᶻ Or spirit

TUESDAY

Scripture Reading
for Today:
Ezekiel 36.24–30

Verse for Today:
Ezekiel 36.26

"*Take Away My Heart of Stone*"

Suddenly I remembered coming home from a meeting in Brooklyn many years ago, sitting in an uncomfortable bus seat facing a few poor people. One of them, a downcast, ragged man, suddenly epitomized for me the desolation, the hopelessness of the destitute, and I began to weep. I had been struck by one of those "beams of love," wounded by it in a most particular way. It was my own condition that I was weeping about—my own hardness of heart, my own sinfulness. I recognized this as a moment of truth, an experience of what the *New Catechism* calls our "tremendous, universal, inevitable and yet inexcusable incapacity to love." I had not read that line when I had that experience, but that is what I felt.

I think that ever since then I have prayed sincerely those Scriptural verses, "Take away my heart of stone and give me a heart of flesh." I had been using this prayer as one of the three acts of faith, hope, and charity. "I believe, help thou my unbelief." "In thee have I hoped, let me never be confounded." "Take away my heart of stone and give me a heart of flesh," so that I may learn how to truly love my brother because in him, in his meanest guise, I am encountering Christ.

—DOROTHY DAY

Go to page 1158 for your next devotional reading.

breath[a] in you, and you shall live; and you shall know that I am the LORD."

7 So I prophesied as I had been commanded; and as I prophesied, suddenly there was a noise, a rattling, and the bones came together, bone to its bone. [8]I looked, and there were sinews on them, and flesh had come upon them, and skin had covered them; but there was no breath in them. [9]Then he said to me, "Prophesy to the breath, prophesy, mortal, and say to the breath:[b] Thus says the Lord GOD: Come from the four winds, O breath,[b] and breathe upon these slain, that they may live." [10]I prophesied as he commanded me, and the breath came into them, and they lived, and stood on their feet, a vast multitude.

11 Then he said to me, "Mortal, these bones are the whole house of Israel. They say, 'Our bones are dried up, and our hope is lost; we are cut off completely.' [12]Therefore prophesy, and say to them, Thus says the Lord GOD: I am going to open your graves, and bring you up from your graves, O my people; and I will bring you back to the land of Israel. [13]And you shall know that I am the LORD, when I open your graves, and bring you up from your graves, O my people. [14]I will put my spirit within you, and you shall live, and I will place you on your own soil; then you shall know that I, the LORD, have spoken and will act, says the LORD."

The Two Sticks

15 The word of the LORD came to me: [16]Mortal, take a stick and write on it, "For Judah, and the Israelites associated with it"; then take another stick and write on it, "For Joseph (the stick of Ephraim) and all the house of Israel associated with it"; [17]and join them together into one stick, so that they may become one in your hand. [18]And when your people say to you, "Will you not show us what you mean by these?" [19]say to them, Thus says the Lord GOD: I am about to take the stick of Joseph (which is in the hand of Ephraim) and the tribes of Israel associated with it; and I will put the stick of Judah upon it,[c] and make them one stick, in order that they may be one in my hand. [20]When the sticks on which you write are in your hand before their eyes, [21]then say to them, Thus says the Lord GOD: I will take the people of Israel from the nations among which they have gone, and will gather them from ev-

ery quarter, and bring them to their own land. [22]I will make them one nation in the land, on the mountains of Israel; and one king shall be king over them all. Never again shall they be two nations, and never again shall they be divided into two kingdoms. [23]They shall never again defile themselves with their idols and their detestable things, or with any of their transgressions. I will save them from all the apostasies into which they have fallen,[d] and will cleanse them. Then they shall be my people, and I will be their God.

24 My servant David shall be king over them; and they shall all have one shepherd. They shall follow my ordinances and be careful to observe my statutes. [25]They shall live in the land that I gave to my servant Jacob, in which your ancestors lived; they and their children and their children's children shall live there forever; and my servant David shall be their prince forever. [26]I will make a covenant of peace with them; it shall be an everlasting covenant with them; and I will bless[e] them and multiply them, and will set my sanctuary among them forevermore. [27]My dwelling place shall be with them; and I will be their God, and they shall be my people. [28]Then the nations shall know that I the LORD sanctify Israel, when my sanctuary is among them forevermore.

Invasion by Gog

38 The word of the LORD came to me: [2]Mortal, set your face toward Gog, of the land of Magog, the chief prince of Meshech and Tubal. Prophesy against him [3]and say: Thus says the Lord GOD: I am against you, O Gog, chief prince of Meshech and Tubal; [4]I will turn you around and put hooks into your jaws, and I will lead you out with all your army, horses and horsemen, all of them clothed in full armor, a great company, all of them with shield and buckler, wielding swords. [5]Persia, Ethiopia,[f] and Put are with them, all of them with buckler and helmet; [6]Gomer and all its troops; Beth-togarmah from the remotest parts of the north with all its troops—many peoples are with you.

7 Be ready and keep ready, you and all

a Or *spirit*   *b* Or *wind* or *spirit*   *c* Heb *I will put them upon it*   *d* Another reading is *from all the settlements in which they have sinned*   *e* Tg: Heb *give*   *f* Or *Nubia;* Heb *Cush*

the companies that are assembled around you, and hold yourselves in reserve for them. 8After many days you shall be mustered; in the latter years you shall go against a land restored from war, a land where people were gathered from many nations on the mountains of Israel, which had long lain waste; its people were brought out from the nations and now are living in safety, all of them. 9You shall advance, coming on like a storm; you shall be like a cloud covering the land, you and all your troops, and many peoples with you.

10 Thus says the Lord God: On that day thoughts will come into your mind, and you will devise an evil scheme. 11You will say, "I will go up against the land of unwalled villages; I will fall upon the quiet people who live in safety, all of them living without walls, and having no bars or gates"; 12to seize spoil and carry off plunder; to assail the waste places that are now inhabited, and the people who were gathered from the nations, who are acquiring cattle and goods, who live at the center*g* of the earth. 13Sheba and Dedan and the merchants of Tarshish and all its young warriors*h* will say to you, "Have you come to seize spoil? Have you assembled your horde to carry off plunder, to carry away silver and gold, to take away cattle and goods, to seize a great amount of booty?"

14 Therefore, mortal, prophesy, and say to Gog: Thus says the Lord God: On that day when my people Israel are living securely, you will rouse yourself*i* 15and come from your place out of the remotest parts of the north, you and many peoples with you, all of them riding on horses, a great horde, a mighty army; 16you will come up against my people Israel, like a cloud covering the earth. In the latter days I will bring you against my land, so that the nations may know me, when through you, O Gog, I display my holiness before their eyes.

Judgment on Gog

17 Thus says the Lord God: Are you he of whom I spoke in former days by my servants the prophets of Israel, who in those days prophesied for years that I would bring you against them? 18On that day, when Gog comes against the land of Israel, says the Lord God, my wrath shall be aroused. 19For in my jealousy and in

my blazing wrath I declare: On that day there shall be a great shaking in the land of Israel; 20the fish of the sea, and the birds of the air, and the animals of the field, and all creeping things that creep on the ground, and all human beings that are on the face of the earth, shall quake at my presence, and the mountains shall be thrown down, and the cliffs shall fall, and every wall shall tumble to the ground. 21I will summon the sword against Gog*j* in*k* all my mountains, says the Lord God; the swords of all will be against their comrades. 22With pestilence and bloodshed I will enter into judgment with him; and I will pour down torrential rains and hailstones, fire and sulfur, upon him and his troops and the many peoples that are with him. 23So I will display my greatness and my holiness and make myself known in the eyes of many nations. Then they shall know that I am the Lord.

Gog's Armies Destroyed

39 And you, mortal, prophesy against Gog, and say: Thus says the Lord God: I am against you, O Gog, chief prince of Meshech and Tubal! 2I will turn you around and drive you forward, and bring you up from the remotest parts of the north, and lead you against the mountains of Israel. 3I will strike your bow from your left hand, and will make your arrows drop out of your right hand. 4You shall fall upon the mountains of Israel, you and all your troops and the peoples that are with you; I will give you to birds of prey of every kind and to the wild animals to be devoured. 5You shall fall in the open field; for I have spoken, says the Lord God. 6I will send fire on Magog and on those who live securely in the coastlands; and they shall know that I am the Lord.

7 My holy name I will make known among my people Israel; and I will not let my holy name be profaned any more; and the nations shall know that I am the Lord, the Holy One in Israel. 8It has come! It has happened, says the Lord God. This is the day of which I have spoken.

9 Then those who live in the towns of Israel will go out and make fires of the weapons and burn them—bucklers and shields, bows and arrows, handpikes and

g Heb *navel*   *h* Heb *young lions*   *i* Gk: Heb *will you not know?*   *j* Heb *him*   *k* Heb *to* or *for*

spears—and they will make fires of them
for seven years. [10]They will not need to
take wood out of the field or cut down
any trees in the forests, for they will make
their fires of the weapons; they will despoil those who despoiled them, and
plunder those who plundered them, says
the Lord GOD.

The Burial of Gog

11 On that day I will give to Gog a
place for burial in Israel, the Valley of the
Travelers[l] east of the sea; it shall block
the path of the travelers, for there Gog and
all his horde will be buried; it shall be
called the Valley of Hamon-gog.[m] [12]Sev-
en months the house of Israel shall spend
burying them, in order to cleanse the
land. [13]All the people of the land shall
bury them; and it will bring them honor
on the day that I show my glory, says the
Lord GOD. [14]They will set apart men to
pass through the land regularly and bury
any invaders[n] who remain on the face of
the land, so as to cleanse it; for seven
months they shall make their search. [15]As
the searchers[n] pass through the land,
anyone who sees a human bone shall set
up a sign by it, until the buriers have buried it in the Valley of Hamon-gog.[m] [16](A
city Hamonah[o] is there also.) Thus they
shall cleanse the land.

17 As for you, mortal, thus says the
Lord GOD: Speak to the birds of every kind
and to all the wild animals: Assemble and
come, gather from all around to the sacrificial feast that I am preparing for you, a
great sacrificial feast on the mountains of
Israel, and you shall eat flesh and drink
blood. [18]You shall eat the flesh of the
mighty, and drink the blood of the
princes of the earth—of rams, of lambs,
and of goats, of bulls, all of them fatlings
of Bashan. [19]You shall eat fat until you
are filled, and drink blood until you are
drunk, at the sacrificial feast that I am preparing for you. [20]And you shall be filled at
my table with horses and charioteers,[p]
with warriors and all kinds of soldiers,
says the Lord GOD.

Israel Restored to the Land

21 I will display my glory among the
nations; and all the nations shall see my
judgment that I have executed, and my
hand that I have laid on them. [22]The
house of Israel shall know that I am the
LORD their God, from that day forward.
[23]And the nations shall know that the
house of Israel went into captivity for
their iniquity, because they dealt treacherously with me. So I hid my face from
them and gave them into the hand of
their adversaries, and they all fell by the
sword. [24]I dealt with them according to
their uncleanness and their transgressions, and hid my face from them.

25 Therefore thus says the Lord GOD:
Now I will restore the fortunes of Jacob,
and have mercy on the whole house of
Israel; and I will be jealous for my holy
name. [26]They shall forget[q] their shame,
and all the treachery they have practiced
against me, when they live securely in
their land with no one to make them
afraid, [27]when I have brought them back
from the peoples and gathered them from
their enemies' lands, and through them
have displayed my holiness in the sight of
many nations. [28]Then they shall know
that I am the LORD their God because I sent
them into exile among the nations, and
then gathered them into their own land. I
will leave none of them behind; [29]and I
will never again hide my face from them,
when I pour out my spirit upon the house
of Israel, says the Lord GOD.

The Vision of the New Temple

40 In the twenty-fifth year of our exile, at the beginning of the year,
on the tenth day of the month, in the
fourteenth year after the city was struck
down, on that very day, the hand of the
LORD was upon me, and he brought me
there. [2]He brought me, in visions of God,
to the land of Israel, and set me down
upon a very high mountain, on which was
a structure like a city to the south. [3]When
he brought me there, a man was there,
whose appearance shone like bronze,
with a linen cord and a measuring reed in
his hand; and he was standing in the gateway. [4]The man said to me, "Mortal, look
closely and listen attentively, and set your
mind upon all that I shall show you, for
you were brought here in order that I
might show it to you; declare all that you
see to the house of Israel."

5 Now there was a wall all around the
outside of the temple area. The length of
the measuring reed in the man's hand was

[l] Or *of the Abarim* [m] That is, *the Horde of Gog* [n] Heb *travelers* [o] That is *The Horde* [p] Heb *chariots* [q] Another reading is *They shall bear*

six long cubits, each being a cubit and a handbreadth in length; so he measured the thickness of the wall, one reed; and the height, one reed. [6]Then he went into the gateway facing east, going up its steps, and measured the threshold of the gate, one reed deep.[r] There were [7]recesses, and each recess was one reed wide and one reed deep; and the space between the recesses, five cubits; and the threshold of the gate by the vestibule of the gate at the inner end was one reed deep. [8]Then he measured the inner vestibule of the gateway, one cubit. [9]Then he measured the vestibule of the gateway, eight cubits; and its pilasters, two cubits; and the vestibule of the gate was at the inner end. [10]There were three recesses on either side of the east gate; the three were of the same size; and the pilasters on either side were of the same size. [11]Then he measured the width of the opening of the gateway, ten cubits; and the width of the gateway, thirteen cubits. [12]There was a barrier before the recesses, one cubit on either side; and the recesses were six cubits on either side. [13]Then he measured the gate from the back[s] of the one recess to the back[s] of the other, a width of twenty-five cubits, from wall to wall.[t] [14]He measured[u] also the vestibule, twenty cubits; and the gate next to the pilaster on every side of the court.[v] [15]From the front of the gate at the entrance to the end of the inner vestibule of the gate was fifty cubits. [16]The recesses and their pilasters had windows, with shutters[v] on the inside of the gateway all around, and the vestibules also had windows on the inside all around; and on the pilasters were palm trees.

17 Then he brought me into the outer court; there were chambers there, and a pavement, all around the court; thirty chambers fronted on the pavement. [18]The pavement ran along the side of the gates, corresponding to the length of the gates; this was the lower pavement. [19]Then he measured the distance from the inner front of[w] the lower gate to the outer front of the inner court, one hundred cubits.[x]

20 Then he measured the gate of the outer court that faced north—its depth and width. [21]Its recesses, three on either side, and its pilasters and its vestibule were of the same size as those of the first gate; its depth was fifty cubits, and its width twenty-five cubits. [22]Its windows, its vestibule, and its palm trees were of the

same size as those of the gate that faced toward the east. Seven steps led up to it; and its vestibule was on the inside.[y] [23]Opposite the gate on the north, as on the east, was a gate to the inner court; he measured from gate to gate, one hundred cubits.

24 Then he led me toward the south, and there was a gate on the south; and he measured its pilasters and its vestibule; they had the same dimensions as the others. [25]There were windows all around in it and in its vestibule, like the windows of the others; its depth was fifty cubits, and its width twenty-five cubits. [26]There were seven steps leading up to it; its vestibule was on the inside.[y] It had palm trees on its pilasters, one on either side. [27]There was a gate on the south of the inner court; and he measured from gate to gate toward the south, one hundred cubits.

28 Then he brought me to the inner court by the south gate, and he measured the south gate; it was of the same dimensions as the others. [29]Its recesses, its pilasters, and its vestibule were of the same size as the others; and there were windows all around in it and in its vestibule; its depth was fifty cubits, and its width twenty-five cubits. [30]There were vestibules all around, twenty-five cubits deep and five cubits wide. [31]Its vestibule faced the outer court, and palm trees were on its pilasters, and its stairway had eight steps.

32 Then he brought me to the inner court on the east side, and he measured the gate; it was of the same size as the others. [33]Its recesses, its pilasters, and its vestibule were of the same dimensions as the others; and there were windows all around in it and in its vestibule; its depth was fifty cubits, and its width twenty-five cubits. [34]Its vestibule faced the outer court, and it had palm trees on its pilasters, on either side; and its stairway had eight steps.

35 Then he brought me to the north gate, and he measured it; it had the same dimensions as the others. [36]Its recesses, its pilasters, and its vestibule were of the same size as the others;[z] and it had win-

r Heb *deep, and one threshold, one reed deep*
s Gk: Heb *roof*   *t* Heb *opening facing opening*
u Heb *made*   *v* Meaning of Heb uncertain
w Compare Gk: Heb *from before*   *x* Heb adds *the east and the north*   *y* Gk: Heb *before them*
z One Ms: Compare verses 29 and 33: MT lacks *were of the same size as the others*

dows all around. Its depth was fifty cubits, and its width twenty-five cubits. [37]Its vestibule[a] faced the outer court, and it had palm trees on its pilasters, on either side; and its stairway had eight steps.

38 There was a chamber with its door in the vestibule of the gate,[b] where the burnt offering was to be washed. [39]And in the vestibule of the gate were two tables on either side, on which the burnt offering and the sin offering and the guilt offering were to be slaughtered. [40]On the outside of the vestibule[c] at the entrance of the north gate were two tables; and on the other side of the vestibule of the gate were two tables. [41]Four tables were on the inside, and four tables on the outside of the side of the gate, eight tables, on which the sacrifices were to be slaughtered. [42]There were also four tables of hewn stone for the burnt offering, a cubit and a half long, and one cubit and a half wide, and one cubit high, on which the instruments were to be laid with which the burnt offerings and the sacrifices were slaughtered. [43]There were pegs, one handbreadth long, fastened all around the inside. And on the tables the flesh of the offering was to be laid.

44 On the outside of the inner gateway there were chambers for the singers in the inner court, one[d] at the side of the north gate facing south, the other at the side of the east gate facing north. [45]He said to me, "This chamber that faces south is for the priests who have charge of the temple, [46]and the chamber that faces north is for the priests who have charge of the altar; these are the descendants of Zadok, who alone among the descendants of Levi may come near to the LORD to minister to him." [47]He measured the court, one hundred cubits deep, and one hundred cubits wide, a square; and the altar was in front of the temple.

The Temple

48 Then he brought me to the vestibule of the temple and measured the pilasters of the vestibule, five cubits on either side; and the width of the gate was fourteen cubits; and the sidewalls of the gate were three cubits[e] on either side. [49]The depth of the vestibule was twenty cubits, and the width twelve[f] cubits; ten steps led up[g] to it; and there were pillars beside the pilasters on either side.

41 Then he brought me to the nave, and measured the pilasters; on each side six cubits was the width of the pilasters.[h] [2]The width of the entrance was ten cubits; and the sidewalls of the entrance were five cubits on either side. He measured the length of the nave, forty cubits, and its width, twenty cubits. [3]Then he went into the inner room and measured the pilasters of the entrance, two cubits; and the width of the entrance, six cubits; and the sidewalls[i] of the entrance, seven cubits. [4]He measured the depth of the room, twenty cubits, and its width, twenty cubits, beyond the nave. And he said to me, This is the most holy place.

5 Then he measured the wall of the temple, six cubits thick; and the width of the side chambers, four cubits, all around the temple. [6]The side chambers were in three stories, one over another, thirty in each story. There were offsets[j] all around the wall of the temple to serve as supports for the side chambers, so that they should not be supported by the wall of the temple. [7]The passageway[k] of the side chambers widened from story to story; for the structure was supplied with a stairway all around the temple. For this reason the structure became wider from story to story. One ascended from the bottom story to the uppermost story by way of the middle one. [8]I saw also that the temple had a raised platform all around; the foundations of the side chambers measured a full reed of six long cubits. [9]The thickness of the outer wall of the side chambers was five cubits; and the free space between the side chambers of the temple [10]and the chambers of the court was a width of twenty cubits all around the temple on every side. [11]The side chambers opened onto the area left free, one door toward the north, and another door toward the south; and the width of the part that was left free was five cubits all around.

12 The building that was facing the temple yard on the west side was seventy cubits wide; and the wall of the building

a Gk Vg Compare verses 26, 31, 34: Heb *pilasters* b Cn: Heb *at the pilasters of the gates*   c Cn: Heb *to him who goes up*   d Heb lacks *one*   e Gk: Heb *and the width of the gate was three cubits* f Gk: Heb *eleven*   g Gk: Heb *and by steps that went up*   h Compare Gk: Heb *tent*   i Gk: Heb *width*   j Gk Compare 1 Kings 6.6: Heb *they entered*   k Cn: Heb *it was surrounded*

was five cubits thick all around, and its depth ninety cubits.

13 Then he measured the temple, one hundred cubits deep; and the yard and the building with its walls, one hundred cubits deep; [14]also the width of the east front of the temple and the yard, one hundred cubits.

15 Then he measured the depth of the building facing the yard at the west, together with its galleries[l] on either side, one hundred cubits.

The nave of the temple and the inner room and the outer[m] vestibule [16]were paneled,[n] and, all around, all three had windows with recessed[o] frames. Facing the threshold the temple was paneled with wood all around, from the floor up to the windows (now the windows were covered), [17]to the space above the door, even to the inner room, and on the outside. And on all the walls all around in the inner room and the nave there was a pattern.[p] [18]It was formed of cherubim and palm trees, a palm tree between cherub and cherub. Each cherub had two faces: [19]a human face turned toward the palm tree on the one side, and the face of a young lion turned toward the palm tree on the other side. They were carved on the whole temple all around; [20]from the floor to the area above the door, cherubim and palm trees were carved on the wall.[q]

21 The doorposts of the nave were square. In front of the holy place was something resembling [22]an altar of wood, three cubits high, two cubits long, and two cubits wide;[r] its corners, its base,[s] and its walls were of wood. He said to me, "This is the table that stands before the LORD." [23]The nave and the holy place had each a double door. [24]The doors had two leaves apiece, two swinging leaves for each door. [25]On the doors of the nave were carved cherubim and palm trees, such as were carved on the walls; and there was a canopy of wood in front of the vestibule outside. [26]And there were recessed windows and palm trees on either side, on the sidewalls of the vestibule.[t]

The Holy Chambers and the Outer Wall

42 Then he led me out into the outer court, toward the north, and he brought me to the chambers that were opposite the temple yard and opposite the building on the north. [2]The length of the building that was on the north side[u] was[v] one hundred cubits, and the width fifty cubits. [3]Across the twenty cubits that belonged to the inner court, and facing the pavement that belonged to the outer court, the chambers rose[w] gallery[x] by gallery[x] in three stories. [4]In front of the chambers was a passage on the inner side, ten cubits wide and one hundred cubits deep,[y] and its[z] entrances were on the north. [5]Now the upper chambers were narrower, for the galleries[x] took more away from them than from the lower and middle chambers in the building. [6]For they were in three stories, and they had no pillars like the pillars of the outer[a] court; for this reason the upper chambers were set back from the ground more than the lower and the middle ones. [7]There was a wall outside parallel to the chambers, toward the outer court, opposite the chambers, fifty cubits long. [8]For the chambers on the outer court were fifty cubits long, while those opposite the temple were one hundred cubits long. [9]At the foot of these chambers ran a passage that one entered from the east in order to enter them from the outer court. [10]The width of the passage[b] was fixed by the wall of the court.

On the south[c] also, opposite the vacant area and opposite the building, there were chambers [11]with a passage in front of them; they were similar to the chambers on the north, of the same length and width, with the same exits[d] and arrangements and doors. [12]So the entrances of the chambers to the south were entered through the entrance at the head of the corresponding passage, from the east, along the matching wall.[x]

13 Then he said to me, "The north chambers and the south chambers opposite the vacant area are the holy chambers, where the priests who approach the LORD shall eat the most holy offerings; there they shall deposit the most holy offerings—the grain offering, the sin offering,

[l] Cn: Meaning of Heb uncertain   [m] Gk: Heb of the court   [n] Gk: Heb the thresholds   [o] Cn Compare Gk 1 Kings 6.4: Meaning of Heb uncertain   [p] Heb measures   [q] Cn Compare verse 25: Heb and the wall   [r] Gk: Heb lacks two cubits wide   [s] Gk: Heb length   [t] Cn: Heb vestibule. And the side chambers of the temple and the canopies   [u] Gk: Heb door   [v] Gk: Heb before the length   [w] Heb lacks the chambers rose   [x] Meaning of Heb uncertain   [y] Gk Syr: Heb a way of one cubit   [z] Heb their   [a] Gk: Heb lacks outer   [b] Heb lacks of the passage   [c] Gk: Heb east   [d] Heb and all their exits

and the guilt offering—for the place is holy. [14]When the priests enter the holy place, they shall not go out of it into the outer court without laying there the vestments in which they minister, for these are holy; they shall put on other garments before they go near to the area open to the people."

15 When he had finished measuring the interior of the temple area, he led me out by the gate that faces east, and measured the temple area all around. [16]He measured the east side with the measuring reed, five hundred cubits by the measuring reed. [17]Then he turned and measured[e] the north side, five hundred cubits by the measuring reed. [18]Then he turned and measured[e] the south side, five hundred cubits by the measuring reed. [19]Then he turned to the west side and measured, five hundred cubits by the measuring reed. [20]He measured it on the four sides. It had a wall around it, five hundred cubits long and five hundred cubits wide, to make a separation between the holy and the common.

The Divine Glory Returns to the Temple

43 Then he brought me to the gate, the gate facing east. [2]And there, the glory of the God of Israel was coming from the east; the sound was like the sound of mighty waters; and the earth shone with his glory. [3]The[f] vision I saw was like the vision that I had seen when he came to destroy the city, and[g] like the vision that I had seen by the river Chebar; and I fell upon my face. [4]As the glory of the LORD entered the temple by the gate facing east, [5]the spirit lifted me up, and brought me into the inner court; and the glory of the LORD filled the temple.

6 While the man was standing beside me, I heard someone speaking to me out of the temple. [7]He said to me: Mortal, this is the place of my throne and the place for the soles of my feet, where I will reside among the people of Israel forever. The house of Israel shall no more defile my holy name, neither they nor their kings, by their whoring, and by the corpses of their kings at their death.[h] [8]When they placed their threshold by my threshold and their doorposts beside my doorposts, with only a wall between me and them, they were defiling my holy name by their abominations that they committed; therefore I have consumed them in my anger.

[9]Now let them put away their idolatry and the corpses of their kings far from me, and I will reside among them forever.

10 As for you, mortal, describe the temple to the house of Israel, and let them measure the pattern; and let them be ashamed of their iniquities. [11]When they are ashamed of all that they have done, make known to them the plan of the temple, its arrangement, its exits and its entrances, and its whole form—all its ordinances and its entire plan and all its laws; and write it down in their sight, so that they may observe and follow the entire plan and all its ordinances. [12]This is the law of the temple: the whole territory on the top of the mountain all around shall be most holy. This is the law of the temple.

The Altar

13 These are the dimensions of the altar by cubits (the cubit being one cubit and a handbreadth): its base shall be one cubit high,[i] and one cubit wide, with a rim of one span around its edge. This shall be the height of the altar: [14]From the base on the ground to the lower ledge, two cubits, with a width of one cubit; and from the smaller ledge to the larger ledge, four cubits, with a width of one cubit; [15]and the altar hearth, four cubits; and from the altar hearth projecting upward, four horns. [16]The altar hearth shall be square, twelve cubits long by twelve wide. [17]The ledge also shall be square, fourteen cubits long by fourteen wide, with a rim around it half a cubit wide, and its surrounding base, one cubit. Its steps shall face east.

18 Then he said to me: Mortal, thus says the Lord GOD: These are the ordinances for the altar: On the day when it is erected for offering burnt offerings upon it and for dashing blood against it, [19]you shall give to the levitical priests of the family of Zadok, who draw near to me to minister to me, says the Lord GOD, a bull for a sin offering. [20]And you shall take some of its blood, and put it on the four horns of the altar, and on the four corners of the ledge, and upon the rim all around; thus you shall purify it and make atonement for it. [21]You shall also take the bull

---

[e] Gk: Heb measuring reed all around. He measured
[f] Gk: Heb Like the vision   [g] Syr: Heb and the visions   [h] Or on their high places   [i] Gk: Heb lacks high

of the sin offering, and it shall be burnt in the appointed place belonging to the temple, outside the sacred area.

22 On the second day you shall offer a male goat without blemish for a sin offering; and the altar shall be purified, as it was purified with the bull. 23When you have finished purifying it, you shall offer a bull without blemish and a ram from the flock without blemish. 24You shall present them before the LORD, and the priests shall throw salt on them and offer them up as a burnt offering to the LORD. 25For seven days you shall provide daily a goat for a sin offering; also a bull and a ram from the flock, without blemish, shall be provided. 26Seven days shall they make atonement for the altar and cleanse it, and so consecrate it. 27When these days are over, then from the eighth day onward the priests shall offer upon the altar your burnt offerings and your offerings of well-being; and I will accept you, says the Lord GOD.

The Closed Gate

44 Then he brought me back to the outer gate of the sanctuary, which faces east; and it was shut. 2The LORD said to me: This gate shall remain shut; it shall not be opened, and no one shall enter by it; for the LORD, the God of Israel, has entered by it; therefore it shall remain shut. 3Only the prince, because he is a prince, may sit in it to eat food before the LORD; he shall enter by way of the vestibule of the gate, and shall go out by the same way.

Admission to the Temple

4 Then he brought me by way of the north gate to the front of the temple; and I looked, and lo! the glory of the LORD filled the temple of the LORD; and I fell upon my face. 5The LORD said to me: Mortal, mark well, look closely, and listen attentively to all that I shall tell you concerning all the ordinances of the temple of the LORD and all its laws; and mark well those who may be admitted to[j] the temple and all those who are to be excluded from the sanctuary. 6Say to the rebellious house,[k] to the house of Israel, Thus says the Lord GOD: O house of Israel, let there be an end to all your abominations 7in admitting foreigners, uncircumcised in heart and flesh, to be in my sanctuary, profaning my temple when you offer to me my food, the fat and the blood. You[l] have broken my covenant with all your abominations. 8And you have not kept charge of my sacred offerings; but you have appointed foreigners[m] to act for you in keeping my charge in my sanctuary.

9 Thus says the Lord GOD: No foreigner, uncircumcised in heart and flesh, of all the foreigners who are among the people of Israel, shall enter my sanctuary. 10But the Levites who went far from me, going astray from me after their idols when Israel went astray, shall bear their punishment. 11They shall be ministers in my sanctuary, having oversight at the gates of the temple, and serving in the temple; they shall slaughter the burnt offering and the sacrifice for the people, and they shall attend on them and serve them. 12Because they ministered to them before their idols and made the house of Israel stumble into iniquity, therefore I have sworn concerning them, says the Lord GOD, that they shall bear their punishment. 13They shall not come near to me, to serve me as priest, nor come near any of my sacred offerings, the things that are most sacred; but they shall bear their shame, and the consequences of the abominations that they have committed. 14Yet I will appoint them to keep charge of the temple, to do all its chores, all that is to be done in it.

The Levitical Priests

15 But the levitical priests, the descendants of Zadok, who kept the charge of my sanctuary when the people of Israel went astray from me, shall come near to me to minister to me; and they shall attend me to offer me the fat and the blood, says the Lord GOD. 16It is they who shall enter my sanctuary, it is they who shall approach my table, to minister to me, and they shall keep my charge. 17When they enter the gates of the inner court, they shall wear linen vestments; they shall have nothing of wool on them, while they minister at the gates of the inner court, and within. 18They shall have linen turbans on their heads, and linen undergarments on their loins; they shall not bind themselves with anything that causes sweat. 19When they go out into the outer court to the people, they shall remove the vestments in which they have been ministering, and

[j] Cn: Heb *the entrance of* [k] Gk: Heb lacks *house*
[l] Gk Syr Vg: Heb *They* [m] Heb lacks *foreigners*

lay them in the holy chambers; and they shall put on other garments, so that they may not communicate holiness to the people with their vestments. 20They shall not shave their heads or let their locks grow long; they shall only trim the hair of their heads. 21No priest shall drink wine when he enters the inner court. 22They shall not marry a widow, or a divorced woman, but only a virgin of the stock of the house of Israel, or a widow who is the widow of a priest. 23They shall teach my people the difference between the holy and the common, and show them how to distinguish between the unclean and the clean. 24In a controversy they shall act as judges, and they shall decide it according to my judgments. They shall keep my laws and my statutes regarding all my appointed festivals, and they shall keep my sabbaths holy. 25They shall not defile themselves by going near to a dead person; for father or mother, however, and for son or daughter, and for brother or unmarried sister they may defile themselves. 26After he has become clean, they shall count seven days for him. 27On the day that he goes into the holy place, into the inner court, to minister in the holy place, he shall offer his sin offering, says the Lord God.

28 This shall be their inheritance: I am their inheritance; and you shall give them no holding in Israel; I am their holding. 29They shall eat the grain offering, the sin offering, and the guilt offering; and every devoted thing in Israel shall be theirs. 30The first of all the first fruits of all kinds, and every offering of all kinds from all your offerings, shall belong to the priests; you shall also give to the priests the first of your dough, in order that a blessing may rest on your house. 31The priests shall not eat of anything, whether bird or animal, that died of itself or was torn by animals.

The Holy District

45 When you allot the land as an inheritance, you shall set aside for the Lord a portion of the land as a holy district, twenty-five thousand cubits long and twenty*n* thousand cubits wide; it shall be holy throughout its entire extent. 2Of this, a square plot of five hundred by five hundred cubits shall be for the sanctuary, with fifty cubits for an open space around it. 3In the holy district you shall measure off a section twenty-five thousand cubits long and ten thousand wide,

in which shall be the sanctuary, the most holy place. 4It shall be a holy portion of the land; it shall be for the priests, who minister in the sanctuary and approach the Lord to minister to him; and it shall be both a place for their houses and a holy place for the sanctuary. 5Another section, twenty-five thousand cubits long and ten thousand cubits wide, shall be for the Levites who minister at the temple, as their holding for cities to live in.*o*

6 Alongside the portion set apart as the holy district you shall assign as a holding for the city an area five thousand cubits wide, and twenty-five thousand cubits long; it shall belong to the whole house of Israel.

7 And to the prince shall belong the land on both sides of the holy district and the holding of the city, alongside the holy district and the holding of the city, on the west and on the east, corresponding in length to one of the tribal portions, and extending from the western to the eastern boundary 8of the land. It is to be his property in Israel. And my princes shall no longer oppress my people; but they shall let the house of Israel have the land according to their tribes.

9 Thus says the Lord God: Enough, O princes of Israel! Put away violence and oppression, and do what is just and right. Cease your evictions of my people, says the Lord God.

Weights and Measures

10 You shall have honest balances, an honest ephah, and an honest bath. *p* 11The ephah and the bath shall be of the same measure, the bath containing one-tenth of a homer, and the ephah one-tenth of a homer; the homer shall be the standard measure. 12The shekel shall be twenty gerahs. Twenty shekels, twenty-five shekels, and fifteen shekels shall make a mina for you.

Offerings

13 This is the offering that you shall make: one-sixth of an ephah from each homer of wheat, and one-sixth of an ephah from each homer of barley, 14and as the fixed portion of oil,*q* one-tenth of a bath from each cor (the cor,*r* like the

n Gk: Heb *ten*   *o* Gk: Heb *as their holding, twenty chambers*   *p* A Heb measure of volume   *q* Cn: Heb *oil, the bath the oil*   *r* Vg: Heb *homer*

homer, contains ten baths); 15and one sheep from every flock of two hundred, from the pastures of Israel. This is the offering for grain offerings, burnt offerings, and offerings of well-being, to make atonement for them, says the Lord God. 16All the people of the land shall join with the prince in Israel in making this offering. 17But this shall be the obligation of the prince regarding the burnt offerings, grain offerings, and drink offerings, at the festivals, the new moons, and the sabbaths, all the appointed festivals of the house of Israel: he shall provide the sin offerings, grain offerings, the burnt offerings, and the offerings of well-being, to make atonement for the house of Israel.

Festivals

18 Thus says the Lord God: In the first month, on the first day of the month, you shall take a young bull without blemish, and purify the sanctuary. 19The priest shall take some of the blood of the sin offering and put it on the doorposts of the temple, the four corners of the ledge of the altar, and the posts of the gate of the inner court. 20You shall do the same on the seventh day of the month for anyone who has sinned through error or ignorance; so you shall make atonement for the temple.

21 In the first month, on the fourteenth day of the month, you shall celebrate the festival of the passover, and for seven days unleavened bread shall be eaten. 22On that day the prince shall provide for himself and all the people of the land a young bull for a sin offering. 23And during the seven days of the festival he shall provide as a burnt offering to the Lord seven young bulls and seven rams without blemish, on each of the seven days; and a male goat daily for a sin offering. 24He shall provide as a grain offering an ephah for each bull, an ephah for each ram, and a hin of oil to each ephah. 25In the seventh month, on the fifteenth day of the month and for the seven days of the festival, he shall make the same provision for sin offerings, burnt offerings, and grain offerings, and for the oil.

Miscellaneous Regulations

46 Thus says the Lord God: The gate of the inner court that faces east shall remain closed on the six working days; but on the sabbath day it shall be opened and on the day of the new moon it shall be opened. 2The prince shall enter by the vestibule of the gate from outside, and shall take his stand by the post of the gate. The priests shall offer his burnt offering and his offerings of well-being, and he shall bow down at the threshold of the gate. Then he shall go out, but the gate shall not be closed until evening. 3The people of the land shall bow down at the entrance of that gate before the Lord on the sabbaths and on the new moons. 4The burnt offering that the prince offers to the Lord on the sabbath day shall be six lambs without blemish and a ram without blemish; 5and the grain offering with the ram shall be an ephah, and the grain offering with the lambs shall be as much as he wishes to give, together with a hin of oil to each ephah. 6On the day of the new moon he shall offer a young bull without blemish, and six lambs and a ram, which shall be without blemish; 7as a grain offering he shall provide an ephah with the bull and an ephah with the ram, and with the lambs as much as he wishes, together with a hin of oil to each ephah. 8When the prince enters, he shall come in by the vestibule of the gate, and he shall go out by the same way.

9 When the people of the land come before the Lord at the appointed festivals, whoever enters by the north gate to worship shall go out by the south gate; and whoever enters by the south gate shall go out by the north gate: they shall not return by way of the gate by which they entered, but shall go out straight ahead. 10When they come in, the prince shall come in with them; and when they go out, he shall go out.

11 At the festivals and the appointed seasons the grain offering with a young bull shall be an ephah, and with a ram an ephah, and with the lambs as much as one wishes to give, together with a hin of oil to an ephah. 12When the prince provides a freewill offering, either a burnt offering or offerings of well-being as a freewill offering to the Lord, the gate facing east shall be opened for him; and he shall offer his burnt offering or his offerings of well-being as he does on the sabbath day. Then he shall go out, and after he has gone out the gate shall be closed.

13 He shall provide a lamb, a yearling, without blemish, for a burnt offering to the Lord daily; morning by morning he shall provide it. 14And he shall provide a

grain offering with it morning by morning regularly, one-sixth of an ephah, and one-third of a hin of oil to moisten the choice flour, as a grain offering to the LORD; this is the ordinance for all time. [15]Thus the lamb and the grain offering and the oil shall be provided, morning by morning, as a regular burnt offering.

16 Thus says the Lord GOD: If the prince makes a gift to any of his sons out of his inheritance,[s] it shall belong to his sons, it is their holding by inheritance. [17]But if he makes a gift out of his inheritance to one of his servants, it shall be his to the year of liberty; then it shall revert to the prince; only his sons may keep a gift from his inheritance. [18]The prince shall not take any of the inheritance of the people, thrusting them out of their holding; he shall give his sons their inheritance out of his own holding, so that none of my people shall be dispossessed of their holding.

19 Then he brought me through the entrance, which was at the side of the gate, to the north row of the holy chambers for the priests; and there I saw a place at the extreme western end of them. [20]He said to me, "This is the place where the priests shall boil the guilt offering and the sin offering, and where they shall bake the grain offering, in order not to bring them

[s] Gk: Heb *it is his inheritance*

THE TRADITION

Keeping Sunday Holy

The people of the land shall bow down at the entrance of that gate before the LORD on the sabbaths and on the new moons.

EZEKIEL 46.3

"TGIF," says modern America as it heads into the weekend. "TGIS," Christians should say as they begin the last day of that weekend. "Thank God It's Sunday!"

What's to celebrate? "Sunday is the day of the Resurrection," Saint Jerome explained. "It is the day of Christians, it is our day."

Setting aside a day a week to rest and re-call God's saving deeds was not someone's bright idea for a well-rounded life. It is one of the commandments God gave the Israelites when he led them out of Egypt: "Remember the sabbath day, and keep it holy" (Exodus 20.8). Prophets such as Ezekiel foretold the dire consequences of ignoring this command; in his vision of a restored Israel, the sabbath is celebrated with great care (see Ezekiel 20.12–13; 46.1–7).

We too are called to celebrate the day of our deliverance, when Jesus won our freedom by rising from the dead. The Lord's Day is "the first of all days, the first of all feasts," and "the foremost holy day of obligation in the universal Church" (*Catechism of the Catholic Church*, 2175, 2177). Getting serious about Sunday means learning to celebrate it in a spirit of praise and joy. We do this especially by participating in the Eucharist, which testifies that we belong to Christ and are members of his body.

And how do we keep holy those Sunday hours not spent at Mass? *Spend time with your family,* says the Church. *Serve the sick and others in need. Do some spiritual reading and reflecting to develop your relationship with God.* Of course, making time for these things means putting other things aside. Work, business concerns, unnecessary shopping trips, activities that interfere with others' observance of the Lord's Day—before plunging in, we should ask ourselves, "Can't this wait till Monday?"

"I would strongly urge everyone to rediscover Sunday," said John Paul II (*On Keeping the Lord's Day Holy,* May 31, 1998, 7). Do not let this "ever new gift" of Christ's love get swallowed up in a secular approach to the weekend. "Do not be afraid to give your time to Christ!"

out into the outer court and so communicate holiness to the people."

21 Then he brought me out to the outer court, and led me past the four corners of the court; and in each corner of the court there was a court— 22in the four corners of the court were small[t] courts, forty cubits long and thirty wide; the four were of the same size. 23On the inside, around each of the four courts[u] was a row of masonry, with hearths made at the bottom of the rows all around. 24Then he said to me, "These are the kitchens where those who serve at the temple shall boil the sacrifices of the people."

Water Flowing from the Temple

47 Then he brought me back to the entrance of the temple; there, water was flowing from below the threshold of the temple toward the east (for the temple faced east); and the water was flowing down from below the south end of the threshold of the temple, south of the altar. 2Then he brought me out by way of the north gate, and led me around on the outside to the outer gate that faces toward the east;[v] and the water was coming out on the south side.

3 Going on eastward with a cord in his hand, the man measured one thousand cubits, and then led me through the water; and it was ankle-deep. 4Again he measured one thousand, and led me through the water; and it was knee-deep. Again he measured one thousand, and led me through the water; and it was up to the waist. 5Again he measured one thousand, and it was a river that I could not cross, for the water had risen; it was deep enough to swim in, a river that could not be crossed. 6He said to me, "Mortal, have you seen this?"

Then he led me back along the bank of the river. 7As I came back, I saw on the bank of the river a great many trees on the one side and on the other. 8He said to me, "This water flows toward the eastern region and goes down into the Arabah; and when it enters the sea, the sea of stagnant waters, the water will become fresh. 9Wherever the river goes,[w] every living creature that swarms will live, and there will be very many fish, once these waters reach there. It will become fresh; and everything will live where the river goes. 10People will stand fishing beside the sea[x] from En-gedi to En-eglaim; it will be a place for the spreading of nets; its fish will be of a great many kinds, like the fish of the Great Sea. 11But its swamps and marshes will not become fresh; they are to be left for salt. 12On the banks, on both sides of the river, there will grow all kinds of trees for food. Their leaves will not wither nor their fruit fail, but they will bear fresh fruit every month, because the water for them flows from the sanctuary. Their fruit will be for food, and their leaves for healing."

The New Boundaries of the Land

13 Thus says the Lord GOD: These are the boundaries by which you shall divide the land for inheritance among the twelve tribes of Israel. Joseph shall have two portions. 14You shall divide it equally; I swore to give it to your ancestors, and this land shall fall to you as your inheritance.

15 This shall be the boundary of the land: On the north side, from the Great Sea by way of Hethlon to Lebo-hamath, and on to Zedad,[y] 16Berothah, Sibraim (which lies between the border of Damascus and the border of Hamath), as far as Hazer-hatticon, which is on the border of Hauran. 17So the boundary shall run from the sea to Hazar-enon, which is north of the border of Damascus, with the border of Hamath to the north.[v] This shall be the north side.

18 On the east side, between Hauran and Damascus; along the Jordan between Gilead and the land of Israel; to the eastern sea and as far as Tamar.[z] This shall be the east side.

19 On the south side, it shall run from Tamar as far as the waters of Meribath-kadesh, from there along the Wadi of Egypt[a] to the Great Sea. This shall be the south side.

20 On the west side, the Great Sea shall be the boundary to a point opposite Lebo-hamath. This shall be the west side.

21 So you shall divide this land among you according to the tribes of Israel. 22You shall allot it as an inheritance for yourselves and for the aliens who reside among you and have begotten children among you. They shall be to you as citi-

t Gk Syr Vg: Meaning of Heb uncertain   u Heb
the four of them   v Meaning of Heb uncertain
w Gk Syr Vg Tg: Heb the two rivers go   x Heb it
y Gk: Heb Lebo-zedad, 16Hamath   z Compare Syr:
Heb you shall measure   a Heb lacks of Egypt

zens of Israel; with you they shall be allotted an inheritance among the tribes of Israel. ²³In whatever tribe aliens reside, there you shall assign them their inheritance, says the Lord GOD.

The Tribal Portions

48 These are the names of the tribes: Beginning at the northern border, on the Hethlon road,[b] from Lebo-hamath, as far as Hazar-enon (which is on the border of Damascus, with Hamath to the north), and[c] extending from the east side to the west,[d] Dan, one portion. ²Adjoining the territory of Dan, from the east side to the west, Asher, one portion. ³Adjoining the territory of Asher, from the east side to the west, Naphtali, one portion. ⁴Adjoining the territory of Naphtali, from the east side to the west, Manasseh, one portion. ⁵Adjoining the territory of Manasseh, from the east side to the west, Ephraim, one portion. ⁶Adjoining the territory of Ephraim, from the east side to the west, Reuben, one portion. ⁷Adjoining the territory of Reuben, from the east side to the west, Judah, one portion.

8 Adjoining the territory of Judah, from the east side to the west, shall be the portion that you shall set apart, twenty-five thousand cubits in width, and in length equal to one of the tribal portions, from the east side to the west, with the sanctuary in the middle of it. ⁹The portion that you shall set apart for the LORD shall be twenty-five thousand cubits in length, and twenty[e] thousand in width. ¹⁰These shall be the allotments of the holy portion: the priests shall have an allotment measuring twenty-five thousand cubits on the northern side, ten thousand cubits in width on the western side, ten thousand in width on the eastern side, and twenty-five thousand in length on the southern side, with the sanctuary of the LORD in the middle of it. ¹¹This shall be for the consecrated priests, the descendants[f] of Zadok, who kept my charge, who did not go astray when the people of Israel went astray, as the Levites did. ¹²It shall belong to them as a special portion from the holy portion of the land, a most holy place, adjoining the territory of the Levites. ¹³Alongside the territory of the priests, the Levites shall have an allotment twenty-five thousand cubits in length and ten thousand in width. The whole length shall be twenty-five thousand cubits and the width twenty[g] thousand. ¹⁴They shall not sell or exchange any of it; they shall not transfer this choice portion of the land, for it is holy to the LORD.

15 The remainder, five thousand cubits in width and twenty-five thousand in length, shall be for ordinary use for the city, for dwellings and for open country. In the middle of it shall be the city; ¹⁶and these shall be its dimensions: the north side four thousand five hundred cubits, the south side four thousand five hundred, the east side four thousand five hundred, and the west side four thousand five hundred. ¹⁷The city shall have open land: on the north two hundred fifty cubits, on the south two hundred fifty, on the east two hundred fifty, on the west two hundred fifty. ¹⁸The remainder of the length alongside the holy portion shall be ten thousand cubits to the east, and ten thousand to the west, and it shall be alongside the holy portion. Its produce shall be food for the workers of the city. ¹⁹The workers of the city, from all the tribes of Israel, shall cultivate it. ²⁰The whole portion that you shall set apart shall be twenty-five thousand cubits square, that is, the holy portion together with the property of the city.

21 What remains on both sides of the holy portion and of the property of the city shall belong to the prince. Extending from the twenty-five thousand cubits of the holy portion to the east border, and westward from the twenty-five thousand cubits to the west border, parallel to the tribal portions, it shall belong to the prince. The holy portion with the sanctuary of the temple in the middle of it, ²²and the property of the Levites and of the city, shall be in the middle of that which belongs to the prince. The portion of the prince shall lie between the territory of Judah and the territory of Benjamin.

23 As for the rest of the tribes: from the east side to the west, Benjamin, one portion. ²⁴Adjoining the territory of Benjamin, from the east side to the west, Simeon, one portion. ²⁵Adjoining the territory of Simeon, from the east side to the west, Issachar, one portion. ²⁶Adjoining the ter-

---

[b] Compare 47.15: Heb *by the side of the way*
[c] Cn: Heb *and they shall be his*   [d] Gk Compare
verses 2-8: Heb *the east side the west*   [e] Compare
45.1: Heb *ten*   [f] One Ms Gk: Heb *of the*
descendants   [g] Gk: Heb *ten*

ritory of Issachar, from the east side to the west, Zebulun, one portion. [27]Adjoining the territory of Zebulun, from the east side to the west, Gad, one portion. [28]And adjoining the territory of Gad to the south, the boundary shall run from Tamar to the waters of Meribath-kadesh, from there along the Wadi of Egypt[h] to the Great Sea. [29]This is the land that you shall allot as an inheritance among the tribes of Israel, and these are their portions, says the Lord GOD.

30 These shall be the exits of the city: On the north side, which is to be four thousand five hundred cubits by measure, [31]three gates, the gate of Reuben, the gate of Judah, and the gate of Levi, the gates of the city being named after the tribes of Israel. [32]On the east side, which is to be four thousand five hundred cubits, three gates, the gate of Joseph, the gate of Benjamin, and the gate of Dan. [33]On the south side, which is to be four thousand five hundred cubits by measure, three gates, the gate of Simeon, the gate of Issachar, and the gate of Zebulun. [34]On the west side, which is to be four thousand five hundred cubits, three gates,[i] the gate of Gad, the gate of Asher, and the gate of Naphtali. [35]The circumference of the city shall be eighteen thousand cubits. And the name of the city from that time on shall be, The LORD is There.

h Heb lacks *of Egypt*   i One Ms Gk Syr: MT *their gates three*

Daniel

The book of Daniel is named after its main character, a young Jew exiled to Babylon (Chaldea) and assigned to the courts of King Nebuchadnezzar. Though none of the king's counselors can correctly interpret the royal dreams, Daniel does so, and his influence at court increases. But though Daniel is living in the courts of the king, he refuses to adopt Babylonian customs that are at odds with his faith. He eats only vegetables and drinks only water rather than defiling himself with the king's food and wine. He refuses to obey an edict forbidding people to pray to anyone but the king. Instead, he follows his custom of praying three times a day.

The book of Daniel contains some of the most memorable stories in the Bible: the three young men in the fiery furnace (see chapter 3), "the writing on the wall" inscribed by disembodied fingers (see chapter 5), and Daniel in the lions' den (see chapter 6). Chapters 13 and 14, which tell the stories of Susanna, Bel, and the Dragon, are found only in the Greek version.

The book of Daniel affirms that God protects those who keep the faith. It also underscores the fact that history belongs to God. Ultimately, he is the one who controls the rise and fall of empires, accomplishing his purposes no matter what happens.

Four Young Israelites at the Babylonian Court

1 In the third year of the reign of King Jehoiakim of Judah, King Nebuchadnezzar of Babylon came to Jerusalem and besieged it. 2The Lord let King Jehoiakim of Judah fall into his power, as well as some of the vessels of the house of God. These he brought to the land of Shinar,*a* and placed the vessels in the treasury of his gods.

3 Then the king commanded his palace master Ashpenaz to bring some of the Israelites of the royal family and of the nobility, 4young men without physical defect and handsome, versed in every branch of wisdom, endowed with knowledge and insight, and competent to serve in the king's palace; they were to be taught the literature and language of the Chaldeans. 5The king assigned them a daily por-

a Gk Theodotion: Heb adds *to the house of his own gods*

tion of the royal rations of food and wine. They were to be educated for three years, so that at the end of that time they could be stationed in the king's court. 6Among them were Daniel, Hananiah, Mishael, and Azariah, from the tribe of Judah. 7The palace master gave them other names: Daniel he called Belteshazzar, Hananiah he called Shadrach, Mishael he called Meshach, and Azariah he called Abednego.

8 But Daniel resolved that he would not defile himself with the royal rations of food and wine; so he asked the palace master to allow him not to defile himself. 9Now God allowed Daniel to receive favor and compassion from the palace master. 10The palace master said to Daniel, "I am afraid of my lord the king; he has appointed your food and your drink. If he should see you in poorer condition than the other young men of your own age, you would endanger my head with the king." 11Then Daniel asked the guard whom the palace master had appointed over Daniel, Hananiah, Mishael, and Azariah: 12"Please test your servants for ten days. Let us be given vegetables to eat and water to drink. 13You can then compare our appearance with the appearance of the young men who eat the royal rations, and deal with your servants according to what you observe." 14So he agreed to this proposal and tested them for ten days. 15At the end of ten days it was observed that they appeared better and fatter than all the young men who had been eating the royal rations. 16So the guard continued to withdraw their royal rations and the wine they were to drink, and gave them vegetables. 17To these four young men God gave knowledge and skill in every aspect of literature and wisdom; Daniel also had insight into all visions and dreams.

18 At the end of the time that the king had set for them to be brought in, the palace master brought them into the presence of Nebuchadnezzar, 19and the king spoke with them. And among them all, no one was found to compare with Daniel, Hananiah, Mishael, and Azariah; therefore they were stationed in the king's court. 20In every matter of wisdom and understanding concerning which the king inquired of them, he found them ten times better than all the magicians and enchanters in his whole kingdom. 21And Daniel continued there until the first year of King Cyrus.

Nebuchadnezzar's Dream

2 In the second year of Nebuchadnezzar's reign, Nebuchadnezzar dreamed such dreams that his spirit was troubled and his sleep left him. 2So the king commanded that the magicians, the enchanters, the sorcerers, and the Chaldeans be summoned to tell the king his dreams. When they came in and stood before the king, 3he said to them, "I have had such a dream that my spirit is troubled by the desire to understand it." 4The Chaldeans said to the king (in Aramaic),b "O king, live forever! Tell your servants the dream, and we will reveal the interpretation." 5The king answered the Chaldeans, "This is a public decree: if you do not tell me both the dream and its interpretation, you shall be torn limb from limb, and your houses shall be laid in ruins. 6But if you do tell me the dream and its interpretation, you shall receive from me gifts and rewards and great honor. Therefore tell me the dream and its interpretation." 7They answered a second time, "Let the king first tell his servants the dream, then we can give its interpretation." 8The king answered, "I know with certainty that you are trying to gain time, because you see I have firmly decreed: 9if you do not tell me the dream, there is but one verdict for you. You have agreed to speak lying and misleading words to me until things take a turn. Therefore, tell me the dream, and I shall know that you can give me its interpretation." 10The Chaldeans answered the king, "There is no one on earth who can reveal what the king demands! In fact no king, however great and powerful, has ever asked such a thing of any magician or enchanter or Chaldean. 11The thing that the king is asking is too difficult, and no one can reveal it to the king except the gods, whose dwelling is not with mortals."

12 Because of this the king flew into a violent rage and commanded that all the wise men of Babylon be destroyed. 13The decree was issued, and the wise men were about to be executed; and they looked for Daniel and his companions, to execute them. 14Then Daniel responded with prudence and discretion to Arioch, the king's chief executioner, who had gone out to execute the wise men of Babylon; 15he

---

b The text from this point to the end of chapter 7 is in Aramaic, except for 3.24-91a, the text of which is in Greek

asked Arioch, the royal official, "Why is the decree of the king so urgent?" Arioch then explained the matter to Daniel. [16]So Daniel went in and requested that the king give him time and he would tell the king the interpretation.

God Reveals Nebuchadnezzar's Dream

17 Then Daniel went to his home and informed his companions, Hananiah, Mishael, and Azariah, [18]and told them to seek mercy from the God of heaven concerning this mystery, so that Daniel and his companions with the rest of the wise men of Babylon might not perish. [19]Then the mystery was revealed to Daniel in a vision of the night, and Daniel blessed the God of heaven.

[20] Daniel said:

"Blessed be the name of God from
    age to age,
  for wisdom and power are his.
[21] He changes times and seasons,
    deposes kings and sets up kings;
  he gives wisdom to the wise
    and knowledge to those who have
      understanding.
[22] He reveals deep and hidden things;
    he knows what is in the darkness,
    and light dwells with him.
[23] To you, O God of my ancestors,
    I give thanks and praise,
  for you have given me wisdom
    and power,
  and have now revealed to me
    what we asked of you,
  for you have revealed to us what
    the king ordered."

Daniel Interprets the Dream

24 Therefore Daniel went to Arioch, whom the king had appointed to destroy the wise men of Babylon, and said to him, "Do not destroy the wise men of Babylon; bring me in before the king, and I will give the king the interpretation."

25 Then Arioch quickly brought Daniel before the king and said to him: "I have found among the exiles from Judah a man who can tell the king the interpretation." [26]The king said to Daniel, whose name was Belteshazzar, "Are you able to tell me the dream that I have seen and its interpretation?" [27]Daniel answered the king, "No wise men, enchanters, magicians, or diviners can show to the king the mystery that the king is asking, [28]but there is a God in heaven who reveals mysteries, and

he has disclosed to King Nebuchadnezzar what will happen at the end of days. Your dream and the visions of your head as you lay in bed were these: [29]To you, O king, as you lay in bed, came thoughts of what would be hereafter, and the revealer of mysteries disclosed to you what is to be. [30]But as for me, this mystery has not been revealed to me because of any wisdom that I have more than any other living being, but in order that the interpretation may be known to the king and that you may understand the thoughts of your mind.

31 "You were looking, O king, and lo! there was a great statue. This statue was huge, its brilliance extraordinary; it was standing before you, and its appearance was frightening. [32]The head of that statue was of fine gold, its chest and arms of silver, its middle and thighs of bronze, [33]its legs of iron, its feet partly of iron and partly of clay. [34]As you looked on, a stone was cut out, not by human hands, and it struck the statue on its feet of iron and clay and broke them in pieces. [35]Then the iron, the clay, the bronze, the silver, and the gold, were all broken in pieces and became like the chaff of the summer threshing floors; and the wind carried them away, so that not a trace of them could be found. But the stone that struck the statue became a great mountain and filled the whole earth.

36 "This was the dream; now we will tell the king its interpretation. [37]You, O king, the king of kings—to whom the God of heaven has given the kingdom, the power, the might, and the glory, [38]into whose hand he has given human beings, wherever they live, the wild animals of the field, and the birds of the air, and whom he has established as ruler over them all— you are the head of gold. [39]After you shall arise another kingdom inferior to yours, and yet a third kingdom of bronze, which shall rule over the whole earth. [40]And there shall be a fourth kingdom, strong as iron; just as iron crushes and smashes everything,[c] it shall crush and shatter all these. [41]As you saw the feet and toes partly of potter's clay and partly of iron, it shall be a divided kingdom; but some of the strength of iron shall be in it, as you saw the iron mixed with the clay. [42]As the toes

---

c Gk Theodotion Syr Vg: Aram adds *and like iron that crushes*

of the feet were part iron and part clay, so the kingdom shall be partly strong and partly brittle. ⁴³As you saw the iron mixed with clay, so will they mix with one another in marriage,ᵈ but they will not hold together, just as iron does not mix with clay. ⁴⁴And in the days of those kings the God of heaven will set up a kingdom that shall never be destroyed, nor shall this kingdom be left to another people. It shall crush all these kingdoms and bring them to an end, and it shall stand forever; ⁴⁵just as you saw that a stone was cut from the mountain not by hands, and that it crushed the iron, the bronze, the clay, the silver, and the gold. The great God has informed the king what shall be hereafter. The dream is certain, and its interpretation trustworthy."

Daniel and His Friends Promoted

46 Then King Nebuchadnezzar fell on his face, worshiped Daniel, and commanded that a grain offering and incense be offered to him. ⁴⁷The king said to Daniel, "Truly, your God is God of gods and Lord of kings and a revealer of mysteries, for you have been able to reveal this mystery!" ⁴⁸Then the king promoted Daniel, gave him many great gifts, and made him ruler over the whole province of Babylon and chief prefect over all the wise men of Babylon. ⁴⁹Daniel made a request of the king, and he appointed Shadrach, Meshach, and Abednego over the affairs of the province of Babylon. But Daniel remained at the king's court.

The Golden Image

3 King Nebuchadnezzar made a golden statue whose height was sixty cubits and whose width was six cubits; he set it up on the plain of Dura in the province of Babylon. ²Then King Nebuchadnezzar sent for the satraps, the prefects, and the governors, the counselors, the treasurers, the justices, the magistrates, and all the officials of the provinces, to assemble and come to the dedication of the statue that King Nebuchadnezzar had set up. ³So the satraps, the prefects, and the governors, the counselors, the treasurers, the justices, the magistrates, and all the officials of the provinces, assembled for the dedication of the statue that King Nebuchadnezzar had set up. When they were standing before the statue that Nebuchadnezzar had set up, ⁴the herald proclaimed aloud, "You

are commanded, O peoples, nations, and languages, ⁵that when you hear the sound of the horn, pipe, lyre, trigon, harp, drum, and entire musical ensemble, you are to fall down and worship the golden statue that King Nebuchadnezzar has set up. ⁶Whoever does not fall down and worship shall immediately be thrown into a furnace of blazing fire." ⁷Therefore, as soon as all the peoples heard the sound of the horn, pipe, lyre, trigon, harp, drum, and entire musical ensemble, all the peoples, nations, and languages fell down and worshiped the golden statue that King Nebuchadnezzar had set up.

8 Accordingly, at this time certain Chaldeans came forward and denounced the Jews. ⁹They said to King Nebuchadnezzar, "O king, live forever! ¹⁰You, O king, have made a decree, that everyone who hears the sound of the horn, pipe, lyre, trigon, harp, drum, and entire musical ensemble, shall fall down and worship the golden statue, ¹¹and whoever does not fall down and worship shall be thrown into a furnace of blazing fire. ¹²There are certain Jews whom you have appointed over the affairs of the province of Babylon: Shadrach, Meshach, and Abednego. These pay no heed to you, O king. They do not serve your gods and they do not worship the golden statue that you have set up."

13 Then Nebuchadnezzar in furious rage commanded that Shadrach, Meshach, and Abednego be brought in; so they brought those men before the king. ¹⁴Nebuchadnezzar said to them, "Is it true, O Shadrach, Meshach, and Abednego, that you do not serve my gods and you do not worship the golden statue that I have set up? ¹⁵Now if you are ready when you hear the sound of the horn, pipe, lyre, trigon, harp, drum, and entire musical ensemble to fall down and worship the statue that I have made, well and good.ᵉ But if you do not worship, you shall immediately be thrown into a furnace of blazing fire, and who is the god that will deliver you out of my hands?"

16 Shadrach, Meshach, and Abednego answered the king, "O Nebuchadnezzar, we have no need to present a defense to you in this matter. ¹⁷If our God whom we serve is able to deliver us from the furnace

---

ᵈ Aram *by human seed*   ᵉ Aram lacks *well and good*

of blazing fire and out of your hand, O king, let him deliver us. *f* ¹⁸But if not, be it known to you, O king, that we will not serve your gods and we will not worship the golden statue that you have set up."

The Fiery Furnace

19 Then Nebuchadnezzar was so filled with rage against Shadrach, Meshach, and

Abednego that his face was distorted. He ordered the furnace heated up seven times more than was customary, ²⁰and ordered some of the strongest guards in his army to bind Shadrach, Meshach, and Abednego and to throw them into the furnace of

f Or If our God whom we serve is able to deliver us, he will deliver us from the furnace of blazing fire and out of your hand, O king.

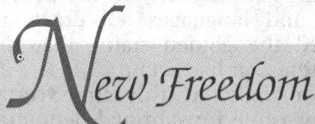 # New Freedom

Four men walking in the white-hot flames. Of course one was an angel so powerful that the king described him as a god. The three young men had no way of knowing they would miraculously survive their fiery ordeal. They refused to dishonor God by bowing down to an idol, and God sent a fireproof angel to protect them as they walked freely in the furnace.

Notice that they were bound when they were cast into the furnace. But the king saw them walking around in the midst of the fire *unbound.* God had sent an angel not only to keep them from burning to death but to unfasten their bonds. In the midst of trial and persecution, they were actually set free. Their story tells us that even in the most desperate circumstances, God can preserve our inner freedom as well as our lives.

No one is likely to command us to kneel before a golden statue today. Our culture promotes more subtle idols that demand our allegiance: sexual icons, success at any price, lust for power, unbridled materialism. The old idols keep popping up, disguised for modern times. Resisting the temptation to give in to these cultural idols often entails great personal sacrifice.

Consider the single man or woman who refuses to give in to the fires of sexual passion, or the husband or wife who resists the temptation to sacrifice family life at the altar of career, or the unmarried woman who hears the dreaded news that she's pregnant but who resists the pressure to solve the "problem" with a quick visit to the local abortion clinic.

None of these are easy choices to make. We will often suffer loss, fear, confusion, and pain in our quest to be faithful to what and whom we believe in. But as we trust God for the outcome, we will experience a new freedom. Perhaps an angel will even stand by our side in the midst of our distress, unbinding and protecting us from the devouring flames that threaten to consume us.

—ANN SPANGLER

Scripture Reading for Today:
Daniel 3.1–23, 91–95

Verse for Today:
Daniel 3.95

Go to page 1166 for your next devotional reading.

blazing fire. [21]So the men were bound, still wearing their tunics,[g] their trousers,[g] their hats, and their other garments, and they were thrown into the furnace of blazing fire. [22]Because the king's command was urgent and the furnace was so overheated, the raging flames killed the men who lifted Shadrach, Meshach, and Abednego. [23]But the three men, Shadrach, Meshach, and Abednego, fell down, bound, into the furnace of blazing fire.

The Prayer of Azariah in the Furnace

24 They walked around in the midst of the flames, singing hymns to God and blessing the Lord. [25]Then Azariah stood still in the fire and prayed aloud:
[26] "Blessed are you, O Lord, God of
>   our ancestors, and worthy of
>   praise;
>   and glorious is your name forever!
[27] For you are just in all you have
>   done;
>   all your works are true and your
>   ways right,
>   and all your judgments are true.
[28] You have executed true judgments in
>   all you have brought upon us
>   and upon Jerusalem, the holy city
>   of our ancestors;
>   by a true judgment you have
>   brought all this upon us
>   because of our sins.
[29] For we have sinned and broken your
>   law in turning away from
>   you;
>   in all matters we have sinned
>   grievously.
[30] We have not obeyed your
>   commandments,
>   we have not kept them or done
>   what you have commanded
>   us for our own good.
[31] So all that you have brought upon
>   us,
>   and all that you have done to us,
>   you have done by a true
>   judgment.
[32] You have handed us over to our
>   enemies, lawless and hateful
>   rebels,
>   and to an unjust king, the most
>   wicked in all the world.
[33] And now we cannot open our
>   mouths;
>   we, your servants who worship
>   you, have become a shame
>   and a reproach.

[34] For your name's sake do not give us
>   up forever,
>   and do not annul your covenant.
[35] Do not withdraw your mercy from
>   us,
>   for the sake of Abraham your
>   beloved
>   and for the sake of your servant
>   Isaac
>   and Israel your holy one,
[36] to whom you promised
>   to multiply their descendants like
>   the stars of heaven
>   and like the sand on the shore of
>   the sea.
[37] For we, O Lord, have become fewer
>   than any other nation,
>   and are brought low this day in
>   all the world because of our
>   sins.
[38] In our day we have no ruler, or
>   prophet, or leader,
>   no burnt offering, or sacrifice, or
>   oblation, or incense,
>   no place to make an offering
>   before you and to find mercy.
[39] Yet with a contrite heart and a
>   humble spirit may we be
>   accepted,
[40] as though it were with burnt
>   offerings of rams and bulls,
>   or with tens of thousands of fat
>   lambs;
>   such may our sacrifice be in your
>   sight today,
>   and may we unreservedly follow
>   you,[h]
>   for no shame will come to those
>   who trust in you.
[41] And now with all our heart we
>   follow you;
>   we fear you and seek your
>   presence.
[42] Do not put us to shame,
>   but deal with us in your patience
>   and in your abundant mercy.
[43] Deliver us in accordance with your
>   marvelous works,
>   and bring glory to your name,
>   O Lord.
[44] Let all who do harm to your
>   servants be put to shame;
>   let them be disgraced and
>   deprived of all power,
>   and let their strength be broken.

---

[g] Meaning of Aram word uncertain   [h] Meaning of Gk uncertain

45 Let them know that you alone are
      the Lord God,
   glorious over the whole world."

The Song of the Three Jews

46 Now the king's servants who threw
them in kept stoking the furnace with
naphtha, pitch, tow, and brushwood.
47And the flames poured out above the
furnace forty-nine cubits, 48and spread
out and burned those Chaldeans who
were caught near the furnace. 49But the
angel of the Lord came down into the furnace to be with Azariah and his companions, and drove the fiery flame out of the
furnace, 50and made the inside of the furnace as though a moist wind were whistling through it. The fire did not touch
them at all and caused them no pain or
distress.

51 Then the three with one voice
praised and glorified and blessed God in
the furnace:
52 "Blessed are you, O Lord, God of
      our ancestors,
   and to be praised and highly
      exalted forever;
   And blessed is your glorious, holy
      name,
   and to be highly praised and
      highly exalted forever.
53 Blessed are you in the temple of
      your holy glory,
   and to be extolled and highly
      glorified forever.
54 Blessed are you who look into the
      depths from your throne on
      the cherubim,
   and to be praised and highly
      exalted forever.
55 Blessed are you on the throne of
      your kingdom,
   and to be extolled and highly
      exalted forever.
56 Blessed are you in the firmament of
      heaven,
   and to be sung and glorified
      forever.

57 "Bless the Lord, all you works of the
      Lord;
   sing praise to him and highly
      exalt him forever.
58 Bless the Lord, you heavens;
   sing praise to him and highly
      exalt him forever.
59 Bless the Lord, you angels of the
      Lord;

   sing praise to him and highly
      exalt him forever.
60 Bless the Lord, all you waters above
      the heavens;
   sing praise to him and highly
      exalt him forever.
61 Bless the Lord, all you powers of the
      Lord;
   sing praise to him and highly
      exalt him forever.
62 Bless the Lord, sun and moon;
   sing praise to him and highly
      exalt him forever.
63 Bless the Lord, stars of heaven;
   sing praise to him and highly
      exalt him forever.

64 "Bless the Lord, all rain and dew;
   sing praise to him and highly
      exalt him forever.
65 Bless the Lord, all you winds;
   sing praise to him and highly
      exalt him forever.
66 Bless the Lord, fire and heat;
   sing praise to him and highly
      exalt him forever.
67 Bless the Lord, winter cold and
      summer heat;
   sing praise to him and highly
      exalt him forever.
68 Bless the Lord, dews and falling
      snow;
   sing praise to him and highly
      exalt him forever.
69 Bless the Lord, ice and cold;
   sing praise to him and highly
      exalt him forever.
70 Bless the Lord, frosts and snows;
   sing praise to him and highly
      exalt him forever.
71 Bless the Lord, nights and days;
   sing praise to him and highly
      exalt him forever.
72 Bless the Lord, light and darkness;
   sing praise to him and highly
      exalt him forever.
73 Bless the Lord, lightnings and
      clouds;
   sing praise to him and highly
      exalt him forever.

74 "Let the earth bless the Lord;
   let it sing praise to him and
      highly exalt him forever.
75 Bless the Lord, mountains and hills;
   sing praise to him and highly
      exalt him forever.

76 Bless the Lord, all that grows in the
     ground;
    sing praise to him and highly
     exalt him forever.
77 Bless the Lord, you springs;
    sing praise to him and highly
     exalt him forever.
78 Bless the Lord, seas and rivers;
    sing praise to him and highly
     exalt him forever.
79 Bless the Lord, you whales and all
     that swim in the waters;
    sing praise to him and highly
     exalt him forever.
80 Bless the Lord, all birds of the air;
    sing praise to him and highly
     exalt him forever.
81 Bless the Lord, all wild animals and
     cattle;
    sing praise to him and highly
     exalt him forever.

82 "Bless the Lord, all people on earth;
    sing praise to him and highly
     exalt him forever.
83 Bless the Lord, O Israel;
    sing praise to him and highly
     exalt him forever.
84 Bless the Lord, you priests of the
     Lord;
    sing praise to him and highly
     exalt him forever.
85 Bless the Lord, you servants of the
     Lord;
    sing praise to him and highly
     exalt him forever.
86 Bless the Lord, spirits and souls of
     the righteous;
    sing praise to him and highly
     exalt him forever.
87 Bless the Lord, you who are holy
     and humble in heart;
    sing praise to him and highly
     exalt him forever.

88 "Bless the Lord, Hananiah, Azariah,
     and Mishael;
    sing praise to him and highly
     exalt him forever.
For he has rescued us from Hades
     and saved us from the
     power[i] of death,
and delivered us from the midst
     of the burning fiery furnace;
from the midst of the fire he has
     delivered us.
89 Give thanks to the Lord, for he is
     good,

for his mercy endures forever.
90 All who worship the Lord, bless the
     God of gods,
    sing praise to him and give thanks
     to him,
for his mercy endures forever."

91 Hearing them sing, and amazed at seeing them alive, King Nebuchadnezzar rose up quickly. He said to his counselors, "Was it not three men that we threw bound into the fire?" They answered the king, "True, O king." 92He replied, "But I see four men unbound, walking in the middle of the fire, and they are not hurt; and the fourth has the appearance of a god."[j] 93Nebuchadnezzar then approached the door of the furnace of blazing fire and said, "Shadrach, Meshach, and Abednego, servants of the Most High God, come out! Come here!" So Shadrach, Meshach, and Abednego came out from the fire. 94And the satraps, the prefects, the governors, and the king's counselors gathered together and saw that the fire had not had any power over the bodies of those men; the hair of their heads was not singed, their tunics[k] were not harmed, and not even the smell of fire came from them. 95Nebuchadnezzar said, "Blessed be the God of Shadrach, Meshach, and Abednego, who has sent his angel and delivered his servants who trusted in him. They disobeyed the king's command and yielded up their bodies rather than serve and worship any god except their own God. 96Therefore I make a decree: Any people, nation, or language that utters blasphemy against the God of Shadrach, Meshach, and Abednego shall be torn limb from limb, and their houses laid in ruins; for there is no other god who is able to deliver in this way." 97Then the king promoted Shadrach, Meshach, and Abednego in the province of Babylon.

Nebuchadnezzar's Second Dream

4 [l] King Nebuchadnezzar to all peoples, nations, and languages that live throughout the earth: May you have abundant prosperity! 2The signs and wonders that the Most High God has worked for me I am pleased to recount.
3 How great are his signs,
    how mighty his wonders!

---

i Gk hand   j Aram *a son of the gods*   k Meaning of Aram word uncertain   l Ch 3.31 in Aram

His kingdom is an everlasting
kingdom,
and his sovereignty is from
generation to generation.

4[m] I, Nebuchadnezzar, was living at
ease in my home and prospering in my
palace. 5I saw a dream that frightened me;
my fantasies in bed and the visions of my
head terrified me. 6So I made a decree that
all the wise men of Babylon should be
brought before me, in order that they
might tell me the interpretation of the
dream. 7Then the magicians, the enchanters, the Chaldeans, and the diviners came
in, and I told them the dream, but they
could not tell me its interpretation. 8At
last Daniel came in before me—he who
was named Belteshazzar after the name of
my god, and who is endowed with a spirit
of the holy gods[n]—and I told him the
dream: 9"O Belteshazzar, chief of the magicians, I know that you are endowed with
a spirit of the holy gods[n] and that no
mystery is too difficult for you. Hear[o] the
dream that I saw; tell me its interpretation.
10[p] Upon my bed this is what I saw;
there was a tree at the center of
the earth,
and its height was great.
11 The tree grew great and strong,
its top reached to heaven,
and it was visible to the ends of
the whole earth.
12 Its foliage was beautiful,
its fruit abundant,
and it provided food for all.
The animals of the field found shade
under it,
the birds of the air nested in
its branches,
and from it all living beings
were fed.

13 "I continued looking, in the visions
of my head as I lay in bed, and there was
a holy watcher, coming down from heav-
en. 14He cried aloud and said:
'Cut down the tree and chop off
its branches,
strip off its foliage and scatter
its fruit.
Let the animals flee from beneath it
and the birds from its branches.
15 But leave its stump and roots in the
ground,
with a band of iron and bronze,
in the tender grass of the field.

Let him be bathed with the dew
of heaven,
and let his lot be with the animals
of the field
in the grass of the earth.
16 Let his mind be changed from that
of a human,
and let the mind of an animal be
given to him.
And let seven times pass
over him.
17 The sentence is rendered by decree
of the watchers,
the decision is given by order of
the holy ones,
in order that all who live may know
that the Most High is sovereign
over the kingdom of mortals;
he gives it to whom he will
and sets over it the lowliest of
human beings.'

18 "This is the dream that I, King Nebuchadnezzar, saw. Now you, Belteshazzar,
declare the interpretation, since all the
wise men of my kingdom are unable to
tell me the interpretation. You are able,
however, for you are endowed with a spirit of the holy gods."[n]

Daniel Interprets the Second Dream

19 Then Daniel, who was called Belteshazzar, was severely distressed for a
while. His thoughts terrified him. The
king said, "Belteshazzar, do not let the
dream or the interpretation terrify you."
Belteshazzar answered, "My lord, may the
dream be for those who hate you, and its
interpretation for your enemies! 20The
tree that you saw, which grew great and
strong, so that its top reached to heaven
and was visible to the end of the whole
earth, 21whose foliage was beautiful and
its fruit abundant, and which provided
food for all, under which animals of the
field lived, and in whose branches the
birds of the air had nests— 22it is you,
O king! You have grown great and strong.
Your greatness has increased and reaches
to heaven, and your sovereignty to the
ends of the earth. 23And whereas the king
saw a holy watcher coming down from
heaven and saying, 'Cut down the tree

m Ch 4.1 in Aram   n Or a holy, divine spirit
o Theodotion: Aram The visions of   p Theodotion
Syr Compare Gk: Aram adds The visions of my
head

and destroy it, but leave its stump and roots in the ground, with a band of iron and bronze, in the grass of the field; and let him be bathed with the dew of heaven, and let his lot be with the animals of the field, until seven times pass over him'— 24this is the interpretation, O king, and it is a decree of the Most High that has come upon my lord the king: 25You shall be driven away from human society, and your dwelling shall be with the wild animals. You shall be made to eat grass like oxen, you shall be bathed with the dew of heaven, and seven times shall pass over you, until you have learned that the Most High has sovereignty over the kingdom of mortals, and gives it to whom he will. 26As it was commanded to leave the stump and roots of the tree, your kingdom shall be re-established for you from the time that you learn that Heaven is sovereign. 27Therefore, O king, may my counsel be acceptable to you: atone for*q* your sins with righteousness, and your iniquities with mercy to the oppressed, so that your prosperity may be prolonged."

Nebuchadnezzar's Humiliation

28 All this came upon King Nebuchadnezzar. 29At the end of twelve months he was walking on the roof of the royal palace of Babylon, 30and the king said, "Is this not magnificent Babylon, which I have built as a royal capital by my mighty power and for my glorious majesty?" 31While the words were still in the king's mouth, a voice came from heaven: "O King Nebuchadnezzar, to you it is declared: The kingdom has departed from you! 32You shall be driven away from human society, and your dwelling shall be with the animals of the field. You shall be made to eat grass like oxen, and seven times shall pass over you, until you have learned that the Most High has sovereignty over the kingdom of mortals and gives it to whom he will." 33Immediately the sentence was fulfilled against Nebuchadnezzar. He was driven away from human society, ate grass like oxen, and his body was bathed with the dew of heaven, until his hair grew as long as eagles' feathers and his nails became like birds' claws.

Nebuchadnezzar Praises God

34 When that period was over, I, Nebuchadnezzar, lifted my eyes to heaven, and my reason returned to me.

I blessed the Most High,
and praised and honored the one
who lives forever.
For his sovereignty is an everlasting
sovereignty,
and his kingdom endures from
generation to generation.
35 All the inhabitants of the earth are
accounted as nothing,
and he does what he wills with
the host of heaven
and the inhabitants of the earth.
There is no one who can stay
his hand
or say to him, "What are you
doing?"

36At that time my reason returned to me; and my majesty and splendor were restored to me for the glory of my kingdom. My counselors and my lords sought me out, I was re-established over my kingdom, and still more greatness was added to me. 37Now I, Nebuchadnezzar, praise and extol and honor the King of heaven,

for all his works are truth,
and his ways are justice;
and he is able to bring low
those who walk in pride.

Belshazzar's Feast

5 King Belshazzar made a great festival for a thousand of his lords, and he was drinking wine in the presence of the thousand.
2 Under the influence of the wine, Belshazzar commanded that they bring in the vessels of gold and silver that his father Nebuchadnezzar had taken out of the temple in Jerusalem, so that the king and his lords, his wives, and his concubines might drink from them. 3So they brought in the vessels of gold and silver*r* that had been taken out of the temple, the house of God in Jerusalem, and the king and his lords, his wives, and his concubines drank from them. 4They drank the wine and praised the gods of gold and silver, bronze, iron, wood, and stone.

The Writing on the Wall

5 Immediately the fingers of a human hand appeared and began writing on the plaster of the wall of the royal palace, next to the lampstand. The king was watching the hand as it wrote. 6Then the king's face

---

q Aram *break off*   *r* Theodotion Vg: Aram lacks *and silver*

turned pale, and his thoughts terrified him. His limbs gave way, and his knees knocked together. 7The king cried aloud to bring in the enchanters, the Chaldeans, and the diviners; and the king said to the wise men of Babylon, "Whoever can read this writing and tell me its interpretation shall be clothed in purple, have a chain of gold around his neck, and rank third in the kingdom." 8Then all the king's wise men came in, but they could not read the writing or tell the king the interpretation. 9Then King Belshazzar became greatly terrified and his face turned pale, and his lords were perplexed.

10 The queen, when she heard the discussion of the king and his lords, came into the banqueting hall. The queen said, "O king, live forever! Do not let your thoughts terrify you or your face grow pale. 11There is a man in your kingdom who is endowed with a spirit of the holy gods.s In the days of your father he was found to have enlightenment, understanding, and wisdom like the wisdom of the gods. Your father, King Nebuchadnezzar, made him chief of the magicians, enchanters, Chaldeans, and diviners,t 12because an excellent spirit, knowledge, and understanding to interpret dreams, explain riddles, and solve problems were found in this Daniel, whom the king named Belteshazzar. Now let Daniel be called, and he will give the interpretation."

The Writing on the Wall Interpreted

13 Then Daniel was brought in before the king. The king said to Daniel, "So you are Daniel, one of the exiles of Judah, whom my father the king brought from Judah? 14I have heard of you that a spirit of the godsu is in you, and that enlightenment, understanding, and excellent wisdom are found in you. 15Now the wise men, the enchanters, have been brought in before me to read this writing and tell me its interpretation, but they were not able to give the interpretation of the matter. 16But I have heard that you can give interpretations and solve problems. Now if you are able to read the writing and tell me its interpretation, you shall be clothed in purple, have a chain of gold around your neck, and rank third in the kingdom."

17 Then Daniel answered in the presence of the king, "Let your gifts be for yourself, or give your rewards to someone else! Nevertheless I will read the writing to the king and let him know the interpretation. 18O king, the Most High God gave your father Nebuchadnezzar kingship, greatness, glory, and majesty. 19And because of the greatness that he gave him, all peoples, nations, and languages trembled and feared before him. He killed those he wanted to kill, kept alive those he wanted to keep alive, honored those he wanted to honor, and degraded those he wanted to degrade. 20But when his heart was lifted up and his spirit was hardened so that he acted proudly, he was deposed from his kingly throne, and his glory was stripped from him. 21He was driven from human society, and his mind was made like that of an animal. His dwelling was with the wild asses, he was fed grass like oxen, and his body was bathed with the dew of heaven, until he learned that the Most High God has sovereignty over the kingdom of mortals, and sets over it whomever he will. 22And you, Belshazzar his son, have not humbled your heart, even though you knew all this! 23You have exalted yourself against the Lord of heaven! The vessels of his temple have been brought in before you, and you and your lords, your wives and your concubines have been drinking wine from them. You have praised the gods of silver and gold, of bronze, iron, wood, and stone, which do not see or hear or know; but the God in whose power is your very breath, and to whom belong all your ways, you have not honored.

24 "So from his presence the hand was sent and this writing was inscribed. 25And this is the writing that was inscribed: MENE, MENE, TEKEL, and PARSIN. 26This is the interpretation of the matter: MENE, God has numbered the days ofv your kingdom and brought it to an end; 27TEKEL, you have been weighed on the scales and found wanting; 28PERES,w your kingdom is divided and given to the Medes and Persians."

29 Then Belshazzar gave the command, and Daniel was clothed in purple, a chain of gold was put around his neck, and a proclamation was made concerning him that he should rank third in the kingdom.

30 That very night Belshazzar, the

s Or a holy, divine spirit   t Aram adds the king your father   u Or a divine spirit   v Aram lacks the days of   w The singular of Parsin

Chaldean king, was killed. [31x] And Darius the Mede received the kingdom, being about sixty-two years old.

The Plot against Daniel

6 It pleased Darius to set over the kingdom one hundred twenty satraps, stationed throughout the whole kingdom, [2]and over them three presidents, including Daniel; to these the satraps gave account, so that the king might suffer no loss. [3]Soon Daniel distinguished himself above all the other presidents and satraps because an excellent spirit was in him, and the king planned to appoint him over the whole kingdom. [4]So the presidents and the satraps tried to find grounds for complaint against Daniel in connection with the kingdom. But they could find no grounds for complaint or any corruption, because he was faithful, and no negligence or corruption could be found in him. [5]The men said, "We shall not find any ground for complaint against this Daniel unless we find it in connection with the law of his God."

[6] So the presidents and satraps conspired and came to the king and said to him, "O King Darius, live forever! [7]All the presidents of the kingdom, the prefects and the satraps, the counselors and the governors are agreed that the king should establish an ordinance and enforce an interdict, that whoever prays to anyone, divine or human, for thirty days, except to you, O king, shall be thrown into a den of lions. [8]Now, O king, establish the interdict and sign the document, so that it cannot be changed, according to the law of the Medes and the Persians, which cannot be revoked." [9]Therefore King Darius signed the document and interdict.

Daniel in the Lions' Den

[10] Although Daniel knew that the document had been signed, he continued to go to his house, which had windows in its upper room open toward Jerusalem, and to get down on his knees three times a day to pray to his God and praise him, just as he had done previously. [11]The conspirators came and found Daniel praying and seeking mercy before his God. [12]Then they approached the king and said concerning the interdict, "O king! Did you not sign an interdict, that anyone who prays to anyone, divine or human, within thirty days except to you, O king, shall be thrown into a den of lions?" The king answered, "The thing stands fast, according to the law of the Medes and Persians, which cannot be revoked." [13]Then they responded to the king, "Daniel, one of the exiles from Judah, pays no attention to you, O king, or to the interdict you have signed, but he is saying his prayers three times a day."

[14] When the king heard the charge, he was very much distressed. He was determined to save Daniel, and until the sun went down he made every effort to rescue him. [15]Then the conspirators came to the king and said to him, "Know, O king, that it is a law of the Medes and Persians that no interdict or ordinance that the king establishes can be changed."

[16] Then the king gave the command, and Daniel was brought and thrown into the den of lions. The king said to Daniel, "May your God, whom you faithfully serve, deliver you!" [17]A stone was brought and laid on the mouth of the den, and the king sealed it with his own signet and with the signet of his lords, so that nothing might be changed concerning Daniel. [18]Then the king went to his palace and spent the night fasting; no food was brought to him, and sleep fled from him.

Daniel Saved from the Lions

[19] Then, at break of day, the king got up and hurried to the den of lions. [20]When he came near the den where Daniel was, he cried out anxiously to Daniel, "O Daniel, servant of the living God, has your God whom you faithfully serve been able to deliver you from the lions?" [21]Daniel then said to the king, "O king, live forever! [22]My God sent his angel and shut the lions' mouths so that they would not hurt me, because I was found blameless before him; and also before you, O king, I have done no wrong." [23]Then the king was exceedingly glad and commanded that Daniel be taken up out of the den. So Daniel was taken up out of the den, and no kind of harm was found on him, because he had trusted in his God. [24]The king gave a command, and those who had accused Daniel were brought and thrown into the den of lions—they, their children, and their wives. Before they reached the bottom of the den the lions overpowered them and broke all their bones in pieces.

x Ch 6.1 in Aram

25 Then King Darius wrote to all peoples and nations of every language throughout the whole world: "May you have abundant prosperity! 26I make a decree, that in all my royal dominion people should tremble and fear before the God of Daniel:

For he is the living God,
    enduring forever.
His kingdom shall never be
        destroyed,
    and his dominion has no end.

27 He delivers and rescues,
    he works signs and wonders in
        heaven and on earth;
    for he has saved Daniel
        from the power of the lions."

28So this Daniel prospered during the reign of Darius and the reign of Cyrus the Persian.

Visions of the Four Beasts

7 In the first year of King Belshazzar of Babylon, Daniel had a dream and vi-

THURSDAY

Scripture Reading
for Today:
Daniel 6.10–24

Verse for Today:
Daniel 6.22

Protection

Daniel was anything but a pragmatist. Why did he have to pray in front of a window, facing toward Jerusalem, flaunting the king's clear command? Daniel simply refused to turn his back on God in order to worship earthly powers. He must have known that even small concessions would have encouraged a greater repression of faith. The initial edict lasted 30 days. What would stop the king from making the order permanent once he got everyone used to the idea?

Despite his regard for Daniel, the king had no choice but to abide by the decree he had issued and to cast him into a den of hungry lions. He entombed Daniel with the raging beasts and placed his signet on the stone. Yet an angel came and clamped the lions' jaws shut, saving Daniel's life.

Centuries later, religious authorities in Jerusalem would place a similar stone over the tomb of Jesus and seal it with a guard of soldiers to make sure no one would tamper with his grave. Once again, mere stones could not stop God's angels. For two angels appeared at the tomb of Jesus and addressed the women who came to anoint Jesus' body: "Why do you look for the living among the dead?"

Both Daniel and Jesus refused to compromise their faith. God preserved the one from death and caused the other to conquer death once and for all. We may not face the kind of persecution that was meted out in the ancient world, but we will surely face pressures to compromise our beliefs in order to fit in with the world around us. When that happens, remember Daniel and Jesus.

Remember, too, that you can sell your soul by making the wrong kinds of compromises. Whatever pressures you face, whether subtle or overt, set your heart at rest by remembering that God protects the blameless.

—ANN SPANGLER

Go to page 1174 for your next devotional reading.

sions of his head as he lay in bed. Then he wrote down the dream: *y* 2I, *z* Daniel, saw in my vision by night the four winds of heaven stirring up the great sea, 3and four great beasts came up out of the sea, different from one another. 4The first was like a lion and had eagles' wings. Then, as I watched, its wings were plucked off, and it was lifted up from the ground and made to stand on two feet like a human being; and a human mind was given to it. 5Another beast appeared, a second one, that looked like a bear. It was raised up on one side, had three tusks*a* in its mouth among its teeth and was told, "Arise, devour many bodies!" 6After this, as I watched, another appeared, like a leopard. The beast had four wings of a bird on its back and four heads; and dominion was given to it. 7After this I saw in the visions by night a fourth beast, terrifying and dreadful and exceedingly strong. It had great iron teeth and was devouring, breaking in pieces, and stamping what was left with its feet. It was different from all the beasts that preceded it, and it had ten horns. 8I was considering the horns, when another horn appeared, a little one coming up among them; to make room for it, three of the earlier horns were plucked up by the roots. There were eyes like human eyes in this horn, and a mouth speaking arrogantly.

Judgment before the Ancient One

9 As I watched,
   thrones were set in place,
     and an Ancient One*b* took
       his throne,
   his clothing was white as snow,
     and the hair of his head like
       pure wool;
   his throne was fiery flames,
     and its wheels were burning fire.
10 A stream of fire issued
   and flowed out from his presence.
   A thousand thousands served him,
     and ten thousand times ten
       thousand stood
       attending him.
   The court sat in judgment,
     and the books were opened.
11I watched then because of the noise of the arrogant words that the horn was speaking. And as I watched, the beast was put to death, and its body destroyed and given over to be burned with fire. 12As for the rest of the beasts, their dominion was taken away, but their lives were prolonged for a season and a time. 13As I watched in the night visions,

   I saw one like a human being*c*
     coming with the clouds of heaven.
   And he came to the Ancient One*d*
     and was presented before him.
14 To him was given dominion
   and glory and kingship,
   that all peoples, nations, and
      languages
   should serve him.
   His dominion is an everlasting
     dominion
     that shall not pass away,
   and his kingship is one
     that shall never be destroyed.

Daniel's Visions Interpreted

15 As for me, Daniel, my spirit was troubled within me,*e* and the visions of my head terrified me. 16I approached one of the attendants to ask him the truth concerning all this. So he said that he would disclose to me the interpretation of the matter: 17"As for these four great beasts, four kings shall arise out of the earth. 18But the holy ones of the Most High shall receive the kingdom and possess the kingdom forever—forever and ever."

19 Then I desired to know the truth concerning the fourth beast, which was different from all the rest, exceedingly terrifying, with its teeth of iron and claws of bronze, and which devoured and broke in pieces, and stamped what was left with its feet; 20and concerning the ten horns that were on its head, and concerning the other horn, which came up and to make room for which three of them fell out— the horn that had eyes and a mouth that spoke arrogantly, and that seemed greater than the others. 21As I looked, this horn made war with the holy ones and was prevailing over them, 22until the Ancient One*d* came; then judgment was given for the holy ones of the Most High, and the time arrived when the holy ones gained possession of the kingdom.

23 This is what he said: "As for the fourth beast,

---

y Q Ms Theodotion: MT adds *the beginning of the words; he said*   *z* Theodotion: Aram *Daniel answered and said, I*   *a* Or *ribs*   *b* Aram *an Ancient of Days*   *c* Aram *one like a son of man*   *d* Aram *the Ancient of Days*   *e* Aram *troubled in its sheath*

there shall be a fourth kingdom
    on earth
  that shall be different from all the
    other kingdoms;
it shall devour the whole earth,
  and trample it down, and break it
    to pieces.

24 As for the ten horns,
  out of this kingdom ten kings
    shall arise,
  and another shall arise after them.
This one shall be different from the
    former ones,
  and shall put down three kings.

25 He shall speak words against the
    Most High,
  shall wear out the holy ones of
    the Most High,
  and shall attempt to change the
    sacred seasons and the law;
and they shall be given into
    his power
for a time, two times,*f* and half a
    time.

26 Then the court shall sit in judgment,
  and his dominion shall be
    taken away,
  to be consumed and totally
    destroyed.

27 The kingship and dominion
  and the greatness of the kingdoms
    under the whole heaven
  shall be given to the people of the
    holy ones of the Most High;
  their kingdom shall be an
    everlasting kingdom,
  and all dominions shall serve and
    obey them."

28 Here the account ends. As for me, Daniel, my thoughts greatly terrified me, and my face turned pale; but I kept the matter in my mind.

Vision of a Ram and a Goat

8 In the third year of the reign of King Belshazzar a vision appeared to me, Daniel, after the one that had appeared to me at first. 2In the vision I was looking and saw myself in Susa the capital, in the province of Elam,*g* and I was by the river Ulai.*h* 3I looked up and saw a ram standing beside the river.*i* It had two horns. Both horns were long, but one was longer than the other, and the longer one came up second. 4I saw the ram charging westward and northward and southward. All beasts were powerless to withstand it, and

no one could rescue from its power; it did as it pleased and became strong.

5 As I was watching, a male goat appeared from the west, coming across the face of the whole earth without touching the ground. The goat had a horn*j* between its eyes. 6It came toward the ram with the two horns that I had seen standing beside the river,*i* and it ran at it with savage force. 7I saw it approaching the ram. It was enraged against it and struck the ram, breaking its two horns. The ram did not have power to withstand it; it threw the ram down to the ground and trampled upon it, and there was no one who could rescue the ram from its power. 8Then the male goat grew exceedingly great; but at the height of its power, the great horn was broken, and in its place there came up four prominent horns toward the four winds of heaven.

9 Out of one of them came another*k* horn, a little one, which grew exceedingly great toward the south, toward the east, and toward the beautiful land. 10It grew as high as the host of heaven. It threw down to the earth some of the host and some of the stars, and trampled on them. 11Even against the prince of the host it acted arrogantly; it took the regular burnt offering away from him and overthrew the place of his sanctuary. 12Because of wickedness, the host was given over to it together with the regular burnt offering;*l* it cast truth to the ground, and kept prospering in what it did. 13Then I heard a holy one speaking, and another holy one said to the one that spoke, "For how long is this vision concerning the regular burnt offering, the transgression that makes desolate, and the giving over of the sanctuary and host to be trampled?"*l* 14And he answered him,*m* "For two thousand three hundred evenings and mornings; then the sanctuary shall be restored to its rightful state."

Gabriel Interprets the Vision

15 When I, Daniel, had seen the vision, I tried to understand it. Then someone appeared standing before me, having the appearance of a man, 16and I heard a human

f Aram *a time, times*   *g* Gk Theodotion: MT Q Ms repeat *in the vision I was looking*   *h* Or *the Ulai Gate*   *i* Or *gate*   *j* Theodotion: Gk *one horn*; Heb *a horn of vision*   *k* Cn Compare 7.8: Heb *one*   *l* Meaning of Heb uncertain   *m* Gk Theodotion Syr Vg: Heb *me*

voice by the Ulai, calling, "Gabriel, help this man understand the vision." ¹⁷So he came near where I stood; and when he came, I became frightened and fell prostrate. But he said to me, "Understand, O mortal,ⁿ that the vision is for the time of the end."

18 As he was speaking to me, I fell into a trance, face to the ground; then he touched me and set me on my feet. ¹⁹He said, "Listen, and I will tell you what will take place later in the period of wrath; for it refers to the appointed time of the end. ²⁰As for the ram that you saw with the two horns, these are the kings of Media and Persia. ²¹The male goat^o is the king of Greece, and the great horn between its eyes is the first king. ²²As for the horn that was broken, in place of which four others arose, four kingdoms shall arise from his^p nation, but not with his power.

23 At the end of their rule,
> when the transgressions have
>> reached their full measure,
> a king of bold countenance
>> shall arise,
>> skilled in intrigue.
²⁴ He shall grow strong in power,^q
> shall cause fearful destruction,
> and shall succeed in what
>> he does.
> He shall destroy the powerful
> and the people of the holy ones.
²⁵ By his cunning
> he shall make deceit prosper
>> under his hand,
> and in his own mind he shall
>> be great.
> Without warning he shall
>> destroy many
> and shall even rise up against the
>> Prince of princes.
> But he shall be broken, and not by
>> human hands.

²⁶The vision of the evenings and the mornings that has been told is true. As for you, seal up the vision, for it refers to many days from now."

27 So I, Daniel, was overcome and lay sick for some days; then I arose and went about the king's business. But I was dismayed by the vision and did not understand it.

Daniel's Prayer for the People

9 In the first year of Darius son of Ahasuerus, by birth a Mede, who became king over the realm of the Chalde-

ans— ²in the first year of his reign, I, Daniel, perceived in the books the number of years that, according to the word of the Lord to the prophet Jeremiah, must be fulfilled for the devastation of Jerusalem, namely, seventy years.

3 Then I turned to the Lord God, to seek an answer by prayer and supplication with fasting and sackcloth and ashes. ⁴I prayed to the Lord my God and made confession, saying,

"Ah, Lord, great and awesome God, keeping covenant and steadfast love with those who love you and keep your commandments, ⁵we have sinned and done wrong, acted wickedly and rebelled, turning aside from your commandments and ordinances. ⁶We have not listened to your servants the prophets, who spoke in your name to our kings, our princes, and our ancestors, and to all the people of the land.

7 "Righteousness is on your side, O Lord, but open shame, as at this day, falls on us, the people of Judah, the inhabitants of Jerusalem, and all Israel, those who are near and those who are far away, in all the lands to which you have driven them, because of the treachery that they have committed against you. ⁸Open shame, O Lord, falls on us, our kings, our officials, and our ancestors, because we have sinned against you. ⁹To the Lord our God belong mercy and forgiveness, for we have rebelled against him, ¹⁰and have not obeyed the voice of the Lord our God by following his laws, which he set before us by his servants the prophets.

11 "All Israel has transgressed your law and turned aside, refusing to obey your voice. So the curse and the oath written in the law of Moses, the servant of God, have been poured out upon us, because we have sinned against you. ¹²He has confirmed his words, which he spoke against us and against our rulers, by bringing upon us a calamity so great that what has been done against Jerusalem has never before been done under the whole heaven. ¹³Just as it is written in the law of Moses, all this calamity has come upon us. We did not entreat the favor of the Lord our God, turning from our iniquities and re-

---

ⁿ Heb *son of man*   ^o Or *shaggy male goat*   ^p Gk Theodotion Vg: Heb *the*   ^q Theodotion and one Gk Ms: Heb repeats (from 8.22) *but not with his power*

flecting on his^r fidelity. ^14So the LORD kept watch over this calamity until he brought it upon us. Indeed, the LORD our God is right in all that he has done; for we have disobeyed his voice.

15 "And now, O Lord our God, who brought your people out of the land of Egypt with a mighty hand and made your name renowned even to this day—we have sinned, we have done wickedly. ^16O Lord, in view of all your righteous acts, let your anger and wrath, we pray, turn away from your city Jerusalem, your holy mountain; because of our sins and the iniquities of our ancestors, Jerusalem and your people have become a disgrace among all our neighbors. ^17Now therefore, O our God, listen to the prayer of your servant and to his supplication, and for your own sake, Lord,^s let your face shine upon your desolated sanctuary. ^18Incline your ear, O my God, and hear. Open your eyes and look at our desolation and the city that bears your name. We do not present our supplication before you on the ground of our righteousness, but on the ground of your great mercies. ^19O Lord, hear; O Lord, forgive; O Lord, listen and act and do not delay! For your own sake, O my God, because your city and your people bear your name!"

The Seventy Weeks

20 While I was speaking, and was praying and confessing my sin and the sin of my people Israel, and presenting my supplication before the LORD my God on behalf of the holy mountain of my God— ^21while I was speaking in prayer, the man Gabriel, whom I had seen before in a vision, came to me in swift flight at the time of the evening sacrifice. ^22He came^t and said to me, "Daniel, I have now come out to give you wisdom and understanding. ^23At the beginning of your supplications a word went out, and I have come to declare it, for you are greatly beloved. So consider the word and understand the vision:

24 "Seventy weeks are decreed for your people and your holy city: to finish the transgression, to put an end to sin, and to atone for iniquity, to bring in everlasting righteousness, to seal both vision and prophet, and to anoint a most holy place.^u ^25Know therefore and understand: from the time that the word went out to restore and rebuild Jerusalem until the time of an anointed prince, there shall

be seven weeks; and for sixty-two weeks it shall be built again with streets and moat, but in a troubled time. ^26After the sixty-two weeks, an anointed one shall be cut off and shall have nothing, and the troops of the prince who is to come shall destroy the city and the sanctuary. Its^v end shall come with a flood, and to the end there shall be war. Desolations are decreed. ^27He shall make a strong covenant with many for one week, and for half of the week he shall make sacrifice and offering cease; and in their place^w shall be an abomination that desolates, until the decreed end is poured out upon the desolator."

Conflict of Nations and Heavenly Powers

10 In the third year of King Cyrus of Persia a word was revealed to Daniel, who was named Belteshazzar. The word was true, and it concerned a great conflict. He understood the word, having received understanding in the vision.

2 At that time I, Daniel, had been mourning for three weeks. ^3I had eaten no rich food, no meat or wine had entered my mouth, and I had not anointed myself at all, for the full three weeks. ^4On the twenty-fourth day of the first month, as I was standing on the bank of the great river (that is, the Tigris), ^5I looked up and saw a man clothed in linen, with a belt of gold from Uphaz around his waist. ^6His body was like beryl, his face like lightning, his eyes like flaming torches, his arms and legs like the gleam of burnished bronze, and the sound of his words like the roar of a multitude. ^7I, Daniel, alone saw the vision; the people who were with me did not see the vision, though a great trembling fell upon them, and they fled and hid themselves. ^8So I was left alone to see this great vision. My strength left me, and my complexion grew deathly pale, and I retained no strength. ^9Then I heard the sound of his words; and when I heard the sound of his words, I fell into a trance, face to the ground.

10 But then a hand touched me and roused me to my hands and knees. ^11He said to me, "Daniel, greatly beloved, pay attention to the words that I am going to

---

^r Heb your   ^s Theodotion Vg Compare Syr: Heb
for the Lord's sake   ^t Gk Syr: Heb He made to
understand   ^u Or thing or one   ^v Or His
^w Cn: Meaning of Heb uncertain

speak to you. Stand on your feet, for I have now been sent to you." So while he was speaking this word to me, I stood up trembling. ¹²He said to me, "Do not fear, Daniel, for from the first day that you set your mind to gain understanding and to humble yourself before your God, your words have been heard, and I have come because of your words. ¹³But the prince of the kingdom of Persia opposed me twenty-one days. So Michael, one of the chief princes, came to help me, and I left him there with the prince of the kingdom of Persia,ˣ ¹⁴and have come to help you understand what is to happen to your people at the end of days. For there is a further vision for those days."

15 While he was speaking these words to me, I turned my face toward the ground and was speechless. ¹⁶Then one in human form touched my lips, and I opened my mouth to speak, and said to the one who stood before me, "My lord, because of the vision such pains have come upon me that I retain no strength. ¹⁷How can my lord's servant talk with my lord? For I am shaking,ʸ no strength remains in me, and no breath is left in me."

18 Again one in human form touched me and strengthened me. ¹⁹He said, "Do not fear, greatly beloved, you are safe. Be strong and courageous!" When he spoke to me, I was strengthened and said, "Let my lord speak, for you have strengthened me." ²⁰Then he said, "Do you know why I have come to you? Now I must return to fight against the prince of Persia, and when I am through with him, the prince of Greece will come. ²¹But I am to tell you what is inscribed in the book of truth. There is no one with me who contends against these princes except Michael, your prince. ¹As for me, in the first year of Darius the Mede, I stood up to support and strengthen him.

11 2 "Now I will announce the truth to you. Three more kings shall arise in Persia. The fourth shall be far richer than all of them, and when he has become strong through his riches, he shall stir up all against the kingdom of Greece. ³Then a warrior king shall arise, who shall rule with great dominion and take action as he pleases. ⁴And while still rising in power, his kingdom shall be broken and divided toward the four winds of heaven, but not to his posterity, nor according to the dominion with which he ruled; for his king-

dom shall be uprooted and go to others besides these.

5 "Then the king of the south shall grow strong, but one of his officers shall grow stronger than he and shall rule a realm greater than his own realm. ⁶After some years they shall make an alliance, and the daughter of the king of the south shall come to the king of the north to ratify the agreement. But she shall not retain her power, and his offspring shall not endure. She shall be given up, she and her attendants and her child and the one who supported her.

"In those times ⁷a branch from her roots shall rise up in his place. He shall come against the army and enter the fortress of the king of the north, and he shall take action against them and prevail. ⁸Even their gods, with their idols and with their precious vessels of silver and gold, he shall carry off to Egypt as spoils of war. For some years he shall refrain from attacking the king of the north; ⁹then the latter shall invade the realm of the king of the south, but will return to his own land.

10 "His sons shall wage war and assemble a multitude of great forces, which shall advance like a flood and pass through, and again shall carry the war as far as his fortress. ¹¹Moved with rage, the king of the south shall go out and do battle against the king of the north, who shall muster a great multitude, which shall, however, be defeated by his enemy. ¹²When the multitude has been carried off, his heart shall be exalted, and he shall overthrow tens of thousands, but he shall not prevail. ¹³For the king of the north shall again raise a multitude, larger than the former, and after some yearsᶻ he shall advance with a great army and abundant supplies.

14 "In those times many shall rise against the king of the south. The lawless among your own people shall lift themselves up in order to fulfill the vision, but they shall fail. ¹⁵Then the king of the north shall come and throw up siegeworks, and take a well-fortified city. And the forces of the south shall not stand, not even his picked troops, for there shall be no strength to resist. ¹⁶But he who comes against him shall take the actions he

ˣ Gk Theodotion: Heb *I was left there with the kings of Persia*   ʸ Gk: Heb *from now*   ᶻ Heb *and at the end of the times years*

pleases, and no one shall withstand him. He shall take a position in the beautiful land, and all of it shall be in his power. [17] He shall set his mind to come with the strength of his whole kingdom, and he shall bring terms of peace[a] and perform them. In order to destroy the kingdom,[b] he shall give him a woman in marriage; but it shall not succeed or be to his advantage. [18] Afterward he shall turn to the coastlands, and shall capture many. But a commander shall put an end to his insolence; indeed,[c] he shall turn his insolence back upon him. [19] Then he shall turn back toward the fortresses of his own land, but he shall stumble and fall, and shall not be found.

20 "Then shall arise in his place one who shall send an official for the glory of the kingdom; but within a few days he shall be broken, though not in anger or in battle. [21] In his place shall arise a contemptible person on whom royal majesty had not been conferred; he shall come in without warning and obtain the kingdom through intrigue. [22] Armies shall be utterly swept away and broken before him, and the prince of the covenant as well. [23] And after an alliance is made with him, he shall act deceitfully and become strong with a small party. [24] Without warning he shall come into the richest parts[d] of the province and do what none of his predecessors had ever done, lavishing plunder, spoil, and wealth on them. He shall devise plans against strongholds, but only for a time. [25] He shall stir up his power and determination against the king of the south with a great army, and the king of the south shall wage war with a much greater and stronger army. But he shall not succeed, for plots shall be devised against him [26] by those who eat of the royal rations. They shall break him, his army shall be swept away, and many shall fall slain. [27] The two kings, their minds bent on evil, shall sit at one table and exchange lies. But it shall not succeed, for there remains an end at the time appointed. [28] He shall return to his land with great wealth, but his heart shall be set against the holy covenant. He shall work his will, and return to his own land.

29 "At the time appointed he shall return and come into the south, but this time it shall not be as it was before. [30] For ships of Kittim shall come against him, and he shall lose heart and withdraw. He shall be enraged and take action against the holy covenant. He shall turn back and pay heed to those who forsake the holy covenant. [31] Forces sent by him shall occupy and profane the temple and fortress. They shall abolish the regular burnt offering and set up the abomination that makes desolate. [32] He shall seduce with intrigue those who violate the covenant; but the people who are loyal to their God shall stand firm and take action. [33] The wise among the people shall give understanding to many; for some days, however, they shall fall by sword and flame, and suffer captivity and plunder. [34] When they fall victim, they shall receive a little help, and many shall join them insincerely. [35] Some of the wise shall fall, so that they may be refined, purified, and cleansed,[e] until the time of the end, for there is still an interval until the time appointed.

36 "The king shall act as he pleases. He shall exalt himself and consider himself greater than any god, and shall speak horrendous things against the God of gods. He shall prosper until the period of wrath is completed, for what is determined shall be done. [37] He shall pay no respect to the gods of his ancestors, or to the one beloved by women; he shall pay no respect to any other god, for he shall consider himself greater than all. [38] He shall honor the god of fortresses instead of these; a god whom his ancestors did not know he shall honor with gold and silver, with precious stones and costly gifts. [39] He shall deal with the strongest fortresses by the help of a foreign god. Those who acknowledge him he shall make more wealthy, and shall appoint them as rulers over many, and shall distribute the land for a price.

The Time of the End

40 "At the time of the end the king of the south shall attack him. But the king of the north shall rush upon him like a whirlwind, with chariots and horsemen, and with many ships. He shall advance against countries and pass through like a flood. [41] He shall come into the beautiful land, and tens of thousands shall fall vic-

---

a Gk: Heb *kingdom, and upright ones with him* b Heb *it* c Meaning of Heb uncertain d Or *among the richest men* e Heb *made them white*

tim, but Edom and Moab and the main part of the Ammonites shall escape from his power. 42He shall stretch out his hand against the countries, and the land of Egypt shall not escape. 43He shall become ruler of the treasures of gold and of silver, and all the riches of Egypt; and the Libyans and the Ethiopians*f* shall follow in his train. 44But reports from the east and the north shall alarm him, and he shall go out with great fury to bring ruin and complete destruction to many. 45He shall pitch his palatial tents between the sea and the beautiful holy mountain. Yet he shall come to his end, with no one to help him.

The Resurrection of the Dead

12 "At that time Michael, the great prince, the protector of your people, shall arise. There shall be a time of anguish, such as has never occurred since nations first came into existence. But at that time your people shall be delivered, everyone who is found written in the book. 2Many of those who sleep in the dust of the earth*g* shall awake, some to everlasting life, and some to shame and everlasting contempt. 3Those who are wise shall shine like the brightness of the sky,*h* and those who lead many to righteousness, like the stars forever and ever. 4But you, Daniel, keep the words secret and the book sealed until the time of the end. Many shall be running back and forth, and evil*i* shall increase."

5 Then I, Daniel, looked, and two others appeared, one standing on this bank of the stream and one on the other. 6One of them said to the man clothed in linen, who was upstream, "How long shall it be until the end of these wonders?" 7The man clothed in linen, who was upstream, raised his right hand and his left hand toward heaven. And I heard him swear by the one who lives forever that it would be for a time, two times, and half a time,*j* and that when the shattering of the power of the holy people comes to an end, all these things would be accomplished. 8I heard but could not understand; so I said, "My lord, what shall be the outcome of these things?" 9He said, "Go your way, Daniel, for the words are to remain secret and sealed until the time of the end. 10Many shall be purified, cleansed, and refined, but the wicked shall continue to act wickedly. None of the wicked shall understand, but those who are wise shall understand. 11From the time that the regular burnt offering is taken away and the abomination that desolates is set up, there shall be one thousand two hundred ninety days. 12Happy are those who persevere and attain the thousand three hundred thirty-five days. 13But you, go your way,*k* and rest; you shall rise for your reward at the end of the days."

Susanna's Beauty Attracts Two Elders

13 There was a man living in Babylon whose name was Joakim. 2He married the daughter of Hilkiah, named Susanna, a very beautiful woman and one who feared the Lord. 3Her parents were righteous, and had trained their daughter according to the law of Moses. 4Joakim was very rich, and had a fine garden adjoining his house; the Jews used to come to him because he was the most honored of them all.

5 That year two elders from the people were appointed as judges. Concerning them the Lord had said: "Wickedness came forth from Babylon, from elders who were judges, who were supposed to govern the people." 6These men were frequently at Joakim's house, and all who had a case to be tried came to them there.

7 When the people left at noon, Susanna would go into her husband's garden to walk. 8Every day the two elders used to see her, going in and walking about, and they began to lust for her. 9They suppressed their consciences and turned away their eyes from looking to Heaven or remembering their duty to administer justice. 10Both were overwhelmed with passion for her, but they did not tell each other of their distress, 11for they were ashamed to disclose their lustful desire to seduce her. 12Day after day they watched eagerly to see her.

13 One day they said to each other, "Let us go home, for it is time for lunch." So they both left and parted from each other. 14But turning back, they met again; and when each pressed the other for the reason, they confessed their lust. Then to-

---

f Or *Nubians;* Heb *Cushites*   *g* Or *the land of dust*
h Or *dome*   *i* Cn Compare Gk: Heb *knowledge*
j Heb *a time, times, and a half*   *k* Gk Theodotion:
Heb adds *to the end*

gether they arranged for a time when they could find her alone.

The Elders Attempt to Seduce Susanna

15 Once, while they were watching for an opportune day, she went in as before with only two maids, and wished to bathe in the garden, for it was a hot day. ¹⁶No one was there except the two elders, who had hidden themselves and were watching her. ¹⁷She said to her maids, "Bring me olive oil and ointments, and shut the garden doors so that I can bathe." ¹⁸They did as she told them: they shut the doors of the garden and went out by the side doors to bring what they had been com-

---

S hine in Us

Scripture Reading for Today:
Daniel 12.1–4

Verse for Today:
Daniel 12.3

Angela of Foligno, a twelfth-century mystic, heard the Lord tell her that he would do "great things" through her. In Daniel 12, we hear God's promise of glory and great things for us too, if we follow and teach his way of wisdom.

Angela was somewhat skeptical of the promise at first. What's your reaction to the prospect of shining like a star for all eternity?

The Lord said to me: "Your whole life, your eating and drinking and sleeping, your whole bodily being, all this is pleasing unto me if you are in the state of love!" And again he spoke: "I shall do great things through you in the eyes of all peoples. Through you my name shall be known far and wide, and shall be glorified, praised, and exalted."

This and many other things of the same kind he said to me. But at his words, I thought of my sinning and my inadequacy and how little I deserved such proof of love. I began to cherish grave doubts of the truth of these words, and my soul answered him who had spoken to me: "If you were, indeed, the Holy Ghost, you would not say such things to me, for they are not so, and do not befit me. And I am, moreover, a frail mortal and might easily fall prey to vanity."

And he answered me: "Now think, and reflect whether it is really possible for you to have vain thoughts because of those words."

And I tried it in order to discover whether what had been spoken to me was the truth and whether he who spoke it was the Holy Ghost. And I gazed out upon the vineyards in order to free myself from the spell of the words. But wherever I gazed, I heard his voice: "Look and observe—all this I have created." And I felt unutterable ecstasy. But while I gazed I again became conscious of how much I had sinned in my life, and I saw within myself nothing but sin and inadequacy, and I was filled with humility as never before.

—ANGELA OF FOLIGNO

Go to page 1182 for your next devotional reading.

manded; they did not see the elders, because they were hiding.

19 When the maids had gone out, the two elders got up and ran to her. 20They said, "Look, the garden doors are shut, and no one can see us. We are burning with desire for you; so give your consent, and lie with us. 21If you refuse, we will testify against you that a young man was with you, and this was why you sent your maids away."

22 Susanna groaned and said, "I am completely trapped. For if I do this, it will mean death for me; if I do not, I cannot escape your hands. 23I choose not to do it; I will fall into your hands, rather than sin in the sight of the Lord."

24 Then Susanna cried out with a loud voice, and the two elders shouted against her. 25And one of them ran and opened the garden doors. 26When the people in the house heard the shouting in the garden, they rushed in at the side door to see what had happened to her. 27And when the elders told their story, the servants felt very much ashamed, for nothing like this had ever been said about Susanna.

The Elders Testify against Susanna

28 The next day, when the people gathered at the house of her husband Joakim, the two elders came, full of their wicked plot to have Susanna put to death. In the presence of the people they said, 29"Send for Susanna daughter of Hilkiah, the wife of Joakim." So they sent for her. 30And she came with her parents, her children, and all her relatives.

31 Now Susanna was a woman of great refinement and beautiful in appearance. 32As she was veiled, the scoundrels ordered her to be unveiled, so that they might feast their eyes on her beauty. 33Those who were with her and all who saw her were weeping.

34 Then the two elders stood up before the people and laid their hands on her head. 35Through her tears she looked up toward Heaven, for her heart trusted in the Lord. 36The elders said, "While we were walking in the garden alone, this woman came in with two maids, shut the garden doors, and dismissed the maids. 37Then a young man, who was hiding there, came to her and lay with her. 38We were in a corner of the garden, and when we saw this wickedness we ran to them. 39Although we saw them embracing, we

could not hold the man, because he was stronger than we, and he opened the doors and got away. 40We did, however, seize this woman and asked who the young man was, 41but she would not tell us. These things we testify."

Because they were elders of the people and judges, the assembly believed them and condemned her to death.

42 Then Susanna cried out with a loud voice, and said, "O eternal God, you know what is secret and are aware of all things before they come to be; 43you know that these men have given false evidence against me. And now I am to die, though I have done none of the wicked things that they have charged against me!"

44 The Lord heard her cry. 45Just as she was being led off to execution, God stirred up the holy spirit of a young lad named Daniel, 46and he shouted with a loud voice, "I want no part in shedding this woman's blood!"

Daniel Rescues Susanna

47 All the people turned to him and asked, "What is this you are saying?" 48Taking his stand among them he said, "Are you such fools, O Israelites, as to condemn a daughter of Israel without examination and without learning the facts? 49Return to court, for these men have given false evidence against her."

50 So all the people hurried back. And the rest of the*l* elders said to him, "Come, sit among us and inform us, for God has given you the standing of an elder." 51Daniel said to them, "Separate them far from each other, and I will examine them."

52 When they were separated from each other, he summoned one of them and said to him, "You old relic of wicked days, your sins have now come home, which you have committed in the past, 53pronouncing unjust judgments, condemning the innocent and acquitting the guilty, though the Lord said, 'You shall not put an innocent and righteous person to death.' 54Now then, if you really saw this woman, tell me this: Under what tree did you see them being intimate with each other?" He answered, "Under a mastic tree."*m* 55And Daniel said, "Very well!

l Gk lacks *rest of the*   *m* The Greek words for *mastic tree* and *cut* are similar, thus forming an ironic wordplay

This lie has cost you your head, for the angel of God has received the sentence from God and will immediately cut[n] you in two."

56 Then, putting him to one side, he ordered them to bring the other. And he said to him, "You offspring of Canaan and not of Judah, beauty has beguiled you and lust has perverted your heart. 57This is how you have been treating the daughters of Israel, and they were intimate with you through fear; but a daughter of Judah would not tolerate your wickedness. 58Now then, tell me: Under what tree did you catch them being intimate with each other?" He answered, "Under an evergreen oak."[o] 59Daniel said to him, "Very well! This lie has cost you also your head, for the angel of God is waiting with his sword to split[o] you in two, so as to destroy you both."

60 Then the whole assembly raised a great shout and blessed God, who saves those who hope in him. 61And they took action against the two elders, because out of their own mouths Daniel had convicted them of bearing false witness; they did to them as they had wickedly planned to do to their neighbor. 62Acting in accordance with the law of Moses, they put them to death. Thus innocent blood was spared that day.

63 Hilkiah and his wife praised God for their daughter Susanna, and so did her husband Joakim and all her relatives, because she was found innocent of a shameful deed. 64And from that day onward Daniel had a great reputation among the people.

Daniel and the Priests of Bel

14 When King Astyages was laid to rest with his ancestors, Cyrus the Persian succeeded to his kingdom. 2Daniel was a companion of the king, and was the most honored of all his Friends.

3 Now the Babylonians had an idol called Bel, and every day they provided for it twelve bushels of choice flour and forty sheep and six measures[p] of wine. 4The king revered it and went every day to worship it. But Daniel worshiped his own God.

So the king said to him, "Why do you not worship Bel?" 5He answered, "Because I do not revere idols made with hands, but the living God, who created heaven and earth and has dominion over all living creatures."

6 The king said to him, "Do you not think that Bel is a living god? Do you not see how much he eats and drinks every day?" 7And Daniel laughed, and said, "Do not be deceived, O king, for this thing is only clay inside and bronze outside, and it never ate or drank anything."

8 Then the king was angry and called the priests of Bel[q] and said to them, "If you do not tell me who is eating these provisions, you shall die. 9But if you prove that Bel is eating them, Daniel shall die, because he has spoken blasphemy against Bel." Daniel said to the king, "Let it be done as you have said."

10 Now there were seventy priests of Bel, besides their wives and children. So the king went with Daniel into the temple of Bel. 11The priests of Bel said, "See, we are now going outside; you yourself, O king, set out the food and prepare the wine, and shut the door and seal it with your signet. 12When you return in the morning, if you do not find that Bel has eaten it all, we will die; otherwise Daniel will, who is telling lies about us." 13They were unconcerned, for beneath the table they had made a hidden entrance, through which they used to go in regularly and consume the provisions. 14After they had gone out, the king set out the food for Bel. Then Daniel ordered his servants to bring ashes, and they scattered them throughout the whole temple in the presence of the king alone. Then they went out, shut the door and sealed it with the king's signet, and departed. 15During the night the priests came as usual, with their wives and children, and they ate and drank everything.

16 Early in the morning the king rose and came, and Daniel with him. 17The king said, "Are the seals unbroken, Daniel?" He answered, "They are unbroken, O king." 18As soon as the doors were opened, the king looked at the table, and shouted in a loud voice, "You are great, O Bel, and in you there is no deceit at all!"

---

[n] The Greek words for *mastic tree* and *cut* are similar, thus forming an ironic wordplay   [o] The Greek words for *evergreen oak* and *split* are similar, thus forming an ironic wordplay   [p] A little more than fifty gallons   [q] Gk *his priests*

19 But Daniel laughed and restrained the king from going in. "Look at the floor," he said, "and notice whose footprints these are." 20The king said, "I see the footprints of men and women and children."

21 Then the king was enraged, and he arrested the priests and their wives and children. They showed him the secret doors through which they used to enter to consume what was on the table. 22Therefore the king put them to death, and gave Bel over to Daniel, who destroyed it and its temple.

Daniel Kills the Dragon

23 Now in that place*r* there was a great dragon, which the Babylonians revered. 24The king said to Daniel, "You cannot deny that this is a living god; so worship him." 25Daniel said, "I worship the Lord my God, for he is the living God. 26But give me permission, O king, and I will kill the dragon without sword or club." The king said, "I give you permission."

27 Then Daniel took pitch, fat, and hair, and boiled them together and made cakes, which he fed to the dragon. The dragon ate them, and burst open. Then Daniel said, "See what you have been worshiping!"

28 When the Babylonians heard about it, they were very indignant and conspired against the king, saying, "The king has become a Jew; he has destroyed Bel, and killed the dragon, and slaughtered the priests." 29Going to the king, they said, "Hand Daniel over to us, or else we will kill you and your household." 30The king saw that they were pressing him hard, and under compulsion he handed Daniel over to them.

Daniel in the Lions' Den

31 They threw Daniel into the lions' den, and he was there for six days. 32There were seven lions in the den, and every day they had been given two human bodies and two sheep; but now they were given nothing, so that they would devour Daniel.

33 Now the prophet Habakkuk was in Judea; he had made a stew and had broken bread into a bowl, and was going into the field to take it to the reapers. 34But the angel of the Lord said to Habakkuk, "Take the food that you have to Babylon, to Daniel, in the lions' den." 35Habakkuk said, "Sir, I have never seen Babylon, and I know nothing about the den." 36Then the angel of the Lord took him by the crown of his head and carried him by his hair; with the speed of the wind*s* he set him down in Babylon, right over the den.

37 Then Habakkuk shouted, "Daniel, Daniel! Take the food that God has sent you." 38Daniel said, "You have remembered me, O God, and have not forsaken those who love you." 39So Daniel got up and ate. And the angel of God immediately returned Habakkuk to his own place.

40 On the seventh day the king came to mourn for Daniel. When he came to the den he looked in, and there sat Daniel! 41The king shouted with a loud voice, "You are great, O Lord, the God of Daniel, and there is no other besides you!" 42Then he pulled Daniel*t* out, and threw into the den those who had attempted his destruction, and they were instantly eaten before his eyes.

r Other ancient authorities lack *in that place*
s Or *by the power of his spirit*   *t* Gk *him*

Hosea

Anyone who has trouble reconciling God's love with his judgment
(and that's most of us) should read the book of Hosea. For Hosea shows
us the other side of the equation. Instead of focusing on how terribly
the people suffered for their sinfulness, Hosea looks at how terribly
God suffered. It is a poignant love story, one between a prophet and a
prostitute, one between God and his people.

Hosea lived in the northern kingdom of Israel and exercised his
prophetic ministry from about 745 B.C. to 722 B.C., just prior to its destruction by the Assyrians. Remarkably, the book begins with God instructing Hosea to marry a prostitute as a way of emphasizing that
Israel has prostituted itself by faithlessly running after other gods. Just
as God loves his wayward people, Hosea loves Gomer, even though
she betrays him. And just as God is ready to forgive his people, Hosea
forgives Gomer.

Hosea reveals a God who is not wrathful, but broken-hearted. He
shows us that God's punishments stem from his love. We suffer, not
because God is throwing a celestial tantrum as a result of our sin, but
because we need strong medicine, shock treatments to bring us to our
senses and drive us back to him.

Hosea not only reveals an important aspect of God's relationship
with his people, he prefigures Jesus, our divine lover, who gave himself
for us despite our wayward hearts.

1 The word of the LORD that came to
Hosea son of Beeri, in the days of
Kings Uzziah, Jotham, Ahaz, and Hezekiah of Judah, and in the days of King Jeroboam son of Joash of Israel.

The Family of Hosea

2 When the LORD first spoke through
Hosea, the LORD said to Hosea, "Go, take
for yourself a wife of whoredom and have
children of whoredom, for the land commits great whoredom by forsaking the
LORD." ³So he went and took Gomer daughter of Diblaim, and she conceived and
bore him a son.

4 And the LORD said to him, "Name

him Jezreel;*a* for in a little while I will punish the house of Jehu for the blood of Jezreel, and I will put an end to the kingdom of the house of Israel. 5On that day I will break the bow of Israel in the valley of Jezreel."

6 She conceived again and bore a daughter. Then the LORD said to him, "Name her Lo-ruhamah,*b* for I will no longer have pity on the house of Israel or forgive them. 7But I will have pity on the house of Judah, and I will save them by the LORD their God; I will not save them by bow, or by sword, or by war, or by horses, or by horsemen."

8 When she had weaned Lo-ruhamah, she conceived and bore a son. 9Then the LORD said, "Name him Lo-ammi,*c* for you are not my people and I am not your God."*d*

The Restoration of Israel

10*e*Yet the number of the people of Israel shall be like the sand of the sea, which can be neither measured nor numbered; and in the place where it was said to them, "You are not my people," it shall be said to them, "Children of the living God." 11The people of Judah and the people of Israel shall be gathered together, and they shall appoint for themselves one head; and they shall take possession of*f* the land, for great shall be the day of Jezreel.

2 *g*Say to your brother,*h* Ammi,*i* and to your sister,*j* Ruhamah.*k*

Israel's Infidelity, Punishment, and Redemption

2 Plead with your mother, plead—
    for she is not my wife,
    and I am not her husband—
  that she put away her whoring from
      her face,
    and her adultery from between
      her breasts,
3 or I will strip her naked
    and expose her as in the day she
      was born,
  and make her like a wilderness,
    and turn her into a parched land,
    and kill her with thirst.
4 Upon her children also I will
      have no pity,
    because they are children of
      whoredom.
5 For their mother has played
      the whore;

she who conceived them has acted
      shamefully.
  For she said, "I will go after
      my lovers;
    they give me my bread and
      my water,
    my wool and my flax, my oil and
      my drink."
6 Therefore I will hedge up her*l* way
      with thorns;
    and I will build a wall against her,
      so that she cannot find her paths.
7 She shall pursue her lovers,
    but not overtake them;
  and she shall seek them,
    but shall not find them.
  Then she shall say, "I will go
    and return to my first husband,
    for it was better with me then
      than now."
8 She did not know
    that it was I who gave her
    the grain, the wine, and the oil,
  and who lavished upon her silver
    and gold that they used for Baal.
9 Therefore I will take back
    my grain in its time,
    and my wine in its season;
  and I will take away my wool and
      my flax,
    which were to cover her
      nakedness.
10 Now I will uncover her shame
    in the sight of her lovers,
    and no one shall rescue her out of
      my hand.
11 I will put an end to all her mirth,
    her festivals, her new moons, her
      sabbaths,
    and all her appointed festivals.
12 I will lay waste her vines and her fig
      trees,
    of which she said,
  "These are my pay,
    which my lovers have given me."
  I will make them a forest,
    and the wild animals shall devour
      them.
13 I will punish her for the festival days
      of the Baals,
    when she offered incense to them

---

a That is *God sows*   *b* That is *Not pitied*   *c* That is *Not my people*   *d* Heb *I am not yours*   *e* Ch 2.1 in Heb   *f* Heb *rise up from*   *g* Ch 2.3 in Heb   *h* Gk: Heb *brothers*   *i* That is *My people*   *j* Gk Vg: Heb *sisters*   *k* That is *Pitied*   *l* Gk Syr: Heb *your*

and decked herself with her ring and
jewelry,
and went after her lovers,
and forgot me, says the LORD.

14 Therefore, I will now allure her,
and bring her into the wilderness,
and speak tenderly to her.
15 From there I will give her her
vineyards,
and make the Valley of Achor a
door of hope.
There she shall respond as in the
days of her youth,
as at the time when she came out
of the land of Egypt.
16On that day, says the LORD, you will call
me, "My husband," and no longer will you
call me, "My Baal."[m] 17For I will remove

the names of the Baals from her mouth,
and they shall be mentioned by name no
more. 18I will make for you[n] a covenant
on that day with the wild animals, the
birds of the air, and the creeping things of
the ground; and I will abolish[o] the bow,
the sword, and war from the land; and I
will make you lie down in safety. 19And I
will take you for my wife forever; I will
take you for my wife in righteousness and
in justice, in steadfast love, and in mercy.
20I will take you for my wife in faithfulness; and you shall know the LORD.
21 On that day I will answer, says
the LORD,
I will answer the heavens

[m] That is, *"My master"*   [n] Heb *them*   [o] Heb
break

THE TRADITION

Solitude

*I will now allure her, and bring her into
the wilderness, and speak tenderly to her.*

HOSEA 2.14

What the Church means by solitude
is not to be confused with what many self-
help books recommend as antidotes to the
frenzied pace of modern life. "Down time"
and a restorative bubble bath may be legiti-
mate responses to hectic days at work,
school, or on the home front, but they do not
qualify as Christian solitude. Neither does
the privacy evoked by the classic Marlene
Dietrich movie line, "I 'vahnt' to be alone."

Solitude is not for relieving stress or doing our own thing. It is our response to a God
who calls us to seek him by leaving routine,
security, and self-concern behind. In solitude
we give him our full attention.

Ever since God led his chosen people out
of Egypt and into 40 years of wooing and
training, the wilderness has been the classic
image for spiritual solitude. Most of us would
have preferred a friendlier, less forbidding
venue—say, the local coffee shop. But the
wilderness experience cannot occur in cir-

cumstances that offer pleasant distractions
and easy escapes.

Only solitude confronts us inescapably
with what most bothers us—our own masks
and fantasies, sins and weaknesses—and hastens the hard process of dying to self. This is
the most radical heart surgery imaginable, but
it is a honeymoon, too, because God is there.

"Therefore, I will now allure her, and bring
her into the wilderness, and speak tenderly
to her." Every day we must choose whether
or not to accept God's invitation into solitude. Will we create a regular discipline of
time to come away with him? Will we respond whenever he calls us into his presence? Will we build a quiet place within—an
inner wilderness where we can meet him all
day long?

If we accept the discipline of solitude, the
stillness of God's own peace will well up in
us like a river, and we will see our desert begin to bloom.

and they shall answer the earth;
22 and the earth shall answer the grain,
    the wine, and the oil,
    and they shall answer Jezreel; *p*
23   and I will sow him*q* for myself in
      the land.
And I will have pity on
    Lo-ruhamah,*r*
and I will say to Lo-ammi,*s*
    "You are my people";
and he shall say, "You are my
    God."

Further Assurances of God's Redeeming Love

3 The LORD said to me again, "Go, love a woman who has a lover and is an adulteress, just as the LORD loves the people of Israel, though they turn to other gods and love raisin cakes." ²So I bought her for fifteen shekels of silver and a homer of barley and a measure of wine.*t* ³And I said to her, "You must remain as mine for many days; you shall not play the whore, you shall not have intercourse with a man, nor I with you." ⁴For the Israelites shall remain many days without king or prince, without sacrifice or pillar, without ephod or teraphim. ⁵Afterward the Israelites shall return and seek the LORD their God, and David their king; they shall come in awe to the LORD and to his goodness in the latter days.

God Accuses Israel

4 Hear the word of the LORD,
    O people of Israel;
for the LORD has an indictment
    against the inhabitants
    of the land.
There is no faithfulness or loyalty,
    and no knowledge of God in
    the land.
2 Swearing, lying, and murder,
    and stealing and adultery
      break out;
    bloodshed follows bloodshed.
3 Therefore the land mourns,
    and all who live in it languish;
together with the wild animals
    and the birds of the air,
    even the fish of the sea are
      perishing.

4 Yet let no one contend,
    and let none accuse,
for with you is my contention,
    O priest.*u*

5 You shall stumble by day;
    the prophet also shall stumble
      with you by night,
    and I will destroy your mother.
6 My people are destroyed for lack of
      knowledge;
because you have rejected
    knowledge,
I reject you from being a priest
    to me.
And since you have forgotten the
    law of your God,
I also will forget your children.

7 The more they increased,
    the more they sinned against me;
they changed*v* their glory
    into shame.
8 They feed on the sin of my people;
    they are greedy for their iniquity.
9 And it shall be like people,
    like priest;
I will punish them for their ways,
    and repay them for their deeds.
10 They shall eat, but not be satisfied;
    they shall play the whore, but not
      multiply;
because they have forsaken the LORD
    to devote themselves to
      11whoredom.

The Idolatry of Israel

Wine and new wine
    take away the understanding.
12 My people consult a piece of wood,
    and their divining rod gives
      them oracles.
For a spirit of whoredom has led
    them astray,
    and they have played the whore,
      forsaking their God.
13 They sacrifice on the tops of the
      mountains,
    and make offerings upon the hills,
under oak, poplar, and terebinth,
    because their shade is good.

Therefore your daughters play
    the whore,
and your daughters-in-law
    commit adultery.

---

p That is *God sows*   *q* Cn: Heb *her*   *r* That is *Not pitied*   *s* That is *Not my people*   *t* Gk: Heb *a homer of barley and a lethech of barley*   *u* Cn: Meaning of Heb uncertain   *v* Ancient Heb tradition: MT *I will change*

Widow of Zarephath

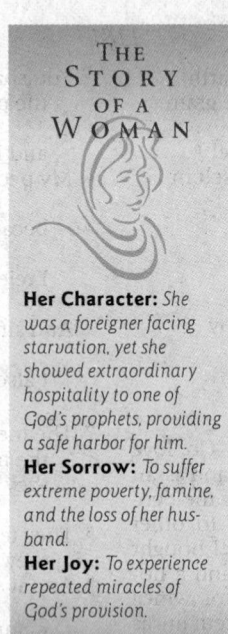

Her Character: *She was a foreigner facing starvation, yet she showed extraordinary hospitality to one of God's prophets, providing a safe harbor for him.*
Her Sorrow: *To suffer extreme poverty, famine, and the loss of her husband.*
Her Joy: *To experience repeated miracles of God's provision.*

Read I Kings 17.8–24

Her arms were spindly and rough, like the dry twigs she had gathered for kindling. She had lived her life a stone's throw from the Mediterranean, at Zarephath, seven miles south of Sidon, in a territory ruled by Jezebel's father. She had always loved the sea, but now its watery abundance only mocked her, reminding her of all she lacked. Every night she hoped for rain, but every morning her depression deepened as she woke to a brilliant sky.

Though she starved herself to feed her child, his distended belly accused her. His need condemned her. She had failed in the most basic ways a mother could, unable to protect and nurture, provide and cherish. These days she stood with shoulders hunched as though to hide her breasts. She had scraped the last bit of flour from the barrel and poured the last drop of oil from the jug.

A stranger had called to her while she gathered sticks for the fire:

"Bring me a little water in a vessel, so that I may drink."

Graciously, she went to fetch it, and then he called after her, "Bring me a morsel of bread in your hand."

Astonished at such a request, she turned on her heel and replied, "As the LORD your God lives, I have nothing baked, only a handful of meal in a jar, and a little oil in a jug; I am now gathering a couple of sticks, so that I may go home and prepare it for myself and my son, that we may eat it, and die" (verse 12).

But the stranger persisted. "Do not be afraid; go and do as you have said; but first make me a little cake of it and bring it to me, and afterwards make something for yourself and your son. For thus says the LORD the God of Israel: The jar of meal will not be emptied and the jug of oil will not fail until the day that the LORD sends rain on the earth" (verses 13–14).

Remarkably, she did exactly as he said, feeding him the food she had reserved for herself and her son.

The woman from Zarephath wasn't an Israelite but a Phoenician. She didn't know the stranger at her door was Elijah, a prophet who had had the gall to inform King Ahab that the drought was God's way of punishing Israel's idolatry. She would have been astonished to learn that Elijah's God had instructed him to "Go now to Zarephath, which belongs to Sidon, and live there; for I have commanded a widow there to feed you" (verse 8).

The widow at Zarephath had felt utterly alone, not knowing that God would provide for her and her child. In truth, she had lacked everything but the one thing she needed—a commodity of the heart called faith. Because of it, her life and her son's life were spared.

Every time she dipped her hand into the flour, every time she poured oil from the jug, she saw another miracle unfold, additional evidence of God's provision. The supply of flour and oil lasted day after day, month after month, never failing until at last the rains came and revived the land. In a time of judgment, God constructed a parable of grace, using a starving woman to display his provision.

Her Legacy of Prayer

"Now I know that you are a man of God, and that the word of the Lord in your mouth is truth."—1 Kings 17.24

Praise God: *For his constant attentiveness.*

Offer Thanks: *For all the ways God has already provided for you and for the ways he will provide in the future.*

Confess: *Any tendency to act as though God really doesn't care about what's happening to you.*

Ask God: *To make you a woman who relies on him daily for her physical, emotional, and spiritual needs.*

Lift Your Heart

Whenever we spin anxious scenarios about the future, we waste precious emotional energy. This kind of worrying represents a negative use of the power of our imagination. As such, it can be a misguided attempt to control the future. But instead of controlling the future, we discover that anxiety soon controls us. Jesus said, "So do not worry about tomorrow, for tomorrow will bring worries of its own. Today's trouble is enough for today" (Matthew 6.34).

Begin to form habits that will help you break the power of worry in your life. Start by thanking God each morning for some small sign of his goodness: a loving friend, a beautiful garden, a child's smile. Gratitude will increase your sense of God's presence in your life. Set aside some time to think about ways God has provided for you in the past. Write them down and make them part of your faith arsenal, so that when you are tempted by anxious thoughts, you can remind yourself of concrete examples of how God has already provided for you.

Father, how easy it is to let anxiety snuff out my gratitude. Help me to linger thankfully in your presence rather than simply rushing on to my next desperate request. Use my weakness and need as a showcase for your strength and provision.

Go to page 1185 for your next devotional reading.

14 I will not punish your daughters
    when they play the whore,
nor your daughters-in-law when
    they commit adultery;
for the men themselves go aside
    with whores,
    and sacrifice with temple
      prostitutes;
thus a people without understanding
    comes to ruin.

15 Though you play the whore,
    O Israel,
    do not let Judah become guilty.
Do not enter into Gilgal,
    or go up to Beth-aven,
    and do not swear, "As the
      LORD lives."
16 Like a stubborn heifer,
    Israel is stubborn;
can the LORD now feed them
    like a lamb in a broad pasture?

17 Ephraim is joined to idols—
    let him alone.
18 When their drinking is ended, they
      indulge in sexual orgies;
they love lewdness more than
    their glory.*w*
19 A wind has wrapped them*x* in
    its wings,
and they shall be ashamed
    because of their altars.*y*

Impending Judgment on Israel and Judah

5 Hear this, O priests!
    Give heed, O house of Israel!
Listen, O house of the king!
    For the judgment pertains to you;
for you have been a snare at
      Mizpah,
    and a net spread upon Tabor,
2 and a pit dug deep in Shittim;*z*
    but I will punish all of them.

3 I know Ephraim,
    and Israel is not hidden from me;
for now, O Ephraim, you have
      played the whore;
    Israel is defiled.
4 Their deeds do not permit them
    to return to their God.
For the spirit of whoredom is within
    them,
and they do not know the LORD.

5 Israel's pride testifies against him;
    Ephraim*a* stumbles in his guilt;

Judah also stumbles with them.
6 With their flocks and herds they
    shall go
to seek the LORD,
but they will not find him;
    he has withdrawn from them.
7 They have dealt faithlessly with the
    LORD;
for they have borne illegitimate
    children.
Now the new moon shall devour
    them along with their fields.

8 Blow the horn in Gibeah,
    the trumpet in Ramah.
Sound the alarm at Beth-aven;
    look behind you, Benjamin!
9 Ephraim shall become a desolation
    in the day of punishment;
among the tribes of Israel
    I declare what is sure.
10 The princes of Judah have become
    like those who remove the
      landmark;
on them I will pour out
    my wrath like water.
11 Ephraim is oppressed, crushed in
      judgment,
because he was determined to go
    after vanity.*b*
12 Therefore I am like maggots to
    Ephraim,
and like rottenness to the house
    of Judah.
13 When Ephraim saw his sickness,
    and Judah his wound,
then Ephraim went to Assyria,
    and sent to the great king.*c*
But he is not able to cure you
    or heal your wound.
14 For I will be like a lion to Ephraim,
    and like a young lion to the
      house of Judah.
I myself will tear and go away;
    I will carry off, and no one
      shall rescue.
15 I will return again to my place
    until they acknowledge their guilt
    and seek my face.

w Cn Compare Gk: Meaning of Heb uncertain
x Heb *her*   *y* Gk Syr: Heb *sacrifices*   *z* Cn:
Meaning of Heb uncertain   *a* Heb *Israel and
Ephraim*   *b* Gk: Meaning of Heb uncertain
c Cn: Heb *to a king who will contend*

In their distress they will beg
    my favor:

A Call to Repentance

6 "Come, let us return to the LORD;
    for it is he who has torn, and he
      will heal us;
  he has struck down, and he will
      bind us up.
² After two days he will revive us;
  on the third day he will raise us up,
    that we may live before him.
³ Let us know, let us press on to know
      the LORD;
  his appearing is as sure as
      the dawn;
  he will come to us like the showers,
    like the spring rains that water the
      earth."

Impenitence of Israel and Judah

⁴ What shall I do with you,
    O Ephraim?
  What shall I do with you,
    O Judah?
  Your love is like a morning cloud,
    like the dew that goes away early.
⁵ Therefore I have hewn them by the
      prophets,
  I have killed them by the words
      of my mouth,
  and my*d* judgment goes forth as
      the light.
⁶ For I desire steadfast love and not
      sacrifice,
  the knowledge of God rather than
      burnt offerings.

d Gk Syr: Heb *your*

MONDAY

Scripture Reading
for Today:
Hosea 6.1–6

Verse for Today:
Hosea 6.6

Jesus Thirsts

"You shall nurse and be carried on her arm, and dandled on her
knees. As a mother comforts her child, so I will comfort you"
(Isaiah 66.12–13).

    Oh, dearest, dearest sister, what is there to do after such
words but stay still and weep with gratitude and love? If people
who are as weak and imperfect as I am only felt what I feel, not
one of them would despair of scaling the summit of the mountain
of love. Jesus does not demand great deeds. All he wants is self-
surrender and gratitude. "I will not accept . . . goats from your
folds. For every wild animal of the forest is mine, the cattle on a
thousand hills. I know all the birds of the air, and all that moves in
the fields is mine. If I were hungry, I would not tell you, for the
world and all that is in it is mine. Do I eat the flesh of bulls, or
drink the blood of goats? *Offer to God a sacrifice of thanksgiving*"
(Psalm 50.9–14).

    That is all Jesus asks from us. He needs nothing from us except
our love. God, who declares he has no need to tell us he is hungry,
does not hesitate to beg a drop of water from the woman of
Samaria. He was thirsty!!! But when he said: "Give me a drink," the
Creator of the universe was asking for the love of the poor thing
he had created. He was thirsty for love! And now more than ever
Jesus thirsts. From the worldly he meets with only ingratitude
and indifference, and even among his disciples there are very few
who surrender fully to the tenderness of his infinite love.

—SAINT THÉRÈSE OF LISIEUX

Go to page 1197 for your next devotional reading.

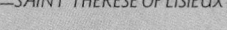

7 But at[e] Adam they transgressed the
covenant;
there they dealt faithlessly
with me.
8 Gilead is a city of evildoers,
tracked with blood.
9 As robbers lie in wait[f] for
someone,
so the priests are banded
together;[g]
they murder on the road to
Shechem,
they commit a monstrous crime.
10 In the house of Israel I have seen a
horrible thing;
Ephraim's whoredom is there,
Israel is defiled.

11 For you also, O Judah, a harvest
is appointed.

When I would restore the fortunes
of my people,
7 1 when I would heal Israel,
the corruption of Ephraim is
revealed,
and the wicked deeds of Samaria;
for they deal falsely,
the thief breaks in,
and the bandits raid outside.
2 But they do not consider
that I remember all their
wickedness.
Now their deeds surround them,
they are before my face.
3 By their wickedness they make the
king glad,
and the officials by their treachery.
4 They are all adulterers;
they are like a heated oven,
whose baker does not need to stir
the fire,
from the kneading of the dough
until it is leavened.
5 On the day of our king the officials
became sick with the heat of
wine;
he stretched out his hand with
mockers.
6 For they are kindled[h] like an oven,
their heart burns
within them;
all night their anger smolders;
in the morning it blazes like a
flaming fire.
7 All of them are hot as an oven,
and they devour their rulers.

All their kings have fallen;
none of them calls upon me.
8 Ephraim mixes himself with
the peoples;
Ephraim is a cake not turned.
9 Foreigners devour his strength,
but he does not know it;
gray hairs are sprinkled upon him,
but he does not know it.
10 Israel's pride testifies against[i] him,
yet they do not return to the LORD
their God,
or seek him, for all this.

Futile Reliance on the Nations

11 Ephraim has become like a dove,
silly and without sense;
they call upon Egypt, they go
to Assyria.
12 As they go, I will cast my net
over them;
I will bring them down like birds
of the air;
I will discipline them according to
the report made to their
assembly.[j]
13 Woe to them, for they have strayed
from me!
Destruction to them, for they have
rebelled against me!
I would redeem them,
but they speak lies against me.

14 They do not cry to me from
the heart,
but they wail upon their beds;
they gash themselves for grain
and wine;
they rebel against me.
15 It was I who trained and
strengthened their arms,
yet they plot evil against me.
16 They turn to that which does not
profit;[f]
they have become like a
defective bow;
their officials shall fall by the sword
because of the rage of their
tongue.
So much for their babbling in the
land of Egypt.

e Cn: Heb *like*   f Cn: Meaning of Heb uncertain
g Syr: Heb *are a company*   h Gk Syr: Heb *brought
near*   i Or *humbles*   j Meaning of Heb
uncertain

Israel's Apostasy

8 Set the trumpet to your lips!
   One like a vulture[k] is over the
      house of the LORD,
because they have broken my
      covenant,
   and transgressed my law.
² Israel cries to me,
   "My God, we—Israel—know you!"
³ Israel has spurned the good;
   the enemy shall pursue him.

⁴ They made kings, but not
      through me;
   they set up princes, but without
      my knowledge.
With their silver and gold they made
      idols
   for their own destruction.
⁵ Your calf is rejected, O Samaria.
   My anger burns against them.
How long will they be incapable of
      innocence?
⁶   For it is from Israel,
an artisan made it;
   it is not God.
The calf of Samaria
   shall be broken to pieces.[l]

⁷ For they sow the wind,
   and they shall reap the whirlwind.
The standing grain has no heads,
   it shall yield no meal;
if it were to yield,
   foreigners would devour it.
⁸ Israel is swallowed up;
   now they are among the nations
      as a useless vessel.
⁹ For they have gone up to Assyria,
   a wild ass wandering alone;
   Ephraim has bargained for lovers.
¹⁰ Though they bargain with
      the nations,
   I will now gather them up.
They shall soon writhe
   under the burden of kings
      and princes.

¹¹ When Ephraim multiplied altars
      to expiate sin,
   they became to him altars for
      sinning.
¹² Though I write for him the
      multitude of my instructions,
   they are regarded as a strange
      thing.
¹³ Though they offer choice sacrifices,[m]

though they eat flesh,
   the LORD does not accept them.
Now he will remember their
      iniquity,
   and punish their sins;
   they shall return to Egypt.
¹⁴ Israel has forgotten his Maker,
      and built palaces;
and Judah has multiplied fortified
      cities;
but I will send a fire upon
      his cities,
   and it shall devour his
      strongholds.

Punishment for Israel's Sin

9 Do not rejoice, O Israel!
   Do not exult[n] as other nations
      do;
for you have played the whore,
   departing from your God.
You have loved a prostitute's pay
   on all threshing floors.
² Threshing floor and wine vat shall
      not feed them,
   and the new wine shall fail them.
³ They shall not remain in the land of
      the LORD;
but Ephraim shall return to Egypt,
   and in Assyria they shall eat
      unclean food.

⁴ They shall not pour drink offerings
      of wine to the LORD,
   and their sacrifices shall not
      please him.
Such sacrifices shall be like
      mourners' bread;
   all who eat of it shall be defiled;
for their bread shall be for their
      hunger only;
   it shall not come to the house of
      the LORD.

⁵ What will you do on the day of
      appointed festival,
   and on the day of the festival of
      the LORD?
⁶ For even if they escape destruction,
   Egypt shall gather them,
   Memphis shall bury them.
Nettles shall possess their precious
      things of silver;[k]
   thorns shall be in their tents.

k Meaning of Heb uncertain   l Or *shall go up in
flames*   m Cn: Meaning of Heb uncertain
n Gk: Heb *To exultation*

7 The days of punishment have come,
     the days of recompense
          have come;
     Israel cries,[o]
  "The prophet is a fool,
     the man of the spirit is mad!"
  Because of your great iniquity,
     your hostility is great.
8 The prophet is a sentinel for my
     God over Ephraim,
  yet a fowler's snare is on all
     his ways,
     and hostility in the house of
          his God.
9 They have deeply corrupted
     themselves
     as in the days of Gibeah;
  he will remember their iniquity,
     he will punish their sins.

10 Like grapes in the wilderness,
     I found Israel.
  Like the first fruit on the fig tree,
     in its first season,
     I saw your ancestors.
  But they came to Baal-peor,
     and consecrated themselves to a
          thing of shame,
     and became detestable like the
          thing they loved.
11 Ephraim's glory shall fly away like a
     bird—
     no birth, no pregnancy, no
          conception!
12 Even if they bring up children,
     I will bereave them until no one
          is left.
  Woe to them indeed
     when I depart from them!
13 Once I saw Ephraim as a young
     palm planted in a lovely
     meadow,[p]
  but now Ephraim must lead out
     his children for slaughter.
14 Give them, O LORD—
     what will you give?
  Give them a miscarrying womb
     and dry breasts.

15 Every evil of theirs began at Gilgal;
     there I came to hate them.
  Because of the wickedness of
     their deeds
  I will drive them out of my
     house.
  I will love them no more;
     all their officials are rebels.

16 Ephraim is stricken,
     their root is dried up,
     they shall bear no fruit.
  Even though they give birth,
     I will kill the cherished offspring
          of their womb.
17 Because they have not listened
     to him,
     my God will reject them;
  they shall become wanderers
     among the nations.

Israel's Sin and Captivity

10 Israel is a luxuriant vine
     that yields its fruit.
  The more his fruit increased
     the more altars he built;
  as his country improved,
     he improved his pillars.
2 Their heart is false;
     now they must bear their
          guilt.
  The LORD[q] will break down
     their altars,
     and destroy their pillars.

3 For now they will say:
     "We have no king,
  for we do not fear the LORD,
     and a king—what could he do
          for us?"
4 They utter mere words;
     with empty oaths they make
          covenants;
  so litigation springs up like
     poisonous weeds
     in the furrows of the field.
5 The inhabitants of Samaria tremble
     for the calf[r] of Beth-aven.
  Its people shall mourn for it,
     and its idolatrous priests shall
          wail[s] over it,
     over its glory that has departed
          from it.
6 The thing itself shall be carried to
     Assyria
     as tribute to the great king.[t]
  Ephraim shall be put to shame,
     and Israel shall be ashamed of his
          idol.[u]

o Cn Compare Gk: Heb *shall know*   p Meaning
of Heb uncertain   q Heb *he*   r Gk Syr: Heb
calves   s Cn: Heb *exult*   t Cn: Heb *to a king
who will contend*   u Cn: Heb *counsel*

7 Samaria's king shall perish
  like a chip on the face of
    the waters.
8 The high places of Aven, the sin
    of Israel,
  shall be destroyed.
Thorn and thistle shall grow up
  on their altars.
They shall say to the mountains,
  Cover us,
and to the hills, Fall on us.

9 Since the days of Gibeah you have
    sinned, O Israel;
  there they have continued.
  Shall not war overtake them in
    Gibeah?
10 I will come[v] against the wayward
    people to punish them;
  and nations shall be gathered
    against them
  when they are punished[w] for
    their double iniquity.

11 Ephraim was a trained heifer
    that loved to thresh,
  and I spared her fair neck;
but I will make Ephraim break the
    ground;
  Judah must plow;
  Jacob must harrow for himself.
12 Sow for yourselves righteousness;
    reap steadfast love;
  break up your fallow ground;
for it is time to seek the LORD,
  that he may come and rain
    righteousness upon you.

13 You have plowed wickedness,
  you have reaped injustice,
  you have eaten the fruit of lies.
Because you have trusted in
    your power
  and in the multitude of your
    warriors,
14 therefore the tumult of war shall rise
    against your people,
  and all your fortresses shall
    be destroyed,
  as Shalman destroyed Beth-arbel on
    the day of battle
  when mothers were dashed in
    pieces with their children.
15 Thus it shall be done to you,
    O Bethel,
  because of your great wickedness.
At dawn the king of Israel
  shall be utterly cut off.

God's Compassion Despite Israel's Ingratitude

11 When Israel was a child, I loved
    him,
  and out of Egypt I called my son.
2 The more I[x] called them,
    the more they went from me;[y]
  they kept sacrificing to the Baals,
    and offering incense to idols.

3 Yet it was I who taught Ephraim to
    walk,
  I took them up in my[z] arms;
  but they did not know that I
    healed them.
4 I led them with cords of human
    kindness,
  with bands of love.
I was to them like those
  who lift infants to their cheeks.[a]
  I bent down to them and
    fed them.

5 They shall return to the land of
    Egypt,
  and Assyria shall be their king,
  because they have refused to
    return to me.
6 The sword rages in their cities,
  it consumes their oracle-priests,
  and devours because of their
    schemes.
7 My people are bent on turning away
    from me.
  To the Most High they call,
  but he does not raise them up
    at all.[b]

8 How can I give you up, Ephraim?
  How can I hand you over,
    O Israel?
How can I make you like Admah?
  How can I treat you like Zeboiim?
My heart recoils within me;
  my compassion grows warm
    and tender.
9 I will not execute my fierce anger;
  I will not again destroy Ephraim;
for I am God and no mortal,
  the Holy One in your midst,
  and I will not come in wrath.[b]

10 They shall go after the LORD,

---

v Cn Compare Gk: Heb *In my desire*   *w* Gk: Heb
bound   *x* Gk: Heb *they*   *y* Gk: Heb *them*   *z* Gk
Syr Vg: Heb *his*   *a* Or *who ease the yoke on their*
jaws   *b* Meaning of Heb uncertain

who roars like a lion;
when he roars,
  his children shall come trembling
    from the west.
11 They shall come trembling like birds
    from Egypt,
  and like doves from the land of
    Assyria;
  and I will return them to their
    homes, says the LORD.

12c Ephraim has surrounded me
    with lies,
  and the house of Israel with
    deceit;
  but Judah still walksd with God,
    and is faithful to the Holy One.

12

Ephraim herds the wind,
  and pursues the east wind all
    day long;
  they multiply falsehood and
    violence;
  they make a treaty with Assyria,
    and oil is carried to Egypt.

The Long History of Rebellion

2 The LORD has an indictment against
    Judah,
  and will punish Jacob according
    to his ways,
  and repay him according to
    his deeds.
3 In the womb he tried to supplant
    his brother,
  and in his manhood he strove
    with God.
4 He strove with the angel and
    prevailed,
  he wept and sought his favor;
he met him at Bethel,
  and there he spoke with him.e
5 The LORD the God of hosts,
  the LORD is his name!
6 But as for you, return to your God,
  hold fast to love and justice,
  and wait continually for
    your God.

7 A trader, in whose hands are false
    balances,
  he loves to oppress.
8 Ephraim has said, "Ah, I am rich,
  I have gained wealth for myself;
in all of my gain
  no offense has been found in me
    that would be sin."f
9 I am the LORD your God
  from the land of Egypt;

I will make you live in tents again,
  as in the days of the appointed
    festival.

10 I spoke to the prophets;
  it was I who multiplied visions,
  and through the prophets I will
    bring destruction.
11 In Gileadg there is iniquity,
  they shall surely come to nothing.
In Gilgal they sacrifice bulls,
  so their altars shall be like
    stone heaps
  on the furrows of the field.
12 Jacob fled to the land of Aram,
  there Israel served for a wife,
  and for a wife he guarded
    sheep.h
13 By a prophet the LORD brought Israel
    up from Egypt,
  and by a prophet he was guarded.
14 Ephraim has given bitter offense,
  so his Lord will bring his crimes
    down on him
  and pay him back for his insults.

Relentless Judgment on Israel

13

When Ephraim spoke, there was
    trembling;
  he was exalted in Israel;
  but he incurred guilt through Baal
    and died.
2 And now they keep on sinning
  and make a cast image for
    themselves,
idols of silver made according to
  their understanding,
  all of them the work of artisans.
"Sacrifice to these," they say.i
  People are kissing calves!
3 Therefore they shall be like the
    morning mist
  or like the dew that goes
    away early,
like chaff that swirls from the
    threshing floor
  or like smoke from a window.

4 Yet I have been the LORD your God
    ever since the land of Egypt;
  you know no God but me,
  and besides me there is no savior.

c Ch 12.1 in Heb   d Heb roams or rules   e Gk
Syr: Heb us   f Meaning of Heb uncertain
g Compare Syr: Heb Gilead   h Heb lacks sheep
i Cn Compare Gk: Heb To these they say sacrifices
of people

5 It was I who fed *j* you in the
    wilderness,
  in the land of drought.
6 When I fed *k* them, they were
    satisfied;
  they were satisfied, and their heart
    was proud;
  therefore they forgot me.
7 So I will become like a lion to them,
  like a leopard I will lurk beside
    the way.
8 I will fall upon them like a bear
    robbed of her cubs,
  and will tear open the covering
    of their heart;
  there I will devour them like a lion,
  as a wild animal would
    mangle them.

9 I will destroy you, O Israel;
  who can help you? *l*
10 Where now is *m* your king, that he
    may save you?
  Where in all your cities are
    your rulers,
  of whom you said,
    "Give me a king and rulers"?
11 I gave you a king in my anger,
  and I took him away in my wrath.

12 Ephraim's iniquity is bound up;
  his sin is kept in store.
13 The pangs of childbirth come
    for him,
  but he is an unwise son;
  for at the proper time he does not
    present himself
    at the mouth of the womb.

14 Shall I ransom them from the power
    of Sheol?
  Shall I redeem them from Death?
  O Death, where are *n* your plagues?
  O Sheol, where is *n* your
    destruction?
  Compassion is hidden from
    my eyes.

15 Although he may flourish among
    rushes, *o*
  the east wind shall come, a blast
    from the LORD,
  rising from the wilderness;
  and his fountain shall dry up,
  his spring shall be parched.
  It shall strip his treasury
    of every precious thing.
16 *p* Samaria shall bear her guilt,

because she has rebelled against
    her God;
they shall fall by the sword,
  their little ones shall be dashed in
    pieces,
  and their pregnant women
    ripped open.

A Plea for Repentance

14 Return, O Israel, to the LORD
    your God,
  for you have stumbled because of
    your iniquity.
2 Take words with you
    and return to the LORD;
  say to him,
    "Take away all guilt;
  accept that which is good,
    and we will offer
    the fruit *q* of our lips.
3 Assyria shall not save us;
    we will not ride upon horses;
  we will say no more, 'Our God,'
    to the work of our hands.
  In you the orphan finds mercy."

Assurance of Forgiveness

4 I will heal their disloyalty;
  I will love them freely,
    for my anger has turned
    from them.
5 I will be like the dew to Israel;
  he shall blossom like the lily,
  he shall strike root like the forests
    of Lebanon. *r*
6 His shoots shall spread out;
  his beauty shall be like the
    olive tree,
  and his fragrance like that of
    Lebanon.
7 They shall again live beneath
    my *s* shadow,
  they shall flourish as a garden; *t*
  they shall blossom like the vine,
  their fragrance shall be like the
    wine of Lebanon.

8 O Ephraim, what have I *u* to do
    with idols?
  It is I who answer and look
    after you. *v*

j Gk Syr: Heb *knew*   *k* Cn: Heb *according to their
pasture*   *l* Gk Syr: Heb *for in me is your help*
m Gk Syr Vg: Heb *I will be*   *n* Gk Syr: Heb *I will
be*   *o* Or *among brothers*   *p* Ch 14.1 in Heb
q Gk Syr: Heb *bulls*   *r* Cn: Heb *like Lebanon*
s Heb *his*   *t* Cn: Heb *they shall grow grain*   *u* Or
What more has Ephraim   *v* Heb *him*

I am like an evergreen cypress;
  your faithfulness[w] comes
    from me.
9 Those who are wise understand
  these things;
  those who are discerning
    know them.

For the ways of the LORD are right,
  and the upright walk in them,
  but transgressors stumble in
    them.

w Heb *your fruit*

Joel

Little is known about the prophet Joel except that he prophesied in Judah. Estimates regarding the dates of his prophetic activity vary widely, from the ninth to the fourth century B.C., though most Catholic scholars date the book from about 400 B.C.

Joel begins by describing a plague of locusts that devour everything in sight. He calls the people to fast and weep for their sins, lest a greater punishment overtake them on the "day of the LORD," a time of judgment in which God finally punishes the wicked and rewards the faithful.

When Jesus' disciples were filled with the Holy Spirit on Pentecost and began speaking in foreign tongues, Peter addressed the astonished crowd, reminding them of a passage from Joel: "I will pour out my spirit on all flesh; your sons and your daughters shall prophesy, your old men shall dream dreams, and your young men shall see visions. Even on the male and female slaves, in those days, I will pour out my spirit" (2.28–29).

One of the shortest books in the Old Testament, Joel's words have left a lasting imprint. They encourage us to entrust ourselves to God "for he is gracious and merciful, slow to anger, and abounding in steadfast love" (2.13).

---

1 The word of the LORD that came to Joel son of Pethuel:

Lament over the Ruin of the Country

2 Hear this, O elders,
　　give ear, all inhabitants of
　　　　the land!
Has such a thing happened in
　　your days,
　　　　or in the days of your ancestors?
3 Tell your children of it,
　　and let your children tell their
　　　　children,
and their children another
　　generation.

4 What the cutting locust left,
　　the swarming locust has eaten.
What the swarming locust left,
　　the hopping locust has eaten,
and what the hopping locust left,
　　the destroying locust has eaten.

5 Wake up, you drunkards, and weep;
　　and wail, all you wine-drinkers,
over the sweet wine,

for it is cut off from your mouth.
6 For a nation has invaded my land,
    powerful and innumerable;
its teeth are lions' teeth,
    and it has the fangs of a lioness.
7 It has laid waste my vines,
    and splintered my fig trees;
it has stripped off their bark and
      thrown it down;
    their branches have turned white.

8 Lament like a virgin dressed in
      sackcloth
    for the husband of her youth.
9 The grain offering and the drink
      offering are cut off
    from the house of the LORD.
The priests mourn,
    the ministers of the LORD.
10 The fields are devastated,
    the ground mourns;
for the grain is destroyed,
    the wine dries up,
    the oil fails.

11 Be dismayed, you farmers,
    wail, you vinedressers,
over the wheat and the barley;
    for the crops of the field
      are ruined.
12 The vine withers,
    the fig tree droops.
Pomegranate, palm, and apple—
    all the trees of the field are
      dried up;
surely, joy withers away
    among the people.

A Call to Repentance and Prayer

13 Put on sackcloth and lament,
    you priests;
    wail, you ministers of the altar.
Come, pass the night in sackcloth,
    you ministers of my God!
Grain offering and drink offering
    are withheld from the house of
      your God.

14 Sanctify a fast,
    call a solemn assembly.
Gather the elders
    and all the inhabitants of the land
to the house of the LORD your God,
    and cry out to the LORD.

15 Alas for the day!
For the day of the LORD is near,

and as destruction from the
    Almighty[a] it comes.
16 Is not the food cut off
    before our eyes,
joy and gladness
    from the house of our God?

17 The seed shrivels under the clods,[b]
    the storehouses are desolate;
the granaries are ruined
    because the grain has failed.
18 How the animals groan!
    The herds of cattle wander about
because there is no pasture for them;
    even the flocks of sheep are
      dazed.[c]

19 To you, O LORD, I cry.
For fire has devoured
    the pastures of the wilderness,
and flames have burned
    all the trees of the field.
20 Even the wild animals cry to you
    because the watercourses are dried
      up,
and fire has devoured
    the pastures of the wilderness.

2 Blow the trumpet in Zion;
    sound the alarm on my holy
      mountain!
Let all the inhabitants of the land
      tremble,
    for the day of the LORD is coming,
      it is near—
2 a day of darkness and gloom,
    a day of clouds and thick
      darkness!
Like blackness spread upon the
      mountains
    a great and powerful army comes;
their like has never been from
      of old,
    nor will be again after them
    in ages to come.

3 Fire devours in front of them,
    and behind them a flame burns.
Before them the land is like the
      garden of Eden,
    but after them a desolate
      wilderness,
    and nothing escapes them.

[a] Traditional rendering of Heb *Shaddai*
[b] Meaning of Heb uncertain   [c] Compare Gk Syr
Vg: Meaning of Heb uncertain

⁴ They have the appearance of horses,
   and like war-horses they charge.
⁵ As with the rumbling of chariots,
   they leap on the tops of the
     mountains,
   like the crackling of a flame of fire
     devouring the stubble,
   like a powerful army
     drawn up for battle.

⁶ Before them peoples are in anguish,
   all faces grow pale.ᵈ
⁷ Like warriors they charge,
   like soldiers they scale the wall.
   Each keeps to its own course,
     they do not swerve fromᵉ
       their paths.
⁸ They do not jostle one another,
   each keeps to its own track;
   they burst through the weapons
     and are not halted.
⁹ They leap upon the city,
   they run upon the walls;
   they climb up into the houses,
     they enter through the windows
       like a thief.

¹⁰ The earth quakes before them,
   the heavens tremble.
   The sun and the moon are
     darkened,
     and the stars withdraw their
       shining.
¹¹ The LORD utters his voice
   at the head of his army;
   how vast is his host!
     Numberless are those who obey
       his command.
   Truly the day of the LORD is great;
     terrible indeed—who can
       endure it?

¹² Yet even now, says the LORD,
   return to me with all your heart,
   with fasting, with weeping, and with
     mourning;
¹³   rend your hearts and not
       your clothing.
   Return to the LORD, your God,
     for he is gracious and merciful,
   slow to anger, and abounding in
     steadfast love,
     and relents from punishing.
¹⁴ Who knows whether he will not
     turn and relent,
     and leave a blessing behind him,
   a grain offering and a drink offering
     for the LORD, your God?

¹⁵ Blow the trumpet in Zion;
     sanctify a fast;
   call a solemn assembly;
¹⁶   gather the people.
   Sanctify the congregation;
     assemble the aged;
   gather the children,
     even infants at the breast.
   Let the bridegroom leave his room,
     and the bride her canopy.

¹⁷ Between the vestibule and the altar
     let the priests, the ministers of the
       LORD, weep.
   Let them say, "Spare your people,
       O LORD,
     and do not make your heritage a
       mockery,
   a byword among the nations.
   Why should it be said among the
       peoples,
   'Where is their God?' "

God's Response and Promise

¹⁸ Then the LORD became jealous for
       his land,
     and had pity on his people.
¹⁹ In response to his people the
       LORD said:
   I am sending you
     grain, wine, and oil,
     and you will be satisfied;
   and I will no more make you
     a mockery among the nations.

²⁰ I will remove the northern army far
       from you,
     and drive it into a parched and
       desolate land,
   its front into the eastern sea,
     and its rear into the western sea;
   its stench and foul smell will
       rise up.
     Surely he has done great things!

²¹ Do not fear, O soil;
     be glad and rejoice,
     for the LORD has done great
       things!
²² Do not fear, you animals of
       the field,
     for the pastures of the wilderness
       are green;
   the tree bears its fruit,

ᵈ Meaning of Heb uncertain   ᵉ Gk Syr Vg: Heb
they do not take a pledge along

the fig tree and vine give their full
yield.

23 O children of Zion, be glad
and rejoice in the LORD your God;
for he has given the early rain *f* for
your vindication,
he has poured down for you
abundant rain,
the early and the later rain,
as before.
24 The threshing floors shall be full
of grain,
the vats shall overflow with wine
and oil.

25 I will repay you for the years

that the swarming locust has eaten,
the hopper, the destroyer, and the
cutter,
my great army, which I sent
against you.

26 You shall eat in plenty and be
satisfied,
and praise the name of the LORD
your God,
who has dealt wondrously with
you.
And my people shall never again be
put to shame.
27 You shall know that I am in the
midst of Israel,

f Meaning of Heb uncertain

THE TRADITION

Lent

Return to me with all your heart, with fasting,
with weeping, and with mourning.

JOEL 2.12

The question so familiar to Catholics arises surprisingly soon after the Christmas ornaments have been packed away. "What are you giving up for Lent?"

The usual suspects file in for review. Movies . . . a favorite TV program . . . chocolate . . . coffee . . . gossip. Or, if the question is phrased in terms of "doing something" for Lent, daily Mass . . . volunteering . . . acts of kindness . . . spiritual reading.

But every discipline, however commendable, is only as good as the spirit and purpose we bring to it. And so, immediately as Lent begins, the very first reading of the Ash Wednesday liturgy (Joel 2.12–18) presents the right perspective: Repent and return to God as if your very life depended on it.

Our great Lenten model of wholehearted surrender and attention to God is Jesus in the wilderness (see Matthew 4.1–11). His 40 days of prayer, fasting, and resisting temptation were not a temporary discipline or foregoing of a few personal indulgences. It ex-

pressed his total commitment to the Father's will. Though Jesus had no sin to wrestle with, he was tested in his calling. Would he carry out his mission as a servant without seeking comfort, acclaim, and power for himself?

Lent gives us the opportunity to reconsider and recommit ourselves to the high calling that we have received through Baptism, as we prayerfully support the catechumens who are to be baptized on holy Saturday. It is a good time for asking ourselves some pointed questions: Am I doing my best to live as a child of God? Do I reject Satan and all his works? Am I pursuing God's will or self-will? To what particular mission is God calling me?

In Lent we imitate the example of Jesus in the wilderness. With his help, we affirm our allegiance to God. We do battle with whatever threatens our true identity and calling. Maybe we give up candy or coffee, but most of all, we give up our very selves.

and that I, the LORD, am your God
and there is no other.
And my people shall never again be
put to shame.

God's Spirit Poured Out

28g Then afterward
I will pour out my spirit on
all flesh;
your sons and your daughters shall
prophesy,
your old men shall dream dreams,
and your young men shall
see visions.
29 Even on the male and female slaves,
in those days, I will pour out
my spirit.

30 I will show portents in the heavens
and on the earth, blood and fire and columns of smoke. 31The sun shall be turned
to darkness, and the moon to blood, before the great and terrible day of the LORD
comes. 32Then everyone who calls on the
name of the LORD shall be saved; for in

Mount Zion and in Jerusalem there shall
be those who escape, as the LORD has said,
and among the survivors shall be those
whom the LORD calls.

3h For then, in those days and at that
time, when I restore the fortunes of
Judah and Jerusalem, 2I will gather all the
nations and bring them down to the valley of Jehoshaphat, and I will enter into
judgment with them there, on account of
my people and my heritage Israel, because
they have scattered them among the nations. They have divided my land, 3and
cast lots for my people, and traded boys
for prostitutes, and sold girls for wine, and
drunk it down.

4 What are you to me, O Tyre and Sidon, and all the regions of Philistia? Are
you paying me back for something? If you
are paying me back, I will turn your deeds
back upon your own heads swiftly and
speedily. 5For you have taken my silver
and my gold, and have carried my rich

g Ch 3.1 in Heb   h Ch 4.1 in Heb

I Will Pour Out My Spirit

Come down upon us,
spirit of God,
spirit of wisdom
and peace and joy;
come as a great wind blowing;
sweep our minds with a storm of light.
Be in us as bright fire burning;
forge our wills to shining swords
in the flame.
Purify our hearts
in the crucible
of the fire of love.
Change our tepid nature
into the warm humanity
of Christ,
as He changed water to wine.
Be in us a stream of life,
as wine in the living vine.

—CARYLL HOUSELANDER

TUESDAY

Scripture Reading
for Today:
Joel 2.23–29

Verses for Today:
Joel 2.28–29

Go to page 1204 for your next devotional reading.

treasures into your temples.ⁱ ⁶You have sold the people of Judah and Jerusalem to the Greeks, removing them far from their own border. ⁷But now I will rouse them to leave the places to which you have sold them, and I will turn your deeds back upon your own heads. ⁸I will sell your sons and your daughters into the hand of the people of Judah, and they will sell them to the Sabeans, to a nation far away; for the LORD has spoken.

Judgment in the Valley of Jehoshaphat

⁹ Proclaim this among the nations:
  Prepare war,^j
    stir up the warriors.
  Let all the soldiers draw near,
    let them come up.
¹⁰ Beat your plowshares into swords,
    and your pruning hooks into
      spears;
    let the weakling say, "I am a
      warrior."

¹¹ Come quickly,^k
    all you nations all around,
    gather yourselves there.
  Bring down your warriors, O LORD.
¹² Let the nations rouse themselves,
    and come up to the valley of
      Jehoshaphat;
    for there I will sit to judge
    all the neighboring nations.

¹³ Put in the sickle,
    for the harvest is ripe.
  Go in, tread,
    for the wine press is full.
  The vats overflow,
    for their wickedness is great.

¹⁴ Multitudes, multitudes,
    in the valley of decision!
  For the day of the LORD is near
    in the valley of decision.
¹⁵ The sun and the moon are
      darkened,

and the stars withdraw their
  shining.

¹⁶ The LORD roars from Zion,
    and utters his voice from
      Jerusalem,
    and the heavens and the earth
      shake.
  But the LORD is a refuge for his
      people,
    a stronghold for the people of
      Israel.

The Glorious Future of Judah

¹⁷ So you shall know that I, the LORD
      your God,
    dwell in Zion, my holy mountain.
  And Jerusalem shall be holy,
    and strangers shall never again
      pass through it.

¹⁸ In that day
    the mountains shall drip sweet wine,
    the hills shall flow with milk,
  and all the stream beds of Judah
    shall flow with water;
  a fountain shall come forth from the
      house of the LORD
    and water the Wadi Shittim.

¹⁹ Egypt shall become a desolation
    and Edom a desolate wilderness,
  because of the violence done to the
      people of Judah,
    in whose land they have shed
      innocent blood.
²⁰ But Judah shall be inhabited forever,
    and Jerusalem to all generations.
²¹ I will avenge their blood, and I will
      not clear the guilty,^l
    for the LORD dwells in Zion.

ⁱ Or *palaces*   ^j Heb *sanctify war*   ^k Meaning of
Heb uncertain   ^l Gk Syr: Heb *I will hold innocent
their blood that I have not held innocent*

Amos

No true prophet has ever been accused of having a honey-coated tongue. This is especially true of Amos, one of whose enemies complained to the king of Israel, saying: "Amos has conspired against you in the very center of the house of Israel; the land is not able to bear all his words" (7.10). Ironically, the name *Amos* actually means "burden bearer." Amos had to bear the burden of speaking words that sounded obnoxious in the ears of the Israelites. He spoke about greed, injustice, religious hypocrisy, complacency, and ruin. His words, spoken by a shepherd to a king, would be repeated over and over by the prophets to God's people.

Amos preached in the northern kingdom of Israel around 750 B.C. His warnings were directed to the surrounding nations as well as to the Israelites. But we are mistaken if we think the words in this book are merely of historical significance. Even now, we may recognize ourselves in some of its pages. If so, we can ask God's forgiveness, confidant of his mercy. Amos 9.11–15 contains a promise of God's restoration.

1 The words of Amos, who was among the shepherds of Tekoa, which he saw concerning Israel in the days of King Uzziah of Judah and in the days of King Jeroboam son of Joash of Israel, two years*a* before the earthquake.

Judgment on Israel's Neighbors

²And he said:
The LORD roars from Zion,
   and utters his voice from
      Jerusalem;
the pastures of the shepherds wither,
   and the top of Carmel dries up.

³ Thus says the LORD:
For three transgressions of
   Damascus,
and for four, I will not revoke the
      punishment;*b*
because they have threshed Gilead
   with threshing sledges of iron.
⁴ So I will send a fire on the house
      of Hazael,
   and it shall devour the
      strongholds of Ben-hadad.
⁵ I will break the gate bars of
      Damascus,
   and cut off the inhabitants from
      the Valley of Aven,
and the one who holds the scepter
      from Beth-eden;

a Or *during two years*   *b* Heb *cause it to return*

and the people of Aram shall go
  into exile to Kir,
  says the LORD.

6 Thus says the LORD:
  For three transgressions of Gaza,
    and for four, I will not revoke the
    punishment;[c]
  because they carried into exile entire
    communities,
  to hand them over to Edom.
7 So I will send a fire on the wall
    of Gaza,
  fire that shall devour its
    strongholds.
8 I will cut off the inhabitants from
    Ashdod,
  and the one who holds the scepter
    from Ashkelon;
  I will turn my hand against Ekron,
  and the remnant of the Philistines
    shall perish,
    says the Lord GOD.

9 Thus says the LORD:
  For three transgressions of Tyre,
    and for four, I will not revoke the
    punishment;[c]
  because they delivered entire
    communities over to Edom,
  and did not remember the
    covenant of kinship.
10 So I will send a fire on the wall
    of Tyre,
  fire that shall devour its
    strongholds.

11 Thus says the LORD:
  For three transgressions of Edom,
    and for four, I will not revoke the
    punishment;[c]
  because he pursued his brother with
    the sword
  and cast off all pity;
  he maintained his anger
    perpetually,[d]
  and kept his wrath[e] forever.
12 So I will send a fire on Teman,
  and it shall devour the
    strongholds of Bozrah.

13 Thus says the LORD:
  For three transgressions of the
    Ammonites,
    and for four, I will not revoke the
    punishment;[c]
  because they have ripped open
    pregnant women in Gilead

in order to enlarge their territory.
14 So I will kindle a fire against the
    wall of Rabbah,
  fire that shall devour its
    strongholds,
  with shouting on the day of battle,
  with a storm on the day of the
    whirlwind;
15 then their king shall go into exile,
  he and his officials together,
    says the LORD.

2 Thus says the LORD:
  For three transgressions of Moab,
    and for four, I will not revoke the
    punishment;[c]
  because he burned to lime
    the bones of the king of Edom.
2 So I will send a fire on Moab,
  and it shall devour the
    strongholds of Kerioth,
  and Moab shall die amid uproar,
  amid shouting and the sound of
    the trumpet;
3 I will cut off the ruler from its
    midst,
  and will kill all its officials
    with him,
    says the LORD.

Judgment on Judah

4 Thus says the LORD:
  For three transgressions of Judah,
    and for four, I will not revoke the
    punishment;[c]
  because they have rejected the law of
    the LORD,
  and have not kept his statutes,
  but they have been led astray by the
    same lies
  after which their ancestors walked.
5 So I will send a fire on Judah,
  and it shall devour the
    strongholds of Jerusalem.

Judgment on Israel

6 Thus says the LORD:
  For three transgressions of Israel,
    and for four, I will not revoke the
    punishment;[c]
  because they sell the righteous
    for silver,
  and the needy for a pair of
    sandals—

---

[c] Heb *cause it to return* [d] Syr Vg: Heb *and his
anger tore perpetually* [e] Gk Syr Vg: Heb *and his
wrath kept*

7 they who trample the head of the
     poor into the dust of
     the earth,
  and push the afflicted out of
     the way;
father and son go in to the
     same girl,
  so that my holy name is profaned;
8 they lay themselves down beside
     every altar
  on garments taken in pledge;
and in the house of their God
     they drink
  wine bought with fines they
     imposed.

9 Yet I destroyed the Amorite
     before them,
  whose height was like the height
     of cedars,
  and who was as strong as oaks;
I destroyed his fruit above,
  and his roots beneath.
10 Also I brought you up out of the
     land of Egypt,
  and led you forty years in
     the wilderness,
  to possess the land of the
     Amorite.
11 And I raised up some of your
     children to be prophets
  and some of your youths to be
     nazirites. *f*
  Is it not indeed so, O people
     of Israel?
          says the LORD.

12 But you made the nazirites *f*
     drink wine,
  and commanded the prophets,
     saying, "You shall not prophesy."

13 So, I will press you down in
     your place,
  just as a cart presses down
     when it is full of sheaves. *g*
14 Flight shall perish from the swift,
     and the strong shall not retain
     their strength,
  nor shall the mighty save
     their lives;
15 those who handle the bow shall
     not stand,
  and those who are swift of foot
     shall not save themselves,
  nor shall those who ride horses
     save their lives;

16 and those who are stout of heart
     among the mighty
  shall flee away naked in that day,
          says the LORD.

Israel's Guilt and Punishment

3 Hear this word that the LORD has spoken against you, O people of Israel,
against the whole family that I brought up
out of the land of Egypt:
2 You only have I known
     of all the families of the earth;
  therefore I will punish you
     for all your iniquities.

3 Do two walk together
     unless they have made an
     appointment?
4 Does a lion roar in the forest,
     when it has no prey?
  Does a young lion cry out from
     its den,
     if it has caught nothing?
5 Does a bird fall into a snare on
     the earth,
  when there is no trap for it?
  Does a snare spring up from
     the ground,
     when it has taken nothing?
6 Is a trumpet blown in a city,
     and the people are not afraid?
  Does disaster befall a city,
     unless the LORD has done it?
7 Surely the Lord GOD does nothing,
     without revealing his secret
     to his servants the prophets.
8 The lion has roared;
     who will not fear?
  The Lord GOD has spoken;
     who can but prophesy?

9 Proclaim to the strongholds
     in Ashdod,
  and to the strongholds in the land
     of Egypt,
  and say, "Assemble yourselves on
     Mount*h* Samaria,
  and see what great tumults are
     within it,
  and what oppressions are in
     its midst."
10 They do not know how to do right,
     says the LORD,

f That is, *those separated* or *those consecrated*
g Meaning of Heb uncertain   *h* Gk Syr: Heb *the*
mountains of

those who store up violence and
robbery in their strongholds.
11 Therefore thus says the Lord GOD:
An adversary shall surround
the land,
and strip you of your defense;
and your strongholds shall be
plundered.

12 Thus says the LORD: As the shepherd rescues from the mouth of the lion two legs, or a piece of an ear, so shall the people of Israel who live in Samaria be rescued, with the corner of a couch and part[i] of a bed.

13 Hear, and testify against the house
of Jacob,
says the Lord GOD, the God
of hosts:
14 On the day I punish Israel for its
transgressions,
I will punish the altars of Bethel,
and the horns of the altar shall
be cut off
and fall to the ground.
15 I will tear down the winter house as
well as the summer house;
and the houses of ivory shall
perish,
and the great houses[j] shall come to
an end,
says the LORD.

4 Hear this word, you cows of Bashan
who are on Mount Samaria,
who oppress the poor, who crush
the needy,
who say to their husbands, "Bring
something to drink!"
2 The Lord GOD has sworn by
his holiness:
The time is surely coming
upon you,
when they shall take you away with
hooks,
even the last of you with
fishhooks.
3 Through breaches in the wall you
shall leave,
each one straight ahead;
and you shall be flung out into
Harmon,[i]
says the LORD.
4 Come to Bethel—and transgress;
to Gilgal—and multiply
transgression;
bring your sacrifices every morning,

your tithes every three days;
5 bring a thank offering of leavened
bread,
and proclaim freewill offerings,
publish them;
for so you love to do, O people
of Israel!
says the Lord GOD.

Israel Rejects Correction

6 I gave you cleanness of teeth in all
your cities,
and lack of bread in all your
places,
yet you did not return to me,
says the LORD.

7 And I also withheld the rain
from you
when there were still three
months to the harvest;
I would send rain on one city,
and send no rain on another city;
one field would be rained upon,
and the field on which it did not
rain withered;
8 so two or three towns wandered
to one town
to drink water, and were not
satisfied;
yet you did not return to me,
says the LORD.

9 I struck you with blight and mildew;
I laid waste[k] your gardens and
your vineyards;
the locust devoured your fig trees
and your olive trees;
yet you did not return to me,
says the LORD.

10 I sent among you a pestilence after
the manner of Egypt;
I killed your young men with
the sword;
I carried away your horses;[l]
and I made the stench of your
camp go up into your
nostrils;
yet you did not return to me,
says the LORD.

11 I overthrew some of you,

---

i Meaning of Heb uncertain   j Or *many houses*
k Cn: Heb *the multitude of*   l Heb *with the
captivity of your horses*

as when God overthrew Sodom
and Gomorrah,
and you were like a brand
snatched from the fire;
yet you did not return to me,
         says the LORD.

12 Therefore thus I will do to you,
O Israel;
because I will do this to you,
prepare to meet your God,
O Israel!

13 For lo, the one who forms the
mountains, creates the wind,
reveals his thoughts to mortals,
makes the morning darkness,
and treads on the heights of
the earth—
the LORD, the God of hosts, is
his name!

A Lament for Israel's Sin

5 Hear this word that I take up over
you in lamentation, O house of Israel:
2 Fallen, no more to rise,
is maiden Israel;
forsaken on her land,
with no one to raise her up.

3 For thus says the Lord GOD:
The city that marched out
a thousand
shall have a hundred left,
and that which marched out
a hundred
shall have ten left.*m*

4 For thus says the LORD to the house
of Israel:
Seek me and live;
5 but do not seek Bethel,
and do not enter into Gilgal
or cross over to Beer-sheba;
for Gilgal shall surely go into exile,
and Bethel shall come to nothing.

6 Seek the LORD and live,
or he will break out against the
house of Joseph like fire,
and it will devour Bethel, with no
one to quench it.
7 Ah, you that turn justice to
wormwood,
and bring righteousness to
the ground!

8 The one who made the Pleiades
and Orion,
and turns deep darkness into
the morning,
and darkens the day into night,
who calls for the waters of the sea,
and pours them out on the
surface of the earth,
the LORD is his name,
9 who makes destruction flash out
against the strong,
so that destruction comes upon
the fortress.

10 They hate the one who reproves
in the gate,
and they abhor the one who
speaks the truth.
11 Therefore because you trample
on the poor
and take from them levies
of grain,
you have built houses of
hewn stone,
but you shall not live in them;
you have planted pleasant vineyards,
but you shall not drink their wine.
12 For I know how many are your
transgressions,
and how great are your sins—
you who afflict the righteous, who
take a bribe,
and push aside the needy in
the gate.
13 Therefore the prudent will keep
silent in such a time;
for it is an evil time.

14 Seek good and not evil,
that you may live;
and so the LORD, the God of hosts,
will be with you,
just as you have said.
15 Hate evil and love good,
and establish justice in the gate;
it may be that the LORD, the God
of hosts,
will be gracious to the remnant of
Joseph.

16 Therefore thus says the LORD, the
God of hosts, the Lord:
In all the squares there shall be
wailing;
and in all the streets they shall
say, "Alas! alas!"

---

m Heb adds to the house of Israel

They shall call the farmers to
       mourning,
and those skilled in lamentation,
       to wailing;
17 in all the vineyards there shall
       be wailing,
for I will pass through the midst
       of you,
                          says the LORD.

The Day of the LORD a Dark Day

18 Alas for you who desire the day of
       the LORD!
Why do you want the day of
       the LORD?

It is darkness, not light;
19   as if someone fled from a lion,
       and was met by a bear;
or went into the house and rested a
       hand against the wall,
       and was bitten by a snake.
20 Is not the day of the LORD darkness,
       not light,
       and gloom with no brightness in it?

21 I hate, I despise your festivals,
       and I take no delight in your
       solemn assemblies.
22 Even though you offer me your
       burnt offerings and grain
       offerings,

Small Sacrifices

WEDNESDAY

Scripture Reading
for Today:
Amos 5.7–15

Verse for Today:
Amos 5.15

It is surprising how many otherwise good, devout Catholics are in the same position as the rich young man, or rather worse. For they are normally not asked to sell all they have, but just to give away a little: to make a small sacrifice to relieve a poor family or friend; or perhaps not even that, but just to lend a trifle to someone who is in need of, say, a bed or a table. But though they may have enough and to spare, they are afraid that just this little thing might be required by themselves, and so they refuse. "So sorry, would have loved to help, but it is so difficult to get things replaced these days, and so I'm sure you'll understand . . ." And what can the poor man or woman do but say: "Oh, it's quite all right. I'm sure I'll be able to manage," and retire in confusion.

And how many of us are never reproached by our conscience if we make undue profit from our neighbor's necessity. Alas! Men and women looked upon as very devout are condemned by rent tribunals for exorbitant charges, and themselves think nothing of underpaying their staff if they can find those who work extra cheap—for example, foreigners in need.

Where a personal relationship is involved, the sin against justice is made all the more poignant by the fact that the virtues of fraternal charity and mercy are also violated. Yet in most of these cases the offender will not be conscious of doing anything wrong.

The reason is not far to seek. We live in a pagan society; and though we are Catholics in church, many of us have the same standards in daily life as our pagan neighbors, or even worse ones, for the corruption of the best is worst.

—HILDA GRAEF

Go to page 1210 for your next devotional reading.

I will not accept them;
and the offerings of well-being of
    your fatted animals
    I will not look upon.
23 Take away from me the noise of
    your songs;
    I will not listen to the melody of
    your harps.
24 But let justice roll down like waters,
    and righteousness like an
        ever-flowing stream.

25 Did you bring to me sacrifices and
offerings the forty years in the wilderness,
O house of Israel? 26You shall take up
Sakkuth your king, and Kaiwan your star-
god, your images,*n* which you made for
yourselves; 27therefore I will take you into
exile beyond Damascus, says the Lord,
whose name is the God of hosts.

Complacent Self-Indulgence Will Be Punished

6 Alas for those who are at ease
    in Zion,
  and for those who feel secure on
    Mount Samaria,
the notables of the first of the
    nations,
  to whom the house of Israel
    resorts!
2 Cross over to Calneh, and see;
  from there go to Hamath
    the great;
  then go down to Gath of the
    Philistines.
Are you better*o* than these
    kingdoms?
  Or is your*p* territory greater than
    their*q* territory,
3 O you that put far away the evil day,
  and bring near a reign of
    violence?

4 Alas for those who lie on beds
    of ivory,
  and lounge on their couches,
and eat lambs from the flock,
  and calves from the stall;
5 who sing idle songs to the sound
    of the harp,
  and like David improvise on
    instruments of music;
6 who drink wine from bowls,
  and anoint themselves with the
    finest oils,

but are not grieved over the ruin
    of Joseph!
7 Therefore they shall now be the first
    to go into exile,
  and the revelry of the loungers
    shall pass away.

8 The Lord God has sworn by himself
    (says the Lord, the God of hosts):
I abhor the pride of Jacob
  and hate his strongholds;
  and I will deliver up the city and
    all that is in it.

9 If ten people remain in one house,
they shall die. 10And if a relative, one who
burns the dead,*r* shall take up the body
to bring it out of the house, and shall say
to someone in the innermost parts of the
house, "Is anyone else with you?" the answer will come, "No." Then the relative*s*
shall say, "Hush! We must not mention
the name of the Lord."

11 See, the Lord commands,
  and the great house shall be
    shattered to bits,
  and the little house to pieces.
12 Do horses run on rocks?
  Does one plow the sea with
    oxen?*t*
But you have turned justice
    into poison
  and the fruit of righteousness into
    wormwood—
13 you who rejoice in Lo-debar,*u*
  who say, "Have we not by our
    own strength
    taken Karnaim*v* for ourselves?"
14 Indeed, I am raising up against you
    a nation,
O house of Israel, says the Lord,
    the God of hosts,
and they shall oppress you from
    Lebo-hamath
    to the Wadi Arabah.

Locusts, Fire, and a Plumb Line

7 This is what the Lord God showed
  me: he was forming locusts at the

---

n Heb *your images, your star-god*   *o* Or *Are they
better*   *p* Heb *their*   *q* Heb *your*   *r* Or *who
makes a burning for him*   *s* Heb *he*   *t* Or *Does
one plow them with oxen*   *u* Or *in a thing of
nothingness*   *v* Or *horns*

time the latter growth began to sprout (it was the latter growth after the king's mowings). ²When they had finished eating the grass of the land, I said,

"O Lord God, forgive, I beg you!
How can Jacob stand?
He is so small!"
³ The Lord relented concerning this;
"It shall not be," said the Lord.

4 This is what the Lord God showed me: the Lord God was calling for a shower of fire,ʷ and it devoured the great deep and was eating up the land. ⁵Then I said,

"O Lord God, cease, I beg you!
How can Jacob stand?
He is so small!"
⁶ The Lord relented concerning this;
"This also shall not be," said the
Lord God.

7 This is what he showed me: the Lord was standing beside a wall built with a plumb line, with a plumb line in his hand. ⁸And the Lord said to me, "Amos, what do you see?" And I said, "A plumb line." Then the Lord said,

"See, I am setting a plumb line
in the midst of my people Israel;
I will never again pass them by;
⁹ the high places of Isaac shall be
made desolate,
and the sanctuaries of Israel shall
be laid waste,
and I will rise against the house
of Jeroboam with the sword."

Amaziah Complains to the King

10 Then Amaziah, the priest of Bethel, sent to King Jeroboam of Israel, saying, "Amos has conspired against you in the very center of the house of Israel; the land is not able to bear all his words. ¹¹For thus Amos has said,

'Jeroboam shall die by the sword,
and Israel must go into exile
away from his land.' "

¹²And Amaziah said to Amos, "O seer, go, flee away to the land of Judah, earn your bread there, and prophesy there; ¹³but never again prophesy at Bethel, for it is the king's sanctuary, and it is a temple of the kingdom."

14 Then Amos answered Amaziah, "I amˣ no prophet, nor a prophet's son; but I amˣ a herdsman, and a dresser of sycamore trees, ¹⁵and the Lord took me from following the flock, and the Lord said to me, 'Go, prophesy to my people Israel.'
16 "Now therefore hear the word of
the Lord.
You say, 'Do not prophesy against
Israel,
and do not preach against the
house of Isaac.'
17 Therefore thus says the Lord:
'Your wife shall become a prostitute
in the city,
and your sons and your daughters
shall fall by the sword,
and your land shall be parceled
out by line;
you yourself shall die in an
unclean land,
and Israel shall surely go into
exile away from its land.' "

The Basket of Fruit

8 This is what the Lord God showed me—a basket of summer fruit.ʸ ²He said, "Amos, what do you see?" And I said, "A basket of summer fruit."ʸ Then the Lord said to me,

"The endᶻ has come upon my
people Israel;
I will never again pass them by.
³ The songs of the templeᵃ shall
become wailings in that day,"
says the Lord God;
"the dead bodies shall be many,
cast out in every place. Be silent!"

4 Hear this, you that trample on
the needy,
and bring to ruin the poor of
the land,
⁵ saying, "When will the new moon
be over
so that we may sell grain;
and the sabbath,
so that we may offer wheat
for sale?
We will make the ephah small and
the shekel great,
and practice deceit with false
balances,
⁶ buying the poor for silver
and the needy for a pair of
sandals,
and selling the sweepings of
the wheat."

ʷ Or for a judgment by fire   ˣ Or was   ʸ Heb qayits   ᶻ Heb qets   ᵃ Or palace

7 The LORD has sworn by the pride
         of Jacob:
    Surely I will never forget any of their
         deeds.
8 Shall not the land tremble on
         this account,
      and everyone mourn who lives in
         it,
    and all of it rise like the Nile,
      and be tossed about and sink
         again, like the Nile of Egypt?

9 On that day, says the Lord GOD,
    I will make the sun go down
         at noon,
      and darken the earth in
         broad daylight.
10 I will turn your feasts into
         mourning,
      and all your songs into
         lamentation;
    I will bring sackcloth on all loins,
      and baldness on every head;
    I will make it like the mourning for
         an only son,
      and the end of it like a bitter day.

11 The time is surely coming, says the
         Lord GOD,
      when I will send a famine on
         the land;
    not a famine of bread, or a thirst for
         water,
      but of hearing the words of
         the LORD.
12 They shall wander from sea to sea,
      and from north to east;
    they shall run to and fro, seeking
         the word of the LORD,
      but they shall not find it.

13 In that day the beautiful young
         women and the young men
      shall faint for thirst.
14 Those who swear by Ashimah
         of Samaria,
      and say, "As your god lives,
         O Dan,"
    and, "As the way of Beer-sheba
         lives"—
      they shall fall, and never
         rise again.

The Destruction of Israel

9 I saw the LORD standing beside[b] the
    altar, and he said:
    Strike the capitals until the
         thresholds shake,

and shatter them on the heads of
         all the people;[c]
    and those who are left I will kill
         with the sword;
    not one of them shall flee away,
      not one of them shall escape.

2 Though they dig into Sheol,
      from there shall my hand
         take them;
    though they climb up to heaven,
      from there I will bring
         them down.
3 Though they hide themselves on the
         top of Carmel,
      from there I will search out and
         take them;
    and though they hide from my sight
         at the bottom of the sea,
      there I will command the
         sea-serpent, and it
         shall bite them.
4 And though they go into captivity in
         front of their enemies,
      there I will command the sword,
         and it shall kill them;
    and I will fix my eyes on them
         for harm and not for good.

5 The Lord, GOD of hosts,
    he who touches the earth and
         it melts,
      and all who live in it mourn,
    and all of it rises like the Nile,
      and sinks again, like the Nile
         of Egypt;
6 who builds his upper chambers in
         the heavens,
      and founds his vault upon
         the earth;
    who calls for the waters of the sea,
      and pours them out upon the
         surface of the earth—
    the LORD is his name.

7 Are you not like the Ethiopians[d]
         to me,
      O people of Israel? says the LORD.
    Did I not bring Israel up from the
         land of Egypt,
      and the Philistines from Caphtor
         and the Arameans from Kir?
8 The eyes of the Lord GOD are upon
         the sinful kingdom,

b Or on   c Heb all of them   d Or Nubians; Heb
Cushites

and I will destroy it from the face
    of the earth
  —except that I will not utterly
    destroy the house of Jacob,
        says the LORD.

9 For lo, I will command,
  and shake the house of Israel
    among all the nations
as one shakes with a sieve,
  but no pebble shall fall to
    the ground.
10 All the sinners of my people shall
    die by the sword,
  who say, "Evil shall not overtake
    or meet us."

The Restoration of David's Kingdom

11 On that day I will raise up
  the booth of David that is fallen,
and repair its*e* breaches,
  and raise up its*f* ruins,
  and rebuild it as in the days of old;
12 in order that they may possess the
    remnant of Edom
  and all the nations who are called
    by my name,
  says the LORD who does this.

13 The time is surely coming, says
    the LORD,
  when the one who plows shall
    overtake the one who reaps,
  and the treader of grapes the one
    who sows the seed;
the mountains shall drip sweet
    wine,
  and all the hills shall flow
    with it.
14 I will restore the fortunes of my
    people Israel,
  and they shall rebuild the ruined
    cities and inhabit them;
they shall plant vineyards and drink
    their wine,
  and they shall make gardens and
    eat their fruit.
15 I will plant them upon their land,
  and they shall never again be
    plucked up
out of the land that I have
    given them,
        says the LORD your God.

e Gk: Heb *their*   *f* Gk: Heb *his*

Obadiah

A mere 21 verses long, Obadiah is the shortest book of the Old Testament. Though nothing is known of the writer, this book was probably written in the fifth century B.C., after Jerusalem and the temple were destroyed by the Babylonians.

Obadiah issues a prophetic warning to the land of Edom, whose inhabitants were descendants of Esau, Jacob's twin brother. Obadiah predicts that God will punish Edom for siding with Babylon and for inhabiting Judah after its people were exiled. It's interesting to note that Herod the Great, who attempted to murder the child Jesus, was descended from the Edomites.

After the destruction of Jerusalem in A.D. 70, the Edomites disappeared from history.

Proud Edom Will Be Brought Low

1 The vision of Obadiah.

Thus says the Lord GOD concerning
    Edom:
We have heard a report from
    the LORD,
    and a messenger has been sent
        among the nations:
"Rise up! Let us rise against it
    for battle!"
2 I will surely make you least among
    the nations;
    you shall be utterly despised.
3 Your proud heart has deceived you,
    you that live in the clefts of
        the rock,a
    whose dwelling is in the heights.
You say in your heart,
    "Who will bring me down to
        the ground?"
4 Though you soar aloft like the eagle,

though your nest is set among the
    stars,
from there I will bring you down,
                says the LORD.

Pillage and Slaughter Will Repay Edom's Cruelty

5 If thieves came to you,
    if plunderers by night
    —how you have been
        destroyed!—
    would they not steal only what
        they wanted?
If grape-gatherers came to you,
    would they not leave gleanings?
6 How Esau has been pillaged,
    his treasures searched out!
7 All your allies have deceived you,
    they have driven you to
        the border;

a Or clefts of Sela

your confederates have prevailed
against you;
those who ate[b] your bread have
set a trap for you—
there is no understanding of it.
8 On that day, says the LORD,
I will destroy the wise out
of Edom,
and understanding out of
Mount Esau.
9 Your warriors shall be shattered,
O Teman,
so that everyone from Mount Esau
will be cut off.

Edom Mistreated His Brother

10 For the slaughter and violence done
to your brother Jacob,
shame shall cover you,
and you shall be cut off forever.
11 On the day that you stood aside,
on the day that strangers carried
off his wealth,
and foreigners entered his gates
and cast lots for Jerusalem,
you too were like one of them.
12 But you should not have gloated[c]
over[d] your brother
on the day of his misfortune;
you should not have rejoiced over
the people of Judah
on the day of their ruin;
you should not have boasted
on the day of distress.

13 You should not have entered the
gate of my people
on the day of their calamity;
you should not have joined in the
gloating over Judah's[e]
disaster
on the day of his calamity;
you should not have looted
his goods
on the day of his calamity.
14 You should not have stood at
the crossings
to cut off his fugitives;
you should not have handed over
his survivors
on the day of distress.

15 For the day of the LORD is near
against all the nations.
As you have done, it shall be done
to you;
your deeds shall return on your
own head.
16 For as you have drunk on my
holy mountain,
all the nations around you
shall drink;
they shall drink and gulp down,[f]
and shall be as though they had
never been.

b Cn: Heb lacks *those who ate*   *c* Heb *But do not gloat* (and similarly through verse 14)   *d* Heb *on the day of*   *e* Heb *his*   *f* Meaning of Heb uncertain

Know Yourself

Knowledge of the self puts us on our knees, and it is very necessary for love. For knowledge of God produces love, and knowledge of the self produces humility. Knowledge of the self is a very important thing in our lives. As Saint Augustine says, "Fill yourselves first, and then only will you be able to give to others."

Knowledge of the self is also a safeguard against pride, especially when you are tempted in life. The greatest mistake is to think you are too strong to fall into temptation. Put your finger in the fire and it will burn. So we have to go through the fire. The temptations are allowed by God. The only thing we have to do is to refuse to give in.

—MOTHER TERESA OF CALCUTTA

Scripture Reading
for Today:
Obadiah 1–4

Verse for Today:
Obadiah 3

Go to page 1214 for your next devotional reading.

Israel's Final Triumph

17 But on Mount Zion there shall be
   those that escape,
   and it shall be holy;
   and the house of Jacob shall take
      possession of those who
      dispossessed them.
18 The house of Jacob shall be a
   fire,
   the house of Joseph a flame,
   and the house of Esau stubble;
   they shall burn them and
      consume them,
   and there shall be no survivor of
      the house of Esau;
         for the LORD has spoken.
19 Those of the Negeb shall possess
   Mount Esau,
   and those of the Shephelah the
      land of the Philistines;
they shall possess the land of
   Ephraim and the land
   of Samaria,
and Benjamin shall possess
   Gilead.
20 The exiles of the Israelites who are
   in Halah *g*
   shall possess*h* Phoenicia as far
      as Zarephath;
   and the exiles of Jerusalem who are
      in Sepharad
   shall possess the towns of
      the Negeb.
21 Those who have been saved*i* shall
   go up to Mount Zion
   to rule Mount Esau;
   and the kingdom shall be
      the LORD's.

g Cn: Heb *in this army* *h* Cn: Meaning of Heb
uncertain *i* Or *Saviors*

Jonah

Even people who have never read a word of Scripture are familiar with the story of Jonah, the man who spent three days and nights in the belly of a gargantuan fish. It all began when God told Jonah to travel northeast to Nineveh, the capital city of Assyria, in order to call the city to repentance. But the Bible's most reluctant prophet immediately jumped onto a ship sailing in the opposite direction. The boat, however, was caught in a storm and the runaway prophet was cast overboard and swallowed by a huge fish. But Jonah prayed for deliverance and before long, the fish belched him out onto the shore. This messy business must have been enough to change his mind for Jonah soon set out for Nineveh.

When he arrived in Nineveh, Jonah marched across the city, shouting: "Forty days more, and Nineveh shall be overthrown!" (3.4). Remarkably, the people repented, and God forgave them. But instead of rejoicing, Jonah sulked because God had done the unthinkable—he had forgiven Israel's enemy.

Full of irony, exaggeration, and humor, the story of Jonah was a pointed message directed to Jews who thought God's forgiveness and mercy could not possibly extend beyond the boundaries of their own nation. It is a classic message that warns of the danger of becoming triumphalistic in our attitudes toward those who do not belong to the community of the faithful.

Jonah Tries to Run Away from God

1 Now the word of the LORD came to Jonah son of Amittai, saying, ²"Go at once to Nineveh, that great city, and cry out against it; for their wickedness has come up before me." ³But Jonah set out to flee to Tarshish from the presence of the LORD. He went down to Joppa and found a ship going to Tarshish; so he paid his fare and went on board, to go with them to Tarshish, away from the presence of the LORD.

4 But the LORD hurled a great wind upon the sea, and such a mighty storm came upon the sea that the ship threatened to break up. ⁵Then the mariners were afraid, and each cried to his god. They threw the cargo that was in the ship into

the sea, to lighten it for them. Jonah, meanwhile, had gone down into the hold of the ship and had lain down, and was fast asleep. [6]The captain came and said to him, "What are you doing sound asleep? Get up, call on your god! Perhaps the god will spare us a thought so that we do not perish."

7 The sailors[a] said to one another, "Come, let us cast lots, so that we may know on whose account this calamity has come upon us." So they cast lots, and the lot fell on Jonah. [8]Then they said to him, "Tell us why this calamity has come upon us. What is your occupation? Where do you come from? What is your country? And of what people are you?" [9]"I am a Hebrew," he replied. "I worship the LORD, the God of heaven, who made the sea and the dry land." [10]Then the men were even more afraid, and said to him, "What is this that you have done!" For the men knew that he was fleeing from the presence of the LORD, because he had told them so.

11 Then they said to him, "What shall we do to you, that the sea may quiet down for us?" For the sea was growing more and more tempestuous. [12]He said to them, "Pick me up and throw me into the sea; then the sea will quiet down for you; for I know it is because of me that this great storm has come upon you." [13]Nevertheless the men rowed hard to bring the ship back to land, but they could not, for the sea grew more and more stormy against them. [14]Then they cried out to the LORD, "Please, O LORD, we pray, do not let us perish on account of this man's life. Do not make us guilty of innocent blood; for you, O LORD, have done as it pleased you." [15]So they picked Jonah up and threw him into the sea; and the sea ceased from its raging. [16]Then the men feared the LORD even more, and they offered a sacrifice to the LORD and made vows.

17[b] But the LORD provided a large fish to swallow up Jonah; and Jonah was in the belly of the fish three days and three nights.

A Psalm of Thanksgiving

2 Then Jonah prayed to the LORD his God from the belly of the fish, [2]saying,

"I called to the LORD out of my
    distress,
  and he answered me;

out of the belly of Sheol I cried,
  and you heard my voice.
[3] You cast me into the deep,
  into the heart of the seas,
  and the flood surrounded me;
all your waves and your billows
    passed over me.
[4] Then I said, 'I am driven away
  from your sight;
how[c] shall I look again
    upon your holy temple?'
[5] The waters closed in over me;
  the deep surrounded me;
weeds were wrapped around
      my head
[6]   at the roots of the mountains.
  I went down to the land
  whose bars closed upon me
      forever;
yet you brought up my life from the
      Pit,
  O LORD my God.
[7] As my life was ebbing away,
  I remembered the LORD;
and my prayer came to you,
  into your holy temple.
[8] Those who worship vain idols
  forsake their true loyalty.
[9] But I with the voice of thanksgiving
  will sacrifice to you;
what I have vowed I will pay.
  Deliverance belongs to the LORD!"
[10]Then the LORD spoke to the fish, and it spewed Jonah out upon the dry land.

Conversion of Nineveh

3 The word of the LORD came to Jonah a second time, saying, [2]"Get up, go to Nineveh, that great city, and proclaim to it the message that I tell you." [3]So Jonah set out and went to Nineveh, according to the word of the LORD. Now Nineveh was an exceedingly large city, a three days' walk across. [4]Jonah began to go into the city, going a day's walk. And he cried out, "Forty days more, and Nineveh shall be overthrown!" [5]And the people of Nineveh believed God; they proclaimed a fast, and everyone, great and small, put on sackcloth.

6 When the news reached the king of Nineveh, he rose from his throne, removed his robe, covered himself with sackcloth, and sat in ashes. [7]Then he had a proclamation made in Nineveh: "By the

a Heb They   b Ch 2.1 in Heb   c Theodotion: Heb surely

decree of the king and his nobles: No human being or animal, no herd or flock, shall taste anything. They shall not feed, nor shall they drink water. ⁸Human beings and animals shall be covered with sackcloth, and they shall cry mightily to God. All shall turn from their evil ways and from the violence that is in their hands. ⁹Who knows? God may relent and change his mind; he may turn from his fierce anger, so that we do not perish."

10 When God saw what they did, how they turned from their evil ways, God changed his mind about the calamity that he had said he would bring upon them; and he did not do it.

Jonah's Anger

4 But this was very displeasing to Jonah, and he became angry. ²He prayed to the LORD and said, "O LORD! Is not this what I said while I was still in my own country? That is why I fled to Tarshish at the beginning; for I knew that you are a gracious God and merciful, slow to anger, and abounding in steadfast love,

and ready to relent from punishing. ³And now, O LORD, please take my life from me, for it is better for me to die than to live." ⁴And the LORD said, "Is it right for you to be angry?" ⁵Then Jonah went out of the city and sat down east of the city, and made a booth for himself there. He sat under it in the shade, waiting to see what would become of the city.

6 The LORD God appointed a bush,ᵈ and made it come up over Jonah, to give shade over his head, to save him from his discomfort; so Jonah was very happy about the bush. ⁷But when dawn came up the next day, God appointed a worm that attacked the bush, so that it withered. ⁸When the sun rose, God prepared a sultry east wind, and the sun beat down on the head of Jonah so that he was faint and asked that he might die. He said, "It is better for me to die than to live."

Jonah Is Reproved

9 But God said to Jonah, "Is it right for

ᵈ Heb *qiqayon*, possibly *the castor bean plant*

Pettiness and Poutiness

FRIDAY

Scripture Reading
for Today:
Jonah 3.1–5; 4.1–4

Verses for Today:
Jonah 4.1–2

What are we to make of this prophet who is angry at God because God is gracious and merciful, slow to anger, rich in clemency, and loath to punish? What are we to think of this prophet who desires death after he successfully converts the entire populace of Nineveh? Perhaps we might try to recognize those Jonah-like attitudes within ourselves. Do we ever place restrictions on how much good we even expect out of other people, particularly those whose values or beliefs are different from our own? Do we ever limit our generosity because we have predetermined just how much we can afford to give freely? Do we ever sulk because God seems to have blessed others in ways that, according to our standards, they do not deserve?

While I suspect that there are many Jonahs among us, can we identify the Jonah within? Can we laugh at our own pettiness, our own "poutiness," and ask God to transform those areas of our lives that prevent us from being gracious and merciful, slow to anger, rich in clemency, and loath to punish?

—MARIBETH HOWELL, O.P.

Go to page 1218 for your next devotional reading.

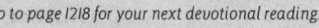

you to be angry about the bush?" And he said, "Yes, angry enough to die." [10]Then the LORD said, "You are concerned about the bush, for which you did not labor and which you did not grow; it came into being in a night and perished in a night. [11]And should I not be concerned about Nineveh, that great city, in which there are more than a hundred and twenty thousand persons who do not know their right hand from their left, and also many animals?"

Micah

Micah came from a small town about 20 miles southwest of Jerusalem. A contemporary of Isaiah, he was appalled by the corruption and arrogance of the political leaders, priests, and prophets who preyed on the poor. He warned of coming judgment upon both Samaria (capital of the northern kingdom) and Jerusalem (capital of the southern kingdom).

Micah 6.8 is a famous passage, summarizing what God requires of every human being: "He has told you, O mortal, what is good; and what does the LORD require of you but to do justice, and to love kindness, and to walk humbly with your God?"

Seven hundred years before Christ, Micah prophesied about the Messiah's birthplace: "But you, O Bethlehem of Ephrathah, who are one of the little clans of Judah, from you shall come forth for me one who is to rule in Israel, whose origin is from of old, from ancient days" (5.2).

As do all the other prophets, Micah speaks of a time of judgment and a time of healing, affirming that God's anger will be replaced by his mercy.

1 The word of the LORD that came to Micah of Moresheth in the days of Kings Jotham, Ahaz, and Hezekiah of Judah, which he saw concerning Samaria and Jerusalem.

Judgment Pronounced against Samaria

2 Hear, you peoples, all of you;
     listen, O earth, and all that is
          in it;
and let the Lord GOD be a witness
          against you,
     the Lord from his holy temple.
3 For lo, the LORD is coming out of his
          place,
     and will come down and tread
          upon the high places of
          the earth.
4 Then the mountains will melt under
          him
     and the valleys will burst open,
like wax near the fire,
     like waters poured down a
          steep place.
5 All this is for the transgression
          of Jacob
     and for the sins of the house
          of Israel.
What is the transgression of Jacob?
     Is it not Samaria?
And what is the high place[a]
          of Judah?
     Is it not Jerusalem?

a Heb *what are the high places*

6 Therefore I will make Samaria a
        heap in the open country,
    a place for planting vineyards.
I will pour down her stones into
        the valley,
    and uncover her foundations.
7 All her images shall be beaten
        to pieces,
    all her wages shall be burned with
        fire,
    and all her idols I will lay waste;
for as the wages of a prostitute she
        gathered them,
    and as the wages of a prostitute
        they shall again be used.

The Doom of the Cities of Judah

8 For this I will lament and wail;
    I will go barefoot and naked;
I will make lamentation like
        the jackals,
    and mourning like the ostriches.
9 For her wound[b] is incurable.
    It has come to Judah;
it has reached to the gate of
        my people,
    to Jerusalem.

10 Tell it not in Gath,
        weep not at all;
    in Beth-leaphrah
        roll yourselves in the dust.
11 Pass on your way,
        inhabitants of Shaphir,
        in nakedness and shame;
    the inhabitants of Zaanan
        do not come forth;
Beth-ezel is wailing
    and shall remove its support
        from you.
12 For the inhabitants of Maroth
        wait anxiously for good,
    yet disaster has come down from the
        LORD
        to the gate of Jerusalem.
13 Harness the steeds to the chariots,
        inhabitants of Lachish;
    it was the beginning of sin
        to daughter Zion,
    for in you were found
        the transgressions of Israel.
14 Therefore you shall give parting gifts
        to Moresheth-gath;
    the houses of Achzib shall be
        a deception
        to the kings of Israel.
15 I will again bring a conqueror
        upon you,

inhabitants of Mareshah;
the glory of Israel
    shall come to Adullam.
16 Make yourselves bald and cut off
        your hair
    for your pampered children;
make yourselves as bald as the eagle,
    for they have gone from you
        into exile.

Social Evils Denounced

2 Alas for those who devise
        wickedness
    and evil deeds[c] on their beds!
When the morning dawns, they
        perform it,
    because it is in their power.
2 They covet fields, and seize them;
        houses, and take them away;
    they oppress householder
        and house,
    people and their inheritance.
3 Therefore thus says the LORD:
    Now, I am devising against this
        family an evil
    from which you cannot remove
        your necks;
and you shall not walk haughtily,
    for it will be an evil time.
4 On that day they shall take up a
        taunt song against you,
    and wail with bitter lamentation,
and say, "We are utterly ruined;
    the LORD[d] alters the inheritance
        of my people;
how he removes it from me!
    Among our captors[e] he parcels
        out our fields."
5 Therefore you will have no one to
        cast the line by lot
    in the assembly of the LORD.

6 "Do not preach"—thus they preach—
    "one should not preach of
        such things;
    disgrace will not overtake us."
7 Should this be said, O house
        of Jacob?
    Is the LORD's patience exhausted?
    Are these his doings?
Do not my words do good
    to one who walks uprightly?
8 But you rise up against my people[f]
        as an enemy;

b Gk Syr Vg: Heb *wounds*   c Cn: Heb *work evil*
d Heb *he*   e Cn: Heb *the rebellious*   f Cn: Heb
But yesterday my people rose

The Shunammite Woman

Her Character: *Generous and hospitable, she was a wealthy and capable woman who showed great kindness to one of God's prophets.*
Her Sorrow: *To lose the son that had been promised her.*
Her Joy: *To experience just how deep God's faithfulness goes.*

Read 2 Kings 4.8–37

Just a few miles north of Jezreel, where Jezebel's story had drawn to its grim conclusion, lived a wealthy Israelite woman whose sharp eye kept track of travelers from Nazareth to Jerusalem. One of the more colorful characters who frequented the road outside her house was Elisha, the prophet who had succeeded Elijah.

One day the Shunammite woman invited Elisha to linger for a meal. Afterward she said to her husband, "Let us make a small roof chamber with walls, and put there for him a bed, a table, a chair, and a lamp, so that he can stay there whenever he comes to us" (4.10).

Moved by her kindness, Elisha inquired, through his servant Gehazi, whether he could use his influence with Israel's king on her behalf. But the woman wasn't looking for favors at court, so Elisha pressed his servant, "What then may be done for her?"

Gehazi merely pointed out the obvious: The woman and her aging husband were childless, without an heir to carry on the family name. So Elisha summoned the woman and promised her: "At this season, in due time, you shall embrace a son."

"No, my lord," she objected, "O man of God; do not deceive your servant."

A year later, just as Elisha had foretold, she held an infant in her arms, laughing as she told others the story of God's surprising gift. Unlike so many of her female forebears— Sarah, Rebekah, Rachel, Tamar, and Hannah—

the Shunammite woman had seemed content without children. Yet God had fulfilled an unspoken desire of her heart.

One morning, however, a servant entered the house with the boy in his arms, explaining that the child had complained of a headache while visiting his father in the fields.

The boy's face was flushed, his forehead hot as she caressed it. But the tighter she held him, the more his spirit seemed to retreat from her. His breathing was labored, his eyes listless. At about noon he died.

Without a word, she carried his small body to the prophet's room, laying it tenderly on Elisha's bed. Closing the door, she summoned a servant and left immediately for Mount Carmel, where she hoped to find Elisha.

As soon as she saw him, she exclaimed: "Did I ask my lord for a son? Did I not say, Do not mislead me?"

So the prophet hurried to Shunem, 25 miles south of Mount Carmel. When Elisha arrived, he found the boy still quiet and cold on his couch. Elisha closed the door behind him. Praying, he stretched his body across the boy's so that hands, mouth, and eyes touched. Gradually he could feel the boy's body warming beneath him. Then he got up and paced the room for a while. At last he stretched himself across the lifeless body again and prayed. The boy's chest lifted. Then he sneezed! Then sneezed again.

Overcome with wonder and joy, the grateful mother fell at Elisha's feet and bowed to the ground. God had been true to his word, fulfilling his promise to her and then preserving it in the face of impossible circumstances.

Praying With the Shunammite Woman

"At this season, in due time, you shall embrace a son."—2 Kings 4.16

Praise God: *That he never overlooks even a small kindness performed out of love for him.*

Offer Thanks: *For the kindness you have experienced at the hands of others.*

Confess: *Your tendency to overlook others' needs because you are so focused on your own.*

Ask God: *To make you eager for opportunities to care for others in basic and practical ways.*

Lift Your Heart

The Shunammite woman is a wonderful example of someone who anticipated Jesus' words to his disciples to "strive first for the kingdom of God and his righteousness, and all these things will be given to you as well" (Matthew 6.33). Like the lilies of the field, she didn't worry about God's provision and so experienced it abundantly. Ask God for an opportunity this week to perform an act of practical kindness for someone else. Consider lending your prayers, your gifts, and your energy on a regular basis to a group or ministry that is working to bring justice to those most in need of it.

Father, show me someone's need today. Help me to break out of my own small world in order to pay attention to the way you want me to show your love to someone else.

Go to page 1221 for your next devotional reading.

you strip the robe from the
peaceful, *g*
from those who pass by trustingly
with no thought of war.
9 The women of my people you
drive out
from their pleasant houses;
from their young children you
take away
my glory forever.
10 Arise and go;
for this is no place to rest,
because of uncleanness that destroys
with a grievous destruction.*h*
11 If someone were to go about
uttering empty falsehoods,
saying, "I will preach to you of
wine and strong drink,"
such a one would be the preacher
for this people!

A Promise for the Remnant of Israel

12 I will surely gather all of you,
O Jacob,
I will gather the survivors
of Israel;
I will set them together
like sheep in a fold,
like a flock in its pasture;
it will resound with people.
13 The one who breaks out will go up
before them;
they will break through and pass
the gate,
going out by it.
Their king will pass on before them,
the LORD at their head.

Wicked Rulers and Prophets

3 And I said:
Listen, you heads of Jacob
and rulers of the house of Israel!
Should you not know justice?—
2 you who hate the good and love
the evil,
who tear the skin off my people,*i*
and the flesh off their bones;
3 who eat the flesh of my people,
flay their skin off them,
break their bones in pieces,
and chop them up like meat *j* in
a kettle,
like flesh in a caldron.

4 Then they will cry to the LORD,
but he will not answer them;

he will hide his face from them at
that time,
because they have acted wickedly.
5 Thus says the LORD concerning
the prophets
who lead my people astray,
who cry "Peace"
when they have something to eat,
but declare war against those
who put nothing into their
mouths.
6 Therefore it shall be night to you,
without vision,
and darkness to you, without
revelation.
The sun shall go down upon
the prophets,
and the day shall be black
over them;
7 the seers shall be disgraced,
and the diviners put to shame;
they shall all cover their lips,
for there is no answer from God.
8 But as for me, I am filled
with power,
with the spirit of the LORD,
and with justice and might,
to declare to Jacob his transgression
and to Israel his sin.

9 Hear this, you rulers of the house of
Jacob
and chiefs of the house of Israel,
who abhor justice
and pervert all equity,
10 who build Zion with blood
and Jerusalem with wrong!
11 Its rulers give judgment for a bribe,
its priests teach for a price,
its prophets give oracles
for money;
yet they lean upon the LORD and say,
"Surely the LORD is with us!
No harm shall come upon us."
12 Therefore because of you
Zion shall be plowed as a field;
Jerusalem shall become a heap
of ruins,
and the mountain of the house a
wooded height.

Peace and Security through Obedience

4 In days to come
the mountain of the LORD's house

g Cn: Heb *from before a garment*   h Meaning of
Heb uncertain   i Heb *from them*   j Gk: Heb *as*

shall be established as the highest of
  the mountains,
  and shall be raised up above
  the hills.
Peoples shall stream to it,
²   and many nations shall come
  and say:
"Come, let us go up to the
  mountain of the Lord,
  to the house of the God of Jacob;
that he may teach us his ways
  and that we may walk in
  his paths."
For out of Zion shall go forth
  instruction,
  and the word of the Lord
  from Jerusalem.

³ He shall judge between many
  peoples,
  and shall arbitrate between strong
  nations far away;
they shall beat their swords into
  plowshares,
  and their spears into pruning
  hooks;
nation shall not lift up sword
  against nation,
  neither shall they learn war
  any more;
⁴ but they shall all sit under their own
  vines and under their own fig
  trees,
  and no one shall make
  them afraid;

Choose the Way of Peace

From a letter from Mother Teresa to the presidents of two countries about to go to war against each other.

I come to you in the name of God, the God that we all love and share, to beg for the innocent ones, our poor of the world, and those who will become poor because of war. They are the ones who will suffer most because they have no means of escape. I plead on bended knee for them. They will suffer and when they do, we will be the ones who are guilty for not having done all in our power to protect and love them.

I plead to you for those who will be left orphaned, widowed, and left alone, because their parents, husbands, brothers, and children have been killed. I beg you please to save them.

I plead for those who will be left with disability and disfigurement. They are God's children. I plead for those who will be left with no home, no food and no love. Please think of them as being your children.

Finally, I plead for those who will have the most precious thing that God can give us, life, taken away from them. I beg you to save our brothers and sisters, yours and ours, because they are given to us by God to love and to cherish. It is not for us to destroy what God has given to us. Please, please let your mind and your will become the mind and will of God.

You have the power to bring war into the world, or to build peace. Please choose the way of peace.

—MOTHER TERESA OF CALCUTTA

Go to page 1223 for your next devotional reading.

MONDAY

Scripture Reading
for Today:
Micah 4.1–5

Verse for Today:
Micah 4.3

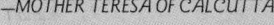

for the mouth of the LORD of hosts
    has spoken.

5 For all the peoples walk,
    each in the name of its god,
but we will walk in the name of the
    LORD our God
    forever and ever.

Restoration Promised after Exile

6 In that day, says the LORD,
    I will assemble the lame
and gather those who have been
    driven away,
    and those whom I have afflicted.
7 The lame I will make the remnant,
    and those who were cast off, a
        strong nation;
and the LORD will reign over them in
    Mount Zion
    now and forevermore.

8 And you, O tower of the flock,
    hill of daughter Zion,
to you it shall come,
    the former dominion shall come,
    the sovereignty of daughter
        Jerusalem.

9 Now why do you cry aloud?
    Is there no king in you?
Has your counselor perished,
    that pangs have seized you like a
        woman in labor?
10 Writhe and groan,[k] O daughter
    Zion,
    like a woman in labor;
for now you shall go forth from
    the city
    and camp in the open country;
    you shall go to Babylon.
There you shall be rescued,
    there the LORD will redeem you
    from the hands of your enemies.

11 Now many nations
    are assembled against you,
saying, "Let her be profaned,
    and let our eyes gaze upon Zion."
12 But they do not know
    the thoughts of the LORD;
they do not understand his plan,
    that he has gathered them as
        sheaves to the threshing floor.
13 Arise and thresh,
    O daughter Zion,
for I will make your horn iron
    and your hoofs bronze;

you shall beat in pieces many
    peoples,
    and shall[l] devote their gain to
        the LORD,
    their wealth to the Lord of the
        whole earth.

5 [m] Now you are walled around with
    a wall;[n]
siege is laid against us;
with a rod they strike the ruler
    of Israel
    upon the cheek.

The Ruler from Bethlehem

20 But you, O Bethlehem of
    Ephrathah,
    who are one of the little clans
        of Judah,
from you shall come forth for me
    one who is to rule in Israel,
whose origin is from of old,
    from ancient days.
3 Therefore he shall give them up
    until the time
    when she who is in labor has
        brought forth;
then the rest of his kindred shall
    return
    to the people of Israel.
4 And he shall stand and feed his
    flock in the strength of
        the LORD,
    in the majesty of the name of the
        LORD his God.
And they shall live secure, for now
    he shall be great
    to the ends of the earth;
5 and he shall be the one of peace.

If the Assyrians come into
    our land
    and tread upon our soil, [p]
we will raise against them seven
    shepherds
    and eight installed as rulers.
6 They shall rule the land of Assyria
    with the sword,
    and the land of Nimrod with the
        drawn sword;[q]
they[r] shall rescue us from the
    Assyrians

---

[k] Meaning of Heb uncertain   [l] Gk Syr Tg: Heb
and I will   [m] Ch 4.14 in Heb   [n] Cn Compare
Gk: Meaning of Heb uncertain   [o] Ch 5.1 in
Heb   [p] Gk: Heb *in our palaces*   [q] Cn: Heb *in its
entrances*   [r] Heb *he*

if they come into our land
or tread within our border.

The Future Role of the Remnant

7 Then the remnant of Jacob,
   surrounded by many peoples,
shall be like dew from the LORD,
   like showers on the grass,
which do not depend upon people
   or wait for any mortal.
8 And among the nations the remnant
   of Jacob,

surrounded by many peoples,
shall be like a lion among the
   animals of the forest,
like a young lion among the
   flocks of sheep,
which, when it goes through,
   treads down
and tears in pieces, with no one
   to deliver.
9 Your hand shall be lifted up over
   your adversaries,
and all your enemies shall be
   cut off.

A New Road

TUESDAY

Scripture Reading
for Today:
Micah 5.2–6

Verse for Today:
Micah 5.2

Many ways led to Bethlehem: Mary and Joseph's long trip from
Nazareth; the shepherds' path over their fields; the wise men's arduous trek across the desert. Jesus' birth causes each of us to set
out on a personal journey—a journey to meet this God who so
humbly and surprisingly came into the world as a child lying in a
manger!

The waiting of the holy family was interrupted by Rome's decree—what inconvenient timing!—so they set off. The way from
Nazareth to Bethlehem was long, 90 miles by donkey and on foot.
Mary had borne the anguish of wondering what Joseph thought
of her pregnancy. We can imagine the two pondering the ancient
prophecies, searching for understanding to ease the questions in
their hearts. Did they share their fears with one another, or were
they calmly silent because it was enough for them to rest in obedience to God's will?

Did Mary fret a bit as she packed, wondering whether to take
the swaddling bands she had made—or would they be back home
in their own village before her time came? Did Joseph cast a last
look longingly back over his shoulder as Nazareth's security
passed out of sight and the way stretched ahead with a pregnant
wife at his side? Yet the same road that led away from familiarity
and comfort led straight to the city where God's promise was to
be fulfilled: "And you, Bethlehem, in the land of Judah, are by no
means least among the rulers of Judah; for from you shall come a
ruler who is to shepherd my people Israel" (Matthew 2.6).

Have I ever experienced something fresh coming to birth in
my circumstances once I have been willing to set out on a new
road, leaving behind my old, familiar routines? *Jesus, may I be just
as willing to follow the road to you as Mary and Joseph were.*

—JEANNE KUN

Go to page 1228 for your next devotional reading.

10 In that day, says the LORD,
  I will cut off your horses from
    among you
  and will destroy your chariots;
11 and I will cut off the cities of
    your land
  and throw down all your
    strongholds;
12 and I will cut off sorceries from your
    hand,
  and you shall have no more
    soothsayers;
13 and I will cut off your images
  and your pillars from among you,
  and you shall bow down no more
    to the work of your hands;
14 and I will uproot your sacred
    poles[s] from among you
  and destroy your towns.
15 And in anger and wrath I will
    execute vengeance
  on the nations that did not obey.

God Challenges Israel

6 Hear what the LORD says:
  Rise, plead your case before
    the mountains,
  and let the hills hear your voice.
2 Hear, you mountains, the
    controversy of the LORD,
  and you enduring foundations of
    the earth;
  for the LORD has a controversy with
    his people,
  and he will contend with Israel.

3 "O my people, what have I done
    to you?
  In what have I wearied you?
    Answer me!
4 For I brought you up from the land
    of Egypt,
  and redeemed you from the house
    of slavery;
  and I sent before you Moses,
    Aaron, and Miriam.
5 O my people, remember now what
    King Balak of Moab devised,
  what Balaam son of Beor
    answered him,
  and what happened from Shittim
    to Gilgal,
  that you may know the saving acts
    of the LORD."

What God Requires

6 "With what shall I come before
    the LORD,

and bow myself before God
    on high?
  Shall I come before him with
    burnt offerings,
  with calves a year old?
7 Will the LORD be pleased with
    thousands of rams,
  with ten thousands of rivers
    of oil?
  Shall I give my firstborn for my
    transgression,
  the fruit of my body for the sin of
    my soul?"
8 He has told you, O mortal, what
    is good;
  and what does the LORD require of
    you
  but to do justice, and to love
    kindness,
  and to walk humbly with
    your God?

Cheating and Violence to Be Punished

9 The voice of the LORD cries to
    the city
  (it is sound wisdom to fear
    your name):
  Hear, O tribe and assembly of
    the city![t]
10 Can I forget[u] the treasures of
    wickedness in the house of
    the wicked,
  and the scant measure that is
    accursed?
11 Can I tolerate wicked scales
  and a bag of dishonest weights?
12 Your[v] wealthy are full of violence;
  your[w] inhabitants speak lies,
  with tongues of deceit in
    their mouths.
13 Therefore I have begun[x] to strike
    you down,
  making you desolate because of
    your sins.
14 You shall eat, but not be satisfied,
  and there shall be a gnawing
    hunger within you;
  you shall put away, but not save,
  and what you save, I will hand
    over to the sword.
15 You shall sow, but not reap;
  you shall tread olives, but not
    anoint yourselves with oil;

---

s Heb *Asherim*   t Cn Compare Gk: Heb *tribe,
and who has appointed it yet?*   u Cn: Meaning of
Heb uncertain   v Heb *Whose*   w Heb *whose*
x Gk Syr Vg: Heb *have made sick*

you shall tread grapes, but not
    drink wine.
16 For you have kept the statutes
        of Omri[y]
    and all the works of the house
        of Ahab,
    and you have followed their
        counsels.
Therefore I will make you a
    desolation, and your[z]
    inhabitants an object
    of hissing;
so you shall bear the scorn of
    my people.

The Total Corruption of the People

7 Woe is me! For I have become like
    one who,
    after the summer fruit has
        been gathered,
    after the vintage has been gleaned,
finds no cluster to eat;
    there is no first-ripe fig for which
        I hunger.
2 The faithful have disappeared from
        the land,
    and there is no one left who
        is upright;
they all lie in wait for blood,
    and they hunt each other
        with nets.
3 Their hands are skilled to do evil;
    the official and the judge ask for a
        bribe,
and the powerful dictate what
        they desire;
    thus they pervert justice.[a]
4 The best of them is like a brier,
    the most upright of them a
        thorn hedge.
The day of their[b] sentinels, of
        their[b] punishment,
    has come;
    now their confusion is at hand.
5 Put no trust in a friend,
    have no confidence in a
        loved one;
guard the doors of your mouth
    from her who lies in your
        embrace;
6 for the son treats the father with
        contempt,
    the daughter rises up against
        her mother,
the daughter-in-law against her
        mother-in-law;
    your enemies are members of
        your own household.

7 But as for me, I will look to
        the LORD,
    I will wait for the God of my
        salvation;
    my God will hear me.

Penitence and Trust in God

8 Do not rejoice over me, O my
        enemy;
    when I fall, I shall rise;
when I sit in darkness,
    the LORD will be a light to me.
9 I must bear the indignation of
        the LORD,
    because I have sinned
        against him,
until he takes my side
    and executes judgment for me.
He will bring me out to the light;
    I shall see his vindication.
10 Then my enemy will see,
    and shame will cover her who
        said to me,
    "Where is the LORD your God?"
My eyes will see her downfall;[c]
    now she will be trodden down
        like the mire of the streets.

A Prophecy of Restoration

11 A day for the building of your walls!
    In that day the boundary shall be
        far extended.
12 In that day they will come to you
        from Assyria to[d] Egypt,
    and from Egypt to the River,
    from sea to sea and from
        mountain to mountain.
13 But the earth will be desolate
    because of its inhabitants,
    for the fruit of their doings.

14 Shepherd your people with
        your staff,
    the flock that belongs to you,
which lives alone in a forest
    in the midst of a garden land;
    let them feed in Bashan and Gilead
        as in the days of old.
15 As in the days when you came out
        of the land of Egypt,
    show us[e] marvelous things.
16 The nations shall see and be
        ashamed

---

y Gk Syr Vg Tg: Heb *the statutes of Omri are kept*
z Heb *its*   a Cn: Heb *they weave it*   b Heb *your*
c Heb lacks *downfall*   d One Ms: MT *Assyria and
cities of*   e Cn: Heb *I will show him*

of all their might;
they shall lay their hands on
their mouths;
their ears shall be deaf;
17 they shall lick dust like a snake,
like the crawling things of
the earth;
they shall come trembling out of
their fortresses;
they shall turn in dread to the
Lord our God,
and they shall stand in fear
of you.

God's Compassion and Steadfast Love

18 Who is a God like you, pardoning
iniquity
and passing over the transgression

of the remnant of your *f*
possession?
He does not retain his anger forever,
because he delights in showing
clemency.
19 He will again have compassion
upon us;
he will tread our iniquities
under foot.
You will cast all our *g* sins
into the depths of the sea.
20 You will show faithfulness to Jacob
and unswerving loyalty to
Abraham,
as you have sworn to our ancestors
from the days of old.

f Heb *his* *g* Gk Syr Vg Tg: Heb *their*

Nahum

Though Jonah tells the story of Nineveh's repentance and God's forgiveness, Nahum prophesies the city's eventual destruction in 612 B.C. Assyria, in fact, had become a terrifying power in the ancient Near East, ruthless in its suppression of other nations. A warlike empire, Assyria overran surrounding nations, leaving behind burnt-out cities, the bodies of enemy soldiers dangling from posts, and the headless corpses of men, women, and children.

Just as many cheered the defeat of the Nazis in World War II, Nahum rejoices in God's long-awaited judgment of this bloody city: "There is no assuaging your hurt, your wound is mortal. All who hear the news about you clap their hands over you" (3.19).

1 An oracle concerning Nineveh. The book of the vision of Nahum of Elkosh.

The Consuming Wrath of God

2 A jealous and avenging God is
    the LORD,
  the LORD is avenging and wrathful;
the LORD takes vengeance on his
    adversaries
  and rages against his enemies.
3 The LORD is slow to anger but great
    in power,
  and the LORD will by no means
    clear the guilty.

His way is in whirlwind and storm,
  and the clouds are the dust of
    his feet.
4 He rebukes the sea and makes it dry,
  and he dries up all the rivers;
Bashan and Carmel wither,
  and the bloom of Lebanon fades.
5 The mountains quake before him,
  and the hills melt;

the earth heaves before him,
  the world and all who live in it.

6 Who can stand before his
    indignation?
  Who can endure the heat of
    his anger?
His wrath is poured out like fire,
  and by him the rocks are broken
    in pieces.
7 The LORD is good,
  a stronghold in a day of trouble;
he protects those who take refuge in
    him,
8   even in a rushing flood.
He will make a full end of his
    adversaries,[a]
  and will pursue his enemies into
    darkness.
9 Why do you plot against the LORD?
  He will make an end;
  no adversary will rise up twice.
10 Like thorns they are entangled,

a Gk: Heb *of her place*

like drunkards they are drunk;
they are consumed like dry straw.

11 From you one has gone out
who plots evil against the LORD,
one who counsels wickedness.

Good News for Judah

12 Thus says the LORD,
"Though they are at full strength
and many,[b]
they will be cut off and pass away.
Though I have afflicted you,
I will afflict you no more.

13 And now I will break off his yoke
from you
and snap the bonds that
bind you."

14 The LORD has commanded
concerning you:

"Your name shall be perpetuated
no longer;
from the house of your gods I will
cut off
the carved image and the
cast image.
I will make your grave, for you
are worthless."

15c Look! On the mountains the feet
of one
who brings good tidings,
who proclaims peace!
Celebrate your festivals, O Judah,
fulfill your vows,
for never again shall the wicked
invade you;
they are utterly cut off.

---

b Meaning of Heb uncertain　　c Ch 2.1 in Heb

God's Jealousy

WEDNESDAY

Scripture Reading
for Today:
Nahum 1.2–7

Verse for Today:
Nahum 1.2

"Jealousy" is a loaded word, and I used to cringe when I would
hear the Ten Commandments begin with the injunction against
idolatry: "You shall not bow down to [idols] or worship them; for I
the LORD your God am a jealous God" (Exodus 20.5). Human jealousy is a sign of fear. Often, it indicates immaturity or a maladap-
tion of the ability to love. God's jealousy is a different matter,
more like mother-love, the protective zeal of a lioness or mother
bear for her young. The word *jealousy* has its root in "zealous,"
denoting extreme enthusiasm and devotion, and God's jealousy retains the word's more positive aspects. It helps us to trust. Who,
after all, would trust a God, a parent, spouse, or lover, who said to
us, "I really love you, but I don't care at all what you do or who
you become"?

Any relationship, to remain alive, requires at least two living
participants. In this case, a God who does not exist as a convenience, magically giving us what we want, or feel we deserve, but
a God who simply *is*—the ground of being, the great "I AM." And
with this God, experienced by the prophet Jeremiah as "the true
God . . . the living God" (Jeremiah 10.10), we can come into our
own, no longer in fear of "being nothing," but people who can listen, who can change, who can be surprised. Even surprised by a
jealous God, who loves us enough to care when we stray. And
who has given us commandments to help us find the way home.

—*KATHLEEN NORRIS*

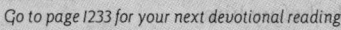

Go to page 1233 for your next devotional reading.

The Destruction of the Wicked City

2 A shatterer[d] has come up
    against you.
  Guard the ramparts;
    watch the road;
gird your loins;
  collect all your strength.

2 (For the LORD is restoring the
    majesty of Jacob,
  as well as the majesty of Israel,
though ravagers have ravaged them
  and ruined their branches.)

3 The shields of his warriors are red;
  his soldiers are clothed in
    crimson.
The metal on the chariots flashes
  on the day when he musters
    them;
  the chargers[e] prance.
4 The chariots race madly through the
    streets,
  they rush to and fro through
    the squares;
their appearance is like torches,
  they dart like lightning.
5 He calls his officers;
  they stumble as they come
    forward;
they hasten to the wall,
  and the mantelet[f] is set up.
6 The river gates are opened,
  the palace trembles.
7 It is decreed[f] that the city[g]
    be exiled,
  its slave women led away,
moaning like doves
  and beating their breasts.
8 Nineveh is like a pool
  whose waters[h] run away.
"Halt! Halt!"—
  but no one turns back.
9 "Plunder the silver,
  plunder the gold!
There is no end of treasure!
  An abundance of every precious
    thing!"

10 Devastation, desolation, and
    destruction!
  Hearts faint and knees tremble,
all loins quake,
  all faces grow pale!
11 What became of the lions' den,
  the cave[i] of the young lions,
where the lion goes,

and the lion's cubs, with no one
  to disturb them?
12 The lion has torn enough for
  his whelps
and strangled prey for his
    lionesses;
he has filled his caves with prey
  and his dens with torn flesh.

13 See, I am against you, says the LORD
of hosts, and I will burn your[j] chariots in
smoke, and the sword shall devour your
young lions; I will cut off your prey from
the earth, and the voice of your messengers shall be heard no more.

Ruin Imminent and Inevitable

3 Ah! City of bloodshed,
  utterly deceitful, full of booty—
    no end to the plunder!
2 The crack of whip and rumble
    of wheel,
  galloping horse and bounding
    chariot!
3 Horsemen charging,
  flashing sword and glittering
    spear,
piles of dead,
  heaps of corpses,
dead bodies without end—
  they stumble over the bodies!
4 Because of the countless
    debaucheries of the prostitute,
  gracefully alluring, mistress
    of sorcery,
who enslaves[k] nations through her
    debaucheries,
  and peoples through her sorcery,
5 I am against you,
  says the LORD of hosts,
and will lift up your skirts over
    your face;
and I will let nations look on your
    nakedness
  and kingdoms on your shame.
6 I will throw filth at you
  and treat you with contempt,
  and make you a spectacle.
7 Then all who see you will shrink
    from you and say,
"Nineveh is devastated; who will
    bemoan her?"

d Cn: Heb *scatterer*   *e* Cn Compare Gk Syr: Heb
cypresses   *f* Meaning of Heb uncertain   *g* Heb
it   *h* Cn Compare Gk: Heb *a pool, from the days
that she has become, and they*   *i* Cn: Heb *pasture*
j Heb *her*   *k* Heb *sells*

Where shall I seek comforters
  for you?

8 Are you better than Thebes[l]
  that sat by the Nile,
with water around her,
  her rampart a sea,
  water her wall?
9 Ethiopia[m] was her strength,
  Egypt too, and that without limit;
  Put and the Libyans were her[n]
    helpers.

10 Yet she became an exile,
  she went into captivity;
even her infants were dashed
    in pieces
  at the head of every street;
lots were cast for her nobles,
  all her dignitaries were bound
    in fetters.
11 You also will be drunken,
  you will go into hiding;[o]
you will seek
  a refuge from the enemy.
12 All your fortresses are like fig trees
  with first-ripe figs—
if shaken they fall
  into the mouth of the eater.
13 Look at your troops:
  they are women in your midst.
The gates of your land
  are wide open to your foes;
  fire has devoured the bars of
    your gates.

14 Draw water for the siege,
  strengthen your forts;

trample the clay,
  tread the mortar,
  take hold of the brick mold!
15 There the fire will devour you,
  the sword will cut you off.
  It will devour you like the locust.

Multiply yourselves like the locust,
  multiply like the grasshopper!
16 You increased your merchants
  more than the stars of the
    heavens.
The locust sheds its skin and
    flies away.
17 Your guards are like grasshoppers,
  your scribes like swarms[o]
    of locusts
settling on the fences
  on a cold day—
when the sun rises, they fly away;
  no one knows where they
    have gone.

18 Your shepherds are asleep,
  O king of Assyria;
  your nobles slumber.
Your people are scattered on the
    mountains
  with no one to gather them.
19 There is no assuaging your hurt,
  your wound is mortal.
All who hear the news about you
  clap their hands over you.
For who has ever escaped
  your endless cruelty?

l Heb *No-amon*   *m* Or *Nubia*; Heb *Cush*
n Gk: Heb *your*   *o* Meaning of Heb uncertain

Habakkuk

Habakkuk preached in Judah around 600 B.C. A century had passed since the northern kingdom of Israel had been conquered by Assyria. And now Assyria had fallen to Babylon (Chaldea). Judah itself was weak, both religiously and politically. Before long the southern kingdom would be overrun by Babylon.

The first two chapters of this book consist of a dialogue between Habakkuk and God. The prophet dares to complain about the way God governs the nations. Why does evil seem to triumph over good, the innocent suffer at the hands of the wicked? Why doesn't God use his power to stop the violence that is spreading everywhere? Instead of chastising Habakkuk for his impertinence, God tells him that he is at work in the midst of Babylon's rise to power. He will use this "fierce and impetuous nation" (1.6) as an instrument of judgment. But Babylon, too, will eventually be judged. As for the righteous, they must live by faith (see 2.4).

The closing verses of Habakkuk affirm that those who believe in God can still find joy in the midst of evil circumstances: "Though the fig tree does not blossom, and no fruit is on the vines; though the produce of the olive fails, and the fields yield no food; though the flock is cut off from the fold, and there is no herd in the stalls, yet I will rejoice in the LORD; I will exult in the God of my salvation" (3.17–18).

1 The oracle that the prophet Habakkuk saw.

The Prophet's Complaint

2 O LORD, how long shall I cry
      for help,
   and you will not listen?
   Or cry to you "Violence!"
      and you will not save?
3 Why do you make me see
      wrongdoing
   and look at trouble?
Destruction and violence are
      before me;
   strife and contention arise.
4 So the law becomes slack
   and justice never prevails.
The wicked surround the
      righteous—
   therefore judgment comes
      forth perverted.

5 Look at the nations, and see!
   Be astonished! Be astounded!

For a work is being done in
your days
that you would not believe if you
were told.
6 For I am rousing the Chaldeans,
that fierce and impetuous nation,
who march through the breadth of
the earth
to seize dwellings not their own.
7 Dread and fearsome are they;
their justice and dignity proceed
from themselves.
8 Their horses are swifter than
leopards,
more menacing than wolves
at dusk;
their horses charge.
Their horsemen come from far away;
they fly like an eagle swift
to devour.
9 They all come for violence,
with faces pressing[a] forward;
they gather captives like sand.
10 At kings they scoff,
and of rulers they make sport.
They laugh at every fortress,
and heap up earth to take it.
11 Then they sweep by like the wind;
they transgress and become guilty;
their own might is their god!

12 Are you not from of old,
O LORD my God, my Holy One?
You[b] shall not die.
O LORD, you have marked them for
judgment;
and you, O Rock, have established
them for punishment.
13 Your eyes are too pure to
behold evil,
and you cannot look on
wrongdoing;
why do you look on the treacherous,
and are silent when the wicked
swallow
those more righteous than they?
14 You have made people like the fish
of the sea,
like crawling things that have
no ruler.

15 The enemy[c] brings all of them up
with a hook;
he drags them out with his net,
he gathers them in his seine;
so he rejoices and exults.
16 Therefore he sacrifices to his net
and makes offerings to his seine;

for by them his portion is lavish,
and his food is rich.
17 Is he then to keep on emptying
his net,
and destroying nations without
mercy?

God's Reply to the Prophet's Complaint

2 I will stand at my watchpost,
and station myself on the rampart;
I will keep watch to see what he will
say to me,
and what he[d] will answer
concerning my complaint.
2 Then the LORD answered me
and said:
Write the vision;
make it plain on tablets,
so that a runner may read it.
3 For there is still a vision for the
appointed time;
it speaks of the end, and does not
lie.
If it seems to tarry, wait for it;
it will surely come, it will
not delay.
4 Look at the proud!
Their spirit is not right in them,
but the righteous live by
their faith.[e]
5 Moreover, wealth[f] is treacherous;
the arrogant do not endure.
They open their throats wide
as Sheol;
like Death they never have
enough.
They gather all nations for
themselves,
and collect all peoples as
their own.

The Woes of the Wicked

6 Shall not everyone taunt such people
and, with mocking riddles, say about
them,
"Alas for you who heap up what is
not your own!"
How long will you load
yourselves with goods taken
in pledge?
7 Will not your own creditors
suddenly rise,
and those who make you tremble
wake up?

a Meaning of Heb uncertain   *b* Ancient Heb
tradition: MT *We*   *c* Heb *He*   *d* Syr: Heb *I*
e Or *faithfulness*   *f* Other Heb Mss read *wine*

Then you will be booty for them.
8 Because you have plundered many
    nations,
  all that survive of the peoples
      shall plunder you—
  because of human bloodshed, and
      violence to the earth,
    to cities and all who live in them.

9 "Alas for you who get evil gain for
      your house,
  setting your nest on high
  to be safe from the reach of
      harm!"
10 You have devised shame for
      your house
  by cutting off many peoples;
  you have forfeited your life.

11 The very stones will cry out from the
      wall,
  and the plaster *g* will respond
      from the woodwork.

12 "Alas for you who build a town by
      bloodshed,
  and found a city on iniquity!"
13 Is it not from the LORD of hosts
      that peoples labor only to feed the
        flames,
  and nations weary themselves for
      nothing?
14 But the earth will be filled

g Or beam

THURSDAY

Scripture Reading
for Today:
Habakkuk 2.1–3

Verse for Today:
Habakkuk 2.3

*S*ometimes I Feel Neglected

So often I question the Lord. I wonder where he is and when he's
going to do something. I grumble and complain, mistaking the severe mercy of God for neglect. I feel forgotten and ignored. I think
my prayers are falling on deaf ears, when all the while he is listening. He is seeing far and deep, often protecting me from my wants,
waiting for my maturity to catch up with my desires. He is patient as my longings mellow to the point where I won't hurt myself and as I learn to desire his will more than mine.

Why is it so difficult for us to understand that God only
wants the best for us? Why is it so hard to take him at his word?
He's never lied to us. He never will lie to us. His promises can never be broken. They have withstood the test of time.

Next time you think you hear nothing in response to your
prayers, don't assume God isn't listening. He may simply want you
to rest in his shadow until he reveals his answer. When you hear a
direct "no," remind yourself there will always be a better "yes."
God is for you. And he will work out everything in conformity
with the purpose of his will. Everything (see Ephesians 1.11).

I pray for you and for myself—that we will both grow in our
faith. That the times we doubt God will grow fewer and fewer and
that the eyes of our hearts will be enlightened. That we may
know God's goodness, real and solid, even in the darkness. May we
come to realize that God is motivated by a love so strong, so
undying and so wise that we have nothing and no one to fear. He
only wants the best, and his best is ours to have. Wait for it.

—KATHY TROCCOLI

Go to page 1235 for your next devotional reading.

with the knowledge of the glory
　　of the Lord,
　　as the waters cover the sea.

15 "Alas for you who make your
　　　neighbors drink,
　　pouring out your wrath[h] until
　　　they are drunk,
　　in order to gaze on their
　　　nakedness!"
16 You will be sated with contempt
　　　instead of glory.
　　Drink, you yourself, and stagger![i]
　　The cup in the Lord's right hand
　　　will come around to you,
　　and shame will come upon
　　　your glory!
17 For the violence done to Lebanon
　　　will overwhelm you;
　　the destruction of the animals will
　　　terrify you—[j]
　　because of human bloodshed and
　　　violence to the earth,
　　to cities and all who live in them.

18 What use is an idol
　　　once its maker has shaped it—
　　a cast image, a teacher of lies?
　　For its maker trusts in what has
　　　been made,
　　　though the product is only an idol
　　　that cannot speak!
19 Alas for you who say to the wood,
　　　"Wake up!"
　　to silent stone, "Rouse yourself!"
　　Can it teach?
　　See, it is gold and silver plated,
　　　and there is no breath in it at all.

20 But the Lord is in his holy temple;
　　let all the earth keep silence
　　　before him!

3 A prayer of the prophet Habakkuk according to Shigionoth.

The Prophet's Prayer

2 O Lord, I have heard of your
　　　renown,
　　and I stand in awe, O Lord, of
　　　your work.
　　In our own time revive it;
　　　in our own time make it known;
　　　in wrath may you remember
　　　mercy.
3 God came from Teman,
　　the Holy One from Mount Paran.
　　　　　　　　　　　　　Selah

His glory covered the heavens,
　　and the earth was full of
　　　his praise.
4 The brightness was like the sun;
　　rays came forth from his hand,
　　where his power lay hidden.
5 Before him went pestilence,
　　and plague followed close behind.
6 He stopped and shook the earth;
　　he looked and made the
　　　nations tremble.
　　The eternal mountains were
　　　shattered;
　　along his ancient pathways
　　the everlasting hills sank low.
7 I saw the tents of Cushan under
　　　affliction;
　　the tent-curtains of the land of
　　　Midian trembled.
8 Was your wrath against the rivers,[k]
　　　O Lord?
　　Or your anger against the rivers,[k]
　　or your rage against the sea,[l]
　　when you drove your horses,
　　　your chariots to victory?
9 You brandished your naked bow,
　　sated[m] were the arrows at your
　　　command.[n]　　　　*Selah*
　　You split the earth with rivers.
10 The mountains saw you,
　　　and writhed;
　　a torrent of water swept by;
　　the deep gave forth its voice.
　　The sun[o] raised high its hands;
11 the moon[p] stood still in its exalted
　　　place,
　　at the light of your arrows
　　　speeding by,
　　at the gleam of your flashing
　　　spear.
12 In fury you trod the earth,
　　in anger you trampled nations.
13 You came forth to save your people,
　　to save your anointed.
　　You crushed the head of the
　　　wicked house,
　　laying it bare from foundation
　　　to roof.[n]　　　　*Selah*
14 You pierced with their[q] own arrows
　　　the head[r] of his warriors,[s]

---

[h] Or *poison*　　[i] Q Ms Gk: MT *be uncircumcised*
[j] Gk Syr: Meaning of Heb uncertain　　[k] Or
against River　　[l] Or *against Sea*　　[m] Cn: Heb
oaths　　[n] Meaning of Heb uncertain　　[o] Heb *It*
[p] Heb *sun, moon*　　[q] Heb *his*　　[r] Or *leader*　　[s] Vg
Compare Gk Syr: Meaning of Heb uncertain

who came like a whirlwind to
   scatter us,[t]
gloating as if ready to devour the
   poor who were in hiding.
15 You trampled the sea with
   your horses,
   churning the mighty waters.

16 I hear, and I tremble within;
   my lips quiver at the sound.
Rottenness enters into my bones,
   and my steps tremble[u]
      beneath me.
I wait quietly for the day of calamity
   to come upon the people who
   attack us.

Trust and Joy in the Midst of Trouble

17 Though the fig tree does not
      blossom,
   and no fruit is on the vines;

though the produce of the olive
      fails,
   and the fields yield no food;
though the flock is cut off from
      the fold,
   and there is no herd in the stalls,
18 yet I will rejoice in the LORD;
   I will exult in the God of my
      salvation.
19 GOD, the Lord, is my strength;
   he makes my feet like the feet of a
      deer,
   and makes me tread upon the
      heights.[v]

To the leader: with stringed[w]
instruments.

t Heb *me*
uncertain   u Cn Compare Gk: Meaning of Heb
   v Heb *my heights*   w Heb *my stringed*

---

*D*isappointment

Scripture Reading
for Today:
Habakkuk 3.17–19

Verses for Today:
Habakkuk 3.17–18

As I stopped to pray today, I brought to Jesus all the hopes and dreams I once held: for my marriage, my children, my parish. My faith was so strong and alive in my youth. Anything seemed possible.

And now? Well, sure, I still believe. I am just a bit disappointed. Our daughter says she has left the church. Our son seems depressed, and I do not know how to help him. Our parish is bravely plugging away, but so many people just do not seem to care. I ask Jesus: what's the point of it all? I have tried so hard to be faithful to you and your people. Why do I feel like such a failure?

Quietly, in the silence of my heart, the answer came as if Jesus were speaking: It was the same for me. It was the same for those first disciples. They had the suffering, the disappointment, the confusion and sense of failure. Don't give up now. You have not lost my path. You are very much on it. Yours is a path to resurrection.

—TERESA PIROLA

Go to page 1238 for your next devotional reading.

Zephaniah

The prophet Zephaniah was active during the reign of King Josiah of
Judah (640–609 B.C.). Josiah's father and grandfather had been vassal
kings under the power of Assyria. Both had embraced pagan worship
practices and allowed Canaanite Baal worship to flourish. As a result,
sacred prostitution and child sacrifice were practiced in Judah. Men and
women bowed to the sun, moon, and stars rather than to Israel's God.

Josiah came to the throne at the age of eight, after his father's as-
sassination. Once grown, he led a religious reform stimulated by reading the book of God's law (probably Deuteronomy) and by the words
of the prophetess Huldah. Though Josiah re-established Jerusalem as
the center of worship and got rid of its pagan priests, Judah reverted to
the old ways after his death.

Zephaniah speaks of the "day of the LORD" as a day of doom so all-
encompassing that birds are swept from the sky and fish vanish from
the sea. Though the nation would suffer, there would also be a day of
judgment for Israel's enemies. As with every true prophet, Zephaniah's
message is one not only of judgment but also of enduring hope: "The
LORD, your God, is in your midst, a warrior who gives victory; he will
rejoice over you with gladness, he will renew you in his love; he will
exult over you with loud singing" (3.17).

1 The word of the LORD that came to
Zephaniah son of Cushi son of Gedaliah son of Amariah son of Hezekiah, in
the days of King Josiah son of Amon of
Judah.

The Coming Judgment on Judah

2 I will utterly sweep away everything
 from the face of the earth, says
 the LORD.
3 I will sweep away humans and
 animals;

I will sweep away the birds of the
 air
 and the fish of the sea.
I will make the wicked stumble.[a]
I will cut off humanity
 from the face of the earth, says
 the LORD.
4 I will stretch out my hand against
 Judah,

---

[a] Cn: Heb *sea, and those who cause the wicked to
stumble*

and against all the inhabitants of
 Jerusalem;
and I will cut off from this place
 every remnant of Baal
and the name of the idolatrous
 priests;[b]
5 those who bow down on the roofs
 to the host of the heavens;
those who bow down and swear to
 the LORD,
 but also swear by Milcom;[c]
6 those who have turned back from
 following the LORD,
 who have not sought the LORD or
 inquired of him.

7 Be silent before the Lord GOD!
 For the day of the LORD is at hand;
the LORD has prepared a sacrifice,
 he has consecrated his guests.
8 And on the day of the LORD's
 sacrifice
I will punish the officials and the
 king's sons
 and all who dress themselves in
 foreign attire.
9 On that day I will punish
 all who leap over the threshold,
who fill their master's house
 with violence and fraud.

10 On that day, says the LORD,
 a cry will be heard from the
  Fish Gate,
a wail from the Second Quarter,
 a loud crash from the hills.
11 The inhabitants of the Mortar wail,
 for all the traders have perished;
 all who weigh out silver are
  cut off.
12 At that time I will search Jerusalem
 with lamps,
and I will punish the people
who rest complacently[d] on
 their dregs,
 those who say in their hearts,
"The LORD will not do good,
 nor will he do harm."
13 Their wealth shall be plundered,
 and their houses laid waste.
Though they build houses,
 they shall not inhabit them;
though they plant vineyards,
 they shall not drink wine
  from them.

The Great Day of the LORD

14 The great day of the LORD is near,

near and hastening fast;
the sound of the day of the LORD
 is bitter,
 the warrior cries aloud there.
15 That day will be a day of wrath,
 a day of distress and anguish,
a day of ruin and devastation,
 a day of darkness and gloom,
a day of clouds and thick darkness,
16 a day of trumpet blast and
  battle cry
against the fortified cities
 and against the lofty battlements.

17 I will bring such distress upon
 people
 that they shall walk like the blind;
because they have sinned against
 the LORD,
their blood shall be poured out
 like dust,
 and their flesh like dung.
18 Neither their silver nor their gold
 will be able to save them
 on the day of the LORD's wrath;
in the fire of his passion
 the whole earth shall be
  consumed;
for a full, a terrible end
 he will make of all the inhabitants
  of the earth.

Judgment on Israel's Enemies

2 Gather together, gather,
 O shameless nation,
2 before you are driven away
 like the drifting chaff,[e]
before there comes upon you
 the fierce anger of the LORD,
before there comes upon you
 the day of the LORD's wrath.
3 Seek the LORD, all you humble of the
 land,
 who do his commands;
seek righteousness, seek humility;
 perhaps you may be hidden
 on the day of the LORD's wrath.
4 For Gaza shall be deserted,
 and Ashkelon shall become a
  desolation;

---

b Compare Gk: Heb *the idolatrous priests with the
priests*   c Gk Mss Syr Vg: Heb *Malcam* (or, *their
king*)   d Heb *who thicken*   e Cn Compare Gk
Syr: Heb *before a decree is born; like chaff a day has
passed away*

Huldah

Her Name Means "Weasel"

THE
STORY
OF A
WOMAN

Read 2 Chronicles 34.22–33

She pressed the leather scroll against her breast, as though cradling a living being. The high priest, Hilkiah, stood before her. King Josiah wanted to know— would the words of the book of the law, which Hilkiah had just discovered in the temple, come to pass?

Holding the scroll by its wooden handles, she unrolled it carefully and began reading:

Her Character: *Trusted by the king with a matter of great importance, she was a prophetess whose word generated a significant religious reform.*
Her Sorrow: *That God's people had refused to respond to him with loving obedience, ignoring repeated warnings about the consequences of their unfaithfulness.*
Her Joy: *As a prophetess, she was privileged to be a messenger of God.*

> You shall love the LORD your God with all your heart, and with all your soul, and with all your might. Keep these words that I am commanding you today in your heart. But if you will not obey the LORD your God by diligently observing all his commandments and decrees, which I am commanding you today, then all these curses shall come upon you and overtake you: Cursed shall you be in the city, and cursed shall you be in the field. Cursed shall be your basket and your kneading bowl. Cursed shall be the fruit of your womb, the fruit of your ground.
>
> (Deuteronomy 6.5–6; 28.15–18)

In her mind, Huldah remembered Judah's terrible offenses. Still holding the scroll, she spoke the searing words:

> Thus says the LORD: I will indeed bring disaster upon this place and upon its inhabitants, all the curses that are written

in the book that was read before the king of Judah. Because they have forsaken me and have made offerings to other gods, so that they have provoked me to anger with all the works of their hands, my wrath will be poured out on this place and will not be quenched.

> (2 Chronicles 34.24–25)

Beyond the brief scene, imaginatively retold above, we know little of Huldah's story— only that God entrusted her with his word in a time of national crisis. She was one of only four women with an authentic prophetic ministry mentioned in the Old Testament (along with Miriam, Deborah, and Isaiah's wife). King Josiah consulted her about the amazing discovery of the book of the law (material that probably forms the core of the book of Deuteronomy) even though prophets like Jeremiah and Zephaniah were also active at the time.

Her words of prophecy confirmed the king's fear. Judah was standing at the brink of a terrible judgment. Across the centuries, God's slow anger had been building to a fiery crescendo. Thirty-five years after Huldah's prophecy, Judah was taken in chains to Babylon and all of its cities were destroyed.

Judgment and mercy, law and grace, punishment and salvation—these are the tensions that characterize the story of God's love affair with his people. Huldah was a woman who understood the paradox and who was not afraid to proclaim the truth— even to a king. She cherished God's Word in a time of spiritual crisis.

Praying With Huldah

When the king heard the words of the law he tore his clothes. Then the king commanded Hilkiah, Ahikam son of Shaphan, Abdon son of Micah, the secretary Shaphan, and the king's servant Asaiah: "Go, inquire of the LORD for me and for those who are left in Israel and in Judah, concerning the words of the book that has been found."—2 Chronicles 34.19–21

Offer Thanks: That God speaks clearly about what he expects from us.

Confess: Any complacency in the face of God's commandments.

Ask God: To help you understand the link between love and obedience.

Lift Your Heart

What a pleasure to have a clean house: The floors are thoroughly scrubbed and waxed, windows shine, and cobwebs have been routed from every nook and cranny. Our hearts can also become sullied by daily wear and tear, by disobedience and disregard for doing things God's way. Set aside a day to conduct a little spring cleaning of your soul. How well have you been doing on the basics—obeying the Ten Commandments? Check Deuteronomy 5.6–21 for a review in case you've forgotten them. Don't be so literal in your reading of the commandments that you forget idolatry can take the form of cherishing money, power, or even a person more than you love God. As you become conscious of your failings, don't wallow in them. Ask God to make your heart an attractive place for his indwelling presence. Then enjoy his forgiveness and take hold of his grace.

Father, may I have ears to hear your Word and a heart to obey it. Cleanse me from my sin and wash me until I am whiter than snow. Make my soul clean and pure, a broad and spacious place for your indwelling Spirit.

Go to page 1243 for your next devotional reading.

Ashdod's people shall be driven out
    at noon,
and Ekron shall be uprooted.

5 Ah, inhabitants of the seacoast,
    you nation of the Cherethites!
The word of the LORD is against you,
    O Canaan, land of the Philistines;
and I will destroy you until no
    inhabitant is left.
6 And you, O seacoast, shall be
    pastures,
meadows for shepherds
    and folds for flocks.
7 The seacoast shall become the
    possession
    of the remnant of the house
    of Judah,
on which they shall pasture,
and in the houses of Ashkelon
    they shall lie down at evening.
For the LORD their God will be
    mindful of them
    and restore their fortunes.

8 I have heard the taunts of Moab
    and the revilings of the
    Ammonites,
how they have taunted my people
    and made boasts against
    their territory.
9 Therefore, as I live, says the LORD of
    hosts,
    the God of Israel,
Moab shall become like Sodom
    and the Ammonites like
    Gomorrah,
a land possessed by nettles and
    salt pits,
    and a waste forever.
The remnant of my people shall
    plunder them,
    and the survivors of my nation
    shall possess them.
10 This shall be their lot in return for
    their pride,
because they scoffed and boasted
against the people of the LORD
    of hosts.
11 The LORD will be terrible
    against them;
he will shrivel all the gods of
    the earth,
and to him shall bow down,
    each in its place,
all the coasts and islands of
    the nations.

12 You also, O Ethiopians,*f*
    shall be killed by my sword.

13 And he will stretch out his hand
    against the north,
    and destroy Assyria;
and he will make Nineveh a
    desolation,
    a dry waste like the desert.
14 Herds shall lie down in it,
    every wild animal;*g*
the desert owl*h* and the
    screech owl*h*
    shall lodge on its capitals;
the owl*i* shall hoot at the window,
    the raven*j* croak on the
    threshold;
for its cedar work will be
    laid bare.
15 Is this the exultant city
    that lived secure,
that said to itself,
    "I am, and there is no one else"?
What a desolation it has become,
    a lair for wild animals!
Everyone who passes by it
    hisses and shakes the fist.

The Wickedness of Jerusalem

3 Ah, soiled, defiled,
    oppressing city!
2 It has listened to no voice;
    it has accepted no correction.
It has not trusted in the LORD;
    it has not drawn near to its God.

3 The officials within it
    are roaring lions;
its judges are evening wolves
    that leave nothing until
    the morning.
4 Its prophets are reckless,
    faithless persons;
its priests have profaned what
    is sacred,
they have done violence to
    the law.
5 The LORD within it is righteous;
    he does no wrong.
Every morning he renders his
    judgment,
    each dawn without fail;
but the unjust knows no shame.

---

f Or *Nubians;* Heb *Cushites*   *g* Tg Compare Gk:
Heb *nation*   *h* Meaning of Heb uncertain
i Cn: Heb *a voice*   *j* Gk Vg: Heb *desolation*

⁶ I have cut off nations;
    their battlements are in ruins;
I have laid waste their streets
    so that no one walks in them;
their cities have been made desolate,
    without people, without
      inhabitants.
⁷ I said, "Surely the city*k* will
    fear me,
    it will accept correction;
it will not lose sight*l*
    of all that I have brought upon it."
But they were the more eager
    to make all their deeds corrupt.

Punishment and Conversion of the Nations

⁸ Therefore wait for me, says the LORD,
    for the day when I arise as
      a witness.
For my decision is to gather nations,
    to assemble kingdoms,
to pour out upon them my
    indignation,
    all the heat of my anger;
for in the fire of my passion
    all the earth shall be consumed.

⁹ At that time I will change the speech
    of the peoples
    to a pure speech,
that all of them may call on the
    name of the LORD
    and serve him with one accord.
¹⁰ From beyond the rivers of
    Ethiopia*m*
my suppliants, my scattered ones,
    shall bring my offering.

¹¹ On that day you shall not be put
    to shame
    because of all the deeds by which
      you have rebelled against me;
for then I will remove from
    your midst
    your proudly exultant ones,
and you shall no longer be haughty
    in my holy mountain.
¹² For I will leave in the midst of you
    a people humble and lowly.
They shall seek refuge in the name
    of the LORD—
¹³   the remnant of Israel;
they shall do no wrong
    and utter no lies,

nor shall a deceitful tongue
    be found in their mouths.
Then they will pasture and lie down,
    and no one shall make them
      afraid.

A Song of Joy

¹⁴ Sing aloud, O daughter Zion;
    shout, O Israel!
Rejoice and exult with all your heart,
    O daughter Jerusalem!
¹⁵ The LORD has taken away the
    judgments against you,
    he has turned away your enemies.
The king of Israel, the LORD, is in
    your midst;
    you shall fear disaster no more.
¹⁶ On that day it shall be said to
    Jerusalem:
Do not fear, O Zion;
    do not let your hands grow weak.
¹⁷ The LORD, your God, is in
    your midst,
    a warrior who gives victory;
he will rejoice over you with
    gladness,
he will renew you*n* in his love;
he will exult over you with
    loud singing
¹⁸   as on a day of festival.*o*
I will remove disaster from you, *p*
    so that you will not bear reproach
      for it.
¹⁹ I will deal with all your oppressors
    at that time.
And I will save the lame
    and gather the outcast,
and I will change their shame
    into praise
    and renown in all the earth.
²⁰ At that time I will bring you home,
    at the time when I gather you;
for I will make you renowned
    and praised
    among all the peoples of
      the earth,
when I restore your fortunes
    before your eyes, says the LORD.

---

k Heb *it*   *l* Gk Syr: Heb *its dwelling will not be cut off*   *m* Or *Nubia*; Heb *Cush*   *n* Gk Syr: Heb *he will be silent*   *o* Gk Syr: Meaning of Heb uncertain   *p* Cn: Heb *I will remove from you; they were*

Haggai

Haggai reminds us of the importance of keeping "first things first."

The Jews had trickled back to Jerusalem after Cyrus of Persia conquered Babylon in 539 B.C. Immersed in the enormous task of rebuilding the city's economy and constructing homes for themselves, they were slow to rebuild the temple. The old men, remembering the beauty of Solomon's temple, had wept when the foundation of the new one was laid. It was so small, so simple, so ordinary. But neighboring Samaritans soon put a stop to the work, and before long the Jews lost heart for their task.

In 520 B.C. Haggai exhorted the people to make the temple their first priority, pointing out that their prosperity was directly linked to their priorities. Without putting God first, all their efforts would be in vain.

Despite considerable opposition from Judah's neighbors, the temple was completed four years after Haggai's prophetic exhortation. Even though the second temple was rustic by comparison to Solomon's, Haggai prophesied: "The latter splendor of this house shall be greater than the former, says the LORD of hosts" (2.9).

Haggai reminds us of the importance of putting God first in everything, reminding us of the first and greatest commandment: "You shall love the Lord your God with all your heart, and with all your soul, and with all your mind" (Matthew 22.37).

The Command to Rebuild the Temple

1 In the second year of King Darius, in the sixth month, on the first day of the month, the word of the LORD came by the prophet Haggai to Zerubbabel son of Shealtiel, governor of Judah, and to Joshua son of Jehozadak, the high priest: ²Thus says the LORD of hosts: These people say the time has not yet come to rebuild the LORD's house. ³Then the word of the LORD came by the prophet Haggai, saying: ⁴Is it a time for you yourselves to live in your paneled houses, while this house lies in ruins? ⁵Now therefore thus says the LORD of hosts: Consider how you have fared. ⁶You have sown much, and harvested little; you eat, but you never have enough; you drink, but you never have your fill; you clothe yourselves, but no

Priorities

MONDAY

Scripture Reading
for Today:
Haggai 1.2–13

Verse for Today:
Haggai 1.2

"Not now. I need to rebuild my house."

"Not now. It's time to plant the barley."

"Not now. I'm exhausted from rebuilding my house and planting my barley."

"The road to hell is paved not only with good intentions but with good reasons," a German preacher once said. And don't our "good reasons" seem so... well... reasonable?

We can easily understand, for example, why the Jews living in Jerusalem in 520 B.C. hadn't given first priority to rebuilding the Lord's temple. Returning home from years of exile in Babylon, they had found their fields neglected, their houses in ruins. Anxious over poor crops and low wages, they put the temple project on indefinite hold as they tried harder to make a better living. *Once things improve, we'll help out... contribute to the building fund...*

Quite reasonable and responsible, we think. But Haggai presents a radically different view: life is hard *because* people are not rebuilding the temple (2.9). In God's eyes, this is the task that has priority. Thus, though it seems to defy human reasoning, now is precisely the *right* time to get the project finished.

Haggai reminds me to scrutinize my own reasoning and priorities. What does God want me to do today... right now? Where is he calling me to put his business before my business?

I don't know about you, but if I don't ask these questions repeatedly, with prayer for the Spirit's guidance, I get towed under quickly by a riptide of personal goals and activities. Some are frivolous, some "reasonable and responsible"; some are even admirable. But to the extent that they are *my* plans and projects, pursuing them means building my own house and neglecting God's. Like the Israelites of Haggai's day, I am putting God off.

"Not now, Lord, I have to scour the sink."

"Not now, Lord, that file needs to be downloaded."

"Not now, Lord, you know I volunteered to help out with that fundraising campaign."

"Now, Louise."

—LOUISE PERROTTA

Go to page 1248 for your next devotional reading.

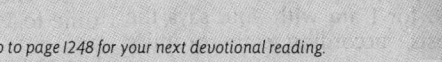

one is warm; and you that earn wages earn wages to put them into a bag with holes.

7 Thus says the LORD of hosts: Consider how you have fared. ⁸Go up to the hills and bring wood and build the house, so that I may take pleasure in it and be honored, says the LORD. ⁹You have looked for much, and, lo, it came to little; and when you brought it home, I blew it away. Why? says the LORD of hosts. Because my house lies in ruins, while all of you hurry off to your own houses. ¹⁰Therefore the heavens above you have withheld the dew, and the earth has withheld its produce. ¹¹And I have called for a drought on the land and the hills, on the grain, the new wine, the oil, on what the soil produces, on human beings and animals, and on all their labors.

12 Then Zerubbabel son of Shealtiel, and Joshua son of Jehozadak, the high priest, with all the remnant of the people, obeyed the voice of the LORD their God, and the words of the prophet Haggai, as the LORD their God had sent him; and the people feared the LORD. ¹³Then Haggai, the messenger of the LORD, spoke to the people with the LORD's message, saying, I am with you, says the LORD. ¹⁴And the LORD stirred up the spirit of Zerubbabel son of Shealtiel, governor of Judah, and the spirit of Joshua son of Jehozadak, the high priest, and the spirit of all the remnant of the people; and they came and worked on the house of the LORD of hosts, their God, ¹⁵on the twenty-fourth day of the month, in the sixth month.

The Future Glory of the Temple

2 In the second year of King Darius, ¹in the seventh month, on the twenty-first day of the month, the word of the LORD came by the prophet Haggai, saying: ²Speak now to Zerubbabel son of Shealtiel, governor of Judah, and to Joshua son of Jehozadak, the high priest, and to the remnant of the people, and say, ³Who is left among you that saw this house in its former glory? How does it look to you now? Is it not in your sight as nothing? ⁴Yet now take courage, O Zerubbabel, says the LORD; take courage, O Joshua, son of Jehozadak, the high priest; take courage, all you people of the land, says the LORD; work, for I am with you, says the LORD of hosts, ⁵according to the promise that I made you when you came out of

Egypt. My spirit abides among you; do not fear. ⁶For thus says the LORD of hosts: Once again, in a little while, I will shake the heavens and the earth and the sea and the dry land; ⁷and I will shake all the nations, so that the treasure of all nations shall come, and I will fill this house with splendor, says the LORD of hosts. ⁸The silver is mine, and the gold is mine, says the LORD of hosts. ⁹The latter splendor of this house shall be greater than the former, says the LORD of hosts; and in this place I will give prosperity, says the LORD of hosts.

A Rebuke and a Promise

10 On the twenty-fourth day of the ninth month, in the second year of Darius, the word of the LORD came by the prophet Haggai, saying: ¹¹Thus says the LORD of hosts: Ask the priests for a ruling: ¹²If one carries consecrated meat in the fold of one's garment, and with the fold touches bread, or stew, or wine, or oil, or any kind of food, does it become holy? The priests answered, "No." ¹³Then Haggai said, "If one who is unclean by contact with a dead body touches any of these, does it become unclean?" The priests answered, "Yes, it becomes unclean." ¹⁴Haggai then said, So it is with this people, and with this nation before me, says the LORD; and so with every work of their hands; and what they offer there is unclean. ¹⁵But now, consider what will come to pass from this day on. Before a stone was placed upon a stone in the LORD's temple, ¹⁶how did you fare?ᵃ When one came to a heap of twenty measures, there were but ten; when one came to the wine vat to draw fifty measures, there were but twenty. ¹⁷I struck you and all the products of your toil with blight and mildew and hail; yet you did not return to me, says the LORD. ¹⁸Consider from this day on, from the twenty-fourth day of the ninth month. Since the day that the foundation of the LORD's temple was laid, consider: ¹⁹Is there any seed left in the barn? Do the vine, the fig tree, the pomegranate, and the olive tree still yield nothing? From this day on I will bless you.

God's Promise to Zerubbabel

20 The word of the LORD came a second time to Haggai on the twenty-fourth day

ᵃ Gk: Heb *since they were*

of the month: [21]Speak to Zerubbabel, governor of Judah, saying, I am about to shake the heavens and the earth, [22]and to overthrow the throne of kingdoms; I am about to destroy the strength of the kingdoms of the nations, and overthrow the chariots and their riders; and the horses and their riders shall fall, every one by the sword of a comrade. [23]On that day, says the LORD of hosts, I will take you, O Zerubbabel my servant, son of Shealtiel, says the LORD, and make you like a signet ring; for I have chosen you, says the LORD of hosts.

Zechariah

Zechariah's prophecies were delivered during 520–518 B.C. Like Haggai, he spoke to the Jewish exiles returning from Babylon, encouraging them in the difficult work of rebuilding the temple in Jerusalem. But unlike Haggai, who speaks directly and plainly, Zechariah's words are highly symbolic, detailing marvelous visions of angels, flying scrolls, golden lampstands, chariots and horses, and various other images. Zechariah's words encouraged the people and buoyed up their leaders, Joshua the high priest and Zerubbabel, a descendent of King David.

Written five hundred years before the birth of Christ, the book of Zechariah contains many Messianic prophecies that were fulfilled in Jesus. Here are just a few:

"Rejoice greatly, O daughter Zion! Shout aloud, O daughter Jerusalem! Lo, your king comes to you; triumphant and victorious is he, humble and riding on a donkey, on a colt, the foal of a donkey" (9.9; see Matthew 21.1–5).

"Then the LORD said to me, 'Throw it into the treasury'—this lordly price at which I was valued by them. So I took the thirty shekels of silver and threw them into the treasury in the house of the LORD" (11.13; see Matthew 26.14–16; 27.3–6).

"When they look on the one whom they have pierced, they shall mourn for him, as one mourns for an only child, and weep bitterly over him, as one weeps over a firstborn" (12.10; see John 19.33–37).

Israel Urged to Repent

1 In the eighth month, in the second year of Darius, the word of the LORD came to the prophet Zechariah son of Berechiah son of Iddo, saying: ²The LORD was very angry with your ancestors. ³Therefore say to them, Thus says the LORD of hosts: Return to me, says the LORD of hosts, and I will return to you, says the LORD of hosts. ⁴Do not be like your ancestors, to whom the former prophets proclaimed, "Thus says the LORD of hosts, Return from your evil ways and from your evil deeds." But they did not hear or heed me, says the LORD. ⁵Your ancestors, where are they? And the prophets, do they live forever? ⁶But my words and my statutes, which I commanded my servants the prophets,

did they not overtake your ancestors? So they repented and said, "The LORD of hosts has dealt with us according to our ways and deeds, just as he planned to do."

First Vision: The Horsemen

7 On the twenty-fourth day of the eleventh month, the month of Shebat, in the second year of Darius, the word of the LORD came to the prophet Zechariah son of Berechiah son of Iddo; and Zechariah[a] said, 8In the night I saw a man riding on a red horse! He was standing among the myrtle trees in the glen; and behind him were red, sorrel, and white horses. 9Then I said, "What are these, my lord?" The angel who talked with me said to me, "I will show you what they are." 10So the man who was standing among the myrtle trees answered, "They are those whom the LORD has sent to patrol the earth." 11Then they spoke to the angel of the LORD who was standing among the myrtle trees, "We have patrolled the earth, and lo, the whole earth remains at peace." 12Then the angel of the LORD said, "O LORD of hosts, how long will you withhold mercy from Jerusalem and the cities of Judah, with which you have been angry these seventy years?" 13Then the LORD replied with gracious and comforting words to the angel who talked with me. 14So the angel who talked with me said to me, Proclaim this message: Thus says the LORD of hosts; I am very jealous for Jerusalem and for Zion. 15And I am extremely angry with the nations that are at ease; for while I was only a little angry, they made the disaster worse. 16Therefore, thus says the LORD, I have returned to Jerusalem with compassion; my house shall be built in it, says the LORD of hosts, and the measuring line shall be stretched out over Jerusalem. 17Proclaim further: Thus says the LORD of hosts: My cities shall again overflow with prosperity; the LORD will again comfort Zion and again choose Jerusalem.

Second Vision: The Horns and the Smiths

18[b]And I looked up and saw four horns. 19I asked the angel who talked with me, "What are these?" And he answered me, "These are the horns that have scattered Judah, Israel, and Jerusalem." 20Then the LORD showed me four blacksmiths. 21And I asked, "What are they coming to do?" He answered, "These are the horns that scattered Judah, so that no head

could be raised; but these have come to terrify them, to strike down the horns of the nations that lifted up their horns against the land of Judah to scatter its people."[c]

Third Vision: The Man with a Measuring Line

2[d] I looked up and saw a man with a measuring line in his hand. 2Then I asked, "Where are you going?" He answered me, "To measure Jerusalem, to see what is its width and what is its length." 3Then the angel who talked with me came forward, and another angel came forward to meet him, 4and said to him, "Run, say to that young man: Jerusalem shall be inhabited like villages without walls, because of the multitude of people and animals in it. 5For I will be a wall of fire all around it, says the LORD, and I will be the glory within it."

Interlude: An Appeal to the Exiles

6 Up, up! Flee from the land of the north, says the LORD; for I have spread you abroad like the four winds of heaven, says the LORD. 7Up! Escape to Zion, you that live with daughter Babylon. 8For thus said the LORD of hosts (after his glory[e] sent me) regarding the nations that plundered you: Truly, one who touches you touches the apple of my eye.[f] 9See now, I am going to raise[g] my hand against them, and they shall become plunder for their own slaves. Then you will know that the LORD of hosts has sent me. 10Sing and rejoice, O daughter Zion! For lo, I will come and dwell in your midst, says the LORD. 11Many nations shall join themselves to the LORD on that day, and shall be my people; and I will dwell in your midst. And you shall know that the LORD of hosts has sent me to you. 12The LORD will inherit Judah as his portion in the holy land, and will again choose Jerusalem.

13 Be silent, all people, before the LORD; for he has roused himself from his holy dwelling.

Fourth Vision: Joshua and Satan

3 Then he showed me the high priest Joshua standing before the angel of

---

a Heb *and he*   b Ch 2.1 in Heb   c Heb *it*
d Ch 2.5 in Heb   e Cn: Heb *after glory he*
f Heb *his eye*   g Or *wave*

the LORD, and Satan[h] standing at his right hand to accuse him. ²And the LORD said to Satan,[h] "The LORD rebuke you, O Satan![h] The LORD who has chosen Jerusalem rebuke you! Is not this man a brand plucked from the fire?" ³Now Joshua was dressed with filthy clothes as he stood before the angel. ⁴The angel said to those who were standing before him, "Take off his filthy clothes." And to him he said, "See, I have taken your guilt away from you, and I will clothe you with festal apparel." ⁵And I said, "Let them put a clean turban on his head." So they put a clean turban on his head and clothed him with the apparel; and the angel of the LORD was standing by.

6 Then the angel of the LORD assured Joshua, saying ⁷"Thus says the LORD of hosts: If you will walk in my ways and keep my requirements, then you shall rule my house and have charge of my courts, and I will give you the right of access among those who are standing here. ⁸Now listen, Joshua, high priest, you and your colleagues who sit before you! For they are an omen of things to come: I am going to bring my servant the Branch. ⁹For on the stone that I have set before Joshua,

on a single stone with seven facets, I will engrave its inscription, says the LORD of hosts, and I will remove the guilt of this land in a single day. ¹⁰On that day, says the LORD of hosts, you shall invite each other to come under your vine and fig tree."

Fifth Vision: The Lampstand and Olive Trees

4 The angel who talked with me came again, and wakened me, as one is wakened from sleep. ²He said to me, "What do you see?" And I said, "I see a lampstand all of gold, with a bowl on the top of it; there are seven lamps on it, with seven lips on each of the lamps that are on the top of it. ³And by it there are two olive trees, one on the right of the bowl and the other on its left." ⁴I said to the angel who talked with me, "What are these, my lord?" ⁵Then the angel who talked with me answered me, "Do you not know what these are?" I said, "No, my lord." ⁶He said to me, "This is the word of the LORD to Zerubbabel: Not by might, nor by power, but by my spirit, says the LORD of hosts. ⁷What

[h] Or the Accuser; Heb the Adversary

TUESDAY

Scripture Reading for Today:
Zechariah 3.1–5

Verse for Today:
Zechariah 3.1

Wise Counsel

I have understood two opposites—one is the wisest thing that anyone may do in this life, the other is the most foolish. The wisest thing is for a person to act according to the will and counsel of his greatest friend. This blessed friend is Jesus. It is his will and counsel that we should stay with him, and hold ourselves closely to him forever, in whatever state we may be; for whether we are clean or foul it is all one to his love.

And then we are made fearful by our enemy and through our own folly and blindness, which say to us, "You know well that you are a wretch, a sinner and faithless. You do not keep the commandments. You are always promising our Lord you will do better, and, starting right away, you fall into the same sin—especially sloth and wasting time." For this is the beginning of sin in my sight, particularly for those who have given themselves to serve God by holding his blessed goodness in their hearts.

—JULIAN OF NORWICH

Go to page 1251 for your next devotional reading.

are you, O great mountain? Before Zerubbabel you shall become a plain; and he shall bring out the top stone amid shouts of 'Grace, grace to it!' "

8 Moreover the word of the Lord came to me, saying, 9"The hands of Zerubbabel have laid the foundation of this house; his hands shall also complete it. Then you will know that the Lord of hosts has sent me to you. 10For whoever has despised the day of small things shall rejoice, and shall see the plummet in the hand of Zerubbabel.

"These seven are the eyes of the Lord, which range through the whole earth." 11Then I said to him, "What are these two olive trees on the right and the left of the lampstand?" 12And a second time I said to him, "What are these two branches of the olive trees, which pour out the oil[i] through the two golden pipes?" 13He said to me, "Do you not know what these are?" I said, "No, my lord." 14Then he said, "These are the two anointed ones who stand by the Lord of the whole earth."

Sixth Vision: The Flying Scroll

5 Again I looked up and saw a flying scroll. 2And he said to me, "What do you see?" I answered, "I see a flying scroll; its length is twenty cubits, and its width ten cubits." 3Then he said to me, "This is the curse that goes out over the face of the whole land; for everyone who steals shall be cut off according to the writing on one side, and everyone who swears falsely[j] shall be cut off according to the writing on the other side. 4I have sent it out, says the Lord of hosts, and it shall enter the house of the thief, and the house of anyone who swears falsely by my name; and it shall abide in that house and consume it, both timber and stones."

Seventh Vision: The Woman in a Basket

5 Then the angel who talked with me came forward and said to me, "Look up and see what this is that is coming out." 6I said, "What is it?" He said, "This is a basket[k] coming out." And he said, "This is their iniquity[l] in all the land." 7Then a leaden cover was lifted, and there was a woman sitting in the basket![k] 8And he said, "This is Wickedness." So he thrust her back into the basket,[k] and pressed the leaden weight down on its mouth. 9Then I looked up and saw two women coming forward. The wind was in their wings; they

had wings like the wings of a stork, and they lifted up the basket[k] between earth and sky. 10Then I said to the angel who talked with me, "Where are they taking the basket?"[k] 11He said to me, "To the land of Shinar, to build a house for it; and when this is prepared, they will set the basket[k] down there on its base."

Eighth Vision: Four Chariots

6 And again I looked up and saw four chariots coming out from between two mountains—mountains of bronze. 2The first chariot had red horses, the second chariot black horses, 3the third chariot white horses, and the fourth chariot dappled gray[m] horses. 4Then I said to the angel who talked with me, "What are these, my lord?" 5The angel answered me, "These are the four winds[n] of heaven going out, after presenting themselves before the Lord of all the earth. 6The chariot with the black horses goes toward the north country, the white ones go toward the west country,[o] and the dappled ones go toward the south country." 7When the steeds came out, they were impatient to get off and patrol the earth. And he said, "Go, patrol the earth." So they patrolled the earth. 8Then he cried out to me, "Lo, those who go toward the north country have set my spirit at rest in the north country."

The Coronation of the Branch

9 The word of the Lord came to me: 10Collect silver and gold[p] from the exiles—from Heldai, Tobijah, and Jedaiah—who have arrived from Babylon; and go the same day to the house of Josiah son of Zephaniah. 11Take the silver and gold and make a crown,[q] and set it on the head of the high priest Joshua son of Jehozadak; 12say to him: Thus says the Lord of hosts: Here is a man whose name is Branch: for he shall branch out in his place, and he shall build the temple of the Lord. 13It is he that shall build the temple of the Lord; he shall bear royal honor, and shall sit upon his throne and rule. There shall be a priest by his throne, with peaceful under-

---

i Cn: Heb gold   j The word falsely added from verse 4   k Heb ephah   l Gk Compare Syr: Heb their eye   m Compare Gk: Meaning of Heb uncertain   n Or spirits   o Cn: Heb go after them p Cn Compare verse 11: Heb lacks silver and gold q Gk Mss Syr Tg: Heb crowns standing between the two of them. ¹⁴And the crown^r shall be in the care of Heldai,^s Tobijah, Jedaiah, and Josiah^t son of Zephaniah, as a memorial in the temple of the LORD.

15 Those who are far off shall come and help to build the temple of the LORD; and you shall know that the LORD of hosts has sent me to you. This will happen if you diligently obey the voice of the LORD your God.

Hypocritical Fasting Condemned

7 In the fourth year of King Darius, the word of the LORD came to Zechariah on the fourth day of the ninth month, which is Chislev. ²Now the people of Bethel had sent Sharezer and Regemmelech and their men, to entreat the favor of the LORD, ³and to ask the priests of the house of the LORD of hosts and the prophets, "Should I mourn and practice abstinence in the fifth month, as I have done for so many years?" ⁴Then the word of the LORD of hosts came to me: ⁵Say to all the people of the land and the priests: When you fasted and lamented in the fifth month and in the seventh, for these seventy years, was it for me that you fasted? ⁶And when you eat and when you drink, do you not eat and drink only for yourselves? ⁷Were not these the words that the LORD proclaimed by the former prophets, when Jerusalem was inhabited and in prosperity, along with the towns around it, and when the Negeb and the Shephelah were inhabited?

Punishment for Rejecting God's Demands

8 The word of the LORD came to Zechariah, saying: ⁹Thus says the LORD of hosts: Render true judgments, show kindness and mercy to one another; ¹⁰do not oppress the widow, the orphan, the alien, or the poor; and do not devise evil in your hearts against one another. ¹¹But they refused to listen, and turned a stubborn shoulder, and stopped their ears in order not to hear. ¹²They made their hearts adamant in order not to hear the law and the words that the LORD of hosts had sent by his spirit through the former prophets. Therefore great wrath came from the LORD of hosts. ¹³Just as, when I^u called, they would not hear, so, when they called, I would not hear, says the LORD of hosts, ¹⁴and I scattered them with a whirlwind among all the nations that they had not

known. Thus the land they left was desolate, so that no one went to and fro, and a pleasant land was made desolate.

God's Promises to Zion

8 The word of the LORD of hosts came to me, saying: ²Thus says the LORD of hosts: I am jealous for Zion with great jealousy, and I am jealous for her with great wrath. ³Thus says the LORD: I will return to Zion, and will dwell in the midst of Jerusalem; Jerusalem shall be called the faithful city, and the mountain of the LORD of hosts shall be called the holy mountain. ⁴Thus says the LORD of hosts: Old men and old women shall again sit in the streets of Jerusalem, each with staff in hand because of their great age. ⁵And the streets of the city shall be full of boys and girls playing in its streets. ⁶Thus says the LORD of hosts: Even though it seems impossible to the remnant of this people in these days, should it also seem impossible to me, says the LORD of hosts? ⁷Thus says the LORD of hosts: I will save my people from the east country and from the west country; ⁸and I will bring them to live in Jerusalem. They shall be my people and I will be their God, in faithfulness and in righteousness.

9 Thus says the LORD of hosts: Let your hands be strong—you that have recently been hearing these words from the mouths of the prophets who were present when the foundation was laid for the rebuilding of the temple, the house of the LORD of hosts. ¹⁰For before those days there were no wages for people or for animals, nor was there any safety from the foe for those who went out or came in, and I set them all against one another. ¹¹But now I will not deal with the remnant of this people as in the former days, says the LORD of hosts. ¹²For there shall be a sowing of peace; the vine shall yield its fruit, the ground shall give its produce, and the skies shall give their dew; and I will cause the remnant of this people to possess all these things. ¹³Just as you have been a cursing among the nations, O house of Judah and house of Israel, so I will save you and you shall be a blessing. Do not be afraid, but let your hands be strong.

14 For thus says the LORD of hosts: Just as I purposed to bring disaster upon you, when your ancestors provoked me to wrath, and I did not relent, says the LORD of hosts, ¹⁵so again I have purposed in these days to do good to Jerusalem and to the house of Judah; do not be afraid. ¹⁶These are the things that you shall do: Speak the truth to one another, render in your gates judgments that are true and make for peace, ¹⁷do not devise evil in your hearts against one another, and love no false oath; for all these are things that I hate, says the LORD.

Joyful Fasting

18 The word of the LORD of hosts came to me, saying: ¹⁹Thus says the LORD of hosts: The fast of the fourth month, and the fast of the fifth, and the fast of the seventh, and the fast of the tenth, shall be seasons of joy and gladness, and cheerful festivals for the house of Judah: therefore love truth and peace.

WEDNESDAY

God With Us

Scripture Reading
for Today:
Zechariah 8.1–8

Verse for Today:
Zechariah 8.6

To a weary people in a desolate city, the prophet Zechariah delivered unbelievable news. The Lord of hosts, who Israel had thought had abandoned them once and for all, was coming back. The return of its powerful God would transform their city, Jerusalem, and the life of its inhabitants. Its streets would be converted from thoroughfares of death, destruction, and fear to avenues of peace and laughter. God would bring back home all the people who had been scattered to other lands. Days of fasting would become occasions for feasting. Zechariah calls this divine program a "sowing of peace" (8.12).

As Christians we believe that we have already begun to live "in these days" described by Zechariah 8.6, that God dwells in the midst of our communities, and even more, that God also dwells within each of us. What Zechariah announced as a future hope, we believe has come to pass. The seeds of peace, sown by God's return to Jerusalem, are now exploding with hidden life in the soil of every space occupied by God's people, cities, parishes, work places, even traffic-filled and violence-ridden streets. The whole cosmos, permeated with divine intentions for our welfare, nourishes these seeds as they grow and makes God's presence among us noticeable to others. Therefore, we no longer fast in mourning. We celebrate.

If we find ourselves thinking that Zechariah describes ideals that are impossible because of the human condition, or that we will never see such things in our lifetime, or that these are marvels reserved for heaven, the Lord continues to ask us, "Even though it seems impossible to the remnant of this people in these days, should it also seem impossible to me?" (8.6). Does the day yet lie in the future when perfect strangers will say to us, "Let us go with you, for we have heard that God is with you" (8.23)?

—*ELIZABETH M. NAGEL*

Go to page 1259 for your next devotional reading.

Many Peoples Drawn to Jerusalem

20 Thus says the LORD of hosts: Peoples shall yet come, the inhabitants of many cities; 21the inhabitants of one city shall go to another, saying, "Come, let us go to entreat the favor of the LORD, and to seek the LORD of hosts; I myself am going." 22Many peoples and strong nations shall come to seek the LORD of hosts in Jerusalem, and to entreat the favor of the LORD. 23Thus says the LORD of hosts: In those days ten men from nations of every language shall take hold of a Jew, grasping his garment and saying, "Let us go with you, for we have heard that God is with you."

Judgment on Israel's Enemies

9   An Oracle.

The word of the LORD is against the
    land of Hadrach
  and will rest upon Damascus.
For to the LORD belongs the capital*ᵛ*
    of Aram,*ʷ*
  as do all the tribes of Israel;
2 Hamath also, which borders on it,
  Tyre and Sidon, though they are
    very wise.
3 Tyre has built itself a rampart,
  and heaped up silver like dust,
  and gold like the dirt of the
    streets.
4 But now, the Lord will strip it of its
    possessions
  and hurl its wealth into the sea,
  and it shall be devoured by fire.

5 Ashkelon shall see it and be afraid;
  Gaza too, and shall writhe in
    anguish;
  Ekron also, because its hopes
    are withered.
The king shall perish from Gaza;
  Ashkelon shall be uninhabited;
6 a mongrel people shall settle
    in Ashdod,
  and I will make an end of the
    pride of Philistia.
7 I will take away its blood from
    its mouth,
  and its abominations from
    between its teeth;
it too shall be a remnant for
    our God;
  it shall be like a clan in Judah,

and Ekron shall be like the
    Jebusites.
8 Then I will encamp at my house as
    a guard,
  so that no one shall march to
    and fro;
no oppressor shall again overrun
    them,
  for now I have seen with my
    own eyes.

The Coming Ruler of God's People

9 Rejoice greatly, O daughter Zion!
  Shout aloud, O daughter
    Jerusalem!
Lo, your king comes to you;
  triumphant and victorious is he,
humble and riding on a donkey,
  on a colt, the foal of a donkey.
10 He*ˣ* will cut off the chariot
    from Ephraim
  and the war-horse from Jerusalem;
and the battle bow shall be cut off,
  and he shall command peace to
    the nations;
his dominion shall be from sea
    to sea,
  and from the River to the ends of
    the earth.

11 As for you also, because of the
    blood of my covenant
    with you,
  I will set your prisoners free from
    the waterless pit.
12 Return to your stronghold,
    O prisoners of hope;
  today I declare that I will restore
    to you double.
13 For I have bent Judah as my bow;
  I have made Ephraim its arrow.
I will arouse your sons, O Zion,
  against your sons, O Greece,
  and wield you like a
    warrior's sword.

14 Then the LORD will appear
    over them,
  and his arrow go forth like
    lightning;
the Lord GOD will sound the
    trumpet
  and march forth in the whirlwinds
    of the south.
15 The LORD of hosts will protect them,

---

v Heb *eye*   *w* Cn: Heb *of Adam* (or *of humankind*)
x Gk: Heb *I*

and they shall devour and tread
   down the slingers;[y]
they shall drink their blood[z]
   like wine,
and be full like a bowl,
   drenched like the corners of
      the altar.

16 On that day the LORD their God will
      save them
   for they are the flock of
      his people;
for like the jewels of a crown
   they shall shine on his land.
17 For what goodness and beauty
      are his!
   Grain shall make the young
      men flourish,
   and new wine the young women.

Restoration of Judah and Israel

10 Ask rain from the LORD
   in the season of the spring rain,
from the LORD who makes the storm
      clouds,
   who gives showers of rain
      to you,[a]
   the vegetation in the field
      to everyone.
2 For the teraphim[b] utter nonsense,
   and the diviners see lies;
the dreamers tell false dreams,
   and give empty consolation.
Therefore the people wander
      like sheep;
   they suffer for lack of a shepherd.

3 My anger is hot against the
      shepherds,
   and I will punish the leaders;[c]
for the LORD of hosts cares for his
      flock, the house of Judah,
   and will make them like his
      proud war-horse.
4 Out of them shall come the
      cornerstone,
   out of them the tent peg,
out of them the battle bow,
   out of them every commander.
5 Together they shall be like warriors
      in battle,
   trampling the foe in the mud of
      the streets;
they shall fight, for the LORD is with
      them,
   and they shall put to shame the
      riders on horses.

6 I will strengthen the house of Judah,
   and I will save the house
      of Joseph.
I will bring them back because I
      have compassion on them,
   and they shall be as though I had
      not rejected them;
for I am the LORD their God and I
      will answer them.
7 Then the people of Ephraim shall
      become like warriors,
   and their hearts shall be glad as
      with wine.
Their children shall see it and
      rejoice,
   their hearts shall exult in the LORD.

8 I will signal for them and gather
      them in,
   for I have redeemed them,
and they shall be as numerous as
      they were before.
9 Though I scattered them among
      the nations,
   yet in far countries they shall
      remember me,
and they shall rear their children
      and return.
10 I will bring them home from the
      land of Egypt,
   and gather them from Assyria;
I will bring them to the land of
      Gilead and to Lebanon,
   until there is no room for them.
11 They[d] shall pass through the sea of
      distress,
   and the waves of the sea shall be
      struck down,
and all the depths of the Nile
      dried up.
The pride of Assyria shall be
      laid low,
   and the scepter of Egypt
      shall depart.
12 I will make them strong in the LORD,
   and they shall walk in his name,
         says the LORD.

11 Open your doors, O Lebanon,
   so that fire may devour
      your cedars!
2 Wail, O cypress, for the cedar
      has fallen,
   for the glorious trees are ruined!

---

y Cn: Heb *the slingstones*   *z* Gk: Heb *shall drink*
a Heb *them*   *b* Or *household gods*   *c* Or *male goats*   *d* Gk: Heb *He*

Wail, oaks of Bashan,
>   for the thick forest has
>   been felled!
3 Listen, the wail of the shepherds,
>   for their glory is despoiled!
> Listen, the roar of the lions,
>   for the thickets of the Jordan
>   are destroyed!

Two Kinds of Shepherds

4 Thus said the LORD my God: Be a shepherd of the flock doomed to slaughter. 5Those who buy them kill them and go unpunished; and those who sell them say, "Blessed be the LORD, for I have become rich"; and their own shepherds have no pity on them. 6For I will no longer have pity on the inhabitants of the earth, says the LORD. I will cause them, every one, to fall each into the hand of a neighbor, and each into the hand of the king; and they shall devastate the earth, and I will deliver no one from their hand.

7 So, on behalf of the sheep merchants, I became the shepherd of the flock doomed to slaughter. I took two staffs; one I named Favor, the other I named Unity, and I tended the sheep. 8In one month I disposed of the three shepherds, for I had become impatient with them, and they also detested me. 9So I said, "I will not be your shepherd. What is to die, let it die; what is to be destroyed, let it be destroyed; and let those that are left devour the flesh of one another!" 10I took my staff Favor and broke it, annulling the covenant that I had made with all the peoples. 11So it was annulled on that day, and the sheep merchants, who were watching me, knew that it was the word of the LORD. 12I then said to them, "If it seems right to you, give me my wages; but if not, keep them." So they weighed out as my wages thirty shekels of silver. 13Then the LORD said to me, "Throw it into the treasury"*e*—this lordly price at which I was valued by them. So I took the thirty shekels of silver and threw them into the treasury*e* in the house of the LORD. 14Then I broke my second staff Unity, annulling the family ties between Judah and Israel.

15 Then the LORD said to me: Take once more the implements of a worthless shepherd. 16For I am now raising up in the land a shepherd who does not care for the perishing, or seek the wandering,*f* or heal the maimed, or nourish the healthy,*g* but devours the flesh of the fat ones, tearing off even their hoofs.
17 Oh, my worthless shepherd,
>   who deserts the flock!
> May the sword strike his arm
>   and his right eye!
> Let his arm be completely withered,
>   his right eye utterly blinded!

Jerusalem's Victory

12

> An Oracle.

The word of the LORD concerning Israel: Thus says the LORD, who stretched out the heavens and founded the earth and formed the human spirit within: 2See, I am about to make Jerusalem a cup of reeling for all the surrounding peoples; it will be against Judah also in the siege against Jerusalem. 3On that day I will make Jerusalem a heavy stone for all the peoples; all who lift it shall grievously hurt themselves. And all the nations of the earth shall come together against it. 4On that day, says the LORD, I will strike every horse with panic, and its rider with madness. But on the house of Judah I will keep a watchful eye, when I strike every horse of the peoples with blindness. 5Then the clans of Judah shall say to themselves, "The inhabitants of Jerusalem have strength through the LORD of hosts, their God."

6 On that day I will make the clans of Judah like a blazing pot on a pile of wood, like a flaming torch among sheaves; and they shall devour to the right and to the left all the surrounding peoples, while Jerusalem shall again be inhabited in its place, in Jerusalem.

7 And the LORD will give victory to the tents of Judah first, that the glory of the house of David and the glory of the inhabitants of Jerusalem may not be exalted over that of Judah. 8On that day the LORD will shield the inhabitants of Jerusalem so that the feeblest among them on that day shall be like David, and the house of David shall be like God, like the angel of the LORD, at their head. 9And on that day I will seek to destroy all the nations that come against Jerusalem.

---

e Syr: Heb *it to the potter*   *f* Syr Compare Gk Vg: Heb *the youth*   *g* Meaning of Heb uncertain

Mourning for the Pierced One

10 And I will pour out a spirit of compassion and supplication on the house of David and the inhabitants of Jerusalem, so that, when they look on the one[h] whom they have pierced, they shall mourn for him, as one mourns for an only child, and weep bitterly over him, as one weeps over a firstborn. 11On that day the mourning in Jerusalem will be as great as the mourning for Hadad-rimmon in the plain of Megiddo. 12The land shall mourn, each family by itself; the family of the house of David by itself, and their wives by themselves; the family of the house of Nathan by itself, and their wives by themselves; 13the family of the house of Levi by itself, and their wives by themselves; the family of the Shimeites by itself, and their wives by themselves; 14and all the families that are left, each by itself, and their wives by themselves.

13 On that day a fountain shall be opened for the house of David and the inhabitants of Jerusalem, to cleanse them from sin and impurity.

Idolatry Cut Off

2 On that day, says the Lord of hosts, I will cut off the names of the idols from the land, so that they shall be remembered no more; and also I will remove from the land the prophets and the unclean spirit. 3And if any prophets appear again, their fathers and mothers who bore them will say to them, "You shall not live, for you speak lies in the name of the Lord"; and their fathers and their mothers who bore them shall pierce them through when they prophesy. 4On that day the prophets will be ashamed, every one, of their visions when they prophesy; they will not put on a hairy mantle in order to deceive, 5but each of them will say, "I am no prophet, I am a tiller of the soil; for the land has been my possession[i] since my youth." 6And if anyone asks them, "What are these wounds on your chest?"[j] the answer will be "The wounds I received in the house of my friends."

The Shepherd Struck, the Flock Scattered

7 "Awake, O sword, against my
   shepherd,
     against the man who is my
        associate,"
           says the Lord of hosts.

Strike the shepherd, that the sheep
   may be scattered;
  I will turn my hand against
     the little ones.
8 In the whole land, says the Lord,
   two-thirds shall be cut off
      and perish,
   and one-third shall be left alive.
9 And I will put this third into
      the fire,
   refine them as one refines silver,
     and test them as gold is tested.
They will call on my name,
   and I will answer them.
I will say, "They are my people";
   and they will say, "The Lord is
      our God."

Future Warfare and Final Victory

14 See, a day is coming for the Lord, when the plunder taken from you will be divided in your midst. 2For I will gather all the nations against Jerusalem to battle, and the city shall be taken and the houses looted and the women raped; half the city shall go into exile, but the rest of the people shall not be cut off from the city. 3Then the Lord will go forth and fight against those nations as when he fights on a day of battle. 4On that day his feet shall stand on the Mount of Olives, which lies before Jerusalem on the east; and the Mount of Olives shall be split in two from east to west by a very wide valley; so that one half of the Mount shall withdraw northward, and the other half southward. 5And you shall flee by the valley of the Lord's mountain,[k] for the valley between the mountains shall reach to Azal;[l] and you shall flee as you fled from the earthquake in the days of King Uzziah of Judah. Then the Lord my God will come, and all the holy ones with him.

6 On that day there shall not be[m] either cold or frost.[n] 7And there shall be continuous day (it is known to the Lord), not day and not night, for at evening time there shall be light.

8 On that day living waters shall flow out from Jerusalem, half of them to the eastern sea and half of them to the west-

---

h Heb on me   i Cn: Heb for humankind has
caused me to possess   j Heb wounds between your
hands   k Heb my mountains   l Meaning of Heb
uncertain   m Cn: Heb there shall not be light
n Compare Gk Syr Vg Tg: Meaning of Heb
uncertain

ern sea; it shall continue in summer as in winter.

9 And the LORD will become king over all the earth; on that day the LORD will be one and his name one.

10 The whole land shall be turned into a plain from Geba to Rimmon south of Jerusalem. But Jerusalem shall remain aloft on its site from the Gate of Benjamin to the place of the former gate, to the Corner Gate, and from the Tower of Hananel to the king's wine presses. 11And it shall be inhabited, for never again shall it be doomed to destruction; Jerusalem shall abide in security.

12 This shall be the plague with which the LORD will strike all the peoples that wage war against Jerusalem: their flesh shall rot while they are still on their feet; their eyes shall rot in their sockets, and their tongues shall rot in their mouths. 13On that day a great panic from the LORD shall fall on them, so that each will seize the hand of a neighbor, and the hand of the one will be raised against the hand of the other; 14even Judah will fight at Jerusalem. And the wealth of all the surrounding nations shall be collected—gold, silver, and garments in great abundance. 15And a plague like this plague shall fall on the horses, the mules, the camels, the donkeys, and whatever animals may be in those camps.

16 Then all who survive of the nations that have come against Jerusalem shall go up year after year to worship the King, the LORD of hosts, and to keep the festival of booths.*o* 17If any of the families of the earth do not go up to Jerusalem to worship the King, the LORD of hosts, there will be no rain upon them. 18And if the family of Egypt do not go up and present themselves, then on them shall*p* come the plague that the LORD inflicts on the nations that do not go up to keep the festival of booths.*o* 19Such shall be the punishment of Egypt and the punishment of all the nations that do not go up to keep the festival of booths.*o*

20 On that day there shall be inscribed on the bells of the horses, "Holy to the LORD." And the cooking pots in the house of the LORD shall be as holy as*q* the bowls in front of the altar; 21and every cooking pot in Jerusalem and Judah shall be sacred to the LORD of hosts, so that all who sacrifice may come and use them to boil the flesh of the sacrifice. And there shall no longer be traders*r* in the house of the LORD of hosts on that day.

o Or *tabernacles*; Heb *succoth*　　*p* Gk Syr: Heb *shall not*　　*q* Heb *shall be like*　　*r* Or *Canaanites*

Malachi

The book of Malachi closes out the 46 books of the Old Testament. Probably written between 486–464 B.C., it predates Nehemiah's arrival in Jerusalem in 445 B.C. and may well have helped him instigate his reforms, particularly those regarding the ban on Jewish men marrying foreign women. Though the temple had been rebuilt, Malachi indicts the Jews for their indifference to God. He recounts the evidence of their complacency—priests who are lax in their duties, men who have divorced their wives to marry pagan women (thus threatening the future of the Jewish community), and those who routinely oppressed the weakest members of the community.

Malachi means "my messenger," and some scholars believe this to be a title rather than a proper name. Perhaps the prophet felt he needed to remain anonymous when pointedly criticizing the ruling powers of Judah.

Malachi closes with a promise: "Lo, I will send you the prophet Elijah before the great and terrible day of the LORD comes. He will turn the hearts of parents to their children and the hearts of children to their parents" (4.5–6). More than four hundred years later, John the Baptist was born. New Testament writers applied this verse to John's role as the prophet who prepared the way for the long-awaited Messiah.

1 An oracle. The word of the LORD to Israel by Malachi.*a*

Israel Preferred to Edom

2 I have loved you, says the LORD. But you say, "How have you loved us?" Is not Esau Jacob's brother? says the LORD. Yet I have loved Jacob ³but I have hated Esau; I have made his hill country a desolation and his heritage a desert for jackals. ⁴If Edom says, "We are shattered but we will rebuild the ruins," the LORD of hosts says:

They may build, but I will tear down, until they are called the wicked country, the people with whom the LORD is angry forever. ⁵Your own eyes shall see this, and you shall say, "Great is the LORD beyond the borders of Israel!"

Corruption of the Priesthood

6 A son honors his father, and servants their master. If then I am a father, where

a Or by my messenger

is the honor due me? And if I am a master, where is the respect due me? says the LORD of hosts to you, O priests, who despise my name. You say, "How have we despised your name?" [7]By offering polluted food on my altar. And you say, "How have we polluted it?"[b] By thinking that the LORD's table may be despised. [8]When you offer blind animals in sacrifice, is that not wrong? And when you offer those that are lame or sick, is that not wrong? Try presenting that to your governor; will he be pleased with you or show you favor? says the LORD of hosts. [9]And now implore the favor of God, that he may be gracious to us. The fault is yours. Will he show favor to any of you? says the LORD of hosts. [10]Oh, that someone among you would shut the temple[c] doors, so that you would not kindle fire on my altar in vain! I have no pleasure in you, says the LORD of hosts, and I will not accept an offering from your hands. [11]For from the rising of the sun to its setting my name is great among the nations, and in every place incense is offered to my name, and a pure offering; for my name is great among the nations, says the LORD of hosts. [12]But you profane it when you say that the Lord's table is polluted, and the food for it[d] may be despised. [13]"What a weariness this is," you say, and you sniff at me,[e] says the LORD of hosts. You bring what has been taken by violence or is lame or sick, and this you bring as your offering! Shall I accept that from your hand? says the LORD. [14]Cursed be the cheat who has a male in the flock and vows to give it, and yet sacrifices to the Lord what is blemished; for I am a great King, says the LORD of hosts, and my name is reverenced among the nations.

2 And now, O priests, this command is for you. [2]If you will not listen, if you will not lay it to heart to give glory to my name, says the LORD of hosts, then I will send the curse on you and I will curse your blessings; indeed I have already cursed them,[f] because you do not lay it to heart. [3]I will rebuke your offspring, and spread dung on your faces, the dung of your offerings, and I will put you out of my presence.[g]

4 Know, then, that I have sent this command to you, that my covenant with Levi may hold, says the LORD of hosts. [5]My covenant with him was a covenant of life and well-being, which I gave him; this called for reverence, and he revered me and stood in awe of my name. [6]True instruction was in his mouth, and no wrong was found on his lips. He walked with me in integrity and uprightness, and he turned many from iniquity. [7]For the lips of a priest should guard knowledge, and people should seek instruction from his mouth, for he is the messenger of the LORD of hosts. [8]But you have turned aside from the way; you have caused many to stumble by your instruction; you have corrupted the covenant of Levi, says the LORD of hosts, [9]and so I make you despised and abased before all the people, inasmuch as you have not kept my ways but have shown partiality in your instruction.

The Covenant Profaned by Judah

10 Have we not all one father? Has not one God created us? Why then are we faithless to one another, profaning the covenant of our ancestors? [11]Judah has been faithless, and abomination has been committed in Israel and in Jerusalem; for Judah has profaned the sanctuary of the LORD, which he loves, and has married the daughter of a foreign god. [12]May the LORD cut off from the tents of Jacob anyone who does this—any to witness[h] or answer, or to bring an offering to the LORD of hosts.

13 And this you do as well: You cover the LORD's altar with tears, with weeping and groaning because he no longer regards the offering or accepts it with favor at your hand. [14]You ask, "Why does he not?" Because the LORD was a witness between you and the wife of your youth, to whom you have been faithless, though she is your companion and your wife by covenant. [15]Did not one God make her?[i] Both flesh and spirit are his.[j] And what does the one God[k] desire? Godly offspring. So look to yourselves, and do not let anyone be faithless to the wife of his youth. [16]For I hate[l] divorce, says the LORD, the God of Israel, and covering one's garment with violence, says the LORD of hosts. So take heed to yourselves and do not be faithless.

---

b Gk: Heb *you* *c* Heb lacks *temple* *d* Compare Syr Tg: Heb *its fruit, its food* *e* Another reading is *at it* *f* Heb *it* *g* Cn Compare Gk Syr: Heb *and he shall bear you to it* *h* Cn Compare Gk: Heb *arouse* *i* Or *Has he not made one?* *j* Cn: Heb *and a remnant of spirit was his* *k* Heb *he* *l* Cn: Heb *he hates*

17 You have wearied the LORD with your words. Yet you say, "How have we wearied him?" By saying, "All who do evil are good in the sight of the LORD, and he delights in them." Or by asking, "Where is the God of justice?"

The Coming Messenger

3 See, I am sending my messenger to prepare the way before me, and the Lord whom you seek will suddenly come to his temple. The messenger of the covenant in whom you delight—indeed, he is coming, says the LORD of hosts. ²But who can endure the day of his coming, and who can stand when he appears?

For he is like a refiner's fire and like fullers' soap; ³he will sit as a refiner and purifier of silver, and he will purify the descendants of Levi and refine them like gold and silver, until they present offer-

*B*efore the Sermon

THURSDAY

Scripture Reading
for Today:
Malachi 2.4–7

Verse for Today:
Malachi 2.7

When you preached on earth, Lord,
you found the divine words
that were able to reach the hearts of your hearers.
Your truth moved them deeply
and prompted them to follow you and to live for you.

Lord, now bless the words of the preacher.
Allow him to forget himself,
his mediocrity, the effect he would like to produce,
so that he can speak solely and in all truth
of you and your doctrine.

So that he can say the things that all his listeners await,
something that truly comes from you,
laden with your love, filled with your wisdom,
which is not the wisdom of this world.

Grant, Lord, that the Holy Spirit may pervade him,
so that he may become a true mediator of your word.
But give to us, his hearers, a good spirit,
so that we may really hear your word
and not simply indulge our mania for criticism—
in our irritation at the mediocrity of what he has said
and at the faulty manner in which he expressed it—
to the point where we see only the preacher
and his weakness, and nothing more of your word
and Spirit.

Instead, let this hour become
a holy hour in which the mediator and the hearer are
united in your Spirit.

—*ADRIENNE VON SPEYR*

Go to page 1260 for your next devotional reading.

ings to the LORD in righteousness.^m ⁴Then the offering of Judah and Jerusalem will be pleasing to the LORD as in the days of old and as in former years.

5 Then I will draw near to you for judgment; I will be swift to bear witness against the sorcerers, against the adulterers, against those who swear falsely, against those who oppress the hired workers in their wages, the widow and the orphan, against those who thrust aside the alien, and do not fear me, says the LORD of hosts.

6 For I the LORD do not change; therefore you, O children of Jacob, have not perished. ⁷Ever since the days of your ancestors you have turned aside from my statutes and have not kept them. Return to me, and I will return to you, says the LORD of hosts. But you say, "How shall we return?"

Do Not Rob God

8 Will anyone rob God? Yet you are robbing me! But you say, "How are we robbing you?" In your tithes and offerings! ⁹You are cursed with a curse, for you are robbing me—the whole nation of you! ¹⁰Bring the full tithe into the storehouse, so that there may be food in my house, and thus put me to the test, says the LORD of hosts; see if I will not open the windows of heaven for you and pour down for you an overflowing blessing. ¹¹I will

^m Or *right offerings to the LORD*

Forgiving Heart

FRIDAY

Scripture Reading for Today:
Malachi 4.4–6

Verses for Today:
Malachi 4.5–6

When my roommate moved in, my first impression was: "This woman cannot be for real!" At twenty-three, Tracy seemed the embodiment of selfless love. She never had a bad word for anyone. If someone wronged her, she patiently excused their behavior. In my cynicism, I labeled her as naive, the product of a sheltered religious upbringing.

That was before I met her father, and the truth dawned. Tracy was no stranger to the school of hard knocks. In fact, she had grown up in an abusive household. Her father, an obsessive personality, did not know what it meant to talk: He could only shout. From early on, this beautiful, intelligent, and faithful young woman had been continually told that she was ugly, stupid, and a financial burden.

Shocked and dismayed by this revelation, I asked Tracy how she came to be so free of bitterness in the face of her upbringing. She winced and was silent for a long while, pondering this painful topic. "My sister became bitter," she said at last. "I started to go that way, too. But then, at sixteen, I made a huge decision: to forgive Dad every day. I think that's what has made the difference. And it is impossible to do so without prayer. I pray every day for a forgiving heart."

Tracy is currently taking Saturday morning classes in German, the language of her father's country of birth. The reason? "I know Dad's heritage means a lot to him," she says. "It might help open up the lines of communication between us."

—TERESA PIROLA

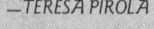

Go to page 1262 for your next devotional reading.

rebuke the locust[n] for you, so that it will not destroy the produce of your soil; and your vine in the field shall not be barren, says the LORD of hosts. 12Then all nations will count you happy, for you will be a land of delight, says the LORD of hosts.

13 You have spoken harsh words against me, says the LORD. Yet you say, "How have we spoken against you?" 14You have said, "It is vain to serve God. What do we profit by keeping his command or by going about as mourners before the LORD of hosts? 15Now we count the arrogant happy; evildoers not only prosper, but when they put God to the test they escape."

The Reward of the Faithful

16 Then those who revered the LORD spoke with one another. The LORD took note and listened, and a book of remembrance was written before him of those who revered the LORD and thought on his name. 17They shall be mine, says the LORD of hosts, my special possession on the day when I act, and I will spare them as parents spare their children who serve them. 18Then once more you shall see the difference between the righteous and the wick-

ed, between one who serves God and one who does not serve him.

The Great Day of the LORD

4[o] See, the day is coming, burning like an oven, when all the arrogant and all evildoers will be stubble; the day that comes shall burn them up, says the LORD of hosts, so that it will leave them neither root nor branch. 2But for you who revere my name the sun of righteousness shall rise, with healing in its wings. You shall go out leaping like calves from the stall. 3And you shall tread down the wicked, for they will be ashes under the soles of your feet, on the day when I act, says the LORD of hosts.

4 Remember the teaching of my servant Moses, the statutes and ordinances that I commanded him at Horeb for all Israel.

5 Lo, I will send you the prophet Elijah before the great and terrible day of the LORD comes. 6He will turn the hearts of parents to their children and the hearts of children to their parents, so that I will not come and strike the land with a curse. [p]

n Heb *devourer*　　o Ch 4.1-6 are Ch 3.19-24 in Heb　　p Or *a ban of utter destruction*

Sarah, the Wife of Tobias

Her Name Means "Chieftainness" or "Princess"

Her Character: *An only child, she was a sensible, courageous, compassionate, and beautiful young woman.*

Her Sorrow: *To have been falsely accused of the murder of her seven husbands, each of whom died on his wedding night.*

Her Joy: *That she lived happily with her eighth husband, who delivered her from the influence of an evil spirit.*

Read Tobit 3.7–17; 7–8

The world is full of love stories, but few are as magical or strange as the story of Sarah and Tobias, who met, fell in love, and married through the help of an angel in disguise.

The only child of devout Jews, Sarah had already been widowed seven times. As the story goes, each of her husbands dropped dead before consummating the marriage. Dismayed by so many deaths, her maid accused her of murder, saying she had strangled them. Sarah was so wounded by these accusations that she asked God to take her life.

Though she didn't know it, a relative by the name of Tobias was about to set out from Nineveh, 325 miles to the northwest. The young man was accompanied by a traveling companion, the angel Raphael. Disguised as a man, the angel was guiding Tobias to Sarah's house and urging him to marry her.

Sarah's story must have been known far and wide because Tobias protested: "I have heard that she already has been married to seven husbands and that they died in the bridal chamber. On the night when they went in to her, they would die. I have heard people saying that it was a demon that killed them. It does not harm her, but it kills anyone who desires to approach her" (6.14–15).

But Raphael prevailed over his young charge, reminding Tobias that his father, Tobit, had commanded him to marry a woman from his own family. And before Tobias even met Sarah, he fell in love with her.

When Tobias proposed marriage as her near kinsman, Sarah's father warned him about so dangerous a bride: "But let me explain to you the true situation more fully, my child. I have given her to seven men of our kinsmen, and all died on the night when they went in to her" (7.10–11).

But Tobias married Sarah that night. Certain he had yet another unlucky bridegroom on his hands, Sarah's father arranged for a grave to be dug so that Tobias's body could be disposed of quietly.

Meanwhile, on the angel's instructions, Tobias performed a strange ritual, burning the liver and heart of a fish he had caught during his journey, creating incense so noxious that it drove away the demon. Rid of this malicious influence, Sarah and Tobias began their life as a couple by praising God and asking the blessing of a long and happy life together.

When Sarah's mother sent a maid to peek into the couple's room, she discovered the newlyweds sleeping peacefully. Sarah's astonished father ordered his servants to fill in the grave before sunrise and then prepared to celebrate the marriage in style.

When Tobias returned to Nineveh with his new bride, the angel Raphael revealed himself to Tobit and Tobias, saying, "It is good to conceal the secret of a king, but to acknowledge and reveal the works of God, and with fitting honor to acknowledge him" (12.7).

Earlier Sarah had been so crushed by circumstances that she had prayed for death. But God answered her with mercy instead, delivering her from a time of sorrow and blessing her with a long life and a husband to love.

Praying With Sarah

"Blessed be God who lives forever, because his kingdom lasts throughout all ages. For he afflicts, and he shows mercy; he leads down to Hades in the lowest regions of the earth, and he brings up from the great abyss." —*Tobit 13.1—2*

Praise God: For his power over any and every kind of evil you will ever encounter.

Offer Thanks: For ways in which God has brought you through times of great suffering, hearing your prayers for mercy.

Confess: Any temptation to despair of God's help or love.

Ask God: For faith to believe his promise—that he will never allow more trials in your life than you can bear.

Lift Your Heart

Some people never tire of reminding us that happiness is fleeting—dependent as it is on changing variables like blue skies, good health, and plenty of money. But the same could be said of sorrow. It won't last forever. If you're tempted to think that suffering has settled over you like a permanent cloud with an endless supply of rainy days, remind yourself of these words from I Corinthians 10.13: "No testing has overtaken you that is not common to everyone. God is faithful, and he will not let you be tested beyond your strength, but with the testing he will also provide the way out so that you may be able to endure it." As long as you are not inviting trouble into your life, you can be confident that God will eventually provide a way out, whether it comes in the shape of an angel, a husband, emotional healing, or even a check in the mail. Count on it; you will not collapse under the weight of your trials.

Father, deliver me from evil and show me your mercy. Open my eyes to your power and love so that I am not blinded by the difficulties I face right now. Even though I can't see you, I believe; help, then, my unbelief.

Go to page 1269 for your next devotional reading.

The New
Testament

The Gospel According to
Matthew

It wasn't until the first generation of Christians was in danger of dying out that a written record of Jesus' life and teaching began to develop. Though the Gospels tell the story of Jesus and are full of historical information, they are not biographies. They are writings that reflect on the meaning of Jesus' life and teaching. There are different theories about who wrote which Gospel and when, but each of the four Gospels reveals much about the life of Christ and the significance of his ministry.

The books of Matthew, Mark, and Luke are known as the Synoptic Gospels because their similarities invite their being viewed together (*syn-optic*, meaning "together viewed"). John's Gospel is distinctive in its concerns and writing style.

The Gospel of Matthew may have been written in Antioch, the capital of the Roman province of Syria. It tells the Good News from a Jewish perspective, presenting Jesus as the fulfillment of Old Testament prophecies. Its primary purpose was to present Jesus as the Messiah and his teachings as the path that Judaism should follow.

By beginning his Gospel with a record of Jesus' family tree (1.1–17), Matthew links Jesus to the whole of Old Testament history. The genealogy contains the names of five female ancestors, three of whose stories involve prostitution, incest, fornication, and murder (Tamar; Rahab; and the wife of Uriah, Bathsheba). Also, three of these women were Gentiles: Tamar, Rahab, and Ruth.

The Genealogy of Jesus the Messiah

1 An account of the genealogy[a] of Jesus the Messiah,[b] the son of David, the son of Abraham.

2 Abraham was the father of Isaac, and Isaac the father of Jacob, and Jacob the father of Judah and his brothers, 3and Judah the father of Perez and Zerah by Tamar, and Perez the father of Hezron, and Hezron the father of Aram, 4and Aram the father of Aminadab, and Aminadab the father of Nahshon, and Nahshon the father of Salmon, 5and Salmon the father of Boaz by Rahab, and Boaz the father of

a Or *birth* *b* Or *Jesus Christ*

Obed by Ruth, and Obed the father of Jesse, [6]and Jesse the father of King David.

And David was the father of Solomon by the wife of Uriah, [7]and Solomon the father of Rehoboam, and Rehoboam the father of Abijah, and Abijah the father of Asaph,[c] [8]and Asaph[c] the father of Jehoshaphat, and Jehoshaphat the father of Joram, and Joram the father of Uzziah, [9]and Uzziah the father of Jotham, and Jotham the father of Ahaz, and Ahaz the father of Hezekiah, [10]and Hezekiah the father of Manasseh, and Manasseh the father of Amos,[d] and Amos[d] the father of Josiah, [11]and Josiah the father of Jechoniah and his brothers, at the time of the deportation to Babylon.

12 And after the deportation to Babylon: Jechoniah was the father of Salathiel, and Salathiel the father of Zerubbabel, [13]and Zerubbabel the father of Abiud, and Abiud the father of Eliakim, and Eliakim the father of Azor, [14]and Azor the father of Zadok, and Zadok the father of Achim, and Achim the father of Eliud, [15]and Eliud the father of Eleazar, and Eleazar the father of Matthan, and Matthan the father of Jacob, [16]and Jacob the father of Joseph the husband of Mary, of whom Jesus was born, who is called the Messiah.[e]

17 So all the generations from Abraham to David are fourteen generations; and from David to the deportation to Babylon, fourteen generations; and from the deportation to Babylon to the Messiah,[e] fourteen generations.

The Birth of Jesus the Messiah

18 Now the birth of Jesus the Messiah[f] took place in this way. When his mother Mary had been engaged to Joseph, but before they lived together, she was found to be with child from the Holy Spirit. [19]Her husband Joseph, being a righteous man and unwilling to expose her to public disgrace, planned to dismiss her quietly. [20]But just when he had resolved to do this, an angel of the Lord appeared to him in a dream and said, "Joseph, son of David, do not be afraid to take Mary as your wife, for the child conceived in her is from the Holy Spirit. [21]She will bear a son, and you are to name him Jesus, for he will save his people from their sins." [22]All this took place to fulfill what had been spoken by the Lord through the prophet:

23 "Look, the virgin shall conceive and
    bear a son,
and they shall name him
    Emmanuel,"

which means, "God is with us." [24]When Joseph awoke from sleep, he did as the angel of the Lord commanded him; he took her as his wife, [25]but had no marital relations with her until she had borne a son;[g] and he named him Jesus.

The Visit of the Wise Men

2 In the time of King Herod, after Jesus was born in Bethlehem of Judea, wise men[h] from the East came to Jerusalem, [2]asking, "Where is the child who has been born king of the Jews? For we observed his star at its rising,[i] and have come to pay him homage." [3]When King Herod heard this, he was frightened, and all Jerusalem with him; [4]and calling together all the chief priests and scribes of the people, he inquired of them where the Messiah[e] was to be born. [5]They told him, "In Bethlehem of Judea; for so it has been written by the prophet:

6 'And you, Bethlehem, in the land
    of Judah,
are by no means least among the
    rulers of Judah;
for from you shall come a ruler
    who is to shepherd[j] my
    people Israel.' "

7 Then Herod secretly called for the wise men[h] and learned from them the exact time when the star had appeared. [8]Then he sent them to Bethlehem, saying, "Go and search diligently for the child; and when you have found him, bring me word so that I may also go and pay him homage." [9]When they had heard the king, they set out; and there, ahead of them, went the star that they had seen at its rising,[i] until it stopped over the place where the child was. [10]When they saw that the star had stopped,[k] they were overwhelmed with joy. [11]On entering the house, they saw the child with Mary his mother; and they knelt down and paid him homage. Then, opening their treasure chests, they offered him gifts of gold, frankincense, and myrrh. [12]And having

---

c Other ancient authorities read *Asa*   d Other
ancient authorities read *Amon*   e Or *the Christ*
f Or *Jesus Christ*   g Other ancient authorities
read *her firstborn son*   h Or *astrologers*; Gk *magi*
i Or *in the East*   j Or *rule*   k Gk *saw the star*

been warned in a dream not to return to Herod, they left for their own country by another road.

The Escape to Egypt

13 Now after they had left, an angel of the Lord appeared to Joseph in a dream and said, "Get up, take the child and his mother, and flee to Egypt, and remain there until I tell you; for Herod is about to search for the child, to destroy him." [14]Then Joseph[l] got up, took the child and his mother by night, and went to Egypt, [15]and remained there until the death of Herod. This was to fulfill what had been spoken by the Lord through the prophet, "Out of Egypt I have called my son."

The Massacre of the Infants

16 When Herod saw that he had been tricked by the wise men,[m] he was infuriat-

[l] Gk *he*   [m] Or *astrologers*; Gk *magi*

Scandalous Birth

Scripture Reading for Today:
Matthew 1.18–25

Verse for Today:
Matthew 1.20

A teenage girl and a young man left their town in Galilee to travel south to Bethlehem, just outside Jerusalem. The trip couldn't have been easy, especially for the young woman whose womb was stretched to bursting with a pregnancy in its ninth month. We know the story well—too well perhaps to be astonished by the scandal of it all.

Certainly it was scandalous that Mary had conceived a child out of wedlock. We know that. But just like the Jews of her day, we miss the deeper "scandal" of divine proportions that was developing in her womb. For God had done the unthinkable—he had fathered a child with a human being. And his child would be born as any other human being—covered in blood, screaming for air, and still attached to his mother by a fleshy cord. Together, God and a young woman had produced a child unique in the history of heaven and earth.

But the scandal didn't end with Jesus' birth. For the God who created the earth allowed Mary and Joseph to take custody of his only Son. Arms that God himself had made would cradle Divinity. The plan and purpose of God would be accomplished through weakness, through human limitation, through dependency— through an infant who was as vulnerable to disaster as any human being who ever lived.

This, indeed, is scandal. It overthrows everything we ever thought about God. No longer is he a God who looks down on us from a lofty height. Instead, he is a tender Father, who cannot bear to be separated from his creatures, who is driven to reveal his true nature by performing the greatest miracle of all—allowing his Son to become one of us, to take us by the hand and lead us out of darkness, to know God even as we are known by him. This is the scandal, this is the miracle, this is the truth that sets us free.

—*ANN SPANGLER*

Go to page 1270 for your next devotional reading.

ed, and he sent and killed all the children in and around Bethlehem who were two years old or under, according to the time that he had learned from the wise men.[n] [17]Then was fulfilled what had been spoken through the prophet Jeremiah:

[18] "A voice was heard in Ramah,
     wailing and loud lamentation,
Rachel weeping for her children;
     she refused to be consoled,
         because they are no more."

The Return from Egypt

[19] When Herod died, an angel of the Lord suddenly appeared in a dream to Jo-seph in Egypt and said, [20]"Get up, take the child and his mother, and go to the land of Israel, for those who were seeking the child's life are dead." [21]Then Joseph[o] got up, took the child and his mother, and went to the land of Israel. [22]But when he heard that Archelaus was ruling over Judea in place of his father Herod, he was afraid to go there. And after being warned in a dream, he went away to the district of Galilee. [23]There he made his home in a town called Nazareth, so that what had been spoken through the prophets might

[n] Or *astrologers*; Gk *magi*   [o] Gk *he*

Flight

TUESDAY

Scripture Reading
for Today:
Matthew 2.13–23

Verse for Today:
Matthew 2.14

We feel it now as a great privilege to have been refugees once, to know what anxiety means. The clatter of the donkey's hooves on the cobblestones of Bethlehem, for instance: Wouldn't that wake up somebody who might report them later? That's why they hurried down the slope into the vineyards and fields to get away as fast as possible. Every sound arouses one's fears. "Maybe they have found out and are on our heels"—that's the constant fear. When the sky grew light, the first cocks began to crow, and the horrid battalion entered the small town, perhaps Mary and Joseph, who were slow travelers, might still have heard the shrieks which rent the air and sent cold chills down their backs. They were still very close to Herod's power. They were still in the neighborhood where they might have been known and identified.

Oh, it is so wrong to picture the flight into Egypt as a nice, smooth hike with angels on all sides ministering to them. The angels certainly were there admiring, adoring, almost unbelieving that the Lord would not have protected his only-begotten Son by means less troublesome than this pitiful flight. Where was the Angel of Death who slew the Egyptians? Where was the angel with the fiery sword at the gates of paradise? But it was obviously the will of the Most High—blessed be his name—that the child and his mother be saved not by supernatural interference, but by the natural means of a tedious flight. We people living in the middle of the twentieth century understand perhaps a little better why: He really has become "like one of us," and we can go to him also during a flight or a persecution, saying full of confidence: "You know how it is."

—MARIA VON TRAPP

Go to page 1273 for your next devotional reading.

be fulfilled, "He will be called a Nazorean."

The Proclamation of John the Baptist

3 In those days John the Baptist appeared in the wilderness of Judea, proclaiming, 2 "Repent, for the kingdom of heaven has come near." *p* 3This is the one of whom the prophet Isaiah spoke when he said,

"The voice of one crying out in
      the wilderness:
'Prepare the way of the Lord,
      make his paths straight.' "

4Now John wore clothing of camel's hair with a leather belt around his waist, and his food was locusts and wild honey. 5Then the people of Jerusalem and all Judea were going out to him, and all the region along the Jordan, 6and they were baptized by him in the river Jordan, confessing their sins.

7 But when he saw many Pharisees and Sadducees coming for baptism, he said to them, "You brood of vipers! Who warned you to flee from the wrath to come? 8Bear fruit worthy of repentance. 9Do not presume to say to yourselves, 'We have Abraham as our ancestor'; for I tell you, God is able from these stones to raise up children to Abraham. 10Even now the ax is lying at the root of the trees; every tree therefore that does not bear good fruit is cut down and thrown into the fire.

11 "I baptize you with*q* water for repentance, but one who is more powerful than I is coming after me; I am not worthy to carry his sandals. He will baptize you with*q* the Holy Spirit and fire. 12His winnowing fork is in his hand, and he will clear his threshing floor and will gather his wheat into the granary; but the chaff he will burn with unquenchable fire."

The Baptism of Jesus

13 Then Jesus came from Galilee to John at the Jordan, to be baptized by him. 14John would have prevented him, saying, "I need to be baptized by you, and do you come to me?" 15But Jesus answered him, "Let it be so now; for it is proper for us in this way to fulfill all righteousness." Then he consented. 16And when Jesus had been baptized, just as he came up from the water, suddenly the heavens were opened to him and he saw the Spirit of God descending like a dove and alighting on him. 17And a voice from heaven said,

"This is my Son, the Beloved,*r* with whom I am well pleased."

The Temptation of Jesus

4 Then Jesus was led up by the Spirit into the wilderness to be tempted by the devil. 2He fasted forty days and forty nights, and afterwards he was famished. 3The tempter came and said to him, "If you are the Son of God, command these stones to become loaves of bread." 4But he answered, "It is written,

'One does not live by bread alone,
      but by every word that comes
            from the mouth of God.' "

5 Then the devil took him to the holy city and placed him on the pinnacle of the temple, 6saying to him, "If you are the Son of God, throw yourself down; for it is written,

'He will command his angels
            concerning you,'
      and 'On their hands they will
            bear you up,
      so that you will not dash your foot
            against a stone.' "

7Jesus said to him, "Again it is written, 'Do not put the Lord your God to the test.' "

8 Again, the devil took him to a very high mountain and showed him all the kingdoms of the world and their splendor; 9and he said to him, "All these I will give you, if you will fall down and worship me." 10Jesus said to him, "Away with you, Satan! for it is written,

'Worship the Lord your God,
      and serve only him.' "

11Then the devil left him, and suddenly angels came and waited on him.

Jesus Begins His Ministry in Galilee

12 Now when Jesus*s* heard that John had been arrested, he withdrew to Galilee. 13He left Nazareth and made his home in Capernaum by the sea, in the territory of Zebulun and Naphtali, 14so that what had been spoken through the prophet Isaiah might be fulfilled:

15 "Land of Zebulun, land of Naphtali,
      on the road by the sea, across the
            Jordan, Galilee of the
            Gentiles—
16 the people who sat in darkness
      have seen a great light,

---

p Or *is at hand*   *q* Or *in*   *r* Or *my beloved Son*
s Gk *he*

and for those who sat in the region
and shadow of death
light has dawned."

17From that time Jesus began to proclaim, "Repent, for the kingdom of heaven has come near."*t*

Jesus Calls the First Disciples

18 As he walked by the Sea of Galilee, he saw two brothers, Simon, who is called Peter, and Andrew his brother, casting a net into the sea—for they were fishermen. 19And he said to them, "Follow me, and I will make you fish for people." 20Immediately they left their nets and followed him. 21As he went from there, he saw two other brothers, James son of Zebedee and his brother John, in the boat with their father Zebedee, mending their nets, and he called them. 22Immediately they left the boat and their father, and followed him.

Jesus Ministers to Crowds of People

23 Jesus*u* went throughout Galilee, teaching in their synagogues and proclaiming the good news*v* of the kingdom and curing every disease and every sickness among the people. 24So his fame spread throughout all Syria, and they brought to him all the sick, those who were afflicted with various diseases and pains, demoniacs, epileptics, and paralytics, and he cured them. 25And great crowds followed him from Galilee, the Decapolis, Jerusalem, Judea, and from beyond the Jordan.

The Beatitudes

5 When Jesus*w* saw the crowds, he went up the mountain; and after he sat down, his disciples came to him. 2Then he began to speak, and taught them, saying:

3 "Blessed are the poor in spirit, for theirs is the kingdom of heaven.

4 "Blessed are those who mourn, for they will be comforted.

5 "Blessed are the meek, for they will inherit the earth.

6 "Blessed are those who hunger and thirst for righteousness, for they will be filled.

7 "Blessed are the merciful, for they will receive mercy.

8 "Blessed are the pure in heart, for they will see God.

9 "Blessed are the peacemakers, for they will be called children of God.

10 "Blessed are those who are persecuted for righteousness' sake, for theirs is the kingdom of heaven.

11 "Blessed are you when people revile you and persecute you and utter all kinds of evil against you falsely*x* on my account. 12Rejoice and be glad, for your reward is great in heaven, for in the same way they persecuted the prophets who were before you.

Salt and Light

13 "You are the salt of the earth; but if salt has lost its taste, how can its saltiness be restored? It is no longer good for anything, but is thrown out and trampled under foot.

14 "You are the light of the world. A city built on a hill cannot be hid. 15No one after lighting a lamp puts it under the bushel basket, but on the lampstand, and it gives light to all in the house. 16In the same way, let your light shine before others, so that they may see your good works and give glory to your Father in heaven.

The Law and the Prophets

17 "Do not think that I have come to abolish the law or the prophets; I have come not to abolish but to fulfill. 18For truly I tell you, until heaven and earth pass away, not one letter,*y* not one stroke of a letter, will pass from the law until all is accomplished. 19Therefore, whoever breaks*z* one of the least of these commandments, and teaches others to do the same, will be called least in the kingdom of heaven; but whoever does them and teaches them will be called great in the kingdom of heaven. 20For I tell you, unless your righteousness exceeds that of the scribes and Pharisees, you will never enter the kingdom of heaven.

Concerning Anger

21 "You have heard that it was said to those of ancient times, 'You shall not murder'; and 'whoever murders shall be liable to judgment.' 22But I say to you that if you are angry with a brother or sister,*a* you will be liable to judgment; and if you insult*b* a brother or sister,*c* you will be

---

t Or *is at hand*   *u* Gk *He*   *v* Gk *gospel*   *w* Gk
he   *x* Other ancient authorities lack *falsely*
y Gk *one iota*   *z* Or *annuls*   *a* Gk *a brother*;
other ancient authorities add *without cause*
b Gk *say Raca to* (an obscure term of abuse)
c Gk *a brother*

liable to the council; and if you say, 'You fool,' you will be liable to the hell[d] of fire. 23So when you are offering your gift at the altar, if you remember that your brother or sister[e] has something against you, 24leave your gift there before the altar and go; first be reconciled to your brother or sister,[e] and then come and offer your gift. 25Come to terms quickly with your accuser while you are on the way to court[f] with him, or your accuser may hand you over to the judge, and the judge to the guard, and you will be thrown into prison. 26Truly I tell you, you will never get out until you have paid the last penny.

Concerning Adultery

27 "You have heard that it was said, 'You shall not commit adultery.' 28But I say to you that everyone who looks at a woman with lust has already committed adultery with her in his heart. 29If your right eye causes you to sin, tear it out and throw it away; it is better for you to lose one of your members than for your whole body to be thrown into hell.[d] 30And if your right hand causes you to sin, cut it off and throw it away; it is better for you to lose one of your members than for your whole body to go into hell.[d]

Concerning Divorce

31 "It was also said, 'Whoever divorces his wife, let him give her a certificate of divorce.' 32But I say to you that anyone who divorces his wife, except on the ground of unchastity, causes her to commit adultery; and whoever marries a divorced woman commits adultery.

d Gk Gehenna   e Gk your brother   f Gk lacks to court

Make Room in Your Soul

WEDNESDAY

Scripture Reading for Today:
Matthew 5.3–12

Verse for Today:
Matthew 5.5

An old priest died. Among his papers was found an ordinary card on which was written, "Every time I look at me, I seem to see only me. Please, Lord, kick me out of me, so that you may find some room for you in me." The people sorting his papers remarked that these few sentences summed up the whole life of this gentle man. He had permitted the Lord to take full possession of him. He had become selfless.

Selflessness! That is the key word for the restoration of the world to Christ. It is part of that new kingdom which he gives us himself in a few simple words: "Blessed are the meek, for they will inherit the earth."

This second beatitude is closely related to the first, for while to be poor in spirit is a passive state, it also means to be full of Christ. And to be full of Christ means also to be active—working with him, by him, for him. Therefore this second beatitude opens a large field to us. Nothing less than the whole world to win for Christ! And it is the meek, the gentle, the kind who are going to do it. But we cannot be any of these things until we are selfless—for how can we be kind to others until we have put selfishness away? Let us, then, begin today on this eviction of self so as to make room for Christ.

—CATHERINE DOHERTY

Go to page 1275 for your next devotional reading.

Concerning Oaths

33 "Again, you have heard that it was said to those of ancient times, 'You shall not swear falsely, but carry out the vows you have made to the Lord.' 34But I say to you, Do not swear at all, either by heaven, for it is the throne of God, 35or by the earth, for it is his footstool, or by Jerusalem, for it is the city of the great King. 36And do not swear by your head, for you cannot make one hair white or black. 37Let your word be 'Yes, Yes' or 'No, No'; anything more than this comes from the evil one. g

Concerning Retaliation

38 "You have heard that it was said, 'An eye for an eye and a tooth for a tooth.' 39But I say to you, Do not resist an evildoer. But if anyone strikes you on the right cheek, turn the other also; 40and if anyone wants to sue you and take your coat, give your cloak as well; 41and if anyone forces you to go one mile, go also the second mile. 42Give to everyone who begs from you, and do not refuse anyone who wants to borrow from you.

Love for Enemies

43 "You have heard that it was said, 'You shall love your neighbor and hate your enemy.' 44But I say to you, Love your enemies and pray for those who persecute you, 45so that you may be children of your Father in heaven; for he makes his sun rise on the evil and on the good, and sends rain on the righteous and on the unrighteous. 46For if you love those who love you, what reward do you have? Do not even the tax collectors do the same? 47And if you greet only your brothers and sisters, h what more are you doing than others? Do not even the Gentiles do the same? 48Be perfect, therefore, as your heavenly Father is perfect.

Concerning Almsgiving

6 "Beware of practicing your piety before others in order to be seen by them; for then you have no reward from your Father in heaven.

2 "So whenever you give alms, do not sound a trumpet before you, as the hypocrites do in the synagogues and in the streets, so that they may be praised by others. Truly I tell you, they have received their reward. 3But when you give alms, do not let your left hand know what your right hand is doing, 4so that your alms may be done in secret; and your Father who sees in secret will reward you. i

Concerning Prayer

5 "And whenever you pray, do not be like the hypocrites; for they love to stand and pray in the synagogues and at the street corners, so that they may be seen by others. Truly I tell you, they have received their reward. 6But whenever you pray, go into your room and shut the door and pray to your Father who is in secret; and your Father who sees in secret will reward you. i

7 "When you are praying, do not heap up empty phrases as the Gentiles do; for they think that they will be heard because of their many words. 8Do not be like them, for your Father knows what you need before you ask him.

9 "Pray then in this way:
Our Father in heaven,
    hallowed be your name.
10   Your kingdom come.
    Your will be done,
        on earth as it is in heaven.
11   Give us this day our daily bread. j
12   And forgive us our debts,
        as we also have forgiven
            our debtors.
13   And do not bring us to the time
            of trial, k
        but rescue us from the
            evil one. l

14For if you forgive others their trespasses, your heavenly Father will also forgive you; 15but if you do not forgive others, neither will your Father forgive your trespasses.

Concerning Fasting

16 "And whenever you fast, do not look dismal, like the hypocrites, for they disfigure their faces so as to show others that they are fasting. Truly I tell you, they have received their reward. 17But when you fast, put oil on your head and wash your face, 18so that your fasting may be seen not by others but by your Father who

g Or evil   h Gk your brothers   i Other ancient authorities add openly   j Or our bread for tomorrow   k Or us into temptation   l Or from evil. Other ancient authorities add, in some form, For the kingdom and the power and the glory are yours forever. Amen.

is in secret; and your Father who sees in secret will reward you.[m]

break in and steal. [21]For where your treasure is, there your heart will be also.

Concerning Treasures

19 "Do not store up for yourselves treasures on earth, where moth and rust[n] consume and where thieves break in and steal; [20]but store up for yourselves treasures in heaven, where neither moth nor rust[n] consumes and where thieves do not

The Sound Eye

22 "The eye is the lamp of the body. So, if your eye is healthy, your whole body will be full of light; [23]but if your eye is

[m] Other ancient authorities add *openly*   [n] Gk *eating*

THURSDAY

Scripture Reading for Today:
Matthew 6.9–15

Verse for Today:
Matthew 6.14

Teach Us to Pray

The "Our Father," the Lord's Prayer, is about universal, incarnational, everlasting things all dear to the heart of God. We pray that God's name is hallowed; God's kingdom comes; God's will is done, on earth, in us, right now. We pray, "Give us this day our daily bread"—enough for everyone. We ask God to forgive us the wrongs we have done as we forgive those who wrong us, so that we live freely in relation to one another with open hands and hearts, sharing bread as sustenance and forgiveness as freedom. Finally, we pray, "Do not bring us to the time of trial, but rescue us from the evil one"—rescue us from all death, especially the death that is most to be feared, the death to hope, to life, to grace, to community and everlasting communion; deliver us from the hinderer, wherever evil is found.

If we knew how to pray this prayer, if we knew how to be drawn into the grid that overlays reality as it is spoken aloud or sighed in silence, we would need no other words, no other prayer. The power and the word would be set in motion and carry us along.

What stops us? Sunk deep in us, like rocks in the soil or saline water that destroys seeds, is our lack of forgiveness, [our] hard-heartedness, cold-bloodedness, refusal to embrace or respect others. We expect, demand even, that God treat us kindly and with unlimited forgiveness. But we do not return the favor to others. Our hard-heartedness short-circuits the words in our hearts, twists and makes them hollow and without meaning, turns them into idle twaddle and nonsense. Jesus is blunt: If we do not forgive others, neither will the Father forgive us.

If we truly attempt to pray, then we will begin to experience a shifting of "tectonic plates" deep within us, for, as Søren Kierkegaard says, "The prayer does not change God, but it changes the one who offers it." Prayer makes us disappear into God.

—*MEGAN MCKENNA*

Go to page 1282 for your next devotional reading.

unhealthy, your whole body will be full of darkness. If then the light in you is darkness, how great is the darkness!

Serving Two Masters

24 "No one can serve two masters; for a slave will either hate the one and love the other, or be devoted to the one and despise the other. You cannot serve God and wealth.*o*

Do Not Worry

25 "Therefore I tell you, do not worry about your life, what you will eat or what you will drink,*p* or about your body, what you will wear. Is not life more than food, and the body more than clothing? 26Look at the birds of the air; they neither sow nor reap nor gather into barns, and yet your heavenly Father feeds them. Are you not of more value than they? 27And can any of you by worrying add a single hour to your span of life?*q* 28And why do you worry about clothing? Consider the lilies of the field, how they grow; they neither toil nor spin, 29yet I tell you, even Solomon in all his glory was not clothed like one of these. 30But if God so clothes the grass of the field, which is alive today and tomorrow is thrown into the oven, will he not much more clothe you—you of little faith? 31Therefore do not worry, saying, 'What will we eat?' or 'What will we drink?' or 'What will we wear?' 32For it is the Gentiles who strive for all these things; and indeed your heavenly Father knows that you need all these things. 33But strive first for the kingdom of God*r* and his*s* righteousness, and all these things will be given to you as well.

34 "So do not worry about tomorrow, for tomorrow will bring worries of its own. Today's trouble is enough for today.

Judging Others

7 "Do not judge, so that you may not be judged. 2For with the judgment you make you will be judged, and the measure you give will be the measure you get. 3Why do you see the speck in your neighbor's*t* eye, but do not notice the log in your own eye? 4Or how can you say to your neighbor,*u* 'Let me take the speck out of your eye,' while the log is in your own eye? 5You hypocrite, first take the log out of your own eye, and then you will see clearly to take the speck out of your neighbor's*t* eye.

Profaning the Holy

6 "Do not give what is holy to dogs; and do not throw your pearls before swine, or they will trample them under foot and turn and maul you.

Ask, Search, Knock

7 "Ask, and it will be given you; search, and you will find; knock, and the door will be opened for you. 8For everyone who asks receives, and everyone who searches finds, and for everyone who knocks, the door will be opened. 9Is there anyone among you who, if your child asks for bread, will give a stone? 10Or if the child asks for a fish, will give a snake? 11If you then, who are evil, know how to give good gifts to your children, how much more will your Father in heaven give good things to those who ask him!

The Golden Rule

12 "In everything do to others as you would have them do to you; for this is the law and the prophets.

The Narrow Gate

13 "Enter through the narrow gate; for the gate is wide and the road is easy*v* that leads to destruction, and there are many who take it. 14For the gate is narrow and the road is hard that leads to life, and there are few who find it.

A Tree and Its Fruit

15 "Beware of false prophets, who come to you in sheep's clothing but inwardly are ravenous wolves. 16You will know them by their fruits. Are grapes gathered from thorns, or figs from thistles? 17In the same way, every good tree bears good fruit, but the bad tree bears bad fruit. 18A good tree cannot bear bad fruit, nor can a bad tree bear good fruit. 19Every tree that does not bear good fruit is cut down and thrown into the fire. 20Thus you will know them by their fruits.

Concerning Self-Deception

21 "Not everyone who says to me, 'Lord, Lord,' will enter the kingdom of

---

o Gk *mammon*   *p* Other ancient authorities lack *or what you will drink*   *q* Or *add one cubit to your height*   *r* Other ancient authorities lack *of God*   *s* Or *its*   *t* Gk *brother's*   *u* Gk *brother*   *v* Other ancient authorities read *for the road is wide and easy*

heaven, but only the one who does the will of my Father in heaven. 22On that day many will say to me, 'Lord, Lord, did we not prophesy in your name, and cast out demons in your name, and do many deeds of power in your name?' 23Then I will declare to them, 'I never knew you; go away from me, you evildoers.'

Hearers and Doers

24 "Everyone then who hears these words of mine and acts on them will be like a wise man who built his house on rock. 25The rain fell, the floods came, and the winds blew and beat on that house, but it did not fall, because it had been founded on rock. 26And everyone who hears these words of mine and does not act on them will be like a foolish man who built his house on sand. 27The rain fell, and the floods came, and the winds blew and beat against that house, and it fell—and great was its fall!"

28 Now when Jesus had finished saying these things, the crowds were astounded at his teaching, 29for he taught them as one having authority, and not as their scribes.

Jesus Cleanses a Leper

8 When Jesus*w* had come down from the mountain, great crowds followed him; 2and there was a leper*x* who came to him and knelt before him, saying, "Lord, if you choose, you can make me clean." 3He stretched out his hand and touched him, saying, "I do choose. Be made clean!" Immediately his leprosy*x* was cleansed. 4Then Jesus said to him, "See that you say nothing to anyone; but go, show yourself to the priest, and offer the gift that Moses commanded, as a testimony to them."

Jesus Heals a Centurion's Servant

5 When he entered Capernaum, a centurion came to him, appealing to him 6and saying, "Lord, my servant is lying at home paralyzed, in terrible distress." 7And he said to him, "I will come and cure him." 8The centurion answered, "Lord, I am not worthy to have you come under my roof; but only speak the word, and my servant will be healed. 9For I also am a man under authority, with soldiers under me; and I say to one, 'Go,' and he goes, and to another, 'Come,' and he comes, and to my slave, 'Do this,' and the slave does it."

10When Jesus heard him, he was amazed and said to those who followed him, "Truly I tell you, in no one*y* in Israel have I found such faith. 11I tell you, many will come from east and west and will eat with Abraham and Isaac and Jacob in the kingdom of heaven, 12while the heirs of the kingdom will be thrown into the outer darkness, where there will be weeping and gnashing of teeth." 13And to the centurion Jesus said, "Go; let it be done for you according to your faith." And the servant was healed in that hour.

Jesus Heals Many at Peter's House

14 When Jesus entered Peter's house, he saw his mother-in-law lying in bed with a fever; 15he touched her hand, and the fever left her, and she got up and began to serve him. 16That evening they brought to him many who were possessed with demons; and he cast out the spirits with a word, and cured all who were sick. 17This was to fulfill what had been spoken through the prophet Isaiah, "He took our infirmities and bore our diseases."

Would-Be Followers of Jesus

18 Now when Jesus saw great crowds around him, he gave orders to go over to the other side. 19A scribe then approached and said, "Teacher, I will follow you wherever you go." 20And Jesus said to him, "Foxes have holes, and birds of the air have nests; but the Son of Man has nowhere to lay his head." 21Another of his disciples said to him, "Lord, first let me go and bury my father." 22But Jesus said to him, "Follow me, and let the dead bury their own dead."

Jesus Stills the Storm

23 And when he got into the boat, his disciples followed him. 24A windstorm arose on the sea, so great that the boat was being swamped by the waves; but he was asleep. 25And they went and woke him up, saying, "Lord, save us! We are perishing!" 26And he said to them, "Why are you afraid, you of little faith?" Then he got up and rebuked the winds and the sea; and there was a dead calm. 27They were amazed, saying, "What sort of man is this, that even the winds and the sea obey him?"

---

w Gk *he*   *x* The terms *leper* and *leprosy* can refer to several diseases   *y* Other ancient authorities read *Truly I tell you, not even*

Jesus Heals the Gadarene Demoniacs

28 When he came to the other side, to the country of the Gadarenes,[z] two demoniacs coming out of the tombs met him. They were so fierce that no one could pass that way. 29Suddenly they shouted, "What have you to do with us, Son of God? Have you come here to torment us before the time?" 30Now a large herd of swine was feeding at some distance from them. 31The demons begged him, "If you cast us out, send us into the herd of swine." 32And he said to them, "Go!" So they came out and entered the swine; and suddenly, the whole herd rushed down the steep bank into the sea and perished in the water. 33The swineherds ran off, and on going into the town, they told the whole story about what had happened to the demoniacs. 34Then the whole town came out to meet Jesus; and when they saw him, they begged him to leave their neighborhood. 1And after getting into a boat he crossed the sea and came to his own town.

Jesus Heals a Paralytic

2 And just then some people were carrying a paralyzed man lying on a bed. When Jesus saw their faith, he said to the paralytic, "Take heart, son; your sins are forgiven." 3Then some of the scribes said to themselves, "This man is blaspheming." 4But Jesus, perceiving their thoughts, said, "Why do you think evil in your hearts? 5For which is easier, to say, 'Your sins are forgiven,' or to say, 'Stand up and walk'? 6But so that you may know that the Son of Man has authority on earth to forgive sins"—he then said to the paralytic— "Stand up, take your bed and go to your home." 7And he stood up and went to his home. 8When the crowds saw it, they were filled with awe, and they glorified God, who had given such authority to human beings.

The Call of Matthew

9 As Jesus was walking along, he saw a man called Matthew sitting at the tax booth; and he said to him, "Follow me." And he got up and followed him.

10 And as he sat at dinner[a] in the house, many tax collectors and sinners came and were sitting[b] with him and his disciples. 11When the Pharisees saw this, they said to his disciples, "Why does your teacher eat with tax collectors and sinners?" 12But when he heard this, he said, "Those who are well have no need of a physician, but those who are sick. 13Go and learn what this means, 'I desire mercy, not sacrifice.' For I have come to call not the righteous but sinners."

The Question about Fasting

14 Then the disciples of John came to him, saying, "Why do we and the Pharisees fast often,[c] but your disciples do not fast?" 15And Jesus said to them, "The wedding guests cannot mourn as long as the bridegroom is with them, can they? The days will come when the bridegroom is taken away from them, and then they will fast. 16No one sews a piece of unshrunk cloth on an old cloak, for the patch pulls away from the cloak, and a worse tear is made. 17Neither is new wine put into old wineskins; otherwise, the skins burst, and the wine is spilled, and the skins are destroyed; but new wine is put into fresh wineskins, and so both are preserved."

A Girl Restored to Life and a Woman Healed

18 While he was saying these things to them, suddenly a leader of the synagogue[d] came in and knelt before him, saying, "My daughter has just died; but come and lay your hand on her, and she will live." 19And Jesus got up and followed him, with his disciples. 20Then suddenly a woman who had been suffering from hemorrhages for twelve years came up behind him and touched the fringe of his cloak, 21for she said to herself, "If I only touch his cloak, I will be made well." 22Jesus turned, and seeing her he said, "Take heart, daughter; your faith has made you well." And instantly the woman was made well. 23When Jesus came to the leader's house and saw the flute players and the crowd making a commotion, 24he said, "Go away; for the girl is not dead but sleeping." And they laughed at him. 25But when the crowd had been put outside, he went in and took her by the hand, and the girl got up. 26And the report of this spread throughout that district.

---

z Other ancient authorities read *Gergesenes*; others, *Gerasenes*   a Gk *reclined*   b Gk *were reclining*   c Other ancient authorities lack *often*   d Gk lacks *of the synagogue*

Jesus Heals Two Blind Men

27 As Jesus went on from there, two blind men followed him, crying loudly, "Have mercy on us, Son of David!" 28When he entered the house, the blind men came to him; and Jesus said to them, "Do you believe that I am able to do this?" They said to him, "Yes, Lord." 29Then he touched their eyes and said, "According to your faith let it be done to you." 30And their eyes were opened. Then Jesus sternly ordered them, "See that no one knows of this." 31But they went away and spread the news about him throughout that district.

Jesus Heals One Who Was Mute

32 After they had gone away, a demoniac who was mute was brought to him. 33And when the demon had been cast out, the one who had been mute spoke; and the crowds were amazed and said, "Never has anything like this been seen in Israel." 34But the Pharisees said, "By the ruler of the demons he casts out the demons."*e*

The Harvest Is Great, the Laborers Few

35 Then Jesus went about all the cities and villages, teaching in their synagogues, and proclaiming the good news of the kingdom, and curing every disease and every sickness. 36When he saw the crowds, he had compassion for them, because they were harassed and helpless, like sheep without a shepherd. 37Then he said to his disciples, "The harvest is plentiful, but the laborers are few; 38therefore ask the Lord of the harvest to send out laborers into his harvest."

e Other ancient authorities lack this verse

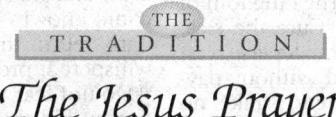

THE TRADITION

The Jesus Prayer

"Have mercy on us, Son of David!"
MATTHEW 9.27

When I try to pray, words fail me. I have no idea how to "pray constantly." Methods of prayer and meditation are too complicated for me.

I want to pray in a way that keeps me focused on the basics.

Can you relate to any of these statements? If so, you might also relate to one of the oldest, simplest, and deepest of Christian spiritual traditions: the Jesus prayer.

"Lord Jesus Christ, Son of God, have mercy on me, a sinner." The prayer appears for the first time in the Gospels, where some version of it is prayed by a collection of needy people—blind beggars, a desperate mother, a despised public official (see Matthew 9.27; 15.22; 20.30; Mark 10.47; Luke 17.13; 18.13, 38).

With a sense of kinship and self-recognition, Christians meditating on the Gospels seize on the prayer as an apt description of our ongoing need for divine mercy. The early spiritual writers recommended this prayer as a way of centering our hearts on God and fulfilling the command to "pray without ceasing" (1 Thessalonians 5.17).

This simple prayer derives its power from "the name that is above every name" (Philippians 2.9) and is often compressed into the single word "Jesus." This says it all. To pray "Jesus" with our lips or in our hearts is to open ourselves to God's mercy. It invites the risen Lord to make his home in us. Gradually, his transforming presence fills us with joy and burning love.

"When I arise in the morning," says one woman who has made the Jesus prayer a part of her life, "it starts me joyfully on a new day. When I travel by air, land, or sea, it sings within my breast ... When I gather my children around me, it murmurs a blessing. And at the end of a weary day, when I lay me down to rest, I give my heart over to Jesus ... I sleep—but my heart as it beats prays on: 'JESUS.'"

The Twelve Apostles

10 Then Jesus *f* summoned his twelve disciples and gave them authority over unclean spirits, to cast them out, and to cure every disease and every sickness. ²These are the names of the twelve apostles: first, Simon, also known as Peter, and his brother Andrew; James son of Zebedee, and his brother John; ³Philip and Bartholomew; Thomas and Matthew the tax collector; James son of Alphaeus, and Thaddaeus; *g* ⁴Simon the Cananaean, and Judas Iscariot, the one who betrayed him.

The Mission of the Twelve

5 These twelve Jesus sent out with the following instructions: "Go nowhere among the Gentiles, and enter no town of the Samaritans, ⁶but go rather to the lost sheep of the house of Israel. ⁷As you go, proclaim the good news, 'The kingdom of heaven has come near.' *h* ⁸Cure the sick, raise the dead, cleanse the lepers, *i* cast out demons. You received without payment; give without payment. ⁹Take no gold, or silver, or copper in your belts, ¹⁰no bag for your journey, or two tunics, or sandals, or a staff; for laborers deserve their food. ¹¹Whatever town or village you enter, find out who in it is worthy, and stay there until you leave. ¹²As you enter the house, greet it. ¹³If the house is worthy, let your peace come upon it; but if it is not worthy, let your peace return to you. ¹⁴If anyone will not welcome you or listen to your words, shake off the dust from your feet as you leave that house or town. ¹⁵Truly I tell you, it will be more tolerable for the land of Sodom and Gomorrah on the day of judgment than for that town.

Coming Persecutions

16 "See, I am sending you out like sheep into the midst of wolves; so be wise as serpents and innocent as doves. ¹⁷Beware of them, for they will hand you over to councils and flog you in their synagogues; ¹⁸and you will be dragged before governors and kings because of me, as a testimony to them and the Gentiles. ¹⁹When they hand you over, do not worry about how you are to speak or what you are to say; for what you are to say will be given to you at that time; ²⁰for it is not you who speak, but the Spirit of your Father speaking through you. ²¹Brother will betray brother to death, and a father his child, and children will rise against parents and have them put to death; ²²and you will be hated by all because of my name. But the one who endures to the end will be saved. ²³When they persecute you in one town, flee to the next; for truly I tell you, you will not have gone through all the towns of Israel before the Son of Man comes.

24 "A disciple is not above the teacher, nor a slave above the master; ²⁵it is enough for the disciple to be like the teacher, and the slave like the master. If they have called the master of the house Beelzebul, how much more will they malign those of his household!

Whom to Fear

26 "So have no fear of them; for nothing is covered up that will not be uncovered, and nothing secret that will not become known. ²⁷What I say to you in the dark, tell in the light; and what you hear whispered, proclaim from the housetops. ²⁸Do not fear those who kill the body but cannot kill the soul; rather fear him who can destroy both soul and body in hell. *j* ²⁹Are not two sparrows sold for a penny? Yet not one of them will fall to the ground apart from your Father. ³⁰And even the hairs of your head are all counted. ³¹So do not be afraid; you are of more value than many sparrows.

32 "Everyone therefore who acknowledges me before others, I also will acknowledge before my Father in heaven; ³³but whoever denies me before others, I also will deny before my Father in heaven.

Not Peace, but a Sword

34 "Do not think that I have come to bring peace to the earth; I have not come to bring peace, but a sword.
35 For I have come to set a man
    against his father,
and a daughter against her mother,
and a daughter-in-law against her
    mother-in-law;
36 and one's foes will be members of
    one's own household.
³⁷Whoever loves father or mother more than me is not worthy of me; and whoev-

---

f Gk *he*   *g* Other ancient authorities read *Lebbaeus,* or *Lebbaeus called Thaddaeus*   *h* Or *is at hand*   *i* The terms *leper* and *leprosy* can refer to several diseases   *j* Gk *Gehenna*

er loves son or daughter more than me is not worthy of me; ³⁸and whoever does not take up the cross and follow me is not worthy of me. ³⁹Those who find their life will lose it, and those who lose their life for my sake will find it.

Rewards

40 "Whoever welcomes you welcomes me, and whoever welcomes me welcomes the one who sent me. ⁴¹Whoever welcomes a prophet in the name of a prophet will receive a prophet's reward; and whoever welcomes a righteous person in the name of a righteous person will receive the reward of the righteous; ⁴²and whoever gives even a cup of cold water to one of these little ones in the name of a disciple—truly I tell you, none of these will lose their reward."

11 Now when Jesus had finished instructing his twelve disciples, he went on from there to teach and proclaim his message in their cities.

Messengers from John the Baptist

2 When John heard in prison what the Messiah*k* was doing, he sent word by his*l* disciples ³and said to him, "Are you the one who is to come, or are we to wait for another?" ⁴Jesus answered them, "Go and tell John what you hear and see: ⁵the blind receive their sight, the lame walk, the lepers*m* are cleansed, the deaf hear, the dead are raised, and the poor have good news brought to them. ⁶And blessed is anyone who takes no offense at me."

Jesus Praises John the Baptist

7 As they went away, Jesus began to speak to the crowds about John: "What did you go out into the wilderness to look at? A reed shaken by the wind? ⁸What then did you go out to see? Someone*n* dressed in soft robes? Look, those who wear soft robes are in royal palaces. ⁹What then did you go out to see? A prophet?*o* Yes, I tell you, and more than a prophet. ¹⁰This is the one about whom it is written,

'See, I am sending my messenger
    ahead of you,
  who will prepare your way
    before you.'

¹¹Truly I tell you, among those born of women no one has arisen greater than John the Baptist; yet the least in the kingdom of heaven is greater than he. ¹²From

the days of John the Baptist until now the kingdom of heaven has suffered violence,*p* and the violent take it by force. ¹³For all the prophets and the law prophesied until John came; ¹⁴and if you are willing to accept it, he is Elijah who is to come. ¹⁵Let anyone with ears*q* listen!

16 "But to what will I compare this generation? It is like children sitting in the marketplaces and calling to one another,

17 'We played the flute for you, and
      you did not dance;
    we wailed, and you did not
      mourn.'

¹⁸For John came neither eating nor drinking, and they say, 'He has a demon'; ¹⁹the Son of Man came eating and drinking, and they say, 'Look, a glutton and a drunkard, a friend of tax collectors and sinners!' Yet wisdom is vindicated by her deeds."*r*

Woes to Unrepentant Cities

20 Then he began to reproach the cities in which most of his deeds of power had been done, because they did not repent. ²¹"Woe to you, Chorazin! Woe to you, Bethsaida! For if the deeds of power done in you had been done in Tyre and Sidon, they would have repented long ago in sackcloth and ashes. ²²But I tell you, on the day of judgment it will be more tolerable for Tyre and Sidon than for you. ²³And you, Capernaum,

  will you be exalted to heaven?
    No, you will be brought down
      to Hades.

For if the deeds of power done in you had been done in Sodom, it would have remained until this day. ²⁴But I tell you that on the day of judgment it will be more tolerable for the land of Sodom than for you."

Jesus Thanks His Father

25 At that time Jesus said, "I thank*s* you, Father, Lord of heaven and earth, because you have hidden these things from the wise and the intelligent and have revealed them to infants; ²⁶yes, Father, for

k Or *the Christ*   *l* Other ancient authorities read *two of his*   *m* The terms *leper* and *leprosy* can refer to several diseases   *n* Or *Why then did you go out? To see someone*   *o* Other ancient authorities read *Why then did you go out? To see a prophet?*   *p* Or *has been coming violently*   *q* Other ancient authorities add *to hear*   *r* Other ancient authorities read *children*   *s* Or *praise*

such was your gracious will.[t] 27All things have been handed over to me by my Father; and no one knows the Son except the Father, and no one knows the Father except the Son and anyone to whom the Son chooses to reveal him.

28 "Come to me, all you that are weary and are carrying heavy burdens, and I will give you rest. 29Take my yoke upon you, and learn from me; for I am gentle and humble in heart, and you will find rest for your souls. 30For my yoke is easy, and my burden is light."

Plucking Grain on the Sabbath

12 At that time Jesus went through the grainfields on the sabbath; his disciples were hungry, and they began to pluck heads of grain and to eat. 2When the Pharisees saw it, they said to him, "Look, your disciples are doing what is not lawful to do on the sabbath." 3He said to them, "Have you not read what David did when he and his companions were hungry? 4He entered the house of God and ate the bread of the Presence, which it was not lawful for him or his companions to eat, but only for the priests. 5Or have you not read in the law that on the sabbath the priests in the temple break the sabbath and yet are guiltless? 6I tell you, something greater than the temple is here. 7But if you had known what this means, 'I desire mercy and not sacrifice,' you would not have condemned the guiltless. 8For the Son of Man is lord of the sabbath."

The Man with a Withered Hand

9 He left that place and entered their synagogue; 10a man was there with a withered hand, and they asked him, "Is it lawful to cure on the sabbath?" so that they might accuse him. 11He said to them, "Suppose one of you has only one sheep and it falls into a pit on the sabbath; will you not lay hold of it and lift it out? 12How much more valuable is a human being than a sheep! So it is lawful to do good on the sabbath." 13Then he said to the man, "Stretch out your hand." He stretched it out, and it was restored, as sound as the other. 14But the Pharisees went out and conspired against him, how to destroy him.

God's Chosen Servant

15 When Jesus became aware of this, he departed. Many crowds[u] followed him, and he cured all of them, 16and he ordered them not to make him known. 17This was to fulfill what had been spoken through the prophet Isaiah:

---

[t] Or *for so it was well-pleasing in your sight*
[u] Other ancient authorities lack *crowds*

FRIDAY

Scripture Reading for Today:
Matthew 11.28–30

Verse for Today:
Matthew 11.28

Finding Rest

"Come to me," cries Jesus. "I will give you rest." I don't know about you, but for me, to speak of eternal joy, delight, bliss, is unreal. I simply cannot imagine unalloyed joy and delight engulfing the whole of me. I know joy, but it is that of sacrifice, of loving God at cost; this is the only joy that means anything to me. But when I think of the more modest term *rest*—yes, then my heart responds.

To be at rest: yearning, struggle, empty longing filled . . . yes, that means something. *I will give you rest because I give you the Father, and you come to me by taking my yoke upon yourself, the yoke of humble, meek, devoted loving.* This is to know the Father, the God of all compassion.

—RUTH BURROWS

Go to page 1284 for your next devotional reading.

18 "Here is my servant, whom I
    have chosen,
  my beloved, with whom my soul
    is well pleased.
  I will put my Spirit upon him,
    and he will proclaim justice to the
    Gentiles.
19 He will not wrangle or cry aloud,
    nor will anyone hear his voice
    in the streets.
20 He will not break a bruised reed
    or quench a smoldering wick
  until he brings justice to victory.
21   And in his name the Gentiles will
    hope."

Jesus and Beelzebul

22 Then they brought to him a demoniac who was blind and mute; and he cured him, so that the one who had been mute could speak and see. 23All the crowds were amazed and said, "Can this be the Son of David?" 24But when the Pharisees heard it, they said, "It is only by Beelzebul, the ruler of the demons, that this fellow casts out the demons." 25He knew what they were thinking and said to them, "Every kingdom divided against itself is laid waste, and no city or house divided against itself will stand. 26If Satan casts out Satan, he is divided against himself; how then will his kingdom stand? 27If I cast out demons by Beelzebul, by whom do your own exorcists*v* cast them out? Therefore they will be your judges. 28But if it is by the Spirit of God that I cast out demons, then the kingdom of God has come to you. 29Or how can one enter a strong man's house and plunder his property, without first tying up the strong man? Then indeed the house can be plundered. 30Whoever is not with me is against me, and whoever does not gather with me scatters. 31Therefore I tell you, people will be forgiven for every sin and blasphemy, but blasphemy against the Spirit will not be forgiven. 32Whoever speaks a word against the Son of Man will be forgiven, but whoever speaks against the Holy Spirit will not be forgiven, either in this age or in the age to come.

A Tree and Its Fruit

33 "Either make the tree good, and its fruit good; or make the tree bad, and its fruit bad; for the tree is known by its fruit. 34You brood of vipers! How can you speak good things, when you are evil? For out of the abundance of the heart the mouth speaks. 35The good person brings good things out of a good treasure, and the evil person brings evil things out of an evil treasure. 36I tell you, on the day of judgment you will have to give an account for every careless word you utter; 37for by your words you will be justified, and by your words you will be condemned."

The Sign of Jonah

38 Then some of the scribes and Pharisees said to him, "Teacher, we wish to see a sign from you." 39But he answered them, "An evil and adulterous generation asks for a sign, but no sign will be given to it except the sign of the prophet Jonah. 40For just as Jonah was three days and three nights in the belly of the sea monster, so for three days and three nights the Son of Man will be in the heart of the earth. 41The people of Nineveh will rise up at the judgment with this generation and condemn it, because they repented at the proclamation of Jonah, and see, something greater than Jonah is here! 42The queen of the South will rise up at the judgment with this generation and condemn it, because she came from the ends of the earth to listen to the wisdom of Solomon, and see, something greater than Solomon is here!

The Return of the Unclean Spirit

43 "When the unclean spirit has gone out of a person, it wanders through waterless regions looking for a resting place, but it finds none. 44Then it says, 'I will return to my house from which I came.' When it comes, it finds it empty, swept, and put in order. 45Then it goes and brings along seven other spirits more evil than itself, and they enter and live there; and the last state of that person is worse than the first. So will it be also with this evil generation."

The True Kindred of Jesus

46 While he was still speaking to the crowds, his mother and his brothers were standing outside, wanting to speak to him. 47Someone told him, "Look, your mother and your brothers are standing outside, wanting to speak to you."*w* 48But to the one who had told him this, Jesus*x* replied, "Who is my mother, and who are

v Gk *sons*   *w* Other ancient authorities lack
verse 47   *x* Gk *he*

Judith

Her Name Means *"Jewess"*

THE STORY OF A WOMAN

Read Judith 10; 13

Judith was a stunning beauty with more true grit than Rooster Cogburn on his best day and more iron in her constitution than the toughest "steel magnolia." Her steady regimen of penance, prayer, and fasting formed a discipline that shaped her soul for the strategic part she would play in Biblical history.

Every day, all day, the Jews of Bethulia begged God's help. Surely he would rescue his people from an army that despised him, calling him no god at all. But the heavens maintained their silent, cloudless gaze as the Assyrian army laid siege to the town: No rain, no miracle from above, no delivering army marching across the horizon. Water jars were emptied. Children fell ill. Men and women fainted. Hope faded.

After 34 days, rank and file Jews clamored for surrender. Bitter that their Mighty God had failed them and convinced he was punishing them, they preferred enslavement at the hand of their enemy rather than a slow and tortured dying. They were ready to surrender to Holofernes, commander-in-chief of Nebuchadnezzar's forces.

But one citizen of Bethulia thought otherwise. The reclusive Judith sent for the elders to speak her mind, berating them for giving in to the people: "Do not try to bind the purposes of the Lord our God; for God is not like a human being, to be threatened, or like a mere mortal, to be won over by pleading.

Her Character: *Wise, courageous, wealthy, and devout, Judith is one of the Old Testament's greatest heroes. Like the young David advancing against Goliath, she single-handedly took on a military power that terrified everyone around her. Many centuries later, Catherine of Siena would follow her example by boldly speaking the truth to leaders of the church who lacked the courage to trust God.*
Her Sorrow: *That the leaders of her people failed to trust God for deliverance.*
Her Joy: *That God defeated his enemy through a woman's hand, revealing his greatness, love, and faithfulness.*

Therefore, while we wait for his deliverance, let us call upon him to help us, and he will hear our voice, if it pleases him . . . Listen to me. I am about to do something that will go down through all generations of our descendants" (8.16–17, 32).

Judith did more than upbraid the town's elders for their lack of faith. She put her own faith into action by slipping into the enemy's camp and killing the great Holofernes.

What gave Judith the courage, the audacity to do what she did? Was it not a certain conviction that God was both faithful and more powerful than any enemy? Through prayer and fasting, she saw what others could not: A daring strategy, unfolding according to a divine timetable, would brilliantly outwit the enemy. The Jews believed God had sent Holofernes to punish them. But Judith had accurately discerned the truth. It was a test, not a punishment. Passing the test meant trusting God and acting courageously to implement his divine plan rather than putting God to the test by losing faith.

If Judith's courage and faith seem impossible to emulate, remember that faith is a gift. It comes as we spend time with God, humbling ourselves, surrendering our fears and sorrows, expecting transforming grace to be given us. Intimacy with God will put us in touch with realities that would otherwise elude us. At times we will be enabled to understand what is really going on in the spiritual realm, helping us deal a resounding blow to our enemies.

Praying With Judith

"But the Lord Almighty has foiled them by the hand of a woman. For their mighty one did not fall by the hands of the young men, nor did the sons of the Titans strike him down, nor did tall giants set upon him; but Judith daughter of Merari with the beauty of her countenance undid him."—*Judith 16.5–6*

Praise God: *For all the ways he has used women to build up the church.*

Offer Thanks: *For whatever way you have already sensed God's calling in your life.*

Confess: *Any lack of faith that God can and will use you.*

Ask God: *For courage to follow his leading.*

Lift Your Heart

We belong to the communion of saints, a body of believers that includes extraordinary women such as Judith, Catherine of Siena, Saint Thérèse of Lisieux, Saint Hildegard of Bingen, Dorothy Day, and Mother Teresa of Calcutta, each of whom God has used to build up the church. Get to know these and other sisters of the faith by reading their individual biographies or by reading their own words and stories in books like *Voices of the Saints* by Bert Ghezzi, *Treasury of Women Saints* by Rhonda Chervin, or *365 Saints* by Woodene Koenig-Bricker. Such women can become our spiritual mentors, their lives instructing, encouraging, and guiding us.

Go to page 1288 for your next devotional reading.

my brothers?" [49]And pointing to his disciples, he said, "Here are my mother and my brothers! [50]For whoever does the will of my Father in heaven is my brother and sister and mother."

The Parable of the Sower

13 That same day Jesus went out of the house and sat beside the sea. [2]Such great crowds gathered around him that he got into a boat and sat there, while the whole crowd stood on the beach. [3]And he told them many things in parables, saying: "Listen! A sower went out to sow. [4]And as he sowed, some seeds fell on the path, and the birds came and ate them up. [5]Other seeds fell on rocky ground, where they did not have much soil, and they sprang up quickly, since they had no depth of soil. [6]But when the sun rose, they were scorched; and since they had no root, they withered away. [7]Other seeds fell among thorns, and the thorns grew up and choked them. [8]Other seeds fell on good soil and brought forth grain, some a hundredfold, some sixty, some thirty. [9]Let anyone with ears[y] listen!"

The Purpose of the Parables

10 Then the disciples came and asked him, "Why do you speak to them in parables?" [11]He answered, "To you it has been given to know the secrets[z] of the kingdom of heaven, but to them it has not been given. [12]For to those who have, more will be given, and they will have an abundance; but from those who have nothing, even what they have will be taken away. [13]The reason I speak to them in parables is that 'seeing they do not perceive, and hearing they do not listen, nor do they understand.' [14]With them indeed is fulfilled the prophecy of Isaiah that says:

'You will indeed listen, but never
      understand,
   and you will indeed look, but
         never perceive.
[15] For this people's heart has
         grown dull,
   and their ears are hard of hearing,
      and they have shut their eyes;
      so that they might not look
         with their eyes,
   and listen with their ears,
   and understand with their heart and
         turn—
   and I would heal them.'
[16]But blessed are your eyes, for they see,

and your ears, for they hear. [17]Truly I tell you, many prophets and righteous people longed to see what you see, but did not see it, and to hear what you hear, but did not hear it.

The Parable of the Sower Explained

18 "Hear then the parable of the sower. [19]When anyone hears the word of the kingdom and does not understand it, the evil one comes and snatches away what is sown in the heart; this is what was sown on the path. [20]As for what was sown on rocky ground, this is the one who hears the word and immediately receives it with joy; [21]yet such a person has no root, but endures only for a while, and when trouble or persecution arises on account of the word, that person immediately falls away.[a] [22]As for what was sown among thorns, this is the one who hears the word, but the cares of the world and the lure of wealth choke the word, and it yields nothing. [23]But as for what was sown on good soil, this is the one who hears the word and understands it, who indeed bears fruit and yields, in one case a hundredfold, in another sixty, and in another thirty."

The Parable of Weeds among the Wheat

24 He put before them another parable: "The kingdom of heaven may be compared to someone who sowed good seed in his field; [25]but while everybody was asleep, an enemy came and sowed weeds among the wheat, and then went away. [26]So when the plants came up and bore grain, then the weeds appeared as well. [27]And the slaves of the householder came and said to him, 'Master, did you not sow good seed in your field? Where, then, did these weeds come from?' [28]He answered, 'An enemy has done this.' The slaves said to him, 'Then do you want us to go and gather them?' [29]But he replied, 'No; for in gathering the weeds you would uproot the wheat along with them. [30]Let both of them grow together until the harvest; and at harvest time I will tell the reapers, Collect the weeds first and bind them in bundles to be burned, but gather the wheat into my barn.' "

y Other ancient authorities add to hear   *z Or mysteries*   *a Gk stumbles*

The Parable of the Mustard Seed

31 He put before them another parable: "The kingdom of heaven is like a mustard seed that someone took and sowed in his field; 32it is the smallest of all the seeds, but when it has grown it is the greatest of shrubs and becomes a tree, so that the birds of the air come and make nests in its branches."

The Parable of the Yeast

33 He told them another parable: "The kingdom of heaven is like yeast that a woman took and mixed in with*b* three measures of flour until all of it was leavened."

The Use of Parables

34 Jesus told the crowds all these things in parables; without a parable he told them nothing. 35This was to fulfill what had been spoken through the prophet:*c*

"I will open my mouth to speak
    in parables;
I will proclaim what has been
    hidden from the foundation
    of the world."*d*

Jesus Explains the Parable of the Weeds

36 Then he left the crowds and went into the house. And his disciples approached him, saying, "Explain to us the parable of the weeds of the field." 37He answered, "The one who sows the good seed is the Son of Man; 38the field is the world, and the good seed are the children of the kingdom; the weeds are the children of the evil one, 39and the enemy who sowed them is the devil; the harvest is the end of the age, and the reapers are angels. 40Just as the weeds are collected and burned up with fire, so will it be at the end of the age. 41The Son of Man will send his angels, and they will collect out of his kingdom all causes of sin and all evildoers, 42and they will throw them into the furnace of fire, where there will be weeping and gnashing of teeth. 43Then the righteous will shine like the sun in the kingdom of their Father. Let anyone with ears*e* listen!

Three Parables

44 "The kingdom of heaven is like treasure hidden in a field, which someone found and hid; then in his joy he goes and sells all that he has and buys that field.

45 "Again, the kingdom of heaven is like a merchant in search of fine pearls; 46on finding one pearl of great value, he went and sold all that he had and bought it.

47 "Again, the kingdom of heaven is like a net that was thrown into the sea and caught fish of every kind; 48when it was full, they drew it ashore, sat down, and put the good into baskets but threw out the bad. 49So it will be at the end of the age. The angels will come out and separate the evil from the righteous 50and throw them into the furnace of fire, where there will be weeping and gnashing of teeth.

Treasures New and Old

51 "Have you understood all this?" They answered, "Yes." 52And he said to them, "Therefore every scribe who has been trained for the kingdom of heaven is like the master of a household who brings out of his treasure what is new and what is old." 53When Jesus had finished these parables, he left that place.

The Rejection of Jesus at Nazareth

54 He came to his hometown and began to teach the people*f* in their synagogue, so that they were astounded and said, "Where did this man get this wisdom and these deeds of power? 55Is not this the carpenter's son? Is not his mother called Mary? And are not his brothers James and Joseph and Simon and Judas? 56And are not all his sisters with us? Where then did this man get all this?" 57And they took offense at him. But Jesus said to them, "Prophets are not without honor except in their own country and in their own house." 58And he did not do many deeds of power there, because of their unbelief.

The Death of John the Baptist

14 At that time Herod the ruler*g* heard reports about Jesus; 2and he said to his servants, "This is John the Baptist; he has been raised from the dead, and for this reason these powers are at work in him." 3For Herod had arrested

---

b Gk *hid in*   *c* Other ancient authorities read *the prophet Isaiah*   *d* Other ancient authorities lack *of the world*   *e* Other ancient authorities add *to hear*   *f* Gk *them*   *g* Gk *tetrarch*

John, bound him, and put him in prison on account of Herodias, his brother Philip's wife,[h] [4]because John had been telling him, "It is not lawful for you to have her." [5]Though Herod[i] wanted to put him to death, he feared the crowd, because they regarded him as a prophet. [6]But when Herod's birthday came, the daughter of Herodias danced before the company, and she pleased Herod [7]so much that he promised on oath to grant her whatever she might ask. [8]Prompted by her mother, she said, "Give me the head of John the Baptist here on a platter." [9]The king was grieved, yet out of regard for his oaths and for the guests, he commanded it to be given; [10]he sent and had John beheaded in the prison. [11]The head was brought on a platter and given to the girl, who brought

h Other ancient authorities read *his brother's wife*
i Gk *he*

Discovery

MONDAY

Scripture Reading
for Today:
Matthew 13.44–46

Verse for Today:
Matthew 13.44

We might assume that he [the man who finds the treasure] is a laborer who was too poor to own land of his own—or at least not enough of it to provide for his family. Such a person would literally have to sell everything in order to buy the field. Sometimes today an Egyptian village boy will decide to sell his ancestral plot to buy a taxi. He hopes to get rich taking tourists around to see the ancient monuments. Such decisions cause an uproar in the village, where land is still the most important thing a peasant can have.

Imagine Jesus' story on the scale of the village—where no behavior goes unnoticed or uncommented upon. The man's action is not trivial even though he does have the motive of the buried treasure. To gain the field, he has had to part with the very substance and security of his life. In addition, the audience knows that the original owner may well sue for part of the treasure. Since the man has sold everything, he will not be able to hide his sudden wealth. What will he do? What do you think happened?

Jesus' story is not as simple as it seems. A cautious person might well not act as this man has done. What little he has would be more security than the treasure. Or would it?

What things do we hold onto with such peasant-like tenacity? What would get us to loosen our hold? The story is not a direct command to sell everything. It presents a striking image of a case in which a person is willing to really change everything about his life. Thus, it can be seen as a positive affirmation of the power of the presence of God to transform our lives. The man does not act out of calculation. He responds to an unexpected discovery. That discovery made it possible for him to launch out beyond the socially ingrained securities of his life. The rule of God is the kind of thing that can provoke such action from those who discover it.

—PHEME PERKINS

Go to page 1289 for your next devotional reading.

it to her mother. 12His disciples came and took the body and buried it; then they went and told Jesus.

Feeding the Five Thousand

13 Now when Jesus heard this, he withdrew from there in a boat to a deserted place by himself. But when the crowds heard it, they followed him on foot from the towns. 14When he went ashore, he saw a great crowd; and he had compassion for them and cured their sick. 15When it was evening, the disciples came to him and said, "This is a deserted place, and the hour is now late; send the crowds away so that they may go into the villages and buy food for themselves." 16Jesus said to them, "They need not go away; you give them something to eat." 17They replied, "We have nothing here but five loaves and two fish." 18And he said, "Bring them here to me." 19Then he ordered the crowds to sit down on the grass. Taking the five loaves and the two fish, he looked up to heaven, and blessed and broke the loaves, and gave them to the disciples, and the disciples gave them to the crowds. 20And all ate and were filled; and they took up what was left over of the broken pieces, twelve baskets full. 21And those who ate were about five thousand men, besides women and children.

Jesus Walks on the Water

22 Immediately he made the disciples get into the boat and go on ahead to the other side, while he dismissed the crowds. 23And after he had dismissed the crowds, he went up the mountain by himself to pray. When evening came, he was there alone, 24but by this time the boat, battered by the waves, was far from the

TUESDAY

Scripture Reading for Today:
Matthew 14:22–33

Verse for Today:
Matthew 14:27

Calming Our Fears

I grew up with water skis on my feet. I loved the exhilarating feeling of the slalom as it beat a staccato rhythm across the water. One summer day, my brother and I hit upon a thrilling idea: We would do without skis altogether and try skiing barefoot instead! Our bold plan involved starting with one ski and then gracefully slipping out of it once the boat built up speed. But there was little grace in our attempt. As soon as we slipped out of the ski, we sank like cement blocks. We hadn't realized that our little motor lacked the power to keep our ski-less feet above the water.

That stormy night on Galilee, Jesus manifested a power beyond anything we can comprehend—not a sorcerer's magic over the elements but the Creator's control over his own creation. His disciples were terrified.

How did Jesus respond to the disciples' fearful cries? Instead of telling them to buck up and stop being babies, he told them to have courage. Then he climbed into the boat and calmed the wind. And that's the way he treats us, speaking a word of courage, climbing into our situation, and calming our souls. We may feel that we are alone on a dark night, in the middle of an angry sea, but the truth is that God sees us no matter where we are or what we are going through. Just as Jesus walked on the water to come to the disciples, he can come to us and calm our fears.

—ANN SPANGLER

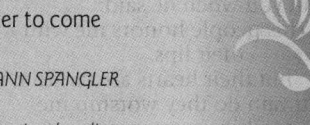

Go to page 1295 for your next devotional reading.

land,[j] for the wind was against them. [25]And early in the morning he came walking toward them on the sea. [26]But when the disciples saw him walking on the sea, they were terrified, saying, "It is a ghost!" And they cried out in fear. [27]But immediately Jesus spoke to them and said, "Take heart, it is I; do not be afraid."

28 Peter answered him, "Lord, if it is you, command me to come to you on the water." [29]He said, "Come." So Peter got out of the boat, started walking on the water, and came toward Jesus. [30]But when he noticed the strong wind,[k] he became frightened, and beginning to sink, he cried out, "Lord, save me!" [31]Jesus immediately reached out his hand and caught him, saying to him, "You of little faith, why did you doubt?" [32]When they got into the boat, the wind ceased. [33]And those in the boat worshiped him, saying, "Truly you are the Son of God."

Jesus Heals the Sick in Gennesaret

34 When they had crossed over, they came to land at Gennesaret. [35]After the people of that place recognized him, they sent word throughout the region and brought all who were sick to him, [36]and begged him that they might touch even the fringe of his cloak; and all who touched it were healed.

The Tradition of the Elders

15 Then Pharisees and scribes came to Jesus from Jerusalem and said, [2]"Why do your disciples break the tradition of the elders? For they do not wash their hands before they eat." [3]He answered them, "And why do you break the commandment of God for the sake of your tradition? [4]For God said,[l] 'Honor your father and your mother,' and, 'Whoever speaks evil of father or mother must surely die.' [5]But you say that whoever tells father or mother, 'Whatever support you might have had from me is given to God,'[m] then that person need not honor the father.[n] [6]So, for the sake of your tradition, you make void the word[o] of God. [7]You hypocrites! Isaiah prophesied rightly about you when he said:

8 'This people honors me with
        their lips,
    but their hearts are far from me;
9 in vain do they worship me,
        teaching human precepts as
    doctrines.' "

Things That Defile

10 Then he called the crowd to him and said to them, "Listen and understand: [11]it is not what goes into the mouth that defiles a person, but it is what comes out of the mouth that defiles." [12]Then the disciples approached and said to him, "Do you know that the Pharisees took offense when they heard what you said?" [13]He answered, "Every plant that my heavenly Father has not planted will be uprooted. [14]Let them alone; they are blind guides of the blind.[p] And if one blind person guides another, both will fall into a pit." [15]But Peter said to him, "Explain this parable to us." [16]Then he said, "Are you also still without understanding? [17]Do you not see that whatever goes into the mouth enters the stomach, and goes out into the sewer? [18]But what comes out of the mouth proceeds from the heart, and this is what defiles. [19]For out of the heart come evil intentions, murder, adultery, fornication, theft, false witness, slander. [20]These are what defile a person, but to eat with unwashed hands does not defile."

The Canaanite Woman's Faith

21 Jesus left that place and went away to the district of Tyre and Sidon. [22]Just then a Canaanite woman from that region came out and started shouting, "Have mercy on me, Lord, Son of David; my daughter is tormented by a demon." [23]But he did not answer her at all. And his disciples came and urged him, saying, "Send her away, for she keeps shouting after us." [24]He answered, "I was sent only to the lost sheep of the house of Israel." [25]But she came and knelt before him, saying, "Lord, help me." [26]He answered, "It is not fair to take the children's food and throw it to the dogs." [27]She said, "Yes, Lord, yet even the dogs eat the crumbs that fall from their masters' table." [28]Then Jesus answered her, "Woman, great is your faith! Let it be done for you as you wish." And her daughter was healed instantly.

---

j Other ancient authorities read *was out on the sea*
k Other ancient authorities read *the wind*
l Other ancient authorities read *commanded, saying*
m Or *is an offering*   n Other ancient authorities add *or the mother*   o Other ancient authorities read *law*; others, *commandment*   p Other ancient authorities lack *of the blind*

Jesus Cures Many People

29 After Jesus had left that place, he passed along the Sea of Galilee, and he went up the mountain, where he sat down. 30Great crowds came to him, bringing with them the lame, the maimed, the blind, the mute, and many others. They put them at his feet, and he cured them, 31so that the crowd was amazed when they saw the mute speaking, the maimed whole, the lame walking, and the blind seeing. And they praised the God of Israel.

Feeding the Four Thousand

32 Then Jesus called his disciples to him and said, "I have compassion for the crowd, because they have been with me now for three days and have nothing to eat; and I do not want to send them away hungry, for they might faint on the way." 33The disciples said to him, "Where are we to get enough bread in the desert to feed so great a crowd?" 34Jesus asked them, "How many loaves have you?" They said, "Seven, and a few small fish." 35Then ordering the crowd to sit down on the ground, 36he took the seven loaves and the fish; and after giving thanks he broke them and gave them to the disciples, and the disciples gave them to the crowds. 37And all of them ate and were filled; and they took up the broken pieces left over, seven baskets full. 38Those who had eaten were four thousand men, besides women and children. 39After sending away the crowds, he got into the boat and went to the region of Magadan.q

The Demand for a Sign

16 The Pharisees and Sadducees came, and to test Jesusr they asked him to show them a sign from heaven. 2He answered them, "When it is evening, you say, 'It will be fair weather, for the sky is red.' 3And in the morning, 'It will be stormy today, for the sky is red and threatening.' You know how to interpret the appearance of the sky, but you cannot interpret the signs of the times.s 4An evil and adulterous generation asks for a sign, but no sign will be given to it except the sign of Jonah." Then he left them and went away.

The Yeast of the Pharisees and Sadducees

5 When the disciples reached the other side, they had forgotten to bring any bread. 6Jesus said to them, "Watch out, and beware of the yeast of the Pharisees and Sadducees." 7They said to one another, "It is because we have brought no bread." 8And becoming aware of it, Jesus said, "You of little faith, why are you talking about having no bread? 9Do you still not perceive? Do you not remember the five loaves for the five thousand, and how many baskets you gathered? 10Or the seven loaves for the four thousand, and how many baskets you gathered? 11How could you fail to perceive that I was not speaking about bread? Beware of the yeast of the Pharisees and Sadducees!" 12Then they understood that he had not told them to beware of the yeast of bread, but of the teaching of the Pharisees and Sadducees.

Peter's Declaration about Jesus

13 Now when Jesus came into the district of Caesarea Philippi, he asked his disciples, "Who do people say that the Son of Man is?" 14And they said, "Some say John the Baptist, but others Elijah, and still others Jeremiah or one of the prophets." 15He said to them, "But who do you say that I am?" 16Simon Peter answered, "You are the Messiah,t the Son of the living God." 17And Jesus answered him, "Blessed are you, Simon son of Jonah! For flesh and blood has not revealed this to you, but my Father in heaven. 18And I tell you, you are Peter,u and on this rockv I will build my church, and the gates of Hades will not prevail against it. 19I will give you the keys of the kingdom of heaven, and whatever you bind on earth will be bound in heaven, and whatever you loose on earth will be loosed in heaven." 20Then he sternly ordered the disciples not to tell anyone that he wasw the Messiah.t

Jesus Foretells His Death and Resurrection

21 From that time on, Jesus began to show his disciples that he must go to Jerusalem and undergo great suffering at the hands of the elders and chief priests and scribes, and be killed, and on the third day be raised. 22And Peter took him aside and began to rebuke him, saying, "God

---

q Other ancient authorities read *Magdala* or *Magdalan*   r Gk *him*   s Other ancient authorities lack 2*When it is . . . of the times*   t Or *the Christ*   u Gk *Petros*   v Gk *petra*   w Other ancient authorities add *Jesus*

forbid it, Lord! This must never happen to you." ²³But he turned and said to Peter, "Get behind me, Satan! You are a stumbling block to me; for you are setting your mind not on divine things but on human things."

The Cross and Self-Denial

24 Then Jesus told his disciples, "If any want to become my followers, let them deny themselves and take up their cross and follow me. ²⁵For those who want to save their life will lose it, and those who lose their life for my sake will find it. ²⁶For what will it profit them if they gain the whole world but forfeit their life? Or what will they give in return for their life? 27 "For the Son of Man is to come with his angels in the glory of his Father,

and then he will repay everyone for what has been done. ²⁸Truly I tell you, there are some standing here who will not taste death before they see the Son of Man coming in his kingdom."

The Transfiguration

17 Six days later, Jesus took with him Peter and James and his brother John and led them up a high mountain, by themselves. ²And he was transfigured before them, and his face shone like the sun, and his clothes became dazzling white. ³Suddenly there appeared to them Moses and Elijah, talking with him. ⁴Then Peter said to Jesus, "Lord, it is good for us to be here; if you wish, Iˣ will make three

ˣ Other ancient authorities read *we*

Peter

"You are Peter, and on this rock I will build my church."
MATTHEW 16.18

I n the popular imagination, the head of the apostles has been typecast as a sort of bouncer at the doors of a celestial supper club—Saint Peter at the pearly gates. Though this picture may make for a few good jokes, it does not fit his actual job description.

Jesus Christ, in fact, is the only one who can judge who will live with him forever. The unique mission that Jesus entrusted to "Simon son of Jonah" when he renamed him Peter (in Greek, "stone," or "boulder") pertains to the *earthly* expression of that kingdom, the Church (see Matthew 16.18). As a sign of Peter's authority, Jesus gives him "the keys of the kingdom of heaven" (verse 19).

Keys are a symbol of power. (Just ask any teenager who obtains the keys to the family car!) Peter's keys, though, signify a supreme authority to govern God's house, the Church.

Jesus confers the keys on Peter alone, then follows up with an amazing promise made to all 12 apostles: to "bind or loose" in heaven— to back up with his own authority—whatever they "bind or loose" on earth (verse 19; see

also 18.18). In union with Peter, the Church's main shepherd on earth, the Eleven have divine backing for the authority they, too, are called to exercise.

As with every aspect of God's dealings with us, Peter's special commissioning reveals the divine willingness to take risks. Impetuous, inconstant, and slow to understand, Peter would not have been a modern headhunter's first choice for a CEO. Yet Peter is the apostle that Jesus commissioned to be his chief personal representative. "Strengthen your brothers," he charged him. "Feed my sheep" (Luke 22.32; John 21.17). Filled with the Spirit at Pentecost, Peter rose to the challenge.

Peter's successors have not always responded as he did. Many popes have been saintly, but others were unscrupulous. Through good times and bad, though, Christ's promised Church perseveres. Precarious though it may appear, the Church built on Peter prevails even over the powers of death because its true foundation and cornerstone is Jesus Christ (1 Corinthians 3.11; 1 Peter 2.4–8).

dwellings y here, one for you, one for Moses, and one for Elijah." 5While he was still speaking, suddenly a bright cloud overshadowed them, and from the cloud a voice said, "This is my Son, the Beloved;z with him I am well pleased; listen to him!" 6When the disciples heard this, they fell to the ground and were overcome by fear. 7But Jesus came and touched them, saying, "Get up and do not be afraid." 8And when they looked up, they saw no one except Jesus himself alone.

9 As they were coming down the mountain, Jesus ordered them, "Tell no one about the vision until after the Son of Man has been raised from the dead." 10And the disciples asked him, "Why, then, do the scribes say that Elijah must come first?" 11He replied, "Elijah is indeed coming and will restore all things; 12but I tell you that Elijah has already come, and they did not recognize him, but they did to him whatever they pleased. So also the Son of Man is about to suffer at their hands." 13Then the disciples understood that he was speaking to them about John the Baptist.

Jesus Cures a Boy with a Demon

14 When they came to the crowd, a man came to him, knelt before him, 15and said, "Lord, have mercy on my son, for he is an epileptic and he suffers terribly; he often falls into the fire and often into the water. 16And I brought him to your disciples, but they could not cure him." 17Jesus answered, "You faithless and perverse generation, how much longer must I be with you? How much longer must I put up with you? Bring him here to me." 18And Jesus rebuked the demon,a and itb came out of him, and the boy was cured instantly. 19Then the disciples came to Jesus privately and said, "Why could we not cast it out?" 20He said to them, "Because of your little faith. For truly I tell you, if you have faith the size of ac mustard seed, you will say to this mountain, 'Move from here to there,' and it will move; and nothing will be impossible for you."d

Jesus Again Foretells His Death and Resurrection

22 As they were gatheringe in Galilee, Jesus said to them, "The Son of Man is going to be betrayed into human hands, 23and they will kill him, and on the third day he will be raised." And they were greatly distressed.

Jesus and the Temple Tax

24 When they reached Capernaum, the collectors of the temple taxf came to Peter and said, "Does your teacher not pay the temple tax?"f 25He said, "Yes, he does." And when he came home, Jesus spoke of it first, asking, "What do you think, Simon? From whom do kings of the earth take toll or tribute? From their children or from others?" 26When Peterg said, "From others," Jesus said to him, "Then the children are free. 27However, so that we do not give offense to them, go to the sea and cast a hook; take the first fish that comes up; and when you open its mouth, you will find a coin;h take that and give it to them for you and me."

True Greatness

18 At that time the disciples came to Jesus and asked, "Who is the greatest in the kingdom of heaven?" 2He called a child, whom he put among them, 3and said, "Truly I tell you, unless you change and become like children, you will never enter the kingdom of heaven. 4Whoever becomes humble like this child is the greatest in the kingdom of heaven. 5Whoever welcomes one such child in my name welcomes me.

Temptations to Sin

6 "If any of you put a stumbling block before one of these little ones who believe in me, it would be better for you if a great millstone were fastened around your neck and you were drowned in the depth of the sea. 7Woe to the world because of stumbling blocks! Occasions for stumbling are bound to come, but woe to the one by whom the stumbling block comes! 8 "If your hand or your foot causes you to stumble, cut it off and throw it away; it is better for you to enter life maimed or lame than to have two hands or two feet and to be thrown into the eternal fire. 9And if your eye causes you to stumble, tear it out and throw it away; it is better

---

y Or tents   z Or my beloved Son   a Gk it or him
b Gk the demon   c Gk faith as a grain of
d Other ancient authorities add verse 21, But this kind does not come out except by prayer and fasting
e Other ancient authorities read living   f Gk didrachma   g Gk he   h Gk stater; the stater was worth two didrachmas

for you to enter life with one eye than to have two eyes and to be thrown into the hell[i] of fire.

The Parable of the Lost Sheep

10 "Take care that you do not despise one of these little ones; for, I tell you, in heaven their angels continually see the face of my Father in heaven.[j] 12What do you think? If a shepherd has a hundred sheep, and one of them has gone astray, does he not leave the ninety-nine on the mountains and go in search of the one that went astray? 13And if he finds it, truly I tell you, he rejoices over it more than over the ninety-nine that never went astray. 14So it is not the will of your[k] Father in heaven that one of these little ones should be lost.

Reproving Another Who Sins

15 "If another member of the church[l] sins against you,[m] go and point out the fault when the two of you are alone. If the member listens to you, you have regained that one.[n] 16But if you are not listened to, take one or two others along with you, so that every word may be confirmed by the evidence of two or three witnesses. 17If the member refuses to listen to them, tell it to the church; and if the offender refuses to listen even to the church, let such a one be to you as a Gentile and a tax collector. 18Truly I tell you, whatever you bind on earth will be bound in heaven, and whatever you loose on earth will be loosed in heaven. 19Again, truly I tell you, if two of you agree on earth about anything you ask, it will be done for you by my Father in heaven. 20For where two or three are gathered in my name, I am there among them."

Forgiveness

21 Then Peter came and said to him, "Lord, if another member of the church[o] sins against me, how often should I forgive? As many as seven times?" 22Jesus said to him, "Not seven times, but, I tell you, seventy-seven[p] times.

The Parable of the Unforgiving Servant

23 "For this reason the kingdom of heaven may be compared to a king who wished to settle accounts with his slaves. 24When he began the reckoning, one who owed him ten thousand talents[q] was brought to him; 25and, as he could not pay, his lord ordered him to be sold, together with his wife and children and all his possessions, and payment to be made. 26So the slave fell on his knees before him, saying, 'Have patience with me, and I will pay you everything.' 27And out of pity for him, the lord of that slave released him and forgave him the debt. 28But that same slave, as he went out, came upon one of his fellow slaves who owed him a hundred denarii;[r] and seizing him by the throat, he said, 'Pay what you owe.' 29Then his fellow slave fell down and pleaded with him, 'Have patience with me, and I will pay you.' 30But he refused; then he went and threw him into prison until he would pay the debt. 31When his fellow slaves saw what had happened, they were greatly distressed, and they went and reported to their lord all that had taken place. 32Then his lord summoned him and said to him, 'You wicked slave! I forgave you all that debt because you pleaded with me. 33Should you not have had mercy on your fellow slave, as I had mercy on you?' 34And in anger his lord handed him over to be tortured until he would pay his entire debt. 35So my heavenly Father will also do to every one of you, if you do not forgive your brother or sister[s] from your heart."

Teaching about Divorce

19 When Jesus had finished saying these things, he left Galilee and went to the region of Judea beyond the Jordan. 2Large crowds followed him, and he cured them there.

3 Some Pharisees came to him, and to test him they asked, "Is it lawful for a man to divorce his wife for any cause?" 4He answered, "Have you not read that the one who made them at the beginning 'made them male and female,' 5and said, 'For this reason a man shall leave his father and mother and be joined to his wife, and the two shall become one flesh'? 6So they are no longer two, but one flesh. Therefore what God has joined together, let no

---

i Gk Gehenna   j Other ancient authorities add verse 11, *For the Son of Man came to save the lost* k Other ancient authorities read *my*   l Gk *If your brother*   m Other ancient authorities lack *against you*   n Gk *the brother*   o Gk *if my brother* p Or *seventy times seven*   q A talent was worth more than fifteen years' wages of a laborer r The denarius was the usual day's wage for a laborer   s Gk *brother*

one separate." ⁷They said to him, "Why then did Moses command us to give a certificate of dismissal and to divorce her?" ⁸He said to them, "It was because you were so hard-hearted that Moses allowed you to divorce your wives, but from the beginning it was not so. ⁹And I say to you, whoever divorces his wife, except for unchastity, and marries another commits adultery."ᵗ

10 His disciples said to him, "If such is

ᵗ Other ancient authorities read *except on the ground of unchastity, causes her to commit adultery;* others add at the end of the verse *and he who marries a divorced woman commits adultery*

Mercy Doesn't Make Sense

Scripture Reading for Today:
Matthew 18.21–35

Verse for Today:
Matthew 18.33

Before I was married I shared an apartment with several other Christian women. One day one of the young women asked to borrow my car to visit her sister. Although I had loaned her my car before, I was very hesitant on this occasion. It was raining hard, and I was afraid both for her safety and for my car. I told her that it would be unwise to drive alone in such a storm and that I'd prefer she wait. But she felt it was important to go immediately, and so she did.

I was eating dinner when she returned some hours later. I can still see her standing in the doorway looking very ashamed.

"Patti, I got in a wreck on the bridge, and your car had to be towed away."

In a flash I knew what mercy was. In my mind's eye I could see myself getting up from the table and embracing her with the words, "Thank God you weren't hurt. It's all right. Don't worry about it." In fact, I believe the Lord was offering me the grace to respond in just that way.

But reason quickly intervened. I thought, "Why should I console her? After all, she wrecked my car. I told her to postpone the trip. It's not reasonable to let her go without some kind of reproach."

I looked at her sullenly and finally mumbled something like, "I told you it wasn't the best time to go."

Meekly she left the room. There I sat alone, knowing I had missed an opportunity to be merciful as my heavenly Father is merciful. At a later time she and I could have discussed the importance of acting responsibly with another person's property. In that moment, however, the merciful thing would have been to console her.

His ways are not our ways. His thoughts are not our thoughts. Mercy will never "make sense" or "seem reasonable." We can rejoice that our Lord never gives us what we truly deserve. "Blessed are the merciful, for they will receive mercy" (Matthew 5.7).

—*PATTI GALLAGHER MANSFIELD*

Go to page 1296 for your next devotional reading.

the case of a man with his wife, it is better not to marry." ¹¹But he said to them, "Not everyone can accept this teaching, but only those to whom it is given. ¹²For there are eunuchs who have been so from birth, and there are eunuchs who have been made eunuchs by others, and there are eunuchs who have made themselves eunuchs for the sake of the kingdom of heaven. Let anyone accept this who can."

Jesus Blesses Little Children

13 Then little children were being brought to him in order that he might lay his hands on them and pray. The disciples spoke sternly to those who brought them; ¹⁴but Jesus said, "Let the little children come to me, and do not stop them; for it is to such as these that the kingdom of heaven belongs." ¹⁵And he laid his hands on them and went on his way.

The Rich Young Man

16 Then someone came to him and said, "Teacher, what good deed must I do to have eternal life?" ¹⁷And he said to him, "Why do you ask me about what is good? There is only one who is good. If you wish to enter into life, keep the commandments." ¹⁸He said to him, "Which ones?" And Jesus said, "You shall not murder; You shall not commit adultery; You shall not steal; You shall not bear false witness; ¹⁹Honor your father and mother; also, You shall love your neighbor as yourself." ²⁰The young man said to him, "I have

*I*mperfect People

THURSDAY

Scripture Reading for Today:
Matthew 19.13–15

Verse for Today:
Matthew 19.13

Jesus had been talking with the crowds about the kingdom. While he was talking, people began to bring children to him to be touched. The disciples apparently saw the children and their need to be touched as bothersome, and they attempted to turn them away. Their rejection of the children is symbolic; [the disciples] are turning away helpless, powerless, needy people, those who have just begun their process of personal growth, those whose strongest needs at this time are for acceptance.

And Jesus became angry [see Mark 10.14], angry because the disciples still didn't understand that the kingdom doesn't reject imperfect, unfinished, even bothersome, people. It embraces them. And so he put his arms around the children. He affirmed their child-level of growth. He hugged their needs. He held all the yearning of their hearts to his. And he said that it is precisely to them that the kingdom belongs.

And what of all of the rest of God's children—insecure adults trying to feel at home, aging women and men still searching for acceptance; people too old to bounce on your lap, needing so badly to be held? What about all of the needy people, those with poor self-esteem and failed dreams? Those who limp through life doing their best to care for others when their own lives reflect such deprivation? What about those who try to slip into the crowd, claim a place of importance, and feel blessed, even for a moment?

It is to such as these that the kingdom belongs.

—FRAN FERDER

Go to page 1301 for your next devotional reading.

kept all these;*u* what do I still lack?"
21Jesus said to him, "If you wish to be perfect, go, sell your possessions, and give the money*v* to the poor, and you will have treasure in heaven; then come, follow me." 22When the young man heard this word, he went away grieving, for he had many possessions.

23 Then Jesus said to his disciples, "Truly I tell you, it will be hard for a rich person to enter the kingdom of heaven. 24Again I tell you, it is easier for a camel to go through the eye of a needle than for someone who is rich to enter the kingdom of God." 25When the disciples heard this, they were greatly astounded and said, "Then who can be saved?" 26But Jesus looked at them and said, "For mortals it is impossible, but for God all things are possible."

27 Then Peter said in reply, "Look, we have left everything and followed you. What then will we have?" 28Jesus said to them, "Truly I tell you, at the renewal of all things, when the Son of Man is seated on the throne of his glory, you who have followed me will also sit on twelve thrones, judging the twelve tribes of Israel. 29And everyone who has left houses or brothers or sisters or father or mother or children or fields, for my name's sake, will receive a hundredfold,*w* and will inherit eternal life. 30But many who are first will be last, and the last will be first.

The Laborers in the Vineyard

20 "For the kingdom of heaven is like a landowner who went out early in the morning to hire laborers for his vineyard. 2After agreeing with the laborers for the usual daily wage,*x* he sent them into his vineyard. 3When he went out about nine o'clock, he saw others standing idle in the marketplace; 4and he said to them, 'You also go into the vineyard, and I will pay you whatever is right.' So they went. 5When he went out again about noon and about three o'clock, he did the same. 6And about five o'clock he went out and found others standing around; and he said to them, 'Why are you standing here idle all day?' 7They said to him, 'Because no one has hired us.' He said to them, 'You also go into the vineyard.' 8When evening came, the owner of the vineyard said to his manager, 'Call the laborers and give them their pay, beginning with the last and then going to the

first.' 9When those hired about five o'clock came, each of them received the usual daily wage.*x* 10Now when the first came, they thought they would receive more; but each of them also received the usual daily wage.*x* 11And when they received it, they grumbled against the landowner, 12saying, 'These last worked only one hour, and you have made them equal to us who have borne the burden of the day and the scorching heat.' 13But he replied to one of them, 'Friend, I am doing you no wrong; did you not agree with me for the usual daily wage?*x* 14Take what belongs to you and go; I choose to give to this last the same as I give to you. 15Am I not allowed to do what I choose with what belongs to me? Or are you envious because I am generous?'*y* 16So the last will be first, and the first will be last."*z*

A Third Time Jesus Foretells His Death and Resurrection

17 While Jesus was going up to Jerusalem, he took the twelve disciples aside by themselves, and said to them on the way, 18"See, we are going up to Jerusalem, and the Son of Man will be handed over to the chief priests and scribes, and they will condemn him to death; 19then they will hand him over to the Gentiles to be mocked and flogged and crucified; and on the third day he will be raised."

The Request of the Mother of James and John

20 Then the mother of the sons of Zebedee came to him with her sons, and kneeling before him, she asked a favor of him. 21And he said to her, "What do you want?" She said to him, "Declare that these two sons of mine will sit, one at your right hand and one at your left, in your kingdom." 22But Jesus answered, "You do not know what you are asking. Are you able to drink the cup that I am about to drink?"*a* They said to him, "We are able." 23He said to them, "You will indeed drink my cup, but to sit at my right hand and at my left, this is not mine to grant, but it is for those

---

u Other ancient authorities add *from my youth*
v Gk lacks *the money*   *w* Other ancient
authorities read *manifold*   *x* Gk *a denarius*
y Gk *is your eye evil because I am good?*   *z* Other
ancient authorities add *for many are called but few
are chosen*   *a* Other ancient authorities add *or to
be baptized with the baptism that I am baptized with?*

for whom it has been prepared by my Father."

24 When the ten heard it, they were angry with the two brothers. 25But Jesus called them to him and said, "You know that the rulers of the Gentiles lord it over them, and their great ones are tyrants over them. 26It will not be so among you; but whoever wishes to be great among you must be your servant, 27and whoever wishes to be first among you must be your slave; 28just as the Son of Man came not to be served but to serve, and to give his life a ransom for many."

Jesus Heals Two Blind Men

29 As they were leaving Jericho, a large crowd followed him. 30There were two blind men sitting by the roadside. When they heard that Jesus was passing by, they shouted, "Lord,*b* have mercy on us, Son of David!" 31The crowd sternly ordered them to be quiet; but they shouted even more loudly, "Have mercy on us, Lord, Son of David!" 32Jesus stood still and called them, saying, "What do you want me to do for you?" 33They said to him, "Lord, let our eyes be opened." 34Moved with compassion, Jesus touched their eyes. Immediately they regained their sight and followed him.

Jesus' Triumphal Entry into Jerusalem

21 When they had come near Jerusalem and had reached Bethphage, at the Mount of Olives, Jesus sent two disciples, 2saying to them, "Go into the village ahead of you, and immediately you will find a donkey tied, and a colt with her; untie them and bring them to me. 3If anyone says anything to you, just say this, 'The Lord needs them.' And he will send them immediately.*c* 4This took place to fulfill what had been spoken through the prophet, saying,

5 "Tell the daughter of Zion,
   Look, your king is coming to you,
      humble, and mounted on
         a donkey,
      and on a colt, the foal of
         a donkey."

6The disciples went and did as Jesus had directed them; 7they brought the donkey and the colt, and put their cloaks on them, and he sat on them. 8A very large crowd*d* spread their cloaks on the road, and others cut branches from the trees and spread them on the road. 9The crowds

that went ahead of him and that followed were shouting,

   "Hosanna to the Son of David!
   Blessed is the one who comes in
      the name of the Lord!
   Hosanna in the highest heaven!"

10When he entered Jerusalem, the whole city was in turmoil, asking, "Who is this?" 11The crowds were saying, "This is the prophet Jesus from Nazareth in Galilee."

Jesus Cleanses the Temple

12 Then Jesus entered the temple*e* and drove out all who were selling and buying in the temple, and he overturned the tables of the money changers and the seats of those who sold doves. 13He said to them, "It is written,

   'My house shall be called a house
      of prayer';
   but you are making it a den
      of robbers."

14 The blind and the lame came to him in the temple, and he cured them. 15But when the chief priests and the scribes saw the amazing things that he did, and heard*f* the children crying out in the temple, "Hosanna to the Son of David," they became angry 16and said to him, "Do you hear what these are saying?" Jesus said to them, "Yes; have you never read,

   'Out of the mouths of infants and
      nursing babies
   you have prepared praise for
      yourself'?"

17He left them, went out of the city to Bethany, and spent the night there.

Jesus Curses the Fig Tree

18 In the morning, when he returned to the city, he was hungry. 19And seeing a fig tree by the side of the road, he went to it and found nothing at all on it but leaves. Then he said to it, "May no fruit ever come from you again!" And the fig tree withered at once. 20When the disciples saw it, they were amazed, saying, "How did the fig tree wither at once?" 21Jesus answered them, "Truly I tell you, if you have faith and do not doubt, not only will you do what has been done to the fig tree, but even if you say to this mountain,

---

b Other ancient authorities lack *Lord*   *c* Or *'The Lord needs them and will send them back immediately.'*   *d* Or *Most of the crowd*   *e* Other ancient authorities add *of God*   *f* Gk lacks *heard*

'Be lifted up and thrown into the sea,' it will be done. 22Whatever you ask for in prayer with faith, you will receive."

The Authority of Jesus Questioned

23 When he entered the temple, the chief priests and the elders of the people came to him as he was teaching, and said, "By what authority are you doing these things, and who gave you this authority?" 24Jesus said to them, "I will also ask you one question; if you tell me the answer, then I will also tell you by what authority I do these things. 25Did the baptism of John come from heaven, or was it of human origin?" And they argued with one another, "If we say, 'From heaven,' he will say to us, 'Why then did you not believe him?' 26But if we say, 'Of human origin,' we are afraid of the crowd; for all regard John as a prophet." 27So they answered Jesus, "We do not know." And he said to them, "Neither will I tell you by what authority I am doing these things.

The Parable of the Two Sons

28 "What do you think? A man had two sons; he went to the first and said, 'Son, go and work in the vineyard today.' 29He answered, 'I will not'; but later he changed his mind and went. 30The father8 went to the second and said the same; and he answered, 'I go, sir'; but he did not go. 31Which of the two did the will of his father?" They said, "The first." Jesus said to them, "Truly I tell you, the tax collectors and the prostitutes are going into the kingdom of God ahead of you. 32For John came to you in the way of righteousness and you did not believe him, but the tax collectors and the prostitutes believed him; and even after you saw it, you did not change your minds and believe him.

The Parable of the Wicked Tenants

33 "Listen to another parable. There was a landowner who planted a vineyard, put a fence around it, dug a wine press in it, and built a watchtower. Then he leased it to tenants and went to another country. 34When the harvest time had come, he sent his slaves to the tenants to collect his produce. 35But the tenants seized his slaves and beat one, killed another, and stoned another. 36Again he sent other slaves, more than the first; and they treated them in the same way. 37Finally he sent his son to them, saying, 'They will respect my son.' 38But when the tenants saw the son, they said to themselves, 'This is the heir; come, let us kill him and get his inheritance.' 39So they seized him, threw him out of the vineyard, and killed him. 40Now when the owner of the vineyard comes, what will he do to those tenants?" 41They said to him, "He will put those wretches to a miserable death, and lease the vineyard to other tenants who will give him the produce at the harvest time."

42 Jesus said to them, "Have you never read in the scriptures:

'The stone that the builders rejected
   has become the cornerstone;h
this was the Lord's doing,
   and it is amazing in our eyes'?
43Therefore I tell you, the kingdom of God will be taken away from you and given to a people that produces the fruits of the kingdom.i 44The one who falls on this stone will be broken to pieces; and it will crush anyone on whom it falls."j

45 When the chief priests and the Pharisees heard his parables, they realized that he was speaking about them. 46They wanted to arrest him, but they feared the crowds, because they regarded him as a prophet.

The Parable of the Wedding Banquet

22 Once more Jesus spoke to them in parables, saying: 2"The kingdom of heaven may be compared to a king who gave a wedding banquet for his son. 3He sent his slaves to call those who had been invited to the wedding banquet, but they would not come. 4Again he sent other slaves, saying, 'Tell those who have been invited: Look, I have prepared my dinner, my oxen and my fat calves have been slaughtered, and everything is ready; come to the wedding banquet.' 5But they made light of it and went away, one to his farm, another to his business, 6while the rest seized his slaves, mistreated them, and killed them. 7The king was enraged. He sent his troops, destroyed those murderers, and burned their city. 8Then he said to his slaves, 'The wedding is ready, but those invited were not worthy. 9Go therefore into the main streets, and invite everyone you find to the wedding banquet.' 10Those slaves went out into the

---

g Gk He   h Or keystone   i Gk the fruits of it
j Other ancient authorities lack verse 44

streets and gathered all whom they found, both good and bad; so the wedding hall was filled with guests.

11 "But when the king came in to see the guests, he noticed a man there who was not wearing a wedding robe, 12and he said to him, 'Friend, how did you get in here without a wedding robe?' And he was speechless. 13Then the king said to the attendants, 'Bind him hand and foot, and throw him into the outer darkness, where there will be weeping and gnashing of teeth.' 14For many are called, but few are chosen."

The Question about Paying Taxes

15 Then the Pharisees went and plotted to entrap him in what he said. 16So they sent their disciples to him, along with the Herodians, saying, "Teacher, we know that you are sincere, and teach the way of God in accordance with truth, and show deference to no one; for you do not regard people with partiality. 17Tell us, then, what you think. Is it lawful to pay taxes to the emperor, or not?" 18But Jesus, aware of their malice, said, "Why are you putting me to the test, you hypocrites? 19Show me the coin used for the tax." And they brought him a denarius. 20Then he said to them, "Whose head is this, and whose title?" 21They answered, "The emperor's." Then he said to them, "Give therefore to the emperor the things that are the emperor's, and to God the things that are God's." 22When they heard this, they were amazed; and they left him and went away.

The Question about the Resurrection

23 The same day some Sadducees came to him, saying there is no resurrection;[k] and they asked him a question, saying, 24"Teacher, Moses said, 'If a man dies childless, his brother shall marry the widow, and raise up children for his brother.' 25Now there were seven brothers among us; the first married, and died childless, leaving the widow to his brother. 26The second did the same, so also the third, down to the seventh. 27Last of all, the woman herself died. 28In the resurrection, then, whose wife of the seven will she be? For all of them had married her."

29 Jesus answered them, "You are wrong, because you know neither the scriptures nor the power of God. 30For in the resurrection they neither marry nor are given in marriage, but are like angels[l] in heaven. 31And as for the resurrection of the dead, have you not read what was said to you by God, 32'I am the God of Abraham, the God of Isaac, and the God of Jacob'? He is God not of the dead, but of the living." 33And when the crowd heard it, they were astounded at his teaching.

The Greatest Commandment

34 When the Pharisees heard that he had silenced the Sadducees, they gathered together, 35and one of them, a lawyer, asked him a question to test him. 36"Teacher, which commandment in the law is the greatest?" 37He said to him, " 'You shall love the Lord your God with all your heart, and with all your soul, and with all your mind.' 38This is the greatest and first commandment. 39And a second is like it: 'You shall love your neighbor as yourself.' 40On these two commandments hang all the law and the prophets."

The Question about David's Son

41 Now while the Pharisees were gathered together, Jesus asked them this question: 42"What do you think of the Messiah?[m] Whose son is he?" They said to him, "The son of David." 43He said to them, "How is it then that David by the Spirit[n] calls him Lord, saying,

44 'The Lord said to my Lord,
   "Sit at my right hand,
      until I put your enemies under
         your feet" '?

45If David thus calls him Lord, how can he be his son?" 46No one was able to give him an answer, nor from that day did anyone dare to ask him any more questions.

Jesus Denounces Scribes and Pharisees

23 Then Jesus said to the crowds and to his disciples, 2"The scribes and the Pharisees sit on Moses' seat; 3therefore, do whatever they teach you and follow it; but do not do as they do, for they do not practice what they teach. 4They tie up heavy burdens, hard to bear,[o] and lay them on the shoulders of others; but they themselves are unwilling to lift a finger to move them. 5They do all their deeds to be

---

k Other ancient authorities read who say that there is no resurrection   l Other ancient authorities add of God   m Or Christ   n Gk in spirit   o Other ancient authorities lack hard to bear

seen by others; for they make their phylac-
teries broad and their fringes long. 6They
love to have the place of honor at banquets and the best seats in the synagogues,
7and to be greeted with respect in the marketplaces, and to have people call them
rabbi. 8But you are not to be called rabbi,
for you have one teacher, and you are all
students.[p] 9And call no one your father
on earth, for you have one Father—the
one in heaven. 10Nor are you to be called
instructors, for you have one instructor,
the Messiah.[q] 11The greatest among you
will be your servant. 12All who exalt themselves will be humbled, and all who humble themselves will be exalted.

13 "But woe to you, scribes and Pharisees, hypocrites! For you lock people out
of the kingdom of heaven. For you do not
go in yourselves, and when others are going in, you stop them.[r] 15Woe to you,
scribes and Pharisees, hypocrites! For you
cross sea and land to make a single convert, and you make the new convert twice
as much a child of hell[s] as yourselves.

16 "Woe to you, blind guides, who
say, 'Whoever swears by the sanctuary is
bound by nothing, but whoever swears by
the gold of the sanctuary is bound by the
oath.' 17You blind fools! For which is
greater, the gold or the sanctuary that has
made the gold sacred? 18And you say,
'Whoever swears by the altar is bound by
nothing, but whoever swears by the gift
that is on the altar is bound by the oath.'
19How blind you are! For which is greater,
the gift or the altar that makes the gift
sacred? 20So whoever swears by the altar,
swears by it and by everything on it; 21and

[p] Gk *brothers* [q] Or *the Christ* [r] Other authorities add here (or after verse 12) verse 14, *Woe to you, scribes and Pharisees, hypocrites! For you devour widows' houses and for the sake of appearance you make long prayers; therefore you will receive the greater condemnation* [s] Gk *Gehenna*

FRIDAY

Scripture Reading for Today:
Matthew 23.1–13

Verse for Today:
Matthew 23.13

Rules and Regulations

Imagine that you are a Pharisee or teacher of the Law in Jesus' day. Get in touch with that feeling of being right. Feel the power in being part of the leadership of your religious community. Savor the feeling of being both right and important.

See yourself approach Jesus in confrontation.

Stand with Jesus while he talks to you about the hypocrisy of keeping rituals but neglecting the most basic acts of human kindness and responsibility. Hear him tell you that the person is more valuable than the Law.

For an instant, you let yourself remember how irksome the Laws have become. Allow yourself to recall the people you have neglected while keeping your religious rituals. You recognize that the great faith of your fathers has deteriorated into obsession with minutiae. This man is speaking truth to you!

You know that you are standing at a difficult crossroad. You can continue what you have always done, straining under the load of keeping hundreds of rules and regulations; or you can give that up and follow this man, Jesus.

Allow the Spirit of Christ to bring to your mind the ways you have hidden in religiosity and neglected love.

—JEANIE MILEY

Go to page 1304 for your next devotional reading.

whoever swears by the sanctuary, swears by it and by the one who dwells in it; 22and whoever swears by heaven, swears by the throne of God and by the one who is seated upon it.

23 "Woe to you, scribes and Pharisees, hypocrites! For you tithe mint, dill, and cummin, and have neglected the weightier matters of the law: justice and mercy and faith. It is these you ought to have practiced without neglecting the others. 24You blind guides! You strain out a gnat but swallow a camel!

25 "Woe to you, scribes and Pharisees, hypocrites! For you clean the outside of the cup and of the plate, but inside they are full of greed and self-indulgence. 26You blind Pharisee! First clean the inside of the cup,*t* so that the outside also may become clean.

27 "Woe to you, scribes and Pharisees, hypocrites! For you are like whitewashed tombs, which on the outside look beautiful, but inside they are full of the bones of the dead and of all kinds of filth. 28So you also on the outside look righteous to others, but inside you are full of hypocrisy and lawlessness.

29 "Woe to you, scribes and Pharisees, hypocrites! For you build the tombs of the prophets and decorate the graves of the righteous, 30and you say, 'If we had lived in the days of our ancestors, we would not have taken part with them in shedding the blood of the prophets.' 31Thus you testify against yourselves that you are descendants of those who murdered the prophets. 32Fill up, then, the measure of your ancestors. 33You snakes, you brood of vipers! How can you escape being sentenced to hell?*u* 34Therefore I send you prophets, sages, and scribes, some of whom you will kill and crucify, and some you will flog in your synagogues and pursue from town to town, 35so that upon you may come all the righteous blood shed on earth, from the blood of righteous Abel to the blood of Zechariah son of Barachiah, whom you murdered between the sanctuary and the altar. 36Truly I tell you, all this will come upon this generation.

The Lament over Jerusalem

37 "Jerusalem, Jerusalem, the city that kills the prophets and stones those who are sent to it! How often have I desired to gather your children together as a hen gathers her brood under her wings, and you were not willing! 38See, your house is left to you, desolate.*v* 39For I tell you, you will not see me again until you say, 'Blessed is the one who comes in the name of the Lord.' "

The Destruction of the Temple Foretold

24 As Jesus came out of the temple and was going away, his disciples came to point out to him the buildings of the temple. 2Then he asked them, "You see all these, do you not? Truly I tell you, not one stone will be left here upon another; all will be thrown down."

Signs of the End of the Age

3 When he was sitting on the Mount of Olives, the disciples came to him privately, saying, "Tell us, when will this be, and what will be the sign of your coming and of the end of the age?" 4Jesus answered them, "Beware that no one leads you astray. 5For many will come in my name, saying, 'I am the Messiah!'*w* and they will lead many astray. 6And you will hear of wars and rumors of wars; see that you are not alarmed; for this must take place, but the end is not yet. 7For nation will rise against nation, and kingdom against kingdom, and there will be famines*x* and earthquakes in various places: 8all this is but the beginning of the birth pangs.

Persecutions Foretold

9 "Then they will hand you over to be tortured and will put you to death, and you will be hated by all nations because of my name. 10Then many will fall away,*y* and they will betray one another and hate one another. 11And many false prophets will arise and lead many astray. 12And because of the increase of lawlessness, the love of many will grow cold. 13But the one who endures to the end will be saved. 14And this good news*z* of the kingdom will be proclaimed throughout the world, as a testimony to all the nations; and then the end will come.

The Desolating Sacrilege

15 "So when you see the desolating

---

t Other ancient authorities add *and of the plate*
u Gk *Gehenna*   *v* Other ancient authorities lack *desolate*   *w* Or *the Christ*   *x* Other ancient authorities add *and pestilences*   *y* Or *stumble*
z Or *gospel*

sacrilege standing in the holy place, as was spoken of by the prophet Daniel (let the reader understand), [16]then those in Judea must flee to the mountains; [17]the one on the housetop must not go down to take what is in the house; [18]the one in the field must not turn back to get a coat. [19]Woe to those who are pregnant and to those who are nursing infants in those days! [20]Pray that your flight may not be in winter or on a sabbath. [21]For at that time there will be great suffering, such as has not been from the beginning of the world until now, no, and never will be. [22]And if those days had not been cut short, no one would be saved; but for the sake of the elect those days will be cut short. [23]Then if anyone says to you, 'Look! Here is the Messiah!'[a] or 'There he is!'—do not believe it. [24]For false messiahs[b] and false prophets will appear and produce great signs and omens, to lead astray, if possible, even the elect. [25]Take note, I have told you beforehand. [26]So, if they say to you, 'Look! He is in the wilderness,' do not go out. If they say, 'Look! He is in the inner rooms,' do not believe it. [27]For as the lightning comes from the east and flashes as far as the west, so will be the coming of the Son of Man. [28]Wherever the corpse is, there the vultures will gather.

The Coming of the Son of Man

29 "Immediately after the suffering of those days

the sun will be darkened,
　　and the moon will not give
　　　　its light;
the stars will fall from heaven,
　　and the powers of heaven will
　　　　be shaken.

[30]Then the sign of the Son of Man will appear in heaven, and then all the tribes of the earth will mourn, and they will see 'the Son of Man coming on the clouds of heaven' with power and great glory. [31]And he will send out his angels with a loud trumpet call, and they will gather his elect from the four winds, from one end of heaven to the other.

The Lesson of the Fig Tree

32 "From the fig tree learn its lesson: as soon as its branch becomes tender and puts forth its leaves, you know that summer is near. [33]So also, when you see all these things, you know that he[c] is near, at the very gates. [34]Truly I tell you, this generation will not pass away until all these things have taken place. [35]Heaven and earth will pass away, but my words will not pass away.

The Necessity for Watchfulness

36 "But about that day and hour no one knows, neither the angels of heaven, nor the Son,[d] but only the Father. [37]For as the days of Noah were, so will be the coming of the Son of Man. [38]For as in those days before the flood they were eating and drinking, marrying and giving in marriage, until the day Noah entered the ark, [39]and they knew nothing until the flood came and swept them all away, so too will be the coming of the Son of Man. [40]Then two will be in the field; one will be taken and one will be left. [41]Two women will be grinding meal together; one will be taken and one will be left. [42]Keep awake therefore, for you do not know on what day[e] your Lord is coming. [43]But understand this: if the owner of the house had known in what part of the night the thief was coming, he would have stayed awake and would not have let his house be broken into. [44]Therefore you also must be ready, for the Son of Man is coming at an unexpected hour.

The Faithful or the Unfaithful Slave

45 "Who then is the faithful and wise slave, whom his master has put in charge of his household, to give the other slaves[f] their allowance of food at the proper time? [46]Blessed is that slave whom his master will find at work when he arrives. [47]Truly I tell you, he will put that one in charge of all his possessions. [48]But if that wicked slave says to himself, 'My master is delayed,' [49]and he begins to beat his fellow slaves, and eats and drinks with drunkards, [50]the master of that slave will come on a day when he does not expect him and at an hour that he does not know. [51]He will cut him in pieces[g] and put him with the hypocrites, where there will be weeping and gnashing of teeth.

The Parable of the Ten Bridesmaids

25 "Then the kingdom of heaven will be like this. Ten brides-

---

[a] Or the Christ　[b] Or christs　[c] Or it　[d] Other ancient authorities lack nor the Son　[e] Other ancient authorities read at what hour　[f] Gk to give them　[g] Or cut him off

Esther

*Her Name May Derive From
"Ishtar," the Babylonian Goddess
of Love or From the Persian Word
for "Star"*

Read Esther 4; 7

Vashti, queen of Persia, had so offended her husband, King Ahasuerus, that a search was conducted for her replacement. Now it happened that many Jews were living in Persia at the time. Exiled from Judah a hundred years earlier, they had been deported to Babylon, which in turn was conquered by Persia. Mordecai and his orphaned cousin Esther were among those living in exile, 650 miles northeast of Jerusalem.

Like many other young virgins, the beautiful Esther was gathered into the king's harem. To refuse the privilege may well have meant her death. As the story goes, Esther so pleased Ahasuerus that she became queen in Vashti's place.

Sometime later, a man named Haman rose to power, who was so highly placed that other officials knelt before him as a sign of respect. One man, however, Esther's cousin Mordecai, refused to kneel. Haman became so angry that he decided to hang him and then eliminate every Jew in the kingdom.

To ascertain the most favorable moment for destroying them, Haman piously consulted his gods by casting a lot (or *pur*). A date 11 months into the future was revealed. Haman immediately persuaded Ahasuerus, who was unaware that his own wife was a Jew, to issue a decree ordering the destruction of the Jews and the confiscation of all their property on that day.

Her Character: *An orphan in a foreign land, she displayed great courage in the midst of a crisis. Prior to risking her life for her people, she humbled herself by fasting, and then put her considerable beauty, social grace, and wisdom in the service of God's plan.*
Her Sorrow: *To learn that her husband, the king, had unwittingly placed her life and the lives of her people in jeopardy.*
Her Joy: *To watch mourning turn to celebration once the Jews enjoyed relief from their enemies.*

Mordecai contacted Esther, asking her to intervene with Ahasuerus. But to come into the king's presence without an invitation meant possible execution, even for the queen. So Esther instructed Mordecai to mobilize all the Jews of the city to fast and pray. She did the same, resolving, "I will go to the king, though it is against the law; and if I perish, I perish" (4.16). On the third day of her fast, Esther approached the king. As soon as Ahasuerus saw her, he held out the golden scepter as a sign of his favor.

Esther then invited the king and Haman to join her for a feast. At the queen's banquet, the king implored Esther to ask for whatever her heart desired. "If I have won your favor, O king," she replied, "and if it pleases the king, let my life be given me—that is my petition—and the lives of my people—that is my request. For we have been sold, I and my people, to be destroyed, to be killed, and to be annihilated."

"Who is he, and where is he, who has presumed to do this?" the king demanded.

"A foe and enemy, this wicked Haman!" (7.3–6).

And so Haman's star, which had risen to so great a height, fell suddenly to earth. He was hanged on the same gallows he had built for Mordecai, and all his property was awarded to Esther. Furthermore, the king issued an edict giving Jews throughout the empire the right to protect themselves, to destroy and plunder every enemy who might raise a hand against them.

The very day Haman's false gods had revealed as a day of reckoning for the Jews became a day of reckoning for their enemies.

Praying With Esther

"Do not think that in the king's palace you will escape any more than all the other Jews. For if you keep silence at such a time as this, relief and deliverance will rise for the Jews from another quarter, but you and your father's family will perish. Who knows? Perhaps you have come to royal dignity for just such a time as this." —*Esther 4.13–14*

Praise God: That he turns the wisdom and the power of the world on its head.

Offer Thanks: That God has purpose for your life.

Confess: Any tendency to view your life in isolation from God's people, to shrink back from some step of faith God may be calling you to take.

Ask God: For the grace to act courageously and wisely.

Lift Your Heart

Many Jewish girls celebrate the Feast of Purim by dressing up as Queen Esther. One way we can emulate Esther today is by fasting. Fasting was a visible sign of her dependency and weakness, an eloquent form of begging God's help. This week, do a little eloquent begging yourself by choosing a day to fast from breakfast and lunch—dinner if you're brave. Drink only water or fruit juice. Perhaps you have a particular need or problem you would like to surrender to God. Use the time you would have spent eating to be alone with him. Tell God that you need him more than you need food. Don't try to manipulate him by your self-sacrifice, but simply allow your weakness to emerge in his presence.

Lord, I need you so much more than food or water. Without your presence, your protection, your wisdom, your gift of faith, I would be lost. Use me in the church and the world around me to accomplish your purposes.

Go to page 1307 for your next devotional reading.

maids[h] took their lamps and went to meet the bridegroom.[i] 2Five of them were foolish, and five were wise. 3When the foolish took their lamps, they took no oil with them; 4but the wise took flasks of oil with their lamps. 5As the bridegroom was delayed, all of them became drowsy and slept. 6But at midnight there was a shout, 'Look! Here is the bridegroom! Come out to meet him.' 7Then all those bridesmaids[h] got up and trimmed their lamps. 8The foolish said to the wise, 'Give us some of your oil, for our lamps are going out.' 9But the wise replied, 'No! there will not be enough for you and for us; you had better go to the dealers and buy some for yourselves.' 10And while they went to buy it, the bridegroom came, and those who were ready went with him into the wedding banquet; and the door was shut. 11Later the other bridesmaids[h] came also, saying, 'Lord, lord, open to us.' 12But he replied, 'Truly I tell you, I do not know you.' 13Keep awake therefore, for you know neither the day nor the hour.[j]

The Parable of the Talents

14 "For it is as if a man, going on a journey, summoned his slaves and entrusted his property to them; 15to one he gave five talents,[k] to another two, to another one, to each according to his ability. Then he went away. 16The one who had received the five talents went off at once and traded with them, and made five more talents. 17In the same way, the one who had the two talents made two more talents. 18But the one who had received the one talent went off and dug a hole in the ground and hid his master's money. 19After a long time the master of those slaves came and settled accounts with them. 20Then the one who had received the five talents came forward, bringing five more talents, saying, 'Master, you handed over to me five talents; see, I have made five more talents.' 21His master said to him, 'Well done, good and trustworthy slave; you have been trustworthy in a few things, I will put you in charge of many things; enter into the joy of your master.' 22And the one with the two talents also came forward, saying, 'Master, you handed over to me two talents; see, I have made two more talents.' 23His master said to him, 'Well done, good and trustworthy slave; you have been trustworthy in a few things, I will put you in charge of many

things; enter into the joy of your master.' 24Then the one who had received the one talent also came forward, saying, 'Master, I knew that you were a harsh man, reaping where you did not sow, and gathering where you did not scatter seed; 25so I was afraid, and I went and hid your talent in the ground. Here you have what is yours.' 26But his master replied, 'You wicked and lazy slave! You knew, did you, that I reap where I did not sow, and gather where I did not scatter? 27Then you ought to have invested my money with the bankers, and on my return I would have received what was my own with interest. 28So take the talent from him, and give it to the one with the ten talents. 29For to all those who have, more will be given, and they will have an abundance; but from those who have nothing, even what they have will be taken away. 30As for this worthless slave, throw him into the outer darkness, where there will be weeping and gnashing of teeth.'

The Judgment of the Nations

31 "When the Son of Man comes in his glory, and all the angels with him, then he will sit on the throne of his glory. 32All the nations will be gathered before him, and he will separate people one from another as a shepherd separates the sheep from the goats, 33and he will put the sheep at his right hand and the goats at the left. 34Then the king will say to those at his right hand, 'Come, you that are blessed by my Father, inherit the kingdom prepared for you from the foundation of the world; 35for I was hungry and you gave me food, I was thirsty and you gave me something to drink, I was a stranger and you welcomed me, 36I was naked and you gave me clothing, I was sick and you took care of me, I was in prison and you visited me.' 37Then the righteous will answer him, 'Lord, when was it that we saw you hungry and gave you food, or thirsty and gave you something to drink? 38And when was it that we saw you a stranger and welcomed you, or naked and gave you clothing? 39And when was it that we saw you sick or in prison and visited you?'

---

h Gk *virgins*   i Other ancient authorities add *and the bride*   j Other ancient authorities add *in which the Son of Man is coming*   k A talent was worth more than fifteen years' wages of a laborer

⁴⁰And the king will answer them, 'Truly I tell you, just as you did it to one of the least of these who are members of my family,ˡ you did it to me.' ⁴¹Then he will say to those at his left hand, 'You that are accursed, depart from me into the eternal fire prepared for the devil and his angels; ⁴²for I was hungry and you gave me no food, I was thirsty and you gave me nothing to drink, ⁴³I was a stranger and you did not welcome me, naked and you did not give me clothing, sick and in prison and you did not visit me.' ⁴⁴Then they also will answer, 'Lord, when was it that we saw you hungry or thirsty or a stranger or naked or sick or in prison, and did not take care of you?' ⁴⁵Then he will answer them, 'Truly I tell you, just as you did not do it to one of the least of these, you did

ˡ Gk *these my brothers*

"*You Did It for Me*"

MONDAY

Scripture Reading
for Today:
Matthew 25.31–46

Verse for Today:
Matthew 25.40

In Christ's human life, there were always a few who made up for the neglect of the crowd. The shepherds did it; their hurrying to the crib atoned for the people who would flee from Christ. The wise men did it; their journey across the world made up for those who refused to stir one hand's breadth from the routine of their lives to go to Christ.

We can do it too, exactly as they did. We are not born too late. We do it by seeing Christ and serving Christ in friends and strangers, in everyone we come in contact with.

Christ himself has proved it for us. For he said that a glass of water given to a beggar was given to him. He made heaven hinge on the way we act toward him in his disguise of commonplace, frail, ordinary humanity.

Did you give me [food] when I was hungry?
Did you give me to drink when I was thirsty?
Did you give me clothes when my own were all rags?
Did you come to see me when I was sick, or in prison, or in trouble?

And to those who say, aghast, that they never had a chance to do such a thing, that they lived two thousand years too late, he will say again what they had the chance of knowing all their lives, that if these things were done for the very least of members of his family, they were done to him.

For a total Christian, the goad of duty is not needed—always prodding one to perform this or that good deed. It is not a duty to help Christ; it is a privilege. Is it likely that Martha and Mary sat back and considered that they had done all that was expected of them—is it likely that Peter's mother-in-law grudgingly served the chicken she had meant to keep till Sunday because she thought it was her "duty"? She did it gladly; she would have served ten chickens if she had had them.

—DOROTHY DAY

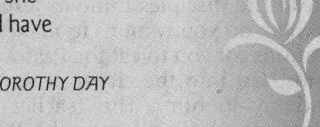

Go to page 1316 for your next devotional reading.

not do it to me.' [46]And these will go away into eternal punishment, but the righteous into eternal life."

The Plot to Kill Jesus

26 When Jesus had finished saying all these things, he said to his disciples, [2]"You know that after two days the Passover is coming, and the Son of Man will be handed over to be crucified."

3 Then the chief priests and the elders of the people gathered in the palace of the high priest, who was called Caiaphas, [4]and they conspired to arrest Jesus by stealth and kill him. [5]But they said, "Not during the festival, or there may be a riot among the people."

The Anointing at Bethany

6 Now while Jesus was at Bethany in the house of Simon the leper,[m] [7]a woman came to him with an alabaster jar of very costly ointment, and she poured it on his head as he sat at the table. [8]But when the disciples saw it, they were angry and said, "Why this waste? [9]For this ointment could have been sold for a large sum, and the money given to the poor." [10]But Jesus, aware of this, said to them, "Why do you trouble the woman? She has performed a good service for me. [11]For you always have the poor with you, but you will not always have me. [12]By pouring this ointment on my body she has prepared me for burial. [13]Truly I tell you, wherever this good news[n] is proclaimed in the whole world, what she has done will be told in remembrance of her."

Judas Agrees to Betray Jesus

14 Then one of the twelve, who was called Judas Iscariot, went to the chief priests [15]and said, "What will you give me if I betray him to you?" They paid him thirty pieces of silver. [16]And from that moment he began to look for an opportunity to betray him.

The Passover with the Disciples

17 On the first day of Unleavened Bread the disciples came to Jesus, saying, "Where do you want us to make the preparations for you to eat the Passover?" [18]He said, "Go into the city to a certain man, and say to him, 'The Teacher says, My time is near; I will keep the Passover at your house with my disciples.' " [19]So the disciples did as Jesus had directed them, and they prepared the Passover meal.

20 When it was evening, he took his place with the twelve;[o] [21]and while they were eating, he said, "Truly I tell you, one of you will betray me." [22]And they became greatly distressed and began to say to him one after another, "Surely not I, Lord?" [23]He answered, "The one who has dipped his hand into the bowl with me will betray me. [24]The Son of Man goes as it is written of him, but woe to that one by whom the Son of Man is betrayed! It would have been better for that one not to have been born." [25]Judas, who betrayed him, said, "Surely not I, Rabbi?" He replied, "You have said so."

The Institution of the Lord's Supper

26 While they were eating, Jesus took a loaf of bread, and after blessing it he broke it, gave it to the disciples, and said, "Take, eat; this is my body." [27]Then he took a cup, and after giving thanks he gave it to them, saying, "Drink from it, all of you; [28]for this is my blood of the[p] covenant, which is poured out for many for the forgiveness of sins. [29]I tell you, I will never again drink of this fruit of the vine until that day when I drink it new with you in my Father's kingdom."

30 When they had sung the hymn, they went out to the Mount of Olives.

Peter's Denial Foretold

31 Then Jesus said to them, "You will all become deserters because of me this night; for it is written,

'I will strike the shepherd,
    and the sheep of the flock will
       be scattered.'

[32]But after I am raised up, I will go ahead of you to Galilee." [33]Peter said to him, "Though all become deserters because of you, I will never desert you." [34]Jesus said to him, "Truly I tell you, this very night, before the cock crows, you will deny me three times." [35]Peter said to him, "Even though I must die with you, I will not deny you." And so said all the disciples.

Jesus Prays in Gethsemane

36 Then Jesus went with them to a

---

m The terms *leper* and *leprosy* can refer to several diseases   n Or *gospel*   o Other ancient authorities add *disciples*   p Other ancient authorities add *new*

place called Gethsemane; and he said to
his disciples, "Sit here while I go over
there and pray." 37He took with him Peter
and the two sons of Zebedee, and began
to be grieved and agitated. 38Then he said
to them, "I am deeply grieved, even to
death; remain here, and stay awake with
me." 39And going a little farther, he threw
himself on the ground and prayed, "My
Father, if it is possible, let this cup pass
from me; yet not what I want but what
you want." 40Then he came to the disciples
and found them sleeping; and he said to
Peter, "So, could you not stay awake with
me one hour? 41Stay awake and pray that
you may not come into the time of trial;[q]
the spirit indeed is willing, but the flesh is
weak." 42Again he went away for the second time and prayed, "My Father, if this
cannot pass unless I drink it, your will be
done." 43Again he came and found them
sleeping, for their eyes were heavy. 44So

[q] Or *into temptation*

THE TRADITION

The Eucharist

While they were eating, Jesus took a loaf of bread, and after blessing it he broke it, gave it to the disciples, and said, "Take, eat; this is my body."

MATTHEW 26.26

He could have told us to do a dramatic reading or to put on a passion play every Sunday. Instead, Jesus told us to share a meal: Take, eat, and drink in memory of me.

The Eucharist is normally celebrated in churches, not dining rooms and restaurants, and is significantly different from every other occasion where we take in nourishment. Still, this sacrament has the form of a meal, a thanksgiving banquet with obvious origins in the Last Supper. There is a table covered with a tablecloth and set with cup, plate, and candles. Hands are washed before the meal and utensils are washed after it. The simplest of menus is prepared and shared.

The Eucharist is a meal that memorializes a death—but not in the manner of funeral luncheons, where the deceased are mourned and eulogized. At every Mass, Jesus and his sacrificial death are not just recalled: They are actually made present. The meal is a memorial of Christ's sacrifice of himself on the cross; we share in his death as we eat the meal.

The connection between eating and dying—strange at first sight—is explained by the symbolism of the Passover meal, celebrated every year in remembrance of the Israelites' deliverance from slavery in Egypt. On the evening of that night passage to freedom, every Jewish household slaughtered a lamb and marked the doorposts with its blood as a sign of God's protection. Then they shared a meal that featured the lamb (see Exodus 12). The Passover as an annual festival of remembrance was instituted by God to be celebrated by the Israelite people every year.

It was at a Passover meal many years after that flight from Egypt that Jesus, the Lamb of God, chose to give himself in a startling new way. On the night of the Passover, he shared that meal with his disciples, but in offering himself on the cross, he took the place of the sacrificial Passover lamb.

Today, when we take part in the Eucharist, Christ's body and blood, offered under the appearances of bread and wine, unite us to him in the new Passover of his death and resurrection. We eat and drink, sharing in Christ's death so as to share in his life.

The *Eucharistic* meal makes present a saving death whose purpose is to prepare another meal—the heavenly banquet where we will sit someday at a table with Jesus in the kingdom of God.

leaving them again, he went away and prayed for the third time, saying the same words. ⁴⁵Then he came to the disciples and said to them, "Are you still sleeping and taking your rest? See, the hour is at hand, and the Son of Man is betrayed into the hands of sinners. ⁴⁶Get up, let us be going. See, my betrayer is at hand."

The Betrayal and Arrest of Jesus

47 While he was still speaking, Judas, one of the twelve, arrived; with him was a large crowd with swords and clubs, from the chief priests and the elders of the people. ⁴⁸Now the betrayer had given them a sign, saying, "The one I will kiss is the man; arrest him." ⁴⁹At once he came up to Jesus and said, "Greetings, Rabbi!" and kissed him. ⁵⁰Jesus said to him, "Friend, do what you are here to do." Then they came and laid hands on Jesus and arrested him. ⁵¹Suddenly, one of those with Jesus put his hand on his sword, drew it, and struck the slave of the high priest, cutting off his ear. ⁵²Then Jesus said to him, "Put your sword back into its place; for all who take the sword will perish by the sword. ⁵³Do you think that I cannot appeal to my Father, and he will at once send me more than twelve legions of angels? ⁵⁴But how then would the scriptures be fulfilled, which say it must happen in this way?" ⁵⁵At that hour Jesus said to the crowds, "Have you come out with swords and clubs to arrest me as though I were a bandit? Day after day I sat in the temple teaching, and you did not arrest me. ⁵⁶But all this has taken place, so that the scriptures of the prophets may be fulfilled." Then all the disciples deserted him and fled.

Jesus before the High Priest

57 Those who had arrested Jesus took him to Caiaphas the high priest, in whose house the scribes and the elders had gathered. ⁵⁸But Peter was following him at a distance, as far as the courtyard of the high priest; and going inside, he sat with the guards in order to see how this would end. ⁵⁹Now the chief priests and the whole council were looking for false testimony against Jesus so that they might put him to death, ⁶⁰but they found none, though many false witnesses came forward. At last two came forward ⁶¹and said, "This fellow said, 'I am able to destroy the temple of God and to build it in three

days.' " ⁶²The high priest stood up and said, "Have you no answer? What is it that they testify against you?" ⁶³But Jesus was silent. Then the high priest said to him, "I put you under oath before the living God, tell us if you are the Messiah,ʳ the Son of God." ⁶⁴Jesus said to him, "You have said so. But I tell you,

From now on you will see the
    Son of Man
seated at the right hand of Power
and coming on the clouds
    of heaven."

⁶⁵Then the high priest tore his clothes and said, "He has blasphemed! Why do we still need witnesses? You have now heard his blasphemy. ⁶⁶What is your verdict?" They answered, "He deserves death." ⁶⁷Then they spat in his face and struck him; and some slapped him, ⁶⁸saying, "Prophesy to us, you Messiah!ʳ Who is it that struck you?"

Peter's Denial of Jesus

69 Now Peter was sitting outside in the courtyard. A servant-girl came to him and said, "You also were with Jesus the Galilean." ⁷⁰But he denied it before all of them, saying, "I do not know what you are talking about." ⁷¹When he went out to the porch, another servant-girl saw him, and she said to the bystanders, "This man was with Jesus of Nazareth."ˢ ⁷²Again he denied it with an oath, "I do not know the man." ⁷³After a little while the bystanders came up and said to Peter, "Certainly you are also one of them, for your accent betrays you." ⁷⁴Then he began to curse, and he swore an oath, "I do not know the man!" At that moment the cock crowed. ⁷⁵Then Peter remembered what Jesus had said: "Before the cock crows, you will deny me three times." And he went out and wept bitterly.

Jesus Brought before Pilate

27 When morning came, all the chief priests and the elders of the people conferred together against Jesus in order to bring about his death. ²They bound him, led him away, and handed him over to Pilate the governor.

The Suicide of Judas

3 When Judas, his betrayer, saw that Jesusᵗ was condemned, he repented and

ʳ Or *Christ*   ˢ Gk *the Nazorean*   ᵗ Gk *he*

brought back the thirty pieces of silver to the chief priests and the elders. [4]He said, "I have sinned by betraying innocent[u] blood." But they said, "What is that to us? See to it yourself." [5]Throwing down the pieces of silver in the temple, he departed; and he went and hanged himself. [6]But the chief priests, taking the pieces of silver, said, "It is not lawful to put them into the treasury, since they are blood money." [7]After conferring together, they used them to buy the potter's field as a place to bury foreigners. [8]For this reason that field has been called the Field of Blood to this day. [9]Then was fulfilled what had been spoken through the prophet Jeremiah,[v] "And they took[w] the thirty pieces of silver, the price of the one on whom a price had been set,[x] on whom some of the people of Israel had set a price, [10]and they gave[y] them for the potter's field, as the Lord commanded me."

Pilate Questions Jesus

11 Now Jesus stood before the governor; and the governor asked him, "Are you the King of the Jews?" Jesus said, "You say so." [12]But when he was accused by the chief priests and elders, he did not answer. [13]Then Pilate said to him, "Do you not hear how many accusations they make against you?" [14]But he gave him no answer, not even to a single charge, so that the governor was greatly amazed.

Barabbas or Jesus?

15 Now at the festival the governor was accustomed to release a prisoner for the crowd, anyone whom they wanted. [16]At that time they had a notorious prisoner, called Jesus[z] Barabbas. [17]So after they had gathered, Pilate said to them, "Whom do you want me to release for you, Jesus[z] Barabbas or Jesus who is called the Messiah?"[a] [18]For he realized that it was out of jealousy that they had handed him over. [19]While he was sitting on the judgment seat, his wife sent word to him, "Have nothing to do with that innocent man, for today I have suffered a great deal because of a dream about him." [20]Now the chief priests and the elders persuaded the crowds to ask for Barabbas and to have Jesus killed. [21]The governor again said to them, "Which of the two do you want me to release for you?" And they said, "Barabbas." [22]Pilate said to them, "Then what should I do with Jesus who is called the Messiah?"[a] All of them said, "Let him be crucified!" [23]Then he asked, "Why, what evil has he done?" But they shouted all the more, "Let him be crucified!"

Pilate Hands Jesus over to Be Crucified

24 So when Pilate saw that he could do nothing, but rather that a riot was beginning, he took some water and washed his hands before the crowd, saying, "I am innocent of this man's blood;[b] see to it yourselves." [25]Then the people as a whole answered, "His blood be on us and on our children!" [26]So he released Barabbas for them; and after flogging Jesus, he handed him over to be crucified.

The Soldiers Mock Jesus

27 Then the soldiers of the governor took Jesus into the governor's headquarters,[c] and they gathered the whole cohort around him. [28]They stripped him and put a scarlet robe on him, [29]and after twisting some thorns into a crown, they put it on his head. They put a reed in his right hand and knelt before him and mocked him, saying, "Hail, King of the Jews!" [30]They spat on him, and took the reed and struck him on the head. [31]After mocking him, they stripped him of the robe and put his own clothes on him. Then they led him away to crucify him.

The Crucifixion of Jesus

32 As they went out, they came upon a man from Cyrene named Simon; they compelled this man to carry his cross. [33]And when they came to a place called Golgotha (which means Place of a Skull), [34]they offered him wine to drink, mixed with gall; but when he tasted it, he would not drink it. [35]And when they had crucified him, they divided his clothes among themselves by casting lots;[d] [36]then they sat down there and kept watch over him. [37]Over his head they put the charge

---

u Other ancient authorities read *righteous*
v Other ancient authorities read *Zechariah* or *Isaiah*   *w* Or *I took*   *x* Or *the price of the precious One*   *y* Other ancient authorities read *I gave*
z Other ancient authorities lack *Jesus*   *a* Or *the Christ*   *b* Other ancient authorities read *this righteous blood*, or *this righteous man's blood*   *c* Gk *the praetorium*   *d* Other ancient authorities add *in order that what had been spoken through the prophet might be fulfilled, "They divided my clothes among themselves, and for my clothing they cast lots."*

against him, which read, "This is Jesus, the King of the Jews."

38 Then two bandits were crucified with him, one on his right and one on his left. [39]Those who passed by derided[e] him, shaking their heads [40]and saying, "You who would destroy the temple and build it in three days, save yourself! If you are the Son of God, come down from the cross." [41]In the same way the chief priests also, along with the scribes and elders, were mocking him, saying, [42]"He saved others; he cannot save himself.[f] He is the King of Israel; let him come down from the cross now, and we will believe in him. [43]He trusts in God; let God deliver him now, if he wants to; for he said, 'I am God's Son.' " [44]The bandits who were crucified with him also taunted him in the same way.

The Death of Jesus

45 From noon on, darkness came over the whole land[g] until three in the afternoon. [46]And about three o'clock Jesus cried with a loud voice, "Eli, Eli, lema sabachthani?" that is, "My God, my God, why have you forsaken me?" [47]When some of the bystanders heard it, they said, "This man is calling for Elijah." [48]At once one of them ran and got a sponge, filled it with sour wine, put it on a stick, and gave it to him to drink. [49]But the others said, "Wait, let us see whether Elijah will come to save him."[h] [50]Then Jesus cried again with a loud voice and breathed his last.[i] [51]At that moment the curtain of the temple was torn in two, from top to bottom. The earth shook, and the rocks were split. [52]The tombs also were opened, and many bodies of the saints who had fallen asleep were raised. [53]After his resurrection they came out of the tombs and entered the holy city and appeared to many. [54]Now when the centurion and those with him, who were keeping watch over Jesus, saw the earthquake and what took place, they were terrified and said, "Truly this man was God's Son!"[j]

55 Many women were also there, looking on from a distance; they had followed Jesus from Galilee and had provided for him. [56]Among them were Mary Magdalene, and Mary the mother of James and Joseph, and the mother of the sons of Zebedee.

The Burial of Jesus

57 When it was evening, there came a rich man from Arimathea, named Joseph, who was also a disciple of Jesus. [58]He went to Pilate and asked for the body of Jesus; then Pilate ordered it to be given to him. [59]So Joseph took the body and wrapped it in a clean linen cloth [60]and laid it in his own new tomb, which he had hewn in the rock. He then rolled a great stone to the door of the tomb and went away. [61]Mary Magdalene and the other Mary were there, sitting opposite the tomb.

The Guard at the Tomb

62 The next day, that is, after the day of Preparation, the chief priests and the Pharisees gathered before Pilate [63]and said, "Sir, we remember what that impostor said while he was still alive, 'After three days I will rise again.' [64]Therefore command the tomb to be made secure until the third day; otherwise his disciples may go and steal him away, and tell the people, 'He has been raised from the dead,' and the last deception would be worse than the first." [65]Pilate said to them, "You have a guard[k] of soldiers; go, make it as secure as you can."[l] [66]So they went with the guard and made the tomb secure by sealing the stone.

The Resurrection of Jesus

28 After the sabbath, as the first day of the week was dawning, Mary Magdalene and the other Mary went to see the tomb. [2]And suddenly there was a great earthquake; for an angel of the Lord, descending from heaven, came and rolled back the stone and sat on it. [3]His appearance was like lightning, and his clothing white as snow. [4]For fear of him the guards shook and became like dead men. [5]But the angel said to the women, "Do not be afraid; I know that you are looking for Jesus who was crucified. [6]He is not here; for he has been raised, as he said. Come, see the place where he[m] lay. [7]Then go quickly and tell his disciples, 'He has been

---

e Or blasphemed   f Or is he unable to save himself?
g Or earth   h Other ancient authorities add And another took a spear and pierced his side, and out came water and blood   i Or gave up his spirit
j Or a son of God   k Or Take a guard   l Gk you know how   m Other ancient authorities read the Lord

raised from the dead,[n] and indeed he is going ahead of you to Galilee; there you will see him.' This is my message for you." [8]So they left the tomb quickly with fear and great joy, and ran to tell his disciples. [9]Suddenly Jesus met them and said, "Greetings!" And they came to him, took hold of his feet, and worshiped him. [10]Then Jesus said to them, "Do not be afraid; go and tell my brothers to go to Galilee; there they will see me."

The Report of the Guard

[11] While they were going, some of the guard went into the city and told the chief priests everything that had happened. [12]After the priests[o] had assembled with the elders, they devised a plan to give a large sum of money to the soldiers, [13]telling them, "You must say, 'His disciples came by night and stole him away while we were asleep.' [14]If this comes to the governor's ears, we will satisfy him and keep you out of trouble." [15]So they took the money and did as they were directed. And this story is still told among the Jews to this day.

The Commissioning of the Disciples

16 Now the eleven disciples went to Galilee, to the mountain to which Jesus had directed them. [17]When they saw him, they worshiped him; but some doubted. [18]And Jesus came and said to them, "All authority in heaven and on earth has been given to me. [19]Go therefore and make disciples of all nations, baptizing them in the name of the Father and of the Son and of the Holy Spirit, [20]and teaching them to obey everything that I have commanded you. And remember, I am with you always, to the end of the age." [p]

[n] Other ancient authorities lack *from the dead*
[o] Gk *they*   [p] Other ancient authorities add *Amen*

The Gospel According to
Mark

Short and to the point—that's how the Gospel of Mark could be summarized. It begins, not with the story of Jesus' birth but with the preaching of John the Baptist, "the voice of one crying out in the wilderness" (1.3). A fast-paced narrative, it focuses more on what Jesus did than on what he taught. Mark emphasized that neither the crowds, the authorities, nor his own disciples truly understood Jesus. Only the crucifixion and resurrection revealed who he really is.

Intended for Gentiles, this Gospel was probably written in Rome during a time of great persecution. The notorious fire of Rome, probably set by Nero and then blamed on the Christians, took place in A.D. 64, instigating a persecution that lasted until A.D. 67. The Gospel of Mark may have been written prior to A.D. 70, on the eve of the destruction of Jerusalem, in order to encourage persecuted believers to stand firm, just as Jesus did while he lived on earth.

The book of Mark emphasizes that Jesus reveals himself to those who follow him no matter how difficult circumstances become.

The Proclamation of John the Baptist

1 The beginning of the good news*a* of Jesus Christ, the Son of God.*b*

2 As it is written in the prophet Isaiah,*c*

"See, I am sending my messenger
　　ahead of you,*d*
who will prepare your way;
3 the voice of one crying out in the
　　wilderness:
　'Prepare the way of the Lord,
　　make his paths straight,' "

4John the baptizer appeared*e* in the wilderness, proclaiming a baptism of repentance for the forgiveness of sins. 5And people from the whole Judean countryside and all the people of Jerusalem were going out to him, and were baptized by him in the river Jordan, confessing their sins. 6Now John was clothed with camel's hair, with a leather belt around his waist, and he ate locusts and wild honey. 7He proclaimed, "The one who is more powerful than I is coming after me; I am not worthy to stoop down and untie the thong of his sandals. 8I have baptized you with*f* water; but he will baptize you with*f* the Holy Spirit."

The Baptism of Jesus

9 In those days Jesus came from Naza-

a Or *gospel*　　*b* Other ancient authorities lack *the Son of God*　　*c* Other ancient authorities read *in the prophets*　　*d* Gk *before your face*　　*e* Other ancient authorities read *John was baptizing*　　*f* Or *in*

reth of Galilee and was baptized by John in the Jordan. [10]And just as he was coming up out of the water, he saw the heavens torn apart and the Spirit descending like a dove on him. [11]And a voice came from heaven, "You are my Son, the Beloved;[g] with you I am well pleased."

The Temptation of Jesus

12 And the Spirit immediately drove him out into the wilderness. [13]He was in the wilderness forty days, tempted by Satan; and he was with the wild beasts; and the angels waited on him.

The Beginning of the Galilean Ministry

14 Now after John was arrested, Jesus came to Galilee, proclaiming the good news[h] of God,[i] [15]and saying, "The time is fulfilled, and the kingdom of God has come near;[j] repent, and believe in the good news."[h]

Jesus Calls the First Disciples

16 As Jesus passed along the Sea of Galilee, he saw Simon and his brother Andrew casting a net into the sea—for they were fishermen. [17]And Jesus said to them, "Follow me and I will make you fish for people." [18]And immediately they left their nets and followed him. [19]As he went a little farther, he saw James son of Zebedee and his brother John, who were in their boat mending the nets. [20]Immediately he called them; and they left their father Zebedee in the boat with the hired men, and followed him.

The Man with an Unclean Spirit

21 They went to Capernaum; and when the sabbath came, he entered the synagogue and taught. [22]They were astounded at his teaching, for he taught them as one having authority, and not as the scribes. [23]Just then there was in their synagogue a man with an unclean spirit, [24]and he cried out, "What have you to do with us, Jesus of Nazareth? Have you come to destroy us? I know who you are, the Holy One of God." [25]But Jesus rebuked him, saying, "Be silent, and come out of him!" [26]And the unclean spirit, convulsing him and crying with a loud voice, came out of him. [27]They were all amazed, and they kept on asking one another, "What is this? A new teaching—with authority! He[k] commands even the unclean spirits, and they obey him." [28]At once his fame

began to spread throughout the surrounding region of Galilee.

Jesus Heals Many at Simon's House

29 As soon as they[l] left the synagogue, they entered the house of Simon and Andrew, with James and John. [30]Now Simon's mother-in-law was in bed with a fever, and they told him about her at once. [31]He came and took her by the hand and lifted her up. Then the fever left her, and she began to serve them.

32 That evening, at sunset, they brought to him all who were sick or possessed with demons. [33]And the whole city was gathered around the door. [34]And he cured many who were sick with various diseases, and cast out many demons; and he would not permit the demons to speak, because they knew him.

A Preaching Tour in Galilee

35 In the morning, while it was still very dark, he got up and went out to a deserted place, and there he prayed. [36]And Simon and his companions hunted for him. [37]When they found him, they said to him, "Everyone is searching for you." [38]He answered, "Let us go on to the neighboring towns, so that I may proclaim the message there also; for that is what I came out to do." [39]And he went throughout Galilee, proclaiming the message in their synagogues and casting out demons.

Jesus Cleanses a Leper

40 A leper[m] came to him begging him, and kneeling[n] he said to him, "If you choose, you can make me clean." [41]Moved with pity,[o] Jesus[p] stretched out his hand and touched him, and said to him, "I do choose. Be made clean!" [42]Immediately the leprosy[m] left him, and he was made clean. [43]After sternly warning him he sent him away at once, [44]saying to him, "See that you say nothing to anyone; but go, show yourself to the priest, and offer for your cleansing what Moses commanded, as a testimony to them." [45]But he went out and began to proclaim it freely, and to spread the word, so that Jesus[p] could no

---

g Or *my beloved Son*   h Or *gospel*   i Other ancient authorities read *of the kingdom*   j Or *is at hand*   k Or *A new teaching! With authority he*   l Other ancient authorities read *he*   m The terms *leper* and *leprosy* can refer to several diseases   n Other ancient authorities lack *kneeling*   o Other ancient authorities read *anger*   p Gk *he*

longer go into a town openly, but stayed out in the country; and people came to him from every quarter.

Jesus Heals a Paralytic

2 When he returned to Capernaum after some days, it was reported that he was at home. ²So many gathered around that there was no longer room for them, not even in front of the door; and he was speaking the word to them. ³Then some people[q] came, bringing to him a paralyzed man, carried by four of them. ⁴And when they could not bring him to Jesus because of the crowd, they removed the roof above him; and after having dug through it, they let down the mat on which the paralytic lay. ⁵When Jesus saw their faith, he said to the paralytic, "Son, your sins are forgiven." ⁶Now some of the

q Gk they

What Do I Really Want?

TUESDAY

Scripture Reading
for Today:
Mark 1.40–45

Verse for Today:
Mark 1.41

Ask yourself: What do I really want when I pray? Do you want to be possessed by God? Or, to put the same question more honestly, do you want to want it? Then you have it. The one point Jesus stressed and repeated and brought up again is that: "Whatever you ask the Father, he will grant it to you" [see John 16.23]. His insistence on faith and perseverance are surely other ways of saying the same thing: You must really want; it must engross you. "Wants" that are passing, faint emotional desires that you do not press with burning conviction, these are things you do not ask "in Jesus' name"; how could you? But what you really want, "with all your heart and soul and mind and strength" [see Luke 10.27], that Jesus pledges himself to see that you are granted.

When you set yourself down to pray, *what do you want?* If you want God to take possession of you, then you are praying. That is all prayer is. There are no secrets, no shortcuts, no methods. Prayer is the utterly ruthless test of your sincerity.

I long to tell myself that the reason why "I can't pray" is that I've never been taught, the right books have passed me by, the holy guru never came down my street. Hence the eager interest in books and articles on prayer—all obscuring from me my lack of true desire.

God's one desire is to come and make his abode with us. Do we believe him or not? Of course, I can cheat. If I choose not to be there for him, and since I am not yet transformed into Jesus, to some extent I always do protect myself against the impact of his love, then that is cause for grief. But it is creative grief. It drives us helpless to Jesus to be healed. We say to him: "If you want to, you can make me clean." But he answers: "I do want to—but do you?" [see John 5.2–8]. That "wanting" is ever the crux of the matter.

—*SISTER WENDY BECKETT*

Go to page 1320 for your next devotional reading.

scribes were sitting there, questioning in their hearts, [7]"Why does this fellow speak in this way? It is blasphemy! Who can forgive sins but God alone?" [8]At once Jesus perceived in his spirit that they were discussing these questions among themselves; and he said to them, "Why do you raise such questions in your hearts? [9]Which is easier, to say to the paralytic, 'Your sins are forgiven,' or to say, 'Stand up and take your mat and walk'? [10]But so that you may know that the Son of Man has authority on earth to forgive sins"—he said to the paralytic— [11]"I say to you, stand up, take your mat and go to your home." [12]And he stood up, and immediately took the mat and went out before all of them; so that they were all amazed and glorified God, saying, "We have never seen anything like this!"

Jesus Calls Levi

13 Jesus[r] went out again beside the sea; the whole crowd gathered around him, and he taught them. [14]As he was walking along, he saw Levi son of Alphaeus sitting at the tax booth, and he said to him, "Follow me." And he got up and followed him.

15 And as he sat at dinner[s] in Levi's[t] house, many tax collectors and sinners were also sitting[u] with Jesus and his disciples—for there were many who followed him. [16]When the scribes of[v] the Pharisees saw that he was eating with sinners and tax collectors, they said to his disciples, "Why does he eat[w] with tax collectors and sinners?" [17]When Jesus heard this, he said to them, "Those who are well have no need of a physician, but those who are sick; I have come to call not the righteous but sinners."

The Question about Fasting

18 Now John's disciples and the Pharisees were fasting; and people[x] came and said to him, "Why do John's disciples and the disciples of the Pharisees fast, but your disciples do not fast?" [19]Jesus said to them, "The wedding guests cannot fast while the bridegroom is with them, can they? As long as they have the bridegroom with them, they cannot fast. [20]The days will come when the bridegroom is taken away from them, and then they will fast on that day.

21 "No one sews a piece of unshrunk cloth on an old cloak; otherwise, the patch pulls away from it, the new from the old, and a worse tear is made. [22]And no one puts new wine into old wineskins; otherwise, the wine will burst the skins, and the wine is lost, and so are the skins; but one puts new wine into fresh wineskins."[y]

Pronouncement about the Sabbath

23 One sabbath he was going through the grainfields; and as they made their way his disciples began to pluck heads of grain. [24]The Pharisees said to him, "Look, why are they doing what is not lawful on the sabbath?" [25]And he said to them, "Have you never read what David did when he and his companions were hungry and in need of food? [26]He entered the house of God, when Abiathar was high priest, and ate the bread of the Presence, which it is not lawful for any but the priests to eat, and he gave some to his companions." [27]Then he said to them, "The sabbath was made for humankind, and not humankind for the sabbath; [28]so the Son of Man is lord even of the sabbath."

The Man with a Withered Hand

3 Again he entered the synagogue, and a man was there who had a withered hand. [2]They watched him to see whether he would cure him on the sabbath, so that they might accuse him. [3]And he said to the man who had the withered hand, "Come forward." [4]Then he said to them, "Is it lawful to do good or to do harm on the sabbath, to save life or to kill?" But they were silent. [5]He looked around at them with anger; he was grieved at their hardness of heart and said to the man, "Stretch out your hand." He stretched it out, and his hand was restored. [6]The Pharisees went out and immediately conspired with the Herodians against him, how to destroy him.

A Multitude at the Seaside

7 Jesus departed with his disciples to the sea, and a great multitude from Galilee followed him; [8]hearing all that he was doing, they came to him in great numbers

r Gk He   s Gk reclined   t Gk his   u Gk reclining   v Other ancient authorities read and   w Other ancient authorities add and drink   x Gk they   y Other ancient authorities lack but one puts new wine into fresh wineskins

from Judea, Jerusalem, Idumea, beyond the Jordan, and the region around Tyre and Sidon. [9]He told his disciples to have a boat ready for him because of the crowd, so that they would not crush him; [10]for he had cured many, so that all who had diseases pressed upon him to touch him. [11]Whenever the unclean spirits saw him, they fell down before him and shouted, "You are the Son of God!" [12]But he sternly ordered them not to make him known.

Jesus Appoints the Twelve

13 He went up the mountain and called to him those whom he wanted, and they came to him. [14]And he appointed twelve, whom he also named apostles,[z] to be with him, and to be sent out to proclaim the message, [15]and to have authority to cast out demons. [16]So he appointed the twelve:[a] Simon (to whom he gave the name Peter); [17]James son of Zebedee and John the brother of James (to whom he gave the name Boanerges, that is, Sons of Thunder); [18]and Andrew, and Philip, and Bartholomew, and Matthew, and Thomas, and James son of Alphaeus, and Thaddae-

[z] Other ancient authorities lack *whom he also named apostles*   [a] Other ancient authorities lack *So he appointed the twelve*

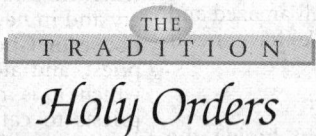

THE TRADITION

Holy Orders

*And he appointed twelve, whom he also named apostles,
to be with him, and to be sent out . . .*

MARK 3.14

Catherine Doherty was an energetic Russian émigré whose love for Christ has inspired many men and women to follow her example of contemplative prayer and service to the poor. While most of those followers are lay people, a striking feature of Catherine's Madonna House apostolate is its "respectful informality" toward Christ's representative, the priest.

"When a priest walks into this house," Catherine said, "*Christ walks in.* We know that in faith."

Wry smiles and retorts often greet such assertions. "Oh sure. Maybe that's true of some priests. But you should see the one in my parish. Can't preach, can't organize, no social skills . . . and he drinks."

"Baloney," Catherine would and did reply. Priests are weak and limited human beings like the rest of us; at the same time, they are one of the greatest signs of God's love. "Christ didn't want to leave us orphans! He comes to us in the disguise of a priest!"

Jesus didn't wait around for 12 perfect men to carry on his mission. He chose a dozen imperfect apostles. Through Holy Orders, Jesus still calls and appoints personal representatives to preach, shepherd, and offer divine worship. The caliber of those deacons, priests, and bishops has not changed significantly over the centuries; they are still flawed. Nonetheless, by the special grace of Holy Orders every priest in his own way represents Jesus. As he serves, "it is Christ himself who is present to his Church as Head of his Body, Shepherd of his flock, high priest of the redemptive sacrifice, Teacher of Truth" (*Catechism of the Catholic Church*, 1548).

We experience this most directly, perhaps, through those sacraments where the priest addresses us in the very words of Christ. "Take, eat, this is my body . . ." or "I absolve you . . ." But in many other ways, too, priests make visible Jesus' ongoing care and presence among his flock.

"And remember, I am with you always, to the end of the age," Jesus assured the disciples (Matthew 28.20). Working through his priests is one way he keeps that promise.

us, and Simon the Cananaean, ¹⁹and Judas Iscariot, who betrayed him.

Jesus and Beelzebul

Then he went home; ²⁰and the crowd came together again, so that they could not even eat. ²¹When his family heard it, they went out to restrain him, for people were saying, "He has gone out of his mind." ²²And the scribes who came down from Jerusalem said, "He has Beelzebul, and by the ruler of the demons he casts out demons." ²³And he called them to him, and spoke to them in parables, "How can Satan cast out Satan? ²⁴If a kingdom is divided against itself, that kingdom cannot stand. ²⁵And if a house is divided against itself, that house will not be able to stand. ²⁶And if Satan has risen up against himself and is divided, he cannot stand, but his end has come. ²⁷But no one can enter a strong man's house and plunder his property without first tying up the strong man; then indeed the house can be plundered.

28 "Truly I tell you, people will be forgiven for their sins and whatever blasphemies they utter; ²⁹but whoever blasphemes against the Holy Spirit can never have forgiveness, but is guilty of an eternal sin"— ³⁰for they had said, "He has an unclean spirit."

The True Kindred of Jesus

31 Then his mother and his brothers came; and standing outside, they sent to him and called him. ³²A crowd was sitting around him; and they said to him, "Your mother and your brothers and sisters[b] are outside, asking for you." ³³And he replied, "Who are my mother and my brothers?" ³⁴And looking at those who sat around him, he said, "Here are my mother and my brothers! ³⁵Whoever does the will of God is my brother and sister and mother."

The Parable of the Sower

4 Again he began to teach beside the sea. Such a very large crowd gathered around him that he got into a boat on the sea and sat there, while the whole crowd was beside the sea on the land. ²He began to teach them many things in parables, and in his teaching he said to them: ³"Listen! A sower went out to sow. ⁴And as he sowed, some seed fell on the path, and the birds came and ate it up. ⁵Other seed fell on rocky ground, where it did not have much soil, and it sprang up quickly, since it had no depth of soil. ⁶And when the sun rose, it was scorched; and since it had no root, it withered away. ⁷Other seed fell among thorns, and the thorns grew up and choked it, and it yielded no grain. ⁸Other seed fell into good soil and brought forth grain, growing up and increasing and yielding thirty and sixty and a hundredfold." ⁹And he said, "Let anyone with ears to hear listen!"

The Purpose of the Parables

10 When he was alone, those who were around him along with the twelve asked him about the parables. ¹¹And he said to them, "To you has been given the secret[c] of the kingdom of God, but for those outside, everything comes in parables; ¹²in order that

'they may indeed look, but not
        perceive,
    and may indeed listen, but not
        understand;
    so that they may not turn again and
        be forgiven.' "

13 And he said to them, "Do you not understand this parable? Then how will you understand all the parables? ¹⁴The sower sows the word. ¹⁵These are the ones on the path where the word is sown: when they hear, Satan immediately comes and takes away the word that is sown in them. ¹⁶And these are the ones sown on rocky ground: when they hear the word, they immediately receive it with joy. ¹⁷But they have no root, and endure only for a while; then, when trouble or persecution arises on account of the word, immediately they fall away.[d] ¹⁸And others are those sown among the thorns: these are the ones who hear the word, ¹⁹but the cares of the world, and the lure of wealth, and the desire for other things come in and choke the word, and it yields nothing. ²⁰And these are the ones sown on the good soil: they hear the word and accept it and bear fruit, thirty and sixty and a hundredfold."

A Lamp under a Bushel Basket

21 He said to them, "Is a lamp brought in to be put under the bushel basket, or under the bed, and not on the lampstand? ²²For there is nothing hidden, except to be

---

b Other ancient authorities lack and sisters   c Or mystery   d Or stumble

disclosed; nor is anything secret, except to come to light. 23Let anyone with ears to hear listen!" 24And he said to them, "Pay attention to what you hear; the measure you give will be the measure you get, and still more will be given you. 25For to those who have, more will be given; and from those who have nothing, even what they have will be taken away."

The Parable of the Growing Seed

26 He also said, "The kingdom of God is as if someone would scatter seed on the ground, 27and would sleep and rise night and day, and the seed would sprout and grow, he does not know how. 28The earth produces of itself, first the stalk, then the head, then the full grain in the head. 29But when the grain is ripe, at once he goes in with his sickle, because the harvest has come."

The Parable of the Mustard Seed

30 He also said, "With what can we compare the kingdom of God, or what parable will we use for it? 31It is like a mustard seed, which, when sown upon the ground, is the smallest of all the seeds on earth; 32yet when it is sown it grows up and becomes the greatest of all shrubs,

WEDNESDAY

Scripture Reading for Today:
Mark 4.1–9

Verse for Today:
Mark 4.8

*S*weet Potential

The milkweed seed—any seed—has immense power, enough to cover a whole hillside with new, young milkweeds, enough power to fill my lawn, and my neighbor's, with dandelions.

Does this feel like a negative power? After all, how many of us yearn for the gold of dandelions in spring? But it may also be a power for good—as Jesus illustrated in his parable—the yield from one seed may be one hundredfold. Think of the multiplied power of the kernels on one cob of corn. I counted them on one such corncob the other day—over one hundred kernels, each bursting with sweet potential. Sown and reproducing themselves—100 x 100 = 10,000. By the next generation of seedtime and harvest, you have a million corn kernels going to work to cover acres of prairie with green cornstalks and yellow silk tassels blowing in the wind.

I'm reminded of the power of other small things in Scripture that had large consequences—individual lives or the fate of nations changing direction. The fruit eaten in the Garden of Eden. The olive leaf glimpsed in the beak of Noah's dove. The drops of lamb's blood painted over the doorways before the first Passover. The voice that the boy Samuel heard in the night. The still, small voice that arrested Elijah in his wilderness despair. The bottomless vessel of oil that saved the widow and her family from starvation. For another widow, the handful of flour—all she had—that she gave to the hungry prophet. The widow's farthing. The coin found in the mouth of a fish. You can think of others. Please, think of others! Or of small events or incidents that have altered the course of your own life. Never despise the power of small things like seeds to transform the landscape of the heart.

—LUCI SHAW

Go to page 1327 for your next devotional reading.

and puts forth large branches, so that the birds of the air can make nests in its shade."

The Use of Parables

33 With many such parables he spoke the word to them, as they were able to hear it; 34he did not speak to them except in parables, but he explained everything in private to his disciples.

Jesus Stills a Storm

35 On that day, when evening had come, he said to them, "Let us go across to the other side." 36And leaving the crowd behind, they took him with them in the boat, just as he was. Other boats were with him. 37A great windstorm arose, and the waves beat into the boat, so that the boat was already being swamped. 38But he was in the stern, asleep on the cushion; and they woke him up and said to him, "Teacher, do you not care that we are perishing?" 39He woke up and rebuked the wind, and said to the sea, "Peace! Be still!" Then the wind ceased, and there was a dead calm. 40He said to them, "Why are you afraid? Have you still no faith?" 41And they were filled with great awe and said to one another, "Who then is this, that even the wind and the sea obey him?"

Jesus Heals the Gerasene Demoniac

5 They came to the other side of the sea, to the country of the Gerasenes.e 2And when he had stepped out of the boat, immediately a man out of the tombs with an unclean spirit met him. 3He lived among the tombs; and no one could restrain him any more, even with a chain; 4for he had often been restrained with shackles and chains, but the chains he wrenched apart, and the shackles he broke in pieces; and no one had the strength to subdue him. 5Night and day among the tombs and on the mountains he was always howling and bruising himself with stones. 6When he saw Jesus from a distance, he ran and bowed down before him; 7and he shouted at the top of his voice, "What have you to do with me, Jesus, Son of the Most High God? I adjure you by God, do not torment me." 8For he had said to him, "Come out of the man, you unclean spirit!" 9Then Jesusf asked him, "What is your name?" He replied, "My name is Legion; for we are many." 10He begged him earnestly not to send

them out of the country. 11Now there on the hillside a great herd of swine was feeding; 12and the unclean spiritsg begged him, "Send us into the swine; let us enter them." 13So he gave them permission. And the unclean spirits came out and entered the swine; and the herd, numbering about two thousand, rushed down the steep bank into the sea, and were drowned in the sea.

14 The swineherds ran off and told it in the city and in the country. Then people came to see what it was that had happened. 15They came to Jesus and saw the demoniac sitting there, clothed and in his right mind, the very man who had had the legion; and they were afraid. 16Those who had seen what had happened to the demoniac and to the swine reported it. 17Then they began to beg Jesush to leave their neighborhood. 18As he was getting into the boat, the man who had been possessed by demons begged him that he might be with him. 19But Jesusf refused, and said to him, "Go home to your friends, and tell them how much the Lord has done for you, and what mercy he has shown you." 20And he went away and began to proclaim in the Decapolis how much Jesus had done for him; and everyone was amazed.

A Girl Restored to Life and a Woman Healed

21 When Jesus had crossed again in the boati to the other side, a great crowd gathered around him; and he was by the sea. 22Then one of the leaders of the synagogue named Jairus came and, when he saw him, fell at his feet 23and begged him repeatedly, "My little daughter is at the point of death. Come and lay your hands on her, so that she may be made well, and live." 24So he went with him.

And a large crowd followed him and pressed in on him. 25Now there was a woman who had been suffering from hemorrhages for twelve years. 26She had endured much under many physicians, and had spent all that she had; and she was no better, but rather grew worse. 27She had heard about Jesus, and came up behind him in the crowd and touched his cloak, 28for she said, "If I but touch his

e Other ancient authorities read *Gergesenes*; others, *Gadarenes*   f Gk *he*   g Gk *they*   h Gk *him*
i Other ancient authorities lack *in the boat*

clothes, I will be made well." 29Immediately her hemorrhage stopped; and she felt in her body that she was healed of her disease. 30Immediately aware that power had gone forth from him, Jesus turned about in the crowd and said, "Who touched my clothes?" 31And his disciples said to him, "You see the crowd pressing in on you; how can you say, 'Who touched me?' " 32He looked all around to see who had done it. 33But the woman, knowing what had happened to her, came in fear and trembling, fell down before him, and told him the whole truth. 34He said to her, "Daughter, your faith has made you well; go in peace, and be healed of your disease."

35 While he was still speaking, some people came from the leader's house to say, "Your daughter is dead. Why trouble the teacher any further?" 36But overhearing*j* what they said, Jesus said to the leader of the synagogue, "Do not fear, only believe." 37He allowed no one to follow him except Peter, James, and John, the brother of James. 38When they came to the house of the leader of the synagogue, he saw a commotion, people weeping and wailing loudly. 39When he had entered, he said to them, "Why do you make a commotion and weep? The child is not dead but sleeping." 40And they laughed at him. Then he put them all outside, and took the child's father and mother and those who were with him, and went in where the child was. 41He took her by the hand and said to her, "Talitha cum," which means, "Little girl, get up!" 42And immediately the girl got up and began to walk about (she was twelve years of age). At this they were overcome with amazement. 43He strictly ordered them that no one should know this, and told them to give her something to eat.

The Rejection of Jesus at Nazareth

6 He left that place and came to his hometown, and his disciples followed him. 2On the sabbath he began to teach in the synagogue, and many who heard him were astounded. They said, "Where did this man get all this? What is this wisdom that has been given to him? What deeds of power are being done by his hands! 3Is not this the carpenter, the son of Mary*k* and brother of James and Joses and Judas and Simon, and are not his sisters here with us?" And they took offense*l* at him. 4Then Jesus said to

them, "Prophets are not without honor, except in their hometown, and among their own kin, and in their own house." 5And he could do no deed of power there, except that he laid his hands on a few sick people and cured them. 6And he was amazed at their unbelief.

The Mission of the Twelve

Then he went about among the villages teaching. 7He called the twelve and began to send them out two by two, and gave them authority over the unclean spirits. 8He ordered them to take nothing for their journey except a staff; no bread, no bag, no money in their belts; 9but to wear sandals and not to put on two tunics. 10He said to them, "Wherever you enter a house, stay there until you leave the place. 11If any place will not welcome you and they refuse to hear you, as you leave, shake off the dust that is on your feet as a testimony against them." 12So they went out and proclaimed that all should repent. 13They cast out many demons, and anointed with oil many who were sick and cured them.

The Death of John the Baptist

14 King Herod heard of it, for Jesus'*m* name had become known. Some were*n* saying, "John the baptizer has been raised from the dead; and for this reason these powers are at work in him." 15But others said, "It is Elijah." And others said, "It is a prophet, like one of the prophets of old." 16But when Herod heard of it, he said, "John, whom I beheaded, has been raised."

17 For Herod himself had sent men who arrested John, bound him, and put him in prison on account of Herodias, his brother Philip's wife, because Herod*o* had married her. 18For John had been telling Herod, "It is not lawful for you to have your brother's wife." 19And Herodias had a grudge against him, and wanted to kill him. But she could not, 20for Herod feared John, knowing that he was a righteous and holy man, and he protected him. When he heard him, he was greatly

---

j Or *ignoring*; other ancient authorities read *hearing*   *k* Other ancient authorities read *son of the carpenter and of Mary*   *l* Or *stumbled*   *m* Gk *his*   *n* Other ancient authorities read *He was*   *o* Gk *he*

perplexed;[p] and yet he liked to listen to him. 21But an opportunity came when Herod on his birthday gave a banquet for his courtiers and officers and for the leaders of Galilee. 22When his daughter Herodias[q] came in and danced, she pleased Herod and his guests; and the king said to the girl, "Ask me for whatever you wish, and I will give it." 23And he solemnly swore to her, "Whatever you ask me, I will give you, even half of my kingdom." 24She went out and said to her mother, "What should I ask for?" She replied, "The head of John the baptizer." 25Immediately she rushed back to the king and requested, "I want you to give me at once the head of John the Baptist on a platter." 26The king was deeply grieved; yet out of regard for his oaths and for the guests, he did not want to refuse her. 27Immediately the king sent a soldier of the guard with orders to bring John's[r] head. He went and beheaded him in the prison, 28brought his head on a platter, and gave it to the girl. Then the girl gave it to her mother. 29When his disciples heard about it, they came and took his body, and laid it in a tomb.

Feeding the Five Thousand

30 The apostles gathered around Jesus, and told him all that they had done and taught. 31He said to them, "Come away to

p Other ancient authorities read *he did many things*
q Other ancient authorities read *the daughter of Herodias herself*   r Gk *his*

THE TRADITION

Anointing of the Sick

They . . . anointed with oil many who were sick and cured them.

MARK 6.13

Older Catholics remember this as the sacrament with the mysterious and somewhat scary title of Extreme Unction, a "final anointing" in preparation for death. Vatican II renamed it to highlight the sacrament's primary purpose, which is to strengthen those who are seriously ill.

We are encouraged to receive the Anointing of the Sick well *before* arriving at death's door. It is fitting to ask for the sacrament even at the very beginning of serious decline due to illness or old age (see the Vatican II document, "The Constitution on the Sacred Liturgy," 73). The danger of death must be real but need not be immediate. It might take the form of a serious surgery or, for an elderly person, a marked decrease in vitality.

The sacrament of Anointing carries on the healing work of Jesus, who went about "curing every disease and every sickness" and commissioned the Twelve to do the same (Matthew 4.23; Mark 6.13). The early Church continued this practice, as we see in the letter of James, that specifies how sick people should seek healing. "They should call for the elders [priests] of the church and have them pray over them, anointing them with oil in the name of the Lord. The prayer of faith will save the sick, and the Lord will raise them up; and anyone who has committed sins will be forgiven" (James 5.14–15).

Anyone can and should pray for the sick, but only priests can administer the sacrament of Anointing. As they lay hands on the sick, pray over them, and anoint them with blessed oil, it is the Divine Physician himself who visits bedside and battlefield, hospital and nursing home.

With what the *Catechism of the Catholic Church* calls his "preferential love for the sick" (1503), Jesus comes bringing strength and courage to endure the difficulties of illness and old age. Sometimes he restores physical health. Sometimes he prepares the soul to enter into glory. Always he offers peace, forgiveness, and the chance to make suffering fruitful by bringing it before his cross.

a deserted place all by yourselves and rest a while." For many were coming and going, and they had no leisure even to eat. [32]And they went away in the boat to a deserted place by themselves. [33]Now many saw them going and recognized them, and they hurried there on foot from all the towns and arrived ahead of them. [34]As he went ashore, he saw a great crowd; and he had compassion for them, because they were like sheep without a shepherd; and he began to teach them many things. [35]When it grew late, his disciples came to him and said, "This is a deserted place, and the hour is now very late; [36]send them away so that they may go into the surrounding country and villages and buy something for themselves to eat." [37]But he answered them, "You give them something to eat." They said to him, "Are we to go and buy two hundred denarii[s] worth of bread, and give it to them to eat?" [38]And he said to them, "How many loaves have you? Go and see." When they had found out, they said, "Five, and two fish." [39]Then he ordered them to get all the people to sit down in groups on the green grass. [40]So they sat down in groups of hundreds and of fifties. [41]Taking the five loaves and the two fish, he looked up to heaven, and blessed and broke the loaves, and gave them to his disciples to set before the people; and he divided the two fish among them all. [42]And all ate and were filled; [43]and they took up twelve baskets full of broken pieces and of the fish. [44]Those who had eaten the loaves numbered five thousand men.

Jesus Walks on the Water

45 Immediately he made his disciples get into the boat and go on ahead to the other side, to Bethsaida, while he dismissed the crowd. [46]After saying farewell to them, he went up on the mountain to pray.

47 When evening came, the boat was out on the sea, and he was alone on the land. [48]When he saw that they were straining at the oars against an adverse wind, he came towards them early in the morning, walking on the sea. He intended to pass them by. [49]But when they saw him walking on the sea, they thought it was a ghost and cried out; [50]for they all saw him and were terrified. But immediately he spoke to them and said, "Take heart, it is I; do not be afraid." [51]Then he got into the boat

with them and the wind ceased. And they were utterly astounded, [52]for they did not understand about the loaves, but their hearts were hardened.

Healing the Sick in Gennesaret

53 When they had crossed over, they came to land at Gennesaret and moored the boat. [54]When they got out of the boat, people at once recognized him, [55]and rushed about that whole region and began to bring the sick on mats to wherever they heard he was. [56]And wherever he went, into villages or cities or farms, they laid the sick in the marketplaces, and begged him that they might touch even the fringe of his cloak; and all who touched it were healed.

The Tradition of the Elders

7 Now when the Pharisees and some of the scribes who had come from Jerusalem gathered around him, [2]they noticed that some of his disciples were eating with defiled hands, that is, without washing them. [3](For the Pharisees, and all the Jews, do not eat unless they thoroughly wash their hands,[t] thus observing the tradition of the elders; [4]and they do not eat anything from the market unless they wash it;[u] and there are also many other traditions that they observe, the washing of cups, pots, and bronze kettles.[v]) [5]So the Pharisees and the scribes asked him, "Why do your disciples not live[w] according to the tradition of the elders, but eat with defiled hands?" [6]He said to them, "Isaiah prophesied rightly about you hypocrites, as it is written,

'This people honors me with
    their lips,
  but their hearts are far from me;
[7] in vain do they worship me,
    teaching human precepts as
        doctrines.'

[8]You abandon the commandment of God and hold to human tradition."

9 Then he said to them, "You have a fine way of rejecting the commandment of God in order to keep your tradition! [10]For Moses said, 'Honor your father and

---

[s] The denarius was the usual day's wage for a laborer   [t] Meaning of Gk uncertain   [u] Other ancient authorities read *and when they come from the marketplace, they do not eat unless they purify themselves*   [v] Other ancient authorities add *and beds*   [w] Gk *walk*

your 'mother'; and, 'Whoever speaks evil of father or mother must surely die.' [11]But you say that if anyone tells father or mother, 'Whatever support you might have had from me is Corban' (that is, an offering to God[x])— [12]then you no longer permit doing anything for a father or mother, [13]thus making void the word of God through your tradition that you have handed on. And you do many things like this."

14 Then he called the crowd again and said to them, "Listen to me, all of you, and understand: [15]there is nothing outside a person that by going in can defile, but the things that come out are what defile."[y]

17 When he had left the crowd and entered the house, his disciples asked him about the parable. [18]He said to them, "Then do you also fail to understand? Do you not see that whatever goes into a person from outside cannot defile, [19]since it enters, not the heart but the stomach, and goes out into the sewer?" (Thus he declared all foods clean.) [20]And he said, "It is what comes out of a person that defiles. [21]For it is from within, from the human heart, that evil intentions come: fornication, theft, murder, [22]adultery, avarice, wickedness, deceit, licentiousness, envy, slander, pride, folly. [23]All these evil things come from within, and they defile a person."

The Syrophoenician Woman's Faith

24 From there he set out and went away to the region of Tyre.[z] He entered a house and did not want anyone to know he was there. Yet he could not escape notice, [25]but a woman whose little daughter had an unclean spirit immediately heard about him, and she came and bowed down at his feet. [26]Now the woman was a Gentile, of Syrophoenician origin. She begged him to cast the demon out of her daughter. [27]He said to her, "Let the children be fed first, for it is not fair to take the children's food and throw it to the dogs." [28]But she answered him, "Sir,[a] even the dogs under the table eat the children's crumbs." [29]Then he said to her, "For saying that, you may go—the demon has left your daughter." [30]So she went home, found the child lying on the bed, and the demon gone.

Jesus Cures a Deaf Man

31 Then he returned from the region of Tyre, and went by way of Sidon towards the Sea of Galilee, in the region of the Decapolis. [32]They brought to him a deaf man who had an impediment in his speech; and they begged him to lay his hand on him. [33]He took him aside in private, away from the crowd, and put his fingers into his ears, and he spat and touched his tongue. [34]Then looking up to heaven, he sighed and said to him, "Ephphatha," that is, "Be opened." [35]And immediately his ears were opened, his tongue was released, and he spoke plainly. [36]Then Jesus[b] ordered them to tell no one; but the more he ordered them, the more zealously they proclaimed it. [37]They were astounded beyond measure, saying, "He has done everything well; he even makes the deaf to hear and the mute to speak."

Feeding the Four Thousand

8 In those days when there was again a great crowd without anything to eat, he called his disciples and said to them, [2]"I have compassion for the crowd, because they have been with me now for three days and have nothing to eat. [3]If I send them away hungry to their homes, they will faint on the way—and some of them have come from a great distance." [4]His disciples replied, "How can one feed these people with bread here in the desert?" [5]He asked them, "How many loaves do you have?" They said, "Seven." [6]Then he ordered the crowd to sit down on the ground; and he took the seven loaves, and after giving thanks he broke them and gave them to his disciples to distribute; and they distributed them to the crowd. [7]They had also a few small fish; and after blessing them, he ordered that these too should be distributed. [8]They ate and were filled; and they took up the broken pieces left over, seven baskets full. [9]Now there were about four thousand people. And he sent them away. [10]And immediately he got into the boat with his disciples and went to the district of Dalmanutha.[c]

x Gk lacks *to God*   y Other ancient authorities add verse 16, "*Let anyone with ears to hear listen*"
z Other ancient authorities add *and Sidon*   a Or *Lord*; other ancient authorities prefix *Yes*   b Gk *he*   c Other ancient authorities read *Mageda* or *Magdala*

The Demand for a Sign

11 The Pharisees came and began to argue with him, asking him for a sign from heaven, to test him. 12And he sighed deeply in his spirit and said, "Why does this generation ask for a sign? Truly I tell you, no sign will be given to this generation." 13And he left them, and getting into the boat again, he went across to the other side.

The Yeast of the Pharisees and of Herod

14 Now the disciples*d* had forgotten to bring any bread; and they had only one loaf with them in the boat. 15And he cautioned them, saying, "Watch out—beware of the yeast of the Pharisees and the yeast of Herod."*e* 16They said to one another, "It is because we have no bread." 17And becoming aware of it, Jesus said to them, "Why are you talking about having no bread? Do you still not perceive or understand? Are your hearts hardened? 18Do you have eyes, and fail to see? Do you have ears, and fail to hear? And do you not remember? 19When I broke the five loaves for the five thousand, how many baskets full of broken pieces did you collect?" They said to him, "Twelve." 20"And the seven for the four thousand, how many baskets full of broken pieces did you collect?" And they said to him, "Seven." 21Then he said to them, "Do you not yet understand?"

Jesus Cures a Blind Man at Bethsaida

22 They came to Bethsaida. Some people*f* brought a blind man to him and begged him to touch him. 23He took the blind man by the hand and led him out of the village; and when he had put saliva on his eyes and laid his hands on him, he asked him, "Can you see anything?" 24And the man*g* looked up and said, "I can see people, but they look like trees, walking." 25Then Jesus*g* laid his hands on his eyes again; and he looked intently and his sight was restored, and he saw everything clearly. 26Then he sent him away to his home, saying, "Do not even go into the village."*h*

Peter's Declaration about Jesus

27 Jesus went on with his disciples to the villages of Caesarea Philippi; and on the way he asked his disciples, "Who do people say that I am?" 28And they answered him, "John the Baptist; and others, Elijah; and still others, one of the prophets." 29He asked them, "But who do you say that I am?" Peter answered him, "You are the Messiah."*i* 30And he sternly ordered them not to tell anyone about him.

Jesus Foretells His Death and Resurrection

31 Then he began to teach them that the Son of Man must undergo great suffering, and be rejected by the elders, the chief priests, and the scribes, and be killed, and after three days rise again. 32He said all this quite openly. And Peter took him aside and began to rebuke him. 33But turning and looking at his disciples, he rebuked Peter and said, "Get behind me, Satan! For you are setting your mind not on divine things but on human things."

34 He called the crowd with his disciples, and said to them, "If any want to become my followers, let them deny themselves and take up their cross and follow me. 35For those who want to save their life will lose it, and those who lose their life for my sake, and for the sake of the gospel,*j* will save it. 36For what will it profit them to gain the whole world and forfeit their life? 37Indeed, what can they give in return for their life? 38Those who are ashamed of me and of my words*k* in this adulterous and sinful generation, of them the Son of Man will also be ashamed when he comes in the glory of his Father with the holy angels." 9 1And he said to them, "Truly I tell you, there are some standing here who will not taste death until they see that the kingdom of God has come with*l* power."

The Transfiguration

2 Six days later, Jesus took with him Peter and James and John, and led them up a high mountain apart, by themselves. And he was transfigured before them, 3and his clothes became dazzling white, such as no one*m* on earth could bleach them. 4And there appeared to them Elijah with Moses, who were talking with Jesus. 5Then Peter said to Jesus, "Rabbi, it is

---

d Gk they   *e* Other ancient authorities read *the Herodians*   *f* Gk They   *g* Gk he   *h* Other ancient authorities add *or tell anyone in the village*   *i* Or *the Christ*   *j* Other ancient authorities read *lose their life for the sake of the gospel*   *k* Other ancient authorities read *and of mine*   *l* Or *in*   *m* Gk *no fuller*

good for us to be here; let us make three dwellings,[n] one for you, one for Moses, and one for Elijah." [6]He did not know what to say, for they were terrified. [7]Then a cloud overshadowed them, and from the cloud there came a voice, "This is my Son, the Beloved;[o] listen to him!" [8]Suddenly when they looked around, they saw no one with them any more, but only Jesus.

The Coming of Elijah

9 As they were coming down the mountain, he ordered them to tell no one about what they had seen, until after the Son of Man had risen from the dead. [10]So they kept the matter to themselves, questioning what this rising from the dead could mean. [11]Then they asked him, "Why do the scribes say that Elijah must come first?" [12]He said to them, "Elijah is indeed coming first to restore all things. How then is it written about the Son of Man, that he is to go through many sufferings and be treated with contempt? [13]But I tell you that Elijah has come, and they did to him whatever they pleased, as it is written about him."

The Healing of a Boy with a Spirit

14 When they came to the disciples, they saw a great crowd around them, and some scribes arguing with them. [15]When the whole crowd saw him, they were immediately overcome with awe, and they ran forward to greet him. [16]He asked them, "What are you arguing about with them?" [17]Someone from the crowd answered him, "Teacher, I brought you my son; he has a spirit that makes him unable to speak; [18]and whenever it seizes him, it dashes him down; and he foams and grinds his teeth and becomes rigid; and I asked your disciples to cast it out, but they could not do so." [19]He answered them, "You faithless generation, how much longer must I be among you? How much longer must I put up with you? Bring him to me." [20]And they brought the boy[p] to him. When the spirit saw him, immediately it convulsed the boy,[p] and he fell on the ground and rolled about, foaming at the mouth. [21]Jesus[q] asked the father, "How long has this been happening to him?" And he said, "From childhood. [22]It has

[n] Or tents   [o] Or my beloved Son   [p] Gk him
[q] Gk He

Why Me?

In a "Hagar the Horrible" comic strip, one of the characters shakes his fist at the sky. "Why me?" he shouts. In the second panel, a voice calls down from the sky, "Why not you?" It's the lesson everyone must learn—that no one is spared suffering, but I tried to duck the lesson just as most people do. When I first read Jesus' words [in Matthew 10.38] that "whoever does not take up the cross and follow me is not worthy of me," I thought it meant that if I committed to Christ, I was stuck with carrying a cross; whereas if I didn't commit, I might be spared the cross. Such naivete! Crosses are always with us, and most are ones we build for ourselves out of choices we make. What Jesus offers is a chance to find a higher meaning in our suffering. Otherwise, we get into the endless cycle of neurotic pain, which has no meaning at all. It's taken me years to understand that the answer to the question "Why me?" is "Why not me?"

—BARBARA BARTOCCI

THURSDAY

Scripture Reading for Today:
Mark 8.34–38

Verse for Today:
Mark 8.35

Go to page 1330 for your next devotional reading.

often cast him into the fire and into the water, to destroy him; but if you are able to do anything, have pity on us and help us." 23Jesus said to him, "If you are able!— All things can be done for the one who believes." 24Immediately the father of the child cried out,ʳ "I believe; help my unbelief!" 25When Jesus saw that a crowd came running together, he rebuked the unclean spirit, saying to it, "You spirit that keeps this boy from speaking and hearing, I command you, come out of him, and never enter him again!" 26After crying out and convulsing him terribly, it came out, and the boy was like a corpse, so that most of them said, "He is dead." 27But Jesus took him by the hand and lifted him up, and he was able to stand. 28When he had entered the house, his disciples asked him privately, "Why could we not cast it out?" 29He said to them, "This kind can come out only through prayer."ˢ

Jesus Again Foretells His Death and Resurrection

30 They went on from there and passed through Galilee. He did not want anyone to know it; 31for he was teaching his disciples, saying to them, "The Son of Man is to be betrayed into human hands, and they will kill him, and three days after being killed, he will rise again." 32But they did not understand what he was saying and were afraid to ask him.

Who Is the Greatest?

33 Then they came to Capernaum; and when he was in the house he asked them, "What were you arguing about on the way?" 34But they were silent, for on the way they had argued with one another who was the greatest. 35He sat down, called the twelve, and said to them, "Whoever wants to be first must be last of all and servant of all." 36Then he took a little child and put it among them; and taking it in his arms, he said to them, 37"Whoever welcomes one such child in my name welcomes me, and whoever welcomes me welcomes not me but the one who sent me."

Another Exorcist

38 John said to him, "Teacher, we saw someoneᵗ casting out demons in your name, and we tried to stop him, because he was not following us." 39But Jesus said, "Do not stop him; for no one who does a deed of power in my name will be able soon afterward to speak evil of me. 40Whoever is not against us is for us. 41For truly I tell you, whoever gives you a cup of water to drink because you bear the name of Christ will by no means lose the reward.

Temptations to Sin

42 "If any of you put a stumbling block before one of these little ones who believe in me,ᵘ it would be better for you if a great millstone were hung around your neck and you were thrown into the sea. 43If your hand causes you to stumble, cut it off; it is better for you to enter life maimed than to have two hands and to go to hell,ᵛ to the unquenchable fire.ʷ 45And if your foot causes you to stumble, cut it off; it is better for you to enter life lame than to have two feet and to be thrown into hell.ᵛ,ʷ 47And if your eye causes you to stumble, tear it out; it is better for you to enter the kingdom of God with one eye than to have two eyes and to be thrown into hell,ᵛ 48where their worm never dies, and the fire is never quenched.

49 "For everyone will be salted with fire.ˣ 50Salt is good; but if salt has lost its saltiness, how can you season it?ʸ Have salt in yourselves, and be at peace with one another."

Teaching about Divorce

10 He left that place and went to the region of Judea andᶻ beyond the Jordan. And crowds again gathered around him; and, as was his custom, he again taught them.

2 Some Pharisees came, and to test him they asked, "Is it lawful for a man to divorce his wife?" 3He answered them, "What did Moses command you?" 4They said, "Moses allowed a man to write a certificate of dismissal and to divorce her." 5But Jesus said to them, "Because of your hardness of heart he wrote this command-

---

ʳ Other ancient authorities add with tears
ˢ Other ancient authorities add and fasting
ᵗ Other ancient authorities add who does not follow us   ᵘ Other ancient authorities lack in me
ᵛ Gk Gehenna   ʷ Verses 44 and 46 (which are identical with verse 48) are lacking in the best ancient authorities   ˣ Other ancient authorities either add or substitute and every sacrifice will be salted with salt   ʸ Or how can you restore its saltiness?   ᶻ Other ancient authorities lack and

ment for you. 6But from the beginning of creation, 'God made them male and female.' 7'For this reason a man shall leave his father and mother and be joined to his wife,*a* 8and the two shall become one flesh.' So they are no longer two, but one flesh. 9Therefore what God has joined together, let no one separate."

10 Then in the house the disciples asked him again about this matter. 11He said to them, "Whoever divorces his wife and marries another commits adultery against her; 12and if she divorces her husband and marries another, she commits adultery."

Jesus Blesses Little Children

13 People were bringing little children to him in order that he might touch them; and the disciples spoke sternly to them. 14But when Jesus saw this, he was indignant and said to them, "Let the little children come to me; do not stop them; for it is to such as these that the kingdom of God belongs. 15Truly I tell you, whoever does not receive the kingdom of God as a little child will never enter it." 16And he took them up in his arms, laid his hands on them, and blessed them.

The Rich Man

17 As he was setting out on a journey, a man ran up and knelt before him, and asked him, "Good Teacher, what must I do to inherit eternal life?" 18Jesus said to him, "Why do you call me good? No one is good but God alone. 19You know the commandments: 'You shall not murder; You shall not commit adultery; You shall not steal; You shall not bear false witness; You shall not defraud; Honor your father and mother.' " 20He said to him, "Teacher, I have kept all these since my youth." 21Jesus, looking at him, loved him and said, "You lack one thing; go, sell what you own, and give the money*b* to the poor, and you will have treasure in heaven; then come, follow me." 22When he heard this, he was shocked and went away grieving, for he had many possessions.

23 Then Jesus looked around and said to his disciples, "How hard it will be for those who have wealth to enter the kingdom of God!" 24And the disciples were perplexed at these words. But Jesus said to them again, "Children, how hard it is*c* to enter the kingdom of God! 25It is easier for a camel to go through the eye of a

needle than for someone who is rich to enter the kingdom of God." 26They were greatly astounded and said to one another,*d* "Then who can be saved?" 27Jesus looked at them and said, "For mortals it is impossible, but not for God; for God all things are possible."

28 Peter began to say to him, "Look, we have left everything and followed you." 29Jesus said, "Truly I tell you, there is no one who has left house or brothers or sisters or mother or father or children or fields, for my sake and for the sake of the good news,*e* 30who will not receive a hundredfold now in this age—houses, brothers and sisters, mothers and children, and fields, with persecutions—and in the age to come eternal life. 31But many who are first will be last, and the last will be first."

A Third Time Jesus Foretells His Death and Resurrection

32 They were on the road, going up to Jerusalem, and Jesus was walking ahead of them; they were amazed, and those who followed were afraid. He took the twelve aside again and began to tell them what was to happen to him, 33saying, "See, we are going up to Jerusalem, and the Son of Man will be handed over to the chief priests and the scribes, and they will condemn him to death; then they will hand him over to the Gentiles; 34they will mock him, and spit upon him, and flog him, and kill him; and after three days he will rise again."

The Request of James and John

35 James and John, the sons of Zebedee, came forward to him and said to him, "Teacher, we want you to do for us whatever we ask of you." 36And he said to them, "What is it you want me to do for you?" 37And they said to him, "Grant us to sit, one at your right hand and one at your left, in your glory." 38But Jesus said to them, "You do not know what you are asking. Are you able to drink the cup that I drink, or be baptized with the baptism that I am baptized with?" 39They replied, "We are able." Then Jesus said to them,

---

a Other ancient authorities lack *and be joined to his wife*   *b* Gk lacks *the money*   *c* Other ancient authorities add *for those who trust in riches*   *d* Other ancient authorities read *to him*   *e* Or *gospel*

"The cup that I drink you will drink; and with the baptism with which I am baptized, you will be baptized; [40]but to sit at my right hand or at my left is not mine to grant, but it is for those for whom it has been prepared."

41 When the ten heard this, they began to be angry with James and John. [42]So Jesus called them and said to them, "You know that among the Gentiles those whom they recognize as their rulers lord it over them, and their great ones are tyrants over them. [43]But it is not so among you; but whoever wishes to become great among you must be your servant, [44]and whoever wishes to be first among you must be slave of all. [45]For the Son of Man came not to be served but to serve, and to give his life a ransom for many."

The Healing of Blind Bartimaeus

46 They came to Jericho. As he and his disciples and a large crowd were leaving Jericho, Bartimaeus son of Timaeus, a blind beggar, was sitting by the roadside. [47]When he heard that it was Jesus of Nazareth, he began to shout out and say, "Jesus, Son of David, have mercy on me!"

The Kingdom of Heaven

FRIDAY

Scripture Reading for Today:
Mark 10.17–25

Verse for Today:
Mark 10.25

"It is easier for a camel to go through the eye of a needle than for someone who is rich to enter the kingdom of God." Any wealthy person who does not behave in accordance with Jesus' will is risking his eternity. But we are all rich, so long as Jesus is not yet fully alive in us.

Even the beggar, carrying a brown bag with nothing but a sandwich in it and cursing anyone who touches it, is no less rich than any other. His heart is set on something which is not God; unless he makes himself poor, in the gospel sense, he will not pass through into the kingdom of heaven.

The road to get there is a narrow one; only nothingness gets through. There are people who are rich in education, and their swollen-headedness blocks their way into the kingdom and the kingdom's entrance into them; the spirit of divine wisdom finds no room in their soul.

Another is rich in haughty conceit, another in human affections; so long as they do not break with all that, they are not with God. Everything must be excised from the heart and replaced with God and with others in their God-given order of importance. There are people who own a wealth of worries; they don't know how to get rid of them by casting them into God's care. They live tortured lives. The joy and peace and charity of the kingdom of heaven are not theirs.

They cannot pass through.

Others' riches are their sins; they torment themselves by weeping over them, instead of incinerating them in the mercy of God and looking ahead, loving God and neighbor to make up for the times when they have not loved.

—CHIARA LUBICH

Go to page 1332 for your next devotional reading.

⁴⁸Many sternly ordered him to be quiet, but he cried out even more loudly, "Son of David, have mercy on me!" ⁴⁹Jesus stood still and said, "Call him here." And they called the blind man, saying to him, "Take heart; get up, he is calling you." ⁵⁰So throwing off his cloak, he sprang up and came to Jesus. ⁵¹Then Jesus said to him, "What do you want me to do for you?" The blind man said to him, "My teacher,ᶠ let me see again." ⁵²Jesus said to him, "Go; your faith has made you well." Immediately he regained his sight and followed him on the way.

Jesus' Triumphal Entry into Jerusalem

11 When they were approaching Jerusalem, at Bethphage and Bethany, near the Mount of Olives, he sent two of his disciples ²and said to them, "Go into the village ahead of you, and immediately as you enter it, you will find tied there a colt that has never been ridden; untie it and bring it. ³If anyone says to you, 'Why are you doing this?' just say this, 'The Lord needs it and will send it back here immediately.'" ⁴They went away and found a colt tied near a door, outside in the street. As they were untying it, ⁵some of the bystanders said to them, "What are you doing, untying the colt?" ⁶They told them what Jesus had said; and they allowed them to take it. ⁷Then they brought the colt to Jesus and threw their cloaks on it; and he sat on it. ⁸Many people spread their cloaks on the road, and others spread leafy branches that they had cut in the fields. ⁹Then those who went ahead and those who followed were shouting,

"Hosanna!
Blessed is the one who comes in
the name of the Lord!
¹⁰ Blessed is the coming kingdom of
our ancestor David!
Hosanna in the highest heaven!"

11 Then he entered Jerusalem and went into the temple; and when he had looked around at everything, as it was already late, he went out to Bethany with the twelve.

Jesus Curses the Fig Tree

12 On the following day, when they came from Bethany, he was hungry. ¹³Seeing in the distance a fig tree in leaf, he went to see whether perhaps he would find anything on it. When he came to it,

he found nothing but leaves, for it was not the season for figs. ¹⁴He said to it, "May no one ever eat fruit from you again." And his disciples heard it.

Jesus Cleanses the Temple

15 Then they came to Jerusalem. And he entered the temple and began to drive out those who were selling and those who were buying in the temple, and he overturned the tables of the money changers and the seats of those who sold doves; ¹⁶and he would not allow anyone to carry anything through the temple. ¹⁷He was teaching and saying, "Is it not written,

'My house shall be called a house of
prayer for all the nations'?
But you have made it a den
of robbers."

¹⁸And when the chief priests and the scribes heard it, they kept looking for a way to kill him; for they were afraid of him, because the whole crowd was spellbound by his teaching. ¹⁹And when evening came, Jesus and his disciplesᵍ went out of the city.

The Lesson from the Withered Fig Tree

20 In the morning as they passed by, they saw the fig tree withered away to its roots. ²¹Then Peter remembered and said to him, "Rabbi, look! The fig tree that you cursed has withered." ²²Jesus answered them, "Haveʰ faith in God. ²³Truly I tell you, if you say to this mountain, 'Be taken up and thrown into the sea,' and if you do not doubt in your heart, but believe that what you say will come to pass, it will be done for you. ²⁴So I tell you, whatever you ask for in prayer, believe that you have receivedⁱ it, and it will be yours. 25 "Whenever you stand praying, forgive, if you have anything against anyone; so that your Father in heaven may also forgive you your trespasses."ʲ

Jesus' Authority Is Questioned

27 Again they came to Jerusalem. As he was walking in the temple, the chief priests, the scribes, and the elders came to him ²⁸and said, "By what authority are you doing these things? Who gave you

The Mother of Maccabees

THE
STORY
OF A
WOMAN

Her Character: *Courageous beyond human understanding, Scripture describes her as "reinforc[ing] her woman's reasoning with a man's courage."*

Her Sorrow: *To have watched all seven of her sons endure agonizing deaths prior to her own death as a martyr.*

Her Joy: *To know that each of her sons loved God more than they loved their own lives. She believed she would be reunited with them in heaven.*

Read 2 Maccabees 7

Antiochus IV (Epiphanes), eighth ruler of the Seleucid dynasty of Syria, was determined to rule his unruly subjects in Palestine by any means necessary—including slaughter, torture, and religious oppression. In order to force the Jews to adopt Hellenistic customs, he defiled the altar in Jerusalem by sacrificing a pig on it. Prostitutes were brought into the temple and two women who had their babies circumcised were murdered along with their children as a horrifying example of what might happen to Jews foolish enough to ignore his commands.

The story is told in 2 Maccabees of a family of martyrs—a mother and her seven sons who were arrested and tortured with whips and scourges to force them to eat pork, contrary to God's law. To obey the king would entail renouncing their faith and, in essence, assenting to all the evils Antiochus had brought upon their people.

One by one, each son refused to give in, affirming his faith in God and then suffering a hideous death. All the while their mother looked on, encouraging her sons with the words of Moses: "Indeed the LORD will vindicate his people, have compassion on his servants, when he sees that their power is gone, neither bond nor free remaining" (Deuteronomy 32.36).

After six of her sons were murdered, the king changed tactics, promising the youngest son power and wealth if he were merely to abandon his customs. At the king's urging, his mother pretended to dissuade him from following the example of his brothers, whispering what must surely have been the most remarkable advice a mother has ever given her child: "My son, have pity on me. I carried you nine months in my womb, and nursed you for three years, and have reared you and brought you up to this point in your life, and have taken care of you. I beg you, my child, to look at the heaven and the earth and see everything that is in them, and recognize that God did not make them out of things that existed. And in the same way the human race came into being. Do not fear this butcher, but prove worthy of your brothers. Accept death, so that in God's mercy I may get you back again along with your brothers" (2 Maccabees 7.27–29).

Her last son suffered a worse death than all the others. Finally, after every child had perished, the mother herself was killed. Each murder but her own is described in gruesome and hideous detail, perhaps because witnessing the torture and death of your children is the most horrifying thing a woman can suffer.

Though remarkable for her courage, the mother described in Maccabees is also notable for her hope, a woman who believed her children belonged ultimately, not to her, but to a loving God who would reunite them in eternity.

Praying With the Mother of Maccabees

"I do not know how you came into being in my womb. It was not I who gave you life and breath, nor I who set in order the elements within each of you. Therefore the Creator of the world, who shaped the beginning of humankind and devised the origin of all things, will in his mercy give life and breath back to you again, since you now forget yourselves for the sake of his laws."

—2 Maccabees 7.22–23

Praise God: *For creating your children, giving them souls that will live forever.*

Offer Thanks: *That each child is his gift to you.*

Confess: *Any tendency to hold onto your children too tightly.*

Ask God: *To remind you of his care and love for your children, not only as their Creator, but as their Father.*

Lift Your Heart

As mothers we want the best for our children. But the truth is we often settle for second best—preferring their happiness, popularity, and success to anything that might cause them grief. This week, take time to pray for your children in the light of eternity. One way to do that is to reflect on the Beatitudes (see Matthew 5.3–12), praying them on behalf of your children. It is impossible to read these words of Jesus without remembering the radical nature of the gospel—a message that turns our world upside down.

Father, give me the grace of remembering that you shaped and created my children while they were still in the womb, numbering their days before they were born. Help me to realize that the best way of loving them is to encourage them to follow Christ whatever the cost.

Go to page 1335 for your next devotional reading.

this authority to do them?" ²⁹Jesus said to them, "I will ask you one question; answer me, and I will tell you by what authority I do these things. ³⁰Did the baptism of John come from heaven, or was it of human origin? Answer me." ³¹They argued with one another, "If we say, 'From heaven,' he will say, 'Why then did you not believe him?' ³²But shall we say, 'Of human origin'?"—they were afraid of the crowd, for all regarded John as truly a prophet. ³³So they answered Jesus, "We do not know." And Jesus said to them, "Neither will I tell you by what authority I am doing these things."

The Parable of the Wicked Tenants

12 Then he began to speak to them in parables. "A man planted a vineyard, put a fence around it, dug a pit for the wine press, and built a watchtower; then he leased it to tenants and went to another country. ²When the season came, he sent a slave to the tenants to collect from them his share of the produce of the vineyard. ³But they seized him, and beat him, and sent him away empty-handed. ⁴And again he sent another slave to them; this one they beat over the head and insulted. ⁵Then he sent another, and that one they killed. And so it was with many others; some they beat, and others they killed. ⁶He had still one other, a beloved son. Finally he sent him to them, saying, 'They will respect my son.' ⁷But those tenants said to one another, 'This is the heir; come, let us kill him, and the inheritance will be ours.' ⁸So they seized him, killed him, and threw him out of the vineyard. ⁹What then will the owner of the vineyard do? He will come and destroy the tenants and give the vineyard to others. ¹⁰Have you not read this scripture:

'The stone that the builders rejected
    has become the cornerstone;ᵏ
¹¹ this was the Lord's doing,
    and it is amazing in our eyes'?"

12 When they realized that he had told this parable against them, they wanted to arrest him, but they feared the crowd. So they left him and went away.

The Question about Paying Taxes

13 Then they sent to him some Pharisees and some Herodians to trap him in what he said. ¹⁴And they came and said to him, "Teacher, we know that you are sincere, and show deference to no one; for you do not regard people with partiality, but teach the way of God in accordance with truth. Is it lawful to pay taxes to the emperor, or not? ¹⁵Should we pay them, or should we not?" But knowing their hypocrisy, he said to them, "Why are you putting me to the test? Bring me a denarius and let me see it." ¹⁶And they brought one. Then he said to them, "Whose head is this, and whose title?" They answered, "The emperor's." ¹⁷Jesus said to them, "Give to the emperor the things that are the emperor's, and to God the things that are God's." And they were utterly amazed at him.

The Question about the Resurrection

18 Some Sadducees, who say there is no resurrection, came to him and asked him a question, saying, ¹⁹"Teacher, Moses wrote for us that if a man's brother dies, leaving a wife but no child, the manˡ shall marry the widow and raise up children for his brother. ²⁰There were seven brothers; the first married and, when he died, left no children; ²¹and the second married the widowᵐ and died, leaving no children; and the third likewise; ²²none of the seven left children. Last of all the woman herself died. ²³In the resurrectionⁿ whose wife will she be? For the seven had married her."

24 Jesus said to them, "Is not this the reason you are wrong, that you know neither the scriptures nor the power of God? ²⁵For when they rise from the dead, they neither marry nor are given in marriage, but are like angels in heaven. ²⁶And as for the dead being raised, have you not read in the book of Moses, in the story about the bush, how God said to him, 'I am the God of Abraham, the God of Isaac, and the God of Jacob'? ²⁷He is God not of the dead, but of the living; you are quite wrong."

The First Commandment

28 One of the scribes came near and heard them disputing with one another, and seeing that he answered them well, he asked him, "Which commandment is the first of all?" ²⁹Jesus answered, "The first is, 'Hear, O Israel: the Lord our God, the Lord is one; ³⁰you shall love the Lord your God with all your heart, and with all your

---

ᵏ Or *keystone*   ˡ Gk *his brother*   ᵐ Gk *her*
ⁿ Other ancient authorities add *when they rise*

soul, and with all your mind, and with all your strength.' ³¹The second is this, 'You shall love your neighbor as yourself.' There is no other commandment greater than these." ³²Then the scribe said to him, "You are right, Teacher; you have truly said that 'he is one, and besides him there is no other'; ³³and 'to love him with all the heart, and with all the understanding, and with all the strength,' and 'to love one's neighbor as oneself,'—this is much more important than all whole burnt offerings and sacrifices." ³⁴When Jesus saw that he answered wisely, he said to him, "You are not far from the kingdom of God." After that no one dared to ask him any question.

The Question about David's Son

35 While Jesus was teaching in the temple, he said, "How can the scribes say that the Messiah° is the son of David?

° Or the Christ

Loving Your Neighbor

MONDAY

Scripture Reading for Today:
Mark 12.28–34

Verses for Today:
Mark 12.30–31

Catherine of Siena was a mystic who recorded some of her conversations with God in her aptly titled book, The Dialogue. *In this excerpt, the speaker is God the Father.*

I would have you know that every virtue of yours and every vice is put into action by means of your neighbors. If you hate me, you harm your neighbors and yourself as well (for you are your chief neighbor), and the harm is both general and particular.

I say general because it is your duty to love your neighbors as your own self [see Leviticus 19.18; Mark 12.33]. In love you ought to help them spiritually with prayer and counsel, and assist them spiritually and materially in their need—at least with your good will if you have nothing else. If you do not love me, you do not love your neighbors, nor will you help those you do not love. But it is yourself you harm most, because you deprive yourself of grace. And you harm your neighbors by depriving them of the prayer and loving desires you should be offering to me on their behalf. Every help you give them ought to come from the affection you bear them for love of me.

In the same way, every evil is done by means of your neighbors, for you cannot love them if you do not love me. This lack of charity for me and for your neighbors is the source of all evils, for if you are not doing good you are necessarily doing evil. And to whom is this evil shown and done? First of all to yourself and then to your neighbors. You do yourself the harm of sin itself, depriving yourself of grace, and there is nothing worse you can do. You harm your neighbors by not giving them the pleasure of the love and charity you owe them, the love with which you ought to be helping them by offering me your prayer and holy desire on their behalf.

—*SAINT CATHERINE OF SIENA*

Go to page 1345 for your next devotional reading.

36David himself, by the Holy Spirit, declared,

'The Lord said to my Lord,
"Sit at my right hand,
until I put your enemies under
your feet." '

37David himself calls him Lord; so how
can he be his son?" And the large crowd
was listening to him with delight.

Jesus Denounces the Scribes

38 As he taught, he said, "Beware of
the scribes, who like to walk around in
long robes, and to be greeted with respect
in the marketplaces, 39and to have the
best seats in the synagogues and places of
honor at banquets! 40They devour widows' houses and for the sake of appearance say long prayers. They will receive
the greater condemnation."

The Widow's Offering

41 He sat down opposite the treasury,
and watched the crowd putting money
into the treasury. Many rich people put in
large sums. 42A poor widow came and put
in two small copper coins, which are
worth a penny. 43Then he called his disciples and said to them, "Truly I tell you,
this poor widow has put in more than all
those who are contributing to the treasury. 44For all of them have contributed
out of their abundance; but she out of her
poverty has put in everything she had, all
she had to live on."

The Destruction of the Temple Foretold

13 As he came out of the temple,
one of his disciples said to him,
"Look, Teacher, what large stones and
what large buildings!" 2Then Jesus asked
him, "Do you see these great buildings?
Not one stone will be left here upon another; all will be thrown down."

3 When he was sitting on the Mount of
Olives opposite the temple, Peter, James,
John, and Andrew asked him privately,
4"Tell us, when will this be, and what will
be the sign that all these things are about
to be accomplished?" 5Then Jesus began to
say to them, "Beware that no one leads
you astray. 6Many will come in my name
and say, 'I am he!'[p] and they will lead
many astray. 7When you hear of wars and
rumors of wars, do not be alarmed; this
must take place, but the end is still to
come. 8For nation will rise against nation,
and kingdom against kingdom; there will
be earthquakes in various places; there
will be famines. This is but the beginning
of the birth pangs.

Persecution Foretold

9 "As for yourselves, beware; for they
will hand you over to councils; and you
will be beaten in synagogues; and you will
stand before governors and kings because
of me, as a testimony to them. 10And the
good news[q] must first be proclaimed to
all nations. 11When they bring you to trial
and hand you over, do not worry beforehand about what you are to say; but say
whatever is given you at that time, for it is
not you who speak, but the Holy Spirit.
12Brother will betray brother to death, and
a father his child, and children will rise
against parents and have them put to
death; 13and you will be hated by all because of my name. But the one who endures to the end will be saved.

The Desolating Sacrilege

14 "But when you see the desolating
sacrilege set up where it ought not to be
(let the reader understand), then those in
Judea must flee to the mountains; 15the
one on the housetop must not go down or
enter the house to take anything away;
16the one in the field must not turn back
to get a coat. 17Woe to those who are pregnant and to those who are nursing infants
in those days! 18Pray that it may not be in
winter. 19For in those days there will be
suffering, such as has not been from the
beginning of the creation that God created
until now, no, and never will be. 20And if
the Lord had not cut short those days, no
one would be saved; but for the sake of
the elect, whom he chose, he has cut short
those days. 21And if anyone says to you at
that time, 'Look! Here is the Messiah!'[r]
or 'Look! There he is!'—do not believe it.
22False messiahs[s] and false prophets will
appear and produce signs and omens, to
lead astray, if possible, the elect. 23But be
alert; I have already told you everything.

The Coming of the Son of Man

24 "But in those days, after that suffering,

the sun will be darkened,
and the moon will not give
its light,

[p] Gk *I am* [q] Gk *gospel* [r] Or *the Christ* [s] Or *christs*

25 and the stars will be falling
    from heaven,
    and the powers in the heavens
       will be shaken.

26Then they will see 'the Son of Man coming in clouds' with great power and glory. 27Then he will send out the angels, and gather his elect from the four winds, from the ends of the earth to the ends of heaven.

The Lesson of the Fig Tree

28 "From the fig tree learn its lesson: as soon as its branch becomes tender and puts forth its leaves, you know that summer is near. 29So also, when you see these things taking place, you know that he[t] is near, at the very gates. 30Truly I tell you, this generation will not pass away until all these things have taken place. 31Heaven and earth will pass away, but my words will not pass away.

The Necessity for Watchfulness

32 "But about that day or hour no one knows, neither the angels in heaven, nor the Son, but only the Father. 33Beware, keep alert;[u] for you do not know when the time will come. 34It is like a man going on a journey, when he leaves home and puts his slaves in charge, each with his work, and commands the doorkeeper to be on the watch. 35Therefore, keep awake—for you do not know when the master of the house will come, in the evening, or at midnight, or at cockcrow, or at dawn, 36or else he may find you asleep when he comes suddenly. 37And what I say to you I say to all: Keep awake."

The Plot to Kill Jesus

14 It was two days before the Passover and the festival of Unleavened Bread. The chief priests and the scribes were looking for a way to arrest Jesus[v] by stealth and kill him; 2for they said, "Not during the festival, or there may be a riot among the people."

The Anointing at Bethany

3 While he was at Bethany in the house of Simon the leper,[w] as he sat at the table, a woman came with an alabaster jar of very costly ointment of nard, and she broke open the jar and poured the ointment on his head. 4But some were there who said to one another in anger, "Why was the ointment wasted in this way?

5For this ointment could have been sold for more than three hundred denarii,[x] and the money given to the poor." And they scolded her. 6But Jesus said, "Let her alone; why do you trouble her? She has performed a good service for me. 7For you always have the poor with you, and you can show kindness to them whenever you wish; but you will not always have me. 8She has done what she could; she has anointed my body beforehand for its burial. 9Truly I tell you, wherever the good news[y] is proclaimed in the whole world, what she has done will be told in remembrance of her."

Judas Agrees to Betray Jesus

10 Then Judas Iscariot, who was one of the twelve, went to the chief priests in order to betray him to them. 11When they heard it, they were greatly pleased, and promised to give him money. So he began to look for an opportunity to betray him.

The Passover with the Disciples

12 On the first day of Unleavened Bread, when the Passover lamb is sacrificed, his disciples said to him, "Where do you want us to go and make the preparations for you to eat the Passover?" 13So he sent two of his disciples, saying to them, "Go into the city, and a man carrying a jar of water will meet you; follow him, 14and wherever he enters, say to the owner of the house, 'The Teacher asks, Where is my guest room where I may eat the Passover with my disciples?' 15He will show you a large room upstairs, furnished and ready. Make preparations for us there." 16So the disciples set out and went to the city, and found everything as he had told them; and they prepared the Passover meal.

17 When it was evening, he came with the twelve. 18And when they had taken their places and were eating, Jesus said, "Truly I tell you, one of you will betray me, one who is eating with me." 19They began to be distressed and to say to him one after another, "Surely, not I?" 20He said to them, "It is one of the twelve, one who is dipping bread[z] into the bowl[a]

---

[t] Or it   [u] Other ancient authorities add *and pray*
[v] Gk *him*   [w] The terms *leper* and *leprosy* can refer to several diseases   [x] The denarius was the usual day's wage for a laborer   [y] Or *gospel*
[z] Gk lacks *bread*   [a] Other ancient authorities read *same bowl*

with me. ²¹For the Son of Man goes as it is written of him, but woe to that one by whom the Son of Man is betrayed! It would have been better for that one not to have been born."

The Institution of the Lord's Supper

22 While they were eating, he took a loaf of bread, and after blessing it he broke it, gave it to them, and said, "Take; this is my body." ²³Then he took a cup, and after giving thanks he gave it to them, and all of them drank from it. ²⁴He said to them, "This is my blood of the*ᵇ* covenant, which is poured out for many. ²⁵Truly I tell you, I will never again drink of the fruit of the vine until that day when I drink it new in the kingdom of God."

Peter's Denial Foretold

26 When they had sung the hymn, they went out to the Mount of Olives. ²⁷And Jesus said to them, "You will all become deserters; for it is written,

'I will strike the shepherd,
    and the sheep will be scattered.'
²⁸But after I am raised up, I will go before you to Galilee." ²⁹Peter said to him, "Even though all become deserters, I will not." ³⁰Jesus said to him, "Truly I tell you, this day, this very night, before the cock crows twice, you will deny me three times." ³¹But he said vehemently, "Even though I must die with you, I will not deny you." And all of them said the same.

Jesus Prays in Gethsemane

32 They went to a place called Gethsemane; and he said to his disciples, "Sit here while I pray." ³³He took with him Peter and James and John, and began to be distressed and agitated. ³⁴And he said to them, "I am deeply grieved, even to death; remain here, and keep awake." ³⁵And going a little farther, he threw himself on the ground and prayed that, if it were possible, the hour might pass from him. ³⁶He said, "Abba,*ᶜ* Father, for you all things are possible; remove this cup from me; yet, not what I want, but what you want." ³⁷He came and found them sleeping; and he said to Peter, "Simon, are you asleep? Could you not keep awake one hour? ³⁸Keep awake and pray that you may not come into the time of trial;*ᵈ* the spirit indeed is willing, but the flesh is weak." ³⁹And again he went away and prayed, saying the same words. ⁴⁰And once more he came and found them sleeping, for their eyes were very heavy; and they did not know what to say to him. ⁴¹He came a third time and said to them, "Are you still sleeping and taking your rest? Enough! The hour has come; the Son of Man is betrayed into the hands of sinners. ⁴²Get up, let us be going. See, my betrayer is at hand."

The Betrayal and Arrest of Jesus

43 Immediately, while he was still speaking, Judas, one of the twelve, arrived; and with him there was a crowd with swords and clubs, from the chief priests, the scribes, and the elders. ⁴⁴Now the betrayer had given them a sign, saying, "The one I will kiss is the man; arrest him and lead him away under guard." ⁴⁵So when he came, he went up to him at once and said, "Rabbi!" and kissed him. ⁴⁶Then they laid hands on him and arrested him. ⁴⁷But one of those who stood near drew his sword and struck the slave of the high priest, cutting off his ear. ⁴⁸Then Jesus said to them, "Have you come out with swords and clubs to arrest me as though I were a bandit? ⁴⁹Day after day I was with you in the temple teaching, and you did not arrest me. But let the scriptures be fulfilled." ⁵⁰All of them deserted him and fled.

51 A certain young man was following him, wearing nothing but a linen cloth. They caught hold of him, ⁵²but he left the linen cloth and ran off naked.

Jesus before the Council

53 They took Jesus to the high priest; and all the chief priests, the elders, and the scribes were assembled. ⁵⁴Peter had followed him at a distance, right into the courtyard of the high priest; and he was sitting with the guards, warming himself at the fire. ⁵⁵Now the chief priests and the whole council were looking for testimony against Jesus to put him to death; but they found none. ⁵⁶For many gave false testimony against him, and their testimony did not agree. ⁵⁷Some stood up and gave false testimony against him, saying, ⁵⁸"We heard him say, 'I will destroy this temple that is made with hands, and in three days I will build another, not made with hands.' " ⁵⁹But even on this point their testimony did not agree. ⁶⁰Then the

---

ᵇ Other ancient authorities add *new*   *ᶜ* Aramaic for *Father*   *ᵈ* Or *into temptation*

high priest stood up before them and asked Jesus, "Have you no answer? What is it that they testify against you?" 61But he was silent and did not answer. Again the high priest asked him, "Are you the Messiah,*e* the Son of the Blessed One?" 62Jesus said, "I am; and

'you will see the Son of Man
     seated at the right hand of
          the Power,'
and 'coming with the clouds
          of heaven.' "

63Then the high priest tore his clothes and said, "Why do we still need witnesses? 64You have heard his blasphemy! What is your decision?" All of them condemned him as deserving death. 65Some began to spit on him, to blindfold him, and to strike him, saying to him, "Prophesy!" The guards also took him over and beat him.

Peter Denies Jesus

66 While Peter was below in the courtyard, one of the servant-girls of the high priest came by. 67When she saw Peter warming himself, she stared at him and said, "You also were with Jesus, the man from Nazareth." 68But he denied it, saying, "I do not know or understand what you are talking about." And he went out into the forecourt.*f* Then the cock crowed.*g* 69And the servant-girl, on seeing him, began again to say to the bystanders, "This man is one of them." 70But again he denied it. Then after a little while the bystanders again said to Peter, "Certainly you are one of them; for you are a Galilean." 71But he began to curse, and he swore an oath, "I do not know this man you are talking about." 72At that moment the cock crowed for the second time. Then Peter remembered that Jesus had said to him, "Before the cock crows twice, you will deny me three times." And he broke down and wept.

Jesus before Pilate

15 As soon as it was morning, the chief priests held a consultation with the elders and scribes and the whole council. They bound Jesus, led him away, and handed him over to Pilate. 2Pilate asked him, "Are you the King of the Jews?" He answered him, "You say so." 3Then the chief priests accused him of many things. 4Pilate asked him again, "Have you no answer? See how many charges they bring

against you." 5But Jesus made no further reply, so that Pilate was amazed.

Pilate Hands Jesus over to Be Crucified

6 Now at the festival he used to release a prisoner for them, anyone for whom they asked. 7Now a man called Barabbas was in prison with the rebels who had committed murder during the insurrection. 8So the crowd came and began to ask Pilate to do for them according to his custom. 9Then he answered them, "Do you want me to release for you the King of the Jews?" 10For he realized that it was out of jealousy that the chief priests had handed him over. 11But the chief priests stirred up the crowd to have him release Barabbas for them instead. 12Pilate spoke to them again, "Then what do you wish me to do*h* with the man you call*i* the King of the Jews?" 13They shouted back, "Crucify him!" 14Pilate asked them, "Why, what evil has he done?" But they shouted all the more, "Crucify him!" 15So Pilate, wishing to satisfy the crowd, released Barabbas for them; and after flogging Jesus, he handed him over to be crucified.

The Soldiers Mock Jesus

16 Then the soldiers led him into the courtyard of the palace (that is, the governor's headquarters*j*); and they called together the whole cohort. 17And they clothed him in a purple cloak; and after twisting some thorns into a crown, they put it on him. 18And they began saluting him, "Hail, King of the Jews!" 19They struck his head with a reed, spat upon him, and knelt down in homage to him. 20After mocking him, they stripped him of the purple cloak and put his own clothes on him. Then they led him out to crucify him.

The Crucifixion of Jesus

21 They compelled a passer-by, who was coming in from the country, to carry his cross; it was Simon of Cyrene, the father of Alexander and Rufus. 22Then they brought Jesus*k* to the place called Golgotha (which means the place of a skull). 23And they offered him wine mixed with

e Or the Christ   f Or gateway   g Other ancient authorities lack Then the cock crowed   h Other ancient authorities read what should I do   i Other ancient authorities lack the man you call   j Gk the praetorium   k Gk him

myrrh; but he did not take it. ²⁴And they crucified him, and divided his clothes among them, casting lots to decide what each should take.

25 It was nine o'clock in the morning when they crucified him. ²⁶The inscription of the charge against him read, "The King of the Jews." ²⁷And with him they crucified two bandits, one on his right and one on his left.*l* ²⁹Those who passed by derided*m* him, shaking their heads and saying, "Aha! You who would destroy the temple and build it in three days, ³⁰save yourself, and come down from the cross!" ³¹In the same way the chief priests, along with the scribes, were also mocking him among themselves and saying, "He saved others; he cannot save himself. ³²Let the Messiah,*n* the King of Israel, come down

from the cross now, so that we may see and believe." Those who were crucified with him also taunted him.

The Death of Jesus

33 When it was noon, darkness came over the whole land*o* until three in the afternoon. ³⁴At three o'clock Jesus cried out with a loud voice, "Eloi, Eloi, lema sabachthani?" which means, "My God, my God, why have you forsaken me?"*p* ³⁵When some of the bystanders heard it, they said, "Listen, he is calling for Elijah." ³⁶And someone ran, filled a sponge with

l Other ancient authorities add verse 28, *And the scripture was fulfilled that says, "And he was counted among the lawless."*   *m* Or *blasphemed*   *n* Or *the Christ*   *o* Or *earth*   *p* Other ancient authorities read *made me a reproach*

The Stations of the Cross

So Pilate . . . handed him over to be crucified.

MARK 15.15

The Stations of the Cross is a devotion that began as a pilgrimage for non-travelers. It is a journey in spirit to the places where Jesus suffered and died. The fact that we generally make this journey while at church or in the comfort of our homes, without the inconveniences of travel, does not make it safe and predictable. Following Jesus always involves risk.

We owe the Stations of the Cross to Franciscan custodians of the holy places in Jerusalem. In the 14th century they organized a devotional walk down the Via Dolorosa, traditionally considered the route Jesus took to Golgotha. Eight "stations," or prayer stops, recalled specific events from Jesus' Passion. Christians returning home from visits to the Holy Land created symbolic representations of the stations as a way of reliving the pilgrimage experience and sharing it with others. Scenes from pious tradition joined scenes from Scripture to form the 14 stations we now travel, especially

on Holy Saturday and the Fridays of Lent.

The Way of the Cross is still a mini-pilgrimage to the sites of Jesus' Passion and death. But it is also a challenging, often disturbing, journey within. As we accompany Jesus to Calvary, we cannot fail to see that he provokes a variety of negative responses from those around him: Cruelty, indifference, outright rejection, mockery, disgust, idle curiosity . . . and some of these reactions, we must admit, live inside us.

The Way of the Cross is a moment of truth. It confronts us with some hard questions about ourselves: *What about our attitudes? What do our ordinary, everyday choices show about where ours heart are? Are we taking up our crosses and following Christ? Are we recognizing and responding to Christ in the suffering of others?* To follow the Way of the Cross in this spirit is to affirm once again our decision to walk the road that leads to life.

sour wine, put it on a stick, and gave it to him to drink, saying, "Wait, let us see whether Elijah will come to take him down." 37Then Jesus gave a loud cry and breathed his last. 38And the curtain of the temple was torn in two, from top to bottom. 39Now when the centurion, who stood facing him, saw that in this way he*q* breathed his last, he said, "Truly this man was God's Son!"*r*

40 There were also women looking on from a distance; among them were Mary Magdalene, and Mary the mother of James the younger and of Joses, and Salome. 41These used to follow him and provided for him when he was in Galilee; and there were many other women who had come up with him to Jerusalem.

The Burial of Jesus

42 When evening had come, and since it was the day of Preparation, that is, the day before the sabbath, 43Joseph of Arimathea, a respected member of the council, who was also himself waiting expectantly for the kingdom of God, went boldly to Pilate and asked for the body of Jesus. 44Then Pilate wondered if he were already dead; and summoning the centurion, he asked him whether he had been dead for some time. 45When he learned from the centurion that he was dead, he granted the body to Joseph. 46Then Joseph*s* bought a linen cloth, and taking down the body,*t* wrapped it in the linen cloth, and laid it in a tomb that had been hewn out of the rock. He then rolled a stone against the door of the tomb. 47Mary Magdalene and Mary the mother of Joses saw where the body*t* was laid.

The Resurrection of Jesus

16 When the sabbath was over, Mary Magdalene, and Mary the mother of James, and Salome bought spices, so that they might go and anoint him. 2And very early on the first day of the week, when the sun had risen, they went to the tomb. 3They had been saying to one another, "Who will roll away the stone for us from the entrance to the tomb?" 4When they looked up, they saw that the stone, which was very large, had already been rolled back. 5As they entered the tomb, they saw a young man, dressed in a white robe, sitting on the right side; and they were alarmed. 6But he said to them, "Do not be alarmed; you are looking for Jesus

of Nazareth, who was crucified. He has been raised; he is not here. Look, there is the place they laid him. 7But go, tell his disciples and Peter that he is going ahead of you to Galilee; there you will see him, just as he told you." 8So they went out and fled from the tomb, for terror and amazement had seized them; and they said nothing to anyone, for they were afraid.*u*

THE SHORTER ENDING OF MARK

[And all that had been commanded them they told briefly to those around Peter. And afterward Jesus himself sent out through them, from east to west, the sacred and imperishable proclamation of eternal salvation.*v*]

THE LONGER ENDING OF MARK

Jesus Appears to Mary Magdalene

9 [Now after he rose early on the first day of the week, he appeared first to Mary Magdalene, from whom he had cast out seven demons. 10She went out and told those who had been with him, while they were mourning and weeping. 11But when they heard that he was alive and had been seen by her, they would not believe it.

Jesus Appears to Two Disciples

12 After this he appeared in another form to two of them, as they were walking into the country. 13And they went back and told the rest, but they did not believe them.

Jesus Commissions the Disciples

14 Later he appeared to the eleven themselves as they were sitting at the table; and he upbraided them for their lack of faith and stubbornness, because they had not believed those who saw him after

---

q Other ancient authorities add *cried out and*
r Or *a son of God*   *s* Gk *he*   *t* Gk *it*   *u* Some of the most ancient authorities bring the book to a close at the end of verse 8. One authority concludes the book with the shorter ending; others include the shorter ending and then continue with verses 9-20. In most authorities verses 9-20 follow immediately after verse 8, though in some of these authorities the passage is marked as being doubtful.   *v* Other ancient authorities add *Amen*

he had risen.[w] [15]And he said to them, "Go into all the world and proclaim the good news[x] to the whole creation. [16]The one who believes and is baptized will be saved; but the one who does not believe will be condemned. [17]And these signs will accompany those who believe: by using my name they will cast out demons; they will speak in new tongues; [18]they will pick up snakes in their hands,[y] and if they drink any deadly thing, it will not hurt them; they will lay their hands on the sick, and they will recover."

The Ascension of Jesus

19 So then the Lord Jesus, after he had spoken to them, was taken up into heaven and sat down at the right hand of God.

[20]And they went out and proclaimed the good news everywhere, while the Lord worked with them and confirmed the message by the signs that accompanied it.[z]‖

w Other ancient authorities add, in whole or in part, *And they excused themselves, saying, "This age of lawlessness and unbelief is under Satan, who does not allow the truth and power of God to prevail over the unclean things of the spirits. Therefore reveal your righteousness now"*—thus they spoke to Christ. And Christ replied to them, *"The term of years of Satan's power has been fulfilled, but other terrible things draw near. And for those who have sinned I was handed over to death, that they may return to the truth and sin no more, that they may inherit the spiritual and imperishable glory of righteousness that is in heaven."* x Or *gospel*   y Other ancient authorities lack *in their hands*   z Other ancient authorities add *Amen*

The Gospel According to
Luke

The longest of the Gospels, Luke is actually part one of a two-part work that includes the Acts of the Apostles. Luke was probably a Gentile writing to Gentiles. Part of the author's purpose is to show that Jesus came to save the entire world, not just the Jews. Interestingly, while the Gospel of Matthew begins with a genealogy that starts with Abraham, the genealogy found in Luke 3 goes all the way back to Adam—again pointing to the universal significance of Jesus' ministry.

The Gospel of Luke is the only one to include the parables of the good Samaritan, the prodigal son, and Lazarus and the rich man. More than any of the other Gospels, Luke presents Jesus as a man who respects the dignity of women and who loves the poor, who raises up the lowly and forgives sinners, even to the point of asking his Father to forgive those who crucified him (see 23.34). No one is outside the circle of his grace.

Dedication to Theophilus

1 Since many have undertaken to set down an orderly account of the events that have been fulfilled among us, [2]just as they were handed on to us by those who from the beginning were eyewitnesses and servants of the word, [3]I too decided, after investigating everything carefully from the very first,[a] to write an orderly account for you, most excellent Theophilus, [4]so that you may know the truth concerning the things about which you have been instructed.

The Birth of John the Baptist Foretold

5 In the days of King Herod of Judea, there was a priest named Zechariah, who belonged to the priestly order of Abijah. His wife was a descendant of Aaron, and her name was Elizabeth. [6]Both of them were righteous before God, living blamelessly according to all the commandments and regulations of the Lord. [7]But they had no children, because Elizabeth was barren, and both were getting on in years.

8 Once when he was serving as priest before God and his section was on duty, [9]he was chosen by lot, according to the custom of the priesthood, to enter the sanctuary of the Lord and offer incense. [10]Now at the time of the incense offering, the whole assembly of the people was praying outside. [11]Then there appeared to

a Or *for a long time*

him an angel of the Lord, standing at the right side of the altar of incense. [12]When Zechariah saw him, he was terrified; and fear overwhelmed him. [13]But the angel said to him, "Do not be afraid, Zechariah, for your prayer has been heard. Your wife Elizabeth will bear you a son, and you will name him John. [14]You will have joy and gladness, and many will rejoice at his birth, [15]for he will be great in the sight of the Lord. He must never drink wine or strong drink; even before his birth he will be filled with the Holy Spirit. [16]He will turn many of the people of Israel to the Lord their God. [17]With the spirit and power of Elijah he will go before him, to turn the hearts of parents to their children, and the disobedient to the wisdom of the righteous, to make ready a people prepared for the Lord." [18]Zechariah said to the angel, "How will I know that this is so? For I am an old man, and my wife is getting on in years." [19]The angel replied, "I am Gabriel. I stand in the presence of God, and I have been sent to speak to you and to bring you this good news. [20]But now, because you did not believe my words, which will be fulfilled in their time, you will become mute, unable to speak, until the day these things occur."

21 Meanwhile the people were waiting for Zechariah, and wondered at his delay in the sanctuary. [22]When he did come out, he could not speak to them, and they realized that he had seen a vision in the sanctuary. He kept motioning to them and remained unable to speak. [23]When his time of service was ended, he went to his home.

24 After those days his wife Elizabeth conceived, and for five months she remained in seclusion. She said, [25]"This is what the Lord has done for me when he looked favorably on me and took away the disgrace I have endured among my people."

The Birth of Jesus Foretold

26 In the sixth month the angel Gabriel was sent by God to a town in Galilee called Nazareth, [27]to a virgin engaged to a man whose name was Joseph, of the house of David. The virgin's name was Mary. [28]And he came to her and said, "Greetings, favored one! The Lord is with you."[b] [29]But she was much perplexed by his words and pondered what sort of greeting this might be. [30]The angel said to

her, "Do not be afraid, Mary, for you have found favor with God. [31]And now, you will conceive in your womb and bear a son, and you will name him Jesus. [32]He will be great, and will be called the Son of the Most High, and the Lord God will give to him the throne of his ancestor David. [33]He will reign over the house of Jacob forever, and of his kingdom there will be no end." [34]Mary said to the angel, "How can this be, since I am a virgin?"[c] [35]The angel said to her, "The Holy Spirit will come upon you, and the power of the Most High will overshadow you; therefore the child to be born[d] will be holy; he will be called Son of God. [36]And now, your relative Elizabeth in her old age has also conceived a son; and this is the sixth month for her who was said to be barren. [37]For nothing will be impossible with God." [38]Then Mary said, "Here am I, the servant of the Lord; let it be with me according to your word." Then the angel departed from her.

Mary Visits Elizabeth

39 In those days Mary set out and went with haste to a Judean town in the hill country, [40]where she entered the house of Zechariah and greeted Elizabeth. [41]When Elizabeth heard Mary's greeting, the child leaped in her womb. And Elizabeth was filled with the Holy Spirit [42]and exclaimed with a loud cry, "Blessed are you among women, and blessed is the fruit of your womb. [43]And why has this happened to me, that the mother of my Lord comes to me? [44]For as soon as I heard the sound of your greeting, the child in my womb leaped for joy. [45]And blessed is she who believed that there would be[e] a fulfillment of what was spoken to her by the Lord."

Mary's Song of Praise

46 And Mary[f] said,
"My soul magnifies the Lord,
[47]   and my spirit rejoices in God
        my Savior,
[48] for he has looked with favor on the
        lowliness of his servant.

b Other ancient authorities add Blessed are you among women   c Gk I do not know a man d Other ancient authorities add of you   e Or believed, for there will be   f Other ancient authorities read Elizabeth

Surely, from now on all
generations will call
me blessed;
49 for the Mighty One has done great
things for me,
and holy is his name.
50 His mercy is for those who fear him
from generation to generation.
51 He has shown strength with his
arm;

When You Don't Feel Blessed

TUESDAY

Scripture Reading
for Today:
Luke 1.26–38

Verse for Today:
Luke 1.28

It must have felt both strange and wonderful to be called "favored" by an angel and then "blessed among women" by her cousin Elizabeth. Yet I wonder if these greetings came back to haunt Mary years later.

Did the terrible irony of Elizabeth's greeting, "blessed are you," pierce her memory as she watched her son stumble through Jerusalem, bearing a cross on his shoulders? Did the angel's promise that her child would be called the "Son of the Most High" ring mockingly in her ears as she stared at the bitter notice nailed to the wood above his head: "Jesus of Nazareth, the King of the Jews"?

Was she tempted to think, "If this is what it means to be blessed, I don't want your blessing, God!"

We don't know. The Scriptures are silent. Yet we do know that Mary was found with the disciples in the upper room when the Holy Spirit descended upon them like fire. Like them, she was praying and seeking God, no doubt searching her own soul but still clinging to his promises.

Mary's tenacity in the face of confusion, anxiety, disappointment, and terrible grief can be a source of comfort and strength. Have you ever received a message from God, a promise or a blessing, only to find that his definition of blessing or his timing and yours were out of sync?

Resist the temptation to let go of whatever God has said to you through his word. Admit that you may not fully understand what he has spoken or promised, but ask him to show you and to give you faith as his word unfolds. Don't become discouraged if you don't feel blessed right away. Have faith in the Father and in his timing. It isn't naive to say that his timing is perfect. It's the simple truth.

Practice the tenacious faith of Mary, of Elizabeth, of Jesus himself. If you do, you may indeed suffer for a time, but you will surely receive great blessings from a gracious God.

—ANN SPANGLER

Go to page 1348 for your next devotional reading.

he has scattered the proud in the
> thoughts of their hearts.
52 He has brought down the powerful
> from their thrones,
> and lifted up the lowly;
53 he has filled the hungry with
> good things,
> and sent the rich away empty.
54 He has helped his servant Israel,
> in remembrance of his mercy,
55 according to the promise he made to
> our ancestors,
> to Abraham and to his
> descendants forever."

56 And Mary remained with her about three months and then returned to her home.

The Birth of John the Baptist

57 Now the time came for Elizabeth to give birth, and she bore a son. 58Her neighbors and relatives heard that the Lord had shown his great mercy to her, and they rejoiced with her.

59 On the eighth day they came to circumcise the child, and they were going to name him Zechariah after his father. 60But his mother said, "No; he is to be called John." 61They said to her, "None of your relatives has this name." 62Then they began motioning to his father to find out what name he wanted to give him. 63He asked for a writing tablet and wrote, "His name is John." And all of them were amazed. 64Immediately his mouth was opened and his tongue freed, and he began to speak, praising God. 65Fear came over all their neighbors, and all these things were talked about throughout the entire hill country of Judea. 66All who heard them pondered them and said, "What then will this child become?" For, indeed, the hand of the Lord was with him.

Zechariah's Prophecy

67 Then his father Zechariah was filled with the Holy Spirit and spoke this prophecy:
68 "Blessed be the Lord God of Israel,
> for he has looked favorably on his
> people and redeemed them.
69 He has raised up a mighty savior[g]
> for us
> in the house of his servant David,
70 as he spoke through the mouth of
> his holy prophets from of
> old,

71 that we would be saved from our
> enemies and from the hand
> of all who hate us.
72 Thus he has shown the mercy
> promised to our ancestors,
> and has remembered his
> holy covenant,
73 the oath that he swore to our
> ancestor Abraham,
> to grant us 74that we, being
> rescued from the hands of
> our enemies,
> might serve him without fear, 75in
> holiness and righteousness
> before him all our days.
76 And you, child, will be called the
> prophet of the Most High;
> for you will go before the Lord to
> prepare his ways,
77 to give knowledge of salvation to his
> people
> by the forgiveness of their sins.
78 By the tender mercy of our God,
> the dawn from on high will break
> upon[h] us,
79 to give light to those who sit in
> darkness and in the shadow
> of death,
> to guide our feet into the way
> of peace."

80 The child grew and became strong in spirit, and he was in the wilderness until the day he appeared publicly to Israel.

The Birth of Jesus

2 In those days a decree went out from Emperor Augustus that all the world should be registered. 2This was the first registration and was taken while Quirinius was governor of Syria. 3All went to their own towns to be registered. 4Joseph also went from the town of Nazareth in Galilee to Judea, to the city of David called Bethlehem, because he was descended from the house and family of David. 5He went to be registered with Mary, to whom he was engaged and who was expecting a child. 6While they were there, the time came for her to deliver her child. 7And she gave birth to her firstborn son and wrapped him in bands of cloth, and laid him in a manger, because there was no place for them in the inn.

g Gk *a horn of salvation*   h Other ancient authorities read *has broken upon*

The Shepherds and the Angels

8 In that region there were shepherds living in the fields, keeping watch over their flock by night. 9Then an angel of the Lord stood before them, and the glory of the Lord shone around them, and they were terrified. 10But the angel said to them, "Do not be afraid; for see—I am bringing you good news of great joy for all the people: 11to you is born this day in the city of David a Savior, who is the Messiah,[i] the Lord. 12This will be a sign for you: you will find a child wrapped in bands of cloth and lying in a manger." 13And suddenly there was with the angel a multitude of the heavenly host,[j] praising God and saying,

14 "Glory to God in the highest heaven,
      and on earth peace among those whom he favors!"[k]

15 When the angels had left them and gone into heaven, the shepherds said to one another, "Let us go now to Bethlehem and see this thing that has taken place, which the Lord has made known to us." 16So they went with haste and found Mary and Joseph, and the child lying in the manger. 17When they saw this, they made known what had been told them about this child; 18and all who heard it were amazed at what the shepherds told them. 19But Mary treasured all these words and pondered them in her heart. 20The shepherds returned, glorifying and praising God for all they had heard and seen, as it had been told them.

Jesus Is Named

21 After eight days had passed, it was time to circumcise the child; and he was called Jesus, the name given by the angel before he was conceived in the womb.

Jesus Is Presented in the Temple

22 When the time came for their purification according to the law of Moses, they brought him up to Jerusalem to present him to the Lord 23(as it is written in the law of the Lord, "Every firstborn male shall be designated as holy to the Lord"), 24and they offered a sacrifice according to what is stated in the law of the Lord, "a pair of turtledoves or two young pigeons."

25 Now there was a man in Jerusalem whose name was Simeon;[l] this man was righteous and devout, looking forward to the consolation of Israel, and the Holy Spirit rested on him. 26It had been revealed to him by the Holy Spirit that he would not see death before he had seen the Lord's Messiah.[m] 27Guided by the Spirit, Simeon[n] came into the temple; and when the parents brought in the child Jesus, to do for him what was customary under the law, 28Simeon[o] took him in his arms and praised God, saying,

29 "Master, now you are dismissing
         your servant[p] in peace,
      according to your word;
30 for my eyes have seen your
         salvation,
31   which you have prepared in the
         presence of all peoples,
32 a light for revelation to the Gentiles
      and for glory to your people
         Israel."

33 And the child's father and mother were amazed at what was being said about him. 34Then Simeon[l] blessed them and said to his mother Mary, "This child is destined for the falling and the rising of many in Israel, and to be a sign that will be opposed 35so that the inner thoughts of many will be revealed—and a sword will pierce your own soul too."

36 There was also a prophet, Anna[q] the daughter of Phanuel, of the tribe of Asher. She was of a great age, having lived with her husband seven years after her marriage, 37then as a widow to the age of eighty-four. She never left the temple but worshiped there with fasting and prayer night and day. 38At that moment she came, and began to praise God and to speak about the child[r] to all who were looking for the redemption of Jerusalem.

The Return to Nazareth

39 When they had finished everything required by the law of the Lord, they returned to Galilee, to their own town of Nazareth. 40The child grew and became strong, filled with wisdom; and the favor of God was upon him.

The Boy Jesus in the Temple

41 Now every year his parents went to

---

i Or the Christ   j Gk army   k Other ancient authorities read peace, goodwill among people
l Gk Symeon   m Or the Lord's Christ   n Gk In the Spirit, he   o Gk he   p Gk slave   q Gk Hanna   r Gk him

Jerusalem for the festival of the Passover. ⁴²And when he was twelve years old, they went up as usual for the festival. ⁴³When the festival was ended and they started to return, the boy Jesus stayed behind in Jerusalem, but his parents did not know it. ⁴⁴Assuming that he was in the group of travelers, they went a day's journey. Then they started to look for him among their relatives and friends. ⁴⁵When they did not find him, they returned to Jerusalem to search for him. ⁴⁶After three days they found him in the temple, sitting among the teachers, listening to them and asking them questions. ⁴⁷And all who heard him were amazed at his understanding and his answers. ⁴⁸When his parents⁵ saw him they were astonished; and his mother said to him, "Child, why have you treated us like this? Look, your father and I have

been searching for you in great anxiety." ⁴⁹He said to them, "Why were you searching for me? Did you not know that I must be in my Father's house?"ᵗ ⁵⁰But they did not understand what he said to them. ⁵¹Then he went down with them and came to Nazareth, and was obedient to them. His mother treasured all these things in her heart.

52 And Jesus increased in wisdom and in years,ᵘ and in divine and human favor.

The Proclamation of John the Baptist

3 In the fifteenth year of the reign of Emperor Tiberius, when Pontius Pilate was governor of Judea, and Herod

⁵ Gk *they*   ᵗ Or *be about my Father's interests?*
ᵘ Or *in stature*

WEDNESDAY

Scripture Reading
for Today:
Luke 2.22–38

Verse for Today:
Luke 2.38

Messengers

Think of it: Anna the aged woman and Mary the very young woman meeting at such a crucial time. How much Mary must have needed her. Anna's early widowhood had given her a fuller understanding of life. She knew what suffering was. Her many years in the temple deepened her relationship with God. She knew what surrender and fidelity meant. Anna came as a sign of hope and a source of strength for Mary. She came as a comfort to this young mother who had just learned that she would have much sorrow in the future.

I have always been struck by the scriptural detail which tells us that Anna came by just "at that moment." Our "Annas" come when we need them. They come "just at the right time" in the form of a phone call, a letter, a person at the door, a compassionate nurse at a bedside. They may not say a lot to us, may not even realize how profoundly they are a messenger of hope to us. But we know . . . and we gain courage from their presence. They bring us a touch of comfort and hope as we embark upon a time of suffering. Our "Annas" are messengers from God. They are compassion-filled people who are not afraid to be with someone who is hurting. They are faith-filled people who bring us encouragement as much by their presence as through their words. They are hope-filled people who bless us by their constant certainty of our ability to overcome adversity.

—*JOYCE RUPP*

Go to page 1351 for your next devotional reading.

was ruler[v] of Galilee, and his brother Philip ruler[v] of the region of Ituraea and Trachonitis, and Lysanias ruler[v] of Abilene, [2]during the high priesthood of Annas and Caiaphas, the word of God came to John son of Zechariah in the wilderness. [3]He went into all the region around the Jordan, proclaiming a baptism of repentance for the forgiveness of sins, [4]as it is written in the book of the words of the prophet Isaiah,

"The voice of one crying out in
        the wilderness:
'Prepare the way of the Lord,
        make his paths straight.
[5] Every valley shall be filled,
        and every mountain and hill shall
                be made low,
    and the crooked shall be made
                straight,
        and the rough ways made smooth;
[6] and all flesh shall see the salvation
                of God.' "

7 John said to the crowds that came out to be baptized by him, "You brood of vipers! Who warned you to flee from the wrath to come? [8]Bear fruits worthy of repentance. Do not begin to say to yourselves, 'We have Abraham as our ancestor'; for I tell you, God is able from these stones to raise up children to Abraham. [9]Even now the ax is lying at the root of the trees; every tree therefore that does not bear good fruit is cut down and thrown into the fire."

10 And the crowds asked him, "What then should we do?" [11]In reply he said to them, "Whoever has two coats must share with anyone who has none; and whoever has food must do likewise." [12]Even tax collectors came to be baptized, and they asked him, "Teacher, what should we do?" [13]He said to them, "Collect no more than the amount prescribed for you." [14]Soldiers also asked him, "And we, what should we do?" He said to them, "Do not extort money from anyone by threats or false accusation, and be satisfied with your wages."

15 As the people were filled with expectation, and all were questioning in their hearts concerning John, whether he might be the Messiah,[w] [16]John answered all of them by saying, "I baptize you with water; but one who is more powerful than I is coming; I am not worthy to untie the thong of his sandals. He will baptize you with[x] the Holy Spirit and fire. [17]His winnowing fork is in his hand, to clear his threshing floor and to gather the wheat into his granary; but the chaff he will burn with unquenchable fire."

18 So, with many other exhortations, he proclaimed the good news to the people. [19]But Herod the ruler,[v] who had been rebuked by him because of Herodias, his brother's wife, and because of all the evil things that Herod had done, [20]added to them all by shutting up John in prison.

The Baptism of Jesus

21 Now when all the people were baptized, and when Jesus also had been baptized and was praying, the heaven was opened, [22]and the Holy Spirit descended upon him in bodily form like a dove. And a voice came from heaven, "You are my Son, the Beloved;[y] with you I am well pleased."[z]

The Ancestors of Jesus

23 Jesus was about thirty years old when he began his work. He was the son (as was thought) of Joseph son of Heli, [24]son of Matthat, son of Levi, son of Melchi, son of Jannai, son of Joseph, [25]son of Mattathias, son of Amos, son of Nahum, son of Esli, son of Naggai, [26]son of Maath, son of Mattathias, son of Semein, son of Josech, son of Joda, [27]son of Joanan, son of Rhesa, son of Zerubbabel, son of Shealtiel,[a] son of Neri, [28]son of Melchi, son of Addi, son of Cosam, son of Elmadam, son of Er, [29]son of Joshua, son of Eliezer, son of Jorim, son of Matthat, son of Levi, [30]son of Simeon, son of Judah, son of Joseph, son of Jonam, son of Eliakim, [31]son of Melea, son of Menna, son of Mattatha, son of Nathan, son of David, [32]son of Jesse, son of Obed, son of Boaz, son of Sala,[b] son of Nahshon, [33]son of Amminadab, son of Admin, son of Arni,[c] son of Hezron, son of Perez, son of Judah, [34]son of Jacob, son of Isaac, son of Abraham, son of Terah, son of Nahor, [35]son of Serug, son of Reu, son of Peleg, son of Eber, son of Shelah, [36]son of Cainan, son of

v Gk tetrarch   w Or the Christ   x Or in   y Or
my beloved Son   z Other ancient authorities read
You are my Son, today I have begotten you   a Gk
Salathiel   b Other ancient authorities read
Salmon   c Other ancient authorities read
Amminadab, son of Aram; others vary widely

Arphaxad, son of Shem, son of Noah, son of Lamech, ³⁷son of Methuselah, son of Enoch, son of Jared, son of Mahalaleel, son of Cainan, ³⁸son of Enos, son of Seth, son of Adam, son of God.

The Temptation of Jesus

4 Jesus, full of the Holy Spirit, returned from the Jordan and was led by the Spirit in the wilderness, ²where for forty days he was tempted by the devil. He ate nothing at all during those days, and when they were over, he was famished. ³The devil said to him, "If you are the Son of God, command this stone to become a loaf of bread." ⁴Jesus answered him, "It is written, 'One does not live by bread alone.' "

5 Then the devil*ᵈ* led him up and showed him in an instant all the king- doms of the world. ⁶And the devil*ᵈ* said to him, "To you I will give their glory and all this authority; for it has been given over to me, and I give it to anyone I please. ⁷If you, then, will worship me, it will all be yours." ⁸Jesus answered him, "It is written,

'Worship the Lord your God,
    and serve only him.' "

9 Then the devil*ᵈ* took him to Jerusa- lem, and placed him on the pinnacle of the temple, saying to him, "If you are the Son of God, throw yourself down from here, ¹⁰for it is written,

'He will command his angels
        concerning you,
    to protect you,'
¹¹and

ᵈ Gk *he*

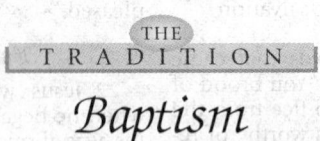

THE TRADITION

Baptism

"You are my Son, the Beloved."
LUKE 3.22

I t is opening day at the playground, and just about every child in the city is testing out the new equipment. Parents sit nearby, chatting through the din of excited shrieks and squeals.

A little girl scrapes her knee and begins to cry, her voice barely audible over the clamor. Immediately, a mother straightens up, eyes moving quickly to a sad little figure in the crowd.

"Amy, what's wrong? Are you hurt?"

Parents have their lapses, but normally they are like this mother: attuned and alert to their children's needs and welfare. Having ac- cepted parenthood, they open their hearts wide to dependent little beings who lay claim to their love and attention. Something similar happens through the sacrament of Baptism.

Baptism opens us to God's love in a new way, drawing us into his family. It tells us we are God's children, with a place in the Father's house and at his table. We become sisters and brothers of Jesus, with a share in his mis- sion and inheritance, and through the gift of the Holy Spirit, we share in Jesus' own inti- mate relationship with the Father.

Baptism represents a dramatic rescue— even more dramatic than those adoptions where children who face a lifetime of sick- ness, poverty, and abuse are whisked away into loving homes. Through that rescue we escape Satan's clutches and sin's power, and we undergo an identity change so radical that it is more rebirth than adoption. "So if anyone is in Christ, there is a new creation" (2 Corinthians 5.17). When we are baptized, we are joined to Jesus—marked as the Father's own, with special claims on his love and at- tention. "My beloved Son," the Father called Jesus. "My beloved daughter," the Father now calls us.

No carefree child on a playground could ever know more confidence and security than we possess as our baptismal birthright!

'On their hands they will bear you up,
  so that you will not dash your
    foot against a stone.' "
12Jesus answered him, "It is said, 'Do not put the Lord your God to the test.' "
13When the devil had finished every test, he departed from him until an opportune time.

The Beginning
of the Galilean Ministry

14 Then Jesus, filled with the power of the Spirit, returned to Galilee, and a report about him spread through all the surrounding country. 15He began to teach in their synagogues and was praised by everyone.

*W*ilderness Faith

THURSDAY

Scripture Reading
for Today:
Luke 4.1–13

Verse for Today:
Luke 4.1

The Holy Spirit initiated a season in Jesus' life in which he would endure testing and temptation. At times, the Spirit will also lead us into the wilderness to endure a time of trial. It may be a wilderness of loneliness, illness, misunderstanding, poverty, failure, or doubt. Whatever the case, we can take courage from this crucial episode in Jesus' life. For Jesus' wilderness experience actually prepared him for his public ministry. The miracles, the preaching, the healings would all characterize the most tremendous ministry the world had ever seen. But not before Jesus engaged in a fierce and terrible spiritual combat.

If you find yourself in the wilderness, perhaps you should be encouraged. God may be preparing you for a time of greater fruitfulness and joy. Such times often do not emerge without a struggle. That struggle may involve facing your own sinfulness and lack of faith. Your enemy wants to convince you that God has abandoned you and that you are good for nothing. In this kind of desert, remember to cling to God. Just as Jesus prayed and fasted, keeping in vital communion with his Father, make sure that you are holding fast to God. You can't possibly face evil on your own and win. But with patience and faith you can emerge stronger and more hopeful than before.

At times you will be tempted to escape the wilderness. If you're lonely, you might find yourself rationalizing an unhealthy relationship. If you're anxious about the future, you might become obsessed with finding ways to protect yourself and your family from financial hardship. If you haven't been able to bear children, you might be tempted to try medical treatments you believe to be unethical in order to conceive. Whatever your temptations, resist the enemy and ask God for the strength to go on.

There will be an end to your wilderness. That will be a time of rejoicing, a time of moving once again in power and confidence, a time of blessing as God continues to fulfill his purpose for your life.

—*ANN SPANGLER*

Go to page 1354 for your next devotional reading.

The Rejection of Jesus at Nazareth

16 When he came to Nazareth, where he had been brought up, he went to the synagogue on the sabbath day, as was his custom. He stood up to read, [17]and the scroll of the prophet Isaiah was given to him. He unrolled the scroll and found the place where it was written:
18 "The Spirit of the Lord is upon me,
        because he has anointed me
            to bring good news to the poor.
    He has sent me to proclaim release
            to the captives
        and recovery of sight to the blind,
            to let the oppressed go free,
19 to proclaim the year of the Lord's
            favor."
[20]And he rolled up the scroll, gave it back to the attendant, and sat down. The eyes of all in the synagogue were fixed on him. [21]Then he began to say to them, "Today this scripture has been fulfilled in your hearing." [22]All spoke well of him and were amazed at the gracious words that came from his mouth. They said, "Is not this Joseph's son?" [23]He said to them, "Doubtless you will quote to me this proverb, 'Doctor, cure yourself!' And you will say, 'Do here also in your hometown the things that we have heard you did at Capernaum.' " [24]And he said, "Truly I tell you, no prophet is accepted in the prophet's hometown. [25]But the truth is, there were many widows in Israel in the time of Elijah, when the heaven was shut up three years and six months, and there was a severe famine over all the land; [26]yet Elijah was sent to none of them except to a widow at Zarephath in Sidon. [27]There were also many lepers[e] in Israel in the time of the prophet Elisha, and none of them was cleansed except Naaman the Syrian." [28]When they heard this, all in the synagogue were filled with rage. [29]They got up, drove him out of the town, and led him to the brow of the hill on which their town was built, so that they might hurl him off the cliff. [30]But he passed through the midst of them and went on his way.

The Man with an Unclean Spirit

31 He went down to Capernaum, a city in Galilee, and was teaching them on the sabbath. [32]They were astounded at his teaching, because he spoke with authority. [33]In the synagogue there was a man who had the spirit of an unclean demon, and he cried out with a loud voice, [34]"Let us alone! What have you to do with us, Jesus of Nazareth? Have you come to destroy us? I know who you are, the Holy One of God." [35]But Jesus rebuked him, saying, "Be silent, and come out of him!" When the demon had thrown him down before them, he came out of him without having done him any harm. [36]They were all amazed and kept saying to one another, "What kind of utterance is this? For with authority and power he commands the unclean spirits, and out they come!" [37]And a report about him began to reach every place in the region.

Healings at Simon's House

38 After leaving the synagogue he entered Simon's house. Now Simon's mother-in-law was suffering from a high fever, and they asked him about her. [39]Then he stood over her and rebuked the fever, and it left her. Immediately she got up and began to serve them.

40 As the sun was setting, all those who had any who were sick with various kinds of diseases brought them to him; and he laid his hands on each of them and cured them. [41]Demons also came out of many, shouting, "You are the Son of God!" But he rebuked them and would not allow them to speak, because they knew that he was the Messiah.[f]

Jesus Preaches in the Synagogues

42 At daybreak he departed and went into a deserted place. And the crowds were looking for him; and when they reached him, they wanted to prevent him from leaving them. [43]But he said to them, "I must proclaim the good news of the kingdom of God to the other cities also; for I was sent for this purpose." [44]So he continued proclaiming the message in the synagogues of Judea.[g]

Jesus Calls the First Disciples

5 Once while Jesus[h] was standing beside the lake of Gennesaret, and the crowd was pressing in on him to hear the word of God, [2]he saw two boats there at the shore of the lake; the fishermen had gone out of them and were washing their nets. [3]He got into one of the boats, the

---

e The terms *leper* and *leprosy* can refer to several diseases   *f* Or *the Christ*   *g* Other ancient authorities read *Galilee*   *h* Gk *he*

one belonging to Simon, and asked him to put out a little way from the shore. Then he sat down and taught the crowds from the boat. 4When he had finished speaking, he said to Simon, "Put out into the deep water and let down your nets for a catch." 5Simon answered, "Master, we have worked all night long but have caught nothing. Yet if you say so, I will let down the nets." 6When they had done this, they caught so many fish that their nets were beginning to break. 7So they signaled their partners in the other boat to come and help them. And they came and filled both boats, so that they began to sink. 8But when Simon Peter saw it, he fell down at Jesus' knees, saying, "Go away from me, Lord, for I am a sinful man!" 9For he and all who were with him were amazed at the catch of fish that they had taken; 10and so also were James and John, sons of Zebedee, who were partners with Simon. Then Jesus said to Simon, "Do not be afraid; from now on you will be catching people." 11When they had brought their boats to shore, they left everything and followed him.

Jesus Cleanses a Leper

12 Once, when he was in one of the cities, there was a man covered with leprosy.*i* When he saw Jesus, he bowed with his face to the ground and begged him, "Lord, if you choose, you can make me clean." 13Then Jesus*j* stretched out his hand, touched him, and said, "I do choose. Be made clean." Immediately the leprosy*i* left him. 14And he ordered him to tell no one. "Go," he said, "and show yourself to the priest, and, as Moses commanded, make an offering for your cleansing, for a testimony to them." 15But now more than ever the word about Jesus*k* spread abroad; many crowds would gather to hear him and to be cured of their diseases. 16But he would withdraw to deserted places and pray.

Jesus Heals a Paralytic

17 One day, while he was teaching, Pharisees and teachers of the law were sitting near by (they had come from every village of Galilee and Judea and from Jerusalem); and the power of the Lord was with him to heal.*l* 18Just then some men came, carrying a paralyzed man on a bed. They were trying to bring him in and lay him before Jesus;*k* 19but finding no way

to bring him in because of the crowd, they went up on the roof and let him down with his bed through the tiles into the middle of the crowd*m* in front of Jesus. 20When he saw their faith, he said, "Friend,*n* your sins are forgiven you." 21Then the scribes and the Pharisees began to question, "Who is this who is speaking blasphemies? Who can forgive sins but God alone?" 22When Jesus perceived their questionings, he answered them, "Why do you raise such questions in your hearts? 23Which is easier, to say, 'Your sins are forgiven you,' or to say, 'Stand up and walk'? 24But so that you may know that the Son of Man has authority on earth to forgive sins"—he said to the one who was paralyzed—"I say to you, stand up and take your bed and go to your home." 25Immediately he stood up before them, took what he had been lying on, and went to his home, glorifying God. 26Amazement seized all of them, and they glorified God and were filled with awe, saying, "We have seen strange things today."

Jesus Calls Levi

27 After this he went out and saw a tax collector named Levi, sitting at the tax booth; and he said to him, "Follow me." 28And he got up, left everything, and followed him.

29 Then Levi gave a great banquet for him in his house; and there was a large crowd of tax collectors and others sitting at the table*o* with them. 30The Pharisees and their scribes were complaining to his disciples, saying, "Why do you eat and drink with tax collectors and sinners?" 31Jesus answered, "Those who are well have no need of a physician, but those who are sick; 32I have come to call not the righteous but sinners to repentance."

The Question about Fasting

33 Then they said to him, "John's disciples, like the disciples of the Pharisees, frequently fast and pray, but your disciples eat and drink." 34Jesus said to them, "You cannot make wedding guests fast while the bridegroom is with them, can you? 35The days will come when the

---

i The terms leper and leprosy can refer to several diseases   j Gk he   k Gk him   l Other ancient authorities read was present to heal them   m Gk into the midst   n Gk Man   o Gk reclining

bridegroom will be taken away from
them, and then they will fast in those
days." 36 He also told them a parable: "No
one tears a piece from a new garment and
sews it on an old garment; otherwise the
new will be torn, and the piece from the
new will not match the old. 37 And no one
puts new wine into old wineskins; otherwise the new wine will burst the skins and
will be spilled, and the skins will be destroyed. 38 But new wine must be put into
fresh wineskins. 39 And no one after drinking old wine desires new wine, but says,
'The old is good.' "[p]

The Question about the Sabbath

6 One sabbath[q] while Jesus[r] was going through the grainfields, his disciples plucked some heads of grain, rubbed
them in their hands, and ate them. 2 But
some of the Pharisees said, "Why are you
doing what is not lawful[s] on the sabbath?" 3 Jesus answered, "Have you not
read what David did when he and his
companions were hungry? 4 He entered
the house of God and took and ate the
bread of the Presence, which it is not lawful for any but the priests to eat, and gave
some to his companions?" 5 Then he said to
them, "The Son of Man is lord of the sabbath."

The Man with a Withered Hand

6 On another sabbath he entered the
synagogue and taught, and there was a
man there whose right hand was withered. 7 The scribes and the Pharisees
watched him to see whether he would
cure on the sabbath, so that they might
find an accusation against him. 8 Even
though he knew what they were thinking,
he said to the man who had the withered
hand, "Come and stand here." He got up
and stood there. 9 Then Jesus said to them,

[p] Other ancient authorities read *better*; others lack verse 39 [q] Other ancient authorities read *On the second first sabbath* [r] Gk *he* [s] Other ancient authorities add *to do*

FRIDAY

Healed, Body and Soul

Scripture Reading for Today: *Luke 5.17–26*

Verse for Today: *Luke 5.20*

Anyone could have spoken a word of false comfort to the paralyzed man, telling him his sins were forgiven, but only God had the power to enable him to get off his mat and walk out the door. Clearly, Jesus had powers over the soul as well as the body.

The people who crowded the house where Jesus was preaching had seen the man's atrophied limbs. But Jesus had seen his atrophied soul. So he dealt with what was inside the man before touching and restoring what was on the outside.

So often, we come to God asking for a miracle: to cure a sick friend, bring back a wayward child, heal an eating disorder, save a troubled marriage. We think we know what will make us whole and happy again. But God always penetrates the surface of our need to deal with the core problem. He is not interested in performing miracles that only display his power. He wants to perform miracles that reveal his love. And so he deals, not just with our pain, but with the source of our pain, not just with the infirmity of our bodies, but with the infirmity of our hearts. Like the paralytic's friends, we are called to pray with faith. As we do, God will forgive our sins.

—ANN SPANGLER

Go to page 1356 for your next devotional reading.

"I ask you, is it lawful to do good or to do harm on the sabbath, to save life or to destroy it?" [10]After looking around at all of them, he said to him, "Stretch out your hand." He did so, and his hand was restored. [11]But they were filled with fury and discussed with one another what they might do to Jesus.

Jesus Chooses the Twelve Apostles

12 Now during those days he went out to the mountain to pray; and he spent the night in prayer to God. [13]And when day came, he called his disciples and chose twelve of them, whom he also named apostles: [14]Simon, whom he named Peter, and his brother Andrew, and James, and John, and Philip, and Bartholomew, [15]and Matthew, and Thomas, and James son of Alphaeus, and Simon, who was called the Zealot, [16]and Judas son of James, and Judas Iscariot, who became a traitor.

Jesus Teaches and Heals

17 He came down with them and stood on a level place, with a great crowd of his disciples and a great multitude of people from all Judea, Jerusalem, and the coast of Tyre and Sidon. [18]They had come to hear him and to be healed of their diseases; and those who were troubled with unclean spirits were cured. [19]And all in the crowd were trying to touch him, for power came out from him and healed all of them.

Blessings and Woes

20 Then he looked up at his disciples and said:
"Blessed are you who are poor,
    for yours is the kingdom of God.
[21] "Blessed are you who are
        hungry now,
    for you will be filled.
"Blessed are you who weep now,
    for you will laugh.
22 "Blessed are you when people hate you, and when they exclude you, revile you, and defame you[t] on account of the Son of Man. [23]Rejoice in that day and leap for joy, for surely your reward is great in heaven; for that is what their ancestors did to the prophets.
24 "But woe to you who are rich,
    for you have received your
        consolation.
25 "Woe to you who are full now,

for you will be hungry.
"Woe to you who are laughing now,
    for you will mourn and weep.
26 "Woe to you when all speak well of you, for that is what their ancestors did to the false prophets.

Love for Enemies

27 "But I say to you that listen, Love your enemies, do good to those who hate you, [28]bless those who curse you, pray for those who abuse you. [29]If anyone strikes you on the cheek, offer the other also; and from anyone who takes away your coat do not withhold even your shirt. [30]Give to everyone who begs from you; and if anyone takes away your goods, do not ask for them again. [31]Do to others as you would have them do to you.
32 "If you love those who love you, what credit is that to you? For even sinners love those who love them. [33]If you do good to those who do good to you, what credit is that to you? For even sinners do the same. [34]If you lend to those from whom you hope to receive, what credit is that to you? Even sinners lend to sinners, to receive as much again. [35]But love your enemies, do good, and lend, expecting nothing in return.[u] Your reward will be great, and you will be children of the Most High; for he is kind to the ungrateful and the wicked. [36]Be merciful, just as your Father is merciful.

Judging Others

37 "Do not judge, and you will not be judged; do not condemn, and you will not be condemned. Forgive, and you will be forgiven; [38]give, and it will be given to you. A good measure, pressed down, shaken together, running over, will be put into your lap; for the measure you give will be the measure you get back."
39 He also told them a parable: "Can a blind person guide a blind person? Will not both fall into a pit? [40]A disciple is not above the teacher, but everyone who is fully qualified will be like the teacher. [41]Why do you see the speck in your neighbor's[v] eye, but do not notice the log in your own eye? [42]Or how can you say to your neighbor,[w] 'Friend,[w] let me take out the speck in your eye,' when you your-

---

[t] Gk *cast out your name as evil*   [u] Other ancient authorities read *despairing of no one*   [v] Gk *brother's*   [w] Gk *brother*

The Woman of Proverbs 31

THE
STORY
OF A
WOMAN

Her Character: *She represents the fulfillment of a life lived in wisdom.*
Her Joy: *To be praised by her husband and children as a woman who surpasses all others.*

Read Proverbs 31.10–31

Proverbs brims with less-than-glowing descriptions of women. There are wayward wives, prostitutes, women with smoother-than-oil lips, strange women, loud women, defiant women, wives who are like a continual drip on a rainy day or rottenness in their husbands' bones, women whose feet never stay home, impudent women, and even a woman so repulsive she is likened to a gold ring in a pig's snout!

Any woman reading Proverbs may be tempted to conclude that its authors blamed women for weaknesses actually rooted in the male psyche, especially when it came to sexual sin. But to balance things out there are at least a few odious descriptions of men, including scoundrels, villains, chattering fools, and sluggards. And Proverbs actually opens and closes with positive portrayals of women: first as wisdom personified and then as a woman who can do no wrong.

But just who is this lady on a pedestal described in Proverbs 31? Is she, as many think, the ideal wife and mother? In traditional Jewish homes, husbands and children recited the poem in Proverbs 31 at the Sabbath table. Written as an acrostic, each line begins with a Hebrew letter in alphabetical sequence, making it easy to memorize. The poem describes a wealthy, aristocratic woman with a large household to direct. She is hard-working, enterprising, capable, strong, wise, skilled, generous, thoughtful of others, dignified, God-fearing, serene—a tremendous credit to her husband. She rises while it is still dark to feed her family. She looks at a field, assesses its value, and purchases it. She weaves cloth and makes linen garments, which she then sells. "Her children rise up and call her happy; her husband too, and he praises her: 'Many women have done excellently, but you surpass them all' " (verses 28–29).

The description of the woman in Proverbs 31 offers a refreshing contrast to other ancient depictions of women, which tend to portray them in more frivolous terms, emphasizing only their charm or beauty. Still, the perfect woman of Proverbs 31 hasn't always been a friend to ordinary women. In fact, she has sometimes been rubbed into the faces of lesser women by critical husbands and preachers unable to resist the temptation. What woman could ever measure up to her? And is a woman's worth to be measured only by what she can accomplish in the domestic sphere? Or was the lady in Proverbs 31 a symbol of all the contributions a woman could make within the culture of her day? Regardless of how you answer these questions, there is more to her story than simply being the ideal wife and mother.

The woman of Proverbs 31 may well be meant to inspire both men and women with a picture of what a virtuous life, male or female, is capable of producing—shelter for others, serenity, honor, prosperity, generosity, confidence about the future—true blessedness. Who wouldn't want to be like such a woman? Who wouldn't sing her praises?

Praying With the Woman of Proverbs 31

For whoever finds [wisdom] finds life and obtains favor from the LORD.
—Proverbs 8.35

Praise God: *For the gift of wisdom, which preserves, blesses, and even prolongs your life.*

Offer Thanks: *For the benefits of wisdom you have already tasted in your daily life.*

Confess: *Any tendency to choose the wisdom of the world over the wisdom of God.*

Ask God: *Every day to make you a woman who longs for wisdom, who prefers it to silver and gold.*

Lift Your Heart

Wisdom has nothing to do with how much "gray matter" you possess. You can be smart as a whip but still full of foolishness. Take a few moments to reflect on this condensed and paraphrased passage from the book of Proverbs: "Blessed is the woman who has found wisdom. She has found something more precious than gold. None of her desires can compare with wisdom. For wisdom brings life, wealth, honor, and peace. Wisdom is a tree of life to be gladly embraced" (3.13–18).

Here are a few vital suggestions for cultivating wisdom in your life:

Pray for it, remembering it is a gift from God.

Read and meditate regularly on Scripture.

Surround yourself with wise friends—listen and learn from them. (Consider meeting regularly with a spiritual director.)

Make quick obedience a hallmark of your spiritual life; it leads to wisdom.

Lord, you are the source of the wisdom that brings life, wealth, honor, and peace. May wisdom be like a growing tree in my life, bearing abundant fruit and providing shelter for others.

Go to page 1360 for your next devotional reading.

self do not see the log in your own eye? You hypocrite, first take the log out of your own eye, and then you will see clearly to take the speck out of your neighbor's[x] eye.

A Tree and Its Fruit

43 "No good tree bears bad fruit, nor again does a bad tree bear good fruit; 44for each tree is known by its own fruit. Figs are not gathered from thorns, nor are grapes picked from a bramble bush. 45The good person out of the good treasure of the heart produces good, and the evil person out of evil treasure produces evil; for it is out of the abundance of the heart that the mouth speaks.

The Two Foundations

46 "Why do you call me 'Lord, Lord,' and do not do what I tell you? 47I will show you what someone is like who comes to me, hears my words, and acts on them. 48That one is like a man building a house, who dug deeply and laid the foundation on rock; when a flood arose, the river burst against that house but could not shake it, because it had been well built.[y] 49But the one who hears and does not act is like a man who built a house on the ground without a foundation. When the river burst against it, immediately it fell, and great was the ruin of that house."

Jesus Heals a Centurion's Servant

7 After Jesus[z] had finished all his sayings in the hearing of the people, he entered Capernaum. 2A centurion there had a slave whom he valued highly, and who was ill and close to death. 3When he heard about Jesus, he sent some Jewish elders to him, asking him to come and heal his slave. 4When they came to Jesus, they appealed to him earnestly, saying, "He is worthy of having you do this for him, 5for he loves our people, and it is he who built our synagogue for us." 6And Jesus went with them, but when he was not far from the house, the centurion sent friends to say to him, "Lord, do not trouble yourself, for I am not worthy to have you come under my roof; 7therefore I did not presume to come to you. But only speak the word, and let my servant be healed. 8For I also am a man set under authority, with soldiers under me; and I say to one, 'Go,' and he goes, and to another, 'Come,' and he comes, and to my slave, 'Do this,' and the slave does it." 9When Jesus heard this he was amazed at him, and turning to the crowd that followed him, he said, "I tell you, not even in Israel have I found such faith." 10When those who had been sent returned to the house, they found the slave in good health.

Jesus Raises the Widow's Son at Nain

11 Soon afterwards[a] he went to a town called Nain, and his disciples and a large crowd went with him. 12As he approached the gate of the town, a man who had died was being carried out. He was his mother's only son, and she was a widow; and with her was a large crowd from the town. 13When the Lord saw her, he had compassion for her and said to her, "Do not weep." 14Then he came forward and touched the bier, and the bearers stood still. And he said, "Young man, I say to you, rise!" 15The dead man sat up and began to speak, and Jesus[z] gave him to his mother. 16Fear seized all of them; and they glorified God, saying, "A great prophet has risen among us!" and "God has looked favorably on his people!" 17This word about him spread throughout Judea and all the surrounding country.

Messengers from John the Baptist

18 The disciples of John reported all these things to him. So John summoned two of his disciples 19and sent them to the Lord to ask, "Are you the one who is to come, or are we to wait for another?" 20When the men had come to him, they said, "John the Baptist has sent us to you to ask, 'Are you the one who is to come, or are we to wait for another?'" 21Jesus[b] had just then cured many people of diseases, plagues, and evil spirits, and had given sight to many who were blind. 22And he answered them, "Go and tell John what you have seen and heard: the blind receive their sight, the lame walk, the lepers[c] are cleansed, the deaf hear, the dead are raised, the poor have good news brought to them. 23And blessed is anyone who takes no offense at me."

24 When John's messengers had gone,

---

x Gk *brother's* y Other ancient authorities read *founded upon the rock* z Gk *he* a Other ancient authorities read *Next day* b Gk *He* c The terms *leper* and *leprosy* can refer to several diseases

Jesus[d] began to speak to the crowds about John:[e] "What did you go out into the wilderness to look at? A reed shaken by the wind? [25]What then did you go out to see? Someone[f] dressed in soft robes? Look, those who put on fine clothing and live in luxury are in royal palaces. [26]What then did you go out to see? A prophet? Yes, I tell you, and more than a prophet. [27]This is the one about whom it is written,

'See, I am sending my messenger
      ahead of you,
   who will prepare your way
      before you.'

[28]I tell you, among those born of women no one is greater than John; yet the least in the kingdom of God is greater than he." [29](And all the people who heard this, including the tax collectors, acknowledged the justice of God,[g] because they had been baptized with John's baptism. [30]But by refusing to be baptized by him, the Pharisees and the lawyers rejected God's purpose for themselves.)

31 "To what then will I compare the people of this generation, and what are they like? [32]They are like children sitting in the marketplace and calling to one another,

'We played the flute for you, and
      you did not dance;
   we wailed, and you did not weep.'

[33]For John the Baptist has come eating no bread and drinking no wine, and you say, 'He has a demon'; [34]the Son of Man has come eating and drinking, and you say, 'Look, a glutton and a drunkard, a friend of tax collectors and sinners!' [35]Nevertheless, wisdom is vindicated by all her children."

A Sinful Woman Forgiven

36 One of the Pharisees asked Jesus[e] to eat with him, and he went into the Pharisee's house and took his place at the table. [37]And a woman in the city, who was a sinner, having learned that he was eating in the Pharisee's house, brought an alabaster jar of ointment. [38]She stood behind him at his feet, weeping, and began to bathe his feet with her tears and to dry them with her hair. Then she continued kissing his feet and anointing them with the ointment. [39]Now when the Pharisee who had invited him saw it, he said to himself, "If this man were a prophet, he would have known who and what kind of

woman this is who is touching him—that she is a sinner." [40]Jesus spoke up and said to him, "Simon, I have something to say to you." "Teacher," he replied, "speak." [41]"A certain creditor had two debtors; one owed five hundred denarii,[h] and the other fifty. [42]When they could not pay, he canceled the debts for both of them. Now which of them will love him more?" [43]Simon answered, "I suppose the one for whom he canceled the greater debt." And Jesus[d] said to him, "You have judged rightly." [44]Then turning toward the woman, he said to Simon, "Do you see this woman? I entered your house; you gave me no water for my feet, but she has bathed my feet with her tears and dried them with her hair. [45]You gave me no kiss, but from the time I came in she has not stopped kissing my feet. [46]You did not anoint my head with oil, but she has anointed my feet with ointment. [47]Therefore, I tell you, her sins, which were many, have been forgiven; hence she has shown great love. But the one to whom little is forgiven, loves little." [48]Then he said to her, "Your sins are forgiven." [49]But those who were at the table with him began to say among themselves, "Who is this who even forgives sins?" [50]And he said to the woman, "Your faith has saved you; go in peace."

Some Women Accompany Jesus

8 Soon afterwards he went on through cities and villages, proclaiming and bringing the good news of the kingdom of God. The twelve were with him, [2]as well as some women who had been cured of evil spirits and infirmities: Mary, called Magdalene, from whom seven demons had gone out, [3]and Joanna, the wife of Herod's steward Chuza, and Susanna, and many others, who provided for them[i] out of their resources.

The Parable of the Sower

4 When a great crowd gathered and people from town after town came to him, he said in a parable: [5]"A sower went out to sow his seed; and as he sowed, some fell on the path and was trampled

[d] Gk he   [e] Gk him   [f] Or Why then did you go out? To see someone   [g] Or praised God   [h] The denarius was the usual day's wage for a laborer   [i] Other ancient authorities read him

on, and the birds of the air ate it up. ⁶Some fell on the rock; and as it grew up, it withered for lack of moisture. ⁷Some fell among thorns, and the thorns grew with it and choked it. ⁸Some fell into good soil, and when it grew, it produced a hundred-fold." As he said this, he called out, "Let anyone with ears to hear listen!"

The Purpose of the Parables

9 Then his disciples asked him what

Women Are Called

MONDAY

Scripture Reading for Today:
Luke 8.1–3

Verses for Today:
Luke 8.2–3

Women were called to follow Jesus. *Yeah, yeah, yeah,* we think. But consider the social pressures women faced in answering Jesus' call to follow. Respectable women in first-century Judaism and society were not to be seen in public; they couldn't speak to a man in public; they could not be taught the Torah; they could never follow a rabbi; they could not make ethical decisions without the supervision of a father or husband. Even if the women didn't know better, Jesus should have known that he wasn't allowed to call women, to speak to them, to teach them, to touch and be touched by them, to eat food they had prepared, to use them as illustrations in stories.

[Nonetheless,] Jesus called women to be his followers. His call to women and his call to men were identical. The primary call to men and women is a call to discipleship.

When Jesus calls women to follow him as disciples, he is calling them to grow up, to take responsibility for their lives. This was a new experience for the women whom Jesus called. They were legally minors, unable to witness in a court of law or make decisions about property. The first-century Jewish woman's spiritual life was really the property of the family—her access to God was through the patriarchal family system.

Jesus defied cultural norms and treated women as adults. He demanded their theological reflection and challenged women to follow him.

Growing up can be frightening. Many women today know the feeling of being less than grown up, the terror of facing the call to maturity. Many women have assumed that someone will look after them; they don't know what to do when the car breaks down or the furnace quits.

We don't care much for the message of Jesus. Martha was a competent cook, for heaven's sake. Why push her into trying to think about theological issues? Why demand that she have a life quest as a disciple in her own right? She was pretty happy—why force her to grow up? Because it's part of the call to follow Jesus as a full disciple.

—*MARY ELLEN ASHCROFT*

Go to page 1364 for your next devotional reading.

this parable meant. [10]He said, "To you it has been given to know the secrets[j] of the kingdom of God; but to others I speak[k] in parables, so that

> 'looking they may not perceive,
>   and listening they may not
>   understand.'

The Parable of the Sower Explained

11 "Now the parable is this: The seed is the word of God. [12]The ones on the path are those who have heard; then the devil comes and takes away the word from their hearts, so that they may not believe and be saved. [13]The ones on the rock are those who, when they hear the word, receive it with joy. But these have no root; they believe only for a while and in a time of testing fall away. [14]As for what fell among the thorns, these are the ones who hear; but as they go on their way, they are choked by the cares and riches and pleasures of life, and their fruit does not mature. [15]But as for that in the good soil, these are the ones who, when they hear the word, hold it fast in an honest and good heart, and bear fruit with patient endurance.

A Lamp under a Jar

16 "No one after lighting a lamp hides it under a jar, or puts it under a bed, but puts it on a lampstand, so that those who enter may see the light. [17]For nothing is hidden that will not be disclosed, nor is anything secret that will not become known and come to light. [18]Then pay attention to how you listen; for to those who have, more will be given; and from those who do not have, even what they seem to have will be taken away."

The True Kindred of Jesus

19 Then his mother and his brothers came to him, but they could not reach him because of the crowd. [20]And he was told, "Your mother and your brothers are standing outside, wanting to see you." [21]But he said to them, "My mother and my brothers are those who hear the word of God and do it."

Jesus Calms a Storm

22 One day he got into a boat with his disciples, and he said to them, "Let us go across to the other side of the lake." So they put out, [23]and while they were sailing he fell asleep. A windstorm swept down on the lake, and the boat was filling with water, and they were in danger. [24]They went to him and woke him up, shouting, "Master, Master, we are perishing!" And he woke up and rebuked the wind and the raging waves; they ceased, and there was a calm. [25]He said to them, "Where is your faith?" They were afraid and amazed, and said to one another, "Who then is this, that he commands even the winds and the water, and they obey him?"

Jesus Heals the Gerasene Demoniac

26 Then they arrived at the country of the Gerasenes,[l] which is opposite Galilee. [27]As he stepped out on land, a man of the city who had demons met him. For a long time he had worn[m] no clothes, and he did not live in a house but in the tombs. [28]When he saw Jesus, he fell down before him and shouted at the top of his voice, "What have you to do with me, Jesus, Son of the Most High God? I beg you, do not torment me"— [29]for Jesus[n] had commanded the unclean spirit to come out of the man. (For many times it had seized him; he was kept under guard and bound with chains and shackles, but he would break the bonds and be driven by the demon into the wilds.) [30]Jesus then asked him, "What is your name?" He said, "Legion"; for many demons had entered him. [31]They begged him not to order them to go back into the abyss.

32 Now there on the hillside a large herd of swine was feeding; and the demons[o] begged Jesus[p] to let them enter these. So he gave them permission. [33]Then the demons came out of the man and entered the swine, and the herd rushed down the steep bank into the lake and was drowned.

34 When the swineherds saw what had happened, they ran off and told it in the city and in the country. [35]Then people came out to see what had happened, and when they came to Jesus, they found the man from whom the demons had gone sitting at the feet of Jesus, clothed and in his right mind. And they were afraid. [36]Those who had seen it told them how

---

[j] Or *mysteries*   [k] Gk lacks *I speak*   [l] Other ancient authorities read *Gadarenes*; others, *Gergesenes*   [m] Other ancient authorities read *a man of the city who had had demons for a long time met him. He wore*   [n] Gk *he*   [o] Gk *they*   [p] Gk *him*

the one who had been possessed by demons had been healed. [37]Then all the people of the surrounding country of the Gerasenes[q] asked Jesus[r] to leave them; for they were seized with great fear. So he got into the boat and returned. [38]The man from whom the demons had gone begged that he might be with him; but Jesus[s] sent him away, saying, [39]"Return to your home, and declare how much God has done for you." So he went away, proclaiming throughout the city how much Jesus had done for him.

A Girl Restored to Life and a Woman Healed

40 Now when Jesus returned, the crowd welcomed him, for they were all waiting for him. [41]Just then there came a man named Jairus, a leader of the synagogue. He fell at Jesus' feet and begged him to come to his house, [42]for he had an only daughter, about twelve years old, who was dying.

As he went, the crowds pressed in on him. [43]Now there was a woman who had been suffering from hemorrhages for twelve years; and though she had spent all she had on physicians,[t] no one could cure her. [44]She came up behind him and touched the fringe of his clothes, and immediately her hemorrhage stopped. [45]Then Jesus asked, "Who touched me?" When all denied it, Peter[u] said, "Master, the crowds surround you and press in on you." [46]But Jesus said, "Someone touched me; for I noticed that power had gone out from me." [47]When the woman saw that she could not remain hidden, she came trembling; and falling down before him, she declared in the presence of all the people why she had touched him, and how she had been immediately healed. [48]He said to her, "Daughter, your faith has made you well; go in peace."

49 While he was still speaking, someone came from the leader's house to say, "Your daughter is dead; do not trouble the teacher any longer." [50]When Jesus heard this, he replied, "Do not fear. Only believe, and she will be saved." [51]When he came to the house, he did not allow anyone to enter with him, except Peter, John, and James, and the child's father and mother. [52]They were all weeping and wailing for her; but he said, "Do not weep; for she is not dead but sleeping." [53]And they laughed at him, knowing that she was dead. [54]But he took her by the hand and called out, "Child, get up!" [55]Her spirit returned, and she got up at once. Then he directed them to give her something to eat. [56]Her parents were astounded; but he ordered them to tell no one what had happened.

The Mission of the Twelve

9 Then Jesus[s] called the twelve together and gave them power and authority over all demons and to cure diseases, [2]and he sent them out to proclaim the kingdom of God and to heal. [3]He said to them, "Take nothing for your journey, no staff, nor bag, nor bread, nor money—not even an extra tunic. [4]Whatever house you enter, stay there, and leave from there. [5]Wherever they do not welcome you, as you are leaving that town shake the dust off your feet as a testimony against them." [6]They departed and went through the villages, bringing the good news and curing diseases everywhere.

Herod's Perplexity

7 Now Herod the ruler[v] heard about all that had taken place, and he was perplexed, because it was said by some that John had been raised from the dead, [8]by some that Elijah had appeared, and by others that one of the ancient prophets had arisen. [9]Herod said, "John I beheaded; but who is this about whom I hear such things?" And he tried to see him.

Feeding the Five Thousand

10 On their return the apostles told Jesus[r] all they had done. He took them with him and withdrew privately to a city called Bethsaida. [11]When the crowds found out about it, they followed him; and he welcomed them, and spoke to them about the kingdom of God, and healed those who needed to be cured.

12 The day was drawing to a close, and the twelve came to him and said, "Send the crowd away, so that they may go into the surrounding villages and countryside, to lodge and get provisions; for we are here in a deserted place." [13]But he said to them, "You give them something to eat."

q Other ancient authorities read *Gadarenes;* others, *Gergesenes*   *r* Gk *him*   *s* Gk *he*   *t* Other ancient authorities lack *and though she had spent all she had on physicians*   *u* Other ancient authorities add *and those who were with him*   *v* Gk *tetrarch*

They said, "We have no more than five loaves and two fish—unless we are to go and buy food for all these people." [14]For there were about five thousand men. And he said to his disciples, "Make them sit down in groups of about fifty each." [15]They did so and made them all sit down. [16]And taking the five loaves and the two fish, he looked up to heaven, and blessed and broke them, and gave them to the disciples to set before the crowd. [17]And all ate and were filled. What was left over was gathered up, twelve baskets of broken pieces.

Peter's Declaration about Jesus

18 Once when Jesus[w] was praying alone, with only the disciples near him, he asked them, "Who do the crowds say that I am?" [19]They answered, "John the Baptist; but others, Elijah; and still others, that one of the ancient prophets has arisen." [20]He said to them, "But who do you say that I am?" Peter answered, "The Messiah[x] of God."

Jesus Foretells His Death and Resurrection

21 He sternly ordered and commanded them not to tell anyone, [22]saying, "The Son of Man must undergo great suffering, and be rejected by the elders, chief priests, and scribes, and be killed, and on the third day be raised."
[23]Then he said to them all, "If any want to become my followers, let them deny themselves and take up their cross daily and follow me. [24]For those who want to save their life will lose it, and those who lose their life for my sake will save it. [25]What does it profit them if they gain the whole world, but lose or forfeit themselves? [26]Those who are ashamed of me and of my words, of them the Son of Man will be ashamed when he comes in his glory and the glory of the Father and of the holy angels. [27]But truly I tell you, there are some standing here who will not taste death before they see the kingdom of God."

The Transfiguration

28 Now about eight days after these sayings Jesus[w] took with him Peter and John and James, and went up on the mountain to pray. [29]And while he was praying, the appearance of his face changed, and his clothes became dazzling white. [30]Suddenly they saw two men, Moses and Elijah, talking to him. [31]They appeared in glory and were speaking of his departure, which he was about to accomplish at Jerusalem. [32]Now Peter and his companions were weighed down with sleep; but since they had stayed awake,[y] they saw his glory and the two men who stood with him. [33]Just as they were leaving him, Peter said to Jesus, "Master, it is good for us to be here; let us make three dwellings,[z] one for you, one for Moses, and one for Elijah"—not knowing what he said. [34]While he was saying this, a cloud came and overshadowed them; and they were terrified as they entered the cloud. [35]Then from the cloud came a voice that said, "This is my Son, my Chosen;[a] listen to him!" [36]When the voice had spoken, Jesus was found alone. And they kept silent and in those days told no one any of the things they had seen.

Jesus Heals a Boy with a Demon

37 On the next day, when they had come down from the mountain, a great crowd met him. [38]Just then a man from the crowd shouted, "Teacher, I beg you to look at my son; he is my only child. [39]Suddenly a spirit seizes him, and all at once he[b] shrieks. It convulses him until he foams at the mouth; it mauls him and will scarcely leave him. [40]I begged your disciples to cast it out, but they could not." [41]Jesus answered, "You faithless and perverse generation, how much longer must I be with you and bear with you? Bring your son here." [42]While he was coming, the demon dashed him to the ground in convulsions. But Jesus rebuked the unclean spirit, healed the boy, and gave him back to his father. [43]And all were astounded at the greatness of God.

Jesus Again Foretells His Death

While everyone was amazed at all that he was doing, he said to his disciples, [44]"Let these words sink into your ears: The Son of Man is going to be betrayed into human hands." [45]But they did not understand this saying; its meaning was concealed from them, so that they could not perceive it. And they were afraid to ask him about this saying.

---

w Gk he   x Or The Christ   y Or but when they were fully awake   z Or tents   a Other ancient authorities read my Beloved   b Or it

True Greatness

46 An argument arose among them as to which one of them was the greatest. 47But Jesus, aware of their inner thoughts, took a little child and put it by his side, 48and said to them, "Whoever welcomes this child in my name welcomes me, and whoever welcomes me welcomes the one who sent me; for the least among all of you is the greatest."

Another Exorcist

49 John answered, "Master, we saw someone casting out demons in your name, and we tried to stop him, because he does not follow with us." 50But Jesus said to him, "Do not stop him; for whoever is not against you is for you."

A Samaritan Village Refuses to Receive Jesus

51 When the days drew near for him to

Glimpses to Keep Us Going

TUESDAY

Scripture Reading for Today:
Luke 9.28–36

Verse for Today:
Luke 9.29

This strange and wonderful scene stands on its own as a significant revelation of Jesus' glory to his disciples, but it is also important to place it in the chronological context of his life. What happened right before the transfiguration and immediately afterward?

Shortly before, Jesus had told his disciples that he was going to suffer, die, and be raised up; he followed this prediction with the challenging conditions of discipleship: Any who would follow Jesus must be willing to lose their lives to gain them. It was then that Peter, James, and John, weighed down by both these announcements, were invited to accompany Jesus as he went to pray and were thus privileged to witness his glorification. Shortly after they descended from the mountain, Jesus predicted his passion a second time.

As Saint Bede commented, "[Our Lord] in a loving concession allowed Peter, James, and John to enjoy for a very short time the contemplation of the happiness that lasts forever, so as to be able to bear adversity with greater fortitude." No doubt the memory of those moments with Jesus on the mountain helped the apostles through many difficult times in their lives.

The flash of God's glory transported them into a state of immense happiness and, beside himself with wonderment, Peter sought to prolong the experience. Though we rarely can stay long on the "mountaintop" before returning to the demands of our everyday lives, how generous of Jesus to give us those moments of consolation to keep going forward when the road gets rough.

Thank you, Lord, for the hope of heaven and those daily graces you give me that encourage and strengthen me here and now.

—*JEANNE KUN*

Go to page 1366 for your next devotional reading.

be taken up, he set his face to go to Jerusalem. ⁵²And he sent messengers ahead of him. On their way they entered a village of the Samaritans to make ready for him; ⁵³but they did not receive him, because his face was set toward Jerusalem. ⁵⁴When his disciples James and John saw it, they said, "Lord, do you want us to command fire to come down from heaven and consume them?"ᶜ ⁵⁵But he turned and rebuked them. ⁵⁶Thenᵈ they went on to another village.

Would-Be Followers of Jesus

57 As they were going along the road, someone said to him, "I will follow you wherever you go." ⁵⁸And Jesus said to him, "Foxes have holes, and birds of the air have nests; but the Son of Man has nowhere to lay his head." ⁵⁹To another he said, "Follow me." But he said, "Lord, first let me go and bury my father." ⁶⁰But Jesusᵉ said to him, "Let the dead bury their own dead; but as for you, go and proclaim the kingdom of God." ⁶¹Another said, "I will follow you, Lord; but let me first say farewell to those at my home." ⁶²Jesus said to him, "No one who puts a hand to the plow and looks back is fit for the kingdom of God."

The Mission of the Seventy

10 After this the Lord appointed seventyᶠ others and sent them on ahead of him in pairs to every town and place where he himself intended to go. ²He said to them, "The harvest is plentiful, but the laborers are few; therefore ask the Lord of the harvest to send out laborers into his harvest. ³Go on your way. See, I am sending you out like lambs into the midst of wolves. ⁴Carry no purse, no bag, no sandals; and greet no one on the road. ⁵Whatever house you enter, first say, 'Peace to this house!' ⁶And if anyone is there who shares in peace, your peace will rest on that person; but if not, it will return to you. ⁷Remain in the same house, eating and drinking whatever they provide, for the laborer deserves to be paid. Do not move about from house to house. ⁸Whenever you enter a town and its people welcome you, eat what is set before you; ⁹cure the sick who are there, and say to them, 'The kingdom of God has come near to you.'ᵍ ¹⁰But whenever you enter a town and they do not welcome you, go out into its streets and say, ¹¹'Even the dust of your town that clings to our feet, we wipe off in protest against you. Yet know this: the kingdom of God has come near.'ʰ ¹²I tell you, on that day it will be more tolerable for Sodom than for that town.

Woes to Unrepentant Cities

13 "Woe to you, Chorazin! Woe to you, Bethsaida! For if the deeds of power done in you had been done in Tyre and Sidon, they would have repented long ago, sitting in sackcloth and ashes. ¹⁴But at the judgment it will be more tolerable for Tyre and Sidon than for you. ¹⁵And you, Capernaum,
will you be exalted to heaven?
No, you will be brought down
to Hades.
16 "Whoever listens to you listens to me, and whoever rejects you rejects me, and whoever rejects me rejects the one who sent me."

The Return of the Seventy

17 The seventyᶠ returned with joy, saying, "Lord, in your name even the demons submit to us!" ¹⁸He said to them, "I watched Satan fall from heaven like a flash of lightning. ¹⁹See, I have given you authority to tread on snakes and scorpions, and over all the power of the enemy; and nothing will hurt you. ²⁰Nevertheless, do not rejoice at this, that the spirits submit to you, but rejoice that your names are written in heaven."

Jesus Rejoices

21 At that same hour Jesusᵉ rejoiced in the Holy Spiritⁱ and said, "I thankʲ you, Father, Lord of heaven and earth, because you have hidden these things from the wise and the intelligent and have revealed them to infants; yes, Father, for such was your gracious will.ᵏ ²²All things have been handed over to me by my Father; and no one knows who the Son is except the Father, or who the Father is ex-

c Other ancient authorities add *as Elijah did*
d Other ancient authorities read *rebuked them, and said, "You do not know what spirit you are of,* ⁵⁶*for the Son of Man has not come to destroy the lives of human beings but to save them."* Then   e Gk *he*
f Other ancient authorities read *seventy-two*   g Or *is at hand for you*   h Or *is at hand*   i Other authorities read *in the spirit*   j Or *praise*   k Or *for so it was well-pleasing in your sight*

cept the Son and anyone to whom the Son chooses to reveal him."

23 Then turning to the disciples, Jesus[l] said to them privately, "Blessed are the eyes that see what you see! 24For I tell you that many prophets and kings desired to see what you see, but did not see it, and to hear what you hear, but did not hear it."

The Parable of the Good Samaritan

25 Just then a lawyer stood up to test Jesus.[m] "Teacher," he said, "what must I do to inherit eternal life?" 26He said to

him, "What is written in the law? What do you read there?" 27He answered, "You shall love the Lord your God with all your heart, and with all your soul, and with all your strength, and with all your mind; and your neighbor as yourself." 28And he said to him, "You have given the right answer; do this, and you will live."

29 But wanting to justify himself, he asked Jesus, "And who is my neighbor?" 30Jesus replied, "A man was going down from Jerusalem to Jericho, and fell into

[l] Gk *he*   [m] Gk *him*

WEDNESDAY

Scripture Reading for Today:
Luke 10.25–37

Verse for Today:
Luke 10.29

*S*tartling Love

The response of Jesus to the question about neighbors is another way to enunciate the Great Commandment to love. This command, the Word of God, is not far away but so near, so neighborly, that it lives on our lips and in our hearts (see Deuteronomy 30.14). The startling love that Jesus asks of us is certainly love of the foreigner, a growing reality in our nation of immigrants at the moment. We are also to love and come very near the beset and beaten among us, the dirty, stripped or ragged of us, the homeless in our neighborhood and the homeless pieces of our own hearts.

The neighbor and the command to love are both embodiments of God's own self. God is so aligned with the outcast that God is like a Samaritan, a hated foreigner come to find us, beaten and abandoned on the way.

The healing Word is God, the Samaritan traveler. We are those who have been thrown to the road in a desert, stripped by sorrows, robbed of joy and peace, perhaps even of our friends who hurry by, busy with their lives. The Word that is very near, our true neighbor, sees us and suffers with us.

Like the Good Samaritan, this traveling God has been tending us and healing us, often unrecognized, all our lives. Sometimes God seems so foreign to us that we do not recognize God, or our wounds, or ourselves. Often, however, God continues to be embodied in those "very near," the ones who love us, the living and dead. In God's hands they have become the very wine and the oil, helping to heal our lives.

Who has been the wine and the oil in your life? Who has provided healing? Who has proved to be a neighbor? And how will you "go and do likewise"?

—REA MCDONNELL, S.S.N.D.

Go to page 1374 for your next devotional reading.

the hands of robbers, who stripped him, beat him, and went away, leaving him half dead. [31]Now by chance a priest was going down that road; and when he saw him, he passed by on the other side. [32]So likewise a Levite, when he came to the place and saw him, passed by on the other side. [33]But a Samaritan while traveling came near him; and when he saw him, he was moved with pity. [34]He went to him and bandaged his wounds, having poured oil and wine on them. Then he put him on his own animal, brought him to an inn, and took care of him. [35]The next day he took out two denarii,[n] gave them to the innkeeper, and said, 'Take care of him; and when I come back, I will repay you whatever more you spend.' [36]Which of these three, do you think, was a neighbor to the man who fell into the hands of the robbers?" [37]He said, "The one who showed him mercy." Jesus said to him, "Go and do likewise."

Jesus Visits Martha and Mary

38 Now as they went on their way, he entered a certain village, where a woman named Martha welcomed him into her home. [39]She had a sister named Mary, who sat at the Lord's feet and listened to what he was saying. [40]But Martha was distracted by her many tasks; so she came to him and asked, "Lord, do you not care that my sister has left me to do all the work by myself? Tell her then to help me." [41]But the Lord answered her, "Martha, Martha, you are worried and distracted by many things; [42]there is need of only one thing.[o] Mary has chosen the better part, which will not be taken away from her."

The Lord's Prayer

11 He was praying in a certain place, and after he had finished, one of his disciples said to him, "Lord, teach us to pray, as John taught his disciples." [2]He said to them, "When you pray, say:

Father,[p] hallowed be your name.
   Your kingdom come.[q]
[3]   Give us each day our daily
      bread.[r]
[4]   And forgive us our sins,
      for we ourselves forgive
      everyone indebted to us.
   And do not bring us to the time
      of trial."[s]

Perseverance in Prayer

5 And he said to them, "Suppose one of you has a friend, and you go to him at midnight and say to him, 'Friend, lend me three loaves of bread; [6]for a friend of mine has arrived, and I have nothing to set before him.' [7]And he answers from within, 'Do not bother me; the door has already been locked, and my children are with me in bed; I cannot get up and give you anything.' [8]I tell you, even though he will not get up and give him anything because he is his friend, at least because of his persistence he will get up and give him whatever he needs.

9 "So I say to you, Ask, and it will be given you; search, and you will find; knock, and the door will be opened for you. [10]For everyone who asks receives, and everyone who searches finds, and for everyone who knocks, the door will be opened. [11]Is there anyone among you who, if your child asks for[t] a fish, will give a snake instead of a fish? [12]Or if the child asks for an egg, will give a scorpion? [13]If you then, who are evil, know how to give good gifts to your children, how much more will the heavenly Father give the Holy Spirit[u] to those who ask him!"

Jesus and Beelzebul

14 Now he was casting out a demon that was mute; when the demon had gone out, the one who had been mute spoke, and the crowds were amazed. [15]But some of them said, "He casts out demons by Beelzebul, the ruler of the demons." [16]Others, to test him, kept demanding from him a sign from heaven. [17]But he knew what they were thinking and said to them, "Every kingdom divided against itself becomes a desert, and house falls on house. [18]If Satan also is divided against himself, how will his kingdom stand? —for you say that I cast out the demons by Beelze-

---

[n] The denarius was the usual day's wage for a laborer   [o] Other ancient authorities read *few things are necessary, or only one*   [p] Other ancient authorities read *Our Father in heaven*   [q] A few ancient authorities read *Your Holy Spirit come upon us and cleanse us.* Other ancient authorities add *Your will be done, on earth as in heaven*   [r] Or *our bread for tomorrow*   [s] Or *us into temptation.* Other ancient authorities add *but rescue us from the evil one* (or *from evil*)   [t] Other ancient authorities add *bread, will give a stone; or if your child asks for*   [u] Other ancient authorities read *the Father give the Holy Spirit from heaven*

bul. [19]Now if I cast out the demons by Beelzebul, by whom do your exorcists[v] cast them out? Therefore they will be your judges. [20]But if it is by the finger of God that I cast out the demons, then the kingdom of God has come to you. [21]When a strong man, fully armed, guards his castle, his property is safe. [22]But when one stronger than he attacks him and overpowers him, he takes away his armor in which he trusted and divides his plunder. [23]Whoever is not with me is against me, and whoever does not gather with me scatters.

The Return of the Unclean Spirit

24 "When the unclean spirit has gone out of a person, it wanders through waterless regions looking for a resting place, but not finding any, it says, 'I will return to my house from which I came.' [25]When it comes, it finds it swept and put in order. [26]Then it goes and brings seven other spirits more evil than itself, and they enter and live there; and the last state of that person is worse than the first."

True Blessedness

27 While he was saying this, a woman in the crowd raised her voice and said to him, "Blessed is the womb that bore you and the breasts that nursed you!" [28]But he said, "Blessed rather are those who hear the word of God and obey it!"

The Sign of Jonah

29 When the crowds were increasing, he began to say, "This generation is an evil generation; it asks for a sign, but no

v Gk *sons*

THE TRADITION

Mary's Role in the Church

"Blessed is the womb that bore you and the breasts that nursed you!"

LUKE 11.27

When a woman in the crowd cried out this blessing in praise of Jesus' mother, Our Lord responded, "Blessed rather are those who hear the word of God and obey it!" (Luke 11.28). While not denying the significance of her motherhood, Jesus was drawing attention to what is *most* commendable about Mary: her faith.

Like Mary's cousin, Elizabeth, we acclaim Mary for believing "that there would be a fulfillment of what was spoken to her by the Lord" (1.45). Mary said yes to a pregnancy that seemed impossible. She waited patiently for God to shed light on unsolved mysteries and advised others to "do whatever he tells you." She traveled with her Son and his ragtag band and stood with Jesus at the cross in what must have been the darkest of all possible nights of faith. Through it all, Mary believed.

Looking at Mary, the first and best of Jesus' disciples, we learn how to believe.

But Mary does not teach like some distant professor up on a podium. She is intimately involved with us because she is essentially a mother—mother of the Redeemer and therefore of the Church, the body of Christ of which we are members.

"Here is your mother" (John 19.27). With these words from the cross, Jesus established a new family and affirmed Mary's maternal role in it. More than a friend, more than an advocate and intercessor, more than a role model, Mary the exemplary disciple has become our spiritual mother.

What a gift we have in Mary's maternal presence and protection! As we discover it, we may find ourselves echoing Elizabeth's words of wonderment when Mary came to visit: "Why has this happened to me, that the mother of my Lord comes to me?" (Luke 1.43).

sign will be given to it except the sign of Jonah. [30]For just as Jonah became a sign to the people of Nineveh, so the Son of Man will be to this generation. [31]The queen of the South will rise at the judgment with the people of this generation and condemn them, because she came from the ends of the earth to listen to the wisdom of Solomon, and see, something greater than Solomon is here! [32]The people of Nineveh will rise up at the judgment with this generation and condemn it, because they repented at the proclamation of Jonah, and see, something greater than Jonah is here!

The Light of the Body

33 "No one after lighting a lamp puts it in a cellar,[w] but on the lampstand so that those who enter may see the light. [34]Your eye is the lamp of your body. If your eye is healthy, your whole body is full of light; but if it is not healthy, your body is full of darkness. [35]Therefore consider whether the light in you is not darkness. [36]If then your whole body is full of light, with no part of it in darkness, it will be as full of light as when a lamp gives you light with its rays."

Jesus Denounces Pharisees and Lawyers

37 While he was speaking, a Pharisee invited him to dine with him; so he went in and took his place at the table. [38]The Pharisee was amazed to see that he did not first wash before dinner. [39]Then the Lord said to him, "Now you Pharisees clean the outside of the cup and of the dish, but inside you are full of greed and wickedness. [40]You fools! Did not the one who made the outside make the inside also? [41]So give for alms those things that are within; and see, everything will be clean for you.

42 "But woe to you Pharisees! For you tithe mint and rue and herbs of all kinds, and neglect justice and the love of God; it is these you ought to have practiced, without neglecting the others. [43]Woe to you Pharisees! For you love to have the seat of honor in the synagogues and to be greeted with respect in the marketplaces. [44]Woe to you! For you are like unmarked graves, and people walk over them without realizing it."

45 One of the lawyers answered him, "Teacher, when you say these things, you insult us too." [46]And he said, "Woe also to you lawyers! For you load people with burdens hard to bear, and you yourselves do not lift a finger to ease them. [47]Woe to you! For you build the tombs of the prophets whom your ancestors killed. [48]So you are witnesses and approve of the deeds of your ancestors; for they killed them, and you build their tombs. [49]Therefore also the Wisdom of God said, 'I will send them prophets and apostles, some of whom they will kill and persecute,' [50]so that this generation may be charged with the blood of all the prophets shed since the foundation of the world, [51]from the blood of Abel to the blood of Zechariah, who perished between the altar and the sanctuary. Yes, I tell you, it will be charged against this generation. [52]Woe to you lawyers! For you have taken away the key of knowledge; you did not enter yourselves, and you hindered those who were entering."

53 When he went outside, the scribes and the Pharisees began to be very hostile toward him and to cross-examine him about many things, [54]lying in wait for him, to catch him in something he might say.

A Warning against Hypocrisy

12 Meanwhile, when the crowd gathered by the thousands, so that they trampled on one another, he began to speak first to his disciples, "Beware of the yeast of the Pharisees, that is, their hypocrisy. [2]Nothing is covered up that will not be uncovered, and nothing secret that will not become known. [3]Therefore whatever you have said in the dark will be heard in the light, and what you have whispered behind closed doors will be proclaimed from the housetops.

Exhortation to Fearless Confession

4 "I tell you, my friends, do not fear those who kill the body, and after that can do nothing more. [5]But I will warn you whom to fear: fear him who, after he has killed, has authority[x] to cast into hell.[y] Yes, I tell you, fear him! [6]Are not five sparrows sold for two pennies? Yet not one of them is forgotten in God's sight. [7]But even the hairs of your head are all counted. Do not be afraid; you are of more value than many sparrows.

w Other ancient authorities add *or under the bushel basket*   *x* Or *power*   *y* Gk Gehenna

8 "And I tell you, everyone who acknowledges me before others, the Son of Man also will acknowledge before the angels of God; 9but whoever denies me before others will be denied before the angels of God. 10And everyone who speaks a word against the Son of Man will be forgiven; but whoever blasphemes against the Holy Spirit will not be forgiven. 11When they bring you before the synagogues, the rulers, and the authorities, do not worry about howz you are to defend yourselves or what you are to say; 12for the Holy Spirit will teach you at that very hour what you ought to say."

The Parable of the Rich Fool

13 Someone in the crowd said to him, "Teacher, tell my brother to divide the family inheritance with me." 14But he said to him, "Friend, who set me to be a judge or arbitrator over you?" 15And he said to them, "Take care! Be on your guard against all kinds of greed; for one's life does not consist in the abundance of possessions." 16Then he told them a parable: "The land of a rich man produced abundantly. 17And he thought to himself, 'What should I do, for I have no place to store my crops?' 18Then he said, 'I will do this: I will pull down my barns and build larger ones, and there I will store all my grain and my goods. 19And I will say to my soul, Soul, you have ample goods laid up for many years; relax, eat, drink, be merry.' 20But God said to him, 'You fool! This very night your life is being demanded of you. And the things you have prepared, whose will they be?' 21So it is with those who store up treasures for themselves but are not rich toward God."

Do Not Worry

22 He said to his disciples, "Therefore I tell you, do not worry about your life, what you will eat, or about your body, what you will wear. 23For life is more than food, and the body more than clothing. 24Consider the ravens: they neither sow nor reap, they have neither storehouse nor barn, and yet God feeds them. Of how much more value are you than the birds! 25And can any of you by worrying add a single hour to your span of life?a 26If then you are not able to do so small a thing as that, why do you worry about the rest? 27Consider the lilies, how they grow: they neither toil nor spin;b yet I tell you,

even Solomon in all his glory was not clothed like one of these. 28But if God so clothes the grass of the field, which is alive today and tomorrow is thrown into the oven, how much more will he clothe you—you of little faith! 29And do not keep striving for what you are to eat and what you are to drink, and do not keep worrying. 30For it is the nations of the world that strive after all these things, and your Father knows that you need them. 31Instead, strive for hisc kingdom, and these things will be given to you as well.

32 "Do not be afraid, little flock, for it is your Father's good pleasure to give you the kingdom. 33Sell your possessions, and give alms. Make purses for yourselves that do not wear out, an unfailing treasure in heaven, where no thief comes near and no moth destroys. 34For where your treasure is, there your heart will be also.

Watchful Slaves

35 "Be dressed for action and have your lamps lit; 36be like those who are waiting for their master to return from the wedding banquet, so that they may open the door for him as soon as he comes and knocks. 37Blessed are those slaves whom the master finds alert when he comes; truly I tell you, he will fasten his belt and have them sit down to eat, and he will come and serve them. 38If he comes during the middle of the night, or near dawn, and finds them so, blessed are those slaves.

39 "But know this: if the owner of the house had known at what hour the thief was coming, hed would not have let his house be broken into. 40You also must be ready, for the Son of Man is coming at an unexpected hour."

The Faithful or the Unfaithful Slave

41 Peter said, "Lord, are you telling this parable for us or for everyone?" 42And the Lord said, "Who then is the faithful and prudent manager whom his master will put in charge of his slaves, to give them their allowance of food at the proper time? 43Blessed is that slave whom his

z Other ancient authorities add *or what* a Or *add a cubit to your stature* b Other ancient authorities read *Consider the lilies; they neither spin nor weave* c Other ancient authorities read *God's* d Other ancient authorities add *would have watched and*

master will find at work when he arrives. [44]Truly I tell you, he will put that one in charge of all his possessions. [45]But if that slave says to himself, 'My master is delayed in coming,' and if he begins to beat the other slaves, men and women, and to eat and drink and get drunk, [46]the master of that slave will come on a day when he does not expect him and at an hour that he does not know, and will cut him in pieces,[e] and put him with the unfaithful. [47]That slave who knew what his master wanted, but did not prepare himself or do what was wanted, will receive a severe beating. [48]But the one who did not know and did what deserved a beating will receive a light beating. From everyone to whom much has been given, much will be required; and from the one to whom much has been entrusted, even more will be demanded.

Jesus the Cause of Division

[49] "I came to bring fire to the earth, and how I wish it were already kindled! [50]I have a baptism with which to be baptized, and what stress I am under until it is completed! [51]Do you think that I have come to bring peace to the earth? No, I tell you, but rather division! [52]From now on five in one household will be divided, three against two and two against three; [53]they will be divided:

father against son
    and son against father,
mother against daughter
    and daughter against mother,
mother-in-law against her
        daughter-in-law
    and daughter-in-law against
        mother-in-law."

Interpreting the Time

[54] He also said to the crowds, "When you see a cloud rising in the west, you immediately say, 'It is going to rain'; and so it happens. [55]And when you see the south wind blowing, you say, 'There will be scorching heat'; and it happens. [56]You hypocrites! You know how to interpret the appearance of earth and sky, but why do you not know how to interpret the present time?

Settling with Your Opponent

[57] "And why do you not judge for yourselves what is right? [58]Thus, when you go with your accuser before a magistrate, on the way make an effort to settle the case,[f] or you may be dragged before the judge, and the judge hand you over to the officer, and the officer throw you in prison. [59]I tell you, you will never get out until you have paid the very last penny."

Repent or Perish

13 At that very time there were some present who told him about the Galileans whose blood Pilate had mingled with their sacrifices. [2]He asked them, "Do you think that because these Galileans suffered in this way they were worse sinners than all other Galileans? [3]No, I tell you; but unless you repent, you will all perish as they did. [4]Or those eighteen who were killed when the tower of Siloam fell on them—do you think that they were worse offenders than all the others living in Jerusalem? [5]No, I tell you; but unless you repent, you will all perish just as they did."

The Parable of the Barren Fig Tree

[6] Then he told this parable: "A man had a fig tree planted in his vineyard; and he came looking for fruit on it and found none. [7]So he said to the gardener, 'See here! For three years I have come looking for fruit on this fig tree, and still I find none. Cut it down! Why should it be wasting the soil?' [8]He replied, 'Sir, let it alone for one more year, until I dig around it and put manure on it. [9]If it bears fruit next year, well and good; but if not, you can cut it down.' "

Jesus Heals a Crippled Woman

[10] Now he was teaching in one of the synagogues on the sabbath. [11]And just then there appeared a woman with a spirit that had crippled her for eighteen years. She was bent over and was quite unable to stand up straight. [12]When Jesus saw her, he called her over and said, "Woman, you are set free from your ailment." [13]When he laid his hands on her, immediately she stood up straight and began praising God. [14]But the leader of the synagogue, indignant because Jesus had cured on the sabbath, kept saying to the crowd, "There are six days on which work ought to be done; come on those days and be cured, and not on the sabbath day." [15]But the Lord answered him and said, "You hypocrites!

---

e Or *cut him off*   *f* Gk *settle with him*

Does not each of you on the sabbath untie his ox or his donkey from the manger, and lead it away to give it water? [16]And ought not this woman, a daughter of Abraham whom Satan bound for eighteen long years, be set free from this bondage on the sabbath day?" [17]When he said this, all his opponents were put to shame; and the entire crowd was rejoicing at all the wonderful things that he was doing.

The Parable of the Mustard Seed

18 He said therefore, "What is the kingdom of God like? And to what should I compare it? [19]It is like a mustard seed that someone took and sowed in the garden; it grew and became a tree, and the birds of the air made nests in its branches."

The Parable of the Yeast

20 And again he said, "To what should I compare the kingdom of God? [21]It is like yeast that a woman took and mixed in with[g] three measures of flour until all of it was leavened."

The Narrow Door

22 Jesus[h] went through one town and village after another, teaching as he made his way to Jerusalem. [23]Someone asked him, "Lord, will only a few be saved?" He said to them, [24]"Strive to enter through the narrow door; for many, I tell you, will try to enter and will not be able. [25]When once the owner of the house has got up and shut the door, and you begin to stand outside and to knock at the door, saying, 'Lord, open to us,' then in reply he will say to you, 'I do not know where you come from.' [26]Then you will begin to say, 'We ate and drank with you, and you taught in our streets.' [27]But he will say, 'I do not know where you come from; go away from me, all you evildoers!' [28]There will be weeping and gnashing of teeth when you see Abraham and Isaac and Jacob and all the prophets in the kingdom of God, and you yourselves thrown out. [29]Then people will come from east and west, from north and south, and will eat in the kingdom of God. [30]Indeed, some are last who will be first, and some are first who will be last."

The Lament over Jerusalem

31 At that very hour some Pharisees came and said to him, "Get away from here, for Herod wants to kill you." [32]He said to them, "Go and tell that fox for me,[i] 'Listen, I am casting out demons and performing cures today and tomorrow, and on the third day I finish my work.' [33]Yet today, tomorrow, and the next day I must be on my way, because it is impossible for a prophet to be killed outside of Jerusalem.' [34]Jerusalem, Jerusalem, the city that kills the prophets and stones those who are sent to it! How often have I desired to gather your children together as a hen gathers her brood under her wings, and you were not willing! [35]See, your house is left to you. And I tell you, you will not see me until the time comes when[j] you say, 'Blessed is the one who comes in the name of the Lord.' "

Jesus Heals the Man with Dropsy

14 On one occasion when Jesus[k] was going to the house of a leader of the Pharisees to eat a meal on the sabbath, they were watching him closely. [2]Just then, in front of him, there was a man who had dropsy. [3]And Jesus asked the lawyers and Pharisees, "Is it lawful to cure people on the sabbath, or not?" [4]But they were silent. So Jesus[k] took him and healed him, and sent him away. [5]Then he said to them, "If one of you has a child[l] or an ox that has fallen into a well, will you not immediately pull it out on a sabbath day?" [6]And they could not reply to this.

Humility and Hospitality

7 When he noticed how the guests chose the places of honor, he told them a parable. [8]"When you are invited by someone to a wedding banquet, do not sit down at the place of honor, in case someone more distinguished than you has been invited by your host; [9]and the host who invited both of you may come and say to you, 'Give this person your place,' and then in disgrace you would start to take the lowest place. [10]But when you are invited, go and sit down at the lowest place, so that when your host comes, he may say to you, 'Friend, move up higher'; then you will be honored in the presence of all who sit at the table with you. [11]For all who exalt themselves will be humbled,

---

g Gk hid in   h Gk He   i Gk lacks for me
j Other ancient authorities lack the time comes when   k Gk he   l Other ancient authorities read a donkey

and those who humble themselves will be exalted."

12 He said also to the one who had invited him, "When you give a luncheon or a dinner, do not invite your friends or your brothers or your relatives or rich neighbors, in case they may invite you in return, and you would be repaid. 13But when you give a banquet, invite the poor, the crippled, the lame, and the blind. 14And you will be blessed, because they cannot repay you, for you will be repaid at the resurrection of the righteous."

The Parable of the Great Dinner

15 One of the dinner guests, on hearing this, said to him, "Blessed is anyone who will eat bread in the kingdom of God!" 16Then Jesus*m* said to him, "Someone gave a great dinner and invited many. 17At the time for the dinner he sent his slave to say to those who had been invited, 'Come; for everything is ready now.' 18But they all alike began to make excuses. The first said to him, 'I have bought a piece of land, and I must go out and see it; please accept my regrets.' 19Another said, 'I have bought five yoke of oxen, and I am going to try them out; please accept my regrets.' 20Another said, 'I have just been married, and therefore I cannot come.' 21So the slave returned and reported this to his master. Then the owner of the house became angry and said to his slave, 'Go out at once into the streets and lanes of the town and bring in the poor, the crippled, the blind, and the lame.' 22And the slave said, 'Sir, what you ordered has been done, and there is still room.' 23Then the master said to the slave, 'Go out into the roads and lanes, and compel people to come in, so that my house may be filled. 24For I tell you,*n* none of those who were invited will taste my dinner.' "

The Cost of Discipleship

25 Now large crowds were traveling with him; and he turned and said to them, 26"Whoever comes to me and does not hate father and mother, wife and children, brothers and sisters, yes, and even life itself, cannot be my disciple. 27Whoever does not carry the cross and follow me cannot be my disciple. 28For which of you, intending to build a tower, does not first sit down and estimate the cost, to see whether he has enough to complete it? 29Otherwise, when he has laid a founda-

tion and is not able to finish, all who see it will begin to ridicule him, 30saying, 'This fellow began to build and was not able to finish.' 31Or what king, going out to wage war against another king, will not sit down first and consider whether he is able with ten thousand to oppose the one who comes against him with twenty thousand? 32If he cannot, then, while the other is still far away, he sends a delegation and asks for the terms of peace. 33So therefore, none of you can become my disciple if you do not give up all your possessions.

About Salt

34 "Salt is good; but if salt has lost its taste, how can its saltiness be restored?*o* 35It is fit neither for the soil nor for the manure pile; they throw it away. Let anyone with ears to hear listen!"

The Parable of the Lost Sheep

15 Now all the tax collectors and sinners were coming near to listen to him. 2And the Pharisees and the scribes were grumbling and saying, "This fellow welcomes sinners and eats with them."

3 So he told them this parable: 4"Which one of you, having a hundred sheep and losing one of them, does not leave the ninety-nine in the wilderness and go after the one that is lost until he finds it? 5When he has found it, he lays it on his shoulders and rejoices. 6And when he comes home, he calls together his friends and neighbors, saying to them, 'Rejoice with me, for I have found my sheep that was lost.' 7Just so, I tell you, there will be more joy in heaven over one sinner who repents than over ninety-nine righteous persons who need no repentance.

The Parable of the Lost Coin

8 "Or what woman having ten silver coins,*p* if she loses one of them, does not light a lamp, sweep the house, and search carefully until she finds it? 9When she has found it, she calls together her friends and neighbors, saying, 'Rejoice with me, for I have found the coin that I had lost.' 10Just so, I tell you, there is joy in the presence

---

m Gk *he*   *n* The Greek word for *you* here is plural   *o* Or *how can it be used for seasoning?*
p Gk *drachmas*, each worth about a day's wage for a laborer

of the angels of God over one sinner who repents."

The Parable of the Prodigal and His Brother

11 Then Jesus[q] said, "There was a man who had two sons. [12]The younger of them said to his father, 'Father, give me the share of the property that will belong to me.' So he divided his property between them. [13]A few days later the younger son gathered all he had and traveled to a distant country, and there he squandered his property in dissolute living. [14]When he had spent everything, a severe famine took place throughout that country, and he began to be in need. [15]So he went and hired himself out to one of the citizens of that country, who sent him to his fields to feed the pigs. [16]He would gladly have filled himself with[r] the pods that the pigs were eating; and no one gave him anything. [17]But when he came to himself he said, 'How many of my father's hired hands have bread enough and to spare, but here I am dying of hunger! [18]I will get up and go to my father, and I will say to him, "Father, I have sinned against heaven and before you; [19]I am no longer worthy to be called your son; treat me like one of your hired hands."' [20]So he set off and went to his father. But while he was still far off, his father saw him and was filled with compassion; he ran and put his arms around him and kissed him. [21]Then the son said to him, 'Father, I have sinned

q Gk *he*   *r* Other ancient authorities read *filled his stomach with*

Come to the Party

Scripture Reading for Today:
Luke 15.11–32

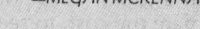

Verse for Today:
Luke 15.21

We must wonder what the younger son did to atone for his actions, to repair the breach in the family, and to honor his father's love. But we can do more than wonder. We can make our response [to this parable] a reality that delights God, our Father.

We can go out to our brothers and sisters whom we have wronged before we feast and enjoy the gracious forgiveness that God has given to us, and we can offer to repair the relationships we have destroyed by our selfishness and greed and thoughtless behavior. Or we can go to those who have returned to God and extend to them a hand of support, of openness, realizing that we too have wronged our Father by acting as though we have spent our whole lives "working like a slave" for God and self-righteously missing the depth of love that our Father has for all his children. We can ask ourselves if we have been living up to our responsibilities as the elder children of the family.

What can we do, with Jesus, to seek reconciliation between our brothers and sisters who refuse to sit down at table and eat together, who refuse to respect all the members of the family, who refuse to confess that we are all sadly in need of clemency, pardon, and some restitution to each other?

Today we need to make sure that we are at any party that God is hosting and that we bring with us anyone God would love to see again. What will God's look of love be like when it is turned on us as we bring them home?

—MEGAN MCKENNA

Go to page 1378 for your next devotional reading.

against heaven and before you; I am no longer worthy to be called your son.'s 22But the father said to his slaves, 'Quickly, bring out a robe—the best one—and put it on him; put a ring on his finger and sandals on his feet. 23And get the fatted calf and kill it, and let us eat and celebrate; 24for this son of mine was dead and is alive again; he was lost and is found!' And they began to celebrate.

25 "Now his elder son was in the field; and when he came and approached the house, he heard music and dancing. 26He called one of the slaves and asked what was going on. 27He replied, 'Your brother has come, and your father has killed the fatted calf, because he has got him back safe and sound.' 28Then he became angry and refused to go in. His father came out and began to plead with him. 29But he answered his father, 'Listen! For all these years I have been working like a slave for you, and I have never disobeyed your command; yet you have never given me even a young goat so that I might celebrate with my friends. 30But when this son of yours came back, who has devoured your property with prostitutes, you killed the fatted calf for him!' 31Then the fathert said to him, 'Son, you are always with me, and all that is mine is yours. 32But we had to celebrate and rejoice, because this brother of yours was dead and has come to life; he was lost and has been found.' "

The Parable of the Dishonest Manager

16 Then Jesust said to the disciples, "There was a rich man who had a manager, and charges were brought to him that this man was squandering his property. 2So he summoned him and said to him, 'What is this that I hear about you? Give me an accounting of your management, because you cannot be my manager any longer.' 3Then the manager said to himself, 'What will I do, now that my master is taking the position away from me? I am not strong enough to dig, and I am ashamed to beg. 4I have decided what to do so that, when I am dismissed as manager, people may welcome me into their homes.' 5So, summoning his master's debtors one by one, he asked the first, 'How much do you owe my master?' 6He answered, 'A hundred jugs of olive oil.' He said to him, 'Take your bill, sit down quickly, and make it fifty.' 7Then he asked

another, 'And how much do you owe?' He replied, 'A hundred containers of wheat.' He said to him, 'Take your bill and make it eighty.' 8And his master commended the dishonest manager because he had acted shrewdly; for the children of this age are more shrewd in dealing with their own generation than are the children of light. 9And I tell you, make friends for yourselves by means of dishonest wealthu so that when it is gone, they may welcome you into the eternal homes.v

10 "Whoever is faithful in a very little is faithful also in much; and whoever is dishonest in a very little is dishonest also in much. 11If then you have not been faithful with the dishonest wealth,u who will entrust to you the true riches? 12And if you have not been faithful with what belongs to another, who will give you what is your own? 13No slave can serve two masters; for a slave will either hate the one and love the other, or be devoted to the one and despise the other. You cannot serve God and wealth."u

The Law and the Kingdom of God

14 The Pharisees, who were lovers of money, heard all this, and they ridiculed him. 15So he said to them, "You are those who justify yourselves in the sight of others; but God knows your hearts; for what is prized by human beings is an abomination in the sight of God.

16 "The law and the prophets were in effect until John came; since then the good news of the kingdom of God is proclaimed, and everyone tries to enter it by force.w 17But it is easier for heaven and earth to pass away, than for one stroke of a letter in the law to be dropped.

18 "Anyone who divorces his wife and marries another commits adultery, and whoever marries a woman divorced from her husband commits adultery.

The Rich Man and Lazarus

19 "There was a rich man who was dressed in purple and fine linen and who feasted sumptuously every day. 20And at his gate lay a poor man named Lazarus, covered with sores, 21who longed to satisfy his hunger with what fell from the rich

---

s Other ancient authorities add *Treat me like one of your hired servants*   t Gk *he*   u Gk *mammon*
v Gk *tents*   w Or *everyone is strongly urged to enter it*

man's table; even the dogs would come and lick his sores. ²²The poor man died and was carried away by the angels to be with Abraham.ˣ The rich man also died and was buried. ²³In Hades, where he was being tormented, he looked up and saw Abraham far away with Lazarus by his side.ʸ ²⁴He called out, 'Father Abraham, have mercy on me, and send Lazarus to dip the tip of his finger in water and cool my tongue; for I am in agony in these flames.' ²⁵But Abraham said, 'Child, remember that during your lifetime you received your good things, and Lazarus in like manner evil things; but now he is comforted here, and you are in agony. ²⁶Besides all this, between you and us a great chasm has been fixed, so that those who might want to pass from here to you cannot do so, and no one can cross from there to us.' ²⁷He said, 'Then, father, I beg you to send him to my father's house— ²⁸for I have five brothers—that he may warn them, so that they will not also come into this place of torment.' ²⁹Abraham replied, 'They have Moses and the prophets; they should listen to them.' ³⁰He said, 'No, father Abraham; but if someone goes to them from the dead, they will repent.' ³¹He said to him, 'If they do not listen to Moses and the prophets, neither will they be convinced even if someone rises from the dead.' "

Some Sayings of Jesus

17 Jesusᶻ said to his disciples, "Occasions for stumbling are bound to come, but woe to anyone by whom they come! ²It would be better for you if a millstone were hung around your neck and you were thrown into the sea than for you to cause one of these little ones to stumble. ³Be on your guard! If another discipleᵃ sins, you must rebuke the offender, and if there is repentance, you must forgive. ⁴And if the same person sins against you seven times a day, and turns back to you seven times and says, 'I repent,' you must forgive."

⁵The apostles said to the Lord, "Increase our faith!" ⁶The Lord replied, "If you had faith the size of aᵇ mustard seed, you could say to this mulberry tree, 'Be uprooted and planted in the sea,' and it would obey you.

⁷ "Who among you would say to your slave who has just come in from plowing or tending sheep in the field, 'Come here

at once and take your place at the table'? ⁸Would you not rather say to him, 'Prepare supper for me, put on your apron and serve me while I eat and drink; later you may eat and drink'? ⁹Do you thank the slave for doing what was commanded? ¹⁰So you also, when you have done all that you were ordered to do, say, 'We are worthless slaves; we have done only what we ought to have done!' "

Jesus Cleanses Ten Lepers

11 On the way to Jerusalem Jesusᶜ was going through the region between Samaria and Galilee. ¹²As he entered a village, ten lepersᵈ approached him. Keeping their distance, ¹³they called out, saying, "Jesus, Master, have mercy on us!" ¹⁴When he saw them, he said to them, "Go and show yourselves to the priests." And as they went, they were made clean. ¹⁵Then one of them, when he saw that he was healed, turned back, praising God with a loud voice. ¹⁶He prostrated himself at Jesus'ᵉ feet and thanked him. And he was a Samaritan. ¹⁷Then Jesus asked, "Were not ten made clean? But the other nine, where are they? ¹⁸Was none of them found to return and give praise to God except this foreigner?" ¹⁹Then he said to him, "Get up and go on your way; your faith has made you well."

The Coming of the Kingdom

20 Once Jesusᶜ was asked by the Pharisees when the kingdom of God was coming, and he answered, "The kingdom of God is not coming with things that can be observed; ²¹nor will they say, 'Look, here it is!' or 'There it is!' For, in fact, the kingdom of God is amongᶠ you."

22 Then he said to the disciples, "The days are coming when you will long to see one of the days of the Son of Man, and you will not see it. ²³They will say to you, 'Look there!' or 'Look here!' Do not go, do not set off in pursuit. ²⁴For as the lightning flashes and lights up the sky from one side to the other, so will the Son of Man be in his day.ᵍ ²⁵But first he must endure much suffering and be rejected by

---

ˣ Gk *to Abraham's bosom*   ʸ Gk *in his bosom*
ᶻ Gk *He*   ᵃ Gk *your brother*   ᵇ Gk *faith as a grain of*   ᶜ Gk *he*   ᵈ The terms *leper* and *leprosy* can refer to several diseases   ᵉ Gk *his*   ᶠ Or *within*   ᵍ Other ancient authorities lack *in his day*

this generation. 26Just as it was in the days of Noah, so too it will be in the days of the Son of Man. 27They were eating and drinking, and marrying and being given in marriage, until the day Noah entered the ark, and the flood came and destroyed all of them. 28Likewise, just as it was in the days of Lot: they were eating and drinking, buying and selling, planting and building, 29but on the day that Lot left Sodom, it rained fire and sulfur from heaven and destroyed all of them 30—it will be like that on the day that the Son of Man is revealed. 31On that day, anyone on the housetop who has belongings in the house must not come down to take them away; and likewise anyone in the field must not turn back. 32Remember Lot's wife. 33Those who try to make their life secure will lose it, but those who lose their life will keep it. 34I tell you, on that night there will be two in one bed; one will be taken and the other left. 35There will be two women grinding meal together; one will be taken and the other left."h 37Then they asked him, "Where, Lord?" He said to them, "Where the corpse is, there the vultures will gather."

The Parable of the Widow and the Unjust Judge

18 Then Jesusi told them a parable about their need to pray always and not to lose heart. 2He said, "In a certain city there was a judge who neither feared God nor had respect for people. 3In that city there was a widow who kept coming to him and saying, 'Grant me justice against my opponent.' 4For a while he refused; but later he said to himself, 'Though I have no fear of God and no respect for anyone, 5yet because this widow keeps bothering me, I will grant her justice, so that she may not wear me out by continually coming.' "j 6And the Lord said, "Listen to what the unjust judge says. 7And will not God grant justice to his chosen ones who cry to him day and night? Will he delay long in helping them? 8I tell you, he will quickly grant justice to them. And yet, when the Son of Man comes, will he find faith on earth?"

The Parable of the Pharisee and the Tax Collector

9 He also told this parable to some who trusted in themselves that they were righteous and regarded others with contempt: 10"Two men went up to the temple to pray, one a Pharisee and the other a tax collector. 11The Pharisee, standing by himself, was praying thus, 'God, I thank you that I am not like other people: thieves, rogues, adulterers, or even like this tax collector. 12I fast twice a week; I give a tenth of all my income.' 13But the tax collector, standing far off, would not even look up to heaven, but was beating his breast and saying, 'God, be merciful to me, a sinner!' 14I tell you, this man went down to his home justified rather than the other; for all who exalt themselves will be humbled, but all who humble themselves will be exalted."

Jesus Blesses Little Children

15 People were bringing even infants to him that he might touch them; and when the disciples saw it, they sternly ordered them not to do it. 16But Jesus called for them and said, "Let the little children come to me, and do not stop them; for it is to such as these that the kingdom of God belongs. 17Truly I tell you, whoever does not receive the kingdom of God as a little child will never enter it."

The Rich Ruler

18 A certain ruler asked him, "Good Teacher, what must I do to inherit eternal life?" 19Jesus said to him, "Why do you call me good? No one is good but God alone. 20You know the commandments: 'You shall not commit adultery; You shall not murder; You shall not steal; You shall not bear false witness; Honor your father and mother.' " 21He replied, "I have kept all these since my youth." 22When Jesus heard this, he said to him, "There is still one thing lacking. Sell all that you own and distribute the moneyk to the poor, and you will have treasure in heaven; then come, follow me." 23But when he heard this, he became sad; for he was very rich. 24Jesus looked at him and said, "How hard it is for those who have wealth to enter the kingdom of God! 25Indeed, it is easier for a camel to go through the eye of

---

h Other ancient authorities add verse 36, "Two will be in the field; one will be taken and the other left." i Gk he j Or so that she may not finally come and slap me in the face k Gk lacks the money

a needle than for someone who is rich to enter the kingdom of God."

26 Those who heard it said, "Then who can be saved?" 27He replied, "What is impossible for mortals is possible for God."

28 Then Peter said, "Look, we have left our homes and followed you." 29And he said to them, "Truly I tell you, there is no one who has left house or wife or brothers or parents or children, for the sake of the kingdom of God, 30who will not get back very much more in this age, and in the age to come eternal life."

A Third Time Jesus Foretells His Death and Resurrection

31 Then he took the twelve aside and said to them, "See, we are going up to Jerusalem, and everything that is written about the Son of Man by the prophets will be accomplished. 32For he will be handed over to the Gentiles; and he will be mocked and insulted and spat upon. 33After they have flogged him, they will kill him, and on the third day he will rise again." 34But they understood nothing about all these things; in fact, what he said

---

FRIDAY

Scripture Reading for Today:
Luke 18.1–8

Verse for Today:
Luke 18.7

*N*ever Give Up

When we feel that God is reluctant and unwilling to come to us, we really are experiencing our own closedness to him. We project what we feel most deeply onto God and think he is holding back. But God never holds back. He gives himself constantly, without the slightest stint. We pull back and hold back; we hesitate and vacillate; we want God one day and forget all about him the next day when his presence is less convenient. We may be thoroughly eaten up by longing for a while; then it fades and we can barely remember how it felt to want God.

These parables [the persistent widow and the friend who asks to borrow bread at midnight (see Luke 11.5–13)] instruct us clearly. No matter how you feel, no matter how difficult or inconvenient or peculiar the way may seem, persist and persist in your inner life! Continue to put one foot before the other on the path to God. Keep going at all costs. If you get sidetracked, come back and keep going.

In these stories, the doors we must beat on are the doors that keep our own heart closed. The reluctant sleeper we must awaken and motivate is the sleeper within our own self. It is our own lack of attention to interior life, our own forgetfulness of God's pervasive presence and constant love. The sleep we must shake off is our own laziness. The judge's disregard for righteousness is our own sloppiness about God's teachings, our own willingness to compromise in favor of our immediate comfort. Rarely is it true that we don't know what we could be doing to help our spiritual life. It is often true that we do not persist in doing what we have begun, inwardly or outwardly.

—MARILYN GUSTIN

Go to page 1380 for your next devotional reading.

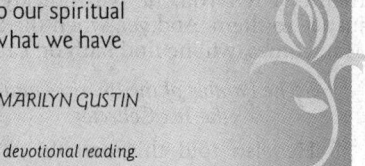

was hidden from them, and they did not grasp what was said.

Jesus Heals a Blind Beggar Near Jericho

35 As he approached Jericho, a blind man was sitting by the roadside begging. 36When he heard a crowd going by, he asked what was happening. 37They told him, "Jesus of Nazareth*l* is passing by." 38Then he shouted, "Jesus, Son of David, have mercy on me!" 39Those who were in front sternly ordered him to be quiet; but he shouted even more loudly, "Son of David, have mercy on me!" 40Jesus stood still and ordered the man to be brought to him; and when he came near, he asked him, 41"What do you want me to do for you?" He said, "Lord, let me see again." 42Jesus said to him, "Receive your sight; your faith has saved you." 43Immediately he regained his sight and followed him, glorifying God; and all the people, when they saw it, praised God.

Jesus and Zacchaeus

19 He entered Jericho and was passing through it. 2A man was there named Zacchaeus; he was a chief tax collector and was rich. 3He was trying to see who Jesus was, but on account of the crowd he could not, because he was short in stature. 4So he ran ahead and climbed a sycamore tree to see him, because he was going to pass that way. 5When Jesus came to the place, he looked up and said to him, "Zacchaeus, hurry and come down; for I must stay at your house today." 6So he hurried down and was happy to welcome him. 7All who saw it began to grumble and said, "He has gone to be the guest of one who is a sinner." 8Zacchaeus stood there and said to the Lord, "Look, half of my possessions, Lord, I will give to the poor; and if I have defrauded anyone of anything, I will pay back four times as much." 9Then Jesus said to him, "Today salvation has come to this house, because he too is a son of Abraham. 10For the Son of Man came to seek out and to save the lost."

The Parable of the Ten Pounds

11 As they were listening to this, he went on to tell a parable, because he was near Jerusalem, and because they supposed that the kingdom of God was to appear immediately. 12So he said, "A nobleman went to a distant country to get royal power for himself and then return. 13He summoned ten of his slaves, and gave them ten pounds,*m* and said to them, 'Do business with these until I come back.' 14But the citizens of his country hated him and sent a delegation after him, saying, 'We do not want this man to rule over us.' 15When he returned, having received royal power, he ordered these slaves, to whom he had given the money, to be summoned so that he might find out what they had gained by trading. 16The first came forward and said, 'Lord, your pound has made ten more pounds.' 17He said to him, 'Well done, good slave! Because you have been trustworthy in a very small thing, take charge of ten cities.' 18Then the second came, saying, 'Lord, your pound has made five pounds.' 19He said to him, 'And you, rule over five cities.' 20Then the other came, saying, 'Lord, here is your pound. I wrapped it up in a piece of cloth, 21for I was afraid of you, because you are a harsh man; you take what you did not deposit, and reap what you did not sow.' 22He said to him, 'I will judge you by your own words, you wicked slave! You knew, did you, that I was a harsh man, taking what I did not deposit and reaping what I did not sow? 23Why then did you not put my money into the bank? Then when I returned, I could have collected it with interest.' 24He said to the bystanders, 'Take the pound from him and give it to the one who has ten pounds.' 25(And they said to him, 'Lord, he has ten pounds!') 26'I tell you, to all those who have, more will be given; but from those who have nothing, even what they have will be taken away. 27But as for these enemies of mine who did not want me to be king over them—bring them here and slaughter them in my presence.' "

Jesus' Triumphal Entry into Jerusalem

28 After he had said this, he went on ahead, going up to Jerusalem.

29 When he had come near Bethphage and Bethany, at the place called the Mount of Olives, he sent two of the disciples, 30saying, "Go into the village ahead of you, and as you enter it you will find tied there a colt that has never been ridden. Untie it and bring it here. 31If anyone

---

l Gk *the Nazorean*   *m* The mina, rendered here by *pound*, was about three months' wages for a laborer

Susanna

Her Name Means
"A White Lily"

THE STORY OF A WOMAN

Her Character: *She is described as a woman of delicate beauty, who trusted God to protect her reputation and her life.*
Her Sorrow: *To be falsely accused and condemned to death.*
Her Joy: *To have her reputation and her life restored and to see justice done.*

Read Daniel 13

Susanna's story reminds us that it really is true: "There's no fool like an old fool."

It happened in Babylon, in a secluded garden, on a balmy day. Susanna was a devout Jewess, married to a highly respected man. Every day at noon she would walk in the garden, accompanied by her maids. One warm day she decided to bathe, not realizing that two old men had concealed themselves in the garden, awaiting their chance to molest her.

These were no ordinary "peeping Toms," but men of position and standing in the community—two elders appointed as judges to govern the people. Associates of her husband, they were accustomed to using their considerable power to get whatever they wanted, especially when it came to women.

As soon as Susanna dismissed her maids, the two old men came out of hiding: "Look, the garden doors are shut, and no one can see us. We are burning with desire for you; so give your consent, and lie with us. If you refuse, we will testify against you that a young man was with you, and this was why you sent your maids away" (13:20–21).

Susanna screamed, but the old men shouted louder, bringing charges against her just as they had threatened. The next day Susanna was brought to trial and condemned to death because of the testimony of the two old liars. The assembly, no doubt composed of men, believed the charges. After all, the accusations had been brought by men of standing, elders and judges.

"O eternal God," Susanna cried out, "you know what is secret and are aware of all things before they come to be; you know that these men have given false evidence against me. And now I am to die, though I have done none of the wicked things that they have charged against me!" (verses 42–43).

As she was being led to her execution, a young boy named Daniel suddenly spoke up: "Are you such fools, O Israelites, as to condemn a daughter of Israel without examination and without learning the facts? Return to court, for these men have given false evidence against her" (verses 48–49).

So the court reconvened and young Daniel was able to question the old men separately: "Now then . . . tell me this: Under what tree did you see them being intimate with each other?" The first man replied that he had seen Susanna and her lover under a mastic tree. The second testified the couple had been under an oak. Their lie couldn't have been more obvious—a mastic tree was small while an oak was large. According to the Law of Moses, the two old men suffered the penalty they had meant to impose on Susanna, forfeiting their lives for their lie.

Susanna's story reminds us of others—of Joseph's encounter with Potiphar's wife and of the stunning reversals in the story of Esther and Mordecai. The weak, the preyed upon, and the oppressed are restored, rescued, and eventually rewarded while their powerful predators are completely destroyed. On the verge of tragedy, God intervened to establish justice and rescue the innocent. He heard the prayer of a woman who trusted him, knowing that he sees every hidden thing.

Praying With Susanna

"O eternal God, you know what is secret and are aware of all things before they come to be; you know that these men have given false evidence against me. And now I am to die, though I have done none of the wicked things that they have charged against me!"—Daniel 13.42–43

Praise God: Because he is all-seeing and all-knowing.
Thank God: For his justice.
Confess: Any temptation to seek revenge on someone who has falsely accused or wronged you.
Ask God: To vindicate and restore you.

Lift Your Heart

In our world the strong often prey upon the weak. For most of history, women have been particularly vulnerable because they have not held positions of power in society. But other groups have also suffered great abuse: the elderly, minorities, children, the poor, the disabled. Whether you have been wounded by someone in power or not, take your mind off yourself this week by praying for justice in an unjust situation that troubles you. It could be occurring at work or at home or even in your neighborhood. Or perhaps you read about it or saw it on the nightly news. Whatever it is, pray Susanna's prayer on behalf of the weak, the powerless, and the innocent, remembering that God can rescue the innocent and establish justice in an instant.

Father, make me sensitive to the hurts of others, male and female, so that I do not ignore the injustices I see in the world around me but confront them through the power of prayer. This week show me one person or group that I can pray for regularly.

Go to page 1386 for your next devotional reading.

asks you, 'Why are you untying it?' just say this, 'The Lord needs it.'" [32]So those who were sent departed and found it as he had told them. [33]As they were untying the colt, its owners asked them, "Why are you untying the colt?" [34]They said, "The Lord needs it." [35]Then they brought it to Jesus; and after throwing their cloaks on the colt, they set Jesus on it. [36]As he rode along, people kept spreading their cloaks on the road. [37]As he was now approaching the path down from the Mount of Olives, the whole multitude of the disciples began to praise God joyfully with a loud voice for all the deeds of power that they had seen, [38]saying,

"Blessed is the king
who comes in the name of
the Lord!
Peace in heaven,
and glory in the highest heaven!"

[39]Some of the Pharisees in the crowd said to him, "Teacher, order your disciples to stop." [40]He answered, "I tell you, if these were silent, the stones would shout out."

Jesus Weeps over Jerusalem

[41] As he came near and saw the city, he wept over it, [42]saying, "If you, even you, had only recognized on this day the things that make for peace! But now they are hidden from your eyes. [43]Indeed, the days will come upon you, when your enemies will set up ramparts around you and surround you, and hem you in on every side. [44]They will crush you to the ground, you and your children within you, and they will not leave within you one stone upon another; because you did not recognize the time of your visitation from God."[n]

Jesus Cleanses the Temple

[45] Then he entered the temple and began to drive out those who were selling things there; [46]and he said, "It is written,
'My house shall be a house
of prayer';
but you have made it a den
of robbers."

[47] Every day he was teaching in the temple. The chief priests, the scribes, and the leaders of the people kept looking for a way to kill him; [48]but they did not find anything they could do, for all the people were spellbound by what they heard.

The Authority of Jesus Questioned

20 One day, as he was teaching the people in the temple and telling the good news, the chief priests and the scribes came with the elders [2]and said to him, "Tell us, by what authority are you doing these things? Who is it who gave you this authority?" [3]He answered them, "I will also ask you a question, and you tell me: [4]Did the baptism of John come from heaven, or was it of human origin?" [5]They discussed it with one another, saying, "If we say, 'From heaven,' he will say, 'Why did you not believe him?' [6]But if we say, 'Of human origin,' all the people will stone us; for they are convinced that John was a prophet." [7]So they answered that they did not know where it came from. [8]Then Jesus said to them, "Neither will I tell you by what authority I am doing these things."

The Parable of the Wicked Tenants

[9] He began to tell the people this parable: "A man planted a vineyard, and leased it to tenants, and went to another country for a long time. [10]When the season came, he sent a slave to the tenants in order that they might give him his share of the produce of the vineyard; but the tenants beat him and sent him away empty-handed. [11]Next he sent another slave; that one also they beat and insulted and sent away empty-handed. [12]And he sent still a third; this one also they wounded and threw out. [13]Then the owner of the vineyard said, 'What shall I do? I will send my beloved son; perhaps they will respect him.' [14]But when the tenants saw him, they discussed it among themselves and said, 'This is the heir; let us kill him so that the inheritance may be ours.' [15]So they threw him out of the vineyard and killed him. What then will the owner of the vineyard do to them? [16]He will come and destroy those tenants and give the vineyard to others." When they heard this, they said, "Heaven forbid!" [17]But he looked at them and said, "What then does this text mean:
'The stone that the builders rejected
has become the cornerstone'?[o]

[18]Everyone who falls on that stone will be broken to pieces; and it will crush anyone on whom it falls." [19]When the scribes and

---

[n] Gk lacks *from God*   [o] Or *keystone*

chief priests realized that he had told this parable against them, they wanted to lay hands on him at that very hour, but they feared the people.

The Question about Paying Taxes

20 So they watched him and sent spies who pretended to be honest, in order to trap him by what he said, so as to hand him over to the jurisdiction and authority of the governor. 21So they asked him, "Teacher, we know that you are right in what you say and teach, and you show deference to no one, but teach the way of God in accordance with truth. 22Is it lawful for us to pay taxes to the emperor, or not?" 23But he perceived their craftiness and said to them, 24"Show me a denarius. Whose head and whose title does it bear?" They said, "The emperor's." 25He said to them, "Then give to the emperor the things that are the emperor's, and to God the things that are God's." 26And they were not able in the presence of the people to trap him by what he said; and being amazed by his answer, they became silent.

The Question about the Resurrection

27 Some Sadducees, those who say there is no resurrection, came to him 28and asked him a question, "Teacher, Moses wrote for us that if a man's brother dies, leaving a wife but no children, the man *p* shall marry the widow and raise up children for his brother. 29Now there were seven brothers; the first married, and died childless; 30then the second 31and the third married her, and so in the same way all seven died childless. 32Finally the woman also died. 33In the resurrection, therefore, whose wife will the woman be? For the seven had married her."

34 Jesus said to them, "Those who belong to this age marry and are given in marriage; 35but those who are considered worthy of a place in that age and in the resurrection from the dead neither marry nor are given in marriage. 36Indeed they cannot die anymore, because they are like angels and are children of God, being children of the resurrection. 37And the fact that the dead are raised Moses himself showed, in the story about the bush, where he speaks of the Lord as the God of Abraham, the God of Isaac, and the God of Jacob. 38Now he is God not of the dead, but of the living; for to him all of them are alive." 39Then some of the scribes an-

swered, "Teacher, you have spoken well." 40For they no longer dared to ask him another question.

The Question about David's Son

41 Then he said to them, "How can they say that the Messiah*q* is David's son? 42For David himself says in the book of Psalms,

'The Lord said to my Lord,
    "Sit at my right hand,
43   until I make your enemies your
            footstool." '

44David thus calls him Lord; so how can he be his son?"

Jesus Denounces the Scribes

45 In the hearing of all the people he said to the*r* disciples, 46"Beware of the scribes, who like to walk around in long robes, and love to be greeted with respect in the marketplaces, and to have the best seats in the synagogues and places of honor at banquets. 47They devour widows' houses and for the sake of appearance say long prayers. They will receive the greater condemnation."

The Widow's Offering

21 He looked up and saw rich people putting their gifts into the treasury; 2he also saw a poor widow put in two small copper coins. 3He said, "Truly I tell you, this poor widow has put in more than all of them; 4for all of them have contributed out of their abundance, but she out of her poverty has put in all she had to live on."

The Destruction of the Temple Foretold

5 When some were speaking about the temple, how it was adorned with beautiful stones and gifts dedicated to God, he said, 6"As for these things that you see, the days will come when not one stone will be left upon another; all will be thrown down."

Signs and Persecutions

7 They asked him, "Teacher, when will this be, and what will be the sign that this is about to take place?" 8And he said, "Beware that you are not led astray; for many will come in my name and say, 'I am

p Gk *his brother*   *q* Or *the Christ*   *r* Other ancient authorities read *his* he!'*s* and, 'The time is near!'*t* Do not go after them.

9 "When you hear of wars and insurrections, do not be terrified; for these things must take place first, but the end will not follow immediately." [10]Then he said to them, "Nation will rise against nation, and kingdom against kingdom; [11]there will be great earthquakes, and in various places famines and plagues; and there will be dreadful portents and great signs from heaven.

12 "But before all this occurs, they will arrest you and persecute you; they will hand you over to synagogues and prisons, and you will be brought before kings and governors because of my name. [13]This will give you an opportunity to testify. [14]So make up your minds not to prepare your defense in advance; [15]for I will give you words*u* and a wisdom that none of your opponents will be able to withstand or contradict. [16]You will be betrayed even by parents and brothers, by relatives and friends; and they will put some of you to death. [17]You will be hated by all because of my name. [18]But not a hair of your head will perish. [19]By your endurance you will gain your souls.

The Destruction of Jerusalem Foretold

20 "When you see Jerusalem surrounded by armies, then know that its desolation has come near.*v* [21]Then those in Judea must flee to the mountains, and those inside the city must leave it, and those out in the country must not enter it; [22]for these are days of vengeance, as a fulfillment of all that is written. [23]Woe to those who are pregnant and to those who are nursing infants in those days! For there will be great distress on the earth and wrath against this people; [24]they will fall by the edge of the sword and be taken away as captives among all nations; and Jerusalem will be trampled on by the Gentiles, until the times of the Gentiles are fulfilled.

The Coming of the Son of Man

25 "There will be signs in the sun, the moon, and the stars, and on the earth distress among nations confused by the roaring of the sea and the waves. [26]People will faint from fear and foreboding of what is coming upon the world, for the powers of the heavens will be shaken. [27]Then they will see 'the Son of Man coming in a

cloud' with power and great glory. [28]Now when these things begin to take place, stand up and raise your heads, because your redemption is drawing near."

The Lesson of the Fig Tree

29 Then he told them a parable: "Look at the fig tree and all the trees; [30]as soon as they sprout leaves you can see for yourselves and know that summer is already near. [31]So also, when you see these things taking place, you know that the kingdom of God is near. [32]Truly I tell you, this generation will not pass away until all things have taken place. [33]Heaven and earth will pass away, but my words will not pass away.

Exhortation to Watch

34 "Be on guard so that your hearts are not weighed down with dissipation and drunkenness and the worries of this life, and that day does not catch you unexpectedly, [35]like a trap. For it will come upon all who live on the face of the whole earth. [36]Be alert at all times, praying that you may have the strength to escape all these things that will take place, and to stand before the Son of Man."

37 Every day he was teaching in the temple, and at night he would go out and spend the night on the Mount of Olives, as it was called. [38]And all the people would get up early in the morning to listen to him in the temple.

The Plot to Kill Jesus

22 Now the festival of Unleavened Bread, which is called the Passover, was near. [2]The chief priests and the scribes were looking for a way to put Jesus*w* to death, for they were afraid of the people.

3 Then Satan entered into Judas called Iscariot, who was one of the twelve; [4]he went away and conferred with the chief priests and officers of the temple police about how he might betray him to them. [5]They were greatly pleased and agreed to give him money. [6]So he consented and began to look for an opportunity to betray him to them when no crowd was present.

The Preparation of the Passover

7 Then came the day of Unleavened

s Gk *I am*   *t* Or *at hand*   *u* Gk *a mouth*   *v* Or *is at hand*   *w* Gk *him*

Bread, on which the Passover lamb had to be sacrificed. [8]So Jesus[x] sent Peter and John, saying, "Go and prepare the Passover meal for us that we may eat it." [9]They asked him, "Where do you want us to make preparations for it?" [10]"Listen," he said to them, "when you have entered the city, a man carrying a jar of water will meet you; follow him into the house he enters [11]and say to the owner of the house, 'The teacher asks you, "Where is the guest room, where I may eat the Passover with my disciples?" ' [12]He will show you a large room upstairs, already furnished. Make preparations for us there." [13]So they went and found everything as he had told them; and they prepared the Passover meal.

The Institution of the Lord's Supper

14 When the hour came, he took his place at the table, and the apostles with him. [15]He said to them, "I have eagerly desired to eat this Passover with you before I suffer; [16]for I tell you, I will not eat it[y] until it is fulfilled in the kingdom of God." [17]Then he took a cup, and after giving thanks he said, "Take this and divide it among yourselves; [18]for I tell you that from now on I will not drink of the fruit of the vine until the kingdom of God comes." [19]Then he took a loaf of bread, and when he had given thanks, he broke it and gave it to them, saying, "This is my body, which is given for you. Do this in remembrance of me." [20]And he did the same with the cup after supper, saying, "This cup that is poured out for you is the new covenant in my blood.[z] [21]But see, the one who betrays me is with me, and his hand is on the table. [22]For the Son of Man is going as it has been determined, but woe to that one by whom he is betrayed!" [23]Then they began to ask one another which one of them it could be who would do this.

The Dispute about Greatness

24 A dispute also arose among them as to which one of them was to be regarded as the greatest. [25]But he said to them, "The kings of the Gentiles lord it over them; and those in authority over them are called benefactors. [26]But not so with you; rather the greatest among you must become like the youngest, and the leader like one who serves. [27]For who is greater,

the one who is at the table or the one who serves? Is it not the one at the table? But I am among you as one who serves.

28 "You are those who have stood by me in my trials; [29]and I confer on you, just as my Father has conferred on me, a kingdom, [30]so that you may eat and drink at my table in my kingdom, and you will sit on thrones judging the twelve tribes of Israel.

Jesus Predicts Peter's Denial

31 "Simon, Simon, listen! Satan has demanded[a] to sift all of you like wheat, [32]but I have prayed for you that your own faith may not fail; and you, when once you have turned back, strengthen your brothers." [33]And he said to him, "Lord, I am ready to go with you to prison and to death!" [34]Jesus[b] said, "I tell you, Peter, the cock will not crow this day, until you have denied three times that you know me."

Purse, Bag, and Sword

35 He said to them, "When I sent you out without a purse, bag, or sandals, did you lack anything?" They said, "No, not a thing." [36]He said to them, "But now, the one who has a purse must take it, and likewise a bag. And the one who has no sword must sell his cloak and buy one. [37]For I tell you, this scripture must be fulfilled in me, 'And he was counted among the lawless'; and indeed what is written about me is being fulfilled." [38]They said, "Lord, look, here are two swords." He replied, "It is enough."

Jesus Prays on the Mount of Olives

39 He came out and went, as was his custom, to the Mount of Olives; and the disciples followed him. [40]When he reached the place, he said to them, "Pray that you may not come into the time of trial."[c] [41]Then he withdrew from them about a stone's throw, knelt down, and prayed, [42]"Father, if you are willing, remove this cup from me; yet, not my will but yours be done." [[43]Then an angel from heaven appeared to him and gave him strength. [44]In his anguish he prayed more

---

[x] Gk he   [y] Other ancient authorities read *never eat it again*   [z] Other ancient authorities lack, in whole or in part, verses 19b-20 (*which is given . . . in my blood*)   [a] Or *has obtained permission*   [b] Gk He   [c] Or *into temptation*

earnestly, and his sweat became like great drops of blood falling down on the ground.]*d* ⁴⁵When he got up from prayer, he came to the disciples and found them sleeping because of grief, ⁴⁶and he said to them, "Why are you sleeping? Get up and pray that you may not come into the time of trial."*e*

The Betrayal and Arrest of Jesus

47 While he was still speaking, suddenly a crowd came, and the one called Judas, one of the twelve, was leading them. He approached Jesus to kiss him; ⁴⁸but Jesus

d Other ancient authorities lack verses 43 and 44
e Or *into temptation*

Praying Through Our Fear

MONDAY

Scripture Reading for Today:
Luke 22.39–46

Verse for Today:
Luke 22.42

Sometimes we make the mistake of thinking everything was easy for Jesus. After all, he was God, wasn't he? He could do anything he wanted—even die on a cross without a word of complaint. Yet Scripture makes it clear that Jesus was filled with fear and agony on the evening before his death.

Though it grieves me to imagine what Jesus must have endured for my sake, it also comforts me. He felt the same fear that prowls inside my soul whenever awful possibilities lurk. Like Jesus, I can honestly cry out to God and ask him to rescue me. And like Jesus, I can tell the Father that whatever happens, I want his will to be done.

The Father answered his Son, not with the response Jesus hoped for, but with the answer he was willing to receive. Instead of a delivering angel, God sent an angel to impart greater courage for the ordeal ahead.

For his part, Jesus urged the disciples to pray they would not fall into temptation. Jesus knew that fear would rule his disciples for a time. After his arrest, Satan would appear to be ascendant. Peter, James, John, and the rest of the lot would lose faith, betray him, and run and hide. None of them would stand when the soldiers came to seize him.

We wonder how the disciples could have been such cowards. Yet we succumb to the same temptations they did. Like Peter, we tell Jesus that we love him and that we are willing to follow him anywhere. Yet we are unwilling to follow him into the darkness of fear and confusion and suffering. Our faith trembles when disaster looms. We want to withdraw, to run and hide, to find a place of ultimate safety.

At such times, we need to echo Jesus' prayer. *"I'm afraid, Lord. Please take this suffering from me. Even so, Father, don't answer my prayer if it contradicts your will."* As we pray, God will answer us. Whether or not he spares us from the suffering we most fear, he will give us courage to face whatever comes.

—*ANN SPANGLER*

Go to page 1389 for your next devotional reading.

said to him, "Judas, is it with a kiss that you are betraying the Son of Man?" [49]When those who were around him saw what was coming, they asked, "Lord, should we strike with the sword?" [50]Then one of them struck the slave of the high priest and cut off his right ear. [51]But Jesus said, "No more of this!" And he touched his ear and healed him. [52]Then Jesus said to the chief priests, the officers of the temple police, and the elders who had come for him, "Have you come out with swords and clubs as if I were a bandit? [53]When I was with you day after day in the temple, you did not lay hands on me. But this is your hour, and the power of darkness!"

Peter Denies Jesus

54 Then they seized him and led him away, bringing him into the high priest's house. But Peter was following at a distance. [55]When they had kindled a fire in the middle of the courtyard and sat down together, Peter sat among them. [56]Then a servant-girl, seeing him in the firelight, stared at him and said, "This man also was with him." [57]But he denied it, saying, "Woman, I do not know him." [58]A little later someone else, on seeing him, said, "You also are one of them." But Peter said, "Man, I am not!" [59]Then about an hour later still another kept insisting, "Surely this man also was with him; for he is a Galilean." [60]But Peter said, "Man, I do not know what you are talking about!" At that moment, while he was still speaking, the cock crowed. [61]The Lord turned and looked at Peter. Then Peter remembered the word of the Lord, how he had said to him, "Before the cock crows today, you will deny me three times." [62]And he went out and wept bitterly.

The Mocking and Beating of Jesus

63 Now the men who were holding Jesus began to mock him and beat him; [64]they also blindfolded him and kept asking him, "Prophesy! Who is it that struck you?" [65]They kept heaping many other insults on him.

Jesus before the Council

66 When day came, the assembly of the elders of the people, both chief priests and scribes, gathered together, and they brought him to their council. [67]They said, "If you are the Messiah, [f] tell us." He replied, "If I tell you, you will not believe; [68]and if I question you, you will not answer. [69]But from now on the Son of Man will be seated at the right hand of the power of God." [70]All of them asked, "Are you, then, the Son of God?" He said to them, "You say that I am." [71]Then they said, "What further testimony do we need? We have heard it ourselves from his own lips!"

Jesus before Pilate

23 Then the assembly rose as a body and brought Jesus [g] before Pilate. [2]They began to accuse him, saying, "We found this man perverting our nation, forbidding us to pay taxes to the emperor, and saying that he himself is the Messiah, a king." [h] [3]Then Pilate asked him, "Are you the king of the Jews?" He answered, "You say so." [4]Then Pilate said to the chief priests and the crowds, "I find no basis for an accusation against this man." [5]But they were insistent and said, "He stirs up the people by teaching throughout all Judea, from Galilee where he began even to this place."

Jesus before Herod

6 When Pilate heard this, he asked whether the man was a Galilean. [7]And when he learned that he was under Herod's jurisdiction, he sent him off to Herod, who was himself in Jerusalem at that time. [8]When Herod saw Jesus, he was very glad, for he had been wanting to see him for a long time, because he had heard about him and was hoping to see him perform some sign. [9]He questioned him at some length, but Jesus [i] gave him no answer. [10]The chief priests and the scribes stood by, vehemently accusing him. [11]Even Herod with his soldiers treated him with contempt and mocked him; then he put an elegant robe on him, and sent him back to Pilate. [12]That same day Herod and Pilate became friends with each other; before this they had been enemies.

Jesus Sentenced to Death

13 Pilate then called together the chief priests, the leaders, and the people, [14]and said to them, "You brought me this man as one who was perverting the people; and here I have examined him in your

---

f Or *the Christ*   *g* Gk *him*   *h* Or *is an anointed king*   *i* Gk *he*

presence and have not found this man guilty of any of your charges against him. [15]Neither has Herod, for he sent him back to us. Indeed, he has done nothing to deserve death. [16]I will therefore have him flogged and release him." [j]

18 Then they all shouted out together, "Away with this fellow! Release Barabbas for us!" [19](This was a man who had been put in prison for an insurrection that had taken place in the city, and for murder.) [20]Pilate, wanting to release Jesus, addressed them again; [21]but they kept shouting, "Crucify, crucify him!" [22]A third time he said to them, "Why, what evil has he done? I have found in him no ground for the sentence of death; I will therefore have him flogged and then release him." [23]But they kept urgently demanding with loud shouts that he should be crucified; and their voices prevailed. [24]So Pilate gave his verdict that their demand should be granted. [25]He released the man they asked for, the one who had been put in prison for insurrection and murder, and he handed Jesus over as they wished.

The Crucifixion of Jesus

26 As they led him away, they seized a man, Simon of Cyrene, who was coming from the country, and they laid the cross on him, and made him carry it behind Jesus. [27]A great number of the people followed him, and among them were women who were beating their breasts and wailing for him. [28]But Jesus turned to them and said, "Daughters of Jerusalem, do not weep for me, but weep for yourselves and for your children. [29]For the days are surely coming when they will say, 'Blessed are the barren, and the wombs that never bore, and the breasts that never nursed.' [30]Then they will begin to say to the mountains, 'Fall on us'; and to the hills, 'Cover us.' [31]For if they do this when the wood is green, what will happen when it is dry?"

32 Two others also, who were criminals, were led away to be put to death with him. [33]When they came to the place that is called The Skull, they crucified Jesus[k] there with the criminals, one on his right and one on his left. [[34]Then Jesus said, "Father, forgive them; for they do not know what they are doing."][l] And they cast lots to divide his clothing. [35]And the people stood by, watching; but the leaders scoffed at him, saying, "He saved

others; let him save himself if he is the Messiah[m] of God, his chosen one!" [36]The soldiers also mocked him, coming up and offering him sour wine, [37]and saying, "If you are the King of the Jews, save yourself!" [38]There was also an inscription over him,[n] "This is the King of the Jews."

39 One of the criminals who were hanged there kept deriding[o] him and saying, "Are you not the Messiah?[m] Save yourself and us!" [40]But the other rebuked him, saying, "Do you not fear God, since you are under the same sentence of condemnation? [41]And we indeed have been condemned justly, for we are getting what we deserve for our deeds, but this man has done nothing wrong." [42]Then he said, "Jesus, remember me when you come into[p] your kingdom." [43]He replied, "Truly I tell you, today you will be with me in Paradise."

The Death of Jesus

44 It was now about noon, and darkness came over the whole land[q] until three in the afternoon, [45]while the sun's light failed;[r] and the curtain of the temple was torn in two. [46]Then Jesus, crying with a loud voice, said, "Father, into your hands I commend my spirit." Having said this, he breathed his last. [47]When the centurion saw what had taken place, he praised God and said, "Certainly this man was innocent."[s] [48]And when all the crowds who had gathered there for this spectacle saw what had taken place, they returned home, beating their breasts. [49]But all his acquaintances, including the women who had followed him from Galilee, stood at a distance, watching these things.

The Burial of Jesus

50 Now there was a good and righteous man named Joseph, who, though a member of the council, [51]had not agreed to their plan and action. He came from

j Here, or after verse 19, other ancient authorities add verse 17, *Now he was obliged to release someone for them at the festival*   *k* Gk *him*   *l* Other ancient authorities lack the sentence *Then Jesus . . . what they are doing*   *m* Or *the Christ*   *n* Other ancient authorities add *written in Greek and Latin and Hebrew* (that is, *Aramaic*)   *o* Or *blaspheming*   *p* Other ancient authorities read *in*   *q* Or *earth*   *r* Or *the sun was eclipsed.* Other ancient authorities read *the sun was darkened*   *s* Or *righteous*

the Jewish town of Arimathea, and he was waiting expectantly for the kingdom of God. 52This man went to Pilate and asked for the body of Jesus. 53Then he took it down, wrapped it in a linen cloth, and laid it in a rock-hewn tomb where no one had ever been laid. 54It was the day of Preparation, and the sabbath was beginning.*t* 55The women who had come with him from Galilee followed, and they saw the tomb and how his body was laid. 56Then they returned, and prepared spices and ointments.

On the sabbath they rested according to the commandment.

The Resurrection of Jesus

24 But on the first day of the week, at early dawn, they came to the tomb, taking the spices that they had prepared. 2They found the stone rolled away from the tomb, 3but when they went in, they did not find the body.*u* 4While they were perplexed about this, suddenly two men in dazzling clothes stood beside them. 5The women*v* were terrified and bowed their faces to the ground, but the men*w* said to them, "Why do you look for the living among the dead? He is not here, but has risen.*x* 6Remember how he told you, while he was still in Galilee, 7that the Son of Man must be handed over to sinners, and be crucified, and on the third day rise again." 8Then they remembered his words, 9and returning from the tomb, they told all this to the eleven and to all the rest. 10Now it was Mary Magda-

t Gk *was dawning*   *u* Other ancient authorities add *of the Lord Jesus*   *v* Gk *They*   *w* Gk *but they*
x Other ancient authorities lack *He is not here, but has risen*

The Killing of God

TUESDAY

Scripture Reading for Today:
Luke 23.33–38

Verse for Today:
Luke 23.33

They mocked and railed on him and smote him; they scourged and crucified him. Well, they were people very remote from ourselves, and no doubt it was all done in the noblest and most beautiful manner. We should not like to think otherwise.

Unhappily, if we think about it at all, we must think otherwise. God was executed by people painfully like us, in a society very similar to our own—in the over-ripeness of the most splendid and sophisticated Empire the world has ever seen. In a nation famous for its religious genius and under a government renowned for its efficiency, he was executed by a corrupt church, a timid politician, and a fickle proletariat led by professional agitators. His executioners made vulgar jokes about him, called him filthy names, taunted him, smacked him in the face, flogged him and hanged him on the common gibbet—a bloody, dusty, sweaty, and sordid business.

If you show people that, they are shocked. So they should be. If that does not shock them, nothing can. If the mere representation of it has an air of irreverence, what is to be said about the deed? It is curious that people who are filled with horrified indignation whenever a cat kills a sparrow can hear that story of the killing of God told Sunday after Sunday and not experience any shock at all.

—DOROTHY SAYERS

Go to page 1390 for your next devotional reading.

lene, Joanna, Mary the mother of James, and the other women with them who told this to the apostles. ¹¹But these words seemed to them an idle tale, and they did not believe them. ¹²But Peter got up and ran to the tomb; stooping and looking in, he saw the linen cloths by themselves; then he went home, amazed at what had happened. *y*

The Walk to Emmaus

13 Now on that same day two of them were going to a village called Emmaus, about seven miles*z* from Jerusalem,

¹⁴and talking with each other about all these things that had happened. ¹⁵While they were talking and discussing, Jesus himself came near and went with them, ¹⁶but their eyes were kept from recognizing him. ¹⁷And he said to them, "What are you discussing with each other while you walk along?" They stood still, looking sad.*a* ¹⁸Then one of them, whose name

y Other ancient authorities lack verse 12   *z* Gk *sixty stadia; other ancient authorities read a hundred sixty stadia*   *a* Other ancient authorities read *walk along, looking sad?"*

"Don't You See?"

WEDNESDAY

Scripture Reading for Today:
Luke 24.13–35

Verse for Today:
Luke 24.25

The story of the disciples going to Emmaus is a work of genius. The two travelers are not just two people who happened to be there that night. They are the Church, they are you and I, because this is Luke's inspired picture of how things are in the Easter Church, the Church of Word and Sacrament: the long journey, the distress and bewilderment, the knowing yet not knowing, the patient tenderness of Christ as he tries to open their minds to understand the Scriptures, their burning hearts, their eventual recognition that they have indeed known the Lord in the breaking of the bread of the Word and the bread of Eucharist. The word is not always clarifying; it is mysterious because it is the presence and self-communication of God. It is not always informative; it is performative, creative: changing and converting and renewing us. And there is something about the journey, the long experience of the road, that makes us able to hear it.

"We had hoped," say the travelers to the Lord. "We had hoped that things would go like this . . . We had our plans, but now . . ." Easter is utterly disconcerting because it is the power and mystery of God taking hold of our frail mortality, our limited hopes. "Don't you see?" their unrecognized fellow-pilgrim asks them. Don't you see that it had to be like that? Was it not written? Isn't it what all the Scriptures are about, from end to end? Don't you understand that the Christ had to suffer and so enter into his glory? Don't you understand that it can't be otherwise for you? You have to jettison your small plans because the Father's plans for you are unthinkably greater and more wonderful. You have to leap into his hands, say an unconditional "Yes," and be born anew. His love exceeds all that you deserve or even desire.

—*MARIA BOULDING*

Go to page 1393 for your next devotional reading.

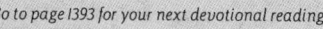

was Cleopas, answered him, "Are you the only stranger in Jerusalem who does not know the things that have taken place there in these days?" [19]He asked them, "What things?" They replied, "The things about Jesus of Nazareth,[b] who was a prophet mighty in deed and word before God and all the people, [20]and how our chief priests and leaders handed him over to be condemned to death and crucified him. [21]But we had hoped that he was the one to redeem Israel.[c] Yes, and besides all this, it is now the third day since these things took place. [22]Moreover, some women of our group astounded us. They were at the tomb early this morning, [23]and when they did not find his body there, they came back and told us that they had indeed seen a vision of angels who said that he was alive. [24]Some of those who were with us went to the tomb and found it just as the women had said; but they did not see him." [25]Then he said to them, "Oh, how foolish you are, and how slow of heart to believe all that the prophets have declared! [26]Was it not necessary that the Messiah[d] should suffer these things and then enter into his glory?" [27]Then beginning with Moses and all the prophets, he interpreted to them the things about himself in all the scriptures.

28 As they came near the village to which they were going, he walked ahead as if he were going on. [29]But they urged him strongly, saying, "Stay with us, because it is almost evening and the day is now nearly over." So he went in to stay with them. [30]When he was at the table with them, he took bread, blessed and broke it, and gave it to them. [31]Then their eyes were opened, and they recognized him; and he vanished from their sight. [32]They said to each other, "Were not our hearts burning within us[e] while he was talking to us on the road, while he was opening the scriptures to us?" [33]That same hour they got up and returned to Jerusalem; and they found the eleven and their companions gathered together. [34]They were saying, "The Lord has risen indeed, and he has appeared to Simon!" [35]Then they told what had happened on the road, and how he had been made known to them in the breaking of the bread.

Jesus Appears to His Disciples

36 While they were talking about this, Jesus himself stood among them and said to them, "Peace be with you."[f] [37]They were startled and terrified, and thought that they were seeing a ghost. [38]He said to them, "Why are you frightened, and why do doubts arise in your hearts? [39]Look at my hands and my feet; see that it is I myself. Touch me and see; for a ghost does not have flesh and bones as you see that I have." [40]And when he had said this, he showed them his hands and his feet.[g] [41]While in their joy they were disbelieving and still wondering, he said to them, "Have you anything here to eat?" [42]They gave him a piece of broiled fish, [43]and he took it and ate in their presence.

44 Then he said to them, "These are my words that I spoke to you while I was still with you—that everything written about me in the law of Moses, the prophets, and the psalms must be fulfilled." [45]Then he opened their minds to understand the scriptures, [46]and he said to them, "Thus it is written, that the Messiah[d] is to suffer and to rise from the dead on the third day, [47]and that repentance and forgiveness of sins is to be proclaimed in his name to all nations, beginning from Jerusalem. [48]You are witnesses[h] of these things. [49]And see, I am sending upon you what my Father promised; so stay here in the city until you have been clothed with power from on high."

The Ascension of Jesus

50 Then he led them out as far as Bethany, and, lifting up his hands, he blessed them. [51]While he was blessing them, he withdrew from them and was carried up into heaven.[i] [52]And they worshiped him,[j] and[j] returned to Jerusalem with great joy; [53]and they were continually in the temple blessing God.[k]

b Other ancient authorities read *Jesus the Nazorean*   c Or *to set Israel free*   d Or *the Christ*   e Other ancient authorities lack *within us*   f Other ancient authorities lack *and said to them, "Peace be with you."*   g Other ancient authorities lack verse 40   h Or *nations. Beginning from Jerusalem* [48]*you are witnesses*   i Other ancient authorities lack *and was carried up into heaven*   j Other ancient authorities lack *worshiped him, and*   k Other ancient authorities add *Amen*

The Gospel According to

John

Tradition has ascribed this Gospel to the apostle John, identifying him as "the disciple whom Jesus loved" (21.20). A number of modern scholars have questioned this identification; perhaps an anonymous disciple was the eyewitness on whose testimony this Gospel was based.

John's Gospel is unique among the four Gospels, with a distinctive structure, style, and emphasis. It contains none of the parables of Jesus but includes certain details the others do not, and it includes more extensive theological reflections on who Jesus is. Beautifully written, it begins with a remarkable prologue that contains many of the themes that will be explored throughout the Gospel.

Why was this book written? The plain and simple answer is found in 20.30–31: "Now Jesus did many other signs in the presence of his disciples, which are not written in this book. But these are written so that you may come to believe that Jesus is the Messiah, the Son of God, and that through believing you may have life in his name."

John tells us that the first witness to the resurrection was a woman. Mary Magdalene, who had stood with the other women at the cross, was the first to proclaim the good news to the other disciples: "I have seen the Lord" (20:18).

The Word Became Flesh

1 In the beginning was the Word, and the Word was with God, and the Word was God. ²He was in the beginning with God. ³All things came into being through him, and without him not one thing came into being. What has come into being ⁴in him was life,ᵃ and the life was the light of all people. ⁵The light shines in the darkness, and the darkness did not overcome it.

6 There was a man sent from God, whose name was John. ⁷He came as a witness to testify to the light, so that all might believe through him. ⁸He himself was not the light, but he came to testify to the light. ⁹The true light, which enlightens everyone, was coming into the world.ᵇ

10 He was in the world, and the world came into being through him; yet the

---

ᵃ Or ³through him. And without him not one thing came into being that has come into being. ⁴In him was life ᵇ Or He was the true light that enlightens everyone coming into the world

world did not know him. ¹¹He came to what was his own,ᶜ and his own people did not accept him. ¹²But to all who received him, who believed in his name, he gave power to become children of God, ¹³who were born, not of blood or of the will of the flesh or of the will of man, but of God.

14 And the Word became flesh and lived among us, and we have seen his glory, the glory as of a father's only son,ᵈ full of grace and truth. ¹⁵(John testified to him and cried out, "This was he of whom I said, 'He who comes after me ranks ahead of me because he was before me.' ") ¹⁶From his fullness we have all received, grace upon grace. ¹⁷The law indeed was given through Moses; grace and truth came through Jesus Christ. ¹⁸No one has ever seen God. It is God the only Son,ᵉ who is close to the Father's heart,ᶠ who has made him known.

The Testimony of John the Baptist

19 This is the testimony given by John when the Jews sent priests and Levites from Jerusalem to ask him, "Who are you?" ²⁰He confessed and did not deny it, but confessed, "I am not the Messiah."ᵍ

²¹And they asked him, "What then? Are you Elijah?" He said, "I am not." "Are you the prophet?" He answered, "No." ²²Then they said to him, "Who are you? Let us have an answer for those who sent us. What do you say about yourself?" ²³He said,

"I am the voice of one crying out
   in the wilderness,
'Make straight the way of the Lord,' "
as the prophet Isaiah said.

24 Now they had been sent from the Pharisees. ²⁵They asked him, "Why then are you baptizing if you are neither the Messiah,ᵍ nor Elijah, nor the prophet?" ²⁶John answered them, "I baptize with water. Among you stands one whom you do not know, ²⁷the one who is coming after me; I am not worthy to untie the thong of his sandal." ²⁸This took place in Bethany across the Jordan where John was baptizing.

The Lamb of God

29 The next day he saw Jesus coming

ᶜ Or *to his own home*   ᵈ Or *the Father's only Son*
ᵉ Other ancient authorities read *It is an only Son, God,* or *It is the only Son*   ᶠ Gk *bosom*   ᵍ Or *the Christ*

Someone Like Us

Scripture Reading for Today:
John 1.1–18

Verse for Today:
John 1.14

A friend of mine was putting her three-year-old son, Eric, to bed. Because he did not want to go to bed, he did everything he could to prolong the conversation with his father and mother. Recognizing a tactic Eric had often used before, his mother said to him, "It is time for you to go to sleep now. Your father and I are going to put out the light after we kiss you goodnight." He responded with the protest, "But I'm afraid in the dark." His mother, whose patience was being tried, said, "There is nothing to be afraid of. God is here with you." Eric looked up at his father and mother and said, "I know that God is here, but I want someone in here with skin on."

A theologian could take Eric's words and form them into a very down-to-earth explanation of the incarnation, the Word made flesh. God knew that we needed someone with "skin on" to walk with us and so he gave us his son, Jesus.

—PAULA RIPPLE COMIN

Go to page 1396 for your next devotional reading.

toward him and declared, "Here is the Lamb of God who takes away the sin of the world! ³⁰This is he of whom I said, 'After me comes a man who ranks ahead of me because he was before me.' ³¹I myself did not know him; but I came baptizing with water for this reason, that he might be revealed to Israel." ³²And John testified, "I saw the Spirit descending from heaven like a dove, and it remained on him. ³³I myself did not know him, but the one who sent me to baptize with water said to me, 'He on whom you see the Spirit descend and remain is the one who baptizes with the Holy Spirit.' ³⁴And I myself have seen and have testified that this is the Son of God."*ʰ*

The First Disciples of Jesus

35 The next day John again was standing with two of his disciples, ³⁶and as he watched Jesus walk by, he exclaimed, "Look, here is the Lamb of God!" ³⁷The two disciples heard him say this, and they followed Jesus. ³⁸When Jesus turned and saw them following, he said to them, "What are you looking for?" They said to him, "Rabbi" (which translated means Teacher), "where are you staying?" ³⁹He said to them, "Come and see." They came and saw where he was staying, and they remained with him that day. It was about four o'clock in the afternoon. ⁴⁰One of the two who heard John speak and followed him was Andrew, Simon Peter's brother. ⁴¹He first found his brother Simon and said to him, "We have found the Messiah" (which is translated Anointed*ⁱ*). ⁴²He brought Simon*ʲ* to Jesus, who looked at

ʰ Other ancient authorities read *is God's chosen one*   *ⁱ* Or *Christ*   *ʲ* Gk *him*

Christmas and Epiphany

And the Word became flesh and lived among us,
and we have seen his glory, the glory as of a father's
only son, full of grace and truth.

JOHN 1.14

*T*his verse from the Gospel reading for Christmas day is a mini-explanation of the great mystery we celebrate during the liturgical season of Christmas and Epiphany. If it sounds abstract, try thinking of it as the hidden caption under every manger scene. *Look, it tells us, this is a real infant. He cries, nurses, drools, and fills his diapers like any other helpless newborn. And this is also the eternal Son—Emmanuel, God with us.*

The revelation of God's humility is one of the profound mysteries of the incarnation. Before Jesus came to us, who could have imagined the Creator becoming so small and dependent? God was all-powerful and majestic. He commanded floods, split the sea, and revealed himself in pillars of fire and mountains that smoked. People quaked with fear in his presence. Everybody knows that God is great. It took a baby in a manger to show us that God is also little.

At Christmas we celebrate the incredible fact that the God who rules the universe became one of us. He didn't just slip into a human body like a disguise; he *became* flesh. He didn't accomplish our salvation from a safe distance: He made his dwelling among us ("pitched his tent," says one translation). Like a new neighbor moving into the house next door, God settled in with us and shared our daily life.

Epiphany points to another cause for celebration: Jesus didn't remain incognito. "We saw his glory." Western rite and Eastern rite Catholics focus on different events here (either the magi's visit or Jesus' baptism), but both highlight the merciful revelation of Jesus' identity and mission.

him and said, "You are Simon son of John. You are to be called Cephas" (which is translated Peter[k]).

Jesus Calls Philip and Nathanael

43 The next day Jesus decided to go to Galilee. He found Philip and said to him, "Follow me." [44]Now Philip was from Bethsaida, the city of Andrew and Peter. [45]Philip found Nathanael and said to him, "We have found him about whom Moses in the law and also the prophets wrote, Jesus son of Joseph from Nazareth." [46]Nathanael said to him, "Can anything good come out of Nazareth?" Philip said to him, "Come and see." [47]When Jesus saw Nathanael coming toward him, he said of him, "Here is truly an Israelite in whom there is no deceit!" [48]Nathanael asked him, "Where did you get to know me?" Jesus answered, "I saw you under the fig tree before Philip called you." [49]Nathanael replied, "Rabbi, you are the Son of God! You are the King of Israel!" [50]Jesus answered, "Do you believe because I told you that I saw you under the fig tree? You will see greater things than these." [51]And he said to him, "Very truly, I tell you,[l] you will see heaven opened and the angels of God ascending and descending upon the Son of Man."

The Wedding at Cana

2 On the third day there was a wedding in Cana of Galilee, and the mother of Jesus was there. [2]Jesus and his disciples had also been invited to the wedding. [3]When the wine gave out, the mother of Jesus said to him, "They have no wine." [4]And Jesus said to her, "Woman, what concern is that to you and to me? My hour has not yet come." [5]His mother said to the servants, "Do whatever he tells you." [6]Now standing there were six stone water jars for the Jewish rites of purification, each holding twenty or thirty gallons. [7]Jesus said to them, "Fill the jars with water." And they filled them up to the brim. [8]He said to them, "Now draw some out, and take it to the chief steward." So they took it. [9]When the steward tasted the water that had become wine, and did not know where it came from (though the servants who had drawn the water knew), the steward called the bridegroom [10]and said to him, "Everyone serves the good wine first, and then the inferior wine after the guests

have become drunk. But you have kept the good wine until now." [11]Jesus did this, the first of his signs, in Cana of Galilee, and revealed his glory; and his disciples believed in him.

12 After this he went down to Capernaum with his mother, his brothers, and his disciples; and they remained there a few days.

Jesus Cleanses the Temple

13 The Passover of the Jews was near, and Jesus went up to Jerusalem. [14]In the temple he found people selling cattle, sheep, and doves, and the money changers seated at their tables. [15]Making a whip of cords, he drove all of them out of the temple, both the sheep and the cattle. He also poured out the coins of the money changers and overturned their tables. [16]He told those who were selling the doves, "Take these things out of here! Stop making my Father's house a marketplace!" [17]His disciples remembered that it was written, "Zeal for your house will consume me." [18]The Jews then said to him, "What sign can you show us for doing this?" [19]Jesus answered them, "Destroy this temple, and in three days I will raise it up." [20]The Jews then said, "This temple has been under construction for forty-six years, and will you raise it up in three days?" [21]But he was speaking of the temple of his body. [22]After he was raised from the dead, his disciples remembered that he had said this; and they believed the scripture and the word that Jesus had spoken.

23 When he was in Jerusalem during the Passover festival, many believed in his name because they saw the signs that he was doing. [24]But Jesus on his part would not entrust himself to them, because he knew all people [25]and needed no one to testify about anyone; for he himself knew what was in everyone.

Nicodemus Visits Jesus

3 Now there was a Pharisee named Nicodemus, a leader of the Jews. [2]He came to Jesus[m] by night and said to him, "Rabbi, we know that you are a teacher who has come from God; for no one can do these signs that you do apart from the

---

k From the word for *rock* in Aramaic (*kepha*) and Greek (*petra*), respectively   l Both instances of the Greek word for *you* in this verse are plural   m Gk *him*

presence of God." ³Jesus answered him, "Very truly, I tell you, no one can see the kingdom of God without being born from above."ⁿ ⁴Nicodemus said to him, "How can anyone be born after having grown old? Can one enter a second time into the mother's womb and be born?" ⁵Jesus answered, "Very truly, I tell you, no one can enter the kingdom of God without being born of water and Spirit. ⁶What is born of the flesh is flesh, and what is born of the Spirit is spirit.ᵒ ⁷Do not be astonished that I said to you, 'Youᵖ must be born from above.'�q ⁸The windᵒ blows where it chooses, and you hear the sound of it, but you do not know where it comes from or where it goes. So it is with everyone who is born of the Spirit." ⁹Nicodemus said to him, "How can these things be?" ¹⁰Jesus answered him, "Are you a teacher of Israel, and yet you do not understand these things?

11 "Very truly, I tell you, we speak of what we know and testify to what we have seen; yet youʳ do not receive our testimony. ¹²If I have told you about earthly things and you do not believe, how can you believe if I tell you about heavenly things? ¹³No one has ascended into heaven except the one who descended from heaven, the Son of Man.ˢ ¹⁴And just as Moses lifted up the serpent in the wilderness, so must the Son of Man be lifted up, ¹⁵that whoever believes in him may have eternal life.ᵗ

16 "For God so loved the world that he gave his only Son, so that everyone who believes in him may not perish but may have eternal life.

17 "Indeed, God did not send the Son into the world to condemn the world, but

---

ⁿ Or *born anew*   ᵒ The same Greek word means both *wind* and *spirit*   ᵖ The Greek word for *you* here is plural   q Or *anew*   ʳ The Greek word for *you* here and in verse 12 is plural   ˢ Other ancient authorities add *who is in heaven*   ᵗ Some interpreters hold that the quotation concludes with verse 15

FRIDAY

Scripture Reading for Today:
John 3.16–21

Verse for Today:
John 3.16

Unimaginable Love

Why did you so dignify us? With unimaginable love you looked upon your creatures within your very self, and you fell in love with us. So it was love that made you create us and give us being just so that we might taste your supreme eternal good.

Then I see how by our sin we lost the dignity you had given us. Rebels that we were, we declared war on your mercy and became your enemies. But stirred by the same fire that made you create us, you decided to give this warring human race a way to reconciliation, bringing great peace out of our war. So you gave us your only-begotten Son, your Word, to be mediator between us and you. He became our justice, taking on himself the punishment for our injustices. He offered you the obedience you required of him in clothing him with our humanity, eternal Father, taking on our likeness and our human nature!

O depth of love! What heart could keep from breaking at the sight of your greatness descending to the lowliness of our humanity? We are your image, and now by making yourself one with us you have become our image, veiling your eternal divinity. And why? For love! You, God, became human and we have been made divine!

—SAINT CATHERINE OF SIENA

Go to page 1398 for your next devotional reading.

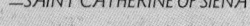

in order that the world might be saved through him. [18]Those who believe in him are not condemned; but those who do not believe are condemned already, because they have not believed in the name of the only Son of God. [19]And this is the judgment, that the light has come into the world, and people loved darkness rather than light because their deeds were evil. [20]For all who do evil hate the light and do not come to the light, so that their deeds may not be exposed. [21]But those who do what is true come to the light, so that it may be clearly seen that their deeds have been done in God."[u]

Jesus and John the Baptist

22 After this Jesus and his disciples went into the Judean countryside, and he spent some time there with them and baptized. [23]John also was baptizing at Aenon near Salim because water was abundant there; and people kept coming and were being baptized [24]—John, of course, had not yet been thrown into prison.

25 Now a discussion about purification arose between John's disciples and a Jew.[v] [26]They came to John and said to him, "Rabbi, the one who was with you across the Jordan, to whom you testified, here he is baptizing, and all are going to him." [27]John answered, "No one can receive anything except what has been given from heaven. [28]You yourselves are my witnesses that I said, 'I am not the Messiah,[w] but I have been sent ahead of him.' [29]He who has the bride is the bridegroom. The friend of the bridegroom, who stands and hears him, rejoices greatly at the bridegroom's voice. For this reason my joy has been fulfilled. [30]He must increase, but I must decrease."[x]

The One Who Comes from Heaven

31 The one who comes from above is above all; the one who is of the earth belongs to the earth and speaks about earthly things. The one who comes from heaven is above all. [32]He testifies to what he has seen and heard, yet no one accepts his testimony. [33]Whoever has accepted his testimony has certified[y] this, that God is true. [34]He whom God has sent speaks the words of God, for he gives the Spirit without measure. [35]The Father loves the Son and has placed all things in his hands. [36]Whoever believes in the Son has eternal life; whoever disobeys the Son will not see life, but must endure God's wrath.

Jesus and the Woman of Samaria

4 Now when Jesus[z] learned that the Pharisees had heard, "Jesus is making and baptizing more disciples than John" [2]— although it was not Jesus himself but his disciples who baptized— [3]he left Judea and started back to Galilee. [4]But he had to go through Samaria. [5]So he came to a Samaritan city called Sychar, near the plot of ground that Jacob had given to his son Joseph. [6]Jacob's well was there, and Jesus, tired out by his journey, was sitting by the well. It was about noon.

7 A Samaritan woman came to draw water, and Jesus said to her, "Give me a drink." [8](His disciples had gone to the city to buy food.) [9]The Samaritan woman said to him, "How is it that you, a Jew, ask a drink of me, a woman of Samaria?" (Jews do not share things in common with Samaritans.)[a] [10]Jesus answered her, "If you knew the gift of God, and who it is that is saying to you, 'Give me a drink,' you would have asked him, and he would have given you living water." [11]The woman said to him, "Sir, you have no bucket, and the well is deep. Where do you get that living water? [12]Are you greater than our ancestor Jacob, who gave us the well, and with his sons and his flocks drank from it?" [13]Jesus said to her, "Everyone who drinks of this water will be thirsty again, [14]but those who drink of the water that I will give them will never be thirsty. The water that I will give will become in them a spring of water gushing up to eternal life." [15]The woman said to him, "Sir, give me this water, so that I may never be thirsty or have to keep coming here to draw water."

16 Jesus said to her, "Go, call your husband, and come back." [17]The woman answered him, "I have no husband." Jesus said to her, "You are right in saying, 'I have no husband'; [18]for you have had five husbands, and the one you have now is not your husband. What you have said is true!" [19]The woman said to him, "Sir, I see that you are a prophet. [20]Our ancestors

---

u Some interpreters hold that the quotation concludes with verse 15   v Other ancient authorities read *the Jews*   w Or *the Christ*
x Some interpreters hold that the quotation continues through verse 36   y Gk *set a seal to*
z Other ancient authorities read *the Lord*
a Other ancient authorities lack this sentence

Gomer

Her Name Means "Completion"

Read Hosea I; 3

The man stood at the door, craning his neck and peering through the half-light. Other than a stray dog curled in a knot against the wall of a neighboring house, he saw nothing. It was too late for a woman to be walking the streets alone. But then, she wouldn't be alone, would she?

He didn't want to go inside yet, to listen to the absence of her chatter, to lie down on the empty bed. By noon the next day, the news of her betrayal would fill every gossip-hungry soul in town like swill in a pig's belly. Hosea, the man who would steer the nation with his prophecies, couldn't control his own wife.

Hosea felt grief and fury like a storm breaking inside him. He had meant to guard his heart. He had never intended to give himself so completely. His pain was the worse for loving her so well. For Gomer had mocked his tenderness and allowed herself to be seduced by other lovers.

Hadn't God warned Hosea and instructed him: "Go, take for yourself a wife of whoredom and have children of whoredom, for the land commits great whoredom by forsaking the LORD" (1.2). And so Hosea had named his children "Jezreel" *(God Sows),* "Lo-ruhama" *(Not pitied),* and "Lo-ammi" *(Not my people).* Each successive child measured the growing rift between husband and wife, mirroring the rift between God and his people. Hosea might even have wondered whether he had fathered the last two.

The word of the Lord that had filled Hosea's mouth now troubled his soul, rushing

Her Character:
Though a married woman, she carried on numerous love affairs, crediting her lovers for the gifts her husband had given her.
Her Sorrow: *To have become the symbol of spiritual adultery—a picture of Israel's unfaithfulness to God.*
Her Joy: *That her husband continued to love her despite her unfaithfulness.*

back with appalling force. So this was how God felt about his own people—bitterly betrayed, cut to the heart, disgusted, outraged. His tender love meant nothing to a people enamored with Canaanite gods. Israel's leaders were the worst whores of all—virtuosos when it came to playing the harlot, cheating the poor and imploring idols to bless them with peace and riches.

If only Israel would learn its lesson and turn back to the Lord before it was too late—if only Gomer would turn back. Hosea wanted to shout in her face, shake her awake to her sin. Enough of patience. Enough of tenderness. She had ignored his threats, shrugging them away as so many flies on a donkey. What choice had he now? He would strip and shame her, punishing her unfaithfulness.

In the midst of his bitter grief, Hosea heard a surprising command, the voice of God instructing him to take back his wife, to love her as the Lord loved the people of Israel. So Hosea took back the wife he couldn't stop loving. And the word of the Lord transformed Lo-ruhama into Ruhama *(Pitied)* and Lo-ammi into Ammi *(My People).*

The story of Gomer and Hosea portrays God's jealousy for his people. For the first time, a prophet dared to speak of God as husband and Israel as his bride. But this is a tangled love story in which God's heart is repeatedly broken. Despite his pleas, regardless of his threats, Israel did not turn back to him until after the northern kingdom was destroyed by Assyria a few years later. Still, the knit-together lives of Hosea and Gomer were a living reminder to the Israelites of both God's judgment and his love.

Praying in Light of the Story of Gomer

On that day, says the LORD, you will call me, "My husband," and no longer will you call me, "My Baal."—Hosea 2:16

Praise God: That he loved you before you ever thought of loving him.

Offer Thanks: For God's mercy.

Confess: Any tendency to love money, pleasure, children, husband, or career more than you love him.

Ask God: To increase your hunger to know him more intimately.

Lift Your Heart

Sometimes couples grow apart, not because either have been unfaithful, but because of sheer busyness. If your relationship with God is bogging down in life's details, why not plan an intimate evening or weekend with him? Let it be a time of quieting your soul in his presence, of hushing life's everyday demands. Spend the day walking a solitary beach, or hidden away at a retreat center or a friend's cottage or cabin. Take your Bible and a book of poetry by Christina Rossetti. Or take Ken Gire's *Intimate Moments with the Savior* or C. S. Lewis's *The Lion, the Witch and the Wardrobe*, or Kathleen Norris's *The Cloister Walk*. If you're artistic, bring paint and art paper and commune with God through the pictures you create. Let it be a time of praising him, of telling him how much you love him, of thanking him for all the ways he has loved you. Don't try to have a great spiritual experience. Just relax and let God know you want to be with him.

Lord, how can I begin to understand how faithfully you've loved me? Draw me into your presence and hold me close. Quiet my noisy heart and speak to me.

Go to page 1403 for your next devotional reading.

worshiped on this mountain, but you[b] say that the place where people must worship is in Jerusalem." [21]Jesus said to her, "Woman, believe me, the hour is coming when you will worship the Father neither on this mountain nor in Jerusalem. [22]You worship what you do not know; we worship what we know, for salvation is from the Jews. [23]But the hour is coming, and is now here, when the true worshipers will worship the Father in spirit and truth, for the Father seeks such as these to worship him. [24]God is spirit, and those who worship him must worship in spirit and truth." [25]The woman said to him, "I know that Messiah is coming" (who is called Christ). "When he comes, he will proclaim all things to us." [26]Jesus said to her, "I am he,[c] the one who is speaking to you."

27 Just then his disciples came. They were astonished that he was speaking with a woman, but no one said, "What do you want?" or, "Why are you speaking with her?" [28]Then the woman left her water jar and went back to the city. She said to the people, [29]"Come and see a man who told me everything I have ever done! He cannot be the Messiah,[d] can he?" [30]They left the city and were on their way to him.

31 Meanwhile the disciples were urging him, "Rabbi, eat something." [32]But he said to them, "I have food to eat that you do not know about." [33]So the disciples said to one another, "Surely no one has brought him something to eat?" [34]Jesus said to them, "My food is to do the will of him who sent me and to complete his work. [35]Do you not say, 'Four months more, then comes the harvest'? But I tell you, look around you, and see how the fields are ripe for harvesting. [36]The reaper is already receiving[e] wages and is gathering fruit for eternal life, so that sower and reaper may rejoice together. [37]For here the saying holds true, 'One sows and another reaps.' [38]I sent you to reap that for which you did not labor. Others have labored, and you have entered into their labor."

39 Many Samaritans from that city believed in him because of the woman's testimony, "He told me everything I have ever done." [40]So when the Samaritans came to him, they asked him to stay with them; and he stayed there two days. [41]And many more believed because of his word. [42]They said to the woman, "It is no longer because of what you said that we believe, for we have heard for ourselves, and we know that this is truly the Savior of the world."

Jesus Returns to Galilee

43 When the two days were over, he went from that place to Galilee [44](for Jesus himself had testified that a prophet has no honor in the prophet's own country). [45]When he came to Galilee, the Galileans welcomed him, since they had seen all that he had done in Jerusalem at the festival; for they too had gone to the festival.

Jesus Heals an Official's Son

46 Then he came again to Cana in Galilee where he had changed the water into wine. Now there was a royal official whose son lay ill in Capernaum. [47]When he heard that Jesus had come from Judea to Galilee, he went and begged him to come down and heal his son, for he was at the point of death. [48]Then Jesus said to him, "Unless you[f] see signs and wonders you will not believe." [49]The official said to him, "Sir, come down before my little boy dies." [50]Jesus said to him, "Go; your son will live." The man believed the word that Jesus spoke to him and started on his way. [51]As he was going down, his slaves met him and told him that his child was alive. [52]So he asked them the hour when he began to recover, and they said to him, "Yesterday at one in the afternoon the fever left him." [53]The father realized that this was the hour when Jesus had said to him, "Your son will live." So he himself believed, along with his whole household. [54]Now this was the second sign that Jesus did after coming from Judea to Galilee.

Jesus Heals on the Sabbath

5 After this there was a festival of the Jews, and Jesus went up to Jerusalem. 2 Now in Jerusalem by the Sheep Gate there is a pool, called in Hebrew[g] Bethzatha,[h] which has five porticoes. [3]In these lay many invalids—blind, lame, and

---

[b] The Greek word for *you* here and in verses 21 and 22 is plural   [c] Gk *I am*   [d] Or *the Christ*   [e] Or *35. . . the fields are already ripe for harvesting.*   [36]*The reaper is receiving*   [f] Both instances of the Greek word for *you* in this verse are plural   [g] That is, *Aramaic*   [h] Other ancient authorities read *Bethesda*, others *Bethsaida*

paralyzed.*[i]* [5]One man was there who had been ill for thirty-eight years. [6]When Jesus saw him lying there and knew that he had been there a long time, he said to him, "Do you want to be made well?" [7]The sick man answered him, "Sir, I have no one to put me into the pool when the water is stirred up; and while I am making my way, someone else steps down ahead of me." [8]Jesus said to him, "Stand up, take your mat and walk." [9]At once the man was made well, and he took up his mat and began to walk.

Now that day was a sabbath. [10]So the Jews said to the man who had been cured, "It is the sabbath; it is not lawful for you to carry your mat." [11]But he answered them, "The man who made me well said to me, 'Take up your mat and walk.' " [12]They asked him, "Who is the man who said to you, 'Take it up and walk'?" [13]Now the man who had been healed did not know who it was, for Jesus had disappeared in*[j]* the crowd that was there. [14]Later Jesus found him in the temple and said to him, "See, you have been made well! Do not sin any more, so that nothing worse happens to you." [15]The man went away and told the Jews that it was Jesus who had made him well. [16]Therefore the Jews started persecuting Jesus, because he was doing such things on the sabbath. [17]But Jesus answered them, "My Father is still working, and I also am working." [18]For this reason the Jews were seeking all the more to kill him, because he was not only breaking the sabbath, but was also calling God his own Father, thereby making himself equal to God.

The Authority of the Son

[19]Jesus said to them, "Very truly, I tell you, the Son can do nothing on his own, but only what he sees the Father doing; for whatever the Father*[k]* does, the Son does likewise. [20]The Father loves the Son and shows him all that he himself is doing; and he will show him greater works than these, so that you will be astonished. [21]Indeed, just as the Father raises the dead and gives them life, so also the Son gives life to whomever he wishes. [22]The Father judges no one but has given all judgment to the Son, [23]so that all may honor the Son just as they honor the Father. Anyone who does not honor the Son does not honor the Father who sent him. [24]Very truly, I tell you, anyone who hears my word and believes him who sent me has eternal life, and does not come under judgment, but has passed from death to life.

[25]"Very truly, I tell you, the hour is coming, and is now here, when the dead will hear the voice of the Son of God, and those who hear will live. [26]For just as the Father has life in himself, so he has granted the Son also to have life in himself; [27]and he has given him authority to execute judgment, because he is the Son of Man. [28]Do not be astonished at this; for the hour is coming when all who are in their graves will hear his voice [29]and will come out—those who have done good, to the resurrection of life, and those who have done evil, to the resurrection of condemnation.

Witnesses to Jesus

[30]"I can do nothing on my own. As I hear, I judge; and my judgment is just, because I seek to do not my own will but the will of him who sent me.

[31]"If I testify about myself, my testimony is not true. [32]There is another who testifies on my behalf, and I know that his testimony to me is true. [33]You sent messengers to John, and he testified to the truth. [34]Not that I accept such human testimony, but I say these things so that you may be saved. [35]He was a burning and shining lamp, and you were willing to rejoice for a while in his light. [36]But I have a testimony greater than John's. The works that the Father has given me to complete, the very works that I am doing, testify on my behalf that the Father has sent me. [37]And the Father who sent me has himself testified on my behalf. You have never heard his voice or seen his form, [38]and you do not have his word abiding in you, because you do not believe him whom he has sent.

[39]"You search the scriptures because you think that in them you have eternal life; and it is they that testify on my behalf. [40]Yet you refuse to come to me to have life. [41]I do not accept glory from human beings. [42]But I know that you do not

---

[i] Other ancient authorities add, wholly or in part, *waiting for the stirring of the water;* [4]*for an angel of the Lord went down at certain seasons into the pool, and stirred up the water; whoever stepped in first after the stirring of the water was made well from whatever disease that person had.*   *[j]* Or *had left because of*   *[k]* Gk *that one*

have the love of God in[l] you. 43I have come in my Father's name, and you do not accept me; if another comes in his own name, you will accept him. 44How can you believe when you accept glory from one another and do not seek the glory that comes from the one who alone is God? 45Do not think that I will accuse you before the Father; your accuser is Moses, on whom you have set your hope. 46If you believed Moses, you would believe me, for he wrote about me. 47But if you do not believe what he wrote, how will you believe what I say?"

Feeding the Five Thousand

6 After this Jesus went to the other side of the Sea of Galilee, also called the Sea of Tiberias.[m] 2A large crowd kept following him, because they saw the signs that he was doing for the sick. 3Jesus went up the mountain and sat down there with his disciples. 4Now the Passover, the festival of the Jews, was near. 5When he looked up and saw a large crowd coming toward him, Jesus said to Philip, "Where are we to buy bread for these people to eat?" 6He said this to test him, for he himself knew what he was going to do. 7Philip answered him, "Six months' wages[n] would not buy enough bread for each of them to get a little." 8One of his disciples, Andrew, Simon Peter's brother, said to him, 9"There is a boy here who has five barley loaves and two fish. But what are they among so many people?" 10Jesus said, "Make the people sit down." Now there was a great deal of grass in the place; so they[o] sat down, about five thousand in all. 11Then Jesus took the loaves, and when he had given thanks, he distributed them to those who were seated; so also the fish, as much as they wanted. 12When they were satisfied, he told his disciples, "Gather up the fragments left over, so that nothing may be lost." 13So they gathered them up, and from the fragments of the five barley loaves, left by those who had eaten, they filled twelve baskets. 14When the people saw the sign that he had done, they began to say, "This is indeed the prophet who is to come into the world."

15 When Jesus realized that they were about to come and take him by force to make him king, he withdrew again to the mountain by himself.

Jesus Walks on the Water

16 When evening came, his disciples went down to the sea, 17got into a boat, and started across the sea to Capernaum. It was now dark, and Jesus had not yet come to them. 18The sea became rough because a strong wind was blowing. 19When they had rowed about three or four miles,[p] they saw Jesus walking on the sea and coming near the boat, and they were terrified. 20But he said to them, "It is I;[q] do not be afraid." 21Then they wanted to take him into the boat, and immediately the boat reached the land toward which they were going.

The Bread from Heaven

22 The next day the crowd that had stayed on the other side of the sea saw that there had been only one boat there. They also saw that Jesus had not got into the boat with his disciples, but that his disciples had gone away alone. 23Then some boats from Tiberias came near the place where they had eaten the bread after the Lord had given thanks.[r] 24So when the crowd saw that neither Jesus nor his disciples were there, they themselves got into the boats and went to Capernaum looking for Jesus.

25 When they found him on the other side of the sea, they said to him, "Rabbi, when did you come here?" 26Jesus answered them, "Very truly, I tell you, you are looking for me, not because you saw signs, but because you ate your fill of the loaves. 27Do not work for the food that perishes, but for the food that endures for eternal life, which the Son of Man will give you. For it is on him that God the Father has set his seal." 28Then they said to him, "What must we do to perform the works of God?" 29Jesus answered them, "This is the work of God, that you believe in him whom he has sent." 30So they said to him, "What sign are you going to give us then, so that we may see it and believe you? What work are you performing? 31Our ancestors ate the manna in the wilderness; as it is written, 'He gave them

---

[l] Or among   [m] Gk of Galilee of Tiberias   [n] Gk Two hundred denarii; the denarius was the usual day's wage for a laborer   [o] Gk the men   [p] Gk about twenty-five or thirty stadia   [q] Gk I am   [r] Other ancient authorities lack after the Lord had given thanks

bread from heaven to eat.' " ³²Then Jesus said to them, "Very truly, I tell you, it was not Moses who gave you the bread from heaven, but it is my Father who gives you the true bread from heaven. ³³For the bread of God is that which⁵ comes down from heaven and gives life to the world." ³⁴They said to him, "Sir, give us this bread always."

35 Jesus said to them, "I am the bread of life. Whoever comes to me will never be hungry, and whoever believes in me will never be thirsty. ³⁶But I said to you that you have seen me and yet do not believe. ³⁷Everything that the Father gives me will come to me, and anyone who comes to me I will never drive away; ³⁸for I have come down from heaven, not to do my own will, but the will of him who sent me. ³⁹And this is the will of him who sent me, that I should lose nothing of all that he has given me, but raise it up on the last

⁵ Or *he who*

$\mathcal{A}$ *Spiritual Anorexic*

MONDAY

Scripture Reading for Today:
John 6.34–40

Verse for Today:
John 6.35

I entered the small chapel feeling anything but happy. Seven wide states separated me from people I had known and cherished all my life. I had moved to the Tucson desert a few months earlier, and though I delighted in the blue-sky beauty of the place, I had yet to feel at home in its encircling nest of mountains.

I entered the quiet noisily—not with out-loud sounds, but with an inner clamor. "Where are you, Lord?" "Why is this so hard?" "Why don't you help me?" I knelt. I sat. I prayed my anxious prayers. Then I noticed the words on the monstrance, encircling the Eucharist: *Ego Sum Panis Vitae.* "I am the Bread of Life." The phrase seemed to mock me. Jesus had uttered these words to unbelieving disciples. Now another disciple of little faith sat in the chapel, wrestling with the words.

I reminded Jesus that he had not said, "I am like the bread of life." No metaphor, this was a literal claim. "If your body is the food that keeps us alive," I wondered, "why do I sometimes feel like a spiritual anorexic?"

The more I reminded Jesus of his words, determined to believe in them, the more I sensed a presence filling me, a new peace settling in. Now, all was quiet—inside and out. God had met me in the confines of the chapel. His Eucharistic Presence had calmed my fears and filled me with renewed hope. I still had questions, but God was in the questions. I still had needs, but God was in the needs. It had only been a few moments, but Christ had banished my emptiness with the sacrament of his presence. My thanks spilled over. I felt full and glad. A fresh sense of wonder brought me to my knees. I knew like never before the truth of Jesus' words: "I am the bread of life. Whoever comes to me will never be hungry, and whoever believes in me will never be thirsty."

—ANN SPANGLER

Go to page 1409 for your next devotional reading.

day. 40This is indeed the will of my Father, that all who see the Son and believe in him may have eternal life; and I will raise them up on the last day."

41 Then the Jews began to complain about him because he said, "I am the bread that came down from heaven." 42They were saying, "Is not this Jesus, the son of Joseph, whose father and mother we know? How can he now say, 'I have come down from heaven'?" 43Jesus answered them, "Do not complain among yourselves. 44No one can come to me unless drawn by the Father who sent me; and I will raise that person up on the last day. 45It is written in the prophets, 'And they shall all be taught by God.' Everyone who has heard and learned from the Father comes to me. 46Not that anyone has seen the Father except the one who is from God; he has seen the Father. 47Very truly, I tell you, whoever believes has eternal life. 48I am the bread of life. 49Your ancestors ate the manna in the wilderness, and they died. 50This is the bread that comes down from heaven, so that one may eat of it and not die. 51I am the living bread that came down from heaven. Whoever eats of this bread will live forever; and the bread that I will give for the life of the world is my flesh."

52 The Jews then disputed among themselves, saying, "How can this man give us his flesh to eat?" 53So Jesus said to them, "Very truly, I tell you, unless you eat the flesh of the Son of Man and drink his blood, you have no life in you. 54Those who eat my flesh and drink my blood have eternal life, and I will raise them up on the last day; 55for my flesh is true food and my blood is true drink. 56Those who eat my flesh and drink my blood abide in me, and I in them. 57Just as the living Father sent me, and I live because of the Father, so whoever eats me will live because of me. 58This is the bread that came down from heaven, not like that which your ancestors ate, and they died. But the one who eats this bread will live forever." 59He said these things while he was teaching in the synagogue at Capernaum.

The Words of Eternal Life

60 When many of his disciples heard it, they said, "This teaching is difficult; who can accept it?" 61But Jesus, being aware that his disciples were complaining about it, said to them, "Does this offend you? 62Then what if you were to see the Son of Man ascending to where he was before? 63It is the spirit that gives life; the flesh is useless. The words that I have spoken to you are spirit and life. 64But among you there are some who do not believe." For Jesus knew from the first who were the ones that did not believe, and who was the one that would betray him. 65And he said, "For this reason I have told you that no one can come to me unless it is granted by the Father."

66 Because of this many of his disciples turned back and no longer went about with him. 67So Jesus asked the twelve, "Do you also wish to go away?" 68Simon Peter answered him, "Lord, to whom can we go? You have the words of eternal life. 69We have come to believe and know that you are the Holy One of God."ᵗ 70Jesus answered them, "Did I not choose you, the twelve? Yet one of you is a devil." 71He was speaking of Judas son of Simon Iscariot,ᵘ for he, though one of the twelve, was going to betray him.

The Unbelief of Jesus' Brothers

7 After this Jesus went about in Galilee. He did not wishᵛ to go about in Judea because the Jews were looking for an opportunity to kill him. 2Now the Jewish festival of Boothsʷ was near. 3So his brothers said to him, "Leave here and go to Judea so that your disciples also may see the works you are doing; 4for no one who wantsˣ to be widely known acts in secret. If you do these things, show yourself to the world." 5(For not even his brothers believed in him.) 6Jesus said to them, "My time has not yet come, but your time is always here. 7The world cannot hate you, but it hates me because I testify against it that its works are evil. 8Go to the festival yourselves. I am notʸ going to this festival, for my time has not yet fully come." 9After saying this, he remained in Galilee.

Jesus at the Festival of Booths

10 But after his brothers had gone to

ᵗ Other ancient authorities read *the Christ, the Son of the living God*   ᵘ Other ancient authorities read *Judas Iscariot son of Simon;* others, *Judas son of Simon from Karyot* (Kerioth)   ᵛ Other ancient authorities read *was not at liberty*   ʷ Or *Tabernacles*   ˣ Other ancient authorities read *wants it*   ʸ Other ancient authorities add *yet*

the festival, then he also went, not publicly but as it were[z] in secret. [11]The Jews were looking for him at the festival and saying, "Where is he?" [12]And there was considerable complaining about him among the crowds. While some were saying, "He is a good man," others were saying, "No, he is deceiving the crowd." [13]Yet no one would speak openly about him for fear of the Jews.

14 About the middle of the festival Jesus went up into the temple and began to teach. [15]The Jews were astonished at it, saying, "How does this man have such learning,[a] when he has never been taught?" [16]Then Jesus answered them, "My teaching is not mine but his who sent me. [17]Anyone who resolves to do the will of God will know whether the teaching is from God or whether I am speaking on my own. [18]Those who speak on their own seek their own glory; but the one who seeks the glory of him who sent him is true, and there is nothing false in him.

19 "Did not Moses give you the law? Yet none of you keeps the law. Why are you looking for an opportunity to kill me?" [20]The crowd answered, "You have a demon! Who is trying to kill you?" [21]Jesus answered them, "I performed one work, and all of you are astonished. [22]Moses gave you circumcision (it is, of course, not from Moses, but from the patriarchs), and you circumcise a man on the sabbath. [23]If a man receives circumcision on the sabbath in order that the law of Moses may not be broken, are you angry with me because I healed a man's whole body on the sabbath? [24]Do not judge by appearances, but judge with right judgment."

Is This the Christ?

25 Now some of the people of Jerusalem were saying, "Is not this the man whom they are trying to kill? [26]And here he is, speaking openly, but they say nothing to him! Can it be that the authorities really know that this is the Messiah?[b] [27]Yet we know where this man is from; but when the Messiah[b] comes, no one will know where he is from." [28]Then Jesus cried out as he was teaching in the temple, "You know me, and you know where I am from. I have not come on my own. But the one who sent me is true, and you do not know him. [29]I know him, because I am from him, and he sent me." [30]Then they tried to arrest him, but no one laid hands on him, because his hour had not yet come. [31]Yet many in the crowd believed in him and were saying, "When the Messiah[b] comes, will he do more signs than this man has done?"[c]

Officers Are Sent to Arrest Jesus

32 The Pharisees heard the crowd muttering such things about him, and the chief priests and Pharisees sent temple police to arrest him. [33]Jesus then said, "I will be with you a little while longer, and then I am going to him who sent me. [34]You will search for me, but you will not find me; and where I am, you cannot come." [35]The Jews said to one another, "Where does this man intend to go that we will not find him? Does he intend to go to the Dispersion among the Greeks and teach the Greeks? [36]What does he mean by saying, 'You will search for me and you will not find me' and 'Where I am, you cannot come'?"

Rivers of Living Water

37 On the last day of the festival, the great day, while Jesus was standing there, he cried out, "Let anyone who is thirsty come to me, [38]and let the one who believes in me drink. As[d] the scripture has said, 'Out of the believer's heart[e] shall flow rivers of living water.' " [39]Now he said this about the Spirit, which believers in him were to receive; for as yet there was no Spirit,[f] because Jesus was not yet glorified.

Division among the People

40 When they heard these words, some in the crowd said, "This is really the prophet." [41]Others said, "This is the Messiah."[b] But some asked, "Surely the Messiah[b] does not come from Galilee, does he? [42]Has not the scripture said that the Messiah[b] is descended from David and comes from Bethlehem, the village where David lived?" [43]So there was a division in the crowd because of him. [44]Some of them wanted to arrest him, but no one laid hands on him.

z Other ancient authorities lack *as it were*   a Or *this man know his letters*   b Or *the Christ*   c Other ancient authorities read *is doing*   d Or *come to me and drink.* 38*The one who believes in me, as*   e Gk *out of his belly*   f Other ancient authorities read *for as yet the Spirit* (others, *Holy Spirit*) *had not been given*

The Unbelief of Those in Authority

45 Then the temple police went back to the chief priests and Pharisees, who asked them, "Why did you not arrest him?" [46]The police answered, "Never has anyone spoken like this!" [47]Then the Pharisees replied, "Surely you have not been deceived too, have you? [48]Has any one of the authorities or of the Pharisees believed in him? [49]But this crowd, which does not know the law—they are accursed." [50]Nicodemus, who had gone to Jesus[g] before, and who was one of them, asked, [51]"Our law does not judge people without first giving them a hearing to find out what they are doing, does it?" [52]They replied, "Surely you are not also from Galilee, are you? Search and you will see that no prophet is to arise from Galilee."

The Woman Caught in Adultery

8 [[53]Then each of them went home, [1]while Jesus went to the Mount of Olives. [2]Early in the morning he came again to the temple. All the people came to him and he sat down and began to teach them. [3]The scribes and the Pharisees brought a woman who had been caught in adultery; and making her stand before all of them, [4]they said to him, "Teacher, this woman was caught in the very act of committing adultery. [5]Now in the law Moses commanded us to stone such women. Now what do you say?" [6]They said this to test him, so that they might have some charge to bring against him. Jesus bent down and wrote with his finger on the ground. [7]When they kept on questioning him, he straightened up and said to them, "Let anyone among you who is without sin be the first to throw a stone at her." [8]And once again he bent down and wrote on the ground.[h] [9]When they heard it, they went away, one by one, beginning with the elders; and Jesus was left alone with the woman standing before him. [10]Jesus straightened up and said to her, "Woman, where are they? Has no one condemned you?" [11]She said, "No one, sir."[i] And Jesus said, "Neither do I condemn you. Go your way, and from now on do not sin again."]][j]

Jesus the Light of the World

12 Again Jesus spoke to them, saying, "I am the light of the world. Whoever follows me will never walk in darkness but will have the light of life." [13]Then the Pharisees said to him, "You are testifying on your own behalf; your testimony is not valid." [14]Jesus answered, "Even if I testify on my own behalf, my testimony is valid because I know where I have come from and where I am going, but you do not know where I come from or where I am going. [15]You judge by human standards;[k] I judge no one. [16]Yet even if I do judge, my judgment is valid; for it is not I alone who judge, but I and the Father[l] who sent me. [17]In your law it is written that the testimony of two witnesses is valid. [18]I testify on my own behalf, and the Father who sent me testifies on my behalf." [19]Then they said to him, "Where is your Father?" Jesus answered, "You know neither me nor my Father. If you knew me, you would know my Father also." [20]He spoke these words while he was teaching in the treasury of the temple, but no one arrested him, because his hour had not yet come.

Jesus Foretells His Death

21 Again he said to them, "I am going away, and you will search for me, but you will die in your sin. Where I am going, you cannot come." [22]Then the Jews said, "Is he going to kill himself? Is that what he means by saying, 'Where I am going, you cannot come'?" [23]He said to them, "You are from below, I am from above; you are of this world, I am not of this world. [24]I told you that you would die in your sins, for you will die in your sins unless you believe that I am he."[m] [25]They said to him, "Who are you?" Jesus said to them, "Why do I speak to you at all?[n] [26]I have much to say about you and much to condemn; but the one who sent me is true, and I declare to the world what I have heard from him." [27]They did not understand that he was speaking to them about the Father. [28]So Jesus said, "When you have lifted up the Son of Man, then you will realize that I am he,[m] and that I do nothing on my own, but I speak these

---

g Gk him   h Other ancient authorities add the sins of each of them   i Or Lord   j The most ancient authorities lack 7.53–8.11; other authorities add the passage here or after 7.36 or after 21.25 or after Luke 21.38, with variations of text; some mark the passage as doubtful.   k Gk according to the flesh   l Other ancient authorities read he   m Gk I am   n Or What I have told you from the beginning

things as the Father instructed me. ²⁹And the one who sent me is with me; he has not left me alone, for I always do what is pleasing to him." ³⁰As he was saying these things, many believed in him.

True Disciples

31 Then Jesus said to the Jews who had believed in him, "If you continue in my word, you are truly my disciples; ³²and you will know the truth, and the truth will make you free." ³³They answered him, "We are descendants of Abraham and have never been slaves to anyone. What do you mean by saying, 'You will be made free'?"

34 Jesus answered them, "Very truly, I tell you, everyone who commits sin is a slave to sin. ³⁵The slave does not have a permanent place in the household; the son has a place there forever. ³⁶So if the Son makes you free, you will be free indeed. ³⁷I know that you are descendants of Abraham; yet you look for an opportunity to kill me, because there is no place in you for my word. ³⁸I declare what I have seen in the Father's presence; as for you, you should do what you have heard from the Father."ᵒ

Jesus and Abraham

39 They answered him, "Abraham is our father." Jesus said to them, "If you were Abraham's children, you would be doingᵖ what Abraham did, ⁴⁰but now you are trying to kill me, a man who has told you the truth that I heard from God. This is not what Abraham did. ⁴¹You are indeed doing what your father does." They said to him, "We are not illegitimate children; we have one father, God himself." ⁴²Jesus said to them, "If God were your Father, you would love me, for I came from God and now I am here. I did not come on my own, but he sent me. ⁴³Why do you not understand what I say? It is because you cannot accept my word. ⁴⁴You are from your father the devil, and you choose to do your father's desires. He was a murderer from the beginning and does not stand in the truth, because there is no truth in him. When he lies, he speaks according to his own nature, for he is a liar and the father of lies. ⁴⁵But because I tell the truth, you do not believe me. ⁴⁶Which of you convicts me of sin? If I tell the truth, why do you not believe me? ⁴⁷Whoever is from God hears the words of

God. The reason you do not hear them is that you are not from God."

48 The Jews answered him, "Are we not right in saying that you are a Samaritan and have a demon?" ⁴⁹Jesus answered, "I do not have a demon; but I honor my Father, and you dishonor me. ⁵⁰Yet I do not seek my own glory; there is one who seeks it and he is the judge. ⁵¹Very truly, I tell you, whoever keeps my word will never see death." ⁵²The Jews said to him, "Now we know that you have a demon. Abraham died, and so did the prophets; yet you say, 'Whoever keeps my word will never taste death.' ⁵³Are you greater than our father Abraham, who died? The prophets also died. Who do you claim to be?" ⁵⁴Jesus answered, "If I glorify myself, my glory is nothing. It is my Father who glorifies me, he of whom you say, 'He is our God,' ⁵⁵though you do not know him. But I know him; if I would say that I do not know him, I would be a liar like you. But I do know him and I keep his word. ⁵⁶Your ancestor Abraham rejoiced that he would see my day; he saw it and was glad." ⁵⁷Then the Jews said to him, "You are not yet fifty years old, and have you seen Abraham?"ᑫ ⁵⁸Jesus said to them, "Very truly, I tell you, before Abraham was, I am." ⁵⁹So they picked up stones to throw at him, but Jesus hid himself and went out of the temple.

A Man Born Blind Receives Sight

9 As he walked along, he saw a man blind from birth. ²His disciples asked him, "Rabbi, who sinned, this man or his parents, that he was born blind?" ³Jesus answered, "Neither this man nor his parents sinned; he was born blind so that God's works might be revealed in him. ⁴Weʳ must work the works of him who sent meˢ while it is day; night is coming when no one can work. ⁵As long as I am in the world, I am the light of the world." ⁶When he had said this, he spat on the ground and made mud with the saliva and spread the mud on the man's eyes, ⁷saying to him, "Go, wash in the pool of Siloam" (which means Sent). Then he went

---

o Other ancient authorities read *you do what you have heard from your father*   *p* Other ancient authorities read *If you are Abraham's children, then do*   *q* Other ancient authorities read *has Abraham seen you?*   *r* Other ancient authorities read *I*   *s* Other ancient authorities read *us*

and washed and came back able to see. [8]The neighbors and those who had seen him before as a beggar began to ask, "Is this not the man who used to sit and beg?" [9]Some were saying, "It is he." Others were saying, "No, but it is someone like him." He kept saying, "I am the man." [10]But they kept asking him, "Then how were your eyes opened?" [11]He answered, "The man called Jesus made mud, spread it on my eyes, and said to me, 'Go to Siloam and wash.' Then I went and washed and received my sight." [12]They said to him, "Where is he?" He said, "I do not know."

The Pharisees Investigate the Healing

13 They brought to the Pharisees the man who had formerly been blind. [14]Now it was a sabbath day when Jesus made the mud and opened his eyes. [15]Then the Pharisees also began to ask him how he had received his sight. He said to them, "He put mud on my eyes. Then I washed, and now I see." [16]Some of the Pharisees said, "This man is not from God, for he does not observe the sabbath." But others said, "How can a man who is a sinner perform such signs?" And they were divided. [17]So they said again to the blind man, "What do you say about him? It was your eyes he opened." He said, "He is a prophet."

18 The Jews did not believe that he had been blind and had received his sight until they called the parents of the man who had received his sight [19]and asked them, "Is this your son, who you say was born blind? How then does he now see?" [20]His parents answered, "We know that this is our son, and that he was born blind; [21]but we do not know how it is that now he sees, nor do we know who opened his eyes. Ask him; he is of age. He will speak for himself." [22]His parents said this because they were afraid of the Jews; for the Jews had already agreed that anyone who confessed Jesus[t] to be the Messiah[u] would be put out of the synagogue. [23]Therefore his parents said, "He is of age; ask him."

24 So for the second time they called the man who had been blind, and they said to him, "Give glory to God! We know that this man is a sinner." [25]He answered, "I do not know whether he is a sinner. One thing I do know, that though I was blind, now I see." [26]They said to him, "What did he do to you? How did he open your eyes?" [27]He answered them, "I have told you already, and you would not listen. Why do you want to hear it again? Do you also want to become his disciples?" [28]Then they reviled him, saying, "You are his disciple, but we are disciples of Moses. [29]We know that God has spoken to Moses, but as for this man, we do not know where he comes from." [30]The man answered, "Here is an astonishing thing! You do not know where he comes from, and yet he opened my eyes. [31]We know that God does not listen to sinners, but he does listen to one who worships him and obeys his will. [32]Never since the world began has it been heard that anyone opened the eyes of a person born blind. [33]If this man were not from God, he could do nothing." [34]They answered him, "You were born entirely in sins, and are you trying to teach us?" And they drove him out.

Spiritual Blindness

35 Jesus heard that they had driven him out, and when he found him, he said, "Do you believe in the Son of Man?"[v] [36]He answered, "And who is he, sir?[w] Tell me, so that I may believe in him." [37]Jesus said to him, "You have seen him, and the one speaking with you is he." [38]He said, "Lord,[w] I believe." And he worshiped him. [39]Jesus said, "I came into this world for judgment so that those who do not see may see, and those who do see may become blind." [40]Some of the Pharisees near him heard this and said to him, "Surely we are not blind, are we?" [41]Jesus said to them, "If you were blind, you would not have sin. But now that you say, 'We see,' your sin remains.

Jesus the Good Shepherd

10 "Very truly, I tell you, anyone who does not enter the sheepfold by the gate but climbs in by another way is a thief and a bandit. [2]The one who enters by the gate is the shepherd of the sheep. [3]The gatekeeper opens the gate for him, and the sheep hear his voice. He calls his own sheep by name and leads them out. [4]When he has brought out all his own, he goes ahead of them, and the sheep follow him because they know his voice. [5]They will not follow a stranger, but

[t] Gk *him*   [u] Or *the Christ*   [v] Other ancient authorities read *the Son of God*   [w] *Sir* and *Lord* translate the same Greek word

they will run from him because they do not know the voice of strangers." [6]Jesus used this figure of speech with them, but they did not understand what he was saying to them.

7 So again Jesus said to them, "Very truly, I tell you, I am the gate for the sheep. [8]All who came before me are thieves and bandits; but the sheep did not listen to them. [9]I am the gate. Whoever enters by me will be saved, and will come in and go out and find pasture. [10]The thief comes only to steal and kill and destroy. I came that they may have life, and have it abundantly.

11 "I am the good shepherd. The good shepherd lays down his life for the sheep. [12]The hired hand, who is not the shepherd and does not own the sheep, sees the wolf coming and leaves the sheep and runs away—and the wolf snatches them and scatters them. [13]The hired hand runs away because a hired hand does not care for the sheep. [14]I am the good shepherd. I know my own and my own know me, [15]just as the Father knows me and I know the Father. And I lay down my life for the sheep. [16]I have other sheep that do not belong to this fold. I must bring them also, and they will listen to my voice. So there will be one flock, one shepherd. [17]For this reason the Father loves me, because I lay down my life in order to take it up again. [18]No one takes[x] it from me, but I lay it down of my own accord. I have power to lay it down, and I have power to take it up again. I have received this command from my Father."

19 Again the Jews were divided because of these words. [20]Many of them were saying, "He has a demon and is out of his mind. Why listen to him?" [21]Others were saying, "These are not the words of one who has a demon. Can a demon open the eyes of the blind?"

[x] Other ancient authorities read *has taken*

*S*helter

Scripture Reading for Today:
John 10.1–5

Verse for Today:
John 10.1

Some years ago I spent several weeks in England. One afternoon we took a drive in the country. A sudden storm came up, so we pulled off the road to wait it out.

In the distance I saw a man standing by a huge rock. He had a large cloak on and a shepherd's crook in his hand. He was calling his sheep. They came, bells tinkling, from different parts of the field. The shepherd never moved in all that rain and lightning, but stood steady for his flock to gather round him.

That scene has been forever engraved on my memory. The shepherd didn't leave his sheep. He didn't abandon them. He didn't let them find refuge of their own. But neither did he take them out of the storm. Instead he bore the storm with them. He provided them with safety and security by his presence.

So God our shepherd desires to do for us. In times of crisis, in the midst of a storm, let us not try to save ourselves. Let us run quickly to the shelter of his arms, where we will find refuge, and stay there until the storm passes by.

For God knows us, and he knows all our needs. He will provide in the midst of the storm. The fruit of such faith is peace and confidence in a God who cares.

—ANN SHIELDS

Go to page 1411 for your next devotional reading.

Jesus Is Rejected by the Jews

22 At that time the festival of the Dedication took place in Jerusalem. It was winter, 23and Jesus was walking in the temple, in the portico of Solomon. 24So the Jews gathered around him and said to him, "How long will you keep us in suspense? If you are the Messiah,*y* tell us plainly." 25Jesus answered, "I have told you, and you do not believe. The works that I do in my Father's name testify to me; 26but you do not believe, because you do not belong to my sheep. 27My sheep hear my voice. I know them, and they follow me. 28I give them eternal life, and they will never perish. No one will snatch them out of my hand. 29What my Father has given me is greater than all else, and no one can snatch it out of the Father's hand.*z* 30The Father and I are one."

31 The Jews took up stones again to stone him. 32Jesus replied, "I have shown you many good works from the Father. For which of these are you going to stone me?" 33The Jews answered, "It is not for a good work that we are going to stone you, but for blasphemy, because you, though only a human being, are making yourself God." 34Jesus answered, "Is it not written in your law,*a* 'I said, you are gods'? 35If those to whom the word of God came were called 'gods'—and the scripture cannot be annulled— 36can you say that the one whom the Father has sanctified and sent into the world is blaspheming because I said, 'I am God's Son'? 37If I am not doing the works of my Father, then do not believe me. 38But if I do them, even though you do not believe me, believe the works, so that you may know and understand*b* that the Father is in me and I am in the Father." 39Then they tried to arrest him again, but he escaped from their hands.

40 He went away again across the Jordan to the place where John had been baptizing earlier, and he remained there. 41Many came to him, and they were saying, "John performed no sign, but everything that John said about this man was true." 42And many believed in him there.

The Death of Lazarus

11 Now a certain man was ill, Lazarus of Bethany, the village of Mary and her sister Martha. 2Mary was the one who anointed the Lord with perfume and wiped his feet with her hair; her brother Lazarus was ill. 3So the sisters sent a message to Jesus,*c* "Lord, he whom you love is ill." 4But when Jesus heard it, he said, "This illness does not lead to death; rather it is for God's glory, so that the Son of God may be glorified through it." 5Accordingly, though Jesus loved Martha and her sister and Lazarus, 6after having heard that Lazarus*d* was ill, he stayed two days longer in the place where he was.

7 Then after this he said to the disciples, "Let us go to Judea again." 8The disciples said to him, "Rabbi, the Jews were just now trying to stone you, and are you going there again?" 9Jesus answered, "Are there not twelve hours of daylight? Those who walk during the day do not stumble, because they see the light of this world. 10But those who walk at night stumble, because the light is not in them." 11After saying this, he told them, "Our friend Lazarus has fallen asleep, but I am going there to awaken him." 12The disciples said to him, "Lord, if he has fallen asleep, he will be all right." 13Jesus, however, had been speaking about his death, but they thought that he was referring merely to sleep. 14Then Jesus told them plainly, "Lazarus is dead. 15For your sake I am glad I was not there, so that you may believe. But let us go to him." 16Thomas, who was called the Twin,*e* said to his fellow disciples, "Let us also go, that we may die with him."

Jesus the Resurrection and the Life

17 When Jesus arrived, he found that Lazarus*d* had already been in the tomb four days. 18Now Bethany was near Jerusalem, some two miles*f* away, 19and many of the Jews had come to Martha and Mary to console them about their brother. 20When Martha heard that Jesus was coming, she went and met him, while Mary stayed at home. 21Martha said to Jesus, "Lord, if you had been here, my brother would not have died. 22But even now I know that God will give you whatever you

y Or *the Christ*   *z* Other ancient authorities read *My Father who has given them to me is greater than all, and no one can snatch them out of the Father's hand*   *a* Other ancient authorities read *in the law*   *b* Other ancient authorities lack *and understand;* others read *and believe*   *c* Gk *him*   *d* Gk *he*   *e* Gk *Didymus*   *f* Gk *fifteen stadia*

ask of him." ²³Jesus said to her, "Your brother will rise again." ²⁴Martha said to him, "I know that he will rise again in the resurrection on the last day." ²⁵Jesus said to her, "I am the resurrection and the life.ᵍ Those who believe in me, even though they die, will live, ²⁶and everyone who lives and believes in me will never die. Do you believe this?" ²⁷She said to him, "Yes, Lord, I believe that you are the Messiah,ʰ the Son of God, the one coming into the world."

Jesus Weeps

28 When she had said this, she went back and called her sister Mary, and told her privately, "The Teacher is here and is

ᵍ Other ancient authorities lack *and the life*
ʰ Or *the Christ*

Jesus Wept and So Do We

WEDNESDAY

Scripture Reading for Today:
John 11.17–44

Verses for Today:
John 11.33–38

It was not an emotionally frozen Messiah who gathered together a small band of followers and called them friends. It was not a sterile God keeping a proper distance who wandered over the Galilean countryside with women and men together. It was not an over-controlled Redeemer who begged for companionship and perspired in agony during his last hours. Jesus did not feel for effect. He felt because feeling is human, and being fully human is not incompatible with being divine.

It is not uncommon today to meet individuals who try, as "good Christians," to transcend their feelings and emotions too quickly. They experience an initial flood of anger or sadness and immediately attempt to dull its intensity. Sometimes this is attempted through prayer. The anxious Christian experiences an emotion judged to be unacceptable and rushes to "give it to God" or "offer it up."

Sometimes, offering up an uncomfortable feeling is not prayer at all, but a religious name for psychological repression. We cannot offer up what we have not fully claimed as our own. We cannot give to God what we have not fully received ourselves. Like Jesus at the tomb of Lazarus, we cannot be deeply moved to transcendent life until we have been deeply moved by present reality. We do not move to the transcendent by skipping over the human, but rather, by knowing it to the full. We will not know the joy of resurrection until we have groaned over death.

As Christians we must be moved with compassion and filled with tenderness. We must churn with anger, struggle with impatience, and cherish joy. We must yearn and want, ache and cry. We must know love.

We may not turn the God-man who entered into human feeling into a stoic savior. We cannot minimize the stories of his emotional expressiveness in order to provide ourselves with an excuse for our own emotional flight.

—*FRAN FERDER*

Go to page 1414 for your next devotional reading.

calling for you." 29And when she heard it, she got up quickly and went to him. 30Now Jesus had not yet come to the village, but was still at the place where Martha had met him. 31The Jews who were with her in the house, consoling her, saw Mary get up quickly and go out. They followed her because they thought that she was going to the tomb to weep there. 32When Mary came where Jesus was and saw him, she knelt at his feet and said to him, "Lord, if you had been here, my brother would not have died." 33When Jesus saw her weeping, and the Jews who came with her also weeping, he was greatly disturbed in spirit and deeply moved. 34He said, "Where have you laid him?" They said to him, "Lord, come and see." 35Jesus began to weep. 36So the Jews said, "See how he loved him!" 37But some of them said, "Could not he who opened the eyes of the blind man have kept this man from dying?"

Jesus Raises Lazarus to Life

38 Then Jesus, again greatly disturbed, came to the tomb. It was a cave, and a stone was lying against it. 39Jesus said, "Take away the stone." Martha, the sister of the dead man, said to him, "Lord, already there is a stench because he has been dead four days." 40Jesus said to her, "Did I not tell you that if you believed, you would see the glory of God?" 41So they took away the stone. And Jesus looked upward and said, "Father, I thank you for having heard me. 42I knew that you always hear me, but I have said this for the sake of the crowd standing here, so that they may believe that you sent me." 43When he had said this, he cried with a loud voice, "Lazarus, come out!" 44The dead man came out, his hands and feet bound with strips of cloth, and his face wrapped in a cloth. Jesus said to them, "Unbind him, and let him go."

The Plot to Kill Jesus

45 Many of the Jews therefore, who had come with Mary and had seen what Jesus did, believed in him. 46But some of them went to the Pharisees and told them what he had done. 47So the chief priests and the Pharisees called a meeting of the council, and said, "What are we to do? This man is performing many signs. 48If we let him go on like this, everyone will believe in him, and the Romans will come

and destroy both our holy place*i* and our nation." 49But one of them, Caiaphas, who was high priest that year, said to them, "You know nothing at all! 50You do not understand that it is better for you to have one man die for the people than to have the whole nation destroyed." 51He did not say this on his own, but being high priest that year he prophesied that Jesus was about to die for the nation, 52and not for the nation only, but to gather into one the dispersed children of God. 53So from that day on they planned to put him to death.

54 Jesus therefore no longer walked about openly among the Jews, but went from there to a town called Ephraim in the region near the wilderness; and he remained there with the disciples.

55 Now the Passover of the Jews was near, and many went up from the country to Jerusalem before the Passover to purify themselves. 56They were looking for Jesus and were asking one another as they stood in the temple, "What do you think? Surely he will not come to the festival, will he?" 57Now the chief priests and the Pharisees had given orders that anyone who knew where Jesus*j* was should let them know, so that they might arrest him.

Mary Anoints Jesus

12 Six days before the Passover Jesus came to Bethany, the home of Lazarus, whom he had raised from the dead. 2There they gave a dinner for him. Martha served, and Lazarus was one of those at the table with him. 3Mary took a pound of costly perfume made of pure nard, anointed Jesus' feet, and wiped them*k* with her hair. The house was filled with the fragrance of the perfume. 4But Judas Iscariot, one of his disciples (the one who was about to betray him), said, 5"Why was this perfume not sold for three hundred denarii*l* and the money given to the poor?" 6(He said this not because he cared about the poor, but because he was a thief; he kept the common purse and used to steal what was put into it.) 7Jesus said, "Leave her alone. She bought it*m* so that she might keep it for the day of my burial. 8You always have

i Or *our temple*; Greek *our place*   *j* Gk *he*   *k* Gk *his feet*   *l* Three hundred denarii would be nearly a year's wages for a laborer   *m* Gk lacks *She bought it*

the poor with you, but you do not always have me."

The Plot to Kill Lazarus

9 When the great crowd of the Jews learned that he was there, they came not only because of Jesus but also to see Lazarus, whom he had raised from the dead. [10]So the chief priests planned to put Lazarus to death as well, [11]since it was on account of him that many of the Jews were deserting and were believing in Jesus.

Jesus' Triumphal Entry into Jerusalem

12 The next day the great crowd that had come to the festival heard that Jesus was coming to Jerusalem. [13]So they took branches of palm trees and went out to meet him, shouting,

"Hosanna!
Blessed is the one who comes in
the name of the Lord—
the King of Israel!"

[14]Jesus found a young donkey and sat on it; as it is written:

[15] "Do not be afraid, daughter of Zion.
Look, your king is coming,
sitting on a donkey's colt!"

[16]His disciples did not understand these things at first; but when Jesus was glorified, then they remembered that these things had been written of him and had been done to him. [17]So the crowd that had been with him when he called Lazarus out of the tomb and raised him from the dead continued to testify.[n] [18]It was also because they heard that he had performed this sign that the crowd went to meet him. [19]The Pharisees then said to one another, "You see, you can do nothing. Look, the world has gone after him!"

Some Greeks Wish to See Jesus

20 Now among those who went up to worship at the festival were some Greeks. [21]They came to Philip, who was from Bethsaida in Galilee, and said to him, "Sir, we wish to see Jesus." [22]Philip went and told Andrew; then Andrew and Philip went and told Jesus. [23]Jesus answered them, "The hour has come for the Son of Man to be glorified. [24]Very truly, I tell you, unless a grain of wheat falls into the earth and dies, it remains just a single grain; but if it dies, it bears much fruit. [25]Those who love their life lose it, and those who hate their life in this world will keep it for eternal life. [26]Whoever serves me must follow me, and where I am, there will my servant be also. Whoever serves me, the Father will honor.

Jesus Speaks about His Death

27 "Now my soul is troubled. And what should I say—'Father, save me from this hour'? No, it is for this reason that I have come to this hour. [28]Father, glorify your name." Then a voice came from heaven, "I have glorified it, and I will glorify it again." [29]The crowd standing there heard it and said that it was thunder. Others said, "An angel has spoken to him." [30]Jesus answered, "This voice has come for your sake, not for mine. [31]Now is the judgment of this world; now the ruler of this world will be driven out. [32]And I, when I am lifted up from the earth, will draw all people[o] to myself." [33]He said this to indicate the kind of death he was to die. [34]The crowd answered him, "We have heard from the law that the Messiah[p] remains forever. How can you say that the Son of Man must be lifted up? Who is this Son of Man?" [35]Jesus said to them, "The light is with you for a little longer. Walk while you have the light, so that the darkness may not overtake you. If you walk in the darkness, you do not know where you are going. [36]While you have the light, believe in the light, so that you may become children of light."

The Unbelief of the People

After Jesus had said this, he departed and hid from them. [37]Although he had performed so many signs in their presence, they did not believe in him. [38]This was to fulfill the word spoken by the prophet Isaiah:

"Lord, who has believed our message,
and to whom has the arm of the
Lord been revealed?"

[39]And so they could not believe, because Isaiah also said,

[40] "He has blinded their eyes
and hardened their heart,
so that they might not look with
their eyes,
and understand with their heart
and turn—
and I would heal them."

---

[n] Other ancient authorities read *with him began to testify that he had called . . . from the dead* [o] Other ancient authorities read *all things* [p] Or *the Christ*

⁴¹Isaiah said this because*q* he saw his glory and spoke about him. ⁴²Nevertheless many, even of the authorities, believed in him. But because of the Pharisees they did not confess it, for fear that they would be put out of the synagogue; ⁴³for they loved human glory more than the glory that comes from God.

Summary of Jesus' Teaching

44 Then Jesus cried aloud: "Whoever believes in me believes not in me but in him who sent me. ⁴⁵And whoever sees me sees him who sent me. ⁴⁶I have come as light into the world, so that everyone who believes in me should not remain in the darkness. ⁴⁷I do not judge anyone who hears my words and does not keep them, for I came not to judge the world, but to save the world. ⁴⁸The one who rejects me and does not receive my word has a judge; on the last day the word that I have spoken will serve as judge, ⁴⁹for I have not spoken on my own, but the Father who sent me has himself given me a commandment about what to say and what to speak. ⁵⁰And I know that his commandment is eternal life. What I speak, therefore, I speak just as the Father has told me."

Jesus Washes the Disciples' Feet

13 Now before the festival of the Passover, Jesus knew that his hour had come to depart from this world and go to the Father. Having loved his

q Other ancient witnesses read when

Receiving

THURSDAY

Scripture Reading
for Today:
John 13.1–17

Verse for Today:
John 13.6

Using your imagination, picture yourself as Peter, with Jesus kneeling before you. Hear yourself arguing about whether he is going to wash your feet. Look deeply into his eyes.

You are a proud person, aren't you? You can do things for yourself—you don't need anyone to do such menial tasks as washing your feet! Feel resistance welling up from deep within. Then hear Jesus' words to you and see the love and compassion on his face.

The moment stands still while Jesus waits for your decision. Hear yourself relenting, asking Jesus to wash not only your feet, but your head and hands as well. Then listen to his patient response. Jesus names the terms of his work with you.

Feel his hands on your feet. Notice his carpenter's hands gently washing your feet. He picks the towel up and gently blots the water. For the first time in a long time, you know what humility is. Perhaps this is the first time in your life you have really known what it was like to be humble enough to receive from someone else.

You want to weep. No, you want to cry like a baby. You want to let long-pent-up tears from your lifetime of self-sufficiency and independence burst into sobs. By this simple act Jesus has touched you at the deepest level of your heart, and you know that you will never be the same.

Ask the living Christ to come to you today to wash your feet. How will you respond?

—JEANIE MILEY

Go to page 1417 for your next devotional reading.

own who were in the world, he loved them to the end. ²The devil had already put it into the heart of Judas son of Simon Iscariot to betray him. And during supper ³Jesus, knowing that the Father had given all things into his hands, and that he had come from God and was going to God, ⁴got up from the table,ʳ took off his outer robe, and tied a towel around himself. ⁵Then he poured water into a basin and began to wash the disciples' feet and to wipe them with the towel that was tied around him. ⁶He came to Simon Peter, who said to him, "Lord, are you going to wash my feet?" ⁷Jesus answered, "You do not know now what I am doing, but later you will understand." ⁸Peter said to him, "You will never wash my feet." Jesus answered, "Unless I wash you, you have no share with me." ⁹Simon Peter said to him, "Lord, not my feet only but also my hands and my head!" ¹⁰Jesus said to him, "One who has bathed does not need to wash, except for the feet,ˢ but is entirely clean. And youᵗ are clean, though not all of you." ¹¹For he knew who was to betray him; for this reason he said, "Not all of you are clean."

12 After he had washed their feet, had put on his robe, and had returned to the table, he said to them, "Do you know what I have done to you? ¹³You call me Teacher and Lord—and you are right, for that is what I am. ¹⁴So if I, your Lord and Teacher, have washed your feet, you also ought to wash one another's feet. ¹⁵For I have set you an example, that you also should do as I have done to you. ¹⁶Very truly, I tell you, servantsᵘ are not greater than their master, nor are messengers greater than the one who sent them. ¹⁷If you know these things, you are blessed if you do them. ¹⁸I am not speaking of all of you; I know whom I have chosen. But it is to fulfill the scripture, 'The one who ate my breadᵛ has lifted his heel against me.' ¹⁹I tell you this now, before it occurs, so that when it does occur, you may believe that I am he.ʷ ²⁰Very truly, I tell you, whoever receives one whom I send receives me; and whoever receives me receives him who sent me."

Jesus Foretells His Betrayal

21 After saying this Jesus was troubled in spirit, and declared, "Very truly, I tell you, one of you will betray me." ²²The dis-

ciples looked at one another, uncertain of whom he was speaking. ²³One of his disciples—the one whom Jesus loved—was reclining next to him; ²⁴Simon Peter therefore motioned to him to ask Jesus of whom he was speaking. ²⁵So while reclining next to Jesus, he asked him, "Lord, who is it?" ²⁶Jesus answered, "It is the one to whom I give this piece of bread when I have dipped it in the dish."ˣ So when he had dipped the piece of bread, he gave it to Judas son of Simon Iscariot.ʸ ²⁷After he received the piece of bread,ᶻ Satan entered into him. Jesus said to him, "Do quickly what you are going to do." ²⁸Now no one at the table knew why he said this to him. ²⁹Some thought that, because Judas had the common purse, Jesus was telling him, "Buy what we need for the festival"; or, that he should give something to the poor. ³⁰So, after receiving the piece of bread, he immediately went out. And it was night.

The New Commandment

31 When he had gone out, Jesus said, "Now the Son of Man has been glorified, and God has been glorified in him. ³²If God has been glorified in him,ᵃ God will also glorify him in himself and will glorify him at once. ³³Little children, I am with you only a little longer. You will look for me; and as I said to the Jews so now I say to you, 'Where I am going, you cannot come.' ³⁴I give you a new commandment, that you love one another. Just as I have loved you, you also should love one another. ³⁵By this everyone will know that you are my disciples, if you have love for one another."

Jesus Foretells Peter's Denial

36 Simon Peter said to him, "Lord, where are you going?" Jesus answered, "Where I am going, you cannot follow me now; but you will follow afterward." ³⁷Peter said to him, "Lord, why can I not follow you now? I will lay down my life for you." ³⁸Jesus answered, "Will you lay

---

ʳ Gk from supper   ˢ Other ancient authorities lack except for the feet   ᵗ The Greek word for you here is plural   ᵘ Gk slaves   ᵛ Other ancient authorities read ate bread with me   ʷ Gk I am   ˣ Gk dipped it   ʸ Other ancient authorities read Judas Iscariot son of Simon; others, Judas son of Simon from Karyot (Kerioth)   ᶻ Gk After the piece of bread   ᵃ Other ancient authorities lack If God has been glorified in him

down your life for me? Very truly, I tell you, before the cock crows, you will have denied me three times.

Jesus the Way to the Father

14 "Do not let your hearts be troubled. Believe[b] in God, believe also in me. [2]In my Father's house there are many dwelling places. If it were not so, would I have told you that I go to prepare a place for you?[c] [3]And if I go and prepare a place for you, I will come again and will take you to myself, so that where I am, there you may be also. [4]And you know the way to the place where I am going."[d] [5]Thomas said to him, "Lord, we do not know where you are going. How can we know the way?" [6]Jesus said to him, "I am the way, and the truth, and the life. No one comes to the Father except through me. [7]If you know me, you will know[e] my Father also. From now on you do know him and have seen him."

8 Philip said to him, "Lord, show us the Father, and we will be satisfied." [9]Jesus said to him, "Have I been with you all this time, Philip, and you still do not know me? Whoever has seen me has seen the Father. How can you say, 'Show us the Father'? [10]Do you not believe that I am in the Father and the Father is in me? The words that I say to you I do not speak on my own; but the Father who dwells in me does his works. [11]Believe me that I am in the Father and the Father is in me; but if you do not, then believe me because of the works themselves. [12]Very truly, I tell you, the one who believes in me will also do the works that I do and, in fact, will do greater works than these, because I am going to the Father. [13]I will do whatever you ask in my name, so that the Father may be glorified in the Son. [14]If in my name you ask me[f] for anything, I will do it.

The Promise of the Holy Spirit

15 "If you love me, you will keep[g] my commandments. [16]And I will ask the Father, and he will give you another Advocate,[h] to be with you forever. [17]This is the Spirit of truth, whom the world cannot receive, because it neither sees him nor knows him. You know him, because he abides with you, and he will be in[i] you.

18 "I will not leave you orphaned; I am coming to you. [19]In a little while the world will no longer see me, but you will see me; because I live, you also will live.

[20]On that day you will know that I am in my Father, and you in me, and I in you. [21]They who have my commandments and keep them are those who love me; and those who love me will be loved by my Father, and I will love them and reveal myself to them." [22]Judas (not Iscariot) said to him, "Lord, how is it that you will reveal yourself to us, and not to the world?" [23]Jesus answered him, "Those who love me will keep my word, and my Father will love them, and we will come to them and make our home with them. [24]Whoever does not love me does not keep my words; and the word that you hear is not mine, but is from the Father who sent me.

25 "I have said these things to you while I am still with you. [26]But the Advocate,[h] the Holy Spirit, whom the Father will send in my name, will teach you everything, and remind you of all that I have said to you. [27]Peace I leave with you; my peace I give to you. I do not give to you as the world gives. Do not let your hearts be troubled, and do not let them be afraid. [28]You heard me say to you, 'I am going away, and I am coming to you.' If you loved me, you would rejoice that I am going to the Father, because the Father is greater than I. [29]And now I have told you this before it occurs, so that when it does occur, you may believe. [30]I will no longer talk much with you, for the ruler of this world is coming. He has no power over me; [31]but I do as the Father has commanded me, so that the world may know that I love the Father. Rise, let us be on our way.

Jesus the True Vine

15 "I am the true vine, and my Father is the vinegrower. [2]He removes every branch in me that bears no fruit. Every branch that bears fruit he prunes[j] to make it bear more fruit. [3]You have already been cleansed[j] by the word that I have spoken to you. [4]Abide in me as I abide in you. Just as the branch cannot bear fruit by itself unless it abides in the

b Or You believe   c Or If it were not so, I would have told you; for I go to prepare a place for you   d Other ancient authorities read Where I am going you know, and the way you know   e Other ancient authorities read If you had known me, you would have known   f Other ancient authorities lack me   g Other ancient authorities read me, keep   h Or Helper   i Or among   j The same Greek root refers to pruning and cleansing

vine, neither can you unless you abide in me. ⁵I am the vine, you are the branches. Those who abide in me and I in them bear much fruit, because apart from me you can do nothing. ⁶Whoever does not abide in me is thrown away like a branch and withers; such branches are gathered, thrown into the fire, and burned. ⁷If you abide in me, and my words abide in you, ask for whatever you wish, and it will be done for you. ⁸My Father is glorified by this, that you bear much fruit and become*ᵏ* my disciples. ⁹As the Father has

loved me, so I have loved you; abide in my love. ¹⁰If you keep my commandments, you will abide in my love, just as I have kept my Father's commandments and abide in his love. ¹¹I have said these things to you so that my joy may be in you, and that your joy may be complete.

12 "This is my commandment, that you love one another as I have loved you. ¹³No one has greater love than this, to lay down one's life for one's friends. ¹⁴You

k Or *be*

FRIDAY

Scripture Reading
for Today:
John 15.1–8

Verse for Today:
John 15.2

*L*etting Go

In our back yard, we have a small grapevine. In the first five years that we lived in this house, nothing was done with it. In fact, except to pull a few grapes from it each September, it was never touched. A friend agreed to prune the vine this summer.

It was horrifying. He cut and snipped and hacked away for a while till there was nothing left, or so it seemed. Only three, skinny, primary shoots remained, and these he raised and draped over the wire. This was my grapevine? It didn't look like it used to at all. Dead wood and weeds I had expected him to remove, but not all that living greenery as well. Within weeks the new growth was apparent. Our most abundant crop of fruit was inevitable.

My expectations for the Lord's pruning work in my life have been adjusted accordingly. In the past few years I have come to understand that he intends to remove more than sin and bad habits, like dead wood and weeds. Lots of good things in my life, like living greenery, may need to go as well. In all things we need interior detachment, but an actual separation is often called for too. Each time I let go—of an activity, an idea, or a person—I experience a form of death. Then I wait for it to kill me.

But what is this? New joy? Greater fruit? New life? All the paradoxes of Christianity become true. "Unless a grain of wheat falls into the earth and dies, it remains just a single grain; but if it dies, it bears much fruit. Those who love their life lose it, and those who hate their life in this world will keep it for eternal life" (John 12.24–25).

We need to let go of many things—worldly ideas and attitudes, material possessions, ungodly desires, and even good plans and activities of our own choosing. If we can't, the Lord will probably pry them loose anyway. It will just hurt more.

—*DOROTHY RANAGHAN*

Go to page 1420 for your next devotional reading.

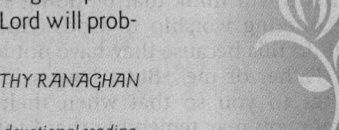

are my friends if you do what I command you. [15]I do not call you servants[l] any longer, because the servant[m] does not know what the master is doing; but I have called you friends, because I have made known to you everything that I have heard from my Father. [16]You did not choose me but I chose you. And I appointed you to go and bear fruit, fruit that will last, so that the Father will give you whatever you ask him in my name. [17]I am giving you these commands so that you may love one another.

The World's Hatred

18 "If the world hates you, be aware that it hated me before it hated you. [19]If you belonged to the world,[n] the world would love you as its own. Because you do not belong to the world, but I have chosen you out of the world—therefore the world hates you. [20]Remember the word that I said to you, 'Servants[o] are not greater than their master.' If they persecuted me, they will persecute you; if they kept my word, they will keep yours also. [21]But they will do all these things to you on account of my name, because they do not know him who sent me. [22]If I had not come and spoken to them, they would not have sin; but now they have no excuse for their sin. [23]Whoever hates me hates my Father also. [24]If I had not done among them the works that no one else did, they would not have sin. But now they have seen and hated both me and my Father. [25]It was to fulfill the word that is written in their law, 'They hated me without a cause.'

26 "When the Advocate[p] comes, whom I will send to you from the Father, the Spirit of truth who comes from the Father, he will testify on my behalf. [27]You also are to testify because you have been with me from the beginning.

16 "I have said these things to you to keep you from stumbling. [2]They will put you out of the synagogues. Indeed, an hour is coming when those who kill you will think that by doing so they are offering worship to God. [3]And they will do this because they have not known the Father or me. [4]But I have said these things to you so that when their hour comes you may remember that I told you about them.

The Work of the Spirit

"I did not say these things to you from the beginning, because I was with you. [5]But now I am going to him who sent me; yet none of you asks me, 'Where are you going?' [6]But because I have said these things to you, sorrow has filled your hearts. [7]Nevertheless I tell you the truth: it is to your advantage that I go away, for if I do not go away, the Advocate[p] will not come to you; but if I go, I will send him to you. [8]And when he comes, he will prove the world wrong about[q] sin and righteousness and judgment: [9]about sin, because they do not believe in me; [10]about righteousness, because I am going to the Father and you will see me no longer; [11]about judgment, because the ruler of this world has been condemned.

12 "I still have many things to say to you, but you cannot bear them now. [13]When the Spirit of truth comes, he will guide you into all the truth; for he will not speak on his own, but will speak whatever he hears, and he will declare to you the things that are to come. [14]He will glorify me, because he will take what is mine and declare it to you. [15]All that the Father has is mine. For this reason I said that he will take what is mine and declare it to you.

Sorrow Will Turn into Joy

16 "A little while, and you will no longer see me, and again a little while, and you will see me." [17]Then some of his disciples said to one another, "What does he mean by saying to us, 'A little while, and you will no longer see me, and again a little while, and you will see me'; and 'Because I am going to the Father'?" [18]They said, "What does he mean by this 'a little while'? We do not know what he is talking about." [19]Jesus knew that they wanted to ask him, so he said to them, "Are you discussing among yourselves what I meant when I said, 'A little while, and you will no longer see me, and again a little while, and you will see me'? [20]Very truly, I tell you, you will weep and mourn, but the world will rejoice; you will have pain, but your pain will turn into joy. [21]When a woman is in labor, she has pain, because her hour has come. But when her child is born, she no longer remembers the an-

---

[l] Gk slaves   [m] Gk slave   [n] Gk were of the world
[o] Gk Slaves   [p] Or Helper   [q] Or convict
the world of

guish because of the joy of having brought a human being into the world. 22So you have pain now; but I will see you again, and your hearts will rejoice, and no one will take your joy from you. 23On that day you will ask nothing of me.*r* Very truly, I tell you, if you ask anything of the Father in my name, he will give it to you.*s* 24Until now you have not asked for anything in my name. Ask and you will receive, so that your joy may be complete.

Peace for the Disciples

25 "I have said these things to you in figures of speech. The hour is coming when I will no longer speak to you in figures, but will tell you plainly of the Father. 26On that day you will ask in my name. I do not say to you that I will ask the Father on your behalf; 27for the Father himself loves you, because you have loved me and have believed that I came from God.*t* 28I came from the Father and have come into the world; again, I am leaving the world and am going to the Father."

29 His disciples said, "Yes, now you are speaking plainly, not in any figure of speech! 30Now we know that you know all things, and do not need to have anyone question you; by this we believe that you came from God." 31Jesus answered them, "Do you now believe? 32The hour is coming, indeed it has come, when you will be scattered, each one to his home, and you will leave me alone. Yet I am not alone because the Father is with me. 33I have said this to you, so that in me you may have peace. In the world you face persecution. But take courage; I have conquered the world!"

Jesus Prays for His Disciples

17 After Jesus had spoken these words, he looked up to heaven and said, "Father, the hour has come; glorify your Son so that the Son may glorify you, 2since you have given him authority over all people,*u* to give eternal life to all whom you have given him. 3And this is eternal life, that they may know you, the only true God, and Jesus Christ whom you have sent. 4I glorified you on earth by finishing the work that you gave me to do. 5So now, Father, glorify me in your own presence with the glory that I had in your presence before the world existed.

6 "I have made your name known to those whom you gave me from the world. They were yours, and you gave them to me, and they have kept your word. 7Now they know that everything you have given me is from you; 8for the words that you gave to me I have given to them, and they have received them and know in truth that I came from you; and they have believed that you sent me. 9I am asking on their behalf; I am not asking on behalf of the world, but on behalf of those whom you gave me, because they are yours. 10All mine are yours, and yours are mine; and I have been glorified in them. 11And now I am no longer in the world, but they are in the world, and I am coming to you. Holy Father, protect them in your name that you have given me, so that they may be one, as we are one. 12While I was with them, I protected them in your name that*v* you have given me. I guarded them, and not one of them was lost except the one destined to be lost,*w* so that the scripture might be fulfilled. 13But now I am coming to you, and I speak these things in the world so that they may have my joy made complete in themselves.*x* 14I have given them your word, and the world has hated them because they do not belong to the world, just as I do not belong to the world. 15I am not asking you to take them out of the world, but I ask you to protect them from the evil one.*y* 16They do not belong to the world, just as I do not belong to the world. 17Sanctify them in the truth; your word is truth. 18As you have sent me into the world, so I have sent them into the world. 19And for their sakes I sanctify myself, so that they also may be sanctified in truth.

20 "I ask not only on behalf of these, but also on behalf of those who will believe in me through their word, 21that they may all be one. As you, Father, are in me and I am in you, may they also be in us,*z* so that the world may believe that you have sent me. 22The glory that you have given me I have given them, so that they may be one, as we are one, 23I in them

---

r Or *will ask me no question*   *s* Other ancient authorities read *Father, he will give it to you in my name*   *t* Other ancient authorities read *the Father*   *u* Gk *flesh*   *v* Other ancient authorities read *protected in your name those whom*   *w* Gk *except the son of destruction*   *x* Or *among themselves*   *y* Or *from evil*   *z* Other ancient authorities read *be one in us*

Elizabeth

Her Name Means
"God Is My Oath"

THE STORY OF A WOMAN

Read Luke 1.5–25, 39–80

Her eyes were a golden brown. Like currants set in pastry, they winked out at the world from cheeks that had baked too long in the sun. Snowy strands of hair straggled from beneath a woolen shawl, tickling her wrinkled face. Small hands rested tenderly on her rounded belly, softly probing for any hint of movement. But all was still. From her vantage point on the roof of the house, she noticed a figure walking up the pathway and wondered who her visitor might be.

She and Zechariah had been content enough in their quiet house these last few months, secluded in their joy. Each morning she had opened her eyes as though waking to a fantastic dream. Sometimes she shook with laughter as she thought about how God had rearranged her life—planting a child in her shriveled up, old-woman's womb.

Six months earlier, Zechariah had been chosen by lot to burn incense before the Most Holy Place, a once-in-a-lifetime privilege. But during his week of priestly service in the temple, he had been frightened half to death by a figure that appeared suddenly next to the altar of incense. "Your wife Elizabeth will bear you a son," the angel told him, "and you will name him John. You will have joy and gladness, and many will rejoice at his birth, for he will be great in the sight of the Lord" (1:13–15).

It was Sarah and Abraham all over again,

Her Character: *A descendant of Aaron, she was a woman the Bible calls "righteous before God." Like very few others, male or female, she is praised for observing all the Lord's commandments and regulations without blame. She was the first person to acknowledge Jesus as Lord.*
Her Sorrow: *To be barren for most of her life.*
Her Joy: *To give birth to John, later known as John the Baptist, the Messiah's forerunner. His name, divinely assigned, meant, "the Lord is gracious."*

Rebekah and Isaac, Rachel and Jacob. God was once again kindling a fire with two dry sticks.

Elizabeth looked down again at the figure advancing up the path, a green sprig of a girl. The older woman stepped carefully down the stairs and into the house to welcome her guest. But with the young woman's words of greeting came something that felt like a gale force wind, shaking the beams and rafters of the house. Steadying herself, the older woman felt suddenly invigorated. Her unborn baby leapt inside her as she shouted out a welcoming response: "Blessed are you among women, and blessed is the fruit of your womb. And why has this happened to me, that the mother of my Lord comes to me? For as soon as I heard the sound of your greeting, the child in my womb leaped for joy. And blessed is she who believed that there would be a fulfillment of what was spoken to her by the Lord" (verses 42–45).

Mary had made the journey all the way from Nazareth to visit her relative Elizabeth. The same angel who had spoken to Zechariah in the temple had whispered the secret of the older woman's pregnancy to the virgin, who was also with child.

The two women held each other, their bonds of kinship now so much stronger than any mere flesh and blood could forge. For Israel's God—the God of Sarah, Rebekah, Rachel, and Hannah—was on the move again, bringing the long-ago promise to fulfillment. And blessed was she who did not doubt that what the Lord had said to her would be accomplished.

Praying With Elizabeth

"Blessed is she who believed that there would be a fulfillment of what was spoken to her by the Lord."—Luke 1.45

Praise God: That he is the Creator who shapes every child in the womb.

Offer Thanks: For the gift of children.

Confess: Any tendency to cheapen the value of human life.

Ask God: To restore your appreciation for the miracle of human life.

Lift Your Heart

Mary's visit to Elizabeth probably occurred when Elizabeth was in her sixth month of pregnancy and Mary was in her first trimester. Take a moment to think about what would have been happening to the children growing in their wombs:

Jesus:

18 days—his nervous system appeared.

30 days—most of his major organ systems had begun to form.

4 weeks—his heart began beating.

7 weeks—his facial features would have been visible.

8 weeks—all his major body structures and organs were present.

10 weeks—tiny teeth were forming in his gums.

12 weeks—his brain was fully formed and he could feel pain. He may have even sucked his thumb.

John:

6 months—he could grasp his hands, kick, do somersaults and hear voices and sounds outside the womb.

You are the Lord and Giver of Life. Help me to respect, protect and nurture life, no matter what color, what age, or what gender.

Go to page 1425 for your next devotional reading.

and you in me, that they may become completely one, so that the world may know that you have sent me and have loved them even as you have loved me. ²⁴Father, I desire that those also, whom you have given me, may be with me where I am, to see my glory, which you have given me because you loved me before the foundation of the world.

25 "Righteous Father, the world does not know you, but I know you; and these know that you have sent me. ²⁶I made your name known to them, and I will make it known, so that the love with which you have loved me may be in them, and I in them."

The Betrayal and Arrest of Jesus

18 After Jesus had spoken these words, he went out with his disciples across the Kidron valley to a place where there was a garden, which he and his disciples entered. ²Now Judas, who betrayed him, also knew the place, because Jesus often met there with his disciples. ³So Judas brought a detachment of soldiers together with police from the

---

Easter and Holy Week

*"I desire that those also, whom you have
given me, may be with me where I am,
to see my glory, which you have given me."*

JOHN 17.24

"Were you there when they crucified my Lord?" asks the Negro spiritual. "Were you there when they laid him in the tomb?" "Were you there when he rose from the dead?"

"We wish!" we exclaim. "If only we could have been with Jesus at supper table, cross, and tomb."

More effectively than time travel, if it were possible, the liturgies of Holy Week and Easter answer this longing. As we gather to celebrate them, we are drawn into the events surrounding Jesus' death and resurrection. We participate in God's mighty deeds just as surely as the first-century eyewitnesses, but on a deeper level than most of them because we know what these events signify.

This is neither wild fancy nor wishful thinking. It is what happens at every Mass: "When the Church celebrates the Eucharist, she commemorates Christ's Passover, and it is made present" (*Catechism of the Catholic Church*, 1364). Christ has been sacrificed and raised up, and we are really witnesses to it. The liturgies of Easter and the Triduum, the three days that precede it, impress this truth on us in a solemn way.

Holy Thursday. We join the apostles for the most momentous meal in history. Jesus washes our dirty feet, then feeds us with bread and wine that he has changed into his own body and blood.

Good Friday. Fasting and repentant, we accompany Jesus as he lays down his life for us. From his agony in Gethsemane to his last breath to his burial, we are with him. We venerate his holy cross and call on the power of his saving blood.

Holy Saturday. In the shadow of the tomb, we fast and wait. This is our hope: that, despite appearances, Jesus has conquered death and "descended into hell" to free the souls of the just.

Easter. On what Saint Augustine called "the mother of all holy vigils," we recall the history of salvation and welcome its triumphant culmination: Jesus breaks the chains of death and arises victorious from the grave. With Mary Magdalene, the apostles, and the Emmaus-bound disciples, we marvel and rejoice.

chief priests and the Pharisees, and they came there with lanterns and torches and weapons. [4]Then Jesus, knowing all that was to happen to him, came forward and asked them, "Whom are you looking for?" [5]They answered, "Jesus of Nazareth."[a] Jesus replied, "I am he."[b] Judas, who betrayed him, was standing with them. [6]When Jesus[c] said to them, "I am he,"[b] they stepped back and fell to the ground. [7]Again he asked them, "Whom are you looking for?" And they said, "Jesus of Nazareth."[a] [8]Jesus answered, "I told you that I am he.[b] So if you are looking for me, let these men go." [9]This was to fulfill the word that he had spoken, "I did not lose a single one of those whom you gave me." [10]Then Simon Peter, who had a sword, drew it, struck the high priest's slave, and cut off his right ear. The slave's name was Malchus. [11]Jesus said to Peter, "Put your sword back into its sheath. Am I not to drink the cup that the Father has given me?"

Jesus before the High Priest

12 So the soldiers, their officer, and the Jewish police arrested Jesus and bound him. [13]First they took him to Annas, who was the father-in-law of Caiaphas, the high priest that year. [14]Caiaphas was the one who had advised the Jews that it was better to have one person die for the people.

Peter Denies Jesus

15 Simon Peter and another disciple followed Jesus. Since that disciple was known to the high priest, he went with Jesus into the courtyard of the high priest, [16]but Peter was standing outside at the gate. So the other disciple, who was known to the high priest, went out, spoke to the woman who guarded the gate, and brought Peter in. [17]The woman said to Peter, "You are not also one of this man's disciples, are you?" He said, "I am not." [18]Now the slaves and the police had made a charcoal fire because it was cold, and they were standing around it and warming themselves. Peter also was standing with them and warming himself.

The High Priest Questions Jesus

19 Then the high priest questioned Jesus about his disciples and about his teaching. [20]Jesus answered, "I have spoken openly to the world; I have always taught in synagogues and in the temple, where all the Jews come together. I have said nothing in secret. [21]Why do you ask me? Ask those who heard what I said to them; they know what I said." [22]When he had said this, one of the police standing nearby struck Jesus on the face, saying, "Is that how you answer the high priest?" [23]Jesus answered, "If I have spoken wrongly, testify to the wrong. But if I have spoken rightly, why do you strike me?" [24]Then Annas sent him bound to Caiaphas the high priest.

Peter Denies Jesus Again

25 Now Simon Peter was standing and warming himself. They asked him, "You are not also one of his disciples, are you?" He denied it and said, "I am not." [26]One of the slaves of the high priest, a relative of the man whose ear Peter had cut off, asked, "Did I not see you in the garden with him?" [27]Again Peter denied it, and at that moment the cock crowed.

Jesus before Pilate

28 Then they took Jesus from Caiaphas to Pilate's headquarters.[d] It was early in the morning. They themselves did not enter the headquarters,[d] so as to avoid ritual defilement and to be able to eat the Passover. [29]So Pilate went out to them and said, "What accusation do you bring against this man?" [30]They answered, "If this man were not a criminal, we would not have handed him over to you." [31]Pilate said to them, "Take him yourselves and judge him according to your law." The Jews replied, "We are not permitted to put anyone to death." [32](This was to fulfill what Jesus had said when he indicated the kind of death he was to die.)

33 Then Pilate entered the headquarters[d] again, summoned Jesus, and asked him, "Are you the King of the Jews?" [34]Jesus answered, "Do you ask this on your own, or did others tell you about me?" [35]Pilate replied, "I am not a Jew, am I? Your own nation and the chief priests have handed you over to me. What have you done?" [36]Jesus answered, "My kingdom is not from this world. If my kingdom were from this world, my followers would be fighting to keep me from being handed over to the Jews. But as it is, my

---

a Gk *the Nazorean*   *b* Gk *I am*   *c* Gk *he*   *d* Gk *the praetorium*

kingdom is not from here." [37]Pilate asked him, "So you are a king?" Jesus answered, "You say that I am a king. For this I was born, and for this I came into the world, to testify to the truth. Everyone who belongs to the truth listens to my voice." [38]Pilate asked him, "What is truth?"

Jesus Sentenced to Death

After he had said this, he went out to the Jews again and told them, "I find no case against him. [39]But you have a custom that I release someone for you at the Passover. Do you want me to release for you the King of the Jews?" [40]They shouted in reply, "Not this man, but Barabbas!" Now Barabbas was a bandit.

19 Then Pilate took Jesus and had him flogged. [2]And the soldiers wove a crown of thorns and put it on his head, and they dressed him in a purple robe. [3]They kept coming up to him, saying, "Hail, King of the Jews!" and striking him on the face. [4]Pilate went out again and said to them, "Look, I am bringing him out to you to let you know that I find no case against him." [5]So Jesus came out, wearing the crown of thorns and the purple robe. Pilate said to them, "Here is the man!" [6]When the chief priests and the police saw him, they shouted, "Crucify him! Crucify him!" Pilate said to them, "Take him yourselves and crucify him; I find no case against him." [7]The Jews answered him, "We have a law, and according to that law he ought to die because he has claimed to be the Son of God."

8 Now when Pilate heard this, he was more afraid than ever. [9]He entered his headquarters[e] again and asked Jesus, "Where are you from?" But Jesus gave him no answer. [10]Pilate therefore said to him, "Do you refuse to speak to me? Do you not know that I have power to release you, and power to crucify you?" [11]Jesus answered him, "You would have no power over me unless it had been given you from above; therefore the one who handed me over to you is guilty of a greater sin." [12]From then on Pilate tried to release him, but the Jews cried out, "If you release this man, you are no friend of the emperor. Everyone who claims to be a king sets himself against the emperor."

13 When Pilate heard these words, he brought Jesus outside and sat[f] on the judge's bench at a place called The Stone Pavement, or in Hebrew[g] Gabbatha.

[14]Now it was the day of Preparation for the Passover; and it was about noon. He said to the Jews, "Here is your King!" [15]They cried out, "Away with him! Away with him! Crucify him!" Pilate asked them, "Shall I crucify your King?" The chief priests answered, "We have no king but the emperor." [16]Then he handed him over to them to be crucified.

The Crucifixion of Jesus

So they took Jesus; [17]and carrying the cross by himself, he went out to what is called The Place of the Skull, which in Hebrew[g] is called Golgotha. [18]There they crucified him, and with him two others, one on either side, with Jesus between them. [19]Pilate also had an inscription written and put on the cross. It read, "Jesus of Nazareth,[h] the King of the Jews." [20]Many of the Jews read this inscription, because the place where Jesus was crucified was near the city; and it was written in Hebrew,[g] in Latin, and in Greek. [21]Then the chief priests of the Jews said to Pilate, "Do not write, 'The King of the Jews,' but, 'This man said, I am King of the Jews.' " [22]Pilate answered, "What I have written I have written." [23]When the soldiers had crucified Jesus, they took his clothes and divided them into four parts, one for each soldier. They also took his tunic; now the tunic was seamless, woven in one piece from the top. [24]So they said to one another, "Let us not tear it, but cast lots for it to see who will get it." This was to fulfill what the scripture says,

"They divided my clothes among
      themselves,
   and for my clothing they cast lots."
[25]And that is what the soldiers did.

Meanwhile, standing near the cross of Jesus were his mother, and his mother's sister, Mary the wife of Clopas, and Mary Magdalene. [26]When Jesus saw his mother and the disciple whom he loved standing beside her, he said to his mother, "Woman, here is your son." [27]Then he said to the disciple, "Here is your mother." And from that hour the disciple took her into his own home.

28 After this, when Jesus knew that all was now finished, he said (in order to fulfill the scripture), "I am thirsty." [29]A jar full of sour wine was standing there. So they

---

e Gk *the praetorium*   *f* Or *seated him*   *g* That is, *Aramaic*   *h* Gk *the Nazorean*

put a sponge full of the wine on a branch of hyssop and held it to his mouth. [30]When Jesus had received the wine, he said, "It is finished." Then he bowed his head and gave up his spirit.

Jesus' Side Is Pierced

31 Since it was the day of Preparation, the Jews did not want the bodies left on the cross during the sabbath, especially because that sabbath was a day of great solemnity. So they asked Pilate to have the legs of the crucified men broken and the bodies removed. [32]Then the soldiers came and broke the legs of the first and of the other who had been crucified with him. [33]But when they came to Jesus and saw that he was already dead, they did not break his legs. [34]Instead, one of the soldiers pierced his side with a spear, and at

once blood and water came out. [35](He who saw this has testified so that you also may believe. His testimony is true, and he knows[i] that he tells the truth.) [36]These things occurred so that the scripture might be fulfilled, "None of his bones shall be broken." [37]And again another passage of scripture says, "They will look on the one whom they have pierced."

The Burial of Jesus

38 After these things, Joseph of Arimathea, who was a disciple of Jesus, though a secret one because of his fear of the Jews, asked Pilate to let him take away the body of Jesus. Pilate gave him permission; so he came and removed his body. [39]Nicodemus, who had at first come to Jesus by

---

i Or *there is one who knows*

A Place Beneath the Cross

MONDAY

Scripture Reading for Today:
John 19.16–27

Verse for Today:
John 19.25

Many of us have stood beneath the cross. Sometimes it is the cross of disease and death. If you have ever accompanied someone dear who went through medical test after test, succumbing to the ravages of cancer, and watched the dwindling and destruction of his or her body, you have been at the foot of the cross with Mary. If you have ever had to place an aging parent with a debilitating disease in a facility for the infirm, you know what it is like to stand beneath the cross. If you have been a parent and had a child die in an unexpected, harsh, or violent way, you have known the heartache of Mary as she watched Jesus die.

The "crosses" we stand by may not always mean that the one who hangs there is physically dying. If you have listened and listened and listened to a friend who is journeying back through old wounds, you have been there beneath the cross. If you have lived with someone so depressed that he or she gave up the desire to live, you have stood on the same hill as Mary. If you have watched someone you love become devoured by drugs or alcohol and heard the denials and false promises, you have had a place beneath the cross. Any time you have been with another person who is suffering and have been unable to take the pain away, you have been at the cross with Mary.

When love is the motivation, one can wait beneath a cross for a very, very long time.

—*JOYCE RUPP*

Go to page 1427 for your next devotional reading.

night, also came, bringing a mixture of myrrh and aloes, weighing about a hundred pounds. ⁴⁰They took the body of Jesus and wrapped it with the spices in linen cloths, according to the burial custom of the Jews. ⁴¹Now there was a garden in the place where he was crucified, and in the garden there was a new tomb in which no one had ever been laid. ⁴²And so, because it was the Jewish day of Preparation, and the tomb was nearby, they laid Jesus there.

The Resurrection of Jesus

20 Early on the first day of the week, while it was still dark, Mary Magdalene came to the tomb and saw that the stone had been removed from the tomb. ²So she ran and went to Simon Peter and the other disciple, the one whom Jesus loved, and said to them, "They have taken the Lord out of the tomb, and we do not know where they have laid him." ³Then Peter and the other disciple set out and went toward the tomb. ⁴The two were running together, but the other disciple outran Peter and reached the tomb first. ⁵He bent down to look in and saw the linen wrappings lying there, but he did not go in. ⁶Then Simon Peter came, following him, and went into the tomb. He saw the linen wrappings lying there, ⁷and the cloth that had been on Jesus' head, not lying with the linen wrappings but rolled up in a place by itself. ⁸Then the other disciple, who reached the tomb first, also went in, and he saw and believed; ⁹for as yet they did not understand the scripture, that he must rise from the dead. ¹⁰Then the disciples returned to their homes.

Jesus Appears to Mary Magdalene

11 But Mary stood weeping outside the tomb. As she wept, she bent over to look*j* into the tomb; ¹²and she saw two angels in white, sitting where the body of Jesus had been lying, one at the head and the other at the feet. ¹³They said to her, "Woman, why are you weeping?" She said to them, "They have taken away my Lord, and I do not know where they have laid him." ¹⁴When she had said this, she turned around and saw Jesus standing there, but she did not know that it was Jesus. ¹⁵Jesus said to her, "Woman, why are you weeping? Whom are you looking for?" Supposing him to be the gardener, she said to

him, "Sir, if you have carried him away, tell me where you have laid him, and I will take him away." ¹⁶Jesus said to her, "Mary!" She turned and said to him in Hebrew,*k* "Rabbouni!" (which means Teacher). ¹⁷Jesus said to her, "Do not hold on to me, because I have not yet ascended to the Father. But go to my brothers and say to them, 'I am ascending to my Father and your Father, to my God and your God.' " ¹⁸Mary Magdalene went and announced to the disciples, "I have seen the Lord"; and she told them that he had said these things to her.

Jesus Appears to the Disciples

19 When it was evening on that day, the first day of the week, and the doors of the house where the disciples had met were locked for fear of the Jews, Jesus came and stood among them and said, "Peace be with you." ²⁰After he said this, he showed them his hands and his side. Then the disciples rejoiced when they saw the Lord. ²¹Jesus said to them again, "Peace be with you. As the Father has sent me, so I send you." ²²When he had said this, he breathed on them and said to them, "Receive the Holy Spirit. ²³If you forgive the sins of any, they are forgiven them; if you retain the sins of any, they are retained."

Jesus and Thomas

24 But Thomas (who was called the Twin*l*), one of the twelve, was not with them when Jesus came. ²⁵So the other disciples told him, "We have seen the Lord." But he said to them, "Unless I see the mark of the nails in his hands, and put my finger in the mark of the nails and my hand in his side, I will not believe."

26 A week later his disciples were again in the house, and Thomas was with them. Although the doors were shut, Jesus came and stood among them and said, "Peace be with you." ²⁷Then he said to Thomas, "Put your finger here and see my hands. Reach out your hand and put it in my side. Do not doubt but believe." ²⁸Thomas answered him, "My Lord and my God!" ²⁹Jesus said to him, "Have you believed because you have seen me? Blessed are those who have not seen and yet have come to believe."

j Gk lacks to look   *k* That is, Aramaic   *l* Gk Didymus

The Purpose of This Book

30 Now Jesus did many other signs in the presence of his disciples, which are not written in this book. [31]But these are written so that you may come to believe[m] that Jesus is the Messiah,[n] the Son of God, and that through believing you may have life in his name.

Jesus Appears to Seven Disciples

21 After these things Jesus showed himself again to the disciples by the Sea of Tiberias; and he showed himself in this way. [2]Gathered there together were Simon Peter, Thomas called the Twin,[o] Nathanael of Cana in Galilee, the sons of Zebedee, and two others of his disciples. [3]Simon Peter said to them, "I am going fishing." They said to him, "We will go with you." They went out and got into the boat, but that night they caught nothing.

4 Just after daybreak, Jesus stood on the beach; but the disciples did not know that it was Jesus. [5]Jesus said to them, "Children, you have no fish, have you?" They answered him, "No." [6]He said to them, "Cast the net to the right side of the boat, and you will find some." So they cast it, and now they were not able to haul it

m Other ancient authorities read *may continue to believe*   n Or *the Christ*   o Gk *Didymus*

*D*o Not Be Afraid

TUESDAY

Scripture Reading for Today:
John 20.11–18

Verse for Today:
John 20.15

Mary Magdalene and another woman had come to the tomb to anoint the body of Jesus with spices [in accordance with] Jewish custom. She had watched him die, his body arching in pain, nailed hand and foot to a Roman cross. Though he had saved her from seven demons, she could do nothing for him.

Now her Messiah was dead. She had come to the tomb, not seeking a miracle, but to show her devotion to a man who had truly loved her. Perhaps she felt the demons encroaching again as she approached the grave just before dawn. She couldn't know then that God had set a limit to her sorrow, that her darkness would soon turn to light.

Sometimes we are like Mary, feeling as though we are living in that desolate time between the crucifixion and the resurrection. Maybe we have been disappointed by life. Or betrayed by someone we love. We have prayed without seeing the slightest evidence that God has heard us. We ache to experience him, but there is nothing.

Mary's disappointment and grief must have given way to bewilderment and then to joy when she encountered, not the corpse of her Savior, but an angel proclaiming him still alive. The man who had overcome the death inside her had himself come back to life.

You may also be looking for Jesus, seeking a deeper assurance of his love and power. Keep looking; stay close to him even when you feel dead inside. Remember the angel's words in Matthew's Gospel: "Do not be afraid . . . he has been raised."

—ANN SPANGLER

Go to page 1430 for your next devotional reading.

in because there were so many fish. [7]That disciple whom Jesus loved said to Peter, "It is the Lord!" When Simon Peter heard that it was the Lord, he put on some clothes, for he was naked, and jumped into the sea. [8]But the other disciples came in the boat, dragging the net full of fish, for they were not far from the land, only about a hundred yards[p] off.

9 When they had gone ashore, they saw a charcoal fire there, with fish on it, and bread. [10]Jesus said to them, "Bring some of the fish that you have just caught." [11]So Simon Peter went aboard and hauled the net ashore, full of large fish, a hundred fifty-three of them; and though there were so many, the net was not torn. [12]Jesus said to them, "Come and have breakfast." Now none of the disciples dared to ask him, "Who are you?" because they knew it was the Lord. [13]Jesus came and took the bread and gave it to them, and did the same with the fish. [14]This was now the third time that Jesus appeared to the disciples after he was raised from the dead.

Jesus and Peter

15 When they had finished breakfast, Jesus said to Simon Peter, "Simon son of John, do you love me more than these?" He said to him, "Yes, Lord; you know that I love you." Jesus said to him, "Feed my lambs." [16]A second time he said to him, "Simon son of John, do you love me?" He said to him, "Yes, Lord; you know that I love you." Jesus said to him, "Tend my sheep." [17]He said to him the third time, "Simon son of John, do you love me?" Peter felt hurt because he said to him the third time, "Do you love me?" And he said

to him, "Lord, you know everything; you know that I love you." Jesus said to him, "Feed my sheep. [18]Very truly, I tell you, when you were younger, you used to fasten your own belt and to go wherever you wished. But when you grow old, you will stretch out your hands, and someone else will fasten a belt around you and take you where you do not wish to go." [19](He said this to indicate the kind of death by which he would glorify God.) After this he said to him, "Follow me."

Jesus and the Beloved Disciple

20 Peter turned and saw the disciple whom Jesus loved following them; he was the one who had reclined next to Jesus at the supper and had said, "Lord, who is it that is going to betray you?" [21]When Peter saw him, he said to Jesus, "Lord, what about him?" [22]Jesus said to him, "If it is my will that he remain until I come, what is that to you? Follow me!" [23]So the rumor spread in the community[q] that this disciple would not die. Yet Jesus did not say to him that he would not die, but, "If it is my will that he remain until I come, what is that to you?"[r]

24 This is the disciple who is testifying to these things and has written them, and we know that his testimony is true. [25]But there are also many other things that Jesus did; if every one of them were written down, I suppose that the world itself could not contain the books that would be written.

---

[p] Gk *two hundred cubits*   [q] Gk *among the brothers*
[r] Other ancient authorities lack *what is that to you*

The *Acts* of the Apostles

Acts is part two of a work whose first half is the Gospel of Luke. It tells the story of the early church's rapid spread from Jerusalem to the rest of the Roman Empire. It begins with Jesus' ascension into heaven and then describes how the disciples were filled with the Holy Spirit on the Feast of Pentecost.

The story of how the church began is filled with dramatic miracles, conflicts, and conversions. Acts stresses the Holy Spirit's role in the formation of the church and follows the ministries of its two primary evangelists: Peter as the leader of the Christian community, and Paul, the Pharisee turned to Christ, who spread Christianity to the Gentiles. Acts describes how the early Christians resolved the nettlesome issue of whether Gentiles could become believers without first becoming Jews.

More than half of Acts is devoted to Paul's missionary journeys. By the end of Paul's ministry, most of the Christian communities were composed of Gentile believers. The book ends with his first imprisonment in Rome.

Though Acts does not comment on the exact nature of Peter or Paul's deaths, both are believed to have been martyred in Rome. As Christians, we owe an enormous debt to two men who patterned their lives and deaths on the Savior they loved.

The Promise of the Holy Spirit

1 In the first book, Theophilus, I wrote about all that Jesus did and taught from the beginning [2]until the day when he was taken up to heaven, after giving instructions through the Holy Spirit to the apostles whom he had chosen. [3]After his suffering he presented himself alive to them by many convincing proofs, appearing to them during forty days and speaking about the kingdom of God. [4]While staying[a] with them, he ordered them not to leave Jerusalem, but to wait there for the promise of the Father. "This," he said, "is what you have heard from me; [5]for John baptized with water, but you will be

a Or *eating*

baptized with[b] the Holy Spirit not many days from now."

The Ascension of Jesus

6 So when they had come together, they asked him, "Lord, is this the time when you will restore the kingdom to Israel?" [7]He replied, "It is not for you to know the times or periods that the Father has set by his own authority. [8]But you will receive power when the Holy Spirit has come upon you; and you will be my witnesses in Jerusalem, in all Judea and Samaria, and to the ends of the earth." [9]When he had said this, as they were watching, he was lifted up, and a cloud took him out of their sight. [10]While he was going and they were gazing up toward heaven, suddenly two men in white robes stood by them. [11]They said, "Men of Galilee, why do you stand looking up toward heaven? This Jesus, who has been taken up from you into heaven, will come in the same way as you saw him go into heaven."

Matthias Chosen to Replace Judas

12 Then they returned to Jerusalem from the mount called Olivet, which is near Jerusalem, a sabbath day's journey away. [13]When they had entered the city, they went to the room upstairs where they were staying, Peter, and John, and James, and Andrew, Philip and Thomas, Bartholomew and Matthew, James son of Alphaeus, and Simon the Zealot, and Judas son of[c] James. [14]All these were constantly devoting themselves to prayer, together with certain women, including Mary the mother of Jesus, as well as his brothers.

15 In those days Peter stood up among the believers[d] (together the crowd numbered about one hundred twenty persons) and said, [16]"Friends,[e] the scripture had to be fulfilled, which the Holy Spirit through David foretold concerning Judas,

[b] Or by   [c] Or the brother of   [d] Gk brothers
[e] Gk Men, brothers

We Are Not Abandoned

WEDNESDAY

Scripture Reading
for Today:
Acts 1.6–11

Verse for Today:
Acts 1.11

I have always looked upon the Feast of the Ascension as a tremendous act of faith in us. Jesus, in leaving us, tells us that we are ready to be the Body of Christ, the Church on earth. Even stronger than his physical departure is the proclamation that if he does not go away, the Spirit cannot come (see John 16.7). When I try to pray and live the Ascension, two images come to my mind: autumn trees and departing friends.

Once, on an autumn day very near the edge of winter, I stood like the friends of Jesus, gazing upward toward an almost empty tree. The leaves seemed to be saying to the tree: Unless we go away, you cannot be renewed. We have to die. We must return to the earth. We have to let go of you so you can be reborn.

And how often in airports I've stood gazing upward toward ascending planes, remembering Jesus' words: "Unless I go away, the Spirit cannot come." Sometimes we have to be left on our own to discover the uniqueness and strength that is ours. It is as though in leaving, whether it be of Jesus, a friend, or a leaf, something of them returns to convince us that we are not alone. We have not been abandoned. We have, perhaps, in that leaving been given the gift of ourselves in a new, deeper, and more lasting way.

—MACRINA WIEDERKEHR

Go to page 1432 for your next devotional reading.
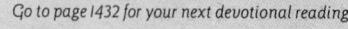

who became a guide for those who arrested Jesus— [17]for he was numbered among us and was allotted his share in this ministry." [18](Now this man acquired a field with the reward of his wickedness; and falling headlong,[f] he burst open in the middle and all his bowels gushed out. [19]This became known to all the residents of Jerusalem, so that the field was called in their language Hakeldama, that is, Field of Blood.) [20]"For it is written in the book of Psalms,

'Let his homestead become desolate,
    and let there be no one to live
        in it';

and

'Let another take his position of
    overseer.'

[21]So one of the men who have accompanied us during all the time that the Lord Jesus went in and out among us, [22]beginning from the baptism of John until the day when he was taken up from us—one of these must become a witness with us to his resurrection." [23]So they proposed two, Joseph called Barsabbas, who was also known as Justus, and Matthias. [24]Then they prayed and said, "Lord, you know everyone's heart. Show us which one of these two you have chosen [25]to take the place[g] in this ministry and apostleship from which Judas turned aside to go to his own place." [26]And they cast lots for them, and the lot fell on Matthias; and he was added to the eleven apostles.

The Coming of the Holy Spirit

2 When the day of Pentecost had come, they were all together in one place. [2]And suddenly from heaven there came a sound like the rush of a violent wind, and it filled the entire house where they were sitting. [3]Divided tongues, as of fire, appeared among them, and a tongue rested on each of them. [4]All of them were filled with the Holy Spirit and began to speak in other languages, as the Spirit gave them ability.

[5] Now there were devout Jews from every nation under heaven living in Jerusalem. [6]And at this sound the crowd gathered and was bewildered, because each one heard them speaking in the native language of each. [7]Amazed and astonished, they asked, "Are not all these who are speaking Galileans? [8]And how is it that we hear, each of us, in our own native language? [9]Parthians, Medes, Elamites, and residents of Mesopotamia, Judea and Cappadocia, Pontus and Asia, [10]Phrygia and Pamphylia, Egypt and the parts of Libya belonging to Cyrene, and visitors from Rome, both Jews and proselytes, [11]Cretans and Arabs—in our own languages we hear them speaking about God's deeds of power." [12]All were amazed and perplexed, saying to one another, "What does this mean?" [13]But others sneered and said, "They are filled with new wine."

Peter Addresses the Crowd

[14] But Peter, standing with the eleven, raised his voice and addressed them, "Men of Judea and all who live in Jerusalem, let this be known to you, and listen to what I say. [15]Indeed, these are not drunk, as you suppose, for it is only nine o'clock in the morning. [16]No, this is what was spoken through the prophet Joel:
[17] 'In the last days it will be, God
        declares,
    that I will pour out my Spirit upon
        all flesh,
        and your sons and your daughters
            shall prophesy,
        and your young men shall
            see visions,
        and your old men shall
            dream dreams.
[18] Even upon my slaves, both men and
        women,
    in those days I will pour out
        my Spirit;
        and they shall prophesy.
[19] And I will show portents in the
        heaven above
    and signs on the earth below,
        blood, and fire, and
            smoky mist.
[20] The sun shall be turned to darkness
        and the moon to blood,
    before the coming of the Lord's
        great and glorious day.
[21] Then everyone who calls on the
        name of the Lord shall
        be saved.'

[22] "You that are Israelites,[h] listen to what I have to say: Jesus of Nazareth,[i] a man attested to you by God with deeds of

---

[f] Or swelling up   [g] Other ancient authorities read the share   [h] Gk Men, Israelites   [i] Gk the Nazorean

power, wonders, and signs that God did
through him among you, as you yourselves know— ²³this man, handed over to
you according to the definite plan and
foreknowledge of God, you crucified and
killed by the hands of those outside the
law. ²⁴But God raised him up, having
freed him from death,ʲ because it was
impossible for him to be held in its power. ²⁵For David says concerning him,
'I saw the Lord always before me,

for he is at my right hand so that
        I will not be shaken;
²⁶ therefore my heart was glad, and my
        tongue rejoiced;
    moreover my flesh will live
        in hope.
²⁷ For you will not abandon my soul
        to Hades,

ʲ Gk *the pains of death*

The Holy Ghost Hole

THURSDAY

Scripture Reading
for Today:
Acts 2.1–13

Verse for Today:
Acts 2.1

Pentecost, or the Festival of Weeks, was originally a Jewish festival, falling fifty days (seven weeks) after Passover. The first fruits
of the grain harvest were offered to the Lord, as commanded in
Deuteronomy 16.10. The giving of the Law to Moses was also celebrated.

It was at this great Jewish festival, when many people were
gathered in Jerusalem, that the Holy Spirit descended on the apostles, Mary, and other disciples of Jesus.

Throughout the Middle Ages, and beyond, in both Catholic
and Protestant countries, Pentecost and the week following it
were holy days and holidays. Pentecost has been considered a
very holy day, one when the Holy Spirit was especially near at
hand. Sometimes people would go to the top of a mountain to
pray. It has been a favorite moment for Baptisms, and the English
name for this feast, Whitsunday, refers to the white robes of the
newly baptized.

The Middle Ages had a strange and delightful way of celebrating the religious meaning of Pentecost. In the ceiling of the
church there would be a large aperture called "the Holy Ghost
Hole." And on Pentecost, to the sound of trumpets or some other
windy noise, down through the hole would be lowered a great
disk, often painted blue with golden rays, and with a white dove,
symbol of the Holy Spirit, painted on it. In some places pigeons or
doves would be released into the church through this hole.
Elsewhere roses were dropped. A few churches tried dropping
burning straw. Alas, unlike the flames described in Acts, this fire
did not hover over the faithful but fell right on them; the practice
was discontinued.

Throughout much of Europe, Pentecost is a traditional time of
communal feasting and family picnicking. It has been curiously neglected in this country. Let's try to remedy that!

—*EVELYN BIRGE VITZ*

Go to page 1435 for your next devotional reading.

or let your Holy One experience
   corruption.
28 You have made known to me the
   ways of life;
   you will make me full of gladness
      with your presence.'

29 "Fellow Israelites,[k] I may say to you confidently of our ancestor David that he both died and was buried, and his tomb is with us to this day. [30]Since he was a prophet, he knew that God had sworn with an oath to him that he would put one of his descendants on his throne. [31]Foreseeing this, David[l] spoke of the resurrection of the Messiah,[m] saying,

'He was not abandoned to Hades,
   nor did his flesh experience
     corruption.'

[32]This Jesus God raised up, and of that all of us are witnesses. [33]Being therefore exalted at[n] the right hand of God, and having received from the Father the promise of the Holy Spirit, he has poured out this that you both see and hear. [34]For David did not ascend into the heavens, but he himself says,

'The Lord said to my Lord,
   "Sit at my right hand,
35   until I make your enemies your
      footstool." '

[36]Therefore let the entire house of Israel know with certainty that God has made him both Lord and Messiah,[o] this Jesus whom you crucified."

The First Converts

37 Now when they heard this, they were cut to the heart and said to Peter and to the other apostles, "Brothers,[k] what should we do?" [38]Peter said to them, "Repent, and be baptized every one of you in the name of Jesus Christ so that your sins may be forgiven; and you will receive the gift of the Holy Spirit. [39]For the promise is for you, for your children, and for all who are far away, everyone whom the Lord our God calls to him." [40]And he testified with many other arguments and exhorted them, saying, "Save yourselves from this corrupt generation." [41]So those who welcomed his message were baptized, and that day about three thousand persons were added. [42]They devoted themselves to the apostles' teaching and fellowship, to the breaking of bread and the prayers.

Life among the Believers

43 Awe came upon everyone, because many wonders and signs were being done by the apostles. [44]All who believed were together and had all things in common; [45]they would sell their possessions and goods and distribute the proceeds[p] to all, as any had need. [46]Day by day, as they spent much time together in the temple, they broke bread at home[q] and ate their food with glad and generous[r] hearts, [47]praising God and having the goodwill of all the people. And day by day the Lord added to their number those who were being saved.

Peter Heals a Crippled Beggar

3 One day Peter and John were going up to the temple at the hour of prayer, at three o'clock in the afternoon. [2]And a man lame from birth was being carried in. People would lay him daily at the gate of the temple called the Beautiful Gate so that he could ask for alms from those entering the temple. [3]When he saw Peter and John about to go into the temple, he asked them for alms. [4]Peter looked intently at him, as did John, and said, "Look at us." [5]And he fixed his attention on them, expecting to receive something from them. [6]But Peter said, "I have no silver or gold, but what I have I give you; in the name of Jesus Christ of Nazareth,[s] stand up and walk." [7]And he took him by the right hand and raised him up; and immediately his feet and ankles were made strong. [8]Jumping up, he stood and began to walk, and he entered the temple with them, walking and leaping and praising God. [9]All the people saw him walking and praising God, [10]and they recognized him as the one who used to sit and ask for alms at the Beautiful Gate of the temple; and they were filled with wonder and amazement at what had happened to him.

Peter Speaks in Solomon's Portico

11 While he clung to Peter and John, all the people ran together to them in the portico called Solomon's Portico, utterly astonished. [12]When Peter saw it, he addressed the people, "You Israelites,[t] why do you wonder at this, or why do you stare at us, as though by our own power or

---

[k] Gk Men, brothers   [l] Gk he   [m] Or the Christ
[n] Or by   [o] Or Christ   [p] Gk them   [q] Or from
house to house   [r] Or sincere   [s] Gk the Nazorean
[t] Gk Men, Israelites

piety we had made him walk? 13The God of Abraham, the God of Isaac, and the God of Jacob, the God of our ancestors has glorified his servant[u] Jesus, whom you handed over and rejected in the presence of Pilate, though he had decided to release him. 14But you rejected the Holy and Righteous One and asked to have a murderer given to you, 15and you killed the Author of life, whom God raised from the dead. To this we are witnesses. 16And by faith in his name, his name itself has made this man strong, whom you see and know; and the faith that is through Jesus[v] has given him this perfect health in the presence of all of you.

17 "And now, friends,[w] I know that you acted in ignorance, as did also your rulers. 18In this way God fulfilled what he had foretold through all the prophets, that his Messiah[x] would suffer. 19Repent therefore, and turn to God so that your sins may be wiped out, 20so that times of refreshing may come from the presence of the Lord, and that he may send the Messiah[y] appointed for you, that is, Jesus, 21who must remain in heaven until the time of universal restoration that God announced long ago through his holy prophets. 22Moses said, 'The Lord your God will raise up for you from your own people[w] a prophet like me. You must listen to whatever he tells you. 23And it will be that everyone who does not listen to that prophet will be utterly rooted out of the people.' 24And all the prophets, as many as have spoken, from Samuel and those after him, also predicted these days. 25You are the descendants of the prophets and of the covenant that God gave to your ancestors, saying to Abraham, 'And in your descendants all the families of the earth shall be blessed.' 26When God raised up his servant,[u] he sent him first to you, to bless you by turning each of you from your wicked ways."

Peter and John before the Council

4 While Peter and John[z] were speaking to the people, the priests, the captain of the temple, and the Sadducees came to them, 2much annoyed because they were teaching the people and proclaiming that in Jesus there is the resurrection of the dead. 3So they arrested them and put them in custody until the next day, for it was already evening. 4But many of those who heard the word believed; and they numbered about five thousand.

5 The next day their rulers, elders, and scribes assembled in Jerusalem, 6with Annas the high priest, Caiaphas, John,[a] and Alexander, and all who were of the high-priestly family. 7When they had made the prisoners[b] stand in their midst, they inquired, "By what power or by what name did you do this?" 8Then Peter, filled with the Holy Spirit, said to them, "Rulers of the people and elders, 9if we are questioned today because of a good deed done to someone who was sick and are asked how this man has been healed, 10let it be known to all of you, and to all the people of Israel, that this man is standing before you in good health by the name of Jesus Christ of Nazareth,[c] whom you crucified, whom God raised from the dead. 11This Jesus[d] is

'the stone that was rejected by you, the builders; it has become the cornerstone.'[e]

12There is salvation in no one else, for there is no other name under heaven given among mortals by which we must be saved."

13 Now when they saw the boldness of Peter and John and realized that they were uneducated and ordinary men, they were amazed and recognized them as companions of Jesus. 14When they saw the man who had been cured standing beside them, they had nothing to say in opposition. 15So they ordered them to leave the council while they discussed the matter with one another. 16They said, "What will we do with them? For it is obvious to all who live in Jerusalem that a notable sign has been done through them; we cannot deny it. 17But to keep it from spreading further among the people, let us warn them to speak no more to anyone in this name." 18So they called them and ordered them not to speak or teach at all in the name of Jesus. 19But Peter and John answered them, "Whether it is right in God's sight to listen to you rather than to God, you must judge; 20for we cannot keep from speaking about what we have seen

---

[u] Or child [v] Gk him [w] Gk brothers [x] Or his Christ [y] Or the Christ [z] Gk While they [a] Other ancient authorities read Jonathan [b] Gk them [c] Gk the Nazorean [d] Gk This [e] Or keystone

and heard." 21After threatening them again, they let them go, finding no way to punish them because of the people, for all of them praised God for what had happened. 22For the man on whom this sign of healing had been performed was more than forty years old.

The Believers Pray for Boldness

23 After they were released, they went to their friends f and reported what the chief priests and the elders had said to them. 24When they heard it, they raised

f Gk *their own*

I Didn't Mean to Be Rude

FRIDAY

Scripture Reading
for Today:
Acts 4.5–12

Verse for Today:
Acts 4.12

Twenty-four years ago I learned something specific. The specificity of what I learned is what makes it, to many, offensive.

Twenty-four years ago a hitchhiking jaunt around Europe brought me one afternoon to a church in Dublin. I was intrigued by Eastern religions at the time, particularly Hinduism, but was theologically open-minded enough to appreciate Christian art and architecture.

The light in the church was dim, and I blinked to adjust my eyes. Wandering toward the back, I encountered a statue of Jesus, who stood marble-white with arms held low, palms open. On his chest the sculptor had depicted his heart, twined with thorns and springing with flames. The base of the statue was inscribed: "Behold the heart that so loved mankind."

Here's the part I can't explain. I remember looking at the statue, but I don't remember falling to my knees. Then I felt an interior presence forming the words, "I am your life."

Twenty-four years ago I learned that Jesus is my Lord. But that's not the offensive part. Soon thereafter, reading Scriptures and learning from other Christians, I discovered that Jesus is everybody's Lord, whether they know it or not.

As I write those words, I think of how rude they sound. It's a hard thing to say; as soon as the idea of objective religious truth is proposed, touchy offense rises up in alarm.

It's hard being thought rude. [Some] Christians may bypass the problem by putting the emphasis on the comfort that Jesus can give: Faith will make you happy. Social strategists may highlight the utility of religious belief: Faith will make you good.

But the real purpose of Jesus' work is more intimate and more deep: Faith will make you his. When Christians say "faith," we don't mean merely acknowledging certain facts about God: "Even the demons believe—and shudder." It's faith as in *having faith in someone*, being faithful to him, following faithfully wherever he leads. Faith doesn't just enlighten us; it transforms us. It does this because it is faith in one true Person, striding over the tumult of lesser gods.

—FREDERICA MATHEWES-GREEN

Go to page 1438 for your next devotional reading.

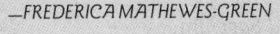

their voices together to God and said, "Sovereign Lord, who made the heaven and the earth, the sea, and everything in them, 25it is you who said by the Holy Spirit through our ancestor David, your servant:*g*

'Why did the Gentiles rage,
    and the peoples imagine vain
        things?
26 The kings of the earth took their
        stand,
    and the rulers have gathered
        together
    against the Lord and against his
        Messiah.'*h*

27For in this city, in fact, both Herod and Pontius Pilate, with the Gentiles and the peoples of Israel, gathered together against your holy servant*g* Jesus, whom you anointed, 28to do whatever your hand and your plan had predestined to take place. 29And now, Lord, look at their threats, and grant to your servants*i* to speak your word with all boldness, 30while you stretch out your hand to heal, and signs and wonders are performed through the name of your holy servant*g* Jesus." 31When they had prayed, the place in which they were gathered together was shaken; and they were all filled with the Holy Spirit and spoke the word of God with boldness.

The Believers Share Their Possessions

32 Now the whole group of those who believed were of one heart and soul, and no one claimed private ownership of any possessions, but everything they owned was held in common. 33With great power the apostles gave their testimony to the resurrection of the Lord Jesus, and great grace was upon them all. 34There was not a needy person among them, for as many as owned lands or houses sold them and brought the proceeds of what was sold. 35They laid it at the apostles' feet, and it was distributed to each as any had need. 36There was a Levite, a native of Cyprus, Joseph, to whom the apostles gave the name Barnabas (which means "son of encouragement"). 37He sold a field that belonged to him, then brought the money, and laid it at the apostles' feet.

Ananias and Sapphira

5 But a man named Ananias, with the consent of his wife Sapphira, sold a piece of property; 2with his wife's knowledge, he kept back some of the proceeds, and brought only a part and laid it at the apostles' feet. 3"Ananias," Peter asked, "why has Satan filled your heart to lie to the Holy Spirit and to keep back part of the proceeds of the land? 4While it remained unsold, did it not remain your own? And after it was sold, were not the proceeds at your disposal? How is it that you have contrived this deed in your heart? You did not lie to us*j* but to God!" 5Now when Ananias heard these words, he fell down and died. And great fear seized all who heard of it. 6The young men came and wrapped up his body,*k* then carried him out and buried him.

7 After an interval of about three hours his wife came in, not knowing what had happened. 8Peter said to her, "Tell me whether you and your husband sold the land for such and such a price." And she said, "Yes, that was the price." 9Then Peter said to her, "How is it that you have agreed together to put the Spirit of the Lord to the test? Look, the feet of those who have buried your husband are at the door, and they will carry you out." 10Immediately she fell down at his feet and died. When the young men came in they found her dead, so they carried her out and buried her beside her husband. 11And great fear seized the whole church and all who heard of these things.

The Apostles Heal Many

12 Now many signs and wonders were done among the people through the apostles. And they were all together in Solomon's Portico. 13None of the rest dared to join them, but the people held them in high esteem. 14Yet more than ever believers were added to the Lord, great numbers of both men and women, 15so that they even carried out the sick into the streets, and laid them on cots and mats, in order that Peter's shadow might fall on some of them as he came by. 16A great number of people would also gather from the towns around Jerusalem, bringing the sick and those tormented by unclean spirits, and they were all cured.

g Or *child*   *h* Or *his Christ*   *i* Gk *slaves*   *j* Gk
to men   *k* Meaning of Gk uncertain

The Apostles Are Persecuted

17 Then the high priest took action; he and all who were with him (that is, the sect of the Sadducees), being filled with jealousy, 18arrested the apostles and put them in the public prison. 19But during the night an angel of the Lord opened the prison doors, brought them out, and said, 20"Go, stand in the temple and tell the people the whole message about this life." 21When they heard this, they entered the temple at daybreak and went on with their teaching.

When the high priest and those with him arrived, they called together the council and the whole body of the elders of Israel, and sent to the prison to have them brought. 22But when the temple police went there, they did not find them in the prison; so they returned and reported, 23"We found the prison securely locked and the guards standing at the doors, but when we opened them, we found no one inside." 24Now when the captain of the temple and the chief priests heard these words, they were perplexed about them, wondering what might be going on. 25Then someone arrived and announced, "Look, the men whom you put in prison are standing in the temple and teaching the people!" 26Then the captain went with the temple police and brought them, but without violence, for they were afraid of being stoned by the people.

27 When they had brought them, they had them stand before the council. The high priest questioned them, 28saying, "We gave you strict orders not to teach in this name,^{l} yet here you have filled Jerusalem with your teaching and you are determined to bring this man's blood on us." 29But Peter and the apostles answered, "We must obey God rather than any human authority.^{m} 30The God of our ancestors raised up Jesus, whom you had killed by hanging him on a tree. 31God exalted him at his right hand as Leader and Savior that he might give repentance to Israel and forgiveness of sins. 32And we are witnesses to these things, and so is the Holy Spirit whom God has given to those who obey him."

33 When they heard this, they were enraged and wanted to kill them. 34But a Pharisee in the council named Gamaliel, a teacher of the law, respected by all the people, stood up and ordered the men to be put outside for a short time. 35Then he said to them, "Fellow Israelites,^{n} consider carefully what you propose to do to these men. 36For some time ago Theudas rose up, claiming to be somebody, and a number of men, about four hundred, joined him; but he was killed, and all who followed him were dispersed and disappeared. 37After him Judas the Galilean rose up at the time of the census and got people to follow him; he also perished, and all who followed him were scattered. 38So in the present case, I tell you, keep away from these men and let them alone; because if this plan or this undertaking is of human origin, it will fail; 39but if it is of God, you will not be able to overthrow them—in that case you may even be found fighting against God!"

They were convinced by him, 40and when they had called in the apostles, they had them flogged. Then they ordered them not to speak in the name of Jesus, and let them go. 41As they left the council, they rejoiced that they were considered worthy to suffer dishonor for the sake of the name. 42And every day in the temple and at home^o they did not cease to teach and proclaim Jesus as the Messiah. ^{p}

Seven Chosen to Serve

6 Now during those days, when the disciples were increasing in number, the Hellenists complained against the Hebrews because their widows were being neglected in the daily distribution of food. 2And the twelve called together the whole community of the disciples and said, "It is not right that we should neglect the word of God in order to wait on tables.^{q} 3Therefore, friends,^{r} select from among yourselves seven men of good standing, full of the Spirit and of wisdom, whom we may appoint to this task, 4while we, for our part, will devote ourselves to prayer and to serving the word." 5What they said pleased the whole community, and they chose Stephen, a man full of faith and the Holy Spirit, together with Philip, Prochorus, Nicanor, Timon, Parmenas, and Nicolaus, a proselyte of Antioch. 6They had

---

^{l} Other ancient authorities read *Did we not give you strict orders not to teach in this name?* ^{m} Gk *than men* ^{n} Gk *Men, Israelites* ^{o} Or *from house to house* ^{p} Or *the Christ* ^{q} Or *keep accounts* ^{r} Gk *brothers*

Mary, the Mother of Jesus

Her Name May Mean "Bitterness"

Her Character: *Her unqualified "yes" to God's plan for her life entailed great personal risk and suffering. She must have endured seasons of confusion, fear, and darkness as events unfolded. She is honored, not only as the mother of Jesus, but as his first disciple.*

Her Sorrow: *To see the son she loved shamed and tortured, left to die like the worst kind of criminal.*

Her Joy: *To see her child raised from the dead; to have received the Holy Spirit along with Jesus' other disciples.*

Read Luke 1.26–38; John 19.26–27
She sat down on the bench and closed her eyes, an old woman silhouetted against the blue Jerusalem sky. These days the memories came unbidden, like a gusty wind carrying her away to other times and places.

A cool breeze teased at her skirts as she balanced the empty jug on her head. But before she could draw water from the spring, a stranger caught her attention:

"Greetings, favored one!" he shouted. "The Lord is with you."

No Nazarene, she was sure, would ever dare greet a maiden like that. But as he approached his words grew bolder, not softer, rushing toward her like water plunging over a cliff:

Do not be afraid, Mary, for you have found favor with God. And now, you will conceive in your womb and bear a son, and you will name him Jesus. He will be great, and will be called the Son of the Most High, and the Lord God will give to him the throne of his ancestor David . . . The Holy Spirit will come upon you, and the power of the Most High will overshadow you; therefore the child to be born will be holy; he will be called Son of God. And now, your relative Elizabeth in her old age has also conceived a son.

(1.30–32, 35–36)

Wave after wave of emotion broke over her as she listened to the angel's words—first confusion and fear, then awe and gratitude, and finally a rush of joy and peace. Then she heard more words, this time cascading from her lips, not his: "Here am I, the servant of the Lord; let it be with me according to your word" (verse 38).

Though the angel departed, her peace remained. The Most High had visited the lowliest of his servants and spoken the promise every Jewish woman longed to hear.

"Woman," Jesus breathed the word softly. His lean arms were flung out on either side of him, as though imploringly. The palms of his hands were pinned with spikes.

She wanted to reach for him with all the might of her love. Would not the God who pitied Abraham also pity her? Would he allow her to suffer what even the patriarch had been spared—the sacrifice of her own child?

"*Eli, Eli, lema sabachthani?*" The cry pierced her like a sword driven through her chest. "My God, my God, why have you forsaken me?" The earth shook as she fell to her knees (see Matthew 27.45–51).

By the time Mary opened her eyes, the setting sun had turned Jerusalem into a golden land. She smiled, wiping the tears from her wrinkled face. Yes, the past was alive inside her, but it was the future that filled her with joy. Soon she would see her son again, and this time it would be his hands that would wipe away the last of her tears.

Praying With Mary

"Greetings, favored one! The Lord is with you."—Luke 1.28

Praise God: *That nothing is impossible with him.*

Offer Thanks: *That a woman's body became the dwelling place of divinity.*

Confess: *Any tendency to devalue yourself as a woman.*

Ask God: *To make you a woman like Mary, who brings Jesus into the world by expressing his character, power, forgiveness, and grace.*

Lift Your Heart

Choose one episode in the life of Mary—her encounter with Gabriel, the birth of her child, the scene with the shepherds, the presentation in the temple, the wise men's visit, the escape to Egypt, her son's agony on the cross, or her presence with the disciples in the upper room. Imagine yourself in her place. What are your struggles, your joys? What thoughts run through your mind? Does anything or anyone take you by surprise? Ask the Holy Spirit to guide your reflections, to help you imagine the sounds, sights, and smells that will bring each scene to life. Let the Scriptures feed your soul with a deeper understanding of God's intention for your life. Pray for the grace to be like the woman who said: "Here am I, the servant of the Lord; let it be with me according to your word."

My soul is full of you, my God, and I cannot hold back my gladness. Everyone who sees me will call me blessed because you have noticed me. You saw my lowliness and my need and filled my emptiness with your presence. Form your likeness in me so that, like Mary, I can bring you into a world that desperately needs your love.

Go to page 1447 for your next devotional reading.

these men stand before the apostles, who prayed and laid their hands on them.

7 The word of God continued to spread; the number of the disciples increased greatly in Jerusalem, and a great many of the priests became obedient to the faith.

The Arrest of Stephen

8 Stephen, full of grace and power, did great wonders and signs among the people. ⁹Then some of those who belonged to the synagogue of the Freedmen (as it was called), Cyrenians, Alexandrians, and others of those from Cilicia and Asia, stood up and argued with Stephen. ¹⁰But they could not withstand the wisdom and the Spirit[s] with which he spoke. ¹¹Then they secretly instigated some men to say, "We have heard him speak blasphemous words against Moses and God." ¹²They stirred up the people as well as the elders and the scribes; then they suddenly confronted him, seized him, and brought him before the council. ¹³They set up false witnesses who said, "This man never stops saying things against this holy place and the law; ¹⁴for we have heard him say that this Jesus of Nazareth[t] will destroy this place and will change the customs that Moses handed on to us." ¹⁵And all who sat in the council looked intently at him, and they saw that his face was like the face of an angel.

Stephen's Speech to the Council

7 Then the high priest asked him, "Are these things so?" ²And Stephen replied:

"Brothers[u] and fathers, listen to me. The God of glory appeared to our ancestor Abraham when he was in Mesopotamia, before he lived in Haran, ³and said to him, 'Leave your country and your relatives and go to the land that I will show you.' ⁴Then he left the country of the Chaldeans and settled in Haran. After his father died, God had him move from there to this country in which you are now living. ⁵He did not give him any of it as a heritage, not even a foot's length, but promised to give it to him as his possession and to his descendants after him, even though he had no child. ⁶And God spoke in these terms, that his descendants would be resident aliens in a country belonging to others, who would enslave

them and mistreat them during four hundred years. ⁷'But I will judge the nation that they serve,' said God, 'and after that they shall come out and worship me in this place.' ⁸Then he gave him the covenant of circumcision. And so Abraham[v] became the father of Isaac and circumcised him on the eighth day; and Isaac became the father of Jacob, and Jacob of the twelve patriarchs.

9 "The patriarchs, jealous of Joseph, sold him into Egypt; but God was with him, ¹⁰and rescued him from all his afflictions, and enabled him to win favor and to show wisdom when he stood before Pharaoh, king of Egypt, who appointed him ruler over Egypt and over all his household. ¹¹Now there came a famine throughout Egypt and Canaan, and great suffering, and our ancestors could find no food. ¹²But when Jacob heard that there was grain in Egypt, he sent our ancestors there on their first visit. ¹³On the second visit Joseph made himself known to his brothers, and Joseph's family became known to Pharaoh. ¹⁴Then Joseph sent and invited his father Jacob and all his relatives to come to him, seventy-five in all; ¹⁵so Jacob went down to Egypt. He himself died there as well as our ancestors, ¹⁶and their bodies[w] were brought back to Shechem and laid in the tomb that Abraham had bought for a sum of silver from the sons of Hamor in Shechem.

17 "But as the time drew near for the fulfillment of the promise that God had made to Abraham, our people in Egypt increased and multiplied ¹⁸until another king who had not known Joseph ruled over Egypt. ¹⁹He dealt craftily with our race and forced our ancestors to abandon their infants so that they would die. ²⁰At this time Moses was born, and he was beautiful before God. For three months he was brought up in his father's house; ²¹and when he was abandoned, Pharaoh's daughter adopted him and brought him up as her own son. ²²So Moses was instructed in all the wisdom of the Egyptians and was powerful in his words and deeds.

23 "When he was forty years old, it came into his heart to visit his relatives,

---

[s] Or *spirit*   [t] Gk *the Nazorean*   [u] Gk *Men, brothers*   [v] Gk *he*   [w] Gk *they*

the Israelites.[x] 24When he saw one of them being wronged, he defended the oppressed man and avenged him by striking down the Egyptian. 25He supposed that his kinsfolk would understand that God through him was rescuing them, but they did not understand. 26The next day he came to some of them as they were quarreling and tried to reconcile them, saying, 'Men, you are brothers; why do you wrong each other?' 27But the man who was wronging his neighbor pushed Moses[y] aside, saying, 'Who made you a ruler and a judge over us? 28Do you want to kill me as you killed the Egyptian yesterday?' 29When he heard this, Moses fled and became a resident alien in the land of Midian. There he became the father of two sons.

30 "Now when forty years had passed, an angel appeared to him in the wilderness of Mount Sinai, in the flame of a burning bush. 31When Moses saw it, he was amazed at the sight; and as he approached to look, there came the voice of the Lord: 32'I am the God of your ancestors, the God of Abraham, Isaac, and Jacob.' Moses began to tremble and did not dare to look. 33Then the Lord said to him, 'Take off the sandals from your feet, for the place where you are standing is holy ground. 34I have surely seen the mistreatment of my people who are in Egypt and have heard their groaning, and I have come down to rescue them. Come now, I will send you to Egypt.'

35 "It was this Moses whom they rejected when they said, 'Who made you a ruler and a judge?' and whom God now sent as both ruler and liberator through the angel who appeared to him in the bush. 36He led them out, having performed wonders and signs in Egypt, at the Red Sea, and in the wilderness for forty years. 37This is the Moses who said to the Israelites, 'God will raise up a prophet for you from your own people[z] as he raised me up.' 38He is the one who was in the congregation in the wilderness with the angel who spoke to him at Mount Sinai, and with our ancestors; and he received living oracles to give to us. 39Our ancestors were unwilling to obey him; instead, they pushed him aside, and in their hearts they turned back to Egypt, 40saying to Aaron, 'Make gods for us who will lead the way for us; as for this Moses who led us out from the land of Egypt, we do not know what has happened to him.' 41At that time they made a calf, offered a sacrifice to the idol, and reveled in the works of their hands. 42But God turned away from them and handed them over to worship the host of heaven, as it is written in the book of the prophets:

'Did you offer to me slain victims
        and sacrifices
    forty years in the wilderness,
        O house of Israel?
43 No; you took along the tent
        of Moloch,
    and the star of your god Rephan,
        the images that you made
            to worship;
    so I will remove you beyond
        Babylon.'

44 "Our ancestors had the tent of testimony in the wilderness, as God[a] directed when he spoke to Moses, ordering him to make it according to the pattern he had seen. 45Our ancestors in turn brought it in with Joshua when they dispossessed the nations that God drove out before our ancestors. And it was there until the time of David, 46who found favor with God and asked that he might find a dwelling place for the house of Jacob.[b] 47But it was Solomon who built a house for him. 48Yet the Most High does not dwell in houses made with human hands;[c] as the prophet says,

49 'Heaven is my throne,
        and the earth is my footstool.
    What kind of house will you build
        for me, says the Lord,
    or what is the place of my rest?
50 Did not my hand make all these
        things?'

51 "You stiff-necked people, uncircumcised in heart and ears, you are forever opposing the Holy Spirit, just as your ancestors used to do. 52Which of the prophets did your ancestors not persecute? They killed those who foretold the coming of the Righteous One, and now you have become his betrayers and murderers. 53You are the ones that received the law as ordained by angels, and yet you have not kept it."

The Stoning of Stephen

54 When they heard these things, they

---

x Gk *his brothers, the sons of Israel*   y Gk *him*
z Gk *your brothers*   a Gk *he*   b Other ancient
authorities read *for the God of Jacob*   c Gk *with
hands*

became enraged and ground their teeth at Stephen.[d] 55But filled with the Holy Spirit, he gazed into heaven and saw the glory of God and Jesus standing at the right hand of God. 56"Look," he said, "I see the heavens opened and the Son of Man standing at the right hand of God!" 57But they covered their ears, and with a loud shout all rushed together against him. 58Then they dragged him out of the city and began to stone him; and the witnesses laid their coats at the feet of a young man named Saul. 59While they were stoning Stephen, he prayed, "Lord Jesus, receive my spirit." 60Then he knelt down and cried out in a loud voice, "Lord, do not hold this sin against them." When he had said 8 this, he died.[e] 1And Saul approved of their killing him.

Saul Persecutes the Church

That day a severe persecution began against the church in Jerusalem, and all except the apostles were scattered throughout the countryside of Judea and Samaria. 2Devout men buried Stephen and made loud lamentation over him. 3But Saul was ravaging the church by entering house after house; dragging off both men and women, he committed them to prison.

Philip Preaches in Samaria

4 Now those who were scattered went from place to place, proclaiming the word. 5Philip went down to the city[f] of Samaria and proclaimed the Messiah[g] to them. 6The crowds with one accord listened eagerly to what was said by Philip, hearing and seeing the signs that he did, 7for unclean spirits, crying with loud shrieks, came out of many who were possessed; and many others who were paralyzed or lame were cured. 8So there was great joy in that city.

9 Now a certain man named Simon had previously practiced magic in the city and amazed the people of Samaria, saying that he was someone great. 10All of them, from the least to the greatest, listened to him eagerly, saying, "This man is the power of God that is called Great." 11And they listened eagerly to him because for a long time he had amazed them with his magic. 12But when they believed Philip, who was proclaiming the good news about the kingdom of God and the name of Jesus Christ, they were baptized, both

men and women. 13Even Simon himself believed. After being baptized, he stayed constantly with Philip and was amazed when he saw the signs and great miracles that took place.

14 Now when the apostles at Jerusalem heard that Samaria had accepted the word of God, they sent Peter and John to them. 15The two went down and prayed for them that they might receive the Holy Spirit 16(for as yet the Spirit had not come[h] upon any of them; they had only been baptized in the name of the Lord Jesus). 17Then Peter and John[i] laid their hands on them, and they received the Holy Spirit. 18Now when Simon saw that the Spirit was given through the laying on of the apostles' hands, he offered them money, 19saying, "Give me also this power so that anyone on whom I lay my hands may receive the Holy Spirit." 20But Peter said to him, "May your silver perish with you, because you thought you could obtain God's gift with money! 21You have no part or share in this, for your heart is not right before God. 22Repent therefore of this wickedness of yours, and pray to the Lord that, if possible, the intent of your heart may be forgiven you. 23For I see that you are in the gall of bitterness and the chains of wickedness." 24Simon answered, "Pray for me to the Lord, that nothing of what you[j] have said may happen to me."

25 Now after Peter and John[k] had testified and spoken the word of the Lord, they returned to Jerusalem, proclaiming the good news to many villages of the Samaritans.

Philip and the Ethiopian Eunuch

26 Then an angel of the Lord said to Philip, "Get up and go toward the south[l] to the road that goes down from Jerusalem to Gaza." (This is a wilderness road.) 27So he got up and went. Now there was an Ethiopian eunuch, a court official of the Candace, queen of the Ethiopians, in charge of her entire treasury. He had come to Jerusalem to worship 28and was returning home; seated in his chariot, he was reading the prophet Isaiah. 29Then

[d] Gk him   [e] Gk fell asleep   [f] Other ancient authorities read a city   [g] Or the Christ   [h] Gk fallen   [i] Gk they   [j] The Greek word for you and the verb pray are plural   [k] Gk after they   [l] Or go at noon

the Spirit said to Philip, "Go over to this chariot and join it." ³⁰So Philip ran up to it and heard him reading the prophet Isaiah. He asked, "Do you understand what you are reading?" ³¹He replied, "How can I, unless someone guides me?" And he invited Philip to get in and sit beside him. ³²Now the passage of the scripture that he was reading was this:

"Like a sheep he was led to the
    slaughter,
and like a lamb silent before
    its shearer,
    so he does not open his mouth.
³³ In his humiliation justice was
    denied him.
Who can describe his generation?
For his life is taken away from
    the earth."

³⁴The eunuch asked Philip, "About whom, may I ask you, does the prophet say this, about himself or about someone else?" ³⁵Then Philip began to speak, and starting with this scripture, he proclaimed to him the good news about Jesus. ³⁶As they were going along the road, they came to some water; and the eunuch said, "Look, here is water! What is to prevent me from being baptized?"ᵐ ³⁸He commanded the chariot to stop, and both of them, Philip and the eunuch, went down into the water, and Philipⁿ baptized him. ³⁹When they came up out of the water, the Spirit of the Lord snatched Philip away; the eunuch saw him no more, and went on his way rejoicing. ⁴⁰But Philip found himself at Azotus, and as he was passing through the region, he proclaimed the good news to all the towns until he came to Caesarea.

The Conversion of Saul

9 Meanwhile Saul, still breathing threats and murder against the disciples of the Lord, went to the high priest ²and asked him for letters to the synagogues at Damascus, so that if he found any who belonged to the Way, men or women, he might bring them bound to Jerusalem. ³Now as he was going along and approaching Damascus, suddenly a light from heaven flashed around him. ⁴He fell to the ground and heard a voice saying to him, "Saul, Saul, why do you persecute me?" ⁵He asked, "Who are you, Lord?" The reply came, "I am Jesus, whom you are persecuting. ⁶But get up and enter the city, and you will be told what you are

to do." ⁷The men who were traveling with him stood speechless because they heard the voice but saw no one. ⁸Saul got up from the ground, and though his eyes were open, he could see nothing; so they led him by the hand and brought him into Damascus. ⁹For three days he was without sight, and neither ate nor drank.

10 Now there was a disciple in Damascus named Ananias. The Lord said to him in a vision, "Ananias." He answered, "Here I am, Lord." ¹¹The Lord said to him, "Get up and go to the street called Straight, and at the house of Judas look for a man of Tarsus named Saul. At this moment he is praying, ¹²and he has seen in a visionᵒ a man named Ananias come in and lay his hands on him so that he might regain his sight." ¹³But Ananias answered, "Lord, I have heard from many about this man, how much evil he has done to your saints in Jerusalem; ¹⁴and here he has authority from the chief priests to bind all who invoke your name." ¹⁵But the Lord said to him, "Go, for he is an instrument whom I have chosen to bring my name before Gentiles and kings and before the people of Israel; ¹⁶I myself will show him how much he must suffer for the sake of my name." ¹⁷So Ananias went and entered the house. He laid his hands on Saulᵖ and said, "Brother Saul, the Lord Jesus, who appeared to you on your way here, has sent me so that you may regain your sight and be filled with the Holy Spirit." ¹⁸And immediately something like scales fell from his eyes, and his sight was restored. Then he got up and was baptized, ¹⁹and after taking some food, he regained his strength.

Saul Preaches in Damascus

For several days he was with the disciples in Damascus, ²⁰and immediately he began to proclaim Jesus in the synagogues, saying, "He is the Son of God." ²¹All who heard him were amazed and said, "Is not this the man who made havoc in Jerusalem among those who invoked this name? And has he not come here for the purpose of bringing them

---

ᵐ Other ancient authorities add all or most of verse 37, *And Philip said, "If you believe with all your heart, you may." And he replied, "I believe that Jesus Christ is the Son of God."*   ⁿ Gk *he*
ᵒ Other ancient authorities lack *in a vision*
ᵖ Gk *him*

bound before the chief priests?" 22Saul became increasingly more powerful and confounded the Jews who lived in Damascus by proving that Jesus*q* was the Messiah.*r*

Saul Escapes from the Jews

23 After some time had passed, the Jews plotted to kill him, 24but their plot became known to Saul. They were watching the gates day and night so that they might kill him; 25but his disciples took him by night and let him down through an opening in the wall,*s* lowering him in a basket.

Saul in Jerusalem

26 When he had come to Jerusalem, he attempted to join the disciples; and they were all afraid of him, for they did not believe that he was a disciple. 27But Barnabas took him, brought him to the apostles, and described for them how on the road he had seen the Lord, who had spoken to him, and how in Damascus he had spoken boldly in the name of Jesus. 28So he went in and out among them in Jerusalem, speaking boldly in the name of the Lord. 29He spoke and argued with the Hellenists; but they were attempting to kill him. 30When the believers*t* learned of it, they brought him down to Caesarea and sent him off to Tarsus.

31 Meanwhile the church throughout Judea, Galilee, and Samaria had peace and was built up. Living in the fear of the Lord and in the comfort of the Holy Spirit, it increased in numbers.

The Healing of Aeneas

32 Now as Peter went here and there among all the believers,*u* he came down also to the saints living in Lydda. 33There he found a man named Aeneas, who had been bedridden for eight years, for he was paralyzed. 34Peter said to him, "Aeneas, Jesus Christ heals you; get up and make your bed!" And immediately he got up. 35And all the residents of Lydda and Sharon saw him and turned to the Lord.

Peter in Lydda and Joppa

36 Now in Joppa there was a disciple whose name was Tabitha, which in Greek is Dorcas.*v* She was devoted to good works and acts of charity. 37At that time she became ill and died. When they had washed her, they laid her in a room up-

stairs. 38Since Lydda was near Joppa, the disciples, who heard that Peter was there, sent two men to him with the request, "Please come to us without delay." 39So Peter got up and went with them; and when he arrived, they took him to the room upstairs. All the widows stood beside him, weeping and showing tunics and other clothing that Dorcas had made while she was with them. 40Peter put all of them outside, and then he knelt down and prayed. He turned to the body and said, "Tabitha, get up." Then she opened her eyes, and seeing Peter, she sat up. 41He gave her his hand and helped her up. Then calling the saints and widows, he showed her to be alive. 42This became known throughout Joppa, and many believed in the Lord. 43Meanwhile he stayed in Joppa for some time with a certain Simon, a tanner.

Peter and Cornelius

10 In Caesarea there was a man named Cornelius, a centurion of the Italian Cohort, as it was called. 2He was a devout man who feared God with all his household; he gave alms generously to the people and prayed constantly to God. 3One afternoon at about three o'clock he had a vision in which he clearly saw an angel of God coming in and saying to him, "Cornelius." 4He stared at him in terror and said, "What is it, Lord?" He answered, "Your prayers and your alms have ascended as a memorial before God. 5Now send men to Joppa for a certain Simon who is called Peter; 6he is lodging with Simon, a tanner, whose house is by the seaside." 7When the angel who spoke to him had left, he called two of his slaves and a devout soldier from the ranks of those who served him, 8and after telling them everything, he sent them to Joppa.

9 About noon the next day, as they were on their journey and approaching the city, Peter went up on the roof to pray. 10He became hungry and wanted something to eat; and while it was being prepared, he fell into a trance. 11He saw the heaven opened and something like a large sheet coming down, being lowered to the ground by its four corners. 12In it were all

q Gk that this   *r* Or the Christ   *s* Gk through the wall   *t* Gk brothers   *u* Gk all of them   *v* The name Tabitha in Aramaic and the name Dorcas in Greek mean *a gazelle*

kinds of four-footed creatures and reptiles and birds of the air. [13]Then he heard a voice saying, "Get up, Peter; kill and eat." [14]But Peter said, "By no means, Lord; for I have never eaten anything that is profane or unclean." [15]The voice said to him again, a second time, "What God has made clean, you must not call profane." [16]This happened three times, and the thing was suddenly taken up to heaven.

17 Now while Peter was greatly puzzled about what to make of the vision that he had seen, suddenly the men sent by Cornelius appeared. They were asking for Simon's house and were standing by the gate. [18]They called out to ask whether Simon, who was called Peter, was staying there. [19]While Peter was still thinking about the vision, the Spirit said to him, "Look, three[w] men are searching for you. [20]Now get up, go down, and go with them without hesitation; for I have sent them." [21]So Peter went down to the men and said, "I am the one you are looking for; what is the reason for your coming?" [22]They answered, "Cornelius, a centurion, an upright and God-fearing man, who is well spoken of by the whole Jewish nation, was directed by a holy angel to send for you to come to his house and to hear what you have to say." [23]So Peter[x] invited them in and gave them lodging.

The next day he got up and went with them, and some of the believers[y] from Joppa accompanied him. [24]The following day they came to Caesarea. Cornelius was expecting them and had called together his relatives and close friends. [25]On Peter's arrival Cornelius met him, and falling at his feet, worshiped him. [26]But Peter made him get up, saying, "Stand up; I am only a mortal." [27]And as he talked with him, he went in and found that many had assembled; [28]and he said to them, "You yourselves know that it is unlawful for a Jew to associate with or to visit a Gentile; but God has shown me that I should not call anyone profane or unclean. [29]So when I was sent for, I came without objection. Now may I ask why you sent for me?"

30 Cornelius replied, "Four days ago at this very hour, at three o'clock, I was praying in my house when suddenly a man in dazzling clothes stood before me. [31]He said, 'Cornelius, your prayer has been heard and your alms have been remembered before God. [32]Send therefore to Joppa and ask for Simon, who is called Peter; he is staying in the home of Simon, a tanner, by the sea.' [33]Therefore I sent for you immediately, and you have been kind enough to come. So now all of us are here in the presence of God to listen to all that the Lord has commanded you to say."

Gentiles Hear the Good News

34 Then Peter began to speak to them: "I truly understand that God shows no partiality, [35]but in every nation anyone who fears him and does what is right is acceptable to him. [36]You know the message he sent to the people of Israel, preaching peace by Jesus Christ—he is Lord of all. [37]That message spread throughout Judea, beginning in Galilee after the baptism that John announced: [38]how God anointed Jesus of Nazareth with the Holy Spirit and with power; how he went about doing good and healing all who were oppressed by the devil, for God was with him. [39]We are witnesses to all that he did both in Judea and in Jerusalem. They put him to death by hanging him on a tree; [40]but God raised him on the third day and allowed him to appear, [41]not to all the people but to us who were chosen by God as witnesses, and who ate and drank with him after he rose from the dead. [42]He commanded us to preach to the people and to testify that he is the one ordained by God as judge of the living and the dead. [43]All the prophets testify about him that everyone who believes in him receives forgiveness of sins through his name."

Gentiles Receive the Holy Spirit

44 While Peter was still speaking, the Holy Spirit fell upon all who heard the word. [45]The circumcised believers who had come with Peter were astounded that the gift of the Holy Spirit had been poured out even on the Gentiles, [46]for they heard them speaking in tongues and extolling God. Then Peter said, [47]"Can anyone withhold the water for baptizing these people who have received the Holy Spirit just as we have?" [48]So he ordered them to be baptized in the name of Jesus Christ. Then they invited him to stay for several days.

---

w One ancient authority reads two; others lack the word   x Gk he   y Gk brothers

Peter's Report to the Church at Jerusalem

11 Now the apostles and the believers[z] who were in Judea heard that the Gentiles had also accepted the word of God. ²So when Peter went up to Jerusalem, the circumcised believers[a] criticized him, ³saying, "Why did you go to uncircumcised men and eat with them?" ⁴Then Peter began to explain it to them, step by step, saying, ⁵"I was in the city of Joppa praying, and in a trance I saw a vision. There was something like a large sheet coming down from heaven, being lowered by its four corners; and it came close to me. ⁶As I looked at it closely I saw four-footed animals, beasts of prey, reptiles, and birds of the air. ⁷I also heard a voice saying to me, 'Get up, Peter; kill and eat.' ⁸But I replied, 'By no means, Lord; for nothing profane or unclean has ever entered my mouth.' ⁹But a second time the voice answered from heaven, 'What God has made clean, you must not call profane.' ¹⁰This happened three times; then everything was pulled up again to heaven. ¹¹At that very moment three men, sent to me from Caesarea, arrived at the house where we were. ¹²The Spirit told me to go with them and not to make a distinction between them and us.[b] These six brothers also accompanied me, and we entered the man's house. ¹³He told us how he had seen the angel standing in his house and saying, 'Send to Joppa and bring Simon, who is called Peter; ¹⁴he will give you a message by which you and your entire household will be saved.' ¹⁵And as I began to speak, the Holy Spirit fell upon them just as it had upon us at the beginning. ¹⁶And I remembered the word of the Lord, how he had said, 'John baptized with water, but you will be baptized with the Holy Spirit.' ¹⁷If then God gave them the same gift that he gave us when we believed in the Lord Jesus Christ, who was I that I could hinder God?" ¹⁸When they heard this, they were silenced. And they praised God, saying, "Then God has given even to the Gentiles the repentance that leads to life."

The Church in Antioch

19 Now those who were scattered because of the persecution that took place over Stephen traveled as far as Phoenicia, Cyprus, and Antioch, and they spoke the word to no one except Jews. ²⁰But among them were some men of Cyprus and Cyrene who, on coming to Antioch, spoke to the Hellenists[c] also, proclaiming the Lord Jesus. ²¹The hand of the Lord was with them, and a great number became believers and turned to the Lord. ²²News of this came to the ears of the church in Jerusalem, and they sent Barnabas to Antioch. ²³When he came and saw the grace of God, he rejoiced, and he exhorted them all to remain faithful to the Lord with steadfast devotion; ²⁴for he was a good man, full of the Holy Spirit and of faith. And a great many people were brought to the Lord. ²⁵Then Barnabas went to Tarsus to look for Saul, ²⁶and when he had found him, he brought him to Antioch. So it was that for an entire year they met with[d] the church and taught a great many people, and it was in Antioch that the disciples were first called "Christians."

27 At that time prophets came down from Jerusalem to Antioch. ²⁸One of them named Agabus stood up and predicted by the Spirit that there would be a severe famine over all the world; and this took place during the reign of Claudius. ²⁹The disciples determined that according to their ability, each would send relief to the believers[z] living in Judea; ³⁰this they did, sending it to the elders by Barnabas and Saul.

James Killed and Peter Imprisoned

12 About that time King Herod laid violent hands upon some who belonged to the church. ²He had James, the brother of John, killed with the sword. ³After he saw that it pleased the Jews, he proceeded to arrest Peter also. (This was during the festival of Unleavened Bread.) ⁴When he had seized him, he put him in prison and handed him over to four squads of soldiers to guard him, intending to bring him out to the people after the Passover. ⁵While Peter was kept in prison, the church prayed fervently to God for him.

Peter Delivered from Prison

6 The very night before Herod was going to bring him out, Peter, bound with two chains, was sleeping between two soldiers, while guards in front of the door

---

[z] Gk *brothers*   [a] Gk lacks *believers*   [b] Or *not to hesitate*   [c] Other ancient authorities read *Greeks*   [d] Or *were guests of*

were keeping watch over the prison. ⁷Suddenly an angel of the Lord appeared and a light shone in the cell. He tapped Peter on the side and woke him, saying, "Get up quickly." And the chains fell off his wrists. ⁸The angel said to him, "Fasten your belt and put on your sandals." He did so. Then he said to him, "Wrap your cloak around you and follow me." ⁹Peter*ᵉ* went out and followed him; he did not realize that what was happening with the angel's help was real; he thought he was seeing a vision. ¹⁰After they had passed the first and the second guard, they came before the iron gate leading into the city. It opened for them of its own accord, and they went outside and walked along a lane, when suddenly the angel left him. ¹¹Then Peter came to himself and said, "Now I am sure that the Lord has sent his angel and rescued me from the hands of Herod and from all that the Jewish people were expecting."

12 As soon as he realized this, he went to the house of Mary, the mother of John whose other name was Mark, where many

ᵉ Gk He

Unchained

MONDAY

Scripture Reading for Today:
Acts 12.6–17

Verse for Today:
Acts 12.7

If you have ever been to Rome, you may have visited Saint Peter in Chains, a church which claims to display the chains mentioned in this passage. Whether these are Peter's chains I couldn't say. But this church reminds us that Peter was freed by an angel while under heavy guard in Jerusalem. It took only one guardian angel to hoodwink four squads of soldiers!

Peter could hardly believe what had happened. He went straight to the house of some believers in the city. What occurred next is one of the more humorous incidents related in the New Testament. When Peter knocked on the door, a maid named Rhoda answered. She was so excited to see him that she left him standing at the door and ran back to tell the others, who promptly told her she was out of her mind. They had prayed for Peter, but they could not believe that God had really answered their prayers. Meanwhile, the fugitive Peter stood on the steps, desperately hoping that someone would let him in.

From Peter's story we learn that our angels possess far greater power than the powers of evil that threaten us. We also learn that God hears the prayers of his people despite their little faith. God had a plan for Peter and for his people that would not be subverted by any evil plan of his enemy. He allowed James to suffer a martyr's death. But Peter's death was postponed through the ministry of an angel.

The gospel is in chains in many parts of the world today, and many believers suffer as a result. We need to pray especially for those who are heralds of the Good News, that God will send his angels to open prison doors so that many more people might come to know his mercy and his forgiveness.

—*ANN SPANGLER*

Go to page 1450 for your next devotional reading.

had gathered and were praying. 13When he knocked at the outer gate, a maid named Rhoda came to answer. 14On recognizing Peter's voice, she was so overjoyed that, instead of opening the gate, she ran in and announced that Peter was standing at the gate. 15They said to her, "You are out of your mind!" But she insisted that it was so. They said, "It is his angel." 16Meanwhile Peter continued knocking; and when they opened the gate, they saw him and were amazed. 17He motioned to them with his hand to be silent, and described for them how the Lord had brought him out of the prison. And he added, "Tell this to James and to the believers." *f* Then he left and went to another place.

18 When morning came, there was no small commotion among the soldiers over what had become of Peter. 19When Herod had searched for him and could not find him, he examined the guards and ordered them to be put to death. Then he went down from Judea to Caesarea and stayed there.

The Death of Herod

20 Now Herod *g* was angry with the people of Tyre and Sidon. So they came to him in a body; and after winning over Blastus, the king's chamberlain, they asked for a reconciliation, because their country depended on the king's country for food. 21On an appointed day Herod put on his royal robes, took his seat on the platform, and delivered a public address to them. 22The people kept shouting, "The voice of a god, and not of a mortal!" 23And immediately, because he had not given the glory to God, an angel of the Lord struck him down, and he was eaten by worms and died.

24 But the word of God continued to advance and gain adherents. 25Then after completing their mission Barnabas and Saul returned to*h* Jerusalem and brought with them John, whose other name was Mark.

Barnabas and Saul Commissioned

13 Now in the church at Antioch there were prophets and teachers: Barnabas, Simeon who was called Niger, Lucius of Cyrene, Manaen a member of the court of Herod the ruler,*i* and Saul. 2While they were worshiping the Lord and fasting, the Holy Spirit said, "Set apart for

me Barnabas and Saul for the work to which I have called them." 3Then after fasting and praying they laid their hands on them and sent them off.

The Apostles Preach in Cyprus

4 So, being sent out by the Holy Spirit, they went down to Seleucia; and from there they sailed to Cyprus. 5When they arrived at Salamis, they proclaimed the word of God in the synagogues of the Jews. And they had John also to assist them. 6When they had gone through the whole island as far as Paphos, they met a certain magician, a Jewish false prophet, named Bar-Jesus. 7He was with the proconsul, Sergius Paulus, an intelligent man, who summoned Barnabas and Saul and wanted to hear the word of God. 8But the magician Elymas (for that is the translation of his name) opposed them and tried to turn the proconsul away from the faith. 9But Saul, also known as Paul, filled with the Holy Spirit, looked intently at him 10and said, "You son of the devil, you enemy of all righteousness, full of all deceit and villainy, will you not stop making crooked the straight paths of the Lord? 11And now listen—the hand of the Lord is against you, and you will be blind for a while, unable to see the sun." Immediately mist and darkness came over him, and he went about groping for someone to lead him by the hand. 12When the proconsul saw what had happened, he believed, for he was astonished at the teaching about the Lord.

Paul and Barnabas in Antioch of Pisidia

13 Then Paul and his companions set sail from Paphos and came to Perga in Pamphylia. John, however, left them and returned to Jerusalem; 14but they went on from Perga and came to Antioch in Pisidia. And on the sabbath day they went into the synagogue and sat down. 15After the reading of the law and the prophets, the officials of the synagogue sent them a message, saying, "Brothers, if you have any word of exhortation for the people, give it." 16So Paul stood up and with a gesture began to speak:

"You Israelites,*j* and others who fear God, listen. 17The God of this people Isra-

f Gk brothers   *g* Gk he   *h* Other ancient authorities read *from*   *i* Gk tetrarch   *j* Gk Men, Israelites

el chose our ancestors and made the people great during their stay in the land of Egypt, and with uplifted arm he led them out of it. [18]For about forty years he put up with[k] them in the wilderness. [19]After he had destroyed seven nations in the land of Canaan, he gave them their land as an inheritance [20]for about four hundred fifty years. After that he gave them judges until the time of the prophet Samuel. [21]Then they asked for a king; and God gave them Saul son of Kish, a man of the tribe of Benjamin, who reigned for forty years. [22]When he had removed him, he made David their king. In his testimony about him he said, 'I have found David, son of Jesse, to be a man after my heart, who will carry out all my wishes.' [23]Of this man's posterity God has brought to Israel a Savior, Jesus, as he promised; [24]before his coming John had already proclaimed a baptism of repentance to all the people of Israel. [25]And as John was finishing his work, he said, 'What do you suppose that I am? I am not he. No, but one is coming after me; I am not worthy to untie the thong of the sandals[l] on his feet.'

26 "My brothers, you descendants of Abraham's family, and others who fear God, to us[m] the message of this salvation has been sent. [27]Because the residents of Jerusalem and their leaders did not recognize him or understand the words of the prophets that are read every sabbath, they fulfilled those words by condemning him. [28]Even though they found no cause for a sentence of death, they asked Pilate to have him killed. [29]When they had carried out everything that was written about him, they took him down from the tree and laid him in a tomb. [30]But God raised him from the dead; [31]and for many days he appeared to those who came up with him from Galilee to Jerusalem, and they are now his witnesses to the people. [32]And we bring you the good news that what God promised to our ancestors [33]he has fulfilled for us, their children, by raising Jesus; as also it is written in the second psalm,

'You are my Son;
    today I have begotten you.'

[34]As to his raising him from the dead, no more to return to corruption, he has spoken in this way,

'I will give you the holy promises
    made to David.'

[35]Therefore he has also said in another psalm,

'You will not let your Holy One
    experience corruption.'

[36]For David, after he had served the purpose of God in his own generation, died,[n] was laid beside his ancestors, and experienced corruption; [37]but he whom God raised up experienced no corruption. [38]Let it be known to you therefore, my brothers, that through this man forgiveness of sins is proclaimed to you; [39]by this Jesus[o] everyone who believes is set free from all those sins[p] from which you could not be freed by the law of Moses. [40]Beware, therefore, that what the prophets said does not happen to you:

[41] 'Look, you scoffers!
    Be amazed and perish,
for in your days I am doing a work,
    a work that you will never believe,
        even if someone tells you.' "

42 As Paul and Barnabas[q] were going out, the people urged them to speak about these things again the next sabbath. [43]When the meeting of the synagogue broke up, many Jews and devout converts to Judaism followed Paul and Barnabas, who spoke to them and urged them to continue in the grace of God.

44 The next sabbath almost the whole city gathered to hear the word of the Lord.[r] [45]But when the Jews saw the crowds, they were filled with jealousy; and blaspheming, they contradicted what was spoken by Paul. [46]Then both Paul and Barnabas spoke out boldly, saying, "It was necessary that the word of God should be spoken first to you. Since you reject it and judge yourselves to be unworthy of eternal life, we are now turning to the Gentiles. [47]For so the Lord has commanded us, saying,

'I have set you to be a light for
    the Gentiles,
so that you may bring salvation to
    the ends of the earth.' "

48 When the Gentiles heard this, they were glad and praised the word of the Lord; and as many as had been destined for eternal life became believers. [49]Thus

---

the word of the Lord spread throughout the region. ⁵⁰But the Jews incited the devout women of high standing and the leading men of the city, and stirred up persecution against Paul and Barnabas, and drove them out of their region. ⁵¹So they shook the dust off their feet in protest against them, and went to Iconium.

Freedom From Sin

TUESDAY

Scripture Reading
for Today:
Acts 13.39–41

Verse for Today:
Acts 13.39

Truth has a way of showing up our lies. Sometimes we keep the sin in our lives well protected, guarded, covered-over with lies. Sometimes we are not free enough to own our sin, so we cannot be healed of it. An unacknowledged wound cannot be healed.

Truth has a way of waiting for us to come forth and confess the lies of our lives. It has a way of gazing at us until we can bear the look of truth no longer. It is then we receive grace to turn to truth and welcome it home. Only when we welcome truth does it have the power to color our lives with honesty.

> The truth stands waiting
> in my lie-filled life
> On the edge of myself it stands
> and looks without interruption
> into my sin-filled heart
> and everywhere its glance falls
> I am dying all the while.
>
> *I have needed to die for so long!*
>
> O Lord, God of life and death
> thank you for this life-giving death
> for this piece of sin
> that I can own
> and claim at last
> and not deny.
> It's mine!
> Mine to weep over
> and acknowledge
> and die to
> and give to you.
>
> I am dying at last
> Truth is falling through my life
> like lightning
> I am losing my life
> I am finding my life.

—*MACRINA WIEDERKEHR*

Go to page 1467 for your next devotional reading.

[52]And the disciples were filled with joy and with the Holy Spirit.

Paul and Barnabas in Iconium

14 The same thing occurred in Iconium, where Paul and Barnabas[s] went into the Jewish synagogue and spoke in such a way that a great number of both Jews and Greeks became believers. [2]But the unbelieving Jews stirred up the Gentiles and poisoned their minds against the brothers. [3]So they remained for a long time, speaking boldly for the Lord, who testified to the word of his grace by granting signs and wonders to be done through them. [4]But the residents of the city were divided; some sided with the Jews, and some with the apostles. [5]And when an attempt was made by both Gentiles and Jews, with their rulers, to mistreat them and to stone them, [6]the apostles[s] learned of it and fled to Lystra and Derbe, cities of Lycaonia, and to the surrounding country; [7]and there they continued proclaiming the good news.

Paul and Barnabas in Lystra and Derbe

8 In Lystra there was a man sitting who could not use his feet and had never walked, for he had been crippled from birth. [9]He listened to Paul as he was speaking. And Paul, looking at him intently and seeing that he had faith to be healed, [10]said in a loud voice, "Stand upright on your feet." And the man[t] sprang up and began to walk. [11]When the crowds saw what Paul had done, they shouted in the Lycaonian language, "The gods have come down to us in human form!" [12]Barnabas they called Zeus, and Paul they called Hermes, because he was the chief speaker. [13]The priest of Zeus, whose temple was just outside the city,[u] brought oxen and garlands to the gates; he and the crowds wanted to offer sacrifice. [14]When the apostles Barnabas and Paul heard of it, they tore their clothes and rushed out into the crowd, shouting, [15]"Friends,[v] why are you doing this? We are mortals just like you, and we bring you good news, that you should turn from these worthless things to the living God, who made the heaven and the earth and the sea and all that is in them. [16]In past generations he allowed all the nations to follow their own ways; [17]yet he has not left himself without a witness in doing good—giving you rains from heaven and fruitful seasons, and filling you with food and your hearts with joy." [18]Even with these words, they scarcely restrained the crowds from offering sacrifice to them.

19 But Jews came there from Antioch and Iconium and won over the crowds. Then they stoned Paul and dragged him out of the city, supposing that he was dead. [20]But when the disciples surrounded him, he got up and went into the city. The next day he went on with Barnabas to Derbe.

The Return to Antioch in Syria

21 After they had proclaimed the good news to that city and had made many disciples, they returned to Lystra, then on to Iconium and Antioch. [22]There they strengthened the souls of the disciples and encouraged them to continue in the faith, saying, "It is through many persecutions that we must enter the kingdom of God." [23]And after they had appointed elders for them in each church, with prayer and fasting they entrusted them to the Lord in whom they had come to believe.

24 Then they passed through Pisidia and came to Pamphylia. [25]When they had spoken the word in Perga, they went down to Attalia. [26]From there they sailed back to Antioch, where they had been commended to the grace of God for the work[w] that they had completed. [27]When they arrived, they called the church together and related all that God had done with them, and how he had opened a door of faith for the Gentiles. [28]And they stayed there with the disciples for some time.

The Council at Jerusalem

15 Then certain individuals came down from Judea and were teaching the brothers, "Unless you are circumcised according to the custom of Moses, you cannot be saved." [2]And after Paul and Barnabas had no small dissension and debate with them, Paul and Barnabas and some of the others were appointed to go up to Jerusalem to discuss this question with the apostles and the elders. [3]So they were sent on their way by the church, and as they passed through both Phoenicia and Samaria, they reported the conversion

---

[s] Gk they   [t] Gk he   [u] Or The priest of Zeus-Outside-the-City   [v] Gk Men   [w] Or committed in the grace of God to the work

of the Gentiles, and brought great joy to all the believers.[x] [4]When they came to Jerusalem, they were welcomed by the church and the apostles and the elders, and they reported all that God had done with them. [5]But some believers who belonged to the sect of the Pharisees stood up and said, "It is necessary for them to be circumcised and ordered to keep the law of Moses."

6 The apostles and the elders met together to consider this matter. [7]After there had been much debate, Peter stood up and said to them, "My brothers,[y] you know that in the early days God made a choice among you, that I should be the one through whom the Gentiles would hear the message of the good news and become believers. [8]And God, who knows the human heart, testified to them by giving them the Holy Spirit, just as he did to us; [9]and in cleansing their hearts by faith he has made no distinction between them and us. [10]Now therefore why are you putting God to the test by placing on the neck of the disciples a yoke that neither our ancestors nor we have been able to bear? [11]On the contrary, we believe that we will be saved through the grace of the Lord Jesus, just as they will."

12 The whole assembly kept silence, and listened to Barnabas and Paul as they told of all the signs and wonders that God had done through them among the Gentiles. [13]After they finished speaking, James replied, "My brothers,[y] listen to me. [14]Simeon has related how God first looked favorably on the Gentiles, to take from among them a people for his name. [15]This agrees with the words of the prophets, as it is written,

[16] 'After this I will return,
    and I will rebuild the dwelling of
        David, which has fallen;
    from its ruins I will rebuild it,
        and I will set it up,
[17] so that all other peoples may seek
        the Lord—
    even all the Gentiles over whom
        my name has been called.
    Thus says the Lord, who has
        been making these things
[18]known from long ago.'[z]

[19]Therefore I have reached the decision that we should not trouble those Gentiles who are turning to God, [20]but we should write to them to abstain only from things polluted by idols and from fornication

and from whatever has been strangled[a] and from blood. [21]For in every city, for generations past, Moses has had those who proclaim him, for he has been read aloud every sabbath in the synagogues."

The Council's Letter to Gentile Believers

22 Then the apostles and the elders, with the consent of the whole church, decided to choose men from among their members[b] and to send them to Antioch with Paul and Barnabas. They sent Judas called Barsabbas, and Silas, leaders among the brothers, [23]with the following letter: "The brothers, both the apostles and the elders, to the believers[x] of Gentile origin in Antioch and Syria and Cilicia, greetings. [24]Since we have heard that certain persons who have gone out from us, though with no instructions from us, have said things to disturb you and have unsettled your minds,[c] [25]we have decided unanimously to choose representatives[d] and send them to you, along with our beloved Barnabas and Paul, [26]who have risked their lives for the sake of our Lord Jesus Christ. [27]We have therefore sent Judas and Silas, who themselves will tell you the same things by word of mouth. [28]For it has seemed good to the Holy Spirit and to us to impose on you no further burden than these essentials: [29]that you abstain from what has been sacrificed to idols and from blood and from what is strangled[e] and from fornication. If you keep yourselves from these, you will do well. Farewell."

30 So they were sent off and went down to Antioch. When they gathered the congregation together, they delivered the letter. [31]When its members[f] read it, they rejoiced at the exhortation. [32]Judas and Silas, who were themselves prophets, said much to encourage and strengthen the believers.[x] [33]After they had been there for some time, they were sent off in peace by the believers[x] to those who had sent

---

[x] Gk brothers   [y] Gk Men, brothers   [z] Other ancient authorities read things. [18]Known to God from of old are all his works.'   [a] Other ancient authorities lack and from whatever has been strangled   [b] Gk from among them   [c] Other ancient authorities add saying, 'You must be circumcised and keep the law,'   [d] Gk men   [e] Other ancient authorities lack and from what is strangled   [f] Gk When they

them. *g* 35But Paul and Barnabas remained in Antioch, and there, with many others, they taught and proclaimed the word of the Lord.

Paul and Barnabas Separate

36 After some days Paul said to Barnabas, "Come, let us return and visit the believers*h* in every city where we proclaimed the word of the Lord and see how they are doing." 37Barnabas wanted to take with them John called Mark. 38But Paul decided not to take with them one who had deserted them in Pamphylia and had not accompanied them in the work. 39The disagreement became so sharp that they parted company; Barnabas took Mark with him and sailed away to Cyprus. 40But Paul chose Silas and set out, the believers*h* commending him to the grace of the Lord. 41He went through Syria and Cilicia, strengthening the churches.

Timothy Joins Paul and Silas

16 Paul*i* went on also to Derbe and to Lystra, where there was a disciple named Timothy, the son of a Jewish woman who was a believer; but his father was a Greek. 2He was well spoken of by the believers*h* in Lystra and Iconium. 3Paul wanted Timothy to accompany him; and he took him and had him circumcised because of the Jews who were in those places, for they all knew that his father was a Greek. 4As they went from town to town, they delivered to them for observance the decisions that had been reached by the apostles and elders who were in Jerusalem. 5So the churches were strengthened in the faith and increased in numbers daily.

Paul's Vision of the Man of Macedonia

6 They went through the region of Phrygia and Galatia, having been forbidden by the Holy Spirit to speak the word in Asia. 7When they had come opposite Mysia, they attempted to go into Bithynia, but the Spirit of Jesus did not allow them; 8so, passing by Mysia, they went down to Troas. 9During the night Paul had a vision: there stood a man of Macedonia pleading with him and saying, "Come over to Macedonia and help us." 10When he had seen the vision, we immediately tried to cross over to Macedonia, being convinced that God had called us to proclaim the good news to them.

The Conversion of Lydia

11 We set sail from Troas and took a straight course to Samothrace, the following day to Neapolis, 12and from there to Philippi, which is a leading city of the district*j* of Macedonia and a Roman colony. We remained in this city for some days. 13On the sabbath day we went outside the gate by the river, where we supposed there was a place of prayer; and we sat down and spoke to the women who had gathered there. 14A certain woman named Lydia, a worshiper of God, was listening to us; she was from the city of Thyatira and a dealer in purple cloth. The Lord opened her heart to listen eagerly to what was said by Paul. 15When she and her household were baptized, she urged us, saying, "If you have judged me to be faithful to the Lord, come and stay at my home." And she prevailed upon us.

Paul and Silas in Prison

16 One day, as we were going to the place of prayer, we met a slave-girl who had a spirit of divination and brought her owners a great deal of money by fortune-telling. 17While she followed Paul and us, she would cry out, "These men are slaves of the Most High God, who proclaim to you*k* a way of salvation." 18She kept doing this for many days. But Paul, very much annoyed, turned and said to the spirit, "I order you in the name of Jesus Christ to come out of her." And it came out that very hour.

19 But when her owners saw that their hope of making money was gone, they seized Paul and Silas and dragged them into the marketplace before the authorities. 20When they had brought them before the magistrates, they said, "These men are disturbing our city; they are Jews 21and are advocating customs that are not lawful for us as Romans to adopt or observe." 22The crowd joined in attacking them, and the magistrates had them stripped of their clothing and ordered them to be beaten with rods. 23After they had given them a severe flogging, they threw them into prison and ordered the

---

g Other ancient authorities add verse 34, *But it seemed good to Silas to remain there*   *h* Gk *brothers*
i Gk *He*   *j* Other authorities read *a city of the first district*   *k* Other ancient authorities read *to us*

jailer to keep them securely. 24Following these instructions, he put them in the innermost cell and fastened their feet in the stocks.

25 About midnight Paul and Silas were praying and singing hymns to God, and the prisoners were listening to them. 26Suddenly there was an earthquake, so violent that the foundations of the prison were shaken; and immediately all the doors were opened and everyone's chains were unfastened. 27When the jailer woke up and saw the prison doors wide open, he drew his sword and was about to kill himself, since he supposed that the prisoners had escaped. 28But Paul shouted in a loud voice, "Do not harm yourself, for we are all here." 29The jailer[l] called for lights, and rushing in, he fell down trembling before Paul and Silas. 30Then he brought them outside and said, "Sirs, what must I do to be saved?" 31They answered, "Believe on the Lord Jesus, and

you will be saved, you and your household." 32They spoke the word of the Lord[m] to him and to all who were in his house. 33At the same hour of the night he took them and washed their wounds; then he and his entire family were baptized without delay. 34He brought them up into the house and set food before them; and he and his entire household rejoiced that he had become a believer in God.

35 When morning came, the magistrates sent the police, saying, "Let those men go." 36And the jailer reported the message to Paul, saying, "The magistrates sent word to let you go; therefore come out now and go in peace." 37But Paul replied, "They have beaten us in public, uncondemned, men who are Roman citizens, and have thrown us into prison; and now are they going to discharge us in secret?

[l] Gk He   [m] Other ancient authorities read *word of God*

THE TRADITION

Apparitions and Visions

> *During the night Paul had a vision.*
> ACTS 16.9

To be a good Catholic you have to believe that Mary appeared at least at Lourdes and Fatima, right?

Wrong.

Apparitions and visions, like dreams and prophetic words or messages, are examples of what the Church calls "private revelation." Through them the Holy Spirit provides direction or encouragement keyed to the needs and situation of particular individuals or groups.

To see how this can work, take a look at Saint Paul's missionary journeys—the one in Acts 16, for example. Paul had been traveling throughout what is now Turkey and had been diverted (we are not told how) from two of his original destinations. One night he had a vision of a man from Macedonia, in Greece, who pleaded for help. Seeing this as a sign from God, Paul took the hint and set off

for Greece. And so began his evangelization of Europe.

Joan of Arc's "voices," the mystical visions of Catherine of Siena, the apparitions of Mary to Juan Diego, Bernadette, and the children of Fatima—how much richer we are because of such private revelations. And yet, no Catholic is ever under any obligation to believe or follow them—not even private revelation the Church has recognized as authentic.

Christian life is a matter of holding fast to God's *public* revelation of himself through Christ, communicated to us in the Church through Scripture and tradition, clarified by the teaching of the Church. Genuine supernatural experiences, whether our own or others', never contradict or distract from these essentials of the faith, but only enrich our understanding of them and guide our response.

Certainly not! Let them come and take us out themselves." [38]The police reported these words to the magistrates, and they were afraid when they heard that they were Roman citizens; [39]so they came and apologized to them. And they took them out and asked them to leave the city. [40]After leaving the prison they went to Lydia's home; and when they had seen and encouraged the brothers and sisters[n] there, they departed.

The Uproar in Thessalonica

17 After Paul and Silas[o] had passed through Amphipolis and Apollonia, they came to Thessalonica, where there was a synagogue of the Jews. [2]And Paul went in, as was his custom, and on three sabbath days argued with them from the scriptures, [3]explaining and proving that it was necessary for the Messiah[p] to suffer and to rise from the dead, and saying, "This is the Messiah,[p] Jesus whom I am proclaiming to you." [4]Some of them were persuaded and joined Paul and Silas, as did a great many of the devout Greeks and not a few of the leading women. [5]But the Jews became jealous, and with the help of some ruffians in the marketplaces they formed a mob and set the city in an uproar. While they were searching for Paul and Silas to bring them out to the assembly, they attacked Jason's house. [6]When they could not find them, they dragged Jason and some believers[n] before the city authorities,[q] shouting, "These people who have been turning the world upside down have come here also, [7]and Jason has entertained them as guests. They are all acting contrary to the decrees of the emperor, saying that there is another king named Jesus." [8]The people and the city officials were disturbed when they heard this, [9]and after they had taken bail from Jason and the others, they let them go.

Paul and Silas in Beroea

[10] That very night the believers[n] sent Paul and Silas off to Beroea; and when they arrived, they went to the Jewish synagogue. [11]These Jews were more receptive than those in Thessalonica, for they welcomed the message very eagerly and examined the scriptures every day to see whether these things were so. [12]Many of them therefore believed, including not a few Greek women and men of high stand-ing. [13]But when the Jews of Thessalonica learned that the word of God had been proclaimed by Paul in Beroea as well, they came there too, to stir up and incite the crowds. [14]Then the believers[n] immediately sent Paul away to the coast, but Silas and Timothy remained behind. [15]Those who conducted Paul brought him as far as Athens; and after receiving instructions to have Silas and Timothy join him as soon as possible, they left him.

Paul in Athens

[16] While Paul was waiting for them in Athens, he was deeply distressed to see that the city was full of idols. [17]So he argued in the synagogue with the Jews and the devout persons, and also in the marketplace[r] every day with those who happened to be there. [18]Also some Epicurean and Stoic philosophers debated with him. Some said, "What does this babbler want to say?" Others said, "He seems to be a proclaimer of foreign divinities." (This was because he was telling the good news about Jesus and the resurrection.) [19]So they took him and brought him to the Areopagus and asked him, "May we know what this new teaching is that you are presenting? [20]It sounds rather strange to us, so we would like to know what it means." [21]Now all the Athenians and the foreigners living there would spend their time in nothing but telling or hearing something new.

[22] Then Paul stood in front of the Areopagus and said, "Athenians, I see how extremely religious you are in every way. [23]For as I went through the city and looked carefully at the objects of your worship, I found among them an altar with the inscription, 'To an unknown god.' What therefore you worship as unknown, this I proclaim to you. [24]The God who made the world and everything in it, he who is Lord of heaven and earth, does not live in shrines made by human hands, [25]nor is he served by human hands, as though he needed anything, since he himself gives to all mortals life and breath and all things. [26]From one ancestor[s] he made all nations to inhabit the whole earth, and he allotted the times of their existence and

---

[n] Gk *brothers*   [o] Gk *they*   [p] Or *the Christ*
[q] Gk *politarchs*   [r] Or *civic center*; Gk *agora*   [s] Gk
From one; other ancient authorities read *From one blood*

the boundaries of the places where they would live, [27]so that they would search for God[t] and perhaps grope for him and find him—though indeed he is not far from each one of us. [28]For 'In him we live and move and have our being'; as even some of your own poets have said,

'For we too are his offspring.'

[29]Since we are God's offspring, we ought not to think that the deity is like gold, or silver, or stone, an image formed by the art and imagination of mortals. [30]While God has overlooked the times of human ignorance, now he commands all people everywhere to repent, [31]because he has fixed a day on which he will have the world judged in righteousness by a man whom he has appointed, and of this he has given assurance to all by raising him from the dead."

32 When they heard of the resurrection of the dead, some scoffed; but others said, "We will hear you again about this." [33]At that point Paul left them. [34]But some of them joined him and became believers, including Dionysius the Areopagite and a woman named Damaris, and others with them.

Paul in Corinth

18 After this Paul[u] left Athens and went to Corinth. [2]There he found a Jew named Aquila, a native of Pontus, who had recently come from Italy with his wife Priscilla, because Claudius had ordered all Jews to leave Rome. Paul[v] went to see them, [3]and, because he was of the same trade, he stayed with them, and they worked together—by trade they were tentmakers. [4]Every sabbath he would argue in the synagogue and would try to convince Jews and Greeks.

5 When Silas and Timothy arrived from Macedonia, Paul was occupied with proclaiming the word,[w] testifying to the Jews that the Messiah[x] was Jesus. [6]When they opposed and reviled him, in protest he shook the dust from his clothes[y] and said to them, "Your blood be on your own heads! I am innocent. From now on I will go to the Gentiles." [7]Then he left the synagogue[z] and went to the house of a man named Titius[a] Justus, a worshiper of God; his house was next door to the synagogue. [8]Crispus, the official of the synagogue, became a believer in the Lord, together with all his household; and many of the Corinthians who heard Paul be-

came believers and were baptized. [9]One night the Lord said to Paul in a vision, "Do not be afraid, but speak and do not be silent; [10]for I am with you, and no one will lay a hand on you to harm you, for there are many in this city who are my people." [11]He stayed there a year and six months, teaching the word of God among them.

12 But when Gallio was proconsul of Achaia, the Jews made a united attack on Paul and brought him before the tribunal. [13]They said, "This man is persuading people to worship God in ways that are contrary to the law." [14]Just as Paul was about to speak, Gallio said to the Jews, "If it were a matter of crime or serious villainy, I would be justified in accepting the complaint of you Jews; [15]but since it is a matter of questions about words and names and your own law, see to it yourselves; I do not wish to be a judge of these matters." [16]And he dismissed them from the tribunal. [17]Then all of them[b] seized Sosthenes, the official of the synagogue, and beat him in front of the tribunal. But Gallio paid no attention to any of these things.

Paul's Return to Antioch

18 After staying there for a considerable time, Paul said farewell to the believers[c] and sailed for Syria, accompanied by Priscilla and Aquila. At Cenchreae he had his hair cut, for he was under a vow. [19]When they reached Ephesus, he left them there, but first he himself went into the synagogue and had a discussion with the Jews. [20]When they asked him to stay longer, he declined; [21]but on taking leave of them, he said, "I[d] will return to you, if God wills." Then he set sail from Ephesus.

22 When he had landed at Caesarea, he went up to Jerusalem[e] and greeted the church, and then went down to Antioch. [23]After spending some time there he departed and went from place to place through the region of Galatia[f] and Phrygia, strengthening all the disciples.

t Other ancient authorities read *the Lord*   u Gk *he*   v Gk *He*   w Gk *with the word*   x Or the *Christ*   y Gk *reviled him, he shook out his clothes*   z Gk *left there*   a Other ancient authorities read *Titus*   b Other ancient authorities read *all the Greeks*   c Gk *brothers*   d Other ancient authorities read *I must at all costs keep the approaching festival in Jerusalem, but I*   e Gk *went up*   f Gk *the Galatian region*

Ministry of Apollos

24 Now there came to Ephesus a Jew named Apollos, a native of Alexandria. He was an eloquent man, well-versed in the scriptures. 25He had been instructed in the Way of the Lord; and he spoke with burning enthusiasm and taught accurately the things concerning Jesus, though he knew only the baptism of John. 26He began to speak boldly in the synagogue; but when Priscilla and Aquila heard him, they took him aside and explained the Way of God to him more accurately. 27And when he wished to cross over to Achaia, the believers*g* encouraged him and wrote to the disciples to welcome him. On his arrival he greatly helped those who through grace had become believers, 28for he powerfully refuted the Jews in public, showing by the scriptures that the Messiah*h* is Jesus.

Paul in Ephesus

19 While Apollos was in Corinth, Paul passed through the interior regions and came to Ephesus, where he found some disciples. 2He said to them, "Did you receive the Holy Spirit when you became believers?" They replied, "No, we have not even heard that there is a Holy Spirit." 3Then he said, "Into what then were you baptized?" They answered, "Into John's baptism." 4Paul said, "John baptized with the baptism of repentance, telling the people to believe in the one who was to come after him, that is, in Jesus." 5On hearing this, they were baptized in the name of the Lord Jesus. 6When Paul had laid his hands on them, the Holy Spirit came upon them, and they spoke in tongues and prophesied— 7altogether there were about twelve of them.

8 He entered the synagogue and for three months spoke out boldly, and argued persuasively about the kingdom of God. 9When some stubbornly refused to believe and spoke evil of the Way before the congregation, he left them, taking the disciples with him, and argued daily in the lecture hall of Tyrannus.*i* 10This continued for two years, so that all the residents of Asia, both Jews and Greeks, heard the word of the Lord.

The Sons of Sceva

11 God did extraordinary miracles through Paul, 12so that when the handker-chiefs or aprons that had touched his skin were brought to the sick, their diseases left them, and the evil spirits came out of them. 13Then some itinerant Jewish exorcists tried to use the name of the Lord Jesus over those who had evil spirits, saying, "I adjure you by the Jesus whom Paul proclaims." 14Seven sons of a Jewish high priest named Sceva were doing this. 15But the evil spirit said to them in reply, "Jesus I know, and Paul I know; but who are you?" 16Then the man with the evil spirit leaped on them, mastered them all, and so overpowered them that they fled out of the house naked and wounded. 17When this became known to all residents of Ephesus, both Jews and Greeks, everyone was awestruck; and the name of the Lord Jesus was praised. 18Also many of those who became believers confessed and disclosed their practices. 19A number of those who practiced magic collected their books and burned them publicly; when the value of these books*j* was calculated, it was found to come to fifty thousand silver coins. 20So the word of the Lord grew mightily and prevailed.

The Riot in Ephesus

21 Now after these things had been accomplished, Paul resolved in the Spirit to go through Macedonia and Achaia, and then to go on to Jerusalem. He said, "After I have gone there, I must also see Rome." 22So he sent two of his helpers, Timothy and Erastus, to Macedonia, while he himself stayed for some time longer in Asia.

23 About that time no little disturbance broke out concerning the Way. 24A man named Demetrius, a silversmith who made silver shrines of Artemis, brought no little business to the artisans. 25These he gathered together, with the workers of the same trade, and said, "Men, you know that we get our wealth from this business. 26You also see and hear that not only in Ephesus but in almost the whole of Asia this Paul has persuaded and drawn away a considerable number of people by saying that gods made with hands are not gods. 27And there is danger not only that this trade of ours may come into disrepute but

g Gk brothers   *h* Or the Christ   *i* Other ancient authorities read *of a certain Tyrannus, from eleven o'clock in the morning to four in the afternoon*   *j* Gk them

also that the temple of the great goddess Artemis will be scorned, and she will be deprived of her majesty that brought all Asia and the world to worship her."

28 When they heard this, they were enraged and shouted, "Great is Artemis of the Ephesians!" 29The city was filled with the confusion; and people*k* rushed together to the theater, dragging with them Gaius and Aristarchus, Macedonians who were Paul's travel companions. 30Paul wished to go into the crowd, but the disciples would not let him; 31even some officials of the province of Asia,*l* who were friendly to him, sent him a message urging him not to venture into the theater. 32Meanwhile, some were shouting one thing, some another; for the assembly was in confusion, and most of them did not know why they had come together. 33Some of the crowd gave instructions to Alexander, whom the Jews had pushed forward. And Alexander motioned for silence and tried to make a defense before the people. 34But when they recognized that he was a Jew, for about two hours all of them shouted in unison, "Great is Artemis of the Ephesians!" 35But when the town clerk had quieted the crowd, he said, "Citizens of Ephesus, who is there that does not know that the city of the Ephesians is the temple keeper of the great Artemis and of the statue that fell from heaven?*m* 36Since these things cannot be denied, you ought to be quiet and do nothing rash. 37You have brought these men here who are neither temple robbers nor blasphemers of our*n* goddess. 38If therefore Demetrius and the artisans with him have a complaint against anyone, the courts are open, and there are proconsuls; let them bring charges there against one another. 39If there is anything further*o* you want to know, it must be settled in the regular assembly. 40For we are in danger of being charged with rioting today, since there is no cause that we can give to justify this commotion." 41When he had said this, he dismissed the assembly.

Paul Goes to Macedonia and Greece

20 After the uproar had ceased, Paul sent for the disciples; and after encouraging them and saying farewell, he left for Macedonia. 2When he had gone through those regions and had given the believers*p* much encouragement, he came to Greece, 3where he stayed for three months. He was about to set sail for Syria when a plot was made against him by the Jews, and so he decided to return through Macedonia. 4He was accompanied by Sopater son of Pyrrhus from Beroea, by Aristarchus and Secundus from Thessalonica, by Gaius from Derbe, and by Timothy, as well as by Tychicus and Trophimus from Asia. 5They went ahead and were waiting for us in Troas; 6but we sailed from Philippi after the days of Unleavened Bread, and in five days we joined them in Troas, where we stayed for seven days.

Paul's Farewell Visit to Troas

7 On the first day of the week, when we met to break bread, Paul was holding a discussion with them; since he intended to leave the next day, he continued speaking until midnight. 8There were many lamps in the room upstairs where we were meeting. 9A young man named Eutychus, who was sitting in the window, began to sink off into a deep sleep while Paul talked still longer. Overcome by sleep, he fell to the ground three floors below and was picked up dead. 10But Paul went down, and bending over him took him in his arms, and said, "Do not be alarmed, for his life is in him." 11Then Paul went upstairs, and after he had broken bread and eaten, he continued to converse with them until dawn; then he left. 12Meanwhile they had taken the boy away alive and were not a little comforted.

The Voyage from Troas to Miletus

13 We went ahead to the ship and set sail for Assos, intending to take Paul on board there; for he had made this arrangement, intending to go by land himself. 14When he met us in Assos, we took him on board and went to Mitylene. 15We sailed from there, and on the following day we arrived opposite Chios. The next day we touched at Samos, and*q* the day after that we came to Miletus. 16For Paul had decided to sail past Ephesus, so that he might not have to spend time in Asia; he was eager to be in Jerusalem, if possible, on the day of Pentecost.

k Gk they   *l* Gk some of the Asiarchs
m Meaning of Gk uncertain   *n* Other ancient authorities read *your*   *o* Other ancient authorities read *about other matters*   *p* Gk *given them*   *q* Other ancient authorities add *after remaining at Trogyllium*

Paul Speaks to the Ephesian Elders

17 From Miletus he sent a message to Ephesus, asking the elders of the church to meet him. [18]When they came to him, he said to them:

"You yourselves know how I lived among you the entire time from the first day that I set foot in Asia, [19]serving the Lord with all humility and with tears, enduring the trials that came to me through the plots of the Jews. [20]I did not shrink from doing anything helpful, proclaiming the message to you and teaching you publicly and from house to house, [21]as I testified to both Jews and Greeks about repentance toward God and faith toward our Lord Jesus. [22]And now, as a captive to the Spirit,[r] I am on my way to Jerusalem, not knowing what will happen to me there, [23]except that the Holy Spirit testifies to me in every city that imprisonment and persecutions are waiting for me. [24]But I do not count my life of any value to myself, if only I may finish my course and the ministry that I received from the Lord Jesus, to testify to the good news of God's grace.

25 "And now I know that none of you, among whom I have gone about proclaiming the kingdom, will ever see my face again. [26]Therefore I declare to you this day that I am not responsible for the blood of any of you, [27]for I did not shrink from declaring to you the whole purpose of God. [28]Keep watch over yourselves and

r Or *And now, bound in the spirit*

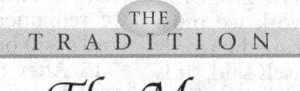

THE
TRADITION

The Mass

On the first day of the week, when we met to break bread . . .
ACTS 20.7

*I*f you were to ask ten ordinary Catholics to describe in one word their experience of Sunday Mass, chances are it wouldn't be "joy."

From all accounts, though, joy is precisely what characterized the early Christians as they "met to break bread" on the first day of each week. The description of the Eucharistic celebration in Acts 20 gives the impression that not even long homilies or accidents dampened their enthusiasm. "Paul talked on and on"—so long that a young man named Eutychus dozed off and fell out a third-story window. What joy that gathering must have experienced when God brought Eutychus back to life through Paul's prayer!

For us, as for the early Christians, gathering together for Mass is an opportunity for joy. One responsorial psalm speaks of coming "to the altar of God, to God my exceeding joy" (Psalm 43.4). Notice that this psalm is not a call to work ourselves into some heightened emotional state. Instead, it is a statement about what happens as we consciously enter into God's presence together.

You might describe it as a journey into joy. The journey begins as we make the decision to leave our cozy beds, our homes, our ordinary lives and routines. It continues as we walk into church—an eclectic assortment of individuals being gathered into a new community to whom the risen Lord will make himself present.

The beauty of singing and ritual, setting, vestments, and vessels signifies that this is no ordinary assembly. Christ has ascended into heaven, and through him we are entering God's presence. "Holy, holy, holy!" Though still on earth, we are also in the heavenly courts, adding our praise to the crescendo of joy arising from the angels and saints before God's throne (see Revelation 4.8).

"Enter into the joy of your master," Jesus says to those who enter his kingdom (see Matthew 25.21, 23). "Come, share my joy," he invites us as we gather for every Eucharist. Because of his presence, the Mass can be for us a foretaste of heaven.

over all the flock, of which the Holy Spirit has made you overseers, to shepherd the church of God[s] that he obtained with the blood of his own Son.[t] [29]I know that after I have gone, savage wolves will come in among you, not sparing the flock. [30]Some even from your own group will come distorting the truth in order to entice the disciples to follow them. [31]Therefore be alert, remembering that for three years I did not cease night or day to warn everyone with tears. [32]And now I commend you to God and to the message of his grace, a message that is able to build you up and to give you the inheritance among all who are sanctified. [33]I coveted no one's silver or gold or clothing. [34]You know for yourselves that I worked with my own hands to support myself and my companions. [35]In all this I have given you an example that by such work we must support the weak, remembering the words of the Lord Jesus, for he himself said, 'It is more blessed to give than to receive.' "

36 When he had finished speaking, he knelt down with them all and prayed. [37]There was much weeping among them all; they embraced Paul and kissed him, [38]grieving especially because of what he had said, that they would not see him again. Then they brought him to the ship.

Paul's Journey to Jerusalem

21 When we had parted from them and set sail, we came by a straight course to Cos, and the next day to Rhodes, and from there to Patara.[u] [2]When we found a ship bound for Phoenicia, we went on board and set sail. [3]We came in sight of Cyprus; and leaving it on our left, we sailed to Syria and landed at Tyre, because the ship was to unload its cargo there. [4]We looked up the disciples and stayed there for seven days. Through the Spirit they told Paul not to go on to Jerusalem. [5]When our days there were ended, we left and proceeded on our journey; and all of them, with wives and children, escorted us outside the city. There we knelt down on the beach and prayed [6]and said farewell to one another. Then we went on board the ship, and they returned home.

7 When we had finished[v] the voyage from Tyre, we arrived at Ptolemais; and we greeted the believers[w] and stayed with them for one day. [8]The next day we left

and came to Caesarea; and we went into the house of Philip the evangelist, one of the seven, and stayed with him. [9]He had four unmarried daughters[x] who had the gift of prophecy. [10]While we were staying there for several days, a prophet named Agabus came down from Judea. [11]He came to us and took Paul's belt, bound his own feet and hands with it, and said, "Thus says the Holy Spirit, 'This is the way the Jews in Jerusalem will bind the man who owns this belt and will hand him over to the Gentiles.' " [12]When we heard this, we and the people there urged him not to go up to Jerusalem. [13]Then Paul answered, "What are you doing, weeping and breaking my heart? For I am ready not only to be bound but even to die in Jerusalem for the name of the Lord Jesus." [14]Since he would not be persuaded, we remained silent except to say, "The Lord's will be done."

15 After these days we got ready and started to go up to Jerusalem. [16]Some of the disciples from Caesarea also came along and brought us to the house of Mnason of Cyprus, an early disciple, with whom we were to stay.

Paul Visits James at Jerusalem

17 When we arrived in Jerusalem, the brothers welcomed us warmly. [18]The next day Paul went with us to visit James; and all the elders were present. [19]After greeting them, he related one by one the things that God had done among the Gentiles through his ministry. [20]When they heard it, they praised God. Then they said to him, "You see, brother, how many thousands of believers there are among the Jews, and they are all zealous for the law. [21]They have been told about you that you teach all the Jews living among the Gentiles to forsake Moses, and that you tell them not to circumcise their children or observe the customs. [22]What then is to be done? They will certainly hear that you have come. [23]So do what we tell you. We have four men who are under a vow. [24]Join these men, go through the rite of purification with them, and pay for the shaving of their heads. Thus all will know

---

[s] Other ancient authorities read *of the Lord*   [t] Or *with his own blood;* Gk *with the blood of his Own*   [u] Other ancient authorities add *and Myra*   [v] Or *continued*   [w] Gk *brothers*   [x] Gk *four daughters, virgins,*

that there is nothing in what they have been told about you, but that you yourself observe and guard the law. 25But as for the Gentiles who have become believers, we have sent a letter with our judgment that they should abstain from what has been sacrificed to idols and from blood and from what is strangled[y] and from fornication." 26Then Paul took the men, and the next day, having purified himself, he entered the temple with them, making public the completion of the days of purification when the sacrifice would be made for each of them.

Paul Arrested in the Temple

27 When the seven days were almost completed, the Jews from Asia, who had seen him in the temple, stirred up the whole crowd. They seized him, 28shouting, "Fellow Israelites, help! This is the man who is teaching everyone everywhere against our people, our law, and this place; more than that, he has actually brought Greeks into the temple and has defiled this holy place." 29For they had previously seen Trophimus the Ephesian with him in the city, and they supposed that Paul had brought him into the temple. 30Then all the city was aroused, and the people rushed together. They seized Paul and dragged him out of the temple, and immediately the doors were shut. 31While they were trying to kill him, word came to the tribune of the cohort that all Jerusalem was in an uproar. 32Immediately he took soldiers and centurions and ran down to them. When they saw the tribune and the soldiers, they stopped beating Paul. 33Then the tribune came, arrested him, and ordered him to be bound with two chains; he inquired who he was and what he had done. 34Some in the crowd shouted one thing, some another; and as he could not learn the facts because of the uproar, he ordered him to be brought into the barracks. 35When Paul[z] came to the steps, the violence of the mob was so great that he had to be carried by the soldiers. 36The crowd that followed kept shouting, "Away with him!"

Paul Defends Himself

37 Just as Paul was about to be brought into the barracks, he said to the tribune, "May I say something to you?" The tribune[a] replied, "Do you know Greek? 38Then you are not the Egyptian who recently stirred up a revolt and led the four thousand assassins out into the wilderness?" 39Paul replied, "I am a Jew, from Tarsus in Cilicia, a citizen of an important city; I beg you, let me speak to the people." 40When he had given him permission, Paul stood on the steps and motioned to the people for silence; and when there was a great hush, he addressed them in the Hebrew[b] language, saying:

22 "Brothers and fathers, listen to the defense that I now make before you."

2 When they heard him addressing them in Hebrew,[b] they became even more quiet. Then he said:

3 "I am a Jew, born in Tarsus in Cilicia, but brought up in this city at the feet of Gamaliel, educated strictly according to our ancestral law, being zealous for God, just as all of you are today. 4I persecuted this Way up to the point of death by binding both men and women and putting them in prison, 5as the high priest and the whole council of elders can testify about me. From them I also received letters to the brothers in Damascus, and I went there in order to bind those who were there and to bring them back to Jerusalem for punishment.

Paul Tells of His Conversion

6 "While I was on my way and approaching Damascus, about noon a great light from heaven suddenly shone about me. 7I fell to the ground and heard a voice saying to me, 'Saul, Saul, why are you persecuting me?' 8I answered, 'Who are you, Lord?' Then he said to me, 'I am Jesus of Nazareth[c] whom you are persecuting.' 9Now those who were with me saw the light but did not hear the voice of the one who was speaking to me. 10I asked, 'What am I to do, Lord?' The Lord said to me, 'Get up and go to Damascus; there you will be told everything that has been assigned to you to do.' 11Since I could not see because of the brightness of that light, those who were with me took my hand and led me to Damascus.

12 "A certain Ananias, who was a devout man according to the law and well spoken of by all the Jews living there, 13came to me; and standing beside me, he

---

[y] Other ancient authorities lack *and from what is strangled*   [z] Gk *he*   [a] Gk *He*   [b] That is, Aramaic   [c] Gk *the Nazorean*

said, 'Brother Saul, regain your sight!' In that very hour I regained my sight and saw him. [14]Then he said, 'The God of our ancestors has chosen you to know his will, to see the Righteous One and to hear his own voice; [15]for you will be his witness to all the world of what you have seen and heard. [16]And now why do you delay? Get up, be baptized, and have your sins washed away, calling on his name.'

Paul Sent to the Gentiles

17 "After I had returned to Jerusalem and while I was praying in the temple, I fell into a trance [18]and saw Jesus*d* saying to me, 'Hurry and get out of Jerusalem quickly, because they will not accept your testimony about me.' [19]And I said, 'Lord, they themselves know that in every synagogue I imprisoned and beat those who believed in you. [20]And while the blood of your witness Stephen was shed, I myself was standing by, approving and keeping the coats of those who killed him.' [21]Then he said to me, 'Go, for I will send you far away to the Gentiles.' "

Paul and the Roman Tribune

22 Up to this point they listened to him, but then they shouted, "Away with such a fellow from the earth! For he should not be allowed to live." [23]And while they were shouting, throwing off their cloaks, and tossing dust into the air, [24]the tribune directed that he was to be brought into the barracks, and ordered him to be examined by flogging, to find out the reason for this outcry against him. [25]But when they had tied him up with thongs,*e* Paul said to the centurion who was standing by, "Is it legal for you to flog a Roman citizen who is uncondemned?" [26]When the centurion heard that, he went to the tribune and said to him, "What are you about to do? This man is a Roman citizen." [27]The tribune came and asked Paul,*d* "Tell me, are you a Roman citizen?" And he said, "Yes." [28]The tribune answered, "It cost me a large sum of money to get my citizenship." Paul said, "But I was born a citizen." [29]Immediately those who were about to examine him drew back from him; and the tribune also was afraid, for he realized that Paul was a Roman citizen and that he had bound him.

Paul before the Council

30 Since he wanted to find out what

Paul*f* was being accused of by the Jews, the next day he released him and ordered the chief priests and the entire council to meet. He brought Paul down and had him stand before them.

23 While Paul was looking intently at the council he said, "Brothers,*g* up to this day I have lived my life with a clear conscience before God." [2]Then the high priest Ananias ordered those standing near him to strike him on the mouth. [3]At this Paul said to him, "God will strike you, you whitewashed wall! Are you sitting there to judge me according to the law, and yet in violation of the law you order me to be struck?" [4]Those standing nearby said, "Do you dare to insult God's high priest?" [5]And Paul said, "I did not realize, brothers, that he was high priest; for it is written, 'You shall not speak evil of a leader of your people.' "

6 When Paul noticed that some were Sadducees and others were Pharisees, he called out in the council, "Brothers, I am a Pharisee, a son of Pharisees. I am on trial concerning the hope of the resurrection*h* of the dead." [7]When he said this, a dissension began between the Pharisees and the Sadducees, and the assembly was divided. [8](The Sadducees say that there is no resurrection, or angel, or spirit; but the Pharisees acknowledge all three.) [9]Then a great clamor arose, and certain scribes of the Pharisees' group stood up and contended, "We find nothing wrong with this man. What if a spirit or an angel has spoken to him?" [10]When the dissension became violent, the tribune, fearing that they would tear Paul to pieces, ordered the soldiers to go down, take him by force, and bring him into the barracks.

11 That night the Lord stood near him and said, "Keep up your courage! For just as you have testified for me in Jerusalem, so you must bear witness also in Rome."

The Plot to Kill Paul

12 In the morning the Jews joined in a conspiracy and bound themselves by an oath neither to eat nor drink until they had killed Paul. [13]There were more than forty who joined in this conspiracy. [14]They went to the chief priests and elders and said, "We have strictly bound our-

---

d Gk *him*   *e* Or *up for the lashes*   *f* Gk *he*
g Gk *Men, brothers*   *h* Gk *concerning hope and resurrection*

selves by an oath to taste no food until we have killed Paul. [15]Now then, you and the council must notify the tribune to bring him down to you, on the pretext that you want to make a more thorough examination of his case. And we are ready to do away with him before he arrives."

16 Now the son of Paul's sister heard about the ambush; so he went and gained entrance to the barracks and told Paul. [17]Paul called one of the centurions and said, "Take this young man to the tribune, for he has something to report to him." [18]So he took him, brought him to the tribune, and said, "The prisoner Paul called me and asked me to bring this young man to you; he has something to tell you." [19]The tribune took him by the hand, drew him aside privately, and asked, "What is it that you have to report to me?" [20]He answered, "The Jews have agreed to ask you to bring Paul down to the council tomorrow, as though they were going to inquire more thoroughly into his case. [21]But do not be persuaded by them, for more than forty of their men are lying in ambush for him. They have bound themselves by an oath neither to eat nor drink until they kill him. They are ready now and are waiting for your consent." [22]So the tribune dismissed the young man, ordering him, "Tell no one that you have informed me of this."

Paul Sent to Felix the Governor

23 Then he summoned two of the centurions and said, "Get ready to leave by nine o'clock tonight for Caesarea with two hundred soldiers, seventy horsemen, and two hundred spearmen. [24]Also provide mounts for Paul to ride, and take him safely to Felix the governor." [25]He wrote a letter to this effect:

26 "Claudius Lysias to his Excellency the governor Felix, greetings. [27]This man was seized by the Jews and was about to be killed by them, but when I had learned that he was a Roman citizen, I came with the guard and rescued him. [28]Since I wanted to know the charge for which they accused him, I had him brought to their council. [29]I found that he was accused concerning questions of their law, but was charged with nothing deserving death or imprisonment. [30]When I was informed that there would be a plot against the man, I sent him to you at once, ordering

his accusers also to state before you what they have against him.*i* "

31 So the soldiers, according to their instructions, took Paul and brought him during the night to Antipatris. [32]The next day they let the horsemen go on with him, while they returned to the barracks. [33]When they came to Caesarea and delivered the letter to the governor, they presented Paul also before him. [34]On reading the letter, he asked what province he belonged to, and when he learned that he was from Cilicia, [35]he said, "I will give you a hearing when your accusers arrive." Then he ordered that he be kept under guard in Herod's headquarters.*j*

Paul before Felix at Caesarea

24 Five days later the high priest Ananias came down with some elders and an attorney, a certain Tertullus, and they reported their case against Paul to the governor. [2]When Paul*k* had been summoned, Tertullus began to accuse him, saying:

"Your Excellency,*l* because of you we have long enjoyed peace, and reforms have been made for this people because of your foresight. [3]We welcome this in every way and everywhere with utmost gratitude. [4]But, to detain you no further, I beg you to hear us briefly with your customary graciousness. [5]We have, in fact, found this man a pestilent fellow, an agitator among all the Jews throughout the world, and a ringleader of the sect of the Nazarenes.*m* [6]He even tried to profane the temple, and so we seized him.*n* [8]By examining him yourself you will be able to learn from him concerning everything of which we accuse him."

9 The Jews also joined in the charge by asserting that all this was true.

Paul's Defense before Felix

10 When the governor motioned to him to speak, Paul replied:

"I cheerfully make my defense, knowing that for many years you have been a judge over this nation. [11]As you can find out, it is not more than twelve days since

I went up to worship in Jerusalem. [12]They did not find me disputing with anyone in the temple or stirring up a crowd either in the synagogues or throughout the city. [13]Neither can they prove to you the charge that they now bring against me. [14]But this I admit to you, that according to the Way, which they call a sect, I worship the God of our ancestors, believing everything laid down according to the law or written in the prophets. [15]I have a hope in God—a hope that they themselves also accept—that there will be a resurrection of both[o] the righteous and the unrighteous. [16]Therefore I do my best always to have a clear conscience toward God and all people. [17]Now after some years I came to bring alms to my nation and to offer sacrifices. [18]While I was doing this, they found me in the temple, completing the rite of purification, without any crowd or disturbance. [19]But there were some Jews from Asia—they ought to be here before you to make an accusation, if they have anything against me. [20]Or let these men here tell what crime they had found when I stood before the council, [21]unless it was this one sentence that I called out while standing before them, 'It is about the resurrection of the dead that I am on trial before you today.' "

22 But Felix, who was rather well informed about the Way, adjourned the hearing with the comment, "When Lysias the tribune comes down, I will decide your case." [23]Then he ordered the centurion to keep him in custody, but to let him have some liberty and not to prevent any of his friends from taking care of his needs.

Paul Held in Custody

24 Some days later when Felix came with his wife Drusilla, who was Jewish, he sent for Paul and heard him speak concerning faith in Christ Jesus. [25]And as he discussed justice, self-control, and the coming judgment, Felix became frightened and said, "Go away for the present; when I have an opportunity, I will send for you." [26]At the same time he hoped that money would be given him by Paul, and for that reason he used to send for him very often and converse with him.

27 After two years had passed, Felix was succeeded by Porcius Festus; and since he wanted to grant the Jews a favor, Felix left Paul in prison.

Paul Appeals to the Emperor

25 Three days after Festus had arrived in the province, he went up from Caesarea to Jerusalem [2]where the chief priests and the leaders of the Jews gave him a report against Paul. They appealed to him [3]and requested, as a favor to them against Paul,[p] to have him transferred to Jerusalem. They were, in fact, planning an ambush to kill him along the way. [4]Festus replied that Paul was being kept at Caesarea, and that he himself intended to go there shortly. [5]"So," he said, "let those of you who have the authority come down with me, and if there is anything wrong about the man, let them accuse him."

6 After he had stayed among them not more than eight or ten days, he went down to Caesarea; the next day he took his seat on the tribunal and ordered Paul to be brought. [7]When he arrived, the Jews who had gone down from Jerusalem surrounded him, bringing many serious charges against him, which they could not prove. [8]Paul said in his defense, "I have in no way committed an offense against the law of the Jews, or against the temple, or against the emperor." [9]But Festus, wishing to do the Jews a favor, asked Paul, "Do you wish to go up to Jerusalem and be tried there before me on these charges?" [10]Paul said, "I am appealing to the emperor's tribunal; this is where I should be tried. I have done no wrong to the Jews, as you very well know. [11]Now if I am in the wrong and have committed something for which I deserve to die, I am not trying to escape death; but if there is nothing to their charges against me, no one can turn me over to them. I appeal to the emperor." [12]Then Festus, after he had conferred with his council, replied, "You have appealed to the emperor; to the emperor you will go."

Festus Consults King Agrippa

13 After several days had passed, King Agrippa and Bernice arrived at Caesarea to welcome Festus. [14]Since they were staying there several days, Festus laid Paul's case before the king, saying, "There is a man here who was left in prison by Felix. [15]When I was in Jerusalem, the chief

---

[o] Other ancient authorities read *of the dead, both of*   [p] Gk *him*

priests and the elders of the Jews informed me about him and asked for a sentence against him. [16]I told them that it was not the custom of the Romans to hand over anyone before the accused had met the accusers face to face and had been given an opportunity to make a defense against the charge. [17]So when they met here, I lost no time, but on the next day took my seat on the tribunal and ordered the man to be brought. [18]When the accusers stood up, they did not charge him with any of the crimes*q* that I was expecting. [19]Instead they had certain points of disagreement with him about their own religion and about a certain Jesus, who had died, but whom Paul asserted to be alive. [20]Since I was at a loss how to investigate these questions, I asked whether he wished to go to Jerusalem and be tried there on these charges.*r* [21]But when Paul had appealed to be kept in custody for the decision of his Imperial Majesty, I ordered him to be held until I could send him to the emperor." [22]Agrippa said to Festus, "I would like to hear the man myself." "Tomorrow," he said, "you will hear him."

Paul Brought before Agrippa

23 So on the next day Agrippa and Bernice came with great pomp, and they entered the audience hall with the military tribunes and the prominent men of the city. Then Festus gave the order and Paul was brought in. [24]And Festus said, "King Agrippa and all here present with us, you see this man about whom the whole Jewish community petitioned me, both in Jerusalem and here, shouting that he ought not to live any longer. [25]But I found that he had done nothing deserving death; and when he appealed to his Imperial Majesty, I decided to send him. [26]But I have nothing definite to write to our sovereign about him. Therefore I have brought him before all of you, and especially before you, King Agrippa, so that, after we have examined him, I may have something to write— [27]for it seems to me unreasonable to send a prisoner without indicating the charges against him."

Paul Defends Himself before Agrippa

26 Agrippa said to Paul, "You have permission to speak for yourself." Then Paul stretched out his hand and began to defend himself:

2 "I consider myself fortunate that it is before you, King Agrippa, I am to make my defense today against all the accusations of the Jews, [3]because you are especially familiar with all the customs and controversies of the Jews; therefore I beg of you to listen to me patiently.

4 "All the Jews know my way of life from my youth, a life spent from the beginning among my own people and in Jerusalem. [5]They have known for a long time, if they are willing to testify, that I have belonged to the strictest sect of our religion and lived as a Pharisee. [6]And now I stand here on trial on account of my hope in the promise made by God to our ancestors, [7]a promise that our twelve tribes hope to attain, as they earnestly worship day and night. It is for this hope, your Excellency,*s* that I am accused by Jews! [8]Why is it thought incredible by any of you that God raises the dead?

9 "Indeed, I myself was convinced that I ought to do many things against the name of Jesus of Nazareth.*t* [10]And that is what I did in Jerusalem; with authority received from the chief priests, I not only locked up many of the saints in prison, but I also cast my vote against them when they were being condemned to death. [11]By punishing them often in all the synagogues I tried to force them to blaspheme; and since I was so furiously enraged at them, I pursued them even to foreign cities.

Paul Tells of His Conversion

12 "With this in mind, I was traveling to Damascus with the authority and commission of the chief priests, [13]when at midday along the road, your Excellency,*s* I saw a light from heaven, brighter than the sun, shining around me and my companions. [14]When we had all fallen to the ground, I heard a voice saying to me in the Hebrew*u* language, 'Saul, Saul, why are you persecuting me? It hurts you to kick against the goads.' [15]I asked, 'Who are you, Lord?' The Lord answered, 'I am Jesus whom you are persecuting. [16]But get up and stand on your feet; for I have appeared to you for this purpose, to appoint you to serve and testify to the things in which you have seen me*v* and to those in

q Other ancient authorities read *with anything*
r Gk *on them*   *s* Gk O *king*   *t* Gk *the Nazorean*
u That is, *Aramaic*   *v* Other ancient authorities
read *the things that you have seen*

which I will appear to you. [17]I will rescue you from your people and from the Gentiles—to whom I am sending you [18]to open their eyes so that they may turn from darkness to light and from the power of Satan to God, so that they may receive forgiveness of sins and a place among those who are sanctified by faith in me.'

Paul Tells of His Preaching

19 "After that, King Agrippa, I was not disobedient to the heavenly vision, [20]but declared first to those in Damascus, then in Jerusalem and throughout the countryside of Judea, and also to the Gentiles, that they should repent and turn to God and do deeds consistent with repentance. [21]For this reason the Jews seized me in the temple and tried to kill me. [22]To this day I have had help from God, and so I stand here, testifying to both small and great, saying nothing but what the prophets and Moses said would take place: [23]that the Messiah[w] must suffer, and that, by being the first to rise from the dead, he would proclaim light both to our people and to the Gentiles."

Paul Appeals to Agrippa to Believe

24 While he was making this defense, Festus exclaimed, "You are out of your mind, Paul! Too much learning is driving you insane!" [25]But Paul said, "I am not out of my mind, most excellent Festus, but I am speaking the sober truth. [26]Indeed the king knows about these things, and to him I speak freely; for I am certain that none of these things has escaped his notice, for this was not done in a corner. [27]King Agrippa, do you believe the prophets? I know that you believe." [28]Agrippa said to Paul, "Are you so quickly persuading me to become a Christian?"[x] [29]Paul replied, "Whether quickly or not, I pray to God that not only you but also all who are listening to me today might become such as I am—except for these chains."

30 Then the king got up, and with him the governor and Bernice and those who had been seated with them; [31]and as they were leaving, they said to one another, "This man is doing nothing to deserve death or imprisonment." [32]Agrippa said to Festus, "This man could have been set free if he had not appealed to the emperor."

Paul Sails for Rome

27 When it was decided that we were to sail for Italy, they transferred Paul and some other prisoners to a centurion of the Augustan Cohort, named Julius. [2]Embarking on a ship of Adramyttium that was about to set sail to the ports along the coast of Asia, we put to sea, accompanied by Aristarchus, a Macedonian from Thessalonica. [3]The next day we put in at Sidon; and Julius treated Paul kindly, and allowed him to go to his friends to be cared for. [4]Putting out to sea from there, we sailed under the lee of Cyprus, because the winds were against us. [5]After we had sailed across the sea that is off Cilicia and Pamphylia, we came to Myra in Lycia. [6]There the centurion found an Alexandrian ship bound for Italy and put us on board. [7]We sailed slowly for a number of days and arrived with difficulty off Cnidus, and as the wind was against us, we sailed under the lee of Crete off Salmone. [8]Sailing past it with difficulty, we came to a place called Fair Havens, near the city of Lasea.

9 Since much time had been lost and sailing was now dangerous, because even the Fast had already gone by, Paul advised them, [10]saying, "Sirs, I can see that the voyage will be with danger and much heavy loss, not only of the cargo and the ship, but also of our lives." [11]But the centurion paid more attention to the pilot and to the owner of the ship than to what Paul said. [12]Since the harbor was not suitable for spending the winter, the majority was in favor of putting to sea from there, on the chance that somehow they could reach Phoenix, where they could spend the winter. It was a harbor of Crete, facing southwest and northwest.

The Storm at Sea

13 When a moderate south wind began to blow, they thought they could achieve their purpose; so they weighed anchor and began to sail past Crete, close to the shore. [14]But soon a violent wind, called the northeaster, rushed down from Crete.[y] [15]Since the ship was caught and could not be turned head-on into the

w Or the Christ   x Or Quickly you will persuade me
to play the Christian   y Gk it

wind, we gave way to it and were driven. [16]By running under the lee of a small island called Cauda[z] we were scarcely able to get the ship's boat under control. [17]After hoisting it up they took measures[a] to undergird the ship; then, fearing that they would run on the Syrtis, they lowered the sea anchor and so were driven. [18]We were being pounded by the storm so violently that on the next day they began to throw the cargo overboard, [19]and on the third day with their own hands they threw the ship's tackle overboard. [20]When neither sun nor stars appeared for many days, and no small tempest raged, all hope of our being saved was at last abandoned.

21 Since they had been without food for a long time, Paul then stood up among them and said, "Men, you should have listened to me and not have set sail from Crete and thereby avoided this damage and loss. [22]I urge you now to keep up your courage, for there will be no loss of life among you, but only of the ship. [23]For last night there stood by me an angel of the God to whom I belong and whom I worship, [24]and he said, 'Do not be afraid, Paul; you must stand before the emperor; and indeed, God has granted safety to all those who are sailing with you.' [25]So keep up your courage, men, for I have faith in God that it will be exactly as I have been told. [26]But we will have to run aground on some island."

27 When the fourteenth night had

[z] Other ancient authorities read *Clauda*   [a] Gk *helps*

Finding Courage

Scripture Reading for Today:
Acts 27.13–26

Verse for Today:
Acts 27.23

Like everyone else aboard that storm-tossed ship, Paul had been terrified when the violent northeaster struck. But an angel calmed his fears and assured him that God would fulfill his purpose for Paul: He would arrive safely in Rome, where he would appear before the emperor and witness to his faith. Not only that, God had granted safe passage to everyone on board.

The angel imparted new courage to Paul. In turn, Paul was able to encourage the others. He was certain that the outcome would be exactly as the angel had told him.

Paul talks about his heavenly encourager as "an angel of the God to whom I belong." His words convey his confidence that his future belongs in God's own hands. The same is true for us. Like Paul, we can expect God to provide both naturally and supernaturally for us. When we find ourselves at sea, not knowing which direction to turn, or when we discover ourselves the victim of some kind of disaster or shipwreck, we can echo the psalmist's words: "I cry to God Most High, to God who fulfills his purpose for me" (Psalm 57.2).

For God has a plan and purpose for each one of us, no matter how stormy our circumstances. Like Paul we can find courage in the word that God speaks to us. And as we grow in courage we can, in turn, encourage those around us. Perhaps the God to whom we belong will send an angel to stand by us in our time of greatest need.

—ANN SPANGLER

Go to page 1471 for your next devotional reading.

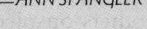

come, as we were drifting across the sea of Adria, about midnight the sailors suspected that they were nearing land. [28]So they took soundings and found twenty fathoms; a little farther on they took soundings again and found fifteen fathoms. [29]Fearing that we might run on the rocks, they let down four anchors from the stern and prayed for day to come. [30]But when the sailors tried to escape from the ship and had lowered the boat into the sea, on the pretext of putting out anchors from the bow, [31]Paul said to the centurion and the soldiers, "Unless these men stay in the ship, you cannot be saved." [32]Then the soldiers cut away the ropes of the boat and set it adrift.

[33] Just before daybreak, Paul urged all of them to take some food, saying, "Today is the fourteenth day that you have been in suspense and remaining without food, having eaten nothing. [34]Therefore I urge you to take some food, for it will help you survive; for none of you will lose a hair from your heads." [35]After he had said this, he took bread; and giving thanks to God in the presence of all, he broke it and began to eat. [36]Then all of them were encouraged and took food for themselves. [37](We were in all two hundred seventy-six[b] persons in the ship.) [38]After they had satisfied their hunger, they lightened the ship by throwing the wheat into the sea.

The Shipwreck

[39] In the morning they did not recognize the land, but they noticed a bay with a beach, on which they planned to run the ship ashore, if they could. [40]So they cast off the anchors and left them in the sea. At the same time they loosened the ropes that tied the steering-oars; then hoisting the foresail to the wind, they made for the beach. [41]But striking a reef,[c] they ran the ship aground; the bow stuck and remained immovable, but the stern was being broken up by the force of the waves. [42]The soldiers' plan was to kill the prisoners, so that none might swim away and escape; [43]but the centurion, wishing to save Paul, kept them from carrying out their plan. He ordered those who could swim to jump overboard first and make for the land, [44]and the rest to follow, some on planks and others on pieces of the ship. And so it was that all were brought safely to land.

Paul on the Island of Malta

28 After we had reached safety, we then learned that the island was called Malta. [2]The natives showed us unusual kindness. Since it had begun to rain and was cold, they kindled a fire and welcomed all of us around it. [3]Paul had gathered a bundle of brushwood and was putting it on the fire, when a viper, driven out by the heat, fastened itself on his hand. [4]When the natives saw the creature hanging from his hand, they said to one another, "This man must be a murderer; though he has escaped from the sea, justice has not allowed him to live." [5]He, however, shook off the creature into the fire and suffered no harm. [6]They were expecting him to swell up or drop dead, but after they had waited a long time and saw that nothing unusual had happened to him, they changed their minds and began to say that he was a god.

[7] Now in the neighborhood of that place were lands belonging to the leading man of the island, named Publius, who received us and entertained us hospitably for three days. [8]It so happened that the father of Publius lay sick in bed with fever and dysentery. Paul visited him and cured him by praying and putting his hands on him. [9]After this happened, the rest of the people on the island who had diseases also came and were cured. [10]They bestowed many honors on us, and when we were about to sail, they put on board all the provisions we needed.

Paul Arrives at Rome

[11] Three months later we set sail on a ship that had wintered at the island, an Alexandrian ship with the Twin Brothers as its figurehead. [12]We put in at Syracuse and stayed there for three days; [13]then we weighed anchor and came to Rhegium. After one day there a south wind sprang up, and on the second day we came to Puteoli. [14]There we found believers[d] and were invited to stay with them for seven days. And so we came to Rome. [15]The believers[d] from there, when they heard of us, came as far as the Forum of Appius and Three Taverns to meet us. On seeing them, Paul thanked God and took courage.

[b] Other ancient authorities read *seventy-six*; others, *about seventy-six*   [c] Gk *place of two seas*   [d] Gk *brothers*

16 When we came into Rome, Paul was allowed to live by himself, with the soldier who was guarding him.

Paul and Jewish Leaders in Rome

17 Three days later he called together the local leaders of the Jews. When they had assembled, he said to them, "Brothers, though I had done nothing against our people or the customs of our ancestors, yet I was arrested in Jerusalem and handed over to the Romans. 18When they had examined me, the Romans*e* wanted to release me, because there was no reason for the death penalty in my case. 19But when the Jews objected, I was compelled to appeal to the emperor—even though I had no charge to bring against my nation. 20For this reason therefore I have asked to see you and speak with you,*f* since it is for the sake of the hope of Israel that I am bound with this chain." 21They replied, "We have received no letters from Judea about you, and none of the brothers coming here has reported or spoken anything evil about you. 22But we would like to hear from you what you think, for with regard to this sect we know that everywhere it is spoken against."

Paul Preaches in Rome

23 After they had set a day to meet with him, they came to him at his lodgings in great numbers. From morning until evening he explained the matter to them, testifying to the kingdom of God and trying to convince them about Jesus both from the law of Moses and from the prophets. 24Some were convinced by what he had said, while others refused to believe. 25So they disagreed with each other; and as they were leaving, Paul made one further statement: "The Holy Spirit was right in saying to your ancestors through the prophet Isaiah,

26 'Go to this people and say,
    You will indeed listen, but never
        understand,
and you will indeed look, but
        never perceive.
27 For this people's heart has
        grown dull,
    and their ears are hard of hearing,
        and they have shut their eyes;
    so that they might not look
        with their eyes,
    and listen with their ears,
    and understand with their heart and
        turn—
    and I would heal them.'

28Let it be known to you then that this salvation of God has been sent to the Gentiles; they will listen."*g*

30 He lived there two whole years at his own expense*h* and welcomed all who came to him, 31proclaiming the kingdom of God and teaching about the Lord Jesus Christ with all boldness and without hindrance.

e Gk *they*   *f* Or *I have asked you to see me and speak with me*   *g* Other ancient authorities add verse 29, *And when he had said these words, the Jews departed, arguing vigorously among themselves*   *h* Or *in his own hired dwelling*

The Letter of Paul to the

Romans

Romans is the longest of Paul's letters and offers the most complete statement of his faith. Paul wrote it about A.D. 57 in order to introduce himself to the Christian community in Rome, which he planned to visit at a future date. But when Paul finally reached Rome, he came in chains, having been arrested in Jerusalem at the instigation of Jews who opposed his preaching.

The epistle to the Romans, written when Paul was still a free man, was addressed to a community primarily composed of Gentile Christians, for Jews had been forced from Rome about A.D. 49 by the Emperor Claudius and did not begin to return until after A.D. 54. Paul's letter stressed that though both Jews and Gentiles are guilty in the sight of God both are candidates for salvation through faith in Jesus Christ. The promise rests not on the law but on grace. Righteousness results not from rigid adherence to the law but from the power of grace at work in us to reconcile us to God.

The letter to the Romans reminds us to resist the temptation to embrace a legalistic version of our faith. Only grace can make us into "little Christs," the people we are called to be through the power of the Holy Spirit.

Salutation

1 Paul, a servant[a] of Jesus Christ, called to be an apostle, set apart for the gospel of God, ²which he promised beforehand through his prophets in the holy scriptures, ³the gospel concerning his Son, who was descended from David according to the flesh ⁴and was declared to be Son of God with power according to the spirit[b] of holiness by resurrection from the dead, Jesus Christ our Lord, ⁵through whom we have received grace and apostleship to bring about the obedi-ence of faith among all the Gentiles for the sake of his name, ⁶including yourselves who are called to belong to Jesus Christ,

7 To all God's beloved in Rome, who are called to be saints:

Grace to you and peace from God our Father and the Lord Jesus Christ.

Prayer of Thanksgiving

8 First, I thank my God through Jesus

a Gk slave   b Or Spirit

Christ for all of you, because your faith is proclaimed throughout the world. ⁹For God, whom I serve with my spirit by announcing the gospelᶜ of his Son, is my witness that without ceasing I remember you always in my prayers, ¹⁰asking that by God's will I may somehow at last succeed in coming to you. ¹¹For I am longing to see you so that I may share with you some spiritual gift to strengthen you— ¹²or rather so that we may be mutually encouraged by each other's faith, both yours and mine. ¹³I want you to know, brothers and sisters,ᵈ that I have often intended to come to you (but thus far have been prevented), in order that I may reap some harvest among you as I have among the rest of the Gentiles. ¹⁴I am a debtor both to Greeks and to barbarians, both to the

wise and to the foolish ¹⁵— hence my eagerness to proclaim the gospel to you also who are in Rome.

The Power of the Gospel

16 For I am not ashamed of the gospel; it is the power of God for salvation to everyone who has faith, to the Jew first and also to the Greek. ¹⁷For in it the righteousness of God is revealed through faith for faith; as it is written, "The one who is righteous will live by faith."ᵉ

The Guilt of Humankind

18 For the wrath of God is revealed from heaven against all ungodliness and

ᶜ Gk *my spirit in the gospel*   ᵈ Gk *brothers*   ᵉ Or
The one who is righteous through faith will live

Encourage Each Other

THURSDAY

Scripture Reading for Today:
Romans 1.8–12

Verses for Today:
Romans 1.11–12

The scene: Two women friends are chatting about life, love, and God. One has stayed committed to the faith and traditions of her Catholic community since the cradle. The other is a "late arrival" to the practice of her faith. Having walked away from the church for many years, she has only recently returned in response to a profound experience of conversion and reconciliation. Their conversation goes something like this:

Cradle Catholic: Your zeal for the faith is amazing. It makes me feel old and tired! The pews are full of people like me. We are so committed, but in many ways we are simply going through the motions. We have lost that fire of conversion.

Returning Catholic: Your constancy is what amazes me. Don't forget that it is only because all you "tired old Catholics" are still here that I have a church to come back to!

Cradle Catholic: Your enthusiasm is refreshing. It challenges us.

Returning Catholic: Your commitment is challenging. It is all very well to be on fire with faith, but now I have to ask myself: Can I hang in there for the long haul?

Cradle Catholic: Sometimes I feel a little envious of your newfound faith. I mean, it seems like you go off and "live it up" for twenty years and then God showers you with blessings!

Returning Catholic: But I also have to live with the things I have done. There are heartaches here which you have been spared because you chose differently.

—*TERESA PIROLA*

Go to page 1473 for your next devotional reading.

wickedness of those who by their wickedness suppress the truth. [19]For what can be known about God is plain to them, because God has shown it to them. [20]Ever since the creation of the world his eternal power and divine nature, invisible though they are, have been understood and seen through the things he has made. So they are without excuse; [21]for though they knew God, they did not honor him as God or give thanks to him, but they became futile in their thinking, and their senseless minds were darkened. [22]Claiming to be wise, they became fools; [23]and they exchanged the glory of the immortal God for images resembling a mortal human being or birds or four-footed animals or reptiles.

24 Therefore God gave them up in the lusts of their hearts to impurity, to the degrading of their bodies among themselves, [25]because they exchanged the truth about God for a lie and worshiped and served the creature rather than the Creator, who is blessed forever! Amen.

26 For this reason God gave them up to degrading passions. Their women exchanged natural intercourse for unnatural, [27]and in the same way also the men, giving up natural intercourse with women, were consumed with passion for one another. Men committed shameless acts with men and received in their own persons the due penalty for their error.

28 And since they did not see fit to acknowledge God, God gave them up to a debased mind and to things that should not be done. [29]They were filled with every kind of wickedness, evil, covetousness, malice. Full of envy, murder, strife, deceit, craftiness, they are gossips, [30]slanderers, God-haters,[f] insolent, haughty, boastful, inventors of evil, rebellious toward parents, [31]foolish, faithless, heartless, ruthless. [32]They know God's decree, that those who practice such things deserve to die—yet they not only do them but even applaud others who practice them.

The Righteous Judgment of God

2 Therefore you have no excuse, whoever you are, when you judge others; for in passing judgment on another you condemn yourself, because you, the judge, are doing the very same things. [2]You say,[g] "We know that God's judgment on those who do such things is in accordance with truth." [3]Do you imagine, whoever you are, that when you judge those who do such things and yet do them yourself, you will escape the judgment of God? [4]Or do you despise the riches of his kindness and forbearance and patience? Do you not realize that God's kindness is meant to lead you to repentance? [5]But by your hard and impenitent heart you are storing up wrath for yourself on the day of wrath, when God's righteous judgment will be revealed. [6]For he will repay according to each one's deeds: [7]to those who by patiently doing good seek for glory and honor and immortality, he will give eternal life; [8]while for those who are self-seeking and who obey not the truth but wickedness, there will be wrath and fury. [9]There will be anguish and distress for everyone who does evil, the Jew first and also the Greek, [10]but glory and honor and peace for everyone who does good, the Jew first and also the Greek. [11]For God shows no partiality.

12 All who have sinned apart from the law will also perish apart from the law, and all who have sinned under the law will be judged by the law. [13]For it is not the hearers of the law who are righteous in God's sight, but the doers of the law who will be justified. [14]When Gentiles, who do not possess the law, do instinctively what the law requires, these, though not having the law, are a law to themselves. [15]They show that what the law requires is written on their hearts, to which their own conscience also bears witness; and their conflicting thoughts will accuse or perhaps excuse them [16]on the day when, according to my gospel, God, through Jesus Christ, will judge the secret thoughts of all.

The Jews and the Law

17 But if you call yourself a Jew and rely on the law and boast of your relation to God [18]and know his will and determine what is best because you are instructed in the law, [19]and if you are sure that you are a guide to the blind, a light to those who are in darkness, [20]a corrector of the foolish, a teacher of children, having in the law the embodiment of knowledge and truth, [21]you, then, that teach others, will you not teach yourself? While you preach against stealing, do you steal? [22]You that forbid adultery, do you com-

[f] Or God-hated   [g] Gk lacks You say

mit adultery? You that abhor idols, do you rob temples? 23You that boast in the law, do you dishonor God by breaking the law? 24For, as it is written, "The name of God is blasphemed among the Gentiles because of you."

25 Circumcision indeed is of value if you obey the law; but if you break the law, your circumcision has become uncircumcision. 26So, if those who are uncircumcised keep the requirements of the law, will not their uncircumcision be regarded as circumcision? 27Then those who are physically uncircumcised but keep the law will condemn you that have the written code and circumcision but break the law. 28For a person is not a Jew who is one outwardly, nor is true circumcision something external and physical. 29Rather, a person is a Jew who is one inwardly, and real circumcision is a matter of the heart—it is spiritual and not literal. Such a person receives praise not from others but from God.

3 Then what advantage has the Jew? Or what is the value of circumcision? 2Much, in every way. For in the first place the Jews*h* were entrusted with the oracles of God. 3What if some were unfaithful? Will their faithlessness nullify the faithful-

ness of God? 4By no means! Although everyone is a liar, let God be proved true, as it is written,

"So that you may be justified in
        your words,
    and prevail in your judging."*i*

5But if our injustice serves to confirm the justice of God, what should we say? That God is unjust to inflict wrath on us? (I speak in a human way.) 6By no means! For then how could God judge the world? 7But if through my falsehood God's truthfulness abounds to his glory, why am I still being condemned as a sinner? 8And why not say (as some people slander us by saying that we say), "Let us do evil so that good may come"? Their condemnation is deserved!

None Is Righteous

9 What then? Are we any better off?*j* No, not at all; for we have already charged that all, both Jews and Greeks, are under the power of sin, 10as it is written:

"There is no one who is righteous,
        not even one;

h Gk *they*   *i* Gk *when you are being judged*   *j* Or *at any disadvantage?*

FRIDAY

Scripture Reading
for Today:
Romans 3.9–20

Verses for Today:
Romans 3.11–12

*W*e All Fall Short

The soul which would remain in peace when another's sin comes to mind must fly as from the pains of hell, asking for God's protection and help.

Looking at another's sin clouds the eye of the soul, hiding for the time being the fair beauty of God—unless we look upon this sinner with contrition with him, compassion on him, and a holy longing to God for him. Otherwise it must harm and disquiet and hinder the soul that looks on these sins.

He who is highest and closest to God may see himself—and needs to do so—as a sinner like me; and I who am the least and lowest who shall be saved may be comforted with him who is the highest.

I saw that all compassion to one's fellow-Christians, exercised in love, is a mark of Christ's indwelling.

—*JULIAN OF NORWICH*

Go to page 1476 for your next devotional reading.

11   there is no one who has
         understanding,
      there is no one who seeks God.
12 All have turned aside, together they
         have become worthless;
      there is no one who shows
         kindness,
      there is not even one."
13 "Their throats are opened graves;
      they use their tongues to deceive."
      "The venom of vipers is under
         their lips."
14   "Their mouths are full of cursing
         and bitterness."
15 "Their feet are swift to shed blood;
16   ruin and misery are in their paths,
17 and the way of peace they have
         not known."
18   "There is no fear of God before
         their eyes."

19 Now we know that whatever the law says, it speaks to those who are under the law, so that every mouth may be silenced, and the whole world may be held accountable to God. 20For "no human being will be justified in his sight" by deeds prescribed by the law, for through the law comes the knowledge of sin.

Righteousness through Faith

21 But now, apart from law, the righteousness of God has been disclosed, and is attested by the law and the prophets, 22the righteousness of God through faith in Jesus Christ[k] for all who believe. For there is no distinction, 23since all have sinned and fall short of the glory of God; 24they are now justified by his grace as a gift, through the redemption that is in Christ Jesus, 25whom God put forward as a sacrifice of atonement[l] by his blood, effective through faith. He did this to show his righteousness, because in his divine forbearance he had passed over the sins previously committed; 26it was to prove at the present time that he himself is righteous and that he justifies the one who has faith in Jesus.[m]

27 Then what becomes of boasting? It is excluded. By what law? By that of works? No, but by the law of faith. 28For we hold that a person is justified by faith apart from works prescribed by the law. 29Or is God the God of Jews only? Is he not the God of Gentiles also? Yes, of Gentiles also, 30since God is one; and he will justify the circumcised on the ground of faith and the uncircumcised through that

same faith. 31Do we then overthrow the law by this faith? By no means! On the contrary, we uphold the law.

The Example of Abraham

4 What then are we to say was gained by[n] Abraham, our ancestor according to the flesh? 2For if Abraham was justified by works, he has something to boast about, but not before God. 3For what does the scripture say? "Abraham believed God, and it was reckoned to him as righteousness." 4Now to one who works, wages are not reckoned as a gift but as something due. 5But to one who without works trusts him who justifies the ungodly, such faith is reckoned as righteousness. 6So also David speaks of the blessedness of those to whom God reckons righteousness apart from works:

7   "Blessed are those whose iniquities
         are forgiven,
      and whose sins are covered;
8   blessed is the one against whom
         Lord will not reckon sin."

9 Is this blessedness, then, pronounced only on the circumcised, or also on the uncircumcised? We say, "Faith was reckoned to Abraham as righteousness." 10How then was it reckoned to him? Was it before or after he had been circumcised? It was not after, but before he was circumcised. 11He received the sign of circumcision as a seal of the righteousness that he had by faith while he was still uncircumcised. The purpose was to make him the ancestor of all who believe without being circumcised and who thus have righteousness reckoned to them, 12and likewise the ancestor of the circumcised who are not only circumcised but who also follow the example of the faith that our ancestor Abraham had before he was circumcised.

God's Promise Realized through Faith

13 For the promise that he would inherit the world did not come to Abraham or to his descendants through the law but through the righteousness of faith. 14If it is the adherents of the law who are to be the heirs, faith is null and the promise is void. 15For the law brings wrath; but

---

k Or through the faith of Jesus Christ   l Or a place of atonement   m Or who has the faith of Jesus   n Other ancient authorities read say about

where there is no law, neither is there violation.

16 For this reason it depends on faith, in order that the promise may rest on grace and be guaranteed to all his descendants, not only to the adherents of the law but also to those who share the faith of Abraham (for he is the father of all of us, [17]as it is written, "I have made you the father of many nations")—in the presence of the God in whom he believed, who gives life to the dead and calls into existence the things that do not exist. [18]Hoping against hope, he believed that he would become "the father of many nations," according to what was said, "So numerous shall your descendants be." [19]He did not weaken in faith when he considered his own body, which was already[o] as good as dead (for he was about a hundred years old), or when he considered the barrenness of Sarah's womb. [20]No distrust made him waver concerning the promise of God, but he grew strong in his faith as he gave glory to God, [21]being fully convinced that God was able to do what he had promised. [22]Therefore his faith[p] "was reckoned to him as righteousness." [23]Now the words, "it was reckoned to him," were written not for his sake alone, [24]but for ours also. It will be reckoned to us who believe in him who raised Jesus our Lord from the dead, [25]who was handed over to death for our trespasses and was raised for our justification.

Results of Justification

5 Therefore, since we are justified by faith, we[q] have peace with God through our Lord Jesus Christ, [2]through whom we have obtained access[r] to this grace in which we stand; and we[s] boast in our hope of sharing the glory of God. [3]And not only that, but we[s] also boast in our sufferings, knowing that suffering produces endurance, [4]and endurance produces character, and character produces hope, [5]and hope does not disappoint us, because God's love has been poured into our hearts through the Holy Spirit that has been given to us.

6 For while we were still weak, at the right time Christ died for the ungodly. [7]Indeed, rarely will anyone die for a righteous person—though perhaps for a good person someone might actually dare to die. [8]But God proves his love for us in that while we still were sinners Christ died for

us. [9]Much more surely then, now that we have been justified by his blood, will we be saved through him from the wrath of God.[t] [10]For if while we were enemies, we were reconciled to God through the death of his Son, much more surely, having been reconciled, will we be saved by his life. [11]But more than that, we even boast in God through our Lord Jesus Christ, through whom we have now received reconciliation.

Adam and Christ

12 Therefore, just as sin came into the world through one man, and death came through sin, and so death spread to all because all have sinned— [13]sin was indeed in the world before the law, but sin is not reckoned when there is no law. [14]Yet death exercised dominion from Adam to Moses, even over those whose sins were not like the transgression of Adam, who is a type of the one who was to come.

15 But the free gift is not like the trespass. For if the many died through the one man's trespass, much more surely have the grace of God and the free gift in the grace of the one man, Jesus Christ, abounded for the many. [16]And the free gift is not like the effect of the one man's sin. For the judgment following one trespass brought condemnation, but the free gift following many trespasses brings justification. [17]If, because of the one man's trespass, death exercised dominion through that one, much more surely will those who receive the abundance of grace and the free gift of righteousness exercise dominion in life through the one man, Jesus Christ.

18 Therefore just as one man's trespass led to condemnation for all, so one man's act of righteousness leads to justification and life for all. [19]For just as by the one man's disobedience the many were made sinners, so by the one man's obedience the many will be made righteous. [20]But law came in, with the result that the trespass multiplied; but where sin increased, grace abounded all the more, [21]so that, just as sin exercised dominion in death, so grace might also exercise dominion

Anna

*Her Name Means "Favor" or
"Grace"*

Her Character: *Married for only seven years, she spent the long years of her widowhood fasting and praying in the temple, abandoning herself entirely to God. A prophetess, she was one of the first people to bear witness to Jesus.*
Her Sorrow: *As a widow, she would probably have been among the most vulnerable members of society.*
Her Joy: *That her own eyes beheld the Messiah she had longed to see.*

Read Luke 2.22–38

A small bird darted past the Court of the Gentiles, flew up to the Court of the Women and then on to the Court of Israel (one of the inner courts of the temple, accessible only to Jewish men). Anna blinked as she watched the beating wings swerve into the sunlight and vanish. She wondered into which privileged corner the little bird had disappeared.

For most of her 84 years, she had been a widow who spent her days praying and fasting in the temple. Though she could not echo the prayer of Jewish men, who praised God for creating them neither Gentiles nor women, she could at least be grateful for the privilege of ascending beyond the Court of the Gentiles to the Court of the Women, where she would be that much closer to the Most Holy Place. Having done so, she bowed her head, rocking back and forth to the rhythm of her prayers:

How lovely is your dwelling place,
  O LORD of hosts! . . .
Even the sparrow finds a home,
  and the swallow a nest for herself,
  where she may lay her young,
at your altars, O LORD of hosts,
  my King and my God.

(Psalm 84.1, 3)

Suddenly a voice interrupted her recitation of the familiar psalm. Old Simeon, she saw, was holding a baby to his breast, shouting out words that thrilled her soul: "Master, now you are dismissing your servant in peace, according to your word; for my eyes have seen your salvation, which you have prepared in the presence of all peoples, a light for revelation to the Gentiles and for glory to your people Israel" (Luke 2.29–32).

Like her, Simeon had lived for nothing but Israel's consolation. Though he had not seen, yet he had hoped. Anna watched as the child's parents hung on the old man's words. Then he handed the infant back to his mother, this time speaking more softly: "This child is destined for the falling and the rising of many in Israel, and to be a sign that will be opposed so that the inner thoughts of many will be revealed—and a sword will pierce your own soul too" (verses 34–35).

Anna placed her arm gently around the young mother's shoulders and gazed at the sleeping infant. Words of thanksgiving spilled from her lips. Her heart felt buoyant, her hope unsinkable. A widow and prophetess from one of the least tribes in Israel had seen the salvation of her God.

Now she, too, felt like a sparrow soaring freely in the house of God. It did not matter that she was forbidden entry into the innermost courts of the temple. God himself was breaking down the dividing walls between Jew and Gentile, male and female, revealing himself to all who hungered for his presence.

That day a child had transformed the Court of the Women into the holiest place of all. More vividly than Jacob, who had dreamed of a ladder full of angels, or Moses, who had beheld a bush burning in the desert, Anna had experienced the very presence of God.

Praying With Anna

She never left the temple but worshiped there with fasting and prayer night and day.—Luke 2.37

Praise God: For men and women who hunger and thirst for God's kingdom.

Offer Thanks: That Jesus is the true bread from heaven, who satisfies the hungry heart.

Confess: Any complacency in your relationship with God.

Ask God: To increase your hunger for his kingdom.

Lift Your Heart

Anna did more than merely long for the coming Messiah. She prayed and fasted daily for the coming of God's kingdom. Even though Christianity has now spread across the globe, there are still many people who suffer from war and injustice, many who have little or nothing to eat, and many more who live in spiritual darkness. This week, stretch yourself beyond your immediate concerns. Look at an atlas, a map, or a globe, and choose a country for which to pray. Read newspaper reports and magazine articles that will help you understand what is going on in that nation. Fast and pray for peace, for daily bread, for freedom and justice, and for Christ's light to shine upon that people.

Jesus, I long for your light to spread across the whole earth so that people from every land will know you. Today, give me a burden for another nation or ethnic group that knows little of you. Show me how to pray in a way that builds your kingdom.

Go to page 1481 for your next devotional reading.

through justification[u] leading to eternal life through Jesus Christ our Lord.

Dying and Rising with Christ

6 What then are we to say? Should we continue in sin in order that grace may abound? ²By no means! How can we who died to sin go on living in it? ³Do you not know that all of us who have been baptized into Christ Jesus were baptized into his death? ⁴Therefore we have been buried with him by baptism into death, so that, just as Christ was raised from the dead by the glory of the Father, so we too might walk in newness of life.

5 For if we have been united with him in a death like his, we will certainly be united with him in a resurrection like his. ⁶We know that our old self was crucified with him so that the body of sin might be destroyed, and we might no longer be enslaved to sin. ⁷For whoever has died is freed from sin. ⁸But if we have died with Christ, we believe that we will also live with him. ⁹We know that Christ, being raised from the dead, will never die again; death no longer has dominion over him. ¹⁰The death he died, he died to sin, once

[u] Or *righteousness*

THE TRADITION

Original Sin

Therefore, just as sin came into the world through one man, and death came through sin, and so death spread to all because all have sinned . . .

ROMANS 5.12

"The only original thing about me is original sin," a young man said of himself.

He must not have been a Catholic.

Catholics may be fuzzy on some aspects of the doctrine, but one thing we do know: Original sin colors every aspect of our lives. We see its pervasiveness in every newspaper, where the occasional report of human goodness is swallowed up in stories of violence, depravity, and pettiness.

Original sin explains the human condition. It is the plight of fallen human beings who aspire to high ideals but are drawn toward sin. "For I do not do the good I want, but the evil I do not want is what I do" (Romans 7.19) is Saint Paul's classic description of this anguished state.

In symbolic language, Genesis 3 presents Adam and Eve's prideful rebellion as the historical event through which original sin entered the world. Their disobedience disrupted God's loving plan, bringing on unparalleled catastrophe and leaving us an oppressive legacy of death, suffering, corrupted human

nature, and alienation from God. We struggle against its effects all our lives.

Unlike our individual acts of personal disobedience, this sin is an inherited state. We receive it from our origins (hence the name "original") in a real but mysterious way.

As theologian Edward O'Connor observes, original sin fits perfectly with another mysterious, fundamental law of humanity: solidarity. In countless ways we are affected by the actions of parents and ancestors, teachers, leaders, neighbors, and even total unknowns in Teheran, Moscow, and Hanoi. Therefore, "it is not arbitrarily, but in accord with the deepest truth of our nature that God treats us in solidarity with one another."

Thanks to that same solidarity, Father O'Connor points out: "We can all be redeemed by the sacrificial death of Jesus, and formed into one body by his Spirit."

In Jesus the solidarity of original sin becomes the holy solidarity of the body of Christ.

for all; but the life he lives, he lives to God. ¹¹So you also must consider yourselves dead to sin and alive to God in Christ Jesus.

12 Therefore, do not let sin exercise dominion in your mortal bodies, to make you obey their passions. ¹³No longer present your members to sin as instruments[v] of wickedness, but present yourselves to God as those who have been brought from death to life, and present your members to God as instruments[v] of righteousness. ¹⁴For sin will have no dominion over you, since you are not under law but under grace.

Slaves of Righteousness

15 What then? Should we sin because we are not under law but under grace? By no means! ¹⁶Do you not know that if you present yourselves to anyone as obedient slaves, you are slaves of the one whom you obey, either of sin, which leads to death, or of obedience, which leads to righteousness? ¹⁷But thanks be to God that you, having once been slaves of sin, have become obedient from the heart to the form of teaching to which you were entrusted, ¹⁸and that you, having been set free from sin, have become slaves of righteousness. ¹⁹I am speaking in human terms because of your natural limitations.[w] For just as you once presented your members as slaves to impurity and to greater and greater iniquity, so now present your members as slaves to righteousness for sanctification.

20 When you were slaves of sin, you were free in regard to righteousness. ²¹So what advantage did you then get from the things of which you now are ashamed? The end of those things is death. ²²But now that you have been freed from sin and enslaved to God, the advantage you get is sanctification. The end is eternal life. ²³For the wages of sin is death, but the free gift of God is eternal life in Christ Jesus our Lord.

An Analogy from Marriage

7 Do you not know, brothers and sisters[x]—for I am speaking to those who know the law—that the law is binding on a person only during that person's lifetime? ²Thus a married woman is bound by the law to her husband as long as he lives; but if her husband dies, she is discharged from the law concerning the husband. ³Accordingly, she will be called an adulteress if she lives with another man while her husband is alive. But if her husband dies, she is free from that law, and if she marries another man, she is not an adulteress.

4 In the same way, my friends,[x] you have died to the law through the body of Christ, so that you may belong to another, to him who has been raised from the dead in order that we may bear fruit for God. ⁵While we were living in the flesh, our sinful passions, aroused by the law, were at work in our members to bear fruit for death. ⁶But now we are discharged from the law, dead to that which held us captive, so that we are slaves not under the old written code but in the new life of the Spirit.

The Law and Sin

7 What then should we say? That the law is sin? By no means! Yet, if it had not been for the law, I would not have known sin. I would not have known what it is to covet if the law had not said, "You shall not covet." ⁸But sin, seizing an opportunity in the commandment, produced in me all kinds of covetousness. Apart from the law sin lies dead. ⁹I was once alive apart from the law, but when the commandment came, sin revived ¹⁰and I died, and the very commandment that promised life proved to be death to me. ¹¹For sin, seizing an opportunity in the commandment, deceived me and through it killed me. ¹²So the law is holy, and the commandment is holy and just and good.

13 Did what is good, then, bring death to me? By no means! It was sin, working death in me through what is good, in order that sin might be shown to be sin, and through the commandment might become sinful beyond measure.

The Inner Conflict

14 For we know that the law is spiritual; but I am of the flesh, sold into slavery under sin.[y] ¹⁵I do not understand my own actions. For I do not do what I want, but I do the very thing I hate. ¹⁶Now if I do what I do not want, I agree that the law is good. ¹⁷But in fact it is no longer I that do it, but sin that dwells within me. ¹⁸For I know that nothing good dwells within

v Or weapons   w Gk the weakness of your flesh
x Gk brothers   y Gk sold under sin

me, that is, in my flesh. I can will what is right, but I cannot do it. [19]For I do not do the good I want, but the evil I do not want is what I do. [20]Now if I do what I do not want, it is no longer I that do it, but sin that dwells within me.

21 So I find it to be a law that when I want to do what is good, evil lies close at hand. [22]For I delight in the law of God in my inmost self, [23]but I see in my members another law at war with the law of my mind, making me captive to the law of sin that dwells in my members. [24]Wretched man that I am! Who will rescue me from this body of death? [25]Thanks be to God through Jesus Christ our Lord!

So then, with my mind I am a slave to the law of God, but with my flesh I am a slave to the law of sin.

Life in the Spirit

8 There is therefore now no condemnation for those who are in Christ Jesus. [2]For the law of the Spirit[z] of life in Christ Jesus has set you[a] free from the law of sin and of death. [3]For God has done what the law, weakened by the flesh, could not do: by sending his own Son in the likeness of sinful flesh, and to deal with sin,[b] he condemned sin in the flesh, [4]so that the just requirement of the law might be fulfilled in us, who walk not according to the flesh but according to the Spirit.[z] [5]For those who live according to the flesh set their minds on the things of the flesh, but those who live according to the Spirit[z] set their minds on the things of the Spirit.[z] [6]To set the mind on the flesh is death, but to set the mind on the Spirit[z] is life and peace. [7]For this reason the mind that is set on the flesh is hostile to God; it does not submit to God's law—indeed it cannot, [8]and those who are in the flesh cannot please God.

9 But you are not in the flesh; you are in the Spirit,[z] since the Spirit of God dwells in you. Anyone who does not have the Spirit of Christ does not belong to him. [10]But if Christ is in you, though the body is dead because of sin, the Spirit[z] is life because of righteousness. [11]If the Spirit of him who raised Jesus from the dead dwells in you, he who raised Christ[c] from the dead will give life to your mortal bodies also through[d] his Spirit that dwells in you.

12 So then, brothers and sisters,[e] we are debtors, not to the flesh, to live ac-

cording to the flesh— [13]for if you live according to the flesh, you will die; but if by the Spirit you put to death the deeds of the body, you will live. [14]For all who are led by the Spirit of God are children of God. [15]For you did not receive a spirit of slavery to fall back into fear, but you have received a spirit of adoption. When we cry, "Abba![f] Father!" [16]it is that very Spirit bearing witness[g] with our spirit that we are children of God, [17]and if children, then heirs, heirs of God and joint heirs with Christ—if, in fact, we suffer with him so that we may also be glorified with him.

Future Glory

18 I consider that the sufferings of this present time are not worth comparing with the glory about to be revealed to us. [19]For the creation waits with eager longing for the revealing of the children of God; [20]for the creation was subjected to futility, not of its own will but by the will of the one who subjected it, in hope [21]that the creation itself will be set free from its bondage to decay and will obtain the freedom of the glory of the children of God. [22]We know that the whole creation has been groaning in labor pains until now; [23]and not only the creation, but we ourselves, who have the first fruits of the Spirit, groan inwardly while we wait for adoption, the redemption of our bodies. [24]For in[h] hope we were saved. Now hope that is seen is not hope. For who hopes[i] for what is seen? [25]But if we hope for what we do not see, we wait for it with patience.

26 Likewise the Spirit helps us in our weakness; for we do not know how to pray as we ought, but that very Spirit intercedes[j] with sighs too deep for words. [27]And God,[k] who searches the heart, knows what is the mind of the Spirit, because the Spirit[l] intercedes for the saints according to the will of God.[m]

28 We know that all things work to-

[z] Or *spirit*   [a] Here the Greek word *you* is singular number; other ancient authorities read *me* or *us*   [b] Or *and as a sin offering*   [c] Other ancient authorities read *the Christ* or *Christ Jesus* or *Jesus Christ*   [d] Other ancient authorities read *on account of*   [e] Gk *brothers*   [f] Aramaic for *Father*   [g] Or [15]*a spirit of adoption, by which we cry, "Abba! Father!"*   [16]*The Spirit itself bears witness*   [h] Or *by*   [i] Other ancient authorities read *awaits*   [j] Other ancient authorities add *for us*   [k] Gk *the one*   [l] Gk *he or it*   [m] Gk *according to God*

gether for good[n] for those who love God, who are called according to his purpose. [29]For those whom he foreknew he also predestined to be conformed to the image of his Son, in order that he might be the firstborn within a large family.[o] [30]And those whom he predestined he also called; and those whom he called he also justified; and those whom he justified he also glorified.

God's Love in Christ Jesus

31 What then are we to say about these things? If God is for us, who is against us? [32]He who did not withhold his own Son, but gave him up for all of us, will he not with him also give us everything else? [33]Who will bring any charge against God's elect? It is God who justifies. [34]Who is to condemn? It is Christ Jesus, who died, yes, who was raised, who is at the right hand of God, who indeed intercedes for us.[p] [35]Who will separate us from the love of Christ? Will hardship, or distress, or persecution, or famine, or nakedness, or peril, or sword? [36]As it is written,

"For your sake we are being killed
      all day long;
    we are accounted as sheep to be
      slaughtered."

[37]No, in all these things we are more than conquerors through him who loved us. [38]For I am convinced that neither death, nor life, nor angels, nor rulers, nor things present, nor things to come, nor powers, [39]nor height, nor depth, nor anything else in all creation, will be able to separate us

---

n Other ancient authorities read *God makes all things work together for good*, or *in all things God works for good*   o Gk *among many brothers*   p Or *Is it Christ Jesus . . . for us?*

MONDAY

Scripture Reading for Today:
Romans 8.28–39

Verse for Today:
Romans 8.28

God Uses Everything

I looked out at the sea of faces, all enrolled in a parish ministry course, and there was Nina. Nina's face, normally so bright and vivacious, told a story of grief. Her baby had died; it was her second miscarriage. A beautiful chapter of life had turned into a nightmare, and Nina was living it, even now, as the group talked about the power of our dreams to make a difference to the mission of the church. My heart sank. *Where are Nina's dreams now?* I thought. How can we speak of power and hope when this woman is facing such debilitating pain?

Yet the Spirit touched Nina in her grief. Within ten weeks she had created a ministry of healing for her own fellow parishioners. Her plan had been simple and straightforward, drawing upon the loving support of her husband and empowered by that rare depth of insight that comes through suffering.

She had gathered some women in the parish who, known to only a few, had also endured a miscarriage. They came together to share one another's silent grief, to pray together and to receive some practical input from a trained counselor whom Nina had contacted through a local church agency.

Nina taught us all something very special about putting our lives at the service of God's kingdom, no matter how impoverished we may feel. With what she had, Nina gave.

—*TERESA PIROLA*

Go to page 1486 for your next devotional reading.

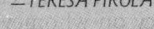

from the love of God in Christ Jesus our Lord.

God's Election of Israel

9 I am speaking the truth in Christ—I am not lying; my conscience confirms it by the Holy Spirit— 2I have great sorrow and unceasing anguish in my heart. 3For I could wish that I myself were accursed and cut off from Christ for the sake of my own people,q my kindred according to the flesh. 4They are Israelites, and to them belong the adoption, the glory, the covenants, the giving of the law, the worship, and the promises; 5to them belong the patriarchs, and from them, according to the flesh, comes the Messiah,r who is over all, God blessed forever.s Amen.

6 It is not as though the word of God had failed. For not all Israelites truly belong to Israel, 7and not all of Abraham's children are his true descendants; but "It is through Isaac that descendants shall be named for you." 8This means that it is not the children of the flesh who are the children of God, but the children of the promise are counted as descendants. 9For this is what the promise said, "About this time I will return and Sarah shall have a son." 10Nor is that all; something similar happened to Rebecca when she had conceived children by one husband, our ancestor Isaac. 11Even before they had been born or had done anything good or bad (so that God's purpose of election might continue, 12not by works but by his call) she was told, "The elder shall serve the younger." 13As it is written,

"I have loved Jacob,
   but I have hated Esau."

14 What then are we to say? Is there injustice on God's part? By no means! 15For he says to Moses,

"I will have mercy on whom I
   have mercy,
and I will have compassion on
   whom I have compassion."

16So it depends not on human will or exertion, but on God who shows mercy. 17For the scripture says to Pharaoh, "I have raised you up for the very purpose of showing my power in you, so that my name may be proclaimed in all the earth." 18So then he has mercy on whomever he chooses, and he hardens the heart of whomever he chooses.

God's Wrath and Mercy

19 You will say to me then, "Why then does he still find fault? For who can resist his will?" 20But who indeed are you, a human being, to argue with God? Will what is molded say to the one who molds it, "Why have you made me like this?" 21Has the potter no right over the clay, to make out of the same lump one object for special use and another for ordinary use? 22What if God, desiring to show his wrath and to make known his power, has endured with much patience the objects of wrath that are made for destruction; 23and what if he has done so in order to make known the riches of his glory for the objects of mercy, which he has prepared beforehand for glory— 24including us whom he has called, not from the Jews only but also from the Gentiles? 25As indeed he says in Hosea,

"Those who were not my people I
   will call 'my people,'
and her who was not beloved I
   will call 'beloved.' "
26 "And in the very place where it was
      said to them, 'You are not
      my people,'
   there they shall be called children
      of the living God."

27 And Isaiah cries out concerning Israel, "Though the number of the children of Israel were like the sand of the sea, only a remnant of them will be saved; 28for the Lord will execute his sentence on the earth quickly and decisively."t 29And as Isaiah predicted,

"If the Lord of hosts had not left
      survivorsu to us,
   we would have fared like Sodom
      and been made like Gomorrah."

Israel's Unbelief

30 What then are we to say? Gentiles, who did not strive for righteousness, have attained it, that is, righteousness through faith; 31but Israel, who did strive for the righteousness that is based on the law, did not succeed in fulfilling that law. 32Why not? Because they did not strive for it on

q Gk my brothers   r Or the Christ   s Or Messiah, who is God over all, blessed forever; or Messiah. May he who is God over all be blessed forever   t Other ancient authorities read for he will finish his work and cut it short in righteousness, because the Lord will make the sentence shortened on the earth   u Or descendants; Gk seed

the basis of faith, but as if it were based on works. They have stumbled over the stumbling stone, 33 as it is written,

"See, I am laying in Zion a stone
  that will make people
  stumble, a rock that will
  make them fall,
and whoever believes in him*v*
  will not be put to shame."

10 Brothers and sisters,*w* my heart's desire and prayer to God for them is that they may be saved. 2 I can testify that they have a zeal for God, but it is not enlightened. 3 For, being ignorant of the righteousness that comes from God, and seeking to establish their own, they have not submitted to God's righteousness. 4 For Christ is the end of the law so that there may be righteousness for everyone who believes.

Salvation Is for All

5 Moses writes concerning the righteousness that comes from the law, that "the person who does these things will live by them." 6 But the righteousness that comes from faith says, "Do not say in your heart, 'Who will ascend into heaven?' " (that is, to bring Christ down) 7 "or 'Who will descend into the abyss?' " (that is, to bring Christ up from the dead). 8 But what does it say?

"The word is near you,
  on your lips and in your heart"
(that is, the word of faith that we proclaim); 9 because*x* if you confess with your lips that Jesus is Lord and believe in your heart that God raised him from the dead, you will be saved. 10 For one believes with the heart and so is justified, and one confesses with the mouth and so is saved. 11 The scripture says, "No one who believes in him will be put to shame." 12 For there is no distinction between Jew and Greek; the same Lord is Lord of all and is generous to all who call on him. 13 For, "Everyone who calls on the name of the Lord shall be saved."

14 But how are they to call on one in whom they have not believed? And how are they to believe in one of whom they have never heard? And how are they to hear without someone to proclaim him? 15 And how are they to proclaim him unless they are sent? As it is written, "How beautiful are the feet of those who bring good news!" 16 But not all have obeyed the good news;*y* for Isaiah says, "Lord, who has believed our message?" 17 So faith comes from what is heard, and what is heard comes through the word of Christ.*z*

18 But I ask, have they not heard? Indeed they have; for

"Their voice has gone out to all
  the earth,
and their words to the ends of the
  world."

19 Again I ask, did Israel not understand? First Moses says,

"I will make you jealous of those
  who are not a nation;
with a foolish nation I will make
  you angry."

20 Then Isaiah is so bold as to say,

"I have been found by those who
  did not seek me;
I have shown myself to those who
  did not ask for me."

21 But of Israel he says, "All day long I have held out my hands to a disobedient and contrary people."

Israel's Rejection Is Not Final

11 I ask, then, has God rejected his people? By no means! I myself am an Israelite, a descendant of Abraham, a member of the tribe of Benjamin. 2 God has not rejected his people whom he foreknew. Do you not know what the scripture says of Elijah, how he pleads with God against Israel? 3 "Lord, they have killed your prophets, they have demolished your altars; I alone am left, and they are seeking my life." 4 But what is the divine reply to him? "I have kept for myself seven thousand who have not bowed the knee to Baal." 5 So too at the present time there is a remnant, chosen by grace. 6 But if it is by grace, it is no longer on the basis of works, otherwise grace would no longer be grace.*a*

7 What then? Israel failed to obtain what it was seeking. The elect obtained it, but the rest were hardened, 8 as it is written,

"God gave them a sluggish spirit,
  eyes that would not see

---

v Or *trusts in it*   *w* Gk *Brothers*   *x* Or *namely, that*   *y* Or *gospel*   *z* Or *about Christ;* other ancient authorities read *of God*   *a* Other ancient authorities add *But if it is by works, it is no longer on the basis of grace, otherwise work would no longer be work*

and ears that would not hear,
 down to this very day."
⁹And David says,
 "Let their table become a snare
 and a trap,
 a stumbling block and a
 retribution for them;
¹⁰ let their eyes be darkened so that
 they cannot see,
 and keep their backs forever bent."

The Salvation of the Gentiles

11 So I ask, have they stumbled so as to fall? By no means! But through their stumbling*ᵇ* salvation has come to the Gentiles, so as to make Israel*ᶜ* jealous. ¹²Now if their stumbling*ᵇ* means riches for the world, and if their defeat means riches for Gentiles, how much more will their full inclusion mean!

13 Now I am speaking to you Gentiles. Inasmuch then as I am an apostle to the Gentiles, I glorify my ministry ¹⁴in order to make my own people*ᵈ* jealous, and thus save some of them. ¹⁵For if their rejection is the reconciliation of the world, what will their acceptance be but life from the dead! ¹⁶If the part of the dough of-

ᵇ Gk transgression   *ᶜ Gk them*   *ᵈ Gk my flesh*

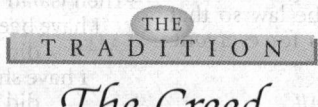

THE TRADITION

The Creed

*If you confess with your lips that Jesus is Lord
and believe in your heart that God raised him from the dead,
you will be saved.*
ROMANS 10.9

Most of us have participated in non-liturgical occasions where people give formal, public expression to something they believe and want to live by. For example, we pledge allegiance to the flag and sing the national anthem. If we belong to the Girl Scouts, Alcoholics Anonymous, or other organizations, we may recite pledges and promises.

Standing up in church to recite the Creed resembles such occasions but is, at heart, radically different from them. When we profess our faith, we are not just giving a mental "yes" to a set of noble ideas and ideals. The Creed summarizes truths that are rooted in history's most important events, the saving acts of God. *Credo.* "I believe." The early Christians summed up the basic article of belief in the watchword, "Jesus is Lord." Gradually they elaborated on it, gathering the essential elements of faith into longer summaries such as the Apostles' Creed (used with the rosary) and the Nicene Creed (said at Sunday Mass).

The Church's creeds, wrote the British author Dorothy Sayers, are "amazing documents" that summarize "the most exciting drama that ever staggered the imagination." Why, then, do so many of us recite them as if in a pious coma? Perhaps, as Sayers suggests, we have not really examined them or have said them too mechanically.

"Dull dogma" comes to life when you see it as your entree into the great ongoing drama of salvation. You hear the gospel and "confess with your lips that Jesus is Lord." But as Saint Paul goes on to explain, saying *credo* involves more than an external expression of faith. You must also "believe in your heart" (Romans 10.9). In other words, to profess the Creed is to express agreement with its truths by committing yourself wholeheartedly to God.

I believe that Jesus is Lord—Lord of the universe, Lord of my life. I believe that he rose from the dead, and that he will raise me up too. I believe that he is at work among his people. Yes, Lord, I believe!

fered as first fruits is holy, then the whole batch is holy; and if the root is holy, then the branches also are holy.

17 But if some of the branches were broken off, and you, a wild olive shoot, were grafted in their place to share the rich root[e] of the olive tree, 18do not boast over the branches. If you do boast, remember that it is not you that support the root, but the root that supports you. 19You will say, "Branches were broken off so that I might be grafted in." 20That is true. They were broken off because of their unbelief, but you stand only through faith. So do not become proud, but stand in awe. 21For if God did not spare the natural branches, perhaps he will not spare you.[f] 22Note then the kindness and the severity of God: severity toward those who have fallen, but God's kindness toward you, provided you continue in his kindness; otherwise you also will be cut off. 23And even those of Israel,[g] if they do not persist in unbelief, will be grafted in, for God has the power to graft them in again. 24For if you have been cut from what is by nature a wild olive tree and grafted, contrary to nature, into a cultivated olive tree, how much more will these natural branches be grafted back into their own olive tree.

All Israel Will Be Saved

25 So that you may not claim to be wiser than you are, brothers and sisters,[h] I want you to understand this mystery: a hardening has come upon part of Israel, until the full number of the Gentiles has come in. 26And so all Israel will be saved; as it is written,

"Out of Zion will come the
     Deliverer;
   he will banish ungodliness
     from Jacob."
27 "And this is my covenant
     with them,
   when I take away their sins."
28As regards the gospel they are enemies of God[i] for your sake; but as regards election they are beloved, for the sake of their ancestors; 29for the gifts and the calling of God are irrevocable. 30Just as you were once disobedient to God but have now received mercy because of their disobedience, 31so they have now been disobedient in order that, by the mercy shown to you, they too may now[j] receive mercy. 32For God has imprisoned all in

disobedience so that he may be merciful to all.

33 O the depth of the riches and wisdom and knowledge of God! How unsearchable are his judgments and how inscrutable his ways!
34 "For who has known the mind of
       the Lord?
   Or who has been his counselor?"
35 "Or who has given a gift to him,
     to receive a gift in return?"
36For from him and through him and to him are all things. To him be the glory forever. Amen.

The New Life in Christ

12 I appeal to you therefore, brothers and sisters,[h] by the mercies of God, to present your bodies as a living sacrifice, holy and acceptable to God, which is your spiritual[k] worship. 2Do not be conformed to this world,[l] but be transformed by the renewing of your minds, so that you may discern what is the will of God—what is good and acceptable and perfect.[m]

3 For by the grace given to me I say to everyone among you not to think of yourself more highly than you ought to think, but to think with sober judgment, each according to the measure of faith that God has assigned. 4For as in one body we have many members, and not all the members have the same function, 5so we, who are many, are one body in Christ, and individually we are members one of another. 6We have gifts that differ according to the grace given to us: prophecy, in proportion to faith; 7ministry, in ministering; the teacher, in teaching; 8the exhorter, in exhortation; the giver, in generosity; the leader, in diligence; the compassionate, in cheerfulness.

Marks of the True Christian

9 Let love be genuine; hate what is evil, hold fast to what is good; 10love one another with mutual affection; outdo one another in showing honor. 11Do not lag in zeal, be ardent in spirit, serve the

---

e Other ancient authorities read *the richness*
f Other ancient authorities read *neither will he spare you*   g Gk lacks *of Israel*   h Gk *brothers*
i Gk lacks *of God*   j Other ancient authorities lack *now*   k Or *reasonable*   l Gk *age*   m Or *what is the good and acceptable and perfect will of God*

Lord.[n] 12Rejoice in hope, be patient in suffering, persevere in prayer. 13Contribute to the needs of the saints; extend hospitality to strangers.

14 Bless those who persecute you; bless and do not curse them. 15Rejoice with those who rejoice, weep with those who weep. 16Live in harmony with one another; do not be haughty, but associate with the lowly;[o] do not claim to be wiser than you are. 17Do not repay anyone evil for evil, but take thought for what is noble in the sight of all. 18If it is possible, so far as

[n] Other ancient authorities read *serve the opportune time*   [o] Or *give yourselves to humble tasks*

Renewing Your Mind

TUESDAY

Scripture Reading for Today:
Romans 12.1–2

Verse for Today:
Romans 12.2

Here is a little test you can take to find out who's in charge—you or your mind.

1. Can you account for what goes on in your mind during the day? While no one can account for sixteen hours of every waking day; nevertheless it can be extremely enlightening to try to remember what you thought about while waiting for a bus, talking on the phone to a long-winded friend, waiting in line for gas, or folding the laundry. Did you choose to think each of those thoughts, or did you just "interrupt" a conversation that was already being carried on in your head?

2. Once you get in touch with some of your thoughts, do you like what you find? Or do you find that you are often critical of others? Does your mind conduct an ongoing analysis of the problems and faults of others? Is it filled with frantic thoughts about what might happen if your child is kidnapped, you lose your job, you aren't able to make ends meet, a man breaks into the house when you're alone? Is it filled with self-concern—with thoughts of me, me, me?

3. Are you building a fantasy life in order to escape present frustration or pain? Are the situations you reflect on real? Are the relationships real? Are the conversations real?

4. Is your mind overactive? Is it always buzzing with thoughts about this or that, flitting from one thing to another? Are you successful when you try to stop a train or pattern of thought? Does your mind do what you want, or does it fight for what it wants to think? Does your mind continually return to a train of thought from which you are trying to divert it?

If you recognize any, some, or all of these typical states of mind, then it's time to take account of your thoughts and the fruit they bear. If you avoid making a decision to retrain your mind, your emotions will only continue to cause frustration and discouragement.

—THERESE CIRNER

Go to page 1488 for your next devotional reading.

it depends on you, live peaceably with all. 19Beloved, never avenge yourselves, but leave room for the wrath of God;*p* for it is written, "Vengeance is mine, I will repay, says the Lord." 20No, "if your enemies are hungry, feed them; if they are thirsty, give them something to drink; for by doing this you will heap burning coals on their heads." 21Do not be overcome by evil, but overcome evil with good.

Being Subject to Authorities

13 Let every person be subject to the governing authorities; for there is no authority except from God, and those authorities that exist have been instituted by God. 2Therefore whoever resists authority resists what God has appointed, and those who resist will incur judgment. 3For rulers are not a terror to good conduct, but to bad. Do you wish to have no fear of the authority? Then do what is good, and you will receive its approval; 4for it is God's servant for your good. But if you do what is wrong, you should be afraid, for the authority*q* does not bear the sword in vain! It is the servant of God to execute wrath on the wrongdoer. 5Therefore one must be subject, not only because of wrath but also because of conscience. 6For the same reason you also pay taxes, for the authorities are God's servants, busy with this very thing. 7Pay to all what is due them—taxes to whom taxes are due, revenue to whom revenue is due, respect to whom respect is due, honor to whom honor is due.

Love for One Another

8 Owe no one anything, except to love one another; for the one who loves another has fulfilled the law. 9The commandments, "You shall not commit adultery; You shall not murder; You shall not steal; You shall not covet"; and any other commandment, are summed up in this word, "Love your neighbor as yourself." 10Love does no wrong to a neighbor; therefore, love is the fulfilling of the law.

An Urgent Appeal

11 Besides this, you know what time it is, how it is now the moment for you to wake from sleep. For salvation is nearer to us now than when we became believers; 12the night is far gone, the day is near. Let us then lay aside the works of darkness and put on the armor of light; 13let us live honorably as in the day, not in reveling and drunkenness, not in debauchery and licentiousness, not in quarreling and jealousy. 14Instead, put on the Lord Jesus Christ, and make no provision for the flesh, to gratify its desires.

Do Not Judge Another

14 Welcome those who are weak in faith,*r* but not for the purpose of quarreling over opinions. 2Some believe in eating anything, while the weak eat only vegetables. 3Those who eat must not despise those who abstain, and those who abstain must not pass judgment on those who eat; for God has welcomed them. 4Who are you to pass judgment on servants of another? It is before their own lord that they stand or fall. And they will be upheld, for the Lord*s* is able to make them stand.

5 Some judge one day to be better than another, while others judge all days to be alike. Let all be fully convinced in their own minds. 6Those who observe the day, observe it in honor of the Lord. Also those who eat, eat in honor of the Lord, since they give thanks to God; while those who abstain, abstain in honor of the Lord and give thanks to God.

7 We do not live to ourselves, and we do not die to ourselves. 8If we live, we live to the Lord, and if we die, we die to the Lord; so then, whether we live or whether we die, we are the Lord's. 9For to this end Christ died and lived again, so that he might be Lord of both the dead and the living.

10 Why do you pass judgment on your brother or sister?*t* Or you, why do you despise your brother or sister?*t* For we will all stand before the judgment seat of God.*u* 11For it is written,

"As I live, says the Lord, every knee
shall bow to me,
and every tongue shall give praise
to*v* God."

12So then, each of us will be accountable to God.*w*

---

p Gk *the wrath*   *q* Gk *it*   *r* Or *conviction*
s Other ancient authorities read *for God*   *t* Gk
brother   *u* Other ancient authorities read *of
Christ*   *v* Or *confess*   *w* Other ancient
authorities lack *to God*

Do Not Make Another Stumble

13 Let us therefore no longer pass judgment on one another, but resolve instead never to put a stumbling block or hindrance in the way of another.[x] 14I know and am persuaded in the Lord Jesus that nothing is unclean in itself; but it is unclean for anyone who thinks it unclean. 15If your brother or sister[y] is being injured by what you eat, you are no longer walking in love. Do not let what you eat cause the ruin of one for whom Christ died. 16So do not let your good be spoken of as evil. 17For the kingdom of God is not food and drink but righteousness and peace and joy in the Holy Spirit. 18The one who thus serves Christ is acceptable to God and has human approval. 19Let us then pursue what makes for peace and for mutual upbuilding. 20Do not, for the sake of food, destroy the work of God. Everything is indeed clean, but it is wrong for you to make others fall by what you eat; 21it is good not to eat meat or drink wine or do anything that makes your brother or sister[y] stumble.[z] 22The faith that you have, have as your own conviction before God. Blessed are those who have no reason to condemn themselves because of what they approve. 23But those who have doubts are condemned if they eat, because

[x] Gk *of a brother*   [y] Gk *brother*   [z] Other ancient authorities add *or be upset or be weakened*

A Dangerous Prayer

WEDNESDAY

Scripture Reading
for Today:
Romans 14.13–19

Verse for Today:
Romans 14.13

If we ask God to root out our pride and sin, he will do it. Some years ago I said a dangerous prayer: "God, I don't want to be judging people rashly, as I do. Whatever you have to do to change me, do it."

The next day I was on a plane, sitting in an aisle seat. A man sitting somewhat in front of me was speaking. He had a cup of hot coffee in his hand and was waving it around.

"Look at him," I thought. "He's going to hit somebody with that cup. Somebody's going to get scalded. You'd think he'd be more careful."

Sure enough, a stewardess walked down the aisle, and the man bumped her. Hot coffee spilled all down her dress. I sat back smugly. "Of course."

About twenty minutes later I felt like having a cup of coffee—which is unusual for me—and I asked her for one. A man across the aisle asked me a question. I am one of those people who cannot talk without using my hands. I began gesturing with the cup of hot coffee. Another stewardess came down the aisle. I bumped her, and hot coffee spilled all over her too. I heard the Lord say, "Ahem."

Ever since I have prayed that prayer, it seems that whenever I have rashly jumped to a negative judgment of someone, before the day is out I have done the very same thing that I have judged them for. God has been intent on removing my pride and giving me his righteousness—and so he is with all of us.

—ANN SHIELDS

Go to page 1490 for your next devotional reading.

they do not act from faith;[a] for whatever does not proceed from faith[a] is sin.[b]

Please Others, Not Yourselves

15 We who are strong ought to put up with the failings of the weak, and not to please ourselves. [2]Each of us must please our neighbor for the good purpose of building up the neighbor. [3]For Christ did not please himself; but, as it is written, "The insults of those who insult you have fallen on me." [4]For whatever was written in former days was written for our instruction, so that by steadfastness and by the encouragement of the scriptures we might have hope. [5]May the God of steadfastness and encouragement grant you to live in harmony with one another, in accordance with Christ Jesus, [6]so that together you may with one voice glorify the God and Father of our Lord Jesus Christ.

The Gospel for Jews and Gentiles Alike

7 Welcome one another, therefore, just as Christ has welcomed you, for the glory of God. [8]For I tell you that Christ has become a servant of the circumcised on behalf of the truth of God in order that he might confirm the promises given to the patriarchs, [9]and in order that the Gentiles might glorify God for his mercy. As it is written,

"Therefore I will confess[c] you
     among the Gentiles,
  and sing praises to your name";
[10]and again he says,
"Rejoice, O Gentiles, with his
     people";
[11]and again,
"Praise the Lord, all you Gentiles,
  and let all the peoples praise him";
[12]and again Isaiah says,
"The root of Jesse shall come,
  the one who rises to rule
     the Gentiles;
in him the Gentiles shall hope."
[13]May the God of hope fill you with all joy and peace in believing, so that you may abound in hope by the power of the Holy Spirit.

Paul's Reason for Writing So Boldly

14 I myself feel confident about you, my brothers and sisters,[d] that you yourselves are full of goodness, filled with all knowledge, and able to instruct one another. [15]Nevertheless on some points I have written to you rather boldly by way

of reminder, because of the grace given me by God [16]to be a minister of Christ Jesus to the Gentiles in the priestly service of the gospel of God, so that the offering of the Gentiles may be acceptable, sanctified by the Holy Spirit. [17]In Christ Jesus, then, I have reason to boast of my work for God. [18]For I will not venture to speak of anything except what Christ has accomplished[e] through me to win obedience from the Gentiles, by word and deed, [19]by the power of signs and wonders, by the power of the Spirit of God,[f] so that from Jerusalem and as far around as Illyricum I have fully proclaimed the good news[g] of Christ. [20]Thus I make it my ambition to proclaim the good news,[g] not where Christ has already been named, so that I do not build on someone else's foundation, [21]but as it is written,

"Those who have never been told of
     him shall see,
  and those who have never heard
     of him shall understand."

Paul's Plan to Visit Rome

22 This is the reason that I have so often been hindered from coming to you. [23]But now, with no further place for me in these regions, I desire, as I have for many years, to come to you [24]when I go to Spain. For I do hope to see you on my journey and to be sent on by you, once I have enjoyed your company for a little while. [25]At present, however, I am going to Jerusalem in a ministry to the saints; [26]for Macedonia and Achaia have been pleased to share their resources with the poor among the saints at Jerusalem. [27]They were pleased to do this, and indeed they owe it to them; for if the Gentiles have come to share in their spiritual blessings, they ought also to be of service to them in material things. [28]So, when I have completed this, and have delivered to them what has been collected,[h] I will set out by way of you to Spain; [29]and I know that when I come to you, I will come in the fullness of the blessing[i] of Christ.

---

[a] Or *conviction*   [b] Other authorities, some ancient, add here 16.25-27   [c] Or *thank*   [d] Gk *brothers*   [e] Gk *speak of those things that Christ has not accomplished*   [f] Other ancient authorities read *of the Spirit* or *of the Holy Spirit*   [g] Or *gospel*   [h] Gk *have sealed to them this fruit*   [i] Other ancient authorities add *of the gospel*

30 I appeal to you, brothers and sisters,[j] by our Lord Jesus Christ and by the love of the Spirit, to join me in earnest prayer to God on my behalf, [31]that I may be rescued from the unbelievers in Judea, and that my ministry[k] to Jerusalem may be acceptable to the saints, [32]so that by God's will I may come to you with joy and be refreshed in your company. [33]The God of peace be with all of you.[l] Amen.

j Gk *brothers*   *k* Other ancient authorities read *my bringing of a gift*   *l* One ancient authority adds 16.25-27 here

Women in Ministry

THURSDAY

Scripture Reading for Today:
Romans 16.1–16

Verses for Today:
Romans 16.1–2

Many women blame Paul's writings for starting the trend of keeping women "in their place" while men run the show. The situation is not that simple. Yes, the writings of Saint Paul have been used by many to promote narrow views. But careful study of the Scriptures shows that Saint Paul was more open-minded than most people imagine.

The New Testament actually shows that Paul worked intimately with women in ministry. Many important members of Paul's churches were women. Some of these women were heads of households: Lydia, for example, who was a wealthy businesswoman, "a dealer in purple cloth." She was one of Paul's first converts in Philippi. In Corinth, a woman named Chloe must have been an important member of the Christian community, for she sent her "people" to Paul with word of dissension among the Corinthians. At the end of Colossians, Paul greets "Nympha and the church in her house," another Christian leader (Colossians 4.15).

Some women were actually coworkers with Paul in ministry. A married couple from Corinth provides one example: "Prisca and Aquila, who work with me in Christ Jesus, and who risked their necks for my life" (Romans 16.3–4). Paul practiced his skill of tentmaking with them in Corinth, and they accompanied him on missionary journeys. One woman, Phoebe, Paul cites as a deacon of the church at Cenchreae, although the exact nature of that ministry in Paul's day is unclear.

Many other names of women appear in the Pauline letters. Romans 16.3–23 records Paul's greetings to numerous women such as Mary, "who has worked very hard among you," Tryphaena and Tryphosa who are called "workers in the Lord," the mother of Rufus whom Paul affectionately regards as "a mother to me also," and Julia and the sister of Nereus.

One might object that these are but names about whom we know little, and thus they are insignificant. But, in fact, we would have to admit the same could be said for most of the twelve apostles!

—*MARIE-ELOISE ROSENBLATT, R.S.M. AND RONALD D. WITHERUP, S.S.*

Go to page 1494 for your next devotional reading.

Personal Greetings

16 I commend to you our sister Phoebe, a deacon[m] of the church at Cenchreae, [2]so that you may welcome her in the Lord as is fitting for the saints, and help her in whatever she may require from you, for she has been a benefactor of many and of myself as well.

3 Greet Prisca and Aquila, who work with me in Christ Jesus, [4]and who risked their necks for my life, to whom not only I give thanks, but also all the churches of the Gentiles. [5]Greet also the church in their house. Greet my beloved Epaenetus, who was the first convert[n] in Asia for Christ. [6]Greet Mary, who has worked very hard among you. [7]Greet Andronicus and Junia,[o] my relatives[p] who were in prison with me; they are prominent among the apostles, and they were in Christ before I was. [8]Greet Ampliatus, my beloved in the Lord. [9]Greet Urbanus, our co-worker in Christ, and my beloved Stachys. [10]Greet Apelles, who is approved in Christ. Greet those who belong to the family of Aristobulus. [11]Greet my relative[q] Herodion. Greet those in the Lord who belong to the family of Narcissus. [12]Greet those workers in the Lord, Tryphaena and Tryphosa. Greet the beloved Persis, who has worked hard in the Lord. [13]Greet Rufus, chosen in the Lord; and greet his mother—a mother to me also. [14]Greet Asyncritus, Phlegon, Hermes, Patrobas, Hermas, and the brothers and sisters[r] who are with them. [15]Greet Philologus, Julia, Nereus and his sister, and Olympas, and all the saints who are with them. [16]Greet one another with a holy kiss. All the churches of Christ greet you.

Final Instructions

17 I urge you, brothers and sisters,[r] to keep an eye on those who cause dissensions and offenses, in opposition to the teaching that you have learned; avoid them. [18]For such people do not serve our Lord Christ, but their own appetites,[s] and by smooth talk and flattery they deceive the hearts of the simple-minded. [19]For while your obedience is known to all, so that I rejoice over you, I want you to be wise in what is good and guileless in what is evil. [20]The God of peace will shortly crush Satan under your feet. The grace of our Lord Jesus Christ be with you.[t]

21 Timothy, my co-worker, greets you; so do Lucius and Jason and Sosipater, my relatives. [p]

22 I Tertius, the writer of this letter, greet you in the Lord.[u]

23 Gaius, who is host to me and to the whole church, greets you. Erastus, the city treasurer, and our brother Quartus, greet you.[v]

Final Doxology

25 Now to God[w] who is able to strengthen you according to my gospel and the proclamation of Jesus Christ, according to the revelation of the mystery that was kept secret for long ages [26]but is now disclosed, and through the prophetic writings is made known to all the Gentiles, according to the command of the eternal God, to bring about the obedience of faith— [27]to the only wise God, through Jesus Christ, to whom[x] be the glory forever! Amen. [y]

m Or *minister*   n Gk *first fruits*   o Or *Junias; other ancient authorities read Julia*   p Or *compatriots*   q Or *compatriot*   r Gk *brothers*   s Gk *their own belly*   t Other ancient authorities lack this sentence   u Or *I Tertius, writing this letter in the Lord, greet you*   v Other ancient authorities add verse 24, *The grace of our Lord Jesus Christ be with all of you. Amen.*   w Gk *the one*   x Other ancient authorities lack *to whom.* The verse then reads, *to the only wise God be the glory through Jesus Christ forever. Amen.*   y Other ancient authorities lack 16.25-27 or include it after 14.23 or 15.33; others put verse 24 after verse 27

1 Corinthians

It is sometimes tempting for modern Christians to wax nostalgic about the early days of the church, as though Christians two thousand years ago were exempt from problems—except those brought on by persecution, of course. Reading Paul's first letter to the Corinthians quickly disposes of such romantic notions. Paul writes as a father to the community he founded in about A.D. 51. This letter was written in Ephesus some five years later.

Like the city they lived in, the Corinthian Christians were plagued with problems regarding improper expressions of sexuality and other acts of immorality. They also suffered from factionalism and various abuses concerning spiritual gifts, worship, and the celebration of the Lord's supper. Paul's letter tries to resolve these matters in order to protect the community of believers and get them back on track. He also addresses such issues as lawsuits, marriage, divorce, food offered to idols, and head coverings worn by women during times of worship.

First Corinthians 13.4–8 is a beautiful passage on the preeminent virtue of love: "Love is patient; love is kind; love is not envious or boastful or arrogant or rude. It does not insist on its own way; it is not irritable or resentful; it does not rejoice in wrongdoing, but rejoices in the truth. It bears all things, believes all things, hopes all things, endures all things.

"Love never ends."

Salutation

1 Paul, called to be an apostle of Christ Jesus by the will of God, and our brother Sosthenes,

2 To the church of God that is in Corinth, to those who are sanctified in Christ Jesus, called to be saints, together with all those who in every place call on the name of our Lord Jesus Christ, both their Lord[a] and ours:

3 Grace to you and peace from God our Father and the Lord Jesus Christ.

4 I give thanks to my[b] God always for

---

[a] Gk *theirs*   [b] Other ancient authorities lack *my*

you because of the grace of God that has been given you in Christ Jesus, [5]for in every way you have been enriched in him, in speech and knowledge of every kind— [6]just as the testimony of[c] Christ has been strengthened among you— [7]so that you are not lacking in any spiritual gift as you wait for the revealing of our Lord Jesus Christ. [8]He will also strengthen you to the end, so that you may be blameless on the day of our Lord Jesus Christ. [9]God is faithful; by him you were called into the fellowship of his Son, Jesus Christ our Lord.

Divisions in the Church

10 Now I appeal to you, brothers and sisters,[d] by the name of our Lord Jesus Christ, that all of you be in agreement and that there be no divisions among you, but that you be united in the same mind and the same purpose. [11]For it has been reported to me by Chloe's people that there are quarrels among you, my brothers and sisters.[e] [12]What I mean is that each of you says, "I belong to Paul," or "I belong to Apollos," or "I belong to Cephas," or "I belong to Christ." [13]Has Christ been divided? Was Paul crucified for you? Or were you baptized in the name of Paul? [14]I thank God[f] that I baptized none of you except Crispus and Gaius, [15]so that no one can say that you were baptized in my name. [16](I did baptize also the household of Stephanas; beyond that, I do not know whether I baptized anyone else.) [17]For Christ did not send me to baptize but to proclaim the gospel, and not with eloquent wisdom, so that the cross of Christ might not be emptied of its power.

Christ the Power and Wisdom of God

18 For the message about the cross is foolishness to those who are perishing, but to us who are being saved it is the power of God. [19]For it is written,
"I will destroy the wisdom of
     the wise,
and the discernment of the
     discerning I will thwart."
[20]Where is the one who is wise? Where is the scribe? Where is the debater of this age? Has not God made foolish the wisdom of the world? [21]For since, in the wisdom of God, the world did not know God through wisdom, God decided, through the foolishness of our proclamation, to save those who believe. [22]For Jews demand signs and Greeks desire wisdom,

[23]but we proclaim Christ crucified, a stumbling block to Jews and foolishness to Gentiles, [24]but to those who are the called, both Jews and Greeks, Christ the power of God and the wisdom of God. [25]For God's foolishness is wiser than human wisdom, and God's weakness is stronger than human strength.

26 Consider your own call, brothers and sisters:[d] not many of you were wise by human standards,[g] not many were powerful, not many were of noble birth. [27]But God chose what is foolish in the world to shame the wise; God chose what is weak in the world to shame the strong; [28]God chose what is low and despised in the world, things that are not, to reduce to nothing things that are, [29]so that no one[h] might boast in the presence of God. [30]He is the source of your life in Christ Jesus, who became for us wisdom from God, and righteousness and sanctification and redemption, [31]in order that, as it is written, "Let the one who boasts, boast in[i] the Lord."

Proclaiming Christ Crucified

2 When I came to you, brothers and sisters,[d] I did not come proclaiming the mystery[j] of God to you in lofty words or wisdom. [2]For I decided to know nothing among you except Jesus Christ, and him crucified. [3]And I came to you in weakness and in fear and in much trembling. [4]My speech and my proclamation were not with plausible words of wisdom,[k] but with a demonstration of the Spirit and of power, [5]so that your faith might rest not on human wisdom but on the power of God.

The True Wisdom of God

6 Yet among the mature we do speak wisdom, though it is not a wisdom of this age or of the rulers of this age, who are doomed to perish. [7]But we speak God's wisdom, secret and hidden, which God decreed before the ages for our glory. [8]None of the rulers of this age understood this; for if they had, they would not have

---

c Or *to*   *d* Gk *brothers*   *e* Gk *my brothers*
f Other ancient authorities read *I am thankful*
g Gk *according to the flesh*   *h* Gk *no flesh*   *i* Or
of   *j* Other ancient authorities read *testimony*
k Other ancient authorities read *the persuasiveness
of wisdom*

Scandalized

FRIDAY

Scripture Reading
for Today:
I Corinthians I.18–25

Verse for Today:
I Corinthians I.18

As I zipped open the cardboard envelope a sweet, heavy fragrance began to spill out. Rifling among the magazine and newspaper clippings I found it, a plastic bag containing a cotton ball. A drop of golden oil was soaked into the cotton. I gently opened the bag, and the scent of roses spilled into the room.

I was in the presence of a miracle—at least, that's what some believe. Eleven years ago, a monk named Father Pangratios was dusting the icons at a Russian Orthodox monastery in the remote Texas hill country. When he came to the icon of the Virgin Mary holding the Christ Child, he noticed drops of liquid on the surface. Beads of fragrant oil were welling up from the eyes of the painted figure and running down the surface of the board.

The news clippings continued the story. Healings. Miracles. One hundred thousand pilgrims a year. Church authorities had examined the simple plank of wood, even slept near it in the chapel all night to make sure there was no human trickery involved. The phenomenon could not be explained.

A lot of people don't like this story. Some are skeptics who don't believe in God, and therefore have an a priori conviction that it's impossible. But there are others who do believe in God, but just can't believe he'd do something like this. It's—to tell the truth—kind of tacky . . .

That's where I think they've missed the point. This is a Christian monastery and giving offense turns out to be a pretty consistent part of the Christian story. Since we believe that Jesus is God in human form, the story begins with God in a diaper—and as Frederick Buechner says, "If you haven't taken that seriously enough to be offended by it, you haven't taken it seriously enough. It proceeds to God on a cross, beaten and bleeding and shamed. It's a brutal story, one that isn't easy to take."

Christian Scriptures speak of the Cross as a stumbling block and a scandal. It breaks our complacency—our notions of dignity—and turns us again to be as children. Even people who aren't Christian can agree that whoever God is, he's going to be outside human control. He's going to do things beyond our comprehension—sometimes, things which seem designed to show us how little we comprehend. Humility before this inscrutable Power seems to be a recurrent theme, no matter what your faith.

Believers describe God in many ways: just, mighty, all-knowing, all-powerful. But no one accuses him of being predictable. The possibility of miracles is something we have to accept—even those which test our taste.

—FREDERICA MATHEWES-GREEN

Go to page 1496 for your next devotional reading.

crucified the Lord of glory. 9But, as it is written,

> "What no eye has seen, nor
>   ear heard,
>   nor the human heart conceived,
>   what God has prepared for those
>   who love him"—

10these things God has revealed to us through the Spirit; for the Spirit searches everything, even the depths of God. 11For what human being knows what is truly human except the human spirit that is within? So also no one comprehends what is truly God's except the Spirit of God. 12Now we have received not the spirit of the world, but the Spirit that is from God, so that we may understand the gifts bestowed on us by God. 13And we speak of these things in words not taught by human wisdom but taught by the Spirit, interpreting spiritual things to those who are spiritual.[l]

14 Those who are unspiritual[m] do not receive the gifts of God's Spirit, for they are foolishness to them, and they are unable to understand them because they are spiritually discerned. 15Those who are spiritual discern all things, and they are themselves subject to no one else's scrutiny.

16 "For who has known the mind
>   of the Lord
>   so as to instruct him?"

But we have the mind of Christ.

On Divisions in the Corinthian Church

3 And so, brothers and sisters,[n] I could not speak to you as spiritual people, but rather as people of the flesh, as infants in Christ. 2I fed you with milk, not solid food, for you were not ready for solid food. Even now you are still not ready, 3for you are still of the flesh. For as long as there is jealousy and quarreling among you, are you not of the flesh, and behaving according to human inclinations? 4For when one says, "I belong to Paul," and another, "I belong to Apollos," are you not merely human?

5 What then is Apollos? What is Paul? Servants through whom you came to believe, as the Lord assigned to each. 6I planted, Apollos watered, but God gave the growth. 7So neither the one who plants nor the one who waters is anything, but only God who gives the growth. 8The one who plants and the one who waters have a common purpose, and each

will receive wages according to the labor of each. 9For we are God's servants, working together; you are God's field, God's building.

10 According to the grace of God given to me, like a skilled master builder I laid a foundation, and someone else is building on it. Each builder must choose with care how to build on it. 11For no one can lay any foundation other than the one that has been laid; that foundation is Jesus Christ. 12Now if anyone builds on the foundation with gold, silver, precious stones, wood, hay, straw— 13the work of each builder will become visible, for the Day will disclose it, because it will be revealed with fire, and the fire will test what sort of work each has done. 14If what has been built on the foundation survives, the builder will receive a reward. 15If the work is burned up, the builder will suffer loss; the builder will be saved, but only as through fire.

16 Do you not know that you are God's temple and that God's Spirit dwells in you?[o] 17If anyone destroys God's temple, God will destroy that person. For God's temple is holy, and you are that temple.

18 Do not deceive yourselves. If you think that you are wise in this age, you should become fools so that you may become wise. 19For the wisdom of this world is foolishness with God. For it is written,

> "He catches the wise in their
>   craftiness,"

20and again,

> "The Lord knows the thoughts of
>   the wise,
>   that they are futile."

21So let no one boast about human leaders. For all things are yours, 22whether Paul or Apollos or Cephas or the world or life or death or the present or the future— all belong to you, 23and you belong to Christ, and Christ belongs to God.

The Ministry of the Apostles

4 Think of us in this way, as servants of Christ and stewards of God's mysteries. 2Moreover, it is required of stewards that they be found trustworthy. 3But with me it is a very small thing that I should be

---

l Or *interpreting spiritual things in spiritual language,* or *comparing spiritual things with spiritual*   m Or *natural*   n Gk *brothers*   o In verses 16 and 17 the Greek word for *you* is plural

The Woman of Samaria

Her Character: *The Jews would have looked down on her because she was a Samaritan. Men would have discounted her because she was a woman. And women would have disdained her because of her many romantic liaisons. She would not have been most people's first choice to advance the gospel in a region where it had not yet been heard.*

Her Sorrow: *To have lived in a way that relegated her to the margins of society.*

Her Joy: *That Jesus broke through barriers of culture, race, gender, and religion in order to reveal himself to her.*

Read John 4.1–42

Every day the woman carried her water jug to Jacob's well just outside Sychar, a town midway between Jerusalem and Nazareth. Even though it was the hottest time of the day, she preferred it to the morning or evening hours, when the other women gathered. How tired she was of their wagging tongues. Better the scorching heat than their sharp remarks.

She was surprised, however, to see that today someone had already arrived at the well. At least she had nothing to fear from his tongue, for Jews did their best to avoid Samaritans, despising them as half-breeds. For once, she was glad to be ignored, grateful that men did not address women in public.

But as she approached the well, the man startled her, breaking the rules she had counted on to protect her. "Give me a drink," he said.

With a toss of her head, she replied, "How is it that you, a Jew, ask a drink of me, a woman of Samaria?" Jews regarded Samaritan women and all they touched as unclean.

But he wouldn't be put off. "If you knew the gift of God, and who it is that is saying to you, 'Give me a drink,' you would have asked him, and he would have given you living water."

"Go," he told her, "call your husband, and come back."

This last request took the wind out of her. Her quick tongue was barely able to reply, "I have no husband."

"You are right in saying, 'I have no husband'; for you have had five husbands, and the one you have now is not your husband," Jesus said.

His words cut her. Shaking off the hurt, she tried changing the subject. "I know that Messiah is coming ... When he comes, he will proclaim all things to us."

Then Jesus declared, "I am he, the one who is speaking to you."

Leaving her water jar, the woman went back to the town and said to the people, "Come and see a man who told me everything I have ever done! He cannot be the Messiah, can he?"

Dodge, counter-dodge—nothing the woman said would keep Jesus at bay. He kept pressing beneath the surface, hemming her in by revealing his knowledge of the most intimate details of her life. Overwhelmed, she finally admitted the truth. And when she did, Jesus startled her with a revelation about himself. He admitted, for the first time, that he was the Messiah.

Jesus had arrived at the well thirsty, hungry, and tired from the journey north to Galilee. But by the time his disciples returned from their shopping trip, he seemed refreshed and restored by his encounter with the woman. As a result of that encounter, many of the Samaritans came to believe in him.

Praying With the Woman of Samaria

Then the woman left her water jar and went back to the city. She said to the people, "Come and see a man who told me everything I have ever done! He cannot be the Messiah, can he?" —*John 4.28–29*

Praise God: *Because in his kingdom, the last shall be first.*

Offer Thanks: *For the way that he has uncovered your need for him.*

Confess: *Any tendency to act as though God cannot work through your weakness but only through your strength.*

Ask God: *To give you the humility to face the depth of your need for grace.*

Lift Your Heart

It's always difficult to admit our sins, particularly if we suffer from the heresy that says God will only love us if we behave well. Though we might never articulate such a thought, it often shapes our theology more than we like to admit. This week, make a list of everything God knows about you that you wish he didn't. Thank him for loving you despite your sins. Then tear up the list, remembering the words of Psalm 103.11–12:

> For as the heavens are high above the earth,
> so great is his steadfast love toward those who fear him;
> as far as the east is from the west,
> so far he removes our transgressions from us.

Lord, you know everything about me, even the things I'm hiding from myself. Give me the grace to admit my sin, believing that though you see me, you still love me. Help me to let go of anything that keeps me from experiencing the living water of your Holy Spirit welling up inside me.

Go to page 1500 for your next devotional reading.

judged by you or by any human court. I do not even judge myself. ⁴I am not aware of anything against myself, but I am not thereby acquitted. It is the Lord who judges me. ⁵Therefore do not pronounce judgment before the time, before the Lord comes, who will bring to light the things now hidden in darkness and will disclose the purposes of the heart. Then each one will receive commendation from God.

6 I have applied all this to Apollos and myself for your benefit, brothers and sisters, ᵖ so that you may learn through us the meaning of the saying, "Nothing beyond what is written," so that none of you will be puffed up in favor of one against another. ⁷For who sees anything different in you?�q What do you have that you did not receive? And if you received it, why do you boast as if it were not a gift?

8 Already you have all you want! Already you have become rich! Quite apart from us you have become kings! Indeed, I wish that you had become kings, so that we might be kings with you! ⁹For I think that God has exhibited us apostles as last of all, as though sentenced to death, because we have become a spectacle to the world, to angels and to mortals. ¹⁰We are fools for the sake of Christ, but you are wise in Christ. We are weak, but you are strong. You are held in honor, but we in disrepute. ¹¹To the present hour we are hungry and thirsty, we are poorly clothed and beaten and homeless, ¹²and we grow weary from the work of our own hands. When reviled, we bless; when persecuted, we endure; ¹³when slandered, we speak kindly. We have become like the rubbish of the world, the dregs of all things, to this very day.

Fatherly Admonition

14 I am not writing this to make you ashamed, but to admonish you as my beloved children. ¹⁵For though you might have ten thousand guardians in Christ, you do not have many fathers. Indeed, in Christ Jesus I became your father through the gospel. ¹⁶I appeal to you, then, be imitators of me. ¹⁷For this reason I sentʳ you Timothy, who is my beloved and faithful child in the Lord, to remind you of my ways in Christ Jesus, as I teach them everywhere in every church. ¹⁸But some of you, thinking that I am not coming to you, have become arrogant. ¹⁹But I will come to you soon, if the Lord wills, and I will find out not the talk of these arrogant people but their power. ²⁰For the kingdom of God depends not on talk but on power. ²¹What would you prefer? Am I to come to you with a stick, or with love in a spirit of gentleness?

Sexual Immorality Defiles the Church

5 It is actually reported that there is sexual immorality among you, and of a kind that is not found even among pagans; for a man is living with his father's wife. ²And you are arrogant! Should you not rather have mourned, so that he who has done this would have been removed from among you?

3 For though absent in body, I am present in spirit; and as if present I have already pronounced judgment ⁴in the name of the Lord Jesus on the man who has done such a thing.ˢ When you are assembled, and my spirit is present with the power of our Lord Jesus, ⁵you are to hand this man over to Satan for the destruction of the flesh, so that his spirit may be saved in the day of the Lord.ᵗ

6 Your boasting is not a good thing. Do you not know that a little yeast leavens the whole batch of dough? ⁷Clean out the old yeast so that you may be a new batch, as you really are unleavened. For our paschal lamb, Christ, has been sacrificed. ⁸Therefore, let us celebrate the festival, not with the old yeast, the yeast of malice and evil, but with the unleavened bread of sincerity and truth.

Sexual Immorality Must Be Judged

9 I wrote to you in my letter not to associate with sexually immoral persons— ¹⁰not at all meaning the immoral of this world, or the greedy and robbers, or idolaters, since you would then need to go out of the world. ¹¹But now I am writing to you not to associate with anyone who bears the name of brother or sisterᵘ who is sexually immoral or greedy, or is an idolater, reviler, drunkard, or robber. Do not even eat with such a one. ¹²For what have I to do with judging those outside? Is it not those who are inside that you are to judge? ¹³God will judge those out-

---

ᵖ Gk *brothers*　　�q Or *Who makes you different from another?*　　ʳ Or *am sending*　　ˢ Or *on the man who has done such a thing in the name of the Lord Jesus*　　ᵗ Other ancient authorities add *Jesus*　　ᵘ Gk *brother*

side. "Drive out the wicked person from among you."

Lawsuits among Believers

6 When any of you has a grievance against another, do you dare to take it to court before the unrighteous, instead of taking it before the saints? ²Do you not know that the saints will judge the world? And if the world is to be judged by you, are you incompetent to try trivial cases? ³Do you not know that we are to judge angels—to say nothing of ordinary matters? ⁴If you have ordinary cases, then, do you appoint as judges those who have no standing in the church? ⁵I say this to your shame. Can it be that there is no one among you wise enough to decide between one believer*v* and another, ⁶but a believer*v* goes to court against a believer*v*—and before unbelievers at that?

7 In fact, to have lawsuits at all with one another is already a defeat for you. Why not rather be wronged? Why not rather be defrauded? ⁸But you yourselves wrong and defraud—and believers*w* at that.

9 Do you not know that wrongdoers will not inherit the kingdom of God? Do not be deceived! Fornicators, idolaters, adulterers, male prostitutes, sodomites, ¹⁰thieves, the greedy, drunkards, revilers, robbers—none of these will inherit the kingdom of God. ¹¹And this is what some of you used to be. But you were washed, you were sanctified, you were justified in the name of the Lord Jesus Christ and in the Spirit of our God.

Glorify God in Body and Spirit

12 "All things are lawful for me," but not all things are beneficial. "All things are lawful for me," but I will not be dominated by anything. ¹³"Food is meant for the stomach and the stomach for food,"*x* and God will destroy both one and the other. The body is meant not for fornication but for the Lord, and the Lord for the body. ¹⁴And God raised the Lord and will also raise us by his power. ¹⁵Do you not know that your bodies are members of Christ? Should I therefore take the members of Christ and make them members of a prostitute? Never! ¹⁶Do you not know that whoever is united to a prostitute becomes one body with her? For it is said, "The two shall be one flesh." ¹⁷But anyone united to the Lord becomes one spirit

with him. ¹⁸Shun fornication! Every sin that a person commits is outside the body; but the fornicator sins against the body itself. ¹⁹Or do you not know that your body is a temple*y* of the Holy Spirit within you, which you have from God, and that you are not your own? ²⁰For you were bought with a price; therefore glorify God in your body.

Directions concerning Marriage

7 Now concerning the matters about which you wrote: "It is well for a man not to touch a woman." ²But because of cases of sexual immorality, each man should have his own wife and each woman her own husband. ³The husband should give to his wife her conjugal rights, and likewise the wife to her husband. ⁴For the wife does not have authority over her own body, but the husband does; likewise the husband does not have authority over his own body, but the wife does. ⁵Do not deprive one another except perhaps by agreement for a set time, to devote yourselves to prayer, and then come together again, so that Satan may not tempt you because of your lack of self-control. ⁶This I say by way of concession, not of command. ⁷I wish that all were as I myself am. But each has a particular gift from God, one having one kind and another a different kind.

8 To the unmarried and the widows I say that it is well for them to remain unmarried as I am. ⁹But if they are not practicing self-control, they should marry. For it is better to marry than to be aflame with passion.

10 To the married I give this command—not I but the Lord—that the wife should not separate from her husband ¹¹(but if she does separate, let her remain unmarried or else be reconciled to her husband), and that the husband should not divorce his wife.

12 To the rest I say—I and not the Lord—that if any believer*v* has a wife who is an unbeliever, and she consents to live with him, he should not divorce her. ¹³And if any woman has a husband who is an unbeliever, and he consents to live with her, she should not divorce him. ¹⁴For the unbelieving husband is made holy through his wife, and the unbeliev-

---

v Gk *brother*   *w* Gk *brothers*   *x* The quotation may extend to the word *other*   *y* Or *sanctuary*

ing wife is made holy through her husband. Otherwise, your children would be unclean, but as it is, they are holy. [15]But if the unbelieving partner separates, let it be so; in such a case the brother or sister is not bound. It is to peace that God has called you.[z] [16]Wife, for all you know, you might save your husband. Husband, for all you know, you might save your wife.

The Life That the Lord Has Assigned

[17] However that may be, let each of you lead the life that the Lord has assigned, to which God called you. This is my rule in all the churches. [18]Was anyone

at the time of his call already circumcised? Let him not seek to remove the marks of circumcision. Was anyone at the time of his call uncircumcised? Let him not seek circumcision. [19]Circumcision is nothing, and uncircumcision is nothing; but obeying the commandments of God is everything. [20]Let each of you remain in the condition in which you were called.

[21] Were you a slave when called? Do not be concerned about it. Even if you can gain your freedom, make use of your present condition now more than ever.[a]

[z] Other ancient authorities read *us*   [a] Or *avail yourself of the opportunity*

Virginity

Perhaps virginity seems a bit cold, even haughty and heartless. But virginity hardly has exclusive claim on those defects, if it has any claims at all. Promiscuity offers a significantly worse fate. I have a very dear friend who, sadly, is more worldly-wise than I am. By libertine feminist standards she ought to be proud of her conquests and ready for more, but frequently she isn't. The most telling insight about the shambles of her heart came to me once in a phone conversation when we were speculating about our futures. Generally they are filled with exotic travel and adventure and Ph.D.'s. This time, however, they were not. She admitted to me that what she really wanted was to be living on a farm in rural Connecticut, raising a horde of children and embroidering tea towels. It is a lovely dream, defiantly unambitious and domestic. But her short, failed sexual relationships haven't taken her any closer to her dream and have left her little hope that she'll ever attain it. I must be honest here: Virginity hasn't landed me on a farm in rural Connecticut, either. Sexual innocence is not a guarantee against heartbreak. But there is a crucial difference: I haven't lost a part of myself to someone who has subsequently spurned it, rejected it, and perhaps never cared for it at all.

I sincerely hope that virginity will not be a lifetime project for me. Quite the contrary, my subversive commitment to virginity serves as preparation for another commitment, for loving one man completely and exclusively. Admittedly, there is a minor frustration in my love: I haven't met the man yet (at least, not to my knowledge). But hope, which does not disappoint, sustains me.

—*SARAH E. HINLICKY*

Go to page 1504 for your next devotional reading.

22For whoever was called in the Lord as a slave is a freed person belonging to the Lord, just as whoever was free when called is a slave of Christ. 23You were bought with a price; do not become slaves of human masters. 24In whatever condition you were called, brothers and sisters,*b* there remain with God.

The Unmarried and the Widows

25 Now concerning virgins, I have no command of the Lord, but I give my opinion as one who by the Lord's mercy is trustworthy. 26I think that, in view of the impending*c* crisis, it is well for you to remain as you are. 27Are you bound to a wife? Do not seek to be free. Are you free from a wife? Do not seek a wife. 28But if you marry, you do not sin, and if a virgin marries, she does not sin. Yet those who marry will experience distress in this life,*d* and I would spare you that. 29I mean, brothers and sisters,*b* the appointed time has grown short; from now on, let even those who have wives be as though they had none, 30and those who mourn as though they were not mourning, and those who rejoice as though they were not rejoicing, and those who buy as though they had no possessions, 31and those who deal with the world as though they had no dealings with it. For the present form of this world is passing away.

32 I want you to be free from anxieties. The unmarried man is anxious about the affairs of the Lord, how to please the Lord; 33but the married man is anxious about the affairs of the world, how to please his wife, 34and his interests are divided. And the unmarried woman and the virgin are anxious about the affairs of the Lord, so that they may be holy in body and spirit; but the married woman is anxious about the affairs of the world, how to please her husband. 35I say this for your own benefit, not to put any restraint upon you, but to promote good order and unhindered devotion to the Lord.

36 If anyone thinks that he is not behaving properly toward his fiancée,*e* if his passions are strong, and so it has to be, let him marry as he wishes; it is no sin. Let them marry. 37But if someone stands firm in his resolve, being under no necessity but having his own desire under control, and has determined in his own mind to keep her as his fiancée,*e* he will do well. 38So then, he who marries his fiancée*e*

does well; and he who refrains from marriage will do better.

39 A wife is bound as long as her husband lives. But if the husband dies,*f* she is free to marry anyone she wishes, only in the Lord. 40But in my judgment she is more blessed if she remains as she is. And I think that I too have the Spirit of God.

Food Offered to Idols

8 Now concerning food sacrificed to idols: we know that "all of us possess knowledge." Knowledge puffs up, but love builds up. 2Anyone who claims to know something does not yet have the necessary knowledge; 3but anyone who loves God is known by him.

4 Hence, as to the eating of food offered to idols, we know that "no idol in the world really exists," and that "there is no God but one." 5Indeed, even though there may be so-called gods in heaven or on earth—as in fact there are many gods and many lords— 6yet for us there is one God, the Father, from whom are all things and for whom we exist, and one Lord, Jesus Christ, through whom are all things and through whom we exist.

7 It is not everyone, however, who has this knowledge. Since some have become so accustomed to idols until now, they still think of the food they eat as food offered to an idol; and their conscience, being weak, is defiled. 8"Food will not bring us close to God." *g* We are no worse off if we do not eat, and no better off if we do. 9But take care that this liberty of yours does not somehow become a stumbling block to the weak. 10For if others see you, who possess knowledge, eating in the temple of an idol, might they not, since their conscience is weak, be encouraged to the point of eating food sacrificed to idols? 11So by your knowledge those weak believers for whom Christ died are destroyed.*h* 12But when you thus sin against members of your family,*i* and wound their conscience when it is weak, you sin against Christ. 13Therefore, if food is a cause of their falling,*j* I will never eat

---

b Gk *brothers*   *c* Or *present*   *d* Gk *in the flesh*
e Gk *virgin*   *f* Gk *falls asleep*   *g* The quotation may extend to the end of the verse   *h* Gk *the weak brother . . . is destroyed*   *i* Gk *against the brothers*   *j* Gk *my brother's falling*

meat, so that I may not cause one of them[k] to fall.

The Rights of an Apostle

9 Am I not free? Am I not an apostle? Have I not seen Jesus our Lord? Are you not my work in the Lord? [2]If I am not an apostle to others, at least I am to you; for you are the seal of my apostleship in the Lord.

[3] This is my defense to those who would examine me. [4]Do we not have the right to our food and drink? [5]Do we not have the right to be accompanied by a believing wife,[l] as do the other apostles and the brothers of the Lord and Cephas? [6]Or is it only Barnabas and I who have no right to refrain from working for a living?

[7]Who at any time pays the expenses for doing military service? Who plants a vineyard and does not eat any of its fruit? Or who tends a flock and does not get any of its milk?

[8] Do I say this on human authority? Does not the law also say the same? [9]For it is written in the law of Moses, "You shall not muzzle an ox while it is treading out the grain." Is it for oxen that God is concerned? [10]Or does he not speak entirely for our sake? It was indeed written for our sake, for whoever plows should plow in hope and whoever threshes should thresh in hope of a share in the crop. [11]If we have sown spiritual good among you,

k Gk cause my brother   *l Gk a sister as wife*

THE TRADITION

Poverty, Chastity, Obedience

*The unmarried woman and the virgin
are anxious about the affairs of the Lord.*

1 CORINTHIANS 7.34

"Take a child to work" day was approaching, and Bobby announced that he was going to spend it with the parish priest. Thrilled at the boy's interest in the priesthood, his mother phoned a friend to announce the good news.

Overhearing her conversation, Johnny set her straight.

"Mom, I don't want to be a priest! I've just always wondered: What is it they *do* all day?"

So much about the life of a parish priest, or any man or woman who lives a consecrated life, goes unseen.

The woman who takes a vow of virginity is called a bride of Christ: Her groom is invisible. Hermits withdraw from the world and, hidden in silence and solitude, do battle for its salvation. Men and women in religious orders express their hope of a coming kingdom by relinquishing the right to marriage, possessions, and some areas of decision-making.

"Not everyone can accept this teaching," Jesus said of the call to celibacy (Matthew

19.11). It is like his challenge to the rich young man to go beyond the demands of the commandments. "If you wish to be perfect, go, sell your possessions, and give the money to the poor ... then come, follow me" (verse 21).

The "evangelical counsels"—poverty, chastity expressed in celibacy, and obedience—are like short cuts; they serve as more direct paths and means for attaining perfect love of God and neighbor. As Vatican II took pains to point out, however, this does not mean that some of us are meant to be holy and some not so holy! *All* are called to "the perfection of charity."

How does God want me to get there? That is the issue.

In a special way, the women and men whom God has called to "get there" by way of the consecrated life are living "pointers" to the reality of the world to come. Committed to a hidden Spouse, they image the destiny of the entire Church, which is even now being prepared to be the bride of Christ.

is it too much if we reap your material benefits? 12If others share this rightful claim on you, do not we still more?

Nevertheless, we have not made use of this right, but we endure anything rather than put an obstacle in the way of the gospel of Christ. 13Do you not know that those who are employed in the temple service get their food from the temple, and those who serve at the altar share in what is sacrificed on the altar? 14In the same way, the Lord commanded that those who proclaim the gospel should get their living by the gospel.

15 But I have made no use of any of these rights, nor am I writing this so that they may be applied in my case. Indeed, I would rather die than that—no one will deprive me of my ground for boasting! 16If I proclaim the gospel, this gives me no ground for boasting, for an obligation is laid on me, and woe to me if I do not proclaim the gospel! 17For if I do this of my own will, I have a reward; but if not of my own will, I am entrusted with a commission. 18What then is my reward? Just this: that in my proclamation I may make the gospel free of charge, so as not to make full use of my rights in the gospel.

19 For though I am free with respect to all, I have made myself a slave to all, so that I might win more of them. 20To the Jews I became as a Jew, in order to win Jews. To those under the law I became as one under the law (though I myself am not under the law) so that I might win those under the law. 21To those outside the law I became as one outside the law (though I am not free from God's law but am under Christ's law) so that I might win those outside the law. 22To the weak I became weak, so that I might win the weak. I have become all things to all people, that I might by all means save some. 23I do it all for the sake of the gospel, so that I may share in its blessings.

24 Do you not know that in a race the runners all compete, but only one receives the prize? Run in such a way that you may win it. 25Athletes exercise self-control in all things; they do it to receive a perishable wreath, but we an imperishable one. 26So I do not run aimlessly, nor do I box as though beating the air; 27but I punish my body and enslave it, so that after proclaiming to others I myself should not be disqualified.

Warnings from Israel's History

10 I do not want you to be unaware, brothers and sisters,*m* that our ancestors were all under the cloud, and all passed through the sea, 2and all were baptized into Moses in the cloud and in the sea, 3and all ate the same spiritual food, 4and all drank the same spiritual drink. For they drank from the spiritual rock that followed them, and the rock was Christ. 5Nevertheless, God was not pleased with most of them, and they were struck down in the wilderness.

6 Now these things occurred as examples for us, so that we might not desire evil as they did. 7Do not become idolaters as some of them did; as it is written, "The people sat down to eat and drink, and they rose up to play." 8We must not indulge in sexual immorality as some of them did, and twenty-three thousand fell in a single day. 9We must not put Christ*n* to the test, as some of them did, and were destroyed by serpents. 10And do not complain as some of them did, and were destroyed by the destroyer. 11These things happened to them to serve as an example, and they were written down to instruct us, on whom the ends of the ages have come. 12So if you think you are standing, watch out that you do not fall. 13No testing has overtaken you that is not common to everyone. God is faithful, and he will not let you be tested beyond your strength, but with the testing he will also provide the way out so that you may be able to endure it.

14 Therefore, my dear friends,*o* flee from the worship of idols. 15I speak as to sensible people; judge for yourselves what I say. 16The cup of blessing that we bless, is it not a sharing in the blood of Christ? The bread that we break, is it not a sharing in the body of Christ? 17Because there is one bread, we who are many are one body, for we all partake of the one bread. 18Consider the people of Israel;*p* are not those who eat the sacrifices partners in the altar? 19What do I imply then? That food sacrificed to idols is anything, or that an idol is anything? 20No, I imply that what pagans sacrifice, they sacrifice to demons and not to God. I do not want you to be partners with demons. 21You cannot drink

---

m Gk *brothers*   *n* Other ancient authorities read *the Lord*   *o* Gk *my beloved*   *p* Gk *Israel according to the flesh*

the cup of the Lord and the cup of demons. You cannot partake of the table of the Lord and the table of demons. 22Or are we provoking the Lord to jealousy? Are we stronger than he?

Do All to the Glory of God

23 "All things are lawful," but not all things are beneficial. "All things are lawful," but not all things build up. 24Do not seek your own advantage, but that of the other. 25Eat whatever is sold in the meat market without raising any question on the ground of conscience, 26for "the earth and its fullness are the Lord's." 27If an un-

believer invites you to a meal and you are disposed to go, eat whatever is set before you without raising any question on the ground of conscience. 28But if someone says to you, "This has been offered in sacrifice," then do not eat it, out of consideration for the one who informed you, and for the sake of conscience— 29I mean the other's conscience, not your own. For why should my liberty be subject to the judgment of someone else's conscience? 30If I partake with thankfulness, why should I be denounced because of that for which I give thanks?

31 So, whether you eat or drink, or

*P*ay the Price

Do not be frightened, Daughters, by the many things you need to consider in order to begin this divine journey [of the practice of prayer], which is the royal road to heaven. A great treasure is gained by traveling this road; no wonder we have to pay what seems to us a high price. The time will come when you will understand how trifling everything is next to so precious a reward.

Now returning to those who want to journey on this road and continue until they reach the end, which is to drink from this water of life, I say that how they are to begin is very important—in fact, all important. They must have a great and very resolute determination to persevere until reaching the end, come what may, happen what may, whatever work is involved, whatever criticism arises, whether they arrive or whether they die on the road, or even if they don't have courage for the trials that are met, or if the whole world collapses. You will hear some persons frequently making objections: "there are dangers"; "so-and-so went astray by such means"; "this other one was deceived"; "another who prayed a great deal fell away"; "it's harmful to virtue"; "it's not for women, for they will be susceptible to illusions"; "it's better they stick to their sewing"; "they don't need these delicacies"; "the Our Father and the Hail Mary are sufficient."

Don't pay any attention to the fears they raise or to the picture of the dangers they paint for you. How many more dangers are there for those who think they obtain this good without following a road? Begin with the assurance that if we don't let ourselves be conquered, we will obtain our goal; this without a doubt, for no matter how small the gain, one will end up being very rich.

—*SAINT TERESA OF AVILA*

TUESDAY

Scripture Reading for Today:
1 Corinthians 9.24–27

Verse for Today:
1 Corinthians 9.24

Go to page 1507 for your next devotional reading.

whatever you do, do everything for the glory of God. ³²Give no offense to Jews or to Greeks or to the church of God, ³³just as I try to please everyone in everything I do, not seeking my own advantage, but that of many, so that they may be saved.

11 ¹Be imitators of me, as I am of Christ.

Head Coverings

2 I commend you because you remember me in everything and maintain the traditions just as I handed them on to you. ³But I want you to understand that Christ is the head of every man, and the husbandq is the head of his wife,r and God is the head of Christ. ⁴Any man who prays or prophesies with something on his head disgraces his head, ⁵but any woman who prays or prophesies with her head unveiled disgraces her head—it is one and the same thing as having her head shaved. ⁶For if a woman will not veil herself, then she should cut off her hair; but if it is disgraceful for a woman to have her hair cut off or to be shaved, she should wear a veil. ⁷For a man ought not to have his head veiled, since he is the image and reflections of God; but woman is the reflections of man. ⁸Indeed, man was not

q The same Greek word means *man* or *husband*
r Or *head of the woman*   s Or *glory*

The Real Presence

The cup of blessing that we bless, is it not a
sharing in the blood of Christ? The bread that we break,
is it not a sharing in the body of Christ?

I CORINTHIANS 10.16

Every time we go to Mass, we hear the priest say the familiar words, "This is my body . . . This is my blood . . ." Do we ever find them odd? Do we ever ask what it means, really, to eat the body and blood of Christ?

Right from the early days of the Church, the very idea of eating the body of Christ made people uneasy. "I am the bread of life," Jesus told a crowd. "My flesh is true food and my blood is true drink. Those who eat my flesh and drink my blood abide in me, and I in them" (John 6.35, 55–56). People grew restless, disconcerted. "Does this shock you?" Jesus asked. It did. "Too hard," said many of Jesus' own disciples, turning away. "Too weird," they might say today.

In some ways it would be more comfortable to explain what goes on at Mass as mere symbolism. But the Catholic Church has always followed Jesus' lead, teaching that the *consecrated* bread and wine are transformed into Jesus' flesh and blood.

Exactly how the substance of bread and wine becomes the substance of Jesus' body is and always will be mystery. But then, so is the incarnation. And isn't the mystery of the Eucharist in perfect continuity with the mystery of "God with us"? How consistent for a God who made a surprise appearance as a baby to continue his physical presence in an equally extraordinary way!

A southern writer told about a little girl from a poor family who had a good grasp of this Real Presence. Given a physical exam by a doctor visiting her slum district school, the child was asked, "Monica, what did the doctor say about you?" The girl reported, "He said that I was a poor miserable specimen of humanity." Then, pirouetting merrily, she added, "But *he* didn't know that I had made my First Communion."

Little Monica knew that she was more than she appeared to be. In the humble bread and wine that hide the presence of divinity—and in Monica and every communicant because of it—there is more than meets the eye.

made from woman, but woman from man. [9]Neither was man created for the sake of woman, but woman for the sake of man. [10]For this reason a woman ought to have a symbol of[t] authority on her head,[u] because of the angels. [11]Nevertheless, in the Lord woman is not independent of man or man independent of woman. [12]For just as woman came from man, so man comes through woman; but all things come from God. [13]Judge for yourselves: is it proper for a woman to pray to God with her head unveiled? [14]Does not nature itself teach you that if a man wears long hair, it is degrading to him, [15]but if a woman has long hair, it is her glory? For her hair is given to her for a covering. [16]But if anyone is disposed to be contentious—we have no such custom, nor do the churches of God.

Abuses at the Lord's Supper

17 Now in the following instructions I do not commend you, because when you come together it is not for the better but for the worse. [18]For, to begin with, when you come together as a church, I hear that there are divisions among you; and to some extent I believe it. [19]Indeed, there have to be factions among you, for only so will it become clear who among you are genuine. [20]When you come together, it is not really to eat the Lord's supper. [21]For when the time comes to eat, each of you goes ahead with your own supper, and one goes hungry and another becomes drunk. [22]What! Do you not have homes to eat and drink in? Or do you show contempt for the church of God and humiliate those who have nothing? What should I say to you? Should I commend you? In this matter I do not commend you!

The Institution of the Lord's Supper

23 For I received from the Lord what I also handed on to you, that the Lord Jesus on the night when he was betrayed took a loaf of bread, [24]and when he had given thanks, he broke it and said, "This is my body that is for[v] you. Do this in remembrance of me." [25]In the same way he took the cup also, after supper, saying, "This cup is the new covenant in my blood. Do this, as often as you drink it, in remembrance of me." [26]For as often as you eat this bread and drink the cup, you proclaim the Lord's death until he comes.

Partaking of the Supper Unworthily

27 Whoever, therefore, eats the bread or drinks the cup of the Lord in an unworthy manner will be answerable for the body and blood of the Lord. [28]Examine yourselves, and only then eat of the bread and drink of the cup. [29]For all who eat and drink[w] without discerning the body,[x] eat and drink judgment against themselves. [30]For this reason many of you are weak and ill, and some have died.[y] [31]But if we judged ourselves, we would not be judged. [32]But when we are judged by the Lord, we are disciplined[z] so that we may not be condemned along with the world.

33 So then, my brothers and sisters,[a] when you come together to eat, wait for one another. [34]If you are hungry, eat at home, so that when you come together, it will not be for your condemnation. About the other things I will give instructions when I come.

Spiritual Gifts

12 Now concerning spiritual gifts,[b] brothers and sisters,[a] I do not want you to be uninformed. [2]You know that when you were pagans, you were enticed and led astray to idols that could not speak. [3]Therefore I want you to understand that no one speaking by the Spirit of God ever says "Let Jesus be cursed!" and no one can say "Jesus is Lord" except by the Holy Spirit.

4 Now there are varieties of gifts, but the same Spirit; [5]and there are varieties of services, but the same Lord; [6]and there are varieties of activities, but it is the same God who activates all of them in everyone. [7]To each is given the manifestation of the Spirit for the common good. [8]To one is given through the Spirit the utterance of wisdom, and to another the utterance of knowledge according to the same Spirit, [9]to another faith by the same Spirit, to another gifts of healing by the one Spirit, [10]to another the working of miracles, to another prophecy, to another the discern-

[t] Gk lacks *a symbol of*   [u] Or *have freedom of choice regarding her head*   [v] Other ancient authorities read *is broken for*   [w] Other ancient authorities add *in an unworthy manner*,   [x] Other ancient authorities read *the Lord's body*   [y] Gk *fallen asleep*   [z] Or *When we are judged, we are being disciplined by the Lord*   [a] Gk *brothers*   [b] Or *spiritual persons*

ment of spirits; to another various kinds of tongues, to another the interpretation of tongues. [11]All these are activated by one and the same Spirit, who allots to each one individually just as the Spirit chooses.

One Body with Many Members

12 For just as the body is one and has many members, and all the members of the body, though many, are one body, so it is with Christ. [13]For in the one Spirit we were all baptized into one body—Jews or Greeks, slaves or free—and we were all made to drink of one Spirit.

14 Indeed, the body does not consist of one member but of many. [15]If the foot would say, "Because I am not a hand, I do not belong to the body," that would not make it any less a part of the body. [16]And

Scripture Reading
for Today:
I Corinthians 12.4–20

Verse for Today:
I Corinthians 12.4

*B*ody of Christ

Many women compare themselves to their sisters in the Lord and, falling short by comparison, say, "It's beyond me—I'll never be as good as they are. Besides, I'm not worth much anyway." This is the plan of the enemy: that we intimidate one another and drive one another into defeatism.

Comparison is the problem. It can form a tool, which the enemy will use against us. It puts our attention on ourselves rather than on the will of the Lord. Therefore we are bound to be mistaken in our judgment.

Fortunately, God does not give up on us as easily as we give up on ourselves. His plan is that we inspire and encourage each other to perfection. In the body of Christ, we are not meant to compare or compete, but to complement each other. "There are varieties of gifts, but the same Spirit" (I Corinthians 12.4). "The body does not consist of one member but of many" (verse 14). Just because I, as a foot in the body, may not have the same function or finesse as a twinkling eye, I don't have the right to say, "I give up. I'll never be as good as that eye anyway." The truth is, the body will limp pretty badly without that foot.

"But," I protest, "I'm such a bad foot; the body is already limping because of me." Okay, then perhaps a corrective shoe is needed. Whether that is formed for me by good teaching, repentance, admonition, those who are authority in my life, or a combination of all of those factors, I receive the corrective shoe gladly and become the most nearly perfect foot I can, pointed straight toward the kingdom of God.

As we start off from a new position of assurance and security, we glance up at the other members of the body to see how we can all move forward together. We should not be surprised to discover that the "eye" we so envied as perfect is now wearing glasses to perfect its vision. We all need improvement, but we are all called to be perfect, to be saints of God.

—*DOROTHY RANAGHAN*

Go to page 1509 for your next devotional reading.

if the ear would say, "Because I am not an eye, I do not belong to the body," that would not make it any less a part of the body. ¹⁷If the whole body were an eye, where would the hearing be? If the whole body were hearing, where would the sense of smell be? ¹⁸But as it is, God arranged the members in the body, each one of them, as he chose. ¹⁹If all were a single member, where would the body be? ²⁰As it is, there are many members, yet one body. ²¹The eye cannot say to the hand, "I have no need of you," nor again the head to the feet, "I have no need of you." ²²On the contrary, the members of the body that seem to be weaker are indispensable, ²³and those members of the body that we think less honorable we clothe with greater honor, and our less respectable members are treated with greater respect; ²⁴whereas our more respectable members do not need this. But God has so arranged the body, giving the greater honor to the inferior member, ²⁵that there may be no dissension within the body, but the members may have the same care for one another. ²⁶If one member suffers, all suffer together with it; if one member is honored, all rejoice together with it.

27 Now you are the body of Christ and individually members of it. ²⁸And God has appointed in the church first apostles, second prophets, third teachers; then deeds of power, then gifts of healing, forms of assistance, forms of leadership, various kinds of tongues. ²⁹Are all apostles? Are all prophets? Are all teachers? Do all work miracles? ³⁰Do all possess gifts of healing? Do all speak in tongues? Do all interpret? ³¹But strive for the greater gifts. And I will show you a still more excellent way.

The Gift of Love

13 If I speak in the tongues of mortals and of angels, but do not have love, I am a noisy gong or a clanging cymbal. ²And if I have prophetic powers, and understand all mysteries and all knowledge, and if I have all faith, so as to remove mountains, but do not have love, I am nothing. ³If I give away all my possessions, and if I hand over my body so that I may boast,*c* but do not have love, I gain nothing.

4 Love is patient; love is kind; love is not envious or boastful or arrogant ⁵or rude. It does not insist on its own way; it is not irritable or resentful; ⁶it does not rejoice in wrongdoing, but rejoices in the truth. ⁷It bears all things, believes all things, hopes all things, endures all things.

8 Love never ends. But as for prophecies, they will come to an end; as for tongues, they will cease; as for knowledge, it will come to an end. ⁹For we know only in part, and we prophesy only in part; ¹⁰but when the complete comes, the partial will come to an end. ¹¹When I was a child, I spoke like a child, I thought like a child, I reasoned like a child; when I became an adult, I put an end to childish ways. ¹²For now we see in a mirror, dimly,*d* but then we will see face to face. Now I know only in part; then I will know fully, even as I have been fully known. ¹³And now faith, hope, and love abide, these three; and the greatest of these is love.

Gifts of Prophecy and Tongues

14 Pursue love and strive for the spiritual gifts, and especially that you may prophesy. ²For those who speak in a tongue do not speak to other people but to God; for nobody understands them, since they are speaking mysteries in the Spirit. ³On the other hand, those who prophesy speak to other people for their upbuilding and encouragement and consolation. ⁴Those who speak in a tongue build up themselves, but those who prophesy build up the church. ⁵Now I would like all of you to speak in tongues, but even more to prophesy. One who prophesies is greater than one who speaks in tongues, unless someone interprets, so that the church may be built up.

6 Now, brothers and sisters,*e* if I come to you speaking in tongues, how will I benefit you unless I speak to you in some revelation or knowledge or prophecy or teaching? ⁷It is the same way with lifeless instruments that produce sound, such as the flute or the harp. If they do not give distinct notes, how will anyone know what is being played? ⁸And if the bugle gives an indistinct sound, who will get ready for battle? ⁹So with yourselves; if in a tongue you utter speech that is not intelligible, how will anyone know what is be-

c Other ancient authorities read *body to be burned*
d Gk *in a riddle*   *e* Gk *brothers*

ing said? For you will be speaking into the air. ¹⁰There are doubtless many different kinds of sounds in the world, and nothing is without sound. ¹¹If then I do not know the meaning of a sound, I will be a foreigner to the speaker and the speaker a foreigner to me. ¹²So with yourselves; since you are eager for spiritual gifts, strive to excel in them for building up the church.

13 Therefore, one who speaks in a tongue should pray for the power to interpret. ¹⁴For if I pray in a tongue, my spirit prays but my mind is unproductive.

¹⁵What should I do then? I will pray with the spirit, but I will pray with the mind also; I will sing praise with the spirit, but I will sing praise with the mind also. ¹⁶Otherwise, if you say a blessing with the spirit, how can anyone in the position of an outsider say the "Amen" to your thanksgiving, since the outsider does not know what you are saying? ¹⁷For you may give thanks well enough, but the other person is not built up. ¹⁸I thank God that I speak in tongues more than all of you; ¹⁹nevertheless, in church I would rather speak five words with my mind, in order

"*My Vocation Is Love*"

THURSDAY

Scripture Reading for Today:
1 Corinthians 13.1–13

Verse for Today:
1 Corinthians 13.13

In chapters twelve and thirteen of the First Epistle to the Corinthians, I read that we cannot all be apostles, prophets, and doctors, that the Church is made up of different members, and that the eye cannot also be the hand. I went on reading and came to: "But strive for the greater gifts. And I will show you a still more excellent way" [12.31]. The apostle explains how even all the most perfect gifts are nothing without love and that charity is the most excellent way of going safely to God. I had found peace at last.

I thought of the Mystical Body of the Church, but I could not recognize myself in any of its members listed by Saint Paul—or, rather, I wanted to recognize myself in them all. Charity gave me the key to my vocation. I realized that if the Church was a body made up of different members, she would not be without the greatest and most essential of them all. I realized that love includes all vocations, that love is all things, and that, because it is eternal, it embraces every time and place.

Swept by an ecstatic joy, I cried: "Jesus, my love! At last I have found my vocation. My vocation is love! I have found my place in the bosom of the Church, and it is you, Lord, who has given it me. In the heart of the Church, who is my Mother, *I will be love.* So I shall be everything, and so my dreams will be fulfilled!" Why do I speak of "ecstatic joy"? It's the wrong phrase to use. Instead, I should speak of peace, that calm, tranquil peace, which the helmsman feels as he sees the beacon, which guides him into the harbor. How brightly this beacon of love burns! And I know how to reach it and make its flames my own.

—*SAINT THÉRÈSE OF LISIEUX*

Go to page 1510 for your next devotional reading.

to instruct others also, than ten thousand words in a tongue.

20 Brothers and sisters,f do not be children in your thinking; rather, be infants in evil, but in thinking be adults. 21In the law it is written,

"By people of strange tongues
　and by the lips of foreigners
I will speak to this people;
　yet even then they will not listen
　　to me,"

says the Lord. 22Tongues, then, are a sign not for believers but for unbelievers, while prophecy is not for unbelievers but for believers. 23If, therefore, the whole church comes together and all speak in tongues, and outsiders or unbelievers enter, will they not say that you are out of your mind? 24But if all prophesy, an unbeliever or outsider who enters is reproved by all and called to account by all. 25After the secrets of the unbeliever's heart are disclosed, that person will bow down before God and worship him, declaring, "God is really among you."

Orderly Worship

26 What should be done then, my friends?f When you come together, each one has a hymn, a lesson, a revelation, a tongue, or an interpretation. Let all things be done for building up. 27If anyone speaks in a tongue, let there be only two or at most three, and each in turn; and let one interpret. 28But if there is no one to interpret, let them be silent in church and

f Gk brothers

FRIDAY

Scripture Reading
for Today:
1 Corinthians 14.13–22

Verse for Today:
1 Corinthians 14.20

Paradox

There are paradoxes here. Echoing in our minds is the Lord's warning, "Unless you change and become like children, you will never enter the kingdom of heaven" [Matthew 18.3]. Yet Saint Paul rebuked the Corinthians for childishness: "I could not speak to you as spiritual people, but rather as people of the flesh, as infants in Christ. I fed you with milk, not solid food, for you were not ready for solid food. Even now you are still not ready, for you are still of the flesh" [1 Corinthians 3.1–3]. Moreover, Jesus put very adult challenges to his friends. We are to take up our cross and follow him, to Calvary and to glory; we are to choose, knowing that heaven and hell are in the balance. These are not children's games.

The paradox, like every other paradox in Christian life, comes back to the person of Christ himself. In his childhood there are qualities of Sonship which he never lost: trust, openness, simplicity, the need to love and be loved. He never lost them, but he transposed them and lived them anew throughout the experiences of maturity.

Our new birth as sons and daughters of God is a share in Christ's Sonship, and we are therefore invited to explore the implications of it as he did. Obedience and simplicity are supposed to be "natural" to childhood; whether they are or not, there is a different obedience and a different simplicity in adult love, the fruit not of natural condition but of deliberate choices made in the power of the Spirit of Sonship.

—MARIA BOULDING

Go to page 1512 for your next devotional reading.

speak to themselves and to God. ²⁹Let two or three prophets speak, and let the others weigh what is said. ³⁰If a revelation is made to someone else sitting nearby, let the first person be silent. ³¹For you can all prophesy one by one, so that all may learn and all be encouraged. ³²And the spirits of prophets are subject to the prophets, ³³for God is a God not of disorder but of peace.

(As in all the churches of the saints, ³⁴women should be silent in the churches. For they are not permitted to speak, but should be subordinate, as the law also says. ³⁵If there is anything they desire to know, let them ask their husbands at home. For it is shameful for a woman to speak in church.ᵍ ³⁶Or did the word of God originate with you? Or are you the only ones it has reached?)

³⁷Anyone who claims to be a prophet, or to have spiritual powers, must acknowledge that what I am writing to you is a command of the Lord. ³⁸Anyone who does not recognize this is not to be recognized. ³⁹So, my friends,ʰ be eager to prophesy, and do not forbid speaking in tongues; ⁴⁰but all things should be done decently and in order.

The Resurrection of Christ

15 Now I would remind you, brothers and sisters,ⁱ of the good newsʲ that I proclaimed to you, which you in turn received, in which also you stand, ²through which also you are being saved, if you hold firmly to the message that I proclaimed to you—unless you have come to believe in vain.

3 For I handed on to you as of first importance what I in turn had received: that Christ died for our sins in accordance with the scriptures, ⁴and that he was buried, and that he was raised on the third day in accordance with the scriptures, ⁵and that he appeared to Cephas, then to the twelve. ⁶Then he appeared to more than five hundred brothers and sistersⁱ at one time, most of whom are still alive, though some have died.ᵏ ⁷Then he appeared to James, then to all the apostles. ⁸Last of all, as to one untimely born, he appeared also to me. ⁹For I am the least of the apostles, unfit to be called an apostle, because I persecuted the church of God. ¹⁰But by the grace of God I am what I am, and his grace toward me has not been in vain. On the contrary, I worked harder than any of them—though it was not I,

but the grace of God that is with me. ¹¹Whether then it was I or they, so we proclaim and so you have come to believe.

The Resurrection of the Dead

12 Now if Christ is proclaimed as raised from the dead, how can some of you say there is no resurrection of the dead? ¹³If there is no resurrection of the dead, then Christ has not been raised; ¹⁴and if Christ has not been raised, then our proclamation has been in vain and your faith has been in vain. ¹⁵We are even found to be misrepresenting God, because we testified of God that he raised Christ—whom he did not raise if it is true that the dead are not raised. ¹⁶For if the dead are not raised, then Christ has not been raised. ¹⁷If Christ has not been raised, your faith is futile and you are still in your sins. ¹⁸Then those also who have diedᵏ in Christ have perished. ¹⁹If for this life only we have hoped in Christ, we are of all people most to be pitied.

20 But in fact Christ has been raised from the dead, the first fruits of those who have died.ᵏ ²¹For since death came through a human being, the resurrection of the dead has also come through a human being; ²²for as all die in Adam, so all will be made alive in Christ. ²³But each in his own order: Christ the first fruits, then at his coming those who belong to Christ. ²⁴Then comes the end,ˡ when he hands over the kingdom to God the Father, after he has destroyed every ruler and every authority and power. ²⁵For he must reign until he has put all his enemies under his feet. ²⁶The last enemy to be destroyed is death. ²⁷For "Godᵐ has put all things in subjection under his feet." But when it says, "All things are put in subjection," it is plain that this does not include the one who put all things in subjection under him. ²⁸When all things are subjected to him, then the Son himself will also be subjected to the one who put all things in subjection under him, so that God may be all in all.

29 Otherwise, what will those people do who receive baptism on behalf of the

---

ᵍ Other ancient authorities put verses 34-35 after verse 40　ʰ Gk *my brothers*　ⁱ Gk *brothers*　ʲ Or *gospel*　ᵏ Gk *fallen asleep*　ˡ Or *Then come the rest*　ᵐ Gk *he*

The Woman Who Lived a Sinful Life

Read Luke 7.36–50

The woman felt as though her world had unraveled in a moment's time. Doors had opened, walls had crumbled, and everything that might yet happen to her no longer frightened, but thrilled her. The weight of an unhappy future had been instantly lifted from her shoulders. She felt clean and whole, innocent as a girl still living in her father's house. Her heart was a wild confusion of sorrow and joy as she followed the rabbi through the doorway of Simon's house.

Her Character: *She was a notorious sinner, possibly a prostitute or adulteress. After having been forgiven, she made a spectacle of herself in a passionate display of love and gratitude.*
Her Sorrow: *That she had offended God so grievously.*
Her Joy: *That Jesus forgave her sins and commended her for her great faith and love.*

Ignoring the stares of the men, she walked over to the place where Jesus was reclining at a table. In her hands she held an alabaster jar of perfume. Trembling, she covered his feet with her kisses and then anointed them with the precious perfume, wiping his feet with her hair. How else could she express her heart to the man who had loved her so well?

Simon the Pharisee was surprised that a sinful woman, even a hungry one, would enter his house. "If this man were a prophet," Simon thought, "he would have known who and what kind of woman this is who is touching him—that she is a sinner" (7:39). All of his questions about Jesus were put to rest by the scene he had just witnessed. His ordered way of looking at the world was safe enough, bolstered by the judgment he had just rendered.

As though he had overheard Simon's secret thoughts, Jesus turned and spoke to him, telling him a parable about two people who

had been forgiven a debt. Then he said,

Do you see this woman? I entered your house; you gave me no water for my feet, but she has bathed my feet with her tears and dried them with her hair. You gave me no kiss, but from the time I came in she has not stopped kissing my feet. You did not anoint my head with oil, but she has anointed my feet with ointment. Therefore, I tell you, her sins, which were many, have been forgiven; hence she has shown great love. But the one to whom little is forgiven, loves little.

(verses 44–47)

The other guests began to say, "Who is this who even forgives sins?"

Jesus said to the woman, "Your faith has saved you; go in peace."

Though the woman was a notorious sinner, she recognized her great need for grace. Repentance turned her world on its head, opening up an entirely new view of things. Simon, by contrast, was a religious man whose habit of judging others had formed a fence around his one-dimensional view of the universe, shielding his neat and orderly life from the unpredictable power of grace.

But Simon and the woman both owed a debt they could not possibly repay. Though his sin was less obvious, it was the more dangerous. He was like a man who was following a map he was certain would lead to heaven. But when heaven came down and walked into his house, he didn't even know it. The woman, on the other hand, realized just how lost she had been. Forgiven much, she loved much.

Praying With the Woman Who Lived a Sinful Life

"Therefore, I tell you, her sins, which were many, have been forgiven; hence she has shown great love. But the one to whom little is forgiven, loves little."
—Luke 7.47

Praise God: For the power of forgiveness in your own life.
Offer Thanks: That God is still ready to forgive you, no matter how frequently or how seriously you have sinned.
Confess: Any self-righteousness that has crept into your life.
Ask God: To protect you against pride.

Lift Your Heart

How long has it been since tears of repentance have washed your soul? Do you find it easier to linger over others' failings than your own? Harsh attitudes toward the notorious sins of others—even the sins of unprincipled politicians or insensitive husbands—will only dry up your love for God.

No matter how long it's been since you committed your life to God, you can still obstruct his grace. Pride has a way of creeping back in, locking you into a black-and-white vision of the universe. This week search your heart for any judgments, large or small, that you have made against others. Make a list of people of whom you've been especially critical. Pray for each one, releasing your judgments and asking God to bless that person. Then tear up the sheet as a sign that you are repenting of the judgments you made. The next time you are tempted to judge someone, quickly repeat this exercise in your mind.

Lord, when others rejected me, you embraced me. What was untouchable in me you touched. Make me a woman who loves much, a woman who is not afraid to fall at your feet, bathing them with her tears.

Go to page 1517 for your next devotional reading.

dead? If the dead are not raised at all, why are people baptized on their behalf?

30 And why are we putting ourselves in danger every hour? [31]I die every day! That is as certain, brothers and sisters,[n] as my boasting of you—a boast that I make in Christ Jesus our Lord. [32]If with merely human hopes I fought with wild animals at Ephesus, what would I have gained by it? If the dead are not raised,

"Let us eat and drink,
for tomorrow we die."

[33]Do not be deceived:
"Bad company ruins good morals."
[34]Come to a sober and right mind, and sin no more; for some people have no knowledge of God. I say this to your shame.

The Resurrection Body

35 But someone will ask, "How are the dead raised? With what kind of body do they come?" [36]Fool! What you sow does not come to life unless it dies. [37]And as for what you sow, you do not sow the body that is to be, but a bare seed, perhaps of wheat or of some other grain. [38]But God gives it a body as he has chosen, and to each kind of seed its own body. [39]Not all flesh is alike, but there is one flesh for human beings, another for animals, another for birds, and another for fish. [40]There are both heavenly bodies and earthly bodies, but the glory of the heavenly is one thing, and that of the earthly is another. [41]There is one glory of the sun, and another glory of the moon, and another glory of the stars; indeed, star differs from star in glory.

42 So it is with the resurrection of the dead. What is sown is perishable, what is raised is imperishable. [43]It is sown in dishonor, it is raised in glory. It is sown in weakness, it is raised in power. [44]It is sown a physical body, it is raised a spiritual body. If there is a physical body, there is also a spiritual body. [45]Thus it is written, "The first man, Adam, became a living being"; the last Adam became a life-giving spirit. [46]But it is not the spiritual that is first, but the physical, and then the spiritual. [47]The first man was from the earth, a man of dust; the second man is[o] from heaven. [48]As was the man of dust, so are those who are of the dust; and as is the man of heaven, so are those who are of heaven. [49]Just as we have borne the image of the man of dust, we will[p] also bear the image of the man of heaven.

50 What I am saying, brothers and sisters,[n] is this: flesh and blood cannot inherit the kingdom of God, nor does the perishable inherit the imperishable. [51]Listen, I will tell you a mystery! We will not all die,[q] but we will all be changed, [52]in a moment, in the twinkling of an eye, at the last trumpet. For the trumpet will sound, and the dead will be raised imperishable, and we will be changed. [53]For this perishable body must put on imperishability, and this mortal body must put on immortality. [54]When this perishable body puts on imperishability, and this mortal body puts on immortality, then the saying that is written will be fulfilled:

"Death has been swallowed up
in victory."

55 "Where, O death, is your victory?
Where, O death, is your sting?"

[56]The sting of death is sin, and the power of sin is the law. [57]But thanks be to God, who gives us the victory through our Lord Jesus Christ.

58 Therefore, my beloved,[r] be steadfast, immovable, always excelling in the work of the Lord, because you know that in the Lord your labor is not in vain.

The Collection for the Saints

16 Now concerning the collection for the saints: you should follow the directions I gave to the churches of Galatia. [2]On the first day of every week, each of you is to put aside and save whatever extra you earn, so that collections need not be taken when I come. [3]And when I arrive, I will send any whom you approve with letters to take your gift to Jerusalem. [4]If it seems advisable that I should go also, they will accompany me.

Plans for Travel

5 I will visit you after passing through Macedonia—for I intend to pass through Macedonia— [6]and perhaps I will stay with you or even spend the winter, so that you may send me on my way, wherever I go. [7]I do not want to see you now just in passing, for I hope to spend some time with you, if the Lord permits. [8]But I will stay in Ephesus until Pentecost, [9]for a wide door for effective work has opened to me, and there are many adversaries.

---

[n] Gk brothers   [o] Other ancient authorities add *the Lord*   [p] Other ancient authorities read *let us*   [q] Gk *fall asleep*   [r] Gk *beloved brothers*

10 If Timothy comes, see that he has nothing to fear among you, for he is doing the work of the Lord just as I am; [11]therefore let no one despise him. Send him on his way in peace, so that he may come to me; for I am expecting him with the brothers.

12 Now concerning our brother Apollos, I strongly urged him to visit you with the other brothers, but he was not at all willing[s] to come now. He will come when he has the opportunity.

Final Messages and Greetings

13 Keep alert, stand firm in your faith, be courageous, be strong. [14]Let all that you do be done in love.

15 Now, brothers and sisters,[t] you know that members of the household of Stephanas were the first converts in Achaia, and they have devoted themselves to the service of the saints; [16]I urge you to put yourselves at the service of such people, and of everyone who works and toils

with them. [17]I rejoice at the coming of Stephanas and Fortunatus and Achaicus, because they have made up for your absence; [18]for they refreshed my spirit as well as yours. So give recognition to such persons.

19 The churches of Asia send greetings. Aquila and Prisca, together with the church in their house, greet you warmly in the Lord. [20]All the brothers and sisters[t] send greetings. Greet one another with a holy kiss.

21 I, Paul, write this greeting with my own hand. [22]Let anyone be accursed who has no love for the Lord. Our Lord, come![u] [23]The grace of the Lord Jesus be with you. [24]My love be with all of you in Christ Jesus.[v]

s *Or it was not at all God's will for him*   t Gk *brothers*   u Gk *Marana tha.* These Aramaic words can also be read *Maran atha,* meaning *Our Lord has come*   v Other ancient authorities add *Amen*

2 Corinthians

The capital of the Roman province of Achaia, Corinth (located in modern-day Greece), was an important commercial hub, one in which every kind of vice seemed to flourish. During his second missionary journey, Paul founded a vigorous church there, meeting up with fellow believers Priscilla and her husband Aquila, tentmakers like him. (These two would later help found the church in Ephesus.)

Paul's first letter to the church in Corinth did not resolve the problems that festered in the fledgling community. Some months after writing it, he addressed the Corinthians again, this time more passionately than ever. Paul speaks of being exhausted and afflicted, even to the point of death. He is upset that false teachers are sowing division and defends himself against accusations that they have leveled against him in his absence. He speaks openly of his sufferings as an apostle (see 11.24–30).

But Paul also mentions mystical experiences, visions and revelations of Christ that elated and sustained him. He speaks, too, of his love and affection for the Corinthians, begging them to listen to him and to live in peace with each other. Paul exhorts them as well to contribute generously to the collection for fellow believers in Jerusalem, reminding them that "the one who sows sparingly will also reap sparingly, and the one who sows bountifully will also reap bountifully" (9.6).

Salutation

1 Paul, an apostle of Christ Jesus by the will of God, and Timothy our brother,

To the church of God that is in Corinth, including all the saints throughout Achaia:

2 Grace to you and peace from God our Father and the Lord Jesus Christ.

Paul's Thanksgiving after Affliction

3 Blessed be the God and Father of our Lord Jesus Christ, the Father of mercies and the God of all consolation, ⁴who consoles us in all our affliction, so that we may be able to console those who are in any affliction with the consolation with which we ourselves are consoled by God. ⁵For just as the sufferings of Christ are

abundant for us, so also our consolation is abundant through Christ. 6If we are being afflicted, it is for your consolation and salvation; if we are being consoled, it is for your consolation, which you experience when you patiently endure the same sufferings that we are also suffering. 7Our hope for you is unshaken; for we know that as you share in our sufferings, so also you share in our consolation.

8 We do not want you to be unaware, brothers and sisters,*a* of the affliction we experienced in Asia; for we were so utterly, unbearably crushed that we despaired of life itself. 9Indeed, we felt that we had received the sentence of death so that we would rely not on ourselves but on God

who raises the dead. 10He who rescued us from so deadly a peril will continue to rescue us; on him we have set our hope that he will rescue us again, 11as you also join in helping us by your prayers, so that many will give thanks on our*b* behalf for the blessing granted us through the prayers of many.

The Postponement of Paul's Visit

12 Indeed, this is our boast, the testimony of our conscience: we have behaved in the world with frankness*c* and godly sincerity, not by earthly wisdom but by

a Gk *brothers*   *b* Other ancient authorities read *your*   *c* Other ancient authorities read *holiness*

Our Need

MONDAY

Scripture Reading for Today:
2 Corinthians 1.3–11

Verse for Today:
2 Corinthians 1.10

Lord, the day is drawing to a close and, like all the other days, it leaves with me the impression of utter defeat. I have done nothing for you: neither have I said conscious prayers, nor performed works of charity, nor any work at all, work that is sacred for every Christian who understands its significance. I have not even been able to control that childish impatience and those foolish rancors that so often occupy the place that should be yours in the "no-man's land" of my emotions. It is in vain that I promise you to do better. I shall be no different tomorrow, nor on the day that follows.

When I retrace the course of my life, I am overwhelmed by the same impression of inadequacy. I have sought you in prayer and in the service of my neighbor, for we cannot separate you from our brothers any more than we can separate our body from our spirit. But in seeking you, do I not find myself? Do I not wish to satisfy myself? Those works that I secretly termed good and saintly dissolve in the light of approaching eternity, and I dare no longer lean on these supports that have lost their stability.

Even actual sufferings bring me no joy because I bear them so badly. Perhaps we are all like this: incapable of discerning anything but our own wretchedness and our own despairing cowardice before the light of the beyond that waxes on our horizon.

But it may be, O Lord, that this impression of privation is part of a divine plan. It may be that, in your eyes, self-complacency is the most obnoxious of all fripperies, and that we must come before you naked so that you, you alone, may clothe us.

—MARGUERITE TEILHARD DE CHARDIN

Go to page 1519 for your next devotional reading.

the grace of God—and all the more toward you. [13]For we write you nothing other than what you can read and also understand; I hope you will understand until the end— [14]as you have already understood us in part—that on the day of the Lord Jesus we are your boast even as you are our boast.

15 Since I was sure of this, I wanted to come to you first, so that you might have a double favor;[d] [16]I wanted to visit you on my way to Macedonia, and to come back to you from Macedonia and have you send me on to Judea. [17]Was I vacillating when I wanted to do this? Do I make my plans according to ordinary human standards,[e] ready to say "Yes, yes" and "No, no" at the same time? [18]As surely as God is faithful, our word to you has not been "Yes and No." [19]For the Son of God, Jesus Christ, whom we proclaimed among you, Silvanus and Timothy and I, was not "Yes and No"; but in him it is always "Yes." [20]For in him every one of God's promises is a "Yes." For this reason it is through him that we say the "Amen," to the glory of God. [21]But it is God who establishes us with you in Christ and has anointed us, [22]by putting his seal on us and giving us his Spirit in our hearts as a first installment.

23 But I call on God as witness against me: it was to spare you that I did not come again to Corinth. [24]I do not mean to imply that we lord it over your faith; rather, we are workers with you for your joy, because you stand firm in the faith. 2 [1]So I made up my mind not to make you another painful visit. [2]For if I cause you pain, who is there to make me glad but the one whom I have pained? [3]And I wrote as I did, so that when I came, I might not suffer pain from those who should have made me rejoice; for I am confident about all of you, that my joy would be the joy of all of you. [4]For I wrote you out of much distress and anguish of heart and with many tears, not to cause you pain, but to let you know the abundant love that I have for you.

Forgiveness for the Offender

5 But if anyone has caused pain, he has caused it not to me, but to some extent—not to exaggerate it—to all of you. [6]This punishment by the majority is enough for such a person; [7]so now instead you should forgive and console him, so that he may not be overwhelmed by excessive sorrow. [8]So I urge you to reaffirm your love for him. [9]I wrote for this reason: to test you and to know whether you are obedient in everything. [10]Anyone whom you forgive, I also forgive. What I have forgiven, if I have forgiven anything, has been for your sake in the presence of Christ. [11]And we do this so that we may not be outwitted by Satan; for we are not ignorant of his designs.

Paul's Anxiety in Troas

12 When I came to Troas to proclaim the good news of Christ, a door was opened for me in the Lord; [13]but my mind could not rest because I did not find my brother Titus there. So I said farewell to them and went on to Macedonia.

14 But thanks be to God, who in Christ always leads us in triumphal procession, and through us spreads in every place the fragrance that comes from knowing him. [15]For we are the aroma of Christ to God among those who are being saved and among those who are perishing; [16]to the one a fragrance from death to death, to the other a fragrance from life to life. Who is sufficient for these things? [17]For we are not peddlers of God's word like so many;[f] but in Christ we speak as persons of sincerity, as persons sent from God and standing in his presence.

Ministers of the New Covenant

3 Are we beginning to commend ourselves again? Surely we do not need, as some do, letters of recommendation to you or from you, do we? [2]You yourselves are our letter, written on our[g] hearts, to be known and read by all; [3]and you show that you are a letter of Christ, prepared by us, written not with ink but with the Spirit of the living God, not on tablets of stone but on tablets of human hearts.

4 Such is the confidence that we have through Christ toward God. [5]Not that we are competent of ourselves to claim anything as coming from us; our competence is from God, [6]who has made us compe-

d Other ancient authorities read *pleasure*   *e* Gk
according to the flesh   *f* Other ancient authorities
read *like the others*   *g* Other ancient authorities
read *your*

tent to be ministers of a new covenant, not of letter but of spirit; for the letter kills, but the Spirit gives life.

7 Now if the ministry of death, chiseled in letters on stone tablets,[h] came in glory so that the people of Israel could not gaze at Moses' face because of the glory of his face, a glory now set aside, [8]how much more will the ministry of the Spirit come in glory? [9]For if there was glory in the ministry of condemnation, much more does the ministry of justification abound in glory! [10]Indeed, what once had glory has lost its glory because of the greater glory; [11]for if what was set aside came through glory, much more has the permanent come in glory!

12 Since, then, we have such a hope, we act with great boldness, [13]not like Moses, who put a veil over his face to keep the people of Israel from gazing at the end of the glory that[i] was being set aside. [14]But their minds were hardened. Indeed, to this very day, when they hear the reading of the old covenant, that same veil is still there, since only in Christ is it set aside. [15]Indeed, to this very day whenever Moses is read, a veil lies over their minds; [16]but when one turns to the Lord, the veil is removed. [17]Now the Lord is the Spirit, and where the Spirit of the Lord is, there is freedom. [18]And all of us, with unveiled faces, seeing the glory of the Lord as though reflected in a mirror, are being transformed into the same image from one degree of glory to another; for this comes from the Lord, the Spirit.

h Gk *on stones*   *i* Gk *of what*

Let God Shine Upon You

TUESDAY

Scripture Reading for Today:
2 Corinthians 3.12–18

Verse for Today:
2 Corinthians 3.18

I encourage everyone to have a special place, a corner or a room, that is reserved for prayer. This special place, with an icon or image of Jesus, will help you leave for a moment the cares of the world and draw you into close communion with the Lord.

I'd like to share a teaching that came to me one day as I sat before the Lord. I was just looking at the Blessed Sacrament and adoring Jesus and telling him I didn't have much to say except that I loved him.

I felt as though the Lord said to me, "Well, don't you know that you don't have to say anything to me? Just be with me. Come into my presence. It's not what you do for me, it's what I want to do for you."

Then I got an image of a person going out of his house and sitting in the sun. As he sat in the sun, he didn't do a thing, but he started to change color. People who saw him knew he had been in the sun because his skin showed it. The man knew it, too, because he felt the effects of the sun: the warmth and the light.

I heard the Lord saying, "So it is when you come into my presence. You will experience the effects of your time spent with me. People will see it in your actions."

It was a great teaching to me, knowing that I didn't always have to be saying things, but all I had to do was be there with Jesus.

—*BRIEGE MCKENNA, O.S.C.*

Go to page 1521 for your next devotional reading.

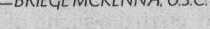

Treasure in Clay Jars

4 Therefore, since it is by God's mercy that we are engaged in this ministry, we do not lose heart. ²We have renounced the shameful things that one hides; we refuse to practice cunning or to falsify God's word; but by the open statement of the truth we commend ourselves to the conscience of everyone in the sight of God. ³And even if our gospel is veiled, it is veiled to those who are perishing. ⁴In their case the god of this world has blinded the minds of the unbelievers, to keep them from seeing the light of the gospel of the glory of Christ, who is the image of God. ⁵For we do not proclaim ourselves; we proclaim Jesus Christ as Lord and ourselves as your slaves for Jesus' sake. ⁶For it is the God who said, "Let light shine out of darkness," who has shone in our hearts to give the light of the knowledge of the glory of God in the face of Jesus Christ.

7 But we have this treasure in clay jars, so that it may be made clear that this extraordinary power belongs to God and does not come from us. ⁸We are afflicted in every way, but not crushed; perplexed, but not driven to despair; ⁹persecuted, but not forsaken; struck down, but not destroyed; ¹⁰always carrying in the body the death of Jesus, so that the life of Jesus may also be made visible in our bodies. ¹¹For while we live, we are always being given up to death for Jesus' sake, so that the life of Jesus may be made visible in our mortal flesh. ¹²So death is at work in us, but life in you.

13 But just as we have the same spirit of faith that is in accordance with scripture—"I believed, and so I spoke"—we also believe, and so we speak, ¹⁴because we know that the one who raised the Lord Jesus will raise us also with Jesus, and will bring us with you into his presence. ¹⁵Yes, everything is for your sake, so that grace, as it extends to more and more people, may increase thanksgiving, to the glory of God.

Living by Faith

16 So we do not lose heart. Even though our outer nature is wasting away, our inner nature is being renewed day by day. ¹⁷For this slight momentary affliction is preparing us for an eternal weight of glory beyond all measure, ¹⁸because we look not at what can be seen but at what cannot be seen; for what can be seen is temporary, but what cannot be seen is eternal.

5 For we know that if the earthly tent we live in is destroyed, we have a building from God, a house not made with hands, eternal in the heavens. ²For in this tent we groan, longing to be clothed with our heavenly dwelling— ³if indeed, when we have taken it off^j we will not be found naked. ⁴For while we are still in this tent, we groan under our burden, because we wish not to be unclothed but to be further clothed, so that what is mortal may be swallowed up by life. ⁵He who has prepared us for this very thing is God, who has given us the Spirit as a guarantee.

6 So we are always confident; even though we know that while we are at home in the body we are away from the Lord— ⁷for we walk by faith, not by sight. ⁸Yes, we do have confidence, and we would rather be away from the body and at home with the Lord. ⁹So whether we are at home or away, we make it our aim to please him. ¹⁰For all of us must appear before the judgment seat of Christ, so that each may receive recompense for what has been done in the body, whether good or evil.

The Ministry of Reconciliation

11 Therefore, knowing the fear of the Lord, we try to persuade others; but we ourselves are well known to God, and I hope that we are also well known to your consciences. ¹²We are not commending ourselves to you again, but giving you an opportunity to boast about us, so that you may be able to answer those who boast in outward appearance and not in the heart. ¹³For if we are beside ourselves, it is for God; if we are in our right mind, it is for you. ¹⁴For the love of Christ urges us on, because we are convinced that one has died for all; therefore all have died. ¹⁵And he died for all, so that those who live might live no longer for themselves, but for him who died and was raised for them.

16 From now on, therefore, we regard no one from a human point of view;^k even though we once knew Christ from a human point of view,^k we know him no

---

^j Other ancient authorities read *put it on according to the flesh*   ^k Gk

longer in that way. [17]So if anyone is in Christ, there is a new creation: everything old has passed away; see, everything has become new! [18]All this is from God, who reconciled us to himself through Christ, and has given us the ministry of reconciliation; [19]that is, in Christ God was reconciling the world to himself,[l] not counting their trespasses against them, and entrusting the message of reconciliation to us. [20]So we are ambassadors for Christ, since God is making his appeal through us; we entreat you on behalf of Christ, be reconciled to God. [21]For our sake he made him to be sin who knew no sin, so that in him we might become the righteousness of God.

6 As we work together with him,[m] we urge you also not to accept the grace of God in vain. [2]For he says,

"At an acceptable time I have
listened to you,
and on a day of salvation I have
helped you."

See, now is the acceptable time; see, now is the day of salvation! [3]We are putting no obstacle in anyone's way, so that no fault may be found with our ministry, [4]but as servants of God we have commended ourselves in every way: through great endurance, in afflictions, hardships, calamities, [5]beatings, imprisonments, riots, labors, sleepless nights, hunger; [6]by purity, knowledge, patience, kindness, holiness of spirit, genuine love, [7]truthful speech, and the power of God; with the weapons of righteousness for the right hand and for

[l] Or *God was in Christ reconciling the world to himself*   [m] Gk *As we work together*

WEDNESDAY

Scripture Reading
for Today:
2 Corinthians 5.1–10

Verse for Today:
2 Corinthians 5.7

*L*ooking Past My Doubts

When I worked as a writer for Hallmark Cards, I wrote this copy for the cover of a Christmas card:

> In the crisp, clear darkness of a December night
> look at the sky and ponder God . . .
> Creator of an infinity of stars
> Millions, billions . . . beyond any number I might count . . .
> Is it not a miracle, indeed, that God
> can look through the stars
> . . . to me?

I was thirty-one when I wrote those words in response to a writer's assignment, and at the time, I didn't believe any of them. Painful life circumstances had shattered my comfortable, take-for-granted faith, and I felt adrift in an existential universe that had no particular meaning. When I looked up at the night sky, all I saw were stars. I didn't see God, nor did it seem as if God saw me. Yet twenty years later, I realize that even though it seemed as if God had abandoned me, it was God's grace that sustained and strengthened me during that anguished period. Gifts of the Spirit were all around me.

While God does look through the stars to see me, sometimes I must look past my own doubts to see God.

—*BARBARA BARTOCCI*

Go to page 1522 for your next devotional reading.

the left; [8]in honor and dishonor, in ill repute and good repute. We are treated as impostors, and yet are true; [9]as unknown, and yet are well known; as dying, and see—we are alive; as punished, and yet not killed; [10]as sorrowful, yet always rejoicing; as poor, yet making many rich; as having nothing, and yet possessing everything.

11 We have spoken frankly to you Corinthians; our heart is wide open to you. [12]There is no restriction in our affections, but only in yours. [13]In return—I speak as to children—open wide your hearts also.

The Temple of the Living God

14 Do not be mismatched with unbelievers. For what partnership is there between righteousness and lawlessness? Or what fellowship is there between light and darkness? [15]What agreement does Christ have with Beliar? Or what does a believer share with an unbeliever? [16]What agreement has the temple of God with idols? For we[n] are the temple of the living God; as God said,

"I will live in them and walk among them,
    and I will be their God,

and they shall be my people.
[17] Therefore come out from them,
    and be separate from them, says the Lord,
and touch nothing unclean;
    then I will welcome you,
[18] and I will be your father,
    and you shall be my sons and daughters,
says the Lord Almighty."

7 Since we have these promises, beloved, let us cleanse ourselves from every defilement of body and of spirit, making holiness perfect in the fear of God.

Paul's Joy at the Church's Repentance

2 Make room in your hearts[o] for us; we have wronged no one, we have corrupted no one, we have taken advantage of no one. [3]I do not say this to condemn you, for I said before that you are in our hearts, to die together and to live together. [4]I often boast about you; I have great pride in you; I am filled with consolation; I am overjoyed in all our affliction.

5 For even when we came into Mace-

[n] Other ancient authorities read *you*   [o] Gk lacks *in your hearts*

THURSDAY

Scripture Reading for Today:
2 Corinthians 6.1–13

Verse for Today:
2 Corinthians 6.2

Living in the Present Moment

[We are to do God's will] in the time given to us: Now, later, tomorrow—carrying out God's will in the present moment, then, in the moment that follows, until we reach the final moment, on which our eternity will depend.

We are not to dwell on the past or dream about the future. The past should be left to God's mercy, since it is no longer ours; and the future will only be fully lived when it becomes the present.

Only the present is in our hands. So that if God is to reign in our lives, we must concentrate our whole mind, heart and strength on the accomplishment of his will here and now.

Just as a traveler in a train would not think of moving forward through the cars so as to get to his destination sooner, but remains seated and lets the train carry him along, so our souls, to get to God, should fulfill, wholeheartedly, his will in the present moment, since time moves forward on its own.

—*CHIARA LUBICH*

Go to page 1525 for your next devotional reading.

donia, our bodies had no rest, but we were afflicted in every way—disputes without and fears within. [6]But God, who consoles the downcast, consoled us by the arrival of Titus, [7]and not only by his coming, but also by the consolation with which he was consoled about you, as he told us of your longing, your mourning, your zeal for me, so that I rejoiced still more. [8]For even if I made you sorry with my letter, I do not regret it (though I did regret it, for I see that I grieved you with that letter, though only briefly). [9]Now I rejoice, not because you were grieved, but because your grief led to repentance; for you felt a godly grief, so that you were not harmed in any way by us. [10]For godly grief produces a repentance that leads to salvation and brings no regret, but worldly grief produces death. [11]For see what earnestness this godly grief has produced in you, what eagerness to clear yourselves, what indignation, what alarm, what longing, what zeal, what punishment! At every point you have proved yourselves guiltless in the matter. [12]So although I wrote to you, it was not on account of the one who did the wrong, nor on account of the one who was wronged, but in order that your zeal for us might be made known to you before God. [13]In this we find comfort.

In addition to our own consolation, we rejoiced still more at the joy of Titus, because his mind has been set at rest by all of you. [14]For if I have been somewhat boastful about you to him, I was not disgraced; but just as everything we said to you was true, so our boasting to Titus has proved true as well. [15]And his heart goes out all the more to you, as he remembers the obedience of all of you, and how you welcomed him with fear and trembling. [16]I rejoice, because I have complete confidence in you.

Encouragement to Be Generous

8 We want you to know, brothers and sisters, [p] about the grace of God that has been granted to the churches of Macedonia; [2]for during a severe ordeal of affliction, their abundant joy and their extreme poverty have overflowed in a wealth of generosity on their part. [3]For, as I can testify, they voluntarily gave according to their means, and even beyond their means, [4]begging us earnestly for the privilege[q] of sharing in this ministry to the saints— [5]and this, not merely as we expected; they gave themselves first to the Lord and, by the will of God, to us, [6]so that we might urge Titus that, as he had already made a beginning, so he should also complete this generous undertaking[r] among you. [7]Now as you excel in everything—in faith, in speech, in knowledge, in utmost eagerness, and in our love for you[s]—so we want you to excel also in this generous undertaking.[r]

8 I do not say this as a command, but I am testing the genuineness of your love against the earnestness of others. [9]For you know the generous act[t] of our Lord Jesus Christ, that though he was rich, yet for your sakes he became poor, so that by his poverty you might become rich. [10]And in this matter I am giving my advice: it is appropriate for you who began last year not only to do something but even to desire to do something— [11]now finish doing it, so that your eagerness may be matched by completing it according to your means. [12]For if the eagerness is there, the gift is acceptable according to what one has— not according to what one does not have. [13]I do not mean that there should be relief for others and pressure on you, but it is a question of a fair balance between [14]your present abundance and their need, so that their abundance may be for your need, in order that there may be a fair balance. [15]As it is written,

"The one who had much did not
        have too much,
  and the one who had little did
        not have too little."

Commendation of Titus

16 But thanks be to God who put in the heart of Titus the same eagerness for you that I myself have. [17]For he not only accepted our appeal, but since he is more eager than ever, he is going to you of his own accord. [18]With him we are sending the brother who is famous among all the churches for his proclaiming the good news;[u] [19]and not only that, but he has also been appointed by the churches to travel with us while we are administering this generous undertaking[r] for the glory of the Lord himself[v] and to show our goodwill. [20]We intend that no one should

p Gk brothers   q Gk grace   r Gk this grace
s Other ancient authorities read your love for us
t Gk the grace   u Or the gospel   v Other ancient
authorities lack himself

blame us about this generous gift that we are administering, 21for we intend to do what is right not only in the Lord's sight but also in the sight of others. 22And with them we are sending our brother whom we have often tested and found eager in many matters, but who is now more eager than ever because of his great confidence in you. 23As for Titus, he is my partner and co-worker in your service; as for our brothers, they are messengers*w* of the churches, the glory of Christ. 24Therefore openly before the churches, show them the proof of your love and of our reason for boasting about you.

The Collection for Christians at Jerusalem

9 Now it is not necessary for me to write you about the ministry to the saints, 2for I know your eagerness, which is the subject of my boasting about you to the people of Macedonia, saying that Achaia has been ready since last year; and your zeal has stirred up most of them. 3But I am sending the brothers in order that our boasting about you may not prove to have been empty in this case, so that you may be ready, as I said you would be; 4otherwise, if some Macedonians come with me and find that you are not ready, we would be humiliated—to say nothing of you—in this undertaking.*x* 5So I thought it necessary to urge the brothers to go on ahead to you, and arrange in advance for this bountiful gift that you have promised, so that it may be ready as a voluntary gift and not as an extortion.

6 The point is this: the one who sows sparingly will also reap sparingly, and the one who sows bountifully will also reap bountifully. 7Each of you must give as you have made up your mind, not reluctantly or under compulsion, for God loves a cheerful giver. 8And God is able to provide you with every blessing in abundance, so that by always having enough of everything, you may share abundantly in every good work. 9As it is written,

"He scatters abroad, he gives to
the poor;
his righteousness*y* endures
forever."

10He who supplies seed to the sower and bread for food will supply and multiply your seed for sowing and increase the harvest of your righteousness.*y* 11You will be enriched in every way for your great generosity, which will produce thanksgiving to God through us; 12for the rendering of this ministry not only supplies the needs of the saints but also overflows with many thanksgivings to God. 13Through the testing of this ministry you glorify God by your obedience to the confession of the gospel of Christ and by the generosity of your sharing with them and with all others, 14while they long for you and pray for you because of the surpassing grace of God that he has given you. 15Thanks be to God for his indescribable gift!

Paul Defends His Ministry

10 I myself, Paul, appeal to you by the meekness and gentleness of Christ—I who am humble when face to face with you, but bold toward you when I am away!— 2I ask that when I am present I need not show boldness by daring to oppose those who think we are acting according to human standards.*z* 3Indeed, we live as human beings,*a* but we do not wage war according to human standards;*z* 4for the weapons of our warfare are not merely human,*b* but they have divine power to destroy strongholds. We destroy arguments 5and every proud obstacle raised up against the knowledge of God, and we take every thought captive to obey Christ. 6We are ready to punish every disobedience when your obedience is complete.

7 Look at what is before your eyes. If you are confident that you belong to Christ, remind yourself of this, that just as you belong to Christ, so also do we. 8Now, even if I boast a little too much of our authority, which the Lord gave for building you up and not for tearing you down, I will not be ashamed of it. 9I do not want to seem as though I am trying to frighten you with my letters. 10For they say, "His letters are weighty and strong, but his bodily presence is weak, and his speech contemptible." 11Let such people understand that what we say by letter when absent, we will also do when present.

12 We do not dare to classify or compare ourselves with some of those who commend themselves. But when they

---

w Gk *apostles*   *x* Other ancient authorities add *of boasting*   *y* Or *benevolence*   *z* Gk *according to the flesh*   *a* Gk *in the flesh*   *b* Gk *fleshly*

measure themselves by one another, and compare themselves with one another, they do not show good sense. 13We, however, will not boast beyond limits, but will keep within the field that God has assigned to us, to reach out even as far as you. 14For we were not overstepping our limits when we reached you; we were the first to come all the way to you with the good news*c* of Christ. 15We do not boast beyond limits, that is, in the labors of others; but our hope is that, as your faith increases, our sphere of action among you may be greatly enlarged, 16so that we may proclaim the good news*c* in lands beyond you, without boasting of work already done in someone else's sphere of action. 17"Let the one who boasts, boast in the Lord." 18For it is not those who commend themselves that are approved, but those whom the Lord commends.

Paul and the False Apostles

11 I wish you would bear with me in a little foolishness. Do bear with me! 2I feel a divine jealousy for you, for I promised you in marriage to one husband, to present you as a chaste virgin to Christ. 3But I am afraid that as the serpent deceived Eve by its cunning, your thoughts will be led astray from a sincere and pure*d* devotion to Christ. 4For if someone comes and proclaims another

c Or *the gospel*   *d* Other ancient authorities lack *and pure*

FRIDAY

Scripture Reading for Today:
2 Corinthians 9.6–15

Verse for Today:
2 Corinthians 9.7

Giving Without Compulsion

Almsgiving is a disciplinary form which so often stops at a hasty or halfhearted solution for the guilt we feel about the world's poor and hungry and an embarrassment at the good things in our own lives. Trapped in our own ego, our alms become grim, stoic gestures.

What we give to others comes best out of a joy and thankfulness of what we have and a desire to share our good fortune. In that spirit we notice all our excesses and learn to balance them. We notice what challenges our love of comfort.

What we share with our brothers and sisters in this world does not always have to be monetary; it does not have to be what we find hard or costly. We can translate our mortifications into actions that are useful and creative and beneficial to those who live with us. For even if we did have the monies to give the world and continued to make our family life miserable, it would be worth very little. We can look to where we are unloving, make the effort to overcome our natural distastes and take the extra step to do things for those who irk us. We might look at and make the effort to curb our own irksome mannerisms, our habitual naggings, our eccentricities which make us difficult to live and work with. We give "alms" to those around us when we attend to those qualities in ourselves that make family life richer rather than poorer, in our renewed efforts at patience, our empathy, our understanding, our tolerance, our creative contributions, our sense of humor and joy.

—*GERTRUD MUELLER NELSON*

Go to page 1526 for your next devotional reading.

The Woman With Hemorrhages

Her Character: *She was so desperate for healing that she ignored the conventions of the day just for the chance to touch Jesus.*

Her Sorrow: *To have suffered a chronic illness that isolated her from others.*

Her Joy: *That after long years of suffering, she finally found peace and freedom.*

Read Luke 8.40–48

The woman hovered at the edge of the crowd. Nobody watched as she melted into the throng of bodies—just one more bee entering the hive. Her shame faded, quickly replaced by a rush of relief. No one had prevented her from joining in. No one had recoiled at her touch.

She pressed closer, but a noisy swarm of men still blocked her view. She could hear Jairus, a ruler of the synagogue, raising his voice above the others, pleading with Jesus to come and heal his daughter before it was too late.

Suddenly the group in front of her shifted, parting like the waters of the Jordan before the children of promise. It was all she needed. Her arm darted through the opening, fingers brushing the tassel on his cloak. Instantly she felt a warmth spread through her, flushing out the pain, clearing out the decay. Her skin prickled and shivered. She felt strong and able, like a young girl coming into her own. She was so glad and giddy, in fact, that her feet wanted to rush her away before she created a spectacle—laughing out loud at her quiet miracle.

But Jesus blocked her escape and silenced the crowd with a curious question: "Who touched me?"

"Who touched him? He must be joking!" voices murmured. "People are pushing and shoving just to get near him!"

Shaking now, the woman fell at his feet: "For 12 years I have been hemorrhaging and have spent all my money on doctors but only grown worse. Today, I knew that if I could just touch your garment, I would be healed." But touching, she knew, meant spreading her defilement—even to the rabbi.

Twelve years of loneliness. Twelve years in which physicians had bled her of all her wealth. Her private affliction a matter of public record. Every cup she handled, every chair she sat on could transmit defilement to others. Even though her impurity was considered a ritual matter rather than an ethical one, it may have rendered her an outcast, making it impossible for her to live with a husband, bear a child, or enjoy the intimacy of friends and family. Surely the rabbi would censure her.

But instead of scolding and shaming her, Jesus praised her: "Daughter, your faith has made you well; go in peace" (verse 48).

His words must have been like water breaching a dam, breaking through her isolation, setting her free. For he had addressed her not harshly but tenderly. Not as *woman* or *sinner*—but rather as *daughter*. She was no longer alone but part of his family by virtue of her faith.

That day countless men and women had brushed against Jesus, but only one had truly touched him. And instead of being defiled by contact with her, his own touch had proven the more contagious, rendering her pure and whole again.

Praying With the Woman With Hemorrhages

Now there was a woman who had been suffering from hemorrhages for twelve years; and though she had spent all she had on physicians, no one could cure her. She came up behind [Jesus] and touched the fringe of his clothes, and immediately her hemorrhage stopped.—*Luke 8.43–44*

Praise God: *That faith produces peace and freedom.*

Offer Thanks: *That faith is a gift that increases with use.*

Confess: *Any tendency to play it so safe that you actually begin to suffocate the faith you have.*

Ask God: *To bring this woman's story to mind the next time you are faced with an opportunity to exercise real faith.*

Lift Your Heart

Trying to live the Christian life without faith is like trying to eat a steak with a straw, or kissing someone without using your lips, or propelling an airplane with foot pedals. It doesn't nourish you, never thrills you, and won't get you anywhere. Before you go to bed each night this week, remind yourself of your need by lighting a small candle at your bedside and praying this prayer:

Father, forgive my little faith.	*No matter how foolish*
Make it big.	*No matter how frightened*
Reduce my ego.	*No matter how strange I feel.*
Make it small.	*Fan my small spark into a brightness*
Give me a chance	*Lighting the way ahead*
To touch you and be touched.	*Amen.*

(Don't forget to blow out the candle before you go to sleep!)

Go to page 1529 for your next devotional reading.

Jesus than the one we proclaimed, or if you receive a different spirit from the one you received, or a different gospel from the one you accepted, you submit to it readily enough. 5I think that I am not in the least inferior to these super-apostles. 6I may be untrained in speech, but not in knowledge; certainly in every way and in all things we have made this evident to you.

7 Did I commit a sin by humbling myself so that you might be exalted, because I proclaimed God's good news*e* to you free of charge? 8I robbed other churches by accepting support from them in order to serve you. 9And when I was with you and was in need, I did not burden anyone, for my needs were supplied by the friends*f* who came from Macedonia. So I refrained and will continue to refrain from burdening you in any way. 10As the truth of Christ is in me, this boast of mine will not be silenced in the regions of Achaia. 11And why? Because I do not love you? God knows I do!

12 And what I do I will also continue to do, in order to deny an opportunity to those who want an opportunity to be recognized as our equals in what they boast about. 13For such boasters are false apostles, deceitful workers, disguising themselves as apostles of Christ. 14And no wonder! Even Satan disguises himself as an angel of light. 15So it is not strange if his ministers also disguise themselves as ministers of righteousness. Their end will match their deeds.

Paul's Sufferings as an Apostle

16 I repeat, let no one think that I am a fool; but if you do, then accept me as a fool, so that I too may boast a little. 17What I am saying in regard to this boastful confidence, I am saying not with the Lord's authority, but as a fool; 18since many boast according to human standards,*g* I will also boast. 19For you gladly put up with fools, being wise yourselves! 20For you put up with it when someone makes slaves of you, or preys upon you, or takes advantage of you, or puts on airs, or gives you a slap in the face. 21To my shame, I must say, we were too weak for that!

But whatever anyone dares to boast of—I am speaking as a fool—I also dare to boast of that. 22Are they Hebrews? So am I. Are they Israelites? So am I. Are they descendants of Abraham? So am I. 23Are they ministers of Christ? I am talking like a madman—I am a better one: with far greater labors, far more imprisonments, with countless floggings, and often near death. 24Five times I have received from the Jews the forty lashes minus one. 25Three times I was beaten with rods. Once I received a stoning. Three times I was shipwrecked; for a night and a day I was adrift at sea; 26on frequent journeys, in danger from rivers, danger from bandits, danger from my own people, danger from Gentiles, danger in the city, danger in the wilderness, danger at sea, danger from false brothers and sisters;*f* 27in toil and hardship, through many a sleepless night, hungry and thirsty, often without food, cold and naked. 28And, besides other things, I am under daily pressure because of my anxiety for all the churches. 29Who is weak, and I am not weak? Who is made to stumble, and I am not indignant?

30 If I must boast, I will boast of the things that show my weakness. 31The God and Father of the Lord Jesus (blessed be he forever!) knows that I do not lie. 32In Damascus, the governor*h* under King Aretas guarded the city of Damascus in order to*i* seize me, 33but I was let down in a basket through a window in the wall,*j* and escaped from his hands.

Paul's Visions and Revelations

12 It is necessary to boast; nothing is to be gained by it, but I will go on to visions and revelations of the Lord. 2I know a person in Christ who fourteen years ago was caught up to the third heaven—whether in the body or out of the body I do not know; God knows. 3And I know that such a person—whether in the body or out of the body I do not know; God knows— 4was caught up into Paradise and heard things that are not to be told, that no mortal is permitted to repeat. 5On behalf of such a one I will boast, but on my own behalf I will not boast, except of my weaknesses. 6But if I wish to boast, I will not be a fool, for I will be speaking the truth. But I refrain from it, so that no one may think better of me than what is

---

e Gk *the gospel of God*   *f* Gk *brothers*   *g* Gk *according to the flesh*   *h* Gk *ethnarch*   *i* Other ancient authorities read *and wanted to*   *j* Gk *through the wall*

seen in me or heard from me, 7even considering the exceptional character of the revelations. Therefore, to keep*k* me from being too elated, a thorn was given me in the flesh, a messenger of Satan to torment me, to keep me from being too elated.*l* 8Three times I appealed to the Lord about this, that it would leave me, 9but he said to me, "My grace is sufficient for you, for power*m* is made perfect in weakness." So, I will boast all the more gladly of my weaknesses, so that the power of Christ may dwell in me. 10Therefore I am content with weaknesses, insults, hardships, persecutions, and calamities for the sake of Christ; for whenever I am weak, then I am strong.

Paul's Concern for the Corinthian Church

11 I have been a fool! You forced me to it. Indeed you should have been the ones commending me, for I am not at all inferior to these super-apostles, even though I am nothing. 12The signs of a true apostle were performed among you with utmost patience, signs and wonders and mighty works. 13How have you been worse off than the other churches, except that I myself did not burden you? Forgive me this wrong!

14 Here I am, ready to come to you this third time. And I will not be a burden, because I do not want what is yours but you; for children ought not to lay up for their parents, but parents for their children. 15I will most gladly spend and be spent for you. If I love you more, am I to be loved less? 16Let it be assumed that I did not burden you. Nevertheless (you say) since I was crafty, I took you in by deceit. 17Did I take advantage of you through any of those whom I sent to you? 18I urged Titus to go, and sent the brother with him. Titus did not take advantage of you, did he? Did we not conduct ourselves with the same spirit? Did we not take the same steps?

19 Have you been thinking all along

k Other ancient authorities read *To keep*   *l* Other ancient authorities lack *to keep me from being too elated*   *m* Other ancient authorities read *my power*

When I Am Weak

MONDAY

Scripture Reading
for Today:
2 Corinthians 12.7–10

Verse for Today:
2 Corinthians 12.9

I don't think there is anyone who needs God's help and grace as much as I do. Sometimes I feel so helpless and weak. I think that is why God uses me. Because I cannot depend on my own strength, I rely on him 24 hours a day. If the day had even more hours, then I would need his help and grace during those hours as well. All of us must cling to God through prayer.

My secret is very simple: I pray. Through prayer I become one in love with Christ. I realize that praying to him is loving him.

In reality, there is only one true prayer, only one substantial prayer: Christ himself. There is only one voice that rises above the face of the earth: the voice of Christ. Perfect prayer does not consist in many words, but in the fervor of the desire which raises the heart to Jesus.

Love to pray. Feel the need to pray often during the day. Prayer enlarges the heart until it is capable of containing God's gift of himself. Ask and seek and your heart will grow big enough to receive him and keep him as your own.

—MOTHER TERESA OF CALCUTTA

Go to page 1532 for your next devotional reading.

that we have been defending ourselves before you? We are speaking in Christ before God. Everything we do, beloved, is for the sake of building you up. 20For I fear that when I come, I may find you not as I wish, and that you may find me not as you wish; I fear that there may perhaps be quarreling, jealousy, anger, selfishness, slander, gossip, conceit, and disorder. 21I fear that when I come again, my God may humble me before you, and that I may have to mourn over many who previously sinned and have not repented of the impurity, sexual immorality, and licentiousness that they have practiced.

Further Warning

13 This is the third time I am coming to you. "Any charge must be sustained by the evidence of two or three witnesses." 2I warned those who sinned previously and all the others, and I warn them now while absent, as I did when present on my second visit, that if I come again, I will not be lenient— 3since you desire proof that Christ is speaking in me. He is not weak in dealing with you, but is powerful in you. 4For he was crucified in weakness, but lives by the power of God. For we are weak in him,*n* but in dealing with you we will live with him by the power of God.

5 Examine yourselves to see whether you are living in the faith. Test yourselves. Do you not realize that Jesus Christ is in you?—unless, indeed, you fail to meet the test! 6I hope you will find out that we have not failed. 7But we pray to God that you may not do anything wrong—not that we may appear to have met the test, but that you may do what is right, though we may seem to have failed. 8For we cannot do anything against the truth, but only for the truth. 9For we rejoice when we are weak and you are strong. This is what we pray for, that you may become perfect. 10So I write these things while I am away from you, so that when I come, I may not have to be severe in using the authority that the Lord has given me for building up and not for tearing down.

Final Greetings and Benediction

11 Finally, brothers and sisters,*o* farewell.*p* Put things in order, listen to my appeal,*q* agree with one another, live in peace; and the God of love and peace will be with you. 12Greet one another with a holy kiss. All the saints greet you.

13 The grace of the Lord Jesus Christ, the love of God, and the communion of*r* the Holy Spirit be with all of you.

n Other ancient authorities read *with him*   *o* Gk *brothers*   *p* Or *rejoice*   *q* Or *encourage one another*   *r* Or *and the sharing in*

The Letter of Paul to the
Galatians

Paul was an itinerant missionary whose travels took him to Galatia (modern-day Turkey) and points beyond. After making converts there, he continued his journey, unaware that other missionaries would soon arrive, intent on undermining the gospel he had preached. These people urged the Galatians to submit to the demands of the Mosaic Law, particularly those regarding circumcision.

Never one to mince words, Paul addresses the converts, calling them "You foolish Galatians!" (3.1). (Another translation says, "O stupid Galatians!") Paul argues that there is nothing they or anyone can do to achieve God's approval. Only faith in Christ will justify them in God's eyes, only faith will lead them to freedom. But that freedom is not to be abused: "For the whole law is summed up in a single commandment, 'You shall love your neighbor as yourself' " (5.14).

Interestingly, Paul points to two Old Testament women who, he says, symbolize the two covenants. Hagar and her children represent those born into slavery under the law while Sarah and her children represent those born into freedom in Christ.

Human beings have always been tempted by "do-it-yourself" brands of religion, but Paul's letter to the Galatians reminds us that Christianity is essentially a "do-it-for us" religion. Though we cooperate with grace, only Christ has the power to save us.

Salutation

1 Paul an apostle—sent neither by human commission nor from human authorities, but through Jesus Christ and God the Father, who raised him from the dead— ²and all the members of God's family*ᵃ* who are with me,

To the churches of Galatia:

3 Grace to you and peace from God our Father and the Lord Jesus Christ, ⁴who gave himself for our sins to set us free from the present evil age, according to the will of our God and Father, ⁵to whom be the glory forever and ever. Amen.

There Is No Other Gospel

6 I am astonished that you are so

ᵃ Gk *all the brothers*

quickly deserting the one who called you in the grace of Christ and are turning to a different gospel— ⁷not that there is another gospel, but there are some who are confusing you and want to pervert the gospel of Christ. ⁸But even if we or an angel*b* from heaven should proclaim to you a gospel contrary to what we proclaimed to you, let that one be accursed! ⁹As we have said before, so now I repeat, if anyone proclaims to you a gospel contrary to what you received, let that one be accursed!

10 Am I now seeking human approval, or God's approval? Or am I trying to please people? If I were still pleasing people, I would not be a servant*c* of Christ.

Paul's Vindication of His Apostleship

11 For I want you to know, brothers

b Or *a messenger*   *c* Gk *slave*

TUESDAY

Scripture Reading for Today:
Galatians 1.6–12

Verse for Today:
Galatians 1.10

*D*on't Beat Around the Bush

Do I give God's people God's Word? Or do I give them what I want to give them and what they want to hear?

I was going to speak at a conference for college-age Christians. Before the conference I read that 35 percent of Catholics in the United States can recall no more than five of the Ten Commandments. This was in my mind as I prayed about the conference. I sensed that I should talk about the Ten Commandments. I cannot say I was enthusiastic at the idea. *What group of college students,* I thought, *wants to hear about the Ten Commandments?*

I felt that God put a question in my mind: Are you going to serve what they want, what you want, or what I want?

"Lord," I said, "I'll do what you want."

So I gave a talk on the Ten Commandments. I talked about God's love and the goodness of his Law, about God's utter determination to make us holy and his punishment of those who scorn his love and break his Law.

At the end of the talk there were young people on their knees weeping. Some came up to me afterwards and asked angrily, "Why didn't anyone make these things clear to us before?"

An hour later a group of youth ministers came up to me, furious. "You just destroyed our program. We've been trying to teach these kids about a God of love and mercy and kindness. You spoke of a God of judgment, a God who causes people to fear."

I told them, "I want young people to know the fullness of God's love and God's mercy. I want them to know the fullness of his life that comes from being his disciples and obeying him."

The youth ministers were not convinced. But three years later some of those same youth ministers came back to me and said that the young people themselves, by the fruit of their lives, had convinced them that it was right to be straightforward with them about God's commandments.

—*ANN SHIELDS*

Go to page 1534 for your next devotional reading.

and sisters,*d* that the gospel that was proclaimed by me is not of human origin; [12]for I did not receive it from a human source, nor was I taught it, but I received it through a revelation of Jesus Christ.

13 You have heard, no doubt, of my earlier life in Judaism. I was violently persecuting the church of God and was trying to destroy it. [14]I advanced in Judaism beyond many among my people of the same age, for I was far more zealous for the traditions of my ancestors. [15]But when God, who had set me apart before I was born and called me through his grace, was pleased [16]to reveal his Son to me,*e* so that I might proclaim him among the Gentiles, I did not confer with any human being, [17]nor did I go up to Jerusalem to those who were already apostles before me, but I went away at once into Arabia, and afterwards I returned to Damascus.

18 Then after three years I did go up to Jerusalem to visit Cephas and stayed with him fifteen days; [19]but I did not see any other apostle except James the Lord's brother. [20]In what I am writing to you, before God, I do not lie! [21]Then I went into the regions of Syria and Cilicia, [22]and I was still unknown by sight to the churches of Judea that are in Christ; [23]they only heard it said, "The one who formerly was persecuting us is now proclaiming the faith he once tried to destroy." [24]And they glorified God because of me.

Paul and the Other Apostles

2 Then after fourteen years I went up again to Jerusalem with Barnabas, taking Titus along with me. [2]I went up in response to a revelation. Then I laid before them (though only in a private meeting with the acknowledged leaders) the gospel that I proclaim among the Gentiles, in order to make sure that I was not running, or had not run, in vain. [3]But even Titus, who was with me, was not compelled to be circumcised, though he was a Greek. [4]But because of false believers*f* secretly brought in, who slipped in to spy on the freedom we have in Christ Jesus, so that they might enslave us— [5]we did not submit to them even for a moment, so that the truth of the gospel might always remain with you. [6]And from those who were supposed to be acknowledged leaders (what they actually were makes no difference to me; God shows no partiality)—those leaders contributed nothing to

me. [7]On the contrary, when they saw that I had been entrusted with the gospel for the uncircumcised, just as Peter had been entrusted with the gospel for the circumcised [8](for he who worked through Peter making him an apostle to the circumcised also worked through me in sending me to the Gentiles), [9]and when James and Cephas and John, who were acknowledged pillars, recognized the grace that had been given to me, they gave to Barnabas and me the right hand of fellowship, agreeing that we should go to the Gentiles and they to the circumcised. [10]They asked only one thing, that we remember the poor, which was actually what I was*g* eager to do.

Paul Rebukes Peter at Antioch

11 But when Cephas came to Antioch, I opposed him to his face, because he stood self-condemned; [12]for until certain people came from James, he used to eat with the Gentiles. But after they came, he drew back and kept himself separate for fear of the circumcision faction. [13]And the other Jews joined him in this hypocrisy, so that even Barnabas was led astray by their hypocrisy. [14]But when I saw that they were not acting consistently with the truth of the gospel, I said to Cephas before them all, "If you, though a Jew, live like a Gentile and not like a Jew, how can you compel the Gentiles to live like Jews?"*h*

Jews and Gentiles Are Saved by Faith

15 We ourselves are Jews by birth and not Gentile sinners; [16]yet we know that a person is justified*i* not by the works of the law but through faith in Jesus Christ.*j* And we have come to believe in Christ Jesus, so that we might be justified by faith in Christ,*k* and not by doing the works of the law, because no one will be justified by the works of the law. [17]But if, in our effort to be justified in Christ, we ourselves have been found to be sinners, is Christ then a servant of sin? Certainly not! [18]But if I build up again the very things that I once tore down, then I demonstrate that I am a transgressor. [19]For through the law I died to the law, so that I might live to God. I have been crucified

d Gk *brothers*   *e* Gk *in me*   *f* Gk *false brothers*
g Or *had been*   *h* Some interpreters hold that the quotation extends into the following paragraph
i Or *reckoned as righteous;* and so elsewhere   *j* Or *the faith of Jesus Christ*   *k* Or *the faith of Christ*

with Christ; [20]and it is no longer I who live, but it is Christ who lives in me. And the life I now live in the flesh I live by faith in the Son of God,[l] who loved me and gave himself for me. [21]I do not nullify the grace of God; for if justification[m] comes through the law, then Christ died for nothing.

Law or Faith

3 You foolish Galatians! Who has bewitched you? It was before your eyes that Jesus Christ was publicly exhibited as crucified! [2]The only thing I want to learn from you is this: Did you receive the Spirit by doing the works of the law or by believing what you heard? [3]Are you so foolish? Having started with the Spirit, are you now ending with the flesh? [4]Did you experience so much for nothing?—if it really was for nothing. [5]Well then, does God[n] supply you with the Spirit and work miracles among you by your doing the works

l Or by the faith of the Son of God   m Or righteousness   n Gk he

Grace Intervenes

WEDNESDAY

Scripture Reading for Today:
Galatians 2.15–21

Verse for Today:
Galatians 2.20

When I moved into my own home in 1985, my goal was to become more efficient in small repairs. A toilet that would not stop running put to the test my do-it-yourself intention. I headed for K-Mart, anticipating no problem. Overcoming my general dislike for hands-on places packed with merchandise and few salespersons, I resolved to find what I needed with a minimum of searching. After twenty minutes, I admitted defeat and slumped over to the customer service phone. Another twenty-minute wait ensued when at last a woman, perhaps forty years old, stormed down the aisle, with an air of resentment as if I were to blame for her bad day. In a disgusted, accusatory tone of voice, she said, "Hey, Lady, what's your problem?"

Everything in me wanted nothing more at that moment than to tell her off. Quickly my mind formulated a cutting remark. I was about to deliver it when grace intervened and restrained my tongue. I saw myself at a crossroads. I could depersonalize another human being or turn the tables in favor of her dignity. Amazingly, not I, but Christ in me, responded to her slur with a heartfelt look of compassion and the words, "You must be having a miserable day." She was taken aback and then blurted out, "How did you know?"

In a lightning flash, there in the hardware section, "Irene" and I had an experience of genuine togetherness. It turned out that she was a single parent with two young children at home under her mother's care. She had been on the floor since opening time without a break. She was needed at home, but her relief was late. Now she had to deal with my plumbing problem. At that we both laughed.

I had been ready to explode. Grace stemmed the vitriolic tide.

—SUSAN MUTO

Go to page 1537 for your next devotional reading.

of the law, or by your believing what you heard?

6 Just as Abraham "believed God, and it was reckoned to him as righteousness," 7so, you see, those who believe are the descendants of Abraham. 8And the scripture, foreseeing that God would justify the Gentiles by faith, declared the gospel beforehand to Abraham, saying, "All the Gentiles shall be blessed in you." 9For this reason, those who believe are blessed with Abraham who believed.

10 For all who rely on the works of the law are under a curse; for it is written, "Cursed is everyone who does not observe and obey all the things written in the book of the law." 11Now it is evident that no one is justified before God by the law; for "The one who is righteous will live by faith."*o* 12But the law does not rest on faith; on the contrary, "Whoever does the works of the law*p* will live by them." 13Christ redeemed us from the curse of the law by becoming a curse for us—for it is written, "Cursed is everyone who hangs on a tree"— 14in order that in Christ Jesus the blessing of Abraham might come to the Gentiles, so that we might receive the promise of the Spirit through faith.

The Promise to Abraham

15 Brothers and sisters,*q* I give an example from daily life: once a person's will*r* has been ratified, no one adds to it or annuls it. 16Now the promises were made to Abraham and to his offspring;*s* it does not say, "And to offsprings,"*t* as of many; but it says, "And to your offspring,"*s* that is, to one person, who is Christ. 17My point is this: the law, which came four hundred thirty years later, does not annul a covenant previously ratified by God, so as to nullify the promise. 18For if the inheritance comes from the law, it no longer comes from the promise; but God granted it to Abraham through the promise.

The Purpose of the Law

19 Why then the law? It was added because of transgressions, until the offspring*s* would come to whom the promise had been made; and it was ordained through angels by a mediator. 20Now a mediator involves more than one party; but God is one.

21 Is the law then opposed to the promises of God? Certainly not! For if a law had been given that could make alive, then righteousness would indeed come through the law. 22But the scripture has imprisoned all things under the power of sin, so that what was promised through faith in Jesus Christ*u* might be given to those who believe.

23 Now before faith came, we were imprisoned and guarded under the law until faith would be revealed. 24Therefore the law was our disciplinarian until Christ came, so that we might be justified by faith. 25But now that faith has come, we are no longer subject to a disciplinarian, 26for in Christ Jesus you are all children of God through faith. 27As many of you as were baptized into Christ have clothed yourselves with Christ. 28There is no longer Jew or Greek, there is no longer slave or free, there is no longer male and female; for all of you are one in Christ Jesus. 29And if you belong to Christ, then you are Abraham's offspring,*s* heirs according to the promise.

4 My point is this: heirs, as long as they are minors, are no better than slaves, though they are the owners of all the property; 2but they remain under guardians and trustees until the date set by the father. 3So with us; while we were minors, we were enslaved to the elemental spirits*v* of the world. 4But when the fullness of time had come, God sent his Son, born of a woman, born under the law, 5in order to redeem those who were under the law, so that we might receive adoption as children. 6And because you are children, God has sent the Spirit of his Son into our*w* hearts, crying, "Abba!*x* Father!" 7So you are no longer a slave but a child, and if a child then also an heir, through God.*y*

Paul Reproves the Galatians

8 Formerly, when you did not know God, you were enslaved to beings that by nature are not gods. 9Now, however, that you have come to know God, or rather to be known by God, how can you turn back again to the weak and beggarly elemental spirits?*z* How can you want to be en-

o Or *The one who is righteous through faith will live*   *p* Gk *does them*   *q* Gk *Brothers*   *r* Or *covenant* (as in verse 17)   *s* Gk *seed*   *t* Gk *seeds*   *u* Or *through the faith of Jesus Christ*   *v* Or *the rudiments*   *w* Other ancient authorities read *your*   *x* Aramaic for *Father*   *y* Other ancient authorities read *an heir of God through Christ*   *z* Or *beggarly rudiments* slaved to them again? [10]You are observing special days, and months, and seasons, and years. [11]I am afraid that my work for you may have been wasted.

[12] Friends,[a] I beg you, become as I am, for I also have become as you are. You have done me no wrong. [13]You know that it was because of a physical infirmity that I first announced the gospel to you; [14]though my condition put you to the test, you did not scorn or despise me, but welcomed me as an angel of God, as Christ Jesus. [15]What has become of the goodwill you felt? For I testify that, had it been possible, you would have torn out your eyes and given them to me. [16]Have I now become your enemy by telling you the truth? [17]They make much of you, but for no good purpose; they want to exclude you, so that you may make much of them. [18]It is good to be made much of for a good purpose at all times, and not only when I am present with you. [19]My little children, for whom I am again in the pain of childbirth until Christ is formed in you, [20]I wish I were present with you now and could change my tone, for I am perplexed about you.

The Allegory of Hagar and Sarah

[21] Tell me, you who desire to be subject to the law, will you not listen to the law? [22]For it is written that Abraham had two sons, one by a slave woman and the other by a free woman. [23]One, the child of the slave, was born according to the flesh; the other, the child of the free woman, was born through the promise. [24]Now this is an allegory: these women are two covenants. One woman, in fact, is Hagar, from Mount Sinai, bearing children for slavery. [25]Now Hagar is Mount Sinai in Arabia[b] and corresponds to the present Jerusalem, for she is in slavery with her children. [26]But the other woman corresponds to the Jerusalem above; she is free, and she is our mother. [27]For it is written,

> "Rejoice, you childless one, you
> who bear no children,
> burst into song and shout, you
> who endure no birth pangs;
> for the children of the desolate
> woman are more numerous
> than the children of the one who
> is married."

[28]Now you,[c] my friends,[d] are children of the promise, like Isaac. [29]But just as at that time the child who was born accord-

ing to the flesh persecuted the child who was born according to the Spirit, so it is now also. [30]But what does the scripture say? "Drive out the slave and her child; for the child of the slave will not share the inheritance with the child of the free woman." [31]So then, friends,[d] we are children, not of the slave but of the free

5 woman. [1]For freedom Christ has set us free. Stand firm, therefore, and do not submit again to a yoke of slavery.

The Nature of Christian Freedom

[2] Listen! I, Paul, am telling you that if you let yourselves be circumcised, Christ will be of no benefit to you. [3]Once again I testify to every man who lets himself be circumcised that he is obliged to obey the entire law. [4]You who want to be justified by the law have cut yourselves off from Christ; you have fallen away from grace. [5]For through the Spirit, by faith, we eagerly wait for the hope of righteousness. [6]For in Christ Jesus neither circumcision nor uncircumcision counts for anything; the only thing that counts is faith working[e] through love.

[7] You were running well; who prevented you from obeying the truth? [8]Such persuasion does not come from the one who calls you. [9]A little yeast leavens the whole batch of dough. [10]I am confident about you in the Lord that you will not think otherwise. But whoever it is that is confusing you will pay the penalty. [11]But my friends,[d] why am I still being persecuted if I am still preaching circumcision? In that case the offense of the cross has been removed. [12]I wish those who unsettle you would castrate themselves!

[13] For you were called to freedom, brothers and sisters;[d] only do not use your freedom as an opportunity for self-indulgence,[f] but through love become slaves to one another. [14]For the whole law is summed up in a single commandment, "You shall love your neighbor as yourself." [15]If, however, you bite and devour one another, take care that you are not consumed by one another.

The Works of the Flesh

[16] Live by the Spirit, I say, and do not

---

a Gk *Brothers*   b Other ancient authorities read
For *Sinai is a mountain in Arabia*   c Other
ancient authorities read *we*   d Gk *brothers*
e Or *made effective*   f Gk *the flesh*

gratify the desires of the flesh. ¹⁷For what the flesh desires is opposed to the Spirit, and what the Spirit desires is opposed to the flesh; for these are opposed to each other, to prevent you from doing what you want. ¹⁸But if you are led by the Spirit, you are not subject to the law.

¹⁹Now the works of the flesh are obvious: fornication, impurity, licentiousness, ²⁰idolatry, sorcery, enmities, strife, jealousy, anger, quarrels, dissensions, factions, ²¹envy, *g* drunkenness, carousing, and

g Other ancient authorities add murder

Jesus, Our Liberator

THURSDAY

Scripture Reading for Today:
Galatians 5.1–6

Verse for Today:
Galatians 5.1

Our real liberator is Jesus Christ. Why is it so important for us to remember this? Because, if we don't remember who our *real* liberator is, we might be led to believe someone or something else is our liberator. And if we do that, we will be living in illusion. We will be living a lie.

Someone might ask, "Who or what else can we think is our liberator?" There are probably many answers to that question. I offer three here.

First, if we don't believe Jesus is our liberator, we could come to believe *we* are our own liberators. We give evidence of living in this illusion every time we find ourselves thinking or saying things like these: "I don't need anyone else. I can go it alone. I'm working really, really hard to earn heaven. No one else can possibly understand what I'm feeling. I have everything under control in my life."

Second, if we don't believe Jesus is our liberator, it might be because we don't even realize we need a liberator. We might think, "Me? Need liberation? From what?" Good question! And one each of us is called to answer for ourselves honestly and often. If we do, we just might discover that we need liberation from one (or some!) of the following: selfishness, pettiness, narrow-mindedness, addictive behaviors, intolerance, a proclivity to violence, dishonesty, discouragement, apathy, fear. Acknowledging one's servitude is the first step toward achieving liberation. Ask anyone in Alcoholics Anonymous.

A third way we can deny that Jesus is our liberator is by assigning that role to someone else—a spouse, a child, a friend, a spiritual director, a favorite spiritual writer, whomever. Expecting another human being to release us from our fears, limitations, and sins is unfair not only to ourselves, but to the other. For we are placing expectations upon him or her that no human being can fulfill. Although other people can and do play significant roles in our liberation, the fact remains: No other human being is our liberator. Only Jesus is.

—MELANNIE SVOBODA

Go to page 1538 for your next devotional reading.

things like these. I am warning you, as I warned you before: those who do such things will not inherit the kingdom of God.

The Fruit of the Spirit

22 By contrast, the fruit of the Spirit is love, joy, peace, patience, kindness, generosity, faithfulness, 23 gentleness, and self-control. There is no law against such things. 24 And those who belong to Christ Jesus have crucified the flesh with its passions and desires. 25 If we live by the Spirit,

let us also be guided by the Spirit. 26 Let us not become conceited, competing against one another, envying one another.

Bear One Another's Burdens

6 My friends,[h] if anyone is detected in a transgression, you who have received the Spirit should restore such a one in a spirit of gentleness. Take care that you yourselves are not tempted. 2 Bear one another's burdens, and in this way you will

h Gk Brothers

FRIDAY

Johnny Appleseed of the Soul

Scripture Reading for Today:
Galatians 5.22–26

Verses for Today:
Galatians 5.22–23

Apple picking . . . It makes me think about the fruit of the Spirit—love, joy, peace, patient endurance, kindness, generosity, faith, mildness, and chastity. Jesus wants me to produce that fruit as abundantly as this tree produces apples. Bearing this kind of fruit doesn't require a talent that others admire. All it requires is yielding to the Holy Spirit and allowing the fruit of holiness to ripen.

A mature tree yields about 40 bushels of apples. A fruit is a mature seed vessel. The seeds of a mature fruit are now capable of becoming trees and bearing their own fruit. I think of that as we eat apples from our bushel.

Applying this to the fruit of the Spirit, I realize more clearly than ever that when I yield to the Spirit and am virtuous, those virtues don't just exist by themselves—they are meant to produce other fruit. When I am loving, mild, patiently enduring, and chaste, I'll be happier as a person, and I'll make others happier to be around me.

But the fruit of the Spirit is not primarily for our benefit, just as a tree doesn't bear fruit to hang there until it drops off and rots. The seeds of our fruit can over time bring forth more fruit in them. My joy can bring forth joy in another. My peace in a situation can help others be peaceful. My act of kindness or generosity can bear fruit in another—even if it may not mature in them for years. In a way, it's a fulfillment of God's commission to Adam and Eve to be fruitful and multiply. Bearing the fruit of the Spirit can bring exponential growth of goodness—and even holiness—to the world.

We are called to be Johnny Appleseeds of the soul, scattering seeds of holiness in our very beings, in our actions, in our words. As the saying goes, "Anyone can count the seeds in an apple, but only God can count the apples in a seed."

—WENDY LEIFELD

Go to page 1542 for your next devotional reading.

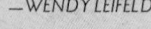

fulfill[i] the law of Christ. [3]For if those who are nothing think they are something, they deceive themselves. [4]All must test their own work; then that work, rather than their neighbor's work, will become a cause for pride. [5]For all must carry their own loads.

6 Those who are taught the word must share in all good things with their teacher.

7 Do not be deceived; God is not mocked, for you reap whatever you sow. [8]If you sow to your own flesh, you will reap corruption from the flesh; but if you sow to the Spirit, you will reap eternal life from the Spirit. [9]So let us not grow weary in doing what is right, for we will reap at harvest time, if we do not give up. [10]So then, whenever we have an opportunity, let us work for the good of all, and especially for those of the family of faith.

Final Admonitions and Benediction

11 See what large letters I make when I am writing in my own hand! [12]It is those who want to make a good showing in the flesh that try to compel you to be circumcised—only that they may not be persecuted for the cross of Christ. [13]Even the circumcised do not themselves obey the law, but they want you to be circumcised so that they may boast about your flesh. [14]May I never boast of anything except the cross of our Lord Jesus Christ, by which[j] the world has been crucified to me, and I to the world. [15]For[k] neither circumcision nor uncircumcision is anything; but a new creation is everything! [16]As for those who will follow this rule—peace be upon them, and mercy, and upon the Israel of God.

17 From now on, let no one make trouble for me; for I carry the marks of Jesus branded on my body.

18 May the grace of our Lord Jesus Christ be with your spirit, brothers and sisters.[l] Amen.

---

i Other ancient authorities read *in this way fulfill*
j Or *through whom*   *k* Other ancient authorities add *in Christ Jesus*   *l* Gk *brothers*

The Letter of Paul to the
Ephesians

Ephesians is known as one of the four "Captivity Letters" (the others are Philippians, Colossians, and Philemon) because in each one the author speaks of being in prison at the time the letter was written. Though ostensibly written by Paul, it may have been composed by one of his disciples, writing after Paul's death.

Much of Ephesians is written in poetic language, perhaps drawn from early Christian hymns and liturgies. Ephesians 6.10–17 includes advice on engaging in spiritual warfare, using the famous metaphor of putting on "the whole armor of God."

The primary message of Ephesians concerns the nature and purpose of the church. It stresses the unity of the church, composed of both Jew and Gentile, with Christ as its Lord. The teaching of this book regarding the church has been summed up by the words: "one, holy, catholic, and apostolic," which is the formulation contained in the Nicene Creed.

Ephesians 4.1–3 tell us how to conduct ourselves within the body of Christ: "I therefore, the prisoner in the Lord, beg you to lead a life worthy of the calling to which you have been called, with all humility and gentleness, with patience, bearing with one another in love, making every effort to maintain the unity of the Spirit in the bond of peace."

Salutation

1 Paul, an apostle of Christ Jesus by the will of God,

To the saints who are in Ephesus and are faithful[a] in Christ Jesus:

2 Grace to you and peace from God our Father and the Lord Jesus Christ.

Spiritual Blessings in Christ

3 Blessed be the God and Father of our Lord Jesus Christ, who has blessed us in Christ with every spiritual blessing in the heavenly places, 4just as he chose us in Christ[b] before the foundation of the world to be holy and blameless before him in love. 5He destined us for adoption as his children through Jesus Christ, according to the good pleasure of his will,

---

a Other ancient authorities lack in Ephesus, reading saints who are also faithful   b Gk in him

[6]to the praise of his glorious grace that he freely bestowed on us in the Beloved. [7]In him we have redemption through his blood, the forgiveness of our trespasses, according to the riches of his grace [8]that he lavished on us. With all wisdom and insight [9]he has made known to us the mystery of his will, according to his good pleasure that he set forth in Christ, [10]as a plan for the fullness of time, to gather up all things in him, things in heaven and things on earth. [11]In Christ we have also obtained an inheritance,[c] having been destined according to the purpose of him who accomplishes all things according to his counsel and will, [12]so that we, who were the first to set our hope on Christ, might live for the praise of his glory. [13]In him you also, when you had heard the word of truth, the gospel of your salvation, and had believed in him, were marked with the seal of the promised Holy Spirit; [14]this[d] is the pledge of our inheritance toward redemption as God's own people, to the praise of his glory.

Paul's Prayer

15 I have heard of your faith in the Lord Jesus and your love[e] toward all the saints, and for this reason [16]I do not cease to give thanks for you as I remember you in my prayers. [17]I pray that the God of our Lord Jesus Christ, the Father of glory, may give you a spirit of wisdom and revelation as you come to know him, [18]so that, with the eyes of your heart enlightened, you may know what is the hope to which he has called you, what are the riches of his glorious inheritance among the saints, [19]and what is the immeasurable greatness of his power for us who believe, according to the working of his great power. [20]God[f] put this power to work in Christ when he raised him from the dead and seated him at his right hand in the heavenly places, [21]far above all rule and authority and power and dominion, and above every name that is named, not only in this age but also in the age to come. [22]And he has put all things under his feet and has made him the head over all things for the church, [23]which is his body, the fullness of him who fills all in all.

From Death to Life

2 You were dead through the trespasses and sins [2]in which you once lived, following the course of this world, follow-

ing the ruler of the power of the air, the spirit that is now at work among those who are disobedient. [3]All of us once lived among them in the passions of our flesh, following the desires of flesh and senses, and we were by nature children of wrath, like everyone else. [4]But God, who is rich in mercy, out of the great love with which he loved us [5]even when we were dead through our trespasses, made us alive together with Christ[g]—by grace you have been saved— [6]and raised us up with him and seated us with him in the heavenly places in Christ Jesus, [7]so that in the ages to come he might show the immeasurable riches of his grace in kindness toward us in Christ Jesus. [8]For by grace you have been saved through faith, and this is not your own doing; it is the gift of God— [9]not the result of works, so that no one may boast. [10]For we are what he has made us, created in Christ Jesus for good works, which God prepared beforehand to be our way of life.

One in Christ

11 So then, remember that at one time you Gentiles by birth,[h] called "the uncircumcision" by those who are called "the circumcision"—a physical circumcision made in the flesh by human hands— [12]remember that you were at that time without Christ, being aliens from the commonwealth of Israel, and strangers to the covenants of promise, having no hope and without God in the world. [13]But now in Christ Jesus you who once were far off have been brought near by the blood of Christ. [14]For he is our peace; in his flesh he has made both groups into one and has broken down the dividing wall, that is, the hostility between us. [15]He has abolished the law with its commandments and ordinances, that he might create in himself one new humanity in place of the two, thus making peace, [16]and might reconcile both groups to God in one body[i] through the cross, thus putting to death that hostility through it.[j] [17]So he came and proclaimed peace to you who were far

---

[c] Or *been made a heritage*   [d] Other ancient authorities read *who*   [e] Other ancient authorities lack *and your love*   [f] Gk *He*   [g] Other ancient authorities read *in Christ*   [h] Gk *in the flesh*   [i] Or *reconcile both of us in one body for God*   [j] Or *in him*, or *in himself*

Herodias

*Her Name, the Female Form of
"Herod," Means "Heroic"*

Her Character: *A proud woman, she used her daughter to manipulate her husband into doing her will.*
Her Shame: *To be rebuked by an upstart prophet for leaving her husband in order to marry his half brother Herod Antipas.*
Her Triumph: *That her scheme to murder her enemy, John the Baptist, worked.*

Read Mark 6.17–29

Her grandfather, Herod the Great, had ruled Judea for 34 years, bringing stability to a troubled region of the Roman Empire. But Herod's reign contained shadows that darkened as the years went on. Herodias knew the stories well— how her grandfather had slaughtered a passel of Jewish brats in Bethlehem, murdered his favorite wife (her own grandmother) and three of his sons for real or imagined intrigues. Nearing the end of his life, Herod was determined that his own death would produce a time of universal mourning rather than celebration. Commanding all the leading Jews to gather in Jericho, he imprisoned them in the hippodrome, ordering them to be executed at the moment of his death. But the king was cheated of his last wish, and his prisoners were set free as soon as he died in the spring of 4 B.C.

Not a nice man, her grandfather. But then kings, she thought, were a rather different order of human beings.

Herodias's husband and his half brother, Herod Antipas, had been lucky survivors of the bloody family. Though Herod Antipas was married to the daughter of King Aretas IV, ruler of Nabatea, to the east, he divorced her in favor of Herodias. In one dicey move, Herod had stolen his brother's wife, compromised his eastern border, and alienated his Jewish subjects, whose law forbade wife-swapping among brothers.

Neither Herod nor Herodias had expected their transgression to become a matter of public agitation. After all, who was there to agitate, except the usual ragtag band of upstarts? A real prophet had not troubled Israel for more than four hundred years.

But trouble was edging toward them in the form of a new Elijah, whom God had been nurturing with locusts and honey in the wilderness that bordered their realm. Caring nothing for diplomacy, John the Baptist upbraided Herod for his unlawful marriage.

Herodias must have been pleased when her husband imprisoned John but upset that he didn't do more. For even Herod had to step carefully lest he ignite an uprising among John's ever-growing number of followers. So John was shut up in Machaerus, a fortress just east of the Dead Sea.

On Herod's birthday a feast was held in his honor and attended by a "who's who" of dignitaries. During the evening, Herodias's young daughter, Salome, performed a dance for Herod and his guests, which so pleased him that he promised his step-daughter anything she desired, up to half his kingdom.

Ever the good daughter, Salome hastened to her mother for advice. When Salome returned to the banquet hall, she surprised Herod with a gruesome demand: "I want you to give me at once the head of John the Baptist on a platter."

Though Herod was distressed by her request, he was even more distressed at the prospect of breaking an oath he had so publicly made. Therefore, in complete disregard for Jewish law, which prohibited execution without trial and decapitation as a form of execution, he immediately ordered John's death.

That night, Herodias must have savored her triumph over the man Jesus referred to as the greatest who had yet lived.

Praying in Light of the Story of Herodias

For John had been telling Herod, "It is not lawful for you to have your brother's wife." And Herodias had a grudge against him, and wanted to kill him.
—Mark 6.18–19

Praise God: *That he gives us opportunities to repent.*
Offer Thanks: *For the men and women in your own life who have had the courage to tell you the truth.*
Confess: *Any tendency to respond defensively to constructive criticism.*
Ask God: *For the grace to respond humbly to correction.*

Lift Your Heart

Most of us hate criticism. Part of our defensiveness stems from our inability to see the connection between brokenness and grace. How differently we would respond if we understood that repentance is like a garden hoe breaking up the soil to make it ready for the seed. If we want to cultivate the fruit of the Spirit in our lives—love, joy, peace, patience, kindness, goodness, faithfulness, gentleness, and self-control—we must cherish the truth however it comes to us. Being receptive to criticism doesn't mean we become women with low self-esteem. It simply means that we will be open about our sins and faults, believing in God's desire to forgive us and help us to change. Is God trying to get your attention about something that is off-kilter in your own life? Is he raising up a prophet in your own family—a child or a husband who is trying to tell you the truth? If so, resist the temptation to make them pay for their words by sulking, holding a grudge, or criticizing them in turn. Instead, be the first to say you're sorry. A habit of repentance will make your heart fertile soil for God's grace.

Father, I know how deceitful the human heart can be. Please give me the courage to be honest and the faith to believe in your forgiveness.

Go to page 1544 for your next devotional reading.

off and peace to those who were near; [18]for through him both of us have access in one Spirit to the Father. [19]So then you are no longer strangers and aliens, but you are citizens with the saints and also members of the household of God, [20]built upon the foundation of the apostles and prophets, with Christ Jesus himself as the cornerstone.[k] [21]In him the whole structure is joined together and grows into a holy temple in the Lord; [22]in whom you also are built together spiritually[l] into a dwelling place for God.

Paul's Ministry to the Gentiles

3 This is the reason that I Paul am a prisoner for[m] Christ Jesus for the sake of you Gentiles— [2]for surely you have already heard of the commission of God's grace that was given me for you, [3]and how the mystery was made known to me by revelation, as I wrote above in a few words, [4]a reading of which will enable you to perceive my understanding of the mystery of Christ. [5]In former generations

k Or keystone   l Gk in the Spirit   m Or of

MONDAY

Scripture Reading for Today:
Ephesians 2.1–10

Verses for Today:
Ephesians 2.8–9

Amazing Grace

The oldest twin, he was socialized into sin at an early age. He often told the story of how he first got drunk when he was two or three years old after he drained the beer bottles left out after one of the many family parties.

He kept the drinking a secret from the beautiful and innocent woman he courted. She never knew until the day he lost his job. She never forgot it because that was the day their first child was born.

Over the years the drinking progressed and so did the consequences. He drank up the weekly paycheck, disappearing for the weekend, but always returning full of remorse and resolutions. When the blackouts started, he was pretty far gone. Caught in the dead-ended trap of addiction and remorse, he was powerless to make the change he so badly desired.

Grace broke through one Saturday morning. He announced to his family that he was going to Alcoholics Anonymous. They wondered what bar that was. It turned out to be a community of grace. The recovery was long and arduous, but he made it out of the dark hole. Surrender to the grace of God's constant presence made the impossible, possible.

As you think about this story of grace, and many others like it, look at your own life story. God yearns to drag us up out of the depths of sin and addiction and suffering. God's grace is ever ready and present if we but give up control, admit our powerlessness, and let God transform us. Write your own story of surrender and grace today. Spend time in silence giving thanks for this generous God. Look at the "now" of your life to uncover new places where God is calling you to "let go and let God."

—CAROL GURA

Go to page 1545 for your next devotional reading.

this mystery[n] was not made known to humankind, as it has now been revealed to his holy apostles and prophets by the Spirit: [6]that is, the Gentiles have become fellow heirs, members of the same body, and sharers in the promise in Christ Jesus through the gospel.

7 Of this gospel I have become a servant according to the gift of God's grace that was given me by the working of his power. [8]Although I am the very least of all the saints, this grace was given to me to bring to the Gentiles the news of the boundless riches of Christ, [9]and to make everyone see[o] what is the plan of the mystery hidden for ages in[p] God who created all things; [10]so that through the church the wisdom of God in its rich variety might now be made known to the rulers and authorities in the heavenly places.

[11]This was in accordance with the eternal purpose that he has carried out in Christ Jesus our Lord, [12]in whom we have access to God in boldness and confidence through faith in him.[q] [13]I pray therefore that you[r] may not lose heart over my sufferings for you; they are your glory.

Prayer for the Readers

14 For this reason I bow my knees before the Father,[s] [15]from whom every family[t] in heaven and on earth takes its name. [16]I pray that, according to the riches of his glory, he may grant that you may be strengthened in your inner being with power through his Spirit, [17]and that

[n] Gk *it*   [o] Other ancient authorities read *to bring to light*   [p] Or *by*   [q] Or *the faith of him*   [r] Or *I*   [s] Other ancient authorities add *of our Lord Jesus Christ*   [t] Gk *fatherhood*

A Love Affair

TUESDAY

Scripture Reading for Today:
Ephesians 3.14–21

Verses for Today:
Ephesians 3.18–19

The greatest tragedy of our world is that men and women do not know, really know, that God loves them. Some believe it in a shadowy sort of way, but their belief in God's love for them is very remote and abstract.

Because of this, they do not know how to love God back. Often they don't even try because it all seems so very difficult and remote. But Christians must realize that the Christian faith, in its essence, is a love affair between God and each human being. Not just a simple love affair: It is a passionate love affair. God so loved each of us that he created us in his image. God so loved each of us that he became human himself, died on a cross, was raised from the dead by the Father, ascended into heaven—and all this in order to bring each of us back to himself, to that heaven which we had lost through our own fault.

Yes, of course the Christian has dogmas and rules, but they all concern love, which is the essence. Dogmas and tenets without love are dead letters, not even worth spelling out. Go love. And where love is, God is.

It is time we awoke from our long sleep, we Christians. It is time we shed our fears of God, or what is worse, our indifference toward him. Then we shall know true peace, true joy. The answers to our international and national problems will come clear in proportion to the amount that we love.

—*CATHERINE DOHERTY*

Go to page 1547 for your next devotional reading.

Christ may dwell in your hearts through faith, as you are being rooted and grounded in love. [18]I pray that you may have the power to comprehend, with all the saints, what is the breadth and length and height and depth, [19]and to know the love of Christ that surpasses knowledge, so that you may be filled with all the fullness of God.

20 Now to him who by the power at work within us is able to accomplish abundantly far more than all we can ask or imagine, [21]to him be glory in the church and in Christ Jesus to all generations, forever and ever. Amen.

Unity in the Body of Christ

4 I therefore, the prisoner in the Lord, beg you to lead a life worthy of the calling to which you have been called, [2]with all humility and gentleness, with patience, bearing with one another in love, [3]making every effort to maintain the unity of the Spirit in the bond of peace. [4]There is one body and one Spirit, just as you were called to the one hope of your calling, [5]one Lord, one faith, one baptism, [6]one God and Father of all, who is above all and through all and in all.

7 But each of us was given grace according to the measure of Christ's gift. [8]Therefore it is said,

"When he ascended on high he
　　made captivity itself a captive;
　he gave gifts to his people."

[9](When it says, "He ascended," what does it mean but that he had also descended[u] into the lower parts of the earth? [10]He who descended is the same one who ascended far above all the heavens, so that he might fill all things.) [11]The gifts he gave were that some would be apostles, some prophets, some evangelists, some pastors and teachers, [12]to equip the saints for the work of ministry, for building up the body of Christ, [13]until all of us come to the unity of the faith and of the knowledge of the Son of God, to maturity, to the measure of the full stature of Christ. [14]We must no longer be children, tossed to and fro and blown about by every wind of doctrine, by people's trickery, by their craftiness in deceitful scheming. [15]But speaking the truth in love, we must grow up in every way into him who is the head, into Christ, [16]from whom the whole body, joined and knit together by every ligament with which it is equipped, as each part is working properly, promotes the body's growth in building itself up in love.

The Old Life and the New

17 Now this I affirm and insist on in the Lord: you must no longer live as the Gentiles live, in the futility of their minds. [18]They are darkened in their understanding, alienated from the life of God because of their ignorance and hardness of heart. [19]They have lost all sensitivity and have abandoned themselves to licentiousness, greedy to practice every kind of impurity. [20]That is not the way you learned Christ! [21]For surely you have heard about him and were taught in him, as truth is in Jesus. [22]You were taught to put away your former way of life, your old self, corrupt and deluded by its lusts, [23]and to be renewed in the spirit of your minds, [24]and to clothe yourselves with the new self, created according to the likeness of God in true righteousness and holiness.

Rules for the New Life

25 So then, putting away falsehood, let all of us speak the truth to our neighbors, for we are members of one another. [26]Be angry but do not sin; do not let the sun go down on your anger, [27]and do not make room for the devil. [28]Thieves must give up stealing; rather let them labor and work honestly with their own hands, so as to have something to share with the needy. [29]Let no evil talk come out of your mouths, but only what is useful for building up,[v] as there is need, so that your words may give grace to those who hear. [30]And do not grieve the Holy Spirit of God, with which you were marked with a seal for the day of redemption. [31]Put away from you all bitterness and wrath and anger and wrangling and slander, together with all malice, [32]and be kind to one another, tenderhearted, forgiving one another, as God in Christ has forgiven you.[w]

5 [1]Therefore be imitators of God, as beloved children, [2]and live in love, as Christ loved us[x] and gave himself up for us, a fragrant offering and sacrifice to God.

---

[u] Other ancient authorities add *first*　　[v] Other ancient authorities read *building up faith*　　[w] Other ancient authorities read *us*　　[x] Other ancient authorities read *you*

Renounce Pagan Ways

3 But fornication and impurity of any kind, or greed, must not even be mentioned among you, as is proper among saints. ⁴Entirely out of place is obscene, silly, and vulgar talk; but instead, let there be thanksgiving. ⁵Be sure of this, that no fornicator or impure person, or one who is greedy (that is, an idolater), has any inheritance in the kingdom of Christ and of God.

6 Let no one deceive you with empty words, for because of these things the wrath of God comes on those who are disobedient. ⁷Therefore do not be associated with them. ⁸For once you were darkness, but now in the Lord you are light. Live as children of light— ⁹for the fruit of the light is found in all that is good and right and true. ¹⁰Try to find out what is pleasing to the Lord. ¹¹Take no part in the unfruitful works of darkness, but instead expose them. ¹²For it is shameful even to mention what such people do secretly;

Time Is Precious

WEDNESDAY

Scripture Reading for Today:
Ephesians 5.6–16

Verses for Today:
Ephesians 5.15–16

Women are called to use their time wisely, just as men are. This means we must defy the way the "world" values time. The world thinks that time spent in prayers and silent communion with God is time wasted. Time spent pursuing Christian growth is wasted. But Jesus in his call to Martha and his affirmation of Mary countered this: Time spent in touch with him, growing in faith, is of crucial importance. The world tells us that our most important time is time spent earning money. Women tend to earn less money, so their time is worth less than men's time, a valuation that does not come from God but from the world. All disciples are to make "the most of the time."

My husband answered the phone while I was writing. It was someone from my children's school, wanting to talk to me, so he handed me the phone. "We really need help on a phone call campaign to get more people out to the Sweetheart Dinner. I wonder if you could help by phoning fifteen people."

"I'm very busy at the moment. With my teaching schedule and a couple of book deadlines, I'm afraid I don't have the time. My husband might have time—"

"Oh, no, I'm sure he's far too busy. I could never ask him. Never mind," she said as she hung up.

To assume the Biblical stance that all are called equally to follow God, to use their time and talents for him and to exercise their callings based on gifts, we have to fight a wealth of cultural biases that tell women their time is cheap and their callings trivial. When a woman begins to sense herself called by Jesus, she may begin to claim the time to do what she needs to do. It may be spent in prayer, in caring for a dying parent, in writing, in going to medical school.

—MARY ELLEN ASHCROFT

Go to page 1549 for your next devotional reading.

¹³but everything exposed by the light becomes visible, ¹⁴for everything that becomes visible is light. Therefore it says,

"Sleeper, awake!
  Rise from the dead,
  and Christ will shine on you."

15 Be careful then how you live, not as unwise people but as wise, ¹⁶making the most of the time, because the days are evil. ¹⁷So do not be foolish, but understand what the will of the Lord is. ¹⁸Do not get drunk with wine, for that is debauchery; but be filled with the Spirit, ¹⁹as you sing psalms and hymns and spiritual songs among yourselves, singing and making melody to the Lord in your hearts, ²⁰giving thanks to God the Father at all times and for everything in the name of our Lord Jesus Christ.

The Christian Household

21 Be subject to one another out of reverence for Christ.

22 Wives, be subject to your husbands as you are to the Lord. ²³For the husband is the head of the wife just as Christ is the head of the church, the body of which he is the Savior. ²⁴Just as the church is subject to Christ, so also wives ought to be, in everything, to their husbands.

25 Husbands, love your wives, just as Christ loved the church and gave himself up for her, ²⁶in order to make her holy by cleansing her with the washing of water by the word, ²⁷so as to present the church to himself in splendor, without a spot or wrinkle or anything of the kind—yes, so that she may be holy and without blemish. ²⁸In the same way, husbands should love their wives as they do their own bodies. He who loves his wife loves himself. ²⁹For no one ever hates his own body, but he nourishes and tenderly cares for it, just as Christ does for the church, ³⁰because we are members of his body.ʸ ³¹"For this reason a man will leave his father and mother and be joined to his wife, and the two will become one flesh." ³²This is a great mystery, and I am applying it to Christ and the church. ³³Each of you, however, should love his wife as himself, and a wife should respect her husband.

Children and Parents

6 Children, obey your parents in the Lord,ᶻ for this is right. ²"Honor your father and mother"—this is the first commandment with a promise: ³"so that it may be well with you and you may live long on the earth."

4 And, fathers, do not provoke your children to anger, but bring them up in the discipline and instruction of the Lord.

Slaves and Masters

5 Slaves, obey your earthly masters with fear and trembling, in singleness of heart, as you obey Christ; ⁶not only while being watched, and in order to please them, but as slaves of Christ, doing the will of God from the heart. ⁷Render service with enthusiasm, as to the Lord and not to men and women, ⁸knowing that whatever good we do, we will receive the same again from the Lord, whether we are slaves or free.

9 And, masters, do the same to them. Stop threatening them, for you know that both of you have the same Master in heaven, and with him there is no partiality.

The Whole Armor of God

10 Finally, be strong in the Lord and in the strength of his power. ¹¹Put on the whole armor of God, so that you may be able to stand against the wiles of the devil. ¹²For ourᵃ struggle is not against enemies of blood and flesh, but against the rulers, against the authorities, against the cosmic powers of this present darkness, against the spiritual forces of evil in the heavenly places. ¹³Therefore take up the whole armor of God, so that you may be able to withstand on that evil day, and having done everything, to stand firm. ¹⁴Stand therefore, and fasten the belt of truth around your waist, and put on the breastplate of righteousness. ¹⁵As shoes for your feet put on whatever will make you ready to proclaim the gospel of peace. ¹⁶With all of these,ᵇ take the shield of faith, with which you will be able to quench all the flaming arrows of the evil one. ¹⁷Take the helmet of salvation, and the sword of the Spirit, which is the word of God.

18 Pray in the Spirit at all times in every prayer and supplication. To that end keep alert and always persevere in suppli-

---

ʸ Other ancient authorities add *of his flesh and of his bones* ᶻ Other ancient authorities lack *in the Lord* ᵃ Other ancient authorities read *your* ᵇ Or *In all circumstances*

cation for all the saints. ¹⁹Pray also for me, so that when I speak, a message may be given to me to make known with boldness the mystery of the gospel,ᶜ ²⁰for which I am an ambassador in chains. Pray that I may declare it boldly, as I must speak.

Personal Matters and Benediction

21 So that you also may know how I am and what I am doing, Tychicus will tell you everything. He is a dear brother and a

ᶜ Other ancient authorities lack *of the gospel*

Mother Love

THURSDAY

Scripture Reading for Today:
Ephesians 6.1–4

Verse for Today:
Ephesians 6.4

Some time ago, I witnessed a scene in New York: A tiny, filthy playground, which had been built among the tall buildings, had no heavy rubber safety pads under the equipment. Tiny tots would climb up a huge slide and, if their mothers didn't catch them at the bottom, would land with a thud on the concrete. I shall never forget the touching sight of toddlers gleefully screeching their way down the slide, while their mamas stood tensely, arms outstretched, faces taut, waiting to rescue them from brain concussions.

This scene became a prime example to me of what philosophers call "contingency." Being finite, fragile human beings, we can be killed instantly by the slightest accident. The fact of contingency poses a difficult and sometimes unbearable problem for those who love others. When we so keenly appreciate the preciousness of another individual—a child, a husband, a parent, a friend—how can we not become worried at the thought of all the dangers that threaten the beloved?

The child sees the world as a wonderful place of possibility, while the mother may come to view it as pure danger. Nagging can be analyzed as a petty way of trying to insure that things go well for loved ones. "Brush your teeth," "comb your hair," "put on your [boots]," etc. All these orders are given to help prevent future suffering such as rotting teeth, social ostracism, or a cold. Nagging or henpecking can become extremely disagreeable to the victim. It is inimical to a free, fun-loving atmosphere.

In possessive smothering, the woman wraps herself like a cocoon around her loved ones. First she holds them safe against the frightening world. Then she tries to mold them into the image that she cherishes for them. Finally, control replaces any respect for their own individuality and freedom.

Personally, I find that only a profound faith in God permits me to accept the myriad possibilities of suffering that threaten those I love. Only by putting them into God's hands can I release them from my own.

—*RONDA DE SOLA CHERVIN*

Go to page 1552 for your next devotional reading.

faithful minister in the Lord. [22]I am sending him to you for this very purpose, to let you know how we are, and to encourage your hearts.

23 Peace be to the whole community,[d] and love with faith, from God the Father and the Lord Jesus Christ. [24]Grace be with all who have an undying love for our Lord Jesus Christ.[e]

[d] Gk *to the brothers*   [e] Other ancient authorities add *Amen*

The Letter of Paul to the
Philippians

Philippi was a city located in northeastern Macedonia, named after Philip II, king of Macedonia and father of Alexander the Great. By midway through the first century, when Paul first visited, it had become a leading city in the Roman province to which it belonged.

One of Paul's first converts in Philippi was a successful businesswoman named Lydia, a dealer in fine cloth, who has the distinction of being his first European convert mentioned in Scripture. The book of Acts tells how an earthquake shook the city when Paul and his companion Silas were imprisoned there (see 16.25–34). Paul felt great affection for the Philippian church, and his letter, commending them and thanking them for their generous support of his ministry, is sometimes called "the letter of joy."

Philippians contains a beautiful hymn about Christ's saving work (2.5–11) and also warns of false teachers who would try to convince the church to submit to the burdens of the Mosaic Law. At the beginning of chapter 4, Paul exhorts two women, Euodia and Syntyche, to resolve their quarrel, identifying them as women leaders in the church who had helped him do the work of the gospel.

Paul sounds a note of rejoicing in this letter, all the more remarkable since he wrote it from prison.

Salutation

1 Paul and Timothy, servants[a] of Christ Jesus,

To all the saints in Christ Jesus who are in Philippi, with the bishops[b] and deacons:[c]

2 Grace to you and peace from God our Father and the Lord Jesus Christ.

Paul's Prayer for the Philippians

3 I thank my God every time I remember you, [4]constantly praying with joy in every one of my prayers for all of you, [5]because of your sharing in the gospel from the first day until now. [6]I am confident of this, that the one who began a good work among you will bring it to completion by the day of Jesus Christ. [7]It is right for me to think this way about all of you, because you hold me in your

---

[a] Gk slaves [b] Or overseers [c] Or overseers and helpers

heart,*d* for all of you share in God's grace*e* with me, both in my imprisonment and in the defense and confirmation of the gospel. 8For God is my witness, how I long for all of you with the compassion of Christ Jesus. 9And this is my prayer, that your love may overflow more and more with knowledge and full insight 10to help you to determine what is best, so that in the day of Christ you may be pure and blameless, 11having produced the harvest of righteousness that comes through Jesus Christ for the glory and praise of God.

Paul's Present Circumstances

12 I want you to know, beloved,*f* that what has happened to me has actually helped to spread the gospel, 13so that it has become known throughout the whole imperial guard*g* and to everyone else that my imprisonment is for Christ; 14and most of the brothers and sisters,*f* having been made confident in the Lord by my

d Or *because I hold you in my heart*   *e* Gk *in grace*   *f* Gk *brothers*   *g* Gk *whole praetorium*

Laundry Prayer

FRIDAY

Scripture Reading for Today:
Philippians 1.3–11

Verses for Today:
Philippians 1.3–4

She loved those Mondays when she was first on the block to get the laundry out drying on the clothesline. Clothes billowing on the line bring back all those memories of Buba—my grandma.

I find her habits ingrained in me. So when I can, I hang out my laundry on Monday mornings. I used to wonder why she loved it so much. It amazed me that "doing laundry" could bring Buba to singing and dancing around the generous kitchen floor. Now I know her secret.

It is all a prayer, that laundry. Not a chore—a task—an automated, get-it-out-of-the-way thing, but an opportunity to appreciate each member of the family. Doing the laundry, I have discovered, is a way to think about the gift of each person in my family. The sheets blowing on the line bring to mind the many moments of togetherness and intimacy shared in our marriage. As I iron the shirts of my husband, I remember his wonderful calming presence in my life. The organized way he goes about his tasks, the logical way he helps me see each crisis encountered come to mind as I press out the pockets and the collars of his shirts. I smooth and fold the jeans of my son, thinking how this artist-child brings new, creative ways of thinking into my world. Large stacks of towels and washcloths are simple reminders of the way my other son's presence is the gift of still and peaceful waters. Folding the underwear and sorting the socks, I remember my oldest daughter. Her depth and spiritual vision have shed light in my own inner life. The youngest child's zest for life comes to mind as my iron traces the fabric of colorful prints. Laundry is a way for me to give thanks for the gifts of my family. I have learned why Buba loved it so much.

—*CAROL GURA*

Go to page 1554 for your next devotional reading.

imprisonment, dare to speak the word[h] with greater boldness and without fear.

15 Some proclaim Christ from envy and rivalry, but others from goodwill. [16]These proclaim Christ out of love, knowing that I have been put here for the defense of the gospel; [17]the others proclaim Christ out of selfish ambition, not sincerely but intending to increase my suffering in my imprisonment. [18]What does it matter? Just this, that Christ is proclaimed in every way, whether out of false motives or true; and in that I rejoice.

Yes, and I will continue to rejoice, [19]for I know that through your prayers and the help of the Spirit of Jesus Christ this will turn out for my deliverance. [20]It is my eager expectation and hope that I will not be put to shame in any way, but that by my speaking with all boldness, Christ will be exalted now as always in my body, whether by life or by death. [21]For to me, living is Christ and dying is gain. [22]If I am to live in the flesh, that means fruitful labor for me; and I do not know which I prefer. [23]I am hard pressed between the two: my desire is to depart and be with Christ, for that is far better; [24]but to remain in the flesh is more necessary for you. [25]Since I am convinced of this, I know that I will remain and continue with all of you for your progress and joy in faith, [26]so that I may share abundantly in your boasting in Christ Jesus when I come to you again.

27 Only, live your life in a manner worthy of the gospel of Christ, so that, whether I come and see you or am absent and hear about you, I will know that you are standing firm in one spirit, striving side by side with one mind for the faith of the gospel, [28]and are in no way intimidated by your opponents. For them this is evidence of their destruction, but of your salvation. And this is God's doing. [29]For he has graciously granted you the privilege not only of believing in Christ, but of suffering for him as well— [30]since you are having the same struggle that you saw I had and now hear that I still have.

Imitating Christ's Humility

2 If then there is any encouragement in Christ, any consolation from love, any sharing in the Spirit, any compassion and sympathy, [2]make my joy complete: be of the same mind, having the same love, being in full accord and of one mind. [3]Do nothing from selfish ambition or conceit, but in humility regard others as better than yourselves. [4]Let each of you look not to your own interests, but to the interests of others. [5]Let the same mind be in you that was[i] in Christ Jesus,

[6] who, though he was in the form
    of God,
  did not regard equality with God
    as something to be exploited,
[7] but emptied himself,
  taking the form of a slave,
  being born in human likeness.
And being found in human form,
[8]   he humbled himself
  and became obedient to the point
    of death—
  even death on a cross.

[9] Therefore God also highly
    exalted him
  and gave him the name
  that is above every name,
[10] so that at the name of Jesus
  every knee should bend,
  in heaven and on earth and under
    the earth,
[11] and every tongue should confess
  that Jesus Christ is Lord,
  to the glory of God the Father.

Shining as Lights in the World

12 Therefore, my beloved, just as you have always obeyed me, not only in my presence, but much more now in my absence, work out your own salvation with fear and trembling; [13]for it is God who is at work in you, enabling you both to will and to work for his good pleasure.

14 Do all things without murmuring and arguing, [15]so that you may be blameless and innocent, children of God without blemish in the midst of a crooked and perverse generation, in which you shine like stars in the world. [16]It is by your holding fast to the word of life that I can boast on the day of Christ that I did not run in vain or labor in vain. [17]But even if I am being poured out as a libation over the sacrifice and the offering of your faith, I am glad and rejoice with all of you— [18]and in the same way you also must be glad and rejoice with me.

Timothy and Epaphroditus

19 I hope in the Lord Jesus to send

---

h Other ancient authorities read *word of God*
i Or *that you have*

The Canaanite Woman

Read Matthew 15.21–28

Her body jerked and twisted, arms thrashing the air. Wide-eyed, the little girl spoke to ghosts her mother could not see, her face changing as rapidly as clouds in a sudden storm. Dark hair stuck in gummy strands against her cheeks.

Her Character:
Though a Gentile, she addressed Jesus as "Lord, Son of David." Her great faith resulted in her daughter's deliverance.
Her Sorrow: *That her child was tormented by an evil spirit.*
Her Joy: *That Jesus freed her daughter from spiritual bondage.*

Her mother wondered what had become of the sweet child who had followed her like a puppy wherever she went. How she missed those soft kisses and the button nose that had nuzzled her cheek. She had hardly slept these last few nights for fear of what her daughter might do to herself.

That morning she caught wind of a Jewish healer who, friends said, had come to Tyre hoping for relief from the crowds that mobbed him in Galilee. It didn't matter that Jews seldom mingled with Gentiles. She would go to him, beg his help, throw a fit herself if necessary.

As soon as she found Jesus, she pleaded, "Have mercy on me, Lord, Son of David; my daughter is tormented by a demon." But he ignored her, saying nothing.

Finally, his disciples said to Jesus, "Send her away, for she keeps shouting after us."

But Jesus knew it would not be that easy to get rid of her. The only way, in fact, would be to answer her prayer.

The woman fell at his feet again, imploring, "Lord, help me."

Then Jesus turned and said, "It is not fair to take the children's food and throw it to the dogs."

"Yes, Lord," she said, "yet even the dogs eat the crumbs that fall from their masters' table."

"Woman, great is your faith! Let it be done for you as you wish," Jesus said. And her daughter was instantly healed.

Scripture doesn't describe the little girl in any detail. It only says she was tormented by a demon. But judging from similar incidents described in Scripture, the signs of demonic manifestation were probably both obvious and frightening.

But why did Jesus seem so rude to the poor mother, ignoring her request and then referring to her and her child as dogs? His response may sound a little less harsh when we realize that the word Jesus used for "dogs" was not the derisive one Jews ordinarily reserved for Gentiles. Instead, it was the term used for little dogs kept as pets. Jesus also made it clear that his primary mission was to the Israelites. Had Jesus performed many miracles in Tyre and Sidon, he would have risked the same kind of mob scenes he had just left behind in Galilee, thus inaugurating a ministry to the Gentiles in advance of his Father's timing.

But the woman couldn't have known the reason for his silence. And it must have tested her faith. Rather than give up or take offense, she exercised her quick wit, revealing both a deep humility and tenacious faith. It was a combination Jesus seemed unable to resist—fertile soil in which to grow a miracle.

Praying With the Canaanite Woman

Then Jesus answered her, "Woman, great is your faith! Let it be done for you as you wish."—*Matthew 15.28*

Praise God: *For his power to deliver us from every form of evil.*
Offer Thanks: *For the deliverance you have already experienced.*
Confess: *Any hopelessness about children or others you love.*
Ask God: *To give you the same "terrier-like" faith that the Canaanite woman had, so that you will never give up praying for the salvation of your loved ones.*

Lift Your Heart

Though most of our children will never suffer this level of demonic torment, all of them are engaged, as we are, in a spiritual battle. As a mother, your prayers and your life play a role in the spiritual protection of your children. This week pray Psalm 46 or Psalm 91 for the spiritual protection of your family. Or take a few moments to pray these verses from Psalm 125:

> Those who trust in the LORD are like Mount Zion,
> which cannot be moved, but abides forever.
> As the mountains surround Jerusalem,
> so the LORD surrounds his people,
> from this time on and forevermore.

Imagine that every member of your family is surrounded by God, just as mountains surround the city of Jerusalem. Offer them to him, placing each one in his care.

Lord, surround my children like the mountains surrounding Jerusalem. Encircle our family with your power and peace. Deliver us from evil now and forever. Amen.

Go to page 1557 for your next devotional reading.

Timothy to you soon, so that I may be cheered by news of you. 20I have no one like him who will be genuinely concerned for your welfare. 21All of them are seeking their own interests, not those of Jesus Christ. 22But Timothy's*j* worth you know, how like a son with a father he has served with me in the work of the gospel. 23I hope therefore to send him as soon as I see how things go with me; 24and I trust in the Lord that I will also come soon.

25 Still, I think it necessary to send to you Epaphroditus—my brother and co-worker and fellow soldier, your messenger*k* and minister to my need; 26for he has been longing for*l* all of you, and has been distressed because you heard that he was ill. 27He was indeed so ill that he nearly died. But God had mercy on him, and not only on him but on me also, so that I would not have one sorrow after another. 28I am the more eager to send him, therefore, in order that you may rejoice at seeing him again, and that I may be less anxious. 29Welcome him then in the Lord with all joy, and honor such people, 30because he came close to death for the work of Christ,*m* risking his life to make up for those services that you could not give me.

3 Finally, my brothers and sisters,*n* rejoice*o* in the Lord.

Breaking with the Past

To write the same things to you is not troublesome to me, and for you it is a safeguard.

2 Beware of the dogs, beware of the evil workers, beware of those who mutilate the flesh! *p* 3For it is we who are the circumcision, who worship in the Spirit of God*q* and boast in Christ Jesus and have no confidence in the flesh— 4even though I, too, have reason for confidence in the flesh.

If anyone else has reason to be confident in the flesh, I have more: 5circumcised on the eighth day, a member of the people of Israel, of the tribe of Benjamin, a Hebrew born of Hebrews; as to the law, a Pharisee; 6as to zeal, a persecutor of the church; as to righteousness under the law, blameless.

7 Yet whatever gains I had, these I have come to regard as loss because of Christ. 8More than that, I regard everything as loss because of the surpassing value of knowing Christ Jesus my Lord. For his sake I have suffered the loss of all things, and I regard them as rubbish, in order that I may gain Christ 9and be found in him, not having a righteousness of my own that comes from the law, but one that comes through faith in Christ,*r* the righteousness from God based on faith. 10I want to know Christ*s* and the power of his resurrection and the sharing of his sufferings by becoming like him in his death, 11if somehow I may attain the resurrection from the dead.

Pressing toward the Goal

12 Not that I have already obtained this or have already reached the goal;*t* but I press on to make it my own, because Christ Jesus has made me his own. 13Beloved,*u* I do not consider that I have made it my own;*v* but this one thing I do: forgetting what lies behind and straining forward to what lies ahead, 14I press on toward the goal for the prize of the heavenly*w* call of God in Christ Jesus. 15Let those of us then who are mature be of the same mind; and if you think differently about anything, this too God will reveal to you. 16Only let us hold fast to what we have attained.

17 Brothers and sisters,*u* join in imitating me, and observe those who live according to the example you have in us. 18For many live as enemies of the cross of Christ; I have often told you of them, and now I tell you even with tears. 19Their end is destruction; their god is the belly; and their glory is in their shame; their minds are set on earthly things. 20But our citizenship*x* is in heaven, and it is from there that we are expecting a Savior, the Lord Jesus Christ. 21He will transform the body of our humiliation*y* that it may be conformed to the body of his glory,*z* by the power that also enables him to make all

4 things subject to himself. 1Therefore, my brothers and sisters,*n* whom I love and long for, my joy and crown,

---

j Gk *his*   *k* Gk *apostle*   *l* Other ancient authorities read *longing to see*   *m* Other ancient authorities read *of the Lord*   *n* Gk *my brothers*   *o* Or *farewell*   *p* Gk *the mutilation*   *q* Other ancient authorities read *worship God in spirit*   *r* Or *through the faith of Christ*   *s* Gk *him*   *t* Or *have already been made perfect*   *u* Gk *Brothers*   *v* Other ancient authorities read *my own yet*   *w* Gk *upward*   *x* Or *commonwealth*   *y* Or *our humble bodies*   *z* Or *his glorious body*

stand firm in the Lord in this way, my beloved.

Exhortations

2 I urge Euodia and I urge Syntyche to be of the same mind in the Lord. ³Yes, and I ask you also, my loyal companion,ᵃ help these women, for they have struggled beside me in the work of the gospel, together with Clement and the rest

of my co-workers, whose names are in the book of life.

4 Rejoiceᵇ in the Lord always; again I will say, Rejoice.ᵇ ⁵Let your gentleness be known to everyone. The Lord is near. ⁶Do not worry about anything, but in everything by prayer and supplication with thanksgiving let your requests be made

a Or *loyal Syzygus*   *b* Or *Farewell*

---

*S*piritual *Achievements*

MONDAY

Scripture Reading
for Today:
Philippians 3.7–11

Verse for Today:
Philippians 3.7

God has given each of us the task of fashioning a beautiful vase for him, which we must carry up the mountain in order to place it in his hands. This vase represents everything we can do to please God: our good works, our prayers, our efforts to grow to maturity; all this God values most highly. Into the making of this vase, then, we put all we have, our whole self. It is for God we are fashioning it, we tell ourselves. When it is finished, we begin our journey up the mountain.

When we reach the top, a double shock awaits us. God is not there—there is silence, no response when we make our arrival known. Secondly, the vase isn't beautiful any more. There it is in our hands, a tawdry, common pot the vase into which we had put our all. A deep instinct is telling us that if we want God, we have to go over the other side of the mountain, and one glance reveals a steep, mist-bound, featureless face. We can't go down there with anything in our hands; we must drop the vase, still precious though so disappointing. We cannot take it with us; we must go to God with nothing in our hands.

Our spiritual achievement is our most precious treasure. It has to go. "For his sake," cries one who understood this, "I have suffered the loss of all things, and I regard them as rubbish, in order that I may gain Christ and be found in him, not having a righteousness of my own that comes from the Law, but one that comes through faith in Christ." Now we can only begin to see the shabbiness of all we have done and do when God shows it to us.

But what matters is that we recognize that it is God who is showing it to us and gladly let it go. The ideas we had formed of God, our working plan of him, so to speak, are destroyed. "Our" God disappears. It is only when he does disappear that we can meet the true God, who is mystery.

—*RUTH BURROWS*

Go to page 1558 for your next devotional reading.

known to God. 7And the peace of God, which surpasses all understanding, will guard your hearts and your minds in Christ Jesus.

8 Finally, beloved,*c* whatever is true, whatever is honorable, whatever is just, whatever is pure, whatever is pleasing, whatever is commendable, if there is any excellence and if there is anything worthy of praise, think about*d* these things. 9Keep on doing the things that you have learned and received and heard and seen in me, and the God of peace will be with you.

Acknowledgment of the Philippians' Gift

10 I rejoice*e* in the Lord greatly that now at last you have revived your concern for me; indeed, you were concerned for me, but had no opportunity to show it.*f* 11Not that I am referring to being in need; for I have learned to be content with whatever I have. 12I know what it is to have little, and I know what it is to have plenty. In any and all circumstances I have learned the secret of being well-fed and of going hungry, of having plenty and of be-

c Gk *brothers*   *d* Gk *take account of*   *e* Gk *I rejoiced*   *f* Gk lacks *to show it*

"*Poor Me!*"

TUESDAY

Scripture Reading for Today:
Philippians 4.10–13

Verse for Today:
Philippians 4.12

I've noticed there are a lot of people walking around with a "poor me" complex, wearing self-pity like a second skin.

There was Regina. Every sentence she uttered was prefaced "With my luck . . ." and the rest of the statement was always bad news. My relative Justine had a way of finding the flip side of all nice things. I bought her an apron, but it was too pretty to wear. I bought her a cake, but it was too fattening to eat. Mary was one who never said a word. She just sighed deep, heavy sighs, regularly. You couldn't mistake what she was saying about her terrible lot in life, even though she minced words.

From my own weaknesses, I've come to understand why some people are chronic complainers, mired in self-pity or on the greed track. It is because basic to our nature as human beings is the desire not just to have, but to have *more*. Some people suffer from a constant condition of subjective poverty. No one denies that objective poverty exists, where people have no shoes or running water, have shabby homes and scanty food. Subjective poverty is different. It is relative. It means feeling poor in relation to others, feeling deprived because we don't have what someone else has, be it money, fame, good looks, good health, and so on.

I remember reading words of wisdom once from Saint Francis de Sales, something I scribbled in a notebook back in my college days. He wrote that truly rich people are the ones who are content with their possessions, not looking over their shoulders to see how much more other people have, and then becoming miserable from the inequality. Truly the choice of being rich or "poor me" is mostly ours to make.

—*ANTOINETTE BOSCO*

Go to page 1562 for your next devotional reading.

ing in need. [13]I can do all things through him who strengthens me. [14]In any case, it was kind of you to share my distress.

15 You Philippians indeed know that in the early days of the gospel, when I left Macedonia, no church shared with me in the matter of giving and receiving, except you alone. [16]For even when I was in Thessalonica, you sent me help for my needs more than once. [17]Not that I seek the gift, but I seek the profit that accumulates to your account. [18]I have been paid in full and have more than enough; I am fully satisfied, now that I have received from Epaphroditus the gifts you sent, a fragrant offering, a sacrifice acceptable and pleas-

ing to God. [19]And my God will fully satisfy every need of yours according to his riches in glory in Christ Jesus. [20]To our God and Father be glory forever and ever. Amen.

Final Greetings and Benediction

21 Greet every saint in Christ Jesus. The friends[g] who are with me greet you. [22]All the saints greet you, especially those of the emperor's household.
23 The grace of the Lord Jesus Christ be with your spirit.[h]

[g] Gk *brothers*   [h] Other ancient authorities add *Amen*

The Letter of Paul to the
Colossians

Colossae was a city in Asia Minor located in an area that is now part of southwestern Turkey. Though Paul had never visited the city, he wrote from prison in order to encourage the Colossians and warn them against false teaching regarding angel worship and various ascetical practices.

Rather than launching a full-scale attack on the falsehoods that threatened the community, Paul begins by asserting Christ's supremacy over all creation. No power, visible or invisible, is greater than Christ, who is the head of the church. Only through Christ are we reconciled to God. Therefore, Christians need not placate the spirits nor slavishly follow religious rules and regulations. Paul urges the Colossians to hold on to the gospel they have received: "Do not let anyone disqualify you, insisting on self-abasement and worship of angels, dwelling on visions, puffed up without cause by a human way of thinking" (2.18).

The book of Colossians reminds us that we needn't waste energy on superstitious beliefs or legalistic practices. Instead, we are to give ourselves to the task of becoming like Christ, imitating his virtues and allowing his peace to rule in our hearts.

Salutation

1 Paul, an apostle of Christ Jesus by the will of God, and Timothy our brother,

2 To the saints and faithful brothers and sisters*a* in Christ in Colossae:

Grace to you and peace from God our Father.

Paul Thanks God for the Colossians

3 In our prayers for you we always thank God, the Father of our Lord Jesus Christ, 4for we have heard of your faith in Christ Jesus and of the love that you have for all the saints, 5because of the hope laid up for you in heaven. You have heard of this hope before in the word of the truth, the gospel 6that has come to you. Just as it is bearing fruit and growing in the whole world, so it has been bearing fruit among yourselves from the day you heard it and truly comprehended the grace of God. 7This you learned from Epaphras, our beloved fellow servant.*b* He is a faithful

a Gk *brothers*   *b* Gk *slave*

minister of Christ on your[c] behalf, [8]and he has made known to us your love in the Spirit.

[9] For this reason, since the day we heard it, we have not ceased praying for you and asking that you may be filled with the knowledge of God's[d] will in all spiritual wisdom and understanding, [10]so that you may lead lives worthy of the Lord, fully pleasing to him, as you bear fruit in every good work and as you grow in the knowledge of God. [11]May you be made strong with all the strength that comes from his glorious power, and may you be prepared to endure everything with patience, while joyfully [12]giving thanks to the Father, who has enabled[e] you[f] to share in the inheritance of the saints in the light. [13]He has rescued us from the power of darkness and transferred us into the kingdom of his beloved Son, [14]in whom we have redemption, the forgiveness of sins.[g]

The Supremacy of Christ

[15] He is the image of the invisible God, the firstborn of all creation; [16]for in[h] him all things in heaven and on earth were created, things visible and invisible, whether thrones or dominions or rulers or powers—all things have been created through him and for him. [17]He himself is before all things, and in[h] him all things hold together. [18]He is the head of the body, the church; he is the beginning, the firstborn from the dead, so that he might come to have first place in everything. [19]For in him all the fullness of God was pleased to dwell, [20]and through him God was pleased to reconcile to himself all things, whether on earth or in heaven, by making peace through the blood of his cross.

[21] And you who were once estranged and hostile in mind, doing evil deeds, [22]he has now reconciled[i] in his fleshly body[j] through death, so as to present you holy and blameless and irreproachable before him— [23]provided that you continue securely established and steadfast in the faith, without shifting from the hope promised by the gospel that you heard, which has been proclaimed to every creature under heaven. I, Paul, became a servant of this gospel.

Paul's Interest in the Colossians

[24] I am now rejoicing in my sufferings for your sake, and in my flesh I am completing what is lacking in Christ's afflictions for the sake of his body, that is, the church. [25]I became its servant according to God's commission that was given to me for you, to make the word of God fully known, [26]the mystery that has been hidden throughout the ages and generations but has now been revealed to his saints. [27]To them God chose to make known how great among the Gentiles are the riches of the glory of this mystery, which is Christ in you, the hope of glory. [28]It is he whom we proclaim, warning everyone and teaching everyone in all wisdom, so that we may present everyone mature in Christ. [29]For this I toil and struggle with all the energy that he powerfully inspires within me.

2 For I want you to know how much I am struggling for you, and for those in Laodicea, and for all who have not seen me face to face. [2]I want their hearts to be encouraged and united in love, so that they may have all the riches of assured understanding and have the knowledge of God's mystery, that is, Christ himself,[k] [3]in whom are hidden all the treasures of wisdom and knowledge. [4]I am saying this so that no one may deceive you with plausible arguments. [5]For though I am absent in body, yet I am with you in spirit, and I rejoice to see your morale and the firmness of your faith in Christ.

Fullness of Life in Christ

[6] As you therefore have received Christ Jesus the Lord, continue to live your lives[l] in him, [7]rooted and built up in him and established in the faith, just as you were taught, abounding in thanksgiving.

[8] See to it that no one takes you captive through philosophy and empty deceit, according to human tradition, according to the elemental spirits of the universe,[m]

---

c Other ancient authorities read *our*   d Gk *his*
e Other ancient authorities read *called*   f Other ancient authorities read *us*   g Other ancient authorities add *through his blood*   h Or *by*
i Other ancient authorities read *you have now been reconciled*   j Gk *in the body of his flesh*   k Other ancient authorities read *of the mystery of God, both of the Father and of Christ*   l Gk *to walk*   m Or *the rudiments of the world*

and not according to Christ. [9]For in him the whole fullness of deity dwells bodily, [10]and you have come to fullness in him, who is the head of every ruler and authority. [11]In him also you were circumcised with a spiritual circumcision,[n] by putting off the body of the flesh in the circumcision of Christ; [12]when you were buried with him in baptism, you were also raised with him through faith in the power of God, who raised him from the dead. [13]And when you were dead in trespasses and the uncircumcision of your flesh, God[o] made you[p] alive together with him, when he forgave us all our trespasses, [14]erasing the record that stood against us with its legal demands. He set this aside, nailing it to the cross. [15]He disarmed[q] the rulers and authorities and made a public example of them, triumphing over them in it.

16 Therefore do not let anyone condemn you in matters of food and drink or of observing festivals, new moons, or sabbaths. [17]These are only a shadow of what is to come, but the substance belongs to Christ. [18]Do not let anyone disqualify you, insisting on self-abasement and worship of angels, dwelling[r] on visions,[s] puffed up without cause by a human way of thinking,[t] [19]and not holding fast to the head, from whom the whole body, nourished and held together by its ligaments and sinews, grows with a growth that is from God.

[n] Gk *a circumcision made without hands*   [o] Gk *he* [p] Other ancient authorities read *made us*; others, *made*   [q] Or *divested himself of*   [r] Other ancient authorities read *not dwelling*   [s] Meaning of Gk uncertain   [t] Gk *by the mind of his flesh*

---

*B*oredom

WEDNESDAY

Scripture Reading for Today:
Colossians 1.24–29

Verse for Today:
Colossians 1.24

Do you know what boredom is? It is a kind of death in a human being. It means that people have let their interior resources dry up and have reached a sort of coma akin to death. Their motivation is at an absolutely low ebb. Boredom is the forerunner of many emotional problems.

But when we are in love with God, it is impossible to be bored! Those who are bored have ceased to love or are in danger of ceasing to be in love. How is it possible to be bored when we believe, as Saint Paul said, we can make up what is "lacking" in the sufferings of Christ? In his infinite mercy, God calls us to become co-redeemers of the world with him! We are co-redeemers with Christ! He has given us an immense power! So our grayish routine isn't gray at all, but resplendent with light—at least it is in our power to make it so.

How does this work in our daily lives? A secretary who "offers up" the tiring task of hitting those typewriter keys is co-redeeming the world with Christ. Cooks making stew, men doing chores, driving trucks, doing repairs—all can save souls from the jaws of hell! How in the name of the All-Holy can you be bored with this typing, cooking, repairing when—in faith—you know everything helps to redeem the world and to render glory to God?

—*CATHERINE DOHERTY*

Go to page 1563 for your next devotional reading.

Warnings against False Teachers

20 If with Christ you died to the elemental spirits of the universe,*u* why do you live as if you still belonged to the world? Why do you submit to regulations, 21"Do not handle, Do not taste, Do not touch"? 22All these regulations refer to things that perish with use; they are simply human commands and teachings. 23These have indeed an appearance of wisdom in promoting self-imposed piety, humility, and severe treatment of the body, but they are of no value in checking self-indulgence.*v*

The New Life in Christ

3 So if you have been raised with Christ, seek the things that are above, where Christ is, seated at the right hand of God. 2Set your minds on things that are above, not on things that are on earth, 3for you have died, and your life is hidden with Christ in God. 4When Christ who is your*w* life is revealed, then you also will be revealed with him in glory.

u Or *the rudiments of the world*   *v* Or *are of no value, serving only to indulge the flesh*   *w* Other authorities read *our*

Of Bigots and Bores

THURSDAY

Scripture Reading for Today: *Colossians 2.6–10*

Verses for Today: *Colossians 2.9–10*

When one says that the unifying idea in our lives, which will give stability and the power of thinking, is God, many shrink back, because they fancy that people who do not think of anything but God must be narrow bigots and bores. As a matter of fact, to be obsessed with God has the very opposite effect from every other obsession; for every other [obsession] excludes everything but itself; it always turns inward and causes us to shut the doors on everything outside. Somehow, the moment the doors of our being are shut, we realize how small and narrow we are, and our obsession rapidly becomes like a spreading and stuffy guest.

There are certain people who, almost as they enter a room, monopolize it, arrange it or disarrange it around themselves, using everything in it for their purpose. "Go on working," they say, "and don't mind me. I always make myself at home." Then they make demands every few minutes, not consciously, maybe, and perhaps only as a bid to keep their host's mind fixed on them, a matter in which they succeed all too well. To be welcome, such guests must have outstanding qualities. They must be lovable, even though selfish; they must have a gift for enchanting conversation and so on. Obsessions have no subject of conversation but self, and they fasten every window against any sound from outside which might interrupt the sound of their own voice.

An obsession with God, however, is the opposite; it flings wide every door opening from the mind and heart, and reaches out, pervading, interweaving everything with his love. It includes everything, and it enlarges the heart so that it can include everything.

—*CARYLL HOUSELANDER*

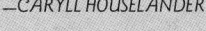

Go to page 1564 for your next devotional reading.

5 Put to death, therefore, whatever in you is earthly: fornication, impurity, passion, evil desire, and greed (which is idolatry). [6]On account of these the wrath of God is coming on those who are disobedient.[x] [7]These are the ways you also once followed, when you were living that life.[y] [8]But now you must get rid of all such things—anger, wrath, malice, slander, and abusive[z] language from your mouth. [9]Do not lie to one another, seeing that you have stripped off the old self with its practices [10]and have clothed yourselves with the new self, which is being renewed in knowledge according to the image of its creator. [11]In that renewal[a] there is no longer Greek and Jew, circumcised and uncircumcised, barbarian, Scythian, slave and free; but Christ is all and in all!

12 As God's chosen ones, holy and beloved, clothe yourselves with compassion, kindness, humility, meekness, and patience. [13]Bear with one another and, if anyone has a complaint against another, forgive each other; just as the Lord[b] has forgiven you, so you also must forgive. [14]Above all, clothe yourselves with love, which binds everything together in perfect harmony. [15]And let the peace of Christ rule in your hearts, to which indeed you were called in the one body. And be thankful. [16]Let the word of Christ[c] dwell in you richly; teach and admonish one another in all wisdom; and with gratitude in your hearts sing psalms, hymns, and spiritual songs to God.[d] [17]And whatever you do, in word or deed, do everything in

---

[x] Other ancient authorities lack *on those who are disobedient* (Gk *the children of disobedience*)   [y] Or *living among such people*   [z] Or *filthy*   [a] Gk *its creator,* [11]*where*   [b] Other ancient authorities read *just as Christ*   [c] Other ancient authorities read *of God,* or *of the Lord*   [d] Other ancient authorities read *to the Lord*

Compassion

FRIDAY

Scripture Reading for Today:
Colossians 3.12–17

Verse for Today:
Colossians 3.12

What a difference a really sisterly feeling among women would make!

I was reminded of an incident told me by a doctor. She does much maternity work, and one day a woman came to the clinic who expected her twelfth baby. She looked a battered wreck, dragging two small children, utterly depressed, unable to face life. The doctor suddenly remembered a very beautiful baby carriage given her by a wealthy patient. It was of a type hardly ever seen today, shining with brilliant paint and chromium, hung on springs and light to push, but with seats for two children and room for parcels besides. As the woman walked away proudly pushing her two children in it, she appeared transformed: How small a thing, the doctor said, can work a change in the outlook of the very poor.

But it was more than merely the baby carriage: This gift typified the just honor shown to her condition. It expressed the compassion of another Catholic woman: that compassion which means suffering with, bearing the burden with, those women who have the courage today to face the fullest weight that a mother can have to bear—a large family to be brought up in a city slum.

—*MAISIE WARD*

Go to page 1566 for your next devotional reading.

the name of the Lord Jesus, giving thanks to God the Father through him.

Rules for Christian Households

18 Wives, be subject to your husbands, as is fitting in the Lord. 19Husbands, love your wives and never treat them harshly.

20 Children, obey your parents in everything, for this is your acceptable duty in the Lord. 21Fathers, do not provoke your children, or they may lose heart. 22Slaves, obey your earthly masters*e* in everything, not only while being watched and in order to please them, but wholeheartedly, fearing the Lord.*e* 23Whatever your task, put yourselves into it, as done for the Lord and not for your masters,*f* 24since you know that from the Lord you will receive the inheritance as your reward; you serve*g* the Lord Christ. 25For the wrongdoer will be paid back for whatever wrong has been done, and there is no partiality. 4 1Masters, treat your slaves justly and fairly, for you know that you also have a Master in heaven.

Further Instructions

2 Devote yourselves to prayer, keeping alert in it with thanksgiving. 3At the same time pray for us as well that God will open to us a door for the word, that we may declare the mystery of Christ, for which I am in prison, 4so that I may reveal it clearly, as I should.

5 Conduct yourselves wisely toward outsiders, making the most of the time.*h* 6Let your speech always be gracious, seasoned with salt, so that you may know how you ought to answer everyone.

Final Greetings and Benediction

7 Tychicus will tell you all the news about me; he is a beloved brother, a faithful minister, and a fellow servant*i* in the Lord. 8I have sent him to you for this very purpose, so that you may know how we are*j* and that he may encourage your hearts; 9he is coming with Onesimus, the faithful and beloved brother, who is one of you. They will tell you about everything here.

10 Aristarchus my fellow prisoner greets you, as does Mark the cousin of Barnabas, concerning whom you have received instructions—if he comes to you, welcome him. 11And Jesus who is called Justus greets you. These are the only ones of the circumcision among my co-workers for the kingdom of God, and they have been a comfort to me. 12Epaphras, who is one of you, a servant*i* of Christ Jesus, greets you. He is always wrestling in his prayers on your behalf, so that you may stand mature and fully assured in everything that God wills. 13For I testify for him that he has worked hard for you and for those in Laodicea and in Hierapolis. 14Luke, the beloved physician, and Demas greet you. 15Give my greetings to the brothers and sisters*k* in Laodicea, and to Nympha and the church in her house. 16And when this letter has been read among you, have it read also in the church of the Laodiceans; and see that you read also the letter from Laodicea. 17And say to Archippus, "See that you complete the task that you have received in the Lord."

18 I, Paul, write this greeting with my own hand. Remember my chains. Grace be with you.*l*

e In Greek the same word is used for *master* and *Lord*   *f* Gk *not for men*   *g* Or *you are slaves of,* or *be slaves of*   *h* Or *opportunity*   *i* Gk *slave*   *j* Other authorities read *that I may know how you are*   *k* Gk *brothers*   *l* Other ancient authorities add *Amen*

Martha

*Her Name, the Feminine Form of
"Lord," Means "Lady"*

**Read Luke 10.38–42 and
John 11.1–12.3**

Martha, Mary, and their brother
Lazarus lived together in
Bethany, a village just two miles
from Jerusalem, on the eastern
slope of the Mount of Olives. All
three were intimate friends of
Jesus.

During one of Jesus' frequent
stays in their home, Martha became annoyed with Mary. Instead
of helping with the considerable
work of feeding and housing
Jesus and his disciples, Mary had
been sitting happily at his feet.
Feeling ignored and unappreciat-
ed, Martha marched over to Jesus and demanded: "Lord, do you not care that my sister
has left me to do the work by myself? Tell her
then to help me."

But Jesus chided her, "Martha, Martha, you
are worried and distracted by many things;
there is need of only one thing. Mary has
chosen the better part, which will not be tak-
en away from her" (Luke 10.40–42).

Jesus' tender rebuke must have embarrassed and startled Martha, calculated as it
was to break the grip of her self-pity and reveal what was really taking place under her
own roof and in her own heart. Martha
seemed confused and distracted, conned into
believing her ceaseless activity would produce something of lasting importance. But
Martha does more than simply instruct
through her mistakes. She shows what it is
like to have a relationship with Jesus so solid
and close that no posturing or hiding is necessary. Where else should she have taken her

Her Character: *Active
and pragmatic, she
seemed never at a loss for
words. Though Jesus
chastened her for allow-
ing herself to become
worried and upset by
small things, she re-
mained his close friend
and follower.*
Her Sorrow: *To have
waited, seemingly in
vain, for Jesus to return in
time to heal her brother
Lazarus.*
Her Joy: *To watch as
Jesus restored her brother
to life.*

frustration and anger, after all,
but to Jesus?

After her brother died, Martha
ran to meet Jesus as soon as she
heard he was near. But her greeting was tinged with complaint:
"Lord, if you had been here, my
brother would not have died."
But faith, too, was present: "Even
now I know that God will give
you whatever you ask of him."

"Your brother will rise again,"
Jesus assured her.

"I know that he will rise
again in the resurrection on the
last day."

"I am the resurrection and the
life," Jesus said. "Those who believe in me, even though they
die, will live, and everyone who
lives and believes in me will
never die. Do you believe this?"
(John 11.25–26).

"Yes, Lord," she told him, "I believe that
you are the Messiah, the Son of God, the one
coming into the world" (verse 27).

But right after her tremendous expression
of faith, Martha's practical side reasserted itself. When Jesus asked for the stone to be removed from Lazarus' tomb, she objected, raising the concern on everyone's mind: "Lord,
already there is a stench because he has been
dead four days." How amazed she must have
been when instead of the stench of death,
Lazarus himself emerged from the tomb.

The more we delve into Martha's story,
the more familiar it seems—as familiar as the
face gazing at us in the bathroom mirror—a
woman who placed too much importance on
her own activity and not enough on sitting
quietly before Jesus, Martha offers a warmly
human portrait of what it means to have
Jesus as a friend, allowing him to stretch her
faith, rebuke her small vision of the world,
and show her what the power of God can do.

Praying With Martha

"Lord, do you not care that my sister has left me to do all the work by myself? Tell her then to help me."—Luke 10.40

Praise God: *For his patience.*

Offer Thanks: *That God meets us where we are, rather than where we "should be."*

Confess: *Any tendency to resent other women.*

Ask God: *For the grace to be completely honest with him.*

Lift Your Heart

Is someone in your life causing you trouble? Your daughter, your mother, your co-worker, your sister in faith, or even a rival? Rather than expressing your grievance to anyone who will listen, take your complaint directly to God. Tell him everything that's bothering you. Ask him to give you understanding about how to respond to this person, even if it means that you, not she, is the one who needs to change.

Father, you know how difficult it is for me to relate to _____. Please help me to know what you think of our difficulties. I ask you for the grace to let go of my own sense of hurt and grievance. If you want me to do anything to try to improve the situation, make me sensitive and obedient to your guidance.

Go to page 1569 for your next devotional reading.

1 Thessalonians

Trouble seemed to chase Paul wherever he preached the gospel. This was certainly the case in Thessalonica, a busy seaport in Macedonia, where a mob formed to oppose his preaching. Soon after leaving the city, Paul arranged for Timothy to return and strengthen the young church, which was primarily made up of Gentiles. Later, Timothy caught up with Paul in Corinth, reporting on conditions at Thessalonica. That report probably motivated Paul to write this letter, the earliest in the New Testament, in A.D. 51, just 20 years after the death and resurrection of Christ.

It is significant that every chapter in I Thessalonians ends with a reference to the second coming of Christ. Paul commends the Thessalonians for their faith and love and encourages them to stand firm in the midst of persecution. He wanted them to be ready for Christ's coming, to live in a way that reflects the work of the Holy Spirit in their lives, enabling them to control their bodies so that they will continue to be pleasing to God.

The book of I Thessalonians reminds us that it is easy to take an extreme position regarding the end times: We either try to predict the end and become obsessed, or we doubt Christ's return and become skeptics. Instead, we are called to believe and be ready.

Salutation

1 Paul, Silvanus, and Timothy,
To the church of the Thessalonians in God the Father and the Lord Jesus Christ:
Grace to you and peace.

The Thessalonians' Faith and Example

2 We always give thanks to God for all of you and mention you in our prayers, constantly ³remembering before our God and Father your work of faith and labor of love and steadfastness of hope in our Lord Jesus Christ. ⁴For we know, brothers and sisters*ª* beloved by God, that he has chosen you, ⁵because our message of the gospel came to you not in word only, but also in power and in the Holy Spirit and with full conviction; just as you know what kind of persons we proved to be among you for your sake. ⁶And you became imitators of us and of the Lord, for in spite of persecution you received the word with

ª Gk brothers

joy inspired by the Holy Spirit, ⁷so that you became an example to all the believers in Macedonia and in Achaia. ⁸For the word of the Lord has sounded forth from you not only in Macedonia and Achaia, but in every place your faith in God has become known, so that we have no need to speak about it. ⁹For the people of those regions^b report about us what kind of welcome we had among you, and how you turned to God from idols, to serve a living and true God, ¹⁰and to wait for his Son from heaven, whom he raised from the dead—Jesus, who rescues us from the wrath that is coming.

Paul's Ministry in Thessalonica

2 You yourselves know, brothers and sisters,^c that our coming to you was not in vain, ²but though we had already

suffered and been shamefully mistreated at Philippi, as you know, we had courage in our God to declare to you the gospel of God in spite of great opposition. ³For our appeal does not spring from deceit or impure motives or trickery, ⁴but just as we have been approved by God to be entrusted with the message of the gospel, even so we speak, not to please mortals, but to please God who tests our hearts. ⁵As you know and as God is our witness, we never came with words of flattery or with a pretext for greed; ⁶nor did we seek praise from mortals, whether from you or from others, ⁷though we might have made demands as apostles of Christ. But we were gentle^d among you, like a nurse tenderly

^b Gk *For they*   ^c Gk *brothers*   ^d Other ancient authorities read *infants*

MONDAY

Scripture Reading for Today:
1 Thessalonians 1.2–10

Verse for Today:
1 Thessalonians 1.2

Prayer of the Teacup

It is one of my favorite morning rituals. I begin my day with a cup of tea or coffee. As the steam from my cup ascends to the heavens, I walk with all my favorite strangers into the heart of God. There is a bit of the stranger in everyone—even friends.

This dawn prayer becomes a sacred moment of yearning. I yearn for God to bless all the peoples of the earth. And so I name my friends to God. Sometimes I do not even name them. I simply see their faces in the ascending steam. I receive the persons who come into my memory, and I give them back to God. So many folks are brought together in my dawn ritual. It is as though we all become one in the heart of God: my family and friends, my community, people who have become a part of my life, those I have worked with in the past, political figures, and church leaders. Often the faces of people whose names I don't even know come to me: people at checkout counters in the stores, folks I've seen during my travels, in the airport, or on the streets. There are the faces of those I read about in the newspapers or see in the evening news. All are strangers. All are friends.

The reason I like my Prayer of the Teacup is that it is so simple. I believe that when we pray for others, we often get bogged down with words. I need few words—just a name or a glance is enough. I simply look at these strangers and friends whom God loves, and I yearn for their good.

—MACRINA WIEDERKEHR

Go to page 1571 for your next devotional reading.
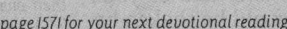

caring for her own children. [8]So deeply do we care for you that we are determined to share with you not only the gospel of God but also our own selves, because you have become very dear to us.

9 You remember our labor and toil, brothers and sisters;[e] we worked night and day, so that we might not burden any of you while we proclaimed to you the gospel of God. [10]You are witnesses, and God also, how pure, upright, and blameless our conduct was toward you believers. [11]As you know, we dealt with each one of you like a father with his children, [12]urging and encouraging you and pleading that you lead a life worthy of God, who calls you into his own kingdom and glory.

13 We also constantly give thanks to God for this, that when you received the word of God that you heard from us, you accepted it not as a human word but as what it really is, God's word, which is also at work in you believers. [14]For you, brothers and sisters,[e] became imitators of the churches of God in Christ Jesus that are in Judea, for you suffered the same things from your own compatriots as they did from the Jews, [15]who killed both the Lord Jesus and the prophets,[f] and drove us out; they displease God and oppose everyone [16]by hindering us from speaking to the Gentiles so that they may be saved. Thus they have constantly been filling up the measure of their sins; but God's wrath has overtaken them at last. [g]

Paul's Desire to Visit the Thessalonians Again

17 As for us, brothers and sisters,[e] when, for a short time, we were made orphans by being separated from you—in person, not in heart—we longed with great eagerness to see you face to face. [18]For we wanted to come to you—certainly I, Paul, wanted to again and again—but Satan blocked our way. [19]For what is our hope or joy or crown of boasting before our Lord Jesus at his coming? Is it not you? [20]Yes, you are our glory and joy!

3 Therefore when we could bear it no longer, we decided to be left alone in Athens; [2]and we sent Timothy, our brother and co-worker for God in proclaiming[h] the gospel of Christ, to strengthen and encourage you for the sake of your faith, [3]so that no one would be shaken by these persecutions. Indeed, you yourselves know that this is what we are destined for. [4]In fact, when we were with you, we told you beforehand that we were to suffer persecution; so it turned out, as you know. [5]For this reason, when I could bear it no longer, I sent to find out about your faith; I was afraid that somehow the tempter had tempted you and that our labor had been in vain.

Timothy's Encouraging Report

6 But Timothy has just now come to us from you, and has brought us the good news of your faith and love. He has told us also that you always remember us kindly and long to see us—just as we long to see you. [7]For this reason, brothers and sisters,[e] during all our distress and persecution we have been encouraged about you through your faith. [8]For we now live, if you continue to stand firm in the Lord. [9]How can we thank God enough for you in return for all the joy that we feel before our God because of you? [10]Night and day we pray most earnestly that we may see you face to face and restore whatever is lacking in your faith.

11 Now may our God and Father himself and our Lord Jesus direct our way to you. [12]And may the Lord make you increase and abound in love for one another and for all, just as we abound in love for you. [13]And may he so strengthen your hearts in holiness that you may be blameless before our God and Father at the coming of our Lord Jesus with all his saints.

A Life Pleasing to God

4 Finally, brothers and sisters,[e] we ask and urge you in the Lord Jesus that, as you learned from us how you ought to live and to please God (as, in fact, you are doing), you should do so more and more. [2]For you know what instructions we gave you through the Lord Jesus. [3]For this is the will of God, your sanctification: that you abstain from fornication; [4]that each one of you know how to control your own body[i] in holiness and honor, [5]not with lustful passion, like the Gentiles who do not know God; [6]that no one wrong or exploit a brother or sister[j] in this matter,

---

[e] Gk brothers   [f] Other ancient authorities read their own prophets   [g] Or completely or forever   [h] Gk lacks proclaiming   [i] Or how to take a wife for himself   [j] Gk brother

because the Lord is an avenger in all these things, just as we have already told you beforehand and solemnly warned you. [7]For God did not call us to impurity but in holiness. [8]Therefore whoever rejects this rejects not human authority but God, who also gives his Holy Spirit to you.

9 Now concerning love of the brothers and sisters,[k] you do not need to have anyone write to you, for you yourselves have been taught by God to love one another; [10]and indeed you do love all the brothers and sisters[k] throughout Macedonia. But we urge you, beloved,[k] to do so more and more, [11]to aspire to live quietly, to mind your own affairs, and to work with your hands, as we directed you, [12]so that you may behave properly toward outsiders and be dependent on no one.

The Coming of the Lord

13 But we do not want you to be uninformed, brothers and sisters,[k] about those who have died,[l] so that you may not grieve as others do who have no hope. [14]For since we believe that Jesus died and

k Gk *brothers*   *l* Gk *fallen asleep*

Miscarriage

TUESDAY

Scripture Reading
for Today:
1 Thessalonians
4.13–18

Verses for Today:
1 Thessalonians
4.13–14

In February, I had suffered a miscarriage. I had believed the event to be resolved on every possible level. But there was deeper spiritual dimension to my pain that lay quiet and untouched until the celebration of All Souls' Day.

That pain had to do with the concreteness of the loss. What happened was not just an event we can abstract by terming it a "miscarriage." It was the death of a very small, very real, very specific person.

And who that was remains a mystery. The question I had asked over and over was not "Why?" but rather, "Who were you?" It was so small, too small to be felt, living within me, closer to me than anyone else, yet I could not answer that question. I hungered for an understanding of who this person was, but such knowledge was beyond my reach. A mystery.

A friend, upon receiving the news of the miscarriage, wrote, "Just keep believing that someday you will meet your sweet baby in heaven." And I do believe it.

If I had not miscarried, that baby would have been in my arms on All Souls' Day. But it did happen, and there I sat, alone. And then again, maybe not so alone. For on that All Souls' Day I finally came to really know my child—not as a frightening mass of tissue that had passed from my body in pain and sorrow back to the earth, but as a person, a part of our family and of the whole human community.

As I listened to the names read out loud and saw those written in the Book of Remembrance, I added one more, one whose name is known only to God.

Someday, I know. Someday.

—AMY WELBORN

Go to page 1572 for your next devotional reading.

rose again, even so, through Jesus, God will bring with him those who have died.[m] 15For this we declare to you by the word of the Lord, that we who are alive, who are left until the coming of the Lord, will by no means precede those who have died.[m] 16For the Lord himself, with a cry of command, with the archangel's call and with the sound of God's trumpet, will descend from heaven, and the dead in Christ will rise first. 17Then we who are alive, who are left, will be caught up in the clouds together with them to meet the Lord in the air; and so we will be with the Lord forever. 18Therefore encourage one another with these words.

5 Now concerning the times and the seasons, brothers and sisters,[n] you do not need to have anything written to you. 2For you yourselves know very well that the day of the Lord will come like a thief in the night. 3When they say, "There

[m] Gk *fallen asleep*   [n] Gk *brothers*

Pray Always

WEDNESDAY

Scripture Reading for Today:
1 Thessalonians 5.14–22

Verses for Today:
1 Thessalonians 5.16–18

Saint Paul repeatedly reminds us to "pray without ceasing" and to "give thanks in all circumstances." When I first read his words, I'd think to myself, "I'll bet he never had to contend with a houseful of kids. Let him wake up to the sound of a dozen eggs dropped on a newly-washed kitchen floor, get a notice of 'head lice' sent home the same day out-of-town company is arriving, or nurse a houseful of tots with the twenty-four hour flu. Then we'll see how practical it is to 'pray always.'"

"Praying always" sounds good in theory, but—let's face it—how realistic is it? Well, I'm here to say that once I began to put prayer into practice (I'm still working on it), the more I understand Saint Paul's instruction. Praying and thanking God for all the circumstances of the day has a way of uplifting and encouraging us. It's like singing when you're down. In addition, we are setting a good example for our children and inspiring them to do the same.

We can praise God in all things by turning every event, every happening, including the unhappy or unpleasant, to God. Yes, it's a little hard to thank God for the bad news as well as the good. But once you get into the habit, it becomes easy.

My kids are now used to hearing me whisper a "Thank you, Jesus" or "Praise God" for the ups as well as the downs of daily life. Granted, I may say it through clenched teeth when it's a fender-bender accident, a houseful of kids passing around the twenty-four hour flu (yuk!), or some unexpected "tragedy"—like having all of the children home from school with a day off when I had plans for lunch.

Yet something happens when you turn an unpleasant situation over to God with praise. Just being thankful "in all circumstances" reminds us that we are God's children and that we refuse to be held hostage or frustrated by any catastrophe that Satan throws our way.

—MARY ANN KUHARSKI

Go to page 1576 for your next devotional reading.

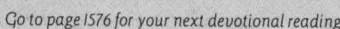

is peace and security," then sudden destruction will come upon them, as labor pains come upon a pregnant woman, and there will be no escape! 4But you, beloved,[o] are not in darkness, for that day to surprise you like a thief; 5for you are all children of light and children of the day; we are not of the night or of darkness. 6So then let us not fall asleep as others do, but let us keep awake and be sober; 7for those who sleep sleep at night, and those who are drunk get drunk at night. 8But since we belong to the day, let us be sober, and put on the breastplate of faith and love, and for a helmet the hope of salvation. 9For God has destined us not for wrath but for obtaining salvation through our Lord Jesus Christ, 10who died for us, so that whether we are awake or asleep we may live with him. 11Therefore encourage one another and build up each other, as indeed you are doing.

Final Exhortations, Greetings, and Benediction

12 But we appeal to you, brothers and sisters,[o] to respect those who labor among you, and have charge of you in the Lord and admonish you; 13esteem them very highly in love because of their work.

Be at peace among yourselves. 14And we urge you, beloved,[o] to admonish the idlers, encourage the fainthearted, help the weak, be patient with all of them. 15See that none of you repays evil for evil, but always seek to do good to one another and to all. 16Rejoice always, 17pray without ceasing, 18give thanks in all circumstances; for this is the will of God in Christ Jesus for you. 19Do not quench the Spirit. 20Do not despise the words of prophets,[p] 21but test everything; hold fast to what is good; 22abstain from every form of evil.

23 May the God of peace himself sanctify you entirely; and may your spirit and soul and body be kept sound[q] and blameless at the coming of our Lord Jesus Christ. 24The one who calls you is faithful, and he will do this.

25 Beloved,[r] pray for us.

26 Greet all the brothers and sisters[o] with a holy kiss. 27I solemnly command you by the Lord that this letter be read to all of them.[s]

28 The grace of our Lord Jesus Christ be with you.[t]

---

o Gk brothers   p Gk despise prophecies   q Or complete   r Gk Brothers   s Gk to all the brothers   t Other ancient authorities add Amen

2 Thessalonians

This letter offers encouragement to the Thessalonians in the midst of persecution, reminding them that God will punish those who afflict them. It also speaks of a forged letter that raised alarm within the church, claiming that the "day of the Lord" had arrived. Second Thessalonians exhorts believers not to be quickly shaken by such false reports and then comforts them by saying that several things had yet to happen before Christ would return.

Later on it warns against those who are "living in idleness, mere busybodies, not doing any work" (3.11) and plainly states the principle that anyone in the community who was unwilling to work should not eat.

Second Thessalonians reminds us that it is impossible to predict the moment of Christ's coming. As Christians, we are not to listen to fear mongers who claim to know the day. For any among us who are confused or afraid about what looms ahead, the prayer in 2.16 is great encouragement: "Now may our Lord Jesus Christ himself and God our Father, who loved us and through grace gave us eternal comfort and good hope, comfort your hearts and strengthen them in every good work and word."

Salutation

1 Paul, Silvanus, and Timothy,
To the church of the Thessalonians in God our Father and the Lord Jesus Christ:
2 Grace to you and peace from God our[a] Father and the Lord Jesus Christ.

Thanksgiving

3 We must always give thanks to God for you, brothers and sisters,[b] as is right, because your faith is growing abundantly, and the love of everyone of you for one another is increasing. 4Therefore we our-selves boast of you among the churches of God for your steadfastness and faith during all your persecutions and the afflictions that you are enduring.

The Judgment at Christ's Coming

5 This is evidence of the righteous judgment of God, and is intended to make you worthy of the kingdom of God, for which you are also suffering. 6For it is indeed just of God to repay with affliction

---

a Other ancient authorities read *the*　　*b* Gk *brothers*

those who afflict you, [7]and to give relief to the afflicted as well as to us, when the Lord Jesus is revealed from heaven with his mighty angels [8]in flaming fire, inflicting vengeance on those who do not know God and on those who do not obey the gospel of our Lord Jesus. [9]These will suffer the punishment of eternal destruction, separated from the presence of the Lord and from the glory of his might, [10]when he comes to be glorified by his saints and to be marveled at on that day among all who have believed, because our testimony to you was believed. [11]To this end we always pray for you, asking that our God will make you worthy of his call and will fulfill by his power every good resolve and work of faith, [12]so that the name of our Lord Jesus may be glorified in you, and you in him, according to the grace of our God and the Lord Jesus Christ.

The Man of Lawlessness

2 As to the coming of our Lord Jesus Christ and our being gathered together to him, we beg you, brothers and sisters,[c] [2]not to be quickly shaken in mind or alarmed, either by spirit or by word or by letter, as though from us, to the effect that the day of the Lord is already here. [3]Let no one deceive you in any way; for that day will not come unless the rebellion comes first and the lawless one[d] is revealed, the one destined for destruction.[e] [4]He opposes and exalts himself above every so-called god or object of worship, so that he takes his seat in the temple of God, declaring himself to be God. [5]Do you not remember that I told you these things when I was still with you? [6]And you know what is now restraining him, so that he may be revealed when his time comes. [7]For the mystery of lawlessness is already at work, but only until the one who now restrains it is removed. [8]And then the lawless one will be revealed, whom the Lord Jesus[f] will destroy[g] with the breath of his mouth, annihilating him by the manifestation of his coming. [9]The coming of the lawless one is apparent in the working of Satan, who uses all power, signs, lying wonders, [10]and every kind of wicked deception for those who are perishing, because they refused to love the truth and so be saved. [11]For this reason God sends them a powerful delusion, leading them to believe what is false, [12]so that all who have not believed the truth but took pleasure in unrighteousness will be condemned.

Chosen for Salvation

[13] But we must always give thanks to God for you, brothers and sisters[c] beloved by the Lord, because God chose you as the first fruits[h] for salvation through sanctification by the Spirit and through belief in the truth. [14]For this purpose he called you through our proclamation of the good news,[i] so that you may obtain the glory of our Lord Jesus Christ. [15]So then, brothers and sisters,[c] stand firm and hold fast to the traditions that you were taught by us, either by word of mouth or by our letter.

[16] Now may our Lord Jesus Christ himself and God our Father, who loved us and through grace gave us eternal comfort and good hope, [17]comfort your hearts and strengthen them in every good work and word.

Request for Prayer

3 Finally, brothers and sisters,[c] pray for us, so that the word of the Lord may spread rapidly and be glorified everywhere, just as it is among you, [2]and that we may be rescued from wicked and evil people; for not all have faith. [3]But the Lord is faithful; he will strengthen you and guard you from the evil one.[j] [4]And we have confidence in the Lord concerning you, that you are doing and will go on doing the things that we command. [5]May the Lord direct your hearts to the love of God and to the steadfastness of Christ.

Warning against Idleness

[6] Now we command you, beloved,[c] in the name of our Lord Jesus Christ, to keep away from believers who are[k] living in idleness and not according to the tradition that they[l] received from us. [7]For you yourselves know how you ought to imitate us; we were not idle when we were with you, [8]and we did not eat anyone's bread without paying for it; but with toil

---

[c] Gk brothers   [d] Gk the man of lawlessness; other ancient authorities read the man of sin   [e] Gk the son of destruction   [f] Other ancient authorities lack Jesus   [g] Other ancient authorities read consume   [h] Other ancient authorities read from the beginning   [i] Or through our gospel   [j] Or from evil   [k] Gk from every brother who is   [l] Other ancient authorities read you

and labor we worked night and day, so that we might not burden any of you. 9This was not because we do not have that right, but in order to give you an example to imitate. 10For even when we were with you, we gave you this command: Anyone unwilling to work should not eat. 11For we hear that some of you are living in idleness, mere busybodies, not doing any work. 12Now such persons we command and exhort in the Lord Jesus Christ to do their work quietly and to earn their own

living. 13Brothers and sisters,m do not be weary in doing what is right.

14 Take note of those who do not obey what we say in this letter; have nothing to do with them, so that they may be ashamed. 15Do not regard them as enemies, but warn them as believers.n

Final Greetings and Benediction

16 Now may the Lord of peace himself

m Gk Brothers   n Gk a brother

THURSDAY

Scripture Reading
for Today:
2 Thessalonians
2.1–5

Verses for Today:
2 Thessalonians
2.1–2

End of the World?

A young man came to see me. He carried a large Bible under his arm. He was a Catholic who was totally consumed by the idea that the end of the world is now, this moment, tomorrow. He also was filled with joy believing that this evil world would at last be destroyed by the almighty power of God.

He began to show me passage after passage in the Bible to prove that now is the end of time and the second coming of Christ. "Now!" he exclaimed with great enthusiasm, "Now people will see the true power of God when he comes to destroy them and this evil world!"

I showed him the Biblical passage wherein our Lord said that no one knows when the end of the world would come. The young man became angry and shouted: "But are you blind? Can you not see all the evil signs that the end is now? Look at the world! Open your eyes. Now is the time for Christ to come in all his power and glory! See how evil everything is!"

I listened to him voice his wild, angry reasons, then I finally said: "Young man, why are you so delighted in going around frightening people and telling them that the end has come? Is it because, for some reason, you yourself find life to be unbearable? Why do you so desperately want the end to be now? You have no right to say that we are living in the time of the end of the world. How do you know what good things God has planned for the world?"

He did not answer my question. Then I added: "Look, if you were to cross a street and if you were killed by a car, then that would be the end of the world for you. Your own life and death should concern you far more than the fact that someday the world will come to an end. If you are well prepared to face God at the moment of your death, that is what counts."

—LOUISE D'ANGELO

Go to page 1577 for your next devotional reading.

give you peace at all times in all ways. The Lord be with all of you.

17 I, Paul, write this greeting with my own hand. This is the mark in every letter of mine; it is the way I write. [18]The grace of our Lord Jesus Christ be with all of you.[o]

o Other ancient authorities add *Amen*

*W*orking

FRIDAY

Scripture Reading for Today:
2 Thessalonians 3.6–13

Verse for Today:
2 Thessalonians 3.12

After I became a Christian I wished for a less worldly career; I wondered why God had not called me to some visibly Christian occupation. As I began to act out my Christianity, it seemed to me that I could do a better job of it if God had "sent" me—to serve the church or my fellow men in some conspicuous way.

Far from choosing his will, I was using my own daydreams about holiness as a way of resisting his will. I thought my wish was to be good for his sake. In fact I was resisting the less conspicuous call to be good in the work I already had. Following the opinion of the world, I doubted whether I could be holy unless I was engaged in some work which the world calls holy. It was some time before I came upon that quotation from Newman, "I shall be a preacher of truth in my own place"; still longer before I could accept or understand it. And the statement of Dorothy Sayers hit me very hard: "The only Christian work is good work well done."

As Christians we are called not only to be converted but also to convert the world. It was difficult for me sometimes to see that I could convert the world by remaining with it rather than by departing from it. I needed to learn, as Merton did after conversion, that the world we wish to be freed from is not "out there" but "in here."

—*EMILIE GRIFFIN*

Go to page 1580 for your next devotional reading.

1 Timothy

First and Second Timothy and Titus are known as the "Pastoral Letters" because they were addressed to individuals rather than communities and focused on issues of pastoral leadership. Whether these were written by Paul or by Pauline disciples is a subject of controversy. For our purposes it is enough to note their important themes.

Before discussing the themes, it helps to understand who Timothy was. The New Testament makes it clear that Timothy's faith was initially shaped by two women—his grandmother Lois and his mother Eunice, who were Jewish believers. His father was Greek, and the family lived in Lystra (located in modern-day Turkey), where Paul founded a church on his first missionary journey. Timothy accompanied Paul on his second and third missionary journeys and eventually became the leader of the church in Ephesus.

This letter addresses certain critical concerns for the early church, such as the importance of sound teaching and the qualifications expected of its leaders. It also instructs Timothy on the way he should conduct himself with older members of the community and offers guidelines to be applied when the church provided for its widows.

In the pages of I Timothy, we glimpse the beginnings of the institutional church at a time in which the first generation of leaders was about to pass the torch to the next.

Salutation

1 Paul, an apostle of Christ Jesus by the command of God our Savior and of Christ Jesus our hope,

2 To Timothy, my loyal child in the faith:

Grace, mercy, and peace from God the Father and Christ Jesus our Lord.

Warning against False Teachers

3 I urge you, as I did when I was on my way to Macedonia, to remain in Ephesus so that you may instruct certain people not to teach any different doctrine, 4and not to occupy themselves with myths and endless genealogies that promote speculations rather than the divine training[a] that is known by faith. 5But the aim of such instruction is love that comes from a pure heart, a good conscience, and sincere

a Or plan

faith. [6]Some people have deviated from these and turned to meaningless talk, [7]desiring to be teachers of the law, without understanding either what they are saying or the things about which they make assertions.

8 Now we know that the law is good, if one uses it legitimately. [9]This means understanding that the law is laid down not for the innocent but for the lawless and disobedient, for the godless and sinful, for the unholy and profane, for those who kill their father or mother, for murderers, [10]fornicators, sodomites, slave traders, liars, perjurers, and whatever else is contrary to the sound teaching [11]that conforms to the glorious gospel of the blessed God, which he entrusted to me.

Gratitude for Mercy

12 I am grateful to Christ Jesus our Lord, who has strengthened me, because he judged me faithful and appointed me to his service, [13]even though I was formerly a blasphemer, a persecutor, and a man of violence. But I received mercy because I had acted ignorantly in unbelief, [14]and the grace of our Lord overflowed for me with the faith and love that are in Christ Jesus. [15]The saying is sure and worthy of full acceptance, that Christ Jesus came into the world to save sinners—of whom I am the foremost. [16]But for that very reason I received mercy, so that in me, as the foremost, Jesus Christ might display the utmost patience, making me an example to those who would come to believe in him for eternal life. [17]To the King of the ages, immortal, invisible, the only God, be honor and glory forever and ever.[b] Amen.

18 I am giving you these instructions, Timothy, my child, in accordance with the prophecies made earlier about you, so that by following them you may fight the good fight, [19]having faith and a good conscience. By rejecting conscience, certain persons have suffered shipwreck in the faith; [20]among them are Hymenaeus and Alexander, whom I have turned over to Satan, so that they may learn not to blaspheme.

Instructions concerning Prayer

2 First of all, then, I urge that supplications, prayers, intercessions, and thanksgivings be made for everyone, [2]for kings and all who are in high positions, so that we may lead a quiet and peaceable life in all godliness and dignity. [3]This is right and is acceptable in the sight of God our Savior, [4]who desires everyone to be saved and to come to the knowledge of the truth. [5]For

> there is one God;
> there is also one mediator
> between God and
> humankind,
> Christ Jesus, himself human,
> 6   who gave himself a ransom for all

—this was attested at the right time. [7]For this I was appointed a herald and an apostle (I am telling the truth,[c] I am not lying), a teacher of the Gentiles in faith and truth.

8 I desire, then, that in every place the men should pray, lifting up holy hands without anger or argument; [9]also that the women should dress themselves modestly and decently in suitable clothing, not with their hair braided, or with gold, pearls, or expensive clothes, [10]but with good works, as is proper for women who profess reverence for God. [11]Let a woman[d] learn in silence with full submission. [12]I permit no woman[d] to teach or to have authority over a man;[e] she is to keep silent. [13]For Adam was formed first, then Eve; [14]and Adam was not deceived, but the woman was deceived and became a transgressor. [15]Yet she will be saved through childbearing, provided they continue in faith and love and holiness, with modesty.

Qualifications of Bishops

3 The saying is sure:[f] whoever aspires to the office of bishop[g] desires a noble task. [2]Now a bishop[h] must be above reproach, married only once,[i] temperate, sensible, respectable, hospitable, an apt teacher, [3]not a drunkard, not violent but gentle, not quarrelsome, and not a lover of money. [4]He must manage his own household well, keeping his children submissive and respectful in every way— [5]for if someone does not know how to manage his own household, how can he take care of God's church? [6]He must not be a recent convert, or he may be puffed up

---

b Gk to the ages of the ages   c Other ancient authorities add in Christ   d Or wife   e Or her husband   f Some interpreters place these words at the end of the previous paragraph. Other ancient authorities read The saying is commonly accepted   g Or overseer   h Or an overseer   i Gk the husband of one wife

Mary of Bethany

Her Name May Mean "Bitterness"

Read Matthew 26.6–13 and John 12.1–8

Jerusalem was swollen with a hundred thousand worshipers, pilgrims who had come to celebrate the annual Passover feast. Every one of them, it seemed, had heard tales of the rabbi Jesus and how he had raised Lazarus from the dead.

The rumors spread quickly, like water coming to a boil. Jesus had disappeared into the countryside, and everywhere people speculated about whether he would return for the Passover celebration. All the while, everyone kept chasing after Mary, inquiring about her brother. Had he really been dead four days? Didn't he smell when he came stumbling out of the tomb?

She could hardly blame them for their crazy questions. Why shouldn't they be curious about the amazing event that had taken place in Bethany several weeks earlier? How could they know that Lazarus was as normal as any other living man? Her own flesh and blood had been called out of darkness by a man who was filled with light. How she longed to see Jesus again!

But shadows framed the edges of her happiness. No amount of celebrating could erase the memory of Jesus weeping that day outside her brother's tomb. Even as others were celebrating the spectacular miracle, he seemed strangely quiet.

When Jesus finally returned to Bethany

THE STORY OF A WOMAN

Her Character: *She appears to have been a single woman who was totally devoted to Jesus. The Gospels portray her, by way of contrast with her sister Martha, as a woman of few words. As Jesus neared the time of his triumphal entry into Jerusalem prior to Passover, she performed a gesture of great prophetic significance.*
Her Sorrow: *She wept at the tomb of her brother, Lazarus, and must have experienced great sorrow at the death of Jesus.*
Her Joy: *To have done something beautiful for Christ.*

before the Passover, Martha served a feast in his honor. As Jesus was reclining at the table with the other guests, Mary entered the room and anointed his head with expensive perfume.

But the disciple Judas Iscariot, failing to appreciate her gesture, objected strenuously: "Why this waste? For this ointment could have been sold for a large sum, and the money given to the poor" (Matthew 26.8–9). Though he cared nothing for the destitute, Judas, a man always looking for a chance to fatten his own pockets, was the keeper of the common purse.

But rather than scolding Mary for her extravagance, Jesus praised her, saying:

Why do you trouble the woman? She has performed a good service for me. For you always have the poor with you, but you will not always have me. By pouring this ointment on my body she has prepared me for burial. Truly I tell you, wherever this good news is proclaimed in the whole world, what she has done will be told in remembrance of her.

(verses 10–13)

From her first encounter with Jesus Christ, Mary seems to have pursued one thing above all—the deepest possible relationship with him. Love gave her insights that others missed. Somehow she must have understood that Jesus would not enter Jerusalem to lasting acclaim but to death and dishonor. While everyone else was busy celebrating his triumph, Mary stood quietly beside him, sharing his grief. She was a prophet whose gesture speaks eloquently even from a distance of two thousand years.

Praying With Mary of Bethany

"Why do you trouble the woman? She has performed a good service for me."
—Matthew 26.10

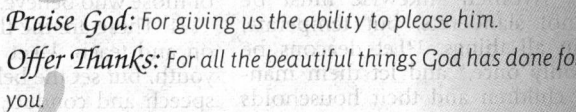

Praise God: For giving us the ability to please him.

Offer Thanks: For all the beautiful things God has done for you.

Confess: Any unwillingness to embrace the difficult parts of the gospel as well as the joyful parts.

Ask God: To give you a greater hunger to live in his presence and to seek his face.

Lift Your Heart

Lovers like nothing better than to please their beloved. Mother Teresa of Calcutta was a woman who loved God extravagantly. Famous for her work with the poorest of the poor in India and throughout the world, she was always looking for a chance to do "something beautiful for God." How easy it is for us to neglect our Divine Lover by always asking him to do beautiful things for us rather than by developing our own capacity to please and delight him. You don't have to travel to the other side of the world to find opportunities. Look for him in the poorest of the poor in your own community: those who are emotionally impoverished, isolated, ill. Find a way to bring the light of God's love into their darkness. Even the smallest gesture can become a beautiful gift for God.

Lord, you have done so many beautiful things for me, pursuing me when I cared nothing for you, restoring my hope, giving me a future worth living for. I want to offer myself generously, not as a miser doling out her favors in hope of a return, but as a woman completely in love with her Maker. Make my life a sweet-smelling fragrance to please you.

Go to page 1583 for your next devotional reading.

with conceit and fall into the condemnation of the devil. [7]Moreover, he must be well thought of by outsiders, so that he may not fall into disgrace and the snare of the devil.

Qualifications of Deacons

8 Deacons likewise must be serious, not double-tongued, not indulging in much wine, not greedy for money; [9]they must hold fast to the mystery of the faith with a clear conscience. [10]And let them first be tested; then, if they prove themselves blameless, let them serve as deacons. [11]Women[j] likewise must be serious, not slanderers, but temperate, faithful in all things. [12]Let deacons be married only once,[k] and let them manage their children and their households well; [13]for those who serve well as deacons gain a good standing for themselves and great boldness in the faith that is in Christ Jesus.

The Mystery of Our Religion

14 I hope to come to you soon, but I am writing these instructions to you so that, [15]if I am delayed, you may know how one ought to behave in the household of God, which is the church of the living God, the pillar and bulwark of the truth. [16]Without any doubt, the mystery of our religion is great:

He[l] was revealed in flesh,
   vindicated[m] in spirit,[n]
     seen by angels,
proclaimed among Gentiles,
   believed in throughout the world,
     taken up in glory.

False Asceticism

4 Now the Spirit expressly says that in later[o] times some will renounce the faith by paying attention to deceitful spirits and teachings of demons, [2]through the hypocrisy of liars whose consciences are seared with a hot iron. [3]They forbid marriage and demand abstinence from foods, which God created to be received with thanksgiving by those who believe and know the truth. [4]For everything created by God is good, and nothing is to be rejected, provided it is received with thanksgiving; [5]for it is sanctified by God's word and by prayer.

A Good Minister of Jesus Christ

6 If you put these instructions before the brothers and sisters,[p] you will be a good servant[q] of Christ Jesus, nourished on the words of the faith and of the sound teaching that you have followed. [7]Have nothing to do with profane myths and old wives' tales. Train yourself in godliness, [8]for, while physical training is of some value, godliness is valuable in every way, holding promise for both the present life and the life to come. [9]The saying is sure and worthy of full acceptance. [10]For to this end we toil and struggle,[r] because we have our hope set on the living God, who is the Savior of all people, especially of those who believe.

11 These are the things you must insist on and teach. [12]Let no one despise your youth, but set the believers an example in speech and conduct, in love, in faith, in purity. [13]Until I arrive, give attention to the public reading of scripture,[s] to exhorting, to teaching. [14]Do not neglect the gift that is in you, which was given to you through prophecy with the laying on of hands by the council of elders.[t] [15]Put these things into practice, devote yourself to them, so that all may see your progress. [16]Pay close attention to yourself and to your teaching; continue in these things, for in doing this you will save both yourself and your hearers.

Duties toward Believers

5 Do not speak harshly to an older man,[u] but speak to him as to a father, to younger men as brothers, [2]to older women as mothers, to younger women as sisters—with absolute purity.

3 Honor widows who are really widows. [4]If a widow has children or grandchildren, they should first learn their religious duty to their own family and make some repayment to their parents; for this is pleasing in God's sight. [5]The real widow, left alone, has set her hope on God and continues in supplications and prayers night and day; [6]but the widow[v] who lives for pleasure is dead even while she lives. [7]Give these commands as well, so that they may be above reproach. [8]And

j Or Their wives, or Women deacons   k Gk be husbands of one wife   l Gk Who; other ancient authorities read God; others, Which   m Or justified   n Or by the Spirit   o Or the last   p Gk brothers   q Or deacon   r Other ancient authorities read suffer reproach   s Gk to the reading   t Gk by the presbytery   u Or an elder, or a presbyter   v Gk she

whoever does not provide for relatives, and especially for family members, has denied the faith and is worse than an unbeliever.

9 Let a widow be put on the list if she is not less than sixty years old and has been married only once;[w] 10she must be well attested for her good works, as one who has brought up children, shown hospitality, washed the saints' feet, helped the afflicted, and devoted herself to doing good in every way. 11But refuse to put younger widows on the list; for when their sensual desires alienate them from Christ, they want to marry, 12and so they incur condemnation for having violated their first pledge. 13Besides that, they learn to be idle, gadding about from house to house; and they are not merely idle, but also gossips and busybodies, saying what they should not say. 14So I would have younger widows marry, bear children, and manage their households, so as to give the adversary no occasion to revile us. 15For some have already turned away to follow Satan. 16If any believing woman[x] has relatives who are really widows, let her assist them; let the church not be burdened, so that it can assist those who are real widows.

17 Let the elders who rule well be considered worthy of double honor,[y] especially those who labor in preaching and teaching; 18for the scripture says, "You

w Gk the wife of one husband   x Other ancient authorities read believing man or woman; others, believing man   y Or compensation

---

"*I* Hate Squash!"

MONDAY

Scripture Reading for Today:
1 Timothy 4.6–16

Verse for Today:
1 Timothy 4.16

I loathe squash. I don't care if you put brown sugar and butter on it. I don't care if you sauté it in virgin olive oil. As far as I'm concerned, it's a repulsive gag-in-the-back-of-the-throat vegetable. As a result of my hostility toward squash, my son is not regularly exposed to it. (Let's be honest: He's never exposed to it.) If he develops a fondness for the vegetable, it will either be because someone else (and I can't imagine who) takes it upon himself or herself to introduce him to it or because (miracles do happen) he has a natural taste for squash and takes to it at first bite. In somewhat the same way, if we do not expose our children to our faith on a regular basis, we can't expect them to find any value in it.

Research by the Search Institute, an organization that examines religious issues as they pertain to youth, indicates that of all the factors leading to a mature acceptance of religion, parents and family top the list. Parents are more important than religion classes, Mass, friends, homilies, or priests. The Institute cites three key elements that make a definite difference in the transference of beliefs: talking about your faith; letting your kids see you practice your convictions by Mass attendance, daily prayer, and Scripture reading; and taking time to live your beliefs through service to others. It comes down to a simple truth: If we want our children to have faith, we must practice our own. We cannot expect our children to embrace that which we ourselves do not value, be it squash or religion.

—WOODENE KOENIG-BRICKER

Go to page 1584 for your next devotional reading.

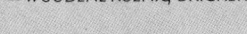

shall not muzzle an ox while it is treading out the grain," and, "The laborer deserves to be paid." [19] Never accept any accusation against an elder except on the evidence of two or three witnesses. [20] As for those who persist in sin, rebuke them in the presence of all, so that the rest also may stand in fear. [21] In the presence of God and of Christ Jesus and of the elect angels, I warn you to keep these instructions without prejudice, doing nothing on the basis of partiality. [22] Do not ordain[z] anyone hastily, and do not participate in the sins of others; keep yourself pure.

23 No longer drink only water, but take a little wine for the sake of your stomach and your frequent ailments.

24 The sins of some people are conspicuous and precede them to judgment, while the sins of others follow them there. [25] So also good works are conspicuous; and even when they are not, they cannot remain hidden.

6 Let all who are under the yoke of slavery regard their masters as worthy of all honor, so that the name of God and the teaching may not be blasphemed. [2] Those who have believing masters must not be disrespectful to them on the ground that they are members of the church;[a] rather they must serve them all the more, since those who benefit by their service are believers and beloved.[b]

---

[z] Gk Do not lay hands on   [a] Gk are brothers
[b] Or since they are believers and beloved, who devote themselves to good deeds

---

Older Women

TUESDAY

Scripture Reading for Today:
1 Timothy 5.3–16

Verse for Today:
1 Timothy 5.5

An old saying claims, "It's better to wear out than rust out." In today's reading we learn of a special "order of widows" within the Church—a group of older women happily ready to "wear out" in service to others.

The list of qualifications required to join this group is similar in spirit to those for bishops and deacons: a woman must be of good character, married only once, hospitable, with a record of good works behind her.

She must also be a "real widow"—one having no relatives to care for her—and over the age of 60. With this latter requirement, Paul is speaking as a seasoned pastor who had evidently experienced some difficulty with younger widows. Perhaps, given material support from the Church, they had too much time on their hands and their idleness proved to be the devil's workshop.

The real widows held an important position in the early Church. They appear to have functioned as deaconesses, exercising great care for the needs of the community. Moreover, they are models of holiness since, in their destitution, they rely on God and spend day and night in prayer.

In a culture that seems to worship youth, today's older women—and men—may feel unneeded. The Church, however, should always value their wisdom, experience, and prayerfulness. If they fulfill this calling, they are the backbone of the Church and a reminder of God's constant care for his people.

—CINDY CAVNAR

Go to page 1587 for your next devotional reading.

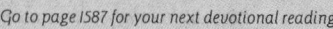

False Teaching and True Riches

Teach and urge these duties. [3]Whoever teaches otherwise and does not agree with the sound words of our Lord Jesus Christ and the teaching that is in accordance with godliness, [4]is conceited, understanding nothing, and has a morbid craving for controversy and for disputes about words. From these come envy, dissension, slander, base suspicions, [5]and wrangling among those who are depraved in mind and bereft of the truth, imagining that godliness is a means of gain.[c] [6]Of course, there is great gain in godliness combined with contentment; [7]for we brought nothing into the world, so that[d] we can take nothing out of it; [8]but if we have food and clothing, we will be content with these. [9]But those who want to be rich fall into temptation and are trapped by many senseless and harmful desires that plunge people into ruin and destruction. [10]For the love of money is a root of all kinds of evil, and in their eagerness to be rich some have wandered away from the faith and pierced themselves with many pains.

The Good Fight of Faith

[11] But as for you, man of God, shun all this; pursue righteousness, godliness, faith, love, endurance, gentleness. [12]Fight the good fight of the faith; take hold of the eternal life, to which you were called and for which you made[e] the good confession in the presence of many witnesses. [13]In the presence of God, who gives life to all things, and of Christ Jesus, who in his testimony before Pontius Pilate made the good confession, I charge you [14]to keep the commandment without spot or blame until the manifestation of our Lord Jesus Christ, [15]which he will bring about at the right time—he who is the blessed and only Sovereign, the King of kings and Lord of lords. [16]It is he alone who has immortality and dwells in unapproachable light, whom no one has ever seen or can see; to him be honor and eternal dominion. Amen.

[17] As for those who in the present age are rich, command them not to be haughty, or to set their hopes on the uncertainty of riches, but rather on God who richly provides us with everything for our enjoyment. [18]They are to do good, to be rich in good works, generous, and ready to share, [19]thus storing up for themselves the treasure of a good foundation for the future, so that they may take hold of the life that really is life.

Personal Instructions and Benediction

[20] Timothy, guard what has been entrusted to you. Avoid the profane chatter and contradictions of what is falsely called knowledge; [21]by professing it some have missed the mark as regards the faith.

Grace be with you.[f]

c Other ancient authorities add *Withdraw yourself from such people*   d Other ancient authorities read *world—it is certain that*   e Gk *confessed*   f The Greek word for *you* here is plural; in other ancient authorities it is singular. Other ancient authorities add *Amen*

2 Timothy

Imagine that you have poured out your life for a cause in which you believe. But instead of living out your last days with a sense of satisfaction as you survey your work, you sit in prison, aware that you may soon be executed—aware, too, that most of your friends have deserted you. Sounds depressing, but this was precisely Paul's situation when he sat in a prison in Rome. Hated by both Jews and Gentiles, he was abandoned by friends who feared to associate with a Roman prisoner.

Yet Paul seems hopeful rather than depressed. He is a man at peace, confident of his future, yet concerned for those he will leave behind. Though this letter may have been completed after his death, it is likely that it contains passages originally written by Paul, who exhorts his protégé, Timothy, to continue to preach and defend the gospel regardless of the personal attacks that will ensue. He wants the younger man to draw encouragement from his example and to consider himself a soldier whose only concern is to serve Christ. For even though everyone else has deserted Paul, the Lord has stood by him. The success of his efforts would be revealed, not in this age, but in eternity. Though Paul is in chains, he reminds Timothy that the gospel can never be chained.

Salutation

1 Paul, an apostle of Christ Jesus by the will of God, for the sake of the promise of life that is in Christ Jesus,

2 To Timothy, my beloved child:

Grace, mercy, and peace from God the Father and Christ Jesus our Lord.

Thanksgiving and Encouragement

3 I am grateful to God—whom I worship with a clear conscience, as my ancestors did—when I remember you constantly in my prayers night and day. 4 Recalling your tears, I long to see you so that I may be filled with joy. 5 I am reminded of your sincere faith, a faith that lived first in your grandmother Lois and your mother Eunice and now, I am sure, lives in you. 6 For this reason I remind you to rekindle the gift of God that is within you through the laying on of my hands; 7 for God did not give us a spirit of cowardice, but rather a spirit of power and of love and of self-discipline.

8 Do not be ashamed, then, of the testimony about our Lord or of me his prisoner, but join with me in suffering for the gospel, relying on the power of God, 9who saved us and called us with a holy calling, not according to our works but according to his own purpose and grace. This grace was given to us in Christ Jesus before the ages began, 10but it has now been revealed through the appearing of our Savior Christ Jesus, who abolished death and brought life and immortality to

Not Ashamed to Look Foolish

WEDNESDAY

Scripture Reading
for Today:
2 Timothy 1.6–16

Verse for Today:
2 Timothy 1.12

Healed of crippling arthritis, Sister Briege McKenna wanted to say "no" when God began leading her into a healing ministry. "I was really worried at being called a faith healer." Then one day in prayer, she received a mental image of herself showing Jesus through a house with many rooms.

Suddenly he came upon a locked door. On the door in large type was PRIVATE PROPERTY—DO NOT ENTER. He asked me, "Briege, why can't I go in this room?"

I replied, "Come now, Jesus, look at all I've given you. I want to keep a little something for myself."

I heard him say, in this image, "You know, Briege, if you do not open that door, you will never know what it means to be truly free."

I remember looking at the image and saying to myself, "Now what is in that room?"

The Lord said, "I'll show you."

Inside that room was my reputation, what others thought of me. I didn't want Jesus in that room because I was preserving my good name and reputation. I wanted to follow Jesus, but I wanted control of my life. I wasn't going to be a fool. Anything to do with the cross, with picking up my cross, that was out of the question.

I heard Jesus saying to me, "I thought you gave me your life."

Clearly the words of my vows came to me. I had promised to give my life to the Lord, for whatever he wanted from me in the Congregation of the Sisters of Saint Clare. I saw myself kneeling before the mother general and the bishop, and I heard myself saying those vows. At the same time, I heard Jesus say, as he pointed to the closed door, "On whose terms did you make that commitment?"

I realized that I had said, "Jesus, I love you and I give you my life—but on my terms." My religious life would never know fully the joy, the peace, the strength, and the courage—all that he wanted to give me—until I abandoned every part of my life and was willing to be a fool for him.

—*BRIEGE MCKENNA, O.S.C.*

Go to page 1590 for your next devotional reading.

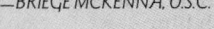

light through the gospel. ¹¹For this gospel I was appointed a herald and an apostle and a teacher,ᵃ ¹²and for this reason I suffer as I do. But I am not ashamed, for I know the one in whom I have put my trust, and I am sure that he is able to guard until that day what I have entrusted to him.ᵇ ¹³Hold to the standard of sound teaching that you have heard from me, in the faith and love that are in Christ Jesus. ¹⁴Guard the good treasure entrusted to you, with the help of the Holy Spirit living in us.

15 You are aware that all who are in Asia have turned away from me, including Phygelus and Hermogenes. ¹⁶May the Lord grant mercy to the household of Onesiphorus, because he often refreshed me and was not ashamed of my chain; ¹⁷when he arrived in Rome, he eagerlyᶜ searched for me and found me ¹⁸—may the Lord grant that he will find mercy from the Lord on that day! And you know very well how much service he rendered in Ephesus.

A Good Soldier of Christ Jesus

2 You then, my child, be strong in the grace that is in Christ Jesus; ²and what you have heard from me through many witnesses entrust to faithful people who will be able to teach others as well. ³Share in suffering like a good soldier of Christ Jesus. ⁴No one serving in the army gets entangled in everyday affairs; the soldier's aim is to please the enlisting officer. ⁵And in the case of an athlete, no one is crowned without competing according to the rules. ⁶It is the farmer who does the work who ought to have the first share of the crops. ⁷Think over what I say, for the Lord will give you understanding in all things.

8 Remember Jesus Christ, raised from the dead, a descendant of David—that is my gospel, ⁹for which I suffer hardship, even to the point of being chained like a criminal. But the word of God is not chained. ¹⁰Therefore I endure everything for the sake of the elect, so that they may also obtain the salvation that is in Christ Jesus, with eternal glory. ¹¹The saying is sure:

If we have died with him, we will
     also live with him;
¹² if we endure, we will also reign with
     him;

if we deny him, he will also
     deny us;
¹³ if we are faithless, he remains
     faithful—
for he cannot deny himself.

A Worker Approved by God

14 Remind them of this, and warn them before Godᵈ that they are to avoid wrangling over words, which does no good but only ruins those who are listening. ¹⁵Do your best to present yourself to God as one approved by him, a worker who has no need to be ashamed, rightly explaining the word of truth. ¹⁶Avoid profane chatter, for it will lead people into more and more impiety, ¹⁷and their talk will spread like gangrene. Among them are Hymenaeus and Philetus, ¹⁸who have swerved from the truth by claiming that the resurrection has already taken place. They are upsetting the faith of some. ¹⁹But God's firm foundation stands, bearing this inscription: "The Lord knows those who are his," and, "Let everyone who calls on the name of the Lord turn away from wickedness."

20 In a large house there are utensils not only of gold and silver but also of wood and clay, some for special use, some for ordinary. ²¹All who cleanse themselves of the things I have mentionedᵉ will become special utensils, dedicated and useful to the owner of the house, ready for every good work. ²²Shun youthful passions and pursue righteousness, faith, love, and peace, along with those who call on the Lord from a pure heart. ²³Have nothing to do with stupid and senseless controversies; you know that they breed quarrels. ²⁴And the Lord's servantᶠ must not be quarrelsome but kindly to everyone, an apt teacher, patient, ²⁵correcting opponents with gentleness. God may perhaps grant that they will repent and come to know the truth, ²⁶and that they may escape from the snare of the devil, having been held captive by him to do his will.ᵍ

Godlessness in the Last Days

3 You must understand this, that in the last days distressing times will come.

ᵃ Other ancient authorities add *of the Gentiles*
ᵇ Or *what has been entrusted to me*   ᶜ Or *promptly*
ᵈ Other ancient authorities read *the Lord*   ᵉ Gk
of these things   ᶠ Gk *slave*   ᵍ Or *by him, to do
his* (that is, God's) *will*

²For people will be lovers of themselves, lovers of money, boasters, arrogant, abusive, disobedient to their parents, ungrateful, unholy, ³inhuman, implacable, slanderers, profligates, brutes, haters of good, ⁴treacherous, reckless, swollen with conceit, lovers of pleasure rather than lovers of God, ⁵holding to the outward form of godliness but denying its power. Avoid them! ⁶For among them are those who make their way into households and captivate silly women, overwhelmed by their sins and swayed by all kinds of desires, ⁷who are always being instructed and can never arrive at a knowledge of the truth. ⁸As Jannes and Jambres opposed Moses, so these people, of corrupt mind and counterfeit faith, also oppose the truth. ⁹But they will not make much progress, because, as in the case of those two men,ʰ their folly will become plain to everyone.

Paul's Charge to Timothy

10 Now you have observed my teaching, my conduct, my aim in life, my faith,

ʰ Gk lacks *two men*

Suffering and Sacrifice

I endure everything for the sake of the elect, so that they may also obtain the salvation that is in Christ Jesus.

2 TIMOTHY 2.10

"Offer it up" is a phrase that used to be part of every Catholic's repertoire, the routine response to sufferings great and small. Admittedly, it was often misused. Addressed to others, it sometimes came across like the routine "How are you?" that doesn't really want to know. Used this way, it was a brisk, dismissive, "spiritual" way to say, "Get over it and don't bother me."

But for many Catholics, "offer it up" was and is a handy reminder—to themselves first of all—that suffering can be fruitful. "Suffering produces endurance," says Saint Paul, "and endurance produces character, and character produces hope, and hope does not disappoint us" (Romans 5.3–5).

This happy result is hardly guaranteed, however. Don't we all know grim stoics and martyr types—embittered, hopeless, and angry people who have not survived suffering so terribly well?

What makes the difference?

It all depends, John Paul II suggested in a 1984 apostolic letter, on what answer you get to that typically human reaction of protest against suffering, "Why?" (*On the Christian Meaning of Human Suffering,* February 11, 1984, 26)

Bring that question to Christ, said the Pope, and you notice that he "is himself suffering and wishes to answer . . . from the cross, from the heart of his own suffering." The answer, growing out of this personal encounter, takes the form of an invitation. "Christ does not explain in the abstract the reasons for suffering, but before all else he says: 'Follow me! Come! Take part through your suffering in this work of saving the world, a salvation achieved through my suffering, through my cross.' "

How exactly our suffering makes us partners with Christ, how God uses it for good is undoubtedly a mystery. But even without fully understanding, we can know that our suffering has meaning. As Paul tells Timothy (see above), it even serves an evangelistic purpose. "I am now rejoicing in my sufferings for your sake, and in my flesh I am completing what is lacking in Christ's afflictions for the sake of his body, that is, the church" (Colossians 1.24).

"Offer it up." What mysteries and what an invitation that simple slogan evokes.

my patience, my love, my steadfastness, [11]my persecutions, and my suffering the things that happened to me in Antioch, Iconium, and Lystra. What persecutions I endured! Yet the Lord rescued me from all of them. [12]Indeed, all who want to live a godly life in Christ Jesus will be persecuted. [13]But wicked people and impostors will go from bad to worse, deceiving others and being deceived. [14]But as for you, continue in what you have learned and firmly believed, knowing from whom you learned it, [15]and how from childhood you have known the sacred writings that are able to instruct you for salvation through faith in Christ Jesus. [16]All scripture is inspired by God and is[i] useful for teaching, for reproof, for correction, and for training in righteousness, [17]so that everyone who belongs to God may be proficient, equipped for every good work.

4 In the presence of God and of Christ Jesus, who is to judge the living and the dead, and in view of his appearing and his kingdom, I solemnly urge you: [2]proclaim the message; be persistent whether

[i] Or *Every scripture inspired by God is also*

*L*oneliness

Scripture Reading for Today:
2 Timothy 4.9–18

Verse for Today:
2 Timothy 4.16

We must not conclude that a spiritual life rescues single persons from the pain of loneliness. It does not. Many times I've been acutely aware of my singleness and really felt lonely: preparing a meal for one, asking for a single table in a restaurant, feeling out of it in the midst of a laughing crowd. Sometimes I wake up at night and wonder what will happen to me when I grow old and sick and no spouse or children, no fellow community members are there to take care of me.

This awareness of my aloneness could cause me to become anxious and depressed. I try to remember the positive, spiritual meaning and the psychological contentment that comes with being single: blessing my quiet apartment at the end of a busy day, staying in or going out as I please, calling a friend or silencing the ring on my phone so I can spend the evening reading and praying. Loneliness slowly changes into solitude also when I recommit myself to the Lord and enjoy his companionship.

In solitude I bring my whole being—physical, emotional, spiritual—before God and ask him for the grace I need to live my single calling joyfully. I do not want to fall into self-pity or madly seek some meaningful encounter. God knows I need his help to live a harmonious inner and outer life, avoiding the either/or extremes that often tempt singles: either too much withdrawal or too much involvement.

Personally, as a Christian, I try to center my singleness in the heart of Jesus, the Single Word spoken by the Father. In the Word made flesh, I am at home with my single calling and united spiritually with all other people, contemplatively present to his will and actively serving the members of his kingdom.

—*SUSAN MUTO*

Go to page 1593 for your next devotional reading.

the time is favorable or unfavorable; convince, rebuke, and encourage, with the utmost patience in teaching. [3]For the time is coming when people will not put up with sound doctrine, but having itching ears, they will accumulate for themselves teachers to suit their own desires, [4]and will turn away from listening to the truth and wander away to myths. [5]As for you, always be sober, endure suffering, do the work of an evangelist, carry out your ministry fully.

6 As for me, I am already being poured out as a libation, and the time of my departure has come. [7]I have fought the good fight, I have finished the race, I have kept the faith. [8]From now on there is reserved for me the crown of righteousness, which the Lord, the righteous judge, will give me on that day, and not only to me but also to all who have longed for his appearing.

Personal Instructions

9 Do your best to come to me soon, [10]for Demas, in love with this present world, has deserted me and gone to Thessalonica; Crescens has gone to Galatia,[j] Titus to Dalmatia. [11]Only Luke is with me. Get Mark and bring him with you, for he is useful in my ministry. [12]I have sent Tychicus to Ephesus. [13]When you come, bring the cloak that I left with Carpus at Troas, also the books, and above all the parchments. [14]Alexander the coppersmith did me great harm; the Lord will pay him back for his deeds. [15]You also must beware of him, for he strongly opposed our message.

16 At my first defense no one came to my support, but all deserted me. May it not be counted against them! [17]But the Lord stood by me and gave me strength, so that through me the message might be fully proclaimed and all the Gentiles might hear it. So I was rescued from the lion's mouth. [18]The Lord will rescue me from every evil attack and save me for his heavenly kingdom. To him be the glory forever and ever. Amen.

Final Greetings and Benediction

19 Greet Prisca and Aquila, and the household of Onesiphorus. [20]Erastus remained in Corinth; Trophimus I left ill in Miletus. [21]Do your best to come before winter. Eubulus sends greetings to you, as do Pudens and Linus and Claudia and all the brothers and sisters.[k]

22 The Lord be with your spirit. Grace be with you.[l]

---

j Other ancient authorities read *Gaul*   k Gk *all the brothers*   l The Greek word for *you* here is plural. Other ancient authorities add *Amen*

The Letter of Paul to

Titus

Paul's co-worker Titus is mentioned 13 times in the New Testament, though never in the book of Acts. A Gentile, he was a disciple and companion of Paul's who traveled with him to Jerusalem and who helped the church at Corinth. The letter to Titus is addressed to him on the island of Crete, where Paul had given him the task of appointing elders and bishops. Titus is instructed to steer clear of men who are arrogant, quick tempered, addicted to wine, violent, or greedy. Instead, he is to look for those who love goodness, who are devout and self-controlled (1.7–8). As in 1 and 2 Timothy, Titus is to protect sound teaching, and he is to instruct the faithful—older men, older women, young women, young men, and slaves—regarding how they are to behave as Christians.

Salutation

1 Paul, a servant[a] of God and an apostle of Jesus Christ, for the sake of the faith of God's elect and the knowledge of the truth that is in accordance with godliness, 2in the hope of eternal life that God, who never lies, promised before the ages began— 3in due time he revealed his word through the proclamation with which I have been entrusted by the command of God our Savior,

4 To Titus, my loyal child in the faith we share:

Grace[b] and peace from God the Father and Christ Jesus our Savior.

Titus in Crete

5 I left you behind in Crete for this reason, so that you should put in order what remained to be done, and should appoint elders in every town, as I directed you: 6someone who is blameless, married only once,[c] whose children are believers, not accused of debauchery and not rebellious. 7For a bishop,[d] as God's steward, must be blameless; he must not be arrogant or quick-tempered or addicted to wine or violent or greedy for gain; 8but he must be hospitable, a lover of goodness, prudent, upright, devout, and self-controlled. 9He must have a firm grasp of the word that is trustworthy in accordance with the teaching, so that he may be able both to preach with sound doctrine and to refute those who contradict it.

10 There are also many rebellious people, idle talkers and deceivers, especially those of the circumcision; 11they must be silenced, since they are upsetting whole families by teaching for sordid gain what it is not right to teach. 12It was one of them, their very own prophet, who said,

a Gk slave   b Other ancient authorities read Grace, mercy,   c Gk husband of one wife   d Or an overseer

"Cretans are always liars, vicious brutes, lazy gluttons." [13]That testimony is true. For this reason rebuke them sharply, so that they may become sound in the faith, [14]not paying attention to Jewish myths or to commandments of those who reject the truth. [15]To the pure all things are pure, but to the corrupt and unbelieving nothing is pure. Their very minds and consciences are corrupted. [16]They profess to know God, but they deny him by their actions. They are detestable, disobedient, unfit for any good work.

Teach Sound Doctrine

2 But as for you, teach what is consistent with sound doctrine. [2]Tell the older men to be temperate, serious, prudent, and sound in faith, in love, and in endurance.

3 Likewise, tell the older women to be reverent in behavior, not to be slanderers or slaves to drink; they are to teach what is good, [4]so that they may encourage the young women to love their husbands, to love their children, [5]to be self-controlled, chaste, good managers of the household, kind, being submissive to their husbands, so that the word of God may not be discredited.

6 Likewise, urge the younger men to be self-controlled. [7]Show yourself in all respects a model of good works, and in your teaching show integrity, gravity, [8]and sound speech that cannot be censured; then any opponent will be put to shame, having nothing evil to say of us.

9 Tell slaves to be submissive to their masters and to give satisfaction in every respect; they are not to talk back, [10]not to pilfer, but to show complete and perfect

Children Are Watching

FRIDAY

Scripture Reading for Today:
Titus 2.1–8

Verses for Today:
Titus 2.4–5

My mother and her friends taught me how to be a friend. They washed dishes and heaped food on plates whenever there was a wedding, graduation, or first communion. They took food to grieving families.

Most mothers worked at home then. They were a neighborhood community, running groups of teens to the high school, or leading Girl Scout troops. They were ready to bake an extra cake or welcome another child or two for the night. They stretched their schedules and their budgets and made room.

Stretching a schedule is more difficult when working for someone else, but mothers still do it. The cakes may be store bought, but mothers still take food to families who have lost someone they love. Their homes still stretch to hold extra children.

Surely Jesus watched his mother carry food to an ailing neighbor and volunteer to watch a few extra children. She helped cook and clean for friends who were celebrating weddings or mourning a death. Mothers have always been doing those things, and children have been watching. I'm glad. I want my daughters to say that their mother and her friends taught them about being a friend.

—MARY VAN BALEN HOLT

Go to page 1598 for your next devotional reading.

fidelity, so that in everything they may be an ornament to the doctrine of God our Savior.

11 For the grace of God has appeared, bringing salvation to all,*e* 12training us to renounce impiety and worldly passions, and in the present age to live lives that are self-controlled, upright, and godly, 13while we wait for the blessed hope and the manifestation of the glory of our great God and Savior,*f* Jesus Christ. 14He it is who gave himself for us that he might redeem us from all iniquity and purify for

himself a people of his own who are zealous for good deeds.

15 Declare these things; exhort and reprove with all authority.*g* Let no one look down on you.

Maintain Good Deeds

3 Remind them to be subject to rulers and authorities, to be obedient, to be ready for every good work, 2to speak evil

e Or *has appeared to all, bringing salvation*   *f* Or *of the great God and our Savior*   *g* Gk *commandment*

Grace

> *But when the goodness and loving kindness of God*
> *our Savior appeared, he saved us, not because*
> *of any works of righteousness that we*
> *had done, but according to his mercy.*
>
> TITUS 3.4–5

What if one day you discovered you had inherited millions from a relative you had never even heard of?

What if you had no medical insurance and someone you had once treated unjustly offered to finance your kidney transplant—and even to donate a kidney?

You would be encountering images of grace.

As a one-word summary of the Christian message, *grace* does nicely. Healing, forgiveness, triumph over death, life with God now and forever—grace covers it all: It is the heart of the Good News of Jesus Christ.

"Grace is favor, the free and undeserved help that God gives us to respond to his call to become children of God" (*Catechism of the Catholic Church*, 1996). Note especially the words *free* and *undeserved*. This is the essence of grace—that it does not depend on any of our "works of righteousness" but on God's mercy (Titus 3.5).

The attitude of favor that we see in God

takes shape in us as "graces"—gifts received. Chief among these is *sanctifying* grace, the radical cleansing and sharing in God's life (see 1 Corinthians 6.11). The effect of the Holy Spirit's abiding presence, sanctifying grace gradually conforms our whole being to the image and likeness of God and fits us "to become participants of the divine nature" (see Genesis 1.26; 2 Peter 1.4).

Actual grace, on the other hand, is the Spirit's help for *acting*, for *doing*—moment-by-moment power to avoid sin and obey God. Tailored to a multitude of passing circumstances, it takes a multitude of changing forms. Wise decisions, good deeds, fruitful personal encounters, temptations overcome—these are traces of actual graces.

Grace is amazing in more ways than we know. Undeserved and unexpected, it is pure gift. All encompassing, it wraps and carries us through life, preparing and making possible our every good thought and deed, our every inclination to do good.

"All is grace," Saint Thérèse of Lisieux used to say. It is no overstatement.

of no one, to avoid quarreling, to be gentle, and to show every courtesy to everyone. ³For we ourselves were once foolish, disobedient, led astray, slaves to various passions and pleasures, passing our days in malice and envy, despicable, hating one another. ⁴But when the goodness and loving kindness of God our Savior appeared, ⁵he saved us, not because of any works of righteousness that we had done, but according to his mercy, through the water*ʰ* of rebirth and renewal by the Holy Spirit. ⁶This Spirit he poured out on us richly through Jesus Christ our Savior, ⁷so that, having been justified by his grace, we might become heirs according to the hope of eternal life. ⁸The saying is sure.

I desire that you insist on these things, so that those who have come to believe in God may be careful to devote themselves to good works; these things are excellent and profitable to everyone. ⁹But avoid stupid controversies, genealogies, dissensions, and quarrels about the law, for they are unprofitable and worthless. ¹⁰After a first and second admonition, have nothing more to do with anyone who causes divisions, ¹¹since you know that such a person is perverted and sinful, being self-condemned.

Final Messages and Benediction

12 When I send Artemas to you, or Tychicus, do your best to come to me at Nicopolis, for I have decided to spend the winter there. ¹³Make every effort to send Zenas the lawyer and Apollos on their way, and see that they lack nothing. ¹⁴And let people learn to devote themselves to good works in order to meet urgent needs, so that they may not be unproductive.

15 All who are with me send greetings to you. Greet those who love us in the faith.

Grace be with all of you.*ⁱ*

ʰ Gk *washing*   *ⁱ* Other ancient authorities add *Amen*

The Letter of Paul to
Philemon

Paul wrote this letter while in prison in Ephesus or possibly in Rome. He addressed it to Philemon and to certain other members of the church, informing Philemon that Onesimus, the slave who apparently robbed him and then ran away, is now a believer in Christ. Paul is sending Onesimus back to Philemon. Though runaway slaves could be executed under Roman law, Paul expresses the hope that Philemon will receive him, not as a slave but as a beloved brother (see verses 15–16). Though Paul does not ask outright for Philemon's freedom, the letter seems to imply that he would like Philemon to free Onesimus so that Onesimus could help Paul preach the gospel (see verses 13–14, 21).

The letter to Philemon reminds us that class distinctions have no place in the church. By virtue of belonging to Christ, we become brothers and sisters in the family of God.

Salutation

1 Paul, a prisoner of Christ Jesus, and Timothy our brother,*a*

To Philemon our dear friend and co-worker, 2to Apphia our sister,*b* to Archippus our fellow soldier, and to the church in your house:

3 Grace to you and peace from God our Father and the Lord Jesus Christ.

Philemon's Love and Faith

4 When I remember you*c* in my prayers, I always thank my God 5because I hear of your love for all the saints and your faith toward the Lord Jesus. 6I pray that the sharing of your faith may become effective when you perceive all the good that we*d* may do for Christ. 7I have indeed received much joy and encouragement from your love, because the hearts of the saints have been refreshed through you, my brother.

Paul's Plea for Onesimus

8 For this reason, though I am bold enough in Christ to command you to do your duty, 9yet I would rather appeal to you on the basis of love—and I, Paul, do this as an old man, and now also as a prisoner of Christ Jesus.*e* 10I am appealing to you for my child, Onesimus, whose father I have become during my imprisonment. 11Formerly he was useless to you, but now he is indeed useful*f* both to you

a Gk *the brother*   *b* Gk *the sister*   *c* From verse 4 through verse 21, *you* is singular   *d* Other ancient authorities read *you* (plural)   *e* Or *as an ambassador of Christ Jesus, and now also his prisoner*   *f* The name Onesimus means *useful* or (compare verse 20) *beneficial*

and to me. [12]I am sending him, that is, my own heart, back to you. [13]I wanted to keep him with me, so that he might be of service to me in your place during my imprisonment for the gospel; [14]but I preferred to do nothing without your consent, in order that your good deed might be voluntary and not something forced. [15]Perhaps this is the reason he was separated from you for a while, so that you might have him back forever, [16]no longer as a slave but more than a slave, a beloved brother—especially to me but how much more to you, both in the flesh and in the Lord.

17 So if you consider me your partner, welcome him as you would welcome me. [18]If he has wronged you in any way, or owes you anything, charge that to my account. [19]I, Paul, am writing this with my own hand: I will repay it. I say nothing about your owing me even your own self. [20]Yes, brother, let me have this benefit from you in the Lord! Refresh my heart in Christ. [21]Confident of your obedience, I am writing to you, knowing that you will do even more than I say.

22 One thing more—prepare a guest room for me, for I am hoping through your prayers to be restored to you.

Final Greetings and Benediction

23 Epaphras, my fellow prisoner in Christ Jesus, sends greetings to you, *g* [24]and so do Mark, Aristarchus, Demas, and Luke, my fellow workers.

25 The grace of the Lord Jesus Christ be with your spirit.*h*

g Here *you* is singular   *h* Other ancient authorities add *Amen*

Salome, Mother of the Sons of Zebedee

Her Name, the Feminine Form of "Solomon," Means "Peace"

Her Character: *A devoted follower of Jesus, her husband ran a fishing business. She shared the common misconception that the Messiah would drive out the Romans and establish a literal kingdom in Palestine. Her name was probably Salome.*

Her Sorrow: *To have stood with other women at the cross, witnessing the death of Jesus of Nazareth.*

Her Joy: *To have seen an angel at Jesus' tomb who proclaimed the resurrection.*

Read Matthew 20.20–24

Salome loved Jesus nearly as much as her own two sons, James and John. She would never forget the day they left their fishing nets to follow him. Lately, she too had come to believe that Jesus was the Messiah of God.

She had smiled when she heard Jesus had nicknamed her boys "the Sons of Thunder." Surely he had recognized the seeds of greatness in the two feisty brothers from Capernaum.

Though she had heard ominous rumors that Jerusalem's men of power hated Jesus, she also knew that the great King David had faced his share of enemies before establishing his kingdom. And hadn't Jesus promised his disciples they would sit on twelve thrones in his kingdom? Even with faith as small as a mustard seed, mountains could be moved.

Salome had left behind her comfortable home on the northwest shore of Galilee to join her sons. Now, as they journeyed up to Jerusalem, she remembered other words Jesus had spoken: "Ask, and it will be given you; search, and you will find; knock, and the door will be opened for you" (Matthew 7.7). She would no longer deny herself the one favor her heart desired. Prostrating herself before him, she begged: "Declare that these two sons of mine will sit, one at your right and one at your left, in your kingdom" (20.21).

But instead of replying to her, Jesus turned to James and John and said, "You do not know what you are asking. Are you able to drink the cup that I am about to drink?"

"We are able," they answered.

Jesus said to them, "You will indeed drink my cup, but to sit at my right hand and at my left, this is not mine to grant, but it is for those for whom it has been prepared by my Father" (verses 22–23).

Like any loving mother, Salome had simply asked for what she thought would make her children happy. But as Jesus' reply and subsequent events proved, she didn't begin to comprehend what she was asking. Soon the man she had approached as a king would himself die on a cross. And she would be one of the women who witnessed his death.

After it was over, she may have remembered the anguished faces of the men who had been crucified with Jesus, one on his right hand and the other on his left—an ironic reminder of her request.

Instead of asking Jesus what he wanted for her sons, Salome acted as though she knew exactly what he needed to do on their behalf. She must have forgotten that Jesus had exhorted his followers to leave behind, not only houses, brothers and sisters, fathers and mothers for his sake, but also children. In Salome's case, it didn't mean turning her back on her children but surrendering them to God. It meant putting Jesus above everything and everyone—loving him better than she loved her own sons. Only then would she understand the meaning of their suffering. Only then would she really know how to pray.

Praying With Salome

"Declare that these two sons of mine will sit, one at your right hand and one at your left, in your kingdom."—*Matthew 20.21*

Praise God: *That his Son has shown us the true meaning of greatness.*

Offer Thanks: *For all the ways, large and small, in which God has served you.*

Confess: *Pride and misguided ambition.*

Ask God: *For the grace to make the connection—that the way down leads to the way up—that it is the humble woman who will be considered great in the kingdom.*

Lift Your Heart

Many women have heard the message of servanthood and internalized it in unhealthy ways. Instead of realizing their inherent dignity as women, they have defined their worth primarily in terms of others. But both men and women are called to model themselves after Jesus Christ, who was not a person who suffered from low self-esteem. His humility wasn't a cover for a sense of unworthiness. If you have made the mistake of living your life through your husband or your children, ask God for the grace to change. Admit you are a human being who needs care, consideration, and replenishment. Ask God to restore balance in your life. But as you go through the process of finding balance, don't eliminate the word *humility* from your vocabulary by embracing a life of selfishness. This week, ask each day for eyes to see another's need. Then ask for grace to serve in a way that truly models the humility of Jesus.

Lord, forgive me for any pride that has crowded you out of my heart. Whenever I am tempted to think or act with selfish ambition, place a check in my spirit. Give me, instead, the courage to be a servant. Make more room in my heart for your love.

Go to page 1601 for your next devotional reading.

The Letter to the
Hebrews

Various authors have been suggested for this book: Paul, Barnabas, Apollos, or Priscilla and Aquila. But it is impossible to tell who wrote what is not really a letter but a written sermon encouraging believers to persevere in their faith. Possibly it was written prior to the destruction of the temple in A.D. 70, and it may have been addressed to Jewish believers who had become wearied by their efforts to live the Christian life.

Whoever wrote Hebrews had an excellent command of Greek and thorough familiarity with the Old Testament. Hebrews reveals Jesus as the perfect high priest who, because he was also human, can sympathize with our weaknesses without himself succumbing to temptation. We are encouraged to persevere as he did and are also to look to the faithful men and women of the old covenant who suffered greatly because of their faith: "Therefore, since we are surrounded by so great a cloud of witnesses, let us also lay aside every weight and the sin that clings so closely, and let us run with perseverance the race that is set before us, looking to Jesus the pioneer and perfecter of our faith, who for the sake of the joy that was set before him endured the cross, disregarding its shame, and has taken his seat at the right hand of the throne of God" (12.1–2).

God Has Spoken by His Son

1 Long ago God spoke to our ancestors in many and various ways by the prophets, ²but in these last days he has spoken to us by a Son,*a* whom he appointed heir of all things, through whom he also created the worlds. ³He is the reflection of God's glory and the exact imprint of God's very being, and he sustains*b* all things by his powerful word. When he had made purification for sins, he sat down at the right hand of the Maj-esty on high, ⁴having become as much superior to angels as the name he has inherited is more excellent than theirs.

The Son Is Superior to Angels

5 For to which of the angels did God ever say,
"You are my Son;
    today I have begotten you"?
Or again,

a Or *the Son*   *b* Or *bears along*

"I will be his Father,
    and he will be my Son"?
⁶And again, when he brings the firstborn
into the world, he says,
"Let all God's angels worship him."
⁷Of the angels he says,
"He makes his angels winds,
    and his servants flames of fire."
⁸But of the Son he says,
"Your throne, O God, is^c forever
    and ever,
and the righteous scepter is the
    scepter of your^d kingdom.

⁹ You have loved righteousness and
    hated wickedness;
therefore God, your God, has
    anointed you
with the oil of gladness beyond
    your companions."
¹⁰And,
"In the beginning, Lord, you
    founded the earth,

^{c} Or *God is your throne* ^{d} Other ancient
authorities read *his*

Raised Up Into Heaven

Angels are everywhere in the New Testament, signaling a closer
rapport between heaven and earth, established by the coming of
Jesus. In fact, the angels couldn't seem to stay away from the man
from Nazareth. Like parentheses encircling a phrase, they were
present at both the beginning and end of Jesus' earthly life.

Notably, the angels were present at his ascension. Few of us
stop to consider the significance of Jesus' reentry into heaven, an
event that is mentioned in the book of Acts and described elsewhere in the Bible. After the Resurrection, Jesus entered heaven as
a victor. But that's not all there is to the story. By becoming
human, Jesus was able to release us from the terrifying bondage of
evil. Having done that, the King of the universe did not shed his
human nature like a worn-out suit. Instead, he chose to reign forever as *both* God and man.

John Chrysostom touches on this amazing truth when he
says that the angels looked on at the ascension because they
wanted "to see the unheard of spectacle of man appearing in
heaven." He goes on to say: "Today we are raised up into heaven,
we who seemed even unworthy of earth. We are exalted above
the heavens; we arrive at the kingly throne. Was it not enough
to be elevated above the heavens? Was not such a glory beyond
all expression? But [Christ] rose above the angels; he passed
the cherubim; he went higher than the seraphim; he bypassed
the thrones; he did not stop until he arrived at the very throne
of God."

The heights to which Jesus has ascended and to which he
invites us are dizzying. The angels look on with awe and so
should we. Higher than the seraphim, more glorious than the
cherubim, our God reigns!

—ANN SPANGLER

Go to page 1603 for your next devotional reading.

MONDAY

Scripture Reading
for Today:
Hebrews 1.1–14

Verses for Today:
Hebrews 1.3–4

and the heavens are the work of
your hands;
11 they will perish, but you remain;
they will all wear out like
clothing;
12 like a cloak you will roll them up,
and like clothing[e] they will be
changed.
But you are the same,
and your years will never end."
13 But to which of the angels has he ever
said,
"Sit at my right hand
until I make your enemies a
footstool for your feet"?
14 Are not all angels[f] spirits in the divine
service, sent to serve for the sake of those
who are to inherit salvation?

Warning to Pay Attention

2 Therefore we must pay greater attention to what we have heard, so that
we do not drift away from it. 2 For if the
message declared through angels was valid, and every transgression or disobedience received a just penalty, 3 how can we
escape if we neglect so great a salvation? It
was declared at first through the Lord, and
it was attested to us by those who heard
him, 4 while God added his testimony by
signs and wonders and various miracles,
and by gifts of the Holy Spirit, distributed
according to his will.

Exaltation through Abasement

5 Now God[g] did not subject the coming world, about which we are speaking,
to angels. 6 But someone has testified
somewhere,
"What are human beings that you
are mindful of them,[h]
or mortals, that you care for
them?[i]
7 You have made them for a little
while lower[j] than the angels;
you have crowned them with
glory and honor,[k]
8   subjecting all things under
their feet."
Now in subjecting all things to them,
God[g] left nothing outside their control.
As it is, we do not yet see everything in
subjection to them, 9 but we do see Jesus,
who for a little while was made lower[l]
than the angels, now crowned with glory
and honor because of the suffering of
death, so that by the grace of God[m] he
might taste death for everyone.

10 It was fitting that God,[g] for whom
and through whom all things exist, in
bringing many children to glory, should
make the pioneer of their salvation perfect
through sufferings. 11 For the one who
sanctifies and those who are sanctified all
have one Father.[n] For this reason Jesus[g]
is not ashamed to call them brothers and
sisters,[o] 12 saying,
"I will proclaim your name to my
brothers and sisters,[o]
in the midst of the congregation I
will praise you."
13 And again,
"I will put my trust in him."
And again,
"Here am I and the children whom
God has given me."
14 Since, therefore, the children share
flesh and blood, he himself likewise
shared the same things, so that through
death he might destroy the one who has
the power of death, that is, the devil,
15 and free those who all their lives were
held in slavery by the fear of death. 16 For
it is clear that he did not come to help
angels, but the descendants of Abraham.
17 Therefore he had to become like his
brothers and sisters[o] in every respect, so
that he might be a merciful and faithful
high priest in the service of God, to make
a sacrifice of atonement for the sins of the
people. 18 Because he himself was tested
by what he suffered, he is able to help
those who are being tested.

Moses a Servant, Christ a Son

3 Therefore, brothers and sisters,[o]
holy partners in a heavenly calling,
consider that Jesus, the apostle and high
priest of our confession, 2 was faithful to
the one who appointed him, just as Moses
also "was faithful in all[p] God's[q] house."
3 Yet Jesus[r] is worthy of more glory than
Moses, just as the builder of a house has
more honor than the house itself. 4 (For

e Other ancient authorities lack like clothing
f Gk all of them   g Gk he   h Gk What is man
that you are mindful of him?   i Gk or the son of
man that you care for him? In the Hebrew of
Psalm 8.4-6 both man and son of man refer to all
humankind   j Or them only a little lower
k Other ancient authorities add and set them over
the works of your hands   l Or who was made a
little lower   m Other ancient authorities read
apart from God   n Gk are all of one   o Gk
brothers   p Other ancient authorities lack all
q Gk his   r Gk this one

every house is built by someone, but the builder of all things is God.) [5]Now Moses was faithful in all God's[s] house as a servant, to testify to the things that would be spoken later. [6]Christ, however, was faithful over God's[s] house as a son, and we are his house if we hold firm[t] the confidence and the pride that belong to hope.

Warning against Unbelief

7 Therefore, as the Holy Spirit says,
"Today, if you hear his voice,
[8] do not harden your hearts as in
         the rebellion,
      as on the day of testing in the
         wilderness,
[9] where your ancestors put me to
         the test,
      though they had seen my works
         [10]for forty years.
   Therefore I was angry with that
         generation,
   and I said, 'They always go astray in
         their hearts,
      and they have not known
         my ways.'
[11] As in my anger I swore,
      'They will not enter my rest.' "
[12]Take care, brothers and sisters,[u] that none of you may have an evil, unbelieving heart that turns away from the living God. [13]But exhort one another every day, as long as it is called "today," so that none of you may be hardened by the deceitfulness of sin. [14]For we have become partners of Christ, if only we hold our first confidence firm to the end. [15]As it is said,
"Today, if you hear his voice,
   do not harden your hearts as in
      the rebellion."
[16]Now who were they who heard and yet were rebellious? Was it not all those who left Egypt under the leadership of Moses? [17]But with whom was he angry forty years? Was it not those who sinned, whose bodies fell in the wilderness? [18]And to whom did he swear that they would not enter his rest, if not to those who were disobedient? [19]So we see that they were unable to enter because of unbelief.

The Rest That God Promised

4 Therefore, while the promise of entering his rest is still open, let us take care that none of you should seem to have

s Gk *his*   *t* Other ancient authorities add *to the end*   *u* Gk *brothers*

TUESDAY

Scripture Reading for Today:
Hebrews 3.5–14

Verse for Today:
Hebrews 3.6

Hold Fast

What you hold, may you [always] hold,
What you do, may you [always] do and never abandon.
But with swift pace, light step,
unswerving feet,
so that even your steps stir up no dust,
may you go forward
securely, joyfully, and swiftly,
on the path of prudent happiness,
not believing anything,
not agreeing with anything
that would dissuade you from this resolution
or that would place a stumbling block for you on the way,
so that you may offer your vows to the Most High
in the pursuit of that perfection
to which the Spirit of the Lord has called you.

—SAINT CLARE OF ASSISI

Go to page 1605 for your next devotional reading.

failed to reach it. [2]For indeed the good news came to us just as to them; but the message they heard did not benefit them, because they were not united by faith with those who listened.[v] [3]For we who have believed enter that rest, just as God[w] has said,

"As in my anger I swore,
'They shall not enter my rest,' "

though his works were finished at the foundation of the world. [4]For in one place it speaks about the seventh day as follows, "And God rested on the seventh day from all his works." [5]And again in this place it says, "They shall not enter my rest." [6]Since therefore it remains open for some to enter it, and those who formerly received the good news failed to enter because of disobedience, [7]again he sets a certain day—"today"—saying through David much later, in the words already quoted,

"Today, if you hear his voice,
do not harden your hearts."

[8]For if Joshua had given them rest, God[w] would not speak later about another day. [9]So then, a sabbath rest still remains for the people of God; [10]for those who enter God's rest also cease from their labors as God did from his. [11]Let us therefore make every effort to enter that rest, so that no one may fall through such disobedience as theirs.

12 Indeed, the word of God is living and active, sharper than any two-edged sword, piercing until it divides soul from spirit, joints from marrow; it is able to judge the thoughts and intentions of the heart. [13]And before him no creature is hidden, but all are naked and laid bare to the eyes of the one to whom we must render an account.

Jesus the Great High Priest

14 Since, then, we have a great high priest who has passed through the heavens, Jesus, the Son of God, let us hold fast to our confession. [15]For we do not have a high priest who is unable to sympathize with our weaknesses, but we have one who in every respect has been tested[x] as we are, yet without sin. [16]Let us therefore approach the throne of grace with boldness, so that we may receive mercy and find grace to help in time of need.

5 Every high priest chosen from among mortals is put in charge of things pertaining to God on their behalf, to offer gifts and sacrifices for sins. [2]He is able to deal gently with the ignorant and wayward, since he himself is subject to weakness; [3]and because of this he must offer sacrifice for his own sins as well as for those of the people. [4]And one does not presume to take this honor, but takes it only when called by God, just as Aaron was.

5 So also Christ did not glorify himself in becoming a high priest, but was appointed by the one who said to him,

"You are my Son,
today I have begotten you";

[6]as he says also in another place,

"You are a priest forever,
according to the order of
Melchizedek."

7 In the days of his flesh, Jesus[w] offered up prayers and supplications, with loud cries and tears, to the one who was able to save him from death, and he was heard because of his reverent submission. [8]Although he was a Son, he learned obedience through what he suffered; [9]and having been made perfect, he became the source of eternal salvation for all who obey him, [10]having been designated by God a high priest according to the order of Melchizedek.

Warning against Falling Away

11 About this[y] we have much to say that is hard to explain, since you have become dull in understanding. [12]For though by this time you ought to be teachers, you need someone to teach you again the basic elements of the oracles of God. You need milk, not solid food; [13]for everyone who lives on milk, being still an infant, is unskilled in the word of righteousness. [14]But solid food is for the mature, for those whose faculties have been trained by practice to distinguish good from evil.

The Peril of Falling Away

6 Therefore let us go on toward perfection,[z] leaving behind the basic teaching about Christ, and not laying again the foundation: repentance from dead works and faith toward God, [2]instruction about baptisms, laying on of hands, resurrection of the dead, and eternal judgment. [3]And we will do[a] this, if

---

[v] Other ancient authorities read *it did not meet with faith in those who listened*   [w] Gk *he*   [x] Or *tempted*   [y] Or *him*   [z] Or *toward maturity*   [a] Other ancient authorities read *let us do*

God permits. ⁴For it is impossible to re-store again to repentance those who have once been enlightened, and have tasted the heavenly gift, and have shared in the Holy Spirit, ⁵and have tasted the goodness of the word of God and the powers of the age to come, ⁶and then have fallen away, since on their own they are crucifying again the Son of God and are holding him up to contempt. ⁷Ground that drinks up the rain falling on it repeatedly, and that produces a crop useful to those for whom it is cultivated, receives a blessing from God. ⁸But if it produces thorns and this-tles, it is worthless and on the verge of being cursed; its end is to be burned over.

9 Even though we speak in this way, beloved, we are confident of better things in your case, things that belong to salva-tion. ¹⁰For God is not unjust; he will not overlook your work and the love that you showed for his sake*b* in serving the saints, as you still do. ¹¹And we want each one of you to show the same diligence so as to realize the full assurance of hope to the very end, ¹²so that you may not be-come sluggish, but imitators of those who through faith and patience inherit the promises.

The Certainty of God's Promise

13 When God made a promise to Abra-ham, because he had no one greater by whom to swear, he swore by himself, ¹⁴saying, "I will surely bless you and mul-tiply you." ¹⁵And thus Abraham,*c* having patiently endured, obtained the promise. ¹⁶Human beings, of course, swear by someone greater than themselves, and an oath given as confirmation puts an end to all dispute. ¹⁷In the same way, when God desired to show even more clearly to the heirs of the promise the unchangeable character of his purpose, he guaranteed it by an oath, ¹⁸so that through two un-changeable things, in which it is impossi-ble that God would prove false, we who have taken refuge might be strongly en-

b Gk *for his name*   *c* Gk *he*

𝒫erfect Obedience

Scripture Reading for Today: *Hebrews 5.7–10*

Verse for Today: *Hebrews 5.8*

Lord, you know that I want to serve you but am always still hanging on to my work and opinion; that again and again I hastily crawl back into myself in order to consider everything from my point of view; that I do this in order to avoid that, wish this and abhor that.

But in your whole life on earth and especially on the cross, you have shown us what it means to do the will of another. For you, this other person was the Father, a Father so perfect that, from the beginning and without forming your own opinion, you considered and accepted each of his decisions as perfect. You did this not through an insight, which would have been the result each time of examination and deliberation, but out of love. Your love for the Father has once and for all taken the place of every personal examination. And this love you also bestowed on your saints.

Give us your filial strength; grant that we learn to love the Father as you love him. Grant that we reach him through you and your attitude, that we become obedient by your perfect obe-dience.

—ADRIENNE VON SPEYR

Go to page 1611 for your next devotional reading.

couraged to seize the hope set before us. [19]We have this hope, a sure and steadfast anchor of the soul, a hope that enters the inner shrine behind the curtain, [20]where Jesus, a forerunner on our behalf, has entered, having become a high priest forever according to the order of Melchizedek.

The Priestly Order of Melchizedek

7 This "King Melchizedek of Salem, priest of the Most High God, met Abraham as he was returning from defeating the kings and blessed him"; [2]and to him Abraham apportioned "one-tenth of everything." His name, in the first place, means "king of righteousness"; next he is also king of Salem, that is, "king of peace." [3]Without father, without mother, without genealogy, having neither beginning of days nor end of life, but resembling the Son of God, he remains a priest forever.

4 See how great he is! Even[d] Abraham the patriarch gave him a tenth of the spoils. [5]And those descendants of Levi who receive the priestly office have a commandment in the law to collect tithes[e] from the people, that is, from their kindred,[f] though these also are descended from Abraham. [6]But this man, who does not belong to their ancestry, collected tithes[e] from Abraham and blessed him who had received the promises. [7]It is beyond dispute that the inferior is blessed by the superior. [8]In the one case, tithes are received by those who are mortal; in the other, by one of whom it is testified that he lives. [9]One might even say that Levi himself, who receives tithes, paid tithes through Abraham, [10]for he was still in the loins of his ancestor when Melchizedek met him.

Another Priest, Like Melchizedek

11 Now if perfection had been attainable through the levitical priesthood—for the people received the law under this priesthood—what further need would there have been to speak of another priest arising according to the order of Melchizedek, rather than one according to the order of Aaron? [12]For when there is a change in the priesthood, there is necessarily a change in the law as well. [13]Now the one of whom these things are spoken belonged to another tribe, from which no one has ever served at the altar. [14]For it is evident that our Lord was descended from

Judah, and in connection with that tribe Moses said nothing about priests.

15 It is even more obvious when another priest arises, resembling Melchizedek, [16]one who has become a priest, not through a legal requirement concerning physical descent, but through the power of an indestructible life. [17]For it is attested of him,

"You are a priest forever,
  according to the order of
    Melchizedek."

[18]There is, on the one hand, the abrogation of an earlier commandment because it was weak and ineffectual [19](for the law made nothing perfect); there is, on the other hand, the introduction of a better hope, through which we approach God.

20 This was confirmed with an oath; for others who became priests took their office without an oath, [21]but this one became a priest with an oath, because of the one who said to him,

"The Lord has sworn
  and will not change his mind,
 'You are a priest forever' "—

[22]accordingly Jesus has also become the guarantee of a better covenant.

23 Furthermore, the former priests were many in number, because they were prevented by death from continuing in office; [24]but he holds his priesthood permanently, because he continues forever. [25]Consequently he is able for all time to save[g] those who approach God through him, since he always lives to make intercession for them.

26 For it was fitting that we should have such a high priest, holy, blameless, undefiled, separated from sinners, and exalted above the heavens. [27]Unlike the other[h] high priests, he has no need to offer sacrifices day after day, first for his own sins, and then for those of the people; this he did once for all when he offered himself. [28]For the law appoints as high priests those who are subject to weakness, but the word of the oath, which came later than the law, appoints a Son who has been made perfect forever.

Mediator of a Better Covenant

8 Now the main point in what we are saying is this: we have such a high

---

[d] Other ancient authorities lack *Even*   [e] Or *a tenth*   [f] Gk *brothers*   [g] Or *able to save completely* [h] Gk lacks *other*

priest, one who is seated at the right hand of the throne of the Majesty in the heavens, [2] a minister in the sanctuary and the true tent[i] that the Lord, and not any mortal, has set up. [3] For every high priest is appointed to offer gifts and sacrifices; hence it is necessary for this priest also to have something to offer. [4] Now if he were on earth, he would not be a priest at all, since there are priests who offer gifts according to the law. [5] They offer worship in a sanctuary that is a sketch and shadow of the heavenly one; for Moses, when he was about to erect the tent,[i] was warned, "See that you make everything according to the pattern that was shown you on the mountain." [6] But Jesus[j] has now obtained a more excellent ministry, and to that degree he is the mediator of a better covenant, which has been enacted through better promises. [7] For if that first covenant had been faultless, there would have been no need to look for a second one.

[8] God[k] finds fault with them when he says:

"The days are surely coming, says
the Lord,
when I will establish a new
covenant with the house
of Israel
and with the house of Judah;
[9] not like the covenant that I made
with their ancestors,
on the day when I took them by
the hand to lead them out
of the land of Egypt;
for they did not continue in
my covenant,
and so I had no concern for them,
says the Lord.
[10] This is the covenant that I will make
with the house of Israel
after those days, says the Lord:
I will put my laws in their minds,
and write them on their hearts,
and I will be their God,
and they shall be my people.
[11] And they shall not teach
one another
or say to each other, 'Know
the Lord,'
for they shall all know me,
from the least of them to
the greatest.
[12] For I will be merciful toward their
iniquities,
and I will remember their sins
no more."

[13] In speaking of "a new covenant," he has made the first one obsolete. And what is obsolete and growing old will soon disappear.

The Earthly and the Heavenly Sanctuaries

9 Now even the first covenant had regulations for worship and an earthly sanctuary. [2] For a tent[i] was constructed, the first one, in which were the lampstand, the table, and the bread of the Presence;[l] this is called the Holy Place. [3] Behind the second curtain was a tent[i] called the Holy of Holies. [4] In it stood the golden altar of incense and the ark of the covenant overlaid on all sides with gold, in which there were a golden urn holding the manna, and Aaron's rod that budded, and the tablets of the covenant; [5] above it were the cherubim of glory overshadowing the mercy seat.[m] Of these things we cannot speak now in detail.

[6] Such preparations having been made, the priests go continually into the first tent[i] to carry out their ritual duties; [7] but only the high priest goes into the second, and he but once a year, and not without taking the blood that he offers for himself and for the sins committed unintentionally by the people. [8] By this the Holy Spirit indicates that the way into the sanctuary has not yet been disclosed as long as the first tent[i] is still standing. [9] This is a symbol[n] of the present time, during which gifts and sacrifices are offered that cannot perfect the conscience of the worshiper, [10] but deal only with food and drink and various baptisms, regulations for the body imposed until the time comes to set things right.

[11] But when Christ came as a high priest of the good things that have come,[o] then through the greater and perfect[p] tent[i] (not made with hands, that is, not of this creation), [12] he entered once for all into the Holy Place, not with the blood of goats and calves, but with his own blood, thus obtaining eternal redemption. [13] For if the blood of goats and bulls, with the sprinkling of the ashes of a heifer, sanctifies those who have been defiled so that their flesh is purified, [14] how

---

i Or *tabernacle*   j Gk *he*   k Gk *He*   l Gk *the presentation of the loaves*   m Or *the place of atonement*   n Gk *parable*   o Other ancient authorities read *good things to come*   p Gk *more perfect*

much more will the blood of Christ, who through the eternal Spirit[q] offered himself without blemish to God, purify our[r] conscience from dead works to worship the living God!

15 For this reason he is the mediator of a new covenant, so that those who are called may receive the promised eternal inheritance, because a death has occurred that redeems them from the transgressions under the first covenant.[s] 16Where a will[s] is involved, the death of the one who made it must be established. 17For a will[s] takes effect only at death, since it is not in force as long as the one who made it is alive. 18Hence not even the first covenant was inaugurated without blood. 19For when every commandment had

been told to all the people by Moses in accordance with the law, he took the blood of calves and goats,[t] with water and scarlet wool and hyssop, and sprinkled both the scroll itself and all the people, 20saying, "This is the blood of the covenant that God has ordained for you." 21And in the same way he sprinkled with the blood both the tent[u] and all the vessels used in worship. 22Indeed, under the law almost everything is purified with

q Other ancient authorities read *Holy Spirit*
r Other ancient authorities read *your*   s The Greek word used here means both *covenant* and *will*   t Other ancient authorities lack *and goats*
u Or *tabernacle*

THE TRADITION

The Crucifix

How much more will the blood of Christ, who through the eternal Spirit offered himself without blemish to God, purify our conscience from dead works to worship the living God!

HEBREWS 9.14

The crucifix is present in every Catholic Church and especially prominent at Mass. Catholics venerate it with a holy kiss on Good Friday. Martyrs have gone to their deaths for refusing to trample it. The sight of it comforts, strengthens, and encourages the sick and dying.

The crucifix, a representation of the cross on which appears an image of Jesus crucified, is an evocative reminder. In wood or stone, glass or metal or paint, it proclaims the reality and the purpose of the incarnation.

The crucifix symbolizes a love we can hardly imagine. "For God so loved the world that he gave his only Son, so that everyone who believes in him may not perish but may have eternal life" (John 3.16).

The crucifix reveals the degree of self-emptying to which a loving God willingly submitted. "Jesus ... endured the cross, disregarding its shame ... He humbled himself and became obedient to the point of death—even

death on a cross" (Hebrews 12.2; Philippians 2.8).

The crucifix recalls a sacrifice so perfect that anyone who believes in it is cleansed and reconciled to God. "I will remember their sins and their lawless deeds no more," (Hebrews 10.17).

The crucifix reminds us that our own suffering, joined to Christ's, has meaning. It reveals a "foolishness" greater than the wisdom of the world. It directs us to a new way of living that centers on "Jesus Christ, and him crucified" (see Colossians 1.24; 1 Corinthians 1.18; 2.2).

We need religious art and objects that feature the resurrection and point us to Christ's triumph and our hope of eternal glory. But, distracted creatures that we are, we also need reminders of what it cost to save us. "What shall I return to the Lord for all his bounty to me?" (Psalm 116.12). This is the question to which every crucifix points.

blood, and without the shedding of blood there is no forgiveness of sins.

Christ's Sacrifice Takes Away Sin

23 Thus it was necessary for the sketches of the heavenly things to be purified with these rites, but the heavenly things themselves need better sacrifices than these. 24For Christ did not enter a sanctuary made by human hands, a mere copy of the true one, but he entered into heaven itself, now to appear in the presence of God on our behalf. 25Nor was it to offer himself again and again, as the high priest enters the Holy Place year after year with blood that is not his own; 26for then he would have had to suffer again and again since the foundation of the world. But as it is, he has appeared once for all at the end of the age to remove sin by the sacrifice of himself. 27And just as it is appointed for mortals to die once, and after that the judgment, 28so Christ, having been offered once to bear the sins of many, will appear a second time, not to deal with sin, but to save those who are eagerly waiting for him.

Christ's Sacrifice Once for All

10 Since the law has only a shadow of the good things to come and not the true form of these realities, it*v* can never, by the same sacrifices that are continually offered year after year, make perfect those who approach. 2Otherwise, would they not have ceased being offered, since the worshipers, cleansed once for all, would no longer have any consciousness of sin? 3But in these sacrifices there is a reminder of sin year after year. 4For it is impossible for the blood of bulls and goats to take away sins. 5Consequently, when Christ*w* came into the world, he said,

"Sacrifices and offerings you have
　　not desired,
　but a body you have prepared
　　for me;
6　in burnt offerings and sin offerings
　　you have taken no pleasure.
7　Then I said, 'See, God, I have come
　　to do your will, O God'
　(in the scroll of the book*x* it is
　　written of me)."

8When he said above, "You have neither desired nor taken pleasure in sacrifices and offerings and burnt offerings and sin offerings" (these are offered according to the law), 9then he added, "See, I have come to do your will." He abolishes the first in order to establish the second. 10And it is by God's will*y* that we have been sanctified through the offering of the body of Jesus Christ once for all.

11 And every priest stands day after day at his service, offering again and again the same sacrifices that can never take away sins. 12But when Christ*z* had offered for all time a single sacrifice for sins, "he sat down at the right hand of God," 13and since then has been waiting "until his enemies would be made a footstool for his feet." 14For by a single offering he has perfected for all time those who are sanctified. 15And the Holy Spirit also testifies to us, for after saying,

16　"This is the covenant that I will
　　make with them
　　after those days, says the Lord:
　I will put my laws in their hearts,
　　and I will write them on
　　　their minds,"
17he also adds,
　"I will remember*a* their sins and
　　their lawless deeds no more."
18Where there is forgiveness of these, there is no longer any offering for sin.

A Call to Persevere

19 Therefore, my friends,*b* since we have confidence to enter the sanctuary by the blood of Jesus, 20by the new and living way that he opened for us through the curtain (that is, through his flesh), 21and since we have a great priest over the house of God, 22let us approach with a true heart in full assurance of faith, with our hearts sprinkled clean from an evil conscience and our bodies washed with pure water. 23Let us hold fast to the confession of our hope without wavering, for he who has promised is faithful. 24And let us consider how to provoke one another to love and good deeds, 25not neglecting to meet together, as is the habit of some, but encouraging one another, and all the more as you see the Day approaching.

26 For if we willfully persist in sin after having received the knowledge of the truth, there no longer remains a sacrifice for sins, 27but a fearful prospect of judg-

v Other ancient authorities read *they*　　*w* Gk *he*
x Meaning of Gk uncertain　　*y* Gk *by that will*
z Gk *this one*　　*a* Gk *on their minds and I will*
remember　　*b* Gk *Therefore, brothers*

ment, and a fury of fire that will consume the adversaries. 28Anyone who has violated the law of Moses dies without mercy "on the testimony of two or three witnesses." 29How much worse punishment do you think will be deserved by those who have spurned the Son of God, profaned the blood of the covenant by which they were sanctified, and outraged the Spirit of grace? 30For we know the one who said, "Vengeance is mine, I will repay." And again, "The Lord will judge his people." 31It is a fearful thing to fall into the hands of the living God.

32 But recall those earlier days when, after you had been enlightened, you endured a hard struggle with sufferings, 33sometimes being publicly exposed to abuse and persecution, and sometimes being partners with those so treated. 34For you had compassion for those who were in prison, and you cheerfully accepted the plundering of your possessions, knowing that you yourselves possessed something better and more lasting. 35Do not, therefore, abandon that confidence of yours; it brings a great reward. 36For you need endurance, so that when you have done the will of God, you may receive what was promised. 37For yet

"in a very little while,
    the one who is coming will come
        and will not delay;
38 but my righteous one will live
        by faith.
    My soul takes no pleasure in
        anyone who shrinks back."

39But we are not among those who shrink back and so are lost, but among those who have faith and so are saved.

The Meaning of Faith

11 Now faith is the assurance of things hoped for, the conviction of things not seen. 2Indeed, by faith*c* our ancestors received approval. 3By faith we understand that the worlds were prepared by the word of God, so that what is seen was made from things that are not visible.*d*

The Examples of Abel, Enoch, and Noah

4 By faith Abel offered to God a more acceptable*e* sacrifice than Cain's. Through this he received approval as righteous, God himself giving approval to his gifts; he died, but through his faith*f* he

still speaks. 5By faith Enoch was taken so that he did not experience death; and "he was not found, because God had taken him." For it was attested before he was taken away that "he had pleased God." 6And without faith it is impossible to please God, for whoever would approach him must believe that he exists and that he rewards those who seek him. 7By faith Noah, warned by God about events as yet unseen, respected the warning and built an ark to save his household; by this he condemned the world and became an heir to the righteousness that is in accordance with faith.

The Faith of Abraham

8 By faith Abraham obeyed when he was called to set out for a place that he was to receive as an inheritance; and he set out, not knowing where he was going. 9By faith he stayed for a time in the land he had been promised, as in a foreign land, living in tents, as did Isaac and Jacob, who were heirs with him of the same promise. 10For he looked forward to the city that has foundations, whose architect and builder is God. 11By faith he received power of procreation, even though he was too old—and Sarah herself was barren—because he considered him faithful who had promised.*g* 12Therefore from one person, and this one as good as dead, descendants were born, "as many as the stars of heaven and as the innumerable grains of sand by the seashore."

13 All of these died in faith without having received the promises, but from a distance they saw and greeted them. They confessed that they were strangers and foreigners on the earth, 14for people who speak in this way make it clear that they are seeking a homeland. 15If they had been thinking of the land that they had left behind, they would have had opportunity to return. 16But as it is, they desire a better country, that is, a heavenly one. Therefore God is not ashamed to be called their God; indeed, he has prepared a city for them.

17 By faith Abraham, when put to the

---

c Gk by this   *d* Or was not made out of visible things   *e* Gk greater   *f* Gk through it   *g* Or By faith Sarah herself, though barren, received power to conceive, even when she was too old, because she considered him faithful who had promised.

test, offered up Isaac. He who had received the promises was ready to offer up his only son, [18]of whom he had been told, "It is through Isaac that descendants shall be named for you." [19]He considered the fact that God is able even to raise someone from the dead—and figuratively speaking, he did receive him back. [20]By faith Isaac invoked blessings for the future on Jacob and Esau. [21]By faith Jacob, when dying, blessed each of the sons of Joseph, "bowing in worship over the top of his staff." [22]By faith Joseph, at the end of his life, made mention of the exodus of the

$\mathcal{E}$*veryday Faith*

THURSDAY

Scripture Reading
for Today:
Hebrews 11.1–7

Verse for Today:
Hebrews 11.1

"Now don't push the term *faith* at me," a lawyer told me bluntly at a dinner party recently. "The word is like a red flag."

"Why such a violent reaction?" I asked.

"Well, because I object to the way people use faith as a theological gimmick to duck all rational problems. At every point where a man wants to understand, they say, 'You just have to have faith,' or, 'Reason only goes so far.' I resent it! I see nothing wrong with 'Prove it to me first, then I'll believe.'"

As we talked, I realized that it had never occurred to this intelligent, well-educated man that in his everyday life he often follows the reverse order—belief and acceptance first, then action. Every day he lives, he acts on faith many times with little proof or none at all, and he does not feel that he is being impractical.

He demonstrates an act of faith each time he boards a plane. He believes that it will take him to his destination, but he has no proof of it. He entrusts life itself to several unknown mechanics who have serviced the plane, as well as to a pilot about whom he knows nothing.

Each time he eats a meal in a restaurant he trusts some unknown cook behind the scenes and eats the food on faith, faith that it is not contaminated.

It is obvious that if we insisted on the "proof first, then faith" order in our daily lives, organized life as we know it would grind to a screeching halt. And since life together among people is possible only by faith, as we act out trust in others, it should not seem odd that the same law applies to our life with God.

In the spiritual realm, when for some reason or other we refuse to act by faith, all activity stops just as completely as it does in the secular realm. There is no way for us even to take the first steps toward the spiritual life except by faith, any more than a baby can get launched on his earthly life without blind baby-trust in his parents and other adults. We accept the fact of a personal relationship with God by faith, even as our young children accept the fact of parental love.

—CATHERINE MARSHALL

Go to page 1613 for your next devotional reading.

Israelites and gave instructions about his burial.[h]

The Faith of Moses

23 By faith Moses was hidden by his parents for three months after his birth, because they saw that the child was beautiful; and they were not afraid of the king's edict.[i] 24By faith Moses, when he was grown up, refused to be called a son of Pharaoh's daughter, 25choosing rather to share ill-treatment with the people of God than to enjoy the fleeting pleasures of sin. 26He considered abuse suffered for the Christ[j] to be greater wealth than the treasures of Egypt, for he was looking ahead to the reward. 27By faith he left Egypt, unafraid of the king's anger; for he persevered as though[k] he saw him who is invisible. 28By faith he kept the Passover and the sprinkling of blood, so that the destroyer of the firstborn would not touch the firstborn of Israel.[l]

The Faith of Other Israelite Heroes

29 By faith the people passed through the Red Sea as if it were dry land, but when the Egyptians attempted to do so they were drowned. 30By faith the walls of Jericho fell after they had been encircled for seven days. 31By faith Rahab the prostitute did not perish with those who were disobedient,[m] because she had received the spies in peace.

32 And what more should I say? For time would fail me to tell of Gideon, Barak, Samson, Jephthah, of David and Samuel and the prophets— 33who through faith conquered kingdoms, administered justice, obtained promises, shut the mouths of lions, 34quenched raging fire, escaped the edge of the sword, won strength out of weakness, became mighty in war, put foreign armies to flight. 35Women received their dead by resurrection. Others were tortured, refusing to accept release, in order to obtain a better resurrection. 36Others suffered mocking and flogging, and even chains and imprisonment. 37They were stoned to death, they were sawn in two,[n] they were killed by the sword; they went about in skins of sheep and goats, destitute, persecuted, tormented— 38of whom the world was not worthy. They wandered in deserts and mountains, and in caves and holes in the ground.

39 Yet all these, though they were commended for their faith, did not receive what was promised, 40since God had provided something better so that they would not, apart from us, be made perfect.

The Example of Jesus

12 Therefore, since we are surrounded by so great a cloud of witnesses, let us also lay aside every weight and the sin that clings so closely,[o] and let us run with perseverance the race that is set before us, 2looking to Jesus the pioneer and perfecter of our faith, who for the sake of[p] the joy that was set before him endured the cross, disregarding its shame, and has taken his seat at the right hand of the throne of God.

3 Consider him who endured such hostility against himself from sinners,[q] so that you may not grow weary or lose heart. 4In your struggle against sin you have not yet resisted to the point of shedding your blood. 5And you have forgotten the exhortation that addresses you as children—

"My child, do not regard lightly the
        discipline of the Lord,
    or lose heart when you are
        punished by him;
6 for the Lord disciplines those whom
        he loves,
    and chastises every child whom he
        accepts."

7Endure trials for the sake of discipline. God is treating you as children; for what child is there whom a parent does not discipline? 8If you do not have that discipline in which all children share, then you are illegitimate and not his children. 9Moreover, we had human parents to discipline us, and we respected them. Should we not be even more willing to be subject to the Father of spirits and live? 10For they disciplined us for a short time as seemed best to them, but he disciplines us for our

---

[h] Gk his bones   [i] Other ancient authorities add By faith Moses, when he was grown up, killed the Egyptian, because he observed the humiliation of his people (Gk brothers)   [j] Or the Messiah   [k] Or because   [l] Gk would not touch them   [m] Or unbelieving   [n] Other ancient authorities add they were tempted   [o] Other ancient authorities read sin that easily distracts   [p] Or who instead of   [q] Other ancient authorities read such hostility from sinners against themselves

good, in order that we may share his holiness. ¹¹Now, discipline always seems painful rather than pleasant at the time, but later it yields the peaceful fruit of righteousness to those who have been trained by it.

12 Therefore lift your drooping hands and strengthen your weak knees, ¹³and make straight paths for your feet, so that what is lame may not be put out of joint, but rather be healed.

Warnings against Rejecting God's Grace

14 Pursue peace with everyone, and the holiness without which no one will see the Lord. ¹⁵See to it that no one fails to obtain the grace of God; that no root of bitterness springs up and causes trouble, and through it many become defiled. ¹⁶See to it that no one becomes like Esau, an immoral and godless person, who sold his birthright for a single meal. ¹⁷You know that later, when he wanted to inher-

*H*olding *Y*ourself in *G*od's *P*resence

FRIDAY

Scripture Reading for Today:
Hebrews 12.5–12

Verse for Today:
Hebrews 12.7

Never give way to the desire to be liberated from your difficulties. This is a privilege, which is from God in order to make you perfect in every virtue. It is a reward and not a punishment, make no doubt of this. What God desires is that you bear this burden patiently, with complete surrender to his holy good pleasure.

Hold your eyes on God and leave the doing to him. That is all the doing you have to worry about, and the only activity which God asks of you and towards which it is he alone who is drawing you.

I may add that it is this that our blessed father [Francis de Sales] would always order me to practice, holding the mind in all simplicity and directness, without act or effort, in that simple gaze upon God and contemplation of God, in total surrender to his will; without a wish to see, or feel, or carry out any work, but merely content to remain in his presence—relaxed, at peace, confident, patient, never inspecting self to see how things are going, nor what one is doing, feeling or enduring. No, you must not inquire what your soul is doing, has done, or will do, nor what may happen to it in any future event or contingency. From this position you must not budge because this sole and single gaze upon God embraces all our duty, especially in a state of suffering. Hold fast to this simple state, and at the instant that you notice your mind drifting away from it, draw yourself back gently, without strain, or looking about, or self-dissection, concerning anything whatever. One thing alone is necessary: It is to have God. In short, then, no matter what is going on, we must hold both our attention and our love on God, not wasting our time in studying what is happening to ourselves, nor what is its cause. Our Lord asks this of us.

—SAINT JEANNE DE CHANTAL

Go to page 1614 for your next devotional reading.

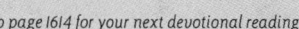

Widow With the Two Coins

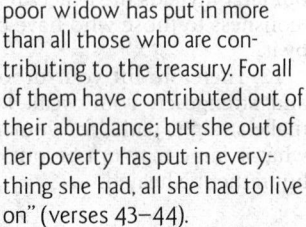

Her Character:
Though extremely poor, she is one of the most great-hearted people in the Bible. Just after warning his disciples to watch out for the teachers of the law who devour widows' houses, Jesus caught sight of her in the temple. He may have called attention to her as a case in point.
Her Sorrow: *To be alone, without a husband to provide for her.*
Her Joy: *To surrender herself to God completely, trusting him to act on her behalf.*

Read Mark 12:41–44

With Passover approaching, the temple was packed with worshipers from all over Israel. Jesus was speaking to his disciples: "Beware of the scribes ... They devour widows' houses and for the sake of appearance say long prayers. They will receive the greater condemnation" (12:38, 40).

Then he sat down opposite the temple treasury, in the Court of the Women. The place was crowded with people dropping their offerings into one of the 13 trumpet-shaped receptacles that hung on the walls. Jesus watched as a widow deposited two small copper coins, less than a day's wages.

Jesus continued, "Truly I tell you, this poor widow has put in more than all those who are contributing to the treasury. For all of them have contributed out of their abundance; but she out of her poverty has put in everything she had, all she had to live on" (verses 43–44).

Here was one of the widows he had just spoken of, pressured, perhaps, by unscrupulous men to give beyond her means. Her faith was such a contrast to their greed.

How easy it would have been for her to conclude that her gift was simply too meager to offer. What need had God for two copper coins anyway? Surely they meant more to her than him.

Perhaps God, in a manner of speaking, did need her offering. Maybe her gesture encouraged his Son, just days away from his passion and death. She had given all she had to live on. Soon, he would give his life. A widow's copper coins, a man's life—everything given for the sake of the kingdom.

Praying With the Widow
With the Two Coins

"Truly I tell you, this poor widow has put in more than all those who are contributing to the treasury. For all of them have contributed out of their abundance; but she out of her poverty has put in everything she had, all she had to live on."—Mark 12.43–44

Praise God: *For judging, not by outward appearances, but as one who sees the heart.*

Offer Thanks: *For blessings of money, time, energy, and emotional resources.*

Confess: *Any tendency to act as though your security depends more on you than it does on God.*

Ask God: *To make you a generous woman with the faith to believe that even small gifts are worth giving.*

Lift Your Heart

This week think of an area of your life that feels particularly empty or impoverished. You may be lonely, financially stretched, worried about the future. Whatever it is, pray about it. Listen for the voice of the Holy Spirit. Is God inviting you to do something to express your trust? What kind of offering would be the most pleasing to him? Once you hear his voice, go ahead and give him what his heart desires.

Father, you are the source of every blessing. This week, help me to give, not only out of my wealth, but out of my poverty. Remind me that I belong to you, body and soul, heart and mind, past, present, and future.

Go to page 1619 for your next devotional reading.

it the blessing, he was rejected, for he found no chance to repent,[r] even though he sought the blessing[s] with tears.

18 You have not come to something[t] that can be touched, a blazing fire, and darkness, and gloom, and a tempest, [19]and the sound of a trumpet, and a voice whose words made the hearers beg that not another word be spoken to them. [20](For they could not endure the order that was given, "If even an animal touches the mountain, it shall be stoned to death." [21]Indeed, so terrifying was the sight that Moses said, "I tremble with fear.") [22]But you have come to Mount Zion and to the city of the living God, the heavenly Jerusalem, and to innumerable angels in festal gathering, [23]and to the assembly[u] of the firstborn who are enrolled in heaven, and to God the judge of all, and to the spirits of the righteous made perfect, [24]and to Jesus, the mediator of a new covenant, and to the sprinkled blood that speaks a better word than the blood of Abel.

25 See that you do not refuse the one who is speaking; for if they did not escape when they refused the one who warned them on earth, how much less will we escape if we reject the one who warns from heaven! [26]At that time his voice shook the earth; but now he has promised, "Yet once more I will shake not only the earth but also the heaven." [27]This phrase, "Yet once more," indicates the removal of what is shaken—that is, created things—so that what cannot be shaken may remain. [28]Therefore, since we are receiving a kingdom that cannot be shaken, let us give thanks, by which we offer to God an acceptable worship with reverence and awe; [29]for indeed our God is a consuming fire.

Service Well-Pleasing to God

13 Let mutual love continue. [2]Do not neglect to show hospitality to strangers, for by doing that some have entertained angels without knowing it. [3]Remember those who are in prison, as though you were in prison with them; those who are being tortured, as though you yourselves were being tortured.[v] [4]Let marriage be held in honor by all, and let the marriage bed be kept undefiled; for God will judge fornicators and adulterers. [5]Keep your lives free from the love of money, and be content with what you

have; for he has said, "I will never leave you or forsake you." [6]So we can say with confidence,

"The Lord is my helper;
    I will not be afraid.
    What can anyone do to me?"

7 Remember your leaders, those who spoke the word of God to you; consider the outcome of their way of life, and imitate their faith. [8]Jesus Christ is the same yesterday and today and forever. [9]Do not be carried away by all kinds of strange teachings; for it is well for the heart to be strengthened by grace, not by regulations about food,[w] which have not benefited those who observe them. [10]We have an altar from which those who officiate in the tent[x] have no right to eat. [11]For the bodies of those animals whose blood is brought into the sanctuary by the high priest as a sacrifice for sin are burned outside the camp. [12]Therefore Jesus also suffered outside the city gate in order to sanctify the people by his own blood. [13]Let us then go to him outside the camp and bear the abuse he endured. [14]For here we have no lasting city, but we are looking for the city that is to come. [15]Through him, then, let us continually offer a sacrifice of praise to God, that is, the fruit of lips that confess his name. [16]Do not neglect to do good and to share what you have, for such sacrifices are pleasing to God.

17 Obey your leaders and submit to them, for they are keeping watch over your souls and will give an account. Let them do this with joy and not with sighing—for that would be harmful to you.

18 Pray for us; we are sure that we have a clear conscience, desiring to act honorably in all things. [19]I urge you all the more to do this, so that I may be restored to you very soon.

Benediction

20 Now may the God of peace, who brought back from the dead our Lord Jesus, the great shepherd of the sheep, by the blood of the eternal covenant, [21]make you complete in everything good so that you may do his will, working among us[y] that which is pleasing in his sight,

r Or no chance to change his father's mind   s Gk it
t Other ancient authorities read a mountain
u Or angels, and to the festal gathering 23and
assembly   v Gk were in the body   w Gk not by
foods   x Or tabernacle   y Other ancient
authorities read you

through Jesus Christ, to whom be the glory forever and ever. Amen.

Final Exhortation and Greetings

22 I appeal to you, brothers and sisters,[z] bear with my word of exhortation, for I have written to you briefly. [23]I want you to know that our brother Timothy has been set free; and if he comes in time, he will be with me when I see you. [24]Greet all your leaders and all the saints. Those from Italy send you greetings. [25]Grace be with all of you.[a]

[z] Gk *brothers*   [a] Other ancient authorities add *Amen*

The Letter of
James

Eusebius, the early church's most prominent historian, called the seven remaining letters found in the New Testament the "Catholic Letters," meaning "catholic" in the sense of "universal." These letters were addressed to a universal audience of believers rather than to a specific group or person like the Pauline letters.

Though this letter could not have come from the apostle James, who died before it was written, it may have been composed by James, the close relative of Jesus who led the Jerusalem council and was martyred in A.D. 62. The letter of James offers a practical guide to Christian living, making no bones about the fact that faith without works is dead. It offers a great deal of helpful teachings:

"The one who doubts is like a wave of the sea, driven and tossed by the wind" (1.6).

"If a brother or sister is naked and lacks daily food, and one of you says to them, 'Go in peace; keep warm and eat your fill,' and yet you do not supply their bodily needs, what is the good of that? So faith by itself, if it has no works, is dead" (2.15–17).

"Resist the devil, and he will flee from you. Draw near to God, and he will draw near to you" (4.7–8).

James 5.13–16 stresses the importance of praying for healing. Verses 14–15 are understood by the Church as a reference to the Sacrament of the Anointing of the Sick.

Salutation

1 James, a servant*a* of God and of the Lord Jesus Christ,

To the twelve tribes in the Dispersion: Greetings.

Faith and Wisdom

2 My brothers and sisters,*b* whenever you face trials of any kind, consider it nothing but joy, 3because you know that the testing of your faith produces endurance; 4and let endurance have its full effect, so that you may be mature and complete, lacking in nothing.

5 If any of you is lacking in wisdom, ask God, who gives to all generously and

a Gk *slave*   *b* Gk *brothers*

ungrudgingly, and it will be given you. ⁶But ask in faith, never doubting, for the one who doubts is like a wave of the sea, driven and tossed by the wind; ⁷, ⁸for the doubter, being double-minded and unstable in every way, must not expect to receive anything from the Lord.

Poverty and Riches

9 Let the believer*c* who is lowly boast in being raised up, ¹⁰and the rich in being brought low, because the rich will disappear like a flower in the field. ¹¹For the sun rises with its scorching heat and withers the field; its flower falls, and its beauty perishes. It is the same way with the rich; in the midst of a busy life, they will wither away.

Trial and Temptation

12 Blessed is anyone who endures temptation. Such a one has stood the test and will receive the crown of life that the Lord*d* has promised to those who love him. ¹³No one, when tempted, should say, "I am being tempted by God"; for God cannot be tempted by evil and he himself tempts no one. ¹⁴But one is tempted by one's own desire, being lured and enticed

by it; ¹⁵then, when that desire has conceived, it gives birth to sin, and that sin, when it is fully grown, gives birth to death. ¹⁶Do not be deceived, my beloved.*e*

17 Every generous act of giving, with every perfect gift, is from above, coming down from the Father of lights, with whom there is no variation or shadow due to change.*f* ¹⁸In fulfillment of his own purpose he gave us birth by the word of truth, so that we would become a kind of first fruits of his creatures.

Hearing and Doing the Word

19 You must understand this, my beloved:*e* let everyone be quick to listen, slow to speak, slow to anger; ²⁰for your anger does not produce God's righteousness. ²¹Therefore rid yourselves of all sordidness and rank growth of wickedness, and welcome with meekness the implanted word that has the power to save your souls.

22 But be doers of the word, and not

c Gk *brother*   *d* Gk *he*; other ancient authorities read *God*   *e* Gk *my beloved brothers*   *f* Other ancient authorities read *variation due to a shadow of turning*

---

*B*e Strong in Trust

MONDAY

Scripture Reading for Today:
James 1.2–8

Verse for Today:
James 1.2

Though we are in such pain, trouble and distress, that it seems to us that we are unable to think of anything except how we are and what we feel, yet as soon as we may, we are to pass lightly over it, and count it as nothing. And why? Because God wills that we should understand that if we know him and love him and reverently fear him, we shall have rest and be at peace. And we shall rejoice in all that he does.

I understood truly that our soul may never find rest in things below, but when it looks through all created things to find its self, it must never remain gazing on its self, but feast on the sight of God its maker who lives within.

He did not say, "You shall not be tempest-tossed; you shall not be work-weary; you shall not be discomforted." But he said, "You shall not be overcome." God wants us to heed these words so that we shall always be strong in trust, both in sorrow and in joy.

—*JULIAN OF NORWICH*

Go to page 1620 for your next devotional reading.

merely hearers who deceive themselves. [23]For if any are hearers of the word and not doers, they are like those who look at themselves[g] in a mirror; [24]for they look at themselves and, on going away, immediately forget what they were like. [25]But those who look into the perfect law, the law of liberty, and persevere, being not hearers who forget but doers who act— they will be blessed in their doing.

26 If any think they are religious, and do not bridle their tongues but deceive their hearts, their religion is worthless. [27]Religion that is pure and undefiled before God, the Father, is this: to care for

orphans and widows in their distress, and to keep oneself unstained by the world.

Warning against Partiality

2 My brothers and sisters,[h] do you with your acts of favoritism really believe in our glorious Lord Jesus Christ?[i] [2]For if a person with gold rings and in fine clothes comes into your assembly, and if a poor person in dirty clothes also comes in, [3]and if you take notice of the one wear-

g Gk at the face of his birth   h Gk My brothers
i Or hold the faith of our glorious Lord Jesus Christ without acts of favoritism

---

Scripture Reading for Today:
James 2.1–9

Verse for Today:
James 2.1

The People We Can't Love

It can easily happen that we pass for very kind people, ever ready to lend a hand or do a good turn, and in our own heart we may think we are. But there will be one or two left out of this benevolent radiance. We shall be courteous to them, for we must not spoil the image we have of ourselves as charitable persons, but we shall be critical, ready to find fault in a discreet way, ready to use them as scapegoats. We shall find it hard to be fair in judgment where they are concerned. We shall come up with rational explanations of why we think as we do, but if we were really honest we would have to admit that in some way these people cut us down to size. In some way they challenge and threaten us. They may seem to undervalue us, perhaps are critical of us, and this makes us feel insecure. We don't like feeling like this so we must find some way of destroying these people—not literally but in so far as they have power over us. We pull them down in our estimation or keep them severely at a distance.

Even the heathen can love those who love them, as our Lord says. His disciples must love their enemies and do them good. Few of us have enemies, but we all have those who hurt us in one way or another, and we can be refusing our love to these. Because we are good people, we don't do outrageous things, and therefore our consciences are kept untroubled. We fail to see the great importance of these small acts of injustice, or attitudes of rejection which we hold. They are sin, and come between us and God. To leave one person out of our love is proof positive—we need no other—that our love for others is not really pure, not the love of Jesus.

—RUTH BURROWS

Go to page 1622 for your next devotional reading.

ing the fine clothes and say, "Have a seat here, please," while to the one who is poor you say, "Stand there," or, "Sit at my feet,"[j] [4]have you not made distinctions among yourselves, and become judges with evil thoughts? [5]Listen, my beloved brothers and sisters.[k] Has not God chosen the poor in the world to be rich in faith and to be heirs of the kingdom that he has promised to those who love him? [6]But you have dishonored the poor. Is it not the rich who oppress you? Is it not they who drag you into court? [7]Is it not they who blaspheme the excellent name that was invoked over you?

[8] You do well if you really fulfill the royal law according to the scripture, "You shall love your neighbor as yourself." [9]But if you show partiality, you commit sin and are convicted by the law as transgressors. [10]For whoever keeps the whole law but fails in one point has become accountable for all of it. [11]For the one who said, "You shall not commit adultery," also said, "You shall not murder." Now if you do not commit adultery but if you murder, you have become a transgressor of the law. [12]So speak and so act as those who are to be judged by the law of liberty. [13]For judgment will be without mercy to anyone who has shown no mercy; mercy triumphs over judgment.

Faith without Works Is Dead

[14] What good is it, my brothers and sisters,[k] if you say you have faith but do not have works? Can faith save you? [15]If a brother or sister is naked and lacks daily food, [16]and one of you says to them, "Go in peace; keep warm and eat your fill," and yet you do not supply their bodily needs, what is the good of that? [17]So faith by itself, if it has no works, is dead.

[18] But someone will say, "You have faith and I have works." Show me your faith apart from your works, and I by my works will show you my faith. [19]You believe that God is one; you do well. Even the demons believe—and shudder. [20]Do you want to be shown, you senseless person, that faith apart from works is barren? [21]Was not our ancestor Abraham justified by works when he offered his son Isaac on the altar? [22]You see that faith was active along with his works, and faith was brought to completion by the works. [23]Thus the scripture was fulfilled that says,

"Abraham believed God, and it was reckoned to him as righteousness," and he was called the friend of God. [24]You see that a person is justified by works and not by faith alone. [25]Likewise, was not Rahab the prostitute also justified by works when she welcomed the messengers and sent them out by another road? [26]For just as the body without the spirit is dead, so faith without works is also dead.

Taming the Tongue

3 Not many of you should become teachers, my brothers and sisters,[k] for you know that we who teach will be judged with greater strictness. [2]For all of us make many mistakes. Anyone who makes no mistakes in speaking is perfect, able to keep the whole body in check with a bridle. [3]If we put bits into the mouths of horses to make them obey us, we guide their whole bodies. [4]Or look at ships: though they are so large that it takes strong winds to drive them, yet they are guided by a very small rudder wherever the will of the pilot directs. [5]So also the tongue is a small member, yet it boasts of great exploits.

How great a forest is set ablaze by a small fire! [6]And the tongue is a fire. The tongue is placed among our members as a world of iniquity; it stains the whole body, sets on fire the cycle of nature,[l] and is itself set on fire by hell.[m] [7]For every species of beast and bird, of reptile and sea creature, can be tamed and has been tamed by the human species, [8]but no one can tame the tongue—a restless evil, full of deadly poison. [9]With it we bless the Lord and Father, and with it we curse those who are made in the likeness of God. [10]From the same mouth come blessing and cursing. My brothers and sisters,[n] this ought not to be so. [11]Does a spring pour forth from the same opening both fresh and brackish water? [12]Can a fig tree, my brothers and sisters,[o] yield olives, or a grapevine figs? No more can salt water yield fresh.

Two Kinds of Wisdom

[13] Who is wise and understanding among you? Show by your good life that your works are done with gentleness born

---

j Gk *Sit under my footstool*   *k* Gk *brothers*   *l* Or *wheel of birth*   *m* Gk *Gehenna*   *n* Gk *My brothers*
o Gk *my brothers*

of wisdom. 14But if you have bitter envy
and selfish ambition in your hearts, do
not be boastful and false to the truth.
15Such wisdom does not come down from
above, but is earthly, unspiritual, devilish.
16For where there is envy and selfish ambition, there will also be disorder and
wickedness of every kind. 17But the wisdom from above is first pure, then peaceable, gentle, willing to yield, full of mercy
and good fruits, without a trace of partiality or hypocrisy. 18And a harvest of righteousness is sown in peace for[p] those
who make peace.

Friendship with the World

4 Those conflicts and disputes among
you, where do they come from? Do
they not come from your cravings that are
at war within you? 2You want something
and do not have it; so you commit murder. And you covet[q] something and cannot obtain it; so you engage in disputes
and conflicts. You do not have, because
you do not ask. 3You ask and do not receive, because you ask wrongly, in order
to spend what you get on your pleasures.
4Adulterers! Do you not know that friendship with the world is enmity with God?
Therefore whoever wishes to be a friend of
the world becomes an enemy of God. 5Or
do you suppose that it is for nothing that
the scripture says, "God[r] yearns jealous-
ly for the spirit that he has made to dwell
in us"? 6But he gives all the more grace;
therefore it says,

"God opposes the proud,
but gives grace to the humble."

7Submit yourselves therefore to God. Resist the devil, and he will flee from you.
8Draw near to God, and he will draw near
to you. Cleanse your hands, you sinners,
and purify your hearts, you double-

[p] Or *by* [q] Or *you murder and you covet*
[r] Gk *He*

Words That Bless

WEDNESDAY

Scripture Reading for Today: *James 3.1–12*

Verse for Today: *James 3.10*

To control speech is to recover its sacredness, to understand that sometimes the words of an innocent "joke," proffered without even thinking, can have disastrous results, can be the "last straw" that pushes a person into ultimate despair and destruction. But our words can also be a witness. A casual conversation across the desk with a colleague can do more for communicating a vision of life, an attitude toward other people or toward work, than formal preaching. It can sow the seeds of a question, of the possibility of a different approach to life, the desire to know more. We have no idea how, in fact, we constantly influence one another by our speech, by the very "tonality" of our personality. And ultimately men and women are converted to God not because someone was able to give brilliant explanations, but because they saw in that person a light, joy, depth, seriousness, and love which alone reveal the presence and the power of God in the world.

As Matthew 12.36–37 says, we shall be judged by our words. We must think about what God's words in the Bible say. And out of this thinking, we must speak words of tenderness, love, pity, compassion, and gentleness because we are men and women of faith; we are Christians.

—*CATHERINE DOHERTY*

Go to page 1623 for your next devotional reading.

minded. [9]Lament and mourn and weep. Let your laughter be turned into mourning and your joy into dejection. [10]Humble yourselves before the Lord, and he will exalt you.

Warning against Judging Another

11 Do not speak evil against one another, brothers and sisters.[s] Whoever speaks evil against another or judges another, speaks evil against the law and judges the law; but if you judge the law, you are not a doer of the law but a judge. [12]There is one lawgiver and judge who is able to save and to destroy. So who, then, are you to judge your neighbor?

Boasting about Tomorrow

13 Come now, you who say, "Today or tomorrow we will go to such and such a town and spend a year there, doing business and making money." [14]Yet you do not even know what tomorrow will bring. What is your life? For you are a mist that appears for a little while and then vanishes. [15]Instead you ought to say, "If the

[s] Gk brothers

THURSDAY

Scripture Reading for Today:
James 4.7–10

Verse for Today:
James 4.7

The Source of Discord

In a collection of children's letters to God compiled by David Heller, I came across this one from a nine-year-old. "To God, How do you know Satan when you see him? Can you give me any clues?" The letter is signed, "Your loyal little girl, Charlene." We do well to follow this child's lead in asking God's help to identify the sources of evil. For if we recognize Satan, the "ruler of the world," we have a much better chance of locking him outside our city gates.

The Church recognizes Satan as "the angel who opposes God" and " 'throws himself across' God's plan and his work of salvation accomplished in Christ." Satan is the "father of lies" through whom sin and death entered the world. At his "definitive defeat" at the end of time, the world will be liberated from sin and death (*Catechism of the Catholic Church*, 2851-52).

What clues do we look for in spotting this arch-deceiver, this unholy adversary, this thorn in our collective side? We will know him by his bulging sack of glossy possessions, vain ambitions, useless fears, seductive control buttons. He works under cover of darkness, and the fruit of his labors is discord. He sets husband against wife, parent against child, black against white, nation against nation, one faith against another.

We oppose Satan best by sticking together, closing ranks around God, our caring Father. "Resist the devil," Saint James advises, "and he will flee from you." Together we raise our shield of prayer against the evil that has been (bombing of innocent people, the Holocaust), that is now (the arms race, child abuse) and that shall be (environmental devastation, media-fed violence). As Church, we plead for the peace the world cannot give.

—GLORIA HUTCHINSON

Go to page 1624 for your next devotional reading.

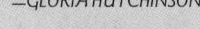

Lord wishes, we will live and do this or that." ¹⁶As it is, you boast in your arrogance; all such boasting is evil. ¹⁷Anyone, then, who knows the right thing to do and fails to do it, commits sin.

Warning to Rich Oppressors

5 Come now, you rich people, weep and wail for the miseries that are coming to you. ²Your riches have rotted, and your clothes are moth-eaten. ³Your gold and silver have rusted, and their rust will be evidence against you, and it will eat your flesh like fire. You have laid up treasure*ᵗ* for the last days. ⁴Listen! The wages of the laborers who mowed your fields, which you kept back by fraud, cry out, and the cries of the harvesters have reached the ears of the Lord of hosts. ⁵You have lived on the earth in luxury and in pleasure; you have fattened your hearts in a day of slaughter. ⁶You have condemned and murdered the righteous one, who does not resist you.

ᵗ Or will eat your flesh, since you have stored up fire

Healing Prayer

I learned to pray with another for healing through my friend, Alex. I had never thought of myself as having a gift for physical healing, and I felt inadequate when Alex asked me to pray for his chronic migraine headaches. As I put my hands on his head, I recalled the loving presence of God that I had always sensed in the created world. Since early childhood, I had frequently experienced leaves, flowers, blades of grass as luminous with the presence of God. It seemed to me that this luminous, loving presence must also fill the cells of our bodies, and so I imagined this presence flowing through the veins, arteries, muscles, and nerves of Alex's head. To my astonishment, Alex's migraine headaches were often relieved when I prayed for him. He told me once, "I think the reason my migraines go away when you pray is because you love every cell for its own sake."

When Jesus went to heal Jairus' daughter, he brought with him his friends Peter, James, and John, and also the girl's parents (see Luke 8.49–56). Perhaps he chose these people because they were the ones who especially loved either him or the little girl.

Sometimes when a sick person asks us for prayer, we, too, choose those who can love that person the most. We usually ask three people to lead the prayer: the sick person's best friend, a person who is suffering from the same sickness, and a person who has been healed of that sickness. We choose these people because they have a natural compassion for the one who is sick. As these three people allow the love of Jesus to move through them, often they, too, are healed. We find that healing occurs more often where there is more love because Jesus, the source of all healing, is love.

—*SHEILA FABRICANT LINN*

Go to page 1628 for your next devotional reading.

FRIDAY

Scripture Reading for Today:
James 5.13–18

Verse for Today:
James 5.15

Patience in Suffering

7 Be patient, therefore, beloved,[u] until the coming of the Lord. The farmer waits for the precious crop from the earth, being patient with it until it receives the early and the late rains. [8]You also must be patient. Strengthen your hearts, for the coming of the Lord is near.[v] [9]Beloved,[w] do not grumble against one another, so that you may not be judged. See, the Judge is standing at the doors! [10]As an example of suffering and patience, beloved,[u] take the prophets who spoke in the name of the Lord. [11]Indeed we call blessed those who showed endurance. You have heard of the endurance of Job, and you have seen the purpose of the Lord, how the Lord is compassionate and merciful.

12 Above all, my beloved,[u] do not swear, either by heaven or by earth or by any other oath, but let your "Yes" be yes and your "No" be no, so that you may not fall under condemnation.

The Prayer of Faith

13 Are any among you suffering? They should pray. Are any cheerful? They should sing songs of praise. [14]Are any among you sick? They should call for the elders of the church and have them pray over them, anointing them with oil in the name of the Lord. [15]The prayer of faith will save the sick, and the Lord will raise them up; and anyone who has committed sins will be forgiven. [16]Therefore confess your sins to one another, and pray for one another, so that you may be healed. The prayer of the righteous is powerful and effective. [17]Elijah was a human being like us, and he prayed fervently that it might not rain, and for three years and six months it did not rain on the earth. [18]Then he prayed again, and the heaven gave rain and the earth yielded its harvest.

19 My brothers and sisters,[x] if anyone among you wanders from the truth and is brought back by another, [20]you should know that whoever brings back a sinner from wandering will save the sinner's[y] soul from death and will cover a multitude of sins.

u Gk brothers   v Or is at hand   w Gk Brothers
x Gk My brothers   y Gk his

1 Peter

The apostle Peter has traditionally been considered the author of this letter, though some scholars have called his authorship into question. Regardless of whether Peter wrote the letter or employed a secretary to write it, or whether it was written by a disciple of Peter's after his death, the Church has always considered it inspired.

Written to Christian communities in Asia Minor (modern Turkey) who were either experiencing or likely to experience persecution, it encourages them to remain faithful to Christ, reminding them that through the resurrection of Jesus Christ they have been given an "inheritance that is imperishable, undefiled, and unfading" (1.4). It offers great comfort to those who are no longer in sync with their culture because they belong to the community of believers.

First Peter also offers practical advice for how Christians should live. For instance, it instructs women to win their husbands to Christ by their exemplary conduct. It also encourages them to focus not on outward appearance but on developing the inward beauty of a gentle and quiet spirit.

Salutation

1 Peter, an apostle of Jesus Christ,
To the exiles of the Dispersion in Pontus, Galatia, Cappadocia, Asia, and Bithynia, [2]who have been chosen and destined by God the Father and sanctified by the Spirit to be obedient to Jesus Christ and to be sprinkled with his blood:

May grace and peace be yours in abundance.

A Living Hope

3 Blessed be the God and Father of our Lord Jesus Christ! By his great mercy he has given us a new birth into a living hope through the resurrection of Jesus Christ from the dead, [4]and into an inheritance that is imperishable, undefiled, and unfading, kept in heaven for you, [5]who are being protected by the power of God through faith for a salvation ready to be revealed in the last time. [6]In this you rejoice,[a] even if now for a little while you have had to suffer various trials, [7]so that the genuineness of your faith—being more precious than gold that, though perishable, is tested by fire—may be found to result in praise and glory and honor when Jesus Christ is revealed. [8]Although you

[a] Or Rejoice in this

have not seen[b] him, you love him; and even though you do not see him now, you believe in him and rejoice with an indescribable and glorious joy, [9]for you are receiving the outcome of your faith, the salvation of your souls.

10 Concerning this salvation, the prophets who prophesied of the grace that was to be yours made careful search and inquiry, [11]inquiring about the person or time that the Spirit of Christ within them indicated when it testified in advance to the sufferings destined for Christ and the subsequent glory. [12]It was revealed to them that they were serving not themselves but you, in regard to the things that have now been announced to you through those who brought you good news by the Holy Spirit sent from heaven—things into which angels long to look!

A Call to Holy Living

13 Therefore prepare your minds for action;[c] discipline yourselves; set all your hope on the grace that Jesus Christ will bring you when he is revealed. [14]Like obedient children, do not be conformed to the desires that you formerly had in ignorance. [15]Instead, as he who called you is holy, be holy yourselves in all your conduct; [16]for it is written, "You shall be holy, for I am holy."

17 If you invoke as Father the one who judges all people impartially according to their deeds, live in reverent fear during the time of your exile. [18]You know that you were ransomed from the futile ways inherited from your ancestors, not with perishable things like silver or gold, [19]but with the precious blood of Christ, like that of a lamb without defect or blemish. [20]He was destined before the foundation of the world, but was revealed at the end of the ages for your sake. [21]Through him you have come to trust in God, who raised him from the dead and gave him glory, so that your faith and hope are set on God.

22 Now that you have purified your souls by your obedience to the truth[d] so that you have genuine mutual love, love one another deeply[e] from the heart.[f] [23]You have been born anew, not of perishable but of imperishable seed, through the living and enduring word of God.[g] [24]For

"All flesh is like grass
    and all its glory like the flower
       of grass.
The grass withers,
    and the flower falls,
[25] but the word of the Lord endures
       forever."
That word is the good news that was announced to you.

The Living Stone and a Chosen People

2 Rid yourselves, therefore, of all malice, and all guile, insincerity, envy, and all slander. [2]Like newborn infants, long for the pure, spiritual milk, so that by it you may grow into salvation— [3]if indeed you have tasted that the Lord is good.

4 Come to him, a living stone, though rejected by mortals yet chosen and precious in God's sight, and [5]like living stones, let yourselves be built[h] into a spiritual house, to be a holy priesthood, to offer spiritual sacrifices acceptable to God through Jesus Christ. [6]For it stands in scripture:
"See, I am laying in Zion a stone,
    a cornerstone chosen and
       precious;
and whoever believes in him[i] will
    not be put to shame."
[7]To you then who believe, he is precious; but for those who do not believe,
"The stone that the builders rejected
    has become the very head of
       the corner,"
[8]and
"A stone that makes them stumble,
    and a rock that makes them fall."
They stumble because they disobey the word, as they were destined to do.

9 But you are a chosen race, a royal priesthood, a holy nation, God's own people,[j] in order that you may proclaim the mighty acts of him who called you out of darkness into his marvelous light.
10 Once you were not a people,
    but now you are God's people;

---

b Other ancient authorities read *known*   c Gk *gird up the loins of your mind*   d Other ancient authorities add *through the Spirit*   e Or *constantly*   f Other ancient authorities read *a pure heart*   g Or *through the word of the living and enduring God*   h Or *you yourselves are being built*   i Or *it*   j Gk *a people for his possession*

Mary Magdalene

Her Name May Mean
"Bitterness"

THE STORY OF A WOMAN

Her Character:
Though mistakenly characterized as a prostitute in many popular writings, the Bible only says that she was tormented by seven demons. She probably suffered a serious mental or physical illness from which Jesus delivered her. She is a beautiful example of a woman whose life was poured out in response to God's extravagant grace.
Her Sorrow: *To watch Jesus' agony at Calvary.*
Her Joy: *To have been the first witness to the resurrection.*

Read John 19.16–42; 20.1–18

She made her way through the shadows to the garden tomb, grateful for the darkness that shrouded her tears. How, she wondered, could the world go on as though nothing had happened? How could the mountains keep from crashing down, the sky resist falling? Had no one noticed that the world had collapsed two days ago?

For the last three years, she had followed the rabbi across Galilee and Judea, providing for him out of her own small purse. Wherever they went, she had felt privileged to tell her story: how Jesus had driven out seven demons, restoring her sanity.

How could Mary not love such a man? How could she not want to do everything for him? She had thought she was living in heaven—to be close to Jesus; to witness healing after healing; to be stirred, surprised, and challenged by his teaching. This indeed was joy to a woman unaccustomed to joy.

But suddenly the religious leaders of Jerusalem had arrested him, turning him over to Pilate, whose soldiers mocked and whipped him nearly to death. His body had hung naked on a Roman cross.

Mary waited through the hours of his agony, unable to look at the spectacle before her, yet unable to turn away. However hideous his suffering, she needed to be near him.

Now that the Sabbath was over, she approached the grave, intending to anoint Jesus' body. But how could she roll away the massive stone? To her surprise the tomb was already open. Strips of linen were lying on the floor and the burial cloth that had been wrapped around Jesus' head was folded up by itself. What had they done with his body, she wondered. To be cheated of this last chance of touching and caring for him was more than she could bear.

So she stood outside the tomb weeping. Then, bending over, she looked inside. Two creatures in white sat on the stony shelf where the body had been laid. "Woman, why are you weeping?" they asked.

"They have taken away my Lord," she said, "and I do not know where they have laid him." Then she turned and saw a man studying her.

"Woman," he said, "why are you weeping? Whom are you looking for?"

Mistaking him for the gardener, she pleaded, "Sir, if you have carried him away, tell me where you have laid him, and I will take him away."

"Mary!" Jesus said.

Startled, she cried out, "Rabbouni!" (meaning Teacher), and then she fell to the ground in awe. The risen Jesus appeared, not to rulers and kings, nor even first of all to his male disciples, but to a woman whose love had held her at the cross and led her to the grave. Mary of Magdala, a person who had been afflicted by demons, whose testimony would not have held up in court because she was a woman, was the first witness of the resurrection. Once again, God had revealed himself to the lowly, and it would only be the humble whose hearing was sharp enough to perceive the message of his love.

Praying With Mary Magdalene

Jesus said to her, "Mary!" She turned and said to him in Hebrew, "Rabbouni!" (which means Teacher).—John 20.16

> **Praise God:** For the death and resurrection of Jesus, his Son and our Savior.
>
> **Offer Thanks:** That the Father has revealed his love so powerfully in Jesus.
>
> **Confess:** Your doubts about God's power or willingness to deliver you from some evil in your life.
>
> **Ask God:** For the grace of deliverance.

Lift Your Heart

One day this week, set your alarm clock so that you wake up a half hour before dawn. Find a spot where you can watch the sunrise. In the early morning shadows, tell God about some area of darkness in your own life or in the life of someone you love. Perhaps it's an illness, a persistent sin, loneliness, a troubled marriage, an addiction, or a wayward child. Whatever it is, surrender it by imagining yourself placing it in the garden tomb next to the body of Jesus. As the sun rises, meditate on that first Easter morning and remember that when Jesus walked out of the tomb, you walked out with him. Ask God for the faith to wait and watch for his delivering power.

Lord, make me a woman like Mary Magdalene, who follows you not because of a legalistic understanding of her faith, but because of an overwhelming sense of gratitude and love for your extravagant grace. Help me surrender my darkness. Flood me with the light of your presence.

Go to page 1630 for your next devotional reading.

once you had not received mercy,
  but now you have received mercy.

Live as Servants of God

11 Beloved, I urge you as aliens and exiles to abstain from the desires of the flesh that wage war against the soul. 12Conduct yourselves honorably among the Gentiles, so that, though they malign you as evildoers, they may see your hon-

orable deeds and glorify God when he comes to judge.[k]

13 For the Lord's sake accept the authority of every human institution,[l] whether of the emperor as supreme, 14or of governors, as sent by him to punish

[k] Gk *God on the day of visitation*   [l] Or *every institution ordained for human beings*

What Is a Saint?

MONDAY

Scripture Reading
for Today:
1 Peter 2.4–10

Verse for Today:
1 Peter 2.9

Saints, according to Scripture, are simply people whom God has chosen for holiness. "You are a chosen race, a royal priesthood, a holy nation."

When most of us think of saints, though, we think of people that the church has officially recognized as outstanding examples of holiness—people that I, for one, am definitely unlike. Some are bruised and bloody. Some have arrows stuck in them until they look like porcupines. Some, oblivious to the world, are lost in rapturous prayer. All of them are dead. What do these certified saints have in common with me, or the rest of the people of God? The key word, I think, is faithfulness. Throughout our lives, God repeatedly calls us to be faithful—to keep the promises our parents and godparents made on our behalf when we were baptized, to reject sin, to believe in and follow Jesus Christ. For Saint Hippolytus of Rome, this meant dying in exile. For Saint Polycarp of Smyrna, it meant being burned at the stake at age 86. For Saint Teresa of Avila, it meant standing up to bishops and inquisitors.

Faithfulness, however, is normally not that dramatic. For my father, Saint Norval of Wheaton, it meant continuing to pray, serve, and rejoice even when so stricken by Alzheimer's that he no longer recognized my mother. For my friend Saint Lucy of Los Angeles, it means patiently teaching inner-city junior-high students, loving them, and listening to them day after day without ever telling them that a rare neurological disorder could at any moment rob her of her mind or her life. For my children Saints Byron and Molly of Houston, it means eight hours or more a day of work they do not especially like so that they can support the children they love very much—and then spending time with those children in the evening when their energy is nearly used up. For my former student Saint Betty of Redlands, it means daily visits to her stroke-impaired father in a nursing home. Sainthood means faithfully doing what has to be done.

—LAVONNE NEFF

Go to page 1632 for your next devotional reading.

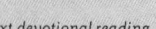

those who do wrong and to praise those who do right. [15]For it is God's will that by doing right you should silence the ignorance of the foolish. [16]As servants[m] of God, live as free people, yet do not use your freedom as a pretext for evil. [17]Honor everyone. Love the family of believers.[n] Fear God. Honor the emperor.

The Example of Christ's Suffering

18 Slaves, accept the authority of your masters with all deference, not only those who are kind and gentle but also those who are harsh. [19]For it is a credit to you if, being aware of God, you endure pain while suffering unjustly. [20]If you endure when you are beaten for doing wrong, what credit is that? But if you endure when you do right and suffer for it, you have God's approval. [21]For to this you have been called, because Christ also suffered for you, leaving you an example, so that you should follow in his steps.
[22] "He committed no sin,
    and no deceit was found in
        his mouth."
[23]When he was abused, he did not return abuse; when he suffered, he did not threaten; but he entrusted himself to the one who judges justly. [24]He himself bore our sins in his body on the cross,[o] so that, free from sins, we might live for righteousness; by his wounds[p] you have been healed. [25]For you were going astray like sheep, but now you have returned to the shepherd and guardian of your souls.

Wives and Husbands

3 Wives, in the same way, accept the authority of your husbands, so that, even if some of them do not obey the word, they may be won over without a word by their wives' conduct, [2]when they see the purity and reverence of your lives. [3]Do not adorn yourselves outwardly by braiding your hair, and by wearing gold ornaments or fine clothing; [4]rather, let your adornment be the inner self with the lasting beauty of a gentle and quiet spirit, which is very precious in God's sight. [5]It was in this way long ago that the holy women who hoped in God used to adorn themselves by accepting the authority of their husbands. [6]Thus Sarah obeyed Abraham and called him lord. You have become her daughters as long as you do what is good and never let fears alarm you.

7 Husbands, in the same way, show consideration for your wives in your life together, paying honor to the woman as the weaker sex,[q] since they too are also heirs of the gracious gift of life—so that nothing may hinder your prayers.

Suffering for Doing Right

8 Finally, all of you, have unity of spirit, sympathy, love for one another, a tender heart, and a humble mind. [9]Do not repay evil for evil or abuse for abuse; but, on the contrary, repay with a blessing. It is for this that you were called—that you might inherit a blessing. [10]For
    "Those who desire life
        and desire to see good days,
    let them keep their tongues
            from evil
        and their lips from speaking
            deceit;
[11] let them turn away from evil and do
            good;
    let them seek peace and pursue it.
[12] For the eyes of the Lord are on
            the righteous,
        and his ears are open to
            their prayer.
    But the face of the Lord is against
        those who do evil."
13 Now who will harm you if you are eager to do what is good? [14]But even if you do suffer for doing what is right, you are blessed. Do not fear what they fear,[r] and do not be intimidated, [15]but in your hearts sanctify Christ as Lord. Always be ready to make your defense to anyone who demands from you an accounting for the hope that is in you; [16]yet do it with gentleness and reverence.[s] Keep your conscience clear, so that, when you are maligned, those who abuse you for your good conduct in Christ may be put to shame. [17]For it is better to suffer for doing good, if suffering should be God's will, than to suffer for doing evil. [18]For Christ also suffered[t] for sins once for all, the righteous for the unrighteous, in order to bring you[u] to God. He was put to death in the flesh, but made alive in the spirit, [19]in which also he went and made a proclamation to the spirits in prison, [20]who in

m Gk slaves   n Gk Love the brotherhood   o Or carried up our sins in his body to the tree
p Gk bruise   q Gk vessel   r Gk their fear   s Or respect   t Other ancient authorities read died
u Other ancient authorities read us

former times did not obey, when God waited patiently in the days of Noah, during the building of the ark, in which a few, that is, eight persons, were saved through water. ²¹And baptism, which this prefigured, now saves you—not as a removal of dirt from the body, but as an appeal to God for ᵛ a good conscience, through the resurrection of Jesus Christ, ²²who has gone into heaven and is at the right hand of God, with angels, authorities, and powers made subject to him.

Good Stewards of God's Grace

4 Since therefore Christ suffered in the flesh, ʷ arm yourselves also with the same intention (for whoever has suffered in the flesh has finished with sin), ²so as to live for the rest of your earthly life ˣ no longer by human desires but by the will of God. ³You have already spent enough time in doing what the Gentiles like to do, living in licentiousness, passions, drunkenness, revels, carousing, and lawless idolatry. ⁴They are surprised that you no longer join them in the same excesses of dissipation, and so they blaspheme. ʸ ⁵But they will have to give an accounting

ᵛ Or *a pledge to God from*   ʷ Other ancient authorities add *for us*; others, *for you*   ˣ Gk *rest of the time in the flesh*   ʸ Or *they malign you*

TUESDAY

Scripture Reading
for Today:
1 Peter 3.1–7

Verses for Today:
1 Peter 3.3–4

*I*nner Beauty

A few weeks ago at a conference, a woman said to me, "You have such a gentle spirit." I was so surprised [that] I wanted to look around for my mother. I've always considered Mom a gentle soul, and I've loved her for it, but never thought that quality would describe me. Especially in work situations, I've been the more assertive, pushy type.

"Who, me?" I answered awkwardly, and if that woman should happen to read this book, I'm openly apologizing to her. I should have said, "thank you."

A few weeks later at a friend's house she said to me, "Judy, there's a real gentleness about you these days," and she meant it as a compliment. Naomi has seen me at my worst, and I couldn't slough off her observation. On the drive home I thought, *Well, maybe I'm finally letting God shine through.* I hadn't been aware of this "gentling," but that is how God works: As we obey what he's telling us, he decorates our character with spiritual beauty.

As God has taught me about surrender, he repeatedly has asked me to relinquish the things I think are best for me—the things that give me identity—and replace them with his purposes and character traits. He's spotlighted how I've patterned my character after the world's standards rather than his, and perhaps that's why I've had to adjust to being called gentle. In the world's eyes, especially in the business world, gentleness is often thought of as wimpy, but God says, "the lasting beauty of a gentle and quiet spirit . . . is very precious in God's sight" (1 Peter 3.4). Gentleness is one of the fruits of the Holy Spirit.

—*JUDITH COUCHMAN*

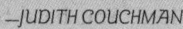

Go to page 1633 for your next devotional reading.

to him who stands ready to judge the living and the dead. ⁶For this is the reason the gospel was proclaimed even to the dead, so that, though they had been judged in the flesh as everyone is judged, they might live in the spirit as God does.

7 The end of all things is near;ᶻ therefore be serious and discipline yourselves for the sake of your prayers. ⁸Above all, maintain constant love for one another, for love covers a multitude of sins. ⁹Be hospitable to one another without complaining. ¹⁰Like good stewards of the manifold grace of God, serve one another with whatever gift each of you has received. ¹¹Whoever speaks must do so as one speaking the very words of God; whoever serves must do so with the strength that God supplies, so that God may be glorified in all things through Jesus Christ.

To him belong the glory and the power forever and ever. Amen.

Suffering as a Christian

12 Beloved, do not be surprised at the fiery ordeal that is taking place among you to test you, as though something strange were happening to you. ¹³But rejoice insofar as you are sharing Christ's sufferings, so that you may also be glad and shout for joy when his glory is revealed. ¹⁴If you are reviled for the name of Christ, you are blessed, because the spirit of glory,ᵃ which is the Spirit of God, is resting on you.ᵇ ¹⁵But let none of you suffer as a murderer, a thief, a criminal, or

z Or *is at hand*   a Other ancient authorities add *and of power*   b Other ancient authorities add *On their part he is blasphemed, but on your part he is glorified*

Let Your Love Be Intense

Scripture Reading for Today:
1 Peter 4.7–11

Verse for Today:
1 Peter 4.8

My friend Laurie told me how, years ago, her husband experienced a peculiar brain disorder that left him unable to feel or express the emotion of love. Laurie kept right on loving him even though he lacked the capacity to show love for her. After nearly two years, he recovered. Was it due to medication—or to the power of her unconditional love? Laurie truly lived the Saint Francis prayer—the part that says, "Help me to love, not to be loved." Today, I say that prayer in new humility, wondering if I could love as Laurie did.

Think about your close relationships. Have you unconsciously created a quid-pro-quo kind of love (I'll do for you, but only as long as you do for me)? For a week, do more for another than that person does for you, and notice how you feel about it. Resentful? Put upon? Pray the Saint Francis prayer, concentrating on the last lines:

O Divine Master, grant that I may not so much seek
to be consoled . . . as to console;
to be understood . . . as to understand;
to be loved . . . as to love.
For it is in giving that we receive,
in pardoning that we are pardoned,
in dying that we are born to eternal life. Amen.

—*BARBARA BARTOCCI*

Go to page 1636 for your next devotional reading.

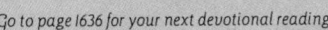

even as a mischief maker. [16]Yet if any of you suffers as a Christian, do not consider it a disgrace, but glorify God because you bear this name. [17]For the time has come for judgment to begin with the household of God; if it begins with us, what will be the end for those who do not obey the gospel of God? [18]And

"If it is hard for the righteous
    to be saved,
  what will become of the ungodly
    and the sinners?"

[19]Therefore, let those suffering in accordance with God's will entrust themselves to a faithful Creator, while continuing to do good.

Tending the Flock of God

5 Now as an elder myself and a witness of the sufferings of Christ, as well as one who shares in the glory to be revealed, I exhort the elders among you [2]to tend the flock of God that is in your charge, exercising the oversight,[c] not under compulsion but willingly, as God would have you do it[d]—not for sordid gain but eagerly. [3]Do not lord it over those in your charge, but be examples to the flock. [4]And when the chief shepherd appears, you will win the crown of glory that never fades away. [5]In the same way, you who are younger must accept the authority of the elders.[e] And all of you must clothe yourselves with humility in your dealings with one another, for

"God opposes the proud,
  but gives grace to the humble."

[6] Humble yourselves therefore under the mighty hand of God, so that he may exalt you in due time. [7]Cast all your anxiety on him, because he cares for you. [8]Discipline yourselves, keep alert.[f] Like a roaring lion your adversary the devil prowls around, looking for someone to devour. [9]Resist him, steadfast in your faith, for you know that your brothers and sisters[g] in all the world are undergoing the same kinds of suffering. [10]And after you have suffered for a little while, the God of all grace, who has called you to his eternal glory in Christ, will himself restore, support, strengthen, and establish you. [11]To him be the power forever and ever. Amen.

Final Greetings and Benediction

[12] Through Silvanus, whom I consider a faithful brother, I have written this short letter to encourage you and to testify that this is the true grace of God. Stand fast in it. [13]Your sister church[h] in Babylon, chosen together with you, sends you greetings; and so does my son Mark. [14]Greet one another with a kiss of love.

Peace to all of you who are in Christ.[i]

---

c Other ancient authorities lack *exercising the oversight*   d Other ancient authorities lack *as God would have you do it*   e Or *of those who are older*   f Or *be vigilant*   g Gk *your brotherhood*   h Gk *She who is*   i Other ancient authorities add *Amen*

2 Peter

The early church was slow to accept Peter as the author of this letter, and many modern scholars believe someone else may have written it sometime after Peter's death, perhaps relying on his sermons. If so, the writer was not committing an act of literary fraud but was merely following a common literary convention by ascribing the piece to a person held in high esteem.

Second Peter warns against false teachers who promote moral laxity and those who scoff at the belief that Christ will come again. It must have been difficult for the readers of this letter, especially in light of the persecutions many Christians faced, to continue to believe in the second coming when they had expected Christ's imminent return.

Second Peter 3.8–9 contains a marvelous reminder for all of us: "But do not ignore this one fact, beloved, that with the Lord one day is like a thousand years, and a thousand years are like one day. The Lord is not slow about his promise, as some think of slowness, but is patient with you, not wanting any to perish, but all to come to repentance." Jesus will come again, but not according to our timetable. No one can know the day or hour, but each of us can live as though today might be the day.

Salutation

1 Simeon[a] Peter, a servant[b] and apostle of Jesus Christ,
To those who have received a faith as precious as ours through the righteousness of our God and Savior Jesus Christ:[c]

2 May grace and peace be yours in abundance in the knowledge of God and of Jesus our Lord.

The Christian's Call and Election

3 His divine power has given us everything needed for life and godliness, through the knowledge of him who called us by[d] his own glory and goodness. 4Thus he has given us, through these things, his precious and very great promises, so that through them you may escape from the corruption that is in the world because of lust, and may become participants of the divine nature. 5For this very reason, you must make every effort to support your faith with goodness, and good-

a Other ancient authorities read *Simon*   b Gk *slave*   c Or *of our God and the Savior Jesus Christ*   d Other ancient authorities read *through*

ness with knowledge, ⁶and knowledge with self-control, and self-control with endurance, and endurance with godliness, ⁷and godliness with mutual*ᵉ* affection, and mutual*ᵉ* affection with love. ⁸For if

these things are yours and are increasing among you, they keep you from being ineffective and unfruitful in the knowledge

ᵉ Gk brotherly

Encouragement

THURSDAY

Scripture Reading
for Today:
2 Peter 1.3–11

Verse for Today:
2 Peter 1.7

Moving from dutiful "devotion" to heartfelt "mutual affection and love" transformed this campus ministry worker's problem-oriented approach to the young women she was counseling.

"Mary: problem with anger"; "Sonja: problem communicating." My approach was comparable to the mentality doctors can develop toward their patients ("Here comes Mrs. O'Brien—lower backache"). For the most part, that was the mentality I had about my own life too.

Then the Lord showed me something. I started to think about what I had experienced in the six or seven years since I had begun a new life as a Christian in college. What I saw startled me. God related to me as a person, his daughter, someone he had called by name and loved personally. Sure, I had problems; but that wasn't what he focused on. He wanted to work on my problems, but even more, he wanted me to know his personal love, to know how pleasing I was to him.

This realization had a tremendous impact on my relationship with God and also with the women I was caring for. I began to think about myself as a sister to these women. A sister is so much more than a counselor. She is a friend, someone who encourages, who rejoices with you when something great happens, who mourns with you in your sadness. She is there to help you with your problems, but even more, to help you become the beautiful woman of God you were meant to be, and to realize how wonderful you are already.

I started talking with each of the women about the strengths each one had, the kinds of things she could do well, what things I loved about the way she was. I put aside my goals and programs and started simply loving her as an older sister would a younger sister. Sometimes the Lord would want me to help her with her problems, but always in the context of personal friendship.

I came to delight in spending time with these women. What a privilege to see others as God sees them, to have the veil of problems removed from my eyes so I can see the image of God that they are!

—DORCEE CLAREY

Go to page 1638 for your next devotional reading.

of our Lord Jesus Christ. [9]For anyone who lacks these things is short-sighted and blind, and is forgetful of the cleansing of past sins. [10]Therefore, brothers and sisters,[f] be all the more eager to confirm your call and election, for if you do this, you will never stumble. [11]For in this way, entry into the eternal kingdom of our Lord and Savior Jesus Christ will be richly provided for you.

12 Therefore I intend to keep on reminding you of these things, though you know them already and are established in the truth that has come to you. [13]I think it right, as long as I am in this body,[g] to refresh your memory, [14]since I know that my death[h] will come soon, as indeed our Lord Jesus Christ has made clear to me. [15]And I will make every effort so that after my departure you may be able at any time to recall these things.

Eyewitnesses of Christ's Glory

16 For we did not follow cleverly devised myths when we made known to you the power and coming of our Lord Jesus Christ, but we had been eyewitnesses of his majesty. [17]For he received honor and glory from God the Father when that voice was conveyed to him by the Majestic Glory, saying, "This is my Son, my Beloved,[i] with whom I am well pleased." [18]We ourselves heard this voice come from heaven, while we were with him on the holy mountain.

19 So we have the prophetic message more fully confirmed. You will do well to be attentive to this as to a lamp shining in a dark place, until the day dawns and the morning star rises in your hearts. [20]First of all you must understand this, that no prophecy of scripture is a matter of one's own interpretation, [21]because no prophecy ever came by human will, but men and women moved by the Holy Spirit spoke from God.[j]

False Prophets and Their Punishment

2 But false prophets also arose among the people, just as there will be false teachers among you, who will secretly bring in destructive opinions. They will even deny the Master who bought them—bringing swift destruction on themselves. [2]Even so, many will follow their licentious ways, and because of these teachers[k] the way of truth will be maligned. [3]And in their greed they will exploit you with deceptive words. Their condemnation, pronounced against them long ago, has not been idle, and their destruction is not asleep.

4 For if God did not spare the angels when they sinned, but cast them into hell[l] and committed them to chains[m] of deepest darkness to be kept until the judgment; [5]and if he did not spare the ancient world, even though he saved Noah, a herald of righteousness, with seven others, when he brought a flood on a world of the ungodly; [6]and if by turning the cities of Sodom and Gomorrah to ashes he condemned them to extinction[n] and made them an example of what is coming to the ungodly;[o] [7]and if he rescued Lot, a righteous man greatly distressed by the licentiousness of the lawless [8](for that righteous man, living among them day after day, was tormented in his righteous soul by their lawless deeds that he saw and heard), [9]then the Lord knows how to rescue the godly from trial, and to keep the unrighteous under punishment until the day of judgment [10]—especially those who indulge their flesh in depraved lust, and who despise authority.

Bold and willful, they are not afraid to slander the glorious ones,[p] [11]whereas angels, though greater in might and power, do not bring against them a slanderous judgment from the Lord.[q] [12]These people, however, are like irrational animals, mere creatures of instinct, born to be caught and killed. They slander what they do not understand, and when those creatures are destroyed,[r] they also will be destroyed, [13]suffering[s] the penalty for doing wrong. They count it a pleasure to revel in the daytime. They are blots and blemishes, reveling in their dissipation[t] while they feast with you. [14]They have eyes full of adultery, insatiable for sin. They entice unsteady souls. They have

f Gk brothers   g Gk tent   h Gk the putting off of my tent   i Other ancient authorities read my beloved Son   j Other ancient authorities read but moved by the Holy Spirit saints of God spoke   k Gk because of them   l Gk Tartaros   m Other ancient authorities read pits   n Other ancient authorities lack to extinction   o Other ancient authorities read an example to those who were to be ungodly   p Or angels; Gk glories   q Other ancient authorities read before the Lord; others lack the phrase   r Gk in their destruction   s Other ancient authorities read receiving   t Other ancient authorities read love-feasts hearts trained in greed. Accursed children! [15]They have left the straight road and have gone astray, following the road of Balaam son of Bosor,[u] who loved the wages of doing wrong, [16]but was rebuked for his own transgression; a speechless donkey spoke with a human voice and restrained the prophet's madness.

17 These are waterless springs and mists driven by a storm; for them the deepest darkness has been reserved. [18]For they speak bombastic nonsense, and with licentious desires of the flesh they entice

[u] Other ancient authorities read *Beor*

Waiting

FRIDAY

Scripture Reading
for Today:
2 Peter 3.8–15

Verse for Today:
2 Peter 3.14

It is Advent, and we are a people, pregnant. Pregnant and waiting. We long for the God/Man to be born, and this waiting is hard. Our whole life is spent, one way or another, in waiting. Information puts us on hold and fills our waiting ear with thin, irritating music. Our order hasn't come in yet. The elevator must be stuck. Our spouse is late. Will the snow never melt, the rain never stop, the paint ever dry? Will anyone ever understand? Will I ever change? Life is a series of hopes, and waitings, and half-fulfillments. With grace and increasing patience and understanding of this human condition of constantly unsatisfied desire, we wait on our incompleted salvation.

Waiting, because it will always be with us, can be made a work of art, and the season of Advent invites us to underscore and understand with a new patience that very feminine state of being, waiting. Our masculine world wants to blast away waiting from our lives. Instant gratification has become our constitutional right, and delay an aberration. We equate waiting with wasting. So we build Concorde airplanes, drink instant coffee, roll out green plastic and call it turf, and reach for the phone before we reach for the pen. The more life asks us to wait, the more we anxiously hurry. The tempo of haste in which we live has less to do with being on time or the efficiency of a busy life—it has more to do with our being unable to wait. But waiting is unpractical time, good for nothing but mysteriously necessary to all that is becoming. As in a pregnancy, nothing of value comes into being without a period of quiet incubation: not a healthy baby, not a loving relationship, not a reconciliation, a new understanding, a work of art, never a transformation. Rather, a shortened period of incubation brings forth what is not whole or strong or even alive. Brewing, baking, simmering, fermenting, ripening, germinating, gestating are the feminine processes of becoming, and they are the symbolic states of being which belong in a life of value, necessary to transformation.

—*GERTRUD MUELLER NELSON*

Go to page 1640 for your next devotional reading.

people who have just[v] escaped from those who live in error. [19]They promise them freedom, but they themselves are slaves of corruption; for people are slaves to whatever masters them. [20]For if, after they have escaped the defilements of the world through the knowledge of our Lord and Savior Jesus Christ, they are again entangled in them and overpowered, the last state has become worse for them than the first. [21]For it would have been better for them never to have known the way of righteousness than, after knowing it, to turn back from the holy commandment that was passed on to them. [22]It has happened to them according to the true proverb,

> "The dog turns back to its
>   own vomit,"

and,

> "The sow is washed only to wallow
>   in the mud."

The Promise of the Lord's Coming

3 This is now, beloved, the second letter I am writing to you; in them I am trying to arouse your sincere intention by reminding you [2]that you should remember the words spoken in the past by the holy prophets, and the commandment of the Lord and Savior spoken through your apostles. [3]First of all you must understand this, that in the last days scoffers will come, scoffing and indulging their own lusts [4]and saying, "Where is the promise of his coming? For ever since our ancestors died,[w] all things continue as they were from the beginning of creation!" [5]They deliberately ignore this fact, that by the word of God heavens existed long ago and an earth was formed out of water and by means of water, [6]through which the world of that time was deluged with water and perished. [7]But by the same word the present heavens and earth have been reserved for fire, being kept until the day of judgment and destruction of the godless.

8 But do not ignore this one fact, beloved, that with the Lord one day is like a thousand years, and a thousand years are like one day. [9]The Lord is not slow about his promise, as some think of slowness, but is patient with you,[x] not wanting any to perish, but all to come to repentance. [10]But the day of the Lord will come like a thief, and then the heavens will pass away with a loud noise, and the elements will be dissolved with fire, and the earth and everything that is done on it will be disclosed.[y]

11 Since all these things are to be dissolved in this way, what sort of persons ought you to be in leading lives of holiness and godliness, [12]waiting for and hastening[z] the coming of the day of God, because of which the heavens will be set ablaze and dissolved, and the elements will melt with fire? [13]But, in accordance with his promise, we wait for new heavens and a new earth, where righteousness is at home.

Final Exhortation and Doxology

14 Therefore, beloved, while you are waiting for these things, strive to be found by him at peace, without spot or blemish; [15]and regard the patience of our Lord as salvation. So also our beloved brother Paul wrote to you according to the wisdom given him, [16]speaking of this as he does in all his letters. There are some things in them hard to understand, which the ignorant and unstable twist to their own destruction, as they do the other scriptures. [17]You therefore, beloved, since you are forewarned, beware that you are not carried away with the error of the lawless and lose your own stability. [18]But grow in the grace and knowledge of our Lord and Savior Jesus Christ. To him be the glory both now and to the day of eternity. Amen.[a]

---

[v] Other ancient authorities read *actually*   [w] Gk *our fathers fell asleep*   [x] Other ancient authorities read *on your account*   [y] Other ancient authorities read *will be burned up*   [z] Or *earnestly desiring*   [a] Other ancient authorities lack *Amen*

Tabitha

*Her Name Means "Gazelle." In
Greek Her Name Was Dorcas.*

Read Acts 9.36–43

The winds roared over the coast,
piling water in noisy heaps along
the rocky shoreline. But though
she lay quietly in the upper room
of her house near the sea, Tabitha
did not hear them. Nor did she
notice the waves of grief that
spilled into the room from the
heart of every woman present.
For once she had nothing to offer,
no word of comfort, no act of
kindness to soften their suffering.
Instead, she lay still as other
women ministered to her, tenderly sponging
her body clean to prepare it for burial.

As Peter approached the house, he could
hear the noise of mourning, a sound more
desolate than the tearing wind. Two men had
summoned him from Lydda, where he had
just healed a paralytic. They urged him to
come quickly because one of the Lord's disciples in Joppa had died.

As soon as he entered the room where
her body lay, the widows surrounded him
with tangible evidence of the woman they
loved, weeping as they held up robes and
other items she had sewn to clothe the poor.
Quickly Peter shooed them from the room as
though to clear the atmosphere of despair.
Then he knelt beside her body.

As Peter prayed, he may have remembered
a startling promise Jesus had made while he

Her Character: *An inhabitant of Joppa, a
town on the Mediter-
ranean coast, 35 miles
northwest of Jerusalem,
she belonged to one of the
earliest Christian congre-
gations. She was a disci-
ple known for her practi-
cal works of mercy.*
Her Sorrow: *To have
suffered a grave illness.*
Her Joy: *To serve Jesus
by serving the poor.*

was on earth: "Very truly, I tell
you, the one who believes in me
will also do the works that I do
and, in fact, will do greater
works than these, because I am
going to the Father. I will do
whatever you ask in my name,
so that the Father may be glorified in the Son. If in my name
you ask me for anything, I will
do it" (John 14.12–14).

His faith rising like the wind
outside, Peter addressed the
dead woman, saying, "Tabitha,
get up." Taking her by the hand,
he actually helped her to her
feet. The story of her miracle
spread quickly through Joppa,
leading many to believe.

The next day she stood
alone on the roof of her house. The shore
was littered with driftwood, trinkets from
yesterday's storm. Tabitha breathed deeply,
inhaling the sea's salty tang, soothed by the
sound of waves lapping the rocks below. But
somehow the view seemed different,
strangely transparent, as though another
world waited just behind the curtain of this
one. Tabitha shaded her eyes with her hand,
peering out at the sea. But she saw nothing
other than the usual collection of fishing
boats bobbing in the waves.

Sighing, she turned and went inside. She
had things to do: clothes to sew, bread to
bake, the poor to feed and clothe. But even in
the midst of her busy preparations, her longing for that other world increased, like hunger
pains before a banquet. Meanwhile, she fed the
longing with her many practical acts of love.

Praying With Tabitha

So Peter got up and went with them; and when he arrived, they took him to the room upstairs. All the widows stood beside him, weeping and showing tunics and other clothing that Dorcas [Tabitha] had made while she was with them.—*Acts 9.39*

Praise God: *For his power over death.*

Offer Thanks: *For answered prayers.*

Confess: *Any habit of limiting the power of prayer.*

Ask God: *To make you a woman whose love for God has practical ramifications for those around her.*

Lift Your Heart

Is there a Tabitha in your life, a good woman or man who is suffering in some way—someone, perhaps, who has been a great support in your own life? Resist the temptation to become depressed about what is happening to them and, instead, spend time this week praying in light of Tabitha's story. Let her miracle increase your faith and shape your prayers. If you have a photograph of the person, paste it to the dashboard of your car, on your refrigerator, or on your computer to remind you to pray. Ask God to bring light out of the darkness of their present circumstances.

Lord, show me how to pray with increasing faith, aware that your Spirit is no less powerful today than two thousand years ago. Act on behalf of your servant, and glorify your name by what you do.

Go to page 1644 for your next devotional reading.

1 John

More a theological treatise than a letter, I John contains many striking similarities to the Gospel of John.

First John asserts the humanity and divinity of Jesus in the face of false teachers who were denying it. This book offers wonderful reassurance concerning God's goodness: "God is light and in him there is no darkness at all" (1.5) and "God is love." (4.16).

Further, I John makes it clear that love is not some vague ideal or emotion. Love is expressed through obedience. Those who love God will also love their brothers and sisters. "Whoever says, 'I am in the light,' while hating a brother or sister, is still in the darkness" (2.9).

The Word of Life

1 We declare to you what was from the beginning, what we have heard, what we have seen with our eyes, what we have looked at and touched with our hands, concerning the word of life— 2this life was revealed, and we have seen it and testify to it, and declare to you the eternal life that was with the Father and was revealed to us— 3we declare to you what we have seen and heard so that you also may have fellowship with us; and truly our fellowship is with the Father and with his Son Jesus Christ. 4We are writing these things so that our*a* joy may be complete.

God Is Light

5 This is the message we have heard from him and proclaim to you, that God is light and in him there is no darkness at all. 6If we say that we have fellowship with him while we are walking in darkness, we lie and do not do what is true; 7but if we walk in the light as he himself is in the light, we have fellowship with one another, and the blood of Jesus his Son cleanses

us from all sin. 8If we say that we have no sin, we deceive ourselves, and the truth is not in us. 9If we confess our sins, he who is faithful and just will forgive us our sins and cleanse us from all unrighteousness. 10If we say that we have not sinned, we make him a liar, and his word is not in us.

Christ Our Advocate

2 My little children, I am writing these things to you so that you may not sin. But if anyone does sin, we have an advocate with the Father, Jesus Christ the righteous; 2and he is the atoning sacrifice for our sins, and not for ours only but also for the sins of the whole world.

3 Now by this we may be sure that we know him, if we obey his commandments. 4Whoever says, "I have come to know him," but does not obey his commandments, is a liar, and in such a person the truth does not exist; 5but whoever obeys his word, truly in this person the love of God has reached perfection. By

a Other ancient authorities read *your*

this we may be sure that we are in him: ⁶whoever says, "I abide in him," ought to walk just as he walked.

A New Commandment

7 Beloved, I am writing you no new commandment, but an old commandment that you have had from the beginning; the old commandment is the word that you have heard. ⁸Yet I am writing you a new commandment that is true in him and in you, because*ᵇ* the darkness is passing away and the true light is already shining. ⁹Whoever says, "I am in the light," while hating a brother or sister,*ᶜ* is still in the darkness. ¹⁰Whoever loves a brother

or sister*ᵈ* lives in the light, and in such a person*ᵉ* there is no cause for stumbling. ¹¹But whoever hates another believer*ᶠ* is in the darkness, walks in the darkness, and does not know the way to go, because the darkness has brought on blindness.
12 I am writing to you, little children,
    because your sins are forgiven on
        account of his name.
13 I am writing to you, fathers,
    because you know him who is
        from the beginning.
I am writing to you, young people,

ᵇ Or *that*   *ᶜ* Gk *hating a brother*   *ᵈ* Gk *loves a brother*   *ᵉ* Or *in it*   *ᶠ* Gk *hates a brother*

THE TRADITION

Sacred Art

> *What we have seen with our eyes, what we have looked at and touched with our hands, concerning the word of life—this life was revealed.*
>
> 1 JOHN 1.1–2

How can you imagine—much less paint or sculpt—the invisible and incomprehensible God, the infinite "One in three Persons"?

You can't. To try would be presumption. This is one reason why the Law of Moses prohibited human attempts to portray God (see Deuteronomy 4.15–16).

It remains true that no human hand will ever capture and convey God's beauty. But when the Son of God took flesh, a new era began—one that opened up grand new vistas for artistic talents and imaginations. The Church Father John Damascene explained the change this way:

> Previously God, who has neither a body nor a face, absolutely could not be represented by an image. But now that he has made himself visible in the flesh and has lived with men, I can make an image of what I have seen of God . . . and contem-

plate the glory of the Lord, his face unveiled.

Using words, the inspired writers of the New Testament bore witness to this reality of "God with us": "We have seen it and testify to it, and declare to you the eternal life that was with the Father and was revealed to us—we declare to you what we have seen and heard" (1 John 1.2–3). In paint, stone, and wood, religious artists do the same. Their handiwork, said the Second Council of Nicaea, "confirms that the incarnation of the Word of God was real and not imaginary."

Images of Jesus renew our sense of wonder that God became one of us. Images of Mary and the saints remind us that he continues his earthly presence through other people. Looking at their images, we see Jesus embodied anew—the pure light of the Holy Spirit refracted in a multitude of human faces.

With eyes of faith, we glimpse what we ourselves are meant to be.

because you have conquered
the evil one.
14 I write to you, children,
because you know the Father.
I write to you, fathers,
because you know him who is
from the beginning.
I write to you, young people,
because you are strong
and the word of God abides
in you,
and you have overcome the
evil one.

15 Do not love the world or the things in the world. The love of the Father is not in those who love the world; 16for all that is in the world—the desire of the flesh, the desire of the eyes, the pride in riches— comes not from the Father but from the world. 17And the world and its desire g are passing away, but those who do the will of God live forever.

Warning against Antichrists

18 Children, it is the last hour! As you have heard that antichrist is coming, so now many antichrists have come. From this we know that it is the last hour. 19They went out from us, but they did not belong to us; for if they had belonged to us, they would have remained with us. But by going out they made it plain that none of them belongs to us. 20But you have been anointed by the Holy One, and all of you have knowledge.h 21I write to you, not because you do not know the truth, but because you know it, and you know that no lie comes from the truth. 22Who is the liar but the one who denies that Jesus is the Christ?i This is the anti-

g Or the desire for it   h Other ancient authorities read you know all things   i Or the Messiah

And It Was Night
(John 13.30)

You stumble unseeing from the upper room
and no number of lanterns and torches can dim
your darkness now, Judas. When did you begin
to guard the hoard and spend starry evenings
behind drawn tent flaps, running the coins
through acquisitive fingers while the company sat
in a circle outside, breaking bread
and talking of light in the crackling campfire?

When did you fine-tune your ears to the clink
of copper and silver and gold, letting
the words of the Master fade out unheeded?
When did you start to begrudge begging hands
and when did you welcome disciples more
for the treasures they gave than the treasures they were?

Now, in the dark of Gethsemane's garden,
you touch greedy lips to the Master's cheek—
a cheap giveaway to your cohorts of night.

—IRENE ZIMMERMAN, O.S.F.

MONDAY

Scripture Reading
for Today:
1 John 2.7–11

Verse for Today:
1 John 2.11

Go to page 1646 for your next devotional reading.

christ, the one who denies the Father and the Son. 23No one who denies the Son has the Father; everyone who confesses the Son has the Father also. 24Let what you heard from the beginning abide in you. If what you heard from the beginning abides in you, then you will abide in the Son and in the Father. 25And this is what he has promised us,*j* eternal life.

26 I write these things to you concerning those who would deceive you. 27As for you, the anointing that you received from him abides in you, and so you do not need anyone to teach you. But as his anointing teaches you about all things, and is true and is not a lie, and just as it has taught you, abide in him.*k*

28 And now, little children, abide in him, so that when he is revealed we may have confidence and not be put to shame before him at his coming.

Children of God

29 If you know that he is righteous, you may be sure that everyone who does right has been born of him. 1See what love the Father has given us, that we should be called children of God; and that is what we are. The reason the world does not know us is that it did not know him. 2Beloved, we are God's children now; what we will be has not yet been revealed. What we do know is this: when he*k* is revealed, we will be like him, for we will see him as he is. 3And all who have this hope in him purify themselves, just as he is pure.

4 Everyone who commits sin is guilty of lawlessness; sin is lawlessness. 5You know that he was revealed to take away sins, and in him there is no sin. 6No one who abides in him sins; no one who sins has either seen him or known him. 7Little children, let no one deceive you. Everyone who does what is right is righteous, just as he is righteous. 8Everyone who commits sin is a child of the devil; for the devil has been sinning from the beginning. The Son of God was revealed for this purpose, to destroy the works of the devil. 9Those who have been born of God do not sin, because God's seed abides in them;*l* they cannot sin, because they have been born of God. 10The children of God and the children of the devil are revealed in this way: all who do not do what is right are not from God, nor are those who do not love their brothers and sisters.*m*

Love One Another

11 For this is the message you have heard from the beginning, that we should love one another. 12We must not be like Cain who was from the evil one and murdered his brother. And why did he murder him? Because his own deeds were evil and his brother's righteous. 13Do not be astonished, brothers and sisters,*n* that the world hates you. 14We know that we have passed from death to life because we love one another. Whoever does not love abides in death. 15All who hate a brother or sister*m* are murderers, and you know that murderers do not have eternal life abiding in them. 16We know love by this, that he laid down his life for us—and we ought to lay down our lives for one another. 17How does God's love abide in anyone who has the world's goods and sees a brother or sister*o* in need and yet refuses help?

18 Little children, let us love, not in word or speech, but in truth and action. 19And by this we will know that we are from the truth and will reassure our hearts before him 20whenever our hearts condemn us; for God is greater than our hearts, and he knows everything. 21Beloved, if our hearts do not condemn us, we have boldness before God; 22and we receive from him whatever we ask, because we obey his commandments and do what pleases him.

23 And this is his commandment, that we should believe in the name of his Son Jesus Christ and love one another, just as he has commanded us. 24All who obey his commandments abide in him, and he abides in them. And by this we know that he abides in us, by the Spirit that he has given us.

Testing the Spirits

4 Beloved, do not believe every spirit, but test the spirits to see whether they are from God; for many false prophets have gone out into the world. 2By this you know the Spirit of God: every spirit that confesses that Jesus Christ has come in the flesh is from God, 3and every spirit that

---

j Other ancient authorities read *you* *k* Or *it*
l Or *because the children of God abide in him*
m Gk *his brother* *n* Gk *brothers* *o* Gk *brother*

does not confess Jesus*ᵖ* is not from God. And this is the spirit of the antichrist, of which you have heard that it is coming; and now it is already in the world. ⁴Little children, you are from God, and have conquered them; for the one who is in you is greater than the one who is in the world. ⁵They are from the world; therefore what they say is from the world, and the world listens to them. ⁶We are from God. Whoever knows God listens to us, and whoever is not from God does not listen to us. From this we know the spirit of truth and the spirit of error.

God Is Love

7 Beloved, let us love one another, because love is from God; everyone who loves is born of God and knows God. ⁸Whoever does not love does not know God, for God is love. ⁹God's love was revealed among us in this way: God sent his only Son into the world so that we might live through him. ¹⁰In this is love, not that we loved God but that he loved us and sent his Son to be the atoning sacrifice for our sins. ¹¹Beloved, since God loved us so much, we also ought to love one another. ¹²No one has ever seen God; if we love one another, God lives in us, and his love is perfected in us.

13 By this we know that we abide in him and he in us, because he has given us of his Spirit. ¹⁴And we have seen and do testify that the Father has sent his Son as the Savior of the world. ¹⁵God abides in those who confess that Jesus is the Son of God, and they abide in God. ¹⁶So we have known and believe the love that God has for us.

God is love, and those who abide in love abide in God, and God abides in them. ¹⁷Love has been perfected among us in this: that we may have boldness on

ᵖ Other ancient authorities read *does away with Jesus* (Gk *dissolves Jesus*)

---

*T*rue Love

Scripture Reading
for Today:
1 John 3.14–18

Verse for Today:
1 John 3.16

To love is essentially to be self-giving. No greater gift can be granted to another person than the gift of self. Already the Old Testament contained these sublime words: "Give me your heart" (Proverbs 23.26). This is what God asks of us. This is why all the exertions, actions, activities, accomplishments, and feats without love are to be counted as nothing (see I Corinthians 13.1–3).

This total donation of self cannot be severed from the readiness to make sacrifices and suffer for the loved one. Indeed, there is no greater love than to give one's life for one's friends. Love and love alone not only makes sacrifices for the one that it loves but even rejoices in doing so.

How eager people are to enjoy with others, and how reluctant they are to make sacrifices for others! And yet, it is from the latter that we can gauge the depth and sublimity of a love.

This is a truth that I had the privilege of understanding at the age of five. I was gravely ill, and I recall my mother bending over my little bed and whispering to me, "Darling, how I wish I could suffer this for you." I was too weak to open my eyes, but I said to myself, "Do not forget this; it is true love." And I have not forgotten it.

—*ALICE VON HILDEBRAND*

Go to page 1647 for your next devotional reading.

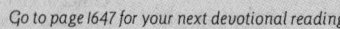

the day of judgment, because as he is, so are we in this world. [18]There is no fear in love, but perfect love casts out fear; for fear has to do with punishment, and who-ever fears has not reached perfection in love. [19]We love[q] because he first loved

q Other ancient authorities add *him*; others add *God*

WEDNESDAY

Scripture Reading
for Today:
1 John 5.13–15

Verse for Today:
1 John 5.14

Asking

Joan Wester Anderson's best-selling Where Miracles Happen *had its beginnings in an experience that took place one sunny autumn afternoon as Joan raked leaves in her backyard. Pausing for a moment, she made a heart-stopping discovery: Her diamond engagement ring and wedding band had fallen off somewhere in the huge leaf piles. Tears filled her eyes. "I would never see the rings again. And not only were they uninsured, they were loved, irreplaceable."*

Joan's neighbor Lynne, appearing on the scene at just that moment, took another approach.

"Let's pray about it," she said, and she knelt right down in the middle of the leaves. And, because she had hold of my hand, so did I.

"God," Lynne began without preamble, "we've got a problem here." Briefly she outlined the situation.

Despite my agitation, I felt a little embarrassed. Yet I was fascinated, too. Lynne was talking to God with easy familiarity, as if he was her real Father, someone who cared so much about her that he would be interested in anything she told him. Well, why not? I thought suddenly. I'm a parent, and there's nothing my children could need that I wouldn't provide. If I were truly his child, wouldn't it work the same way?

Lynne was finishing her discussion. "We need a miracle, God," I heard her say. "Please let us find the rings." She sat back on her heels, wordlessly surveying the yard.

Her eyes traveled across the orange and yellow piles. Slowly she stood up and walked past several deep mounds. When she reached one on the other side of the yard, she stopped, bent over, plunged her hand into it, and then straightened. "Here they are," she said, looking into her palm. "Here are your rings."

Something great seemed to tremble in the air, something awesome and wondrous. Was this what it meant to trust? Like two little girls, we had approached our Father, placed a broken toy in his lap, and asked with complete assurance (at least on Lynne's part), "Daddy, fix it."

Why should I have been surprised when he did?

—JOAN WESTER ANDERSON

Go to page 1650 for your next devotional reading.

us. [20]Those who say, "I love God," and hate their brothers or sisters,[r] are liars; for those who do not love a brother or sister[s] whom they have seen, cannot love God whom they have not seen. [21]The commandment we have from him is this: those who love God must love their brothers and sisters[r] also.

Faith Conquers the World

5 Everyone who believes that Jesus is the Christ[t] has been born of God, and everyone who loves the parent loves the child. [2]By this we know that we love the children of God, when we love God and obey his commandments. [3]For the love of God is this, that we obey his commandments. And his commandments are not burdensome, [4]for whatever is born of God conquers the world. And this is the victory that conquers the world, our faith. [5]Who is it that conquers the world but the one who believes that Jesus is the Son of God?

Testimony concerning the Son of God

6 This is the one who came by water and blood, Jesus Christ, not with the water only but with the water and the blood. And the Spirit is the one that testifies, for the Spirit is the truth. [7]There are three that testify:[u] [8]the Spirit and the water and the blood, and these three agree. [9]If we receive human testimony, the testimony of God is greater; for this is the testimony of God that he has testified to his Son. [10]Those who believe in the Son of God have the testimony in their hearts. Those who do not believe in God[v] have made him a liar by not believing in the testimony that God has given concerning his Son. [11]And this is the testimony: God gave us eternal life, and this life is in his Son.

[12]Whoever has the Son has life; whoever does not have the Son of God does not have life.

Epilogue

13 I write these things to you who believe in the name of the Son of God, so that you may know that you have eternal life.

14 And this is the boldness we have in him, that if we ask anything according to his will, he hears us. [15]And if we know that he hears us in whatever we ask, we know that we have obtained the requests made of him. [16]If you see your brother or sister[w] committing what is not a mortal sin, you will ask, and God[x] will give life to such a one—to those whose sin is not mortal. There is sin that is mortal; I do not say that you should pray about that. [17]All wrongdoing is sin, but there is sin that is not mortal.

18 We know that those who are born of God do not sin, but the one who was born of God protects them, and the evil one does not touch them. [19]We know that we are God's children, and that the whole world lies under the power of the evil one. [20]And we know that the Son of God has come and has given us understanding so that we may know him who is true;[y] and we are in him who is true, in his Son Jesus Christ. He is the true God and eternal life.

21 Little children, keep yourselves from idols.[z]

---

[r] Gk brothers   [s] Gk brother   [t] Or the Messiah
[u] A few other authorities read (with variations)
[7]There are three that testify in heaven, the Father, the Word, and the Holy Spirit, and these three are one.
[8]And there are three that testify on earth: [v] Other ancient authorities read in the Son   [w] Gk your brother   [x] Gk he   [y] Other ancient authorities read know the true God   [z] Other ancient authorities add Amen

2 John

During the first two centuries, the gospel was spread by traveling evangelists, who would stay in the homes of those receptive to their message. Gnostic teachers also followed this custom, thus spreading false doctrine wherever they went. Second John was probably addressed to the church in or near Ephesus at the end of the first century and was written in order to encourage believers to love each other and to adhere to sound teaching about Jesus Christ. In order to protect the community from false teaching, believers were instructed not to provide hospitality to traveling missionaries who spread false teaching.

Salutation

1 The elder to the elect lady and her children, whom I love in the truth, and not only I but also all who know the truth, ²because of the truth that abides in us and will be with us forever:

3 Grace, mercy, and peace will be with us from God the Father and from*a* Jesus Christ, the Father's Son, in truth and love.

Truth and Love

4 I was overjoyed to find some of your children walking in the truth, just as we have been commanded by the Father. ⁵But now, dear lady, I ask you, not as though I were writing you a new commandment, but one we have had from the beginning, let us love one another. ⁶And this is love, that we walk according to his commandments; this is the commandment just as you have heard it from the beginning—you must walk in it.

7 Many deceivers have gone out into the world, those who do not confess that Jesus Christ has come in the flesh; any such person is the deceiver and the antichrist! ⁸Be on your guard, so that you do not lose what we*b* have worked for, but may receive a full reward. ⁹Everyone who does not abide in the teaching of Christ, but goes beyond it, does not have God; whoever abides in the teaching has both the Father and the Son. ¹⁰Do not receive into the house or welcome anyone who comes to you and does not bring this teaching; ¹¹for to welcome is to participate in the evil deeds of such a person.

Final Greetings

12 Although I have much to write to you, I would rather not use paper and ink; instead I hope to come to you and talk with you face to face, so that our joy may be complete.

13 The children of your elect sister send you their greetings.*c*

a Other ancient authorities add *the Lord*
b Other ancient authorities read *you*   *c* Other ancient authorities add *Amen*

Let Us Love

THURSDAY

Scripture Reading
for Today:
2 John 5–6

Verse for Today:
2 John 5

Some time ago a man came to our house and said: "Mother, there is a Hindu family that has eight children. They have not eaten for a long time. Do something for them." So I took some rice and went. When I arrived at their house, I could see the hunger in the children's eyes. Their eyes were shining with hunger. I gave the rice to the mother. She took it and divided it into two, and then she went out. When she came back, I asked her, "Where did you go?" She said, "They are hungry also." Her neighbors were also hungry. What struck me most was not that she gave the rice but that she knew they were hungry. Because she knew, she shared. I did not bring more rice that night. I waited until the next morning so that they could experience the joy of sharing and loving.

Love, to be true, has to hurt, and this woman who was hungry—she knew that her neighbor was also hungry. That family happened to be a Mohammedan family. It was so touching, so real. This is where we are most unjust to our poor—we don't know them. We don't know how great they are, how lovable, how hungry for that understanding love. Today God loves the world through you and through me. Are we that love and that compassion? God proves that Christ loves us—that he has come to be his Father's compassion. Today God is loving the world through you and through me and through all those who are his love and compassion in the world.

—*MOTHER TERESA OF CALCUTTA*

Go to page 1652 for your next devotional reading.

3 John

This letter spotlights the tensions that sometimes developed in the early church between those conducting missionary activities and leaders of the local church. Addressed to Gaius, who is commended for receiving the missionaries that the writer of 3 John sent to him, it criticizes a leader by the name of Diotrephes, who refused the missionaries and expelled anyone in the church who extended hospitality to them. Ironically, Diotrephes's actions are in line with the instructions in 2 John forbidding the community to welcome false teachers, though the letter gives no indication of his motive except to say that he "likes to put himself first" and "does not acknowledge our authority" (verse 9).

Salutation

1 The elder to the beloved Gaius, whom I love in truth.

Gaius Commended for His Hospitality

2 Beloved, I pray that all may go well with you and that you may be in good health, just as it is well with your soul. [3]I was overjoyed when some of the friends[a] arrived and testified to your faithfulness to the truth, namely how you walk in the truth. [4]I have no greater joy than this, to hear that my children are walking in the truth.

5 Beloved, you do faithfully whatever you do for the friends,[a] even though they are strangers to you; [6]they have testified to your love before the church. You will do well to send them on in a manner worthy of God; [7]for they began their journey for the sake of Christ,[b] accepting no support from non-believers.[c] [8]Therefore we ought to support such people, so that we may become co-workers with the truth.

Diotrephes and Demetrius

9 I have written something to the church; but Diotrephes, who likes to put himself first, does not acknowledge our authority. [10]So if I come, I will call attention to what he is doing in spreading false charges against us. And not content with those charges, he refuses to welcome the friends,[a] and even prevents those who want to do so and expels them from the church.

11 Beloved, do not imitate what is evil but imitate what is good. Whoever does good is from God; whoever does evil has

---

[a] Gk brothers   [b] Gk for the sake of the name
[c] Gk the Gentiles

not seen God. [12]Everyone has testified favorably about Demetrius, and so has the truth itself. We also testify for him,[d] and you know that our testimony is true.

Final Greetings

13 I have much to write to you, but I

would rather not write with pen and ink; [14]instead I hope to see you soon, and we will talk together face to face.

15 Peace to you. The friends send you their greetings. Greet the friends there, each by name.

[d] Gk lacks for him

FRIDAY

Scripture Reading for Today:
3 John

Verse for Today:
3 John 5

Hospitality of the Heart

What the world needs most today is the hospitality of the heart. Hospitality of the heart means accepting all others as they are, allowing them to make themselves at home in one's heart.

To be at home in another person's heart means touching love, the love of a brother or sister in Christ. Touching the love of another means realizing that God loves us. For it is through the other—our neighbor, our brother or sister—that we can begin to understand the love of God.

This is especially necessary in our strange technological loneliness that has separated us so thoroughly not only from our neighbors, but from our fathers, mothers, grandparents, in short, from our relations. Yes, our technological age has begotten a terrible loneliness! We must begin to give the hospitality of the heart. In other words, we must open ourselves to a sharing of friendship that is rooted in the very heart of Christ whom we call our friend.

We have to shed our "stiff upper lips." We have to be open to the other, share with the other, express our love for the other. This can only be done if we open the doors of our hearts. Let us do that now, before the doors of our hearts are frozen shut by some new technological achievement!

—CATHERINE DOHERTY

Go to page 1656 for your next devotional reading.

The Letter of
Jude

The letter of Jude was written to warn against false teaching regarding what has sometimes been called "cheap grace." Apparently, the community was threatened by teachers who proclaimed that God's grace allowed them to sin freely. Jude calls such people waterless clouds; trees without fruit, twice dead; wild waves of the sea; and wandering stars, for whom the deepest darkness will be reserved (see verses 12–13).

Salutation

1 Jude,[a] a servant[b] of Jesus Christ and brother of James,

To those who are called, who are beloved[c] in[d] God the Father and kept safe for[d] Jesus Christ:

2 May mercy, peace, and love be yours in abundance.

Occasion of the Letter

3 Beloved, while eagerly preparing to write to you about the salvation we share, I find it necessary to write and appeal to you to contend for the faith that was once for all entrusted to the saints. 4For certain intruders have stolen in among you, people who long ago were designated for this condemnation as ungodly, who pervert the grace of our God into licentiousness and deny our only Master and Lord, Jesus Christ.[e]

Judgment on False Teachers

5 Now I desire to remind you, though you are fully informed, that the Lord, who once for all saved[f] a people out of the land of Egypt, afterward destroyed those who did not believe. 6And the angels who did not keep their own position, but left their proper dwelling, he has kept in eternal chains in deepest darkness for the judgment of the great day. 7Likewise, Sodom and Gomorrah and the surrounding cities, which, in the same manner as they, indulged in sexual immorality and pursued unnatural lust, [g] serve as an example by undergoing a punishment of eternal fire.

8 Yet in the same way these dreamers also defile the flesh, reject authority, and slander the glorious ones.[h] 9But when the archangel Michael contended with the devil and disputed about the body of Moses, he did not dare to bring a condemnation of slander[i] against him, but said, "The Lord rebuke you!" 10But these people slander whatever they do not understand, and they are destroyed by those things that, like irrational animals, they know by instinct. 11Woe to them! For they go the way of Cain, and abandon themselves to Balaam's error for the sake of gain, and perish in Korah's rebellion. 12These are blemishes[j] on your love-feasts, while they feast with you without fear, feeding

a Gk Judas   b Gk slave   c Other ancient authorities read sanctified   d Or by   e Or the only Master and our Lord Jesus Christ   f Other ancient authorities read though you were once for all fully informed, that Jesus (or Joshua) who saved   g Gk went after other flesh   h Or angels; Gk glories   i Or condemnation for blasphemy   j Or reefs

themselves.[k] They are waterless clouds carried along by the winds; autumn trees without fruit, twice dead, uprooted; [13]wild waves of the sea, casting up the foam of their own shame; wandering stars, for whom the deepest darkness has been reserved forever.

14 It was also about these that Enoch, in the seventh generation from Adam, prophesied, saying, "See, the Lord is coming[l] with ten thousands of his holy ones, [15]to execute judgment on all, and to convict everyone of all the deeds of ungodliness that they have committed in such an ungodly way, and of all the harsh things that ungodly sinners have spoken against him." [16]These are grumblers and malcontents; they indulge their own lusts; they are bombastic in speech, flattering people to their own advantage.

Warnings and Exhortations

17 But you, beloved, must remember the predictions of the apostles of our Lord Jesus Christ; [18]for they said to you, "In the last time there will be scoffers, indulging their own ungodly lusts." [19]It is these worldly people, devoid of the Spirit, who are causing divisions. [20]But you, beloved, build yourselves up on your most holy faith; pray in the Holy Spirit; [21]keep yourselves in the love of God; look forward to the mercy of our Lord Jesus Christ that leads to[m] eternal life. [22]And have mercy on some who are wavering; [23]save others by snatching them out of the fire; and have mercy on still others with fear, hating even the tunic defiled by their bodies.[n]

Benediction

24 Now to him who is able to keep you from falling, and to make you stand without blemish in the presence of his glory with rejoicing, [25]to the only God our Savior, through Jesus Christ our Lord, be glory, majesty, power, and authority, before all time and now and forever. Amen.

[k] Or *without fear. They are shepherds who care only for themselves*   [l] Gk *came*   [m] Gk *Christ to*   [n] Gk *by the flesh*. The Greek text of verses 22-23 is uncertain at several points

Revelation

The book of Revelation is a form of apocalyptic writing popular in the two centuries before and after Christ. Probably written at the end of the first century, it employs symbolic and allegorical language in order to convey the secret purposes of God regarding times of persecution. Revelation, like other instances of apocalyptic literature, has its roots in Old Testament prophecy, drawing particularly from Ezekiel, Daniel, and Zechariah. It was written during a time of persecution in the Roman Empire, and its main theme is that Christ has already won the decisive victory over Satan.

One of the Bible's most fascinating and most misunderstood books, Revelation does not provide a map of current or future events and is best read with the help of a commentary. It contains an extended vision given to John on the island of Patmos, a vision described in highly symbolic and allegorical terms, not to be interpreted literally. For instance, *Babylon* refers not to an ancient city located in modern-day Iraq, but to the Roman Empire. The number seven stands for completeness and one thousand means a multitude.

The book of Revelation contains themes and truths that have endured throughout the centuries. Though addressing a crisis in the early church, it has meaning for our own day and implications for the future. Just as Genesis, the first book of the Bible, reveals God's original intention for the world, Revelation offers us a glimpse of how he will fully accomplish his purposes.

Introduction and Salutation

1 The revelation of Jesus Christ, which God gave him to show his servants[a] what must soon take place; he made[b] it known by sending his angel to his servant[c] John, 2who testified to the word of God and to the testimony of Jesus Christ, even to all that he saw.

3 Blessed is the one who reads aloud the words of the prophecy, and blessed are those who hear and who keep what is written in it; for the time is near.

a Gk slaves   *b Gk and he made*   *c Gk slave*

Lydia

Her Name Signifies That She Was a Woman from Lydia, the Region in Asia Minor in Which Thyatira Lay

THE STORY OF A WOMAN

Her Character: *A Gentile adherent of Judaism from Thyatira in Asia Minor, she was a successful businesswoman who sold a type of cloth prized for its purple color. As head of her household, she may have been either widowed or single.*
Her Sorrow: *To see Paul and Silas beaten and thrown into prison for the sake of the gospel she had embraced.*
Her Joy: *That God's Spirit directed Paul and his companions to Macedonia, enabling her and others at Philippi to hear the gospel for the first time.*

Read Acts 16.6–40

The wind rustled the branches overhead, making them a swaying canopy for the circle of women bowed in prayer. The river's edge had become their place of worship, a green sanctuary where they gathered each Sabbath to pray.

Lydia listened as a stranger from Tarsus invoked the familiar words of the *shema:* "Hear, O Israel: The LORD is our God, the LORD alone. You shall love the LORD your God with all your heart, and with all your soul, and with all your might" (Deuteronomy 6.4–5). But Paul did not stop with the traditional *shema.* Instead, he spoke of a God whose son had been murdered for love. His name was Jesus. And he had risen from the grave after suffering the most agonizing death imaginable. He was Messiah, the merciful and holy one who had come to save God's people.

Lydia felt a great wind rushing over her even though the branches overhead had grown still. Tears rolled down her cheeks, though she felt more like singing than crying. Afterward, she and her household were baptized in the river, and Lydia insisted that Paul and his companions accept her hospitality.

Still, Philippi seemed an unlikely place to plant the gospel. A prosperous Roman colony, it didn't even have enough Jews to provide the ten men required to form a synagogue. Even so, Philippi had its group of praying women.

Paul had originally planned to preach the gospel in Asia when he felt constrained by the Holy Spirit to turn aside. Soon after he had a vision in which a Macedonian begged him, "Come over to Macedonia and help us." Days later he found himself on the riverbank preaching to the women who had gathered for prayer.

Shortly after Lydia's conversion, she heard news that Paul and Silas had been whipped and thrust into prison for the crime of driving an evil spirit from a slave girl. The girl's owners dragged Paul and Silas before the city magistrates, claiming, "These men are disturbing our city; they are Jews and are advocating customs that are not lawful for us as Romans to adopt or observe" (Acts 16.20–21).

After their release, Paul returned to Lydia's home for a short while. As Lydia said goodbye to the apostle and his companions, she may have remembered the words of his accusers. Paul and Silas had indeed disturbed the citizens of Philippi, throwing the city into an uproar. In fact the gospel had thrown the entire region into an uproar from which it would never recover.

Lydia was Paul's first convert in Europe and the first member of the church at Philippi, a community that later became a source of great consolation to the apostle when he was imprisoned. A Gentile who had turned to Judaism and had moved to Philippi from Thyatira, Lydia was a prominent businesswoman who sold fine cloth to those who could afford it. Perhaps her prayers, joined with those of the other women gathered at the riverbank, helped prepare the way for the gospel to be planted in Europe.

Praying With Lydia

On the sabbath day we went outside the gate by the river, where we supposed
there was a place of prayer; and we sat down and spoke to the women who
had gathered there.—*Acts 16.13*

Praise God: *For sending messengers of the gospel.*
Offer Thanks: *That God enables us to believe by first opening
our hearts to faith.*
Confess: *Any way you may have neglected prayer, especially
in community with other believers.*
Ask God: *To help you make prayer a greater priority in your
life.*

Lift Your Heart

It's interesting to note that the Holy Spirit directed Paul to Macedonia and ultimately to a group of women who had already gathered for prayer. Perhaps their
faithfulness in prayer was a magnet that attracted God's Spirit. This week, invite a few friends to pray with you. Gather in your home or find your own
"green sanctuary" outdoors. Sing hymns and ask God for a fresh outpouring of
his Spirit in your churches, homes, neighborhoods, and nation. Pray for a
greater opening for the gospel. Perhaps God will create an "uproar" in your city
as a result of your prayers.

*Lord, Scripture says that you inhabit the praises of your people. Come now
and dwell with us as we seek your face. Let the fresh wind of your Holy Spirit
fall on us. May our churches, homes, and neighborhoods become places of
prayer, shaking the world around us in a way that brings you glory.*

Go to page 1661 for your next devotional reading.

4 John to the seven churches that are in Asia:

Grace to you and peace from him who is and who was and who is to come, and from the seven spirits who are before his throne, 5and from Jesus Christ, the faithful witness, the firstborn of the dead, and the ruler of the kings of the earth.

To him who loves us and freed*d* us from our sins by his blood, 6and made*e* us to be a kingdom, priests serving*f* his God and Father, to him be glory and dominion forever and ever. Amen.

7 Look! He is coming with the clouds;
   every eye will see him,
   even those who pierced him;
   and on his account all the tribes
      of the earth will wail.
So it is to be. Amen.

8 "I am the Alpha and the Omega," says the Lord God, who is and who was and who is to come, the Almighty.

A Vision of Christ

9 I, John, your brother who share with you in Jesus the persecution and the kingdom and the patient endurance, was on the island called Patmos because of the word of God and the testimony of Jesus. *g* 10I was in the spirit*h* on the Lord's day, and I heard behind me a loud voice like a trumpet 11saying, "Write in a book what you see and send it to the seven churches, to Ephesus, to Smyrna, to Pergamum, to Thyatira, to Sardis, to Philadelphia, and to Laodicea."

12 Then I turned to see whose voice it was that spoke to me, and on turning I saw seven golden lampstands, 13and in the midst of the lampstands I saw one like the Son of Man, clothed with a long robe and with a golden sash across his chest. 14His head and his hair were white as white wool, white as snow; his eyes were like a flame of fire, 15his feet were like burnished bronze, refined as in a furnace, and his voice was like the sound of many waters. 16In his right hand he held seven stars, and from his mouth came a sharp, two-edged sword, and his face was like the sun shining with full force.

17 When I saw him, I fell at his feet as though dead. But he placed his right hand on me, saying, "Do not be afraid; I am the first and the last, 18and the living one. I was dead, and see, I am alive forever and ever; and I have the keys of Death and of Hades. 19Now write what you have seen,

what is, and what is to take place after this. 20As for the mystery of the seven stars that you saw in my right hand, and the seven golden lampstands: the seven stars are the angels of the seven churches, and the seven lampstands are the seven churches.

The Message to Ephesus

2 "To the angel of the church in Ephesus write: These are the words of him who holds the seven stars in his right hand, who walks among the seven golden lampstands:

2 "I know your works, your toil and your patient endurance. I know that you cannot tolerate evildoers; you have tested those who claim to be apostles but are not, and have found them to be false. 3I also know that you are enduring patiently and bearing up for the sake of my name, and that you have not grown weary. 4But I have this against you, that you have abandoned the love you had at first. 5Remember then from what you have fallen; repent, and do the works you did at first. If not, I will come to you and remove your lampstand from its place, unless you repent. 6Yet this is to your credit: you hate the works of the Nicolaitans, which I also hate. 7Let anyone who has an ear listen to what the Spirit is saying to the churches. To everyone who conquers, I will give permission to eat from the tree of life that is in the paradise of God.

The Message to Smyrna

8 "And to the angel of the church in Smyrna write: These are the words of the first and the last, who was dead and came to life:

9 "I know your affliction and your poverty, even though you are rich. I know the slander on the part of those who say that they are Jews and are not, but are a synagogue of Satan. 10Do not fear what you are about to suffer. Beware, the devil is about to throw some of you into prison so that you may be tested, and for ten days you will have affliction. Be faithful until death, and I will give you the crown of life. 11Let anyone who has an ear listen to what the Spirit is saying to the churches.

d Other ancient authorities read *washed*   *e* Gk *and he made*   *f* Gk *priests to*   *g* Or *testimony to Jesus*   *h* Or *in the Spirit*

Whoever conquers will not be harmed by the second death.

The Message to Pergamum

12 "And to the angel of the church in Pergamum write: These are the words of him who has the sharp two-edged sword:
13 "I know where you are living, where Satan's throne is. Yet you are holding fast to my name, and you did not deny your faith in me[i] even in the days of Antipas my witness, my faithful one, who was killed among you, where Satan lives. 14But I have a few things against you: you have some there who hold to the teaching of Balaam, who taught Balak to put a stumbling block before the people of Israel, so that they would eat food sacrificed to idols and practice fornication. 15So you also have some who hold to the teaching of the Nicolaitans. 16Repent then. If not, I will come to you soon and make war against them with the sword of my mouth. 17Let anyone who has an ear listen to what the Spirit is saying to the churches. To everyone who conquers I will give some of the hidden manna, and I will give a white stone, and on the white stone is written a new name that no one knows except the one who receives it.

The Message to Thyatira

18 "And to the angel of the church in Thyatira write: These are the words of the Son of God, who has eyes like a flame of fire, and whose feet are like burnished bronze:
19 "I know your works—your love, faith, service, and patient endurance. I know that your last works are greater than the first. 20But I have this against you: you tolerate that woman Jezebel, who calls herself a prophet and is teaching and beguiling my servants[j] to practice fornication and to eat food sacrificed to idols. 21I gave her time to repent, but she refuses to repent of her fornication. 22Beware, I am throwing her on a bed, and those who commit adultery with her I am throwing into great distress, unless they repent of her doings; 23and I will strike her children dead. And all the churches will know that I am the one who searches minds and hearts, and I will give to each of you as your works deserve. 24But to the rest of you in Thyatira, who do not hold this teaching, who have not learned what some call 'the deep things of Satan,' to

you I say, I do not lay on you any other burden; 25only hold fast to what you have until I come. 26To everyone who conquers and continues to do my works to the end,

I will give authority over
   the nations;
27 to rule[k] them with an iron rod,
   as when clay pots are shattered—
28even as I also received authority from my Father. To the one who conquers I will also give the morning star. 29Let anyone who has an ear listen to what the Spirit is saying to the churches.

The Message to Sardis

3 "And to the angel of the church in Sardis write: These are the words of him who has the seven spirits of God and the seven stars:
"I know your works; you have a name of being alive, but you are dead. 2Wake up, and strengthen what remains and is on the point of death, for I have not found your works perfect in the sight of my God. 3Remember then what you received and heard; obey it, and repent. If you do not wake up, I will come like a thief, and you will not know at what hour I will come to you. 4Yet you have still a few persons in Sardis who have not soiled their clothes; they will walk with me, dressed in white, for they are worthy. 5If you conquer, you will be clothed like them in white robes, and I will not blot your name out of the book of life; I will confess your name before my Father and before his angels. 6Let anyone who has an ear listen to what the Spirit is saying to the churches.

The Message to Philadelphia

7 "And to the angel of the church in Philadelphia write:
  These are the words of the holy one,
    the true one,
  who has the key of David,
  who opens and no one will shut,
    who shuts and no one opens:
8 "I know your works. Look, I have set before you an open door, which no one is able to shut. I know that you have but little power, and yet you have kept my word and have not denied my name. 9I will make those of the synagogue of Satan who say that they are Jews and are not, but are lying—I will make them come and

i Or deny my faith   j Gk slaves   k Or to shepherd

bow down before your feet, and they will learn that I have loved you. [10]Because you have kept my word of patient endurance, I will keep you from the hour of trial that is coming on the whole world to test the inhabitants of the earth. [11]I am coming soon; hold fast to what you have, so that no one may seize your crown. [12]If you conquer, I will make you a pillar in the temple of my God; you will never go out of it. I will write on you the name of my God, and the name of the city of my God, the new Jerusalem that comes down from my God out of heaven, and my own new name. [13]Let anyone who has an ear listen to what the Spirit is saying to the churches.

The Message to Laodicea

14 "And to the angel of the church in Laodicea write: The words of the Amen, the faithful and true witness, the origin[l] of God's creation:

15 "I know your works; you are neither cold nor hot. I wish that you were either cold or hot. [16]So, because you are lukewarm, and neither cold nor hot, I am about to spit you out of my mouth. [17]For you say, 'I am rich, I have prospered, and I need nothing.' You do not realize that you are wretched, pitiable, poor, blind, and naked. [18]Therefore I counsel you to buy from me gold refined by fire so that you may be rich; and white robes to clothe you and to keep the shame of your nakedness from being seen; and salve to anoint your eyes so that you may see. [19]I reprove and discipline those whom I love. Be earnest, therefore, and repent. [20]Listen! I am standing at the door, knocking; if you hear my voice and open the door, I will come in to you and eat with you, and you with me. [21]To the one who conquers I will give a place with me on my throne, just as I myself conquered and sat down with my Father on his throne. [22]Let anyone who has an ear listen to what the Spirit is saying to the churches."

The Heavenly Worship

4 After this I looked, and there in heaven a door stood open! And the first voice, which I had heard speaking to me like a trumpet, said, "Come up here, and I will show you what must take place after this." [2]At once I was in the spirit,[m] and there in heaven stood a throne, with one seated on the throne! [3]And the one seated there looks like jasper and carnelian, and around the throne is a rainbow that looks like an emerald. [4]Around the throne are twenty-four thrones, and seated on the thrones are twenty-four elders, dressed in white robes, with golden crowns on their heads. [5]Coming from the throne are flashes of lightning, and rumblings and peals of thunder, and in front of the throne burn seven flaming torches, which are the seven spirits of God; [6]and in front of the throne there is something like a sea of glass, like crystal.

Around the throne, and on each side of the throne, are four living creatures, full of eyes in front and behind: [7]the first living creature like a lion, the second living creature like an ox, the third living creature with a face like a human face, and the fourth living creature like a flying eagle. [8]And the four living creatures, each of them with six wings, are full of eyes all around and inside. Day and night without ceasing they sing,

"Holy, holy, holy,
    the Lord God the Almighty,
    who was and is and is to come."

[9]And whenever the living creatures give glory and honor and thanks to the one who is seated on the throne, who lives forever and ever, [10]the twenty-four elders fall before the one who is seated on the throne and worship the one who lives forever and ever; they cast their crowns before the throne, singing,

11 "You are worthy, our Lord and God,
    to receive glory and honor
        and power,
    for you created all things,
        and by your will they existed and
        were created."

The Scroll and the Lamb

5 Then I saw in the right hand of the one seated on the throne a scroll written on the inside and on the back, sealed[n] with seven seals; [2]and I saw a mighty angel proclaiming with a loud voice, "Who is worthy to open the scroll and break its seals?" [3]And no one in heaven or on earth or under the earth was able to open the scroll or to look into it. [4]And I began to weep bitterly because no one

[l] Or beginning   [m] Or in the Spirit   [n] Or written on the inside, and sealed on the back

was found worthy to open the scroll or to look into it. ⁵Then one of the elders said to me, "Do not weep. See, the Lion of the tribe of Judah, the Root of David, has conquered, so that he can open the scroll and its seven seals."

6 Then I saw between the throne and the four living creatures and among the elders a Lamb standing as if it had been slaughtered, having seven horns and seven eyes, which are the seven spirits of God sent out into all the earth. ⁷He went and took the scroll from the right hand of the one who was seated on the throne. ⁸When

At Home in Your Soul

MONDAY

Scripture Reading for Today:
Revelation 3.20–22

Verse for Today:
Revelation 3.20

We all know the woman who is exaggeratedly house-proud, who concentrates on the neatness, cleanliness, beauty of her house, to the exclusion of its comfort. Her house is not a home; nothing must ever be left about, out of place. To come in with muddy shoes is a crime; it is a crime to disarrange the cushions! In such a house one can neither work nor rest, one is never at home, because it is not a home.

There are many women who are "soul-proud" in the same way. They spend their whole time cleaning up their soul, turning out the rubbish, dusting and polishing. Like the house-proud woman they become nervous, tired; there is nothing left in them to give; they have wasted themselves on the silver, the curtains, the ornaments.

Christ wants to be at home in your soul. He will not go away and leave you if the house is chilly and uncomfortable; he loves you too much to leave you, but how often, how tragically often, he must say nowadays:

"The Son of Man has nowhere to lay his head."

Christ asks for a home in your soul, where he can be at rest with you, where he can talk easily to you, where you and he, alone together, can laugh and be silent and be delighted with one another.

"Listen," he says, "I am standing at the door, knocking." Christ never goes away, never forgets, all day long, wherever you are, whoever you are, whatever you are doing, his whole heart is concentrated upon you. He watches you with the eye of a mother watching an only child. He sees not the surface things, not the imperfections inevitable to human frailty, but the truly lovable in you, your dependence on him, your need of him. Does a mother love her child less when its hair is tousled, does she love her child less because it has fallen and bruised itself? No, indeed; only, if that is possible, more!

What then must we do?

Listen. Be silent. Let Christ speak to you.

—CARYLL HOUSELANDER

Go to page 1662 for your next devotional reading.

he had taken the scroll, the four living creatures and the twenty-four elders fell before the Lamb, each holding a harp and golden bowls full of incense, which are the prayers of the saints. 9They sing a new song:

"You are worthy to take the scroll
    and to open its seals,
for you were slaughtered and by
        your blood you ransomed
        for God
    saints from*o* every tribe and
        language and people
        and nation;
10 you have made them to be a
        kingdom and priests serving*p*
        our God,
    and they will reign on earth."

11 Then I looked, and I heard the voice of many angels surrounding the throne and the living creatures and the elders; they numbered myriads of myriads and thousands of thousands, 12singing with full voice,

"Worthy is the Lamb that was
        slaughtered

to receive power and wealth and
        wisdom and might
and honor and glory and blessing!"
13Then I heard every creature in heaven and on earth and under the earth and in the sea, and all that is in them, singing,

"To the one seated on the throne
        and to the Lamb
be blessing and honor and glory and
        might
forever and ever!"

14And the four living creatures said, "Amen!" And the elders fell down and worshiped.

The Seven Seals

6 Then I saw the Lamb open one of the seven seals, and I heard one of the four living creatures call out, as with a voice of thunder, "Come!"*q* 2I looked, and there was a white horse! Its rider had a bow; a crown was given to him, and he came out conquering and to conquer.

o Gk *ransomed for God from*   *p* Gk *priests to*
q Or *"Go!"*

A Vision

When, during adoration, I repeated the prayer, "Holy God" several times, a vivid presence of God suddenly swept over me, and I was caught up in spirit before the majesty of God. I saw how the Angels and the Saints of the Lord give glory to God. The glory of God is so great that I dare not try to describe it, because I would not be able to do so, and souls might think that what I have written is all there is. Saint Paul, I understand now why you did not want to describe heaven, but only said that eye has not seen, nor ear heard, nor the human heart conceived what God has prepared for those who love him [see I Corinthians 2.9; 2 Corinthians 12.1–7].

Yes, that is indeed so. And all that has come forth from God returns to him in the same way and gives him perfect glory. Now I have seen the way in which I adore God; oh, how miserable it is! And what a tiny drop it is in comparison to that perfect heavenly glory. *O my God, how good you are to accept my praise as well, and to turn your face to me with kindness and let us know that our prayer is pleasing to you.*

—FAUSTINA KOWALSKA

Go to page 1667 for your next devotional reading.

TUESDAY

Scripture Reading for Today:
Revelation 4.1–11

Verse for Today:
Revelation 4.8

3 When he opened the second seal, I heard the second living creature call out, "Come!"[r] [4]And out came[s] another horse, bright red; its rider was permitted to take peace from the earth, so that people would slaughter one another; and he was given a great sword.

5 When he opened the third seal, I heard the third living creature call out, "Come!"[r] I looked, and there was a black horse! Its rider held a pair of scales in his hand, [6]and I heard what seemed to be a voice in the midst of the four living creatures saying, "A quart of wheat for a day's pay,[t] and three quarts of barley for a day's pay,[t] but do not damage the olive oil and the wine!"

7 When he opened the fourth seal, I heard the voice of the fourth living creature call out, "Come!"[r] [8]I looked and there was a pale green horse! Its rider's name was Death, and Hades followed with him; they were given authority over a fourth of the earth, to kill with sword, famine, and pestilence, and by the wild animals of the earth.

9 When he opened the fifth seal, I saw under the altar the souls of those who had been slaughtered for the word of God and for the testimony they had given; [10]they cried out with a loud voice, "Sovereign Lord, holy and true, how long will it be before you judge and avenge our blood on the inhabitants of the earth?" [11]They were each given a white robe and told to rest a little longer, until the number would be complete both of their fellow servants[u] and of their brothers and sisters,[v] who were soon to be killed as they themselves had been killed.

12 When he opened the sixth seal, I looked, and there came a great earthquake; the sun became black as sackcloth, the full moon became like blood, [13]and the stars of the sky fell to the earth as the fig tree drops its winter fruit when shaken by a gale. [14]The sky vanished like a scroll rolling itself up, and every mountain and island was removed from its place. [15]Then the kings of the earth and the magnates and the generals and the rich and the powerful, and everyone, slave and free, hid in the caves and among the rocks of the mountains, [16]calling to the mountains and rocks, "Fall on us and hide us from the face of the one seated on the throne and from the wrath of the Lamb; [17]for the great day of their wrath has come, and who is able to stand?"

The 144,000 of Israel Sealed

7 After this I saw four angels standing at the four corners of the earth, holding back the four winds of the earth so that no wind could blow on earth or sea or against any tree. [2]I saw another angel ascending from the rising of the sun, having the seal of the living God, and he called with a loud voice to the four angels who had been given power to damage earth and sea, [3]saying, "Do not damage the earth or the sea or the trees, until we have marked the servants[u] of our God with a seal on their foreheads."

4 And I heard the number of those who were sealed, one hundred forty-four thousand, sealed out of every tribe of the people of Israel:

5 From the tribe of Judah twelve thousand sealed,
   from the tribe of Reuben twelve thousand,
   from the tribe of Gad twelve thousand,
6 from the tribe of Asher twelve thousand,
   from the tribe of Naphtali twelve thousand,
   from the tribe of Manasseh twelve thousand,
7 from the tribe of Simeon twelve thousand,
   from the tribe of Levi twelve thousand,
   from the tribe of Issachar twelve thousand,
8 from the tribe of Zebulun twelve thousand,
   from the tribe of Joseph twelve thousand,
   from the tribe of Benjamin twelve thousand sealed.

The Multitude from Every Nation

9 After this I looked, and there was a great multitude that no one could count, from every nation, from all tribes and peoples and languages, standing before the throne and before the Lamb, robed in white, with palm branches in their hands. [10]They cried out in a loud voice, saying,

r Or "Go!"   s Or went   t Gk *a denarius*   u Gk
slaves   v Gk brothers

"Salvation belongs to our God who
    is seated on the throne, and
    to the Lamb!"

[11]And all the angels stood around the
throne and around the elders and the four
living creatures, and they fell on their
faces before the throne and worshiped
God, [12]singing,

"Amen! Blessing and glory
    and wisdom
and thanksgiving and honor
    and power and might
be to our God forever and ever!
    Amen."

13 Then one of the elders addressed
me, saying, "Who are these, robed in
white, and where have they come from?"
[14]I said to him, "Sir, you are the one that
knows." Then he said to me, "These are
they who have come out of the great ordeal; they have washed their robes and
made them white in the blood of the
Lamb.

15 For this reason they are before the
        throne of God,
    and worship him day and night
        within his temple,
    and the one who is seated on the
        throne will shelter them.
16 They will hunger no more, and
        thirst no more;
    the sun will not strike them,
        nor any scorching heat;
17 for the Lamb at the center of the
        throne will be their shepherd,
    and he will guide them to springs
        of the water of life,
    and God will wipe away every tear
        from their eyes."

The Seventh Seal and the Golden Censer

8 When the Lamb opened the seventh
    seal, there was silence in heaven for
about half an hour. [2]And I saw the seven
angels who stand before God, and seven
trumpets were given to them.

3 Another angel with a golden censer
came and stood at the altar; he was given
a great quantity of incense to offer with
the prayers of all the saints on the golden
altar that is before the throne. [4]And the
smoke of the incense, with the prayers of
the saints, rose before God from the hand
of the angel. [5]Then the angel took the censer and filled it with fire from the altar and
threw it on the earth; and there were peals
of thunder, rumblings, flashes of lightning, and an earthquake.

The Seven Trumpets

6 Now the seven angels who had the
seven trumpets made ready to blow them.

7 The first angel blew his trumpet, and
there came hail and fire, mixed with
blood, and they were hurled to the earth;
and a third of the earth was burned up,
and a third of the trees were burned
up, and all green grass was burned up.

8 The second angel blew his trumpet,
and something like a great mountain,
burning with fire, was thrown into the
sea. [9]A third of the sea became blood, a
third of the living creatures in the sea
died, and a third of the ships were destroyed.

10 The third angel blew his trumpet,
and a great star fell from heaven, blazing
like a torch, and it fell on a third of the
rivers and on the springs of water. [11]The
name of the star is Wormwood. A third of
the waters became wormwood, and many
died from the water, because it was made
bitter.

12 The fourth angel blew his trumpet,
and a third of the sun was struck, and a
third of the moon, and a third of the stars,
so that a third of their light was darkened;
a third of the day was kept from shining,
and likewise the night.

13 Then I looked, and I heard an eagle
crying with a loud voice as it flew in midheaven, "Woe, woe, woe to the inhabitants of the earth, at the blasts of the other
trumpets that the three angels are about to
blow!"

9 And the fifth angel blew his trumpet,
    and I saw a star that had fallen from
heaven to earth, and he was given the key
to the shaft of the bottomless pit; [2]he
opened the shaft of the bottomless pit,
and from the shaft rose smoke like the
smoke of a great furnace, and the sun and
the air were darkened with the smoke
from the shaft. [3]Then from the smoke
came locusts on the earth, and they were
given authority like the authority of scorpions of the earth. [4]They were told not to
damage the grass of the earth or any green
growth or any tree, but only those people
who do not have the seal of God on their
foreheads. [5]They were allowed to torture
them for five months, but not to kill
them, and their torture was like the torture of a scorpion when it stings someone.
[6]And in those days people will seek death

but will not find it; they will long to die, but death will flee from them.

7 In appearance the locusts were like horses equipped for battle. On their heads were what looked like crowns of gold; their faces were like human faces, [8]their hair like women's hair, and their teeth like lions' teeth; [9]they had scales like iron breastplates, and the noise of their wings was like the noise of many chariots with horses rushing into battle. [10]They have tails like scorpions, with stingers, and in their tails is their power to harm people for five months. [11]They have as king over them the angel of the bottomless pit; his name in Hebrew is Abaddon,[w] and in Greek he is called Apollyon.[x]

12 The first woe has passed. There are still two woes to come.

13 Then the sixth angel blew his trumpet, and I heard a voice from the four[y] horns of the golden altar before God, [14]saying to the sixth angel who had the trumpet, "Release the four angels who are bound at the great river Euphrates." [15]So the four angels were released, who had been held ready for the hour, the day, the month, and the year, to kill a third of humankind. [16]The number of the troops of cavalry was two hundred million; I heard their number. [17]And this was how I saw

w That is, *Destruction*   x That is, *Destroyer*
y Other ancient authorities lack *four*

THE TRADITION

Incense

The smoke of the incense, with the prayers of the saints, rose before God from the hand of the angel.

REVELATION 8.4

Altar servers may not realize it, but producing aromatic clouds of incense continues a liturgical practice that goes back to the book of Exodus. There, God instructed Moses in the particulars of the public rituals and sacrifices by which the Israelites were to worship him. Burning incense twice a day was one of them.

Morning and evening, the high priest was to offer specially prepared incense on an altar built for this purpose (Exodus 30.1–8, 34–38). By New Testament times, ordinary priests were carrying out this duty. Luke tells us that Zechariah was burning the evening incense at the temple when the angel Gabriel appeared to announce the birth of John the Baptist (see Luke 1.8–11).

"Do not be afraid, Zechariah, for your prayer has been heard" (Luke 1.13). What prayer is Gabriel referring to? Zechariah's priestly prayer for the people? A personal prayer of sorrow about being childless? Luke leaves the statement ambiguous. Either way, though, John's birth is a clear answer from

God. Offered with the evening incense, carried by it into the heavenly courts, Zechariah's prayer moved God to act and advance his kingdom.

Peeking into those courts with the author of Revelation, we find the same association of incense and effective prayer. Whether the incense *is* the "prayers of the saints" or is mixed in with them (see Revelation 5.8; 8.4), the offering precipitates action. In highly symbolic language, God is portrayed bending the evils of history to his purposes in response to his people's prayers.

Incense is a good symbol for our lives, as well as our prayers. Like Saint Paul we ourselves are to be "the aroma of Christ to God" (2 Corinthians 2.15). Like Jesus we are to present our lives as "a fragrant offering and sacrifice to God" (Ephesians 5.2).

"Let my prayer be counted as incense before you," the psalmist prayed (Psalm 141.2). To which we might add: "Let my life be counted as incense before you—and through it, may your kingdom come!"

the horses in my vision: the riders wore breastplates the color of fire and of sapphire[z] and of sulfur; the heads of the horses were like lions' heads, and fire and smoke and sulfur came out of their mouths. 18By these three plagues a third of humankind was killed, by the fire and smoke and sulfur coming out of their mouths. 19For the power of the horses is in their mouths and in their tails; their tails are like serpents, having heads; and with them they inflict harm.

20 The rest of humankind, who were not killed by these plagues, did not repent of the works of their hands or give up worshiping demons and idols of gold and silver and bronze and stone and wood, which cannot see or hear or walk. 21And they did not repent of their murders or their sorceries or their fornication or their thefts.

The Angel with the Little Scroll

10 And I saw another mighty angel coming down from heaven, wrapped in a cloud, with a rainbow over his head; his face was like the sun, and his legs like pillars of fire. 2He held a little scroll open in his hand. Setting his right foot on the sea and his left foot on the land, 3he gave a great shout, like a lion roaring. And when he shouted, the seven thunders sounded. 4And when the seven thunders had sounded, I was about to write, but I heard a voice from heaven saying, "Seal up what the seven thunders have said, and do not write it down." 5Then the angel whom I saw standing on the sea and the land
raised his right hand to heaven
6   and swore by him who lives
      forever and ever,
who created heaven and what is in it, the earth and what is in it, and the sea and what is in it: "There will be no more delay, 7but in the days when the seventh angel is to blow his trumpet, the mystery of God will be fulfilled, as he announced to his servants[a] the prophets."

8 Then the voice that I had heard from heaven spoke to me again, saying, "Go, take the scroll that is open in the hand of the angel who is standing on the sea and on the land." 9So I went to the angel and told him to give me the little scroll; and he said to me, "Take it, and eat; it will be bitter to your stomach, but sweet as honey in your mouth." 10So I took the little scroll

from the hand of the angel and ate it; it was sweet as honey in my mouth, but when I had eaten it, my stomach was made bitter.

11 Then they said to me, "You must prophesy again about many peoples and nations and languages and kings."

The Two Witnesses

11 Then I was given a measuring rod like a staff, and I was told, "Come and measure the temple of God and the altar and those who worship there, 2but do not measure the court outside the temple; leave that out, for it is given over to the nations, and they will trample over the holy city for forty-two months. 3And I will grant my two witnesses authority to prophesy for one thousand two hundred sixty days, wearing sackcloth."

4 These are the two olive trees and the two lampstands that stand before the Lord of the earth. 5And if anyone wants to harm them, fire pours from their mouth and consumes their foes; anyone who wants to harm them must be killed in this manner. 6They have authority to shut the sky, so that no rain may fall during the days of their prophesying, and they have authority over the waters to turn them into blood, and to strike the earth with every kind of plague, as often as they desire.

7 When they have finished their testimony, the beast that comes up from the bottomless pit will make war on them and conquer them and kill them, 8and their dead bodies will lie in the street of the great city that is prophetically[b] called Sodom and Egypt, where also their Lord was crucified. 9For three and a half days members of the peoples and tribes and languages and nations will gaze at their dead bodies and refuse to let them be placed in a tomb; 10and the inhabitants of the earth will gloat over them and celebrate and exchange presents, because these two prophets had been a torment to the inhabitants of the earth.

11 But after the three and a half days, the breath[c] of life from God entered them, and they stood on their feet, and those who saw them were terrified. 12Then they[d] heard a loud voice from heaven

z Gk hyacinth   a Gk slaves   b Or allegorically; Gk spiritually   c Or the spirit   d Other ancient authorities read I

saying to them, "Come up here!" And they went up to heaven in a cloud while their enemies watched them. ¹³At that moment there was a great earthquake, and a tenth of the city fell; seven thousand people were killed in the earthquake, and the rest were terrified and gave glory to the God of heaven.

14 The second woe has passed. The third woe is coming very soon.

The Seventh Trumpet

15 Then the seventh angel blew his trumpet, and there were loud voices in heaven, saying,

"The kingdom of the world has
become the kingdom of
our Lord
and of his Messiah,*e*
and he will reign forever and ever."

16 Then the twenty-four elders who sit on their thrones before God fell on their faces and worshiped God, ¹⁷singing,

"We give you thanks, Lord
God Almighty,
who are and who were,

for you have taken your great power
and begun to reign.
¹⁸ The nations raged,
but your wrath has come,
and the time for judging the dead,
for rewarding your servants, *f*
the prophets
and saints and all who fear
your name,
both small and great,
and for destroying those who
destroy the earth."

19 Then God's temple in heaven was opened, and the ark of his covenant was seen within his temple; and there were flashes of lightning, rumblings, peals of thunder, an earthquake, and heavy hail.

The Woman and the Dragon

12 A great portent appeared in heaven: a woman clothed with the sun, with the moon under her feet, and on her head a crown of twelve stars. ²She was pregnant and was crying out in birth

e Gk *Christ*   *f* Gk *slaves*

Lurking Dragons

WEDNESDAY

Scripture Reading
for Today:
Revelation 12.1–6

Verse for Today:
Revelation 12.1

The woman who faces the dragon in Revelation is traditionally believed to be Mary. Her child is Jesus, and the dragon is identified as Satan. While the imagery in the last book of the Bible is metaphorical and poetic, the sense of impending evil is real.

Every age has its dragons. From the Black Plague to AIDS, from Attila the Hun to Hitler, from the Ice Age to the Atomic Age, dragons wait to devour us. In the late 300s, Saint Gregory Nazianzus penned words that resonate in our souls some sixteen hundred years later: "Alas, dear Christ, the Dragon is here again. Alas, he is here: Terror has seized me, and fear."

It's only natural, given all the lurking dragons, for us to be seized by terror. Yet the message that [is presented] is not one of fear, but one of love. Despite appearances, we have nothing to fear, for in the words of Scripture, "There is no fear in love, but perfect love casts out fear" (1 John 4.18). If you love, you need not be afraid of dragons.

What am I most afraid of?
What dragon is breathing fire in my life right now?
—WOODENE KOENIG-BRICKER

Go to page 1676 for your next devotional reading.

pangs, in the agony of giving birth. [3]Then another portent appeared in heaven: a great red dragon, with seven heads and ten horns, and seven diadems on his heads. [4]His tail swept down a third of the stars of heaven and threw them to the earth. Then the dragon stood before the woman who was about to bear a child, so that he might devour her child as soon as it was born. [5]And she gave birth to a son, a male child, who is to rule[g] all the nations with a rod of iron. But her child was snatched away and taken to God and to his throne; [6]and the woman fled into the wilderness, where she has a place prepared by God, so that there she can be nourished for one thousand two hundred sixty days.

Michael Defeats the Dragon

7 And war broke out in heaven; Michael and his angels fought against the dragon. The dragon and his angels fought back, [8]but they were defeated, and there was no longer any place for them in heaven. [9]The great dragon was thrown down, that ancient serpent, who is called the Devil and Satan, the deceiver of the whole world—he was thrown down to the earth, and his angels were thrown down with him.

10 Then I heard a loud voice in heaven, proclaiming,

"Now have come the salvation and
        the power
    and the kingdom of our God
    and the authority of his
        Messiah,[h]
for the accuser of our comrades[i]
        has been thrown down,
    who accuses them day and night
        before our God.
[11] But they have conquered him by the
        blood of the Lamb
    and by the word of their
        testimony,
for they did not cling to life even in
        the face of death.
[12] Rejoice then, you heavens
    and those who dwell in them!
But woe to the earth and the sea,
    for the devil has come down
        to you
with great wrath,
    because he knows that his time
        is short!"

The Dragon Fights Again on Earth

13 So when the dragon saw that he had been thrown down to the earth, he pursued[j] the woman who had given birth to the male child. [14]But the woman was given the two wings of the great eagle, so that she could fly from the serpent into the wilderness, to her place where she is nourished for a time, and times, and half a time. [15]Then from his mouth the serpent poured water like a river after the woman, to sweep her away with the flood. [16]But the earth came to the help of the woman; it opened its mouth and swallowed the river that the dragon had poured from his mouth. [17]Then the dragon was angry with the woman, and went off to make war on the rest of her children, those who keep the commandments of God and hold the testimony of Jesus.

The First Beast

18 Then the dragon[k] took his stand on the sand of the seashore. 13 [1]And I saw a beast rising out of the sea, having ten horns and seven heads; and on its horns were ten diadems, and on its heads were blasphemous names. [2]And the beast that I saw was like a leopard, its feet were like a bear's, and its mouth was like a lion's mouth. And the dragon gave it his power and his throne and great authority. [3]One of its heads seemed to have received a death-blow, but its mortal wound[l] had been healed. In amazement the whole earth followed the beast. [4]They worshiped the dragon, for he had given his authority to the beast, and they worshiped the beast, saying, "Who is like the beast, and who can fight against it?"

5 The beast was given a mouth uttering haughty and blasphemous words, and it was allowed to exercise authority for forty-two months. [6]It opened its mouth to utter blasphemies against God, blaspheming his name and his dwelling, that is, those who dwell in heaven. [7]Also it was allowed to make war on the saints and to conquer them.[m] It was given authority over every tribe and people and language and nation, [8]and all the inhabitants of the earth will worship it, everyone whose

g Or to shepherd   h Gk Christ   i Gk brothers
j Or persecuted   k Gk Then he; other ancient
authorities read Then I stood   l Gk the plague of
its death   m Other ancient authorities lack this
sentence

name has not been written from the foundation of the world in the book of life of
the Lamb that was slaughtered.[n]
9 Let anyone who has an ear listen:
10 If you are to be taken captive,
into captivity you go;
if you kill with the sword,
with the sword you must be
killed.
Here is a call for the endurance and faith
of the saints.

The Second Beast

11 Then I saw another beast that rose
out of the earth; it had two horns like a
lamb and it spoke like a dragon. 12It exercises all the authority of the first beast on
its behalf, and it makes the earth and its
inhabitants worship the first beast, whose
mortal wound[o] had been healed. 13It
performs great signs, even making fire
come down from heaven to earth in the
sight of all; 14and by the signs that it is
allowed to perform on behalf of the beast,
it deceives the inhabitants of earth, telling
them to make an image for the beast that
had been wounded by the sword[p] and
yet lived; 15and it was allowed to give
breath[q] to the image of the beast so that
the image of the beast could even speak
and cause those who would not worship
the image of the beast to be killed. 16Also
it causes all, both small and great, both
rich and poor, both free and slave, to be
marked on the right hand or the forehead,
17so that no one can buy or sell who does
not have the mark, that is, the name of the
beast or the number of its name. 18This
calls for wisdom: let anyone with understanding calculate the number of the
beast, for it is the number of a person. Its
number is six hundred sixty-six.[r]

The Lamb and the 144,000

14 Then I looked, and there was the
Lamb, standing on Mount Zion!
And with him were one hundred forty-
four thousand who had his name and his
Father's name written on their foreheads.
2And I heard a voice from heaven like the
sound of many waters and like the sound
of loud thunder; the voice I heard was like
the sound of harpists playing on their
harps, 3and they sing a new song before
the throne and before the four living creatures and before the elders. No one could
learn that song except the one hundred
forty-four thousand who have been redeemed from the earth. 4It is these who
have not defiled themselves with women,
for they are virgins; these follow the Lamb
wherever he goes. They have been redeemed from humankind as first fruits for
God and the Lamb, 5and in their mouth
no lie was found; they are blameless.

The Messages of the Three Angels

6 Then I saw another angel flying in
midheaven, with an eternal gospel to proclaim to those who live[s] on the earth—to
every nation and tribe and language and
people. 7He said in a loud voice, "Fear
God and give him glory, for the hour of
his judgment has come; and worship him
who made heaven and earth, the sea and
the springs of water."
8 Then another angel, a second, followed, saying, "Fallen, fallen is Babylon
the great! She has made all nations drink
of the wine of the wrath of her fornication."
9 Then another angel, a third, followed
them, crying with a loud voice, "Those
who worship the beast and its image, and
receive a mark on their foreheads or on
their hands, 10they will also drink the
wine of God's wrath, poured unmixed
into the cup of his anger, and they will be
tormented with fire and sulfur in the presence of the holy angels and in the presence of the Lamb. 11And the smoke of
their torment goes up forever and ever.
There is no rest day or night for those who
worship the beast and its image and for
anyone who receives the mark of its
name."
12 Here is a call for the endurance of
the saints, those who keep the commandments of God and hold fast to the faith
of[t] Jesus.
13 And I heard a voice from heaven
saying, "Write this: Blessed are the dead
who from now on die in the Lord." "Yes,"
says the Spirit, "they will rest from their
labors, for their deeds follow them."

Reaping the Earth's Harvest

14 Then I looked, and there was a
white cloud, and seated on the cloud was

[n] Or *written in the book of life of the Lamb that was slaughtered from the foundation of the world* [o] Gk *whose plague of its death* [p] Or *that had received the plague of the sword* [q] Or *spirit* [r] Other ancient authorities read *six hundred sixteen* [s] Gk *sit* [t] Or *to their faith in*

one like the Son of Man, with a golden crown on his head, and a sharp sickle in his hand! ¹⁵Another angel came out of the temple, calling with a loud voice to the one who sat on the cloud, "Use your sickle and reap, for the hour to reap has come, because the harvest of the earth is fully ripe." ¹⁶So the one who sat on the cloud swung his sickle over the earth, and the earth was reaped.

17 Then another angel came out of the temple in heaven, and he too had a sharp sickle. ¹⁸Then another angel came out from the altar, the angel who has authority over fire, and he called with a loud voice to him who had the sharp sickle, "Use your sharp sickle and gather the clusters of the vine of the earth, for its grapes are ripe." ¹⁹So the angel swung his sickle over the earth and gathered the vintage of the earth, and he threw it into the great wine press of the wrath of God. ²⁰And the wine press was trodden outside the city, and blood flowed from the wine

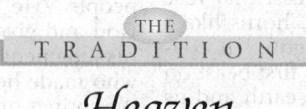

THE TRADITION

Heaven

Then I looked, and there was the Lamb, standing on Mount Zion!
REVELATION 14.1

An old woman, the organized type, was making her funeral arrangements.

"I want an open casket," she told the undertaker. "Make me look nice. But here's the important thing: Put a fork in my right hand."

"A fork?" *Now I've heard everything,* he thought.

"I don't care if it sounds crazy," the woman went on. "All my life I've looked forward to the part of the meal where they take away your plate and say, 'Keep your fork.' That means dessert is coming, and I love dessert! Well, I want to keep my fork one last time as my statement that the best is yet to come."

Who can adequately describe the reward for faithful disciples of Jesus? "Heaven," we call it, "paradise," or "the kingdom of God." Jesus spoke of it using images of a banquet and a house with many rooms.

What images would *you* use to describe heaven? A never-ending vacation with beloved family and friends? The honeymoon period of a marriage that is guaranteed to get better and better with each passing day? A recapturing of childhood's joy and wonder, of first discoveries untarnished by disappointments? A homecoming to a beloved native land?

The book of Revelation describes this wondrous life to come with the rich image of the holy city, the new Jerusalem (see especially chapters 21 and 22). This city blazes with God's glory, light more radiant than the sun. Sparkling with gold and precious stones, it is a cube—absolute symmetry indicating absolute perfection. The cube is also intended to recall the shape of the inner chamber of the temple in the earthly Jerusalem. This was a spot so holy that only the high priest could enter, and then only once a year. In the heavenly Jerusalem, the whole city is God's temple and throne room. We have access to God, seeing him face-to-face.

Even the most visionary among us can only grasp at images to express what heaven is like, and so John's picture is hardly a photograph. Still, it is a gripping portrayal of the perfect peace and joy that come from communion with God and with those who love him.

But we don't have to wait for death to start tasting this dessert! Even now we are called to experience something of the union with God that we will know fully in the heavenly Jerusalem. And so, as Saint Catherine of Siena used to say, "All the way to heaven is heaven."

press, as high as a horse's bridle, for a distance of about two hundred miles.ᵘ

The Angels with the Seven Last Plagues

15 Then I saw another portent in heaven, great and amazing: seven angels with seven plagues, which are the last, for with them the wrath of God is ended.

2 And I saw what appeared to be a sea of glass mixed with fire, and those who had conquered the beast and its image and the number of its name, standing beside the sea of glass with harps of God in their hands. ³And they sing the song of Moses, the servantᵛ of God, and the song of the Lamb:

"Great and amazing are your deeds,
    Lord God the Almighty!
Just and true are your ways,
    King of the nations!ʷ
⁴ Lord, who will not fear
    and glorify your name?
For you alone are holy.
    All nations will come
    and worship before you,
for your judgments have been
        revealed."

5 After this I looked, and the temple of the tentˣ of witness in heaven was opened, ⁶and out of the temple came the seven angels with the seven plagues, robed in pure bright linen,ʸ with golden sashes across their chests. ⁷Then one of the four living creatures gave the seven angels seven golden bowls full of the wrath of God, who lives forever and ever; ⁸and the temple was filled with smoke from the glory of God and from his power, and no one could enter the temple until the seven plagues of the seven angels were ended.

The Bowls of God's Wrath

16 Then I heard a loud voice from the temple telling the seven angels, "Go and pour out on the earth the seven bowls of the wrath of God."

2 So the first angel went and poured his bowl on the earth, and a foul and painful sore came on those who had the mark of the beast and who worshiped its image.

3 The second angel poured his bowl into the sea, and it became like the blood of a corpse, and every living thing in the sea died.

4 The third angel poured his bowl into the rivers and the springs of water, and they became blood. ⁵And I heard the angel of the waters say,

"You are just, O Holy One, who are
        and were,
    for you have judged these things;
⁶ because they shed the blood of
        saints and prophets,
    you have given them blood to
        drink.
    It is what they deserve!"
⁷And I heard the altar respond,
    "Yes, O Lord God, the Almighty,
    your judgments are true and just!"

8 The fourth angel poured his bowl on the sun, and it was allowed to scorch people with fire; ⁹they were scorched by the fierce heat, but they cursed the name of God, who had authority over these plagues, and they did not repent and give him glory.

10 The fifth angel poured his bowl on the throne of the beast, and its kingdom was plunged into darkness; people gnawed their tongues in agony, ¹¹and cursed the God of heaven because of their pains and sores, and they did not repent of their deeds.

12 The sixth angel poured his bowl on the great river Euphrates, and its water was dried up in order to prepare the way for the kings from the east. ¹³And I saw three foul spirits like frogs coming from the mouth of the dragon, from the mouth of the beast, and from the mouth of the false prophet. ¹⁴These are demonic spirits, performing signs, who go abroad to the kings of the whole world, to assemble them for battle on the great day of God the Almighty. ¹⁵("See, I am coming like a thief! Blessed is the one who stays awake and is clothed,ᶻ not going about naked and exposed to shame.") ¹⁶And they assembled them at the place that in Hebrew is called Harmagedon.

17 The seventh angel poured his bowl into the air, and a loud voice came out of the temple, from the throne, saying, "It is done!" ¹⁸And there came flashes of lightning, rumblings, peals of thunder, and a violent earthquake, such as had not occurred since people were upon the earth, so violent was that earthquake.

ᵘ Gk one thousand six hundred stadia   ᵛ Gk slave
ʷ Other ancient authorities read the ages   ˣ Or tabernacle   ʸ Other ancient authorities read stone
ᶻ Gk and keeps his robes

[19]The great city was split into three parts, and the cities of the nations fell. God remembered great Babylon and gave her the wine-cup of the fury of his wrath. [20]And every island fled away, and no mountains were to be found; [21]and huge hailstones, each weighing about a hundred pounds,[a] dropped from heaven on people, until they cursed God for the plague of the hail, so fearful was that plague.

The Great Whore and the Beast

17 Then one of the seven angels who had the seven bowls came and said to me, "Come, I will show you the judgment of the great whore who is seated on many waters, [2]with whom the kings of the earth have committed fornication, and with the wine of whose fornication the inhabitants of the earth have become drunk." [3]So he carried me away in the spirit[b] into a wilderness, and I saw a woman sitting on a scarlet beast that was full of blasphemous names, and it had seven heads and ten horns. [4]The woman was clothed in purple and scarlet, and adorned with gold and jewels and pearls, holding in her hand a golden cup full of abominations and the impurities of her fornication; [5]and on her forehead was written a name, a mystery: "Babylon the great, mother of whores and of earth's abominations." [6]And I saw that the woman was drunk with the blood of the saints and the blood of the witnesses to Jesus.

When I saw her, I was greatly amazed. [7]But the angel said to me, "Why are you so amazed? I will tell you the mystery of the woman, and of the beast with seven heads and ten horns that carries her. [8]The beast that you saw was, and is not, and is about to ascend from the bottomless pit and go to destruction. And the inhabitants of the earth, whose names have not been written in the book of life from the foundation of the world, will be amazed when they see the beast, because it was and is not and is to come.

[9]"This calls for a mind that has wisdom: the seven heads are seven mountains on which the woman is seated; also, they are seven kings, [10]of whom five have fallen, one is living, and the other has not yet come; and when he comes, he must remain only a little while. [11]As for the beast that was and is not, it is an eighth but it belongs to the seven, and it goes to destruction. [12]And the ten horns that you saw are ten kings who have not yet received a kingdom, but they are to receive authority as kings for one hour, together with the beast. [13]These are united in yielding their power and authority to the beast; [14]they will make war on the Lamb, and the Lamb will conquer them, for he is Lord of lords and King of kings, and those with him are called and chosen and faithful."

15 And he said to me, "The waters that you saw, where the whore is seated, are peoples and multitudes and nations and languages. [16]And the ten horns that you saw, they and the beast will hate the whore; they will make her desolate and naked; they will devour her flesh and burn her up with fire. [17]For God has put it into their hearts to carry out his purpose by agreeing to give their kingdom to the beast, until the words of God will be fulfilled. [18]The woman you saw is the great city that rules over the kings of the earth."

The Fall of Babylon

18 After this I saw another angel coming down from heaven, having great authority; and the earth was made bright with his splendor. [2]He called out with a mighty voice,

"Fallen, fallen is Babylon the great!
    It has become a dwelling place
        of demons,
    a haunt of every foul spirit,
    a haunt of every foul bird,
    a haunt of every foul and
        hateful beast.[c]
[3] For all the nations have drunk[d]
        of the wine of the wrath of her
            fornication,
    and the kings of the earth have
            committed fornication
            with her,
    and the merchants of the earth
        have grown rich from the
            power[e] of her luxury."

4 Then I heard another voice from heaven saying,

"Come out of her, my people,

---

[a] Gk *weighing about a talent*   [b] Or *in the Spirit*
[c] Other ancient authorities lack the words *a haunt of every foul beast* and attach the words *and hateful* to the previous line so as to read *a haunt of every foul and hateful bird*   [d] Other ancient authorities read *She has made all nations drink*   [e] Or *resources*

so that you do not take part
    in her sins,
and so that you do not share in her
    plagues;
5 for her sins are heaped high
    as heaven,
  and God has remembered
    her iniquities.
6 Render to her as she herself
    has rendered,
  and repay her double for
    her deeds;
  mix a double draught for her
    in the cup she mixed.
7 As she glorified herself and lived
    luxuriously,
  so give her a like measure of
    torment and grief.
Since in her heart she says,
  'I rule as a queen;
I am no widow,
  and I will never see grief,'
8 therefore her plagues will come in a
    single day—
    pestilence and mourning
      and famine—
  and she will be burned with fire;
    for mighty is the Lord God who
      judges her."
9 And the kings of the earth, who committed fornication and lived in luxury with her, will weep and wail over her when they see the smoke of her burning; 10they will stand far off, in fear of her torment, and say,
"Alas, alas, the great city,
  Babylon, the mighty city!
For in one hour your judgment
  has come."

11 And the merchants of the earth weep and mourn for her, since no one buys their cargo anymore, 12cargo of gold, silver, jewels and pearls, fine linen, purple, silk and scarlet, all kinds of scented wood, all articles of ivory, all articles of costly wood, bronze, iron, and marble, 13cinnamon, spice, incense, myrrh, frankincense, wine, olive oil, choice flour and wheat, cattle and sheep, horses and chariots, slaves—and human lives.*f*

14 "The fruit for which your soul
    longed
  has gone from you,
  and all your dainties and
    your splendor
  are lost to you,
    never to be found again!"

15The merchants of these wares, who gained wealth from her, will stand far off, in fear of her torment, weeping and mourning aloud,
16 "Alas, alas, the great city,
  clothed in fine linen,
    in purple and scarlet,
  adorned with gold,
    with jewels, and with pearls!
17 For in one hour all this wealth has
    been laid waste!"

And all shipmasters and seafarers, sailors and all whose trade is on the sea, stood far off 18and cried out as they saw the smoke of her burning,
"What city was like the great city?"
19And they threw dust on their heads, as they wept and mourned, crying out,
"Alas, alas, the great city,
  where all who had ships at sea
    grew rich by her wealth!
For in one hour she has been
    laid waste."

20 Rejoice over her, O heaven, you saints and apostles and prophets! For God has given judgment for you against her.

21 Then a mighty angel took up a stone like a great millstone and threw it into the sea, saying,
"With such violence Babylon the
    great city
  will be thrown down,
  and will be found no more;
22 and the sound of harpists and
      minstrels and of flutists and
      trumpeters
  will be heard in you no more;
and an artisan of any trade
  will be found in you no more;
and the sound of the millstone
  will be heard in you no more;
23 and the light of a lamp
  will shine in you no more;
and the voice of bridegroom
    and bride
  will be heard in you no more;
for your merchants were the
    magnates of the earth,
  and all nations were deceived by
    your sorcery.
24 And in you*g* was found the blood
    of prophets and of saints,
  and of all who have been
    slaughtered on earth."

f Or chariots, and human bodies and souls
g Gk her

The Rejoicing in Heaven

19 After this I heard what seemed to be the loud voice of a great multitude in heaven, saying,

"Hallelujah!
Salvation and glory and power
    to our God,
2   for his judgments are true
        and just;
he has judged the great whore
    who corrupted the earth with her
        fornication,
and he has avenged on her the
    blood of his servants."[h]

3 Once more they said,

"Hallelujah!
The smoke goes up from her forever
    and ever."

4 And the twenty-four elders and the four living creatures fell down and worshiped God who is seated on the throne, saying,

"Amen. Hallelujah!"

5 And from the throne came a voice saying,

"Praise our God,
    all you his servants,[h]
and all who fear him,
    small and great."

6 Then I heard what seemed to be the voice of a great multitude, like the sound of many waters and like the sound of mighty thunderpeals, crying out,

"Hallelujah!
For the Lord our God
    the Almighty reigns.
7 Let us rejoice and exult
    and give him the glory,
for the marriage of the Lamb
        has come,
    and his bride has made
        herself ready;
8 to her it has been granted to
        be clothed
    with fine linen, bright and pure"—

for the fine linen is the righteous deeds of the saints.

9 And the angel said[i] to me, "Write this: Blessed are those who are invited to the marriage supper of the Lamb." And he said to me, "These are true words of God." 10 Then I fell down at his feet to worship him, but he said to me, "You must not do that! I am a fellow servant[j] with you and your comrades[k] who hold the testimony of Jesus.[l] Worship God! For the testimony of Jesus[l] is the spirit of prophecy."

The Rider on the White Horse

11 Then I saw heaven opened, and there was a white horse! Its rider is called Faithful and True, and in righteousness he judges and makes war. 12 His eyes are like a flame of fire, and on his head are many diadems; and he has a name inscribed that no one knows but himself. 13 He is clothed in a robe dipped in[m] blood, and his name is called The Word of God. 14 And the armies of heaven, wearing fine linen, white and pure, were following him on white horses. 15 From his mouth comes a sharp sword with which to strike down the nations, and he will rule[n] them with a rod of iron; he will tread the wine press of the fury of the wrath of God the Almighty. 16 On his robe and on his thigh he has a name inscribed, "King of kings and Lord of lords."

The Beast and Its Armies Defeated

17 Then I saw an angel standing in the sun, and with a loud voice he called to all the birds that fly in midheaven, "Come, gather for the great supper of God, 18 to eat the flesh of kings, the flesh of captains, the flesh of the mighty, the flesh of horses and their riders—flesh of all, both free and slave, both small and great." 19 Then I saw the beast and the kings of the earth with their armies gathered to make war against the rider on the horse and against his army. 20 And the beast was captured, and with it the false prophet who had performed in its presence the signs by which he deceived those who had received the mark of the beast and those who worshiped its image. These two were thrown alive into the lake of fire that burns with sulfur. 21 And the rest were killed by the sword of the rider on the horse, the sword that came from his mouth; and all the birds were gorged with their flesh.

The Thousand Years

20 Then I saw an angel coming down from heaven, holding in his hand the key to the bottomless pit and a great chain. 2 He seized the dragon, that ancient serpent, who is the Devil and Satan, and bound him for a thousand years, 3 and threw him into the pit, and locked and sealed it over him, so that he would

---

h Gk *slaves*   *i* Gk *he said*   *j* Gk *slave*   *k* Gk *brothers*   *l* Or *to Jesus*   *m* Other ancient authorities read *sprinkled with*   *n* Or *will shepherd*

deceive the nations no more, until the thousand years were ended. After that he must be let out for a little while.

4 Then I saw thrones, and those seated on them were given authority to judge. I also saw the souls of those who had been beheaded for their testimony to Jesus[o] and for the word of God. They had not worshiped the beast or its image and had not received its mark on their foreheads or their hands. They came to life and reigned with Christ a thousand years. 5(The rest of the dead did not come to life until the thousand years were ended.) This is the first resurrection. 6Blessed and holy are those who share in the first resurrection. Over these the second death has no power, but they will be priests of God and of Christ, and they will reign with him a thousand years.

Satan's Doom

7 When the thousand years are ended, Satan will be released from his prison 8and will come out to deceive the nations at the four corners of the earth, Gog and Magog, in order to gather them for battle; they are as numerous as the sands of the sea. 9They marched up over the breadth of the earth and surrounded the camp of the saints and the beloved city. And fire came down from heaven[p] and consumed them. 10And the devil who had deceived them was thrown into the lake of fire and sulfur, where the beast and the false prophet were, and they will be tormented day and night forever and ever.

The Dead Are Judged

11 Then I saw a great white throne and the one who sat on it; the earth and the heaven fled from his presence, and no place was found for them. 12And I saw the dead, great and small, standing before the throne, and books were opened. Also another book was opened, the book of life. And the dead were judged according to their works, as recorded in the books. 13And the sea gave up the dead that were in it, Death and Hades gave up the dead that were in them, and all were judged according to what they had done. 14Then Death and Hades were thrown into the lake of fire. This is the second death, the lake of fire; 15and anyone whose name was not found written in the book of life was thrown into the lake of fire.

The New Heaven and the New Earth

21 Then I saw a new heaven and a new earth; for the first heaven and the first earth had passed away, and the sea was no more. 2And I saw the holy city, the new Jerusalem, coming down out of heaven from God, prepared as a bride adorned for her husband. 3And I heard a loud voice from the throne saying,

"See, the home[q] of God is among
    mortals.
He will dwell[r] with them;
they will be his peoples,[s]
and God himself will be
    with them;[t]
4 he will wipe every tear from
    their eyes.
Death will be no more;
mourning and crying and pain
    will be no more,
for the first things have passed away."

5 And the one who was seated on the throne said, "See, I am making all things new." Also he said, "Write this, for these words are trustworthy and true." 6Then he said to me, "It is done! I am the Alpha and the Omega, the beginning and the end. To the thirsty I will give water as a gift from the spring of the water of life. 7Those who conquer will inherit these things, and I will be their God and they will be my children. 8But as for the cowardly, the faithless,[u] the polluted, the murderers, the fornicators, the sorcerers, the idolaters, and all liars, their place will be in the lake that burns with fire and sulfur, which is the second death."

Vision of the New Jerusalem

9 Then one of the seven angels who had the seven bowls full of the seven last plagues came and said to me, "Come, I will show you the bride, the wife of the Lamb." 10And in the spirit[v] he carried me away to a great, high mountain and showed me the holy city Jerusalem coming down out of heaven from God. 11It has the glory of God and a radiance like a very rare jewel, like jasper, clear as crystal.

---

o Or *for the testimony of Jesus*   p Other ancient authorities read *from God, out of heaven,* or *out of heaven from God*   q Gk *the tabernacle*   r Gk *will tabernacle*   s Other ancient authorities read *people*   t Other ancient authorities add *and be their God*   u Or *the unbelieving*   v Or *in the Spirit*

¹²It has a great, high wall with twelve gates, and at the gates twelve angels, and on the gates are inscribed the names of the twelve tribes of the Israelites; ¹³on the east three gates, on the north three gates, on the south three gates, and on the west three gates. ¹⁴And the wall of the city has twelve foundations, and on them are the twelve names of the twelve apostles of the Lamb.

15 The angel*w* who talked to me had a measuring rod of gold to measure the city and its gates and walls. ¹⁶The city lies foursquare, its length the same as its width; and he measured the city with his rod, fifteen hundred miles;*x* its length and width and height are equal. ¹⁷He also measured its wall, one hundred forty-four cubits*y* by human measurement, which the angel was using. ¹⁸The wall is built of jasper, while the city is pure gold, clear as glass. ¹⁹The foundations of the wall of the city are adorned with every jewel; the first was jasper, the second sapphire, the third agate, the fourth emerald, ²⁰the fifth onyx, the sixth carnelian, the seventh chrysolite, the eighth beryl, the ninth topaz, the tenth chrysoprase, the eleventh jacinth, the twelfth amethyst. ²¹And the twelve gates are twelve pearls, each of the gates is a single pearl, and the street of the city is pure gold, transparent as glass.

22 I saw no temple in the city, for its temple is the Lord God the Almighty and the Lamb. ²³And the city has no need of sun or moon to shine on it, for the glory of God is its light, and its lamp is the Lamb.

w Gk *He*   *x* Gk *twelve thousand stadia*   *y* That is, almost seventy-five yards

*T*ransparency

THURSDAY

Scripture Reading for Today:
Revelation 21.9–14, 22–27

Verse for Today:
Revelation 21.23

Painfully we have to unlearn our mistaken notions about glory, so that we can learn Christ's values and learn discipleship, consenting to serve and to be emptied and to let the light shine through us. For Christ's first nine months on earth, Mary was his only visible medium; he shone only through her, as the sunlight shines with a special color through the windows at Chartres. Today, believers are his transparencies. If the light is to come through we have to be servants of the covenant-love, wherever and in whatever way may be required, not for our own aggrandizement but in self-forgetting; and this is indeed glorious, although it does not feel like it.

Jerusalem stands not only for the Church as whole, but for every lover of God; "and the city has no need of sun or moon to shine on it, for the glory of God is its light, and its lamp is the Lamb." It is not your glory but his, and you have to consent to be transparent, to be the lantern not the light, like John the Baptist. Are you prepared to let this glory shine through you, through your unselfish loving, your smiling, your unselfseeking service and humility? Are you prepared to let the joy of the Lord radiate to others through you? In no other way "the glory of the LORD shall be revealed, and all people shall see it together" [Isaiah 40.5]. It will be visible only if we allow Christ to be born in our lives and shine through us.

—*MARIA BOULDING*

Go to page 1677 for your next devotional reading.

Come, Lord Jesus

FRIDAY

Scripture Reading
for Today:
Revelation 22.12–21

Verse for Today:
Revelation 22.17

At the origin of all things, O Lord,
God the Father summoned you:
"Come!" and you came.

This summons, which you heard
and which you answered,
you also place in us,
so that it may possess in us the living force
truly to summon you.

You allow even us
to summon you: "Come!"
And by allowing us this, you show us
that you will to answer the summons
and to come,
that you are even now coming,
that we need only call you,
that we are permitted to expect you.

You hear. You hand over to us this summons
with the whole force of your divine will:
you place yourself completely at the disposition
of this summons that you suggest to us.
As if you were the servant
and we the ones in command.
In this "Come!" you give away
to us your secret. The secret that you never hear
a question
without answering it.
You allow us, in whatever state we may be in, to call
for you,
and you come.

Lord, grant that each of us, grant that your whole
Church,
grant that all who have not yet found the way
to you and to your Church
may learn—each one separately and all together,
particularly all in your Church—
to let your summons ring out.

Teach us to say: "Come!"
In the same spirit of prayer
that you poured into our hearts
when in our midst you began to pray:

Father, thy kingdom come! *Amen.*

—*ADRIENNE VON SPEYR*

Go to page 1678 for your next devotional reading.

Priscilla

Her Name, the Diminutive of "Prisca," Means "Worthy" or "Venerable"

THE
STORY
OF A
WOMAN

Her Character: *One of the first missionaries and a leader of the early church, along with her husband Aquila, she was a woman whose understanding of the faith helped build up the church.*
Her Sorrow: *To experience opposition to the gospel from both Jews and Gentiles.*
Her Joy: *To spread the gospel and nurture the church.*

Read Acts 18.1–4, 18–28; 19
How good it was to have Paul back again, she thought. Ephesus was on fire with the gospel, their young church growing stronger each day. Paul's preaching and miracles had brought many to faith. Even the touch of his handkerchief had healed illnesses and delivered people from evil spirits.

Priscilla couldn't help laughing when she heard the story of Sceva's seven sons, Jewish exorcists who had tried to duplicate such wonders by driving out an evil spirit with a magic invocation, associating themselves with Jesus and Paul.

But the spirit had merely mocked them: "Jesus I know, and Paul I know; but who are you?" (19.15). Then the man they were trying to deliver beat them so soundly they ran bleeding and naked from the house.

Priscilla's faith had been planted years earlier in an atmosphere of strife and controversy, first in Rome and later in Corinth. The latter was a commercial center, famous for its appetite for vice, hardly a place to nurture the faith of a new believer. Yet that was where God transplanted her, along with her husband Aquila, after Claudius expelled Jews from Rome in A.D. 49.

After the couple had been in Corinth for about a year, they met a man who would involve them in yet more controversy. Paul of Tarsus was a Jew who had ruthlessly persecuted Jesus' followers until his own dramatic conversion. Lately he had been traveling in Asia Minor and Macedonia, preaching the gospel wherever he went. When he arrived in Corinth, he probably met the couple through their common trade as tentmakers. Priscilla and Aquila invited Paul to stay in their home and work with them. After eighteen months, Paul set sail for Ephesus, taking Priscilla and Aquila with him.

The three missionaries must have been eager to see a city that ranked in importance with Rome, Corinth, Antioch, and Alexandria. True to form, Paul's preaching soon resulted in a riot from which he escaped with his life, thanks to the wise counsel of other believers, possibly including Priscilla. When Paul left Ephesus, Priscilla and Aquila took charge of the church that met in their home.

Before long another Jew arrived, preaching eloquently about Jesus to the Jews at Ephesus. But Apollos had grasped only a shadow of the gospel, one more in keeping with the message of John the Baptist than of Jesus. Rather than denouncing him, Priscilla and Aquila merely took him aside and instructed him in the faith. They did their job so well that Apollos eventually went on to Corinth, where he advanced the work Paul had begun.

Priscilla must have been a spiritually mature woman, whose gifts equipped her for leadership. Her name actually precedes Aquila's four out of the six times they are mentioned together in the New Testament, probably signifying her greater abilities as a leader or the fact that her family may have hailed from a higher social strata. Priscilla's role in instructing Apollos and leading the early church is remarkable. She helped the early church flourish in a culture steeped in paganism.

Praying With Priscilla

Greet Prisca [Priscilla] and Aquila, who work with me in Christ Jesus, and who risked their necks for my life, to whom not only I give thanks, but also all the churches of the Gentiles.—Romans 16.3–4

Praise God: *For using both women and men to spread the gospel of Jesus Christ.*

Offer Thanks: *For women whose faith have nourished yours.*

Confess: *Any tendency to live out your own faith in a half-hearted manner, limiting the way God wants to use you.*

Ask God: *To make you unafraid of the controversy that is generated by a faithful life.*

Lift Your Heart

It's a Wonderful Life is a movie that tells the heartwarming story of George Bailey's Christmas Eve visit with an angel, who cures his depression by showing him just how valuable his life has been. Like George Bailey, most of us have affected others in more positive ways than we might guess.

Our lives are meant to have a rippling effect, so that others feel the influence of our gifts and faith. This week, snatch a quiet moment on your knees or in your favorite chair, and close your eyes. Imagine yourself as a stone in the hand of God. Watch him throw you out into the water. What kind of ripples do you see? Are they large or small? Perhaps your brother is a Christian because you shared your faith with him. Maybe a child has responded to God's forgiveness because she first experienced yours. Pray that God will make waves with your faith, even rocking a few boats along the way.

Father, I don't want to settle for the status quo, professing belief in you and then acting as though everything good in life comes from the world around me. Let the ripple effect of my faith build up your church.

Go to page 2 for your next devotional reading.

24The nations will walk by its light, and the kings of the earth will bring their glory into it. 25Its gates will never be shut by day—and there will be no night there. 26People will bring into it the glory and the honor of the nations. 27But nothing unclean will enter it, nor anyone who practices abomination or falsehood, but only those who are written in the Lamb's book of life.

The River of Life

22 Then the angel*z* showed me the river of the water of life, bright as crystal, flowing from the throne of God and of the Lamb 2through the middle of the street of the city. On either side of the river is the tree of life*a* with its twelve kinds of fruit, producing its fruit each month; and the leaves of the tree are for the healing of the nations. 3Nothing accursed will be found there any more. But the throne of God and of the Lamb will be in it, and his servants*b* will worship him; 4they will see his face, and his name will be on their foreheads. 5And there will be no more night; they need no light of lamp or sun, for the Lord God will be their light, and they will reign forever and ever.

6 And he said to me, "These words are trustworthy and true, for the Lord, the God of the spirits of the prophets, has sent his angel to show his servants*b* what must soon take place."

7 "See, I am coming soon! Blessed is the one who keeps the words of the prophecy of this book."

Epilogue and Benediction

8 I, John, am the one who heard and saw these things. And when I heard and saw them, I fell down to worship at the feet of the angel who showed them to me; 9but he said to me, "You must not do that! I am a fellow servant*c* with you and your comrades*d* the prophets, and with those who keep the words of this book. Worship God!"

10 And he said to me, "Do not seal up the words of the prophecy of this book, for the time is near. 11Let the evildoer still do evil, and the filthy still be filthy, and the righteous still do right, and the holy still be holy."

12 "See, I am coming soon; my reward is with me, to repay according to everyone's work. 13I am the Alpha and the Omega, the first and the last, the beginning and the end."

14 Blessed are those who wash their robes,*e* so that they will have the right to the tree of life and may enter the city by the gates. 15Outside are the dogs and sorcerers and fornicators and murderers and idolaters, and everyone who loves and practices falsehood.

16 "It is I, Jesus, who sent my angel to you with this testimony for the churches. I am the root and the descendant of David, the bright morning star."

17 The Spirit and the bride say, "Come."
And let everyone who hears say,
"Come."
And let everyone who is thirsty
come.
Let anyone who wishes take the
water of life as a gift.

18 I warn everyone who hears the words of the prophecy of this book: if anyone adds to them, God will add to that person the plagues described in this book; 19if anyone takes away from the words of the book of this prophecy, God will take away that person's share in the tree of life and in the holy city, which are described in this book.

20 The one who testifies to these things says, "Surely I am coming soon."
Amen. Come, Lord Jesus!

21 The grace of the Lord Jesus be with all the saints. Amen.*f*

z Gk he   *a* Or *the Lamb.* 2*In the middle of the street of the city, and on either side of the river, is the tree of life*   *b* Gk *slaves*   *c* Gk *slave*   *d* Gk *brothers*   *e* Other ancient authorities read *do his commandments*   *f* Other ancient authorities lack *all;* others lack *the saints;* others lack *Amen*

Study
Helps

Topical Index

Acknowledgements

Biographies

Lectionary

Topical Index

The devotional articles, the character sketches, and the "Tradition" articles in this Bible contain a wide variety of topics that may be of interest to you, ranging from practical help on priorities to guidance on prayer to mediations on God's presence. This index is designed to help you find those topics easily and quickly.

Acknowledgements

Page 2. Taken from *Words Made Flesh* by Fran Ferder. Copyright © 1986 by Ave Maria Press, Notre Dame, IN 46556. Used by permission of the publisher.

Page 5. Copyright © 1998 by Carol Gura. Used by permission of the publisher. Thomas More Publishing, 200 East Bethany Drive, Allen, Texas 75002. All rights reserved.

Page 6. Taken from *My Life Is in Your Hands* by Kathy Troccoli. Copyright © by Kathy Troccoli. Used by permission of Zondervan Publishing House.

Page 7. Taken from *How to Read and Pray the Parables* by Marilyn Gustin. Copyright © 1992 by Ligouri Publications. Used by permission of the author.

Page 12. Taken from *Where Miracles Happen* by Joan Wester Anderson. Copyright © 1994, Brett Books, Inc., Brooklyn NY 11229-0011. Used by permission.

Page 20. Taken from *Dear Heart, Come Home.* Copyright © 1997 by The Crossroad Publishing Company. Used by permission.

Page 21. Taken from "Life with the Beavers." *Our Sunday Visitor* (August 9, 1998). Copyright © 1998 by Lisa Ferguson. Used by permission.

Page 25. Taken from *Sister Wendy's Book of Meditations* by Lara Maiklen and Patricia Wright. Copyright © 1998 by DK Publishing, Inc.

Page 39. Taken from *Amazing Grace* by Kathleen Norris. Copyright © 1998 by Kathleen Norris. Used by permission of G.P. Putnam's Sons, a division of Penguin Putnam, Inc.

Page 44. Taken from *A Miracle a Day* by Ann Spangler. Copyright © 1996 by Ann Spangler. Used by permission of Zondervan Publishing House.

Page 52. Taken from *Revelations of Divine Mercy, Daily Readings from the Diary of Blessed Faustina Kowalski* by George Kosicki. Copyright © 1996. Used by permission.

Page 55. Taken from "Seventy Times Seven." *New Covenant Magazine* (July/August 1991). Used by permission of the author.

Page 65. Taken from "What's in God's Name?" *New Covenant Magazine* (April 1991). Used by permission of the author.

Page 68. Quote by Dorothy Day taken from "The Mystery of the Poor." *The Catholic Worker,* April 1964, p. 2.

Page 70. Taken from *A Miracle a Day* by Ann Spangler. Copyright © 1996 by Ann Spangler. Used by permission of Zondervan Publishing House.

Page 76. Taken from *Hildegard of Bingen,* translated by Mother Columba Hart and Jane Bishop. Copyright © 1990 by the Abbey of Regina Laudis: Benedictine Congregation Regina Laudis of the Strict Observance, Inc. Used by permission of Paulist Press.

Page 97. Taken from *Full of Grace: Women and the Abundant Life.* Copyright © 1998 by Johnnette S. Benkovic. Published by Servant Publications, Box 8617, Ann Arbor, Michigan, 48107. Used by permission.

Page 102. Taken from an article by Roma Bourassa. Used by permission of the author.

Page 107. Taken from *365 Mary: A Daily Guide to Mary's Wisdom and Comfort* by Woodeene Koenig-Bricker. Copyright © 1997 Harper Collins Publishers, New York.

Page 110. Taken from *365 Mary: A Daily Guide to Mary's Wisdom and Comfort* by Woodeene Koenig-Bricker. Copyright © 1997 Harper Collins Publishers, New York.

Page 128. Taken from *Miracles Do Happen* by Briege McKenna and Henry Libersat. Copyright © 1987 by Briege McKenna and Henry Libersat. Published by Servant Publications, Box 8617, Ann Arbor, Michigan. 48107. Used by permission.

Page 158. Taken from *Lent, Reflections and Stories on the Daily Readings*. Copyright © 1996 by Orbis Books. Used by permission.

Page 174. Taken from *Traits of a Healthy Family* by Dolores Curran. Copyright © 1983. Used by permission of the author.

Page 191. Taken from *Seasons of Your Heart* by Macrina Wiederkehr. Copyright © 1991 by Harper San Francisco.

Page 199. Taken from *Quiltless Catholic Parenting from A to Y*. Copyright © 1995 by Bert Ghezzi. Published by Servant Publications, Box 8617, Ann Arbor, Michigan, 48107. Used by permission.

Page 201. Taken from "Starry-eyed Ideal." *St. Anthony Messenger* (April 1990). Used by permission of the author.

Page 214. Taken from *The Celtic Way of Prayer* by Esther de Waal. Copyright © 1997 by Doubleday.

Page 225. Taken from "The Other Side of Fear." *Ligourian* (September 1998). Used by permission of the publisher.

Page 231. Taken from *Graham Crackers, Galoshes, and God* by Bernadette McCarver Snyder. Copyright © 1995 by Ligouri Publications. Used by permission of the publisher.

Page 248. Taken from *We Have Been Friends Together* by Raissa Maritain. Copyright © 1942. All rights reserved.

Page 258. Taken from *Graham Crackers, Galoshes, and God* by Bernadette McCarver Snyder. Copyright © 1995 by Ligouri Publications. Used by permission of the publisher.

Page 278. Taken from *By Grief Refined, Letters to a Widow* by Alice von Hildebrand. Copyright © 1994 by Franciscan University Press. Used by permission.

Page 281. Copyright © 1998 by Carol Gura. Used by permission of Thomas More Publishing, 200 East Bethany Drive, Allen, Texas 75002. All rights reserved.

Page 287. Taken from *God's Word Today* (August 1998). Copyright © God's Word Today, 2115 Summit Avenue, St. Paul, MN 55105-1082. Used by permission.

Page 295. Taken from *Midlife Awakenings: Discovering the Gifts Life Has Given Us* by Barbara Bartocci. Copyright © 1998 by Ave Maria Press, Notre Dame, IN 46556. Used by permission of the publisher.

Page 301. Taken from *Balancing Act* by Mary Ellen Ashcroft. Copyright © 1996 by Mary Ellen Ashcroft. Used by permission of InterVarsity Press, P.O. Box 1400, Downers Grove, IL 60515.

Page 305. Taken from *A Miracle a Day* by Ann Spangler. Copyright © 1996 by Ann Spangler. Used by permission of Zondervan Publishing House.

Page 331. Taken from *Seasons of Your Heart* by Macrina Wiederkehr. Copyright © 1991 by Harper San Francisco.

Page 337. Taken from *The School of Charity: Meditations on the Christian Creed* by Evelyn Underhill. Copyright © 1991 by Darton, Longman & Todd LTD., London.

Page 344. Taken from *Walking on Water* by Madeleine L'Engle. Copyright © 1991 by Harold Shaw Publishers.

Page 354. Taken from *My Life Is in Your Hands* by Kathy Troccoli. Copyright © by Kathy Troccoli. Used by permission of Zondervan Publishing House.

Page 366. Copyright © 2000 by Louise Perotta. Used by permission.

Page 377. Taken from *A Miracle a Day* by Ann Spangler. Copyright © 1996 by Ann Spangler. Used by permission of Zondervan Publishing House.

Page 378. Taken from *The Pummeled Heart: Finding Peace through Pain* by Antoinette Bosco. Copyright © 1994, Twenty-Third Publications, Mystic, CT 06355. Used by permission of the publisher.

Page 388. Taken from *A Miracle a Day* by Ann Spangler. Copyright © 1996 by Ann Spangler. Used by permission of Zondervan Publishing House.

Page 391. Taken from *An Angel a Day* by Ann Spangler. Copyright © 1994 by Ann Spangler. Used by permission of Zondervan Publishing House.

Page 409. Taken from *Celebrating the Single Life* by Dr. Susan Muto. Copyright © 1982 by Epiphany Association 2000, 947 Tropical Avenue, Pittsburgh, PA 15216-3031. Used by permission of Dr. Muto and Epiphany Association. All rights reserved.

Page 418. Taken from *God's Word Today* (September 1, 1997). Used by permission of the author.

Page 444. Taken from *The Bible Today*, January 1986. Published by The Liturgical Press. Copyright © 1986 by Irene Nowell, O.S.B. Used by permission of the author.

Page 447. Taken from *Refresh Your Life in the Spirit*. Copyright © 1997 by Babsie Bleasdell with Henry Libersat. Published by Servant Publications, Box 8617, Ann Arbor, Michigan, 48017. Used by permission.

Page 453. Taken from *The Collected Works of St. Teresa of Avila, Vol. 2*, translated by Kieran Kavanaugh, O.C.D. and Otilio Rodriguez, O.C.D. Copyright © 1976 by ICS Publications. Used by permission of the publisher.

Page 483. Taken from *Enfolded in Love, Daily Readings with Julian of Norwich* by Julian of Norwich. Copyright © 1980 by Darton, Longman and Todd, LTD., London, England.

Page 494. Reprinted by permission from *U.S. Catholic* magazine, Claretian Publications.

Page 501. Used by permission of *Our Sunday Visitor*, 200 Noll Plaza, Huntington, IN, 46750. All rights reserved.

Page 508. Copyright © 2000 by Louise Perotta. Used by permission.

Page 519. Taken from *Around the Year with the Trapp Family*. Used by permission of the Trapp Family Estate, Johannes von Trapp, President.

Page 524. Taken from *Walking on Water* by Madeleine L'Engle. Copyright © 1991 by Harold Shaw Publishers.

Page 535. Taken from *The Bible Today* (January 1986). Published by The Liturgical Press. Copyright © 1986 by Irene Nowell, O.S.B. Used by permission of the author.

Page 538. Taken from *Mystics, Visionaries, and Prophets* by Shawn Madigan. Used by permission.

Page 543. Taken from *God's Word Today* (September 1994). Copyright © 1994 by Cindy Cavnar. Used by permission.

Page 551. Taken from *The Kiss from the Cross: Saints for Every Kind of Suffering*. Copyright © 1994 by Ronda De Sola Chervin. Published by Servant Publications, Box 8617, Ann Arbor, Michigan, 48107. Used by permission.

Page 556. Taken from *The Soul Afire: Revelations of the Mystics*, edited by H. A. Reinhold. Copyright © 1973 by Pantheon Books. Used by permission.

Page 562. Taken from *Dorothy Day: Selected Writings* edited by Robert Ellsberg. Copyright © 1983, 1992 by Robert Ellsbert and Tamar Hennessey. Published in 1992 by Orbis Books, Maryknoll, New York 10545.

Page 588. Taken from *A Life-Giving Way* by Esther De Waal. Copyright © 1995 by Liturgical Press. Used by permission.

Page 601. Taken from *Land of Crosses* by Michael Bourdeaux. Copyright © 1979. All rights reserved.

Page 615. Taken from *Dorothy Day: Selected Writings* edited by Robert Ellsberg. Copyright © 1983, 1992 by Robert Ellsbert and Tamar Hennessey. Published in 1992 by Orbis Books, Maryknoll, New York 10545.

Page 621. Taken from *The Comforting of Christ* by Caryll Houselander. Copyright © 1947 by Sheed & Ward. All rights reserved.

Page 628. Taken from *Graham Crackers, Galoshes, and God* by Bernadette McCarver Snyder. Copyright © 1995 by Ligouri Publications. Used by permission of the publisher.

Page 652. Taken from *The Irrational Season* by Madeleine L'Engle. Copyright © 1977 by Madeleine L'Engle. All rights reserved.

Page 656. Taken from "What Job Learned." *New Covenant Magazine* (November 1991). Used by permission of the author.

Page 662. Taken from *God's Word Today* (July 4, 1998). Used by permission of author.

Page 671. Taken from *From Union Square to Rome* by Dorothy Day. Copyright © 1978. Used by Permission.

Page 673. Taken from *An Angel a Day* by Ann Spangler. Copyright © 1994 by Ann Spangler. Used by permission of Zondervan Publishing House.

Page 675. Taken from *God's Word Today* (July 27, 1998). Used by permission of the author.

Page 678. Taken from *New Covenant Magazine* (July 1981). Copyright © 1980 by Dorothy Ranagan. Used by permission.

Page 688. Taken from *Pathways of Spiritual Living* by Susan Annette Muto. Copyright © 1984 by St. Bede's Publications. Used by permission.

Page. 692. Quote taken from *The Cloister Walk* by Kathleen Norris. Riverhead Books, New York, 1996.

Page 694. Taken from *Praying Our Goodbyes* by Joyce Rupp, O.S.M. Copyright © 1988 by Ave Maria Press, Notre Dame, IN 46556. Used with permission of the publisher.

Page 697. Taken from *Dreams and Miracles* by Ann Spangler. Copyright © 1997 by Ann Spangler. Used by permission of Zondervan Publishing House.

Page 700. Taken from *Turning, Reflections on the Experience of Conversion* by Emilie Griffin. Copyright © 1980 by Doubleday.

Page 710. Taken from *Elizabeth Seton: Selected Writings* by Dr. Ellin M. Kelly and Dr. Annabelle M. Melville. Copyright © 1987 by Paulist Press. Used by permission of the publisher.

Page 714. Taken from *Towards Evening* by Mary Hope. Copyright © 1997 by Paraclete Press. Used by permission.

Page 731. Taken from *A Tree Full of Angels* by Macrina Wiederkehr. Copyright © 1988 by Harper Collins Publishers, New York.

Page 735. Taken from *A Life-Giving Way* by Esther De Waal. Copyright © 1995 by Liturgical Press. Used by permission.

Page 739. Taken from *My Life Is in Your Hands* by Kathy Troccoli. Copyright © by Kathy Troccoli. Used by permission of Zondervan Publishing House.

Page 742. Taken from *Full of Grace: Women and the Abundant Life*. Copyright © 1998 by Johnnette S. Benkovic. Published by Servant Publications, Box 8617, Ann Arbor, Michigan, 48107. Used by permission.

Page 747. Taken from *God's Word Today* (December 1998). Used by permission of the author.

Page 759. Taken from *Catherine of Siena, The Dialogue* by Suzanne Noffke. Copyright © 1980 by Paulist Press. Used by permission of the publisher.

Page 762. Taken from *Pastoral Renewal* magazine (October 1985). Copyright © by Sister Ann Shields. Used by permission of the author.

Page 764. Taken from *The Coming of God* by Maria Boulding. Copyright © 1986 by Collins & Collins, UK.

Page 765. Taken from *All Earth is Crammed with Heaven: Daily Reflections for Mothers* by Mary van Balen Holt. Copyright © 1996, Servant Publications. Used by permission of the author.

Page 772. Taken from *A Tree Full of Angels* by Macrina Wiederkehr. Copyright © 1988 by Harper Collins Publishers, New York.

Page 780. Taken from *Refresh Your Life in the Spirit*. Copyright © 1997 by Babsie Bleasdell with Henry Libersat. Published by Servant Publications, Box 8617, Ann Arbor, Michigan, 48017. Used by permission.

Page 782. Taken from *Midlife Awakenings: Discovering the Gifts Life Has Given Us* by Barbara Bartocci. Copyright © 1998 by Ave Maria Press, Notre Dame, IN 46556. Used by permission of the publisher.

Page 791. Taken from *A Tree Full of Angels* by Macrina Wiederkehr. Copyright © 1988 by Harper Collins Publishers, New York.

Page 795. Taken from "A Kind Answer." *New Covenant Magazine* (February 1985). Used by permission of the author.

Page 803. Taken from *Traits of a Healthy Family* by Dolores Curran. Copyright © 1983 by the author. Used by permission of the author.

Page 818. Taken from *New Covenant Magazine* (May 1980). Copyright © 1980 by Dorothy Ranagan. Used by permission.

Page 1010. Story taken from *Inspired* by Joanna Laufer and Kenneth S. Lewis. Doubleday, New York, 1998.

Page 1019. Taken from *Guiltless Catholic Parenting from A to Y*. Copyright © 1995 by Bert Ghezzi. Published by Servant Publications, Box 8617, Ann Arbor, Michigan, 48107. Used by permission.

Page 1025. Taken from *Sister Thea Bowman Shooting Star* by Thea Bowman. Copyright © 1993 by Celestine Cepress, FSPA, Ph.D. Used by permission of Franciscan Sisters of Perpetual Adoration, La Crosse, WI.

Page 1036. Taken from *Womanspirit: Reclaiming the Deep Feminine in our Human Spirituality* by Susan Annette Muto. Copyright © 1999 by The Crossroad Publishing Company. Used by permission.

Page 1045. Taken from *How to Read and Pray the Parables* by Marilyn Gustin. Copyright © 1992 by Ligouri Publications. Used by permission of the author.

Page 1050. Taken from *The Soul Afire: Revelations of the Mystics*, edited by H. A. Reinhold. Copyright © 1973 by Pantheon Books. Used by permission.

Page 1065. Taken from *No Greater Love* by Mother Teresa. Copyright © 1997. Used by permission of New World Library, Novato, CA. 94949.

Page 1080. Taken from *Healing the Wounds of Divorce: A Spiritual Guide to Recovery* by Barbara Leahy Shlemon. Copyright © 1992 by Ave Maria Press, Notre Dame, IN 46556. Used by permission of the publisher.

Page 1084. Taken from *God's Word Today* (July 8, 1998). Used by permission of the author.

Page 1090. Taken from *Miracles Do Happen*. Copyright © 1987 by Briege McKenna and Henry Libersat. Published by Servant Publications, Box 8617, Ann Arbor, Michigan. 48107. Used by permission.

Page 1092. Taken from *Celine* by Stephane-Joseph Piat, O.F.M. Copyright © 1997 by Ignatius Press. Used by permission.

Page 1123. Taken from *Full of Grace: Women and the Abundant Life*. Copyright © 1998 by Johnnette S. Benkovic. Published by Servant Publications, Box 8617, Ann Arbor, Michigan, 48107. Used by permission.

Page 1139. Taken from *Dorothy Day: Selected Writings* edited by Robert Ellsberg. Copyright © 1983, 1992 by Robert Ellsbert and Tamar Hennessey. Published in 1992 by Orbis Books, Maryknoll, New York 10545.

Page 1158. Taken from *An Angel a Day* by Ann Spangler. Copyright © 1994 by Ann Spangler. Used by permission of Zondervan Publishing House.

Page 1166. Taken from *An Angel a Day* by Ann Spangler. Copyright © 1994 by Ann Spangler. Used by permission of Zondervan Publishing House.

Page 1174. Taken from *The Soul Afire: Revelations of the Mystics*, edited by H. A. Reinhold. Copyright © 1973 by Pantheon Books. Used by permission.

Page 1185. Taken from *The Autobiography of St. Therese of Lisieux, The Story of a Soul*, by John Beevers. Copyright © 1957 Doubleday.

Page 1197. Taken from *The Splendor of the Rosary* by Maisie Ward. Copyright © 1945. All rights reserved.

Page 1204. Taken from *God in Our Daily Life* by Hilda C. Graef.

Page 1210. Taken from *No Greater Love* by Mother Teresa. Copyright © 1997. Used by permission of New World Library, Novato, CA. 94949.

Page 1214. Taken from "A Prophet Who Pouts." *The Bible Today* (March 1995). Used by permission of the author.

Page 1221. Taken from *Suffering into Joy, What Mother Teresa Teaches about True Joy*. Copyright © 1994 by Eileen Egan and Kathleen Egan, O.S.B. Published by Servant Publications, Box 8617, Ann Arbor, Michigan, 48107. Used by permission.

Page 1223. Taken from *God's Word Today* (December 24, 1998). Used by permission of the author.

Page 1228. Taken from *Amazing Grace* by Kathleen Norris. Copyright © 1998 by Kathleen Norris. Used by permission of G.P. Putnam's Sons, a division of Penguin Putnam, Inc.

Page 1233. Taken from *My Life Is in Your Hands* by Kathy Troccoli. Copyright © by Kathy Troccoli. Used by permission of Zondervan Publishing House.

Page 1235. Taken from *100 Inspiring Stories* by Teresa Pirola. Copyright © 1998 by David Lovell Publishers, Fairfield, Australia.

Page 1243. Copyright © 2000 by Louise Perotta. Used by permission.

Page 1248. Taken from *Enfolded in Love, Daily Readings with Julian of Norwich* by Julian of Norwich. Copyright © 1980 by Darton, Longman and Todd, LTD, London, England.

Page 1251. Taken from *The Bible Today* (September 1996). Published by Liturgical Press. Copyright © by Elizabeth M. Nagel. Used by permission.

Page 1259. Taken from *With God and With Men* by Adrienne von Speyr, translated by Adrian Walker. Copyright © 1992 by Ignatius Press. Used by permission.

Page 1260. Taken from *100 Inspiring Stories* by Teresa Pirola. Copyright © 1998 by David Lovell Publishers, Fairfield, Australia.

Page 1269. Taken from *A Miracle a Day* by Ann Spangler. Copyright © 1996 by Ann Spangler. Used by permission of Zondervan Publishing House.

Page 1270. Taken from *Yesterday, Today, and Forever* by Maria Augusta Trapp. Used by permission of the Trapp Family Estate, Johannes von Trapp, President.

Page 1273. Taken from *Grace in Every Season: Through the Year with Catherine Doherty* by Mary Achterhoff Bezzett. Copyright © 1992 by Madonna House Publications, 2888 Dafoe Rd., Combermere, ON, K0J 1L0, Canada. Used by permission.

Page 1275. Taken from *Lent, Reflections and Stories on the Daily Readings.* Copyright © 1996 by Orbis Books. Used by permission.

Page 1282. Taken from *Through Him, With Him, In Him* by Ruth Burrows. Copyright © 1987 by Dimension Books Inc., Denville, NJ 07834. Used by permission.

Page 1288. Taken from *Hearing the Parables of Jesus* by Pheme Perkins. Copyright © 1981 by Pheme Perkins. Used by permission of Paulist Press.

Page 1289. Taken from *A Miracle a Day* by Ann Spangler. Copyright © 1996 by Ann Spangler. Used by permission of Zondervan Publishing House.

Page 1295. Taken from "Quality of Mercy." *New Covenant Magazine* (June 1985). Used by permission of the author.

Page 1296. Taken from *Words Made Flesh* by Fran Ferder. Copyright © 1986 by Ave Maria Press, Notre Dame, IN 46556. Used by permission of the publisher.

Page 1301. Taken from *Becoming Fire: Experience the Power of Jesus Every Day.* Copyright © 1998 by Smyth & Helwys Publishing, Inc. Used by permission.

Page 1307. Taken from *Dorothy Day: Selected Writings* edited by Robert Ellsberg. Copyright © 1983, 1992 by Robert Ellsbert and Tamar Hennessey. Published in 1992 by Orbis Books, Maryknoll, New York 10545.

Page 1316. Taken from *The Mystery of Love: Saints in Art through the Centuries* by Wendy Beckett. Copyright © 1996 by HarperCollinsReligious in Great Britain.

Page 1318. Quote from Catherine Doherty taken from *Grace in Every Season* edited by Mary Achterhoff. Servant Publications, Ann Arbor, MI, 1992.

Page 1320. Taken from *Water My Soul* by Luci Shaw. Copyright © 1998 by Luci Shaw. Used by permission of Zondervan Publishing House.

Page 1327. Taken from *Midlife Awakenings: Discovering the Gifts Life Has Given Us* by Barbara Bartocci. Copyright © 1998 by Ave Maria Press, Notre Dame, IN 46556. Used by permission of the publisher.

Page 1330. Taken from *Christian Living Today* by Chiara Lubich. Copyright © 1997 by New City Press. Used by permission of the publisher.

Page 1335. Taken from *Catherine of Siena, The Dialogue* by Suzanne Noffke. Copyright © 1980 by Paulist Press. Used by permission of the publisher.

Page 1447. Taken from *An Angel a Day* by Ann Spangler. Copyright © 1994 by Ann Spangler. Used by permission of Zondervan Publishing House.

Page 1450. Taken from *Seasons of Your Heart* by Macrina Wiederkehr. Copyright © 1991 by Harper San Francisco.

Page 1467. Taken from *An Angel a Day* by Ann Spangler. Copyright © 1994 by Ann Spangler. Used by permission of Zondervan Publishing House.

Page 1471. Taken from *100 Inspiring Stories* by Teresa Pirola. Copyright © 1998 by David Lovell Publishers, Fairfield, Australia.

Page 1473. Taken from *Enfolded in Love, Daily Readings with Julian of Norwich* by Julian of Norwich, Copyright © 1980 by Darton, Longman and Todd, LTD., London, England.

Page 1478. Quote taken from "The Catholic Vision" by Edward D. O'Connor, C.S.C. *Our Sunday Visitor*, Huntington, IN, 1992.

Page 1481. Taken from *100 Inspiring Stories* by Teresa Pirola. Copyright © 1998 by David Lovell Publishers, Fairfield, Australia.

Page 1484. Quote taken from *Creed or Chaos?* by Dorothy Sayers. Harcourt, Brace, and Co., New York, 1949.

Page 1486. Taken from *The Facts About Your Feelings*. Copyright © 1982. Used by permission of the author. All rights reserved.

Page 1488. Taken from *Pastoral Renewal Magazine* (November 1986). Copyright © by Sister Ann Shields. Used by permission of the author.

Page 1490. Taken from "Was St. Paul Sexist?" by Marie-Eloise Rosenblatt, R.S.M., and Ronald D. Witherup, S.S., *Catholic Update* C0496, (April 1996). Used by permission of St. Anthony Messenger Press, 1615 Republic St., Cincinnati, OH 45210.

Page 1494. Taken from *The Possibility of Miracles* by Frederica Mathewes-Green. Used by permission of the author.

Page 1500. Taken from "Subversive Virginity." *First Things* (October 1998). Used by permission of the publisher.

Page 1504. Taken from *The Collected Works of St. Teresa of Avila, Vol. 2*, translated by Kieran Kavanaugh, O.C.D. and Otilio Rodriguez, O.C.D. Copyright © 1976 by ICS Publications. Used by permission of the publisher.

Page 1507. Taken from *New Covenant Magazine* (September 1979). Copyright © 1980 by Dorothy Ranagan. Used by permission.

Page 1509. Taken from *The Autobiography of St. Therese of Lisieux, The Story of a Soul*, by John Beevers. Copyright © 1957 by Doubleday.

Page 1510. Taken from *The Coming of God* by Maria Boulding. Copyright © 1986 by Collins & Collins, UK.

Page 1517. Taken from *Stumbling Blocks or Stepping Stones?* by Benedict J. Groeschel, C.F.R. Copyright © 1987 by Benedict J. Groeschel. Used by permission of Paulist Press.

Page 1519. Taken from *Miracles Do Happen*. Copyright © 1987 by Briege McKenna and Henry Libersat. Published by Servant Publications, Box 8617, Ann Arbor, Michigan. 48107. Used by permission.

Page 1521. Taken from *Midlife Awakenings: Discovering the Gifts Life Has Given Us* by Barbara Bartocci. Copyright © 1998 by Ave Maria Press, Notre Dame, IN 46556. Used by permission of the publisher.

Page 1522. Taken from *May They All Be One* by Chiara Lubich. Copyright © 1968, 1990 by New City Press. Used by permission of the publisher.

Page 1525. Taken from *To Dance with God* by Gertrud Mueller Nelson. Copyright © 1986 by Paulist Press. Used by permission of the publisher.

Page 1529. Taken from *No Greater Love* by Mother Teresa. Copyright © 1997. Used by permission of New World Library, Novato, CA. 94949.

Page 1532. Taken from *Pastoral Renewal* magazine (November 1986). Copyright © by Sister Ann Shields. Used by permission of the author.

Page 1534. Taken from *Womanspirit: Reclaiming the Deep Feminine in our Human Spirituality* by Susan Annette Muto. Copyright © 1999 by The Crossroad Publishing Company. Used by permission.

Page 1537. Taken from "Jesus, Our Real Liberator" by Melannie Svoboda, in *Praying Magazine* (March 1, 1999). Copyright © 1999 by Melannie Svoboda. Used by permission.

Page 1538. Taken from "The Apples in a Seed" by Wendy Leifield. *New Covenant Magazine* (October 1994).

Page 1544. Copyright © 1998 by Carol Gura. Reprinted by permission of Thomas More Publishing, 200 East Bethany Drive, Allen, Texas 75002. All rights reserved.

Page 1545. Taken from *Grace in Every Season: Through the Year with Catherine Doherty* by Mary Achterhoff Bezzett. Copyright © 1992 by Madonna House Publications, 2888 Dafoe Rd., Combermere, ON, K0J 1L0, Canada. Used by permission.

Page 1547. Taken from *Balancing Act* by Mary Ellen Ashcroft. Copyright © 1996 by Mary Ellen Ashcroft. Used by permission of InterVarsity Press, P.O. Box 1400, Downers Grove, IL 60515.

Page 1549. Taken from *Feminine, Free, and Faithful* by Ronda Chervin. Copyright © 1986. Used by permission.

Page 1552. Copyright © 1998 by Carol Gura. Reprinted by permission of Thomas More Publishing, 200 East Bethany Drive, Allen, Texas 75002. All rights reserved.

Page 1557. Taken from *To Believe in Jesus* by Ruth Burrows. Copyright © 1981, 1978 by Dimension Books, Inc., Denville, NJ 07834. Used by permission.

Page 1558. Taken from *The Pummeled Heart: Finding Peace through Pain* by Antoinette Bosco. Copyright © 1994 by Twenty-Third Publications, Mystic, CT 06355. Used by permission of the publisher.

Page 1562. Taken from *Grace in Every Season: Through the Year with Catherine Doherty* by Mary Achterhoff Bezzett. Copyright © 1992 by Madonna House Publications, 2888 Dafoe Rd., Combermere, ON, K0J 1L0, Canada. Used by permission.

Page 1563. Taken from *The Comforting of Christ* by Caryll Houselander. Copyright © 1947 by Sheed & Ward. All rights reserved.

Page 1564. Taken from *Be Not Solicitous* by Maisie Ward. Copyright © 1953 by Sheed & Ward. All rights reserved.

Page 1569. Taken from *Seasons of Your Heart* by Macrina Wiederkehr. Copyright © 1991 by Harper San Francisco.

Page 1571. Taken from *For the Soul That Was Within Me* by Amy Welborn. Copyright © 1998 by Amy Welborn. Used by permission of the author.

Page 1572. Permission by *Our Sunday Visitor*, 200 Noll Plaza, Huntington, IN, 46750. All rights reserved.

Page 1576. Taken from *Come Home ... The Door is Open* by Louise D'Angelo. Copyright © 1982. Used by permission.

Page 1577. Taken from *Turning, Reflections on the Experience of Conversion* by Emilie Griffin. Copyright © 1980 by Doubleday.

Page 1583. Taken from *U.S. Catholic* magazine. Published by Claretian Publications.

Page 1584. Taken from *God's Word Today* (October 1995). Copyright © 1995 by Cindy Cavnar. Used by permission of the author.

Page 1587. Taken from *Miracles Do Happen.* Copyright © 1987 by Briege McKenna and Henry Libersat. Published by Servant Publications, Box 8617, Ann Arbor, Michigan. 48107. Used by permission.

Page 1590. Taken from *Celebrating the Single Life* by Dr. Susan Muto. Copyright © 1982 by Epiphany Association 2000, 947 Tropical Avenue, Pittsburgh, PA 15216-3031. Used by permission of Dr. Muto and Epiphany Association. All rights reserved.

Page 1593. Taken from *All Earth is Crammed with Heaven: Daily Reflections for Mothers* by Mary van Balen Holt. Copyright © 1996, Servant Publications. Used by permission of the author.

Page 1601. Taken from *An Angel a Day* by Ann Spangler. Copyright © 1994 by Ann Spangler. Used by permission of Zondervan Publishing House.

Page 1603. Taken from *Clare of Assisi, Early Documents* by Regis Armstrong, O.F.M., Cap. Copyright © 1988 by Paulist Press. Used by permission.

Page 1605. Taken from *Prayers of the Women Mystics.* Copyright © 1992 by Ronda De Sola Chervin. Published by Servant Publications, Box 8617, Ann Arbor, Michigan, 48107. Used by permission.

Page 1611. Taken from *Beyond Ourselves* by Catherine Marshall. Copyright © 1961 by Chosen Books.

Page 1613. Taken from *St. Chantal on Prayer* by Rev. A. Durand. Used by permission.

Page 1619. Taken from *Enfolded in Love, Daily Readings with Julian of Norwich* by Julian of Norwich. Copyright © 1980 by Darton, Longman and Todd, LTD., London, England.

Page 1620. Taken from *To Believe in Jesus* by Ruth Burrows. Copyright © 1981, 1978 by Dimension Books, Inc., Denville, NJ 07834. Used by permission.

Page 1622. Taken from *Grace in Every Season: Through the Year with Catherine Doherty* by Mary Achterhoff Bezzett. Copyright © 1992 by Madonna House Publications, 2888 Dafoe Rd., Combermere, ON, K0J 1L0, Canada. Used by permission.

Page 1623. Taken from "Our Father: The Prayer Jesus Taught Us," by Gloria Hutchinson, *Catholic Update* C1296 (December 1996). Reprinted by permission of St. Anthony Messenger Press, 1615 Republic St., Cincinnati, OH 45210.

Page 1624. Taken from *Simple Ways to Pray for Healing* by Matthew Linn, Sheila Fabricant Linn, and Dennis Linn. Copyright © 1998 by Paulist Press. Used by permission.

Page 1630. Taken from *U.S. Catholic* magazine. Published by Claretian Publications.

Page 1632. Taken from *The Woman Behind the Mirror.* Copyright © 1997 by Broadman & Holman Publishers. Used by permission.

Page 1633. Taken from *Midlife Awakenings: Discovering the Gifts Life Has Given Us* by Barbara Bartocci. Copyright © 1998 by Ave Maria Press, Notre Dame, IN 46556. Used by permission of the publisher.

Page 1636. Taken from *My Problem Was My Problem-Oriented Approach* by Dorcee Clarey. Copyright © 1979 by Dorcee Clarey. Used by permission of the author.

Page 1638. Taken from *To Dance with God* by Gertrud Mueller Nelson. Copyright © 1986 by Paulist Press. Used by permission of the publisher.

Page 1644. Taken from *Woman Un-Bent* by Irene Zimmerman, O.S.F. Copyright © 1999 by Saint Mary's Press, Winona, MN. Used by permission of the publisher.

Page 1646. Taken from *By Grief Refined, Letters to a Widow* by Alice von Hildebrand. Copyright © 1994 by Franciscan University Press. Used by permission.

Page 1647. Taken from *Where Miracles Happen* by Joan Wester Anderson. Copyright © 1994 by Brett Books, Inc., Brooklyn NY 11229-0011. Used by permission.

Page 1650. Taken from *Mother Teresa, Contemplative in the Heart of the World* by Brother Angelo Devananda Scolozzi. Copyright © 1985 by Servant Books.

Page 1652. Taken from *Grace in Every Season: Through the Year with Catherine Doherty* by Mary Achterhoff Bezzett. Copyright © 1992 by Madonna House Publications, 2888 Dafoe Rd., Combermere, ON, K0J 1L0, Canada. Used by permission.

Page 1661. Taken from *The Comforting of Christ* by Caryll Houselander. Copyright © 1947 by Sheed & Ward. All rights reserved.

1662. Taken from *Revelations of Divine Mercy, Daily Readings from the Diary of Blessed Faustina Kowalski,* by George Kosicki. Copyright © 1996. Used by permission.

Page 1667. Taken from *365 Mary: A Daily Guide to Mary's Wisdom and Comfort* by Woodeene Koenig-Bricker. Copyright © 1997 by Harper Collins Publishers, New York.

Page 1676. Taken from *The Coming of God* by Maria Boulding. Copyright © by 1986 by Collins & Collins, UK.

Biographies

Joan Wester Anderson's writing career began in 1973 with a series of family humor articles for local newspapers and parenting magazines. Since that time, her work, totaling ten books and more than one thousand articles and stories, have been published nationally in numerous magazines and newspapers, and she is a frequent guest on television and radio shows. Her *New York Times* national bestseller *Where Angels Walk* has sold over a million copies in the United States and, to date, has been translated into nine foreign languages. Other popular books by Joan include *Where Miracles Happen, The Power of Miracles*, and *An Angel to Watch over Me*. Joan and her husband live in a Chicago suburb. They have five grown children and one grandchild.

Angela of Foligno (1248–1309) married young, had seven children, and was by her own account an unusually sinful woman until her late thirties. At that point she had a radical conversion while on a pilgrimage to the birthplace of Saint Francis of Assisi. She became a Third Order Franciscan and, after her entire family died (probably of the plague), lived a penitential life of prayer and service to the sick. Gifted with many visions, Angela described her relationship with God in *The Book of Divine Consolation*, which made her one of the most popular mystical writers of Europe.

Mary Ellen Ashcroft has served as associate professor of English at Bethel College in St. Paul, Minnesota, since 1989. She lectures and leads workshops on numerous topics including religious experience, language and metaphors for God, calling and vocation, women in the New Testament, and the life and work of Dorothy Sayers. A popular speaker, Mary Ellen has also written and directed a number of plays, as well as articles for various Christian publications. Among her books are *Balancing Act, Temptations Women Face, The Magdalene Gospel*, and *The Beginning of Wisdom*. Mary Ellen and her three teenage children are active in St. Stephen's Episcopal Church in Minneapolis, where her husband, Eric, serves as rector.

Ann Ball has taught elementary and high school students, worked as a private investigator, and now owns and directs a security services company. She studied journalism at the University of Texas and has written many books, including *Modern Saints: Their Lives and Faces, Catholic Traditions in Cooking, A Litany of Saints, A Handbook of Catholic Sacramentals*, and *Faces of Holiness*. Ann and her family live in Houston.

Barbara Bartocci, a professional speaker and writer, leads workshops on career development, creative writing, and spiritual growth through midlife. Her varied career includes work as a college trustee, radio talk show host, managing editor, advertising executive, and public relations director. Her articles have appeared in a host of popular magazines, and she is the author of three books: *My Angry Son, Unexpected Answers*, and *Midlife Awakenings*.

Sister Wendy Beckett is a member of the Notre Dame sisters, a teaching order. Educated at St. Anne's College, Oxford, she taught in South Africa, then returned to England in 1970 to take up the life of a contemplative nun. An art lover all her life, Sister Wendy has become well known to television viewers for her insightful and humorous commentaries on art history and specific works of art. Her books include *Sister Wendy's Story of Painting*, a guide to eight hundred years of Western painting, *Sister Wendy's Book of Saints*, and the series *Sister Wendy's Meditations on Joy ... Peace ... Love ... Silence*.

Johnette Benkovic is the founder and director of "Living His Life Abundantly," a non-profit Catholic communications ministry. Johnette is the host of a weekday radio program and hosts and produces a number of television programs in association with Eternal Word Television Network. She is the author of *Full of Grace: Women and the Abundant Life*.

Babsie Bleasdell is an internationally acclaimed speaker and storyteller with a gift for communicating the Gospel with drama and humor. Born and raised in a Catholic family in Trinidad, where she still makes her home, Babsie worked as an office manager and a politician before devoting herself full-time to Church renewal movements. She is a leader of the Word of Life Prayer Community and has authored and coauthored a number of articles and books, including *Refresh Your Life in the Spirit*. She has two daughters.

Antoinette Bosco is the executive director of the *Litchfield County Times* and a member of the advisory board of *Woman* magazine, both located in Connecticut. A syndicated columnist for the Catholic News Service since 1974, she is the author of more than 200 magazine articles and several thousand newspaper columns and stories. Among her six books are *The Pummeled Heart, Coincidences*, and *Successful Single Parenting*.

Maria Boulding is a contemplative Benedictine nun at the Stanbrook Abbey in Worcester, England. She is the author of *The Coming of God, Marked for Life*, and *Prayer, Our Journey Home*, and has edited and translated Saint Augustine's *Confessions*.

Roma Bourassa, a retired home economics teacher, is an enthusiastic quilter and piano student. Roma and her husband, Roger, a retired dentist turned woodcarver and gardener, have been involved in many types of parish and community service during their fifty-four years of married life. They live in Maine and have three children, twelve grandchildren, and seven great-grandchildren.

Sister Thea Bowman (1937–1990) was a teacher, a singer, a dancer, and a lecturer who tirelessly spread the Good News and promoted pride in black culture. A Franciscan Sister of Perpetual Adoration, she received her doctorate in English from Catholic University of America and chaired the English department at Viterbo College in LaCrosse, Wisconsin. She helped found the Institute of Black Catholic Studies at Xavier University, New Orleans.

Ruth Burrows is prioress of a Carmelite monastery in England and author of a number of books on the contemplative life. These include *Guidelines for Mystical Prayer, Ascent to Love, Interior Castle Explored, To Believe in Jesus*, and *Through Him, With Him, In Him*.

Concepción Cabrera de Armida (1862–1937), known to her friends as Conchita, was born in San Luis Potosí, Mexico, one of twelve children in a devout, well-to-do family. Lively, attractive, and deeply prayerful, she had a following of twenty-two suitors and chose her husband on the basis of his dedication to Christ. His sudden death, after nine children and sixteen happy years of marriage was a hard blow, but Conchita carried on, taking over the household and combining her life of motherhood with the heights of mystical experience. With the help of a saintly priest, she founded an order of priests, two orders of nuns, and several apostolates for lay people. Conchita's published writings include part of her copious spiritual diary, letters to her children, and *Before the Altar*, a still-popular booklet for Eucharistic adoration.

Floretta Miller Calmeyn's battle with cancer ended on May 18, 1998. Her final prayer to family and friends was this: "May you walk in beauty. May you soar like the eagle. May you find God in the very ground of your being and heights of your dreams. May you dance and sing, laugh and cry, through the seasons of your life. Spirit freeing, loving seeing at each heartfelt meeting."

Saint Catherine of Siena (1347–1380) was born in Italy, the twenty-fourth in a family of twenty-five children. At eighteen she joined a branch of the Dominican order whose members stayed in their own homes and gave themselves to prayer and good works. Catherine's deep prayer and service to the sick and poor attracted attention and drew a motley crowd of disciples; religious and secular rulers sought her advice. An international political figure, Catherine was a "mystic activist" whose intimate union with God—revealed in her mystical work, *The Dialogue*—directed all her activity. She was declared one of only three women Doctors of the Church in 1970.

Cindy Cavnar is a writer, editor, and religious education professional. She has published many articles and booklets, especially about the saints, and is the author of *Prayers and Meditations of Thérèse of Lisieux*. Cindy and her husband, Nick, are the parents of three children and live in Kansas.

Therese Cirner and her husband, Randall, are the parents of five children and live in Steubenville, Ohio. They are coauthors of *Ten Weeks to a Better Marriage* and have traveled extensively, giving talks and leading workshops on marriage and family life. Therese's published writings include magazine articles and a book, *The Facts About Your Feelings*.

Saint Clare of Assisi (1193–1253), born into a prominent family, was expected to make an illustrious marriage. Instead, at eighteen, she slipped away by night to become a follower of Saint Francis, whose preaching had stirred her desire for a consecrated celibate life of poverty and penance. Other women joined Clare (her sister and eventually her mother among them); so began the religious order of Poor Clares. Known for healings and miracles, Clare twice saved Assisi from invading armies. She was canonized just two years after her death.

Dorcee Clarey is an elementary school teacher with many years of experience in counseling and campus ministry. She is a member of a religious community in Ann Arbor, Michigan, "the Servants of God's Love."

Paula Ripple Comin is a former college teacher and dean of students and was the first executive director of the North American Conference of Separated and Divorced Catholics. She worked eight years with children at shelters for battered women in Wisconsin and Florida. Since 1992 Paula has been presenting retreats and workshops throughout the U.S. and Canada for Retreats International Summer Institute for Retreat and Pastoral Ministry. Her books include *The Pain and the Possibility, Called to Be Friends, Walking with Loneliness, Growing Strong at the Broken Places,* and *Mixed Blessings.*

Judith Couchman is an award-winning author and speaker who owns Judith & Company, a writing and consulting business. She was the founding editor-in-chief of *Clarity,* a magazine for Christian and spiritually seeking women. Judith is the author/compiler of many books, including *The Woman Behind the Mirror, Shaping a Woman's Soul,* and *Designing a Woman's Life.* She lives in Colorado and speaks to women's and professional groups around the country.

Dolores Curran has written on family and parenting issues for many years. She is a syndicated columnist for diocesan newspapers and author of many articles and books. Her *Traits of a Healthy Family* won a Christopher Award and has been called a contemporary classic; her next work was another best seller, *Stress and the Healthy Family.* Dolores lectures widely in the U.S. and abroad.

Louise D'Angelo is founder of the Maryheart Crusaders, a national group of laypeople that seeks to reunite fallen-away Catholics with the Church and stimulate lukewarm Catholics toward a fuller spiritual life. Her books include *Come Home… The Door Is Open* and *Too Busy For God? Think Again!*

Dorothy Day (1897–1980) intended to change the world to a certain extent—to make it "a little simpler for people to feed, clothe, and shelter themselves as God intended"—by working for justice, living with the poor, and establishing "little cells of joy and peace in a harried world." Co-founder with Peter Maurin of the Catholic Worker movement, she combined social activism and contemplation, as her many writings show. Among them: *On Pilgrimage, From Union Square to Rome,* and *The Long Loneliness.*

Ronda De Sola Chervin has been a university professor in California and Ohio and is the author or contributor to about fifty books including *Prayers of the Women Mystics, Treasury of Women Saints, Quotable Saints, Woman to Woman, A Widow's Walk, The Kiss from the Cross,* and, with her daughter, *Catholic Customs and Traditions.*

Esther de Waal has lectured and published widely on monastic and Celtic spirituality. Her books include *The Celtic Way of Prayer, Rediscovering the Celtic Tradition, A Seven Day Journey with Thomas Merton, Seeking God: The Way of St. Benedict,* and *A Life-Giving Way: A Commentary on the Rule of St. Benedict.*

Catherine Doherty (1896–1985), a Russian who fled her homeland and emigrated to Canada after the Communist Revolution, abandoned a promising career in response to Christ's invitation to "sell all, give it to the poor, follow me." Moving into the slums, she served the needs of the poor by establishing "Friendship House" centers in places like Toronto, Chicago, and Harlem. Today hundreds of men and women follow her example of prayer and outreach to the needy by participating in Madonna House Apostolate, which she founded with her husband, Eddie. Her extensive writings include *Poustinia, The Gospel without Compromise, Fragments of My Life,* and a collection of daily reflections, *Grace in Every Season.*

Rena Duff has a master's degree in religious education and serves her parish in St. Clairsville, Ohio, as coordinator of adult and high school religious education. She has written guides for Bible study and has led Bible study groups for years.

Fran Ferder, a member of the Franciscan Sisters of Perpetual Adoration, holds a doctorate in clinical psychology and another in ministry. She is codirector of Therapy and Renewal Associates, a ministerial counseling and consultation service for the archdiocese of Seattle. A nationally known speaker, she is also the author or coauthor of several books including *Words Made Flesh*.

Lisa Ferguson has written for *New Covenant*, *Our Sunday Visitor*, and other publications. She lives in Steubenville, Ohio.

Hilda Graef's many books include *God in Our Daily Life*, *Adult Christianity*, *Mystics of Our Times*, and *The Devotion to Our Lady*, and studies of Edith Stein and John Henry Newman.

Cecile Gray is a pastoral associate in campus ministry at the St. Thomas More Newman Center at Ohio State University. She has a degree in Scripture (she occasionally teaches Hebrew) and a doctorate in literature and psychology from the University of Dallas.

Emilie Griffin has worked extensively as a retreat and workshop leader with Christians of many denominations and is an award-winning writer, editor, and marketing consultant. Her books on the spiritual life include *Wilderness Time: The Experience of Retreat*, *Turning*, *Chasing the Kingdom*, *Homeward Voyage: Reflections on Life-Changes*, and *The Reflective Executive*. Emilie and her husband, William, are founding members of the Chrysostom Society, a Christian writers group, and members of the Catholic Commission on Intellectual and Cultural Affairs. They have three grown children and live in New Orleans.

Carol Gura, former director of evangelization for the diocese of Cleveland for nine years, is a free-lance writer and international presenter. The thrust of her work is retreats, workshops, and publications that assist people in linking faith and daily life. Married and mother of four young adults, Carol lives with her husband outside Cleveland and enjoys quilting and gardening. Her books include *Ministering to Young Adults*, *Transforming Parish Life*, and *Crossing the River*.

Marilyn Gustin has written many books centering on Scripture and Christian living. Among them are *How to Read and Pray the Gospels*, *How to Read and Pray the Parables*, *Choosing Joy for Lent*, *The Inward Journey*, and *From Victim to Decision-Maker*.

Saint Hildegard of Bingen (1098–1179) was a German abbess who combined mystical gifts with scholarship and diplomatic skills. Known as the "Sybil of the Rhine" for her powers of prophecy, she exerted great influence on both secular and religious leaders. At forty-three she began writing: poetry, drama, history, liturgical songs, works on politics, herbal medicine, and even a diagnosis of psychological disorders. Her best-known work, *Scivias*, (its full Latin title means *Know the Ways of the Lord*) recounts twenty-six of her visions. At sixty Hildegard undertook preaching tours aimed at church reform.

Sarah E. Hinlicky, a writer living in New York City, is an editorial assistant at *First Things*.

Mary van Balen Holt is a free-lance writer, teacher, and mother of three children. She is the author of *Marriage: A Covenant of Seasons*, *All Earth Is Crammed with Heaven*, and *A Dwelling Place Within*.

Mary Hope is the name under which Daisy Haywood Moseley (1892–1979) published part of her spiritual journal, *Towards Evening*. A devout Southern Catholic and caregiver to her aged aunt and mother, Daisy spent much of her childhood in Italy, France, and England. She was a prolific writer whose articles frequently appeared in religious magazines; she also authored a collection of saints' biographies for young people and a life of the English martyr Robert Southwell. Daisy's diaries, correspondence, and other writings are in the Southern Historical Collection at the University of North Carolina, Chapel Hill.

Kathleen Spears Hopkins holds a B.A. in English literature and a master's degree in theological studies. Married and the mother of three, she has performed many roles in her church community, from pastoral team member to choir conductor.

Caryll Houselander (1901–1954), born in Bath, England, expressed her artistic talents in a variety of occupations: doing layouts in an ad agency, carving crib figures and stations of the cross for a church decorator, illustrating books, sculpting, decorating houses, and writing and illustrating stories for religious magazines. Known for her compassion and psychological insight, she counseled many spiritually needy people and did occupational therapy with child victims of World War II. Caryll's powerful, original writings on the Christian life include *The Reed of God*, *The Com-*

forting of Christ, *The Passion of the Child Christ*, children's stories, and her autobiography, *A Rocking-Horse Catholic*.

Maribeth Howell, O.P., is an Adrian Dominican Sister who teaches Scripture at Kenrick Seminary in Saint Louis. She studied at Saint Paul University (Ottawa, Ontario) and received both a Ph.D. and an S.T.D. from The Catholic University of Louvain in Belgium.

Gloria Hutchinson is a former teacher, catechist, and religious education coordinator who writes extensively on the spiritual life. Her books include *Jesus and John*, *Six Ways to Pray from Six Great Saints*, a series on retreats with saints and near-saints, and reflections on the rosary and the stations of the cross. She and her family live in northern Maine.

Saint Jeanne de Chantal (1572–1641), a French baroness, enjoyed eight happy years of marriage before her husband was killed in a hunting accident. Overcome with grief, she learned to lean on God, patiently enduring the hardships involved in being dependent on relatives as she cared for her four children. After developing a life of prayer and service to the poor, Jeanne prayed for a good spiritual director and was given a vision of Saint Francis de Sales—who had had a vision of *her* as the woman who would help him found a religious order for women, the Visitation.

Julian of Norwich (1342–after 1413), an English woman whose real name is unknown, received a series of sixteen visions of Our Lord during a severe illness in May 1373. She became an anchoress, a woman dedicated to religious life, living permanently alone in a cell attached to Saint Julian's Church in Norwich. After twenty years of meditating on the visions she had received, Julian recorded them and their meaning in *The Revelations of Divine Love*. This is the first book known to be written by a woman in English and is acknowledged as one of the great classics of spiritual literature.

Woodene Koenig-Bricker is the author of *365 Saints*, *365 Mary*, and *Prayers of the Saints*. The editor of *Catholic Parent* magazine, she has written extensively in the Catholic and secular press about spirituality and the family. She and her husband are parents of a teenage son.

Faustina Kowalska (1905–1938), one of eight children born to poor and pious parents in central Poland, was deeply prayerful from childhood. Un-

able to obtain her parents' permission to become a nun, Faustina diverted herself with social activities. One evening during a dance, she had a vision of Jesus who asked, "How long will you keep putting me off?" Spurred to action, she left home and entered the Sisters of Our Lady of Mercy. Her challenging but simple life changed forever after her February 1931 vision of Jesus and his invitation to become "an apostle of Divine Mercy." She worked tirelessly to spread this devotion until her death from tuberculosis. Pope John Paul II declared her the first saint of the new millenium on April 30, 2000.

Mary Ann Kuharski is a full-time homemaker and mother of thirteen children, six of whom are adopted and of mixed races. She is a right-to-life activist and a free-lance writer whose work has appeared in *Newsweek*, *Our Sunday Visitor*, *Christianity Today*, and many other publications. She is the author of *Raising Catholic Children*, *How to Talk to Your Children About Prayer*, and *Parenting with Prayer*. She and her husband, John, and their family live in Minneapolis, Minnesota.

Jeanne Kun is an editor, writer, and graphic artist whose articles have appeared in a number of Christian publications. She is on the staff of the Catholic Bible study magazine, *The Word Among Us*.

Wendy Leifeld has been a columnist and contributor for many Catholic publications and is the author of *Mothers of the Saints*. She and her husband, Martin, have four children and live in Wisconsin.

Madeleine L'Engle, a graduate of Smith College and Columbia University, is an internationally acclaimed author who has also been active in theater and teaching. Widowed after forty years of marriage to the actor Hugh Franklin, she travels widely from her home base in New York, leading retreats, lecturing at writers' conferences, and addressing church and student groups in the U.S. and abroad. Her approximately forty books include award-winning children's novels (*A Wrinkle in Time*, *A Swiftly Tilting Planet*), reflections on Christian living (*The Irrational Season*, *Walking on Water*), explorations of the Bible (*The Genesis Trilogy*), and autobiographical works (*Two-Part Invention: The Story of a Marriage*).

Sheila Fabricant Linn and her husband, Dennis, work as a team giving presentations on healing with Matt Linn, who lives in a Jesuit community in Minneapolis. The three have taught courses in over forty countries and in many universities and hospitals, including a course to doctors that is accredited by the American Medical Association. Sheila has co-authored ten books with Dennis and Matt: among them, *Simple Ways to Pray for Healing*, *Healing the Greatest Hurt*, and *Don't Forgive Too Soon: Extending the Two Hands That Heal*. The team's books have sold over a million copies in English and have been translated into more than fifteen languages. Sheila and her husband and son live in Colorado.

Cora Lombardo, A.S.C.J., has written for *Our Sunday Visitor* and other publications and lives in New Castle, Pennsylvania.

Chiara Lubich was born in 1920, in Trent, Italy, a city that was heavily bombed during World War II. She and her friends spent much of 1943 and 1944 in air raid shelters—a time for reading the Gospels and for considering the true meaning of life. Out of this experience came a resolution to "make God our life's ideal" and a movement: Focolare, which now numbers four million supporters worldwide and emphasizes spiritual renewal and Christian unity. Chiara has written more than thirty books, which have appeared in twenty-six languages, and has received many awards including the Templeton Prize for Progress in Religion (1977) and the UNESCO Prize for Peace Education (1996).

Patti Gallagher Mansfield and Al, her husband, are internationally recognized leaders in the Catholic charismatic renewal. A popular conference speaker and workshop leader, Patti has been a magazine columnist and is the author of *Proclaim His Marvelous Deeds* and *As By a New Pentecost*. Patti, Al, and their four children live in Louisiana.

Raïssa Maritain (1883–1960) was born in Russia to devout Jewish parents who emigrated to Paris when she was ten. Searching for the meaning of life as a Sorbonne university student, she met her future husband, Jacques, who had grown up in a liberal French Protestant family. The lectures of the philosopher Henri Bergson and especially the friendship of the writer Léon Bloy opened the couple to the grace of faith: They were received into the Catholic Church in 1906. Jacques went on to become a prominent philosopher, especially known for his understanding of Thomas Aquinas. Raïssa discovered a call to contemplative prayer. Author of *We Have Been Friends Together*, *Adventures in Grace*, and *Raïs-*

sa's Journal, she also collaborated with Jacques on books on prayer, liturgy, and poetry. In France and then the U.S., Raïssa and Jacques practiced an evangelistic hospitality, opening heart and home to countless persons, especially artists and writers.

Catherine Marshall was one of America's best-known inspirational writers. Her novel, *Christy*, based on her mother's life, became a popular CBS television series. Her many books include *Beyond Ourselves*, *The Helper*, and *A Man Called Peter*. She died in 1983.

Céline Martin (1869–1959), closest sister of Thérèse of Lisieux and a Carmelite nun in the same monastery as the saint, was also Thérèse's confidante and witness to the work of grace in her soul.

A gifted photographer, archivist, and student of Scripture, she produced the first version of Thérèse's autobiographical *Story of a Soul*. Céline was a convinced follower of her sister's "little way" to God and saw herself as living proof that Thérèse's doctrine of "spiritual childhood" was not just for the young and tractable.

Céline lived to be almost ninety and struggled all her life to overcome her headstrong, opinionated tendencies: "daughter of thunder," she called herself.

Frederica Mathewes-Green is a columnist for *Christianity Today*. She is also a regular commentator on National Public Radio's "All Things Considered" and the Odyssey Television Network's "News Odyssey." A popular retreat leader, speaker, and lecturer at writers' conferences, she is the author of *Facing East: A Pilgrim's Journey into the Mysteries of Orthodoxy*. She has raised three children.

Sandy Mayrand is a wife and mother who lives in Ohio.

Rea McDonnell, S.S.N.D., is a pastoral counselor and spiritual director at the Consultation Center, Silver Spring, Maryland. She has coauthored two books with Rachel Callahan: *Hope for Healing: Good News for Adult Children of Alcoholics* and *Wholing the Heart: Good News for Those Who Grew Up in Troubled Families*.

Briege McKenna, O.S.C., was born in County Armagh, Ireland, and admitted to the Congregation of the Sisters of Saint Clare on her fifteenth birthday. Diagnosed with crippling rheumatoid arthritis in 1965, she underwent many painful treatments before being miraculously healed—deformed feet and all—at a prayer meeting in 1970. She tells the story in *Miracles Do Happen*, and also at rallies, retreats and conferences worldwide. Through her ministry of healing and evangelism, as well as a special outreach to priests, many people have come to physical and spiritual health.

Megan McKenna, well known for her workshops, retreats, and cassette series, received her doctorate from the Graduate Theological Union, Berkeley, California. She has taught in Chicago, San Francisco, Dublin, and Albuquerque. Her numerous books include *Parables, Not Counting Women and Children*, and *Mary: Shadow of Grace*.

Elizabeth McNamer teaches religious studies at Rocky Mountain College in Billings, Montana. She is an archaeologist, lecturer, free-lance writer, and editor of the Bible study newsletter, *Scripture from Scratch*. Elizabeth and her husband have five grown children.

Saint Mechtild of Magdeburg (1207–1282?) was touched by the Holy Spirit when she was twelve. At twenty she joined the Béguines, a group of widows and single holy women living together without vows and devoted to prayer and works of mercy. Later, in flight from enemies who resented her criticisms of laxity in the Church, she fled to the Benedictine monastery of Helfta.

Mechtild's book, *The Overflowing Light of the Godhead*, describes some of her joyful mystical experiences and revelations and ranks her among the greatest medieval German writers. She was never canonized, but her feast is observed in many Benedictine convents.

Alice Meynell (1847–1922) was an English poet and essayist. She was a working journalist throughout her life, writing newspaper essays and simple, sincere poems that enjoyed great popularity. Alice converted to Catholicism around 1872 and married Wilfrid Meynell five years later; they had eight children. Her poetry collections include *Preludes* and *Last Poems*.

Jeanie Miley is executive director of Growth Options, an organization that helps people grow closer to Christ through seminars and spiritual direction. For the past ten years she has been involved in healing retreats, workshops, and Bible studies, with an emphasis on contemplative

prayer and spiritual formation. A graduate of the Spiritual Direction Institute at the Cenacle Retreat Center in Washington, D.C., Jeanie has written several books: *The Spiritual Art of Creative Silence*, *Shared Splendor*, and *Becoming Fire*. She lives in San Angelo, Texas, with her husband and three children.

Hazel Miller lives in New York and works as a flight attendant.

Dame Gertrude More (1606–1633), the great-great-granddaughter of Saint Thomas More, was born in England and entered the Benedictine monastery of Cambrai, Flanders. Under the guidance of Dom Augustine Baker, a well-known Benedictine spiritual director and writer of ascetical works, she developed a deep prayer life—as revealed in her books, *Spiritual Exercises* and *Practices of Divine Love*, both published after her death.

Susan Muto is the executive director of Epiphany Association, an ecumenical lay center in Pittsburgh, and past director of Duquesne University's former Institute of Formative Spirituality.

An expert in literature and spirituality, she has lectured in the fields of formative spirituality and formation theology at a number of seminaries, colleges, and other institutes of higher learning. Susan is a popular speaker who offers conferences, seminars, and workshops on lay formation throughout the U.S. and abroad. She has written many articles, and her books include *Celebrating the Single Life*, *Womanspirit*, *Pathways of Spiritual Living*, and *Blessings That Make Us Be*.

Elizabeth M. Nagel is assistant professor of Scripture at Saint Charles Borromeo Seminary (Wynnewood, Pennsylvania). She holds a doctorate in Sacred Scripture from the Pontifical Biblical Institute in Rome and is especially interested in evangelization.

LaVonne Neff, an editor at Loyola Press in Chicago, has written many articles and reviews for a variety of Christian publications. Her books include *Breakfast with the Saints*; *A Life for God: A Mother Teresa Reader*; *One of a Kind: Making the Most of Your Child*; *A Prayer Book for Catholic Families*; and books for children. She and her husband, David, who is editor of *Christianity Today*, have two adult children and two grandchildren.

Gertrud Mueller Nelson was born in Cologne, Germany, and raised in St. Paul, Minnesota. She has been involved in Montessori education, studied clip art in Germany, and attended the C.G. Jung Institute in Zurich. Her clip art adorns many parish liturgical and educational bulletins. She lives in Del Mar, California, with her psychiatrist husband and three children.

Kathleen Norris is an award-winning poet and author of the *New York Times* bestseller *The Cloister Walk, Amazing Grace, Dakota: A Spiritual Geography, The Quotidian Mysteries,* and three volumes of poetry. Her poetry and essays have appeared in numerous magazines and anthologies. A recipient of grants from the Bush and Guggenheim foundations, she has been in residence twice at the Institute for Religious and Cultural Research at St. John's Abbey in Collegeville, Minnesota, and has been, for ten years, an oblate of Assumption Abbey in North Dakota. She and her husband, the poet David Dwyer, live in South Dakota.

Irene Nowell, O.S.B., is director of community formation at Mount Saint Scholastica, in Atchison, Kansas. She holds a doctorate in biblical studies from The Catholic University of America and has published many articles and books, including *Women in the Old Testament* and *Sing a New Song,* a study of the responsorial psalms in the Sunday liturgy.

Pheme Perkins holds a doctorate in New Testament and Christian origins from Harvard University and is professor of New Testament at Boston College. She is a past president of the Catholic Biblical Association and has served on the board of the *Catholic Biblical Quarterly Monograph Series.* She is the author of many published works, and her commentaries on various New Testament books can be found in the *New Jerome Biblical Commentary* and the *Collegeville Bible Commentary.*

Saint Perpetua (181–203) was born in Carthage, North Africa, the daughter of a pagan father and, most probably, a Christian mother. At twenty-two, after marrying a prominent man and giving birth to a son, she began receiving instructions in the faith. Just then, the emperor Severus launched a persecution against anyone who refused to worship him as a god. Perpetua and four other Christians were arrested, tried, and thrown to wild animals in an arena as public entertainment. Her account of the group's last days, completed by an eyewitness, report of their heroic deaths and is moving and gripping.

Louise Perrotta has been a missionary, youth worker, editor, and writer. Her published work includes the book *All You Need to Know about Prayer You Can Learn from the Poor.* Contributing editor for the *Catholic Women's Devotional Bible,* she and her husband, Kevin, live in Minnesota, and have five children and five grandchildren.

Teresa Pirola has been a writer and publisher of religious education materials for parishes, schools, and diocesan agencies in Sydney, Australia, since 1991. Through her organization, The Story Source, she shares the vision that ordinary people can and do proclaim the gospel in extraordinary ways.

Dorothy Ranaghan and her husband, Kevin, wrote *As the Spirit Leads Us,* a pioneering book on the Catholic charismatic renewal and have themselves been leaders in the movement since the early seventies. A gifted speaker and writer, Dorothy was for many years a regular columnist for *New Covenant* magazine. She and her family live in Indiana.

Harriet Gillum Robinet is a writer in Oak Park, Illinois. She is the author of books of historical fiction for middle-grade children.

Marie-Eloise Rosenblatt, R.S.M., a Sister of Mercy, is assistant professor of Religious Studies at Santa Clara University and the author of *Paul the Accused.*

Joyce Rupp is well known for her work as a writer and retreat and conference speaker. A member of the Servite (Servants of Mary) community, she has led retreats throughout North America, as well as in Europe, Asia, and Africa. Joyce is the author of eight books, among them, *Your Sorrow Is My Sorrow, The Cup of Life, Praying Our Goodbyes,* and *Dear Heart, Come Home.*

Nijole Sadunaite, a Lithuanian Catholic, was arrested in August 1974 by the Soviet secret police for the "crime" of helping to circulate the *Chronicle of the Catholic Church in Lithuania,* an underground journal which records the heroism of the Church behind the Iron Curtain. Refusing to betray her Catholic contacts, she was sentenced to three years in prison camps and three years exile in Siberia. She endured her ordeal with heroic trust in God and a love that embraced both her fellow prisoners and her persecutors.

Dorothy Sayers (1893–1957) was an English dramatist, novelist, poet, essayist, and translator of Dante. Brought up in a Church of England home, she was a convert to Catholicism and was particularly concerned to make Jesus accessible and real to the ordinary person, which is the goal of her popular radio play, *The Man Born to Be King*. She is also known for her clever detective stories featuring Lord Peter Wimsey and for many thought-provoking essays including those collected in *The Mind of the Maker*, *Unpopular Opinions*, and *Creed or Chaos?*

Saint Elizabeth Ann Seton (1774–1821) was raised in a prominent Episcopalian family in New York City, married a businessman, and had five children. Widowed in 1803, she became a Catholic through the influence of her husband's business friends, a devout Italian family. Years of hardship and poverty followed, as she struggled to raise and support her children. Eventually she was invited to found a teaching order and open a school for girls in Maryland. From her labors came the first American religious society, the Sisters of Charity, and the foundations of the parochial school system. In 1975 Mother Seton became the first American-born saint to be canonized.

Luci Shaw is past president of Harold Shaw Publishers. Her first book of prose, *God in the Dark*, met with critical acclaim, and her workbook on keeping a journal, *Lifepath*, is the text for workshops she leads across the continent. Luci is the author of many other books including *Listen to the Green*, *Writing the River*, and *Water My Soul*. A speaker, teacher, poet, editor, and writer, she lives in Bellingham, Washington.

Ann Shields is an evangelist, author, and popular conference speaker with many years' experience in teaching, counseling, and youth ministry. She has published a number of articles on spiritual renewal and written a book, *Fire in My Heart*. She currently serves with Renewal Ministries and belongs to the Servants of God's Love, a religious community in Ann Arbor, Michigan.

Barbara Leahy Shlemon has been involved in the healing ministry since 1965. A registered nurse, she has traveled nationally and internationally, directing retreats and workshops, and addressing conferences and conventions. Her books include *Healing Prayer*, *Healing the Hidden Self*, and *Healing the Wounds of Divorce*, as well as an audio program, *Beloved Child*. She has five children.

Bernadette McCarver Snyder has been a regular columnist and has published widely in the Catholic press for many years. Her books include humorous reflections on everyday Christian living (*Graham Crackers, Galoshes, and God*) and children's books (*365 Fun Facts for Catholic Kids*, *Fun Facts Dictionary*, *150 Fun Facts from the Bible*).

Ann Spangler is the former vice-president and editorial director for Servant Publications and a former senior acquisitions editor for Zondervan Publishing House. She is the author of *An Angel a Day*, *A Miracle a Day*, *Dreams and Miracles*, and co-author, with Jean Syswerda, of *Women of the Bible*. General editor of the *Catholic Women's Devotional Bible*, she and her daughters live in Michigan.

Melannie Svoboda, a Sister of Notre Dame of Chardon, Ohio, is on the formation team of the Detroit and Chicago Jesuit provinces. She frequently gives talks and retreats around the country and is the author of five books, among them, *Everyday Epiphanies* and *Traits of a Healthy Spirituality*. She is a regular columnist for *Praying* magazine.

Marguerite Teilhard de Chardin, an invalid by age 20, died in 1936 after serving ten years as president of the Catholic Association of the Sick. Her brother, Pierre, the well-known Jesuit scientist and theologian, wrote that she fought for health but sought always "to find God in the heart of human infirmity" and to prove by her example that, in Christ, suffering is transfigured. To know Marguerite, he said, was "to perceive that hidden in the depth of suffering lies a power that can dissipate egoism, bring tenderness to the heart, clarify the understanding, and reveal God."

Saint Teresa of Avila (1515–1582) was twenty when she entered a Carmelite convent in Avila, Spain. By her own account, she was lax in her spiritual life for the next two decades, indulging in "one pastime, one vanity, and one occasion of sin after another." After her religious awakening she made up for lost time, working diligently to reform the Carmelite order, founding many small monasteries, and writing important books on contemplative prayer: *Life*, *The Way of Perfection*, and *The Interior Castle*. Saint Teresa was declared one of only three women Doctors of the Church in 1970.

Mother Teresa of Calcutta (1910–1997) was born in Skopje, Yugoslavia, into a close-knit and religious Albanian family. At eighteen she left home forever, first to train as a Sister of Loreto in Dublin, then to teach at a girls' school in Calcutta. Eighteen years later, after hearing Jesus' call to live and serve among the "poorest of the poor," she received permission to leave her convent and found a new order, the Missionary Sisters of Charity. Recipient of the Nobel Peace Prize, Mother Teresa authored many books of simple wisdom, among them *A Gift for God, My Life for the Poor, The Life of Christ, Spiritual Counsel,* and *Seeking the Heart of God.*

Saint Thérèse of Lisieux (1873–1897), youngest of five daughters who all became nuns, was born of saintly middle-class parents in northern France. Admitted into the Carmelite order at fifteen, Thérèse experienced no visions, ecstasies, or revelations but made steady progress in holiness by approaching routine annoyances and her own imperfections in a spirit of deep trust and burning love for God. After her painful, heroically endured death from tuberculosis, Thérèse's "little way" to God was popularized through her *Story of a Soul,* a slim but profound book which has become a spiritual classic and influenced countless readers. Thérèse was canonized in 1925, named a patron of the missions (she had dreamed of being a missionary and corresponded with two priests in China), and declared one of only three women Doctors of the Church.

Kathy Troccoli is a singer-songwriter who has garnered four pop radio hits as well as two Grammy nominations and thirteen Dove award nominations. She tours nationally and has appeared on *The Tonight Show* with Jay Leno, *Live with Regis and Kathie Lee, Entertainment Tonight,* and other TV programs. She has written a book of meditations, *My Life Is in Your Hands.*

Evelyn Underhill (1875–1941) was an articulate Anglican poet and writer who, following a 1907 conversion experience, devoted much of her time and abilities to studying Christian mysticism. Her books—among them, *Mysticism, the Mystic Way,* and *The Essentials of Mysticism*—helped establish mystical theology as a reputable discipline for contemporary study. Evelyn also wrote about other aspects of the Christian Life—for example, *The School of Charity, The Mystery of Sacrifice,* and *The Spiritual Life*—and was a popular spiritual counselor, retreat-giver and lecturer.

Sigrid Undset (1882–1949) grew up in Norway, one of two daughters of a cultured Danish mother and an internationally respected archaeologist father, who died when Sigrid was eleven. Lacking funds for college, she worked ten years as a secretary in an engineering firm, laboring late at night and on weekends at what she *really* liked: writing. Her literary debut came when she was twenty-five—a short novel on adultery—and she soon gained an enthusiastic readership. In 1909 Sigrid met a Norwegian artist who divorced his wife to marry her; three children and seven years later, their marriage also collapsed. Sigrid's ensuing crisis of faith led her from being a free-thinking skeptic to a committed Catholic—a conversion that was seen as sensational and scandalous in Norway, where Catholics were virtually unknown. Of her thirty-six books, perhaps the best known is *Kristin Lavransdatter,* one of the powerful novels set in medieval Norway, for which she won the Nobel prize for literature in 1928.

Evelyn Birge Vitz was educated at Smith College and Yale University and is professor of French and director of medieval and Renaissance studies at New York University. Raised a Presbyterian and for many years an atheist, she was received into the Catholic Church with her husband in 1979. She is the author of *A Continual Feast: A Cookbook to Celebrate the Joys of Family and Faith throughout the Christian Year.* Evelyn and her husband, Paul, a psychology professor at N.Y.U., have three girls and three boys. They live in Greenwich Village.

Barbara Vogel lives in Buffalo, New York.

Alice von Hildebrand received her doctorate in philosophy from Fordham University, where she studied under Dietrich von Hildebrand. She mastered his thought, collaborated with him, and later became his wife. Since her retirement from Hunter College (CUNY), where she taught philosophy for thirty-seven years, she has spoken and written extensively on women's issues. Her works include *By Love Refined, By Grief Refined, Women and the Priesthood,* and, with her husband, *The Art of Living.*

Adrienne von Speyr (1902–1967), born into a Swiss Protestant family of doctors and clergymen, persevered despite great obstacles to become a skilled and empathetic physician who helped many patients resolve family crises and treated the poor for free. She married a widowed history professor and became stepmother to his children; after his death, she married another historian, Werner Kaegi. Adrienne had already had many experiences of mystical prayer when, in 1940, she met the Swiss theologian Hans Urs von Balthasar, through whom she came into the Catholic Church. Adrienne's many writings, the fruit of her contemplative prayer, include her classic about Our Lady, *Handmaid of the Lord*, meditative studies of Scripture, and collections of prayers.

Maria von Trapp (1905–1987) was born on a train to Vienna and entrusted to an elderly cousin two years later when her mother died. It was a lonely, strict, and atheistic upbringing. Not until Maria heard a Jesuit preaching one day (she had wandered into a church looking for a Bach concert) did she realize that the Bible was not "legends and inventions," as she had always been told. She became a Catholic, entered a convent, left for reasons of health, and became a tutor in the von Trapp family. Her marriage to the widowed Baron Georg von Trapp and the emergence of the Trapp Family Singers is told in *The Sound of Music*, which is loosely based on one of Maria's books. After fleeing the Nazis by walking over the Alps to Italy in 1938, the Trapp family came to the U.S. as "poor refugees," eventually settling in Stowe, Vermont, where they opened the Trapp Family Music Camp and Lodge.

Lisa and Steve Walker are parents and nationally recognized youth ministers who speak frequently at conferences and consult with parishes and dioceses. They are cofounders of the Catholic Work Camps, which aim to give young Catholics an experience of serving others, and coauthors of *Are We Having Fun Yet?* Lisa's most recent book is *Women in Youth Ministry*.

Maisie Ward (1889–1975) came from a bookish family of English Catholics: Her father wrote biographies of Cardinals Newman and Wiseman; her mother wrote several novels. Maisie's own books include *Caryll Houselander, Be Not Solicitous, Saints Who Made History, They Saw His Glory*, and *The Splendor of the Rosary*. With her

husband, Frank, she founded the influential publishing house Sheed & Ward and did street evangelism with the Catholic Evidence Guild. Among her many efforts to assist the poor and disadvantaged was cofounding the Catholic Housing Aid Society, the first housing aid group in Britain; in her eighties, she raised money to benefit India's lowest caste "untouchables." Wilfrid, one of Maisie and Frank's two children, is himself a well-known novelist and essayist.

Amy Welborn lives in Lakeland, Florida, with her three children. In addition to leading pro-life workshops and teaching theology in a Catholic high school, she has been writing in the Catholic press for more than a decade. Her column appears regularly in *Our Sunday Visitor*.

Macrina Wiederkehr is a member of the Benedictine community of St. Scholastica, Fort Smith, Arkansas. She is retreat director of the Benedictine Retreat Center and leader of retreats and days of renewal in parishes throughout the United States. She is a poet and author of books of prayers and reflections including *Seasons of Your Heart, Gold in Your Memories*, and *A Tree Full of Angels*.

Ronald D. Witherup, S.S., holds a doctorate in Biblical studies from Union Theological Seminary, Richmond, Virginia. Among his books are *Conversion in the Old Testament; The Bible Companion: a Handbook for Beginners*; and a commentary on the gospel of Matthew.

Irene Zimmerman, O.S.F., a School Sister of Saint Francis, grew up among many siblings on a farm near Westphalia, Iowa. She began writing poetry intermittently—as a child, and later as she taught high school English and French in Milwaukee. She has worked in a boarding school, in various clerical positions, and most recently as part of the academic support staff at Alverno College.

Lectionary

Many Catholics would like to
read the passages of Scripture
that will be read aloud in church
for the daily and Sunday Masses,
but they lack a schedule that will
quickly guide them to the readings for the day. They wonder
whether they are in Year A, B,
or C on the Sunday schedule or
Year I or II on the daily cycle of
readings. The schedule that
follows makes it easy to find the
correct readings simply by looking at the calendar date. The
liturgical years (beginning with
the first Sunday of Advent—
usually occurring late in November) are also clearly marked so
that readers can follow the
church calendar as well.

Please keep in mind that
although the passages cited in
the following schedule match
the readings of the daily and
Sunday Masses, the translation
of Scripture read at Mass is different than the NRSV.

Advent, *Liturgical year 2001*

WEEK 1, ADVENT

Sun, Dec 3, 2000	Jeremiah 33.14-16
	Psalms 25.4-5, 8-9, 10, 14
	1 Thessalonians 3.12—4.2
	Luke 21.25-28, 34-36
Mon, Dec 4	Isaiah 2.1-5
	Psalms 122.1-2, 3-4, 8-9
	Matthew 8.5-11
Tue, Dec 5	Isaiah 11.1-10
	Psalms 72.1, 7-8, 12-13, 17
	Luke 10.21-24
Wed, Dec 6	Isaiah 25.6-10
	Psalms 23.1-3, 3-4, 5, 6
	Matthew 15.29-37
Thu, Dec 7	Isaiah 26.1-6
	Psalms 118.1, 8-9, 19-21, 25-27
	Matthew 7.21, 24-27
Fri, Dec 8 *Immaculate Conception of the Virgin Mary— Solemnity*	Genesis 3.9-15, 20
	Psalms 98.1, 2-3, 3-4
	Ephesians 1.3-6, 11-12
	Luke 1.26-38
Sat, Dec 9	Isaiah 30.19-21, 23-26
	Psalms 147.1-2, 3-4, 5-6
	Matthew 9.35—10.1, 6-8

WEEK 2, ADVENT

Sun, Dec 10	Baruch 5.1-9
	Psalms 126.1-2, 2-3, 4-5, 6
	Philippians 1.4-6, 8-11
	Luke 3.1-6
Mon, Dec 11	Isaiah 35.1-10
	Psalms 85.9-10, 11-12, 13-14
	Luke 5.17-26
Tue, Dec 12 *Our Lady of Guadalupe— Feast*	Zechariah 2.14-17
	Psalms 45.11-12, 14-17
	Romans 8.28-30
	Luke 2.15-19
Wed, Dec 13	Isaiah 40.25-31
	Psalms 103.1-2, 3-4, 8, 10
	Matthew 11.28-30
Thu, Dec 14	Isaiah 41.13-20
	Psalms 145.1, 9, 10-11, 12-13
	Matthew 11.11-15
Fri, Dec 15	Isaiah 48.17-19
	Psalms 1.1-2, 3, 4, 6
	Matthew 11.16-19
Sat, Dec 16	Sirach 48.1-4, 9-11
	Psalms 80.2-3, 15-16, 18-19
	Matthew 17.10-13

WEEK 3, ADVENT

Sun, Dec 17
Zephaniah 3.14-18
Isaiah 12.2-3, 4, 5-6
Philippians 4.4-7
Luke 3.10-18

Mon, Dec 18
Jeremiah 23.5-8
Psalms 72.1, 12-13, 18-19
Matthew 1.18-24

Tue, Dec 19
Judges 13.2-7, 24-25
Psalms 71.3-4, 5-6, 16-17
Luke 1.5-25

Wed, Dec 20
Isaiah 7.10-14
Psalms 24.1-2, 3-4, 5-6
Luke 1.26-38

Thu, Dec 21
Song of Songs 2.8-14
Psalms 33.2-3, 11-12, 20-21
Luke 1.39-45

Fri, Dec 22
I Samuel 1.24-28
I Samuel 2.1, 4-5, 6-7, 8
Luke 1.46-56

Sat, Dec 23
Malachi 3.1-4, 23-24
Psalms 25.4-5, 8-9, 10, 14
Luke 1.57-66

WEEK 4, ADVENT

Sun, Dec 24
Micah 5.1-4
Psalms 80.2-3, 15-16, 18-19
Hebrews 10.5-10
Luke 1.39-45

Christmas Season

Mon, Dec 25
Christmas—
Solemnity
Isaiah 9.1-6
Psalms 96.1-2, 2-3, 11-12, 13
Titus 2.11-14
Luke 2.1-14

Tue, Dec 26
Saint Stephen,
first martyr—
Feast
Acts 6.8-10; 7.54-59
Psalms 31.3-4, 6, 7, 8, 17, 21
Matthew 10.17-22

Wed, Dec 27
Saint John, apostle
and evangelist—
Feast
I John 1.1-4
Psalms 97.1-2, 5-6, 11-12
John 20.2-8

Thu, Dec 28
The Holy Innocents,
martyrs—
Feast
I John 1.5—2.2
Psalms 124.2-3, 4-5, 7-8
Matthew 2.13-18

Fri, Dec 29
I John 2.3-11
Psalms 96.1-2, 2-3, 5-6
Luke 2.22-35

Sat, Dec 30
I John 2.12-17
Psalms 96.7-8, 8-9, 10
Luke 2.36-40

Sun, Dec 31
The Holy Family—
Feast
Sirach 3.2-6, 12-14
Psalms 128.1-2, 3, 4-5
Colossians 3.12-21
Luke 2.41-52

Mon, Jan 1, 2001
Mary, Mother
of God—
Solemnity
Numbers 6.22-27
Psalms 67.2-3, 5, 6, 8
Galatians 4.4-7
Luke 2.16-21

Tue, Jan 2
I John 2.22-28
Psalms 98.1, 2-3, 3-4
John 1.19-28

Wed, Jan 3
I John 2.29—3.6
Psalms 98.1, 3-4, 5-6
John 1.29-34

Thu, Jan 4
I John 3.7-10
Psalms 98.1, 7-8, 9
John 1.35-42

Fri, Jan 5
I John 3.11-21
Psalms 100.1-2, 3, 4, 5
John 1.43-51

Sat, Jan 6
I John 5.5-13
Psalms 147.12-13, 14-15, 19-20
Mark 1.7-11

Sun, Jan 7
Epiphany
of the Lord—
Solemnity
Isaiah 60.1-6
Psalms 72.1-2, 7-8, 10-11, 12-13
Ephesians 3.2-3, 5-6
Matthew 2.1-12

Ordinary Time

WEEK 1

Mon, Jan 8
Baptism
of the Lord—
Feast
Isaiah 42.1-4, 6-7
Psalms 29.1-2, 3-4, 3, 9-10
Acts 10.34-38
Luke 3.15-16, 21-22

Tue, Jan 9
Hebrews 2.5-12
Psalms 8.2, 5, 6-7, 8-9
Mark 1.21-28

Wed, Jan 10
Hebrews 2.14-18
Psalms 105.1-2, 3-4, 6-7, 8-9
Mark 1.29-39

Thu, Jan 11
Hebrews 3.7-14
Psalms 95.6-7, 8-9, 10-11
Mark 1.40-45

Fri, Jan 12
Hebrews 4.1-5, 11
Psalms 78.3, 4, 6-7, 8
Mark 2.1-12

Sat, Jan 13
Hebrews 4.12-16
Psalms 19.8, 9, 10, 15
Mark 2.13-17

WEEK 2

Sun, Jan 14   Isaiah 62.1-5
Psalms 96.1-2, 2-3, 7-8, 9-10
I Corinthians 12.4-11
John 2.1-12

Mon, Jan 15   Hebrews 5.1-10
Psalms 110.1, 2, 3, 4
Mark 2.18-22

Tue, Jan 16   Hebrews 6.10-20
Psalms 111.1-2, 4-5, 9-10
Mark 2.23-28

Wed, Jan 17   Hebrews 7.1-3, 15-17
Psalms 110.1, 2, 3, 4
Mark 3.1-6

Thu, Jan 18   Hebrews 7.25—8.6
Psalms 40.7-8, 8-9, 10, 17
Mark 3.7-12

Fri, Jan 19   Hebrews 8.6-13
Psalms 85.8, 10, 11-12, 13-14
Mark 3.13-19

Sat, Jan 20   Hebrews 9.2-3, 11-14
Psalms 47.2-3, 6-7, 8-9
Mark 3.20-21

WEEK 3

Sun, Jan 21   Nehemiah 8.2-4, 5-6, 8-10
Psalms 19.8, 9, 10, 15
I Corinthians 12.12-30
Luke 1.1-4, 4.14-21

Mon, Jan 22   Hebrews 9.15, 24-28
Psalms 98.1, 2-3, 3-4, 5-6
Mark 3.22-30

Tue, Jan 23   Hebrews 10.1-10
Psalms 40.2, 4, 7-8, 10, 11
Mark 3.31-35

Wed, Jan 24   Hebrews 10.11-18
Psalms 110.1, 2, 3, 4
Mark 4.1-20

Thu, Jan 25   Acts 9.1-22
Psalms 117.1, 2
Mark 16.15-18

Fri, Jan 26   Hebrews 10.32-39
Psalms 37.3-4, 5-6, 23-24,
39-40
Mark 4.26-34

Sat, Jan 27   Hebrews 11.1-2, 8-19
Luke 1.69-70, 71-72, 73-75
Mark 4.35-41

WEEK 4

Sun, Jan 28   Jeremiah 1.4-5, 17-19
Psalms 71.1-2, 3-4, 5-6, 15-17
I Corinthians 12.31—13.13
Luke 4.21-30

Mon, Jan 29   Hebrews 11.32-40
Psalms 31.20, 21, 22, 23, 24
Mark 5.1-20

Tue, Jan 30   Hebrews 12.1-4
Psalms 22.26-27, 28, 30, 31-32
Mark 5.21-43

Wed, Jan 31   Hebrews 12.4-7, 11-15
Psalms 103.1-2, 13-14, 17-18
Mark 6.1-6

Thu, Feb 1   Hebrews 12.18-19, 21-24
Psalms 48.2-3, 3-4, 9, 10-11
Mark 6.7-13

Fri, Feb 2   Malachi 3.1-4
Presentation   Psalms 24.7, 8, 9, 10
of the Lord—   Hebrews 2.14-18
Feast   Luke 2.22-40

Sat, Feb 3   Hebrews 13.15-17, 20-21
Psalms 23.1-3, 3-4, 5, 6
Mark 6.30-34

WEEK 5

Sun, Feb 4   Isaiah 6.1-2, 3-8
Psalms 138.1-2, 2-3, 4-5, 7-8
I Corinthians 15.1-11
or 15.3-8, 11
Luke 5.1-11

Mon, Feb 5   Genesis 1.1-19
Psalms 104.1-2, 5-6, 10, 12, 24, 35
Mark 6.53-56

Tue, Feb 6   Genesis 1.20—2.4
Psalms 8.4-5, 6-7, 8-9
Mark 7.1-13

Wed, Feb 7   Genesis 2.5-9, 15-17
Psalms 104.1-2, 27-28, 29-30
Mark 7.14-23

Thu, Feb 8   Genesis 2.18-25
Psalms 128.1-2, 3, 4-5
Mark 7.24-30

Fri, Feb 9   Genesis 3.1-8
Psalms 32.1-2, 5, 6, 7
Mark 7.31-37

Sat, Feb 10   Genesis 3.9-24
Psalms 90.2, 3-4, 5-6, 12-13
Mark 8.1-10

WEEK 6

Sun, Feb 11
Jeremiah 17.5-8
Psalms 1.1-2, 3, 4, 6
1 Corinthians 15.12, 16-20
Luke 6.17, 20-26

Mon, Feb 12
Genesis 4.1-15, 25
Psalms 50.1, 8, 16-17, 20-21
Mark 8.11-13

Tue, Feb 13
Genesis 6.5-8; 7.1-5, 10
Psalms 29.1-2, 3-4, 8, 9-10
Mark 8.14-21

Wed, Feb 14
Genesis 8.6-13, 20-22
Psalms 116.12-13, 14-15, 18-19
Mark 8.22-26

Thu, Feb 15
Genesis 9.1-13
Psalms 102.16-18, 19-21, 29, 22-23
Mark 8.27-33

Fri, Feb 16
Genesis 11.1-9
Psalms 33.10-11, 12-13, 14-15
Mark 8.34—9.1

Sat, Feb 17
Hebrews 11.1-7
Psalms 145.2-3, 4-5, 10-11
Mark 9.2-13

WEEK 7

Sun, Feb 18
1 Samuel 26.2, 7-9, 12-13, 22-23
Psalms 103.1-2, 3-4, 8, 10, 12-13
1 Corinthians 15.45-49
Luke 6.27-38

Mon, Feb 19
Sirach 1.1-10
Psalms 93.1, 1-2, 5
Mark 9.14-29

Tue, Feb 20
Sirach 2.1-11
Psalms 37.3-4, 18-19, 27-28, 39-40
Mark 9.30-37

Wed, Feb 21
Sirach 4.11-19
Psalms 119.165, 168, 171, 172, 174, 175
Mark 9.38-40

Thu, Feb 22
Chair of Saint Peter, apostle—Feast
1 Peter 5.1-4
Psalms 23.1-3, 3-4, 5, 6
Matthew 16.13-19

Fri, Feb 23
Sirach 6.5-17
Psalms 119.12, 16, 18, 27, 34, 35
Mark 10.1-12

Sat, Feb 24
Sirach 17.1-15
Psalms 103.13-14, 15-16, 17-18
Mark 10.13-16

WEEK 8

Sun, Feb 25
Sirach 27.4-7
Psalms 92.2-3, 13-14, 15-16
1 Corinthians 15.54-58
Luke 6.39-45

Mon, Feb 26
Sirach 17.19-27
Psalms 32.1-2, 5, 6, 7
Mark 10.17-27

Tue, Feb 27
Sirach 35.1-12
Psalms 50.5-6, 7-8, 14, 23
Mark 10.28-31

Lent

Wed, Feb 28
Ash Wednesday
Joel 2.12-18
Psalms 51.3-4, 5-6, 12-13, 14, 17
2 Corinthians 5.20—6.2
Matthew 6.1-6, 16-18

Thu, Mar 1
Deuteronomy 30.15-20
Psalms 1.1-2, 3, 4, 6
Luke 9.22-25

Fri, Mar 2
Isaiah 58.1-9
Psalms 51.3-4, 5-6, 18-19
Matthew 9.14-15

Sat, Mar 3
Isaiah 58.9-14
Psalms 86.1-2, 3-4, 5-6
Luke 5.27-32

WEEK I, LENT

Sun, Mar 4
Deuteronomy 26.4-10
Psalms 91.1-2, 10-11, 12-13, 14-15
Romans 10.8-13
Luke 4.1-13

Mon, Mar 5
Leviticus 19.1-2, 11-18
Psalms 19.8, 9, 10, 15
Matthew 25.31-46

Tue, Mar 6
Isaiah 55.10-11
Psalms 34.4-5, 6-7, 16-17, 18-19
Matthew 6.7-15

Wed, Mar 7
Jonah 3.1-10
Psalms 51.3-4, 12-13, 18-19
Luke 11.29-32

Thu, Mar 8
Esther C.12, 14-16, 23-25
Psalms 138.1-2, 2-3, 7-8
Matthew 7.7-12

Fri, Mar 9
Ezekiel 18.21-28
Psalms 130.1-2, 3-4, 5-6, 7-8
Matthew 5.20-26

Sat, Mar 10
Deuteronomy 26.16-19
Psalms 119.1-2, 4-5, 7-8
Matthew 5.43-48

WEEK 2, LENT

Sun, Mar 11
Genesis 15.5-12, 17-18
Psalms 27.1, 7-8, 8-9, 13-14
Philippians 3.17—4.1
or 3.20—4.1
Luke 9.28-36

Mon, Mar 12
Daniel 9.4-10
Psalms 79.8, 9, 11, 13
Luke 6.36-38

Tue, Mar 13
Isaiah 1.10, 16-20
Psalms 50.8-9, 16-17, 21, 23
Matthew 23.1-12

Wed, Mar 14
Jeremiah 18.18-20
Psalms 31.5-6, 14, 15-16
Matthew 20.17-28

Thu, Mar 15
Jeremiah 17.5-10
Psalms 1.1-2, 3, 4, 6
Luke 16.19-31

Fri, Mar 16
Genesis 37.3-4, 12-13, 17-18
Psalms 105.16-17, 18-19, 20-21
Matthew 21.33-43, 45-46

Sat, Mar 17
Micah 7.14-15, 18-20
Psalms 103.1-2, 3-4, 9-10, 11-12
Luke 15.1-3, 11-32

WEEK 3, LENT

Sun, Mar 18
Exodus 3.1-8, 13-15
Psalms 103.1-2, 3-4, 6-7, 8, 11
1 Corinthians 10.1-6, 10-12
Luke 13.1-9

Mon, Mar 19
Saint Joseph, Husband
of Mary—Solemnity
2 Samuel 7.4-5, 12-14, 16
Psalms 89.2-3, 4-5, 27, 29
Romans 4.13, 16-18, 22
Matthew 1.16, 18-21, 24

Tue, Mar 20
Daniel 3.25, 34-43
Psalms 25.4-5, 6-7, 8-9
Matthew 18.21-35

Wed, Mar 21
Deuteronomy 4.1, 5-9
Psalms 147.12-13, 15-16, 19-20
Matthew 5.17-19

Thu, Mar 22
Jeremiah 7.23-28
Psalms 95.1-2, 6-7, 8-9
Luke 11.14-23

Fri, Mar 23
Hosea 14.2-10
Psalms 81.6-8, 8-9, 10-11, 14, 17
Mark 12.28-34

Sat, Mar 24
Annunciation
of the Lord—
Solemnity
Isaiah 7.10-14
Psalms 40.7-8, 8-9, 10, 11
Hebrews 10.4-10
Luke 1.26-38

WEEK 4, LENT

Sun, Mar 25
Joshua 5.9, 10-12
Psalms 34.2-3, 4-5, 6-7
2 Corinthians 5.17-21
Luke 15.1-3, 11-32

Mon, Mar 26
Isaiah 65.17-21
Psalms 30.2, 4, 5-6, 11-13
John 4.43-54

Tue, Mar 27
Ezekiel 47.1-9, 12
Psalms 46.2-3, 5-6, 8-9
John 5.1-3, 5-16

Wed, Mar 28
Isaiah 49.8-15
Psalms 145.8-9, 13-14, 17-18
John 5.17-30

Thu, Mar 29
Exodus 32.7-14
Psalms 106.19-20, 21-22, 23
John 5.31-47

Fri, Mar 30
Wisdom 2.1, 12-22
Psalms 34.17-18, 19-20, 21, 23
John 7.1-2, 10, 25-30

Sat, Mar 31
Jeremiah 11.18-20
Psalms 7.2-3, 9-10, 11-12
John 7.40-53

WEEK 5, LENT

Sun, Apr 1
Isaiah 43.16-21
Psalms 126.1-2, 2-3, 4-5, 6
Philippians 3.8-14
John 8.1-11

Mon, Apr 2
Daniel 13.1-9, 15-17, 19-30, 33-62
Psalms 23.1-3, 3-4, 5, 6
John 8.12-20

Tue, Apr 3
Numbers 21.4-9
Psalms 102.2-3, 16-18, 19-21
John 8.21-30

Wed, Apr 4
Daniel 3.14-20, 91-92, 95
Daniel 3.52, 53, 54, 55, 56
John 8.31-42

Thu, Apr 5
Genesis 17.3-9
Psalms 105.4-5, 6-7, 8-9
John 8.51-59

Fri, Apr 6
Jeremiah 20.10-13
Psalms 18.2-3, 3-4, 5-6, 7
John 10.31-42

Sat, Apr 7
Ezekiel 37.21-28
Jeremiah 31.10, 11-12, 13
John 11.45-57

HOLY WEEK

Sun, Apr 8
Passion (Palm) Sunday
Isaiah 50.4-7
Psalms 22.8-9, 17-18, 19-20, 23-24
Philippians 2.6-11
Luke 22.14—23.56

Mon, Apr 9
Isaiah 42.1-7
Psalms 27.1, 2, 3, 13-14
John 12.1-11

Tue, Apr 10
Isaiah 49.1-6
Psalms 71.1-2, 3-4, 5-6, 15, 17
John 13.21-33, 36-38

Wed, Apr 11
Isaiah 50.4-9
Psalms 69.8-10, 21-22, 31, 33-34
Matthew 26.14-25

Thu, Apr 12
Holy Thursday
Exodus 12.1-8, 11-14
Psalms 116.12-13, 15-16, 17-18
1 Corinthians 11.23-26
John 13.1-15

Fri, Apr 13
Good Friday
Isaiah 52.13—53.12
Psalms 31.2, 6, 12-13, 15-16, 17, 25
Hebrews 4.14-16; 5.7-9
John 18.1—19.42

Sat, Apr 14
Holy Saturday
Genesis 1.1—2.2
Psalms 104.1-2, 5-6, 10, 12, 13-14, 24, 35
Genesis 22.1-18
Psalms 16.5, 8, 9-10, 11
Exodus 14.15—15.1
Exodus 15.1-2, 3-4, 5-6, 17-18
Isaiah 54.5-14
Psalms 30.2, 4, 5-6, 11-12, 13
Isaiah 55.1-11
Isaiah 12.2-3, 4, 5-6
Baruch 3.9-15, 32—4.4
Psalms 19.8, 9, 10, 11
Ezekiel 36.16-28
Psalms 42.3, 5; 43.3, 4
Romans 6.3-11
Psalms 118.1-2, 16, 17, 22-23
Luke 24.1-12

Easter

WEEK 1, EASTER

Sun, Apr 15
Easter Sunday
Acts 10.34, 37-43
Psalms 118.1-2, 16-17, 22-23
Colossians 3.1-4
John 20.1-9

Mon, Apr 16
Acts 2.14, 22-32
Psalms 16.1-2, 5, 7-8, 9-10, 11
Matthew 28.8-15

Tue, Apr 17
Acts 2.36-41
Psalms 33.4-5, 18-19, 20, 22
John 20.11-18

Wed, Apr 18
Acts 3.1-10
Psalms 105.1-2, 3-4, 6-7, 8-9
Luke 24.13-35

Thu, Apr 19
Acts 3.11-26
Psalms 8.2, 5, 6-7, 8-9
Luke 24.35-48

Fri, Apr 20
Acts 4.1-12
Psalms 118.1-2, 4, 22-24, 25-27
John 21.1-14

Sat, Apr 21
Acts 4.13-21
Psalms 118.1, 14-15, 16-18, 19-21
Mark 16.9-15

WEEK 2, EASTER

Sun, Apr 22
Acts 5.12-16
Psalms 118.2-4, 13-15, 22-24
Revelation 1.9-11, 12-13, 17-19
John 20.19-31

Mon, Apr 23
Acts 4.23-31
Psalms 2.1-3, 4-6, 7-9
John 3.1-8

Tue, Apr 24
Acts 4.32-37
Psalms 93.1, 1-2, 5
John 3.7-15

Wed, Apr 25
1 Peter 5.5-14
Psalms 89.2-3, 6-7, 16-17
Mark 16.15-20

Thu, Apr 26
Acts 5.27-33
Psalms 34.2, 9, 17-18, 19-20
John 3.31-36

Fri, Apr 27
Acts 5.34-42
Psalms 27.1, 4, 13-14
John 6.1-15

Sat, Apr 28
Acts 6.1-7
Psalms 33.1-2, 4-5, 18-19
John 6.16-21

WEEK 3, EASTER

Sun, Apr 29
Acts 5.27-32, 40-41
Psalms 30.2, 4, 5-6, 11-12, 13
Revelation 5.11-14
John 21.1-19

Mon, Apr 30
Acts 6.8-15
Psalms 119.23-24, 26-27, 29-30
John 6.22-29

Tue, May 1
Acts 7.51—8.1
Psalms 31.3-4, 6, 7, 8, 17, 21
John 6.30-35

Wed, May 2
Acts 8.1-8
Psalms 66.1-3, 4-5, 6-7
John 6.35-40

Thu, May 3
Saints Philip and
James, apostles—Feast
I Corinthians 15.1-8
Psalms 19.2-3, 4-5
John 14.6-14

Fri, May 4
Acts 9.1-20
Psalms 117.1, 2
John 6.52-59

Sat, May 5
Acts 9.31-42
Psalms 116.12-13, 14-15, 16-17
John 6.60-69

WEEK 4, EASTER

Sun, May 6
Acts 13.14, 43-52
Psalms 100.1-2, 3, 5
Revelation 7.9, 14-17
John 10.27-30

Mon, May 7
Acts 11.1-18
Psalms 42.2-3; 43.3, 4
John 10.1-10

Tue, May 8
Acts 11.19-26
Psalms 87.1-3, 4-5, 6-7
John 10.22-30

Wed, May 9
Acts 12.24—13.5
Psalms 67.2-3, 5, 6, 8
John 12.44-50

Thu, May 10
Acts 13.13-25
Psalms 89.2-3, 21-22, 25, 27
John 13.16-20

Fri, May 11
Acts 13.26-33
Psalms 2.6-7, 8-9, 10-11
John 14.1-6

Sat, May 12
Acts 13.44-52
Psalms 98.1, 2-3, 3-4
John 14.7-14

WEEK 5, EASTER

Sun, May 13
Acts 14.21-27
Psalms 145.8-9, 10-11, 12-13
Revelation 21.1-5
John 13.31-33, 34-35

Mon, May 14
Saint Matthias,
apostle—Feast
Acts 1.15-17, 20-26
Psalms 113.1-2, 3-4, 5-6, 7-8
John 15.9-17

Tue, May 15
Acts 14.19-28
Psalms 145.10-11, 12-13, 21
John 14.27-31

Wed, May 16
Acts 15.1-6
Psalms 122.1-2, 3-4, 4-5
John 15.1-8

Thu, May 17
Acts 15.7-21
Psalms 96.1-2, 2-3, 10
John 15.9-11

Fri, May 18
Acts 15.22-31
Psalms 57.8-9, 10-12
John 15.12-17

Sat, May 19
Acts 16.1-10
Psalms 100.1-2, 3, 5
John 15.18-21

WEEK 6, EASTER

Sun, May 20
Acts 15.1-2, 22-29
Psalms 67.2-3, 5, 6, 8
Revelation 21.10-14, 22-23
John 14.23-29

Mon, May 21
Acts 16.11-15
Psalms 149.1-2, 3-4, 5-6, 9
John 15.26—16.4

Tue, May 22
Acts 16.22-34
Psalms 138.1-2, 2-3, 7-8
John 16.5-11

Wed, May 23
Acts 17.15, 22—18.1
Psalms 148.1-2, 11-12, 13, 14
John 16.12-15

Thu, May 24
Ascension of the Lord
Acts 1.1-11
Psalms 47.2-3, 6-7, 8-9
Ephesians 1.17-23
Luke 24.46-53

Fri, May 25
Acts 18.9-18
Psalms 47.2-3, 4-5, 6-7
John 16.20-23

Sat, May 26
Acts 18.23-28
Psalms 47.2-3, 8-9, 10
John 16.23-28

WEEK 7, EASTER

Sun, May 27
Acts 7.55-60
Psalms 97.1-2, 6-7, 9
Revelation 22.12-14, 16-17, 20
John 17.20-26

Mon, May 28
Acts 19.1-8
Psalms 68.2-3, 4-5, 6-7
John 16.29-33

Tue, May 29
Acts 20.17-27
Psalms 68.10-11, 20-21
John 17.1-11

Wed, May 30
Acts 20.28-38
Psalms 68.29-30, 33-35, 35-36
John 17.11-19

Thu, May 31
Visitation of the Virgin Mary to Elizabeth—Feast
Zephaniah 3.14-18
Isaiah 12.2-3, 4, 5-6
Luke 1.39-56

Fri, June 1
Acts 25.13-21
Psalms 103.1-2, 11-12, 19-20
John 21.15-19

Sat, June 2
Acts 28.16-20, 30-31
Psalms 11.4, 5, 7
John 21.20-25

Sun, June 3
Pentecost—Solemnity
Acts 2.1-11
Psalms 104.1, 24, 29-30, 31, 34
1 Corinthians 12.3-7, 12-13
John 20.19-23

Ordinary Time
WEEK 9

Mon, June 4
Tobit 1.1, 2; 2.1-9
Psalms 112.1-2, 3-4, 5-6
Mark 12.1-12

Tue, June 5
Tobit 2.9-14
Psalms 112.1-2, 7-8, 9
Mark 12.13-17

Wed, June 6
Tobit 3.1-11, 16
Psalms 25.2-4, 4-5, 6-7, 8-9
Mark 12.18-27

Thu, June 7
Tobit 6.11; 7.1, 9-14; 8.4-7
Psalms 128.1-2, 3, 4-5
Mark 12.28-34

Fri, June 8
Tobit 11.5-15
Psalms 146.2, 7, 8-9, 9-10
Mark 12.35-37

Sat, June 9
Tobit 12.1, 5-15, 20
Tobit 13.2, 6
Mark 12.38-44

WEEK 10

Sun, June 10
The Holy Trinity— Solemnity
Proverbs 8.22-31
Psalms 8.4-5, 6-7, 8-9
Romans 5.1-5
John 16.12-15

Mon, June 11
Saint Barnabas, apostle—Memorial
Acts 11.21-26; 13.1-3
Psalms 98.1, 2-3, 3-4, 5-6
Matthew 10.7-13

Tue, June 12
2 Corinthians 1.18-22
Psalms 119.129, 130, 131, 132, 133, 135
Matthew 5.13-16

Wed, June 13
2 Corinthians 3.4-11
Psalms 99.5, 6, 7, 8, 9
Matthew 5.17-19

Thu, June 14
2 Corinthians 3.15—4.1, 3-6
Psalms 85.9-10, 11-12, 13-14
Matthew 5.20-26

Fri, June 15
2 Corinthians 4.7-15
Psalms 116.10-11, 15-16, 17-18
Matthew 5.27-32

Sat, June 16
2 Corinthians 5.14-21
Psalms 103.1-2, 3-4, 8-9, 11-12
Matthew 5.33-37

WEEK 11

Sun, June 17
The Body and Blood of Christ (Corpus Christi)—Solemnity
Genesis 14.18-20
Psalms 110.1, 2, 3, 4
1 Corinthians 11.23-26
Luke 9.11-17

Mon, June 18
2 Corinthians 6.1-10
Psalms 98.1, 2-3, 3-4
Matthew 5.38-42

Tue, June 19
2 Corinthians 8.1-9
Psalms 146.2, 5-6, 7, 8-9
Matthew 5.43-48

Wed, June 20
2 Corinthians 9.6-11
Psalms 112.1-2, 3-4, 9
Matthew 6.1-6, 16-18

Thu, June 21
2 Corinthians 11.1-11
Psalms 111.1-2, 3-4, 7-8
Matthew 6.7-15

Fri, June 22
Sacred Heart of Jesus— Solemnity
Ezekiel 34.11-16
Psalms 23.1-3, 3-4, 5, 6
Romans 5.5-11
Luke 15.3-7

Sat, June 23
2 Corinthians 12.1-10
Psalms 34.8-9, 10-11, 12-13
Matthew 6.24-34

WEEK 12

Sun, June 24
Birth of Saint John
the Baptist—
Solemnity

Isaiah 49.1-6
Psalms 139.1-3, 13-14, 14-15
Acts 13.22-26
Luke 1.57-66, 80

Mon, June 25

Genesis 12.1-9
Psalms 33.12-13, 18-19, 20, 22
Matthew 7.1-5

Tue, June 26

Genesis 13.2, 5-18
Psalms 15.2-3, 3-4, 5
Matthew 7.6, 12-14

Wed, June 27

Genesis 15.1-12, 17-18
Psalms 105.1-2, 3-4, 6-7, 8-9
Matthew 7.15-20

Thu, June 28

Genesis 16.1-12, 15-16
Psalms 106.1-2, 3-4, 4-5
Matthew 7.21-29

Fri, June 29
Saints Peter and Paul,
apostles—Solemnity

Acts 12.1-11
Psalms 34.2-3, 4-5, 6-7, 8-9
2 Timothy 4.6-8, 17-18
Matthew 16.13-19

Sat, June 30

Genesis 18.1-15
Luke 1.46-47, 48-49, 50, 53,
54-55
Matthew 8.5-17

WEEK 13

Sun, July 1

1 Kings 19.16-21
Psalms 16.1-2, 5, 7-8, 9-10, 11
Galatians 5.1, 13-18
Luke 9.51-62

Mon, July 2

Genesis 18.16-33
Psalms 103.1-2, 3-4, 8-9, 10-11
Matthew 8.18-22

Tue, July 3
Saint Thomas,
apostle—Feast

Ephesians 2.19-22
Psalms 117.1, 2
John 20.24-29

Wed, July 4

Genesis 21.5, 8-20
Psalms 34.7-8, 10-11, 12-13
Matthew 8.28-34

Thu, July 5

Genesis 22.1-19
Psalms 115.1-2, 3-4, 5-6, 8-9
Matthew 9.1-8

Fri, July 6

Genesis 23.1-4, 19; 24.1-8, 62-67
Psalms 106.1-2, 3-4, 4-5
Matthew 9.9-13

Sat, July 7

Genesis 27.1-5, 15-29
Psalms 135.1-2, 3-4, 5-6
Matthew 9.14-17

WEEK 14

Sun, July 8

Isaiah 66.10-14
Psalms 66.1-3, 4-5, 6-7, 16, 20
Galatians 6.14-18
Luke 10.1-12, 17-20

Mon, July 9

Genesis 28.10-22
Psalms 91.1-2, 3-4, 14-15
Matthew 9.18-26

Tue, July 10

Genesis 32.23-33
Psalms 17.1, 2-3, 6-7, 8, 15
Matthew 9.32-38

Wed, July 11

Genesis 41.55-57; 42.5-7, 17-24
Psalms 33.2-3, 10-11, 18-19
Matthew 10.1-7

Thu, July 12

Genesis 44.18-21, 23-29; 45.1-5
Psalms 105.16-17, 18-19, 20-21
Matthew 10.7-15

Fri, July 13

Genesis 46.1-7, 28-30
Psalms 37.3-4, 18-19, 27-28,
39-40
Matthew 10.16-23

Sat, July 14

Genesis 49.29-33; 50.15-24
Psalms 105.1-2, 3-4, 6-7
Matthew 10.24-33

WEEK 15

Sun, July 15

Deuteronomy 30.10-14
Psalms 69.14, 17, 30-31, 33-34,
36, 37
Colossians 1.15-20
Luke 10.25-37

Mon, July 16

Exodus 1.8-14, 22
Psalms 124.1-3, 4-6, 7-8
Matthew 10.34—11.1

Tue, July 17

Exodus 2.1-15
Psalms 69.3, 14, 30-31, 33-34
Matthew 11.20-24

Wed, July 18

Exodus 3.1-6, 9-12
Psalms 103.1-2, 3-4, 6-7
Matthew 11.25-27

Thu, July 19

Exodus 3.11-20
Psalms 105.5, 8-9, 24-25, 26-27
Matthew 11.28-30

Fri, July 20

Exodus 11.10—12.14
Psalms 116.12-13, 15-16, 17-18
Matthew 12.1-8

Sat, July 21

Exodus 12.37-42
Psalms 136.1, 23-24, 10-12, 13-15
Matthew 12.14-21

WEEK 16

Sun, July 22	Genesis 18.1-10
	Psalms 15.2-3, 3-4, 5
	Colossians 1.24-28
	Luke 10.38-42
Mon, July 23	Exodus 14.5-18
	Exodus 15.1-2, 3-4, 5-6
	Matthew 12.38-42
Tue, July 24	Exodus 14.21—15.1
	Exodus 15.8-9, 10, 12, 17
	Matthew 12.46-50
Wed, July 25	2 Corinthians 4.7-15
Saint James,	Psalms 126.1-2, 2-3, 4-5, 6
apostle—Feast	Matthew 20.20-28
Thu, July 26	Sirach 44.1, 10-15
Saints Joachim and	Psalms 132.11, 13-14, 17-18
Ann, parents of	Matthew 13.16-17
Mary—Memorial	
Fri, July 27	Exodus 20.1-17
	Psalms 19.8, 9, 10, 11
	Matthew 13.18-23
Sat, July 28	Exodus 24.3-8
	Psalms 50.1-2, 5-6, 14-15
	Matthew 13.24-30

WEEK 17

Sun, July 29	Genesis 18.20-32
	Psalms 138.1-2, 2-3, 6-7, 7-8
	Colossians 2.12-14
	Luke 11.1-13
Mon, July 30	Exodus 32.15-24, 30-34
	Psalms 106.19-20, 21-22, 23
	Matthew 13.31-35
Tue, July 31	Exodus 33.7-11; 34.5-9, 28
	Psalms 103.6-7, 8-9, 10-11, 12-13
	Matthew 13.35-43
Wed, Aug 1	Exodus 34.29-35
	Psalms 99.5, 6, 7, 9
	Matthew 13.44-46
Thu, Aug 2	Exodus 40.16-21, 34-38
	Psalms 84.3, 4, 5-6, 8, 11
	Matthew 13.47-53
Fri, Aug 3	Leviticus 23.1, 4-11, 15-16, 27, 34-37
	Psalms 81.3-4, 5-6, 10-11
	Matthew 13.54-58
Sat, Aug 4	Leviticus 25.1, 8-17
	Psalms 67.2-3, 5, 7-8
	Matthew 14.1-12

WEEK 18

Sun, Aug 5	Ecclesiastes 1.2; 2.21-23
	Psalms 95.1-2, 6-7, 8-9
	Colossians 3.1-5, 9-11
	Luke 12.13-21
Mon, Aug 6	Daniel 7.9-10, 13-14
Transfiguration	Psalms 97.1-2, 5-6, 9
of the Lord—	2 Peter 1.16-19
Feast	Luke 9.28-36
Tue, Aug 7	Numbers 12.1-13
	Psalms 51.3-4, 5-6, 6-7, 12-13
	Matthew 14.22-36
Wed, Aug 8	Numbers 13.1-2, 25—14.1, 26-29, 34-35
	Psalms 106.6-7, 13-14, 21-22, 23
	Matthew 15.21-28
Thu, Aug 9	Numbers 20.1-13
	Psalms 95.1-2, 6-7, 8-9
	Matthew 16.13-23
Fri, Aug 10	2 Corinthians 9.6-10
Saint Lawrence,	Psalms 112.1-2, 5-6, 7-8, 9
deacon and	John 12.24-26
martyr—Feast	
Sat, Aug 11	Deuteronomy 6.4-13
	Psalms 18.2-3, 3-4, 47, 51
	Matthew 17.14-20

WEEK 19

Sun, Aug 12	Wisdom 18.6-9
	Psalms 33.1, 12, 18-19, 20-22
	Hebrews 11.1-2, 8-19
	or 11.1-2, 8-12
	Luke 12.32-48
Mon, Aug 13	Deuteronomy 10.12-22
	Psalms 147.12-13, 14-15, 19-20
	Matthew 17.22-27
Tue, Aug 14	Deuteronomy 31.1-8
	Deuteronomy 32.3-4, 7, 8, 9, 12
	Matthew 18.1-5, 10, 12-14
Wed, Aug 15	Revelation 11.19; 12.1-6, 10
Assumption of the	Psalms 45.10, 11, 12, 16
Virgin Mary into	1 Corinthians 15.20-26
Heaven—Solemnity	Luke 1.39-56
Thu, Aug 16	Joshua 3.7-10, 11, 13-17
	Psalms 114.1-2, 3-4, 5-6
	Matthew 18.21—19.1
Fri, Aug 17	Joshua 24.1-13
	Psalms 136.1-3, 16-18, 21-22, 24
	Matthew 19.3-12
Sat, Aug 18	Joshua 24.14-29
	Psalms 16.1-2, 5, 7-8, 11
	Matthew 19.13-15

WEEK 20

Sun, Aug 19
Jeremiah 38.4-6, 8-10
Psalms 40.2, 3, 4, 18
Hebrews 12.1-4Luke 12.49-53

Mon, Aug 20
Judges 2.11-19
Psalms 106.34-35, 36-37, 39-40, 43, 44
Matthew 19.16-22

Tue, Aug 21
Judges 6.11-24
Psalms 85.9, 11-12, 13-14
Matthew 19.23-30

Wed, Aug 22
Judges 9.6-15
Psalms 21.2-3, 4-5, 6-7
Matthew 20.1-16

Thu, Aug 23
Judges 11.29-39
Psalms 40.5, 7-8, 8-9, 10
Matthew 22.1-14

Fri, Aug 24
Saint Bartholomew, apostle—Feast
Revelation 21.9-14
Psalms 145.10-11, 12-13, 17-18
John 1.45-51

Sat, Aug 25
Ruth 2.1-3, 8-11; 4.13-17
Psalms 128.1-2, 3, 4, 5
Matthew 23.1-12

WEEK 21

Sun, Aug 26
Isaiah 66.18-21
Psalms 117.1, 2
Hebrews 12.5-7, 11-13
Luke 13.22-30

Mon, Aug 27
1 Thessalonians 1.2-5, 8-10
Psalms 149.1-2, 3-4, 5-6, 9
Matthew 23.13-22

Tue, Aug 28
1 Thessalonians 2.1-8
Psalms 139.1-3, 4-5
Matthew 23.23-26

Wed, Aug 29
Beheading of Saint John the Baptist, martyr—Memorial
Jeremiah 1.17-19
Psalms 71.1-2, 3-4, 5-6, 15, 17
Mark 6.17-29

Thu, Aug 30
1 Thessalonians 3.7-13
Psalms 90.3-4, 12-13, 14, 17
Matthew 24.42-51

Fri, Aug 31
1 Thessalonians 4.1-8
Psalms 97.1, 2, 5-6, 10, 11-12
Matthew 25.1-13

Sat, Sept 1
1 Thessalonians 4.9-12
Psalms 98.1, 7-8, 9
Matthew 25.14-30

WEEK 22

Sun, Sept 2
Sirach 3.17-18, 20, 28-29
Psalms 68.4-5, 6-7, 10-11
Hebrews 12.18-19, 22-24
Luke 14.1, 7-14

Mon, Sept 3
1 Thessalonians 4.13-18
Psalms 96.1, 3, 4-5, 11-12, 13
Luke 4.16-30

Tue, Sept 4
1 Thessalonians 5.1-6, 9-11
Psalms 27.1, 4, 13-14
Luke 4.31-37

Wed, Sept 5
Colossians 1.1-8
Psalms 52.10, 11
Luke 4.38-44

Thu, Sept 6
Colossians 1.9-14
Psalms 98.2-3, 3-4, 5-6
Luke 5.1-11

Fri, Sept 7
Colossians 1.15-20
Psalms 100.1, 2, 3, 4, 5
Luke 5.33-39

Sat, Sept 8
Birth of the Virgin Mary—Feast
Micah 5.1-4
Psalms 13.6, 6
Matthew 1.1-16, 18-23

WEEK 23

Sun, Sept 9
Wisdom 9.13-18
Psalms 90.3-4, 5-6, 12-13, 14-17
Philemon 1.9-10, 12-17
Luke 14.25-33

Mon, Sept 10
Colossians 1.24—2.3
Psalms 62.6-7, 9
Luke 6.6-11

Tue, Sept 11
Colossians 2.6-15
Psalms 145.1-2, 8-9, 10-11
Luke 6.12-19

Wed, Sept 12
Colossians 3.1-11
Psalms 145.2-3, 10-11, 12-13
Luke 6.20-26

Thu, Sept 13
Colossians 3.12-17
Psalms 150.1-2, 3-4, 5-6
Luke 6.27-38

Fri, Sept 14
Triumph of the Holy Cross— Feast
Numbers 21.4-9
Psalms 78.1-2, 34-35, 36-37, 38
Philippians 2.6-11
John 3.13-17

Sat, Sept 15
Our Lady of Sorrows— Memorial
Hebrews 5.7-9
Psalms 31.2-3, 3-4, 5-6, 15-16, 20
John 19.25-27

WEEK 24

Sun, Sept 16
Exodus 32.7-11, 13-14
Psalms 51.3-4, 12-13, 17, 19
1 Timothy 1.12-17
Luke 15.1-32

Mon, Sept 17
1 Timothy 2.1-8
Psalms 28.2, 7, 8-9
Luke 7.1-10

Tue, Sept 18
1 Timothy 3.1-13
Psalms 101.1-2, 2-3, 5, 6
Luke 7.11-17

Wed, Sept 19
1 Timothy 3.14-16
Psalms 111.1-2, 3-4, 5-6
Luke 7.31-35

Thu, Sept 20
1 Timothy 4.12-16
Psalms 111.7-8, 9, 10
Luke 7.36-50

Fri, Sept 21
Saint Matthew,
apostle and
evangelist—Feast
Ephesians 4.1-7, 11-13
Psalms 19.2-3, 4-5
Matthew 9.9-13

Sat, Sept 22
1 Timothy 6.13-16
Psalms 100.2, 3, 4, 5
Luke 8.4-15

WEEK 25

Sun, Sept 23
Amos 8.4-7
Psalms 113.1-2, 4-6, 7-8
1 Timothy 2.1-8
Luke 16.1-13

Mon, Sept 24
Ezra 1.1-6
Psalms 126.1-2, 2-3, 4-5, 6
Luke 8.16-18

Tue, Sept 25
Ezra 6.7-8, 12, 14-20
Psalms 122.1-2, 3-4, 4-5
Luke 8.19-21

Wed, Sept 26
Ezra 9.5-9
Tobit 13.2, 3-4, 6, 7-8
Luke 9.1-6

Thu, Sept 27
Haggai 1.1-8
Psalms 149.1-2, 3-4, 5-6, 9
Luke 9.7-9

Fri, Sept 28
Haggai 1.15—2.9
Psalms 43.1, 2, 3, 4
Luke 9.18-22

Sat, Sept 29
Michael, Gabriel, and
Raphael, archangels—
Feast
Daniel 7.9-10, 13-14
Psalms 138.1-2, 2-3, 4-5
John 1.47-51

WEEK 26

Sun, Sept 30
Amos 6.1, 4-7
Psalms 146.7, 8-9, 9-10
1 Timothy 6.11-16
Luke 16.19-31

Mon, Oct 1
Zechariah 8.1-8
Psalms 102.16-18, 19-23, 29
Luke 9.46-50

Tue, Oct 2
Guardian Angels—
Memorial
Exodus 23.20-23
Psalms 91.1-2, 3-4, 5-6, 10-11
Matthew 18.1-5, 10

Wed, Oct 3
Nehemiah 2.1-8
Psalms 137.1-2, 3, 4-5, 6
Luke 9.57-62

Thu, Oct 4
Nehemiah 8.1-4, 5-6, 7-12
Psalms 19.8, 9, 10, 11
Luke 10.1-12

Fri, Oct 5
Baruch 1.15-22
Psalms 79.1-2, 3-5, 8, 9
Luke 10.13-16

Sat, Oct 6
Baruch 4.5-12, 27-29
Psalms 69.33-35, 36-37
Luke 10.17-24

WEEK 27

Sun, Oct 7
Habakkuk 1.2-3; 2.2-4
Psalms 95.1-2, 6-7, 8-9
2 Timothy 1.6-8, 13-14
Luke 17.5-10

Mon, Oct 8
Jonah 1.1—2.1, 11
Psalms 2.2, 3, 4, 5, 8
Luke 10.25-37

Tue, Oct 9
Jonah 3.1-10
Psalms 130.1-2, 3-4, 7-8
Luke 10.38-42

Wed, Oct 10
Jonah 4.1-11
Psalms 86.3-4, 5-6, 9-10
Luke 11.1-4

Thu, Oct 11
Malachi 3.13-20
Psalms 1.1-2, 3, 4, 6
Luke 11.5-13

Fri, Oct 12
Joel 1.13-15; 2.1-2
Psalms 9.2-3, 6, 8-9, 16
Luke 11.15-26

Sat, Oct 13
Joel 4.12-21
Psalms 97.1-2, 5-6, 11-12
Luke 11.27-28

WEEK 28

Sun, Oct 14
2 Kings 5.14-17
Psalms 98.1, 2-3, 3-4
2 Timothy 2.8-13
Luke 17.11-19

Mon, Oct 15
Romans 1.1-7
Psalms 98.1, 2-3, 3-4
Luke 11.29-32

Tue, Oct 16
Romans 1.16-25
Psalms 19.2-3, 4-5
Luke 11.37-41

Wed, Oct 17
Romans 2.1-11
Psalms 62.2-3, 6-7, 9
Luke 11.42-46

Thu, Oct 18
2 Timothy 4.9-17
Saint Luke, evangelist—Psalms 145.10-11, 12-13, 17-18
Feast   Luke 10.1-9

Fri, Oct 19
Romans 4.1-8
Psalms 32.1-2, 5, 11
Luke 12.1-7

Sat, Oct 20
Romans 4.13, 16-18
Psalms 105.6-7, 8-9, 42-43
Luke 12.8-12

WEEK 29

Sun, Oct 21
Exodus 17.8-13
Psalms 121.1-2, 3-4, 5-6, 7-8
2 Timothy 3.14—4.2
Luke 18.1-8

Mon, Oct 22
Romans 4.20-25
Luke 1.69-70, 71-72, 73-75
Luke 12.13-21

Tue, Oct 23
Romans 5.12, 15, 17-19, 20-21
Psalms 40.7-8, 8-9, 10, 17
Luke 12.35-38

Wed, Oct 24
Romans 6.12-18
Psalms 124.1-3, 4-6, 7-8
Luke 12.39-48

Thu, Oct 25
Romans 6.19-23
Psalms 1.1-2, 3, 4, 6
Luke 12.49-53

Fri, Oct 26
Romans 7.18-25
Psalms 119.66, 68, 76, 77, 93, 94
Luke 12.54-59

Sat, Oct 27
Romans 8.1-11
Psalms 24.1-2, 3-4, 5-6
Luke 13.1-9

WEEK 30

Sun, Oct 28
Sirach 35.12-14, 16-18
Psalms 34.2-3, 17-18, 19, 23
2 Timothy 4.6-8, 16-18
Luke 18.9-14

Mon, Oct 29
Romans 8.12-17
Psalms 68.2, 4, 6-7, 20-21
Luke 13.10-17

Tue, Oct 30
Romans 8.18-25
Psalms 126.1-2, 2-3, 4-5, 6
Luke 13.18-21

Wed, Oct 31
Romans 8.26-30
Psalms 13.4-5, 6
Luke 13.22-30

Thu, Nov 1
All Saints   Revelation 7.2-4, 9-14
Solemnity   Psalms 24.1-2, 3-4, 5-6
1 John 3.1-3
Matthew 5.1-12

Fri, Nov 2
Commemoration of   Wisdom 3.1-9
All the Faithful   Psalms 27.1, 4, 7, 8, 9, 13-14
Departed (All Souls)—   Romans 6.3-9
Solemnity   Matthew 25.31-46

Sat, Nov 3
Romans 11.1-2, 11-12, 25-29
Psalms 94.12-13, 14-15, 17-18
Luke 14.1, 7-11

WEEK 31

Sun, Nov 4
Wisdom 11.22—12.1
Psalms 145.1-2, 8-9, 10-11, 13, 14
2 Thessalonians 1.11—2.2
Luke 19.1-10

Mon, Nov 5
Romans 11.29-36
Psalms 69.30-31, 33-34, 36-37
Luke 14.12-14

Tue, Nov 6
Romans 12.5-16
Psalms 131.1, 2, 3
Luke 14.15-24

Wed, Nov 7
Romans 13.8-10
Psalms 112.1-2, 4-5, 9
Luke 14.25-33

Thu, Nov 8
Romans 14.7-12
Psalms 27.1-4, 13-14
Luke 15.1-10

Fri, Nov 9
Dedication of the   Genesis 28.11-18
Basilica of St. John   Psalms 84.3, 4, 5-6, 8, 11
Lateran in Rome—   1 Corinthians 3.9-13, 16-17
Feast   Luke 19.1-10

Sat, Nov 10
Romans 16.3-9, 16, 22-27
Psalms 145.2-3, 4-5, 10-11
Luke 16.9-15

WEEK 32

Sun, Nov 11	2 Maccabees 7.1-2, 9-14 Psalms 17.1, 5-6, 8, 15 2 Thessalonians 2.16—3.5 Luke 20.27-38
Mon, Nov 12	Wisdom 1.1-7 Psalms 139.1-3, 4-6, 7-8, 9-10 Luke 17.1-6
Tue, Nov 13	Wisdom 2.23—3.9 Psalms 34.2-3, 16-17, 18-19 Luke 17.7-10
Wed, Nov 14	Wisdom 6.2-11 Psalms 82.3-4, 6-7 Luke 17.11-19
Thu, Nov 15	Wisdom 7.22—8.1 Psalms 119.89, 90, 91, 130, 135, 175 Luke 17.20-25
Fri, Nov 16	Wisdom 13.1-9 Psalms 19.2-3, 4-5 Luke 17.26-37
Sat, Nov 17	Wisdom 18.14-16; 19.6-9 Psalms 105.2-3, 36-37, 42-43 Luke 18.1-8

WEEK 33

Sun, Nov 18	Malachi 3.19-20 Psalms 98.5-6, 7-8, 9 2 Thessalonians 3.7-12 Luke 21.5-19
Mon, Nov 19	1 Maccabees 1.10-15, 41-43, 54-57, 62-63 Psalms 119.53, 61, 134, 150, 155, 158 Luke 18.35-43
Tue, Nov 20	2 Maccabees 6.18-31 Psalms 3.2-3, 4-5, 6-8 Luke 19.1-10
Wed, Nov 21	2 Maccabees 7.1, 20-31 Psalms 17.1, 5-6, 8, 15 Luke 19.11-28
Thu, Nov 22	1 Maccabees 2.15-29 Psalms 50.1-2, 5-6, 14-15 Luke 9.41-44
Fri, Nov 23	1 Maccabees 4.36-37, 52-59 1 Chronicles 29.10, 11, 11-12, 12 Luke 19.45-48
Sat, Nov 24	1 Maccabees 6.1-13 Psalms 9.2-3, 4, 6, 16, 19 Luke 20.27-40

WEEK 34

Sun, Nov 25 *Christ the King—* *Solemnity*	2 Samuel 5.1-3 Psalms 122.1-2, 3-4, 4-5 Colossians 1.12-20 Luke 23.35-43
Mon, Nov 26	Daniel 1.1-6, 8-20 Daniel 3.52, 53, 54, 55, 56 Luke 21.1-4
Tue, Nov 27	Daniel 2.31-45 Daniel 3.57, 58, 59, 60, 61 Luke 21.5-11
Wed, Nov 28	Daniel 5.1-6, 13-14, 16-17, 23-28 Daniel 3.62, 63, 64, 65, 66, 67 Luke 21.12-19
Thu, Nov 29	Daniel 6.12-28 Daniel 3.68, 69, 70, 71, 72, 73, 74 Luke 21.20-28
Fri, Nov 30 *Saint Andrew,* *apostle—Feast*	Romans 10.9-18 Psalms 19.2-3, 4-5 Matthew 4.18-22
Sat, Dec 1	Daniel 7.15-27 Daniel 3.82, 83, 84, 85, 86, 87 Luke 21.34-36

Advent, Liturgical year 2002

WEEK 1, ADVENT

Sun, Dec 2, 2001	Isaiah 2.1-5 Psalms 122.1-2, 3-4, 4-5, 6-7, 8-9 Romans 13.11-14 Matthew 24.37-44
Mon, Dec 3	Isaiah 4.2-6 Psalms 122.1-2, 3-4, 4-5, 6-7, 8-9 Matthew 8.5-11
Tue, Dec 4	Isaiah 11.1-10 Psalms 72.1, 7-8, 12-13, 17 Luke 10.21-24
Wed, Dec 5	Isaiah 25.6-10 Psalms 23.1-3, 3-4, 5, 6 Matthew 15.29-37
Thu, Dec 6	Isaiah 26.1-6 Psalms 118.1, 8-9, 19-21, 25-27 Matthew 7.21, 24-27
Fri, Dec 7	Isaiah 29.17-24 Psalms 27.1, 4, 13-14 Matthew 9.27-31
Sat, Dec 8 *Immaculate* *Conception of the* *Virgin Mary—* *Solemnity*	Genesis 3.9-15, 20 Psalms 98.1, 2-3, 3-4 Ephesians 1.3-6, 11-12 Luke 1.26-38

WEEK 2, ADVENT

Sun, Dec 9
Isaiah 11.1-10
Psalms 72.1-2, 7-8, 12-13, 17
Romans 15.4-9
Matthew 3.1-12

Mon, Dec 10
Isaiah 35.1-10
Psalms 85.9-10, 11-12, 13-14
Luke 5.17-26

Tue, Dec 11
Isaiah 40.1-11
Psalms 96.1-2, 3, 10, 11-12, 13
Matthew 18.12-14

Wed, Dec 12
Our Lady of
Guadalupe—
Feast
Zechariah 2.14-17
Psalms 45.11-12, 14-17
Romans 8.28-30
Luke 2.15-19

Thu, Dec 13
Isaiah 41.13-20
Psalms 145.1, 9, 10-11, 12-13
Matthew 11.11-15

Fri, Dec 14
Isaiah 48.17-19
Psalms 1.1-2, 3, 4, 6
Matthew 11.16-19

Sat, Dec 15
Sirach 48.1-4, 9-11
Psalms 80.2-3, 15-16, 18-19
Matthew 17.10-13

WEEK 3, ADVENT

Sun, Dec 16
Isaiah 35.1-6, 10
Psalms 146.6-7, 8-9, 9-10
James 5.7-10
Matthew 11.2-11

Mon, Dec 17
Genesis 49.2, 8-10
Psalms 72.3-4, 7-8, 17
Matthew 1.1-17

Tue, Dec 18
Jeremiah 23.5-8
Psalms 72.1, 12-13, 18-19
Matthew 1.18-24

Wed, Dec 19
Judges 13.2-7, 24-25
Psalms 71.3-4, 5-6, 16-17
Luke 1.5-25

Thu, Dec 20
Isaiah 7.10-14
Psalms 24.1-2, 3-4, 5-6
Luke 1.26-38

Fri, Dec 21
Song of Songs 2.8-14
Psalms 33.2-3, 11-12, 20-21
Luke 1.39-45

Sat, Dec 22
1 Samuel 1.24-28
1 Samuel 2.1, 4-5, 6-7, 8
Luke 1.46-56

WEEK 4, ADVENT

Sun, Dec 23
Isaiah 7.10-14
Psalms 24.1-2, 3-4, 5-6
Romans 1.1-7
Matthew 1.18-24

Mon, Dec 24
2 Samuel 7.1-5, 8-11, 16
Psalms 89.2-3, 4-5, 27, 29
Luke 1.67-79

Christmas

Tue, Dec 25
Christmas
Solemnity
Isaiah 62.11-12
Psalms 97.1, 6, 11-12
Titus 3.4-7
Luke 2.15-20

Wed, Dec 26
Saint Stephen,
first martyr—Feast
Acts 6.8-10; 7.54-59
Psalms 31.3-4, 6, 7, 8, 17, 21
Matthew 10.17-22

Thu, Dec 27
Saint John, apostle
and evangelist—Feast
1 John 1.1-4
Psalms 97.1-2, 5-6, 11-12
John 20.2-8

Fri, Dec 28
The Holy Innocents,
martyrs—Feast
1 John 1.5—2.2
Psalms 124.2-3, 4-5, 7-8
Matthew 2.13-18

Sat, Dec 29
1 John 2.3-11
Psalms 96.1-2, 2-3, 5-6
Luke 2.22-35

Sun, Dec 30
The Holy Family—
Feast
Sirach 3.2-6, 12-14
Psalms 128.1-2, 3, 4-5
Colossians 3.12-21
Matthew 2.13-15, 19-23

Mon, Dec 31
1 John 2.18-21
Psalms 96.1-2, 11-12, 13
John 1.1-18

Tue, Jan 1, 2002
Mary, Mother of God—
Solemnity
Numbers 6.22-27
Psalms 67.2-3, 5, 6, 8
Galatians 4.4-7
Luke 2.16-21

Wed, Jan 2
1 John 2.22-28
Psalms 98.1, 2-3, 3-4
John 1.19-28

Thu, Jan 3
1 John 2.29—3.6
Psalms 98.1, 3-4, 5-6
John 1.29-34

Fri, Jan 4
1 John 3.7-10
Psalms 98.1, 7-8, 9
John 1.35-42

Sat, Jan 5
1 John 3.11-21
Psalms 100.1-2, 3, 4, 5
John 1.43-51

Sun, Jan 6
Epiphany of the Lord—
Solemnity
Isaiah 60.1-6
Psalms 72.1-2, 7-8, 10-11, 12-13
Ephesians 3.2-3, 5-6
Matthew 2.1-12

Mon, Jan 7
1 John 3.22—4.6
Psalms 2.7-8, 10-11
Matthew 4.12-17, 23-25

Tue, Jan 8
1 John 4.7-10
Psalms 72.1-2, 3-4, 7-8
Mark 6.34-44

Wed, Jan 9
1 John 4.11-18
Psalms 72.1-2, 10, 12-13
Mark 6.45-52

Thu, Jan 10
1 John 4.19—5.4
Psalms 72.1-2, 14-15, 17
Luke 4.14-22

Fri, Jan 11
1 John 5.5-13
Psalms 147.12-13, 14-15, 19-20
Luke 5.12-16

Sat, Jan 12
1 John 5.14-21
Psalms 149.1-2, 3-4, 5-6, 9
John 3.22-30

Ordinary Time

WEEK 1

Sun, Jan 13
Baptism of the Lord—
Feast
Isaiah 42.1-4, 6-7
Psalms 29.1-2, 3-4, 3, 9-10
Acts 10.34-38
Matthew 3.13-17

Mon, Jan 14
1 Samuel 1.1-8
Psalms 116.12-13, 14-17, 18-19
Mark 1.14-20

Tue, Jan 15
1 Samuel 1.9-20
1 Samuel 2.1, 4-5, 6-7, 8
Mark 1.21-28

Wed, Jan 16
1 Samuel 3.1-10, 19-20
Psalms 40.2-5, 7-8, 8-9, 10
Mark 1.29-39

Thu, Jan 17
1 Samuel 4.1-11
Psalms 44.10-11, 14-15, 25-26
Mark 1.40-45

Fri, Jan 18
1 Samuel 8.4-7, 10-22
Psalms 89.16-17, 18-19
Mark 2.1-12

Sat, Jan 19
1 Samuel 9.1-4, 17-19; 10.1
Psalms 21.2-3, 4-5, 6-7
Mark 2.13-17

WEEK 2

Sun, Jan 20
Isaiah 49.3, 5-6
Psalms 40.2, 4, 7-8, 8-9, 10
1 Corinthians 1.1-3
John 1.29-34

Mon, Jan 21
1 Samuel 15.16-23
Psalms 50.8-9, 16-17, 21, 23
Mark 2.18-22

Tue, Jan 22
1 Samuel 16.1-13
Psalms 89.20, 21-22, 27-28
Mark 2.23-28

Wed, Jan 23
1 Samuel 17.32-33, 37, 40-51
Psalms 144.1, 2, 9-10
Mark 3.1-6

Thu, Jan 24
1 Samuel 18.6-9; 19.1-7
Psalms 56.2-3, 9-10, 10-12, 13-14
Mark 3.7-12

Fri, Jan 25
Acts 9.1-22
Psalms 117.1, 2
Mark 16.15-18

Sat, Jan 26
2 Samuel 1.1-4, 11-12, 19, 23-27
Psalms 80.2-3, 5-7
Mark 3.20-21

WEEK 3

Sun, Jan 27
Isaiah 8.23—9.3
Psalms 27.1, 4, 13-14
1 Corinthians 1.10-13, 17
Matthew 4.12-23
or 4.12-17

Mon, Jan 28
2 Samuel 5.1-7, 10
Psalms 89.20, 21-22, 25-26
Mark 3.22-30

Tue, Jan 29
2 Samuel 6.12-15, 17-19
Psalms 24.7, 8, 9, 10
Mark 3.31-35

Wed, Jan 30
2 Samuel 7.4-17
Psalms 89.4-5, 27-28, 29-30
Mark 4.1-20

Thu, Jan 31
2 Samuel 7.18-19, 24-29
Psalms 132.1-2, 3-5, 11, 12, 13-14
Mark 4.21-25

Fri, Feb 1
2 Samuel 11.1-4, 5-10, 13-17
Psalms 51.3-4, 5-6, 6-7, 10-11
Mark 4.26-34

Sat, Feb 2
Presentation
of the Lord—
Feast
Malachi 3.1-4
Psalms 24.7, 8, 9, 10
Hebrews 2.14-18
Luke 2.22-40

WEEK 4

Sun, Feb 3
Zephaniah 2.3; 3.12-13
Psalms 146.6-7, 8-9, 9-10
I Corinthians 1.26-31
Matthew 5.1-12

Mon, Feb 4
2 Samuel 15.13-14, 30; 16.5-13
Psalms 3.2-3, 4-5, 6-7
Mark 5.1-20

Tue, Feb 5
2 Samuel 18.9-10, 14, 24-25,
30—19.3
Psalms 86.1-2, 3-4, 5-6
Mark 5.21-43

Wed, Feb 6
2 Samuel 24.2, 9-17
Psalms 32.1-2, 5, 6, 7
Mark 6.1-6

Thu, Feb 7
I Kings 2.1-4, 10-12
I Chronicles 29.10, 11, 11-12, 12
Mark 6.7-13

Fri, Feb 8
Sirach 47.2-11
Psalms 18.31, 47, 50, 51
Mark 6.14-29

Sat, Feb 9
I Kings 3.4-13
Psalms 119.9, 10, 11, 12, 13, 14
Mark 6.30-34

WEEK 5

Sun, Feb 10
Isaiah 58.7-10
Psalms 112.4-5, 6-7, 8-9
I Corinthians 2.1-5
Matthew 5.13-16

Mon, Feb 11
I Kings 8.1-7, 9-13
Psalms 132.6-7, 8-10
Mark 6.53-56

Tue, Feb 12
I Kings 8.22-23, 27-30
Psalms 84.3, 4, 5, 10, 11
Mark 7.1-13

Lent

Wed, Feb 13
Ash Wednesday
Joel 2.12-18
Psalms 51.3-4, 5-6, 12-13, 14, 17
2 Corinthians 5.20—6.2
Matthew 6.1-6, 16-18

Thu, Feb 14
Deuteronomy 30.15-20
Psalms 1.1-2, 3, 4, 6
Luke 9.22-25

Fri, Feb 15
Isaiah 58.1-9
Psalms 51.3-4, 5-6, 18-19
Matthew 9.14-15

Sat, Feb 16
Isaiah 58.9-14
Psalms 86.1-2, 3-4, 5-6
Luke 5.27-32

WEEK 1, LENT

Sun, Feb 17
Genesis 2.7-9; 3.1-7
Psalms 51.3-4, 5-6, 12-13, 14, 17
Romans 5.12-19
or 5.12, 17-19
Matthew 4.1-11

Mon, Feb 18
Leviticus 19.1-2, 11-18
Psalms 19.8, 9, 10, 15
Matthew 25.31-46

Tue, Feb 19
Isaiah 55.10-11
Psalms 34.4-5, 6-7, 16-17, 18-19
Matthew 6.7-15

Wed, Feb 20
Jonah 3.1-10
Psalms 51.3-4, 12-13, 18-19
Luke 11.29-32

Thu, Feb 21
Esther C.12, 14-16, 23-25
Psalms 138.1-2, 2-3, 7-8
Matthew 7.7-12

Fri, Feb 22
Chair of Saint Peter,
apostle—Feast
I Peter 5.1-4
Psalms 23.1-3, 3-4, 5, 6
Matthew 16.13-19

Sat, Feb 23
Deuteronomy 26.16-19
Psalms 119.1-2, 4-5, 7-8
Matthew 5.43-48

WEEK 2, LENT

Sun, Feb 24
Genesis 12.1-4
Psalms 33.4-5, 18-19, 20, 22
2 Timothy 1.8-10
Matthew 17.1-9

Mon, Feb 25
Daniel 9.4-10
Psalms 79.8, 9, 11, 13
Luke 6.36-38

Tue, Feb 26
Isaiah 1.10, 16-20
Psalms 50.8-9, 16-17, 21, 23
Matthew 23.1-12

Wed, Feb 27
Jeremiah 18.18-20
Psalms 31.5-6, 14, 15-16
Matthew 20.17-28

Thu, Feb 28
Jeremiah 17.5-10
Psalms 1.1-2, 3, 4, 6
Luke 16.19-31

Fri, Mar 1
Genesis 37.3-4, 12-13, 17-18
Psalms 105.16-17, 18-19, 20-21
Matthew 21.33-43, 45-46

Sat, Mar 2
Micah 7.14-15, 18-20
Psalms 103.1-2, 3-4, 9-10, 11-12
Luke 15.1-3, 11-32

WEEK 3, LENT

Sun, Mar 3
Exodus 17.3-7
Psalms 95.1-2, 6-7, 8-9
Romans 5.1-2, 5-8
John 4.5-42

Mon, Mar 4
2 Kings 5.1-15
Psalms 42.2, 3; 43.3, 4
Luke 4.24-30

Tue, Mar 5
Daniel 3.25, 34-43
Psalms 25.4-5, 6-7, 8-9
Matthew 18.21-35

Wed, Mar 6
Deuteronomy 4.1, 5-9
Psalms 147.12-13, 15-16, 19-20
Matthew 5.17-19

Thu, Mar 7
Jeremiah 7.23-28
Psalms 95.1-2, 6-7, 8-9
Luke 11.14-23

Fri, Mar 8
Hosea 14.2-10
Psalms 81.6-8, 8-9, 10-11, 14, 17
Mark 12.28-34

Sat, Mar 9
Hosea 6.1-6
Psalms 51.3-4, 18-19, 20-21
Luke 18.9-14

WEEK 4, LENT

Sun, Mar 10
1 Samuel 16.1, 6-7, 10-13
Psalms 23.1-3, 3-4, 5, 6
Ephesians 5.8-14
John 9.1-41

Mon, Mar 11
Isaiah 65.17-21
Psalms 30.2, 4, 5-6, 11-13
John 4.43-54

Tue, Mar 12
Ezekiel 47.1-9, 12
Psalms 46.2-3, 5-6, 8-9
John 5.1-3, 5-16

Wed, Mar 13
Isaiah 49.8-15
Psalms 145.8-9, 13-14, 17-18
John 5.17-30

Thu, Mar 14
Exodus 32.7-14
Psalms 106.19-20, 21-22, 23
John 5.31-47

Fri, Mar 15
Wisdom 2.1, 12-22
Psalms 34.17-18, 19-20, 21, 23
John 7.1-2, 10, 25-30

Sat, Mar 16
Jeremiah 11.18-20
Psalms 7.2-3, 9-10, 11-12
John 7.40-53

WEEK 5, LENT

Sun, Mar 17
Ezekiel 37.12-14
Psalms 130.1-2, 3-4, 5-6, 7-8
Romans 8.8-11
John 11.1-45

Mon, Mar 18
Daniel 13.1-9, 15-17, 19-30, 33-62
Psalms 23.1-3, 3-4, 5, 6
John 8.1-11

Tue, Mar 19
Saint Joseph,
Husband of Mary—
Solemnity
2 Samuel 7.4-5, 12-14, 16
Psalms 89.2-3, 4-5, 27, 29
Romans 4.13, 16-18, 22
Luke 2.41-51

Wed, Mar 20
Daniel 3.14-20, 91-92, 95
Daniel 3.52, 53, 54, 55, 56
John 8.31-42

Thu, Mar 21
Genesis 17.3-9
Psalms 105.4-5, 6-7, 8-9
John 8.51-59

Fri, Mar 22
Jeremiah 20.10-13
Psalms 18.2-3, 3-4, 5-6, 7
John 10.31-42

Sat, Mar 23
Ezekiel 37.21-28
Jeremiah 31.10, 11-12, 13
John 11.45-57

HOLY WEEK

Sun, Mar 24
Passion
(Palm)
Sunday
Isaiah 50.4-7
Psalms 22.8-9, 17-18, 19-20, 23-24
Philippians 2.6-11
Matthew 26.14—27.66

Mon, Mar 25
Isaiah 42.1-7
Psalms 27.1, 2, 3, 13-14
John 12.1-11

Tue, Mar 26
Isaiah 49.1-6
Psalms 71.1-2, 3-4, 5-6, 15, 17
John 13.21-33, 36-38

Wed, Mar 27
Isaiah 50.4-9
Psalms 69.8-10, 21-22, 31, 33-34
Matthew 26.14-25

Thu, Mar 28
Holy Thursday
Exodus 12.1-8, 11-14
Psalms 116.12-13, 15-16, 17-18
1 Corinthians 11.23-26
John 13.1-15

Fri, Mar 29
Good Friday
Isaiah 52.13—53.12
Psalms 31.2, 6, 12-13, 15-16, 17, 25
Hebrews 4.14-16; 5.7-9
John 18.1—19.42

Sat, Mar 30
Holy Saturday
Genesis 1.1—2.2
Psalms 104.1-2, 5-6, 10, 12, 13-14, 24, 35
Genesis 22.1-18
Psalms 16.5, 8, 9-10, 11

Sat, Mar 30
Holy Saturday

Exodus 14.15—15.1
Exodus 15.1-2, 3-4, 5-6, 17-18
Isaiah 54.5-14
Psalms 30.2, 4, 5-6, 11-12, 13
Isaiah 55.1-11
Isaiah 12.2-3, 4, 5-6
Baruch 3.9-15, 32—4.4
Psalms 19.8, 9, 10, 11
Ezekiel 36.16-28
Psalms 42.3, 5; 43.3, 4
Romans 6.3-11
Psalms 118.1-2, 16, 17, 22-23
Matthew 28.1-10

Easter
WEEK 1, EASTER

Sun, Mar 31
Easter Sunday

Acts 10.34, 37-43
Psalms 118.1-2, 16-17, 22-23
I Corinthians 5.6-8
John 20.1-9

Mon, Apr 1

Acts 2.14, 22-32
Psalms 16.1-2, 5, 7-8, 9-10, 11
Matthew 28.8-15

Tue, Apr 2

Acts 2.36-41
Psalms 33.4-5, 18-19, 20, 22
John 20.11-18

Wed, Apr 3

Acts 3.1-10
Psalms 105.1-2, 3-4, 6-7, 8-9
Luke 24.13-35

Thu, Apr 4

Acts 3.11-26
Psalms 8.2, 5, 6-7, 8-9
Luke 24.35-48

Fri, Apr 5

Acts 4.1-12
Psalms 118.1-2, 4, 22-24, 25-27
John 21.1-14

Sat, Apr 6

Acts 4.13-21
Psalms 118.1, 14-15, 16-18, 19-21
Mark 16.9-15

WEEK 2, EASTER

Sun, Apr 7

Acts 2.42-47
Psalms 118.2-4, 13-15, 22-24
I Peter 1.3-9
John 20.19-31

Mon, Apr 8
*Annunciation
of the Lord—
Solemnity*

Isaiah 7.10-14
Psalms 40.7-8, 8-9, 10, 11
Hebrews 10.4-10
Luke 1.26-38

Tue, Apr 9

Acts 4.32-37
Psalms 93.1, 1-2, 5
John 3.7-15

Wed, Apr 10

Acts 5.17-26
Psalms 34.2-3, 4-5, 6-7, 8-9
John 3.16-21

Thu, Apr 11

Acts 5.27-33
Psalms 34.2, 9, 17-18, 19-20
John 3.31-36

Fri, Apr 12

Acts 5.34-42
Psalms 27.1, 4, 13-14
John 6.1-15

Sat, Apr 13

Acts 6.1-7
Psalms 33.1-2, 4-5, 18-19
John 6.16-21

WEEK 3, EASTER

Sun, Apr 14

Acts 2.14, 22-28
Psalms 16.1-2, 5, 7-8, 9-10, 11
I Peter 1.17-21
Luke 24.13-35

Mon, Apr 15

Acts 6.8-15
Psalms 119.23-24, 26-27, 29-30
John 6.22-29

Tue, Apr 16

Acts 7.51—8.1
Psalms 31.3-4, 6, 7, 8, 17, 21
John 6.30-35

Wed, Apr 17

Acts 8.1-8
Psalms 66.1-3, 4-5, 6-7
John 6.35-40

Thu, Apr 18

Acts 8.26-40
Psalms 66.8-9, 16-17, 20
John 6.44-51

Fri, Apr 19

Acts 9.1-20
Psalms 117.1, 2
John 6.52-59

Sat, Apr 20

Acts 9.31-42
Psalms 116.12-13, 14-15, 16-17
John 6.60-69

WEEK 4, EASTER

Sun, Apr 21
Acts 2.14, 36-41
Psalms 23.1-3, 3-4, 5, 6
I Peter 2.20-25
John 10.1-10

Mon, Apr 22
Acts 11.1-18
Psalms 42.2-3; 43.3, 4
John 10.11-18

Tue, Apr 23
Acts 11.19-26
Psalms 87.1-3, 4-5, 6-7
John 10.22-30

Wed, Apr 24
Acts 12.24—13.5
Psalms 67.2-3, 5, 6, 8
John 12.44-50

Thu, Apr 25
Saint Mark,
evangelist—Feast
I Peter 5.5-14
Psalms 89.2-3, 6-7, 16-17
Mark 16.15-20

Fri, Apr 26
Acts 13.26-33
Psalms 2.6-7, 8-9, 10-11
John 14.1-6

Sat, Apr 27
Acts 13.44-52
Psalms 98.1, 2-3, 3-4
John 14.7-14

WEEK 5, EASTER

Sun, Apr 28
Acts 6.1-7
Psalms 33.1-2, 4-5, 18-19
I Peter 2.4-9
John 14.1-12

Mon, Apr 29
Acts 14.5-18
Psalms 115.1-2, 3-4, 15-16
John 14.21-26

Tue, Apr 30
Acts 14.19-28
Psalms 145.10-11, 12-13, 21
John 14.27-31

Wed, May 1
Acts 15.1-6
Psalms 122.1-2, 3-4, 4-5
John 15.1-8

Thu, May 2
Acts 15.7-21
Psalms 96.1-2, 2-3, 10
John 15.9-11

Fri, May 3
Saints Philip and
James, Apostles—Feast
I Corinthians 15.1-8
Psalms 19.2-3, 4-5
John 14.6-14

Sat, May 4
Acts 16.1-10
Psalms 100.1-2, 3, 5
John 15.18-21

WEEK 6, EASTER

Sun, May 5
Acts 8.5-8, 14-17
Psalms 66.1-3, 4-5, 6-7, 16, 20
I Peter 3.15-18
John 14.15-21

Mon, May 6
Acts 16.11-15
Psalms 149.1-2, 3-4, 5-6, 9
John 15.26—16.4

Tue, May 7
Acts 16.22-34
Psalms 138.1-2, 2-3, 7-8
John 16.5-11

Wed, May 8
Acts 17.15, 22—18.1
Psalms 148.1-2, 11-12, 13, 14
John 16.12-15

Thu, May 9
Ascension of the Lord
Acts 1.1-11
Psalms 47.2-3, 6-7, 8-9
Ephesians 1.17-23
Matthew 28.16-20

Fri, May 10
Acts 18.9-18
Psalms 47.2-3, 4-5, 6-7
John 16.20-23

Sat, May 11
Acts 18.23-28
Psalms 47.2-3, 8-9, 10
John 16.23-28

WEEK 7, EASTER

Sun, May 12
Acts 1.12-14
Psalms 27.1, 4, 7-8
I Peter 4.13-16
John 17.1-11

Mon, May 13
Acts 19.1-8
Psalms 68.2-3, 4-5, 6-7
John 16.29-33

Tue, May 14
Saint Matthias,
apostle—Feast
Acts 1.15-17, 20-26
Psalms 113.1-2, 3-4, 5-6, 7-8
John 15.9-17

Wed, May 15
Acts 20.28-38
Psalms 68.29-30, 33-35, 35-36
John 17.11-19

Thu, May 16
Acts 22.30; 23.6-11
Psalms 16.1-2, 5, 7-8, 9-10, 11
John 17.20-26

Fri, May 17
Acts 25.13-21
Psalms 103.1-2, 11-12, 19-20
John 21.15-19

Sat, May 18
Acts 28.16-20, 30-31
Psalms 11.4, 5, 7
John 21.20-25

Sun, May 19
Pentecost
Acts 2.1-11
Psalms 104.1, 24, 29-30, 31, 34
I Corinthians 12.3-7, 12-13
John 20.19-23

Ordinary Time

WEEK 7

Mon, May 20
James 3.13-18
Psalms 19.8, 9, 10, 15
Mark 9.14-29

Tue, May 21
James 4.1-10
Psalms 55.7-8, 9-10, 10-11, 23
Mark 9.30-37

Wed, May 22
James 4.13-17
Psalms 49.2-3, 6-7, 8-10, 11
Mark 9.38-40

Thu, May 23
James 5.1-6
Psalms 49.14-15, 15-16, 17-18, 19-20
Mark 9.41-50

Fri, May 24
James 5.9-12
Psalms 103.1-2, 3-4, 8-9, 11-12
Mark 10.1-12

Sat, May 25
James 5.13-20
Psalms 141.1-2, 3, 8
Mark 10.13-16

WEEK 8

Sun, May 26
The Holy Trinity—
Solemnity
Exodus 34.4-6, 8-9
Daniel 3.52, 53, 54, 55, 56
2 Corinthians 13.11-13
John 3.16-18

Mon, May 27
1 Peter 1.3-9
Psalms 111.1-2, 5-6, 9, 10
Mark 10.17-27

Tue, May 28
1 Peter 1.10-16
Psalms 98.1, 2-3, 3-4
Mark 10.28-31

Wed, May 29
1 Peter 1.18-25
Psalms 147.12-13, 14-15, 19-20
Mark 10.32-45

Thu, May 30
1 Peter 2.2-5, 9-12
Psalms 100.2, 3, 4, 5
Mark 10.46-52

Fri, May 31
Visitation of the
Virgin Mary to
Elizabeth—Feast
Romans 12.9-16
Isaiah 12.2-3, 4, 5-6
Luke 1.39-56

Sat, June 1
Jude 1.17, 20-25
Psalms 63.2, 3-4, 5-6
Mark 11.27-33

WEEK 9

Sun, June 2
The Body and Blood
of Christ (Corpus
Christi)—Solemnity
Deuteronomy 8.2-3, 14-16
Psalms 147.12-13, 14-15, 19-20
1 Corinthians 10.16-17
John 6.51-58

Mon, June 3
2 Peter 1.2-7
Psalms 91.1-2, 14-15, 15-16
Mark 12.1-12

Tue, June 4
2 Peter 3.12-15, 17-18
Psalms 90.2, 3-4, 10, 14, 16
Mark 12.13-17

Wed, June 5
2 Timothy 1.1-3, 6-12
Psalms 123.1-2, 2
Mark 12.18-27

Thu, June 6
2 Timothy 2.8-15
Psalms 25.4-5, 8-9, 10, 14
Mark 12.28-34

Fri, June 7
Sacred Heart of Jesus—
Solemnity
Deuteronomy 7.6-11
Psalms 103.1-2, 3-4, 6-7, 8, 10
1 John 4.7-16
Matthew 11.25-30

Sat, June 8
2 Timothy 4.1-8
Psalms 71.8-9, 14-15, 16-17, 22
Mark 12.38-44

WEEK 10

Sun, June 9
Hosea 6.3-6
Psalms 50.1, 8, 12-13, 14-15
Romans 4.18-25
Matthew 9.9-13

Mon, June 10
1 Kings 17.1-7
Psalms 121.1-2, 3-4, 5-6, 7-8
Matthew 5.1-12

Tue, June 11
Saint Barnabas,
apostle—Memorial
Acts 11.21-26; 13.1-3
Psalms 98.1, 2-3, 3-4, 5-6
Matthew 10.7-13

Wed, June 12
1 Kings 18.20-39
Psalms 16.1-2, 4, 5, 8, 11
Matthew 5.17-19

Thu, June 13
1 Kings 18.41-46
Psalms 65.10, 10-11, 12-13
Matthew 5.20-26

Fri, June 14
1 Kings 19.9, 11-16
Psalms 27.7-8, 8-9, 13-14
Matthew 5.27-32

Sat, June 15
1 Kings 19.19-21
Psalms 16.1-2, 5, 7-8, 9-10
Matthew 5.33-37

WEEK 11

Sun, June 16
Exodus 19.2-6
Psalms 100.1-2, 3, 5
Romans 5.6-11
Matthew 9.36—10.8

Mon, June 17
1 Kings 21.1-16
Psalms 5.2-3, 5-6, 7
Matthew 5.38-42

Tue, June 18
1 Kings 21.17-29
Psalms 51.3-4, 5-6, 11, 16
Matthew 5.43-48

Wed, June 19
2 Kings 2.1, 6-14
Psalms 31.20, 21, 24
Matthew 6.1-6, 16-18

Thu, June 20
Sirach 48.1-14
Psalms 97.1-2, 3-4, 5-6, 7
Matthew 6.7-15

Fri, June 21
2 Kings 11.1-4, 9-18, 20
Psalms 132.11, 12, 13-14, 17-18
Matthew 6.19-23

Sat, June 22
2 Chronicles 24.17-25
Psalms 89.4-5, 29-30, 31-32, 33-34
Matthew 6.24-34

WEEK 12

Sun, June 23
Jeremiah 20.10-13
Psalms 69.8-10, 14, 17, 33-35
Romans 5.12-15
Matthew 10.26-33

Mon, June 24
Birth of Saint John the Baptist— Solemnity
Isaiah 49.1-6
Psalms 139.1-3, 13-14, 14-15
Acts 13.22-26
Luke 1.57-66, 80

Tue, June 25
2 Kings 19.9-11, 14-21, 31-35, 36
Psalms 48.2-3, 3-4, 10-11
Matthew 7.6, 12-14

Wed, June 26
2 Kings 22.8-13; 23.1-3
Psalms 119.33, 34, 35, 36, 37, 40
Matthew 7.15-20

Thu, June 27
2 Kings 24.8-17
Psalms 79.1-2, 3-5, 8, 9
Matthew 7.21-29

Fri, June 28
2 Kings 25.1-12
Psalms 137.1-2, 3, 4-5, 6
Matthew 8.1-4

Sat, June 29
Saints Peter and Paul, apostles— Solemnity
Acts 12.1-11
Psalms 34.2-3, 4-5, 6-7, 8-9
2 Timothy 4.6-8, 17-18
Matthew 16.13-19

WEEK 13

Sun, June 30
2 Kings 4.8-11, 14-16
Psalms 89.2-3, 16-17, 18-19
Romans 6.3-4, 8-11
Matthew 10.37-42

Mon, July 1
Amos 2.6-10, 13-16
Psalms 50.16-17, 18-19, 20-21, 22-23
Matthew 8.18-22

Tue, July 2
Amos 3.1-8; 4.11-12
Psalms 5.4-6, 6-7, 8
Matthew 8.23-27

Wed, July 3
Saint Thomas. apostle—Feast
Ephesians 2.19-22
Psalms 117.1, 2
John 20.24-29

Thu, July 4
Amos 7.10-17
Psalms 19.8, 9, 10, 11
Matthew 9.1-8

Fri, July 5
Amos 8.4-6, 9-12
Psalms 119.2, 10, 20, 30, 40, 131
Matthew 9.9-13

Sat, July 6
Amos 9.11-15
Psalms 85.9, 11-12, 13-14
Matthew 9.14-17

WEEK 14

Sun, July 7
Zechariah 9.9-10
Psalms 145.1-2, 8-9, 10-11, 13-14
Romans 8.9, 11-13
Matthew 11.25-30

Mon, July 8
Hosea 2.16, 17-18, 21-22
Psalms 145.2-3, 4-5, 6-7, 8-9
Matthew 9.18-26

Tue, July 9
Hosea 8.4-7, 11-13
Psalms 115.3-4, 5-6, 7-8, 9-10
Matthew 9.32-38

Wed, July 10
Hosea 10.1-3, 7-8, 12
Psalms 105.2-3, 4-5, 6-7
Matthew 10.1-7

Thu, July 11
Hosea 11.1, 3-4, 8-9
Psalms 80.2, 3, 15-16
Matthew 10.7-15

Fri, July 12
Hosea 14.2-10
Psalms 51.3-4, 8-9, 12-13, 14, 17
Matthew 10.16-23

Sat, July 13
Isaiah 6.1-8
Psalms 93.1, 1-2, 5
Matthew 10.24-33

WEEK 15

Sun, July 14
Isaiah 55.10-11
Psalms 65.10, 11, 12-13, 14
Romans 8.18-23
Matthew 13.1-23

Mon, July 15
Isaiah 1.10-17
Psalms 50.8-9, 16-17, 21, 23
Matthew 10.34—11.1

Tue, July 16
Isaiah 7.1-9
Psalms 48.2-3, 3-4, 5-6, 7-8
Matthew 11.20-24

Wed, July 17
Isaiah 10.5-7, 13-16
Psalms 94.5-6, 7-8, 9-10, 14-15
Matthew 11.25-27

Thu, July 18
Isaiah 26.7-9, 12, 16-19
Psalms 102.13-14, 15, 16-18, 19-21
Matthew 11.28-30

Fri, July 19
Isaiah 38.1-6, 21-22, 7-8
Isaiah 38.10, 11, 12, 16
Matthew 12.1-8

Sat, July 20
Micah 2.1-5
Psalms 10.1-2, 3-4, 7-8, 14
Matthew 12.14-21

WEEK 16

Sun, July 21
Wisdom 12.13, 16-19
Psalms 86.5-6, 9-10, 15-16
Romans 8.26-27
Matthew 13.24-43

Mon, July 22
Saint Mary
Magdalene—
Memorial
2 Corinthians 5.14-17
Psalms 63.2, 3-4, 5-6, 8-9
John 20.1-2, 11-18

Tue, July 23
Micah 7.14-15, 18-20
Psalms 85.2-4, 5-6, 7-8
Matthew 12.46-50

Wed, July 24
Jeremiah 1.1, 4-10
Psalms 71.1-2, 3-4, 5-6, 15, 17
Matthew 13.1-9

Thu, July 25
Saint James, apostle—
Feast
2 Corinthians 4.7-15
Psalms 126.1-2, 2-3, 4-5, 6
Matthew 20.20-28

Fri, July 26
Saints Joachim and
Ann, parents of
Mary—Memorial
Sirach 44.1, 10-15
Psalms 132.11, 13-14, 17-18
Matthew 13.16-17

Sat, July 27
Jeremiah 7.1-11
Psalms 84.3, 4, 5-6, 8, 11
Matthew 13.24-30

WEEK 17

Sun, July 28
1 Kings 3.5, 7-12
Psalms 119.57, 72, 76-77,
   127-128, 129-130
Romans 8.28-30
Matthew 13.44-52

Mon, July 29
Saint Martha—
Memorial
Proverbs 31.10-13, 19-20, 30-31
Psalms 112.1-2, 3-4, 5-6, 7-8,
Luke 10.38-42

Tue, July 30
Jeremiah 14.17-22
Psalms 79.8, 9, 11, 13
Matthew 13.35-43

Wed, July 31
Jeremiah 15.10, 16-21
Psalms 59.2-3, 4, 10-11, 17, 18
Matthew 13.44-46

Thu, Aug 1
Jeremiah 18.1-6
Psalms 146.1-2, 2-4, 5-6
Matthew 13.47-53

Fri, Aug 2
Jeremiah 26.1-9
Psalms 69.6, 8-10, 14
Matthew 13.54-58

Sat, Aug 3
Jeremiah 26.11-16, 24
Psalms 69.15-16, 30-31, 33-34
Matthew 14.1-12

WEEK 18

Sun, Aug 4
Isaiah 55.1-3
Psalms 145.8-9, 15-16, 17-18
Romans 8.35, 37-39
Matthew 14.13-21

Mon, Aug 5
Jeremiah 28.1-17
Psalms 119.29, 43, 79, 80, 95, 102
Matthew 14.13-21

Tue, Aug 6
Transfiguration
of the Lord—
Feast
Daniel 7.9-10, 13-14
Psalms 97.1-2, 5-6, 9
2 Peter 1.16-19
Matthew 17.1-9

Wed, Aug 7
Jeremiah 31.1-7
Jeremiah 31.10, 11-12, 13
Matthew 15.21-28

Thu, Aug 8
Jeremiah 31.31-34
Psalms 51.12-13, 14-15, 18-19
Matthew 16.13-23

Fri, Aug 9
Nahum 2.1, 3; 3.1-3, 6-7
Deuteronomy 32.35-36, 39, 41
Matthew 16.24-28

Sat, Aug 10
2 Corinthians 9.6-10
Psalms 112.1-2, 5-6, 7-8, 9
John 12.24-26

WEEK 19

Sun, Aug 11
I Kings 19.9, 11-13
Psalms 85.9, 10, 11-12, 13-14
Romans 9.1-5
Matthew 14.22-33

Mon, Aug 12
Ezekiel 1.2-5, 24-28
Psalms 148.1-2, 11-12, 12-14, 14
Matthew 17.22-27

Tue, Aug 13
Ezekiel 2.8—3.4
Psalms 119.14, 24, 72, 103, 111, 131
Matthew 18.1-5, 10, 12-14

Wed, Aug 14
Ezekiel 9.1-7; 10.18-22
Psalms 113.1-2, 3-4, 5-6
Matthew 18.15-20

Thu, Aug 15
Assumption of the
Virgin Mary into
Heaven—Solemnity
Revelation 11.19; 12.1-6, 10
Psalms 45.10, 11, 12, 16
I Corinthians 15.20-26
Luke 1.39-56

Fri, Aug 16
Ezekiel 16.1-15, 60, 63
Isaiah 12.2-3, 4, 5-6
Matthew 19.3-12

Sat, Aug 17
Ezekiel 18.1-10, 13, 30-32
Psalms 51.12-13, 14-15, 18-19
Matthew 19.13-15

WEEK 20

Sun, Aug 18
Isaiah 56.1, 6-7
Psalms 67.2-3, 5, 6, 8
Romans 11.13-15, 29-32
Matthew 15.21-28

Mon, Aug 19
Ezekiel 24.15-24
Deuteronomy 32.18-19, 20, 21
Matthew 19.16-22

Tue, Aug 20
Ezekiel 28.1-10
Deuteronomy 32.26-27, 27-28,
    30, 35-36
Matthew 19.23-30

Wed, Aug 21
Ezekiel 34.1-11
Psalms 23.1-3, 3-4, 5, 6
Matthew 20.1-16

Thu, Aug 22
Ezekiel 36.23-28
Psalms 51.12-13, 14-15, 18-19
Matthew 22.1-14

Fri, Aug 23
Ezekiel 37.1-14
Psalms 107.2-3, 4-5, 6-7, 8-9
Matthew 22.34-40

Sat, Aug 24
Saint Bartholomew,
apostle—Feast
Revelation 21.9-14
Psalms 145.10-11, 12-13, 17-18
John 1.45-51

WEEK 21

Sun, Aug 25
Isaiah 22.15, 19-23
Psalms 138.1-2, 2-3, 6, 8
Romans 11.33-36
Matthew 16.13-20

Mon, Aug 26
2 Thessalonians 1.1-5, 11-12
Psalms 96.1-2, 2-3, 4-5
Matthew 23.13-22

Tue, Aug 27
2 Thessalonians 2.1-3, 14-16
Psalms 96.10, 11-12, 13
Matthew 23.23-26

Wed, Aug 28
2 Thessalonians 3.6-10, 16-18
Psalms 128.1-2, 4-5
Matthew 23.27-32

Thu, Aug 29
Beheading of
Saint John the Baptist,
martyr—Memorial
Jeremiah 1.17-19
Psalms 71.1-2, 3-4, 5-6, 15, 17
Mark 6.17-29

Fri, Aug 30
I Corinthians 1.17-25
Psalms 33.1-2, 4-5, 10, 11
Matthew 25.1-13

Sat, Aug 31
I Corinthians 1.26-31
Psalms 33.12-13, 18-19, 20-21
Matthew 25.14-30

WEEK 22

Sun, Sept 1
Jeremiah 20.7-9
Psalms 63.2, 3-4, 5-6, 8-9
Romans 12.1-2
Matthew 16.21-27

Mon, Sept 2
I Corinthians 2.1-5
Psalms 119.97, 98, 99, 100,
    101, 102
Luke 4.16-30

Tue, Sept 3
I Corinthians 2.10-16
Psalms 145.8-9, 10-11, 12-13, 13-14
Luke 4.31-37

Wed, Sept 4
I Corinthians 3.1-9
Psalms 33.12-13, 14-15, 20-21
Luke 4.38-44

Thu, Sept 5
I Corinthians 3.18-23
Psalms 24.1-2, 3-4, 5-6
Luke 5.1-11

Fri, Sept 6
I Corinthians 4.1-5
Psalms 37.3-4, 5-6, 27-28, 39-40
Luke 5.33-39

Sat, Sept 7
I Corinthians 4.9-15
Psalms 145.17-18, 19-20, 21
Luke 6.1-5

WEEK 23

Sun, Sept 8	Ezekiel 33.7-9
	Psalms 95.1-2, 6-7, 8-9
	Romans 13.8-10
	Matthew 18.15-20
Mon, Sept 9	I Corinthians 5.1-8
	Psalms 5.5-6, 7, 12
	Luke 6.6-11
Tue, Sept 10	I Corinthians 6.1-11
	Psalms 149.1-2, 3-4, 5-6, 9
	Luke 6.12-19
Wed, Sept 11	I Corinthians 7.25-31
	Psalms 45.11-12, 14-15, 16-17
	Luke 6.20-26
Thu, Sept 12	I Corinthians 8.1-7, 11-13
	Psalms 139.1-3, 13-14, 23-24
	Luke 6.27-38
Fri, Sept 13	I Corinthians 9.16-19, 22-27
	Psalms 84.3, 4, 5-6, 8, 12
	Luke 6.39-42
Sat, Sept 14	Numbers 21.4-9
Triumph of the	Psalms 78.1-2, 34-35, 36-37, 38
Holy Cross—	Philippians 2.6-11
Feast	John 3.13-17

WEEK 24

Sun, Sept 15	Sirach 27.30—28.7
	Psalms 103.1-2, 3-4, 9-10, 11-12
	Romans 14.7-9
	Matthew 18.21-35
Mon, Sept 16	I Corinthians 11.17-26, 33
	Psalms 40.7-8, 8-9, 10, 17
	Luke 7.1-10
Tue, Sept 17	I Corinthians 12.12-14, 27-31
	Psalms 100.1-2, 3, 4, 5
	Luke 7.11-17
Wed, Sept 18	I Corinthians 12.31—13.13
	Psalms 33.2-3, 4-5, 12, 22
	Luke 7.31-35
Thu, Sept 19	I Corinthians 15.1-11
	Psalms 118.1-2, 16-17, 28
	Luke 7.36-50
Fri, Sept 20	I Corinthians 15.12-20
	Psalms 17.1, 6-7, 8, 15
	Luke 8.1-3
Sat, Sept 21	Ephesians 4.1-7, 11-13
	Psalms 19.2-3, 4-5
	Matthew 9.9-13

WEEK 25

Sun, Sept 22	Isaiah 55.6-9
	Psalms 145.2-3, 8-9, 17-18
	Philippians 1.20-24, 27
	Matthew 20.1-16
Mon, Sept 23	Proverbs 3.27-34
	Psalms 15.2-3, 3-4, 5
	Luke 8.16-18
Tue, Sept 24	Proverbs 21.1-6, 10-13
	Psalms 119.1, 27, 30, 34, 35, 44
	Luke 8.19-21
Wed, Sept 25	Proverbs 30.5-9
	Psalms 119.29, 72, 89, 101,
	104, 163
	Luke 9.1-6
Thu, Sept 26	Ecclesiastes 1.2-11
	Psalms 90.3-4, 5-6, 12-13, 14, 17
	Luke 9.7-9
Fri, Sept 27	Ecclesiastes 3.1-11
	Psalms 144.1-2, 3-4
	Luke 9.18-22
Sat, Sept 28	Ecclesiastes 11.9—12.8
	Psalms 90.3-4, 5-6, 12-13, 14, 17
	Luke 9.43-45

WEEK 26

Sun, Sept 29	Ezekiel 18.25-28
	Psalms 25.4-5, 6-7, 8-9
	Philippians 2.1-11
	or 2.1-5
	Matthew 21.28-32
Mon, Sept 30	Job 1.6-22
	Psalms 17.1, 2-3, 6-7
	Luke 9.46-50
Tue, Oct 1	Job 3.1-3, 11-17, 20-23
	Psalms 88.2-3, 4-5, 6, 7-8
	Luke 9.51-56
Wed, Oct 2	Exodus 23.20-23
Guardian Angels—	Psalms 91.1-2, 3-4, 5-6, 10-11
Memorial	Matthew 18.1-5, 10
Thu, Oct 3	Job 19.21-27
	Psalms 27.7-8, 8-9, 13-14
	Luke 10.1-12
Fri, Oct 4	Job 38.1, 12-21; 40.3-5
	Psalms 139.1-3, 7-8, 9-10, 13-14
	Luke 10.13-16
Sat, Oct 5	Job 42.1-3, 5-6, 12-16
	Psalms 119.66, 71, 75, 91, 125, 130
	Luke 10.17-24

WEEK 27

Sun, Oct 6
Isaiah 5.1-7
Psalms 80.9, 12, 13-14, 15-16,
19-20
Philippians 4.6-9
Matthew 21.33-43

Mon, Oct 7
Galatians 1.6-12
Psalms 111.1-2, 7-8, 9, 10
Luke 10.25-37

Tue, Oct 8
Galatians 1.13-24
Psalms 139.1-3, 13-14, 14-15
Luke 10.38-42

Wed, Oct 9
Galatians 2.1-2, 7-14
Psalms 117.1, 2
Luke 11.1-4

Thu, Oct 10
Galatians 3.1-5
Luke 1.69-70, 71-72, 73-75
Luke 11.5-13

Fri, Oct 11
Galatians 3.7-14
Psalms 111.1-2, 3-4, 5-6
Luke 11.15-26

Sat, Oct 12
Galatians 3.22-29
Psalms 105.2-3, 4-5, 6-7
Luke 11.27-28

WEEK 28

Sun, Oct 13
Isaiah 25.6-10
Psalms 23.1-3, 3-4, 5, 6
Philippians 4.12-14, 19-20
Matthew 22.1-14

Mon, Oct 14
Galatians 4.22-24, 26-27,
31—5.1
Psalms 113.1-2, 3-4, 5, 6-7
Luke 11.29-32

Tue, Oct 15
Galatians 5.1-6
Psalms 119.41, 43, 44, 45, 47, 48
Luke 11.37-41

Wed, Oct 16
Galatians 5.18-25
Psalms 1.1-2, 3, 4, 6
Luke 11.42-46

Thu, Oct 17
Ephesians 1.3-10
Psalms 98.1, 2-3, 3-4, 5-6
Luke 11.47-54

Fri, Oct 18
Saint Luke,
evangelist—Feast
2 Timothy 4.9-17
Psalms 145.10-11, 12-13, 17-18
Luke 10.1-9

Sat, Oct 19
Ephesians 1.15-23
Psalms 8.2-3, 4-5, 6-7
Luke 12.8-12

WEEK 29

Sun, Oct 20
Isaiah 45.1, 4-6
Psalms 96.1, 3, 4-5, 7-8, 9-10
1 Thessalonians 1.1-5
Matthew 22.15-21

Mon, Oct 21
Ephesians 2.1-10
Psalms 100.2, 3, 4, 5
Luke 12.13-21

Tue, Oct 22
Ephesians 2.12-22
Psalms 85.9-10, 11-12, 13-14
Luke 12.35-38

Wed, Oct 23
Ephesians 3.2-12
Isaiah 12.2-3, 4, 5-6
Luke 12.39-48

Thu, Oct 24
Ephesians 3.14-21
Psalms 33.1-2, 4-5, 11-12, 18-19
Luke 12.49-53

Fri, Oct 25
Ephesians 4.1-6
Psalms 24.1-2, 3-4, 5-6
Luke 12.54-59

Sat, Oct 26
Ephesians 4.7-16
Psalms 122.1-2, 3-4, 4-5
Luke 13.1-9

WEEK 30

Sun, Oct 27
Exodus 22.20-26
Psalms 18.2-3, 3-4, 47, 51
1 Thessalonians 1.5-10
Matthew 22.34-40

Mon, Oct 28
Saints Simon and Jude,
Apostles—Feast
Ephesians 2.19-22
Psalms 19.2-3, 4-5
Luke 6.12-16

Tue, Oct 29
Ephesians 5.21-33
Psalms 128.1-2, 3, 4-5
Luke 13.18-21

Wed, Oct 30
Ephesians 6.1-9
Psalms 145.10-11, 12-13, 13-14
Luke 13.22-30

Thu, Oct 31
Ephesians 6.10-20
Psalms 144.1, 2, 9-10
Luke 13.31-35

Fri, Nov 1
All Saints—Solemnity
Revelation 7.2-4, 9-14
Psalms 24.1-2, 3-4, 5-6
1 John 3.1-3
Matthew 5.1-12

Sat, Nov 2
Commemoration of
All the Faithful
Departed (All Souls)—
Solemnity
Isaiah 25.6, 7-9
Psalms 27.1, 4, 7, 8, 9, 13-14,
Romans 6.3-9
Matthew 25.31-46

WEEK 31

Sun, Nov 3
Malachi 1.14—2.2, 8-10
Psalms 131.1, 2, 3
I Thessalonians 2.7-9, 13
Matthew 23.1-12

Mon, Nov 4
Philippians 2.1-4
Psalms 131.1, 2, 3
Luke 14.12-14

Tue, Nov 5
Philippians 2.5-11
Psalms 22.26-27, 28-30, 31-32
Luke 14.15-24

Wed, Nov 6
Philippians 2.12-18
Psalms 27.1, 4, 13-14
Luke 14.25-33

Thu, Nov 7
Philippians 3.3-8
Psalms 105.2-3, 4-5, 6-7
Luke 15.1-10

Fri, Nov 8
Philippians 3.17—4.1
Psalms 122.1-2, 3-4, 4-5
Luke 16.1-8

Sat, Nov 9
Dedication of the Basilica of St. John Lateran in Rome— Feast
Genesis 28.11-18
Psalms 84.3, 4, 5-6, 8, 11
I Corinthians 3.9-13, 16-17
Luke 19.1-10

WEEK 32

Sun, Nov 10
Wisdom 6.12-16
Psalms 63.2, 3-4, 5-6, 7-8
I Thessalonians 4.13-17
Matthew 25.1-13

Mon, Nov 11
Titus 1.1-9
Psalms 24.1-2, 3-4, 5-6
Luke 17.1-6

Tue, Nov 12
Titus 2.1-8, 11-14
Psalms 37.3-4, 18, 23, 27, 29
Luke 17.7-10

Wed, Nov 13
Titus 3.1-7
Psalms 23.1-3, 3-4, 5, 6
Luke 17.11-19

Thu, Nov 14
Philemon 1.7-20
Psalms 146.7, 8-9, 9-10
Luke 17.20-25

Fri, Nov 15
2 John 1.4-9
Psalms 119.1, 2, 10, 11, 17, 18
Luke 17.26-37

Sat, Nov 16
3 John 1.5-8
Psalms 112.1-2, 3-4, 5-6
Luke 18.1-8

WEEK 33

Sun, Nov 17
Proverbs 31.10-13, 19-20, 30-31
Psalms 128.1-2, 3, 4-5
I Thessalonians 5.1-6
Matthew 25.14-30

Mon, Nov 18
Revelation 1.1-4; 2.1-5
Psalms 1.1-2, 3, 4, 6
Luke 18.35-43

Tue, Nov 19
Revelation 3.1-6, 14-22
Psalms 15.2-3, 3-4, 5
Luke 19.1-10

Wed, Nov 20
Revelation 4.1-11
Psalms 150.1-2, 3-4, 5-6
Luke 19.11-28

Thu, Nov 21
Revelation 5.1-10
Psalms 149.1-2, 3-4, 5-6, 9
Luke 9.41-44

Fri, Nov 22
Revelation 10.8-11
Psalms 119.14, 24, 72, 103, 111, 131
Luke 19.45-48

Sat, Nov 23
Revelation 11.4-12
Psalms 144.1, 2, 9-10
Luke 20.27-40

WEEK 34

Sun, Nov 24
Christ the King— Solemnity
Ezekiel 34.11-12, 15-17
Psalms 23.1-2, 2-3, 5, 6
I Corinthians 15.20-26, 28
Matthew 25.31-46

Mon, Nov 25
Revelation 14.1-3, 4-5
Psalms 24.1-2, 3-4, 5-6
Luke 21.1-4

Tue, Nov 26
Revelation 14.14-19
Psalms 96.10, 11-12, 13
Luke 21.5-11

Wed, Nov 27
Revelation 15.1-4
Psalms 98.1, 2-3, 7-8, 9
Luke 21.12-19

Thu, Nov 28
Revelation 18.1-2, 21-23; 19.1-3, 9
Psalms 100.2, 3, 4, 5
Luke 21.20-28

Fri, Nov 29
Revelation 20.1-4, 11—21.2
Psalms 84.3, 4, 5-6, 8
Luke 21.29-33

Sat, Nov 30
Saint Andrew, apostle—Feast
Romans 10.9-18
Psalms 19.2-3, 4-5
Matthew 4.18-22

Advent, Liturgical year 2003

WEEK 1, ADVENT

Sun, Dec 1, 2002
Isaiah 63.16-17, 19
Psalms 80.2-3, 15-16, 18-19
1 Corinthians 1.3-9
Mark 13.33-37

Mon, Dec 2
Isaiah 2.1-5
Psalms 122.1-2, 3-4, 4-5, 6-7, 8-9
Matthew 8.5-11

Tue, Dec 3
Isaiah 11.1-10
Psalms 72.1, 7-8, 12-13, 17
Luke 10.21-24

Wed, Dec 4
Isaiah 25.6-10
Psalms 23.1-3, 3-4, 5, 6
Matthew 15.29-37

Thu, Dec 5
Isaiah 26.1-6
Psalms 118.1, 8-9, 19-21, 25-27
Matthew 7.21, 24-27

Fri, Dec 6
Isaiah 29.17-24
Psalms 27.1, 4, 13-14
Matthew 9.27-31

Sat, Dec 7
Isaiah 30.19-21, 23-26
Psalms 147.1-2, 3-4, 5-6
Matthew 9.35—10.1, 6-8

WEEK 2, ADVENT

Sun, Dec 8
Isaiah 40.1-5, 9-11
Psalms 85.9-10, 11-12, 13-14
2 Peter 3.8-14
Mark 1.1-8

Mon, Dec 9
*Immaculate
Conception of the
Virgin Mary—
Solemnity*
Genesis 3.9-15, 20
Psalms 98.1, 2-3, 3-4
Ephesians 1.3-6, 11-12
Luke 1.26-38

Tue, Dec 10
Isaiah 40.1-11
Psalms 96.1-2, 3, 10, 11-12, 13
Matthew 18.12-14

Wed, Dec 11
Isaiah 40.25-31
Psalms 103.1-2, 3-4, 8, 10
Matthew 11.28-30

Thu, Dec 12
*Our Lady of
Guadalupe—
Feast*
Zechariah 2.14-17
Psalms 45.11-12, 14-17
Romans 8.28-30
Luke 2.15-19

Fri, Dec 13
Isaiah 48.17-19
Psalms 1.1-2, 3, 4, 6
Matthew 11.16-19

Sat, Dec 14
Sirach 48.1-4, 9-11
Psalms 80.2-3, 15-16, 18-19
Matthew 17.10-13

WEEK 3, ADVENT

Sun, Dec 15
Isaiah 61.1-2, 10-11
Luke 1.46-48, 49-50, 53-54
1 Thessalonians 5.16-24
John 1.6-8, 19-28

Mon, Dec 16
Numbers 24.2-7, 15-17
Psalms 25.4-5, 6-7, 8-9
Matthew 21.23-27

Tue, Dec 17
Genesis 49.2, 8-10
Psalms 72.3-4, 7-8, 17
Matthew 1.1-17

Wed, Dec 18
Jeremiah 23.5-8
Psalms 72.1, 12-13, 18-19
Matthew 1.18-24

Thu, Dec 19
Judges 13.2-7, 24-25
Psalms 71.3-4, 5-6, 16-17
Luke 1.5-25

Fri, Dec 20
Isaiah 7.10-14
Psalms 24.1-2, 3-4, 5-6
Luke 1.26-38

Sat, Dec 21
Song of Songs 2.8-14
Psalms 33.2-3, 11-12, 20-21
Luke 1.39-45

WEEK 4, ADVENT

Sun, Dec 22
2 Samuel 7.1-5, 8-11, 16
Psalms 89.2-3, 4-5, 27, 29
Romans 16.25-27
Luke 1.26-38

Mon, Dec 23
Malachi 3.1-4, 23-24
Psalms 25.4-5, 8-9, 10, 14
Luke 1.57-66

Tue, Dec 24
2 Samuel 7.1-5, 8-11, 16
Psalms 89.2-3, 4-5, 27, 29
Luke 1.67-79

Christmas

Wed, Dec 25
Christmas—Solemnity
Isaiah 62.11-12
Psalms 97.1, 6, 11-12
Titus 3.4-7
Luke 2.15-20

Thu, Dec 26
*Saint Stephen, first
martyr—Feast*
Acts 6.8-10; 7.54-59
Psalms 31.3-4, 6, 7, 8, 17, 21
Matthew 10.17-22

Fri, Dec 27
*Saint John, apostle
and evangelist—Feast*
1 John 1.1-4
Psalms 97.1-2, 5-6, 11-12
John 20.2-8

Sat, Dec 28
*The Holy Innocents,
martyrs—Feast*
1 John 1.5—2.2
Psalms 124.2-3, 4-5, 7-8
Matthew 2.13-18

Sun, Dec 29
The Holy Family—
Feast

Sirach 3.2-6, 12-14
Psalms 128.1-2, 3, 4-5
Colossians 3.12-21
Luke 2.22-40 or 2.22, 39-40

Mon, Dec 30

I John 2.12-17
Psalms 96.7-8, 8-9, 10
Luke 2.36-40

Tue, Dec 31

I John 2.18-21
Psalms 96.1-2, 11-12, 13
John 1.1-18

Wed, Jan 1, 2003
Mary, Mother of God—
Solemnity

Numbers 6.22-27
Psalms 67.2-3, 5, 6, 8
Galatians 4.4-7
Luke 2.16-21

Thu, Jan 2

I John 2.22-28
Psalms 98.1, 2-3, 3-4
John 1.19-28

Fri, Jan 3

I John 2.29—3.6
Psalms 98.1, 3-4, 5-6
John 1.29-34

Sat, Jan 4

I John 3.7-10
Psalms 98.1, 7-8, 9
John 1.35-42

Sun, Jan 5
Epiphany of the Lord—
Solemnity

Isaiah 60.1-6
Psalms 72.1-2, 7-8, 10-11, 12-13
Ephesians 3.2-3, 5-6
Matthew 2.1-12

Mon, Jan 6

I John 3.22—4.6
Psalms 2.7-8, 10-11
Matthew 4.12-17, 23-25

Tue, Jan 7

I John 3.22—4.6
Psalms 2.7-8, 10-11
Matthew 4.12-17, 23-25

Wed, Jan 8

I John 4.7-10
Psalms 72.1-2, 3-4, 7-8
Mark 6.34-44

Thu, Jan 9

I John 4.11-18
Psalms 72.1-2, 10, 12-13
Mark 6.45-52

Fri, Jan 10

I John 4.19—5.4
Psalms 72.1-2, 14-15, 17
Luke 4.14-22

Sat, Jan 11

I John 5.5-13
Psalms 147.12-13, 14-15, 19-20
Luke 5.12-16

Ordinary Time

WEEK 1

Sun, Jan 12
Baptism of the Lord—
Feast

Isaiah 42.1-4, 6-7
Psalms 29.1-2, 3-4, 3, 9-10
Acts 10.34-38
Mark 1.7-11

Mon, Jan 13

Hebrews 1.1-6
Psalms 97.1-2, 6-7, 9
Mark 1.14-20

Tue, Jan 14

Hebrews 2.5-12
Psalms 8.2, 5, 6-7, 8-9
Mark 1.21-28

Wed, Jan 15

Hebrews 2.14-18
Psalms 105.1-2, 3-4, 6-7, 8-9
Mark 1.29-39

Thu, Jan 16

Hebrews 3.7-14
Psalms 95.6-7, 8-9, 10-11
Mark 1.40-45

Fri, Jan 17

Hebrews 4.1-5, 11
Psalms 78.3, 4, 6-7, 8
Mark 2.1-12

Sat, Jan 18

Hebrews 4.12-16
Psalms 19.8, 9, 10, 15
Mark 2.13-17

WEEK 2

Sun, Jan 19

I Samuel 3.3-10, 19
Psalms 40.2, 4, 7-8, 8-9, 10
I Corinthians 6.13-15, 17-20
John 1.35-42

Mon, Jan 20

Hebrews 5.1-10
Psalms 110.1, 2, 3, 4
Mark 2.18-22

Tue, Jan 21

Hebrews 6.10-20
Psalms 111.1-2, 4-5, 9-10
Mark 2.23-28

Wed, Jan 22

Hebrews 7.1-3, 15-17
Psalms 110.1, 2, 3, 4
Mark 3.1-6

Thu, Jan 23

Hebrews 7.25—8.6
Psalms 40.7-8, 8-9, 10, 17
Mark 3.7-12

Fri, Jan 24

Hebrews 8.6-13
Psalms 85.8, 10, 11-12, 13-14
Mark 3.13-19

Sat, Jan 25
Conversion of Saint
Paul, apostle—Feast

Acts 9.1-22
Psalms 117.1, 2
Mark 16.15-18

WEEK 3

Sun, Jan 26
Jonah 3.1-5, 10
Psalms 25.4-5, 6-7, 8-9
I Corinthians 7.29-31
Mark 1.14-20

Mon, Jan 27
Hebrews 9.15, 24-28
Psalms 98.1, 2-3, 3-4, 5-6
Mark 3.22-30

Tue, Jan 28
Hebrews 10.1-10
Psalms 40.2, 4, 7-8, 10, 11
Mark 3.31-35

Wed, Jan 29
Hebrews 10.11-18
Psalms 110.1, 2, 3, 4
Mark 4.1-20

Thu, Jan 30
Hebrews 10.19-25
Psalms 24.1-2, 3-4, 5-6
Mark 4.21-25

Fri, Jan 31
Hebrews 10.32-39
Psalms 37.3-4, 5-6, 23-24,
     39-40
Mark 4.26-34

Sat, Feb 1
Hebrews 11.1-2, 8-19
Luke 1.69-70, 71-72, 73-75
Mark 4.35-41

WEEK 4

Sun, Feb 2
*Presentation
of the Lord—
Feast*
Malachi 3.1-4
Psalms 24.7, 8, 9, 10
Hebrews 2.14-18
Luke 2.22-40

Mon, Feb 3
Hebrews 11.32-40
Psalms 31.20, 21, 22, 23, 24
Mark 5.1-20

Tue, Feb 4
Hebrews 12.1-4
Psalms 22.26-27, 28, 30, 31-32
Mark 5.21-43

Wed, Feb 5
Hebrews 12.4-7, 11-15
Psalms 103.1-2, 13-14, 17-18
Mark 6.1-6

Thu, Feb 6
Hebrews 12.18-19, 21-24
Psalms 48.2-3, 3-4, 9, 10-11
Mark 6.7-13

Fri, Feb 7
Hebrews 13.1-8
Psalms 27.1, 3, 5, 8-9
Mark 6.14-29

Sat, Feb 8
Hebrews 13.15-17, 20-21
Psalms 23.1-3, 3-4, 5, 6
Mark 6.30-34

WEEK 5

Sun, Feb 9
Job 7.1-4, 6-7
Psalms 147.1-2, 3-4, 5-6
I Corinthians 9.16-19, 22-23
Mark 1.29-39

Mon, Feb 10
Genesis 1.1-19
Psalms 104.1-2, 5-6, 10, 12, 24, 35
Mark 6.53-56

Tue, Feb 11
Genesis 1.20—2.4
Psalms 8.4-5, 6-7, 8-9
Mark 7.1-13

Wed, Feb 12
Genesis 2.5-9, 15-17
Psalms 104.1-2, 27-28, 29-30
Mark 7.14-23

Thu, Feb 13
Genesis 2.18-25
Psalms 128.1-2, 3, 4-5
Mark 7.24-30

Fri, Feb 14
Genesis 3.1-8
Psalms 32.1-2, 5, 6, 7
Mark 7.31-37

Sat, Feb 15
Genesis 3.9-24
Psalms 90.2, 3-4, 5-6, 12-13
Mark 8.1-10

WEEK 6

Sun, Feb 16
Leviticus 13.1-2, 44-46
Psalms 32.1-2, 5, 11
I Corinthians 10.31—11.1
Mark 1.40-45

Mon, Feb 17
Genesis 4.1-15, 25
Psalms 50.1, 8, 16-17, 20-21
Mark 8.11-13

Tue, Feb 18
Genesis 6.5-8; 7.1-5, 10
Psalms 29.1-2, 3-4, 8, 9-10
Mark 8.14-21

Wed, Feb 19
Genesis 8.6-13, 20-22
Psalms 116.12-13, 14-15, 18-19
Mark 8.22-26

Thu, Feb 20
Genesis 9.1-13
Psalms 102.16-18, 19-21, 29,
     22-23
Mark 8.27-33

Fri, Feb 21
Genesis 11.1-9
Psalms 33.10-11, 12-13, 14-15
Mark 8.34—9.1

Sat, Feb 22
*Chair of Saint Peter,
apostle—Feast*
I Peter 5.1-4
Psalms 23.1-3, 3-4, 5, 6
Matthew 16.13-19

WEEK 7

Sun, Feb 23
Isaiah 43.18-19, 21-22, 24-25
Psalms 41.2-3, 4-5, 13-14
2 Corinthians 1.18-22
Mark 2.1-12

Mon, Feb 24
Sirach 1.1-10
Psalms 93.1, 1-2, 5
Mark 9.14-29

Tue, Feb 25
Sirach 2.1-11
Psalms 37.3-4, 18-19, 27-28, 39-40
Mark 9.30-37

Wed, Feb 26
Sirach 4.11-19
Psalms 119.165, 168, 171, 172, 174, 175
Mark 9.38-40

Thu, Feb 27
Sirach 5.1-8
Psalms 1.1-2, 3-4, 6
Mark 9.41-50

Fri, Feb 28
Sirach 6.5-17
Psalms 119.12, 16, 18, 27, 34, 35
Mark 10.1-12

Sat, Mar 1
Sirach 17.1-15
Psalms 103.13-14, 15-16, 17-18
Mark 10.13-16

WEEK 8

Sun, Mar 2
Hosea 2.15-17, 21-22
Psalms 103.1-2, 3-4, 8, 10, 12-13
2 Corinthians 3.1-6
Mark 2.18-22

Mon, Mar 3
Sirach 17.19-27
Psalms 32.1-2, 5, 6, 7
Mark 10.17-27

Tue, Mar 4
Sirach 35.1-12
Psalms 50.5-6, 7-8, 14, 23
Mark 10.28-31

Lent

Wed, Mar 5
Ash Wednesday
Joel 2.12-18
Psalms 51.3-4, 5-6, 12-13, 14, 17
2 Corinthians 5.20—6.2
Matthew 6.1-6, 16-18

Thu, Mar 6
Deuteronomy 30.15-20
Psalms 1.1-2, 3, 4, 6
Luke 9.22-25

Fri, Mar 7
Isaiah 58.1-9
Psalms 51.3-4, 5-6, 18-19
Matthew 9.14-15

Sat, Mar 8
Isaiah 58.9-14
Psalms 86.1-2, 3-4, 5-6
Luke 5.27-32

WEEK 1, LENT

Sun, Mar 9
Genesis 9.8-15
Psalms 25.4-5, 6-7, 8-9
1 Peter 3.18-22
Mark 1.12-15

Mon, Mar 10
Leviticus 19.1-2, 11-18
Psalms 19.8, 9, 10, 15
Matthew 25.31-46

Tue, Mar 11
Isaiah 55.10-11
Psalms 34.4-5, 6-7, 16-17, 18-19
Matthew 6.7-15

Wed, Mar 12
Jonah 3.1-10
Psalms 51.3-4, 12-13, 18-19
Luke 11.29-32

Thu, Mar 13
Esther C.12, 14-16, 23-25
Psalms 138.1-2, 2-3, 7-8
Matthew 7.7-12

Fri, Mar 14
Ezekiel 18.21-28
Psalms 130.1-2, 3-4, 5-6, 7-8
Matthew 5.20-26

Sat, Mar 15
Deuteronomy 26.16-19
Psalms 119.1-2, 4-5, 7-8
Matthew 5.43-48

WEEK 2, LENT

Sun, Mar 16
Genesis 22.1-2, 9, 10-13, 15-18
Psalms 116.10, 15, 16-17, 18-19
Romans 8.31-34
Mark 9.2-10

Mon, Mar 17
Daniel 9.4-10
Psalms 79.8, 9, 11, 13
Luke 6.36-38

Tue, Mar 18
Isaiah 1.10, 16-20
Psalms 50.8-9, 16-17, 21, 23
Matthew 23.1-12

Wed, Mar 19
Saint Joseph, Husband of Mary—Solemnity
2 Samuel 7.4-5, 12-14, 16
Psalms 89.2-3, 4-5, 27, 29
Romans 4.13, 16-18, 22
Luke 2.41-51

Thu, Mar 20
Jeremiah 17.5-10
Psalms 1.1-2, 3, 4, 6
Luke 16.19-31

Fri, Mar 21
Genesis 37.3-4, 12-13, 17-18
Psalms 105.16-17, 18-19, 20-21
Matthew 21.33-43, 45-46

Sat, Mar 22
Micah 7.14-15, 18-20
Psalms 103.1-2, 3-4, 9-10, 11-12
Luke 15.1-3, 11-32

WEEK 3, LENT

Sun, Mar 23
Exodus 20.1-17
Psalms 19.8, 9, 10, 11
I Corinthians 1.22-25
John 2.13-25

Mon, Mar 24
2 Kings 5.1-15
Psalms 42.2, 3; 43.3, 4
Luke 4.24-30

Tue, Mar 25
Annunciation of the Lord— Solemnity
Isaiah 7.10-14
Psalms 40.7-8, 8-9, 10, 11
Hebrews 10.4-10
Luke 1.26-38

Wed, Mar 26
Deuteronomy 4.1, 5-9
Psalms 147.12-13, 15-16, 19-20
Matthew 5.17-19

Thu, Mar 27
Jeremiah 7.23-28
Psalms 95.1-2, 6-7, 8-9
Luke 11.14-23

Fri, Mar 28
Hosea 14.2-10
Psalms 81.6-8, 8-9, 10-11, 14, 17
Mark 12.28-34

Sat, Mar 29
Hosea 6.1-6
Psalms 51.3-4, 18-19, 20-21
Luke 18.9-14

WEEK 4, LENT

Sun, Mar 30
2 Chronicles 36.14-17, 19-23
Psalms 137.1-2, 3, 4-5, 6
Ephesians 2.4-10
John 3.14-21

Mon, Mar 31
Isaiah 65.17-21
Psalms 30.2, 4, 5-6, 11-13
John 4.43-54

Tue, Apr 1
Ezekiel 47.1-9, 12
Psalms 46.2-3, 5-6, 8-9
John 5.1-3, 5-16

Wed, Apr 2
Isaiah 49.8-15
Psalms 145.8-9, 13-14, 17-18
John 5.17-30

Thu, Apr 3
Exodus 32.7-14
Psalms 106.19-20, 21-22, 23
John 5.31-47

Fri, Apr 4
Wisdom 2.1, 12-22
Psalms 34.17-18, 19-20, 21, 23
John 7.1-2, 10, 25-30

Sat, Apr 5
Jeremiah 11.18-20
Psalms 7.2-3, 9-10, 11-12
John 7.40-53

WEEK 5, LENT

Sun, Apr 6
Jeremiah 31.31-34
Psalms 51.3-4, 12-13, 14-15
Hebrews 5.7-9
John 12.20-33

Mon, Apr 7
Daniel 13.1-9, 15-17, 19-30, 33-62
Psalms 23.1-3, 3-4, 5, 6
John 8.1-11

Tue, Apr 8
Numbers 21.4-9
Psalms 102.2-3, 16-18, 19-21
John 8.21-30

Wed, Apr 9
Daniel 3.14-20, 91-92, 95
Daniel 3.52, 53, 54, 55, 56
John 8.31-42

Thu, Apr 10
Genesis 17.3-9
Psalms 105.4-5, 6-7, 8-9
John 8.51-59

Fri, Apr 11
Jeremiah 20.10-13
Psalms 18.2-3, 3-4, 5-6, 7
John 10.31-42

Sat, Apr 12
Ezekiel 37.21-28
Jeremiah 31.10, 11-12, 13
John 11.45-57

HOLY WEEK

Sun, Apr 13
Passion (Palm) Sunday
Isaiah 50.4-7
Psalms 22.8-9, 17-18, 19-20, 23-24
Philippians 2.6-11
Mark 14.1—15.47

Mon, Apr 14
Isaiah 42.1-7
Psalms 27.1, 2, 3, 13-14
John 12.1-11

Tue, Apr 15
Isaiah 49.1-6
Psalms 71.1-2, 3-4, 5-6, 15, 17
John 13.21-33, 36-38

Wed, Apr 16
Isaiah 50.4-9
Psalms 69.8-10, 21-22, 31, 33-34
Matthew 26.14-25

Thu, Apr 17
Holy Thursday
Exodus 12.1-8, 11-14
Psalms 116.12-13, 15-16, 17-18
I Corinthians 11.23-26
John 13.1-15

Fri, Apr 18
Good Friday
Isaiah 52.13—53.12
Psalms 31.2, 6, 12-13, 15-16, 17, 25
Hebrews 4.14-16; 5.7-9
John 18.1—19.42

Sat, Apr 19
Genesis 1.1—2.2
 or 1.1, 26-31
Psalms 104.1-2, 5-6, 10, 12, 13-14, 24, 35
Genesis 22.1-18
 or 22.1-2, 9, 10-13, 15-18

Sat, Apr 19   Psalms 16.5, 8, 9-10, 11
                      Exodus 14.15—15.1
                      Exodus 15.1-2, 3-4, 5-6, 17-18
                      Isaiah 54.5-14
                      Psalms 30.2, 4, 5-6, 11-12, 13
                      Isaiah 55.1-11
                      Isaiah 12.2-3, 4, 5-6
                      Baruch 3.9-15, 32—4.4
                      Psalms 19.8, 9, 10, 11
                      Ezekiel 36.16-28
                      Psalms 42.3, 5; 43.3, 4
                      Romans 6.3-11
                      Psalms 118.1-2, 16, 17, 22-23
                      Mark 16.1-8

Easter

WEEK 1, EASTER

Sun, Apr 20   Acts 10.34, 37-43
Easter Sunday   Psalms 118.1-2, 16-17, 22-23
                      1 Corinthians 5.6-8
                      John 20.1-9

Mon, Apr 21   Acts 2.14, 22-32
                      Psalms 16.1-2, 5, 7-8, 9-10, 11
                      Matthew 28.8-15

Tue, Apr 22   Acts 2.36-41
                      Psalms 33.4-5, 18-19, 20, 22
                      John 20.11-18

Wed, Apr 23   Acts 3.1-10
                      Psalms 105.1-2, 3-4, 6-7, 8-9
                      Luke 24.13-35

Thu, Apr 24   Acts 3.11-26
                      Psalms 8.2, 5, 6-7, 8-9
                      Luke 24.35-48

Fri, Apr 25   1 Peter 5.5-14
Saint Mark,   Psalms 89.2-3, 6-7, 16-17
evangelist—Feast   Mark 16.15-20

Sat, Apr 26   Acts 4.13-21
                      Psalms 118.1, 14-15, 16-18, 19-21
                      Mark 16.9-15

WEEK 2, EASTER

Sun, Apr 27   Acts 4.32-35
                      Psalms 118.2-4, 13-15, 22-24
                      1 John 5.1-6
                      John 20.19-31

Mon, Apr 28   Acts 4.23-31
                      Psalms 2.1-3, 4-6, 7-9
                      John 3.1-8

Tue, Apr 29   Acts 4.32-37
                      Psalms 93.1, 1-2, 5
                      John 3.7-15

Wed, Apr 30   Acts 5.17-26
                      Psalms 34.2-3, 4-5, 6-7, 8-9
                      John 3.16-21

Thu, May 1   Acts 5.27-33
                      Psalms 34.2, 9, 17-18, 19-20
                      John 3.31-36

Fri, May 2   Acts 5.34-42
                      Psalms 27.1, 4, 13-14
                      John 6.1-15

Sat, May 3   1 Corinthians 15.1-8
Saints Philip and   Psalms 19.2-3, 4-5
James, apostles—   John 14.6-14
Feast

WEEK 3, EASTER

Sun, May 4   Acts 3.13-15, 17-19
                      Psalms 4.2, 4, 7-8, 9
                      1 John 2.1-5
                      Luke 24.35-48

Mon, May 5   Acts 6.8-15
                      Psalms 119.23-24, 26-27, 29-30
                      John 6.22-29

Tue, May 6   Acts 7.51—8.1
                      Psalms 31.3-4, 6, 7, 8, 17, 21
                      John 6.30-35

Wed, May 7   Acts 8.1-8
                      Psalms 66.1-3, 4-5, 6-7
                      John 6.35-40

Thu, May 8   Acts 8.26-40
                      Psalms 66.8-9, 16-17, 20
                      John 6.44-51

Fri, May 9   Acts 9.1-20
                      Psalms 117.1, 2
                      John 6.52-59

Sat, May 10   Acts 9.31-42
                      Psalms 116.12-13, 14-15, 16-17
                      John 6.60-69

WEEK 4, EASTER

Sun, May 11
Acts 4.8-12
Psalms 118.1, 8-9, 21-23, 26,
21, 29
1 John 3.1-2
John 10.11-18

Mon, May 12
Acts 11.1-18
Psalms 42.2-3; 43.3, 4
John 10.1-10

Tue, May 13
Acts 11.19-26
Psalms 87.1-3, 4-5, 6-7
John 10.22-30

Wed, May 14
Saint Matthias,
apostle—Feast
Acts 1.15-17, 20-26
Psalms 113.1-2, 3-4, 5-6, 7-8
John 15.9-17

Thu, May 15
Acts 13.13-25
Psalms 89.2-3, 21-22, 25, 27
John 13.16-20

Fri, May 16
Acts 13.26-33
Psalms 2.6-7, 8-9, 10-11
John 14.1-6

Sat, May 17
Acts 13.44-52
Psalms 98.1, 2-3, 3-4
John 14.7-14

WEEK 5, EASTER

Sun, May 18
Acts 9.26-31
Psalms 22.26-27, 28, 30, 31-32
1 John 3.18-24
John 15.1-8

Mon, May 19
Acts 14.5-18
Psalms 115.1-2, 3-4, 15-16
John 14.21-26

Tue, May 20
Acts 14.19-28
Psalms 145.10-11, 12-13, 21
John 14.27-31

Wed, May 21
Acts 15.1-6
Psalms 122.1-2, 3-4, 4-5
John 15.1-8

Thu, May 22
Acts 15.7-21
Psalms 96.1-2, 2-3, 10
John 15.9-11

Fri, May 23
Acts 15.22-31
Psalms 57.8-9, 10-12
John 15.12-17

Sat, May 24
Acts 16.1-10
Psalms 100.1-2, 3, 5
John 15.18-21

WEEK 6, EASTER

Sun, May 25
Acts 10.25-26, 34-35, 44-48
Psalms 98.1, 2-3, 3-4
1 John 4.7-10
John 15.9-17

Mon, May 26
Acts 16.11-15
Psalms 149.1-2, 3-4, 5-6, 9
John 15.26—16.4

Tue, May 27
Acts 16.22-34
Psalms 138.1-2, 2-3, 7-8
John 16.5-11

Wed, May 28
Acts 17.15, 22—18.1
Psalms 148.1-2, 11-12, 13, 14
John 16.12-15

Thu, May 29
Ascension of the Lord
Acts 1.1-11
Psalms 47.2-3, 6-7, 8-9
Ephesians 1.17-23
Mark 16.15-20

Fri, May 30
Acts 18.9-18
Psalms 47.2-3, 4-5, 6-7
John 16.20-23

Sat, May 31
Visitation of the
Virgin Mary to
Elizabeth—Feast
Zephaniah 3.14-18
Isaiah 12.2-3, 4, 5-6
Luke 1.39-56

WEEK 7, EASTER

Sun, June 1
Acts 1.15-17, 20-26
Psalms 103.1-2, 11-12, 19-20
1 John 4.11-16
John 17.11-19

Mon, June 2
Acts 19.1-8
Psalms 68.2-3, 4-5, 6-7
John 16.29-33

Tue, June 3
Acts 20.17-27
Psalms 68.10-11, 20-21
John 17.1-11

Wed, June 4
Acts 20.28-38
Psalms 68.29-30, 33-35, 35-36
John 17.11-19

Thu, June 5
Acts 22.30; 23.6-11
Psalms 16.1-2, 5, 7-8, 9-10, 11
John 17.20-26

Fri, June 6
Acts 25.13-21
Psalms 103.1-2, 11-12, 19-20
John 21.15-19

Sat, June 7
Acts 28.16-20, 30-31
Psalms 11.4, 5, 7
John 21.20-25

Sun, June 8
Pentecost
Acts 2.1-11
Psalms 104.1, 24, 29-30, 31, 34
1 Corinthians 12.3-7, 12-13
John 20.19-23

Ordinary Time

WEEK 10

Mon, June 9 — 2 Corinthians 1.1-7
Psalms 34.2-3, 4-5, 6-7, 8-9
Matthew 5.1-12

Tue, June 10 — 2 Corinthians 1.18-22
Psalms 119.129, 130, 131, 132, 133, 135
Matthew 5.13-16

Wed, June 11
Saint Barnabas, apostle—Memorial
Acts 11.21-26; 13.1-3
Psalms 98.1, 2-3, 3-4, 5-6
Matthew 10.7-13

Thu, June 12 — 2 Corinthians 3.15—4.1, 3-6
Psalms 85.9-10, 11-12, 13-14
Matthew 5.20-26

Fri, June 13 — 2 Corinthians 4.7-15
Psalms 116.10-11, 15-16, 17-18
Matthew 5.27-32

Sat, June 14 — 2 Corinthians 5.14-21
Psalms 103.1-2, 3-4, 8-9, 11-12
Matthew 5.33-37

WEEK 11

Sun, June 15
The Holy Trinity— Solemnity
Deuteronomy 4.32-34, 39-40
Psalms 33.4-5, 6, 9, 18-19, 20, 22
Romans 8.14-17
Matthew 28.16-20

Mon, June 16 — 2 Corinthians 6.1-10
Psalms 98.1, 2-3, 3-4
Matthew 5.38-42

Tue, June 17 — 2 Corinthians 8.1-9
Psalms 146.2, 5-6, 7, 8-9
Matthew 5.43-48

Wed, June 18 — 2 Corinthians 9.6-11
Psalms 112.1-2, 3-4, 9
Matthew 6.1-6, 16-18

Thu, June 19 — 2 Corinthians 11.1-11
Psalms 111.1-2, 3-4, 7-8
Matthew 6.7-15

Fri, June 20 — 2 Corinthians 11.18, 21-30
Psalms 34.2-3, 4-5, 6-7
Matthew 6.19-23

Sat, June 21 — 2 Corinthians 12.1-10
Psalms 34.8-9, 10-11, 12-13
Matthew 6.24-34

WEEK 12

Sun, June 22
The Body and Blood of Christ (Corpus Christi)—Solemnity
Exodus 24.3-8
Psalms 116.12-13, 15-16, 17-18
Hebrews 9.11-15
Mark 14.12-16, 22-26

Mon, June 23 — Genesis 12.1-9
Psalms 33.12-13, 18-19, 20, 22
Matthew 7.1-5

Tue, June 24
Birth of Saint John the Baptist—Solemnity
Isaiah 49.1-6
Psalms 139.1-3, 13-14, 14-15
Acts 13.22-26
Luke 1.57-66, 80

Wed, June 25 — Genesis 15.1-12, 17-18
Psalms 105.1-2, 3-4, 6-7, 8-9
Matthew 7.15-20

Thu, June 26 — Genesis 16.1-12, 15-16
Psalms 106.1-2, 3-4, 4-5
Matthew 7.21-29

Fri, June 27
Sacred Heart of Jesus— Solemnity
Hosea 11.1, 3-4, 8-9
Isaiah 12.2-3, 4, 5-6
Ephesians 3.8-12, 14-19
John 19.31-37

Sat, June 28 — Genesis 18.1-15
Luke 1.46-47, 48-49, 50, 53, 54-55
Matthew 8.5-17

WEEK 13

Sun, June 29
Saints Peter and Paul, apostles—Solemnity
Acts 12.1-11
Psalms 34.2-3, 4-5, 6-7, 8-9
2 Timothy 4.6-8, 17-18
Matthew 16.13-19

Mon, June 30 — Genesis 18.16-33
Psalms 103.1-2, 3-4, 8-9, 10-11
Matthew 8.18-22

Tue, July 1 — Genesis 19.15-29
Psalms 26.2-3, 9-10, 11-12
Matthew 8.23-27

Wed, July 2 — Genesis 21.5, 8-20
Psalms 34.7-8, 10-11, 12-13
Matthew 8.28-34

Thu, July 3
Saint Thomas, apostle—Feast
Ephesians 2.19-22
Psalms 117.1, 2
John 20.24-29

Fri, July 4 — Genesis 23.1-4, 19; 24.1-8, 62-67
Psalms 106.1-2, 3-4, 4-5
Matthew 9.9-13

Sat, July 5 — Genesis 27.1-5, 15-29
Psalms 135.1-2, 3-4, 5-6
Matthew 9.14-17

WEEK 14

Sun, July 6
Ezekiel 2.2-5
Psalms 123.1-2, 2, 3-4
2 Corinthians 12.7-10
Mark 6.1-6

Mon, July 7
Genesis 28.10-22
Psalms 91.1-2, 3-4, 14-15
Matthew 9.18-26

Tue, July 8
Genesis 32.23-33
Psalms 17.1, 2-3, 6-7, 8, 15
Matthew 9.32-38

Wed, July 9
Genesis 41.55-57; 42.5-7, 17-24
Psalms 33.2-3, 10-11, 18-19
Matthew 10.1-7

Thu, July 10
Genesis 44.18-21, 23-29; 45.1-5
Psalms 105.16-17, 18-19, 20-21
Matthew 10.7-15

Fri, July 11
Genesis 46.1-7, 28-30
Psalms 37.3-4, 18-19, 27-28,
39-40
Matthew 10.16-23

Sat, July 12
Genesis 49.29-33; 50.15-24
Psalms 105.1-2, 3-4, 6-7
Matthew 10.24-33

WEEK 15

Sun, July 13
Amos 7.12-15
Psalms 85.9-10, 11-12, 13-14
Ephesians 1.3-14 or 1.3-10
Mark 6.7-13

Mon, July 14
Exodus 1.8-14, 22
Psalms 124.1-3, 4-6, 7-8
Matthew 10.34—11.1

Tue, July 15
Exodus 2.1-15
Psalms 69.3, 14, 30-31, 33-34
Matthew 11.20-24

Wed, July 16
Exodus 3.1-6, 9-12
Psalms 103.1-2, 3-4, 6-7
Matthew 11.25-27

Thu, July 17
Exodus 3.11-20
Psalms 105.5, 8-9, 24-25, 26-27
Matthew 11.28-30

Fri, July 18
Exodus 11.10—12.14
Psalms 116.12-13, 15-16, 17-18
Matthew 12.1-8

Sat, July 19
Exodus 12.37-42
Psalms 136.1, 23-24, 10-12, 13-15
Matthew 12.14-21

WEEK 16

Sun, July 20
Jeremiah 23.1-16
Psalms 23.1-3, 3-4, 5, 6
Ephesians 2.13-18
Mark 6.30-34

Mon, July 21
Exodus 14.5-18
Exodus 15.1-2, 3-4, 5-6
Matthew 12.38-42

Tue, July 22
*Saint Mary
Magdalene—
Memorial*
2 Corinthians 5.14-17
Psalms 63.2, 3-4, 5-6, 8-9
John 20.1-2, 11-18

Wed, July 23
Exodus 16.1-5, 9-15
Psalms 78.18-19, 23-24, 25-26,
27-28
Matthew 13.1-9

Thu, July 24
Exodus 19.1-2, 9-11, 16-20
Daniel 3.52, 53, 54, 55, 56
Matthew 13.10-17

Fri, July 25
*Saint James,
apostle—Feast*
2 Corinthians 4.7-15
Psalms 126.1-2, 2-3, 4-5, 6
Matthew 20.20-28

Sat, July 26
*Saints Joachim and
Ann, parents of
Mary—Memorial*
Sirach 44.1, 10-15
Psalms 132.11, 13-14, 17-18
Matthew 13.16-17

WEEK 17

Sun, July 27
2 Kings 4.42-44
Psalms 145.10-11, 15-16, 17-18
Ephesians 4.1-6
John 6.1-15

Mon, July 28
Exodus 32.15-24, 30-34
Psalms 106.19-20, 21-22, 23
Matthew 13.31-35

Tue, July 29
*Saint Martha—
Memorial*
Proverbs 31.10-13, 19-20, 30-31
Psalms 112.1-2, 3-4, 5-6, 7-8, 9
John 11.19-27

Wed, July 30
Exodus 34.29-35
Psalms 99.5, 6, 7, 9
Matthew 13.44-46

Thu, July 31
Exodus 40.16-21, 34-38
Psalms 84.3, 4, 5-6, 8, 11
Matthew 13.47-53

Fri, Aug 1
Leviticus 23.1, 4-11, 15-16, 27,
34-37
Psalms 81.3-4, 5-6, 10-11
Matthew 13.54-58

Sat, Aug 2
Leviticus 25.1, 8-17
Psalms 67.2-3, 5, 7-8
Matthew 14.1-12

WEEK 18

Sun, Aug 3
Exodus 16.2-4, 12-15
Psalms 78.3-4, 23-24, 25, 54
Ephesians 4.17, 20-24
John 6.24-35

Mon, Aug 4
Numbers 11.4-15
Psalms 81.12-13, 14-15, 16-17
Matthew 14.13-21

Tue, Aug 5
Numbers 12.1-13
Psalms 51.3-4, 5-6, 6-7, 12-13
Matthew 14.22-36

Wed, Aug 6
Transfiguration
of the Lord—
Feast
Daniel 7.9-10, 13-14
Psalms 97.1-2, 5-6, 9
2 Peter 1.16-19
Mark 9.2-10

Thu, Aug 7
Numbers 20.1-13
Psalms 95.1-2, 6-7, 8-9
Matthew 16.13-23

Fri, Aug 8
Deuteronomy 4.32-40
Psalms 77.12-13, 14-15, 16, 21
Matthew 16.24-28

Sat, Aug 9
Deuteronomy 6.4-13
Psalms 18.2-3, 3-4, 47, 51
Matthew 17.14-20

WEEK 19

Sun, Aug 10
1 Kings 19.4-8
Psalms 34.2-3, 4-5, 6-7, 8-9
Ephesians 4.30—5.2
John 6.41-51

Mon, Aug 11
Deuteronomy 10.12-22
Psalms 147.12-13, 14-15, 19-20
Matthew 17.22-27

Tue, Aug 12
Deuteronomy 31.1-8
Deuteronomy 32.3-4, 7, 8, 9, 12
Matthew 18.1-5, 10, 12-14

Wed, Aug 13
Deuteronomy 34.1-12
Psalms 66.1-3, 5, 8, 16-17
Matthew 18.15-20

Thu, Aug 14
Joshua 3.7-10, 11, 13-17
Psalms 114.1-2, 3-4, 5-6
Matthew 18.21—19.1

Fri, Aug 15
Assumption of the
Virgin Mary into
Heaven—Solemnity
Revelation 11.19; 12.1-6, 10
Psalms 45.10, 11, 12, 16
1 Corinthians 15.20-26
Luke 1.39-56

Sat, Aug 16
Joshua 24.14-29
Psalms 16.1-2, 5, 7-8, 11
Matthew 19.13-15

WEEK 20

Sun, Aug 17
Proverbs 9.1-6
Psalms 34.2-3, 10-11, 12-13, 14-15
Ephesians 5.15-20
John 6.51-58

Mon, Aug 18
Judges 2.11-19
Psalms 106.34-35, 36-37, 39-40,
43, 44
Matthew 19.16-22

Tue, Aug 19
Judges 6.11-24
Psalms 85.9, 11-12, 13-14
Matthew 19.23-30

Wed, Aug 20
Judges 9.6-15
Psalms 21.2-3, 4-5, 6-7
Matthew 20.1-16

Thu, Aug 21
Judges 11.29-39
Psalms 40.5, 7-8, 8-9, 10
Matthew 22.1-14

Fri, Aug 22
Ruth 1.1, 3-6, 14-16, 22
Psalms 146.5-6, 7, 8-9, 9-10
Matthew 22.34-40

Sat, Aug 23
Ruth 2.1-3, 8-11; 4.13-17
Psalms 128.1-2, 3, 4, 5
Matthew 23.1-12

WEEK 21

Sun, Aug 24
Joshua 24.1-2, 15-17, 18
Psalms 34.2-3, 16-17, 18-19,
20-21, 22-23
Ephesians 5.21-32
John 6.60-69

Mon, Aug 25
1 Thessalonians 1.2-5, 8-10
Psalms 149.1-2, 3-4, 5-6, 9
Matthew 23.13-22

Tue, Aug 26
1 Thessalonians 2.1-8
Psalms 139.1-3, 4-5
Matthew 23.23-26

Wed, Aug 27
1 Thessalonians 2.9-13
Psalms 139.7-8, 9-10, 11-12
Matthew 23.27-32

Thu, Aug 28
1 Thessalonians 3.7-13
Psalms 90.3-4, 12-13, 14, 17
Matthew 24.42-51

Fri, Aug 29
Beheading of
Saint John the Baptist,
martyr—Memorial
Jeremiah 1.17-19
Psalms 71.1-2, 3-4, 5-6, 15, 17
Mark 6.17-29

Sat, Aug 30
1 Thessalonians 4.9-12
Psalms 98.1, 7-8, 9
Matthew 25.14-30

WEEK 22

Sun, Aug 31

Deuteronomy 4.1-2, 6-8
Psalms 15.2-3, 3-4, 4-5
James 1.17-18, 21-22, 27
Mark 7.1-8, 14-15, 21-23

Mon, Sept 1

I Thessalonians 4.13-18
Psalms 96.1, 3, 4-5, 11-12, 13
Luke 4.16-30

Tue, Sept 2

I Thessalonians 5.1-6, 9-11
Psalms 27.1, 4, 13-14
Luke 4.31-37

Wed, Sept 3

Colossians 1.1-8
Psalms 52.10, 11
Luke 4.38-44

Thu, Sept 4

Colossians 1.9-14
Psalms 98.2-3, 3-4, 5-6
Luke 5.1-11

Fri, Sept 5

Colossians 1.15-20
Psalms 100.1, 2, 3, 4, 5
Luke 5.33-39

Sat, Sept 6

Colossians 1.21-23
Psalms 54.3-4, 6, 8
Luke 6.1-5

WEEK 23

Sun, Sept 7

Isaiah 35.4-7
Psalms 146.7, 8-9, 9-10
James 2.1-5
Mark 7.31-37

Mon, Sept 8
Birth of the
Virgin Mary—Feast

Micah 5.1-4
Psalms 13.6
Matthew 1.1-16, 18-23
or 1.18-23

Tue, Sept 9

Colossians 2.6-15
Psalms 145.1-2, 8-9, 10-11
Luke 6.12-19

Wed, Sept 10

Colossians 3.1-11
Psalms 145.2-3, 10-11, 12-13
Luke 6.20-26

Thu, Sept 11

Colossians 3.12-17
Psalms 150.1-2, 3-4, 5-6
Luke 6.27-38

Fri, Sept 12

I Timothy 1.1-2, 12-14
Psalms 16.1-2, 5, 7-8, 11
Luke 6.39-42

Sat, Sept 13

I Timothy 1.15-17
Psalms 113.1-2, 3-4, 5, 6-7
Luke 6.43-49

WEEK 24

Sun, Sept 14
Triumph of the
Holy Cross—
Feast

Numbers 21.4-9
Psalms 78.1-2, 34-35, 36-37, 38
Philippians 2.6-11
John 3.13-17

Mon, Sept 15
Our Lady of Sorrows—
Memorial

Hebrews 5.7-9
Psalms 31.2-3, 3-4, 5-6, 15-16, 20
John 19.25-27

Tue, Sept 16

I Timothy 3.1-13
Psalms 101.1-2, 2-3, 5, 6
Luke 7.11-17

Wed, Sept 17

I Timothy 3.14-16
Psalms 111.1-2, 3-4, 5-6
Luke 7.31-35

Thu, Sept 18

I Timothy 4.12-16
Psalms 111.7-8, 9, 10
Luke 7.36-50

Fri, Sept 19

I Timothy 6.2-12
Psalms 49.6-7, 8-10, 17-18, 19-20
Luke 8.1-3

Sat, Sept 20

I Timothy 6.13-16
Psalms 100.2, 3, 4, 5
Luke 8.4-15

WEEK 25

Sun, Sept 21

Wisdom 2.17-20
Psalms 54.3-4, 5, 6-8
James 3.16—4.3
Mark 9.30-37

Mon, Sept 22

Ezra 1.1-6
Psalms 126.1-2, 2-3, 4-5, 6
Luke 8.16-18

Tue, Sept 23

Ezra 6.7-8, 12, 14-20
Psalms 122.1-2, 3-4, 4-5
Luke 8.19-21

Wed, Sept 24

Ezra 9.5-9
Tobit 13.2, 3-4, 6, 7-8, 6
Luke 9.1-6

Thu, Sept 25

Haggai 1.1-8
Psalms 149.1-2, 3-4, 5-6, 9
Luke 9.7-9

Fri, Sept 26

Haggai 1.15—2.9
Psalms 43.1, 2, 3, 4
Luke 9.18-22

Sat, Sept 27

Zechariah 2.5-9, 14-15
Jeremiah 31.10, 11-12, 13
Luke 9.43-45

WEEK 26

Sun, Sept 28 Numbers 11.25-29
Psalms 19.8, 10, 12-13, 14
James 5.1-6
Mark 9.38-43, 45, 47-48

Mon, Sept 29 Revelation 12.7-12
Michael, Gabriel, and Psalms 138.1-2, 2-3, 4-5
Raphael, archangels— John 1.47-51
Feast

Tue, Sept 30 Zechariah 8.20-23
Psalms 87.1-3, 4-5, 6-7
Luke 9.51-56

Wed, Oct 1 Nehemiah 2.1-8
Psalms 137.1-2, 3, 4-5, 6
Luke 9.57-62

Thu, Oct 2 Exodus 23.20-23
Guardian Angels— Psalms 91.1-2, 3-4, 5-6, 10-11
Memorial Matthew 18.1-5, 10

Fri, Oct 3 Baruch 1.15-22
Psalms 79.1-2, 3-5, 8, 9
Luke 10.13-16

Sat, Oct 4 Baruch 4.5-12, 27-29
Psalms 69.33-35, 36-37
Luke 10.17-24

WEEK 27

Sun, Oct 5 Genesis 2.18-24
Psalms 128.1-2, 3, 4-5, 6
Hebrews 2.9-11
Mark 10.2-16

Mon, Oct 6 Jonah 1.1—2.1, 11
Psalms 2.2, 3, 4, 5, 8
Luke 10.25-37

Tue, Oct 7 Jonah 3.1-10
Psalms 130.1-2, 3-4, 7-8
Luke 10.38-42

Wed, Oct 8 Jonah 4.1-11
Psalms 86.3-4, 5-6, 9-10
Luke 11.1-4

Thu, Oct 9 Malachi 3.13-20
Psalms 1.1-2, 3, 4, 6
Luke 11.5-13

Fri, Oct 10 Joel 1.13-15; 2.1-2
Psalms 9.2-3, 6, 16, 8-9
Luke 11.15-26

Sat, Oct 11 Joel 4.12-21
Psalms 97.1-2, 5-6, 11-12
Luke 11.27-28

WEEK 28

Sun, Oct 12 Wisdom 7.7-11
Psalms 90.12-13, 14-15, 16-17
Hebrews 4.12-13
Mark 10.17-30

Mon, Oct 13 Romans 1.1-7
Psalms 98.1, 2-3, 3-4
Luke 11.29-32

Tue, Oct 14 Romans 1.16-25
Psalms 19.2-3, 4-5
Luke 11.37-41

Wed, Oct 15 Romans 2.1-11
Psalms 62.2-3, 6-7, 9
Luke 11.42-46

Thu, Oct 16 Romans 3.21-29
Psalms 130.1-2, 3-4, 5-6
Luke 11.47-54

Fri, Oct 17 Romans 4.1-8
Psalms 32.1-2, 5, 11
Luke 12.1-7

Sat, Oct 18 2 Timothy 4.9-17
Saint Luke, Psalms 145.10-11, 12-13, 17-18
evangelist—Feast Luke 10.1-9

WEEK 29

Sun, Oct 19 Isaiah 53.10-11
Psalms 33.4-5, 18-19, 20, 22
Hebrews 4.14-16
Mark 10.35-45

Mon, Oct 20 Romans 4.20-25
Luke 1.69-70, 71-72, 73-75
Luke 12.13-21

Tue, Oct 21 Romans 5.12, 15, 17-19, 20-21
Psalms 40.7-8, 8-9, 10, 17
Luke 12.35-38

Wed, Oct 22 Romans 6.12-18
Psalms 124.1-3, 4-6, 7-8
Luke 12.39-48

Thu, Oct 23 Romans 6.19-23
Psalms 1.1-2, 3, 4, 6
Luke 12.49-53

Fri, Oct 24 Romans 7.18-25
Psalms 119.66, 68, 76, 77, 93, 94
Luke 12.54-59

Sat, Oct 25 Romans 8.1-11
Psalms 24.1-2, 3-4, 5-6
Luke 13.1-9

WEEK 30

Sun, Oct 26	Jeremiah 31.7-9
	Psalms 126.1-2, 2-3, 4-5, 6
	Hebrews 5.1-6
	Mark 10.46-52
Mon, Oct 27	Romans 8.12-17
	Psalms 68.2, 4, 6-7, 20-21
	Luke 13.10-17
Tue, Oct 28	Ephesians 2.19-22
Saints Simon and	Psalms 19.2-3, 4-5
Jude, apostles—Feast	Luke 6.12-16
Wed, Oct 29	Romans 8.26-30
	Psalms 13.4-5, 6
	Luke 13.22-30
Thu, Oct 30	Romans 8.31-39
	Psalms 109.21-22, 26-27, 30-31
	Luke 13.31-35
Fri, Oct 31	Romans 9.1-5
	Psalms 147.12-13, 14-15, 19-20
	Luke 14.1-6
Sat, Nov 1	Revelation 7.2-4, 9-14
	Psalms 24.1-2, 3-4, 5-6
	1 John 3.1-3
	Matthew 5.1-12

WEEK 31

Sun, Nov 2	Isaiah 25.6, 7-9
Commemoration	Psalms 103.8, 10, 13-14, 15-16,
of All the Faithful	17-18
Departed (All Souls)	1 Corinthians 15.20-24, 25-28
—Solemnity	John 11.17-27
Mon, Nov 3	Romans 11.29-36
	Psalms 69.30-31, 33-34, 36-37
	Luke 14.12-14
Tue, Nov 4	Romans 12.5-16
	Psalms 131.1, 2, 3
	Luke 14.15-24
Wed, Nov 5	Romans 13.8-10
	Psalms 112.1-2, 4-5, 9
	Luke 14.25-33
Thu, Nov 6	Romans 14.7-12
	Psalms 27.1-4, 13-14
	Luke 15.1-10
Fri, Nov 7	Romans 15.14-21
	Psalms 98.1, 2-3, 3-4
	Luke 16.1-8
Sat, Nov 8	Romans 16.3-9, 16, 22-27
	Psalms 145.2-3, 4-5, 10-11
	Luke 16.9-15

WEEK 32

Sun, Nov 9	Genesis 28.11-18
Dedication of the	Psalms 84.3, 4, 5-6, 8, 11
Basilica of St. John	1 Corinthians 3.9-13, 16-17
Lateran in Rome—	Luke 19.1-10
Feast	
Mon, Nov 10	Wisdom 1.1-7
	Psalms 139.1-3, 4-6, 7-8, 9-10
	Luke 17.1-6
Tue, Nov 11	Wisdom 2.23—3.9
	Psalms 34.2-3, 16-17, 18-19
	Luke 17.7-10
Wed, Nov 12	Wisdom 6.2-11
	Psalms 82.3-4, 6-7
	Luke 17.11-19
Thu, Nov 13	Wisdom 7.22—8.1
	Psalms 119.89, 90, 91, 130,
	135, 175
	Luke 17.20-25
Fri, Nov 14	Wisdom 13.1-9
	Psalms 19.2-3, 4-5
	Luke 17.26-37
Sat, Nov 15	Wisdom 18.14-16; 19.6-9
	Psalms 105.2-3, 36-37, 42-43
	Luke 18.1-8

WEEK 33

Sun, Nov 16	Daniel 12.1-3
	Psalms 16.5, 8, 9-10, 11
	Hebrews 10.11-14, 18
	Mark 13.24-32
Mon, Nov 17	1 Maccabees 1.10-15, 41-43,
	54-57, 62-63
	Psalms 119.53, 61, 134, 150,
	155, 158
	Luke 18.35-43
Tue, Nov 18	2 Maccabees 6.18-31
	Psalms 3.2-3, 4-5, 6-8
	Luke 19.1-10
Wed, Nov 19	2 Maccabees 7.1, 20-31
	Psalms 17.1, 5-6, 8, 15
	Luke 19.11-28
Thu, Nov 20	1 Maccabees 2.15-29
	Psalms 50.1-2, 5-6, 14-15
	Luke 9.41-44
Fri, Nov 21	1 Maccabees 4.36-37, 52-59
Presentation of the	1 Chronicles 29.10, 11, 11-12, 12
Virgin Mary—	Luke 19.45-48
Memorial	
Sat, Nov 22	1 Maccabees 6.1-13
	Psalms 9.2-3, 4, 6, 16, 19
	Luke 20.27-40

WEEK 34

Sun, Nov 23
Christ the King—
Solemnity

Daniel 7.13-14
Psalms 93.1, 1-2, 5
Revelation 1.5-8
John 18.33-37

Mon, Nov 24

Daniel 1.1-6, 8-20
Daniel 3.52, 53, 54, 55, 56
Luke 21.1-4

Tue, Nov 25

Daniel 2.31-45
Daniel 3.57, 58, 59, 60, 61
Luke 21.5-11

Wed, Nov 26

Daniel 5.1-6, 13-14, 16-17, 23-28
Daniel 3.62, 63, 64, 65, 66, 67
Luke 21.12-19

Thu, Nov 27

Daniel 6.12-28
Daniel 3.68, 69, 70, 71, 72, 73, 74
Luke 21.20-28

Fri, Nov 28

Daniel 7.2-14
Daniel 3.75, 76, 77, 78, 79, 80, 81
Luke 21.29-33

Sat, Nov 29

Daniel 7.15-27
Daniel 3.82, 83, 84, 85, 86, 87
Luke 21.34-36

Advent, Liturgical year 2004

WEEK I, ADVENT

Sun, Nov 30, 2003

Jeremiah 33.14-16
Psalms 25.4-5, 8-9, 10, 14
1 Thessalonians 3.12—4.2
Luke 21.25-28, 34-36

Mon, Dec I

Isaiah 2.1-5
Psalms 122.1-2, 3-4, 4-5, 6-7, 8-9
Matthew 8.5-11

Tue, Dec 2

Isaiah 11.1-10
Psalms 72.1, 7-8, 12-13, 17
Luke 10.21-24

Wed, Dec 3

Isaiah 25.6-10
Psalms 23.1-3, 3-4, 5, 6
Matthew 15.29-37

Thu, Dec 4

Isaiah 26.1-6
Psalms 118.1, 8-9, 19-21, 25-27
Matthew 7.21, 24-27

Fri, Dec 5

Isaiah 29.17-24
Psalms 27.1, 4, 13-14
Matthew 9.27-31

Sat, Dec 6

Isaiah 30.19-21, 23-26
Psalms 147.1-2, 3-4, 5-6
Matthew 9.35—10.1, 6-8

WEEK 2, ADVENT

Sun, Dec 7

Baruch 5.1-9
Psalms 126.1-2, 2-3, 4-5, 6
Philippians 1.4-6, 8-11
Luke 3.1-6

Mon, Dec 8
Immaculate
Conception of the
Virgin Mary—
Solemnity

Genesis 3.9-15, 20
Psalms 98.1, 2-3, 3-4
Ephesians 1.3-6, 11-12
Luke 1.26-38

Tue, Dec 9

Isaiah 40.1-11
Psalms 96.1-2, 3, 10, 11-12, 13
Matthew 18.12-14

Wed, Dec 10

Isaiah 40.25-31
Psalms 103.1-2, 3-4, 8, 10
Matthew 11.28-30

Thu, Dec II

Isaiah 41.13-20
Psalms 145.1, 9, 10-11, 12-13
Matthew 11.11-15

Fri, Dec 12
Our Lady of
Guadalupe—
Feast

Zechariah 2.14-17
Psalms 45.11-12, 14-17
Romans 8.28-30
Luke 2.15-19

Sat, Dec 13

Sirach 48.1-4, 9-11
Psalms 80.2-3, 15-16, 18-19
Matthew 17.10-13

WEEK 3, ADVENT

Sun, Dec 14

Zephaniah 3.14-18
Isaiah 12.2-3, 4, 5-6
Philippians 4.4-7
Luke 3.10-18

Mon, Dec 15

Numbers 24.2-7, 15-17
Psalms 25.4-5, 6-7, 8-9
Matthew 21.23-27

Tue, Dec 16

Zephaniah 3.1-2, 9-13
Psalms 34.2-3, 6-7, 17-18, 19, 23
Matthew 21.28-32

Wed, Dec 17

Genesis 49.2, 8-10
Psalms 72.3-4, 7-8, 17
Matthew 1.1-17

Thu, Dec 18

Jeremiah 23.5-8
Psalms 72.1, 12-13, 18-19
Matthew 1.18-24

Fri, Dec 19

Judges 13.2-7, 24-25
Psalms 71.3-4, 5-6, 16-17
Luke 1.5-25

Sat, Dec 20

Isaiah 7.10-14
Psalms 24.1-2, 3-4, 5-6
Luke 1.26-38

WEEK 4, ADVENT

Sun, Dec 21
Micah 5.1-4
Psalms 80.2-3, 15-16, 18-19
Hebrews 10.5-10
Luke 1.39-45

Mon, Dec 22
I Samuel 1.24-28
I Samuel 2.1, 4-5, 6-7, 8
Luke 1.46-56

Tue, Dec 23
Malachi 3.1-4, 23-24
Psalms 25.4-5, 8-9, 10, 14
Luke 1.57-66

Wed, Dec 24
2 Samuel 7.1-5, 8-11, 16
Psalms 89.2-3, 4-5, 27, 29
Luke 1.67-79

Christmas

Thu, Dec 25
Christmas—
Solemnity
Isaiah 52.7-10
Psalms 98.1, 2-3, 3-4, 5-6
Hebrews 1.1-6
John 1.1-18
    or 1.1-5, 9-14

Fri, Dec 26
Saint Stephen, first
martyr—Feast
Acts 6.8-10; 7.54-59
Psalms 31.3-4, 6, 7, 8, 17, 21
Matthew 10.17-22

Sat, Dec 27
Saint John, apostle
and evangelist—
Feast
I John 1.1-4
Psalms 97.1-2, 5-6, 11-12
John 20.2-8

Sun, Dec 28
The Holy Family—
Feast
Sirach 3.2-6, 12-14
Psalms 128.1-2, 3, 4-5
Colossians 3.12-21
Luke 2.41-52

Mon, Dec 29
I John 2.3-11
Psalms 96.1-2, 2-3, 5-6
Luke 2.22-35

Tue, Dec 30
I John 2.12-17
Psalms 96.7-8, 8-9, 10
Luke 2.36-40

Wed, Dec 31
I John 2.18-21
Psalms 96.1-2, 11-12, 13
John 1.1-18

Thu, Jan 1, 2004
Mary, Mother of God—
Solemnity
Numbers 6.22-27
Psalms 67.2-3, 5, 6, 8
Galatians 4.4-7
Luke 2.16-21

Fri, Jan 2
I John 2.22-28
Psalms 98.1, 2-3, 3-4
John 1.19-28

Sat, Jan 3
I John 2.29—3.6
Psalms 98.1, 3-4, 5-6
John 1.29-34

Sun, Jan 4
Epiphany
of the Lord—
Solemnity
Isaiah 60.1-6
Psalms 72.1-2, 7-8, 10-11, 12-13
Ephesians 3.2-3, 5-6
Matthew 2.1-12

Mon, Jan 5
I John 3.22—4.6
Psalms 2.7-8, 10-11
Matthew 4.12-17, 23-25

Tue, Jan 6
I John 4.7-10
Psalms 72.1-2, 3-4, 7-8
Mark 6.34-44

Wed, Jan 7
I John 3.22—4.6
Psalms 2.7-8, 10-11
Matthew 4.12-17, 23-25

Thu, Jan 8
I John 4.7-10
Psalms 72.1-2, 3-4, 7-8
Mark 6.34-44

Fri, Jan 9
I John 4.11-18
Psalms 72.1-2, 10, 12-13
Mark 6.45-52

Sat, Jan 10
I John 4.19—5.4
Psalms 72.1-2, 14-15, 17
Luke 4.14-22

Ordinary Time

WEEK 1

Sun, Jan 11
Baptism of the Lord—
Feast
Isaiah 42.1-4, 6-7
Psalms 29.1-2, 3-4, 3, 9-10
Acts 10.34-38
Luke 3.15-16, 21-22

Mon, Jan 12
I Samuel 1.1-8
Psalms 116.12-13, 14-17, 18-19
Mark 1.14-20

Tue, Jan 13
I Samuel 1.9-20
I Samuel 2.1, 4-5, 6-7, 8
Mark 1.21-28

Wed, Jan 14
I Samuel 3.1-10, 19-20
Psalms 40.2-5, 7-8, 8-9, 10
Mark 1.29-39

Thu, Jan 15
I Samuel 4.1-11
Psalms 44.10-11, 14-15, 25-26
Mark 1.40-45

Fri, Jan 16
I Samuel 8.4-7, 10-22
Psalms 89.16-17, 18-19
Mark 2.1-12

Sat, Jan 17
I Samuel 9.1-4, 17-19; 10.1
Psalms 21.2-3, 4-5, 6-7
Mark 2.13-17

WEEK 2

Sun, Jan 18
Isaiah 62.1-5
Psalms 96.1-2, 2-3, 7-8, 9-10
I Corinthians 12.4-11
John 2.1-12

Mon, Jan 19
I Samuel 15.16-23
Psalms 50.8-9, 16-17, 21, 23
Mark 2.18-22

Tue, Jan 20
I Samuel 16.1-13
Psalms 89.20, 21-22, 27-28
Mark 2.23-28

Wed, Jan 21
I Samuel 17.32-33, 37, 40-51
Psalms 144.1, 2, 9-10
Mark 3.1-6

Thu, Jan 22
I Samuel 18.6-9; 19.1-7
Psalms 56.2-3, 9-10, 10-12, 13-14
Mark 3.7-12

Fri, Jan 23
I Samuel 24.3-21
Psalms 57.2, 3-4, 6, 11
Mark 3.13-19

Sat, Jan 24
2 Samuel 1.1-4, 11-12, 19, 23-27
Psalms 80.2-3, 5-7
Mark 3.20-21

WEEK 3

Sun, Jan 25
Nehemiah 8.2-4, 5-6, 8-10
Psalms 19.8, 9, 10, 15
I Corinthians 12.12-30
Luke 1.1-4; 4.14-21

Mon, Jan 26
2 Samuel 5.1-7, 10
Psalms 89.20, 21-22, 25-26
Mark 3.22-30

Tue, Jan 27
2 Samuel 6.12-15, 17-19
Psalms 24.7, 8, 9, 10
Mark 3.31-35

Wed, Jan 28
2 Samuel 7.4-17
Psalms 89.4-5, 27-28, 29-30
Mark 4.1-20

Thu, Jan 29
2 Samuel 7.18-19, 24-29
Psalms 132.1-2, 3-5, 11, 12, 13-14
Mark 4.21-25

Fri, Jan 30
2 Samuel 11.1-4, 5-10, 13-17
Psalms 51.3-4, 5-6, 6-7, 10-11
Mark 4.26-34

Sat, Jan 31
2 Samuel 12.1-7, 10-17
Psalms 51.12-13, 14-15, 16-17
Mark 4.35-41

WEEK 4

Sun, Feb 1
Jeremiah 1.4-5, 17-19
Psalms 71.1-2, 3-4, 5-6, 15-17
I Corinthians 12.31—13.13
Luke 4.21-30

Mon, Feb 2
Presentation
of the Lord—
Feast
Malachi 3.1-4
Psalms 24.7, 8, 9, 10
Hebrews 2.14-18
Luke 2.22-40
  or 2.22-32

Tue, Feb 3
2 Samuel 18.9-10, 14, 24-25,
  30—19.3
Psalms 86.1-2, 3-4, 5-6
Mark 5.21-43

Wed, Feb 4
2 Samuel 24.2, 9-17
Psalms 32.1-2, 5, 6, 7
Mark 6.1-6

Thu, Feb 5
I Kings 2.1-4, 10-12
I Chronicles 29.10, 11, 11-12, 12
Mark 6.7-13

Fri, Feb 6
Sirach 47.2-11
Psalms 18.31, 47, 50, 51
Mark 6.14-29

Sat, Feb 7
I Kings 3.4-13
Psalms 119.9, 10, 11, 12, 13, 14
Mark 6.30-34

WEEK 5

Sun, Feb 8
Isaiah 6.1-2, 3-8
Psalms 138.1-2, 2-3, 4-5, 7-8
I Corinthians 15.1-11
  or 15.3-8, 11
Luke 5.1-11

Mon, Feb 9
I Kings 8.1-7, 9-13
Psalms 132.6-7, 8-10
Mark 6.53-56

Tue, Feb 10
I Kings 8.22-23, 27-30
Psalms 84.3, 4, 5, 10, 11
Mark 7.1-13

Wed, Feb 11
I Kings 10.1-10
Psalms 37.5-6, 30-31, 39-40
Mark 7.14-23

Thu, Feb 12
I Kings 11.4-13
Psalms 106.3-4, 35-36, 37, 40
Mark 7.24-30

Fri, Feb 13
I Kings 11.29-32; 12.19
Psalms 81.10-11, 12-13, 14-15
Mark 7.31-37

Sat, Feb 14
I Kings 12.26-32; 13.33-34
Psalms 106.6-7, 19-20, 21-22
Mark 8.1-10

WEEK 6

Sun, Feb 15
Jeremiah 17.5-8
Psalms 1.1-2, 3, 4, 6
1 Corinthians 15.12, 16-20
Luke 6.17, 20-26

Mon, Feb 16
James 1.1-11
Psalms 119.67, 68, 71, 72, 75, 76
Mark 8.11-13

Tue, Feb 17
James 1.12-18
Psalms 94.12-13, 14-15, 18-19
Mark 8.14-21

Wed, Feb 18
James 1.19-27
Psalms 15.2-3, 3-4, 5
Mark 8.22-26

Thu, Feb 19
James 2.1-9
Psalms 34.2-3, 4-5, 6-7
Mark 8.27-33

Fri, Feb 20
James 2.14-24, 26
Psalms 112.1-2, 3-4, 5-6
Mark 8.34—9.1

Sat, Feb 21
James 3.1-10
Psalms 12.2-3, 4-5, 7-8
Mark 9.2-13

WEEK 7

Sun, Feb 22
1 Samuel 26.2, 7-9, 12-13, 22-23
Psalms 103.1-2, 3-4, 8, 10, 12-13
1 Corinthians 15.45-49
Luke 6.27-38

Mon, Feb 23
James 3.13-18
Psalms 19.8, 9, 10, 15
Mark 9.14-29

Tue, Feb 24
James 4.1-10
Psalms 55.7-8, 9-10, 10-11, 23
Mark 9.30-37

Lent

Wed, Feb 25
Ash Wednesday
Joel 2.12-18
Psalms 51.3-4, 5-6, 12-13, 14, 17
2 Corinthians 5.20—6.2
Matthew 6.1-6, 16-18

Thu, Feb 26
Deuteronomy 30.15-20
Psalms 1.1-2, 3, 4, 6
Luke 9.22-25

Fri, Feb 27
Isaiah 58.1-9
Psalms 51.3-4, 5-6, 18-19
Matthew 9.14-15

Sat, Feb 28
Isaiah 58.9-14
Psalms 86.1-2, 3-4, 5-6
Luke 5.27-32

WEEK 1, LENT

Sun, Feb 29
Deuteronomy 26.4-10
Psalms 91.1-2, 10-11, 12-13, 14-15
Romans 10.8-13
Luke 4.1-13

Mon, Mar 1
Leviticus 19.1-2, 11-18
Psalms 19.8, 9, 10, 15
Matthew 25.31-46

Tue, Mar 2
Isaiah 55.10-11
Psalms 34.4-5, 6-7, 16-17, 18-19
Matthew 6.7-15

Wed, Mar 3
Jonah 3.1-10
Psalms 51.3-4, 12-13, 18-19
Luke 11.29-32

Thu, Mar 4
Esther C.12, 14-16, 23-25
Psalms 138.1-2, 2-3, 7-8
Matthew 7.7-12

Fri, Mar 5
Ezekiel 18.21-28
Psalms 130.1-2, 3-4, 5-6, 7-8
Matthew 5.20-26

Sat, Mar 6
Deuteronomy 26.16-19
Psalms 119.1-2, 4-5, 7-8
Matthew 5.43-48

WEEK 2, LENT

Sun, Mar 7
Genesis 15.5-12, 17-18
Psalms 27.1, 7-8, 8-9, 13-14
Philippians 3.17—4.1
Luke 9.28-36

Mon, Mar 8
Daniel 9.4-10
Psalms 79.8, 9, 11, 13
Luke 6.36-38

Tue, Mar 9
Isaiah 1.10, 16-20
Psalms 50.8-9, 16-17, 21, 23
Matthew 23.1-12

Wed, Mar 10
Jeremiah 18.18-20
Psalms 31.5-6, 14, 15-16
Matthew 20.17-28

Thu, Mar 11
Jeremiah 17.5-10
Psalms 1.1-2, 3, 4, 6
Luke 16.19-31

Fri, Mar 12
Genesis 37.3-4, 12-13, 17-18
Psalms 105.16-17, 18-19, 20-21
Matthew 21.33-43, 45-46

Sat, Mar 13
Micah 7.14-15, 18-20
Psalms 103.1-2, 3-4, 9-10, 11-12
Luke 15.1-3, 11-32

WEEK 3, LENT

Sun, Mar 14
Exodus 3.1-8, 13-15
Psalms 103.1-2, 3-4, 6-7, 8, 11
I Corinthians 10.1-6, 10-12
Luke 13.1-9

Mon, Mar 15
2 Kings 5.1-15
Psalms 42.2, 3; 43.3, 4
Luke 4.24-30

Tue, Mar 16
Daniel 3.25, 34-43
Psalms 25.4-5, 6-7, 8-9
Matthew 18.21-35

Wed, Mar 17
Deuteronomy 4.1, 5-9
Psalms 147.12-13, 15-16, 19-20
Matthew 5.17-19

Thu, Mar 18
Jeremiah 7.23-28
Psalms 95.1-2, 6-7, 8-9
Luke 11.14-23

Fri, Mar 19
Saint Joseph, Husband
of Mary—Solemnity
2 Samuel 7.4-5, 12-14, 16
Psalms 89.2-3, 4-5, 27, 29
Romans 4.13, 16-18, 22
Matthew 1.16, 18-21, 24,
or Luke 2.41-51

Sat, Mar 20
Hosea 6.1-6
Psalms 51.3-4, 18-19, 20-21
Luke 18.9-14

WEEK 4, LENT

Sun, Mar 21
Joshua 5.9, 10-12
Psalms 34.2-3, 4-5, 6-7
2 Corinthians 5.17-21
Luke 15.1-3, 11-32

Mon, Mar 22
Isaiah 65.17-21
Psalms 30.2, 4, 5-6, 11-13
John 4.43-54

Tue, Mar 23
Ezekiel 47.1-9, 12
Psalms 46.2-3, 5-6, 8-9
John 5.1-3, 5-16

Wed, Mar 24
Isaiah 49.8-15
Psalms 145.8-9, 13-14, 17-18
John 5.17-30

Thu, Mar 25
Annunciation
of the Lord—
Solemnity
Isaiah 7.10-14
Psalms 40.7-8, 8-9, 10, 11
Hebrews 10.4-10
Luke 1.26-38

Fri, Mar 26
Wisdom 2.1, 12-22
Psalms 34.17-18, 19-20, 21, 23
John 7.1-2, 10, 25-30

Sat, Mar 27
Jeremiah 11.18-20
Psalms 7.2-3, 9-10, 11-12
John 7.40-53

WEEK 5, LENT

Sun, Mar 28
Isaiah 43.16-21
Psalms 126.1-2, 2-3, 4-5, 6
Philippians 3.8-14
John 8.1-11

Mon, Mar 29
Daniel 13.1-9, 15-17, 19-30, 33-62
Psalms 23.1-3, 3-4, 5, 6
John 8.12-20

Tue, Mar 30
Numbers 21.4-9
Psalms 102.2-3, 16-18, 19-21
John 8.21-30

Wed, Mar 31
Daniel 3.14-20, 91-92, 95
Daniel 3.52, 53, 54, 55, 56
John 8.31-42

Thu, Apr 1
Genesis 17.3-9
Psalms 105.4-5, 6-7, 8-9
John 8.51-59

Fri, Apr 2
Jeremiah 20.10-13
Psalms 18.2-3, 3-4, 5-6, 7
John 10.31-42

Sat, Apr 3
Ezekiel 37.21-28
Jeremiah 31.10, 11-12, 13
John 11.45-57

HOLY WEEK

Sun, Apr 4
Passion
(Palm)
Sunday
Isaiah 50.4-7
Psalms 22.8-9, 17-18, 19-20,
23-24
Philippians 2.6-11
Luke 22.14—23.56
or 23.1-49

Mon, Apr 5
Isaiah 42.1-7
Psalms 27.1, 2, 3, 13-14
John 12.1-11

Tue, Apr 6
Isaiah 49.1-6
Psalms 71.1-2, 3-4, 5-6, 15, 17
John 13.21-33, 36-38

Wed, Apr 7
Isaiah 50.4-9
Psalms 69.8-10, 21-22, 31, 33-34
Matthew 26.14-25

Thu, Apr 8
Holy Thursday
Exodus 12.1-8, 11-14
Psalms 116.12-13, 15-16, 17-18
I Corinthians 11.23-26
John 13.1-15

Fri, Apr 9
Good Friday
Isaiah 52.13—53.12
Psalms 31.2, 6, 12-13, 15-16, 17, 25
Hebrews 4.14-16; 5.7-9
John 18.1—19.42

Sat, Apr 10
Holy Saturday
Genesis 1.1—2.2
Psalms 104.1-2, 5-6, 10, 12, 13-14,
24, 35
Genesis 22.1-18
or 22.1-2, 9, 10-13, 15-18

Sat, Apr 10
Holy Saturday

Psalms 16.5, 8, 9-10, 11
Exodus 14.15—15.1
Exodus 15.1-2, 3-4, 5-6, 17-18
Isaiah 54.5-14
Psalms 30.2, 4, 5-6, 11-12, 13
Isaiah 55.1-11
Isaiah 12.2-3, 4, 5-6
Baruch 3.9-15, 32—4.4
Psalms 19.8, 9, 10, 11
Ezekiel 36.16-28
Psalms 42.3, 5; 43.3, 4
Romans 6.3-11
Psalms 118.1-2, 16, 17, 22-23
Luke 24.1-12

Easter

WEEK 1, EASTER

Sun, Apr 11
Easter Sunday

Acts 10.34, 37-43
Psalms 118.1-2, 16-17, 22-23
1 Corinthians 5.6-8
John 20.1-9

Mon, Apr 12

Acts 2.14, 22-32
Psalms 16.1-2, 5, 7-8, 9-10, 11
Matthew 28.8-15

Tue, Apr 13

Acts 2.36-41
Psalms 33.4-5, 18-19, 20, 22
John 20.11-18

Wed, Apr 14

Acts 3.1-10
Psalms 105.1-2, 3-4, 6-7, 8-9
Luke 24.13-35

Thu, Apr 15

Acts 3.11-26
Psalms 8.2, 5, 6-7, 8-9
Luke 24.35-48

Fri, Apr 16

Acts 4.1-12
Psalms 118.1-2, 4, 22-24, 25-27
John 21.1-14

Sat, Apr 17

Acts 4.13-21
Psalms 118.1, 14-15, 16-18, 19-21
Mark 16.9-15

WEEK 2, EASTER

Sun, Apr 18

Acts 5.12-16
Psalms 118.2-4, 13-15, 22-24
Revelation 1.9-11, 12-13, 17-19
John 20.19-31

Mon, Apr 19

Acts 4.23-31
Psalms 2.1-3, 4-6, 7-9
John 3.1-8

Tue, Apr 20

Acts 4.32-37
Psalms 93.1, 1-2, 5
John 3.7-15

Wed, Apr 21

Acts 5.17-26
Psalms 34.2-3, 4-5, 6-7, 8-9
John 3.16-21

Thu, Apr 22

Acts 5.27-33
Psalms 34.2, 9, 17-18, 19-20
John 3.31-36

Fri, Apr 23

Acts 5.34-42
Psalms 27.1, 4, 13-14
John 6.1-15

Sat, Apr 24

Acts 6.1-7
Psalms 33.1-2, 4-5, 18-19
John 6.16-21

WEEK 3, EASTER

Sun, Apr 25

Acts 5.27-32, 40-41
Psalms 30.2, 4, 5-6, 11-12, 13
Revelation 5.11-14
John 21.1-19

Mon, Apr 26

Acts 6.8-15
Psalms 119.23-24, 26-27, 29-30
John 6.22-29

Tue, Apr 27

Acts 7.51—8.1
Psalms 31.3-4, 6, 7, 8, 17, 21
John 6.30-35

Wed, Apr 28

Acts 8.1-8
Psalms 66.1-3, 4-5, 6-7
John 6.35-40

Thu, Apr 29

Acts 8.26-40
Psalms 66.8-9, 16-17, 20
John 6.44-51

Fri, Apr 30

Acts 9.1-20
Psalms 117.1, 2
John 6.52-59

Sat, May 1

Acts 9.31-42
Psalms 116.12-13, 14-15, 16-17
John 6.60-69

WEEK 4, EASTER

Sun, May 2
Acts 13.14, 43-52
Psalms 100.1-2, 3, 5
Revelation 7.9, 14-17
John 10.27-30

Mon, May 3
Saints Philip and
James, Apostles—
Feast
I Corinthians 15.1-8
Psalms 19.2-3, 4-5
John 14.6-14

Tue, May 4
Acts 11.19-26
Psalms 87.1-3, 4-5, 6-7
John 10.22-30

Wed, May 5
Acts 12.24—13.5
Psalms 67.2-3, 5, 6, 8
John 12.44-50

Thu, May 6
Acts 13.13-25
Psalms 89.2-3, 21-22, 25, 27
John 13.16-20

Fri, May 7
Acts 13.26-33
Psalms 2.6-7, 8-9, 10-11
John 14.1-6

Sat, May 8
Acts 13.44-52
Psalms 98.1, 2-3, 3-4
John 14.7-14

WEEK 5, EASTER

Sun, May 9
Acts 14.21-27
Psalms 145.8-9, 10-11, 12-13
Revelation 21.1-5
John 13.31-33, 34-35

Mon, May 10
Acts 14.5-18
Psalms 115.1-2, 3-4, 15-16
John 14.21-26

Tue, May 11
Acts 14.19-28
Psalms 145.10-11, 12-13, 21
John 14.27-31

Wed, May 12
Acts 15.1-6
Psalms 122.1-2, 3-4, 4-5
John 15.1-8

Thu, May 13
Acts 15.7-21
Psalms 96.1-2, 2-3, 10
John 15.9-11

Fri, May 14
Saint Matthias,
apostle—Feast
Acts 1.15-17, 20-26
Psalms 113.1-2, 3-4, 5-6, 7-8
John 15.9-17

Sat, May 15
Acts 16.1-10
Psalms 100.1-2, 3, 5
John 15.18-21

WEEK 6, EASTER

Sun, May 16
Acts 15.1-2, 22-29
Psalms 67.2-3, 5, 6, 8
Revelation 21.10-14, 22-23
John 14.23-29

Mon, May 17
Acts 16.11-15
Psalms 149.1-2, 3-4, 5-6, 9
John 15.26—16.4

Tue, May 18
Acts 16.22-34
Psalms 138.1-2, 2-3, 7-8
John 16.5-11

Wed, May 19
Acts 17.15, 22—18.1
Psalms 148.1-2, 11-12, 13, 14
John 16.12-15

Thu, May 20
Ascension of the Lord
Acts 1.1-11
Psalms 47.2-3, 6-7, 8-9
Ephesians 1.17-23
Luke 24.46-53

Fri, May 21
Acts 18.9-18
Psalms 47.2-3, 4-5, 6-7
John 16.20-23

Sat, May 22
Acts 18.23-28
Psalms 47.2-3, 8-9, 10
John 16.23-28

WEEK 7, EASTER

Sun, May 23
Acts 7.55-60
Psalms 97.1-2, 6-7, 9
Revelation 22.12-14, 16-17, 20
John 17.20-26

Mon, May 24
Acts 19.1-8
Psalms 68.2-3, 4-5, 6-7
John 16.29-33

Tue, May 25
Acts 20.17-27
Psalms 68.10-11, 20-21
John 17.1-11

Wed, May 26
Acts 20.28-38
Psalms 68.29-30, 33-35, 35-36
John 17.11-19

Thu, May 27
Acts 22.30; 23.6-11
Psalms 16.1-2, 5, 7-8, 9-10, 11
John 17.20-26

Fri, May 28
Acts 25.13-21
Psalms 103.1-2, 11-12, 19-20
John 21.15-19

Sat, May 29
Acts 28.16-20, 30-31
Psalms 11.4, 5, 7
John 21.20-25

Sun, May 30
Pentecost
Acts 2.1-11
Psalms 104.1, 24, 29-30, 31, 34
I Corinthians 12.3-7, 12-13
John 20.19-23

Ordinary Time

WEEK 9

Mon, May 31
Visitation of the
Virgin Mary to
Elizabeth—Feast

Zephaniah 3.14-18
Isaiah 12.2-3, 4, 5-6
Luke 1.39-56

Tue, June 1

2 Peter 3.12-15, 17-18
Psalms 90.2, 3-4, 10, 14, 16
Mark 12.13-17

Wed, June 2

2 Timothy 1.1-3, 6-12
Psalms 123.1-2, 2
Mark 12.18-27

Thu, June 3

2 Timothy 2.8-15
Psalms 25.4-5, 8-9, 10, 14
Mark 12.28-34

Fri, June 4

2 Timothy 3.10-17
Psalms 119.157, 160, 161, 165,
  166, 168
Mark 12.35-37

Sat, June 5

2 Timothy 4.1-8
Psalms 71.8-9, 14-15, 16-17, 22
Mark 12.38-44

WEEK 10

Sun, June 6
The Holy Trinity—
Solemnity

Proverbs 8.22-31
Psalms 8.4-5, 6-7, 8-9
Romans 5.1-5
John 16.12-15

Mon, June 7

1 Kings 17.1-7
Psalms 121.1-2, 3-4, 5-6, 7-8
Matthew 5.1-12

Tue, June 8

1 Kings 17.7-16
Psalms 4.2-3, 4-5, 7-8
Matthew 5.13-16

Wed, June 9

1 Kings 18.20-39
Psalms 16.1-2, 4, 5, 8, 11
Matthew 5.17-19

Thu, June 10

1 Kings 18.41-46
Psalms 65.10, 10-11, 12-13
Matthew 5.20-26

Fri, June 11
Saint Barnabas,
apostle—Memorial

Acts 11.21-26; 13.1-3
Psalms 98.1, 2-3, 3-4, 5-6
Matthew 10.7-13

Sat, June 12

1 Kings 19.19-21
Psalms 16.1-2, 5, 7-8, 9-10
Matthew 5.33-37

WEEK 11

Sun, June 13
The Body and Blood
of Christ (Corpus
Christi)—Solemnity

Genesis 14.18-20
Psalms 110.1, 2, 3, 4
1 Corinthians 11.23-26
Luke 9.11-17

Mon, June 14

1 Kings 21.1-16
Psalms 5.2-3, 5-6, 7
Matthew 5.38-42

Tue, June 15

1 Kings 21.17-29
Psalms 51.3-4, 5-6, 11, 16
Matthew 5.43-48

Wed, June 16

2 Kings 2.1, 6-14
Psalms 31.20, 21, 24
Matthew 6.1-6, 16-18

Thu, June 17

Sirach 48.1-14
Psalms 97.1-2, 3-4, 5-6, 7
Matthew 6.7-15

Fri, June 18
Sacred Heart of Jesus—
Solemnity

Ezekiel 34.11-16
Psalms 23.1-3, 3-4, 5, 6
Romans 5.5-11
Luke 15.3-7

Sat, June 19

2 Chronicles 24.17-25
Psalms 89.4-5, 29-30, 31-32,
  33-34
Matthew 6.24-34

WEEK 12

Sun, June 20

Zechariah 12.10-11
Psalms 62.2, 3-4, 5-6, 8-9
Galatians 3.26-29
Luke 9.18-24

Mon, June 21

2 Kings 17.5-8, 13-15, 18
Psalms 60.3, 4-5, 12-13
Matthew 7.1-5

Tue, June 22

2 Kings 19.9-11, 14-21, 31-35, 36
Psalms 48.2-3, 3-4, 10-11
Matthew 7.6, 12-14

Wed, June 23

2 Kings 22.8-13; 23.1-3
Psalms 119.33, 34, 35, 36, 37, 40
Matthew 7.15-20

Thu, June 24
Birth of Saint John
the Baptist—
Solemnity

Isaiah 49.1-6
Psalms 139.1-3, 13-14, 14-15
Acts 13.22-26
Luke 1.57-66, 80

Fri, June 25

2 Kings 25.1-12
Psalms 137.1-2, 3, 4-5, 6
Matthew 8.1-4

Sat, June 26

Lamentations 2.2, 10-14, 18-19
Psalms 74.1-2, 3-5, 5-7, 20-21
Matthew 8.5-17

WEEK 13

Sun, June 27
I Kings 19.16-21
Psalms 16.1-2, 5, 7-8, 9-10, 11
Galatians 5.1, 13-18
Luke 9.51-62

Mon, June 28
Amos 2.6-10, 13-16
Psalms 50.16-17, 18-19, 20-21,
22-23
Matthew 8.18-22

Tue, June 29
Saints Peter and Paul,
apostles—Solemnity
Acts 12.1-11
Psalms 34.2-3, 4-5, 6-7, 8-9
2 Timothy 4.6-8, 17-18
Matthew 16.13-19

Wed, June 30
Amos 5.14-15, 21-24
Psalms 50.7, 8-9, 10-11, 12-13,
16-17
Matthew 8.28-34

Thu, July 1
Amos 7.10-17
Psalms 19.8, 9, 10, 11
Matthew 9.1-8

Fri, July 2
Amos 8.4-6, 9-12
Psalms 119.2, 10, 20, 30, 40, 131
Matthew 9.9-13

Sat, July 3
Saint Thomas,
apostle—Feast
Ephesians 2.19-22
Psalms 117.1, 2
John 20.24-29

WEEK 14

Sun, July 4
Isaiah 66.10-14
Psalms 66.1-3, 4-5, 6-7, 16, 20
Galatians 6.14-18
Luke 10.1-12, 17-20

Mon, July 5
Hosea 2.16, 17-18, 21-22
Psalms 145.2-3, 4-5, 6-7, 8-9
Matthew 9.18-26

Tue, July 6
Hosea 8.4-7, 11-13
Psalms 115.3-4, 5-6, 7-8, 9-10
Matthew 9.32-38

Wed, July 7
Hosea 10.1-3, 7-8, 12
Psalms 105.2-3, 4-5, 6-7
Matthew 10.1-7

Thu, July 8
Hosea 11.1, 3-4, 8-9
Psalms 80.2, 3, 15-16
Matthew 10.7-15

Fri, July 9
Hosea 14.2-10
Psalms 51.3-4, 8-9, 12-13, 14, 17
Matthew 10.16-23

Sat, July 10
Isaiah 6.1-8
Psalms 93.1, 1-2, 5
Matthew 10.24-33

WEEK 15

Sun, July 11
Deuteronomy 30.10-14
Psalms 69.14, 17, 30-31, 33-34,
36, 37
Colossians 1.15-20
Luke 10.25-37

Mon, July 12
Isaiah 1.10-17
Psalms 50.8-9, 16-17, 21, 23
Matthew 10.34—11.1

Tue, July 13
Isaiah 7.1-9
Psalms 48.2-3, 3-4, 5-6, 7-8
Matthew 11.20-24

Wed, July 14
Isaiah 10.5-7, 13-16
Psalms 94.5-6, 7-8, 9-10, 14-15
Matthew 11.25-27

Thu, July 15
Isaiah 26.7-9, 12, 16-19
Psalms 102.13-14, 15, 16-18, 19-21
Matthew 11.28-30

Fri, July 16
Isaiah 38.1-6, 21-22, 7-8
Isaiah 38.10, 11, 12, 16
Matthew 12.1-8

Sat, July 17
Micah 2.1-5
Psalms 10.1-2, 3-4, 7-8, 14
Matthew 12.14-21

WEEK 16

Sun, July 18
Genesis 18.1-10
Psalms 15.2-3, 3-4, 5
Colossians 1.24-28
Luke 10.38-42

Mon, July 19
Micah 6.1-4, 6-8
Psalms 50.5-6, 8-9, 16-17, 21, 23
Matthew 12.38-42

Tue, July 20
Micah 7.14-15, 18-20
Psalms 85.2-4, 5-6, 7-8
Matthew 12.46-50

Wed, July 21
Jeremiah 1.1, 4-10
Psalms 71.1-2, 3-4, 5-6, 15, 17
Matthew 13.1-9

Thu, July 22
Saint Mary
Magdalene—
Memorial
Song of Songs 3.1-4
Psalms 63.2, 3-4, 5-6, 8-9
John 20.1-2, 11-18

Fri, July 23
Jeremiah 3.14-17
Jeremiah 31.10, 11-12, 13
Matthew 13.18-23

Sat, July 24
Jeremiah 7.1-11
Psalms 84.3, 4, 5-6, 8, 11
Matthew 13.24-30

WEEK 17

Sun, July 25
Genesis 18.20-32
Psalms 138.1-2, 2-3, 6-7, 7-8
Colossians 2.12-14
Luke 11.1-13

Mon, July 26
Saints Joachim and
Ann, parents of
Mary—Memorial
Sirach 44.1, 10-15
Psalms 132.11, 13-14, 17-18
Matthew 13.16-17

Tue, July 27
Jeremiah 14.17-22
Psalms 79.8, 9, 11, 13
Matthew 13.35-43

Wed, July 28
Jeremiah 15.10, 16-21
Psalms 59.2-3, 4, 10-11, 17, 18
Matthew 13.44-46

Thu, July 29
Saint Martha—
Memorial
Proverbs 31.10-13, 19-20, 30-31
Psalms 112.1-2, 3-4, 5-6, 7-8, 9
Luke 10.38-42

Fri, July 30
Jeremiah 26.1-9
Psalms 69.6, 8-10, 14
Matthew 13.54-58

Sat, July 31
Jeremiah 26.11-16, 24
Psalms 69.15-16, 30-31, 33-34
Matthew 14.1-12

WEEK 18

Sun, Aug 1
Ecclesiastes 1.2; 2.21-23
Psalms 95.1-2, 6-7, 8-9
Colossians 3.1-5, 9-11
Luke 12.13-21

Mon, Aug 2
Jeremiah 28.1-17
Psalms 119.29, 43, 79, 80, 95, 102
Matthew 14.13-21

Tue, Aug 3
Jeremiah 30.1-2, 12-15, 18-22
Psalms 102.16-18, 19-23, 29
Matthew 15.1-2, 10-14

Wed, Aug 4
Jeremiah 31.1-7
Jeremiah 31.10, 11-12, 13
Matthew 15.21-28

Thu, Aug 5
Jeremiah 31.31-34
Psalms 51.12-13, 14-15, 18-19
Matthew 16.13-23

Fri, Aug 6
Transfiguration
of the Lord—
Feast
Daniel 7.9-10, 13-14
Psalms 97.1-2, 5-6, 9
2 Peter 1.16-19
Luke 9.28-36

Sat, Aug 7
Habakkuk 1.12—2.4
Psalms 9.8-9, 10-11, 12-13
Matthew 17.14-20

WEEK 19

Sun, Aug 8
Wisdom 18.6-9
Psalms 33.1, 12, 18-19, 20-22
Hebrews 11.1-2, 8-19
or 11.1-2, 8-12
Luke 12.32-48

Mon, Aug 9
Ezekiel 1.2-5, 24-28
Psalms 148.1-2, 11-12, 12-14, 14
Matthew 17.22-27

Tue, Aug 10
Saint Lawrence,
deacon and martyr—
Feast
2 Corinthians 9.6-10
Psalms 112.1-2, 5-6, 7-8, 9
John 12.24-26

Wed, Aug 11
Ezekiel 9.1-7; 10.18-22
Psalms 113.1-2, 3-4, 5-6
Matthew 18.15-20

Thu, Aug 12
Ezekiel 12.1-12
Psalms 78.56-57, 58-59, 61-62
Matthew 18.21—19.1

Fri, Aug 13
Ezekiel 16.1-15, 60, 63
Isaiah 12.2-3, 4, 5-6
Matthew 19.3-12

Sat, Aug 14
Ezekiel 18.1-10, 13, 30-32
Psalms 51.12-13, 14-15, 18-19
Matthew 19.13-15

WEEK 20

Sun, Aug 15
Assumption of the
Virgin Mary into
Heaven—Solemnity
Revelation 11.19; 12.1-6, 10
Psalms 45.10, 11, 12, 16
1 Corinthians 15.20-26
Luke 1.39-56

Mon, Aug 16
Ezekiel 24.15-24
Deuteronomy 32.18-19, 20, 21
Matthew 19.16-22

Tue, Aug 17
Ezekiel 28.1-10
Deuteronomy 32.26-27, 27-28, 30, 35-36
Matthew 19.23-30

Wed, Aug 18
Ezekiel 34.1-11
Psalms 23.1-3, 3-4, 5, 6
Matthew 20.1-16

Thu, Aug 19
Ezekiel 36.23-28
Psalms 51.12-13, 14-15, 18-19
Matthew 22.1-14

Fri, Aug 20
Ezekiel 37.1-14
Psalms 107.2-3, 4-5, 6-7, 8-9
Matthew 22.34-40

Sat, Aug 21
Ezekiel 43.1-7
Psalms 85.9-10, 11-12, 13-14
Matthew 23.1-12

WEEK 21

Sun, Aug 22
Isaiah 66.18-21
Psalms 117.1, 2
Hebrews 12.5-7, 11-13
Luke 13.22-30

Mon, Aug 23
2 Thessalonians 1.1-5, 11-12
Psalms 96.1-2, 2-3, 4-5
Matthew 23.13-22

Tue, Aug 24
Saint Bartholomew,
apostle—Feast
Revelation 21.9-14
Psalms 145.10-11, 12-13, 17-18
John 1.45-51

Wed, Aug 25
2 Thessalonians 3.6-10, 16-18
Psalms 128.1-2, 4-5
Matthew 23.27-32

Thu, Aug 26
1 Corinthians 1.1-9
Psalms 145.2-3, 4-5, 6-7
Matthew 24.42-51

Fri, Aug 27
1 Corinthians 1.17-25
Psalms 33.1-2, 4-5, 10, 11
Matthew 25.1-13

Sat, Aug 28
1 Corinthians 1.26-31
Psalms 33.12-13, 18-19, 20-21
Matthew 25.14-30

WEEK 22

Sun, Aug 29
Sirach 3.17-18, 20, 28-29
Psalms 68.4-5, 6-7, 10-11
Hebrews 12.18-19, 22-24
Luke 14.1, 7-14

Mon, Aug 30
1 Corinthians 2.1-5
Psalms 119.97, 98, 99, 100, 101, 102
Luke 4.16-30

Tue, Aug 31
1 Corinthians 2.10-16
Psalms 145.8-9, 10-11, 12-13, 13-14
Luke 4.31-37

Wed, Sept 1
1 Corinthians 3.1-9
Psalms 33.12-13, 14-15, 20-21
Luke 4.38-44

Thu, Sept 2
1 Corinthians 3.18-23
Psalms 24.1-2, 3-4, 5-6
Luke 5.1-11

Fri, Sept 3
1 Corinthians 4.1-5
Psalms 37.3-4, 5-6, 27-28, 39-40
Luke 5.33-39

Sat, Sept 4
1 Corinthians 4.9-15
Psalms 145.17-18, 19-20, 21
Luke 6.1-5

WEEK 23

Sun, Sept 5
Wisdom 9.13-18
Psalms 90.3-4, 5-6, 12-13, 14-17
Philemon 1.9-10, 12-17
Luke 14.25-33

Mon, Sept 6
1 Corinthians 5.1-8
Psalms 5.5-6, 7, 12
Luke 6.6-11

Tue, Sept 7
1 Corinthians 6.1-11
Psalms 149.1-2, 3-4, 5-6, 9
Luke 6.12-19

Wed, Sept 8
Birth of the
Virgin Mary—Feast
Romans 8.28-30
Psalms 13.6, 6
Matthew 1.1-16, 18-23

Thu, Sept 9
1 Corinthians 8.1-7, 11-13
Psalms 139.1-3, 13-14, 23-24
Luke 6.27-38

Fri, Sept 10
1 Corinthians 9.16-19, 22-27
Psalms 84.3, 4, 5-6, 8, 12
Luke 6.39-42

Sat, Sept 11
1 Corinthians 10.14-22
Psalms 116.12-13, 17-18
Luke 6.43-49

WEEK 24

Sun, Sept 12
Exodus 32.7-11, 13-14
Psalms 51.3-4, 12-13, 17, 19
1 Timothy 1.12-17
Luke 15.1-32
 or 15.1-10

Mon, Sept 13
1 Corinthians 11.17-26, 33
Psalms 40.7-8, 8-9, 10, 17
Luke 7.1-10

Tue, Sept 14
Triumph of the
Holy Cross—
Feast
Numbers 21.4-9
Psalms 78.1-2, 34-35, 36-37, 38
Philippians 2.6-11
John 3.13-17

Wed, Sept 15
Our Lady of Sorrows—
Memorial
Hebrews 5.7-9
Psalms 31.2-3, 3-4, 5-6, 15-16, 20
John 19.25-27, or Luke 2.33-35

Thu, Sept 16
1 Corinthians 15.1-11
Psalms 118.1-2, 16-17, 28
Luke 7.36-50

Fri, Sept 17
1 Corinthians 15.12-20
Psalms 17.1, 6-7, 8, 15
Luke 8.1-3

Sat, Sept 18
1 Corinthians 15.35-37, 42-49
Psalms 56.10-12, 13-14
Luke 8.4-15

WEEK 25

Sun, Sept 19

Amos 8.4-7
Psalms 113.1-2, 4-6, 7-8
1 Timothy 2.1-8
Luke 16.1-13

Mon, Sept 20

Proverbs 3.27-34
Psalms 15.2-3, 3-4, 5
Luke 8.16-18

Tue, Sept 21
St. Matthew, apostle
and evangelist—Feast

Ephesians 4.1-7, 11-13
Psalms 19.2-3, 4-5
Matthew 9.9-13

Wed, Sept 22

Proverbs 30.5-9
Psalms 119.29, 72, 89, 101,
    104, 163
Luke 9.1-6

Thu, Sept 23

Ecclesiastes 1.2-11
Psalms 90.3-4, 5-6, 12-13, 14, 17
Luke 9.7-9

Fri, Sept 24

Ecclesiastes 3.1-11
Psalms 144.1-2, 3-4
Luke 9.18-22

Sat, Sept 25

Ecclesiastes 11.9—12:8
Psalms 90.3-4, 5-6, 12-13, 14, 17
Luke 9.43-45

WEEK 26

Sun, Sept 26

Amos 6.1, 4-7
Psalms 146.7, 8-9, 9-10
1 Timothy 6.11-16
Luke 16.19-31

Mon, Sept 27

Job 1.6-22
Psalms 17.1, 2-3, 6-7
Luke 9.46-50

Tue, Sept 28

Job 3.1-3, 11-17, 20-23
Psalms 88.2-3, 4-5, 6, 7-8
Luke 9.51-56

Wed, Sept 29
Michael, Gabriel, and
Raphael, archangels—
Feast

Daniel 7.9-10, 13-14
Psalms 138.1-2, 2-3, 4-5
John 1.47-51

Thu, Sept 30

Job 19.21-27
Psalms 27.7-8, 8-9, 13-14
Luke 10.1-12

Fri, Oct 1

Job 38.1, 12-21; 40.3-5
Psalms 139.1-3, 7-8, 9-10, 13-14
Luke 10.13-16

Sat, Oct 2
Guardian Angels—
Memorial

Exodus 23.20-23
Psalms 91.1-2, 3-4, 5-6, 10-11
Matthew 18.1-5, 10

WEEK 27

Sun, Oct 3

Habakkuk 1.2-3, 2.2-4
Psalms 95.1-2, 6-7, 8-9
2 Timothy 1.6-8, 13-14
Luke 17.5-10

Mon, Oct 4

Galatians 1.6-12
Psalms 111.1-2, 7-8, 9, 10
Luke 10.25-37

Tue, Oct 5

Galatians 1.13-24
Psalms 139.1-3, 13-14, 14-15
Luke 10.38-42

Wed, Oct 6

Galatians 2.1-2, 7-14
Psalms 117.1, 2
Luke 11.1-4

Thu, Oct 7

Galatians 3.1-5
Luke 1.69-70, 71-72, 73-75
Luke 11.5-13

Fri, Oct 8

Galatians 3.7-14
Psalms 111.1-2, 3-4, 5-6
Luke 11.15-26

Sat, Oct 9

Galatians 3.22-29
Psalms 105.2-3, 4-5, 6-7
Luke 11.27-28

WEEK 28

Sun, Oct 10

2 Kings 5.14-17
Psalms 98.1, 2-3, 3-4
2 Timothy 2.8-13
Luke 17.11-19

Mon, Oct 11

Galatians 4.22-24, 26-27,
    31—5.1
Psalms 113.1-2, 3-4, 5, 6-7
Luke 11.29-32

Tue, Oct 12

Galatians 5.1-6
Psalms 119.41, 43, 44, 45, 47, 48
Luke 11.37-41

Wed, Oct 13

Galatians 5.18-25
Psalms 1.1-2, 3, 4, 6
Luke 11.42-46

Thu, Oct 14

Ephesians 1.3-10
Psalms 98.1, 2-3, 3-4, 5-6
Luke 11.47-54

Fri, Oct 15

Ephesians 1.11-14
Psalms 33.1-2, 4-5, 12-13
Luke 12.1-7

Sat, Oct 16

Ephesians 1.15-23
Psalms 8.2-3, 4-5, 6-7
Luke 12.8-12

WEEK 29

Sun, Oct 17
Exodus 17.8-13
Psalms 121.1-2, 3-4, 5-6, 7-8
2 Timothy 3.14—4.2
Luke 18.1-8

Mon, Oct 18
Saint Luke,
evangelist—Feast
2 Timothy 4.9-17
Psalms 145.10-11, 12-13, 17-18
Luke 10.1-9

Tue, Oct 19
Ephesians 2.12-22
Psalms 85.9-10, 11-12, 13-14
Luke 12.35-38

Wed, Oct 20
Ephesians 3.2-12
Isaiah 12.2-3, 4, 5-6
Luke 12.39-48

Thu, Oct 21
Ephesians 3.14-21
Psalms 33.1-2, 4-5, 11-12, 18-19
Luke 12.49-53

Fri, Oct 22
Ephesians 4.1-6
Psalms 24.1-2, 3-4, 5-6
Luke 12.54-59

Sat, Oct 23
Ephesians 4.7-16
Psalms 122.1-2, 3-4, 4-5
Luke 13.1-9

WEEK 30

Sun, Oct 24
Sirach 35.12-14, 16-18
Psalms 34.2-3, 17-18, 19, 23
2 Timothy 4.6-8, 16-18
Luke 18.9-14

Mon, Oct 25
Ephesians 4.32—5.8
Psalms 1.1-2, 3, 4, 6
Luke 13.10-17

Tue, Oct 26
Ephesians 5.21-33
Psalms 128.1-2, 3, 4-5
Luke 13.18-21

Wed, Oct 27
Ephesians 6.1-9
Psalms 145.10-11, 12-13, 13-14
Luke 13.22-30

Thu, Oct 28
Saints Simon and
Jude, apostles—Feast
Ephesians 2.19-22
Psalms 19.2-3, 4-5
Luke 6.12-16

Fri, Oct 29
Philippians 1.1-11
Psalms 111.1-2, 3-4, 5-6
Luke 14.1-6

Sat, Oct 30
Philippians 1.18-26
Psalms 42.2, 3, 5
Luke 14.1, 7-11

WEEK 31

Sun, Oct 31
Wisdom 11.22—12.1
Psalms 145.1-2, 8-9, 10-11, 13, 14
2 Thessalonians 1.11—2.2
Luke 19.1-10

Mon, Nov 1
All Saints—Solemnity
Revelation 7.2-4, 9-14
Psalms 24.1-2, 3-4, 5-6
1 John 3.1-3
Matthew 5.1-12

Tue, Nov 2
Commemoration of
All the Faithful
Departed (All Souls)—
Solemnity
Wisdom 3.1-9 or 3.1-6, 9
Psalms 27.1, 4, 7, 8, 9, 13-14
Romans 6.3-9 or 6.3-4, 8-9
Matthew 25.31-46

Wed, Nov 3
Philippians 2.12-18
Psalms 27.1, 4, 13-14
Luke 14.25-33

Thu, Nov 4
Philippians 3.3-8
Psalms 105.2-3, 4-5, 6-7
Luke 15.1-10

Fri, Nov 5
Philippians 3.17—4.1
Psalms 122.1-2, 3-4, 4-5
Luke 16.1-8

Sat, Nov 6
Philippians 4.10-19
Psalms 112.1-2, 5-6, 8, 9
Luke 16.9-15

WEEK 32

Sun, Nov 7
2 Maccabees 7.1-2, 9-14
Psalms 17.1, 5-6, 8, 15
2 Thessalonians 2.16—3.5
Luke 20.27-38

Mon, Nov 8
Titus 1.1-9
Psalms 24.1-2, 3-4, 5-6
Luke 17.1-6

Tue, Nov 9
Dedication of the
Basilica of St. John
Lateran in Rome—
Feast
Genesis 28.11-18
Psalms 84.3, 4, 5-6, 8, 11
1 Corinthians 3.9-13, 16-17
Luke 19.1-10

Wed, Nov 10
Titus 3.1-7
Psalms 23.1-3, 3-4, 5, 6
Luke 17.11-19

Thu, Nov 11
Philemon 1.7-20
Psalms 146.7, 8-9, 9-10
Luke 17.20-25

Fri, Nov 12
2 John 1.4-9
Psalms 119.1, 2, 10, 11, 17, 18
Luke 17.26-37

Sat, Nov 13
3 John 1.5-8
Psalms 112.1-2, 3-4, 5-6
Luke 18.1-8

WEEK 33

Sun, Nov 14

Malachi 3.19-20
Psalms 98.5-6, 7-8, 9
2 Thessalonians 3.7-12
Luke 21.5-19

Mon, Nov 15

Revelation 1.1-4; 2.1-5
Psalms 1.1-2, 3, 4, 6
Luke 18.35-43

Tue, Nov 16

Revelation 3.1-6, 14-22
Psalms 15.2-3, 3-4, 5
Luke 19.1-10

Wed, Nov 17

Revelation 4.1-11
Psalms 150.1-2, 3-4, 5-6
Luke 19.11-28

Thu, Nov 18

Revelation 5.1-10
Psalms 149.1-2, 3-4, 5-6, 9
Luke 9.41-44

Fri, Nov 19

Revelation 10.8-11
Psalms 119.14, 24, 72, 103, 111, 131
Luke 19.45-48

Sat, Nov 20

Revelation 11.4-12
Psalms 144.1, 2, 9-10
Luke 20.27-40

WEEK 34

Sun, Nov 21
Christ the King—
Solemnity

2 Samuel 5.1-3
Psalms 122.1-2, 3-4, 4-5
Colossians 1.12-20
Luke 23.35-43

Mon, Nov 22

Revelation 14.1-3, 4-5
Psalms 24.1-2, 3-4, 5-6
Luke 21.1-4

Tue, Nov 23

Revelation 14.14-19
Psalms 96.10, 11-12, 13
Luke 21.5-11

Wed, Nov 24

Revelation 15.1-4
Psalms 98.1, 2-3, 7-8, 9
Luke 21.12-19

Thu, Nov 25

Revelation 18.1-2, 21-23; 19.1-3, 9
Psalms 100.2, 3, 4, 5
Luke 21.20-28

Fri, Nov 26

Revelation 20.1-4, 11—21.2
Psalms 84.3, 4, 5-6, 8
Luke 21.29-33

Sat, Nov 27

Revelation 22.1-7
Psalms 95.1-2, 3-5, 6-7
Luke 21.34-36

Advent, *Liturgical year 2005*

WEEK 1, ADVENT

Sun, Nov 28, 2004

Isaiah 2.1-5
Psalms 122.1-2, 3-4, 4-5, 6-7, 8-9
Romans 13.11-14
Matthew 24.37-44

Mon, Nov 29

Isaiah 4.2-6
Psalms 122.1-2, 3-4, 8-9
Matthew 8.5-11

Tue, Nov 30
Saint Andrew,
apostle—Feast

Romans 10.9-18
Psalms 19.2-3, 4-5
Matthew 4.18-22

Wed, Dec 1

Isaiah 25.6-10
Psalms 23.1-3, 3-4, 5, 6
Matthew 15.29-37

Thu, Dec 2

Isaiah 26.1-6
Psalms 118.1, 8-9, 19-21, 25-27
Matthew 7.21, 24-27

Fri, Dec 3

Isaiah 29.17-24
Psalms 27.1, 4, 13-14
Matthew 9.27-31

Sat, Dec 4

Isaiah 30.19-21, 23-26
Psalms 147.1-2, 3-4, 5-6
Matthew 9.35—10.1, 6-8

WEEK 2, ADVENT

Sun, Dec 5

Isaiah 11.1-10
Psalms 72.1-2, 7-8, 12-13, 17
Romans 15.4-9
Matthew 3.1-12

Mon, Dec 6

Isaiah 35.1-10
Psalms 85.9-10, 11-12, 13-14
Luke 5.17-26

Tue, Dec 7

Isaiah 40.1-11
Psalms 96.1-2, 3, 10, 11-12, 13
Matthew 18.12-14

Wed, Dec 8
Immaculate
Conception of the
Virgin Mary—
Solemnity

Genesis 3.9-15, 20
Psalms 98.1, 2-3, 3-4
Ephesians 1.3-6, 11-12
Luke 1.26-38

Thu, Dec 9

Isaiah 41.13-20
Psalms 145.1, 9, 10-11, 12-13
Matthew 11.11-15

Fri, Dec 10

Isaiah 48.17-19
Psalms 1.1-2, 3, 4, 6
Matthew 11.16-19

Sat, Dec 11

Sirach 48.1-4, 9-11
Psalms 80.2-3, 15-16, 18-19
Matthew 17.10-13

WEEK 3, ADVENT

Sun, Dec 12   Isaiah 35.1-6, 10
Psalms 146.6-7, 8-9, 9-10
James 5.7-10
Matthew 11.2-11

Mon, Dec 13   Numbers 24.2-7, 15-17
Psalms 25.4-5, 6-7, 8-9
Matthew 21.23-27

Tue, Dec 14   Zephaniah 3.1-2, 9-13
Psalms 34.2-3, 6-7, 17-18, 19, 23
Matthew 21.28-32

Wed, Dec 15   Isaiah 45.6-8, 18, 21-25
Psalms 85.9-10, 11-12, 13-14
Luke 7.18-23

Thu, Dec 16   Isaiah 54.1-10
Psalms 30.2, 4, 5-6, 11-12, 13
Luke 7.24-30

Fri, Dec 17   Genesis 49.2, 8-10
Psalms 72.3-4, 7-8, 17
Matthew 1.1-17

Sat, Dec 18   Jeremiah 23.5-8
Psalms 72.1, 12-13, 18-19
Matthew 1.18-24

WEEK 4, ADVENT

Sun, Dec 19   Isaiah 7.10-14
Psalms 24.1-2, 3-4, 5-6
Romans 1.1-7
Matthew 1.18-24

Mon, Dec 20   Isaiah 7.10-14
Psalms 24.1-2, 3-4, 5-6
Luke 1.26-38

Tue, Dec 21   Zephaniah 3.14-18
Psalms 33.2-3, 11-12, 20-21
Luke 1.39-45

Wed, Dec 22   1 Samuel 1.24-28
1 Samuel 2.1, 4-5, 6-7, 8
Luke 1.46-56

Thu, Dec 23   Malachi 3.1-4, 23-24
Psalms 25.4-5, 8-9, 10, 14
Luke 1.57-66

Fri, Dec 24   2 Samuel 7.1-5, 8-11, 16
Psalms 89.2-3, 4-5, 27, 29
Luke 1.67-79

Christmas

Sat, Dec 25   Isaiah 62.11-12
Christmas—Solemnity   Psalms 97.1, 6, 11-12
Titus 3.4-7
Luke 2.15-20

Sun, Dec 26   Sirach 3.2-6, 12-14
The Holy Family—   Psalms 128.1-2, 3, 4-5
Feast   Colossians 3.12-21
Matthew 2.13-15, 19-23

Mon, Dec 27   1 John 1.1-4
Saint John, apostle   Psalms 97.1-2, 5-6, 11-12
and evangelist—Feast   John 20.2-8

Tue, Dec 28   1 John 1.5—2.2
The Holy Innocents,   Psalms 124.2-3, 4-5, 7-8
martyrs—Feast   Matthew 2.13-18

Wed, Dec 29   1 John 2.3-11
Psalms 96.1-2, 2-3, 5-6
Luke 2.22-35

Thu, Dec 30   1 John 2.12-17
Psalms 96.7-8, 8-9, 10
Luke 2.36-40

Fri, Dec 31   1 John 2.18-21
Psalms 96.1-2, 11-12, 13
John 1.1-18

Sat, Jan 1, 2005   Numbers 6.22-27
Mary, Mother of God—   Psalms 67.2-3, 5, 6, 8
Solemnity   Galatians 4.4-7
Luke 2.16-21

Sun, Jan 2   Isaiah 60.1-6
Epiphany of the Lord—   Psalms 72.1-2, 7-8, 10-11, 12-13
Solemnity   Ephesians 3.2-3, 5-6
Matthew 2.1-12

Mon, Jan 3   1 John 3.22—4.6
Psalms 2.7-8, 10-11
Matthew 4.12-17, 23-25

Tue, Jan 4   1 John 4.7-10
Psalms 72.1-2, 3-4, 7-8
Mark 6.34-44

Wed, Jan 5   1 John 4.11-18
Psalms 72.1-2, 10, 12-13
Mark 6.45-52

Thu, Jan 6   1 John 4.19—5.4
Psalms 72.1-2, 14-15, 17
Luke 4.14-22

Fri, Jan 7   1 John 3.22—4.6
Psalms 2.7-8, 10-11
Matthew 4.12-17, 23-25

Sat, Jan 8   1 John 4.7-10
Psalms 72.1-2, 3-4, 7-8
Mark 6.34-44

Ordinary Time

WEEK I

Sun, Jan 9
Baptism of the Lord—
Feast
Isaiah 42.1-4, 6-7
Psalms 29.1-2, 3-4, 3, 9-10
Acts 10.34-38
Matthew 3.13-17

Mon, Jan 10
Hebrews 1.1-6
Psalms 97.1-2, 6-7, 9
Mark 1.14-20

Tue, Jan II
Hebrews 2.5-12
Psalms 8.2, 5, 6-7, 8-9
Mark 1.21-28

Wed, Jan 12
Hebrews 2.14-18
Psalms 105.1-2, 3-4, 6-7, 8-9
Mark 1.29-39

Thu, Jan 13
Hebrews 3.7-14
Psalms 95.6-7, 8-9, 10-11
Mark 1.40-45

Fri, Jan 14
Hebrews 4.1-5, 11
Psalms 78.3, 4, 6-7, 8
Mark 2.1-12

Sat, Jan 15
Hebrews 4.12-16
Psalms 19.8, 9, 10, 15
Mark 2.13-17

WEEK 2

Sun, Jan 16
Isaiah 49.3, 5-6
Psalms 40.2, 4, 7-8, 8-9, 10
I Corinthians 1.1-3
John 1.29-34

Mon, Jan 17
Hebrews 5.1-10
Psalms 110.1, 2, 3, 4
Mark 2.18-22

Tue, Jan 18
Hebrews 6.10-20
Psalms 111.1-2, 4-5, 9-10
Mark 2.23-28

Wed, Jan 19
Hebrews 7.1-3, 15-17
Psalms 110.1, 2, 3, 4
Mark 3.1-6

Thu, Jan 20
Hebrews 7.25—8.6
Psalms 40.7-8, 8-9, 10, 17
Mark 3.7-12

Fri, Jan 21
Hebrews 8.6-13
Psalms 85.8, 10, 11-12, 13-14
Mark 3.13-19

Sat, Jan 22
Hebrews 9.2-3, 11-14
Psalms 47.2-3, 6-7, 8-9
Mark 3.20-21

WEEK 3

Sun, Jan 23
Isaiah 8.23—9.3
Psalms 27.1, 4, 13-14
I Corinthians 1.10-13, 17
Matthew 4.12-23

Mon, Jan 24
Hebrews 9.15, 24-28
Psalms 98.1, 2-3, 3-4, 5-6
Mark 3.22-30

Tue, Jan 25
Acts 22.3-16,
   or Acts 9.1-22
Psalms 117.1, 2
Mark 16.15-18

Wed, Jan 26
Hebrews 10.11-18
Psalms 110.1, 2, 3, 4
Mark 4.1-20

Thu, Jan 27
Hebrews 10.19-25
Psalms 24.1-2, 3-4, 5-6
Mark 4.21-25

Fri, Jan 28
Hebrews 10.32-39
Psalms 37.3-4, 5-6, 23-24,
   39-40
Mark 4.26-34

Sat, Jan 29
Hebrews 11.1-2, 8-19
Luke 1.69-70, 71-72, 73-75
Mark 4.35-41

WEEK 4

Sun, Jan 30
Zephaniah 2.3; 3.12-13
Psalms 146.6-7, 8-9, 9-10
I Corinthians 1.26-31
Matthew 5.1-12

Mon, Jan 31
Hebrews 11.32-40
Psalms 31.20, 21, 22, 23, 24
Mark 5.1-20

Tue, Feb I
Hebrews 12.1-4
Psalms 22.26-27, 28, 30, 31-32
Mark 5.21-43

Wed, Feb 2
Presentation
of the Lord—
Feast
Malachi 3.1-4
Psalms 24.7, 8, 9, 10
Hebrews 2.14-18
Luke 2.22-40
   or 2.22-32

Thu, Feb 3
Hebrews 12.18-19, 21-24
Psalms 48.2-3, 3-4, 9, 10-11
Mark 6.7-13

Fri, Feb 4
Hebrews 13.1-8
Psalms 27.1, 3, 5, 8-9
Mark 6.14-29

Sat, Feb 5
Hebrews 13.15-17, 20-21
Psalms 23.1-3, 3-4, 5, 6
Mark 6.30-34

WEEK 5

Sun, Feb 6
Isaiah 58.7-10
Psalms 112.4-5, 6-7, 8-9
I Corinthians 2.1-5
Matthew 5.13-16

Mon, Feb 7
Genesis 1.1-19
Psalms 104.1-2, 5-6, 10, 12, 24, 35
Mark 6.53-56

Tue, Feb 8
Genesis 1.20—2.4
Psalms 8.4-5, 6-7, 8-9
Mark 7.1-13

Lent

Wed, Feb 9
Ash Wednesday
Joel 2.12-18
Psalms 51.3-4, 5-6, 12-13, 14, 17
2 Corinthians 5.20—6.2
Matthew 6.1-6, 16-18

Thu, Feb 10
Deuteronomy 30.15-20
Psalms 1.1-2, 3, 4, 6
Luke 9.22-25

Fri, Feb 11
Isaiah 58.1-9
Psalms 51.3-4, 5-6, 18-19
Matthew 9.14-15

Sat, Feb 12
Isaiah 58.9-14
Psalms 86.1-2, 3-4, 5-6
Luke 5.27-32

WEEK 1, LENT

Sun, Feb 13
Genesis 2.7-9; 3.1-7
Psalms 51.3-4, 5-6, 12-13, 14, 17
Romans 5.12-19
or 5.12, 17-19
Matthew 4.1-11

Mon, Feb 14
Leviticus 19.1-2, 11-18
Psalms 19.8, 9, 10, 15
Matthew 25.31-46

Tue, Feb 15
Isaiah 55.10-11
Psalms 34.4-5, 6-7, 16-17, 18-19
Matthew 6.7-15

Wed, Feb 16
Jonah 3.1-10
Psalms 51.3-4, 12-13, 18-19
Luke 11.29-32

Thu, Feb 17
Esther C.12, 14-16, 23-25
Psalms 138.1-2, 2-3, 7-8
Matthew 7.7-12

Fri, Feb 18
Ezekiel 18.21-28
Psalms 130.1-2, 3-4, 5-6, 7-8
Matthew 5.20-26

Sat, Feb 19
Deuteronomy 26.16-19
Psalms 119.1-2, 4-5, 7-8
Matthew 5.43-48

WEEK 2, LENT

Sun, Feb 20
Genesis 12.1-4
Psalms 33.4-5, 18-19, 20, 22
2 Timothy 1.8-10
Matthew 17.1-9

Mon, Feb 21
Daniel 9.4-10
Psalms 79.8, 9, 11, 13
Luke 6.36-38

Tue, Feb 22
Chair of Saint Peter,
apostle—Feast
I Peter 5.1-4
Psalms 23.1-3, 3-4, 5, 6
Matthew 16.13-19

Wed, Feb 23
Jeremiah 18.18-20
Psalms 31.5-6, 14, 15-16
Matthew 20.17-28

Thu, Feb 24
Jeremiah 17.5-10
Psalms 1.1-2, 3, 4, 6
Luke 16.19-31

Fri, Feb 25
Genesis 37.3-4, 12-13, 17-18
Psalms 105.16-17, 18-19, 20-21
Matthew 21.33-43, 45-46

Sat, Feb 26
Micah 7.14-15, 18-20
Psalms 103.1-2, 3-4, 9-10, 11-12
Luke 15.1-3, 11-32

WEEK 3, LENT

Sun, Feb 27
Exodus 17.3-7
Psalms 95.1-2, 6-7, 8-9
Romans 5.1-2, 5-8
John 4.5-42

Mon, Feb 28
2 Kings 5.1-15
Psalms 42.2, 3; 43.3, 4
Luke 4.24-30

Tue, Mar 1
Daniel 3.25, 34-43
Psalms 25.4-5, 6-7, 8-9
Matthew 18.21-35

Wed, Mar 2
Deuteronomy 4.1, 5-9
Psalms 147.12-13, 15-16, 19-20
Matthew 5.17-19

Thu, Mar 3
Jeremiah 7.23-28
Psalms 95.1-2, 6-7, 8-9
Luke 11.14-23

Fri, Mar 4
Hosea 14.2-10
Psalms 81.6-8, 8-9, 10-11, 14, 17
Mark 12.28-34

Sat, Mar 5
Hosea 6.1-6
Psalms 51.3-4, 18-19, 20-21
Luke 18.9-14

WEEK 4, LENT

Sun, Mar 6
I Samuel 16.1, 6-7, 10-13
Psalms 23.1-3, 3-4, 5, 6
Ephesians 5.8-14
John 9.1-41

Mon, Mar 7
Isaiah 65.17-21
Psalms 30.2, 4, 5-6, 11-13
John 4.43-54

Tue, Mar 8
Ezekiel 47.1-9, 12
Psalms 46.2-3, 5-6, 8-9
John 5.1-3, 5-16

Wed, Mar 9
Isaiah 49.8-15
Psalms 145.8-9, 13-14, 17-18
John 5.17-30

Thu, Mar 10
Exodus 32.7-14
Psalms 106.19-20, 21-22, 23
John 5.31-47

Fri, Mar 11
Wisdom 2.1, 12-22
Psalms 34.17-18, 19-20, 21, 23
John 7.1-2, 10, 25-30

Sat, Mar 12
Jeremiah 11.18-20
Psalms 7.2-3, 9-10, 11-12
John 7.40-53

WEEK 5, LENT

Sun, Mar 13
Ezekiel 37.12-14
Psalms 130.1-2, 3-4, 5-6, 7-8
Romans 8.8-11
John 11.1-45
    or 11.3-7, 17, 20-27, 33-45

Mon, Mar 14
Daniel 13.1-9, 15-17, 19-30, 33-62
Psalms 23.1-3, 3-4, 5, 6
John 8.1-11

Tue, Mar 15
Numbers 21.4-9
Psalms 102.2-3, 16-18, 19-21
John 8.21-30

Wed, Mar 16
Daniel 3.14-20, 91-92, 95
Daniel 3.52, 53, 54, 55, 56
John 8.31-42

Thu, Mar 17
Genesis 17.3-9
Psalms 105.4-5, 6-7, 8-9
John 8.51-59

Fri, Mar 18
Jeremiah 20.10-13
Psalms 18.2-3, 3-4, 5-6, 7
John 10.31-42

Sat, Mar 19
Saint Joseph,
Husband of Mary—
Solemnity
2 Samuel 7.4-5, 12-14, 16
Psalms 89.2-3, 4-5, 27, 29
Romans 4.13, 16-18, 22
Luke 2.41-51

HOLY WEEK

Sun, Mar 20
Passion
(Palm)
Sunday
Isaiah 50.4-7
Psalms 22.8-9, 17-18, 19-20,
    23-24
Philippians 2.6-11
Matthew 26.14—27.66

Mon, Mar 21
Isaiah 42.1-7
Psalms 27.1, 2, 3, 13-14
John 12.1-11

Tue, Mar 22
Isaiah 49.1-6
Psalms 71.1-2, 3-4, 5-6, 15, 17
John 13.21-33, 36-38

Wed, Mar 23
Isaiah 50.4-9
Psalms 69.8-10, 21-22, 31, 33-34
Matthew 26.14-25

Thu, Mar 24
Holy Thursday
Exodus 12.1-8, 11-14
Psalms 116.12-13, 15-16, 17-18
I Corinthians 11.23-26
John 13.1-15

Fri, Mar 25
Good Friday
Isaiah 52.13—53.12
Psalms 31.2, 6, 12-13, 15-16, 17, 25
Hebrews 4.14-16; 5.7-9
John 18.1—19.42

Sat, Mar 26
Holy Saturday
Genesis 1.1—2.2
Psalms 33.4-5, 6-7, 12-13, 20-22
Genesis 22.1-18
Psalms 16.5, 8, 9-10, 11
Exodus 14.15—15.1
Exodus 15.1-2, 3-4, 5-6, 17-18
Isaiah 54.5-14
Psalms 30.2, 4, 5-6, 11-12, 13
Isaiah 55.1-11
Isaiah 12.2-3, 4, 5-6
Baruch 3.9-15, 32—4.4
Psalms 19.8, 9, 10, 11
Ezekiel 36.16-28
Psalms 51.12-13, 14-15, 18-19
Romans 6.3-11
Psalms 118.1-2, 16, 17, 22-23
Matthew 28.1-10

Easter

WEEK 1, EASTER

Sun, Mar 27
Easter Sunday
Acts 10.34, 37-43
Psalms 118.1-2, 16-17, 22-23
I Corinthians 5.6-8
John 20.1-9

Mon, Mar 28
Acts 2.14, 22-32
Psalms 16.1-2, 5, 7-8, 9-10, 11
Matthew 28.8-15

Tue, Mar 29
Acts 2.36-41
Psalms 33.4-5, 18-19, 20, 22
John 20.11-18

Wed, Mar 30
Acts 3.1-10
Psalms 105.1-2, 3-4, 6-7, 8-9
Luke 24.13-35

Thu, Mar 31
Acts 3.11-26
Psalms 8.2, 5, 6-7, 8-9
Luke 24.35-48

Fri, Apr 1
Acts 4.1-12
Psalms 118.1-2, 4, 22-24, 25-27
John 21.1-14

Sat, Apr 2
Acts 4.13-21
Psalms 118.1, 14-15, 16-18, 19-21
Mark 16.9-15

WEEK 2, EASTER

Sun, Apr 3
Acts 2.42-47
Psalms 118.2-4, 13-15, 22-24
I Peter 1.3-9
John 20.19-31

Mon, Apr 4
Annunciation
of the Lord—
Solemnity
Isaiah 7.10-14
Psalms 40.7-8, 8-9, 10, 11
Hebrews 10.4-10
Luke 1.26-38

Tue, Apr 5
Acts 4.32-37
Psalms 93.1, 1-2, 5
John 3.7-15

Wed, Apr 6
Acts 5.17-26
Psalms 34.2-3, 4-5, 6-7, 8-9
John 3.16-21

Thu, Apr 7
Acts 5.27-33
Psalms 34.2, 9, 17-18, 19-20
John 3.31-36

Fri, Apr 8
Acts 5.34-42
Psalms 27.1, 4, 13-14
John 6.1-15

Sat, Apr 9
Acts 6.1-7
Psalms 33.1-2, 4-5, 18-19
John 6.16-21

WEEK 3, EASTER

Sun, Apr 10
Acts 2.14, 22-28
Psalms 16.1-2, 5, 7-8, 9-10, 11
I Peter 1.17-21
Luke 24.13-35

Mon, Apr 11
Acts 6.8-15
Psalms 119.23-24, 26-27, 29-30
John 6.22-29

Tue, Apr 12
Acts 7.51—8.1
Psalms 31.3-4, 6, 7, 8, 17, 21
John 6.30-35

Wed, Apr 13
Acts 8.1-8
Psalms 66.1-3, 4-5, 6-7
John 6.35-40

Thu, Apr 14
Acts 8.26-40
Psalms 66.8-9, 16-17, 20
John 6.44-51

Fri, Apr 15
Acts 9.1-20
Psalms 117.1, 2
John 6.52-59

Sat, Apr 16
Acts 9.31-42
Psalms 116.12-13, 14-15, 16-17
John 6.60-69

WEEK 4, EASTER

Sun, Apr 17
Acts 2.14, 36-41
Psalms 23.1-3, 3-4, 5, 6
I Peter 2.20-25
John 10.1-10

Mon, Apr 18
Acts 11.1-18
Psalms 42.2-3; 43.3, 4
John 10.11-18

Tue, Apr 19
Acts 11.19-26
Psalms 87.1-3, 4-5, 6-7
John 10.22-30

Wed, Apr 20
Acts 12.24—13.5
Psalms 67.2-3, 5, 6, 8
John 12.44-50

Thu, Apr 21
Acts 13.13-25
Psalms 89.2-3, 21-22, 25, 27
John 13.16-20

Fri, Apr 22
Acts 13.26-33
Psalms 2.6-7, 8-9, 10-11
John 14.1-6

Sat, Apr 23
Acts 13.44-52
Psalms 98.1, 2-3, 3-4
John 14.7-14

WEEK 5, EASTER

Sun, Apr 24
Acts 6.1-7
Psalms 33.1-2, 4-5, 18-19
I Peter 2.4-9
John 14.1-12

Mon, Apr 25
Saint Mark,
evangelist—Feast
I Peter 5.5-14
Psalms 89.2-3, 6-7, 16-17
Mark 16.15-20

Tue, Apr 26
Acts 14.19-28
Psalms 145.10-11, 12-13, 21
John 14.27-31

Wed, Apr 27
Acts 15.1-6
Psalms 122.1-2, 3-4, 4-5
John 15.1-8

Thu, Apr 28
Acts 15.7-21
Psalms 96.1-2, 2-3, 10
John 15.9-11

Fri, Apr 29
Acts 15.22-31
Psalms 57.8-9, 10-12
John 15.12-17

Sat, Apr 30
Acts 16.1-10
Psalms 100.1-2, 3, 5
John 15.18-21

WEEK 6, EASTER

Sun, May 1
Acts 8.5-8, 14-17
Psalms 66.1-3, 4-5, 6-7, 16, 20
I Peter 3.15-18
John 14.15-21

Mon, May 2
Acts 16.11-15
Psalms 149.1-2, 3-4, 5-6, 9
John 15.26—16.4

Tue, May 3
Saints Philip and
James, apostles—Feast
I Corinthians 15.1-8
Psalms 19.2-3, 4-5
John 14.6-14

Wed, May 4
Acts 17.15, 22—18.1
Psalms 148.1-2, 11-12, 13, 14
John 16.12-15

Thu, May 5
Ascension of the Lord
Acts 1.1-11
Psalms 47.2-3, 6-7, 8-9
Ephesians 1.17-23
Matthew 28.16-20

Fri, May 6
Acts 18.9-18
Psalms 47.2-3, 4-5, 6-7
John 16.20-23

Sat, May 7
Acts 18.23-28
Psalms 47.2-3, 8-9, 10
John 16.23-28

WEEK 7, EASTER

Sun, May 8
Acts 1.12-14
Psalms 27.1, 4, 7-8
I Peter 4.13-16
John 17.1-11

Mon, May 9
Acts 19.1-8
Psalms 68.2-3, 4-5, 6-7
John 16.29-33

Tue, May 10
Acts 20.17-27
Psalms 68.10-11, 20-21
John 17.1-11

Wed, May 11
Acts 20.28-38
Psalms 68.29-30, 33-35, 35-36
John 17.11-19

Thu, May 12
Acts 22.30; 23.6-11
Psalms 16.1-2, 5, 7-8, 9-10, 11
John 17.20-26

Fri, May 13
Acts 25.13-21
Psalms 103.1-2, 11-12, 19-20
John 21.15-19

Sat, May 14
Saint Matthias,
apostle—Feast
Acts 1.15-17, 20-26
Psalms 113.1-2, 3-4, 5-6, 7-8
John 15.9-17

Sun, May 15
Pentecost
Acts 2.1-11
Psalms 104.1, 24, 29-30, 31, 34
I Corinthians 12.3-7, 12-13
John 20.19-23

Ordinary Time

WEEK 7

Mon, May 16
Sirach 1.1-10
Psalms 93.1, 1-2, 5
Mark 9.14-29

Tue, May 17
Sirach 2.1-11
Psalms 37.3-4, 18-19, 27-28, 39-40
Mark 9.30-37

Wed, May 18
Sirach 4.11-19
Psalms 119.165, 168, 171, 172, 174, 175
Mark 9.38-40

Thu, May 19
Sirach 5.1-8
Psalms 1.1-2, 3-4, 6
Mark 9.41-50

Fri, May 20
Sirach 6.5-17
Psalms 119.12, 16, 18, 27, 34, 35
Mark 10.1-12

Sat, May 21
Sirach 17.1-15
Psalms 103.13-14, 15-16, 17-18
Mark 10.13-16

WEEK 8

Sun, May 22
The Holy Trinity—
Solemnity

Exodus 34.4-6, 8-9
Daniel 3.52, 53, 54, 55, 56
2 Corinthians 13.11-13
John 3.16-18

Mon, May 23

Sirach 17.19-27
Psalms 32.1-2, 5, 6, 7
Mark 10.17-27

Tue, May 24

Sirach 35.1-12
Psalms 50.5-6, 7-8, 14, 23
Mark 10.28-31

Wed, May 25

Sirach 36.5-6, 10-17
Psalms 79.8, 9, 11, 13
Mark 10.32-45

Thu, May 26

Sirach 42.15-25
Psalms 33.2-3, 4-5, 6-7, 8-9
Mark 10.46-52

Fri, May 27

Sirach 44.1, 9-13
Psalms 149.1-2, 3-4, 5-6, 9
Mark 11.11-26

Sat, May 28

Sirach 51.12-20
Psalms 19.8, 9, 10, 11
Mark 11.27-33

WEEK 9

Sun, May 29
The Body and Blood of
Christ (Corpus Christi)
—Solemnity

Deuteronomy 8.2-3, 14-16
Psalms 147.12-13, 14-15, 19-20
1 Corinthians 10.16-17
John 6.51-58

Mon, May 30

Tobit 1.1, 2; 2.1-9
Psalms 112.1-2, 3-4, 5-6
Mark 12.1-12

Tue, May 31
Visitation of the
Virgin Mary to
Elizabeth—Feast

Romans 12.9-16
Isaiah 12.2-3, 4, 5-6
Luke 1.39-56

Wed, June 1

Tobit 3.1-11, 16
Psalms 25.2-4, 4-5, 6-7, 8-9
Mark 12.18-27

Thu, June 2

Tobit 6.11; 7.1, 9-14; 8.4-7
Psalms 128.1-2, 3, 4-5
Mark 12.28-34

Fri, June 3
Sacred Heart of Jesus—
Solemnity

Deuteronomy 7.6-11
Psalms 103.1-2, 3-4, 6-7, 8, 10
1 John 4.7-16
Matthew 11.25-30

Sat, June 4

Tobit 12.1, 5-15, 20
Tobit 13.2, 6
Mark 12.38-44

WEEK 10

Sun, June 5

Hosea 6.3-6
Psalms 50.1, 8, 12-13, 14-15
Romans 4.18-25
Matthew 9.9-13

Mon, June 6

2 Corinthians 1.1-7
Psalms 34.2-3, 4-5, 6-7, 8-9
Matthew 5.1-12

Tue, June 7

2 Corinthians 1.18-22
Psalms 119.129, 130, 131, 132,
133, 135
Matthew 5.13-16

Wed, June 8

2 Corinthians 3.4-11
Psalms 99.5, 6, 7, 8, 9
Matthew 5.17-19

Thu, June 9

2 Corinthians 3.15—4.1, 3-6
Psalms 85.9-10, 11-12, 13-14
Matthew 5.20-26

Fri, June 10

2 Corinthians 4.7-15
Psalms 116.10-11, 15-16, 17-18
Matthew 5.27-32

Sat, June 11
Saint Barnabas,
apostle—Memorial

Acts 11.21-26; 13.1-3
Psalms 98.1, 2-3, 3-4, 5-6
Matthew 10.7-13

WEEK 11

Sun, June 12

Exodus 19.2-6
Psalms 100.1-2, 3, 5
Romans 5.6-11
Matthew 9.36—10.8

Mon, June 13

2 Corinthians 6.1-10
Psalms 98.1, 2-3, 3-4
Matthew 5.38-42

Tue, June 14

2 Corinthians 8.1-9
Psalms 146.2, 5-6, 7, 8-9
Matthew 5.43-48

Wed, June 15

2 Corinthians 9.6-11
Psalms 112.1-2, 3-4, 9
Matthew 6.1-6, 16-18

Thu, June 16

2 Corinthians 11.1-11
Psalms 111.1-2, 3-4, 7-8
Matthew 6.7-15

Fri, June 17

2 Corinthians 11.18, 21-30
Psalms 34.2-3, 4-5, 6-7
Matthew 6.19-23

Sat, June 18

2 Corinthians 12.1-10
Psalms 34.8-9, 10-11, 12-13
Matthew 6.24-34

WEEK 12

Sun, June 19
Jeremiah 20.10-13
Psalms 69.8-10, 14, 17, 33-35
Romans 5.12-15
Matthew 10.26-33

Mon, June 20
Genesis 12.1-9
Psalms 33.12-13, 18-19, 20, 22
Matthew 7.1-5

Tue, June 21
Genesis 13.2, 5-18
Psalms 15.2-3, 3-4, 5
Matthew 7.6, 12-14

Wed, June 22
Genesis 15.1-12, 17-18
Psalms 105.1-2, 3-4, 6-7, 8-9
Matthew 7.15-20

Thu, June 23
Genesis 16.1-12, 15-16
   or 16.6-12, 15-16
Psalms 106.1-2, 3-4, 4-5
Matthew 7.21-29

Fri, June 24
Birth of Saint John the
Baptist—Solemnity
Isaiah 49.1-6
Psalms 139.1-3, 13-14, 14-15
Acts 13.22-26
Luke 1.57-66, 80

Sat, June 25
Genesis 18.1-15
Luke 1.46-47, 48-49, 50, 53,
   54-55
Matthew 8.5-17

WEEK 13

Sun, June 26
2 Kings 4.8-11, 14-16
Psalms 89.2-3, 16-17, 18-19
Romans 6.3-4, 8-11
Matthew 10.37-42

Mon, June 27
Genesis 18.16-33
Psalms 103.1-2, 3-4, 8-9, 10-11
Matthew 8.18-22

Tue, June 28
Genesis 19.15-29
Psalms 26.2-3, 9-10, 11-12
Matthew 8.23-27

Wed, June 29
Saints Peter and Paul,
apostles—Solemnity
Acts 12.1-11
Psalms 34.2-3, 4-5, 6-7, 8-9
2 Timothy 4.6-8, 17-18
Matthew 16.13-19

Thu, June 30
Genesis 22.1-19
Psalms 115.1-2, 3-4, 5-6, 8-9
Matthew 9.1-8

Fri, July 1
Genesis 23.1-4, 19; 24.1-8, 62-67
Psalms 106.1-2, 3-4, 4-5
Matthew 9.9-13

Sat, July 2
Genesis 27.1-5, 15-29
Psalms 135.1-2, 3-4, 5-6
Matthew 9.14-17

WEEK 14

Sun, July 3
Zechariah 9.9-10
Psalms 145.1-2, 8-9, 10-11, 13-14
Romans 8.9, 11-13
Matthew 11.25-30

Mon, July 4
Genesis 28.10-22
Psalms 91.1-2, 3-4, 14-15
Matthew 9.18-26

Tue, July 5
Genesis 32.23-33
Psalms 17.1, 2-3, 6-7, 8, 15
Matthew 9.32-38

Wed, July 6
Genesis 41.55-57; 42.5-7, 17-24
Psalms 33.2-3, 10-11, 18-19
Matthew 10.1-7

Thu, July 7
Genesis 44.18-21, 23-29; 45.1-5
Psalms 105.16-17, 18-19, 20-21
Matthew 10.7-15

Fri, July 8
Genesis 46.1-7, 28-30
Psalms 37.3-4, 18-19, 27-28,
   39-40
Matthew 10.16-23

Sat, July 9
Genesis 49.29-33; 50.15-24
Psalms 105.1-2, 3-4, 6-7
Matthew 10.24-33

WEEK 15

Sun, July 10
Isaiah 55.10-11
Psalms 65.10, 11, 12-13, 14
Romans 8.18-23
Matthew 13.1-23
   or 13.1-9

Mon, July 11
Exodus 1.8-14, 22
Psalms 124.1-3, 4-6, 7-8
Matthew 10.34—11.1

Tue, July 12
Exodus 2.1-15
Psalms 69.3, 14, 30-31, 33-34
Matthew 11.20-24

Wed, July 13
Exodus 3.1-6, 9-12
Psalms 103.1-2, 3-4, 6-7
Matthew 11.25-27

Thu, July 14
Exodus 3.11-20
Psalms 105.5, 8-9, 24-25, 26-27
Matthew 11.28-30

Fri, July 15
Exodus 11.10—12.14
Psalms 116.12-13, 15-16, 17-18
Matthew 12.1-8

Sat, July 16
Exodus 12.37-42
Psalms 136.1, 23-24, 10-12, 13-15
Matthew 12.14-21

WEEK 16

Sun, July 17
Wisdom 12.13, 16-19
Psalms 86.5-6, 9-10, 15-16
Romans 8.26-27
Matthew 13.24-43

Mon, July 18
Exodus 14.5-18
Exodus 15.1-2, 3-4, 5-6
Matthew 12.38-42

Tue, July 19
Exodus 14.21—15.1
Exodus 15.8-9, 10, 12, 17
Matthew 12.46-50

Wed, July 20
Exodus 16.1-5, 9-15
Psalms 78.18-19, 23-24, 25-26,
   27-28
Matthew 13.1-9

Thu, July 21
Exodus 19.1-2, 9-11, 16-20
Daniel 3.52, 53, 54, 55, 56
Matthew 13.10-17

Fri, July 22
Saint Mary
Magdalene—Memorial
Song of Songs 3.1-4
Psalms 63.2, 3-4, 5-6, 8-9
John 20.1-2, 11-18

Sat, July 23
Exodus 24.3-8
Psalms 50.1-2, 5-6, 14-15
Matthew 13.24-30

WEEK 17

Sun, July 24
I Kings 3.5, 7-12
Psalms 119.57, 72, 76-77,
   127-128, 129-130
Romans 8.28-30
Matthew 13.44-52

Mon, July 25
Saint James, apostle—
Feast
2 Corinthians 4.7-15
Psalms 126.1-2, 2-3, 4-5, 6
Matthew 20.20-28

Tue, July 26
Saints Joachim and
Ann, parents of
Mary—Memorial
Sirach 44.1, 10-15
Psalms 132.11, 13-14, 17-18
Matthew 13.16-17

Wed, July 27
Exodus 34.29-35
Psalms 99.5, 6, 7, 9
Matthew 13.44-46

Thu, July 28
Exodus 40.16-21, 34-38
Psalms 84.3, 4, 5-6, 8, 11
Matthew 13.47-53

Fri, July 29
Saint Martha—
Memorial
Proverbs 31.10-13, 19-20, 30-31
Psalms 112.1-2, 3-4, 5-6, 7-8, 9
John 11.19-27

Sat, July 30
Leviticus 25.1, 8-17
Psalms 67.2-3, 5, 7-8
Matthew 14.1-12

WEEK 18

Sun, July 31
Isaiah 55.1-3
Psalms 145.8-9, 15-16, 17-18
Romans 8.35, 37-39
Matthew 14.13-21

Mon, Aug 1
Numbers 11.4-15
Psalms 81.12-13, 14-15, 16-17
Matthew 14.13-21

Tue, Aug 2
Numbers 12.1-13
Psalms 51.3-4, 5-6, 6-7, 12-13
Matthew 14.22-36

Wed, Aug 3
Numbers 13.1-2, 25—14.1, 26-29,
   34-35
Psalms 106.6-7, 13-14, 21-22, 23
Matthew 15.21-28

Thu, Aug 4
Numbers 20.1-13
Psalms 95.1-2, 6-7, 8-9
Matthew 16.13-23

Fri, Aug 5
Deuteronomy 4.32-40
Psalms 77.12-13, 14-15, 16, 21
Matthew 16.24-28

Sat, Aug 6
Transfiguration
of the Lord—
Feast
Daniel 7.9-10, 13-14
Psalms 97.1-2, 5-6, 9
2 Peter 1.16-19
Matthew 17.1-9

WEEK 19

Sun, Aug 7
I Kings 19.9, 11-13
Psalms 85.9, 10, 11-12, 13-14
Romans 9.1-5
Matthew 14.22-33

Mon, Aug 8
Deuteronomy 10.12-22
Psalms 147.12-13, 14-15, 19-20
Matthew 17.22-27

Tue, Aug 9
Deuteronomy 31.1-8
Deuteronomy 32.3-4, 7, 8, 9, 12
Matthew 18.1-5, 10, 12-14

Wed, Aug 10
Saint Lawrence,
deacon and martyr—
Feast
2 Corinthians 9.6-10
Psalms 112.1-2, 5-6, 7-8, 9
John 12.24-26

Thu, Aug 11
Joshua 3.7-10, 11, 13-17
Psalms 114.1-2, 3-4, 5-6
Matthew 18.21—19.1

Fri, Aug 12
Joshua 24.1-13
Psalms 136.1-3, 16-18, 21-22, 24
Matthew 19.3-12

Sat, Aug 13
Joshua 24.14-29
Psalms 16.1-2, 5, 7-8, 11
Matthew 19.13-15

WEEK 20

Sun, Aug 14
Isaiah 56.1, 6-7
Psalms 67.2-3, 5, 6, 8
Romans 11.13-15, 29-32
Matthew 15.21-28

Mon, Aug 15
Assumption of the
Virgin Mary into
Heaven—Solemnity
Revelation 11.19; 12.1-6, 10
Psalms 45.10, 11, 12, 16
I Corinthians 15.20-26
Luke 1.39-56

Tue, Aug 16
Judges 6.11-24
Psalms 85.9, 11-12, 13-14
Matthew 19.23-30

Wed, Aug 17
Judges 9.6-15
Psalms 21.2-3, 4-5, 6-7
Matthew 20.1-16

Thu, Aug 18
Judges 11.29-39
Psalms 40.5, 7-8, 8-9, 10
Matthew 22.1-14

Fri, Aug 19
Ruth 1.1, 3-6, 14-16, 22
Psalms 146.5-6, 7, 8-9, 9-10
Matthew 22.34-40

Sat, Aug 20
Ruth 2.1-3, 8-11; 4.13-17
Psalms 128.1-2, 3, 4, 5
Matthew 23.1-12

WEEK 21

Sun, Aug 21
Isaiah 22.15, 19-23
Psalms 138.1-2, 2-3, 6, 8
Romans 11.33-36
Matthew 16.13-20

Mon, Aug 22
I Thessalonians 1.2-5, 8-10
Psalms 149.1-2, 3-4, 5-6, 9
Matthew 23.13-22

Tue, Aug 23
I Thessalonians 2.1-8
Psalms 139.1-3, 4-5
Matthew 23.23-26

Wed, Aug 24
Saint Bartholomew,
apostle—Feast
Revelation 21.9-14
Psalms 145.10-11, 12-13, 17-18
John 1.45-51

Thu, Aug 25
I Thessalonians 3.7-13
Psalms 90.3-4, 12-13, 14, 17
Matthew 24.42-51

Fri, Aug 26
I Thessalonians 4.1-8
Psalms 97.1, 2, 5-6, 10, 11-12
Matthew 25.1-13

Sat, Aug 27
I Thessalonians 4.9-12
Psalms 98.1, 7-8, 9
Matthew 25.14-30

WEEK 22

Sun, Aug 28
Jeremiah 20.7-9
Psalms 63.2, 3-4, 5-6, 8-9
Romans 12.1-2
Matthew 16.21-27

Mon, Aug 29
Beheading of
Saint John the Baptist,
martyr—Memorial
Jeremiah 1.17-19
Psalms 71.1-2, 3-4, 5-6, 15, 17
Mark 6.17-29

Tue, Aug 30
I Thessalonians 5.1-6, 9-11
Psalms 27.1, 4, 13-14
Luke 4.31-37

Wed, Aug 31
Colossians 1.1-8
Psalms 52.10, 11
Luke 4.38-44

Thu, Sept 1
Colossians 1.9-14
Psalms 98.2-3, 3-4, 5-6
Luke 5.1-11

Fri, Sept 2
Colossians 1.15-20
Psalms 100.1, 2, 3, 4, 5
Luke 5.33-39

Sat, Sept 3
Colossians 1.21-23
Psalms 54.3-4, 6, 8
Luke 6.1-5

WEEK 23

Sun, Sept 4
Ezekiel 33.7-9
Psalms 95.1-2, 6-7, 8-9
Romans 13.8-10
Matthew 18.15-20

Mon, Sept 5
Colossians 1.24—2.3
Psalms 62.6-7, 9
Luke 6.6-11

Tue, Sept 6
Colossians 2.6-15
Psalms 145.1-2, 8-9, 10-11
Luke 6.12-19

Wed, Sept 7
Colossians 3.1-11
Psalms 145.2-3, 10-11, 12-13
Luke 6.20-26

Thu, Sept 8
Birth of the
Virgin Mary—
Feast
Micah 5.1-4,
    or Romans 8.28-30
Psalms 13.6, 6
Matthew 1.1-16, 18-23
    or 1.18-23

Fri, Sept 9
I Timothy 1.1-2, 12-14
Psalms 16.1-2, 5, 7-8, 11
Luke 6.39-42

Sat, Sept 10
I Timothy 1.15-17
Psalms 113.1-2, 3-4, 5, 6-7
Luke 6.43-49

WEEK 24

Sun, Sept 11
Sirach 27.30—28.7
Psalms 103.1-2, 3-4, 9-10, 11-12
Romans 14.7-9
Matthew 18.21-35

Mon, Sept 12
1 Timothy 2.1-8
Psalms 28.2, 7, 8-9
Luke 7.1-10

Tue, Sept 13
1 Timothy 3.1-13
Psalms 101.1-2, 2-3, 5, 6
Luke 7.11-17

Wed, Sept 14
Triumph
of the Holy Cross—
Feast
Numbers 21.4-9
Psalms 78.1-2, 34-35, 36-37, 38
Philippians 2.6-11
John 3.13-17

Thu, Sept 15
Our Lady of Sorrows—
Memorial
Hebrews 5.7-9
Psalms 31.2-3, 3-4, 5-6, 15-16, 20
John 19.25-27

Fri, Sept 16
1 Timothy 6.2-12
Psalms 49.6-7, 8-10, 17-18, 19-20
Luke 8.1-3

Sat, Sept 17
1 Timothy 6.13-16
Psalms 100.2, 3, 4, 5
Luke 8.4-15

WEEK 25

Sun, Sept 18
Isaiah 55.6-9
Psalms 145.2-3, 8-9, 17-18
Philippians 1.20-24, 27
Matthew 20.1-16

Mon, Sept 19
Ezra 1.1-6
Psalms 126.1-2, 2-3, 4-5, 6
Luke 8.16-18

Tue, Sept 20
Ezra 6.7-8, 12, 14-20
Psalms 122.1-2, 3-4, 4-5
Luke 8.19-21

Wed, Sept 21
Saint Matthew,
apostle and
evangelist—Feast
Ephesians 4.1-7, 11-13
Psalms 19.2-3, 4-5
Matthew 9.9-13

Thu, Sept 22
Haggai 1.1-8
Psalms 149.1-2, 3-4, 5-6, 9
Luke 9.7-9

Fri, Sept 23
Haggai 1.15—2.9
Psalms 43.1, 2, 3, 4
Luke 9.18-22

Sat, Sept 24
Zechariah 2.5-9, 14-15
Jeremiah 31.10, 11-12, 13
Luke 9.43-45

WEEK 26

Sun, Sept 25
Ezekiel 18.25-28
Psalms 25.4-5, 6-7, 8-9
Philippians 2.1-11
or 2.1-5
Matthew 21.28-32

Mon, Sept 26
Zechariah 8.1-8
Psalms 102.16-18, 19-21, 29, 22-23
Luke 9.46-50

Tue, Sept 27
Zechariah 8.20-23
Psalms 87.1-3, 4-5, 6-7
Luke 9.51-56

Wed, Sept 28
Nehemiah 2.1-8
Psalms 137.1-2, 3, 4-5, 6
Luke 9.57-62

Thu, Sept 29
Michael, Gabriel, and
Raphael, archangels—
Feast
Revelation 12.7-12
Psalms 138.1-2, 2-3, 4-5
John 1.47-51

Fri, Sept 30
Baruch 1.15-22
Psalms 79.1-2, 3-5, 8, 9
Luke 10.13-16

Sat, Oct 1
Baruch 4.5-12, 27-29
Psalms 69.33-35, 36-37
Luke 10.17-24

WEEK 27

Sun, Oct 2
Isaiah 5.1-7
Psalms 80.9, 12, 13-14, 15-16, 19-20
Philippians 4.6-9
Matthew 21.33-43

Mon, Oct 3
Jonah 1.1—2.1, 11
Psalms 2.2, 3, 4, 5, 8
Luke 10.25-37

Tue, Oct 4
Jonah 3.1-10
Psalms 130.1-2, 3-4, 7-8
Luke 10.38-42

Wed, Oct 5
Jonah 4.1-11
Psalms 86.3-4, 5-6, 9-10
Luke 11.1-4

Thu, Oct 6
Malachi 3.13-20
Psalms 1.1-2, 3, 4, 6
Luke 11.5-13

Fri, Oct 7
Joel 1.13-15; 2.1-2
Psalms 9.2-3, 6, 16, 8-9
Luke 11.15-26

Sat, Oct 8
Joel 4.12-21
Psalms 97.1-2, 5-6, 11-12
Luke 11.27-28

WEEK 28

Sun, Oct 9
Isaiah 25.6-10
Psalms 23.1-3, 3-4, 5, 6
Philippians 4.12-14, 19-20
Matthew 22.1-14
or 22.1-10

Mon, Oct 10
Romans 1.1-7
Psalms 98.1, 2-3, 3-4
Luke 11.29-32

Tue, Oct 11
Romans 1.16-25
Psalms 19.2-3, 4-5
Luke 11.37-41

Wed, Oct 12
Romans 2.1-11
Psalms 62.2-3, 6-7, 9
Luke 11.42-46

Thu, Oct 13
Romans 3.21-29
Psalms 130.1-2, 3-4, 5-6
Luke 11.47-54

Fri, Oct 14
Romans 4.1-8
Psalms 32.1-2, 5, 11
Luke 12.1-7

Sat, Oct 15
Romans 4.13, 16-18
Psalms 105.6-7, 8-9, 42-43
Luke 12.8-12

WEEK 29

Sun, Oct 16
Isaiah 45.1, 4-6
Psalms 96.1, 3, 4-5, 7-8, 9-10
I Thessalonians 1.1-5
Matthew 22.15-21

Mon, Oct 17
Romans 4.20-25
Luke 1.69-70, 71-72, 73-75
Luke 12.13-21

Tue, Oct 18
Saint Luke,
evangelist—Feast
2 Timothy 4.9-17
Psalms 145.10-11, 12-13, 17-18
Luke 10.1-9

Wed, Oct 19
Romans 6.12-18
Psalms 124.1-3, 4-6, 7-8
Luke 12.39-48

Thu, Oct 20
Romans 6.19-23
Psalms 1.1-2, 3, 4, 6
Luke 12.49-53

Fri, Oct 21
Romans 7.18-25
Psalms 119.66, 68, 76, 77, 93, 94
Luke 12.54-59

Sat, Oct 22
Romans 8.1-11
Psalms 24.1-2, 3-4, 5-6
Luke 13.1-9

WEEK 30

Sun, Oct 23
Exodus 22.20-26
Psalms 18.2-3, 3-4, 47, 51
I Thessalonians 1.5-10
Matthew 22.34-40

Mon, Oct 24
Romans 8.12-17
Psalms 68.2, 4, 6-7, 20-21
Luke 13.10-17

Tue, Oct 25
Romans 8.18-25
Psalms 126.1-2, 2-3, 4-5, 6
Luke 13.18-21

Wed, Oct 26
Romans 8.26-30
Psalms 13.4-5, 6
Luke 13.22-30

Thu, Oct 27
Romans 8.31-39
Psalms 109.21-22, 26-27, 30-31
Luke 13.31-35

Fri, Oct 28
Saints Simon and
Jude, apostles—Feast
Ephesians 2.19-22
Psalms 19.2-3, 4-5
Luke 6.12-16

Sat, Oct 29
Romans 11.1-2, 11-12, 25-29
Psalms 94.12-13, 14-15, 17-18
Luke 14.1, 7-11

WEEK 31

Sun, Oct 30
Malachi 1.14—2.2, 8-10
Psalms 131.1, 2, 3
I Thessalonians 2.7-9, 13
Matthew 23.1-12

Mon, Oct 31
Romans 11.29-36
Psalms 69.30-31, 33-34, 36-37
Luke 14.12-14

Tue, Nov 1
All Saints—Solemnity
Revelation 7.2-4, 9-14
Psalms 24.1-2, 3-4, 5-6
I John 3.1-3
Matthew 5.1-12

Wed, Nov 2
Commemoration of
All the Faithful
Departed (All Souls)—
Solemnity
Wisdom 3.1-9 or 3.1-6, 9
Psalms 27.1, 4, 7, 8, 9, 13-14
Romans 6.3-9
Matthew 25.31-46

Thu, Nov 3
Romans 14.7-12
Psalms 27.1-4, 13-14
Luke 15.1-10

Fri, Nov 4
Romans 15.14-21
Psalms 98.1, 2-3, 3-4
Luke 16.1-8

Sat, Nov 5
Romans 16.3-9, 16, 22-27
Psalms 145.2-3, 4-5, 10-11
Luke 16.9-15

WEEK 32

Sun, Nov 6
Wisdom 6.12-16
Psalms 63.2, 3-4, 5-6, 7-8
I Thessalonians 4.13-17
  or 4.13-14
Matthew 25.1-13

Mon, Nov 7
Wisdom 1.1-7
Psalms 139.1-3, 4-6, 7-8, 9-10
Luke 17.1-6

Tue, Nov 8
Wisdom 2.23—3.9
Psalms 34.2-3, 16-17, 18-19
Luke 17.7-10

Wed, Nov 9
Dedication of the
Basilica of St. John
Lateran in Rome—
Feast
Genesis 28.11-18
Psalms 84.3, 4, 5-6, 8, 11
I Corinthians 3.9-13, 16-17
Luke 19.1-10

Thu, Nov 10
Wisdom 7.22—8.1
Psalms 119.89, 90, 91, 130, 135, 175
Luke 17.20-25

Fri, Nov 11
Wisdom 13.1-9
Psalms 19.2-3, 4-5
Luke 17.26-37

Sat, Nov 12
Wisdom 18.14-16; 19.6-9
Psalms 105.2-3, 36-37, 42-43
Luke 18.1-8

WEEK 33

Sun, Nov 13
Proverbs 31.10-13, 19-20, 30-31
Psalms 128.1-2, 3, 4-5
I Thessalonians 5.1-6
Matthew 25.14-30
  or 25.14-15, 19-20

Mon, Nov 14
I Maccabees 1.10-15, 41-43,
  54-57, 62-63
Psalms 119.53, 61, 134, 150,
  155, 158
Luke 18.35-43

Tue, Nov 15
2 Maccabees 6.18-31
Psalms 3.2-3, 4-5, 6-8
Luke 19.1-10

Wed, Nov 16
2 Maccabees 7.1, 20-31
Psalms 17.1, 5-6, 8, 15
Luke 19.11-28

Thu, Nov 17
I Maccabees 2.15-29
Psalms 50.1-2, 5-6, 14-15
Luke 9.41-44

Fri, Nov 18
I Maccabees 4.36-37, 52-59
I Chronicles 29.10, 11, 11-12, 12
Luke 19.45-48

Sat, Nov 19
I Maccabees 6.1-13
Psalms 9.2-3, 4, 6, 16, 19
Luke 20.27-40

WEEK 34

Sun, Nov 20
Christ the King—
Solemnity
Ezekiel 34.11-12, 15-17
Psalms 23.1-2, 2-3, 5, 6
I Corinthians 15.20-26, 28
Matthew 25.31-46

Mon, Nov 21
Daniel 1.1-6, 8-20
Daniel 3.52, 53, 54, 55, 56
Luke 21.1-4

Tue, Nov 22
Daniel 2.31-45
Daniel 3.57, 58, 59, 60, 61
Luke 21.5-11

Wed, Nov 23
Daniel 5.1-6, 13-14, 16-17, 23-28
Daniel 3.62, 63, 64, 65, 66, 67
Luke 21.12-19

Thu, Nov 24
Daniel 6.12-28
Daniel 3.68, 69, 70, 71, 72, 73, 74
Luke 21.20-28

Fri, Nov 25
Daniel 7.2-14
Daniel 3.75, 76, 77, 78, 79, 80, 81
Luke 21.29-33

Sat, Nov 26
Daniel 7.15-27
Daniel 3.82, 83, 84, 85, 86, 87
Luke 21.34-36

Advent, *Liturgical year 2006*

WEEK I, ADVENT

Sun, Nov 27, 2005
Isaiah 63.16-17, 19
Psalms 80.2-3, 15-16, 18-19
I Corinthians 1.3-9
Mark 13.33-37

Mon, Nov 28
Isaiah 2.1-5
Psalms 122.1-2, 3-4, 4-5, 6-7, 8-9
Matthew 8.5-11

Tue, Nov 29
Isaiah 11.1-10
Psalms 72.1, 7-8, 12-13, 17
Luke 10.21-24

Wed, Nov 30
Saint Andrew,
apostle—Feast
Romans 10.9-18
Psalms 19.2-3, 4-5
Matthew 4.18-22

Thu, Dec 1
Isaiah 26.1-6
Psalms 118.1, 8-9, 19-21, 25-27
Matthew 7.21, 24-27

Fri, Dec 2
Isaiah 29.17-24
Psalms 27.1, 4, 13-14
Matthew 9.27-31

Sat, Dec 3
Isaiah 30.19-21, 23-26
Psalms 147.1-2, 3-4, 5-6
Matthew 9.35—10.1, 6-8

WEEK 2, ADVENT

Sun, Dec 4
Isaiah 40.1-5, 9-11
Psalms 85.9-10, 11-12, 13-14
2 Peter 3.8-14
Mark 1.1-8

Mon, Dec 5
Isaiah 35.1-10
Psalms 85.9-10, 11-12, 13-14
Luke 5.17-26

Tue, Dec 6
Isaiah 40.1-11
Psalms 96.1-2, 3, 10, 11-12, 13
Matthew 18.12-14

Wed, Dec 7
Isaiah 40.25-31
Psalms 103.1-2, 3-4, 8, 10
Matthew 11.28-30

Thu, Dec 8
*Immaculate
Conception of the
Virgin Mary—
Solemnity*
Genesis 3.9-15, 20
Psalms 98.1, 2-3, 3-4
Ephesians 1.3-6, 11-12
Luke 1.26-38

Fri, Dec 9
Isaiah 48.17-19
Psalms 1.1-2, 3, 4, 6
Matthew 11.16-19

Sat, Dec 10
Sirach 48.1-4, 9-11
Psalms 80.2-3, 15-16, 18-19
Matthew 17.10-13

WEEK 3, ADVENT

Sun, Dec 11
Isaiah 61.1-2, 10-11
Luke 1.46-48, 49-50, 53-54
1 Thessalonians 5.16-24
John 1.6-8, 19-28

Mon, Dec 12
*Our Lady of
Guadalupe—
Feast*
Zechariah 2.14-17
Psalms 45.11-12, 14-17
Romans 8.28-30
Luke 2.15-19

Tue, Dec 13
Zephaniah 3.1-2, 9-13
Psalms 34.2-3, 6-7, 17-18, 19, 23
Matthew 21.28-32

Wed, Dec 14
Isaiah 45.6-8, 18, 21-25
Psalms 85.9-10, 11-12, 13-14
Luke 7.18-23

Thu, Dec 15
Isaiah 54.1-10
Psalms 30.2, 4, 5-6, 11-12, 13
Luke 7.24-30

Fri, Dec 16
Isaiah 56.1-3, 6-8
Psalms 67.2-3, 5, 7-8
John 5.33-36

Sat, Dec 17
Genesis 49.2, 8-10
Psalms 72.3-4, 7-8, 17
Matthew 1.1-17

WEEK 4, ADVENT

Sun, Dec 18
2 Samuel 7.1-5, 8-11, 16
Psalms 89.2-3, 4-5, 27, 29
Romans 16.25-27
Luke 1.26-38

Mon, Dec 19
Judges 13.2-7, 24-25
Psalms 71.3-4, 5-6, 16-17
Luke 1.5-25

Tue, Dec 20
Isaiah 7.10-14
Psalms 24.1-2, 3-4, 5-6
Luke 1.26-38

Wed, Dec 21
Song of Songs 2.8-14
Psalms 33.2-3, 11-12, 20-21
Luke 1.39-45

Thu, Dec 22
1 Samuel 1.24-28
1 Samuel 2.1, 4-5, 6-7, 8
Luke 1.46-56

Fri, Dec 23
Malachi 3.1-4, 23-24
Psalms 25.4-5, 8-9, 10, 14
Luke 1.57-66

Sat, Dec 24
2 Samuel 7.1-5, 8-11, 16
Psalms 89.2-3, 4-5, 27, 29
Luke 1.67-79

Christmas

Sun, Dec 25
Christmas—Solemnity
Isaiah 62.11-12
Psalms 97.1, 6, 11-12
Titus 3.4-7
Luke 2.15-20

Mon, Dec 26
*Saint Stephen, first
martyr—Feast*
Acts 6.8-10; 7.54-59
Psalms 31.3-4, 6, 7, 8, 17, 21
Matthew 10.17-22

Tue, Dec 27
*Saint John, apostle
and evangelist—Feast*
1 John 1.1-4
Psalms 97.1-2, 5-6, 11-12
John 20.2-8

Wed, Dec 28
*The Holy Innocents,
martyrs—Feast*
1 John 1.5—2.2
Psalms 124.2-3, 4-5, 7-8
Matthew 2.13-18

Thu, Dec 29
1 John 2.3-11
Psalms 96.1-2, 2-3, 5-6
Luke 2.22-35

Fri, Dec 30
*The Holy Family—
Feast*
Sirach 3.2-6, 12-14
Psalms 128.1-2, 3, 4-5
Colossians 3.12-21
Luke 2.22-40

Sat, Dec 31
1 John 2.18-21
Psalms 96.1-2, 11-12, 13
John 1.1-18

Sun, Jan 1, 2006   Numbers 6.22-27
Mary, Mother of God— Psalms 67.2-3, 5, 6, 8
Solemnity   Galatians 4.4-7
      Luke 2.16-21

Mon, Jan 2   I John 2.22-28
      Psalms 98.1, 2-3, 3-4
      John 1.19-28

Tue, Jan 3   I John 2.29—3.6
      Psalms 98.1, 3-4, 5-6
      John 1.29-34

Wed, Jan 4   I John 3.7-10
      Psalms 98.1, 7-8, 9
      John 1.35-42

Thu, Jan 5   I John 3.11-21
      Psalms 100.1-2, 3, 4, 5
      John 1.43-51

Fri, Jan 6   I John 5.5-13
      Psalms 147.12-13, 14-15, 19-20
      Mark 1.7-11

Sat, Jan 7   I John 5.14-21
      Psalms 149.1-2, 3-4, 5, 6, 9
      John 2.1-12

Sun, Jan 8   Isaiah 60.1-6
Epiphany of the Lord— Psalms 72.1-2, 7-8, 10-11, 12-13
Solemnity   Ephesians 3.2-3, 5-6
      Matthew 2.1-12

Ordinary Time
WEEK I

Mon, Jan 9   Isaiah 42.1-4, 6-7
Baptism of the Lord— Psalms 29.1-2, 3-4, 3, 9-10
Feast   Acts 10.34-38
      Mark 1.7-11

Tue, Jan 10   I Samuel 1.9-20
      I Samuel 2.1, 4-5, 6-7, 8
      Mark 1.21-28

Wed, Jan 11   I Samuel 3.1-10, 19-20
      Psalms 40.2-5, 7-8, 8-9, 10
      Mark 1.29-39

Thu, Jan 12   I Samuel 4.1-11
      Psalms 44.10-11, 14-15, 25-26
      Mark 1.40-45

Fri, Jan 13   I Samuel 8.4-7, 10-22
      Psalms 89.16-17, 18-19
      Mark 2.1-12

Sat, Jan 14   I Samuel 9.1-4, 17-19; 10.1
      Psalms 21.2-3, 4-5, 6-7
      Mark 2.13-17

WEEK 2

Sun, Jan 15   I Samuel 3.3-10, 19
      Psalms 40.2, 4, 7-8, 8-9, 10
      I Corinthians 6.13-15, 17-20
      John 1.35-42

Mon, Jan 16   I Samuel 15.16-23
      Psalms 50.8-9, 16-17, 21, 23
      Mark 2.18-22

Tue, Jan 17   I Samuel 16.1-13
      Psalms 89.20, 21-22, 27-28
      Mark 2.23-28

Wed, Jan 18   I Samuel 17.32-33, 37, 40-51
      Psalms 144.1, 2, 9-10
      Mark 3.1-6

Thu, Jan 19   I Samuel 18.6-9; 19.1-7
      Psalms 56.2-3, 9-10, 10-12, 13-14
      Mark 3.7-12

Fri, Jan 20   I Samuel 24.3-21
      Psalms 57.2, 3-4, 6, 11
      Mark 3.13-19

Sat, Jan 21   2 Samuel 1.1-4, 11-12, 19, 23-27
      Psalms 80.2-3, 5-7
      Mark 3.20-21

WEEK 3

Sun, Jan 22   Jonah 3.1-5, 10
      Psalms 25.4-5, 6-7, 8-9
      I Corinthians 7.29-31
      Mark 1.14-20

Mon, Jan 23   2 Samuel 5.1-7, 10
      Psalms 89.20, 21-22, 25-26
      Mark 3.22-30

Tue, Jan 24   2 Samuel 6.12-15, 17-19
      Psalms 24.7, 8, 9, 10
      Mark 3.31-35

Wed, Jan 25   Acts 9.1-22
Conversion of   Psalms 117.1, 2
Saint Paul, apostle— Mark 16.15-18
Feast

Thu, Jan 26   2 Samuel 7.18-19, 24-29
      Psalms 132.1-2, 3-5, 11, 12, 13-14
      Mark 4.21-25

Fri, Jan 27   2 Samuel 11.1-4, 5-10, 13-17
      Psalms 51.3-4, 5-6, 6-7, 10-11
      Mark 4.26-34

Sat, Jan 28   2 Samuel 12.1-7, 10-17
      Psalms 51.12-13, 14-15, 16-17
      Mark 4.35-41

WEEK 4

Sun, Jan 29

Deuteronomy 18.15-20
Psalms 95.1-2, 6-7, 7-9
I Corinthians 7.32-35
Mark 1.21-28

Mon, Jan 30

2 Samuel 15.13-14, 30; 16.5-13
Psalms 3.2-3, 4-5, 6-7
Mark 5.1-20

Tue, Jan 31

2 Samuel 18.9-10, 14, 24-25,
30—19.3
Psalms 86.1-2, 3-4, 5-6
Mark 5.21-43

Wed, Feb 1

2 Samuel 24.2, 9-17
Psalms 32.1-2, 5, 6, 7
Mark 6.1-6

Thu, Feb 2
*Presentation
of the Lord—
Feast*

Malachi 3.1-4
Psalms 24.7, 8, 9, 10
Hebrews 2.14-18
Luke 2.22-40

Fri, Feb 3

Sirach 47.2-11
Psalms 18.31, 47, 50, 51
Mark 6.14-29

Sat, Feb 4

I Kings 3.4-13
Psalms 119.9, 10, 11, 12, 13, 14
Mark 6.30-34

WEEK 5

Sun, Feb 5

Job 7.1-4, 6-7
Psalms 147.1-2, 3-4, 5-6
I Corinthians 9.16-19, 22-23
Mark 1.29-39

Mon, Feb 6

I Kings 8.1-7, 9-13
Psalms 132.6-7, 8-10
Mark 6.53-56

Tue, Feb 7

I Kings 8.22-23, 27-30
Psalms 84.3, 4, 5, 10, 11
Mark 7.1-13

Wed, Feb 8

I Kings 10.1-10
Psalms 37.5-6, 30-31, 39-40
Mark 7.14-23

Thu, Feb 9

I Kings 11.4-13
Psalms 106.3-4, 35-36, 37, 40
Mark 7.24-30

Fri, Feb 10

I Kings 11.29-32; 12.19
Psalms 81.10-11, 12-13, 14-15
Mark 7.31-37

Sat, Feb 11

I Kings 12.26-32; 13.33-34
Psalms 106.6-7, 19-20, 21-22
Mark 8.1-10

WEEK 6

Sun, Feb 12

Leviticus 13.1-2, 44-46
Psalms 32.1-2, 5, 11
I Corinthians 10.31—11.1
Mark 1.40-45

Mon, Feb 13

James 1.1-11
Psalms 119.67, 68, 71, 72, 75, 76
Mark 8.11-13

Tue, Feb 14

James 1.12-18
Psalms 94.12-13, 14-15, 18-19
Mark 8.14-21

Wed, Feb 15

James 1.19-27
Psalms 15.2-3, 3-4, 5
Mark 8.22-26

Thu, Feb 16

James 2.1-9
Psalms 34.2-3, 4-5, 6-7
Mark 8.27-33

Fri, Feb 17

James 2.14-24, 26
Psalms 112.1-2, 3-4, 5-6
Mark 8.34—9.1

Sat, Feb 18

James 3.1-10
Psalms 12.2-3, 4-5, 7-8
Mark 9.2-13

WEEK 7

Sun, Feb 19

Isaiah 43.18-19, 21-22, 24-25
Psalms 41.2-3, 4-5, 13-14
2 Corinthians 1.18-22
Mark 2.1-12

Mon, Feb 20

James 3.13-18
Psalms 19.8, 9, 10, 15
Mark 9.14-29

Tue, Feb 21

James 4.1-10
Psalms 55.7-8, 9-10, 10-11, 23
Mark 9.30-37

Wed, Feb 22
*Chair of Saint Peter,
apostle—Feast*

I Peter 5.1-4
Psalms 23.1-3, 3-4, 5, 6
Matthew 16.13-19

Thu, Feb 23

James 5.1-6
Psalms 49.14-15, 15-16, 17-18,
19-20
Mark 9.41-50

Fri, Feb 24

James 5.9-12
Psalms 103.1-2, 3-4, 8-9, 11-12
Mark 10.1-12

Sat, Feb 25

James 5.13-20
Psalms 141.1-2, 3, 8
Mark 10.13-16

WEEK 8

Sun, Feb 26
Hosea 2.15-17, 21-22
Psalms 103.1-2, 3-4, 8, 10, 12-13
2 Corinthians 3.1-6
Mark 2.18-22

Mon, Feb 27
I Peter 1.3-9
Psalms 111.1-2, 5-6, 9, 10
Mark 10.17-27

Tue, Feb 28
I Peter 1.10-16
Psalms 98.1, 2-3, 3-4
Mark 10.28-31

Lent

Wed, Mar 1
Ash Wednesday
Joel 2.12-18
Psalms 51.3-4, 5-6, 12-13, 14, 17
2 Corinthians 5.20—6.2
Matthew 6.1-6, 16-18

Thu, Mar 2
Deuteronomy 30.15-20
Psalms 1.1-2, 3, 4, 6
Luke 9.22-25

Fri, Mar 3
Isaiah 58.1-9
Psalms 51.3-4, 5-6, 18-19
Matthew 9.14-15

Sat, Mar 4
Isaiah 58.9-14
Psalms 86.1-2, 3-4, 5-6
Luke 5.27-32

WEEK 1, LENT

Sun, Mar 5
Genesis 9.8-15
Psalms 25.4-5, 6-7, 8-9
I Peter 3.18-22
Mark 1.12-15

Mon, Mar 6
Leviticus 19.1-2, 11-18
Psalms 19.8, 9, 10, 15
Matthew 25.31-46

Tue, Mar 7
Isaiah 55.10-11
Psalms 34.4-5, 6-7, 16-17, 18-19
Matthew 6.7-15

Wed, Mar 8
Jonah 3.1-10
Psalms 51.3-4, 12-13, 18-19
Luke 11.29-32

Thu, Mar 9
Esther C.12, 14-16, 23-25
Psalms 138.1-2, 2-3, 7-8
Matthew 7.7-12

Fri, Mar 10
Ezekiel 18.21-28
Psalms 130.1-2, 3-4, 5-6, 7-8
Matthew 5.20-26

Sat, Mar 11
Deuteronomy 26.16-19
Psalms 119.1-2, 4-5, 7-8
Matthew 5.43-48

WEEK 2, LENT

Sun, Mar 12
Genesis 22.1-2, 9, 10-13, 15-18
Psalms 116.10, 15, 16-17, 18-19
Romans 8.31-34
Mark 9.2-10

Mon, Mar 13
Daniel 9.4-10
Psalms 79.8, 9, 11, 13
Luke 6.36-38

Tue, Mar 14
Isaiah 1.10, 16-20
Psalms 50.8-9, 16-17, 21, 23
Matthew 23.1-12

Wed, Mar 15
Jeremiah 18.18-20
Psalms 31.5-6, 14, 15-16
Matthew 20.17-28

Thu, Mar 16
Jeremiah 17.5-10
Psalms 1.1-2, 3, 4, 6
Luke 16.19-31

Fri, Mar 17
Genesis 37.3-4, 12-13, 17-18
Psalms 105.16-17, 18-19, 20-21
Matthew 21.33-43, 45-46

Sat, Mar 18
Saint Joseph,
Husband of Mary—
Solemnity
2 Samuel 7.4-5, 12-14, 16
Psalms 89.2-3, 4-5, 27, 29
Romans 4.13, 16-18, 22
Matthew 1.16, 18-21, 24,
  or Luke 2.41-51

WEEK 3, LENT

Sun, Mar 19
Exodus 20.1-17
  or 20.1-3, 7-8, 12-17
Psalms 19.8, 9, 10, 11
I Corinthians 1.22-25
John 2.13-25

Mon, Mar 20
2 Kings 5.1-15
Psalms 42.2, 3; 43.3, 4
Luke 4.24-30

Tue, Mar 21
Daniel 3.25, 34-43
Psalms 25.4-5, 6-7, 8-9
Matthew 18.21-35

Wed, Mar 22
Deuteronomy 4.1, 5-9
Psalms 147.12-13, 15-16, 19-20
Matthew 5.17-19

Thu, Mar 23
Jeremiah 7.23-28
Psalms 95.1-2, 6-7, 8-9
Luke 11.14-23

Fri, Mar 24
Hosea 14.2-10
Psalms 81.6-8, 8-9, 10-11, 14, 17
Mark 12.28-34

Sat, Mar 25
Annunciation
of the Lord—
Solemnity
Isaiah 7.10-14
Psalms 40.7-8, 8-9, 10, 11
Hebrews 10.4-10
Luke 1.26-38

WEEK 4, LENT

Sun, Mar 26   2 Chronicles 36.14-17, 19-23
Psalms 137.1-2, 3, 4-5, 6
Ephesians 2.4-10
John 3.14-21

Mon, Mar 27   Isaiah 65.17-21
Psalms 30.2, 4, 5-6, 11-13
John 4.43-54

Tue, Mar 28   Ezekiel 47.1-9, 12
Psalms 46.2-3, 5-6, 8-9
John 5.1-3, 5-16

Wed, Mar 29   Isaiah 49.8-15
Psalms 145.8-9, 13-14, 17-18
John 5.17-30

Thu, Mar 30   Exodus 32.7-14
Psalms 106.19-20, 21-22, 23
John 5.31-47

Fri, Mar 31   Wisdom 2.1, 12-22
Psalms 34.17-18, 19-20, 21, 23
John 7.1-2, 10, 25-30

Sat, Apr 1   Jeremiah 11.18-20
Psalms 7.2-3, 9-10, 11-12
John 7.40-53

WEEK 5, LENT

Sun, Apr 2   Jeremiah 31.31-34
Psalms 51.3-4, 12-13, 14-15
Hebrews 5.7-9
John 12.20-33

Mon, Apr 3   Daniel 13.1-9, 15-17, 19-30, 33-62
Psalms 23.1-3, 3-4, 5, 6
John 8.1-11

Tue, Apr 4   Numbers 21.4-9
Psalms 102.2-3, 16-18, 19-21
John 8.21-30

Wed, Apr 5   Daniel 3.14-20, 91-92, 95
Daniel 3.52, 53, 54, 55, 56
John 8.31-42

Thu, Apr 6   Genesis 17.3-9
Psalms 105.4-5, 6-7, 8-9
John 8.51-59

Fri, Apr 7   Jeremiah 20.10-13
Psalms 18.2-3, 3-4, 5-6, 7
John 10.31-42

Sat, Apr 8   Ezekiel 37.21-28
Jeremiah 31.10, 11-12, 13
John 11.45-57

HOLY WEEK

Sun, Apr 9
Passion
(Palm)
Sunday
Isaiah 50.4-7
Psalms 22.8-9, 17-18, 19-20, 23-24
Philippians 2.6-11
Mark 14.1—15.47

Mon, Apr 10   Isaiah 42.1-7
Psalms 27.1, 2, 3, 13-14
John 12.1-11

Tue, Apr 11   Isaiah 49.1-6
Psalms 71.1-2, 3-4, 5-6, 15, 17
John 13.21-33, 36-38

Wed, Apr 12   Isaiah 50.4-9
Psalms 69.8-10, 21-22, 31, 33-34
Matthew 26.14-25

Thu, Apr 13
Holy Thursday
Exodus 12.1-8, 11-14
Psalms 116.12-13, 15-16, 17-18
I Corinthians 11.23-26
John 13.1-15

Fri, Apr 14
Good Friday
Isaiah 52.13—53.12
Psalms 31.2, 6, 12-13, 15-16, 17, 25
Hebrews 4.14-16; 5.7-9
John 18.1—19.42

Sat, Apr 15
Holy Saturday
Genesis 1.1—2.2
Psalms 104.1-2, 5-6, 10, 12, 13-14, 24, 35
Genesis 22.1-18
Psalms 16.5, 8, 9-10, 11
Exodus 14.15—15.1
Exodus 15.1-2, 3-4, 5-6, 17-18
Isaiah 54.5-14
Psalms 30.2, 4, 5-6, 11-12, 13
Isaiah 55.1-11
Isaiah 12.2-3, 4, 5-6
Baruch 3.9-15, 32—4.4
Psalms 19.8, 9, 10, 11
Ezekiel 36.16-28
Psalms 51.12-13, 14-15, 18-19
Romans 6.3-11
Psalms 118.1-2, 16, 17, 22-23
Mark 16.1-8

Easter

WEEK 1, EASTER

Sun, Apr 16
Easter Sunday
Acts 10.34, 37-43
Psalms 118.1-2, 16-17, 22-23
1 Corinthians 5.6-8
John 20.1-9

Mon, Apr 17
Acts 2.14, 22-32
Psalms 16.1-2, 5, 7-8, 9-10, 11
Matthew 28.8-15

Tue, Apr 18
Acts 2.36-41
Psalms 33.4-5, 18-19, 20, 22
John 20.11-18

Wed, Apr 19
Acts 3.1-10
Psalms 105.1-2, 3-4, 6-7, 8-9
Luke 24.13-35

Thu, Apr 20
Acts 3.11-26
Psalms 8.2, 5, 6-7, 8-9
Luke 24.35-48

Fri, Apr 21
Acts 4.1-12
Psalms 118.1-2, 4, 22-24, 25-27
John 21.1-14

Sat, Apr 22
Acts 4.13-21
Psalms 118.1, 14-15, 16-18, 19-21
Mark 16.9-15

WEEK 2, EASTER

Sun, Apr 23
Acts 4.32-35
Psalms 118.2-4, 13-15, 22-24
1 John 5.1-6
John 20.19-31

Mon, Apr 24
Acts 4.23-31
Psalms 2.1-3, 4-6, 7-9
John 3.1-8

Tue, Apr 25
Saint Mark,
evangelist—Feast
1 Peter 5.5-14
Psalms 89.2-3, 6-7, 16-17
Mark 16.15-20

Wed, Apr 26
Acts 5.17-26
Psalms 34.2-3, 4-5, 6-7, 8-9
John 3.16-21

Thu, Apr 27
Acts 5.27-33
Psalms 34.2, 9, 17-18, 19-20
John 3.31-36

Fri, Apr 28
Acts 5.34-42
Psalms 27.1, 4, 13-14
John 6.1-15

Sat, Apr 29
Acts 6.1-7
Psalms 33.1-2, 4-5, 18-19
John 6.16-21

WEEK 3, EASTER

Sun, Apr 30
Acts 3.13-15, 17-19
Psalms 4.2, 4, 7-8, 9
1 John 2.1-5
Luke 24.35-48

Mon, May 1
Acts 6.8-15
Psalms 119.23-24, 26-27, 29-30
John 6.22-29

Tue, May 2
Acts 7.51—8.1
Psalms 31.3-4, 6, 7, 8, 17, 21
John 6.30-35

Wed, May 3
Saints Philip and
James, apostles—Feast
1 Corinthians 15.1-8
Psalms 19.2-3, 4-5
John 14.6-14

Thu, May 4
Acts 8.26-40
Psalms 66.8-9, 16-17, 20
John 6.44-51

Fri, May 5
Acts 9.1-20
Psalms 117.1, 2
John 6.52-59

Sat, May 6
Acts 9.31-42
Psalms 116.12-13, 14-15, 16-17
John 6.60-69

WEEK 4, EASTER

Sun, May 7
Acts 4.8-12
Psalms 118.1, 8-9, 21-23, 26, 21, 29
1 John 3.1-2
John 10.11-18

Mon, May 8
Acts 11.1-18
Psalms 42.2-3; 43.3, 4
John 10.1-10

Tue, May 9
Acts 11.19-26
Psalms 87.1-3, 4-5, 6-7
John 10.22-30

Wed, May 10
Acts 12.24—13.5
Psalms 67.2-3, 5, 6, 8
John 12.44-50

Thu, May 11
Acts 13.13-25
Psalms 89.2-3, 21-22, 25, 27
John 13.16-20

Fri, May 12
Acts 13.26-33
Psalms 2.6-7, 8-9, 10-11
John 14.1-6

Sat, May 13
Acts 13.44-52
Psalms 98.1, 2-3, 3-4
John 14.7-14

WEEK 5, EASTER

Sun, May 14
Acts 9.26-31
Psalms 22.26-27, 28, 30, 31-32
1 John 3.18-24
John 15.1-8

Mon, May 15
Acts 14.5-18
Psalms 115.1-2, 3-4, 15-16
John 14.21-26

Tue, May 16
Acts 14.19-28
Psalms 145.10-11, 12-13, 21
John 14.27-31

Wed, May 17
Acts 15.1-6
Psalms 122.1-2, 3-4, 4-5
John 15.1-8

Thu, May 18
Acts 15.7-21
Psalms 96.1-2, 2-3, 10
John 15.9-11

Fri, May 19
Acts 15.22-31
Psalms 57.8-9, 10-12
John 15.12-17

Sat, May 20
Acts 16.1-10
Psalms 100.1-2, 3, 5
John 15.18-21

WEEK 6, EASTER

Sun, May 21
Acts 10.25-26, 34-35, 44-48
Psalms 98.1, 2-3, 3-4
1 John 4.7-10
John 15.9-17

Mon, May 22
Acts 16.11-15
Psalms 149.1-2, 3-4, 5-6, 9
John 15.26—16.4

Tue, May 23
Acts 16.22-34
Psalms 138.1-2, 2-3, 7-8
John 16.5-11

Wed, May 24
Acts 17.15, 22—18.1
Psalms 148.1-2, 11-12, 13, 14
John 16.12-15

Thu, May 25
Ascension of the Lord
Acts 1.1-11
Psalms 47.2-3, 6-7, 8-9
Ephesians 1.17-23
Mark 16.15-20

Fri, May 26
Acts 18.9-18
Psalms 47.2-3, 4-5, 6-7
John 16.20-23

Sat, May 27
Acts 18.23-28
Psalms 47.2-3, 8-9, 10
John 16.23-28

WEEK 7, EASTER

Sun, May 28
Acts 1.15-17, 20-26
Psalms 103.1-2, 11-12, 19-20
1 John 4.11-16
John 17.11-19

Mon, May 29
Acts 19.1-8
Psalms 68.2-3, 4-5, 6-7
John 16.29-33

Tue, May 30
Acts 20.17-27
Psalms 68.10-11, 20-21
John 17.1-11

Wed, May 31
Visitation of the Virgin Mary to Elizabeth—Feast
Romans 12.9-16
Isaiah 12.2-3, 4, 5-6
Luke 1.39-56

Thu, June 1
Acts 22.30; 23.6-11
Psalms 16.1-2, 5, 7-8, 9-10, 11
John 17.20-26

Fri, June 2
Acts 25.13-21
Psalms 103.1-2, 11-12, 19-20
John 21.15-19

Sat, June 3
Acts 28.16-20, 30-31
Psalms 11.4, 5, 7
John 21.20-25

Sun, June 4
Pentecost
Acts 2.1-11
Psalms 104.1, 24, 29-30, 31, 34
1 Corinthians 12.3-7, 12-13
John 20.19-23

Ordinary Time

WEEK 9

Mon, June 5
2 Peter 1.2-7
Psalms 91.1-2, 14-15, 15-16
Mark 12.1-12

Tue, June 6
2 Peter 3.12-15, 17-18
Psalms 90.2, 3-4, 10, 14, 16
Mark 12.13-17

Wed, June 7
2 Timothy 1.1-3, 6-12
Psalms 123.1-2, 2
Mark 12.18-27

Thu, June 8
2 Timothy 2.8-15
Psalms 25.4-5, 8-9, 10, 14
Mark 12.28-34

Fri, June 9
2 Timothy 3.10-17
Psalms 119.157, 160, 161, 165, 166, 168
Mark 12.35-37

Sat, June 10
2 Timothy 4.1-8
Psalms 71.8-9, 14-15, 16-17, 22
Mark 12.38-44

WEEK 10

Sun, June 11
The Holy Trinity—
Solemnity

Deuteronomy 4.32-34, 39-40
Psalms 33.4-5, 6, 9, 18-19, 20, 22
Romans 8.14-17
Matthew 28.16-20

Mon, June 12

I Kings 17.1-7
Psalms 121.1-2, 3-4, 5-6, 7-8
Matthew 5.1-12

Tue, June 13

I Kings 17.7-16
Psalms 4.2-3, 4-5, 7-8
Matthew 5.13-16

Wed, June 14

I Kings 18.20-39
Psalms 16.1-2, 4, 5, 8, 11
Matthew 5.17-19

Thu, June 15

I Kings 18.41-46
Psalms 65.10, 10-11, 12-13
Matthew 5.20-26

Fri, June 16

I Kings 19.9, 11-16
Psalms 27.7-8, 8-9, 13-14
Matthew 5.27-32

Sat, June 17

I Kings 19.19-21
Psalms 16.1-2, 5, 7-8, 9-10
Matthew 5.33-37

WEEK 11

Sun, June 18
The Body and Blood of
Christ (Corpus Christi)
—Solemnity

Exodus 24.3-8
Psalms 116.12-13, 15-16, 17-18
Hebrews 9.11-15
Mark 14.12-16, 22-26

Mon, June 19

I Kings 21.1-16
Psalms 5.2-3, 5-6, 7
Matthew 5.38-42

Tue, June 20

I Kings 21.17-29
Psalms 51.3-4, 5-6, 11, 16
Matthew 5.43-48

Wed, June 21

2 Kings 2.1, 6-14
Psalms 31.20, 21, 24
Matthew 6.1-6, 16-18

Thu, June 22

Sirach 48.1-14
Psalms 97.1-2, 3-4, 5-6, 7
Matthew 6.7-15

Fri, June 23
Sacred Heart of Jesus—
Solemnity

Hosea 11.1, 3-4, 8-9
Isaiah 12.2-3, 4, 5-6
Ephesians 3.8-12, 14-19
John 19.31-37

Sat, June 24
Birth of Saint John
the Baptist—
Solemnity

Isaiah 49.1-6
Psalms 139.1-3, 13-14, 14-15
Acts 13.22-26
Luke 1.57-66, 80

WEEK 12

Sun, June 25

Job 38.1, 8-11
Psalms 107.23-24, 25-26, 28-29,
30-31
2 Corinthians 5.14-17
Mark 4.35-41

Mon, June 26

2 Kings 17.5-8, 13-15, 18
Psalms 60.3, 4-5, 12-13
Matthew 7.1-5

Tue, June 27

2 Kings 19.9-11, 14-21, 31-35, 36
Psalms 48.2-3, 3-4, 10-11
Matthew 7.6, 12-14

Wed, June 28

2 Kings 22.8-13; 23.1-3
Psalms 119.33, 34, 35, 36, 37, 40
Matthew 7.15-20

Thu, June 29
Saints Peter and Paul,
apostles—Solemnity

Acts 12.1-11
Psalms 34.2-3, 4-5, 6-7, 8-9
2 Timothy 4.6-8, 17-18
Matthew 16.13-19

Fri, June 30

2 Kings 25.1-12
Psalms 137.1-2, 3, 4-5, 6
Matthew 8.1-4

Sat, July 1

Lamentations 2.2, 10-14, 18-19
Psalms 74.1-2, 3-5, 5-7, 20-21
Matthew 8.5-17

WEEK 13

Sun, July 2

Wisdom 1.13-15; 2.23-24
Psalms 30.2, 4, 5-6, 11, 12, 13
2 Corinthians 8.7, 9, 13-15
Mark 5.21-43
or 5.21-24, 35-43

Mon, July 3
Saint Thomas,
apostle—Feast

Ephesians 2.19-22
Psalms 117.1, 2
John 20.24-29

Tue, July 4

Amos 3.1-8; 4.11-12
Psalms 5.4-6, 6-7, 8
Matthew 8.23-27

Wed, July 5

Amos 5.14-15, 21-24
Psalms 50.7, 8-9, 10-11, 12-13,
16-17
Matthew 8.28-34

Thu, July 6

Amos 7.10-17
Psalms 19.8, 9, 10, 11
Matthew 9.1-8

Fri, July 7

Amos 8.4-6, 9-12
Psalms 119.2, 10, 20, 30, 40, 131
Matthew 9.9-13

Sat, July 8

Amos 9.11-15
Psalms 85.9, 11-12, 13-14
Matthew 9.14-17

WEEK 14

Sun, July 9
Ezekiel 2.2-5
Psalms 123.1-2, 2, 3-4
2 Corinthians 12.7-10
Mark 6.1-6

Mon, July 10
Hosea 2.16, 17-18, 21-22
Psalms 145.2-3, 4-5, 6-7, 8-9
Matthew 9.18-26

Tue, July 11
Hosea 8.4-7, 11-13
Psalms 115.3-4, 5-6, 7-8, 9-10
Matthew 9.32-38

Wed, July 12
Hosea 10.1-3, 7-8, 12
Psalms 105.2-3, 4-5, 6-7
Matthew 10.1-7

Thu, July 13
Hosea 11.1, 3-4, 8-9
Psalms 80.2, 3, 15-16
Matthew 10.7-15

Fri, July 14
Hosea 14.2-10
Psalms 51.3-4, 8-9, 12-13, 14, 17
Matthew 10.16-23

Sat, July 15
Isaiah 6.1-8
Psalms 93.1, 1-2, 5
Matthew 10.24-33

WEEK 15

Sun, July 16
Amos 7.12-15
Psalms 85.9-10, 11-12, 13-14
Ephesians 1.3-14
or 1.3-10
Mark 6.7-13

Mon, July 17
Isaiah 1.10-17
Psalms 50.8-9, 16-17, 21, 23
Matthew 10.34—11.1

Tue, July 18
Isaiah 7.1-9
Psalms 48.2-3, 3-4, 5-6, 7-8
Matthew 11.20-24

Wed, July 19
Isaiah 10.5-7, 13-16
Psalms 94.5-6, 7-8, 9-10, 14-15
Matthew 11.25-27

Thu, July 20
Isaiah 26.7-9, 12, 16-19
Psalms 102.13-14, 15, 16-18, 19-21
Matthew 11.28-30

Fri, July 21
Isaiah 38.1-6, 21-22, 7-8
Isaiah 38.10, 11, 12, 16
Matthew 12.1-8

Sat, July 22
Saint Mary
Magdalene—Memorial
2 Corinthians 5.14-17
Psalms 63.2, 3-4, 5-6, 8-9
John 20.1-2, 11-18

WEEK 16

Sun, July 23
Jeremiah 23.1-16
Psalms 23.1-3, 3-4, 5, 6
Ephesians 2.13-18
Mark 6.30-34

Mon, July 24
Micah 6.1-4, 6-8
Psalms 50.5-6, 8-9, 16-17, 21, 23
Matthew 12.38-42

Tue, July 25
Saint James,
apostle—Feast
2 Corinthians 4.7-15
Psalms 126.1-2, 2-3, 4-5, 6
Matthew 20.20-28

Wed, July 26
Saints Joachim and
Ann, parents of Mary—
Memorial
Sirach 44.1, 10-15
Psalms 132.11, 13-14, 17-18
Matthew 13.16-17

Thu, July 27
Jeremiah 2.1-3, 7-8, 12-13
Psalms 36.6-7, 8-9, 10-11
Matthew 13.10-17

Fri, July 28
Jeremiah 3.14-17
Jeremiah 31.10, 11-12, 13
Matthew 13.18-23

Sat, July 29
Saint Martha—
Memorial
Proverbs 31.10-13, 19-20, 30-31
Psalms 112.1-2, 3-4, 5-6, 7-8, 9
Luke 10.38-42

WEEK 17

Sun, July 30
2 Kings 4.42-44
Psalms 145.10-11, 15-16, 17-18
Ephesians 4.1-6
John 6.1-15

Mon, July 31
Jeremiah 13.1-11
Deuteronomy 32.18-19, 20, 21
Matthew 13.31-35

Tue, Aug 1
Jeremiah 14.17-22
Psalms 79.8, 9, 11, 13
Matthew 13.35-43

Wed, Aug 2
Jeremiah 15.10, 16-21
Psalms 59.2-3, 4, 10-11, 17, 18
Matthew 13.44-46

Thu, Aug 3
Jeremiah 18.1-6
Psalms 146.1-2, 2-4, 5-6
Matthew 13.47-53

Fri, Aug 4
Jeremiah 26.1-9
Psalms 69.6, 8-10, 14
Matthew 13.54-58

Sat, Aug 5
Jeremiah 26.11-16, 24
Psalms 69.15-16, 30-31, 33-34
Matthew 14.1-12

WEEK 18

Sun, Aug 6
Transfiguration
of the Lord—
Feast

Daniel 7.9-10, 13-14
Psalms 97.1-2, 5-6, 9
2 Peter 1.16-19
Mark 9.2-10

Mon, Aug 7

Jeremiah 28.1-17
Psalms 119.29, 43, 79, 80, 95, 102
Matthew 14.13-21

Tue, Aug 8

Jeremiah 30.1-2, 12-15, 18-22
Psalms 102.16-18, 19-23, 29
Matthew 15.1-2, 10-14

Wed, Aug 9

Jeremiah 31.1-7
Jeremiah 31.10, 11-12, 13
Matthew 15.21-28

Thu, Aug 10
Saint Lawrence,
deacon and martyr—
Feast

2 Corinthians 9.6-10
Psalms 112.1-2, 5-6, 7-8, 9
John 12.24-26

Fri, Aug 11

Nahum 2.1, 3; 3.1-3, 6-7
Deuteronomy 32.35-36, 39, 41
Matthew 16.24-28

Sat, Aug 12

Habakkuk 1.12—2.4
Psalms 9.8-9, 10-11, 12-13
Matthew 17.14-20

WEEK 19

Sun, Aug 13

1 Kings 19.4-8
Psalms 34.2-3, 4-5, 6-7, 8-9
Ephesians 4.30—5.2
John 6.41-51

Mon, Aug 14

Ezekiel 1.2-5, 24-28
Psalms 148.1-2, 11-12, 12-14, 14
Matthew 17.22-27

Tue, Aug 15
Assumption of the
Virgin Mary into
Heaven—Solemnity

Revelation 11.19; 12.1-6, 10
Psalms 45.10, 11, 12, 16
1 Corinthians 15.20-26
Luke 1.39-56

Wed, Aug 16

Ezekiel 9.1-7; 10.18-22
Psalms 113.1-2, 3-4, 5-6
Matthew 18.15-20

Thu, Aug 17

Ezekiel 12.1-12
Psalms 78.56-57, 58-59, 61-62
Matthew 18.21—19.1

Fri, Aug 18

Ezekiel 16.1-15, 60, 63
Isaiah 12.2-3, 4, 5-6
Matthew 19.3-12

Sat, Aug 19

Ezekiel 18.1-10, 13, 30-32
Psalms 51.12-13, 14-15, 18-19
Matthew 19.13-15

WEEK 20

Sun, Aug 20

Proverbs 9.1-6
Psalms 34.2-3, 10-11, 12-13, 14-15
Ephesians 5.15-20
John 6.51-58

Mon, Aug 21

Ezekiel 24.15-24
Deuteronomy 32.18-19, 20, 21
Matthew 19.16-22

Tue, Aug 22

Ezekiel 28.1-10
Deuteronomy 32.26-27, 27-28,
30, 35-36
Matthew 19.23-30

Wed, Aug 23

Ezekiel 34.1-11
Psalms 23.1-3, 3-4, 5, 6
Matthew 20.1-16

Thu, Aug 24
Saint Bartholomew,
apostle—Feast

Revelation 21.9-14
Psalms 145.10-11, 12-13, 17-18
John 1.45-51

Fri, Aug 25

Ezekiel 37.1-14
Psalms 107.2-3, 4-5, 6-7, 8-9
Matthew 22.34-40

Sat, Aug 26

Ezekiel 43.1-7
Psalms 85.9-10, 11-12, 13-14
Matthew 23.1-12

WEEK 21

Sun, Aug 27

Joshua 24.1-2, 15-17, 18
Psalms 34.2-3, 16-17, 18-19,
20-21, 22-23
Ephesians 5.21-32
John 6.60-69

Mon, Aug 28

2 Thessalonians 1.1-5, 11-12
Psalms 96.1-2, 2-3, 4-5
Matthew 23.13-22

Tue, Aug 29
Beheading of
Saint John the Baptist,
martyr—Memorial

Jeremiah 1.17-19
Psalms 71.1-2, 3-4, 5-6, 15, 17
Mark 6.17-29

Wed, Aug 30

2 Thessalonians 3.6-10, 16-18
Psalms 128.1-2, 4-5
Matthew 23.27-32

Thu, Aug 31

1 Corinthians 1.1-9
Psalms 145.2-3, 4-5, 6-7
Matthew 24.42-51

Fri, Sept 1

1 Corinthians 1.17-25
Psalms 33.1-2, 4-5, 10, 11
Matthew 25.1-13

Sat, Sept 2

1 Corinthians 1.26-31
Psalms 33.12-13, 18-19, 20-21
Matthew 25.14-30

WEEK 22

Sun, Sept 3

Deuteronomy 4.1-2, 6-8
Psalms 15.2-3, 3-4, 4-5
James 1.17-18, 21-22, 27
Mark 7.1-8, 14-15, 21-23

Mon, Sept 4

I Corinthians 2.1-5
Psalms 119.97, 98, 99, 100,
     101, 102
Luke 4.16-30

Tue, Sept 5

I Corinthians 2.10-16
Psalms 145.8-9, 10-11, 12-13, 13-14
Luke 4.31-37

Wed, Sept 6

I Corinthians 3.1-9
Psalms 33.12-13, 14-15, 20-21
Luke 4.38-44

Thu, Sept 7

I Corinthians 3.18-23
Psalms 24.1-2, 3-4, 5-6
Luke 5.1-11

Fri, Sept 8
Birth of the
Virgin Mary—
Feast

Micah 5.1-4
Psalms 13.6
Matthew 1.1-16, 18-23
     or 1.18-23

Sat, Sept 9

I Corinthians 4.9-15
Psalms 145.17-18, 19-20, 21
Luke 6.1-5

WEEK 23

Sun, Sept 10

Isaiah 35.4-7
Psalms 146.7, 8-9, 9-10
James 2.1-5
Mark 7.31-37

Mon, Sept 11

I Corinthians 5.1-8
Psalms 5.5-6, 7, 12
Luke 6.6-11

Tue, Sept 12

I Corinthians 6.1-11
Psalms 149.1-2, 3-4, 5-6, 9
Luke 6.12-19

Wed, Sept 13

I Corinthians 7.25-31
Psalms 45.11-12, 14-15, 16-17
Luke 6.20-26

Thu, Sept 14
Triumph of the
Holy Cross—
Feast

Numbers 21.4-9
Psalms 78.1-2, 34-35, 36-37, 38
Philippians 2.6-11
John 3.13-17

Fri, Sept 15
Our Lady of Sorrows—
Memorial

Hebrews 5.7-9
Psalms 31.2-3, 3-4, 5-6, 15-16, 20
Luke 2.33-35

Sat, Sept 16

I Corinthians 10.14-22
Psalms 116.12-13, 17-18
Luke 6.43-49

WEEK 24

Sun, Sept 17

Isaiah 50.4-9
Psalms 116.1-2, 3-4, 5-6, 8-9
James 2.14-18
Mark 8.27-35

Mon, Sept 18

I Corinthians 11.17-26, 33
Psalms 40.7-8, 8-9, 10, 17
Luke 7.1-10

Tue, Sept 19

I Corinthians 12.12-14, 27-31
Psalms 100.1-2, 3, 4, 5
Luke 7.11-17

Wed, Sept 20

I Corinthians 12.31—13.13
Psalms 33.2-3, 4-5, 12, 22
Luke 7.31-35

Thu, Sept 21
Saint Matthew,
apostle and
evangelist—Feast

Ephesians 4.1-7, 11-13
Psalms 19.2-3, 4-5
Matthew 9.9-13

Fri, Sept 22

I Corinthians 15.12-20
Psalms 17.1, 6-7, 8, 15
Luke 8.1-3

Sat, Sept 23

I Corinthians 15.35-37, 42-49
Psalms 56.10-12, 13-14
Luke 8.4-15

WEEK 25

Sun, Sept 24

Wisdom 2.17-20
Psalms 54.3-4, 5, 6-8
James 3.16—4.3
Mark 9.30-37

Mon, Sept 25

Proverbs 3.27-34
Psalms 15.2-3, 3-4, 5
Luke 8.16-18

Tue, Sept 26

Proverbs 21.1-6, 10-13
Psalms 119.1, 27, 30, 34, 35, 44
Luke 8.19-21

Wed, Sept 27

Proverbs 30.5-9
Psalms 119.29, 72, 89, 101,
     104, 163
Luke 9.1-6

Thu, Sept 28

Ecclesiastes 1.2-11
Psalms 90.3-4, 5-6, 12-13, 14, 17
Luke 9.7-9

Fri, Sept 29
Michael, Gabriel, and
Raphael, archangels—
Feast

Daniel 7.9-10, 13-14
Psalms 138.1-2, 2-3, 4-5
John 1.47-51

Sat, Sept 30

Ecclesiastes 11.9—12.8
Psalms 90.3-4, 5-6, 12-13, 14, 17
Luke 9.43-45

WEEK 26

Sun, Oct 1
Numbers 11.25-29
Psalms 19.8, 10, 12-13, 14
James 5.1-6
Mark 9.38-43, 45, 47-48

Mon, Oct 2
Guardian Angels—
Memorial
Exodus 23.20-23
Psalms 91.1-2, 3-4, 5-6, 10-11
Matthew 18.1-5, 10

Tue, Oct 3
Job 3.1-3, 11-17, 20-23
Psalms 88.2-3, 4-5, 6, 7-8
Luke 9.51-56

Wed, Oct 4
Job 9.1-12, 14-16
Psalms 88.10-11, 12-13, 14-15
Luke 9.57-62

Thu, Oct 5
Job 19.21-27
Psalms 27.7-8, 8-9, 13-14
Luke 10.1-12

Fri, Oct 6
Job 38.1, 12-21; 40.3-5
Psalms 139.1-3, 7-8, 9-10, 13-14
Luke 10.13-16

Sat, Oct 7
Job 42.1-3, 5-6, 12-16
Psalms 119.66, 71, 75, 91, 125, 130
Luke 10.17-24

WEEK 27

Sun, Oct 8
Genesis 2.18-24
Psalms 128.1-2, 3, 4-5, 6
Hebrews 2.9-11
Mark 10.2-16

Mon, Oct 9
Galatians 1.6-12
Psalms 111.1-2, 7-8, 9, 10
Luke 10.25-37

Tue, Oct 10
Galatians 1.13-24
Psalms 139.1-3, 13-14, 14-15
Luke 10.38-42

Wed, Oct 11
Galatians 2.1-2, 7-14
Psalms 117.1, 2
Luke 11.1-4

Thu, Oct 12
Galatians 3.1-5
Luke 1.69-70, 71-72, 73-75
Luke 11.5-13

Fri, Oct 13
Galatians 3.7-14
Psalms 111.1-2, 3-4, 5-6
Luke 11.15-26

Sat, Oct 14
Galatians 3.22-29
Psalms 105.2-3, 4-5, 6-7
Luke 11.27-28

WEEK 28

Sun, Oct 15
Wisdom 7.7-11
Psalms 90.12-13, 14-15, 16-17
Hebrews 4.12-13
Mark 10.17-30

Mon, Oct 16
Galatians 4.22-24, 26-27,
31—5.1
Psalms 113.1-2, 3-4, 5, 6-7
Luke 11.29-32

Tue, Oct 17
Galatians 5.1-6
Psalms 119.41, 43, 44, 45, 47, 48
Luke 11.37-41

Wed, Oct 18
Saint Luke,
evangelist—Feast
2 Timothy 4.9-17
Psalms 145.10-11, 12-13, 17-18
Luke 10.1-9

Thu, Oct 19
Ephesians 1.3-10
Psalms 98.1, 2-3, 3-4, 5-6
Luke 11.47-54

Fri, Oct 20
Ephesians 1.11-14
Psalms 33.1-2, 4-5, 12-13
Luke 12.1-7

Sat, Oct 21
Ephesians 1.15-23
Psalms 8.2-3, 4-5, 6-7
Luke 12.8-12

WEEK 29

Sun, Oct 22
Isaiah 53.10-11
Psalms 33.4-5, 18-19, 20, 22
Hebrews 4.14-16
Mark 10.35-45
or 10.42-45

Mon, Oct 23
Ephesians 2.1-10
Psalms 100.2, 3, 4, 5
Luke 12.13-21

Tue, Oct 24
Ephesians 2.12-22
Psalms 85.9-10, 11-12, 13-14
Luke 12.35-38

Wed, Oct 25
Ephesians 3.2-12
Isaiah 12.2-3, 4, 5-6
Luke 12.39-48

Thu, Oct 26
Ephesians 3.14-21
Psalms 33.1-2, 4-5, 11-12, 18-19
Luke 12.49-53

Fri, Oct 27
Ephesians 4.1-6
Psalms 24.1-2, 3-4, 5-6
Luke 12.54-59

Sat, Oct 28
Saints Simon and
Jude, apostles—Feast
Ephesians 2.19-22
Psalms 19.2-3, 4-5
Luke 6.12-16

WEEK 30

Sun, Oct 29   Jeremiah 31.7-9
Psalms 126.1-2, 2-3, 4-5, 6
Hebrews 5.1-6
Mark 10.46-52

Mon, Oct 30   Ephesians 4.32—5.8
Psalms 1.1-2, 3, 4, 6
Luke 13.10-17

Tue, Oct 31   Ephesians 5.21-33
Psalms 128.1-2, 3, 4-5
Luke 13.18-21

Wed, Nov 1
All Saints—Solemnity   Revelation 7.2-4, 9-14
Psalms 24.1-2, 3-4, 5-6
I John 3.1-3
Matthew 5.1-12

Thu, Nov 2
Commemoration of
All the Faithful
Departed (All Souls)
—Solemnity   Isaiah 25.6, 7-9
Psalms 103.8, 10, 13-14, 15-16, 17-18
I Corinthians 15.20-24, 25-28
John 11.17-27

Fri, Nov 3   Philippians 1.1-11
Psalms 111.1-2, 3-4, 5-6
Luke 14.1-6

Sat, Nov 4   Philippians 1.18-26
Psalms 42.2, 3, 5
Luke 14.1, 7-11

WEEK 31

Sun, Nov 5   Deuteronomy 6.2-6
Psalms 18.2-3, 3-4, 47, 57
Hebrews 7.23-28
Mark 12.28-34

Mon, Nov 6   Philippians 2.1-4
Psalms 131.1, 2, 3
Luke 14.12-14

Tue, Nov 7   Philippians 2.5-11
Psalms 22.26-27, 28-30, 31-32
Luke 14.15-24

Wed, Nov 8   Philippians 2.12-18
Psalms 27.1, 4, 13-14
Luke 14.25-33

Thu, Nov 9
Dedication of the
Basilica of St. John
Lateran in Rome—
Feast   Genesis 28.11-18
Psalms 84.3, 4, 5-6, 8, 11
I Corinthians 3.9-13, 16-17
Luke 19.1-10

Fri, Nov 10   Philippians 3.17—4.1
Psalms 122.1-2, 3-4, 4-5
Luke 16.1-8

Sat, Nov 11   Philippians 4.10-19
Psalms 112.1-2, 5-6, 8, 9
Luke 16.9-15

WEEK 32

Sun, Nov 12   I Kings 17.10-16
Psalms 146.7, 8-9, 9-10
Hebrews 9.24-28
Mark 12.38-44

Mon, Nov 13   Titus 1.1-9
Psalms 24.1-2, 3-4, 5-6
Luke 17.1-6

Tue, Nov 14   Titus 2.1-8, 11-14
Psalms 37.3-4, 18, 23, 27, 29
Luke 17.7-10

Wed, Nov 15   Titus 3.1-7
Psalms 23.1-3, 3-4, 5, 6
Luke 17.11-19

Thu, Nov 16   Philemon 1.7-20
Psalms 146.7, 8-9, 9-10
Luke 17.20-25

Fri, Nov 17   2 John 1.4-9
Psalms 119.1, 2, 10, 11, 17, 18
Luke 17.26-37

Sat, Nov 18   3 John 1.5-8
Psalms 112.1-2, 3-4, 5-6
Luke 18.1-8

WEEK 33

Sun, Nov 19   Daniel 12.1-3
Psalms 16.5, 8, 9-10, 11
Hebrews 10.11-14, 18
Mark 13.24-32

Mon, Nov 20   Revelation 1.1-4; 2.1-5
Psalms 1.1-2, 3, 4, 6
Luke 18.35-43

Tue, Nov 21   Revelation 3.1-6, 14-22
Psalms 15.2-3, 3-4, 5
Luke 19.1-10

Wed, Nov 22   Revelation 4.1-11
Psalms 150.1-2, 3-4, 5-6
Luke 19.11-28

Thu, Nov 23   Revelation 5.1-10
Psalms 149.1-2, 3-4, 5-6, 9
Luke 9.41-44

Fri, Nov 24   Revelation 10.8-11
Psalms 119.14, 24, 72, 103, 111, 131
Luke 19.45-48

Sat, Nov 25   Revelation 11.4-12
Psalms 144.1, 2, 9-10
Luke 20.27-40

WEEK 34

Sun, Nov 26
Christ the King—
Solemnity

Daniel 7.13-14
Psalms 93.1, 1-2, 5
Revelation 1.5-8
John 18.33-37

Mon, Nov 27

Revelation 14.1-3, 4-5
Psalms 24.1-2, 3-4, 5-6
Luke 21.1-4

Tue, Nov 28

Revelation 14.14-19
Psalms 96.10, 11-12, 13
Luke 21.5-11

Wed, Nov 29

Revelation 15.1-4
Psalms 98.1, 2-3, 7-8, 9
Luke 21.12-19

Thu, Nov 30
Saint Andrew,
apostle—Feast

Romans 10.9-18
Psalms 19.2-3, 4-5
Matthew 4.18-22

Fri, Dec 1

Revelation 20.1-4, 11—21.2
Psalms 84.3, 4, 5-6, 8
Luke 21.29-33

Sat, Dec 2

Revelation 22.1-7
Psalms 95.1-2, 3-5, 6-7
Luke 21.34-36

NOTES

NOTES

NOTES

NOTES

NOTES

Catholic Women's Devotional Bible

Ann Spangler, General Editor

Louise Perrotta, Contributing Editor

[For a list of authors and contributors,
see the Biographical Index]

Project management and editorial by Shari TeSlaa

Editorial assistance by Ruth DeJager, Donna Huisjen,
and Julie Zahm

Production management by Phil Herich

Art direction by Jamie DeBruyn

Cover design by Jamie DeBruyn

Interior design by Sharon Wright, Belmont, MI

Interior proofreading by Peachtree Editorial
and Proofreading Service, Peachtree City, GA

Literary agency by Wolgemuth & Associates, Brentwood, TN

Interior typesetting by Auto-graphics, Inc., Pomona, CA

Guarantee

Care

We suggest loosening the binding of your new Bible
by gently pressing on a small section of pages at a time
from the center. To ensure against breakage of the spine,
it is best not to bend the cover backward around the
spine or to carry study notes, church bulletins, pens, etc., inside
the cover. Because a felt-tipped marker will "bleed" through
the pages, we recommend use of a ball-point pen or
pencil to underline favorite passages. Your Bible should
not be exposed to excessive heat, cold or humidity. Protecting
the gold or silver edges of the paper from moisture
will avoid spotting, streaking or fading.